Principles of

Animal Physiology

THIRD EDITION

Christopher D. Moyes, Ph.D.
Queen's University

Patricia M. Schulte, Ph.D.
University of British Columbia

PEARSON

Toronto

1007557488

VP, Cross Media & Publishing Services: Gary Bennett
Editorial Director: Claudine O'Donnell
Executive Editor: Lisa Rahn
Marketing Manager: Kimberly Teska
Program Manager: Darryl Kamo
Project Manager: Richard di Santo
Senior Developmental Editor: Lise Dupont
Production Services: Roxanne Klaas, S4Carlisle Publishing Services
Permissions Project Manager: Erica Mojzes
Photo Permissions Research: Carolyn Arcabascio, PreMediaGlobal
Text Permissions Research: Haydee Hidalgo, Electronic Publishing Services, Inc.
Art Director: Zena Denchik
Cover and Interior Designer: Anthony Leung
Cover image: GettyImages

Original edition published by Pearson Education, Inc., publishing as Benjamin Cummings, San Francisco, CA, USA. Copyright © 2008 Pearson Education, Inc.

Library and Archives Canada Cataloguing in Publication
Moyes, Christopher D., 1960-, author
  Principles of animal physiology / Christopher D. Moyes, Ph.D.
(Queen's University), Patricia M. Schulte, Ph.D. (University of British
Columbia). — Third edition.
  Includes bibliographical references and index.
  ISBN 978-0-321-83817-9 (pbk.)
  1. Physiology—Textbooks.   I. Schulte, Patricia M., 1965-, author   II. Title.
QP31.2.M69 2014   571.1   C2014-906141-2

4 5 6 7 8 9 10 V011 18 17 16 15

PEARSON

Brief Contents

Part One
Introduction to Physiology 2

Photo source: Scott Nielsen/Bruce Coleman Inc.

Part Two
The Cellular Basis of Animal Physiology 98

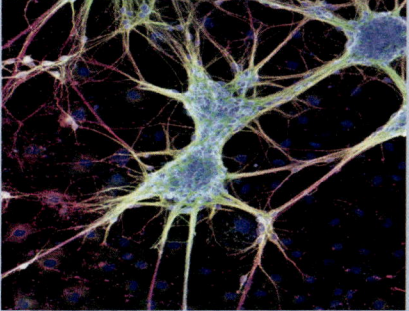

Photo source: Francois Paquet-Durand / Science Source

Part Three
Integrating Physiological Systems 256

Photo source: Image Quest Marine

About the Authors

Christopher D. Moyes, Ph.D.
Queen's University

Chris Moyes received his Ph.D. in Zoology from the University of British Columbia in the area of comparative muscle physiology. After postdoctoral fellowships in molecular physiology at the U.S. National Institutes of Health and Simon Fraser University, he took a position at Queen's University, where he is a Full Professor in the Department of Biology, and Department Head (2013–2015). He teaches a spectrum of courses in animal physiology, comparative biochemistry, and cell biology. Using a wide range of comparative and traditional models, his research addresses questions in molecular physiology and metabolic biochemistry. One major theme of his research is the study of the evolutionary and developmental origins of variation in muscle structure and function. Another major area of his research is the response of animals to environmental stress. In all of his research he emphasizes the integration of physiological processes, from molecular to organismal levels.

Dr. Moyes is a recipient of the Ontario Premier's Research Excellence Award. He is a member of the American Physiological Society and the Canadian Society of Zoologists and has served on research grant panels for the Natural Science and Engineering Research Council of Canada and the U.S. National Science Foundation. He is also Editor-in-Chief of *Comparative Biochemistry and Physiology B Biochemistry*.

He has published more than 100 peer-reviewed papers, including contributions to four books.

More of his research is detailed on his homepage at http://post.queensu.ca/~cdm2/.

Patricia M. Schulte, Ph.D.
University of British Columbia

Trish Schulte received her Ph.D. in Biological Sciences from Stanford University in the area of evolutionary physiology. After graduating, she took a position as an assistant professor in the Department of Biology at the University of Waterloo, and then moved to the Department of Zoology at the University of British Columbia in Vancouver where she is currently a Full Professor.

Research in her laboratory focuses on the mechanisms that fish use to respond to environmental stressors such as high temperature, hypoxia, and altered salinity. She is particularly interested in understanding how genetic variation among individuals contributes to variation in their stress response across multiple levels of biological organization, and assessing the consequences of this variation for performance and fitness in variable environments. Dr. Schulte's research group also conducts applied research in fisheries, aquaculture, and aquatic toxicology. She has published over 100 peer-reviewed papers, including contributions to several books.

Dr. Schulte was the President of the Canadian Society of Zoologists (2007–2008), and is a member of the Society for Integrative and Comparative Biology, The Society for Experimental Biology, and the American Physiological Society. She was the co-editor in chief of the journal *Physiological and Biochemical Zoology* (2009–2014), and is a member of the editorial board of the journal *Comparative Biochemistry and Physiology*.

Dr. Schulte has taught physiology courses at multiple levels, including introductory physiology, comparative physiology, and human physiology. She is a recipient of a several teaching awards, including the UBC Science Undergraduate Society Award for Excellence in Teaching and the Faculty of Science Achievement Award for Teaching. She is currently the departmental director for Life Sciences for the Carl Wieman Science Education Initiative at UBC, which is dedicated to promoting the use of evidence-based approaches to science education for undergraduates.

You can learn more about her research and teaching activities on her homepage at http://www.zoology.ubc.ca/person/pschulte.

Dedication

Thanks to our families, friends, colleagues, and students for their influence and support during the development of this textbook. We dedicate this textbook to the memory of Peter Hochachka, an inspiration to comparative physiologists and valued mentor to both of us.

CHAPTER 3

Chemistry, Biochemistry, and Cell Physiology   38

PART TWO THE CELLULAR BASIS OF ANIMAL PHYSIOLOGY 98

CHAPTER 4

Cell Signaling and Endocrine Regulation 98

CHAPTER 5
Neuron Structure and Function   154

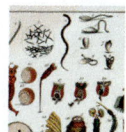

CHAPTER 6

Cellular Movement and Muscles   208

PART THREE INTEGRATING PHYSIOLOGICAL SYSTEMS 256

CHAPTER 7

Sensory Systems 256

CHAPTER 8

Functional Organization of Nervous Systems   310

CHAPTER 9

Circulatory Systems   356

CHAPTER 10

Immune Systems   414

CHAPTER 11

Respiratory Systems   442

CHAPTER 12

Locomotion 498

CHAPTER 13

Ion and Water Balance   542

CHAPTER 14

Digestion and Energy Metabolism 592

CHAPTER 15

Thermal Physiology   634

CHAPTER 16

Reproductive Physiology   668

Preface

The 21st century is an incredibly exciting time to be a biologist. Animal biologists now have access to data from a range of complete animal genomes covering a broad spectrum of the diversity of animals. At the time of writing this preface, complete genomes already exist for several hundred species of invertebrates and over two hundred species of vertebrates; in the next few years, we expect that genome sequences will be available for thousands of species of animals. But the fundamental questions about how the genes in these genomes work together to allow animals to perform their diverse physiological functions and to go about their daily lives are still largely unanswered. Animal physiologists are at the forefront of integrating this new genome sequence information into a functional and evolutionary framework as part of their efforts to understand how animals work. Our goal in writing this textbook is to convey a sense of this excitement to students who are approaching the study of animal physiology for the first time.

One of the challenges that students face when they approach their first course in physiology is the great breadth and diversity of the subject matter. Physiology is among the most integrative of the life sciences, drawing on ideas from chemistry, physics, mathematics, molecular biology, and cell biology for its conceptual underpinnings. In addition, to fully appreciate the physiological diversity of animals, students must have a working knowledge of environmental biology, ecology, systematics, and evolutionary biology. We have written this book to give students a well-organized and engaging treatment of the fundamental principles of animal physiology. Throughout the book, we integrate concepts from all levels of biological organization to explore the nature of diversity in biological molecules, cells, physiological systems, and whole animals. We hope that this approach will spark the interest of all students, whatever their background preparation.

KEY THEMES

Students are sometimes so focused on remembering the "facts" of physiology that they are unable to place these facts into a well-developed conceptual framework. To help students get past this difficult barrier, we organized this book around several key themes and fundamental principles that are highlighted in each chapter and strove to present this material in an accessible fashion that engages student learning.

A Focus on Unifying Principles. In Chapter 1, we introduce four unifying themes in animal physiology:

- Physiology integrates across levels of biological organization from molecules to populations.

- Physiological processes are based in the laws of chemistry and physics.

- Physiological diversity among animals is the result of evolutionary processes.

- Physiological processes are homeostatically regulated.

Every chapter revisits these key themes, providing a unifying thread that ties together our concept of animal physiology.

Orientation Around Learning. To promote comprehension, each chapter begins with *Learning Objectives* that connect directly with the headings in the chapter and with the Review Questions at the end of the chapter. To assist with the integration of material across chapters, many chapters feature a new *Looking Back* section that identifies the critical background material found in earlier chapters.

An Emphasis on Animal Diversity and Evolution. We are strongly committed to the importance of teaching about the physiological diversity of animals, because we feel that this diversity is a fundamental property of the natural world. We also believe that books focusing only on humans can cause students to form the erroneous impression that physiological processes in humans are typical of those in all animals, and thus we provide diverse examples in their evolutionary context. As a result, we include extensive discussion of physiological processes in both vertebrates and invertebrates throughout the book and attempt to interweave evolutionary thinking into these discussions. Our new Chapter 2 discusses the major events in the evolution of animals, with a focus on the evolution of physiologically significant traits and how they contributed to the evolutionary diversification of the major animal groups.

Attention to the Integrative Nature of Animal Physiology. Throughout the book, we emphasize the integrative nature of physiology in a number of ways. Each chapter begins with an opening essay that provides a short, engaging vignette that places the system under discussion into its environmental or evolutionary framework. Together, these features help to build student understanding of how physiological systems interrelate and depend on each other.

Integration of Physiology with Cell and Molecular Biology. We divided this book into three main sections. In Part One, we provide an overview of the basic principles of animal physiology, identifying the common themes in the discipline and emphasizing the role of evolution in animal diversity.

In Part Two, we discuss the cellular basis of animal physiology. The goal of Part Two is to provide students with a general context for understanding animal physiology and to show how, at a cellular level, animals are both similar to and different from other organisms. We hope that this treatment will help students begin to see how the somewhat abstract processes that they study in other courses have direct relevance to the understanding of animal physiology.

Providing a strong foundation in cellular and molecular physiology is critical for students because our understanding of animal physiology has changed dramatically in the last 10 years due to advances in fields such as genomics, transcriptomics, proteomics, and cell biology, and a solid understanding of these disciplines is central to the modern concept of physiology.

In Part Three, we discuss how cells and tissues interact to form the integrative physiological systems of animals. We consider each of the major physiological systems in turn, building on the twin themes of conservation and diversity to address the question: How do different animals use fundamentally similar building blocks to construct unique physiological systems to meet the challenges imposed by the environment? Throughout the third part of this book, we integrated the discussion of the cellular and molecular processes that underpin physiological processes, at a depth that will encourage students to understand the relevance of these disciplines to animal physiology.

Integrated Treatment of Endocrine Regulation. The treatment of endocrine systems is one unique element in the book's organization. Rather than relegating these systems to a single isolated chapter, we discuss endocrinology in Part Two in the context of the various means of cellular signaling and communication, and then integrate the presentation of its various physiological roles throughout the chapters in Part Two. We find that students better understand how hormones control systems once they have been introduced to all the diverse ways in which cells send and receive signals. By establishing the foundation of cellular control early in the text, we are able to discuss the impact of specific hormones and glands in the context of each physiological system, increasing the integrative nature of the discussion. This approach places the endocrine system in its appropriate evolutionary framework—as one of several means of intercellular communication that are available to multicellular organisms—and clearly demonstrates how communication and coordination are critical for the functioning of essentially every organ system.

NEW FOR THE 3rd EDITION

For the 3rd Edition, we expanded the pedagogical features throughout the text to facilitate students' learning. New

for the 3rd Edition, you will find the following in each chapter:

- A short and engaging chapter-opening essay that introduces an animal or scenario that epitomizes the importance of the physiological system discussed in the chapter.
- Learning Objectives that organize ideas into major themes for students.
- Looking Back sections that direct students to specific material earlier in the text.
- More succinct chapter summaries that focus on the major points.

From Chapter 4 onward, each chapter showcases these feature boxes:

- **Math in Physiology** takes a quantitative approach to physiological principles.
- **Challenges to Homeostasis** discusses how animals respond to physiological challenges.
- **Applications** addresses how physiology can be used or studied to solve real-world problems.

In addition, we revised the narrative and the figures extensively with the goal of helping students to master some of the most difficult concepts in physiology. The highlights of these changes in the 3rd Edition include:

Chapter 1, Introduction to Physiological Principles

- A new opening feature on Porcelain crabs to emphasize environmental physiology and the applications of physiology to conservation biology.
- A new focus on exploring the unifying themes that tie together both the basic and applied aspects of the discipline of animal physiology.
- An expanded discussion of the relationship between form and function, the concepts of homology and analogy, and scaling as a unifying principle in physiology, including several new Figures

Chapter 2, Physiological Evolution of Animals

- **New to the 3rd Edition!** This chapter provides a survey of animal diversity, focusing on the origins of physiological traits and the significance of phylogenies.
- This chapter introduces the critical events in animal evolution and the role of environment in the selective process.

Chapter 3, Chemistry, Biochemisty, and Cell Physiology

- A more refined discussion of energetics, including an explanation of chemical energy transfers, bonds, solubility, and thermal effects, clearing up ambiguity about these topics.

- A reorganized and expanded discussion of metabolic rate determinants, collecting information from disparate 2nd Edition chapters into a single section.

- A more complete discussion of the membrane potential/Nernst equation/Goldman equation, with this important information in the body of the chapter, rather than in a boxed feature.

- A discussion of tissue types and the roles and regulation of epithelial tissues, including transport and transporters.

Chapter 4, Cell Signaling and Endocrine Regulation

- A substantial reorganization of the second half of the chapter to provide a more focused discussion of the fundamental shared principles of endocrine regulation, using selected examples from vertebrates to illustrate these principles.

- An expanded section discussing endocrine systems and how they evolved, including a new Figure showing the major endocrine glands of mammals.

- A new section on the evolution of the vertebrate pituitary gland.

Chapter 5, Neuron Structure and Function

- A more comprehensive explanation of the Nernst and Goldman equations, including a new Figure and boxed feature.

- A revised discussion of saltatory conduction, including a new Figure.

- An expanded discussion of molecular events at the synapse.

- An updated discussion of the evolution of neurons that reflects the recent cloning of bacterial voltage-gated Na^+ channels.

Chapter 6, Cellular Movement and Muscles

- New Figures to illustrate topics including (1) skeletal muscle structure, explaining how all of the muscles fit together; (2) the impact of arrangement (series versus parallel) on muscle structure; and (3) muscle fiber mosaics.

- An expanded feature on force and work, which consolidates the force/work/power material in a single location.

- New and revised Figures that help distinguish between muscle fiber types, expanding the discussion of smooth muscle.

- A reorganization of the discussion of EC coupling that more clearly distinguishes between cardiac and skeletal muscle.

- A new feature on muscle remodeling in exercise, combining the themes of structural changes and cellular regulation.

Chapter 7, Sensory Systems

- New sections on topics including nociception, hearing in whales and dolphins, and the photoreceptors involved in circadian rhythms.

- A new boxed feature on using pheromones to alter behavior.

- An expanded discussion of electroreception, including a new Figure.

- An updated discussion of magnetoreception.

Chapter 8, Functional Organization of Nervous Systems

- An expanded treatment of the organization and evolution of nervous systems.

- Increased coverage of the general anatomy of the central nervous system, with more information about the spinal cord.

- New boxed features examining (1) the scaling of brain size, neuron number, and behavioral complexity; (2) how ocean acidification affects fish behavior by disturbing brain homeostasis; and (3) functional magnetic resonance imaging and brain plasticity.

- New sections on the corpus callosum, mirror neurons, and language acquisition in birds.

- An expanded discussion of the enteric nervous system.

- A new section focusing on the role of the hypothalamus in regulating bodily functions such as circadian rhythms and sleep-wake cycles.

Chapter 9, Circulatory Systems

- New discussions of orthostatic hypotension and space flight, physiology of dinosaur circulatory systems, the development of the human heart, and the coevolution of circulatory and respiratory systems.

- Revised and clarified discussion of the evolution of the lymphatic system, amphibian circulatory systems, ion channels and pacemaker currents, and the cardiovascular physiology of giraffes.

- A new boxed feature dealing with the use of EKG technology to diagnose heart conditions.

- New Figures to illustrate the evolution of vertebrate circulatory systems and cardiac anatomy, the development of the mammalian heart, and the effect of elevated blood pressure on risk of cardiovascular disease.

Chapter 10, Immune Systems

- **New** to the 3rd Edition! This chapter discusses comparative immunology, with a focus on evolutionary diversity of the innate and adaptive immune systems.

- It includes discussion of the molecular mechanisms that organisms use to detect foreign molecules and the roles of the various immune cells, particularly B cells and T cells.

- The addition of a chapter on immunology provides context for the interaction between immunity and other physiological processes, particularly the circulatory, thermal, and digestive systems.

Chapter 11, Respiratory Systems

- A new discussion of the potential for unidirectional ventilation in crocodile lungs.

- A revised discussion of Root effect hemoglobins, emphasizing recent research suggesting a role for these hemoglobins in delivery of oxygen to systemic tissues in fish.

- A new section on the evolution of myoglobin in diving mammals.

- New boxed features dealing with (1) the treatment of respiratory distress syndrome in premature infants, (2) pulmonary function tests, and (3) adaptations to high altitude in bar-headed geese.

Chapter 12, Locomotion

- An expanded discussion of the importance of animal athletes as models for understanding physiological evolution.

- New features on type II diabetes and migration.

- An expanded discussion of the regulation of homeostasis in muscle.

- A new feature on the cost of transport and a revised discussion of work loops that deconstruct positive and negative work to help students understand the biophysical basis of locomotion.

Chapter 13, Ion and Water Balance

- An expanded discussion of osmotic strategies used by animals, highlighting the important transitions that arose in the context of animal evolution.

- A reorganized section on kidney function and regulation, focusing on the four main homeostatic functions: ion balance, osmotic balance, pH balance, and blood pressure regulation.

- A new feature that delves into the quantitative analysis of renal clearance, including an explicit discussion of the concept of a "virtual volume."

- A new feature, "Conservation Physiology of Salmon," highlighting recent work showing how ionoregulatory physiology influences the survival of animals in nature.

Chapter 14, Digestion and Energy Metabolism

- A change in the scope of the chapter to also include energy metabolism and its regulation.

- A reorganization of the section on regulation of digestion to discuss processes along a linear timeline.

- A new *Applications* feature focusing on the gut microbiome, with appropriate cross-referencing to the new Immune Systems chapter.

- A new feature focusing on obesity as a homeostatic challenge.

- A more consistent treatment of the many hormones that regulate digestion and metabolic rate.

Chapter 15, Thermal Physiology

- An expanded discussion of thermal biology to better consider physiological ecology, including a new Applications feature on thermal tolerance and conservation biology of Atlantic cod, an expanded discussion of the impact of temperature on metabolism, and new material on thermal effects on aerobic scope and the OCLTT hypothesis.

- Revised discussion of the evolution of uncoupling proteins, including introduction of a **Challenges to Homeostasis** feature on the evolution and development of thermogenin and brown adipose tissue.

- Revised treatment of the ectotherm/endotherm, poikilotherm/homeotherm distinctions, with a revised Figure.

- A new summary Figure on the diversity in futile cycles.

- A modified discussion of Arrhenius plots to include more student-driven calculations as part of a Math in Physiology feature.

Chapter 16, Reproductive Physiology

- A new feature on pesticides targeting insect-specific pathways addresses how pesticides can be used to target insect development and reproduction.

- A Math in Physiology feature combines the concepts of allometry with the constraints on milk production.

We hope that you enjoy using this textbook. Please feel free to contact us at the email addresses below if you have any comments or suggestions on how we could make this book an even better tool to help you learn or teach animal physiology.

Chris Moyes
Queen's University
chris.moyes@queensu.ca

Trish Schulte
University of British Columbia
pschulte@zoology.ubc.ca

Supplements

COMPANION WEBSITE

This student resource features answers to the Review Questions and Concept Checks that appear in the text, chapter-specific quizzes, links to physiology labs and other relevant websites, an interactive glossary, and more. Please visit www.pearsoncanada.ca/moyes.

COMPUTERIZED TEST BANK

Pearson's computerized test banks allow instructors to filter and select questions to create quizzes, tests, or homework. Instructors can revise questions or add their own, and may be able to choose print or online options. These questions are also available in Microsoft Word format.

COURSESMART FOR STUDENTS

CourseSmart goes beyond traditional expectations—providing instant, online access to the required textbooks and course materials at an average savings of 60%. With instant access from any computer and the ability to search your text, you will find the content you need quickly, no matter where you are. And with online tools like highlighting and note-taking, you can save time and study efficiently. See all the benefits at www.coursesmart.com/students.

COURSESMART FOR INSTRUCTORS

CourseSmart goes beyond traditional expectations—providing instant, online access to the textbooks and course materials you need at a lower cost for students. And even as students save money, you can save time and hassle with a digital eTextbook that allows you to search for the most relevant content at the very moment you need it. Whether it's evaluating textbooks or creating lecture notes to help students with difficult concepts, CourseSmart can make life a little easier. See how when you visit www.coursesmart.com/instructors.

TECHNOLOGY SPECIALISTS

Pearson's Technology Specialists work with faculty and campus course designers to ensure that Pearson technology products, assessment tools, and online course materials are tailored to meet your specific needs. This highly qualified team is dedicated to helping schools take full advantage of a wide range of educational resources, by assisting in the integration of a variety of instructional materials and media formats. Your local Pearson Canada sales representative can provide you with more details on this service program.

PEARSON CUSTOM LIBRARY

For enrollments of at least 25 students, you can create your own textbook by choosing the chapters that best suit your own course needs. To begin building your custom text, visit www.pearsoncustomlibrary.com. You may also work with a dedicated Pearson Custom editor to create your ideal text—publishing your own original content or mixing and matching Pearson content. Contact your local Pearson Representative to get started.

Acknowledgments

Preparing the 3rd Edition of our textbook required a team of dedicated people to bring it to fruition. The Pearson Canada team conducted the extensive research needed to identify the strengths and weaknesses of our 2nd Edition. They also helped us revise the chapters, developing the manuscript into the finished product. A team of three editors managed the three-year revision process. Maurice Esses, Lise Dupont, and Lisa Rahn managed to keep us on track, successfully maintaining the delicate balance between motivation and persistence. It is impossible to imagine how the 3rd Edition could have been completed without their support.

The 3rd Edition continues to benefit from the work done by the developmental team in place for the 1st and 2nd Editions, notably Catherine Murphy, the developmental editor, Laura Southworth, our art development editor, and Susan Malloy and Marie Beaugureau, our project editors at Benjamin Cummings.

We would particularly like to thank various friends and colleagues who have provided input and suggestions on specific chapters. CDM would like to thank his colleagues at Queen's for their contributions to the new chapters on evolution of physiological systems (Steve Lougheed, Vicki Freisen) and comparative immunology (Bill Bendena, Virginia Walker), and to thank Doug Symes (University of Calgary) for his advice on the Cost of Transport feature. PMS would like to thank her colleagues in the comparative physiology group at UBC for their advice and support throughout this project, with particular thanks to Tony Farrell for suggestions regarding cardiac physiology, Bill Milsom for his advice on respiratory physiology, and Doug Altshuler for helpful discussions regarding ways to approach teaching neurophysiology and the nervous system.

REVIEWERS

We would also like to thank the instructors who reviewed the 3rd Edition manuscript:

Eli Asem, *Purdue University*
Adam Oliver Brown, *University of Ottawa*
Julian Christians, *Simon Fraser University*
Reyniel Cruz-Aguado, *Douglas College*
Rosa da Silva, *McMaster University*
Jeff W. Dawson, *Carleton University*
Heidi Englehardt, *University of Waterloo*
David H. Evans, *University of Florida*
Corey Flynn, *University of Calgary*
Wei Ge, *Chinese University of Hong Kong*
Kathleen Gilmour, *University of Ottawa*
Helga Guderley, *Université Laval*
Raymond P. Henry, *Auburn University*
Kelly S. Johnson, *Ohio University*
Kevin S. Kinney, *Depauw University*
Heather Koopman, *University of North Carolina at Wilmington*
Roswitha Marx, *University of Victoria*
Joanne Nash, *University of Toronto at Scarborough*
Linda Ogren, *University of California, Santa Cruz*
Robert J. Omeljaniuk, *Lakehead University*
Sushama Pavgi-Denver, *University of Michigan*
Scott D. Reid, *University of British Columbia*
Gregory Schmaltz, *University of the Fraser Valley*
Jason Schreer, *State University of New York at Potsdam*
James Staples, *University of Western Ontario*
Jonathon Stillman, *San Francisco State University*
Marva Sweeney-Nixon, *University of Prince Edward Island*
Steven Swoap, *Williams College*
Keith Tierney, *University of Alberta*
Helene Volkoff, *Memorial University*
Tracy L. E. Wagner, *Washburn University*

Principles of

Animal Physiology

THIRD EDITION

CHAPTER 1

Introduction to Physiological Principles

Learning Objectives

After reading this chapter, you should be able to:

1. Describe the levels of biological organization studied by physiologists.

2. Use examples to show how the laws of chemistry and physics are relevant to understanding physiological systems.

3. Outline how evolution results in diversity of both form and function and strong links between them in animals.

4. Discuss the processes involved in physiological regulation at multiple time scales.

FIGURE 1.1   Porcelain crab (Genus *Petrolisthes*)

Photo source: Frogkick/Fotolia.

I f you have ever been to the seashore, you will have noticed the intertidal zone—the area that is covered and uncovered by the tides each day. What you may not have realized is that the intertidal zone is one of the most challenging habitats on Earth. The cycle of tides can cause huge changes in the characteristics of the environment as the tide moves in and out. On hot days when the tide moves out, the temperature of an isolated tidepool in the high intertidal can more than double, while on cold winter days at northern latitudes the temperature can drop almost to freezing. During the day, oxygen levels may rise to several times normal due to the oxygen produced by photosynthesizing algae. At night, oxygen consumption due to respiration by the plants and animals in the tidepool can cause oxygen to drop to almost undetectable levels. These daily cycles of photosynthesis and respiration can also cause wide swings in the pH of the water, which can range from slightly acidic to very alkaline. Similarly, the salinity of a tidepool can increase on hot days as water evaporates, or decrease to nearly the salinity of freshwater on a very rainy day. For intertidal animals that live outside of tidepools, desiccation can be an important challenge, especially on sunny days in exposed areas of the habitat. All of these environmental changes are physically challenging for animals, and animals that live in the intertidal zone have physiological specializations that help them cope with their harsh environment.

Despite the challenging environmental conditions in the high intertidal zone, this zone is teeming with life. For example, Porcelain crabs—similar to the one shown in Figure 1.1—are common inhabitants of both the high intertidal and nearby subtidal zones in the rocky intertidal areas of many of the world's oceans. Animal physiologists seek to understand the mechanisms that allow species such as Porcelain crabs to survive and thrive in these highly variable conditions. The large variations in abiotic environmental parameters in high intertidal habitats are very different from the relatively constant conditions in the nearby subtidal habitats. Because subtidal habitats are always beneath the surface of the water, temperature, oxygen levels, salinity, and pH remain fairly constant both within a day and across seasons. Despite the radical differences in environmental conditions between subtidal and intertidal habitats, these habitats may be only a few meters apart in space. This feature makes the intertidal zone an intriguing place to study the physiological adaptations of the animals that live there.

Porcelain crabs are particularly useful animals for studying environmental adaptation because there are many related species that live in habitats ranging from the warm and constant conditions of the subtidal zone in the tropics to the extremely variable conditions of the high intertidal in the temperate zone. In fact, the largest genus of Porcelain crabs (genus *Petrolisthes*) contains over 100 species. By comparing the physiology of species from different habitats, it may be possible to understand the key processes that allow species to thrive in the challenging intertidal environment.

In *Petrolisthes*, there is a strong correlation between the maximum temperature of the habitat in which a species is found and the highest temperature at which the heart can beat. Species of Porcelain crabs that are found in the high intertidal in the hot tropics are able to maintain cardiac function at substantially higher temperatures than are species that are found in much cooler and more constant temperate subtidal habitats. These data suggest that the physiology of the cardiovascular system may play a role in setting the geographical distribution of Porcelain crabs.

In addition to helping to understand the present-day distribution of species such as Porcelain crabs, research in animal physiology can also help to make predictions about the likely responses of animals to environmental change. You might predict that the less hardy subtidal crabs found in the cool temperate zones would be the most likely to be vulnerable to the extreme heat waves associated with global warming, but instead the crabs that live in the hottest environments may be the species at the most risk. These high intertidal crabs are already living right at the edge of their thermal tolerance range, and they have limited ability to adjust their thermal tolerance between seasons compared with their temperate zone relatives. For these high intertidal tropical species even a small increase in extreme temperatures that they experience during a heat wave is likely to be fatal. In fact, there is already evidence suggesting that some species of Porcelain crabs have disappeared from the southern edge of their species range over the last hundred years.

The example of Porcelain crabs illustrates the important role that animal physiologists can play in addressing both fundamental biological questions as well as applied questions with practical implications. In this chapter we explore some of the unifying themes that tie together both the basic and applied aspects of the discipline of animal physiology. We return to these themes throughout this book as we explore the fascinating science of how animals work. ◾

▌OVERVIEW

In the words of the renowned physiologist Knut Schmidt-Nielsen, animal physiology is *"the study of how animals work."* Animal physiologists study the structure and function of the various parts of an animal, and how these parts work together to allow animals to perform their normal behaviors and to respond to their environments. Almost a million different species of animals have been described by scientists, and it is estimated that as many as 7 million may currently live on Earth. Each of these species has acquired countless unique properties through **evolution**. Animal physiologists are interested in both the *causes* and the *consequences* of this great diversity.

Physiology is a central discipline in biology linking the underlying molecular and cellular mechanisms to characteristics of whole organisms such as performance and fitness (Figure 1.2). The physiological properties of an animal are aspects of the animal's **phenotype**, which includes all of the observable traits of an organism at all levels of biological organization, from the biochemistry of the cell to the anatomy, physiology, and behavior of the animal. Physiological traits, like other characteristics of animals, are determined in large part by the **genes** of the genome—the **genotype**—but are also influenced by the way the genes are regulated, particularly in response to external conditions. Thus, both the genotype of an organism and its environment interact through development to produce the phenotype of the adult organism.

Physiologists must be able to understand how processes occurring at the molecular, cellular, tissue, organ, and organ system levels of organization interact to influence the physiological phenotype. Each physiological process is a product of the activities of complex tissues, organs, and systems that can arise through complex patterns of genetic regulation of countless cells. The phenotype is itself the product of processes at many levels of biological organization, including the biochemical, cellular, tissue, organ, and organ system levels. Together these processes interact to produce complex behaviors and physiological responses.

An individual genotype can have the capacity to produce more than one phenotype. Although the same genes

---

FIGURE 1.2 **Physiology is a central discipline in biology**

Morphology, physiology, and behavior are key components of the phenotype of an adult organism. These phenotypes are the result of interactions between the genotype and the environment acting on processes at all levels of biological organization. Variation in morphology, physiology, and behavior can influence performance and reproductive success. Thus, physiology has implications for evolutionary change in the genotype of a population over time.

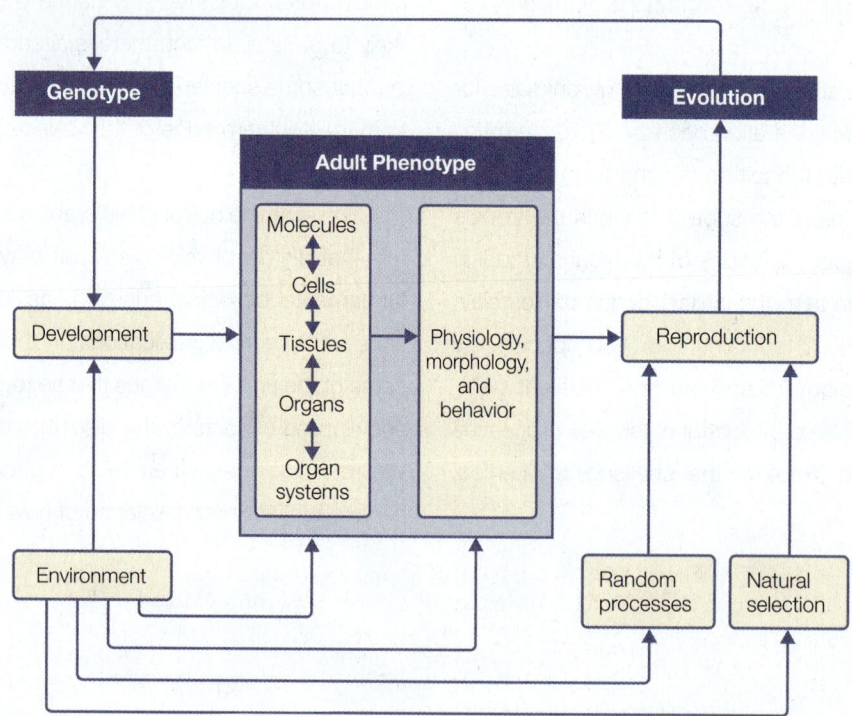

are found in each cell, they are regulated in combinations to allow animals to develop distinct tissues.

In addition to orchestrating the normal developmental program, the genotype controls the way animals can alter their phenotype in response to physiological and environmental conditions. For example, if identical twins were raised in different places, it is possible that one twin might grow taller than the other due to differences in diet. Every individual genotype has a capacity to differ in complex, often unpredictable ways because of the way the genes respond to external conditions. Throughout this book you will encounter examples of the many ways in which organisms alter their physiological systems to respond to environmental change.

Ultimately, the phenotype (**morphology,** physiology, and behavior) of an animal influences its reproductive success. Differential survival of organisms with distinct phenotypes may result in evolutionary change in the genotype of a population over many generations. As a result, animal physiologists also consider how evolution shapes physiological phenotypes.

Evolutionary change is the ultimate cause of the enormous diversity of animal species. Despite this diversity, there are important commonalities in the physiological functioning of all animals. In this chapter we examine some of the unifying themes that are common to all of physiology. Throughout this book, we will return to these themes as we examine how animals work.

UNIFYING THEMES IN PHYSIOLOGY

Despite the great diversity of organisms on Earth, there are many commonalities within physiology—unifying themes that apply to all physiological processes. It is possible to outline the common themes in physiology in a number of ways. We have chosen to highlight four fundamental themes that we focus on throughout this book (Table 1.1).

Integration in Physiology

Biologists often organize the living world by dividing it into what are termed *levels of biological organization* (Figure 1.3). Processes at each level of organization interact to produce the processes at the next level of organization. For example, atoms interact to form molecules, and molecules can be assembled into macromolecules. Macromolecules are organized into biochemical pathways and networks, and these biochemical interactions are grouped together into cells, which are the lowest level of biological organization capable of independent life. In multicellular organisms such as animals, cells are assembled into tissues, organs, and organ systems, which work together to allow the whole organism to perform its functions. Organisms interact in populations, and groups of interbreeding populations form species. Species interact to form communities, ecosystems, and ultimately the entire biosphere.

Table 1.1 Unifying themes in animal physiology	
Unifying Theme	**Related Ideas**
Physiology is integrative.	Animal physiologists study phenomena at multiple levels of organization, from molecules to ecosystems. Animal physiologists address both basic and applied questions.
Physiological processes obey the laws of physics and chemistry.	The mechanical properties of materials influence physiological processes. Electrical laws are needed to understand the functions of membranes in all cells, including excitable cells such as neurons and muscle. Chemical laws, which govern interactions between biological molecules, help to explain the effects of temperature on physiological processes. Physical laws can be used to explain why body size affects many physiological processes.
Physiological processes are shaped by evolution.	Natural selection can cause a relationship between form and function. Differences among taxa can be adaptations as a result of evolution by natural selection, or can result from random processes. Similarity among traits can be due to homology (shared ancestry) or homoplasy (independent evolution).
Physiological processes are usually regulated.	Negative feedback loops help maintain homeostasis. Positive feedback loops generate an explosive response. Acclimation and acclimatization allow longer term, but usually reversible, adjustments to environmental change. Irreversible phenotypic adjustments can also occur during development and some can be passed across generations.

FIGURE 1.3 **Levels of biological organization**

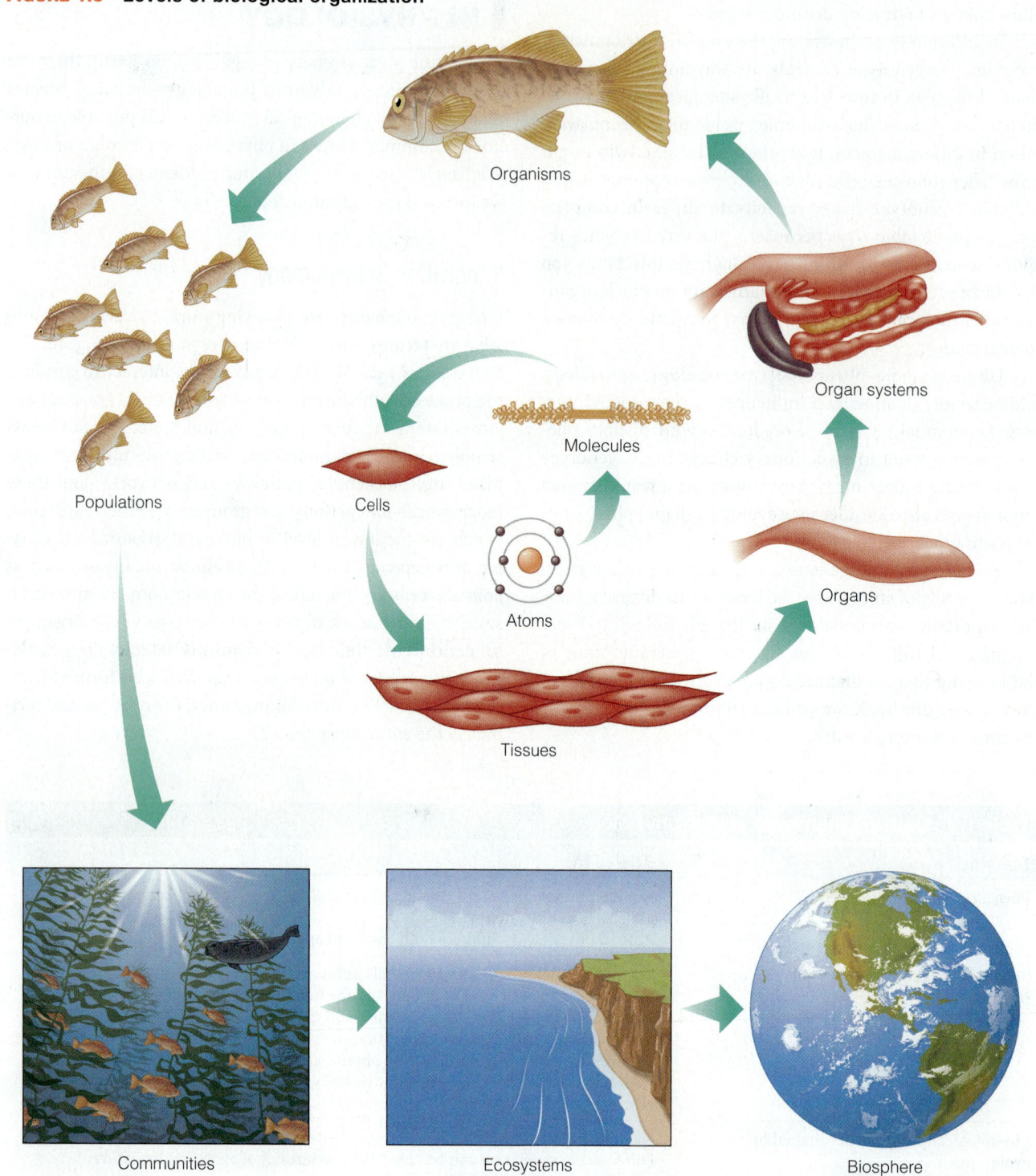

Organisms

Populations

Cells

Molecules

Atoms

Organ systems

Organs

Tissues

Communities

Ecosystems

Biosphere

Animal physiologists study phenomena at multiple levels of organization

Although animal physiology is characterized by its focus on how individual organisms function, physiologists usually consider multiple levels of organization as they strive to understand how animals work. Often a physiologist interested in a process at one level of organization also studies its function at a lower level. For example, someone studying how a salmon can live in salt water during part of its life and freshwater during another part might study the patterns of changes in ion levels in the blood and also study the cellular mechanisms in the gills that control those processes. This approach, known as **reductionism**, assumes that we can learn about a system by studying the function of its parts.

Reductionist approaches can be extremely illuminating, and have been the basis of many important biological discoveries, but ultimately many processes have characteristics that are not apparent simply by examining the component parts. This feature of complex systems is called **emergence**, which is just another way of saying that the whole is often more than the sum of its parts. The **emergent properties** of a system are properties that can be observed at one level of biological organization and that are due to the interactions of the component parts of the system. These emergent properties can be difficult to predict by studying each part in isolation. Physiologists are usually interested in emergent properties, and thus physiologists study how molecules, cells, and tissues interact to produce the complex system that is an organism.

Animal physiologists also think about how physiological processes acting in an individual organism affect the function of the organism within populations and communities. Thus, animal physiologists also are concerned about the ecological consequences of physiological processes.

Animal physiologists address basic and applied questions

Animal physiologists ask a wide range of questions that include aspects of both basic and applied biology. Basic research in animal physiology provides profound insights into how animals work and the evolutionary causes and consequences of variation in physiological processes. Animal physiologists ask questions such as: How can animals live in extreme environments? How do processes at the cellular and molecular level influence the performance of animals in the environment? Physiology also has enormous practical importance. To emphasize the practical importance of the study of animal physiology, each chapter of this book after the first three introductory chapters includes a box (Applications) that highlights an application of physiology to a real-world problem.

For example, there are important applications of physiology in conservation biology and ecology. As we saw with the Porcelain crabs that are the subject of the opening essay of this chapter, understanding the physiological functions of animals can help us predict their responses to environmental changes such as pollution, climate warming, and ocean acidification.

Another area in which animal physiology plays an important practical role is in understanding human health and disease. Medical doctors need a very strong understanding of physiology to understand and treat diseases and conditions such as heart disease, obesity, and diabetes that are very common in modern societies. Similarly, veterinary medicine relies on physiological knowledge for the treatment of diseases in animals. Agricultural production of animals for food

also requires substantial knowledge of animal physiology to help develop optimal rearing practices to maintain health and promote the growth of farm animals.

Much of our medical knowledge is gained from research on animals, and thus understanding animal physiology is crucial for those involved in medical research. Such research is often performed on what are termed "**model organisms**," or species that are chosen because they have features that make them particularly suitable for specific experiments. This approach of using an animal model with features that are favorable for scientific study is known as the **August Krogh principle**: *For every biological problem there is an organism on which it can be most conveniently studied.*

Model organisms are studied by a wide community of researchers because (1) they have features that are conducive to experimentation and (2) understanding a process in the model provides insight into how the process works in other species of interest. Perhaps the most famous example of such a model system in physiology is the squid. Unlike mammals, squid have some specialized neurons that are large enough to be easily seen and readily manipulated. The use of squid as a model system was critical in the development of our understanding of how neurons work in all animals.

> ## CONCEPT CHECK
>
> 1. How would you define physiology?
> 2. What is a model organism in the context of physiological research?

Physics and Chemistry: The Basis of Physiology

The integrative nature of physiology is particularly evident when we consider the role of chemistry and physics in physiology. Animals are constructed from natural materials and thus obey the same physical and chemical laws that apply to everything that we see around us. Physiologists often borrow concepts and techniques from the physical and chemical sciences, including engineering, to help them understand how animals work. As a result of this focus on chemistry and physics, physiology is a quantitative science. To emphasize the quantitative nature of physiology, each chapter of this book after the first three introductory chapters includes a box (Math in Physiology) that highlights an application of quantitative reasoning in physiology. You will also find a series of quantitative questions at the end of each chapter to help you practice these skills.

The laws of diffusion help to explain the evolution of animal form and function

The process of diffusion affects almost every physiological process, so understanding the physical laws that govern diffusion provides insights into the form, function, and physiology of animals. The eminent medical physiologist and physicist Adolf Fick developed what are now known as Fick's Laws of diffusion, which you will encounter at multiple points throughout this book. Fick's first law demonstrates that substances diffuse from areas of high concentration to areas of low concentration. This law is a special case of a much more general principle in physics and physiology: that substances move from areas of high potential energy to areas of low potential energy. This movement is a consequence of the second law of thermodynamics, which states that isolated systems spontaneously move toward a state of maximum **entropy**. This means that over time, differences in concentration, charge, temperature, or pressure will tend to equalize within a system, unless energy is added to maintain this difference.

A concentration gradient can be thought of as a source of potential energy that can be used to drive diffusion. Similarly, a voltage gradient, which represents a source of electrical potential energy, can drive the movement of charged particles. The fact that both concentration and voltage gradients can drive movements of substances is important in physiology because many important physiological processes, such as signaling in neurons and muscle cells and the active transport of materials into cells, involve the movement of charged molecules such as sodium across membranes. For these charged particles both the concentration gradient and the electrical gradient are important for determining the extent and rate of diffusion.

The same principles that apply to the diffusion of substances apply to the conduction of **heat**. Heat flows from areas of high temperature to areas of low temperature. As you will see in Chapter 15, the form and function of many animals is shaped by the need to regulate heat loss or gain. Pressure gradients also act as sources of potential energy that can move substances. Substances will move from areas of high pressure to areas of low pressure. As you will see in Chapters 9 and 11, this relationship is fundamental to understanding the functioning of the circulatory and respiratory systems in animals.

Fick's second law considers the amount of diffusion that occurs across a surface such as a cell membrane or an epithelial tissue. This law summarizes the idea that the amount of a substance that diffuses across a surface is proportional to the area of that surface and inversely proportional to the distance across which the substance must diffuse. Fick's second law is critical for understanding the form and function of epithelia such as the lungs and the gut that are involved in the exchange of substances by diffusion. These epithelia must have as large a surface area as possible and be as thin as possible to maximize the exchange of materials.

In addition, we can demonstrate from considering Brownian motion, or the random movement of particles in a solution, that the time needed for a particle to diffuse across a given distance is proportional to the square of the distance. The practical consequence of this relationship is that diffusion is rapid across short distances, but extremely slow across long distances. For example, a molecule such as sodium can diffuse across the width of a typical cell membrane (~10 nanometers) in less than 25 nanoseconds, but would take almost 30 days to diffuse across 10 centimeters and more than 15 years to diffuse across one meter (the approximate distance from the heart to the feet in an adult human) under typical physiological conditions. The limitations of diffusion across long distances help to explain why gas exchange surfaces such as lungs and gills are extremely thin, and why animals that are larger than a few millimeters in diameter must have **circulatory systems** to move substances around their bodies.

Mechanical theory helps us understand how organisms work

Each material has physical properties that are useful in some contexts but not others. It would be a mistake for an engineer to design a skyscraper from Styrofoam, or a kite of concrete. Likewise, biological materials, or biomaterials—**proteins, carbohydrates**, and **lipids**—also have characteristic physical properties that make them useful for some processes but not others. The physicochemical characteristics of these biomaterials are determined by their molecular properties. For example, the **aorta**, which is one of the largest blood vessels in a vertebrate, contains high levels of the protein collagen. This strong structural protein helps the aorta withstand the high **pressure** generated by the heart. Smaller blood vessels such as the capillaries that are not exposed to such high mechanical forces have much less collagen in their walls, which allows them to be thin to maximize the exchange of materials by diffusion.

Differences in the molecular properties of proteins may be a result of differences in the sequences of the proteins, but they can also be the result of the modification of an existing protein. The protein **keratin** provides an example of a network of proteins that can be made more rigid by the addition of bonds that cross-link multiple keratin proteins together. The keratin present in fingernails is heavily cross-linked, which helps to make it stronger and less likely to bend. The keratin in hair has fewer cross-links, which allows it to be more flexible.

In addition to mechanical properties, other engineering concepts such as flow, pressure, resistance, stress, and strain play important roles in physiology. For example, understanding how the heart pumps blood through the blood vessels has many parallels with understanding how mechanical plumbing systems work. Both physiologists and engineers must take into account factors such as pressure gradients, the power of the pump, and the resistance in the plumbing. Thus, the principles of physics that apply to engineering also apply to physiological systems.

Electrical potentials are a fundamental physiological currency

Just as we use electricity to power many of the machines we use in our daily lives, animals use electricity to power cellular activities. Cells establish a charge difference across biological membranes by moving ions and molecules to create ion and electrical gradients. All cells and many organelles within cells rely on this potential difference, or **membrane potential**, to drive processes that are needed for survival such as the movement of essential molecules across membranes. Animals also use changes in electrical potentials to send signals within and between cells, helping to coordinate the complex processes of the body. Muscle cells and neurons, two cell types that are found only in animals, use changes in membrane potential to send signals. Thus, electrical theory has played an important role in helping physiologists to understand the way that neurons and muscles work.

Temperature affects physiological processes

Because physiological processes have their basis in physical and chemical laws, they are profoundly affected by temperature. The rate of most chemical reactions increases as temperature increases. Increasing the temperature increases the energy of molecules and causes an increase in the number of collisions between molecules in a closed system. Most reactions involve the breakage or formation of chemical bonds, which can occur only if molecules are close to each other. So the more molecular collisions occur, the faster the rate of a chemical reaction. However, at high temperatures many of the intermolecular interactions that stabilize proteins begin to break down and protein function declines. Because most biochemical reactions involve proteins as **catalysts**, when these catalysts break down, the rate of the reaction falls. The effects of temperature on molecular events combine to influence the way animals interact with environmental temperature. Thus, temperature has a profound effect on processes at all levels of biological organization.

Biochemical and physiological patterns are influenced by body size

From tiny zooplankton weighing less than a milligram to blue whales weighing over 100,000 kilograms, animals vary greatly in body size, and these differences have profound effects on both the shape of an organism and on the physiological processes that allow them to perform their functions. The relationships between anatomical or physiological traits and body size are termed **scaling** relationships. When morphology or physiology change in direct proportion to body mass, the scaling relationship is said to be **isometric** (from the Greek *iso* = same, and *metric* = measure). However, it has long been known that many structures and processes do not increase proportionately with body mass. In fact, this phenomenon was first discussed by Galileo Galilei in 1638, when he described how the **bones** of larger animals are proportionately thicker than the bones of smaller animals. Figure 1.4 shows a comparison of the skeleton of a cat and an elephant, drawn at the same body size so that you can easily compare the relative thickness of the bones. Note how the bones of an elephant are much thicker than the bones of a cat. When body shape or physiology changes disproportionately as body size increases, the relationship is said to be **allometric** (from the Greek *allo* = different, and *metric* = measure).

FIGURE 1.4   A cat skeleton and an elephant skeleton, drawn at the same size

Note the proportionally thicker limb bones of the elephant.

Cat   Elephant

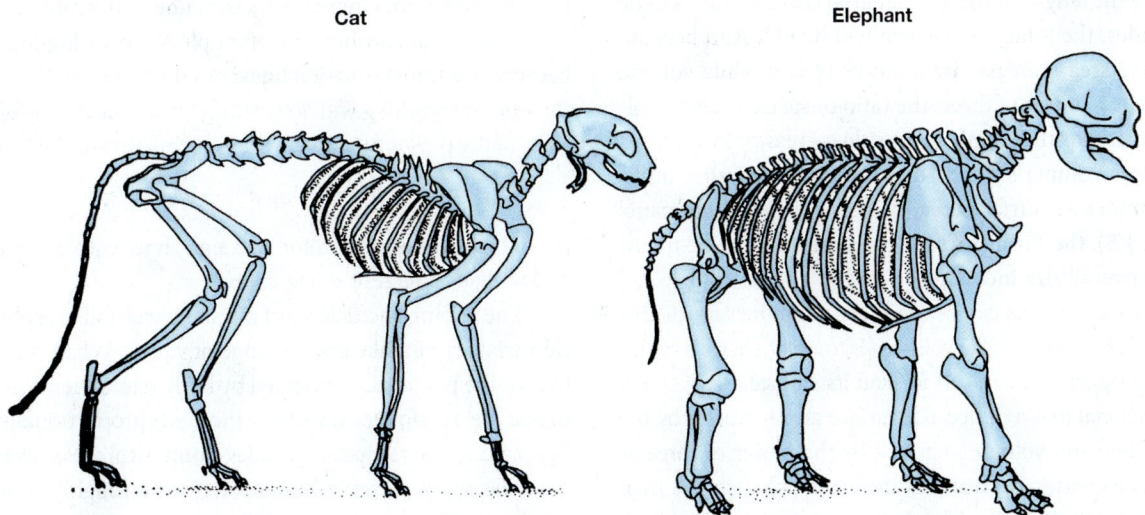

Figure source: Pough, F. Harvey; Janis, Christine M.; Heiser, John B., *Vertebrate Life*, 9th Ed" ©2013, p. 174. Reprinted and Electronically reproduced by permission of Pearson Education, Inc., Upper Saddle River, New Jersey.

FIGURE 1.5   The surface area-to-volume ratio of an object decreases as size increases

Surface area-to-volume ratio can be maintained if a larger object is made up of multiple smaller objects, each with its own surface area.

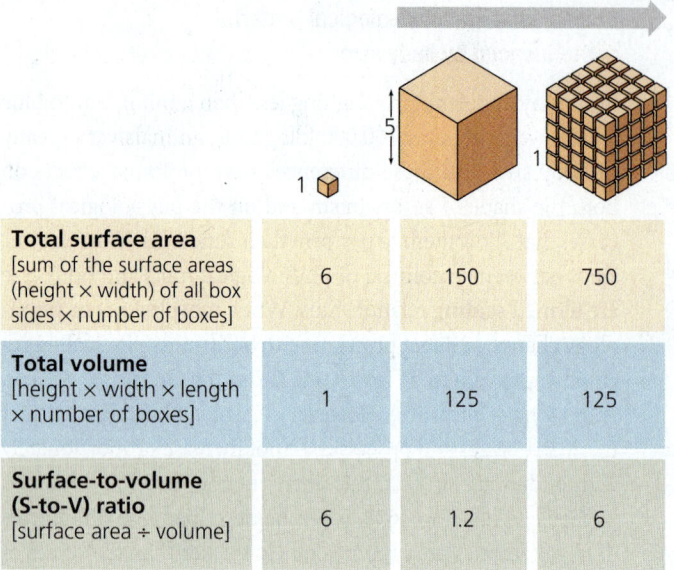

Surface area increases while total volume remains constant

Total surface area [sum of the surface areas (height × width) of all box sides × number of boxes]	6	150	750
Total volume [height × width × length × number of boxes]	1	125	125
Surface-to-volume (S-to-V) ratio [surface area ÷ volume]	6	1.2	6

Figure source: Reece, Jane B.; Urry, Lisa A.; Cain, Michael L; Wasserman, Steven A.; Minorsky, Peter V.; Jackson, Robert B., *Campbell Biology*, 9th Ed., ©2011, p. 99. Reprinted and Electronically reproduced by permission of Pearson Education, Inc., Upper Saddle River, New Jersey.

The fundamental reason why the bones of an elephant are proportionately thicker than the bones of a cat has to do with the relationship between area and volume (Figure 1.5). Consider a hypothetical animal shaped like a cube. The volume of a cube is equal to the length of the side of the cube to the third power (L^3). The surface area of each side of the cube is equal to the length of the side squared (L^2). Because a cube has six sides, the total surface area will be $6L^2$. And because the surface area increases by a power of two while volume increases by a power of three, the ratio of surface area to volume decreases as the length of the side increases. In contrast, if the larger volume is made up of repeating smaller units, each with its own surface area (as shown in the right panel of Figure 1.5), the surface area-to-volume ratio can be maintained as overall size increases.

Similar arguments can be made based on the surface area and volume of a sphere. The volume (V) of a sphere with radius r will be proportional to $(4/3) \pi r^3$ and its surface area (A) will be proportional to $4 \pi r^2$. Because surface area increases by the power of two and volume increases by the power of three as the radius increases, surface area increases by much less than volume as body size rises. This is relevant to the size of limb bones because the strength of a bone is related to its cross-sectional area (πr^2), but the weight that the bone must support

is directly related to the animal's volume, which increases as $(4/3) \pi r^3$. If animal skeletons scaled isometrically, the bones would not be sufficiently strong to support the weight of a large animal, because the cross-sectional area of the bone (its strength) would not increase as fast as would the weight of the animal. Thus, larger animals have thicker bones than would be expected based on the proportions of smaller animals, as can be seen in Figure 1.4.

Surface area-to-volume relationships apply to more than just limb bones. In fact, these relationships are pervasive in biology. The surface of an organism, whether unicellular or multicellular, is involved in exchange of materials with the environment, while the volume of the organism is responsible for the processing and use of those materials. Because volume increases more than does surface area as radius increases, the surface available for exchange of materials quickly becomes limiting. Of course, one way to get around this limitation is to have a different shape. For example, a very long thin cell would have a much higher surface area-to-volume ratio than would a spherical cell. In multicellular organisms such as animals, exchange surfaces are often highly folded to maximize surface area.

We can describe scaling relationships mathematically using a power function, which takes the form:

$$y = aM^b$$

In this case $y =$ surface area, M is the body mass (or volume), a is a constant, and b is a term called the **scaling coefficient**. For a cube or a sphere, this power function would be:

$$y = aM^{2/3}$$

The scaling coefficient for a cube or a sphere is 2/3 (or 0.67) because surface area increases as the square of the radius, while volume increases as the cube of the radius.

Scaling relationships are often plotted on a log-log scale, because this transformation linearizes the equation. Because of the rules for working with logarithms, if we take the log of both sides of the power function, we get an equation of the form:

$$\log y = \log a + b \log M$$

This is the equation for a straight line, with a slope of b and with an intercept of $\log a$.

The scaling coefficients of physiological and morphological variables can take a wide range of values. When b is equal to zero the process is unaffected by body size. When b is equal to one the physiological variable increases proportionally with body mass, and the process scales isometrically. For example, the mass of the heart in humans follows a roughly isometric relationship with body mass. When b is negative, the variable decreases with body size. The heart rate of mammals is an example of a physiological process with negative b. Thus, the heart rate of an elephant is much lower than the heart rate of a shrew. The claws of fiddler crabs provide an example of a trait that scales with a scaling coefficient greater than one. Larger fiddler crabs have claws that are even larger than you would predict based on the increase in their body size alone.

Many physiological processes have a scaling coefficient that is between zero and one. Metabolic rate is an important example of a physiological process that has a positive scaling coefficient that is less than one. The scaling of metabolic rate has been the subject of intense interest from physiologists. In the late 1800s Max Rubner reported that the metabolic rate of dogs of various sizes was constant when body surface area was taken into account, suggesting that metabolism has a scaling coefficient of 0.67. In other words, this observation means that the metabolic rate of one gram of tissue from a large dog is lower than the metabolic rate of one gram of tissue from a small dog. Rubner developed a hypothesis about heat dissipation to explain this rather puzzling observation. Mammals such as dogs are **endotherms** that maintain a relatively constant body temperature by generating metabolic heat. If metabolism scaled isometrically with body size, Rubner suggested that large dogs would generate too much heat to dissipate across their relatively small surface area, and thus they must have lower metabolic rates per gram of tissue than small dogs.

Rubner's hypothesis explaining the allometric scaling of metabolic rate was widely accepted until the 1930s when Max Kleiber assembled a much larger data set relating body size and metabolic rate in a variety of species of birds and mammals. Kleiber's work suggested the value of the scaling coefficient was closer to 0.75 (3/4) rather than the value of 0.67 (2/3) expected from Rubner's studies, implying that surface area-to-volume ratios cannot explain metabolic scaling relationships. This discrepancy has resulted in a long-standing controversy in physiology. Normally reticent physiologists have been inspired to engage in animated—sometimes vitriolic—arguments about both the exact value of b and the underlying mechanisms associated with the scaling of various physiological processes. We discuss the scaling of metabolism in more detail later in this book.

CONCEPT CHECK

3. Why do the rates of biochemical reactions increase as temperature increases? Do they do so infinitely?

4. What is allometric scaling?

Form, Function, and Evolution

One of the major unifying themes of physiology is that form and function are connected. It is impossible to understand physiology (function) without an understanding of form (anatomy) and vice versa. The relationship between structure and function is often so strong that it is possible to make inferences about function simply by looking at structure. For example, Figure 1.6 shows the anatomy of the digestive systems of a coyote (*Canis latrans*) and a koala (*Phascolarctos cinereus*). These mammals are of similar size but have very different feeding strategies. Coyotes are omnivores, but they have a strong preference for meat. They cannot eat tough or fibrous plant material, such as leaves and grasses. Koalas are obligate herbivores that eat a plant-based diet mostly consisting of the leaves of certain kinds of *Eucalyptus* trees. *Eucalyptus* leaves contain compounds that are toxic to most animals. The leaves are also extremely fibrous and have low nutritional quality.

The **cellulose** and other fibrous material in plant tissues such as eucalyptus leaves are much more difficult to digest than are animal flesh and softer plant material such as fruits. Because the diet of a coyote is relatively simple to digest, these animals have a shorter intestinal tract than do herbivores such as koalas. The koala has a much longer digestive tract because its extremely fibrous diet takes much longer to digest.

One major physiological challenge for animals such as koalas that eat a diet of very fibrous plant materials is that no animals express the **enzymes** that are needed to digest compounds such as cellulose, which are a major component of fibrous plant tissues. Koalas are able to use fibrous material such as eucalyptus leaves for food because the cellulose in the leaves is digested by symbiotic bacteria that live within the koala's gut. Most of the cellulose-digesting bacteria are found within the cecum of the gut. From Figure 1.6 you can see that the cecum of a koala is much larger than the cecum of a coyote. In general, carnivores and most omnivores have a relatively small cecum, whereas many herbivores have a very large cecum.

The relationship between the form and the function of the digestive tract is very clear in all mammals. If you came across an unfamiliar mammal, you would likely be able to make a fairly accurate prediction about the type of diet it consumes simply by examining the structure of its digestive tract.

Form and function are the products of evolution

One of the fundamental challenges of animal physiology is to understand and account for the great diversity of animal body forms and the strategies that animals use to cope with their environments. Consider the neck of a giraffe, which, in relation to its body size, is far longer than the neck of its closest living relative, the okapi. When a physiologist thinks about the neck of a giraffe, what question first springs to mind? A respiratory physiologist might wonder: *How* can a giraffe breathe through such a long neck? A cardiovascular physiologist might wonder: How can a giraffe's heart pump blood all the way up to its head? These mechanistic questions are amenable to the experimental methods of physiology and can be addressed using many of

FIGURE 1.6   **Form and function in the vertebrate digestive system**

The digestive systems of omnivores such as a coyote (*Canis latrans*) are typically much shorter than those of herbivores such as a koala (*Phascolarctos cinereus*). Also note the difference in size of the cecum between these species. The cecum is home to symbiotic bacteria that help to digest the cellulose in the eucalyptus leaves that form a major part of a koala's diet.

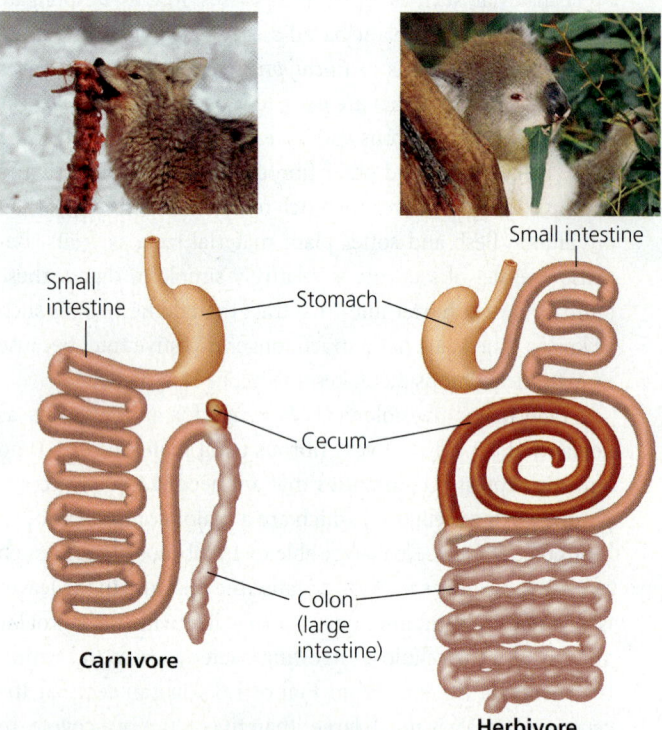

Carnivore

Herbivore

Small intestine

Small intestine

Stomach

Cecum

Colon (large intestine)

Figure source: Urry, Lisa A.; Cain, Michael L; Wasserman, Steven A.; Minorsky, Peter V.; Jackson, Robert B.; Reece, Jane B., *Campbell Biology In Focus*, 1st Ed., ©2014, p. 677. Reprinted and Electronically reproduced by permission of Pearson Education, Inc., Upper Saddle River, New Jersey. *Photo source:* (koala) Tom Brakefield/Getty Images; (coyote) Blickwinkel/ Alamy.

the techniques and conceptual approaches we discuss in this book. In contrast, an evolutionary physiologist might wonder: *Why* does a giraffe have a long neck? This question actually encompasses two different kinds of thinking. If we wish to address the **proximate cause** of the giraffe's long neck, which involves the immediate physiological or biochemical basis of this trait, we might examine the genes that specify the size or number of vertebrae in the skeleton. Alternatively, we might wish to understand the **ultimate cause** of the giraffe's long neck: whether long necks provided an evolutionary advantage to the ancestors of the giraffe. To address these ultimate questions we need to consider the impact of evolutionary change and the adaptive significance of the physiological traits that we study. The form and function, and thus the physiology, of animals are the products of evolution, and can only be fully understood when this evolutionary history is taken into account.

Animals have many traits in common

Although it is easy to be overwhelmed by the diversity in animal form and function, animal biologists strive to understand the nature of this diversity. One of the best ways to understand how an animal works is to establish in which ways the animal is similar to other organisms. Some animal traits are shared among all organisms, some among all animals, and some among related animals (lineages). Other traits are truly unique to the species being studied.

When a new species of insect is discovered deep in the Amazon jungle, we already know many of its features. Like all eukaryotic organisms, it will possess a genome of DNA, proteins of the same 20 **amino acids**, and phospholipid membranes. Like other animals, its cells will be connected to each other with proteins such as collagen and elastin, and it will have nerves and muscles that allow it to sense the world around it and move from place to place. Like other invertebrates, it will lack a spinal cord. Like other arthropods, it will have an exoskeleton of chitin. Like other insects, it will have six legs and paired wings. We can be reasonably certain of these features because the new species of insect has an evolutionary history that included, at some point in the last billion years, ancestors that it shared with other insects, invertebrates, **metazoans**, and ultimately all eukaryotic organisms. Thus, species that are closely related to each other are likely to share more features and species that are distantly related are likely to share fewer features.

Disentangling the complex interrelationships among the great diversity of physiological processes in animals requires a solid understanding of the processes that generate evolutionary change in organisms.

What is adaptation?

The word **adaptation** has two distinct meanings within the context of physiology. Many evolutionary biologists argue that the word *adaptation* should *only* be used to refer to the product or process of evolution by natural selection, that is, a change in a population or group of organisms over evolutionary time. However, physiologists often use the word *adaptation* as a synonym for the word *remodeling*. For example, a medical physiologist might discuss exercise adaptations: the changes in the muscles and heart that occur during exercise training. In this book, the word *adaptation* is used strictly to refer to evolutionary adaptation, but it is important that you learn to make the distinction between this definition and the way the term is sometimes used by other scientists and the general community.

To an evolutionary physiologist, an adaptation is a trait that arose via a process such as natural selection that conveys an increase in reproductive success. Thus, an evolutionary adaptation is the result of processes that occur over generations, rather than within the lifetime of a single individual. The evolution of insecticide resistance in insects provides an excellent example of the principles of adaptive evolution. Over the last 50 years, chemical insecticides such as organophosphates have been used to kill insects that harm crops or carry disease. Organophosphates kill insects by inhibiting acetylcholinesterase, an enzyme that is vital for neuronal transmission. When we use an organophosphate insecticide, it kills off most of the insects in a population, but the few rare individuals with beneficial mutations survive and reproduce. This differential survival changes the structure of the population.

We can see examples of the evolution of insecticide resistance in *Culex pipiens* (the common house mosquito). Some mosquitoes have mutations in the *acetylcholinesterase* gene that make the enzyme more tolerant of the insecticide. Other mosquitoes have extra copies of the **esterase** gene, which encodes an enzyme that converts the organophosphate into a less toxic form. These mutations are vital for survival in the presence of the insecticide, but in the absence of insecticide the individuals carrying these mutations are at a disadvantage. Mosquitoes that overproduce the esterase protein use energy that could serve other physiological functions; those with the mutated acetylcholinesterase have an enzyme that does not function quite as well as the nonmutant (or *wild-type*) protein. Thus, the insecticide-resistant genotypes are superior to wild-type genotypes only when the insecticides are present.

We can distill several general principles about the process of evolutionary adaptation from the example of insecticide tolerance in mosquitoes. For adaptive evolution to occur:

1. There must be variation among individuals in the trait under consideration.
2. The trait must be heritable—genetically determined and passed on to offspring.
3. The trait must increase the fitness (reproductive success) of the individuals that have the trait.
4. The relative fitness of the different genotypes depends on the environment. If the environment changes, the trait may no longer be beneficial.

Not all differences are evolutionary adaptations

Not all evolution is adaptive. For example, **genetic drift**, or random changes in the frequency of particular genotypes in a population over time, can result in substantial differences in the phenotype of two populations, independent of any adaptive evolution. Genetic drift is most likely to occur in small populations and is a result of happenstance, not of differences in fitness. If a forest fire kills most of the individuals of a population, the few survivors may happen to display a different genotype frequency than the ancestral

population. After a number of generations, the derived population may differ from the ancestral population, but not for any reason related to natural selection and fitness. This example of genetic drift is known as the **founder effect**. Genetic drift and selection can also act in opposition. For example, beneficial mutations can be lost from a population simply due to genetic drift. Genetic drift is one example of processes that result in **neutral evolution**, or changes in populations that are not due to differences in fitness.

Because of the potential for random changes to occur in populations over time, physiologists must always be careful to avoid assuming that a particular difference between species or populations has a function that has been shaped by adaptive evolution. When comparing physiological traits among species, it is important to consider the evolutionary history of the groups being compared. For example, llamas (*Lama glama*) and vicuñas (*Vicugna vicugna*) are mammals that live in high-altitude habitats in South America. Their hemoglobin, a molecule that helps to carry oxygen in the blood, has a very high **affinity** for oxygen compared with that of lowland mammals such as cows and sheep. This high affinity for oxygen is potentially advantageous at high altitude where the partial pressure of oxygen is low, as it could allow the animal to extract oxygen from the air more efficiently. This match between the phenotype of the llama hemoglobin and the environment in which llamas live has been used as evidence that their high-affinity hemoglobin may have arisen as an adaptation to high altitude. However, llamas and vicuñas are members of the family Camelidae. Other members of this family, such as the one-humped camel, or dromedary (*Camelus dromedarius*), also have hemoglobin with very high oxygen affinity, but do not live at high altitudes. The lowland-living shared ancestor of llamas and dromedaries likely had high-affinity hemoglobin; therefore the high oxygen affinity of llama hemoglobin is unlikely to be a specific adaptation to high altitude. Instead, the high oxygen affinity may be a preadaptation, or exaptation, that may have allowed them to colonize high-altitude habitats.

From these examples it is clear that physiologists must be extremely careful when exploring the ultimate cause of difference between populations or species. It can be tempting to develop adaptive explanations to account for differences among populations or species that could have arisen via a variety of mechanisms. Seemingly plausible adaptive explanations of traits are called "just so stories" by analogy to the famous children's book by Rudyard Kipling that contains stories such as "How the Camel Got His Hump." In order to rigorously argue that a particular physiological phenotype is adaptive, it is necessary to demonstrate that the phenotype is heritable, that it had a function that has been shaped by natural selection in the ancestors of the modern animals being studied, and that it increases the fitness of individuals carrying the phenotype.

Phenotypes may be homologous or analogous

As we discussed for the example of hemoglobins in camels and llamas, phenotypic traits can be similar among organisms due to **homology**, because of inheritance from a shared ancestor. However, structures that are not obviously similar can still be homologous. The classic example of such homologies is the limbs of vertebrates (Figure 1.7). Despite their diverse shapes, the flippers of a marine mammal, the wings of a bird, the legs of a dog, and the arms of a human all share a common ancestry, and have many underlying structural similarities. They all contain similar bones, but the shapes and relative sizes of these bones are altered in the different groups, resulting in substantial differences in the overall shape of the limb.

Not all traits that are similar are homologous. Analogous traits are those that share a similar function but do not share a common evolutionary history. The wings of an insect and the wings of a bird are analogous, not homologous. Homology and analogy can be a little difficult to tease apart. For example, consider the wings of birds and the wings of bats. Both are derived from the forelimbs of their shared ancestor among the tetrapods, and so they are homologous structures as forelimbs. However, their function as wings was derived independently in each case from a flightless ancestor so they are functionally analogous as wings.

The concept of analogy in biology falls within the broader concept of **homoplasy**, or the independent evolution of similar traits. Homoplasy often arises due to convergent evolution. The camera-type **eyes** of vertebrates and of cephalopod mollusks are a classic example of homoplasy, as they are structurally similar organs that have independent evolutionary origins. Both cephalopods and vertebrates have a camera-type eye with an adjustable lens that is capable of forming a focused image. Cephalopods and vertebrates do not share a recent common ancestor, and in each case closely related taxa lack camera-type eyes.

Homoplasy can evolve in a variety of ways. **Convergent evolution** of unrelated taxa toward similar phenotypes can occur because particular shapes or functions are favored in a specific environment. The wings of birds and bats and the eyes of cephalopods and vertebrates provide clear examples of convergent evolution. The term **parallel evolution** describes the situation in which a shared underlying trait evolves in the same way independently in different lineages.

Stickleback fish provide a clear example of parallel evolution. Following the last glaciation, threespine sticklebacks (*Gasterosteus aculeatus*) invaded the freshwater lakes and streams in the northern hemisphere as the glaciers retreated. Marine populations of sticklebacks are heavily armored and have large spines in various locations on their body. Many freshwater populations have lost most of the armor and have much smaller spines. This loss of armor plating has occurred repeatedly and independently in multiple freshwater populations. Similar changes have occurred in physiological traits in sticklebacks. For example, marine populations perform better than do freshwater populations when tested for their ability to swim aerobically for long periods. Associated with this difference in performance, the marine sticklebacks have larger swimming muscles, and these muscles contain more **aerobic** fibers. These differences have been found across multiple marine and freshwater populations, suggesting parallel evolution of these traits. The selective factors associated with the repeated loss of armor and aerobic swimming performance in freshwater sticklebacks compared with the ancestral populations that had these traits are poorly understood. However, the observation of repeated loss of these traits strongly suggests that these changes are adaptive.

Although the camera eyes of vertebrates and cephalopod mollusks are clearly homoplastic traits in that each evolved from independent ancestral groups that lacked a camera-type eye, the eyes of these two groups share some underlying

FIGURE 1.7 Homology and analogy

(a) The limbs of vertebrates are homologous structures that are derived from a shared common ancestor, despite their diverse shapes. **(b)** The camera-type eyes of vertebrates and cephalopod mollusks are analogous structures that arose independently via convergent evolution.

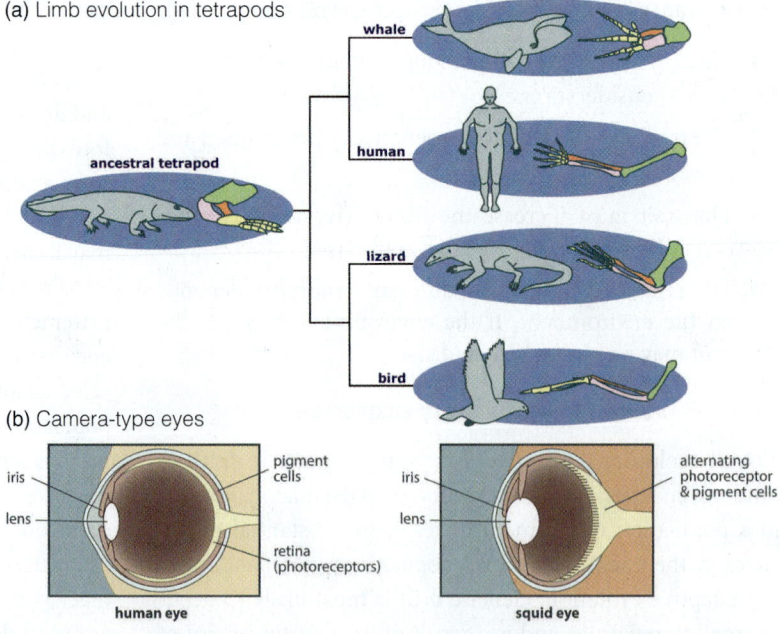

Figure source: Adapted from Thanukos, A. (2008). Top two tetrapod components appeared as Figure 1 on p. 499, Bringing homologies into focus. Evolution: Education and Outreach 1:498–504. Bottom two eye components appeared as Figure 3 on p. 500., DOI 10.1007/s12052-008-0080-5. Springer. ISSN: 1936-6434 (electronic version). *Understanding Evolution.* 2014. University of California Museum of Paleontology, 2014

similarities. For example, a transcription factor called *Pax6* is involved in the development of the eyes in both cephalopods and vertebrates. In fact, *Pax6* is present in all animals and controls eye development in organisms such as insects that have an entirely different kind of eye. *Pax6* is even expressed in the single-celled photoreceptors of certain types of jellyfish. These data suggest that *Pax6* is a gene that has been associated with photoreceptors since the early evolution of animals. Thus, the role of *Pax6* in eye development is homologous and shared among all animals, but the camera-type eyes of vertebrates and cephalopods are independently derived from the non–camera-type eyes of their ancestors and are thus homoplastic. This pattern has been termed "*deep homology*" because it arises from shared molecular traits among all animals and may underlie many examples of convergent evolution.

Similar deep homologies have been detected in other physiological systems. In *Drosophila*, a gene called *Tinman* controls heart development. Researchers named this gene after the Wizard of Oz character of the tin woodsman, who lacks a heart. Flies that lack the gene *Tinman* never develop a heart. In mice, a gene in a family called *Nkx* is needed for heart development. Mice that have mutated versions of the *Nkx* genes have defects in cardiac development. *Nkx* and *Tinman* make very similar proteins, and these genes clearly share the same evolutionary origin. Similarly, an *Nkx/Tinman* homologue has been discovered in the lancelet (*Branchiostoma*, formerly called *Amphioxus*), an invertebrate chordate. This gene is expressed in the developing tubelike heart of these animals. This high degree of conservation suggests a common evolutionary origin of these very diverse hearts. Indeed, animals that lack a heart, such as Cnidarians, also express a gene similar to *Tinman*, which is expressed around the base of the gastrovascular cavity, in a region that is involved in pumping fluids through the body. Thus, there may be a very deep homology among tissues involved in pumping fluids despite their great diversity and separate evolutionary histories.

CONCEPT CHECK

5. What is an adaptation?
6. Distinguish between homology and analogy.

Regulation and Homeostasis

Most organisms are faced with environmental variation. Temperature, food availability, and the physicochemical environment around an animal can change as an animal moves around the landscape and with changes in the time of day, the season, or across years. Animals utilize a variety of mechanisms to compensate for these environmental changes across different time scales and at different levels of biological organization. On a minute-to-minute basis, physiological regulatory networks control the functioning of many systems. For example,

animals alter their heart rate and ventilation to rapidly adjust to changing oxygen demand in the transition from rest to exercise. On longer time scales, organisms can adjust the rates of transcription, translation, and protein degradation to adjust protein amounts, resulting in functional changes in cells, organs, and organ systems. For example, with repeated aerobic exercise your heart, muscles, and skeletal system all change in both morphology and function, improving your exercise performance. Throughout this book you will encounter examples of physiological regulation at many time scales.

Animals can be physiological conformers or regulators

Multicellular animals can be classified according to the strategies they use to cope with changing conditions. **Conformers** allow internal conditions to change when faced with variation in external conditions. For example, the body temperature of a fish will be low in cold water and high in warm water. Thus, each of the cells in a fish's body must cope with the effects of changes in external temperature.

Regulators maintain relatively constant internal conditions regardless of the conditions in the external environment. Your body temperature is likely to be approximately 37°C whether you are in a warm room or standing outside on a very cold day. Your body has mechanisms to maintain its internal temperature, and thus the vast majority of the cells in your body do not have to cope with the effects of changes in ambient temperature. Animals may be regulators with respect to one internal parameter, but conformers with respect to another parameter. For example, lizards conform to external temperature but regulate their internal salt concentrations within a narrow range.

Each strategy has its benefits and costs. Because physiological responses demand metabolic energy, conforming can be less expensive than regulating. However, environmental changes can have deleterious effects on physiology, so regulating provides a much more stable internal environment.

Homeostasis is the maintenance of internal constancy

The maintenance of internal conditions in the face of environmental perturbations is referred to as **homeostasis**, a concept promoted by Walter Cannon in 1929 (Figure 1.8). The word *homeostasis* does not imply that there is no change in the organism, only that the animal initiates specific responses to control or regulate a particular vital variable. For example, your body temperature remains relatively constant only because numerous physiological processes actively change, adjusting the rates of heat production and heat loss. For example, when you stand in the cold air, your muscles may shiver to produce heat that replaces the heat lost to the environment. Even though one physiological process, such as muscle activity, changes, this serves to maintain a physiological state within a normal range.

FIGURE 1.8 **Homeostasis**

This polar bear (*Ursus maritimus*) maintains a relatively constant internal body temperature that is much higher than its habitat temperature despite the large daily and seasonal fluctuations in environmental temperatures.

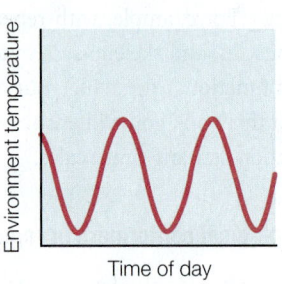

Photo source: st__iv/Fotolia.

Because of the importance of the concept of homeostasis in physiology, each chapter of this book after the first three introductory chapters includes a box (Challenges to Homeostasis) that highlights the mechanisms animals use to cope with environmental change.

Intrinsic to the original concept of homeostasis is the idea that some physiological systems must change their activity to permit constancy of function in others. However, some researchers have coined the term **allostasis** (the process of achieving homeostasis through change) to emphasize that the regulatory mechanisms themselves may change through time. For example, many northern mammals shed their brown summer fur and grow a thicker white winter fur. This process would be considered an allostatic response. Similarly, metabolism changes throughout the reproductive cycle of an organism. For example, when a female mammal lactates, metabolism is adjusted to a new level to cope with the demands of producing milk. Metabolism is still homeostatically regulated, but at a new level. The concept of allostasis explicitly takes into account this constantly shifting baseline, and emphasizes the costs of the processes required to do so.

The nature of the physiological response to an environmental change depends on many factors. Short-term challenges can often be dealt with using existing physiological systems. When a dog is too hot, it can move to a cooler location or pant to shed heat in its breath. These are effective short-term behavioral and physiological approaches to reducing thermal stress. However, they are not effective long-term strategies. Instead, dogs cope with long-term changes in temperature, such as seasonal cycles, by growing fur in the autumn and shedding fur in the spring.

This example illustrates several principles that govern physiological changes. First, some physiological strategies are effective in the short term but less useful for the long term. Holding your breath may be fine for a brief dive to the bottom of a lake, but it will not help you cope with low oxygen levels while you climb Mount Everest. Second, some strategies require a significant investment in resources and need longer to take effect. Hair growth, for instance, is a relatively slow process that requires metabolic energy. Third, some stressors are sufficiently predictable that animals remodel physiology in anticipation of the stress, and often in predictable cycles. Many physiological processes change daily, showing a **circadian rhythm**. Some changes are seasonal, such as the growth and shedding of fur. Other patterns, such as coral reef spawning, are linked to the lunar cycle. In some cases, cyclical physiological changes proceed without any environmental input, but generally they arise in response to specific environmental cues, such as temperature or photoperiod.

Feedback loops control physiological pathways

To maintain homeostasis, animals must (1) detect external conditions and (2) if necessary initiate compensatory responses that (3) keep vital areas buffered against unfavorable change. Animals most often maintain homeostasis using a **reflex control pathway**. A change in the internal or external environment provides a stimulus. The stimulus then causes a response. For instance, when you depress the gas pedal of your car (the stimulus), the car accelerates (the response). If you take your foot off the gas (remove the stimulus), the car will slow down.

FIGURE 1.9 Antagonistic controls

Your body temperature is held relatively constant by antagonistic loops. If cold conditions cause a decrease in your body temperature, this triggers an increase in heat production and a reduction in heat dissipation. When body temperature increases, heat production pathways are inhibited and heat dissipation pathways are stimulated, correcting body temperature.

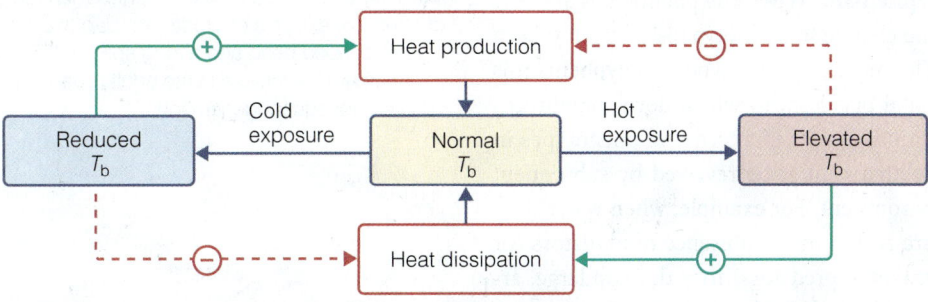

Animals fine-tune physiological responses by using **antagonistic controls**: independent regulators that exert opposite effects on a step or pathway (Figure 1.9). In the car analogy above, the gas pedal and the brake are examples of antagonistic controls. You can cause the car to decelerate by taking your foot off the gas or depressing the brake, but the car's response will be greater if you use both in combination. For example, animals control body temperature by regulating both heat production and heat dissipation (Figure 1.9). As we discuss in detail in Chapter 4: Cell Signaling and Endocrine Regulation and Chapter 8: Nervous Systems, the **endocrine** and nervous systems play an important role in the feedback regulation of many physiological processes.

Negative feedback loops maintain homeostasis

In a **negative feedback loop**, the response sends a signal back to the stimulus, reducing the intensity of the stimulus. For example, when you eat, the incoming food causes the stomach to swell. The change in stomach volume and early **digestion** products trigger a negative feedback loop, acting through your brain, to reduce your appetite.

Many physiological systems have a **set point**, a preferred physiological state defended through feedback loops. Your body temperature has a set point of approximately 37°C. When temperature rises, your body may sweat to cool you down, whereas a decrease in body temperature may trigger shivering to warm you back to your set point. Although the set point for human body temperature is close to 37°C, the exact body temperature set point varies between individuals and changes throughout the day.

Positive feedback loops cause explosive responses

Some physiological systems are controlled by **positive feedback loops**. Unlike negative feedback loops, which minimize changes in the regulated variable, positive feedback loops maximize changes in the regulated variable. For example, the muscles in the **stomach** are normally regulated to contract and relax in a regular pattern to gently mix food. However, when a toxin is detected, a positive **feedback** loop is triggered to induce forceful contractions that propel the food back up the esophagus to induce vomiting. Pathways involving positive feedback loops begin slowly but rapidly increase in intensity. In a positive feedback loop there must also be a signal that allows the animal to stop the process at the proper time, so that the action does not spiral out of control.

Acclimation and acclimatization result in reversible phenotypic changes

Most animals are able to remodel their physiological machinery in response to external conditions. The word **acclimation** refers to the process of change in response to a controlled environmental variable (usually in a laboratory setting), while the word **acclimatization** refers to the process of change in response to natural environmental variation. For example, if you take a fish from water at 15°C and transfer it to water at 5°C, over time you will observe a variety of changes in muscle biochemistry, metabolic rate, and other physiological parameters. This process would be referred to as acclimation. In contrast, if you compare a fish that you capture in the summer from a lake with a mean temperature of 15°C with a fish that you capture in winter from a lake at 5°C, you will observe many of the same changes, but in this case the process would be termed acclimatization. Acclimatization may be the result not just of the temperature change, but also of changes in day length, food availability, and any other environmental parameters that vary between summer and winter. In general, both acclimation and acclimatization are reversible physiological changes.

Animals can also irreversibly alter their phenotype

Acclimation and acclimatization are special cases of a general phenomenon called **phenotypic plasticity**, or the ability of an organism to alter its phenotype in response to environmental conditions. The term phenotypic plasticity encompasses a wide range of changes in phenotype, some reversible and some irreversible. When a particular phenotype exists in two or more discrete forms, the change is referred to as **polyphenism**. When the phenotypes are part of a continuum, the change in phenotype is referred to as a **reaction norm**. The most common type of polyphenism is due to developmental plasticity, in which development under different conditions results in alternative phenotypes in the adult organism that cannot be reversed by subsequent changes in the environment. For example, when water fleas (*Daphnia pulex*) are reared in the presence of predators (or even chemical extracts of predators) they develop large, armored, helmet-shaped heads and an elongated spiny tail. When they are reared in the absence of predators, they develop with much smaller heads and a shorter, less spiky tail (Figure 1.10). Adult water fleas retain these morphologies even if predator extracts are subsequently removed from or added to the water.

Some acquired traits can even be passed on to subsequent generations via a mechanism called **epigenetic inheritance**. For example, some populations of killifish (*Fundulus heteroclitus*) live in highly polluted sites and have high tolerance of pollutants such as PCBs. If you rear the offspring of these fish in the lab, the offspring also have high tolerance. However, if you then breed these offspring to form an F2 generation and rear them in the lab, this generation has lower tolerance. These data suggest that at least some part of the increased tolerance of killifish from polluted sites is the result of epigenetic mechanisms that can be inherited across one generation, but are then reset. The study of the epigenetic inheritance of physiological traits is still in its infancy, and it is not yet clear how common these types of examples may be. However, it is clear that animals have many mechanisms by which they can reversibly or irreversibly alter their physiological phenotypes to respond to environmental change.

FIGURE 1.10 **Developmental plasticity or polyphenism**

Alternative morphs of the water flea, *Daphnia pulex*. When genetically identical individuals are reared in the absence of predator extracts, these features are absent. When reared in the presence of chemical extracts of predators, *Daphnia pulex* have a large helmet-shaped head and a long spiky tail. These developmental changes are irreversible in the adult organism, but are not inherited by subsequent generations.

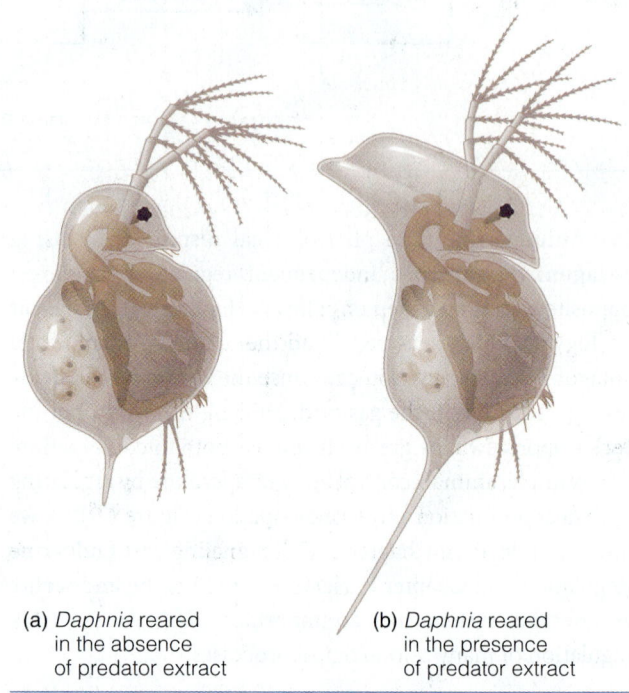

(a) *Daphnia* reared in the absence of predator extract

(b) *Daphnia* reared in the presence of predator extract

CONCEPT CHECK

7. What is homeostasis?
8. Distinguish between acclimation, polyphenism, and phenotypic plasticity.

SUMMARY

Animal physiology is the study of how animals work. Because of physiology's central position in biology, animal physiologists study both the causes and the consequences of physiological processes. Mechanisms at multiple levels of biological organization act together to allow animals to function as an integrated whole. Although the enormous diversity of life on Earth may seem bewildering at first, there are a few fundamental themes that unify physiology as the study of how animals work.

1. Animal physiology is an integrative discipline that examines processes at a variety of levels of biological organization. Because of this integrative perspective, animal physiologists can address a wide range of both basic and applied questions, ranging from the molecular details of particular diseases to the consequences of climate change for animal populations.

2. Because animal physiologists are interested in mechanisms, they make extensive use of principles from physics and chemistry, because animals are constrained by the same chemical and physical laws that govern all the processes in our universe.

3. Because animal life has arisen through the process of evolution, understanding the evolutionary history of organisms is fundamental to understanding the relationships between anatomy and physiology.

4. Animal physiologists have fundamental focus on the control mechanisms that regulate physiological function. These control mechanisms operate on a variety of time scales and involve complex feedback loops. Acclimation, acclimatization, and other forms of phenotypic plasticity are some of the complex responses that animals use to cope with environmental variation.

REVIEW QUESTIONS

1. **LO①** Where would organelles such as the mitochondrion fit in the levels of organization shown in Figure 1.3?

2. **LO②** What is the Krogh principle, and why is it useful for animal physiologists?

3. **LO②** All organisms have a maximum temperature at which they can function. Suggest a possible physical basis for this observation.

4. **LO②** How might size-related changes in surface area-to-volume ratios affect physiological functions?

5. **LO③** What are three fundamental requirements for adaptive evolution of a trait to occur?

6. **LO③** Are the eyes of vertebrates and cephalopod mollusks homologous or analogous? Justify your answer.

7. **LO④** What is the main benefit of having antagonistic controls in physiological systems?

8. **LO④** Explain why a positive feedback loop is unlikely to be involved in a control system that maintains homeostasis.

SYNTHESIS QUESTIONS

1. What physical, chemical, or physiological constraints might lead to allometric scaling?

2. Why do physiologists need to understand evolution?

3. Compare and contrast adaptive evolution and genetic drift.

4. When might an adaptation become detrimental?

5. Home heating systems such as a furnace are regulated via negative feedback. Describe how such a system might work.

6. Make an argument for or against adopting the use of the term allostasis.

7. Dogs typically shed some hair in the spring. Is this an example of acclimation or acclimatization? How might you experimentally distinguish between these two possibilities?

CHAPTER

2

Physiological Evolution of Animals

Learning Objectives

After reading this chapter, you should be able to:

1. Explain the evolutionary relationship between protozoans and metazoans.
2. Demonstrate familiarity with the evolutionary relationships among animals.
3. Identify the major events in animal evolution.
4. Discuss the evolutionary origins of specific physiological abilities.

FIGURE 2.1   **Yeti Crab (*Kiwa hirsuta*)**

Photo source: Ifremer, A. Fifis/AP Images.

T he diversity of life on Earth inspires many to learn more about biology. Whether your awareness of animals comes from your own experience or watching nature shows on television, you have some appreciation for the breadth of animal diversity. Remarkably, there are a great many living animals yet to be discovered, and paleontologists regularly uncover new types of animals in the fossil record. One challenge for scientists is to figure out how all of these animals are related, and thus what they tell us about the evolutionary origins of animals.

More than 10 years ago the Census of Marine Life began a project of exploring the world to catalog the many animals living in oceans, as well as to find new species. The strange animals the Census found, such as the "fur"-covered Yeti crab (Figure 2.1), spark the imagination about the as-yet undiscovered life forms that likely exist on the planet. Though living animals are indeed remarkably diverse, those alive today represent only a snapshot in time.

A far richer world is evident from explorations of the fossil record. In the early 1900s, a paleontologist named Charles Walcott uncovered an extraordinary fossil bed in the Canadian Rockies. The deposit was remarkable because of the richness of the collection of soft-bodied animals, of types that had largely escaped preservation in other fossil beds. Analysis of this Burgess Shale collection reveals a rich diversity in animals present in the area around 500 mya (million years ago). When the fossils were discovered, Walcott assigned each to the most similar groups of extant animals. As it turned out, many of the original taxonomic assignments are now thought to be wrong, and the confusion about evolutionary affinities led Stephen J. Gould to prepare his 1990 book, *Wonderful Life: The Burgess Shale and the Nature of History*, in which he proposed that many of the Burgess Shale fossils were members of phyla that are now extinct. A more conservative interpretation is that these fossils all belong to extant phyla. Though many lineages within the phyla may have disappeared entirely, this approach assumes that the number of phyla has not changed markedly.

An awareness of the evolutionary origins and phylogenetic diversity of animals is essential for an understanding of the conservation and divergence in animal traits, including physiological traits. In this chapter, we provide a survey of animal diversity, albeit a general one, focusing on the origins of physiological traits. ■

■ INTRODUCTION

About 4.5 bya (billion years ago) the planet Earth coalesced from clumps of debris floating through space after the Big Bang that occurred about 14 bya. For another billion years, Earth's surface was a harsh place: Asteroid bombardment and volcanic eruptions were constantly remodeling the surface of the planet. Yet it was during this tumultuous period that life on Earth began. Some researchers believe that organic molecules arose from a "primordial soup" of methane, **ammonia,** and water, energized by atmospheric electrical discharges. Others believe that the first organic molecules arose from chemical reactions of products of deep-sea volcanoes. Regardless of the origins of the first small organic molecules, the pathway to living organisms required the formation of larger macromolecules with the capacity for **catalysis** and self-replication. At some point around 4 bya, these purely chemical processes produced the earliest life form, the **progenote**. The progenote was likely a chemoautolithotroph, capable of surviving without oxygen and living on inorganic sources of energy and carbon. The closest living relatives to the progenote are likely the Archaea. The modern Archaea are **extremophiles**, able to survive in the harshest environments that exist on Earth, such as sulfuric hot springs and deep-sea vents.

The progenote was the ancestor to all organisms on the planet and, as a result, it is likely that many of the biological features that are shared by all currently living organisms arose in the progenote. These shared features include dependence on water, the role of nucleic acids, the use of only 20 amino acids in proteins, and the basic pathways of intermediary metabolism.

Within the next billion years, the progenote's descendants diverged to form three distinct groups of organisms: Eubacteria, Archaea, and Eukaryota. Each lineage diversified independently over the next 3 billion years. The two prokaryote lineages, Eubacteria and Archaea, remained single-celled organisms with little intracellular organization. In contrast, the ancestral eukaryotes experienced evolutionary changes that resulted in the production of membranous, subcellular compartments, thereby increasing intracellular organization. This is thought to have begun when the earliest eukaryotes found a way to package their DNA into a membrane-bound compartment: the nucleus. Later, around 3 bya, a eukaryote engulfed a bacterium that likely resembled a modern purple bacterium. Although the purple bacterium was probably ingested as food, it developed a symbiotic relationship with its host, replicating within the host cell. Over time, the bacterial endosymbiont lost its capacity to exist outside the cell, and the host cell became reliant on the metabolic contributions of the endosymbiont, the ancestor of mitochondria. By 2 bya, all of the diverse groups of unicellular organisms were established, including the many lineages of single-celled eukaryotes, collectively known as **protists**.

The origins of animals can be traced back about 600 mya, with the appearance of sponges. In the time since, animal evolution occurred in concert with changing environmental conditions (Figure 2.2). We cannot understand the basis of animal diversity without an awareness of the evolutionary origins of animals in a changing environment. On the one hand, many cellular processes are similar across major taxa, so what we learn from studies on model species of fungi and

FIGURE 2.2 **Biotic and abiotic events over geologic time**

Many evolutionary events coincide with periods of environmental change over the geological record. The colors reflect periods of global warmth (red) and cold (blue).

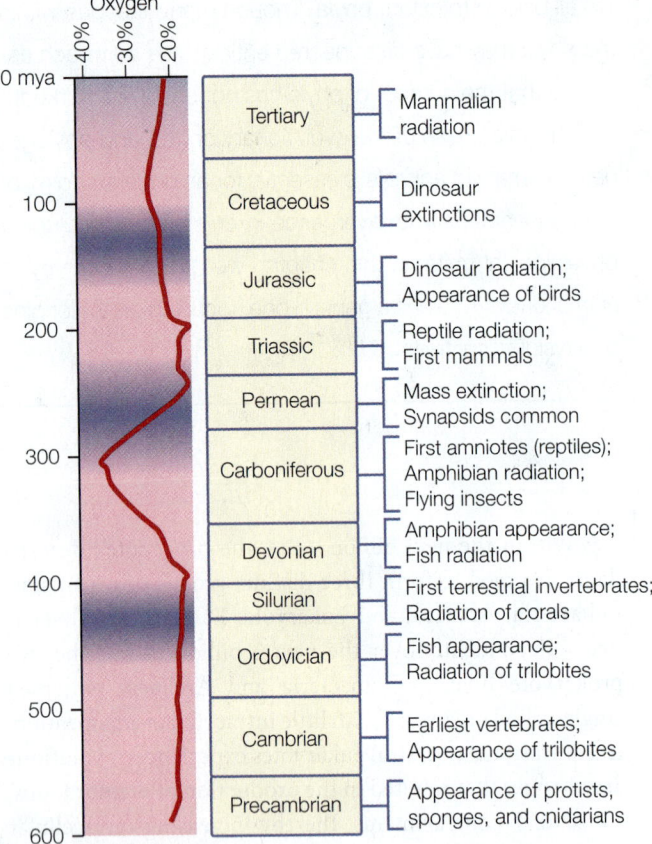

Figure source: Oxygen patterns are based on Berner, R. A. (1999). Atmospheric oxygen over Phanerozoic time. *Proceedings of the National Academy of Sciences USA, 96,* 10955–10957.

plants tells us a lot about how these features work in animals. On the other hand, each lineage often evolved novel ways of using similar machinery to face the chemical and physical stresses imposed by the environment. By understanding how different taxa solved similar problems, we can better understand the constraints on animal cell function and physiological evolution. Modern animal physiology builds upon studies of organisms in diverse taxa to understand the cellular origins of diversity in animals.

ANIMAL EVOLUTION AND PHYSIOLOGY

The starting point for any discussion of the evolutionary origin of animals must be the protists. They are single-celled organisms (although some can form colonies) that share the properties characteristic of eukaryotes: a membrane-bound nucleus and organelles. Protists are a collection of only distantly related organisms containing more than 50 different phyla. The most familiar protists are *Euglena* (with features of both animals and plants), *Plasmodium* (the single-celled flagellate parasites of blood that cause malaria), *Paramecium* (ciliated hunters), and amoebas (cells that are the namesake of amoeboid movement). Early researchers recognized that some protists were able to move from place to place, and because locomotion was deemed to be a unique trait of animals, the mobile protists were at one point considered to be the ancestors of animals, giving rise to the term **protozoan**. The term continues to be used in some contexts, but it has no meaningful evolutionary basis. The protist phyla emerged prior to the origins of the three main eukaryote kingdoms: plants, fungi, and animals. The term **metazoan**, which arose originally to distinguish multicellular animals from the single-celled protozoans, is now used synonymously with "animal."

The earliest steps in animal evolution involved the formation of a multicellular entity, though the mechanisms by which this occurred remain uncertain. The colonial hypothesis suggests that genetically identical individual cells remained associated as colonies, a phenomenon that is common in flagellated protists. Amongst the protists, genetic studies show that the **choanoflagellates** are the protists most closely related to metazoans. They are single-celled organisms that possess a flagellum emerging from a cup-shaped collar extending from a more spherical cell body. Remarkably, they are very similar in appearance to **choanocytes**, a flagellated cell in sponges (Figure 2.3).

There is not much difference between a colony of genetically identical cells and a multicellular organism. The

FIGURE 2.3 **Choanoflagellates and choanocytes**

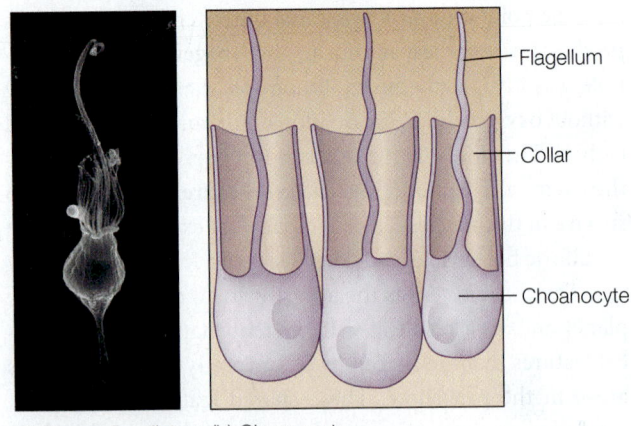

(a) Choanoflagellate   (b) Choanocyte

Photo source: Mark J Dayel (2012) Choanoflagellates and animal multicellularity. url: http://www.dayel.com/choanoflagellates/ (visited on 01/01/2013).

real distinction arose when select cells of the colony divested themselves of certain capacities, becoming specialized for specific functions on behalf of the colony. Upon achieving a division of labor amongst its cells, the organism is able to grow to larger size, and evolve in ways that permit greater colonial/organismal complexity. When faced with environmental challenges, single-celled organisms generally rely on biochemical solutions, whereas in multicellular organisms, specialized cells can make different contributions to the solution, which may involve biochemical or anatomical processes. The integration of these functions occurring in separate regions of an organism is the essence of physiology.

The approach taken in this chapter is to weave together the themes of animal **phylogeny** and physiological evolution. To be able to compare the physiological properties of animals, you need to appreciate the phylogenetic relationships among animals (Figure 2.4). Many of the animals we discuss in this text may be unfamiliar to students, so we introduce them briefly here. Interested readers should consult any of the many excellent zoology textbooks for additional details about individual groups. The approach also offers insights to students with interests more aligned with human biology. The evolutionary relationships permit nonhuman animals to be used as experimental models to study diseases and physiological dysfunction.

Multicellularity and the Invention of Tissues

Many groups of unicellular organisms have independently evolved their own versions of multicellularity through formation of colonies. The transition from single-celled organisms to true multicellular organisms occurred independently in the ancestors of plants, fungi, and animals. Each lineage found different solutions to the challenge of building the multicellular collections known as **tissues**.

Fungi and plants evolved from separate ancestors, each of which had a cell wall. Whether composed of chitin (in fungi) or cellulose (in plants), the rigid cell wall provided resistance to osmotic swelling, and tissues arose from connections between

FIGURE 2.4 **Animal phylogenetic relationships**

In this tree we summarize the major lineages of animals. The lengths of the various horizontal branches have no meaning. Where multiple horizontal branches emerge from a single vertical branch (polytomy), there is uncertainty about the underlying phylogenetic relationships. Our understanding of the relationships among animal groups is still being actively researched, and updated phylogenetic trees appear regularly. The tree presented here, and those that follow, is intended to provide an overview of phylogenetic relatedness among groups, and is not the final or definitive statement of these relationships.

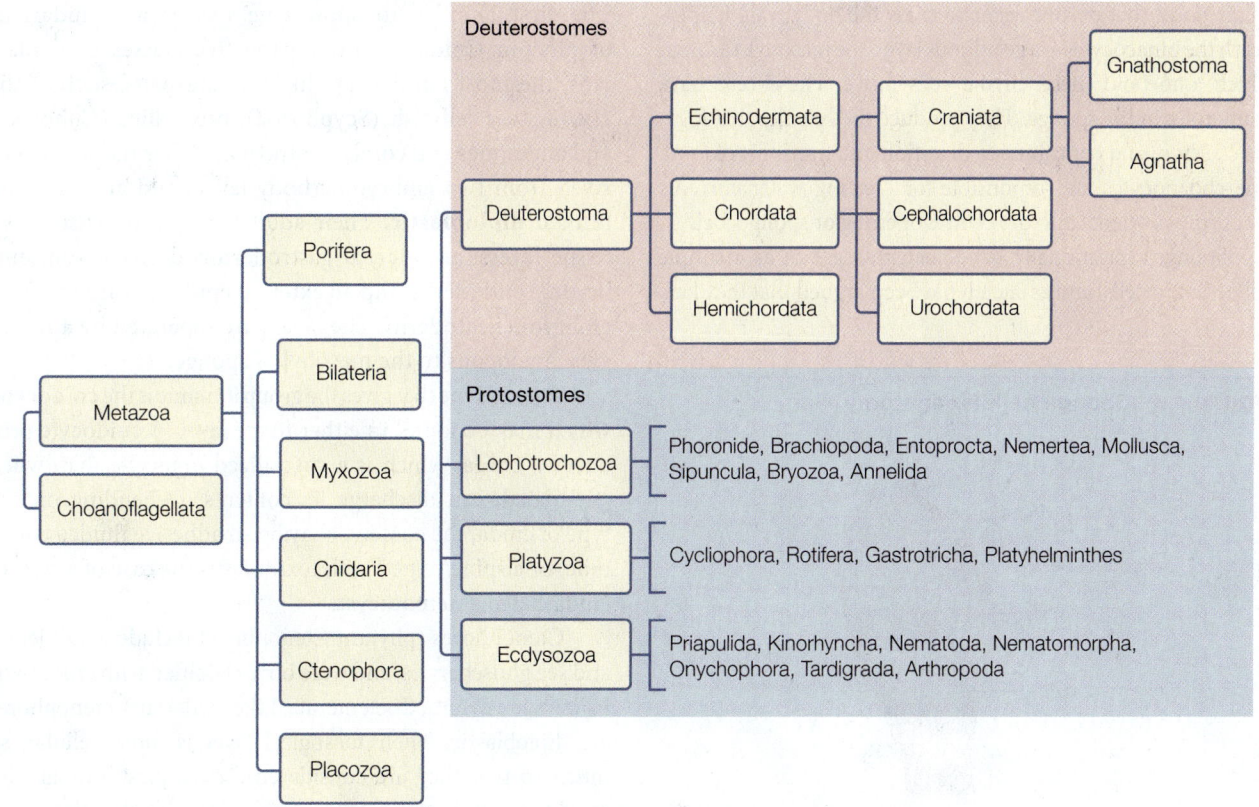

adjacent cell walls. Animal cells, in contrast, evolved from protists that lacked a cell wall. Thus, their evolutionary path required solutions to the physical problems that, in plants and fungi, were solved by the presence of the cell wall. The sodium-potassium pump (Na^+/K^+ **ATPase**) appeared early in animal evolution, enabling animal cells to regulate cell volume, ionic balance, and osmotic balance. **Collagen**, one of the vital extracellular matrix proteins used to construct tissues, also arose very early in metazoan evolution. Once these physical associations between cells were established, more elaborate pathways for intercellular communication became possible and necessary. Though plants and fungi use chemical messengers to communicate, animals possess much more complicated mechanisms for cell-to-cell signaling. We will discuss these milestones later in this chapter, but we begin by charting the origins of tissues. In the earliest stages of animal evolution we see the first appearance of some degree of cellular specialization, the formation of tissues, and greater anatomical sophistication.

Placozoans and sponges lack discrete tissues

Sponges (phylum Porifera) are the simplest of animals, and their unusual anatomy leads some taxonomists to separate sponges from true animals, or **Eumetazoans**.

Sponges are a collection of only three cell types: choanocytes, mesenchyme cells, and pinacocytes (Figure 2.5). The pinacocytes are the flat cells that form much of the body. Some pinacocytes can become specialized to form porocytes, which create pores that permit water to cross the body wall. Underneath the pinacocytes is a gelatinous layer, the mesohyl, through which amoeboid mesenchyme cells move. These cells have many roles in the sponge. They produce the spicules that form the skeleton, and contribute to digestion and transport of food. The choanocytes are responsible for creating water currents that bring nutrients into the central opening or spongocoel.

Sponges traditionally have been thought of as a simple collection of cells, and as such it has been argued that they lack discrete tissues. Many sponges possess some of the hallmarks of a tissue, with simple cell-to-cell connections and connective tissue underlying the cells. There is some cellular division of labor, but the cells are not quite as specialized as in other animals. With ill-defined tissues, the requirements for basic physiology processes—nutrition, excretion, and gas exchange—fall to individual cells. The responsibilities for reproduction are distributed between cell types. Choanocytes and mesenchyme cells are both involved in sexual and **asexual reproduction**.

One of the simplest eumetazoans is *Trichoplax adhaerens*, the only living species of Placozoa, literally "flat animal." It consists of a sheet of cells about 1 millimeter in diameter, with the underside of the cell layer possessing **flagella**, enabling the animal to glide over the substrate. Its discovery placed it at an important transition point in early animal evolution, but its exact relationship to other animals remains unclear. Some phylogeneticists place the group basal to sponges, because of the anatomical simplicity. It lacks tissues or organs and has very few cellular specializations. Though it is clearly the simplest of metazoans in structure, it is not known if this trait is a reflection of an evolutionary **reduction** in complexity, as is seen in many parasitic metazoans. Thus, some phylogeneticists consider sponges more ancient, and place the placozoans as sister taxa to more recent groups.

Cnidarians possess true tissues

The first animals to show true tissues are cnidarians of phylum Cnidaria. Among the five classes of cnidarians, the most familiar are likely hydrazoans, such as the *Hydra*, true jellyfish (Scyphozoa), box jellies (Cubozoa), and anemones and corals (Anthozoa). Their tissues are derived from two embryonic body layers and are therefore termed **diploblastic**. Their adult forms also possess two tissue layers: an internal gastrodermis derived from embryonic endoderm, and an external epidermis arising from embryonic ectoderm. The layers are separated by a mesoglea, analogous to the mesohyl of sponges.

The cell type that gives the group its name is the **cnidocyte**, which may be found in either tissue layer. A cnidocyte produces a **cnida**, which is a specialized organelle that, when stimulated, can discharge its contents. Depending on the type of cnida, the contents may be an adhesive fluid, a coiled tube, or a spine tipped with toxins, as is the case of a type of cnida called a **nematocyst**.

Ctenophores (phylum Ctenophora) include comb jellies and sea gooseberries, and were once classified with cnidarians in a single phylum, Coelenterata. Like cnidarians, ctenophores are diploblastic. Their mesogleal layer is more cellular, so much so that they are considered the simplest animals derived from three embryonic tissue layers (triploblastic).

FIGURE 2.5   **Sponge cellular anatomy**

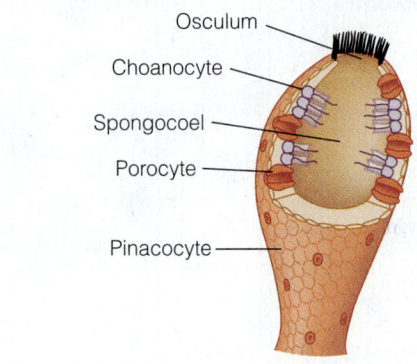

Osculum

Choanocyte

Spongocoel

Porocyte

Pinacocyte

Cnidarians are the simplest of animals with true muscle cells. Anemones use longitudinal muscle to shorten the body stalk, and circular muscles to narrow the body cavity, causing the stalk to lengthen. In Chapter 6 you will learn about the evolutionary and cellular origins of muscles. Cnidarians and ctenophores each have what appear to be smooth and striated muscles, but recent evidence suggests that these lineages may have evolved muscles through different routes than did other animals. Some of the molecular machinery needed to make muscle occurs in protists that predate animals, whereas some components of muscles, such as titin and troponin, do not occur in cnidarians and ctenophores.

Bilaterians are triploblastic with some degree of cephalization

One aspect of body plan that we have not yet discussed is symmetry. Most sponges are considered asymmetrical. Cnidarians and ctenophores show **radial symmetry**. An animal is radially symmetrical if any plane through the animal from oral/anterior to aboral/posterior generates mirror images. The groups of animals that emerged after cnidarians share a number of features that represent important steps in the evolution of body plans and physiology. They have **bilateral symmetry**, which means they can be cut into identical halves by only one plane. They are also **triploblastic**, with tissues arising from three embryonic layers: endoderm, **mesoderm**, and ectoderm. These animals also show the first evidence of **cephalization**, which is an evolutionary trend toward the centralization of nervous and sensory functions at the anterior end of the body.

There are approximately 25 phyla of animals more complex than cnidarians. Though any new species discovered can usually be assigned to one of these phyla with little difficulty, the evolutionary relationship between phyla is extraordinarily difficult to establish. There is no single set of taxonomic groupings that is definitive, though there are a number of commonly used terms used to lump phyla into groups based on different combinations of shared attributes.

The simplest approach to subdividing the triploblastic bilaterians is to distinguish between **protostomes** and *deuterostomes*. As we discuss in a subsequent section, these groups differ in terms of the embryonic origin of the mouth. In some cases, protostomes are subdivided into two groups: Ecdysozoa and Lophotrochozoa. The ecdysozoans share an ability to molt. Thus, nematodes, tardigrades, and arthropods are all ecdysozoans. Though lophotrochozoans do not molt, they are defined by the presence of either of two anatomic features. The term lopho-, from Greek *lophos,* meaning ridge, refers to a fan of ciliated tentacles around the mouth of some members of this group. The term troche-, from the Greek *trochiska,* meaning small wheel, refers to bands of **cilia** that circle the body of the **larva**. Mollusks and annelids are the largest groups of lophotrochozoans. Many of the phyla grouped with lophotrochozoans have more ambiguous relationships, and in some evolutionary trees, select lophotrochozoans are separated to form a third group, the platyzoans (see Figure 2.3).

Protostomes and deuterostomes differ in the embryonic origins of the mouth and anus

During early gastrulation, a region of the **blastula** (a hollow ball of cells) migrates inward, causing first a depression and then a pit called the blastopore. In animals classified as protostomes ("first mouth") the blastopore becomes the mouth, and the **anus** forms at a distant site. Arthropods, annelids, and mollusks are all protostomes. In deuterostomes ("second mouth"), the anus arises from the blastopore, and the mouth is formed second. Deuterostomes include chordates, hemichordates, and echinoderms (Figure 2.6).

Amniotes (birds, mammals, and reptiles) differ somewhat from the typical deuterostome pattern. In birds and mammals the blastula is not round but disk shaped (a blastodisc) and during gastrulation, birds and mammals produce a longitudinal groove (primitive streak) rather than a circular pore, but the invagination is homologous to the blastopore.

A coelom forms by enterocoely or schizocoely

Another approach used to categorize bilaterian phyla is the appearance and nature of an internal body cavity known as the **coelom**. To be considered a coelom, the cavity must arise

FIGURE 2.6 Gastrulation in protostomes and deuterostomes

The main distinction between protostomes and deuterostomes is the fate of the first invagination, typically the blastopore. In protostomes it forms the mouth, whereas in deuterostomes it forms the anus.

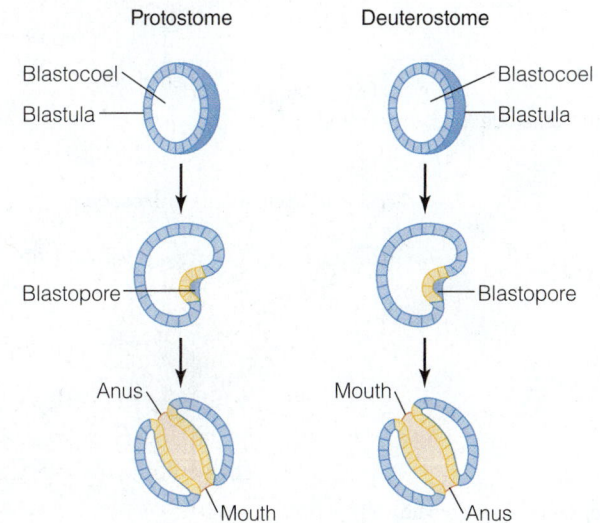

between tissues. Recall that sponges have no true tissues, and hence no gaps between tissues; diploblasts may have an acellular layer between tissue layers, but there is no true gap. The appearance of three embryonic tissue layers permitted the development of gaps between tissues, which in turn facilitated greater diversity in tissue organization. Some triploblastic animals (nemerteans and flatworms) lack an internal body cavity and are called *acoelomates* (Figure 2.7a). However, most triploblasts possess some form of coelom. In *pseudocoelomates*, a gap appears between the endoderm and mesoderm (Figure 2.7b). *Coelomates* possess a true coelom, which forms within the mesoderm layer (Figure 2.7c).

FIGURE 2.7 Acoelomates, pseudocoelomates, and coelomates

Triploblastic animals can be distinguished on the basis of the presence and nature of the coelom. **(a)** Acoelomates lack a coelom. **(b)** The coelom appears between endoderm and mesoderm in pseudocoelomates, and **(c)** between two mesodermal layers in coelomates.

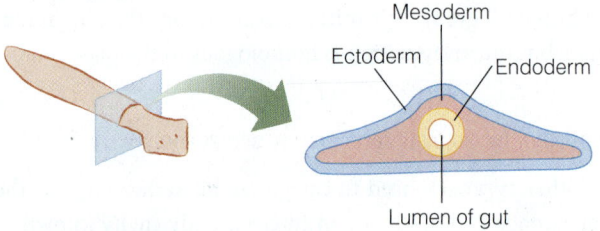

(a) Flatworm (acoelomate)

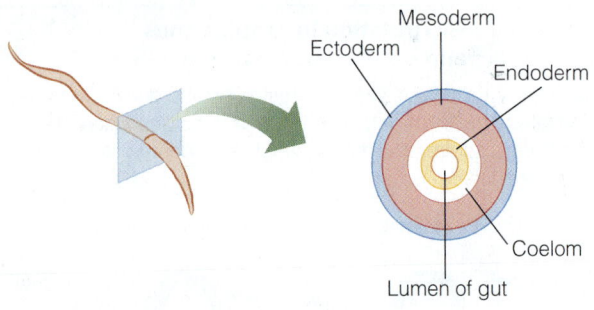

(b) Nematode (pseudocoelomate)

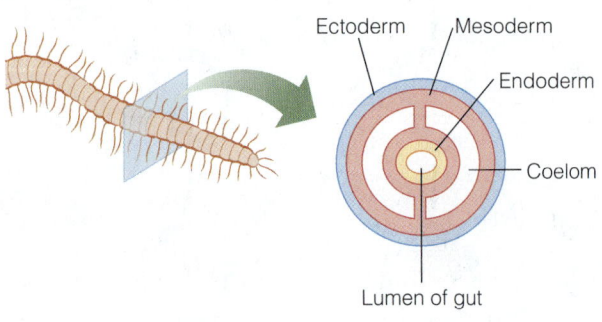

(c) Annelid (coelomate)

One would expect that such an important distinction would be definitive, but in many species the nature of a cavity is ambiguous and can even change during development. For example, nemerteans were long considered acoelomates, but it is now known that reduced cavities within the circulatory system are derived from a true coelom.

The appearance of the coelom was important in the evolution of physiology because it allows greater specialization of internal organs. The coelom arises early in embryonic development, though it originates by different routes in protostomes and deuterostomes. It may form when the mesoderm splits to form an internal compartment (*schizocoely*) or when layers of mesoderm pinch off from the gut (*enterocoely*). Protostomes generally display schizocoely and deuterostomes enterocoely, though chordates show schizocoely. The developmental processes can be used to help distinguish between animal groups, but there is little obvious significance for the physiology of the animal.

In the following sections, we survey the major groups of bilaterian, triploblastic organisms, focusing on those we discuss in more detail in later chapters.

Platyhelminthes include parasitic and free-living worms

The phylum Platyhelminthes (Figure 2.8) includes four classes of flatworms. Turbellaria includes free-living flatworms such as the familiar planaria. Monogenea are ectoparasitic flukes of fish, and Trematoda are endoparasitic flukes. Cestoda,

---

FIGURE 2.8 Platyhelminthes

Photo source: Image Quest Marine.

better known as tapeworms, are endoparasites that sometimes reach extraordinary lengths in the gastrointestinal tract of vertebrates.

Platyhelminthes are among the simplest of organisms to possess a simple digestive tract, although it is incomplete, lacking an anus. The digestive tract has been secondarily lost in a group of the cestodes. All platyhelminthes possess a primitive **kidney**, or **protonephridium**, that enables excretion of nitrogenous waste and water. A primitive brain exists in the anterior region, and longitudinal nerves and transverse nerves run throughout the body. They have sensory cells all over their body, with cells capable of detecting light, touch, water currents, and gravity. Their dorsoventral flattening permits gas exchange over the entire body; they lack circulatory or respiratory systems. The body wall is composed of muscle cells running circularly and longitudinally to change body length, and obliquely to enable the body to twist. The epidermis possesses cells that secrete lubricants and adhesives.

Mollusks possess a calcareous shell

The phylum Mollusca includes six classes, though we discuss only three in this text: Gastropoda are snails and slugs; Bivalvia are clams and oysters; and Cephalopoda include squid, octopus, and the chambered nautilus. These share an anatomic division of a head-foot region and visceral mass. Their mantle is a tissue that secretes some form of calcium-based shell, though this is greatly reduced in cephalopods and some gastropods, such as slugs and nudibranchs. Though they have a coelom, it is reduced to small cavities around the heart, kidney, and gonads.

Mollusks are a very diverse group of animals, with a number of unusual traits in some species. They are aquatic except for select gastropods that have invaded land, many of which have acquired an ability to survive severe dehydration. Many bivalve mollusks are capable of surviving great fluctuations in external salinity and oxygen levels. Most mollusks are "sluggish" animals, living at a "snail's pace," which makes the sensory, circulatory, and locomotor specializations of cephalopods all the more impressive.

Annelids have segmented bodies

Annelida is a large phylum of worms, the most common of which is the earthworm. The feature that distinguishes this group is an elongated, wormlike body composed of segments bearing paired bristles, or setae. The body of an annelid is divided into repeating segments, each of which is called a **metamer**. Metamerism is an important step in evolution and development because the simplest segments are duplications, each of which has a similar range of functions. What follows from this redundancy is the potential for regional specializations. **Tagmata** is the term for a series of segments that become grouped together to collaborate on a specific

function. Though annelids have some degree of anterior–posterior tagmatization, most of the metamers are very similar to each other. The physiology of annelids depends on the segmental nature of the body. You will learn about the unusual features of the annelid circulatory system in Chapter 9, and the nature of their locomotion in Chapter 12.

The phylum Annelida has traditionally been divided into subphyla Clitellata and Polychaeta. The Clitellata include earthworms (oligochaetes) and leeches (hirudineans). Polychaetes, however, are a dubious subphylum. It is likely that Polychaeta is a combination of several distantly related groups. There are also groups that were once considered separate phyla, such as the siboglinids, which include the pogonophoran tube worms found in deep-sea thermal vents (Figure 2.9). As you will discover in Chapter 14, pogonophorans lack a mouth and instead possess an internal sac of symbiotic bacteria that use the chemical energy from the toxic emissions from the vents to produce organic compounds used by the worms.

Arthropods show metamerism and tagmatization

The phylum Arthropoda, the first group of ecdysozoans we have discussed, is the largest group of animals in existence, encompassing more than 60 percent of named species. The group includes four extant subphyla: Chelicerata (spiders, horseshoe crabs), Crustacea (lobsters, barnacles, and brine shrimp), Myriapoda (millipedes and centipedes), and Hexapoda (insects). The remarkable diversity in this group means that they appear often throughout this textbook. Like annelids, arthropods are metameric, with a body plan consisting of repeating segments, though the specialization of segments (tagmatization) is much more pronounced than in annelids.

Arthropods have a chitin-based exoskeleton that they may shed between life history stages. They possess an open circulatory system, which is contiguous with the coelom and termed the **hemocoel**. They also experience **metamorphosis**, which

FIGURE 2.9 The deep-sea vent worm *Riftia*

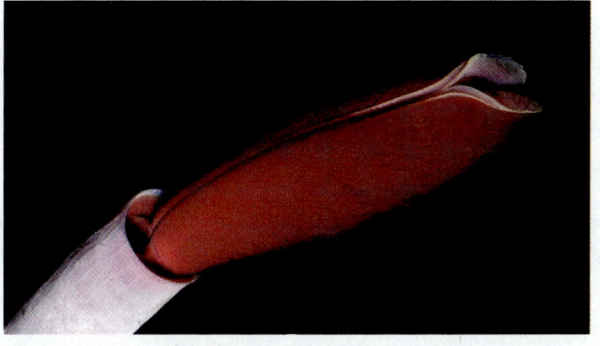

Photo source: Image Quest Marine.

is a major change in body plan that accompanies maturation. These traits underlie much of the variation in the physiology of arthropods, and their success in inhabiting so many of the ecological niches on Earth. The external covering was essential to permit members of the lineage to invade land (Chapter 13). The presence of the hemocoel alters the relationship between the circulatory and respiratory systems in these animals (Chapters 9 and 11). The capacity for metamorphosis affects many aspects of their physiology. Metamorphosis means that life stages rely on different foods (Chapter 14) and move in different ways (Chapter 12); the control of metamorphosis has important ramifications for reproduction (Chapter 16).

Deuterostomes include echinoderms and chordates

The most ancient of the deuterostomes is the phylum Echinodermata. Sea stars (class Asteroidea), brittle stars (Ophiuroidea), sea urchins (Echinoidea), and sea cucumbers (Holothuroidea) are all echinoderms. They share a calcium-based endoskeleton, pentaradial symmetry, and a water-vascular system of canals.

The phylum Chordata includes the early chordates of the subphyla Urochordata (tunicates) and Cephalochordata (lancelets), as well as the much larger and more diverse subphylum Craniata. Chordates are bilaterally symmetrical, with four traits present at some point in development. They possess a notochord, dorsal nerve cord, postanal tail, and pharyngeal slits. These traits are obvious in the early chordates, but also evident in the more familiar groups of craniates, including vertebrates.

The transitions from early chordates to Craniata included a number of important physiological transitions that have profound implications for vertebrate diversity: increasing complexity of the nervous system with the formation of a large three-part brain, a solid backbone derived from the notochord, segmental muscles, major blood vessels, and an endoskeleton with cranium. The pharyngeal structures that serve as filter-feeding organs in lancelets and tunicates evolved to become many anterior structures in vertebrates, including the gills of fish, jawbones and muscles, ear bones, nerves, and blood vessels. The feeding groove, or endostyle, of urochordates and cephalochordates is homologous to a similar structure in larval lampreys, which during metamorphosis becomes the thyroid gland. Obviously, a great deal of physiology relies on these structures, and variations in how they have evolved and how they develop account for much of the diversity seen in vertebrates.

CONCEPT CHECK

1. Distinguish between the terms protist, protozoan, metazoan, and eumetazoan.
2. What is a coelom?
3. Distinguish between metamers and tagmata.

Vertebrates

In 1983 Carl Gans and Glenn Northcutt proposed that the success of vertebrates was attributable in large part to a new way of building a head. Their position was that the transition from early chordates to vertebrates was accompanied by a series of changes in embryonic development that led to greater cephalization. In metazoans, the nervous system arises from embryonic ectoderm, and it is the fate of these cells that determines the nature of the nervous system. Whereas early chordates have a fairly diffuse nerve sensory network, vertebrates have a much more concentrated and elaborate centralized nervous system. Muscle, connective tissue, and the skeleton arise from embryonic mesoderm. In early chordates, the head is the terminus of the notochord, but in vertebrates the notochord-derived tissues terminate at the base of the skull. The musculoskeletal features of the vertebrate head arise from the neural crest region of the embryo. In many respects, it appears as if the vertebrate head is derived from structures "added on" to the early chordate skeleton. Gans and Northcutt argue that the "new head" may have arisen in response to a lifestyle that became progressively more predatory. Though the specific elements of the "new head" hypothesis continue to be discussed and challenged, many of the distinguishing physiological features of the various vertebrate classes are linked directly or indirectly to processes that involve specializations of the head.

Different agnathan ancestors gave rise to modern agnathans and fish

Approximately 400 mya, the seas of the world were rich in diverse fishlike vertebrates, many of which have since disappeared. Some groups exist now only as fossils, whereas others are represented by extant species. The collection of fossils gives insights into the morphology of the extinct animals, which can be compared with the morphology of living species to construct evolutionary trees that explain the origins of vertebrates. More recently, genetic tools have been used to study the relationships between living fish. Unfortunately, the conclusions from morphological and genetic approaches offer many conflicting versions of early vertebrate evolution. One version of the phylogeny of the early vertebrates is depicted in Figure 2.10.

The earliest of the vertebrates lacked a jaw, and they are collectively considered agnathans (*gnathos* means jaws in Greek). Agnathans include a number of only distantly related groups, including the extinct ostracoderms (osteostracans and heterostracans) and the two extant agnathan groups, hagfish and lamprey. Lamprey and hagfish appear to have shared a common ancestor around 480 mya. The exact relationship between these groups is still vigorously debated, fueled in part by the remarkable anatomical and physiological divergence between hagfish and lamprey, such as the distinctions between their osmoregulatory strategies

FIGURE 2.10 **Phylogeny of early vertebrates**

Extinct groups are presented in *italics*.

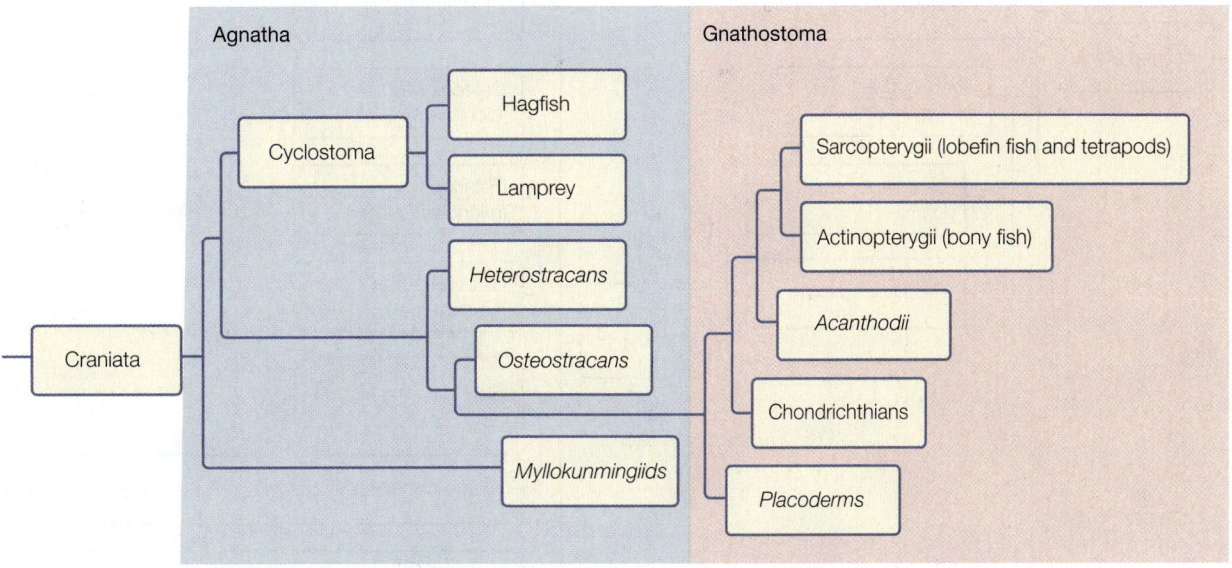

(Chapter 13). However, they share a cartilaginous skeleton, internal gill pouches, and a rudimentary digestive tract, but both lack paired fins. It is now thought that the last common ancestor of lamprey and hagfish was far more complex than either of the derived groups. In other words, hagfish and lamprey became much simpler over evolution, but did so by different routes, accounting for the morphological divergence between these two groups.

Though vertebrates arose from agnathans, they did not evolve from the hagfish/lamprey lineage, but rather from other agnathans, likely a branch related to the ostracoderms. These extinct vertebrates possessed mineralized bone and used gills for respiration rather than filter feeding. Though they lacked paired fins, lateral extensions likely helped stabilize them in swimming.

Cartilaginous fish evolved from placoderms

The transition from ostracoderms to jawed fish involved a repurposing of one of the gill arches to form a jaw. One of the earliest groups of jawed fish, now extinct, are the placoderms. These armor-plated fish possessed well-developed jaws, with hard projections that served as teeth. Somewhere around 425 mya, a placoderm group served as ancestors for cartilaginous fish, class Chondrichthyes. This group includes elasmobranchs (sharks, skates) and holocephalans (ratfish), though these two lineages diverged shortly after the earliest chondrichthyians appeared around 400 mya. They share a cartilaginous skeleton, but differ in other respects. The ratfish is also called a chimaera because it has features of both sharks and bony fish. Elasmobranchs have hard, placoid scales but ratfish lack scales. Elasmobranchs have gill slits that permit

water to reach the internalized gills, whereas ratfish have a gill cover, or operculum, as does a bony fish. Elasmobranchs have replaceable teeth derived from modified scales, whereas ratfish teeth are hard, permanent plates.

Several groups of bony fish evolved in the Devonian period

Around 400 mya, there was a proliferation in the diversity of bony fish (Osteichthyes), including the main groups of ray-finned fish (Actinopterygii) and lobe-finned fish (Sarcopterygii). They likely shared a common ancestor with a group of fish known as Acanthodii.

Actinopterygians are an extraordinarily diverse group, comprising more than 25,000 species of fish inhabiting every major aquatic ecosystem. Early attempts to subdivide actinopterygians relied on three groups: Chondrostei (sturgeons, paddlefish), Holostei (gar, bowfin), and Teleostei (most ray-finned fish). However, the classification scheme changes regularly, particularly in response to new genetic information. A current phylogeny of actinopterygians is provided in Figure 2.11, focusing on lineages mentioned elsewhere in the text. This group of fish is remarkable in its diversity. There are some exceptionally athletic species such as tuna (Chapter 12), some of which are able to regulate their body temperature (Chapter 15). They have evolved strategies for living in niches spanning freshwater to hypersaline water, and some are even capable of invading land (Chapter 13). They have also evolved unusual abilities to produce electricity and heat (Chapter 6).

Sarcopterygians are currently represented by only a few fish groups, including coelocanths (Coelocanthomorpha) and lungfish (Dipnoi), as well as a third lineage that were the ancestors of tetrapods (Figure 2.12). These share lobe-shaped, fleshy

FIGURE 2.11 **Actinopterygian fish**

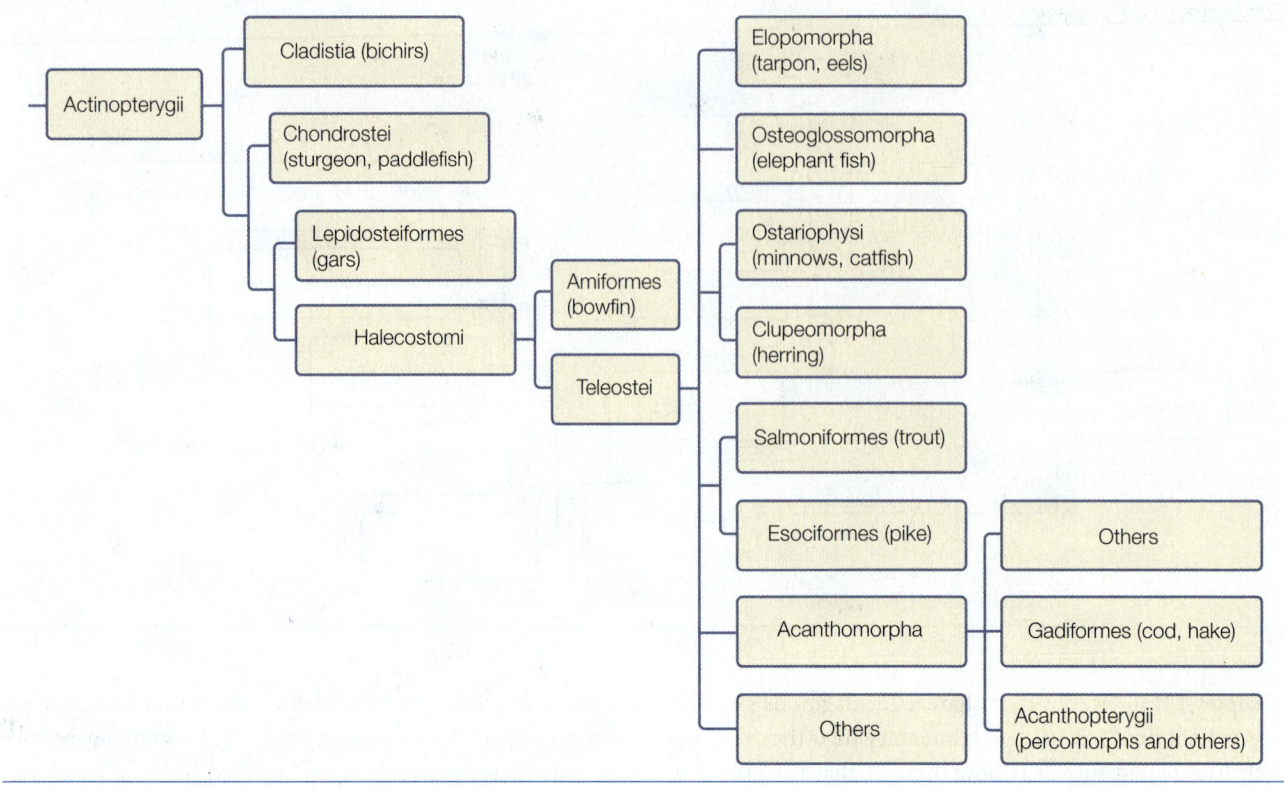

FIGURE 2.12 **Sarcopterygian phylogeny**

The major groups of animals in the tetrapod lineages are shown. The figure does not identify or distinguish between the many extinct groups of tetrapods found in the fossil record. Major extant groups are shown in **bold**, and extinct groups are in *italics*.

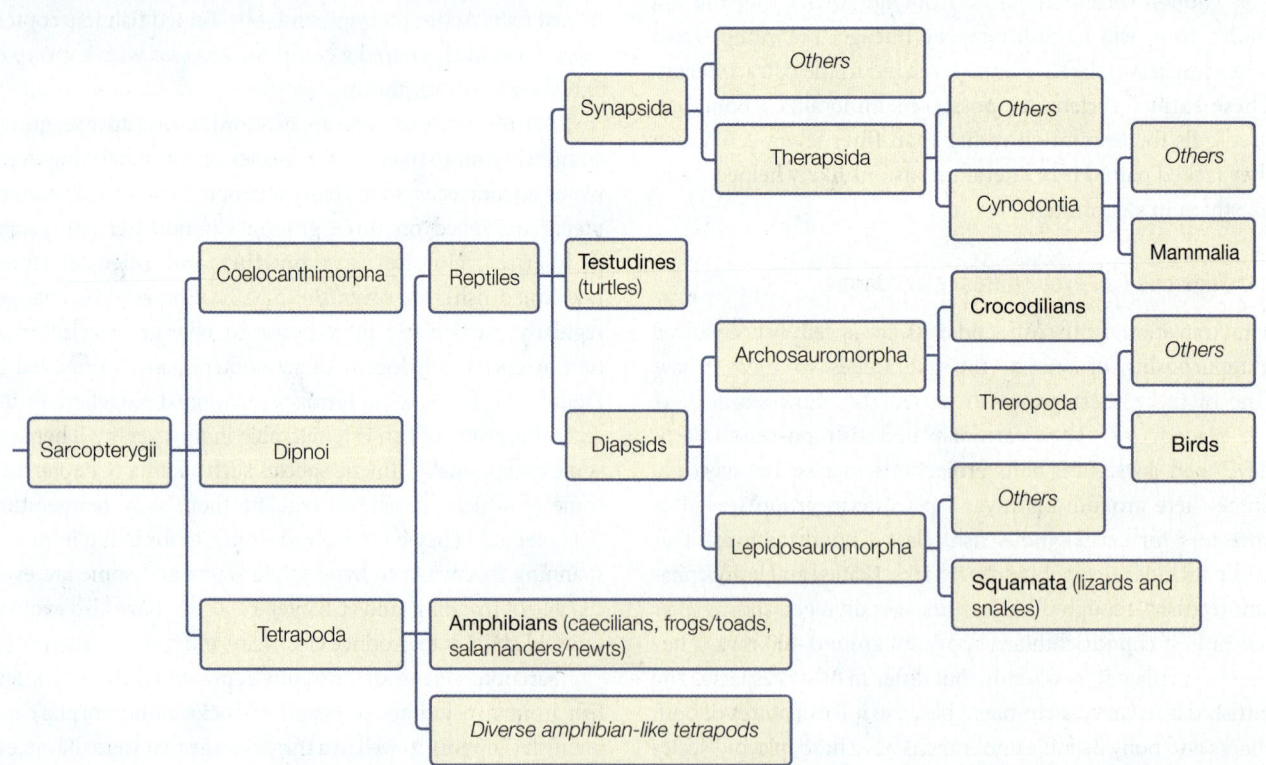

fins that connect to the trunk by a single bone. This contrasts to the situation with ray-finned fish, where the connections are much more complex. Their teeth are covered in enamel, the same material that covers our teeth. The two lineages, lungfish and coelocanths, last shared a common ancestor around 400 mya. Though the coelacanth lineage remained in seawater, the Dipnoi lineage invaded freshwater. The divergence contributed to the distinctions in their osmotic strategies (Chapter 13). The lungfish lineage evolved modified appendages, which may have facilitated their movement in waters with heavy vegetation, and a primitive lung, which may have facilitated their ability to move from water to land. One claim to fame for lungfish is their ability to survive severe dehydration by forming a **mucus** cocoon (Chapter 13).

Sarcopterygians gave rise to tetrapods

The transition from mostly aquatic to mostly terrestrial vertebrates began in sarcopterygians and occurred in the late Devonian, around 370 mya. The exact group that led to the tetrapods may never be known, but sarcopterygians as a group show a collection of adaptations that appear to have laid the foundation for the invasion of land. The extinct *Tiktaalik* is a genus of sarcopterygian that appears intermediate between fish and tetrapod. It had tetrapod-like lungs, distinct from the lungs of lungfish, and a rib structure and neck joint arrangement characteristic of the tetrapods.

Amphibians must return to water to breed

Amphibians are the first group of vertebrates to have made a home on land. Their name is derived from their ability to move between land and water, as does a frog, or from a requirement to spend part of the life in water, as does a toad. These are the most ancient of the extant **tetrapods**: animals with four legs (Figure 2.12). The group shares the following traits, which distinguish it from fish: a loss of the select bones in the skull, neck, and opercular region; a regression of the notochord and a more rigid spinal column; pelvic and pectoral appendicular modifications with greater musculature and replacement of fin rays with digits; and the fusion of the vertebral column with the pelvis via sacral vertebrae. Many of these features become more specialized in later tetrapods.

Amphibians differ from other tetrapods in that they are not amniotes. Amphibian eggs are simple in structure, with an embryo growing inside a layer of gelatinous material that must remain in water. In contrast, embryos of amniotes possess a set of four extraembryonic membranes: amnion, allantois, chorion, and yolk sac. The differences between amphibians and other tetrapods relate to the amphibian dependence on water. This group arose in the Carboniferous period, when life abounded in warm and humid swampy areas.

Amphibians are an intriguing group to study in terms of physiology. They are intermediate between fish and reptiles in many ways. Their larvae are aquatic and, like fish, respire through gills. As adults, most amphibians develop lungs and breathe air, although many rely in part on gas exchange across the external skin (cutaneous) or lining of the mouth (buccal). When in water, they face the same sort of osmotic challenges as do freshwater fish, with mechanisms to minimize ion loss across the body surface. Unlike fish, they excrete urea as a nitrogenous waste. Like reptiles, amphibians possess robust skeletal musculature that supports the animals while on land. Some amphibians, such as toads, possess a thickened body surface to limit evaporative water loss, though it is not as well developed as that of reptiles.

Reptiles and their ancestors have dominated land for 300 million years

Around 350 mya, the amniotes appeared on the scene. **Amniotes** (mammals, birds, and reptiles) possess extraembryonic membranes in the developing embryo. The exact origin of amniotes is unclear because even the earliest of reptilian fossils reflect two lineages. One lineage included the earliest of amniotes, and diverged to include modern mammals (synapsids) and an extinct group of reptiles (anapsids). The second lineage (diapsids) includes all extant reptiles and birds. The distinction between these groups is the number of openings in the side of the skull near the temple, which serves as an attachment point for jaw muscles. Synapsids have a single opening on each side; anapsids have no openings; and diapsids have paired openings (Figure 2.13). The exact phylogenetic relationship between turtles (Testudines) and other reptiles is debated; the turtle skull has anapsid morphology, but comparative genetics suggest a much closer relationship with diapsids.

As you will see in Chapter 16, the extraembryonic membranes have a profound impact on embryonic development, and lay the foundation for the placental development seen in

FIGURE 2.13 **Skulls from a synapsid and a diapsid**

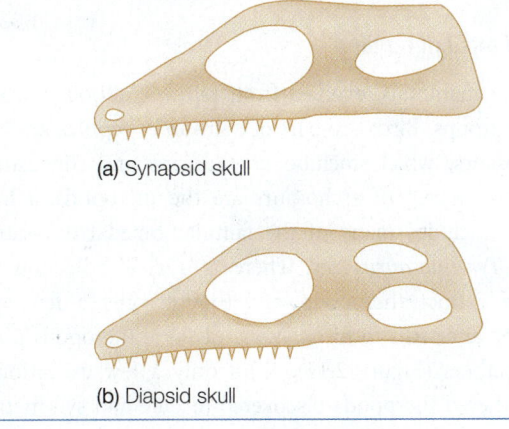

(a) Synapsid skull

(b) Diapsid skull

most mammals. In reptiles and birds, the nature of the egg-shell was essential for the complete transition to a terrestrial existence in amniotes. This commitment to land was also accompanied by modifications of the external body covering. As discussed in Chapter 13, the outer layer of skin, the *stratum corneum*, is a vital osmotic barrier that allows amniotes to resist water loss.

Mammals evolved from therapsid reptiles

Synapsids were an abundant group of reptiles in the Carboniferous period, and many of the familiar reptilian fossils belong to this group, including sail-backs (e.g., *Dimetrodon*). One of the more derived groups of synapsids was the therapsids. This group was the earliest to begin a transition toward a more upright posture, with appendages moving from the sides to a more ventral position. Many features of these early reptiles suggest an elevated metabolic rate. The sail of *Dimetrodon* and its relatives was thought to be a mechanism for warming the body. This is also the first group that evolved a secondary palate, which separates oral and nasal chambers. From these therapsid reptiles arose three lineages: dicynodonts, therocephalians, and cynodonts. Members of the latter group grew progressively smaller in body size, accompanied by changes in habits and diet, relying more on grazing and small prey, such as insects. Around 220 mya, the first of the mammal-like reptiles arose from small cynodonts, about the size of a mouse. By 210 mya, many of the synapsids had disappeared, but the early mammals that evolved from cynodonts thrived.

It is not yet known when the distinguishing features of mammals arose. Fur is thought to have appeared in early mammals, and there is little evidence of fur in cynodonts. In Chapter 16 we discuss the evolution of mammary glands and **lactation**, though the ancestral state of ill-defined mammary glands is seen in the most ancient of the living mammals, the monotremes. The transition from egg laying to live bearing was also an event that happened only after the early mammals evolved. Monotremes retain the egg-laying (**oviparous**) mode of their reptilian ancestors, whereas marsupials and placental mammals give live birth (**viviparous**).

Birds are modern reptiles

Birds, like mammals, evolved from reptiles, although from different groups. Birds are part of a group of reptiles known as archosaurs, which include crocodilians and dinosaurs. Within this group of archosaurs are the theropods, a lineage that includes many of the familiar bipedal dinosaurs such as *Tyrannosaurus rex*. There is a rich collection of fossils of extinct theropods, and though only a few appear to be ancestors to birds, many of these theropods possessed feathers (Figure 2.14). With only a few exceptions, most feathered theropods discovered to date had symmetrical feathers. As you will learn in Chapter 15, feathers must be

FIGURE 2.14 **Theropod fossil**

Photo source: Scott Nielsen/Bruce Coleman Inc.

asymmetrical to create the airflow patterns necessary to generate lift. The feather structure, in combination with other anatomical specializations, suggests that many of these theropods were able to maintain elevated body temperatures, with feathers serving as **insulation**. The birds are the only remaining representatives from the theropod lineage, and they remain distinctive from other reptiles in their thermal biology. Like mammals, birds are endotherms (see Chapter 15), though their distinct ancestries mean this is an example of convergent physiological evolution. Apart from feathers, most aspects of bird biology are similar to that of reptiles and distinct from that of mammals, including many skeletal features of the skull, vertebral column, and lower jaw.

CONCEPT CHECK

4. Which group of fish gave rise to the tetrapod lineage?
5. What is an amniote?
6. What is the phylogenetic relationship between mammals, birds, and reptiles?

EVOLUTIONARY CONSERVATION AND CONVERGENCE IN ANIMAL PHYSIOLOGY

Phylogenies create a framework for understanding why specific animals display their sets of physiological properties. The observation that some aspects of animal physiology are shared broadly is due in part to the common ancestry of animals. For example, much of the structural support for respiratory and **cardiovascular systems** evolved as a means to get oxygen to mitochondria, which appeared in ancient protists long before the origins of animals. Other physiological traits are innovations that arose in specific lineages, and in many cases arose repeatedly and independently by distinct mechanisms. For example, many taxa have representatives that are warm-bodied, an adaptation that is thought to increase physiological capacities. By comparing and contrasting the convergent physiology of warm-bodied insects, fish, mammals, and birds, physiologists can identify common themes and mechanisms.

Molecular Innovations

In a seminal paper in 1970, Susumu Ohno proposed that duplications of entire genomes occurred early in the evolution of vertebrates. Often, if a particular gene is found in a single copy in an invertebrate, there are four copies (or **isoforms**) in vertebrates. This "rule of four" reflects ancestral genome duplications; each single gene locus was duplicated, giving two copies of all genes, then reduplicated, giving four copies of all genes. The individual genes within the duplicated genomes underwent mutation, selection, and genetic drift to diverge into distantly related gene families. After a period of divergence, some individual genes duplicated again. The newly duplicated genes are more closely related to each other than to their distant ancestors, creating clusters of genes of similar origin.

When did these genome duplications occur? A possible answer comes from phylogenetic analyses of a family of genes involved in development, the *Hox* family. The first genome duplication probably occurred just before the agnathans diverged from the vertebrate lineage. The second duplication coincided with the development of jaws. The primitive chordates such as amphioxus have a single cluster of *Hox* genes; the agnathan lamprey has two or sometimes three clusters; and the more recent jawed vertebrates, from sharks to humans, possess at least four clusters of *Hox* genes. In each case, genome duplications coincided with important revolutions in morphological and physiological complexity. In later chapters, where we discuss the remarkable physiological complexity of vertebrates, recognize that this is enabled by whole-genome duplications and the subsequent diversity in important families of proteins. In the following sections, we explore some examples in which gene duplications and divergence played a central role in physiological evolution.

The myosin gene family divergence underlies much of animal diversity

As you will learn in Chapter 6, myosin is a molecular motor found in all eukaryotic organisms, suggesting that it first appeared more than 1 bya. Over the course of evolution, each lineage experienced complex, independent genetic events that resulted in an expansion of the myosin repertoire. Present-day eukaryotes produce more than 30 different classes of myosins, distinguished by major differences in structural organization and amino acid sequence. A myosin tree can be created using data from representatives of the multicellular eukaryotes (Figure 2.15). Plants greatly expanded the myosin 8 and 11 families, which are absent in fungi and animals. Animals possess many duplicated genes for myosin 2 (myosin II). While other eukaryotes have myosin II, only animals use it to build muscle.

One of the earliest events in animal evolution was the divergence of class II myosin into two subclasses. One type is used to build striated muscle. The other is used in smooth muscle and nonmuscle tissues. Each group of animals expanded myosin gene families in different ways. For example, *Drosophila* has only one gene of each myosin II subclass, but it can make many different myosin II isoforms by alternative gene splicing. Mammals have 15 different genes for myosin II. How did they get so many genes? How do they differ? What are the advantages of each isoform?

One of the reasons that vertebrates possess such large myosin II gene families can be traced back to the two rounds of whole-genome duplications that occurred more than 300 mya. This gave the ancestral vertebrates redundant copies of genes. Some mutations affected the promoter of the gene, which influenced when the gene was expressed. Some myosin II isoforms, such as perinatal and embryonic isoforms, are expressed only in specific tissues or during particular developmental windows. Some mutations occurred in the coding region of the gene, leading to a change in functional or structural properties. In Chapter 6 we discuss the kinetic differences between cardiac α-myosin and β-myosin. Cardiac α-myosin has greater maximal rates of ATP **hydrolysis** and shortening velocity, but cardiac β-myosin permits greater contractile efficiency, particularly at low contraction velocities. The modest structural differences in these two genes provide an opportunity to tailor **cardiac muscle** to the physiological challenges. In general, myosin diversification provided vertebrates with the opportunity to build specialized muscles, and respond more effectively to environmental, physiological, and developmental conditions.

Na$^+$/K$^+$ ATPase is essential for ion homeostasis and excitable tissues

Na$^+$ pumps are found in many taxa as a solution to the challenge of high external Na$^+$ concentrations. Though absent from higher plants, simple plants (mosses, algae) and fungi possess Na$^+$ pumps that allow these multicellular eukaryotes to export Na$^+$ from their cells.

The animal Na$^+$ pump is the **Na$^+$/K$^+$ ATPase**, better known as the **sodium-potassium pump**. It is a multimeric protein, though its functional features are linked to the structure of its alpha subunit. It belongs to the P-type ATPase family, and the IIC subfamily. Many taxa possess IIC subfamily ion pumps, including algae, fungi, and many protists, and thus its origin is likely prokaryotic. This ancestral gene evolved to generate

FIGURE 2.15 **Myosin gene family**

This tree shows the origins and diversity in myosin family members of eukaryotes, including plants (*Arabidopsis thaliana*), fungi (fission yeast, *Schizosaccharomyces pombe*), invertebrates (nematodes, *C. elegans*), and vertebrates (ricefish, *Oryzias* *latipes*). Note the expansion of the members of the myosin 2 gene family in animals. The names of myosin families are identified with Arabic numbers in this figure for simplicity; elsewhere in this text they are identified using Roman numerals.

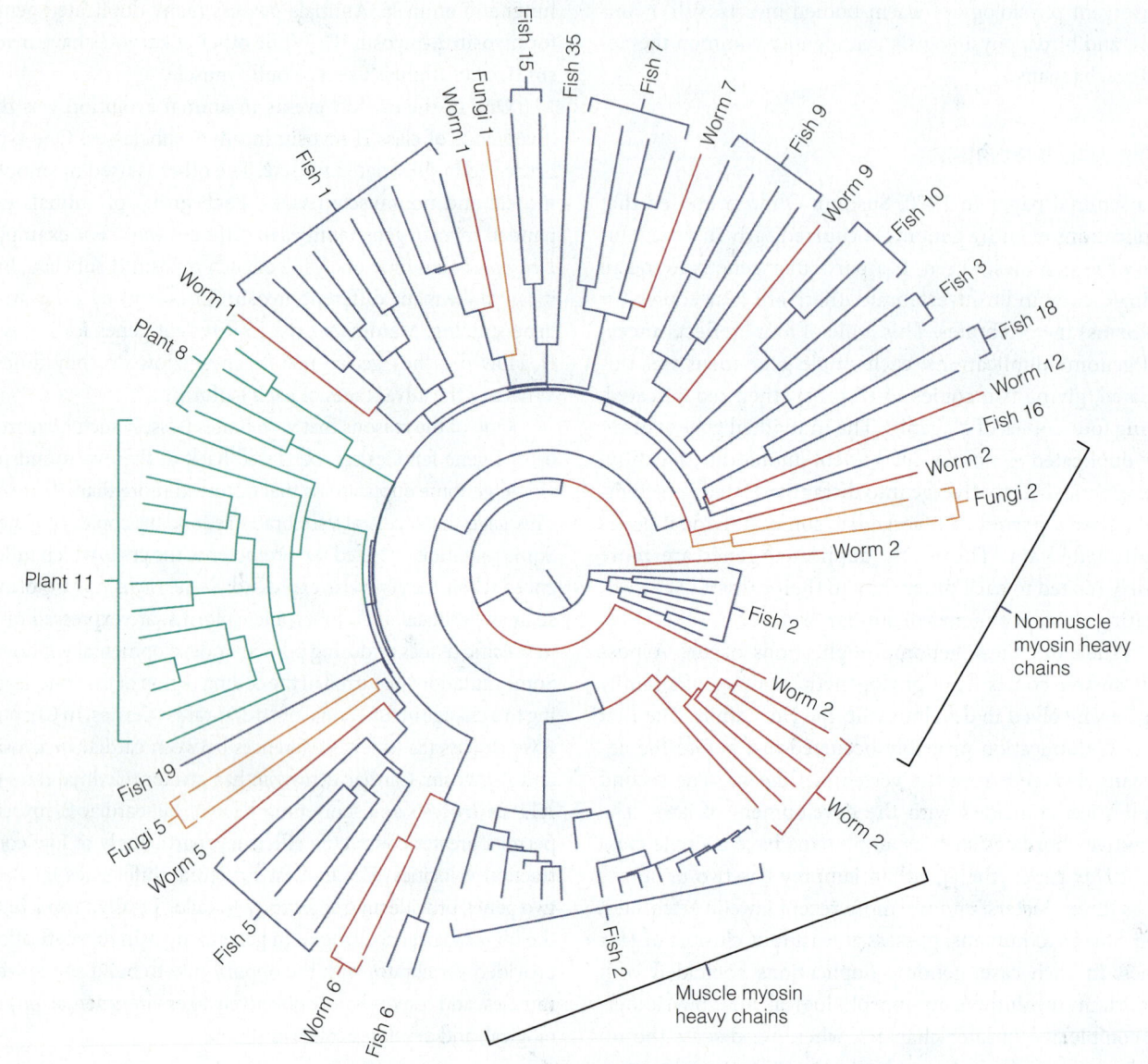

many types of ion-pumping ATPases, including many that appear in later chapters, such as Ca^{2+} ATPases, H^+ ATPase, K^+ ATPases, and Na^+/K^+ ATPase. However, only animals possess gene variants that are able to exchange Na^+ for K^+, making the Na^+/K^+ ATPase unique to animals. Appearing early in metazoan evolution, the alpha gene duplicated repeatedly through both gene and genome duplication, with the greatest diversity in isoforms seen in vertebrates. At some point prior to the origin of vertebrates, ancestral deuterostomes likely possessed a single copy of a Na^+/K^+ ATPase gene, which duplicated and evolved into the H^+/K^+ ATPase that is essential for the production of an acidic stomach.

Within animals, there are many examples of how evolution of Na^+/K^+ ATPase genes contributes to adaptations in relation to osmoregulation. Individuals change the expression of Na^+/K^+ ATPase genes when changing environments; the ability to alter the expression undoubtedly contributes to the ability of fish to move between freshwater and seawater at different life stages. Lineages alter **constitutive** expression of the genes with evolutionary isolation in a novel environment; copepods that evolved in marine environments experience changes in gene expression as they become established as an invasive species in freshwater. There is also evolution of the structure of Na^+/K^+ ATPase subunits. Many plants have toxins that impair the

Na$^+$/K$^+$ ATPase of animals that feed on them. In turn, many lineages of plant-feeding insects have evolved genes with amino acid differences that prevent the toxin from binding.

The Na$^+$/K$^+$ ATPase enables animal cells to create an electrical potential across the cell membrane. As you will see in later chapters, neurons (Chapter 5) and muscles (Chapter 6) depend on rapid changes in polarity of the cell membrane to trigger excitation. Though the rapid transitions (depolarization, repolarization) are due to ion channels, the Na$^+$/K$^+$ ATPase has an important role in maintaining membrane ion gradients.

The appearance of collagen coincided with tissue formation

Multicellular organisms have evolved mechanisms that enable collections of cells to be arranged in three-dimensional space. A cell wall is produced in both plants and fungi, though the composition differs between these kingdoms. In plants, the cell wall is cellulose and in fungi, it is chitin. A cell wall prevents the plant and fungal cells from swelling beyond tolerable limits. The rigid structure also acts as a barrier to contact between cell membranes. The unicellular ancestors of animals lacked a cell wall, a distinction that had a number of consequences. First, it permitted cells to interact via their cell membranes using specific transmembrane adhesion proteins, such as cadherins. Choanoflagellates, the closest protist ancestor to animals, possess a rich repertoire of cadherins.

In addition to membrane receptor proteins, even the earliest animal cells were able to secrete proteins into the extracellular space to construct the macromolecular network known as the extracellular matrix. The extracellular matrix protein collagen was one of the earliest innovations in animals. Some collagens can be used to form fibrils, which have important roles in connective tissue (Figure 2.16). Other non–fibril-forming collagens can be used to make sheets, such as the basal lamina that forms the foundation of many tissues. Even sponges possess at least two genes for collagens, one fibrillar and one nonfibrillar. The animals that evolved from the basal metazoans have each benefited from diversification of collagen genes.

Most anatomic features of animals can be traced back to their extracellular matrix. Complex tissues are constructed on a platform of the basal lamina, a fibrous sheet that is both a cellular support and a physical barrier. Muscles rely on connective tissue to connect myocytes to each other, as well as muscle to bone (via tendons), and bone to bone (via ligaments). The lack of a cell wall permits a direct connection between a cell and its extracellular fluid, which is also essential for efficient communication between cells.

Hormones extended the range of cell-to-cell signaling

The exquisite complexity of cell communication in animals evolved from an ancient capacity to sense external conditions.

FIGURE 2.16 **Collagen fibrils**

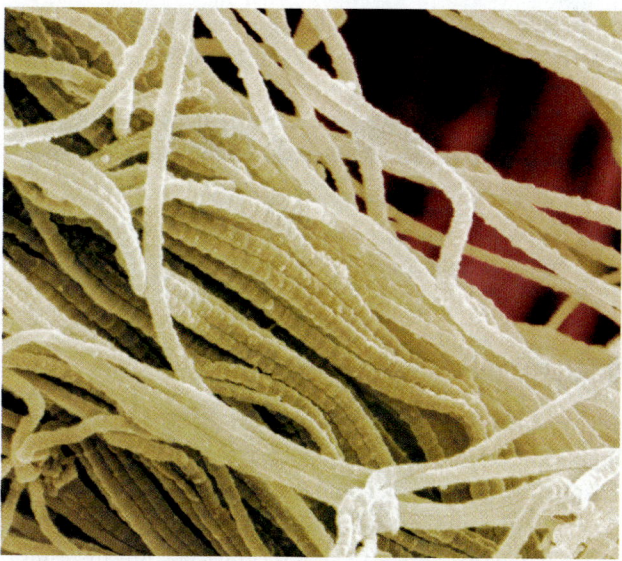

Photo source: Paul Gunning/Science Source.

In single-celled protists, the main purpose of sensory abilities is to detect potential food and avoid potential risks, both of which serve to ensure that the single autonomous cell survives. In multicellular organisms, the nature of cellular communication became more diverse and more specialized, incorporating internal signaling molecules. Animals began to produce chemical messengers that could be released and detected elsewhere. Local autocrine and paracrine signals were sufficient in small, simple animals, but as body size and complexity grew, a more sophisticated set of signals was needed for communication across greater distances. The evolution of an internal circulation permitted the use of this system for sending chemical signals to distant locations (endocrine signaling). A **hormone** is a signaling factor that transmits messages from one part of the body to a distant site. Though other multicellular organisms use hormones, their signaling pathways are best developed in animals.

For an endocrine signal to function, there must have been both the ability to make a signaling molecule and a receptor that detects the signal. Thus, the evolution of hormone-receptor interactions provides insight into how complex systems arose via natural selection. For example, **aldosterone** is a **steroid hormone** that is produced only in tetrapods, where it plays a role in water and mineral balance. How could the ability to produce aldosterone as a signal evolve in the absence of a receptor for aldosterone? In early vertebrates, there was a single receptor for a group of steroid hormones known as corticoids. Just prior to the divergence of cartilaginous fish and bony fish, a genomic event duplicated the corticoid receptor. The receptors diverged to provide different routes of regulating glucocorticoid and mineralocorticoids. Once the ability to produce aldosterone arose in tetrapods, they had already evolved a receptor capable of binding and responding to it. With the ability to both produce and respond to aldosterone, changes to the sensitivity and downstream targets could evolve to provide greater discrimination between the ancestral receptors.

CONCEPT CHECK

7. Did myosin evolve as a muscle protein?
8. When did collagen evolve and what is its significance?
9. What are cadherins?

Integrative Processes

Many of the anatomical and physiological specializations of animals relate in one way or another to the acquisition of nutrients. The diet provides both the raw material for biosynthesis and the energy to support metabolic demands. As a result, much of physiological evolution is connected directly or indirectly to the acquisition and processing of nutrients.

The evolution of complexity was accompanied by an increase in cephalization

The earliest animals had a very simple nervous system, with sensory receptors scattered around the body and little in the way of central processing of information. The nerve nets of cnidarians, for example, permitted coordination of muscles needed for movement and sensory input for environmental factors such as light. With the evolution of complexity, and the appearance of bilateralism, there was a trend toward concentrating sensory and nervous systems in the anterior part of the animal. Animals used this orientation to move directionally, with their most sensitive regions moving forward, ready to follow attractants, find food, or recognize threats. As the nervous system itself grew in complexity, the importance of the head grew in parallel. In arthropods, evolution led to an increase in the number of segments incorporated into the head region, perhaps permitting more extravagant sensory and feeding structures. With vertebrates, and the appearance of a notochord and corresponding nerve cord, a more elaborate head was formed. In mammals, it sometimes appears that most physiological processes serve to ensure the health of the brain. The central nervous system is responsible for controlling almost everything: feeding, breathing, reflexes, sensory processing, thermoregulation, movement, and even reproduction.

Terrestriality arose in multiple lineages

The ability to control internal osmolarity independent of external conditions was essential for the success of the animal lineages that invaded land. The earliest of many waves of terrestrial invaders were invertebrates. First the ancient myriapods, then their arthropod predators, invaded land more than 420 mya. Later, around 400 mya, the first tetrapods ventured onto land. Other groups of animals have select lineages that have invaded land, including several taxa of worms, such as nematodes and earthworms.

The study of the physiological adaptations of animals that have succeeded on land reveals many common themes, and some unique approaches. A terrestrial existence puts animals at risk for desiccation, and species that successfully invaded land demonstrate evolutionary adaptations that reduce water loss. These animals need a body surface that is more resistant to desiccation than is found in their aquatic relatives (Chapter 13). No longer able to excrete metabolic wastes directly into the water, they also need an alternative way to produce and dispose of nitrogenous waste (Chapter 13). Locomotor systems have evolved in ways that compensate for the greater effects of gravity (Chapter 12). Respiratory systems, though still focused on collecting oxygen, must have ways of dealing with differences in the O_2/CO_2 content and the viscosity of the respiratory fluids, while also ensuring that the respiratory surface has the appropriate structural support (Chapter 11), all while ensuring that it is not working to the detriment of water balance (Chapter 13) and **thermoregulation** (Chapter 15).

Metabolic pathways are broadly conserved, though metabolic rate varies widely

Prokaryotes (Eubacteria and Archaea) distinguish themselves by the remarkable capacity to use biochemical adaptations to solve environmental challenges. Animals, in contrast, rely much more on physiological evolution, where anatomy and functional properties contribute to evolutionary success. Biochemical variation between animals does occur, but the general patterns are much more similar among animals than among bacteria. Many of the unique biochemical capabilities in animals, such as the ability to digest cellulose (Chapter 14), in fact rely on symbiotic organisms, taking advantage of their biochemical capacities. Nonetheless, there is one area of biochemistry where animals show remarkable variation, and that is the realm of **metabolic rate** variation.

Metabolism is the sum of all biochemical processes; metabolic rate is measured as heat production per unit time. Many physiological studies identify differences in metabolic rate between animals and control of metabolic rate within animals. Of course, there are differences among animals that relate to lifestyle, such as mode of locomotion (Chapter 12) and diet (Chapter 14). One of the longest standing controversies in physiology is the mechanism that accounts for differences in metabolic rate in relation to body size (Chapters 1 and 14). There are phylogenetic differences related to physiological traits, such as body temperature, where species that maintain a high body temperature do so at the expense of metabolic energy (Chapter 15). Within many taxa, there are individual groups of animals that show a capacity to induce **metabolic depression** under adverse conditions. Later in this text you will learn that tardigrades, rotifers, and brine shrimp depress metabolic rate to barely detectible rates when they experience severe dehydration; insects and frogs undergo metabolic arrest during freezing (Chapter 13); and birds and mammals cool their bodies in the cold as a means of sparing metabolic energy (Chapter 14). Understanding the phylogenetic separation between these various groups prompts questions about the properties of animals that permit select groups to converge on evolutionary strategies to control metabolism.

CONCEPT CHECK

10. What is cephalization?
11. Why is metabolism more diverse in bacteria than in animals?

SUMMARY

Understanding the diversity of animals and phylogenetic relatedness is essential to exploring physiological evolution. In the evolution of metazoans, solutions to the challenges of multicellularity were constrained by the traits of protist ancestors, primarily the lack of a cell wall. The trajectory of animal physiological evolution included milestones such as the formation of tissues, the three-dimensional complexity permitted by the evolution of a coelom, and the acquisition of lineage-specific novel traits through evolution, development, and their interactions. Multiple rounds of genome duplications facilitated the radiation of vertebrates. The redundancy of duplicated copies of critical genes permitted evolutionary divergence in the form of anatomical and physiological specialization.

REVIEW QUESTIONS

1. **LO①** What is the significance of the similarity between choanoflagellates and choanocytes?

2. **LO①** Why aren't protozoans considered animals?

3. **LO②** Which animals are diploblasts?

4. **LO②** Explain why arthropods are considered Ecdysozoans.

5. **LO②** Did all jawed animals evolve from the same agnathan ancestors?

6. **LO③** How many times did terrestriality arise in animal lineages?

7. **LO③** What is meant by the term "a new head"?

8. **LO④** What is the significance of the evolution of the Na^+/K^+ ATPase?

9. **LO④** When did endothermy arise in animal evolution?

10. **LO④** Which came first, hormones or hormone receptors?

SYNTHESIS QUESTIONS

1. Speculate on how animals might have evolved if the ancestral protist possessed a cell wall.

2. What critical events led to the origin and diversification of tetrapods?

3. Would you expect the underlying metabolic pathways to be similar or different in animal models of metabolic arrest?

3

Chemistry, Biochemistry, and Cell Physiology

FIGURE 3.1 **Wood frog (*Lithobates sylvaticus*) in the frozen state**

Photo source: Ted Kinsman/Science Source.

A nimals are collections of chemical reactions, organized into compartments—organelles, cells, tissues—and as such, they behave in ways that are consistent with the laws of chemistry and physics. Physiological processes of animals reflect strategies to regulate chemistry to support the animal. This may seem overly simplistic, but consider the plight of the wood frog, *Lithobates sylvaticus*, (Figure 3.1) from the perspective of a biochemist.

Like many animals, frogs do not control their body temperature. As their environment cools, so does their body. As temperature decreases, the wood frog has to cope with multiple effects of temperature. Metabolic demand decreases as temperatures drop, due to reduced movement, slower heart rate, and slower rates of digestion and respiration. Metabolic rate drops by about half with each 10°C decrease in temperature. In parallel with the reduced metabolic demand is a lower rate of energy production. All of these metabolic changes can be attributed to direct or indirect changes in chemical reactions in response to changes in temperature.

In addition to reductions in chemical reaction rates, the frog tissues change in their physical properties. The membranes that surround cells and organelles become less liquid and more solid. This affects many membrane-dependent processes such as transport, which in turn affect the activities of muscles and nerves, tissues that depend upon regulated changes in membrane electrochemical gradients.

As winter approaches, the frog prepares for a more drastic change. The wood frog buries itself under the leaf debris and prepares to be frozen. Organs produce high levels of sugars that will help protect tissues. Slowly its extremities freeze, then its body core, and its organs begin to shrivel as water is drawn from the inside of cells to become incorporated into ice in the blood. The frog enters a period of suspended animation, where its metabolic reactions slow to undetectable levels.

All is not lost for this frozen frog. With the onset of spring, the frog begins to thaw. Within a very short period of time, it will be hopping again across the forest floor, heading to water and preparing to mate. It is easy enough to simply appreciate the remarkable life of a wood frog, but to understand how this animal is able to survive these transitions depends upon an awareness of the rules of chemistry and biochemistry.

This chapter presents an overview of the basic rules of physics, chemistry, biochemistry, cell biology, and evolution, each discussed within the context of animal biology. It serves as a foundation for later chapters, and (if you are lucky) will be a review of material covered in prerequisites and previous courses. More likely, it will become a useful reference to understand how the basic properties of cells account for the more complex physiological properties of organisms. ∎

OVERVIEW

Physiology is the study of how animals work and how they solve the challenges of surviving in the natural environment. Though we often think of animal physiology as a study of organs, systems, and whole animals, it is important to recognize that reasons for many of these features can be traced back to underlying rules of chemistry, biochemistry, and cell biology. Many of the properties of organs and systems emerge from regulation of cellular processes, such as energy production, membrane transport, cellular anatomy, and gene expression. While the physiology of an animal is much more than the sum of these molecular and cellular processes, an awareness of how cells work is vital to understanding complex physiological processes.

CHEMISTRY

In the purely chemical world, chemical reactions proceed according to the rules of *thermodynamics*. The first law of thermodynamics, also called the law of conservation of energy, states that energy can be converted from one form to another but the total amount of energy in the universe is constant. The second law, also called the law of entropy, states that the universe is becoming more chaotic. Both laws describe the constraints that exist when energy is transferred between systems. With any spontaneous transfer of energy, some energy is diverted in a way that increases the randomness (entropy) of a system, another form of energy. Although each chemical reaction conforms to these principles, living organisms are able to delay the inevitable increase in entropy. The survival of living organisms depends upon an ability to impede the natural processes that lead to chemical breakdown.

Energy

Energy is the ability to do work. In our world, gasoline is an important form of chemical energy. We know that if the fuel tank of a car is full of gasoline, we have the potential to use this fuel to move the car from place to place. Burning the gasoline causes the pistons in the engine to move, turning the drive shaft and ultimately the wheels. This familiar analogy illustrates many important principles that govern energy transfers, or **energetics**. The gasoline in the tank has **potential energy** trapped within its chemical structure. When gasoline is ignited, the resulting explosion releases heat and carbon dioxide, moving the piston in its cylinder. This type of energy is **kinetic energy**, the energy of movement.

The standard SI (Système International) unit of energy is the **joule**, although the imperial unit, the **calorie**, persists in the scientific literature. A joule is defined in many ways, depending on the circumstances. In electrical terms, a joule (J) is the amount of energy used when 1 watt of power (W) is expended for the period of 1 second (1 J = 1 W sec). Conversely, a watt is defined as a joule per second. You are probably most familiar with the units of energy from your household electrical bill, with energy consumption expressed in kilowatt hours (1 kW · h = 3.6 × 10^6 J). In more biological terms, a piece of toast with butter has about 300 kJ of energy, which is enough energy to allow you to run for about 6 minutes or light a 100-watt bulb for about 50 minutes.

All energy is kinetic energy, potential energy, or a combination of both. However, in the context of biological systems it is more useful to classify types of energy by other categories (Figure 3.2).

- **Radiant energy** is energy that is released from an object and transmitted to another object by waves or particles. The sun is the most obvious source of radiant energy, emitting light that serves as an energy source for photosynthetic organisms. Other forms of radiant energy occur in animals, such as the infrared radiation given off by warm-bodied objects, which can be detected by animals such as snakes.
- **Mechanical energy** is a combination of potential and kinetic energy that can be used to move objects from place to place. A flying bird uses its wings to produce the mechanical energy necessary for flight. A kangaroo uses its legs to store mechanical energy in the form of elastic storage energy. Recoil of these "springs" helps the kangaroo hop. Many forms of mechanical energy have important roles in animal locomotion.
- **Electrical energy** is a combination of potential and kinetic energy that results from the movement of charged particles down a charge gradient. Excitable tissues, such as neurons and muscle, rely on electrical signals across the cell membrane.
- **Thermal energy** is a form of kinetic energy that is reflected in the movement of particles, and serves to increase temperature. Animals can capture thermal energy arising from chemical reactions, and use physiological mechanisms to control thermal energy exchanges with the environment.
- **Chemical energy** is a form of potential energy that is held within the bonds of chemical structures. It is important in all metabolic reactions, including transport processes such as ion pumping.

Food webs transfer energy

Most biological processes are essentially transfers of energy from one form to another. When you see and smell a rose, the perception is essentially a cascade of chemical and electrical energy transfers between the sensory system and the brain.

FIGURE 3.2 Biological energy

The five main forms of energy relevant to biological systems, with examples of physiological processes that depend upon them.

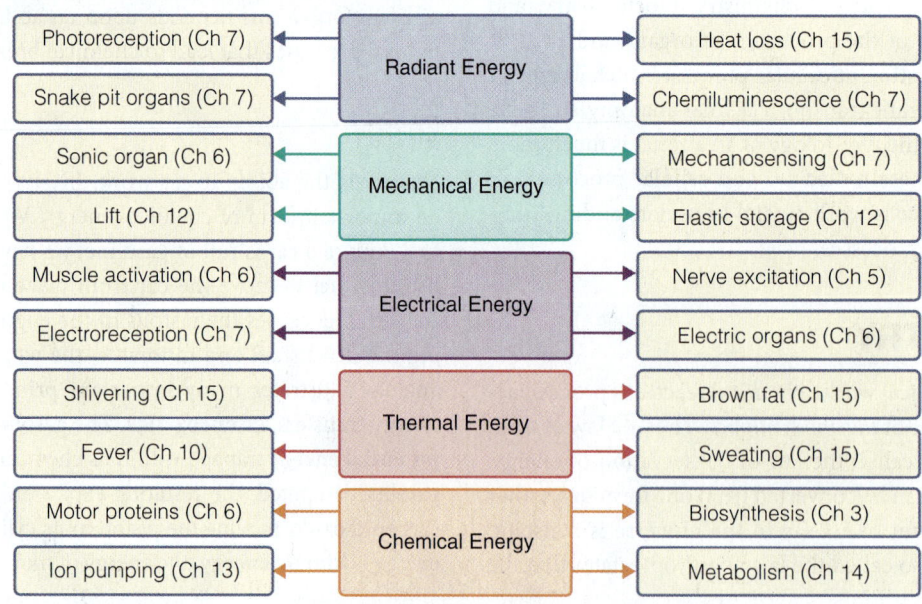

We are more familiar with the concept of energy transfers in the context of food webs. Plants capture the energy of **photons** and use it to create sugars. Herbivorous animals eat the plants, and carnivores eat the herbivores. At each level, some potential energy in the diet is assimilated to form animal tissues. Some potential energy is converted to heat, which is either lost to the environment or retained within the animal. Dietary potential energy is also transferred to kinetic energy, when animals use nutrients to fuel locomotion. A portion of the potential energy in the diet is locked in chemical structures that can't be liberated by the animal, and is excreted in waste products. Light is the ultimate source of dietary energy for most animals; it also provides the energy that allows animals to use vision and perceive color.

The chemical energy transferred between trophic levels is stored within molecules in the bonds between atoms. Chemical reactions liberate energy from one bond in order to produce other bonds. We discuss the nature of chemical bonds and the role of energy in bond formation a bit later in this chapter. However, other forms of energy are also critical components of biological function.

Energy is stored in electrochemical gradients

Molecules within a system tend to disperse or *diffuse* randomly within the available space. Two aspects of **diffusion** govern the properties of many biological processes. First, diffusion is certain to lead to a random distribution of molecules, but the rate of diffusion can be slow. Many physiological systems function to reduce the reliance on slow rates of diffusion. Second, the tendency of molecules to diffuse is a source of energy that cells can use to drive other processes. Living

organisms can invest energy to delay the inevitable tendency toward randomness. Similarly, biological systems can invest energy to move molecules out of a random distribution. The resulting **diffusion gradient** is a form of energy storage that the cell can use for other purposes. Diffusion gradients are often created across biological membranes (Figure 3.3).

A **chemical gradient** arises when one type of molecule occurs at a higher concentration on one side of a membrane. The **absolute** concentrations on either side of a membrane are less important than the relative concentrations. Chemical gradients are typically expressed as a ratio of the concentrations of the specific molecule on either side of the membrane. For example, you might say that a given molecule is tenfold more concentrated outside the cell.

An **electrical gradient** arises if the distribution of charged molecules is unequal on either side of an electrical barrier in a circuit. The electrical gradient across the barrier is dependent on the distributions of all the charged molecules combined. The strength of the electrical gradient is expressed in the electrical unit of volts. In cells, membranes are the electrical barrier and the electrical gradient is called the *membrane potential*.

The nature of the molecule determines whether the potential energy of the gradient is primarily electrical or chemical. If a molecule is uncharged, then it can only form a chemical gradient. A charged molecule can form a chemical gradient and can influence the electrical gradient. In animal cells, the concentration of Na^+ is much greater outside the cell than inside; there is both an electrical gradient (more positive charges outside the cell) and a chemical gradient (more Na^+ ions outside the cell). Transmembrane gradients are often discussed as **electrochemical gradients**.

FIGURE 3.3 **Storage of potential energy in electrochemical gradients**
Animals can use the energy stored as **(a)** chemical gradients or **(b)** electrical gradients, or membrane potential.

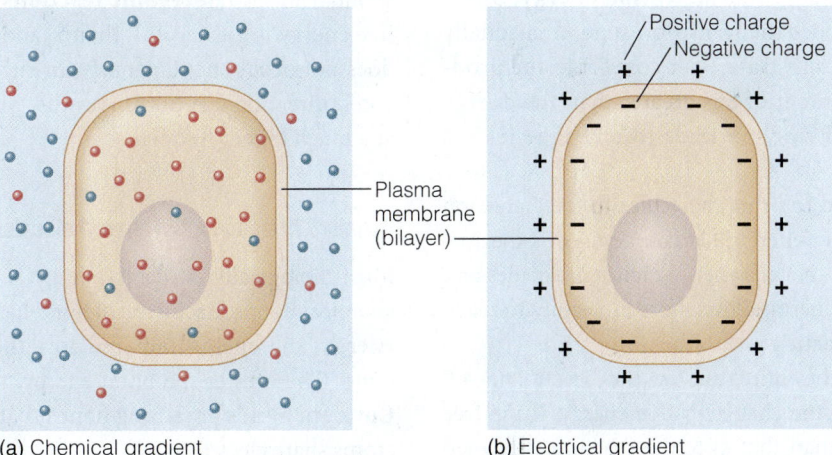

(a) Chemical gradient

(b) Electrical gradient

Chemical energy is transferred in chemical reactions

Every chemical has a characteristic energy associated with its structure. The energy is associated with the bonds between atoms. Bond strengths differ depending on the properties of the atoms, the distance between electrons and the nucleus, and the number of electrons shared when forming a bond. The energy of bonds, or bond strength, is measured in joules. For example, an H–H bond has an energy of 435 kJ per mol, or about 0.7 attojoules per bond. This is the energy that is required to break the bond, or the energy that must be invested to make the bond.

Most chemical reactions involve changes in energy, which arise when bonds are made and broken. Let's consider a simple reaction in which a single substrate, S, becomes a single product, P:

$$S \rightarrow P$$

At any given time, each molecule of S is vibrating in solution, experiencing subtle changes in its structure. A single molecule of S at times moves quickly (lots of kinetic energy) and at other times moves slowly (less kinetic energy). At any point in time, the collection of S molecules would have different energy contents, depicted in Figure 3.4a as a frequency distribution. Occasionally, a molecule of S has so much energy that it is able to assume a specific structure that is vulnerable to a more significant change: the chemical reaction. This structure of S changes to a **transition state**, something that is intermediate between S and P. Thus, the equation of the reaction should take into account the transition state (S*), and be written as

$$S \rightarrow S^* \rightarrow P$$

Discussion about energetic transitions in reactions revolve around **free energy** (G), which we discuss in more detail in a later section. The progression of the reaction from S to P, expressed in terms of energy content, is shown in Figure 3.4b. The free energy required for a molecule to reach the transition state is the **activation energy**, or E_A. Once a molecule reaches the transition state, it is equally likely to revert to the substrate, S, or convert to the product, P. The energy content of S is greater than the energy of P, so the chemical reaction leads to a change in free energy (ΔG).

Energy is required to bring molecules to the transition state, and one source of energy that can be used is thermal energy. An infusion of thermal energy excites molecules and the additional kinetic energy allows more molecules to reach E_A, accelerating the reaction.

When looking at the entire reaction, the direction (S → P or P → S) depends on the change in free energy. If the free energy of P is lower than that of S, the reaction is termed

FIGURE 3.4   Chemical reactions, substrates, products, and thermal energy

(a) A collection of substrate molecules, S, possesses an average energy level and an average arrangement of electrons around its nucleus. But at any given time, some S molecules are energy rich and others energy poor. **(b)** Occasionally a molecule of S might absorb enough energy from the surroundings (perhaps from a molecular collision) that it achieves the transition state. At this point it could revert to S, or change into a novel product, P.

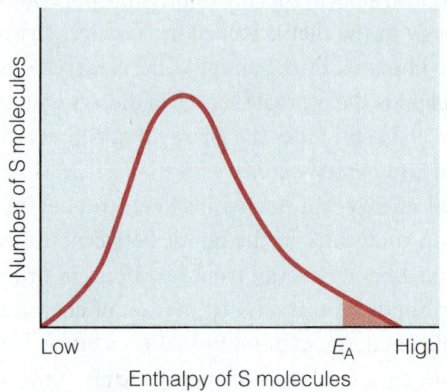

(a)

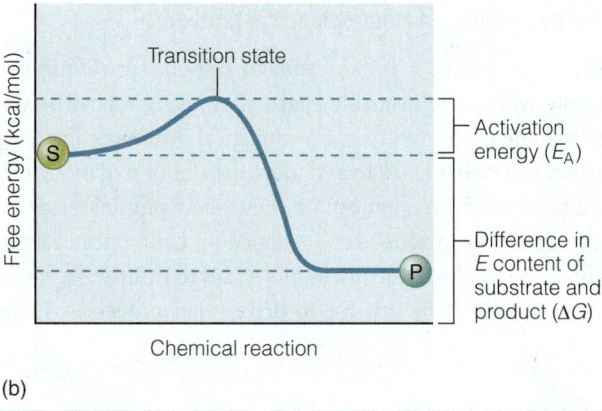

(b)

exergonic; it is thermodynamically possible and can occur spontaneously. **Endergonic reactions** are those in which the free energy is greater in P than S, and the forward direction does not occur spontaneously. In either scenario, the unfavored direction can occur, but the favored direction occurs at a much higher frequency.

Covalent bonds involve shared electrons

Most biologically available energy is stored in the form of chemical bonds. Each type of bond has a characteristic **bond energy**, the energy required to either form or break the bond. The greater the bond energy, the stronger the bond. **Covalent bonds** are strong bonds that are formed when two atoms share electrons.

Each element has a characteristic arrangement of electrons that influences the types of bonds it can form. Specifically, for the six common biological elements (H, C, O, S, P, N), each atom has at least one unpaired electron in its outer electron shell. Atoms with unpaired electrons can readily form covalent bonds with other atoms with unpaired electrons. These atoms share electrons so readily that they are rarely present in elemental form. Atoms with more than one unpaired electron can form multiple covalent bonds. For instance, molecular oxygen has two oxygen atoms joined by a double covalent bond. Large molecules are built from a collection of individual atoms attached by covalent bonds.

Several of the most common bonds are shown in Figure 3.5, which also shows molecular combinations, or functional groups, that recur in biological chemistry.

FIGURE 3.5 **Important functional groups and bonds**

Although there are many types of bonds and functional groups, those illustrated here are particularly common in macromolecular structure.

Functional groups		Covalent bonds	
O‖ —C—OH	Carboxyl	—S—S—	Disulfide
H| —N—H	Amino	—C—O—‖ O	Ester
—OH	Hydroxyl	O‖ O‖ —P—O—P—|OH |OH	Phosphodiester
H| —C—H|H	Methyl	—C—S—‖ O	Thioester
O‖ —P—OH|OH	Phosphoryl	—C—O—C—	Ether
—SH	Sulfhydryl	H| —N—C—‖ O	Peptide

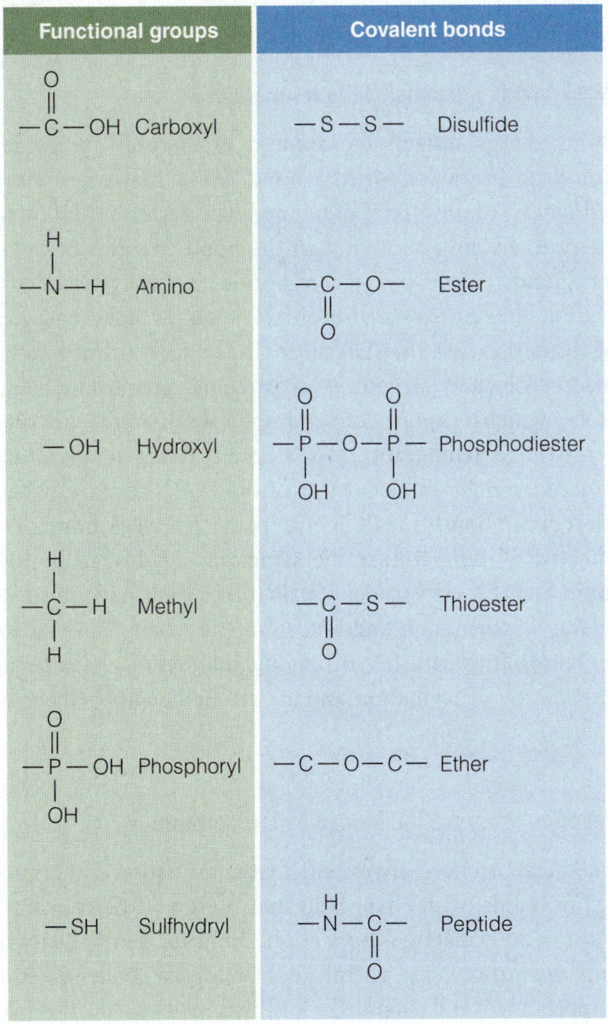

Weak bonds control macromolecular structure

Noncovalent bonds organize molecules into three-dimensional structures. In general, noncovalent bonds are called **weak bonds** or sometimes weak interactions to further distinguish them from strong bonds.

Weak bonds arise between atoms with asymmetrical distributions of electrons either within the atom or between atoms. Four types of weak bonds can be distinguished based on how they form molecular interactions: hydrogen bonds, van der Waals forces, ionic bonds, and **hydrophobic** interactions (Figure 3.6).

To understand the nature of most weak bonds, we start with the behavior of the electrons that orbit the nucleus. Some atoms have a nucleus so adept at attracting electrons that when a bond between atoms breaks, an electron from one atom remains with the other to create ions. Free sodium, for example, has lost one of its electrons, creating Na^+, a positively charged ion, or **cation**. Free chloride possesses an extra electron, creating Cl^-, an electrically charged ion, or **anion**. When an anion interacts with a cation, they can form a compound held together by an **ionic bond**. Most of the molecules we think of as salts, acids, and bases rely on ionic bonds to join anions and cations.

Within a molecule, a covalent bond arises when electrons are shared between two atoms. When two atoms are the same, the electrons of the bond are shared equally between them. When the atoms are dissimilar, the electrons in a bond can be shared unequally. This asymmetry in electron distribution creates a polarity, or **dipole**, within the

FIGURE 3.6 **Weak bonds**

Four types of weak bonds are van der Waals forces, hydrogen bonds, ionic bonds, and hydrophobic interactions.

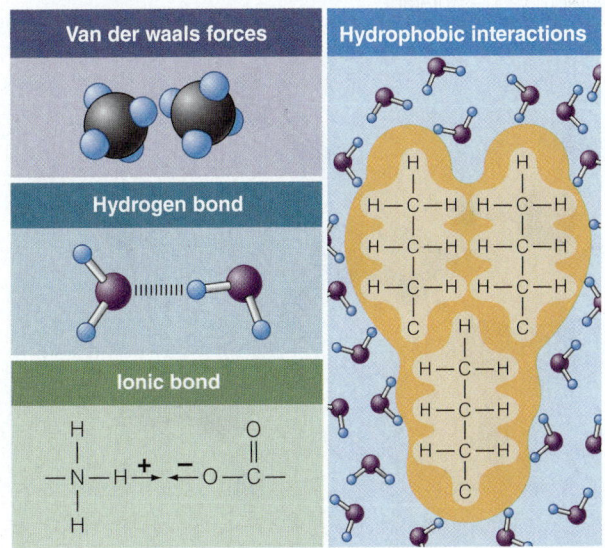

molecular structure. One region is slightly negative (δ^-) and the other is slightly positive (δ^+). In a water molecule, the electrons in the O–H covalent bond are not shared equally: The oxygen atom more strongly attracts the electron, giving the oxygen a δ^- and the hydrogen a δ^+. This asymmetry can arise in molecules that have a bond between a hydrogen and nitrogen, fluorine, or oxygen, each a strongly electronegative element.

If two molecules possessing dipoles encounter each other, the atom with the δ^- can become attracted to the hydrogen with the δ^+. This attraction constitutes a **hydrogen bond**. Many of the properties of water can be attributed to the hydrogen bonds formed between the δ^+ of hydrogen of one water molecule and the δ^- of oxygen in another water molecule (Figure 3.7). Hydrogen bonds are also critical to the three-dimensional structure of nucleic acids and proteins.

The dipoles arising across a covalent bond between H and O are relatively strong, but bonds between H and less electronegative atoms, such as carbon (C), can form small, transient dipoles. When an atom with a transient dipole encounters another atom, the distribution of electrons in the second atom is altered. The weak interaction between the two dipoles is the **van der Waals force**. Van der Waals forces are effective only over a very narrow range of atomic distances. When two atoms are far away, the dipole of one atom has no effect on the electron cloud of the other. As the atoms approach, the attraction between the atoms increases.

When the atoms get too close, their electron shells repel each atom away from the other, creating a dispersion force. The van der Waals radius is the distance at which the attractive force is at its greatest. Each atom has a characteristic van der Waals radius. The shape of molecules influences the strength of the dipoles. Long, thin molecules, such as fatty acids, can produce greater dipoles than short, bulky molecules with the same number of atoms and electrons. This allows the long, thin molecules to arrange themselves closer together. The van der Waals forces between fatty acids of the cell membrane are responsible for the flat, leaf-like arrangement of the lipid bilayer.

Van der Waals forces, hydrogen bonds, and ionic bonds form the basis of mutual attraction between two charged or slightly charged atoms. However, **hydrophobic interactions** form between atoms because of a mutual aversion to water. Whole molecules or specific regions of large molecules can be hydrophobic ("water-fearing"). The bonds within hydrophobic molecules share electrons equally and therefore do not possess significant dipoles. With little internal charge, they cannot interact effectively with the more polar molecules such as water.

Weak bonds are sensitive to temperature

Bond energy reflects the amount of thermal energy required to break (or form) a bond. Weak bonds are more vulnerable to the effects of temperature because their bond energies are much lower than the bond energies of covalent bonds. Whereas covalent bonds have energies of formation of 200–900 kcal/mol, weak bonds have energies of formation less than 5 kcal/mol. The three-dimensional macromolecular structures of proteins, membranes, and DNA, which primarily depend upon weak bonds, are also sensitive to temperature. As a result, rising temperature can cause macromolecules to unfold, or *denature,* when these weak bonds break. However, not all weak bonds are affected by temperature the same way. Hydrogen bonds, ionic bonds, and van der Waals forces each have positive energy of formation and tend to break when temperature increases. In contrast, hydrophobic interactions have negative energy of formation and are strengthened by thermal energy.

Reaction rates are influenced by temperature

Chemical reactions are essentially the formation and breakage of bonds, with changes in free energy of the reactants. Most of these reactions have implications for thermal energy and when discussing chemical or biological processes, it is important to understand the distinctions between thermal

FIGURE 3.7 **Water dipole and hydrogen bonds**
Oxygen atoms in water strongly attract the electron of the hydrogen atom. The result is a small charge difference (δ). The hydrogen atom is slightly positive (δ^+) and the oxygen atom is slightly negative (δ^-). These charges influence the way that water molecules interact.

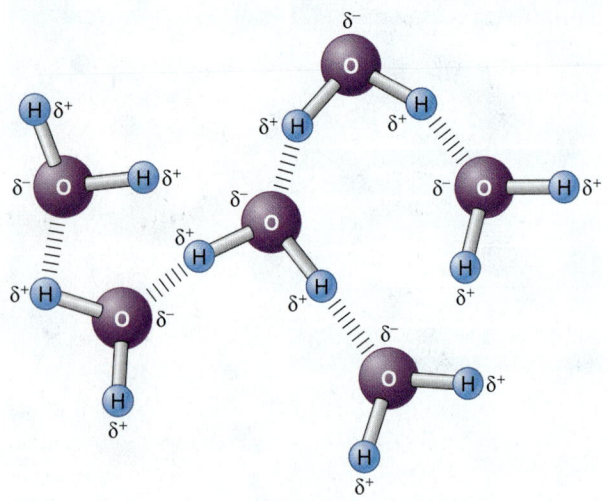

energy, temperature, and heat. Thermal energy is actually a rather ill-defined term, though it is often equated with kinetic energy of a system. Temperature is a measure of the average thermal energy of a system. Heat is the transfer of thermal energy from a system with high temperature to one with lower temperature.

Thermal energy can be considered the sum of the kinetic energies within a system. By kinetic energy, we mean the energy associated with molecular movement: rotation, vibration, and translation. When a system gains thermal energy, there is an increase in the movement of molecules within that system. This type of movement has a profound effect on molecular reactivity and the rate of chemical reactions.

In most chemical reactions, some energy is either gained or lost in the form of thermal energy. As a result, the progression of chemical reactions has thermal implications for an animal, and the thermal biology of the animal in turn affects its chemical reactions.

Most spontaneous chemical reactions (though not all) tend to occur faster at high temperatures. At higher temperatures, molecules have more kinetic energy and they are more likely to reach activation energy. For reactions with multiple substrates, the increase in movement also increases the likelihood that molecules will encounter each other. Thus, physiological strategies that permit some animals to elevate body temperature above the ambient temperature confer advantages to processes that depend on chemical reactions.

The release of thermal energy in reactions tends to increase the temperature of the solution in which the reaction occurs. Within a cell, the thermal energy warms the **cytoplasm**, and heat is transferred to the **extracellular** fluid, and ultimately to the rest of the animal. Depending on the thermal physiology of the animal, this heat may serve to maintain a body temperature higher than the environment. This in turn allows chemical reactions to proceed at faster rates.

CONCEPT CHECK

1. What are the five main forms of energy used by animals? Provide biological and nonbiological examples of processes that represent conversion of energy from one form to another.
2. What is the difference between thermal energy, heat, and temperature?
3. How are weak bonds affected by temperature?

Properties of Water

Most cells are composed primarily of water. Aquatic organisms also live in water, and even the cells of terrestrial organisms are bathed in the aquatic environment of their extracellular fluids. Many physiological processes arose to meet the challenges of the physical and chemical properties of water.

The properties of water are unique

A **solvent** is the liquid in which other molecules (SOLUTES) are dissolved. Collectively, the solutes and solvents constitute the **solution**. In biological systems, the solvent is usually water. Water's unusual combination of physicochemical properties, which can be attributed to its ability to form hydrogen bonds, has special significance in biological processes and constrains the direction of biological evolution. Liquid water is actually a network of interconnected water molecules. Each water molecule interacts strongly with other water molecules through H bonds, creating internal cohesiveness. At the interface between air and water, the attraction between water molecules creates a force called **surface tension**. This prevents most water molecules from spontaneously escaping to the air. Many animals take advantage of surface tension to move over water. Their mass exerts a force on the water, but it is not great enough to disrupt the molecular interactions between water molecules.

The organization of water molecules changes in relation to temperature. At high temperatures, the water molecules possess enough thermal energy to escape the restraining force of surface tension. At this point, the water "boils," and water molecules can escape as gaseous water (steam). In contrast, low temperatures stabilize water structure as a result of the formation of additional hydrogen bonds. Water solidifies, or freezes, when each water molecule forms four hydrogen bonds to create a stable lattice of water molecules.

Changes in temperature also influence the density of water. Although frozen water molecules incorporate more hydrogen bonds, the geometry is such that the water molecules are held further apart than in liquid water. Consequently, ice is less dense than liquid water and tends to float. These physical properties of water have important effects on aquatic ecosystems. In temperate regions of Earth, a layer of ice forms on the surface of lakes in early winter. The ice layer insulates the lake water from the air conditions, creating a more stable environment for aquatic organisms. Temperature also alters the density of liquid water. Because the density of water is greatest at 4°C, the deepest parts of large water bodies tend to be a constant 4°C, whereas surface waters can be colder or warmer, depending on the latitude and season.

Other physical properties of water have an important impact on biological processes. Water has a lower **melting point** (0°C) and a higher boiling point (100°C) than other solvents. In most habitable locations on Earth, then, water is a very stable liquid. Water's high **heat of vaporization**, the amount of energy required to cause liquid water to boil or evaporate, makes sweating an effective cooling strategy for mammals. A great deal of energy is absorbed when liquid water vaporizes. Water on the skin absorbs a lot of thermal energy from the body in the process of evaporation.

Solubility determines how much solute can dissolve in water

Every molecule exposed to a liquid has the potential to dissolve in the solvent. Whether the collection of molecules is in a gas, liquid, or solid phase, some fraction of the population will dissolve and enter the solvent. The fraction of the population of molecules that enter the solution is determined by the solubility of the molecule, which is dependent on the properties of the molecule and the solution.

In a simple system of a solute and solvent, the fraction that can enter solution is expressed as a **solubility coefficient**. It is derived **empirically** by adding increasing amounts of solute to a given solvent. Once a point is reached where no additional solute will dissolve, the solution is said to be *saturated* with the solute. The solubility coefficient of a solid is expressed as the amount of solute (in grams or moles) per amount of solvent, typically expressed in units of mass (grams), moles, or volume (ml).

In a more complex system, solutes often have a choice of entering one of two solvents. For example, solutes in a cell may dissolve in the aqueous cytoplasm or the lipid membrane. The **partition coefficient** describes what fraction of a solute dissolves in which solution. For example, oxygen is 4.4 times more soluble in lipid membranes of a cell than in the aqueous cytoplasm. Oxygen has a membrane to aqueous partition coefficient of 4.4.

When the system consists of a gas and a liquid, **Henry's Law** defines the amount of the gas that will dissolve. The concentration of a gas in a solution (c) equals the partial pressure of the gas (p) divided by the Henry's Law constant (k_H).

$$c = p/k_H$$

At a constant temperature, the amount of a given gas that dissolves in a given type and volume of liquid is directly proportional to the partial pressure of that gas in equilibrium with that liquid.

Solutes influence the physical properties of water

Many solutes can dissolve in water because they can form hydrogen bonds with water molecules. Water-soluble molecules in solution are often surrounded by a coat of water molecules called the **hydration shell**. The hydration shell increases the functional size of the molecule, and influences how the solute interacts with other molecules in complex biological systems.

In the tissues of most animals, the most common solutes are **inorganic ions**. K^+ is the most abundant cation inside cells, and Na^+ is the most abundant cation in the extracellular fluid. However, in some species, particularly marine animals, the most abundant solutes are organic ones such as urea, amino acids, and sugars. Each type of solute can exert specific, distinct effects on the chemical properties of other molecules within the solution. However, all solutes, regardless of their chemical nature, exhibit four basic properties, known as **colligative properties**. Solutes reduce the freezing point of the solution, and increase the boiling point, the vapor pressure, and the osmotic pressure of the solution. The colligative properties depend only on the concentration of solutes, not their size or charge.

In a solution with high concentrations of solutes, cooling to 0°C will not induce freezing. The thermal energy of the system is low enough to form the extra hydrogen bonds, but the solutes block the formation of hydrogen bonds necessary to form the ice crystal. When solutes are present, the solution must be cooled below 0°C before the extra hydrogen bonds can form. The freezing point of biological fluids, such as cytoplasm or blood, is always lower than freshwater, and sometimes even as low as seawater. The difference in the freezing point of body fluids and the aquatic environment has important ramifications for aquatic animals.

Similar mechanisms are responsible for the effects of solutes on the vapor pressure and boiling point of water. A water molecule can escape liquid water only at the water-gas interface. When solute molecules are also present at the surface, they reduce the likelihood that a water molecule will escape. We discuss the fourth colligative property, osmotic pressure, after we discuss a related concept: diffusion.

Solutes move through water by diffusion

The ability of solutes to move throughout a solution is termed the **diffusivity**. The direction of diffusion of molecules in a solution depends on the concentration gradient, but the rate of diffusion depends on many additional factors. Molecules move more rapidly when the gradients are steeper. The properties of the solute itself also influence the rate of diffusion. If solute molecules are relatively large, they have a more difficult time moving through the restrictive structure of water. Large molecules like proteins diffuse much more slowly than small molecules like K^+. The hydration shell that forms around many molecules enlarges the functional size of the molecule, restricting its mobility. Other factors that influence how the solute interacts with the solvent, such as charge and solubility, also affect the rate of diffusion. Each solute has an experimentally determined **diffusion coefficient** (D_s), which is influenced by the structural properties of the solute. The rate of diffusion of a solute (dQ_s/dt) depends on the diffusion coefficient of the solute (D_s), the diffusion area (A), and the concentration gradient (dC/dX). The relationship between these parameters is defined by the **Fick equation**:

$$\frac{dQ_s}{dt} = D_s \times A \times \frac{dC}{dX}$$

Small solutes, such as inorganic ions, are able to traverse the width of the cell, typically about 10 micrometers (μm), in a fraction of a second. The time required for a molecule to diffuse a given distance increases with the square of the distance. If a molecule takes 1 second to diffuse 0.1 millimeter, it would take about 3 hours to diffuse 1 centimeter. Many biological processes depend on diffusion, such that physiological and anatomical strategies have evolved to prevent these processes from becoming "diffusion limited."

Solutes in biological systems impose osmotic pressure

The **semipermeable membranes** of cells allow some molecules to cross while restricting the movement of others. Imagine a situation where two identical solutions of pure water exist on either side of a membrane that allows free movement of water molecules only (Figure 3.8). On each side of the membrane is approximately 55.5 mol of water per liter. Water molecules freely cross the membrane in both directions. If you added NaCl to one side of the membrane, a concentration gradient would be created for Na^+ and Cl^-. Because the membrane is permeable to water alone, only water molecules could move across to equalize the concentration gradients. There would be a net movement of water molecules from the side with pure water to the side with solutes. This would increase the volume on the side with solutes. Eventually, the net movement of water would stop when the force generated by the movement of water equaled the force of gravity, which prevents the water column from getting any higher. In cells, the movement of water is restricted not by gravity but by the flexibility of the cell membrane. In either case, the force associated with the movement of water is the **osmotic pressure**, the fourth colligative property of solutes.

The ability of solutions to induce water to cross a membrane is expressed as the **osmolarity**, expressed in units of **osmoles** per liter (OsM). Osmolarity is analogous in many respects to **molarity** (M). Whereas molarity is a reflection of the concentration of specific molecules in a solution, osmolarity depends on the total concentration of particles in solution. The osmolarity of a solution of known molarity can be calculated on the basis of the number of particles derived from each molecule. In the context of osmolarity, solutes are often called **osmolytes**. If a solution has only one osmolyte, and that osmolyte does not dissociate, then molarity and osmolarity are equivalent. For instance, 1 mol/l (or 1 M) glucose solution has an osmolarity of 1 osmol/l (or 1 OsM). Some compounds dissociate into multiple particles. Each mole of NaCl produces 1 mol of Na^+ and 1 mol of Cl^-. Thus, a 1 M NaCl solution has an osmolarity of 2 OsM. Knowledge of the concentration and valency of the osmolytes would allow you to estimate osmolarity, but in reality the osmolarity is somewhat less. Some of the salt does not dissociate, and

---

FIGURE 3.8 Osmotic pressure

The two solutions differing in solute concentration are separated by a semipermeable membrane. The movement of water creates osmotic pressure. Movement will continue until the force of gravity is equal to the osmotic pressure.

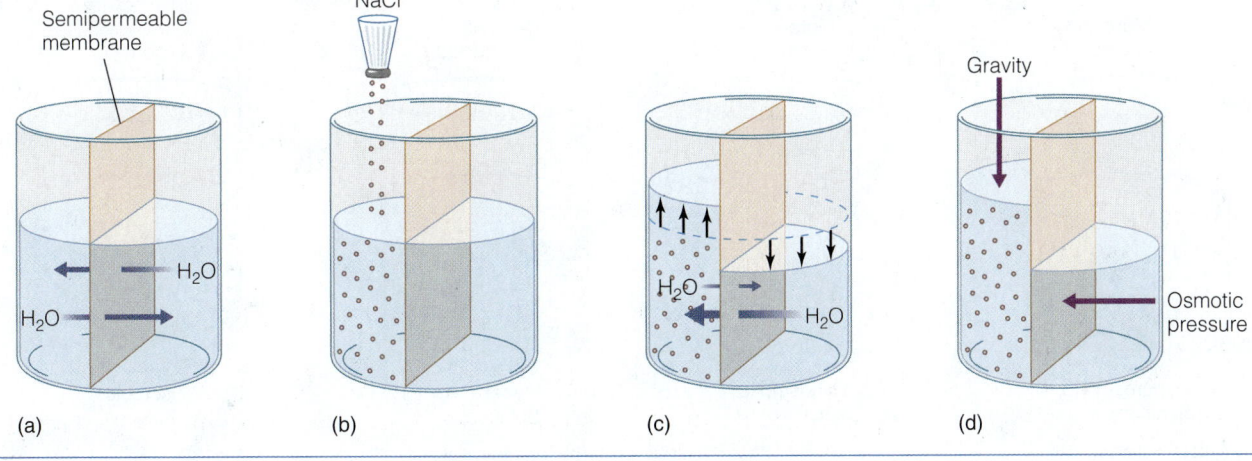

some of the water molecules become associated with the hydration shell of the ions. The osmolarity and osmotic pressure of a solution are physical properties of a solution. However, in a biological setting the absolute osmolarity is often less important than the osmolarity of an extracellular fluid relative to the osmolarity of the intracellular fluid (Figure 3.9a). If a cell is placed in a solution with greater osmolarity, then the solution is considered **hyperosmotic** (relative to the cell). Similarly, if a cell is placed in pure water, the solution is **hyposmotic**. When the osmolarity is the same on both sides of the cell membrane, the solution is **isosmotic**.

Differences in osmolarity can alter cell volume

Biologists usually make distinctions between osmolarity, which is related to the osmotic pressure, and **tonicity**, which is the effect of a solution on cell volume. Tonicity depends on differences in osmolarity, but also on the types of solutes and the permeability of the membrane to those solutes.

To understand the distinction between osmolarity and tonicity, consider the following example (Figure 3.9b). A cell that is placed in an isosmotic salt solution neither shrinks nor swells (an **isotonic** solution). If more salt is added, the cell loses water and shrinks. Thus, this solution is both hyperosmotic and **hypertonic**. Imagine now that small amounts of urea, a permeant solute, are added to the isotonic salt solution. The urea would equilibrate across the cell membrane, and thus prevent the net movement of water in or out of the cell; this is an isotonic solution. Of course, if the cell were placed in a solution containing only urea, the movement of urea into the cell, combined with the high internal salt concentration, would draw water into the cell, causing it to swell or even burst; this is a **hypotonic** solution.

FIGURE 3.9 **Osmolarity versus tonicity**

(a) A cell is in an isosmotic solution when the solution has an osmotic pressure equal to that of the cell cytoplasm. If salt is added to the solution it becomes a hyperosmotic solution. Water leaves the cell, causing the cell volume to shrink, until the osmotic pressures are again equal. If the salt concentration is reduced, as would be the case if more water was added, the solution becomes hyposmotic. Water flows into the cell, causing

it to swell. **(b)** The effects of solutes on cell volume depend on the ability of the solute to enter the cell. If NaCl is added to an isosmotic solution, the cell shrinks and the solution is considered hypertonic. If urea is added to the solution, there is little change in cell volume because urea can cross the cell membrane. Thus, adding urea to this solution makes it hyperosmotic, but it is also isotonic.

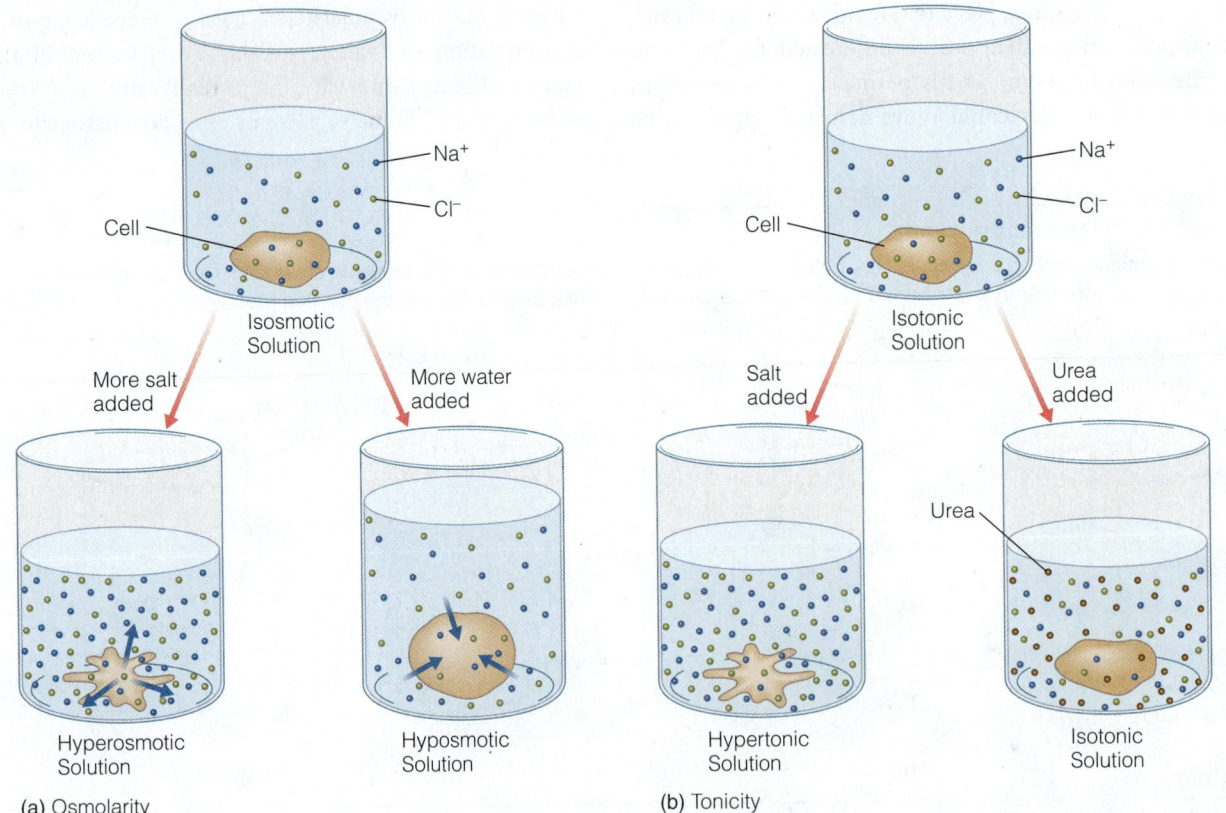

(a) Osmolarity

(b) Tonicity

Acids and bases alter the pH of water

A small proportion of the H_2O molecules in any solution dissociates into ions by breaking one of the covalent bonds between oxygen and hydrogen, resulting in a proton (H^+) and a **hydroxyl ion (OH^-)**.

$$H_2O \leftrightarrow H^+ + OH^-$$

The dissociation of water into ions is reversible. Both the forward reaction (water dissociation) and the reverse direction (water formation) occur simultaneously. Only a very small proportion of water molecules are dissociated at any given time, about 1 in 555,000,000 water molecules at room temperature (25°C). Under these conditions (pure water at 25°C), the concentration of protons arising from water dissociation is 10^{-7} M. For the sake of convenience, the concentration of protons is usually converted to the **pH scale**. The pH of a solution is calculated as the negative logarithm of proton concentration (denoted as $[H^+]$). Thus, the pH of pure water at 25°C is pH 7 (log 10^{-7}). As we see later in this chapter, the negative logarithmic scale, designated by the prefix p, is also a convenient way to express low concentrations of other ions, such as pOH for $[OH^-]$ and pCa for $[Ca^{2+}]$.

A solution is considered **neutral** when $[H^+] = [OH^-]$, or pH = pOH. Pure water at 25°C possesses 10^{-7} M concentrations of both H^+ and OH^-: pH = 7 and pOH = 7. The temperature of a solution of pure water alters the proportion of water molecules with enough thermal energy to break the covalent O–H bond. For instance, at 45°C almost twice as many H_2O molecules dissociate, lowering the pH to 6.72. At 5°C, about half as many H_2O molecules dissociate, raising the pH to 7.28. In each of these situations, water remains neutral (pH=pOH), but the pH at neutrality, or **pN**, varies inversely with temperature. In practice, pure water changes its pH at a rate of −0.014 units per degree Celsius.

Pure water is never anything but neutral. However, ionizable solutes can influence the pH of a solution. An **acid** releases one or more protons. Hydrochloric acid (HCl) is an acid because it dissociates into H^+ and Cl^-. A **base** causes a reduction in the $[H^+]$ of the solution. When the base sodium hydroxide (NaOH) is dissolved into water, it rapidly dissociates into Na^+ and OH^-. The extra OH^- arising from NaOH dissociation rapidly interacts with H^+ to form H_2O, reducing the $[H^+]$ and increasing pH.

The degree to which acids and bases change the pH of a solution depends on the ease with which the molecule dissociates under physiological conditions. Inorganic acids such as HCl and H_2SO_4 are considered strong acids because they readily release their protons to the solution. Similarly, NaOH and KOH are strong bases because they readily dissociate to release OH^-. Many biological molecules are weak acids or weak bases, which are only partially ionized under physiological conditions.

If an acid is defined as something that releases a proton, then we can discuss acids with the general formula of HA. Dissociation of the acid HA produces H^+ and the anion, A^-. We can describe a reversible chemical reaction with the equation

$$HA \leftrightarrow H^+ + A^-$$

The relationship between the substrate (HA) and products (H^+ and A^-) is the **mass action ratio**, expressed as:

$$\text{Mass action ratio} = \frac{[H^+] \times [A^-]}{[HA]}$$

To understand how these parameters change, consider an experiment where the acid, HA, is added to pure water. When first added to water, HA remains intact and $[A^-]$ is equal to zero; the mass action ratio is also close to zero. However, very quickly at least some of the acid dissociates. There is an increase in both $[H^+]$ and $[A^-]$, and as a result an increase in the mass action ratio. At some point the reaction slows, with $[HA]$ reaching a minimum and $[H^+]$ and $[A^-]$ reaching a maximum. When this occurs, the reaction is at equilibrium. It is important to recognize that although there is no net change in the concentrations of reactants, both forward and reverse reactions continue, but at equal rates. When the reaction is at equilibrium, the mass action ratio attains a specific value, K_{eq}, the **equilibrium constant**. Under most circumstances, the equilibrium constant is converted to its negative log ($\log_{10} K_{eq}$), analogous to the way we converted $[H^+]$ to pH. Thus, the equilibrium equation can be rewritten after log transformation as

$$pK = pH - \log \frac{[A^-]}{[HA]}$$

Put another way, the pK is the pH at which half the acid is dissociated, $[A^-] = [HA]$, $[A^-]/[HA] = 1$, and log $[A^-]/[HA] = 0$.

This simple equation is useful for understanding many different biochemical and physiological principles. For example, the pK value reflects the strength of acids and bases. A strong acid will give up its proton even when the concentration of protons in the surrounding area is very high (low pH). Thus, the pH must be very low to prevent a strong acid from dissociating. The pK value is low for a strong acid—less than 3 for hydrochloric acid and sulfuric acid. Similarly, strong bases, such as sodium hydroxide and ammonium hydroxide, have pK values greater than 11. The pK values for some common biological acids and bases are shown in Table 3.1.

The equilibrium equation is a powerful tool for analyzing biological solutions. Once we know the values of three

Table 3.1 Acids and bases

Acid	Reaction	pK
Carbonic acid	$H_2CO_3 \rightarrow HCO_3^- + H^+$	3.8
	$HCO_3^- \rightarrow CO_3^{2-} + H^+$	10.2
Phosphoric acid	$H_3PO_4 \rightarrow H_2PO_4^- + H^+$	3.1
	$H_2PO_4^- \rightarrow HPO_4^{2-} + H^+$	6.9
	$HPO_4^{2-} \rightarrow PO_4^{3-} + H^+$	12.4
Ammonium	$NH_4^+ \rightarrow NH_3 + H^+$	9.3
Acetic acid	$CH_3COOH \rightarrow CH_3COO^- + H^+$	4.8
Glycine (amino)	$R-NH_3^+ \rightarrow R-NH_2 + H^+$	2.3
Glycine (carboxy)	$R-COOH \rightarrow R-COO^- + H^+$	9.6

Histidine (imidazole) — 6.0

of the four parameters, we can calculate the one that is unknown. To determine pH, we can rearrange the equation into the form

$$pH = pK + \log \frac{[A^-]}{[HA]}$$

This rearrangement is known as the **Henderson-Hasselbalch equation**, named after the researchers who used the relationship to explain the behavior of CO_2 (HA) and HCO_3^- (A^-), which is important in respiratory physiology (see Chapter 11: Respiratory Systems).

Both pH and temperature affect the ionization of biological molecules

Changes in pH can alter the dissociation of other molecules with ionizable groups. Let's look at the amino acid glycine to explore how pH affects its structure. Glycine has a carboxyl group that can be protonated ($-COOH$) or deprotonated ($-COO^-$). It has an amino group that can be deprotonated ($-NH_2$) or protonated ($-NH_3^+$). The protonation state of the carboxyl and amino groups in a molecule of glycine depends on the pH of the solution.

We can observe the effects of pH on glycine structure and charge. For a solution of glycine at very low pH, where $[H^+]$ is high, both amino and carboxyl groups are protonated. The carboxyl group is uncharged ($-COOH$) and the amino group has a positive charge ($-NH_3^+$), giving glycine

a net positive charge. Adding base to this solution to increase pH causes a series of changes in the protonation state of both of these groups. First, the carboxyl groups become deprotonated ($-COOH \rightarrow -COO_2^- + H^+$). At pH 2.3, exactly half of the carboxyl groups in the glycine molecule are ionized. This pH value is the equilibrium constant for the carboxyl group of the glycine molecule, or its pK_{COOH}. Adding more base causes deprotonation of the amino group. At pH 9.6, exactly half the amino groups are protonated. This pH value is the equilibrium constant for the amino group of glycine, or its pK_{NH2}. At still higher pH values, the carboxyl groups remain charged and the amino groups are fully deprotonated, giving the glycine molecule a net negative charge. Midway between the two pK values, the glycine molecule has no net charge, as the charges on the carboxyl group (COO^-) balance the charges on the amino group (NH_3^+). Glycine and other molecules that have both negative and positive charges are called **zwitterions**.

The ionization state of molecules is very sensitive to temperature. Let's return to the previous example of a glycine solution at different pH values. At pH 2.3, which is the pK_{COOH}, half of the carboxyl groups have lost their proton. If we increased the temperature, more protons would dissociate as the weak bond between O and H breaks. Thus, at a higher temperature, a lower pH is needed to achieve a 50 percent ionized state. In other words, the pK value decreases as temperature increases. Each ionizable group has a characteristic sensitivity to temperature, expressed as $\Delta pK/°C$. For example, the ionization of the carboxyl group of glycine is relatively insensitive to temperature ($\Delta pK/°C = -0.0025$), whereas the ionization of the **imidazole group** of histidine is more sensitive to temperature ($\Delta pK/°C = -0.017$).

The protonation state of many molecules can have important effects on molecular processes. Many of the effects of temperature and pH on cells can be traced to the effects on the protonation state of critical molecules. For example, many proteins form structures that depend on particular ionization states of amino acids. Changes in pH or temperature can affect how these proteins fold and function. By actively regulating temperature and pH, animals diminish the debilitating effects of changes in protonation state.

Buffers limit changes in pH

A variety of mechanisms help cells regulate pH. The first level of defense is a **buffer**. A buffer is a chemical found in a solution that dampens the effect of added acid or base on the pH of the solution. Buffers are often described as if they were single molecules. In reality we should think of them as buffer systems, because they are mixtures of at least two forms of a molecule, typically protonated and deprotonated.

If we add a buffer to the solution, the protons liberated from the acid can associate with the buffer. As a result, the addition of acid has less effect on pH than it does in the absence of buffer. Most buffer systems rely on weak acids, present in both the acid form (HA) and the anion form (A$^-$). Furthermore, a buffer works only over a particular range of pH values. Acetic acid is a weak acid that can be used as a buffer. The effects of an acetic acid/acetate buffer are illustrated by the titration curve shown in Figure 3.10. If you started your titration at low pH, most of the acetic acid would be in the protonated form (HA). If you added small volumes of NaOH, the pH would increase proportionately. Below pH 3.75, acetic acid would remain mostly protonated (HA). If you add more base, the increase in pH would induce some acetic acid (HA) to become deprotonated (HA → H$^+$ + A$^-$). Because some of the protons are liberated from acetic acid, the added NaOH has a reduced effect on the pH of the solution. This buffering effect is evident over the pH range of about 3.75 to 5.75, where the titration curve is quite shallow. Once pH reaches 5.75, most of the acetic acid is in the deprotonated form (A$^-$), which cannot act as a buffer. This pH range corresponds to the greatest buffering capacity of the solution, and is centered on the pK value for the buffer, about 4.75, where about half of the buffer is protonated (HA) and half deprotonated (A$^-$).

Animals use a variety of different molecules as buffers. The best buffers in animal cells have pK values that approach the pH of the compartment in which they are used. Phosphate ($H_2PO_4^-/HPO_4^{2-}$) is an important buffer in the cytoplasm of most cells, with a pK$_A$ of 6.9. The amino acid histidine contributes to buffering in many animal cells because the pK value of its imidazole side chain is very close to intracellular pH. Histidine residues within large proteins help buffer the cytoplasm against changes in pH. Many species use amino acids with imidazole groups to produce dipeptides that serve as important intracellular buffers. The dipeptides carnosine (histidine and β-alanine), anserine (1-methylhistidine and β-alanine), and ophidine (3-methylhistidine and β-alanine) are important buffers in the muscle of many species.

In air-breathing animals, the most important extracellular buffer is bicarbonate/CO$_2$, but it works by a different mechanism than a simple A$^-$/HA buffer pair. In a closed test tube, bicarbonate/CO$_2$ would have little buffering capacity at physiological pH because its pK is much too low (3.8). It works as a biological buffer because animals can expire CO$_2$. As [H$^+$] increases, bicarbonate is consumed and carbonic acid is produced (H_2CO_3), which in turn forms H_2O and CO_2.

$$H^+ + HCO_3^- \rightarrow H_2CO_3 \rightarrow H_2O + CO_2$$

When an animal expires CO$_2$ as a gas, it is essentially eliminating a weak acid from the body, buffering against a change in pH. You will learn more about the interaction between CO$_2$ and acid-base balance in Chapter 11: Respiratory Systems.

CONCEPT CHECK

4. What change in pH has a greater effect on proton concentration: pH 6 to 7 or pH 7 to 8?

5. Describe a cup of coffee (no milk, one sugar) in terms of solute, solvent, and solution.

6. What is the difference between osmolarity and tonicity?

BIOCHEMISTRY

Animals control the inner workings of cells through the use of enzymes, which interconvert macromolecules to create building blocks and control the flow of chemical energy. A metabolic pathway is a series of consecutive enzymatic reactions that catalyze the conversion of substrates to products, with multiple stable intermediates. Flow through the pathway is called **metabolic flux**. Metabolic pathways can be either synthetic (**anabolic**), degradative (**catabolic**), or a combination of both (**amphibolic**). **Energy metabolism** revolves around production of ATP. **Metabolism** is the sum of all these metabolic pathways within the cell, tissue, or organism.

In the following sections, we discuss the nature of enzymes and metabolic energy, and the metabolism of three of the four major classes of biological macromolecules: proteins, carbohydrates, and lipids. The fourth class of macromolecules, nucleic acids, is discussed later in this chapter when we consider genetics.

FIGURE 3.10 **Effects of buffers on changes in pH**
Buffers blunt the effects of added bases (or acid) on the pH of a solution.

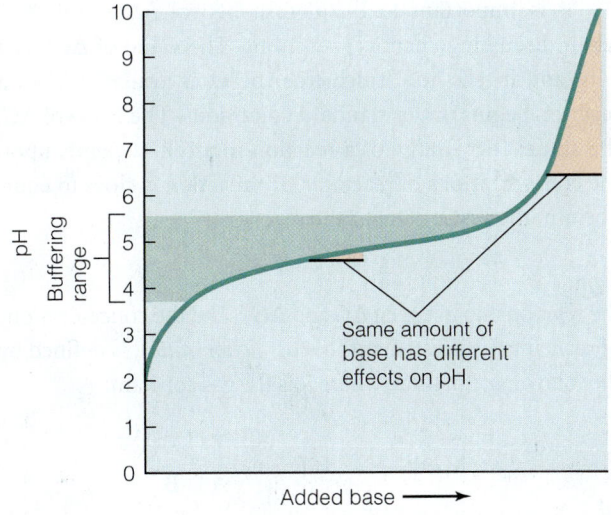

pH

Buffering range

Same amount of base has different effects on pH.

Added base →

Enzymes

Enzymes are biological catalysts that convert a substrate to a product. Enzymes, like other types of catalysts, have three properties: (1) they are active at very low concentrations within the cell; (2) they increase the rate of reactions but they themselves are not altered in the process; (3) they do not change the nature of the products.

Although some enzymes, called ribozymes, are made of **RNA**, most enzymes are composed of protein. Many enzymes possess nonprotein components, called **cofactors**. A cofactor that is covalently bonded into the enzyme is called a **prosthetic group**. Some enzymes use cofactors that are metals, such as copper, iron, magnesium, zinc, and selenium. Organic cofactors, or **coenzymes**, are usually derived from **vitamins; coenzyme A** is derived from pantothenic acid, FAD from riboflavin, and NAD from niacin. Many of the life-threatening diseases we associate with vitamin deficiencies can be traced back to perturbations of metabolism due to loss of function of specific enzymes.

Enzyme function is studied using two complementary and interrelated approaches. **Thermodynamics**, literally the movement of heat, is the study of how energy is transferred between chemical reactants. **Enzyme kinetics** is the study of the parameters that affect enzymatic rates. When considering a chemical reaction, thermodynamics can explain the direction of a spontaneous reaction, whereas kinetics describes the rate at which the reaction occurs.

All chemical reactions are governed by the laws of thermodynamics

The first law of thermodynamics deals with conservation of energy. The energy within a substrate is either transferred to the product or released. The first law doesn't tell us if the reaction will go forward or backward, only that the energy transformations must be balanced. The second law of thermodynamics provides a way of predicting if a reaction is likely to occur. It says that spontaneous processes occur in the direction that will increase randomness, or **entropy** (S). Throughout this chapter we discuss many examples of increases in entropy. When table salt dissolves in water or ice melts, the molecules that were once in a well-ordered crystal begin to disperse. Diffusion also illustrates the principle of spontaneous increases in entropy. Solutes at high concentration tend to disperse to regions of lower concentration. Collectively, these laws tell us that the total energy of the universe is constant but that it tends toward randomness.

What does this mean for chemical reactions? Consider a "system" to be a pool of chemicals that can interact. The individual chemicals possess energy, and the total energy of

this system is called the **enthalpy** (H). The total includes a component that can be used to elevate temperature (T) or alternatively to increase the randomness, or **entropy** (S), in the system. The balance is available for other purposes, and is called free energy (G). The equation that relates these parameters was first proposed by J. Willard Gibbs in 1878.

$$H = G + TS$$

When monitoring chemical reactions, it is less useful to know the energy content of a system than to follow how the energy content changes in the system. When constraining the system to a constant temperature, the equation can be expressed as:

$$\Delta H = \Delta G + T\,\Delta S$$

In biological systems, what is most important is the value of ΔG, because the change in free energy is the energy that is available for other purposes.

$$\Delta G = \Delta H - T\,\Delta S$$

If ΔG is negative this means that energy is available, and given the right machinery, can be applied to other systems. If ΔG is positive, this means that the reaction won't occur spontaneously. As you may have guessed, reactions that have a positive ΔG can be linked to reactions with a larger negative ΔG, permitting the pair of reactions to proceed.

Chemists evaluate these parameters under **standard conditions**. The standard free energy, or $\Delta G°$, is value of ΔG when measured at 25°C, with each reactant present at a concentration of 1 M. This constraint applies even if the reactants include H^+, which would equate to pH 0, a value that is not relevant to biological systems. When we use the laws of thermodynamics to discuss biological systems, the parameters must be altered to reflect normal cellular conditions. When biochemists adjust $\Delta G°$ for standard conditions, they assume a pH of 7.0 and denote the change in free energy as $\Delta G°'$.

It is important to distinguish between ΔG and $\Delta G°'$ when discussing chemical reactions. The value of $\Delta G°'$ is a constant. It tells how much free energy is available when a reaction begins under standard conditions. The value of ΔG, the actual free energy of a reaction in a cell, depends upon the concentrations of reactants. If a reaction is close to equilibrium, then $\Delta G = 0$. For the reaction

$$A + B \leftrightarrow Y + Z$$

the relationship between ΔG and $\Delta G°'$, and the concentrations of reactants (expressed as the *mass action ratio*), is defined by the following equation, where R is the gas constant:

$$\Delta G - \Delta G°' + RT \ln \frac{[Y][Z]}{[A][B]}$$

When the reaction is at equilibrium, $\Delta G = 0$, the mass action ratio is equal to K_{eq}, and the equation is reduced to

$$0 = \Delta G^{\circ'} + RT \ln K_{eq}$$

or

$$\Delta G^{\circ'} = -RT \ln K_{eq}$$

We can measure K_{eq} directly by letting the reaction reach equilibrium. The value of $\Delta G^{\circ'}$ can be calculated from the equation above. Now, knowing K_{eq} and $\Delta G^{\circ'}$, we can calculate the amount of actual free energy ΔG available for a reaction at any concentration of reactants. This allows you to predict whether a reaction will occur under any conditions you define.

Remember that ΔG represents the maximal amount of free energy theoretically available from a reaction, under a constant temperature and pressure that approximates conditions found in the cell. Cells use enzymes to mediate chemical reactions and transfer as much energy as possible to other useful forms. Some enzymes mediate reactions that store energy as chemical energy, such as ATP or NADH. Free energy can also be used to create electrochemical gradients. The ability to divert free energy into useful forms is central to the success of living organisms.

Enzymes accelerate reactions by reducing the reaction activation energy

The laws of thermodynamics that govern chemical reactions in test tubes also apply to chemical reactions in living cells. Enzymes do not determine whether or not a chemical reaction is thermodynamically possible. However, enzymes do have the ability to accelerate thermodynamically feasible reactions by factors of 10^8 to 10^{12}.

Previously we discussed how substrate molecules in an uncatalyzed reaction must obtain sufficient energy to meet the activation energy (E_A) barrier. Once the E_A is met, the substrate can adopt the transition state and then spontaneously change into the product. Although an enzymatic reaction uses the same substrate and yields the same product as an uncatalyzed reaction, it produces a different intermediate at the transition state. First, the enzyme (E) and substrate (S) bind to form the ES complex. After conversion to transition states (ES*, EP*), the final product (P) is formed and then is released by the enzyme. This is represented as shown:

$$S + E \leftrightarrow ES \leftrightarrow ES^* \leftrightarrow EP^* \leftrightarrow EP \leftrightarrow E + P$$

The energy required to reach this intermediate state is lower than in the uncatalyzed reaction (Figure 3.11). With a lower energy barrier, more of the substrate molecules possess enough energy to reach the transition state, and the reaction

FIGURE 3.11 Enzymes and E_A

Enzymes are biological catalysts that accelerate reactions without changing the nature of the product. When the substrate (S) binds the enzyme (E), the enzyme-substrate complex (ES) is formed. The enzyme alters the substrate through a series of transition states. The enzyme-product complex (EP) is formed, and product (P) is released. The rate is faster than the uncatalyzed rate because of the lower activation energy (E_A).

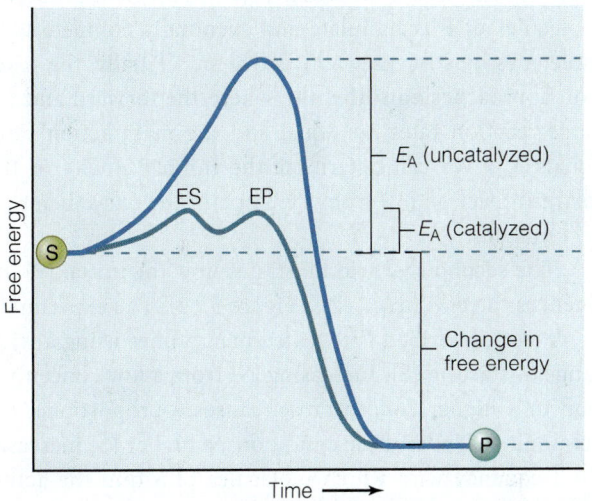

is accelerated. Like other chemical reactions, enzyme reactions are reversible, proceeding through the same set of reaction intermediates.

An enzymatic reaction begins with the substrate binding at a specific location called the **active site**. Think of the active site as a pocket into which the substrate fits. The enzyme can bind the substrate only if it possesses the proper conformation. The three-dimensional folding of the enzyme, maintained by weak bonds, forms the active site.

Once it binds the substrate, the enzyme induces a change in the molecular structure of the substrate, perhaps as subtle as a shift in the distribution of electrons across a particular bond or a twist in the substrate molecule. By inducing these subtle structural changes in the substrate, the enzyme makes the substrate more likely to spontaneously undergo more significant changes. Many enzymes require two or more substrates. These enzymes may accelerate reactions by bringing destabilized reactants in close proximity. All together, these changes increase the probability that the substrate will undergo a major change in structure toward the formation of EP*.

Enzyme kinetics describe enzymatic properties

Thermodynamics explain why reactions occur, but *enzyme kinetics* explains the rate at which reactions occur. Cells regulate enzymes to ensure that reactions occur, not at the fastest possible rate, but at the appropriate rate.

The simplest way to influence an enzymatic reaction is to change the concentration of substrates (S) or products (P). We use the reaction S → P to illustrate the importance of substrate concentration ([S]) in two experimental scenarios.

The first scenario illustrates how the buildup of [P] influences the rate of the forward reaction. When the reaction begins, there is no product ([P] = 0). As it proceeds, molecules of P accumulate and eventually compete with molecules of S for the same active site. Finally, the reaction approaches **equilibrium**, where the forward and reverse reaction rates are equal and the mass action ratio equals K_{eq}. We can determine the initial velocity of the forward reaction (V) from the slope of the curve before P accumulates.

The second scenario illustrates how the initial [S] influences the enzymatic rate (Figure 3.12). The experiment previously described is repeated many times using a wide range of starting [S]. Increasing [S] from a low concentration to a higher concentration causes a proportional increase in V. Under these conditions, a higher [S] increases the frequency with which molecules of S find the active site. However, after a point, increases in [S] no longer cause a proportional increase in V. The higher abundance of S molecules still increases the probability of a collision with E. However, if S encounters E in the midst of a reaction cycle, the enzyme is unable to bind S. Eventually, E is saturated with S molecules and further increases in [S] do not increase V beyond a maximal rate (V_{max}). When enzymes are at V_{max}, each molecule of enzyme has a characteristic number of catalytic cycles per unit time, known as **catalytic constant** (k_{cat}), or turnover number.

A high rate of enzymatic activity could be achieved by a cell, in principle, in either of two ways. Some enzymes work very fast, and show a high k_{cat}. The cell does not need many molecules of the enzyme because each molecule works quickly. The fastest enzymes can undergo more than 40,000,000 catalytic cycles each second. Alternatively, cells could make many copies of an enzyme with a low k_{cat}. The relative importance of each strategy—faster enzymes versus more enzymes—depends on the nature of the reaction and the nature of the enzyme.

The relationship between [S] and V was first described mathematically by the biochemists Leonor Michaelis and Maud Menten as a rectangular hyperbola. The **Michaelis-Menten equation** is

$$V = V_{max} \times \frac{[S]}{[S] + K_m}$$

The value for the Michaelis-Menten constant (K_m) is the concentration of substrate [S] required to obtain an initial velocity (V) that is half the maximal velocity (V_{max}). K_m is an indicator of the affinity of an enzyme for a substrate. A low K_m means that the enzyme has high affinity for the substrate, and little substrate is needed to drive the reaction at a high rate.

Traditionally, experimental derivation of the kinetic constants, K_m and V_{max} required manipulation of the Michaelis-Menton equation into a form that generates a linear equation. Rearranging the equation as into the **Lineweaver-Burk equation** generates a straight line on a graph of $1/V$ (y axis) and $1/[S]$ (x axis):

$$1/V = K_m/V_{max} \text{ x } 1/[S] + 1/V_{max}$$

The kinetic constants can be calculated from the X intercept ($-1/K_m$) and Y intercept ($1/V_{max}$). Other linear transformations of the Michaelis-Menten equation exist, each of which has its own strengths and weaknesses in accurately estimating the kinetic constants.

Not all enzymes demonstrate hyperbolic Michaelis-Menten kinetics. For instance, homotropic enzymes show a sigmoidal relationship between V and [S] (Figure 3.13). Homotropic enzymes typically have multiple subunits that can each bind a substrate molecule. At low [S], each active site has a low affinity for S. The enzyme does not bind S very well and the reaction velocity is slow. Once one subunit binds one molecule of S, it undergoes a change in conformation that in turn alters the ability of other subunits to bind a substrate

FIGURE 3.12 **The Michaelis-Menten rectangular hyperbola**

Each point on the curve represents the initial velocity (V). The maximal velocity (V_{max}) is the velocity at which the curve reaches an asymptote. The K_m is the [S] required to reach a velocity that is one-half of the maximal velocity.

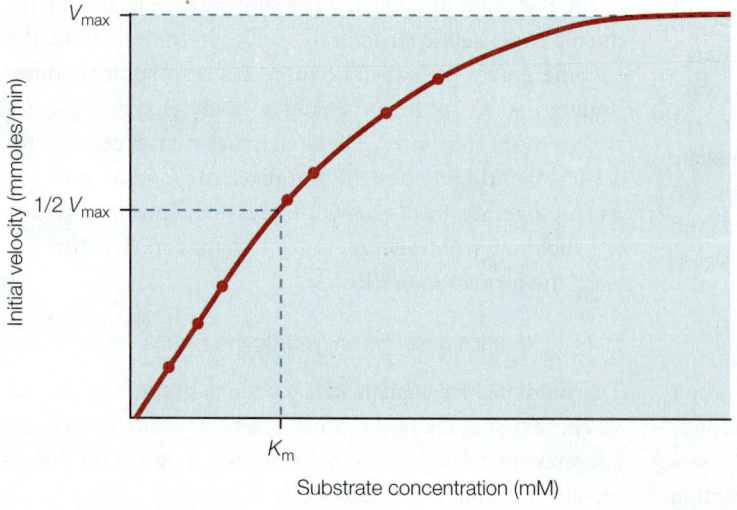

FIGURE 3.13 Homotropic enzymes and sigmoidal kinetics

Not all enzymes obey Michaelis-Menten kinetics. Homotropic enzymes show sigmoidal kinetics. The enzymes usually possess multiple active sites. When the enzyme binds one molecule of S, the changes in conformation increase the ability to bind a second molecule of S. The slope of the linear range of the curve indicates the degree of cooperativity. The slope of this region provides the Hill coefficient.

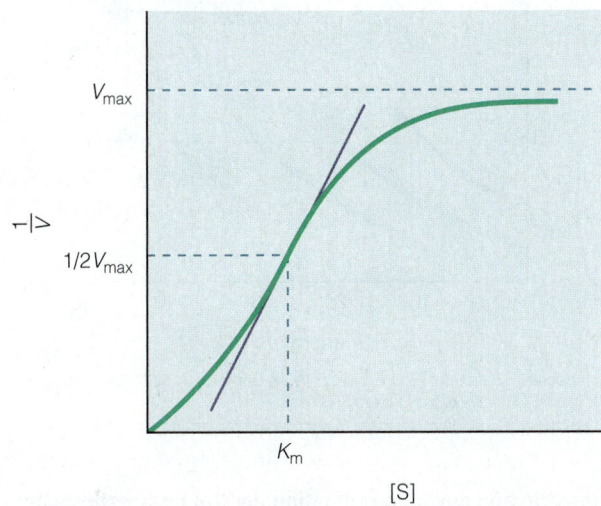

The physicochemical environment alters enzyme kinetics

Every enzyme has a characteristic optimal activity under a specific set of environmental conditions (Figure 3.14). Enzyme kinetics are influenced by environmental conditions, such as temperature, pH, salt concentration, and hydrostatic pressure. While these factors generally have little impact on human metabolism, such environmental factors can influence the metabolic biochemistry of other species.

Some enzymes function optimally under conditions that resemble normal cellular conditions. For instance,

FIGURE 3.14 Effects of salt and temperature on enzyme kinetics

Most enzymes function optimally under physiologically realistic conditions. **(a)** The activity of mammalian enzymes changes in response to the concentration of the salt KCl. Maximal activity occurs at concentrations that approximate those found within the cell ($100-150$ mM K^+). **(b)** Increasing temperature accelerates enzymes. Beyond an optimal temperature, the enzyme denatures and loses catalytic activity.

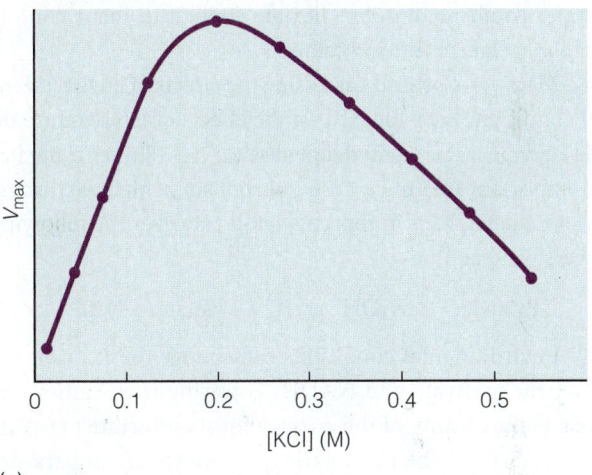

(a)

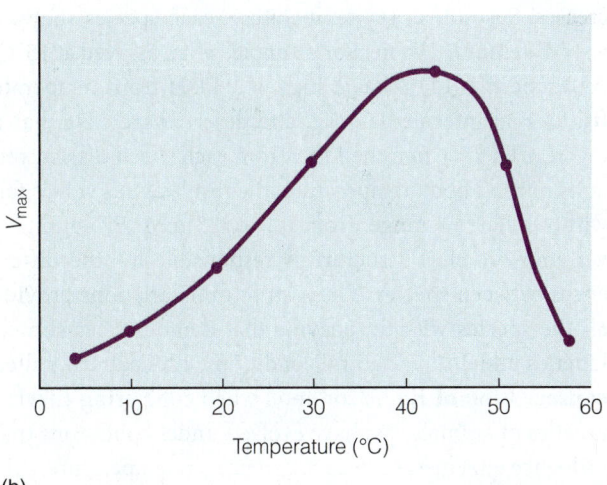

(b)

molecule. As a result, doubling of [S] more than doubles V, a phenomenon called *cooperativity*. The degree of cooperativity is described by the *Hill coefficient*, which is the slope of relationship at the point of inflection.

Enzyme kinetics are assessed under carefully controlled experimental conditions that do not approximate normal cellular conditions. Interpreting the impact of enzyme kinetics in living cells is often difficult. The conditions necessary to evaluate V_{max} require [P] to be zero, which never occurs in living cells. Thus, enzymes in cells almost never could proceed at V_{max}. As with other chemical reactions, the rate and direction of the enzymatic reaction depend on the difference between the mass action ratio, which is calculated from the actual [S] and [P], and the K_{eq} value, which is the expected [S] and [P] when the reaction reaches equilibrium. In a **near-equilibrium reaction**, the mass action ratio is close to K_{eq}; the forward and reverse directions continue at equal rates, with little net change in [S] or [P]. Most enzyme reactions are far from equilibrium in cells. If the mass action ratio is lower than K_{eq}, then the reaction will proceed in the forward direction. When the mass action ratio is higher than K_{eq}, the reaction will tend to favor the reverse direction. By altering the concentrations of substrates and products, cells can regulate enzyme activities and metabolic pathways.

mammalian enzymes often function optimally at normal body temperatures of 37−40°C. However, the optimal conditions for many enzymes bear little similarity to normal cellular conditions; the optimal temperature for some mammalian enzymes is well above normal body temperatures.

Environmental conditions typically influence enzyme kinetics through effects on weak bonds. First, changes in weak bonds can alter the three-dimensional structure of the enzyme. For instance, warm temperatures could break bonds that are necessary to form the active site. Second, environmental conditions can alter the ionization state of critical amino acids within the active site. For instance, the amino acid histidine is important in many active sites, and changes in pH can alter its protonation state and consequently substrate affinity (K_m). Any environmentally induced change in K_m, either an increase or a decrease, can be disruptive to a cell. Third, environmental conditions can alter the ability of the enzyme to undergo structural changes necessary for catalysis. Enzymes must be rigid enough to maintain the proper conformation, but flexible enough to incur conformational changes during catalysis.

Many of the studies assessing the effects of environmental conditions have focused on the effects of temperature on the enzyme lactate **dehydrogenase** (LDH). This enzyme has an important role in glucose metabolism, which we discuss in more detail later in this chapter. It catalyzes the following reversible reaction:

$$\text{Pyruvate} + \text{NADH}^+ + \text{H}^+ \leftrightarrow \text{lactate} + \text{NAD}^+$$

Environmental conditions can change the K_m value of LDH for pyruvate and NADH. Lowering temperature increases the affinity of the enzyme for its substrate pyruvate (Figure 3.15). When comparing the effects of temperature on K_m in different species, several patterns emerge. First, in every species, the K_m value decreases as temperature decreases. Second, at any temperature, each species shows a very different K_m value. For example, when assayed at 15°C, Antarctic fish LDH has a high K_m, LDH from temperate fish has an intermediate K_m, and desert lizard LDH has a low K_m. Third, when the LDH from each species is assayed at its normal body temperature, the resulting K_m values fall within a narrow range, from 0.1 to 0.3 mM. Evolutionary variation in LDH structure is responsible for the differences between species. These structural variations provide all the species with an enzyme that demonstrates similar kinetics under their natural conditions. This pattern, called **conservation of K_m,** is common when comparing enzyme kinetics of animals that have evolved under conditions that influence enzymes, such as differences in temperature, salt, and hydrostatic pressure.

FIGURE 3.15 **Conservation of K_m**

The K_m of an enzyme often changes with temperature. For a number of unrelated species, the K_m of LDH for pyruvate increases with an increase in temperature; that is, at warmer temperatures LDH is less able to bind pyruvate. However, when you examine the kinetic values that would occur at the actual body temperatures for the animal, you find that the K_m values are very similar across species.

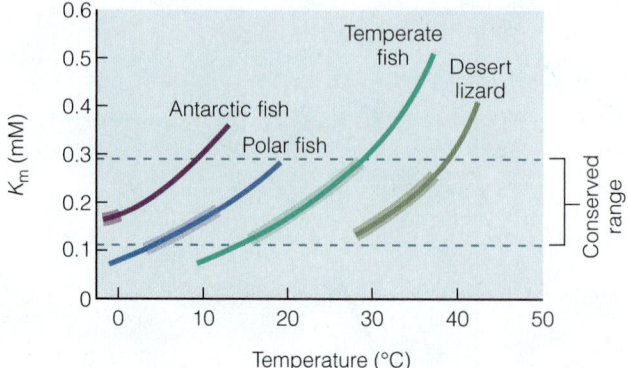

Figure source: Data from Hochachka, P. W., & Somero, G. N. (2002). *Biochemical adaptation.* Oxford: Oxford University Press.

Allosteric and covalent regulation control enzymatic rates

Molecules that do not participate directly in catalysis can also alter enzyme kinetics. **Competitive inhibitors** are molecules that can bind to the active site, preventing substrate molecules from binding. The effectiveness of a competitive inhibitor depends on [S]. When [S] is low, the inhibitor outcompetes S for the active site, reducing the reaction rate. At a very high [S], the inhibition by the competitor is greatly reduced. Thus, a competitive inhibitor increases K_m but doesn't affect V_{max}.

Allosteric regulators are molecules that alter enzyme kinetics by binding to the protein at locations far away from the active site. The allosteric regulator alters the three-dimensional structure of the enzyme, inducing complex changes in enzyme kinetics. For example, an allosteric activator could increase the affinity of the enzyme for the substrate. Allosteric effectors can activate or inhibit enzyme activity, changing either K_m or V_{max}. Enzymes often possess multiple sites for different allosteric regulators. Enzymes controlled by allosteric regulators are often larger and more complex than other enzymes. Typically, each metabolic pathway is regulated by one or more key allosteric enzymes.

Enzymes can also be regulated by the **covalent modification** of critical amino acid residues within the protein. The most common type of covalent modification is protein **phosphorylation**, in which a specific **protein kinase** transfers the phosphate group from ATP to an amino acid of the target enzyme. For instance, tyrosine kinase is a regulatory enzyme that phosphorylates target proteins at specific tyrosine residues. Another common class of protein kinases is specific for threonine and serine residues. Protein phosphorylation is reversible. Cells possess suites of **protein phosphatases** that cleave phosphate groups from phosphorylated amino acid residues. Phosphorylation might stimulate an enzyme or inhibit it.

Enzymes convert nutrients to reducing energy

Enzymes transfer energy from nutrients to molecules that function as energy stores. These energy-rich molecules are a type of energy currency, acting as substrates and products for hundreds of different enzymes. Cells store chemical energy in two main forms: reducing energy and high-energy molecules.

Many enzymatic reactions exchange energy between molecules using cofactors, such as NAD, NADP, FAD, and FMN. These reactions are catalyzed by enzymes with the common names dehydrogenase, reductase, and oxidase. When an enzymatic reaction transfers an electron to the oxidized form, NAD^+ or $NADP^+$, the reduced forms, NADH or NADPH, are produced and can be used to drive other reactions. In other words, energy can be stored by reducing a molecule and this energy can be recovered, in part, by oxidizing the reduced compound. The reduced forms of these cofactors are call **reducing equivalents**.

Consider the nonenzymatic and enzymatic reactions for lactate **oxidation**. Without an enzyme, lactate is oxidized to form pyruvate with the following reaction:

$$\text{Lactate}^- \rightarrow \text{pyruvate}^- + 2H^+ + 2e^- \quad \Delta G^{o\prime} = -36 \text{ kJ/mol}$$

The negative standard free energy ($\Delta G^{o\prime}$) means that energy is liberated in this reaction, and without an enzyme the energy released would be lost as heat. Cells possess the enzyme LDH, introduced earlier in this chapter, which couples lactate oxidation to NAD^+ reduction. The NAD^+ reduction reaction has a positive $\Delta G^{o\prime}$.

$$NAD^+ + 2e^- + 2H^+ \rightarrow NADH + H^+ \quad \Delta G^{o\prime} = +62 \text{ kJ/mol}$$

By coupling lactate oxidation to NAD reduction, the enzymatic reaction captures free energy from lactate oxidation in the form of NADH.

$$\text{Lactate}^- + NAD^+ \rightarrow NADH + H^+ + \text{pyruvate}^- \quad \Delta G^{o\prime} = +26 \text{ kJ/mol}$$

Note that the enzymatic reaction for lactate oxidation has a positive $\Delta G^{o\prime}$, which means the reverse direction of this reaction (lactate formation) is normally favored.

The most important reducing equivalent in energy metabolism is NADH. The reducing energy within the cell, or **redox status**, is best expressed as $[NADH]/[NAD^+]$. This ratio is high when a cell is rich in reducing energy, and low when cells are energy poor. NAD is a reactant in many enzymes of energy metabolism, but other enzymes are allosterically regulated by NAD. Whether acting through mass action effects or allosteric regulation, enzymes sensitive to $[NADH]/[NAD^+]$ allow metabolic pathways to respond to the energy state.

ATP is a carrier of free energy

Cells use many types of molecules to store energy (Figure 3.16), but ATP is the most versatile of these high-energy molecules and participates in countless reactions. ATP synthesis requires energy, and ATP breakdown liberates energy.

$$ADP^{3-} + HPO_4^{2-} + H^+ \rightarrow ATP^{4-} + H_2O$$
$$\Delta G^{o\prime} = -30.5 \text{ kJ/mol}$$

FIGURE 3.16 **Molecules that serve as energy carriers**

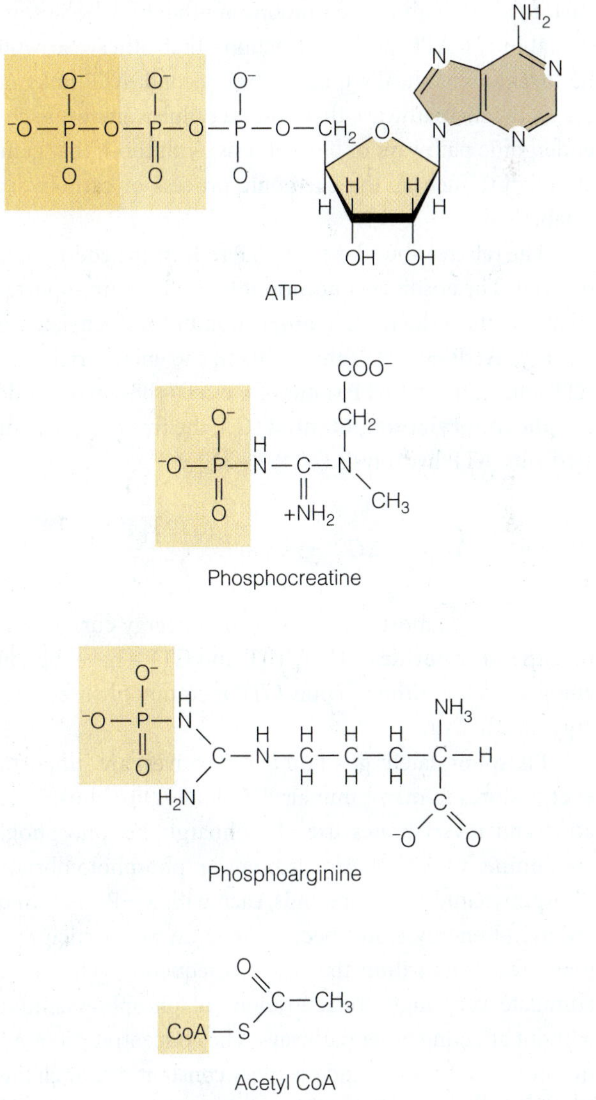

ATP

Phosphocreatine

Phosphoarginine

Acetyl CoA

ATP possesses two phosphodiester bonds ($-P-O-P-$). Some enzymes break the bond between the second and third phosphate groups, forming ADP. In some cases the inorganic phosphate (P_i) is released as a product, but often the P_i is transferred to another molecule. Other enzymes target the bond between the first and second phosphate groups, forming AMP and pyrophosphate (PP_i). Because these energy exchange reactions involve a breakdown of a phosphodiester bond, they are often called high-energy bonds. It is important to realize that the energy is not stored in the bond *per se*, but is released when ATP hydrolysis occurs—a reaction with large, negative free energy. If the concentrations of ADP and phosphate were very high and ATP very low, the thermodynamics for ATP breakdown would be unfavorable and there would be no energy associated with the breaking of the phosphodiester bond.

The importance of utilizing a metabolite like ATP is, first, to avoid high concentrations of other metabolites; participation of ATP permits reactions that otherwise would be thermodynamically unfavorable. Second, ATP links major metabolic pathways that require cellular energy, such as endergonic pathways of biosynthesis, with those that generate energy, such as the exergonic process of carbohydrate catabolism.

The relative abundance of ATP reflects the energy status of a cell. The absolute concentration of ATP is unimportant; what counts is the relative proportion of the adenylate pool (ATP + ADP + AMP) that exists in the energy-rich forms ATP and ADP. The ATP status of the cell is best expressed by the **phosphorylation potential** (G_p), the free energy associated with ATP hydrolysis (ATP → ADP + P_i):

$$\Delta G_p = \Delta G^{\circ\prime} + RT \ln \frac{[\,ADP\,][\,P_i\,]}{[\,ATP\,]}$$

ATP is the most common form of energy currency, but the other **nucleotides**—GTP, TTP, and CTP—have the same energetic value, although only GTP is commonly used in energy metabolism.

Phosphorylated guanidine derivatives are important energy stores in many animals. Vertebrates use phosphocreatine and invertebrates use phosphoarginine, phosphoglycocyamine, phosphotaurocyamine, or phospholombricine. Phosphoguanidine compounds, each with a $-P-N-$ bond, are useful energy stores because they do not participate in many reactions within the cell. Consequently, cells can accumulate very high concentrations of phosphoguanidines without affecting other pathways. The concentration of ATP, in contrast, is kept low and relatively constant. Major changes in ATP concentration would have kinetic consequences for countless enzymes that use ATP as a substrate or product.

For instance, the ATP concentration in vertebrate muscle is typically about 5 mM, whereas phosphocreatine concentrations might be 10−50 mM. Animal tissues use these high-energy compounds when the need for ATP temporarily outstrips the capacity to produce ATP. When ATP levels decline, the energy within phosphoguanidine is transferred to ADP to form ATP. In vertebrates, creatine phosphokinase (CPK) catalyzes this reaction.

$$\text{Phosphocreatine} + \text{ADP} \leftrightarrow \text{ATP} + \text{creatine}$$

Acetyl coenzyme A, or **acetyl CoA**, is another important high-energy store. Energy is released in reactions that hydrolyze its thioester bond ($-O-S-$). As we see later in this chapter, many pathways of biosynthesis and energy metabolism intersect at acetyl CoA. Collectively, reducing energy and high-energy compounds provide the energetic support for many cellular processes.

CONCEPT CHECK

7. Distinguish between allosteric and covalent regulation of enzymes.
8. Distinguish between the following types of reactions: anabolic, catabolic, and amphibolic.
9. Why is ATP considered a "high-energy" molecule?

Proteins

Proteins play many important roles in cell structure and function. Almost all enzymes are proteins (though many have nonprotein components). Proteins form the internal skeleton of a cell (cytoskeleton) as well the extracellular matrix needed to organize cells into complex tissues. The diversity in protein structure is afforded by the use of 20 amino acids that can be strung together in countless combinations. The blueprint for all proteins in a cell is in the form of DNA, which is transcribed into RNA and translated to form the appropriate proteins at the right time.

Proteins are polymers of amino acids

Animals build proteins from combinations of 20 amino acids. As the name implies, amino acids share the general structure of an amino group ($-NH_2$) and a carboxylic acid group ($-COOH$). They are called α-amino acids because both the amino and carboxyl groups are located on the first, or α, carbon.

Amino acids are distinguished from one another by their side groups (R). The R groups of polar amino acids form hydrogen bonds with water. Some polar amino acids are uncharged at physiological pH values (serine, threonine, cysteine, tyrosine, asparagine, glutamine), while others possess R groups with side chains that can become charged. Acidic amino acids (aspartate, glutamate) are negatively charged at physiological pH when carboxyl groups become deprotonated ($-COOH \rightarrow -COO^- + H^+$). Basic amino acids (arginine, lysine) take on a positive charge when amino groups become protonated ($-NH_2 + H^+ \rightarrow -NH_3^+$). Many amino acids are **nonpolar** because their R groups are aliphatic chains (alanine, valine, leucine, isoleucine, methionine) or aromatic rings (phenylalanine, tryptophan) that do not readily interact with water. The collection of amino acids, with their unique properties of side chain length, shape, charge, and polarity, provides cells with the building blocks necessary to construct thousands of different proteins.

Proteins are folded into three-dimensional shapes

Amino acids are polymerized into linear chains by covalent **peptide** bonds that link the amino group ($-NH_3$) of one amino acid to the carboxyl group ($-COOH$) of another amino acid.

$$R_2-N-\underset{\underset{H}{|}}{\overset{\overset{H}{|}}{N}}\boxed{H + H-O}-\overset{\overset{O}{||}}{C}-R_2 \rightarrow R_2-\overset{\overset{H}{|}}{N}-\overset{\overset{O}{||}}{C}-R_2 + H_2O$$

Two amino acids in a chain is a dipeptide. Polypeptides are longer chains of amino acids. At one end of the **polymer**, called the C terminus, the amino acid has an unbonded carboxyl group. At the other end, the N terminus, the amino

acid has an unbonded amino group. The linear sequence of amino acids in a protein is called the **primary structure**.

Once the primary structure is established, proteins are organized into more complex three-dimensional conformations (Figure 3.17). In many cases, the three-dimensional arrangement is a natural consequence of the primary structure, arising automatically when the protein is made. The overall structure is, however, also labile. The weak bonds discussed earlier in this chapter control the structure of proteins, and their vulnerability to physical and chemical factors means protein structure changes in response to specific environments.

First, the protein folds onto itself to assume its **secondary structure**. The information for proper folding is contained directly in the primary structure. The size, charge, and polarity of the side groups influence the interactions between amino acids in the chain. Secondary structures arise when side groups of amino acids interact to form a structure that is more stable than the simple linear conformation. The two most common protein secondary structural motifs are the α-helix and the β-sheet. In the α-helix, the protein is twisted into a spiral with 3.6 amino acids per turn and side chains extending outward. The structure is stabilized in two ways. First, hydrogen bonds form between the C=O of one amino acid and the N−H of the amino acid four positions along the chain. Second, the α-helix structure is stabilized when opposing side chains can interact. With the period of 3.6 amino acids, a side chain is exposed to the side chain of the amino acid three or four positions away. For example, if two aromatic amino acids are three positions apart, when the protein twists into an α-helix the structure will be

FIGURE 3.17   Protein structural levels
The amino acid sequence of a protein is its primary structure. This polypeptide can then be folded and organized into three-dimensional conformations.

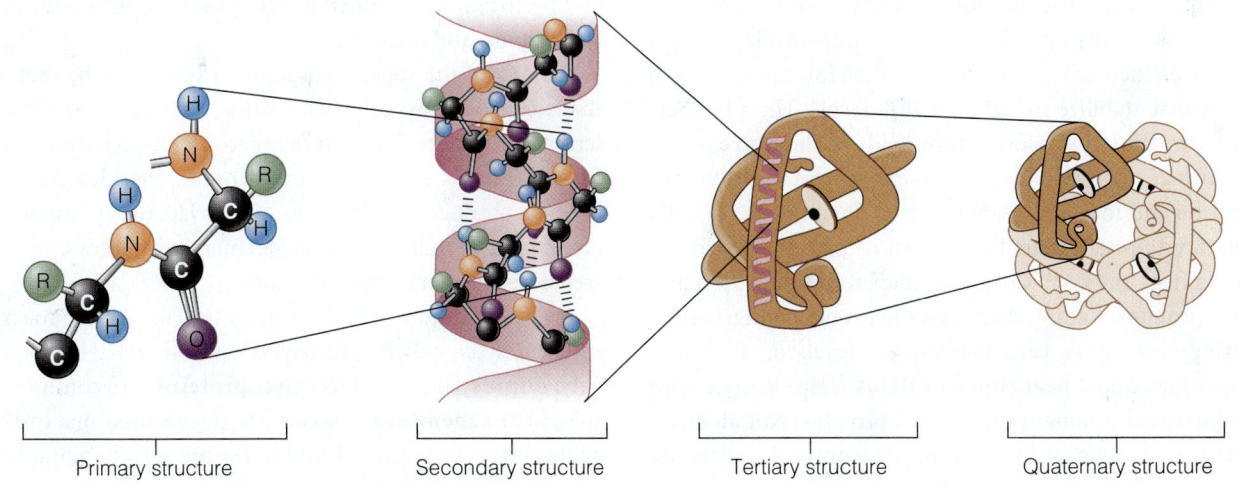

| Primary structure | Secondary structure | Tertiary structure | Quaternary structure |

stabilized by the hydrophobic interactions between the side chains. Similarly, negatively charged amino acids are often found three residues away from positively charged amino acids. Their electrostatic interactions stabilize the protein. The other common type of secondary structure, the β-sheet, forms when linear regions of a protein align side by side and form hydrogen bonds. In this conformation, the side chains extend above and below the face of the sheet.

Once a protein forms its secondary structure, the different regions fold together to create its **tertiary structure**. If the protein folds in a way that allows two adjacent cysteine residues to come into close proximity, their sulfhydryl groups ($-SH$) can form a covalent bond ($-S-S-$), called a **disulfide** bond or bridge. Multiple weak bonds link various amino acids and side chains to stabilize three-dimensional structure. Many proteins assume a globular structure when hydrophobic interactions form between regions scattered throughout the protein. By pulling together hydrophobic regions, a hydrophobic core is formed that stabilizes the structure of the protein.

A protein can achieve a quaternary structure when multiple subunits, or **polypeptide** chains, are brought together. Proteins with two subunits are called **dimers—a homodimer** if the **monomers** are identical, otherwise a **heterodimer**. Proteins can be composed of even larger numbers of subunits, such as **trimers** (three subunits) and tetramers (four subunits).

Molecular chaperones help proteins fold

Proteins can function properly only when they are folded into the correct conformation. Many proteins can use the information within the primary sequence to fold spontaneously, but others require the help of **molecular chaperones**. Each cell contains different chaperones to ensure that proteins are properly folded. They work by forcing the protein into a conformation that allows the appropriate weak bonds to form.

Environmental conditions, such as temperature, can alter weak bonds and disrupt three-dimensional protein structure. Increasing temperature weakens the hydrogen bonds that stabilize α-helices and β-sheets. High temperature can cause the protein to unfold, or **denature**. Once denatured, a protein can no longer perform its proper function and may even damage cells. Therefore, a partially denatured protein must be refolded or destroyed before it can damage the cell. Molecular chaperones bind to denatured proteins, folding them into the proper configuration. During heat stress, cells increase the levels of molecular chaperones called **heat shock proteins** (Hsp) to cope with the increased number of denatured proteins. Not all chaperones are responsive to heat, but by convention they are often identified as an Hsp. For example, cells have many chaperones related to Hsp70, which are produced in various subcellular compartments under unstressed conditions. These chaperones are essential in ensuring that newly formed proteins are properly folded.

CONCEPT CHECK

10. Distinguish between primary, secondary, tertiary, and quaternary structure.
11. Why does temperature affect the three-dimensional structure of proteins?
12. What is a molecular chaperone?

Carbohydrates

Carbohydrates share a preponderance of hydroxyl ($-OH$), or alcohol, groups, and for this reason they are often called *polyols*. For any animal, the diet is a vital source of the carbohydrates used to build and fuel cells. Glucose, the most common carbohydrate in animal diets, is central to cellular energy metabolism and biosynthesis because of its metabolic versatility. Cells can break glucose down for energy, or store it for later consumption, or use it to build other carbohydrates needed by the cell.

Animals use monosaccharides for energy and biosynthesis

Monosaccharides are small carbohydrates that have from three to seven carbons. The most common monosaccharides are the six-carbon sugars (**hexoses**), including glucose, fructose, and galactose (Figure 3.18). Glucose and galactose, as well as mannose, can be modified by the addition of acidic groups, amino groups, and modified amino groups. These sugar derivatives serve many purposes in the cell, primarily as modifications of other macromolecules, including proteins, lipids, and nucleic acids.

Many of the sugars that animals obtain in the diet are **disaccharides**, two monosaccharides connected by a covalent bond (Figure 3.19). In order to use disaccharides, animals first break them down into monosaccharides. Animals can also produce disaccharides such as lactose, an important component of milk in mammalian mammary secretions, and trehalose, an energy store and solute.

The addition of carbohydrates to other macromolecules is called **glycosylation**. Glycosylated lipids (**glycolipids**) and proteins (**glycoproteins**) are common in the **plasma membrane** of cells. A glycosylated macromolecule displays an altered molecular profile, changing how

FIGURE 3.18 **Common monosaccharides**

These structural models of monosaccharides show how side groups extend above and below the plane of the ring structures. The α and β forms of glucose differ in the orientation of the hydroxy group on C-1.

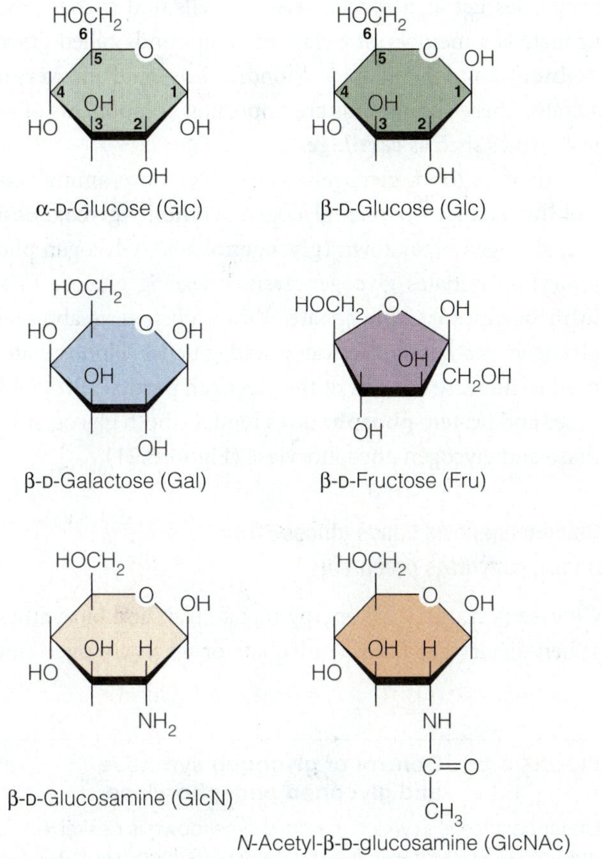

α-D-Glucose (Glc)

β-D-Glucose (Glc)

β-D-Galactose (Gal)

β-D-Fructose (Fru)

β-D-Glucosamine (GlcN)

N-Acetyl-β-D-glucosamine (GlcNAc)

it interacts with other macromolecules and reducing its susceptibility to degradation.

Complex carbohydrates perform many functional and structural roles

Complex carbohydrates, or **polysaccharides**, are larger polymers of carbohydrates that serve in energy storage and structure. Polysaccharides can be composed of long chains of a single type of monosaccharide or combinations of two alternating monosaccharides. Common polysaccharides important in metabolism and structure are shown in Figure 3.20.

Polymers of glucose are important forms of stored energy in plants and animals. Long chains are created when α-D-glucose molecules are attached between carbons 1 and 4 (α1,4 glycoside bonds). Plant starch is a mixture of amylose, which has few branches, and amylopectin, which has a side branch approximately every thirty glucose molecules. Starch is used by the plant for glucose storage, but it is an important dietary source of energy for many animals. **Glycogen** is like amylopectin but with branches approximately every ten glucose molecules. Acting as an internal energy store for most animals, glycogen is central to the energy metabolism of an animal and is a nutrient for animals that eat other animals.

Cellulose, another plant-derived glucose polymer, is essentially indigestible in animals because the glucose units are connected by β1,4 glycoside bonds. Cellulose, in most animals, provides dietary fiber. However, some animals, such as ruminants and termites, possess gastrointestinal symbionts that can degrade cellulose for energy.

FIGURE 3.19 **Common disaccharides**

Both trehalose and maltose are made from two glucose molecules but with bonds forming between different pairs of carbons.

Sucrose and maltose are synthesized in plants; animals obtain them by eating the plants.

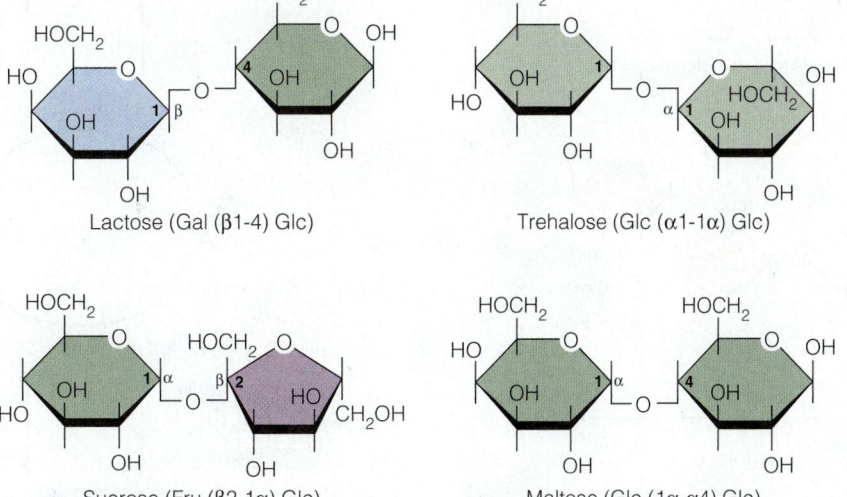

Lactose (Gal (β1-4) Glc)

Trehalose (Glc (α1-1α) Glc)

Sucrose (Fru (β2-1α) Glc)

Maltose (Glc (1α-α4) Glc)

FIGURE 3.20 **Polysaccharides**

(a) Plants and animals use polymers of glucose as energy stores. Amylose and amylopectin are the two polysaccharides that compose starch, an important dietary source of energy for animals. Animals produce glycogen, which resembles the plant polysaccharides but with much greater branching.
(b) Animals build many polysaccharides from combinations of monosaccharides and amino sugars, such as N-acetyl-glucosamine (GlcNAc). Chitin is a polymer of N-acetyl-glucosamine, whereas hyaluronate is a polymer of N-acetyl-glucosamine and glucuronic acid (GlcA).

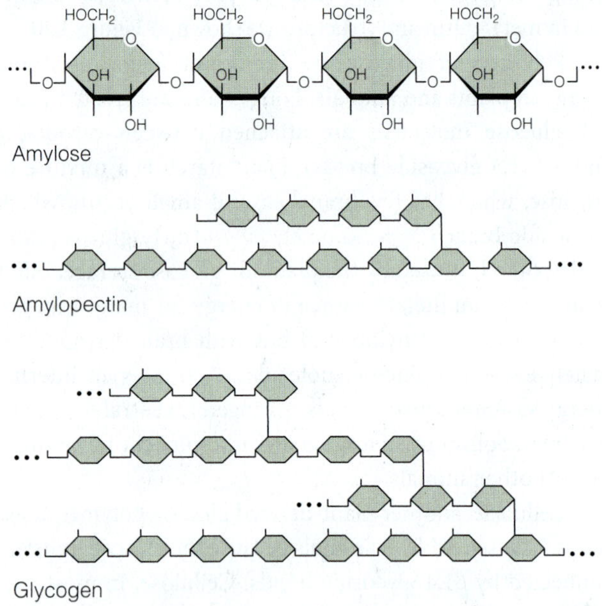

Amylose

Amylopectin

Glycogen

(a) Glucose polymers

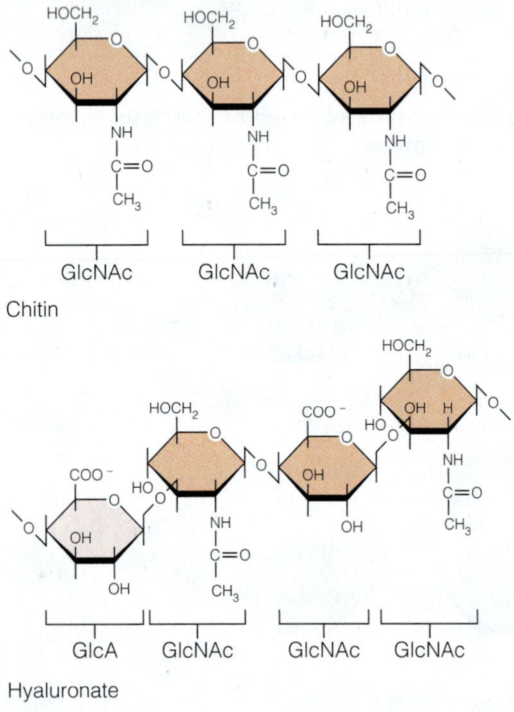

Chitin

Hyaluronate

(b) Glucose and amino sugar polymers

Polysaccharides are also critical structural components of animal cells. Arthropods build their exoskeletons with **chitin**, a polysaccharide of N-acetyl-glucosamine. Vertebrates secrete hyaluronate, a polymer of N-acetyl-glucosamine and glucuronic acid, into the extracellular space, where its gel-like properties act as a spacer between cells and tissues. Hyaluronate is a member of a class of compounds called **glycosaminoglycans** that include chondroitin sulfate and **keratan** sulfate. These compounds are important components of animal tissues such as **cartilage**.

In order to use glycogen as an energy store, animals control the balance between glycogen synthesis (**glycogenesis**) and glycogen breakdown (**glycogenolysis**). Glycogen phosphorylase initiates glycogenolysis, releasing glucose in the form of glucose 1-phosphate. When glucose is abundant, glycogen synthase is activated and glucose 1-phosphate is used to increase the size of the glycogen particle. Protein kinases and protein **phosphatases** regulate both glycogen synthase and glycogen phosphorylase (Figure 3.21).

Gluconeogenesis builds glucose from noncarbohydrate precursors

Glucose is essential for energy metabolism and biosynthesis. When dietary glucose is inadequate or when glycogen stores

FIGURE 3.21 **Control of glycogen synthase and glycogen phosphorylase**

Under conditions in which glycogen breakdown is desirable, both glycogen synthase and glycogen phosphorylase are phosphorylated by protein kinases. Phosphorylation inhibits glycogen synthase but stimulates glycogen phosphorylase. Similarly, dephosphorylation of these two enzymes by protein phosphatases favors glycogen synthesis.

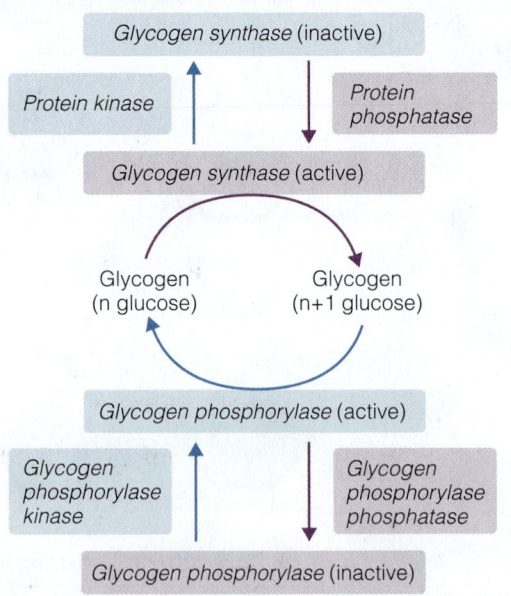

are compromised, animals can produce glucose from noncarbohydrate precursors via **gluconeogenesis**. The gluconeogenic pathway (Figure 3.22) using mitochondrial pyruvate as a starting point has the following overall reaction:

$$2\text{pyruvate} + 4\text{ATP} + 2\text{GTP} + 2\text{NADH} + 4H_2O \rightarrow \text{glucose} + 4\text{ADP} + 2\text{GDP} + 6\text{Pi} + 2\text{NAD}^+ + 2H^+$$

Gluconeogenesis begins in the mitochondria, where pyruvate carboxylase converts pyruvate to oxaloacetate, the substrate for PEP carboxykinase (PEPCK). In species with a mitochondrial PEPCK, PEP is transported to the cytoplasm; if PEPCK is cytoplasmic, the mitochondria convert oxaloacetate to malate, export it, and then resynthesize oxaloacetate within the cytoplasm. A series of reactions produces glucose 6-phosphate, which can be used to produce glycogen, or in some tissues converted to glucose by glucose 6-phosphatase. Because gluconeogenesis requires a great deal of energy, cells stimulate gluconeogenesis only when they have excess energy available. The metabolic indicators of energy status, such as acetyl CoA and adenylates (AMP, ADP, and ATP), regulate the gluconeogenic rate. The pathway is controlled mainly by availability of gluconeogenic substrates and allosteric regulation of pyruvate carboxylase and fructose 1,6-bisphosphatase (FBPase).

Many substrates can be used to produce glucose. Anything that can be made into pyruvate, such as lactate and some amino acids (alanine, serine, and glycine), can utilize the gluconeogenic pathway described above. Many other amino acids can enter the TCA cycle and be converted into oxaloacetate, then utilize this pathway. However, animal cells cannot use fatty acids as gluconeogenic substrates.

Glycolysis is a low-efficiency, high-velocity pathway

Glycolysis is the pathway that breaks down glucose obtained from the blood and glucose 6-phosphate derived from processing the glucose 1-phosphate liberated from stored glycogen. This pathway is a vital source of ATP because it can proceed in the absence of oxygen (anoxia) and can produce ATP very rapidly (albeit for brief periods).

Although glycolysis is usually discussed from the perspective of glucose or glycogen breakdown, other carbohydrates derived from the diet are also processed into hexoses that can enter glycolysis. Disaccharides are first broken down into monosaccharides: trehalose into two glucose, lactose into glucose and galactose, sucrose into glucose and fructose. The glycolytic pathway (Figure 3.23) using glucose as the initial substrate has the following overall reaction:

$$\text{Glucose} + 2\text{ADP} + 2\text{NAD}^+ \rightarrow 2\text{ATP} + 2\text{pyruvate} + 2\text{NADH} + 2H^+$$

When glucose is carried into the cell, the enzyme hexokinase rapidly phosphorylates it, using a molecule of ATP.

Because glucose 6-phosphate is not readily transported across the cell membrane, phosphorylation of glucose traps glucose within the cell. The next steps in glycolysis are a series of enzymatic reactions that convert the glucose backbone to fructose, which is then hydrolyzed to form two trioses that are ultimately converted to pyruvate. Seven of the ten glycolytic reactions are freely reversible, and catalyzed by the enzymes shared with the gluconeogenic pathway. The three irreversible glycolytic reactions—hexokinase, phosphofructokinase (PFK), and pyruvate kinase (PK)—are important sites of regulation for the pathway, acting via mass action effects, allosteric regulation, and covalent modification. During periods of high energy demand, much of the ATP is broken down to ADP and AMP, affecting the mass action ratios for all three regulatory enzymes. Both ADP and AMP are powerful activators of PFK enzymatic activity, whereas ATP inhibits PFK as well as PK. When cells do not need energy, glycolysis is inhibited at PFK and PK. With PFK inhibited, glucose 6-phosphate is diverted into glycogen synthesis. Thus, the fate of the glucose 6-phosphate—glycolysis or glycogen synthesis—is linked to energy status through regulation of PFK. This is an example of **negative feedback regulation**, in which an increase in the concentration of products inhibits the pathway.

In addition to the 2 mol of ATP per glucose, glycolysis produces 2 mol of pyruvate and NADH. Glycolysis can continue only if the cell can remove the pyruvate and NADH produced. The fate of these products depends on two factors: the metabolic demands of the cell and the availability of oxygen.

When energy is required and oxygen abundant, pyruvate produced in glycolysis enters the mitochondria for further oxidation. First, the enzyme pyruvate dehydrogenase (PDH) produces acetyl CoA, which is further oxidized to produce CO_2. The reducing energy (4 NADH and 1 $FADH_2$) and nucleotides (1 GTP) allow mitochondria to produce the equivalent of 15 ATP from pyruvate. Because the cytoplasmic production of pyruvate produces only 1 ATP per pyruvate, considerably more energy is produced by glucose oxidation (glucose $\rightarrow$ CO_2) than by glycolysis (glucose $\rightarrow$ pyruvate).

Mitochondria also dispose of the cytoplasmic NADH produced in glycolysis. Although they cannot oxidize NADH directly, mitochondria use two **redox shuttles** to obtain the reducing energy of cytoplasmic NADH. In the α-glycerophosphate shuttle, cytoplasmic NADH is first oxidized by the enzyme α-glycerophosphate dehydrogenase (α-GPDH), embedded within the mitochondrial inner membrane. Oxidation of glycolytic NADH in the α-glycerophosphate shuttle generates two ATP. In the malate-aspartate shuttle, malate dehydrogenase oxidizes NADH and

FIGURE 3.22 **Gluconeogenesis**

Cells convert pyruvate to glucose and glycogen using the enzymes of gluconeogenesis. The exact route of phosphoenolpyruvate synthesis depends upon tissue and species. Some species use a mitochondrial PEPCK to produce phosphoenolpyruvate.

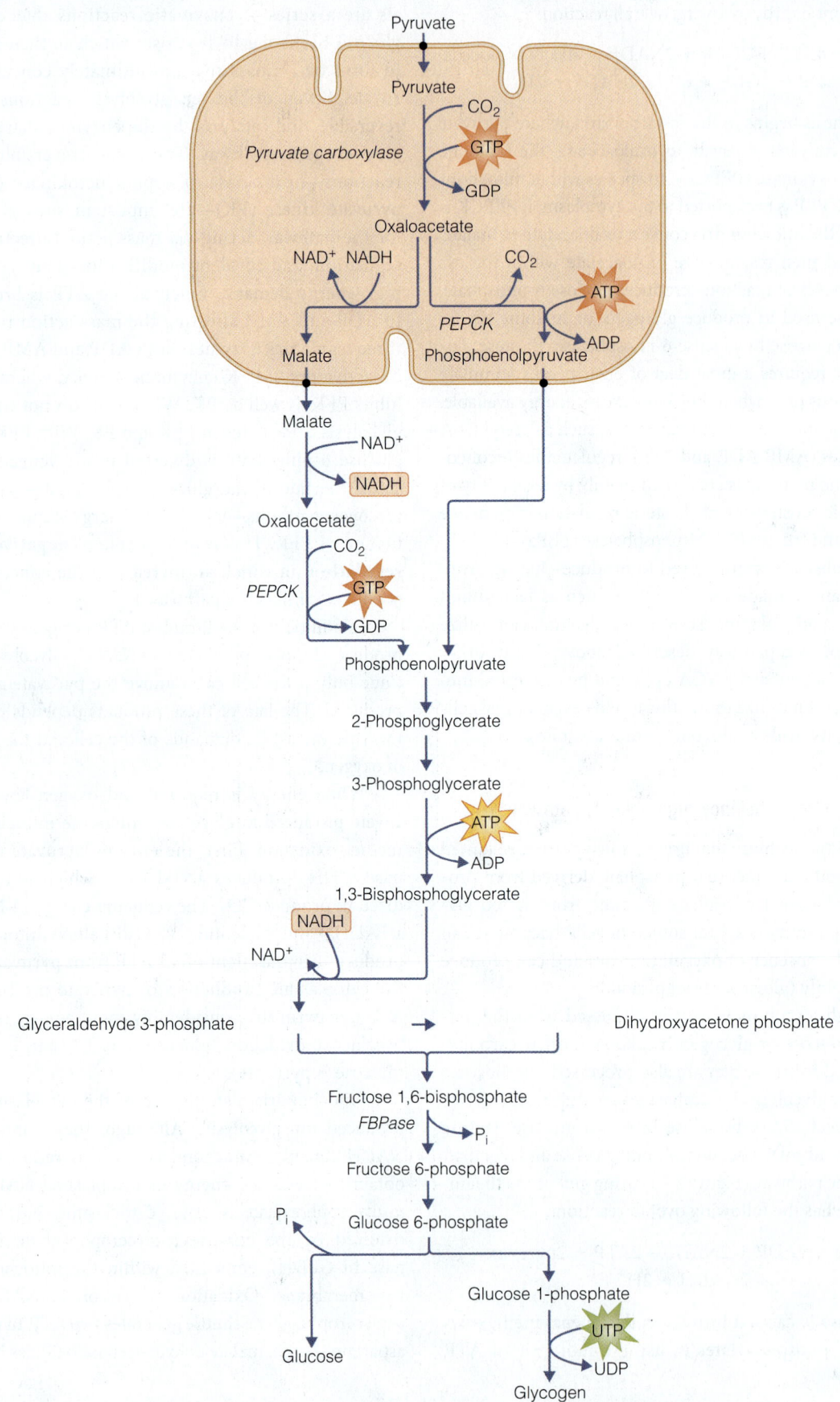

FIGURE 3.23 **Glycolysis**

Glycolysis is a series of cytoplasmic enzymes that breaks down glucose or glycogen to produce ATP. Because ATP is required by hexokinase, glycolysis from glycogen produces more ATP (three ATP per glucosyl) than it does from glucose (two ATP per glucose). The other important products of glycolysis are pyruvate and NADH. The three irreversible reactions are highlighted.

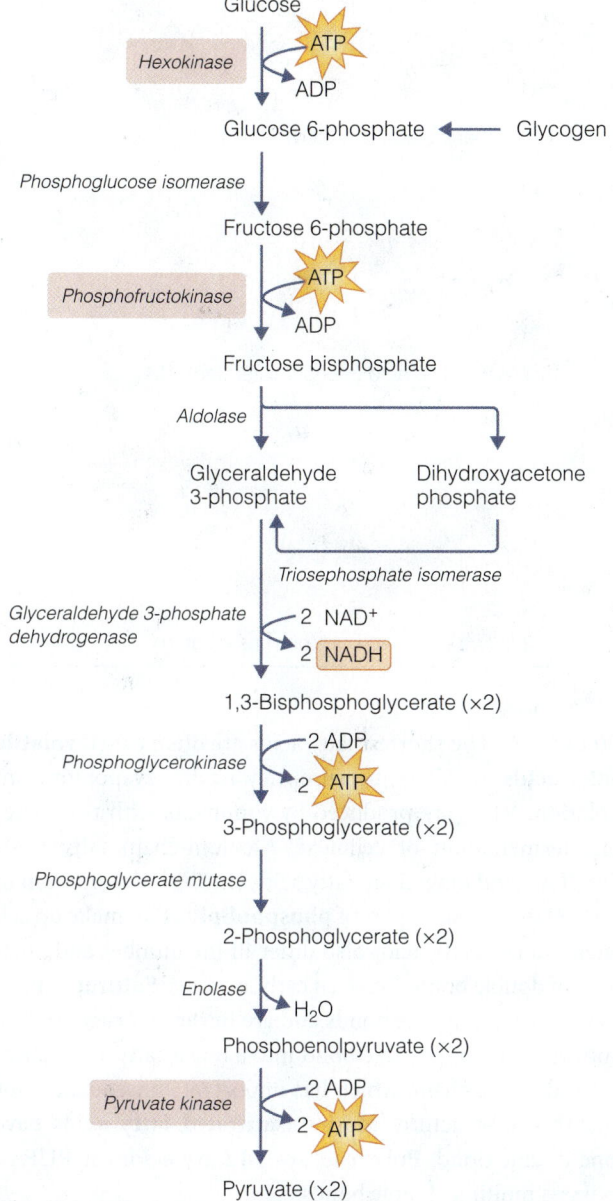

produces malate, which can be transported into mitochondria where it is oxidized by another malate dehydrogenase, regenerating NADH within the mitochondria.

Terminal dehydrogenases oxidize NADH under anaerobic conditions

Because mitochondria require oxygen to process pyruvate and NADH, the nature of the end products of glycolysis depends on the availability of oxygen. Environmental hypoxia arises when external oxygen levels fall below critical levels for prolonged periods. Intertidal bivalves may close their shells during tidal cycles, inducing hours of hypoxia, whereas parasites of the gastrointestinal tract live perpetually under hypoxia. Functional anoxia can arise when tissue oxygen demands outstrip oxygen delivery from the blood. For example, muscle can become hypoxic during intense exercise. Diving animals gradually deplete their onboard oxygen stores, causing short-term hypoxia in some tissues. In each of these situations, animals depend on glycolysis for energy and must be able to oxidize NADH to allow glycolysis to continue. One of the most common pathways for NAD^+ regeneration is through the activity of LDH, an enzyme we introduced earlier in this chapter.

$$Pyruvate + NADH + H^+ \leftrightarrow lactate + NAD^+$$

This reaction regenerates NAD^+ and disposes of pyruvate, permitting glycolysis to continue. For many species, lactate production is a strong indication of glycolytic flux. Once produced in the LDH reaction, lactate can either be retained in the tissue or exported from the cell into extracellular fluid. Although lactate is slightly toxic, it can be tolerated for short periods. When the anoxia bout ends, lactate is metabolized, and is often used as a substrate to regenerate glucose and glycogen.

The most hypoxia-tolerant and anoxia-tolerant animals use three general mechanisms to extend survival. One is to reduce their metabolic demands to extend the life of their energy stores by entering some form of **dormancy** or reducing the metabolic demands of specific tissues. For example, a turtle can depress its metabolic rate at the onset of a dive. Second, animals can extend hypoxic survival by storing high levels of glycogen. Almost half the dry weight of some bivalve mollusks, for example, is glycogen, providing many days of anoxia tolerance. Third, some anoxia-tolerant organisms alter the nature of glycolysis to produce an alternative end product that is less toxic than lactate. Some mollusks produce strombine, alanopine, or octopine. Some species of fish can convert lactate to ethanol, which is then excreted into the water. This additional reaction spares them the toxicity of lactate, but in the process they lose a valuable source of energy. Bivalve mollusks and some endoparasites also produce alternate end products, but gain extra energy along the way. Phosphoenolpyruvate (PEP) can be diverted from glycolysis to produce succinate (4 ATP/glucose) or propionate (6 ATP/glucose). The various alternative pathways and **anaerobic** end products are summarized in Figure 3.24. Collectively, these variations of glycolysis allow animals to succeed in anoxic environments that are toxic to other species.

FIGURE 3.24 **Anaerobic end products of glycolysis**

Animals collectively have many different ways to oxidize NADH when oxygen is limiting. Many animals and tissues rely on lactate dehydrogenase, but other pathways occur in hypoxia-tolerant animals. Some anaerobic end products can lead to production of extra ATP.

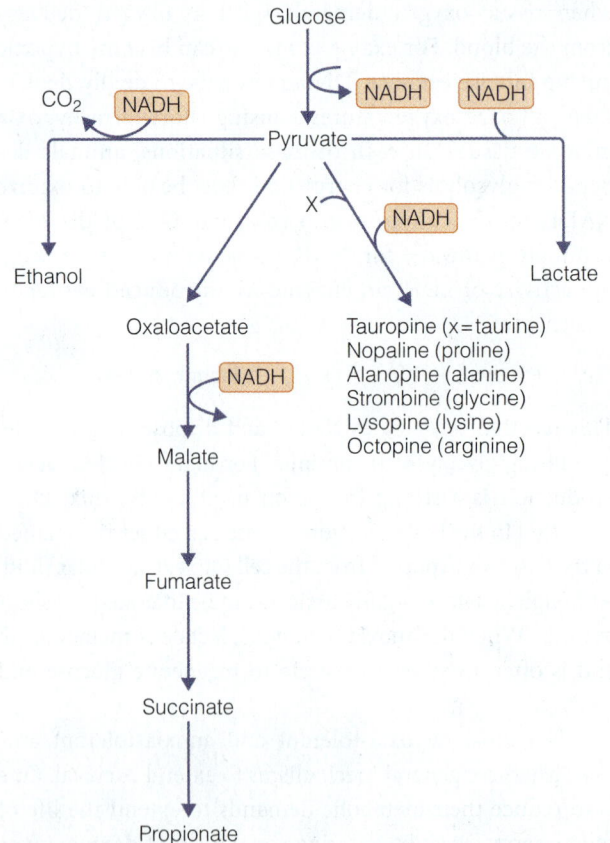

Lipids

Lipids are a class of hydrophobic organic molecules including fatty acids, triglycerides, phospholipids, steroids, and steroid derivatives. They have many roles in animal cells, acting as substrates for energy production, building blocks for membranes, and signaling molecules.

Fatty acids are long aliphatic chains produced from acetyl CoA

Fatty acids are long chains of carbon atoms (aliphatic) ending with a carboxyl group (Figure 3.25). They can vary in chain length from two carbons, as with acetate, to more than

FIGURE 3.25 **Fatty acids**

Saturated fats such as stearic acid (18:0) are linear in structure. Addition of a double bond, as shown with the monounsaturated fatty acid oleic acid (18:1), introduces a bend in the structure. The second double bond shown in the polyunsaturated acid linoleic acid (18:2) causes further disruption of the linear structure.

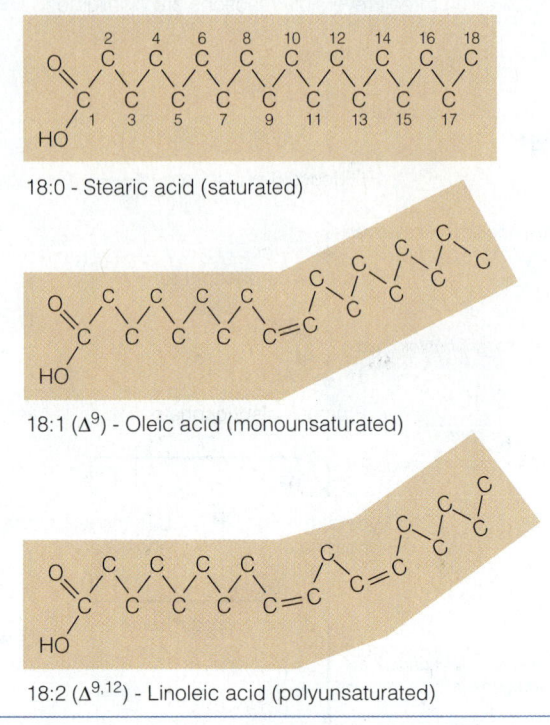

18:0 - Stearic acid (saturated)

18:1 (Δ^9) - Oleic acid (monounsaturated)

18:2 ($\Delta^{9,12}$) - Linoleic acid (polyunsaturated)

30 carbons. The shortest fatty acids are often called **volatile fatty acids**, or VFAs, because they readily evaporate from solution. VFAs are produced by ruminants with the bacterial fermentation of cellulose. Medium-chain fatty acids (MCFAs) and long-chain fatty acids (LCFAs) are common in energy stores and as part of **phospholipids** that make up cell membranes. Fatty acids also differ in the number and position of double bonds between carbon atoms. **Saturated fatty acids** have no double bonds and are linear in structure. The introduction of a double bond into a linear fatty acid causes a bend in the chain, which has important consequences for membrane structure. **Monounsaturated fatty acids** have one double bond. **Polyunsaturated fatty acids**, or PUFAs, possess multiple double bonds.

Fatty acid nomenclature considers both the chain length and the number of bonds. Palmitic acid is denoted as 16:0, meaning it is 16 carbons long and has no double bonds. There are two naming systems to denote fatty acids, which differ in how they identify the location of the first double bond. In the delta (Δ) system, a number corresponds to location of the double bond relative to the carboxyl carbon; in the omega (ω) system, the number refers to the distance from the methyl end of the fatty acid. Thus, the 18-carbon fatty acid oleic acid can be either 18:1 Δ^9 or 18:1 ω9. Linoleic acid is denoted as either 18:2 $\Delta^{9,12}$ or 18:2 ω6.

Animals can produce many fatty acids using the enzyme fatty acid synthase, which cyclically adds two-carbon units to the fatty acid. Though fatty acids grow by adding acetyl groups, malonyl CoA, a three-carbon activated fatty acid is the actual substrate for the enzyme fatty acid synthase. Malonyl CoA is produced by acetyl CoA carboxylase. Using the reducing energy of NADPH, fatty acid synthase repeatedly adds acetyl CoA groups to the fatty acid. After seven cycles, when the fatty acid has grown to 16 carbons, palmitate has been produced and is released by the enzyme. The overall reaction for palmitate synthesis is

$$\text{Acetyl CoA} + 7\text{malonyl CoA} + 7\text{NADPH} + 7\text{H}^+$$
$$\rightarrow \text{palmitate} + 7\text{NADP}^+$$

Though palmitate is the product of fatty acid synthase, accessory enzymes process much of it to produce other fatty acids. These enzymes elongate the carbon chain and introduce double bonds to produce the other important fatty acids, such as oleic acid. Many animals can produce all of the fatty acids needed for growth, but some animals are incapable of producing specific fatty acids and must obtain these in the diet. For example, humans have a dietary requirement for linoleic acid (18:2 ω6) and linolenic acid (18:3 ω3).

Fatty acids are oxidized in mitochondrial β-oxidation

Fatty acids are an important fuel for many tissues, such as the mammalian heart, which typically derives more than 70 percent of its energy from fatty acid oxidation. The fatty acid oxidation pathway occurs primarily in the mitochondria and results in the production of acetyl CoA. Depending on the conditions, this acetyl CoA can be oxidized by mitochondria or be diverted to other pathways. Fatty acids can have many structures, differing in chain length, branching patterns, and desaturation. These variations require side reactions to convert the fatty acids to forms that can enter β-oxidation. We will focus on the pathway for oxidation of palmitate, but along the way we will identify some of the alternate pathways used to process other fatty acids.

Because the actual substrate for β-oxidation is fatty acyl CoA, cells must first convert fatty acids to their CoA esters using a fatty acyl CoA synthase. Short- and medium-chain fatty acids are able to enter the mitochondria directly, where they are activated by a mitochondrial fatty acyl CoA synthase. Palmitate, which cannot cross into mitochondria, is oxidized by the mitochondria by a multistep process involving activation and transport. The fatty acid is converted to fatty acyl CoA. Next, the enzyme carnitine palmitoyl transferase-1, or CPT-1, replaces the CoA with carnitine, forming fatty acyl carnitine, which is carried into the mitochondria, where another enzyme, CPT-2, converts it back to fatty acyl CoA. This elaborate transport scheme provides an extra level of control over long-chain fatty acid oxidation. By regulating the activity of CPT-1, cells control how much fatty acid can enter the mitochondria for catabolism.

Once inside the mitochondria, fatty acids enter the β-oxidation pathway (Figure 3.26). This is a cyclical pathway

FIGURE 3.26 Fatty acid oxidation
Fatty acids are activated in the cytoplasm to form fatty acyl CoA. Once transported into mitochondria, fatty acyl CoA enters the β-oxidation pathway. Oxidation, hydration, oxidation, and thiolysis produce acetyl CoA, reducing equivalents, and a fatty acyl CoA shortened by two carbons. The shortened fatty acyl CoA reenters the β-oxidation pathway and the cycle repeats until the fatty acid is reduced to acetyl CoA units.

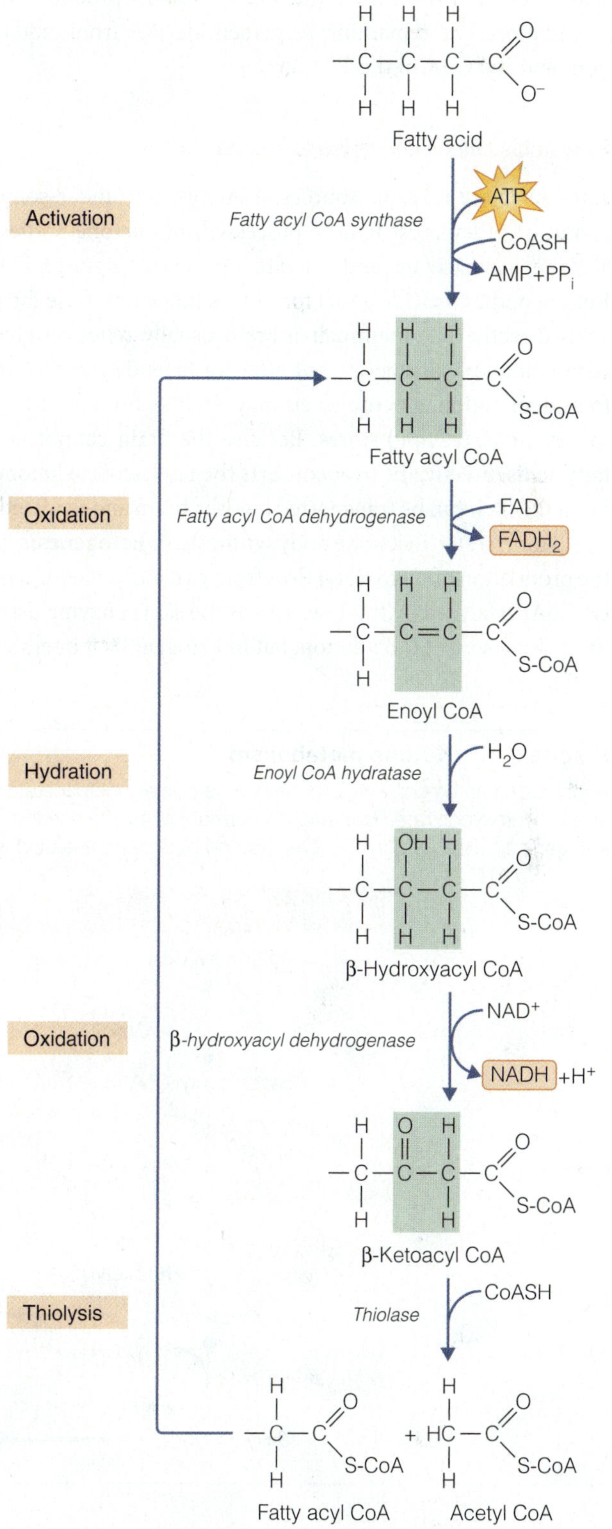

that sequentially cuts pairs of carbons off the end of the fatty acid in the form of acetyl CoA. The shortened fatty acid returns to the pathway, and the cycle is repeated until the entire fatty acid is broken down to acetyl CoA. With each trip through the pathway, reducing equivalents are produced at two enzymatic steps: fatty acyl CoA dehydrogenase produces $FADH_2$, and β-hydroxyacyl CoA dehydrogenase produces NADH. About 30 percent of the energy liberated from fatty acids is derived from the reducing equivalents produced in β-oxidation. The remaining 70 percent derives from oxidation of acetyl CoA in the TCA cycle.

Fatty acids can be converted to ketone bodies

Fatty acids are valuable sources of energy, but under some conditions they must first be processed into ketone bodies: acetone, acetoacetate, and β-hydroxybutyrate (Figure 3.27). Ketone bodies provide a fuel for tissues that cannot use fatty acids directly. The mammalian brain usually relies on glucose oxidation for energy, but after an extended period of food deprivation, glucose levels may decline, forcing tissues to rely more on lipid stores. Because the brain cannot use fatty acids directly, the liver converts the fatty acids to ketone bodies, which can be transported into the brain and oxidized.

The first step in ketone body synthesis, or **ketogenesis**, is the production of acetoacetyl CoA from two molecules of acetyl CoA, catalyzed by thiolase. This is the same enzyme used in the final step of β-oxidation, but in ketogenesis it operates in the reverse direction. After condensation with another acetyl CoA and subsequent hydrolysis, acetoacetate is formed. Acetoacetate can then be converted to β-hydroxybutyrate by the enzyme β-hydroxybutyrate dehydrogenase (β-HBDH), or it can break down spontaneously to form acetone. In the target tissues, **ketolysis** reconverts β-hydroxybutyrate and acetoacetate to acetyl CoA. Acetoacetate is activated into the CoA ester, then hydrolyzed by thiolase to form two acetyl CoA molecules.

Ketone bodies are a useful alternative to fatty acids for many animals. Although some energy is lost in the complete cycle of ketogenesis and ketolysis, for some tissues, particularly under starvation conditions, ketone bodies are the only metabolic energy source available. Chondrichthians (sharks and their relatives) in fact appear biochemically predisposed to using ketone bodies as their "lipid" fuel. Unlike other vertebrates, their muscles are unable to use fatty acids directly, instead relying on ketone bodies as a fuel for energy.

Triglyceride is the major form of lipid storage

Most fatty acids in animal cells are esterified to a glycerol backbone. A **monoacylglyceride** has a single fatty acid esterified to glycerol, typically at the first position of the glycerol molecule. Diacylglyceride has fatty acids esterified to the first and second position of glycerol. **Triglyceride** has three fatty acids esterified to the glycerol backbone (Figure 3.28). Each of these terms—monoacylglycerides, diacylglycerides,

---

FIGURE 3.27 **Ketone metabolism**

Acetyl CoA can be converted to the ketone bodies acetoacetate and β-hydroxybutyrate. This reaction normally occurs in specific ketogenic tissues, such as the liver. Ketone bodies are released through the blood for uptake by ketolytic tissues, such as the brain. Acetyl CoA is resynthesized at the cost of 1 GTP to regenerate the substrate succinyl CoA.

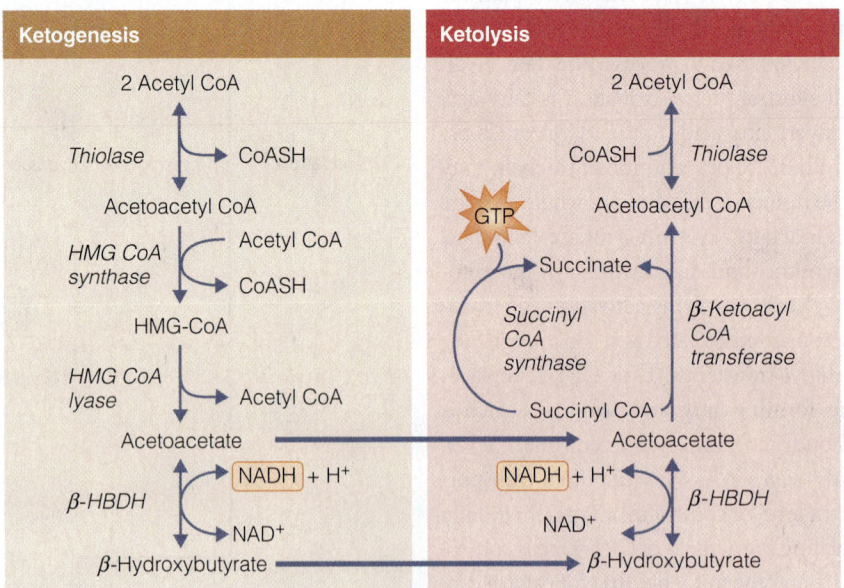

FIGURE 3.28 Triglycerides

Triglycerides are composed of three fatty acids esterified to a glycerol backbone. Fatty acids can vary in chain length and number of double bonds.

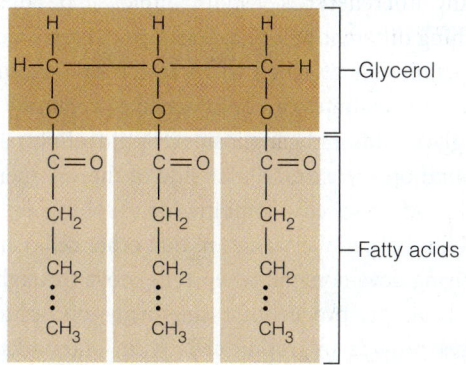

FIGURE 3.29 Triglyceride synthesis

Glycerol 3-phosphate, produced from glycolysis (dihydroxyacetone phosphate) or glycerol, is the acceptor for two sequential additions of activated fatty acids (fatty acyl CoA). The formation of triglyceride requires dephosphorylation and addition of another fatty acid group to the third and last position on the glycerol backbone.

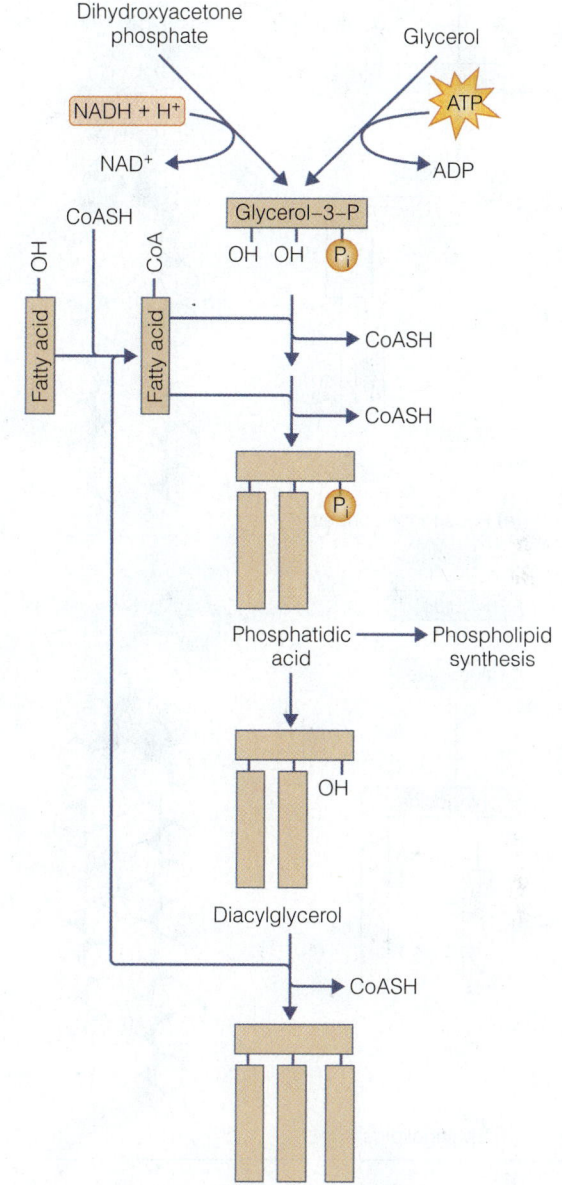

and triglycerides—refers to a class of molecules. For example, hundreds of chemically distinct triglyceride molecules can be constructed by using different fatty acids in each of the three positions on the glycerol backbone.

Triglycerides are vital energy stores for animals, and can be found in high concentrations in lipid-storage tissues in the form of lipid droplets. In insects, a tissue called the fat body is the main site of lipid storage. Many other invertebrates, such as mollusks and crustaceans, store lipid in a large **hepatopancreas**. Vertebrates store triglyceride in liver, muscle, and **adipose tissue**, such as **blubber**. Adipocytes, the cells within adipose tissue, store triglyceride when an animal is well fed, then release lipids when the animal needs extra fuel.

Triglyceride synthesis, or **lipogenesis**, is a multistep process overlapping with phospholipid synthesis (Figure 3.29). Each fatty acid is activated into its CoA ester by fatty acyl CoA synthase. Starting with glycerol 3-phosphate, the fatty acids are added sequentially to carbon 1, then carbon 2, forming a phosphatide. After removal of the phosphate group, diacylglycerol is formed. Addition of a third fatty acid completes the triglyceride molecule.

Triglyceride breakdown, or **lipolysis**, requires enzymes called **lipases** that attack the triglyceride molecule, breaking the bond between the fatty acid and the glycerol backbone. Hormone-sensitive lipase liberates fatty acids from triglycerides and diacylglycerides. Another lipase, monoacylglyceride lipase, completes the breakdown of the triglyceride by releasing the last fatty acid from the glycerol backbone. The liberated fatty acids are either used directly within the cell or transferred to the circulation for uptake by other tissues that use them for energy metabolism.

The balance between triglyceride synthesis and degradation is carefully controlled within animals. Lipolysis does not directly generate energy, but lipogenesis requires energy. As

with other pathways we have discussed, if both synthesis and degradation occurred simultaneously, cells would waste energy.

Phospholipids predominate in biological membranes

In addition to their role in energy metabolism, fatty acids are vital components of the phospholipids used to produce biological membranes. Animal cells produce two classes of phospholipids: phosphoglycerides and sphingolipids (Figure 3.30).

FIGURE 3.30 **Phospholipids**

Phospholipids, including **(a)** phosphoglycerides and **(b)** sphingolipids, share a similar three-dimensional structure. They are built on different backbones: glycerol for phosphoglycerides and sphingosine for sphingolipids.

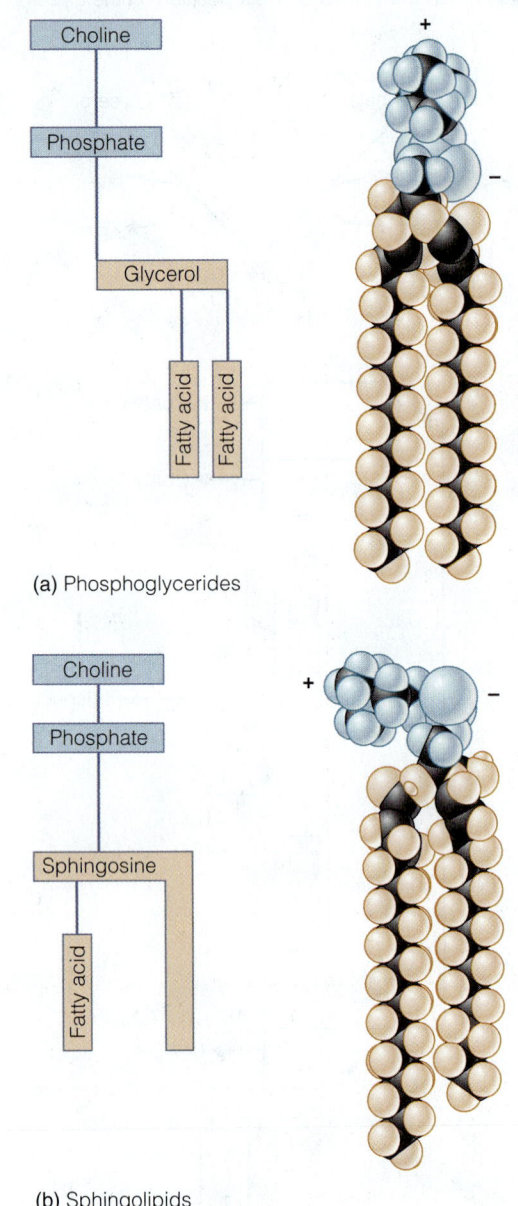

(a) Phosphoglycerides

(b) Sphingolipids

shapes. The backbone of a sphingolipid is sphingosine. With its long aliphatic chain, its structure is similar to monoacylglycerol. Ceramide is formed when a fatty acid is esterified to sphingosine, creating a structure that resembles diacylglycerol. Many different types of sphingolipid can be constructed by attaching different polar head groups to ceramide. When phosphocholine is attached to ceramide, sphingomyelin is formed. Carbohydrates can be attached to ceramide to form neutral glycolipids and gangliosides. Sphingolipids are most often found on the extracellular side of the cell membrane. Each cell makes a specific combination of sphingolipids, providing a kind of cellular signature that other cells can recognize. During development, when cells move throughout the body to begin the process of tissue formation, sphingolipid signatures provide migrating cells with landmarks. When the migrating cells find the correct sphingolipid signature, they cease migration and differentiate to form tissues.

Phospholipids are broken down by **phospholipases**, many of which are important in cell-signaling cascades. Each type of phospholipase attacks a specific region of a phospholipid molecule. Phospholipase A (PLA) breaks the ester bonds that connect the fatty acids to the glycerol backbone. PLA_1 releases the fatty acid from the first carbon of glycerol, whereas PLA_2 releases the fatty acid from the second position. Phospholipases B and C break different phosphodiester bonds between the polar head group and the glycerol backbone. When PLB attacks phosphatidyl inositol, inositol and phosphatide are produced. When PLC attacks the same phospholipid, inositol phosphate and diacylglyceride are released. Regulation of PLC, an important enzyme in signal transduction pathways of many cells, will be discussed in more detail in Chapter 4: Hormones and Cell Signaling.

Steroids share a multiple ring structure

Steroids are a collection of lipid molecules that share a basic aromatic structure of four hydrocarbon rings. The steroid **cholesterol** is found in many **cellular membranes** and is part of the lipoprotein complexes that transport lipids through the blood. It is also a precursor for synthesis of the vertebrate steroid hormones. Although invertebrates don't possess steroid hormones, some use a steroidlike hormone, **ecdysone**, to control maturation and development.

The pathways of steroid synthesis involve nonsteroid intermediates (Figure 3.31). Steroid synthesis begins when acetate is used to produce mevalonate, the precursor for activated isoprene. Activated isoprene is the precursor for many familiar molecules, such as carotenoids and vitamins A, E, and K. Ubiquinone, a type of quinone, is an important component in mitochondrial energy production. Activated isoprene is also used to produce isoprenoids that act as hormones, including insect juvenile hormone and pheromones.

Phosphoglycerides are constructed from phosphatides, an intermediate in triglyceride synthesis. In phosphogylceride synthesis, the phosphate group links the phosphatide to a polar head group, such as serine, choline, ethanolamine, and inositol. The physical properties of a phosphoglyceride are determined by the properties of both the fatty acids (chain length, saturation) and the polar head group.

Although **sphingolipids** are chemically very different from phosphoglycerides, they have similar three-dimensional

FIGURE 3.31 **Steroid biosynthesis**

This simplified pathway of steroid synthesis illustrates the many intermediates that are used by cells.

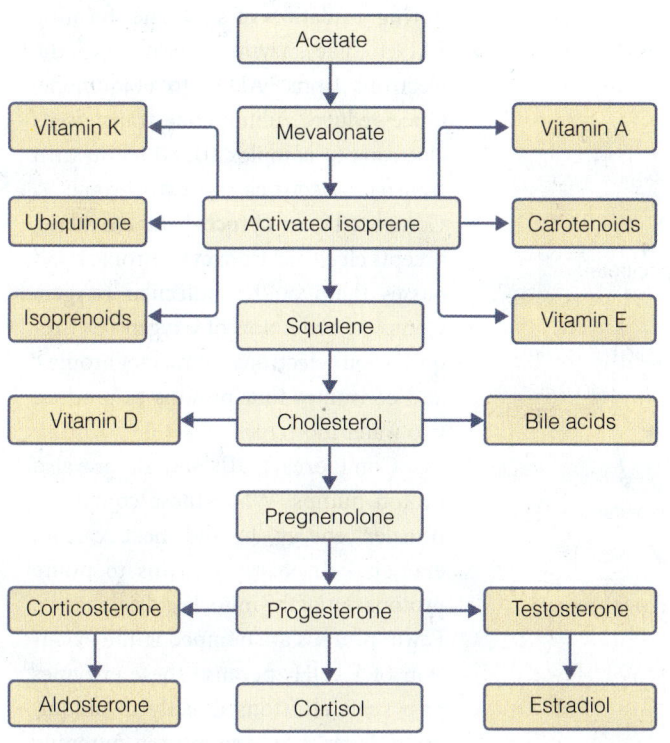

Further along the pathway of cholesterol synthesis is squalene, a steroid used by sharks to aid in buoyancy. Cholesterol is the precursor for many steroid hormones, discussed in later chapters (see Figure 4.8).

CONCEPT CHECK

16. How is energy derived from triglyceride breakdown?
17. What are the products of triglyceride breakdown?
18. What are the main classes of phospholipid?

Mitochondrial Metabolism

Mitochondria process metabolites generated in the cytoplasm, breaking them down to capture their chemical energy in the form of ATP. The main point of entry for mitochondrial energy-producing pathways is acetyl CoA, which as you've learned earlier in this chapter is produced in many pathways (Figure 3.32). Acetyl CoA enters the cyclical **tricarboxylic acid cycle (TCA cycle)** and is oxidized to form reducing equivalents (NADH, FADH$_2$), which provide the fuel for mitochondrial ATP production.

FIGURE 3.32 **Acetyl CoA production from diverse metabolites**

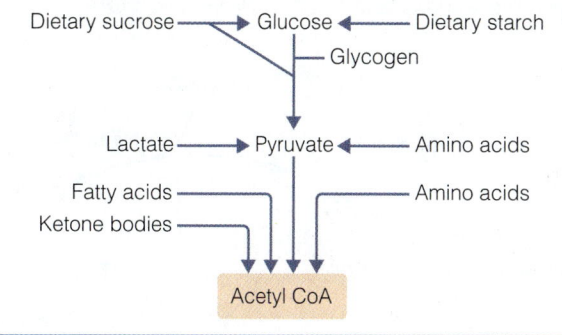

The TCA cycle uses acetyl CoA to generate reducing equivalents

Once acetyl CoA is produced within mitochondria, its fate depends on intracellular conditions. When cells need energy, acetyl CoA enters the TCA cycle, where its oxidation ultimately leads to ATP production. The TCA cycle (Figure 3.33) consists of eight enzymes that collectively catalyze the following reaction:

$$\text{Acetyl CoA} + 3\text{NAD}^+ + \text{GDP} + P_i + \text{FAD} \rightarrow 2\text{CO}_2 + 3\text{NADH} + \text{FADH}_2 + \text{GTP}$$

The four dehydrogenases in the TCA cycle produce reducing equivalents: NADH is produced by isocitrate dehydrogenase, 2-oxoglutarate dehydrogenase, and malate dehydrogenase; FADH$_2$ is produced by succinate dehydrogenase. Most of the ATP produced through acetyl CoA oxidation comes from the subsequent oxidation of NADH and FADH$_2$. The TCA cycle also produces one molecule of GTP, which is energetically equivalent to ATP. This reaction, catalyzed by succinyl CoA synthase, is an example of **substrate-level phosphorylation**. The TCA cycle is not an isolated pathway so much as a collection of enzymes acting on a pool of metabolites exchanged with other pathways. When intermediates are removed for other reactions, cells use **anaplerotic pathways** to regenerate the intermediates.

Cells control the rate of the TCA cycle in three ways: by regulating the concentrations of reactants (substrates and products), the levels of the enzymes, and the catalytic activity of enzymes. Tissues that use a lot of energy, such as the heart and brain, have high levels of the TCA enzymes. In many tissues, the flux through the TCA cycle is affected by the levels of acetyl CoA and oxaloacetate, as well as other intermediates in the cycle. When tissues have abundant energy, they typically use acetyl CoA and intermediates as biosynthetic substrates. Acetyl CoA is an important substrate in fatty acid synthesis, and oxaloacetate is a substrate for glucose synthesis. When biosynthetic reactions deplete these substrates, the rate of the TCA cycle declines. Allosteric effectors also

FIGURE 3.33 **Tricarboxylic acid cycle**

The enzymes of the TCA cycle oxidize acetyl CoA to release its energy in the form of reducing equivalents (3 NADH, 1 FADH$_2$) and 1 GTP.

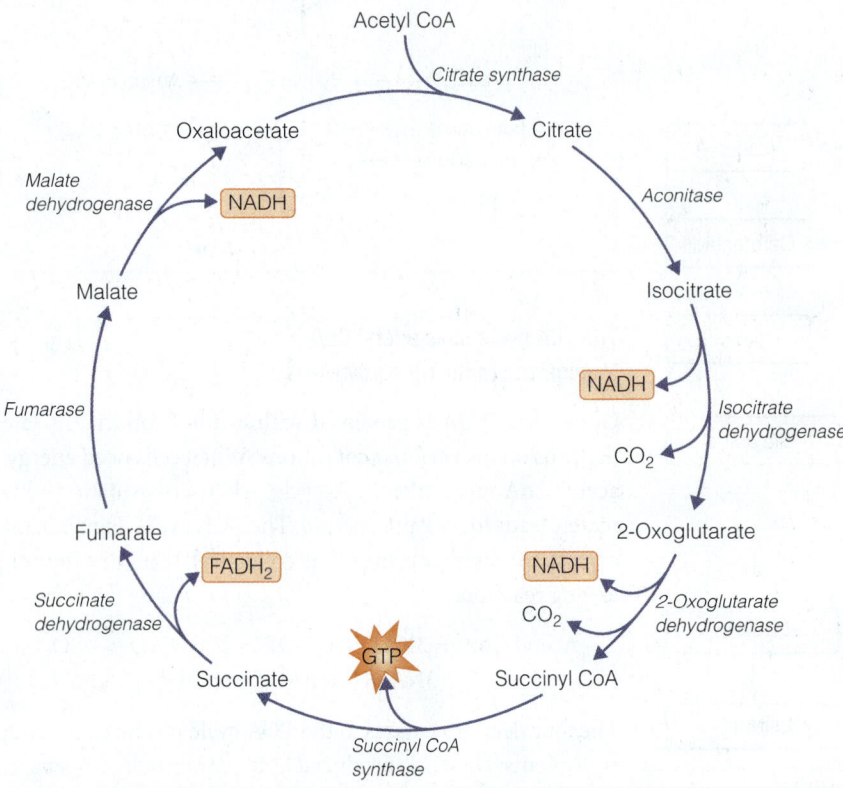

regulate the TCA cycle. Calcium, frequently elevated during periods of high metabolic demand, stimulates isocitrate dehydrogenase and 2-oxoglutarate dehydrogenase, increasing the rate of NADH production to help the cell meet its energy demands.

The ETS generates a proton gradient, heat, and reactive oxygen species

Mitochondria use reducing equivalents as the substrate for **oxidative phosphorylation (OXPHOS)**, a complex pathway that combines oxidation by the **electron transport system (ETS)** with phosphorylation (Figure 3.34). The ETS builds an electrochemical gradient that can be used to drive ATP synthesis and energy-dependent transport processes. Found within the inner mitochondrial membrane, the ETS consists of four multisubunit proteins (complexes I, II, III, and IV) and two electron carriers (ubiquinone, cytochrome *c*).

Although electrons can enter the ETS in several ways, each pathway converges on the first mobile carrier, ubiquinone. The NADH produced in the TCA cycle passes electrons to complex I, which in turn reduces ubiquinone. Several FADH$_2$-linked enzymes found in the inner mitochondrial

membrane pass electrons directly to ubiquinone. For example, the TCA cycle enzyme succinate dehydrogenase is actually complex II of the ETS. An FAD group within its structure becomes reduced during oxidation of succinate, forming FADH$_2$. The enzyme in turn passes the electrons from FADH$_2$ to ubiquinone. Once reduced, ubiquinone transfers its electrons to complex III, which in turn transfers electrons to cytochrome *c*. Complex IV, or **cytochrome** *c* oxidase, accepts electrons from cytochrome *c* and passes them on to molecular oxygen. Complete reduction of oxygen (O$_2$) requires four electrons from cytochrome *c* and consumes four protons to produce two water molecules.

Complexes I, III, and IV are also proton pumps. When these complexes transfer energy to the next carrier, enough free energy remains to pump protons out of the mitochondrial matrix. Fewer protons are pumped in the oxidation of FADH$_2$ because these enzymes pass their electrons directly to ubiquinone, bypassing the proton-pumping complex I. The proton gradient formed by the ETS has both electrical and chemical components: a pH gradient (pH) and a membrane potential ($\Delta\psi$). This **proton motive force**, or δp, is potential energy that can be used to drive other processes, such as ATP synthesis.

The ETS converts much of the energy liberated from NADH oxidation to the proton motive force. Some energy is "lost" in the formation of two by-products: heat and **reactive oxygen species (ROS)**. Conditions that increase electron flow and oxygen consumption also increase heat production. ROS production is an inevitable consequence of electron movement through the ETS. Usually more than 99 percent of the electrons that enter the ETS make the journey all the way to the end of the chain, forming water. However, a few are stolen from the ETS by molecular oxygen to form superoxide (O$_2^-$), a potent ROS that can attack chemical bonds, damaging macromolecules such as lipids, proteins, and DNA. Cells possess vigorous antioxidant defense mechanisms to inactivate superoxide before it can cause damage. The enzyme superoxide dismutase, or SOD, consumes superoxide to produce hydrogen peroxide (H$_2$O$_2$), which is less toxic than superoxide. Other antioxidant enzymes, such as catalase and glutathione peroxidase, consume H$_2$O$_2$, preventing it from causing cellular damage.

FIGURE 3.34 **Oxidative phosphorylation**

Complex I collects electrons from NADH produced by various mitochondrial dehydrogenases. Complex II, or succinate dehydrogenase, transfers electrons from succinate to FAD. Both complex I and II, as well as other FAD-linked dehydrogenases not shown, transfer electrons to ubiquinone (Q). Electron transfer continues through complex III, cytochrome *c*, and finally complex IV, cytochrome oxidase. During electron transport, complexes I, III, and IV also pump protons out of the mitochondrial matrix, creating the proton motive force (Δp). The mitochondrial F_1F_o ATPase (complex V) uses Δp to fuel ATP synthesis.

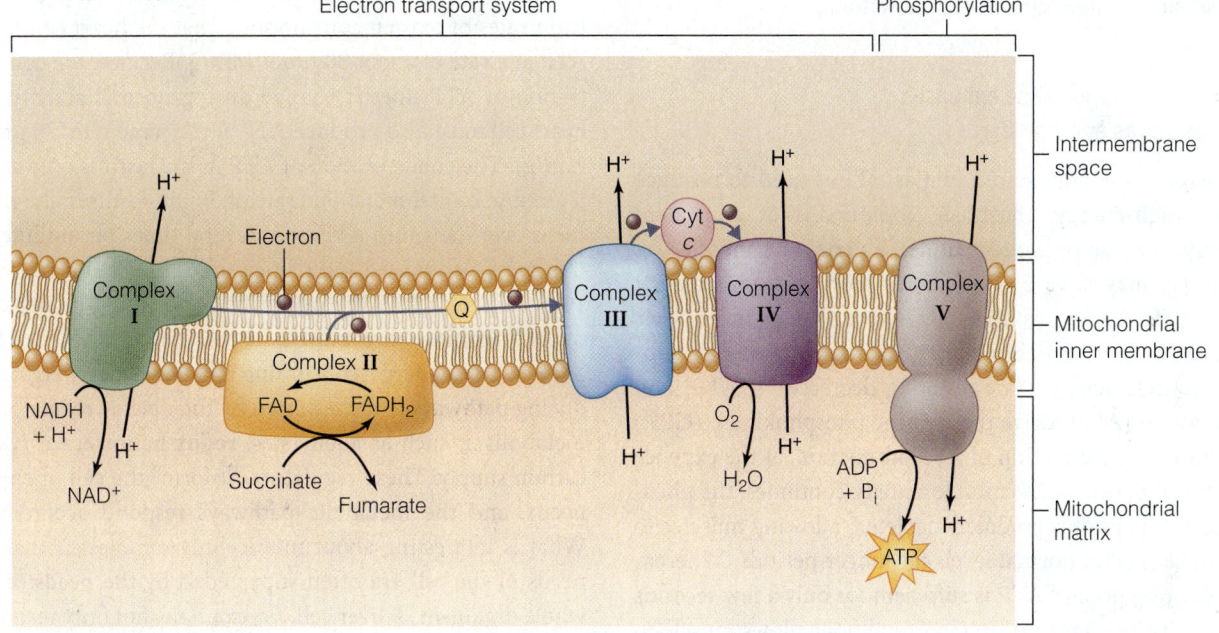

The F_1F_o ATPase uses the proton motive force to generate ATP

To this point we have discussed how mitochondria build *p* but not how it is used to produce ATP. Mitochondria possess an ATP synthase, usually called the F_1F_o ATPase, that uses the energy contained in *p* to drive the phosphorylation of ADP. (Although it normally functions in the direction of ATP synthesis, the F_1F_o ATPase is reversible and able to break down ATP under some conditions.) The F_1F_o ATPase possesses a proton-pumping region and a catalytic region. When protons pass through the enzyme, which spans the mitochondrial inner membrane, the energy is used to catalyze the synthesis of ATP. Oxidative phosphorylation is the combination of oxidation by the ETS and phosphorylation by F_1F_o ATPase. Note that there is no physical linkage between oxidation and phosphorylation; the two processes are functionally coupled through a mutual dependence on *p*.

The rate of ATP synthesis by the F_1F_o ATPase depends on the magnitude of *p* and the availability of the substrates ADP and inorganic phosphate (P_i). When cells are rapidly hydrolyzing ATP, [ADP] and [P_i] increase, accelerating the rate of the F_1F_o ATPase reaction. To understand how this process is regulated, consider what happens in a muscle that goes from rest to exercise. At rest, the rate of ATP breakdown is slow and [ATP] builds up while [ADP] and [P_i] decline. The ETS builds δp to its maximum because the ATPase, the major drain on the gradient, is inhibited. With little flux through the ETS, the rate of respiration is low. This is the biochemical reason why you breathe less when resting. When muscle activity begins, ATP is hydrolyzed and the concentrations of ADP and P_i increase. With the stimulation of the ATP synthase, δp is depleted and ETS accelerates to replenish the gradient. We increase our oxygen consumption during exercise because of this linkage between ATP synthesis and oxidation.

The functional linkage between oxidation and phosphorylation (**coupling**) depends on the integrity of the inner mitochondrial membrane. All membranes are somewhat permeable to protons, but the inner mitochondrial membrane is relatively resistant to proton leak. If the protons pumped out of the mitochondria by the ETS were to leak back into the mitochondria, δp would be dissipated, causing two effects on oxidative phosphorylation. First, the ETS would continue at a high rate, pumping protons and consuming oxygen in a futile effort to rebuild δp. Second, the reduction in δp would prevent the mitochondria from producing ATP. Mitochondria that show high rates of respiration with no ATP production are considered uncoupled.

Whereas this state is disastrous for energy production, it is an important mechanism by which to produce heat. Some mammals have specific proteins that facilitate the movement of protons across the inner membrane. As you will learn in Chapter 15: Thermal Physiology, these **uncoupling proteins** are important in mammals that experience cold stress, such as newborns and hibernators.

Creatine phosphokinase enhances energy stores and transfer

Some of the energy stored first as ATP is used to produce other high-energy phosphate compounds of equivalent energy, such as phosphocreatine. A vertebrate muscle, for example, may have 5 to 10 times more phosphocreatine than ATP, serving as an energy store. When the muscle begins to work at high intensity, ATP is consumed to support muscle activity. The resulting decrease in [ATP] and increase in [ADP] drive the creatine phosphokinase (CPK) reaction in the direction of ATP production, at the expense of phosphocreatine. As muscle activity continues, the phosphocreatine pool is gradually depleted, allowing muscles to preserve ATP at normal levels for longer periods. Whereas the existing pool of ATP is sufficient for only a few seconds of activity, the large phosphocreatine pool allows muscle to maintain ATP levels and sustain contractions for a much longer duration.

In addition to bolstering energy stores, phosphocreatine is a component of the phosphocreatine shuttle, a pathway that improves the efficiency of energy transfer within the cell. The cycle begins with ATP produced by the mitochondria. CPK on the outer mitochondrial membrane uses this ATP to phosphorylate creatine. The phosphocreatine diffuses from the mitochondria to the myofibrils, where another CPK uses the phosphocreatine to regenerate ATP. This CPK shuttle improves the efficiency of energy transfer in two ways. First, creatine and phosphocreatine are smaller molecules than the adenylates and have higher diffusion coefficients. Second, the absolute concentrations of creatine and phosphocreatine are much greater than those of the adenylates, allowing much steeper intracellular gradients to form, which accelerates the rates of diffusion.

CONCEPT CHECK

19. Which molecule is at the convergence of pathways for oxidation of fatty acids, carbohydrate, lactate, and some amino acids?
20. What is the proton motive force?
21. How is oxidation coupled to phosphorylation in mitochondrial oxidative phosphorylation?

Integration of Pathways of Energy Metabolism

The metabolic traits exhibited by whole animals can be traced back to the cellular pathways of energy metabolism. Put simply, in order to remain in energetic balance, cells must produce ATP at rates that match the ATP demand. Consider the situation in a mammalian heart cell. We know from rates of oxygen consumption that the heart consumes ATP at a rate of about 30 μmol/min/g. Because the concentration of ATP doesn't change during normal activity, the heart cell must also produce ATP at the same rate (30 μmol/min/g). The concentration of ATP in the heart is only about 5 μmol/g, so at a metabolic rate of 30 μmol/min/g the heart turns over the entire ATP pool several times per minute. At this **turnover rate**, a cell that produces ATP at a rate only 10 percent less than the rate of demand would be depleted of ATP within two minutes. At the cellular level, the balance between energy-consuming pathways and energy-producing pathways is orchestrated by the diverse regulators of metabolism, such as adenylates, **redox balance**, Ca^{2+}, and carbon supply. These regulators "inform" the cell of energy needs, and the metabolic pathways respond accordingly. What is interesting about multicellular animals is that the needs of the cell are often superceded by the needs of the whole organism. A liver cell, for example, not only responds to its own metabolic needs but also produces energy substrates for the entire animal. When glucose levels are low, the liver increases the rates of gluconeogenesis and glycogenolysis, releasing glucose to the blood for use in other tissues. This altruistic response is imposed on the liver cell by hormones that affect the catalytic properties of the enzymes of intermediary metabolism, largely through covalent modification, such as phosphorylation. We will discuss the nature of hormones in the next chapter, Cell Signaling and Endocrine Regulation.

The sum of the cellular metabolic properties yields the whole-animal metabolic patterns. Variations in animal metabolic rate are central to many problems in animal physiology. In other chapters you will learn how body size affects metabolic rates, and how animals control metabolic rate to survive environmental challenges, such as hypoxia, **hypothermia**, and dehydration. Metabolic strategies in animals address the constant fluctuations in nutrient availability, energy demand, and environmental conditions. Ensuring the correct flow of energy requires exquisite control of the pathways of intermediary metabolism. Opposing pathways must be reciprocally regulated to avoid a **futile cycle**: simultaneous synthesis and degradation of a metabolite. Similarly, the various alternatives must be utilized in a way that takes into consideration the advantages and disadvantages of each class of fuel. These choices are also influenced by long-term and short-term metabolic priorities of the cells and organisms.

Oxygen and ATP control the balance between glycolysis and oxidative phosphorylation

Glycolysis produces 2 mol of ATP for every mol of glucose, but complex oxidation of glucose yields 36 mol of ATP per mol. Despite the differences in energy yield, glycolysis and oxidative phosphorylation both play important roles in energy metabolism. Glycolysis, in addition to being able to operate without oxygen, can produce ATP at much greater rates than can oxidative metabolism. The conditions that allow such high rates also require the pathway to be somewhat inefficient. In contrast, oxidative metabolism is very efficient in conserving chemical energy, but to do so, it is necessarily slow. Think of glycolysis as a high-performance sports car—useful to get somewhere fast but not the best car for gas mileage. Oxidative metabolism, by contrast, is the fuel-efficient compact car. Like some suburban families, the cell maintains both types of engines in working order, to be called upon for different needs.

Physical properties of fuels influence fuel selection

Each of the major metabolic fuels displays physical properties that influence how the fuel is stored and used. Carbohydrate is stored as large granules of glycogen, coated with water molecules that make up its hydration shell. Glycogen particles can be so large that they interfere with cellular processes. Some tissues, such as the mantle of bivalve mollusks, can safely accumulate high levels of glycogen, but if glycogen reached this high level in a muscle it would prevent the muscle from contracting normally. Although glycogen is readily mobilized, its physical properties prevent most cells from storing high levels. In contrast, lipid is stored at much higher levels in the form of anhydrous, amorphous droplets of triglyceride. These physical differences, coupled with the energy content of a given mass of stored fuel, affect fuel selection. Cells can obtain about 10 times more ATP from lipid than from the same mass of hydrated glycogen particles. Given the advantage of lipid as an energy store, you might wonder why animals use glycogen at all. Glycogen can be mobilized much faster than lipid, and plays a vital role under conditions in which energy is required very quickly, as in the "fight-or-flight" response. Most cells use a combination of lipid and carbohydrate fuels to balance the advantages and disadvantages of each fuel.

The main way the cells regulate the balance between fatty acids and carbohydrates is through the mitochondrial enzyme pyruvate dehydrogenase (PDH). This enzyme is regulated allosterically by ATP, acetyl CoA, and NADH. When cells have fatty acids available, their oxidation increases concentrations of ATP, NADH, and acetyl CoA. These metabolites inhibit PDH, sparing pyruvate for gluconeogenesis. When energy stores are depleted, the concentrations of NADH, ATP, and acetyl CoA tend to decrease, which lessens the inhibition of PDH. These same metabolites also influence the phosphorylation state of PDH by regulating the activities of PDH kinase (PDHK) and PDH phosphatase (PDHP). ATP, NADH, and acetyl CoA each activate PDHK, causing PDH to be converted to its inactive, phosphorylated form. The activity of PDHP, in contrast, is governed primarily by Ca^{2+}. High $[Ca^{2+}]$ stimulates PDHP, converting PDH to its active dephosphorylated form.

Fuel selection can be calculated from the respiratory quotient

Each pathway for oxidation of fuels demonstrates characteristic relationships between the amount of (1) ATP produced, (2) oxygen consumed, and (3) CO_2 generated. The reason these parameters differ among fuels can be traced back to the pathways of degradation. Ratios of different combinations of these three parameters provide important information about fuel selection. The differences in the ratio of ATP produced to oxygen consumed (the ATP/O ratio) can be traced to the reliance on FAD-linked enzymes. Each time an NADH molecule is produced in the mitochondria, oxidative phosphorylation can produce 3 molecules of ATP and consume 1 atom of oxygen (ATP/O = 3). When a molecule of $FADH_2$ is produced, only 2 molecules of ATP can be generated while consuming the same 1 atom of oxygen (ATP/O = 2). Carbohydrate oxidation uses predominantly NADH-linked enzymes, whereas lipid oxidation relies more heavily on FAD-linked enzymes. Because of this difference, carbohydrate yields more ATP for a given volume of oxygen. This difference has an effect on the fuel preference of at least some animals that live at low oxygen levels. For example, the heart of most humans uses lipid as a major fuel. In contrast, humans that have adapted to high altitude, such as the natives of the high Andes, rely more heavily on glucose oxidation. Of course, in more extreme hypoxia and anoxia, animals have little choice but to rely on glycolysis.

Differences in the ratio of CO_2 produced to O_2 consumed, known as the **respiratory quotient (RQ)**, arise from the pathways of oxidation. Glucose has six carbons, and oxidizing it completely to 6 CO_2 yields 2 NADH in the cytoplasm, 2 NADH via PDH, 6 NADH via the TCA cycle, and 2 $FADH_2$ via succinate dehydrogenase. The 12 reducing equivalents consume 12 atoms of oxygen, or 6 molecules of O_2. Thus, carbohydrate oxidation yields an RQ of 1 (6 mol of CO_2 to 6 mol of O_2). In contrast, oxidation of fatty acids generates an RQ of about 0.7, although the exact number depends on the specific fatty acid. Consider the pathway of palmitate oxidation. As a 16-carbon fatty acid, it generates 16 mol of CO_2 per mol of palmitate. Seven cycles of β-oxidation are required to break palmitate into 8 molecules of acetyl CoA, yielding 7 $FADH_2$ and 7 NADH. Oxidation of the 8 acetyl CoA in the TCA cycle yields 24 NADH and 8 $FADH_2$. Oxidation of the 46 reducing equivalents consumes 23 mol of O_2, giving an RQ of 0.7 (16 mol of CO_2 to 23 mol of O_2). Because of these characteristic relationships between RQ and fuel oxidation, measurement of CO_2 production and O_2 consumption of whole animals can provide important insight into the pathways that are being used to support energy metabolism.

Energetic intermediates regulate the balance between anabolism and catabolism

A cell activates pathways of energy production when it needs energy, but when energy is abundant it stimulates **anabolic pathways**, storing nutrients or producing building blocks for cell growth or cell division. How do cells actually sense the need for energy and regulate the transition between catabolism and anabolism? Many of the pathways we have discussed are sensitive to the cellular indices of energetic status, primarily acetyl CoA, adenylates, and NADH. Changes in the concentration of these products reflect energy status and cause compensatory changes in metabolic pathways. When cells are "energy rich," the concentrations of acetyl CoA, NADH, and ATP are relatively high and the concentrations of CoA, NAD^+, ADP, and AMP are low. Consider how these metabolites stimulate gluconeogenesis while inhibiting glycolysis (Figure 3.35). By matching the rates of ATP synthesis with rates of ATP utilization, cells are able to defend ATP concentrations within a narrow range.

Animals also use other metabolites to reciprocally regulate opposing pathways. When metabolic conditions induce cells to commit to fatty acid synthesis, the increases in the levels of malonyl CoA block fatty acid oxidation by inhibiting CPT-1. Cells further separate anabolism and catabolism using tissue specializations. The liver has the enzymes for ketogenesis but cannot break down ketone bodies. Muscles have the enzymes for ketolysis but cannot synthesize ketone bodies. In fact, the control of energy metabolism in complex animals reflects a division of labor such that some tissues become servile to others. Liver and adipose tissue perform important functions for whole-animal metabolic balance, giving lower priority to their own cellular and metabolic needs.

Metabolic rate is the sum of all chemical reactions

In a living cell, tissue, or organism, the combination of anabolic and catabolic processes can be expressed as the metabolic rate. The concept of metabolic rate is straightforward, but its calculation is a bit more problematic, and differs depending on the ultimate reason for estimating it. From an

FIGURE 3.35 **Reciprocal regulation of glucose metabolism**

High-energy compounds, such as ATP, acetyl CoA, and NADH, inhibit glycolysis and stimulate gluconeogenesis at key regulatory enzymes.

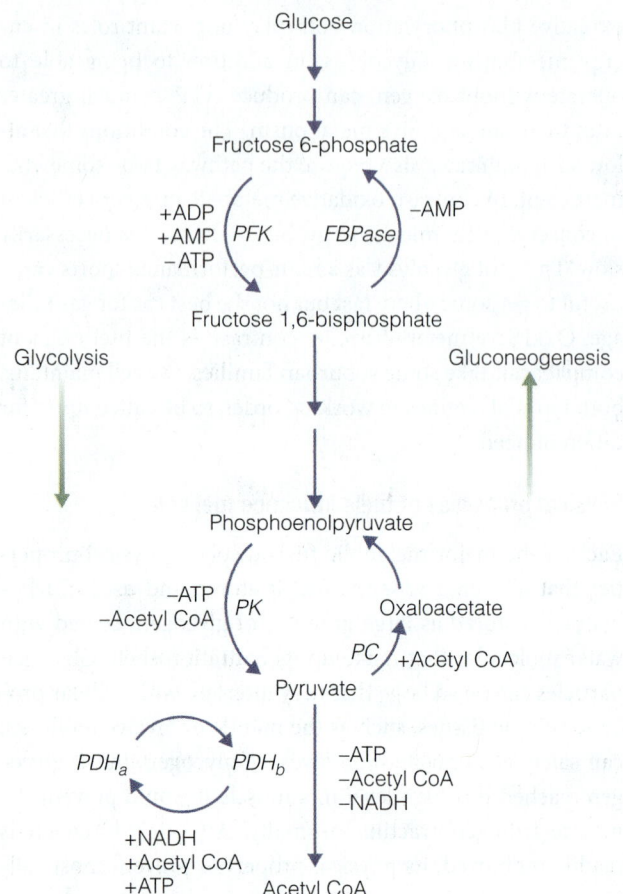

energy budget perspective, metabolic rate is best expressed as a change in energy content, essentially the heat released from the system, measured in joules. The metabolic rate of a biological system is measured via direct **calorimetry**, using instruments that measure heat production. The metabolic rate can also be estimated by measuring oxygen consumption, with the assumption that the moles of oxygen consumed faithfully reflect the amount of heat produced. A conversion factor, or oxycaloric coefficient, translates oxygen consumption into joules (Table 3.2).

Fuels differ in the specific pathways for degradation, the nature of the end products, and the relative importance of NADH vs FADH-linked reactions. As a result, energetic parameters such as energy content and oxycaloric coefficients, as with RQ values, depend on which specific fuels are in use.

Many aspects of animal physiology incorporate energetic perspectives, and many evolutionary strategies and physiological responses to environmental challenges involve some form of regulation of metabolism and metabolic rate (see Chapter 14: Digestion and Energy Metabolism).

Table 3.2 Energy content, oxycaloric coefficients, and respiratory quotients in relation to metabolic fuel

Fuel	Energy Content (Joules/mg)	Oxycaloric Coefficient (Joules/mmol O_2)	Respiratory Quotient
Carbohydrate	18	482	1.00
Protein	19	444	0.83–1.00
Lipid	38	448	0.72

Source: Data from Gnaiger, E. (1983). Calculation of energetic and biochemical equivalents of respiratory oxygen consumption. In E. Gnaiger & H. Forstner (Eds.), *Polarographic oxygen sensors.* Berlin: Springer.

CONCEPT CHECK

22. How does glucose catabolism differ under (a) high versus low energy conditions and (b) normal versus low oxygen conditions.
23. Under what conditions is it more advantageous to use carbohydrate rather than lipid as a metabolic fuel?
24. What is a respiratory quotient?

■ CELL PHYSIOLOGY

In the opening essay, we discussed how the evolutionary origins of animals required a new relationship between cells to foster multicellular relationships. Cellular membranes[1] perform two main roles that are central to multicellularity and cellular function. First, they allow cells to isolate themselves from the environment, giving them control over intracellular conditions. Second, membranes help cells organize intracellular pathways into discrete subcellular compartments, including organelles. Separation of processes also requires specific mechanisms to transfer molecules across the membranes. Many complex physiological properties and responses depend on cellular transport and transfers between subcellular compartments. Ultimately, the cellular properties that determine physiological function are controlled through regulation of gene expression.

Membrane Structure and Transport

Cellular membranes are composed of phospholipids, other lipids, and diverse proteins. The membrane is a lipid bilayer, each of which is a sheet of lipid molecules arranged side by side. The surfaces of the lipid bilayer are composed of the polar head groups of phospholipids, and the internal hydrophobic core is composed of long fatty acid chains of the phospholipids attached through van der Waals forces.

[1]Cellular membranes refer to all of the membranes within a cell, including the plasma membrane (or cell membrane) that surrounds the cell and the membranes that form the organelles.

The lipid profile affects membrane properties

Animals produce specialized membranes with unique molecular signatures by varying the structures and proportions of the different types of lipid. Much of the variation can be attributed to the profile of **phosphoglycerides**, the most abundant of which are phosphatidylcholine (PC), phosphatidylserine (PS), and phosphatidylethanolamine (PE). Recall from earlier in this chapter that each of these phospholipids is really a class of molecules with constituent fatty acids that differ in chain length and saturation. Although phosphoglycerides are the most abundant molecules in the bilayer, membranes also possess other lipids, including sphingolipids, glycolipids, and cholesterol, as well as many proteins. Glycolipids resemble phospholipids, but with complex carbohydrate modifications that impart a negative charge to the polar head group. Nerve cells possess high concentrations of sphingolipids and glycolipids because they alter the electrical properties of the membrane. Glycolipids are also important in communication between cells.

Cholesterol has an unusual role in membranes. Although it is absent from some membranes, such as mitochondrial membranes, cholesterol can compose almost half the lipid component of other membranes. Cholesterol influences membrane properties in complex ways because of the way it integrates into the **lipid bilayer** (Figure 3.36). One end of the molecule interacts with phospholipids near the polar head groups, filling gaps between phospholipids to reduce the **permeability** to low-molecular-weight solutes. Cholesterol also disrupts the interactions between fatty acids, enhancing membrane **fluidity**. The unusual ability of cholesterol to increase fluidity while decreasing permeability provides animals with an important mechanism for controlling membrane properties.

Lipid membranes are heterogeneous

While the **fluid mosaic model** illustrates the general relationships between lipid and protein variation in membrane proteins, it underemphasizes the spatial variation seen in membrane lipids (Figure 3.37). The inner and outer layers of the phospholipid bilayer typically possess different types of lipids. PE and PS are found almost exclusively in the inner

FIGURE 3.36 **Unusual membrane properties of cholesterol**

Cholesterol strengthens the interactions between phospholipid polar head groups while disrupting the interactions between fatty acid tails.

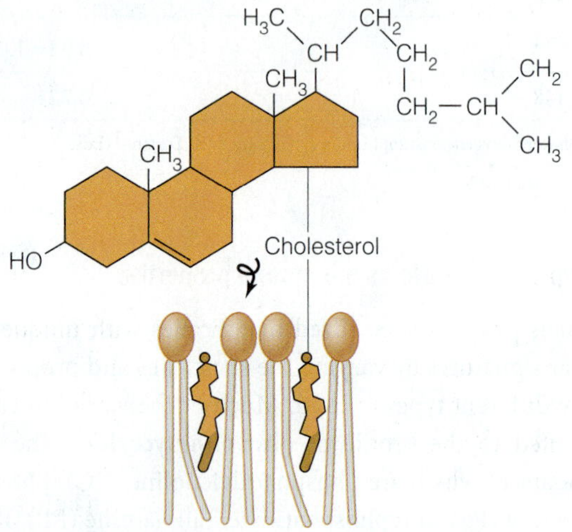

H₃C, CH₂, CH, CH₃, CH₂, CH₂, CH₂—CH, CH₂, CH₃

HO — Cholesterol

leaflet, whereas PC is concentrated in the outer leaflet. Glycolipids are found only in the outer leaflet of the membrane. Membranes also possess discrete regions that are enriched in cholesterol and glycolipids. These **lipid rafts** serve two important functions. Their molecular composition causes a slight thickening of the lipid bilayer, which recruits phospholipids with longer chain fatty acids and proteins with relatively long transmembrane domains. Because of the distinct molecular composition of lipid rafts, they can act as microcompartments within the cell, providing an additional way to spatially organize pathways.

FIGURE 3.37 **Membrane heterogeneity**

Cellular membranes are heterogeneous in composition. Most cells maintain distinct profiles in inner and outer monolayers, sometimes exchanging phospholipids between layers. Lipid rafts are regions of the plasma membrane that accumulate cholesterol and glycolipids, thickening the membrane. These thicker regions preferentially recruit proteins with longer transmembrane domains.

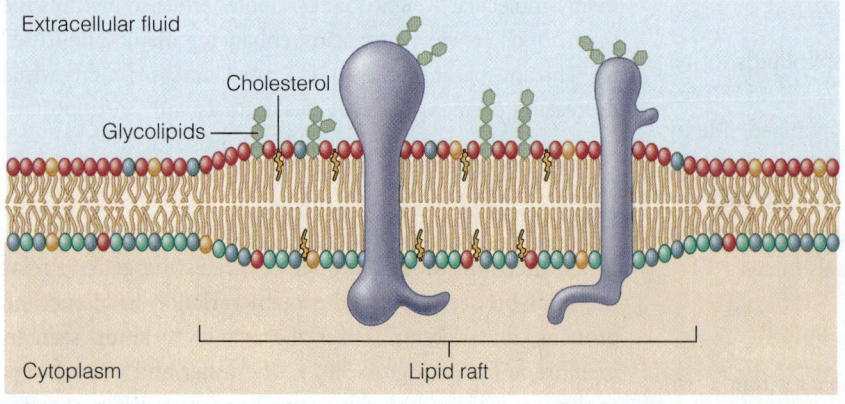

Extracellular fluid

Cholesterol

Glycolipids

Cytoplasm — Lipid raft

Environmental stress can alter membrane fluidity

An essential component of the fluid mosaic model is the ability of the constituents to move throughout the membrane. Phospholipids and proteins can rotate in position as well as move laterally through the membrane. Membrane fluidity depends on the properties of the membrane lipids, which are influenced by the physical environment. Cells regulate the fluidity of the membrane by controlling the nature of lipids to achieve the appropriate degree of molecular movement. Low temperature, for example, can strengthen the van der Waals forces between membrane lipids, restricting molecular movement within the membrane (Figure 3.38). Because this can adversely affect membrane function, many animals actively remodel their membranes to compensate for the effects of the physical environment. By altering the membrane lipid profile, they can keep membrane fluidity constant. We will discuss this pattern of membrane regulation, called **homeoviscous adaptation**, in Chapter 15: Thermal Physiology.

Membranes possess integral and peripheral proteins

Protein is an important constituent of most cellular membranes, in some cases making up more than half the mass of the membrane. **Integral membrane proteins** are tightly bound to the membrane, either embedded in the bilayer or spanning the entire membrane. **Peripheral membrane proteins** have a weaker association with the lipid bilayer, typically binding to integral membrane proteins or glycolipids. The different relationships between the bilayer and membrane proteins are shown in Figure 3.39.

Membrane proteins have important structural and regulatory roles within cells. They contribute to structural support by linking the intracellular cytoskeleton to the extracellular matrix. Many of the intrinsic membrane proteins are receptors that are part of complex signaling pathways. Because membranes are physical barriers to the free movement of many vital organic and inorganic solutes, cells use integral proteins to transport molecules across membranes.

Many molecules must move across cellular membranes

Many cellular processes depend on the ability to transport molecules across membranes. The three main classes of membrane transport are passive diffusion, facilitated diffusion, and active transport. These classes of transport are distinguished by the direction of transport, the nature of the carriers, and the role of energy in the process (Figure 3.40).

FIGURE 3.38 **Temperature and membrane fluidity**

Temperature alters the fluidity of membranes by changing the interactions between phospholipids.

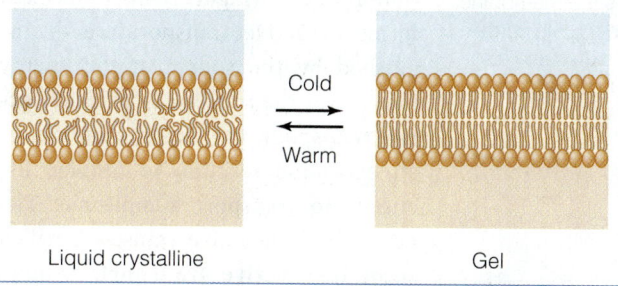

Liquid crystalline   Gel

FIGURE 3.39 **Integral membrane proteins**

Membrane proteins can demonstrate many different types of relationships with membranes. Each membrane protein has within its structure hydrophobic regions that interact favorably with the bilayer. Depending on the protein, these regions can be α-helices or β-barrels. Transmembrane proteins span the entire bilayer, exposing regions to both sides of the membrane. Often these exposed regions possess modifications, such as the carbohydrate chains of glycoproteins. Peripheral membrane proteins are not embedded within the membrane but associate with exposed regions of integral membrane proteins.

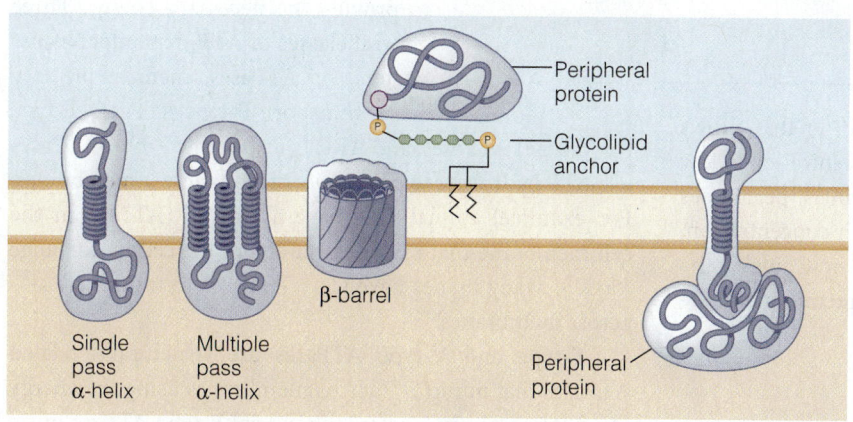

Single pass α-helix

Multiple pass α-helix

β-barrel

Peripheral protein

Glycolipid anchor

Peripheral protein

Some hydrophobic molecules can freely cross biological membranes by **passive diffusion**. Many molecules, such as steroid hormones, are freely soluble in lipid. When these molecules encounter a cell membrane, they dissolve into the lipid bilayer and escape to the other side. Both influx and **efflux** occur simultaneously, but the net movement (influx minus efflux) depends on the concentration gradient. The net movement of molecules is from high concentration to low concentration. The steeper the concentration gradient, the greater the rate of movement across the membrane. No specific transporters are required, and no energy, beyond the concentration gradient itself, is required.

Membrane proteins can facilitate the diffusion of impermeant molecules

Hydrophilic molecules cross membranes by other pathways that involve specific transport proteins. If the concentration gradient is favorable, the molecule may cross the membrane by **facilitated diffusion**. As with passive diffusion, no energy beyond that of the concentration gradient is required to drive transport, but with facilitated diffusion a protein is required to carry the molecule across the membrane. Three main types of proteins carry out facilitated diffusion: ion channels, porins, and permeases (see Figure 3.41).

Ion channels are membrane proteins that form pores through which only specific ions may pass, and only when the channel is open. The channels are specific to one or sometimes two ions. Calcium ion (Ca^{2+}) channels, for instance, possess a structure that allows the free movement of Ca^{2+}, but does not allow other cations such as Mg^{2+}, K^+, or Na^+ to cross at appreciable rates. The specificity of transport is due to a structural component of the channel known as the **selectivity filter**. The channel can be opened in response to cellular conditions. **Ligand-gated channels** are opened when specific regulatory molecules bind. One important ligand-gated channel is the Ca^{2+} channel sensitive to inositol triphosphate (IP_3); this channel induces the release of Ca^{2+} stores when its ligand, IP_3, is present. **Voltage-gated channels** are opened or closed in response to membrane potential. For example, K^+ channels in muscle and neurons open when the membrane depolarizes. **Mechanogated channels** are regulated through interactions with the subcellular proteins that make up the cytoskeleton. Changes in cell shape, such as cell swelling, alter the arrangement of the cytoskeleton. Upon sensing the changes in the cytoskeleton, mechanogated channels may open or close.

Porins are large channels that function in ways similar to ion channels but permit the passage of much larger molecules. Mitochondria have a porin in the outer membrane that facilitates the transfer of low-molecular-weight molecules from the cytoplasm to the mitochondria. **Aquaporins** are water channels in the plasma membranes; each aquaporin molecule can transport 3 billion water molecules per second. Some aquaporins, called *aquaglyceroporins*, are also capable of transporting nonwater molecules, such as glycerol and possibly urea. Aquaporins may also be involved in transport of gases across membranes.

The third type of protein that facilitates diffusion is a **permease**. Rather than creating a pore for a molecule, a permease functions more like an enzyme. It binds the substrate and then undergoes a conformation change that causes the carrier to release the substrate to the other side. Several

FIGURE 3.40   **Modes of membrane transport**

The mechanisms of transport across cellular membranes depend on the lipid solubility of the solute as well as the direction and magnitude of the concentration gradient. Passive diffusion needs no carrier, as lipid-soluble solutes move freely across the membrane. Facilitated diffusion carries impermeant solutes across the membrane on protein carriers, including channels (either ion channels or porins) and permeases. Solutes can also be transported by active transport, which can move molecules against a concentration gradient.

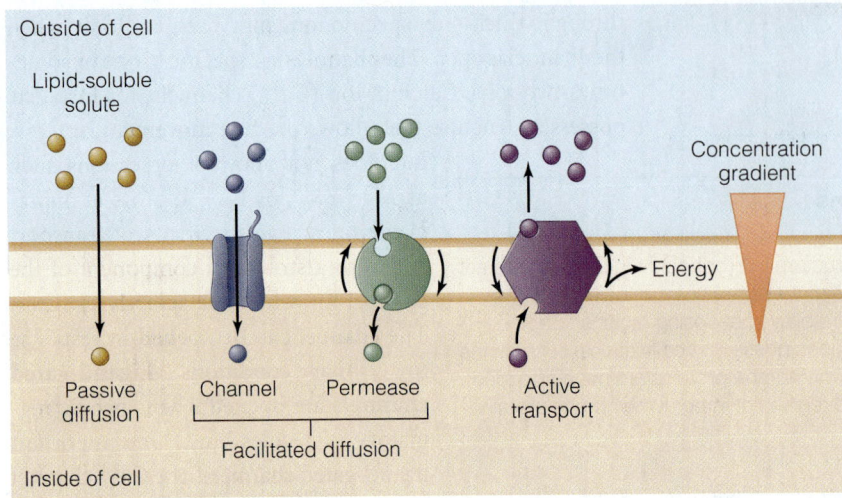

Passive diffusion — Channel — Permease — Active transport
Facilitated diffusion
Outside of cell / Inside of cell
Lipid-soluble solute
Concentration gradient
Energy

tissues possess glucose permease, a transporter that allows glucose to enter cells, passing from high concentration to low concentration. Unlike porins and ion channels, permeases can become saturated with substrate at high concentration, such that the transport process depends on how quickly the permease can carry its substrate across the membrane.

Active transporters use energy to pump molecules against gradients

In passive and facilitated diffusion, uncharged molecules can move only from areas of high concentration to areas of low concentration. In contrast, cells use **active transport** to move molecules across membranes against concentration gradients (Figure 3.42). Two main forms of active transport are distinguished by the source of the energy that drives the process. In **primary active transport**, the carrier protein uses an exergonic reaction to provide the energy to transport a molecule. The other form of active transport, called **secondary active transport**, couples the movement of one molecule to the movement of a second molecule. The kinetic properties of a transporter are similar to those of enzymes, with an affinity constant (K_m) and a maximal rate, which for the transporter is (J_{max}).

The most common primary active transporters use the hydrolysis of ATP to provide the necessary energy. Three general classes of ATP-dependent transporters, or ATPases, mediate primary active transport: P-type ATPases, F-type (or V-type) ATPases, and ABC transporters. P-type ATPases use ATP hydrolysis to pump specific ions across membranes. For example, animal cells have a Na^+/K^+ ATPase in the cell membrane that extrudes Na^+ from the cell in exchange for K^+. Many tissues have Ca^{2+} ATPases to transport Ca^{2+} across membranes.

F-type and V-type ATPases are structurally related ATPases that pump H^+ across membranes using the energy of ATP hydrolysis. The mitochondrial F-type ATPase operates in reverse, using H^+ movements down electrochemical gradients to provide the energy for ATP synthesis. The

FIGURE 3.41   **Ion channels**

Channels are proteins that mediate facilitated diffusion of ions and other metabolites. Channels typically exist in either a closed or an open conformation. They are opened by specific triggers, including specific ligands, voltage conditions, or physical associations with structural elements.

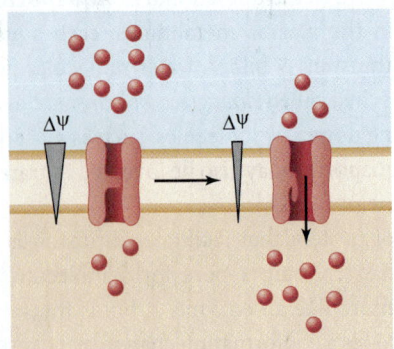

(a) Voltage-gated

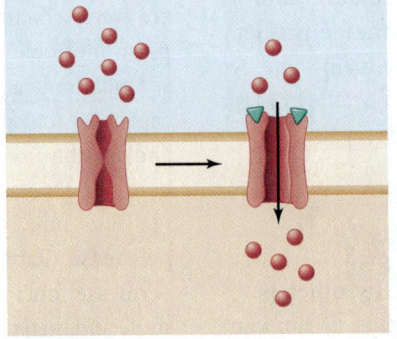
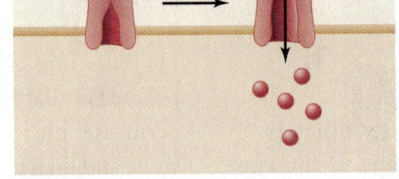

(b) Ligand-gated

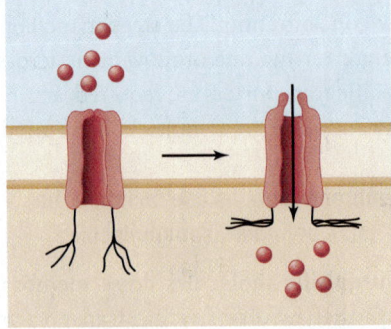

(c) Mechanogated

FIGURE 3.42 Active transport

Active transporters use energy to transport ions and metabolites against concentration gradients. Primary active transporters use the energy of ATP hydrolysis. Secondary active transporters use the energy associated with the electrochemical gradient of one molecule to drive the transport of another.

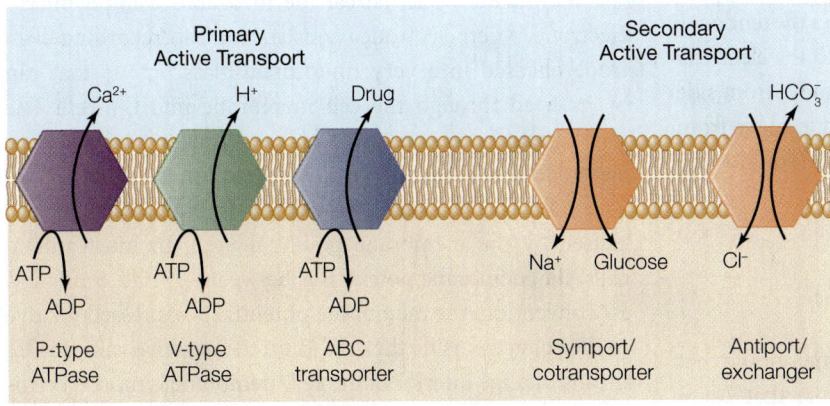

V-type ATPases allow cells and organelles to extrude protons to acidify a compartment, such as the lumen of the lysosome or the inside of the stomach.

The ABC transporters carry large organic molecules across the cell membrane. Cells often use ABC transporters to export toxins from the cell. The multidrug resistance protein, an important ABC transporter, is often linked to types of cancers that become resistant to chemotherapy. Some cancerous cells survive chemotherapy by transporting the toxic drug out of the cell before the chemotherapeutic agent can kill it.

Secondary active transport uses the energy held in the electrochemical gradient of one molecule to provide the energy to drive another molecule against its gradient. If the molecules move in opposite directions, the carrier is called an **antiport**, or **exchanger**. For example, red blood cells use a Cl^-/HCO_3^- exchanger (also called *band 3*) to drive the transport of these ions across the membrane. The direction of ion movement by this carrier depends on the relative gradients of the two ions. Alternatively, a **symport**, or **cotransporter**, is used to move molecules in the same direction. For example, intestinal cells use a Na^+-glucose cotransporter to import glucose against its concentration gradient, driven by a greater inward Na^+ electrochemical gradient.

All of these transport processes influence chemical gradients across membranes, but only a subset of transporters affect the electrical gradient. Carriers that transport uncharged molecules, such as the glucose permease, are termed **electroneutral** carriers. Similarly, carriers such as the Cl^-/HCO_3^- exchanger that exchange two ions of the same charge are also electroneutral. In contrast, the carriers that transfer a charge across the membrane are called **electrogenic** carriers. When we discuss Na^+/K^+ ATPase throughout this text, keep in mind that it is an electrogenic carrier because it exchanges 3 Na^+ for 2 K^+ ions.

The movement of charged molecules depends on the electrochemical gradient

For uncharged molecules, we only need to consider the concentration gradient to determine whether movement across a membrane is via diffusion or active transport. For charged molecules, however, the situation is more complex. Movement of charged molecules is influenced by the electrochemical gradient, which involves both a concentration gradient and an electrical gradient. For example, imagine a charged molecule X^+ that is found on two sides of a semipermeable membrane. X^+ is at higher concentration on side A of the membrane than on side B. Thus, the concentration gradient will tend to cause X^+ to move down its concentration gradient from side A to side B via diffusion (assuming that the membrane is permeable to X^+ because of the presence of open ion channels). However, if there is a charge difference between side A and side B of the membrane, then the movement of X^+ becomes more difficult to predict.

Imagine that side B of the membrane is positively charged compared with side A. Like charges repel, so the positive charges on side B will repel X^+, opposing its movement down its concentration gradient. In essence, the electrical gradient opposes the concentration gradient and could potentially prevent X^+ from moving down its concentration gradient, or might even cause it to move against its concentration gradient. Whether X^+ moves from side A to side B, or in the other direction, depends on the relative strengths of the concentration gradient and the electrical gradient. By comparing these two gradients, it is possible to predict the direction in which a charged molecule will move passively by diffusion.

The relative strengths of the chemical and electrical gradients are reflected in a quantity called the **electrochemical potential difference ($\Delta\mu$)**, which can be represented mathematically as follows:

$$\Delta\mu = RT \ln\frac{[X^+]_O}{[X^+]_I} + zF(E_O - E_I)$$

Where:

R = the ideal gas constant (8.315 joules/K.mol)

T = temperature in Kelvin

$[X^+]_O$ = the concentration of ion X^+ on side O of the membrane

$[X^+]_I$ = the concentration of ion X^+ on side I of the membrane

z = the valence of the ion

F = Faraday's constant (96,485 joules/Volt.mol)

$(E_O - E_I)$ = the electrical potential difference across the membrane

The first part of this equation describes the tendency of ion X^+ to move across the membrane due to the concentration gradient, and the second part of the equation describes the tendency of ion X^+ to move across the membrane due to the electrical gradient. If $\Delta\mu$ is positive, then X^+ will tend to move from side A to side B. If $\Delta\mu$ is negative, then X^+ will tend to move from side B to side A; and if $\Delta\mu$ is zero, then the ion is in equilibrium and will not tend to move toward either side.

The Nernst equation allows calculation of the equilibrium potential

The electrical potential difference across the membrane that exactly balances the concentration gradient so that $\Delta\mu$ is zero is termed the **equilibrium potential** for that ion (E_{ion}). For a given concentration gradient, it is possible to calculate the equilibrium potential for an ion using the Nernst equation:

$$E_{ion} = \frac{RT}{zF} \ln \frac{[X]_{outside}}{[X]_{inside}}$$

where R is the gas constant, T is the temperature (Kelvin), z is the valence of the ion, F is the Faraday constant, and $[X]$ is the molar concentration of the ion. Note that the Nernst equation is simply the equation for the electrochemical potential solved for the point at which $\Delta\mu = 0$. We can use the Nernst equation to determine the membrane potential required to oppose a given concentration gradient. For example, if $[X^+]_{outside} = 10\,mM$ and $[X^+]_{inside} = 100\,mM$, $E_X = -60\,mV$. In other words, the force driving the outward movement of X^+ resulting from its tenfold concentration gradient can be exactly balanced by a 60 mV excess of negative charge inside the membrane. At this electrical gradient, there would be no net movement of X^+ across the membrane.

Cells maintain a resting membrane potential

All animal cells maintain a voltage difference across their cell membranes, and voltage differences also occur across some organelle membranes, such as the mitochondrial membrane. These voltage differences represent a source of potential energy that cells can harness to move molecules across membranes. The voltage difference is termed the *resting membrane potential difference*, or the **membrane potential**, for short. In addition to using the membrane potential as a source of energy, **excitable cells** use changes in membrane potential as communication signals. As we discuss in Chapters 5 and 6, this property is particularly important for nerve and muscle

cells, and thus the membrane potential is critical for allowing the coordinated movements of cells and organisms. Electrical signaling is not, however, a unique property of nerve and muscle cells. Several other types of cells use electrical signals, including fertilized eggs and hormone-secreting cells.

Membrane potential can be measured using a microelectrode. Microelectrodes consist of a thin recording electrode encased in a very fine-tipped glass pipette that can be inserted through the cell membrane into the cell. The microelectrode is connected via a voltmeter to a reference electrode that is immersed in the solution outside the cell. The voltmeter measures the voltage drop across the circuit caused by the membrane potential (V_m). In most animal cells, the membrane potential is between -5 and -100 mV. By convention, the membrane potential is expressed relative to the voltage outside the cell. Thus, the negative value for V_m means that the interior of the cell membrane is more electronegative than the exterior of the cell membrane.

The Na$^+$/K$^+$ ATPase establishes concentration gradients

Active pumping of Na$^+$ and K$^+$ ions by the electrogenic Na$^+$/K$^+$ATPase is responsible for establishing the concentration gradients for these ions across the cell membrane. Ultimately it is these concentration gradients (along with the selective permeability of the membrane) that establish the membrane potential. The Na$^+$/K$^+$ATPase is also responsible for maintaining the resting membrane potential. Although most membranes are only sparingly permeable to Na$^+$ at rest, a small amount of Na$^+$ does leak into the cell down its electrochemical gradient, while K$^+$ leaks out. Without appropriate compensation, these ion movements would result in the dissipation of the Na$^+$ and K$^+$ concentration gradients that are needed to establish the membrane potential. Cells use the Na$^+$/K$^+$ ATPase to compensate for the leakage of Na$^+$ and K$^+$ ions. If you poison the Na$^+$/K$^+$ ATPase with a drug called ouabain, the membrane potential difference of the cell slowly decays over the course of a few hours, eventually reaching a value close to 0 mV.

The membrane potential represents a balance between equilibrium potentials

If the membrane potential differs from the equilibrium potential for an ion, that ion will tend to move across the cell membrane (assuming that the membrane is permeable to that ion). These ion movements will continue until the membrane potential reaches the equilibrium potential for the ion. Thus, a permeant ion will tend to drive the membrane potential toward its own equilibrium potential, if no other forces are acting. If the membrane is permeable to only a single ion, then the membrane potential will quickly reach the equilibrium potential for that ion. However, real cell membranes are permeable to more than one ion. In fact, most cell membranes have appreciable permeability to K^+, Na^+, and Cl^-, so these are the main ions that influence the membrane potential. The more permeable the membrane is to a particular ion, the more that ion will force the membrane potential toward its own equilibrium potential.

For example, in a typical neuron, the equilibrium potential for Na^+ is around +55 mV and the equilibrium potential for K^+ is around −90 mV (as calculated using the Nernst equation), but the membrane potential is −70 mV. The membrane potential is much closer to the equilibrium potential for K^+ because at rest the neuronal cell membrane is much more permeable to K^+ than to Na^+. However, the membrane potential does not entirely reach the equilibrium potential for K^+ because of the influence of Na^+. Membranes are also quite permeable to Cl^-, and the equilibrium potential of Cl^- in a typical neuron is around −70 mV, very close to the measured resting membrane potential. However, there are no active transporters maintaining a concentration gradient for Cl^- ions. The Cl^- ions passively distribute themselves across the membrane in response to the membrane potential established by the Na^+ and K^+ ions.

The Goldman equation can be used to calculate membrane potential

The Nernst equation calculates the relationship between membrane potential and the concentration gradients of individual ions. The membrane potential, however, is a weighted average of the equilibrium potentials of the permeant ions, using a weighting factor that takes into account the relative permeabilities of these ions. The Goldman-Hodgkin-Katz Constant Field equation (usually referred to as the **Goldman equation**) can be used to calculate this weighted average. Its estimation of the membrane potential is based on the concentrations, valences, and relative permeabilities of a series of ions. Because most plasma membranes under resting conditions have appreciable permeability only to potassium, sodium, and chloride, the Goldman equation can be written as follows:

$$E_m = \frac{RT}{F} \ln \frac{P_K[K^+]_o + P_{Na}[Na^+]_o + P_{Cl}[Cl^-]_i}{P_K[K^+]_i + P_{Na}[Na^+]_i + P_{Cl}[Cl^-]_o}$$

where P_{ion} is the permeability of the membrane to that ion and $[ion]_o$ and $[ion]_i$ represent the extracellular and intracellular concentrations, respectively, of a given ion. Note that the inside and outside concentrations for the Cl^- ion are reversed. This is due to the fact that chloride has a negative valence, while K^+ and Na^+ have positive valence. Thus, an electrical force that would tend to move K^+ out of the cell would tend to move Cl^- into the cell.

From the Goldman equation, the impact of ion permeability on the membrane potential is clear. Any ion with a low permeability has little effect on the membrane potential, even if there is a large concentration gradient across the membrane for that ion.

Consider the situation when the permeability of the membrane for an ion is zero. In this case, the term for that ion drops out of the equation. For example, if the membrane is permeable only to K^+, the Goldman equation simplifies to

$$E_m = \frac{RT}{F} \ln \frac{P_K[K^+]_o}{P_K[K^+]_i}$$

The two terms for K^+ permeability also cancel out, leaving an equation that is equivalent to the Nernst equation for potassium (with the exception of the valence term, z, which is neglected because potassium has a valence of +1). When the membrane is permeable only to a single ion, the membrane potential will be equal to the equilibrium potential for that ion.

In addition to providing an estimate of the resting membrane potential, the Goldman equation allows the estimation of the membrane potential during electrical signaling. For example, when a large number of Na^+ channels open within the membrane (as is the case during signaling in nerve cells), the permeability of the membrane to Na^+ increases greatly. In the case of neural signaling, this increase in Na^+ permeability is so large that P_{Na} becomes much greater than P_K and P_{Cl}. Under these conditions, the Goldman equation is dominated by the term for Na^+, and the membrane potential approaches the equilibrium potential for Na^+ as calculated by the Nernst equation.

Changes in membrane permeability alter membrane potential

Because ion permeability is a major factor involved in establishing the resting membrane potential, changes in ion permeability cause changes in membrane potential (Figure 3.43). Excitable cells such as neurons and muscle cells alter the permeability of their membranes to generate changes in membrane potentials. We can use the Nernst equation to predict the nature of the ion movements following changes in membrane permeabilities. For example, in mammalian neurons the concentration of Na^+ is typically about tenfold greater outside the cell, so E_{Na} = +58 mV. In contrast, K^+ concentration outside the cell is only about 1/40 of that inside the cell, so E_K = −90 mV. The resting membrane potential of neurons is typically about −70 mV. If the Na^+ permeability of the membrane increases (as a result of the opening of Na^+ channels), Na^+ will enter the cell, because both the electrical and concentration gradients favor inward Na^+ movement until the membrane potential reaches

FIGURE 3.43 **Hyperpolarization and depolarization**

The gradients of Na$^+$ and K$^+$ across the cell membrane largely determine the resting membrane potential. When specific ion channels open, the movement of ions changes the membrane potential. If K$^+$ moves out of the cell, the magnitude of the membrane potential increases (hyperpolarization). If Na$^+$ moves into the cell, the magnitude of the membrane potential decreases (depolarization).

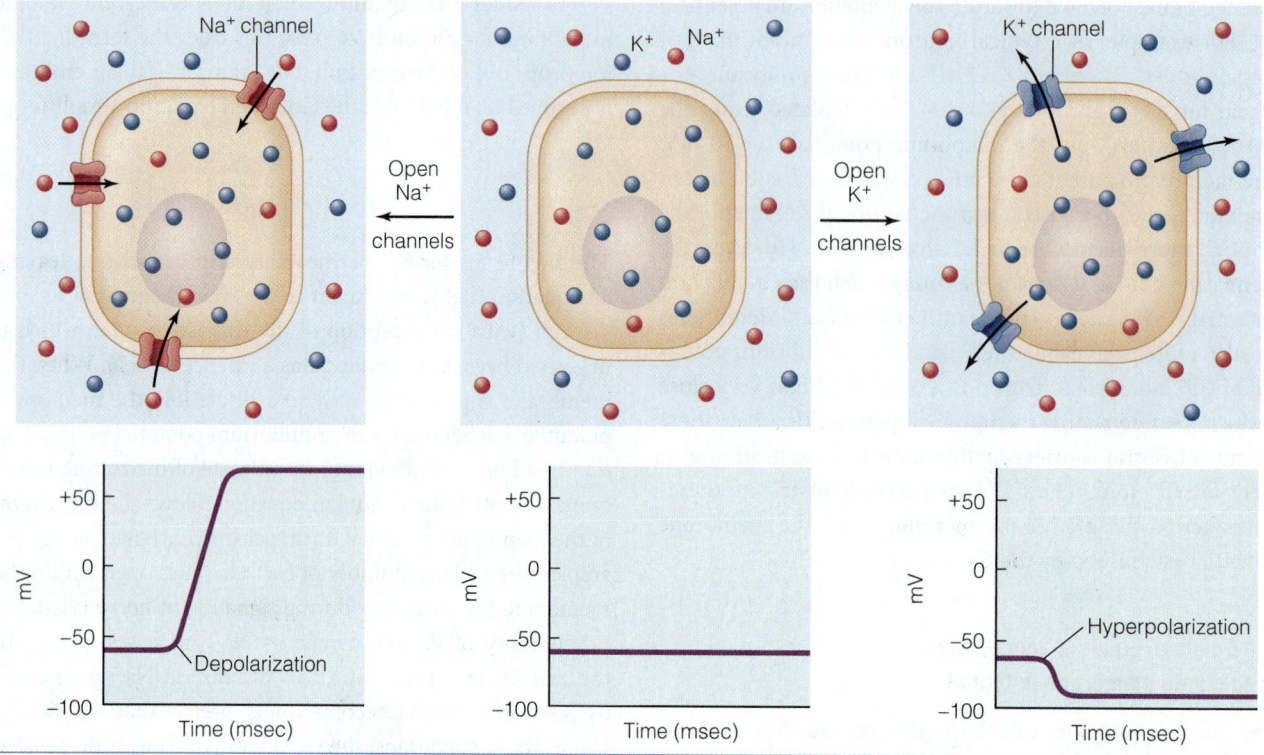

the equilibrium potential for Na$^+$ of $+58$ mV. The resulting inward Na$^+$ movement causes a reduction in the magnitude of the membrane potential termed a **depolarization**. In contrast, if the K$^+$ permeability of the membrane increases (as a result of the opening of K$^+$ channels), K$^+$ will move out of the cell, because both its concentration and electrical gradients favor outward K$^+$ movement until the membrane potential reaches the equilibrium potential for K$^+$ of -90 mV. The loss of positive charges from the interior of the cell results in a **hyperpolarization**. As we discuss in later chapters, many cells use cycles of depolarization, hyperpolarization, and repolarization as communication signals.

CONCEPT CHECK

25. Discuss the composition of biological membranes.

26. How can cells alter the fluidity of membranes, and why is this capacity important to cellular function?

27. What is the relationship between the Nernst equation and the equilibrium potential?

28. Distinguish between depolarization, repolarization, and hyperpolarization.

Cellular Organization

Eukaryotes rely on complex intracellular organization to orchestrate the many processes required for life. Central to the diversity in physiological function is the ability of individual cells to perform specific roles for the tissue and the whole animal. We gain a clearer understanding of complex physiological systems by studying the role of the various cellular compartments that contribute to the process.

Mitochondria are the powerhouse of the cell

Mitochondria are complex organelles, possessing intricate networks of membranes. The innermost compartment is the mitochondrial matrix, delimited by the inner mitochondrial membrane. The outer mitochondrial membrane surrounds the organelle and creates another compartment called the intermembrane space. Each of these compartments has its own complement of enzymes and performs different functions for the mitochondria and the cell. The matrix houses the enzymes and metabolites of the TCA cycle. The inner mitochondrial membrane, which is often highly convoluted, holds the enzymes of oxidative phosphorylation and all the transporters necessary to move metabolites in and out of the mitochondria. About 80 percent of the mass of the inner membrane is protein, the highest protein content of any biological membrane in animals. Mitochondria organize the inner membrane into layers, or **lamellae**, that are tightly folded. In some tissues, as much as 70 m^2 of mitochondrial inner membrane can be folded into a 1-cm^3 volume of mitochondria.

Mitochondrial structure varies greatly among cell types. Many cells, such as liver, contain hundreds of individual oblong mitochondria scattered throughout the cell. These individual mitochondria are rapidly transported throughout the cell. Some cells organize their mitochondria into networks of interconnected organelles called the *mitochondrial reticulum*, which is constantly remodeled by enzymes that mediate its fission and fusion.

Earlier in this chapter you learned that mitochondria possess the enzymes of oxidative phosphorylation, and make most of the ATP a cell requires. Cells frequently respond to changes in energy demand by altering their levels of mitochondria, using both biosynthetic and degradative pathways. Most of the genes required for synthesis of mitochondrial proteins are located in the nucleus. Mitochondrial biogenesis requires that each of these genes be expressed in unison to produce the hundreds of proteins needed for new mitochondria or an extension of the mitochondrial reticulum. Mitochondrial biogenesis also requires replication of mitochondrial DNA (mtDNA) and synthesis of additional mitochondrial membranes. Degradative pathways control the levels of mitochondria and mitochondrial proteins. Damaged mitochondrial fragments are engulfed by autophagosomes and degraded in lysosomes. Cells that fail to destroy defective mitochondria suffer energy shortfalls and eventually cell death.

The cytoskeleton controls cell shape and directs intracellular movement

The **cytoskeleton** is a network of protein-based fibers that extends throughout the cell. It has an important role in maintaining cell structure, acting as a frame upon which the cell membrane is mounted. It gives the cell its characteristic external shape and also supports and organizes intracellular membranes. Organelle networks such as the endoplasmic reticulum and Golgi apparatus are mounted on the cytoskeleton. The cytoskeleton is dynamic in structure, under constant reorganization. Apart from its structural roles, the cytoskeleton is an important participant in many cellular processes, including signal transduction.

The cytoskeleton is constructed from three types of fibers: **microfilaments**, **microtubules**, and **intermediate filaments**. These proteins are long strings of monomers connected end to end to form a polymer. Microtubules are large, stiff tubes composed of the protein **tubulin**. Microfilaments are small, flexible chains of **actin**. Intermediate filaments, so named because they are intermediate in size, are composed of many types of monomers. Most cells possess each of these cytoskeletal elements, but many cells are richer in one particular type. For example, the tails of sperm are largely microtubules, muscles are largely actin polymers, and skin is rich in the intermediate filament keratin.

Other proteins work in conjunction with the cytoskeleton to conduct many types of movement. These proteins, called **motor proteins**, are mechanoenzymes that use the energy of ATP hydrolysis to walk along the cytoskeleton. **Myosin** is the motor protein that walks along actin polymers; **kinesin** and **dynein** move on microtubules. In Chapter 6: Cellular Movement and Muscles, we discuss the structure and function of the cytoskeleton and motor proteins in the context of cellular and intracellular movement.

The endoplasmic reticulum and Golgi apparatus mediate vesicular traffic

Cells have layers of membranous organelles extending around the nucleus to the periphery of the cell (Figure 3.44). The first layer, the **endoplasmic reticulum (ER)**, is the gateway to the other compartments. Proteins are made in the ER, folded, and then sent to their final destinations in the plasma membrane, the Golgi apparatus, **lysosomes**, and endosomes. The vehicle that carries proteins between compartments is a **vesicle**, a small membrane-bound organelle. Some vesicles are surrounded by a shell of coat proteins, such as **clathrin**, coat protein complex I (COP-I), and COP-II. These proteins help form the vesicle, but they also have an important influence on where the vesicle is sent.

Cells are often illustrated in ways that suggest that vesicles drift freely throughout the cytoplasm. In reality, vesicles are carried throughout the cell by motor proteins moving on cytoskeletal tracks. For example, vesicles coated with COP-I may be carried toward the Golgi apparatus, whereas vesicles coated with COP-II may be sent to the ER. Coat proteins and other vesicle membrane proteins influence which motor protein is bound. If a vesicle binds myosin it will be carried on microfilaments, but if it binds dynein it will be carried on microtubules. Protein kinases and protein phosphatases regulate vesicular traffic by altering the cytoskeleton, motor proteins, or vesicle proteins. These processes ensure that vesicles and their contents are sent to the correct location at the correct time.

Many types of intracellular sorting pathways use the ER-Golgi network. Most cells produce proteins, and sometimes other molecules, for release from the cell. This process, called **exocytosis**, begins in the ER. Proteins are made here and packaged into vesicles that move through the Golgi apparatus, ultimately fusing to the plasma membrane to release the vesicle contents to the extracellular space. In the reverse pathway,

FIGURE 3.44   **Intracellular traffic**

Vesicles move throughout the cell, transferring membranes and vesicle contents between compartments.

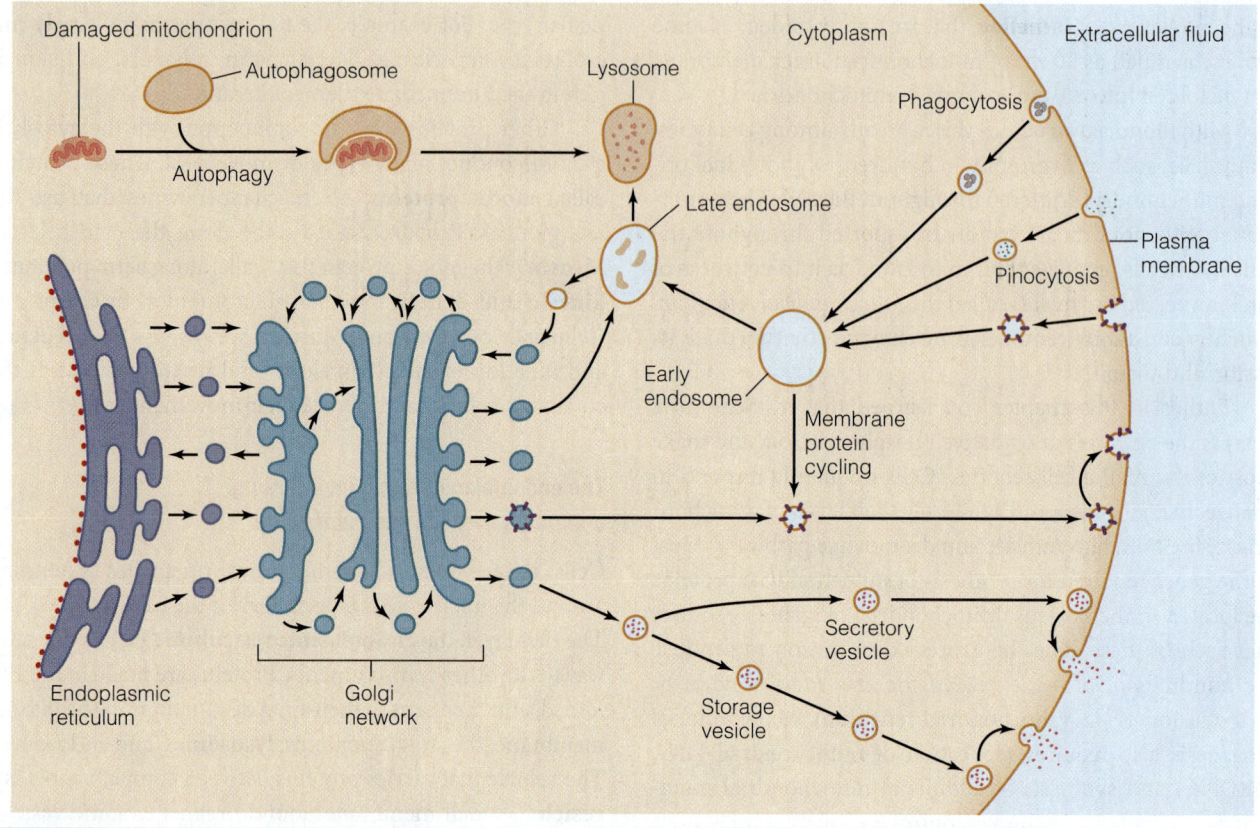

endocytosis, vesicles form at the plasma membrane, engulfing liquid droplets (**pinocytosis**) or large particles (**phagocytosis**). The same pathways of endocytosis and exocytosis regulate the proteins found in the plasma membrane, such as membrane transporters and channels. When transporters are no longer needed, they can be removed from the membrane and stored in vesicles until needed again. Conversely, when a secretory vesicle fuses to the plasma membrane, its internal contents are expelled but the vesicle membrane, both lipid and integral proteins, disperses into the plasma membrane. Cells control the numbers and types of proteins in the plasma membrane through endocytosis and exocytosis. Vesicles rich in transporters fuse to the plasma membrane to increase transport capacity. Conversely, regions of the plasma membrane are extracted during vesicle formation to remove transporters for storage or degradation. Vesicles in transit can be directed to other compartments to assist in processing their contents. Endosomes act as clearinghouses for vesicles, collecting them and then redistributing their contents and membrane proteins into new vesicles that are sent to their correct locations. They send damaged proteins and foreign materials to lysosomes for proteolytic degradation. Once vesicles reach

their destination, another series of proteins mediate the fusion of vesicles with target membranes.

The pathways of intracellular sorting allow animal cells to control many of the processes we have considered throughout this chapter, including secretion, ingestion, and membrane transport. Another function of these pathways, specifically the secretory pathway, is to build and maintain a fibrous network outside the cells: the extracellular matrix.

The extracellular matrix mediates interactions between cells

Cells are organized into a three-dimensional tissue by a network of fibers called the **extracellular matrix**. The proteins used to build the matrix are synthesized by the ER, packaged into vesicles, and sent out of the cell using the secretory pathway. During transit through the **Golgi apparatus**, suites of enzymes modify the proteins, adding branched chains of sugars. As you learned earlier in this chapter, glycosylation alters the properties of the proteins in many ways. In the extracellular matrix, water binds to the hydrophilic sugars to create a gel-like coating that fills the space between cells.

Extracellular matrix macromolecules can be proteins, simple glycoproteins, glycosaminoglycans, or combinations of both, known as proteoglycans (Figure 3.45). **Collagen** is a long, stiff fiber formed as a triple helix of three separate collagen glycoprotein monomers. Elastin is a small protein that is linked together into an intricate web. When the network is stretched it acts like a rubber band, providing the tissue with elasticity. Many extracellular matrix components are linked together by the glycoprotein fibronectin. Each fibronectin molecule binds other fibronectins as well as different matrix components to form a fibrous network.

Hyaluronan is a glycosaminoglycan composed of thousands of repeats of the disaccharide glucuronic acid-N-acetylglucosamine. With its hydration shell, it forms a noncompressible gel that acts as a cushion between cells. Hyaluronan fills the spaces between joints of land animals, easing movement. Other glycosaminoglycans, such as chondroitin sulfate and keratan[2] sulfate, are covalently attached to proteins to form **proteoglycans**. Cartilage is composed primarily of aggrecan, a proteoglycan that incorporates more than 100 glycosaminoglycans into its structure. Many proteoglycans link the different extracellular matrix proteins together to form a network.

The extracellular matrix can be simple in structure and composed of only a few proteins, or it can be organized into an extensive network. The extracellular matrix is more than just the cement that connects cells together. Many specialized structures such as the insect exoskeleton, vertebrate skeleton, and molluscan shells are modified extracellular matrices secreted by specific cells. For example, bone and cartilage are tissues formed from the extracellular matrix of osteoblasts and chondroblasts, respectively. The **basal lamina** (Figure 3.46), or **basement membrane**, is a type of extracellular matrix found in many tissues, where it acts as a solid support that helps anchor cells. It is designed and maintained primarily by specialized cells called **fibroblasts**.

Cells use various strategies to modulate both the matrix properties and their relationship with the matrix. First, most types of extracellular matrix components can be made many ways. For instance, mammals have 20 different collagen genes, so in principle a collagen trimer can be constructed $8,000$ (20^3) ways. Even though most of these possible variants are never constructed, it illustrates the potential for variation in one of the many components of the extracellular matrix. Second, variations occur in the type and position of carbohydrate groups of simple glycoproteins and proteoglycans. Each variation influences the physical properties of the extracellular matrix protein. By controlling which proteins are made and how they are modified by glycosylation, cells determine which building blocks are available to build the extracellular matrix. Cells control which proteins are released to the extracellular space using the secretory pathway discussed in the previous section.

Secreting the extracellular matrix components from the cell is really only one step in building a tissue. The cells also produce integral membrane proteins called matrix receptors to connect them to the extracellular matrix. **Integrins** are an important class of plasma membrane receptors that bind the cytoskeleton on the inside of cells and bind the extracellular matrix on the outside of cells. A cell changes its association with

FIGURE 3.45 Extracellular matrix components

The extracellular matrix is composed of combinations of proteins and glycoproteins, glycosaminoglycans (GAGs) and proteoglycans. Many of the individual molecules, shown in the left column, can be combined into more complex macromolecules, shown on the right. The protein components are shown in green and the GAG components in blue.

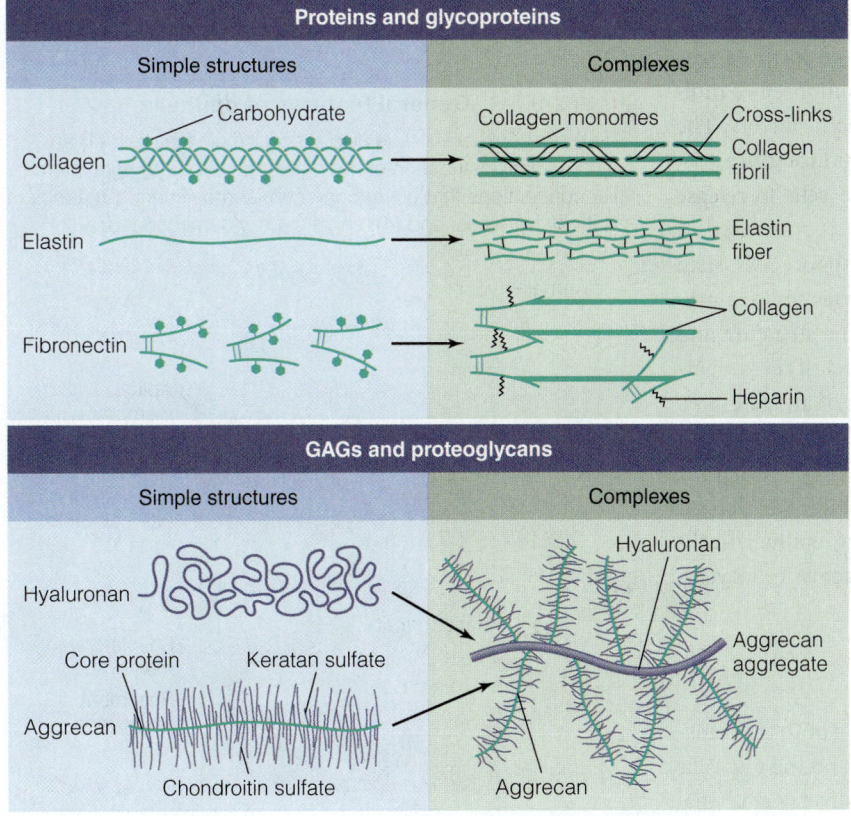

[2]Do not confuse *keratan,* with *keratin,* which is an intermediate filament protein of the cytoskeleton.

FIGURE 3.46   Basal lamina

In many tissues, fibroblasts produce a thick layer of extracellular matrix called the basal lamina. Some cells use the basal lamina as a foundation, but other cells and blood vessels use it as a porous frame.

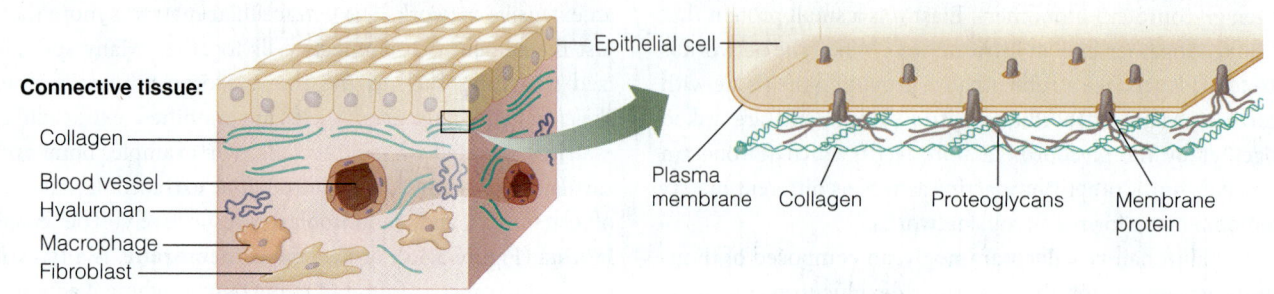

Connective tissue:
Collagen
Blood vessel
Hyaluronan
Macrophage
Fibroblast

Epithelial cell

Plasma membrane   Collagen   Proteoglycans   Membrane protein

the extracellular matrix by changing the types of integrins in its membrane, mediated by endocytosis and exocytosis.

Cells can also break down the extracellular matrix by secreting **proteases** called matrix **metalloproteinases**. By controlling both the production of the matrix and its degradation, cells can regulate their ability to move throughout a tissue. For example, when blood vessels grow, they use matrix metalloproteinases to break down the extracellular matrix of the local cells to allow the blood vessels to penetrate into new regions of the tissue.

Most tissues are composed of multiple cell types

Cell-to-cell connections in combination with an extracellular matrix allows cells to come together to form tissues. Glands (discussed in Chapter 4) are each composed of multiple types of cells specialized to release specific factors. The pancreas (Figure 4.35) has alpha cells to produce **glucagon**, beta cells to produce insulin, and exocrine cells to release **digestive enzymes**. The brain (Chapter 7) is composed of many types of neurons as well as multiple support cells, such as glia. Muscles (Chapter 6) possess myocytes, muscle precursor cells, and fibroblasts. In each case, the structure and function of the tissue depends upon the ability of cells to perform their specific functions in the context of an integrated tissue. All of this depends on the abilities of cells to interconnect and communicate.

One tissue type that plays a role in multiple physiological systems is **epithelium**. Most commonly, epithelial cells play a role in transport, moving molecules across cell layers.

Epithelial tissues share four specialized properties that affect solute movements

The properties of epithelial tissues depend on both the transport properties of individual epithelial cells and the way cells are interconnected to form the tissue. The diverse epithelial tissues, from frog skin to insect Malpighian tubule, share four general features (Figure 3.47).

First, epithelial cell function depends on the asymmetric distribution of transporters within the cell. The **apical** cell membrane, exposed to the outside world, has a different profile of proteins than the basolateral cell membrane, which faces inward. This cellular topography arises because cells insert proteins in the correct location and restrict their movement in the lipid bilayer. In part, the proteins are collected together in chemically distinct regions of the membrane, such as the lipid rafts. Once in membranes, they are anchored in position by attachment to the cytoskeleton.

FIGURE 3.47   General features of epithelia

The typical epithelial tissue displays four main features: **(1)** an asymmetrical distribution of membrane proteins; **(2)** tight intercellular connections that govern paracellular movement; **(3)** a multiplicity of cell types; and **(4)** a high density of mitochondria.

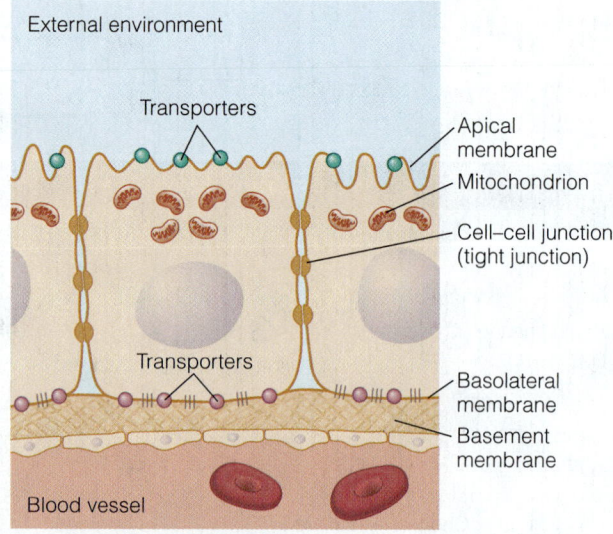

External environment

Transporters

Apical membrane
Mitochondrion
Cell–cell junction (tight junction)

Transporters

Basolateral membrane
Basement membrane

Blood vessel

Second, epithelial cells are interconnected by protein linkages that convert the collection of cells to an impermeable sheet of tissue. Recall that **tight junctions** are formed when membrane proteins of one cell connect to a specific protein in an adjacent cell. The interaction between adjacent cells limits the movement of solutes and water around cells. These intercellular connections also create a kind of protein belt around the circumference of the epithelial cell, restricting the free movement of membrane proteins between apical and basolateral membrane regions to maintain the cellular topography.

Third, epithelial tissues consist of many types of cells. This diversity is most extreme in the digestive system, which we discuss in the next chapter. However, even relatively simple tissues, such as the fish gill, are composed of several cell types, each with important roles, such as providing specific transport capabilities or structural support.

Fourth, ion transport demands a great deal of energy. Most epithelial cells with a major role in transport possess abundant mitochondria to produce ATP. In some cases, mitochondria are in close proximity to the regions of the plasma membrane that conduct the transport processes. In other cases, motor proteins and the cytoskeleton actively transport mitochondria to these regions when metabolic demands increase. The energetic costs of ion transport may account for almost half of the metabolic rate of the tissue.

Solutes move across epithelial tissues by paracellular and transcellular transport

Although epithelial tissues transport some solutes for their own purposes, most transport processes serve to transfer solutes from one side of the tissue to the other. Epithelial tissues use two main routes of transport across the cell (Figure 3.48). **Transcellular transport** is the movement of solutes (or water) through epithelial cells. For example, solutes can diffuse from the extracellular fluid that bathes the cells and move across the basolateral membrane, through the cytoplasm, and across the apical membrane into the external environment (either the open water or the lumen of an organ that communicates with the external environment). Conversely, the movement of solutes (or water) *between* adjacent cells is **paracellular transport**. For example, molecules diffuse from the blood, through the extracellular fluid, and into the narrow confines of the interstitial fluid between adjacent cells. From here, the molecules pass through the tight junctions that connect epithelial cells into sheets. The neighboring cells can secrete molecules into the interstitial space to control its nature in ways that create gradients that drive paracellular movements. Although the tight junction can prevent large molecules from

FIGURE 3.48 **Transcellular and paracellular transport**
(a) Tight epithelia can transfer solutes across the cell using transporters on the apical and basolateral plasma membrane. **(b)** In leaky epithelia, small solutes can also move between cells, passing through the tight junctions that interconnect cells.

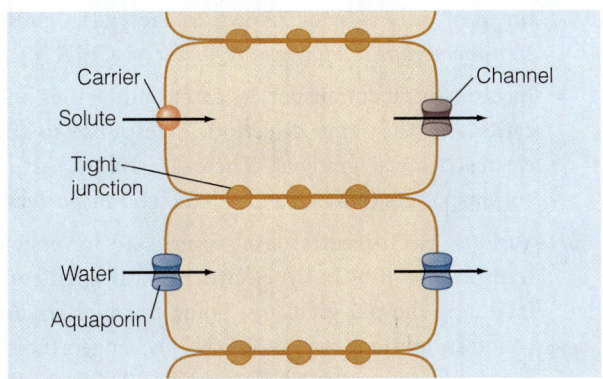

(a) Transcellular transport

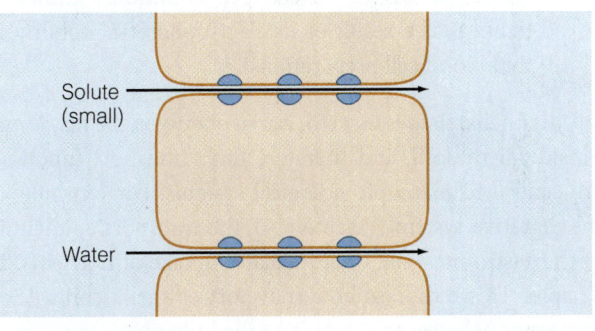

(b) Paracellular transport

crossing, small molecules (water, ions) can cross through the protein connections. Tissues that permit paracellular transport are frequently called **leaky epithelia**. Tissues that conduct minimal paracellular transport are called **tight epithelia**.

Epithelial tissues possess suites of transporters, including the following transporters frequently implicated in ion and water balance. Though many of these transporters have acquired common names, typically as a result of how they were first discovered, we use the more descriptive names throughout this text to better demonstrate their function.

- ATPases are central to ion movements. The Na^+/K^+ ATPase, or sodium pump, is a primary active transporter that uses the energy of ATP hydrolysis to export three Na^+ in exchange for importing two K^+. Some tissues use a H^+ ATPase to pump protons to change pH, a driving force for other transport processes. Ca^{2+} ATPases reestablish Ca^{2+} gradients across cellular membranes.

- Various ion channels (Cl^-, K^+, and Na^+) can open or close in response to mechanical, electrical, or chemical signals to permit specific ions to flow down electrochemical gradients. The Cl^- channel most commonly implicated in transfer of Cl^- across the apical membrane of cells is better known as the *cystic fibrosis transmembrane conductance regulator*, or *CFTR*.

- Electroneutral cotransporters carry both anions and cations in the same direction in response to the electrochemical gradient. There are Na^+-K^+-$2Cl^-$ cotransporters (NKCC) and K^+-Cl^- cotransporters.

- Various electroneutral exchangers are reversible transporters driven by electrochemical gradients, including the pH gradients. Some transporters are cation antiporters, such as Na^+/H^+ exchangers (commonly abbreviated as NHE) and NH_4^+/H^+ exchangers. Other transporters are anion antiporters, such as the Cl^-/HCO_3^- exchanger (commonly known as *band 3* as a result of its electrophoretic mobility in red blood cell preparations).

Epithelial tissues form the barrier between the inside and outside of the cell, and therefore their transport functions are central to many physiological systems. For example, in the digestive system (Chapter 14), the transport epithelium of the gastrointestinal tract mediates uptake of nutrients. In Chapter 13 we discuss how transport epithelia control ion and water balance, particularly in the kidney.

CONCEPT CHECK

29. Summarize the roles of the different subcellular compartments within a cell, and discuss how they influence physiological function.
30. What does the Na^+/K^+ ATPase do in a typical cell?
31. Distinguish between paracellular transport and transcellular transport.

Physiological Genetics and Genomics

The nature of physiological diversity, whether in the response of an individual or in the variations arising over evolutionary time, resides in the genes: how they differ between species and how they are regulated in individual cells. Homeostatic regulation depends on the ability of the cell to put the right protein in the proper place at the proper time with the appropriate activity. Cells have many mechanisms to control the rates of synthesis of specific proteins. RNA polymerases read the genes, producing mRNA in the process of **transcription**. Once RNA is made, it is used as a template to produce protein in the process of **translation**. Cells can control the levels of both RNA and protein using mechanisms that target rates of synthesis and degradation.

Nucleic acids are polymers of nucleotides

The two types of nucleic acids, **deoxyribonucleic** acid (DNA) and ribonucleic acid (RNA), are structurally similar but perform different functions within the cell. DNA is the genetic blueprint for building cells. RNA reads the information encoded by the DNA and interprets it to make proteins. Cells produce three main forms of RNA: transfer RNA (**tRNA**), ribosomal RNA (**rRNA**), and messenger RNA (**mRNA**). Certain molecules of RNA complex with proteins to form riboproteins.

Both RNA and DNA are polymers of nucleotides. All nucleotides are composed of a nitrogenous base attached to a sugar linked to a phosphate. RNA and DNA differ in the type of sugar in the nucleotide: Ribonucleotides contain ribose, whereas deoxyribonucleotides possess deoxyribose. Both RNA and DNA are synthesized from combinations of four types of nucleotides that differ in the nature of their nitrogenous bases. Three of the four nitrogenous bases, the **pyrimidine cytosine** and the purines **adenine** and **guanine**, are found in nucleotides of both RNA and DNA. The fourth nitrogenous base is another pyrimidine: uracil in RNA and thymine in DNA. The ribonucleotides are ATP, UTP, CTP, and GTP. The deoxyribonucleotides are dATP, dTTP, dCTP, and dGTP. In many cases, the nucleotide sequence in DNA and RNA is represented using one-letter codes. Thus, A refers to the residue derived from the nucleotide ATP (in RNA) or dATP (in DNA), C is CTP/dCTP, G is GTP/dGTP, T is dTTP, and U is UTP.

Nucleic acids form from long polymers of nucleotides linked by phosphodiester bonds that form between the phosphate of one nucleotide and the sugar of the adjacent nucleotide. The end of the polymer that terminates with a phosphate group is deemed the 5-prime end (5′); the other end terminates with a sugar and is the 3′ end. The nucleic acid has a polarity, conferred by its 5′ and 3′ ends, that is an important consideration when discussing the biochemical processes involved in nucleic acid function.

DNA is a double-stranded α-helix packaged into chromosomes

DNA usually exists within cells as a double-stranded polymer (Figure 3.49) in which hydrogen bonds connect the two strands. Each specific nucleotide can form hydrogen bonds with only one other nucleotide. Three hydrogen bonds form between G and C, whereas two hydrogen bonds form between A and T. When one strand of DNA encounters another complementary strand, hydrogen bonds form between the strands, creating a double-stranded molecule. The two strands *anneal* in an antiparallel arrangement, with the 5′ end of one strand associated with the 3′ end of the other strand.

Double-stranded DNA twists into an α-helix with two topological features: a minor groove and a major groove. The two strands of DNA appear as ridges, separated by a trough. These contours between two strands compose the minor groove. The

FIGURE 3.49 **DNA structure**

Each strand of DNA binds to another, complementary strand. Hydrogen bonds form between specific base pairs. Two bonds form between A and T. Three bonds form between C and G. The double-stranded DNA is twisted into an α-helix, forming a minor groove between strands. The major groove reflects the period of the twisting of the helix.

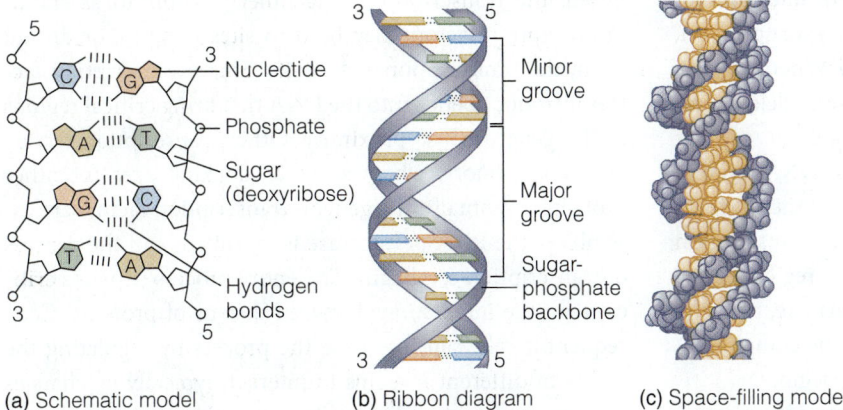

(a) Schematic model (b) Ribbon diagram (c) Space-filling model

major groove results from the twisting pattern of the α-helix. Every 10 base pairs, a distance of about 3.6 nm, the helix completes a full turn, forming the major groove that resembles a saddle. Variations in nucleotide sequence cause subtle regional alterations in the shape of DNA and the topology of the major and minor grooves. This structural variation is information that is used by the DNA-binding proteins to attach to the correct location to regulate expression of specific genes.

The DNA in animal cells is highly compressed into tight structures with the aid of DNA-binding proteins called **histones**. If you were to unwind the DNA in a single mammalian cell, the strands would stretch several meters. The long strands of DNA wrap twice around the barrel-shaped histones until a structure resembling a strand of pearls is formed. These strands are then twisted and folded into highly compressed arrangements, which has two main advantages to cells. First, it allows the cell to fit large amounts of DNA into the small volume. Second, coating DNA with histones helps reduce the damage caused by radiation and chemicals. However, in this compressed configuration DNA is biochemically inert; it cannot function as a template for RNA synthesis (transcription) or DNA synthesis (replication). Cells must use histone-modifying enzymes to release histones from DNA, thereby regulating gene expression.

DNA is organized into genomes

The entire collection of DNA within a cell is called the **genome**. Within the nucleus, the genome is divided into separate segments of DNA called **chromosomes**. Within chromosomes are the genes, which possess the DNA sequences that are used to produce all the different types of RNA, including the mRNA that encodes proteins. Each gene also possesses regions of DNA called promoters that determine when the gene is expressed. Many genes are divided into multiple sections

on the same chromosome. The sections that encode RNA are known as **exons**, and the interspersed DNA sections are called **introns** (Figure 3.50).

In most animals, genes account for less than half of the genome. The majority of the genome is a mixture of different types of random and repetitious DNA, much of which serves no known function and is often called junk DNA.

Across the animal kingdom, genome size ranges more than 6,000-fold. The smallest genome is found in one of the simplest animals: Placozoans, a relative of sponges, have only about 0.02 pg of DNA per cell. The largest genome in animals, about 133 pg/cell, belongs to the African marbled lungfish. Surprisingly, there is little relationship between the size of the genome and the complexity of the animal. For example, both the largest and the smallest vertebrate genomes are found in fish. The pufferfish genome is only about 0.3 percent the size of the lungfish genome. There is also no relationship between the number of chromosomes and the complexity of the animal. Humans possess 46 chromosomes. Some deer have only 6, whereas carp may have more than 100.

Transcriptional control acts at gene regulatory regions

The rate of synthesis for many proteins is proportional to the levels of mRNA. Historically, mRNA levels were measured

FIGURE 3.50 **Chromosomes and genes**

Chromosomes possess structural regions, such as centromeres and telomeres, in addition to noncoding regions and genes.

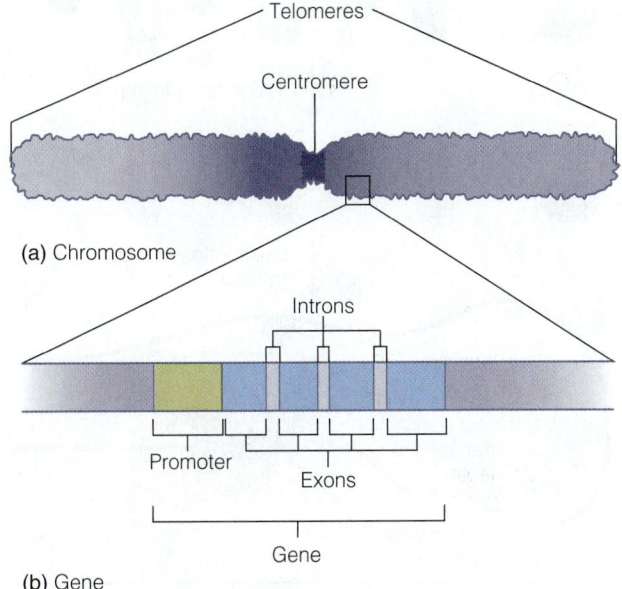

(a) Chromosome

(b) Gene

using northern blots, but recent advances in genomics and engineering have led to the development of techniques for assessing complex changes in the levels of mRNA for thousands of genes simultaneously.

At any point in time, most of the genome of a cell is wrapped around histones and rolled into nucleosomes (Figure 3.51). Under these conditions the genes are quiescent, unable to bind the transcriptional machinery. When the gene product is required, the chromatin must be remodeled to allow transcriptional activators access to the regulatory regions of the gene. Transcriptional regulators, both DNA-binding proteins and coactivators, associate with each other to form regulatory complexes on the promoter. The transcription initiation complex assembles near a specific region of the promoter designated as the transcription start site, typically a sequence of TATA (the TATA box). Once the complex assembles, the process of mRNA synthesis can begin.

Cells can regulate the rate of mRNA synthesis by altering the conformation of the gene and changing the ability of the transcriptional machinery to assemble. Sometimes gene expression is induced by stimulation of the enzymes that remodel chromatin. These enzymes work by altering the structure of the histones that organize DNA into nucleosomes. Histones can be modified by acetylation, methylation, and phosphorylation. For example, when a histone acetyl transferase (HAT)

adds an acetyl group to a critical lysine in a histone, this induces a change in structure that permits remodeling of chromatin to favor gene expression. The gene can be silenced by a histone deacetylase (HDAC) that removes the acetyl group.

Once the regulatory regions within the gene are exposed, the transcriptional machinery is able to assemble. Transcription factors may bind to sites close to, or distant from, the transcriptional start site. Some transcription factors introduce bends into the DNA that bring critical regions of the gene in close proximity. Other transcription factors bind coactivators, which serve as docking sites for other proteins. Eventually, the general transcription factors are assembled, the RNA polymerase is recruited, and the process of transcription can begin. The entire process depends critically on the interactions between dozens of proteins. Consequently, cells can fine-tune the process by regulating the ability of different proteins to interact, typically by changes in protein phosphorylation. The phosphorylation state can affect the transfer of a transcription factor between the cytoplasm and the nucleus. It can also alter the ability of transcriptional regulators to interact with DNA or other proteins, both stimulatory and inhibitory proteins. Because each gene is regulated by dozens of transcription factors, the combinations of regulatory conditions are endless.

The primary mRNA transcript possesses sequences that will eventually code for the protein (exons) as well as other sequences that are interspersed between exons (introns). It must first be processed in a way that removes introns and splices together exons. Next, the spliced RNA must be polyadenylated; long strings of 200 or more ATP residues are added to the 5′ end of the transcript to produce the poly A$^+$ tail that is characteristic of mRNA. Once these post-transcriptional modifications are completed, the mature mRNA is exported to the cytoplasm.

RNA degradation influences RNA levels

Controlling transcription is one important mechanism for cells to alter RNA levels; another is to vary the rate of RNA degradation. RNA is degraded by **nucleases** called **RNases**. An RNase can attack the end of the RNA (exonucleases) or internal sites (endonucleases), preventing the mRNA from acting as a template for protein synthesis.

Cells have ways to preferentially degrade or protect individual mRNAs. A long poly A$^+$ tail protects an mRNA from degradation. Soon after release into the cytoplasm, exonucleases nibble off the ends of the poly A$^+$ tail. The mRNA can still be translated into protein at this point. Once the exonucleases shorten the tail to about 30 bases, the RNA is attacked by an endonuclease, causing enough damage to prevent the protein from being translated.

Other processes accelerate the rate of mRNA degradation. Some mRNAs are unstable, existing in the cytoplasm for

FIGURE 3.51 **Transcriptional regulation**

Quiescent DNA is tightly wrapped around histones. Remodeling of chromatin gives DNA-binding proteins access to gene control regions. The general transcription factors allow RNA polymerase II to bind to initiate transcription. Other DNA regulatory proteins, such as the activators and coactivators shown here, increase the likelihood that the transcriptional machinery will assemble.

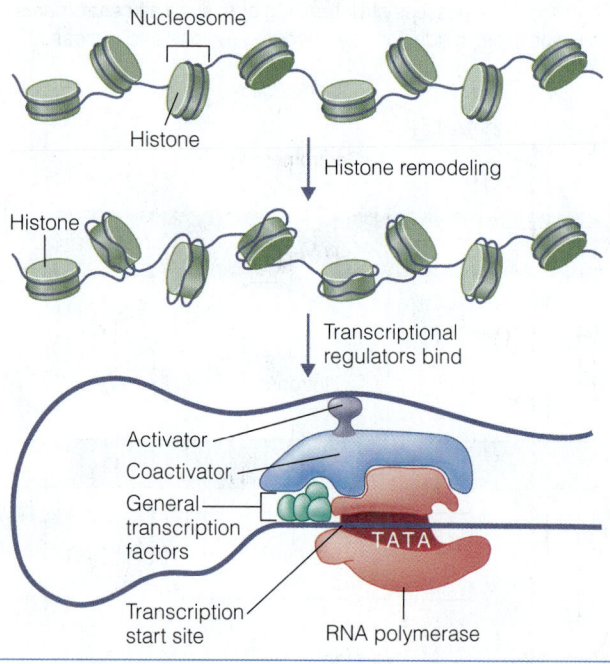

only a few minutes before becoming degraded. These unstable mRNAs have long stretches of A and U bases within their 3′ untranslated regions (3′-UTR). These AU-rich regions recruit proteins that accelerate mRNA degradation. The ability to accelerate RNA degradation is essential in many cells, particularly those that produce regulatory proteins. Once a signaling protein is no longer needed, the RNase machinery can rapidly degrade the mRNA to prevent it from being translated. More recently, another mechanism of transcript-specific RNA degradation has been identified. Small micro-RNAs are gene products that are transcribed and bind to mRNA molecules. The RNA:RNA hybrid may be rapidly degraded, lowering the mRNA levels and thereby reducing protein synthesis.

Cells can also reduce the rate of RNA degradation. Stabilizing proteins can bind to specific regions in the poly A$^+$ tail or other regions of the mRNA to prevent RNase attack. Some microRNAs bind mRNA, acting to both resist degradation and prevent translation. These mechanisms allow the cell to maintain a pool of preformed mRNA available for immediate use if cellular conditions demand the gene product.

Global changes in translation control many pathways

Once an mRNA arrives in the cytoplasm, the process of translation can begin with the assistance of **ribosomes** and amino acyl tRNAs. Ribosomes, complexes of rRNA and proteins, catalyze the formation of peptide bonds between amino acids in the growing protein. The amino acids are provided in the form of amino acyl tRNA. Each amino acid uses a specific tRNA that can bind to a specific set of three nucleotides on the mRNA called a codon. The 5′ end of the mRNA recruits proteins called initiation factors, in combination with a methionine tRNA (tRNA$_{MET}$) and a ribosome. The complex moves down the mRNA chain until it reaches the sequence AUG, which is the start codon. Another amino acyl tRNA is recruited, and the ribosome catalyzes the formation of a peptide bond between the amino acids to begin the process of elongation. In most circumstances, proteins called elongation factors enter the ribosome and accelerate the catalytic cycle. In a typical animal cell, each individual ribosome can add an amino acid to the chain at a rate of one to two per second. The process continues until the ribosomal complex reaches a stop codon, a nucleotide sequence that is incapable of binding any amino acyl tRNA. At any point in time, a single mRNA may be translated by many ribosomes bound all along the mRNA.

Cells can control the rate of translation using nonspecific mechanisms that affect all translation within the cell, as well as specific mechanisms that influence only a subset of mRNAs. Many of the initiation factors and elongation factors are regulated through protein phosphorylation. In addition, each of these factors can bind inhibitory proteins. Such mechanisms allow cells to mount global changes in translation rates. Many types of mRNA possess sequences that act to regulate their translation. For example, sequences in the 3′ UTR and 5′ UTR bind proteins that alter the ability of the mRNA to be translated.

Cells rapidly reduce protein levels through protein degradation

Once proteins are synthesized, they remain in the cell until they are degraded. Just as cells use degradation to control mRNA levels, they use protein degradation to control protein levels. Some proteins are removed only when they sustain enough damage to become dysfunctional. The structural changes in damaged proteins recruit enzymes that mark the protein for degradation. These enzymes transfer a small protein called **ubiquitin** to the damaged protein. Once the ubiquitination machinery has attached a ubiquitin chain to the damaged protein, the protein is bound by a multiprotein complex called the **proteasome**. Proteolytic enzymes within the proteasome degrade the ubiquitin-tagged proteins to amino acids.

Earlier we discussed how some types of mRNA are preferentially degraded. Many of these unstable mRNAs encode proteins that are also subject to accelerated degradation. Proteins such as cell cycle regulators and transcription factors can be ubiquitinated even in the absence of structural damage. Characteristic amino acid sequences within the proteins recruit the ubiquitination machinery. Often the recognition sequences can be phosphorylated, altering their ability to be subjected to rapid degradation.

Collectively, cells use these regulatory processes to control the levels of mRNA and protein. They enable cells to modify cellular properties in response to changing environmental and physiological conditions. Cells are also able to modulate their physiological response by altering the types of proteins they express. Animals, particularly vertebrates, can draw upon isoforms of proteins with subtly different properties that provide cells with alternative strategies to meet environmental and physiological challenges.

Protein variants arise through gene duplications and rearrangements

Protein isoforms provide a cell with flexibility in structure and function. A suite of proteins can be created with distinct properties. Isoforms can be produced through multiple mechanisms involving single genes, different alleles, or different genes (Figure 3.52).

Variations in protein structure can arise when the primary mRNA from a gene is connected together using different combinations of exons, a process known as **alternative splicing**. For example, more than 40 different isoforms of fibronectin can result from a single gene. Each isoform of fibronectin binds different combinations of extracellular matrix molecules.

FIGURE 3.52 **Origins of protein variants**

Cells are able to produce protein isoforms in many different ways. Cells can splice exons in different combinations to create distinct proteins. Often the same gene can occur in different sequences within a population. Some individuals can have two different versions of the same gene (*A* or *a*) on chromosomes inherited from each parent. Gene duplications can lead to extra gene copies in different loci. These genes can diverge to encode different enzymes (A and B).

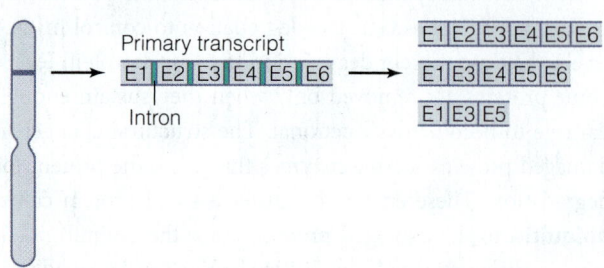

(a) Alternate splicing

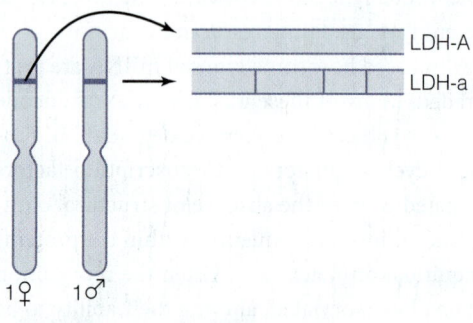

(b) Allelic variation

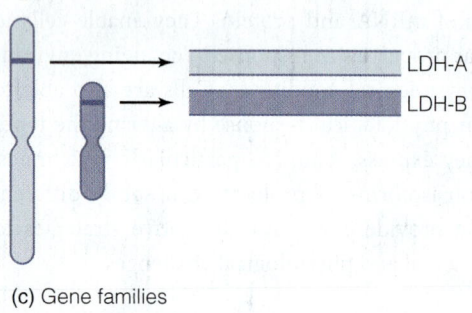

(c) Gene families

FIGURE 3.53 **Gene duplications**

Gene recombination can provide cells with extra copies of genes. In contrast to equal crossover, **(a)** where homologous regions of chromosomes are exchanged, unequal crossover **(b)** provides one chromosome with extra genetic material. **(c)** Cells also possess many different kinds of mobile elements that can move or duplicate genes between chromosomes.

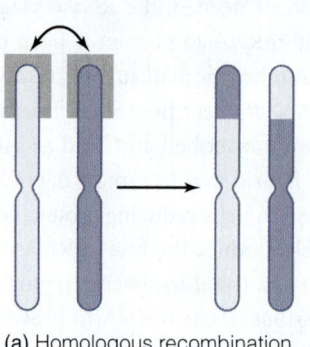

(a) Homologous recombination
(equal crossover)

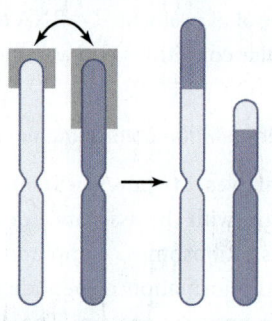

(b) Unequal crossover

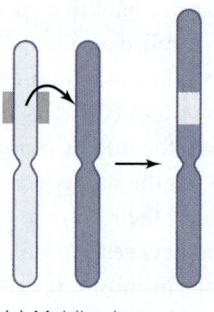

(c) Mobile elements

Within any population of animals, there is some variation in the exact sequence of specific genes. As a consequence, a diploid individual may possess two different versions of the same gene, one arising from the mother and one from the father. These different forms of the same gene are **alleles**. If the gene encodes an enzyme, the isoforms are also called **allozymes**. Often the differences in allozyme structure have little effect on function. Because they are functionally neutral, natural selection does not remove them from the population. However, in some cases the regulatory or catalytic properties of allozymes may be subtly different. Often different allozymes predominate in two populations of animals. For example, if a specific allozyme functions better in the cold, that gene might occur at a higher frequency in populations of animals exposed to the cold.

Other types of isoforms are encoded by separate genes that arose from ancestral **gene duplications**. Figure 3.53 shows some of the ways that genes can become duplicated. During the process of meiosis, long stretches of DNA may be transferred from one chromosome to another. In most cases, two chromosomes exchange homologous regions and no gain or loss of genes occurs. This process of shuffling gene combinations is one of the advantages of sexual reproduction. Occasionally, the machinery of homologous recombination misidentifies homologous regions. Unequal crossover results, and one chromosome donates an end to another chromosome. The progeny derived from the gamete that lost the chromosomal region would not likely survive. However, the progeny from the recipient gamete will be endowed with extra copies of the duplicated genes. These extra copies could kill the cell or, if neutral or beneficial, get transmitted to the next generation. As a result of these gene duplication processes, many genes occur as **paralogs** in an individual; two versions of a gene with a shared ancestry but divergent functions.

Another way that genes can become duplicated is through **mobile elements**. Many organisms possess genes that are capable of jumping from one chromosome to another. In most cases, the mobile element encodes a transposase, the enzyme required to cut the DNA from one strand and insert it into another. Occasionally, other genes become trapped in the mobile elements. When the mobile elements move, the other genes are carried along, endowing the recipient chromosome with the extra copy.

Genetic recombination does not always lead to production of extra copies of entire genes. In some cases, fragments of genes are moved from one gene and inserted into a completely different gene. A protein may possess domains within its structure that resemble regions of otherwise unrelated proteins. For instance, hundreds of different proteins can bind ATP using a protein structure called an **ATP-binding cassette**. This motif appears in the ABC transporters we discussed early in this chapter. This structure, which appears in all living organisms, probably arose only once, or perhaps a few times, billions of years ago. Its appearance in so many different genes and in all taxa is likely due to genetic recombination events that moved this region from one gene to another.

Ancient genome duplications contribute to physiological diversity

The ancestral animal was endowed with a set of genes that have been transmitted to subsequent generations and are present in most animals. The collection of genes arising in different species but from a common ancestor are **orthologs**. When comparing the simplest of animals to the most complex, we see that orthologous genes have diverged in structure and function; however, they can be recognized as having a common ancestor.

At several points in animal evolution, genes and genomes have undergone duplication events. These provide organisms with extra copies of redundant DNA that can accumulate mutations and diverge to endow the organisms with novel capacities. The key to achieving the opportunity for specialization is obtaining the raw material: a nonlethal extra copy of a gene.

At several points in the evolution of animals, whole genomes were duplicated. Many of the duplicated genes were eventually lost, but many were retained and diverged to form gene families. Many of the anatomical and functional specializations of vertebrates are a result of these genomic duplications. Often, if a particular gene is found in a single copy in an invertebrate, there are four isoforms in vertebrates. This "rule-of-four" reflects ancestral genome duplications; each single gene locus was duplicated, giving two copies of all genes, then reduplicated, giving four copies of all genes. The individual genes within the duplicated genomes underwent mutation, selection, and drift to diverge into distantly related genes. After a period of divergence, some individual genes duplicated again. The newly duplicated genes were more closely related to each other than to their distant ancestors, creating gene clusters. When did these genome duplications occur? A possible answer comes from phylogenetic analyses of a family of genes involved in development, the *Hox* family. The first genome duplication probably occurred just before the jawless vertebrates, or agnathans, diverged from the vertebrate lineage. The second duplication coincided with the development of jaws. The primitive chordates such as amphioxus have a single cluster of *Hox* genes, the agnathan lamprey has two or sometimes three clusters, and the more recent jawed vertebrates, from sharks to humans, possess at least four clusters of *Hox* genes. In each case, genome duplications coincided with important revolutions in morphological and physiological complexity.

These original genome duplications in the vertebrate lineage probably occurred more than 300 million years ago. Many modern animals have experienced relatively recent genome duplications, including many examples of frogs and fish that gained an extra set of chromosomes to become tetraploids. In some cases, tetraploid populations exist within diploid species; not nearly enough time has passed within the tetraploid lineage for the duplicated genes to diverge. The common carp, however, became tetraploid about 15 million years ago. Its closest relative, the grass carp, has half the number of chromosomes. Many genes that are in single copy in other vertebrates are found in pairs in common carp. Although the pairs have diverged in structure, they have not yet become different in function.

Over many generations, the duplicated genes can follow many fates. The duplicated gene might incur mutations in the promoter or coding region that prevent it from being transcribed, rendering it a pseudogene. In some cases, one copy of the gene mutates and diverges, resulting in a protein with distinct properties. In other cases, both copies mutate and diverge, resulting in a pair of proteins with overlapping functions.

These genetic processes, originating early in animal evolution and operating at the level of individual cells, provide animals with physiological flexibility. The integration of different cell types into complex physiological systems is an important reason why animals have radiated into so many diverse species over the course of evolution.

SUMMARY

Biological systems, from molecules to organisms, depend upon the rules of physics and chemistry. Many biological processes are essentially transfers of energy. Biochemical structures and reactions depend on chemical potential energy, and are directly influenced by temperature. Solution chemistry influences movement and activity of water and ions, including protons; differences across membranes create electrochemical gradients that drive many biological processes.

Enzymes are organic catalysts that speed reactions by reducing the activation energy barrier. Enzyme reaction velocity (V) and substrate affinity (K_m) depend on the physicochemical environment, such as the temperature, ion composition, and pH of the solution. Cells control reaction rates by changing the concentration of reactants, the levels or activities of enzymes, and the concentration of substrates, products, and regulators. Enzymes control the interconversions of macromolecules that are essential for structure and metabolism.

Carbohydrates (glucose, glycogen) can be produced from noncarbohydrate precursors using gluconeogenesis, or broken down to pyruvate (glycolysis), which may be further oxidized to CO_2. In the absence of oxygen, most animals use lactate dehydrogenase to balance redox and dispose of pyruvate. Anoxia-tolerant animals can use other pathways for oxidizing NADH in the absence of oxygen, some of which provide additional ATP.

Phospholipids, including phosphoglycerides and sphingolipids, are used to make cell membranes. Steroids and their precursors fulfill many roles within cells, and steroid hormones are particularly important in cell signaling. Fatty acids can be synthesized by the enzyme fatty acid synthase, for use in biosynthesis or energy storage. When energy is needed, lipases can break down triglycerides to release the fatty acids, which can be oxidized by the mitochondrial β-oxidation pathway.

Most oxidative fuels can be converted to acetyl CoA within mitochondria. When acetyl CoA enters the tricarboxylic acid cycle, acetyl CoA is oxidized to produce reducing equivalents, NADH and $FADH_2$. Oxidation of reducing equivalents by the electron transport system generates a proton gradient, heat, and reactive oxygen species. The mitochondria F_1F_o ATPase, or ATP synthase, uses the proton motive force to generate ATP. Phosphorylation is coupled to oxidation through a shared dependence on the proton motive force. Under some circumstances, mitochondria can become uncoupled, leading to the production of heat instead of ATP.

The balance between biosynthesis and catabolism is regulated by energetic intermediates such as ATP, NADH, and acetyl CoA. Without this regulation, the two processes could occur simultaneously, leading to loss of energy in futile cycles. Metabolic regulation also determines which fuels are oxidized under which conditions.

Membranes allow cells to create permeability barriers that help them to define environments. Membranes are heterogeneous combinations of phospholipids, cholesterol, and numerous integral and peripheral proteins. The nature of the lipid membrane influences fluidity, an important determinant of protein function.

While some hydrophobic molecules can cross membranes by passive diffusion, membrane proteins are required for transport of most molecules. Some transporters, such as ion channels, facilitate the diffusion of impermeant molecules down concentration gradients by creating pores. Active transporters use energy to pump molecules against gradients.

The electrochemical gradients that exist across cellular membranes are produced by active transporters and used to drive diverse physiological processes. The interior of the plasma membrane is electronegative, with a membrane potential between 5 and 100 mV. Potassium gradients are the most important component of the resting membrane potential. Changes in membrane permeability alter the membrane potential in ways that cells use to communicate.

The basic structure of cells—including the mitochondria, cytoskeleton, extracellular matrix, and secretory networks—can be regulated and remodeled to serve many purposes. The ability to follow developmental programs, or respond to physiological and environmental challenges, resides in the genes. Physiological change begins in many cases with the ways cells control genes. Cells and tissues are remodeled using processes from transcriptional control to post-translational regulation. Evolutionary processes, including gene and genome duplications, provide the raw material for achieving physiological diversity.

REVIEW QUESTIONS

1. **LO❶** What are the four types of weak bonds and how do they differ from each other and from covalent bonds?

2. **LO❶** Why are reaction rates influenced by temperature?

3. **LO❷** How does the density of water change in relation to temperature? How do these properties affect animals that live in marine and freshwater environments?

4. **LO❷** Discuss the mechanism by which cells can use transporters to change their osmotic and ionic properties.

5. **LO❸** Distinguish between the types of polysaccharides relevant to animals.

6. **LO❸** Compare the structures of phospholipids.

7. **LO④** If the enzymatic reaction $A + B \leftrightarrow C + D$ is near equilibrium, then the mass action ratio is close to the equilibrium constant. What happens to the mass action ratio if you add more enzyme? What happens when you add more of A? What do you need to know to predict what would happen if temperature changed?

8. **LO④** Distinguish between the parameters that describe enzyme kinetics and discuss the ways that cells control enzyme kinetics.

9. **LO⑤** What metabolic conditions can affect the values of the respiratory quotient? What metabolic conditions affect the relationship between ATP produced and oxygen consumed?

10. **LO⑤** How do the pathways of gluconeogenesis and glycolysis overlap?

11. **LO⑥** Discuss the ways in which a cell is able to alter its interactions with other cells.

12. **LO⑥** Discuss the mechanism by which cells can use transporters to change their osmotic and ionic properties.

13. **LO⑦** Many physiological processes require a change in the levels of proteins, such as membrane transporters. Discuss the processes that cells can use to change the protein levels. Discuss how the subcellular compartment influences this pathway.

14. **LO⑦** Other physiological processes require changes in the *activities* of proteins. While this can arise through changes in the *levels* of proteins, it can also change through regulation of protein function. Discuss the various ways that cells can alter the activity of enzymes or transporters.

15. **LO⑧** Discuss the origins of genetic variation.

16. **LO⑧** How does genetic variation provide physiological flexibility?

SYNTHESIS QUESTIONS

1. Describe, in chemical terms, how antacids work.

2. Why do your hands get wrinkled if you spend too much time in the bathtub? Would the same thing happen when you swim in the ocean? Describe these environments using the terminology of osmolarity and tonicity.

3. What is the relationship between pK and pH? How does temperature influence the pK of water? What might this mean for animals that experience changes in body temperature?

4. A type of protein comes in six different forms. Each form can dimerize with the other. How many unique homodimers and heterodimers can be formed from these six proteins?

5. Many animals maintain metabolites at concentrations near the K_m value for metabolic enzymes. For example, the concentration of pyruvate is often close to the K_m value for LDH. Why might this be advantageous, in terms of kinetic regulation?

6. Trace the path of a protein hormone, such as insulin, from its gene in the nucleus to secretion out of the cell.

7. Discuss the ways in which a cell is able to alter its interactions with other cells.

QUANTITATIVE QUESTIONS

1. What is the proton concentration of a solution at pH 7.4? At what temperature would this solution be neutral?

2. Calculate the basis for an $RQ = 1$ for carbohydrate oxidation. Why does palmitate oxidation give an $RQ = 0.7$?

3. What rate of oxygen consumption would you expect in a tissue with a metabolic rate of 30 μmol ATP/g/min?

CHAPTER

4

Cell Signaling and Endocrine Regulation

Learning Objectives

After reading this chapter, you should be able to:

1. Summarize the shared features of signaling systems.

2. Compare and contrast the major chemical classes of signaling molecules.

3. Explain how chemical messengers communicate their signals to a target cell.

4. Compare the general features of signal transduction via intracellular receptors, ligand-gated ion channels, receptor enzymes, and G protein–coupled receptors.

5. Compare the different signal transduction pathways associated with G protein–coupled receptors.

6. Outline some of the ways that endocrine systems are organized using selected examples.

7. Outline some of the major patterns in the evolution of endocrine systems.

FIGURE 4.1 **Cell signaling is critical in the bioluminescence of the Hawaiian bobtail squid, *Euprymna scolopes***

Photo source: Image Quest Marine.

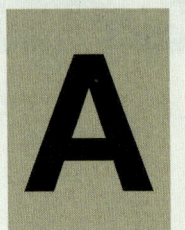

At every level of organization, life depends on communication. Animals send signals to each other in the form of sounds, scents, and visual cues. Within an animal, organs, tissues, and cells communicate with each other using chemical and electrical signals. Even within a single cell there is constant communication of information among organelles.

In all organisms, cellular communication systems involve sending and receiving a signal, often in the form of a chemical messenger. We can see the fundamentals of these mechanisms even in single-celled organisms. For example, the marine bacterium *Vibrio fischeri* is capable of producing light. These bacteria produce a signaling chemical that binds to a specific receptor within the bacterial cell. Binding of the signal causes the receptor to change shape and act as a transcription factor that induces the transcription of the genes involved in light production.

V. fischeri seldom reach high enough densities to produce large amounts of the inducing chemical when they are free-living, and as a result, the free-living bacteria generally do not glow, or only emit dim light. However, these bacteria are also found in a mutualistic relationship with a species of squid—*Euprymna scolopes* (Figure 4.1), the Hawaiian bobtail squid. The bacteria colonize specialized organs on the underside of the squid that provide an ideal home for the bacteria, allowing them to grow to a very high density. Under these conditions, the amount of signaling chemical increases in the environment, allowing the bacteria to glow brightly.

The light produced by the bacteria glows from these so-called "light organs" on the underside of the squid. This **bioluminescence** allows the predatory squid to blend in with the light descending through the water from the surface, making them invisible from below. Thus, the glowing bacteria act as camouflage that helps the squid to catch their prey.

Squid are not born with bacteria in their light organ. Instead, the bacteria colonize the light organ as the squid develop. This process of colonization involves complex communication between the squid and the bacteria. For example, the squid detects and recognizes the type of bacteria that enter the light organ. Only *V. fischeri* can colonize the light organ, while other bacterial species are rejected. The bacteria also influence the development of the squid, as squid reared in the laboratory in the absence of the bacteria do not develop a complete light organ. These observations suggest that the complex mutualistic relationship between the bacteria and the squid depends both on cellular signaling among the bacteria and on signaling between the bacteria and the squid.

This example of cellular communication between a prokaryote and an animal illustrates the shared features of cellular communication in all living things: the production of a signal in a cell, the transport of that signal to another cell, and the transduction of that signal into a response. In this chapter, we begin by exploring each of these steps in cell signaling, looking at the molecular and cellular details of how signaling systems function. We then examine the systems-level functioning of signaling systems, using the endocrine systems of animals as an example to illustrate the ways in which signaling systems are organized. ■

■ OVERVIEW

Everything that an animal does involves communication among cells. Moving, digesting food, and even reading this chapter all require the coordinated action of thousands of individual cells engaging in constant communication. Communication between cells occurs when a signaling cell sends a signal to a *target cell*, usually in the form of a chemical messenger. Figure 4.2 summarizes the principal types of cell signaling in animals. Adjacent cells can communicate via direct contact between extracellular matrix and membrane proteins, in a process termed juxtacrine communication, or through channels called **gap junctions** that span the membranes of two adjacent cells. However, the majority of cells do not make direct physical contact with each other. Thus, most cell signaling is indirect, and begins when one cell releases a chemical messenger into its environment. The chemical messenger then travels through the extracellular fluids until it reaches the target cell. At the target cell, the chemical messenger binds to a **receptor**, changing the shape of the receptor and activating **signal transduction pathways** that cause a response within the target cell. Interactions between chemical messengers and receptors are highly specific, allowing precise communication of signals between cells.

Chemical messengers can travel from a signaling cell to nearby target cells by diffusion in a process called **paracrine** communication. These messengers can even affect the signaling cell, in a process called **autocrine** communication. But, as we discussed in Chapter 1: Introduction to Physiological Principles, the rate of diffusion is limited by distance, and thus diffusion is insufficient to carry signals to distant target cells. For long-distance cell-to-cell communication, animals use the **endocrine system** and the **nervous system**. In

FIGURE 4.2 **An overview of cell signaling within an individual**

Cells communicate either directly, via aqueous pores that connect adjacent cells, or indirectly, when the signaling cell releases a chemical messenger into the extracellular environment. **(a)** Direct cell signaling can occur through pores called gap junctions. **(b)** Paracrine signaling occurs when chemical messengers diffuse from the signaling cell to nearby target cells, where they bind to receptors and initiate signal transduction pathways that cause a response. Autocrine signaling is similar except that the chemical messenger causes a response in the signaling cell. **(c)** Endocrine signaling occurs when chemical messengers called

hormones travel long distances via the circulatory system. When the hormone reaches the target cell it binds to a receptor, initiates signal transduction pathways, and causes a response. **(d)** In neural signaling, electrical signals travel across long distances within a single cell. The electrical signal then either passes directly to the target cell via gap junctions, or triggers the release of a chemical messenger called a neurotransmitter. The neurotransmitter carries the signal to the target cell by diffusing across a short distance, where it binds to receptors on the target cell, initiates signal transduction pathways, and causes a response.

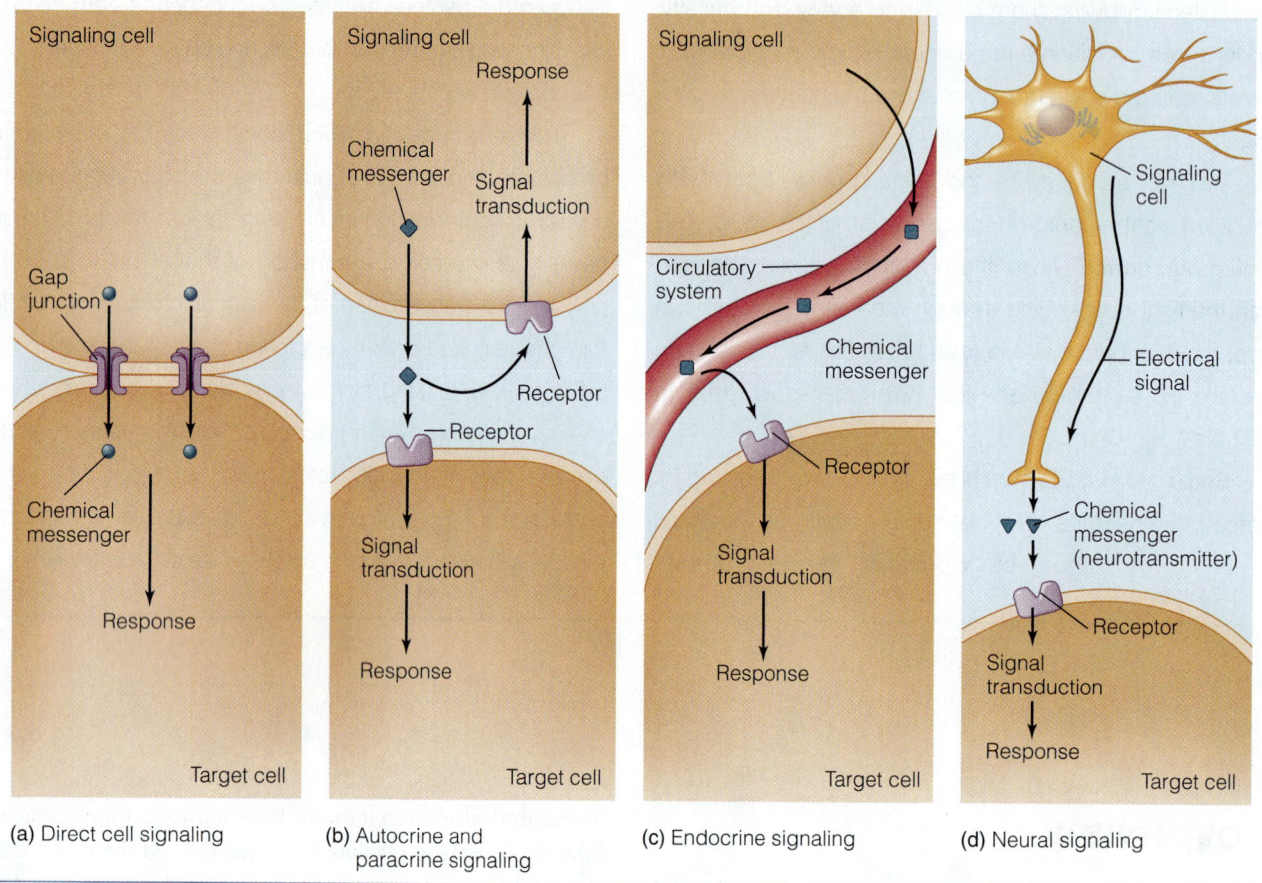

(a) Direct cell signaling

(b) Autocrine and paracrine signaling

(c) Endocrine signaling

(d) Neural signaling

the endocrine system, the circulatory system carries the chemical messenger from the signaling cell to the target cell. These endocrine messengers are called **hormones**. In the nervous system, an electrical signal travels within a single cell (the neuron), potentially across long distances. This electrical signal can be directly transferred to an adjacent cell via gap junctions, but in many neurons, the electrical signal results in the release of a chemical messenger called a **neurotransmitter** that diffuses to the target cell over a very short distance. There are also some neurons that release their neurotransmitters into the circulation. In this case the signaling molecule is called a **neurohormone**. Animals can also send chemical messengers into the external

environment, where they can be detected by other organisms. When this inter-individual communication occurs between members of the same species, the chemical messengers are termed **pheromones**, and when it occurs between members of different species, the chemical messengers are termed **allelochemicals** or *allelomones*.

Although these systems appear to be rather distinct, they actually share many features at the biochemical level. In this chapter, we first examine the biochemical basis of cell signaling, outlining the shared features of different signaling systems. We look at how cells release chemical messengers, how these messengers travel to the target cell, how they bind to receptors, and how they exert their effects through signal transduction pathways. We devote much of this chapter to a discussion of the fundamental properties of receptors and signal transduction mechanisms, not only because these processes are involved in the regulation of every physiological system, but also because you will encounter receptors and signal transduction mechanisms many times throughout this book. We then step back from the cellular details of communications mechanisms to take a closer look at one of the important cellular communication systems in animals: the endocrine system.

THE BIOCHEMICAL BASIS OF CELL SIGNALING

Cells are separated from their environment by a phospholipid membrane. Thus, any chemical messenger traveling between two cells must first pass from the aqueous cytoplasm of the signaling cell, through its lipid membrane, and into the aqueous extracellular fluid. At the target cell the messenger must then get its signal across the lipid membrane of the target cell into its aqueous cytoplasm. Because most chemicals are either soluble in aqueous solutions (hydrophilic) or soluble in lipids (hydrophobic), sending a chemical messenger from one cell to another presents a substantial challenge. For example, hydrophobic chemical messengers can pass through cell membranes, but do not dissolve well in aqueous fluids such as cytoplasm or blood. Hydrophilic chemical messengers are soluble in the cytoplasm and extracellular fluids, but do not pass through cell membranes. These fundamental chemical properties pose a problem that cells must solve in order to communicate with each other.

General Features of Cell Signaling

Cells can circumvent the problem of moving a hydrophilic chemical messenger through the lipid environment of the membrane by communicating via gap junctions. Gap junctions are specialized protein complexes that connect the cytoplasms of two adjacent cells (Figure 4.3). Gap junctions are composed of interlocking cylindrical proteins (called connexins in vertebrates, or innexins in invertebrates) assembled in groups of four or six to form doughnut-like pores (hemichannels or connexons) in the cell membrane. The hemichannels of two adjacent cells come together to form a pore between the two cells. Gap junctions are permeable to a variety of small hydrophilic molecules, including Ca^{2+} and **cAMP** (cyclic **adenosine** monophosphate), as well as some other small hydrophilic signaling molecules. Thus, some hydrophilic chemical messengers can travel from the signaling cell to the target cell via gap

junctions without having to pass through the lipids of the membrane.

We can demonstrate that two cells are connected via gap junctions by injecting a fluorescent dye that cannot cross the cell membrane into one of the cells. If gap junctions connect two cells, dye that is injected into one cell will diffuse through the gap junctions into the adjacent cell (if the dye is small enough to pass through the pore), and both cells will start to fluoresce. If no gap junctions are present, the dye will remain in the first cell because it is unable to cross the membrane, and the second cell will not fluoresce.

In most physiological situations, direct communication via gap junctions involves the movement of ions between cells. The movement of ions into or out of a cell can act as a signal by causing a change in the membrane potential (see Chapter 3: Chemistry, Biochemistry, and Cell Physiology) that triggers a response in the target cell. This rapid communication of signals between adjacent cells is a simple way to coordinate cellular responses. As we see in later chapters, the movement of ions through gap junctions helps to coordinate the contraction of smooth and cardiac muscle, and is involved in the transmission of electrical signals between some nerve cells. Other small molecules can also move between

FIGURE 4.3 The structure of gap junctions

Gap junctions are protein complexes that form aqueous pores between adjacent cells. Proteins called connexins (in vertebrates) or innexins (in invertebrates) form the structure of the gap junction.

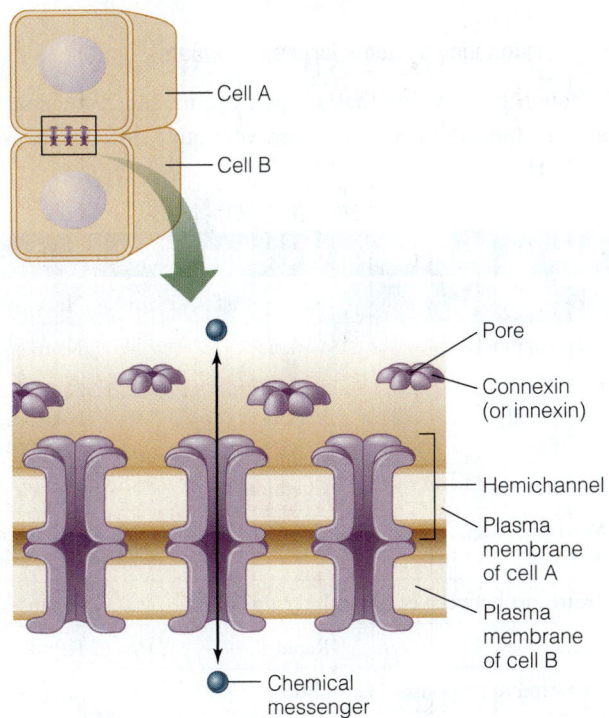

cells via gap junctions, including a variety of intracellular signaling molecules such as cAMP. However, gap junctions are not simply passive pores. They are relatively selective and allow only certain molecules to move between cells. The ability of a substance to pass through a gap junction depends on its molecular weight, its shape, its net charge, and specific interactions between the substance and the connexins that make up the gap junctions in a given cell. By allowing certain molecules to pass directly from one cell to another, gap junctions play a critical role in coordinating physiological responses at the tissue level. Gap junctions can also be opened and closed to regulate communication of substances between cells. Increased intracellular calcium and decreased intracellular pH both cause gap junctions to close. The number of gap junctions connecting two cells can also be regulated on a physiological time scale.

Direct communication via gap junctions is a very efficient way to send signals, but gap junctions can only form between adjacent cells. Animals need other strategies for sending signals to more distant cells, or to neighboring cells that are not connected by gap junctions. This kind of signaling is called *indirect cell signaling*, and involves three steps:

1. Release of a chemical messenger from the signaling cell into the extracellular environment

2. Transport of the chemical messenger through the extracellular environment to the target cell

3. Communication of the signal to the target cell via receptor binding

Indirect signaling systems form a continuum

Although the systems that animals use for indirect signaling are often discussed as if they were quite different from each other, they are actually just specialized ways of achieving the same result. Table 4.1 shows some of the similarities and differences between the various types of cellular communication. In general, autocrine, paracrine, neural, endocrine, and inter-individual chemical communication systems differ largely in the type of cell involved in messenger secretion and in the way that the messenger is transported to the target cell. In contrast, the mechanisms governing the release of the chemical messenger from the signaling cell, the types of chemical messengers utilized, and the mechanisms for communicating the signal to the target cell are very similar among systems.

The most important distinction between types of signaling is in their maximum signaling distance. Diffusion occurs very slowly across long distances (see Chapter 1: Introduction to Physiological Principles). Because autocrine and paracrine signals move by diffusion, their maximum signaling distance is short. The nervous system and the endocrine systems use different mechanisms to overcome this limitation of diffusion. The endocrine system uses the circulatory system to transport molecules across long distances. In contrast, cell-to-cell communication in the nervous system occurs by diffusion across short distances at a structure called the **synapse**. Long-distance communication in the nervous system occurs within a single neuronal cell, using electrical signals. The unique structure of neurons, and the properties of the electrical signals called **action potentials**, allow signals to be communicated across long distances within a single cell. These properties are discussed in more detail in Chapter 5: Neuron Structure and Function. However, the distinction between nervous and endocrine communication is somewhat blurry, as some neurons can secrete neurotransmitters into the circulatory system, in which case the messenger is termed a **neurohormone**.

Table 4.1 Comparison of systems for cell-to-cell communication				
	Autocrine/Paracrine	**Nervous**	**Endocrine**	**Inter-Individual**
Secretory cell	Various	Neural	Endocrine	Exocrine and various epithelial cells
Target cell	Various	Neuron, muscle, adipose, endocrine, exocrine	Various	Sensory and neural
Signal type	Chemical	Electrical and chemical	Chemical	Chemical
Maximum signaling distance	Short	Can be long intracellularly, short across synapse	Long	Very long
Transport between cells	Interstitial fluid	Synapse	Circulatory fluids	External environment
Speed	Rapid	Rapid	Slower	Various
Duration of response	Short	Short	Longer	Various

Most neural cells make specific contact with their target cells at a synapse, insuring that the signal reaches the correct target cell. In contrast, once a hormone is released into the circulation by an endocrine cell, it has the potential to contact almost every tissue in the body. However, endocrine communication is also extremely specific because only target cells that express appropriate receptors respond to a circulating hormone, while cells that lack the receptor do not.

The hormones of the endocrine system are secreted by a variety of tissues. In the vertebrates, many hormones are secreted by specialized **endocrine glands**. These glands lack ducts and release hormones directly into the extracellular fluid. The hormones then move across the walls of the blood vessels into the circulatory system for transport around the body (Figure 4.4). Endocrine hormones play a wide variety of physiological roles, including regulating reproduction, growth and development, maintaining homeostasis, and responding to the environment. We discuss the roles of the endocrine system in more detail later in the chapter.

The longest-distance chemical communication occurs between individuals via pheromones and allelochemicals. Pheromones are important sexual signals that are involved in attracting mates in many species (see Chapter 7: Sensory Systems and Chapter 16: Reproductive Physiology for more information about pheromones). In many species, pheromones are produced in **exocrine glands** (Figure 4.4) that secrete chemicals into ducts that lead to the surface of the body (including the skin, the respiratory surfaces, and the surface of the gut). Exocrine glands also produce secretions in addition to pheromones that perform a variety of physiological roles. For example, **saliva** and pancreatic secretions are involved in digesting food. Pheromones can also be released by a variety of nonglandular tissues. For example, urine contains a wide variety of pheromones in many species of vertebrates.

Although each type of cell-to-cell communication can easily be distinguished based on the maximum distance of signaling (Table 4.1), these types of communication have many features in common at the biochemical level. Therefore, in the next sections we begin our consideration of the biochemical basis of cell signaling without separating the different types of signaling used by animals. In this way, we can clearly see how cells have solved the general problem of sending chemical signals across the cell membrane when direct communication is not possible.

The structure of the messenger determines the type of signaling mechanism

The chemical structure of the messenger is the critical property that affects the way in which indirect signaling is accomplished. Hydrophobic messengers use different mechanisms

---

FIGURE 4.4 The structure of exocrine and endocrine glands

Exocrine glands secrete chemicals into ducts that lead to the surface of the body, whereas endocrine glands secrete hormones directly into the extracellular fluid where they diffuse into the circulatory system.

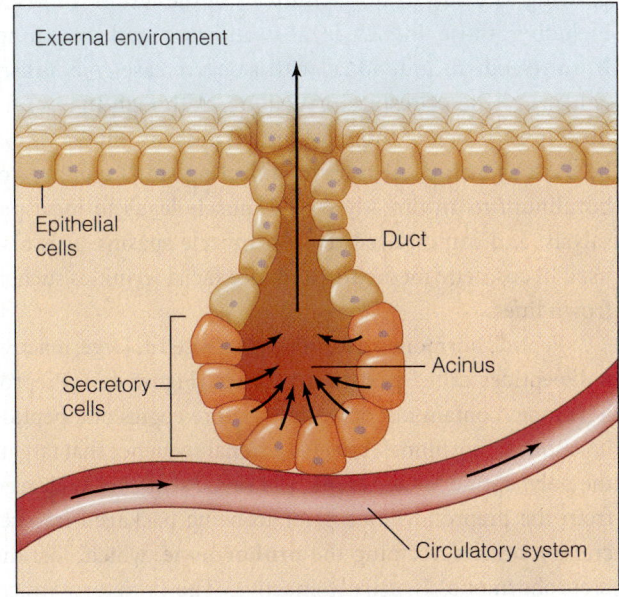

(a) Exocrine gland

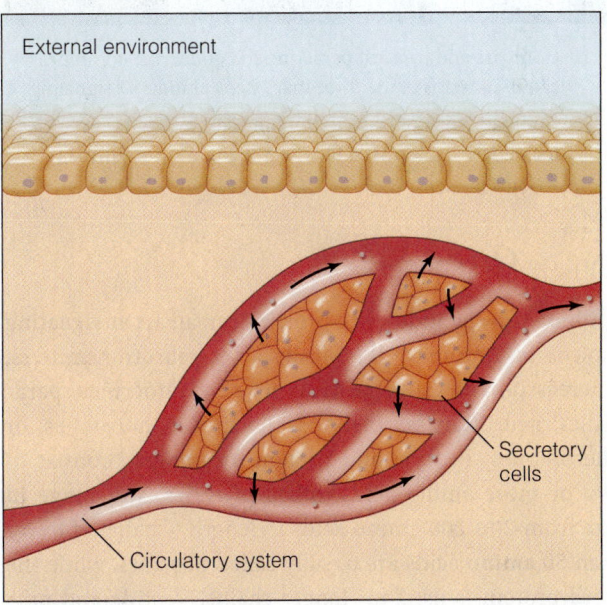

(b) Endocrine gland

Table 4.2   A comparison of hydrophilic and hydrophobic chemical messengers

	Hydrophilic Messengers	Hydrophobic Messengers
Storage	Intracellular vesicles	Synthesized on demand
Secretion	Exocytosis	Diffusion across membrane
Transport	Dissolved in extracellular fluids	Short distances: dissolved in extracellular fluid Long distances: bound to carrier proteins
Receptor	Transmembrane	Intracellular or transmembrane
Effects	Rapid	Slower or rapid

for signaling than do hydrophilic messengers, because hydrophobic messengers can diffuse freely across cell membranes, whereas hydrophilic messengers cannot. Table 4.2 summarizes the similarities and differences between hydrophilic and hydrophobic chemical messengers in each step of indirect cell signaling.

There are six main classes of chemicals that are known to participate in cellular signaling in animals: peptides, steroids, amines, fatty acid derivatives, purines, and gases. Almost all of the known vertebrate hormones are peptides, steroids, or amines, whereas there are examples of all six classes of messengers acting as autocrine messengers, paracrine messengers, or neurotransmitters. In the next sections we look at each of these main classes of chemical messengers to see how their biochemical properties affect their release from the signaling cell, transport through the extracellular fluid, and actions on the target cell.

CONCEPT CHECK

1. Compare and contrast paracrine and endocrine communication in terms of the three main steps of indirect signaling.
2. Compare and contrast hydrophilic and hydrophobic messengers in terms of the three main steps of indirect signaling.

Peptide Messengers

Amino acids, peptides, and proteins can all act as signaling molecules. Amino acids typically act as neurotransmitters, whereas peptides and proteins may be autocrines, paracrines, neurotransmitters, neurohormones, hormones, or pheromones. Peptide and protein messengers consist of two or more amino acids linked in series, and range in size from 2 to 200 amino acids in length. Chains of fewer than 50 amino acids are usually called peptides, while the word protein is used for longer chains. Peptide and protein messengers are hydrophilic chemicals that cannot diffuse across the membranes, but are soluble in aqueous solutions.

Peptide messengers are released by exocytosis

Peptide and protein messengers are synthesized on the rough endoplasmic reticulum along with most of the other proteins destined for secretion from the cell. The peptides are then packaged into vesicles for either immediate release or storage for later use. Most of the peptide hormones and neurotransmitters and many paracrine messengers are synthesized in advance and stored for later release, whereas paracrine peptides such as the **cytokines** are synthesized only on demand. We can see the importance of regulated exocytosis of stored messengers by examining the effects of botulinum toxin, a protein produced by the bacterium *Clostridium botulinum*. This protein blocks the regulated exocytosis of neurotransmitters traveling between nerves and muscles, preventing muscle contraction and causing paralysis. Exposure to a large dose of this toxin causes the disease botulism, which is characterized by weakness and paralysis, generally starting in the area of the head and progressing to paralysis of the muscles of the rest of the body, including those involved in swallowing and breathing. If untreated, an individual with a severe case of botulism is likely to die of respiratory failure. Although the botulinum toxin is one of the most potent poisons known, it can be used as a medical therapy. Injecting small amounts of botulinum toxin directly into a muscle leads to local paralysis, and can be used to treat muscle spasms. It is also used in cosmetic medicine to reduce facial wrinkles such as frown lines.

Peptide hormones are often synthesized as large, inactive polypeptides called **preprohormones** (Figure 4.5). Preprohormones contain not only one or more copies of a peptide hormone or hormones, but also a signal sequence that targets the polypeptide for secretion. The signal sequence is cleaved from the preprohormone prior to being packaged into secretory vesicles, forming the **prohormone**, which, like the preprohormone, is usually inactive. The secretory vesicle contains proteolytic enzymes that cut the prohormone into the active hormone or hormones. The signaling cell then releases the active peptide hormone by exocytosis.

FIGURE 4.5 **Synthesis of peptide hormones**

Peptide hormones are synthesized by ribosomes on the rough endoplasmic reticulum, often as large preprohormones. The preprohormone enters the rough endoplasmic reticulum, where the signal sequence is cleaved off. The resulting prohormone is packaged into vesicles that move to the Golgi apparatus for further processing and sorting. In the Golgi apparatus, the prohormone is packaged into secretory vesicles, where it is cleaved into active hormone and one or more peptide fragments. The secretory vesicle fuses with the plasma membrane, releasing its contents by exocytosis.

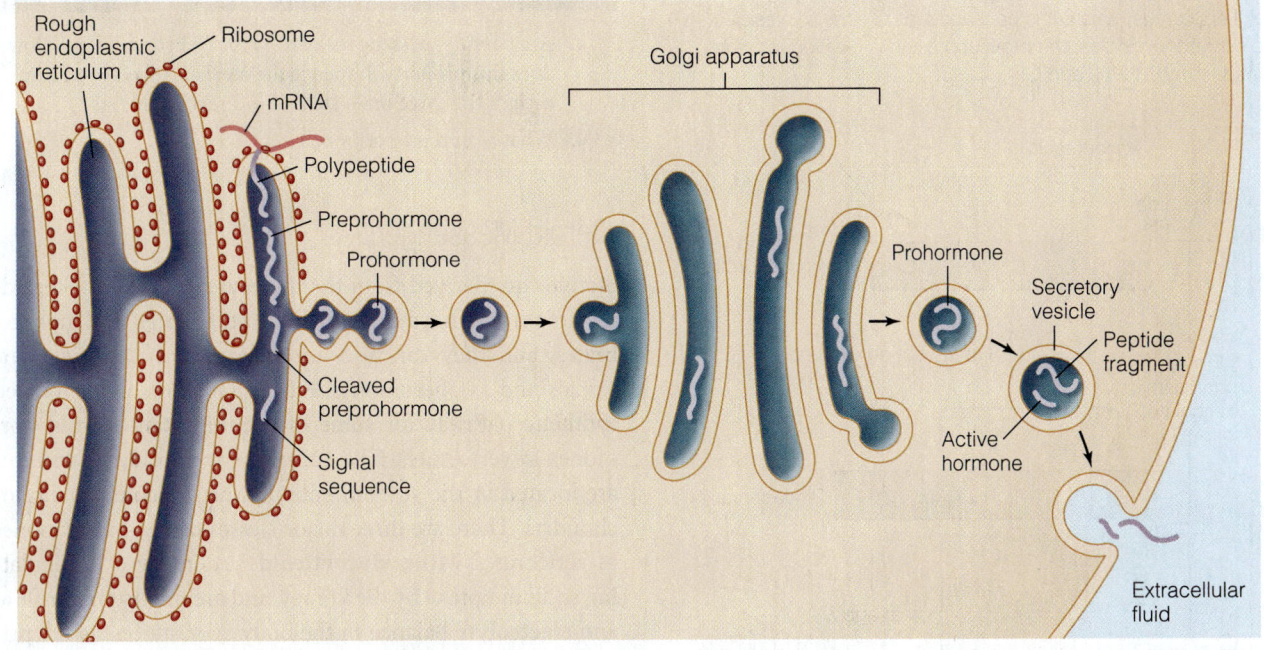

Figure 4.6 shows an example of a preprohormone, the one containing arginine vasopressin (AVP), also known as **antidiuretic** hormone (ADH). Ribosomes on the exterior of the rough endoplasmic reticulum translate the preprovasopressin mRNA into protein. The signal peptide directs the newly synthesized polypeptide to the interior of the rough endoplasmic reticulum. The signal peptide is then cleaved off, forming provasopressin, which is packaged into secretory vesicles. In the secretory vesicles it is cleaved into three different peptides: vasopressin, neurophysin, and a glycoprotein. Vasopressin is a hormone that acts on the kidney to regulate the reabsorption of water (see Chapter 13: Ion and Water Balance). The functions of neurophysin and the glycoprotein are not yet well understood, but they may be involved in the proper sorting and secretion of arginine vasopressin.

Peptide messengers dissolve in extracellular fluids

Once released from the signaling cell, a chemical messenger must move through the extracellular fluid to the target cell. Hydrophilic chemical messengers such as peptides and proteins dissolve well in aqueous solutions and can easily move from the signaling cell to the target cell, either by diffusion or carried by the circulatory system. Peptide messengers are usually broken down and removed from extracellular fluids by proteolytic enzymes. The rate of this breakdown can be measured as the messenger's **half-life**—the time taken to reduce the concentration of the messenger by half. Peptide messengers generally have half-lives ranging from a few seconds to a few hours. As a result of these short half-lives, the signaling cell must continually produce messengers in order to cause a sustained response in a target cell.

Peptides bind to transmembrane receptors

Hydrophilic signaling molecules such as peptides and proteins cannot pass through the membrane of the target cell, but instead bind to **transmembrane receptors** (Figure 4.7). The extracellular portion of a transmembrane receptor contains the *ligand-binding domain*. **Ligand** is the general term for any molecule that binds specifically to a protein. Thus, a peptide chemical messenger acts as a ligand for a transmembrane receptor protein. Transmembrane receptors also have a membrane-spanning (*transmembrane*) domain and an *intracellular domain*. When a ligand binds to the ligand-binding domain of a transmembrane receptor, the receptor changes shape, communicating the signal carried by the ligand across the cell membrane, without the ligand itself needing to cross the lipid-rich membrane. Transmembrane

FIGURE 4.6 **The synthesis of arginine vasopressin (AVP)**

AVP is synthesized on the rough endoplasmic reticulum as a large polypeptide, preprovasopressin, which contains a signal peptide (SP), AVP, neurophysin (NPH), and a glycoprotein (GP). In the rough endoplasmic reticulum the signal peptide is cleaved off, producing provasopressin. The provasopressin passes to the Golgi apparatus, where it is packaged into secretory vesicles. In the secretory vesicles, the provasopressin is cleaved into three peptides: AVP, NPH, and GP.

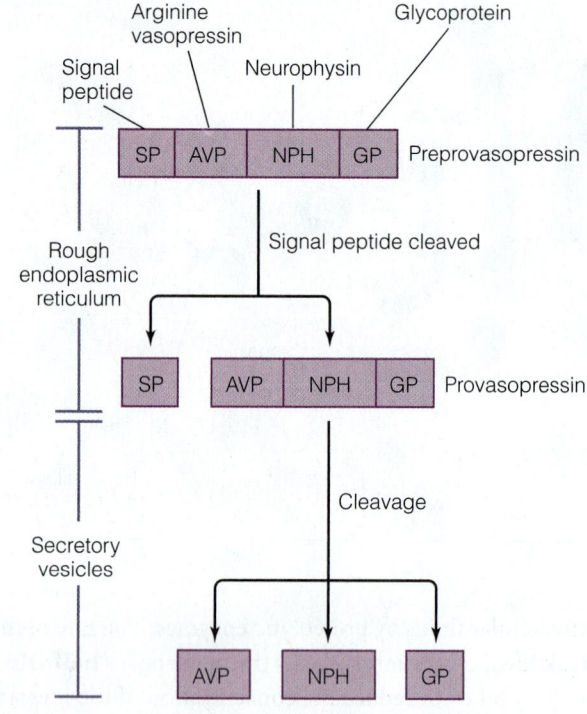

FIGURE 4.7 **The structure of a transmembrane receptor**

(a) Transmembrane receptors have an extracellular ligand-binding domain, a membrane-spanning domain, and an intracellular domain. **(b)** When the messenger (ligand) binds to the receptor, the conformation of the receptor changes.

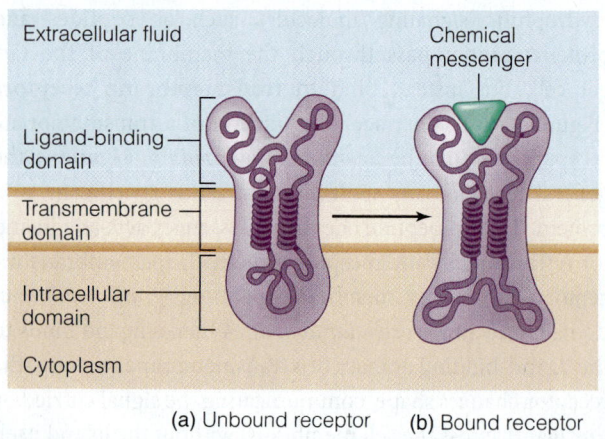

(a) Unbound receptor   (b) Bound receptor

receptors activate cytoplasmic signal transduction pathways that cause rapid changes in the activity of the target cell, usually by altering membrane potential, or phosphorylating and modifying the activity of existing proteins.

CONCEPT CHECK

3. Are peptide messengers hydrophilic or hydrophobic? How does this property influence the mechanisms involved in each of the three main steps of indirect signaling?
4. What is a preprohormone?

Steroid Messengers

Steroids are derived from the molecule cholesterol. Steroids are important hormones in both vertebrates and invertebrates, and they can also act as paracrine and autocrine signals and as pheromones. Figure 4.8 shows a generalized synthetic pathway for some of the important steroid hormones in vertebrates. The enzymes for steroid biosynthesis are located in the smooth endoplasmic reticulum or mitochondria. There are three major classes of steroid hormones in vertebrates. **Mineralocorticoids** are involved in regulating sodium uptake by the kidney, and are important for fluid and **electrolyte** balance in the body. Aldosterone is the primary mineralocorticoid in mammals. We discuss the mineralocorticoids in more detail in Chapter 13: Ion and Water Balance. The **glucocorticoids** (**cortisol**, cortisone, and corticosterone), also called the stress hormones, have widespread actions including increasing glucose production, increasing the breakdown of proteins into amino acids, increasing the release of fatty acids from adipose tissue, and regulating the immune system and inflammatory responses. The *reproductive hormones* (**estrogens**, **progesterone**, **testosterone**), which we discuss in Chapter 16: Reproductive Physiology, regulate sex-specific characteristics and reproduction.

The principal steroids in invertebrates are the *ecdysteroids,* which play an important role in the regulation of molting in arthropods. Much less is known about the role of these steroids in other invertebrate phyla, but they are thought to play a role in development and reproduction.

Because all steroids contain several carbon rings, some synthetic chemicals with similar structures bind to steroid receptors and mimic or block the action of the natural hormone. Environmental exposures to chemicals such as the insecticide DDT have been associated with low sperm counts and increased incidence of breast and prostate cancer in humans, developmental abnormalities such as reduced penis size and feminization in animals including fish and alligators, and interference with molting in crustaceans. Chemicals such as DDT bind to and activate the receptor for estrogen, and other chemicals

FIGURE 4.8 Synthetic pathways for some of the biologically active steroids in vertebrates

Cholesterol is the precursor for the three main classes of vertebrate steroids: the glucocorticoids (including cortisol and corticosterone), the mineralocorticoids (including aldosterone), and the sex steroids (including testosterone and estradiol).

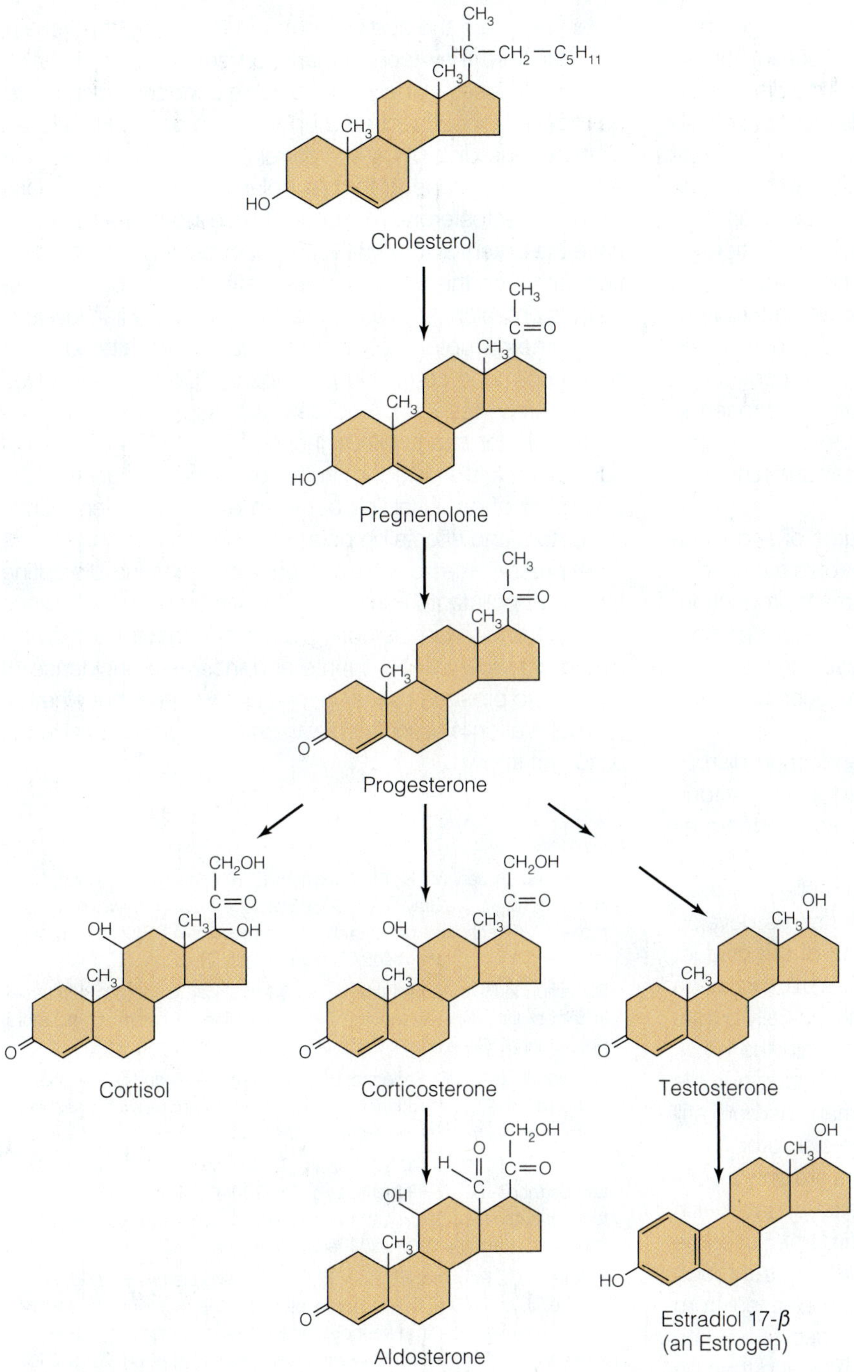

Cholesterol

Pregnenolone

Progesterone

Cortisol

Corticosterone

Testosterone

Aldosterone

Estradiol 17-β
(an Estrogen)

such as some pesticides interfere with other aspects of steroid metabolism—a phenomenon called **endocrine disruption**. In addition to synthetic chemicals such as DDT, human waste can also be an important source of endocrine disruptors. See

Box 4.1: Challenges to Homeostasis: Endocrine Disruptors for more details about this important environmental issue.

Steroids bind to carrier proteins

Because steroids can easily pass through biological membranes, they cannot be stored within the cell, and thus must be synthesized on demand. They then diffuse across the membrane of the signaling cell and into the extracellular fluid. Steroids can diffuse across short distances dissolved in extracellular fluids, but for long-distance transport they are usually bound to **carrier proteins**. Some steroids have specific carrier proteins (termed binding globulins), while others bind nonspecifically to generalized carrier proteins, such as **albumin**, the principal carrier protein in vertebrate blood. Carrier proteins help hydrophobic chemical messengers dissolve in aqueous solutions by surrounding the hydrophobic messenger and isolating it from the aqueous solution. Hydrophobic chemical messengers bind reversibly to their carrier proteins, resulting in an equilibrium between free and bound messengers. As described by the law of mass action (see Chapter 3: Chemistry, Biochemistry, and Cell Physiology), in an equilibrium system the amounts of reactants and products are always in balance. Thus, you can describe the equilibrium between a chemical messenger and its carrier protein using the following equation:

$$M + C \leftrightarrow MC$$

where M is the concentration of unbound messenger, C is the concentration of carrier protein, and MC is the concentration of messenger bound to carrier protein. If the amount of free messenger increases, the equilibrium will shift to the right, increasing the amount of messenger bound to carrier protein. If the amount of free messenger decreases, the equilibrium will shift to the left, decreasing the amount of messenger bound to carrier protein.

CHALLENGES TO HOMEOSTASIS 4.1

ENDOCRINE DISRUPTORS

A sewage outfall (the place where a sewer or sewage treatment plant discharges into a river, lake, or the ocean) acts as a point source of pollution. Close to the outfall the discharged sewage can contain high levels of chemicals that have physiological effects on animals. For example, populations of teleost fish naturally contain low levels of so-called *intersex* individuals that have both male and female sexual characteristics. Scientists in England discovered that populations of fish living close to sewage outfalls have a higher proportion of intersex individuals than populations located farther from the outfalls. Sewage coming from the outfalls contains high levels of estrogens excreted by women on birth control pills or hormone replacement therapy. Exposure to estrogen in the water coming out of the sewage outfalls tends to feminize the male fish, causing them to be intersex and rendering them sterile.

Agricultural runoff provides another source of endocrine disruptors. In many countries, anabolic steroids are used in livestock to improve growth and increase meat production. These steroids and their breakdown products are present in the urine of the animals and thus are present in the runoff from agricultural operations. This runoff has been shown to masculinize female fish.

Industrial chemicals can also act as endocrine disruptors. For example, tributyltin is widely used as an antifouling agent in marine paint, because it prevents invertebrates such as barnacles from settling on the hulls of ships. Unfortunately, tributyltin causes a condition called imposex in mollusks such as snails. Imposex female snails develop a penis that grows and blocks the opening of the oviduct preventing the release of eggs. In mild cases, reproduction is reduced, but in extreme cases the female actually bursts due to the pressure of the growing eggs within the body. Tributyltin is now banned for use on smaller boats, but it is still used on large ships, and the water in many harbors still contains detectable levels of this endocrine disruptor.

You might think that endocrine disruptors are only a concern for populations living in polluted areas (such as fish near sewage outfalls or snails in polluted harbors), but some of these chemicals can travel very long distances through the atmosphere and the ocean. Pollutants released from sources in the highly populated and developed temperate regions of the globe can travel via these routes and then be deposited and accumulate even in very distant locations. For example, a wide variety of endocrine disruptors, including polychlorinated biphenyls (PCBs) and DDT, have been found in the tissues of Arctic marine mammals and seabirds, including that iconic Arctic mammal, the polar bear.

Polar bears are the apex predator in the Arctic food chain, and because they feed primarily on seal blubber, they receive high doses of these lipid-soluble endocrine disruptors, as they are bioconcentrated up the food chain. High levels of endocrine disruptors are correlated with increased levels of progesterone in female polar bears and decreased levels of testosterone in males. These hormonal changes have the potential to negatively impact polar bear reproduction, although the population-level effects of endocrine disruptors on polar bears are currently unknown. High levels of endocrine disruptors are also associated with altered levels of the hormone cortisol in polar bears. Cortisol is involved in the stress response and can also supress the immune system. Polar bears with higher levels of PCBs in their tissues have a disrupted immune response, suggesting the possibility of a causal link between exposure to endocrine disruptors and effects on polar bear health.

At present, the possible existence of endocrine-disrupting effects of pollutants in humans is controversial. High tissue levels of endocrine-disrupting chemicals have been associated with low sperm counts and increased incidence of breast and prostate cancer in men and women, but whether this correlation is associated with an underlying causal effect is not yet known.

References

- Ankley, G. T., Jensen, K. M., Makynen, E. A., Kahl, M. D., Korte, J. J., Hornung, M. W., . . . Gray, L. E. (2003). Effects of the androgenic growth promoter 17-β-trenbolone on fecundity and reproductive endocrinology of the fathead minnow. *Environmental Toxicology and Chemistry, 22*, 1350–1360.

- Bahamonde P. A., Munkittrick, K. R., & Martyniuk, C. J. (2013). Intersex in teleost fish: Are we distinguishing endocrine disruption from natural phenomena? *General and Comparative Endocrinology, 192*, 25–35.

- Jenssen, B. M. (2006). Endocrine-disrupting chemicals and climate change: A worse-case combination for Arctic marine mammals and seabirds? *Environmental Health Perspectives, 114* (Supp.1), 76–80.

- Orlando, E. F., Kolok, A. S., Binzcik, G. A., Gates, J. L., Horton, M. K., Lambright, C. S., . . . Guillette, L. J., Jr. (2004). Endocrine-disrupting effects of cattle feedlot effluent on an aquatic sentinel species, the fathead minnow. *Environmental Health Perspectives 112*, 353–358.

- Oskam, I. C., Ropstad, E., Dahl, E., Lie, E., Derocher, A. E., Wiig, O., . . . Skaare, J. U. (2003). Organochlorines affect the major androgenic hormone, testosterone, in male polar bears (*Ursus maritimus*) at Svalbard. *Journal of Toxicology and Environmental Health Part A, 66*, 2119–2139.

- Sonne, C. (2010). Health effects from long-range transported contaminants in Arctic top predators: An integrated review based on studies of polar bears and relevant model species. *Environment International, 36*, 461–491.

- Titley-O'Neal, C. P., Munkittrick, K.R., & Macdonald, B. A. (2011). The effects of organotin on female gastropods. *Journal of Environmental Monitoring, 13*, 2360–2388.

The binding of a hydrophobic messenger to its carrier proteins is outlined in Figure 4.9. When a signaling cell releases a chemical messenger into the extracellular fluid, the free concentration of the messenger is high in the local environment, and the messenger will tend to bind to its carrier protein. For most hydrophobic chemical messengers, more than 99 percent of the messenger binds to its carrier protein, but a small fraction of the messenger is always free in solution. Both free and bound messengers travel through the circulatory system to the target cell. At the target cell, the free messenger diffuses into the cell and binds to its receptor. The binding of the messenger to its receptor reduces the concentration of free messenger in the extracellular fluid adjacent to the target cell. The resulting low concentration of free messenger causes the bound messenger to dissociate from the carrier protein (because of the law of mass action), delivering the messenger to the target cell.

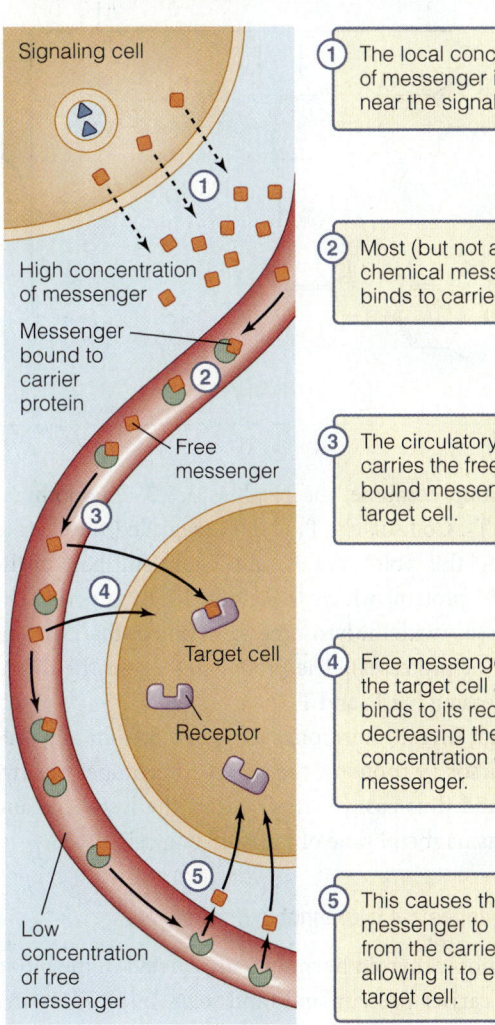

FIGURE 4.9 Transport of hydrophobic chemical messengers

Signaling cell

High concentration of messenger

Messenger bound to carrier protein

Free messenger

Target cell

Receptor

Low concentration of free messenger

1. The local concentration of messenger is high near the signaling cell.

2. Most (but not all) of the chemical messenger binds to carrier proteins.

3. The circulatory system carries the free and bound messenger to the target cell.

4. Free messenger enters the target cell and binds to its receptor, decreasing the concentration of free messenger.

5. This causes the bound messenger to dissociate from the carrier protein, allowing it to enter the target cell.

Because free and bound chemical messengers are in equilibrium, changes in the concentration of any of the reactants or products influence the concentrations of the others. Thus, increases in the amount of messenger that is released from the signaling cell will increase the amount of messenger delivered to the target cell. Conversely, increases in the concentration of the carrier protein will tend to decrease the concentration of free chemical messenger, whereas decreases in the concentration of carrier protein will increase the concentration of free messenger. As we discuss in the next section, the amount of free messenger influences the response of the target cell. Thus, changes in both the amount of messenger and the amount of carrier protein can affect cell signaling.

Steroids bind to intracellular receptors

The **lipophilic** steroids can easily cross the membrane of the target cell, and thus they can bind either to transmembrane receptors or to receptors inside the cell. The intracellular receptors are the best-studied class of steroid receptor. Once they bind to a steroid, intracellular steroid receptors act as transcription factors, controlling the expression of target genes. Because this pathway relies on changes in transcription and translation, there is a detectable lag time between binding of the messenger and observation of the initial effects. In contrast, when a steroid messenger binds to a transmembrane receptor, it activates a cytoplasmic signal transduction pathway, which causes rapid *nongenomic* effects that do not require changes in transcription or translation.

CONCEPT CHECK

5. What are the three main classes of steroid hormones in vertebrates?

6. Why are steroids usually bound to carrier proteins when transported in the blood?

Biogenic Amines

Amines are chemicals that possess an amine ($-NH_2$) group attached to a carbon atom. Amines that function in cellular signaling are termed **biogenic amines**. Many amines are synthesized from amino acids. The **catecholamines** (dopamine, norepinephrine, and epinephrine) are synthesized from the amino acid tyrosine. **Dopamine**, which is found in all animal taxa, acts as a neurotransmitter. **Norepinephrine** and **epinephrine** are known only from vertebrates, and can act as neurotransmitters, paracrines, and hormones. *Octopamine* and *tyramine*, which are also synthesized from the amino acid tyrosine, are important neurotransmitters in invertebrates. Although octopamine and tyramine have activity when administered to vertebrates, their physiological role in vertebrates is not clear. The **thyroid hormones** are synthesized from a polypeptide containing the amino acid tyrosine. These messengers are found only in vertebrates, and act as hormones. They are not thought to function as neurotransmitters or paracrines. **Serotonin**, which is synthesized from the amino acid tryptophan, is a neurotransmitter found in all animal taxa. **Melatonin**, which is also synthesized from the amino acid tryptophan, is found in almost all organisms and acts as a neurotransmitter and a hormone. In vertebrates, melatonin plays a critical role in regulating sleep-wake cycles and seasonal rhythms. Although melatonin is found in most invertebrate taxa, its role in these organisms is not well understood. As is the case in vertebrates, most evidence suggests that it is involved in the regulation of activity patterns. **Histamine** is synthesized from the amino acid histidine. This biogenic amine functions as a neurotransmitter and a paracrine signaling molecule in both vertebrates and invertebrates. Histamine plays an important role in immune responses and allergic reactions. **Acetylcholine**, a neurotransmitter found in all animals, is synthesized from choline, an amine that is not an amino acid, and acetyl-coenzyme A. It is the primary neurotransmitter at the neuromuscular junction of vertebrates, and because of its importance, and the fact that it is not synthesized from an amino acid, it is sometimes classified separately from the other biogenic amines.

Most biogenic amines are hydrophilic molecules that are packaged into vesicles and released into the extracellular fluid by exocytosis. They can either be synthesized on demand or be stored for later release. Because they are important neurotransmitters, we discuss the mechanisms for the synthesis and release of the catecholamines, acetylcholine, and serotonin in more detail in Chapter 5: Neuron Structure and Function. Here, we focus on the thyroid hormones, which are an interesting exception to the general rules governing the synthesis and release of biogenic amines.

Thyroid hormones diffuse across the membrane

Thyroid hormone synthesis begins when the enzyme iodinase adds one or more iodine molecules to tyrosine residues in the protein thyroglobulin (Figure 4.10). If a particular tyrosine residue is iodinated once, the resulting compound is called monoiodotyrosine (MIT). If a particular tyrosine residue is iodinated twice, the resulting compound is called diiodotyrosine (DIT). The iodinated tyrosine residues in the thyroglobulin molecule are then coupled via a covalent bond. If two DIT groups combine, the result is $3,5,3',5'$-tetraiodothyronine, called T_4 (or thyroxine). Alternatively, if one DIT group and

FIGURE 4.10 **Synthetic pathways for the thyroid hormones**

Thyroid hormone synthesis begins when the enzyme iodinase adds one or more iodine molecules to the amino acid tyrosine within the protein thyroglobulin. Monoiodotyrosine (MIT) has a single iodine molecule added per tyrosine residue; diiodotyrosine (DIT) has two iodine molecules per tyrosine residue. If one molecule of MIT and one molecule of DIT combine, they form triiodothyronine (T_3). Adding an additional molecule of DIT forms tetraiodothyronine (T_4), also known as thyroxine. Collectively, T_3 and T_4 are termed the thyroid hormones.

one MIT group combine, the result is $3,5,3'$ triiodothyronine, called T_3. Collectively, T_3 and T_4 are called the thyroid hormones. At this point, the T_3 and T_4 are still part of the thyroglobulin protein, which is packaged into vesicles. The vesicles then fuse with the lysosome, an organelle that contains proteinases (or proteases). The proteinases digest the thyroglobulin, releasing the T_3 and T_4.

Although thyroid hormones are derived from a hydrophilic precursor (a protein), the thyroid hormones are hydrophobic and thus easily diffuse out of the lysosome and cross the plasma membrane of the signaling cell.

Thyroid hormones are hydrophobic messengers

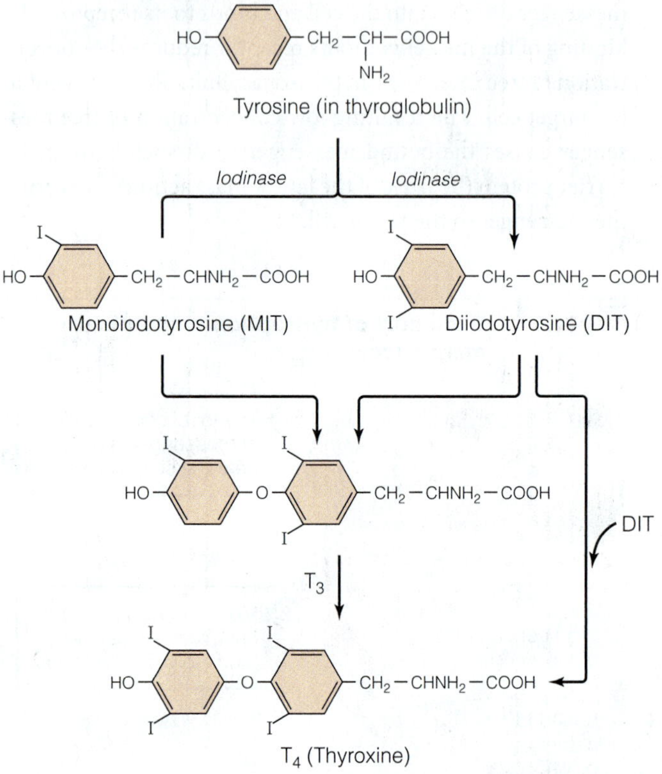

The hydrophobic thyroid hormones are carried in the blood bound to a carrier protein, and bind to an intracellular receptor in the target cell. Like all intracellular receptors for chemical messengers, the thyroid hormone receptor acts as a transcription factor when bound to thyroid hormone, altering the transcription of target genes. Thus, although thyroid hormones are derived from a protein, they behave more like steroid hormones than like peptide hormones. Thyroid hormones play an important role in setting metabolic rate and regulating body temperature in mammals (Chapter 15: Thermal Physiology).

> ### CONCEPT CHECK
>
> 7. Are amines hydrophilic or hydrophobic messengers? How does this affect their release, transport, and signaling?
> 8. Outline the ways in which thyroid hormone release, transport, and signaling differ from that of other biogenic amines.

Other Classes of Messenger

All hormones are peptides, steroids, or amines, but a number of other classes of molecules can act as neurotransmitters or paracrine chemical messengers, including certain lipids, purines, and even gases. Many of these molecules have only recently been identified as important chemical signaling molecules, but research in these areas is extremely active, because these molecules are involved in many important disease-related processes in humans, including **inflammation**, pain, and vascular disease.

Eicosanoids are lipid messengers

A class of lipids known as the **eicosanoids** can act as neurotransmitters and paracrine chemical messengers. The hydrophobic eicosanoids diffuse out of the membrane of the signaling cell and diffuse to the target cell, where they bind to transmembrane receptors. Most eicosanoids have an extremely short half-life in extracellular fluids, and degrade within a few seconds. As a result, they cannot be transported across long distances, and thus cannot act as hormones. Most eicosanoids are derivatives of arachidonic acid, a 20-carbon fatty acid common in plasma membrane phospholipids. The pathway for eicosanoid synthesis is shown in Figure 4.11. Eicosanoid synthesis proceeds through either the lipoxygenase pathway, which produces the *leukotrienes* and *lipoxins*, or the cyclooxygenase pathway, which produces

prostaglandins, *prostacyclins*, and *thromboxanes*. Prostaglandins are one of the most studied groups of eicosanoids because they are involved in pain perception. Many common painkillers (including aspirin and ibuprofen) work by blocking prostaglandin synthesis.

Eicosanoids can also function as neurotransmitters. For example, one of the eicosanoids is thought to bind to the cannabinoid receptor in the brain. These receptors were so named because they also bind to the drug tetrahydrocannabinoid (THC), a lipid that is the bioactive component of the marijuana plant, *Cannabis sativa*.

There are three known gaseous chemical messengers

Only three gases are known to act as chemical messengers in animals: nitric oxide, carbon monoxide, and hydrogen sulfide. **Nitric oxide** (NO) was the first gas identified as a chemical messenger, and a great deal is now known about its mechanisms of action. Nitric oxide is produced by the enzyme *nitric oxide synthase* (NOS), which catalyzes the reaction of the amino acid arginine with oxygen to produce nitric oxide and citrulline (another amino acid). Animals have several isoforms of NOS, some of which are **inducible** (synthesized in response to specific signals), and some of which are constitutive (present all the time). Like the eicosanoids, nitric oxide has an extremely short half-life (2–30 seconds) in extracellular fluids and thus can act as a paracrine messenger

FIGURE 4.11 **Synthetic pathway for eicosanoids**

Phospholipase A_2 catalyzes the cleavage of membrane phospholipids to form arachidonic acid, the substrate for eicosanoid synthesis. The cyclooxygenase pathway produces prostaglandins, prostacyclins, and thromboxanes. The lipoxygenase pathway produces leukotrienes.

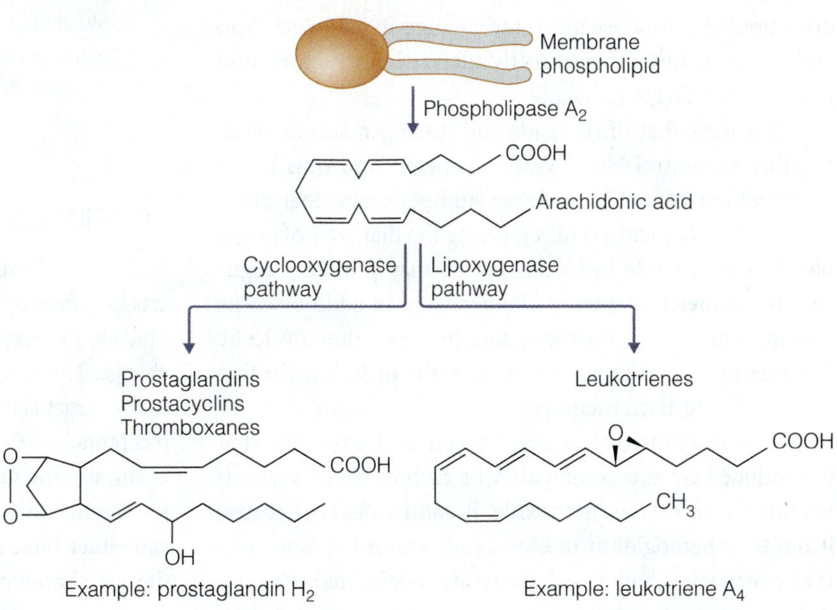

or neurotransmitter but cannot act as a hormone. Nitric oxide plays a critical role in regulating many physiological functions because it is a *vasodilator*. It causes the smooth muscle around blood vessels to relax, increasing the diameter of the blood vessel and causing more blood to flow into the local area. Nitric oxide is also important for paracrine communication in the immune system.

Because it is a gas, nitric oxide can freely diffuse across the cell membrane from the signaling cell to the target cell. Nitric oxide can act within the cell in several ways. One important action of nitric oxide is to bind to and activate the intracellular enzyme guanylate cyclase. Guanylate cyclase catalyzes the formation of cyclic cGMP, which then activates a specific protein kinase, which goes on to phosphorylate a variety of target proteins. The cGMP produced by guanylate cyclase is quickly removed from the cell by a series of enzymes termed **phosphodiesterases** (PDE), thus terminating the nitric oxide signal. Drugs such as Viagra block the isoform of PDE that is found in the smooth muscle cells surrounding blood vessels of the penis. Blocking PDE results in prolonged elevation of cGMP within the cell, causing the cells to relax and the blood vessels to vasodilate. The net result of this vasodilation is increased blood flow to the penis, which (as we discuss in Chapter 16: Reproductive Physiology) is necessary to sustain erection.

Like nitric oxide, hydrogen sulfide is a gaseous signaling molecule that is involved in the regulation of blood pressure. Hydrogen sulfide is produced from the amino acid cysteine by several enzymes that are present in the kidney, brain, and liver. Hydrogen sulfide relaxes the smooth muscle surrounding blood vessels by altering the function of a potassium channel on the muscle cell membrane. Hydrogen sulfide is an unusual signaling molecule in that it does not bind to a receptor and change its conformation and activity. Instead it directly alters the structure and function of a target molecule.

The ways that nitric oxide and hydrogen sulfide work together to control blood vessel diameter (and thus blood pressure) are not yet clear. Some studies suggest that nitric oxide is mainly involved in regulating the diameter of larger blood vessels, while hydrogen sulfide may primarily regulate the diameter of smaller blood vessels. In addition to its role in vasodilation, hydrogen sulfide is also thought to be involved in various processes in the brain, including the formation of long-term memory.

Carbon monoxide is best known as a toxic gas that is produced by the combustion of carbon-based fuels. If we breathe in carbon monoxide, it can be deadly because it binds to hemoglobin in blood cells and inhibits oxygen transport (see Chapter 11: Respiratory Systems). Despite its dangerous reputation, carbon monoxide is an important

signaling molecule that is produced naturally as a product of the degradation of heme molecules by the heme-oxygenase enzyme system. Like the other gaseous neurotransmitters, carbon monoxide is involved in blood vessel dilation. It plays a particularly important role in the blood vessels of the heart. Carbon monoxide is also synthesized in the nervous system. In the brain, it functions as a neurotransmitter and regulates a variety of functions, including the hypothalamo-pituitary axis of the endocrine system that we discuss later in this chapter.

Purines can act as neurotransmitters and paracrines

A variety of purines, including adenosine, adenosine monophosphate (AMP), **adenosine triphosphate** (ATP), and the guanine nucleotides, are known to act as neurotransmitters, **neuromodulators**, or paracrines. A neuromodulator is a cellular signaling molecule that alters the activity of other signaling molecules, such as neurotransmitters. Purines have a very wide range of functions. For example, adenosine acts on the immune system to promote wound healing, can change the rhythm of the heartbeat in vertebrates, and is a potent calming neurotransmitter in the brain. Purines are released from signaling cells via a variety of mechanisms. Adenosine can be moved across the membrane by specific proteins termed **nucleoside** transporters. Other purines are packaged into secretory vesicles, often along with other classes of neurotransmitters, and released by exocytosis. When involved in cellular signaling, purines bind to transmembrane receptors known as *purinergic* receptors.

CONCEPT CHECK

9. What are eicosanoids?
10. Name three gaseous signaling molecules, and one function that they share.

Communication of the Signal to the Target Cell

Each of the classes of chemical messengers described above exerts its effects by binding to a receptor protein. When a ligand binds to its receptor, the receptor undergoes a conformational change. This change in the shape of the receptor sends a signal to the target cell. Hydrophilic ligands bind to transmembrane receptors, and the conformational change of that receptor communicates the signal to the inside of the cell without the need for the ligand to cross the membrane. Hydrophobic ligands can either bind to transmembrane receptors or pass through the membrane of the target cell and bind to intracellular receptors. Because intracellular receptors are located within the cell (either in the cytoplasm or nucleus), changes in the shape of intracellular receptors can easily be communicated to other biochemical pathways inside the cell.

Ligand-receptor interactions are specific

Ligand-receptor interactions are extremely specific, because the ligand-binding site of a receptor has a particular shape, allowing only molecules sharing related structures to bind efficiently to the receptor. Just as only the correctly shaped key will open the lock on your door, only the correctly shaped ligand can bind to a given receptor (Figure 4.12a). Some chemicals with structures similar to the natural ligand can mimic the action of a ligand on its receptor. Chemicals that bind to and activate receptors are termed receptor **agonists** (Figure 4.12b). Chemicals that bind to but do not activate receptors are termed receptor **antagonists** because they prevent the binding of the natural ligand (Figure 4.12c). Many drugs are receptor agonists or antagonists. For example, tubocurarine is a plant compound that is the active ingredient in poison darts used by South American indigenous hunters to paralyze their prey. Tubocurarine binds to a receptor at the neuromuscular junction. Because tubocurarine is a receptor antagonist, binding of tubocurarine blocks the receptor, which prevents communication from nerves to muscles and causes paralysis.

Receptor type determines the cellular response

A target cell can respond to a ligand only if the appropriate receptor is expressed on or in the target cell. Two cells side by side in the body may be bathed in a chemical signal, but only the cell that possesses the appropriate receptor will respond. Thus, chemical signaling is a bit like a radio signal. Two people jogging side by side along a city street are both exposed to radio waves, but only the person who has a portable radio (the appropriate receptor for radio waves) can receive the information signal carried by the broadcast.

The hundreds of chemical messengers found in animals can be used in millions of combinations. But any given cell responds to only a fraction of these signals, depending on the types of receptors that are present in the cell. Although no cells in the body are capable of responding to all possible ligands, most cells express receptors for many types of ligands. It is the particular combination of receptors expressed by a cell that generates the specificity of cellular responses to different combinations of chemical signals.

Receptors have several domains

Receptors are large proteins that are composed of several domains. The ligand-binding domain contains the binding site for the chemical messenger. The remaining domains of

FIGURE 4.12 Ligand-receptor interactions

A ligand is a small molecule that binds specifically to a receptor, causing a response in the target cell. Both agonists and antagonists can bind to a receptor, but only agonists cause a response.

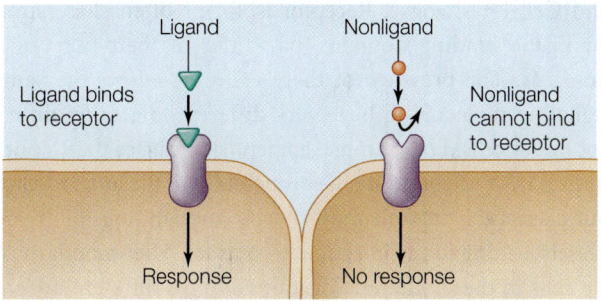

(a) Ligand binding causes a response

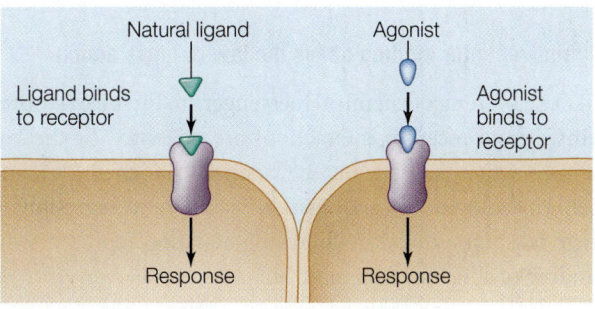

(b) Agonist binding causes a response

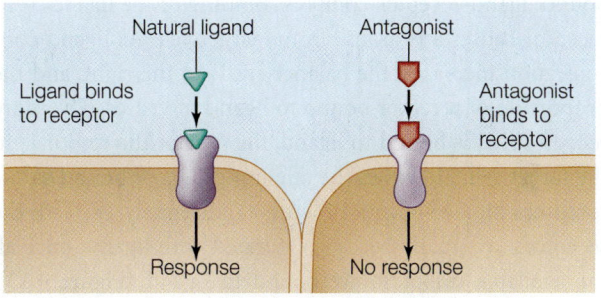

(c) Antagonist binding does not cause a response

the protein convey its functional activity by interacting with signal transduction molecules within the cell. The structure of the ligand-binding domain determines the nature of the ligands that can interact with the receptor. The remaining functional domains determine the nature of the effects of that receptor on the target cell. For many receptors it is possible to construct recombinant proteins with the ligand-binding domain of one receptor and the functional domains of another. The types of functional domains present in the recombinant protein determine the nature of the response in the target cell, not the type of ligand-binding domain.

A ligand may bind to more than one receptor

Many receptors are part of large gene families. These genes are transcribed into similar proteins, termed isoforms, with distinct properties (see Chapter 3: Chemistry, Biochemistry, and Cell Physiology). Receptor isoforms often share similar ligand-binding domains, but differ in their functional domains. The presence of these isoforms allows the same signaling molecule to have very different effects on different target cells. For example, epinephrine causes the smooth muscle cells surrounding the bronchioles of the lung to relax, but causes the smooth muscle cells surrounding the blood vessels leading to the intestine to contract. The smooth muscle cells in these different locations express different **adrenergic receptor** isoforms (different versions of the receptor for epinephrine).

Ligand-receptor binding obeys the law of mass action

Like the binding of chemical messengers to their carrier proteins, ligand-receptor interactions are governed by the law of mass action (see Chapter 3: Chemistry, Biochemistry, and Cell Physiology). Natural ligands usually bind reversibly to their receptors; thus, the following equation represents the binding of a ligand to its receptor:

$$L + R \leftrightarrow LR \rightarrow \text{response}$$

where L is the free ligand, R is the receptor, and LR is the bound ligand-receptor complex. Binding of the ligand to its receptor causes a response in the target cell. As ligand concentration increases, the balance shifts to the right, and the proportion of receptor bound to ligand increases. The more receptor that is bound to ligand, the greater the response in the target cell. However, the amount of ligand bound to the receptors on a cell cannot increase indefinitely. Instead, the receptors eventually become saturated with ligand, once all the available receptors are bound to ligand (Figure 4.13). Once the saturation point is reached, adding more ligand will not increase the response in the target cell.

Receptor number can vary

Target cells vary in the number of receptors they possess. The more receptors on a cell, the more likely it is that a ligand will bind to the receptor at any given concentration of ligand (Figure 4.14a), and the greater the response in the target cell. Target cells with high concentrations of receptors will be more sensitive to the presence of the ligand than target cells with lower concentrations of the receptor.

The number of receptors on a target cell can change over time. These effects can easily be observed following the administration of certain drugs. For example, opiate drugs (opium, morphine, codeine, and heroin) bind to and activate

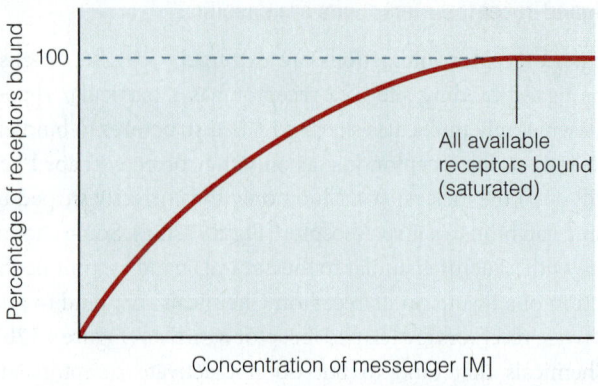

FIGURE 4.13 **Effects of messenger concentration**
As messenger concentration increases, the percentage of receptors bound to messenger increases up to the saturation point, at which all available receptors are bound to messenger.

All available receptors bound (saturated)

Percentage of receptors bound

100

Concentration of messenger [M]

opiate receptors that are found on cells throughout the body, and particularly in the brain. The normal function of these receptors is to induce pleasure and block pain. When a person regularly consumes a drug such as heroin, the number of opiate receptors on the target cells decreases which reduces the intensity of the pleasure signal—a phenomenon termed **down-regulation**. As a result, heroin users must consume more and more of the drug in order to achieve the same effects. When a habitual heroin user stops taking the drug, the low levels of opiate receptors in the brain reduce the brain's sensitivity to endorphins, the natural ligands of the opiate receptors. The reduced signal from the endorphins causes withdrawal symptoms, including nausea, vomiting, muscle pain, and bone pain, when an addicted individual stops taking the drug. After a period of time without heroin, receptor numbers return to normal, and the withdrawal symptoms gradually abate.

Receptors can also be **up-regulated**. For example, caffeine (the active ingredient in coffee) binds to receptors for the neurotransmitter adenosine. Adenosine is an inhibitory neurotransmitter, so when it binds to its receptor it tends to reduce brain activity, producing a calming effect. Caffeine is an antagonist for these receptors, binding but not activating them. The net result is that caffeine acts as a stimulant by removing the calming effects of adenosine. The brain responds to the removal of this calming signal by increasing the number of adenosine receptors on these brain cells. Up-regulation results in increased sensitivity to the naturally occurring adenosine, and thus homeostatically regulates brain activity, restoring brain activity to normal by balancing out the effects of the ingested caffeine. As a result of this up-regulation, coffee drinkers must drink more and more coffee over time to obtain the same stimulatory effect. Habitual coffee drinkers may need several cups of coffee just

FIGURE 4.14 **Effects of receptor concentration and affinity on the percentage of bound receptors**

(a) Cells that have a higher concentration of receptors have a larger number of bound receptors at any given concentration of messenger, and these cells respond to the messenger more strongly than cells with fewer receptors.
(b) At a given concentration of messenger, cells with high-affinity receptors have a higher percentage of bound receptors, and a greater response than cells with low-affinity receptors, as long as the messenger concentration is low. At messenger concentrations where all receptors are saturated, there is no difference in response between the cells if the total number of receptors is similar. The dissociation constant (K_d), or the concentration of messenger at which the receptor is 50 percent saturated, is an indication of the affinity of the receptor for the messenger. Receptors with high K_d have low affinity for the messenger, whereas receptors with low K_d have high affinity for the messenger. Alternatively, affinity can be expressed using the affinity constant (K_a), which is the inverse of K_d.

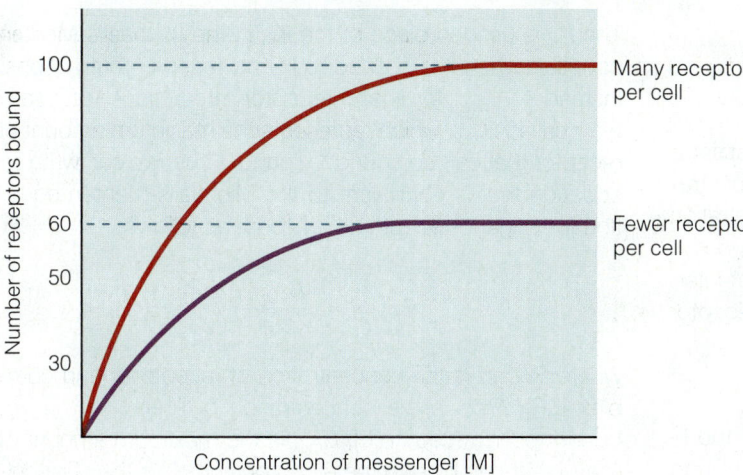

(a) Effect of receptor concentration

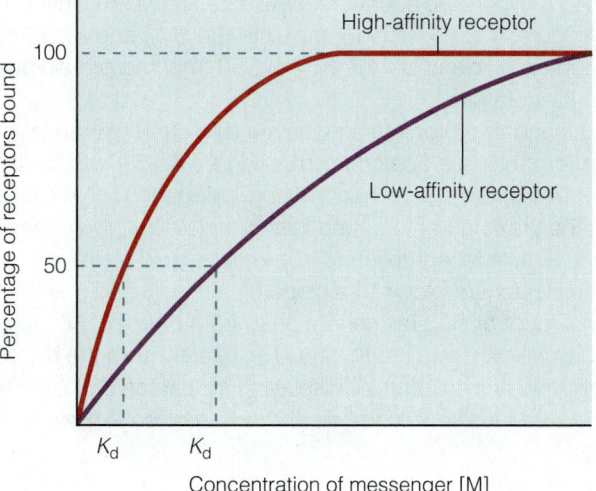

(b) Effect of receptor affinity

these individuals to be unusually sensitive to naturally occurring adenosine in their system, and thus they will tend to feel sleepy without their morning coffee.

Receptor affinity for a ligand can vary

Receptors can also vary in the strength with which they bind a ligand. The strength of binding between a ligand and a receptor can be expressed using the **dissociation constant (K_d)** for that receptor. The dissociation constant is defined as the concentration of messenger at which half of the receptors on the cell surface are bound to ligand (Figure 4.14b). Thus receptors with high affinity have a low dissociation constant, and receptors with low affinity have a high dissociation constant. Alternatively, we can express the strength of receptor-ligand interactions with the **affinity constant (K_a)** (also called the association constant), which is defined as the inverse of the dissociation constant (or the inverse of the concentration of messenger at which half of the receptors are bound). The larger the K_a value, the higher the affinity, and the more tightly the ligand binds to the receptor. Figure 4.14b illustrates the effects of differences in the affinity constant. A high-affinity receptor causes greater activity in the target cell at low ligand concentration than does a low-affinity receptor. High-affinity receptors also saturate at lower ligand concentrations.

The affinity constants of some hormone receptors are very large ($> 10^8$ l/mol). Thus, a receptor can bind to these messengers even when they are present at very low concentrations. In contrast, the affinity constants for some neurotransmitter and paracrine receptors are lower ($\sim 10^4$ l/mol), requiring higher concentrations of messenger to stimulate their receptors.

See Box 4.2: Math in Physiology: Ligand-Receptor Interactions for further discussion of the mathematics used to describe ligand-receptor interactions.

Ligand signaling must be inactivated

As long as a ligand remains bound to its receptor, it will continue to activate that receptor and cause a response in the target cell. This signal must be terminated in order for the body to be able to respond to changing conditions. The activity of ligand-receptor complexes can be regulated in a variety of ways (Figure 4.16). The simplest

to fully wake up in the morning because they need higher levels of caffeine to cancel out the effects of adenosine on their highly sensitive up-regulated target cells. If habitual coffee drinkers attempt to suddenly stop drinking coffee, the high levels of adenosine receptor in the brain cause

LIGAND-RECEPTOR INTERACTIONS

Ligand-receptor interactions are very similar to enzyme-substrate interactions (discussed in Chapter 3: Chemistry, Biochemistry, and Cell Physiology), and thus they also follow the law of mass action. As a result, the approaches developed for analyzing enzyme-substrate interactions are directly applicable to ligand-receptor interactions. Recall that the Michaelis-Menten equation can be used to describe the hyperbolic curve that represents the effect of substrate concentration on reaction rate. This equation is written as:

$$Velocity = \frac{V_{max[S]}}{Km + S}$$

Where **V_{max}** is the **maximum velocity** of the reaction at saturating substrate concentration, [S] is the substrate concentration, and K_m is the **Michaelis constant** (or the concentration at which the reaction velocity is half of the maximum velocity). To work out the equivalent terms for a ligand-receptor interaction we need to examine the equation for a ligand-receptor interaction, which we can write out as follows:

$$L + R \leftrightarrow LR$$

Where L is the ligand, R is the receptor, and LR is the ligand-receptor complex (i.e., a receptor with ligand bound to it). From basic biochemistry we know that for equilibrium reactions, the rate of formation of the product can be described using the **rate constant** of the forward reaction (K_f) multiplied by the concentration of the reactants (K_f[L][R]), while the rate of formation of the reactants can be described using the rate constant of the reverse reaction (K_r) multiplied by the concentration of the product (K_r[LR]). When the reaction reaches equilibrium, the rate of formation of the product equals the rate of formation of the reactant according to the equation below:

$$K_f[L][R] = K_r[LR]$$

We can rearrange this equation to give:

$$K_f = [LR]$$
$$K_r \, [L][R]$$

The term K_f/K_r is called the equilibrium constant (K_{eq}) of the reaction. For ligand-receptor interactions, we usually use the term *affinity constant* (K_a), rather than equilibrium constant, but the principle is exactly the same. Recall that the dissociation constant (K_d) is simply the inverse of the affinity constant:

$$K_d = [L][R]$$
$$[LR]$$

The K_d is used in place of the K_m in the Michaelis-Menten equation when it is applied to ligand-receptor interactions. Instead of V_{max}, for ligand-receptor interactions we use a term called B_{max}, which represents the maximum amount of receptor that can be bound to ligand. Thus, we can write an equation that is equivalent to the Michaelis-Menten equation for a ligand-receptor interaction, as follows:

$$Bound = \frac{B_{max \times Free}}{Kd + Free}$$

where *Bound* is the concentration of receptor-ligand complex [LR], *Free* is the concentration of ligand that is not bound to the receptor [L], B_{max} is the maximum amount of ligand that can bind to the receptor, and K_d is the dissociation constant. This equation can be used to describe the shape of curves such as the one shown in Figure 4.15a. By fitting a hyperbolic equation to the data shown in panel A of the figure, it is possible to calculate the B_{max} and K_d of the receptor. In this case, the B_{max} is 550 fmol/mg protein and the K_d is 25 pM.

Ligand-receptor interactions are also often plotted in linear form using a *Scatchard plot* (Figure 4.15b), which has the ratio of the concentration of bound ligand to free ligand on the y-axis and the bound ligand concentration on the x-axis. Simple receptor-ligand interactions yield a straight line on a Scatchard plot with a slope of $-1/K_d$ (or $-K_a$) and an x-intercept at $B_{max,}$ as can be seen from the plot. Although today we calculate the K_d and B_{max} directly from the hyperbolic equation in panel A, displaying a Scatchard plot is still useful because examining its shape can reveal a number of

way to terminate signaling is to remove the ligand from the extracellular fluid (Figure 4.16a). For example, enzymes in the liver and kidney degrade many circulating hormones. When hormone levels fall in the blood, they will also fall in the fluid surrounding a cell, causing bound hormone to

dissociate from its receptor (according to the law of mass action). When the receptor is no longer bound to the hormone, signaling terminates.

Removal of a hormone from the blood is a relatively slow process, requiring several minutes to hours. Most

FIGURE 4.15 **Determining the K_d and B_{max} of a receptor**

(a) The effect of ligand concentration on the amount of bound receptor; **(b)** a Scatchard plot showing the same data; and **(c)** a Scatchard plot showing a hypothetical case where two receptors are expressed on the same cell. Receptor 1 has high affinity but low B_{max} and Receptor 2 has low affinity but high B_{max}. The black line shows the shape of the combined curve for both receptors that is obtained in the experiment.

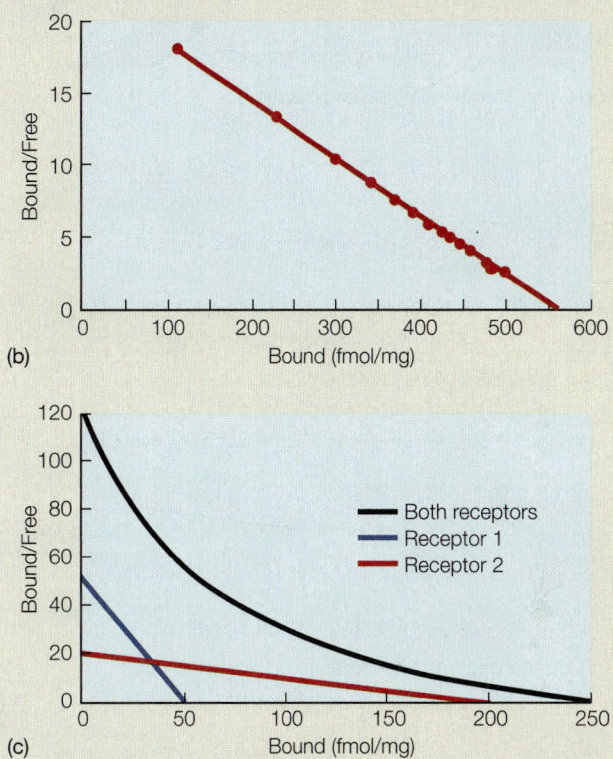

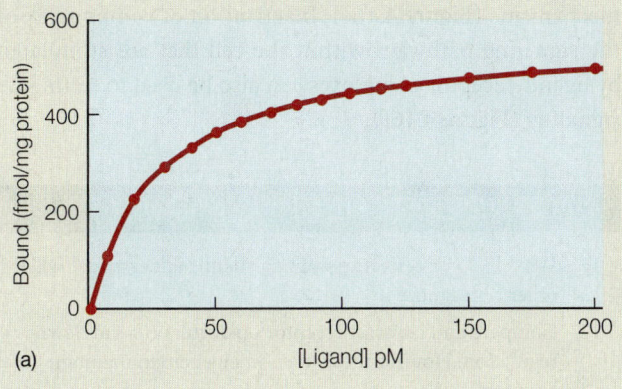

interesting features of ligand-receptor interactions. For example, Figure 4.15c shows a Scatchard plot from a hypothetical experiment examining the receptors for a hormone on a specific target tissue. In this case, the Scatchard plot that was obtained (shown in black) is not linear. The most common reason for obtaining a nonlinear Scatchard plot is if there is more than one type of receptor for a particular ligand expressed on a cell. In Figure 4.15c this nonlinear Scatchard plot is the result of the presence of two different receptors for the ligand being expressed on the cell. One of

the receptors binds the ligand with low affinity, but is present at a high concentration and thus has a high B_{max}. The other receptor binds the ligand with high affinity, but is present at a low concentration on the cell and thus has a low B_{max}. Each individual receptor produces a linear Scatchard plot reflecting its own K_a and B_{max}, but with both present in the sample, you observe a curve that is a combination of the two underlying linear functions. Thus, simply looking at the Scatchard plot can tell an experimenter quite a bit about the nature of the receptors expressed on a tissue.

signaling molecules must be regulated over much shorter time periods. These molecules can be inactivated or removed in several ways. Adjacent cells can take up signaling molecules from the extracellular fluid (Figure 4.16b), thus reducing the concentration of the signaling molecule

and causing them to dissociate from the receptor. This is a common mechanism for the removal of neurotransmitters from the synapse. This process is the target of a number of drug therapies. For example, drugs called selective serotonin reuptake inhibitors (SSRIs) inhibit the reuptake of

FIGURE 4.16 **Termination of ligand-receptor signaling**

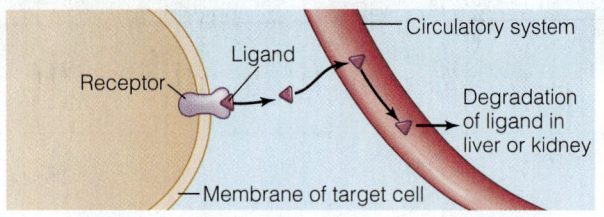

(a) Ligand removed by distant tissues

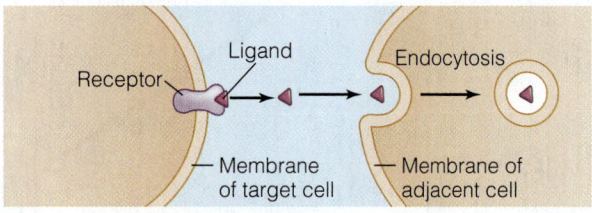

(b) Ligand taken up by adjacent cells

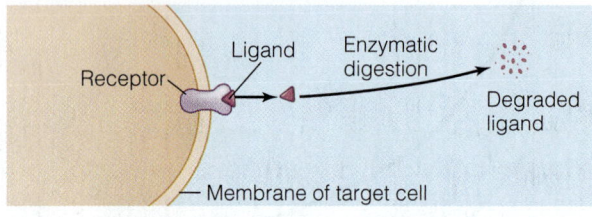

(c) Ligand degraded by extracellular enzymes

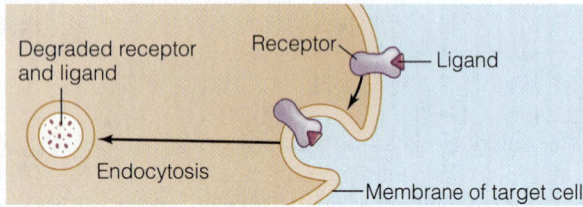

(d) Ligand-receptor complex removed by endocytosis

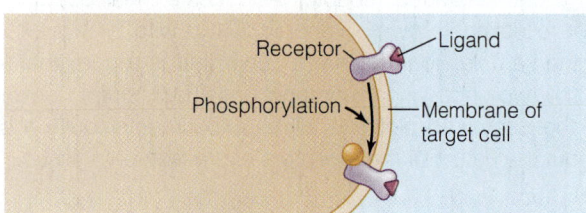

(e) Receptor inactivation

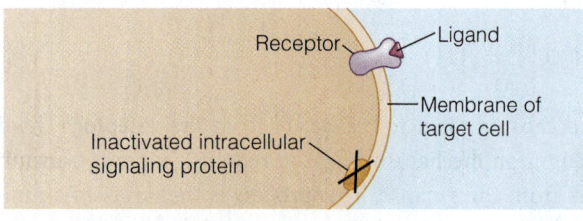

(f) Inactivation of signal transduction pathway

serotonin from the synapse, increasing the concentration of serotonin in the synapse, which causes increased binding of serotonin to its receptors. SSRIs are commonly used to treat depression. An alternative means of removing a signaling molecule from its receptor is to use enzymes that degrade the signaling molecule (Figure 4.16c). The ligand-receptor complex can also be removed from the membrane by endocytosis (Figure 4.16d). Internalized receptors can then either be degraded (resulting in receptor down-regulation) or recycled to the cell membrane, once the ligand has been removed. Intracellular enzymes can degrade hydrophobic chemical messengers that diffuse into cells. Receptors can also be inactivated by phosphorylation or other similar mechanisms (Figure 4.16e). Inactivation of components of the signaling pathways within the cell that are stimulated by ligand-receptor complexes can also be used to terminate signaling (Figure 4.16f).

CONCEPT CHECK

11. Why do some cells respond to a chemical messenger while other cells ignore it?

12. Compare and contrast receptor up-regulation and down-regulation. How do these phenomena help to maintain homeostasis?

SIGNAL TRANSDUCTION PATHWAYS

So far, we have seen that the type and concentration of both the ligand and receptor can affect the response of the target cell, but we have not yet discussed the details of how the binding of the ligand to the receptor causes a response in the target cell. When a ligand binds to a receptor, the receptor undergoes a conformational change. But how does a simple signal like the change in the shape of a protein get converted into a complex response in the target cell? The cell uses signal transduction pathways to convert the change in the shape of a receptor to a complex response. Transducers are devices that convert signals from one form to another. Signal transduction in the cell is analogous to signal transduction in familiar transducing devices like a radio. All transducers have four important components: a receiver, a transducer, an amplifier, and a responder. In the cell, the ligand-binding domain of the receptor acts as a receiver, receiving the signal by binding to the incoming chemical messenger. The ligand-binding domain, together with other domains within the receptor, acts as a transducer by undergoing a conformational change that activates a signal transduction pathway. The signal transduction pathway as a whole acts as an amplifier, increasing the number of molecules affected by the signal. The responders in signal transduction pathways can be one or more of a wide variety of cellular functions, such as the expression of a gene, the activity of a protein, or the permeability of the cell membrane.

All signal transduction pathways have the same general structure (Figure 4.17). When a ligand binds to its receptor, the receptor undergoes a conformational change. The conformational change in the receptor acts as a signal that converts an inactive substance (A) to its active form. The activated substance A in turn activates substance B, which activates substance C, and so on, until the end of the cascade. The change in conformation of a single receptor caused by the binding of a single molecule of chemical messenger can result in the conversion of many molecules of substance A to their active forms. Each one of these many molecules of substance A can then go on to activate many molecules of substance B, and so on down the chain, potentially producing millions of molecules of the final product. As a result, signal transduction cascades greatly amplify the original signal caused by binding of a molecule of chemical messenger. The longer the signal transduction cascade, the greater the degree of signal **amplification**.

Cells have many signal transduction pathways, some of them very complex. In this book we focus on the signal transduction pathways that are the most important in regulating physiological processes. These signal transduction pathways are associated with intracellular receptors, ligand-gated ion channels, **receptor-enzymes**, and G protein–coupled receptors (Figure 4.18). As the name suggests, **intracellular receptors** are located inside the cell, and interact with hydrophobic chemical messengers. Hydrophilic chemical messengers generally interact with transmembrane receptors. **Ligand-gated ion channels** initiate a response in the target cell by changing the ion permeability of the membrane. **Receptor-enzymes** induce a response by activating or inactivating intracellular enzymes. **G protein–coupled receptors** send signals to an associated **G protein**, which then initiates a signal transduction pathway that causes a response in the target cell.

Intracellular Receptors

When a ligand binds to an intracellular receptor, the receptor changes shape and becomes activated (Figure 4.19). Activated intracellular receptors act as transcription factors that regulate the transcription of target genes by binding to specific DNA sequences, and increasing or decreasing mRNA production from the target gene. Intracellular receptors have three domains: a *ligand-binding domain*, a *DNA-binding domain*, and a *transactivation domain*, each of which performs specific steps in signal transduction. Once a hydrophobic ligand has diffused across the cell membrane, the ligand binds to the ligand-binding site. Ligand binding causes a conformational change in the receptor that activates it. Some intracellular receptors are located in the cytoplasm, and only move to the nucleus once they bind to the ligand. Other intracellular receptors are found in the nucleus, already bound to DNA and ready to be activated.

The DNA-binding domain of an intracellular receptor binds to specific sequences, termed *response elements*, adjacent to their target genes. Because the DNA-binding domain of each intracellular receptor recognizes

FIGURE 4.17 Amplification by signal transduction pathways

When a single molecule of ligand binds to a single receptor, the receptor undergoes a conformational change. The change in shape of the receptor converts inactive substance A to active substance A*. As long as the ligand remains bound to the receptor, it will continue to activate substance A. Thus, a single molecule of ligand can activate many molecules of substance A into A*. Substance A* then goes on to activate substance B, and so on down the chain. At each step, one molecule of a substance can activate many molecules of the next substance in the chain. Thus, signal transduction cascades can greatly amplify the signal.

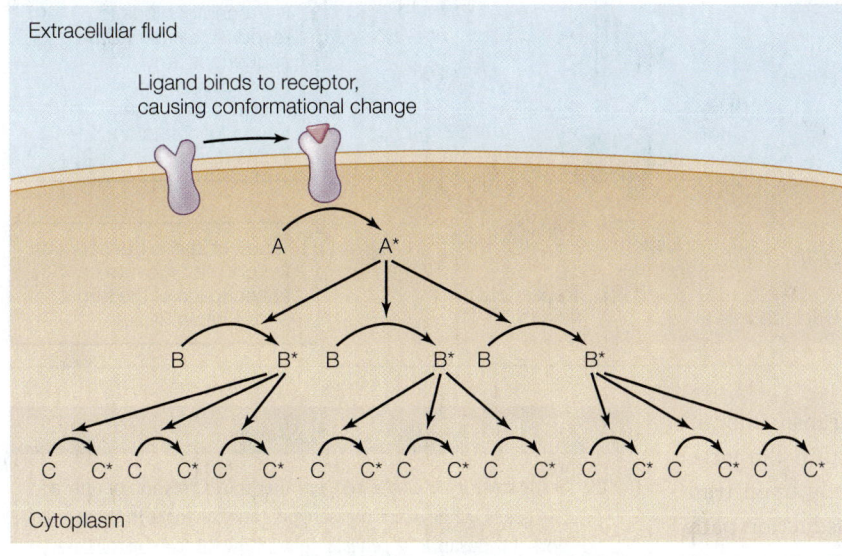

a specific response element, and only the intended target genes contain appropriate response element sequences, intracellular receptors bind only to their target genes and not to other genes in the genome. Once the receptor is bound to the response element, the transactivation domain of the receptor interacts with other transcription factors to regulate the transcription of the target genes, increasing or decreasing the production of mRNA. Together, the DNA-binding domain and the transactivation domain act as the transducer in this signal transduction pathway. Many important endocrine hormones bind to intracellular receptors, including estrogen, testosterone, and the glucocorticoid stress hormones.

The changes in transcription initiated by the binding of a ligand to its receptor set off a cascade of events within the target cell (Figure 4.20). The first step of the response is often activation of a small number of specific genes, usually coding for other transcription factors. The gene products then go on to activate other genes. This cascade of gene regulation acts as the amplifier in the signal transduction pathway. The interactions between activated intracellular receptors and transcription factors vary among genes, and the same receptor may increase the transcription of some genes while decreasing the transcription of others. In this way, a hydrophobic ligand can have complex effects on a target cell. Because these ligands exert their effects by altering transcription, the response of the target cell is generally slow, with the first effects detectable within about 30 minutes and the secondary effects occurring over hours or days.

Hydrophobic ligands can also bind to transmembrane receptors, in which case the responses within the target cell are very rapid, because they do not rely upon transcription. However, the specific signal transduction pathways involved in these rapid *nongenomic* responses are not well understood.

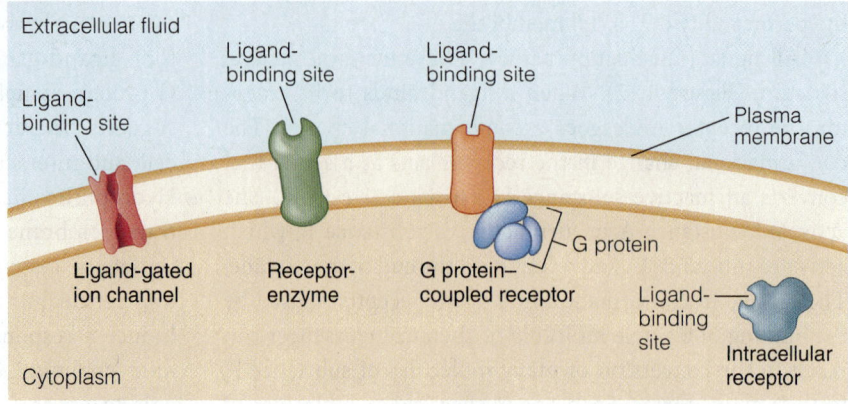

FIGURE 4.18 **Types of receptors in animals**

Some of the physiologically important receptors in animals are intracellular receptors, ligand-gated ion channels, receptor-enzymes, and G protein–coupled receptors.

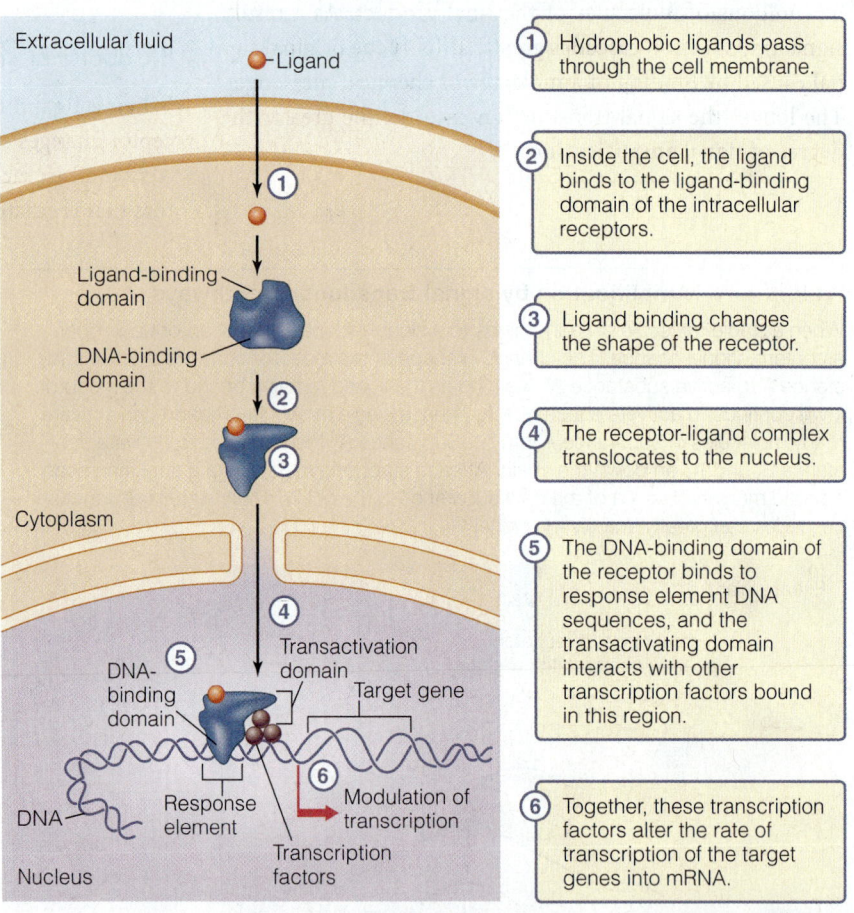

FIGURE 4.19 **Signal transduction by intracellular receptors**

1. Hydrophobic ligands pass through the cell membrane.

2. Inside the cell, the ligand binds to the ligand-binding domain of the intracellular receptors.

3. Ligand binding changes the shape of the receptor.

4. The receptor-ligand complex translocates to the nucleus.

5. The DNA-binding domain of the receptor binds to response element DNA sequences, and the transactivating domain interacts with other transcription factors bound in this region.

6. Together, these transcription factors alter the rate of transcription of the target genes into mRNA.

CONCEPT CHECK

13. Some hydrophobic messengers alter the expression of only a few genes, while other messengers cause changes in the regulation of thousands of genes. Explain how this can be the case.

14. Some responses to hydrophobic ligands are termed nongenomic responses. How do they differ from the typical responses to a hydrophobic ligand?

FIGURE 4.20 Transcriptional cascades initiated by intracellular receptors

In the first step of signal transduction by intracellular receptors, the messenger-receptor complex binds to target gene A at a specific response element, altering its transcription. The product of target gene A then goes on to interact with DNA and regulate the transcription of additional genes. The products of these additional genes may also act as transcription factors or go on to have effects on many biochemical pathways.

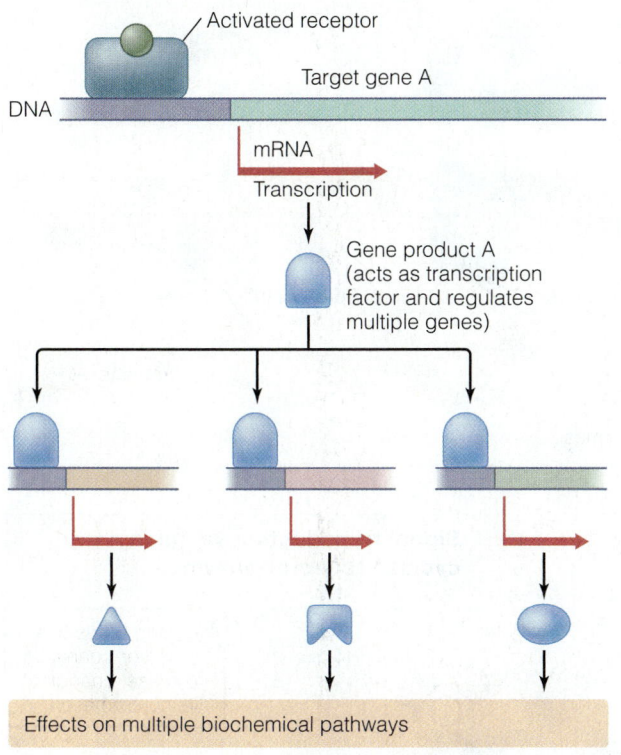

Ligand-Gated Ion Channels

Signal transduction by ligand-gated ion channels is relatively simple and direct compared with signal transduction by other receptors. When a ligand binds to a ligand-gated ion channel, the protein undergoes a conformational change, opening an ion channel within the protein—a route for ions to move across the cell membrane (Figure 4.21). When the ion channel opens, ions move into or out of the cell, as dictated by their electrochemical gradients, altering the membrane potential of the cell (Chapter 3: Chemistry, Biochemistry, and Cell Physiology). The resulting change in membrane potential acts as a signal within the target cell. Changes in membrane potential as a result of the opening of ligand-gated ion channels are very rapid, and a single molecule of chemical messenger can open an ion channel that could allow many individual ions to cross the cell membrane, allowing for some signal amplification.

CONCEPT CHECK

15. What is the primary response of a cell when a ligand binds to a ligand-gated ion channel?

16. Which would you predict to be faster, signaling via a ligand-gated ion channel or signaling via an intracellular receptor? Justify your answer.

Signal Transduction via Receptor-Enzymes

Receptor-enzymes contain an extracellular ligand-binding domain, a transmembrane domain, and an intracellular catalytic domain (Figure 4.22a). The ligand-binding domain contains a region that binds specifically to a chemical messenger. When ligand binds to the ligand-binding domain, the receptor changes shape, and the transmembrane domain transmits this shape change across the membrane, activating the catalytic domain of the enzyme. The catalytic domains of receptor-enzymes act as enzymatic catalysts that initiate the next link in the signal transduction cascade. The signal transduction pathways of receptor-enzymes involve *phosphorylation cascades* in which proteins at each step phosphorylate or dephosphorylate other proteins within the target cell. **Phosphorylation** cascades amplify the original signal, causing a response in the target cell.

Receptor-enzymes are named based on the reaction catalyzed by the intracellular catalytic domain. In this book, we discuss three types of receptor-enzymes: (1) receptor guanylate cyclases, (2) receptor tyrosine kinases, and (3) receptor

FIGURE 4.21 The structure and function of ligand-gated ion channels

(a) When no ligand is bound to the receptor, the ion channel is closed and ions cannot cross the membrane. **(b)** When a ligand binds to the ion channel, the channel changes conformation and the ion channel opens, allowing ions to cross the membrane. Although this figure shows a situation where ligand binding opens a closed channel, it is also possible for the opposite to occur. For some ligand-gated ion channels, ligand binding causes an open channel to close.

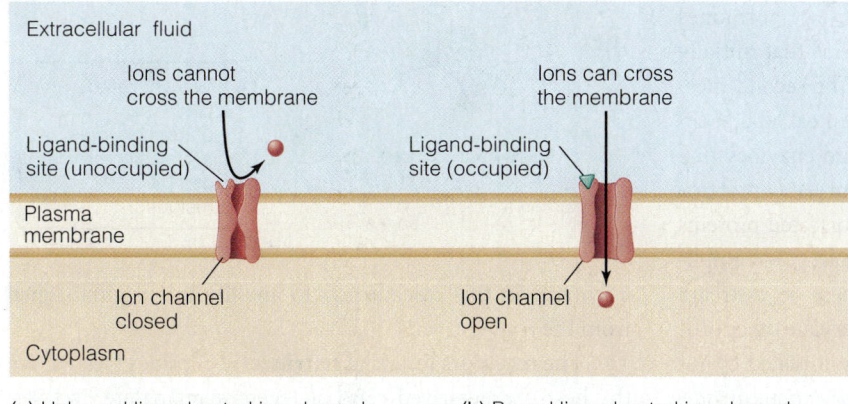

(a) Unbound ligand-gated ion channel (b) Bound ligand-gated ion channel

FIGURE 4.22 **Receptor-enzymes**

(a) Structure of a receptor-enzyme. A receptor-enzyme has an extracellular ligand-binding domain, a transmembrane domain, and an intracellular catalytic (enzyme) domain. **(b)** Three types of receptor-enzymes in animals. Receptor guanylate cyclases convert GTP to cGMP. Receptor tyrosine kinases phosphorylate tyrosine residues in proteins. Receptor serine/threonine kinases phosphorylate serine or threonine residues in proteins.

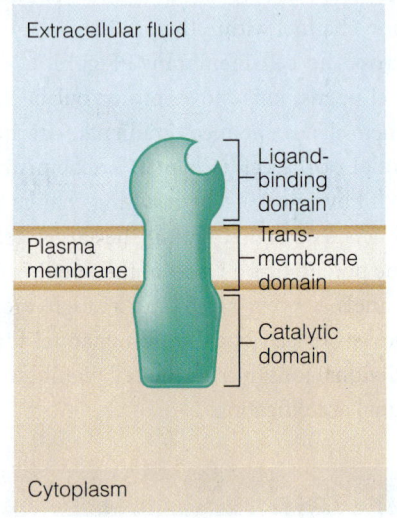

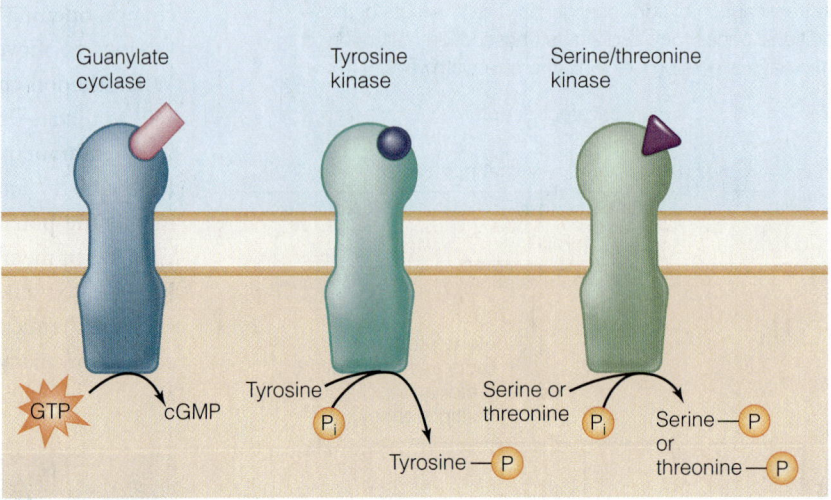

(a) Structure of a receptor-enzyme (b) Types of receptor-enzymes

serine/threonine kinases (Figure 4.22b). In animals, the majority of known receptor-enzymes are tyrosine kinases. Animals also have many forms of receptor serine/threonine kinase, some of which play important roles in growth and development and in the response to environmental stressors. Only a few receptor guanylate cyclases are known.

Receptor guanylate cyclases generate cyclic GMP

When a ligand binds to a receptor guanylate cyclase, the receptor undergoes a conformational change, activating the guanylate cyclase domain of the receptor (Figure 4.23). The activated guanylate cyclase produces cyclic **guanosine** monophosphate (cGMP). The cGMP acts as a **second messenger** within the cell. Second messengers are low-molecular-weight diffusible molecules that act as part of signal transduction pathways to communicate signals within the cell. (The name second messenger was coined to distinguish between these intracellular messengers and the extracellular messengers (e.g., hormones and paracrines) that are the "first messengers" that initially activate the signal transduction pathway.) The second messenger cGMP binds to and activates a protein called cGMP-dependent protein kinase (PKG). Kinases are enzymes that phosphorylate other proteins. PKG phosphorylates proteins at serine or threonine residues. The phosphorylated proteins then go on to activate other proteins, propagating and amplifying the signal through the cell. Many of these downstream proteins are also protein kinases that phosphorylate other proteins. Thus, the signal transduction pathway initiated by receptor guanylate cyclases is termed a *phosphorylation cascade*.

FIGURE 4.23 **Signal transduction via guanylate cyclase receptor-enzymes**

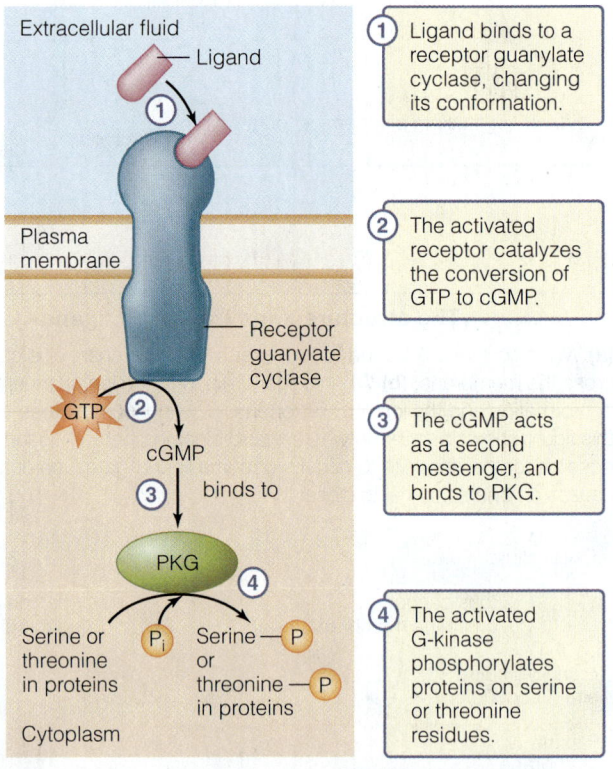

1. Ligand binds to a receptor guanylate cyclase, changing its conformation.

2. The activated receptor catalyzes the conversion of GTP to cGMP.

3. The cGMP acts as a second messenger, and binds to PKG.

4. The activated G-kinase phosphorylates proteins on serine or threonine residues.

Each step in this cascade acts to amplify the original signal from the receptor.

The receptors for atrial **natriuretic** peptides (ANPs) are the best-characterized class of receptor guanylate cyclases.

ANPs are a group of closely related peptides that are produced by muscle cells in the heart in response to increases in blood pressure. As we see in Chapter 13: Ion and Water Balance, ANPs trigger vasodilation and induce the kidney to reduce blood volume.

Receptor tyrosine kinases signal through Ras proteins

There are more than 50 known receptor tyrosine kinases, most of which bind to chemical messengers that are critical for cellular growth and proliferation, such as insulin, epidermal **growth factor**, and vascular endothelial growth factor. When a chemical messenger binds to a receptor tyrosine kinase, the bound receptor associates with other tyrosine kinase receptors in the membrane to form dimers (Figure 4.24). The dimerized receptors then phosphorylate each other on multiple tyrosine residues, a process called autophosphorylation. The phosphorylated receptors interact with and activate one of many intracellular signaling molecules, most of which are protein kinases.

In the case of the growth factor receptors, these activated kinases signal to the Ras protein, which acts as the next step in the signal transduction pathway. Ras proteins bind to and hydrolyze GTP and function as switches by cycling between the **active state**, when GTP is bound, and the inactive state, when GDP is bound. Because of this GTPase activity, the Ras proteins are members of a protein family known as the small G-protein. They are distinct from the heterotrimeric G proteins that we discuss later in the chapter. GTPase-activating proteins (GAPs) and guanine nucleotide–releasing proteins (GNRPs) catalyze the transition between active and inactive Ras. Receptor tyrosine kinases signal through GAPs and GNRPs to regulate Ras.

Ras activates a serine/threonine phosphorylation cascade that sends a signal through the cell. There are many serine/threonine phosphorylation cascades in animal cells, but one particularly important one involves the mitogen activated protein kinases (MAP kinases) (Figure 4.25). Activated Ras signals to a MAP-kinase-kinase-kinase (MAPKKK), which phosphorylates a MAP-kinase-kinase (MAPKK). In turn, the MAP-kinase-kinase phosphorylates a MAP kinase (MAPK). The MAP kinase then phosphorylates other protein kinases, cellular proteins, and the transcription factors Elk-1 and Jun. These transcription factors regulate the transcription of other transcription factors, which regulate the transcription of various genes. Thus, the phosphorylation cascades triggered by receptor tyrosine kinases greatly amplify the original chemical signal. Because they activate extensive phosphorylation cascades within the cell, the Ras proteins have wide-ranging effects on cellular growth and metabolism. Approximately 30 percent of human cancers involve mutations in the genes encoding Ras. These mutations turn the Ras protein "on" constitutively so that it is active even in the absence of a ligand. The activated Ras sends a strong signal to the cell, stimulating it to grow and divide uncontrollably, causing cancer.

The insulin receptor is another example of a critically important tyrosine kinase receptor. Like other tyrosine kinase receptors, the insulin receptor functions as a dimer. Binding of insulin to the extracellular ligand-binding domain (also called the alpha subunit) causes the receptor to dimerize. Dimerization causes the intracellular domains (also called the beta subunits) to autophosphorylate each other on their tyrosine residues and become active. The intracellular domains of the receptor dimer also act as a tyrosine kinase

---

FIGURE 4.24 **Signal transduction via receptor tyrosine kinases**

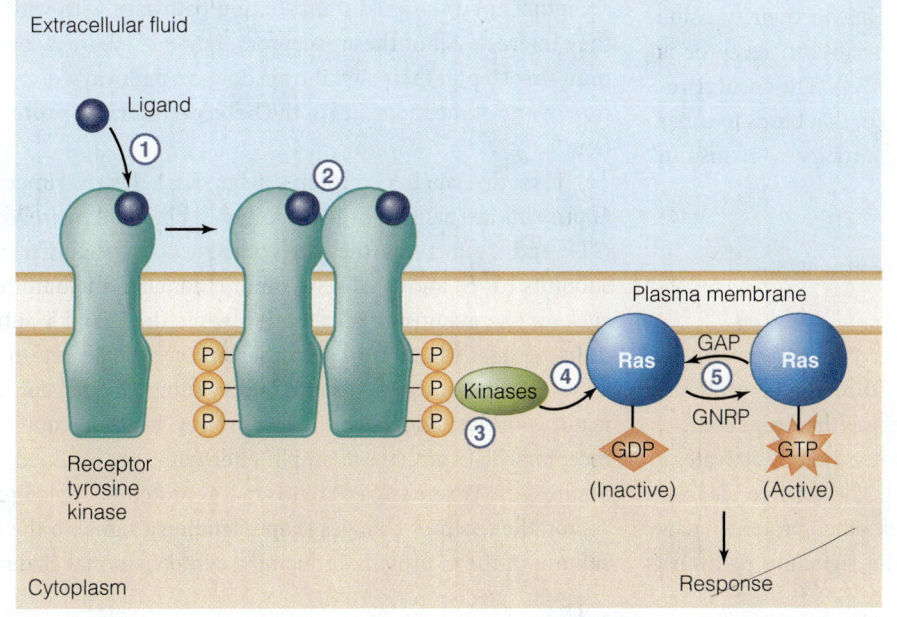

Extracellular fluid

Ligand

① Ligand binds to receptor.

② Receptors dimerize and autophosphorylate.

Plasma membrane

③ Phosphorylated receptors interact with protein kinases.

Ras GAP Ras

Kinases ④ ⑤

GDP GNRP GTP

④ Protein kinases signal to Ras protein.

Receptor tyrosine kinase

(Inactive) (Active)

Cytoplasm

Response

⑤ Ras switches between the active and inactive forms.

FIGURE 4.25 **Signal transduction via the MAP-kinase phosphorylation cascade**

The Ras proteins that are activated by receptor tyrosine kinases phosphorylate MAP-kinase-kinase-kinase, and the phosphorylated MAPKKK then phosphorylates a MAP-kinase-kinase, which in turn phosphorylates a MAP kinase, which then phosphorylates other protein kinases, transcription factors, and diverse cellular proteins.

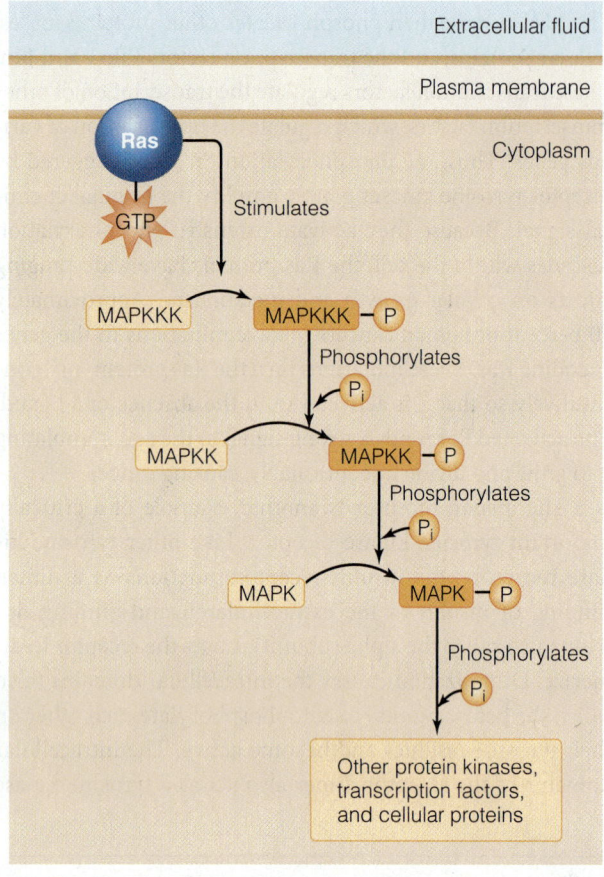

that phosphorylates other target proteins on their tyrosine residues. The best-known target of the insulin receptor is called the insulin receptor substrate (IRS). The insulin receptor substrate acts as a docking protein that binds to other intracellular signaling proteins that participate in insulin signal transduction.

Receptor serine/threonine kinases directly activate phosphorylation cascades

Receptor serine/threonine kinases directly activate phosphorylation cascades, without working through Ras proteins. When a ligand binds to a receptor serine/threonine kinase, the conformational change in the receptor directly activates a serine/threonine kinase (Figure 4.26a). The activated serine/threonine kinase then phosphorylates other proteins, activating a phosphorylation cascade. The signaling pathways

activated by receptor serine/threonine kinases are not yet fully understood, but are similar to the pathways used by receptor tyrosine kinases in that they involve phosphorylation cascades that greatly amplify the signal in the target cell.

The *transforming growth factor* (TGF-β) receptors are among the most intensively studied receptor serine/threonine kinases, because mutations in TGF-β receptors and the associated signal transduction pathways have been implicated in the development of human cancers. TGF-β receptors are present as a complex consisting of two distinct proteins, called TGF-β Type I and Type II receptors (Figure 4.26b). The ligand TGF-β first binds to the Type II receptor, which causes the Type I receptor to associate with the TGF-β Type II receptor complex. The Type II receptor then phosphorylates the Type I receptor, activating the intracellular catalytic domain of the Type I receptor. The catalytic domain of the activated Type I receptor then phosphorylates a series of target proteins called SMADs on specific serine and threonine residues. The phosphorylated SMADs move to the nucleus where they interact with other proteins to regulate the transcription of target genes.

CONCEPT CHECK

17. What are the three main parts of a receptor-enzyme?
18. How do receptor-enzymes amplify incoming signals?

Signal Transduction via G Protein–Coupled Receptors

G protein–coupled receptors are a large family of membrane-spanning proteins with seven transmembrane domains. G protein–coupled receptors control many critical physiological functions, and there is enormous diversity in these receptors and the signal transduction pathways with which they interact. All of these receptors, however, share a common first step in their signal transduction pathways: activation of one of the members of the **heterotrimeric G protein** family.

Like the small G proteins (e.g., Ras), heterotrimeric G proteins are named for their ability to bind and hydrolyze GTP, and the fact that they are composed of three different subunits (α, β, and γ). The α subunit contains the binding sites for the guanosine nucleotides, while the β and γ subunits are tightly bound to each other, and are usually referred to as a single functional group, the βγ subunit. The general features of the signaling pathways from G protein–coupled receptors via G proteins to amplifier enzymes are outlined in Figure 4.27. When a ligand binds to a G protein–coupled receptor, the receptor changes shape, sending a signal to the α subunit of the G protein, inducing a conformational change

FIGURE 4.26 Signal transduction via receptor serine/threonine kinases

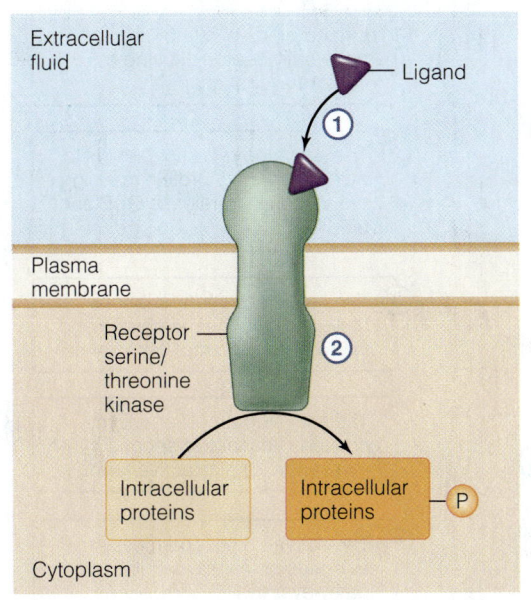

1. Ligand binds to a receptor serine/threonine kinase, changing its conformation.

2. The conformational change activates the serine/threonine kinase domain of the receptor.

3. The serine/threonine kinase phosphorylates proteins on serine or threonine residues.

(a) General structure of receptor serine/threonine kinase

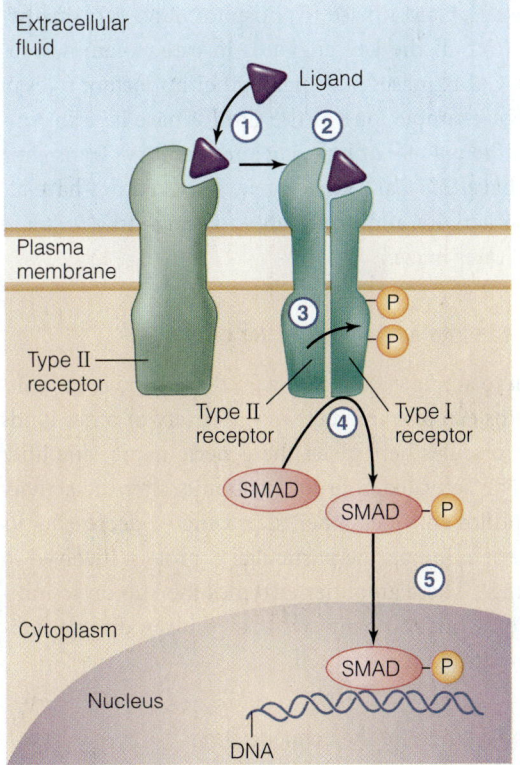

1. Ligand binds to the Type II TGF–β receptor.

2. The bound receptor dimerizes with the Type I receptor.

3. The Type II receptor phosphorylates the Type I receptor, activating it.

4. The activated receptor phosphorylates a SMAD protein.

5. The activated SMADs enter the nucleus and regulate gene expression.

(b) Signal transduction by TGF-β receptors

The best-characterized targets of the βγ subunit are ion channels. Interaction with the βγ subunit causes these ion channels to open, allowing ions to move into or out of the cell, depending on their electrical and concentration gradients. Ion movements cause changes in membrane potential, which act as signals within the cell. Thus, G protein signaling via ion channels is a relatively direct pathway to generate a response in the cell.

G protein–coupled receptors are extremely diverse

G protein signaling is involved in cell-to-cell communication in a wide variety of organisms, including fungi, plants, and animals, but the number and diversity of G protein–coupled receptors have greatly increased during the evolution of the metazoans. The single-cell budding yeast *Saccharomyces cerevisiae* has only three G protein–coupled receptors, but even relatively simple metazoans have hundreds of different G protein–coupled receptors. For example, the genome of the nematode *Caenorhabditis elegans* contains almost 1,100 different genes with sequences similar to G protein–coupled receptors. Although we do not yet know whether all of these sequences encode functional receptors, it is likely that at least several hundred of these genes function in cell-to-cell communication in nematodes. This high diversity of G protein–coupled receptors is not unique to nematodes. In fact, in all of the animal genomes that have been fully sequenced to date, somewhere between 1 percent and 5 percent of the entire protein-coding part of the genome consists of sequences similar to G protein–coupled receptors.

G protein–coupled receptors recognize many different ligands and stimuli, including light, odors, and chemical messengers, and thus play an important part in both environmental sensing and cell-to-cell communication in multicellular organisms. The human genome, for example, contains approximately 1,000 sequences related to the G protein–coupled receptors. Approximately

in the G protein. The conformational change causes the α subunit of the G protein to release GDP, bind a molecule of GTP, and become active. The activated subunit then dissociates from the βγ subunit. Both the βγ and α subunits can then go on to interact with downstream targets.

FIGURE 4.27 **Signal transduction via G protein–coupled receptors**

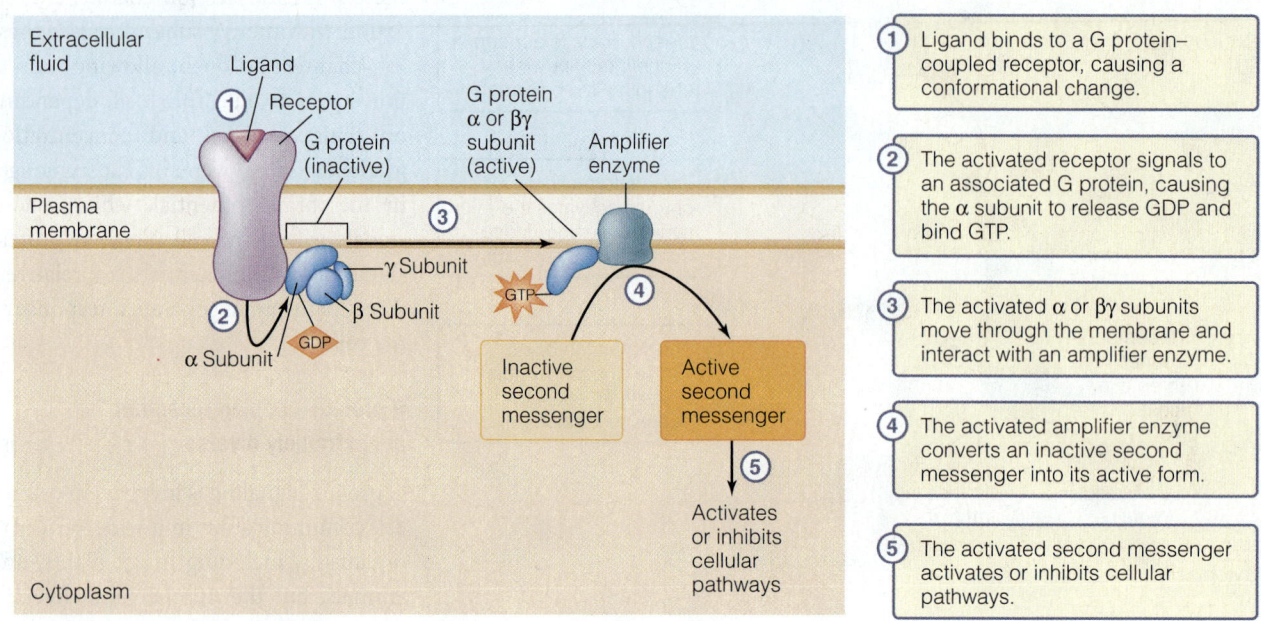

Extracellular fluid
Ligand
(1) Receptor
G protein (inactive)
G protein α or βγ subunit (active)
Amplifier enzyme
Plasma membrane
(3)
γ Subunit
β Subunit
(2)
α Subunit
GDP
GTP
(4)
Cytoplasm
Inactive second messenger
Active second messenger
(5)
Activates or inhibits cellular pathways

1. Ligand binds to a G protein–coupled receptor, causing a conformational change.
2. The activated receptor signals to an associated G protein, causing the α subunit to release GDP and bind GTP.
3. The activated α or βγ subunits move through the membrane and interact with an amplifier enzyme.
4. The activated amplifier enzyme converts an inactive second messenger into its active form.
5. The activated second messenger activates or inhibits cellular pathways.

700 of these are involved in the senses of smell and taste, or other chemosensory functions. The remaining 300 likely interact with chemical signaling molecules, and are thus involved in cell-to-cell communication. Of the G protein–coupled receptors that are involved in cell signaling, approximately 140 have no known ligand or function, and are termed **orphan receptors**. Evolutionary analyses suggest that all of the G protein–coupled receptor genes in animals have a common ancestor, and arose by duplication and descent with modification over evolution to perform different roles in complex multicellular animals.

G proteins can act through Ca²⁺-calmodulin

If a G protein interacts with and opens a Ca^{2+} channel, the resulting increase in cytoplasmic $[Ca^{2+}]$ initiates signal transduction cascades within the target cell. Most Ca^{2+}-mediated signal transduction cascades act through the protein **calmodulin**, a Ca^{2+}-binding protein that is present in every eukaryotic cell. Calmodulin has four binding sites for Ca^{2+}. Binding of Ca^{2+} to all four sites activates the protein, which then interacts with numerous other proteins. Calmodulin is known to interact with and regulate over 100 different cellular proteins. One important group of these target proteins is a diverse family of serine/threonine kinases called the Ca^{2+}-calmodulin-dependent protein kinases (CaM kinases). One of the best-studied examples of a CaM kinase is CaM kinase II, which is found in high concentration in neurons that secrete neurotransmitters called catecholamines. When cytoplasmic Ca^{2+} increases in these neurons, the change in Ca^{2+} concentration activates

CaM kinase II. CaM kinase II phosphorylates tyrosine hydroxylase (one of the key enzymes in catecholamine biosynthesis). CaM kinases play many other important roles in animals. For example, one of the CaM kinase genes is implicated in the process of learning and memory. Transgenic mice that have this CaM kinase gene knocked out have altered brain activity and are unable to learn how to swim through a water maze.

G proteins can interact with amplifier enzymes

In addition to acting via ion channels, the βγ and α subunits of G proteins can also interact with a variety of other kinds of target molecules here given the generic name "amplifier enzyme." The activated G protein subunits alter the activity of the amplifier enzyme, either increasing or decreasing its activity (depending on the particular G protein involved in the signaling). These amplifier enzymes then go on to initiate signal transduction pathways that result in diverse indirect effects within the target cell.

Amplifier enzymes alter the concentration of second messengers

Amplifier enzymes catalyze the conversion of a small molecule second messenger between its inactive and active forms. A single molecule of activated amplifier enzyme can catalyze the conversion of thousands of molecules of second messenger, greatly amplifying the signal. Second messengers then go on to activate or inhibit a variety of pathways within the cell.

Table 4.3 Second messengers of G protein-coupled receptors

Second Messenger	Synthesized by	Action	Effects
Ca^{2+}	None	Binds to calmodulin	Alters enzyme activity
cGMP	Guanylate cyclase	Activates protein kinases (usually protein kinase G)	Phosphorylates proteins Opens and closes ion channels
cAMP	Adenylate cyclase	Activates protein kinases (usually protein kinase A)	Phosphorylates proteins Opens and closes ion channels
Phosphatidylinositol (IP_3)/ diacylglycerol (DAG)	Phospholipase C	Activates protein kinase C Stimulates Ca^{2+} release from intracellular stores	Alters enzyme activity Phosphorylates proteins

Despite the enormous diversity of G protein–coupled receptors, all G proteins act through one of only four second messengers: Ca^{2+}, **cyclic GMP**, phosphatidylinositol/diacylglycerol, and **cyclic adenosine monophosphate (cAMP)**. Table 4.3 summarizes the similarities and differences between these second messenger cascades. All of these cascades amplify the signal within the target cell, inducing responses that may occur in milliseconds or hours.

Guanylate cyclase generates cGMP

Most of the G proteins that use cGMP as a second messenger activate the amplifier enzyme guanylate cyclase, which catalyzes the conversion of GTP to cGMP. The cGMP then goes on to activate PKG, which goes on to phosphorylate many other proteins. In addition, some G protein–coupled receptors use a different signal transduction pathway. When a ligand binds to these G protein–coupled receptors, the α subunit of the associated G protein moves laterally within the membrane and binds to and activates the amplifier enzyme **phosphodiesterase**. The activated phosphodiesterase catalyzes the conversion of cGMP to GMP, causing cGMP levels in the cytoplasm to drop. The decrease in cytoplasmic cGMP causes cGMP to dissociate from Na^+ channels in the membrane, closing them. The closing of the Na^+ channels prevents Na^+ from entering the cell, which changes the membrane potential and thus transduces the chemical signal into an electrical signal. This signal transduction pathway plays a part in vertebrate vision. We discuss signal transduction in the cells of both invertebrate and vertebrate eyes in more detail in Chapter 7: Sensory Systems.

Phospholipase C generates phosphatidylinositol

The inositol-phospholipid signaling pathway (Figure 4.28) was first discovered as the signal transduction pathway responsible for regulating secretion from the salivary glands of insects, but a huge variety of G protein–coupled receptors that signal through the inositol-phospholipid pathway are now known from most animal taxa. These pathways regulate a diversity of physiological functions, including smooth muscle contraction, glycogen degradation in the liver, water reabsorption by the vertebrate kidney, and many aspects of immune function.

When a chemical messenger binds to one of these receptors, the activated receptor stimulates a G protein called G_q, which in turn activates inositide-specific phospholipase C (phospholipase C-β). In less than a second, this enzyme cleaves a phosphorylated membrane phospholipid, called phosphatidylinositol bisphosphate (PIP_2). Cleavage of PIP_2 produces two products: **inositol trisphosphate (IP_3)** and **diacylglycerol (DAG)**. Both IP_3 and DAG act as second messengers in two branches of the phosphatidylinositol signal transduction cascade.

The IP_3 produced by PIP_2 hydrolysis is water soluble and rapidly leaves the plasma membrane by diffusion. IP_3 binds to IP_3-gated Ca^{2+} release channels in the membrane of the endoplasmic reticulum, activating them. The activated channels open, allowing Ca^{2+} efflux from the endoplasmic reticulum. The increased cytoplasmic Ca^{2+} concentration further activates the channel, causing an even greater Ca^{2+} efflux. Increases in cytoplasmic Ca^{2+} act as a third messenger, causing diverse effects within the cell.

IP_3 is rapidly inactivated by specific phosphatases, and the Ca^{2+} is quickly removed from the cytoplasm by active transport, terminating the response. The actions of IP_3 generally last less than a second after the chemical messenger dissociates from the receptor. Some of the IP_3 can be further phosphorylated to form $1,3,4,5$-tetrakisphosphate (IP_4), which mediates slower and more prolonged responses in the cell.

DAG, the other cleavage product of PIP_2, initiates two different signal transduction pathways. Unlike IP_3, DAG remains in the membrane and can be cleaved to form arachidonic acid, which is the substrate for the synthesis of eicosanoids—a type of chemical messenger. Alternatively,

FIGURE 4.28   The inositol-phospholipid signaling pathway

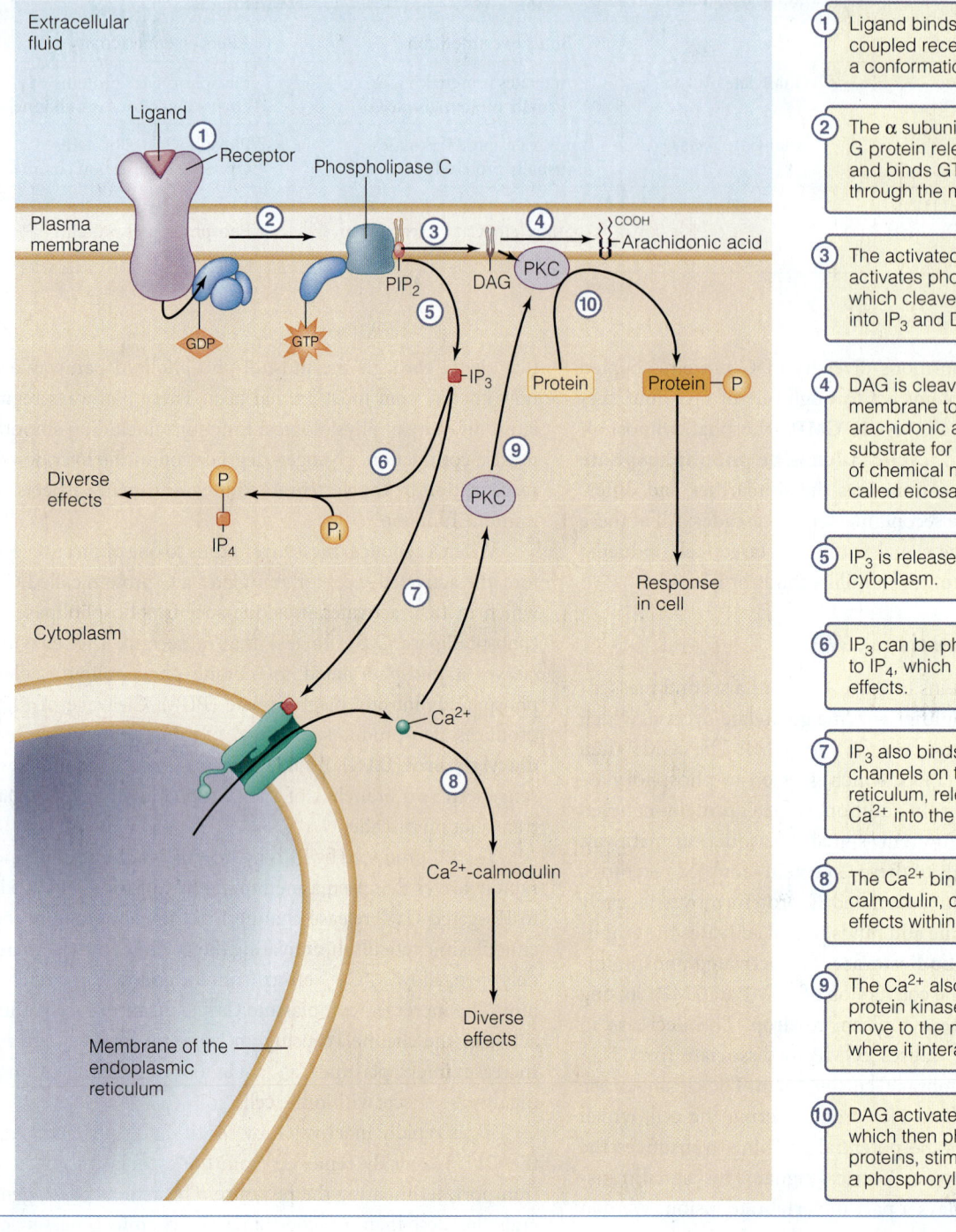

DAG can activate protein kinase C (PKC), a Ca^{2+}-dependent kinase. An increase in cytoplasmic Ca^{2+} (caused by signals from IP_3) triggers PKC to move to the membrane, where it interacts with DAG. At the membrane, DAG activates PKC. Activated PKC phosphorylates serine and threonine residues on a variety of proteins including MAP kinase, which we have already discussed. Through these pathways,

activated PKC can alter the activities of existing proteins and influence the transcription of genes and thus the production of new proteins.

Cyclic AMP was the first second messenger discovered

Many physiologically important processes involve G proteins that signal via the **adenylate cyclase**–cyclic AMP system, using cAMP as a second messenger. Cyclic AMP was the first intracellular second messenger identified, and as a result we know a great deal about these signal transduction pathways. Two types of G proteins interact with the cAMP signal transduction pathway: stimulatory G proteins (G_s) and inhibitory G proteins (G_i) (Figure 4.29). G_s and G_i proteins differ in their subunits, although their β and γ subunits can be similar. Both G_i and G_s proteins interact with the amplifier enzyme adenylate cyclase, which catalyzes the conversion of ATP to cAMP. When a ligand binds to a receptor that interacts with a G_s protein, the α_s subunit of the activated G_s protein binds to and activates the membrane-bound enzyme adenylate cyclase. When a ligand binds to a receptor that interacts with a G_i protein, the α_i subunits of the G_i protein inhibit adenylate cyclase. G_i and G_s proteins act together to regulate intracellular cAMP levels.

In the next step of the cAMP signal transduction pathway, cAMP binds to protein kinase A (PKA) at sites on the regulatory subunit of the inactive kinase. Binding of cAMP alters the conformation of the regulatory subunits, causing them to dissociate from the catalytic subunits. The unbound catalytic subunits are active, and catalyze the phosphorylation of specific proteins. Protein phosphorylation causes a response in the target cell.

Cells have mechanisms to rapidly dephosphorylate the proteins phosphorylated by PKA, ensuring that cAMP-dependent signals persist only for short periods (seconds to minutes). Serine/threonine phosphatases remove the phosphates added by PKA. The activity of proteins regulated by phosphorylation depends on the balance between the activities of PKA and the serine/threonine phosphatases. When cAMP stimulates PKA activity, the balance of the reaction tends to swing toward phosphorylation of the target proteins.

FIGURE 4.29 G protein signal transduction via adenylate cyclase

G protein–coupled signal transduction through adenylate cyclase can be either stimulatory or inhibitory.

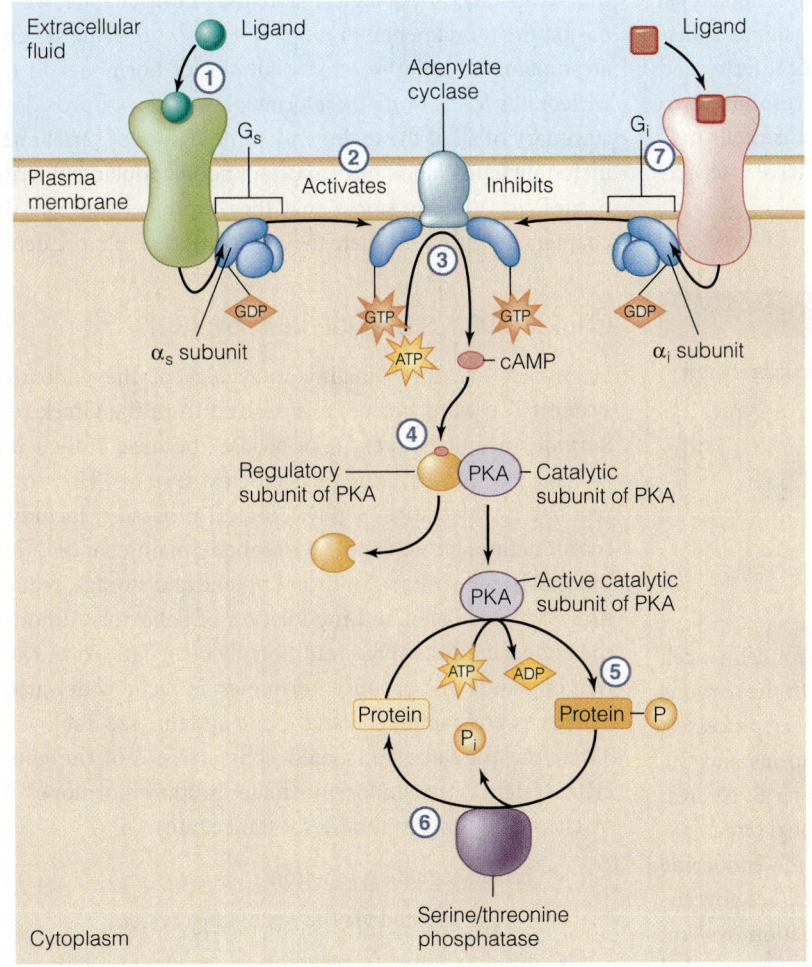

① Ligand binds to a G_s protein–coupled receptor, causing a conformational change.

② The α_s subunit releases GDP, binds GTP, moves through the membrane, and activates adenylate cyclase.

③ Activated adenylate cyclase catalyzes the conversion of ATP to cAMP.

④ cAMP binds to the regulatory subunit of protein kinase A (PKA), which dissociates from the catalytic subunit, activating it.

⑤ The activated catalytic subunit phosphorylates proteins, causing a response.

⑥ The phosphorylated proteins are rapidly dephosphorylated by serine/threonine phosphatases, terminating the response.

⑦ When ligand binds to a G_i protein–coupled receptor, the α_i subunit inhibits adenylate cyclase, inhibiting the signal transduction pathway.

In contrast, when cAMP levels are low, the balance of the reaction tends to swing toward the dephosphorylation of the target proteins.

Signal transduction pathways can interact

Ca^{2+} and cAMP signal transduction pathways interact with each other at several levels. For example, Ca^{2+}-calmodulin interacts with adenylate cyclase. Adenylate cyclase is the first amplifier enzyme of the cAMP-mediated signal transduction pathway, and catalyzes the production of cAMP. Similarly, Ca^{2+}-calmodulin also interacts with cAMP phosphodiesterase, the enzyme that breaks down cAMP. Therefore, Ca^{2+} plays a role in regulating the cAMP signaling pathway. Conversely, PKA, one of the steps in the cAMP signaling pathway, can phosphorylate Ca^{2+} channels and pumps, altering their activity. Thus, the cAMP signaling pathway can regulate the Ca^{2+}-calmodulin pathway. Both protein kinase A and CaM kinase often phosphorylate different sites on the same target proteins. From this example, it is clear that signal transduction cascades in the cell are not simple linear connections from the binding of a chemical messenger, through several amplification steps, culminating in a cellular response. Instead, signal transduction in the cell acts more like a network of intertwined threads that combine to generate complex responses. **In vivo**, the network is even more complex, because cells may receive multiple signals, many of which may have interacting effects.

CONCEPT CHECK

19. Outline the five main steps in G protein–coupled receptor signaling.
20. What is a second messenger?

INTRODUCTION TO ENDOCRINE SYSTEMS

The endocrine system is an important system for cell-to-cell communication in many animals. Together with the nervous system, it regulates essentially all physiological processes. We discuss the structure and function of neurons and the nervous system in subsequent chapters (Chapter 5: Neuron Structure and Function and Chapter 8: Functional Organization of Nervous Systems). Here, we focus on the endocrine system to provide an introduction to the principles governing the operation of this critical communication system. Throughout this book, we return to both the nervous and endocrine systems as we discuss how physiological systems

are regulated. Therefore, it is important to develop a clear understanding of how both the nervous and endocrine systems are organized and how they function before beginning to study the functions of the other systems.

Endocrine systems evolved along with the circulatory systems of animals. Thus, the structure and function of endocrine systems varies a great deal, particularly among the invertebrates, which represent more than 98 percent of the species on Earth. Consistent with the diverse body plans of invertebrates (see Chapter 2: Physiological Evolution of Animals), their endocrine systems are extremely diverse. In contrast, the body plans of vertebrate taxa are much more similar to each other and their endocrine systems have many features in common. In this chapter, we begin by focusing on the endocrine systems of the vertebrates, and then provide a brief introduction to invertebrate endocrinology in the context of our general discussion of the evolution of endocrine systems later in this chapter.

Because of the diversity of animal hormones, within the scope of this chapter it would be impossible to examine all of the hormones in all animal groups in any detail. Instead, we defer treatment of most hormones to later chapters, where they will be discussed in the context of their role in the regulation of specific physiological systems. In this chapter, we focus on the fundamental principles of how endocrine systems are organized, using selected examples of hormones in the vertebrates to illustrate these principles. Table 4.4 provides a summary of all of the major endocrine tissues of vertebrates, including both glands and important nonglandular endocrine tissues, and the hormones that they produce, and lists the chapters in this book where they are discussed in more detail.

Characteristics of Endocrine Systems

Hormones are the signaling molecules of the endocrine system. The word hormone is derived from the Greek root *hormao,* meaning "to excite or arouse," because of their important role in activating physiological systems. Hormones regulate a wide range of physiological processes, including reproduction, growth and development, maintenance of homeostasis, regulation of nutrient uptake and storage, regulation of metabolism, and modulation of behavior. Although the endocrine system has traditionally been defined as a system of glands that produce hormones, in fact a wide variety of tissues are part of the endocrine system (see Table 4.4). Thus, the fundamental shared characteristic of the endocrine system is that endocrine tissues produce hormones. To be classified as a hormone, a substance must:

- Have a signaling function
- Be transported via the circulatory system
- Bind to a specific receptor
- Exert its effects at extremely low concentrations

Table 4.4 The major hormones of vertebrates				
Secretory Tissue	**Hormone**	**Chemical Class**	**Effects**	**For More Details, See**
Pineal gland	Melatonin	Amine	Circadian and seasonal rhythms	Chapter 7
Hypothalamus (clusters of secretory neurons)	Tropic hormones (see Figure 4.33)	Peptides	Regulation of anterior pituitary	Chapter 4 Chapter 8 Chapter 13 Chapter 16
Posterior pituitary (extensions of hypothalamic neurons)	Oxytocin	Peptide	Breast and uterus in mammals	Chapter 16
	Vasopressin (mammals)	Peptide	Water reabsorption in excretory system	Chapter 13
	Vasotocin, isotocin, mesotocin (fish, amphibians, reptiles, birds)	Peptide	Activities similar to both oxytocin and vasopressin	Chapter 13
Anterior pituitary gland	Prolactin (PRL)	Peptide	Milk production in mammals, behavior, osmoregulation in fish	Chapter 16 Chapter 13
	Growth hormone (GH)	Peptide	Metabolism, growth	Chapter 13 Chapter 14
	Adrenocorticotropic hormone (ACTH)	Peptide	Release of corticosteroids	Chapter 4 Chapter 8 Chapter 13
	Thyroid-stimulating hormone (TSH)	Peptide	Synthesis and release of thyroid hormones	Chapter 8
	Follicle-stimulating hormone (FSH)	Peptide	Egg or sperm production; sex hormone production	Chapter 16
	Luteinizing hormone (LH)	Peptide	Sex hormone production; egg or sperm production	Chapter 16
Thyroid gland	Triiodothyronine (T_3) and thyroxine (T_4)	Amines	Metabolism, growth, and development	Chapter 13
	Calcitonin	Peptide	Regulation of plasma Ca^{2+} (in nonhuman vertebrates)	Chapter 13 Chapter 14
Parathyroid gland	Parathyroid hormone	Peptide	Regulation of plasma Ca^{2+} and phosphate	Chapter 13
Thymus gland	Thymosin, thymopoietin	Peptide	Immune system development	Chapter 10
Heart (individual cells in atrium)	Atrial natriuretic peptide (ANP)	Peptide	Regulation of sodium levels and blood pressure	Chapter 9 Chapter 13
Liver (various cells)	Angiotensin (secreted as precursor molecule angiotensinogen)	Peptide	Regulation of aldosterone; regulation of blood pressure	Chapter 9 Chapter 13
	Insulin-like growth factor (IGF)	Peptide	Growth, metabolism	Chapter 13 Chapter 14
Stomach and small intestine (various cells)	Gastrin, cholecystokinin (CCK), secretin, ghrelin, and many others	Peptides	Digestion and absorption of nutrients; regulation of food intake	Chapter 14
Pancreas	Insulin	Peptide	Regulation of blood glucose	Chapter 4 Chapter 14
	Glucagon	Peptide	Regulation of blood glucose	Chapter 4 Chapter 14

(continued)

Table 4.4 **The major hormones of vertebrates** (*continued*)

Secretory Tissue	Hormone	Chemical Class	Effects	For More Details, See
	Somatostatin	Peptide	Regulation of blood glucose and other nutrients; growth; metabolism	Chapter 4 Chapter 14
	Pancreatic polypeptide	Peptide	Regulation of pancreas; glucose regulation	Chapter 14
Adrenal gland (cortex) in mammals; dispersed cells in other vertebrates	Aldosterone (in tetrapods, but not in fish)	Steroid	Ion regulation	Chapter 13
	Glucocorticoids (e.g., cortisol)	Steroid	Ion regulation; stress response; nutrient uptake and storage; behavior	Chapter 4 Chapter 8 Chapter 13
	Precursors of androgens	Steroids	Sex drive in females; bone growth at puberty in males	Chapter 16
Adrenal gland (medulla) in mammals; chromaffin cells in other vertebrates	Epinephrine, norepinephrine	Amines	Stress response; regulation of cardiovascular system	Chapter 4 Chapter 8 Chapter 9
Corpuscles of Stannius (fish); various tissues in mammals	Stanniocalcin	Peptide	Plasma calcium regulation in fish; function in mammals poorly understood	Chapter 13
Kidney (various cells)	Erythropoietin (EPO)	Peptide	Red blood cell production	Chapter 9 Chapter 11
Adipose tissue (various cells)	Leptin	Peptide	Food intake; metabolism; reproduction	Chapter 14
Testes (male)	Inhibin	Peptide	Regulation of sex hormones	Chapter 16
	Androgens	Steroid	Sperm production; secondary sexual characteristics	Chapter 16
Ovaries (female)	Inhibin	Peptide	Regulation of sex hormones	Chapter 16
	Estrogens and progesterone	Steroid	Egg production; secondary sexual characteristics	Chapter 16
Placenta (pregnant female mammals only)	Estrogens and progesterone	Steroids	Fetal and maternal development	Chapter 16
	Chorionic gonadotropin (CG) (Independently evolved in anthropoid primates (monkeys, apes, humans) and horses only)	Peptide	Fetal and maternal development	Chapter 16
	Chorionic somatomammotropin (CS) (also called placental lactogen) (Independently evolved in primates, rodents, and ruminants only)	Peptide	Fetal and maternal development	Chapter 16

A single hormone may influence multiple physiological processes. For example, glucocorticoid hormones are important in regulating metabolism, nutrient uptake and storage, and behavior, and they also affect immune function. Hormones also interact to affect physiological processes. For example, the hormones insulin and glucagon work together to regulate blood glucose levels.

Like other signaling molecules, hormones exert their effects by binding to receptors expressed by the target cell. Like the interactions between all signaling molecules and their receptors, the interaction between a hormone and its receptor is highly specific, and only tissues that express the appropriate receptor will respond to a particular hormone. A single hormone can also have very distinct effects on different target cells because target cells can express alternative forms of receptor for a particular hormone that are coupled to different signal transduction pathways. For example, the hormone epinephrine causes blood vessels in the gut to constrict and causes blood vessels in **skeletal muscles** to dilate. Hormone levels in the blood must be tightly regulated for them to act as controllers of physiological systems. This regulation is accomplished using feedback loops.

Hormone levels are regulated by feedback loops

Feedback loops contain a *sensor* that detects the state or level of a regulated variable and sends that information to an **integrating center** that evaluates the incoming information and sends out a signal that provokes an appropriate response in an **effector**—a target tissue that causes (effects) a change in the regulated variable.

In a **negative feedback loop** a change in the regulated variable causes a response in the effector that tends to return the regulated variable back to its original value. In this way, a negative feedback loop tends to hold the regulated variable close to a particular **set point** and maintain homeostasis. In a **positive feedback loop** the system responds to a change in the regulated variable by causing further deviation from the set point. Positive feedback loops amplify changes in the regulated variable and cause large, rapid, physiological changes. A key feature of positive feedback loops is that they require an additional factor to control the loop and stop the positive feedback, which otherwise could continue amplifying the signal indefinitely.

The actions of insulin illustrate the principle of negative feedback

Most animals maintain some level of homeostatic regulation over the concentration of sugars in their extracellular fluids. Mammals have particularly precise control over the glucose levels in their blood, because the mammalian brain is entirely reliant on glucose as a fuel. If glucose levels fall too low, the brain cannot function. In contrast, if glucose levels rise too high, the osmotic balance of the blood will be disturbed. This precise homeostatic regulation is governed by negative feedback control.

Insulin is one of several hormones involved in the homeostatic regulation of blood glucose in mammals. In mammals, a gland called the **pancreas** secretes the peptide hormone insulin when blood glucose rises. The pancreas is a complex gland with both exocrine and endocrine functions. The exocrine pancreas secretes digestive enzymes into the gut (see Chapter 14: Digestion and Energy Metabolism). Dispersed among the exocrine tissue are small clumps of cells, termed the **islets of Langerhans**, that perform the endocrine functions of the pancreas. **Pancreatic beta cells** within these islets secrete insulin when blood glucose rises.

Increases in blood glucose cause the metabolic rate of the cell to increase, resulting in an increase in ATP levels within the cell. The increased [ATP] sends a signal to an ATP-dependent potassium (K_{ATP}) channel, causing it to close. Closing of a K^+ channel will cause the cell to depolarize (see Chapter 3: Chemistry, Biochemistry, and Cell Physiology). This change in membrane potential causes a voltage-gated Ca^{2+} channel to open, causing Ca^{2+} to enter the cell. The increase in intracellular Ca^{2+} acts as a signal to cause the exocytosis of vesicles containing insulin. The insulin released from the cell travels through blood to target cells in the liver, adipose tissue, and muscle. At the target cells, insulin binds to and activates its receptor, which, as we have already discussed, is a receptor tyrosine kinase (see Figure 4.24). The activated receptor is then autophosphorylated, initiating a complex network of signal transduction pathways. The ultimate effect of these signal transduction pathways is to promote the uptake and storage of glucose, resulting in a decrease in blood glucose levels. The decrease in blood glucose removes the signal for the pancreatic cell to release insulin, and insulin levels decline, in an example of negative feedback regulation.

The actions of oxytocin illustrate the principle of postive feedback

Most hormonal regulation involves negative feedback loops, but **oxytocin** is an example of a hormone that is involved in a positive feedback pathway. Oxytocin has a wide range of functions, and is both a neurotransmitter and a hormone. In mammals, one of its important endocrine functions involves regulation of uterine contraction (see Chapter 16: Reproductive Physiology). At the onset of *parturition,* the process of expelling a fetus from the uterus at birth, the fetus changes position, putting pressure on the cervix (the opening of the uterus). Stretch-sensitive cells in the cervix send a signal to the brain that causes the release of oxytocin from the posterior pituitary. Oxytocin binds to receptors on the smooth muscle cells of the uterus, causing them to contract. Uterine contractions push the fetus against the cervix, increasing the stimulus on the stretch-sensitive cells. This increases the signal and causes even more oxytocin to be released. This positive feedback loop continues until the fetus is delivered, releasing the pressure on the cervix and terminating the signal.

Feedback loops can be complex

The feedback loop regulating insulin secretion involves a relatively straightforward direct feedback loop (Figure 4.30a). In a direct feedback loop the endocrine cell itself senses a change in the extracellular environment and releases a chemical messenger that acts on target cells elsewhere in the body. Thus, the endocrine cell acts as the integrating center that interprets the change in the stimulus variable. The response of the target cell to the secreted hormone then brings the stimulus variable back into the normal range. Atrial natriuretic peptide (ANP) is another example of a hormone involved in a direct feedback loop. Stretch-sensitive cells in the atrium of the mammalian heart sense the increased tension caused by increased blood pressure within the atrium. These cells then secrete ANP, which travels to target cells in the blood vessels and kidneys and causes responses that lower blood pressure. The lowered blood pressure feeds back by reducing the tension on the atrial cells, reducing the release of ANP.

First-order feedback loops provide a slightly more sophisticated level of regulation, involving the nervous system (Figure 4.30b). In these types of pathways, a sensory organ perceives a stimulus and sends a signal via the nervous system

---

FIGURE 4.30 **Feedback regulatory systems in animals**

(a) Direct feedback loops involve only the endocrine system, and the endocrine gland acts both as the integrating center and as the tissue that communicates with the target organ. **(b)** First-order feedback loops have one step (a neuron that releases a neurotransmitter or a neurohormone) between the integrating center and the target organ. **(c)** Second-order feedback loops have two steps (a neuron and an endocrine gland) between the integrating center and the target organ. **(d)** Third-order feedback loops contain an additional endocrine gland in the pathway, providing a third point of feedback regulation.

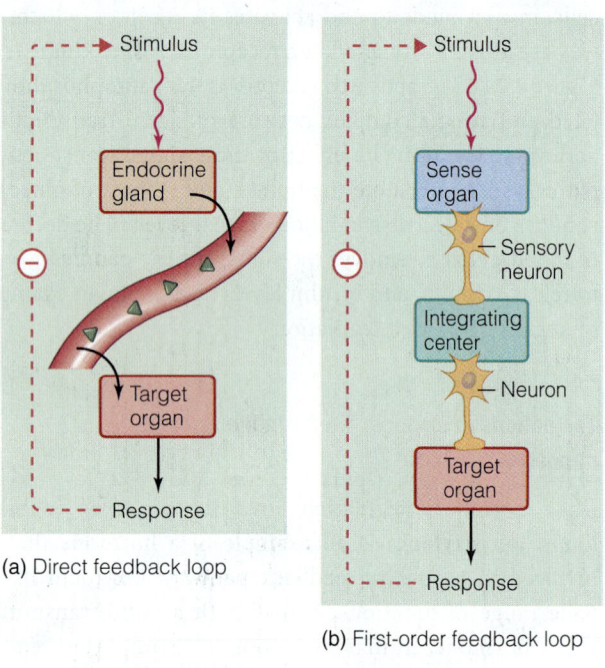

(a) Direct feedback loop

(b) First-order feedback loop

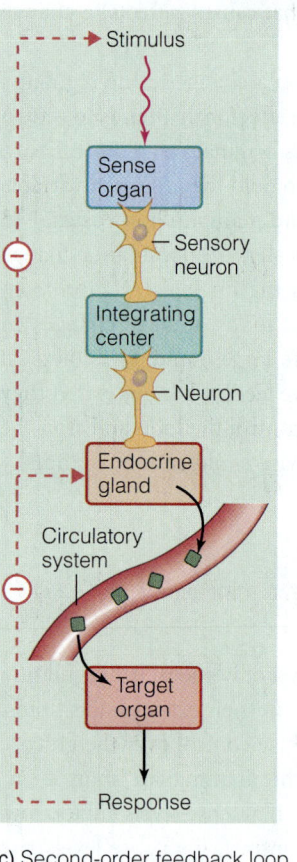

(c) Second-order feedback loop

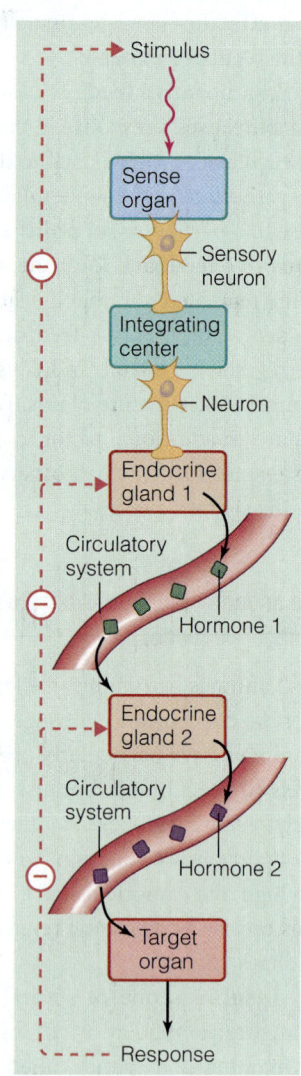

(d) Third-order feedback loop

to an integrating center (such as the brain) that interprets the signal. Neurons then transmit the signal (in the form of either a neurotransmitter or a neurohormone) to a specific target organ, causing a response. Neural and neurohormonal pathways are both termed first-order response pathways because only a single step links the integrating center and the response.

Most endocrine pathways in vertebrates, however, are more complicated than direct or first-order pathways, and involve both the nervous and endocrine systems. These pathways can be classified as either second- or third-order feedback loops. Every step in a response loop may act as a control point over the pathway. Thus, direct and first-order response pathways can be regulated at only one control point; second-order pathways can be regulated at two points; and third-order pathways can be regulated at three points. Third-order feedback loops provide the most sophisticated and tightly regulated feedback.

Figure 4.30c shows a typical second-order feedback loop. In this case, a sense organ perceives a stimulus and sends a signal to the integrating center, which sends a signal via a neuron that secretes either a neurohormone or a neurotransmitter that acts on an endocrine gland. The endocrine gland then secretes a hormone into the blood. The hormone travels to the target cell, causing a response.

In third-order feedback loops (Figure 4.30d), a sense organ perceives a stimulus and sends a signal to the integrating center. The integrating center then sends a signal via a neuron that secretes either a neurohormone or a neurotransmitter that acts on an endocrine gland. The endocrine gland then secretes a hormone that binds to a receptor on a second endocrine gland and triggers the secretion of a second hormone, which then induces a response in the target cells.

Pituitary hormones provide examples of several types of feedback loops

The vertebrate pituitary gland secretes many important hormones that regulate growth, reproduction, and metabolism. Pituitary hormones also control the release of hormones from other important endocrine glands, including the thyroid gland, the adrenal glands, and the endocrine cells of the gonads. As a result, the pituitary is often considered the "master gland" of vertebrates.

The pituitary gland is present in all vertebrates, and its structure, function, and embryonic origins have many similarities in all vertebrate groups, suggesting that the pituitary gland evolved in the earliest vertebrates. However, as we discuss at the end of this chapter, there is also substantial variation in pituitary structure among vertebrate taxa. Here we focus on the structure of the mammalian pituitary to provide an introduction to this critical endocrine gland. The pituitary gland is divided into two distinct sections: the *neurohypophysis*, or

posterior pituitary, and the *adenohypophysis*, which includes the **anterior pituitary**. The neurohypophysis is embryologically derived from neural ectoderm, and is an extension of a part of the brain called the hypothalamus. The adenohypophysis has a different embryological origin, as it is derived from a portion of the ectoderm of the roof of the mouth called Rathke's pouch. The adenohypophysis also includes a region called the intermediate lobe, which is a part of the adenohypophysis adjacent to the posterior pituitary. In adult mammals, this region is simply a thin sheet of cells that cannot be easily distinguished from the anterior lobe of the pituitary, but it can be quite large in other vertebrates. The intermediate lobe secretes melanocyte-stimulating hormone (MSH). The hormones of the pituitary provide examples of many types of feedback loops, including first-, second-, and third-order feedback loops.

Neurohormones from the posterior pituitary are involved in first-order feedback loops

The posterior pituitary is not really an independent organ but is instead an extension of the hypothalamus via a stalk called the *infundibulum* (Figure 4.31). Neurons that originate in the hypothalamus travel through the infundibulum to terminate in the posterior pituitary. In the hypothalamus, the cell bodies of these neurons synthesize the hormones oxytocin and vasopressin and package them into secretory vesicles. The vesicles are transported along the neuron via a process called **axonal transport** (see Chapters 5 and 6). The neural endings of these hypothalamic neurons, which are located in the posterior pituitary, secrete the hormones from these vesicles into the blood. Thus these posterior pituitary hormones are examples of neurohormones. Because only a single step (a hypothalamic neuron that secretes a neurohormone) connects the integrating center and the effector organs, oxytocin and vasopressin are examples of neurohormones involved in first-order feedback loops.

The hypothalamus regulates the secretion of anterior pituitary hormones

In all vertebrates, the hypothalamus controls the secretion of hormones from the anterior pituitary. In hagfish, lampreys, and **teleost fishes**, this control is accomplished by paracrine communication of chemical messengers released by hypothalamic neurons that are located close to the cells of the anterior pituitary. In other vertebrates, however, the connection between the hypothalamus and the anterior pituitary is indirect. Hypothalamic neurons secrete neurohormones into a specialized microcirculation, called the **hypothalamic-pituitary portal system** (Figure 4.32). A **portal system** is an arrangement of blood vessels with two capillary beds separated by a **portal vein**. The hypothalamic-pituitary portal

FIGURE 4.31 **The hypothalamus and the posterior pituitary gland of mammals**

The pituitary gland is located at the base of the brain, and is divided into the anterior pituitary and the posterior pituitary. The infundibulum connects the hypothalamus—a part of the brain—and the posterior pituitary, which is made up of the endings of neurons that originate in the hypothalamus. The nerve endings of the posterior pituitary secrete neurohormones into the blood. The anterior pituitary secretes hormones into the blood, under the control of neurohormones released by the hypothalamus.

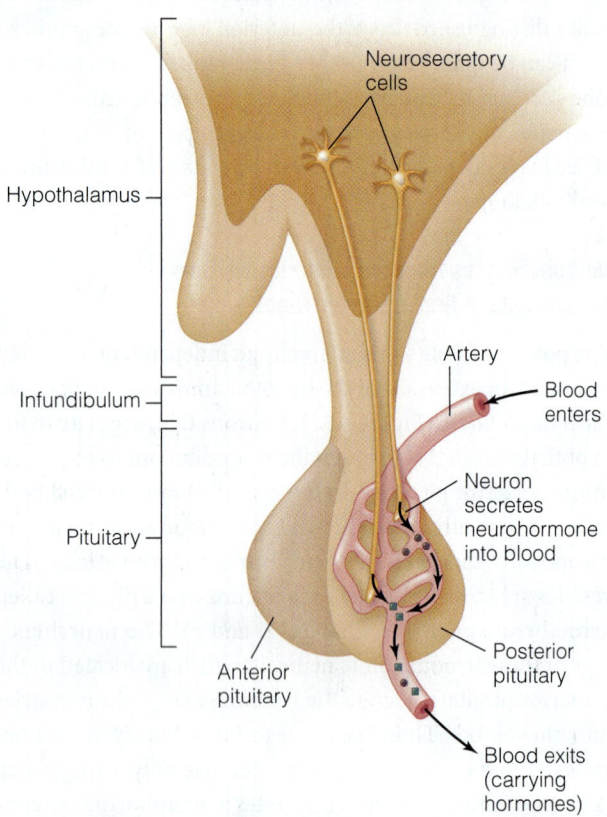

FIGURE 4.32 **The anterior pituitary and the hypothalamic-pituitary portal system**

Neurons from the hypothalamus secrete neurohormones into the hypothalamic-pituitary portal circulatory system. The portal vein carries the neurohormones to the anterior pituitary, where they stimulate endocrine cells to release hormones into the blood. The blood exits from the pituitary, carrying the hormones throughout the body via the circulatory system.

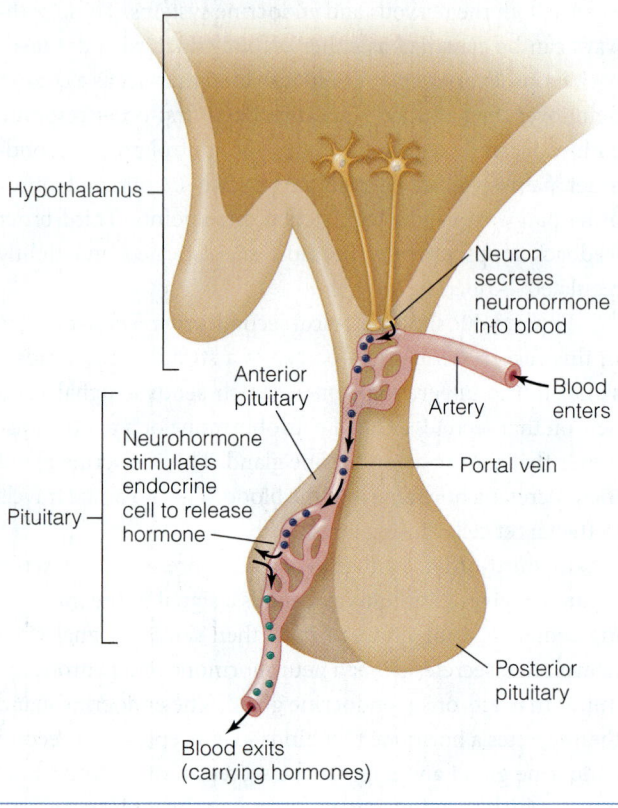

system carries the neurohormones secreted by the hypothalamus to the anterior pituitary, where they stimulate or inhibit the release of pituitary hormones. The hypothalamic-pituitary portal system allows neurohormones to be carried from the hypothalamus to the pituitary without being diluted in the general circulation.

Prolactin is an anterior pituitary hormone involved in a second-order feedback loop

Figure 4.33 shows the relationship between the hypothalamic neurohormones and the hormones of the anterior pituitary. Prolactin is the only anterior pituitary hormone that participates in a second-order feedback loop. The brain acts as the integrating center that regulates the secretion of prolactin, stimulating the hypothalamus to release the neurohormones prolactin-releasing hormone or prolactin-inhibiting hormone

into the hypothalamic-pituitary portal system. These neurohormones regulate the release of **prolactin**, which has direct effects on its target tissues. Prolactin is best known for regulating the secretion of milk from the mammary glands in mammals, but it also has diverse effects on sexual behavior and growth. It is also involved in the regulation of larval development and ion and water balance in some nonmammalian vertebrates.

Many anterior pituitary hormones participate in third-order pathways

In contrast to prolactin, the majority of anterior pituitary hormones can go on to regulate the release of yet more hormones, and thus they participate in third-order feedback loops. Hormones that cause the release of other hormones are called **tropic (or trophic) hormones**, from the Greek root *tropos*, "to turn toward." (The alternate term, which is often heard, is from the Greek root *trophikos*, "nourishment.") For example, the neurohormone corticotropin-releasing

FIGURE 4.33 **The relationship between the hypothalamic neurohormones and the hormones of the anterior pituitary**

The hypothalamus secretes releasing or inhibiting neurohormones into the hypothalamic-pituitary portal system. These neurohormones act on the endocrine cells of the anterior pituitary to stimulate or inhibit the release of the pituitary hormones. The circulatory system carries these hormones to their target tissues, causing a response. Some of these target tissues are endocrine glands, which secrete hormones into the blood. The circulatory system carries these hormones to their target tissues, causing a response.

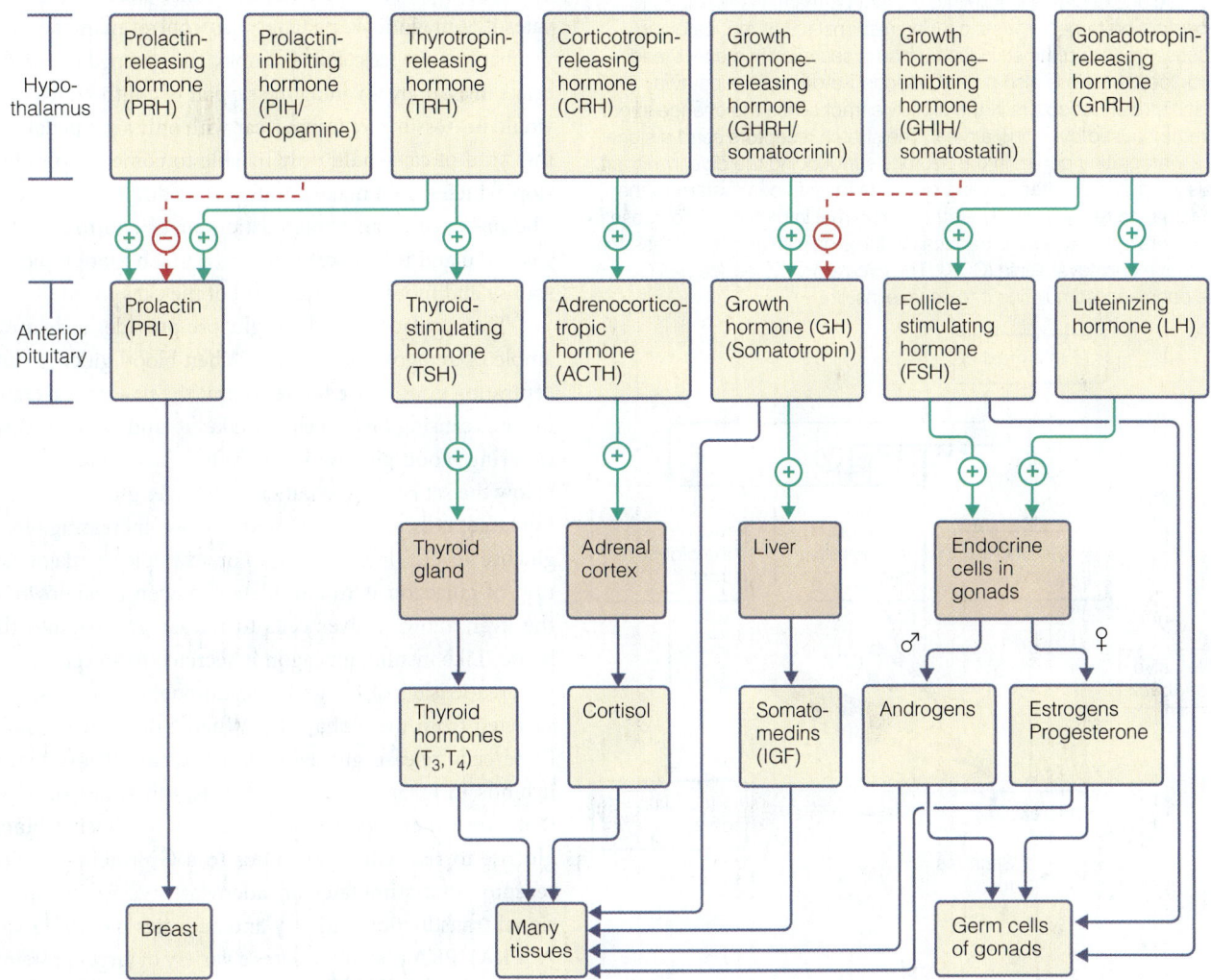

hormone from the hypothalamus regulates the secretion of adrenocorticotropic hormone (ACTH) from the pituitary, which in turn causes the release of glucocorticoid hormones from the adrenal **cortex**, which goes on to affect the activity of many target tissues. Third-order feedback loops are subject to very complex regulation because changes in the concentration of any of the hormones in the hypothalamic-pituitary axis can regulate the concentrations of other hormones in the pathway, generally via negative feedback.

A single hormone can be regulated by multiple types of feedback pathways

Hormones can be regulated in a variety of ways, using different types of feedback pathways. Figure 4.34 summarizes some of the ways in which insulin levels are regulated in mammals, as an example of this complexity. Stretch receptors in the gut can detect the presence of food in the digestive tract, and send a signal to an integrating center in the enteric nervous system (the neurons surrounding the digestive system; see Chapter 8: Functional Organization of Nervous Systems). The enteric nervous system then sends a neural signal directly to the pancreas, causing an increase in the secretion of insulin even before blood glucose starts to rise. This kind of direct control of hormone secretion by the nervous system is an example of a second-order feedback loop. In addition, the pancreas secretes insulin in response to the hormone cholecystokinin (CCK), which is secreted by the gut. The gut releases CCK when glucose-sensitive cells in the gut detect the presence of glucose in a meal. Note that the CCK-mediated pathway does not fit neatly into our classification of pathway types, as it involves two hormones but does not

FIGURE 4.34 **Interaction of some of the pathways regulating insulin secretion**

Insulin is an example of a hormone that is regulated by several feedback pathways. A direct stimulus-response pathway (pathway 1) regulates insulin synthesis. The pancreas senses increases in blood glucose and secretes insulin into the bloodstream. Insulin binds to receptors on target organs, causing responses that reduce blood glucose, reducing the stimulus for insulin secretion in a direct feedback loop. Insulin is also part of a second-order control pathway 3, in which stretch receptors in the digestive tract sense the change in gut volume caused by eating a meal. The stretch receptors send a signal to an integrating center in the neurons surrounding the digestive tract. This integrating center sends a signal via the nervous system to the pancreas to release insulin. At the same time, in pathway 2, glucose receptors in the digestive tract cause the digestive tract to release the hormone cholecystokinin (CCK). The circulatory system carries CCK to the pancreas, stimulating it to secrete insulin.

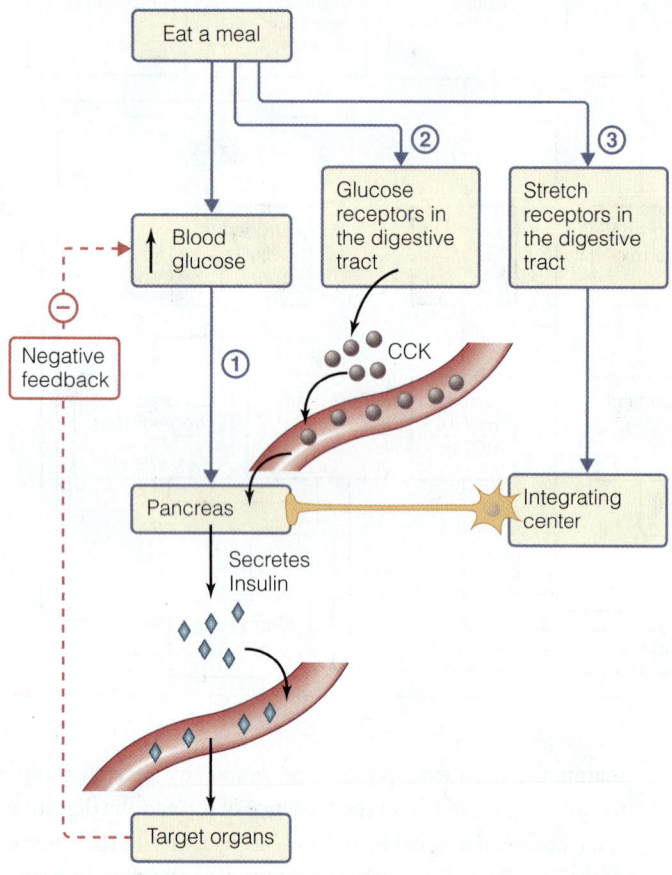

utilize the central nervous system. This example emphasizes the concept that pathways of feedback regulation represent a continuum of design, rather than discrete organizational systems, and that many of these pathways can interact to form even more-complex regulatory networks. In the case of insulin, many pathways interact to regulate insulin secretion, only some of which are shown in Figure 4.34. These interacting pathways allow the homeostatic regulation of blood glucose to be extremely responsive to environmental conditions.

Antagonistic hormone pairs provide precise regulation

The endocrine system can maintain extremely precise control over physiological processes by using antagonistic pairs of hormones. In an antagonistic pair, one hormone activates a process, whereas the other hormone inactivates it. Antagonistic pairings also control many familiar mechanical devices. For example, the gas pedal and the brake in a car are an antagonistic pair of control devices. It would be possible to design a car with only a gas pedal, but this kind of car would only be able to come to a gradual stop, which would make it much more difficult to control. The presence of an antagonistic pair of controllers (the gas pedal and the brake) provides a much more rapid response and more precise control of the car's speed.

The regulation of blood glucose provides a clear example of antagonistic pairing. When blood glucose concentration rises above the set point, the pancreas secretes insulin, causing target cells to take up and store glucose, lowering blood glucose levels. When blood glucose falls below the set point, the pancreas secretes glucagon, causing target cells to release stored glucose, increasing blood glucose levels (Figure 4.35). For example, a major action of glucagon is to stimulate glycogen breakdown in the liver, allowing liver cells to release glucose into the blood. Like insulin, glucagon is secreted from cells in the pancreatic islets of Langerhans, although in this case it is secreted from the alpha cells. When blood glucose falls, these cells release glucagon into the circulation, where it binds to receptors on target cells, initiating pathways that cause them to release glucose, thus causing blood glucose to rise. Glucagon binds to a G protein–coupled receptor that stimulates an adenylate cyclase–mediated signal transduction pathway and activates protein kinase A (PKA). PKA phosphorylates a variety of target proteins, causing biochemical changes that ultimately promote the release of glucose into the blood. By acting together, insulin and glucagon maintain blood glucose levels within a very narrow range.

Another clear example of an antagonistic hormone pair is provided by the hormones that regulate Ca^{2+} levels in the blood. The **parathyroid glands** sense blood Ca^{2+} levels. When Ca^{2+} levels fall, these glands produce **parathyroid hormone**, which stimulates Ca^{2+} release from bone, increases the absorption of Ca^{2+} by the intestine, and increases Ca^{2+} reabsorption by the kidneys. Together, these responses increase blood Ca^{2+} levels. Thus parathyroid hormone is involved in the negative feedback regulation of blood Ca^{2+} levels. **Calcitonin** antagonizes the actions of parathyroid hormone by inhibiting the release of Ca^{2+} from the bones and reducing the reabsorption of Ca^{2+} by the kidneys, resulting in loss of Ca^{2+} in the urine. Together these responses

FIGURE 4.35 **Antagonistic regulation of blood glucose by insulin and glucagon**

Increases in plasma glucose stimulate the beta cells of the pancreas to increase insulin secretion. At the same time, this causes the alpha cells of the pancreas to decrease glucagon secretion. Increased insulin stimulates its target tissues to increase glucose uptake. Decreased glucagon causes its target tissues to decrease glucose release. Together these actions decrease plasma glucose in a negative feedback loop. Similarly, if plasma glucose declines, insulin secretion decreases and glucagon secretion increases, stimulating glucose release into the plasma.

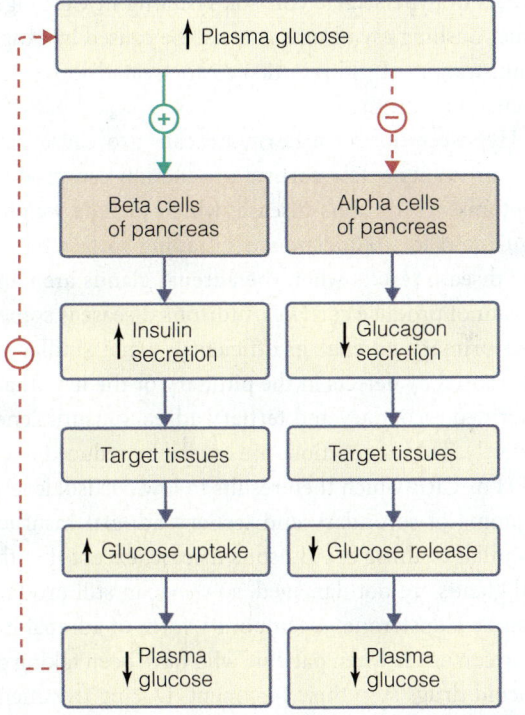

FIGURE 4.36 **Additivity and synergism**

Infusion of cortisol, glucagon, or epinephrine into dogs results in an increase in blood glucose. These effects are larger when the hormones are injected in combination. Infusion of epinephrine and glucagon results in additive effects on blood glucose. Infusion of all three hormones in combination has a synergistic effect.

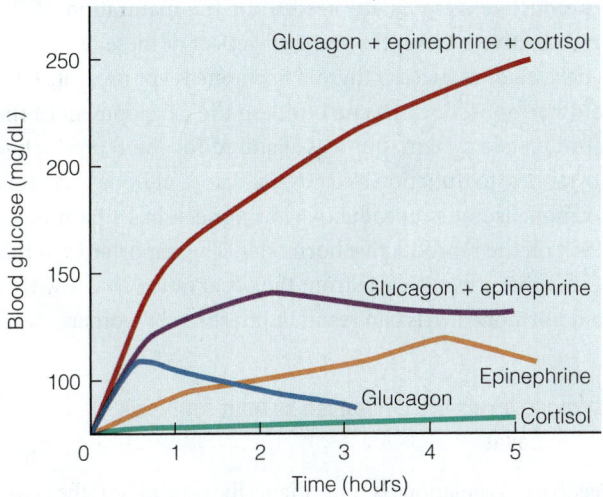

Figure source: Data from Eigler, N., Saccà, L., & Sherwin, R. S. (1979, January 1). Synergistic interactions of physiologic increments of glucagon, epinephrine, and cortisol in the dog: A model for stress-induced hyperglycemia. *Journal of Clinical Investigation, 63* (1),114–123. doi:10.1172/JCI109264. Copyright © 1979, The American Society for Clinical Investigation.

cause plasma Ca^{2+} to decrease. As we discuss later in this chapter, calcitonin is less important for calcium regulation in mammals than it is in other vertebrates.

Hormones can demonstrate additivity and synergism

Hormones can also interact positively to increase the activity of a physiological system. These positive interactions can be *additive*, in which case the effect of the hormones in combination is equivalent to the sum of the effects of each hormone in isolation. The regulation of blood glucose provides an example of the additive effects of hormones. Like glucagon, the hormones epinephrine (also called adrenalin) and cortisol can increase blood glucose. Figure 4.36 illustrates the results of an experiment in which glucagon, epinephrine, cortisol, or combinations of these hormones were injected into dogs. Alone, injection of glucagon, epinephrine, or cortisol causes an increase in blood glucose. When both glucagon and epinephrine are injected together,

the increase in blood glucose is larger, and is equivalent to the sum of the increase in blood glucose in response to epinephrine plus the increase in blood glucose in response to glucagon.

Epinephrine binds to a G protein–coupled receptor in the cell membrane of liver cells. This receptor signals via an adenylate cyclase–mediated signal transduction pathway that activates PKA. This is similar to glucagon signaling, which also occurs via activation of PKA. Thus, although these two hormones bind to different G protein–coupled receptors, they both activate PKA, and the effect of the hormones in combination is equal to the sum of the actions of each hormone alone.

Sometimes a combination of hormones can have an effect greater than the sum of the effects of the hormones alone. This type of interactive effect is referred to as **synergism**. Figure 4.37 also provides an example of a synergistic effect. Cortisol causes an increase in blood glucose, but this effect is smaller than the responses to glucagon or epinephrine. When cortisol, glucagon, and epinephrine are injected in combination, however, the net effect is much greater than the sum of the effects observed when any one hormone is injected alone. As a steroid hormone, cortisol interacts with an intracellular receptor, and thus exerts its effects through a different signal transduction pathway than does either epinephrine or glucagon, which allows this synergistic effect.

Hormones can also have a *permissive* effect, which occurs when the complete effects of one hormone are dependent on the presence of another hormone. For example, reproductive hormones such as **gonadotropins** and the reproductive steroids are needed for the maturation of the reproductive system. However, the effect of these hormones is delayed or reduced if thyroid hormone is not present. Thyroid hormone alone has no effect on the development of the reproductive system, but it is required for the reproductive hormones to function effectively. Thus, although thyroid hormone is not a reproductive hormone, it has a permissive effect on the reproductive hormones. The importance of this permissive effect is clear from the observation that low thyroid hormone levels can result in infertility in women.

Hormone levels are influenced by both synthesis and removal

Feedback regulation is important in controlling the rates of synthesis and release of a hormone, which is a critical regulator of hormone levels, but the levels of a hormone in the blood can also be regulated by the rate of hormone removal. Hormones can be removed from the circulation by being (1) degraded by the target tissue, (2) degraded by enzymes in the liver and excreted in the **bile**, or (3) degraded by enzymes present in the liver or kidneys and excreted via the urine. If rates of degradation increase, hormone levels in the blood will decrease, whereas if the rates of degradation decrease, hormone levels will increase.

Hydrophobic hormones such as steroids can be regulated by yet another factor. These hormones are transported in the blood bound to carrier proteins. It is the unbound fraction that is thought to be biologically active. High concentrations of carrier proteins reduce the amount of unbound hormone in the blood, reducing the effective concentration of the hormone, while low levels of the carrier protein increase the effective concentration. For example, sex hormone–binding globulin is the carrier for sex hormones such as estrogen and testosterone. Low levels of sex hormone–binding globulin are associated with an increased risk of breast cancer, an effect that is thought to be mediated by an increase in the effective concentration of estrogen.

Endocrine pathologies occur when hormone levels are dysregulated

Hypersecretion of a hormone can cause a variety of pathological changes in an organism. For example, Cushing's syndrome in mammals (including humans) is caused by excessive secretion of the glucocorticoid hormone cortisol. The cortisol acts on its target tissues to produce the symptoms of Cushing's syndrome, which include rapid weight gain, particularly on the back and face. Cushing's syndrome can be caused by a tumor of the adrenal gland that causes elevated secretion of cortisol or by a tumor of the **pituitary gland** that releases large amounts of ACTH, which causes the adrenal glands to produce large amounts of cortisol (see Figure 4.36). Occasionally, tumors elsewhere in the body can begin to spontaneously produce ACTH in an uncontrolled manner, which causes the adrenals to hypersecrete cortisol, resulting in Cushing's syndrome. Cushing's syndrome can also be caused by exogenous administration of glucocorticoids to treat diseases such as rheumatoid arthritis.

Hyposecretion of a hormone can also cause pathologies. For example, low cortisol production can produce the symptoms of Addison's disease, which include weight loss, fatigue, and low blood pressure leading to fainting. Addison's disease results when the adrenal glands are damaged and cannot produce cortisol. Addison's disease is sometimes called primary adrenal insufficiency, while similar conditions caused by defects in the pituitary or the hypothalamus are termed secondary and tertiary adrenal insufficiency, respectively. These conditions are caused by reduced release of ACTH or CRF, which then results in low cortisol levels. The symptoms of secondary and tertiary adrenal insufficiency are similar to those of Addison's disease, except that the adrenal glands are not damaged, so they can still produce the hormone aldosterone. A temporary form of adrenal insufficiency can occur when patients who have been taking glucocorticoid drugs stop their treatment. During treatment, the high levels of glucocorticoids in the blood act via a negative feedback loop to suppress the secretion of ACTH from the pituitary and CRF from the hypothalamus (see Figure 4.36), and the adrenal glands may start to **atrophy** because they do not need to produce their own cortisol. When the glucocorticoid drugs are withdrawn, it can take some time for the hypothalamo-pituitary-adrenal (HPA) axis to return to normal, causing temporary symptoms of adrenal insufficiency.

The responsiveness of the target cell can vary

Although the effective concentration of a hormone in the blood is an important determinant of its activity, the responsiveness of the target cell can also alter the effects of a hormone. The most important mechanism of regulation at the target cell is at the level of the receptor. As we have already discussed, the number of receptors on a target cell can change over time through the processes of down-regulation and up-regulation. The action of the reproductive hormones progesterone and estrogen on the uterus of mammals provides examples of both receptor up-regulation and down-regulation.

CELL-TO-CELL COMMUNICATION AND DIABETES MELLITUS

Diabetes mellitus, one of the most common diseases in the Western world, results when the body fails to either secrete or respond to insulin. There are two major types of diabetes: type 1 and type 2. Gestational diabetes, which occurs when pregnant women with no previous history of diabetes develop high blood glucose, is also fairly common and occurs in 5–10 percent of all pregancies.

Diabetes of all types is caused by failures in cell-to-cell communication, although in type 1 diabetes the primary defect is in the signaling cell, whereas in type 2 diabetes and gestational diabetes the problem is in the target cells. In type 1 diabetes, the body does not produce sufficient insulin in response to increases in blood glucose. In type 2 diabetes and gestational diabetes, the target cells do not fully respond to insulin, even if it is present. Type 2 diabetes is by far the most common type of diabetes. Currently, over 90 percent of North Americans with diabetes have type 2, and the incidence of type 2 diabetes in Western populations is growing as millions more people with type 2 diabetes are diagnosed every year. Particularly alarming is the rapid rate of increase in type 2 diabetes in teenagers. Diabetes can also occur in mammals other than humans, and can be quite prevalent in domestic pets such as cats and dogs. Type 1 diabetes appears to be most common in dogs, while the diabetes in cats may be more similar to human type 2 diabetes.

Type 2 diabetes is a progressive disease that begins with defects in the signal transduction pathway for insulin. The initial symptoms of the disease are usually mild, and may involve frequent urination, thirst, and fatigue. In the early stages of the disease, diabetes can be controlled with a careful diet and a limited intake of glucose, but as the disease progresses, the pancreas secretes more and more insulin in response to the reduced activation of the target tissues. Eventually, the pancreas loses its ability to secrete high amounts of insulin, and insulin levels fall. At this point, the disease must be treated with injections of insulin to regulate blood glucose. Untreated diabetes has many serious complications, including blindness, vascular disease, kidney failure, heart attack, and stroke.

The signal transduction pathways for insulin are rather complex and have only recently been identified. When insulin binds to its receptor (a tyrosine kinase), the receptor is autophosphorylated and the tyrosine kinase domain then phosphorylates a protein called the insulin receptor substrate (IRS). Phosphorylated IRS activates the phosphatidylinositol and MAP-kinase signal transduction pathways. The phosphatidylinositol pathway stimulates glucose uptake from the blood, while the MAP-kinase pathway stimulates cell growth. Because so many different proteins are involved in insulin signal transduction, the precise defect associated with type 2 diabetes is not yet known, and may vary from person to person or among tissues.

Obesity is a major risk factor for type 2 diabetes, and most patients with type 2 diabetes are obese when diagnosed. Lack of exercise and a diet high in simple carbohydrates such as sugars also predispose a person to type 2 diabetes. Genetic factors also contribute to type 2 diabetes, so having a close relative with type 2 diabetes indicates an increased risk that a person will develop the disease. Scientists do not yet understand why obesity is related to increased risk of type 2 diabetes, but studies in mice have shown that adipocytes (fat cells) release a hormone called resistin, and levels of resistin are elevated in obese mice. Resistin is thought to down-regulate the insulin signal transduction pathway, suggesting the possibility of a link between obesity and type 2 diabetes.

References

- Bevan, P. (2001). Insulin signaling. *Journal of Cell Science, 114.* 1429–1430.
- Frojdo, S., Vidal, H., & Pirola, L. (2009). Alterations of insulin signaling in type 2 diabetes: A review of the current evidence from humans. *Biochimica et Biophysica Acta, 1792*, 83–92.
- Leney, S. E., & Tavare, J. M. (2009). The molecular basis of insulin-stimulated glucose uptake: Signaling, trafficking and potential drug targets. *Journal of Endocrinology, 203*, 1–18.
- Steppan, C. M., Bailey, S. T., Bhat, S., Brown, E. J., Banerjee, R. R., Wright, C. M., . . . Lazar, M. A. (2001). The hormone resistin links obesity to diabetes. *Nature, 409*, 307–312.
- White, M. F. (2002). IRS proteins and the common path to diabetes. *American Journal of Physiology: Endocrinology and Metabolism, 283*, E413–E422.

During the reproductive cycle of mammals, levels of estrogen and progesterone change over time (see Chapter 16: Reproductive Physiology). As an egg develops in the ovary, the ovary produces estrogen. This estrogen binds to estrogen receptors on uterine cells, and causes them to up-regulate the expression of receptors for progesterone. Progesterone is made by the corpus luteum of the ovary beginning at **ovulation**. Progesterone down-regulates the estrogen receptor in the uterine epithelium and increases the activity of an enzyme that metabolizes estrogen into an inactive form, causing the uterus to be less responsive to estrogen. Progesterone also down-regulates its own receptor in the epithelial cells

FIGURE 4.37 **The vertebrate stress response**

When an organism perceives a stimulus such as the presence of a predator, sensory neurons send various signals to the brain, which acts as an integrating center to decide whether these stimuli represent a stressful event. If the brain interprets the stimuli as stressful, it sends out signals to various target tissues using three main pathways. **(1)** It stimulates the sympathetic nervous system, which directly regulates the activity of a variety of tissues. **(2)** The stimulated sympathetic nervous system also stimulates the release of epinephrine and norepinephrine from the adrenal medulla. These hormones then act on a variety of target tissues. **(3)** The brain also sends signals to the hypothalamus, causing it to release corticotropin-releasing hormone (CRH). The CRH binds to receptors on the anterior pituitary, causing it to release adrenocorticotropic hormone (ACTH). The ACTH then binds to receptors on cells in the adrenal cortex, causing them to release glucocorticoid hormones, which have diverse effects on a variety of target tissues.

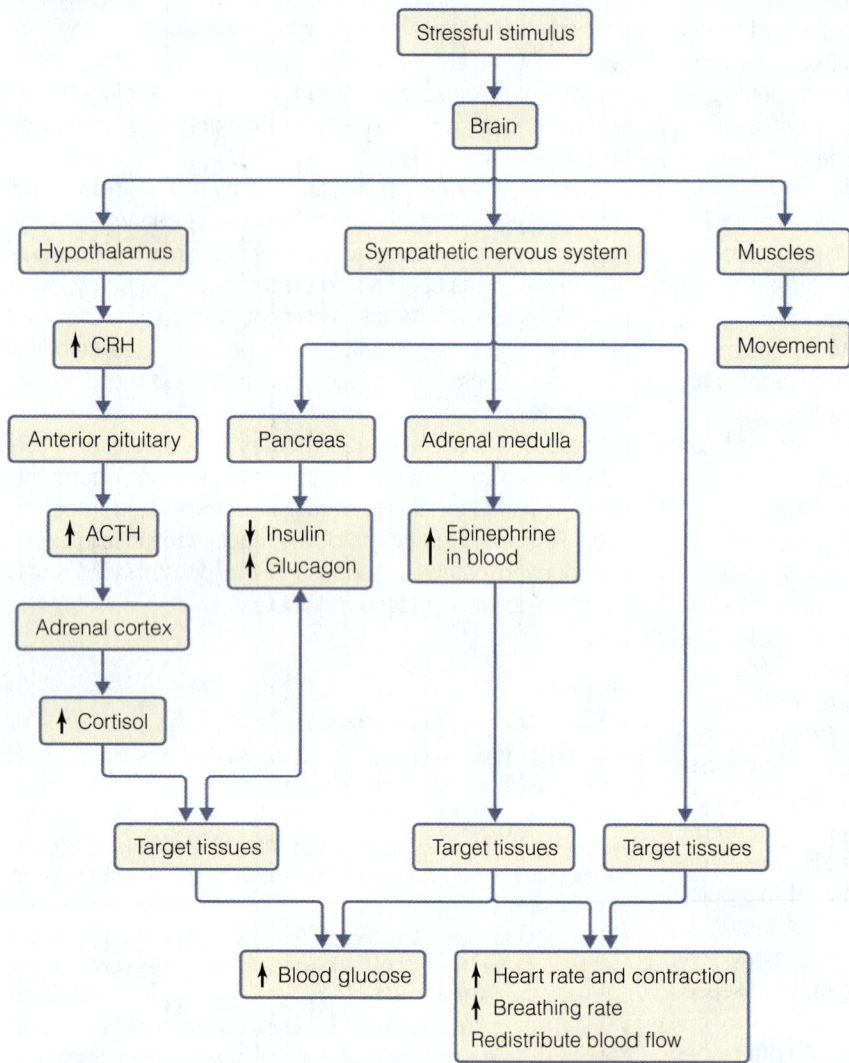

hormone in a wide variety of animals, including humans and fishes. In fishes, it is also involved in the physiological response to increases in environmental salinity (see Chapter 13: Ion and Water Balance). During acclimation to seawater, this hormone sends a signal to the gills to undergo a change in cell morphology and biochemistry that helps the animal cope with the change in external ions and osmolarity. The process of seawater acclimation is associated with an increase in the number of cortisol receptors on the gill, making these cells more responsive to the cortisol signal.

The responsiveness of the target cell can also be modified by alterations in any step of the signal transduction pathways involved in hormone signaling. Many diseases and drugs target signal transduction pathways. Type 2 **diabetes mellitus** provides an example of a disease that is caused by defects in signal transduction pathways (see Box 4.3: Application: Cell-to-Cell Communication and Diabetes Mellitus on page 141).

The nervous and endocrine systems interact in the stress response

The nervous system and the endocrine system interact to control many physiological processes. The response of the body to stressful stimuli is a particularly clear example of this interaction. When the sense organs of a vertebrate perceive an alarming stimulus (such as the presence of a predator), the organism initiates a complex set of behavioral and physiological responses that are often called the "fight-or-flight" response (see Chapter 8: Functional Organization of Nervous Systems). The fight-or-flight response involves both the endocrine system and the nervous system acting together to coordinate this complex but critically important behavioral and physiological response (Figure 4.37).

of the uterus, but not in the cells of the underlying stromal tissue. This decrease in responsivity to estrogen and transfer of progesterone responsiveness from the epithelium to the stroma allows the embryo to implant following fertilization. These changes in receptor expression are absolutely critical in maintaining a healthy pregnancy.

The glucocorticoid hormone cortisol provides another example of receptor up-regulation. Cortisol is a stress

When an animal detects the presence of an alarming stimulus (such as a predator), sensory nerves send a signal to the brain. The brain acts as an integrating center that takes information from the various senses and makes a decision regarding the "threat level" of the stimulus. If the brain decides that the stimulus represents a threat, it sends out a signal via motor neurons, which causes muscles to contract, causing the animal to run away or fight, as necessary. At the same time, the hypothalamus activates a portion of the nervous system termed the *sympathetic nervous system* (see Chapter 8: Functional Organization of Nervous Systems). The sympathetic nervous system sends out signals to target organs including the heart, vascular smooth muscle, and other tissues. These responses help to increase blood flow and redirect it toward the working muscles and away from tissues such as the gut. The sympathetic nervous system also increases the rate and depth of breathing. Together these responses help to provide the skeletal muscles with the oxygen they need to contract and thus engage in the fight-or-flight response.

In addition to the target tissues discussed above, the sympathetic nervous system also affects the activity of several endocrine glands. For example, stimulation of the sympathetic nervous system reduces the release of insulin from the pancreas and increases the release of glucagon. Target tissues respond to the change in insulin and glucagon levels by increasing blood glucose, which can be used as an energy source during the fight-or-flight response. The sympathetic nervous system also stimulates the **adrenal glands**. In mammals, the adrenal glands are compact organs located adjacent to each kidney, and consist of two types of tissue. The **adrenal cortex**, on the outside of the gland, is composed of interrenal tissue, and secretes mineralocorticoid and glucocorticoid hormones such as aldosterone and cortisol. The inside of the adrenal gland is called the **adrenal medulla** and is composed of **chromaffin cells** that secrete the catecholamines, epinephrine and norepinephrine.

The sympathetic nervous system releases the neurotransmitter acetylcholine onto chromaffin cells of the adrenal medulla. These cells then release either norepinephrine or epinephrine into the circulatory system. The ratio of norepinephrine to epinephrine that is released varies among species. In dogfish sharks, norepinephrine is the only catecholamine released by chromaffin cells, whereas in frogs norepinephrine makes up about 55–70 percent of the released catecholamines. In contrast, mammals release mostly epinephrine.

As we have already discussed, epinephrine and norepinephrine bind to members of a family of G protein–coupled receptors, termed the adrenergic receptors, that activate signal transduction pathways that alter the activity of existing proteins. Thus, epinephrine and norepinephrine have very rapid effects within their target cells. Epinephrine and norepinephrine interact with many target organs, including the heart, lungs, and muscles, to galvanize the body into action.

The hypothalamo-pituitary axis is involved in the stress response

The fight-or-flight response also involves the activation of the hypothalamo-pituitary endocrine response (see Figures 4.36 and 4.37). When the hypothalamus is activated by a stressful stimulus, it increases the secretion of corticotropin-releasing hormone (CRH) into the hypothalamic-pituitary portal system. CRH binds to its receptors on target cells in the anterior pituitary and causes them to release adrenocorticotropic hormone (ACTH) into the bloodstream (see Figure 4.37). ACTH binds to G protein–coupled receptors in the membranes of cells in the adrenal cortex. Activation of this receptor stimulates adenylate cyclase, which catalyzes the formation of cAMP. The cAMP activates protein kinase A, which phosphorylates and activates an enzyme that causes cholesterol to be released from intracellular stores. This cholesterol is transported to the mitochondria, where it is used as a substrate for the synthesis of glucocorticoid hormones. In humans and fish, cortisol is the primary glucocorticoid hormone, whereas the structurally similar corticosterone is the primary glucocorticoid hormone in rats and mice. In all these species, however, the effects of glucocorticoids in the stress response are similar.

As hydrophobic hormones, glucocorticoids bind to an intracellular receptor located in the cytoplasm of target cells. Glucocorticoid binding induces a conformational change that causes the hormone-receptor complex to move to the nucleus and regulate transcription. Glucocorticoids have diverse functions, including the breakdown of lipids and proteins, and increasing blood glucose. Because these effects are mediated through changes in transcription and translation, in contrast to the rapid effects of epinephrine, which acts through cytoplasmic signal transduction pathways, the effects of glucocorticoids are much slower, and are involved in recovery from the effects of the immediate fight-or-flight response. The glucocorticoids' metabolic functions help the body to restore energy balance following the energetically costly fight-or-flight response.

CONCEPT CHECK

21. Compare and contrast negative feedback and positive feedback. Which type of control allows maintenance of homeostasis?

22. What are antagonistic pairings? What are the advantages of this organization of control systems?

23. Provide an example of a hormone controlled by a third-order endocrine pathway, and outline each step in the regulatory cascade.

Evolution of Endocrine Systems

As we saw with the example of the bacterium *Vibrio fischeri* at the beginning of this chapter, even unicellular organisms have the ability to communicate using chemical signals, but with the origin of multicellularity the ability of cells to communicate with each other became increasingly critical for survival. As we discussed in Chapter 2: Physiological Evolution of Animals, the sponges have the simplest body organization of all extant metazoans, with epithelial tissue but no nervous or muscle tissue. However, sponges are still able to mount a coordinated response to stimuli, suggesting that they have mechanisms that allow communication among cells. Although the mechanisms of cell signaling that coordinate these responses remain poorly understood, they appear to involve electrical signals within cells in some species, as well as a variety of paracrine chemical signals including glutamate, GABA, and possibly nitric oxide.

All metazoans other than sponges possess nervous tissue. In fact, as we discuss in later chapters, there are substantial similarities in the structure and function of nervous systems across animal taxa that suggest that the nervous systems of bilaterians are likely to be derived from that of a common ancestor (see Chapter 5: Neuron Structure and Function and Chapter 8: Functional Organization of Nervous Systems). In contrast, the organization of endocrine systems is quite diverse among animal taxa. Unlike nervous systems, which were present in the common ancestor of the Bilateria, endocrine systems could only arise from the ancestral paracrine communication systems following the evolution of a circulatory system that could carry hormones from one part of the body to another. Because circulatory systems are thought to have arisen independently several times in different bilaterian animal groups, we can conclude that endocrine systems have arisen multiple times and that the endocrine systems of, for example, vertebrates and arthropods are not directly related.

Although there are substantial differences in the organization of animal endocrine systems, there are also substantial similarities. These similarities likely stem from the evolution of endocrine systems from a shared set of basic signal transduction mechanisms involved in paracrine communication in the ancestral metazoans. Over time, however, animal cell-to-cell communication mechanisms have diverged and diversified into the complex endocrine systems we see in various taxa. In all animals, however, endocrine systems rely upon a similar set of chemical messengers, receptors, and signal transduction pathways.

Endocrine systems vary in complexity among animal phyla

The organization of endocrine systems varies between invertebrates and vertebrates. Compared with the vertebrates, invertebrates have relatively few endocrine glands, and most endocrine signaling utilizes neurohormones rather than hormones. Within the invertebrates, there is a correlation between the complexity of the endocrine system and the complexity of body form or organization. For example, invertebrates with relatively simply body plans (such as platyhelminths) have a limited number of neurohormones that are mostly involved with regulating growth and development. They appear to have few physiologically active hormones. In contrast, invertebrate phyla with more complex body plans (such as the annelids, mollusks, and arthropods) have complex neuroendocrine pathways that regulate most physiological processes, although there are relatively few classical hormones compared with the large number of hormones in vertebrates. The increase in complexity of the endocrine system across animal phyla is related to the increase in complexity of the circulatory system that allows hormones to be transported across long distances in these groups.

Hyperglycemic hormones are an example of an invertebrate neurohormone

The regulation of glucose in crustaceans provides an example of the similarities and differences between vertebrate and invertebrate endocrine systems. As is the case in vertebrates, many invertebrates use chemical signaling mechanisms to maintain homeostasis in extracellular glucose levels. However, in invertebrates this regulation is typically performed by a neurohormone, rather than hormones such as insulin and glucagon that are used for glucose regulation in vertebrates. For example, in crustaceans (crabs, prawns, and shrimp) a neurohormone termed *crustacean hyperglycemic hormone* (CHH) plays a principal role in glucose regulation. CHH was first discovered when researchers injected crabs with extracts of tissues from the eyestalks of other crabs and found that these extracts caused **hyperglycemia**—an increase in circulating glucose. CHH is synthesized in the cell bodies of secretory neurons that are clustered into an area termed the X-organ within the crustacean eyestalk. Projections from these cell bodies extend into a region called the sinus gland, which acts as a storage and release site for the neurohormone. Because CHH is released by neural tissue, it is considered a neurohormone or **neuropeptide**. The sinus gland releases CHH into the circulatory system, which carries the neurohormone to target cells throughout the body. At the target cell, CHH binds to a transmembrane receptor that activates guanylate cyclase and increases the concentration of cGMP within the target cell. The cGMP acts as a second messenger, activating a signaling pathway that causes the breakdown of glycogen into glucose, causing the release of glucose from the target cell

FIGURE 4.38 **Regulation of circulating glucose by crustacean hyperglycemic hormone**

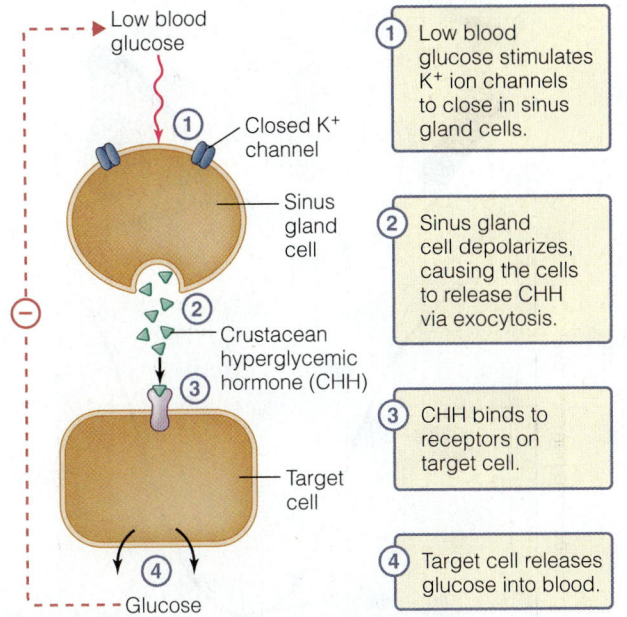

① Low blood glucose stimulates K^+ ion channels to close in sinus gland cells.

② Sinus gland cell depolarizes, causing the cells to release CHH via exocytosis.

③ CHH binds to receptors on target cell.

④ Target cell releases glucose into blood.

into the circulatory system. This increase in glucose results in the hyperglycemia that gives the hormone its name.

CHH regulates blood glucose via a negative feedback mechanism (Figure 4.38). When blood glucose levels are high, a K^+ channel on the membrane of the neurosecretory cells within the sinus gland is in the open conformation, allowing K^+ to leave the cell. This hyperpolarizes the membrane (makes the inside of the cell more negative; see Chapter 3: Chemistry, Biochemistry, and Cell Physiology). When blood glucose levels drop, this K^+ channel closes, and the cell depolarizes. Depolarization causes the cells to release CHH. The CHH then travels through the circulatory system and causes target cells to release glucose into the circulation, causing glucose levels to return to normal. As is the case for many hormones, other factors can also modulate the release of CHH. For example, inputs from the nervous system alter the activity of the sinus gland cells in response to external cues such as season, time of day, temperature, and changes in environmental salinity. CHH also has other functions in addition to the regulation of circulating glucose, including the regulation of lipid metabolism.

Although CHH is primarily regulated via negative feedback from circulating glucose levels, crustacean hyperglycemic hormone can also be regulated by positive feedback. When CHH binds to its receptor on target cells, the activated receptor increases flux through glycolysis. One of the end products of glycolysis is a three-carbon unit called lactate (see Chapter 3: Chemistry, Biochemistry, and Cell

Physiology). When stimulated by CHH, target cells produce lactate, which is released into the circulation. The **neurosecretory cells** of the X-organ–sinus gland complex are sensitive to circulating lactate, which causes them to release more CHH in a positive feedback loop. The signals from lactate and glucose work together to regulate CHH secretion.

The major steroid hormones differ between vertebrates and arthropods

All vertebrates, including the jawless lampreys and hagfish, use a series of related steroid hormones as chemical messengers, including estrogens, androgens, and glucocorticoids. A number of these vertebrate-like steroids have been detected in the tissues of invertebrates, but their physiological role remains unclear. The best evidence for a role of vertebrate-like steroids in invertebrates comes from mollusks. Mollusks respond to exogenously applied steroids, but they appear to lack the complete suite of enzymes necessary to synthesize vertebrate-like steroids, and vertebrate-like steroids may not be the natural ligand of the single steroid receptor gene that has been identified in mollusks. Thus, the role of vertebrate-like steroids in the endocrinology of mollusks is unclear and remains an active area of research.

There is little evidence to suggest that vertebrate-like steroids play a physiological role in arthropods. Instead, a different series of steroid hormones called the **ecdysteroids** are important. These hormones are derived from the steroid **ecdysone**. The structure of ecdysone is similar to that of the vertebrate steroid hormones, but it contains more hydroxyl groups (Figure 4.39). The ecdysteroids play an important role in regulating reproduction and development in insects and crustaceans. Ecdysone also plays a role in regulating molting in some (but not all) species of nematode worms. Ecdysteroid receptors have also recently been discovered in mollusks and polychaete worms, although the physiological role of the ecdysteroid receptors in these invertebrate groups remains unknown.

FIGURE 4.39 **The structure of ecdysone, a precursor of arthropod steroid hormones**

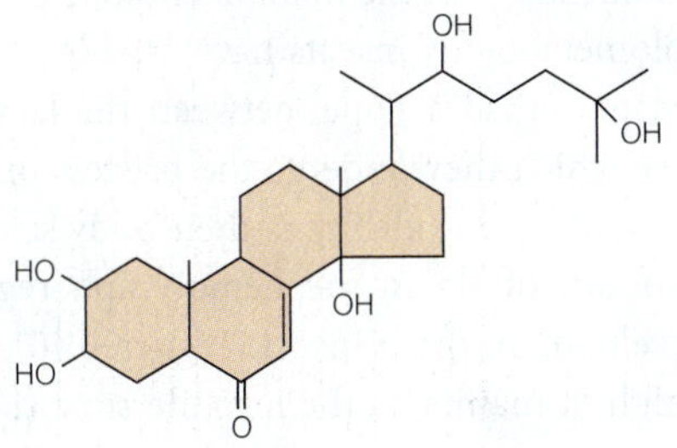

Ecdysone

The role of ecdysone in regulating reproduction and development is best understood for insects. In insect larvae, ecdysone secretion is regulated by a neurohormone called prothoracicotropic hormone (PTTH) that is produced by the insect brain. This neurohormone stimulates a gland called the **prothoracic gland** to secrete ecdysone. Ecdysone is actually a prohormone, and is rapidly converted to the active hormone 20-hydroxyecdysone (also called ecdysterone) by enzymes found in the hemolymph and various peripheral tissues. Like the vertebrate steroid hormones, 20-hydroxyecdysone binds to an intracellular receptor that regulates gene expression by binding to a hormone-responsive element. The role of 20-hydroxyecdysone in regulating molting in insect larvae is discussed in more detail in Chapter 16: Reproductive Physiology.

Although 20-hydroxyecdysone is structurally similar to vertebrate steroids, it does not appear to be biologically active in the vertebrates, and does not have detectable effects on the vertebrate reproductive system. However, a few studies have reported that ecdysterone has anabolic effects in vertebrates, increasing muscle growth and lean muscle mass.

Arthropods also use other terpenoids as hormones

Terpenoids are a group of extremely diverse naturally occurring lipid-soluble compounds that contain multiples of a five-carbon isoprene unit. The steroids form one subgroup of the terpenoids. The steroids are the only known class of terpenoid signaling molecule in vertebrates, but invertebrates use a variety of classes of terpenoid as hormones. For example, **juvenile hormone** (JH) and *methyl farnesoate* are important terpenoid hormones that control the process of molting in insects and crustaceans, respectively.

All arthropods have a rigid exoskeleton, a hard outer covering that provides both protection and support. In order to grow, an arthropod must shed its exoskeleton by molting. In the hemimetabolous insects, the larval and adult stages resemble each other, although the juvenile stages lack wings and reproductive organs. In contrast, the adults of the holometabolous insects differ radically in shape from their larvae. Caterpillars and butterflies, for example, are the larval and adult stages of the holometabolous Lepidopteran insects. Holometabolous insects have an additional developmental stage, called a pupa, between the larva and the adult, during which they undergo the process of metamorphosis—a complete remodeling of their body structures.

The amount of JH in the hemolymph regulates the stage of development of an insect (Figure 4.40). When JH levels are high, it maintains the juvenile state (i.e., the larval stage of holometabolous insects). JH levels gradually decrease during development, and when they drop below

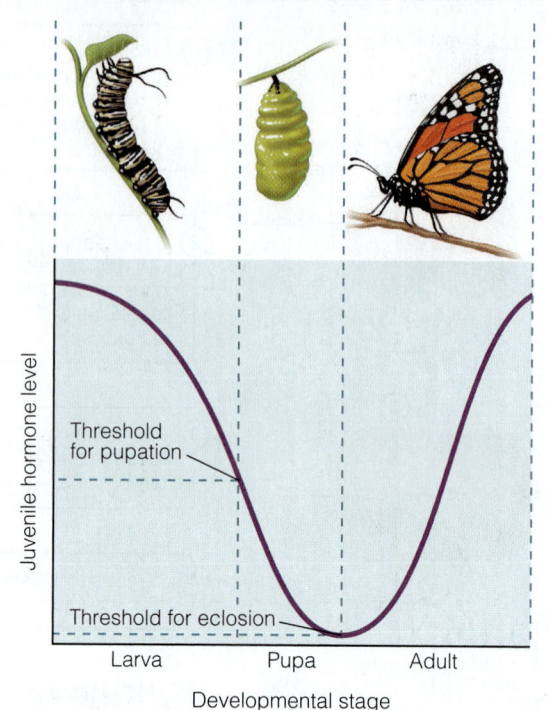

FIGURE 4.40 **Levels of juvenile hormone during development of a holometabolous insect**

a critical threshold, the larva will pupate and begin the process of metamorphosis. Once JH levels drop almost to zero, the pupa will eclose and emerge as an adult insect, at which point JH levels start rising again.

A variety of hormones and neurohormones, including JH, ecdysteroids, **eclosion** hormone, and bombyxin, are involved in regulating molting in insects. We discuss these hormones and their relationships in more detail in Chapter 16: Reproductive Physiology.

The structure and function of many hormones is highly conserved in vertebrates

Compared with the great diversity of hormonal pathways in invertebrates, many vertebrate hormone pathways are homologous (have a shared ancestry; see Chapter 1: Introduction to Physiological Principles) and maintain a common function throughout the vertebrates. As a result, a hormone that is extracted from one vertebrate species is often biologically active in another species. For example, the insulin used to treat diabetes in humans was traditionally obtained by extracting it from the pancreas of slaughtered livestock, such as sheep, cows, or pigs. Similarly, an estrogen-containing drug called Premarin that is used for hormone replacement therapy in postmenopausal women is derived from the urine of pregnant mares (female horses). Hormones often have conserved functions even between mammals and nonmammalian vertebrates. For example, when mammalian growth hormone is injected into fish it causes increased growth. However, this conservatism of the structure and function of vertebrate hormones is not always the case. For example, there is a difference in the number of disulfide bonds in the hormone prolactin beween fish and mammals. There are two disulfide bonds in the prolactin of teleost fish and three in the prolactin of animals such as lungfish and tetrapods. These hormones have different functional properties. Unfortunately, many of the earliest studies on the role of prolactin in teleost fishes were performed using hormone purified from cows and sheep, before the fundamental difference in structure in teleost and tetrapod prolactin was known.

Some hormonal pathways have evolved via gene duplication

Gene and genome duplications have been important in the evolution of vertebrate form and function (see Chapter 2: Physiological Evolution of Animals), and the endocrine system is no exception to this rule. Many genes encoding hormone receptors and peptide hormones have undergone gene duplications during vertebrate evolution. For example, vasopressin and oxytocin are related peptide hormones that are released by the posterior pituitary in mammals. Jawless fishes (lampreys and hagfish) have only one member of this gene family. Many lines of evidence suggest that a whole-genome duplication occurred during the early evolution of the jawed vertebrates (the gnathostomes). The ancestral single copy of a vasopressinlike gene in this ancestor was duplicated, and then the two copies diverged in sequence and function into vasopressin and oxytocin.

Corticosteroid hormones provide another example of the role of gene duplication during the evolution of endocrine systems. The extant jawless vertebrates (lampreys and hagfish) have only a single receptor that responds to corticosteroids. In contrast, all jawed vertebrates have two related receptors that bind corticosteroids: a glucocorticoid receptor (GR) and a mineralocorticoid receptor (MR). The GR is involved in the stress response and the homeostatic regulation of glucose, while the MR regulates sodium and water balance. The genes encoding these receptors are similar in structure and sequence, which suggests that they are the result of the whole-genome duplication that occurred in the lineage leading to the jawed vertebrates.

In lampreys, 11-deoxycortisol is the main steroid that binds to their single corticosteroid receptor. In all jawed vertebrates one of two very similar steroid hormones (cortisol or corticosterone) binds to and activates the GR. Cortisol is the primary glucocorticoid hormone in teleost fish and in most mammals, while corticosterone is the primary glucocorticoid hormone in most amphibians, reptiles, and birds (and in rodents, among the mammals). The situation is rather different for the MR. In teleost fishes a hormone called deoxycorticosterone binds to the MR, whereas in all tetrapods the MR is activated by aldosterone, a hormone that is not present in physiologically relevant concentration in teleost fishes. Interestingly, both the MR of teleost fishes and the corticosteroid receptor of lampreys and hagfish are capable of binding aldosterone, despite the fact that these groups do not produce significant amounts of this hormone.

Prolactin and **growth hormone** provide another example of hormone genes that arose via gene duplication in the common ancestor of the vertebrates. Extant jawless fish produce growth hormone, but not prolactin. Thus the growth hormone and prolactin genes are likely the result of the whole-genome duplication in the lineage leading to the jawed vertebrates. Shortly after the lineage of teleost fish arose, another gene duplication event occurred, creating a third protein, *somatolactin*. In mammalian lineages, there have been additional gene duplication events that have led to gene families of prolactin-like proteins. Ruminants and rodents independently experienced multiple duplications of the prolactin gene, creating families of prolactin-like proteins. Throughout most tetrapods, the structure of prolactin is highly conserved, though a few lineages have experienced periods of accelerated evolution leading to structural divergence. In most cases where they have been studied in sufficient detail, the prolactin-like proteins appear to have roles similar to that of prolactin. Many of these prolactin relatives are expressed in tissues other than the anterior pituitary, though usually in tissues involved in reproduction, such as the mammalian **placenta** and uterus.

Gene copies can also be lost following genome duplications. The gonadotropin-releasing hormones (gnRH) provide an interesting example of genes that have experienced multiple rounds of duplication and loss. Recent data from the genome sequence of lampreys suggest that two ancient genome duplications prior to the divergence of the gnathostomes and the lampreys resulted in the presence of four ancestral gnRH genes, one of which was lost early in vertebrate evolution. The remaining three major classes of gnRH genes (types I, II, and III) then underwent selective gene losses such that type III gnRH was lost in the ancestor of all the tetrapods, and the type II gnRH was lost in many species of mammals (including rodents). The functional significance of these gene losses remains largely unknown.

Some hormones have acquired new functions during vertebrate evolution

Prolactin is an excellent example of a signaling molecule with a function that diversified over the course of vertebrate evolution. Across vertebrates, prolactin has been shown to have roles in (1) water and electrolyte balance, (2) reproduction, (3) growth and development, (4) metabolism, (5) brain and behavior, and (6) immunoregulation. In fishes, the main role of prolactin is in the control of water and Na^+ movements across the epithelia of the gill, gut, and kidney. Prolactin also plays a role in osmoregulation of amphibians, but its most dominant function appears to be in growth and development in this group of animals. It promotes growth while inhibiting metamorphosis in amphibian larvae by antagonizing the actions of thyroid hormone. Prolactin surges also induce amphibians to return to the water to breed, perhaps foreshadowing the increasing importance of prolactin as a reproductive hormone in tetrapods. Prolactin plays a relatively minor role in osmoregulation in birds and mammals. With a diminished role in osmoregulation, prolactin gained a greater role in control of reproductive physiology of mammals.

As the name suggests, prolactin's primary function in mammals is to stimulate milk production in the mammary gland. It stimulates the growth of the mammary gland epithelial cells, and induces the expression of genes for milk proteins and metabolic enzymes needed for synthesis of milk sugars and fats. Prolactin also affects the maintenance and function of the reproductive tracts of female (uterus and ovary) and male (prostate, seminal vesicles, epididymis, Sertoli cells, and Leydig cells) mammals. Prolactin also controls parental behavior in numerous species of mammals, birds, and even fish, often interacting with glucocorticoids and androgens.

Some hormone pathways are reduced in humans

There are a number of hormone pathways that are important in nonmammalian vertebrates that appear to play a reduced role in mammals, and particularly in humans. The hormone calcitonin provides a useful example of such a hormone. In fish and amphibians, calcitonin plays an important role in fluid regulation, ion balance, and acid-base balance, and is particularly important in regulating plasma calcium levels. In mammals, calcitonin plays some role in decreasing plasma calcium and phosphate levels, mostly through suppressing the loss of calcium phosphate from bone and by inhibiting the reabsorption of calcium and phosphate from the urine. The role of calcitonin in humans appears to be minor, as surgical removal of the thyroid gland (the primary site of calcitonin synthesis) does not cause any alteration in plasma calcium levels. Although humans (and many other mammals) naturally synthesize only very low levels of calcitonin, mammalian tissues can respond to calcitonin if it is injected in high doses. For example, calcitonin is prescribed to treat osteoporosis (brittle bones) in postmenopausal women because it increases bone mineralization.

The hormone **stanniocalcin** provides another example of an important hormone in fish that has undergone a shift in roles in mammals. Stanniocalcin is involved in regulating plasma calcium in fish. It is released from a small endocrine gland on the ventral surface of the kidney of fish called the corpuscles of Stannius. Mammals lack the corpuscles of Stannius, and for many years they were thought not to produce stanniocalcin, because it cannot be detected in mammalian blood, and because parathyroid hormone plays the main role in calcium regulation in mammals. However, many mammalian tissues, including the kidney, produce stanniocalcin. It is thought to act as a paracrine regulator of a variety of processes, including tissue growth.

Melanocyte-stimulating hormone (MSH) is a third example of a hormone that plays a reduced role in humans compared with other vertebrates. MSH is secreted from the intermediate lobe of the pituitary gland (which is located between the anterior and posterior pituitary in nonmammalian vertebrates). MSH plays an important role in regulating skin coloration in amphibians and reptiles by changing the location of pigment granules in cells called *melanocytes* in the skin. However, in birds and in adult mammals, and particularly in humans, the intermediate lobe of the pituitary is reduced to a thin layer of cells, and levels of MSH in the blood are extremely low. However, MSH still plays an important role in humans as a paracrine regulator in a variety of tissues, including the skin and the brain. In the skin, MSH is responsible for the darkening of skin in response to sunlight. **Ultraviolet** light striking the cell induces a signal transduction pathway that results in the production of MSH. The MSH is released from the skin cells and binds to receptors on the surface of nearby melanocytes, which respond by increasing the synthesis of the pigment melanin. In the brain, MSH is synthesized by neurons and acts to suppress appetite. In fact, some forms of obesity are associated with defects in the MSH receptor.

The structure of endocrine glands varies among the vertebrates

The adrenal glands provide an example of a trend toward consolidation of endocrine tissues into compact glands during vertebrate evolution (Figure 4.41). Mammals have a compact and highly organized adrenal gland. The adrenal glands of reptiles and birds are also quite compact, as they are in mammals, but the interrenal (glucocorticoid-secreting) and chromaffin (epinephrine-secreting) tissues are intermingled, rather than being separated into a distinct cortex and medulla. The interrenal and chromaffin cells of amphibians are intermingled in a diffuse stripe along the kidney. In **elasmobranch fish**, the interrenal cells form a fairly compact organ that is located on the kidney, but the chromaffin cells are found in the body cavity anterior to the kidney,

FIGURE 4.41 **Comparative anatomy of adrenal tissues in vertebrates**

Chromaffin cells (shown in gray) and interrenal cells (shown in black) are associated with the kidneys of vertebrates. In mammals, birds, and reptiles they form discrete adrenal glands, while in fishes and amphibians the cells are in isolated clusters.

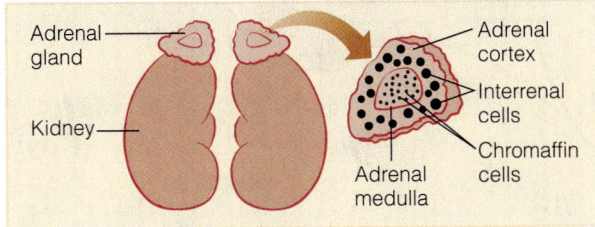

(a) Mammal (e.g., human)

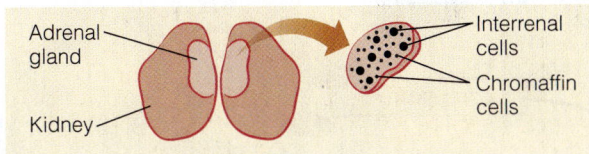

(b) Bird (e.g., Herring gull)

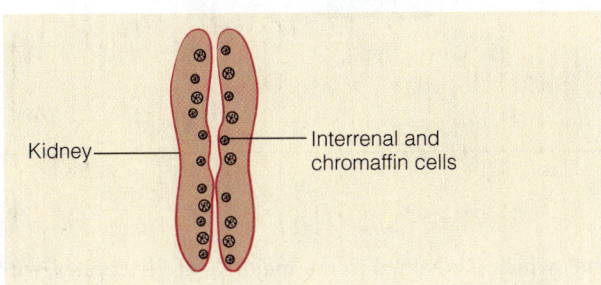

(c) Amphibian (e.g., *Necturus*)

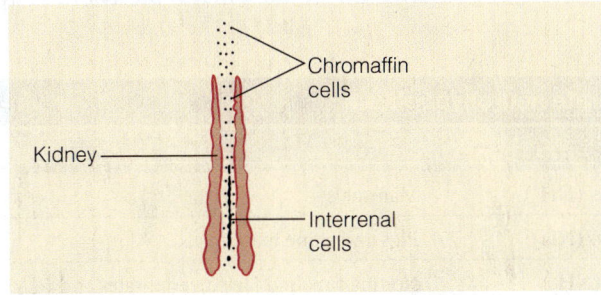

(d) Elasmobranch (e.g., shark)

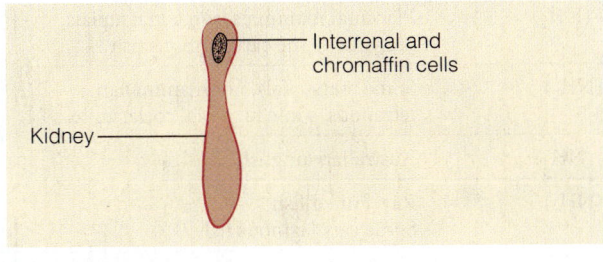

(e) Bony fish (e.g., trout)

grouped into loose clusters. Bony fish entirely lack a discrete adrenal gland; their interrenal cells are generally located in a single layer around the blood vessels of the anterior kidney, while the chromaffin cells vary in location, often being associated with interrenal cells. However, despite these differences in the structure of the target organs among vertebrates, the overall organization and functions of the stress response are similar. This transition from a dispersed group of hormone-secreting cells toward a compact and organized gland is a general trend in the evolution of endocrine systems in both vertebrates and invertebrates.

The structure of the pituitary differs among vertebrates

The pituitary provides another example of an important endocrine gland whose structure varies among the vertebrates. As we discussed earlier in the chapter, the relationship between the hypothalamus and the anterior pituitary differs among vertebrates groups, as does the structure of the pituitary gland itself. Figure 4.42 summarizes the typical pituitary anatomy of some of the major vertebrate groups. The relative sizes of the three major parts of the pituitary (the anterior pituitary, the posterior pituitary, and the intermediate lobe) vary substantially among groups. The size of the intermediate lobe is greatly reduced in birds and mammals, reflecting the lesser importance of melanocyte-stimulating hormone in these animals. The other important anatomical difference in the pituitary among vertebrates is the lack of a portal blood circulation connecting the hypothalamus and the anterior pituitary in agnathans and teleost fishes. In the agnathans and the teleosts, the neurohypophysis (posterior pituitary) has fingerlike projections that extend into the adenohypophysis. The hypothalamic neurons within the neurohypophysis release their messengers into the interstitial fluid of the adenohypophysis. These paracrine messengers then reach their target tissues in the adenohypophysis by diffusion. In contrast, the cartilaginous fishes, the nonteleost bony fishes, and the tetrapods have a pituitary portal blood system, so the hypothalamic neurohormones are carried to the adenohypophysis by the circulatory system.

The neurohormones of the posterior pituitary vary among vertebrates

As we discussed earlier in the chapter, the posterior pituitary of mammals secretes the neurohormones oxytocin and vasopressin into the main circulatory system, where they act on various tissues. The neurohormones of the posterior pituitary are nonapeptides (short peptides made up of only nine amino acids) that are members of a superfamily of related peptides that differ from each other by only one or two amino acids (Table 4.5). The jawless vertebrates, such as hagfish and lampreys, possess only a single pituitary

FIGURE 4.42   The anatomy of the pituitary in the major vertebrate groups

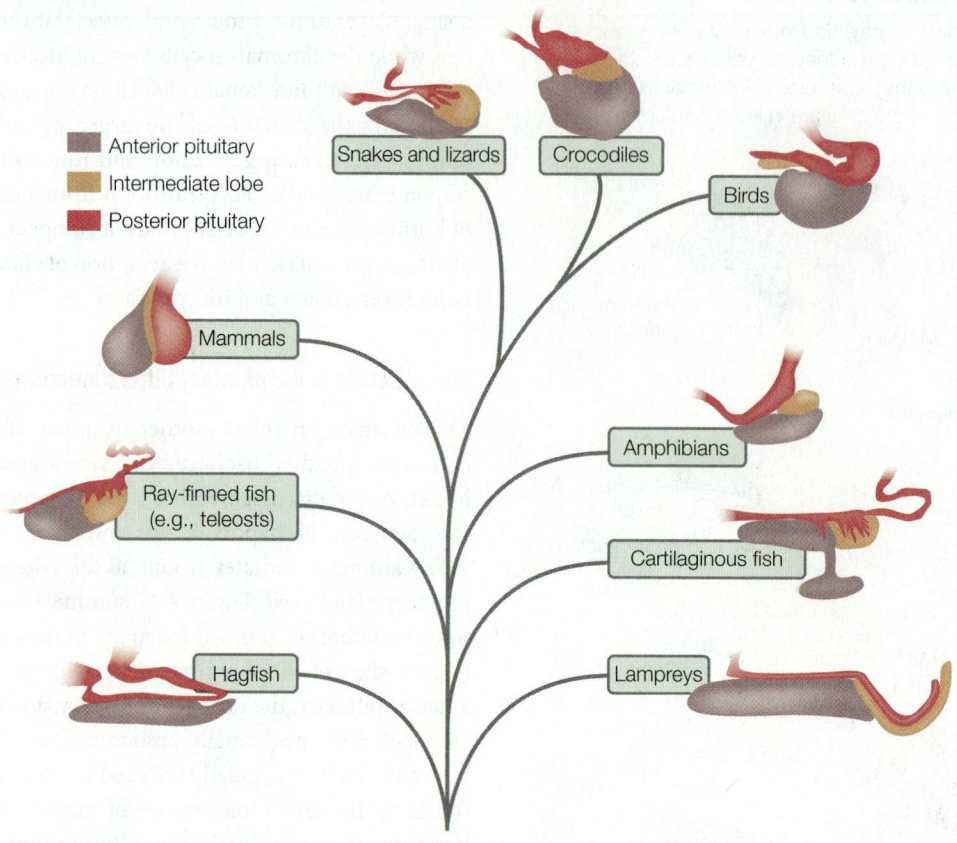

nonapeptide, called vasotocin. The whole-genome duplication in the ancestor of the jawed vertebrates resulted in the formation of two families of related nonapeptides. One of these gene families descended from the original vasotocin gene, which is retained in the majority of vertebrates, with divergent forms (arginine vasopressin and lysine vasopressin) found only in mammals. The ancestral member of the oxytocin gene family is the isotocin that is present in bony

Table 4.5   The major nonapeptide hormones of the vertebrate neurohypophysis

Vasopressin Family		
Arginine vasopressin	Cys-Tyr-Phe-Gln-Asn-Cys-Pro-Arg-Gly- (NH$_2$)	Mammals
Lysine vasopressin	Cys-Tyr-Phe-Gln-Asn-Cys-Pro-Lys-Gly- (NH$_2$)	Pigs and some marsupials
Vasotocin	Cys-Tyr-Ile-Gln-Asn-Cys-Pro-Arg-Gly- (NH$_2$)	Nonmammalian jawed vertebrates and agnathans
Oxytocin Family		
Oxytocin	Cys-Tyr-Ile-Gln-Asn-Cys-Pro-Leu-Gly- (NH$_2$)	Placental mammals, some marsupials, platypus, some cartilaginous fish
Mesotocin	Cys-Tyr-Ile-Gln-Asn-Cys-Pro-Ile-Gly- (NH$_2$)	Some marsupials, nonmammalian tetrapods, some lungfish, coelacanths
[Phe2]mesotocin	Cys-Phe-Ile-Gln-Asn-Cys-Pro-Ile-Gly- (NH$_2$)	Australian lungfish
Isotocin	Cys-Tyr-Ile-Ser-Asn-Cys-Pro-Ile-Gly -(NH$_2$)	Ray-finned fish Some cartilaginous fish

Note: (Highlighting indicates the amino acids that differ from the sequence of the ancestral vasotocin.)

fishes. At some point prior to the colonization of land by vertebrates, this gene diverged to form the mesotocin that is found in coelocanths, lungfish, and most nonmammalian tetrapods. A mutation that resulted in a switch from isoleucine to leucine occurred in the lineage leading to mammals, resulting in the formation of oxytocin. Note that some cartilaginous fishes also have oxytocin, but this is the result of an independent mutation at the same site. In fact, there has been a great deal of diversification in the oxytocin family within cartilaginous fish, and at least eight different pituitary nonapeptides related to oxytocin are found in various species of cartilaginous fishes. For simplicity, these peptides are not shown in Table 4.5, as the functional significance of this variation is poorly understood.

The members of the vasopressin family of hormones are involved in the regulation of water balance and blood pressure in all vertebrates, and they also have a variety of behavioral effects, particularly for behaviors associated with reproduction. For example, injection of vasotocin induces spawning behavior in teleost fish and courtship and mating behavior in amphibians.

The oxytocin-like hormones released by the pituitary also have a wide variety of roles. In female mammals, oxytocin stimulates the contraction of the uterus at birth, and after birth stimulates contraction of smooth muscles in the breasts, causing milk to be ejected into the ducts of the breasts, which facilitates suckling by the newborn

(see Table 4.4). In male mammals, the oxytocin released by the posterior pituitary may facilitate sperm transport within the reproductive system. In fish, isotocin is thought to be involved in regulating ion and water balance, and appears to play some role in regulating drinking and a variety of social and reproductive behaviors, although its actions are not as well studied as those of vasotocin. Mesotocin may play a role in regulating egg laying in reptiles and birds, and it has been shown to play an important social role in birds by facilitating group behaviors such as pair bonding and flocking.

In addition to being released by the posterior pituitary, members of the oxytocin and vasopressin families are also released locally within the brain, where they have profound effects on behavior. These brain nonapeptides are particularly important in regulating social and mating behavior in species ranging from fish to mammals.

CONCEPT CHECK

24. What are the major differences between invertebrate and vertebrate endocrine systems?

25. How have gene duplications played a role in the evolution of the vertebrate endocrine system? Support your answer with at least two examples.

SUMMARY

There are many types of cell-to-cell communication in animals, including direct, autocrine, paracrine, neural, endocrine, and inter-individual. These types of communication vary in the distance that the chemical messengers travel from one cell to another. Indirect cell signaling involves three steps: (1) release of the messenger from the signaling cell, (2) transport through the extracellular environment, and (3) communication with the target cell. The mechanisms involved in these steps of indirect cell signaling differ depending on whether the signaling molecule is hydrophobic or hydrophilic.

Communicating a signal to the target cell involves a highly specific interaction between the chemical messenger and a receptor protein. Binding of the ligand results in a change in the conformation of the receptor that triggers a signal transduction pathway within the target cell. Ultimately, these signal transduction pathways result in modifications to the cell, including changes in protein activity, changes in gene expression, or changes in membrane properties.

Cells express numerous types of receptors, and thus several signal transduction cascades can be activated at any given time. Thus, signal transduction cascades in living cells operate as complex

networks that integrate the various signals and convert them into appropriate physiological responses.

Endocrine systems are important communications networks in animals that are responsible for maintaining homeostatis and regulating growth, development, and reproduction. Endocrine hormones are regulated by a variety of feedback loops, including negative feedback loops that assist in the maintenance of homeostasis and positive feedback loops that allow explosive responses. Hormones are often grouped into antagonistic pairs that allow extremely precise homeostatic regulation, and can also work additively or synergistically.

Vertebrate and invertebrate endocrine systems are not homologous, but instead arose independently from paracrine or neural signaling mechanisms. In invertebrates, most endocrine signaling is accomplished by neurohormones, while classical endocrine hormones are common in vertebrates. Although vertebrate endocrine systems share a single evolutionary origin and have many features in common, there has also been substantial divergence in the structure and function of the vertebrate endocrine system.

REVIEW QUESTIONS

1. **LO❶** What are the main types of indirect signaling, and what is the primary feature that distinguishes them?

2. **LO❶** What are the three major steps involved in indirect chemical signaling?

3. **LO❷** You read an article in the newspaper about the discovery of a new steroid hormone. What can you predict about how it is synthesized and/or stored by the signaling cell, how it is transported through the blood, and how it acts on the target cell?

4. **LO❷** If the newspaper article in Question #3 were about a peptide hormone, how would your predictions change?

5. **LO❸** From the perspective of the target cell, is there a fundamental difference between a paracrine signal and an endocrine signal? Why or why not?

6. **LO❸** What are the three main domains of a transmembrane receptor, and what are their functions?

7. **LO❹** Compare and contrast the signal transduction cascades initiated by intracellular receptors and G protein–coupled receptors.

8. **LO❹** Compare and contrast the functions of intracellular and transmembrane steroid receptors.

9. **LO❺** Compare and contrast the function of heterotrimeric G proteins and a small soluble G protein such as Ras.

10. **LO❺** What is the difference between signaling through G_s and G_i?

11. **LO❻** Which classes of chemical messenger are utilized for endocrine communication? Give one example of a hormone from each class.

12. **LO❻** Compare and contrast positive and negative feedback. Provide an example from the endocrine system of vertebrates for each type of feedback.

13. **LO❼** Are the endocrine systems of vertebrates and invertebrates homologous? Justify your answer.

14. **LO❼** Compare and contrast the insulin/glucagon system for blood glucose regulation in vertebrates with the function and regulation of crustacean hyperglycemic hormone (CHH).

SYNTHESIS QUESTIONS

1. Epinephrine and glucagon both act to increase blood glucose, but they act on a different subset of tissues. What characteristics are likely to determine whether a particular tissue responds to epinephrine, glucagon, or to both hormones?

2. People who do not regularly drink coffee often feel much greater effects when they ingest modest doses of caffeine than do heavy coffee drinkers. Explain at a molecular level why this might be so.

3. The anticancer drug tamoxifen binds to the estrogen receptor. Tamoxifen inhibits the growth of breast tissue but promotes growth of uterine tissues, thus reducing the risk of breast cancer but potentially increasing the risk of uterine cancer. Explain how the same chemical messenger could have opposite effects in two different tissues.

4. What are the advantages of a multistep signal transduction pathway in cell-to-cell communication?

5. Epinephrine binds to a G protein–coupled receptor that signals via G_s. Acetylcholine binds to a G protein–coupled receptor that signals via G_i. You construct a recombinant receptor with the extracellular domain of the acetylcholine receptor and the intracellular domain of the epinephrine receptor, and transfect it into cultured cells. Your preliminary experiments indicate that the receptor is processed correctly, and inserted into the plasma membrane. If you applied acetylcholine to your transfected cells, what would you expect to happen to intracellular cAMP levels? What would happen if you applied epinephrine? Explain your answers.

6. Why are peptide messengers released by exocytosis? Why are steroid hormones not released in this way?

7. Why do selective serotonin reuptake inhibitors (SSRIs) affect the response of a target cell to serotonin?

8. How does increasing the amount of a receptor on a target cell affect the B_{max} and K_d of the ligand-receptor interaction? What would be the effect of this change on the response of a target cell to the ligand?

9. Thinking about the evolution of endocrine systems, what evolutionary patterns result in the phenomenon of "endocrine disruption" observed when male fish living in sewage outfalls are feminized by artificial human contraceptives and hormone replacement therapies in the effluent?

10. What are the major parts of any control system (mechanical or biological)? Choose an example of a biological control system and show how it fits the general description of control systems that you provided.

QUANTITATIVE QUESTIONS

1. The graph below outlines the results of an experiment to determine the binding characteristics of a ligand to its receptor on the surface of adipocytes (fat cells).

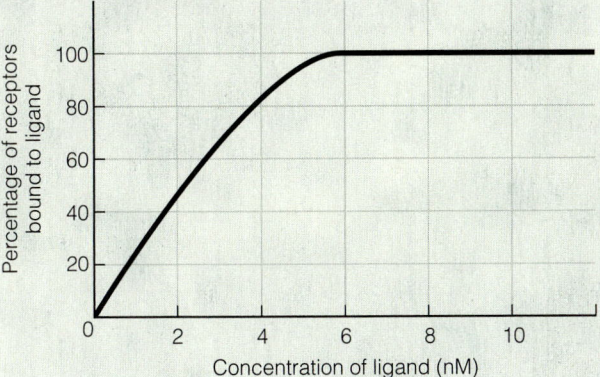

(a) What is the minimum concentration of ligand at which the receptor is saturated?
(b) What is the affinity constant of the receptor?
(c) If the receptor number on the adipocytes were doubled, what would be the predicted maximum binding of the ligand?
(d) If the receptor number on the adipocytes were doubled, would the affinity constant of the receptor change?

2. In insects, the Malpighian tubules are involved in the maintenance of ion and water balance. When a peptide hormone called diuretic hormone is applied to Malpighian tubules isolated from the blood-sucking insect *Rhodnius prolixus*, the tubule epithelium begins to secrete fluid at a rate of approximately 5 nL/min. The biogenic amine serotonin has similar effects, causing secretion at a rate of approximately 4 nL/min. When both chemical messengers are applied together, however, fluid secretion occurs at a rate of approximately 45 nL/min. Is this an example of additivity, synergism, or antagonism? Justify your answer.

CHAPTER

5

Neuron Structure and Function

Learning Objectives

After reading this chapter, you should be able to:

❶ Predict the effects of changes in membrane permeability on ion movements and electrical events in a neuron, using the Nernst and Goldman equations.

❷ Describe the properties of graded potentials in the dendrites, cell body, and axon hillock of a neuron.

❸ Explain how the opening and closing of voltage-gated ion channels influences the properties of action potentials.

❹ Describe the regulation of neurotransmitter release at a chemical synapse.

❺ Categorize neurons and glial cells into structural or functional types.

❻ Explain how changes in axon diameter and myelination influence the speed of action potential conduction.

❼ Compare and contrast the actions of different classes of neurotransmitters.

❽ Describe the unique features of electrical communication in metazoans compared with all other organisms.

FIGURE 5.1 **The longfin squid (*Doryteuthis pealeii*)**

Photo source: Jeff Rotman/Alamy.

t first glance a squid such as the one shown in Figure 5.1 appears to be an unlikely creature to have sparked a revolution in neurobiology, but much of what we know about how neurons work was derived from studies using this species. Alan Hodgkin and Andrew Huxley used squid for their pioneering experiments demonstrating that neurons send electrical signals by selectively allowing ions to cross the cell membrane in a voltage-dependent fashion. The Hodgkin-Huxley theory of the action potential is the basis for much of our current understanding of neurophysiology.

Like most cephalopod mollusks, squid have complex brains and nervous systems, but the critical feature that made squid an ideal species for Hodgkin and Huxley's experiments is the presence of neurons with axons that have a very large diameter compared with neurons in most other animals. These so-called **giant axons** can be up to a millimeter in diameter, whereas most axons are only a few micrometers in diameter. The giant axons are projections from the neurons that stimulate muscle contraction in the main body wall, or *mantle*, of the squid. A squid can expand and contract its mantle, drawing water into the mantle cavity and rapidly expelling it through a tubelike tissue called the siphon. This stream of water provides a kind of jet propulsion that pushes squid rapidly through the water. Squid are active predators, and jet propulsion allows them to capture fast-moving prey such as fish. The signal from the brain that controls the contraction of the mantle is carried by the giant axons. As we will see later in the chapter, the large diameter of these axons allows extremely rapid conduction of electrical signals, allowing the squid to have an extremely rapid reaction time.

Squid giant axons are the largest known axons in any animal. They are hundreds of times larger in diameter than a typical mammalian axon, and as much as 50 times larger than giant axons in other invertebrates. When Hodgkin and Huxley were performing their experiments, which began while Huxley was still an undergraduate student, the only available recording electrodes were far too large to fit into a typical mammalian axon. By using squid giant axons, Hodgkin and Huxley were able to make electrical recordings from the inside of a single cell that would have been impossible if they had tried to use other species. The squid is thus an excellent illustration of the power of the Krogh principle and the selection of an appropriate model system, which we discussed in Chapter 1. Their detailed experimental work using the squid giant axon allowed Hodgkin and Huxley to formulate a model that could explain action potentials in terms of known electrical theory. Their data and model were published in a classic series of papers in the early 1950s, and in 1963 they received the Nobel Prize for Medicine for this work.

Using neurons for rapid, long-distance electrical communication is a unique feature of animals. In this chapter, we explore the fundamental cellular basis of how neurons work. We focus on the biophysics of electrical signaling, and examine how these electrical signals can be transduced into chemical signals that are sent between cells. ■

LOOKING BACK 5

Before you begin this chapter, you may find it helpful to review Chapter 3: Chemistry, Biochemistry, and Cell Physiology, where we describe the structure of biological membranes and the molecular mechanisms of transport across them. Recall that all animal cells and some subcellular organelles maintain an electrochemical gradient across their membrane that can be used to drive the transport of substances (Chapter 1: Introduction to Physiological Principles). This electrochemical gradient is critical to the function of neurons, and we explore it in more depth here. Signaling at a chemical synapse of a neuron shares many features in common with other signaling systems, such as hormonal communication, so you may need to review Chapter 4: Cell Signaling and Endocrine Regulation, where we discuss the general features of communication among cells in animals, the biochemical basis of cell signaling, and signal transduction pathways.

▌OVERVIEW

As we discussed in Chapter 3: Chemistry, Biochemistry, and Cell Physiology, animal cells use active transport of ions to maintain a voltage difference across their cell membranes, termed the **membrane potential**. Certain classes of cells, termed **excitable cells**, can rapidly alter their membrane potential by altering the distribution of ions across the membrane. These excitable cells use the resulting changes in the membrane potential as communication signals. The best-known excitable cells are **neurons**—cells that are specialized to carry electrical signals, often across long distances. In this chapter we explore the structure and function of neurons, looking at how they use electrical signals for communication.

Neurons vary in their structure and properties, but all neurons use the same basic mechanisms to send signals. Figure 5.2 uses a vertebrate **motor neuron**, the neurons that communication from the central nervous system to the muscles, an example of this signaling function. The first functional zone of a motor neuron consists of the **dendrites** and **cell body** (or **soma**). Dendrites are fine, branching extensions of the neuron, originating at the cell body. The word

FIGURE 5.2   Structure and function of a typical vertebrate motor neuron

Like other neurons, motor neurons can be divided into four functional zones that are involved in signal reception, integration, conduction, and transmission.

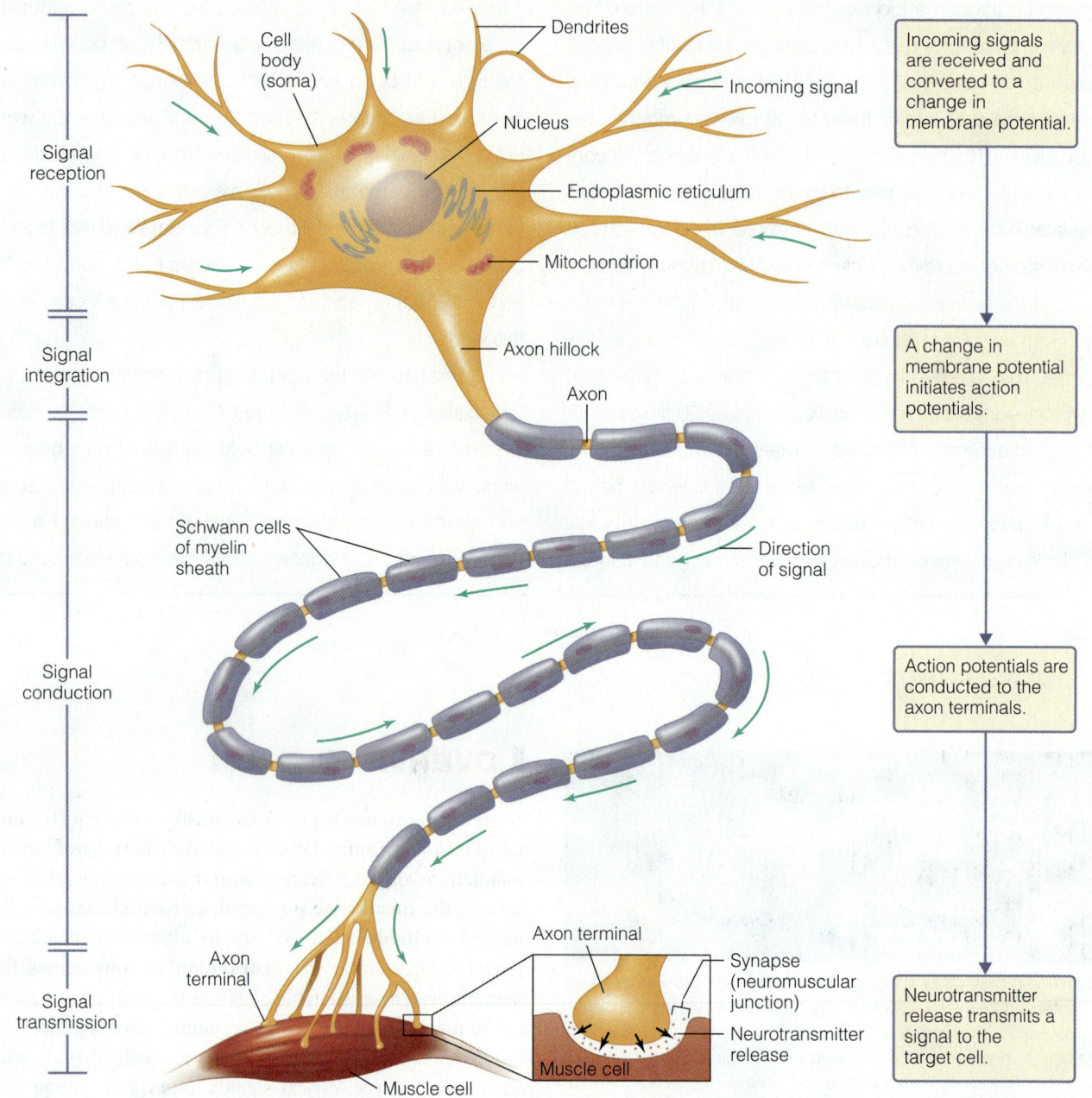

Signal reception

Signal integration

Signal conduction

Signal transmission

Cell body (soma)

Dendrites

Incoming signal

Nucleus

Endoplasmic reticulum

Mitochondrion

Axon hillock

Axon

Schwann cells of myelin sheath

Direction of signal

Axon terminal

Axon terminal

Synapse (neuromuscular junction)

Neurotransmitter release

Muscle cell

Muscle cell

Incoming signals are received and converted to a change in membrane potential.

A change in membrane potential initiates action potentials.

Action potentials are conducted to the axon terminals.

Neurotransmitter release transmits a signal to the target cell.

dendrite is derived from the Greek word for tree (*dendron*) because of the highly branched appearance of the dendrites of many neurons. The dendrites are responsible for sensing incoming signals, converting these signals to an electrical signal in the form of a change in the membrane potential, and transmitting the signal to the cell body. The cell body contains the nucleus and the protein synthetic machinery of the cell, as well as most of the organelles, although mitochondria are also found in the dendrites and at the axon terminal.

Like the dendrites, the plasma membrane of the cell body often also contains receptors, and thus can participate in detecting incoming signals.

The second functional zone of a motor neuron, which is specialized for signal integration, consists of the **axon hillock**. The axon hillock is located at the junction of the cell body and the axon. Incoming signals from dendrites and the cell body are conducted to the axon hillock. If the signal at the axon hillock is sufficiently large, a specialized electrical signal, termed the **action potential**, is initiated. Action potentials occur in the **axon**, a long slender extension leading off the cell body at the axon hillock.

The axon forms the third functional zone of the neuron, and is specialized for signal conduction. Axons are often quite short (just a few millimeters), but the axons of some neurons, such as motor neurons in large mammals, can be several meters long. For example, consider the neurons in the neck of a giraffe. The axons of these neurons are about three meters long, but this is relatively short in comparison to the axons of some neurons in blue whales, which may be as much as 25 meters long. Each neuron has only a single axon, although the axon may branch into several *collaterals*. Vertebrate motor neurons are wrapped in a **myelin sheath** that increases the speed of conduction of electrical impulses to the **axon terminals**.

The axon terminals make up the fourth functional zone of the neuron, which is specialized for signal transmission to target cells. In a motor neuron, the end of the axon branches to form several axon terminals. Each axon terminal is a swelling of the end of the axon that forms a **synapse** with the target skeletal muscle cell. At the axon terminal of a motor neuron the electrical signal is transduced into a chemical signal in the form of a chemical neurotransmitter. The neurotransmitter diffuses across the synapse and binds to specific receptors on the muscle cell membrane, initiating a signal in the muscle cell and causing the muscle to contract.

We begin the chapter by exploring the basics of how neurons maintain a membrane potential, and then we examine how changes in the membrane potential act as signals in each of the four functional zones of a neuron. Using a generalized vertebrate motor neuron as an example, we follow a signal as it travels from one end of the motor neuron to the other, discussing the features of the electrical signals in each part of the cell, and how the neuron transmits signals to its target cells, vertebrate skeletal muscles.

In the second half of the chapter, we look at how each of these steps has been modified and specialized in different neurons and in neurons from different kinds of organisms. We first discuss variation in the structure of neurons, and then address variation in the functional properties of neurons. We end the chapter with a discussion of the evolution of neurons.

SIGNALING IN A VERTEBRATE MOTOR NEURON

The overall process of signaling in a vertebrate motor neuron involves receiving an incoming signal, converting that signal to a change in the membrane potential, triggering action potentials that conduct the signal across long distances, and then transmitting the signal to target cells in the form of a neurotransmitter. In the following sections we first consider the fundamental nature of electrical signals in neurons, and then we examine the types of signals that occur in each of the functional zones of a motor neuron.

Electrical Signals in Neurons

As excitable cells, neurons can rapidly alter their membrane potential in response to an incoming signal, and these changes in membrane potential can act as electrical signals. As we discussed in Chapter 3: Chemistry, Biochemistry, and Cell Physiology, neurons are not the only excitable cells. Muscle cells, some endocrine cells, fertilized eggs, some types of plant cells, and many unicellular organisms also have the capacity to rapidly alter their membrane potentials. However, neurons are the only cells that are specialized to use changes in membrane potential to communicate signals across long distances. It is the property of excitability that gives neurons the ability to store, recall, and distribute information, and which is the main subject of this chapter.

Like most animal cells, neurons maintain a voltage difference across their cell membranes. In excitable cells such as neurons, when the cell is not involved in sending an electrical signal, this voltage difference is termed the *resting membrane potential difference*, or the **resting membrane potential** (V_m), for short. Most neurons have a resting membrane potential of approximately $-70\,\text{mV}$. Recall, from our discussion of membrane potentials in Chapter 3: Chemistry, Biochemistry, and Cell Physiology, that the membrane potential is expressed relative to the voltage outside the cell. Thus, this value of V_m means that the inside of the cell membrane is about 70 mV more negatively charged than the outside of the membrane.

Ionic concentration gradients and permeability establish membrane potential

Only two factors are required to establish a potential difference across a membrane: a concentration gradient for an ion and a membrane that is permeable to that ion. Consider a situation where two solutions are separated by a membrane that is impermeable to ions (Figure 5.3). Assume that the interior of the cell contains 100 mM KCl and 10 mM NaCl, and the extracellular fluid contains 100 mM NaCl and 10 mM KCl. The concentration gradient for K^+ (100 mM inside the cell and 10 mM outside the cell) favors outward movement, whereas the concentration gradient for Na^+ (100 mM outside and 10 mM inside the cell) favors inward movement. There is no gradient for the movement of Cl^- (because the concentration of Cl^- is 110 mM both inside and outside the cell). The solutions on either side of

FIGURE 5.3   The equilibrium potential

To understand the equilibrium potential, consider a hypothetical cell. If the membrane is impermeable, there would be no voltage difference. If the membrane became permeable to an ion, that ion would move across the membrane down its concentration gradient. Ion movements would continue until a charge gradient built up that exactly counterbalanced the chemical gradient, resulting in an equilibrium at which there is no further net movement of the ion.

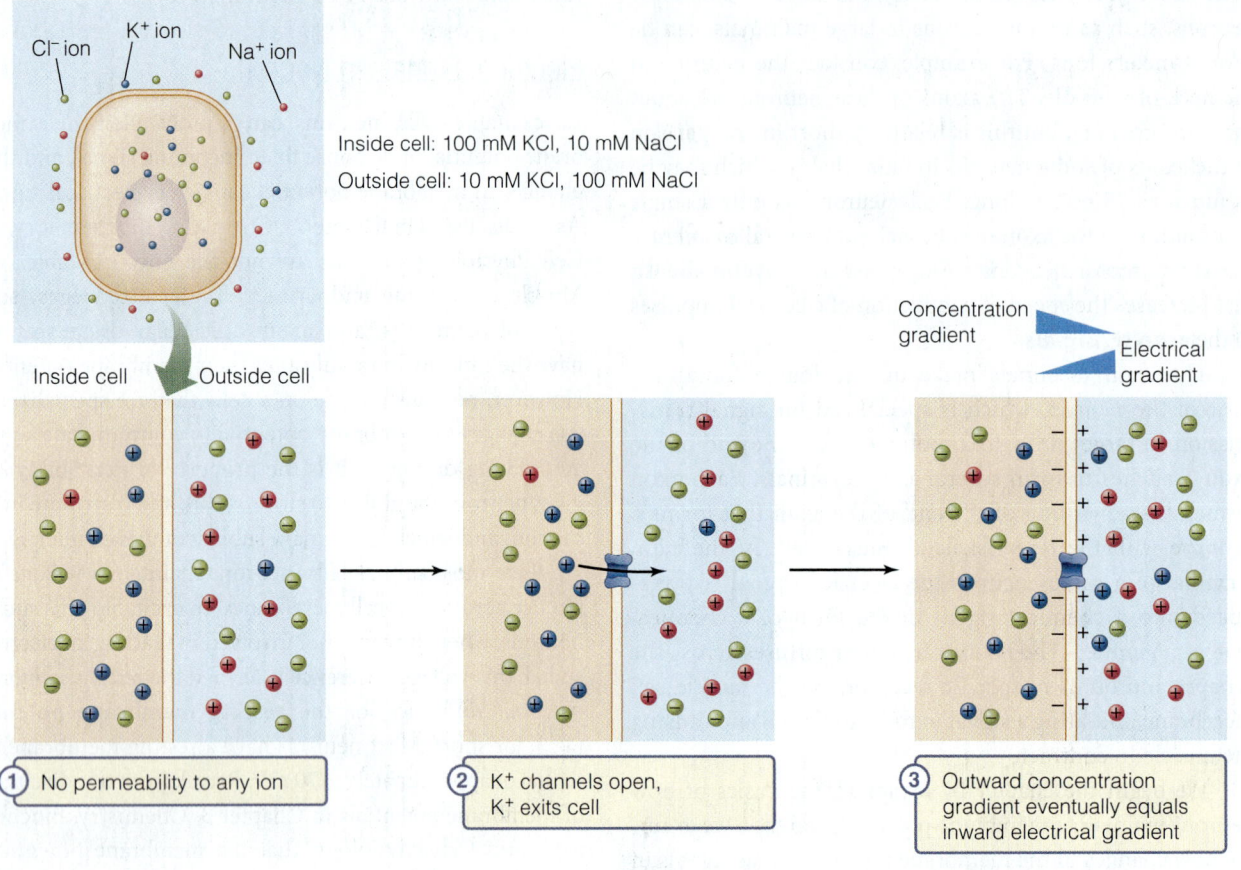

Inside cell: 100 mM KCl, 10 mM NaCl

Outside cell: 10 mM KCl, 100 mM NaCl

① No permeability to any ion

② K⁺ channels open, K⁺ exits cell

③ Outward concentration gradient eventually equals inward electrical gradient

the membrane are also electroneutral, with equal numbers of anions and cations.

Imagine now that we insert channels into the membrane that allow the passage of K^+, but no other ion. The concentration gradient will cause K^+ to move out of the cell along the concentration gradient, creating a local region of electronegativity on the inner face of the membrane (where K^+ left) and a local region of electropositivity on the outer face of the membrane (where K^+ appeared). This excess negative charge at the inside face of the membrane generates an electrical force that tends to draw positive charges back into the cell. As more K^+ leaves the cell, the electrical force gradually increases to a level that exactly balances the driving force from the K^+ concentration gradient. Potassium ions continue to move across the membrane, but their inward and outward fluxes exactly balance each other. The potential difference across the membrane under these equilibrium conditions is termed the **equilibrium potential** for that ion (E_{ion}). Because only a single ion can move across the membrane in this hypothetical example, the equilibrium potential is equivalent to the resting membrane potential ($E_{ion} = V_m$).

The Nernst equation can be used to calculate the equilibrium potential of an ion

We can calculate the equilibrium potential (E_{ion}) for any ion using the **Nernst equation**. The Nernst equation is usually written as follows:

$$E_{ion} = \frac{RT}{zF} \ln \frac{[\,X\,]_{outside}}{[\,X\,]_{inside}}$$

where R is the gas constant (8.315 joules/K.mol), T is the temperature (Kelvin), z is the valence of the ion, F is the Faraday constant (96,485 joules/Volt.mol), and [X] is the molar concentration of the ion.

In our hypothetical example in Figure 5.3, $[K^+]_{outside} = 10$ mM and $[K^+]_{inside} = 100$ mM, resulting in $E_K = -60$ mV. In other words, the force driving the outward movement of K^+ resulting from its tenfold concentration gradient can be exactly balanced by -60 mV excess of negative charge inside the membrane.

The equilibrium potential for a particular ion is also called the **reversal potential** for that ion, because the direction of ion movement across the membrane changes when the voltage difference across the membrane exceeds this level. In the case of our hypothetical example in Figure 5.3, net K^+ flux was down its concentration gradient from the inside to the outside of the cell until the membrane potential difference reached -60 mV, at which point there was no additional net movement of K^+. If the membrane potential were to become even more negative, the net movement of K^+ would be from the outside of the cell back to the inside—against its concentration gradient. This reversal of ion movement occurs because under these conditions the force due to the electrical gradient is greater than the force due to the concentration gradient.

It is important to emphasize that the charge difference across the membrane (i.e., the membrane potential) is the result of extremely small differences in the number of charged molecules immediately adjacent to the membrane, and that changes in the membrane potential can be caused by the movements of relatively small numbers of ions—a number that is too small to detectably change the overall ion concentration of the cytoplasm or extracellular fluid. In our example in Figure 5.3 the actual number of ions that needed to move across the membrane before the system reached the equilibrium potential was less than 1/100,000 of the total K^+ ions within a typical cell. This would not result in a measurable change in the overall K^+ concentration either inside or outside the cell.

The localization of the charge difference immediately adjacent to the membrane arises because the cell membrane acts as a *capacitor*. A capacitor is a device containing two electrically conductive materials separated by an *insulator*, a very thin layer of a nonconducting material. Electrical charges can interact with each other across the insulator if the layer is sufficiently thin. In a cell, the cytoplasm and the extracellular fluid are conducting materials, whereas the lipid bilayer of the cell membrane is the insulator. The excess positive charge along the outside of the membrane attracts the excess negative charge along the intracellular face of the membrane. These electrical interactions can only occur across very small distances, and do not affect ions in the **bulk phase** of the cytoplasm or extracellular fluid. Thus, the membrane potential occurs only in the area immediately adjacent to the membrane, and the bulk of the fluid in the cytoplasm and extracellular fluid is not electrically charged.

The Goldman equation is used to calculate the membrane potential

In our hypothetical example in Figure 5.3, neither Na^+ nor Cl^- affected the membrane potential because the membrane was not permeable to either of these ions. As a result, the membrane potential was equal to the equilibrium potential for potassium. Of course, the situation in real cells is not so simple, since there are several ions that differ in concentration between the inside and the outside of the cell, and real membranes have varying degrees of permeability to multiple ions.

For most cells, the primary ions that affect the membrane potential are K^+, Na^+, and Cl^- because they can move across membranes and there are differences in their intracellular and extracellular concentrations. As we discussed in Chapter 3: Chemistry, Biochemistry, and Cell Physiology, a modification of the Nernst equation, the Goldman-Hodgkin-Katz Constant Field equation (usually referred to as the **Goldman equation**) can be used to calculate the resting membrane potential based on the concentrations and permeabilities of all of the relevant ions.

The Goldman equation represents the sum of the equilibrium potentials for all of the relevant ions, with a weighting factor that takes into account the relative permeabilities of the ions (P_{ion}).

$$E_m = \frac{RT}{F} \ln \frac{P_K[K^+]_o + P_{Na}[Na^+]_o + P_{Cl}[Cl^-]_i}{P_K[K^+]_i + P_{Na}[Na^+]_i + P_{Cl}[Cl^-]_o}$$

In this equation, $[ion]_o$ and $[ion]_i$ represent the extracellular and intracellular concentrations, respectively, of a given ion. Notice that the ratio of intracellular and extracellular ion concentrations is reversed for chloride compared with sodium and potassium. This is because chloride has a valence of negative one, while sodium and potassium have a valence of positive one. The Goldman equation is typically written to include terms for K^+, Na^+, and Cl^- because the membrane at rest has very low permeability for most other ions.

The influence of each ion on the overall membrane potential is proportional to its permeability. For example, resting neurons are more permeable to K^+ than to the other ions, and as a result, K^+ plays the major role in setting the value of the resting membrane potential of neurons.

Experimentally, it is easier to measure the relative permeability of ions, rather than the absolute permeability. Hence, the Goldman equation is often rewritten using relative permeabilities (essentially by dividing each permeability term by P_K).

$$E_m = \frac{RT}{F} \ln \frac{[K^+]_o + P_{Na}/P_K[Na^+]_o + P_{Cl}/P_K[Cl^-]_i}{[K^+]_i + P_{Na}/P_K[Na^+]_i + P_{Cl}/P_K[Cl^-]_o}$$

If the permeability of the membrane for an ion is zero, then the term for that ion drops out of the Goldman equation. For example, if the membrane that is impermeable to Na^+ and Cl^- (like our hypothetical example in Figure 5.3), the Goldman equation simplifies to the Nernst equation for K^+.

$$E_m = \frac{RT}{F} \ln \frac{P_K[K^+]_o}{P_K[K^+]_i}$$

The Na$^+$/K$^+$ ATPase maintains the membrane potential

As we discussed in Chapter 3: Chemistry, Biochemistry, and Cell Physiology, the Na$^+$/K$^+$ ATPase is an electrogenic pump that pumps three Na^+ ions out of the cell for every two K^+ ions that it pumps into the cell. However, this electrogenic

USING THE NERNST AND GOLDMAN EQUATIONS

We can use the Nernst and Goldman equations to predict the nature of the ion movements as a result of changes in membrane permeabilities, such as those that occur during electrical signaling in neurons. Below are the ion concentrations and permeabilities for a squid giant axon.

$[K^+]_i = 400$ mM and $[K^+]_o = 20$ mM

$[Na^+]_i = 50$ mM and $[Na^+]_o = 440$ mM

$[Cl^-]_i = 51$ mM and $[Cl^-]_o = 560$ mM

$P_{Na} / P_K = 0.04$

$P_{Cl} / P_K = 0.45$

R = 8.315 joules/K.mol

F = 96,485 joules/Volt.mol

Assume that the operating temperature for a squid is 20°C, which can be converted to the Kelvin scale by adding 273.15.

Substituting these values into the Goldman equation gives a value for the resting membrane potential of the squid giant axon of −60 mV, which is a good approximation of the measured resting membrane potential.

Returning to the Nernst equation, we can also calculate the equilibrium potentials for each of these ions. Under the conditions above, the equilibrium potential is −76 mV for K^+, +55 mV for Na^+, and −61 mV for Cl^-. These equilibrium potentials establish the "boundary conditions" for the membrane potential. That is, the

membrane potential cannot be more negative than −76 mV or more positive than +55 mV because there are no chemical gradients large enough to produce larger membrane potential differences.

At rest, the membrane does not quite reach the equilibrium potential for K^+ because of the competing effects of Na^+, but because Na^+ permeability is relatively low its influence is small, and the membrane potential is close to the K^+ equilibrium potential. Note that the squid giant axon also has appreciable permeability to Cl^- (about half that of K^+). In fact, some cell membranes (for example, in muscle cells) are more permeable to Cl^- than they are to K^+. However, even in this case, K^+ plays the major role in establishing the membrane potential. The Na^+/K^+ ATPase actively pumps Na^+ and K^+ ions to establish their concentration gradients. The K^+ concentration gradient sets the resting membrane potential difference, and Cl^- ions passively distribute themselves across the membrane in response. Thus, in the case of Cl^- ions, the intracellular and extracellular Cl^- levels are a consequence rather than a cause of the resting membrane potential.

In addition to providing an estimate of the resting membrane potential, the Nernst and Goldman equations allow the estimation of the membrane potential during electrical signaling. For example, when a large number of Na^+ channels open within the membrane (as is the case during signaling in nerve cells), the permeability of the membrane to Na^+ increases greatly. In the case of neuronal signaling, this increase in Na^+ permeability is so large that P_{Na}

component contributes to only a small part of the resting membrane potential (approximately −10 mV). The primary contributors to the resting membrane potential are the concentration gradients for these ions in combination with the differential permeability of the membrane. However, the Na^+/K^+ ATPase plays a very important role in maintaining the membrane potential. Cell membranes have an intrinsic permeability to ions, even at rest, due to the presence of **leak channels**. Ions will tend to move down their electrochemical gradients (toward their equilibrium potential) through these leak channels. Active pumping by the Na^+/K^+ ATPase is needed to compensate for the leakage of Na^+ and K^+ ions. If the activity of the Na^+/K^+ ATPase is inhibited (for example, with drugs such as ouabain or digitalis), the membrane potential of the cell will slowly decay. If the Na^+/K^+ ATPase is completely inhibited, membrane potential will eventually reach a value of 0 mV over the course of a few hours. Active

pumping by the Na^+/K^+ ATPase is particularly important for maintaining the resting membrane potential in electrically excitable cells, because these cells undergo large increases in membrane permeability during signaling.

Changes in membrane permeability cause electrical signals

Neurons alter the permeability of their membranes to generate changes in membrane potential that act as electrical signals. The changes in membrane permeability in neurons are the result of opening and closing of specific ion channels in the membrane.

During **depolarization**, the charge difference between the inside and outside of the cell membrane decreases, and the membrane potential becomes less negative (Figure 5.5). Either positively charged ions entering the cell or negatively charged ions moving out of the cell can make the inside of

becomes much greater than P_K and P_{Cl}. If you substitute permeabilities of essentially zero for K^+ and Cl^- into the Goldman equation, these parts of the equation drop out and the Goldman equation simplifies to the Nernst equation for Na^+.

As a result, when the permeability for Na^+ is extremely high relative to the permeabilities for K^+ and Cl^-, the Goldman equation is dominated by the term for Na^+, and the membrane potential approaches the equilibrium potential for Na^+ as calculated by the Nernst equation.

Thus, when Na^+ channels open in this neuron, membrane potential will tend to go toward the equilibrium potential for Na^+, which is +55 mV, because both the electrical and concentration gradients favor its movement (Figure 5.4a). Because Na^+ is a positively charged ion, it must be moving into the cell in this case because the membrane potential goes toward +55 mV from the resting membrane potential of around −60 mV (that is, the interior of the cell becomes more positively charged). This entry of positive charges into the cell results in a depolarization.

In contrast, if K^+ channels open, the membrane potential will tend to go toward the equilibrium potential for K^+, which is −75 mV (Figure 5.4b). Because K^+ is a positively charged ion, this change in membrane potential must be caused by K^+ moving out of the cell. Both its concentration and electrical gradients favor outward K^+ movement until the membrane potential reaches the equilibrium potential for K^+ of −75 mV. This loss of positive charges from the interior of the cell results in a hyperpolarization.

FIGURE 5.4   **Depolarization or hyperpolarization due to opened ion channels**

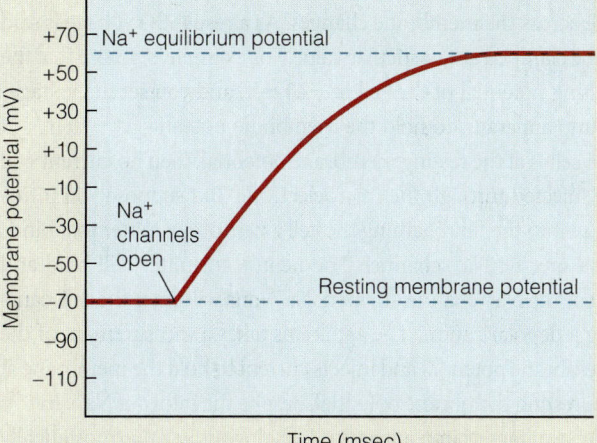

(a) Opening of Na^+ channels depolarizes the membrane

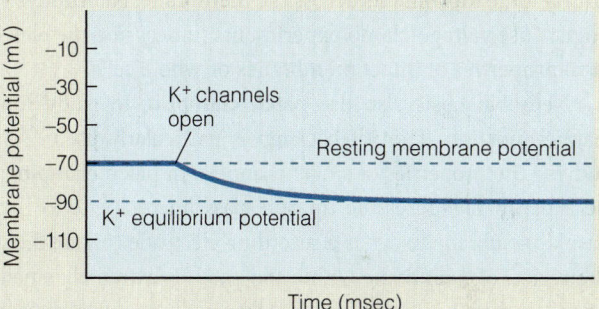

(b) Opening of K^+ channels hyperpolarizes the membrane

the cell membrane less negatively charged, causing depolarization. During **hyperpolarization**, the membrane potential becomes more negative. Either negatively charged ions entering the cell or positively charged ions moving out of the cell can make the inside of the cell membrane more negative, causing hyperpolarization. During repolarization, the cell membrane returns toward the resting membrane potential, following a depolarization or hyperpolarization. It is possible to use the Nernst and Goldman equations to predict the direction of movement of any ion during neural signaling (Box 5.1: Math in Physiology: Using the Nernst and Goldman Equations).

FIGURE 5.5   **A recording of changes in membrane potential in a neuron**

Resting membrane potential of a neuron is usually about −70 mV. During depolarization, the membrane potential becomes less negative. During repolarization, the membrane returns to the resting membrane potential. During hyperpolarization, membrane potential becomes more negative.

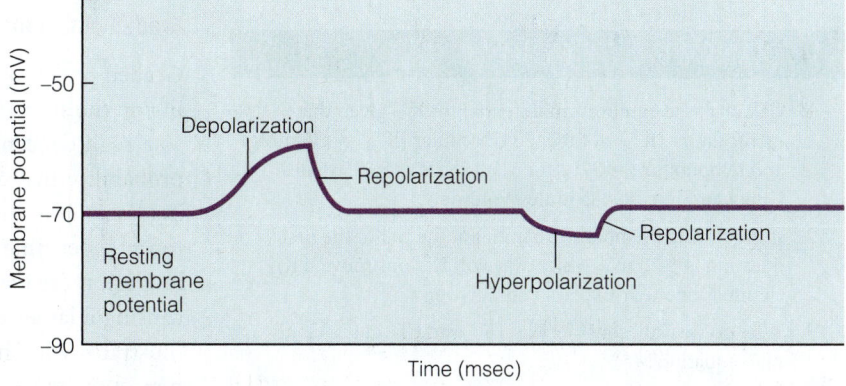

Ion channel function can be studied using the voltage clamp

Depolarization and hyperpolarization of a neuron is caused by the opening and closing of ion channels. One of the most widely used methods for studying ion channels in single cells is the **voltage clamp**. The basic idea of a voltage-clamp experiment is to hold the voltage across a membrane at a constant level by injecting current into the cell via a **microelectrode** any time the voltage across the membrane changes. As a result, the voltage is said to be clamped at a particular value. For example, suppose that the resting potential of the cell is −70 mV, and you set the voltage-clamp apparatus to hold the membrane potential at −70 mV. If the cell is at the resting membrane potential, then no current will be injected through the microelectrode. But suppose you introduce into the fluid bathing the cell a neurotransmitter that binds to a specific Na^+ channel. The neurotransmitter will bind and cause the Na^+ channel to open. Na^+ ions will enter the cell, causing a depolarization. The apparatus takes a measurement of the membrane potential and injects current to hold the membrane at the resting membrane potential, despite the influx of Na^+. In this way, a voltage-clamp apparatus is analogous to a thermostatically controlled heater operating by negative feedback.

The amount of injected current is a direct measure of natural ionic movements across the membrane. Neurophysiologists use voltage-clamp experiments to describe the electrical properties of intact membranes or whole cells.

Neurobiologists also use **patch clamping** to study ion channel function. The patch clamp is particularly useful for studying the properties of single channels. In patch clamping, the experimenter fuses the tip of a glass micropipette to the plasma membrane to act as a recording electrode (Figure 5.6). The region of membrane within the patch is extremely small (often less than 1 micron), and usually contains a relatively low number of ion channels. In fact, some of the patches will contain only a single ion channel, as shown in the figure. The experimenter can then voltage-clamp this small region of membrane and record the extremely small currents generated by a single ion channel (they are measured in picoamperes; pico = 10^{-12}). Patch clamping allows neurobiologists to study the properties of a single ion-channel molecule, while voltage-clamping a whole cell, or a large region of a membrane, provides information about the behavior of populations of ion channels.

CONCEPT CHECK

1. Calculate the equilibrium potential for K^+, given that extracellular $[K^+]$ = 4 mM; intracellular $[K^+]$ = 135 mM, and temperature = 37°C, or 310.15K. R = 8.315 joules/K.mol and F = 96,485 joules/Volt.mol.

2. If the resting membrane potential of the cell in the first question is −70 mV, which way will K^+ ions move if K^+ channels opened? Explain your answer.

3. Why do we only consider Na^+, K^+ and Cl^- in the Goldman equation?

FIGURE 5.6 **Patch clamping**

In a patch-clamp experiment, a glass micropipette is fused to a tiny region of the membrane. This pipette can be used as an electrode to record the tiny currents flowing through one or a small number of individual channel proteins.

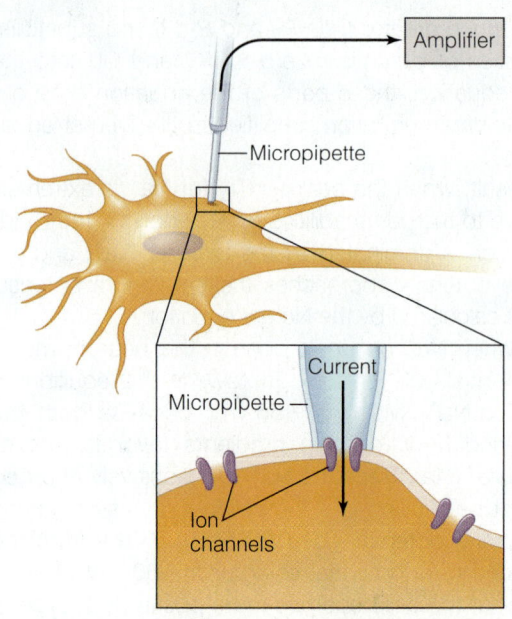

Signals in the Dendrites and Cell Body

Vertebrate motor neurons receive incoming signals in the form of a chemical neurotransmitter. Membrane-bound receptors in the dendrites or cell body transduce (convert) this incoming chemical signal into an electrical signal in the form of a change in the membrane potential. In Chapter 4: Cell Signaling and Endocrine Regulation, we discussed how receptors in many cells, including neurons, transduce incoming chemical signals into electrical signals. Recall that binding of neurotransmitter to a specific ligand-gated receptor causes ion channels in the membrane to open or close, changing the permeability of the membrane and altering the movement of ions. This change in permeability alters the membrane potential and causes an electrical signal. In the dendrites and cell bodies of neurons, these electrical signals are called **graded potentials**.

Graded potentials vary in magnitude

Graded potentials vary in magnitude (are graded) depending on the strength of the stimulus. A strong stimulus, such as a high concentration of neurotransmitter, increases the probability that a given ion channel will open, thus causing more ion channels to open, and keeping them open for a longer time. If more ion channels open (or stay open longer), more ions will move across the plasma membrane, causing a larger change in membrane potential. Figure 5.7 illustrates what happens when different concentrations of neurotransmitter are present near the dendrite of a neuron.

FIGURE 5.7 Stimulus strength and graded potentials

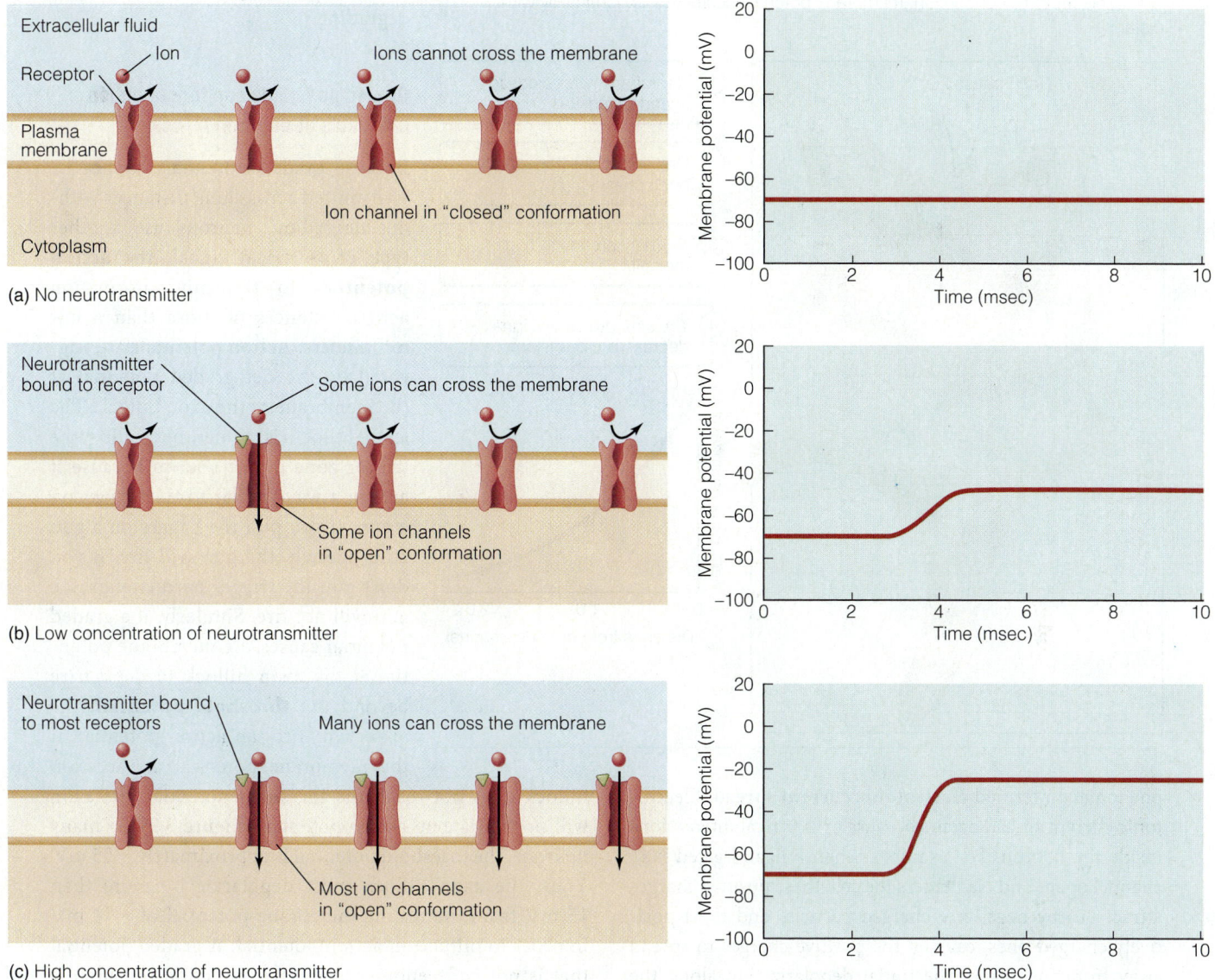

(a) No neurotransmitter

(b) Low concentration of neurotransmitter

(c) High concentration of neurotransmitter

When no neurotransmitter is present, the ligand-gated ion channels on the surface of the dendrite remain closed, no ions can move across the membrane through those channels, and the membrane potential stays the same. When the neurotransmitter is present at low concentrations, a few ion channels open, allowing a small number of ions to cross the membrane, causing a small change in membrane potential. When a high concentration of the neurotransmitter is present, many ion channels open, and stay open longer, allowing more ions to cross the membrane, causing a large change in membrane potential. Thus, the amplitude of the graded potential directly reflects the strength of the incoming stimulus.

As we discussed above, graded potentials can either hyperpolarize or depolarize the cell, depending on the type of ion channel that is opened or closed. The most important ion channels in the dendrites and cell body of a neuron are

Na^+, K^+, Cl^-, and Ca^{2+} channels. From the Nernst equation we can calculate that opening Na^+ or Ca^{2+} channels will depolarize a typical neuron, while opening K^+ or Cl^- channels will hyperpolarize a neuron.

Graded potentials are short-distance signals

Graded potentials can travel through the cell, but they decrease in strength as they get farther away from the opened ion channel, a phenomenon called *conduction with decrement*. Figure 5.8 shows a neuron with a ligand-gated Na^+ channel on the membrane. When neurotransmitter (the ligand) binds to a ligand-gated Na^+ channel, the channel opens and Na^+ ions move into the cell. Na^+ entry causes a local depolarization in a small area of the membrane surrounding the opened channel. This positive charge then spreads along the inside of the membrane, causing depolarization, a

FIGURE 5.8 **Conduction with decrement**

During electrotonic conduction, membrane potential decreases exponentially with distance.

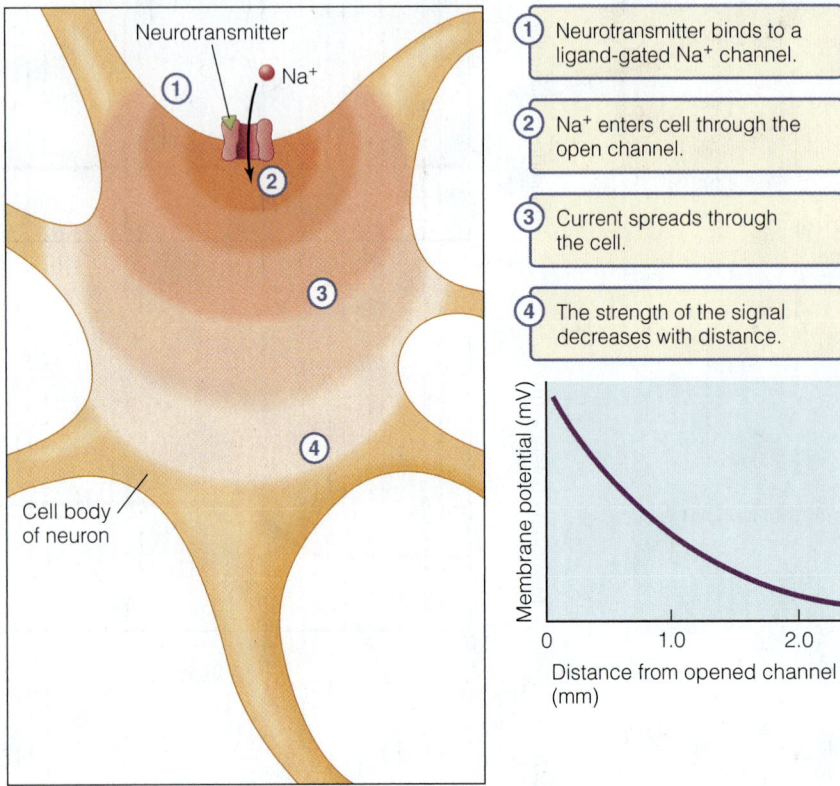

① Neurotransmitter binds to a ligand-gated Na⁺ channel.

② Na⁺ enters cell through the open channel.

③ Current spreads through the cell.

④ The strength of the signal decreases with distance.

Neurotransmitter

Na⁺

Cell body of neuron

Membrane potential (mV)

Distance from opened channel (mm)

the dendrites to the axon hillock, they cannot travel longer distances without degrading.

Graded potentials can trigger action potentials at the axon hillock

Because graded potentials cannot be transmitted across long distances without degrading, neurons use another type of electrical signal, the **action potential**, to transmit information across distances of more than a few millimeters. Action potentials are triggered by the net graded potential at the membrane of the axon hillock. The axon hillock is sometimes called the trigger zone of the neuron because it acts in a way similar to the trigger on a gun. If you pull the trigger on a gun hard enough, the gun will fire. If you don't pull the trigger hard enough the gun will not fire. Similarly, if a graded potential causes the membrane potential at the axon hillock to depolarize beyond the **threshold potential**, the axon will "fire" an action potential. If the membrane potential at the axon hillock does not reach the threshold potential, the axon will not initiate an action potential (Figure 5.9). In many neurons, the threshold potential is approximately −55 mV. Thus, the axon hillock must depolarize by more than 15 mV from the resting membrane potential of −70 mV in order to initiate an action potential. A graded potential that is not large enough to trigger an action potential is called a *subthreshold potential*. Graded potentials that are even larger than needed to trigger an action potential are called *suprathreshold potentials*.

Because the axon hillock must reach the threshold potential in order to generate an action potential, graded potentials can either increase or decrease the likelihood of an action potential firing in the axon. A depolarizing graded potential moves the membrane potential at the axon hillock closer to the threshold potential. A hyperpolarizing graded potential moves the membrane potential at the axon hillock farther from the threshold potential. A depolarizing graded potential is called an **excitatory potential** because it makes an action potential more likely to occur by bringing the membrane potential closer to the threshold potential. A hyperpolarizing graded potential makes an action

phenomenon termed **electrotonic current spread**. Electrotonic current spread occurs because of electrical interactions inside the neuron. For example, when a ligand-gated Na⁺ channel opens and Na⁺ enters the cell, these positive charges attract nearby negatively charged particles and repel positively charged ones, causing the positive charges to spread away from the site of the initial depolarization along the membrane. This causes the depolarization to move along the membrane in all directions.

The extent of the depolarization decreases as it moves farther and farther from the opened channels, just as ripples in a pond decrease in strength as they move farther away from their source. The signal is conducted, but it gets fainter and fainter as it travels. With ripples in a pond, the ripples decrease in size with distance due to the frictional resistance of the water. As we discuss in more detail later in the chapter, several features of the neuron influence why a graded potential decreases as it travels through the cell, including leakage of charged ions across the cell membrane, the **electrical resistance** of the cytoplasm, and the electrical properties of the membrane. As a result of these features, although graded potentials can travel the short distance from

FIGURE 5.9 **Subthreshold and suprathreshold potentials**

The resting membrane potential of most neurons is around −70 mV and the threshold potential is −55 mV. **(a)** Subthreshold graded potentials (less than +15 mV) do not trigger an action potential. **(b)** Graded potentials that are at or above the threshold potential (greater than +15 mV) trigger an action potential.

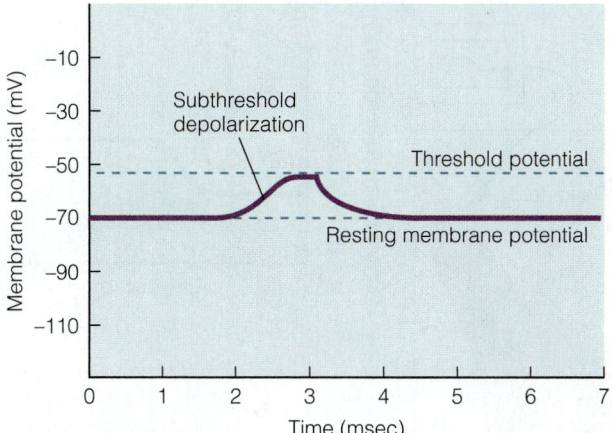

(a) Subthreshold graded potential

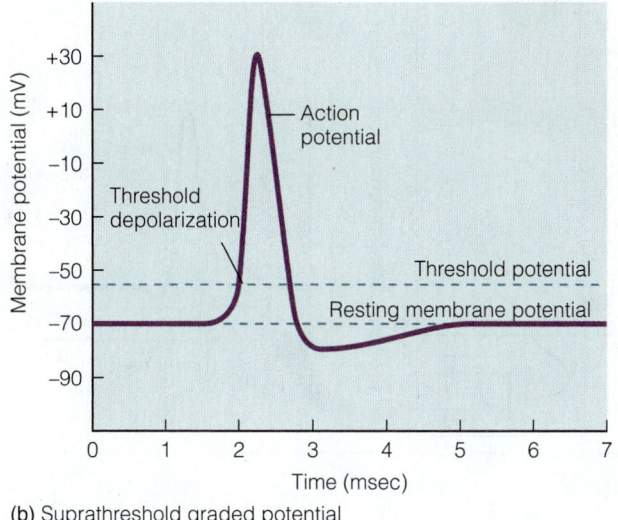

(b) Suprathreshold graded potential

potential less likely to occur (by taking the membrane potential farther from the threshold potential), and so is called an **inhibitory potential**.

Graded potentials can be integrated across time and space

The dendrites and cell body of a neuron have receptors at many sites on the membrane, and each neuron may have multiple kinds of receptors and ion channels. Thus,

neurons can generate many graded potentials simultaneously. Graded potentials from different sites can interact with each other to influence the net change in membrane potential at the axon hillock; this phenomenon is called **spatial summation**. In the example of spatial summation shown in Figure 5.10, a neurotransmitter opens ligand-gated Na^+ channels in one dendrite, causing Na^+ to enter the dendrite and depolarizing that area of the membrane, but alone this depolarization is not sufficient to trigger an action potential. Similarly, in the other dendrite, a neurotransmitter also opens a ligand-gated Na^+ channel, but again this depolarization is not sufficient to trigger an action potential. Both of these depolarizations travel to the axon hillock, and when they meet, they sum together to result in a net depolarization that exceeds the threshold potential and triggers an action potential. It is important to note that the phenomenon of spatial summation can also prevent action potential generation. Imagine a situation in which a suprathreshold depolarization as the result of the opening of a ligand-gated Na^+ channel occurs at the same time that, in the other dendrite, a neurotransmitter opens ligand-gated K^+ channels. Opening of K^+ channels causes K^+ to leave the dendrite, and hyperpolarizes that area of the membrane. These two graded potentials travel through the cell to the axon hillock. In this example there is no change in membrane potential at the axon hillock despite the changes in membrane potential in the dendrites, because change in membrane potential caused by the movement of Na^+ into the cell in one dendrite exactly balances the change in membrane potential caused by the movement of K^+ out of the cell in the other dendrite. Thus, the net change in membrane potential at the axon hillock reflects the relative strengths and sign of the signals in the dendrites.

Depolarizations that occur at two slightly different times can also combine to determine the net change in membrane potential at the axon hillock, a phenomenon called **temporal summation** (Figure 5.11). Consider two depolarizations, E_1 and E_2, each of 10 mV. If depolarization E_2 occurs after depolarization E_1 has died out, then the maximum depolarization is 10 mV, which is not large enough to trigger an action potential. In contrast, if depolarization E_2 occurs before E_1 has died out, the two depolarizations build on each other and result in an increased net depolarization to a maximum of 20 mV, bringing the cell from the resting membrane potential of −70 mV beyond the threshold potential of −55 mV, triggering an action potential.

The axon hillock acts as a decision point for the neuron. The neuron will fire an action potential in the axon only if the combination of all the graded potentials in the dendrites

FIGURE 5.10   **Spatial summation**

Graded potentials from different locations can interact to influence the net change in membrane potential at the axon hillock. In the neuron shown below, neurotransmitter binds to a ligand-gated Na⁺ channel in dendrite A, opening the channel, and causing a subthreshold depolarizing graded potential. At the same time, neurotransmitter binds to a ligand-gated Na⁺ channel in dendrite B, also causing a subthreshold depolarizing graded potential. Both graded potentials travel electrotonically through the cell. At the axon hillock, these subthreshold depolarizations add together, causing a suprathreshold depolarization that triggers an action potential in the axon.

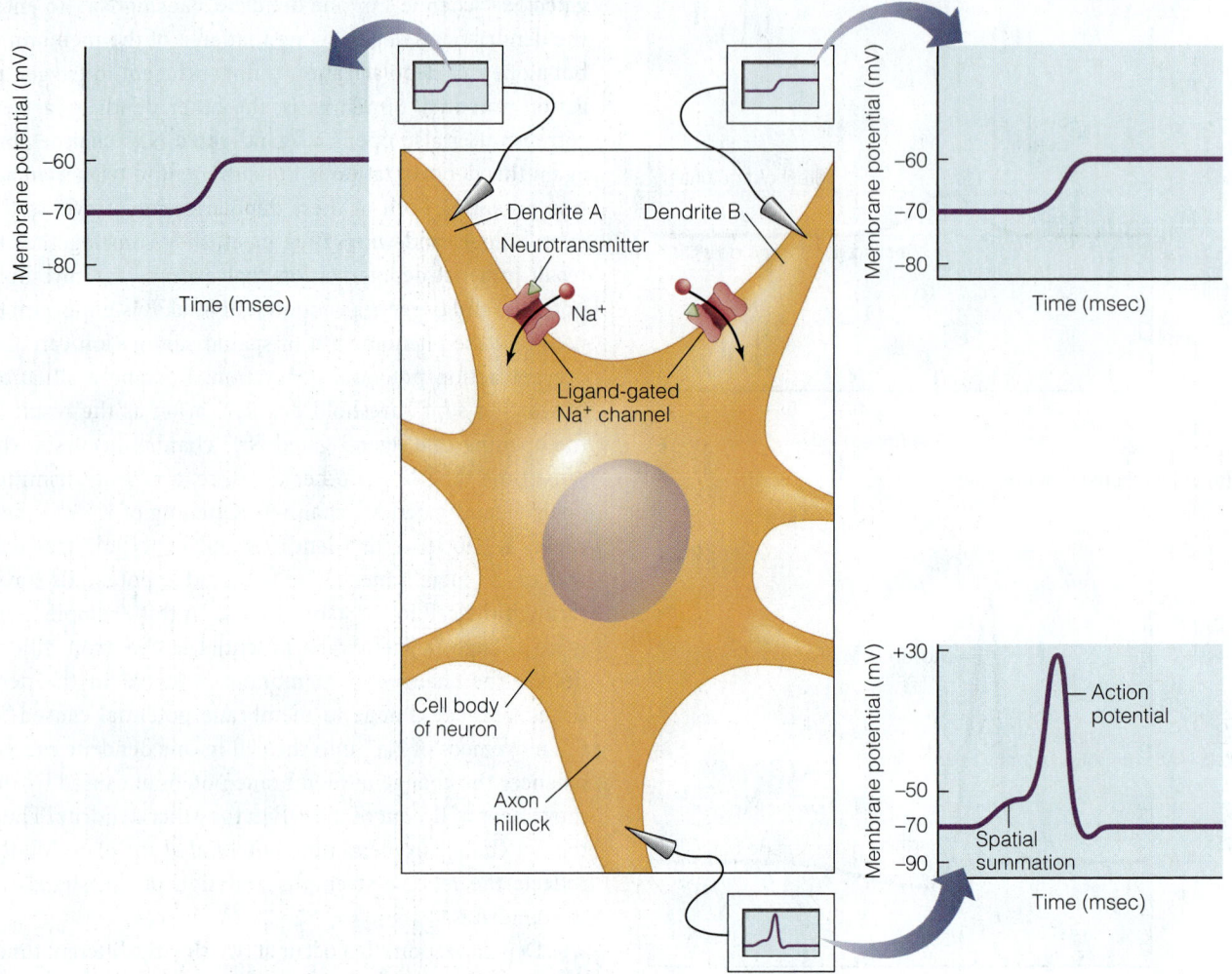

and cell body causes the axon hillock to depolarize beyond threshold. Spatial and temporal summation of graded potentials allow a neuron to integrate inputs from many different stimuli, and determine whether the axon hillock is depolarized beyond threshold and if an action potential will occur in the axon.

CONCEPT CHECK

4. What causes graded potentials to vary in magnitude?
5. Explain electrotonic current spread.
6. What is the difference between temporal and spatial summation? Can spatial summation occur without temporal summation?

Signals in the Axon

Action potentials are stereotyped changes in membrane potential that can be transmitted across long distances without degrading. They differ from graded potentials in many respects (Table 5.1). Action potentials typically have three phases (Figure 5.12a). The **depolarization phase** of the action potential is triggered when the membrane potential at the axon hillock reaches threshold (as a result of the summed graded potential at the axon hillock). Once the axon hillock reaches threshold, the adjacent axonal membrane quickly depolarizes, reaching a positive membrane potential of about +30 mV. The depolarization phase is followed by a **repolarization phase**, during which the membrane potential rapidly returns to the resting membrane potential. Following repolarization,

FIGURE 5.11 Temporal summation

Graded potentials occurring at slightly different times can interact to influence the net graded potential. **(a)** Subthreshold depolarizations (E_1 and E_2) of 10 mV that do not overlap in time do not trigger an action potential. **(b)** Subthreshold depolarizations that occur at slightly different times may sum, if they overlap in time. If the net change in membrane potential exceeds the threshold, they will trigger an action potential.

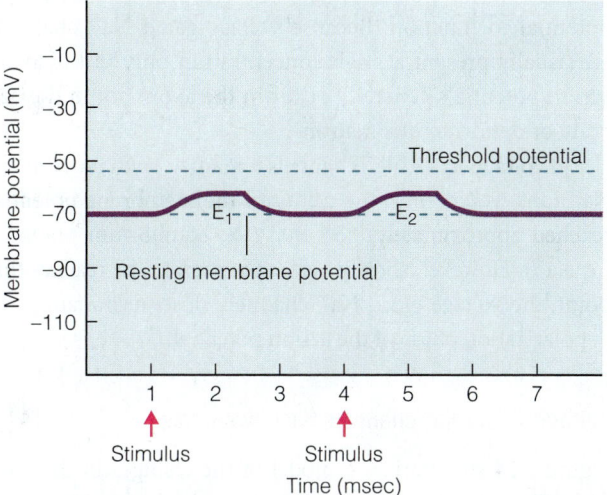

(a) No summation

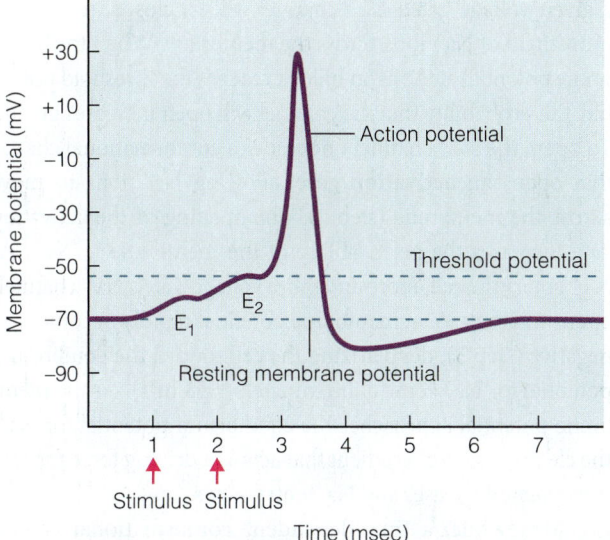

(b) Temporal summation resulting in an action potential

the membrane potential becomes even more negative than the resting membrane potential, and may approach the K^+ equilibrium potential. The duration and size of this **after-hyperpolarization phase** varies greatly among neurons, typically lasting between 2 and 15 msec, at which point the membrane returns to the resting membrane potential.

The ability of an axon to generate new action potentials varies during the phases of the action potential. During the **absolute refractory period**, which coincides with the depolarization and repolarization phases, the axon is incapable of generating a new action potential, no matter how strong the stimulus. During the **relative refractory period**, which coincides with the after-hyperpolarization phase, a new action potential can be generated, but only by very large stimuli.

Voltage-gated channels generate the action potential

Opening and closing of **voltage-gated ion channels** cause the characteristic phases of the action potential. Just as the binding of a neurotransmitter changes the shape of a ligand-gated ion channel, changes in membrane potential change the shape of voltage-gated ion channels, allowing ions to move across the membrane. Because there is some variation in the ion channels involved in the action potential in axons from different species, here we concentrate on the model of the action potential developed for the giant axon of the squid, which also applies to neurons such as vertebrate motor neurons. Opening of voltage-gated Na^+ channels causes the depolarization phase of the action potential, and opening of voltage-gated K^+ channels initiates the repolarization and hyperpolarization phases in these neurons (Figure 5.12a).

Voltage-gated Na^+ channels open at the threshold potential

When the membrane potential at the axon hillock approaches the threshold potential (typically around -55 mV), voltage-gated Na^+ channels in the axon hillock begin to open, changing the permeability of the membrane to Na^+ ions (Figure 5.12b), allowing Na^+ ions to move across the

Table 5.1 Differences between graded potentials and action potentials	
Graded Potentials	**Action Potentials**
Vary in magnitude	Always the same size and shape (in a given cell type)
Vary in duration	Always the same duration (in a given cell type)
Decay with distance	Do not decay with distance
Occur in dendrites and cell body	Occur in axons of neurons (also in muscle cells)
Caused by opening and closing of many kinds of ion channels	Caused by opening and closing of voltage-gated ion channels

FIGURE 5.12 **The phases of a typical action potential**
(a) Changes in membrane potential during an action potential.
(b) Changes in membrane permeability during an action potential.

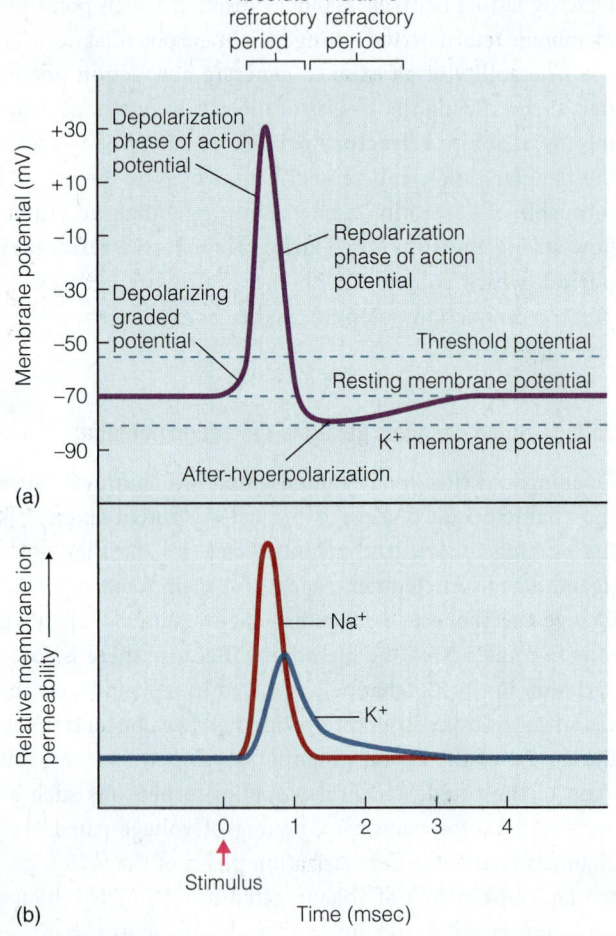

more Na^+ ions to enter the cell. This mechanism, termed the *Hodgkin cycle*, represents an example of a positive feedback loop (Figure 5.13). The positive feedback loop of Na^+ entry reinforces itself, resulting in an extremely rapid change in membrane Na^+ permeability, and accounting for the rapid depolarization phase of the action potential. The density of voltage-gated Na^+ channels in the membrane must be high in order for the positive feedback mechanism of the action potential to function. Because voltage-gated Na^+ channels are usually present at high concentration only in the axon, action potentials generally occur in the axon, not in the cell body or dendrites of a neuron.

If voltage-gated Na^+ channels remained open indefinitely, Na^+ ions would enter the cell until the membrane potential reached approximately +55 mV (the equilibrium potential for Na^+). However, shortly before the membrane reaches this point, the voltage-gated Na^+ channels close, terminating the depolarization phase of the action potential.

Voltage-gated Na^+ channels have two gates

Figure 5.14 summarizes a model of the changes in the conformation of voltage-gated Na^+ channels during the action potential. When the membrane of the neuron is at the resting membrane potential (step 1), there is a high probability that a given voltage-gated Na^+ channel will be closed, preventing movement of Na^+ ions across the membrane. When the membrane potential at the axon hillock reaches the threshold potential, the probability that the channel will open increases greatly. To open, the Na^+ channel undergoes a conformational change that opens an **activation gate**, allowing Na^+ ions to move across the membrane (step 2). The opening of the activation gate increases the permeability of the membrane to Na^+. As Na^+ enters the cell, more and more voltage-gated Na^+ channels open, and the axonal membrane potential rapidly becomes less negative (step 3), depolarizing the cell toward the equilibrium potential for Na^+ ions (approximately +55 mV). As the membrane potential approaches the equilibrium potential for Na^+, the electrochemical gradient that acts as a driving force for Na^+ movement decreases and Na^+ entry slows.

Meanwhile, a time-dependent conformational change occurs in the channel, closing an **inactivation gate** (step 4 in Figure 5.14). With the inactivation gate closed, no more Na^+ can enter the cell, terminating the depolarization phase of the action potential. During this phase, the voltage-gated Na^+ channel cannot be opened even by a suprathreshold depolarizing stimulus. This corresponds to the absolute **refractory period** of the action potential. Over several milliseconds, in response to changes in the membrane potential caused by the actions of the voltage-gated K^+ channels, the inactivation gate resets, and the channel returns to its initial conformation (activation gate closed, inactivation gate open), ready to initiate another action potential (step 5 in Figure 5.14).

membrane. The probability that a given voltage-gated Na^+ channel will be open (termed the open probability of the channel) depends on the size of the graded potential. An excitatory graded potential that depolarizes the membrane toward the threshold potential increases the probability that a voltage-gated Na^+ channel will be open. Thus, at the threshold potential, more voltage-gated Na^+ channels will be open than when the axon hillock is at the resting membrane potential, increasing the permeability of the membrane to Na^+.

A positive feedback loop drives the depolarization phase

The Na^+ influx from the first voltage-gated channels to open in response to the graded potential further depolarizes the local region of the membrane, further increasing the probability that voltage-gated Na^+ channels will open. More voltage-gated Na^+ channels open as a result, further increasing the permeability of the membrane, allowing even

FIGURE 5.13 **The Hodgkin cycle: A positive feedback loop due to voltage-gated Na⁺ channels**

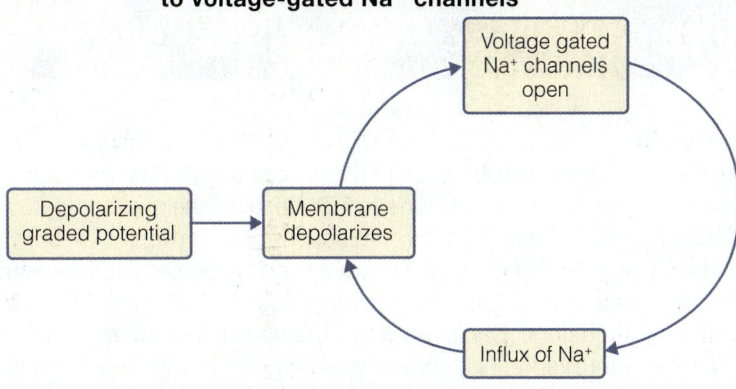

Because voltage-gated Na⁺ channels are critical for the depolarizing phase of the action potential, drugs and toxins that interfere with this channel prevent action potential generation and block the conduction of signals along neurons. See Box 5.2: Applications: Voltage-Gated Na⁺ Channel Blockers for more information about these fascinating compounds.

Voltage-gated K⁺ channels open slowly

In addition to increasing the open probability of voltage-gated Na⁺ channels, threshold depolarization of the membrane at the axon hillock increases

FIGURE 5.14 **A model for the action of voltage-gated Na⁺ channels**

① When the neuron is at the resting membrane potential the activation gate closes voltage-gated Na⁺ channels, preventing Na⁺ entry.

② A suprathreshold depolarizing graded potential causes the activation gate to open, allowing Na⁺ to enter the cell.

③ Increased Na⁺ entry further depolarizes the cell, opening even more voltage-gated Na⁺ channels in a positive feedback loop, causing the rapid depolarization phase of the action potential.

④ The inactivation gate of the channel closes as the membrane approaches +30 mV, preventing Na⁺ entry.

⑤ Over time, in response to the rapid repolarization of the membrane, the channel returns to its original state.

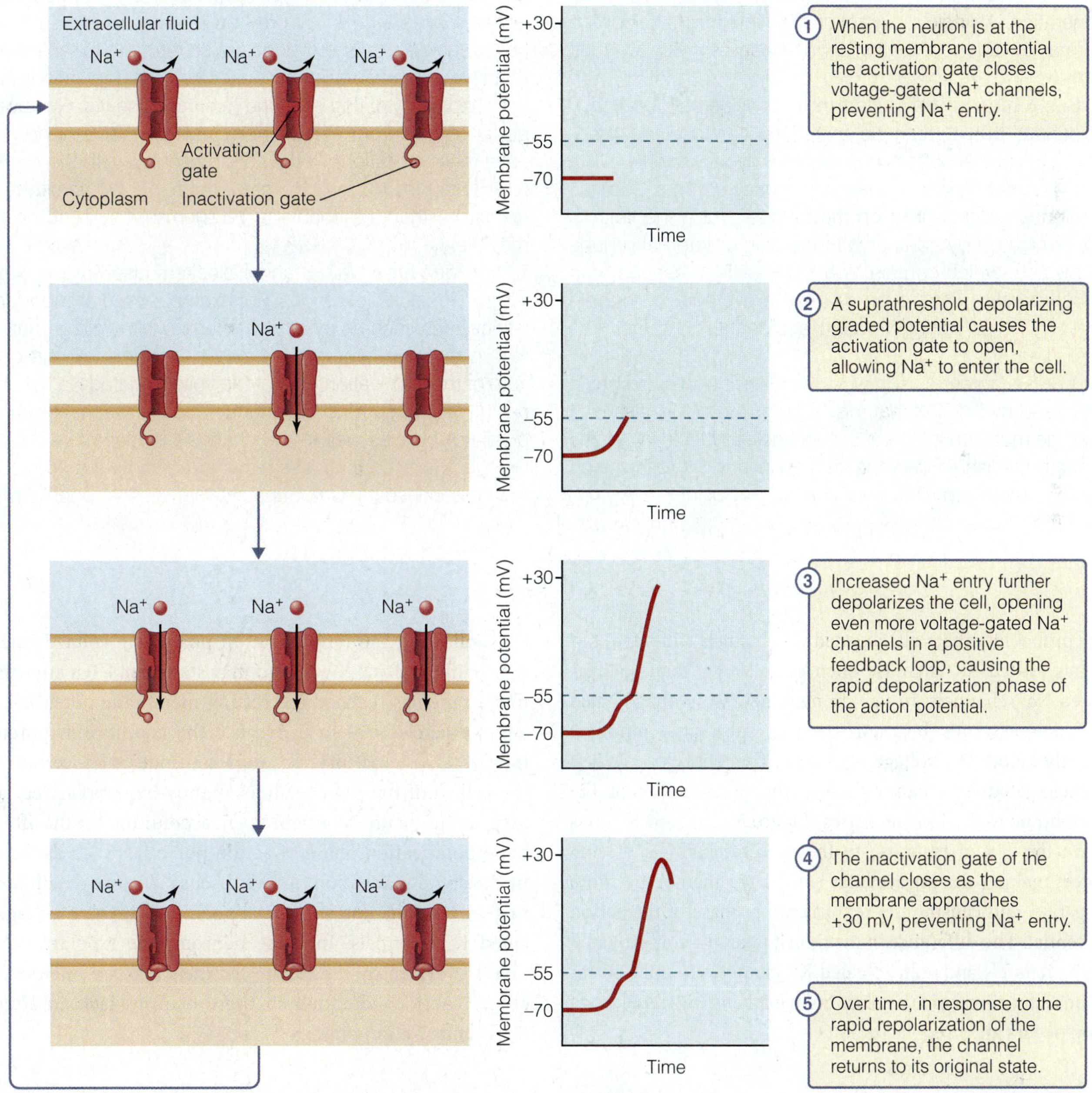

VOLTAGE-GATED NA⁺ CHANNEL BLOCKERS

Many animals, including fish, snakes, and marine invertebrates, contain toxins that block voltage-gated Na⁺ channels and abolish action potentials. Because these toxins interfere with electrical signaling in neurons, and can cause paralysis or death when ingested, they can act as potent antipredator defenses. For example, the tissues of various species of pufferfish (order Tetraodontiformes) contain a toxin called tetrodotoxin (TTX). Pufferfish do not actually synthesize TTX. Instead, they accumulate it from symbiotic bacteria living in their guts. TTX blocks voltage-gated Na⁺ channels by binding to a pocket at the mouth of the channel, blocking Na⁺ entry and preventing action potential generation. A single milligram of TTX would be lethal for the normal predators of pufferfish, and can even kill an adult human.

Sushi made from pufferfish is considered a delicacy in Japan, but it must be extremely carefully prepared. The flesh of the pufferfish contains only very low levels of TTX, and eating it produces very mild symptoms, such as numbness and tingling on the tongue. But if the flesh is contaminated by contact with the skin or internal organs of the fish, which contain high levels of TTX, eating it can cause paralysis and even death. On average, 50 people die of TTX poisoning through accidental contamination every year.

TTX is a potent poison, so how do pufferfish avoid being paralyzed by the TTX that they accumulate in their tissues? A single mutation in one of the voltage-gated Na⁺ channels of the pufferfish renders the channel insensitive to inhibition by TTX, and the pufferfish immune to the toxin.

Like pufferfish, California newts (*Taricha torosa*) also sequester high levels of TTX for protection against predators. The newts are immune to TTX because their voltage-gated Na⁺ channels contain mutations that prevent TTX binding. In the case of the newts, however, natural selection has also shaped the voltage-gated Na⁺ channels of their predators. Garter snakes (*Thamnopis sirtalis*) are important predators of newts in some portions of their species range. Populations of garter snakes from regions where the newts are present have a high frequency of individuals with mutations in their voltage-gated Na⁺ channels. These mutations make the channels insensitive to TTX, and these garter snakes will readily prey on the newts. Interestingly, garter snakes in some regions are so resistant to the newts that even the least resistant snakes in these populations are not affected by eating even the most toxic newts. However, garter snakes from areas where newts are absent do not have these mutations. If they are presented with the newts experimentally, they will try to eat them, but will vomit them up, and if they are unable to rid themselves of the newt, they die.

Voltage-gated Na⁺ channel blockers also have a wide range of useful applications. For example, several important insecticides such as pyrethrins interfere with voltage-gated Na⁺ channels. Pyrethrins are thought to impede the closure of the inactivation gate of the voltage-gated Na⁺ channel in insects, causing continuous depolarization. Pyrethrin does not bind as well to the channels in mammals, so although it is toxic, it is less lethal in humans and livestock than it is in insects. Unfortunately, many insect populations

---

the probability that voltage-gated K⁺ channels will open. But voltage-gated K⁺ channels open more slowly than voltage-gated Na⁺ channels. In fact, in most neurons, voltage-gated K⁺ channels only begin to open in substantial numbers shortly before the voltage-gated Na⁺ channels close. When voltage-gated K⁺ channels open, the permeability of the membrane to K⁺ ions increases (Figure 5.12b), and K⁺ ions leave the cell in response to their electrochemical driving force, making the intracellular side of the membrane more negative, and causing the repolarization phase of the action potential. The difference in the time it takes for voltage-gated Na⁺ channels and voltage-gated K⁺ channels to open in response to a threshold depolarization explains why repolarization occurs after depolarization.

Following the repolarization phase, the voltage-gated K⁺ channels close slowly, and may stay open even after the membrane has reached the resting membrane potential of approximately −70 mV. Because the equilibrium potential for K⁺ is −90 mV, K⁺ ions continue to move out of the cell until the membrane is slightly hyperpolarized, as long as the channels remain open, accounting for the after-hyperpolarization phase of action potentials such as those in the squid giant axon. As we discuss in more detail later in this chapter, not all action potentials involve voltage-gated K⁺ channels. In these neurons, the repolarization phase is driven by the "leak" channels that are open even at rest. Action potentials in these neurons lack an after-hyperpolarization phase.

FIGURE 5.15 **A toxic species: the Japanese pufferfish (*Takifugu rubripes*)**

Photo source: Jerry Young/DK Images.

have undergone adaptive evolution in their voltage-gated Na$^+$ channel genes, accumulating mutations that cause resistance, which makes pyrethrin-based insecticides less useful.

Several anesthetics are voltage-gated Na$^+$ channel blockers. For example, the local anesthetic Lidocaine blocks the pore of the voltage-gated Na$^+$ channel, impeding the flow of ions when the channel is activated, and reducing action potential generation. Lidocaine is commonly used to numb the mouth during dental procedures. By blocking electrical signals from pain-sensitive neurons, lidocaine acts as an anesthetic. But if both Lidocaine and TTX act as blockers of the voltage-gated Na$^+$ channel, why does

Lidocaine simply act as a mild anesthetic, while TTX can kill you? One important difference between these two toxins is that Lidocaine is only effective at very high doses. Ingesting small amounts of Lidocaine will not cause any broad-based systematic effects on the nervous system, although large doses can be fatal. When Lidocaine is applied on the skin or gums it does not enter the circulation in doses high enough to be fatal, and instead it primarily acts locally to cause temporary numbness. In contrast, tetrodotoxin is active at very low concentrations, so ingesting even small amounts of this toxin can be devastating.

References

- Feldman, C. R., E. D. Brodie, Jr., E. D. Brodie, III, & M. E. Pfrender. 2012. Constraint shapes convergence in tetrodotoxin-resistant sodium channels of snakes. *Proceedings of the National Academy of Sciences (USA)*, *109*, 4556–4561.
- Geffeney S. L., E. Fujimoto, E. D. Brodie III, E. D. Brodie, Jr., & P. C. Ruben. 2005. Evolutionary diversification of TTX-resistant sodium channels in a predator–prey interaction. *Nature, 434*, 759–763.
- Hanifin, C. T., E. D. Brodie, Jr., & E. D. Brodie III. 2008. Phenotypic mismatches reveal escape from arms race coevolution. *PLoS Biology*, 6:e60.
- Venkatesh, B., S. Q. Lu, N. Dandona, S. L. See, S. Brenner, & T. W. Soong. 2005. Genetic basis of tetrodotoxin resistance in pufferfishes. *Current Biology*, 15, 2069–2072.
- Zakon, H. H. 2012. Adaptive evolution of voltage-gated sodium channels: The first 800 million years. *Proceedings of the National Academy of Sciences (USA)*, 109, Supplement 1:10619–10625.

Both Na$^+$ and K$^+$ shape the action potential

Figure 5.16 summarizes the relationship between the voltage-gated Na$^+$ and K$^+$ channels and how they produce the action potential. When the axon hillock depolarizes beyond the threshold potential, both the Na$^+$ and K$^+$ channels receive a signal to open. The voltage-gated Na$^+$ channels open very quickly, allowing Na$^+$ to enter the cell, causing further depolarization. This greater depolarization opens even more Na$^+$ channels, causing even greater depolarization in a positive feedback cycle. As the axon hillock approaches the equilibrium potential for Na$^+$, ion entry slows, and the voltage-gated Na$^+$ channels close, preventing further Na$^+$ entry, and terminating the positive feedback loop of the depolarization phase. At about the same time, the

voltage-gated K$^+$ channels begin to open, K$^+$ leaves the cell, and the intracellular side of the membrane becomes more negative, initiating the repolarization phase of the action potential.

At the end of an action potential, some Na$^+$ ions have entered the cell and some K$^+$ ions have moved out, leaving the cell in a slightly different state from the starting point. From the preceding discussion, you might think that large numbers of ions must move across the cell membrane during an action potential. In fact, the number of ions moving across the membrane is extremely small compared with the total number of ions in the intracellular and extracellular fluids. As a result, the changes in membrane potential during the action potential are not associated with any measurable changes in

FIGURE 5.16 **Relationship of voltage-gated Na⁺ and K⁺ channels during an action potential**

A suprathreshold graded potential stimulates both Na⁺ and K⁺ channels to open. Na⁺ channels open immediately, and the resulting influx of Na⁺ causes even more Na⁺ channels to open, in a positive feedback loop. K⁺ channels open more slowly, becoming fully opened around the time that the Na⁺ channels close and causing an efflux of K⁺ ions that repolarizes the membrane. K⁺ ions may continue to leave the cell and cause the membrane to hyperpolarize. Repolarization and hyperpolarization remove the stimulus to open K⁺ channels, causing them to close.

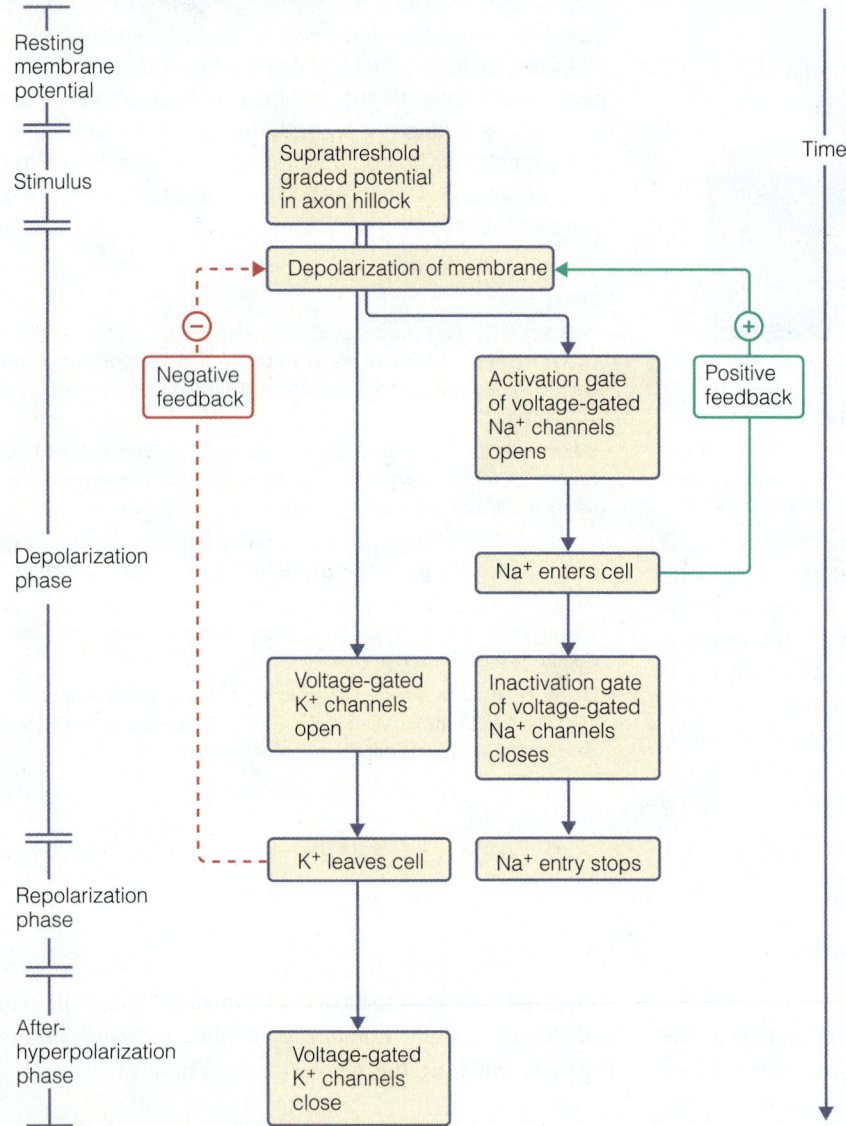

Action potentials transmit signals across long distances

Up to this point we have discussed how an action potential occurs at the axon hillock, but we have not considered how action potentials are involved in signaling along the axon. One property of the action potential, which is sometimes termed its *"all-or-none"* nature, is crucial in allowing neurons to transmit electrical signals across long distances. Action potentials are often described as all-or-none phenomena because once an action potential has been initiated (by the opening of a sufficient number of voltage-gated Na⁺ channels), it always proceeds to its conclusion; it never stops halfway through, or fails to reach its peak depolarization. But how does this property allow action potentials to send signals along the axon, potentially across long distances?

In fact, individual action potentials do not actually travel along the axon. Instead, an action potential in one part of the axon triggers other action potentials in adjacent areas of the axonal membrane. The conduction of an action potential along the axon is similar to what happens when you knock over the first in a long line of dominoes. The first domino that is knocked over starts the next domino falling, which starts the next domino, and so on down to the end of the line. In neurons, the first action potential at the axon hillock causes another action potential farther down the axon, and so on down to the axon terminal. Just as the last domino in a series of falling dominoes is identical to the first domino, the last action potential at the axon terminal is identical to the first action potential at the axon hillock. Thus, action potentials can be conducted across long distances without decaying.

Figure 5.17 summarizes the mechanism of action potential conduction along the axon. Conduction of an action potential along the axon represents a combination of action potentials occurring at specific points along the axon, and local flow of ions and electrical current along the axon, which triggers action potentials further downstream.

ion concentrations inside or outside the cell. However, even though only relatively small numbers of ions actually move across the membrane during a single action potential, thousands of repeated action potentials would eventually cause the Na⁺ and K⁺ gradients of the resting cell membrane to dissipate, changing the resting membrane potential of the cell, unless ion gradients were restored. As you might expect from its role in establishing the resting membrane potential, the Na⁺/K⁺ ATPase plays a primary role in restoring ion gradients following repeated action potentials.

FIGURE 5.17 **Conduction of action potentials**

Na^+ that enters the axon through voltage-gated Na^+ channels induces a local depolarization. This local depolarization spreads along the axon via electrotonic conduction, triggering additional action potentials further down the axon. This process of electrotonic current spread and new action potential initiation continues down to the end of the axon. Each action potential is essentially the same as the preceding ones, resulting in conduction without decrement.

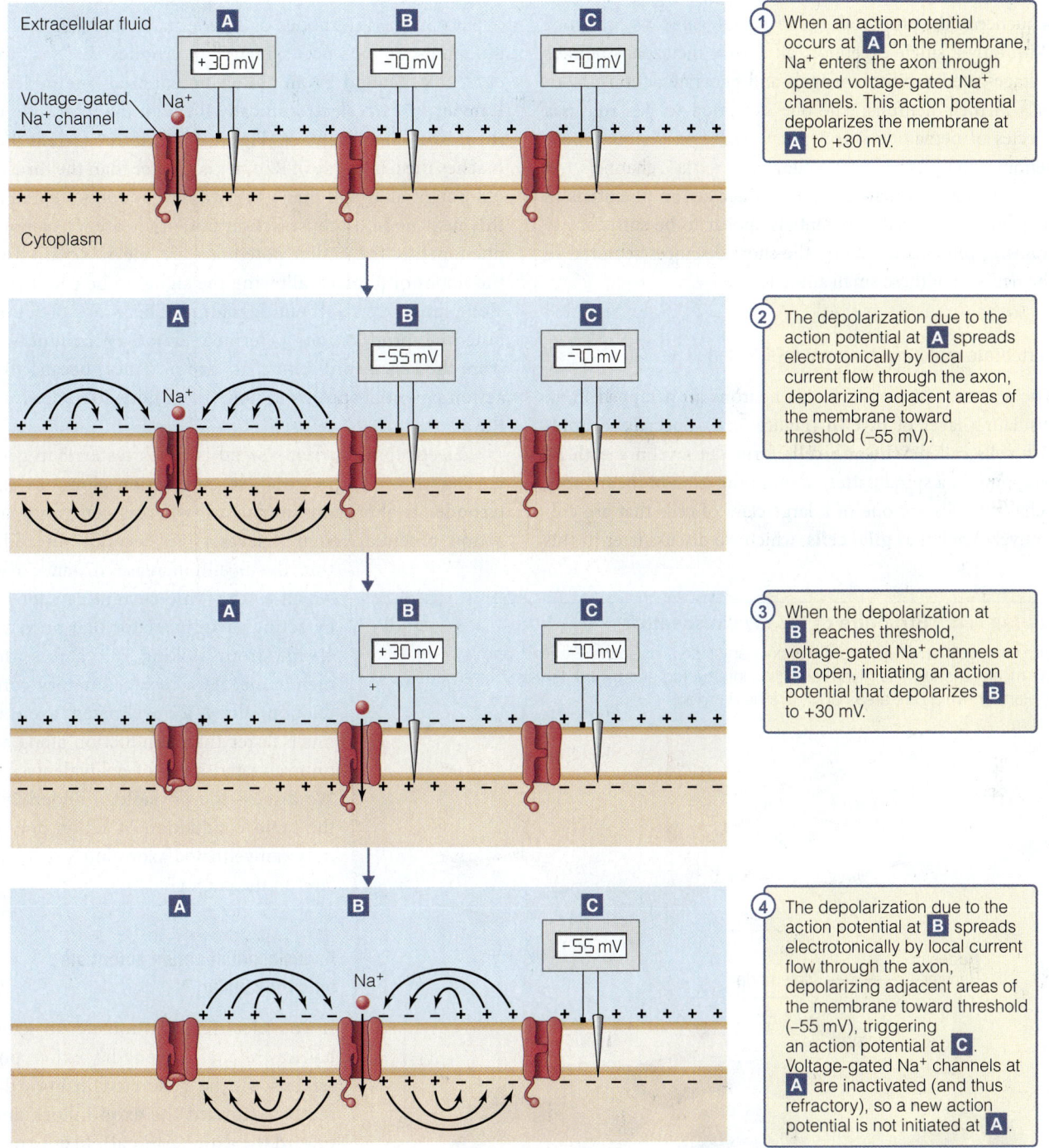

1. When an action potential occurs at **A** on the membrane, Na^+ enters the axon through opened voltage-gated Na^+ channels. This action potential depolarizes the membrane at **A** to +30 mV.

2. The depolarization due to the action potential at **A** spreads electrotonically by local current flow through the axon, depolarizing adjacent areas of the membrane toward threshold (−55 mV).

3. When the depolarization at **B** reaches threshold, voltage-gated Na^+ channels at **B** open, initiating an action potential that depolarizes **B** to +30 mV.

4. The depolarization due to the action potential at **B** spreads electrotonically by local current flow through the axon, depolarizing adjacent areas of the membrane toward threshold (−55 mV), triggering an action potential at **C**. Voltage-gated Na^+ channels at **A** are inactivated (and thus refractory), so a new action potential is not initiated at **A**.

During an action potential, the Na^+ ions entering via the voltage-gated Na^+ channels depolarize the section of the membrane immediately surrounding the channel. This depolarization can then spread along the axon by electrotonic current spread, just as the depolarizations associated with graded potentials spread through the dendrites and cell body. When the membrane in the adjacent region of the axon reaches the threshold potential, voltage-gated Na^+

channels in this region open and trigger another action potential. The cycle of ion entry, current spread, and triggering of an action potential continues along the axon from the axon hillock to the axon terminal, causing action potential to spread like a wave along the axon.

The ability of action potentials to boost signals is a consequence of the properties of the voltage-gated Na$^+$ channel. With only a single exception, all known metazoans possess voltage-gated sodium channels and generate action potentials in their neurons. The one exception to this rule is a species of nematode worm, *Caenorhabditis elegans,* whose genome completely lacks voltage-gated Na$^+$ channels. As a result, these animals do not produce action potentials in their neurons. Graded potentials appear to be sufficient to transmit information along the short distances required in the neurons of these small animals.

Vertebrate motor neurons are myelinated

The axons of vertebrate motor neurons are wrapped in an insulating layer of **myelin** (Figure 5.18). Specialized lipid-rich cells called **Schwann cells** form the myelin sheath by wrapping in a spiral pattern around the axon of the neuron. Schwann cells are one of a large class of cells that are collectively known as **glial cells**, which we discuss later in this chapter. Several Schwann cells may wrap long axons, separated by areas of exposed axonal membrane called **nodes of Ranvier** that contain high densities of voltage-gated channels. In contrast, the myelinated regions of the axons are termed the **internodes**.

Voltage-gated channels are present at extremely low density in the internodes of a myelinated axon, so action potentials do not occur in the internodes. Instead, the current generated by an action potential at one node of Ranvier spreads electrotonically through the internode to the next node of Ranvier (Figure 5.19). If the current that reaches the next node of Ranvier is greater than the threshold potential, it will then trigger a new action potential at this next node. Because action potentials are all-or-none phenomena, the action potentials are the same at all of the nodes of Ranvier, allowing the signal to be conducted along long axons without degrading. This mode of action potential propagation is termed **saltatory conduction** from the Latin word *saltare* (to leap or dance) because the action potential appears to jump from node to node along the axon.

Electrotonic current spread is much faster than generating an action potential, so conduction along the internodes is almost instantaneous, whereas generating an action potential requires several milliseconds. In addition, the myelin increases distance over which electrotonic current can spread by acting as an insulator that prevents charge from leaking out across the membrane. As a result, saltatory conduction along a myelinated axon is much faster than conduction along an unmyelinated axon of equivalent size. We discuss the physiology underlying the rapid conduction of action potentials in myelinated axons in more detail later in the chapter.

FIGURE 5.18   Structure of the myelin sheath

Schwann cells wrap around the axon many times, insulating the axon and forming the myelin sheath. The myelin sheath is interrupted at regular intervals by the nodes of Ranvier, which are areas of unmyelinated axon.

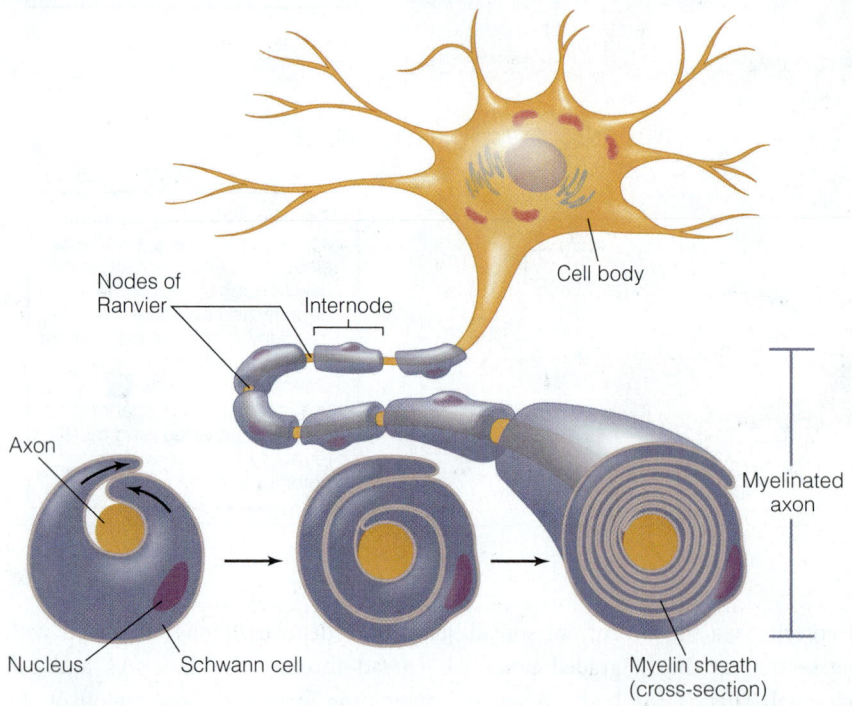

Nodes of Ranvier

Internode

Cell body

Axon

Nucleus

Schwann cell

Myelinated axon

Myelin sheath (cross-section)

Axons conduct action potentials unidirectionally

If you electrically stimulate an axon halfway along its length, action potentials will be generated in both directions (toward the axon hillock and toward the axon terminal). In a natural action potential, however, the stimulus always starts at the axon hillock and travels toward the axon terminal, with little or no conduction in the reverse direction. Because the depolarization caused by the Na$^+$ entering

FIGURE 5.19 Conduction along a myelinated axon

The depolarization at one node of Ranvier is transmitted quickly via electrotonic current spread through the internodes, and triggers an action potential at the next node of Ranvier. Generating an action potential is much slower than electrotonic current spread, so the signal is conducted more slowly at the node of Ranvier than through the internodes.

(a) Myelinated axons are wrapped by a series of accessory cells.

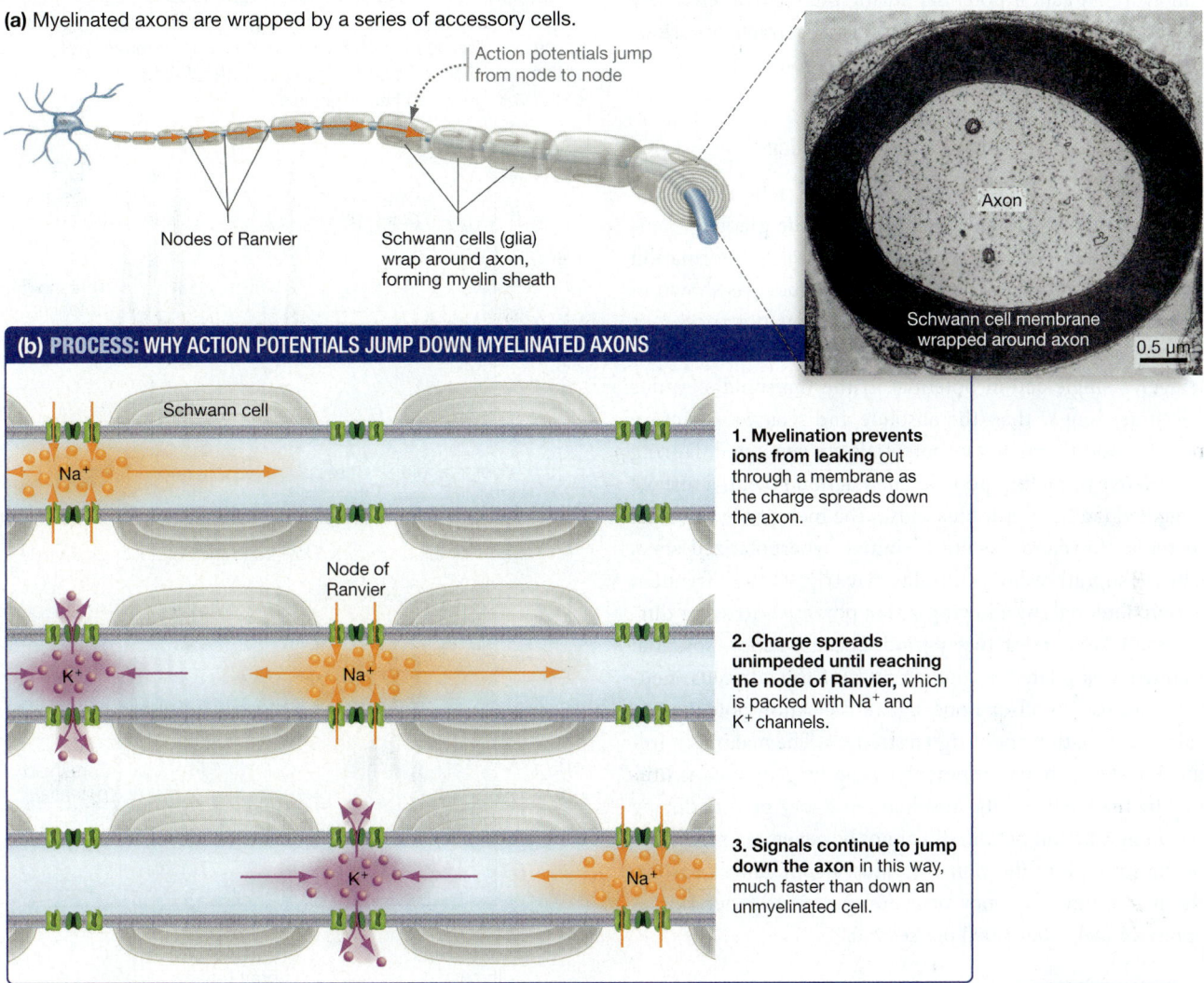

Action potentials jump from node to node

Nodes of Ranvier

Schwann cells (glia) wrap around axon, forming myelin sheath

Axon

Schwann cell membrane wrapped around axon

0.5 μm

(b) PROCESS: WHY ACTION POTENTIALS JUMP DOWN MYELINATED AXONS

Schwann cell

Na^+

1. Myelination prevents ions from leaking out through a membrane as the charge spreads down the axon.

Node of Ranvier

K^+ Na^+

2. Charge spreads unimpeded until reaching the node of Ranvier, which is packed with Na^+ and K^+ channels.

K^+ Na^+

3. Signals continue to jump down the axon in this way, much faster than down an unmyelinated cell.

Figure source: Freeman, Scott., Quillin, Kim., Allison, Lizabeth, *Biological Science*, 5th Ed., ©2014, P. 937. Reprinted And Electronically Reproduced By Permission of Pearson Education, Inc., Upper Saddle River, New Jersey.

through voltage-gated Na^+ channels spreads in all directions along the axon, why do action potentials occur only in the downstream direction (toward the axon terminal) rather than also spreading backward toward the axon hillock? If you examine a natural action potential (that started at the axon hillock and is being transmitted toward the axon terminal), at any point along the membrane the region just upstream of the point you are observing must have recently produced an action potential. As a result, the voltage-gated Na^+ channels in this upstream region of the axon are in a conformation in which they are unable to open in response to change in the membrane potential (i.e., with their activation gate open and their inactivation

gate closed, as illustrated in Figure 5.14, step 4). During this time, which corresponds to the absolute refractory period (see Figure 5.12), voltage-gated Na^+ channels are incapable of generating additional action potentials. This prevents backward (*retrograde*) conduction of action potentials. The absolute refractory period also prevents summation of action potentials, because a new action potential can only be triggered once the absolute refractory period is completed.

Following the absolute refractory period, the membrane enters the relative refractory period (see Figure 5.12). During the relative refractory period, the voltage-gated Na^+ channels have reset to their original configuration and are capable of initiating another action potential, but new action potentials are more difficult to generate because the membrane is hyperpolarized. As a result, a larger depolarization is required to reach threshold. Only a very strong stimulus can cause an action potential during the relative refractory period. Together, the absolute and relative refractory periods prevent retrograde conduction of action potentials.

Action potential frequency carries information

How can an all-or-none signal like the action potential carry information about the strength of the graded potential in the cell body? Action potentials carry information by changing frequency rather than amplitude. As shown in Figure 5.20, a **subthreshold stimulus** does not trigger an action potential, whereas a brief stimulus at threshold might trigger a single action potential. If the threshold stimulus continues longer than the absolute and relative refractory periods, additional action potentials are generated. During the relative refractory period, a new action potential may be triggered if a large stimulus causes the membrane potential to reach threshold despite its initial hyperpolarized state. Thus, a suprathreshold stimulus may trigger more frequent action potentials by allowing action potentials to occur during the relative refractory period. Because action potential frequency is related to the strength of the stimulus, neurons can use an all-or-none signal, the action potential, to carry information about signal strength. The maximum frequency at which action potentials can be generated is limited by the length of the absolute refractory period, during which new action potentials cannot be generated regardless of the strength of the signal. In most mammalian neurons, the maximum frequency of action potential generation is approximately 500–1,000 per second.

> ### CONCEPT CHECK
>
> 7. Compare and contrast action potentials and graded potentials.
> 8. Why does the membrane potential become positive during the depolarization phase of the action potential?
> 9. Why can action potentials conduct signals across long distances along the axon without degrading, whereas graded potentials die out within a few millimeters?

Signals Across the Synapse

Once the action potential reaches the axon terminal, the fourth important functional zone of a neuron, the neuron must transmit the signal carried by the action potential across the synapse to the target cell. The cell that transmits the signal is referred to as the **presynaptic cell**, and the cell receiving the signal is called the **postsynaptic cell**. The space

Action potential frequency relates to stimulus frequency. **(a)** A weak stimulus triggers a low frequency of action potentials. **(b)** A sustained suprathreshold stimulus triggers more frequent action potentials. A sufficiently large suprathreshold stimulus can trigger a new action potential during the relative refractory period of the previous action potential. The maximum frequency of action potentials is limited by the absolute refractory period of the voltage-gated Na^+ channels.

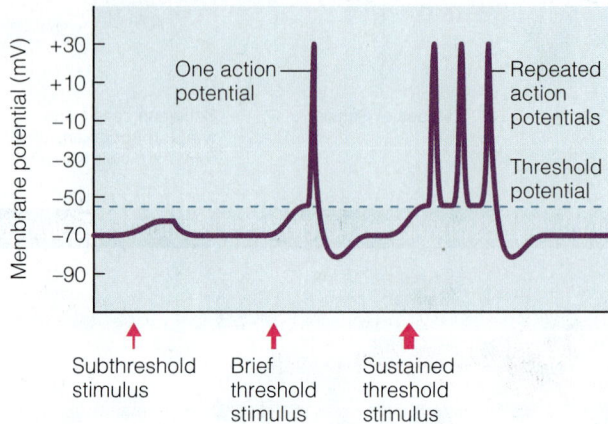

(a) A weak stimulus triggers a low frequency of action potentials

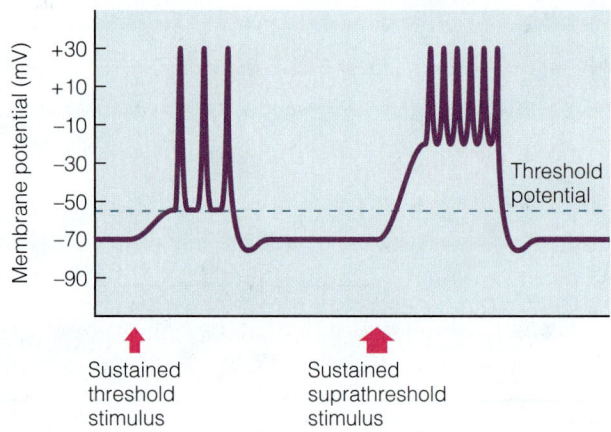

(b) A suprathreshold stimulus triggers a high frequency of action potentials

between the presynaptic and the postsynaptic cell is referred to as the **synaptic cleft**. Together, these three components make up the synapse. Neurons can form synapses with themselves, with other neurons, and with many other kinds of postsynaptic cells, including muscle and endocrine cells. The synapse between a motor neuron and a skeletal muscle cell, which we discuss in detail in this part of the chapter, is termed the **neuromuscular junction**.

Intracellular Ca^{2+} regulates neurotransmitter release

Much of what we know about the biochemical events at the synapse has been learned from studying the neuromuscular junction. The mechanism of **synaptic transmission** at the

FIGURE 5.21 **Events of signal transmission at a chemical synapse**

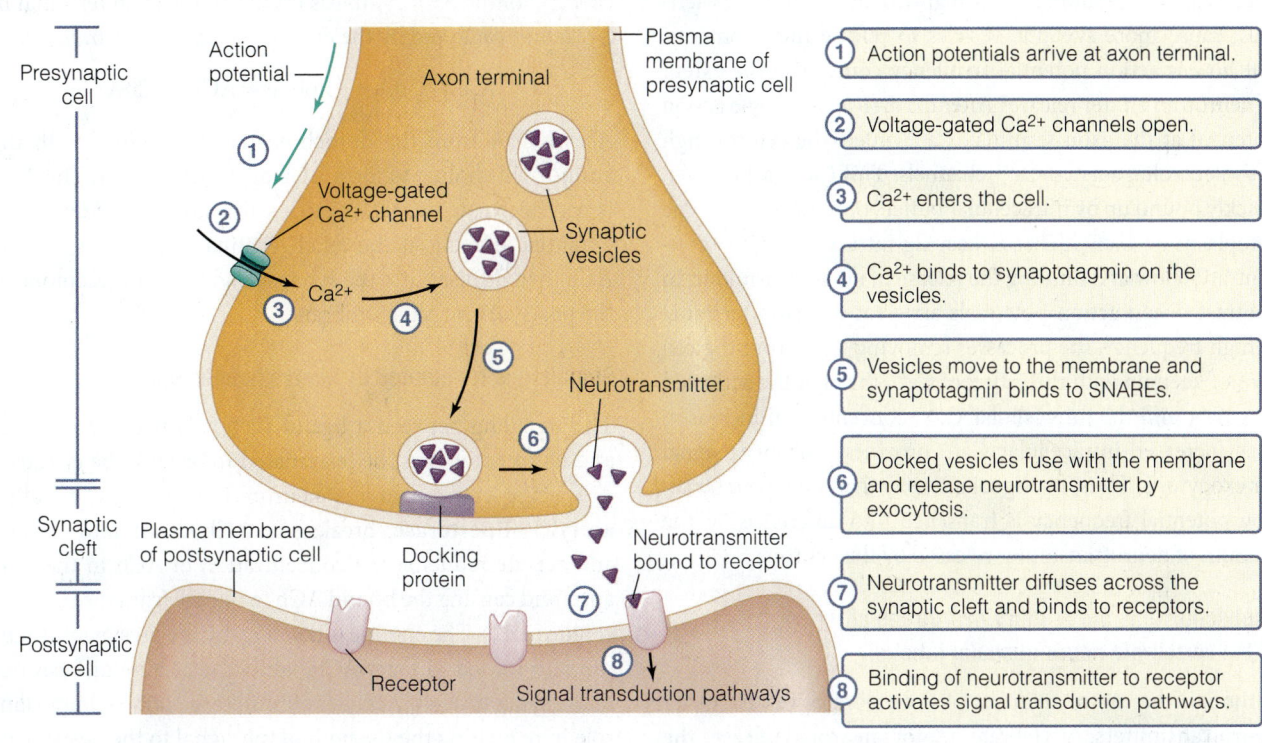

1. Action potentials arrive at axon terminal.

2. Voltage-gated Ca^{2+} channels open.

3. Ca^{2+} enters the cell.

4. Ca^{2+} binds to synaptotagmin on the vesicles.

5. Vesicles move to the membrane and synaptotagmin binds to SNAREs.

6. Docked vesicles fuse with the membrane and release neurotransmitter by exocytosis.

7. Neurotransmitter diffuses across the synaptic cleft and binds to receptors.

8. Binding of neurotransmitter to receptor activates signal transduction pathways.

neuromuscular junction is outlined in Figure 5.21. When an action potential reaches the membrane of the presynaptic axon terminal of the neuromuscular junction, the resulting depolarization triggers the opening of voltage-gated Ca^{2+} channels on the cell membrane of the axon terminal. The concentration of Ca^{2+} inside the neuron is much lower than the concentration of Ca^{2+} outside the neuron; the equilibrium potential for Ca^{2+} is $+130$ mV (as calculated using the Nernst equation for a typical mammalian neuron); and the resting membrane potential is -70 mV. Thus, both concentration and electrical gradients favor the movement of Ca^{2+} into the cell. The resulting increased Ca^{2+} concentration inside the axon terminal acts as a signal to neurotransmitter-containing **synaptic vesicles**.

Synaptic vesicles are not randomly distributed within the synapse. Instead, they are grouped into at least two distinct pools: a readily releasable pool, and a storage pool. The readily releasable pool of vesicles is located at the active zone of the synapse, bound to docking proteins called **SNAREs** at the synaptic membrane, ready to release their contents by exocytosis. The storage pool, in contrast, consists of vesicles bound to the cytoskeleton, and not docked to the membrane.

The Ca^{2+} that enters the synapse via the voltage-gated Ca^{2+} channels binds to a protein called **synaptotagmin** on the membranes of vesicles in the active zone of the synapse. Binding of Ca^{2+} changes the conformation of synaptotagmin, allowing it to interact with the **SNARE** complex and the synaptic membrane. These interactions cause the vesicles to

fuse with the synaptic membrane and release their contents by regulated exocytosis, in a process similar to the release of other intercellular signaling molecules. The Ca^{2+} signal also causes vesicles from the storage pool to move to the active zone of the plasma membrane and bind to docking proteins, ready for release following subsequent action potentials.

Each vesicle contains many molecules of neurotransmitter, and the number of molecules of neurotransmitter within a vesicle is similar for all vesicles within a neuron. With increasing action potential frequency, more and more vesicles move to the membrane and release their contents by exocytosis. Because each vesicle contains many molecules of neurotransmitter, the amount of neurotransmitter a neuron releases increases in a steplike fashion, with each step corresponding to the contents of a vesicle, rather than increasing in a smoothly graded fashion as would happen if neurotransmitter were released one molecule at a time. This pattern of release is termed the *quantal* release of neurotransmitter. However, under normal physiological conditions most neurons release many synaptic vesicles when stimulated, so the quantal release of transmitter is not generally apparent.

Action potential frequency influences neurotransmitter release

The amount of neurotransmitter released at a synapse is related to the frequency of action potentials at the axon terminal. Weak signals, resulting from low-frequency action potentials, cause fewer synaptic vesicles to release their contents, whereas strong signals, resulting from high-frequency action potentials, cause more synaptic vesicles to release their contents. But how is action potential frequency coupled to the extent of neurotransmitter release? After the arrival of a single action potential at the axon terminal, Ca^{2+} enters the cell through activated voltage-gated Ca^{2+} channels. This Ca^{2+} is, however, quickly bound up by intracellular buffers or removed from the cytoplasm by Ca^{2+} ATPases, keeping intracellular Ca^{2+} concentration low and limiting the release of neurotransmitter. In contrast, when action potentials arrive at the axon terminal at high frequency, the processes removing Ca^{2+} from the cell cannot keep up with the influx of Ca^{2+} through the activated channels, and the intracellular Ca^{2+} concentration increases. This increased intracellular Ca^{2+} provides a stronger signal for exocytosis. Thus, the signal intensity that was coded by action potential frequency is translated into differences in the amount of neurotransmitter released by the neuron.

Acetylcholine is the primary neurotransmitter at the vertebrate neuromuscular junction

Although the motor neurons of invertebrates release other neurotransmitters, vertebrate motor neurons release the neurotransmitter **acetylcholine** (ACh) into the synapse. ACh is a biogenic amine (see Chapter 4: Cell Signaling and Endocrine Regulation) that is synthesized from a compound called choline. ACh synthesis occurs in the axon terminal in a reaction catalyzed by the enzyme *choline acetyl transferase*:

$$Acetyl\ CoA + choline \rightarrow ACh + CoA$$

Acetyl CoA from the mitochondria is combined with the amino acid choline to form ACh and coenzyme A. The ACh is packaged into synaptic vesicles and stored until an action potential arriving at the axon terminal triggers its release. ACh then diffuses into the synapse and binds to receptors on the postsynaptic cell membrane.

Signaling is terminated by acetylcholinesterase

The signaling between a ligand such as a neurotransmitter and its receptor must be terminated in order to be effective. A specific enzyme in the neuromuscular synapse, called **acetylcholinesterase**, breaks the ACh down into choline and acetate reducing the concentration of ACh in the synapse, and causing the bound ACh to release from the receptor (Figure 5.22). The choline is taken up by the presynaptic neuron and reused to form ACh, while the acetate diffuses out of the synaptic cleft. Acetylcholinesterase plays an important role in regulating the strength of the signal to the postsynaptic cell by regulating the concentration of neurotransmitter at the synapse.

FIGURE 5.22 **Synthesis and recycling of acetylcholine (ACh) at the synapse**

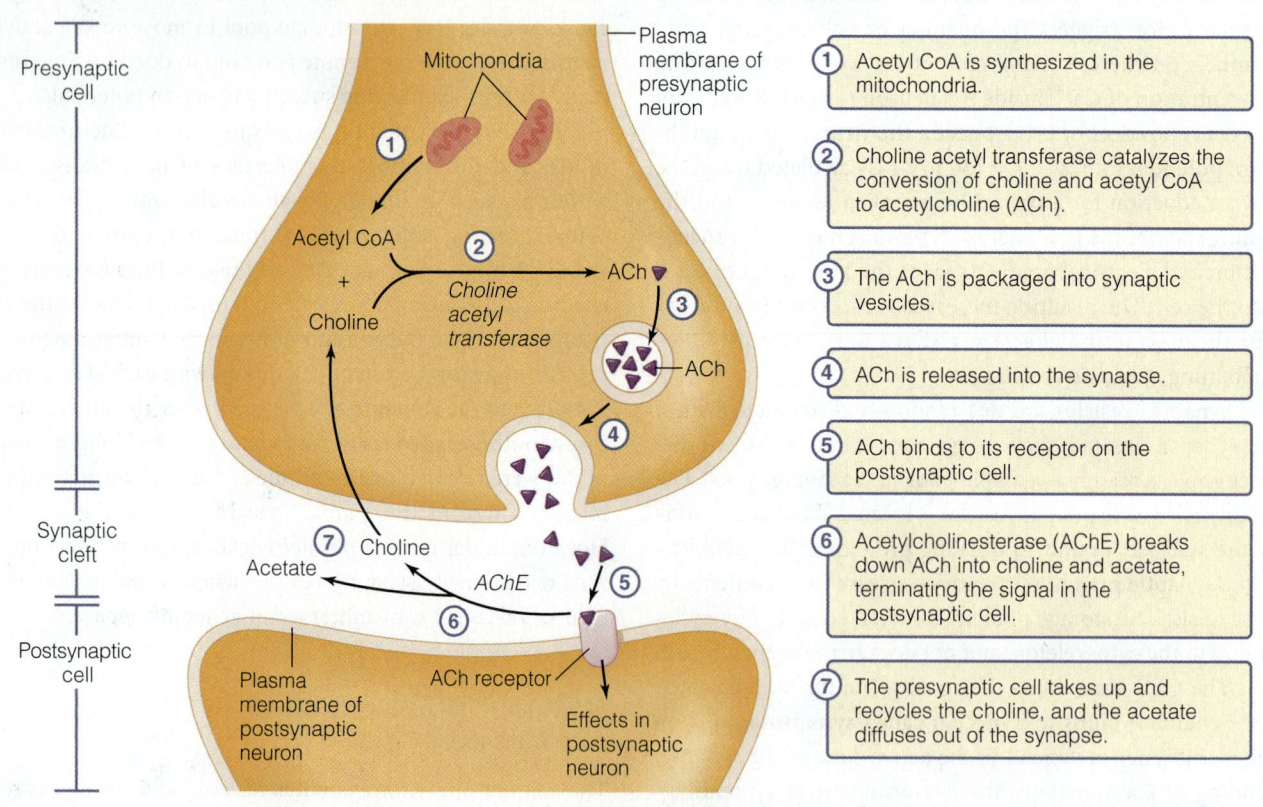

1. Acetyl CoA is synthesized in the mitochondria.

2. Choline acetyl transferase catalyzes the conversion of choline and acetyl CoA to acetylcholine (ACh).

3. The ACh is packaged into synaptic vesicles.

4. ACh is released into the synapse.

5. ACh binds to its receptor on the postsynaptic cell.

6. Acetylcholinesterase (AChE) breaks down ACh into choline and acetate, terminating the signal in the postsynaptic cell.

7. The presynaptic cell takes up and recycles the choline, and the acetate diffuses out of the synapse.

Postsynaptic cells express specific receptors

The responses of postsynaptic cells to neurotransmitters are similar to the responses of target cells to hormones and other chemical messengers, discussed in Chapter 4: Cell Signaling and Endocrine Regulation. Postsynaptic cells detect neurotransmitters using specific cell-surface receptors. When a neurotransmitter binds to its receptor, the receptor changes shape. This change in shape of the receptor acts as a signal in the target cell. Skeletal muscle cells express a class of receptor called **nicotinic ACh receptors**, which were named because of their ability to bind to the drug nicotine (the active ingredient in tobacco). Nicotinic ACh receptors are ligand-gated ion channels. When ACh binds to a nicotinic receptor, the receptor changes shape, opening a pore in the middle of the receptor that allows ions to cross the membrane. Nicotinic ACh receptors contain a relatively nonselective channel that is permeable to Na^+, K^+, and to a lesser extent Ca^{2+}; however, graded potentials in the postsynaptic cell caused by these channels are dominated by Na^+ ions because of the high driving force for Na^+ influx relative to K^+ efflux (as predicted by the Nernst equation). ACh binding to nicotinic receptors on skeletal muscle cells always causes a rapid excitatory postsynaptic potential because the resulting influx of Na^+ depolarizes the postsynaptic muscle cell. As we discuss in more detail in Chapter 6: Cellular Movement and Muscles, these excitatory potentials initiate muscle contraction.

Neurotransmitter amount and receptor activity influence signal strength

As for all ligand-receptor interactions, both the amount of neurotransmitter present in the synapse and the number of receptors on the postsynaptic cell influence the strength of signal in the target cell. Small amounts of neurotransmitter provoke relatively small responses in the postsynaptic cell. As neurotransmitter concentration increases, the response of the postsynaptic cell increases up to the point that all of the available receptors are saturated.

The concentration of neurotransmitter in the synapse is a result of the balance between the rate of neurotransmitter release from the presynaptic cell and the rate of removal of the neurotransmitter from the synapse. As we have already discussed, the amount of neurotransmitter that is released from the presynaptic cell is largely a function of the frequency of action potentials at the presynaptic axon terminal. In contrast, the removal of neurotransmitter from the synapse depends on three main processes: (1) Neurotransmitters can simply diffuse passively out of the synapse. (2) Surrounding cells, including presynaptic neurons, can also take up neurotransmitter. These cells act as important regulators of many neurotransmitters. (3) Enzymes present in the synapse can degrade neurotransmitters. As we have

already discussed, at the neuromuscular junction acetylcholinesterase activity is the most important determinant of ACh concentration.

At any given amount of neurotransmitter, the response of the postsynaptic cell is also dependent on the number of receptors present on the target cell. As you would expect, a postsynaptic cell can only respond if it has the appropriate receptors in the cell membrane. If there is a very low density of receptors on the postsynaptic membrane, neurotransmitter will cause a weak response. If the density of receptors on the postsynaptic membrane is very high, the response will be larger. The density of receptors on the postsynaptic cell can be regulated by a variety of factors, including genetic variation among individuals, the metabolic state of the postsynaptic cell, and specific drugs and disease states.

The human disorder *myasthenia gravis* is an example of a disease state caused by alterations in receptor number on muscle cells. People with myasthenia gravis experience muscle weakness and increased susceptibility to muscle fatigue, particularly in muscles that are used repeatedly. These symptoms are the result of an autoimmune condition in which antibodies from a person's immune system destroy ACh receptors at the neuromuscular junction. The decrease in receptor number reduces the intensity of the signal in the postsynaptic muscle cell at any given level of acetylcholine release, which reduces the strength of muscle contractions and causes muscle weakness.

The symptoms of myasthenia gravis can be treated with a class of drugs called *acetylcholinesterase inhibitors*. By partially inhibiting the enzyme acetylcholinesterase, these drugs reduce the rate of removal of ACh from its receptors, increasing the concentration of ACh in the synapse. This increase in ACh prolongs the effects of this neurotransmitter, partially compensating for the decreased number of ACh receptors in patients with myasthenia gravis. Thus, these drugs can help to reduce the symptoms of muscle weakness and fatigue. However, the dosage of acetylcholinesterase inhibitors must be carefully controlled because at high levels they can be deadly. Indeed, organophosphate pesticides and chemical weapons such as the nerve gas sarin are acetylcholinesterase inhibitors that work by inhibiting the degradation of ACh by acetylcholinesterase. At high doses, these agents greatly increase the concentration of ACh in the synapse. At the neuromuscular junction, these large increases in ACh lead to overexcitation of the muscle, causing twitching and other forms of uncoordinated muscle contraction, potentially leading to muscle fatigue, paralysis, severe difficulty in breathing, and ultimately death because of increasing fatigue and paralysis of the respiratory muscles. Lower doses of these agents also cause a range of other symptoms because ACh acts as a neurotransmitter not just at the neuromuscular junction but also at many other synapses, causing a wide variety of effects.

DIVERSITY OF NEURAL SIGNALING

Now that we have examined how signals travel from one end of a motor neuron to the other, we can begin to address some of the enormous diversity in these processes among neurons from a single organism, and among neurons from different kinds of organisms. The diversity of neuron structure and function allows neurons to play many roles. Some neurons (including the motor neurons that we have already discussed) are specialized to transmit signals very rapidly across long distances, while other neurons are specialized to integrate many incoming signals and process them to produce a response. We begin this section by examining the structural diversity of neurons, looking at how neuron structure relates to neuron function. We then look at some of the important processes performed by neurons to see how they vary among neurons that perform different physiological roles in a variety of animal species.

Neurons perform three distinct functions. They receive and integrate incoming signals, they conduct these signals through the cell, and they transmit these signals to other cells. In the first part of the chapter we discussed how vertebrate motor neurons detect incoming signals in the form of neurotransmitters. Many chemical substances can act as neurotransmitters, and we discuss some of this diversity later in the chapter in our consideration of the diversity of synaptic transmission. But neurons are also capable of detecting many kinds of incoming signals in addition to chemical signals in the form of neurotransmitters. Some neurons are specialized to detect incoming signals such as temperature, pressure, light, or environmental chemicals. The mechanisms that neurons use to detect these signals are extremely diverse, but they share one fundamental characteristic. Whatever the incoming signal, membrane-bound receptors in the dendrites of the sensory neuron receive the signal and transduce it into

an electrical signal in the form of a change in the membrane potential. Because of the diversity and complexity of these processes, we do not consider them in detail here. Instead, we devote Chapter 7: Sensory Systems to these fascinating issues. In this chapter we focus on the diversity of signal conduction and transmission, looking first at the diversity of the action potential and the conduction velocity of action potentials along the axon. Then we examine some of the enormous diversity of synaptic transmission. We conclude the chapter with a discussion of the evolution of neurons.

Structural Diversity of Neurons

Although most neurons have dendrites, a cell body, and an axon, the details of neuron structure vary greatly at the cellular level. Some neurons have relatively simple structures, while others have complex, highly branched structures (Figure 5.23a). There is no clear correlation between the complexity of an organism and the complexity of its neurons. Instead, the structure of a neuron relates to the function of that particular neuron. For example, neurons within the mammalian brain typically have large numbers of dendrites, but may lack an obvious axon. The many dendrites of these neurons allow them to integrate an enormous number of incoming signals from other neurons. In contrast, the dendrites and axon of a motor neuron can easily be distinguished, as the axon is typically much longer than the dendrites. These neurons are specialized for rapid, long-distance electrical signaling.

Neurons can be classified based on their function

As we discuss in more detail in Chapter 8: Functional Organization of Nervous Systems, neurons can be divided into one of three classes, depending on their functions (Figure 5.23b). **Sensory** (or **afferent**) **neurons** convey sensory information from the body to the central nervous system (which consists of the brain and spinal cord in vertebrates). **Interneurons** are located within the central nervous system, and convey signals from one neuron to another. **Efferent neurons** convey signals from the central nervous system to effector organs. The motor neurons that we have already discussed are one class of efferent neuron. In the case of motor neurons the effector is always a skeletal muscle, but other types of efferent neurons communicate with a variety of effector organs, including smooth muscles and endocrine glands.

Neurons can be classified based on their structure

Although there is substantial diversity in the structure of neurons, most of this diversity falls within one of three major structural types (Figure 5.23c). The vertebrate motor neurons

FIGURE 5.23 **Variation in neuron structure and function**

(a) Structural diversity of neurons. Neurons always have a cell body, one axon, and at least one dendrite, but the number of dendrites, the position of the cell body, and the length of the axon can vary. **(b)** Functional classes of neurons. Sensory neurons detect incoming signals. Interneurons form connections among neurons. Efferent neurons convey signals from the nervous system to effector organs. **(c)** Structural classes of neurons. Multipolar neurons have one obvious axon and multiple dendrites. Bipolar neurons have a single branched dendrite and an obvious axon. Unipolar neurons have a single large axon that branches into two main processes. Note the variation in the location of the integrating center among these neurons.

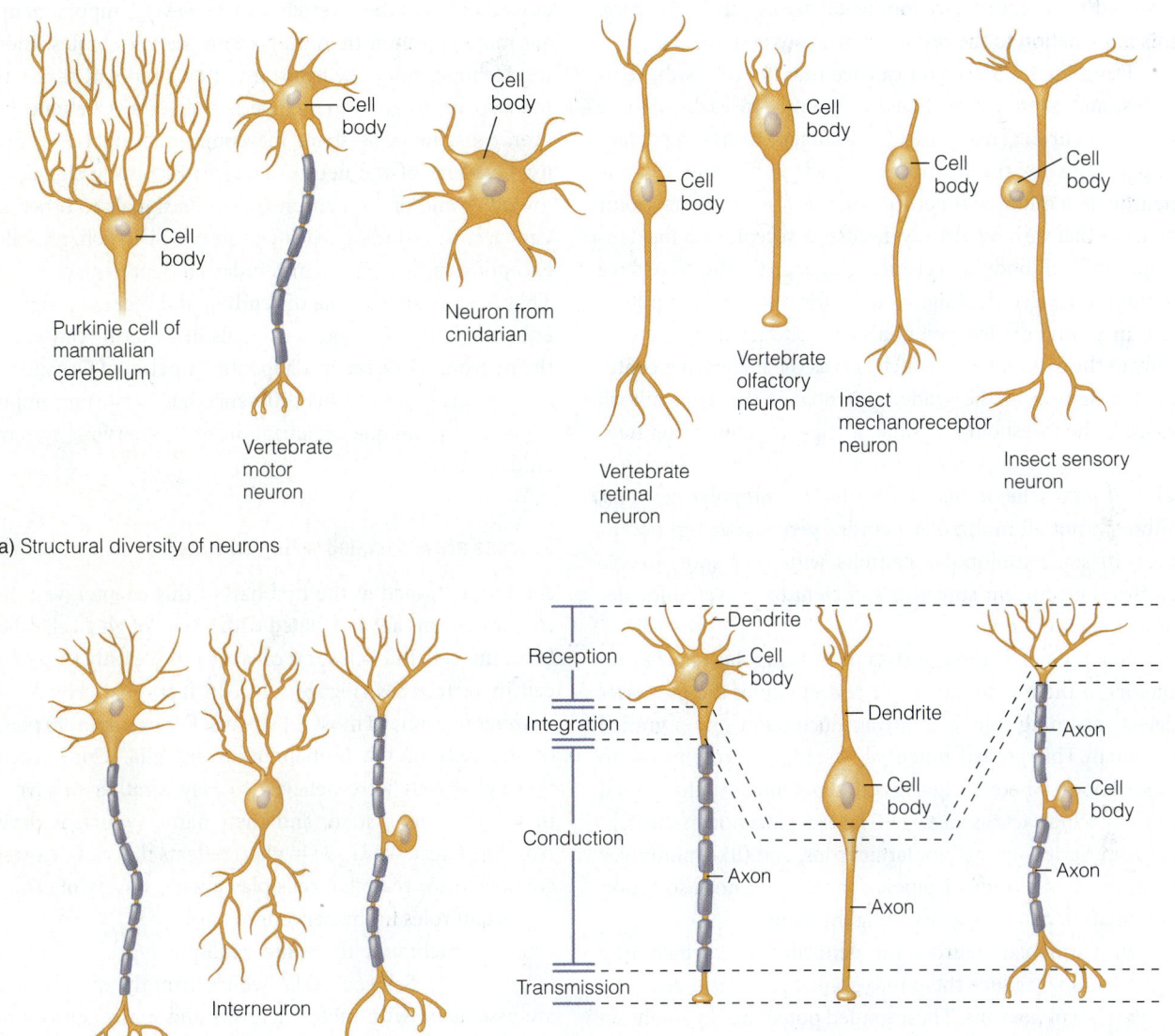

(a) Structural diversity of neurons

(b) Functional classes of neurons

(c) Structural classes of neurons

that we discussed in the first part of this chapter are examples of **multipolar neurons**. These neurons have many cellular extensions (or processes) that originate at the cell body. Only one of these processes is an axon, whereas the remaining processes are dendrites. Multipolar neurons are the most common type of neuron in vertebrates. **Bipolar neurons** have two main processes extending from the cell body, one of which is highly branched and conveys signals to the cell body, and thus is functionally similar to a dendrite, and the other of which conveys signals away from the cell body, and thus acts as an axon. As discussed in Chapter 6, some sensory neurons, such as retinal cells and olfactory cells, are bipolar neurons. However, few other vertebrate neurons have this form, and bipolar neurons are thus the least common type of neuron in the vertebrate nervous system. A **unipolar neuron** has a single process from the cell body. In most unipolar neurons, however, this process splits into two main branches. As a result, these cells are sometimes termed *pseudo-unipolar*. One of these two branches conveys signals toward the cell body, and the other conveys signals away from the cell body. Unipolar neurons are generally sensory neurons that are involved in detecting environmental signals and conveying this information to the rest of the nervous system.

From Figure 5.23c you can see that the cell body, dendrites, and axon are arranged differently in each of these types of neuron. This change in arrangement has important implications for the functions of each of the zones of the neuron. In a multipolar neuron, such as the vertebrate motor neurons that we have already discussed, receptors in the dendrites and cell body detect incoming signals and transduce them into an electrical signal in the form of a graded potential. Incoming graded potentials are conducted electrotonically to the axon hillock, which acts as the integrating center for the neuron. If the graded potential at the axon hillock exceeds the threshold potential, it triggers action potentials, which are conducted along the axon to the axon terminal. This general scheme fits well for most multipolar neurons, although not all multipolar neurons generate action potentials. In some multipolar neurons with very short axons, electrotonic current spread is sufficient to convey information along the axon.

In a bipolar neuron, just as in a multipolar neuron, receptors in the membrane at the end of one of the processes detect incoming signals and transduce them into a graded potential. This graded potential spreads electrotonically to the cell body, where it triggers action potentials in the second process, which acts as an axon. The exact location of the trigger zone varies among bipolar neurons, and (like multipolar neurons) some kinds of bipolar neurons do not use action potentials to convey signals along the axon.

In a unipolar neuron, the dendrites detect incoming signals and transduce them into graded potentials, as in the other types of neurons. These graded potentials do not, however, travel directly to the cell body. Instead, they travel only as far as the beginning (or initial segment) of the process that leads to the cell body. If the graded potential in this initial segment exceeds threshold, it will trigger an action potential. These action potentials then travel toward the cell body, and onward to the axon terminal. As a result of this arrangement, there has been some disagreement as to whether to call the first of these long extensions of a unipolar neuron an axon or a dendrite, because it is functionally similar to an axon in that it can generate action potentials, but it conducts impulses toward the cell body rather than away from the cell body and thus is functionally similar to a dendrite. For our purposes, we will refer to both of the processes of a unipolar neuron as axons. The important point to keep in mind, however, is that the integrating center is located in a very different position in a unipolar neuron compared with a multipolar neuron.

Neurons from invertebrates can also be grouped into these main structural classifications, and are organized in ways similar to the vertebrate neurons that we have discussed so far. In the invertebrates, however, unipolar neurons are more common than they are in the vertebrates. Indeed, invertebrate motor neurons are often unipolar, rather than multipolar. Whether in an invertebrate or a vertebrate, however, most neurons share the common property of polarity. One end of the neuron receives incoming signals, and the other end of the neuron transmits signals to other cells. Cnidarians, including sea anemones and jellyfish, provide an exception to this rule. Some cnidarian neurons lack polarity. That is, they are capable of sending and receiving signals at either end and can conduct signals in either direction along the neuron. As we see in Chapter 8: Functional Organization of Nervous Systems, this difference has important implications for the unique organization of the nervous system in cnidarians.

Neurons are associated with glial cells

As we mentioned in the first half of this chapter, vertebrate motor neurons are associated with a type of glial cell called a Schwann cell. But Schwann cells are not the only type of glial cell in vertebrates (Figure 5.24). In fact, glial cells far outnumber neurons in most organisms. For example, 90 percent of the cells in the human brain are glia. Until recently, these glial cells were believed to play a rather passive role in the nervous system, and their name (which is derived from the Greek word *glia* = glue) reflects this view. However, we now know that glial cells play a wide variety of critically important roles in the nervous system.

In vertebrates, there are multiple types of glial cells (Figure 5.24). Schwann cells, which form the myelin sheath, are associated with motor neurons and many sensory neurons. Schwann cells play an important role in neural signaling by increasing the conduction speed of action potentials along the axon. They are also essential for the regeneration and regrowth of damaged sensory and motor neurons. When a neuron is damaged, Schwann cells digest the damaged axon and provide a pathway for neuronal regrowth. **Oligodendrocytes** form a myelin sheath for neurons in the central nervous system (CNS). A single oligodendrocyte may wrap around the axons of several neurons, and thus differs from a Schwann cell, which always enwraps a single neuron. **Astrocytes** have large stellate (star-shaped) cell bodies and many processes. They are located in the central nervous system and play a variety of roles, including transporting nutrients

FIGURE 5.24 **Some of the primary glial cells of vertebrates**

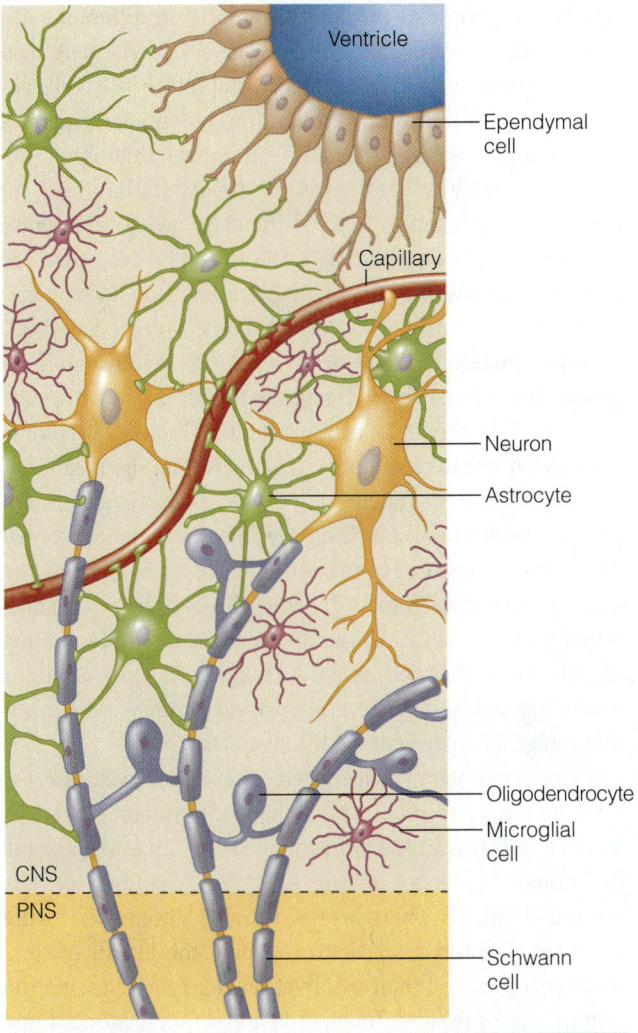

Ventricle

Ependymal cell

Capillary

Neuron

Astrocyte

Oligodendrocyte

Microglial cell

CNS

PNS

Schwann cell

the neurons of the gut. These glial cells are thought to perform functions similar to those of astrocytes in the CNS. *Radial* glia are found in the central nervous system during development and play an important role in structuring the developing nervous system.

Although glial cells maintain a resting membrane potential, they do not generate action potentials, nor do they form obvious chemical synapses. However, despite their lack of obvious chemical synapses, glial cells can take up neurotransmitters, and thus they can regulate neurotransmitter concentration at the synapse, which can have important effects on neurons. In addition, some glial cells in the central nervous system, such as astrocytes, form connections with each other and with neurons via gap junctions. Astrocytes actively communicate with each other through these gap junctions using intracellular Ca^{2+} and other signaling molecules. The presence of gap junctions suggests a complex interchange of signals between neurons and glia, which may be important in regulating the function of the nervous system. Recently it has also been shown that some types of glial cells, including astrocytes, release neurotransmitterlike molecules termed **gliotransmitters** that can influence the activity of neurons and synapses. Some common gliotransmitters include glutamate, GABA, and ATP—molecules that can also act as neurotransmitters when released by neurons.

Glial cells in invertebrates have a wide range of morphologies, depending on their location in the organism and the species being examined. Invertebrate glial cells are often termed **gliocytes**, and appear to be functionally similar to astrocytes, as they intimately ensheathe synapses. Invertebrates lack a true myelin sheath, but axons of peripheral neurons may still be wrapped in several layers of glial cell membrane. In general, the layers of membrane in invertebrate wrapping are not as closely stacked as they are in a vertebrate myelin sheath. Also, the proteins involved in the structure of the myelin sheath of vertebrates and the wrappings of invertebrates differ, suggesting that the molecular machinery involved in invertebrate wrappings is fundamentally different from that of the myelin sheath of vertebrates, and likely evolved independently. However, despite these potentially independent evolutionary origins, the functions of glial cells are thought to be similar in both vertebrates and invertebrates.

to neurons, removing debris, guiding neuronal development, and regulating the contents of the extracellular space around neurons (including regulating synaptic neurotransmitter levels). In fact, astrocytes in the brain often enwrap synapses and may play an important role in regulating synaptic communication by regulating neurotransmitter levels. **Microglia** are involved in neuronal maintenance. Microglia are the smallest glial cells. They are similar to the macrophages of the immune system, and they function to remove debris and dead cells from the central nervous system. Microglia are most active following trauma or during disease. **Ependymal cells** line the fluid-filled cavities of the central nervous system. They often have cilia, which they use to circulate the **cerebrospinal fluid** that bathes the central nervous system of vertebrates. **Satellite cells** are a specific type of glial cell that are found in the ganglia of the peripheral nervous system (PNS), and *enteric glia* are associated with

---

CONCEPT CHECK

13. Is a typical vertebrate efferent (motor) neuron (as shown in Figure 5.23b) multipolar, bipolar, or unipolar?

14. Describe the primary types of glial cells in vertebrates. What are their functions?

Diversity of Signal Conduction

We have already seen that axons can conduct signals either electrotonically or using a combination of electrotonic current spread and regenerating action potentials, but there is additional diversity in signal conduction among neurons that we have yet to consider. Both the shape of the action potential and the speed of action potential conduction along the axon vary among neurons. In the first half of the chapter we considered the shape of an action potential in a squid giant axon, and most action potentials have this general form. However, the exact shape of the action potential can vary among neurons from different organisms, between types of neurons from the same organism, and even among action potentials within the same neuron under different physiological conditions. The variations in the shapes of action potentials are the result of the diversity of the molecular properties of the voltage-gated Na$^+$ and K$^+$ channels among these neurons. In fact, some neurons do not use voltage-gated K$^+$ channels to repolarize the neuron following the depolarization phase of the action potential. In these neurons the repolarization phase of the action potential is carried out by K$^+$ movements through K$^+$ leak channels that are open at all times. As you might expect, neurons of this type do not exhibit an after-hyperpolarization phase following the action potential.

Voltage-gated ion channels are encoded by multiple genes

Many ion channels exist as multiple isoforms: slightly different molecular variants of the same protein, encoded by different genes (see Chapter 3: Chemistry, Biochemistry, and Cell Physiology). Sequence variation among the isoforms of voltage-gated ion channels can lead to functional differences that change the way neurons work. In mammals, at least 18 separate genes encode voltage-gated K$^+$ channels, and over 50 distinct types of voltage-gated K$^+$ channels have been characterized among all animal

species. Voltage-gated K$^+$ channels cause the repolarizing phase of the action potential in most neurons. Thus, their diverse isoforms result in a diversity of shapes during the repolarizing phase of the action potential in different cells, tissues, and organisms. Voltage-gated K$^+$ channels also have a strong influence on the excitability of the cell, action potential duration, and action potential frequency. For example, voltage-gated K$^+$ channels that open extremely quickly in response to depolarization tend to make action potentials more difficult to generate, because K$^+$ ions leave the cell at the same time that Na$^+$ ions are entering, countering the depolarization due to voltage-gated Na$^+$ channels. In contrast, some voltage-gated K$^+$ channels are referred to as *delayed rectifiers*, because they respond relatively slowly to changes in membrane potential, increasing the length of the action potential. Table 5.2 lists some examples of the diversity of K$^+$ channels. The significance of this diversity for the functioning of the whole organism is not yet fully understood, but it clearly influences the functional diversity of neurons. Having multiple copies of genes is not the only way that animals generate diversity in K$^+$ channel function. Box 5.3: Challenges to Homeostasis: RNA Editing of Potassium Channels as an Adaptation to Cold Environments highlights some recent work on another mechanism that can generate diversity in K$^+$ channels.

Compared with voltage-gated K$^+$ channels, voltage-gated Na$^+$ channels are much less diverse. Mammals express at least 11 isoforms of the voltage-gated Na$^+$ channel, but the functional differences among these Na$^+$ channel isoforms are rather minor. There are measurable differences in the exact time required for them to open, the length of time they stay open, and their inactivation characteristics, but the importance of these differences is not yet understood. Only two voltage-gated Na$^+$ channel genes have been identified in *Drosophila* and squid, compared with the 11 isoforms in mammals. The significance of the increase in isoform number as the complexity of the nervous system increases is also

Table 5.2 Diversity of K$^+$ channels	
Channel Type	**Function**
Delayed rectifier	Opens slowly in response to changes in membrane potential; closes slowly; responsible for repolarizing axonal membrane following an action potential
A channel (K$_A$ channel)	Opens when membrane is depolarized; closes rapidly; influences neuron excitability
Inward rectifier (K$_{IR}$ channel)	Opens when membrane is hyperpolarized; influences duration of action potential
Ca^{2+} activated (K$_{Ca}$ channel)	Opens in the presence of Ca^{2+}; influences excitability of neuron
M channel (K$_M$ channel)	Opens when membrane is depolarized; closes slowly; regulated by neurotransmitters
ACh channel (K$_{ACh}$ channel)	Opens when membrane is exposed to ACh; involved in regulating heartbeat

poorly understood, but it may be important in the functioning of complex mammalian nervous systems.

The density of voltage-gated Na$^+$ channels also has a profound effect on the function of a neuron. All else being equal, neurons that have a higher density of voltage-gated Na$^+$ channels will have a lower threshold than neurons with a lower density of voltage-gated Na$^+$ channels. A higher density means more Na$^+$ channels are available to open at a given stimulus intensity, and more Na$^+$ will enter the cell. As a result, the balance point between the dissipation and influx of Na$^+$ ions is more easily reached at a lower level of depolarization. Thus, a smaller graded potential can excite a neuron with high densities of voltage-gated Na$^+$ channels. Similarly, the density of voltage-gated Na$^+$ channels can also influence the length of the relative refractory period. Neurons with higher densities of voltage-gated Na$^+$ channels tend to have shorter relative refractory periods because of the decrease in the threshold potential.

The many isoforms of voltage-gated channels have only recently been identified, and neurobiologists still do not entirely understand the role that these isoforms play in generating functional diversity in the nervous system. In general, there is a correlation between the complexity of the nervous system and the total number of isoforms of voltage-gated ion channels, which suggests (but does not prove) that more diverse voltage-gated channels are required to build a highly complex nervous system. Variants in ion channels can be mixed and matched to generate even larger numbers of combinations. There are millions of possible combinations of isoforms of voltage-gated channels, neurotransmitters, and receptors, and thus millions of possible types of neuron. The human nervous system, one of the most complex nervous systems of any animal, contains billions of individual neurons, many with unique properties and functions. Biologists are only just beginning to probe the complexities of these interactions, and many important questions have yet to be addressed. The role of isoforms in generating diversity in neural signaling is thus an area of intensive current research.

Voltage-gated Ca^{2+} channels can also be involved in action potentials

In some neurons, voltage-gated Ca^{2+} channels are involved in the action potential. In neurons that have voltage-gated Ca^{2+} channels in the axon, these channels open at the same time as (or instead of) voltage-gated Na$^+$ channels. This results in Ca^{2+} entry into the cell, causing a depolarization. Generally, the depolarization caused by Ca^{2+} influx is slower and more sustained than the depolarization from Na$^+$ influx. A sustained depolarization phase slows down the rate at which action potentials can be generated by prolonging the refractory period. For example, the action potentials that control rhythmic swimming in jellyfish have a sustained depolarization phase due to Ca^{2+} influx, and last about 10 times longer than a typical vertebrate action potential. As we discuss in Chapter 6, voltage-gated Ca^{2+} channels are also important in establishing the shape of action potentials in excitable tissues other than neurons, including cardiac muscle.

Conduction speed varies among axons

In addition to differences in the shape of the action potential, the speed of action potential conduction along the axon varies greatly among neurons (Table 5.3). Some neurons conduct action potentials very quickly, while action potentials in other neurons are conducted rather slowly. Animals use two main strategies for increasing the speed of action potential conduction: **myelination** and increasing the diameter of the axon. The axons of some neurons, including the vertebrate motor neurons that we have already mentioned, are myelinated. Other neurons with high conduction velocity have unusually large-diameter axons termed **giant axons**. The fastest nerve conduction is always observed in either large-diameter or myelinated neurons. In the next sections we examine how the properties of the axon influence conduction speed, and see how these properties are modified in giant axons and myelinated axons.

The cable properties of the axon influence current flow

To understand how the properties of the axon influence the speed of action potential conduction, we need to review some basic physics and take a closer look at electrical currents in the axon. The physical principles that govern the extent of current flow along an axon are similar to the physical principles governing the conduction of electrical current through transatlantic telephone cables. Thus, the properties of the axon that dictate current flow along the axon are often called the **cable properties** of the axon. Current, whether in an electrical wire or in an axon, is simply a measure of the amount of charge moving past a point in a given amount of time, and is a function of the drop in voltage across the circuit and the resistance of the circuit. Ohm's law (a principle that you should be familiar with from introductory physics courses) describes this relationship between current and voltage. Ohm's law is often written in the form

$$V = IR$$

where I is the current, V is the voltage drop across the circuit, and R is the resistance of the circuit. Voltage is a measure of the energy carried by a unit of charge. Thus, the difference in voltage between two points is a measure of the energy available to move charge from one point to the other, just as potential energy is a measure of the energy available to move an

RNA EDITING OF POTASSIUM CHANNELS AS AN ADAPTATION TO COLD ENVIRONMENTS

The common octopus (*Octopus vulgaris*) shown in Figure 5.25 is found worldwide in shallow tropical and temperate habitats, while other species of octopuses are restricted to specific habitats. For example, octopuses in the genus *Pareledone* are found only in the waters around Antarctica. Like all mollusks, octopuses are ectotherms that have a body temperature similar to their habitat temperature, so an *O. vulgaris* on a tropical reef would have a body

temperature around 30°C, while a *Pareledone* in the waters of the Antarctic Ocean would have a body temperature around −1.8°C.

Temperature has a profound effect on the rate of all biochemical reactions, including the opening and closing of voltage-gated ion channels. Specifically, it has been shown that the closing of voltage-gated K^+ channels is extremely temperature sensitive. Thus, low temperatures will tend to slow the closing of this channel and prolong the action potential.

One way that octopuses such as *Pareledone* might compensate for the effects of their cold habitat could be to have a voltage-gated K^+ channel with a different protein sequence that allows it to work more rapidly in the cold. Dr. Joshua Rosenthal at the University of Puerto Rico set out to test this hypothesis by cloning and sequencing the gene encoding the voltage-gated K^+ channel from *Pareledone* and *O. vulgaris*. Contrary to the original hypothesis, however, the sequences of the genes from these two species were identical, and they were both very similar to the sequence for the gene in squid. In addition, when these sequences were expressed in *Xenopus* oocytes, they had identical functional properties. Because the genes from these two species encoded functionally identical proteins, these data suggested that if these proteins were working at the respective body temperatures

FIGURE 5.25 **The common octopus (*Octopus vulgaris*)**

Photo source: Michal Adamczyk/Fotolia.

Organism/Nerve	Diameter (µm)	Myelination	Speed of Propagation (m/sec)
Squid/giant axon	50–1000	No	30 (at 15°C)
Crayfish/leg	36	No	8 (at 20°C)
Lumbricus (worm) lateral	60	No	11.3 (at 20°C)
Frog/sciatic nerve, A fibers	18	Yes	42 (at 20°C)
Frog/sciatic nerve, B fibers	2	Yes	4 (at 20°C)
Frog/sciatic nerve, C fibers	2.5	No	0.3 (at 20°C)
Cat/saphenous nerve, A fibers	22	Yes	120 (at 37°C)
Cat/saphenous nerve, B fibers	3	Yes	15 (at 37°C)
Cat/saphenous nerve, C fibers	1	No	2 (at 37°C)

Table 5.3 **Conduction velocities in axons from various species**

of the two species, then the potassium channels in *Pareledone* should open about 14 times more slowly and close about 60 times more slowly than would be the case in *O. vulgaris*.

Although it is possible that *Pareledone* simply live at a slower pace of life than do octopuses from warmer habitats, Dr. Rosenthal and his graduate student Sandra Garrett thought that there might be more to the story. They hypothesized that the RNA encoding the K⁺ channel in octopuses might be modified after it was transcribed in a way that was not occurring when the channels were expressed in *Xenopus* oocytes. They found that although the octopus genome contains a single gene for this channel, there were multiple different RNA sequences expressed in octopus tissues, which generated diversity in ion channel sequences from this single gene.

The diversity of RNA sequences occurs because of a process termed RNA editing, which has been shown to be common in squid K⁺ channels. One common form of RNA editing is performed by a group of enzymes called ADARs (adenosine deaminases that act on RNA). These enzymes replace adenosines in RNA with inosines, which are read by the translational machinery as guanosines. Depending on exactly where in the sequence these replacements take place, this may change the amino acid sequence of the protein.

RNA editing occurred in both *O. vulgaris* and *Pareledone* K⁺ channels. In *O. vulgaris* the proteins from the edited RNAs opened and closed more slowly than the unedited version by about 30 to 60 percent. In *Pareledone*, the proteins from the edited RNAs closed much faster than the unedited version. In particular, a single substitution in a region of the molecule that lies at the interface between the voltage sensor and the ion pore (site I321V) caused the edited version to close twice as fast as the unedited version.

To test the hypothesis that this specific RNA edit represents an adaptation to life in the cold, Dr. Rosenthal and his student sequenced this gene (and all of its edited versions) in two Arctic species, two additional tropical species, and two species from the temperate waters around California. Many of the previously identified editing sites varied among species, but the edited sequence at site I321V was the most closely correlated with habitat temperature.

Reference

- Garrett, S., & Rosenthal, J. J. C. (2012). RNA editing underlies temperature adaptation in K⁺ channels from polar octopuses. *Science, 335,* 848–851.

object from one point to another. In contrast, **resistance** is a measure of the force opposing the flow of electrical current. Thus, by rearranging the equation, you can see that current is proportional to the voltage drop across a circuit, and inversely proportional to the resistance.

Current flows through an electrical circuit only when the circuit is complete. You can think of an axon as behaving like a simple electrical circuit in which current flows as shown in Figure 5.26a. Ions moving through voltage-gated channels cause a current across the membrane. This introduced current spreads electrotonically along the axon. Some of this current leaks out of the axon, and a current flows "backward" along the outside of the axon, completing the circuit. Each compartment of the axon has an associated resistance, which impedes the flow of the current.

Thus, we can think of each small area of the axon as consisting of an electrical circuit with three resistors (the extracellular fluid, the membrane, and the cytoplasm), as shown in Figure 5.26b.

Notice that in addition to the membrane resistance (designated R_m), intracellular resistance (designated R_i), and extracellular resistance (designated R_e), there is an additional element in this circuit diagram, designated C_m. The parallel bar symbol in the circuit diagram indicates the presence of a capacitor. Thus, the part of the circuit that crosses the membrane is actually represented by a resistor and a capacitor arranged in parallel. Capacitors are devices that can store electrical charge that consist of two conducting materials separated by an insulating layer. In the case of the cell membrane, the intracellular fluid and extracellular fluid are the conducting layers of the capacitor, while the phospholipids of the cell membrane are the insulating layer.

The circuit shown in Figure 5.26b describes what is happening in a small patch of the axon, but recall that axons can be very long. In order to fully model the axon, we need to think about the axon as a series of these small circuits connected together to form a much larger electrical circuit along the axon (Figure 5.26c). With this simplified model of the axon as an electrical circuit in mind, we can begin to see how these circuit elements affect the speed of action potential conduction along the axon.

Intracellular and membrane resistance influence conduction speed

When a region of the membrane is depolarized, the inside of the membrane becomes more positively charged than adjacent regions of membrane, while the outside of the membrane becomes more negatively charged than adjacent regions. As a result, current spreads along the axon (on both the inner and outer surfaces) by electrotonic conduction. As this electrotonic current spreads along the axon, it depolarizes these adjacent regions of the membrane. However, as we mentioned in the first part of the chapter, the change in membrane potential (measured as the voltage drop across the membrane) decreases with distance, a phenomenon called *conduction with decrement*. But why does voltage decrease with distance? Recall that resistance is a force that impedes current flow. Thus, in a simple electrical conductor the decrease in voltage is a direct result of the resistance of the material. Because resistance is cumulative with distance, we would expect to see the voltage drop with distance, according to Ohm's law. For electrotonic current spread, we need to consider the resistance of both the extracellular and intracellular fluids. If the resistance of these materials is high, voltage will drop quickly with distance.

However, an axon is not just a simple conductor, and we need to consider more than just the intracellular and extracellular resistances. Most membranes contain *K⁺ leak channels*, which, unlike voltage-gated channels, are essentially always open. Thus, as current travels along the axon, some positive charge leaks out through these channels, decreasing the current as it flows along the axon. The extent of loss of this positive charge depends upon the resistance of the membrane. When membrane resistance is high, current flow across the membrane will be low, and less charge will be lost. When membrane resistance is low, current flow across the membrane will be large, and more charge will be lost, resulting in greater dissipation of the axonal current with distance.

The effects of membrane resistance, extracellular resistance, and intracellular resistance on the distance an electrical

FIGURE 5.26   Model of the current flow in an axon
(a) Electrotonic current spread. Introduced current (for example, due to Na⁺ influx) spreads electrotonically through the axon, but some of this current leaks out through the membrane and flows "backward" along the outside of the axon. **(b)** An electrical circuit model for a patch of membrane. The axon consists of three compartments: the extracellular fluid, the membrane, and the cytoplasm with an associated electrical resistance. The cell membrane also acts as a capacitor, and can be modeled as a resistor and capacitor arranged in parallel. **(c)** An electrical circuit model for a segment of an axon. An actual axon can be modeled as a series of smaller circuits connected together.

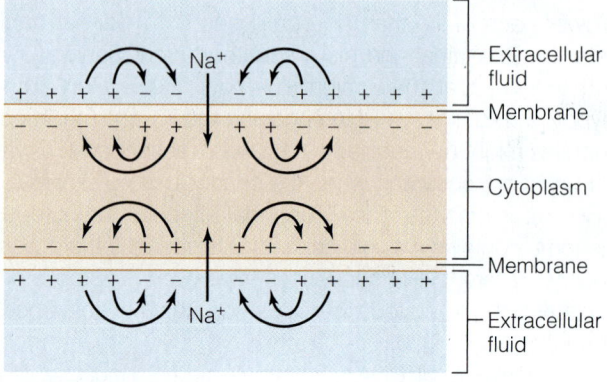

(a) Current flow in axon

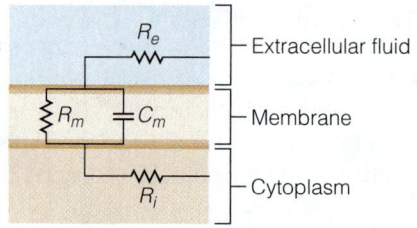

(b) An electrical circuit model for a patch of membrane

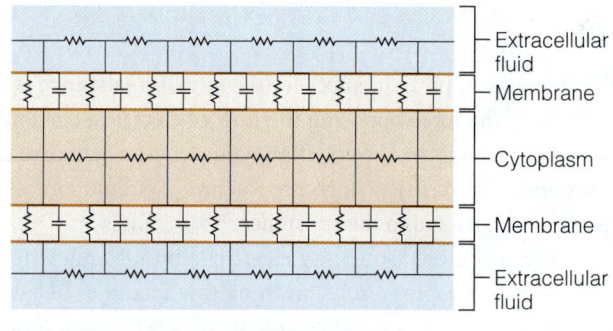

(c) An electrical circuit model for the axon

signal can travel are summarized by a parameter termed the **length constant (λ)** of the membrane. The length constant is defined as the distance over which a change in membrane potential will decrease to 37 percent of its original value. This may seem to be an arbitrary value, but it is a consequence of the fact that a change in membrane potential decreases

FIGURE 5.27 The relationship between membrane potential, distance along the axon, and the length constant

When the length constant is large, the change in membrane potential as a result of an introduced current decays slowly with the distance traveled by electrotonic current spread. When the length constant is small, the membrane potential decays rapidly with distance. V_{max} = maximum change in membrane potential at the stimulus point. x = distance from the initial stimulus. V = change in membrane potential at a distance (x) from the initial stimulus. λ = length constant of the membrane.

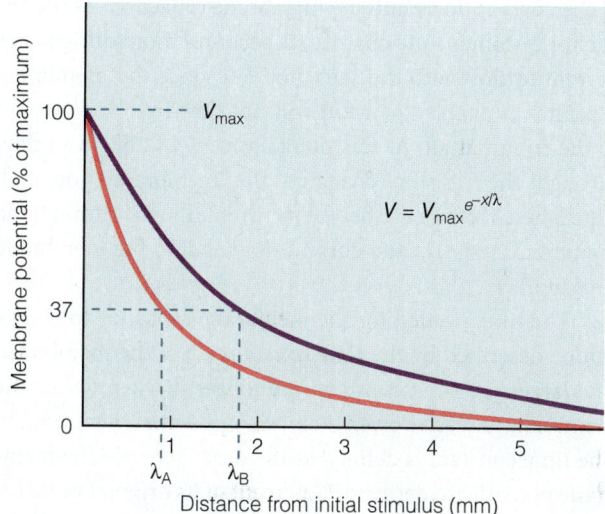

$$V = V_{max}e^{-x/\lambda}$$

spread essentially instantaneously along the axon. A neuron that used only electrotonic current flow would transmit signals very rapidly. In fact, neurons with very short axons often use only electrotonic conduction to carry electrical signals, but electrotonic current spread is effective only up to a distance of 2 or 3 millimeters in most organisms. In longer axons, action potentials must be generated to "boost" the signal before it dies out because of the decrease in voltage with distance. However, the ability to signal over long distances using the action potential comes with a cost—a reduced speed of signal conduction. Because electrotonic currents spread along the axon extremely rapidly, the farther a threshold depolarization can spread along the axon, the shorter the length of time it will take for an impulse to reach the end of the axon. Thus, increasing the length constant of the axon increases the speed of signal conduction along the neuron by allowing the signal to be carried farther by the more rapid electrotonic conduction rather than by repeated generation of action potentials.

Membrane capacitance influences the speed of conduction

As we have already mentioned, biological membranes act as electrical capacitors. You can observe the presence of the membrane capacitor by examining what happens when you inject current into a neuron (Figure 5.28). A rectangular pulse of current does not result in an immediate change in the membrane potential of the cell. Instead, there is a lag caused by the presence of the membrane capacitor. When a capacitor is present in an electrical circuit (whether in a manufactured electrical circuit or a biological membrane), it will accumulate a charge difference across its insulating surface. For example, consider a simple electrical circuit that consists of a switch, a battery, a capacitor, and a resistor arranged in series. When we close the switch on the circuit, the voltage difference between the poles of the battery causes electrons to try to flow from the negative pole (cathode) of the battery to the positive pole (anode) of the battery. But the capacitor acts as an insulator, so negative charges cannot flow across the capacitor and instead "pile up" on one side. Recall from basic physics that like charges repel and opposite charges attract. As a result of this attraction (which occurs across the thin insulating layer of the capacitor), the negative charges on one side of the capacitor "pull" positive charges toward the capacitor and repel negative charges, causing current to flow through the circuit. Note that current does not actually flow across the insulating layer of the capacitor. Instead, electrostatic forces acting across the insulating layer of the capacitor induce a current in the circuit.

As more and more charges build up on the capacitor, they increasingly repel each other, and it becomes more and

exponentially with distance (37 percent is equivalent to $1/e$). As shown in Figure 5.27, when the length constant is large, the change in membrane potential degrades less with distance, whereas if the length constant is small, change in membrane potential degrades quickly with distance. The length constant can be calculated as follows:

$$\lambda = \sqrt{r_m/(r_i + r_o)}$$

where r_m = membrane resistance, r_i = intracellular resistance, and r_o = extracellular resistance. The extracellular resistance is usually assumed to be low and constant, and is often neglected in these calculations, so the equation can be rewritten as

$$\lambda = \sqrt{r_m/r_i}$$

From this equation, it is easy to see that the length constant of the membrane will be largest when membrane resistance is high and intracellular resistance is low.

So why does the length constant of a membrane influence the speed of conduction along the axon? Recall that conduction along an axon represents a combination of electrotonic conduction along the axon and action potential generation at specific points on the axon. Electrotonic conduction is very rapid compared with the speed of opening and closing voltage-gated channels during an action potential; in fact, for our purposes electrotonic currents can be considered to

FIGURE 5.28 **Response of a membrane to a rectangular pulse of introduced current**

When a neuronal membrane is exposed to a rectangular pulse of current, the membrane potential does not change instantaneously. Instead, due to the capacitance of the membrane, membrane potential increases gradually with injected current, and then decreases gradually when the stimulus is removed.

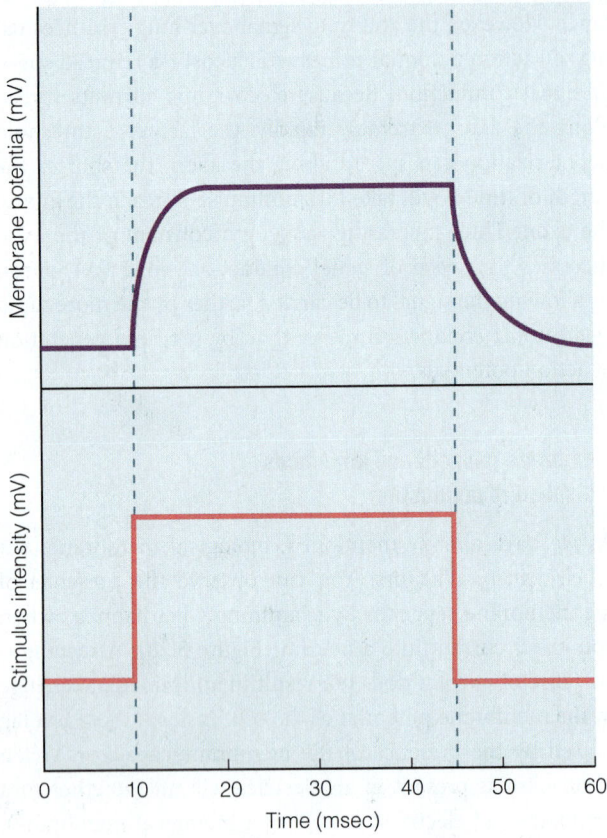

the area and thickness of the membrane. The larger the area of the capacitor, the greater the capacitance, while the thicker the insulating layer, the lower the capacitance.

So why is the membrane capacitor important for the function of an axon? In the case of the axonal membrane, which we can model as a resistor and a capacitor arranged in parallel as shown in Figure 5.26, when you introduce an electrical current into an axon (for example, by opening voltage-gated Na^+ channels), the membrane voltage will change, but more slowly than expected because initially most of the current flows into the membrane capacitor. As the capacitor becomes fully charged, it becomes more difficult for current to flow into the capacitor, and once the membrane capacitor is charged, current will not flow into this portion of the circuit at all. At this point, current will begin to flow through the resistor, changing the membrane potential. Thus, there is a balance between current flowing through the membrane resistors and current flowing into the membrane capacitor.

The time needed for the membrane capacitor to charge can be described by the *time constant* (τ) of the membrane. The larger the time constant, the longer it will take for the membrane to reach a given membrane potential (Figure 5.29). The time constant is defined as the time taken for the membrane potential to decay to 37 percent of its original value (or to reach 63 percent of its maximal value). As was the case with the length constant of the membrane, these numbers are not arbitrary, but instead reflect the observation that there is an exponential increase in membrane potential. The relationship

more difficult for additional charges to be deposited on the capacitor. Eventually, the charge on the capacitor will equal the driving force coming from the voltage drop across the battery, and no more current will flow. The point at which current stops flowing across a particular capacitor is determined by a parameter called *capacitance*. You can think of capacitance as the quantity of charge needed to create a potential difference between the two surfaces of the capacitor. Thus, a capacitor with high capacitance is able to store large amounts of charge, and a capacitor with low capacitance is only able to store relatively small amounts of charge. Capacitance depends on three features of the capacitor: the material properties of the capacitor, the area of the two conducting surfaces, and the thickness of the insulating layer. The electrical properties of biological membranes don't change that much from one cell to another, so we only need to consider

FIGURE 5.29 **The time constant of the membrane**

When the time constant (τ) of the membrane is large, it takes longer for the membrane to reach the maximum potential difference. The time constant (τ) is a reflection of the capacitance (c_m). When capacitance is large, the time constant will be large.

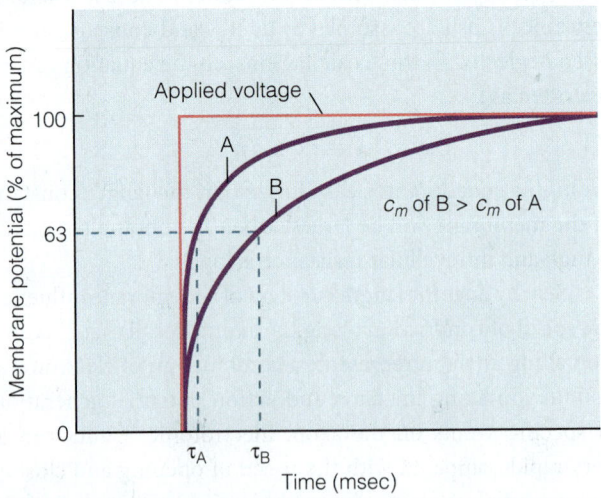

between electrical properties of the membrane and the time constant of the membrane is described as follows:

$$\tau = r_m c_m$$

where r_m = membrane resistance and c_m = membrane capacitance. Increases in either membrane resistance or membrane capacitance will increase the time constant of the membrane, delaying current flow across the membrane.

The time constant of the membrane has important consequences for temporal summation in neuronal cell bodies. Imagine two graded potentials occurring at the same time in a presynaptic cell that sum to provide a suprathreshold potential. What will happen if these two graded potentials occur at slightly different times? The time constant of the membrane helps us to determine the answer to this question. If the time constant is small, these potentials will decay rapidly, and they are less likely to be able to sum to provide a suprathreshold potential. In contrast, if the time constant is large, these potentials will decay slowly, making them more likely to overlap in time, and thus to sum to a suprathreshold potential.

It is clear that the time constant of the membrane is important in temporal summation, but how does changing the time constant of the membrane affect the speed of conduction along the axon? As current spreads electrotonically along the axon, some of the voltage must first be used in order to charge the membrane capacitor. Only once the capacitor is fully charged does current begin to flow across the membrane and alter membrane potential. As a result, electrotonic current spread is delayed. The smaller the time constant of the membrane, the faster the membrane can depolarize by a given amount and the greater the rate of electrotonic current spread and action potential propagation.

To summarize our discussion so far, three main factors influence the speed of action potential propagation. The first factor is the kinetics of the voltage-gated channels. For example, all things being equal, action potentials typically propagate faster at higher temperatures than at lower temperatures (within physiological limits) because the channels open faster at warmer temperatures. This observation suggests that the speed of opening of the voltage-gated channels sets limits on the speed of action potential propagation. In fact, voltage-gated channels open and close very slowly compared with the speed of electrotonic current spread, so any factors that can increase the speed or distance of electrotonic current spread will increase the speed of conduction. Electrotonic current spread is, in turn, dependent on the length constant and the time constant of the axon. In the next sections we address how myelination and increasing the diameter of the axon, as in giant axons, alter these properties of the axon and thus conduction velocity.

Giant axons have high conduction speed

Giant axons have evolved independently many times, and are found in both vertebrates and invertebrates, although they are absent in mammals. Giant axons are easily visible to the naked eye and can be up to a millimeter in diameter, much larger than most mammalian axons, which are typically less than 5 μm in diameter. We have already discussed the giant axons of squid (see Figure 5.1), which are involved in signaling to the **mantle cavity** so that it contracts and allows the squid to use "jet propulsion" to swim (Figure 5.30). Some parts of the mantle are much farther away from the central nervous system of the squid than others. In order to reach all parts of the mantle at the same time, action potentials must be conducted faster in the neurons that innervate the distant parts of the mantle than in neurons with short axons. Axons that activate muscles at the far end of the mantle cavity have very large diameters, while axons that activate muscles in the region of the mantle cavity closest to the central nervous system have smaller diameters. Combining axons of varying diameters allows the near-simultaneous contraction of the entire mantle by speeding up conduction to the most distant part of the body.

The effects of membrane resistance and intracellular resistance on the length constant of the membrane explain why large-diameter axons, such as giant axons, conduct signals more rapidly than small axons. Recall that the length constant of the membrane increases as membrane resistance increases, but decreases as intracellular resistance increases. So what happens to membrane resistance and intracellular resistance as axon diameter increases? Membrane resistance is inversely proportional to the surface area of the membrane. As surface area increases so does the number of leak channels, allowing greater ion flow across the membrane so that membrane resistance decreases. Assuming that the axon is roughly cylindrical in shape, the surface area of the membrane is related to the radius of the axon via the following formula:

$$\text{Surface area} = 2\pi r h$$

where r is the radius of the axon, and h is the length. Thus, the membrane resistance is inversely proportional to the radius of the axon. As axon radius, and thus diameter, increases, membrane resistance decreases.

Intracellular resistance, however, is related to the volume of the axon. As volume increases, intracellular resistance decreases. The volume of the axon can be approximated with the formula for the volume of a cylinder:

$$\text{Volume} = \pi r^2 h$$

Thus, intracellular resistance decreases in proportion to the radius of the axon *squared*. So what are the effects of

FIGURE 5.30 **Schematic diagram of part of the nervous system of the squid (*Loligo pealei*)**

When squid want to move rapidly, they expel water out of their siphon by rapidly contracting the mantle muscles. To ensure that the entire mantle contracts rapidly in a coordinated way, axons of neurons that innervate distant parts of the mantle have much larger diameter axons than neurons that innervate parts of the mantle close to the stellate ganglion. These giant axons conduct action potentials much more rapidly than smaller diameter axons.

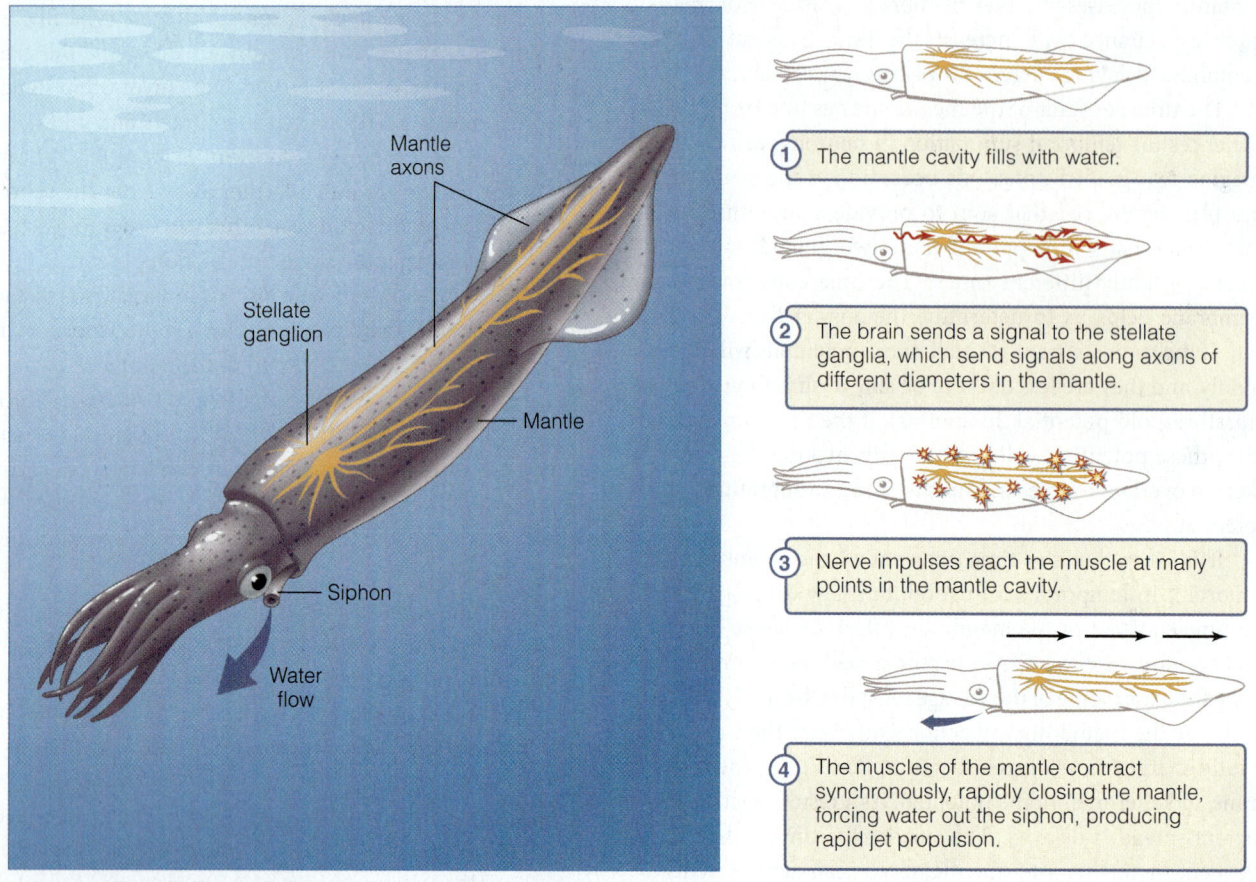

Mantle axons

Stellate ganglion

Mantle

Siphon

Water flow

1 The mantle cavity fills with water.

2 The brain sends a signal to the stellate ganglia, which send signals along axons of different diameters in the mantle.

3 Nerve impulses reach the muscle at many points in the mantle cavity.

4 The muscles of the mantle contract synchronously, rapidly closing the mantle, forcing water out the siphon, producing rapid jet propulsion.

membrane resistance and intracellular resistance on the length constant of the membrane? As axon radius increases, both membrane resistance and intracellular resistance decrease. From the definition of the length constant ($\lambda = \sqrt{r_m/r_i}$), we can see that decreasing the intracellular resistance will increase the length constant of the membrane, increasing conduction speed. However, decreasing membrane resistance will tend to decrease the length constant, slowing conduction speed. So why do these two effects not simply cancel each other out? Remember that the intracellular resistance decreases in proportion to the radius of the axon squared, while membrane resistance decreases in direct proportion to the radius of the axon. Thus, increasing the radius of an axon has a much greater effect on the intracellular resistance than on the membrane resistance. Therefore, the net effect of increasing the radius of an axon is to increase the speed of conduction (Figure 5.31).

The capacitance of the membrane also changes as axon diameter increases, but this has only a marginal effect on the time constant of the membrane. We have already seen that membrane resistance decreases as membrane area increases. In contrast, membrane capacitance increases with membrane area. Thus, the effects of membrane resistance and membrane capacitance on the time constant of the membrane have a tendency to cancel each other out. Therefore, changes in the time constant of the membrane have a relatively small effect on local current flow as axon diameter increases.

Myelinated neurons evolved in the vertebrates

Although increasing axon diameter provides substantial increases in conduction velocity, there are two main disadvantages to using large axons to increase conduction velocity. Large axons take up more space, and this may limit the number of neurons that can be packed into the nervous system. Organisms such as mammals, with very complex nervous systems, do not have giant axons. Instead, they use myelination to increase the speed of action

FIGURE 5.31 **Why giant axons conduct action potentials rapidly**

The geometry of the axon influences the length constant (λ) of the membrane and explains why larger-diameter axons conduct signals more rapidly than small-diameter axons. A longer length constant means that local currents can flow farther without degrading, so signal conduction will be faster. The length constant of the membrane is directly proportional to the membrane resistance, and inversely proportional to the intracellular resistance. The membrane resistance (r_m) is inversely proportional to axon radius, whereas intracellular resistance (r_i) is inversely proportional to axon radius *squared*. An axon with radius 1 will have a length constant proportional to 0.7, while an axon with radius 5 will have a length constant proportional to 1.6, and the larger axon will conduct signals faster.

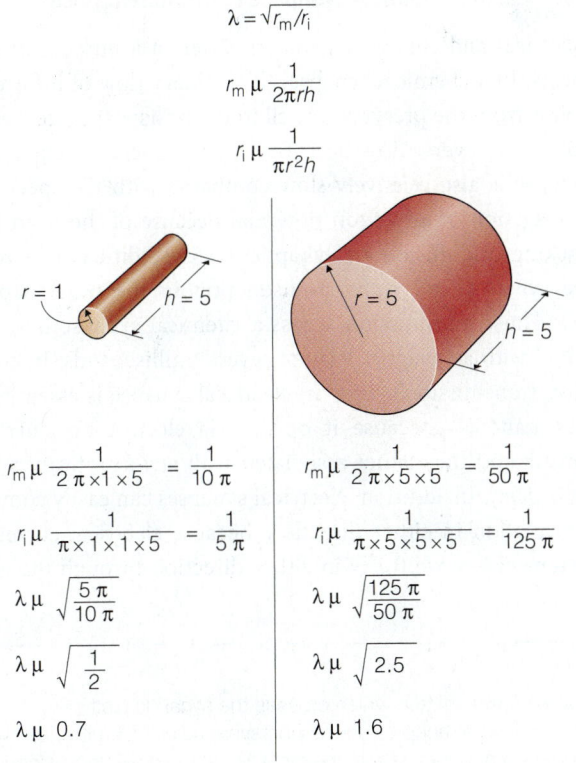

$$\lambda = \sqrt{r_m / r_i}$$

$$r_m \propto \frac{1}{2\pi r h}$$

$$r_i \propto \frac{1}{\pi r^2 h}$$

$r = 1$ $h = 5$

$r = 5$ $h = 5$

$$r_m \propto \frac{1}{2\,\pi \times 1 \times 5} = \frac{1}{10\,\pi}$$

$$r_i \propto \frac{1}{\pi \times 1 \times 1 \times 5} = \frac{1}{5\,\pi}$$

$$\lambda \propto \sqrt{\frac{5\,\pi}{10\,\pi}}$$

$$\lambda \propto \sqrt{\frac{1}{2}}$$

$$\lambda \propto 0.7$$

$$r_m \propto \frac{1}{2\,\pi \times 5 \times 5} = \frac{1}{50\,\pi}$$

$$r_i \propto \frac{1}{\pi \times 5 \times 5 \times 5} = \frac{1}{125\,\pi}$$

$$\lambda \propto \sqrt{\frac{125\,\pi}{50\,\pi}}$$

$$\lambda \propto \sqrt{2.5}$$

$$\lambda \propto 1.6$$

potential conduction. Large-diameter axons also have a much larger volume of cytoplasm per unit length, making them energetically expensive to produce and maintain. As a result, you would expect that giant axons would be used only when extremely high-speed conduction is a necessity for survival. In squid, giant axons are present only in the neurons controlling escape and prey-capture behaviors. Similarly, giant axons are associated with startle and escape responses in other organisms (including both vertebrates and invertebrates).

Myelinated neurons are found in most vertebrates. Only lampreys and hagfish (jawless vertebrates) lack multilayered myelin sheaths. As we have already discussed, certain invertebrate neurons also have axons that are wrapped in multiple layers of cell membrane, although these wrappings differ in structure from the true myelin sheath found in vertebrates, and may not be as effective in increasing the rate of signal conduction. The myelin sheath is an important evolutionary innovation, allowing rapid signal conduction in a compact space, which may have provided the conditions necessary for the evolution of the complex nervous systems of the vertebrates.

Myelination increases conduction speed

As we mentioned earlier in the chapter, all else being equal, myelinated neurons conduct signals more rapidly than unmyelinated neurons because a greater proportion of the signal conduction occurs electrotonically, which is much faster than generating action potentials. The myelin sheath increases the length over which electrotonic current can spread before it drops below the threshold potential required to generate an action potential at the next node of Ranvier.

The myelin sheath acts as insulation for the axon, reducing current loss through leak channels and thus increasing membrane resistance. Reducing ion leakage increases the length constant of the membrane, increasing the distance that local current can travel electrotonically before degrading. Thus, reducing ion leakage increases overall conduction velocity. The presence of the myelin sheath also decreases the capacitance of the membrane, because capacitance is inversely proportional to the thickness of the insulating layer in a capacitor. The many layers of cell membrane of the myelin sheath act together as a single insulator. Thus, although each membrane alone has the same thickness, the effective thickness of the many-layered myelin sheath is much greater. The increase in the thickness of the membrane decreases the capacitance, reducing the time constant of the membrane and thus increasing the speed of electrotonic conduction in the internodes.

Note that the placement of the nodes of Ranvier is critical for the function of a myelinated axon. The nodes cannot be placed too far apart or the signal will not be sufficient to depolarize the neuron beyond threshold at the next node, because current inevitably decreases with distance, although less so in a myelinated axon than in an unmyelinated axon. Typically, the length of the internodes is about 100 times the diameter of the axon, ranging from about 200 μm to 2 mm. Indeed, in some neurons, electrotonic spread can carry a suprathreshold depolarization past several nodes of Ranvier, which then appear to fire "simultaneously."

The high density of voltage-gated channels at the nodes of Ranvier is also important in the conduction of signals in myelinated neurons. This high density of channels decreases the threshold potential for firing of action potentials in this region, decreasing the size of the electrotonic current needed to trigger an action potential.

Diversity of Synaptic Transmission

Once the wave of depolarization reaches the axon terminal, this electrical signal must be transferred to the postsynaptic cell. In the first half of the chapter, we saw how vertebrate motor neurons release the neurotransmitter acetylcholine to send signals across the synapse. But synaptic transmission is incredibly diverse, and can be accomplished via a variety of mechanisms. For example, unlike the vertebrate motor neurons that we discussed in the first half of the chapter, some neurons do not release chemical neurotransmitters onto their target cells. Instead, these neurons have gap junctions that directly connect them to their target cells (Figure 5.32). Gap junctions are composed of a series of proteins that form small pores in the membranes of two adjacent cells, allowing ions and other small molecules to travel directly from cell to cell. Synapses in which the presynaptic and postsynaptic cells are connected via gap junctions are termed **electrical synapses**, because the electrical signal in the presynaptic cell is directly transferred to the postsynaptic cell through the gap junctions. Most neurons, however, do not form gap junctions with their target cells. Instead, these neurons form **chemical synapses**. As we saw in the case of a vertebrate motor neuron, at a chemical synapse the presynaptic neuron converts its electrical signal to a chemical signal in the form of one or more neurotransmitters, which diffuses across the synapse to the postsynaptic cell and binds to receptors on the postsynaptic membrane.

Electrical and chemical synapses play different roles

Electrical and chemical synapses differ in a number of respects. In a chemical synapse, the primary flow of information is from the presynaptic cell to the postsynaptic cell, and not in the reverse direction. Transmission across a chemical synapse is also relatively slow compared with the speed of propagation of an action potential because of the need for docking and fusion of synaptic vesicles, diffusion across the synapse, and signal transduction in the postsynaptic cell. Thus, transmission across a chemical synapse is associated with a synaptic delay of several milliseconds. In contrast, transmission across an electrical synapse is essentially instantaneous, because it occurs via electrotonic current spread, and thus is not associated with any significant synaptic delay. In addition, electrical synapses can easily convey information in either direction, because electrical currents or ions can move freely in either direction through the gap

FIGURE 5.32 **Electrical and chemical synapses.**
(a) In an electrical synapse, the electrical signal is directly transmitted from the presynaptic cell to the postsynaptic cell via gap junctions. **(b)** In a chemical synapse, the electrical signal in the presynaptic cell is converted to a chemical signal, in the form of a neurotransmitter, which crosses the synaptic cleft and binds to a receptor on the postsynaptic cell membrane. The receptor converts the chemical signal to an electrical signal in the postsynaptic cell.

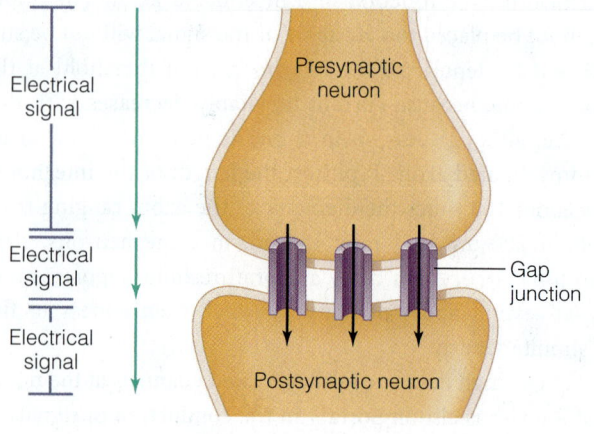

(a) Electrical synapse

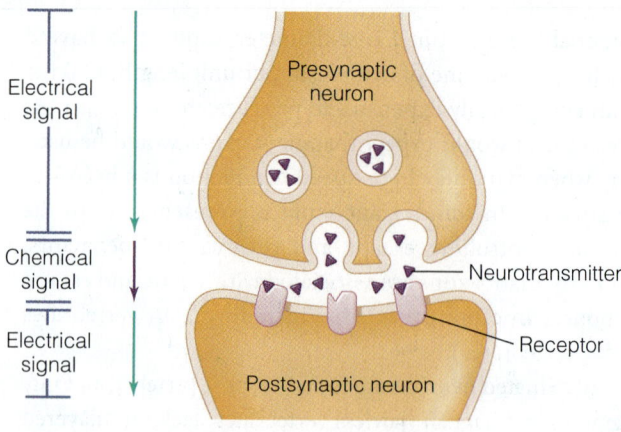

(b) Chemical synapse

junctions connecting the cells (although some gap junctions have specialized structures that ensure unidirectional signal transmission).

Although signal transmission across an electrical synapse is much more rapid than across a chemical synapse, chemical synapses have one substantial advantage over electrical synapses. In an electrical synapse, the signal in the postsynaptic cell is always similar to the signal sent by the presynaptic cell, because direct transfer of ions or current causes the postsynaptic signal. In a chemical synapse, the signal in the postsynaptic cell is not necessarily the same as in the presynaptic cell. For example, a series of action potentials in a presynaptic cell could result in the release of a neurotransmitter that causes the postsynaptic cell to hyperpolarize, inhibiting it from firing action potentials. Chemical synapses provide an additional level of regulation for the nervous system; in comparison, direct electrical coupling across an electrical synapse limits the diversity of the signal in the postsynaptic cell.

Electrical synapses are present in neural pathways involved in escape behaviors in some organisms, presumably because they increase the speed of the escape response. For example, the neurons involved in the escape response of crayfish are connected via electrical synapses.

The proportion of electrical to chemical synapses in the nervous system also varies among organisms. For example, organisms with relatively simple nervous systems, such as cnidarians (jellyfish, sea anemones, and related animals), often have electrical synapses between their neurons, whereas organisms with more complex neural pathways generally make more use of chemical synapses. As we discuss in Chapter 8: Functional Organization of Nervous Systems, from these more complex neural pathways and networks emerge more sophisticated and plastic animal behaviors. However, electrical synapses also play an important role in organisms with more complex nervous systems. In the mammalian brain, electrical synapses among neurons may be important in synchronizing brain function. For example, the hormone-secreting cells of the hypothalamus (see Chapter 4: Cell Signaling and Endocrine Regulation) are connected by electrical synapses. These electrical synapses coordinate the action potentials in these neurons, causing them to secrete neurohormones into the pituitary portal system at the same time, causing neurohormones to be released from multiple cells in a single burst.

Chemical synapses have diverse structures

There is substantial diversity in the morphology of chemical synapses (Figure 5.33a). We have already examined the morphology of the neuromuscular junction, the chemical synapse between a motor neuron and a muscle. The axon of a motor neuron splits into several terminal branches, and each branch terminates in a swelling called the axon terminal (or sometimes the *terminal bouton* or *synaptic knob*). The synapses formed at axon terminals are highly structured, and the postsynaptic cell membrane contains increased densities of neurotransmitter receptors in close proximity to the axon terminal. Axon terminals are found at the ends of many types of neurons, in addition to the motor neurons that we have already encountered. Alternatively, some neurons form synapses at **axon varicosities**, or swellings along the axon that can be arranged like beads on a string. Each of these swellings contains vesicles filled with molecules of neurotransmitter, which are released onto the target cell. As we will see in Chapter 8, certain types of neurons in the peripheral nervous system, called *autonomic neurons*, form synapses with their effector organs at axon varicosities. These *neuroeffector junctions* differ from true synapses in that the postsynaptic cell membrane at the junction is not specialized, and does not contain a high concentration of receptors. Instead, neurotransmitter diffuses broadly and contacts receptors located across large areas of the target organ. Neurons in the central nervous system can form a similar type of synapse, called an *en passant synapse*, that consists of a swelling along the axon of the presynaptic neuron. These synapses differ from neuroeffector junctions in that the postsynaptic membrane may be specialized and contain high densities of receptors. Another common type of synapse in the central nervous system is termed a *spine synapse*. In these synapses, the presynaptic cell connects with a specialized structure, termed a **dendritic** *spine*, on the dendrite of the postsynaptic cell.

Neuron-to-neuron synapses can form at a variety of locations (Figure 5.33b). **Axodendritic synapses** form between the axon terminal of one neuron and the dendrite of another, while **axosomatic synapses** form between the axon terminal of one neuron and the cell body of another. Axodendritic and axosomatic synapses are the most common types of neuron-to-neuron synapses. **Dendrodendritic synapses** form between the dendrites of two neurons, and are often electrical synapses that allow communication of information in both directions between neurons. **Axoaxonic synapses** form between an axon terminal of a presynaptic neuron and the axon of a postsynaptic neuron. Axoaxonic synapses are rare relative to axodendritic and axosomatic synapses, but are most often found at the axon hillock or the axon terminal of the postsynaptic neuron. At the axon terminal, they play a role in regulating neurotransmitter release from the postsynaptic neuron, often by altering Ca^{2+} influx. We discuss some examples of axoaxonic synapses at axon terminals in Chapter 8: Functional Organization of Nervous Systems. By modulating the release of neurotransmitter from neurons within the nervous system, these axoaxonic synapses play a role in regulating learned behaviors.

FIGURE 5.33 **Variation in the structure and location of synapses**

(a) Structural diversity of chemical synapses. There are four main types of chemical synapses. **(b)** Diversity in the location of neuron-to-neuron synapses. Synapses can be axodendritic, axosomatic, dendrodendritic, or axoaxonic.

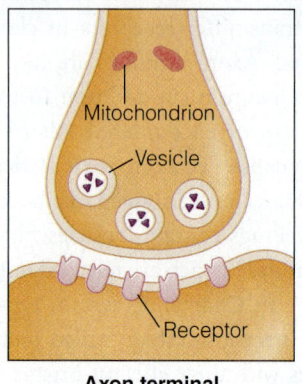

Axon terminal

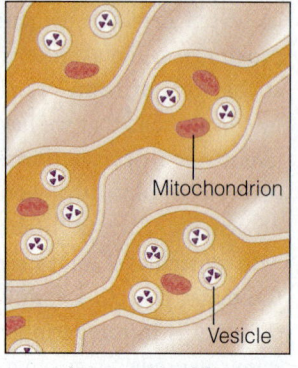

Axon varicosities

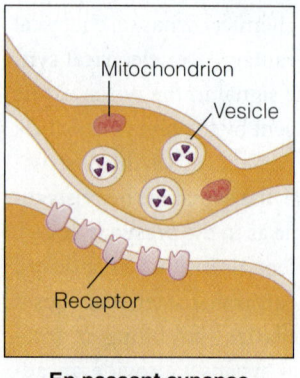

En passant synapse

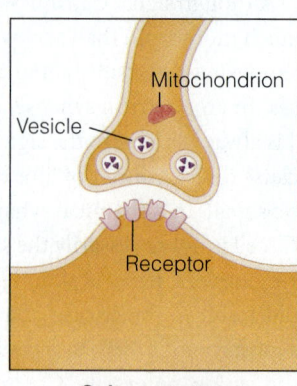

Spine synapse

(a) Types of synapses

(b) Locations of neuron-to-neuron synapses

There are many types of neurotransmitters

Neurons that form chemical synapses with their target cells can communicate in diverse ways in part because of the large number of different chemical substances that act as neurotransmitters. Neurobiologists have discovered more than 50 substances that act as neurotransmitters (Table 5.4), and these neurotransmitters have diverse effects on postsynaptic cells.

To be classified as a neurotransmitter, a substance must meet several criteria. It must be synthesized in neurons. It must be released at the presynaptic cell membrane following depolarization, and it must bind to a postsynaptic receptor and cause a detectable effect. Neurobiologists often group neurotransmitters into five major classes: amino acids, neuropeptides, biogenic amines, acetylcholine, and a grab-bag class consisting of neurotransmitters that do not fit into any of the other groups.

Many of these classes of molecules can also act as hormones or paracrine signals, and thus neurotransmission is part of a continuum of chemical communication systems in animals.

Four amino acids have been shown to act as neurotransmitters: glutamate, aspartate, glycine, and gamma-aminobutyric acid (**GABA**). Glutamate, aspartate, and glycine are also used for protein synthesis; GABA is a derivative of glutamate. Animals can synthesize all four of the amino acids that act as chemical messengers, although they may also obtain these amino acids from food. Once synthesized, amino acid neurotransmitters are packaged into vesicles, and stored until they are released by exocytosis.

The neuropeptides, also called neuroactive peptides or peptide neurotransmitters, are composed of short chains of amino acids. Neuropeptides are synthesized in the rough

Table 5.4 A summary of neurotransmitters

Neurotransmitter	Receptor	Receptor Type	Receptor Location	Effect
Acetylcholine	Nicotinic	Ionotropic	Skeletal muscles, autonomic neurons, CNS (central nervous system)	Excitatory
	Muscarinic	Metabotropic	Smooth and cardiac muscle, endocrine and exocrine glands, CNS	Excitatory or inhibitory
Amino Acids				
Glycine	Glycine	Ionotropic	CNS	Inhibitory
Aspartate	Aspartate	Ionotropic	CNS	Excitatory
Glutamate	AMPA	Ionotropic	CNS	Excitatory
	NMDA	Ionotropic	CNS	Excitatory
	mGlu1-8	Metabotropic	CNS	Excitatory or inhibitory
GABA	GABA-A	Ionotropic	CNS	Inhibitory
	GABA-B	Metabotropic	CNS	Generally inhibitory
Biogenic Amines				
Dopamine	Dopamine	Metabotropic	CNS	Excitatory or inhibitory
Norepinephrine	α and β adrenergic	Metabotropic	CNS and peripheral nervous system (PNS), cardiac muscle, smooth muscle	Excitatory or inhibitory
Epinephrine	α and β adrenergic	Metabotropic	Cardiac muscle, smooth muscle, CNS	Excitatory or inhibitory
Peptides				
Endorphins	Opiate	Metabotropic	CNS	Generally inhibitory
Neuropeptide Y	NPY	Metabotropic	CNS	Excitatory or inhibitory
Other				
Adenosine	Purine	Metabotropic	CNS	Generally inhibitory
Nitric oxide	Soluble guanylyl cyclase	N/A	CNS, smooth muscle	N/A

endoplasmic reticulum, which synthesizes all secreted peptides. In neurons, the rough endoplasmic reticulum is generally found in the cell body. Vesicles containing peptide neurotransmitters are then transported from the cell body to the axon terminal along a complex network of microtubules, via a process called **fast axonal transport**. However, neurobiologists have recently discovered that some neurons in the brains of invertebrates such as snails can synthesize peptide neurotransmitters in both the axon and axon terminal, suggesting an additional layer of functional complexity.

Acetylcholine and the biogenic amines play particularly important roles in integrating physiological functions because they are important neurotransmitters that communicate with many kinds of tissues. You will encounter these neurotransmitters repeatedly as you read this book, because they are involved in the homeostatic regulation of many physiological systems. We have already discussed the role of acetylcholine at the neuromuscular junction, but this neurotransmitter plays many other roles in the nervous system. Because of their physiological importance, we discuss acetylcholine and the biogenic amines in more detail in later sections.

Some neurotransmitters do not fit into any simple chemical class. These neurotransmitters include **purines** such as ATP, which is important in energy metabolism, and the gas nitric oxide. The gaseous neurotransmitters, such as nitric oxide (NO), are not packaged into vesicles. Instead, after they are synthesized at the axon terminal, they diffuse freely out of the presynaptic neuron in all directions into every nearby cell. Because NO diffuses freely across membranes, it cannot be stored, and must be synthesized as needed.

Neurotransmitters can be excitatory or inhibitory

The response of a target cell depends on the type of receptors it expresses. Thus, depending on the nature of its receptor, a neurotransmitter can cause the postsynaptic cell to either depolarize or hyperpolarize. *Inhibitory neurotransmitters* generally cause hyperpolarization, making the postsynaptic cell less likely to generate an action potential. The resulting changes in membrane potential are often referred to as **inhibitory postsynaptic potentials (IPSPs)**. Excitatory neurotransmitters generally cause depolarization, making the postsynaptic cell more likely to generate an action potential. These depolarizations are termed **excitatory postsynaptic potentials (EPSPs)**.

Neurotransmitter receptors can be ionotropic or metabotropic

The binding of a neurotransmitter to its receptor can cause either a fast or a slow response within the postsynaptic cell, depending on the signal transduction cascade associated with the receptor. Neurotransmitter receptors are often classified as either ionotropic or metabotropic. **Ionotropic receptors** are ligand-gated ion channels. When a neurotransmitter or other chemical signaling molecule binds to an ionotropic receptor, the conformation of the protein changes, opening a pore within the receptor protein that allows ions to move across the cell membrane (Figure 5.34a). Because binding of the neurotransmitter directly causes changes in the shape of the protein to result in ion movement, ionotropic receptors initiate rapid changes in the membrane potential of the postsynaptic cell. The nicotinic ACh receptors that we have already encountered are an example of an ionotropic receptor.

When a neurotransmitter binds to a **metabotropic receptor**, there is a change in the conformation of the receptor (Figure 5.34b) that sends a signal via a second messenger, initiating a signaling cascade within the postsynaptic cell. We have already discussed the organization and function of various signal transduction pathways in Chapter 4: Cell Signaling and Endocrine Regulation, and metabotropic receptors work through similar mechanisms. Many metabotropic receptors are G protein–coupled receptors, although some work through other pathways. A signaling cascade activated by a metabotropic receptor ultimately sends a message to ion channel proteins, modulating the activity of ion channels on the postsynaptic cell membrane and thus altering membrane potential. Metabotropic receptors tend to cause slower-acting changes in the postsynaptic cell than do ionotropic receptors because of the complex signaling pathways between binding of the neurotransmitter to the receptor and the opening of ion channels. Metabotropic receptors often also cause long-term changes in the postsynaptic cell by affecting the transcription or translation of receptors and ion channels.

FIGURE 5.34 **Ionotropic and metabotropic receptors**

(a) Structure and function of an ionotropic receptor. When there is no neurotransmitter bound to an ionotropic receptor, the ion channel within the protein is closed, and ions cannot cross the cell membrane. When neurotransmitter binds to an ionotropic receptor, the gated ion channel opens, which allows ions to cross the membrane and cause a response in the postsynaptic cell. **(b)** Structure and function of a metabotropic receptor. When neurotransmitter binds to a metabotropic receptor, the receptor changes shape, sending a signal that activates a signal transduction pathway. The signal transduction pathway can open or close ion channels, modify existing ion channel proteins, or activate or repress gene expression, causing a coordinated cellular response.

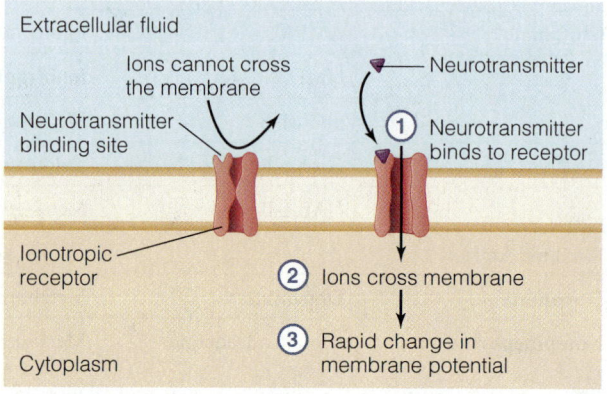

(a) Ionotropic receptors

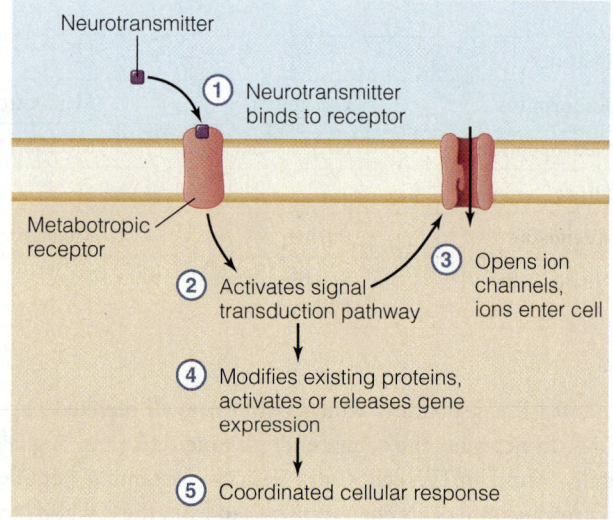

(b) Metabotropic receptors

Acetylcholine receptors can be ionotropic or metabotropic

We have already discussed the role of acetylcholine (ACh) in carrying signals across the neuromuscular junction, but acetylcholine is also a neurotransmitter at many other synapses, including synapses in the autonomic nervous system and the brain in vertebrates (see Chapter 8 for a discussion of the physiology of these systems). Receptors for acetylcholine are termed the **cholinergic receptors**. There are two major classes of cholinergic receptors: the *nicotinic* and the *muscarinic* receptors. As we have already discussed, nicotinic receptors are ionotropic receptors that cause a rapid response in the target cell, whereas muscarinic receptors are metabotropic receptors that cause slower responses in the target cell.

The nicotinic receptor is made up of a variety of combinations of the five possible subunits: α, β, γ, δ, and ε, each of which is encoded by several isoforms. The nicotinic acetylcholine receptor was first studied intensively in the electric organ of the ray *Torpedo californica*, which generates a strong electrical current that these rays use to stun their prey. The electric organ is a modified muscle that has high levels of the nicotinic acetylcholine receptor. Figure 5.35 shows the combination of subunits of the ACh receptor expressed in the *Torpedo* electric organ. These subunits are arranged like the staves of a barrel around a central pore. The subunit composition of nicotinic receptors differs between skeletal muscle, the autonomic nervous system, and the brain. The nicotinic receptors in the autonomic nervous system are made up of an α3 subunit, an α5 subunit, an α7 subunit, a β2 subunit, and a β4 subunit, while the receptors in the brain are predominantly composed of combinations of α4 and β2 subunits. These different subunit and isoform combinations confer differing properties, adding to the complexity of the vertebrate nervous system.

Muscarinic ACh receptors are metabotropic receptors that are indirectly coupled to ion channels through G proteins. Muscarinic receptors are named because the drug muscarine binds to them and not to nicotinic receptors. They are found on a variety of tissues, including the brain, the heart, the gut, and the bronchial passages. Stimulation of muscarinic receptors causes a slower response in the postsynaptic cell than does stimulation of nicotinic receptors, and the response can be either excitatory or inhibitory, depending on the cell type. Thus, although metabotropic receptors (such as the muscarinic receptors) cause slower responses than ionotropic receptors (such as the nicotinic receptors), they are capable of generating more diverse responses. Table 5.5 summarizes some of the similarities and differences between types of cholinergic receptors.

The biogenic amines play diverse physiological roles

Amines are chemicals that possess an amino ($-NH_2$) group; those that can act as chemical messengers are referred to as the biogenic amines. Several biogenic amines act as neurotransmitters, including the **catecholamines** (dopamine, norepinephrine, and epinephrine), and serotonin. All of these biogenic amines are synthesized in the axon terminal using an amino acid as a precursor. Acetylcholine also contains an NH_2 group, and thus potentially could be considered a biogenic amine. But because ACh is not synthesized from an amino acid precursor, and because the NH_2 group is in the center of the molecule rather than at one end, ACh is usually classified separately from the biogenic amines.

The catecholamines are synthesized via a common pathway from the amino acid tyrosine (Figure 5.36). Serotonin is synthesized from the amino acid tryptophan via a common pathway with the hormone melatonin. Dopamine and serotonin are primarily involved in signaling within the central nervous system and are discussed in more detail in Chapter 8: Functional Organization of Nervous Systems. Epinephrine and norepinephrine (also called adrenaline and noradrenaline) play an important role in the peripheral nervous system and are involved in regulating many important physiological processes, including heart rate and breathing, which we discuss in more detail in later chapters.

Receptors for norepinephrine and epinephrine are termed the **adrenergic receptors** (derived from the word *adrenaline*). There are two major classes of adrenergic receptors: alpha (α) and beta (β). Both norepinephrine and epinephrine bind to α receptors, although epinephrine binding to α receptors is weak. In contrast, β receptors bind strongly to both neurotransmitters. In mammals, several variants of each receptor type are present (α1, α2; β1, β2, etc.). The great diversity of receptor types allows norepinephrine and epinephrine to have opposing effects on different tissues, depending on the particular receptor that is present. For example, when norepinephrine binds to β2 receptors on the smooth muscles surrounding the bronchioles (passages leading to the lungs), the muscle relaxes. Muscle relaxation increases the diameter of the bronchiole, making it easier to breathe. In contrast, when norepinephrine binds to α1 adrenergic receptors on the smooth muscles surrounding blood vessels, the muscles contract. Muscle contraction decreases the diameter of the blood vessel, increasing blood pressure. The diversity of adrenergic receptors and their associated

FIGURE 5.35 A schematic diagram of a nicotinic ACh receptor from the electric organ of *Torpedo*

The nicotinic ACh receptor is an ionotropic receptor made up of five subunits arranged around a central pore that forms a Na^+ channel. Each receptor has two binding sites for ACh, formed by the α subunit at the junction of the γ or δ subunits.

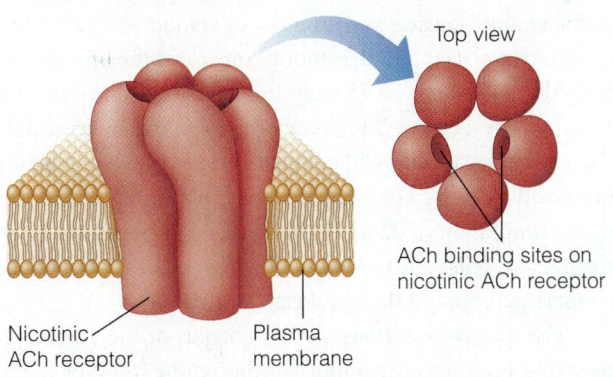

Top view

ACh binding sites on nicotinic ACh receptor

Nicotinic ACh receptor

Plasma membrane

Table 5.5 Cholinergic receptor subtypes

Receptor Subtype	Location	Effect of Binding	Second Messenger Pathway	Agonists	Antagonists
Nicotinic	Neuromuscular junctions, ganglionic neurons, adrenal medulla	Excitation	Ion influx	ACh, nicotine, carbachol	Curare
Muscarinic	Gut	Excitation	G protein coupled	ACh, muscarine, carbachol	Atropine, scopolamine
	Heart	Inhibition			
	Bronchioles (lung)	Excitation			
	Sweat glands	Activation			
	Blood vessels of skeletal muscle	Inhibition			

signal transduction pathways accounts for the opposing effects of norepinephrine and epinephrine on different tissues.

Isoforms of the same class of receptor may activate very different signal transduction cascades within a target cell. Figure 5.37 provides an example of this phenomenon by outlining the primary signal transduction pathways associated with the most physiologically significant adrenergic receptors in mammals.

The binding of norepinephrine to α1 adrenergic receptors activates a signal transduction cascade involving a G protein (called G_q) that activates phospholipase C, which in turn breaks down the molecule phosphatidyl (PIP) into a molecule of diacylglycerol (DAG) and inositol triphosphate (IP_3). Activation of α1 adrenergic receptors causes the smooth muscles surrounding the blood vessels leading to the skin and internal organs to contract, causing vasoconstriction (Table 5.6). In these smooth muscle cells, the DAG activates the enzyme protein kinase C (PKC), which phosphorylates and activates voltage-gated Ca^{2+} channels on the cell membrane, allowing Ca^{2+} to enter the cell from the extracellular space. The IP_3 binds to and opens Ca^{2+} channels on the sarcoplasmic reticulum that cause the release of Ca^{2+} from intracellular stores. Together the Ca^{2+} from the extracellular space and from intracellular stores causes the muscle to contract, causing vasoconstriction.

The binding of the norepinephrine to α2 adrenergic receptors activates a G protein called G_i (for inhibitory G protein), which inactivates the enzyme adenylate cyclase. The inactivation of adenylate cyclase causes cyclic AMP (cAMP) levels to decrease. This decrease in cAMP inactivates the enzyme protein kinase A. Because PKA is inactivated, the voltage-gated Ca^{2+} channels that are present on these cells are no longer being phosphorylated, which makes them more difficult to open. The α2 adrenergic receptor is found at the axon terminal of adrenergic neurons on the presynaptic side of the adrenergic synapse (Table 5.6). Reducing the activity of the voltage-gated

Ca^{2+} channel in these presynaptic neurons causes them to release less neurotransmitter. In this way, norepinephrine acts as a negative feedback signal inhibiting its own release.

The binding of the epinephrine or norephinephrine to β1 adrenergic receptors activates a G protein called G_s (for stimulatory G protein), which activates adenylate cyclase, causing cAMP to increase. The increased cAMP activates PKA, which phosphorylates a variety of target proteins. β1 adrenergic receptors are particularly important in heart cells (Table 5.6). In these cells one of the important proteins phosphorylated by PKA are the voltage-gated Ca^{2+} channels on the cell membrane. Phosphorylation makes these voltage-gated Ca^{2+} channels easier to open, and increases Ca^{2+} levels in the cell. Activation of the β1 adrenergic receptor also activates a Ca^{2+} channel on the sarcoplasmic reticulum, causing it to release Ca^{2+} from internal stores, which further increases intracellular calcium. As we discuss in more detail in Chapters 6 and 9, these effects increase the rate and strength of cardiac muscle contraction.

β2 adrenergic receptors work via a similar signal transduction pathway to β1 adrenergic receptors, signaling through G_s and adenylate cyclase, but stimulation of β2 has very different effects from stimulation of β1 receptors. β2 adrenergic receptors are found primarily in smooth muscle, particularly in the smooth muscle surrounding the blood vessels leading to skeletal muscles and the smooth muscle of the bronchioles of the lungs (Table 5.6). In smooth muscle the cAMP formed by adenylate cyclase inhibits a protein called myosin light chain kinase. Myosin light chain kinase activates contraction in smooth muscle. Thus, by inhibiting myosin light chain kinase, stimulation of β2 adrenergic receptors causes the muscle to relax. This causes dilation of the bronchial passages and an increase in blood flow to skeletal muscle.

The variety of actions of the subtypes of the adrenergic receptors is particularly important during the "fight or flight" response. Norepinephrine and epinephrine are released in

FIGURE 5.36 The synthetic pathway for the catecholamines

The catecholamines norepinephrine (NE) and epinephrine (E) are synthesized via a common pathway with dopamine from the amino acid tyrosine. L-dopa, DOPA, NE, and E are biogenic amines: chemical messengers containing an amine group (NH_2).

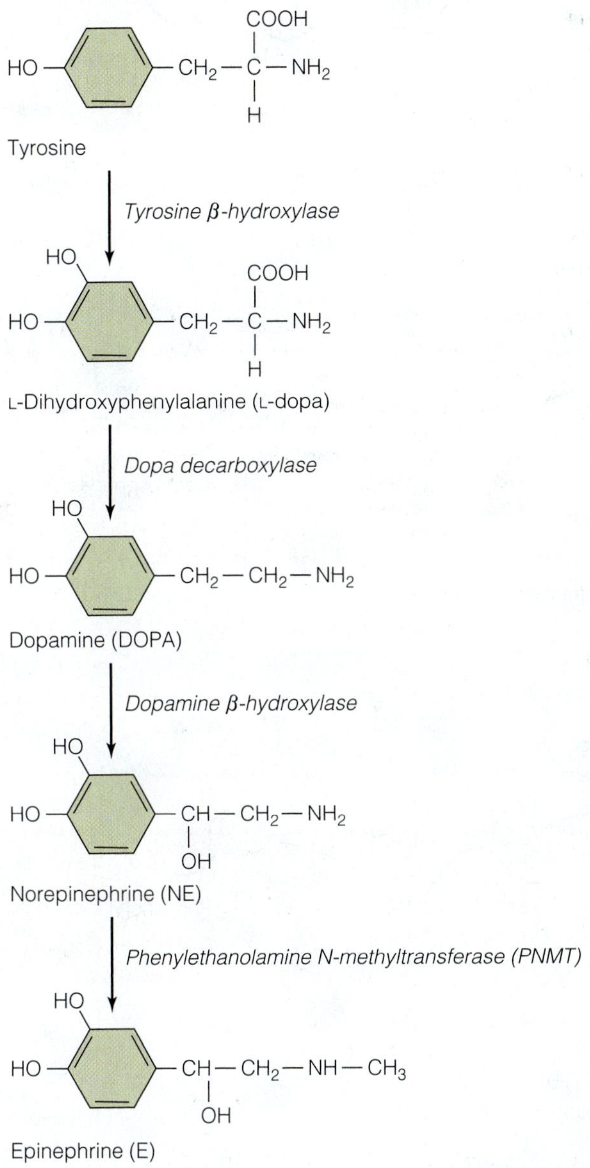

Tyrosine

Tyrosine β-hydroxylase

L-Dihydroxyphenylalanine (L-dopa)

Dopa decarboxylase

Dopamine (DOPA)

Dopamine β-hydroxylase

Norepinephrine (NE)

Phenylethanolamine N-methyltransferase (PNMT)

Epinephrine (E)

The adrenergic receptors provide an example of a much more general principle: that the effects of a single neurotransmitter can differ depending on the particular receptor that is present on the target tissue and on the signal transduction pathways within that tissue.

Neurons can synthesize more than one kind of neurotransmitter

For many years it was believed that a neuron could secrete only a single kind of neurotransmitter, but now it is known that a single neuron can secrete several different neurotransmitters. For example, many neurons synthesize both a small molecule neurotransmitter (like ACh or norepinephrine) and one or more neuropeptides. It is still not entirely clear how a neuron controls which neurotransmitter it releases, but different neurotransmitters appear to be released from a single axon terminal at different stimulus frequencies. For example, low-frequency stimulation might release ACh, whereas high-frequency stimulation might release a neuropeptide. It is likely that separate groups of synaptic vesicles reside in a single neuron, each containing a different neurotransmitter, and each releasing its contents in response to different stimulus frequencies.

Neurotransmitter release varies depending on physiological state

In addition to its substantial diversity among neurons and across species, synaptic transmission also varies within a single neuron, depending on the physiological state of that neuron. We have already discussed how action potential frequency relates to neurotransmitter release, but most neurons have another layer of functional complexity because neurotransmitter release can vary depending on the past history of action potentials at that axon terminal. As we will see in Chapter 7, this **synaptic plasticity**, or the ability of a synapse to change its function in response to patterns of use, underlies many important brain functions, including learning and memory. The vast majority of neurons exhibit at least some degree of synaptic plasticity.

Figure 5.38 illustrates some features of synaptic plasticity at the neuromuscular junction. An increase in neurotransmitter release in response to repeated action potentials is termed **synaptic facilitation**. Synaptic facilitation occurs because the accumulation of intracellular Ca^{2+} following each action potential allows more neurotransmitter to be released by subsequent action potentials. In contrast, **synaptic depression**, which is a decrease in neurotransmitter release with repeated action potentials, occurs because of the progressive depletion of the readily accessible pool of synaptic vesicles that is available for fusion and exocytosis of neurotransmitter.

Post-tetanic potentiation (**PTP**) occurs after a train of high-frequency action potentials in the presynaptic neuron.

response to immediately stressful stimuli, which prepares the animal to respond by either running away or fighting, if necessary. These signaling molecules cause relaxation of smooth muscles in the bronchi and in blood vessels leading to the skeletal muscles, allowing the animal to breathe more easily and causing more blood flow to the working muscles. At the same time, these signaling molecules increase the rate and strength of cardiac contraction, helping to pump more blood to the working muscles, and they also cause contraction in the smooth muscles leading to the skin and internal organs, directing blood flow away from the sites that are less immediately important.

FIGURE 5.37 **Binding of norepinephrine to different receptor subtypes**

Norepinephrine can bind to several types of receptor, causing opposing responses in the target cell. **(a)** When norepinephrine binds to an α1 adrenergic receptor, the receptor changes shape and activates a G_q protein, signaling to the enzyme phospholipase C (PLC), which catalyzes the breakdown of phosphatidylinositol-phosphate (PIP) into diacylglycerol (DAG) and inositol triphosphate (IP_3). The DAG activates the enzyme protein kinase C, which then phosphorylates and activates Ca^{2+} channels. In smooth muscle, this causes vasoconstriction. **(b)** When norepinephrine binds to an α2 adrenergic receptor, the receptor activates a G_i protein that inactivates the enzyme adenylate cyclase (AC). This reduces the production of cAMP from ATP, reducing intracellular cAMP levels. The reduced cAMP inactivates protein kinase A (PKA), preventing the phosphorylation of Ca^{2+} channels and inactivating them. In adrenergic neurons, this reduces the release of norepinephrine. **(c)** When norepinephrine binds to a β1 receptor, the change in shape of the receptor activates a G_s protein, which activates adenylate cyclase (AC), which increases the conversion of ATP to cAMP, increasing intracellular cAMP. The cAMP signals to protein kinase A (PKA), which then phosphorylates and activates Ca^{2+} channels, which increases the rate and strength of muscle contraction in the heart. **(d)** When norepinephrine binds to a β1 receptor, G_s activates adenylate cyclase (AC), increasing cAMP and activating PKA. In smooth muscle, the PKA inactivates myosin light chain kinase (MLCK), which reduces muscle contraction and causes vasodilation. Thus, the same neurotransmitter can have opposing effects in different postsynaptic cells, depending on the type of receptor that is present.

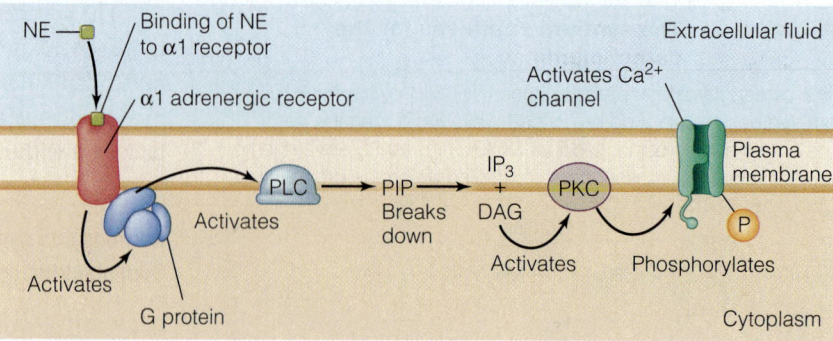

(a) Binding of NE to α1 adrenergic receptors

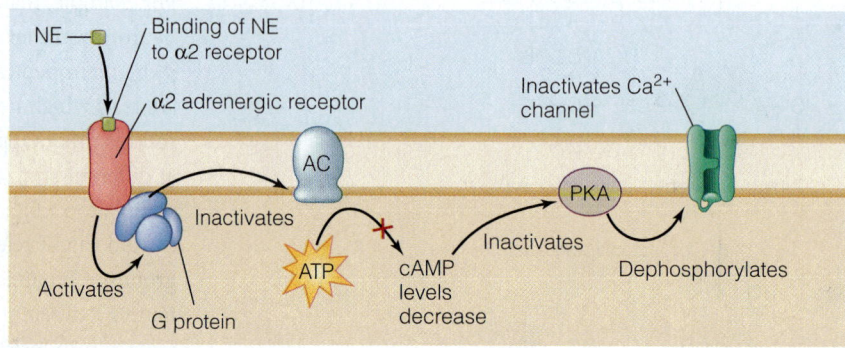

(b) Binding of NE to α2 adrenergic receptors

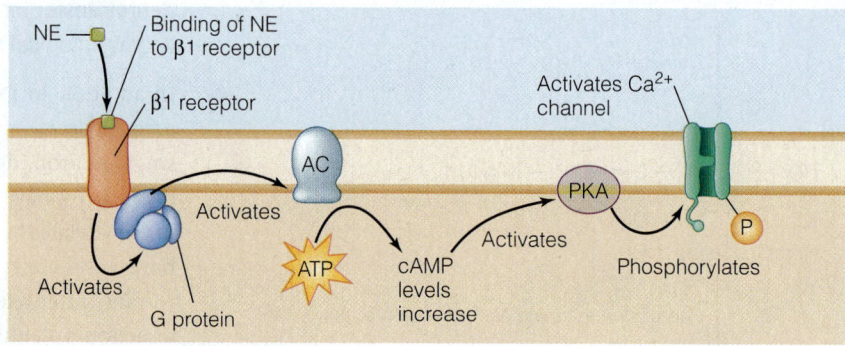

(c) Binding of NE to β1 receptors

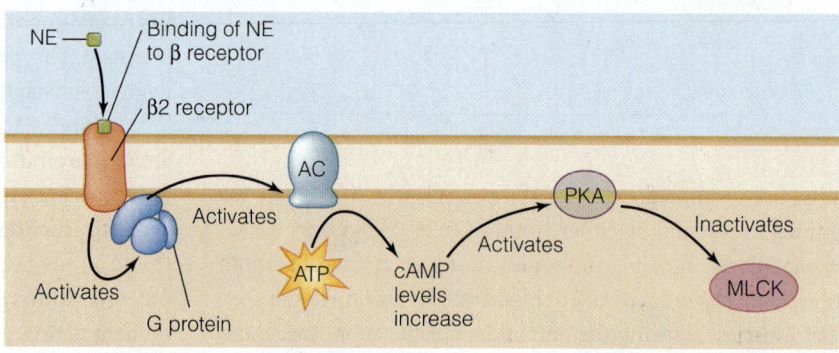

(d) Binding of NE to β2 receptors

Table 5.6	Summary of some major adrenergic receptor subtypes			
Receptor Subtype	**Location (in humans)**	**Effect (in humans)**	**Second Messenger System**	**Sensitivity**
α1	Smooth muscle of blood vessels of skin, gut, kidneys, salivary glands	Vasoconstriction	G protein activates phospholipase C	NE > E
α2	Membrane of adrenergic axon terminals	Inhibits release of NE	G protein inactivates adenylate cyclase, inhibits cAMP production	NE > E
β1	Heart	Increases the strength of cardiac contraction and increases heart rate	G protein activates adenylate cyclase, activates cAMP production	NE = E
β2	Lungs Smooth muscle of blood vessels leading to skeletal and cardiac muscle	Dilates bronchial passages Vasodilation	G protein activates adenylate cyclase, cAMP production	E > NE

FIGURE 5.38 Synaptic plasticity

If a motor neuron is stimulated several times in succession, the membrane potential change in the postsynaptic cell may increase in amplitude with each succeeding stimulus, a process called synaptic facilitation. After a long period of high-frequency stimulation, the amplitude of the change in membrane potential in the postsynaptic cell will eventually decrease, a process called synaptic depression. If the stimulus is removed, and the neuron is allowed a brief interval (up to several minutes) without stimulation, the amplitude of the potential evoked by the next stimulus is increased, a process called post-tetanic potentiation.

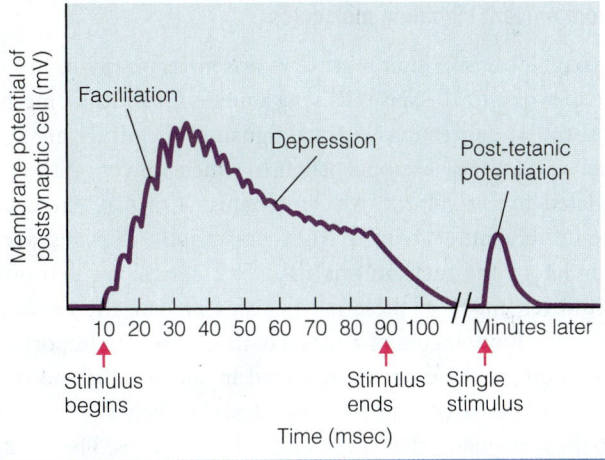

For several seconds or minutes following a burst of action potentials, a subsequent action potential will result in increased release of neurotransmitter. The mechanisms underlying PTP differ from those involved in synaptic facilitation, and are thought to involve a Ca^{2+}-dependent increase in the available pool of neurotransmitter-containing vesicles. Synaptic facilitation and post-tetanic potentiation result in only brief changes in the activity of the synapse, but as we shall see in Chapter 8, neurons have other mechanisms that allow them to undergo long-term changes in synaptic activity.

Evolution of Neural Signaling

Neurons and muscle cells, which rely on electrical signals for their function, evolved very early in the radiation of the metazoans, more than 650 million years ago. One way of examining the evolution of this signaling is to compare the structure and function of neurons in various metazoan groups to attempt to identify the core complement of proteins required for electrical signaling in neurons, which should provide clues into the nature of neurons in the last common ancestor of the animals. Alternatively, although neurons are unique to metazoans, many organisms use electrical signals for communication. Studying the mechanisms of electrical communication in other organisms could provide clues as to the evolution of the metazoan neuron.

Many organisms use electrical signaling

Green algae and plants can produce action potentials, and they use these action potentials as signals for communication throughout the body. Plants do not have a specialized tissue for conducting action potentials to specific locations over long distances. The action potential in plants appears to propagate through the vascular tissues of the plant: the xylem or phloem vessels. The electrical signals can thus propagate through the vascular tissue to the entire plant. Most of the work on action potentials in plants has concentrated on the response to wounding, but even a stimulus as simple as turning on a light can provoke an action potential in plants such as a tomato. Carnivorous plants such as the Venus fly trap (*Dionaea muscipula*) use action potentials to coordinate the movement of specialized structures that they use to trap insects. Similarly, the folding of the leaves of the so-called sensitive plant (*Mimosa pudica*) is coordinated using action potentials as signals.

Algae from the family Characeae, such as *Chara corallina*, have giant cells that are capable of generating action potentials. Single cells in this species can be up to a millimeter in diameter and several centimeters in length. Early neurobiologists sometimes used this species as an experimental model when squid were not available, as these algae produce an action potential that has a shape similar to those observed in the squid giant axon. The action potentials in these algae are used to coordinate cytoplasmic streaming within their giant cells.

Action potentials in nonmetazoans involve Ca²⁺

At a molecular level the action potential in *Chara* is very different from the action potential in the neurons of animals. It results from ion movements through Cl^- channels that are activated in a Ca^{2+}-dependent manner. An increase in Ca^{2+} influx through a voltage-gated ion channel takes place at the beginning of the action potential, which initiates a signal transduction pathway that opens Cl^- channels, causing Cl^- ions to leave the cell. The influx of Ca^{2+} and efflux of Cl^- depolarizes the cell, resulting in an action potential. Therefore, the action potential in *Chara* is not solely due to a voltage-gated channel, although a voltage-gated channel triggers it. The action potential in *Chara* shares some features with metazoan action potentials, although it differs in many respects. It acts in an all-or-none fashion, but is conducted about 1,000 times more slowly than a typical vertebrate action potential.

The nature and ionic basis of the plant action potential is not yet well understood because plant cells are more difficult to work with than animal cells, since they have a rigid cell wall and multiple intracellular compartments with varying ionic composition. However, it is known that action potentials are conducted without decrement in plants, and that the action potential may involve Ca^{2+} ions.

Paramecium, a ciliate protist, swims via the coordinated beating of the cilia that cover its exterior. If a *Paramecium* makes contact with a solid object while swimming, it will back up by reversing the direction in which the cilia beat. This reversal is the result of opening voltage-gated Ca^{2+} channels, which causes an action potential. Mutant *Paramecium* that do not contain a functional copy of the gene for this voltage-gated Ca^{2+} channel can only swim forward. In general, action potentials in protists appear to be Ca^{2+} dependent; a single species, *Actinocoryne contractilis*, has been demonstrated to have both Ca^{2+}- and Na^+-dependent action potentials.

Animals have unique voltage-gated Na⁺ channels

Metazoans have a unique family of voltage-gated Na^+ channels that is thought to have been one of the key evolutionary innovations associated with the evolution of the action potential as a long-distance electrical signal. Essentially all metazoans have at least one gene that codes for a voltage-gated Na^+ channel. In fact, as we have already discussed, many metazoan genomes contain multiple genes that code for slightly different isoforms of voltage-gated Na^+ channels. The DNA sequences of voltage-gated Na^+ channel genes from all metazoans share many features, suggesting that the voltage-gated Na^+ channel arose only once, in a common ancestor of the metazoans. A voltage-gated Na^+ channel was recently discovered in bacteria, but this channel is rather different from the voltage-gated Na^+ channels of metazoans, and its evolutionary relationship to them remains unclear.

Current evidence suggests that the most likely ancestor of the metazoan voltage-gated Na^+ channel was a voltage-gated channel that generated both Na^+- and Ca^{2+}-dependent signals (perhaps a channel similar to the one discovered in *Actinocoryne contractilis*, discussed above). Ca^{2+} plays an important role in intracellular signaling in many cell types, and it is possible that this limits its utility as an ion that can be used to carry long-distance electrical signals.

Neurotransmitters evolved from ancient signaling molecules

Synaptic transmission must have arisen very early in metazoan evolution, because all living animals have similar mechanisms for converting electrical signals to chemical signals at the synapse. For example, jellyfish, which are very distantly related to vertebrates, have mechanisms of Ca^{2+}-induced neurotransmitter release from presynaptic neurons very similar to the mechanisms used by mammalian neurons. However, many of these mechanisms predate the metazoans, and homologues of a subset of the genes with important functions at the synapse are found in single-celled eukaryotes such as yeast. Choanoflagellates, the likely sister group to the metazoans, share even more of these genes. These data suggest that synaptic transmission arose as a modification of the mechanisms for cell-to-cell communication present in many organisms.

Many neurotransmitters are simple molecules, such as amino acids, that are found in all living things. Even acetylcholine has been detected in bacteria, algae, protozoans, and plants (organisms that do not have nervous systems). So it is apparent that most neurotransmitters did not originally evolve to perform their neural signaling role. Metazoans appear to have taken ancient molecules and used them for a new function: cell-to-cell signaling in the nervous system.

As nervous systems have become more elaborate, the number and complexity of neurotransmitter-receptor interactions has increased. For example, *Branchiostoma lanceolatum* —the lancelet (or amphioxus)—a cephalochordate (the sister group to the vertebrates), has only one catecholamine receptor gene, and uses dopamine but not norepinephrine as a neurotransmitter. Lampreys and hagfish have two catecholamine receptor genes, and both dopamine and norepinephrine are used as neurotransmitters. In contrast, in mammals there are five different dopamine receptors, nine α adrenergic receptors, and three β adrenergic receptors. The increased complexity of neurotransmitter-receptor interactions may be involved in the evolution of increasing complexity in vertebrate nervous systems.

CONCEPT CHECK

21. Compare the ionic basis of the action potential in metazoans to those of *Chara*.

22. Why might having action potentials with a depolarization phase based on Na^+ be advantageous compared to an action potential with a depolarization phase based on Ca^{2+}?

SUMMARY

Neurons use a combination of graded potentials and action potentials to send electrical signals. Graded potentials spread through the cell via electrotonic conduction, which allows rapid conduction of electrical potentials, but causes them to degrade with distance. Graded potentials can sum to trigger action potentials, which can be used to boost the electrical signal in the axon, allowing long-distance signal propagation.

Action potentials are generated by voltage-gated channels. An initial depolarization triggers the opening of a voltage-gated Na^+ channel, resulting in a positive feedback cycle that causes the phases of the action potential to occur in an "all-or-none" fashion. Action potentials take time, because they involve the opening and closing of ions channels. The depolarization due to the action potential spreads very rapidly due to electrotonic current spread. This current then triggers a new action potential farther along the axon.

Although action potentials can vary in shape among different neurons, as a result of differences in the properties or density of voltage-gated Na^+ and K^+ channels, each action potential in a given axon is identical, so the signal at the axon terminal is identical to the initial signal at the axon hillock. This property of action potentials allows electrical signals to be conducted across long distances without degrading.

The cable properties of the axon influence the speed at which current is conducted along the axon. Large-diameter axons conduct signals more rapidly than small-diameter axons. The cable properties of axons can also be used to understand the role of myelination and saltatory conduction in axons. Myelination increases membrane resistance and increases the distance over which graded potentials can propagate before they have to be regenerated with an action potential. Because action potentials are relatively slow compared to electrotonic current spread, myelinated neurons conduct signals faster than do unmyelinated neurons of equivalent size.

When an action potential reaches the axon terminal, the signal is transmitted to other cells across the synapse. At chemical synapses, action potentials trigger the opening of voltage-gated Ca^{2+} channels, and the resulting Ca^{2+} influx causes vesicles to fuse with the membrane and release neurotransmitter. Neurotransmitters bind to receptors on the postsynaptic cell, triggering a response. Over the course of evolution, the number and diversity of ion channels and neurotransmitters in metazoans has increased with increasing complexity of the nervous system.

REVIEW QUESTIONS

1. **LO①** Why does the opening of a Na^+ channel cause a neuron to depolarize?

2. **LO①** Why do only the ions Na^+, K^+, and Cl^- appear in the Goldman equation as formulated for a neuron at rest?

3. **LO②** Why can't graded potentials be propagated across long distances in neurons?

4. **LO②** What is the difference between temporal and spatial summation? Can spatial summation occur without temporal summation?

5. **LO③** Draw a diagram to illustrate the relationship between the states of the various voltage-gated ion channels, membrane permeability, and the phases and refractory periods of the action potential.

6. **LO③** What molecular properties of the ion channels involved in action potentials cause unidirectional propagation of action potentials along the axon, and why?

7. **LO④** You have discovered a drug that blocks voltage-gated Ca^{2+} channels. What are the likely effects of this drug at the synapse?

8. **LO④** Describe the processes at a chemical synapse that make acetylcholinesterase inhibitors effective in the treatment of myasthenia gravis.

9. **LO⑤** What are the four main functional zones of a neuron?

10. **LO⑤** Which type of neuron would you expect to have more dendrites, an afferent (sensory) neuron or an interneuron? Justify your answer.

11. LO⑥ Explain why a myelinated neuron conducts signals more rapidly than an equivalent unmyelinated neuron.

12. LO⑥ Explain how changes in the length constant of the membrane cause increases in the speed of signal propagation as axon diameter increases.

13. LO⑦ Compare and contrast the signal transduction pathways initiated by binding of norepinephrine to the various types of adrenergic receptors.

14. LO⑦ How can a single neurotransmitter be excitatory in some cells but inhibitory in others?

15. LO⑧ The giant cells of the alga *Chara* generate an action potential that consists of a depolarization phase and a repolarization phase, as in metazoan neurons. The resting membrane potential of these cells is −170 mV. The table below gives the extracellular and intracellular concentrations of ions in these giant cells. Using this information, calculate the equilibrium potentials for each ion, and use these data to suggest which ions could be responsible for the depolarization phase and the repolarization phase of the action potential. Assume that the temperature is 20°C.

Compartment	[K^+]	[Na^+]	[Ca^{2+}]	[Cl^-]
Extracellular (pond water)	0.1	0.1	0.1	0.4
Intracellular (cytoplasm)	110	5	0.001	22

16. LO⑧ Could a *Paramecium* generate an action potential if placed in water that lacked Ca^{2+}? Justify your answer.

SYNTHESIS QUESTIONS

1. Explain in your own words why increasing the density of voltage-gated Na^+ channels decreases the threshold potential of a neuron.

2. Draw a diagram of the shape of an action potential in a neuron that expresses voltage-gated K^+ channels compared with the action potential in a neuron that does not express voltage-gated K^+ channels, assuming that all other factors are similar between the neurons. Explain the reasoning behind any differences that you indicate in shape between the two action potentials.

3. Ouabain is a poison that selectively binds to the Na^+/K^+ ATPase and inhibits it. What would happen over the course of a few hours to the resting membrane potential of a neuron that was poisoned with ouabain?

4. Immediately after the application of ouabain, would the neuron in question 3 still be able to generate an action potential? Why or why not?

5. A student is eating at the lab bench (in clear violation of laboratory policy), and mistakenly sprinkles tetrodotoxin on his fries. Given that this substance inhibits voltage-gated Na^+ channels, indicate whether the following statements concerning this student are true or false. Explain your answers, and consider the time course of the response.
   (a) It will be more difficult for the student's neurons to generate action potentials.
   (b) The student's neurons will fire more frequently, because membrane potential will be brought closer to threshold.
   (c) The effect on the membrane potential of the student's neurons could be predicted by the Nernst equation, which factors in the effects of both ion concentration and ion permeability.

6. Describe the relationship between the after-hyperpolarization phase of the action potential and the relative refractory period. Why is the relative refractory period important for neural signaling?

7. What would happen if you experimentally stimulated an axon close to both the axon hillock and the axon terminal at the same time? Justify your answer.

8. What would happen to action potential generation in an axon if you applied a drug that caused voltage-gated K^+ channels to remain open constantly?

9. Imagine a postsynaptic neuron that is contacted by two different excitatory presynaptic neurons. One of these presynaptic neurons (neuron A) contacts the cell body of the postsynaptic cell next to the axon hillock, whereas the other presynaptic neuron (B) contacts a dendrite of the postsynaptic cell on the side of the cell body farthest away from the axon hillock. Explain why repeated firing of neuron A at slightly below the threshold potential could cause the postsynaptic neuron to initiate an action potential, while firing of neuron B at exactly the same intensity and frequency might not.

10. Drugs called selective serotonin reuptake inhibitors (SSRIs), which affect the reuptake of neurotransmitter by presynaptic cells, are used for the treatment of depression. Serotonin normally causes an excitatory postsynaptic potential. What effect would the administration of an SSRI have on the response of these postsynaptic cells, and why?

QUANTITATIVE QUESTIONS

1. Use the table below and the Goldman equation to calculate the resting membrane potential of a neuron at 37°C. (Temperature in Kelvin = Temperature in °C + 273.15). Please report your answer in millivolts.

Ion	Intracellular Concentration (mM)	Extracellular Concentration (mM)	Membrane Permeability at rest
K^+	140	4	1
Na^+	15	145	0.05
Cl^-	4	110	0.1
Ca^{2+}	0.0001	5	0

2. The neuron described in question 1 contains ligand-gated Ca^{2+} channels. What will happen to the membrane potential of this neuron if neurotransmitter binds to these channels? Provide an estimate of the maximum possible change in membrane potential when Ca^{2+} channels open.

3. During extreme dehydration, plasma K^+ can increase to as high as 10 mM.
   (a) What would the membrane potential of this neuron be under these conditions? (Assume there are no other changes in ion concentrations.)
   (b) What would happen to the ability of this neuron to generate action potentials during extreme dehydration? Why might this be problematic?

4. Twelve neurons synapse on one postsynaptic neuron. At the axon hillock of the postsynaptic neuron, 10 of the presynaptic neurons produce EPSPs of 2 mV each and the other two produce IPSPs of 4 mV each. The threshold potential of the postsynaptic cell is −60 mV (resting membrane potential is −70 mV). Will an action potential be produced? Justify your answer.

5. Calculate the relative conduction velocities in two different axons, one with a diameter of 2 μm and another with a diameter of 50 μm, assuming that all other factors are the same between the two axons.

6

Cellular Movement and Muscles

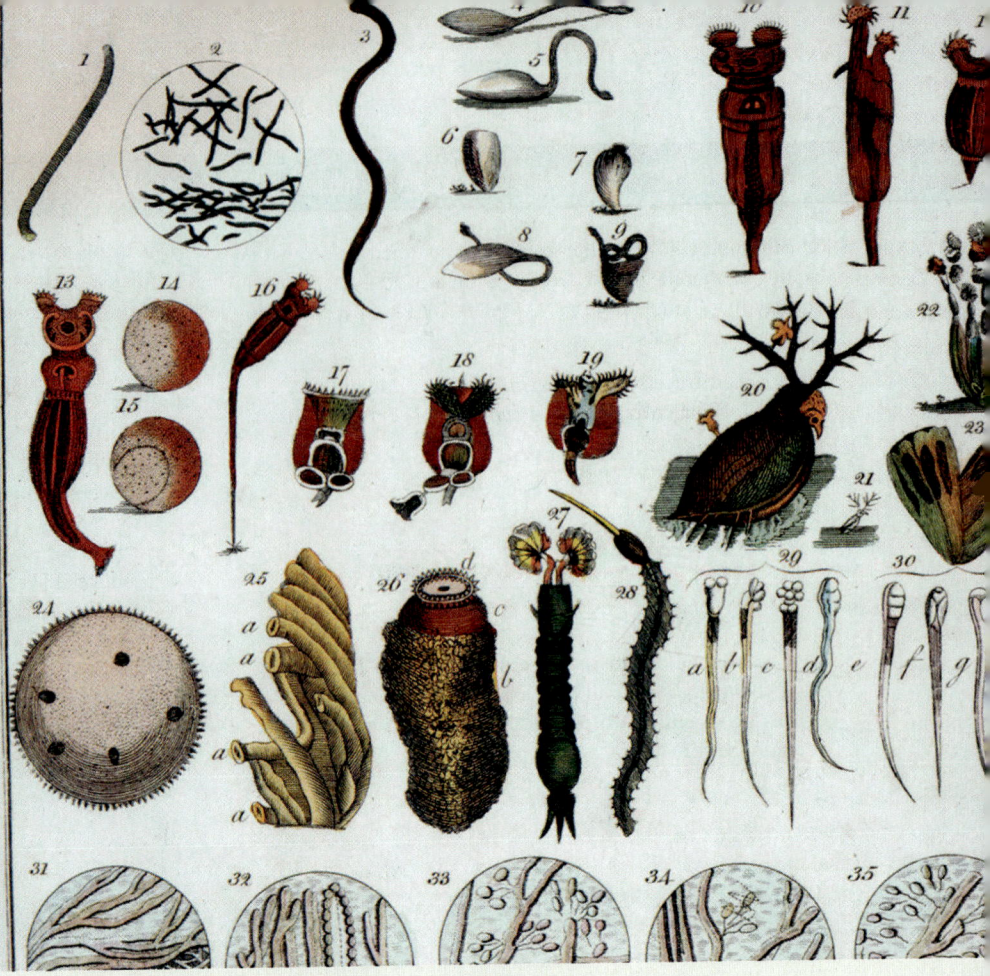

FIGURE 6.1 van Leeuwenhoek's animalcules

Photo source: Art HIP/Art Resource, NY.

Learning Objectives

After reading this chapter, you should be able to:

1. Describe the components of the cytoskeleton, comparing and contrasting microtubule- and actin-based systems.

2. Discuss the roles of the cytoskeleton in different types of movement and physiological processes.

3. Compare and contrast the properties of myosin and actin in the context of intracellular movement versus muscle contraction.

4. Identify muscle cell components and explain the relationships among them.

5. Compare and contrast the mechanisms of regulation of cardiac, skeletal, and smooth muscle types.

6. Discuss the anatomical and physiological differences between muscle types, including modified muscles.

More than 300 years ago a Dutch dry-goods merchant named Anton van Leeuwenhoek became one of the earliest cell biologists. Utilizing his flair for glasswork, van Leeuwenhoek created a homemade lens that allowed him to discover the microscopic organisms inhabiting pond water. He was struck by how these small creatures swam forward and backward through the water. Even then, *movement was synonymous with life*, and he recognized that these microscopic "animalcules," as he called them, were alive (Figure 6.1). Over the next 200 years, the quality of microscopes improved. By the late 1800s, microscopists were able to look inside living cells, allowing them to see organelles move rapidly throughout large algal cells. Even the cytoplasm itself seemed to flow beneath the margins of the plasma membrane.

We now realize that all eukaryotic organisms show some form of movement, either within cells, by cells, or by organisms. However, animals are the only group of multicellular organisms that are able to actively move from place to place, courtesy of a distinctive cell type found only in animals: the muscle cell, or *myocyte*. A study of the evolutionary and developmental origins of muscles reveals a paradox of unity and diversity. At the molecular level, most muscle proteins have homologues in fungi, plants, and other eukaryotes. Although muscles are constructed from the same cytoskeletal elements shared by all organisms, the distinct features of the homologues in animals enable them to construct muscle.

We begin this chapter examining the mechanisms that enable cells to conduct intracellular transport. Apart from important roles in cellular physiology, such as cellular movement, vesicle transport, endocytosis, and exocytosis, the cytoskeletal hardware for intracellular movement is the raw material for muscle. It is important to appreciate the evolutionary origins of muscle to understand why it is built and regulated as it is. When you think of muscle, the first function that likely springs to mind is its role in locomotion. Apart from locomotion, muscles play important roles in virtually all physiological systems. Therefore, we approach this chapter considering just the basic features of muscle cells, leaving for later chapters a discussion of their roles and regulation in each physiological system. ∎

LOOKING BACK 6

You may find it helpful to review Chapter 3, where we describe the nature of energy (pp. 40–42), the fundamentals of energy metabolism (pp. 57–58, 71–77), the biochemical basis of molecular structures, including proteins (pp. 58–70), and the intracellular organization of organelles and the need for intracellular sorting (pp. 84–90). Also, Chapter 5 describes the basic properties of neurons and how motor neurons regulate muscle.

∎ OVERVIEW

Every physiological process, be it intracellular transport, changes in cell shape, cell motility, or muscle-dependent animal locomotion, depends in some way on movement. Regardless of the type of movement, the same intracellular machinery underlies each one: the *cytoskeleton* and its *motor proteins*. Recall from Chapter 3: Chemistry, Biochemistry, and Cell Physiology that eukaryotic cells possess a cytoskeleton composed of microtubules, microfilaments, and intermediate filaments. Of these, only microtubules and microfilaments have important roles in cellular movement. Microtubules work in conjunction with the motor proteins kinesin and dynein. Myosin, in contrast, is the actin-dependent motor protein. The diversity in cellular movement is possible because these basic elements can be arranged and used in many combinations.

There are four general ways that cells use these elements to conduct movement, which can be distinguished by whether the cytoskeleton, the motor protein, or both can move (Figure 6.2). In the first scenario, movement is driven by active reorganization of the cytoskeletal network (Figure 6.2a). If you think of the cytoskeleton as a frame on which the cell membrane is mounted, cells can move themselves by adding to cytoskeleton, pushing the cell membrane outward. This type of movement, often called amoeboid movement, is common in many motile cells. For example, white blood cells can use amoeboid movement to move over the surface of blood vessels, and force themselves between the cells that make up the lining of the capillaries. Cells regulate this type of movement by controlling the rate and direction of growth of cytoskeletal fibers.

In the second scenario, the motor protein is anchored in the membrane and the cytoskeleton can be moved (Figure 6.2b). The ratcheting action of the motor protein pulls the cytoskeleton in one direction. For example, the cells that line the digestive tract have projections known as microvilli, which are extensions of the cytoskeleton (see Chapter 14: Digestion and Energy Metabolism). The cytoskeleton can be pushed outward by the action of motor proteins embedded in the cell membrane. Cells regulate this type of movement by turning the motor proteins on or off.

In the third scenario, the cytoskeleton is stationary, and motor proteins are free to move (Figure 6.2c). The motor proteins pick up cargo, such as vesicles or organelles, and walk along the complex cytoskeletal networks to different locations. Cells mediate this movement, or intracellular traffic, by controlling where it builds the cytoskeleton, regulating what cargo gets carried, and which direction the motor proteins move. For example, the precision of the cell signaling pathways we

FIGURE 6.2 Four ways to use the cytoskeleton for movement

In each panel, the motor protein is shown in blue, cytoskeleton in red. **(a)** Cells can use a cytoskeleton as an intracellular support, using reorganization of the cytoskeletal elements to change cell shape. This approach need not involve motor proteins. **(b)** Cells use the motor protein like a lever, pulling the cytoskeleton backward. **(c)** Cells can use the cytoskeleton as a track for motor proteins to move along, often carrying intracellular cargo. **(d)** Cells can arrange the motor proteins and cytoskeleton such that motor proteins pull the ends of the cell together.

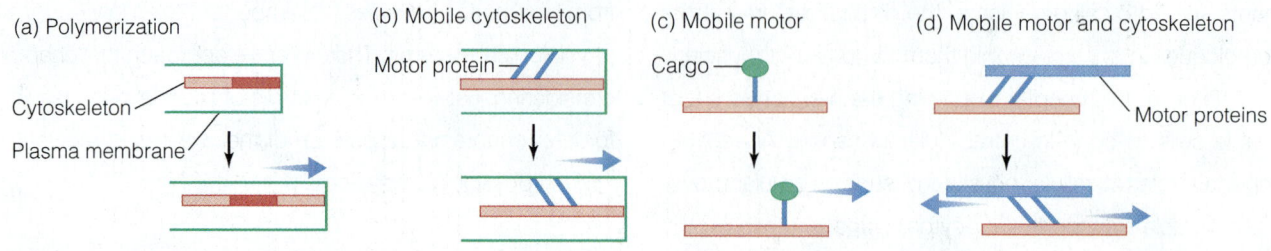

discussed in Chapter 4: Cell Signaling and Endocrine Regulation depends on motor proteins being able to carry secretory vesicles from sites of synthesis to the plasma membrane for exocytosis. If a vesicle is carried to the wrong place or released at the wrong time, dangerous miscommunications can result.

The final scenario we consider is when the cytoskeleton and motor proteins are arranged in complex arrays (Figure 6.2d). When motor proteins are activated, the cytoskeletal elements slide over each other to cause a change in cell shape. Cells then organize the cytoskeleton in a way that translates this tugging action into movement. As you will see later in this chapter, these cytoskeletal superstructures are the foundation of cilia, flagella, and muscle. Cells primarily regulate this type of movement by controlling the activity of the motor protein.

CYTOSKELETON AND MOTOR PROTEINS

The cytoskeleton and motor proteins work in conjunction to enable animals to mediate intracellular trafficking, changes in cell shape, and cellular movement. Three general explanations exist for the variations seen in the cellular movement in animal cells. First, most animals possess multiple isoforms of critical cytoskeletal and motor proteins. This arsenal of genetic variation allows metazoans to build specialized types of cells. Second, animal cells can use a single set of building blocks to organize the cytoskeleton in different ways. Third, animals can regulate an existing suite of proteins in real time; hormones bind to receptors, triggering regulatory cascades that alter enzyme activity that modifies the properties of the cytoskeleton and motor proteins. These three aspects of diversity account for the distinct ways animal cells build and use the cytoskeleton and motor proteins for movement. The capacity to be different at a cellular level is central to the animals' ability to generate specific types of cells, as well as to adapt to evolutionary challenges. As we proceed through this textbook, you will see that these cellular processes underlie many important physiological systems.

Microtubules

Microtubules are intracellular rodlike structures that radiate throughout the cell, performing many functions (see Table 6.1).

Table 6.1 Microtubules and animal physiology	
Cellular Process	**Physiological Function**
Cytokinesis	Development and growth: All cells need to divide, and microtubules ensure that chromosomes are equally divided after mitosis.
Axon structure	Nervous system: Microtubules support the long axons.
Vesicle transport	Hormones and cell signaling: Microtubules carry hormones and neurohormones from sites of synthesis to sites of release.
Pigment dispersion	Adaptive coloration: Microtubules control the distribution of pigment granules throughout the cell to affect animal color.
Flagellar movement	Reproduction: Flagella allow sperm to swim toward the egg.
Ciliary movement	Respiration, digestion: Cilia propel mucus and other fluids over the epithelial surface.

Cells can organize microtubules in many arrangements. Most cells gather the ends of microtubules near the nucleus of the cell at the **microtubule-organizing center (MTOC)** (Figure 6.3). The microtubules radiate from the MTOC like spokes of a wheel that extend to all margins of the cell. The outward ends of microtubules are anchored to integral proteins embedded within the plasma membrane. This microtubule network is vital to intracellular traffic, as motor proteins can move either toward the central MTOC or to the periphery of the cell.

Cells use their microtubule network to control the movement of subcellular components, such as vesicles and organelles. Microtubule systems also mediate the rapid changes in skin color seen in some animals that use cryptic coloration, such as the African claw-toed frog, *Xenopus laevis* (Figure 6.4). Skin color is determined by the distribution of dark pigment granules within cells called *melanophores*. When the pigment granules are concentrated near the MTOC, the skin is pale in color. When the granules are dispersed throughout the cell, the skin darkens. Changes in the

FIGURE 6.3 Microtubule network of cells
Many cells organize microtubules into a network, with the minus ends gathered near the center of the cell at the microtubule-organizing center (MTOC).

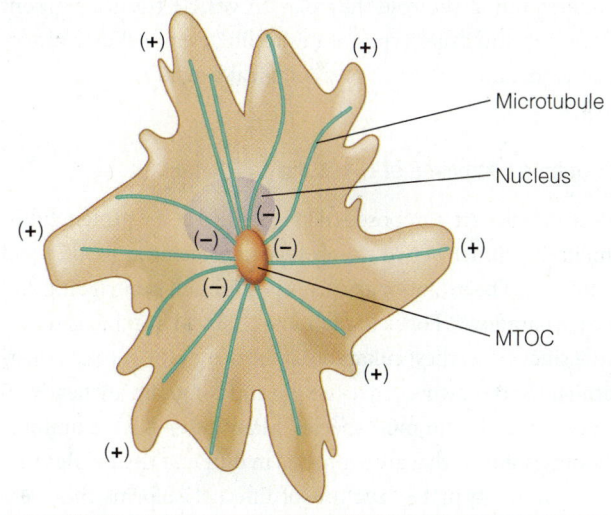

FIGURE 6.4 Movement of pigment granules
Melanophores from the African claw-toed frog *Xenopus* allow rapid changes in color. Arrays of microtubules radiating from the central MTOC carry pigment granules throughout the cell. Actin filaments, not shown here, also play a role in controlling local pigment distribution. Pigment granules aggregate in response to the hormone melatonin, and disperse in response to melanophore-stimulating hormone, MSH.

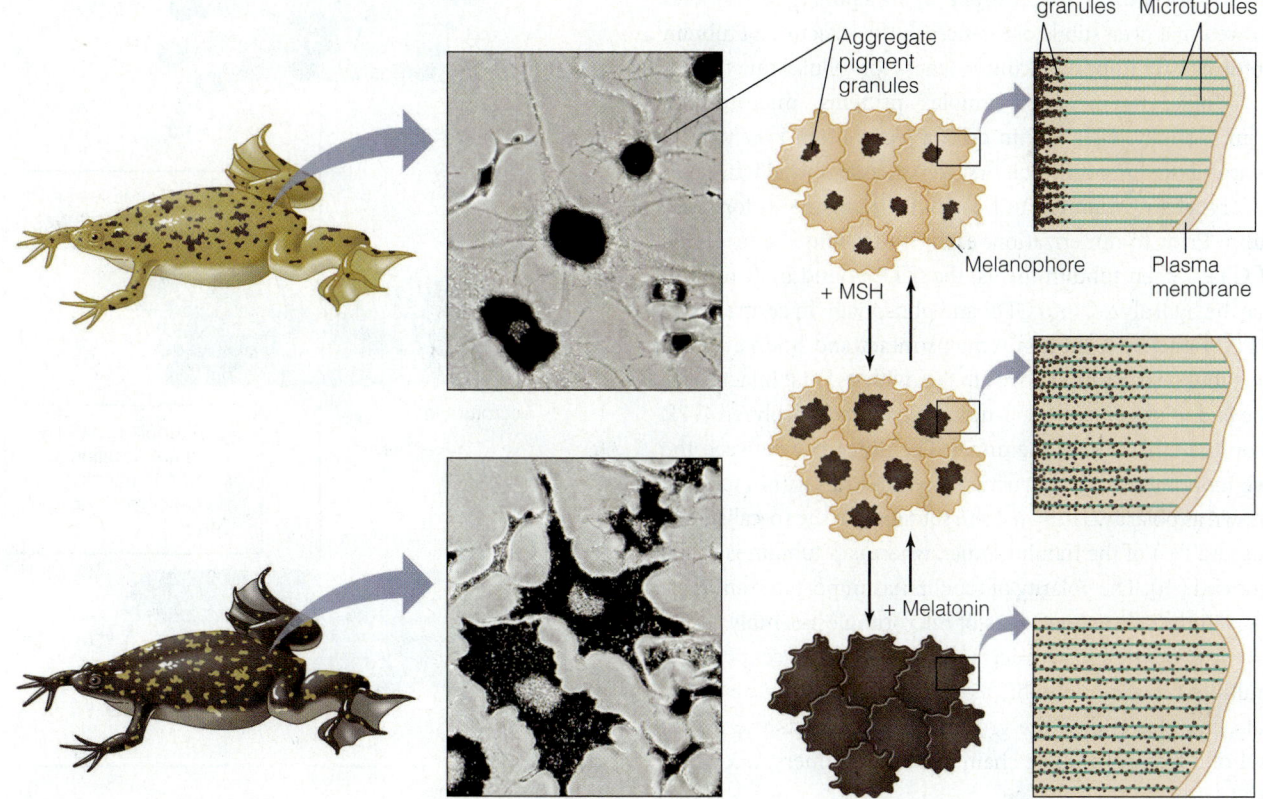

Figure source: Micrographs courtesy of V. Gelfand, University of Illinois.

directional movement of pigment granules along microtubule tracks within the melanophore, controlled and triggered by hormones, create adaptive coloration in animals. A closer look at how microtubules are built will lay the foundation for understanding the role they play in vesicle traffic, pigment dispersal, and other types of intracellular and cellular movements that are central to physiological function.

Tubulin is composed of α-tubulin and β-tubulin

Microtubules are composed of long strings of the protein tubulin, itself a dimer of two closely related proteins: α-tubulin and β-tubulin. The evolutionary history of tubulin is intriguing and rich in paradoxes. For example, tubulin genes have changed very little since the earliest eukaryotes. The α-tubulin of yeast is very similar to your own; even α-tubulin and β-tubulin are nearly 40 percent identical in most species. Many animals have multiple tubulin isoforms that are expressed in different tissues. Because of the similarity in the structures of different isoforms, they were believed to be interchangeable—for example, one α-tubulin isoform could be replaced with another α-tubulin isoform without obvious consequences. The importance of the subtle differences in tubulin structure between species, as well as within a species, has only recently been appreciated. In one instance, when nematodes (*C. elegans*) were genetically modified to express a different isoform of β-tubulin in their touch neurons, the mutant worms had sensory dysfunction. These studies showed that even subtle differences in the structure of tubulin isoforms have important consequences for cellular function.

Unlike many large, complex proteins, microtubules form spontaneously within cells, a feature that is central to microtubule function. The first step of assembly (Figure 6.5) occurs when α-tubulin and β-tubulin combine to form tubulin. Prior to dimerization, each subunit binds a molecule of GTP. When tubulin forms, the GTP bound by β-tubulin may be hydrolyzed into GDP and phosphate. In contrast, the GTP bound by α-tubulin remains intact and bound within the tubulin structure. The α-tubulin, with its GTP intact, is on one end of the dimer; the β-tubulin, with its hydrolyzed GTP, is on the other end of the dimer. The difference between the two monomers creates structural asymmetries within tubulin, known as polarity. The α-tubulin subunit is at the so-called minus end (−) of the tubulin dimer, whereas β-tubulin is at the plus end (+). The polarity of tubulin has important ramifications in the subsequent steps of microtubule assembly.

The next step in microtubule assembly occurs when multiple tubulins assemble end to end. Like a line of magnets, the plus end of the growing chain attracts the minus end of a free dimer. The chain of tubulin dimers, known as

FIGURE 6.5 Microtubule assembly

Microtubules are composed of repeating units of the protein tubulin, a dimer of two GTP-binding proteins, α-tubulin and β-tubulin. Tubulin dimers connect end to end to begin the construction of a protofilament. The protofilaments join side by side to start the formation of a sheet. Once the sheet reaches a critical width, it rolls into a tube to form the microtubules. Microtubules grow by adding tubulin and shrink by losing tubulin.

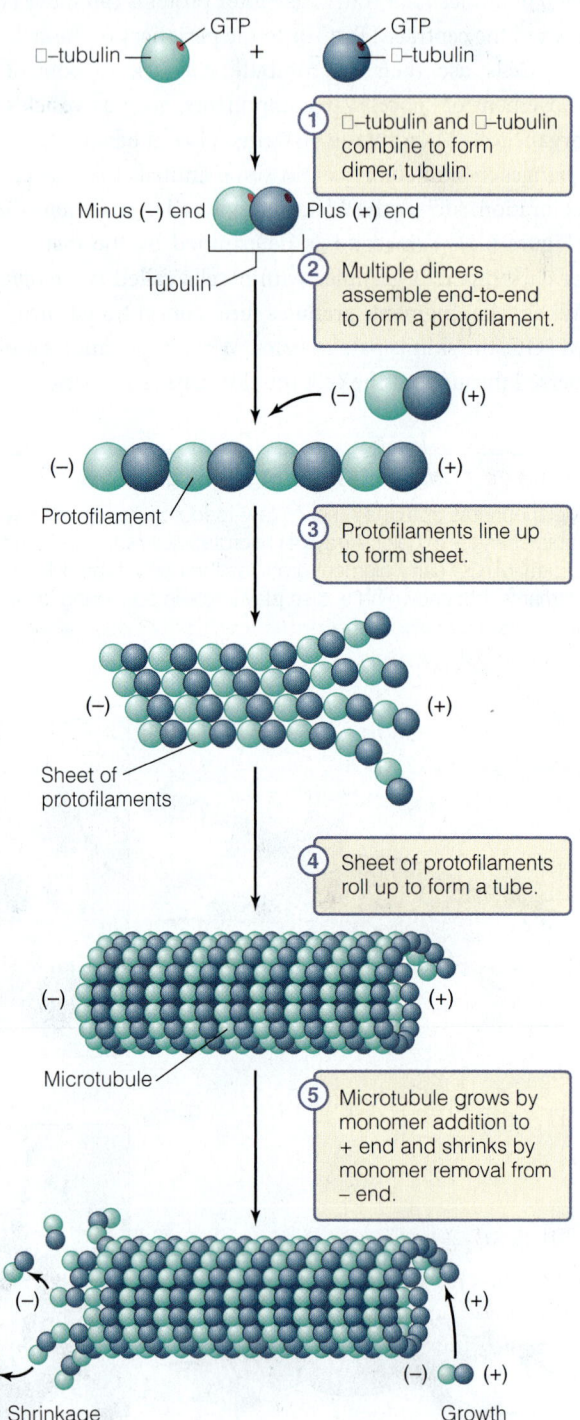

1. α–tubulin and β–tubulin combine to form dimer, tubulin.
2. Multiple dimers assemble end-to-end to form a protofilament.
3. Protofilaments line up to form sheet.
4. Sheet of protofilaments roll up to form a tube.
5. Microtubule grows by monomer addition to + end and shrinks by monomer removal from − end.

FIGURE 6.6 **Microtubule dynamics**

Whether a microtubule grows or shrinks depends on tubulin concentration. Below a critical concentration (C_c) the microtubule is more likely to shrink. Above C_c it will likely grow. Although both ends can add or lose tubulin, the plus end has a lower C_c. This means at any particular tubulin concentration, the plus end is more likely to grow than is the minus end.

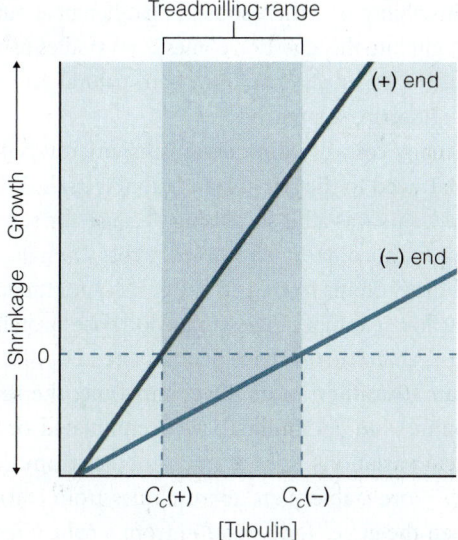

a **protofilament**, grows until it reaches a critical length. The protofilaments then line up side by side to form a sheet that eventually rolls into a tube to form the microtubule. Because the angle between adjacent protofilaments is about 28°, 13 protofilaments are required to form a complete tube. Once the microtubule is formed, it can continue to grow by incorporating more dimers, or it may shrink by shedding dimers.

Microtubules show dynamic instability

Microtubule dynamics, such as the rates of growth and shrinkage, regulate many cellular functions. The balance between growth and shrinkage determines the length of the microtubule (Figure 6.6). Many factors influence microtubule dynamics, but the most important is the local concentration of tubulin. If one end of the microtubule is exposed to a high concentration of tubulin, it will tend to grow. At low tubulin concentrations, however, microtubules tend to lose tubulin dimers and shrink. At a specific critical concentration (C_c), growth and shrinkage are in balance and there is no net change in length. However, several factors complicate this simple pattern of concentration-dependent regulation. First, the C_c value at the plus end is lower than at the minus end. This means that if *both ends* are exposed to the *same tubulin concentration*, the plus end is more likely to grow and

the minus end is more likely to shrink. However, if you were to follow the position of an individual tubulin dimer, you would see it move progressively from the plus end toward the minus end, a process called treadmilling. Some drugs disrupt microtubule dynamics by binding to free tubulin, preventing it from incorporating into microtubules, or binding to the microtubules, where they may disrupt polymerization or prevent depolymerization.

The second feature that distinguishes microtubule growth is known as dynamic instability. Even when the tubulin concentration exceeds C_c, the microtubule will grow for a few seconds, then spontaneously shrink for a few seconds. This concentration-independent transition is due to a change in the GTP bound by β-tubulin. Once incorporated into a microtubule, the β-tubulin subunit may or may not hydrolyze GTP. As long as the GTP in β-tubulin remains intact, the microtubule tends to grow. Alternatively, if the GTP is hydrolyzed, the microtubule will tend to shrink. Microtubules maintain their constant length by balancing growth and shrinkage, while hydrolyzing a lot of GTP in the process. This may at first seem to be a waste of the cell's energy, but it is a necessary cost. Dynamic instability, despite its energetic costs, enhances the ability of the cell to regulate microtubule growth in space and time. Systems in motion are much easier to alter than static systems.

Microtubule dynamics are also regulated by **microtubule-associated proteins**, or MAPs (Figure 6.7). These proteins bind to the surface of microtubules, stabilizing or destabilizing the microtubule structure. Some MAPs bind to the plus end of microtubules and prevent the transition from growth to shrinkage. A group of MAPs called stable-tubule only polypeptides, or STOPs, are used by many cell types that need long, stable microtubules. For instance, STOPs are abundant in nerves where microtubules are important for the development of long axons and dendrites. Other MAPs act as protein cross-linkers. MAPs can join microtubules together into bundles, or link the microtubules to other cellular structures, such as membrane receptors. However, not all MAPs stabilize microtubules. For example, katanin (Japanese for "sword") is a MAP that severs microtubules. Normal cell function depends on the regulation of both assembly and disassembly of microtubules. Preventing microtubules from dissociating impairs many cellular processes, including cell division.

The activities of MAPs are regulated by protein kinases and protein phosphatases. Changes in MAP phosphorylation can alter its subcellular location, change its ability to bind a microtubule, or alter its functional properties. Many signaling pathways target MAPs to alter microtubule structure. For example, the hormones that regulate cell division, known as cytokines, induce changes in microtubule structure by

Microtubules are connected to each other and to membrane proteins by microtubule-associated proteins, or MAPs.

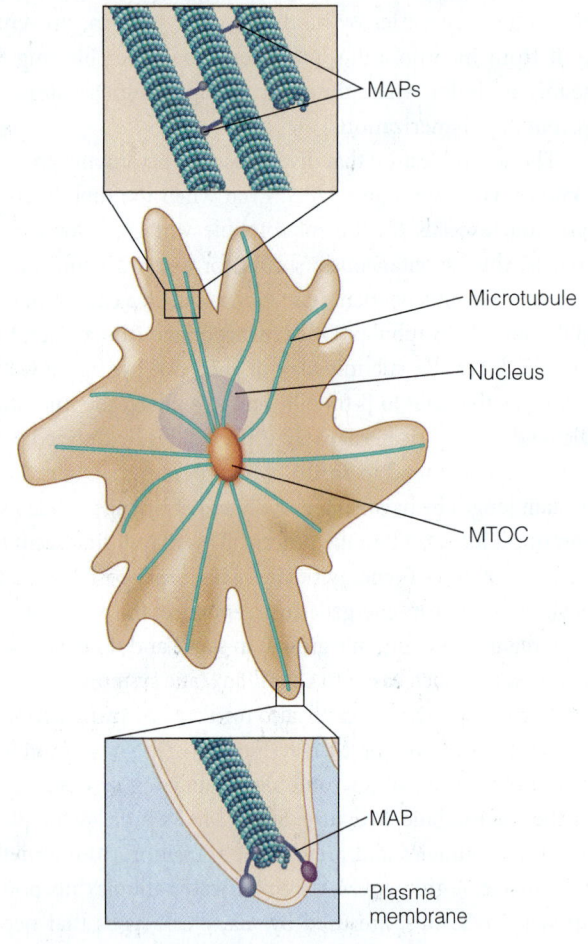

MAPs

Microtubule

Nucleus

MTOC

MAP

Plasma membrane

regulating the MAP structure and activity. The subsequent changes in the microtubule network ensure that cellular constituents are equally divided between daughter cells.

Chemicals that disrupt microtubule dynamics can be potent poisons, and many plants have evolved the ability to produce or concentrate microtubule poisons as feeding deterrents. Many of these microtubule toxins have been developed as therapeutic agents (see Box 6.1: Applications: Pharmaceutical Uses of Microtubule Disruptors).

Temperature is another parameter that affects microtubule dynamics. Early experiments showed that isolated microtubules could assemble and disassemble spontaneously in test tubes. When microtubules were cooled to 25°C, for example, they disassembled. Although this is a useful laboratory technique to study microtubule dynamics, what does it mean for animals? Temperature-induced disassembly is not physiologically relevant for most endothermic animals, such as mammals and birds, because they maintain body temperatures well above the threshold temperature. However, many ectothermic animals must endure temperatures low enough to disrupt the microtubules of a mammal.

The thermal instability of microtubules presents a conundrum. If mammalian microtubules spontaneously disassemble at 25°C, what is different about the microtubules of animals that live at even colder temperatures? Many mammalian tissues can stabilize microtubules using a number of microtubule-binding proteins, such as STOPs, MAPs, and capping proteins. Do cold-dwelling organisms use these same proteins to prevent thermal instability, or is there something different about tubulin itself? Insight into this question comes from studies using models in which differences arise from both natural selection and genetic engineering approaches.

For many cold-dwelling organisms, microtubule stability can be traced to the structure of tubulin itself. When first discovered, this was a bit surprising because the sequence of tubulin is extraordinarily conserved across animals. Isolated microtubule proteins from cold-water fish spontaneously assemble at lower temperatures than do those proteins from mammals. Antarctic fish have been isolated in polar seas for more than 10 million years. Over this time, the sequences of α-tubulins and β-tubulins have accumulated only a few amino acid variations, yet the microtubules from these fish are much more stable than microtubules from warm-water fish. When the genes for β-tubulin from a cold-tolerant cod were transfected into cultured human cells, the microtubules from the transgenic cells were stable in the cold. These studies show that very subtle differences in tubulin structure, even one or two amino acids, can result in profound differences in cold stability. Researchers studied microtubules produced by yeast in which the β-tubulin gene was subtly mutated; a single cysteine was mutated to alanine. This simple mutation made the microtubules cold stable. Unfortunately for the yeast, the structural changes that increased cold stability also dramatically impaired processes that depend on microtubule dynamic instability, such as growth and cell replication. These studies illustrate two important aspects of microtubules. First, microtubule function is critically dependent upon maintaining a dynamic balance between assembly and disassembly, or stability and instability. Second, even modest changes in microtubule structure, arising through evolution or genetic engineering, can produce a microtubule with very different properties. Whether these subtle mutations are adaptive or lethal depends on how the specific mutation affects the proteins, and how the structural change influences function in the context of environmental conditions.

Microtubule polarity determines the direction of movement

The extensive microtubule networks within cells provide a complex roadway for the motor proteins. But how do motor proteins identify which road to ride? Once on the road, how do they decide which way to go? Recall that the orientation of the dimers endows a microtubule with a structural polarity, where microtubules have a plus end and a minus end.

PHARMACEUTICAL USES OF MICROTUBULE DISRUPTORS

Many normal cellular processes incorporate reorganization of microtubules, and, not surprisingly, chemicals that disrupt microtubule dynamics have profound effects on cells. The most famous of the microtubule disruptors are each **alkaloids** that are thought to have evolved in plants to deter grazing. The Pacific yew tree (*Taxus*) produces taxol; the periwinkle plant (*Vinca*) produces vinblastine; and the autumn crocus (*Colchicum*) produces colchicine.

Because of their ability to affect microtubules, many of these plant defense agents have been developed as drugs to treat human ailments. The drugs influence different aspects of microtubule dynamics. When taxol, and its natural and synthetic relatives, binds to microtubules at a site on β-tubulin, it promotes polymerization and stabilization of the microtubule network. Vinblastine also binds the β-tubulin subunit, but suppresses microtubule dynamic action. At effective doses, it doesn't change the mass of microtubules, but prevents changes. Colchicine binds onto free tubulin and prevents microtubule growth, indirectly promoting depolymerization.

Each of these drugs affects microtubules, yet they differ profoundly in the types of applications they can treat. Each has proven useful in the lab as an agent to explore microtubule dynamics. Vinblastine and taxol are useful as anticancer drugs. Not only do they kill the rapidly dividing tumor cells by disrupting the changes in the mitotic spindle, they also kill the cells that line blood vessels, depriving tumors of blood flow. However, these two drugs affect different types of tumors: Taxol is effective against solid tumors of the breast and ovary, whereas vinblastine works best in blood cancers. By contrast, colchicine has limited antitumor properties, but it is effective against gout. Though each of these drugs targets microtubules, the diversity in effects can be attributed to differences between cell types in the many other proteins that regulate microtubule dynamics. In tumors, differences in sensitivity to these drugs relate to the ability of the cell to excrete the drug through ABC transporters (see Chapter 3).

Though this feature focuses on the utility of drugs that target microtubules, it is also fascinating to consider what may be different in those few animals that can feed on plants that are toxic enough to rapidly kill most grazers. *Vinca*, for example, is eaten by fluid-feeding insects, such as aphids and white flies. There are many anecdotes about herbivores such as cattle and moose feeding on ornamental yew bushes, then promptly dropping dead. However, white-tail deer are an established pest of the species; the gut bacteria of deer may degrade the toxins before they can affect the animal.

Further Reading

- Yue, Q.-X., Liu, X., & Guo, D.-A. (2010). Microtubule-binding natural products for cancer therapy. *Planta Medica 76*, 1037–1043.
- Dumontet, C., & Jordan, M. A. (2010). Microtubule-binding agents: A dynamic field of cancer therapeutics. *Nature Reviews Drug Discovery, 9*, 790–803.

Because cells organize microtubules by collecting the minus ends at the MTOC, the plus ends are found at the periphery. Motor proteins recognize microtubule polarity, and each motor protein moves in a characteristic direction; **kinesin** moves along the microtubule in the plus direction, whereas **dynein** moves in the minus direction.

The polarity of the microtubules and the directional movement of the motor proteins allow cells to transport cargo to the right place. Consider how a neuron uses this network to transport neurotransmitter vesicles (Figure 6.8). Kinesin can pick up vesicles filled with neurotransmitters in the cell body, and walk along microtubules toward the plus ends at the synapse. Once the vesicles release their neurotransmitters, endocytosis returns empty vesicles to the cell. Dynein then carries the endocytic vesicle to the cell body, moving along the microtubule toward the minus end. This simple example illustrates why directional movements of neurosecretory vesicles are necessary for nerve function.

Most cells possess countless types of vesicles that need to be transported to many locations. How do cells ensure that each of these diverse vesicles goes to the correct location? At least part of the answer lies in the structural diversity of motor proteins themselves. Large gene families encode multiple isoforms of kinesin, dynein, and their respective regulatory proteins. Each combination of isoforms imparts different transport characteristics.

Kinesin and dynein move along microtubules

Although kinesin and dynein are unrelated proteins, they work in similar ways. Both undergo conformational changes, where they stretch out to grab a tubulin dimer, then bend to pull themselves along the microtubule. Likewise, in both, the structural changes in the motor protein are fueled by ATP hydrolysis, the rate of movement of kinesin and dynein along the microtubule is determined primarily by the ATPase

FIGURE 6.8   **Vesicle traffic in a neuron**
Vesicle traffic depends on the polarity of the microtubules. Kinesin carries vesicles of neurotransmitters to the synapse, whereas dynein carries empty vesicles back to the MTOC.

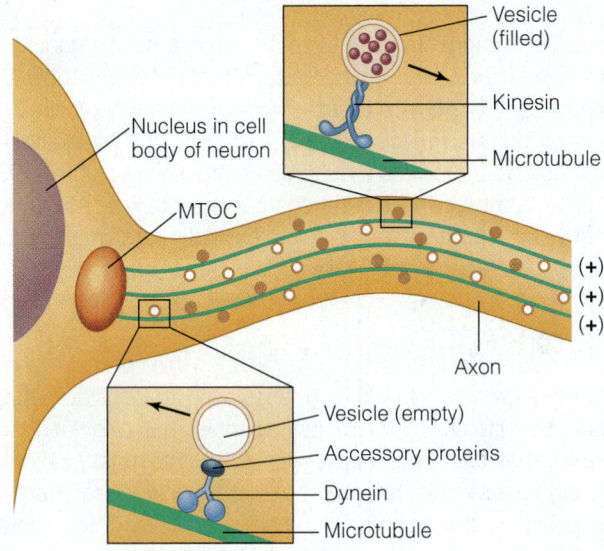

dyneins are dimers of two identical subunits (heavy chains) with a number of associated smaller proteins. **Axonemal dyneins** are the driving force behind movements generated by cilia and flagella.

Cilia and flagella are composed of microtubules

Cilia and flagella are similar structures with diverse roles in animal physiology. For example, flagella propel sperm toward the egg, while cilia allow epithelial cells to push mucus over the cell surface, as occurs in the respiratory tract.

Cilia differ from flagella in their arrangement and the way they move. Flagella normally occur singly or in pairs, whereas cilia are more abundant. In addition, flagella move in a whiplike manner, whereas cilia move with a wavelike motion. Microtubules in cilia and flagella are arranged into a structure called an **axoneme,** which is wrapped in an extension of the plasma membrane in the form of a membranous sheath.

A cross-section through a flagellum reveals a structure that resembles a wagon wheel (Figure 6.9). At the hub of the wheel are two single microtubules interconnected by a protein bridge. Around the edge are nine pairs of microtubules or doublets, connected to each other by the protein nexin. Protein spokes then radiate from the two singlets toward the nine doublets. Almost 10 years before microtubules were first identified, this "nine + two" arrangement in axonemes was understood to underlie the structure of all flagella and cilia seen in animals.

How does dynein power microtubule movement in cilia and flagella? Each doublet has a series of dynein motors that are attached to one doublet, extending their heads toward the neighboring doublet. At rest, the dynein sits inactive in this structure. When the cell receives a signal, protein kinases phosphorylate critical proteins associated with dynein to activate the ATPase. Once activated, dynein walks along the neighboring microtubule toward the minus end of the microtubule located at the base of the axoneme. The waving of cilia and whipping of flagella result from asymmetric activation of dyneins on opposing sides of the axoneme. When dyneins on one side of the axoneme are activated, the tip of the flagellum bends in that direction. These cycles of activation and inactivation of dynein along the entire length of the axoneme generate movement. If all of the dyneins were activated simultaneously, no movement would occur.

domain of the proteins, and regulatory proteins that associate with the motor protein control the rate of movement. Despite these similarities, kinesin and dynein have important differences that affect how cells use them to move along microtubules.

Let's first consider the structure and function of kinesin. Each kinesin molecule has a long neck, a fanlike tail, and a globular head that possesses ATPase activity. The tail is responsible for attaching to cargo, whereas the head attaches to the microtubule. Phylogenetic analyses have revealed a very large and diverse family of kinesins. Some members of the kinesin superfamily are active as monomers. Other kinesins assemble into dimers, either homodimers or heterodimers. These kinesin dimers may in turn interact with regulatory proteins called kinesin-associated proteins. Some kinesin-associated proteins can alter the kinetics of movement, such as the rate of ATP hydrolysis, while some influence the type of cargo kinesin binds. Many of these kinesin-associated proteins are themselves members of multigene families, which enable cells to fine-tune microtubule-based movements.

Like kinesin, dynein has a globular head, a neck, and a tail. The head has ATPase activity and mediates binding to the microtubule. Dynein is larger than kinesin, and can move along microtubules about five times faster. Unlike kinesin, dynein does not attach directly to its cargo. Instead, this interaction is mediated by large multiprotein complexes of accessory proteins, providing another layer of regulation of microtubule movement. The many isoforms of dyneins fall into two classes: cytoplasmic and axonemal. *Cytoplasmic*

CONCEPT CHECK

1. Which motor proteins work with microtubules?
2. Which plant alkaloids disrupt animal cytoskeleton function? What do they do for the plants? Why might they have no effect on the cytoskeleton in the plants?

Structure of the flagellum

The tail of a sperm is constructed from microtubules arranged into a complex network called an axoneme. The core structure is composed of nine doublets of microtubules, connected by the linker protein nexin. Radial spokes extend from this outer ring toward a central pair of single microtubules. Dynein arms extend from one doublet to the adjacent doublet.

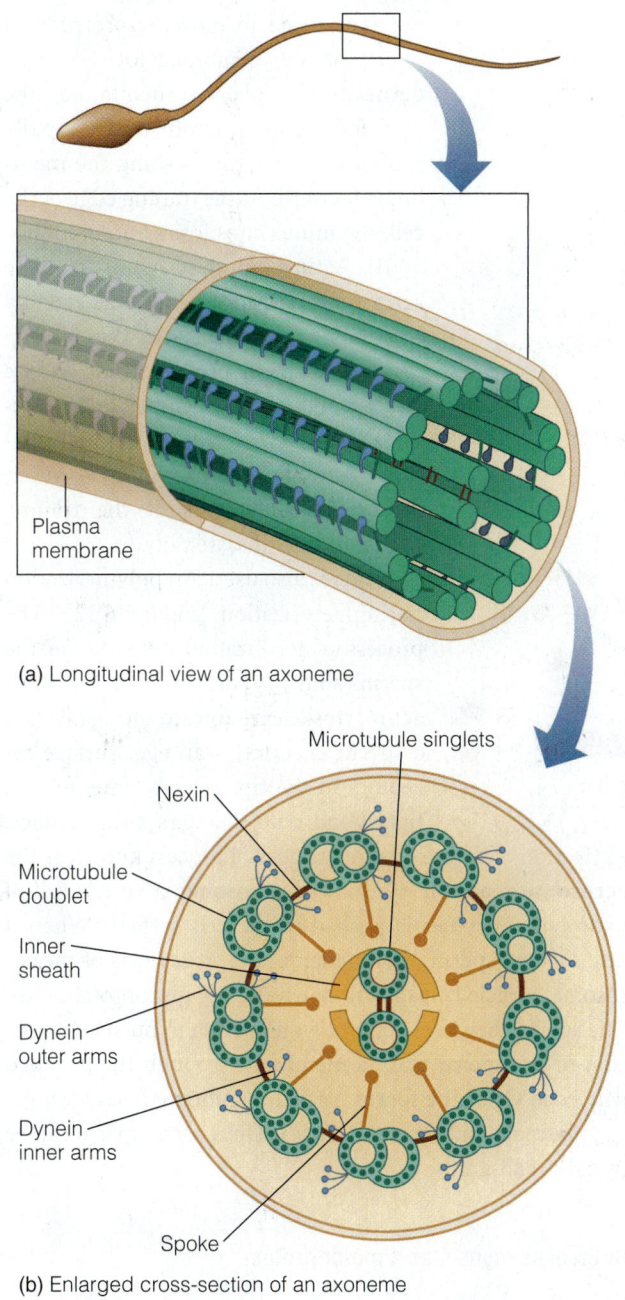

(a) Longitudinal view of an axoneme

(b) Enlarged cross-section of an axoneme

Microfilaments

Microfilaments are the other type of cytoskeletal fiber used in movement. Like microtubules, microfilaments play important roles in the transport of vesicles throughout cells.

In addition, microfilament-based movement also allows cells to change shape and move from place to place. The elements of microfilament-based movement, actin and its motor protein myosin, are found in all eukaryotic cells; the organization of these elements enables diverse types of cellular movement. In some cases, cellular movement arises simply from the polymerization of actin. More often, however, actin-based movement involves the motor protein myosin. Let's look at the many ways in which microfilaments drive movement.

Microfilaments are polymers of actin

Microfilaments are composed of long strings of the protein actin. These actin monomers are called *G-actin*, because of the globular structure of the protein. When G-actin assembles into filaments, however, it is referred to as *F-actin* (Figure 6.10). As with microtubules, microfilaments have an intrinsic polarity that is linked to the organization of the monomers. Actin can spontaneously assemble and disassemble without an energy investment. It polymerizes spontaneously when its concentration is above a threshold critical concentration, C_c. Each actin filament can grow from both plus and minus ends, but growth is six to ten times faster at the plus end. If the growth at the plus end exactly balances the shrinkage at the minus end, the total length of the microfilament is constant. As with microtubules, actin filaments can undergo treadmilling; if you were to follow the position of an individual actin monomer, you would see it move progressively from the plus end toward the minus end. As with microtubules, accessory proteins can modulate the rate of microfilament growth. One way that a cell increases the length of a microfilament is by stabilizing the minus end, preventing it from disassembling. To do that, cells use capping proteins that bind on the end of microfilaments to stabilize the structure.

Cells can arrange microfilaments in many ways, often with the help of actin-binding proteins that cross-link microfilaments (Figure 6.11). Microfilaments can be arranged in tangled networks, linked together by long, flexible actin-binding proteins such as filamin, or aligned in parallel into stiff bundles, cross-linked by short actin-binding proteins such as fascin. Actin bundles run throughout the cell, providing support. In some instances, these stiff actin fibers push the margins of the cell outward. For example, they provide the foundation for microvilli, the fingerlike extensions of digestive epithelia. Whether actin forms long, unbranched filaments or highly branched filaments is determined by the relative levels of formin and actin-related protein (ARP). The bundles and networks of microfilaments comprising the actin cytoskeleton are connected to the plasma membrane by specific anchoring proteins such as dystrophin.

FIGURE 6.10 Structure of actin and microfilaments

G-actin monomers join together to initiate the formation of F-actin. After this process of nucleation, the microfilament elongates by incorporating more G-actin into the plus end. Growth is more favorable at the plus end, and the minus end is more likely to lose monomers. This pattern results in the process called treadmilling, where an individual monomer (shown in purple) travels down the length of the filament, from + to −, even if the total length remains constant. If the minus end of the microfilament is stabilized, by a capping protein for instance, the microfilaments can lengthen.

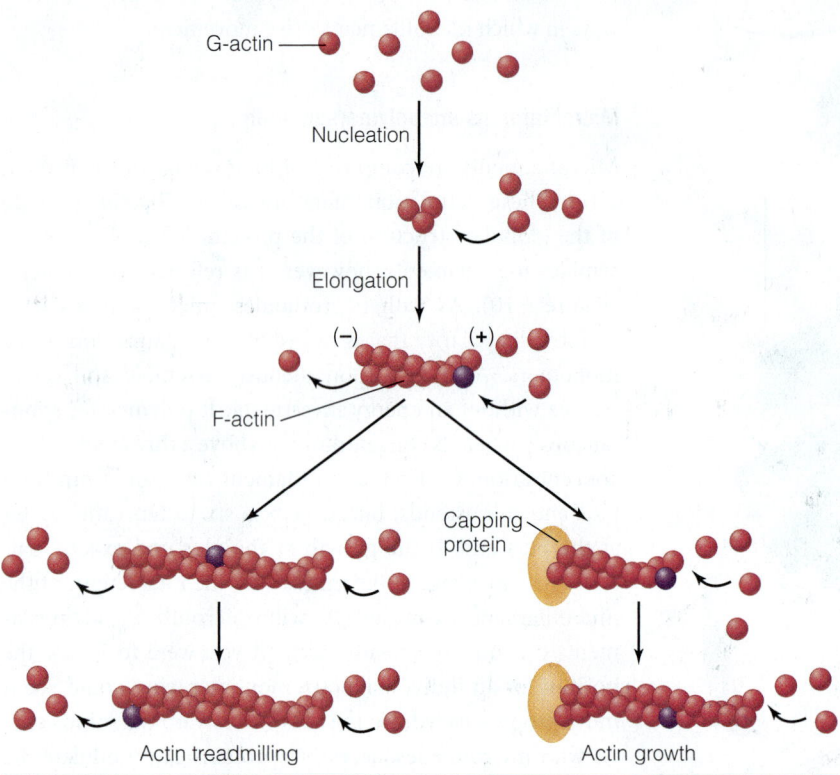

Actin polymerization can generate movement

Although most types of microfilament-based movement rely on myosin, the actual polymerization of actin can mediate some forms of movement. Though biologists do not yet fully understand how it works, actin polymerization is important in two kinds of amoeboid movement in animals. **Filopodia** are thin rodlike extensions of cells formed by actin fibers. Cells build filopodia for many purposes. For example, nerve cells use filopodia to make physical contact with neighboring cells, which is an important step in the embryonic development of the nervous system. Digestive epithelia use filopodia to build microvilli, protrusions that increase the surface area of the plasma membrane. In contrast, some metazoan cells move using actin-based extensions called lamellipodia. **Lamellipodia** resemble the pseudopodia found in protists, but they are thinner and more sheetlike. The nature of the amoeboid protrusions in animals depends upon how the newly synthesized microfilaments are integrated into fibers. Filopodia result when the microfilaments are limited to simple fibers. Lamellipodia arise from sheetlike networks of microfilaments.

In a stationary cell, the actin network extends around the cell's periphery, attached at many points to plasma membrane receptors, forming a structure called the cell cortex. When this cell is induced to move, it protrudes a region of the membrane forward. Underneath the plasma membrane, the plus ends of the microfilaments rapidly incorporate G-actin, pushing the membrane forward. At the trailing edge of the cell, the minus ends lose G-actin monomers. Actin-binding proteins regulate actin polymerization, and consequently amoeboid movement. At the leading edge, the protein profilin binds to free G-actin monomers, helping them integrate into the plus end of the microfilament. Another protein, cofilin, however, breaks microfilaments at the trailing edge to trigger disassembly.

Sperm also use actin polymerization during fertilization (Figure 6.12). The process of fertilization depends on the sperm's ability to control the growth of its actin cytoskeleton toward the egg. When a sperm encounters an egg, surface receptors in the tip, or acrosome, form a tight bond with the egg's outer surface. Activation of these receptors triggers a process known as the **acrosome reaction**. Within the **acrosome**, a vesicle full of hydrolytic enzymes is pushed to the cell surface. When it binds to the sperm plasma membrane, exocytosis of the acrosomal vesicle helps break down the egg glycoprotein coat. The sperm then uses actin polymerization to push an extension of the sperm plasma membrane through the softened jelly coat. Once the sperm plasma membrane fuses with the egg plasma membrane, the nuclear DNA of the sperm can be transferred into the egg.

Actin uses myosin as a motor protein

Although some cells use actin polymerization to generate movement, in most situations microfilaments are used in combination with myosin. Different arrangements of actin and myosin enable cells to transport vesicles and organelles, change shape, and even move from place to place. As was the case with microtubule-based movements, diversity in both the motor protein and associated regulatory proteins provides cells with the regulatory precision needed to control

FIGURE 6.11 Actin networks

Actin microfilaments can be arranged in many different conformations, often using cross-linking proteins for stabilization. Microfilaments can grow from their plus ends, causing cellular extensions. Actin bundles form when parallel arrays are cross-linked together.

The microfilaments can be attached to integral membrane proteins by cross-linking proteins such as dystrophin. Actin can also be arranged into complex networks stabilized by cross-linking proteins such as filamin and fascin.

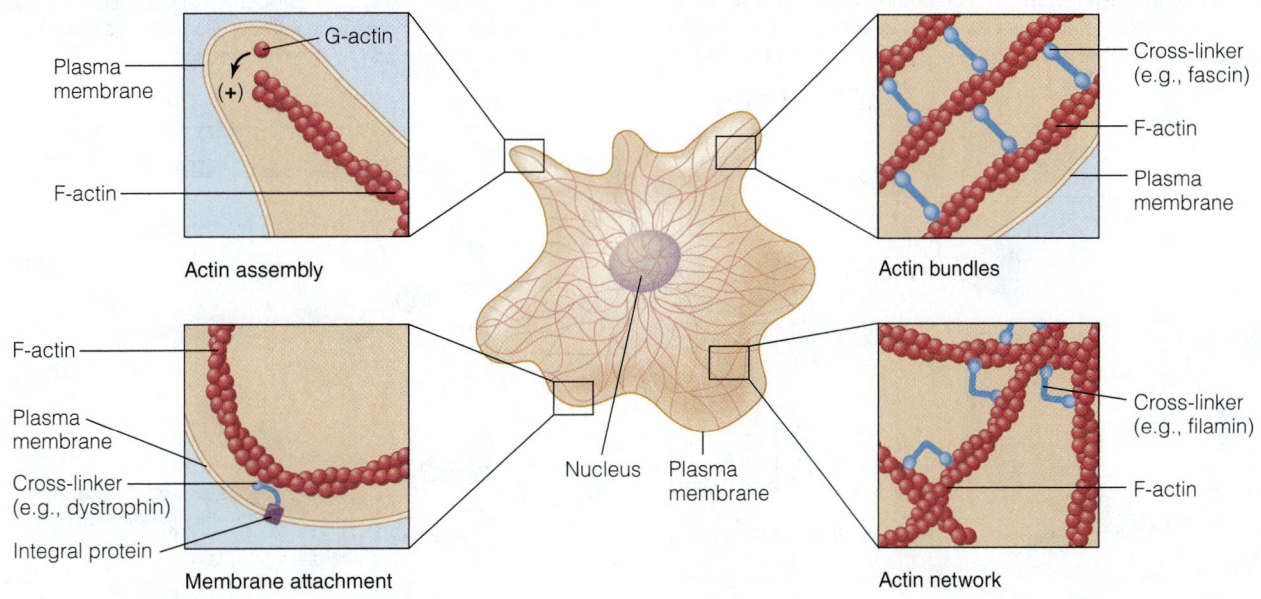

intracellular traffic. Many aspects of actin- and myosin-based movement are similar throughout eukaryotes. For example, muscle uses a unique arrangement of actin and myosin, in combination with novel isoforms of myosin and its regulatory proteins. Let's begin by examining myosin structure and consider how it controls movement.

The myosin gene family of eukaryotes is very large, with at least 17 different classes of myosins (I–XVII) distinguished by differences in their structural properties. The most common myosins studied in animals are in classes I, II, and V. Myosin II is sometimes called **muscle myosin**, although it also occurs in nonmuscle tissues. Myosins I and V are most important in intracellular traffic. Most animals possess multiple isoforms of myosins within each class, adding to the repertoire of myosin functions available in animal cells.

Despite their structural differences, each myosin isoform shares a general organization, with a head, a tail, and a neck (Figure 6.13). The head possesses ATPase activity, which provides the energy for movement. The tail allows myosin to bind cargo, such as vesicles, organelles, or even the plasma membrane. In addition, the tail structure of some myosin isoforms can cause the individual myosin proteins to assemble into dimers. Whereas myosin I remains as a monomer, both myosin II and myosin V normally dimerize. The neck regulates the activity of the myosin head directly, and also mediates the effects of proteins that associate with the neck, known as **myosin light chains**. Myosin II, for example,

has two different myosin light chains: an essential light chain and a regulatory light chain. Myosin light chains are regulated by reversible phosphorylation. Phosphorylation by **myosin light chain kinase (MLCK)** may alter the catalytic activity of the myosin head or induce a structural change that permits myosin to interact with actin. Many of the hormones and other signaling factors that regulate myosin function target either MLCK or **myosin light chain phosphatase (MLCP)**, which dephosphorylates the myosin light chain.

The sliding filament model describes actino-myosin activity

Despite the great diversity in myosin, the basic mechanism that defines its interaction with microfilaments is shared by all isoforms. Myosin, like all the motor proteins we have discussed, is an ATPase that converts the energy released from ATP hydrolysis into mechanical energy. To understand this process we must consider both the chemical events associated with the enzymatic head of the myosin, as well as the structural changes throughout the myosin that culminate in movement. The two processes are integrated in the **sliding filament model**. This general model, first proposed almost 70 years ago by Hugh Huxley, shows how a myosin head walks along an actin polymer. This model can be used to explain all the different types of movement mediated by myosin. For example, a model involving a single myosin can be used to describe vesicular transport. The sliding filament model can also be used

FIGURE 6.12   Acrosome of sperm

Once the sperm finds the egg, activation of membrane receptors in the sperm triggers the exocytosis of the acrosomal vesicle and the polymerization of microfilaments. The acrosomal enzymes help dissolve the physical barriers around the egg. The growing microfilaments push the sperm membrane through the jelly coat into contact with the egg plasma membrane. After membrane fusion, the sperm DNA moves into the egg to complete fertilization.

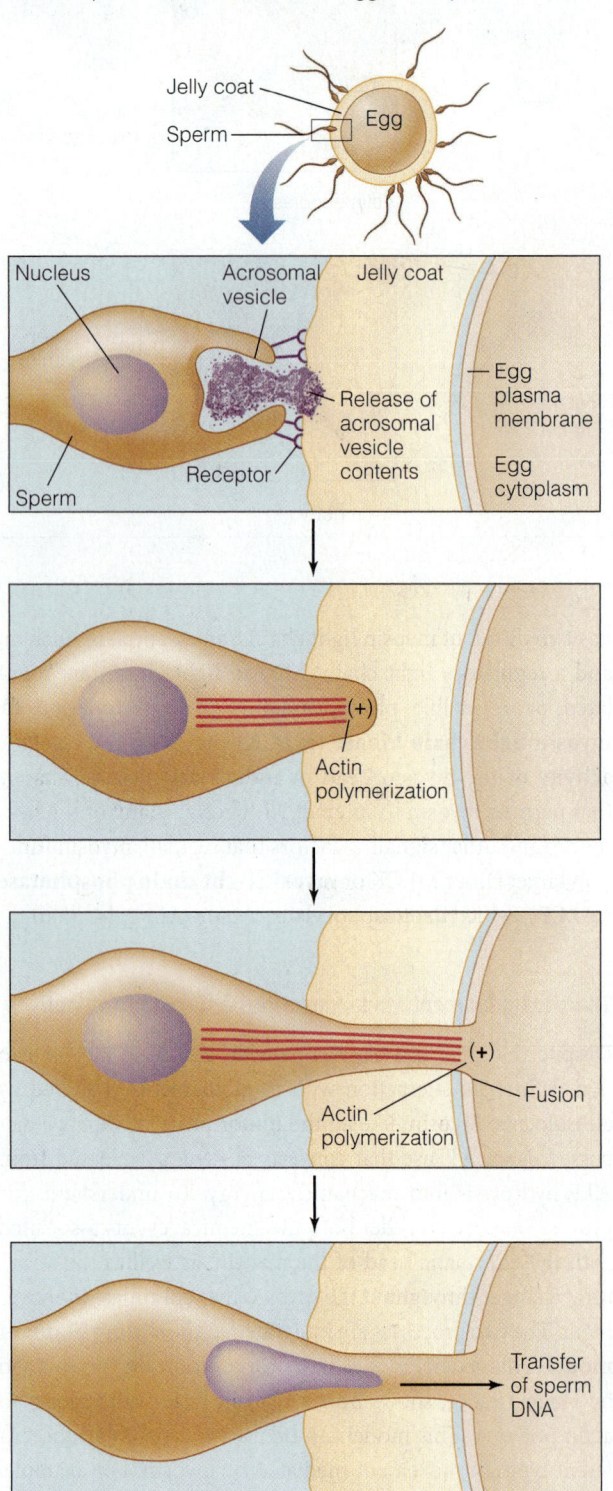

FIGURE 6.13   Myosin structures

Each myosin isoform possesses a catalytic head, a regulatory neck, and a tail region that interacts with other proteins. Regulatory proteins, such as light chains and calmodulin, can bind the neck region. Differences in structures of myosin and its regulatory proteins account for the specific properties of each isoform. Myosins I and V are used primarily in intracellular traffic. Myosin II is involved in cytokinesis and muscle contraction.

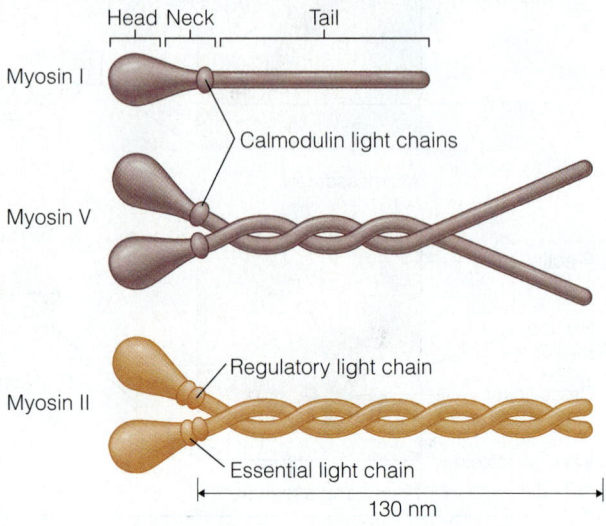

to describe how myosin and actin interact during muscle contraction, discussed later in this chapter.

Many of the principles explained by the sliding filament model can be illustrated through the following analogy. Imagine a rope stretching across the floor of a room, attached to the wall. Now think about how you would pull yourself across the room using your arm. You start by extending your arm forward to grasp the rope, then bend your extended arm, pulling yourself forward. Next, you release the rope, extend your arm, grasp the rope again, and bend your arm. As you make your way across the room, your arm undergoes cycles of extension, grasping, and bending. Although each part of the cycle costs energy, the most demanding step in the cycle is when you bend your arm to pull yourself forward. In the sliding filament model, myosin acts very much like your arm, and actin is the equivalent of the rope. The myosin molecule extends by straightening its neck, pushing the head forward. The myosin head then forms a bond with actin, just as your hand grasps the rope. This strong interaction between myosin and actin is called a **cross-bridge**. Myosin bends, pulling the actin toward its tail. This step is called the **power stroke**. The cross-bridge cycle includes the formation of the cross-bridge, the power stroke, and the return to the resting, unattached position.

The mechanical changes in the cross-bridge cycle are driven by chemical and structural changes occurring within the myosin catalytic head (Figure 6.14). As previously discussed, myosin is an ATPase; the breakdown of ATP provides the energy for the mechanical changes. At the beginning of the cycle, myosin is tightly bound to actin and the ATP binding site is empty. If no ATP is available, the myosin remains firmly attached. However, once ATP binds, myosin loses its affinity for actin, and the cross-bridge is broken. Release of actin activates the myosin ATPase to break ATP down to ADP and phosphate. The hydrolysis of ATP causes myosin to extend forward to grasp further up the actin microfilament. (Although the ATP molecule within the myosin head has been chemically changed to ADP and phosphate, the energy that had been stored within the ATP remains stored within the myosin head as an energy-rich conformation.) Once myosin binds again, it first releases phosphate and then ADP. Upon phosphate release, myosin uses the stored energy to pull the actin microfilament in the power stroke. The myosin head remains attached to the actin until another ATP molecule finds its empty nucleotide-binding site and the cycle repeats. If no

ATP is available, myosin remains firmly attached to actin, creating a condition known as **rigor**. When an animal dies, the ATP levels decline and muscles become locked in *rigor mortis*.

The actual movement that happens within the cell during a cross-bridge cycle depends upon the structural arrangements of actin and myosin, specifically which of the two is free to move. Returning to our earlier analogy, if the rope is tied to the wall, your arms pull you across the room. However, if the rope is not attached to the wall, your arm actions move the rope. Within the cell, actino-myosin movement depends on which of the elements, actin or myosin, is immobilized. If the actin microfilament is immobile, then myosin walks along the microfilament. This is analogous to myosin carrying a vesicle throughout the cell. Conversely, if myosin is immobile, the actin filament moves. In some cases, myosin is attached to the plasma membrane; in this situation, cross-bridge cycling pulls the actin microfilament over the surface of the plasma membrane. This arrangement allows cells to change shape. We will consider a third scenario

---

FIGURE 6.14 Sliding filament model

In this figure, we follow a single myosin head as it progresses through a cross-bridge cycle. In the absence of ATP, the myosin head remains attached to the microfilament. Once ATP binds (step 1), myosin releases the microfilament. ATP hydrolysis induces myosin to extend toward the plus end of the microfilament (step 2), although the energy remains trapped in the myosin head.

Upon release of the phosphate, the stored energy is used to bend myosin, pulling the filament back in the power stroke (step 3). Once the movement is complete, ADP is released (step 4) and the ATP binding site remains vacant until ATP binds to initiate another cross-bridge cycle.

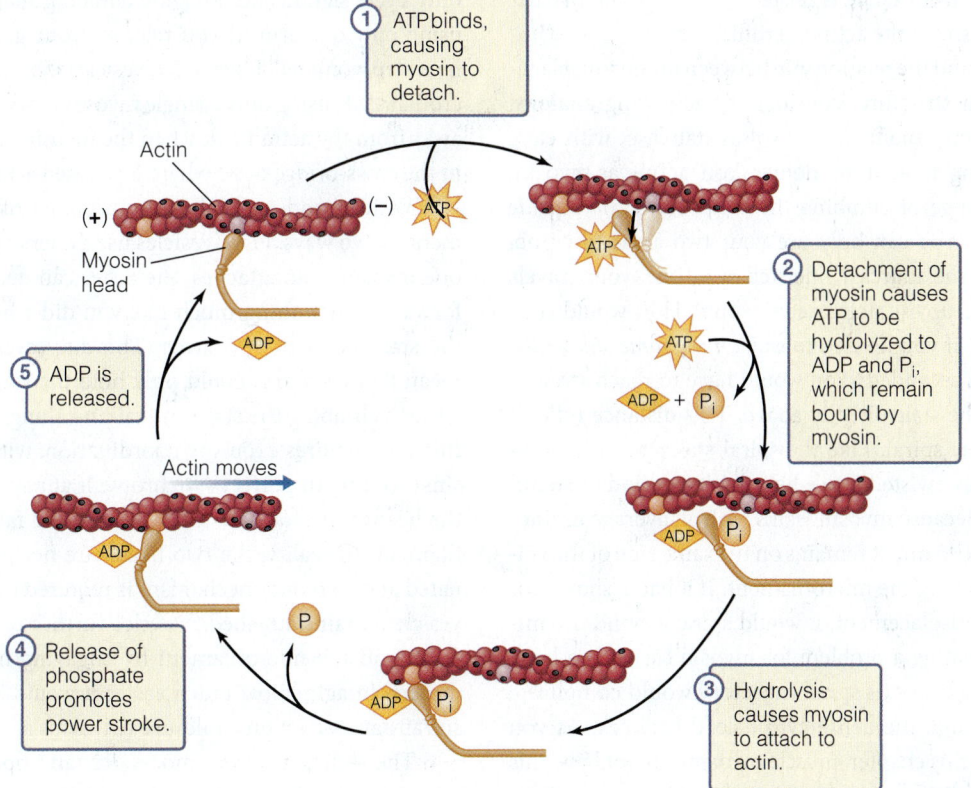

1 ATP binds, causing myosin to detach.

2 Detachment of myosin causes ATP to be hydrolyzed to ADP and P_i, which remain bound by myosin.

3 Hydrolysis causes myosin to attach to actin.

4 Release of phosphate promotes power stroke.

5 ADP is released.

Actin
Myosin head
(+) (−)
Actin moves

later in this chapter when we discuss how the sliding filament model applies in muscle, where both the actin and myosin are organized into a three-dimensional superstructure. The various muscles differ in terms of the event that initiates the actino-myosin activity, but the basic cross-bridge cycling is similar among all actin and myosin interactions.

Myosin activity is influenced by unitary displacement and duty cycle

The sliding filament model provides the context for understanding two features of actino-myosin–based movement: duty cycle and unitary displacement. These properties are most easily understood using the myosins involved in intracellular trafficking as an example.

Unitary displacement corresponds to the distance myosin steps during each cross-bridge cycle. Returning to our rope-pulling analogy, the unitary displacement is the distance you are able to move with each cycle of release, extend, grasp, and pull. In this analogy, the unitary displacement depends on the length of one's arm. With myosin, the step size depends on the length of the neck. Optical studies show that the actual distance moved with each step is not fixed; for example, the unitary displacement of a myosin V monomer may range anywhere from 5 nm to a maximum distance of about 20 nm. The myosin V dimer uses both of its monomers in tandem, walking along actin with an average unitary displacement of about 36 nm. This distance is related to an important structural characteristic of the actin microfilament.

To understand the relationship between unitary displacement and actin structure, consider the following analogy. Think of the actin filament as a spiral staircase, with each step representing an actin monomer. You, acting as myosin, have the challenge of climbing the stairs from the *outside of the staircase*. You can only use your two arms to climb. If you climbed the staircase one step at a time, your travels would carry you up the staircase in a spiral. How would your strategy change if you needed to stay *on the same side of the staircase* as you ascended? You would have to reach straight up as high as the stair directly above. This distance reflects the *period* of the spiral. Like the spiral staircase, microfilaments are spirals, twisted into a helix with a period of 36 nm (Figure 6.15). Because myosin walks with an average unitary displacement of 36 nm, it remains on the same side of the spiral as it travels along the microfilament. If it had a shorter or longer unitary displacement, it would spiral around the microfilament, creating a problem for myosin carrying a large vesicle or organelle, as its spiral trajectory would complicate movement through the dense cytoskeletal network. As you will see later in this chapter, muscle myosins do not have this 36-nm unitary displacement; nonetheless, they avoid these problems in other ways.

FIGURE 6.15   **Unitary displacement**

Myosin V walks along the actin filament in steps of about 36 nm, which corresponds to the period of the actin filament.

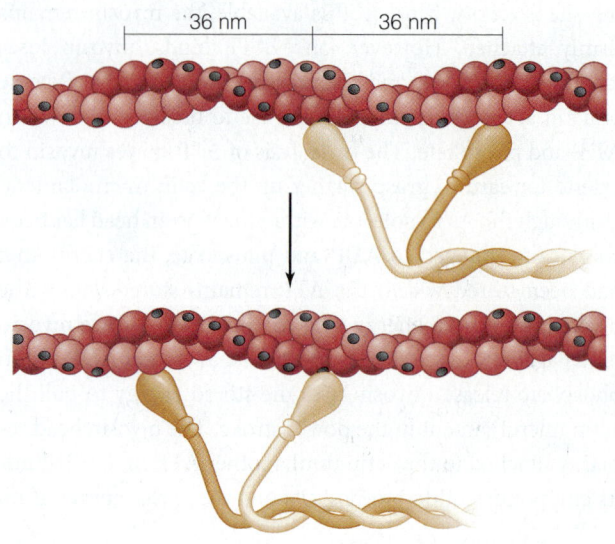

The second parameter that describes myosin activity is **duty cycle**, the proportion of time in each cross-bridge cycle that myosin is attached to actin. Most nonmuscle myosins have duty cycles of about 0.5. This means that myosin is tightly bound to actin for only half of each cross-bridge cycle. Why is duty cycle significant? Imagine climbing that spiral staircase using only one arm. If you released your grasp to reach the next step, you'd fall. Likewise, if vesicles were carried along microfilaments using only a single myosin head, they would float away from the actin track when the myosin reached the point in the cross-bridge cycle where it released actin.

Vesicles and organelles avoid falling off the microfilament in two ways. First, vesicles use dimers of myosin. When one myosin head attaches, the other can detach and extend forward, functioning much like you did when you climbed the staircase with two arms. The duty cycle of 0.5 would mean that each arm could only hold the stair half the time. Clearly, climbing the stairs or walking along a microfilament this way requires exquisite coordination, with the two myosins working in perfect synchrony. If at any point neither of the heads was attached, the vesicle would fall off the microfilament. In reality, the two heads are not perfectly coordinated and a second mechanism is required to ensure that the vesicle remains attached. Vesicles further reduce the risk of falling off the microfilament by engaging multiple myosin dimers. Imagine how much easier it would be to climb that spiral staircase if you could use two arms as well as two legs.

The sliding filament model was an important advancement in our understanding of how myosin moves along actin. Its general features apply to most types of actino-myosin

Table 6.2 Actin and myosin function in animal physiology

Cellular Process	Physiological Function
Vesicle transport	Hormones and cell signaling: Microfilaments carry hormones, neurotransmitters, and neurohormones from sites of synthesis to sites of release.
Microvilli	Digestion: Actin supports the fingerlike extensions of the cells of the intestinal epithelium.
Amoeboid movement	Immunology: White blood cells use amoeboid movement to invade damaged tissue.
Skeletal muscle contraction	Locomotion: Muscles provide the contractile force for movement. Respiratory physiology: Trunk muscles help move air over the respiratory surface.
Cardiac muscle contraction	Circulatory physiology: Cardiac muscles pump blood.
Smooth muscle contraction	Circulatory physiology: Vascular smooth muscle controls the diameter of blood vessels. Digestion: Visceral smooth muscle forces food down the intestinal lumen.

activity in all eukaryotes. However, the exact values of duty cycle, unitary displacement, and other kinetic features of **actinomyosin** change in different situations. For example, the kinetics differ depending on whether myosin and actin are immobilized or free to move. The mechanical properties of actinomyosin influence the enzymatic features, and vice versa.

Actin and myosin perform diverse and important functions in animal cells (Table 6.2). Many of their responsibilities in animal cells are little different from their roles in other eukaryotes. Over hundreds of millions of years, animals evolved novel isoforms of myosin, and arranged actin and myosin in different ways, providing the foundation for a specialized contractile tissue: muscle.

> ### CONCEPT CHECK
>
> 3. What factors influence the assembly and disassembly of microtubules and microfilaments?
> 4. What is meant by polarity with respect to microfilaments and microtubules? Why is it important to structure and function?

▌ MUSCLE

Earlier in this chapter we discussed how the cytoskeleton and motor proteins mediate diverse types of intracellular and cellular movement. Animals use these same elements to build muscle cells, or **myocytes**. A "muscle," such as skeletal muscle or heart muscle, is composed of many types of cells, each of which contributes to tissue structure and function. In addition to the myocytes, which confer the contractile properties of muscle, there are also endothelial cells that make up capillaries, immune cells for defense, pluripotent stem cells to rebuild damaged myocytes, and fibroblasts to produce the extracellular matrix and connective tissue that holds the muscle together. In a heart, for example, there are more nonmuscle cells than muscle cells, though the larger myocytes make the greatest contribution to mass.

Muscles provide the contractile force needed in many multicellular tissues and physiological systems. We are most familiar with their role in animal locomotion, where skeletal muscles move the body trunk and appendages. However, muscles play many roles in animal physiology beyond locomotion. In the circulatory system, for example, muscles provide the pumping power of the heart and give blood vessels control over their diameter. In subsequent chapters, we will also discuss how muscles are used by the respiratory system to pump gases; by the digestive system to move food along the gut; and by the reproductive system to expel gametes and embryos.

As you will see later in this chapter, animals use these basic elements to produce many types of muscles with unique structural and functional features. One important dichotomy in muscle biology is the distinction between smooth and striated muscle (Figure 6.16). Muscles such as cardiac and skeletal muscle have a striped appearance, giving rise to the name **striated muscle**. In contrast, the muscles that line blood vessels and viscera do not appear striped, and are called **smooth muscle**. The difference in microscopic appearance in these muscle types can be traced to the way thick and thin filaments are organized inside the cell. In the next section, we begin by discussing how striated muscle is constructed and regulated, returning to structure and function of smooth muscle later in this section. Although we focus on vertebrate muscles, most of the basic features apply equally well to invertebrates.

General Features of Striated Muscles

The remainder of this chapter focuses on the *cellular aspects of muscle function*: how muscle cells are built, how they are controlled, and how the elements have been fine-tuned at the cellular level to achieve diversity in function. Although there

FIGURE 6.16 **Smooth and striated muscle**

(a) Striated muscle has a striped microscopic appearance due to the regular arrangement of thick and thin filaments. **(b)** Smooth muscle lacks striations. This image shows a low layer of smooth muscle cut longitudinally, and an upper layer in cross section.

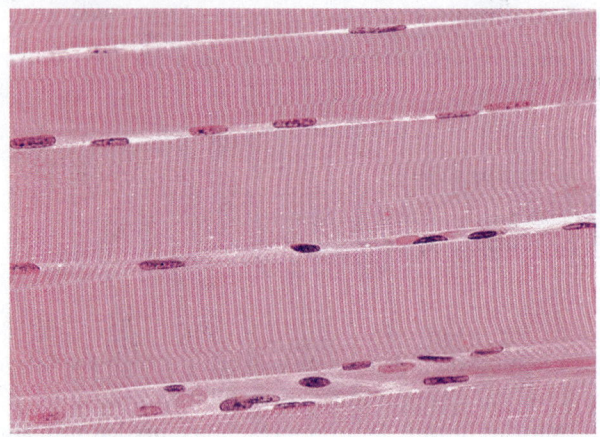

(a)

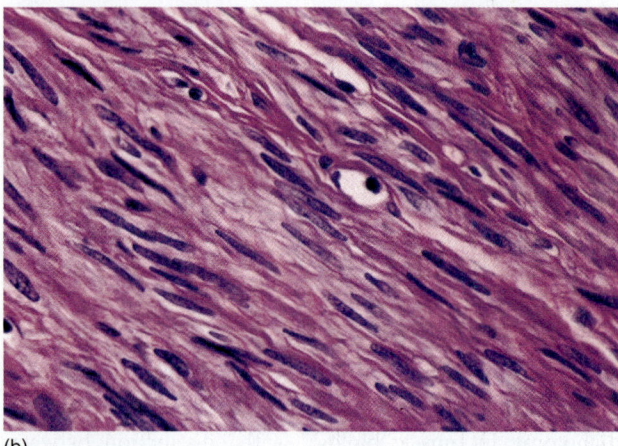

(b)

Photo source: (a): Pearson Education/PH College; (b): Melba Photo Agency/ Alamy.

is extraordinary diversity in the way muscles are constructed and used, some features are shared among all muscle types and species. In beginning our discussion of muscle with the subcellular components, it is important to keep in mind how the various components work together to produce a muscle (Figure 6.17). A solid foundation in how a muscle cell works is required to understand how muscle cells regulate other physiological systems.

Muscle cells possess thick and thin filaments

Earlier in this chapter we discussed the importance of actin and myosin in movement of eukaryotic cells. Muscle cells use variations on these molecules to create an internal network that underlies muscle contraction. Instead of relying

on individual myosin molecules, muscle makes polymers of myosin, brought together to form a superstructure known as the **thick filament**. Muscle cells also convert a dynamic actin microfilament network into a static structure known as a **thin filament** (Figure 6.18). All muscles rely on thick and thin filaments, but the arrangement of these components within cells differs between muscle types.

The basis of interaction between the thick and thin filaments, the sliding filament model, discussed earlier in this chapter, applies equally well to other actino-myosin interactions. However, the application of the sliding filament model to muscle is more complicated because of the unique properties of muscle myosin, its arrangement into a thick filament, and the integration of thick and thin filaments into a three-dimensional lattice.

In most areas of cell biology, "myosin" refers to the motor protein itself, such as monomeric myosin I or dimeric myosin V. When physiologists discuss muscle, however, "myosin" refers to a hexamer consisting of two myosin II motor proteins, or **myosin heavy chains**, and four myosin light chains. About 150 myosins are collected together by the tail to create an assembly that resembles a bouquet of flowers; the thick filament is composed of two bouquets arranged end to end. The two ends of the thick filament appear bushy from the myosin heads extending outward, while the tails of the two bouquets are located in the center of the thick filament, in a region devoid of myosin heads. A thick filament is composed of about 300 myosin hexamers, providing about 300 myosin heads on each end.

Thin filaments are similar in structure to cytoskeletal microfilaments, but they are constructed with different actin isoforms. Microfilaments are polymers of β-actin; thin filaments are made from α-actin. As we learned earlier in this chapter, microfilaments constantly assemble and disassemble. In contrast, thin filaments are stabilized in a way that prevents spontaneous growth or shrinkage, and arranged in a fixed array.

Striated muscle thick and thin filaments are arranged into sarcomeres

Striated muscles arrange their thick and thin filaments in highly organized arrays. The end of each thick filament is surrounded by an array of thin filaments, typically six. A single thick filament has this array on either end, and the combination of two thin filament arrays around a single thick filament is known as a **sarcomere**. The sarcomeres are repeated in parallel and in series to create the myofibril. While the structure of the sarcomere is relevant to striated muscles, the principles of contraction apply broadly to all muscles.

FIGURE 6.17 **Composition of skeletal muscle**

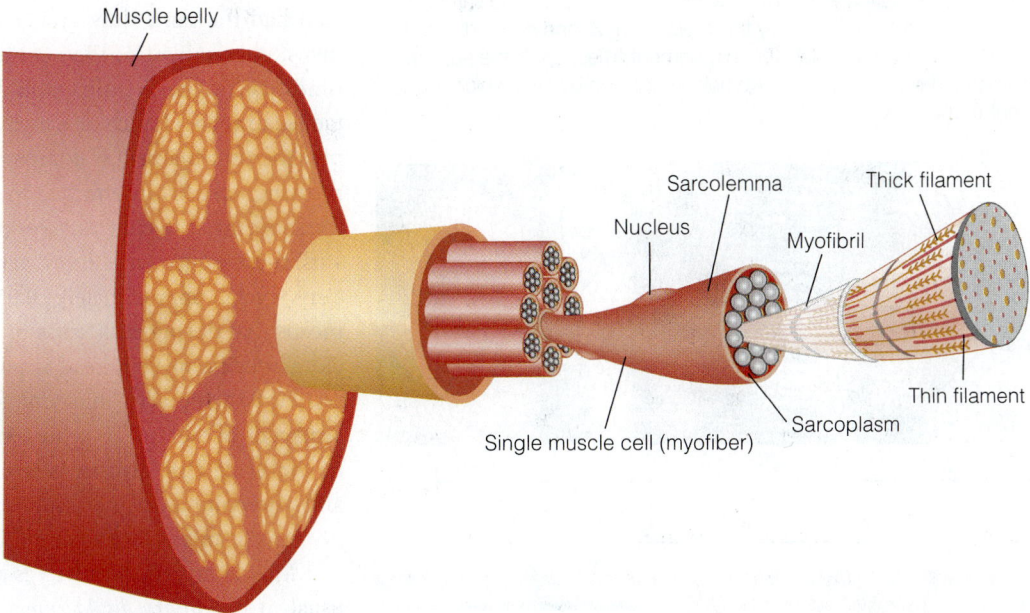

FIGURE 6.18 **Thick and thin filaments**

Muscle is composed of thick filaments and thin filaments. **(a)** Thick filaments consist mainly of myosin molecules connected by the tail with heads extending radially. **(b)** Thin filaments are mainly actin, though numerous actin-binding proteins (not shown) influence thin filament function.

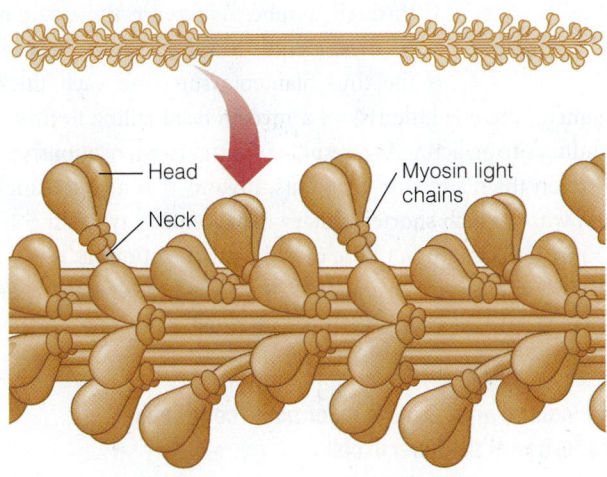

(a) Thick filament

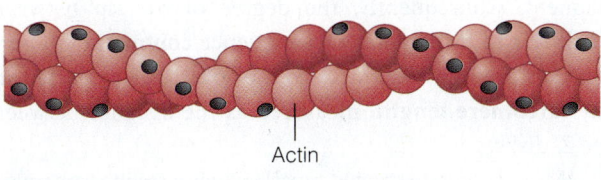

(b) Thin filament

The microscopic appearance of striated muscle is rooted in sarcomere structure (Figure 6.19). The end of each sarcomere is a protein plate called the **Z-disk**. Recall that thin filaments, like microfilaments, possess polarity, with a plus and minus end. The plus end of the thin filament is attached to the Z-disk and the minus end is directed toward the center of the sarcomere. The double-headed thick filaments are arranged between Z-disks, spanning two opposing thin filament arrays. The region of a sarcomere where thick filaments occur forms a dark region called the **A-band (or anisotropic band)**. The narrower **I-band (or isotropic band)** region spans a Z-disk, and includes the portion of the thin filaments without overlap with thick filaments. The **M-line** is the central region of the sarcomere between the two minus ends of the thin filament. In this region, the thick filaments do not overlap with thin filaments.

Specific proteins maintain these structural relationships within the sarcomere. For example, nebulin runs along the length of the thin filament, twisting around the actin filament; the length of nebulin determines the length of the thin filament. The thick filament is held in position by the protein **titin**, which connects the end of the thick filaments to the Z-disks. Because the distance between the end of the thick filament and Z-disk changes with contraction, titin must be compressible. Although we discuss sarcomere features based on its two-dimensional microscopic appearance, you should remember the three-dimensional arrangement of thick filament and thin filaments (Figure 6.20). The thin filaments are arrayed in a cylinder around the thick filament, while the thick filament is held

FIGURE 6.19 **The sarcomere**

Thick and thin filaments, in association with structural proteins, comprise the sarcomere. Each thin filament is anchored into the Z-disk by the protein CapZ, and capped at the minus end by tropomodulin. Nebulin parallels the thin filament to establish the appropriate length of each filament. The thick filaments are held in position by titin, which anchors the thick filament to the Z-disk.

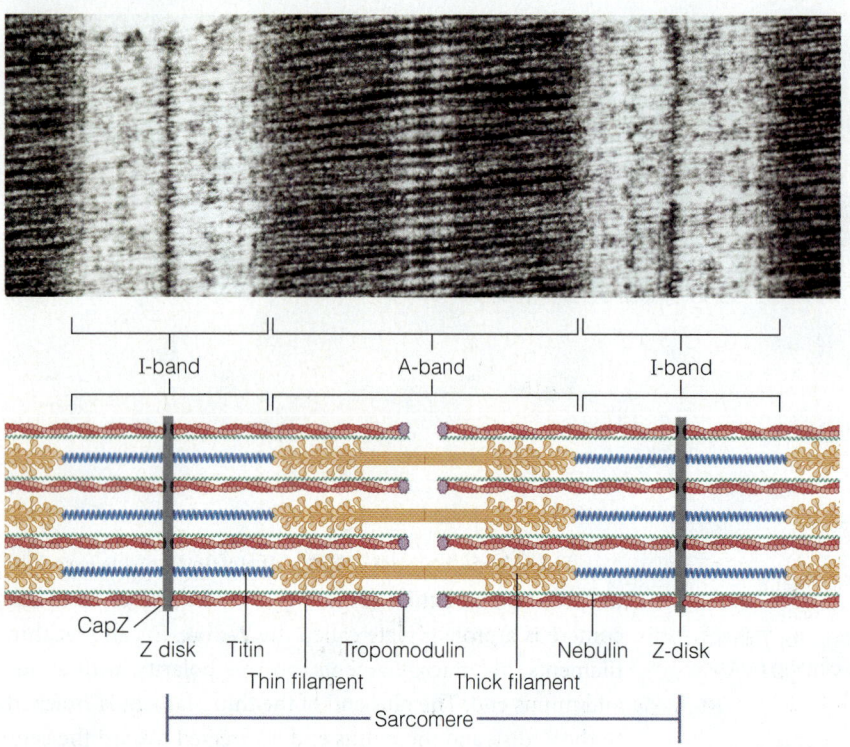

Photo source: C. F. Armstrong/Science Source.

Consider these structural relationships in the context of *duty cycle*. If muscle myosin had the same duty cycle as vesicle myosins, roughly 0.5, then at any given time half of the myosins would be attached to actin. How could a myosin head pull the thin filament if dozens of other myosins were firmly attached to actin at the same time? In contrast to other myosins, muscle myosin II has a very short duty cycle, approximately 0.05. That means that during each cross-bridge cycle, a specific myosin head is physically attached to the actin filament for only 5 percent of the time. For the remainder of the cycle this myosin is unattached and therefore does not impede other myosins from pulling the thin filament.

Muscle myosin II activity is also unusual in its *unitary displacement*. Earlier in this chapter we discussed how a unitary displacement of 36 nm was critical for a vesicular myosin to walk along the one plane of an actin filament, much like an acrobat crosses a tightrope. In reality, muscle myosins behave much less like a tightrope walker than like an octopus pulling itself through a tube. Wherever the octopus reaches, it finds a wall to grasp. Because the thin filaments surround each thick filament, there is little risk of a myosin head failing to find a binding site on actin. As a result of the structural relationships between thick and thin filaments, myosin II is able to function with a much shorter unitary displacement, typically 5 to 15 nm. You can think of the molecular interactions in muscle actino-myosin activity as a series of myosin heads taking turns pulling along the thin filaments with small, quick tugs.

at a constant location near the center of the thin filament array. In vertebrate striated muscle, six thin filaments surround each thick filament; each thin filament interacts with three separate thick filaments; and the resulting ratio of thick filaments to thin filaments is 1:2.

Myosin II has a unique duty cycle and unitary displacement

The sarcomeric structure, maintained by suites of proteins, ensures that bouquets of myosin heads are kept in a location where they are able to bind actin. The interaction between actin and myosin in muscle is very similar to the sliding filament model we discussed earlier. However, the structural organization, coupled with unique properties of muscle myosin, complicates the simple model described earlier involving a single myosin head.

The distinct features of muscle actino-myosin activity are linked to the sarcomeric organization. First, unlike the situation in vesicle traffic, when myosin detaches from actin it cannot drift away. Myosin heads on the thick filament are held in position opposite actin. Second, hundreds of myosin molecules are attached together in the thick filament.

Sarcomeric organization determines contractile properties of the muscle cell

Thick filament movement is the sum of many individual cross-bridge events. Cross-bridges can only form where myosin heads are in a position that can contact the thin filament. Consequently, the degree of overlap between thick and thin filaments can influence contractile properties. For any muscle, the degree of overlap is reflected in the **sarcomere length**, measured as the distance between the Z-disks.

Most vertebrate striated muscles show a resting sarcomere length of about 2.0 μm. The amount of force generated by a sarcomere is maximal over this range because there is an optimal

FIGURE 6.20 **Arrangement of thick and thin filaments**

Each thick filament is surrounded by an array of thin filaments. This arrangement ensures that myosin heads are able to find a microfilament at all times.

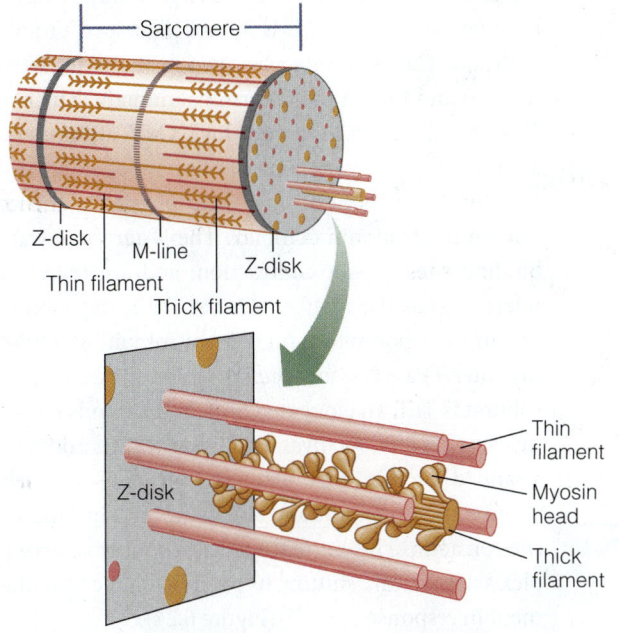

FIGURE 6.21 **Sarcomere length-force relationship**

The ability of a sarcomere to contract depends upon the degree of overlap of thick and thin filaments. Maximal force can be generated within a narrow range of sarcomere lengths, characteristic of the muscle type. When contraction begins at a point where sarcomeres are stretched to a length that is optimal for force generation, force production declines but remains high as the sarcomere shortens (1). When contraction begins at a point where sarcomeres are stretched beyond their optimal length, activation causes the sarcomere to shorten, which permits more myosin heads to be engaged (2). This means force production increases with shortening, but the total force is still lower than when the sarcomere starts at its optimal length.

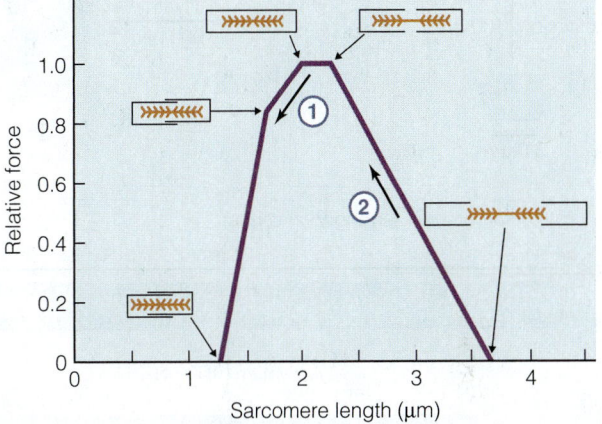

Figure source: Adapted from Bers, D. M. (1991). Figure 15 from *Excitation-contraction coupling and cardiac contractile force.* Dordrecht, the Netherlands: Kluwers Academic.

overlap between thick and thin filaments (Figure 6.21). Muscle cells can be stretched, however, changing sarcomere length enough to influence the degree of overlap. If a muscle cell is stretched beyond a sarcomere length of about 2.5 μm, some of the myosin heads near the midpoint of the thick filament cannot connect with the thin filament. If it is stretched to beyond about 3.5 μm, there is little overlap between thick and thin filaments; no cross-bridges can form and no shortening can occur. The contraction is also weakened if the sarcomere length is much shorter than about 2 μm. At this point, the thin filaments from adjacent Z-disks start to overlap, physically impeding cross-bridge formation. Below a sarcomere length of about 1.65 μm, thick filaments collide with the Z-disk and no further contraction is possible. Sarcomeric proteins such as titin and nebulin help maintain sarcomere lengths within a useful range.

In Figure 6.20, we depict sarcomere length using only a single thick filament and two of the thin filaments of the array. Each sarcomere is a collection of a small number of thick filaments and their thin filament arrays. The exact number differs among muscles, but Figure 6.21 shows about 20 arrays. The shape is similar to a barrel about 2.5 μm long and 1–2 μm in diameter. These barrels are in turn arranged end to end to form a **myofibril**. Within a muscle, the myofibril runs the length of the cell; the number of sarcomeres in a myofibril depends on the length of the muscle but it may range from hundreds to thousands of sarcomeres. The diameter of a muscle cell depends on the number of myofibrils arranged

side by side. When muscle cells grow in length, they add more sarcomeres to the ends of each myofibril, and when they grow in diameter, more myofibrils are added, typically by splitting existing myofibrils longitudinally then rebuilding the halves into two complete myofibrils.

The three-dimensional organization of myofibrils influences the contractile properties of the striated muscle, such as force generation, shortening, and contraction velocity. The amount of force that a sarcomere can generate is proportional to its cross-sectional area (about 10 Newtons (N) per cm^2). Consider the impact of building a muscle using sarcomeres arranged in series versus parallel (Figure 6.22). Sarcomeres arranged in parallel are good at generating force but do so without much shortening. Conversely, sarcomeres arranged in series generate less force but are adept at shortening, both shortening more and shortening faster. These simple examples illustrate how anatomic variations can allow muscles to be optimized for different types of contraction: maximal shortening versus maximal force.

The sarcomere properties, including thick and thin filament composition, and the arrangement of the sarcomeres determine the nature of force and shortening of the muscle when activated. In the following section, we begin our discussion of

FIGURE 6.22 **Sarcomere arrangements**

(a) Consider each sarcomere of a myofibril to be a cylinder 2.5 μm long, and when activated able to generate 100 pN force and shorten by 0.5 μm. **(b)** 10 sarcomeres in parallel would be 25 μm long but have 10 times the cross-sectional area. When activated, they would shorten only 0.5 μm but generate 10 times the force of a single sarcomere. **(c)** When arranged in series, the 10 sarcomeres would shorten the string by about 5 μm, but only generate about 100 pN force.

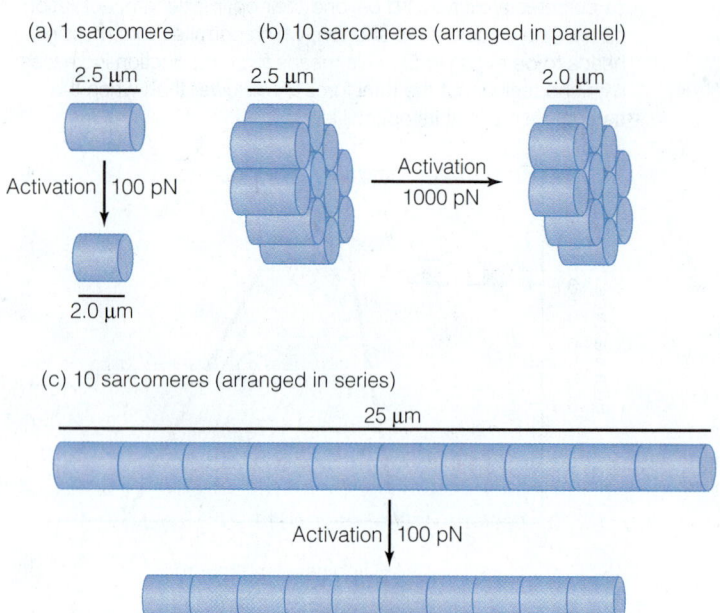

the factors that determine when myocytes are activated, turning our attention to the processes that control interaction between thick and thin filaments.

Actino-myosin activity is activated by Ca²⁺

Muscle cells, or **myofibers**, are composed of bundles of myofibrils, each of which is constructed from sarcomeres, which are in turn composed of arrays of thick and thin filaments. For muscle cells to contract, the interaction between thick and thin filaments must be regulated; inhibited at rest and activated when the muscle cell is stimulated. In striated muscle, actino-myosin activity is activated when intracellular levels of Ca^{2+} rise. The Ca^{2+} signal is transmitted to the contractile apparatus by the thin filament regulatory proteins **troponin** and **tropomyosin** (Figure 6.23).

When $[Ca^{2+}]$ is low, the troponin-tropomyosin complex sits on the thin filament in a position that blocks actin's binding site for myosin. When $[Ca^{2+}]$ rises, they roll out of the way, allowing myosin to bind to actin to initiate the cross-bridge cycle. To understand how these processes are regulated, we must consider in more detail the structures of troponin and tropomyosin, focusing on how they respond to $[Ca^{2+}]$.

The troponin component is composed of three subunits: TnC, TnI, and TnT. Each subunit contributes to Ca^{2+}-dependent regulation of contraction. The first subunit, TnC, is the Ca^{2+} sensor (the *C* in TnC stands for *calcium*). It is a member of a large family of Ca^{2+}-binding proteins. TnC is a dumbbell-shaped protein with four Ca^{2+}-binding sites, two in the N-terminal domain and two in the C-terminal domain. The two C-terminal sites have a very high Ca^{2+} affinity and are probably always occupied. They are often termed structural sites because they help physically anchor TnC in the troponin complex. The N-terminal Ca^{2+} binding sites trigger contraction, and are therefore referred to as the regulatory *sites*. TnI is the subunit that links troponin to actin, thereby inhibiting actino-myosin ATPase (*I* is for *inhibitory*). The third troponin subunit is TnT, an elongated protein that binds tropomyosin (*T* is for *tropomyosin*). Tropomyosin is a double-stranded protein that extends over approximately seven actin monomers and blocks the myosin-binding sites on actin. The entire troponin-tropomyosin complex acts as a unit, shifting its position on the thin filament in response to Ca^{2+} (Figure 6.24).

In a typical resting muscle, Ca^{2+} is maintained at a very low concentration, typically below 200 nM. At this concentration, the TnC regulatory sites are unable to bind Ca^{2+}. With the regulatory sites vacant, TnC assumes a particular structure that restricts its interactions with TnI. As a result, TnI binds actin, and the entire troponin-tropomyosin complex remains in an inhibitory position. When the muscle is activated, cytoplasmic Ca^{2+} levels can rise 100-fold. This allows the regulatory sites to bind Ca^{2+}, causing a structural change within TnC that exposes a hydrophobic region in the protein. Once uncovered, the hydrophobic

FIGURE 6.23 **Troponin and tropomyosin**

Troponin, a trimer of TnC, TnI, and TnT, binds to every seventh actin on the thin filament. Tropomyosin extends from troponin over seven actins. Its position on the thin filament in relation to the myosin binding site either permits or inhibits actino-myosin activity.

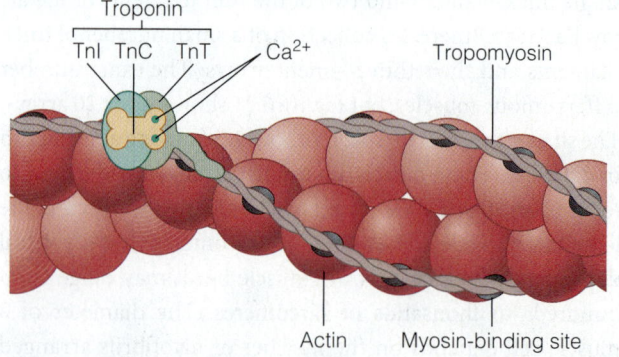

FIGURE 6.24 **Regulation of actino-myosin contraction by thin filament proteins**

Calcium binding to the low-affinity sites of TnC triggers a structural reorganization of troponin-tropomyosin, sliding it off the myosin-binding site of actin, into the major groove of the thin filament.

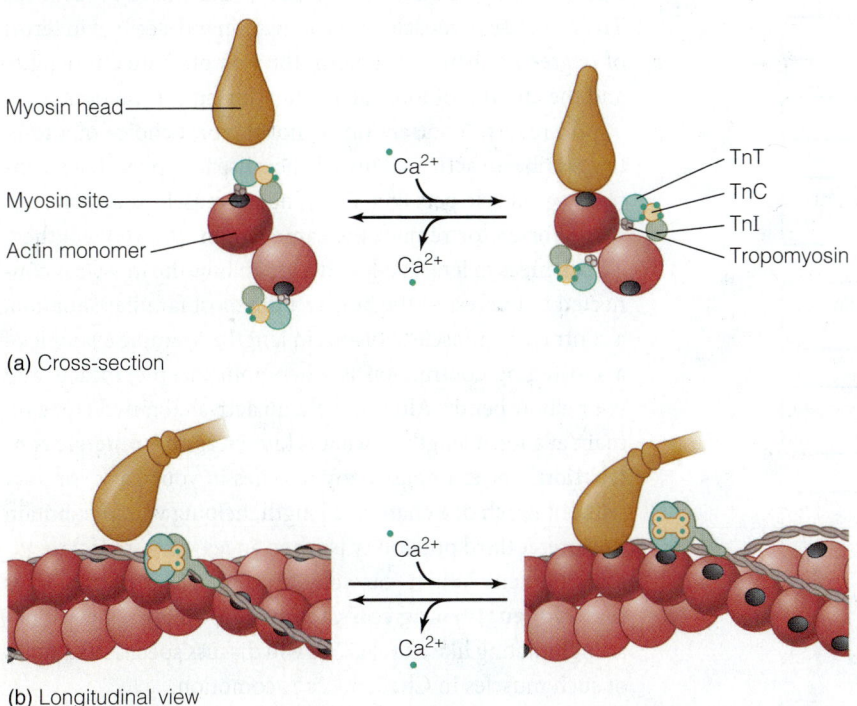

(a) Cross-section

(b) Longitudinal view

Thick filaments also influence contractile properties

The composition and properties of thick filaments also influence muscle contraction. Animals have the potential to build different types of thick filaments by drawing upon the large myosin II gene family. Vertebrates have eight different myosin II genes, each producing a myosin heavy chain with distinct structural or functional properties (Table 6.3). Because muscle myosins combine as homodimers or heterodimers, vertebrates can potentially make 32 different myosin II dimers from their eight genes. Although 32 combinations are possible, each muscle cell normally expresses only a subset of the myosin II genes.

Vertebrate heart muscle uses two myosin II genes (α and β) to make three different dimers (αα, αβ, ββ). Each of these combinations has a distinctive actino-myosin ATPase rate: The αα combination has the fastest ATPase, whereas ββ has the slowest. Animals alter the myosin heavy chain profile in response to changes in activity level. Exercise training may cause cardiac muscle to shift from β- to α-myosin isoforms. The relationship with activity level is also reflected in interspecies comparisons. Some species, such as rabbits, typically express their β-myosin II genes, whereas species with higher heart rates, such as rats, express their α-myosin II genes.

Myosin isoform shifts also occur in skeletal muscle, which can express seven different myosins (I, IIa, IIb, IIx/d, perinatal, embryonic, and extraocular). Many of these skeletal isoforms vary in their ATPase rates, whereas others differ in noncatalytic aspects of myosin function, such as the ability to interact with regulatory or structural proteins. Some isoforms are expressed at discrete points in development, as skeletal muscle progresses from embryonic, through perinatal, and then finally to muscle-specific adult isoforms. It is not yet known how each myosin II isoform influences muscle function during development. In fact, some muscles in the jaw and neck continue to use embryonic or perinatal myosin II isoforms into adulthood.

Adult skeletal myofibers in vertebrates are categorized as type I, IIa, IIb, or IIx/d on the basis of the myosin II isoform. The catalytic properties of myosins are matched to the contractile demands of the muscle. Slow-twitch skeletal muscle uses predominantly β-myosin II, the "cardiac" isoform with low velocity and high efficiency. Fast-twitch

patch on TnC can bind a corresponding hydrophobic region in TnI. Strengthening the TnC-TnI interaction causes a weakening in the TnI-actin interaction, allowing troponin to slide into the groove in actin. The strong TnT-tropomyosin interaction ensures that troponin and tropomyosin move as a complex. In this position, myosin is now free to bind actin and induce actino-myosin ATPase activity. Cross-bridge cycling can continue as long as the troponin-tropomyosin complex remains locked in this permissive position, and there is sufficient ATP to supply the actino-myosin ATPase.

The actino-myosin activity stops when $[Ca^{2+}]$ falls to resting levels and the structural changes are reversed. The regulatory sites on troponin lose their Ca^{2+}. The TnC bends to hide its hydrophobic TnI binding site. TnI reestablishes its connection with actin, and the troponin-tropomyosin complex returns to its inhibitory position. The molecular processes involved in contraction are summarized in Figure 6.25.

This general model of Ca^{2+}-induced contraction applies to all striated muscles. However, there is a great deal of diversity in contraction kinetics. We attribute much of this diversity to the control of cytoplasmic $[Ca^{2+}]$. The strength of contraction depends on $[Ca^{2+}]$ because it influences how many troponin-tropomyosin complexes are affected; the duration of contraction is influenced by how long $[Ca^{2+}]$ remains elevated.

FIGURE 6.25 Summary of ionic events in actino-myosin activation

Contraction begins when the Ca^{2+} levels within the muscle cell cytoplasm rise in response to excitation. Relaxation begins when the cytosolic Ca^{2+} levels decline, through the actions of ion pumps.

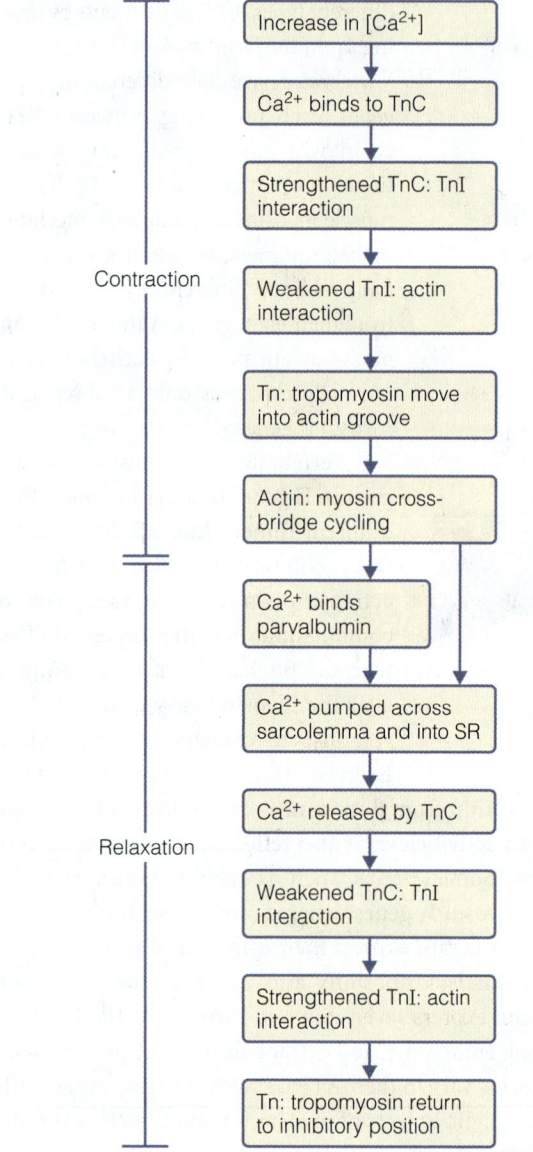

skeletal muscle, in contrast, uses IIb-myosin II, which has faster velocity but lower efficiency. Although each myofiber expresses a single myosin isoform, a muscle can be made up of myofibers expressing different myosin II isoforms. An example of the diversity in muscle myosins is shown in Figure 6.26. The largest diameter (black) fibers are type IIb, specialized for force generation. The smallest (orange) fibers are type I, specialized for efficiency. We will consider the importance of **muscle fiber** types in more detail in Chapter 12: Locomotion.

Muscle contraction can generate force

Activation of actino-myosin ATPase in muscle can be considered in terms of molecular interactions, but in terms of animal physiology the important factor is how these molecular events translate into changes at the whole-tissue level. The response of muscle upon activation is described in terms of degree of change in length, the rate of change in length, and the amount of force generated during contraction.

In reality, "contraction" is not the best choice of a term to describe an activated muscle because it implies that a contracting muscle gets smaller. When a muscle is activated, it may shorten, or remain the same length, or even lengthen. The changes in length depend a lot on how the muscle is connected to the rest of the body. In the most familiar situation, a contracting muscle shortens in length. A simple example of a shortening contraction is when your bicep contracts and your elbow bends. Alternatively, an activated muscle may remain at a fixed length in what is known as an **isometric contraction**. For example, many muscles in your back contract without much of a change in length, helping you to maintain posture. A third possibility is when an activated muscle actually lengthens. When you walk down stairs some leg muscles undergo **lengthening contractions**, slowing the rate of descent by acting like a brake. We will discuss specific examples of such muscles in Chapter 12: Locomotion.

In many fields of muscle biology, the terms *eccentric* and *concentric* are used to describe the nature of changes in length in relation to contraction. Concentric literally means "having the same center," whereas eccentric means "not having the same center." The problem with these terms is that, in some fields, they have been used in ways that can be misleading, given the strict definition of the term. Cardiovascular physiologists use concentric and eccentric in an appropriate way when describing the orientation of contraction with respect to the center of the chamber. For example, a normal heart produces a concentric contraction because it contracts symmetrically around the center of the chamber. If one wall of the heart hypertrophies and gets stronger, the contraction may be eccentric, or "off center." However, exercise physiologists use concentric to describe a shortening contraction, with the term chosen because the ends of the muscle move toward the center. Likewise, eccentric contractions are used synonymously with lengthening contractions, as if the term meant "away from center." While the use of these terms is more common in the exercise literature, they are more accurately used in describing cardiac physiology. To avoid confusion, we use the more descriptive terms: shortening, isometric, and lengthening contractions.

In the accompanying feature, we discuss how variation in shortening and force generation arises at the level of

Table 6.3	Myosin isoform properties in mammals
Isoform	**Properties**
α	This fast cardiac isoform is expressed in cardiac muscle, in species with faster heart rates, or in response to activity.
β (= I)	This slow cardiac/slow oxidative isoform is expressed in cardiac muscle of species with slower heart rates, type I (slow oxidative) skeletal fibers.
IIa	Found in **fast oxidative-glycolytic fibers**. ATPase rates intermediate between I and IIx/d.
IIx/d	Found in **fast glycolytic fibers**. ATPase rates intermediate between IIa and IIb.
IIb	Found in fast glycolytic fibers, this displays the fastest ATPase rates.
Embryonic	Expressed in skeletal muscles in early embryonic development, as well as some adult muscle.
Perinatal	Expressed in skeletal muscles in late embryonic development, as well as some adult muscle.
Extraocular	Expressed in eye muscles.

FIGURE 6.26 **Mosaic of fibers in tetrapod muscle**

Most tetrapods possess muscles that are mosaics of different fiber types. In the rat diaphragm muscle shown below, the fiber types are distinguished by immunohistochemistry, using fluorescent antibodies that bind to specific myosin heavy chain isoforms. Type I fibers are shown in orange, Type IIa in green, Type IIb in blue, and Type IIx/d in black.

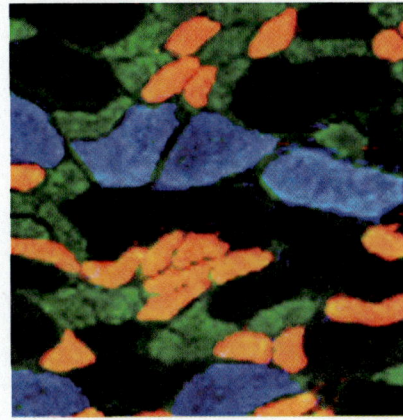

Photo source: Dr. Gary Sieck.

the sarcomeres and cross-bridge kinetics (Box 6.2: Math in Physiology: Factors Affecting Force, Work, and Power).

Cardiac and skeletal muscle cells differ in some structural properties

In the preceding sections, we did not distinguish between cardiac and skeletal muscle in describing the basic structure of muscle. They are both considered striated muscle because they share the basic sarcomeric organization that gives rise to the microscopic striped appearance. They have a great deal of similarity in the structure and organization of their contractile apparatus. However, there are important differences

that should be considered before discussing their regulation, where there is a great deal more divergence between cardiac and skeletal muscle.

Cellular dimensions: A skeletal muscle cell, or myofiber, possesses long myofibrils, but skeletal muscles differ widely in the length. Because myofibrils usually run the length of the muscle, they are short in small muscles and long in larger muscles. The smallest muscle in humans, the 1.3-mm-long stapedius, controls the movement of small bones in the middle ear. The longest muscle in humans is the sartorius, which stretches about 60 centimeters from the outside of the hip to the inside of the knee, winding around the thigh. The greater size of the skeletal myofiber is possible because it is produced by the fusion of many individual cells. A cardiac muscle cell, or **cardiomyocyte**, possesses myofibrils that are typically about 100 sarcomeres in length. Thus, a typical mammalian ventricular cardiomyocyte is about 0.2 millimeters in length. Most vertebrate cardiomyocytes are individual cells, though some have undergone an additional round of the cell cycle (without cell division) and possess two nuclei.

Regulatory proteins: Though the basic structure of the filaments, sarcomeres, and myofibrils are similar in striated muscles, the muscles are required to perform very different types of contractions. The mechanistic basis of these differences in contractile properties is due in part to the specific proteins used to make thick and thin filaments. There are heart-specific and skeleton-specific isoforms of regulatory proteins, such as troponins and tropomyosins, and different myosin heavy chains and light chains. Though the thick and thin filaments appear similar, they differ in many properties that influence contractile properties.

Thus, there is a general similarity in the way vertebrates build striated muscle. Despite the similarity in structure of types of striated myocytes, there are remarkable differences

FACTORS AFFECTING FORCE, WORK, AND POWER

Though you have probably encountered the terms force, work, and power in your everyday life, it is likely that the terms have been misused. In muscle physiology, they have specific definitions, and the distinctions are important in understanding how muscles are able to convert actinomyosin activity into useful movements.

Force is something that has the tendency to cause movement, or creates stress in a system that does not move. You exert force when you push a ball to move it, or push against a wall. In the context of muscle physiology, force is synonymous with tension. At the molecular level, force is generated by the cross-bridge cycle of actinomyosin ATPase. When activated, each myosin head generates about 5 pN of force during a cross-bridge cycle. A thick filament has about 600 heads, but when the sarcomere is activated, only about 5 percent are generating force at any timepoint. Thus, a single thick filament can generate a maximal force of about 150 pN force (600 × 5 pN × 5%), if all of the myosin heads are participating.

There are a number of biological factors that influence force production. First, at the level of the myofiber, a muscle can activate different proportions of the myosin heads, and the easiest way to do this is by varying Ca^{2+} release. If the cell released few Ca^{2+} ions into the cytoplasm, few troponin-tropomyosin complexes would be induced to move, and few cross-bridges would form. Muscle contractile elements show a sigmoidal relationship between $[Ca^{2+}]$ and muscle force (Figure 6.27a). This strategy of altering Ca^{2+} levels to regulate force is important in cardiac muscle, but most skeletal muscles release enough Ca^{2+} during each contraction to induce near-maximal force.

Another factor that affects force production is the rate of shortening. Or put another way, why can you lift a feather faster than a brick? In classic experiments performed almost 80 years ago, A. V. Hill established the factors that affect contraction velocity (V) when a muscle is activated. It depends on force generated by the contraction (P), the maximal force the muscle could generate at a given length (F_o) and two constants, one related to velocity (b) and another related to force (c). The equation, shown below, can be used to predict the contraction velocity under different conditions.

$$V = b \, (F_o - F) \, / \, (F + c)$$

Consider how the relationship develops when you ask your biceps muscle to contract to lift different objects. V would be lowest when you try to lift an object too heavy to move; you would exert maximal force ($F = F_o$), making the numerator approach zero. V would be highest when you try to move an object of negligible mass, such as a feather. F approaches

zero, the numerator ($b \, F_o$) is at its maximum, the denominator ($F + c$) approaches a minimum, and velocity is at its maximum. Continuing the experiment between these two extremes generates the force velocity curve (Figure 6.27b).

What is the mechanistic basis of this relationship in terms of molecular events in the sarcomere? The same number of cross-bridges will be involved whether the situation generates maximal force or maximal velocity of shortening. In 1957, Andrew Huxley explained the force-velocity relationship in terms of cross-bridge kinetics. The difference between force generation and shortening lies in the structural changes in the myosin head. When we think of the cross-bridge cycle in terms of a single myosin molecule, we see how it reaches forward and pulls the thin filament. When you factor into this model the hundreds of other myosin heads, things get a bit more complicated. Each individual myosin can only bind the thin filament when

FIGURE 6.27 **Force, Ca^{2+}, and contraction velocity**

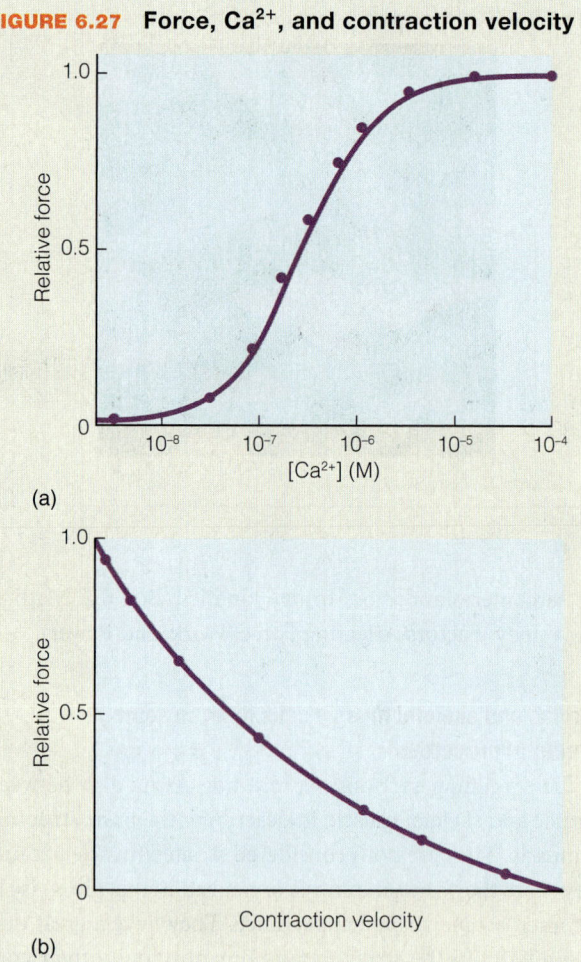

(a)

(b)

it reaches forward looking for a binding site on actin. Once it binds, several chemical steps must occur before the head can generate force in its power stroke. If shortening is fast, other myosin heads can pull the thin filament back before the myosin head has a chance to undergo its power stroke. The sliding filament bends myosin into the position that it would have assumed had it been given the time to undertake its power stroke. Although the chemical events in the power stroke (ADP and P_i release) still happen, the structural changes in the myosin head have already occurred. Consequently, this cross-bridge cycle generates no force. Put simply, a very high contraction velocity prevents many cross-bridges from generating force. Now consider what happens when a muscle generates its maximal force, such as when it lifts the heaviest object possible. During a cross-bridge cycle, the tension on the muscle prevents the thin filament from moving appreciably and each myosin head in a cross-bridge remains in a form that allows it to generate force.

Translating between force production and other biomechanical parameters enables researchers to understand how contraction affects how a muscle is used in an integrated organism. **Work** (W) is a unit of energy, measured in Joules (or calories). Mathematically, it is the product of force (F) and distance (d).

$$W = F \times d$$

As a unit of energy, it can be directly compared to metabolic energy. It costs you a certain number of joules to move a kilometer, but it does not matter whether you walk or run that kilometer—the total energy costs are similar. Of course, you expend that energy faster when you run, but the total energy required to cover the distance isn't affected.

The rate of doing work is the **power** (P).

$$P = W/t$$

Because $W = F \times d$, P can also be expressed as the product of force (F) and shortening velocity (V):

$$P = FV$$

We learned earlier that a thick muscle generates more force than a muscle with the same number of sarcomeres arranged in series (see Figure 6.22). However, the two muscles generate similar power: The thick muscle generates lots of force but at low shortening velocities, whereas the thin muscle generates rapid shortening but little force.

An animal can alter the power output of a muscle by changing either the force generation or the velocity of shortening. Consider the following example to understand the

trade-offs between these parameters and how they affect power. You can throw a ball by contracting your triceps muscle in the back of your arm. You can maximize force by trying to throw a very heavy ball. Your arm might generate a great deal of force, but the ball is so heavy that you can barely move your arm (your triceps has high force but little shortening). Alternatively, you can maximize shortening velocity. The way to move your arm the fastest is by choosing a very light ball; very little force is generated but you can move your arm very quickly. Neither of these situations generates significant power because in each situation one of the parameters—force or shortening velocity—approaches zero. Power is greatest at an intermediate velocity (Figure 6.28). Most

FIGURE 6.28 **Power, efficiency, and velocity**

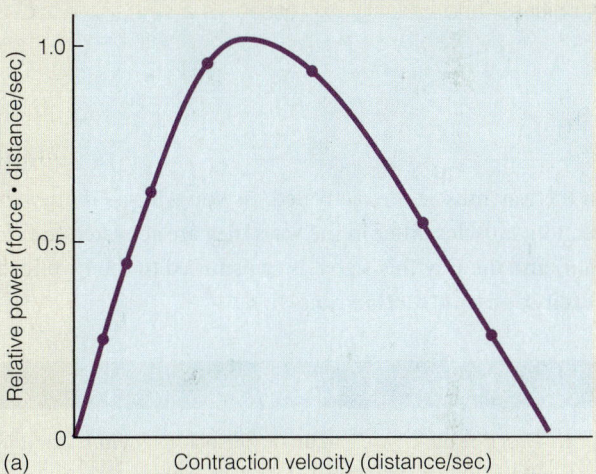

(a)

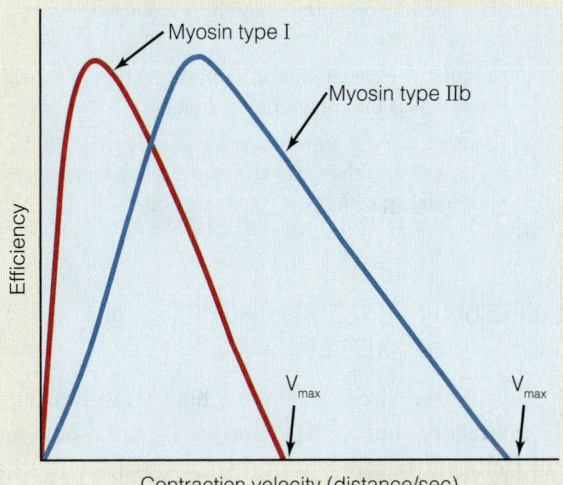

(b)

FACTORS AFFECTING FORCE, WORK, AND POWER

muscles generate maximal power when contraction velocity is 30–40 percent of the maximal shortening velocity.

Mechanical power is the most important parameter in most forms of locomotion. Animals apply the power generated by a muscle to the environment to generate movement. The arm throws a ball by transferring the power generated in contraction to forward movement of the ball. The power you generate with a leg contraction allows you to jump. The contraction must be forceful and rapid, or you will not leave the ground. Many muscles are built, arranged, and used in ways that maximize power output.

One final parameter to consider in muscle design is mechanical efficiency. It is the ratio of power output and metabolic demands. It is a reflection of how effective the system is at converting metabolic energy into power. Because power is the rate of doing work (J/sec) and metabolic rate is the rate of consuming energy (J/sec), the ratio is unitless, and typically expressed as a percent. A typical

muscle working at its optimal rate may have a mechanical efficiency of 25 percent. The muscle may become less efficient when power output is not maximal. Based on Figure 6.28a, this would occur when shortening velocity is either too high or too low. When you use your biceps to lift an object, there is an optimal rate for lifting it. Moving either faster or slower reduces the power output, and therefore the efficiency. Earlier in this chapter, we discussed how muscles can alter myosins as part of a strategy to optimize contractile properties. Though myosin types differ in maximal velocity (V_{max}), they also differ in their efficiency. Myosin type I has its optimal efficiency at shorter velocities, whereas type IIb has its optimal efficiency at faster velocities (Figure 6.28b).

Reference

• Huxley, A. F. (2000). Cross-bridge action: Present views, prospects, and unknowns. *Journal of Biomechanics, 33,* 1189–1195.

---

in the way muscles are activated. As you will see in the next section, muscles differ in the ways they are activated (*excitation*) and the way this signal is transmitted to the myofibrils (**excitation-contraction** *coupling*).

CONCEPT CHECK

5. Describe duty cycle and unitary displacement in relation to nonmuscle and muscle myosin activity.

6. How does the organization of the sarcomere influence contractile force?

7. Compare the constraints on myosin function in vesicle traffic versus the contractile apparatus.

8. Is muscle activity more accurately described as cellular movement or a change in cell shape? What types of cells need to move within the vertebrate body?

Excitation in Vertebrate Skeletal and Cardiac Muscles

So far, we have discussed the machinery involved in muscle contraction, but we have not yet discussed how muscle contraction is triggered. In all striated muscles, (i) excitation begins with depolarization of the muscle cell membrane, or sarcolemma; (ii) contraction ensues when cytosolic

$[Ca^{2+}]$ increases; and (iii) thin filament regulatory proteins (troponin-tropomyosin) change their position to permit myosin to bind actin. Where types of striated muscle differ is (i) in the trigger for **sarcolemmal** depolarization, (ii) the pattern of change in membrane potential over time, (iii) the propagation of depolarization along the sarcolemma, (iv) the link between depolarization and Ca^{2+} release, and (v) the cellular origins of Ca^{2+}. This capacity for animals to make different types of muscles makes it difficult to make generalizations about a "typical" skeletal muscle, for example. Thus, for each step of the pathway, we consider first the mechanisms used by the average skeletal muscle, then consider the variations on the theme.

Striated muscles are all activated by an action potential

The action potential, first described in Chapter 3, is also the signal for contraction of most muscle cells. The resting membrane potential of the sarcolemma is about -70 mV. Upon activation, muscles experience a rapid depolarization, followed by repolarization and hyperpolarization. The properties of the muscle action potential, such as rates of depolarization and repolarization and action potential duration, are determined by the density and activities of various channels in the sarcolemma.

As with other cell types, depolarization is induced when Na$^+$ channels are opened. In a skeletal muscle, these channels are opened when a neurotransmitter binds onto a channel and causes it to open, permitting the inflow of Na$^+$. In skeletal muscles of vertebrates, the excitatory neurotransmitter from motor nerves is typically acetylcholine, which opens a ligand-gated Na$^+$/K$^+$ channel. The inward rush of Na$^+$ causes a rapid depolarization, causing voltage-sensitive Ca^{2+} channels to open, which allows the influx of Ca^{2+} into the cell from the extracellular space. After a period, Na$^+$ channels and Ca^{2+} channels begin to close and voltage-sensitive K$^+$ channels open, causing the cell to repolarize. The density and kinetic properties of these various ion channels determine the features of the action potential: the rate of depolarization, the rate of repolarization, and, consequently, the duration of the action potential. This general pattern of an action potential, depolarization, and repolarization is similar among vertebrate striated muscles. However, muscles show very important differences in the time course, or kinetics, of the change in membrane potential.

The concept of all or none, first discussed in the context of neurons, can also be applied to myofibers, with some caveats. Like neurons, the action potential of striated muscles is all or none. This electrical all-or-none event does not necessarily translate to an all-or-none contractile event. We have discussed how the pattern of change in [Ca^{2+}] over time (Ca^{2+} transient), may differ in a myofiber and that this can alter contractile properties. In the next section we will discuss contractile summation, where an individual skeletal myofiber is capable of generating additional force at higher frequency because of an incomplete Ca^{2+} transient. Later we consider the concept of recruitment. Muscles are composed of multiple myofibers, each with its own contractile control. Changes in force of the muscle can arise as different **motor units** are activated.

Striated muscles differ in the time course of the action potential

Specializations in the nature of the action potential permit types of muscle to contract at different rates (measured as changes in force or length per second) and different frequencies (contraction-relaxation cycles per second). Consider the differences in the action potential seen in three striated muscles: a very fast skeletal muscle, a slow skeletal muscle, and a cardiac muscle, each stimulated to contract once (Figure 6.29). The two skeletal muscles differ in terms of the time required to fully depolarize. Faster skeletal muscles reach their peak depolarization faster. This is possible because the faster muscle may have more channels that permit inward movement of Na$^+$ or Ca^{2+}, or they may possess channels that open faster or stay open longer.

The action potentials depicted in Figure 6.29 also differ in the rate of repolarization. One factor that affects the rate of repolarization is how long the depolarizing channels remain

FIGURE 6.29 Action potentials in striated muscle
The time course of change in action potential and force are shown for **(a)** fast skeletal muscle, **(b)** slow skeletal muscle, and **(c)** cardiac muscle. Skeletal muscles may differ in the rate of depolarization, the time required to complete an action potential, and length of contraction cycle. Cardiac muscle differs from slow skeletal muscles in terms of the action potential. In this example, the contraction profiles are similar, but the action potential in cardiac muscle is prolonged. This is attributed to voltage-sensitive Ca^{2+} channels remaining open for longer periods.

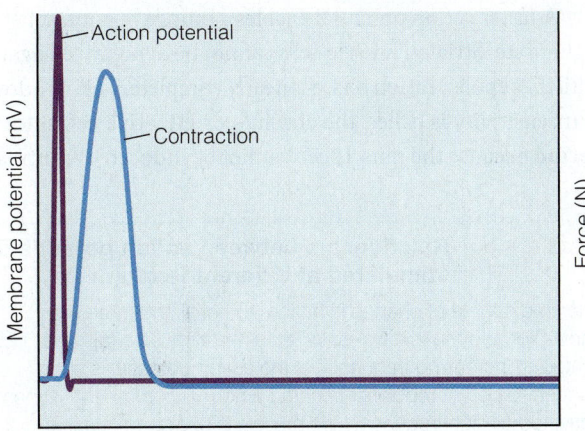

(a) Fast skeletal muscle

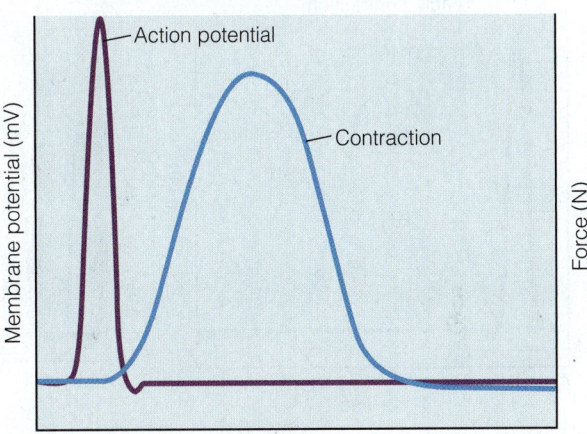

(b) Slow skeletal muscle

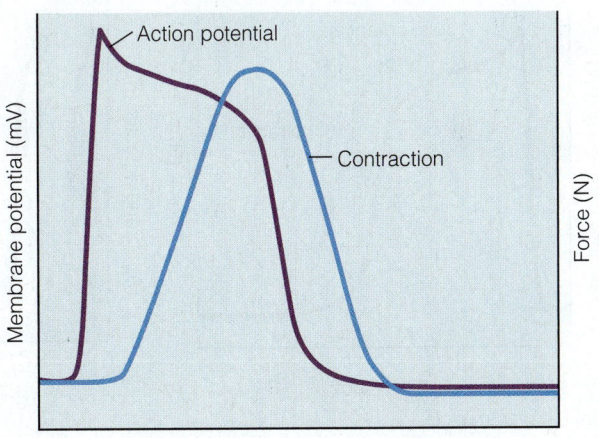

(c) Cardiac muscle

open. The long plateau phase seen in the cardiac muscle action potential is due to Ca^{2+} channels that remain open for longer periods. Repolarization is due to the opening of K^+ channels, and not surprisingly, K^+ channels are the targets of hormones and drugs that regulate contraction rate. For example, acetylcholine and adenosine can each modulate the properties of K^+ channels and affect the rate of repolarization. A wide variety of neurotransmitters and neurohormones can affect contraction kinetics through similar mechanisms.

A faster action potential enables a muscle to contract at a higher rate. Striated muscle cells cannot be depolarized again until the repolarization phase is nearly complete. This window of insensitivity is called the absolute or **effective refractory period** because the muscle cell cannot be induced to contract

again by normal physiological regulators. However, once a muscle cell is partially repolarized, it is able to respond to a second stimulus. This phase of the action potential is called the **relative refractory period**. Whereas skeletal muscle cells have very short effective and relative refractory periods, cardiac muscle has a prolonged relative refractory period. This electrical property has important consequences for how each muscle is used.

Cardiac and skeletal muscles differ in refractory periods

Figure 6.30 depicts an action potential and contraction-relaxation cycle for a slow skeletal muscle and a cardiac muscle. Each muscle is shown responding to a stimulation

FIGURE 6.30 **Relationship between action potentials and contraction in skeletal and cardiac muscle stimulated at different frequencies**

The time course of change in action potential and force are shown for two muscle types. When skeletal muscle **(a)** is activated at increasing frequencies, the action potential is short enough to permit repolarization and a normal contraction. When activated at high frequency, the muscle is unable to relax, and a sustained contraction occurs. When cardiac muscle **(b)** is stimulated at higher frequency, a point is reached where stimulation occurs while the action potential is in the refractory period. Contractions may or may not occur, and the normal frequency is lost (arrhythmia).

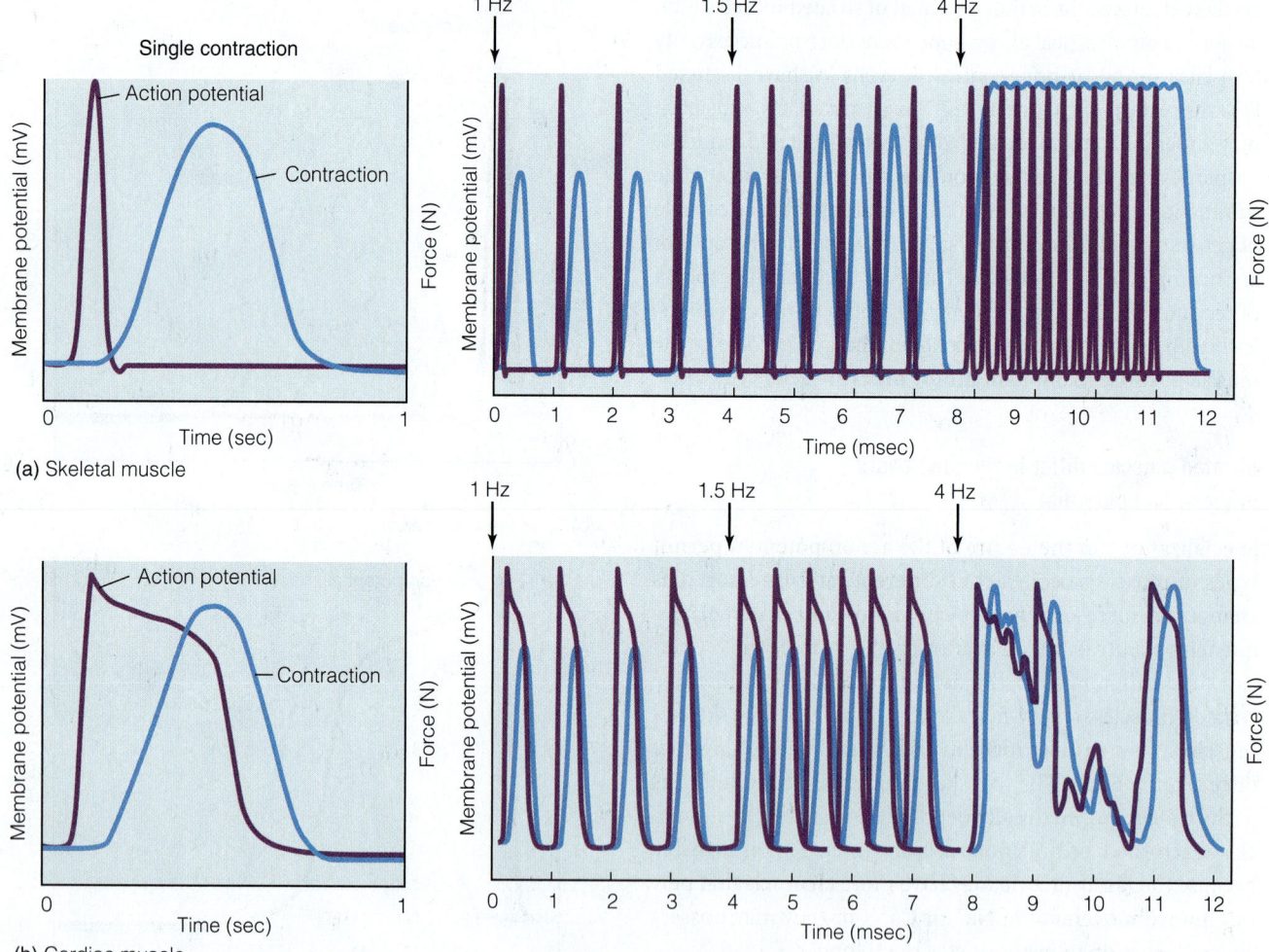

frequency of 1 Hz (1 per second). We next increase the frequency of stimulation to 1.5 Hz. Note that in each case, the muscle responds by increasing the frequency of action potentials, and the frequency of complete contraction and relaxation. When the frequency of stimulation is increased further to 4 Hz, differences in the contraction pattern emerge. The skeletal muscle is able to trigger a second action potential before the contraction is complete, and a greater contraction is induced. In contrast, high-frequency stimulation causes a heart to take up a chaotic pattern as the consequence of stimulation depends on whether it arrives during the effective or relative refractory periods.

When skeletal muscles are stimulated at high frequency, they are able to alter the magnitude of the contraction. This process is called **contractile summation**, where contractions add on to the previous contraction. (Do not confuse the summation that occurs in muscle contraction with spatial and temporal summation of graded potentials that occurs in neurons.) It is also possible to stimulate skeletal muscle at such a high frequency that the contraction is maximal and sustained, a condition called **tetanus**. In cardiac muscle, the long refractory periods prevent the heart from experiencing either summation or tetanus. The cardiac muscle must relax before it can contract. When frequency of stimulation is too great, the frequency of contraction becomes erratic, and the heart loses its natural rhythm. This condition, known as *arrhythmia*, prevents the heart from properly filling and emptying. In Chapter 9 you will explore how the regulation of the heart rate depends on the manner of stimulation of cardiomyocytes.

Skeletal muscle excitation is triggered by neurotransmitters

Most vertebrate skeletal muscles are **neurogenic muscles**, and receive signals from a *motor neuron*. The motor neuron axon termini are located in a region of the sarcolemma called the **motor end plate** (Figure 6.31). The sarcolemma at the motor end plate is rich in receptors for the neurotransmitter released by the motor neuron: acetylcholine. Upon stimulation of a motor neuron, acetylcholine is released from synaptic vesicles into the neuromuscular synapse. It crosses the synapse and binds nicotinic acetylcholine receptors within the sarcolemma. As we discussed in Chapter 5: Neuron Structure and Function, these ligand-gated ion channels are Na^+ channels. If enough nicotinic acetylcholine receptors are activated, the depolarization at the motor end plate initiates a wave of depolarization along the sarcolemma: the action potential. The passage of the action potential along the sarcolemma induces an all-or-none contraction.

Twitch muscles are neurogenic skeletal muscles that are innervated by one or, occasionally, a few motor neurons. In these muscles the action potential spreads rapidly along the

FIGURE 6.31 **Twitch muscles**

(a) Motor neurons innervate individual myofibers, shown here in longitudinal section. **(b)** A neuron terminus (bouton) sends signals to the muscle at its motor end plate. Neurotransmitter, typically acetycholine, binds to its receptor, a ligand-gated Na^+ channel. Upon opening, the inward flow of Na^+ depolarizes the muscle (excitation).

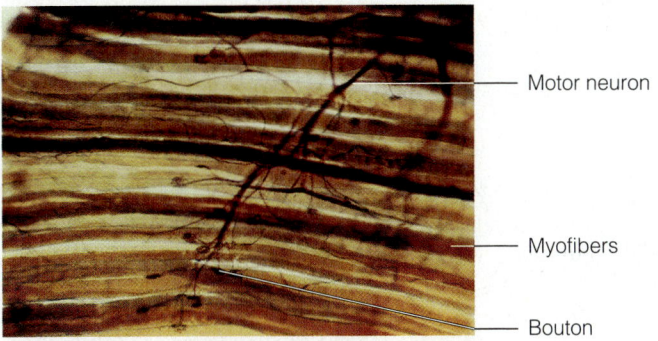

Motor neuron

Myofibers

Bouton

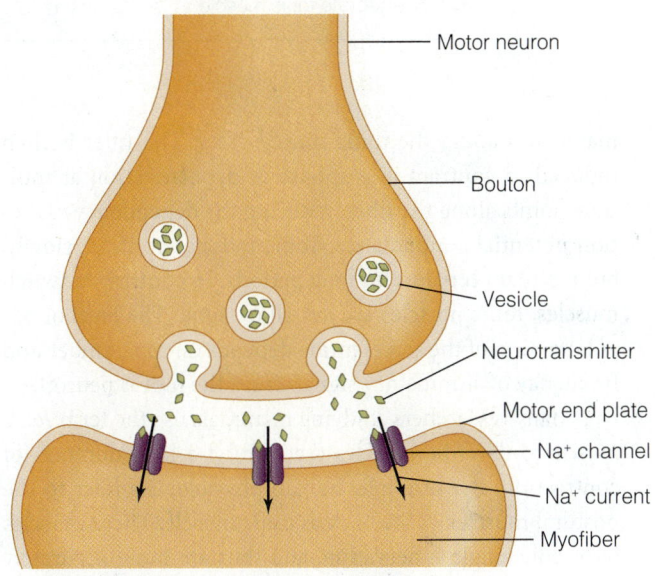

Motor neuron

Bouton

Vesicle

Neurotransmitter

Motor end plate

Na^+ channel

Na^+ current

Myofiber

Photo source: Astrid & Hanns-Frieder Michler/Science Source.

sarcolemma, causing a uniform contraction along the length of the myofiber. Because of their electrical nature, action potentials move rapidly, but in many muscles passive conductance from the motor end plate is inadequate to ensure that the signal reaches the entire muscle essentially simultaneously. There are two main ways that muscles are able to ensure that the entire sarcolemma is depolarized uniformly in space and time: through multiple innervations (tonic muscle) and through invaginations of the sarcolemma (T-tubules).

One way in which the challenge of uniform contraction is met in some neurogenic muscles is through multiple innervations. Vertebrate striated muscle with multiple innervations is called **tonic muscle** (Figure 6.32). When motor neurons are stimulated, neurotransmitter release occurs at

FIGURE 6.32   Tonic muscle

Unlike twitch myofibers, tonic myofibers are controlled by multiple nerves. **(a)** In vertebrates, a tonic muscle is typically controlled by a single nerve synapsing at multiple locations along a single tonic muscle cell. **(b)** Invertebrate tonic muscle may have multiple nerves controlling a single muscle cell, and each of those nerves may form synapses at multiple sites.

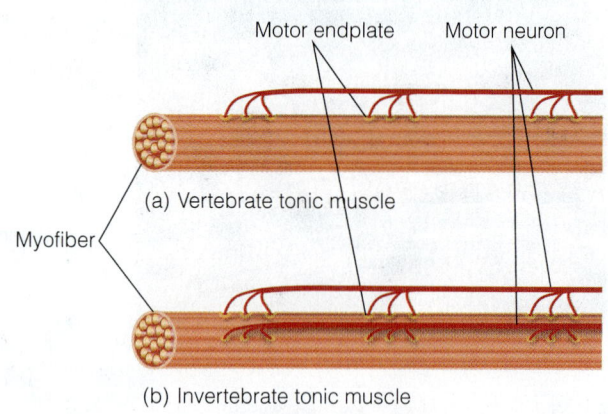

(a) Vertebrate tonic muscle

(b) Invertebrate tonic muscle

FIGURE 6.33   T-tubules

Many types of muscle have T-tubules, invaginations of the sarcolemma that penetrate deep into the muscle cell to speed the spread of the action potential.

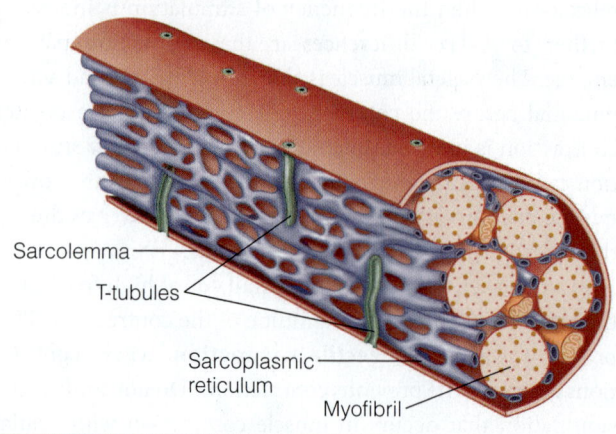

many sites along the tonic muscle fiber. The fiber is then induced to contract in response to depolarization at multiple points along the fiber, reducing the dependency on action potential conductance. Tonic muscles contract slowly, but maintain **tension** for long periods. In contrast to twitch muscles, tonic muscles are not all or none. The level of depolarization of the sarcolemma depends on the number and frequency of stimulatory signals from the motor neuron.

Many researchers studying mammals use the term *tonic muscle* to describe muscles that exhibit a long duration of contraction. For example, human physiologists refer to the postural muscles of the back as tonic muscle. These muscles have only single innervation, and thus are more accurately described as slow-twitch muscle. Mammals do have a few true tonic muscles, located around the eye (extraocular), in the ear, and in the esophagus.

T-tubules enhance action potential penetration into the myocyte

Central to activation of muscle is the propagation of the action potential along the surface of the sarcolemma. Many muscles possess modifications of the sarcolemma that penetrate deep into the muscle cell. These invaginations are called transverse tubules, or **T-tubules** (Figure 6.33). When the sarcolemma depolarizes, the action potential follows the T-tubules deep into the muscle fiber.

The T-tubules allow for more efficient transmission of the action potential and, not surprisingly, they are most common in muscles that must respond rapidly to stimulation.

Muscles that do not need to contract quickly may lack T-tubules entirely, relying solely on the sarcolemma for excitation. However, the T-tubule system is extensive in large or quick-contracting muscles, such as vertebrate fast-twitch skeletal muscles. T-tubules also exist in the cardiac muscle of mammals and some birds, although in generally less developed form than in the skeletal muscle of the same species.

Cardiac muscle cells are stimulated by other muscle cells

Unlike skeletal muscles, the vertebrate heart contracts in response to stimulation from other muscle cells. Because the entire heart contracts without neuronal input, each of the myocytes of the heart is considered a **myogenic muscle**. In the intact heart, some specialized myocytes depolarize spontaneously. These **pacemaker cells** transmit their electrical signal throughout the heart and cause other cardiomyocytes to depolarize and contract.

Pacemaker cells are unusual in that they show an unstable resting membrane potential. These cells possess an unusual ion channel, the funny channel or *f-channel,* that is permeable to both Na^+ and K^+. When the channel is open, an imbalance in Na^+ influx and K^+ efflux leads to a slow depolarization. Once the pacemaker cell membrane depolarizes to a critical voltage, the *threshold voltage,* voltage-sensitive Ca^{2+} channels open to initiate the action potential. Though the f-channels close during the action potential, hyperpolarization of the pacemaker cells at the end of the action potential reactivates the f-channels, causing the cells to slowly depolarize again. Many of the factors that regulate heart rate, such as adenosine, acetylcholine, and catecholamines, alter the kinetic properties of the f-channels.

The action potential of the pacemaker cells induces an action potential in the myocytes to which they are connected through cell-to-cell connections called gap junctions. These permit the electrical excitation to be transmitted from cell to cell. In contrast to pacemaker cells, depolarization of non-pacemaker cardiomyocytes is due to the opening of voltage-dependent Na^+ channels, much like the situation seen in other excitable cells. Interestingly, a normal cardiomyocyte has the ability to contract spontaneously, much like a pacemaker cell. In an intact heart, these cardiomyocytes would receive an excitatory signal from a pacemaker before they would experience their own spontaneous contraction. However, if the pacemaker cells become damaged, other cardiomyocytes can become the pacemaker to determine the rate of cardiac contraction. Some cases of arrhythmia arise from a faulty pacemaker. Surgical interventions can destroy the defective pacemaker cells, and permit other cardiomyocytes to adapt and become a new pacemaker. We discuss the function of the heart in greater detail in Chapter 9.

CONCEPT CHECK

9. What channels determine depolarization and repolarization in muscles?
10. How does the refractory period differ between skeletal and cardiac muscle? Why is this important to the function of the muscle?

Excitation-Contraction Coupling in Striated Muscles

The process of excitation ends when the muscle cell membrane is depolarized. The next steps in the process, the mechanism by which excitation triggers contraction, are collectively known as excitation-contraction coupling, or **EC coupling**. As with other steps, the mechanisms of EC coupling differ among muscle types, and again there are many clear dichotomies between skeletal and cardiac muscle.

Depolarization leads to an increase in cytoplasmic [Ca^{2+}]

In all vertebrate striated muscles, the action potential across the sarcolemma triggers an increase in [Ca^{2+}] in the muscle cell cytoplasm. Some Ca^{2+} flows into the cell from the extracellular space, and some enters the cytoplasm from intracellular stores. The main storage site for Ca^{2+} in the cell is the muscle endoplasmic reticulum, known as the

FIGURE 6.34 Terminal cisternae

Many striated muscles possess enlargements of the sarcoplasmic reticulum (SR) near the region of the T-tubules. In mammals, the terminal cisternae are most extensive in muscles that contract at high frequencies.

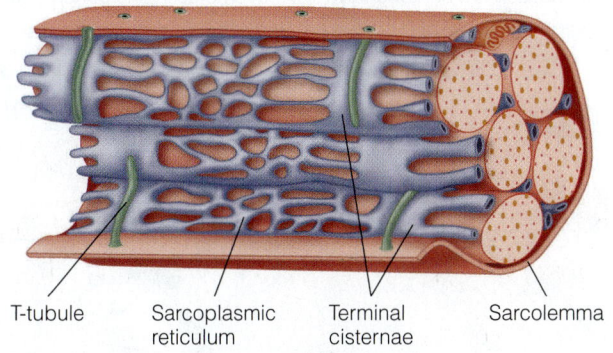

T-tubule   Sarcoplasmic   Terminal   Sarcolemma
reticulum   cisternae

sarcoplasmic reticulum, or SR. In striated muscle, the SR frequently has enlargements, called **terminal cisternae** (Figure 6.34) that increase the capacity for Ca^{2+} storage and localize it to discrete regions within the muscle cell. Because terminal cisternae ensure rapid Ca^{2+} delivery, they are well developed in muscles that contract quickly, such as fast-twitch skeletal muscle. Muscles are able to accumulate Ca^{2+} to very high levels within the SR, often bound to the Ca^{2+}-binding protein **calsequestrin**. In all striated muscles, contraction begins when Ca^{2+} levels rise, and Ca^{2+} binds troponin C to initiate the movement of the troponin-tropomyosin complex. As it rolls into the groove in the thin filament, the myosin engages actin and cross-bridge cycling begins.

Control of EC coupling in muscles, and variation seen between muscles, is due to differences in the sources of Ca^{2+} and the rates of movement into and out of the sarcoplasm. These transport processes are mediated by carriers, depicted in Figure 6.35.

FIGURE 6.35 Transporters and channels involved in EC coupling

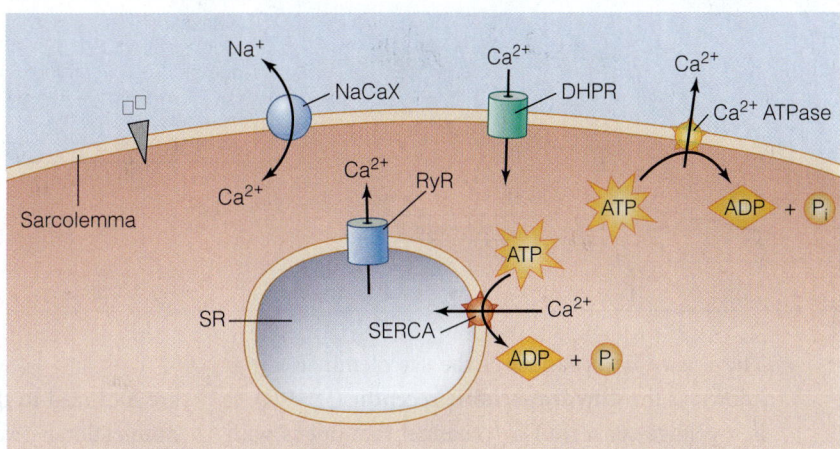

FIGURE 6.36 **Depolarization-induced Ca²⁺ release**

The upper panel shows the various transporters involved in the Ca²⁺ transient. Note that the DHPR and RyR interact physically in skeletal muscle. Subsequent panels show events in relaxation (1) Ca²⁺ release (2) and relaxation (3). In each row, the left image depicts a time point (red arrow) during the action potential (purple) and contraction (blue). The image in the center shows ion movements in this phase of the contractile cycle.

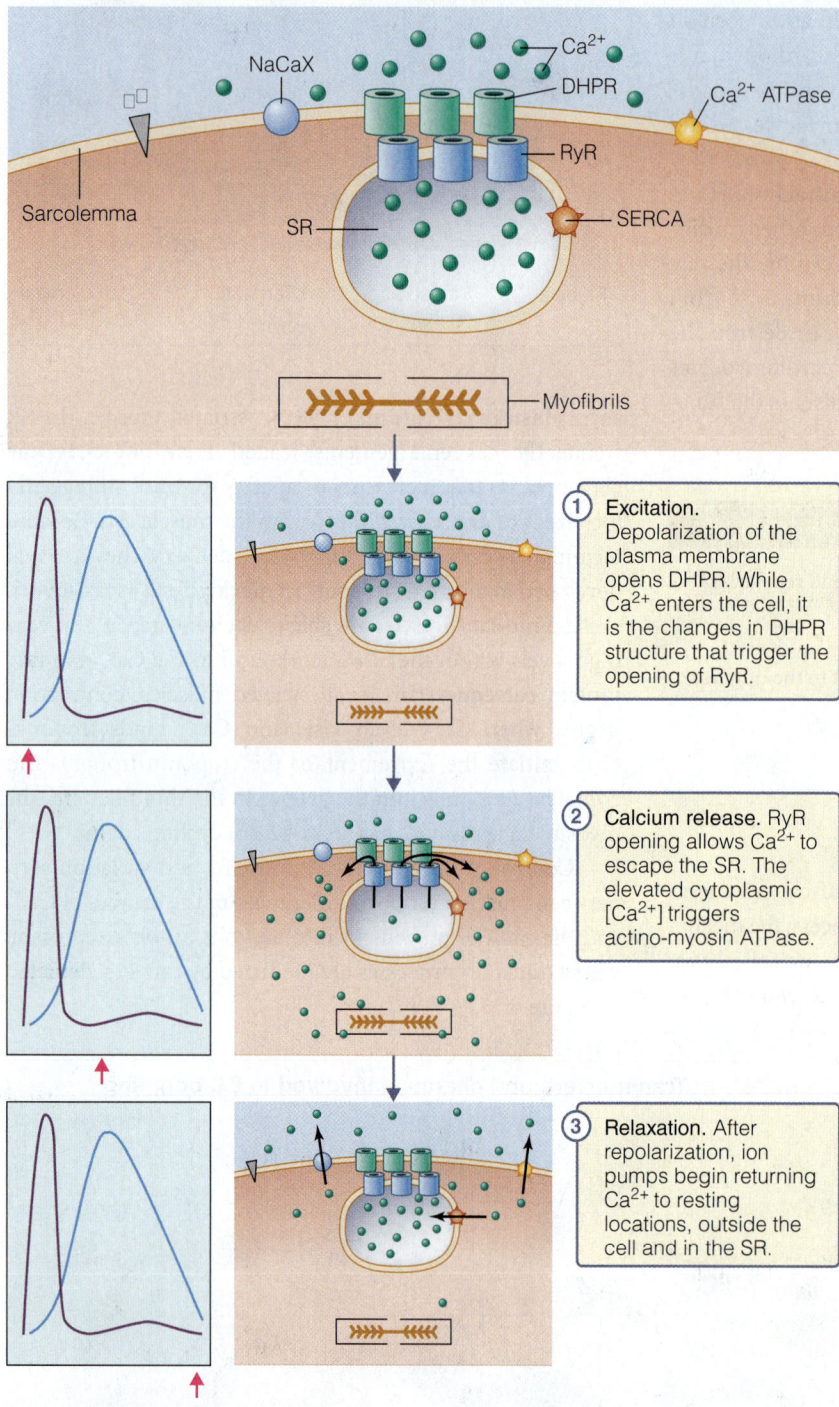

① **Excitation.** Depolarization of the plasma membrane opens DHPR. While Ca²⁺ enters the cell, it is the changes in DHPR structure that trigger the opening of RyR.

② **Calcium release.** RyR opening allows Ca²⁺ to escape the SR. The elevated cytoplasmic [Ca²⁺] triggers actino-myosin ATPase.

③ **Relaxation.** After repolarization, ion pumps begin returning Ca²⁺ to resting locations, outside the cell and in the SR.

- The main Ca²⁺ channel of the sarcolemma (SL) is known as the **dihydropyridine receptor (DHPR)**. It is a voltage-sensitive Ca²⁺ channel that opens with depolarization.

- The sodium-calcium exchanger (**NaCaX**) is a reversible transporter of the SL that exchanges Na⁺ for Ca²⁺. It is reversible and can work to allow Ca²⁺ into a cell or expel it from the cell, depending on the electrochemical gradients for each ion and the membrane potential.

- The Ca²⁺ ATPase is an active transporter in the SL that expels Ca²⁺ from the cell during relaxation.

- The Ca²⁺ channel of the SR is called the **ryanodine receptor (RyR)**. When open, it permits the release of Ca²⁺ from the SR stores into the sarcoplasm.

- **SERCA** is a Ca²⁺ ATPase found in the SR (and ER of nonmuscle cells), and pumps Ca²⁺ from the sarcoplasm into the SR.

DHPR activation induces Ca²⁺ release from the SR

Regardless of the type of striated muscle, depolarization opens the voltage-sensitive Ca²⁺ channel (DHPR). Whether this movement is sufficient to trigger contraction depends on the type of muscle, and the rates of contraction.

In striated muscles that contract slowly, inward Ca²⁺ movement through the DHPR is sufficient to elevate sarcoplasmic Ca²⁺ high enough to trigger contraction. For example, many lower vertebrates, such as fish, rely primarily on Ca²⁺ movements from the ECF across the SL to induce contraction. In such animals, T-tubules are reduced and there is minimal SR.

In striated muscles that contract more rapidly, there is greater reliance on the SR as a source of Ca²⁺. Typically, the SR is more elaborate and organized into terminal cisternae. As well, the sarcolemma has many T-tubules to enhance the propagation of the action potential. Finally, in faster muscles, the T-tubules of the SL and terminal cisternae of the SR are localized to the same region, which improves the communication between the SL and the SR. Where muscles differ is in the nature of the interaction between the SR and the SL.

In skeletal muscle, the DHPR and RyR Ca^{2+} channels are physically associated with each other (Figure 6.36). While depolarization induces DHPR to open and permit Ca^{2+} inflow, it is the accompanying structural change in the DHPR that is important. The close association between the DHPR and RyR allows the RyR to detect the depolarization-induced structural changes in DHPR. Activation of DHPR opens the RyR, and allows the SR Ca^{2+} stores to be released into the sarcoplasm. This pattern of EC coupling is called **depolarization-induced Ca^{2+} release**.

Cardiac muscles of birds and mammals use a different process to link DHPR and RyR activation. In **Ca^{2+}-induced Ca^{2+} release**, the open DHPR allows extracellular Ca^{2+} to enter the cell. Because DHPR are localized near terminal cisternae, local $[Ca^{2+}]$ can increase in the small space between the SL and the terminal cisternae (Figure 6.37). The high local $[Ca^{2+}]$ triggers the opening of cardiac muscle RyR, and the SR Ca^{2+} stores are released into the muscle cytoplasm. This pathway also appears to be important in the hearts of some lower vertebrates with high cardiac rates. For example, unlike most fish, high-performance species such as tuna rely on Ca^{2+}-induced Ca^{2+} release for EC coupling.

Relaxation follows removal of Ca^{2+} from the cytoplasm

Once contraction is complete, the muscle must reverse the steps to permit relaxation. To this point, we have discussed the mechanisms that lead to depolarization and the subsequent increase in cytoplasmic $[Ca^{2+}]$ that induce contraction. These ion movements across membranes must be reversed to allow relaxation to occur. As mentioned previously, the duration of the action potential determines how quickly a muscle can relax. Once the membrane repolarizes, the muscle can start to reestablish Ca^{2+} gradients. In vertebrate striated muscle, relaxation requires a suite of transporters to pump Ca^{2+} out of the cytoplasm, back across the sarcolemma, or into the SR. Both the sarcolemma and the SR possess active Ca^{2+} ATPases that pump Ca^{2+} out of the

cell using the energy of ATP hydrolysis. The efflux of Ca^{2+} is augmented by the sarcolemmal NaCaX, which exchanges Ca^{2+} for Na^+. During excitation, this reversible exchanger can allow extracellular Ca^{2+} to enter the cell in exchange for

FIGURE 6.37 **Ca^{2+}-induced Ca^{2+} release**

As with Figure 6.36, the upper panel shows the various transporters involved in the Ca^{2+} transient. Note that the DHPR and RyR are not physically associated. Subsequent panels show events in relaxation (1) Ca^{2+} release (2) and relaxation (3). In each row, the left image depicts a time point (red arrow) during the action potential (purple) and contraction (blue). The image in the center shows ion movements in this phase of the contractile cycle.

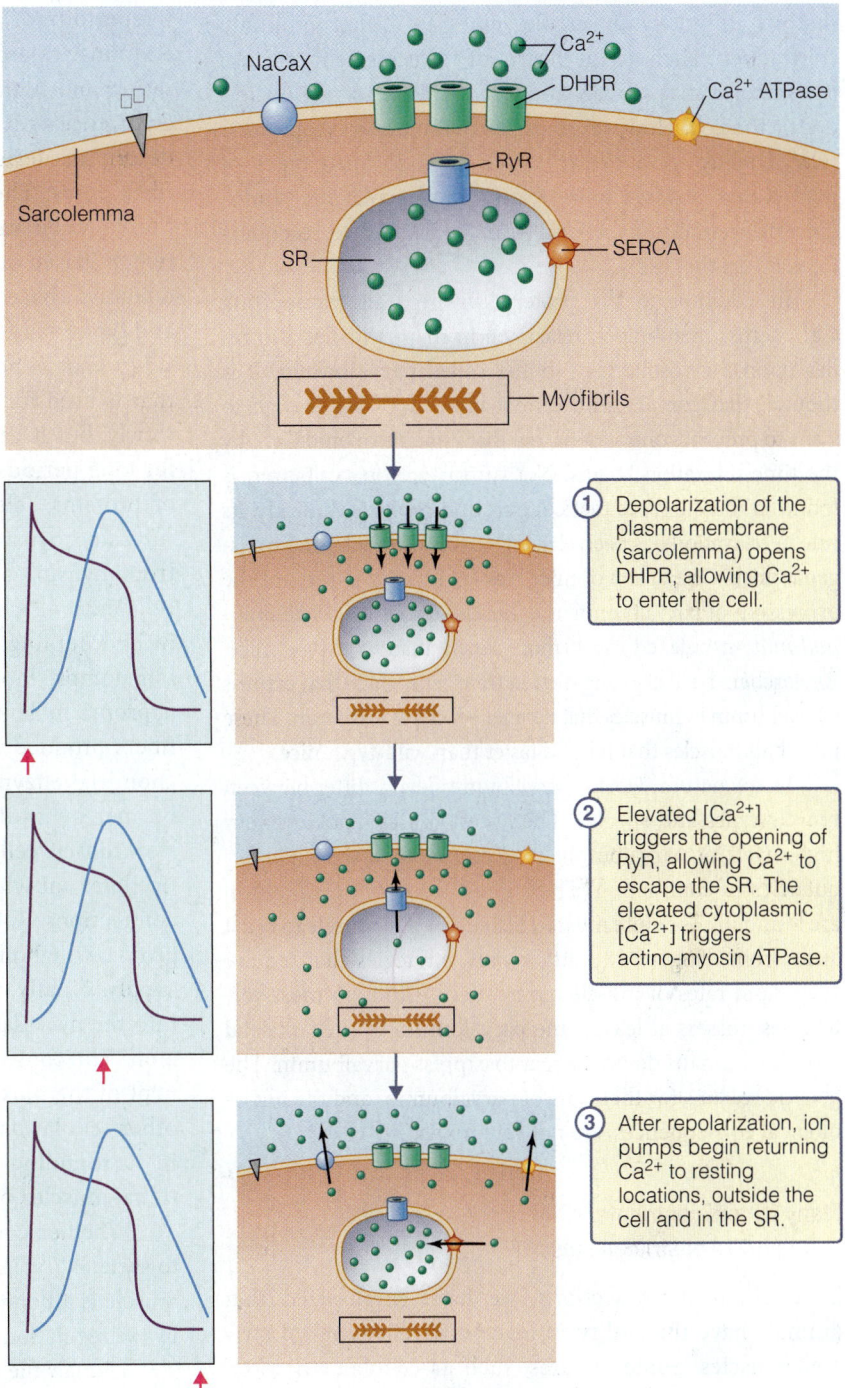

1. Depolarization of the plasma membrane (sarcolemma) opens DHPR, allowing Ca^{2+} to enter the cell.

2. Elevated $[Ca^{2+}]$ triggers the opening of RyR, allowing Ca^{2+} to escape the SR. The elevated cytoplasmic $[Ca^{2+}]$ triggers actino-myosin ATPase.

3. After repolarization, ion pumps begin returning Ca^{2+} to resting locations, outside the cell and in the SR.

intracellular Na^+. However, it is most important during relaxation, where Ca^{2+} efflux is coupled to Na^+ influx. As in other Na^+-driven transport processes, muscles ultimately use the Na^+/K^+ ATPase to reestablish Na^+ gradients.

The role of each specific Ca^{2+} transporter depends upon the way Ca^{2+} is used to induce contraction. Muscles that primarily rely on sarcolemmal Ca^{2+} influx to initiate contraction, such as the hearts of lower vertebrates, use the sarcolemmal NaCaX and Ca^{2+} ATPase to pump Ca^{2+} out of the cell. However, muscles that elevate cytoplasmic $[Ca^{2+}]$ using intracellular stores, such as most types of mammalian striated muscle, use the sarcoplasmic (endoplasmic) reticulum Ca^{2+} ATPase, or SERCA, to resequester Ca^{2+} in the SR.

In addition to the proteins involved in transporting Ca^{2+} across membranes, relaxation in many muscles also relies upon a cytosolic Ca^{2+} buffer called **parvalbumin**. It is thought that parvalbumin cannot bind Ca^{2+} fast enough to Ca^{2+} to prevent contractions, but that it is able to bind Ca^{2+} by the time relaxation begins. Not surprisingly, parvalbumin is found in muscle types that contract and relax very quickly. Its role in relaxation has been elegantly demonstrated using transgenic mice. One group of mice was engineered to prevent the expression of parvalbumin; the muscles of these *parvalbumin-null mutants* relaxed much more slowly than wild-type mice. Researchers have also engineered transgenic mice that express parvalbumin in muscles that normally lack parvalbumin. These mice had muscles that relaxed faster than wild-type mice.

In the natural world, parvalbumin levels differ between muscle types and species. The fastest muscles possess very high levels of parvalbumin to accommodate the high frequencies of contraction. The highest levels of parvalbumin are found in fish white muscle. Fish use white muscle to burst away from danger or to attack prey, strategies that require very rapid rates of muscle contraction. Although most vertebrates possess at least some parvalbumin in their skeletal muscles, humans do not appear to express parvalbumin. The genetic reasons for their loss of parvalbumin, and the physiological consequences, are not yet known.

Many factors contribute to differences in properties of striated muscles

Throughout these sections, we have emphasized that animals have the ability to make different types of striated muscles. Some features, such as cellular structure, are very similar, though differences in thick and thin filaments may subtly alter contractile properties. Distinct types of muscles may differ in complex ways related to excitation and EC coupling. Though striated muscles can be constructed many ways, the differences in composition and regulation have important functional consequences. The ability to produce skeletal muscles with different contractile properties is essential in constructing a locomotor system capable of carrying out different types of movement. The result of such a specialization process is a repertoire of muscle fiber types. Some vertebrate skeletal muscles are specialized for burst activity (short duration and high intensity), whereas others are suited to endurance activity (long duration, low intensity). Various descriptive terms are used to distinguish between these fiber types. They may be called white and red muscle (based upon **myoglobin** content), fast twitch and slow twitch (based on the speed of contraction), glycolytic and oxidative (based on metabolic specialization), or type II and type I (based on myosin heavy chain isoforms). Consider what is necessary to produce a specialized muscle that is used for low-frequency contractions. It contracts slowly, but it can continue contraction-relaxation cycles for long periods. Slow muscle cells express specific *types* of proteins: "slow" isoforms of thick filament proteins (myosin, myosin light chains), thin filaments (troponin, tropomyosin), and ion transport machinery. Slow muscle cells must also regulate the *amounts* of proteins involved in EC coupling, such as parvalbumin, ion channels, and ion pumps. Fiber-type specialization also demands the appropriate levels of metabolic proteins. Slow muscle fibers produce very high levels of myoglobin and mitochondrial enzymes to ensure that the ATP demands can be met by oxidative phosphorylation. In addition, the slow muscle cell must be integrated into a complex, multicellular muscle. The appropriate motor neurons make connections with the motor end plates. The blood vessels grow throughout the tissue to ensure an adequate blood supply. Finally, the slow muscle must also be connected into the necessary biomechanical framework of the skeleton. The contractile machinery is an important component of the muscle phenotype, but as you can see, many other cellular processes, both in the muscle cell itself and in surrounding cells, are necessary to construct a functional muscle.

Whether comparing skeletal muscle types, or cardiac to skeletal (Table 6.4), it is important to recognize that each muscle is a point on a continuum of possibilities, endowed by the regulation of an animal's genome.

Though the basic features of a given muscle are determined in early development, mature animals also retain a capacity to remodel muscles in response to physiological needs. Hearts can become stronger and leg muscles can become faster; this ability to modify muscle properties is an example of

Table 6.4   Comparing mammalian cardiac and skeletal striated muscles

	Cardiac	Skeletal
Cell morphology	Single cells (cardiomyocytes) about 10 to 20 μm in diameter and 100 μm in length	Multiple cells fused into large myofibers that are 10 to 100 μm in diameter and 1 to 100 mm in length
Excitation	Myogenic and involuntary	Neurogenic and usually voluntary
Action potential	Slow repolarization, with long refractory period	Fast repolarization, with short refractory period
EC coupling	Ca^{2+}-induced Ca^{2+} release	Depolarization-induced Ca^{2+} release
Sarcoplasmic reticulum	Well-developed terminal cisternae in birds and mammals. Poorly developed SR in lower vertebrates.	Amount of terminal cisternae depends on fiber type.

phenotypic plasticity. In the accompanying feature (Box 6.3: Challenges to Homeostasis: Remodeling Muscle in Response to Changing Conditions) we discuss the underlying mechanisms that permit a muscle cell to alter its structure and function in response to a change in activity.

CONCEPT CHECK

11. What is the role of T-tubules? Which type of muscle would have abundant T-tubules?

12. What is the role of terminal cisternae? Which type of muscle would have abundant terminal cisternae?

13. Distinguish between depolarization-induced Ca^{2+} release and Ca^{2+}-induced Ca^{2+} release.

14. What role do Ca^{2+}-binding proteins play in contraction and relaxation?

DIVERSITY IN MUSCLE STRUCTURE AND FUNCTION

Muscle cells first arose in cnidarians, such as the familiar *Hydra*. Myoepithelial cells combined to form fibers that worked in conjunction with their internal hydrostatic skeleton to extend the body stalk. True muscle first appeared in a related group of animals called ctenophores. These animals, which include sea walnuts and sea gooseberries, have true smooth muscle cells in the body wall.

The animals within the various worm phyla, including flatworms, nematodes, and annelids, have more elaborate muscle systems. Nematodes move using longitudinal muscles in the body wall, whereas annelids possess complex longitudinal and circular smooth muscles. Worms also use muscle for nonlocomotor functions. Nematodes have pharyngeal muscles used for feeding, and annelids have thickened regions of blood vessels that act as pumping hearts.

Although these ancient animals have several discrete types of muscle, more complex recent animals display much greater diversity in muscle anatomy and physiology.

One of the most important factors driving the diversity of muscle types in more complex animals was the trend toward larger bodies. Whereas small animals can survive using simple diffusion of respiratory gases, large animals have low surface area-to-volume ratios, and simple diffusion cannot meet their metabolic demands. Thus, the genes for muscle proteins evolved in combination with primitive respiratory and circulatory systems. For example, mollusks possess well-developed muscular hearts, and their multiple types of muscle are used in locomotion and feeding. Likewise, arthropods have complex muscles that control ventilation and movement.

The greatest diversity in muscle types, however, occurs in the vertebrates. More than 300 million years ago, the early vertebrate ancestors experienced two rounds of genome duplications. The extra copies of genes for critical muscle proteins allowed for the evolution of highly specialized muscle types. Instead of only having single genes for important muscle proteins, as found in the invertebrates and protochordates, genome duplication and later gene duplications in ancestors of more complex animals created extra copies of these genes, providing fertile ground for the evolution of specialized muscle protein isoforms. Invertebrates employ only one or two muscle myosin genes to build all muscles; vertebrates possess at least 15 different myosin genes and use eight of them in muscle. With the transition to land and the challenges of movement under the full weight of gravity, muscle genes rapidly evolved, allowing muscle specialization and diversification.

Smooth Muscle

As discussed above, the earliest muscles to evolve were smooth muscles; striated muscle is more complex in organization, but

REMODELING MUSCLE IN RESPONSE TO CHANGING CONDITIONS

The ability of an animal to remodel its muscles is central to homeostasis. The process for remodeling a heart or a skeletal muscle involves changes in the muscle cells and the other cell types that support tissue function. When you undertake endurance exercise training, for example, your heart gets stronger and your heart rate declines. This involves changes in the channels that govern heart rate (pacemaker cells), changes in the connective tissue by fibroblasts, and changes in the cardiomyocytes as individual cells become longer. At the same time, the muscles of the leg are remodeled to become more efficient in metabolism, in contrast to strength training, in which the muscles grow in size to generate more force. The capacity to remodel muscles depends on the muscle being able to sense the demand, and control the expression of genes that permit coordinated changes in muscle construction.

The remodeling process of the muscle cells is under control of hormonal and nonhormonal mechanisms of cell signaling (Figure 6.38). One hormone that is thought to be important is thyroid hormone. Thyroid hormones influence the pattern of myosin isoform expression. Thyroid hormone enters the cell through a transporter (1) and binds to its receptor located in the nucleus (2). The receptor is located on gene promoters at specific regions called thyroid hormone responsive elements. Once it binds to a hormone, the activated receptor recruits other proteins to form a multiprotein complex that can increase or decrease the rate of transcription (3). Thyroid hormone treatment has reciprocal effects on myosin gene expression in cardiac myocytes; it represses the expression of the β-myosin II gene, while inducing the expression of the α-myosin II gene. If the average levels of thyroid hormones remain high over a few weeks, the contractile machinery is gradually remodeled with α-myosin II replacing β-myosin II in the thick filament. As mentioned previously, α-myosin dimers exhibit the fastest actino-myosin ATPase rates. Thyroid hormones regulate many of the genes involved in muscle synthesis, as well as many other genes in other tissues. By using a circulating endocrine hormone like thyroid hormone to respond to physiological challenges, animals are able to coordinate the remodeling of many tissues and physiological functions.

Mechanoreceptors in muscle cells can detect physical changes in muscle shape and trigger changes in signaling pathways (4). When a muscle cell is stretched, for example, a signal cascade can be activated, typically involving a protein kinase (5). Phosphorylation of transcription factors alters the expression of suites of genes that influence muscle remodeling (6). One such protein is the protein *insulin-like growth factor II*, which is synthesized (7), then secreted into the extracellular space (8). The IGF II binds to receptors on muscle plasma membranes to trigger signaling pathways that alter the expression of genes encoding muscle proteins (9). This is an example of *autocrine* stimulation, in which the muscle cell stimulates itself.

Changes in muscle activity also alter the intracellular environment, causing changes in the average concentration of Ca^{2+} or metabolites. For example, increases in Ca^{2+} can stimulate Ca-dependent enzymes such as calmodulin-dependent protein kinase (CamK). Increases in the concentration of AMP, an indication of energetic shortfalls, can

smooth muscle plays more diverse roles in animals. Many tissues use multiple layers of smooth muscle, arranged in circular and longitudinal orientations (Figure 6.39).

Smooth muscle is efficient at inducing a slow regular contraction, or maintaining a degree of contraction for long periods. The functional flexibility makes it useful in many physiological systems. In many tissues, smooth muscle is organized in circular and longitudinal arrangements. Activation of the circular layer reduces the diameter and increases the length of the tube, whereas activation of the longitudinal layer shortens the tube but makes it wider.

Smooth muscle lines the walls of blood vessels, controlling blood flow by regulating the diameter of the blood vessels. Smooth muscle works in a similar fashion in the respiratory system of terrestrial vertebrates to control the diameter of airways. Circular and longitudinal layers of smooth muscle in the digestive tract propel food down the gut and control the length of the gastrointestinal tract. Reproductive function also depends on smooth muscle to propel gametes or offspring along the reproductive tract. Although it shares many features with striated muscle, such as the basic interaction between actin and myosin, it has important differences that provide the smooth muscle cell with remarkable flexibility in contraction dynamics and distinct pathways of EC coupling regulation.

Smooth muscle lacks organized sarcomeres

Although smooth muscle cells are composed of the same contractile elements as striated muscle, animals can organize

stimulate AMP-dependent protein kinase (AMPK). These protein kinases can phosphorylate their own target proteins, including transcription factors, contributing to the remodeling process.

In the case of muscle damage, the repair process may include stimulation of satellite cells. These pluripotent stem cells reside in muscle, awaiting a signal from myofibers that they are required. When myofibers secrete signaling factors, this induces the satellite cells to move to the affected area, fuse with muscle, and contribute additional nuclei to the multicellular myofiber. This is an example of *paracrine* stimulation.

Collectively, these diverse pathways allow muscles to sense and respond to changes in muscle activity, and permit phenotypic remodeling of the muscle to permit it to become better able to meet the demands placed upon it.

FIGURE 6.38 **Control of gene expression in response to physiological changes**

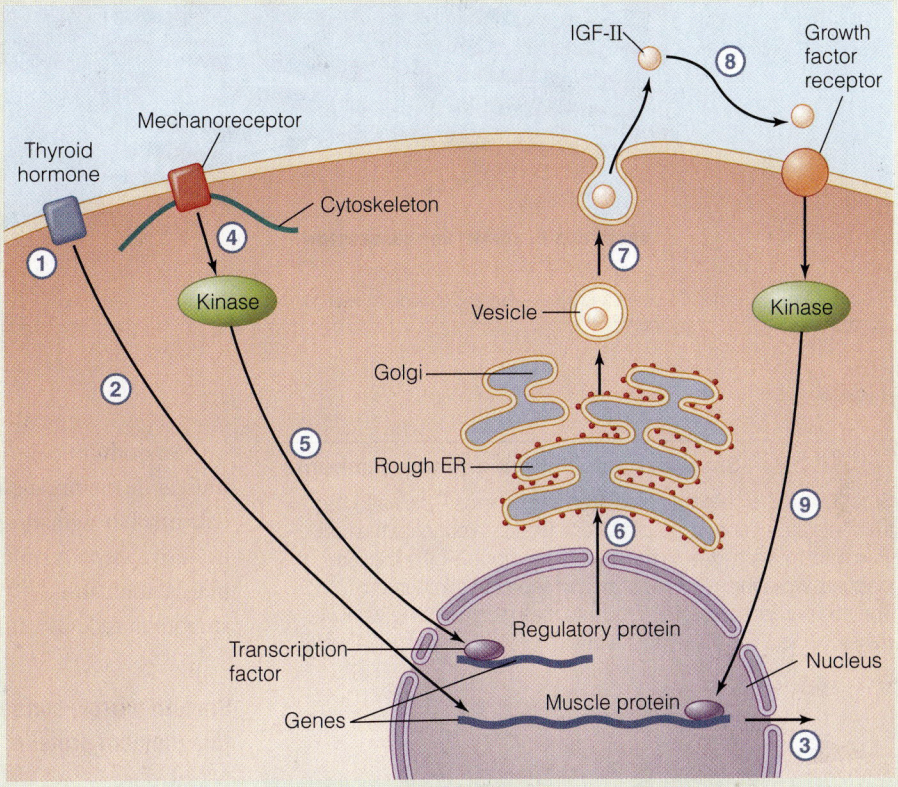

and regulate smooth muscle in various ways. Striated muscles arrange their thick and thin filaments into sarcomeres, producing their characteristic striped appearance. Smooth muscle also has thin filaments and thick filaments, but they are not organized into sarcomeres. At the cellular level, smooth muscle is a collection of individual cells that are organized into a functional network. Gap junctions between smooth muscle cells allow them to communicate and exert a common response to local regulators, creating a functional group that acts as a unit. This cellular organization is reminiscent of the organization of cardiac muscle. One or more functional groups may be physically linked together by connective tissue, but regulated independently within that tissue. In the circulatory system, for example, a layer of smooth muscle surrounds the blood vessels. The smooth

muscle cells may be induced to contract in unison in one region, while a neighboring region remains relaxed. Many organs have layers of smooth muscle arranged in a way that allows contraction in different planes. For example, the gastrointestinal tract has an inner layer of circular muscle that regulates circumference, and a layer of longitudinal muscle that regulates length.

The main difference between smooth and striated muscle is in the organization of the thick and thin filaments. Instead of parallel arrays of sarcomeres, smooth muscle scatters clusters of thick and thin filaments throughout the cytoplasm (Figure 6.40). The aggregated filaments interconnect with each other to form a network within the cytoplasm, and attach to the plasma membrane at specific regions called **adhesion plaques**. This three-dimensional arrangement of

FIGURE 6.39 Circular and longitudinal layers of smooth muscle

This micrograph highlights the cellular arrangement in a tissue where two layers of muscle run at 90° angles, as with circular and longitudinal muscle.

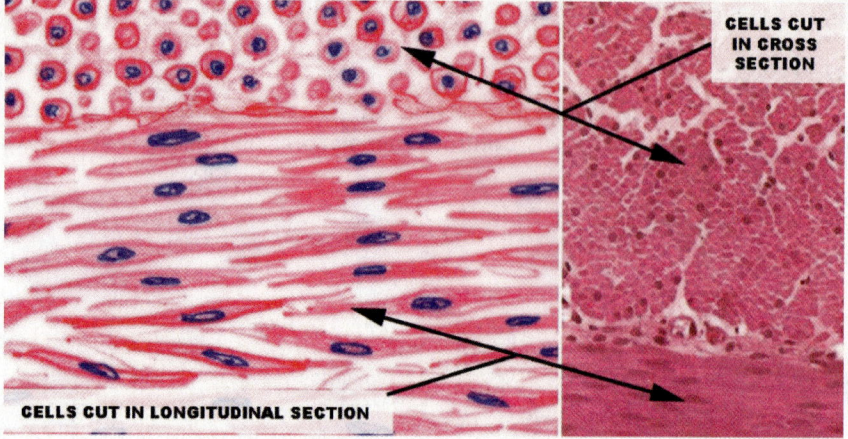

Photo source: © Thomas Caceci/2014 Virginia-Maryland College of Veterinary Medicine.

FIGURE 6.40 Smooth muscle thick and thin filaments

Smooth muscle cells lack organized sarcomeres. Thick and thin filaments are arranged in complex networks throughout the cell: Thin filaments are fixed to the plasma membrane by adhesion plaques, while thick filaments overlap separate thin filaments. The thin filaments are integrated into the cytoskeletal network via dense bodies, which are points of attachment with microfilaments.

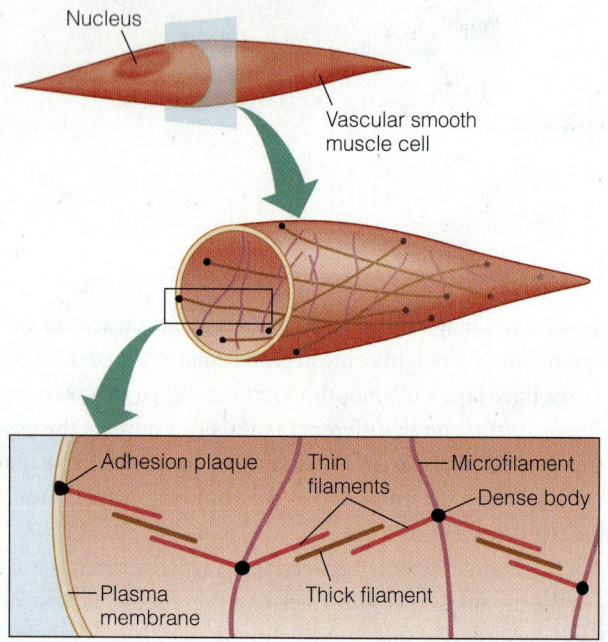

thick and thin filaments allows smooth muscle cells to contract in all dimensions. In contrast to striated muscle, with twice as many thin filaments as thick filaments, smooth muscle has about 15 thin filaments for each thick filament.

Smooth muscle also differs in structure from striated muscle in membrane organization. It lacks the elaborate sarcolemmal invaginations called T-tubules, and does not have an extensive sarcoplasmic reticulum. Because these structures aid in excitation and Ca^{2+} delivery, it should not be surprising that smooth muscle also differs from striated muscle in EC coupling.

Smooth muscle contraction is regulated by both thick and thin filament proteins

Regulation of contraction is much more complex in smooth muscle than in striated muscle. Smooth muscle contractility is regulated by nerves, hormones, and physical conditions, such as stretch. As in striated muscle activation, many regulators of smooth muscle contractility exert their effects by changing $[Ca^{2+}]$. In smooth muscle, however, $[Ca^{2+}]$ exerts its effect on both thick filaments and thin filaments. Furthermore, many types of smooth muscle alter contractility by changing the *sensitivity* to Ca^{2+}, rather than $[Ca^{2+}]$. In many of the subsequent chapters, we consider the specific mechanisms by which regulators influence smooth muscle contractility. In the next section, we consider in general terms some of the more common regulatory cascades that affect smooth muscle contraction through Ca^{2+}-dependent and Ca^{2+}-independent mechanisms.

In contrast to striated muscle, smooth muscle lacks troponin; the effects of Ca^{2+} are mediated via other regulatory proteins. **Caldesmon** is an actin-binding protein that binds to the thin filament and prevents myosin from binding to actin. In this sense, caldesmon in smooth muscle functionally replaces TnC. Caldesmon moves out of this inhibitory position in response to Ca^{2+}, but it does not directly bind Ca^{2+}. When the [Ca^{2+}] increases, the soluble protein calmodulin binds to Ca^{2+}, then binds to caldesmon. The calmodulin-caldesmon complex dissociates from actin and allows the formation of a cross-bridge between myosin and actin. When Ca^{2+} levels fall, the Ca^{2+}-calmodulin-caldesmon complex dissociates and caldesmon returns to its inhibitory site on actin. Many hormones that act on smooth muscle mediate their effects by regulating the Ca^{2+}-dependent effects of caldesmon. These hormones alter signaling cascades that stimulate protein kinases and protein phosphatases. For instance, when caldesmon is phosphorylated by a MAP kinase, it is unable to bind to actin, even though Ca^{2+} levels may fall. Thus, caldesmon phosphorylation sustains contractions in a manner that is independent of Ca^{2+}.

Much of the regulation of vertebrate smooth muscle is mediated via the thick filament proteins. Recall that muscle myosin is a hexamer of two myosin heavy chains with four myosin light chains. In smooth muscle, the myosin light chains regulate the ability of the myosin heavy chain heads to form a cross-bridge. Many agents that alter smooth muscle contractility act by changing the phosphorylation state of myosin light chains. When phosphorylated by myosin light chain kinase (MLCK), the myosin light chain enhances the ability of myosin to bind to actin. When dephosphorylated by myosin light chain phosphatase (MLCP), myosin light chain prevents the myosin heavy chain from forming the cross-bridge, thereby allowing the smooth muscle to relax.

Many of the effectors that regulate smooth muscle contractility induce their effects via regulation of the activity of MLCK or MLCP. For example, Ca^{2+} can stimulate MLCK and thereby favor contraction. The effects of Ca^{2+} on MLCK are mediated indirectly by calmodulin. Thus, Ca^{2+} exerts effects on both the thin filament (Ca^{2+}-calmodulin-caldesmon) and the thick filament (MLCK-myosin light chain). The two main pathways of Ca^{2+}-dependent regulation of smooth muscle are summarized in Figure 6.41. Many of these factors alter Ca^{2+} levels in a very complex manner. One hormone may cause a small but rapid increase in Ca^{2+} throughout the cell, whereas another hormone might cause a greater Ca^{2+} increase that is localized near the plasma membrane. These complex spatial and temporal patterns of Ca^{2+}, known as Ca^{2+} signatures, affect different signaling cascades. Once a hormone binds to its receptor on the smooth muscle membrane, it may exert effects directly on one or more components of the smooth muscle signaling pathway.

Many signaling factors act in ways that do not cause changes in [Ca^{2+}] but rather by activating or inhibiting MLCK and MLCP. For example, nitric oxide stimulates smooth muscle relaxation by stimulating guanylate cyclase. The increase in cGMP levels activates cGMP-dependent protein kinase (PKG), which phosphorylates and activates MLCP. The effect of these cellular changes is to permit

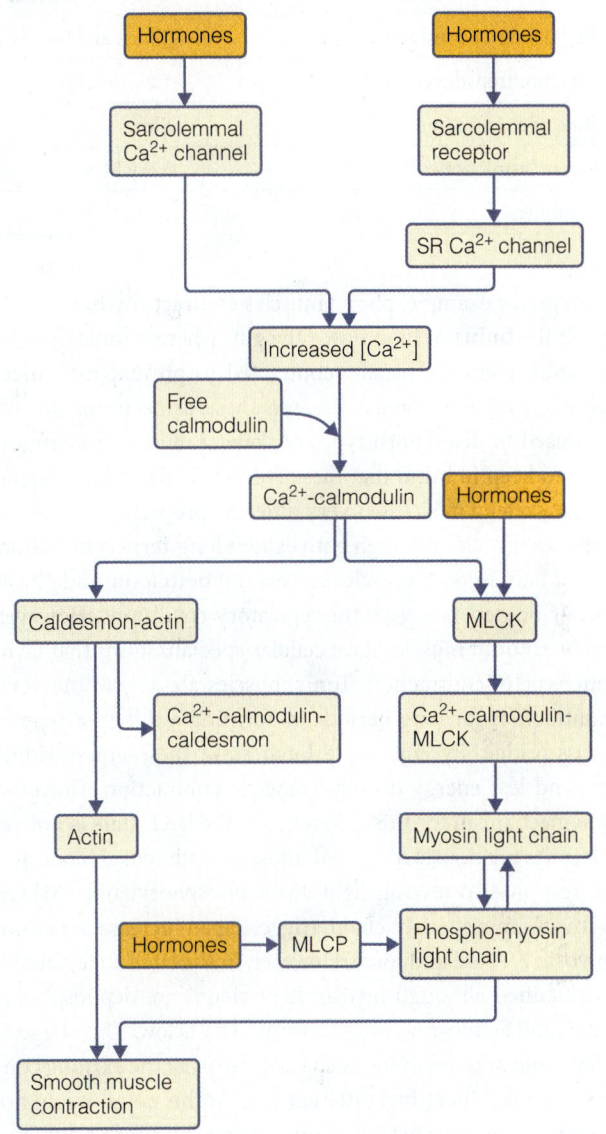

FIGURE 6.41 **Control of smooth muscle contraction** Smooth muscle contraction is regulated by pathways that target both thick and thin filament proteins. Many signaling factors impinge on this pathway, including hormones (shown above), neurotransmitters, and neurohormones.

vasodilation. In later chapters, we will discuss the pathways by which diverse neural and hormonal factors regulate smooth muscle function in specific physiological systems.

Latch cross-bridges maintain smooth muscle contraction for long periods

The contractile properties of smooth muscle differ widely in terms of force generation, as well as contraction and relaxation rates. Smooth muscles are often broadly divided into tonic and phasic smooth muscles. Tonic muscles are those that remain contracted for a long period, whereas **phasic muscles** contract and relax frequently. Within the digestive

Table 6.5 Comparing smooth and striated muscle

	Smooth	Striated
Ca^{2+} source	Primarily extracellular	Primarily intracellular
Thick and thin filaments	Not arranged into sarcomeres	Arranged as sarcomeres
Regulation of contraction	Thick and thin filaments	Mainly thin filament
Calcium transducer	Calmodulin	Troponin
Rate of contraction	Slow	Faster
Sarcoplasmic reticulum	Very little	Can be abundant
T-tubules	None	Can be abundant

system, for example, phasic muscles contract rhythmically to push the **bolus** of food down the gut, whereas tonic muscles in **sphincters** are usually contracted to prevent movement between compartments. Because these same terms are often used to distinguish types of skeletal muscle, it is important to keep in mind that these are simply descriptive terms. Tonic skeletal muscle has very different properties from tonic smooth muscle, although both exhibit long-term contraction.

Many smooth muscles can exhibit both tonic and phasic behavior, depending on the regulatory conditions. However, some smooth muscles have cellular specializations that favor one type of contraction. Tonic muscles are able to maintain contraction for long periods by forming a different type of cross-bridge. By entering a **latch state** these cross-bridges expend less energy during isometric contraction. However, the mechanism for this difference in the latch state is not yet clear. As previously discussed, most smooth muscle contracts in response to myosin light chain phosphorylation. MLCK activates myosin light chain, triggering an increase in actino-myosin ATPase and force. However, in the latch state, force is maintained although myosin light chains are dephosphory-lated and actino-myosin ATPase activity is low. This suggests that tonic muscles in the latch state are using the existing contractile machinery in a different way. At this point, we do not know for certain what factors are responsible for this different type of cross-bridge activity. Some researchers believe that the entire process of cross-bridge cycling slows. Others believe that the cytoskeleton itself interacts with actin and myosin to strengthen the physical interactions in this tonic state.

A summary of the differences between smooth and striated muscle is given in Table 6.5.

CONCEPT CHECK

15. Does smooth muscle have actin and myosin? Does it have thick and thin filaments? Does it have sarcomeres?
16. Discuss the regulation of smooth muscle contractile properties through Ca^{2+} and Ca^{2+}-independent mechanisms.

Invertebrate Muscles

All muscles share the features of myosin-based thick filaments and actin-based thin filaments, but the variation in the arrangement of filaments and regulation of contraction is much more pronounced in the invertebrates than the vertebrates. Researchers have studied the structural diversity in muscle of invertebrates for many years, identifying many variations in myofibrillar organization and muscle design. More recently, studies of common invertebrate model species (*Drosophila*, *C. elegans*) have furthered the understanding of the molecular basis of muscle development and regulation through functional genomics. As discussed in Chapter 2, it is now known that striated muscle has evolved at least twice in animals, once in cnidarians and once more in bilateran animals.

Many invertebrates possess obliquely striated muscle

As in vertebrates, some invertebrate muscles are smooth (lacking sarcomeres) or striated, with numerous sarcomeres attached end to end to form long myofibrils. Unlike vertebrates, invertebrates show many muscle forms that are intermediate between smooth and striated. There is also a great deal of variation in the arrangement of thick and thin filaments, with ratios ranging from 1:3 to 1:10 in different muscles and species.

Recall that vertebrate striated muscle is composed of sarcomeres attached end to end to form a myofibril that is attached to the sarcolemma at each end. The cross-striated pattern arises because the sarcomeres are attached side by side, perpendicular to the sarcolemma (Figure 6.42). **Obliquely striated muscle**, found in many invertebrates, differs from striated muscle in two respects. First, the sarcomeres are not connected side by side, disrupting the pattern of cross-striation. Second, instead of long myofibrils of sarcomeres, each individual sarcomere is attached to a pinnacle-shaped structure called a dense body, extending perpendicularly through the thin muscle cell. They are similar in many respects to the dense bodies of smooth muscle. The dense

FIGURE 6.42 Obliquely striated muscle

The body wall of *C. elegans* is constructed from obliquely striated muscle.

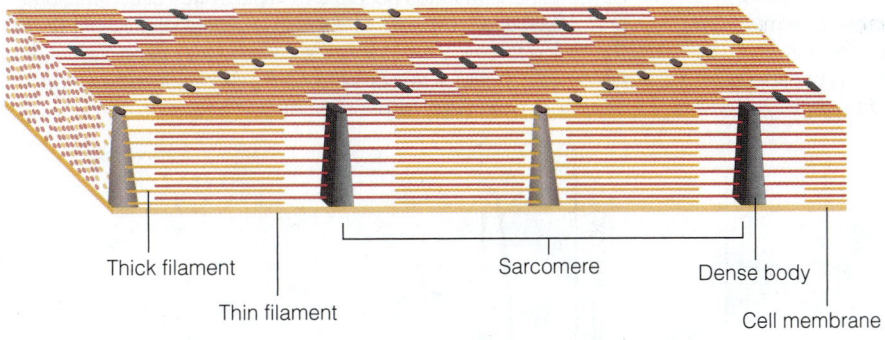

Thick filament

Thin filament

Sarcomere

Dense body

Cell membrane

bodies are attached to the inside of the sarcolemma, which is in turn connected via receptors to the extracellular matrix proteins to the basal lamina, which in turn is connected to the cuticle. When obliquely striated muscle contracts, it pulls on the dense bodies, causing a local shortening of the body. In the case of *C. elegans*, the obliquely striated muscle runs under the cuticle, such that contraction causes the body to bend at that point.

Invertebrate muscles contract in response to graded excitatory postsynaptic potentials

The vertebrate striated muscles we have discussed to this point all contract when the sarcolemmal membrane potential briefly depolarizes. In the case of a neurogenic skeletal muscle, activation of the motor neurons controlling that myofiber induces depolarization of that cell and a subsequent contraction. The main way that vertebrate twitch muscles can produce graded contractions is by recruiting different numbers of motor units. Stronger contractions result when many motor neurons are stimulated to activate many myofibers within the muscle.

Some invertebrate muscles have a different way of translating excitatory information from the nervous system into a graded muscle contraction. Unlike vertebrate twitch muscle, these invertebrate myofibers do not contract in an all-or-none manner. In the simplest system, a single muscle fiber is innervated by a single motor neuron that controls the myofiber at multiple motor end plates, much like a vertebrate tonic muscle. When the neuron fires a single impulse, the muscle experiences a minor depolarization. The muscle responds with a small elevation of Ca^{2+} and a weak contraction. Because this depolarization favors an excitation of the muscle, it is called an **excitatory postsynaptic potential**, or EPSP (Figure 6.43). This system is able to achieve a graded contraction because EPSPs can summate. When the nerve sends two rapid impulses, the neurotransmitters affect a broader area of the sarcolemma and induce a greater depolarization,

which in turn causes a greater release of Ca^{2+}. The strongest contractions result when multiple impulses trigger a very large depolarization and maximal Ca^{2+} release.

In many cases, these muscles are innervated by multiple neurons, each with a different effect on the muscle membrane potential. One excitatory neuron may induce a strong depolarization with a single impulse, acting in many ways like a motor neuron in a twitch fiber. Other excitatory neurons may innervate the same muscle cell but exert smaller effects on membrane potential, acting primarily through the summation of EPSPs.

The muscle may also be innervated by inhibitory neurons. When these neurons fire, they hyperpolarize the membrane. These inhibitory postsynaptic potentials (IPSPs) make it more difficult to induce a contraction. This is another distinction between invertebrate and vertebrate striated muscle, which can only receive excitatory input. In general, the invertebrates use complex innervation to control simple muscles, whereas vertebrates use a multiplicity of fibers with more straightforward innervation.

Asynchronous insect flight muscles do not use Ca^{2+} transients

As we have seen, many muscles rely on the Ca^{2+} transient to trigger cycles of contraction and relaxation. In the fastest of vertebrate skeletal muscles, the toadfish sonic muscle, Ca^{2+} transients occur as fast as one hundred times a second (100 Hz). However, vertebrate muscles cannot be induced to contract faster than this due to the limits of the vertebrate EC coupling machinery. The sonic muscles of the cicada are unusual in that their mode of EC coupling is fundamentally similar to that of vertebrate skeletal muscles, yet they are able to contract and relax much faster. The flight muscles of many insects are even faster. The high-frequency buzz of flying insects arises when the wings beat in the range of 250 to 1,000 Hz. They are able to contract at these remarkable frequencies by using a different mode of EC coupling.

Recall that vertebrate muscles contract in response to a single spike of Ca^{2+} arising from a single action potential. To relax, these muscles must reduce Ca^{2+} to low levels to inactivate the actino-myosin ATPase. Insect flight muscles differ from this model in the linkage between neuronal stimulation and contraction (Figure 6.44). As with other neurogenic muscles, the insect first activates the flight muscle by a single neuronal stimulation. However, unlike other muscles, a single action potential is followed by a long series of contraction

FIGURE 6.43 **Graded excitatory postsynaptic potentials in invertebrate muscles**

Invertebrate muscles receive impulses from motor neurons. The degree of depolarization depends on the number of stimuli from the neurons. A single stimulus causes a small depolarization, or excitatory postsynaptic potential (EPSP), which is capable of triggering a small contraction. Multiple stimuli trigger a greater depolarization and stronger contraction.

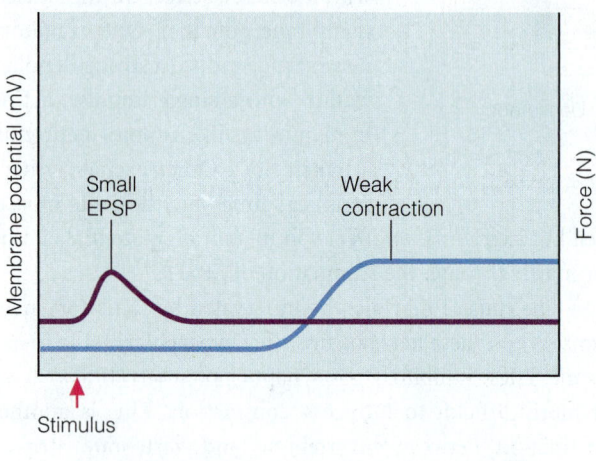

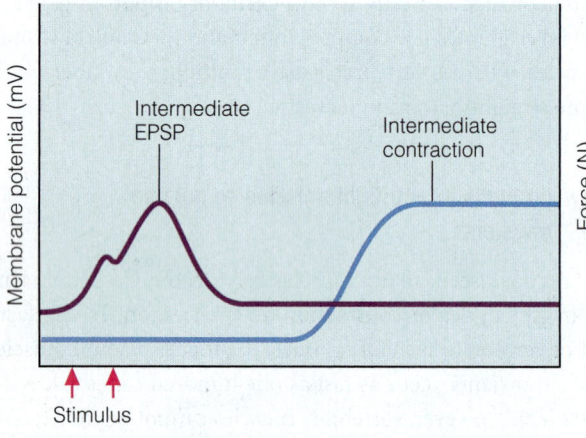

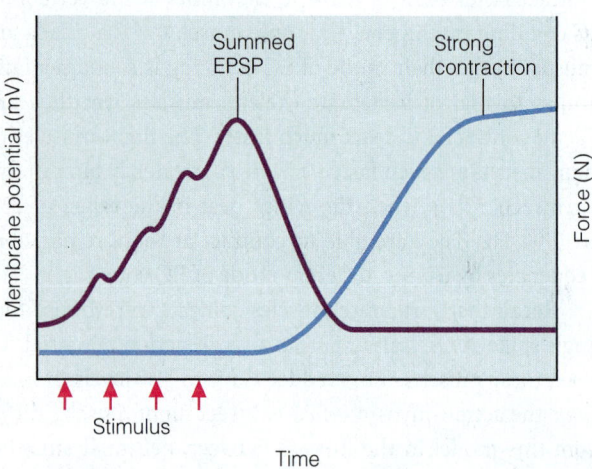

FIGURE 6.44 **Stretch-activated asynchronous muscles**

Asynchronous muscles generate multiple cycles of contraction and relaxation in response to a single neuronal stimulation. During the period following excitation, Ca^{2+} levels likely remain elevated. Relaxation occurs in response to contraction-induced inactivation. Contraction is in response to stretch activation.

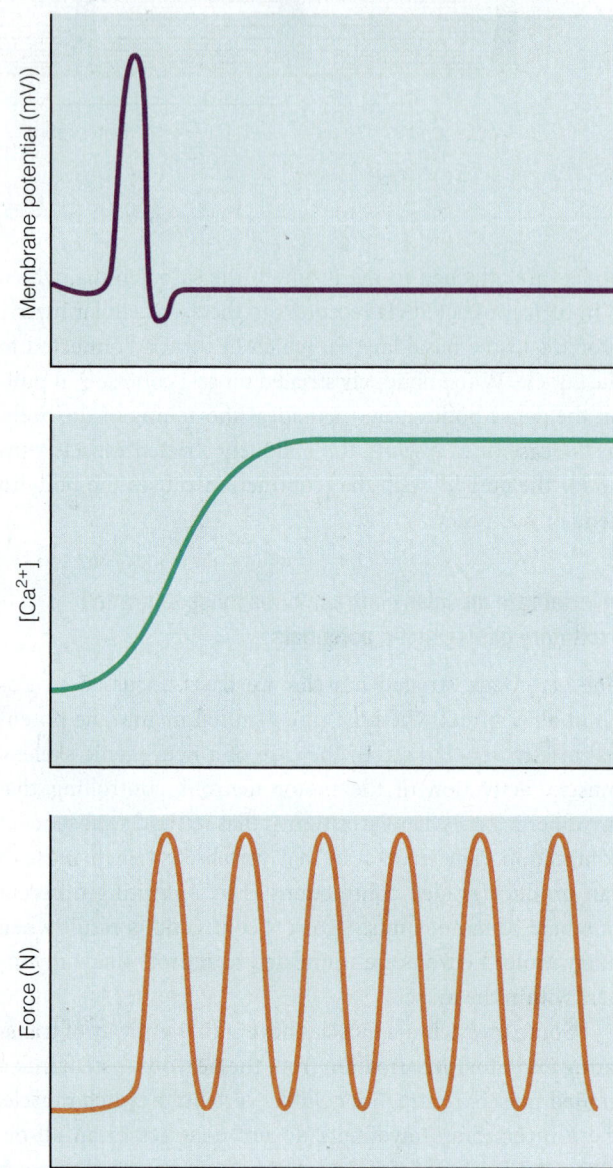

flight muscle because nervous stimulation is not synchronized with contraction. Most flying insects use asynchronous flight muscles to fly, although many also incorporate synchronous flight muscles, particularly to control the fine movements required for navigation.

Asynchronous flight muscle is able to contract and relax at high frequency because it has a different relationship between Ca^{2+}, TnC, and contraction. Though many questions remain, it appears that this type of flight muscle possesses two

and relaxation cycles. During flight, multiple action potentials occur but the frequency is much lower than the wing beat frequency. This type of muscle is called **asynchronous**

different TnC isoforms. One is regulated in a Ca^{2+}-dependent manner, whereas another is part of a pathway in which stretch of the muscle activates contraction. Once contraction occurs, the stretch-activation pathway is inactivated, permitting the muscle to relax. The muscle is stretched again through the actions of other thoracic muscles, repeating the cycle. Although the phenomenon of stretch activation–contraction inactivation has been recognized for decades, the molecular basis remains a bit obscure. It appears that flight is made possible by careful regulation of both the Ca^{2+}-sensitive and stretch-sensitive pathways.

Mollusk catch muscles maintain contraction for long periods

Bivalve mollusks (clams, oysters, and mussels) possess a most remarkable muscle that is capable of generating long-duration contractions while expending remarkably little energy. The muscles, often adductor muscles, are responsible for rapidly closing the shells and maintaining this state for very long periods, protecting the animal from predators or harsh external conditions.

These muscles possess a thick and thin filament structure similar in many respects to that of vertebrate smooth muscle, but with important differences. A large dimeric protein, *paramyosin,* forms the core of the thick filament, around which a monolayer of myosin molecules is attached. This myosin is distinct from vertebrate myosins, and can be regulated directly by Ca^{2+}. (Recall that the thick filament of vertebrate smooth muscle is also regulated by Ca^{2+}, though indirectly.)

When the catch muscle is stimulated by cholinergic nerves, the acetylcholine triggers an increase in sarcoplasmic $[Ca^{2+}]$ (Figure 6.45). When Ca^{2+} binds myosin, cross-bridge cycling occurs and the muscle contracts. Sustained cholinergic activity for a time ensures that $[Ca^{2+}]$ remains elevated and force is generated. After a time, Ca^{2+} and ACh levels decline, yet the catch muscle remains contracted. It is not until serotonergic nerves release serotonin that the muscle relaxes, without changes in $[Ca^{2+}]$. Remarkably, during this period of sustained contraction, the muscle consumes very little energy, suggesting that cross-bridge cycling has ceased.

The mechanisms by which the catch muscle sustains contraction remain unclear, but it is thought that the changes

FIGURE 6.45 Molluscan catch muscle contraction and relaxation

Upon stimulation by cholinergic nerves, the increase in acetylcholine induces contraction of the mollusk adductor muscle. Even though Ca^{2+} levels decline, the muscle remains contracted in the catch state, where little energy is consumed. Relaxation ensues after serotonergic nerves fire. The changes in catch state coincide with changes in phosphorylation of the protein twitchin.

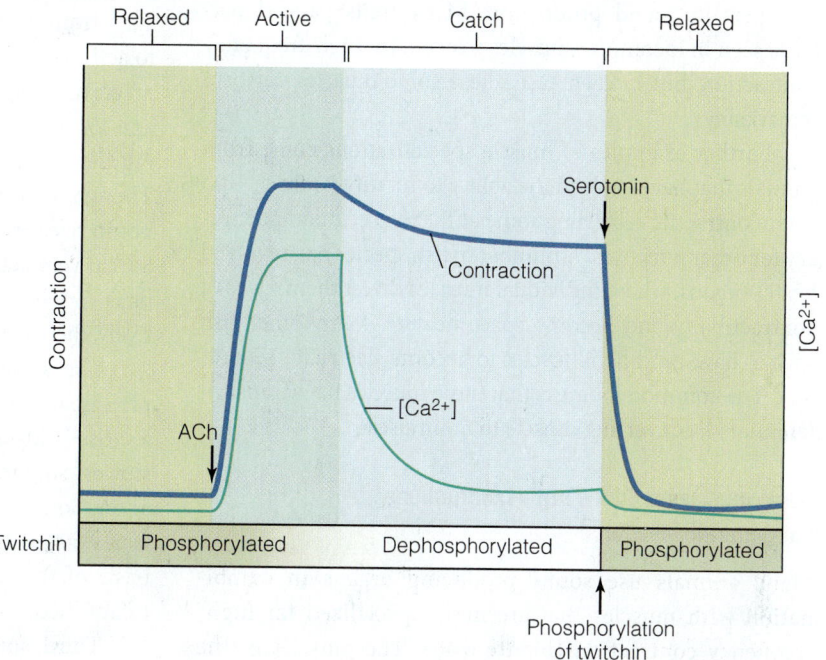

Figure source: Adapted from Twitchin as a regulator of catch contraction in molluscan smooth muscle. *Journal of muscle research and cell motility, 26*(6–8):455–60, Figure 1. Funabara D, Kanoh S, Siegman MJ, Butler TM, Hartshorne DJ, & Watabe S. ©2005. With permission of Springer Science+Business Media.

are related to phosphorylation of another unusual protein, *twitchin.* This protein is related to titin, the enormous protein that controls the length of a sarcomere. When twitchin is phosphorylated, the muscle is capable of twitch activity: contracting and relaxing. However, when the catch muscle is engaged, twitchin becomes progressively dephosphorylated, likely via the action of a calmodulin-sensitive protein phosphatase calcineurin. The dephosphorylation of twitchin coincides with the entry into the catch state. Upon exit from the catch state, serotonin activates protein kinase A (PKA), which phosphorylates twitchin. It remains unclear how dephosphorylated twitchin works to attain the catch state. It is possible that the protein strengthens the actino-myosin cross-bridges or, alternately, creates other types of interactions between thick and thin filaments.

CONCEPT CHECK

17. Compare and contrast EC coupling in synchronous and asynchronous insect flight muscles.
18. What are EPSPs?

Specialized Muscles and Transdifferentiated Muscle

Muscle is a remarkable tissue, with the capacity to undertake many types of activity. There have been many examples of convergent evolution whereby muscles have evolved to take part in sound production. Many traits parallel patterns seen in locomotor muscles selected for high-frequency contraction, but in each case, these sonic muscles perform remarkably.

Further examples of muscle specializations come from animals that have evolved the ability to modify a muscle into a noncontractile cell, using some of the intracellular machinery for other purposes. A number of fish species have evolved heater organs, where individual muscles divest themselves of contractibility and become space heaters. Many other fish species have modified muscles to become electricity generators. The common theme is that these muscles have transdifferentiated, converting muscle to nonmuscle.

Sonic muscles produce rapid contractions but generate less force

Many animals use sound-producing organs in combination with muscles that are more specialized for high-frequency contraction (Figure 6.46). The muscles of the shaker organ in a rattlesnake tail contract 100 times per second (100 Hz). The cicada is an insect that buzzes by bending a region of its exoskeleton, called a tymbal, about 200 times a second. The toadfish produces a shrill, whistlelike sound using a sonic muscle that vibrates its swim bladder at more than 200 Hz. What is striking about each of these muscles is the way in which the animal modifies the muscle machinery to operate at such frequencies, often 10 times faster than the fastest locomotor muscles in the same animal. Surprisingly, the contractile machinery of sonic muscles is not very different from that of locomotor muscle. Typically, **sonic muscles** are built using fast skeletal isoforms of thick and thin filament proteins, resulting in cross-bridge cycling rates and ATPase rates that are similar to fast-**twitch fibers**. So what makes a sonic muscle able to contract and relax so quickly?

First, the muscles have a very fast Ca^{2+} transient. Sonic muscles have very abundant SR. Upon excitation, the flood of Ca^{2+} from the SR rapidly saturates the regulatory sites of TnC to activate contraction. Flooding the cytoplasm with Ca^{2+} is a great way to speed contraction, but it presents a bit of a problem for relaxation. Sonic muscles speed relaxation by removing Ca^{2+} from the myofibril and the sarcoplasm very quickly. Though the structural basis remains unclear, sonic muscle troponin releases Ca^{2+} faster than skeletal muscle troponin. The SR has very active Ca^{2+} uptake machinery. These muscles also have very high levels of the Ca^{2+} buffer parvalbumin. Collectively, these processes allow for a very fast Ca^{2+} transient.

The second property necessary for rapid contraction rates is fast cross-bridge cycling. The myosin head must form a cross-bridge, undergo the power stroke, then detach. The slowest step in this cycle is the detachment of myosin from actin. Sonic muscle myosin detachment rates are about six times faster than toadfish fast-twitch fibers. The molecular basis of this difference in cross-bridge kinetics is not yet established.

Third, some muscles are able to shorten sarcomeres beyond the limit seen in most muscles. As shown in Figure 6.21, the minimum sarcomere length for most muscles is achieved when the ends of the thick filament butt up against the Z-disk. In some sonic muscles, the Z-disk has perforations that allow the thick filaments to penetrate into the adjacent sarcomeres. It is thought that this ability to change length to such a dramatic degree is important in achieving the high frequency–low force contraction in sonic muscles.

We know that the mechanical properties of the sound-producing structures also impinge on the muscle contractile performance. The muscle designs that enable these high-frequency contractions also limit their ability to generate force.

FIGURE 6.46 Animals with sonic muscles
(a) Rattlesnake **(b)** Cicada **(c)** Toadfish

(a)　　　　　　　　(b)　　　　　　　　(c)

Photo source: (a) Steve Byland/Fotolia; (b) Rubik Oleg/Fotolia; (c) Joe Quinn/Shutterstock.

Sound-producing organs use elements that are made in such a way that they can be vibrated or bent with relatively little force. They are dedicated structures that can change radically without affecting other physiological systems. In contrast, animals that use the respiratory system for vocalization face constraints on just how radically the sound-producing machinery can be modified in evolution. Any adaptations in these animals must adequately serve the dual purposes of the structures, namely respiration and sound production. It is possible that the specialized muscle properties seen in toadfish, rattlesnakes, and cicadas were made possible because they evolved in combination with dedicated sound-producing organs.

Heater organs and electric organs are modified muscles

Genetic diversity in contractile proteins affords animals the opportunity to produce muscles with unique contractile properties. These capacities arise through relatively modest changes in the profile or arrangement of muscle proteins. Although the diverse muscle fiber types may have differences in contractile properties, each muscle remains recognizable as a muscle. In some cases, a muscle may undergo transdifferentiation, in which it is diverted from a typical developmental program to create a tissue endowed with novel properties. Let's examine two situations that occur in fish, when embryonic muscle undergoes transdifferentiation to create a tissue with a noncontractile function.

This first example of a transdifferentiated muscle is found in billfish, a group that includes marlin and swordfish. These fish possess a transdifferentiated eye muscle that functions as a heater organ. By warming the optical sensory system, billfish are thought to maintain visual function even when pursuing prey into deep, cold waters. We can gain some insight into the mechanism of heat generation by examining how the cellular structure of this heater organ differs from that of a conventional muscle. Heater organs have few myofibrils, but abundant SR and mitochondria. To understand how heater organs function, let's consider how normal muscles produce heat. All muscles produce some heat as a by-product of muscle metabolism, and all tissues produce heat in the reactions that lead to ATP production, as well as the reactions that lead to ATP hydrolysis. As in most tissues, considerable heat is produced by mitochondria during oxidative phosphorylation. In muscles, ATP is hydrolyzed by the ATPase reactions at the myofibrils during cross-bridge cycling, and at the ion-pumping ATPases required in EC coupling. Heater organs are thought to generate heat by cycling Ca^{2+} in and out of the SR (Figure 6.47). Activation allows Ca^{2+} to escape the SR through RyR into the cytoplasm. Ca^{2+} is then pumped back into the SR using the Ca^{2+} ATPase, fueled by mitochondrial ATP. The entire process of Ca^{2+} cycling and mitochondrial energy metabolism

FIGURE 6.47 **Billfish heater organ**

Billfish, such as marlin and swordfish, **(a)** possess heater organs. They are modified muscles found near the eye **(b)**, where they are thought to warm the optical system to maintain optical function in cold water. **(c)** Heat is generated by futile cycling of Ca^{2+} in and out of the SR, fueled by mitochondrial oxidative phosphorylation.

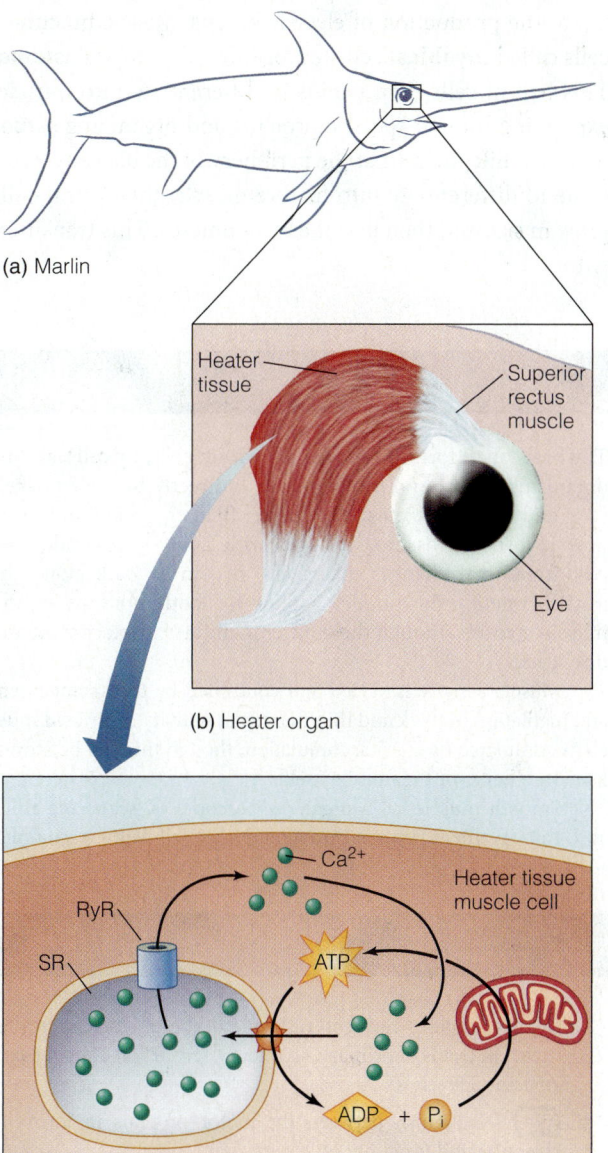

(a) Marlin

(b) Heater organ

(c) Ca^{2+} cycling

constitutes a **futile cycle**. Metabolic energy is expended to produce ATP, which is then hydrolyzed to pump Ca^{2+}. This generates enough heat to warm the eye and optical nerves. We will consider other examples of heat-producing futile cycles in Chapter 15.

A second type of transdifferentiated muscle is the **electric organ**, a tissue with modified muscle cells called electrocytes. These cells produce an electrical discharge in response to neuronal stimulation. Large fish like the electric eel can produce enough electricity to shock a predator or stun prey. Smaller species that live in dark, murky waters may use weak electrical signals to communicate. Electric organs have a polyphyletic origin, meaning they have arisen independently in many distant groups of fish. Researchers have been able to follow the developmental processes that led to the production of electric organs. Muscle precursor cells called **myoblasts** cluster together to form a **blastema**. This ball of cells then begins to differentiate into muscle, expressing muscle-specific proteins and organizing sarcomeres. While the cells at the periphery of the blastema continue to differentiate into mature muscle, the central cells grow in size and then lose their sarcomeres. This transition

probably occurs when the muscle becomes innervated by specialized electromotor neurons. These cells eventually become the electrocytes. We will revisit the electric organs in Chapter 7: Sensory Systems when we discuss their role in sensory pathways.

CONCEPT CHECK

19. Briefly describe three different muscles that are able to maintain a contraction for long periods: tonic muscle, smooth muscle (latch), and a mollusk catch muscle.

20. Why are heater organs and electric organs considered modified muscles?

SUMMARY

The basis of all forms of movement within cells, by cells, and by organisms can be traced directly or indirectly to the cytoskeleton and motor proteins. The sliding filament model describes how myosin forms cross-bridges with actin, then undergoes conformational changes that cause myosin to walk along the microfilament. This model applies for both nonmuscle and muscle myosins, though these differ in unitary displacement and duty cycle.

Muscle activity is varied and controlled by the arrangement and regulation of thick and thin filaments. Activity in striated muscle is stimulated by Ca^{2+} accumulation, though this can be stimulated by a nerve or the muscle itself.

Smooth muscle lacks organized sarcomeres, scattering thick and thin filament arrays throughout the cell with a complex geometry. Its contraction is controlled in both Ca^{2+}-dependent and Ca^{2+}-independent ways, acting at both the thick and thin filaments.

Invertebrate muscles differ from vertebrate striated muscle in many ways. Some insect muscles can exhibit graded contractions, with the strength of contraction dependent on summation of postsynaptic potentials, either excitatory (EPSP) or inhibitory (IPSP). Asynchronous insect flight muscles use a stretch-activation pathway, which permits rapid contraction rates. Bivalve catch muscles sustain contraction by reinforcing thick and thin filament interactions, without expending ATP.

Muscle can be modified in ways that permit specialization for function. Sonic muscles contract at very high frequency. Muscle can also be used to make specialized tissues, such as heater organs and electric organs.

REVIEW QUESTIONS

1. **LO 1** Compare and contrast microtubules and microfilaments in terms of primary, secondary, tertiary, and quaternary structural levels.

2. **LO 1** Distinguish between the motor proteins in terms of structure and function.

3. **LO 2** What is the role of energy in construction and use of the cytoskeleton?

4. **LO 2** Describe the different ways the actin cytoskeleton can be used to control cell structure and shape.

5. **LO 3** Contrast the properties exhibited by myosins that walk on microfilaments with those of thin filaments.

6. **LO 3** Discuss the structure and function of myosin within the thick filament.

7. **LO 4** What is the relationship between muscle filaments (thick and thin), sarcomeres, myofibrils, and myofibers?

8. **LO 4** Discuss the role of Ca^{2+}-binding proteins in muscle contraction.

9. **LO 5** What are the main differences between cardiac and skeletal muscle?

10. **LO 5** Contrast the ways smooth and striated muscle rely on thick versus thin filament regulation.

11. **LO 6** Compare the contractile properties of sonic and locomotor muscles of fish.

12. **LO 6** What are muscle fiber types? How do animals alter muscle fiber types in response to physiological challenges?

SYNTHESIS QUESTIONS

1. What genomic and genetic events might have contributed to the expansion of the myosin II family in vertebrates?

2. What enables the cell to produce so many configurations of actin filaments, given that microfilaments and thin filaments are composed of simple repeats of actin?

3. Describe the molecular processes of neuromuscular excitation, from the sites of neurotransmitter synthesis to Ca^{2+} release within the muscle.

4. How do animals use muscle in physiological systems?

5. Hummingbird hearts beat extremely quickly, at about 30 Hz. Predict what you would find if you examined the structure of a hummingbird cardiomyocyte.

6. The main pathways of energy production are glycolysis and mitochondrial oxidative phosphorylation. Discuss how these metabolic pathways integrate into the EC coupling patterns of different muscles.

7. Striated muscle cells are postmitotic and can live for the lifetime of the organism. Discuss how this property affects muscle biology, both normally and in disease.

QUANTITATIVE QUESTIONS

1. Many cellular structures require metabolic energy to build and maintain. Calculate the cost of building the microtubule support for the axon of a motor neuron. Assume that the axon is 1 m long and 1 μm in diameter, with 50 microtubules aligned in parallel. If a tubulin monomer is 8 nm long, how many tubulins are needed to produce the microtubules of the axon? How many moles of GTP and GDP are tied up in the structure of this microtubule?

2. Most skeletal muscles generate 10–20 N of force per cm^2 of cross-sectional area. If a myosin head generates 5 pN of force, and a thick filament has about 600 myosin heads, how many thick filaments appear per cm^2 of cross-sectional area?

CHAPTER

7

Sensory Systems

Learning Objectives

After reading this chapter, you should be able to:

1. Classify sensory receptors based on stimulus location and modality.

2. Explain how incoming sensory stimuli are encoded as action potentials such that information about stimulus modality, location, intensity, and duration is preserved.

3. Compare and contrast olfactory mechanisms in vertebrates and invertebrates.

4. Compare the signal transduction mechanisms involved in gustation in vertebrates and invertebrates.

5. Explain how mechanoreceptors underlie the senses of touch and proprioception.

6. Compare the mechanisms involved in the senses of equilibrium and hearing in vertebrates and invertebrates.

7. Compare the structure and function of photoreceptors across animal taxa.

8. Explain how mammalian eyes form a crisply focused image and can detect complex environmental features such as depth and color.

9. Outline the mechanisms involved in sensory modalities such as thermoreception, electroreception, and magnetoreception and compare them with the other sensory modalities.

FIGURE 7.1 **A little big-eared bat (*Micronycteris megalotis*) and a katydid (*Copiphora gorgonensis*)**

Photo source: (top) Barry Mansell/SuperStock; (bottom) Daniel Robert/Fernando Montealegre-Z/AP Images.

ou might not think that the bat and the katydid shown in Figure 7.1 have a lot in common, but these animals have a close ecological relationship that involves sound. Little big-eared bats are nocturnal animals that use **echolocation** to navigate around their environment and detect their prey. During echolocation, bats produce pulses of high-frequency sounds that reflect off objects in the environment, causing echoes. By determining how long it takes the echoes to return to their ears, bats can estimate the distance to an object, and also get a sense of its size and the direction in which it is moving. The large external ears of these bats are one of the many adaptations that give them the extremely sensitive hearing they need to catch prey items using echolocation.

It is clear that hearing is useful for bats, but what about the katydids? From Figure 7.1 it might not even be obvious that katydids have ears, but in fact, katydids have excellent hearing. Katydids' ears are located in the bend on their front legs in a region where the cuticle (the exoskeleton of the insect) is thin. This thin region of the cuticle vibrates in response to sound waves. Sensory neurons detect these vibrations and transduce them into changes in membrane potential that trigger action potentials in the insects' nervous system, allowing them to detect sounds.

Katydids use their ears to detect the mating calls of other members of their species, and they also listen for the echolocation calls of bats so that they can take evasive action to escape being eaten. Thus, the sense of hearing plays an important role in the ecology of both bats and katydids and is an important part of the relationship between them.

In this chapter we explore the many sensory systems that animals use to monitor their internal and external environments, looking at the structure and function of sensory receptors ranging in size from single cells to complex organs like the ears of bats and katydids. ■

LOOKING BACK 7

Sensory cells use a variety of signal transduction pathways to convert incoming sensory information into changes in membrane potential. Before reading this chapter, you should review Chapter 4: Cell Signaling and Endocrine Regulation to make sure that you understand the general features of signal transduction pathways and their organization. Because the ultimate effect of these signaling pathways in sensory receptors is a change in the membrane potential, you also should review Chapter 5: Neuron Structure and Function to ensure that you have a solid understanding of the nature of the membrane potential and the ways that cells can use alterations in membrane potential as signals. Sensory systems must communicate incoming sensory information to the brain for processing, so you should also make sure that you understand how action potentials can communicate signals across long distances by reviewing the appropriate sections of Chapter 5: Neuron Structure and Function.

▌ OVERVIEW

Animals have a diverse array of sensory systems that they use to monitor their internal and external environments. When we think of these sensory systems, we often imagine the complex ears of vertebrates, or the multifaceted eyes of insects. Complex sensory organs such as eyes and ears contain a large number of sensory cells and accessory tissues, but animal sensory systems can be as simple as an isolated sensory cell that sends information to the brain for processing.

Sensory receptor cells are typically specialized to detect a single type of stimulus, but no matter what kind of stimulus they detect, all sensory receptor cells work via mechanisms that are broadly similar to those used by cells to detect incoming chemical signals that we discussed in Chapter 4: Cell Signaling and Endocrine Regulation.

Sensory receptor cells take incoming stimuli of various types and transduce (convert) them into changes in membrane potential (Figure 7.2). In most sensory receptor cells, specialized receptor proteins in the membrane absorb the energy of the incoming stimulus and undergo a conformational change. The conformational change in the receptor protein then activates a signal transduction pathway that, directly or indirectly, opens or closes ion channels in the cell membrane, changing the membrane potential.

The change in membrane potential caused by the detection of the incoming stimulus ultimately sends a signal onward to integrating centers such as the brain. The integrating centers must then interpret this incoming sensory information and elicit appropriate responses. Thus, sensory reception is a process with many steps, including (1) reception of the signal, (2) transduction of the signal, (3) transmission of the signal to the integrating center, and (4) perception of the stimulus at the integrating center. In this chapter we begin by discussing some of the general features of sensory reception, and then we examine how specific sensory systems perform the steps of sensory reception.

▌ GENERAL PROPERTIES OF SENSORY RECEPTION

The terminology used in the field of sensory physiology can be confusing, because similar terms can be used for very different structures. In this chapter, we use the term sense organ to describe a complex structure consisting of multiple tissues that work together to allow an organism to detect an incoming stimulus. The eyes of vertebrates are an example of a sense organ. We use the term **sensory receptor** to refer to a cell that is specialized to detect incoming sensory stimuli.

FIGURE 7.2 An overview of sensory receptors

Sensory receptors detect incoming stimuli of many kinds.
(a) Chemoreceptors detect chemical stimuli. For most chemoreceptors, chemicals bind to the receptor, causing a conformational change and activating a signal transduction pathway that opens or closes ion channels, which alters the membrane potential of the sensory cell. **(b)** Mechanoreceptors detect stretch or tension on the cell membrane. When a pressure stimulus distorts the cell membrane, it changes the conformation of the mechanoreceptor protein, opening ion channels and changing the membrane potential of the sensory cell. **(c)** Photoreceptors detect light by absorbing the energy carried by the incoming light stimulus, and changing shape, activating a transduction pathway that opens or closes ion channels, resulting in a change in the membrane potential of the sensory cell.

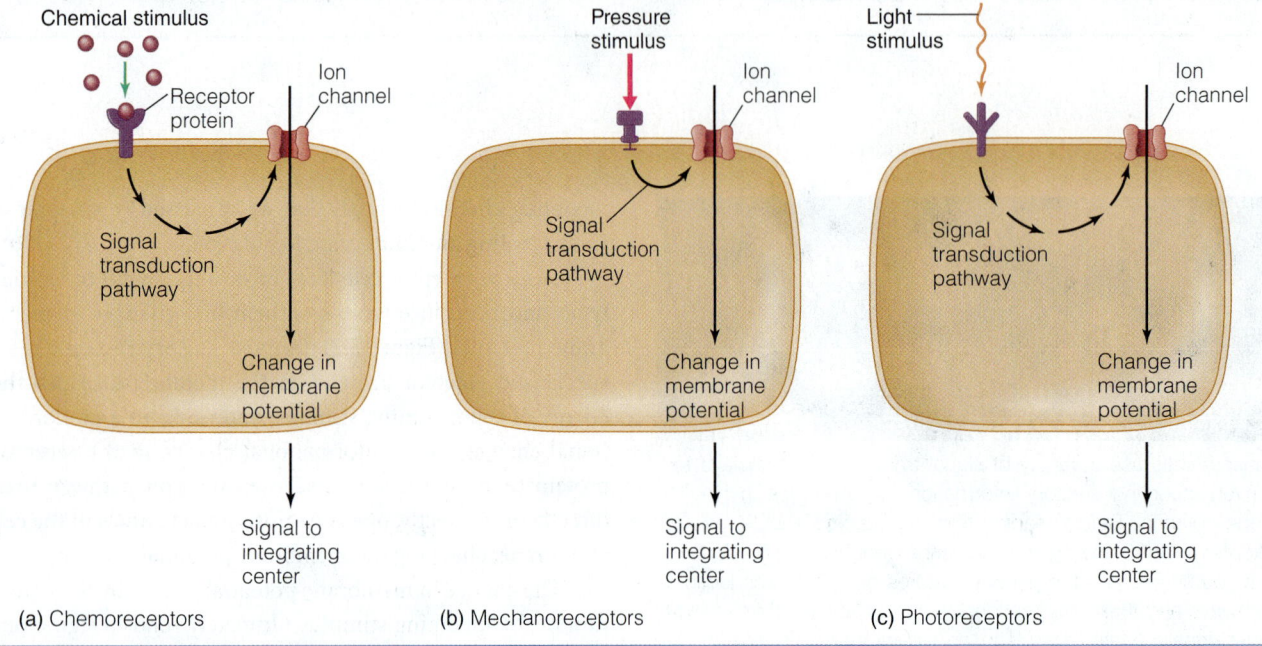

(a) Chemoreceptors   (b) Mechanoreceptors   (c) Photoreceptors

Sensory receptor cells can be found within complex sensory organs, as is the case for the light-sensitive cells in the retina of vertebrate eyes. Other sensory receptors are isolated cells embedded within a nonsensory tissue, as is the case for many of the touch-sensitive cells in the skin of vertebrates. The membranes of sensory receptor cells contain specific **receptor proteins** that are specialized to detect incoming sensory signals. A change in the conformation of these proteins activates signal transduction pathways within the sensory receptor, causing a change in membrane potential that can act as a signal in the nervous system.

Afferent neurons, as you will recall from Chapter 5: Neuron Structure and Function, send signals in the form of action potentials from the periphery to integrating centers such as the brain. Some sensory receptors are themselves afferent neurons. These afferent neurons detect incoming signals and transduce them into action potentials that can be sent to the integrating center. This type of sensory receptor is termed a **sensory neuron** (Figure 7.3a). Other sensory receptors are epithelial cells that send a signal to a separate afferent neuron that then sends signals in the form of action potentials to the integrating center (Figure 7.3b). In the case of a sensory neuron, a receptor protein in the dendrite of the neuron detects the incoming sensory signal, and changes conformation. The change in the conformation of the receptor protein alters the activity of a signal transduction pathway that ultimately results in a change in the membrane potential of the receptor. This change in membrane potential is a type of graded potential (see Chapter 5: Neuron Structure and Function) that is termed a **generator potential**. The generator potential spreads along the membrane to the spike-initiating (trigger) zone of the neuron, where it will generate action potentials in the axon, if the generator potential exceeds the threshold potential for the neuron. Recall from Chapter 5: Neuron Structure and Function that the spike-initiating zone of a sensory neuron need not be located in the axon hillock of the neuron. Sensory neurons are often bipolar or unipolar neurons, with their spike-initiating zones located at the **distal** end of the neuron between the dendrites and the axon. The action potentials are then conducted along the axon to the axon terminals of the neuron, where they cause the release of a neurotransmitter. This neurotransmitter conveys the signal to other neurons and onward to integrating centers such as the brain, where they are interpreted.

FIGURE 7.3 **The types of sensory receptor cells**

(a) An incoming stimulus activates a receptor protein in the sensory neuron, causing a depolarization called a generator potential. The generator potential triggers action potentials in the axon of the neuron. **(b)** An incoming stimulus activates a receptor protein on the surface of the receptor cell, causing a receptor potential. The receptor potential opens voltage-gated Ca^{2+} channels, causing the release of neurotransmitter onto the primary afferent neuron. The stimulated afferent neuron generates action potentials that are conducted to integrating centers.

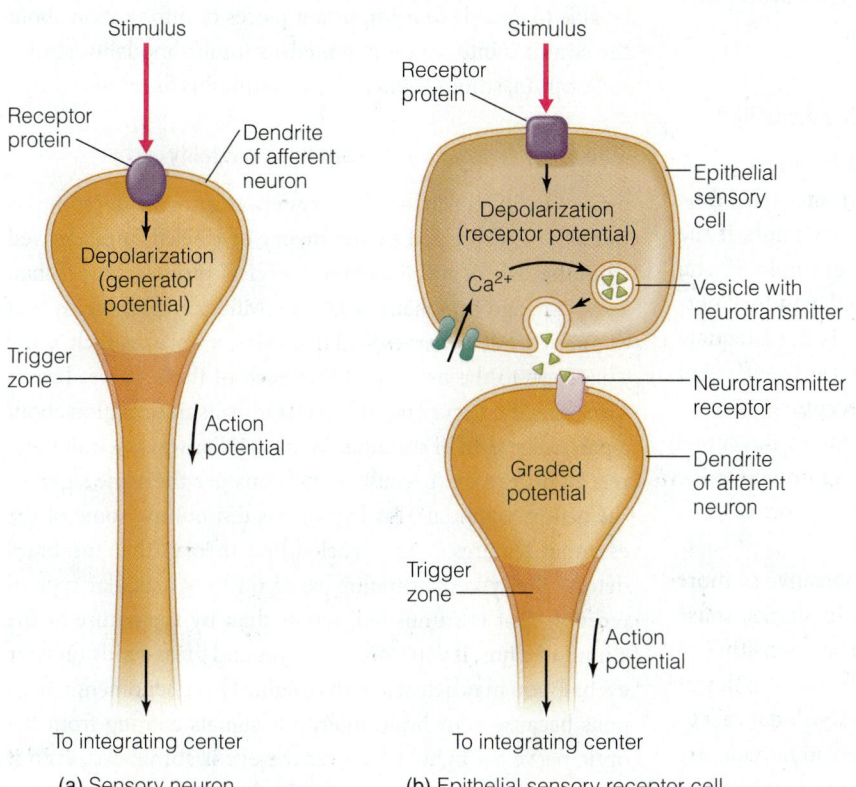

(a) Sensory neuron

(b) Epithelial sensory receptor cell

When the sensory receptor cell is separate from the afferent sensory neuron, the initial graded potential in the sensory receptor cell is called a **receptor potential**. The receptor potential spreads across the sensory receptor cell to the site of the synapse with the afferent neuron, where it triggers the release of neurotransmitter. The neurotransmitter then binds to receptors on the primary afferent neuron and causes a postsynaptic graded potential. This potential then travels to the trigger zone of the afferent neuron, where it initiates action potentials if it exceeds threshold. The action potentials are conducted along the axon to the axon terminals of the afferent neuron, causing the release of neurotransmitter and communicating the signal to the nervous system.

Whether a sensory receptor is a neuron or an epithelial cell, however, its function is to detect an incoming stimulus and transduce it into changes in membrane potential that convey information about the signal to integrating centers.

Classification of Sensory Receptors

Sensory receptors and sense organs can be classified in a number of ways. In elementary school, you probably learned about the five senses (touch, taste, smell, hearing, and vision). This classification, first developed by Aristotle over 2,000 years ago, is an explicitly human-centered system that focuses only on the senses that we consciously employ, ignores some obvious senses such as our ability to detect temperature changes, and entirely neglects sensory information that we are not consciously aware of, such as internal environmental parameters like blood pressure and blood oxygenation. This classification scheme also neglects the wide range of sensory systems in other animals. Many animals have senses that humans do not appear to possess, such as the ability to detect electric or magnetic fields. Similarly, some animals lack one or more of the five senses defined for humans.

Receptors can be classified based on stimulus location or modality

An alternative way of classifying sensory receptors is by the location of the stimulus. In this classification, telereceptors (or teleceptors) detect stimuli coming from locations at some distance from the body. Vision and hearing are good examples of telereceptive senses. Exteroceptors detect stimuli occurring on the outside of the body, such as pressure and temperature, and interoceptors detect stimuli occurring inside the body, such as blood pressure and blood oxygen. **Proprioceptors** provide information about the position and orientation of your body, and include generalized receptors in the skin and muscles as well as specialized receptors such as the vestibular apparatus of the inner ears of vertebrates. This classification is of limited utility to physiologists, however, because it tells us little or nothing about how the receptors work.

The most physiologically meaningful classification of sensory receptors is based on the type of stimulus that the receptor can detect, which is sometimes called the stimulus modality. **Chemoreceptors** detect chemical signals. They form the basis of the senses of smell and taste and are important in sensing components of the internal environment such as blood oxygen and pH. Pressure and movement stimulate **mechanoreceptors**, which are involved in the senses of touch, hearing, and balance, as well as in *proprioception*, or the sense of body position. Mechanoreceptors are also involved in detecting many important internal body parameters, such as blood pressure. **Photoreceptors** detect light, and are the basis for the sense of vision. **Thermoreceptors** sense temperature. **Electroreceptors** and **magnetoreceptors** sense electric and magnetic fields, respectively.

Receptors may detect more than one stimulus modality

Although most receptors have a preferred (or most sensitive) stimulus modality, called the **adequate stimulus**, some receptors can also be excited by other stimuli, if the incoming signal is sufficiently large. For example, if you press on your eyelid when your eye is closed, you may perceive a bright spot of light. Although light is the adequate stimulus for the photoreceptors of your eyes, sufficient pressure can also stimulate these photoreceptors, causing them to send a signal to your brain. Your brain interprets this signal as a light, because it has been programmed to interpret any signal coming from the photoreceptors of your eyes as a light stimulus.

A few types of receptors are naturally sensitive to more than one stimulus modality. For example, in sharks, sense organs called the **ampullae of Lorenzini** are sensitive to electricity, touch, and temperature. Receptors that can detect more than one class of stimulus are called **polymodal receptors**. The most common polymodal receptors in humans are the **nociceptors**, which detect extremely strong, potentially damaging stimuli of various kinds. They are responsible for the sensation of pain in humans and many other animals. Some nociceptors are specific for a particular stimulus such as extreme high or low temperature, strong mechanical stimuli, or damaging chemicals, but other nociceptors appear to be polymodal, and can detect more than one type of stimulus. For example, some nociceptors are stimulated both by high temperature and strong mechanical stimulation, while other nociceptors respond to thermal, mechanical, and chemical stimuli.

CONCEPT CHECK

1. For the following stimuli, determine whether the receptor involved is a mechanoreceptor, a chemoreceptor, or a photoreceptor: (a) blood oxygen, (b) acceleration, (c) light, (d) sound waves, (e) blood glucose.
2. For the following stimuli, determine whether the receptor involved is an interocepter, proprioceptor, or exteroceptor: (a) blood oxygen, (b) acceleration, (c) light, (d) sound waves, (e) blood glucose.

Stimulus Encoding in Sensory Systems

Whatever the type of stimulus, sensory receptors ultimately convert the signal to a series of action potentials in an afferent neuron. Because all action potentials are essentially the same, how can an organism differentiate among stimuli, or detect the strength of a signal? In order for an organism to interpret an incoming signal in a coherent way, a sensory receptor must be able to encode four important pieces of information about the stimulus into action potentials: stimulus modality, stimulus location, stimulus intensity, and stimulus duration.

Sensory pathways encode stimulus modality

One way in which sensory systems can encode stimulus modality is described by the theory of labeled lines, derived from the "law of specific nerve energies" proposed more than 150 years ago by Johannes Müller. Müller hypothesized that different kinds of nerves lead from sensory organs such as the ear or eye to the brain, and that each of these nerves has its own "specific nerve energy" that transmits information about a particular kind of stimulus. While Müller was not quite correct in his theory (because all neurons use the same signal—the action potential), his hypothesis did outline some of the essential features of the labeled-line theory: that the brain detects the type of stimulus based on the particular type of receptor that is stimulated, rather than by the nature of the stimulus. Thus, if you close your eyes and press gently on your eyeball, you may detect a flash of light. This phenomenon happens because your brain interprets signals coming from the optic nerve as "light" whenever the eye is stimulated, even if the stimulus is actually pressure on the eyeball. Because most sensory receptors are maximally sensitive to only one type of stimulus, and a sensory receptor is part of or synapses with a particular afferent neuron, signals in that afferent neuron in the brain makes the assumption that the signal must represent a specific stimulus modality. The brain appears to interpret stimulus modality based on a labeled line. Sensory systems are often organized into **sensory units** consisting of multiple sensory receptors that form synapses with a single afferent neuron. In general, all of the sensory receptors associated with a single afferent neuron are of the same type, and thus the theory of labeled-line perception can, in most cases, account for our ability to distinguish among different stimulus modalities.

The fundamental assumption of the labeled-line theory is that there is a specific pathway from a sensory cell to the integrating center. However, it is clear that not all information about stimulus modality can be encoded in this way. For example, recall the ampullae of Lorenzini, receptors in sharks that are sensitive to electricity, pressure, and temperature. How could such a receptor encode information regarding stimulus modality? A receptor sensitive to more than one sensory modality likely encodes information in the temporal pattern of its action potentials. For example, bursts of action potentials could convey a different message than a continuous series. In addition, the relative firing patterns of several adjacent sensory cells may carry information regarding stimulus modality. For example, imagine a situation in which each sensory cell is sensitive to more than one type of stimulus, but their relative sensitivities vary (for example, the first receptor might be very sensitive to stimulus A, but less sensitive to stimulus B, while a second receptor has the opposite pattern). By comparing the relative intensity of the signal coming from the two receptors, an afferent neuron could code information regarding the stimulus modality. The mechanisms underlying this "cross-fiber" coding of information are not yet entirely understood, but may be important for the coding of information from senses such as taste in vertebrates.

Receptive fields provide information about stimulus location

Sensory systems must also encode the location of the stimulus. The task of encoding stimulus location varies among receptors. We discuss how sensory systems such as vision and hearing encode the location of a stimulus later in the chapter. But for many sensory systems, the main factor coding stimulus location is the location of the stimulated receptor on the body. Thus, the labeled-line theory, which in part accounts for coding of stimulus modality, can also explain how these sensory systems code for stimulus location.

In this section, we use the sense of touch in vertebrates as an example of how a sensory system can encode the location of a stimulus. Afferent neurons involved in the sense of touch have a **receptive field**, which corresponds to the region of the skin that causes a response in that particular afferent neuron. The size of the receptive field varies among neurons. Neurons with large receptive fields detect stimuli across a larger area than neurons with small receptive fields, and thus neurons with small receptive fields provide more precise localization of the stimulus, or greater **acuity**, than neurons with large receptive fields. However, the information from a single afferent neuron can only signal whether a stimulus has occurred within the receptive field, and cannot provide more precise localization. Animals improve their ability to localize stimuli by having afferent neurons with overlapping receptive fields. A stimulus that causes both neuron A and neuron B to respond must be located within the area of overlap between the receptive fields of the two afferent neurons. This is an example of a phenomenon termed **population coding**, in which information about the stimulus is encoded in the pattern of firing of multiple neurons.

Many sensory systems take advantage of a phenomenon termed **lateral inhibition** to further improve acuity. In the simplified example shown in Figure 7.4, a weak stimulus such as a gentle touch across the receptive fields of neurons A, B, and C would cause each neuron to release a small amount of neurotransmitter onto its second-order neuron, stimulating all three of the second-order neurons (A_1, B_1, and C_1). In contrast, a strong stimulus such as a pin pushing into the skin in the center of the receptive field of neuron B causes it to release a large amount of neurotransmitter onto its second-order neuron (B_2). This pin prick also causes the skin to bend slightly in the area of the receptive fields for the adjacent neurons A and C, weakly stimulating them. A weak stimulus to neurons A and C would ordinarily cause them to release a small amount of neurotransmitter onto their second-order neurons (A_2 and C_2). But in the example shown here, there are lateral interneurons that form synapses between the axon terminals of neuron B and neurons A and C. The strong response of neuron B causes it to release neurotransmitter onto these lateral interneurons. These interneurons release an inhibitory neurotransmitter that prevents the release of neurotransmitter from neurons A and C onto their second-order neurons. Thus, rather than exhibiting a weak response, neurons A_2 and C_2 do not fire. Lateral inhibition increases the contrast between the signals from neurons at the center of the stimulus and neurons on the edge, allowing finer discrimination.

Sensory receptors have a dynamic range

Action potentials are all-or-none electrical events that do not usually code intensity through changes in magnitude. Instead, action potentials code stimulus intensity through changes in frequency. Strong stimuli typically trigger high-frequency series (or trains) of action potentials, whereas weaker stimuli trigger lower-frequency trains of action potentials.

Most sensory receptor cells are able to encode stimuli over a relatively limited range of intensities, called the **dynamic range** of the receptor (Figure 7.5a). The weakest stimulus that produces a response in a receptor 50 percent of the time is termed the **threshold of detection**. Many sensory receptors are extremely sensitive and can detect signals that are close to the theoretical detection limits for the stimulus. For example, some of the photoreceptors in the human eye can detect a single photon of light, and some mechanoreceptors on human fingertips can detect depression of the skin of less than 0.1 micron. Below the threshold stimulus intensity, the receptor cell fails to initiate action potentials. At the top of the dynamic range, the receptor cell is saturated and cannot increase its response even if the signal strength increases. In principle, any of the steps in **sensory transduction** can set the top of the dynamic range of a receptor. A receptor reaches the top of its dynamic range if all of the available receptor proteins become saturated. The receptor could also reach the top of its

FIGURE 7.4 **Determining the location of a stimulus with multiple receptors**

A stimulus at the center of the receptive field of neuron B strongly stimulates this neuron, and weakly stimulates the adjacent neurons A and C. Neuron B forms synapses with lateral interneurons that make connections with the axon terminals of neurons A and C. These lateral interneurons release an inhibitory neurotransmitter onto neurons A and C, reducing the amount of neurotransmitter that they release. As a result, neuron B_1 receives a strong stimulus that triggers action potentials, while neurons A_1 and C_1 receive a weak stimulus that does not trigger action potentials. Lateral inhibition increases the contrast between the signals in neurons A_1, B_1, and C_1, improving the ability to discriminate between stimuli.

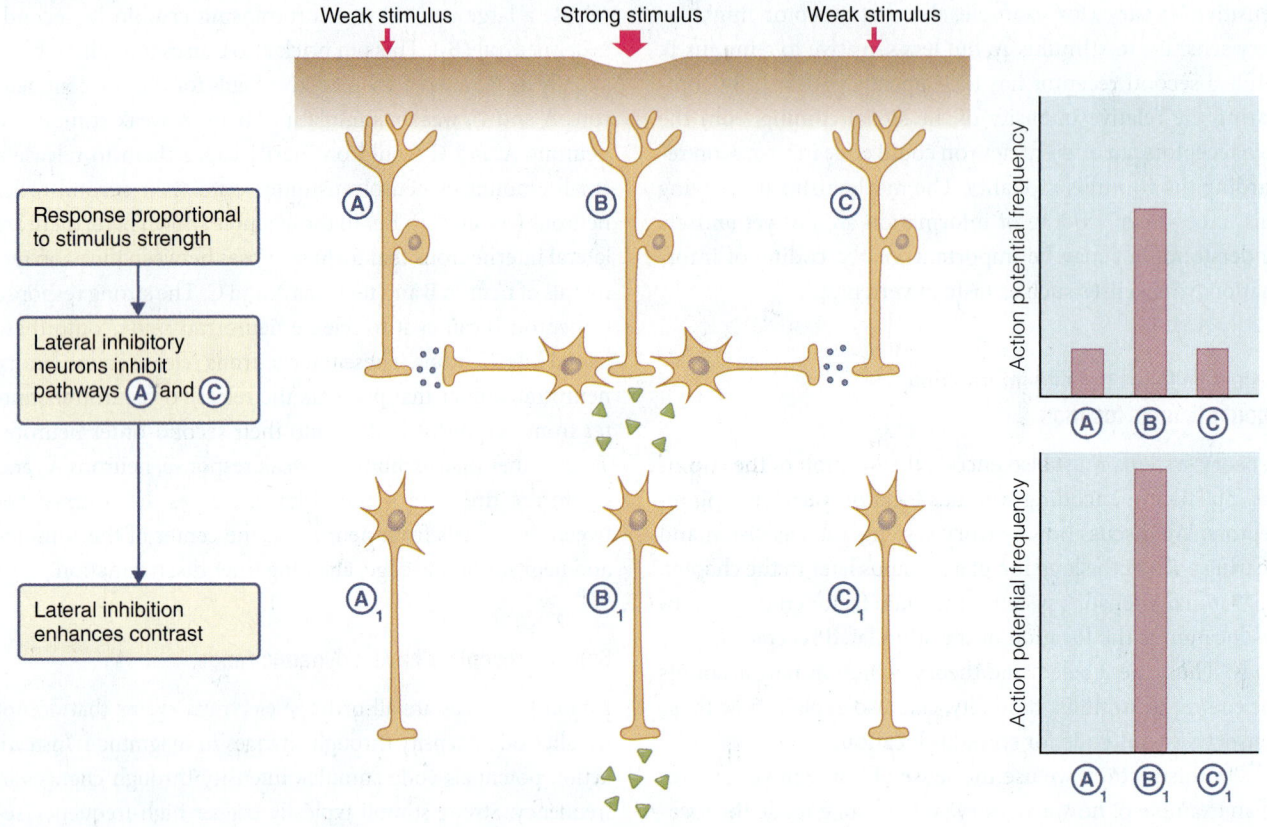

dynamic range if all available ion channels have opened or closed. The receptor will also reach the top of its dynamic range if the membrane potential reaches the equilibrium potential for the particular ion involved in the receptor or generator potential (because no net ion movement will occur beyond this point). The maximum rate of release of neurotransmitter from the receptor cell, or the maximum frequency of action potentials in the afferent neuron, can also set the top of the dynamic range.

There is a trade-off between dynamic range and discrimination

Figure 7.5b illustrates two hypothetical receptors with varying dynamic ranges. Receptor A has a large dynamic range and can detect both very weak and very strong stimuli. In contrast, receptor B can only detect very weak stimuli, and becomes saturated at moderate stimulus levels. Because the range of stimulus intensities is large and the range of action

potential frequencies is limited, receptor A has relatively low power to discriminate among differences in intensity. A relatively large change in stimulus intensity causes only a small change in the response of receptor A, whereas a relatively small change in stimulus intensity causes a large change in the response of receptor B. Receptor B is sensitive to only a small portion of the possible range of stimulus intensities, but it has the ability to provide very fine discrimination within that range.

Range fractionation increases sensory discrimination

One way to improve sensory discrimination is to use populations of receptors. Groups of receptors, each sensitive to a different range of stimulus intensities, can work together to provide fine discrimination across a wider range of intensities. With this strategy, called **range fractionation**, individual receptor cells are sensitive to only a small portion of the possible range of intensities, but multiple receptors

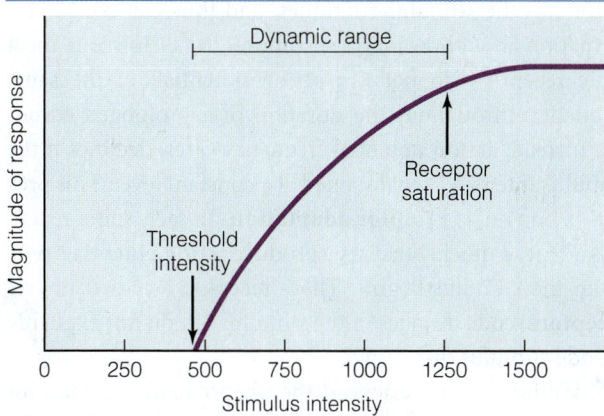

(a) Dynamic range of a receptor

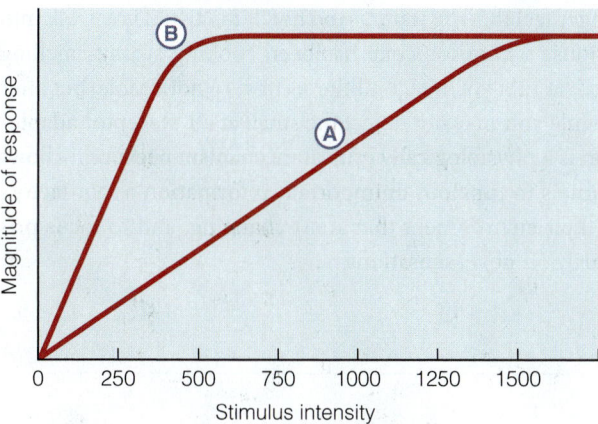

(b) Varying sensitivity

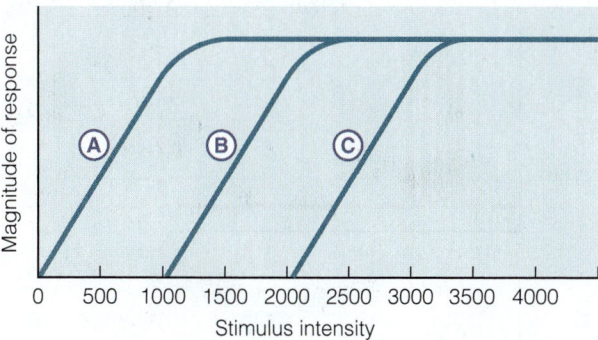

(c) Range fractionation

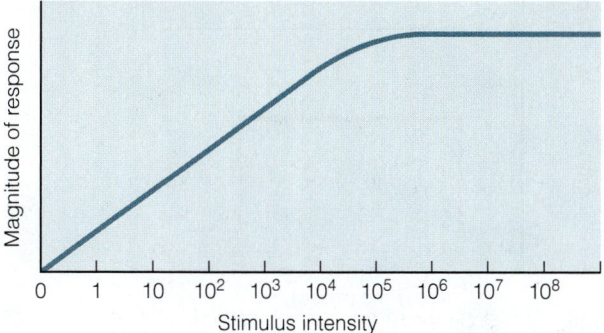

(d) Logarithmic encoding

cover different parts of the range (Figure 7.5c). In a system designed in this way, stimulus intensity is actually coded through the behavior of populations of sensory receptors.

Sense organs can have a very large dynamic range

The upper limit of the frequency of action potentials is set by the refractory periods of the voltage-gated channels involved in the action potential (see Chapter 5: Neuron Structure and Function). The lowest action potential frequency that is likely to be physiologically meaningful is on the order of one per second, and the maximum frequency of action potentials in most neurons is around 1,000 per second, yielding a dynamic range of approximately a thousandfold. In contrast, the intensity of many environmental stimuli varies across a much larger range. For example, a jet engine is about 1.4 million times as loud as the faintest sound that a human being can hear. So how can a sensory receptor code for such a wide range of stimulus intensities with such a small range of action potential frequencies? Range fractionation can extend the dynamic range of a receptor, but many receptors use another strategy.

Many receptors encode signals logarithmically

It is possible to encode a wide range of stimulus intensities using a single sensory receptor cell, without resorting to range fractionation. Figure 7.5d shows a hypothetical example of a receptor that encodes stimuli logarithmically so that the response increases linearly with the logarithm of the stimulus intensity. In this relationship there is a large increase in the response to changes in stimulus intensity when stimulus intensity is low, providing fine discrimination, but when stimulus intensity is high there is only a limited change in the response even when there is a very large change in the stimulus. Thus, there is only coarse discrimination at high stimulus intensities. This type of curve represents a compromise between a broad dynamic range and fine discrimination

FIGURE 7.5 Stimulus-response relationships in sensory receptors

(a) Sensory receptors have a dynamic range over which the response of the receptor increases with increasing stimulus intensity. **(b)** Receptors with varying dynamic range. Receptor A is saturated at high intensity, but has a relatively small change in response for each change in stimulus intensity. Receptor B is saturated at low stimulus intensity, but has a large change in response for each change in stimulus intensity. **(c)** Using the strategy of range fractionation, several receptors can work together to provide fine discrimination across a wide range of stimulus intensities. **(d)** Some receptors encode signals logarithmically, allowing fine discrimination at low stimulus intensities and coarser discrimination at high stimulus intensities.

between similar stimulus intensities. Logarithmic coding allows a receptor to have a constant response to a given percentage change in stimulus intensity.

Many of our sensory systems employ this kind of strategy. For example, if you stand in a darkened room and light a candle, it is easy to notice the change in light intensity, but if you do the same thing in a bright room, you are unlikely to notice the difference. You have the ability to make fine discriminations between intensities at low light levels, but cannot make fine discriminations at high light levels. Similarly, if you help a friend to move furniture, you're unlikely to notice the change in weight if someone puts a book on top of the sofa, but you could easily detect the weight of the book if that was the only object you were holding. This logarithmic relationship between actual and perceived stimulus intensity is known as the Weber-Fechner relationship. Sensations such as brightness, loudness, and weight all obey the Weber-Fechner relationship.

Tonic and phasic receptors encode stimulus duration

Two functional classes of sensory receptors code stimulus duration (Figure 7.6). **Tonic receptors** fire action potentials

as long as the stimulus continues, and thus can convey information about how long the stimulus lasts. However, most tonic receptors do not fire action potentials at the same frequency throughout the duration of a prolonged stimulus. Instead, action potential frequency often declines if the stimulus intensity is maintained at a constant level. This process is known as **receptor adaptation**. In fact, some receptors adapt so quickly that they produce action potentials only when the stimulus begins. These receptors, termed **phasic receptors**, code changes in the stimulus but do not explicitly encode stimulus duration.

We have all experienced the phenomenon of receptor adaptation. When you first step into a hot bath, the water may feel uncomfortably warm, but very soon you will no longer feel that the water is too hot. Similarly, if you walk into a house where someone has been cooking strong-smelling food, at first you may find the scent very noticeable, but after a while you may not detect the smell at all. Receptor adaptation is a physiologically critical mechanism because it allows animals to tune out unimportant information about factors in their environment that aren't changing, and to focus primarily on novel sensations.

FIGURE 7.6 Phasic and tonic receptors

(a) Tonic receptors remain depolarized throughout the duration of a stimulus. Many tonic receptors show the phenomenon of adaptation, in which the response declines with time. **(b)** Phasic receptors adapt very rapidly, and thus depolarize only at the beginning of a stimulus.

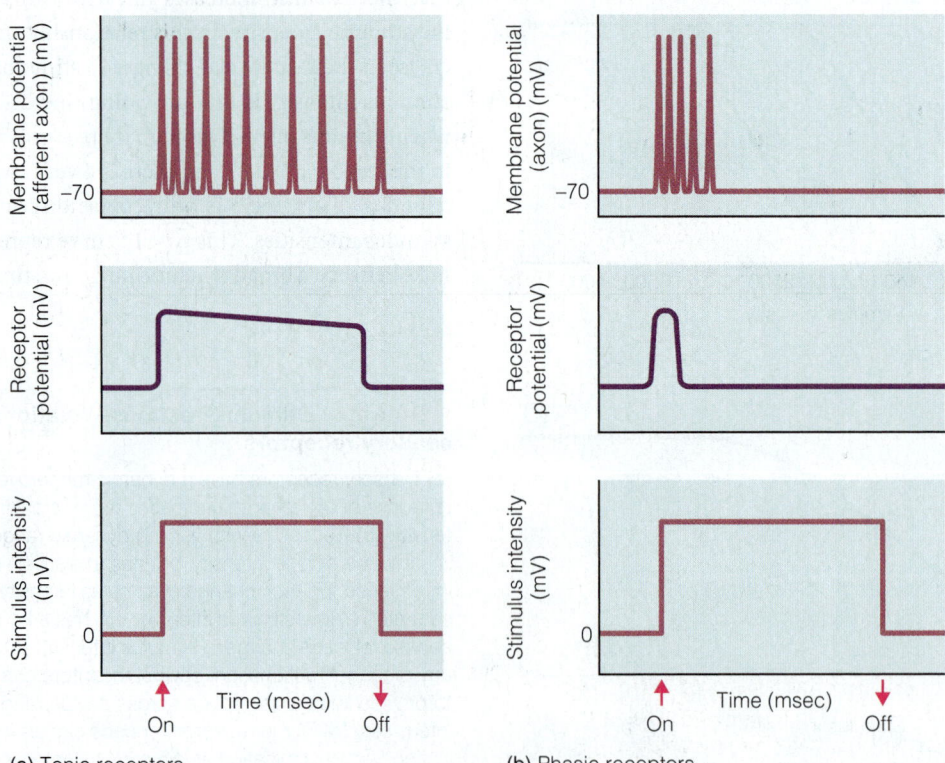

(a) Tonic receptors

(b) Phasic receptors

CHEMORECEPTION

Most cells can sense incoming chemical signals, and animals have many types of chemoreceptors that they use to sense their external and internal chemical environments. Here we focus on the senses of smell and taste, which multicellular organisms use to sense chemicals in their external environment. For terrestrial animals, **olfaction**, or the sense of smell, is generally defined as the detection of chemicals carried in air. Thus, olfaction provides the ability to sense chemicals whose source is located at some distance from the body. This is in contrast to the sense of taste, or **gustation**, which allows the detection of dissolved chemicals emitted from ingested food. Although it is easy to distinguish between gustation and olfaction for terrestrial organisms, it is more difficult to make this distinction in aquatic organisms. In aquatic vertebrates, gustation always involves detecting sensations involving food, whereas olfaction involves detecting a wide variety of environmental chemicals, including those associated with food, predators, potential mates, and particular locations. In vertebrates (whether aquatic or terrestrial), olfaction and gustation are also distinct from one another based on structural criteria: They are performed by different sense organs, use different signal transduction mechanisms, and separate integrating centers process the incoming information from the senses of taste and smell.

The Olfactory System

The ancestors of all animals undoubtedly possessed chemoreceptors, and vertebrates and insects share many similarities in the mechanisms of olfaction. However, current evidence suggests that the olfactory systems of vertebrates and insects evolved independently. We first discuss the mechanisms underlying olfaction in vertebrates. We then briefly compare and contrast the analogous mechanisms in insects.

The vertebrate olfactory system can distinguish thousands of odorants

Vertebrate olfactory systems have an enormous capacity to distinguish among **odorants**, the chemicals detected by the olfactory system. Studies on humans indicate that most people can distinguish among tens of thousands of different odorants, and even a very small change in the structure of an odorant can cause a huge difference in the subjective perception of an odor. For example, humans perceive the compound octanol as smelling like oranges or roses, and describe the compound octanoic acid as smelling rancid or sweaty. The only difference between octanoic acid and octanol is that octanoic acid ends with a carboxylic acid group, whereas octanol ends in a hydroxyl group.

The vertebrate olfactory system is located in the roof of the nasal cavity (Figure 7.7). Olfaction begins when an odorant molecule comes in contact with the mucus layer that lines and moistens the olfactory epithelium of the nose. The mucus contains **odorant-binding proteins**, which are thought to be involved in allowing lipophilic odorant molecules to dissolve in the aqueous mucus layer. Vertebrate olfactory receptor cells are bipolar neurons with one end in the olfactory epithelium and another end that passes through holes in the bony cribriform plate and forms synapses with neurons in the olfactory bulb of the brain. On the outer surface of the olfactory epithelium the membrane of the olfactory receptor cell is highly modified and covered in cilia, which project into the mucus layer lining the inside of the nose. The cilia on the olfactory receptor neurons are nonmotile, and thus they do not beat, but they contain **odorant receptor proteins**, which are the receptor proteins involved in detecting incoming chemical signals.

Odorant receptors are G protein coupled

Odorant receptor proteins are G protein–coupled receptors, similar in many respects to those involved in hormonal communication (see Chapter 4: Cell Signaling and Endocrine Regulation). Odorant receptor proteins are members of a large multigene family, and all of the vertebrate genomes that have been sequenced so far contain many genes coding for odorant receptors (for example, the mouse genome contains at least 1,000 potential odorant receptor genes). Each odorant receptor cell expresses only a single kind of odorant receptor protein out of this wide range of possible proteins.

When an odorant molecule binds to an odorant receptor, the receptor undergoes a conformational change that sends a signal to an associated G protein, G_{olf}. Activated G_{olf} signals via adenylate cyclase, activating a signal transduction pathway (shown in Figure 7.8) that ultimately causes a depolarizing generator potential. If the depolarization is sufficiently large, action potentials will be triggered in the dendrite of the olfactory receptor neuron. Note that these action potentials travel *toward* the cell body of this bipolar neuron, in contrast to the arrangement found in a motor neuron, in which the action potential always travels away from the cell body. These action potentials are ultimately transmitted to the other end of the neuron, where the axon terminals form synapses with the neurons of the olfactory bulb in the brain.

FIGURE 7.7 **The olfactory organ of a dog**

The olfactory epithelium of mammals, located in the nasal cavity, contains supporting cells and olfactory receptor neurons. These bipolar sensory neurons have one end that forms synapses within the olfactory bulb of the brain. These neurons then pass through holes in the bony cribriform plate so that the ciliated end of the neuron is located in the olfactory epithelium. The cilia of the bipolar neurons contain the odorant receptor proteins that detect incoming chemical stimuli. These cilia project into a mucus layer containing odorant-binding proteins that coats the olfactory epithelium.

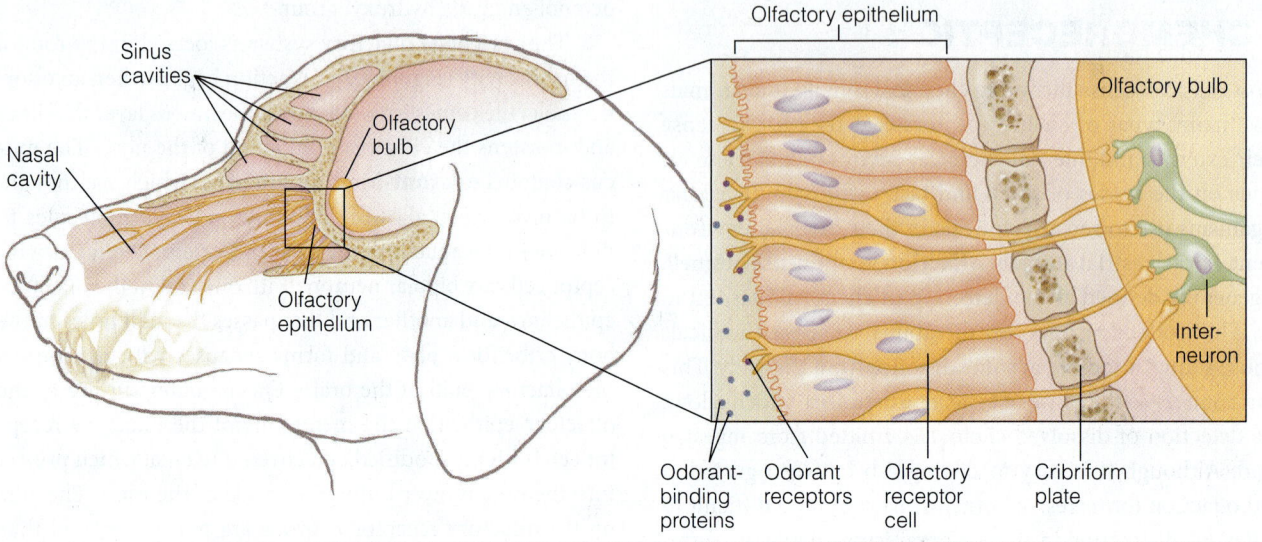

FIGURE 7.8 **Signal transduction in an olfactory receptor cell**

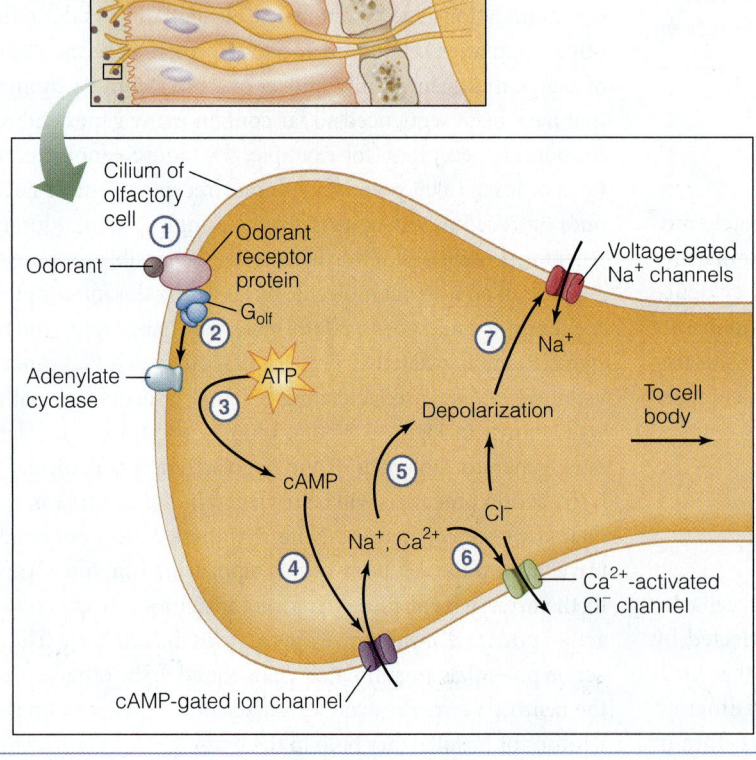

1. Binding of odorant to an odorant receptor causes a conformational change.

2. The activated G protein, G_{olf}, moves through the membrane and activates adenylate cyclase.

3. Adenylate cyclase converts ATP into cAMP.

4. cAMP opens cAMP-gated ion channels.

5. Ca^{2+} and Na^+ enter the cell, causing a generator potential.

6. The Ca^{2+} also opens Ca^{2+}-activated Cl^- channels, causing Cl^- to leave the cell, increasing the depolarization.

7. The generator potential opens voltage-gated Na^+ channels, triggering action potentials.

Recent evidence suggests that additional signal transduction pathways may also play a role in odorant detection in mammals. For example, some odorant receptors are coupled to G proteins that activate a phospholipase C (PLC)–mediated signal transduction cascade, in which PLC hydrolyzes phosphatidylinositol-4,5-bisphosphate (PIP_2) in the plasma membrane, producing inositol trisphosphate (IP_3) and diacylglycerol (DAG), which results in an increase in intracellular Ca^{2+}, causing plasma membrane Cl^- channels to open. However, just as with the cAMP-mediated signal transduction cascade, the ultimate result of the PLC-mediated signal transduction cascade is to depolarize the cell, triggering action potentials.

Although vertebrate genomes contain up to a thousand genes coding for odorant receptor proteins, the total number of odors that an animal can distinguish is even larger, possibly numbering in the tens of thousands. Experiments in mammals such as rats and humans indicate that each olfactory neuron expresses only one odorant receptor gene, but that each odorant receptor can recognize more than one odorant. Thus, a given odorant excites multiple olfactory neurons, but to different degrees. As a result, each odorant excites a unique combination of olfactory neurons. The number of distinct odorants that can be discriminated using such a combinatorial code is extremely large. Even if each odorant were coded by a combination of only three different receptors, there would be approximately 1 billion potential combinations. The code for each odor actually involves more than three receptors, and thus the potential for odor discrimination by the vertebrate olfactory system may be much larger than a billion combinations.

An alternative chemosensory system detects pheromones

Terrestrial vertebrates use an organ called the **vomeronasal organ** to detect a particular class of environmental chemicals, termed **pheromones**. Pheromones are chemical signals that are released by an animal that affect the behavior of another animal of the same species. Pheromones play an important role in maintaining social hierarchies and stimulating reproduction in many animals (see Chapter 16: Reproductive Physiology). The vomeronasal organ is an accessory olfactory organ that is structurally and molecularly distinct from the primary olfactory epithelium (Figure 7.9). In mammals, the paired vomeronasal organs are found on each side of the base of the nasal cavity near the nasal septum (the tissue that separates the two nostrils). In reptiles, the vomeronasal organ (often called Jacobson's organ, after the scientist who discovered it) is found on an analogous location on the palate. A narrow tube leads from the vomeronasal organ to either the oral cavity or the nasal cavity, depending on the species. For example, in snakes this tube is located in the oral cavity,

FIGURE 7.9 **Vomeronasal organs**

(a) In mammals, the vomeronasal organ, which detects pheromones, is located at the base of the nasal cavity and is connected to the mouth via the nasopalatine duct. **(b)** In reptiles, the vomeronasal organ (called Jacobson's organ) is located in the palate.

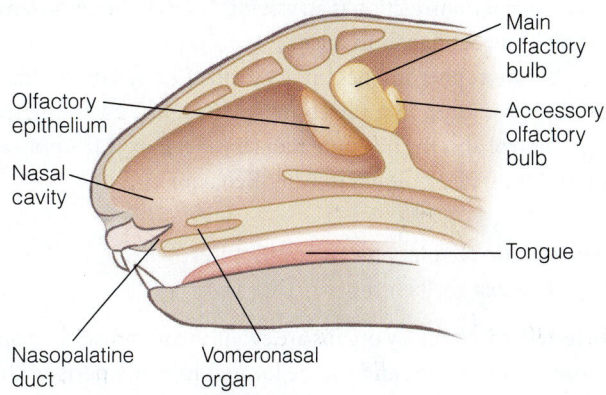

(a) Vomeronasal organ of mammals

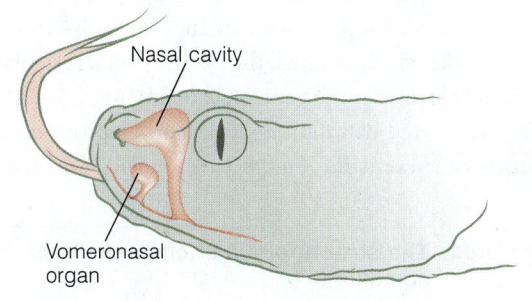

(b) Vomeronasal (Jacobson's) organ of reptiles

and a snake can use its tongue to transfer pheromones to the vomeronasal organ by flicking its tongue into its mouth.

Like the olfactory epithelium, the epithelium of the vomeronasal organ expresses chemoreceptors. However, the pheromone receptors of the vomeronasal organ differ from the odorant receptors of the olfactory epithelium. The G protein–coupled receptors of the vomeronasal organ (VR1 and VR2) activate a phospholipase C–based signal transduction system, while most olfactory receptors activate an adenylate cyclase–cAMP signal transduction pathway. The VR signal transduction pathway ultimately causes an ion channel in the transient receptor potential (TRP) family to open, altering membrane potential and causing an electrical signal in the vomeronasal receptor sensory neuron. The importance of the TRP2 gene in pheromone reception has been clearly demonstrated using mice in which the TRP2 gene is knocked out. Mice are normally quite aggressive and territorial mammals. If you put a male mouse alone in a cage for a day or two, it will establish the entire cage as its territory and attack any new males that you introduce. Normal male mice do not attack intruder females, and they ignore castrated males. However, if urine from an intact male mouse is applied to a castrated mouse, the resident male mouse will attack the castrated male intruder, just as it would an intact male. If a TRP2 **knockout** male establishes a territory, it ignores introduced castrated male mice swabbed with the urine of an intact male. It also mates indiscriminately with both females and males. These data demonstrate that TRP2 signal transduction is an essential part of the communication of sexual signals in mice.

Because pheromones affect behavior, scientists have used pheromones in a variety of applications, including insect control and the perfume industry (see Box 7.1: Applications: Using Pheromones to Alter Behavior).

Invertebrate olfactory mechanisms differ from those in vertebrates

Invertebrate olfactory organs are evolutionarily distinct from those in vertebrates and can be located in many parts of the body, although they are most often concentrated at the anterior end, on or near the head. In arthropods (such as insects and crustaceans), the invertebrates in which olfaction has been most intensively studied, the primary olfactory organs are generally located on the antennae or antennules. The antennae are covered with hundreds of hairlike projections of the cuticle called **sensilla** (Figure 7.10). Sensilla are complex

---

FIGURE 7.10 **The structure of a chemosensitive sensillum**

Insect sensilla are complex sensory organs that can contain both chemoreceptive and mechanoreceptive sensory neurons. Sensilla are involved in olfaction, detection of pheromones, gustation, and the senses of touch and hearing in insects.

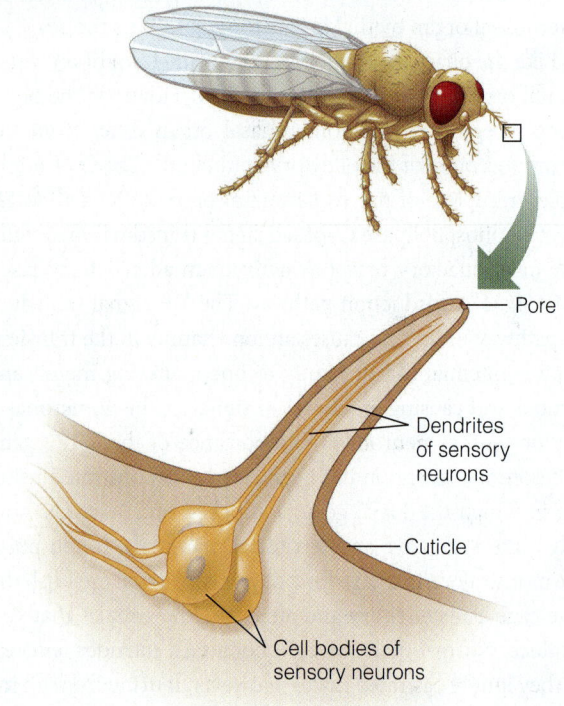

Pore

Dendrites of sensory neurons

Cuticle

Cell bodies of sensory neurons

---

sensory organs that have a variety of morphologies and functions, including both mechanosensory and chemosensory transduction. Olfactory sensilla have a small pore at their tip to allow odorants to cross the exoskeleton. Olfactory sensilla also contain odorant receptor neurons. As in vertebrates, these neurons express odorant receptor proteins.

The signal transduction mechanisms activated by odorant receptor proteins have been studied in only a few species of invertebrates, but they generally involve cAMP as a second messenger, just as in the vertebrates. Similarly, odorant-binding proteins and G protein–coupled odorant receptors have been detected in every species of invertebrate examined so far. However, the odorant receptors of invertebrates share little sequence similarity with mammalian odorant receptors, and are likely independently derived from G protein–coupled receptors found in the common ancestor of all animals. Even within the invertebrates, odorant receptors share little similarity among groups. For example, the odorant receptors in *Drosophila* (a fruit fly) are unlike those found in *Caenorhabditis elegans* (a nematode).

Although the odorant code has not yet been deciphered for any invertebrate, the mechanisms of signal processing likely differ among invertebrate groups. In *Drosophila*, as in vertebrates, each olfactory neuron expresses a single odorant receptor, and olfactory neurons likely code odorant information combinatorially. In contrast, in *C. elegans,* each olfactory neuron expresses several different odorant receptors, and thus the "odorant code" cannot be a simple combinatorial system like that found in mammals.

As discussed in Box 7.1: Applications: Using Pheromones to Alter Behavior, many invertebrates also detect pheromones. Aquatic invertebrates are thought to use essentially the same system for detecting both odorants and pheromones, but in terrestrial invertebrates such as insects these two systems are separated. Insects have specialized pheromone-sensitive sensilla on their antennae that are similar in structure to those that detect odors, but their numbers and distributions differ between males and females. The sensory neurons of these sensilla are exceptionally sensitive and highly selective. In fact, the pheromone-sensitive sensilla of the silk moth *Bombyx mori* can detect as little as a single molecule of the pheromone bombykol.

CONCEPT CHECK

5. The olfactory system codes information by using what is termed a combinatorial code. What are the advantages of using a combinatorial code to detect incoming chemical stimuli?

6. What would happen to the ability to smell if a drug that inhibited adenylate cyclase were applied to the olfactory epithelium of a vertebrate? Would this drug affect the sensing of pheromones if applied to the vomeronasal epithelium? Justify your answer.

USING PHEROMONES TO ALTER BEHAVIOR

Pheromones are chemicals released from an animal that elicit a *specific response* from another member of the same species. Many pheromones fall into the category of *sex pheromones:* chemicals that are released to detect or attract potential mates. Animals can often detect sex pheromones in extremely low quantities, and this property of pheromones makes them an attractive target for developing products that can be used to influence behavior.

Insect pheromones are routinely used as biocontrol agents. For example, codling moths are an important pest on apples; the "worm" in an apple is often the larval stage of this moth (Figure 7.11). To control codling moths, farmers take advantage of a pheromone that female codling moths use to attract males. Farmers can hang small dispensers containing this pheromone on their apple trees, and the dispensers gradually release the pheromone throughout the orchard. The widespread pheromone makes it difficult for the male moths to locate the trail emanating from a female, and prevents the females from mating and laying eggs that would develop into larvae on the apples.

Pheromones can also be used to attract beneficial insects. For example, honeybee pheromones can be sprayed onto crops to attract worker bees as pollinators. Similarly, the pheromone that tells worker bees that larvae are present in the hive and need to be fed can be introduced into a beehive to increase the drive of the workers to go and collect pollen. By using this pheromone, farmers can increase the rate at which their crops are pollinated.

It is not just humans that have co-opted pheromone signals for their own purposes. Some predatory spiders emit a chemical that mimics the pheromones used by specific moth species; the male moths are lured to the spider and trapped in the web. Some species of orchids have evolved to produce chemicals that mimic insect pheromones to attract them as pollinators.

Because pheromones play an important role in regulating the behavior of animals ranging from insects to mice, it leads to the question of whether pheromones might also play a role in humans. Indeed many experiments suggest that chemical cues can influence human physiology and behavior. For example, exposing women to swabs from the underarms of other women can alter the timing of their menstrual cycles and mood. But no studies have convincingly demonstrated the physiological basis of pheromone sensing in humans. The vomeronasal organ is greatly reduced in size in adult humans compared to its size in the human fetus and in other adult mammals. Humans also lack an accessory olfactory bulb, the part of the brain responsible for interpreting pheromone signals in other animals. In addition, the majority of the genes encoding vomeronasal receptors contain deletions or other changes that would likely make them nonfunctional, and humans do not have a copy of the TRP2 ion channel. Together, these data suggest that pheromone signaling via the vomeronasal organ is unlikely in humans.

The reduction or loss of vomeronasal signaling appears to have occurred in the Old World primates. The TRP2 gene is present in the prosimians and the New World monkeys, but is mutated or absent in the Old World monkeys and the apes. Interestingly, the loss of pheromone-based signaling in the Old World monkeys roughly coincides with the evolution of color vision. It may be that Old World monkeys, apes, and humans rely more on visual signals than on pheromones for detecting gender.

Although humans don't appear to use the vomeronasal organ for detecting pheromones, this is not the only potential site of pheromone detection and signaling. For example, rodents have been shown to use both the olfactory epithelium and the vomeronasal epithelium to detect pheromones, leaving open the possibility that the olfactory epithelium can be used as a pheromone detection pathway in humans.

Despite the lack of strong evidence for pheromone-mediated signaling in humans, a number of companies in the perfume industry have attempted to manufacture and market perfumes containing potential human pheromones, but there are no clinical studies supporting their effectiveness at this time.

References

- Gomez-Dias, C., & Benton, R. (2013). The joy of sex pheromones. *EMBO Reports. 10*, 874–883.

- Liman, E. R., & Innan, H. (2003). Relaxed selective pressure on an essential component of pheromone transduction in primate evolution. *Proceedings of the National Academy of Science USA,* 100, 3328–3332.

- Young, J. M., Massa, H.F., Hsu, L., & Trask, B. J. (2010). Extreme variability among mammalian V1R gene families. *Genome Research, 20*, 10–18.

- Zhang, J. Z., & Webb, D.M. (2003). Evolutionary deterioration of the vomeronasal pheromone transduction pathway in catarrhine primates. *Proceedings of the National Academy of Science USA, 100*, 8337–8341.

FIGURE 7.11   **The larva of a codling moth emerging from an apple**

Photo source: Graphic Science/Alamy.

The Gustatory System

Unlike the olfactory system, the gustatory system (or sense of taste) is not able to discriminate among thousands of different molecules. Instead, at least in humans, tastes can be grouped into one of five classes: salty, sweet, bitter, sour, and umami. Umami is a word coined by a Japanese scientist from the words *umai* (delicious) and *mi* (essence), and corresponds to a savory or meaty sensation. Sweet, umami, and salty tastes indicate nutritionally important carbohydrates, proteins, and ions, whereas bitter and sour tastes generally reflect potentially toxic substances.

Taste buds are vertebrate gustatory receptors

In terrestrial vertebrates, taste receptor cells are found on the tongue, soft palate, larynx, and esophagus and are clustered into groups known as **taste buds** (Figure 7.12). In aquatic vertebrates, taste buds can also be located on the external surface of the body. For example, many fish have taste buds on the barbells (whiskerlike projections from the lower jaw). The sea robin even has taste buds on the tips of its fins, which are useful because these fish use their fins to probe in the mud for food. Although the shapes, sizes, and distributions of taste buds vary among

FIGURE 7.12 **Structure of a vertebrate taste bud**

A taste bud consists of a pore containing sensory receptor cells and support cells. The apical surface of the receptor cells is covered with microvilli that project into a pore open to the surface of the body. Receptor proteins on these microvilli detect tastants dissolved in saliva or other fluids.

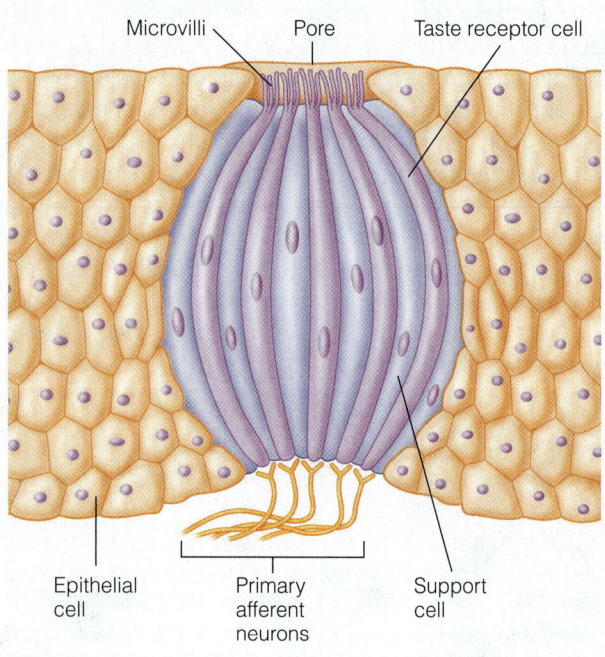

vertebrate species, all taste buds have certain common features. Taste buds are onion-shaped structures that contain multiple taste receptor cells (in humans each bud contains between 50 and 100 taste receptor cells), with a pore that opens out to the surface of the body. Dissolved chemicals from food, termed **tastants**, enter through this pore and contact the taste receptor cell. The apical surface of the taste cell is folded into numerous microvilli, which contain the receptors and ion channels that mediate the transduction of the taste signal.

Vertebrate taste receptors use diverse signal transduction mechanisms

Figure 7.13 summarizes the signal transduction mechanisms used by taste receptor proteins for salty, sour, sweet, and bitter tastes, respectively. Salty tastes are conveyed by Na^+ ions in food, while sour tastes are conveyed by H^+ ions. Sugars and related organic molecules convey sweet tastes, while amino acids and related molecules convey the sensation umami. In contrast, a wide range of organic molecules can convey a bitter taste, including compounds like caffeine, nicotine, and quinine.

The receptor protein for salty substances is not actually a receptor at all, but instead a Na^+ ion channel (Figure 7.13a). These Na^+ channels are also permeable to H^+ ions, and thus may play a role in the perception of sour tastes. Because Na^+ and H^+ compete for access to the channel, however, these channels are probably important for the perception of "sourness" only in species with relatively low Na^+ levels in their saliva. Thus, hamsters, which have low saliva Na^+, use these channels to detect sourness, while humans and rats, which have relatively high saliva Na^+, taste sourness through other mechanisms.

A number of sour-taste transduction mechanisms have been proposed, depending on the species being investigated. Figure 7.13b summarizes one of these potential mechanisms, which was first described in the taste receptor cells of salamanders. These taste receptor cells sense sourness via an apically localized K^+ channel that is blocked directly by protons. Blocking these K^+ channels leads to depolarization of the taste cells, by decreasing K^+ permeability and altering the resting membrane potential, as described by the Goldman equation. This depolarization ultimately causes neurotransmitter release. In contrast, in frogs, taste cells contain H^+-gated Ca^{2+} channels and H^+ transporters that are believed to be involved in detecting sourness, although the specific proteins involved have not yet been sequenced. Recent molecular studies in mammals have suggested that acid-sensing ion channels (ASICs) may be important for detection of sourness. These

FIGURE 7.13 Signal transduction in taste receptor cells

(a) Signal transduction for salty substances. **(b)** Signal transduction for sour substances. **(c)** Signal transduction for sweet substances. **(d)** Signal transduction for bitter substances. Note that Umami tastes are detected via a variety of mechanisms, some of which resemble those for sweet substances.

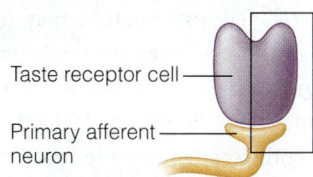

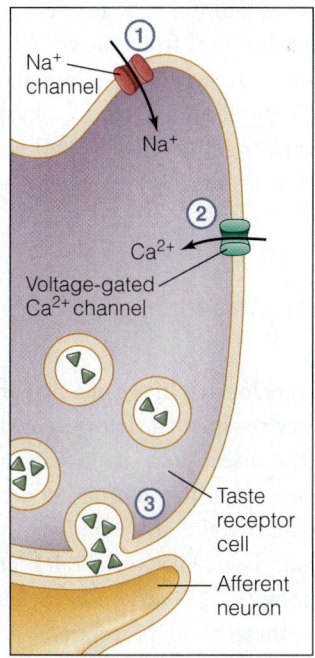

1 Na^+ from salty food enters through a Na^+ channel.

2 The resulting depolarization opens voltage-gated Ca^{2+} channels.

3 The influx of Ca^{2+} causes neurotransmitter release.

(a) Salty

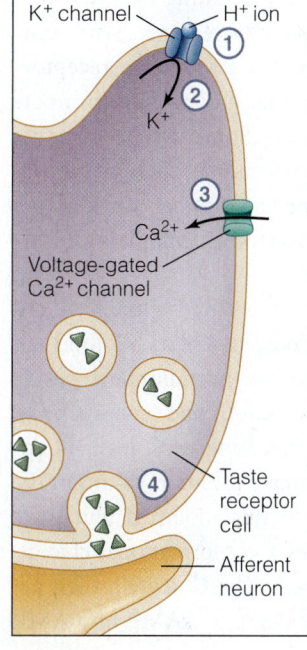

1 H^+ ions from sour foods block the K^+ channel.

2 This blockage prevents K^+ from leaving the cell.

3 The resulting depolarization opens voltage-gated Ca^{2+} channels.

4 The influx of Ca^{2+} causes neurotransmitter release.

(b) Sour

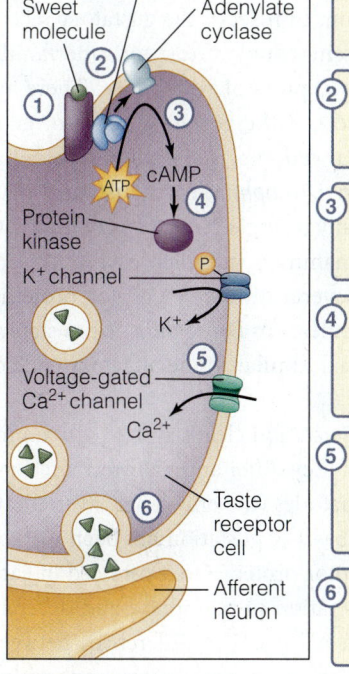

1 A sweet substance binds to its receptor, causing a conformational change.

2 The activated G protein, gustducin, activates adenylate cyclase.

3 Adenylate cyclase catalyzes the conversion of ATP to cAMP.

4 The cAMP activates a protein kinase that phosphorylates and closes a K^+ channel.

5 The resulting depolarization opens voltage-gated Ca^{2+} channels.

6 The influx of Ca^{2+} causes neurotransmitter release.

(c) Sweet

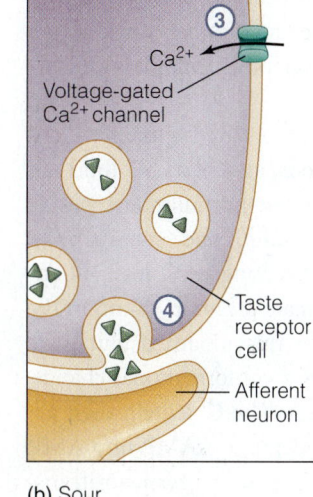

1 A bitter substance binds to its receptor, causing a conformational change.

2 The activated G protein, transducin, activates phospholipase C (PLC).

3 PLC catalyzes the conversion of PIP_2 into the second messenger IP_3.

4 IP_3 causes the release of Ca^{2+} from intracellular stores.

5 The influx of Ca^{2+} causes neurotransmitter release.

(d) Bitter

channels appear to be Na$^+$ channels that open in response to changes in pH.

The signal transduction pathway for sweet-taste receptors is summarized in Figure 7.13c. Sweet substances such as sugars bind to G protein–coupled receptors at the apical cell surface, and activate the G protein **gustducin**, which signals through an adenylate cyclase signal transduction pathway. The receptors for "sweetness" have recently been identified in mice. These receptors are sensitive to many kinds of sweet substances, including monosaccharides, polysaccharides, high-potency sweeteners, and some amino acids. This suggests that the sweet-taste receptors are broad-spectrum receptors that do not discriminate among alternative sweet substances. Some sweet substances (in particular, strong artificial sweeteners such as saccharine) may also activate an IP$_3$-mediated signal transduction cascade, which leads to the closing of K$^+$ channels and depolarization of the receptor cell.

The taste umami, which is caused by L-glutamate and other amino acids present in foods, as well as the food additive MSG, appears to be detected by multiple types of G protein–coupled receptors, including one that is similar to the receptors responsible for detecting sweetness and another that is similar to the glutamate receptors found in the brain. When glutamate binds to this modified glutamate receptor, the receptor undergoes a conformational change, activating an associated G protein. The G protein then activates a phosphodiesterase that degrades cAMP into AMP. The decreases in cAMP are thought to trigger neurotransmitter release, although the precise pathways involved have not yet been identified.

Bitter-taste receptors appear to be much more complex and specific than sweet-taste receptors. Humans have at least 25 genes coding for bitter-taste receptors, and each taste cell that is sensitive to "bitterness" expresses many of these genes. The way in which this complex pattern of expression is translated into the perception of bitterness is still unknown, although the signal transduction mechanisms within the bitter-taste receptor cells have been worked out (Figure 7.13d).

Coding differs between the olfactory and gustatory systems

There is considerable debate among sensory neurobiologists as to how the perception of a taste is coded in the brain. Taste receptor proteins act through a variety of signal transduction mechanisms, unlike odor receptor proteins, which are always coupled to G proteins. Each taste receptor cell expresses more than one kind of taste receptor protein, unlike olfactory neurons, which each express only a single olfactory receptor protein. Unlike olfactory receptor cells, which are bipolar sensory neurons, taste receptor cells are epithelial cells that release neurotransmitter onto a primary afferent neuron, and a single taste neuron may synapse with more than one taste receptor cell, suggesting that coding of taste information may be very complex. Thus, coding in the gustatory system is unlikely to operate via a mechanism in which a neuron is responsible for a single particular taste sensation. Instead, it is probable that each taste is coded by the complex pattern of activity across many neurons, and the code for perception of tastants must be quite different from the code for perception of odorants. However, despite the fact that olfaction and gustation are very different from a physiological perspective, they work together closely, and our perception of the taste of a substance is dependent on our sense of smell.

Taste reception differs between vertebrates and invertebrates

Taste receptors in arthropods are located in sensilla that are structurally similar to olfactory sensilla. Gustatory sensilla are found on many parts of the insect body, including the outside of the **proboscis** or mouth, in the internal mouthparts (pharynx), along the wing margin, at the ends of the legs, and in the female vaginal plates. Like vertebrates, arthropods can distinguish among the primary tastants, but the mechanisms underlying these taste perceptions are quite different from those in the vertebrates. Arthropod taste receptor cells are bipolar sensory neurons, similar to the neurons involved in olfaction in the vertebrates, and unlike the epithelial cells that synapse with a sensory neuron in vertebrate gustation. In insects, the gustatory receptors belong to the G protein–coupled receptor superfamily, similar to the olfactory receptors of vertebrates. There are approximately 60 members of the gustatory receptor gene family in the *Drosophila* genome, suggesting substantial functional complexity. In *Drosophila*, each gustatory neuron appears to express only a single receptor protein, quite unlike the situation in mammals in which each gustatory receptor cell expresses several different receptor proteins. These data suggest that, at least in *Drosophila*, the gustatory code may be combinatorial, similar to the olfactory code of mammals.

The mechanisms of gustation clearly differ between insects and vertebrates, and they differ among invertebrates as well. For example, in nematodes (the only other invertebrate for which the molecular basis of gustation has been worked out in detail), many receptor proteins are expressed in each neuron, similar to the situation in mammals, and different from the mechanisms in insects. The differences between the mechanisms of gustation in vertebrates and among invertebrates suggest that gustatory organs must have evolved independently several times.

Nociceptors detect noxious chemical stimuli

Animals are also able to detect and respond to external and internal chemical stimuli that are potentially damaging. Nociceptors that detect harmful environmental chemicals are concentrated in the mouth, sinuses, airways, and mucous membranes. Chemicals such as capsaicin (from hot peppers), mustard oil (in mustard seeds and wasabi), and acrolein (the acrid ingredient in tobacco smoke and vehicle exhaust) stimulate these nociceptors and can cause a painful, burning sensation. The nociceptors that detect these chemicals express a specific member of the TRP (transient receptor potential) family of ion channels, called TRPA1. Similar TRP channels also respond to a variety of internal chemical stimuli associated with inflammation. Nociceptor neurons expressing these TRP channels are found throughout the body, and are particularly numerous on the skin. The TRPA1 channel is found in animals as diverse as insects, mollusks, and vertebrates. This phylogenetic pattern suggests that the ability to detect noxious chemicals is phylogenetically ancient and highly conserved.

FIGURE 7.14 **Mechanosensory protein complexes**

(a) *C. elegans* touch receptors contain mechanosensory neurons with ENaC-type channels in their membranes. **(b)** *Drosophila* touch receptors contain mechanosensory neurons with TRP-type channels in their membranes. In both cases, mechanical stimuli cause the extracellular anchors to move relative to the cytoskeleton, pulling on the channel and causing a conformational change that opens or closes the channel, changing the membrane potential of the cell.

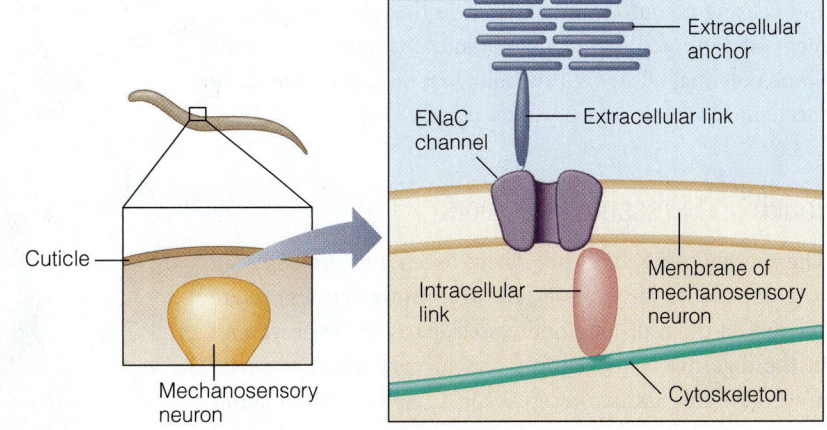

(a) ENaC channels in a *C. elegans* touch receptor

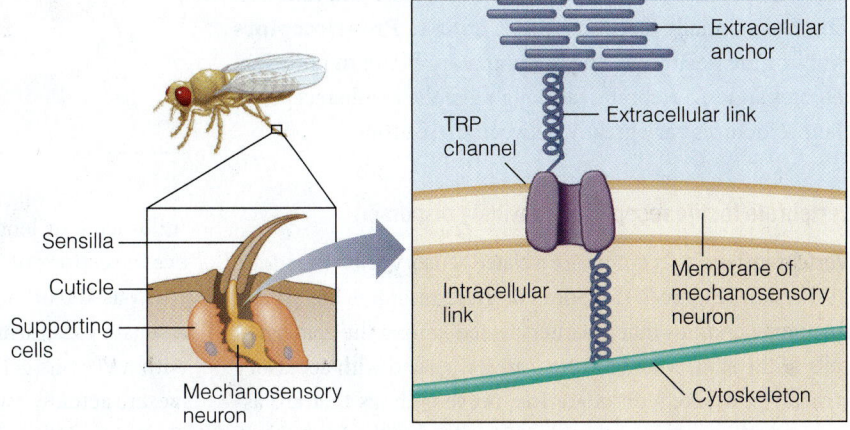

(b) TRP channels in a *Drosophila* touch receptor

CONCEPT CHECK

7. Compare and contrast olfaction and gustation in vertebrates.

8. How would the response of a taste receptor cell differ between a food that is slightly salty and a food that is very salty? How would this affect action potential generation in the afferent neuron?

MECHANORECEPTION

Mechanoreceptors are specialized cells or organs that can transform mechanical stimuli, such as pressure changes, into electrical signals that can then be interpreted by the rest of the nervous system. All organisms, and probably all cells, have the ability to sense and respond to mechanical stimuli. Mechanoreception is important for cell volume control, and the senses of touch, hearing, and balance, and it plays a critical role in regulating blood pressure in vertebrates. Most mechanoreceptor cells are small and widely dispersed, making it challenging to use traditional biochemical approaches to isolate the proteins responsible for mechanosensory transduction. Thus, despite decades of investigation, the mechanisms by which a mechanoreceptor converts a mechanical stimulus to an electrical stimulus are only now being elucidated.

Genetic studies in *Drosophila* and *C. elegans* have demonstrated that there are two main types of mechanoreceptor proteins in animals: ENaC (epithelial sodium channels) and TRP (transient receptor potential) channels (Figure 7.14). Although these channels were first identified in invertebrates, they have recently been isolated from the mechanoreceptors in the ears and skin of vertebrates, suggesting that they play an important role in all forms of mechanoreception. Both ENaC and TRP mechanoreceptor proteins are attached to the cytoskeleton and to extracellular matrix proteins. Mechanical stimuli such as touch and pressure move the extracellular anchoring proteins, pulling on the ion channel and causing a conformational change that alters the movement of ions across the membrane, changing the membrane potential of the cell, and allowing the cell to transduce mechanical signals into electrical signals.

Touch and Pressure Receptors

The mechanoreceptors that detect touch and pressure can be grouped into three classes. **Baroreceptors** detect pressure changes in the walls of blood vessels, parts of the heart, and in the digestive, reproductive, and urinary tracts of vertebrates. We discuss baroreceptors in Chapter 9: Circulatory Systems. **Tactile receptors** detect touch, pressure, and vibration on the body surface. Both vertebrates and invertebrates have tactile receptors, although their structure and function vary substantially between these groups. **Proprioceptors** monitor the position of the body, and are found in both vertebrates and invertebrates, although like the tactile receptors, their structures vary greatly between these groups.

Vertebrate tactile receptors are widely dispersed

Vertebrate tactile receptors are isolated sensory cells embedded in the skin (Figure 7.15). Some of these receptors are simply free nerve endings that are interspersed among the epidermal cells of the skin, whereas others are associated with accessory structures. Merkel's disks are free nerve endings that are associated with an enlarged epidermal cell called the Merkel cell. These receptors have a very small receptive field, and are used for fine tactile discrimination. Both the free nerve endings and Merkel's disks are slowly adapting tonic receptors that are most sensitive to indentation of the skin, and are thus important for sensing light touch and pressure on the surface of the skin. We use the Merkel's disks in our skin when we perform tasks such as reading Braille letters that require very fine discrimination.

The nerve endings of the root hair plexus, which are wrapped around the base of hair follicles, monitor movements across the body surface. When a hair is displaced, the movement of the hair follicle causes the sensory nerve endings to stretch, stimulating mechanoreceptor proteins on the dendritic membrane. These receptors are rapidly adapting phasic receptors, so they are most sensitive to changes in movement. For example, you can often sense when an insect crawls across your skin, but you may not detect an insect that is not moving.

Pacinian corpuscles are located deep within the skin and in the muscles, joints, and internal organs. At almost a

FIGURE 7.15 **Touch and pressure receptors in vertebrate skin**

Skin mechanoreceptors may be free nerve endings or sensory neurons associated with complex accessory structures.

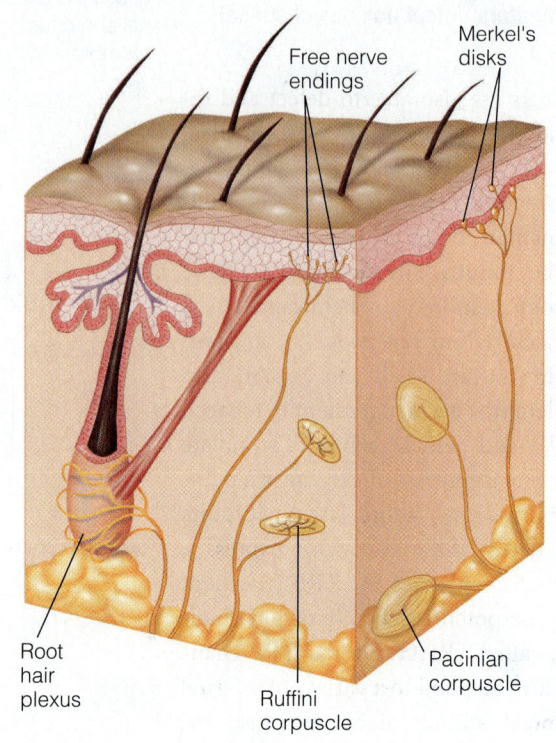

Free nerve endings

Merkel's disks

Root hair plexus

Ruffini corpuscle

Pacinian corpuscle

millimeter in length, they are actually visible to the naked eye in sections of skin, and a typical human hand contains as many as 400 of these receptors. **Pacinian corpuscles** contain a sensory dendrite surrounded by up to 70 layers of tissue with a viscous gel between them. These layers, called lamellae, are actually modified Schwann cells and layers of connective tissue. When something presses on a Pacinian corpuscle, the lamellae change shape, changing the shape of the sensory dendrite and initiating a change in the membrane potential. The viscous gel quickly returns to its original position, even in the presence of continuous pressure, returning the membrane potential to its resting level. As a result, the sensation of pressure disappears even though the pressure is still present at the surface of the skin. When the pressure is removed, the connective tissue layers return to their normal shape, pulling on the nerve ending, which causes another change in membrane potential, and another stimulus. Thus, Pacinian corpuscles are rapidly adapting sensory receptors that are sensitive to both the beginning and end of a stimulus. This property makes Pacinian corpuscles especially sensitive to vibrations. So when you feel your cell phone vibrating, it is your Pacinian corpuscles that detect the incoming call. Pacinian corpuscles have relatively large receptive fields, and thus do not allow for fine-scale discrimination of touch sensations.

Ruffini corpuscles are located in the connective tissue of the skin and of the limbs and joints. They are slowly adapting receptors that are sensitive to stretching of the skin and movement of the joints as we move around. Ruffini corpuscles work together with other proprioceptors to help an animal determine the location of its body in space. When you hit the snooze button on your alarm clock without even opening your eyes, it is your Ruffini corpuscles that helped you do so!

Vertebrate proprioceptors monitor body position

In addition to touch and pressure receptors such as Ruffini corpuscles, there are three major groups of vertebrate proprioceptors associated with the joints and limbs:

1. **Muscle spindles** on the surface of skeletal muscles monitor the length of the muscle. Each muscle spindle consists of modified muscle fibers called intrafusal fibers enclosed in a connective tissue capsule.

2. Golgi tendon organs are located at the junction between a skeletal muscle and a tendon. These receptors are stimulated by changes in the tension in the tendon.

3. Joint capsule receptors are located in the capsules that enclose the joints. Several types of receptors are in this category, including receptors similar to free nerve endings, Pacinian corpuscles, and Golgi tendon organs. These receptors detect pressure, tension, and movement in the joint.

Proprioceptors typically do not adapt to stimuli, and thus constantly send information to the central nervous system regarding body position. Another class of more rapidly adapting receptors is responsible for detecting movement, and provides the sense of *kinesthesia*.

Insects have several types of tactile and proprioceptors

Insects and other arthropods are encased in a hard exoskeleton, so their sense of touch cannot function via free nerve endings in the body surface, as is the case for the touch receptors in vertebrates. Instead, most insect touch receptors are grouped into complex organs called trichoid sensilla that consist of a hairlike projection of the cuticle associated with a bipolar sensory neuron (Figure 7.16a). When the hair bends in the socket of a trichoid sensillum (as a result of a touch or vibration), accessory structures transfer the movement to the tip of the bipolar sensory neuron located beneath the hairlike projection. The movement opens stretch-sensitive TRP ion channels in the membrane of the mechanoreceptor neuron, changing the membrane potential, and sending a signal in the form of action potentials to the insect's nervous system. Trichoid sensilla can be extremely sensitive, detecting even small changes in air movements. Insects use their trichoid sensilla to detect the air movements caused by the motion of

FIGURE 7.16 **Variation in the structure of insect sensilla**

(a) A trichoid sensillum is associated with a hairlike projection of the cuticle. **(b)** A campaniform sensillum is associated with a dome-shaped projection of the cuticle.

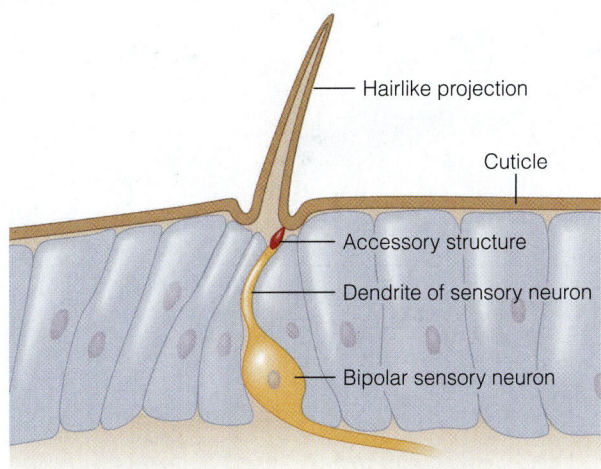

(a) Trichoid sensilla

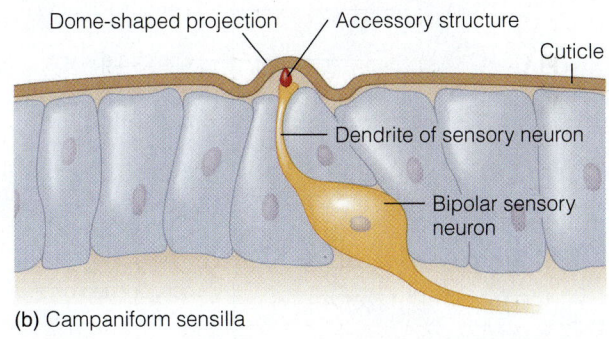

(b) Campaniform sensilla

a predator, and can use this information to take evasive actions (explaining why it is so difficult to swat a fly!).

Insects use another type of sensillum on the external surface of the cuticle, called a campaniform sensillum, for proprioception (Figure 7.16b). Campaniform sensilla resemble trichoid sensilla except that they lack the hair shaft and instead are covered with a dome-shaped section of thin cuticle. They are usually found in clusters, particularly on or near the joints of the limbs, and detect the deformation of the cuticle as an insect moves. Thus, campaniform sensilla are critical in allowing an insect to make coordinated movements.

Insects also have a proprioceptor that can detect bending of the cuticle. These proprioceptors are organized into functional units called scolopidia (Figure 7.17), which consist of a specialized bipolar sensory neuron and a complex accessory cell (the scolopale) that surrounds the ciliated sensory dendrite at one end. This structure is attached to the cuticle via a ligament or attachment cell. These mechanoreceptors can exist as isolated cells or may be grouped to form complex organs called chordotonal organs, which form the basis for the sense of hearing in some insects.

FIGURE 7.17 **Structure of an insect scolopidium**

Scolopidia are associated with the internal surface of the cuticle. The bipolar sensory neuron of the scolopidium is surrounded by sheath cells and scolopale cells. The attachment (or cap) cell links the complex to the cuticle.

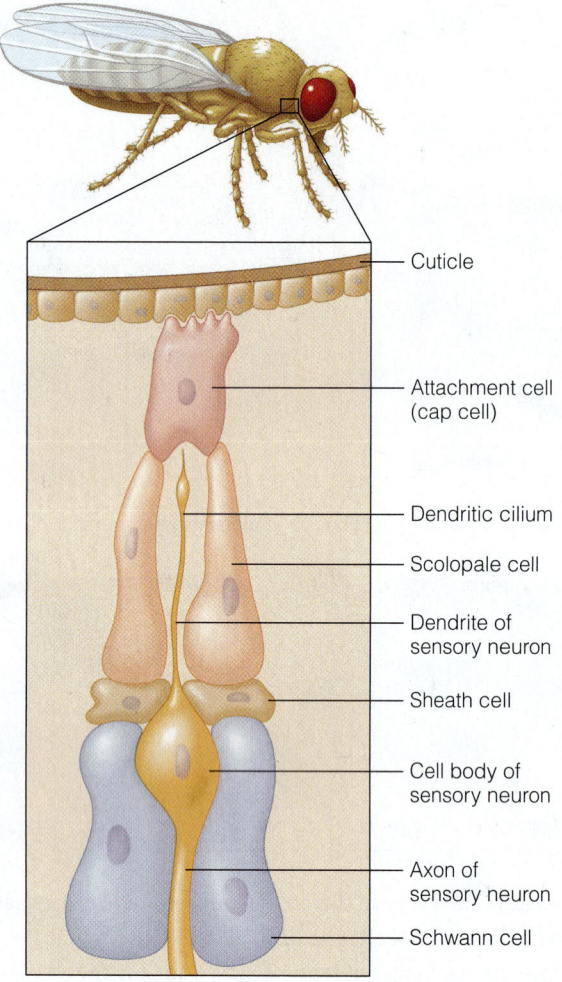

— Cuticle

— Attachment cell (cap cell)

— Dendritic cilium

— Scolopale cell

— Dendrite of sensory neuron

— Sheath cell

— Cell body of sensory neuron

— Axon of sensory neuron

— Schwann cell

Insects also have a variety of internal mechanoreceptors that function as stretch receptors and proprioceptors. Unlike the mechanoreceptors associated with the cuticle, these receptors are not organized into complex organs, and do not contain ciliated bipolar neurons. Instead, these mechanoreceptors are usually isolated multipolar neurons associated with muscle and connective tissue. These mechanoreceptors use ENaC channels for signal transduction.

CONCEPT CHECK

9. What are possible advantages of having both tonic and phasic touch receptors in the skin of vertebrates?

10. Why do insects have complex touch organs, rather than isolated sensory neurons associated with the body surface as in mammals?

Equilibrium and Hearing

In addition to detecting touch, pressure, and the location of the limbs, mechanoreceptors are involved in the senses of equilibrium and hearing. The sense of equilibrium, sometimes called the sense of balance in humans, involves detecting the position of the body relative to the force of gravity. The sense of hearing involves detecting and interpreting sound waves. In vertebrates the ear is the organ responsible for both equilibrium and hearing. In invertebrates, however, the organs of equilibrium are entirely separate from the organs of hearing.

Statocysts are the organ of equilibrium for invertebrates

Many invertebrates have organs called **statocysts** that they use to detect the orientation of their bodies with respect to gravity (Figure 7.18). Statocysts are hollow, fluid-filled cavities that are lined with mechanosensory neurons, and contain dense particles of calcium carbonate called **statoliths**. When the orientation of the animal changes, the statolith moves across the sheet of mechanoreceptors. This movement stimulates the mechanoreceptive cells, sending a signal to the nervous system. This signal provides a cue about the position of the body. Most marine invertebrates have relatively simple statocysts (as shown in Figure 7.18a), but cephalopod mollusks, such as the octopus, have a particularly complicated statocyst system (Figure 7.18b). An octopus has two statocysts, one on each side of the head. Each statocyst is composed of a globelike structure called the macula, and three **cristae**, each oriented in a different plane. The cristae and macula contain statoliths that move in response to mechanical stimuli. The crista detects angular acceleration, or the turning of the body, while the macula detects linear acceleration, or the degree of forward motion. This system is analogous to the organs of equilibrium in the vertebrates.

Insects use a variety of organs for hearing

There is a great deal of variation in the ability to hear among insect species; some species lack specialized organs for detecting sound, while others have specialized "ears" in several locations. The simplest type of insect ear is composed of groups of modified trichoid sensilla. Sound waves (vibrations carried in air) cause these thin sensilla to bend, and send a signal to a bipolar sensory neuron. However, this type of ear is not particularly sensitive, and most insect ears are derived from the chordotonal organs that insects use for proprioception.

Many insects, including cockroaches, honeybees, and water striders, use a modified chordotonal organ called the subgenual organ to detect vibrations carried through the ground (or the surface of the water, in the case of a water

FIGURE 7.18 Invertebrate organs of equilibrium

Statocysts contain ciliated sensory neurons and calcified stato-liths. When a mechanical stimulus such as a change in body orientation disturbs the statoliths, their motion stimulates receptor proteins on the cilia of the sensory neurons, depolarizing the cell. **(a)** Most invertebrates have simple statocysts. **(b)** Cephalopod mollusks have complex statocysts that consist of three cristae, oriented in different planes, with a sac called the macula at the base. The cristae detect angular acceleration, while the macula detects forward acceleration, providing the cephalopod with detailed information about body position and movement.

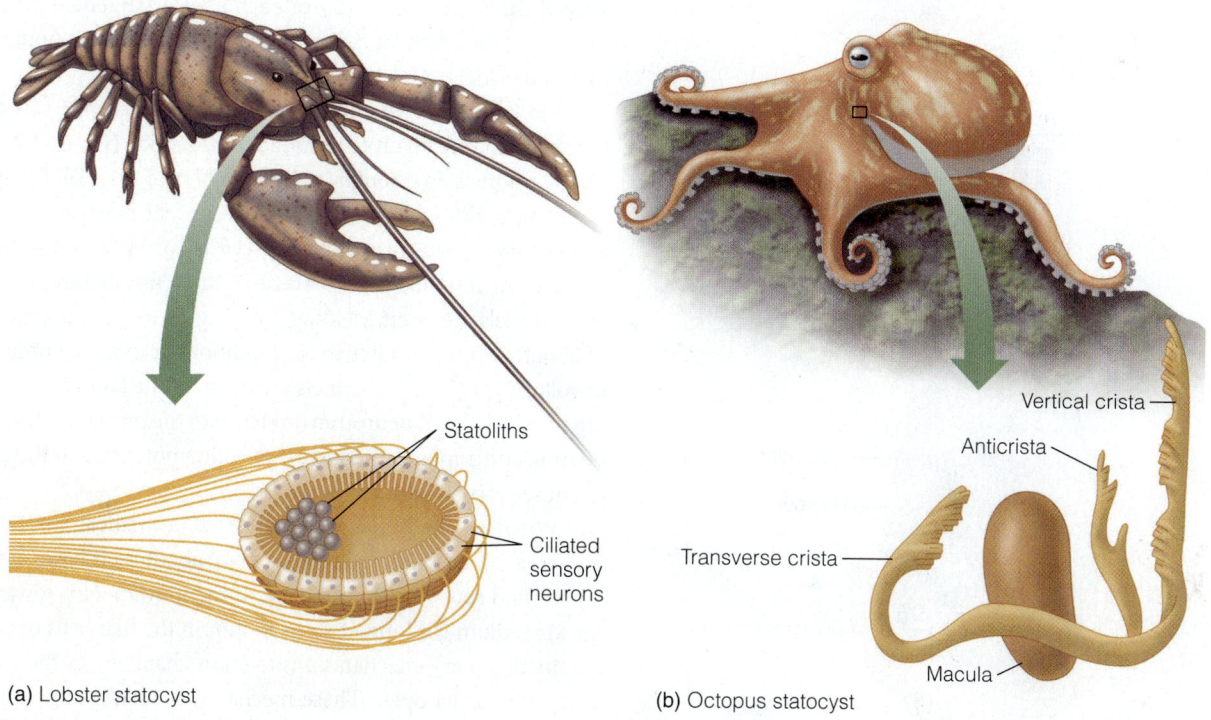

(a) Lobster statocyst

Statoliths

Ciliated sensory neurons

(b) Octopus statocyst

Vertical crista

Anticrista

Transverse crista

Macula

strider), and in at least some species, these subgenual organs may also be able to detect sound waves. Subgenual organs are located inside the insect leg. Vibrations of the leg cause the subgenual organ to vibrate, opening a mechanosensitive ion channel on the sensory neuron within the chordotonal organ, initiating action potentials that send a signal to the integrating centers of the nervous system.

An alternative type of insect ear is a modified chordo-tonal organ called the Johnston's organ, which is located at the base of the antennae of many insects, including moths, fruit flies, honeybees, and mosquitoes. Sound waves bend fine hairs on the antennae, stretching the membrane of the cells within the underlying chordotonal organ, opening mechanosensitive ion channels, and initiating action potentials in the mechanosensory neuron. These insects use John-ston's organ to detect sounds such as mating calls.

The most sensitive insect ears are called **tympanal organs**. A tympanal organ consists of a very thin region of the cuticle, called the *tympanum*, located over an air space similar to the air space in a drum. Sound waves cause the thin tympanum to vibrate, causing the air within the air space to vibrate. A chordotonal organ in this air space detects these vibrations, and sends signals in the form of action potentials

to the nervous system. Tympanal organs are found on many locations on the insect body, including the legs, abdomen, thorax, and wing base.

Katydids (relatives of grasshoppers and crickets) have particularly sophisticated hearing. The tympanum is con-nected to a series of stiff, leverlike structures that run through an air-filled space and connect to an inner, fluid-filled cham-ber that contains the mechanosensitive cells. This functional organization is similar to that of the mammalian ear, which we discuss later in the chapter, providing a striking example of convergent evolution.

Vertebrate organs of hearing and equilibrium contain hair cells

The vertebrate organs that are involved in the senses of hear-ing and equilibrium contain multiple mechanosensory cells and accessory structures. Unlike the mechanoreceptor cells that we have discussed so far, in these organs the mechanore-ceptor cells are not themselves sensory neurons, but instead contain modified epithelial cells that synapse with a sensory neuron. These highly specialized sensory receptor cells have extensive extracellular structures associated with them and

FIGURE 7.19   **The structure of a vertebrate hair cell**

Vertebrate hair cells (except those in the ears of adult mammals) have a long kinocilium and several short stereocilia. The kinocilia and stereocilia are connected to each other via tip links and a variety of other structures that cause the stereocilia to work together as a bundle.

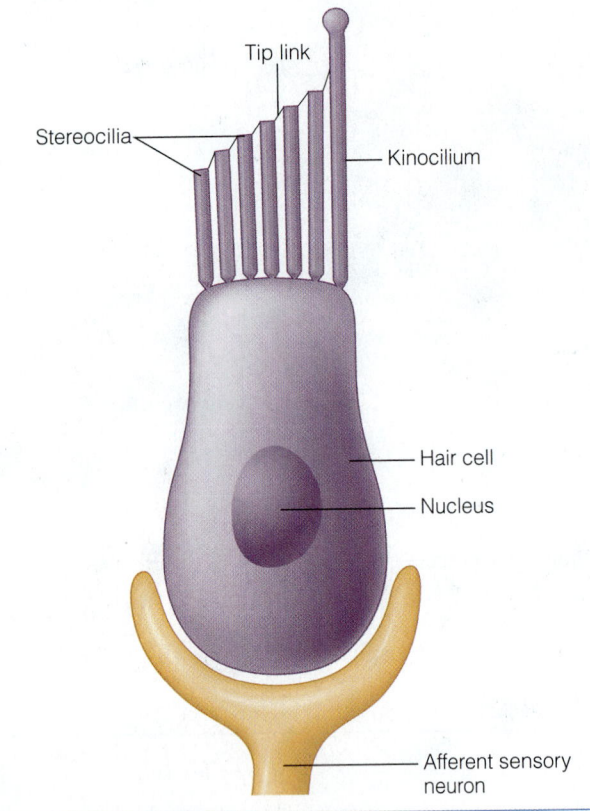

are termed **hair cells** because of the prominent cilia that extend from the apical end of each cell (Figure 7.19).

Most vertebrate hair cells have a single long cilium, the **kinocilium**, and many shorter projections, called **stereocilia**. Invertebrates also have mechanoreceptors that are similar to hair cells, but these cells can contain between 1 and 700 kinocilia. The kinocilium of a vertebrate hair cell is a true cilium with a 9 + 2 arrangement of microtubules (see Chapter 6: Cellular Movement and Muscles), although it is nonmotile, but the stereocilia are actually microvilli that contain polymerized actin molecules. There are hundreds of actin filaments along most of the length of a stereocilium, but there are far fewer (only a few dozen) at the base of the stereocilium. As a result, stereocilia taper at their bases, having the appearance of pencils balanced on their points.

The hair cells in the ears of adult mammals lack the kinocilium, suggesting that the kinocilium is not necessary for mechanoreception. Instead, the stereocilia play a critical role in mechanosensory transduction. The stereocilia and kinocilium (when present) are arranged in a tight bundle, with the shortest stereocilia placed farthest away from the kinocilium in the bundle, and with the stereocilia gradually becoming taller the closer they are to the kinocilium. The stereocilia are connected to each other and the kinocilium by a series of small fibers that cause the bundle of **hair cells** to act as a single unit. One particular type of these fibers, called a **tip link**, connects the top of each shorter stereocilium to the side of the adjacent taller one. These tip links are thought to play a critical role in sound transduction.

Mechanosensitive ion channels localized near the tips of the stereocilia are involved in sound transduction (Figure 7.20). These channels are thought to be members of the TRP family of channels, although the precise identity of the mechanosensitive channel in the vertebrate hair cell is currently somewhat debated. At rest, about 15 percent of these mechanosensitive ion channels are open, yielding a resting membrane potential of about -60 mV. Under these conditions, a modest number of voltage-gated Ca^{2+} channels are open on the hair cell, causing some release of neurotransmitter onto the primary afferent neuron, and a modest frequency of action potentials in the afferent sensory neuron.

When a hair cell is exposed to a mechanical stimulus such as a vibration, the stereocilia pivot about their bases, acting as rigid rods that do not bend. If the movement is toward the kinocilium (or longest stereocilium in the hair cells of the mammalian ear), mechanosensitive ion channels on the tips of the stereocilia open. These mechanosensitive channels are relatively nonselective, and allow the passage of a variety of ions, including K^+ and Ca^{2+}. However, at least in the hair cells of the vertebrate ear, the extracellular fluid around the hair cell is very high in K^+. As a result, K^+ enters the hair cell down its concentration gradient, causing the hair cell to depolarize by about 20 mV. This depolarization opens voltage-gated Ca^{2+} channels on the membrane of the hair cell, allowing additional Ca^{2+} to enter the cell (compared with the resting state), increasing the exocytosis of neurotransmitter from the hair cell onto the afferent neuron, and increasing the frequency of action potentials in the afferent neuron.

If the movement of the stereocilia is in the other direction, the mechanosensitive channels that were open at rest close. The closed channels prevent K^+ from entering the cell and cause the hair cell to hyperpolarize by about 5 mV (relative to the resting state), decreasing the release of neurotransmitter and the frequency of action potentials in the sensory neuron. Note that these sensory neurons associated with a hair cell fire action potentials all the time; neurotransmitter release from the hair cell simply increases or decreases the frequency of these action potentials depending on the direction that the stereocilia move. Thus, hair cells can detect not just movement, but the direction of that movement. The change in the membrane potential of the hair cell is also asymmetric—the change is larger in one direction than the other.

FIGURE 7.20 **Signal transduction in a vertebrate hair cell**

(a) At rest the hair cell is slightly depolarized and releases moderate amounts of neurotransmitter onto the primary afferent neuron, causing an intermediate frequency of action potentials. **(b)** When a pressure signal causes the stereocilia to pivot toward the kinocilium, mechanically gated channels on the stereocilia open, allowing additional K^+ to enter the cell from the extracellular fluid, which has a high concentration of K^+. The resulting depolarization opens voltage-gated Ca^{2+} channels, allowing Ca^{2+} to enter the cell. The influx of Ca^{2+} causes increased release of neurotransmitter onto the primary afferent neuron, increasing the frequency of action potentials. **(c)** When a pressure signal causes the stereocilia to pivot away from the kinocilium, the mechanically gated channels on the stereocilia close, hyperpolarizing the cell and closing voltage-gated Ca^{2+} channels. The resulting reduction in intracellular Ca^{2+} decreases the release of neurotransmitter onto the primary afferent neuron, reducing the frequency of action potentials.

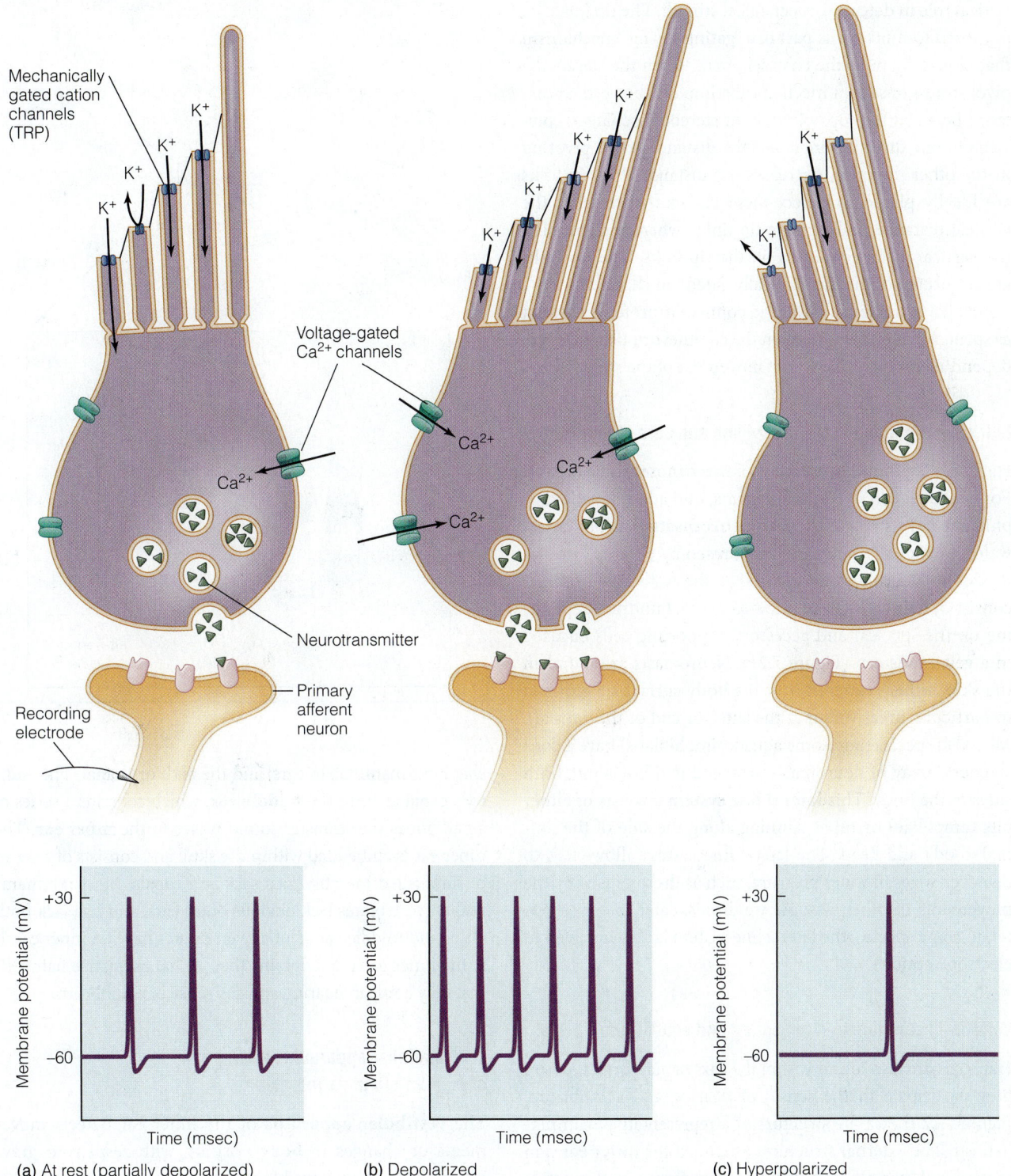

Mechanically gated cation channels (TRP)

K^+

Voltage-gated Ca^{2+} channels

Ca^{2+}

Neurotransmitter

Recording electrode

Primary afferent neuron

(a) At rest (partially depolarized)

(b) Depolarized

(c) Hyperpolarized

Membrane potential (mV)

+30

−60

Time (msec)

Tip links are critical for mechanosensory transduction

So far, we have not discussed how the mechanosensitive channels on the stereocilia are opened and closed by the pivoting movement of the stereocilia. Experiments using chemicals that destroy the tip links that connect adjacent stereocilia indicate that removing the tip links abolishes mechanosensory transduction, and that transduction is restored once the tip links regenerate. These results suggest that the tip links play a critical role in detecting mechanical stimuli. The tip links are proposed to function as part of a "gating spring" mechanism that physically pulls the channel open. When the stereocilia pivot in response to a mechanical stimulus, the vertical distance between the tops of adjacent stereocilia changes; pivoting in one direction increases the distance, while pivoting in the other direction decreases the distance. The tip links are ideally placed to detect these changes. Increasing the vertical distance pulls on the tip links, whereas decreasing the vertical distance pushes on the tip links. The tip links are connected to the mechanically gated ion channels on the stereocilia via a series of elastic connector proteins that act as springs that either pull open the channel or push it closed, depending on the direction of movement of the stereocilia.

Hair cells are found in the lateral line and ears of fish

Hair cells are found in a variety of mechanosensitive organs. For example, fish, larval amphibians, and adult aquatic amphibians have structures called **neuromasts** that can detect water movements, such as those caused by potential predators or prey as they move through the water. Neuromasts consist of hair cells (from a few to over a hundred, depending on the species) and accessory supporting cells encased in a gelatinous cap (Figure 7.21). Neuromasts are found in the skin, either scattered over the body surface or grouped in particular areas (often at the anterior end of the animal). Most fish species (and some aquatic amphibians) have a conspicuous array of neuromasts arranged in a line along both sides of the body. This **lateral line system** consists of either pits (ampullae) or tubes running along the side of the animal's body and head. The lateral line system allows fish to detect changes in water pressure, such as those caused by the movements of other fish. As we discuss later in this chapter, in some species, the lateral line system is also involved in electroreception.

Vertebrate ears function in hearing and equilibrium

Hair cells are also found within the ears of vertebrates, where they participate in the senses of hearing and equilibrium. Figure 7.22 shows the structure of a representative mammalian ear. The external structures are called the **outer ear** and in mammals consist of the **pinna**, which forms the distinctive

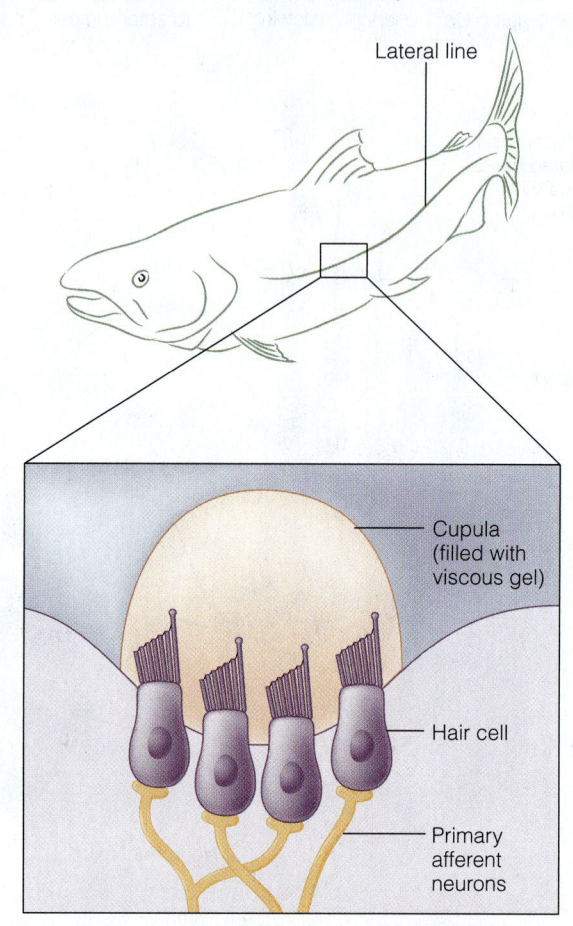

FIGURE 7.21 **Structure of a vertebrate neuromast**
Neuromasts are cup-shaped sensory organs. In aquatic organisms, neuromasts are found either scattered across the surface of the skin or grouped into structures such as the lateral line. When a mechanical stimulus contacts the cupula of a neuromast, the gel within the cupula shifts, stimulating the hair cells. The hair cells release neurotransmitter onto primary afferent neurons, sending a signal to the rest of the nervous system.

Lateral line

Cupula (filled with viscous gel)

Hair cell

Primary afferent neurons

shapes of mammalian ears, and the auditory canal. The auditory canal leads to the **middle ear**, which contains a series of small bones that transfer sound waves to the **inner ear**. The inner ear is embedded within the skull and consists of a series of fluid-filled membranous sacs and canals. Most nonmammalian vertebrates lack obvious outer ears, and fish lack both outer and middle ears, but all vertebrates have an inner ear. It is the inner ear that contains the mechanosensitive hair cells that play a role in hearing and the sense of equilibrium.

The vestibular apparatus is the organ of equilibrium in vertebrates

The **vestibular apparatus** of the inner ear detects movements or changes in body position with respect to gravity and is thus responsible for the sense of equilibrium or

FIGURE 7.22 The structure of the mammalian ear

Mammalian ears consist of an outer ear, a middle ear, and an inner ear.

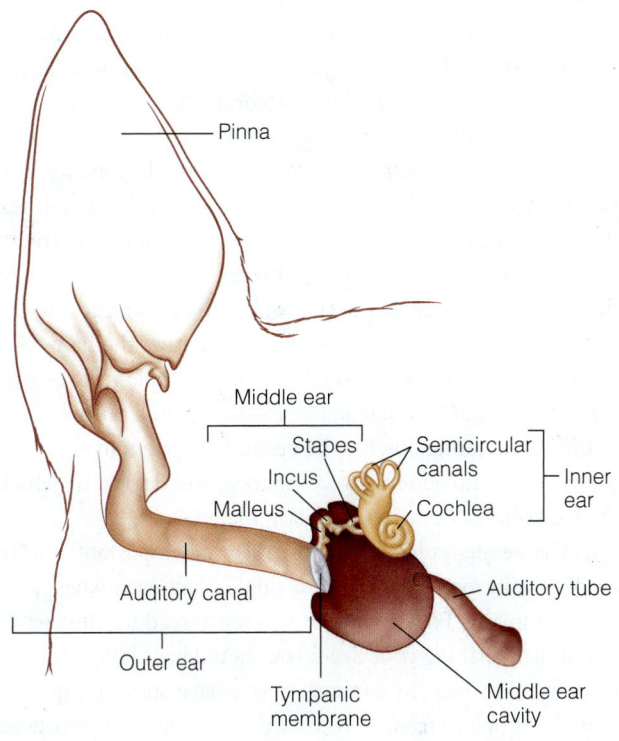

FIGURE 7.23 Vertebrate inner ears

The inner ear in most vertebrates consists of three semicircular canals arranged in planes at right angles joined at their base by a swelling called the ampulla, and a series of sacs including the utricle and the saccule. In many vertebrates, the floor of the saccule contains a small pocket called the lagena. In birds and mammals, the lagena is greatly extended to form the cochlear duct or cochlea.

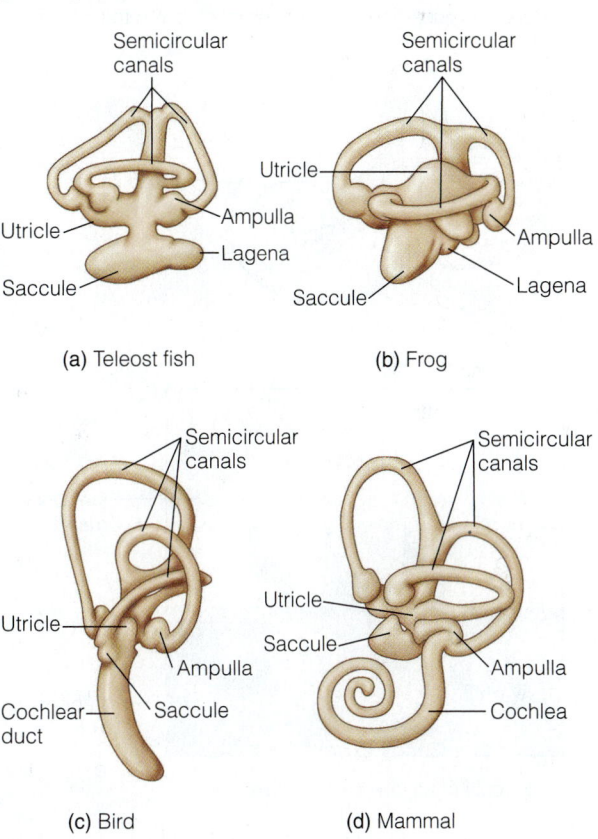

(a) Teleost fish

(b) Frog

(c) Bird

(d) Mammal

balance. In all craniates, except the lampreys and hagfish, the vestibular apparatus consists of three **semicircular canals** with an enlarged region at one end (called the **ampulla**), and two saclike swellings called the **utricle** and the **saccule** (Figure 7.23). In most vertebrates, the saccule also contains a small extension called the **lagena**. In birds and mammals, the lagena is greatly extended and is called the **cochlear duct** (in birds), or the **cochlea** (in mammals). The utricle, saccule, and the ampullae of the semicircular canals contain mechanoreceptive hair cells that are involved in the sense of equilibrium. The cochlea also contains hair cells, but it is involved in hearing and is not a part of the vestibular apparatus.

The mechanoreceptors of the ampullae and the vestibular sacs differ. The utricle and saccule contain a series of mineralized **otoliths** suspended in a gelatinous matrix above a membrane called the macula that is densely covered with more than 100,000 hair cells (Figure 7.24). The ampullae of the semicircular canals lack otoliths, and instead contain cristae that consist of hair cells located within a cup-shaped gelatinous mass called the cupula. The cristae of semicircular canals detect angular acceleration, and motion in circular patterns, such as when you shake your head. In contrast, the maculae of the vestibular sacs detect linear acceleration, or motion along a line, and are stimulated when the body is in a tilted position.

When you move your head to one side, the otoliths and the gelatinous masses of the maculae in the utricle and saccule induce a drag on the hair cells, stimulating them. The macula of the utricle is oriented horizontally in the ear, and can detect motion in the horizontal plane (Figure 7.25a–d). The macula of the saccule is oriented vertically, so it can detect motion in the vertical plane. Within the utricle and saccule, the hair cells are oriented in two different directions so that a single sheet of hair cells can detect motion forward and back or side to side, covering two dimensions of movement. The utricle can also detect tilting of the head (Figure 7.25e). When you tilt your head, gravity pulls on the gelatinous mass of the sacs, which stimulates particular subsets of the hair cells, depending on the direction of the tilt. Because different hair cells are stimulated by a forward and a backward tilt, the brain can determine the direction of the tilt. The intensity of the hair cell response is related to the angle of tilt, so the brain can also determine the degree of tilt. The vestibular sacs play an important role in maintaining the orientation of

FIGURE 7.24 **The mechanoreceptors of the inner ear**

(a) The mechanoreceptors of the utricle and saccule are found in structures called maculae. The hair cells of each macula are embedded in a gelatinous matrix that is overlain with a series of otoliths. **(b)** The mechanoreceptors of the semicircular canals are located in the ampullae in structures called cristae. Cristae are similar in structure to the neuromasts shown in Figure 7.21, consisting of hair cells embedded in a cup-shaped gelatinous mass called the cupula.

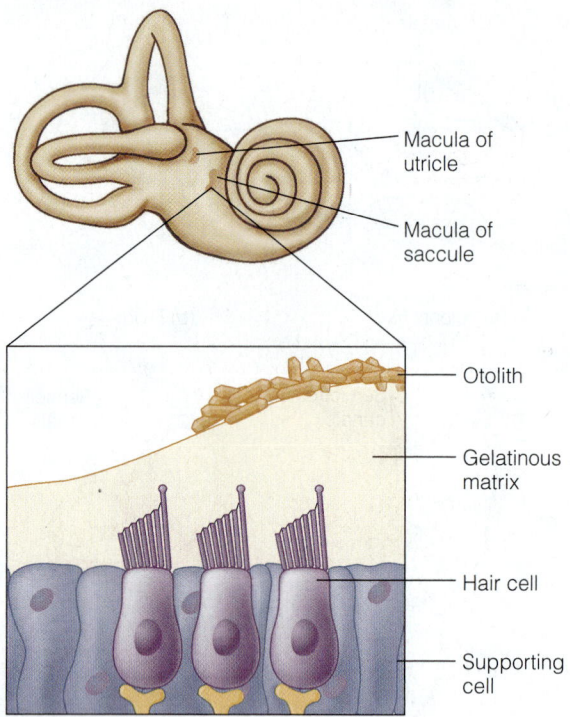

Macula of utricle

Macula of saccule

Otolith

Gelatinous matrix

Hair cell

Supporting cell

(a) Macula of an utricle or saccule

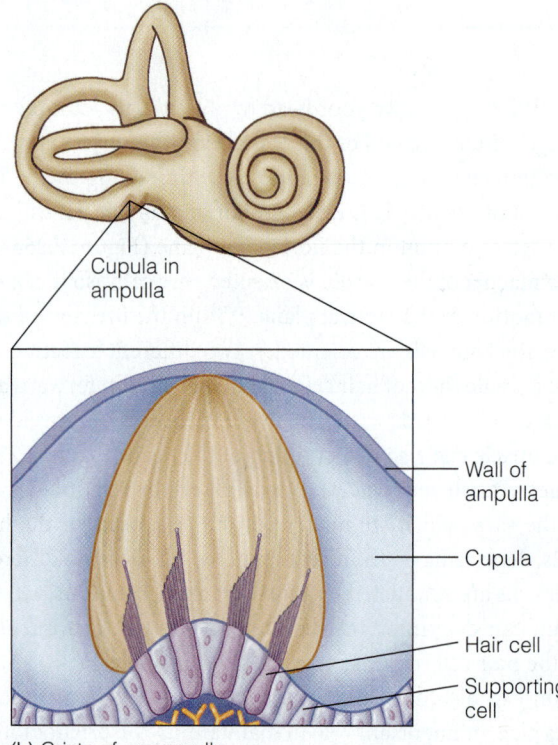

Cupula in ampulla

Wall of ampulla

Cupula

Hair cell

Supporting cell

(b) Crista of an ampulla

the body with respect to gravity. If your head and body start to tilt, the vestibular sacs send a signal to the brain, which automatically compensates by altering posture in order to maintain your position.

In contrast to the vestibular sacs, which detect whether the body is tilted, the semicircular canals detect angular acceleration (Figure 7.26). Most vertebrates have three semicircular canals that are arranged perpendicular to each other, so that each canal detects acceleration in a single plane. When you turn your head in the plane of a particular canal, the fluid in that canal is set in motion. Because of the inertia of the fluid there is a difference between the movement of the fluid and the movement of the wall of the canal, causing the fluid to slosh against the ampulla, stimulating the hair cells. Because each canal is oriented in a different plane, acceleration of the fluid in a particular canal depends on the plane of the movement, allowing the vestibular system to sense the direction of movement by comparing the degree to which the hair cells in each canal are stimulated.

The semicircular canals also play an important role in keeping your eyes oriented on a single point even when your head is moving. For example, if you try to read this text while nodding or shaking your head, you should have little difficulty reading the words. In contrast, if you have someone quickly move the book in front of your face while you hold your head still, you will likely find it difficult to read the words.

Balance and body orientation depend on inputs from the visual system, proprioceptors, and the inner ear. You can observe this effect if you ask someone to try to stand still with his or her eyes closed. It is almost impossible to do—you will notice that your subject makes small movements and rocks back and forth. When signals from the vestibular and visual systems conflict, it can cause what is called motion sickness.

The inner ear detects sounds

In addition to detecting body position, the inner ear detects sounds. In fish, incoming sound waves cause the otoliths in the vestibular sacs to move, causing the stereocilia of the hair cells to pivot, and stimulating the auditory neurons. Some fish use their swim bladder to help amplify the sounds coming to the inner ear. The clupeids (fish in the herring family) have a gas duct that connects the swim bladder to the hearing system. Sounds cause the swim bladder to vibrate, and this vibration is passed through the gas duct to the ear. Clupeid fish such as shad use their excellent hearing to detect the echolocation sounds produced by whales and dolphins (their main predators).

In carp, the swim bladder is connected to the inner ear via a system of bones called the Weberian ossicles (Figure 7.27). Carp have excellent hearing because the Weberian ossicles transmit sounds to the inner ear.

FIGURE 7.25 **Functions of the utricles in mammals**

(a) The hair cells of the utricles are overlain with a gelatinous layer topped with bony otoliths. **(b)** At rest or during constant motion, the hair cells are partially depolarized. **(c)** During forward acceleration, the hair cells pivot toward the longest stereocilium (recall that mammalian hair cells lack a kinocilium). This bending activates mechanogated channels on the stereocilia, which depolarizes the cell, increasing its release of neurotransmitter and thus increasing the frequency of action potentials in the primary afferent neurons. **(d)** During backward acceleration or **(e)** forward tilt of the head, the stereocilia pivot away from the longest stereocilium, reducing the frequency of action potentials.

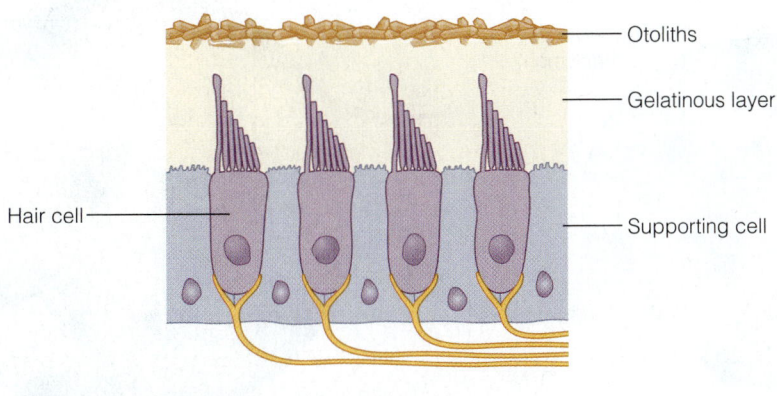

(a) Hair cells of the utricle

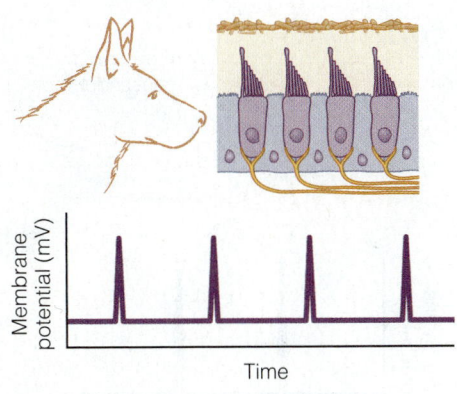

(b) Rest or constant motion

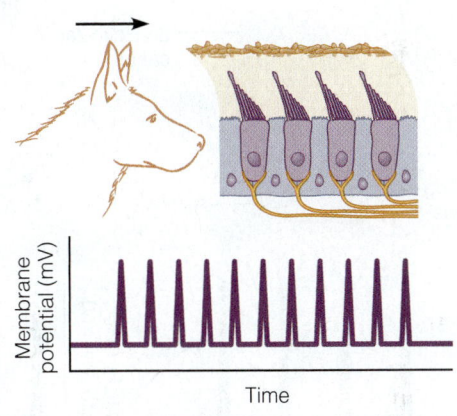

(c) Forward acceleration

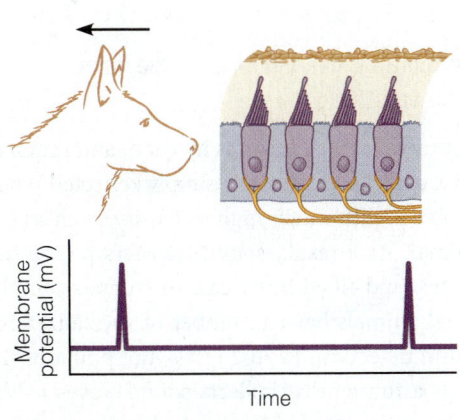

(d) Backward acceleration

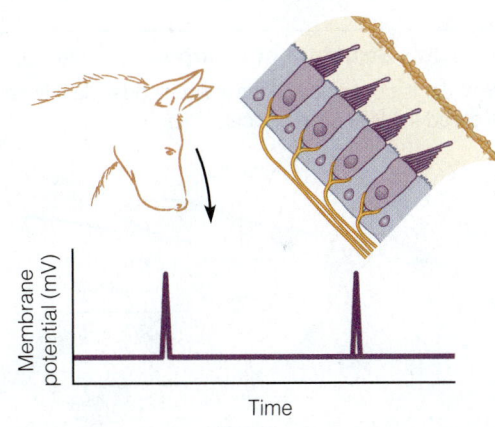

(e) Head tilted forward

FIGURE 7.26 Functions of the semicircular canals

(a) A semicircular canal consists of a fluid-filled tube with a swelling, termed the ampulla, at the bottom. **(b)** The ampulla contains a neuromast that senses pressure. **(c)** At rest, the hair cells of the neuromast are partially depolarized. When the head is rotated in one direction, the fluid in the semicircular canal exerts pressure in

the opposite direction, causing the stereocilia of the hair cells to pivot. Depending on the orientation of the hair cells, this will either **(d)** hyperpolarize the hair cell, decreasing the frequency of action potentials, or **(e)** depolarize the hair cell, increasing the frequency of action potentials.

Semicircular canal (filled with endolymph)

Cupula

Hair cell

Ampulla

(a) Semicircular canal

Cupula

Neuromast

Stereocilia

Hair cell

Afferent sensory neuron

(b) Ampulla

Semicircular canal

Recording electrode

Ampulla

Membrane potential (mV)

Time

(c) Rest

Head rotation

Pressure from endolymph

Membrane potential (mV)

Time

(d) Acceleration to the left

Head rotation

Pressure from endolymph

Membrane potential (mV)

Time

(e) Acceleration to the right

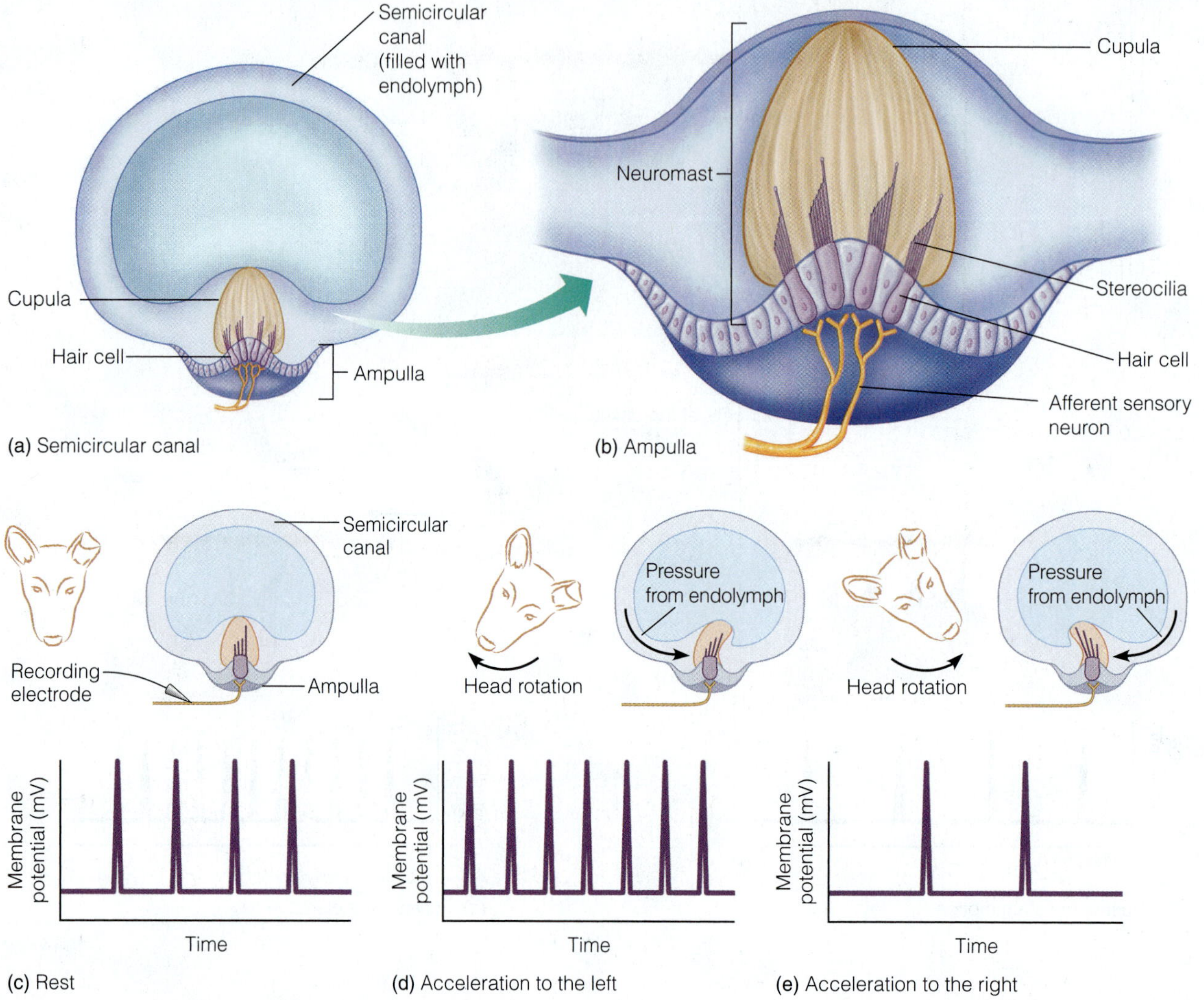

FIGURE 7.27 Structure of a carp ear

The inner ear is connected to the swim bladder via a series of bones called the Weberian ossicles.

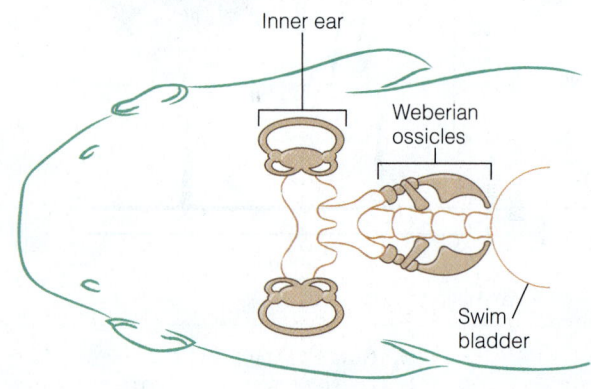

Inner ear

Weberian ossicles

Swim bladder

In terrestrial vertebrates, hearing involves the inner, middle, and outer ears

Sound does not travel as well in air as in water, and much of the sound that travels through air is simply reflected when it contacts an object with much higher density, such as the body of an animal. As a result, sound transfers poorly between air and the fluid-filled inner ear. To compensate, the ears of terrestrial animals have a number of specializations to increase sound detection. In mammals, the pinna of the outer ear acts as a funnel that collects sound waves in the air from a large area, concentrating them onto the auditory canal. Ears with a larger pinna capture more of the sound wave for a given sound intensity and hence receive more sound energy, so animals with large external ears typically have excellent hearing. While passing the pinna, sound also goes through a filtering process. For example, in humans sounds are enhanced in the frequency range where human speech is normally found. The filtering process also adds directional information.

The middle ear plays the most important role in improving detection of sounds in air. Although the details of middle ear structure vary substantially between groups of organisms, the fundamental design principles are similar. The air-filled middle ear is separated from the outer ear by the **tympanic membrane** and from the fluid-filled inner ear by the **oval window** (Figure 7.28a). Within the middle ear are one or more small bones that together span the space from the tympanic membrane to the oval window. Mammals have three of these bones, called the **malleus** (**hammer**), the **incus** (anvil), and the **stapes** (stirrup). Sound waves traveling through the auditory canal cause the thin tympanic membrane to vibrate. Vibration of the tympanic membrane causes the first of the bones (the malleus in mammals) to vibrate. The vibration is transferred through the bones (from the malleus to the incus to the stapes in mammals) to the oval window. Vibrations of the oval window transfer the sound stimulus to the fluid-filled inner ear. The structure of the middle ear is specialized to amplify sound. For example, the tympanic membrane has a surface area about 20 times that of the oval window. Thus the energy from the vibration of the tympanic membrane is concentrated into a smaller area in the oval window, amplifying the sound. The malleus, incus, and stapes of mammals are connected to each other with the biological equivalent of hinges, which allows these bones to act as levers that amplify the vibrations. Similar principles apply to the middle ears of reptiles and birds, and although these animals have different numbers and shapes of middle ear bones than do mammals, the arrangement and connections of these bones also allow them to act as amplifiers. Together, the arrangement of the bones and the difference in the relative sizes of the tympanic membrane and oval window cause such good amplification that a vibration of a mammalian tympanic membrane as small as 0.1 angstrom (less than the size of a hydrogen atom) can cause a response large enough to stimulate the hair cells of the inner ear.

FIGURE 7.28 Anatomy of the mammalian middle and inner ear

(a) The middle ear contains three small bones (the malleus, incus, and stapes) that transmit sound waves from the tympanic membrane to the oval window of the cochlea. **(b)** When the cochlea is illustrated uncoiled, it becomes apparent that it consists of a bent tube leading from the oval window to the round window. The top portion of the tube is called the vestibular duct and is lined with the vestibular membrane. The bottom of the tube is called the tympanic duct and is lined with the organ of Corti, which contains hair cells embedded in the basilar membrane.

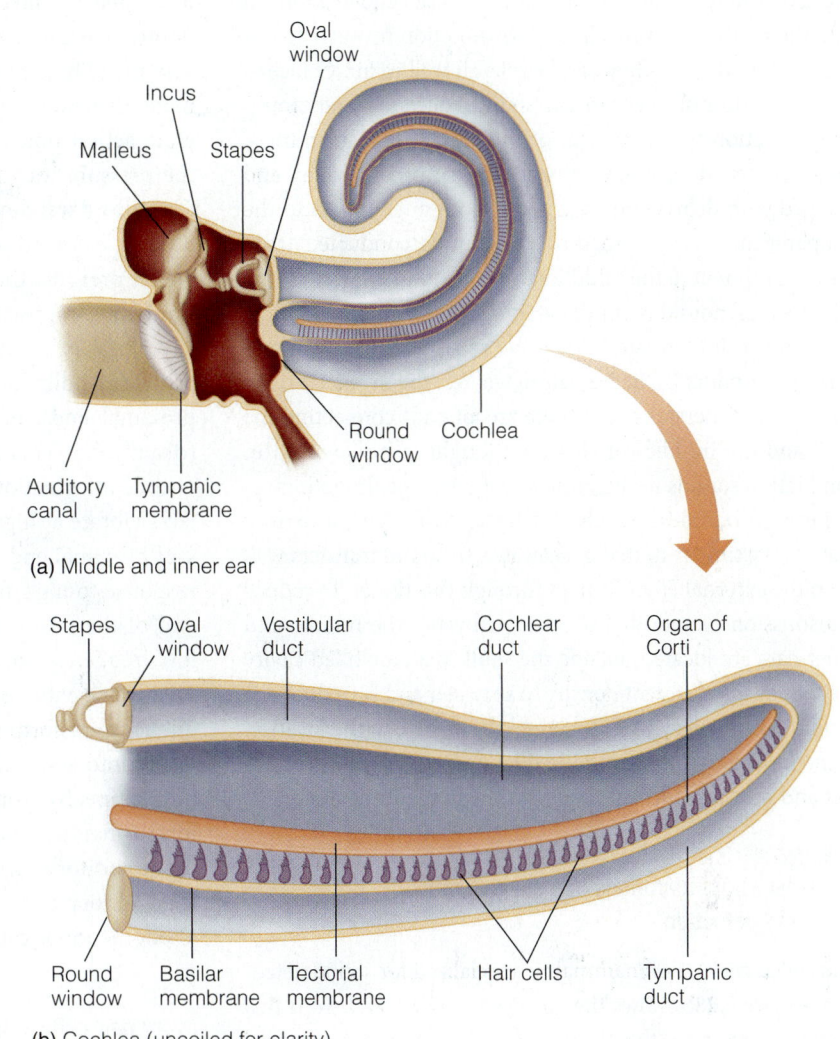

(a) Middle and inner ear

(b) Cochlea (uncoiled for clarity)

Cetaceans have highly modified ears

The aquatic environment can be dark and murky, and thus it is not always possible to use vision to navigate underwater. Instead, whales use echolocation (similar to the bats that were discussed at the beginning of this chapter) to navigate through their environment and catch their prey. Although sounds travel farther and faster in water than in air, if you have ever tried to listen to sounds while you are swimming underwater, you will have noticed that sounds seem muffled and blurry. This is because human ears are specialized for detecting sounds in air. The sound seems muffled and blurry because sounds are easily transferred from water through the tissues of the body to the inner ear, rather than solely through the middle ear, making it difficult to detect sound direction. The ears of cetaceans have specializations relative to the standard mammalian plan that allow them to hear effectively underwater so that they can use echolocation. In fact, their ears are so specialized for function in water that it is not clear whether they can hear at all well in air. Cetacean outer ears do not perform the sound collecting and amplifying function that is typical of the ears of land mammals. Cetacean ears do not have pinnae, the ear canal is small and plugged with debris and wax, and it does not connect to the tympanic membrane. So how are sounds conducted from the environment to the middle ear? In the toothed whales (the odontocetes) sound is conducted to the tympanic membrane through specialized fatty tissues in the jaw. The mechanisms of sound conduction in the baleen whales (the mysticetes) are not as well understood, but there are fat pads connecting the skull and the middle ear that are thought to be involved in conducting sounds to the tympanic membrane. In both mysticetes and odontocetes, these fatty deposits have a density that is very similar to that of seawater, so sound transfers well from the external environment through this tissue. To reduce transmission of sounds via other pathways, the middle and inner ears are located outside the skull in an air-filled cavity that has a very different density to seawater and thus does not conduct sound very well. Together, the change in the location of the inner ear and the modified fat pads allow whales to detect and precisely localize sounds transmitted underwater.

The inner ear of mammals has specializations for sound detection

The coiled cochlea of mammals is specialized for sound detection. Figure 7.28b shows the cochlea uncoiled, and from this diagram you can see that the two outer compartments (the vestibular and tympanic ducts) are actually one continuous tube, although early anatomists gave them two different names because they appear to be distinct structures in the tightly coiled cochlea. The vestibular and tympanic ducts are filled with a fluid called **perilymph**, which is similar in composition to other extracellular fluids. The cochlear duct is filled with a fluid called **endolymph** that is quite different from other extracellular fluids, being high in K^+ and low in Na^+. The **organ of Corti** contains the hair cells and sits on the **basilar membrane** that lines one side of the cochlear duct. Vertebrate inner ears contain several types of hair cells that perform slightly different auditory functions. In mammals, these types are called the **inner hair cells** and the **outer hair cells**. Inner hair cells detect sounds, and outer hair cells help to amplify sounds.

Incoming sounds cause the oval window of the inner ear to vibrate, causing waves in the perilymph of the vestibular duct. These waves in the perilymph push on the basilar membrane, causing it to vibrate. The stereocilia on the inner hair cells of the organ of Corti pivot in response to the vibrations of the basilar membrane. As with the hair cells in the lateral line of a fish, the tip links connecting the stereocilia pull open the mechanosensitive ion channels in the membrane of the inner hair cells, causing them to depolarize. The inner hair cells then release a neurotransmitter, glutamate, that excites sensory neurons and causes them to generate action potentials. In this way, the cochlea transduces the pressure waves in the perilymph into electrical signals. The **round window** of the cochlea serves as a pressure valve, bulging outward as fluid pressure rises in the inner ear, which prevents the waves from doubling back through the fluid, thus improving sound clarity.

The basilar membrane is stiff and narrow near its attachment point close to the round and oval windows (the proximal end), but wider and more flexible at the other (distal) end. This differential stiffness helps the cochlea to encode information about the frequency of a sound. Stiff objects vibrate at higher frequencies than flexible objects. The stiff proximal end of the basilar membrane vibrates most in response to high-frequency sounds, while the flexible distal end of the basilar membrane vibrates most in response to low-frequency sounds. Thus, different areas of the basilar membrane vibrate in response to sounds of different frequency, transforming a frequency signal carried by the sound waves into a spatial signal coded by location on the basilar membrane. Neurons from each part of the basilar membrane form synaptic connections with neurons in particular areas in the auditory cortex of the brain; therefore, specific areas of the auditory cortex respond to particular frequencies. This phenomenon is called **place coding**.

Outer hair cells amplify sounds

Inner hair cells code for sound loudness in much the same way as do other mechanosensory cells. Loud noises cause greater movement of the basilar membrane, and greater depolarization of the hair cell, which in turn generates a higher frequency of action potentials in the afferent sensory neurons. The outer hair cells also play an important role in the loudness of sounds. Current theories of sound transduction in the inner ear suggest that the outer hair cells amplify sounds by increasing the movement of the basilar membrane for a sound of a given loudness, thus causing a larger stimulus to the inner hair cells.

Outer hair cells perform this amplification function because, unlike inner hair cells, outer hair cells change *shape* in response to sound waves, rather than releasing neurotransmitter. When the stereocilia of an outer hair cell pivot in response to a sound wave, the mechanosensory channels on the stereocilia open, allowing K^+ to enter the cell. The resulting depolarization acts as a signal to a voltage-sensitive motor protein, which causes the cell to change shape and pull on the basilar membrane, increasing the amount the basilar membrane moves in response to a particular sound. The protein responsible for this change in shape of the outer hair cells has been identified, and if the gene that codes for this protein (called prestin) is knocked out in mice, the animals are born profoundly deaf. Certain types of deafness in humans are also caused by mutations in the prestin gene.

Outer hair cells make contact with very few afferent neurons that carry signals to the brain. Instead, they form synapses with efferent neurons that carry signals from the brain to the ear. These efferent neurons are part of a feedback loop; they release the neurotransmitter acetylcholine onto the outer hair cells in response to loud noises, reducing the response of the outer hair cells. Because outer hair cells normally amplify sounds, this feedback loop acts as a protective mechanism for the inner hair cells, which can be damaged by loud noises.

The ears can detect sound location

The brain uses information from both ears to estimate the location of the stimulus, including the time lag and differences in sound intensity. If a sound comes from one side, the sound waves will not reach both ears at the same time because the distance from the sound source is slightly different between the two ears. The brain registers the time lag, helping to localize the sound. Sounds coming from one side must also pass through the head to reach the other ear, altering the intensity of the sound in that ear. The discrepancy between the sound in the two ears helps to pinpoint the sound location. If a sound does not come from the sides, but rather from above, below, or immediately in front of the face, there is no time lag or discrepancy in intensity between the ears, and it is more difficult to determine the location of a sound. In mammals, the outer ears also help in localizing sounds. However, this mechanism is not particularly efficient, so most animals move their head or rotate their outer ears in order to better localize the source of a sound.

CONCEPT CHECK

11. What would happen to sound transduction if the endolymph of the vertebrate inner ear had high [Na^+] and low [K^+]?

12. How does the structure of the basilar membrane of the mammalian ear allow fine discrimination of different sound frequencies?

PHOTORECEPTION

Photoreception is the ability to detect a small portion of the electromagnetic spectrum from the near ultraviolet to the near infrared, that is, wavelengths of approximately 300 nm to just greater than 1,000 nm, although most species detect only a portion of this range (humans can only detect wavelengths from approximately 350 to 750 nm; Figure 7.29a). Animals lack the ability to detect other wavelengths of electromagnetic radiation such as radio waves. This concentration on a very narrow band of the electromagnetic spectrum supports the idea that animals evolved in water. The wavelengths that represent visible light travel relatively well through water, whereas water blocks most other wavelengths. Figure 7.29b shows the degree of attenuation, or the amount of signal lost, for an electromagnetic signal that passes through a meter of water. From this figure, you can see that water is relatively transparent to violet, blue, and green light, but that it quickly becomes rather opaque to yellow, orange, and particularly to red light. A meter of water almost completely blocks far red and near infrared light. Only at the other end of the electromagnetic spectrum, at very long wavelengths, are signals able to pass through water effectively. Thus, animals living in water can use only a narrow range of the electromagnetic spectrum. The degree of attenuation of light also varies depending on the presence of light-absorbing compounds in the water. Some aquatic animals, particularly those living in light-poor habitats, have poor vision, and have instead developed the ability to sense electric fields. We discuss this electroreceptive sense in more detail later in the chapter.

Photoreceptors

Photoreceptive organs range in complexity from single light-sensitive cells to complex eyes that can form sharp, focused images. In this section, we first consider the structure of individual photoreceptive cells, and look at the signal transduction mechanisms they use to convert an incoming photon of light to a change in the membrane potential of the cell. Then we look at how these cells are put together into complex photoreceptive organs such as eyes. Finally, we examine how the interaction of multiple photoreceptive cells in complex eyes allows the formation of images and the detection of complex image properties such as color.

The structure of photoreceptor cells differs among animals

Two major types of photoreceptor cells are found in animals (Figure 7.30). **Ciliary photoreceptors** have a single cilium protruding from the cell, often with a highly folded ciliary membrane that forms lamellae or disks that contain

(a) The types of electromagnetic radiation. **(b)** Most wavelengths of electromagnetic radiation do not travel well through water. Only visible light and very long wavelength electromagnetic radiation penetrate into deeper water. Animals detect a narrow band of the electromagnetic spectrum in the visible light range, which suggests the possibility that photoreceptors evolved in aquatic organisms.

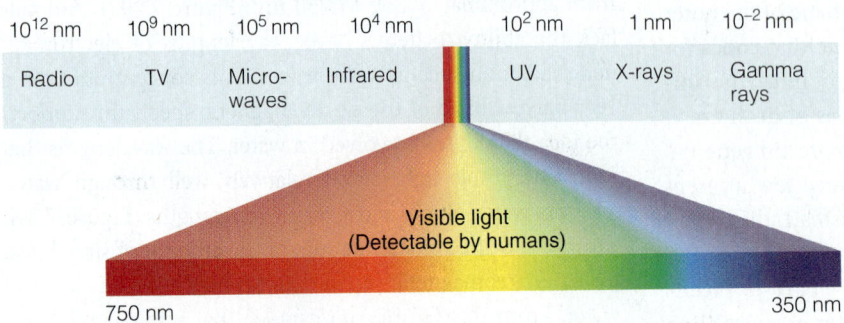

(a) The electromagnetic spectrum

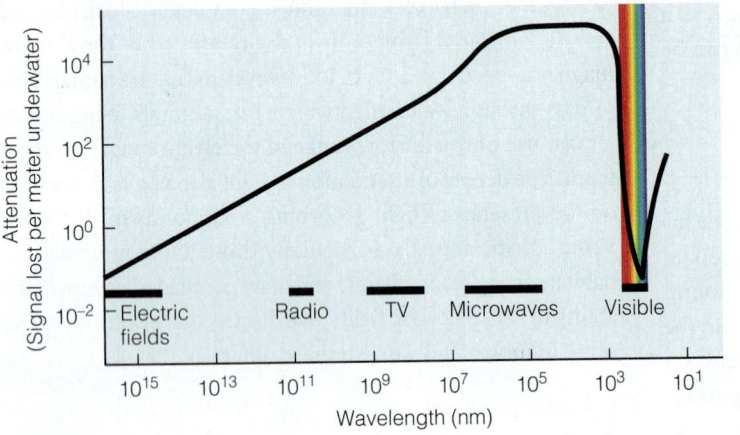

(b) Attenuation of electromagnetic radiation in water

are located outside the main eyes, or they are present only in larval forms and are absent from adult animals. The only known exceptions to the predominance of rhabdomeric eyes among the protostome invertebrates (worms, mollusks, and arthropods) are a few species of mollusk, such as the bay scallop *Pecten irradians* and the file clam *Lima scabra*, in which the adults have eyes that contain both rhabdomeric and ciliary photoreceptors. The picture in the deuterostomes (echinoderms, such as sea urchins, and chordates, such as the vertebrates) is also unclear. Most deuterostomes have rhabdomeric eyes, similar to those of the protostome invertebrates. The major exception to this rule is the vertebrates, which have only ciliary photoreceptors in their eyes. The cnidarians (jellyfish and related organisms) also have only ciliary photoreceptors. This phylogenetic pattern is difficult to interpret based on what we know about the relationships among living organisms. A recent discovery that rhabdomeric photoreceptors in some invertebrates pass through a developmental stage in which they have cilia suggests the possibility that all photoreceptor cells are derived from an ancestral ciliated cell. Alternatively, the bilateral ancestor of the protostomes and deuterostomes may have already possessed two types of photoreceptors, one of which may have been lost in some evolutionary lineages (such as the one leading to the vertebrates). Until the mechanisms of photoreception are studied in more animal taxa, particularly among the invertebrates, the evolution of animal photoreceptor cells is likely to remain an open question.

Mammals have two types of photoreceptor cells

Although all vertebrate photoreceptor cells are ciliary photoreceptors, in mammals they can be divided into two subclasses, **rods** and **cones** (Figure 7.31). Although rods and cones have different shapes, they share similar features. Both have an outer segment composed of a series of membranous disks that contain the photopigments. A connecting cilium joins the outer segment to the inner segment that contains the nucleus. The other end of this cell forms synaptic connections with other cells of the vertebrate eye.

In addition to their morphological differences, mammalian rods and cones differ functionally in a number of respects

photopigments, the molecules specialized for absorbing the energy coming from incoming photons. In contrast, in **rhabdomeric photoreceptors** (also called microvillus photoreceptors) the apical surface that contains the photopigments is elaborated into multiple outfoldings called microvillar projections. In addition to these structural differences, ciliary and rhabdomeric photoreceptor cells also differ in that they use distinct signal transduction mechanisms for converting the energy carried by incoming photons to a change in the membrane potential of the receptor cell.

Both rhabdomeric and ciliary photoreceptors are widely distributed in most animal groups, but the pattern of the distributions of these types of photoreceptors among organisms presents a rather confusing picture (Figure 7.30). The majority of invertebrate groups have rhabdomeric photoreceptors in their eyes. Some invertebrate groups (such as the mollusks and the platyhelminths) also have some ciliary photoreceptors, but these are generally present only as small, isolated photoreceptors, or in very simple photoreceptive organs that

FIGURE 7.30 **Phylogenetic distribution of ciliary and rhabdomeric photoreceptors**

There is no clear pattern in the phylogenetic distribution of ciliary photoreceptors (shown in orange) and rhabdomeric photoreceptors (shown in blue). Many groups have both kinds of photoreceptors. Vertebrates have only ciliary photoreceptors, and arthropods have only rhabdomeric photoreceptors.

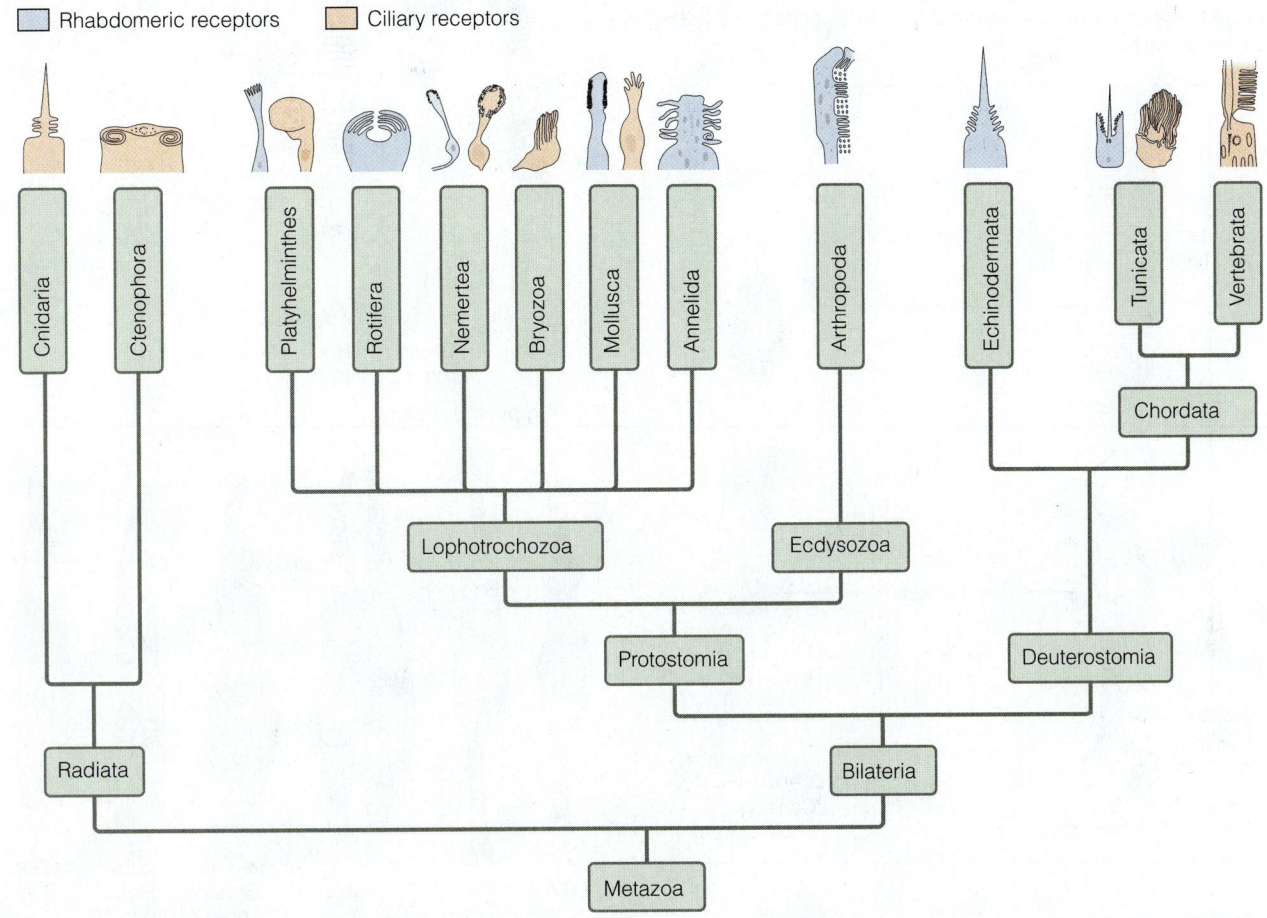

(Table 7.1). In comparison to cones, rods typically have more photopigment than do cones, have a much slower response time, and integrate signals over a longer period. As a result, rods have a very high sensitivity compared with cones, but saturate at relatively low light levels. Because of these differences between rods and cones, rods function best in dim light, while cones function best in bright light. In fact, in mammals, rods are so sensitive that they can respond even to a single photon. Many **nocturnal** mammals have relatively higher numbers of rod cells in their eyes for better vision in dim light.

Many vertebrates have more than one type of cone photoreceptor, each having a slightly different photopigment that is maximally sensitive to a particular wavelength of light. As we discuss in detail later in the chapter, integrating centers compare the relative signals from these receptors to allow detection of colors. You have probably noticed that in dim light (such as at twilight), the world appears in shades of gray. You use your cones for color vision in bright light, and your rods for noncolor vision in dim light.

There is substantial diversity among vertebrates in the shape of the rods and cones (Figure 7.32). In fact, in many species it can be difficult to distinguish between rods and cones based on cell shape alone. For example, frogs have several types of rod-shaped photoreceptors in their eyes that

Table 7.1 Mammalian rods and cones		
Feature	**Rods**	**Cones**
Class of photoreceptor	Ciliary	Ciliary
Shape	Outer segment rod shaped	Outer segment cone shaped
Sensitivity	Sensitive to very dim light	Sensitive to brighter light

FIGURE 7.31   **Structure of mammalian ciliary photoreceptors—the rods and cones**

Although they differ in shape, rods and cones have the same structural components: an outer segment consisting of a series of disks containing the photopigments, an inner segment containing the cell body, and synaptic terminals that make connections with neurons in the retina.

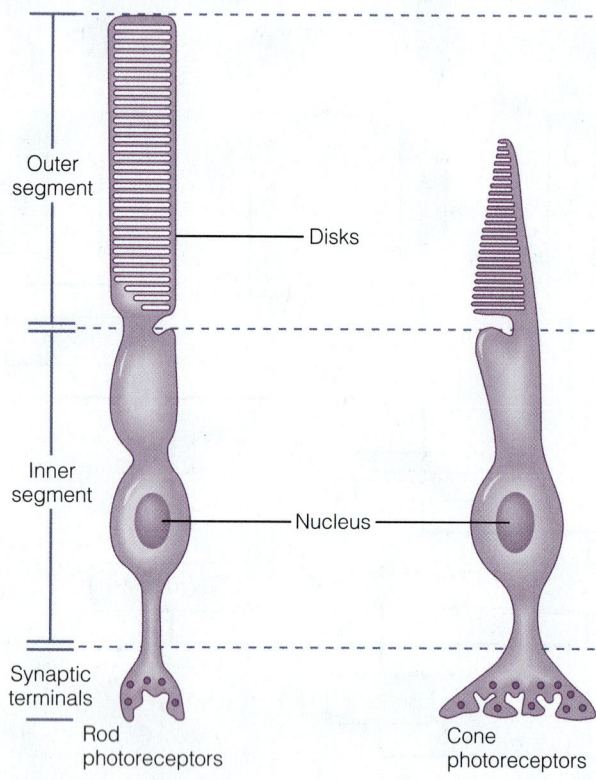

FIGURE 7.32   **Structural diversity of vertebrate photoreceptors**

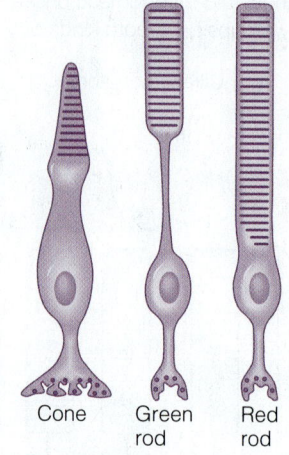

(a) Frog photoreceptors

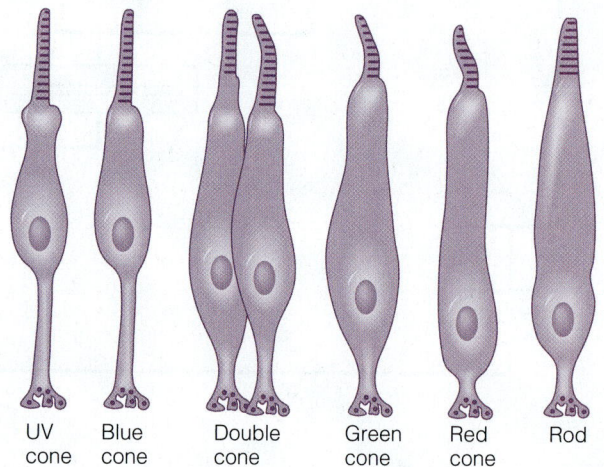

(b) Turtle photoreceptors

they use to see colors. Thus, the shape of the photoreceptor cell is not the important characteristic that determines whether it is involved in color vision or dim-light vision. Instead, the properties of a photoreceptor cell depend on the properties of the photopigment that it contains.

Chromophores allow photoreceptors to absorb light

Photopigments consist of a pigment called a **chromophore** associated with a specific photoreceptor protein. In the vast majority of photoreceptors, the chromophore is a derivative of vitamin A, such as **retinal**, and the associated protein is a member of the **opsin** gene family. Opsins are G protein–coupled receptors that are covalently linked to the chromophore. Depending on the particular photoreceptive cell, the photopigment complex is called by different names, including **rhodopsin**, iodopsin, porphyropsin, melanopsin, pinopsin, and VA opsin, among others. All of these photopigments, however, consist of a vitamin A–derived chromophore bound to a G protein in the opsin gene family. The sensitivity of the chromophore-opsin complex to particular parts of the light spectrum differs among these photopigments as a result of

differences in the amino acid sequence of the opsin protein. Differences in the spectral sensitivity of the chromophore-opsin combination underlie color vision.

Although the specific structures of the photopigments vary among photoreceptors, the general pattern of their chemical activation is similar. In the unactivated state, the chromophore is present in the *cis* conformation. When the chromophore absorbs the energy of incoming light, it undergoes a conformational change, rotating the molecule to an all-*trans* conformation. For example, absorbing light converts the chromophore 11-*cis* retinal to all-*trans* retinal (Figure 7.33). In the *cis* conformation, the chromophore binds to opsin, but when it is converted to the *trans* conformation, it no longer binds to opsin, and is released in a process known as **bleaching**. The chromophore is then reconverted to the *cis* isomer by isomerase enzymes in an ATP-requiring process that takes several minutes. In the photoreceptors of vertebrates, the all-*trans* retinal is exported from the photoreceptor cell to nearby epithelial cells, where it is converted to 11-*cis* retinal and then reimported

FIGURE 7.33 Isomerization of retinal

The molecule 11-*cis* retinal absorbs a photon of light and rotates to form all-*trans* retinal.

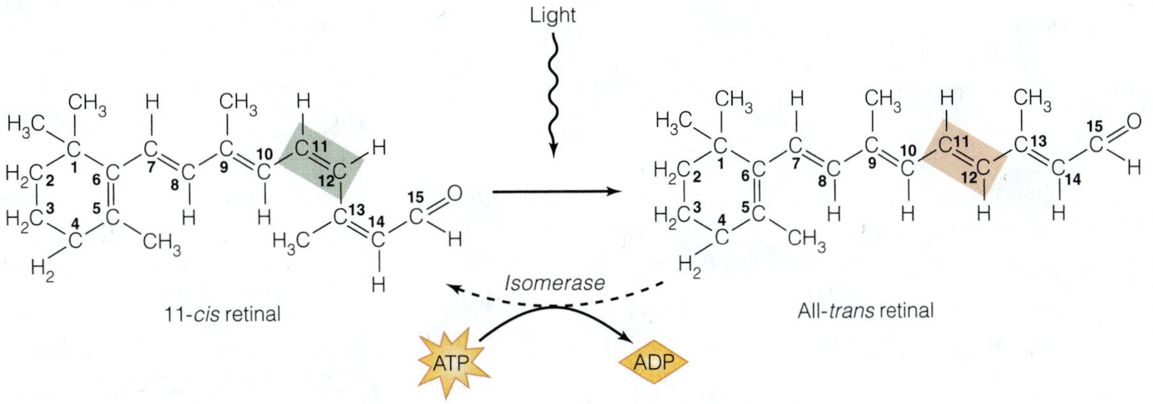

11-*cis* retinal   All-*trans* retinal

Isomerase

ATP   ADP

into the photoreceptor, whereas in invertebrates this process typically takes place within the photoreceptor cell.

The mechanisms of phototransduction differ among organisms

When the chromophore dissociates from opsin, the opsin undergoes a conformational change and becomes activated. Like other G protein–coupled receptors, the activated opsin signals to an associated G protein that activates a downstream signal transduction cascade. Animal photoreceptors generally utilize one of two signal transduction cascades: either phospholipase C (PLC) or cGMP. The opsins found in rhabdomeric photoreceptors, such as those present in most invertebrates, signal through a G_q protein that activates a phospholipase C (PLC)-mediated signal transduction cascade (Figure 7.34a). PLC catalyzes the breakdown of phosphatidyl-4,5-bisphosphate (PIP_2) into two intracellular messengers, inositol triphosphate (IP_3) and diacylglycerol (DAG). These signaling molecules initiate signal transduction pathways that open nonselective cation channels, and Ca^{2+} and Na^+ enter the cell, resulting in a depolarizing receptor potential. This depolarizing receptor potential causes an increase in neurotransmitter release from the photoreceptor, sending a signal to the nervous system that is ultimately interpreted as light.

In contrast, the opsins found in ciliary photoreceptors, such as those in vertebrates, signal through an inhibitory G_i protein called **transducin**, initiating a cyclic GMP-mediated signal transduction cascade (Figure 7.34b). Transducin activates a phosphodiesterase (PDE) enzyme that hydrolyzes cGMP to GMP. This decrease in cGMP concentration closes a cGMP-gated Na^+ channel in the photoreceptor membrane, and Na^+ influx slows or stops. Reduced Na^+ influx coupled with continuing K^+ efflux hyperpolarizes the cell, causing a receptor potential. The hyperpolarization decreases the release of neurotransmitter from the photoreceptor cell onto the associated afferent neuron, sending a signal to the

nervous system that the brain ultimately interprets as light. In the dark, cGMP levels in the cell are high, cGMP binds to the channels, and most of the channels will be open, keeping the cell depolarized and sending a constant signal to the afferent sensory neuron. Dim light causes a slight decrease in cGMP, causing a few channels to close, whereas bright light causes a larger decrease in cGMP, causing all or most of the Na^+ channels to close. Thus, the response of the cell is graded, depending on the light intensity.

CONCEPT CHECK

13. Compare and contrast phototransduction in rhabdomeric and ciliary photoreceptors.
14. Compare and contrast the structure and function of rods and cones. Do all vertebrates have these photoreceptors?

The Structure and Function of Eyes

Although an individual photoreceptor cell can detect the relative brightness of a light source, an eye can obtain a great deal of additional information from an incoming light stimulus. The minimum criterion for calling a structure an eye, rather than simply a photoreceptor, is the ability to detect the direction from which light has entered the organ. Eyespots are single cells (or regions of a cell) that contain a photosensitive pigment and a shading pigment that helps provide directional information by shading light coming from some directions. For example, the eyespot of the protist *Euglena* is located at its anterior end, and consists of a light-sensitive swelling of the cell membrane that is associated with a red pigment. *Euglena*, which is a photosynthesizer, uses this eyespot to orient itself toward the light.

Eyes, however, are much more complex organs consisting of groups of cells specialized for different functions, and often include both multiple photoreceptor cells and separate

FIGURE 7.34 **Phototransduction in invertebrates and vertebrates**

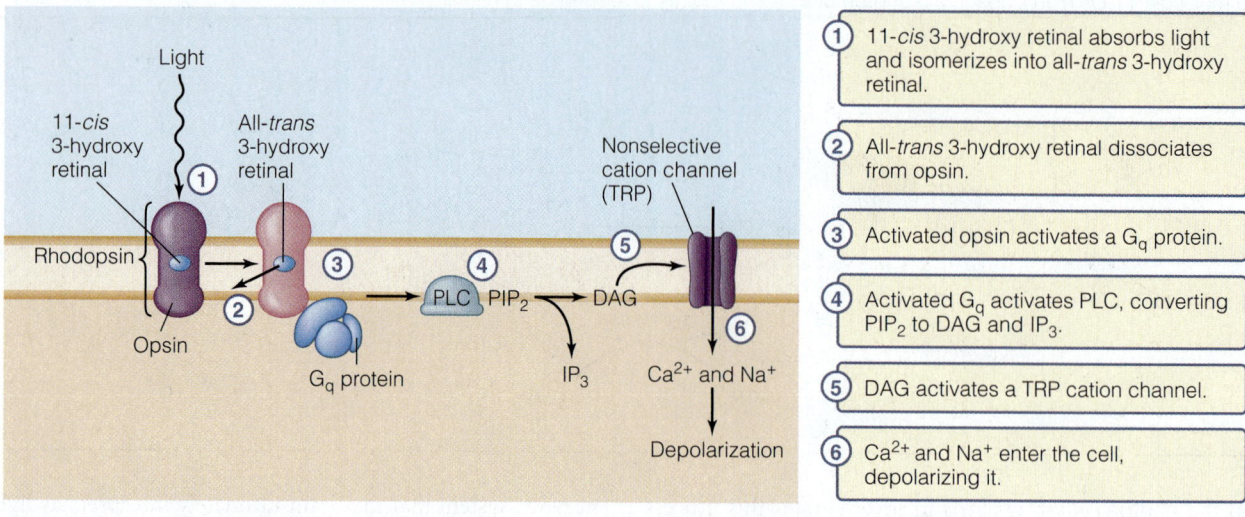

(a) Phototransduction in rhabdomeric photoreceptors

1. 11-*cis* 3-hydroxy retinal absorbs light and isomerizes into all-*trans* 3-hydroxy retinal.

2. All-*trans* 3-hydroxy retinal dissociates from opsin.

3. Activated opsin activates a G_q protein.

4. Activated G_q activates PLC, converting PIP_2 to DAG and IP_3.

5. DAG activates a TRP cation channel.

6. Ca^{2+} and Na^+ enter the cell, depolarizing it.

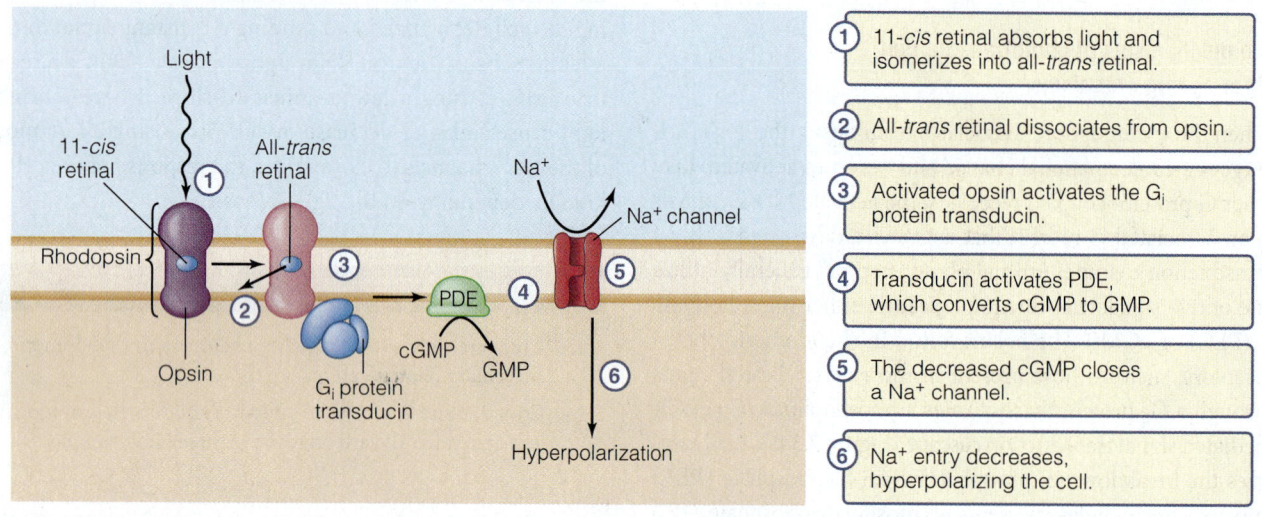

(b) Phototransduction in vertebrate photoreceptors

1. 11-*cis* retinal absorbs light and isomerizes into all-*trans* retinal.

2. All-*trans* retinal dissociates from opsin.

3. Activated opsin activates the G_i protein transducin.

4. Transducin activates PDE, which converts cGMP to GMP.

5. The decreased cGMP closes a Na^+ channel.

6. Na^+ entry decreases, hyperpolarizing the cell.

pigment cells. Eyes can provide information such as light direction and contrasts between light and dark, and some eyes can form focused images. Among multicellular animals, there are four main types of eyes (Figure 7.35).

Flat-sheet eyes (Figure 7.35a) contain a layer of photoreceptor cells that form a primitive **retina** lined with a pigmented epithelium. These eyes provide some sense of light direction, and may allow the detection of contrasts between light and dark. Many animal groups have eyes of this type, although they are most often seen in larval forms or as accessory eyes in adults. However, the limpet *Patella* has a simple patch of pigmented cells that serve as its primary eyes.

Cup-shaped eyes (Figure 7.35b) are similar to flat-sheet eyes, except that the retinal sheet is folded to form a narrow aperture. These eyes provide much better discrimination of light direction and intensity, and allow improved

detection of contrasts between light and dark. The most advanced cup-shaped eyes, such as those of the *Nautilus*, a cephalopod, have extremely small, pinhole-sized openings. The pinhole blocks most of the light from entering the eye so that an incoming point light source illuminates a single point on the retina, forming an image. This design is similar to a primitive type of camera called a pinhole camera. Pinhole camera eyes can form images, although the resolution is poor and the image is dim. In order to form a crisp image, the aperture (pinhole) must be small, but a small aperture lets in only a small amount of light, resulting in a dim image. Thus, there is a compromise between image clarity and image intensity.

Vesicular eyes (Figure 7.35c) and modern cameras solve this conflict by inserting a lens into the pinhole aperture. A lens takes multiple sources of light and refracts them,

FIGURE 7.35 **Structure of the major types of animal eyes**

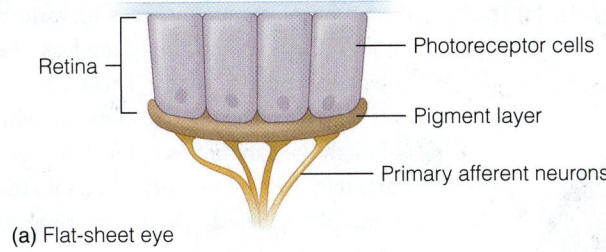

Retina
Photoreceptor cells
Pigment layer
Primary afferent neurons

(a) Flat-sheet eye

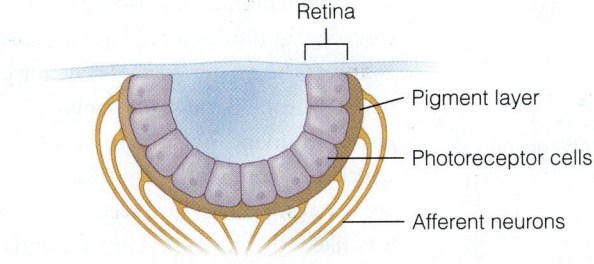

Retina
Pigment layer
Photoreceptor cells
Afferent neurons

(b) Cup-shaped eye

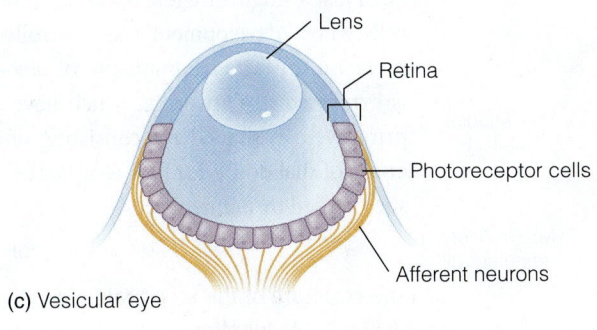

Lens
Retina
Photoreceptor cells
Afferent neurons

(c) Vesicular eye

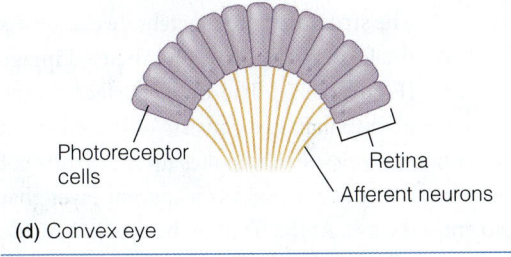

Photoreceptor cells
Retina
Afferent neurons

(d) Convex eye

focusing the light from a single source onto a single point on the retina. The challenge in developing a good vesicular eye is that the lens must fit precise specifications in order to provide a clear image. However, even a bad lens is better than no lens at all, and provides an improvement over a pinhole camera–type eye. Vesicular eyes are found in some mollusks, but only the cephalopod mollusks have the capacity to alter the shape or position of the lens to focus the image. Like cephalopods, vertebrates have complex vesicular eyes with a lens that can be used to generate a sharp, focused image.

Convex eyes (Figure 7.35d) are present in many annelids, mollusks, and arthropods. In these eyes, the individual photoreceptors radiate outward from the base, forming a convex, rather than a concave, light-gathering surface.

The most complex convex eyes are the **compound eyes** of the arthropods (Figure 7.36). Compound eyes are composed of many **ommatidia** arranged radially to form the convex light-gathering surface. The number of ommatidia in a compound eye varies greatly among species. For example, worker ants of the genus *Pomera* have only a single ommatidium per eye, while the eye of the dragonfly contains over 25,000 ommatidia arranged in a hexagonal pattern. The structure of an ommatidium also varies among species, although it generally consists of a modified region of the cuticle called the **cornea** overlying a crystalline cone that forms a lens. Immediately below this lens is a group of photoreceptive cells, called retinular cells, in a tubular arrangement. The retinular cells are rhabdomeric photoreceptor cells, as is typical for invertebrates. The microvilli of these photoreceptors project toward a central area called the rhabdom. Thus, in cross section, the ommatidium resembles a slice through an orange.

There are two major types of compound eyes in arthropods

Compound eyes form images in two rather different ways. Apposition compound eyes, which are found in many diurnal insects, consist of ommatidia that are each surrounded by a pigment cell. In an apposition compound eye each ommatidium operates essentially independently, and detects only a small part of the world directly in front of the ommatidium. However, the afferent neurons leading from the eye make many interconnections, so animals with apposition compound eyes are able to generate an integrated image. In contrast, super-position compound eyes have ommatidia that work together to produce a bright, superimposed image on the retina. Eyes of this type, found in nocturnal insects and crustaceans, function well in dim light. Compound eyes do not provide the resolving power of the camera eyes of vertebrates, but can still provide quite detailed visual discrimination.

There are two ways to increase the resolving power of a compound eye: reducing the size of each ommatidium or increasing the number of ommatidia. However, diffraction due to the wave properties of light limits the minimum size of an ommatidium. Once this size is reached, the only way to increase visual acuity is to increase the number of ommatidia, and thus the size of the compound eye. In fact, in order to have the average resolving power of the human eye, an insect eye would have to be nearly a meter in diameter.

Although insect eyes have limited resolving power, they are very proficient at capturing images from many directions. For example, a dragonfly can see almost 360 degrees around itself, except for a small blind spot caused by its body. In addition, insects generally have powerful close-up vision,

FIGURE 7.36 **Structure of an insect compound eye and ommatidium**

(a) The compound eye of *Drosophila melanogaster.* **(b)** A compound eye is composed of a cornea and many ommatidia. **(c)** Each ommatidium consists of a cornea, a crystalline cone, and several rhabdomeric photoreceptors called retinular cells. **(d)** The retinular cells are arranged radially, with their microvilli pointing inward to form a structure called the rhabdom.

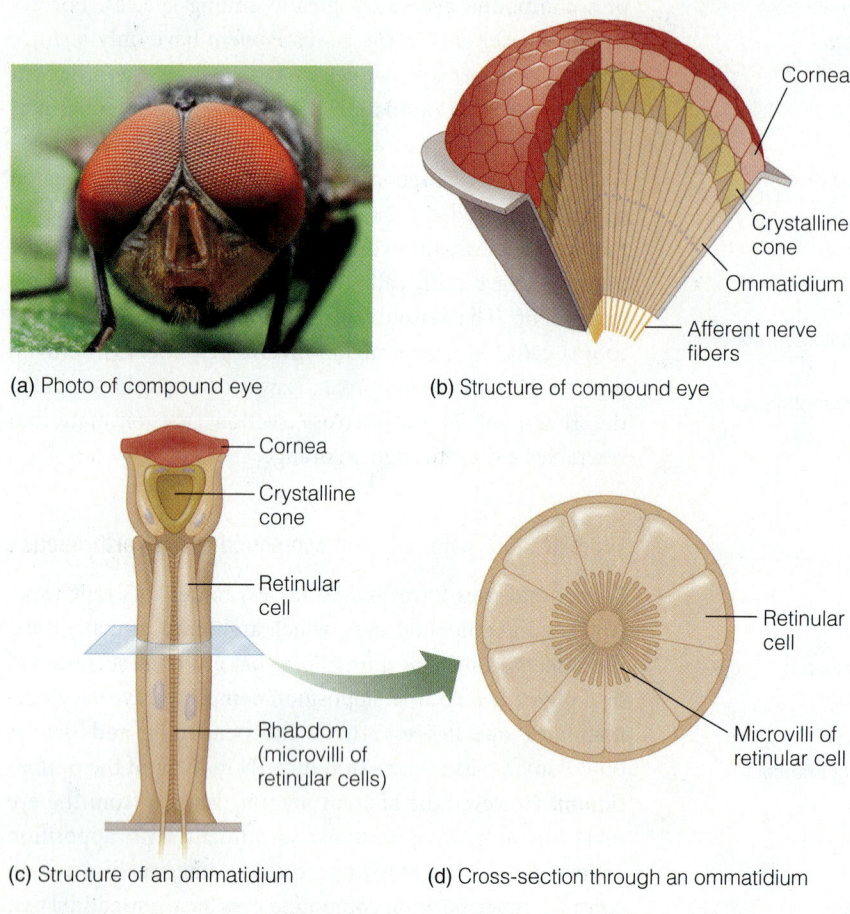

(a) Photo of compound eye

(b) Structure of compound eye

(c) Structure of an ommatidium

(d) Cross-section through an ommatidium

Photo source: jayvee18/Fotolia.

and they can see objects for which we would need a microscope. However, most insects can see only a few millimeters away from their body. Dragonflies have the best distance vision among insects, and can see objects up to a meter away.

Structurally diverse eyes share underlying molecular similarity

Although the structure of eyes is very diverse across animals, at a molecular level the genes that control eye formation are surprisingly similar. For example, loss-of-function mutations in the gene coding for the transcription factor *pax-6* cause reduced or absent eye structures in both vertebrates and invertebrates. In humans, *pax-6* mutation causes the inherited disease aniridia, in which the iris of the eye is missing or misformed. In *Drosophila*, mutation of the *pax-6* gene causes the mutant phenotype called eyeless. Thus, the *pax-6* gene is responsible for the development of the eye in a wide variety of animals.

In *Drosophila*, ectopic expression of *pax-6* (turning the gene on in tissues where it is not normally present) results in the formation of compound eyes in various parts of the body, including the legs, the antennae, and the wings. These ectopic eyes have been shown to respond to light, although they are not functional eyes because they are not correctly wired into the brain. Nevertheless, these experiments demonstrate that *pax-6* functions like an on switch, initiating a developmental cascade that results in eye formation, and acting as the master control gene for eye development. Because homologues of *pax-6* are found not just in *Drosophila*, which has compound eyes, but also in vertebrates, which have vesicular eyes, it is likely that all eyes share a common ancestor. This ancestral eye may have been just a single or a few photoreceptive cells whose development was controlled by *pax-6*. In fact, a homologue of *pax-6* is expressed in flatworms, which have a primitive cup-shaped eye consisting of a group of rhabdomeric photoreceptor cells surrounded by pigment cells.

The structure of the vertebrate eye relates to its function

The structure of the vertebrate eye allows the formation of a bright, focused image (Figure 7.37). The outer surface of the mammalian eye consists of the **sclera**, a tough layer of connective tissue that makes up the "white" of the eye in humans, and the cornea, a transparent layer that allows light to enter the eye. At the front of the eye, just inside the cornea, are the **iris**, the **ciliary body**, and the **lens**. The iris consists of two layers of pigmented smooth muscle surrounding an opening called the **pupil**. The iris can constrict or dilate, controlling the amount of light that enters the eye. The iris dilates in dim light, increasing the size of the pupil, and allowing more light to enter the eye. In bright light, the iris constricts, reducing the size of the pupil, and limiting the amount of light that enters the eye. The lens is held in place behind the pupil by suspensory ligaments that are attached to the ciliary body, which contains the **ciliary muscles**. The iris and ciliary body divide the eye into two compartments. The anterior chamber contains a fluid called the **aqueous humor**. Aqueous humor is secreted by the ciliary body and circulates into the anterior chamber via the pupil. The lens is suspended in the posterior chamber, which contains a

FIGURE 7.37 Structure of a mammalian eye

Light entering the eye passes through the cornea, the aqueous humor, the pupil, the lens, and the vitreous humor before striking the retina.

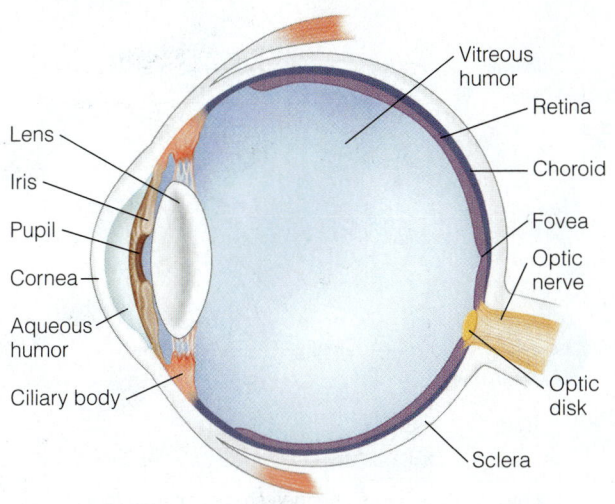

gelatinous mass called the **vitreous humor**. The vitreous humor assists in stabilizing the eye and provides support for the retina. Lining the inside surface of the eye is the retina, which contains the photoreceptor cells and several layers of interneurons that help to process the incoming visual signals. Immediately under the retina is the retinal pigment epithelium, which contains the cells that regenerate all-*trans* retinal back into the 11-*cis* conformation following light absorption. Just under the retinal pigment epithelium is a highly pigmented layer of tissue called the **choroid**. The choroid contains blood vessels, providing nourishment to the eye. In most diurnal animals, such as humans, the choroid also absorbs light that reaches the back of the eye so that it is not reflected, which might cause distortion of the visual image. The choroids of nocturnal animals such as cats are slightly different from those of humans. They contain a layer called the **tapetum** that reflects light instead of absorbing it, amplifying the light and allowing nocturnal animals to see better than diurnal animals in dim light. Light reflected off the tapetum can make a cat's eyes appear to glow in the dark.

The lens focuses light on the retina

Both the cornea and lens have a convex shape, and thus act as converging lenses that focus the light on the retina (Figure 7.38). Converging lenses work by bending light rays toward each other, a process called **refraction**. Light refracts as it passes through objects of differing optical densities. In terrestrial vertebrates, the degree of refraction is much greater between the air and the cornea than between the cornea and the lens because of the large difference in optical density between the

air and corneal tissue. Thus, the cornea of terrestrial vertebrates plays the greatest role in focusing the image, whereas the lens only fine-tunes the focus. You can observe this effect for yourself; when you open your eyes underwater, you will find that it is difficult to bring objects into focus, because the cornea has a similar optical density to water and no longer refracts light in the same way as it does in the air. The cornea is less important than the lens for focusing images in the eyes of aquatic vertebrates because of this effect. The importance of the cornea in humans can be demonstrated by the success of laser eye surgery for correcting some vision problems.

The point at which the light waves converge after passing through a lens is called the *focal point*. The distance from the center of a lens to its focal point is called the *focal length*. A sharp image can be formed only at the focal point of a lens. Thus, incoming light rays must converge at the retina, not behind it or in front of it, in order to produce a clear image. The focal length of an image changes, depending on the distance between the object and the eye. As shown in Figure 7.38a, light rays reflected off a distant object are nearly parallel when they pass through the lens, but light rays reflected off a nearby object are not parallel when they pass through the lens (Figure 7.38b). As a result of this difference in angle, the focal lengths for nearby and distant images differ. In order to produce focused images of objects at various distances, the eye must ensure that the focal point falls on the retina, a process termed **accommodation**. Because the location and shape of the cornea are fixed, the cornea does not participate in accommodation. Instead, the lens must either change position relative to the retina, or change shape.

Some polychaete worms change focal length by changing the volume of fluid in the eye, which alters the size of the eye and thus the distance between the lens and the retina. Many invertebrates and vertebrates alter focal length by moving the lens forward or backward. In contrast, lizards, birds, and mammals alter their focal length by changing the shape of the lens (Figure 7.38). To focus on nearby objects, the ciliary muscles contract, which increases their width and loosens the tension on the suspensory ligaments, causing the lens to become more rounded. To focus on distant objects, the ciliary muscles relax. This reduces the width of the ciliary muscles, increasing the tension on the suspensory ligaments, which pulls on the lens and flattens it. A more spherical lens aids in focusing on nearby objects, whereas a flatter lens brings distant objects into focus on the retina.

Vertebrate retinas have multiple layers

In addition to containing the photoreceptor cells that transduce incoming light energy into an electrical signal, vertebrate retinas contain many interneurons that play an important role in the processing of visual signals (Figure 7.39a). The rods and cones are actually located at the back of the retina,

FIGURE 7.38 **Image formation and accommodation by the mammalian eye**

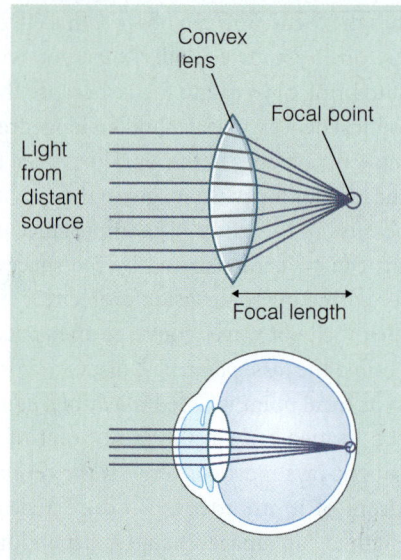
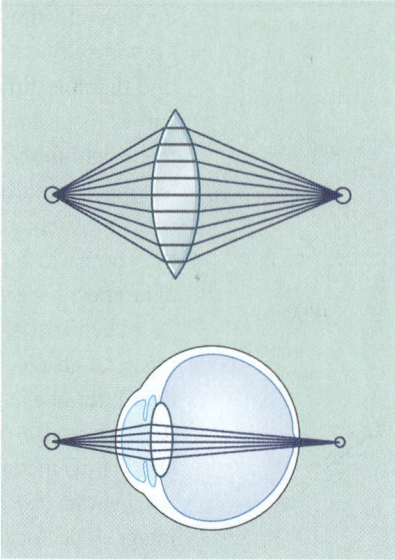
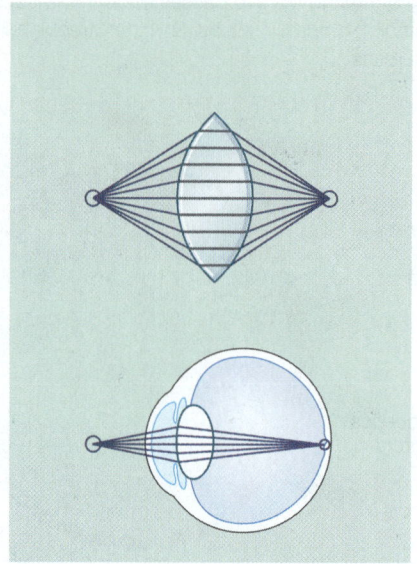

(a) Light rays from a distant object are parallel when they strike the eye, and focal length is short.

(b) Light rays from a nearby object are not parallel. Focal length increases and image is not focused on the retina.

(c) Lens changes shape, altering focal length and bringing image of nearby object into focus on the retina in the process of accommodation.

oriented with their tips embedded in the pigment epithelium at the back of the eye. The rods and cones form synapses with a layer of bipolar cells, and these bipolar cells in turn form synapses with a layer of retinal ganglion cells. In the same layers as the bipolar and ganglion cells are two additional classes of interneuron: the *horizontal cells* and the amacrine cells. The axons of the ganglion cells run along the surface of the retina, joining together to form the optic nerve, which exits the retina at a point slightly off the center of the retina. This area, called the optic disk, contains no photoreceptor cells, causing a "blind spot."

Because the photoreceptors of the vertebrate retina are located in its deepest layer, light entering the eye must travel through the ganglion and bipolar cells before reaching the photoreceptor cells. The only exception to this rule is an area called the fovea or the visual streak. The fovea is a circular region located roughly in the middle of the eye. Most non-mammalian vertebrates, as well as some mammals (including humans and other primates), have a fovea in each eye. In contrast, the majority of mammals, and some nonmammalian vertebrates, have a visual streak, which is a narrow strip along the retina arranged in the plane of the horizon. In both the fovea and the visual streak, the overlying bipolar and ganglion cells are pushed to one side, allowing light to strike the photoreceptors without passing through several layers of neurons. As a result, vision is sharpest in these regions.

The retina of cephalopods is arranged rather differently than the retina of vertebrates. In the cephalopods, the photoreceptors are located on the surface of the retina, rather than at the back (Figure 7.39b). Supporting cells are located between the photoreceptor cells, but there are no additional layers of cells. The axons of the photoreceptors come together to form the optic nerve, rather than forming synapses with interneurons within the retina. Thus, the cephalopod retina has far fewer parts than a vertebrate retina, and little signal processing occurs in the retina itself.

Information from rods and cones is processed differently

The vertebrate retina processes information coming from rods and cones differently (Figure 7.40). Rod signaling path-ways are organized using the principle of convergence. Many rods synapse with a single bipolar cell, and many of these bipolar cells can synapse with a **ganglion cell**. As a result, as many as 100 rods may connect with a single retinal ganglion cell. In contrast, a cone located within the **fovea** connects to a single bipolar cell, and that bipolar cell connects to a single ganglion cell. Thus, a single pathway carries a signal from a cone cell to the visual centers of the brain. Toward the edge of the retina, cones participate in somewhat more convergent pathways, but never to the extent seen with rods. These differences in wiring result in differences in the size of the receptive fields of retinal ganglion cells. A retinal ganglion cell that is associated with only one or a few photoreceptors has a small receptive field, processing information from only a small area of the retina. In contrast, a retinal ganglion cell that is associated with many photoreceptors has a large receptive field, and processes information from a larger area of the retina. Thus, retinal ganglion cells that are associated

FIGURE 7.39 **Organization of the retina in vertebrates and cephalopods**

(a) In the vertebrate retina, the photoreceptors are located toward the back. Light must pass through several layers of cells before striking the photoreceptors. The middle layers of the retina also contain interneurons that are important for signal processing within the vertebrate retina. **(b)** The cephalopod retina consists of a single layer of photoreceptor and supporting cells. Light entering the eye strikes the photoreceptors directly without passing through multiple retinal layers. There are no interneurons, and little or no signal processing occurs within the retina.

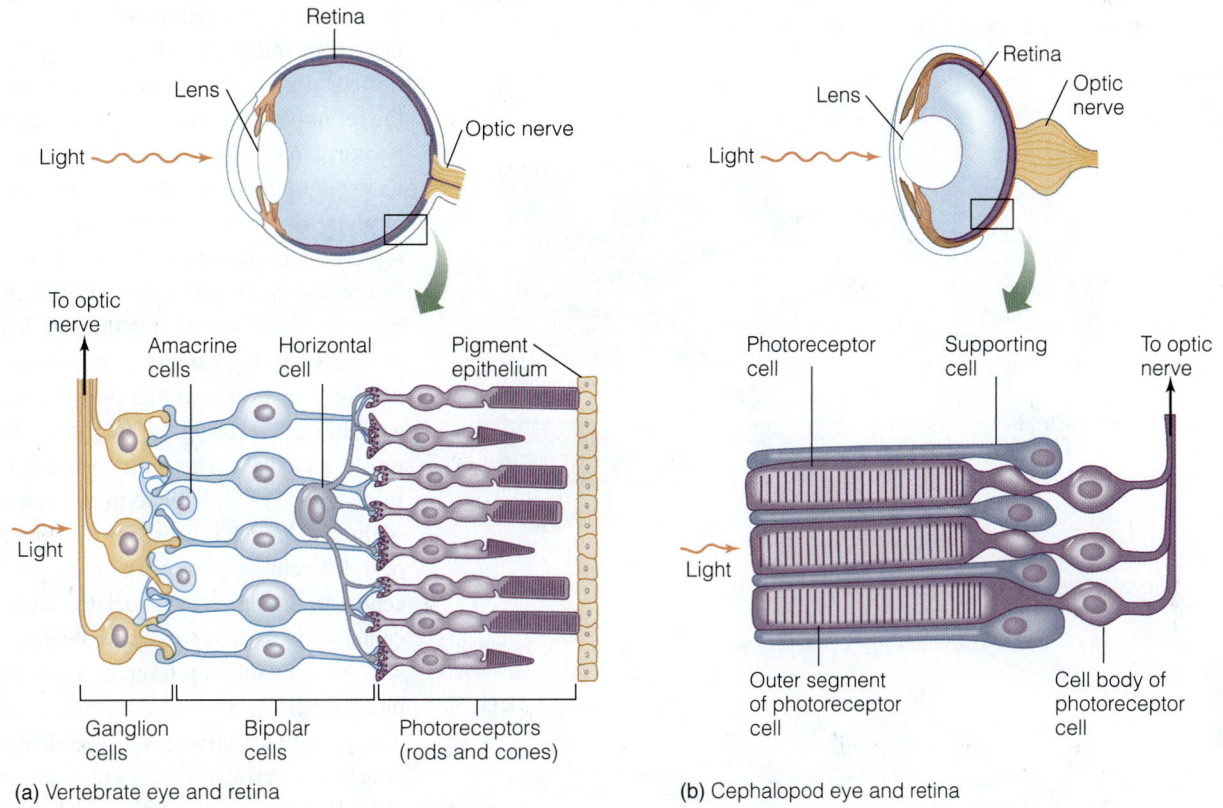

(a) Vertebrate eye and retina

(b) Cephalopod eye and retina

with cones located in the fovea have very small receptive fields and can provide a detailed, high-resolution image. In contrast, the receptive field of a retinal ganglion cell that receives inputs from rod photoreceptors is much larger, and thus rods provide less detailed images.

Signal processing in the retina enhances contrast

Vertebrate retinas are organized such that they enhance the perception of borders and contrast, using the process of lateral inhibition that we discussed at the beginning of this chapter. In fact, a point light source causes a greater response in a retinal ganglion cell than does evenly distributed diffuse illumination of the same intensity. This phenomenon occurs because the receptive fields of retinal ganglion cells have a *center-surround* organization, consisting of a central region surrounded by a concentric ring that each have different responses to light (Figure 7.41). For example, an "on-center" retinal ganglion cell increases action potential frequency in response to illumination of the center of the receptive field, and decreases action potential frequency in response to illumination of the surround region of the receptive field.

An "off-center" retinal ganglion cell shows the opposite response. The horizonatal and amacrine cells of the retina play the major role in establishing the center-surround organization of a retinal ganglion cell.

To see how this works, let's trace the events in the retina when light strikes the receptive field of a retinal ganglion cell with an on-center organization (Figure 7.41, left side). When a bright light is shone onto photoreceptors in the center region of the receptive field, the energy from the incoming light converts 11-*cis* retinal to all-*trans* retinal, activating the G protein transducin, which decreases cGMP within the photoreceptor cell. The decrease in cGMP closes Na^+ channels, hyperpolarizing the cell. This hyperpolarizing graded potential reduces the release of the neurotransmitter glutamate from the photoreceptor cell. Glutamate is an inhibitory neurotransmitter for the bipolar cell, so a decrease in the inhibitory neurotransmitter glutamate stimulates the bipolar cell, causing it to depolarize. The depolarization increases the release of neurotransmitter from the bipolar cell, stimulating the ganglion cell to depolarize.

Now let's look at what happens when a more diffuse light is shone onto the receptive field such that it

FIGURE 7.40 **Convergence in the vertebrate retina**

(a) The signaling pathways of rods show convergence. Many rods can form synapses with one bipolar cell, and several bipolar cells may form synapses with a single ganglion cell. Thus, the receptive fields of these retinal ganglion cells include input from many photoreceptor cells. **(b)** The signaling pathways of cones in the fovea do not converge. A single cone forms a synapse with a single bipolar cell, which forms synapses with a single ganglion cell. Thus, the receptive fields of these ganglion cells include input from only a single photoreceptor cell.

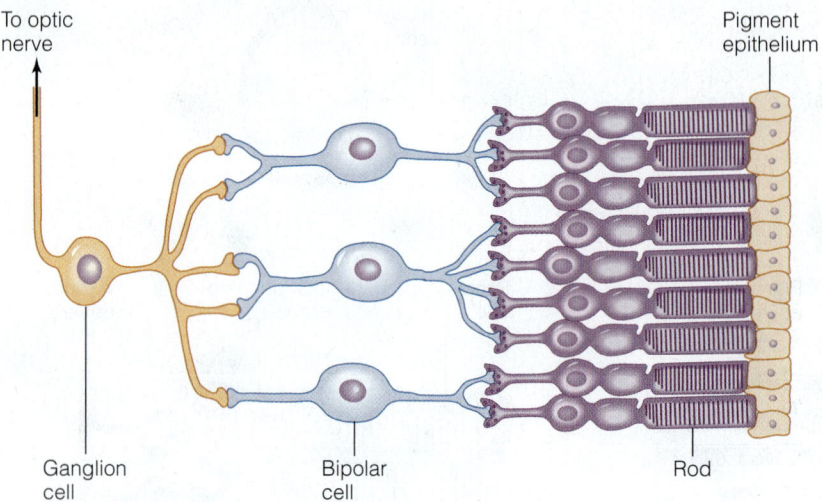

(a) Signal processing from rod photoreceptors

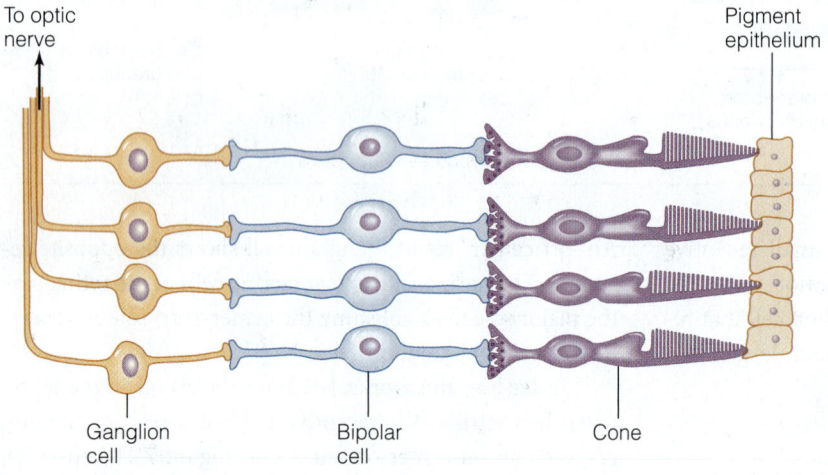

(b) Signal processing from cone photoreceptors

response to diffuse light compared with a point of light in the center of the receptive field.

Similar processes occur for retinal ganglion cells with an off-center organization, but in this case, glutamate released from the photoreceptor cells acts as an excitatory neurotransmitter for bipolar cells connected to photoreceptors in the center of the receptive field. When light strikes these photoreceptors, it causes the photoreceptor to hyperpolarize and decrease the release of glutamate, just as in the case of a photoreceptor in an on-center receptive field. In the case of an off-center receptive field, however, this decrease in glutamate hyperpolarizes the bipolar cell and reduces the release of neurotransmitter onto the retinal ganglion cell, causing the frequency of action potentials in the retinal ganglion cell to decline. The difference in the response of the bipolar cell is caused by the presence of a different isoform of the glutamate receptor in bipolar cells associated with on-center and off-center receptive fields.

To add another layer of complexity, bipolar cells do not always form synapses directly with ganglion cells. Instead, bipolar cells form electrical synapses with amacrine cells. Depolarization of the bipolar cell is communicated directly to the amacrine cell via gap junctions. The amacrine cell integrates and modifies the inputs from several bipolar cells, ultimately altering the release of neurotransmitter from the amacrine cell onto the ganglion cell. These extremely complex relationships are particularly prevalent in the highly convergent pathways involved with rod photoreceptors.

illuminates photoreceptors in both the center and surround regions. In addition to forming synapses with bipolar cells, photoreceptors in the surround region of the receptive field form synapses with horizontal cells (Figure 7.42). When stimulated, these horizontal cells inhibit the activity of the bipolar cells that are connected to the photoreceptors at the center of the receptive field. Thus, bipolar cells that form synapses with photoreceptors in the center of the receptive field receive two conflicting inputs: a stimulatory input from the center photoreceptors and an inhibitory input from the surround photoreceptors (via the horizontal cells). These two conflicting inputs cause the bipolar cell to send a much weaker signal to the retinal ganglion cell, reducing its

The brain processes the visual signal

We can define a region called the **visual field**, which consists of the entire area that can be seen without moving the eyes. Depending on the position of the eyes on the head, each eye sees a somewhat different part of the visual field. In animals with their eyes on the sides of their heads, there is little overlap between the visual fields of the right and left eyes, whereas in animals with eyes placed toward the front of their heads there is a great deal of overlap between the visual fields of the right and left eyes, in an area called the **binocular zone**. Figure 7.43 illustrates the visual field of a human. Human eyes are on the front of the head, and the binocular zone is large.

FIGURE 7.41 Receptive fields of retinal ganglion cells

Retinal ganglion cells have complex receptive fields that are divided into regions with different responses to light. Ganglion cells with an on-center receptive field fire action potentials at higher frequency in response to light focused on the center of the receptive field and fire action potentials at a decreased frequency in response to light focused on the surrounding region of the receptive field. When light strikes both the center (on) region and the surround (off) region at the same time, the two effects partially cancel out and the frequency of action potentials increases only slightly. The opposite pattern holds for retinal ganglion cells with an off-center organization.

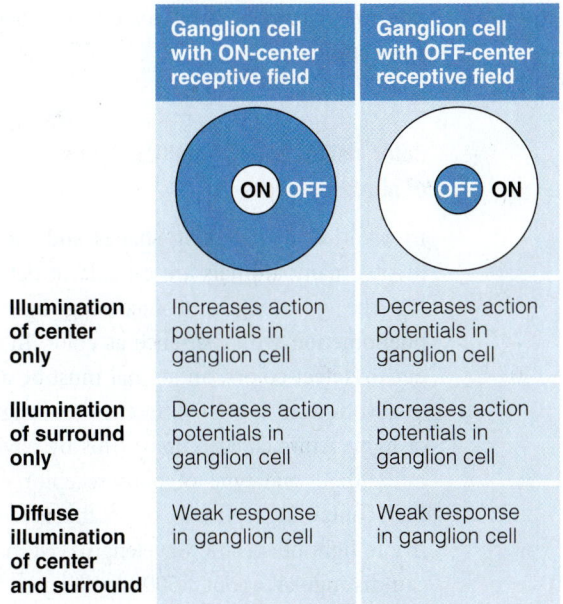

	Ganglion cell with ON-center receptive field	Ganglion cell with OFF-center receptive field
Illumination of center only	Increases action potentials in ganglion cell	Decreases action potentials in ganglion cell
Illumination of surround only	Decreases action potentials in ganglion cell	Increases action potentials in ganglion cell
Diffuse illumination of center and surround	Weak response in ganglion cell	Weak response in ganglion cell

FIGURE 7.42 Lateral inhibition in the vertebrate retina

Photoreceptors communicate with both bipolar cells and horizontal cells. Excited horizontal cells inhibit neighboring bipolar cells—the process of lateral inhibition.

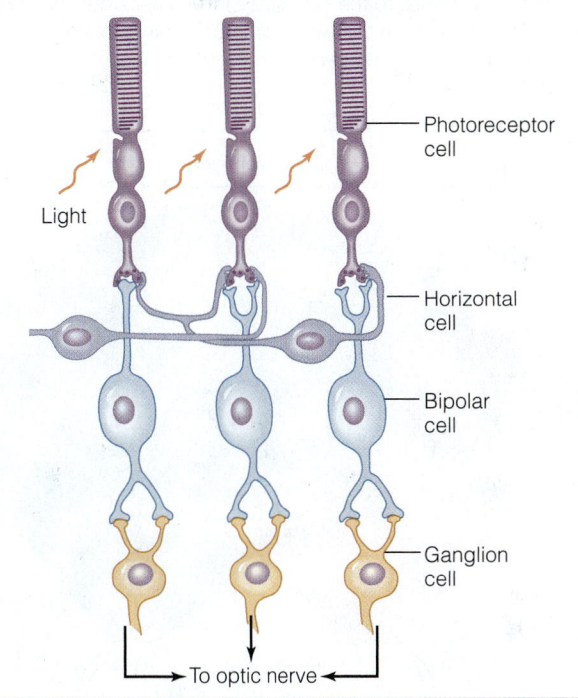

Each part of the retina detects a different portion of the visual field. Light from the left part of the visual field strikes the right part of the retina of each eye, whereas light from the right part of the visual field strikes the left part of the retina of each eye. In fact, we can divide the human retina down the middle (roughly at the fovea) and define two regions of each retina: the temporal half (toward the outside of the face) and the nasal half (toward the center of the face). The temporal retina of the right eye detects the left visual field, and the nasal retina detects the right visual field. In contrast, the temporal retina of the left eye detects the right visual field, and the nasal retina of the left eye detects the left visual field.

The two optic nerves carrying information from the right and left eyes converge in a region called the **optic chiasm** (Figure 7.43). Most of the neurons then form synapses in a part of the brain called the *lateral geniculate nucleus*, which in turn sends processes to the **visual cortex**, which is responsible for the final processing of visual information (see Chapter 8: Functional Organization of Nervous Systems).

Neurons coming from the temporal retina of the right eye send projections to the right lateral geniculate nucleus, whereas neurons coming from the temporal retina of the left eye send projections to the left lateral geniculate nucleus. In contrast, neurons coming from the nasal retinas of the right and left eyes cross over at the optic chiasm to form synapses with the lateral geniculate nucleus on the opposite side of the brain. As a result, the right half of the brain processes signals from the left part of the visual field, and the left half of the brain processes signals from the right half of the visual field. The right and left sides of the visual field overlap in the binocular zone, and thus signals from the binocular zone are processed on both sides of the brain. Animals can compare the properties of the images in the binocular zone coming from each eye to provide information such as the distance of an object from the body. This is one of the processes that underlie depth perception.

In general, the degree of crossing of neurons in the optic chiasm is related to the degree of overlap between the left and right visual fields. In fish and amphibians with eyes located at the extreme sides of the head, the left and right visual fields do not overlap. These animals lack a binocular zone, and most of the neurons in the optic nerve from the right eye send projections to the left side of the brain, whereas the optic nerve from the left eye sends projections to the right side of the brain. Similarly, in mice, which also have a limited overlap between their right and left visual fields, about 97 percent of the fibers cross over to the other side of the brain, while only 3 percent of the fibers are uncrossed. Although animals (such as fish and rodents) with eyes on each

In humans, about half of the neurons coming from each eye cross over each other in the optic chiasm. Neurons sending signals from the right side of the field of view from both the left and right eyes send processes to the left half of the brain, whereas neurons sending signals from the left side of the field of view from both the right and left eyes send processes to the right side of the brain. Thus, each side of the brain receives information from both eyes. Comparing these two views provides stereopsis, which enhances depth perception.

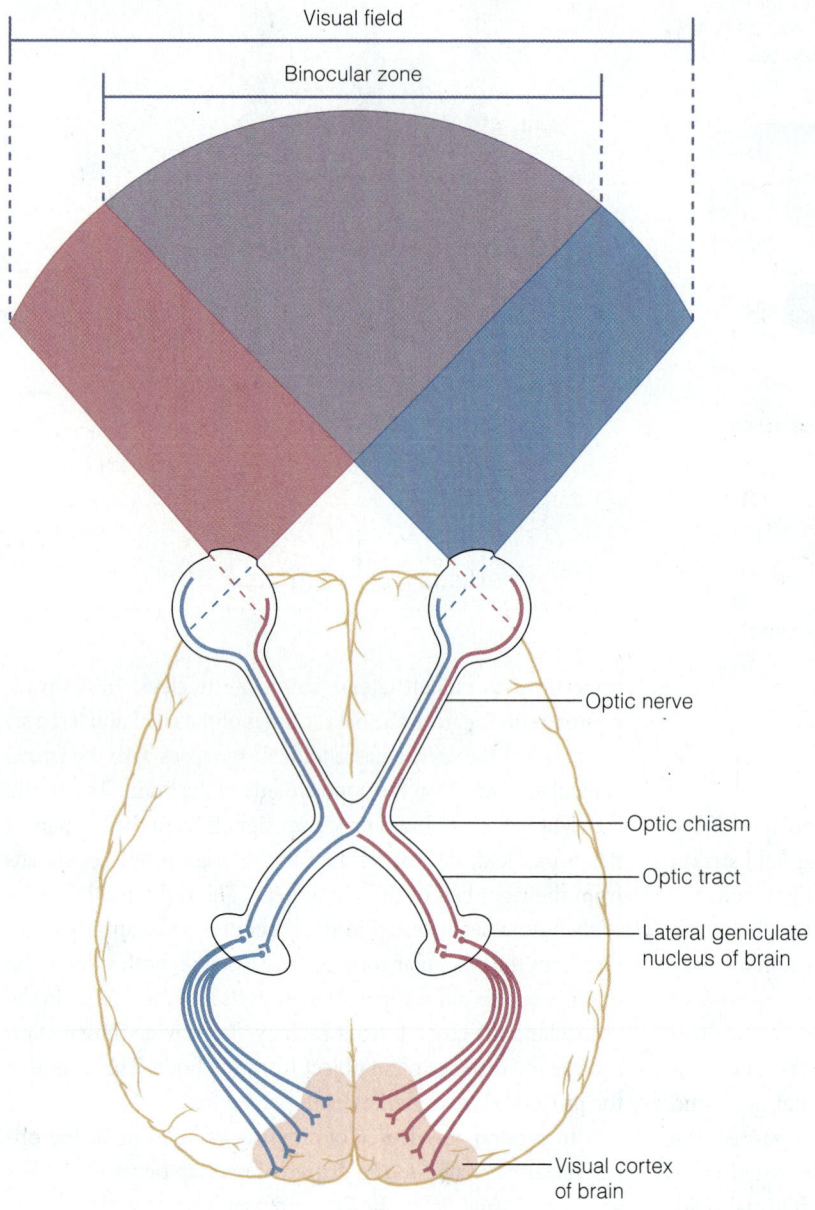

Visual field

Binocular zone

Optic nerve

Optic chiasm

Optic tract

Lateral geniculate
nucleus of brain

Visual cortex
of brain

to have roughly equal amounts of crossed and uncrossed fibers, allowing easy comparison of signals from each eye on both sides of the brain. Owls, which have eyes at the front of their heads, and excellent depth perception, are an exception to this rule because all of their optic neurons cross at the optic chiasm. The two sides of an owl's brain communicate with each other in other parts of the visual pathway, allowing both sides of the brain to process images from both eyes, and providing the necessary conditions for effective depth perception.

Color vision requires multiple types of photoreceptors

In addition to detecting shapes and movements, many animals are capable of detecting the wavelength of incoming light, a phenomenon we experience as color. In order to detect colors, an animal must be able to distinguish among different wavelengths of light. Animals accomplish this by having more than one type of photoreceptor cell, each containing a photopigment that is sensitive to light of specific wavelengths. Humans can distinguish about 1,500 wavelengths between 400 nm (blue) and 700 nm (red). This might suggest that humans would need several thousand different photopigments and photoreceptor cells; however, humans have only three different cone photoreceptors, with maximum sensitivities of approximately 440 nm (blue), 530 nm (green), and 565 nm (red) (Figure 7.44). Light of a given wavelength stimulates more than one type of cone, but to different degrees. The retina and brain then compare the output from each type of cone and infer the color of the stimulus.

Each cone photoreceptor is maximally sensitive to a particular wavelength of light, but can also be stimulated by light of other wavelengths. So how can the brain distinguish between a low-intensity stimulus at the peak wavelength and a strong stimulus at another wavelength? Clearly, a single cone photoreceptor cannot provide information about the wavelength of incoming light. The outputs of all types of cones must be used to estimate the wavelength of the incoming light. The first stage of this processing occurs in the horizontal and ganglion cells of the retina, where lateral inhibition by horizontal cells plays an important role in the initial processing of color information. This system, called

side of the head tend to have poor depth perception, these animals have excellent panoramic vision, often having an almost 360-degree view of the world. Humans have a large binocular zone, and about 60 percent of the fibers in the optic nerve cross over to the other side of the brain at the optic chiasm, while 40 percent of the fibers are uncrossed. This cross-fiber organization plays a part in generating **stereopsis**, in which comparison of the information by the two eyes assists in depth perception. In general, animals with superior stereopsis tend

FIGURE 7.44 **The absorbance spectra of human rods and cones**

Humans typically have one type of rod photopigment and three types of cone photopigment. Although the absorbance spectra of the photopigments overlap, each has a unique absorbance maximum. By comparing the signals coming from each type of photoreceptor, the brain can distinguish over 1,000 different wavelengths of light.

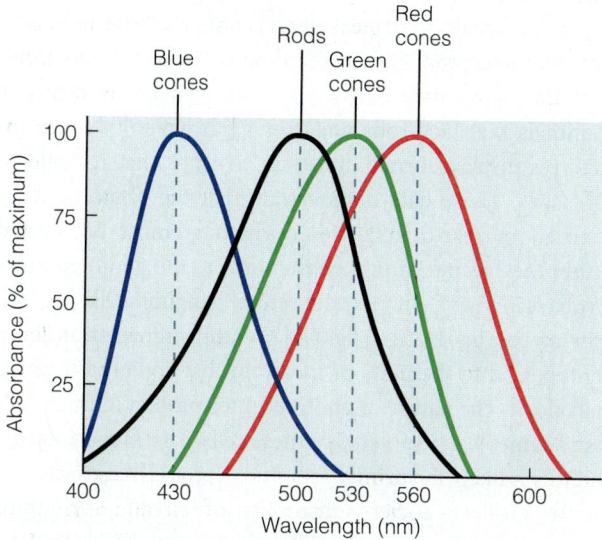

Color vision evolved secondarily in primates

All of the Old World primates (humans, apes, and Old World monkeys) have trichromatic color vision similar to that found in humans. In contrast, the New World monkeys vary greatly in their ability to see colors. Most species are dichromatic; a few species have trichromatic females but dichromatic males; and only the howler monkeys are true trichromats. The genetics of these different visual systems have now been worked out, and their evolution has been studied in detail.

Humans and the other Old World primates have classic trichromatic color vision, with three opsin genes in the genome: one coding for a blue-sensitive photopigment, one coding for a green-sensitive photopigment, and one coding for a red-sensitive photopigment. The "green" and "red" opsins are coded by very similar DNA sequences, and differ by only 11 amino acids. This degree of differentiation suggests, based on the approximate mutation rate of genes in the vertebrates, that these genes began to diverge from each other about 40 million years ago. It appears that an ancestral "green" opsin gene was duplicated at that time, during the early evolution of the Old World primates, and the two genes began to diverge. In humans, these two genes are located very close together on the X chromosome, further suggesting that they arose through an ancestral duplication in this part of the genome.

Some species of New World primate, such as the owl monkey, a nocturnal animal, are monochromats and are thus color-blind. But most other species of New World monkeys have a form of trichromatic color vision. These monkeys have only two opsin genes in their genome—a "blue" opsin and a "green" opsin. As in the Old World primates, the "green" opsin gene is found on the X chromosome, but in this case the gene has not been duplicated. Instead, in some species of New World monkeys, two different alleles of this one gene are present in the population. One of the alleles is sensitive to green light, and the other is more sensitive to red light. An individual that is heterozygous for these alleles (having one copy of the "green" allele and one copy of its "red" variant) is functionally trichromatic, expressing a "blue" opsin, a "green" opsin, and a "red" opsin. Because the "green" opsin gene is found on the X chromosome, males of these species cannot have trichromatic color vision, because they have only one copy of the X chromosome, plus a Y chromosome that lacks the opsin gene. Thus, males of these species are always homozygous at the "green" opsin gene, and are functionally dichromatic and are red/green color-blind. Females can be either red/green color-blind or trichromats, depending on whether they are homozygous or heterozygous at the "green" opsin gene.

Of all the New World primates, only the howler monkeys deviate from this system. In howler monkeys, the "green" opsin gene has been duplicated, similar to the situation in the Old World primates. Thus, both male and female howler monkeys are true trichromats, and have color vision similar

trichromatic color vision, allows humans to see a wide range of colors using only three types of cone photoreceptors.

Birds, reptiles, and shallow-water fishes can be trichromatic, tetrachromatic, or even pentachromatic (depending on the species). It is difficult for us to understand the visual world of a pentachromatic animal. The additional photoreceptors likely allow these species to discriminate among colors that appear the same to humans, and some species can detect light in the ultraviolet (UV) or infrared ranges that humans cannot detect. Most mammals are **dichromats**, having only middle (green) and short (blue) wavelength cones (in addition to rods) in their retinas. Because dichromats lack the "red" cone, these animals cannot distinguish between red colors and green colors, which is similar to a human who is red/green color-blind. Many marine mammals and a few nocturnal rodents and carnivores have secondarily lost one of these pigments and become monochromats that cannot distinguish colors at all.

Because ancient reptilelike creatures with at least trichromatic color vision are the probable ancestors of the mammals, we can infer that mammals must have lost one or more of the ancestral photopigment genes. Mammals are thought to have evolved primarily as nocturnal creatures (first appearing during the time of the dinosaurs), and at that time some of the genes needed for color vision may have been lost because they were not needed for vision in dim light. Trichromacy was subsequently restored only in the primates.

to that in humans. Because the New World monkeys diverged from the Old World monkeys prior to the evolution of the primates, the gene duplication in the howler monkeys is independent from that shared by all of the Old World primates. It also appears to be somewhat more recent, as the "green" and "red" opsins of the howler monkeys differ from each other by only eight amino acids (compared with the 11 amino acid differences in the Old World primates). Thus, true trichromacy has evolved at least twice in the primates, once in the lineage leading to the Old World primates (including humans), and once in the ancestors of the howler monkeys. Multiple independent evolution of a phenotypic trait strongly suggests that this trait has been selected over evolutionary time for some important function. For example, being able to distinguish many shades of red and green might allow primates to easily find ripe fruit in a background of leaves.

Some photoreceptors are not involved in vision

Photoreceptors play a variety of roles in addition to their role in vision. For example, animals use photoreceptors to regulate circadian and circannual rhythms. A circadian rhythm is a roughly 24-hour cycle of changes in physiological processes, while in a circannual rhythm a physiological process varies with a period of approximately a year. Circadian and circannual rhythms are endogenous (meaning they are generated within the body) via an internal clock mechanism, so they persist even when an organism is kept in constant darkness. External cues, and particularly information about light and dark, help to entrain these rhythms. For example, circadian rhythms tend to diverge from a period of 24 hours if an animal is held in constant dark, but the clock can be reset if an animal is exposed to a predictable day length, or **photoperiod**.

Both visual and nonvisual photoreceptors are involved in resetting circadian rhythms in many animals. Many insects, for example, have photoreceptors deep within the brain, in addition to the ones in the eyes. These deep-brain photoreceptor cells contain a photopigment called **cryptochrome** that is thought to be the primary light detector involved in entraining circadian rhythms. Photoreceptors in the eyes also play a role in detecting light and communicating with the circadian clock in some insect species.

In most nonmammalian vertebrates, a part of the brain termed the **pineal gland** is directly sensitive to light and contains its own biological clock. The opsin-related protein **melanopsin** is the primary photoreceptor pigment in the pineal gland. The pineal organ of nonmammalian vertebrates rests on top of the brain, and in some species the skull over the pineal gland is very thin, allowing substantial light to penetrate to the pineal organ. In fact, in some extinct vertebrates, the pineal organ apparently formed a third eye with a lens to focus light. In living organisms, only the lamprey and some lizards retain the remnants of this third eye.

Nonmammalian vertebrates also have structures that are called deep-brain photoreceptors, although the role of these photoreceptors remains enigmatic. For example, recent studies in zebrafish indicate that larvae that lack eyes or a pineal gland can still respond to light. This light response appears to be dependent on cells within the hypothalamus that express two types of opsin: melanopsin and a generalized opsin that is found in many tissues.

In mammals, the pineal gland is unlikely to be an important photoreceptor. In fact, mammals that lack eyes cannot reset their circadian clocks. However, genetically defective mammals that lack rods and cones but have otherwise intact eyes display normal circadian rhythms that respond to light cues. These data demonstrate that the photoreceptors involved in resetting circadian rhythms must be located within the eye, but cannot be the same as the photoreceptors involved in vision. In fact, the retinal ganglion cells play the primary role in detecting light and sending information about photoperiod to the parts of the brain that contain the circadian clock. The nature of photoreceptor protein in these cells is still somewhat disputed, but these cells express melanopsin, and this is likely the primary photoreceptor in these cells.

In modern society, disorders of circadian rhythms are common, and underlie phenomena such as jet lag (see Box 7.2: Challenges to Homeostasis: Circadian Rhythms in the Modern World).

CONCEPT CHECK

15. What are the advantages of a vesicular eye compared with a pinhole-type eye?
16. Would you expect laser eye surgery (which affects the shape of the cornea) to be effective in an aquatic vertebrate? Why or why not?

Other Sensory Modalities

In addition to the classic five senses of touch, taste, hearing, smell, and vision, animals can detect a variety of other types of stimuli. For example, all animals are able to detect differences in temperature. In addition, many species can detect a variety of forms of electromagnetic radiation, including electrical and magnetic fields, although humans appear to lack these **sensory modalities**. In this section we provide a brief introduction to these other sensory modalities, highlighting some of the taxa that have particularly refined abilities.

Thermoreceptors detect temperature

Animals have central thermoreceptors, located in the hypothalamus of the brain, that monitor their internal temperature, and peripheral thermoreceptors that monitor environmental temperature. There are three types of

CIRCADIAN RHYTHMS IN THE MODERN WORLD

Many people are familiar with the phenomenon of jet lag, which is a feeling of excessive sleepiness during the day coupled with difficulty falling asleep at night. Jet lag occurs because your internal circadian clock does not reset immediately when you travel rapidly across multiple time zones, and so ends up out of sync with the external cues of light and dark. As a result, your body prepares itself for sleep at the wrong time of day, and your alertness suffers. It takes several days or a week for your internal clock to reset itself to the new photoperiod, at which point the symptoms of jet lag disappear. Shift workers can experience similar problems because they are required to be active at night when their circadian clock is signaling that they should be entering a period of reduced activity and sleep. Disruptions of circadian rhythms can lead to a variety of adverse health consequences, including obesity, diabetes, and cardiovascular problems such as high blood pressure.

Unfortunately, almost all people in modern societies may be experiencing some form of circadian rhythm disruption. Epidemiological studies indicate that the length of time that people sleep (sleep duration) is decreasing over time, and that sleep patterns are changing. So what is the cause of this disruption?

One possible cause of sleep disruption in modern societies is electric lighting. Artificial electric light is a pervasive part of modern life, and as a result, most people experience a longer period of light than is normal across 24 hours. But does this increased light exposure cause sleep disruption? In an intriguing study, Wright et al. (2013) addressed this question by measuring the sleep cycle and sleep duration of eight individuals under typical modern-day conditions. The participants were allowed to maintain their normal routines of school, work, and socializing. Like most people in modern societies, the study participants spent most of the day indoors, and used artificial light after sunset to allow them to remain active after dark. The study authors then took their test subjects camping in a region where there was no access to artificial light. Participants spent the day outdoors and were not allowed to use flashlights or personal electronic devices, so that they had no artificial light after dark except for campfires.

To determine sleep-wake cycles, all the participants wore activity monitors throughout the study. At the end of a week of exposure to either modern-day conditions or camping, the researchers took the participants into a dimly lit room in the lab and measured levels of the hormone **melatonin** across a day to assess the circadian cycle in this hormone. Melatonin is associated with sleep-wake cycles in humans, and its levels are high at night and lower during the day.

When they were exposed to modern-day conditions the participants tended to get up later and stay up later than under natural conditions. The rhythm in melatonin also differed between treatments, and the relationship between sleep-wake cycles and melatonin rhythms changed. In particular, melatonin levels (which are an indicator of sleepiness) remained high for about two hours after waking under modern-day conditions, while under natural conditions, melatonin levels started to drop about an hour before waking. Thus, under modern-day conditions these subjects appear to be chronically tired in the mornings.

Interestingly, the total amount of sleep was not significantly different between groups. The main difference between them was in the timing of their sleep-wake cycle relative to their circadian rhythm in melatonin. This study was conducted during the summer, when natural day length is the longest, suggesting that differences in sleep patterns might have been even greater had the study been performed in the wintertime.

There were also individual differences in the extent of this effect. Survey data in modern societies suggest that human sleep patterns vary along a continuum defined by two major *chronotypes*, or individuals with somewhat different sleep windows. So-called "larks" are early risers who tend to go to bed early. So-called "night-owls" tend to get up late and go to bed late. In this experiment, the "night-owls" experienced the greatest change in their sleep patterns between modern-day conditions and camping, suggesting that they may be experiencing greater sleep disruption than are "larks."

Surveys suggest that almost 80 percent of the adult population in the developed world uses an alarm clock to wake up on weekdays. This loss of sleep is often compensated by sleeping for longer on the weekends. The phenomenon of sleeping for different amounts of time on weekdays and weekends is termed "social jet lag." Unfortunately, as with traveler's jet lag and shift work, this pattern is associated with adverse health consequences.

So what can we do to better match our sleep-wake cycles to our circadian rhythm? Maintaining a regular pattern of bedtime throughout the week is one important component. It is also important to get some exposure to bright, natural light in the morning, and to make sure not to be exposed to too much light in the evening.

References

- Kantermann, T. (2013). Circadian biology: Sleep-styles shaped by light-styles. *Current Biology, 23*, R689–R690.
- Roenneberg, T., Kantermann, T., Juda, M., Vetter, C., & Allebrandt, K.V. (2013). Light and the human circadian clock. *Handbook of Experimental Pharmacology 217*, 311–331.
- Wright, K. P. Jr., McHill, A. W., Birks, B. R., Griffin, B. R., Rusterholz, T., & Chinoy, E.D. (2013). Entrainment of the human circadian clock to the natural light-dark cycle. *Current Biology, 23*, 1554–1558.

peripheral thermoreceptors: warm-sensitive thermoreceptors, cold-sensitive thermoreceptors, and thermoreceptors that are specialized for detecting painfully hot stimuli. In mammals, warm-sensitive neurons start to fire action potentials when the skin temperature is raised above 30°C, and firing frequency increases with increasing temperature up to a saturating value. In contrast, cold receptors are extremely sensitive to small (0.5°C) decreases in temperature, but they respond mostly to temperature change, rather than the absolute value of the temperature. The thermal nociceptors detect painful heat and burns, and start to fire only at higher, painful temperatures (starting at around 45°C in mammals). These neurons increase their firing frequency in parallel with increasing pain sensation.

Thermoreception begins when specific thermoreceptor proteins in the free nerve endings of thermoreceptor neurons are activated. These receptors, which are found in both vertebrates and invertebrates, are called thermoTRPs and, like some mechanoreceptors and chemoreceptors, express members of the TRP family of ion channels. Individual thermoTRPs are specialized to detect distinct temperature ranges; some thermoTRPs are activated by heat, others by cold. Capsaicin, the "hot" ingredient in peppers, stimulates warm-sensitive neurons, while menthol, the ingredient that makes mints taste "cool," stimulates cold-sensitive neurons.

Some animals have highly specialized sensory organs that allow them to detect heat radiating from objects at a distance. For example, pit vipers (a group that includes rattlesnakes) have specialized **pit organs** that are cup-shaped depressions found between the eye and nostril on either side of the head (Figure 7.45). Other snakes such as the boa constrictor have labial pits along the upper and lower jaws. Pit organs and labial pits are extremely sensitive thermoreceptors that allow snakes to detect mammalian prey and to select thermally appropriate

habitats. The cup shape of these organs in pit vipers allows the formation of a somewhat blurry and low contrast, but recognizable, image similar to that of a pinhole camera. This image allows snakes such as rattlesnakes to use temperature cues to locate particularly vulnerable regions of their prey.

The thermoreceptive neurons in the pit organs can detect temperature changes as small as 0.003°C (compare this with the 0.5°C discrimination of human thermoreceptors). Pit organ thermoreceptors are sensitive to capsaicin, and express TRPA1 channels, suggesting that they work on the same principles as do the temperature-sensitive nociceptors that are found in all animals. However, the TRPA1 channels in the pit organs of snakes are the most thermally sensitive of all the TRP channels that have currently been described.

Electroreceptors detect electrical fields

All animals produce weak electric fields as a result of the actions of their muscles and nerves. Similarly, the flow of water over objects causes a static electrical discharge. Thus, electrical fields can provide information about the biotic and abiotic environment to organisms with appropriate sensory receptors. However, air is a poor conductor of electricity, so terrestrial animals do not generally make use of electroreception.

Electroreception appears to have evolved in the early vertebrates, as jawless fish such as lampreys have electroreceptors. The electroreceptors in fishes are derived from the lateral line, and contain modified hair cells, although these cells lack cilia and detect electrical fields rather than pressure waves.

Cartilagenous fishes such as sharks have particularly elaborate electrosensory organs that are located in a series of pores distributed across the head. These pores, termed the ampullae of Lorenzini after the Italian anatomist who first described them in 1678, are filled with an electrically conductive jelly and lined with modified hair cells. A net negative charge inside the ampulla causes an electrical change in each hair cell, triggering the release of neurotransmitters to adjacent clusters of afferent sensory neurons. For example, the electrosensitive great hammerhead shark (*Sphyrna mokarran*) can detect buried stingrays by sweeping its wide head over the bottom of the ocean like a metal detector. Scalloped hammerhead sharks (*Sphyrna lewini*) can detect electric fields of less than 0.1 nV/cm, equivalent to the electric field of a flashlight battery connected to electrodes over 16,000 kilometers apart in the ocean.

Electroreception appears to have been lost in the ancestors of teleost fishes. However, two distantly related groups of freshwater teleosts (the osteoglossomorphs and the ostariophysans) appear to have independently evolved electroreception.

Some species of amphibians also possess an electroreceptive sense, as do the monotremes (the egg-laying mammals,

FIGURE 7.45 **Pit organs of snakes**
The pit organ of this fer de lance pit viper is clearly visible as a large pit between the small nostril and the eye.

Photo source: Ingo Schulz/imageBROKER/Alamy.

including the echidna and platypus). In the platypus, the electroreceptors are located in the bill. They are bipolar sensory neurons, rather than modified epithelial (hair) cells as in fish.

No species of reptile or bird has been shown to utilize electroreception, and placental mammals were generally thought to lack the ability to detect electrical fields as well. However, a recent report suggests that the Guiana dolphin (*Sotalia guianensis*) may detect electrical fields using small sensory organs derived from the follicles of the vibrissae, or whiskers, that are mechanoreceptive organs in other mammals.

All of these species use what is termed "passive" electroreception; they detect the electrical fields associated with other organisms or objects in the environment. In contrast, the weakly electric fish have an "active" electrical sense. They have a specialized electric organ that can produce electrical discharges that they use for communication and electrolocation. Objects or other animals in the environment alter the shape of the electric field generated by the weakly electric fish (Figure 7.46). Nonconducting objects such as a stone decrease the density of the field lines, while conducting or capacitive objects such as small animals increase the density of the field lines. Electric fish then detect these perturbations of the electric field and use this information to locate the object, in a process analogous to echolocation in bats. For further insight into the electrical sense of these intriguing fish, see Box 7.3: Math in Physiology: Communication in Weakly Electric Fish.

Magnetoreceptors detect magnetic fields

Magnetoreception, or the ability to detect magnetic fields (also called magnetoception), is widely distributed throughout the animal kingdom. Migratory birds, **homing** salmon, and many other organisms use Earth's magnetic field to help them navigate, although humans apparently lack this sense. Magnetoreception has been extensively studied, but the mechanisms of magnetoreception are not understood for any animal, and it remains the most elusive of sensory modalities.

Scientists have identified specific neurons in the olfactory epithelium of rainbow trout that respond to magnetic fields. These neurons contain particles that resemble **magnetite** when examined under a microscope. Magnetite is a natural mineral that responds to magnetic fields, and thus could be the basis for magnetoreception in animals. The magnetite particles in trout olfactory neurons are arranged in a chain within the cell, similar to a compass needle, strongly suggesting that trout use a magnetite-based mechanism for detecting magnetic fields. A similar mechanism is used by some species of bacteria that can orient themselves in a magnetic field. However, the mechanism by which magnetoreceptive sensory neurons in trout respond to changes in the position of the magnetite is still unknown. Not all animals that can respond to magnetic fields have detectable magnetite crystals, so it is unlikely that this mechanism is found in all magnetoreceptors.

Another proposed mechanism of magnetoreception, which has been extensively investigated in both migratory birds and in *Drosophila*, involves a group of proteins known as cryptochromes. Cryptochromes are light-sensitive pigments that are involved in light sensing in many animals, playing a key role in regulating biological rhythms such as circadian and circannual rhythms. For example, corals use cryptochromes to sense the duration and color of moonlight, and use this information to synchronize their spawning. In vertebrates, cryptochromes are found in cells in the retina. When blue light strikes a cryptochrome, it transfers one of its electrons to a molecule of flavin adenine dinucleotide (FAD). As a result, cryptochrome and FAD each end up with an unpaired electron. The unpaired electrons on cryptochrome and FAD interact with each other, influencing a property of the electrons that is termed "spin." In the electron pair, the two electrons can either spin in the same direction or in opposite directions, and the pair can flip between the two states. The surrounding magnetic field can influence the flips between these two states, which could affect the outcome of reactions that are dependent on this electron pair. This change

---

FIGURE 7.46 Active electrolocation in a weakly electric fish

Weakly electric fish produce electrical discharges from the electric organ located in the tail (shown in black). These electrical discharges result in an electric field around the fish. Objects in the environment distort this electric field. Nonconducting objects (such as the stone shown above the fish) decrease the density of the electric field, while conducting objects (such as the worm shown below the fish) increase the density of the field lines. The fish detects these distortions in the electric field and can identify the positions of objects in their environment, as well as their electrical properties.

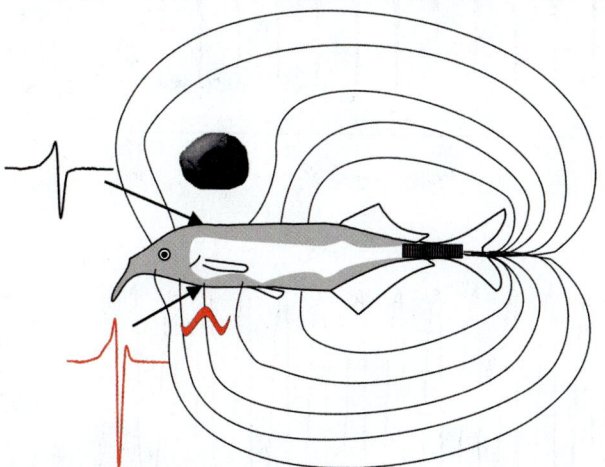

Figure source: From Non-visual environmental imaging and object detection through active electrolocation in weakly electric fish. Journal of Comparative Physiology A: Volume 192, Issue 6, pp 601–612, Figure 1, p. 603. Von der Emde, G. © 2006. With permission of Springer Science+Business Media.

Although many species of fish are electroreceptive, only about 350 of the approximately 30,000 species of fish alive today are able to produce electrical discharges. These fishes have a specialized electric organ that consists of highly derived nerve or muscle cells that are called electrocytes. These electrocytes are activated simultaneously to produce a coordinated electrical discharge that results in an electrical field around the fish. Some species of electric fish, such as the electric eel (*Electrophorus electricus*) can produce an electrical discharge up to about 600 V, which is strong enough to deliver a nasty electric shock, but most electric fish are so-called weakly electric fish that generate electrical discharges on the order of 1 volt. If you put your hand in a tank containing these fish you would not even notice the slightest tingle, but we can detect the electrical discharges of these fish with appropriate equipment. Weakly electric fish use their electric organ discharge (EOD) for electrolocation and for communication.

There are two major groups of weakly electric fish: the African elephantnose fish (Mormyriformes; Figure 7.47a) and the South American knifefish (Gymnotiformes; Figure 7.47b). Most species of Mormyriformes have what are termed "pulse-type" EODs, which are short bursts of electrical activity followed by longer pauses between discharges. The intervals between the pulses contain substantial information, and both the shape and frequency of the pulses varies between species and even between sexes within a species.

Many species within the Gymnotiformes have an alternative form of electrical discharge, which is termed "wave type." In a wave-type EOD the pauses between discharges are about the same length as the discharge itself, resulting in a continuous sine wave–type discharge. Although the continuous discharge from their electric organ should provide excellent electrolocation, it could potentially pose a problem for communication among these fish. Having a continuous electrical discharge must be a little bit like talking nonstop while simultaneously trying to listen to a conversation going on around you.

So how do wave-type electric fish discriminate incoming signals from other fish from the background of their

---

FIGURE 7.47 **The electric discharges of weakly electric fish**

(a) Almost all African Mormyriformes, such as the elephantnose fish (*Gnathonemus petersii*), have pulse-type discharges from their electric organs. **(b)** Many of the South American Gymnotiformes, such as the black ghost knifefish (*Apteronotus albifrons*), have wave-type discharges from their electric organs.

(a) An elephantnose fish with a pulse-type electric organ discharge.

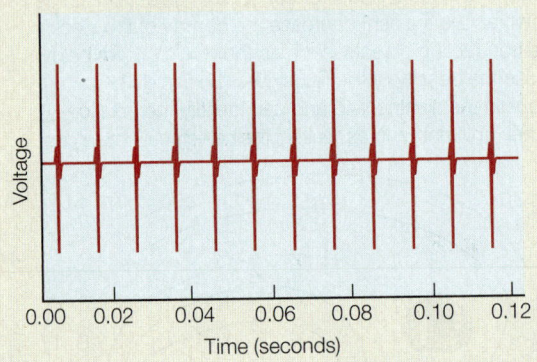

(b) Black ghost knifefish with a wave-type electric organ discharge.

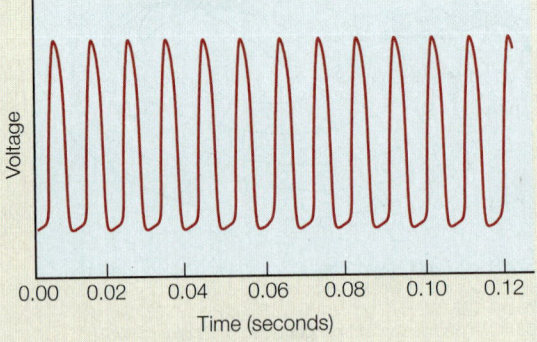

Photo source: (a) Jerry Young/DK Images. (b) Reinhard, H./picture alliance/Arco Images G/Newscom.

own strong signals? Interestingly, rather than interfering with electrical communication, wave-type electric fish rely on the presence of their own EOD for detecting incoming signals from other electric fish. If you surgically abolish the ability of a wave-type electric fish to generate an EOD, their ability to detect other members of their species drops precipitously.

To understand this apparently paradoxical result, it is necessary to appreciate some of the mathematics and physics associated with the interaction between waves such as sound waves or electromagnetic waves. Let's begin by considering two waves with the same amplitude, but slightly different frequency (Figure 7.48). When the two waves encounter each other their amplitudes sum. In this example, the two waves start off synchronized, so their summed amplitude is double their initial amplitude, but if the two waves differ in frequency the two waves will gradually get out of phase. At some point the crest of one wave will occur at the same time as the trough of the other wave. When this happens, the two waves cancel out, and the amplitude of the resulting wave is near zero. Thus, when two waves with constant amplitude but slightly different frequencies interact, they produce a new wave with varying amplitude. Each high-amplitude part of the new wave is called a "beat," and the timing between beats is called the beat frequency. If the two initial waves are very similar in frequency, the resulting beat frequency will be low because it takes a long time for the waves to get fully out of phase, whereas if the two waves are more different in frequency, the resulting beat frequency will be high because it takes less time for the two waves to get fully out of phase.

When two wave-type electric fish encounter each other, their electrical signals interact and produce beats. The fish detect the beats, and the beat frequency helps them to interpret the signals coming from other electric fish. The high sensitivity of electric fish to the beats generated by interacting electrical signals explains why these electric fish must be producing an EOD in order to easily detect signals from other electric fish.

Although beats are useful for electrical communication between wave-type electric fish, they can also interfere with

FIGURE 7.48 Interactions between sine waves

When two sine waves (y_1 and y_2) with slightly different frequencies interact, they produce a new wave with varying amplitude. These amplitude variations are called beats.

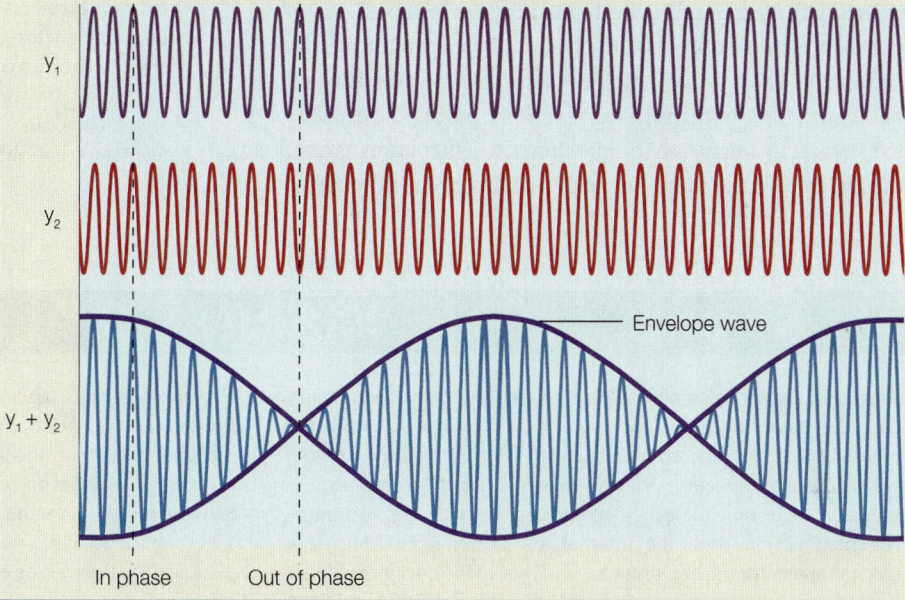

electrolocation if the beat frequency is similar to the signal from prey items. To avoid confusion, many species of wave-type electric fish express a behavior termed the jamming avoidance response. When two fish whose EODs have similar frequencies encounter each other, each fish will shift the frequency of its electrical discharge away from the frequency produced by the other individual. By doing this, they increase the frequency of the resulting beats and avoid generating low-frequency beats that are similar to the electric field disruption caused by prey items.

References

• Krahe, R., & Fortune, E. S. (2013). Electric fishes: Neural systems, behaviour and evolution. *Journal of Experimental Biology, 216*, 2363–2364.

• Kramer, B. (1999). Waveform discrimination, phase sensitivity and jamming avoidance in a wave-type electric fish. *Journal of Experimental Biology, 202*, 1387–1398.

• Rose, G. J. (2004). Insights into neural mechanisms and evolution of behaviour from electric fish. *Nature Reviews Neuroscience, 5*, 943–951.

• Sawtell, N. B., Williams, A., & Bell, C. C. (2005). From sparks to spikes: Information processing in the electrosensory systems of fish. *Current Opinion in Neurobiology, 15*, 437–443.

• Yu, N., Hupé, G. J., Garfinkle, C., Lewis, J. E., & Longtin, A. (2012). Coding conspecific identity and motion in the electric sense. *PLoS Computational Biology, 8*, e1002564.

in the activity of cryptochrome is hypothesized to influence the sensitivity of the retinal neurons, changing visual perception. In this way, it is possible that birds may "see" magnetic fields.

Because all animals possess cryptochromes, this opens the possibility that all animals have some ability to detect magnetic fields. When the cryptochrome gene in *Drosophila* is knocked out, the mutant flies are unable to orient in a magnetic field. Their ability to orient to the magnetic field can be restored by inserting the gene coding for human cryptochrome. This experiment demonstrates that the human cryptochrome has the capacity to act as a magnetic-field detector. However, it is not known whether humans have the sensory processing capacity to interpret this signal, so the question of whether humans have the ability to sense magnetic fields remains open, although to date most of the available evidence suggests that we are unable to navigate based on detection of magnetic fields.

CONCEPT CHECK

17. If the pit organs of a pit viper use the same receptor (TRPA1) as do nociceptors, why doesn't the viper detect pain rather than heat when it is tracking its prey?

18. The human retina contains functional cryptochromes that can rescue cryptochrome mutants in *Drosophila* and restore magnetoreception. But humans do not appear to have the ability to detect magnetic fields. In fact, in the absence of other directional cues, humans tend to walk in circles. How can we have functional cryptochromes but no magnetoreception?

SUMMARY

Animals have a variety of sensory receptors that they use to transduce the energy from incoming signals into changes in membrane potential that can be communicated to other parts of the nervous system. Sensory receptors can be classified based on the stimulus modality that they detect: Chemoreceptors sense environmental chemicals in both the internal and external environments; mechanoreceptors sense pressure changes; photoreceptors detect light; thermoreceptors detect temperature; electroreceptors detect electrical currents, and magnetoreceptors detect magnetic fields. Most receptors specifically detect only a single stimulus modality, but some receptors (including many of the pain-receptive nociceptors) are polymodal and can detect more than one type of stimulus. Sensory receptors can be as simple as a single cell embedded within a tissue such as skin, or can be organized into complex sensory organs such as the eyes or ears of vertebrates.

REVIEW QUESTIONS

1. **LO 1** What is the difference between a sense organ and a sensory receptor?

2. **LO 1** What are the primary stimulus modalities detected by animal sensory receptors?

3. **LO 2** Explain labeled-line coding and give an example of the kinds of sensory information that can be encoded by this method.

4. **LO 2** What is the relationship between the intensity of a stimulus and the response of the primary afferent neuron? How do neurons encode changes in stimulus intensity?

5. **LO 2** Many sensory systems encode stimuli logarithmically. Compare and contrast this approach with range fractionation.

6. **LO 3** Outline the similarities and differences between the receptors involved in the detection of odorants and the receptors involved in the detection of pheromones in mammals.

7. **LO 3** Outline the similarities and differences between the receptors involved in odorant detection in mammals and insects.

8. **LO 4** Compare and contrast the signal transduction mechanisms used by gustatory receptors to detect the primary types of tastants.

9. **LO 4** Compare the mammalian gustatory system with that in insects.

10. **LO 5** What are the major families of mechanoreceptor proteins involved in touch, proprioception, and hearing?

11. **LO 5** List four major types of vertebrate touch receptors and identify them as either slowly adapting or rapidly adapting receptors.

12. **LO 6** Using the vertebrate ear as an example, outline some of the ways in which sensory systems amplify environmental stimuli.

13. **LO 6** Outer hair cells respond to sounds, but they do not make synaptic connections with afferent neurons that carry sound information to the brain. What is their role in hearing?

14. **LO 7** Outline two possible scenarios for the evolution of animal photoreceptors.

15. **LO 7** Explain how the properties of vertebrate rods make them suitable for photoreception in dim light.

16. **LO 8** Explain the role of the following types of cells in the mammalian retina, using one or two sentences for each answer: rods, cones, horizontal cells, bipolar cells, amacrine cells, retinal ganglion cells.

17. **LO 8** Explain how changing the shape of the mammalian lens allows objects at different distances to be brought into focus.

18. **LO 9** Compare the receptors found in the pit organs of some snakes to the thermoreceptors found in other vertebrates.

19. **LO 9** Compare active electrolocation with echolocation.

SYNTHESIS QUESTIONS

1. Mechanoreceptors do not depolarize in response to light, no matter how intense the stimulus, but the eye responds to a mechanical stimulus (such as pressing on the eyeball) if the stimulus is sufficiently large. Why might this be?

2. Do taste receptors use labeled-line coding? Why or why not?

3. Receptors for fine touch are typically located in the shallow layers of the skin, while receptors for stronger touch stimuli are typically located in deeper layers. Why might this be so?

4. Hair cells have prominent cilia on their apical surface. Why do these cilia increase the sensitivity of a hair cell to mechanical stimuli?

5. Why do the inner ears of most vertebrates have three semicircular canals and not just one?

6. Peripheral vision is the ability to detect objects outside the center of the visual field. Vertebrates vary in the extent of their peripheral vision. What differences would you expect in the retina of an animal with excellent peripheral vision, compared to one with poor peripheral vision?

7. Humans have only three types of cone photoreceptors, but can distinguish thousands of colors. How is this possible?

8. What predictions could you make about what would happen to vision in an individual with a degenerative disease that destroyed the horizontal cells of the retina?

QUANTITATIVE QUESTIONS

1. You are studying a sensory receptor and find that the amplitude of the receptor (generator) potential increases linearly with the log of the stimulus intensity. The generator potential results in a train of action potentials whose frequency increases linearly with increasing generator potential (above the threshold value). You also observe that above a certain level, additional increases in stimulus intensity do not result in increases in action potential frequency.
   (a) Graph the results for generator potential amplitude and action potential frequency.
   (b) What do these results tell you about how this receptor encodes stimulus intensity?

2. One way in which the vertebrate auditory system detects the location of a sound is to compare the time at which a sound reaches one ear to the time at which that sound reaches the other ear.
   (a) How long would it take for a sound reaching the left side of the head to reach the right ear, assuming that the distance between the ears is approximately 12 cm and that the speed at which a sound travels through the head is approximately 1,000 m/s?
   (b) Neurotransmission takes approximately 10–20 milliseconds. Using this information and the value you calculated in part a, what are the implications for the localization of a sound?

3. The vertebrate olfactory system uses a combinatorial coding scheme in which each odorant receptor cell expresses only a single G protein–coupled odorant receptor, but in which each receptor can detect several odorants. You are a scientist working on a little-known vertebrate, the schmoo, and have discovered 100 functional olfactory G protein–coupled receptors in the schmoo genome. Assuming a simple combinatorial code, how many potential odorants could a schmoo distinguish if each receptor could detect 3 different odorants? What if each receptor could detect 5 different odorants? What is the minimum number of genes required to discriminate among 10,000 different odorants if each receptor can detect 2 different odorants?

8

Functional Organization of Nervous Systems

Learning Objectives

After reading this chapter, you should be able to:

1. Describe the organization of the nervous systems of the major animal phyla.

2. Outline the anatomy of the vertebrate central nervous system.

3. Describe the main functional regions of the vertebrate brain and the variation in these structures among vertebrate taxa.

4. Describe how the sympathetic, parasympathetic, and enteric branches of the autonomic nervous system work together to regulate body functions.

5. Compare and contrast somatic motor pathways and autonomic pathways.

6. Compare and contrast the mechanisms controlling involuntary and voluntary behaviors.

7. Explain the mechanisms involved in short- and long-term memory and learning.

8. Discuss how the brain helps to maintain homeostasis in many physiological systems.

FIGURE 8.1 **Bottlenose dolphins (*Tursiops truncatus*)**

Photo source: Canoneer/Fotolia.

Have you ever tried to stay up all night to study for an exam? With enough caffeine you could probably do it, but missing sleep is unlikely to lead to high achievement. After one night of missed sleep you will notice irritability, decreased alertness, and reduced performance on complex tasks such as exams. After two days without sleep most people are unable to concentrate, they become physically clumsy, and they begin to make mistakes even on simple tasks. After three days without any sleep, a person is likely to experience hallucinations and may start to lose their grasp on reality. Although we do not fully understand the functions of sleep, it is clear that sleep is somehow required to maintain brain function, and that the effects of sleep deprivation demonstrate the critical role that the brain plays in coordinating behavior.

Although all vertebrates require sleep to maintain effective brain function, bottlenose dolphins such as the ones shown in Figure 8.1 are able to stay awake, alert, and continuously active for fifteen days, without any decline in performance on complex tasks. Dolphins avoid the effects of sleep deprivation by letting one half of their brain sleep while the other half remains active. The half of the brain that stays alert is sufficient to coordinate behavior, and this allows the other half of the brain to benefit from the restorative properties of sleep. Although this type of sleep is found in several bird species, it is a very unusual ability in mammals, and is known only from marine mammals such as dolphins.

Maintaining a constant level of alertness may help dolphins to avoid predators, to maintain contact with other members of their social group so that they do not drift apart while asleep, or to avoid accidental drowning. Whatever the reason for this unusual sleep pattern, however, it serves to remind us that the complex behaviors of animals are coordinated by the nervous system, as are many involuntary physiological functions, and demonstrates the important role of the brain as a control center in animal nervous systems.

In this chapter we explore the evolution of nervous systems and how they control the diverse functions of the body, with a focus on the important role of the brain as a primary control center. ∎

LOOKING BACK 8

Before you begin this chapter, you should review Chapter 5: Neuron Structure and Function to ensure that you have a robust understanding of the mechanisms involved in electrical and chemical communication among neurons. You should also be familiar with the types of glial cells in different parts of the nervous system and their roles. Because the nervous system and the endocrine system interact in a variety of ways, you may also wish to review Chapter 4: Cell Signaling and Endocrine Regulation. In the current chapter we explore how signals from sensory systems are integrated by the nervous system to allow an animal to modify physiology and behavior, so you may also find it helpful to review Chapter 7: Sensory Systems, where we discuss the mechanisms that animals use to monitor their internal and external environments.

∎ OVERVIEW

The nervous system is one of the body's homeostatic control systems, helping to regulate physiological processes and coordinate behavior. But how do the many individual neurons that make up the nervous system work together to perform these complex tasks? Like other homeostatic control systems, the nervous system contains sensors, integrating centers, and output pathways (Figure 8.2). In Chapter 7: Sensory Systems, we discussed how sensory receptors detect incoming stimuli and convert the signal to a change in membrane potential. Afferent sensory neurons carry these signals to one or more *integrating centers*, such as a brain or ganglion. Integrating centers typically contain many **interneurons**, which (as the name suggests) form synaptic connections among neurons. The more interneurons that are added to a neural pathway, the greater the possibilities for interconnections, and the greater the ability to integrate information. The complex behavioral and physiological control systems of animals result from these multistep neural pathways, which find their most elaborate form in large integrating centers such as the mammalian brain. For example, an average human brain contains more than 80 billion neurons connected via trillions of synapses. Integrating centers ultimately send an output signal via **efferent neurons** to effector organs, including skeletal muscles, glands, and internal organs. Thus, the nervous system acts to sense environmental information, integrate this information, and coordinate the response.

In this chapter we first examine the general principles underlying the organization of nervous systems and survey the diversity of nervous systems among animal taxa. We then focus on the nervous systems of vertebrates, taking a closer look at the functions of the principal integrating centers of vertebrates—the brain and spinal cord—using mammals as an example. Next, we examine the vertebrate peripheral nervous system, looking at the organization of the efferent pathways that carry signals to effector organs. Finally, we end the chapter with a consideration of the integrated functions of nervous systems, addressing how sensory receptors, afferent neurons, integrating centers, and efferent pathways work together to allow organisms to perform complex behaviors and maintain physiological homeostasis.

FIGURE 8.2 **An overview of the organization of nervous systems**

Nervous systems contain sensors, integrating centers, and output pathways. Sensory receptors convert the energy from incoming stimuli of various kinds to changes in the membrane potential. Afferent neurons conduct these signals in the form of action potentials to integrating centers such as the brain or ganglia. Interneurons within the integrating centers process the information and send out signals via efferent neurons to effectors such as the muscles and internal organs, resulting in changes in behavior or physiological processes.

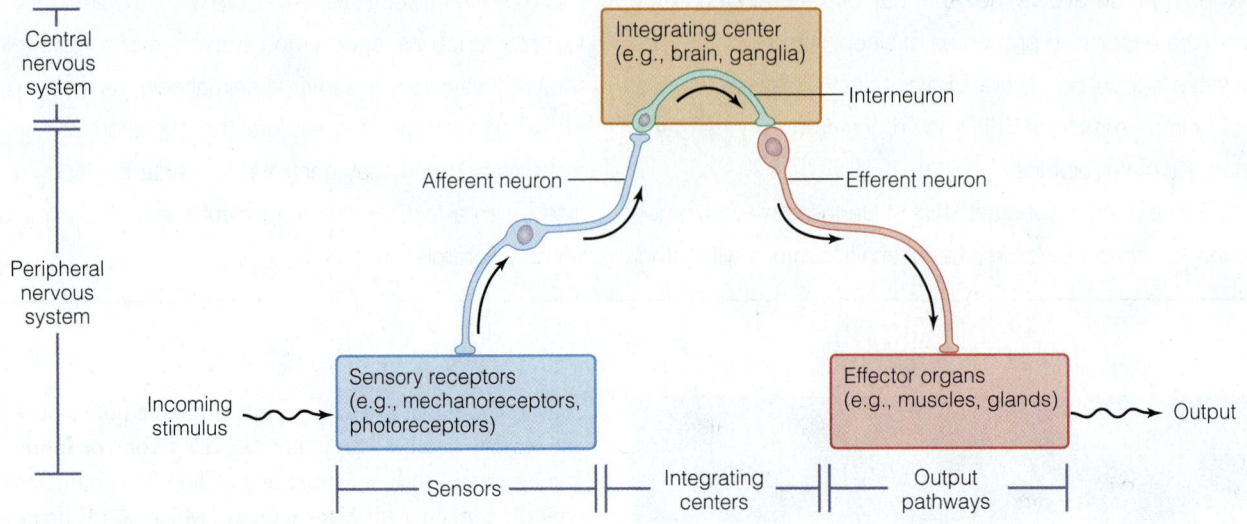

ORGANIZATION AND EVOLUTION OF NERVOUS SYSTEMS

Most nervous systems are organized into three functional divisions: an afferent sensory division; integrating centers; and an efferent division. In many organisms, the afferent and efferent divisions can be grouped together as the **peripheral nervous system**, while the integrating centers can be grouped together as the **central nervous system**. This distinction between the central and peripheral nervous systems arose in bilaterally symmetrical animals.

Figure 8.3 provides an overview of the organization of the nervous system of vertebrates. The central nervous system consists of the *brain* and the *spinal cord*, which are encased in a cartilaginous or bony covering. The **afferent division** of the peripheral nervous system carries signals from the periphery into the central nervous system. The brain and spinal cord integrate these signals and send out commands to the body via the **efferent division** of the peripheral nervous system. The efferent division can itself be divided into the **somatic nervous system**, which innervates skeletal muscle, and the **autonomic nervous system**, which innervates all other parts of the body. Vertebrates also have an **enteric nervous system** associated with the gut, which is regulated independently and also by the brain via the autonomic nervous system.

In general, organisms with more complex nervous systems have more neurons than organisms with less complex nervous systems. However, the total number of neurons is not necessarily larger in species with more complex integrating centers. For example, some species of flatworms have several thousand neurons, despite lacking an obvious brain. In contrast, the entire nervous system of the nematode *Caenorhabditis elegans* contains only 302 neurons and about 6,000 synapses, despite having a clearly recognizable brain. Thus, the relationship between the number of neurons and the organization of the nervous system is not always clear cut.

Evolution of Nervous Systems

Figure 8.4 shows the organization of nervous systems in the major animal phyla. Cnidarians are radially symmetrical animals with nervous systems that are interconnected into a large web (or **nerve net**) with neurons distributed throughout the body. Unlike the cnidarians, most animals are bilaterally symmetrical with sense organs and nervous integrating centers clustered at the anterior end of the body. This pattern of locating sense organs and nervous integrating centers at the anterior end of the body, known as **cephalization**, becomes increasingly apparent in more complex nervous systems. The radially symmetrical echinoderms represent the only exception to this pattern.

The nervous systems of bilaterally symmetrical animals typically contain one or more **ganglia**, which are groupings of neuronal cell bodies interconnected by synapses. Ganglia function as integrating centers for the nervous system. In many species, the ganglia in the anterior region of the body are grouped together into larger clusters

FIGURE 8.3 **Major divisions of vertebrate nervous systems**

Vertebrate nervous systems can be divided into the central nervous system (consisting of the brain and spinal cord) and the peripheral nervous system (consisting of afferent and efferent pathways). The efferent pathways of the peripheral nervous system can be further separated into two systems: the somatic motor division that initiates movement by stimulating skeletal muscles, and the autonomic division that regulates physiological functions. The autonomic division is divided into the sympathetic and parasympathetic nervous systems. The enteric nervous system, which regulates the digestive organs, is also considered part of the autonomic division, but it functions as a semi-autonomous nervous system.

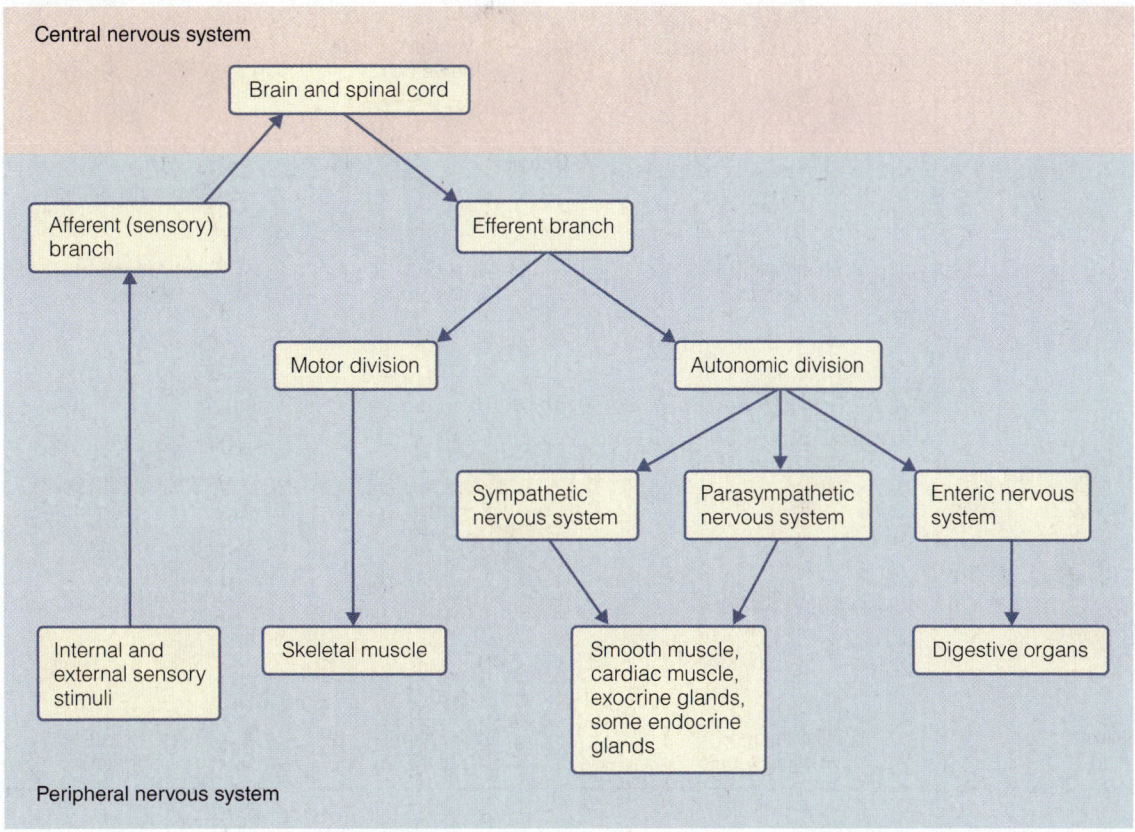

forming a **brain**, which is a complex integrating center. The degree of cephalization varies greatly among the bilaterally symmetrical invertebrates, although most species have a well-developed brain, several ganglia, and one or more nerve cords (Figure 8.4).

In invertebrates, bundles of axons that connect ganglia or run between a ganglion and the brain are called *connectives* or *commissures*. Within the brains of both vertebrates and invertebrates, groupings of neuronal cell bodies are termed **nuclei**, which are the functional equivalent of ganglia, and groupings of neuronal axons are called **tracts**. Outside of the integrating centers, the axons of afferent and efferent neurons are usually organized into structures called **nerves**, which are the functional equivalent of the tracts in the integrating centers.

Nerves can be complex structures. Figure 8.5 illustrates the structure of a vertebrate nerve, which consists of parallel bundles of myelinated and unmyelinated axons enclosed in several layers of connective tissue. Within a nerve, individual axons and their myelin sheaths (if present) are surrounded by the endoneurium. Individual axons within a nerve are often called nerve fibers. Many axons are bundled together into structures called fascicles by another layer of connective tissue, the perineurium. Several fascicles and blood vessels are grouped together, enclosed by a fibrous layer of connective tissue called the epineurium, forming the nerve. Most nerves contain axons of both afferent and efferent neurons, and are thus termed mixed nerves, although there are some purely afferent or purely efferent nerves.

Sponges lack a nervous system

The phylum Porifera (the sponges) is the only group of metazoans to lack neurons and a nervous system. However, in some sponges there is evidence of coordinated behavioral responses caused by electrical communication among cells. Sponges feed by generating a current of water through their body using the cilia of the choanocyte cells (see Chapter 2).

FIGURE 8.4 **Organization of the nervous system in representative animal groups**

The cnidarians have a nerve net, while all other groups (with the exception of the radially symmetrical echinoderms) display some degree of cephalization.

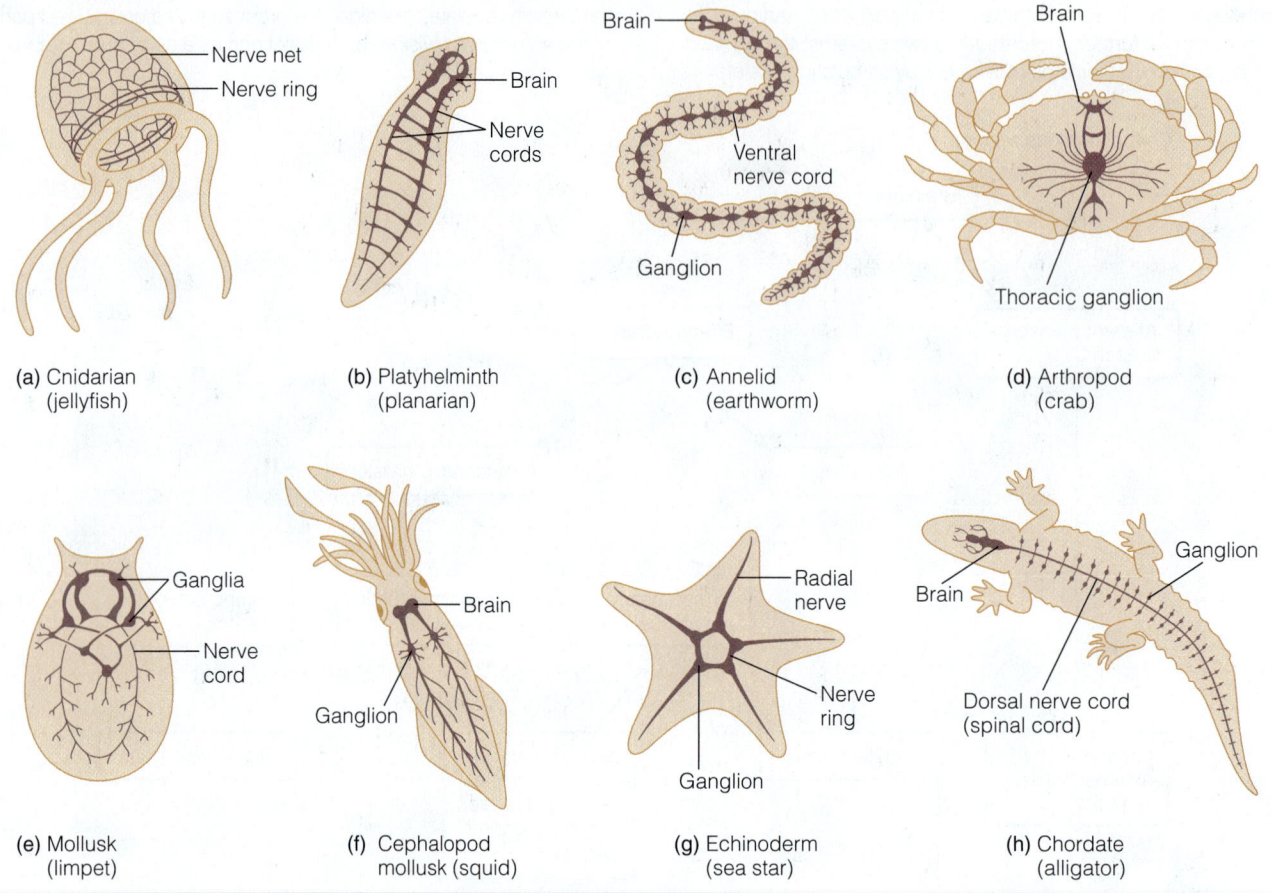

(a) Cnidarian (jellyfish)

(b) Platyhelminth (planarian)

(c) Annelid (earthworm)

(d) Arthropod (crab)

(e) Mollusk (limpet)

(f) Cephalopod mollusk (squid)

(g) Echinoderm (sea star)

(h) Chordate (alligator)

Electrical or mechanical stimuli cause this beating to stop in a coordinated fashion as a result of a signal carried by action potentials through a tissue called the *trabecular reticulum*, a thin, strandlike network of cells. These cells form a **syncytium**—a group of cells whose cytoplasms are functionally connected either directly or via gap junctions. Transmission of action potentials in sponges is slow compared with transmission of action potentials in a neuron, so electrical signals can take as much as a minute to travel through the trabecular reticulum, resulting in a substantial lag between signal and response in these animals.

Cnidarian nerve nets allow complex behaviors

Unlike the neurons in most other organisms, the neurons of the cnidarian nerve net (Figure 8.4a) are not specialized but can function as sensory neurons, interneurons, or efferent neurons, and can communicate synaptically at several points along their length. Cnidarian neurons often form *en passant* synapses (see Chapter 5: Neuron Structure and Function), allowing information to be passed in either direction across

the synapse. In fact, many cnidarian neurons are functionally bipolar, in that a stimulus at any point on the organism triggers an impulse that radiates out from the stimulus site in every direction.

The organization of the nerve net varies among cnidarians, with species such as the freshwater *Hydra* having relatively diffuse nerve nets, whereas in other species the neurons are organized into linear tracts or circular nerve rings. The nerve rings can be concentrated around the oral opening, or in other locations. The groupings of neurons within the nerve net are thought to act as integrating centers. In some species the nerve net is broken down into several pathways with characteristic conduction speeds that control different behavioral responses. In fact, in many species of cnidarians epithelial cells can also generate action potentials, and are connected via gap junctions, adding yet another layer of complexity. However, no species of cnidarian has a grouping of neurons equivalent to a large ganglion or brain.

Despite lacking an obvious brain, cnidarians can perform some rather complex behaviors. For example, the sea

FIGURE 8.5 **The structure of a vertebrate nerve**

A nerve is composed of groups of axons from many neurons surrounded by successive layers of connective tissue (the endoneurium, perineurium, and epineurium).

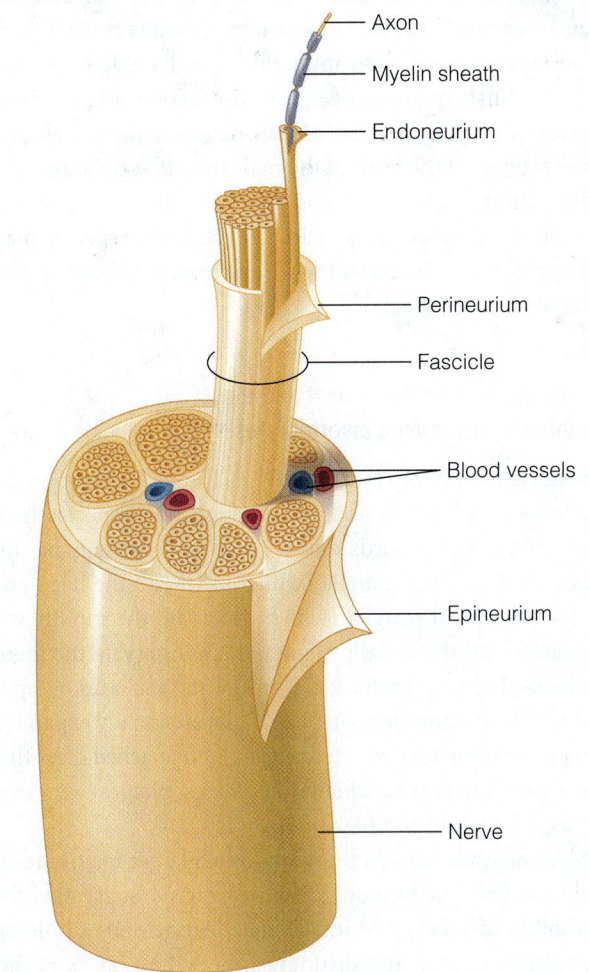

- Axon
- Myelin sheath
- Endoneurium
- Perineurium
- Fascicle
- Blood vessels
- Epineurium
- Nerve

(Figure 8.4b) as well as one or more plexuses. Depending on the species, there may be additional nerve cords as well. Some species of flatworms lack an obvious brain, while others have a well-developed brain that allows them to perform complex behaviors and even learn tasks such as navigating a maze.

Nematodes and annelids show substantial cephalization

Nemertine, nematode, and annelid worms have a more structured nervous system than flatworms, with a well-developed brain, ganglia in each body segment, and one or more nerve cords that communicate information between the tissues and the various integrating centers, which gives their nervous systems a ladderlike appearance (Figure 8.4c). The nematode *C. elegans* is an important model system for the study of nervous system development, and their nervous systems are particularly well understood. The hermaphroditic form of this species has a total of 959 cells in the adult body, of which 302 are neurons. Even with this small nervous system, *C. elegans* is capable of quite complex behaviors, including locomotion, foraging, feeding, and moving toward or away from specific stimuli such as chemicals, odorants, food sources, temperatures, and other nematodes.

Unlike in the vertebrates (and many other organisms) the developmental trajectory of the *C. elegans* nervous system is fixed, which means that the neural anatomy of *C. elegans* is very similar among individuals. This property has allowed researchers to map out all of the connections among the neurons in the nervous system. The nervous system is divided into two sections: a pharyngeal nervous system and a somatic nervous system (with 20 and 282 neurons, respectively, in hermaphrodites). There are approximately 6,400 chemical synapses, 900 gap junction synapses, and 1,500 neuromuscular junctions. Consistent with the trend of cephalization, the cell bodies of the neurons of both nervous systems are concentrated in the head region, organized into a series of ganglia surrounding the pharynx.

THE ARTHROPOD NERVOUS SYSTEM CONTAINS SEGMENTAL GANGLIA

The arthropod nervous system (Figure 8.4d) contains a brain, a ventral nerve cord, and a series of segmental ganglia. In some species there is a ganglion in each body segment, giving the nervous system a ladderlike appearance, while in other species the ganglia from several body segments may be fused. For example, in crabs such as the one shown in Figure 8.4d the segmental ganglia are concentrated in two major integrating centers: the brain and the thoracic ganglion.

anemone *Calliactis parasitica* attaches its tentacles onto a mollusk shell and somersaults onto the shell (Figure 8.6), a behavior that involves detecting a shell, using its tentacles to grab onto the shell, detaching its foot from the substrate, making coordinated movements of the whole body to somersault up onto the shell, and reattaching its foot onto the shell. Thus, the apparent simplicity of the cnidarian nerve net hides substantial complexities.

Nervous system complexity varies among flatworms

Flatworms (phylum Platyhelminthes) are the simplest of the bilaterally symmetrical animals. There is substantial diversity in the complexity of the nervous system among the 20,000 species of flatworms. Some species have only a nerve net, or **plexus**, and no obvious ganglia or brain. In other species of flatworms, the nervous system is arranged in a ladderlike pattern with two longitudinal nerve cords connected by commissures

FIGURE 8.6 **Nerve nets and complex behaviors**

(a) Cutaway view of a sea anemone, showing the nervous system. The cnidarian nervous system is diffuse, composed of a loosely organized nerve net. **(b)** Shell-climbing behavior in a sea anemone, *Calliactis parasitica.* Despite their seemingly simple nervous systems, cnidarians can perform complex behaviors.

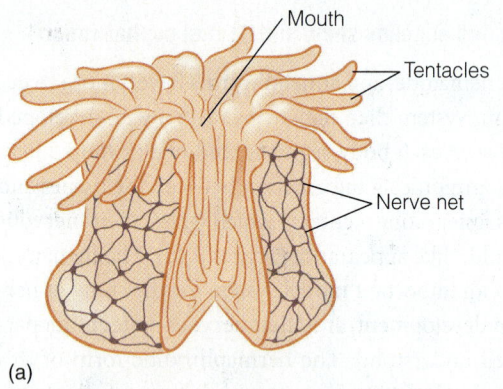

Mouth

Tentacles

Nerve net

(a)

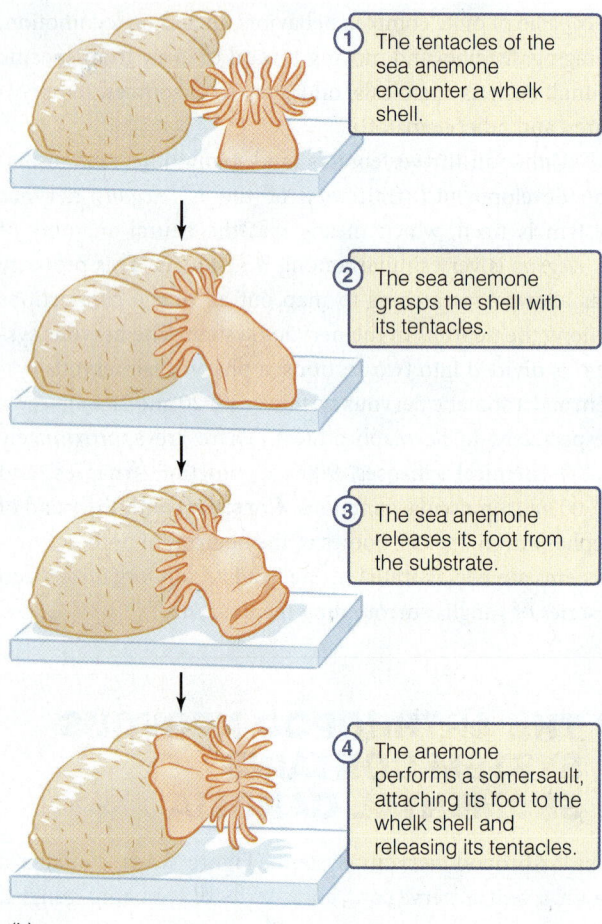

1 The tentacles of the sea anemone encounter a whelk shell.

2 The sea anemone grasps the shell with its tentacles.

3 The sea anemone releases its foot from the substrate.

4 The anemone performs a somersault, attaching its foot to the whelk shell and releasing its tentacles.

(b)

Insects conform to the general nervous system plan of other arthropods. All insects have a dorsally located brain at the anterior end connected to a ventral nerve cord and a series of segmental ganglia. The number of ganglia varies among species. For example, in the house fly *Musca domestica,* all of the ganglia in the chest and abdomen are joined together in a single thoracic ganglion.

The ganglia in each segment play a major role in coordinating behaviors associated with the body parts of that segment. As a result, the nervous system of an insect tends to be quite decentralized, with individual ganglia able to control and coordinate quite complex behaviors. For example, in one species of praying mantis (*Mantis religiosa*) the female frequently bites off the head of the male during copulation. The male mantis continues to copulate with the female mantis even in the absence of its head. In fact, in this species mating may be more successful when the male is beheaded than when its head is intact.

Cephalopods have the largest and most complex brains among invertebrates

The nervous system varies greatly in complexity among the mollusks (Figure 8.4e and f), although most species have dual ventral nerve cords and a series of large ganglia, including the cerebral ganglia (which innervate the head and neck), the buccal ganglia (which innervate the mouth and stomach), and the pedal ganglia (which innervate the foot). In the cephalopod mollusks (a group that includes octopus and squid), the anterior pairs of ganglia are greatly expanded and placed close together to create a tightly packed mass that lies between the eyes and encircles the esophagus—in other words, a large and complex brain.

An octopus has a brain that is much larger relative to its body size than the brain of a fish or a reptile, suggesting the possibility of substantial intelligence. An octopus can learn to navigate a maze and distinguish between objects of different shapes, sizes, and degrees of brightness. Some studies indicate that an octopus can even learn by simply watching another octopus perform a task. Although an octopus has a very large brain, it has another important integrating center: Each arm has a large ganglion that controls arm movements and that can function essentially independently of the brain. When researchers severed the connections between the brain and the arm of an octopus and then stimulated the skin on the arm, the arm behaved exactly as it would have in an intact octopus. Thus, the integrating center of an octopus is actually highly distributed and involves both the brain and the ganglia.

The echinoderms lack an obvious brain

The echinoderms (sea stars and their relatives) are one of the few exceptions to the general trend of increasing cephalization in animals (Figure 8.4g). These radially symmetrical animals lack an obvious brain, and instead have a series of ganglia and several nerve rings. Echinoderms are descended from a bilaterally symmetrical ancestor that likely had some cephalization. Presumably, present-day echinoderms lost this ancestral cephalization during the transition to a radially symmetrical body plan. In fact, many modern echinoderm groups have bilaterally symmetrical larvae that develop radial symmetry during metamorphosis to the adult form.

Vertebrates have a hollow dorsal nerve cord

Unlike the solid, ventrally located nerve cords found in most invertebrates, the chordates have a hollow nerve cord located on the dorsal side of the body (Figure 8.4h). The chordate nerve cord is hollow because it forms from a sheet of ectoderm that is rolled into a tube that ultimately develops into the brain, at the anterior end, and the **spinal cord** in the body. Although the developmental trajectory and structure of vertebrate and invertebrate nerve cords is very different, recent molecular evidence suggests that the molecular underpinnings of central nervous system development are very similar. These data reveal a deep homology between the central nervous systems of vertebrates and invertebrates and suggest that the common ancestor of both protostomes and deuterostomes may have had a nervous system that was organized into central and peripheral divisions.

Vertebrates are among the most highly cephalized organisms, with large and complex brains relative to their body size. Large mammals such as whales and elephants may have as many as 10^{11} neurons in their brains.

CONCEPT CHECK

1. Do cnidarians have clearly defined afferent neurons, interneurons, and efferent neurons?
2. What is cephalization?
3. What is the difference between a neuron and a nerve?

THE CNS OF VERTEBRATES

The central nervous system (CNS) acts as the primary integrating center and plays a major role in coordinating behavior and helping to maintain homeostasis. In vertebrates, the CNS consists of the spinal cord and brain.

Anatomy of the Vertebrate CNS

Both the brain and the spinal cord are made up of layers of neural tissue surrounding a fluid-filled central cavity that is lined with an epithelium. As we discussed in Chapter 5: Neuron Structure and Function, the neurons of the CNS are associated with glial cells. In fact, glial cells outnumber neurons in the vertebrate CNS. About 65 percent of the cells in the brain of a mouse, about 90 percent of the cells in a human brain, and 97 percent of the cells in an elephant brain are glia.

In vertebrates, the delicate neural tissue of the CNS is protected in a variety of ways:

1. It is encased in bone or cartilage.
2. It is surrounded by a protective membrane called the **meninges**.
3. It floats in a cushioning fluid called **cerebrospinal fluid** (CSF).
4. It is physiologically separated from the rest of the body by the **blood-brain barrier**.

The vertebrate CNS is encased in cartilage or bone

In the vertebrates, the brain is enclosed within the **skull**, and the spinal cord is located within the **vertebral column** (Figure 8.7). In cartilaginous fish, such as sharks, skates, and rays, the skull and vertebral column are made of cartilage, but in most vertebrates they are constructed of bone. The **cranial nerves** exit the central nervous system directly from the braincase, whereas the **spinal nerves** emerge from the spinal cord at regular intervals. Some of the cranial nerves bring in afferent information from the sense organs, whereas other nerves send efferent signals out to effector organs, such as muscles, glands, and organs.

The spinal nerves are named based on the region of the spine where they originate. The cervical spinal nerves emerge from the spinal cord in the region of the neck and innervate the head, neck, arms, hands, and **diaphragm**. The thoracic spinal nerves emerge from the spinal cord in the chest region, and innervate the intercostal muscles (involved in breathing) and the heart. The lumbar, sacral, and coccygeal spinal nerves emerge in the lower back and pelvis and innervate the legs, pelvis, bladder, and bowel.

Although the spinal nerves emerge from the vertebral column along its entire length, the spinal cord itself does not reach all the way down into the lumbar region in humans. Instead, the lumbar, sacral, and coccygeal nerves branch out from the spinal cord and travel down the vertebral column to the point where they exit. Thus, the bottom third of the vertebral column contains spinal nerves but no spinal cord.

The meninges surround the CNS

One or more protective layers of connective tissue called the **meninges** (singular: meninx) surround the brain and spinal cord (Figure 8.8). Fish have only a single thin meninx, whereas amphibians, reptiles, and birds have two: a thick outer layer called the dura mater and a thin secondary meninx. Mammals have three meninges. Like the other tetrapods they have the dura mater, but the secondary meninx is divided into a weblike middle layer called the arachnoid mater and a

FIGURE 8.7 **Structure of the vertebrate central nervous system**

(a) The brain and spinal cord. The central nervous system is composed of the brain and spinal cord, enclosed in a cartilaginous or bony covering (the skull and spine). The cranial nerves emerge from the braincase, whereas the spinal nerves emanate from the spinal cord at regular intervals. These nerves are part of the peripheral nervous system. **(b)** Cross-section of a mammalian spinal cord. The spinal cord contains both gray and white matter. Afferent sensory neurons enter the spinal cord on the dorsal side, and efferent neurons exit the spinal cord on the ventral side.

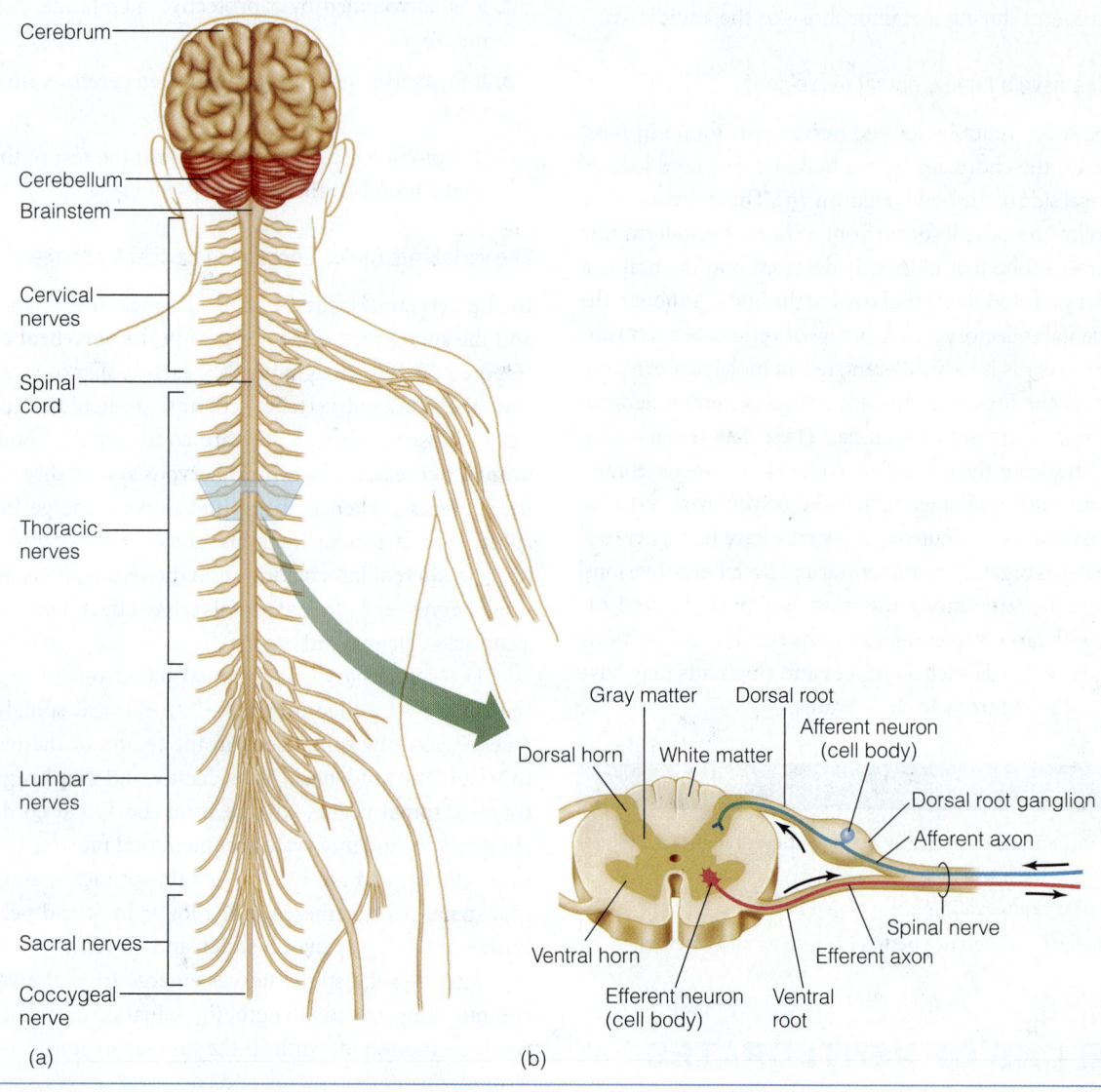

(a)

Cerebrum
Cerebellum
Brainstem
Cervical nerves
Spinal cord
Thoracic nerves
Lumbar nerves
Sacral nerves
Coccygeal nerve

(b)

Gray matter   Dorsal root
Dorsal horn   White matter
Afferent neuron (cell body)
Dorsal root ganglion
Afferent axon
Ventral horn
Spinal nerve
Efferent axon
Efferent neuron (cell body)   Ventral root

thin inner layer called the *pia mater*. Within the meninges, the brain and spinal cord float in a plasmalike fluid called **cerebrospinal fluid (CSF)** that acts as a shock absorber and cushions the delicate tissues of the central nervous system.

The CNS is physiologically separated from the rest of the body

The vertebrate central nervous system is also physiologically separated from the rest of the body. The **blood-brain barrier**, which is formed by tight junctions between the endothelial cells lining the brain capillaries, prevents materials from leaking out of the bloodstream and into the central nervous system via paracellular pathways (between the cells). In addition, these cells do not perform pinocytosis, so the only ways that substances can move into the brain are by directly dissolving in the membrane or by catalyzed transport via a protein exchanger, channel, or pump. Small, lipid-soluble molecules such as ethanol and some barbiturate drugs can cross directly into the central nervous system, but most substances are excluded. However, a number of specialized carrier transport systems allow the brain to

FIGURE 8.8 **The meninges**

The meninges are protective membranes that surround the brain. Mammals have three meninges, whereas other species have fewer.

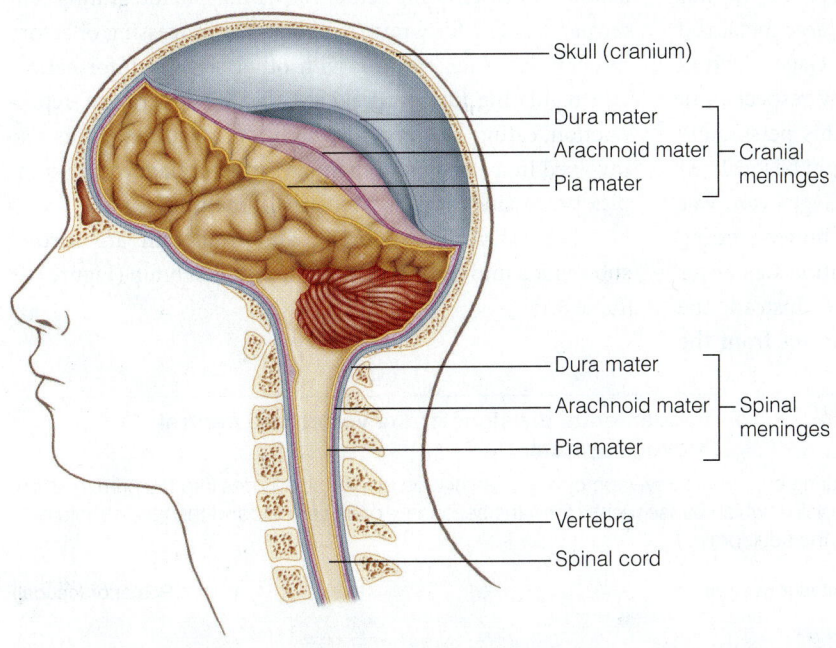

- Skull (cranium)
- Dura mater ⎫
- Arachnoid mater ⎬ Cranial meninges
- Pia mater ⎭
- Dura mater ⎫
- Arachnoid mater ⎬ Spinal meninges
- Pia mater ⎭
- Vertebra
- Spinal cord

is similar to that seen in the spinal cord. In mammals this pattern is reversed, and the gray matter in the brain is found on the surface, while the inner parts of the brain are mostly composed of white matter, except for the **basal nuclei**, which are regions of gray matter deep within the brain. The pattern of gray and white matter in birds is more complex, and differs from that of both reptiles and mammals.

The fact that we can see distinct regions of gray and white matter in the CNS indicates that the cell bodies of neurons are located in clusters in specific regions of the brain. Computational modeling suggests that this arrangement may maximize computational complexity by allowing the large numbers of connections among neurons, while simultaneously maximizing the speed of signal conduction.

The spinal cord mediates information flow between the brain and body

The spinal cord is the primary pathway for information flow between the brain and the rest of the body. In addition, the spinal cord also contains a number of complete neural circuits (afferent pathways, interneurons, and efferent pathways) that can control behavior independently of the brain.

In cross-section, the gray matter of the spinal cord often has a butterfly-shaped appearance, a pattern that is particularly evident in humans (see Figure 8.7). The "wings" of this butterfly are termed the **dorsal** and **ventral horns**. Afferent sensory neurons from the periphery terminate in the dorsal horn, where they synapse on interneurons or efferent neurons. The cell bodies of these unipolar sensory neurons are located outside the spinal cord in the **dorsal root ganglia**. Efferent neurons originate in the ventral horn of the spinal cord and exit through the *ventral root*.

take up circulating nutrients such as glucose and amino acids. Thus, the blood-brain barrier protects the brain from harmful substances while allowing useful molecules to enter. There are several areas of the brain where the blood-brain barrier is more permeable. In particular, the regions around the pineal gland, the pituitary gland, and parts of the hypothalamus are quite permeable, allowing secreted molecules such as hormones to leave the brain and enter the circulatory system, and allowing receptors in the brain to monitor the composition of the blood.

The CNS contains gray and white matter

At a macroscopic level the CNS appears to consist of two types of tissue, the **gray matter** and the **white matter**. White matter consists of bundles of axons and their associated myelin sheaths. The fatty tissue of the myelin sheath gives white matter its color. Gray matter is composed of neuronal cell bodies and dendrites and a variety of associated glial cells, such as astrocytes and oligodendrocytes, which lack the characteristic fatty deposits of the myelin sheath and thus appear gray.

The separation of the CNS into gray and white matter is found in all vertebrates. In the spinal cord the gray matter is found in the center of the spinal cord, with white matter to the outside. The positioning of the white and gray matter in the brain differs among vertebrates. In fish, amphibians, and reptiles, the organization of the white and gray matter in the brain

CONCEPT CHECK

4. Compare and contrast the meninges and the blood-brain barrier.
5. Compare and contrast gray matter and white matter.

The Vertebrate Brain

Our earliest understanding of the function of the brain was derived from studies of individuals who survived traumatic brain injuries, tumors, or strokes. Observation of such individuals suggested that injuries to specific parts of the brain resulted in specific functional deficits. One of the most famous cases of this sort was that of Phineas Gage, who suffered a brain injury when a blasting charge that he was preparing accidentally exploded and drove a large metal rod called a tamping iron into his skull in 1848. Gage survived the accident and was still functional in many respects, but his brain injuries were reputed to have left his personality changed, suggesting that personality traits might be localized to a specific region of the brain. Although Gage's case was famous, it only indirectly contributed to our understanding of brain regionalization, as his medical condition was never fully documented in the scientific literature. Instead, the careful work of multiple scientists and physicians from the mid-1800s to the present has gradually revealed the important functions of the different regions of the brain.

Vertebrate brains have three main regions

During embryonic development, both the brain and the spinal cord of vertebrates are formed from a simple hollow tube of ectoderm-derived cells called the neural tube. The posterior portion of the neural tube forms the spinal cord, while the anterior end of the neural tube develops three swellings that ultimately form the brain (Figure 8.9). These three regions, which are found in all vertebrate brains, are called the **hindbrain**, or *rhombencephalon*, the **midbrain**, or *mesencephalon*, and the **forebrain**, or *prosencephalon*. As the brain continues to develop, the primary brain vesicles form the secondary vesicles, which ultimately lead to the major regions of the brain. Because the vertebrate brain is simply an extension of the spinal cord, it is also hollow on the inside. These central cavities are called the **ventricles**, and they are filled with cerebrospinal fluid. Ciliated ependymal cells, a type of glial cell (see Chapter 5: Neuron Structure and Function), circulate the cerebrospinal fluid through the ventricles and the spinal cord.

The hindbrain controls most reflex responses and regulates involuntary behaviors such as breathing and the maintenance of body position. The midbrain

is predominantly involved in coordinating visual, auditory, and sensory information from touch and pressure receptors (although in mammals, as we shall see later in the chapter, it acts largely as a routing center rather than an integrating center per se). The forebrain is involved in processing olfactory information, integrating it with other sensory information, and regulating functions such as body temperature, reproduction, eating, sleeping, and emotion. The forebrain is also involved in learning and memory, and performs other complex processing tasks, particularly in mammals.

The forebrain, midbrain, and hindbrain are further subdivided into specific regions in the adult brain (Figure 8.9; Table 8.1).

FIGURE 8.9 Fundamental divisions of the vertebrate central nervous system

During embryonic development, the neural tube quickly subdivides into the primary brain vesicles, which subsequently form the secondary brain vesicles and then the structures of the adult brain.

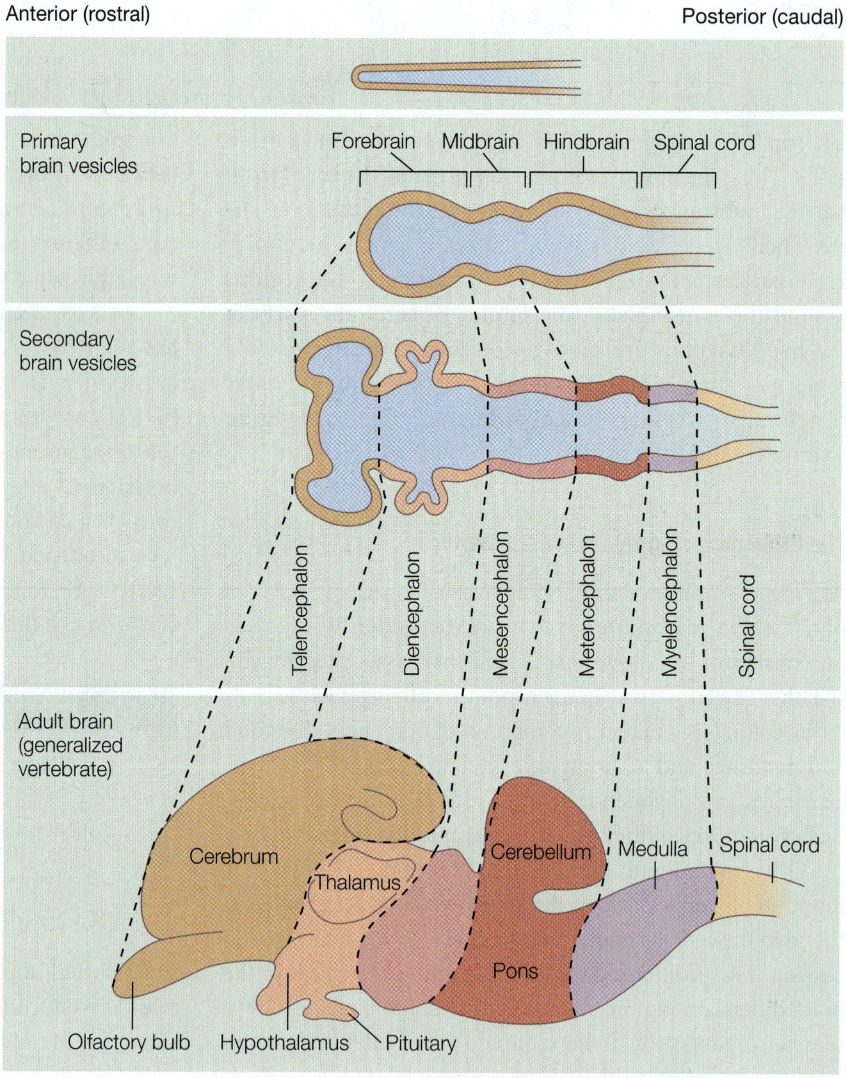

Table 8.1 The parts of the vertebrate brain and their functions

Structure	Function
Forebrain: Telencephalon	
Cerebrum	Information processing
• Basal ganglia	• Movements
• Amygdala	• Emotions
• Hippocampus	• Memory
Olfactory bulb	Sense of smell
Accessory olfactory bulb	Detection of pheromones
Forebrain: Diencephalon	
Thalamus	Integrates sensory information
Hypothalamus, pituitary	Homeostatic regulation (e.g., body temperature, feeding, reproduction, hunger and thirst), circadian rhythms, sleep-wake cycles
Epithalamus	Melatonin secretion, circadian rhythms, regulation of limbic system
Midbrain	
Tectum (optic lobes)	Processes visual, auditory, and touch information
Tegmentum	Reflex responses to visual, auditory, and touch information
Hindbrain	
Medulla oblongata	Generates rhythmic breathing, regulates heart rate and blood pressure
Pons	Regulates breath-holding, integrates among areas
Cerebellum	Maintains body posture, coordinates locomotion, integrates information from proprioceptors

Brain size varies among vertebrates

Brain size varies greatly among vertebrates (Figure 8.10), but much of this variation can be accounted for by differences in body size because larger animals tend to have larger brains. But at any given body size, brain size can differ substantially among taxa. In particular, birds and mammals have unusually large brains for their body size—six to ten times larger than those of similarly sized reptiles. Presumably, organisms with large brains relative to their body size have more complex integrating centers and an expanded repertoire of behaviors. Box 8.1: Math in Physiology: Brain Size and Brain Complexity explores these issues in more detail.

FIGURE 8.10 Brain size and body mass

The relationship between brain size and body mass for representative animal groups is plotted on a double logarithmic scale. Each polygon encloses data from a major vertebrate group. For each group, the polygon rises toward the right, showing that brain size tends to increase with body size.

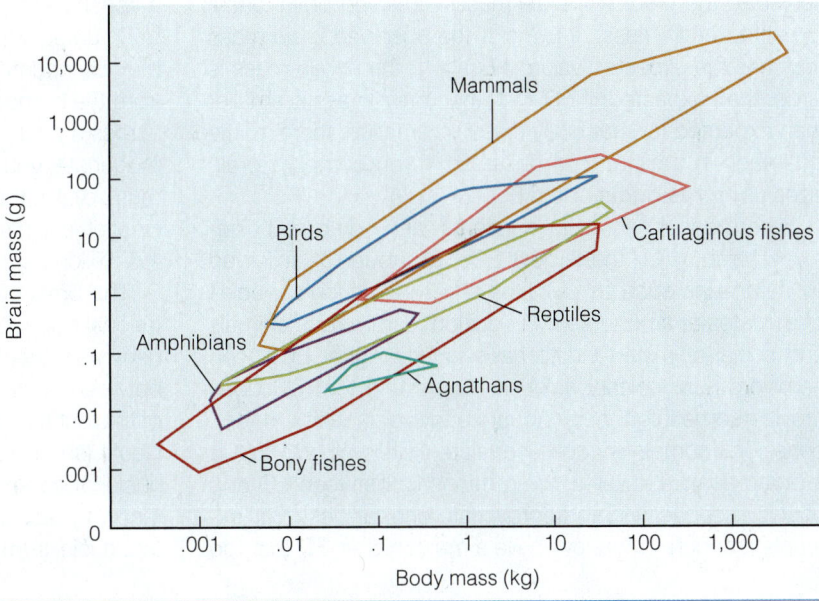

BRAIN SIZE AND BRAIN COMPLEXITY

Mammalian brains range from less than 0.05 grams in the smallest shrews to as much as 9 kilograms in sperm whales, but the functional significance of this variation is very poorly understood. Are larger brains more complex? Do they provide greater cognitive capacity? The answers to these questions have been surprisingly difficult to obtain, as it is not at all clear how best to compare brains among species.

One way to compare brains would be to simply look at the size of the brain. However, there is no correlation between the absolute size of the brain and the cognitive ability of a mammal. For example, although the mass of a rhesus macaque's brain is about 95 grams and a cow's brain is around 450 grams, monkeys have much higher cognitive capacity than do cows.

One way to factor out the body mass effect when comparing brain sizes would be to use the concept of allometry (see Chapter 1: Introduction to Physiological Principles). Many anatomical and physiological factors increase with body size according to a power function of the form:

$$y = aM^b$$

In the case of the relationship between brain mass and body mass, y = brain mass, M = body mass, a is a constant, and b is the scaling coefficient. By taking the log of both sides of the equation, you obtain the equation for a straight line with the scaling coefficient as the slope. ($\log y = b \log M + \log a$).

This scaling equation can be used to determine the predicted mass of the brain of an animal of a given mass. Neuroanatomists then used this value to compute the **encephalization quotient (EQ)**, which is the ratio of the observed to the predicted brain mass (Observed brain mass: Expected brain mass). If EQ is 1, the observed brain mass matches the expected value; if EQ > 1, then brain mass is larger than expected; if EQ < 1, then brain mass is smaller than expected for that body mass. In practice, there is little difference in the patterns observed if you compare brain sizes using **residuals** or the EQ.

When encephalization quotients are compared, humans have by far the largest EQs, at around 7, followed by cetaceans such as dolphins at 5, and various species of primates at around 2–3. In addition, carnivorous animals and social animals tend to have slightly higher EQs than herbivorous or solitary animals, suggesting that EQ does provide some information about cognitive capacity. In fact, behavioral complexity does correlate quite well with EQ at a broad scale. However, the relationship between EQ and cognitive capacity is an approximate one, at best. For example, capuchin monkeys have a much higher EQ than do

gorillas, but gorillas are thought to have much higher cognitive capacity.

One of the problems with calculating EQs is that the value obtained depends on the taxa used to calculate the regression line. For example, in primates the scaling coefficient of the regression of brain mass against body mass is close to 1.0, while in cetaceans it is 0.38, and for all mammalian orders considered together it is closer to 0.75. If you used the scaling coefficient for primates, you would find that the human brain is about 10 percent larger than the expected value for a primate, whereas if you use the scaling coefficient for all mammals, the human brain is two to three times as big as those of other primates.

The data used to generate the regression can also be a problem. Each data point in the regression represents an entire species, but we seldom have reliable data on the average brain mass and body mass of a species. Also, body mass can vary greatly between, or even within, individuals. Consider a human being that gains weight so that his or her body mass changes from 75 kilograms to 150 kilograms. A change in weight does not change cognitive capacity, but the EQ of this person would drop from 6.56 to 4.14.

Perhaps a better way to compare brain complexity would be to directly measure the number of neurons in the brains of different species. Unfortunately, until recently it was very difficult to accurately estimate the number of neurons in a vertebrate brain. A new technique pioneered by Dr. Suzana Herculano-Houzel and her colleagues has changed this.

Dr. Herculano-Houzel's technique involves taking a whole brain and gently homogenizing it to disrupt the cell membranes but not the nuclei. If you stain the nuclei with a specific stain called DAPI, the number of nuclei can then be counted using a fluorescent microscope or flow cytometer. By counting the number of nuclei in multiple samples from the homogenate, taking the average number of nuclei across samples, and multiplying by the total volume of homogenate, you can estimate the total number of nuclei (and thus cells) in the brain. Using this technique, Dr. Herculano-Houzel estimates that the human brain contains about 170 billion cells.

The brain contains both neurons and glia, and computational capacity is likely to be a function of the number of neurons rather than the total number of cells. To distinguish between neurons and glia, the technique takes advantage of the fact that the nuclei of neurons contain a protein called NeuN (short for neuronal nuclei) that is not present in the nuclei of non-neural cells. You can stain nuclei using a fluorescently labeled antibody against NeuN to specifically detect nuclei from neurons. Of the 170 billion cells in the brain, about 86 billion are neurons and 84 billion are non-neuronal cells such as glia.

Dr. Herculano-Houzel has used this technique to compare the number of neurons in the brains of primates and rodents (Figure 8.11). It has long been known that primates have larger brains for their body size than do rodents, but Dr. Herculano-Houzel's data revealed a surprise. If we compare rodents and primates with similar-sized brains, the primates have far more neurons per gram of brain than do rodents. Taking these two factors together, a 3-kilogram capuchin monkey has more than double the number of neurons in the brain than does a 50-kilogram capybara.

Counting the number of neurons in the brain also revealed that the scaling rules for the brain differ between rodents and primates. In rodents, neuron density decreases with body size. The brain of an agouti has about 48 million neurons per gram of brain, while the brain of a capybara has about 21 million neurons per gram of brain. In contrast, in primates the slope of the scaling relationship is much shallower, so larger brains have a similar number of neurons per gram as do smaller brains.

Dr. Herculano-Houzel's data indicate that primate brains are built more economically than are the brains of rodents, with more neurons per unit area. The resulting tighter packing of neurons could account for the high cognitive capacity of primate brains by allowing more synapses to form. The human brain, however, is not particularly exceptional for a primate brain. Our brains have more neurons compared with that of a rhesus macaque (86 billion versus 64 billion neurons), but this is what would be expected for a primate of our size.

But what about the great apes? Gorillas and orangutans have body sizes similar to or larger than those of humans, but their brains are only about one-third the size of ours and contain about 29 billion neurons. The lower number of neurons in the brains of gorillas and orangutans compared with humans is associated with their lower level of cognitive complexity. The relationship between brain size and neuron number in gorillas and orangutans is similar to that in all primates, but their brains are much smaller than would be expected based on their body size. These data suggest that the brains of great apes are not unusual for primates, but that their bodies are much bigger than would be expected.

FIGURE 8.11 Body size, brain size, and neuron numbers in rodents and primates with similar brain sizes

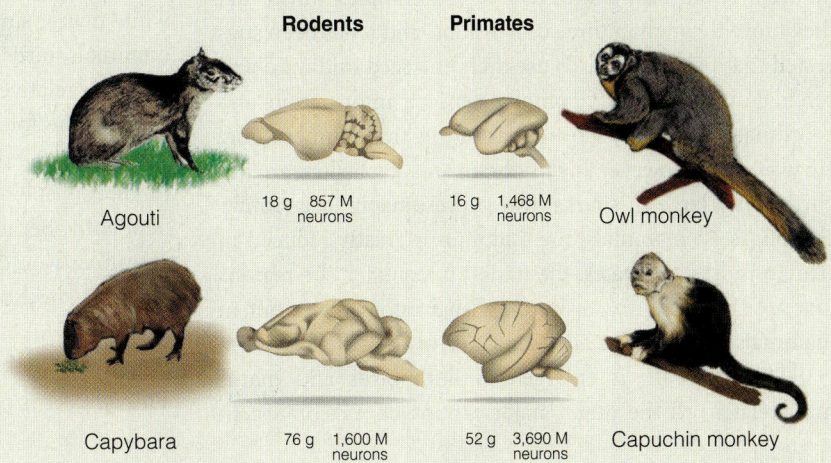

Rodents	Primates

Agouti — 18 g 857 M neurons

Owl monkey — 16 g 1,468 M neurons

Capybara — 76 g 1,600 M neurons

Capuchin monkey — 52 g 3,690 M neurons

Figure source: Herculano-Houzel, S. (2009). The human brain in numbers: a linearly scaled-up primate brain. *Front. Hum. Neurosci.* 3:31. doi: 10.3389/neuro.09.031.2009. (c) 2009.

It is possible that great apes have undergone selection for increased body size, possibly due to sexual selection or male-male competition.

At present, the number of neurons in the brain has only been measured for a relatively small number of species, so it remains to be seen whether neuron number is a strong predictor of cognitive complexity across a broader sample of mammals. However, this approach of counting neurons holds the promise of helping to reveal some of the mysteries of cognition and brain complexity.

References

1. Herculano-Houzel, S. (2009). The human brain in numbers: A linearly scaled-up primate brain. *Frontiers in Neuroscience, 31*, 1–11.

2. Herculano-Houzel, S. (2012). The remarkable, yet not extraordinary, human brain as a scaled-up primate brain and its associated cost. *Proceedings of the National Academy of Sciences USA, 109*, Supplement 1, 10661–10668.

3. Herculano-Houzel, S., Collins, C. E., Wong, P., & Kaas, H. (2007). Cellular scaling rules for primate brains. *Proceedings of the National Academy of Sciences USA, 104*, 3562–3567.

4. Herculano-Houzel, S., & Kaas, J. H. (2011). Gorilla and orangutan brains conform to the primate cellular scaling rules: Implications for human evolution. *Brain, Behavior and Evolution, 77*, 33–44.

5. Herculano-Houzel, S., & Lent, R. (2005). Isotropic fractionator: A simple, rapid method for the quantification of total cell and neuron numbers in the brain. *Journal of Neuroscience, 25*, 2518–2521.

The relative sizes of brain regions vary among vertebrates

Variation in brain size among taxa is largely a result of changes in the relative sizes of different parts of the brain, rather than in the development of entirely new structures (Figure 8.12). For example, bony fishes and birds have a relatively large midbrain and cerebellum—the parts of the brain involved in the interpretation of sensory signals and coordinating motion. Fish and birds live in a complex world that they move through in three dimensions, and it has been suggested that fishes and birds use their enlarged midbrain and cerebellum to interpret complex sensory information and coordinate their body movements in this three-dimensional environment. However, the midbrain and cerebellum are not particularly large in sharks, which presumably face similar challenges. In mammals, the midbrain is greatly reduced in size. In most vertebrates, the midbrain contains the regions that are involved in interpreting visual information, but in mammals this function has been taken over by the forebrain.

The forebrain is enlarged in both birds and mammals relative to the other major groups of vertebrates. In mammals, the outer layer of the forebrain is enlarged and reorganized, forming the **isocortex** (also called the neocortex). The isocortex is made up of gray matter, whereas the majority of the internal parts of the mammalian brain are made up of white matter, except for the basal nuclei—clusters of gray matter deep within the cerebrum. Thus, the mammalian brain is fundamentally reorganized compared with the brains of other vertebrates, which have an outer layer of white matter surrounding an inner core of gray matter. Like mammals, birds have large forebrains; however, in birds the cortex is relatively thin and undeveloped. In contrast, other parts of the forebrain are enlarged, particularly in a structure called the dorsoventricular ridge *(DVR)*. The enlarged forebrains of birds and mammals presumably evolved independently, because the last common ancestor of birds and mammals would have had a small forebrain, as is typical for reptiles. The isocortex of mammals and the DVR of birds perform similar functions, and are thought to have evolved independently from similar structures in the reptilian brain. This subject is of more than just academic interest, because

FIGURE 8.12 **Brain structure in representative vertebrate groups**
Most groups of vertebrates have the same major brain structures, although these structures vary greatly in relative size.

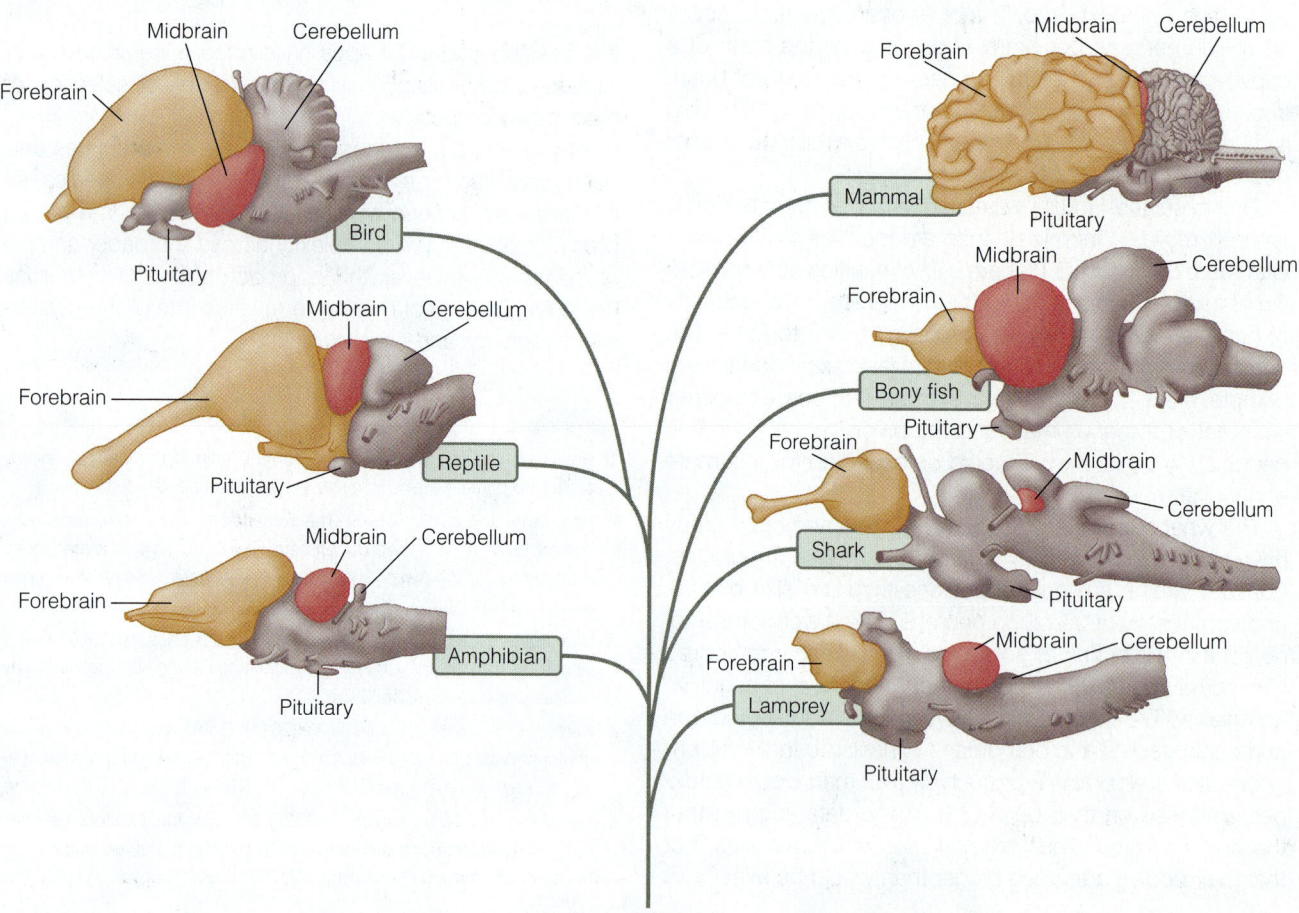

both birds and mammals are capable of performing complex, learned behaviors, and thus the evolution of brain structures may shed light on the evolution of intelligence, a process governed by the isocortex in mammals.

In addition to variation in brain size and structure among major groups of vertebrates, there is also substantial variation in brain size within groups. For example, mormyrid fish have unusually large midbrains relative to other fish. Mormyrids are weakly electric fish that use electric fields for navigation and communication. The midbrain is involved in sensory processing, and processing electrosensory information likely requires sophisticated neural circuitry. Similarly, within mammals, humans and dolphins have very large brains and highly folded cortices compared with other mammals. This morphology is consistent with their high intelligence. In addition, in marine mammals, the large size of the brain may be associated with their use of echolocation.

The hindbrain supports basic functions

The hindbrain is located between the spinal cord and the remainder of the brain, and contains three structurally and functionally distinct regions, the *pons*, the *cerebellum*, and the *medulla oblongata*, which function collectively to support vital bodily processes such as breathing, circulation, and movement.

The **medulla oblongata** (often referred to simply as the medulla) is located at the anterior end of the spinal cord, and contains reflex centers regulating breathing, heart rate, and the diameter of blood vessels, thus regulating blood pressure, as we discuss in detail in Chapter 9: Circulatory Systems. The medulla oblongata also contains neural pathways that communicate between the spinal cord and the brain. Many of these pathways cross over each other in the medulla such that the left side of the brain controls the right side of the body and the right side of the brain controls the left side of the body. Because it regulates such important survival systems, damage to the medulla is almost always fatal.

The **pons** (which means "bridge" in Latin) is located immediately anterior to the medulla, and is an important pathway that communicates information between the medulla, the cerebellum, and the forebrain. The pons also contains centers that control alertness and initiate states such as sleep and dreaming, and it regulates reflex activities such as breathing by influencing the activity of the medulla oblongata.

The **cerebellum** is located at the back of the brain, and consists of two highly folded hemispheres. The cerebellum integrates sensory input from the eyes, ears, and muscle with motor commands from the forebrain, and thus is responsible for motor coordination. In humans, damage to this area during birth can cause cerebral palsy, a disorder characterized by uncontrollable tremors. The cerebellum may also play a role in speech, learning, emotions, and attention. Although the cerebellum makes up only 10 percent of the weight of the human brain, it contains as many neurons as the rest of the brain combined.

The midbrain is greatly reduced in mammals

In fish and amphibians, the midbrain coordinates reflex responses to auditory and visual stimuli and is the primary center for coordinating and initiating behavioral responses. In contrast, in mammals it is much smaller relative to the rest of the brain and primarily serves as a relay center. In non-mammalian vertebrates, the roof of the midbrain, called the **tectum**, contains a pair of brain centers called **optic lobes** that coordinate sensory input from the eyes. In mammals these regions are called the superior colliculi, and are much smaller than in other vertebrates, functioning only in reflex optical responses such as orienting the eyes toward visual stimuli or adjusting focus, while the forebrain takes over the majority of visual processing. The tectum also contains the paired *inferior colliculi*, nuclei that are involved in hearing. Neurons conducting signals from the inner ear form synapses in this region. The posterior part of the midbrain is called the **tegmentum**, and contains regions that help with fine control of muscles. Lesions in this area of the brain can lead to Parkinson's disease, a condition associated with muscle tremors. In mammals the midbrain is sometimes grouped together with the pons and medulla oblongata and termed the **brainstem**.

The forebrain controls complex processes

In mammals, the forebrain is involved in processing and integrating sensory information, and in coordinating behavior. The forebrain consists of the *cerebrum*, the *thalamus*, the *epithalamus*, and the *hypothalamus*. The **cerebrum**, whose outer layer is the cortex, is divided into two **cerebral hemispheres** (Figure 8.13). The left hemisphere controls the right half of the body, and the right hemisphere controls the left half of the body. Although the right and left hemispheres seem to be mirror images, they are not functionally identical. For example, in most humans the areas that control speech are located in the left hemisphere, and areas that govern perception of spatial relationships are found in the right hemisphere.

The corpus callosum allows communication between hemispheres

The two hemispheres of the forebrain are connected by bundles of white matter called commissures that allow them to communicate with each other. In mammals, the

FIGURE 8.13 **A coronal section through the human cerebrum**

The cerebrum is divided into two hemispheres connected via the corpus callosum. A thin layer of gray matter (the cerebral cortex) surrounds a large mass of white matter. Embedded within this white matter are more areas of gray matter (the epithalamus, thalamus, hypothalamus, basal nuclei, and amygdala).

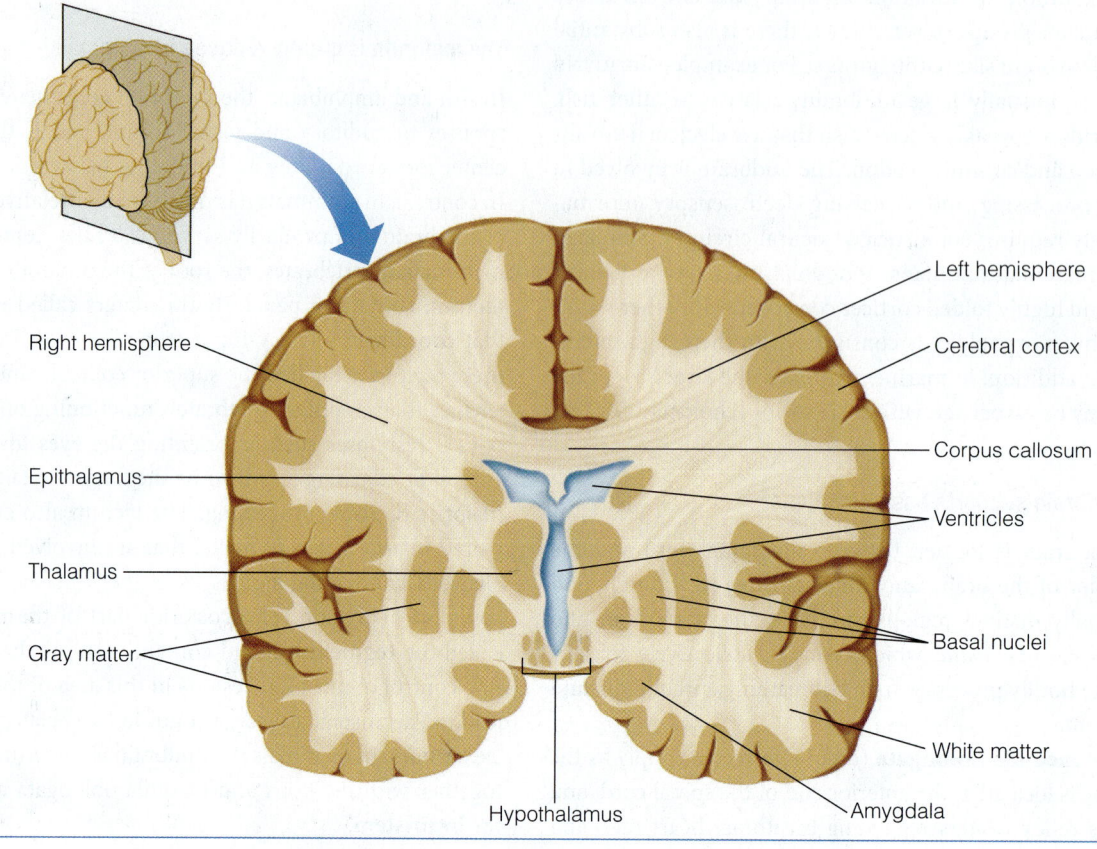

largest of these commissures is called the **corpus callosum**. Experiments in which the corpus callosum is cut have revealed some of the important functional differences between the two brain hemispheres. Roger Sperry was a pioneer in this area. In experiments using cats, Sperry demonstrated that cutting the corpus callosum caused no obvious changes in behavior, but that subtle changes could be detected using specialized equipment. Recall that sensory information from the right eye is processed in the left hemisphere of the brain and sensory information from the left eye is processed in the right hemisphere of the brain (see Chapter 7: Sensory Systems). When Sperry severed the optic chiasm and corpus callosum of a cat, and then covered its left eye and taught it a simple conditioned behavior, the cat could not perform this task when its right eye was covered instead of the left. It was as if only one side of the brain learned to perform the task, and could not communicate this learning to the other side of the brain. Sperry termed this phenomenon the split-brain syndrome.

Similar observations have been made in human patients following brain surgery designed to reduce the severity of epileptic seizures. In this surgery, a patient's corpus callosum is cut so that an epileptic seizure in one side of the brain cannot spread to the other hemisphere. Sperry was able to demonstrate that these patients had a subtle form of split-brain syndrome. Sperry presented images or words to either the right or left visual field of these patients, and then asked the subjects a series of simple questions or had them perform basic tasks. For example, in one experiment, the word *key* was presented to the left visual field (which is processed by the right hemisphere of the brain), while the word *ring* was simultaneously presented to the right visual field (which is processed by the left hemisphere of the brain). Normal subjects report seeing the word *keyring*. Patients whose corpus callosum had been severed reported seeing the word *ring* that had been projected to the right visual field and processed by the left hemisphere. They appeared to be unaware that the word *key* had been presented to the left visual field and processed by the right hemisphere, although some subjects occasionally reported that they saw a flash of light on the left side of the screen.

In most humans, the ability to communicate using language is localized in the left hemisphere of the brain, while the right hemisphere lacks language ability. Thus, the right hemisphere was unable to communicate that the light observed in the left visual field represented a word. Control subjects could verbalize both the words *key* and *ring* because the intact corpus callosum could transfer the information between the two hemispheres. This difference between normal subjects and "split-brain" patients is not obvious in everyday life because we seldom look at objects using only one eye. We can easily move our eyes or turn our heads so that both halves of the brain receive complete sensory information.

Although the right hemisphere does not have the ability to speak, it can still reason and communicate in other ways. For example, Sperry asked the split-brain subjects to reach behind a curtain and choose the object whose name had just been projected on the screen. They could not see the objects, but had to distinguish them by touch. When split-brain patients were asked to use their left hand (which is under the control of the right hemisphere), they chose the key, even though they had denied seeing the word. Thus, the right hemisphere had seen the word *key* and recognized its meaning, but was simply unable to communicate this information verbally. Interestingly, when asked to name the object they had just touched with their left hand, split-brain subjects responded by saying "ring"—the word observed by the left hemisphere.

Together, these and many subsequent studies have demonstrated that mammalian brains, and particularly the brains of humans, are highly lateralized with differing functions performed in each hemisphere.

The hypothalamus maintains homeostasis

The **hypothalamus** is located at the base of the forebrain just below the thalamus. The hypothalamus controls the internal organs and interacts with the autonomic nervous system, which we discuss later in this chapter. In addition, it regulates the secretion of pituitary hormones (see Chapter 4: Cell Signaling and Endocrine Regulation). The hypothalamus plays an important role in regulating the endocrine system and thus serves as a crucial link between the nervous and endocrine systems. Indeed, the primary function of the hypothalamus is to maintain the body's homeostatic balance. The hypothalamus regulates body temperature, fluid balance, blood pressure, body weight, and many bodily sensations such as hunger, thirst, pleasure, and sex drive.

The limbic system influences emotions

The hypothalamus is part of the **limbic system**, a network of connected structures that lie along the border between the cortex and the rest of the brain (Figure 8.14). These regions work together to influence many processes, including emotions, motivation, and memory. Thus, the limbic system is sometimes called the "emotional brain" because it controls emotions, decisions, and motivation. The limbic system includes several structures in addition to the hypothalamus.

The **amygdala** is involved in emotional responses, particularly those of aggression and fear. Electrical stimulation of the amygdala causes aggressive behavior, while removal of the amygdala results in decreased aggression and fear. For example, rats with damage to the amygdala will readily approach cats. Monkeys with damage to the amygdala are more eager to approach and interact with novel objects or unknown monkeys, suggesting that the amygdala controls fear reactions in primates. However, a different response is observed if the amygdala is damaged in infant monkeys. These monkeys are unable to develop normal social interactions, suggesting that the amygdala performs other roles in addition to simply regulating fear and aggression, at least in primates. For example, humans with damage to the amygdala are unable to accurately interpret facial expressions, particularly those associated with negative emotions such as fear or anger. The amygdala is also involved in maintaining memories of the emotional effects of an event.

The **hippocampus** converts short-term memories to long-term memories. For example, if you look up a

---

FIGURE 8.14 Anatomy of the limbic system

The limbic system consists of structures including the thalamus, hypothalamus, hippocampus, amygdala, and olfactory bulb.

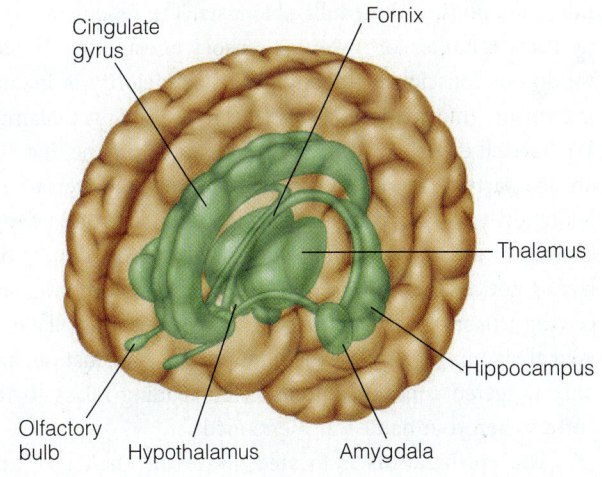

telephone number, you can keep the number in your short-term memory by repeating it a few times, but the memory of this number usually fades quickly once you have placed the call. If you want to remember the number for a long time, the hippocampus must convert this short-term memory to a lasting one. A person with a damaged hippocampus cannot build lasting memories. He or she can remember new facts for a short time, but will forget them within a few minutes. In contrast, memories from before the time of damage are unaffected. We discuss how the hippocampus helps to form lasting memories later in this chapter.

The **olfactory bulb**, which also forms part of the limbic system, is important for the sense of smell. Sensory neurons from the olfactory epithelium connect directly to the olfactory bulb, rather than being routed through the midbrain, as is the case for most other incoming sensory information. The olfactory bulb then integrates the signals from the olfactory neurons and transmits them to the cortex for processing. As we discuss later in the chapter, all other sensory information is first processed by the thalamus before being sent to the cortex. In contrast, olfactory information bypasses the thalamus and instead takes a more direct route. The olfactory bulb is also connected to the amygdala and hippocampus, and thus odors tend to provoke strong emotions and memories in humans.

The thalamus acts as a relay station

The **thalamus** is a large grouping of gray matter located deep within the forebrain, immediately above the hypothalamus. The thalamic nuclei receive input from the limbic system and from every sensory modality except olfaction. In fact, some researchers consider it part of the limbic system itself. The thalamus integrates and relays this information to the cortex. The thalamus is part of a structure called the reticular formation. The reticular formation is a net of neurons extending from the thalamus down through the brainstem, including parts of the midbrain, pons, and medulla oblongata. The reticular formation acts as a filter for incoming sensory information. In fact, we do not consciously attend to the vast majority of incoming sensory information. Instead, it is filtered by the thalamus. We have all experienced this phenomenon. Imagine that you are at a party, surrounded by the buzz of many conversations. Suddenly, you hear your name spoken behind you and you become aware that someone is talking about you, despite not having noticed the conversation before. Although you were receiving sensory information about this conversation all along, your thalamus filtered out the unimportant information, and only triggered conscious attention by sending relays to the cortex when your name was mentioned.

The **epithalamus** is located above the thalamus, and contains the habenular nuclei and the **pineal complex**. The habenular nuclei communicate with the tegmentum

of the midbrain, while the pineal is involved in establishing circadian rhythms and secretes the hormone melatonin (see Chapter 7: Sensory Systems).

The cortex integrates and interprets information

The outer layer of the mammalian cerebrum integrates and interprets sensory information and initiates voluntary movements, and thus has taken over many of the functions that are performed by the midbrain in other vertebrates. This region, called the cortex, is necessary for cognition and all other so-called higher functions, including the ability to concentrate, reason, and think in abstract form. In some mammals, the cortex is smooth (Figure 8.15a), whereas in other species it is folded so that the surface of the brain has a walnutlike appearance (Figure 8.15b). The outer, visible regions of these folds are called **gyri** (singular: gyrus), and the grooves are called **sulci** (singular: sulcus). These folds greatly increase the surface area of the cortex, increasing the number of neurons and their interconnections, and thus increasing the functional complexity of the forebrain. The cortex varies in surface area by a factor of 125 between the least cortical mammals, such as hedgehogs, and the most cortical mammals, such as primates and cetaceans. The degree of folding of the cortex appears to be correlated with the functional complexity of the brain and the intelligence of the organism.

The cortex of mammals is rather distinct in structure compared with the cortex of other vertebrates. Because of its unusual organization, the mammalian cortex is often referred to as the neocortex or isocortex. The isocortex is organized into six functionally distinct layers with neuronal processes and cell bodies distributed within the layers in a specific fashion (Figure 8.16). The main visible difference between the layers is the shape and density of the neurons located in each layer. The outermost layer (I) contains few cell bodies and few connections among cells. Layers II and III are involved in integrating signals within the cortex, while the remaining layers contain neurons that communicate with other parts of the brain, including the thalamus, brainstem, and spinal cord. The cortex is thought to be organized into functional units called columns that are oriented vertically within the cortex and extend through all six of the cortical layers, although the functional significance of this vertical organization is still a matter of debate. Indeed, the degree of columnar organization appears to vary among parts of the cortex and among species. Columns may be further broken down into minicolumns of less than a millimeter in diameter, containing only about 100 neurons. There are numerous interconnections between neurons within a column, and although there are fewer connections among columns, these connections can extend far across the cortex, or into subcortical areas such as the thalamus. Thus, the cortex may act as

FIGURE 8.15 **Structural variation in mammalian brains**

In some species the cortex is relatively smooth, whereas in others it is folded into a series of elaborate gyri and sulci.

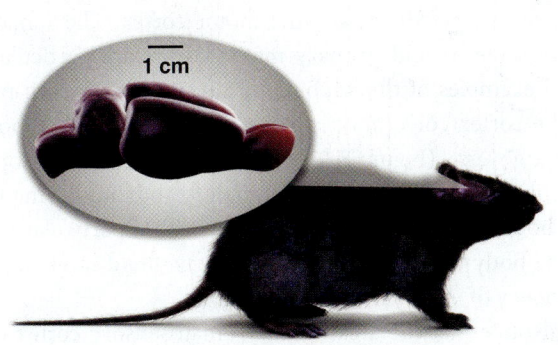

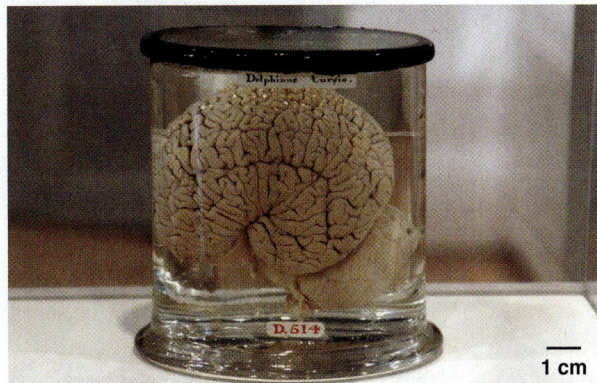

(a) Rat brain

(b) Dolphin brain

Photo source: (a) Science Picture Company/Science Picture Co./Corbis; (b) Richard Gardner/Rex Features/AP Images

FIGURE 8.16 **Layers of the human cortex**

The cerebral cortex is arranged in six distinct layers, although the cellular composition of these layers varies depending on the particular area of the cortex.

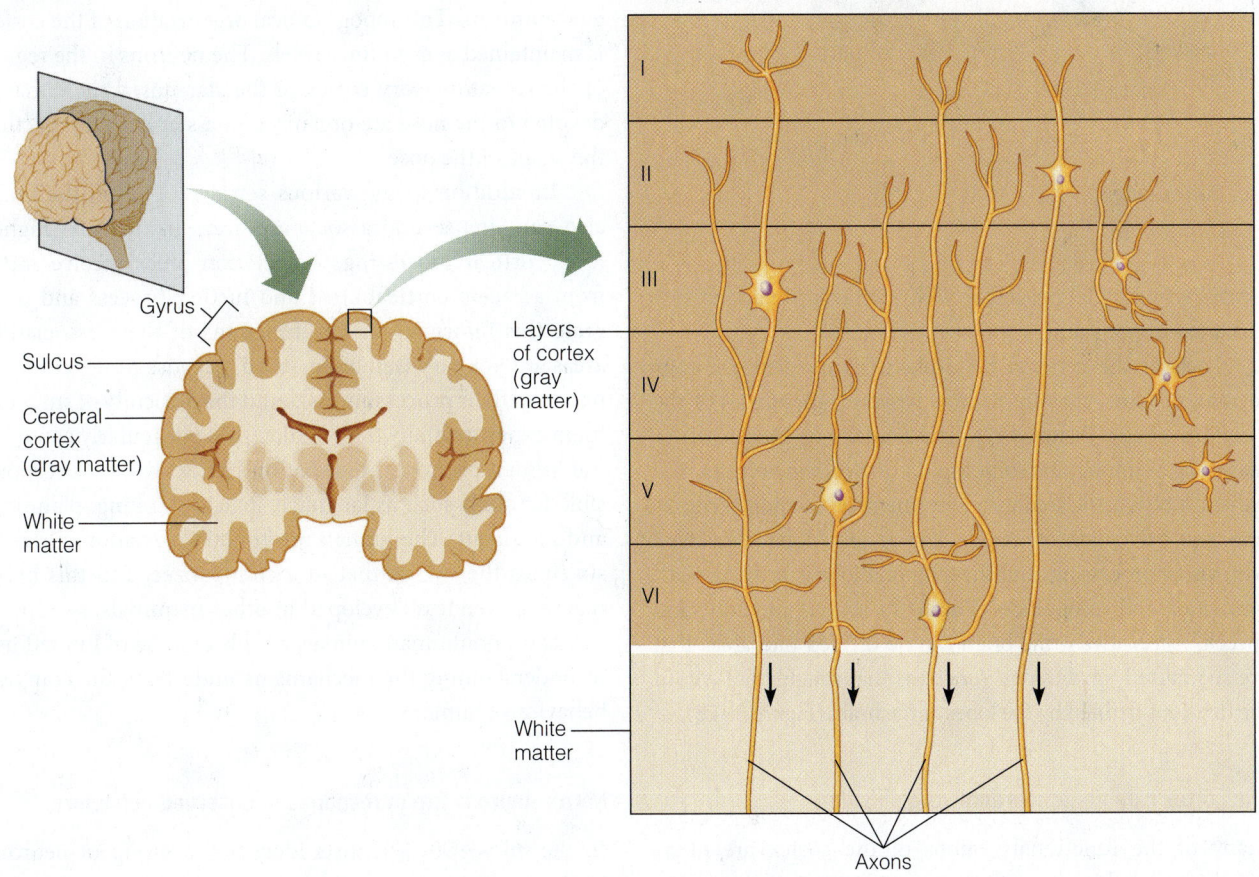

FIGURE 8.17 **Lobes, cortices, and association areas of the human brain**

(a) The cerebrum can be divided into several lobes, each named after the overlying bones. **(b)** The cerebrum can also be divided into functional regions called cortical areas, each involved in coordinating a different function.

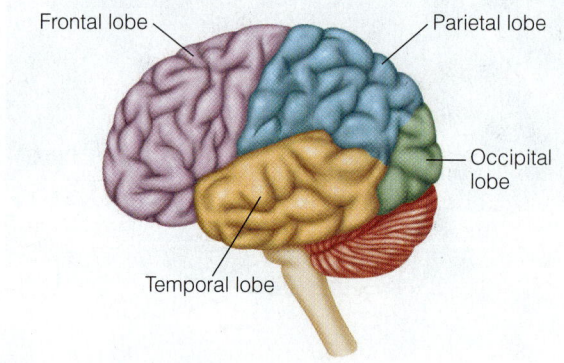

(a) Lobes of the brain

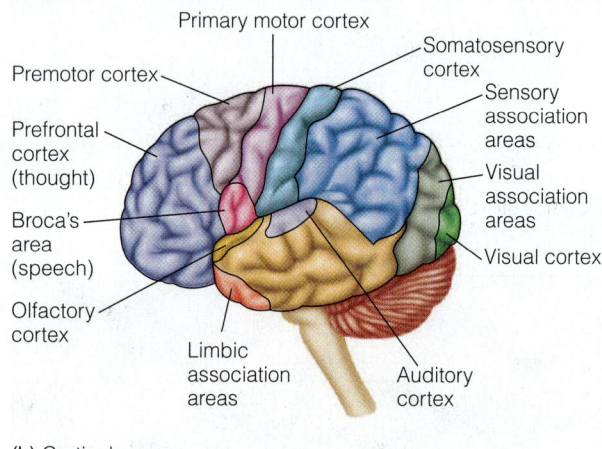

(b) Cortical areas

a massively parallel processor with each column acting as a semiautonomous unit.

Each of the cerebral hemispheres is divided into four regions, or lobes, that are defined based on the names of the overlying bones (Figure 8.17). The frontal lobe is involved in reasoning, planning, and some aspects of speech in humans. The parietal lobe is associated with movement, orientation, recognition, and perception of stimuli. The occipital lobe is involved with visual processing, and the temporal lobe is involved with perception and recognition of auditory stimuli, memory, and speech. Alternatively, the brain can be divided into areas that are specialized for different functions that roughly fall within the divisions defined by the lobes of the brain (Figure 8.17b).

The cortex exhibits topographic organization

Many of the functional regions of the cortex are organized topographically, such that specific areas of the cortex

correspond to particular functions. This arrangement echoes the concept of labeled lines, which we encountered when discussing sensory systems (see Chapter 7: Sensory Systems), and applies to the visual cortex, the auditory cortex, the somatosensory cortex, and the motor cortex. The somatosensory cortex and primary motor cortex are particularly good examples of this topographic arrangement: each part of the cortex corresponds to the specific part of the body that it governs (Figure 8.18). The significance of this topographic arrangement is not well understood, but having the cell bodies of the neurons associated with a particular part of the body close together in the cortex could increase the efficiency of information processing.

Notice that the areas of the somatosensory cortex devoted to various parts of the body are disproportionate. For example, the face and hands take up more than half the map of both the sensory cortex and motor cortex in humans. The size of the cortical region typically reflects the number of sensory or motor neurons present in a particular body part, rather than the size of the body part itself. Thus, the amount of cortex devoted to inputs from a particular part of the body differs among species, reflecting the relative importance of various parts of the body for sensation and movement. For example, the nose takes up a disproportionate amount of the somatosensory cortex in the star-nosed mole. These animals live in burrows and use their sensitive noses to probe their environments. This topographical organization of the cortex is maintained at even finer levels: The neurons in the region of the somatosensory cortex of the star-nosed mole that is devoted to the nose are organized in a star shape, reflecting the shape of the nose.

In addition to the various sensory cortices, the brain also contains several association areas involved in higher level cortical processing. Association areas receive input from adjacent cortical areas and further process and integrate this information. The functions of these association areas are not very well understood, because of the complex nature of their processing tasks and the difficulty of studying them experimentally. This difficulty is particularly acute for the human prefrontal association cortex, which is responsible for skills such as language, logical thinking, planning, and judgment. The human prefrontal association cortex is six times the size of that in a chimpanzee, and this brain region is even less developed in other mammals, so experiments on nonhuman animals are likely to be of limited use in understanding the mechanisms underlying the complex behavior of humans.

Mirror neurons fire in response to observed behaviors

In the mid-1990s scientists identified a group of neurons in the premotor cortex, somatosensory cortex, and several

FIGURE 8.18 **Somatosensory maps**

The area of the cortex devoted to a given body part depends on the importance of that body part to the organism. **(a)** Body proportions of a human and a star-nosed mole. **(b)** Proportion of the somatosensory cortex devoted to particular body parts. In humans, a disproportionate area of the cortex is devoted to sensory input from the hands and mouth. In star-nosed moles, a disproportionate amount of the cortex is devoted to the front paws and nose.

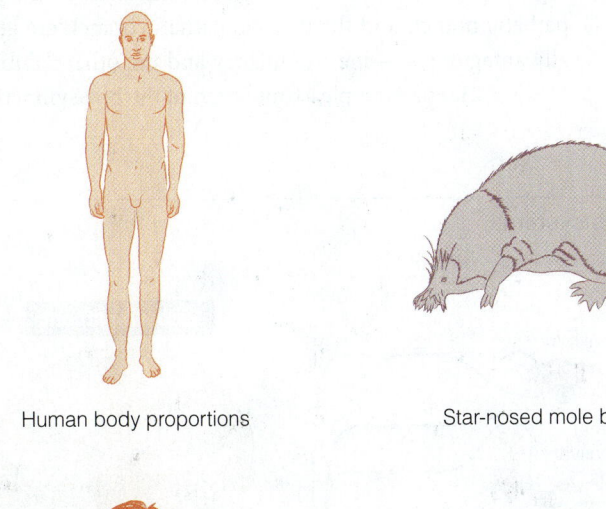

Human body proportions   Star-nosed mole body proportions

(a)

Human sensory homunculus   Star-nosed mole sensory homunculus

(b)

THE PERIPHERAL NERVOUS SYSTEM OF VERTEBRATES

The peripheral nervous system of vertebrates includes all portions of the nervous system other than the brain and spinal cord (i.e., all parts of the nervous system that are outside the skull and vertebral column). We have already discussed the afferent division of the peripheral nervous system (see Chapter 7: Sensory Systems). Here we concentrate on the efferent division, which is divided into the autonomic and somatic nervous systems.

The Autonomic Nervous System

The autonomic nervous system of vertebrates is involved in the homeostatic regulation of most physiological functions, including heart rate, blood pressure, breathing, and many other processes that are critical for life. These functions are not usually under conscious control, and thus this nervous system is sometimes referred to as the involuntary nervous system. The autonomic division can be differentiated into three branches. The **sympathetic nervous system** is most active during periods of stress or physical activity, whereas the **parasympathetic nervous system** is most active during periods of rest. Thus, the parasympathetic branch is sometimes referred to as the "resting and digesting" system, because it is mainly concerned with redirecting energy toward quiet activities such as digestion. In contrast, the sympathetic branch is sometimes called the "fight-or-flight" system. Stimulating the sympathetic nervous system causes increases in heart rate, deeper breathing, and diversion of blood from the digestive system to the working muscles. Although the action of the sympathetic branch is most obvious during the fight-or-flight response, which we discussed in Chapter 4: Cell Signaling and Endocrine Regulation, it also plays an important role in daily activities, in particular in regulating blood pressure and blood flow to tissues. The enteric nervous system, which is located in the walls of the gut, has typically been considered part of the autonomic nervous system. However, it may be appropriate to consider it a separate division of the peripheral nervous system because it operates independently of

other cortical areas that fired not only when a monkey performed an action, but also when the monkey saw or heard other monkeys or humans performing that action. These neurons, termed **mirror neurons**, have now been identified in both primates and birds. The functional role of mirror neurons remains elusive, but they have been suggested to be involved in our understanding of the goals and intentions of others, in imitation and mimicry, as well as more complex processes such as empathy and language.

CONCEPT CHECK

6. What type of symptoms would you expect in an individual who had a stroke that damaged part of the cerebellum?

7. Compare and contrast the function of the midbrain in mammals with its function in other vertebrates.

the other two branches, although the parasympathetic and sympathetic branches can regulate its activity. The enteric branch is entirely concerned with digestion, and innervates the gastrointestinal tract, pancreas, and **gallbladder**.

The sympathetic and parasympathetic branches act together to maintain homeostasis

The autonomic nervous system maintains homeostasis by balancing the activity of the sympathetic and parasympathetic nervous systems and their effects on their target organs.

Three important features of the autonomic nervous system underlie its ability to maintain homeostasis: dual innervation, antagonistic action, and basal tone. As you can see from Figure 8.19, most internal organs receive input from both the sympathetic and parasympathetic nervous systems. Through this process of dual innervation, the two branches can work together to regulate effector organs. The effects of the sympathetic branch and the parasympathetic branch are generally antagonistic—one stimulatory and the other inhibitory (Table 8.2). For example, stimulation of the parasympathetic

FIGURE 8.19 **Dual innervation in the autonomic nervous system**

Most organs receive input from both the parasympathetic and sympathetic nervous systems.

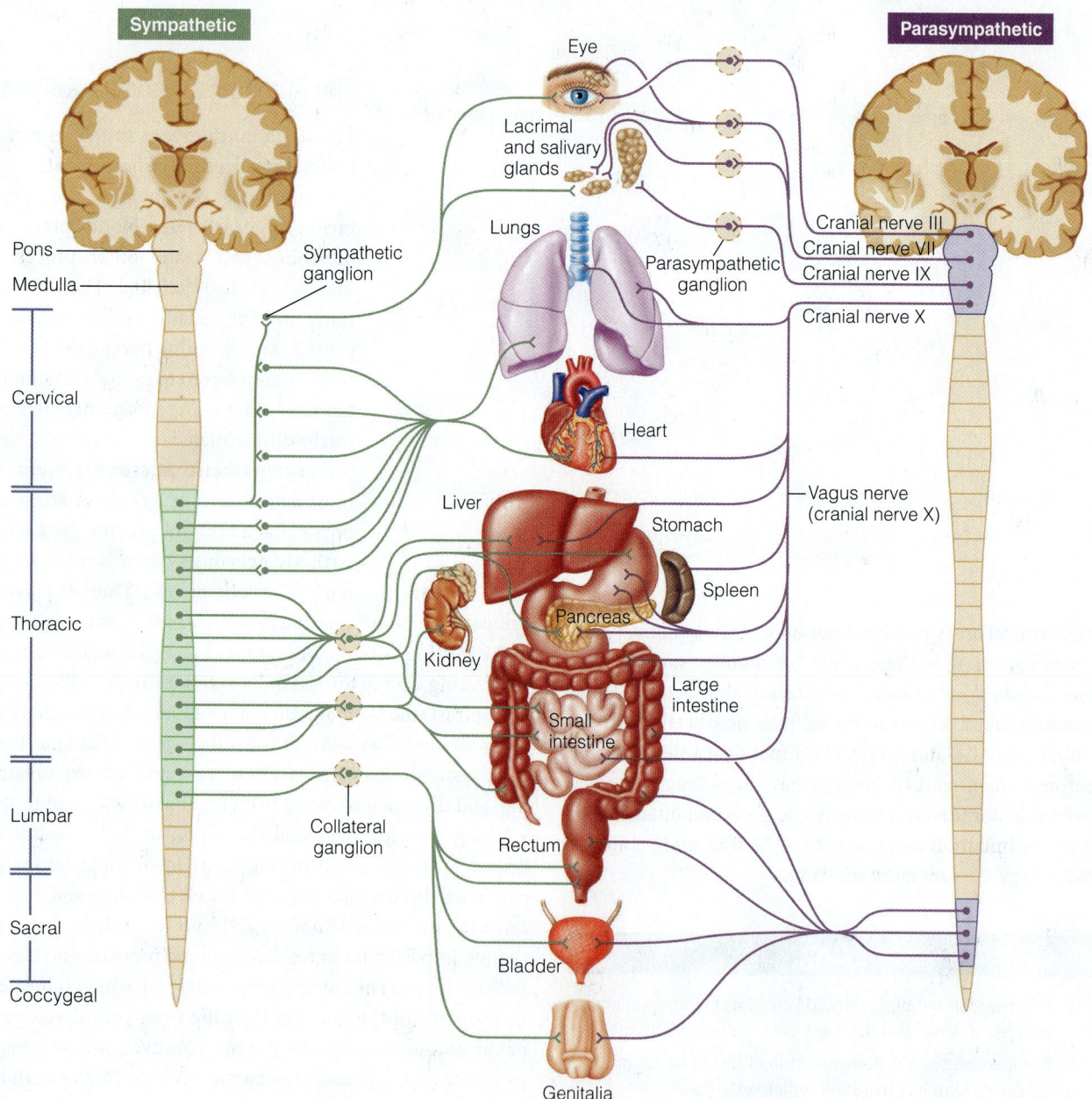

Table 8.2 Actions of the sympathetic and parasympathetic nervous systems in humans

Effector Organ	Parasympathetic Stimulation	Sympathetic Stimulation	Adrenergic Receptor
Pupil of eye	Constricts	Dilates	α
Lacrimal glands of eyes	Stimulates secretion	None	None
Salivary gland	Watery secretion	Thick secretion	α, β2
Heart	Slows heart rate	Increases rate and force	β1
Arterioles	None	Constricts	α
Nasal glands	Stimulates secretion	None	None
Bronchioles of lungs	Constricts	Dilates	β2
Digestive tract	Increased motility and secretion	Decreased motility and secretion	α, β2
Exocrine pancreas	Increases enzyme secretion	Decreases enzyme secretion	α
Endocrine pancreas	Stimulates insulin secretion	Inhibits insulin secretion	α
Adrenal medulla	None	Secretes epinephrine	None
Kidney	None	Increases renin secretion	β1
Bladder	Release of urine	Retention of urine	α, β2
Adipose tissue	None	Fat breakdown	β1
Sweat glands	General sweating	Localized sweating	α
Arrector pili muscles of skin	None	Contract, causing hair to stand on end	α
Male sex organs	Erection	Ejaculation	α
Uterus	Depends on stage of cycle	Depends on stage of cycle	α, β2

nervous system causes the bronchioles of the lung to constrict by causing the associated smooth muscle to contract. In contrast, stimulation of the sympathetic nervous system causes bronchioles to dilate through relaxation of the associated smooth muscle. Finally, both the parasympathetic and sympathetic nervous systems have basal tone (or basal tonic activity), such that even under resting conditions autonomic neurons produce action potentials. Thus, both increases and decreases in action potential frequency can alter the response of the target organ, similar to the volume control on a radio. Together these three organizing principles allow the autonomic nervous system to exert precise control and to maintain homeostasis by balancing the input of the parasympathetic and sympathetic branches of the autonomic nervous system.

A single preganglionic neuron generally synapses with several postganglionic neurons, and may also make contact with *intrinsic neurons* that are located entirely within the ganglion, allowing for relatively complex integration of function within the ganglion itself. At the effector organ, the postganglionic neuron releases neurotransmitter from specialized structures called varicosities, as discussed in Chapter 4: Cell Signaling and Endocrine Regulation. The axons of postganglionic autonomic neurons have a series of swellings at their distal end arranged in series along the surface of the effector organ, like beads on a string. Each varicosity acts as a synapse with the effector organ, releasing neurotransmitter in response to action potentials. The underlying membrane of the effector organ is not specialized and does not contain high concentrations of receptors. Instead, the neuron simply releases neurotransmitter into the extracellular fluid. The neurotransmitter then diffuses to receptors distributed across the membrane of the effector organ.

The anatomy of the sympathetic and parasympathetic branches differs

All autonomic pathways contain two neurons in series (Figure 8.20). The cell body of the first, or **preganglionic neuron**, is located within the central nervous system. This neuron synapses with a second, or **postganglionic**, efferent neuron in peripheral structures called **autonomic ganglia** that contain many such synapses. There are three main

FIGURE 8.20 **Structure and neurotransmitters of the sympathetic and parasympathetic nervous systems**

The parasympathetic nervous system has a long preganglionic neuron and a short postganglionic neuron, while the sympathetic nervous system has a short preganglionic neuron and a long postganglionic neuron.

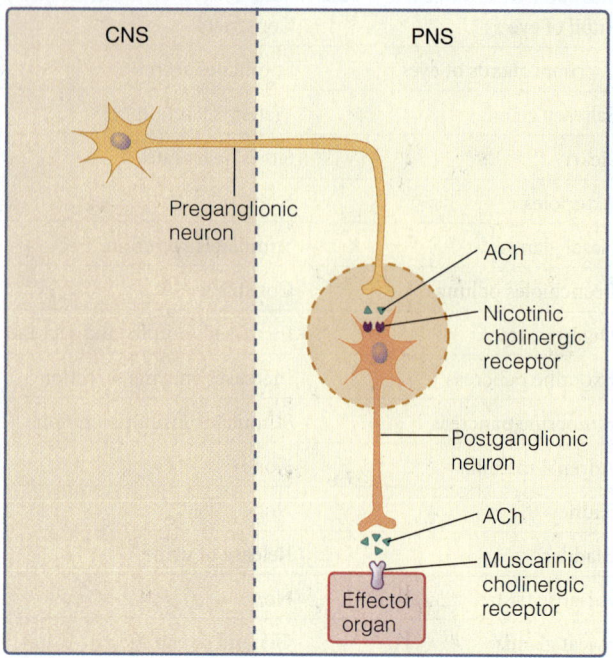

(a) Sympathetic nervous system

(b) Parasympathetic nervous system

anatomical differences between the sympathetic and parasympathetic branches of the autonomic nervous system.

- The cell bodies of most preganglionic sympathetic neurons are located in the thoracic and lumbar regions of the spinal cord, while most of the parasympathetic pathways originate either in the hindbrain or in the sacral region of the spinal cord (see Figure 8.19).

- Sympathetic ganglia are found in a chain that runs close to the spinal cord, while parasympathetic ganglia are located close to the effector organ. Thus, most sympathetic pathways have short preganglionic neurons and long postganglionic neurons, while parasympathetic pathways have long preganglionic neurons and short postganglionic neurons.

- In the sympathetic nervous system, a preganglionic sympathetic neuron forms synapses with 10 or more postganglionic neurons. In the parasympathetic system, a preganglionic neuron forms synapses with three or fewer postganglionic neurons. Stimulation of a single sympathetic preganglionic neuron will thus have rather widespread effects, while stimulation of a preganglionic parasympathetic neuron typically causes a much more localized response.

The neurotransmitters of the sympathetic and parasympathetic systems differ

In both the sympathetic and parasympathetic divisions, the preganglionic neuron releases the neurotransmitter acetylcholine (ACh), and the postganglionic neuron has nicotinic receptors that bind the ACh. Nicotinic acetylcholine receptors are ligand-gated ion channels, and binding of ACh allows Na^+ to enter and rapidly depolarize the postganglionic cell. The effects of nicotinic receptors are always stimulatory.

In the parasympathetic nervous system, the postganglionic cell releases ACh, but the target organ has muscarinic rather than nicotinic ACh receptors. Muscarinic ACh receptors are coupled to G proteins, and thus typically cause somewhat slower responses than do nicotinic receptors. There are several types of muscarinic receptors, and binding of ACh can be either stimulatory or inhibitory, depending on the type of receptor present on the target cell.

In contrast, in the sympathetic nervous system, postganglionic cells typically release the neurotransmitter norepinephrine, which binds to adrenergic receptors on the effector organ. The various types of adrenergic receptors work through different second messenger pathways and cause a variety of responses in the target cell. Differences in receptor subtypes among effector organs explain the diverse effects of sympathetic and parasympathetic stimulation of various tissues. These differences are important clinically in predicting the effects of many drugs. In general, binding of norepinephrine to receptors is stimulatory, while binding to receptors is inhibitory. A few classes of postganglionic sympathetic neurons, including those innervating the sweat glands of the skin, release ACh rather than norepinephrine, but these neurons are much less numerous than the adrenergic neurons.

Table 8.3 summarizes some of the similarities and differences between the sympathetic and parasympathetic nervous systems.

Some effectors receive only sympathetic innervation

Although the principle of dual innervation applies to most of the target organs of the autonomic nervous system, some organs—including the sweat glands, the arrector pili muscles of the skin, the adrenal medulla, the kidneys, and most blood vessels—are only innervated by sympathetic neurons (see Table 8.3). The effects of sympathetic stimulation on the sweat glands and arrector pili muscles are obvious. Humans commonly sweat during stressful situations, and in many mammals fear causes the hair (or fur) to stand on end, because of the actions of the arrector pili muscles.

The adrenal medulla, the core of the adrenal gland, is also involved in the response to stressful situations. The adrenal glands are paired glands located immediately above the kidneys. The adrenal medulla is actually a highly modified sympathetic ganglion. Preganglionic sympathetic neurons terminate in the adrenal medulla, but the postganglionic neurons do not go on to innervate a target organ (Figure 8.21). Instead, they are modified into neurosecretory cells called chromaffin cells that release epinephrine and norepinephrine directly into

the circulation, producing widespread excitatory effects. As we discussed in Chapter 4: Cell Signaling and Endocrine Regulation, we can easily see the origins of the adrenal glands as sympathetic ganglia by looking at fish, which lack a discrete adrenal gland. In elasmobranchs (sharks and rays), these neurosecretory cells are directly associated with the autonomic ganglia. In bony fish, these cells are dispersed throughout the anterior part of the kidney, similar to the location in mammals, although they are not grouped into a discrete gland. This progression

FIGURE 8.21 Sympathetic innervation of the adrenal medulla

The adrenal medulla receives innervation from a preganglionic sympathetic neuron, and is thus equivalent to a sympathetic ganglion.

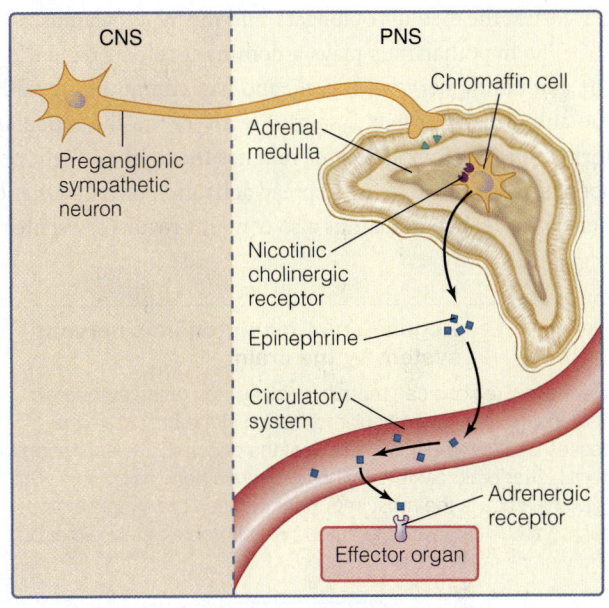

Table 8.3 Similarities and differences between the sympathetic and parasympathetic nervous systems

Characteristic	Sympathetic	Parasympathetic
Number of neurons in chain	Two	Two
Location of cell bodies of the preganglionic neuron	Thoracic and lumbar regions of spinal cord	Hindbrain Sacral region of spinal cord
Location of ganglia	Close to spinal cord	Close to effector organ
Preganglionic neuron	Short	Long
Postganglionic neuron	Long	Short
Synapses per preganglionic neuron	Many	Few
Neurotransmitter released by preganglionic neuron	ACh	ACh
Neurotransmitter released by postganglionic neuron	NE	ACh

from a clear ganglionic structure to dispersed cells to a non-ganglionic tissue (the adrenal medulla) suggests the likely evolutionary origin of this unusual structure.

The central nervous system regulates the autonomic nervous system

The central nervous system exerts control over the autonomic nervous system at several levels, including the spinal cord, brainstem, hypothalamus, and cortex. The relationship between these brain regions and the autonomic nervous system is outlined in Figure 8.22. Many of the inputs from the central nervous system reach the autonomic nervous system via the reticular formation, a set of neurons located in the brainstem. Although the reticular formation can itself act as an integrating center, its main role is to communicate signals coming from the cortex, the medulla oblongata, and the hypothalamus.

The hypothalamus plays a dominant role in regulating the autonomic nervous system, and can communicate with the autonomic nervous system directly or via the reticular formation. The hypothalamus initiates the fight-or-flight response, which involves widespread activation of sympathetic neurons. The hypothalamus also contains regulatory centers for body temperature, food intake, and water balance, all of which are homeostatically regulated via the autonomic nervous system. The medulla oblongata contains centers that control heart rate, blood pressure, and breathing by influencing the activity of the autonomic nervous system.

Most of these changes in the activity of the autonomic nervous system occur at the unconscious level via **reflex arcs**, simple neural circuits that do not involve the conscious centers of the brain. Figure 8.23 shows an example of such a reflex arc, one involved in regulating blood pressure. When blood pressure falls, receptors located in various parts of the body detect the decrease. These receptors send a signal to the cardiovascular control center in the medulla oblongata via afferent sensory neurons. The cardiovascular control center then influences the activity of the autonomic nervous system, increasing sympathetic activity and decreasing parasympathetic activity. These resulting changes in autonomic output cause adjustments in heart rate, stroke volume, and vasoconstriction, returning blood pressure back to normal in a negative feedback loop.

The limbic system, which governs emotions, also has a profound effect on the activity of the autonomic nervous system. Blushing, fainting at the sight of blood, and "butterflies" in the stomach are all examples of the response of the autonomic nervous system to emotions.

FIGURE 8.22 Regulation of the autonomic nervous system by the brain

Many brain regions can modulate the activity of the autonomic nervous system. The reticular formation in the brainstem processes and communicates most of the descending information from higher brain centers to the autonomic nervous system. The hypothalamus is the most important of these brain regions and can communicate with the autonomic nervous system either directly or via the reticular formation.

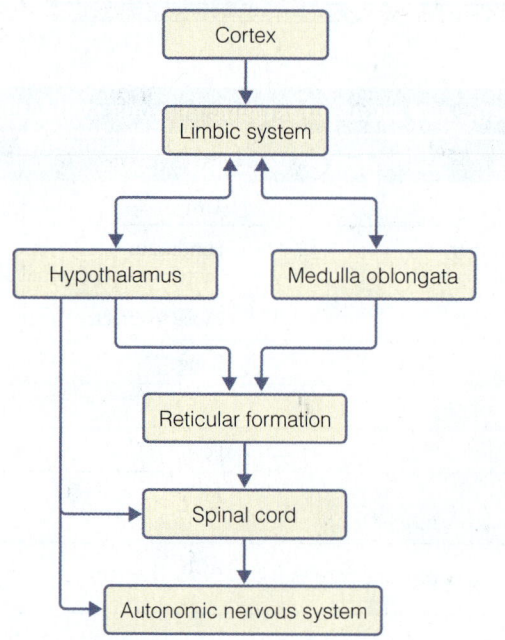

FIGURE 8.23 An example of an autonomic reflex arc: the reflex control of blood pressure

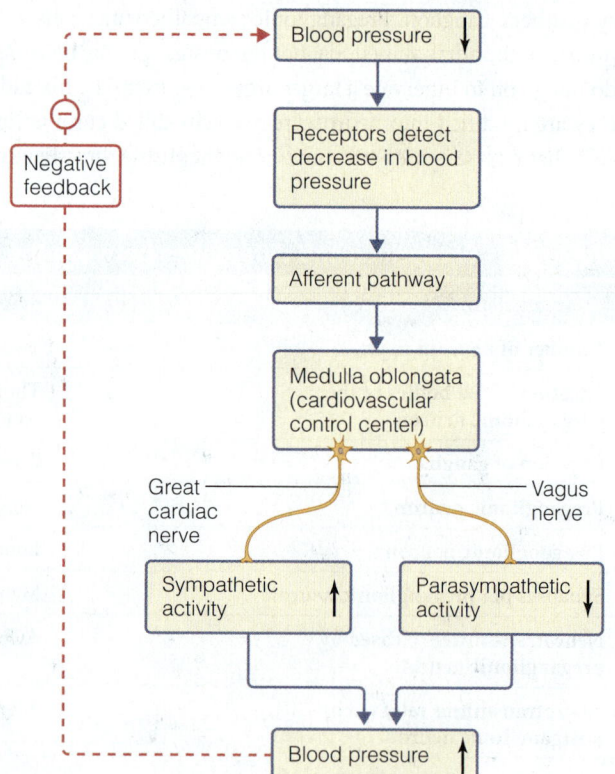

The enteric nervous system regulates the gut

The enteric nervous system is organized as a large *plexus*, or nerve net, located in the walls of the gut. It has traditionally been considered a division of the autonomic nervous system. However, it is a complete semi-independent nervous system with afferent neurons, interneurons, and efferent neurons. Because of this organization, the enteric nervous system has complete reflex arcs that are independent of the central nervous system. There is substantial communication between the central nervous system and the enteric nervous system, and this communication runs in both directions. Signals are sent from the central nervous system to the enteric nervous system and from the enteric nervous system to the central nervous system via the autonomic nervous system (particularly the parasympathetic nervous system). In fact, 90 percent of the fibers in the **vagus nerve**, an important cranial nerve that contains afferent, motor, and parasympathetic components, are afferent fibers from the enteric nervous system. Although the role of the enteric nervous system in regulating the motility of the gut has been appreciated for many decades, we are only just starting to understand its many other functions.

CONCEPT CHECK

8. Compare and contrast the sympathetic and parasympathetic nervous systems.
9. What is the significance of having dual innervation of many organs by both the sympathetic and parasympathetic nervous systems?
10. What sort of receptors would you expect the neurosecretory chromaffin cells of the adrenal medulla to express?

Somatic Motor Pathways

Somatic motor pathways control skeletal muscles, which are usually under conscious control. Thus, the motor pathways are sometimes called the "voluntary nervous system." However, some efferent motor pathways are not under conscious control, and instead represent reflex responses—rapid involuntary movements in response to a stimulus. For example, if you sit with your legs crossed and tap sharply just under your kneecap, your leg will kick out, in the patellar (knee-jerk) reflex. Efferent motor pathways can be distinguished from autonomic pathways in seven ways.

1. Efferent motor neurons control only one type of effector organ—skeletal muscle.
2. The cell bodies of motor neurons are located in the central nervous system in vertebrates, and never within ganglia outside of the central nervous system.

3. Efferent motor pathways are monosynaptic—there is only a single synapse between the central nervous system and the effector organ. As a result, efferent motor neurons can be among the longest neurons in the vertebrate body, with axons that can span several meters in large animals.
4. The morphology of the synapse differs between the autonomic and motor pathways. At the neuromuscular junction, a motor neuron splits into a cluster of axon terminals that branch out over the motor end plate, unlike autonomic neurons, which have several synaptic varicosities arranged in series like a string of beads.
5. The synaptic cleft between the motor neuron and the muscle cell membrane is much narrower than that between autonomic neurons and their effector cells. Thus, neurotransmitters typically diffuse across the neuromuscular junction more rapidly than across the synaptic cleft of autonomic neurons, and motor neurons tend to communicate more rapidly with their effectors.
6. All vertebrate motor neurons release acetylcholine at the neuromuscular junction, whereas sympathetic neurons release epinephrine and parasympathetic neurons release acetylcholine. In many invertebrates, motor neurons release glutamate.
7. The effect of acetylcholine on vertebrate skeletal muscle is always excitatory, whereas autonomic neurons may be excitatory or inhibitory. Stimulation of an efferent motor neuron leads to the contraction of skeletal muscle, and muscles relax only when the associated motor neurons are at rest.

CONCEPT CHECK

11. Compare and contrast the somatic and autonomic divisions of the autonomic nervous system.
12. What is a reflex arc? Provide an example from the somatic division of the peripheral nervous system.

INTEGRATIVE FUNCTIONS OF NERVOUS SYSTEMS

Neurobiologists are only beginning to understand how integrating centers such as the brain take information from sensory systems and integrate this information to allow animals to respond to their environments in a dynamic way. In this section we discuss some of the important topics relating to how nervous systems function, beginning with simple behaviors, and then examining some of the more complex functions of the nervous system.

Coordination of Behavior

Multicellular animals are capable of diverse forms of behavior, which are made possible by the complexity of nervous system organization and function. Animal behaviors can be loosely grouped into three categories: reflex behaviors, rhythmic behaviors, and voluntary behaviors. **Reflex behaviors** are involuntary responses to stimuli, and are among the simplest types of animal behaviors. Many animals also have a series of rhythmic behaviors, and these rhythms underlie such important processes as locomotion, breathing, and the function of the heart. Voluntary behaviors range greatly in complexity, from apparently simple acts such as mating or fighting, to complex behaviors such as reading and writing. In this section we discuss each of these kinds of behaviors in turn, working from the simplest to the most complex.

Reflex arcs control many involuntary behaviors

The least complex integrated response of the nervous system is the reflex arc, which controls the simplest type of animal behavior—reflexes, or rapid involuntary responses to stimuli. In principle, a reflex arc could involve as few as two neurons (Figure 8.24): a sensory afferent neuron that detects the stimulus and an efferent neuron that carries the output to an effector cell (such as a muscle). This reflex arc is called a monosynaptic reflex arc, because it contains only a single neuron-to-neuron synapse in the chain from sensory neuron to effector neuron. A monosynaptic reflex arc may contain more than two neurons, as long as there is only one neuron-to-neuron synapse along any path from the stimulus to the response. Indeed, most monosynaptic reflex arcs contain many neurons.

Neurons in a reflex arc can be arranged in two fundamentally different ways. Figure 8.25a illustrates the principle of **convergence**, in which multiple afferent neurons synapse with a single efferent neuron. A convergent arrangement of neurons allows spatial summation. For example, the activity of a single afferent neuron may be insufficient to excite the efferent neuron, but the simultaneous activity of many afferent neurons may be sufficient to cause a response. This effect occurs as a result of spatial summation. Convergence can also allow the comparison and integration of sensory signals from

FIGURE 8.25 Convergence and divergence in a monosynaptic reflex arc

(a) In a convergent arrangement, many presynaptic neurons interact with a single postsynaptic neuron. **(b)** In a divergent arrangement, a single presynaptic neuron forms synapses with many postsynaptic neurons. R = sensory receptor; E = effector organ.

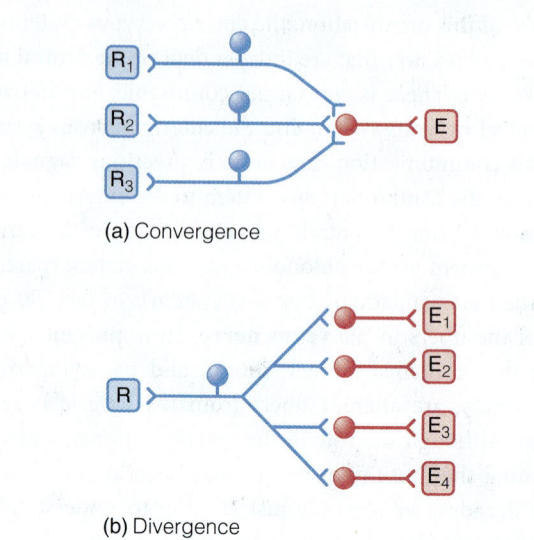

(a) Convergence

(b) Divergence

multiple parts of the body, increasing the complexity of information processing. For example, we have already discussed the significance of a convergent arrangement of neurons in the mammalian retina (see Chapter 7: Sensory Systems).

Figure 8.25b illustrates an alternative organization, called **divergence**. In this arrangement, a single afferent neuron forms synapses with more than one efferent neuron. Divergence allows a single signal to control multiple independent processes, and is a way to amplify the effect of a signal. Divergent functional arrangements allow the nervous system to engage in parallel processing, which allows very rapid integration of inputs and responses. The autonomic nervous system shows high levels of divergence. A single neural pathway from the autonomic nervous system may make connections with many target organs, allowing a coordinated and amplified response.

Note that all of the reflex arcs illustrated in Figure 8.25 are monosynaptic reflex arcs, because they contain only a single synapse in the chain between stimulus and response. Most reflex arcs have a more complex structure, and are called **polysynaptic** reflex arcs, because they contain synapses between more than two types of neurons. A simple polysynaptic reflex arc is shown in Figure 8.26, and includes a sensory cell, an afferent sensory neuron, an interneuron, an efferent neuron, and an effector cell. This type of reflex arc is illustrated by the reflex response to touch in *C. elegans*, which is governed by six touch receptors, five pairs of interneurons, and 69 motor neurons. Adding interneurons to a

FIGURE 8.24 A two-neuron reflex arc

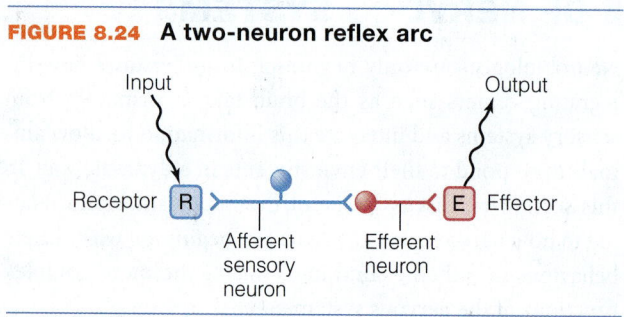

FIGURE 8.26 **A polysynaptic reflex arc**

A polysynaptic reflex arc includes a sensory receptor (R), an afferent neuron, an interneuron, one or more efferent neurons, and one or more effector organs (E).

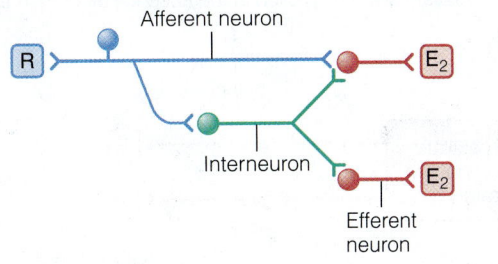

reflex arc greatly increases the potential responses of the arc and the complexity of the processing.

Pattern generators initiate rhythmic behaviors

Pattern generators govern many important physiological processes and simple rhythmic behaviors such as chewing, walking, swimming, and breathing. Pattern generators are groups of neurons that produce self-sustaining patterns of depolarization, independent of sensory input. Pattern generators can be organized in two different ways. The simplest form of organization involves a **pacemaker cell**. A pacemaker cell generates a spontaneous rhythmic depolarization, and thus controls the firing of all the cells in the network. Pacemaker cells are common in biological systems. For example, as we discuss in Chapter 9: Circulatory Systems, spontaneous pacemaker cells initiate the heartbeat in many kinds of animals. Pattern generators can also be made up of neurons that do not, as individuals, generate rhythmic depolarizations. Instead, the rhythm is an emergent property of the network that manifests itself because of the organization of the neurons in the network, rather than being an intrinsic property of the neurons themselves.

To get a sense of how pattern generators operate, consider a two-neuron pair. In this neuron pair, neither neuron generates a rhythm by itself, but when the first neuron (A) fires, it inhibits the other neuron (B) from firing until a defined period elapses, at which point neuron B fires. Neuron B then inhibits neuron A for a defined period of time, after which point it fires, and the loop continues. Imagine two robots programmed to hit if they are hit first. If robot A hits robot B, then robot B will respond by hitting back, which will cause robot A to hit back, and so on. The trick in this kind of network is getting it started in the first place. Once the chain of events is established, it will continue indefinitely, and it is no longer possible to determine where the behavior was initiated. Various mechanisms can start the rhythmic oscillations. Often, input from a sensory receptor is needed in order to start the

rhythm. Thus, the distinction between reflex arcs and pattern generators is not precise. Instead, these two types of control pathways interact to produce the complex behavior and physiological responses of animals.

Pattern generators govern swimming behavior in the leech

One approach to understanding the neurobiology underlying complex behaviors is to study simple behaviors in organisms with less complex nervous systems than those found in mammals. One such organism is the medicinal leech, *Hirudo medicinalis*. Like other members of the phylum Annelida, leeches are segmented worms with a brain, a ventral nerve cord, and a series of ganglia located in each body segment. Each segmental ganglion contains approximately 400 neurons, and this simple nervous organization makes the leech an excellent experimental model system. Leeches are ectoparasitic—they attach themselves to vertebrate hosts and feed on their blood. When a leech bites into the skin it injects a local anesthetic and anticoagulant to keep the blood running freely and to avoid detection by the host. A leech can consume up to 15 ml of blood during a single blood meal, or 10 times its unfed body size. Up to the middle of the nineteenth century, leeches were commonly used in a medical treatment called "bloodletting" in which physicians would apply leeches to the skin and allow them to suck the patient's blood. This therapy was thought to be helpful for a wide range of illnesses, including fever, headaches, and even obesity. Bloodletting is no longer a common therapy, but leeches are still occasionally used during surgical procedures, such as skin or tissue grafting. For example, leech therapy is particularly useful during finger or ear reattachment surgery to prevent pooling of blood, which can damage the newly grafted tissue.

In its natural habitat, a leech detects its prey by sensing the waves made by a prey animal as it moves about in the water. The leech then swims toward the potential prey, using a rhythmic undulatory motion. Over the last 30 years, neurobiologists have unraveled many components of the neural network that regulates this behavior (Figure 8.27). Swimming begins when mechanoreceptors in the skin sense a stimulus such as the waves made by a prey animal. These mechanoreceptors send an afferent sensory signal to the swim trigger interneuron, which makes a synaptic connection with the swim gating interneuron. When stimulated, the swim gating interneuron activates a network of neurons that forms a central pattern generator called the swim oscillator. This central pattern generator sends out rhythmic signals to motor neurons that stimulate muscles in the body wall to initiate rhythmic swimming. The circuit diagram of the swim oscillator is not yet fully worked out, but it involves at least seven oscillator interneurons and four motor neurons. Leeches can also initiate swimming behavior in the absence of a touch stimulus.

FIGURE 8.27 **The neural circuit governing swimming behavior in the leech**

A sensory signal from skin mechanoreceptors stimulates a swim trigger interneuron that stimulates a swim gating interneuron and a swim excitor interneuron. These interneurons activate the group of neurons that makes up the swim oscillator central pattern generator.

The central pattern generator then sends out a rhythmic signal to the swimming musculature. The swim excitor interneurons also process descending information from the leech brain, allowing the leech to initiate swimming even in the absence of a touch stimulus.

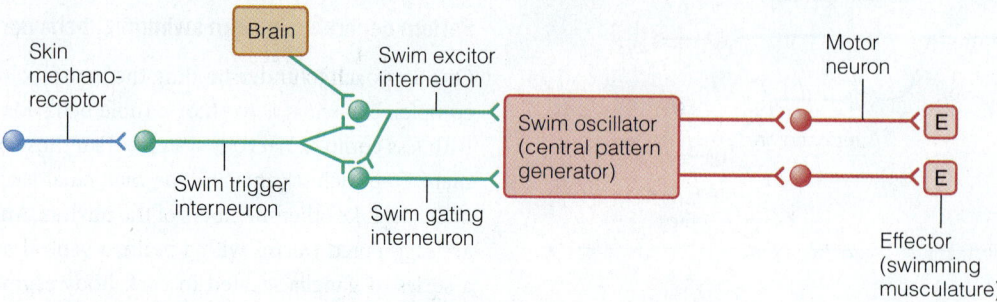

An additional neuron in the circuit, sometimes called the swim excitor interneuron, can modulate the activity of the swim gating neuron or the central pattern generator itself in response to signals from the leech brain, but the pathways involved in this higher level of control are not yet understood.

Pattern generators and reflexes are involved in tetrapod locomotion

Four-limbed (tetrapod) vertebrates move by swinging their legs in stereotyped patterns that we call gaits (such as running, walking, or trotting). Gaits such as walking involve rhythmic back-and-forth movements of the legs. Even the seemingly simple movements involved in walking or running require the coordinated contraction of many muscles so that each joint moves just the right distance at just the right time. In some ways, the mechanisms underlying locomotion in four-limbed vertebrates bear a striking resemblance to the control of swimming behavior in leeches. The brainstem (particularly the pons and medulla) usually initiates the command to begin locomotion (Figure 8.28). The brainstem then sends a signal to a network of neurons in the spinal cord that acts as a central pattern generator, similar to the pattern generator in the leech ganglia. The pattern generator then sends coordinated motor output signals to the muscles that control the movement of the limbs, initiating rhythmic movements. Unlike the pattern generator that controls swimming in leeches, the structure and neural connections of this pattern generator are not yet known, and even their location within the spinal cord remains somewhat elusive. However, a variety of experiments have demonstrated that a pattern generator must exist within the spinal cord.

In addition to generating rhythmic limb movements, animals must be able to respond to obstacles as they walk or run by dynamically changing their movements in response to changes in the contours of the ground. Stretch receptors and proprioceptors in the limbs sense information about the position of the limbs and the impact of the feet on the ground

FIGURE 8.28 **The neural circuit governing locomotion in mammals**

The brainstem sends a signal to the spinal cord central pattern generator. The central pattern generator then sends a rhythmic motor output signal to skeletal muscles. Sensory feedback from proprioceptors and vision travels to the pattern generator, the cerebellum, and the cerebral cortex (via the thalamus), modifying the output of the central pattern generator.

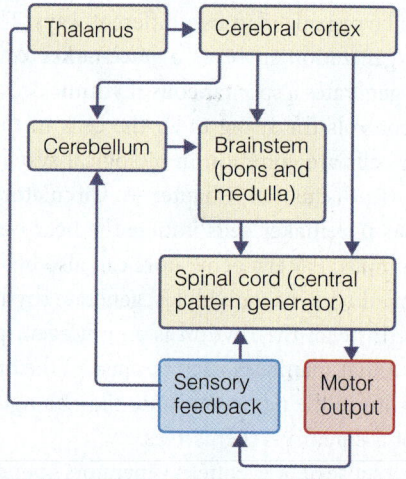

during walking or running. These receptors send sensory feedback to the pattern generator, allowing the pattern generator to modify its output in response to changing environmental demands. Thus, reflex arcs play an important role in regulating locomotory movements. However, these afferent inputs are not necessary to initiate rhythmic locomotion. For example, if you apply a drug such as curare, which paralyzes the muscles without interfering with nervous system function, and then record electrical activity in the motor neurons leading to the limb musculature, you will observe a phenomenon called fictive locomotion. If you stimulate the central pattern generator, the motor neurons will produce rhythmic firing patterns much as they would during normal locomotion, even in the complete absence of any movement-related feedback from the paralyzed muscles. Thus, sensory feedback is not necessary to generate rhythmic locomotory patterns, but simply modifies the output of the pattern generator.

The brain regulates and coordinates the activity of the spinal cord pattern generators, controlling the speed and smoothness of locomotion and adjusting locomotion in response to visual stimuli. Three parts of the brain (the brainstem, the cortex, and the cerebellum) have important roles to play in regulating locomotion. Centers in the brainstem regulate speed. By placing electrodes into the brains of experimental animals, neuroscientists have been able to demonstrate that weakly stimulating this part of the brain initiates walking. Increasing the stimulus intensity increases walking speed and eventually causes trotting and then galloping. The cortex plays an important role in guiding locomotion in complex environments, and in coordinating visual signals with locomotion. For example, a cat with damage to the premotor cortex can still walk on a smooth surface, or even on an inclined plane, but cannot step over objects. Sensory feedback from the working muscles and from other senses, such as vision, enters the cerebral cortex via the thalamus. The cerebral cortex then sends signals to the brainstem and spinal cord to modify locomotion.

The cerebellum fine-tunes locomotion by regulating the timing and intensity of signals to the spinal cord pattern generator. Humans or experimental animals with damage to the cerebellum walk in an uncoordinated way that resembles a drunken gait; their movements are jerky and uncoordinated, and they may stumble. In normal animals the cerebellum receives inputs from the stretch receptors and proprioceptors in the limbs, compares these signals to the intended movement, and then sends signals to the brainstem to correct the movement if necessary, thus coordinating locomotion.

The brain coordinates voluntary movements

Although reflex responses and central pattern generators play an important role in animal behavior, most vertebrates (and many invertebrates) can perform much more complex behavioral tasks. These voluntary behaviors are consciously planned and coordinated by the brain, and can be finely regulated in response to environmental circumstances. Figure 8.30 shows a schematic diagram of the parts of the vertebrate nervous system that are involved in regulating voluntary movements. First, an animal must decide to make a motion. This decision is made in the cerebral cortex of the brain, and includes inputs from the supplementary motor cortex, the association cortex, the visual cortex, and the limbic system. The decision to move is then developed into a program for movement in the primary motor cortex. This motor program is independent of the actual muscles that execute the program. For example, a person who knows how to write his or her name can easily (although a little clumsily) write it by holding a pencil between the toes. Similar regions of the brain are activated in each case, demonstrating that

the "program" for writing your name is independent of the specific controls of the muscles of your hands (or feet).

The primary motor cortex executes the motor program by sending signals along a series of tracts (groups of axons) to the spinal cord. Two main pathways are involved in voluntary movements. The pyramidal tracts are direct pathways from the primary motor cortex to the spinal cord and are so named because they pass through a portion of the medulla called the medullary pyramids. The pyramidal tracts play the major role in directing voluntary movements. These tracts cross over each other in the medulla, and thus the left side of the brain controls the right side of the body and vice versa. The extrapyramidal tracts are indirect pathways to motor neurons that, unlike the pyramidal tracts, make numerous synaptic connections within the brain prior to entering the spinal cord. They control the muscle groups that regulate posture and balance. For example, when you sign your name, the pyramidal tracts control the fine movements of your hands and arms, while the extrapyramidal tracts maintain your body position and orientation, although there is some overlap in function between the two systems.

The axons in the pyramidal and extrapyramidal tracts synapse with motor neurons within the spinal cord, and these motor neurons cause the appropriate muscles to contract in order to initiate movements. Just as with rhythmic locomotion, sensory afferent neurons return feedback from stretch receptors and proprioceptors in the muscles to the cerebellum. The cerebellum also receives sensory information from other sensory receptors such as the vestibular apparatus of the ear, which is involved in the sense of balance. The cerebellum integrates these inputs and sends a signal to the cortex (via the thalamus) to refine and adjust the descending motor output in order to complete the planned movement successfully.

Voluntary movements are complex behaviors that can easily be disrupted by changes to brain homeostasis. For example, alcohol consumption affects communication between the brain regions responsible for visual and motor control. The disruption of brain function by alcohol explains why intoxicated individuals have poor hand-eye coordination and emphasizes why drinking and driving is a bad idea. Box 8.2: Challenges to Homeostasis provides another example of the effects of changes in brain homeostasis on behavior.

Communication is a complex behavior

Communication is the transfer of information from one organism to another such that an action on the part of one organism alters the behavior of another organism. Many animals have the ability to communicate with each other, but human communication is particularly sophisticated. Language processing functions are carried out by the **cerebral cortex**, and particularly by two association areas called **Broca's area** and **Wernicke's area**, after the physicians that first described the roles of these areas. Wernicke's area is involved in language comprehension, while

OCEAN ACIDIFICATION AFFECTS FISH BEHAVIOR BY DISTURBING BRAIN HOMEOSTASIS

Voluntary movements require careful integration of multiple processes coordinated by the central nervous system, so even a modest disturbance of brain homeostasis has the potential to cause major disruptions in these behaviors. One interesting example of this phenomenon comes from studies of the effects of ocean acidification on the behavior of tropical reef fish.

Ocean acidification occurs when the CO_2 produced from burning fossil fuels dissolves in water, causing a reduction in the pH of the ocean. Although ocean pH was fairly stable over the last 600,000 years, since the industrial revolution human use of fossil fuels has already caused a decline in ocean pH of about 0.1 units, and by 2100 ocean pH is predicted to decrease by another 0.3 to 0.5 units. Although this does not seem like a particularly large change, the pH scale is logarithmic, so a 0.5 unit change in pH represents a very large change in H^+ ion concentration. If the pH of the ocean dropped from the current levels of around 8.07 down to 7.57, this would result in triple the concentration of hydrogen ions in the water.

We are only just beginning to understand the potential effects of ocean acidification on marine life, but it is expected to cause many changes in ocean ecosystems. For example, ocean acidification makes it more difficult for species with calcium carbonate in their exoskeleton, such as sea urchins, crabs, oysters, and reef-building corals, to grow and develop because the reduced pH reduces the availability of the calcium carbonate that they need to make their hard external shell or exoskeleton.

Because fish have efficient and effective homeostatic mechanisms for regulating the CO_2 levels and pH of their blood and interstitial fluid, they were not considered to be at much direct risk from ocean acidification. Although even for fish, ecosystem changes would have the potential to cause indirect harm by interfering with food sources or other interspecies interactions. Recently, however, scientists have

FIGURE 8.29 **An orange clownfish (*Amphiprion percula*)**

Photo source: cbpix/Fotolia.

discovered that ocean acidification has several important direct effects on fish behavior.

Orange clownfish (*Amphiprion percula*), like the one shown in Figure 8.29, typically live in association with sea anemones on coral reefs around tropical islands with lush vegetation. Clownfish larvae float in the water column until it is time to settle and grow to adulthood. The larvae of clownfish locate suitable settlement habitat using both olfactory and auditory cues, and ocean acidification has been shown to interfere with both processes.

Clownfish are strongly attracted to the scent of the sea anemones in which they live, and to the scent of the leaves of tropical rainforest trees (such as *anthostemon chrysanthus*), which indicates the presence of a suitable island and reef. On the other hand, they strongly avoid the scent of the leaves of a tropical swamp tree (*Melaleuca nervosa*), which would indicate unsuitable swampy habitat. When clownfish

Broca's area is involved in the production of speech sounds. In more than 95 percent of humans, both Broca's area and Wernicke's area are found in the left hemisphere, and the parallel regions of the right hemisphere are not involved in language processing. In addition to these classic association areas, more recent studies demonstrate that the basal ganglia are also important for language processing, and particularly for language acquisition—the process of learning language.

One particularly important feature of human language is the fact that our language is not innate. We can learn and use many different languages. Only bats, dolphins, elephants, and sea lions, and a few types of birds (e.g., zebra finches, crows, parrots, and hummingbirds) have the ability to learn and use new combinations of vocal sounds. The mechanisms involved in vocal learning in humans and songbirds are thought to be similar, in that both have a critical period during early life

larvae are raised in acidified ocean water, they are less attracted to the scent of anemones and rainforest trees, and instead they are strongly attracted to the scent of the swamp tree. This change in voluntary behavior in larvae exposed to ocean acidification could cause them to select unsuitable habitat that would not allow them to grow to adulthood.

Ocean acidification also disrupts the ability of orange clownfish larvae to detect and avoid predators using olfactory cues. In fact, orange clownfish that are reared in acidified ocean water are strongly attracted to the odor of predators, instead of avoiding predator odors. This change in behavior has obvious potential for negative consequences.

These changes in clownfish behavior could involve changes in the function of the sensory organs or changes in the function of the brain. Recent research suggests that changes in brain homeostasis as a result of ocean acidification may be the culprit. When fish are exposed to high CO_2, they homeostatically regulate the acid-base balance of the blood by accumulating bicarbonate (HCO_3^-), which helps to neutralize the blood. They take up this HCO_3^- in exchange for Cl^-, so this process causes reductions in extracellular Cl^-. These changes in Cl^- balance have the potential to interfere with neuronal signaling that involves chloride channels.

The GABA-A receptor is a ligand-gated chloride channel (see Chapter 5: Neuron Structure and Function) that is an important neurotransmitter-receptor in the brain. Normally, opening of GABA-A receptors results in movement of Cl^- into the cell down its electrochemical gradient. Movement of a negatively charged ion into a postsynaptic neuron would result in hyperpolarization, and thus an inhibitory postsynaptic potential. Because of this effect, GABA acts as an inhibitory neurotransmitter in the brain.

Dr. Goran Nilsson, from the University of Oslo, working with a team from James Cook University in Australia headed by Dr. Philip Munday, hypothesized that ocean acidification might be interfering with GABA-A receptor function by reversing the direction of Cl^- movement. If extracellular Cl^- levels are abnormally low in fish exposed to ocean acidification (because of the homeostatic regulation of extracellular pH), then instead of entering the cell when GABA-A receptors opened, Cl^- might leave the cell because of a reversal in the electrochemical gradient. This would cause GABA to be an excitatory rather than an inhibitory neurotransmitter.

To test this hypothesis, Dr. Nilsson treated clownfish with gabazine, an antagonist of the GABA-A receptor, which blocks its function. Clownfish reared in normal seawater could detect and avoid the odor of a predator, and gabazine did not interfere with this function. Clownfish reared in acidified seawater were strongly attracted to the odor of a predator, and gabazine reversed this behavior and caused them to avoid the predator. These data strongly suggest that the effects of ocean acidification on the behavior of clownfish are due to changes in brain homeostasis that affect the function of the GABA-A receptor, thus demonstrating just how sensitive voluntary behavior may be to small changes in brain chemistry.

References

- Dixson, D. L., Munday, P. L., & Jones, G. P. (2010). Ocean acidification disrupts the innate ability of fish to detect predator olfactory cues. *Ecology Letters, 13*, 68–75.
- Munday, P. L., Dixson, D. L., Donelson, J. M., Jones, G. P., Pratchett, M. S., Devitsina, G. V., & Døving, K. B. (2009). Ocean acidification impairs olfactory discrimination and homing ability of a marine fish. *Proceedings of the National Academy of Sciences USA, 106*, 1848–1852.
- Nilsson, G. E., Dixson, D. L., Domenici, P., McCormick, M. I., Sorensen, C., Watson, S. A., & Munday, P. L. (2012). Near-future carbon dioxide levels alter fish behaviour by interfering with neurotransmitter function. *Nature Climate Change, 2*, 201–204.
- Simpson, S. D., Munday, P. L., Wittenrich, M. L., Manassa, R., Dixson, D. L., Gagliano, M., & Yan, H. Y. (2011). Ocean acidification erodes crucial auditory behaviour in a marine fish. *Biology Letters, 7*, 917–920.

in which vocal communication is learned, and both require regular practice and feedback. Vocal learning in humans and songbirds also has some parallels at the level of the brain. Vocal learning in songbirds involves a region called Area X, which is the homologue of the mammalian basal ganglia. In birds, knockdown of a gene called *FOXP* in Area X results in impaired vocal learning. In humans, mutations of the *FOXP* gene cause severe speech and language disorders.

CONCEPT CHECK

13. What is the difference between a monosynaptic reflex arc and a polysynaptic reflex arc?

14. What kinds of behaviors involve pattern generators?

15. What is the location of the pattern generator governing walking in vertebrates?

FIGURE 8.30 **Control of voluntary movement in mammals**

The cerebral cortex initiates voluntary movements. The motor cortex then initiates a motor program by sending efferent signals via the direct pyramidal tract and the indirect extrapyramidal tract. The neurons of the pyramidal tract proceed directly from the cortex to the spinal cord without forming any intermediate synapses, sending a signal via motor neurons to the muscles of the limbs to control movement. The extrapyramidal tract is a multineuron chain that forms synapses in many brain areas before reaching the spinal cord and sending signals via motor neurons to the muscles of posture and balance.

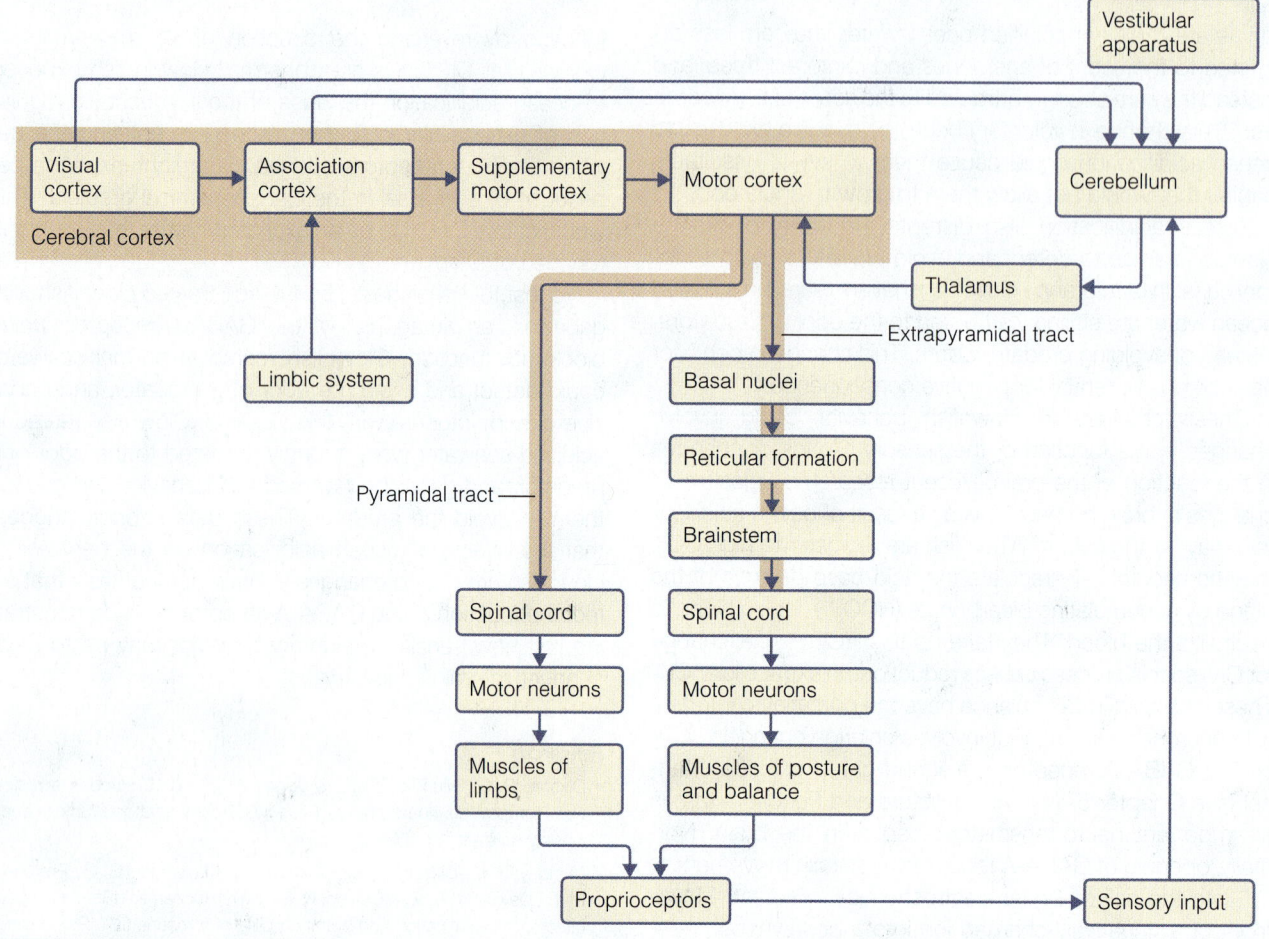

Learning and Memory

In addition to performing complex behaviors, most animals can remember experiences, and modify their behavior accordingly. Although learning and memory are related concepts, these words describe two distinct tasks. Learning refers to the process of acquiring new information, while memory refers to the retention and retrieval of that learned information. The vast majority of animals have the ability to form memories and to learn. Learning and memory are possible because of the **plasticity** of the nervous system—the ability to change both synaptic connections and functional properties of neurons in response to stimuli.

Invertebrates show simple learning and memory

Aplysia californica, the sea slug, is used as a model system for studying learning and memory. Like other mollusks, *Aplysia* has a fairly simple nervous system consisting of about 20,000 neurons organized into a series of ganglia. *Aplysia* demonstrates a simple kind of learning called **habituation**—a decline in the tendency to respond to a stimulus due to repeated exposure. Humans also show habituation. For example, if you live near a construction site, at first the noise of the construction may be very disturbing, and you may have difficulty concentrating or studying, but after a while you "get used to" the noise and easily ignore it—you have become habituated to the stimulus. Habituation is an important property of nervous systems, because it allows animals to ignore unimportant routine stimuli and pay more attention to novel, potentially dangerous ones. If you gently touch *Aplysia* on its siphon (a fleshy spout above the gill used to expel seawater), the animal will withdraw its gills and siphon into the mantle cavity (Figure 8.31). However, after repeated gentle touches, *Aplysia* will reduce gill withdrawal by about one-third. If you repeatedly touch the siphon 10 or 15 times over the course of a few minutes, the habituation response lasts

FIGURE 8.31 The gill-withdrawal reflex in *Aplysia californica*

(a) Dorsal view of *Aplysia californica*. **(b)** The neural circuit governing the gill-withdrawal reflex. Sensory neurons in the skin of the siphon detect a mechanical stimulus. These sensory neurons form synapses with interneurons and motor neurons. These motor neurons send an efferent signal that causes the gill to withdraw. Habituation of the reflex occurs because of functional changes at the synapse between the sensory and motor neuron as a result of repeated stimulation.

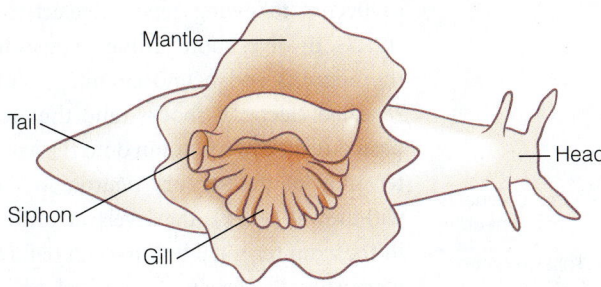

(a) *Aplysia californica*, dorsal view

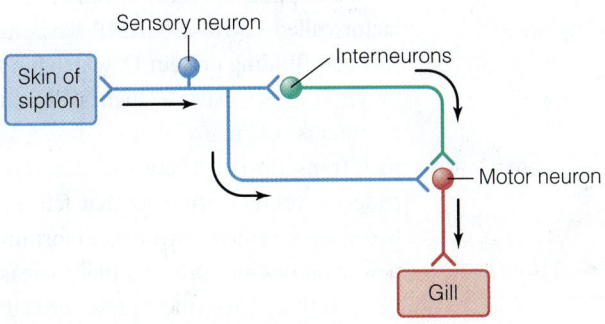

(b) The neural circuit governing the gill-withdrawal reflex

FIGURE 8.32 The neural network involved in sensitization in *Aplysia*

Sensitization of the gill-withdrawal reflex involves a second neural circuit from the skin of the tail. An electrical shock to the tail sends an afferent signal along a sensory neuron that makes a synaptic connection with a facilitating interneuron. This facilitating interneuron makes synaptic connections with the neurons involved in the gill-withdrawal reflex, modifying their response to touch stimuli.

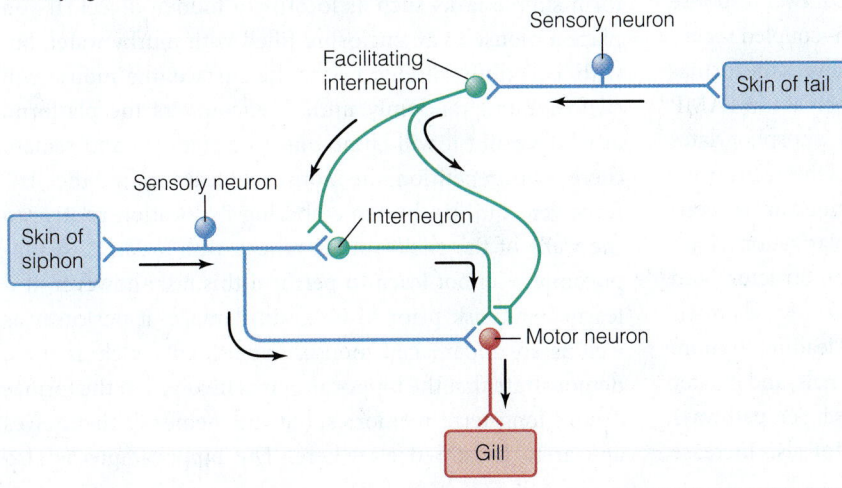

for about a day, a phenomenon called short-term habituation. If you repeat this stimulation protocol on several consecutive days, the habituation lasts for three or four weeks, a phenomenon called long-term habituation.

Habituation occurs because of functional changes at the synapse between the sensory neuron and the motor neuron. In short-term habituation, a Ca^{2+} channel in the membrane of the presynaptic axon terminal of the sensory neuron is inactivated. Touching the siphon still generates an action potential in the sensory neuron, but when the action potential reaches the axon terminal, less Ca^{2+} flows into the axon terminal, because of the partial inactivation of the voltage-gated Ca^{2+} channels. Neurotransmitter release depends on the influx of Ca^{2+} into the axon terminals, and therefore habituated animals release less neurotransmitter. In addition, there are some morphological changes in the presynaptic axon terminal, including changes in the number and location of neurotransmitter-containing vesicles. Long-term habituation results in similar changes in the presynaptic axon terminal, but to a greater degree. Although the molecular mechanisms involved in the inactivation of the voltage-gated Ca^{2+} channels and the changes in vesicle distribution are not yet known, it is clear that changes in the presynaptic axon terminal of sensory neurons that contact motor neurons cause habituation in *Aplysia*.

Aplysia also demonstrates a kind of learning called **sensitization** (Figure 8.32). In contrast to habituation, sensitization is an increase in the response to a gentle stimulus after exposure to a strong stimulus. For example, imagine being alone in your house in the middle of the night. You suddenly hear a loud noise coming from the basement. For the next little while you will probably be acutely aware of all the sounds around you—you will be sensitized to your environment. You can demonstrate the phenomenon of sensitization in *Aplysia* by delivering an electrical shock to the tail. If you gently touch *Aplysia* on its siphon after this electrical shock, the gill-withdrawal reflex will be much larger and last longer than in an unsensitized animal. The effects of a single shock die out after about an hour, but multiple strong shocks will affect the gill-withdrawal response for a week or more.

As with habituation, during sensitization physiological changes occur in the presynaptic axon terminal of the sensory neuron from the siphon. However, in the case of sensitization there is an increase in Ca^{2+} entry, and increased neurotransmitter release, rather than a reduction. The mechanism underlying this increase in neurotransmitter release

FIGURE 8.33 The molecular mechanism of sensitization in *Aplysia*

The facilitating interneuron releases serotonin onto the axon terminal of the sensory neurons involved in the gill-withdrawal reflex. Serotonin binds to a G protein–coupled receptor that increases intracellular cAMP, activating protein kinase A (PKA), which inactivates voltage-gated K^+ channels. When these K^+ channels are inactivated, action potentials last longer, leading to more Ca^{2+} influx through voltage-gated Ca^{2+} channels, and greater neurotransmitter release from the sensory neuron onto the cell body of the motor neuron.

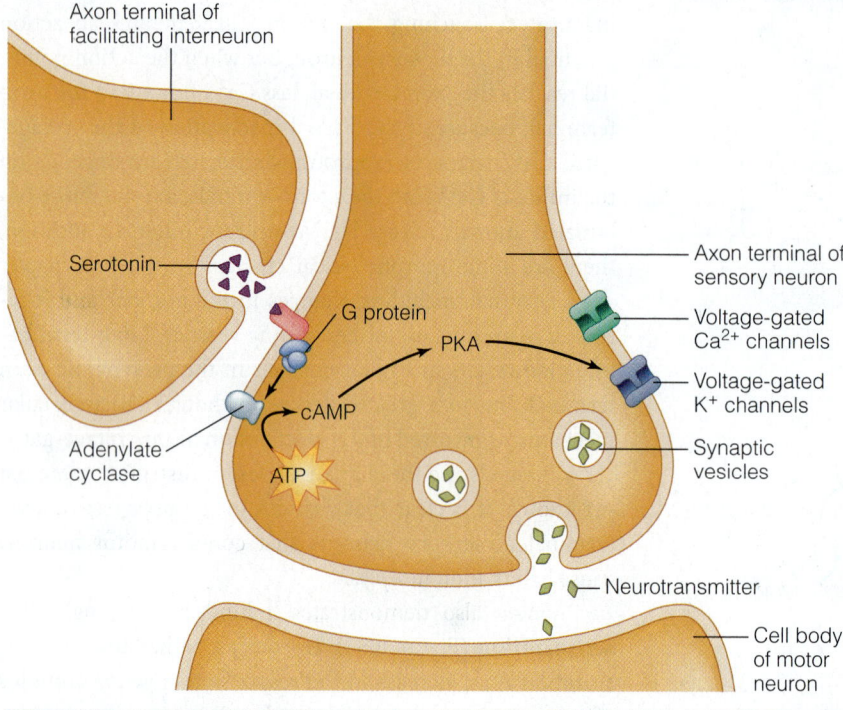

the number and location of neurotransmitter vesicles and activate another Ca^{2+} channel, allowing more Ca^{2+} to enter the cell, further increasing neurotransmitter release. These direct effects of serotonin are relatively short-lived and account for the short-term sensitization of the gill-withdrawal reflex.

Longer-term sensitization, such as occurs following repeated electrical shocks, involves more lasting changes to the neurons and neural circuitry. With repeated electrical shocks (and thus repeated release of serotonin onto the axon terminal of the sensory neuron in the withdrawal reflex), the levels of cAMP in the axon terminal become still higher, increasing the levels of activated PKA. Some of the activated PKA enters the nucleus and phosphorylates a transcription factor called CREB-1 (cAMP Response Element Binding protein 1), which binds to cAMP-responsive sequences in the promoters of many genes, increasing their transcription. These activated genes code for protein products that fall into two classes: proteins involved in forming new synapses and proteins that increase PKA activity. Together these proteins increase the number of synaptic connections and their responsiveness, leading to long-term sensitization of the gill-withdrawal reflex.

involves a second neural circuit: a sensory neuron from the tail that makes a synaptic connection with several interneurons (only one interneuron is shown in Figure 8.32 for clarity). In turn, these interneurons make synaptic connections on the axon terminal of the sensory neuron involved in the gill-withdrawal response. An electrical shock to the tail sends an afferent signal to the interneurons, which then release the neurotransmitter serotonin onto the axon terminal of the sensory neuron involved in the gill-withdrawal response (Figure 8.33). Serotonin binds to a G protein–coupled receptor that activates adenylate cyclase, which catalyzes the formation of the second messenger cAMP. The increase in cAMP activates protein kinase A (PKA), which phosphorylates voltage-gated K^+ channels in the membrane of the axon terminal, inactivating them. Voltage-gated K^+ channels are responsible for repolarizing the cell after the depolarization phase of an action potential (see Chapter 5: Neuron Structure and Function for details of this process). When these K^+ channels are inactivated, action potentials last longer, leading to more Ca^{2+} influx through voltage-gated Ca^{2+} channels, and greater neurotransmitter release. The second messenger pathways activated when serotonin binds to its receptor also increase

The hippocampus is important for memory formation in mammals

Memory formation has also been extensively studied in mammals. For example, rats and mice can be trained to perform simple tasks such as locating a hidden object. If you place a mouse in an enclosure filled with murky water, but with a platform hidden below the surface, the mouse will swim around randomly until it encounters the platform, at which point it will climb onto the platform and remain there. With repetition, the mouse will learn to find the platform very quickly, by remembering its location relative to the walls of the enclosure. A mouse with a damaged hippocampus cannot learn to perform this task; however, if it learned the task prior to its brain damage, it performs as well as an undamaged mouse. Experiments such as these demonstrate that the hippocampus is involved in the formation of long-term memories, but the memories themselves appear to be stored elsewhere. The hippocampus is also

FUNCTIONAL MAGNETIC RESONANCE IMAGING AND BRAIN PLASTICITY

Brain-imaging technology is revolutionizing the way in which physiologists study the functions of the brain and has revealed an astonishing level of plasticity. For example, scientists have been able to determine that the brains of taxi drivers working in London, England, differ from those of other people. In order to get a license to drive a taxi in London, drivers must pass a difficult test that assesses their ability to find their way. The streets of London are not laid out in a grid pattern, which makes navigating in London without a map difficult. London taxi drivers have an enlarged hippocampus, a part of the brain known to be involved in spatial relationships and memory.

But are these differences the result of training, or are people with these unusual brain structures simply attracted to professions in which they can excel? A technique called functional magnetic resonance imaging (fMRI) is providing a way to address this question. An MRI machine emits a powerful magnetic field that can be directed at the brain (or at other parts of the body). This magnetic field causes the hydrogen atoms in water molecules to realign with the magnetic field, just as a compass aligns with Earth's magnetic field. The MRI machine then sends out a pulse of radio energy. This pulse briefly knocks the hydrogen atoms out of alignment. As the hydrogen atoms return to their aligned position they emit energy, which the MRI machine can detect and interpret. Because the amount of water (and hence hydrogen atoms) varies in different structures of the brain, an MRI machine can provide detailed brain images. Functional MRI is a simple modification of this technique. Parts of the brain that are working harder require more oxygen than parts of the brain that are resting and thus tend to have higher levels of blood flow. Thus the MRI signal changes as a subject uses different parts of the brain. If you make a series of MRI images while asking a subject to perform a mental task, you generate an fMRI image, in which you can observe changes in blood flow (and thus changes in activity) in different parts of the brain. For example, listening to music activates a part of the brain involved in processing incoming auditory information, whereas speaking activates different parts of the brain. Studies using fMRI are revealing the truly dynamic nature of the brain. For example, there are observable changes in the brains of adults when they are taught a new alphabet.

As for the London taxi drivers, recent studies have shown that the differences in their brain structure and activity are a result of practice, not an accident of birth. The brain can alter its structure and function in response to training, and thus there is a physiological basis for the adage, "Practice makes perfect."

References
- Maguire, E. A., Spiers, H. J., Good, C. D., Hartley, T., Frackowiak, R. S., & Burgess, N. (2003). Navigation expertise and the human hippocampus: A structural brain imaging analysis. *Hippocampus, 13,* 250–259.
- Maguire, E. A., Gadian, D. G., Johnsrude, I. S., Good, C. D., Ashburner, J., Frackowiak, R. S., & Frith, C. D. (2000). Navigation-related structural change in the hippocampi of taxi drivers. *Proceedings of the National Academy of Sciences USA, 97,* 4398–4403.

associated with memory formation in humans (see Box 8.3: Applications: Functional Magnetic Resonance Imaging and Brain Plasticity).

The cellular and molecular mechanisms underlying memory formation in the hippocampus have been examined **in vitro** using recording electrodes placed into thin slices of hippocampal tissue. In these preparations, repetitive stimulation of a particular presynaptic neuron eventually leads to an increase in the response of the postsynaptic neuron, a phenomenon called **long-term potentiation**. Over time, a particular level of presynaptic stimulation is converted to a larger postsynaptic output. Long-term potentiation is thought to be important in memory formation because it provides a mechanism in which repetitive activity of a particular neural pathway can leave a record of itself even after the activity has stopped. Although long-term potentiation

can occur in several parts of the brain, it is easiest to demonstrate in the hippocampus, further suggesting that the hippocampus is important in memory formation.

Long-term potentiation likely occurs via several mechanisms, but the best-studied mechanism involves changes in certain specific postsynaptic neurons in the hippocampus, the so-called CA1 cells (Figure 8.34). Note that this is in contrast to habituation and sensitization in *Aplysia*, which involve changes in presynaptic neurons. These postsynaptic CA1 cells express two different types of receptors for the neurotransmitter glutamate: AMPA receptors and NMDA receptors (which are so named because they selectively bind the drugs AMPA and NMDA). NMDA receptors are ligand-gated Ca^{2+} channels, so when glutamate binds to NMDA receptors, Ca^{2+} enters the cell. AMPA receptors are ligand-gated Na^+ channels, so when glutamate binds to AMPA

FIGURE 8.34 **Long-term potentiation in hippocampal neurons**

(a) Low-frequency stimulation of the presynaptic cell results in moderate release of glutamate. Glutamate released from the presynaptic cell binds to the AMPA and NMDA receptors on the postsynaptic cell. Na^+ enters through the AMPA receptor, causing depolarization, but the presence of Mg^{2+} in the NMDA receptor prevents Ca^{2+} from entering the cell. **(b)** High-frequency stimulation of the presynaptic cell results in greater release of glutamate. Glutamate binds to both receptor types on the postsynaptic cell. Increased glutamate causes increased Na^+ entry through AMPA

receptors, causing a greater depolarization. This greater depolarization displaces Mg^{2+} from the NMDA receptor, allowing Ca^{2+} to enter the cell. The influx of Ca^{2+} activates protein kinases (CaMKII and PKC), phosphorylating the AMPA receptor, increasing its sensitivity to glutamate. CaMKII also phosphorylates proteins that target additional AMPA receptors to the synaptic cleft, and together these mechanisms increase the sensitivity of the postsynaptic cell to glutamate. CaMKII is also thought to trigger the release of paracrine factors that cause the presynaptic cell to release more glutamate.

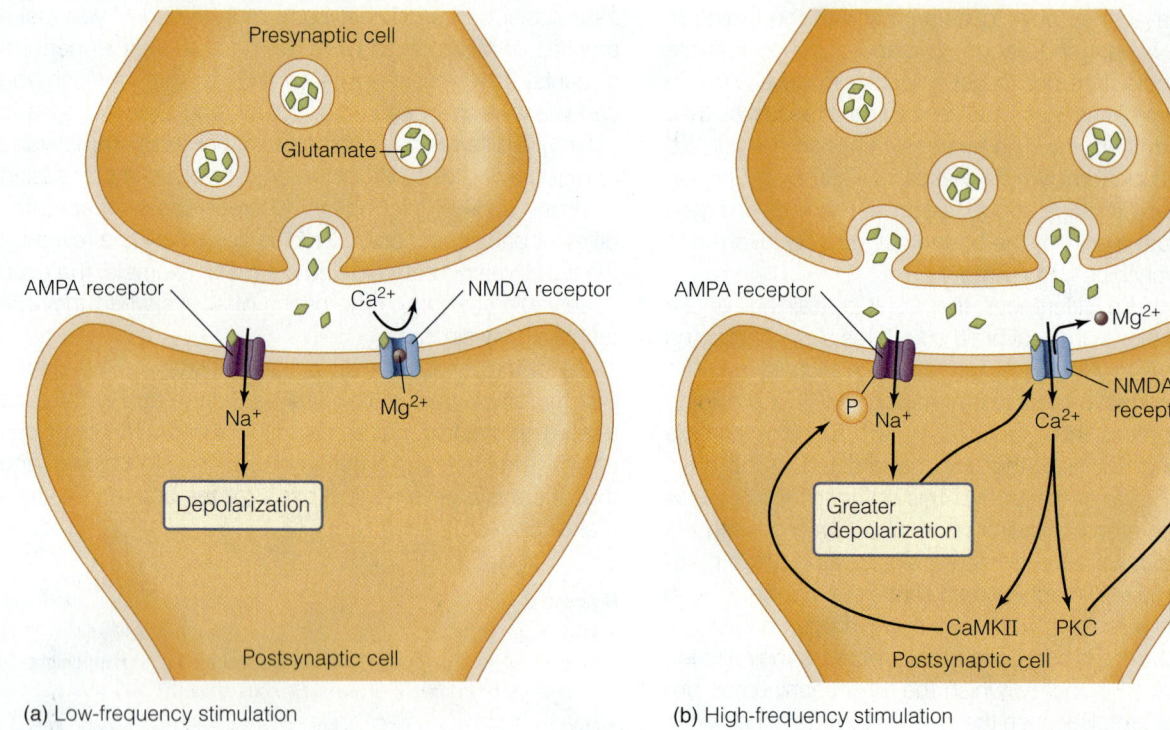

(a) Low-frequency stimulation

(b) High-frequency stimulation

receptors, Na^+ enters the cell. Low-frequency stimulation of the presynaptic neuron causes moderate release of glutamate into the synapse, and only the AMPA receptors open, because Mg^{2+} blocks the NMDA ion channels (Figure 8.34a).

High-frequency stimulation of the presynaptic neuron causes greater release of glutamate, and the resulting greater depolarization of the postsynaptic membrane displaces the magnesium ions from the channel of the NMDA receptor (Figure 8.34b). With the Mg^{2+} gone and the ion channel open, Ca^{2+} enters the postsynaptic cell via the NMDA receptor. The increase in intracellular calcium levels activates calcium-calmodulin-dependent protein kinase II (CaMKII) and protein kinase C (PKC), which phosphorylate a variety of proteins. For example, in CA1 cells CaMKII phosphorylates the AMPA receptor, making it more sensitive to glutamate, and also increases the number of AMPA receptors on the postsynaptic membrane by relocating receptors from intracellular stores. PKC activates a paracrine signaling pathway

that causes the presynaptic cell to produce more glutamate. The net effect of these changes is more glutamate acting on more sensitive postsynaptic neurons, increasing the response to subsequent stimuli, and improving memory formation.

Transgenic mice have been used to test this mechanism of long-term potentiation and its relationship to memory formation. For example, transgenic mice that lack the CaMKII gene do not show long-term potentiation and have more trouble finding a hidden platform under murky water than do normal mice, while transgenic mice that produce too much CaMKII show greater long-term potentiation and perform better on hidden-platform tests and other tests of learning and memory. Similarly, transgenic mice that lack NMDA receptor expression in hippocampal neurons have more difficulty learning to find their way through a maze, or to find a hidden underwater platform. These results strongly indicate that long-term potentiation is involved in at least some kinds of memory formation in vertebrates.

Regulation and Homeostasis

Although many parts of the brain help to coordinate homeostatic processes, the hypothalamus is the key player in homeostatic regulation. The hypothalamus integrates input from many brain regions. It also directly monitors important internal parameters such as temperature, osmolarity, and hormone levels in the blood. When the hypothalamus detects deviations from normal set points, it sends out signals that restore homeostasis. The hypothalamus can send signals using the autonomic nervous system and/or using the endocrine system via the pituitary. The hypothalamus is thus a particularly critical region of the brain because it serves as a link between the nervous system and the endocrine system.

Multiple brain regions send inputs to the hypothalamus

A variety of brain regions send inputs to the hypothalamus. The nucleus of the solitary tract in the medulla oblongata collects sensory input from the vagus nerve, which carries sensory information from the internal organs, including input from the digestive system and the enteric nervous system. The reticular formation in the brainstem sends signals from the spinal cord, including information from inputs such as skin temperature. The hypothalamus also receives information from the forebrain, and particularly from the other parts of the limbic system (including the amygdala, the hippocampus, and the olfactory cortex), providing information about emotional state and motivation.

Although most of the CNS is physiologically separated from the rest of the body by the blood-brain barrier, this barrier is modified in regions of the hypothalamus called the circumventricular organs. The capillaries in these regions are termed fenestrated, because they contain pores through which substances such as hormones can diffuse (*fenestra* = window in Latin). The circumventricular organs contain osmoreceptors and receptors for a variety of hormones, allowing the hypothalamus to directly monitor these parameters.

The hypothalamus helps maintain ion and water balance

As we discuss in more detail in Chapter 13: Ion and Water Balance, vertebrates maintain the osmolarity and ion composition of body fluids within a narrow range. The hypothalamus receives inputs from the circumventricular organs that directly monitor blood osmolarity as well as inputs from sensors in the circulatory system that monitor blood pressure and thus blood volume (see Chapter 9: Circulatory Systems). When blood osmolarity rises or blood pressure declines, the hypothalamus signals to the pituitary to release a hormone called antidiuretic hormone (or vasopressin) that causes the kidneys to reabsorb water from the urine. In addition, the hypothalamus triggers the sensation of thirst, resulting in increased drinking if water is available. Sensors in the gut then provide sensory feedback to the hypothalamus to inhibit drinking as the gut fills.

The hypothalamus regulates body temperature

As we discuss in more detail in Chapter 15: Thermal Physiology, the hypothalamus, along with the spinal cord (particularly in birds), plays a major role in the regulation of body temperature in both ectotherms and endotherms. The hypothalamus is one of the few brain regions that contains neurons that are directly sensitive to temperature. In addition, the hypothalamus receives inputs from thermoreceptors in the periphery, allowing it to integrate information about temperature in all parts of the body. The hypothalamus then sends out signals that alter behavior and a variety of physiological systems to maintain body temperature within appropriate limits.

The hypothalamus regulates food intake

As we discuss in more detail in Chapter 14: Digestion and Energy Metabolism, the ventromedial nucleus of the hypothalamus regulates appetite and feeding behavior. For example, electrical stimulation of parts of the ventromedial nucleus in rats triggers feeding behavior even when the rat has just finished eating to the point of satiation. Similarly, destroying other parts of the ventromedial nucleus causes complete cessation of feeding. Data such as these suggest that the hypothalamus contains regions that stimulate feeding and regions that cause feeding to stop, and that the balance of the activity of these different parts of the hypothalamus regulates feeding behavior.

The ways in which the hypothalamus stimulates and inhibits feeding remain poorly understood, but likely involve sensing of fat and glucose levels and of a variety of hormones such as insulin and leptin that are released by the gut, adipose, and other tissues.

The hypothalamus is involved in the stress response

The stress response has two main components: activation of the sympathetic nervous system and activation of the endocrine system (see Chapter 4: Cell Signaling and Endocrine Regulation). Both of these components are controlled by the limbic system of the brain, including the amygdala and hypothalamus. The amygdala is responsible for activating the sympathetic nervous system, while the hypothalamus activates the endocrine system. When activated by a stressful stimulus, the hypothalamus releases corticotropin-releasing hormone (CRH) into the hypothalamic-pituitary portal blood system, causing the pituitary to release adrenocorticotropic hormone (ACTH) into the circulation. The ACTH binds to receptors on the adrenal cortex (a part of the adrenal gland, surrounding the adrenal medulla). The adrenal cortex then releases glucocorticoid hormones, such as cortisol, into the blood.

Cortisol is a steroid hormone, and it mediates many of its actions by altering gene transcription in its target cells. Thus, cortisol typically acts fairly slowly, over the course of an hour or so. Because of the generally slow time course of the cortisol response, the role of the glucocorticoid hormones in the immediate response to stress is not entirely understood. Cortisol may, however, be important in preparing an animal to respond to a subsequent stressor, or to recover from the previous one.

The brain integrates sensory information associated with potentially stressful stimuli using two different pathways. In one pathway, the incoming sensory information travels from the thalamus to the sensory cortex, where it is integrated. If the cortex concludes that the sensory stimulus is dangerous, its sends a signal to the limbic system. At the same time, using a second pathway, the thalamus can send signals directly to the limbic system without any sophisticated processing, by-passing the sensory cortex. For example, if you are startled and frightened by a sudden noise in the night, you may initiate a stress response before you consciously realize what caused the noise.

Although the stress response is a vital survival tool that allows vertebrates to respond to stressful situations quickly and efficiently, chronic activation of this response can have deleterious consequences. Chronic stress can result in a weakened immune system, elevated blood cholesterol levels, high blood pressure, and even impaired growth. In addition, chronic stress can affect the brain. In particular, chronic elevation of stress hormones interferes with long-term potentiation in the hippocampus. Indeed, long-term exposure to high levels of glucocorticoids can cause the hippocampus to atrophy, decreasing the total number of neurons in this area of the brain, eventually causing irreversible memory loss. Single episodes of stress (acute stress), on the other hand, are associated with increased growth of neurons in the hippocampus and improved memory. Various stress-coping strategies, including the formation of strong social networks, have been shown to be protective against the negative effects of chronic social stress in primates, such as baboons and humans.

The hypothalamus regulates circadian rhythms

Circadian rhythms are predictable daily variations in physiological parameters that are linked with the daily cycle of light and dark. Almost every aspect of behavior and physiology undergoes a circadian rhythm, including processes such as metabolic rate, activity, and digestion. Circadian rhythms persist even when an organism is kept in constant darkness; however, without environmental cues these rhythms tend to be somewhat longer or shorter than 24 hours—giving rise to the name circadian (*circa* = about; *dies* = day). External environmental cues such as the pattern of light and dark help to keep the intrinsic circadian clock in sync with the natural environment.

In mammals, the circadian clock is located in the hypothalamus, or more specifically within the **suprachiasmatic nucleus (SCN)**, a grouping of about 10,000 neurons within the hypothalamus. The circadian clock within the SCN is generated by a rhythmic cycle of changes in gene expression in a subset of these neurons. Although the SCN is found only in vertebrates, circadian clocks are found in all animals, and appear to work via similar mechanisms.

The rhythmic cycle of gene expression in the SCN is caused by a negative feedback loop involving gene regulation (Figure 8.35). The transcription factors BMAL1 and CLOCK heterodimerize and bind to an activator sequence called an E-box within the promoters of several genes in the gene families period (*per*) and cryptochrome (*cry*). The resulting protein products (PERs and CRYs) heterodimerize in the cytoplasm. The PER:CRY dimers are then translocated back to the nucleus, where they inhibit the activity of the CLOCK:BMAL1 heterodimer, and thus inhibit their own transcription. As a result of the time lags between these events, the levels of PER and CRY increase and decrease cyclically. Although the exact mechanisms by which changes in PER and CRY initiate changes in the activity of the clock neurons are not fully understood, mutations in these genes result in changes in the rhythms of electrical activity.

The pattern of cyclic gene expression is a common pattern in the circadian clocks of all animals, although the details of the transcriptional regulatory circuit can differ. In fruit flies (*Drosophila melanogaster*), a gene called cycle (*cyc*) is the homologue of the mammalian gene BMAL1, and *Drosophila* have *per* genes as well. But fruit flies use a gene called timeless (*tim*) instead of the cryptochromes (*cry*), and their homologue of the cryptochromes is used as a light sensor that helps to entrain the circadian rhythm to the cycles of day and night, rather than as part of the clock itself.

The suprachiasmatic nucleus communicates its rhythmic electrical signal to other parts of the brain and to many physiological systems via the pituitary, resulting in circadian rhythms in many biological processes (Figure 8.36). The suprachiasmatic nucleus also sends signals to the pineal gland,

FIGURE 8.35 **Gene regulation and the circadian clock in mammals**

Circadian clocks are caused by oscillating patterns of gene expression in neurons within the SCN. The proteins BMAL1 and CLOCK heterodimerize and activate the transcription of the *per* and *cry* gene families, by binding to an E-box in their promoters.

The mRNA is translated in the cytoplasm and the resulting PER and CRY proteins dimerize and are translocated back to the nucleus, where they inhibit the activity of the BMAL1:CLOCK heterodimer.

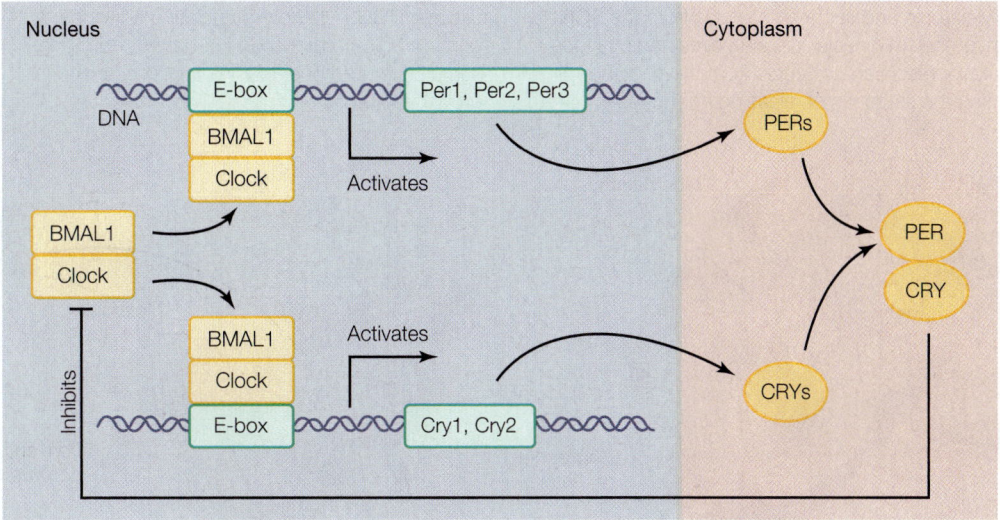

in a neighboring part of the brain. The pineal gland secretes the hormone melatonin into the cerebrospinal fluid and the blood in a circadian rhythm. In humans, melatonin secretion is high at night and low during the day. Most tissues of the body have receptors for melatonin, so although the effects of this hormone are not yet fully understood, they are likely to be widespread. The suprachiasmatic nucleus and parts of the anterior pituitary have particularly high levels of melatonin receptors, so melatonin likely plays a role in feedback regulation of the circadian clock. In fact, administration of melatonin can shift the circadian clock, or improve entrainment to environmental cues. Because of these effects, melatonin is increasingly used as a nutritional supplement to reduce the severity of jet lag, although its effectiveness is controversial.

Mammals must be able to sense external cycles of light and dark to keep their circadian clock entrained with the day-night cycle. Ganglion cells within the retina of the eye that can sense light make synaptic connections with neurons in the SCN, providing information about the external light conditions to the circadian clock neurons.

Nonmammalian vertebrates have a more complex system for regulating circadian rhythms. They have pacemakers not just in the SCN, but also in the retina and the pineal gland, and all are capable of taking in light input. All three structures communicate with each other via neurons and hormones to coordinate the circadian rhythm of the animal. However, the relative importance of each of these structures varies among species. For example, even within lizards, removing the pineal has different effects on circadian rhythms in different species.

The hypothalamus regulates sleep-wake cycles

Although the existence of sleep in invertebrates is a matter of debate, all vertebrates exhibit sleeplike behaviors, or periods of time in which there is decreased response to external stimuli and changes in brain activity. However, most of what we know about sleep has been learned in studies with mammals. In mammals, a balance between the activities of arousal centers and sleep centers in the brain determines the state of wakefulness. The arousal centers are found in several regions in the brainstem and the hypothalamus. These arousal centers send signals to the cortex that promote alertness. One of the hypothalamic arousal centers (the tuberomammillary nucleus) is known to release histamine as one of its neurotransmitters. This may be why "anti-histamine" medicines, which block the actions of histamine, cause sleepiness.

The sleep center is located in a specific region of the hypothalamus called the ventrolateral preoptic nucleus (VLPO). The VLPO uses the inhibitory neurotransmitter GABA to decrease the activity of various regions in the hypothalamus and cortex. A number of drugs that are prescribed for insomnia (such as Ambien, Lunesta, and benzodiazepams) work by increasing the effect of GABA on GABA receptors in the brain.

The arousal centers and the VLPO exhibit mutual inhibition. When the arousal centers are active, they inhibit the activity of the VLPO and when the VLPO is active it inhibits the arousal centers. This antagonistic arrangement allows animals to transition from waking to sleeping with few intermediate states. Various factors, including circadian rhythms

FIGURE 8.36 The brain regulates circadian rhythms by controlling the endocrine system

(a) The organs involved in circadian rhythms in mammals. **(b)** The endocrine system and circadian rhythms. A light signal from the retinal ganglion cells entrains the circadian clock in the suprachiasmatic nucleus (SCN) of the hypothalamus. The SCN sends a signal to the pineal gland, altering the release of melatonin on a circadian cycle. Melatonin and secreted proteins from the SCN affect the other hypothalamic nuclei, causing circadian changes in the release of vasopressin and oxytocin from the posterior pituitary, and affecting the secretion of releasing hormones into the pituitary portal system. The releasing hormones in turn affect the secretion of the pituitary hormones, which go on to have direct effects on a variety of tissues, as well as influencing the release of hormones from other endocrine glands. Melatonin from the pineal gland also enters the bloodstream and has effects on many tissues. (TSH = thyroid-stimulating hormone; ACTH = adrenocorticotropic hormone; GH = growth hormone; FSH = follicle-stimulating hormone; LH = luteinizing hormone; IGF = insulinlike growth factor).

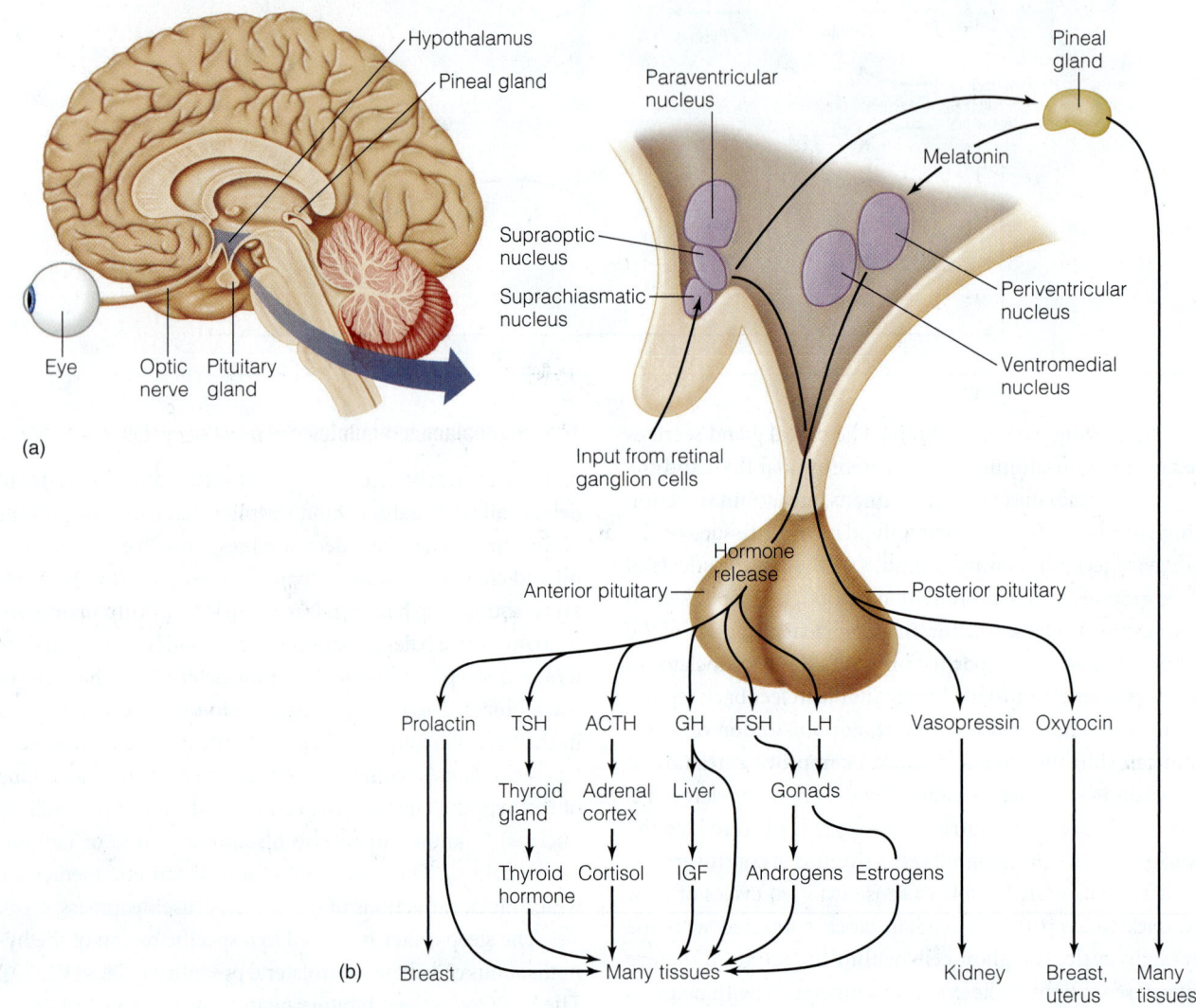

and environmental context, influence the relative activity of the arousal centers and the VLPO. In diurnal mammals such as humans, the arousal centers are most active during the day and the sleep centers are most active at night. Because our circadian rhythms do not shift immediately when we travel across time zones, we experience the phenomenon of jet lag because our natural rhythms of activity in the sleep and arousal centers are offset relative to the external cycles of night and day. It is difficult to fall asleep when our circadian rhythm is maintaining high activity in the arousal centers,

and we feel sleepy during the day because the sleep centers are highly active at that time. As we previously discussed, administration of melatonin may help to reset the circadian clock and shorten the period of jet lag.

If you stay awake for long enough, you will eventually experience a very strong drive to sleep, no matter what time of day it is or what you are doing. In fact, sleep is essential for mammals, and they die if deprived of sleep for long periods. The exact mechanisms that cause increased sleepiness over time are not known, but sleepiness is associated with an increase in the levels of the neurotransmitter adenosine in the cerebrospinal fluid. Caffeine blocks the binding of adenosine to its receptor, which accounts for the stimulant effects of this drug.

Sleep is divided into phases

Sleep is characterized by particular patterns of brain activity that can be detected as changes in electrical activity in the skin of the head. The electrical activity of the neurons in the brain propagates through the cerebrospinal fluid through the meninges and skull to the skin, where it can be detected as minute changes in voltage that represent the summed activity of billions of neurons. An electroencephalogram (EEG) is a recording of these electrical signals.

Sleep in mammals is divided into two major phases that have characteristic EEG patterns: REM (rapid eye movement) sleep and non-REM sleep, which is itself typically divided into four stages of increasing depth. Normal humans alternate through phases of non-REM and REM sleep every 90 to 120 minutes, with episodes of REM sleep lasting between 10 minutes and an hour at a time (Figure 8.37). The percentage of REM sleep is highest in infants, but declines as we age. Sleep begins in the non-REM phase, progressing through several stages of ever deeper sleep to slow-wave sleep. Slow-wave sleep is accompanied by slow breathing and heart rate and lowered body temperature. From slow-wave sleep, humans normally progress to less deep stages of non-REM sleep and then to REM sleep, and cycle back and forth between them through the night.

REM sleep is characterized by very rapid movements of the eyes, increased breathing frequency, and increased brain activity. During REM sleep the brain can be even more active than when we are awake, which may account for the dreams that occur during this stage. During REM sleep we lose muscle tone as a result of signals from the brain that inhibit the somatic motor system innervating the major body muscles. Thus, during REM sleep the arms and legs are essentially paralyzed so that we do not act on our dreams.

Recently, functional magnetic resonance imaging (fMRI, see Box 8.3: Applications: Functional Magnetic Resonance Imaging and Brain Plasticity) has been used to determine exactly what parts of the brain are active during the various phases of sleep. During all stages of non-REM sleep the frontal, parietal, and temporal lobes of the cortex, and the thalamus all show decreased levels of activity, with further reductions in activity in the hippocampus during slow-wave sleep. During REM sleep, however, the cortex is active, as are selected regions of the brainstem and limbic system. In fact, the limbic system has higher activity than is typical during wakefulness.

The purpose of sleep, and particularly of REM sleep, is not well understood. REM sleep has been suggested to be involved in memory consolidation, and brain development and plasticity, or it may be required to stimulate activity in the brain. However, the evidence for these various possibilities is generally poor.

All vertebrates sleep, but little is known about the nature of sleep in fish, amphibians, or reptiles. Sleep in birds is similar to that observed in mammals, with periods of REM and non-REM sleep. However, their cycles of REM and non-REM sleep are extremely short compared with those in mammals, with episodes of REM sleep lasting only a few seconds. Many bird species are capable of uni-hemispheric sleep in which only one side of the brain sleeps at a time. In birds, as in mammals, the right side of the brain controls the left side of the body, and vice versa, so when the right hemisphere is asleep the bird shuts its left eye, and when the left hemisphere is asleep the bird shuts its right eye. Uni-hemispheric sleep occurs only during non-REM sleep.

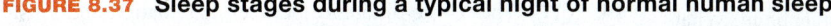

FIGURE 8.37 **Sleep stages during a typical night of normal human sleep**

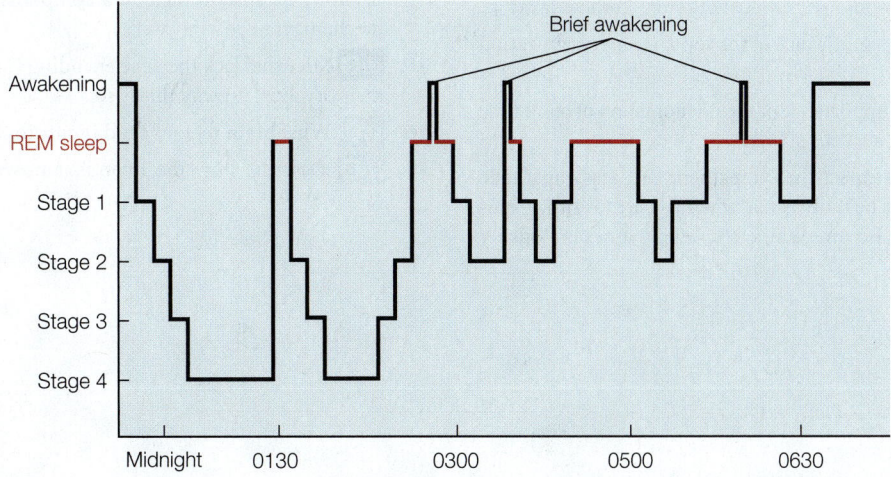

Different species of mammals sleep for different amounts of time, at different times of day, and have different amounts of REM sleep. Carnivores tend to sleep for longer periods, and tend to sleep more deeply and have longer and more frequent episodes of REM sleep than do herbivores. Uni-hemispheric sleep is rare in mammals and has only been documented in marine mammals such as the dolphins we discussed at the beginning of the chapter.

CONCEPT CHECK

19. Describe how the hypothalamus is able to directly sense the osmolarity of the blood, despite the presence of the blood-brain barrier.

20. What are the main differences between REM and non-REM sleep?

SUMMARY

Except for the nervous systems of cnidarians, which are arranged as nerve nets that allow conduction of information in all directions, animal nervous systems generally consist of functionally distinct afferent sensory pathways, integrating centers, and efferent pathways. Although nervous systems vary in complexity among animals, an evolutionary trend toward cephalization is associated with an increase in the size and importance of the brain in the bilaterian animals.

Although the overall organization of the brain is similar within the vertebrates, the size of the brain and the relative sizes of brain regions vary among groups. For example, in mammals, the forebrain has taken over many of the sensory integration functions of the midbrain, and also controls more complex processes such as reasoning and the control of voluntary behavior.

The brain and spinal cord of vertebrates send signals to the efferent division of the peripheral nervous system, including both motor and autonomic pathways, to control behavior and maintain homeostasis. Many involuntary behaviors are controlled by reflex arcs through the spinal cord, and pattern generators initiate rhythmic behaviors, including apparently complex behaviors such as swimming in animals like leeches and locomotion in mammals. Voluntary movements require coordination by more complex integrating centers such as the higher centers of the brain.

The hypothalamus is a part of the forebrain that maintains homeostasis and helps to coordinate many aspects of the endocrine system as well as being involved in complex processes such as circadian rhythms and sleep-wake cycles in all vertebrates.

REVIEW QUESTIONS

1. **LO①** How do the nervous systems of cnidarians differ from those of other animals?

2. **LO①** Compare and contrast the terms "brain" and "ganglion."

3. **LO②** How are the delicate tissues of the brain and spinal cord protected in vertebrates?

4. **LO②** What are spinal nerves?

5. **LO③** What are the main regions of the vertebrate brain?

6. **LO③** If you compared a reptile and a mammal of the same body size, which would be likely to have the larger brain? What part of the brain would be the most different in these taxa?

7. **LO③** What is the significance of the topographic organization of the cortex?

8. **LO④** What is the importance of the phenomenon of basal tone in the autonomic nervous system?

9. **LO④** Would you expect the sympathetic or parasympathetic nervous system to be more active when you are (a) sitting quietly, (b) studying for an exam, or (c) taking an exam? Justify your answers.

10. **LO⑤** List the major similarities and differences between the somatic and autonomic nervous systems.

11. **LO⑤** Why is the autonomic nervous system sometimes called the involuntary nervous system?

12. **LO⑥** What is a pattern generator? Explain how a neural circuit can form a pattern generator.

13. **LO⑥** What is the limbic system? How is it important in behavior?

14. **LO⑦** What is the difference between habituation and sensitization? Be sure to include a comparison of the underlying mechanism in your answer.

15. **LO⑦** Mice that lack the gene encoding CaMKII have impaired memory. Explain why this is so.

16. **LO⑧** What brain regions send inputs to the hypothalamus?

17. **LO⑧** Describe how the hypothalamus regulates sleep-wake cycles.

SYNTHESIS QUESTIONS

1. You can surgically remove large parts of the forebrain from a mammal, and the animal will survive. However, destruction of even relatively small parts of the hindbrain usually causes death. Why might that be so?

2. What is the functional significance of the highly folded and grooved appearance of the surface of the brain in some mammals?

3. Injury to the spinal cord can cause paralysis, but the extent of the paralysis (for example, whether only the arms or both the arms and the legs are paralyzed) depends on the location of the spinal cord injury. Explain why this is the case.

4. Nicotinic acetylcholine receptors are found on muscle cells, and on postganglionic neurons in the sympathetic nervous system (among other places in the body). Use this information to explain why chewing nicotine-containing gum can cause a rapid heart rate and tremors in the hands of nonsmokers.

5. Would the autonomic nervous system function if the preganglionic neurotransmitters were different between the sympathetic and parasympathetic nervous systems but the postganglionic neurotransmitters were the same?

6. Nerve gases such as sarin act as acetylcholinesterase inhibitors. What effects would sarin have on functions controlled by the parasympathetic nervous system? Use your answer to predict some of the symptoms of sarin poisoning. What other parts of the nervous system would you predict to be affected by sarin?

7. Compare the role of presynaptic and postsynaptic mechanisms in habituation and sensitization.

QUANTITATIVE QUESTIONS

1. Herculano-Houzel et al. (2007) estimate that in primates, the mass of the brain is linearly related to the number of neurons in the brain according to the following equation:

Brain mass $= -3.127 + 1.372 \times 10^{-8}$ (Number of neurons)

A human brain weighs approximately 1,500 grams. According to this equation, how many neurons would it be expected to contain? An elephant brain weighs approximately 4,200 grams. If elephant brains scale by the same rules as primate brains, how many neurons would an elephant brain be expected to contain?

2. If elephant brains scale according to the scaling rules for rodent brains (Herculano-Houzel, 2006), then an elephant brain would be expected to contain 23 billion neurons. Compare this result to your calculation from the previous question based on the scaling rules for primates. Do you think elephant brains are more likely to scale by the primate rules or by the rodent rules? Defend your answer.

3. The knee-jerk reflex is a monosynaptic reflex arc that takes about 32 milliseconds to occur in humans. This time delay occurs because it takes about 1 millisecond for the receptor to sense stretch and initiate an electrical signal, about 6 milliseconds to conduct the afferent signal to the spinal cord, 1 millisecond for synaptic transmission to the efferent neuron, 10 milliseconds for conduction through the efferent neuron, 2 milliseconds for neurotransmission to the muscle, and 12 milliseconds between the muscle action potential and the onset of contraction. Imagine that instead of being a monosynaptic reflex arc, the knee-jerk reflex was due to a polysynaptic reflex arc. How would this affect the time needed to complete the reflex? Provide a quantitative estimate of the change in the time needed for the reflex, if any. What might be an advantage of a polysynaptic reflex arc?

CHAPTER

9

Circulatory Systems

FIGURE 9.1　**A pygmy shrew (*Sorex minutus*)**

Photo source: creativenature.nl/Fotolia.

The heart of an adult blue whale (*Balaenoptera musculus*) can weigh over 600 kilograms and is the size of a small car (such as a Volkswagen Beetle or Mini Cooper). Compare this to the size of a heart in an adult human, which weighs about 300 grams (similar to the weight of a large orange), or the heart of an adult pygmy shrew (*Sorex minutus;* Figure 9.1), which weighs less than 0.04 gram (or about the same as a grain of rice). So which animal has the biggest heart? This seems like a simple question, and in absolute terms the heart of the blue whale is clearly the largest of these three hearts (and, in fact, the blue whale heart is the largest heart of any animal that has ever lived). But relative to body weight, the heart of a blue whale is not particularly exceptional. Across mammals, heart size is proportional to body weight, with a "typical" mammal having a heart that is approximately 0.6 percent of its body weight. Both blue whales and humans conform to this relationship fairly well, but the pygmy shrew's heart takes up about 1.3 percent of its body weight of 3 grams, making its heart more than twice as large as would be expected based on its small body size. So the tiny pygmy shrew arguably has a much larger heart (in relative terms) than does the massive blue whale.

Heart rate also varies predictably with body weight among mammals, but in this case it decreases exponentially as body weight increases. The tiny heart of a shrew beats more than 600 times per minute, while a human heart at rest beats about 70 times per minute, and the huge heart of a blue whale is estimated to beat approximately 6 times per minute or less at rest. Note that the values of heart rate for blue whales are only estimates, because they have never successfully been measured in nature, but the heart rates of other large whales, such as humpback whales (*Megaptera novaeangliae*), have been measured and are in this range. Again, we can ask the question: Which animal has the fastest heart rate? The shrew's heart rate is clearly the fastest in absolute terms, but relative to its body mass it is actually rather slow compared with the heart rate of other mammals.

What accounts for the unusual properties of the heart of a shrew? Why is it unusually large, with an unusually slow heart rate, given the size of the animal? One possible explanation is that during exercise the heart rate of a shrew approaches the maximum that is physically possible, given the speed at which cardiac muscle can contract and electrical impulses can be conducted through the heart. Perhaps shrews are reaching an absolute limitation on heart rate, and instead compensate by having a heart that is large for their body size that pumps more blood with each beat, so that the total cardiac output (the amount of blood pumped times the number of beats per minute) is maintained.

In this chapter, you will learn about the structure and function of animal circulatory systems, with a special focus on the role of the heart, and you will see how this critical physiological system is regulated to meet the demands of the body. ▪

LOOKING BACK 9

In this chapter we examine the structure, function, and evolution of circulatory systems. Before beginning this chapter be sure to review Chapter 1: Introduction to Physiological Principles to make sure that you understand why the limitations of diffusion make circulatory systems so important. You may also find it helpful to review Chapter 2: Physiological Evolution of Animals to help you understand the phylogenetic relationships among animal groups, which is critical in appreciating the evolution of circulatory systems. To understand how the heartbeat is initiated and regulated it is important to be familiar with the concept of electrical excitability of cells, which is introduced in Chapter 3: Chemistry, Biochemistry, and Cell Physiology and further developed in Chapter 5: Neuron Structure and Function. The pumping of the heart is the result of contraction of cardiac muscle, so you should also be familiar with the basics of muscle contraction, which are explained in Chapter 6: Cellular Movement and Muscles. At the end of the chapter we discuss how the nervous system regulates the circulatory system, so it may also be useful to review Chapter 8: Functional Organization of Nervous Systems.

▪ OVERVIEW

Unicellular organisms and some small metazoans lack circulatory systems and instead rely on diffusion to transport molecules from place to place. Although diffusion can be rapid over short distances (such as across a cell membrane or within a single cell), it is slow across long distances (Figure 9.2a). In fact, the time (t) needed for a molecule to diffuse between two points is proportional to the square of the distance (x) over which diffusion occurs ($t \propto x^2$). This relationship is a simplified form of Einstein's diffusion equation (which is also called the second law of diffusion). The second law of diffusion can be used to predict that at 37°C a small molecule such as glucose in aqueous solution would take about 5 seconds to diffuse across 100 microns (the size of an average cell) but would take more than 60 years to diffuse across several meters (the distance from the heart to the feet and back again in an average-sized human).

Because of this limitation on the rate of diffusion, larger animals move fluids through their bodies by a process called **bulk flow**, or *convective transport*. The bulk flow of fluids can transport substances across long distances far faster than would be possible by diffusion alone. For example, the human circulatory system can move a milliliter of blood from the heart to the feet and back again in about 60 seconds, rather than the 60 years that would be needed for a substance to diffuse across this distance!

As stated in Newton's second law of motion (force = mass × acceleration), if we exert sufficient force on an object, it will start moving (or accelerate, if it is already in motion). Thus, bulk flow of a fluid occurs when an external force is applied to the fluid, setting it in motion. In circulatory systems, the fluid is confined within a series of chambers and tubes (Figure 9.2b). By pressing down on this confined fluid, you increase the pressure in the immediate area. The fluid then flows from this area of high pressure to any adjacent areas of lower pressure. In many circulatory systems, one-way valves help to ensure that the fluid flows in one direction around the system.

In this chapter, we begin by looking at the common features of all circulatory systems, and then provide a survey of the structure of circulatory systems in the major animal phyla to demonstrate the various solutions to the problem of moving substances across long distances. We then focus on the vertebrate circulatory systems as an example of how flow through a circulatory system can be regulated.

UNITY AND DIVERSITY OF CIRCULATORY SYSTEMS

Animal circulatory systems are structurally diverse, ranging in complexity from the relatively simple circulatory systems of insects to the highly branched circulatory systems of animals such as decapod crustaceans and vertebrates. Despite this structural diversity, all animal circulatory systems transport substances using the bulk flow of fluids. Bulk flow allows circulatory systems to rapidly transport oxygen and nutrients to actively metabolizing tissues, and to remove carbon dioxide and other waste products. Bulk flow in circulatory systems helps to coordinate physiological processes by transporting signaling molecules from place to place within the body, and assists in the defense of the body by transporting immune cells to the site of invasion by foreign organisms. In some animals, the circulatory system even plays a role in temperature regulation, by conveying heat from the working muscles out to the surface of the body where it can be lost to the environment.

General Characteristics of Circulatory Systems

Despite the apparent diversity of animal circulatory systems, every animal circulatory system is made up of three important components:

1. One or more pumps or other propulsive structures that apply a force to drive fluid flow, often in combination with one-way valves to ensure unidirectional flow

2. A system of tubes, channels, or other spaces through which the fluid can flow

3. A fluid that circulates through the system

There is, however, substantial diversity among animals in the structure and organization of each of these components.

Circulatory systems use diverse pumping structures

All circulatory systems have some type of pumping structure that propels fluids around the system. We are most familiar with the pumping action of contractile chambers such as the vertebrate **heart** (Figure 9.3a). Chambered hearts are found in both vertebrates and invertebrates. Muscular contraction of the heart increases the pressure within the heart chambers. When the pressure in the heart exceeds that in the rest of the circulatory system, blood flows down this pressure gradient out into the circulatory system. One-way valves help to ensure unidirectional flow.

FIGURE 9.2 Diffusion and bulk flow

(a) Diffusion is rapid over short distances, but the time needed for diffusion increases exponentially with distance. To transport substances rapidly across long distances, animals use the bulk flow of fluids. **(b)** Increased local pressure in one area of the circulatory system drives flow from the area of high pressure to any adjacent areas of lower pressure, a phenomenon known as bulk flow. One-way valves are often present to ensure that this flow is unidirectional.

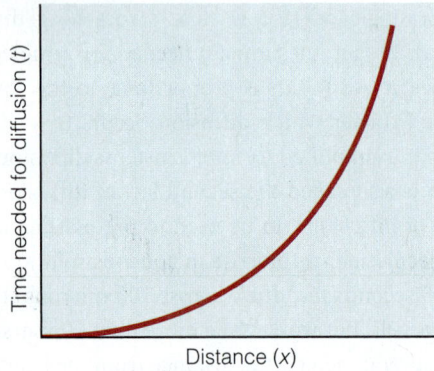

(a) Diffusion

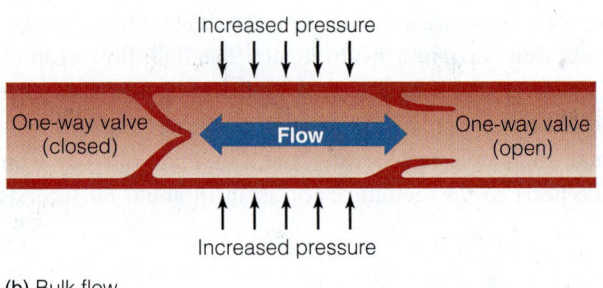

(b) Bulk flow

FIGURE 9.3 **Types of pumping structures in animal circulatory systems**

(a) Contractile chambers such as the vertebrate heart increase blood pressure in a closed chamber through contractions of their muscular walls. As pressure increases, valves open, allowing fluid to flow down the resulting pressure gradient. One-way valves are required to ensure unidirectional flow. **(b)** Structures such as skeletal muscles can act as pumps. Contraction and relaxation of skeletal muscles alternatively compress and expand a blood vessel, forcing the fluid along the vessel. One-way valves ensure unidirectional flow. **(c)** Contractile blood vessels and peristaltic hearts push blood using waves of rhythmic contraction. These vessels may contain valves to ensure unidirectional flow, but the direction of contraction is often sufficient to cause flow to be largely unidirectional.

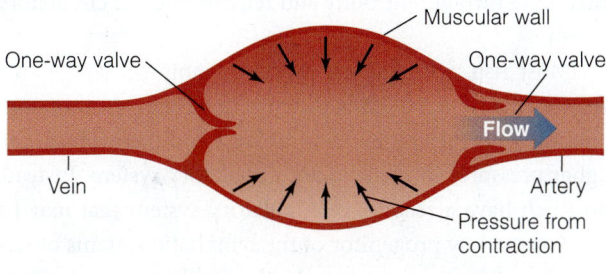

(a) Contractile chamber

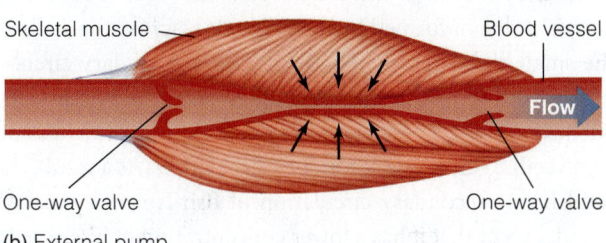

(b) External pump

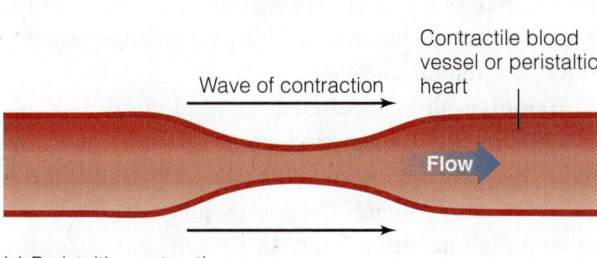

(c) Peristaltic contraction

Chambered hearts often have more than one chamber. The chambers that the circulatory fluid first enters are typically called **atria** (singular: atrium). Animal hearts may have one or more atria, and these chambers function both as reservoirs and as pumps. Fluid flows from the atria into an even more muscular chamber, called the **ventricle**, which acts as the primary pump.

Chambered hearts are not the only type of pumping structures found in animal circulatory systems. Organs that are not strictly associated with the circulatory system, such as skeletal muscles, can be used to develop pressure gradients

(Figure 9.3b). For example, in terrestrial vertebrates the actions of the leg muscles help to push blood back to the heart. Similarly, in many arthropods, normal body movements propel blood around the body. In these systems, the blood vessels generally contain one-way valves to maintain the unidirectional flow of the circulatory fluid.

Pulsating or contractile blood vessels and tubelike hearts, which are found in some invertebrates and the early embryos of vertebrates, move blood by **peristalsis** (Figure 9.3c). Peristaltic contractions are rhythmic waves of muscle contraction that proceed in a coordinated fashion from one end of a tube to the other. Similar to squeezing toothpaste from its tube, peristaltic contractions squeeze blood through the pumping structure and into the circulatory system. Because peristaltic contractions usually occur in a specific direction, these pumps can cause unidirectional flow even when no valves are present.

Circulatory systems can be open or closed

Circulatory fluids flow either through enclosed **blood vessels** that have walls with a specialized lining that separates the circulatory fluid from the tissues, or through open spaces called sinuses that allow the circulatory fluid to make direct contact with the tissues. In a **closed circulatory system**, the circulatory fluid remains within blood vessels at all points in the circulatory system. Thus, substances must diffuse across the walls of the blood vessels to enter the tissues in animals with closed circulatory systems. In an **open circulatory system**, the circulating fluid enters a sinus at least at one point in the circulatory system and thus comes into direct contact with the tissues, allowing the circulating fluid to mix with extracellular fluids. In general, closed circulatory systems generate higher pressures than open circulatory systems.

Open circulatory systems usually contain both blood vessels and sinuses, and sinuses can have complex, highly branched structures. As a result, the difference between open and closed circulatory systems is not absolute. For example, the circulatory systems of decapod crustaceans such as crabs and lobsters are usually described as open, because they contain sinuses. However, as can be seen in Figure 9.4, these animals have a very complex network of blood vessels, and the sinuses through which blood returns to the heart are made up of small, very well-defined channels that are functionally similar to blood vessels, despite the lack of a specialized lining. In addition, the decapod crustacean circulatory system can generate pressures similar to those of some lower vertebrates. Thus, in many respects decapod crustacean circulatory systems are very similar to closed systems from a functional perspective, although they are usually classified as open systems because the sinuses lack the specialized lining typical of blood vessels.

FIGURE 9.4 **Resin cast of the circulatory system of a decapod crustacean, *Cancer magister***

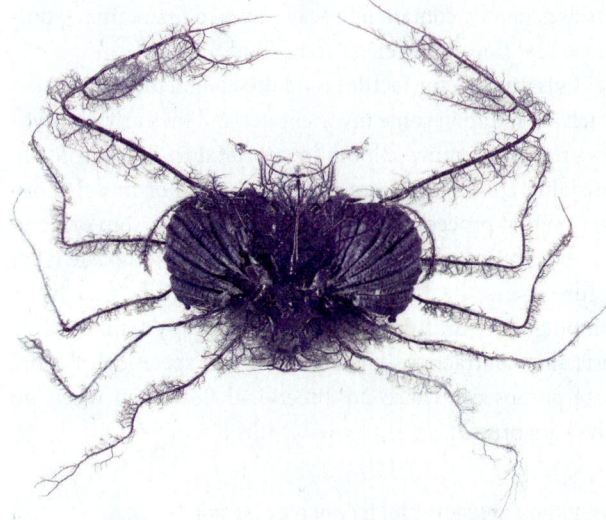

Photo source: Iain J. McGaw and Carl L. Reiber.

Circulatory systems pump several types of fluids

The fluids moved around the body of an animal by the circulatory system play a variety of roles, providing a relatively constant internal environment and transporting nutrients, oxygen, waste products, immune cells, and signaling molecules around the body. As we discuss in later chapters, these fluids can also play noncirculatory roles. For example, the hydrostatic pressure exerted by the circulating fluid of arthropods helps spiders to extend their limbs. Similarly, earthworms and other annelids use a hydrostatic skeleton for locomotion (see Chapter 12: Locomotion). In insects, increases in the hydrostatic pressure of the circulation are involved in molting and the unfurling of the wings as an insect emerges from its pupa.

There is some disagreement among comparative physiologists about the terminology that should be used for circulatory fluids, but here we distinguish several major types of fluids. We use the term **interstitial fluid** for the extracellular fluid that directly bathes the tissues of either vertebrates or invertebrates. Even animals that lack a specialized circulatory system are usually able to propel interstitial fluid around their bodies by bulk flow due to movement of the body. We define **blood** as the fluid that circulates within a closed circulatory system, such as that of a vertebrate. Blood is a complex tissue that has multiple components. It contains proteins and a variety of cells suspended in a fluid called **plasma**.

Most vertebrates have a secondary circulatory system, in addition to the cardiovascular system, that circulates a fluid called **lymph** around the body. Lymph is similar in composition to blood except that it lacks blood cells and large proteins. It is formed from blood by a process called **ultrafiltration** in the small blood vessels. The pressure difference across the walls of the small blood vessels forces fluid out of the blood and into the interstitial space around the cells, where it mixes with the interstitial fluid. Blood cells and large molecules such as proteins cannot pass across the walls of most of the small blood vessels, but these walls are quite permeable to small molecules and water. The walls of the small blood vessels thus act as a filter, forming a lymphatic fluid that is similar in composition to plasma, but contains few proteins or cells. The **lymphatic system** pumps this **ultrafiltrate** through the body and returns it to the circulatory system.

Most fish, with the exception of lungfish, lack a true lymphatic system, which is thought to have evolved in conjunction with the colonization of land and the evolution of higher pressures in the primary circulatory system. Instead, most fish have a secondary circulatory system that may be the evolutionary progenitor of the lymphatic systems of terrestrial vertebrates. Like lymph, the fluid in the secondary circulatory system of fish is derived from blood, but (unlike lymph) it is not formed by ultrafiltration across the walls of the small blood vessels. Fluid enters the secondary circulatory system of fish through openings from the primary circulatory system. These openings allow plasma, proteins, and some cells to enter the secondary circulation. As a result, the fluid in the secondary circulation of fish is very similar to blood, except that it has a lower concentration of blood cells. The functions of the secondary circulatory system of fish are poorly understood, but may include gas exchange, osmoregulation, and immune defense.

Hemolymph is the circulating fluid of open circulatory systems. In an open circulatory system, hemolymph flows through blood vessels, but when it enters the sinuses it directly contacts the tissues, and thus is continuous with the interstitial fluid. As a result, it is difficult to distinguish between blood, lymph, and interstitial fluid in these organisms. Indeed, the word *hemolymph* was coined to imply this combination of blood and lymph (*hema* is the Greek root for blood). The sinuses of open circulatory systems are sometimes referred to collectively as the **hemocoel**.

Blood and hemolymph are primarily composed of water containing dissolved ions and organic solutes and are thus similar in composition to interstitial fluid. However, these circulatory fluids also contain blood cells and relatively high concentrations of proteins. Many animals maintain the composition of their blood and interstitial fluid in strict separation from the external environment, homeostatically regulating the composition of the blood. However, in some animals the composition of body fluids varies in concert with the environment.

Blood and hemolymph contain proteins

The interstitial fluid of vertebrates typically has a low protein concentration (ranging from 0.2 to 2.0 g/l). In contrast, the circulatory fluids of animals with closed circulatory systems often contain a rather high concentration of proteins. For example, protein concentration may be 10–90 g/l in the hemolymph of decapod crustaceans, 30–80 g/l in the blood of vertebrates, and up to 110 g/l in the blood of cephalopod mollusks. In many invertebrate taxa, these proteins are primarily **respiratory pigments** that are used to transport or store oxygen (see Chapter 11: Respiratory Systems for more on the structure and function of respiratory pigments). In the vertebrates, the respiratory pigments are located within cells, and thus the principal proteins dissolved in the circulatory fluids are carrier proteins such as **albumin** and the **globulins**, and proteins involved in blood clotting.

Blood and hemolymph contain cells

The diverse cell types found in the circulatory fluid of many animals are called **hemocytes**. Hemocytes perform a wide variety of functions in different animals, including oxygen transport or storage, nutrient transport or storage, phagocytosis of damaged cells, immune defense, and blood clotting.

Figure 9.5 compares the hemocytes of insects and vertebrates to provide an overview of the great variety of these cells. Although the hemocytes of vertebrates and insects appear to be quite distinct, developmental biologists have recently discovered that in both of these taxa, a group of transcription factors called the GATA factors are involved in the development of these cells. This similarity suggests that blood cells may have a common origin in all animals. We discuss the functioning of immune cells in more detail in Chapter 10: Immune Systems, and erythrocytes in more detail in Chapter 11: Respiratory Systems.

Vertebrate blood has three main components

When vertebrate blood is centrifuged, it separates into three main components (Figure 9.6). The fluid portion, or plasma, makes up approximately 55 percent of the whole blood volume in normal humans. The other major component of the blood is the red blood cells, or **erythrocytes** (approximately 45 percent of blood volume in humans), which are involved in oxygen transport. The other blood cells, consisting of the various immune and blood-clotting cells, make up a small fraction of the blood. The fraction of the blood that is made up of erythrocytes is termed the **hematocrit**. Hematocrit varies substantially among vertebrates (from 20 to 65 percent), and can vary within an individual depending on physiological condition. For example, acclimation of humans to high altitude causes an increase in hematocrit.

FIGURE 9.5 **Hemocytes**

Left: Insects such as *Drosophila* have three main classes of hemocytes. Plasmatocytes are small cells that use phagocytosis to engulf foreign invaders. Lamellocytes are large cells produced in response to parasitic infections. Crystal cells contain enzymes that they use to lyse foreign invaders. Right: Vertebrate hemocytes can be divided into erythrocytes, or cells that contain hemoglobin, and leukocytes, which do not. Lymphocytes are involved in adaptive (or specific) immunity. Monocytes and granulocytes are immune cells that engulf or destroy invading particles using enzymes. Thrombocytes are involved in blood clotting. In mammals, the most important thrombocytes are small cell fragments called platelets.

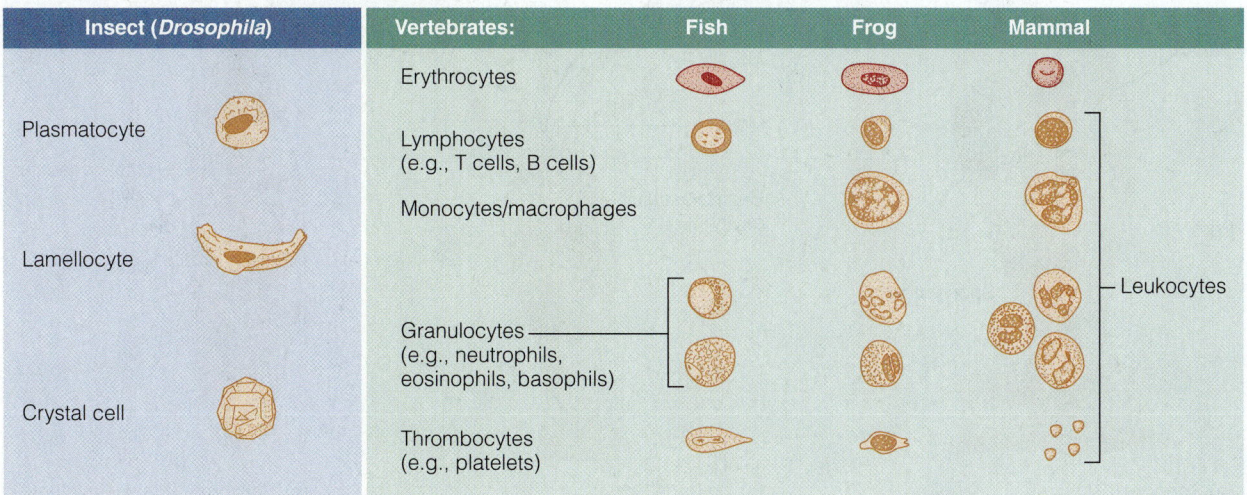

FIGURE 9.6   The composition of vertebrate blood

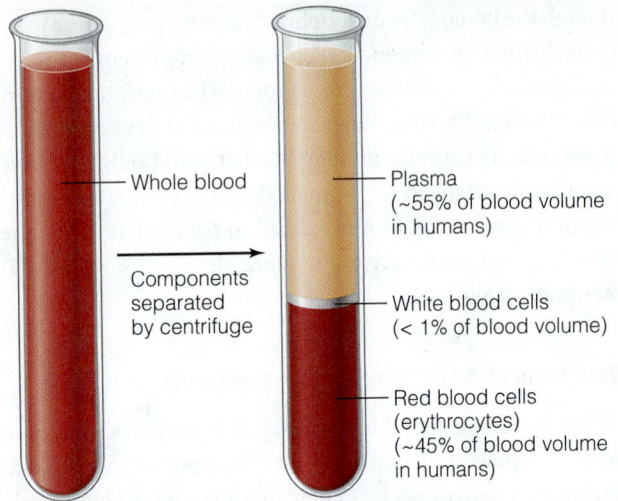

Whole blood

Components separated by centrifuge

Plasma (~55% of blood volume in humans)

White blood cells (< 1% of blood volume)

Red blood cells (erythrocytes) (~45% of blood volume in humans)

The size and structure of erythrocytes varies greatly among vertebrates. For example, the largest vertebrate erythrocyte (that of the salamander *Amphiuma*) is almost 2,000 times larger than the smallest erythrocyte (that of the lesser mouse deer, *Tragulus javanicus*). In most vertebrates, erythrocytes have nuclei and other organelles. However, mammals, some fish, and some amphibians have enucleated erythrocytes. In fact, mammalian erythrocytes lack nuclei, mitochondria, and other organelles including ribosomes. As a result, a mature mammalian erythrocyte cannot perform protein synthesis or cell division.

Erythrocytes are generally round or oval in shape, although mammalian erythrocytes are shaped like biconcave disks (disks with indentations on both sides). The biconcave shape increases the surface area of the erythrocyte, possibly facilitating oxygen transfer.

CONCEPT CHECK

1. What are the three main types of pumping structures in animal circulatory systems?
2. What is the difference between an open circulatory system and a closed circulatory system?
3. Distinguish between blood, lymph, and hemolymph.

Circulatory Plans of the Major Animal Phyla

There is substantial diversity in the structure of circulatory systems among animals. Animals such as sponges, cnidarians, and flatworms lack a circulatory system that transports an internal fluid, but all of these animals have mechanisms for propelling fluids around their bodies (Figure 9.7). For example, sponges propel water through their bodies using *choanocytes*, specialized cells with rhythmically beating flagellae. Cnidarians propel water from the external medium through their mouths into a **gastrovascular cavity** using muscular contractions, and pump the water down to their tentacles, carrying oxygen and digested food along with it. Flatworms also have a gastrovascular cavity, which in many species is

FIGURE 9.7   Bulk flow in animals that lack circulatory systems

(a) The body wall of a sponge is full of pores that lead into an inner cavity called the spongocoel. The beating of flagellated choanocytes propels water through the pores into the spongocoel and out the osculum. (b) Cnidarians use muscular contractions to propel water into the mouth and through the gastrovascular cavity. (c) Platyhelminths and nematodes use contractions of a muscular pharynx to propel fluid through their gastrovascular cavity.

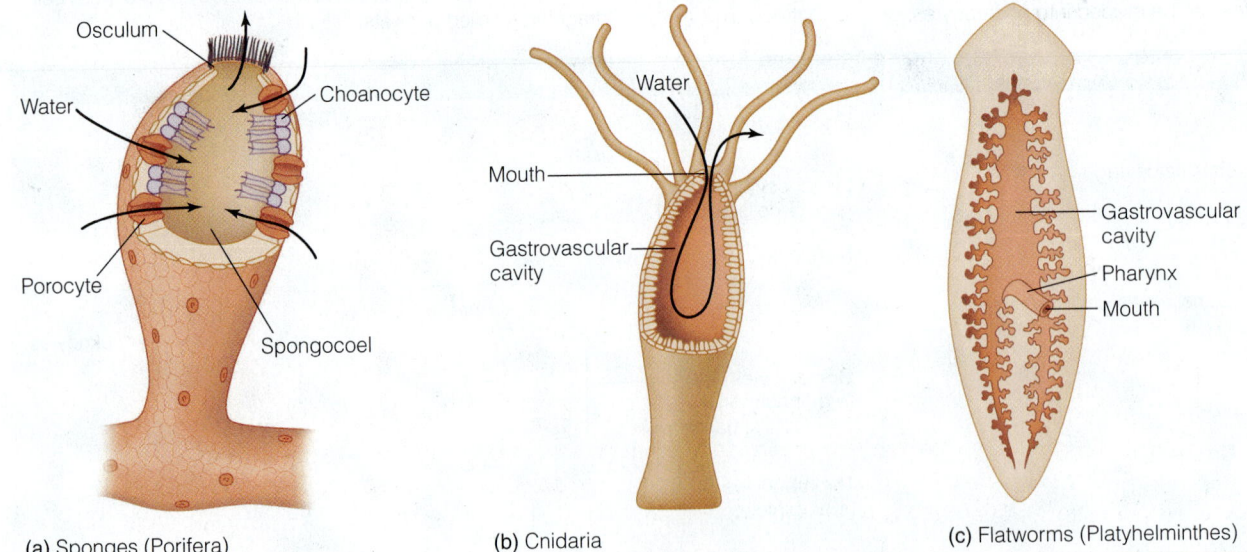

Osculum

Water

Choanocyte

Porocyte

Spongocoel

(a) Sponges (Porifera)

Water

Mouth

Gastrovascular cavity

(b) Cnidaria

Gastrovascular cavity

Pharynx

Mouth

(c) Flatworms (Platyhelminthes)

lined with ciliated **flame cells** whose beating propels water containing food particles to all parts of the body. In all these species, the bulk flow of fluids is part of a combined respiratory, digestive, and circulatory system.

Nematodes (phylum Nematoda) and horsehair worms (phylum Nematomorpha) also lack specialized circulatory systems, but they can move interstitial fluid through their body cavity (called a *pseudocoelom*) by bulk flow powered by contractions of the muscles in their body walls. Nematodes and horsehair worms are seldom more than a millimeter thick (although some species can be up to 30 meters long), and they obtain oxygen by diffusion across the entire body surface. As a result, these animals probably have little need for a circulatory system to transport oxygen. Instead, bulk flow of interstitial fluid is most important for transporting signaling molecules and immune cells.

Most annelids have closed circulatory systems

Phylum Annelida is divided into three main branches: class Polychaeta (e.g., tube worms), class Oligochaeta (e.g., earthworms), and class Hirudinea (leeches). The circulatory systems of leeches are different from those of the other annelids, and we do not discuss them further here. All polychaetes and oligochaetes are able to circulate interstitial fluid using either cilia or muscular contractions of the body wall. Some polychaetes rely solely on this system, but most polychaetes and oligochaetes have a system of blood vessels that circulates a specialized fluid containing oxygen carrier proteins. This system may have an open design, as in some polychaetes (Figure 9.8a), but the majority of polychaetes and all oligochaetes have closed circulatory systems that circulate blood through the body (Figure 9.8b).

Oligochaetes such as earthworms have a series of small blood vessels connecting the large dorsal and ventral blood vessels that run the length of the animal. The dorsal vessel is contractile, and moves blood toward the head using rhythmic waves of peristaltic contraction. The blood then flows through five pairs of muscular contractile tubes (or simple tubelike hearts) that pump blood from the dorsal to the ventral blood vessel. The blood travels back along the body through the ventral blood vessel. Small connecting blood vessels carry the blood from the tissues back to the dorsal vessel.

Most mollusks have open circulatory systems

The circulatory systems of mollusks are extremely diverse, consistent with the enormous diversity in body form within this phylum. All mollusks have hearts or contractile organs of some sort, and most groups have at least some blood vessels, with some species having extensive vascular networks.

FIGURE 9.8 Circulatory systems of annelids

(a) Some polychaetes have open circulatory systems. **(b)** Most polychaetes and all oligochaetes have closed circulatory systems.

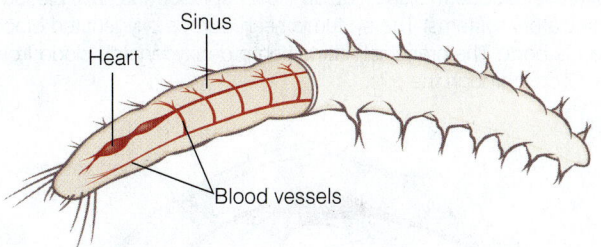

(a) Open circulatory system of annelid (polychaete)

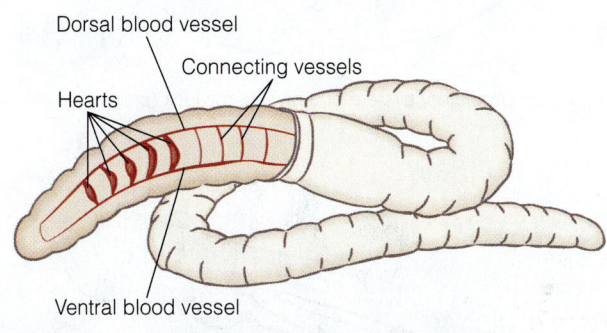

(b) Closed circulatory system of annelid (oligochaete)

However, almost all mollusks have open circulatory systems (Figure 9.9). Only the cephalopods (squid, octopus, and cuttlefish) have completely closed circulatory systems.

The closed circulatory system of cephalopods evolved from an open circulatory system, likely one similar to those in cephalopods such as the *Nautilus*. In nautiloids, blood returning from the gills enters the atria of the heart, and then is pumped by the ventricle through blood vessels that empty into a large sinus. Contractile blood vessels then pump blood across the gills and back to the heart. In contrast, squid and octopuses have a closed circulatory system and three muscular chambered hearts (Figure 9.9b). The *systemic heart* pumps oxygenated blood to the body. After passing through the body tissues, the deoxygenated blood flows into the two *branchial hearts* that pump blood through the gills. From the gills, the oxygenated blood flows back into the systemic heart.

Arthropod circulatory systems vary in complexity

Almost all arthropods have one or more hearts and at least some blood vessels, but no arthropod lineages have evolved a completely closed circulatory system. The circulatory systems of crustaceans vary from quite simple in smaller and less active species to extremely complex in large, active

FIGURE 9.9 Circulatory systems of mollusks

(a) The circulatory system of a bivalve such as a clam. Most mollusks have open circulatory systems. **(b)** The circulatory system of a cephalopod mollusk (squid). Most cephalopods have closed circulatory systems. The systemic heart pumps oxygenated blood to the body. The branchial hearts pump deoxygenated blood from the body through the gills.

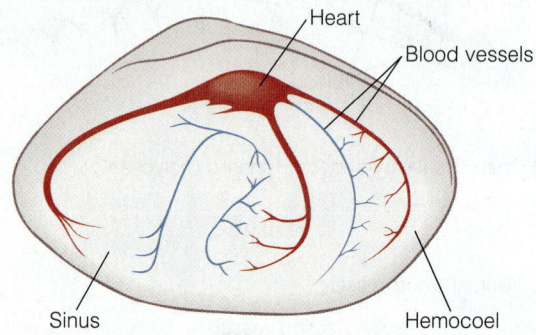

(a) Open circulatory system of a bivalve mollusk (clam)

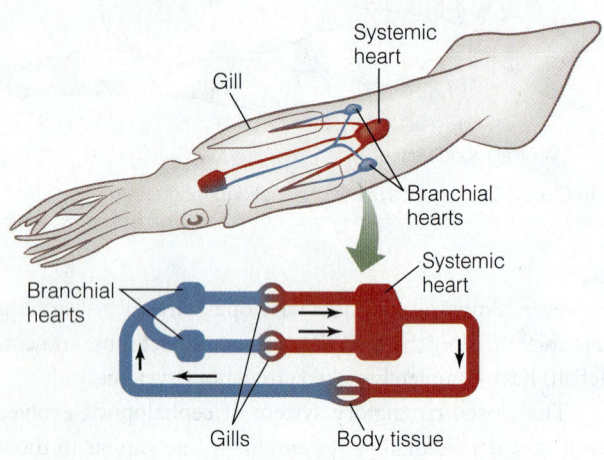

(b) Closed circulatory system of a cephalopod mollusk (squid)

FIGURE 9.10 Circulatory systems in crustaceans

(a) Circulation in a brachiopod crustacean. Brachiopods such as fairy shrimp have simple circulatory systems with few blood vessels and a long tubular heart. **(b)** Circulation in a decapod crustacean. Decapod crustaceans have elaborate open circulatory systems with arteries and capillary beds and a muscular, chamberlike heart. The heart pumps the circulatory fluid through the arteries into successively smaller blood vessels that drain into small channels within the head and body tissues. The fluid returns to the heart via a set of ostia.

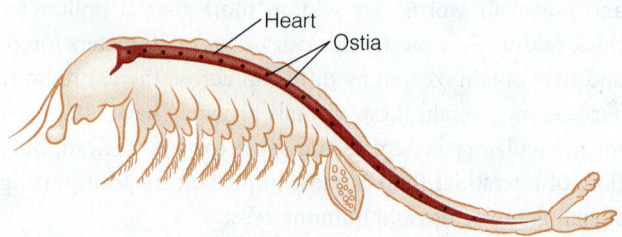

(a) Brachiopod crustacean (fairy shrimp)

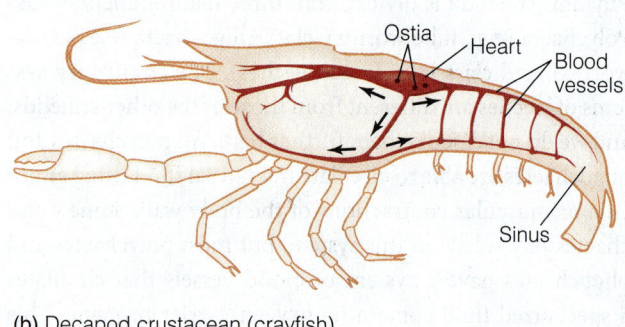

(b) Decapod crustacean (crayfish)

passes into veins that empty into the pericardial sinus, entering the heart via small holes called **ostia** that can be opened or closed to regulate flow.

Decapods have among the most sophisticated open circulatory systems of any invertebrate, and many of their blood vessels have muscular valves that they can use to control the amount of blood flowing to particular tissues. The sinuses are very small in some species, and act functionally as blood vessels. Thus, although crustacean circulatory systems are structurally open, they are functionally similar to closed systems.

Crustacean hearts are both suction and pressure pumps

Although the shape and size of the heart varies greatly among crustaceans, their hearts share a number of features in common. Crustacean hearts generally pump hemolymph out into the circulation via arteries, and blood returns to the heart via a series of holes, or ostia. Muscular valves at the junction between the heart and the arteries can be opened and closed, actively regulating the direction of flow

species (Figure 9.10). Brachiopod crustaceans such as the fairy shrimp (also known as "sea monkeys" to generations of North American children) have a simple tubular heart that may extend almost the entire length of the body, and relatively few blood vessels. In contrast, decapod crustaceans such as lobsters, crabs, and crayfish have a very muscular heart that acts as a contractile chamber, and an extensive network of blood vessels (Figure 9.10b). These animals have a single heart encased in a sac called the *pericardial sinus.* Several branching arteries lead out of the heart to many parts of the body, ultimately emptying out into sinuses deep within the tissues. The arteries leading from the heart contain valves that regulate flow to the tissues. After passing through the tissues, the blood drains into a sinus located along the ventral side of the body. This sinus leads to the gills, where the blood is reoxygenated prior to its return to the heart. The blood

of hemolymph to the tissues. The heart itself is suspended within the body cavity via a series of ligaments. Figure 9.11 illustrates the stages of cardiac contraction in decapod crustaceans, which have particularly strong and muscular hearts. The hearts of most arthropods, including crustaceans, are **neurogenic**—they contract in response to signals from the nervous system (see Chapter 6: Cellular Movement and Muscles). The neurons of the cardiac ganglion, located on the surface of the heart and among the **cardiomyocytes** (the heart cells), are the primary rhythm generator. These neurons undergo spontaneous rhythmic depolarizations that initiate the rhythmic contraction of the heart (see Chapter 8: Functional Organization of Nervous Systems for a discussion of neural rhythm generators). The neurons of the cardiac ganglion send a signal to close the ostia of the heart and initiate the heartbeat. As the cardiomyocytes contract, they decrease the volume of the heart chamber, exerting pressure on the circulatory fluid. This increase in pressure causes blood to squirt out of the heart and into the circulatory system via the arteries; the closed valves guarding the ostia prevent flow in the other direction.

The contraction of the heart also pulls on the ligaments that connect the heart to the body wall, stretching them. When the heart relaxes, the ligaments spring back, pulling apart the walls of the heart. This elastic recoil increases the volume of the heart, reducing the pressure in the internal chambers. This decrease in pressure sucks fluid into the heart via the opened ostia. Backflow from the arteries into the heart is prevented by muscular valves at the entrance to the arteries. Thus, arthropod hearts act as both suction and pressure pumps. They fill by suction, and they empty as a result of increasing pressure.

Insects have simple open circulatory systems

Although most insects are metabolically very active, they have extremely simple open circulatory systems. In many insects the only obvious structure in the circulatory system is a large dorsal vessel that extends along most of the body (Figure 9.12). Insects can maintain high metabolic rates despite this simple circulatory system because, unlike most other animals, the insect circulatory system does not play a major role in oxygen transport. As we discuss in Chapter 11: Respiratory Systems, insects have a specialized *tracheal system* that consists of a series of blind-ended air-filled tubes that conduct oxygen directly to the tissues in gaseous form, bypassing the circulatory system. As a result, the circulatory

FIGURE 9.11 Heart function in decapod crustaceans
(a) When the heart contracts, the ostia close, and blood flows out via the arteries. The contraction pulls on the elastic suspensory ligaments, which store this potential energy. **(b)** As the heart relaxes, the suspensory ligaments recoil, increasing the volume of the heart. The ostia open, and the low pressure sucks blood into the heart through the opened ostia.

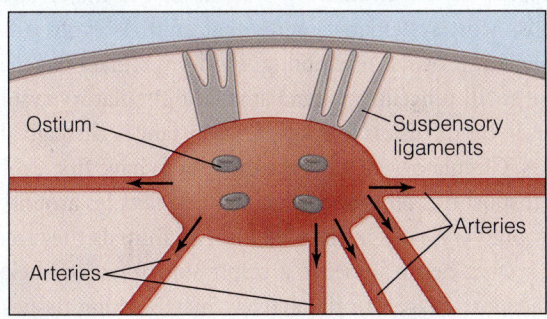

(a) Systole

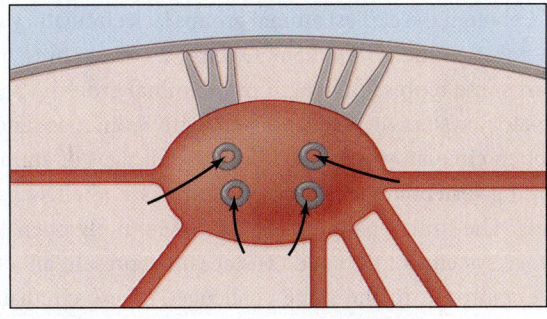

(b) Diastole

FIGURE 9.12 Circulatory system of insects
Insects have relatively simple open circulatory systems. The contractile dorsal blood vessel is elaborated into a series of hearts found along the body, often with one in each body segment. These hearts and the contractile dorsal blood vessel push blood using peristaltic contractions from the posterior end to the anterior end of the body. The circulatory fluid then discharges into the open hemocoel and percolates back through the sinuses of the body, assisted by normal body movements.

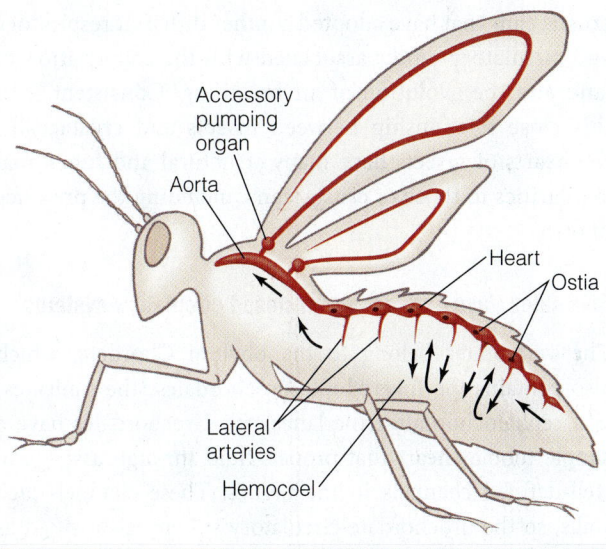

system is not needed for oxygen transport, and instead is involved primarily in delivering nutrients, immune cells, and signaling molecules. This observation highlights the important coevolutionary relationship between the circulatory and respiratory systems.

Insect circulatory systems can contain multiple pumping structures. For example, the posterior part of the dorsal vessel is contractile and is often divided into several discrete pumping organs that function as hearts, one per abdominal segment. The anterior part of the dorsal vessel is less muscular and is termed the **aorta**. The dorsal blood vessel contains mutiple ostia. The *incurrent ostia* are slitlike openings that allow hemolymph to enter the dorsal blood vessel. In general, these incurrent ostia open when the blood vessel relaxes, allowing blood to enter the dorsal vessel and close when the blood vessel contracts, preventing backflow. In most insects, contractions of the hearts pump hemolymph toward the head, although in some species pumping either toward the head or toward the abdomen is possible. The hemolymph empties into a sinus in the region of the brain, and then percolates back to the abdomen, via another sinus. In some species *excurrent ostia* are also present in the dorsal blood vessel. These excurrent ostia allow hemolymph to leave the dorsal blood vessel in places other than the head, and in some species these ostia can be used to adjust the volume of hemolymph flow to different parts of the body. Normal body movements help to move the hemolymph through the sinuses, returning the blood to the heart via the incurrent ostia, as in other arthropods. Many insects also have accessory pulsatile organs (simple hearts) in their antennae, wings, and limbs. In fact, some species have dozens of these small hearts, which help to propel hemolymph through their long, narrow appendages.

Recent genomic analyses suggest that the taxon Hexapoda (the insects) is, in fact, nested within the crustaceans. This pattern suggests that the insects are highly derived crustaceans that have adopted a rather different respiratory and circulatory mode, associated with the colonization of land and the evolution of air breathing. Consistent with this close relationship between insects and crustaceans, the hearts of insects have many structural and functional similarities to those of crustaceans, including the presence of ostia.

Chordates have both open and closed circulatory systems

The vertebrates belong to the phylum Chordata, which also contains the invertebrate urochordates (the tunicates) and cephalochordates (the lancelets). Urochordates have a simple tubular heart that propels fluid through a series of well-defined channels in the tissues. These channels lack walls, so the urochordate circulatory system is classified as

open. The heart is located at the base of the digestive tract in the posterior part of the body and pumps fluid through the body using peristaltic contractions. In some tunicates such as *Ciona*, the direction of these contractions reverses periodically, causing the direction of blood flow to reverse. The physiological significance of this flow pattern is not yet understood, although some authors have suggested that it serves to disperse nutrient-gathering cells around the body.

Cephalochordates such as the lancelet (formerly called *Amphioxus*) lack an obvious chambered heart and instead have a long tubular heart or contractile blood vessel located at the base of the digestive tract and additional pulsatile blood vessels in other locations within the circulatory system that assist in pumping blood through the circulatory system. The circulatory system is largely closed, with blood vessels emptying into sinuses in only a few locations in the body.

Vertebrates have closed circulatory systems in which the blood remains within blood vessels at all points in its passage through the body. We discuss the structure, function, and evolution of vertebrate circulatory systems in subsequent sections of this chapter.

Closed circulatory systems evolved multiple times in animals

From the examples outlined above, it is clear that there is substantial diversity in the structure and organization of animal circulatory systems, and that there are many alternate evolutionary solutions to the problem of moving fluids around the body by bulk flow. Figure 9.13 summarizes the properties of the circulatory systems of the major animal groups. Most systematists agree that animals evolved from flagellated protists resembling modern choanoflagellates. These small unicellular organisms lack circulatory systems, and rely on diffusion to transport substances through their bodies. Circulatory systems are thought to have first evolved to transport nutrients and other small molecules around the body, but very early in the evolution of animals the circulatory system began to serve a respiratory function, helping to transport oxygen to the actively metabolizing tissues. In most animal groups, this respiratory function has been a major force shaping the evolution of circulatory systems.

Although the earliest animal groups lack circulatory systems, most animals have them. Open systems are present in at least some representatives of most animal groups. Closed circulatory systems evolved independently from these ancestral open circulatory systems in several lineages of animals, including vertebrates, cephalopod mollusks, and oligochaete worms. The functionally closed, but structurally open, circulatory systems of decapod crustaceans represent an alternative approach to the same challenges. These circulatory systems differ in structure but are functionally similar, and

FIGURE 9.13 **Evolution of animal circulatory systems**

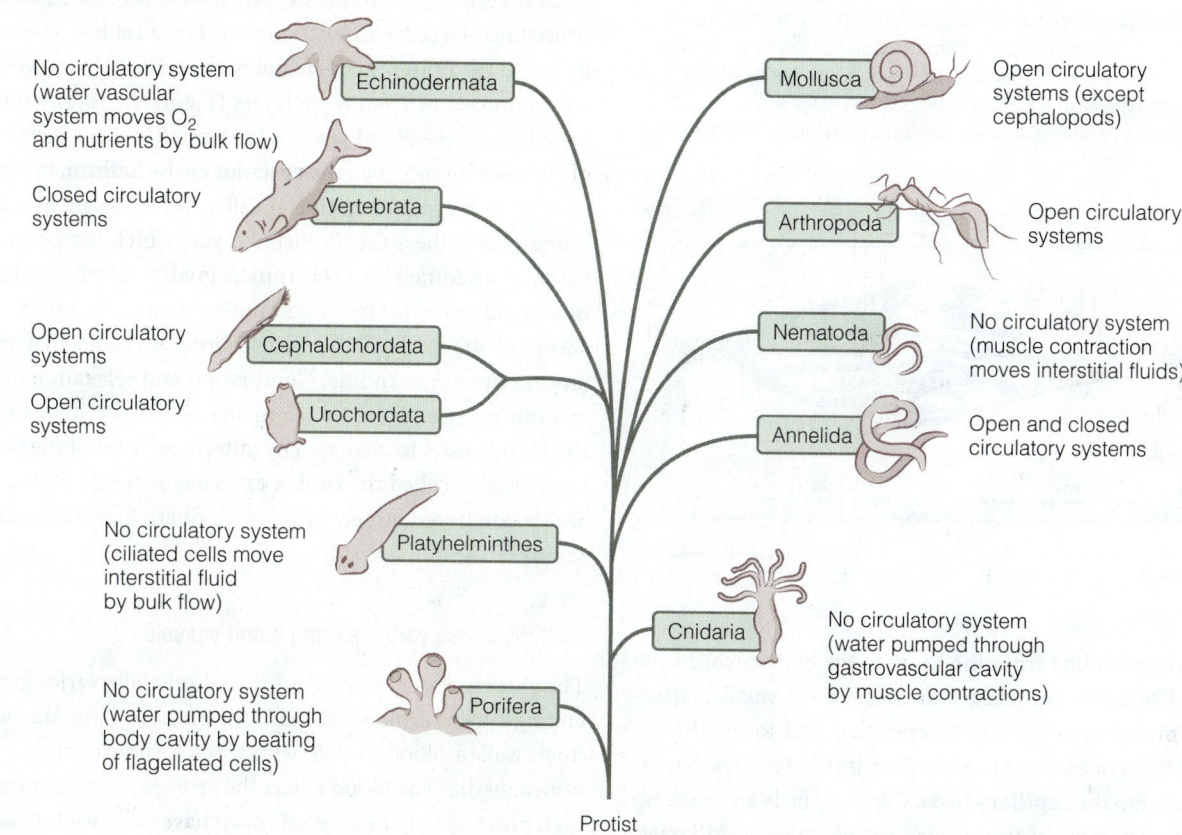

No circulatory system (water vascular system moves O_2 and nutrients by bulk flow) — Echinodermata

Closed circulatory systems — Vertebrata

Open circulatory systems — Cephalochordata

Open circulatory systems — Urochordata

No circulatory system (ciliated cells move interstitial fluid by bulk flow) — Platyhelminthes

No circulatory system (water pumped through body cavity by beating of flagellated cells) — Porifera

Mollusca — Open circulatory systems (except cephalopods)

Arthropoda — Open circulatory systems

Nematoda — No circulatory system (muscle contraction moves interstitial fluids)

Annelida — Open and closed circulatory systems

Cnidaria — No circulatory system (water pumped through gastrovascular cavity by muscle contractions)

Protist

are thus examples of convergent evolution. Closed circulatory systems provide several advantages over open circulatory systems, including the ability to generate high pressure and flow and the ability to better control and direct blood flow to specific tissues.

The high pressure and flow generated by closed circulatory systems are particularly important for oxygen delivery to actively metabolizing tissues. Consistent with this idea, closed circulatory systems are usually found in highly active organisms with high demands for oxygen, or those living in oxygen-limited environments where oxygen supply is low. The main exception to this pattern is the simple open circulatory system of the highly active insects. As we have already discussed, insects do not use the circulatory system as their primary means of gas transport and instead have a tracheal system that delivers oxygen in gaseous form to the tissues. In this case, high flow rates and pressure in the circulatory system may not be required, so a closed circulatory system is not necessary, despite the high metabolic rate of these animals. Taken together, the patterns we observe in the structure and function of circulatory systems across animal phyla support a strong coevolutionary relationship between the circulatory and respiratory systems.

CONCEPT CHECK

4. Do all animals have a circulatory system?
5. Do all annelids have a closed circulatory system? Provide examples to support your answer.
6. What is the major factor involved in the evolution of closed circulatory systems? Do all animals fit with this general rule?

The Circulatory Plan of Vertebrates

Because much of our understanding of the structure and function of circulatory systems has come from research on the closed circulatory systems of vertebrates (and particularly on mammals), here we examine the circulatory plan of these animals in greater detail. All jawed vertebrates have a closed circulatory system with a common circulatory plan in which the blood remains within blood vessels with specialized walls throughout the circulation (Figure 9.14). All vertebrates have a primary systemic heart that pumps blood to a large blood vessel termed an **artery**. The word artery is the general term for blood vessels that carry blood away from the heart. The

FIGURE 9.14   **The vertebrate circulatory plan**

Vertebrates share a common circulatory plan in which the heart pumps blood to a large artery, then through successively smaller arteries to the arterioles that lead to the capillary beds, where substances diffuse to the tissues across the walls of the capillaries. Capillaries coalesce into venules and then veins, which return blood to the heart.

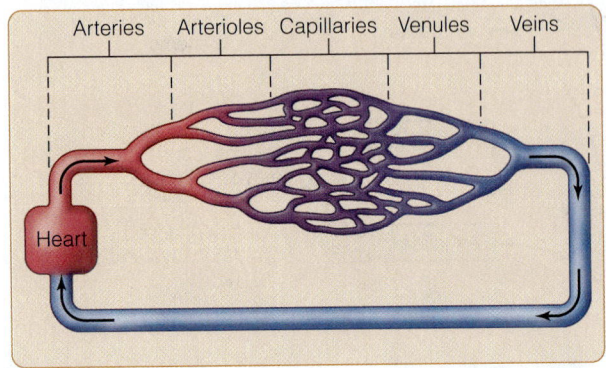

large artery leading from the heart to the body is called the aorta. The aorta branches into successively smaller arteries, culminating in the feed arteries that lead to the tissues. Within the tissues, the arteries branch into **arterioles** that direct flow into the **capillary beds**. Capillary beds are made up of dense networks of thin-walled vessels called **capillaries**, which are the primary site of diffusion of materials into the tissues. At the end of the capillary beds, capillaries coalesce into small vessels called **venules**, which in turn coalesce into larger vessels called **veins** that return blood to the heart.

Although this general circulatory plan provides a good overview of the route of blood through the vertebrate circulatory system, actual circulatory systems are rather more complex. For example, arteries do not always simply branch to form progressively smaller vessels. Arteries can also form **anastomoses** (singular: anastomosis), which are connections from one blood vessel to another. Anastomoses provide an alternate pathway for blood to flow if one route is blocked. For example, the arteries in the joints contain numerous anastomoses, allowing blood to flow even if the bending of the joint closes off one of the arteries. Anastomoses become more frequent the farther you get from the heart so that arterioles and capillaries tend to form dense interconnected networks. In addition, venous shunts and arteriovenous anastomoses allow blood to be redirected to avoid a particular capillary bed if necessary. Similarly, many vertebrates have more than one pumping structure arranged in series rather than the single heart shown in Figure 9.14.

Vertebrate blood vessels have complex walls

A defining feature of the closed circulatory systems of vertebrates is the presence of blood vessels that prevent the circulating blood from coming into direct contact with the tissues. Vertebrate blood vessels are hollow tubular structures consisting of a complex wall surrounding a central open cavity called the **lumen**. In vertebrates, the walls of blood vessels are composed of up to three layers (Figure 9.15). The innermost layer of the blood vessel is the **tunica intima**. It consists of an inner lining called the **vascular endothelium**, made up of a smooth sheet of epithelial cells, and a basement membrane called the subendothelial layer, which supports the vascular endothelium. The **tunica media**, or middle layer, of a blood vessel is largely composed of smooth muscle and sheets of the extracellular matrix protein elastin that wrap around the tunica intima. Contraction and relaxation of the smooth muscle of the tunica media allows the diameter of the blood vessel to change. The outermost layer of the blood vessel wall is called the **tunica externa**, or *tunica adventitia*, and is composed largely of collagen fibers that support and reinforce the blood vessel.

Wall thickness varies among blood vessels

The thickness of the layers of the vessel walls varies greatly among types of blood vessels. Arteries are large-diameter, thick-walled blood vessels with a thick tunica externa and tunica media. The blood enters the arteries from the heart at high pressures, so these vessels must have thick walls to avoid bursting. The arteries closest to the heart have a particularly thick tunica externa, which makes them highly elastic. Arteries farther from the heart tend to have a thicker tunica media, and are sometimes called muscular arteries. Arterioles have thinner walls and lack an extensive tunica externa. Larger arterioles have a relatively extensive tunica media, composed of thick layers of smooth muscle, but in the smallest arterioles, the tunica media consists of a single layer of smooth muscle arranged in a spiral pattern around the endothelium. The smooth muscle cells allow the arterioles to change diameter, regulating the flow of blood to specific capillary beds. Arterioles are the primary site of regulation of blood flow to the tissues. During **vasoconstriction**, the diameter of an arteriole decreases, reducing flow through the arteriole to the capillary bed of a tissue. During **vasodilation**, the diameter of an arteriole increases, increasing flow through the arteriole into the capillary bed of a tissue.

Capillaries lack the tunica media and tunica externa and have extremely thin walls composed of a single sheet of endothelial cells, wrapped in an occasional contractile **pericyte cell**. These thin walls allow substances to pass between the blood and the tissues. Substances can move across the capillary walls in several ways. Lipid-soluble substances can move across the cell membrane by simple diffusion. Vesicles transport large water-soluble substances such as proteins across the cell in a process called **transcytosis**. Small molecules such as water and ions can move across the capillary wall via

FIGURE 9.15 **Variation in the structure of vertebrate blood vessels**

Representative portions of blood vessels from the systemic circuit of a mammalian circulatory system are shown in cross section. Arteries and veins are composed of three layers (the tunica externa, tunica media, and tunica intima) of varying thickness, lined with an endothelium. Smaller vessels such as arterioles, capillaries, and venules lack one or more of these layers.

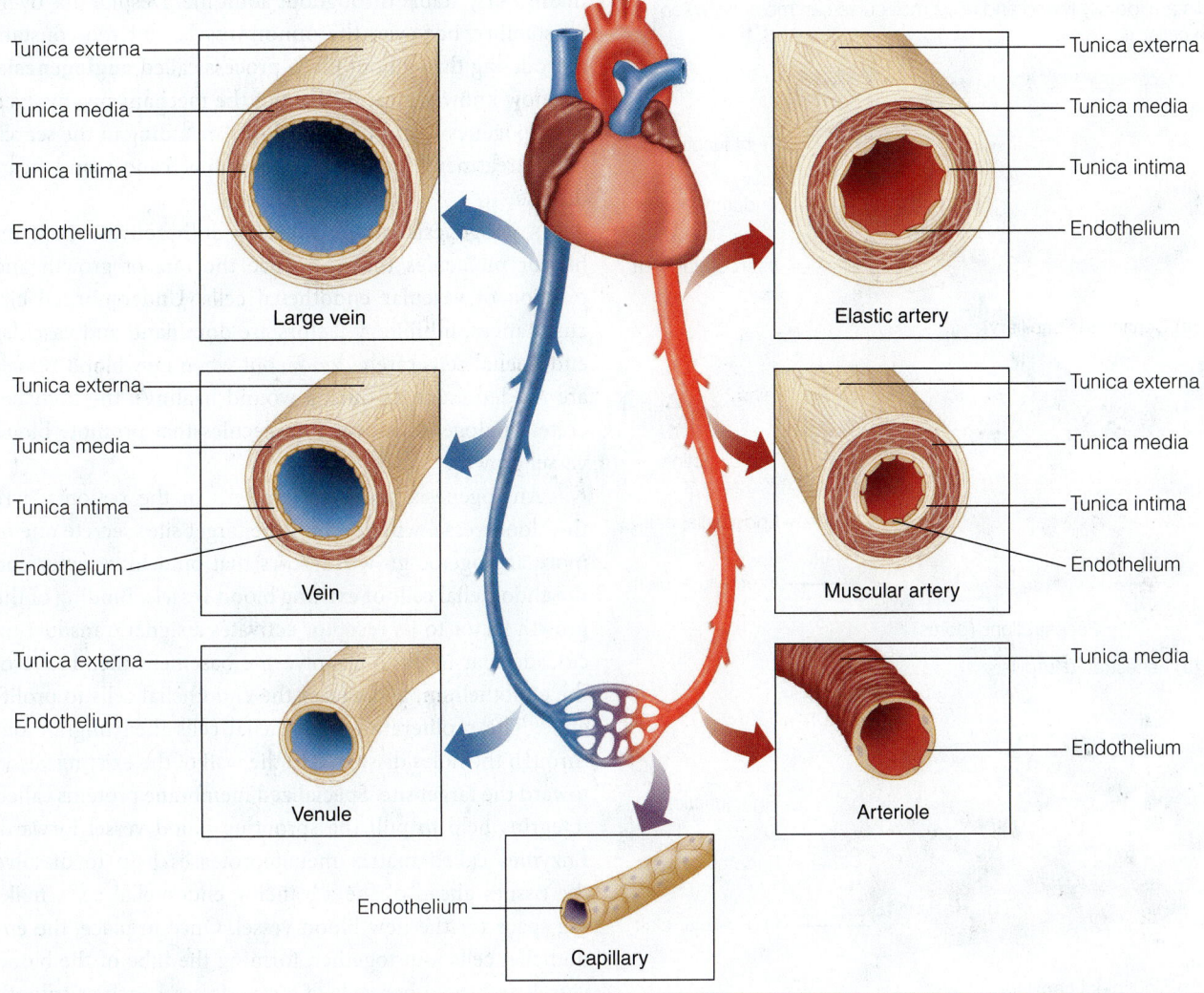

a **paracellular pathway**, through pores between the cells of the capillary wall. Capillaries have very small diameters, and are often just large enough for blood cells to squeeze through.

The structure of the tunica intima varies among capillaries (Figure 9.16). The cells of the vascular endothelium of capillaries are held together with tight junctions. As we discussed in Chapter 8: Functional Organization of Nervous Systems, the capillaries of the central nervous system are particularly tightly joined, allowing few molecules to pass; this forms the blood-brain barrier. **Continuous capillaries** are found in the skin and muscle. The seal between the cells of a continuous capillary is not usually complete, leaving areas of unjoined membrane that allow fluids and small molecules to pass from the blood to the interstitial fluid. **Fenestrated capillaries** are similar to continuous capillaries except that the cells of the vascular endothelium contain numerous pores

covered with a thin diaphragm. Small molecules and fluids can pass easily through these pores, and thus fenestrated capillaries are found in areas of the body that are specialized for the exchange of substances, such as parts of the kidney, the endocrine organs, and the intestine. **Sinusoidal capillaries** are the most porous of all capillaries, and are found only in very specialized organs such as the liver and bone marrow. They have fewer tight junctions and more spaces between the cells. This structure allows large proteins to move across the capillary wall.

Capillaries empty into venules, which lead into the veins that return blood to the heart. A vein usually has a thinner wall and larger lumen than a similarly sized artery. As a result, veins can be easily stretched. When blood enters the veins it is under much lower pressure than when it enters the arteries, so exceptionally thick walls are not needed. In

FIGURE 9.16 **Variation in capillary structure**

(a) In a continuous capillary, the endothelial cells are connected via tight junctions. **(b)** In a fenestrated capillary, the endothelial cells have many oval pores (fenestrations) that allow the regulated movement of solutes. **(c)** In a sinusoidal capillary, the endothelial cells are loosely linked and large molecules can move between the cells.

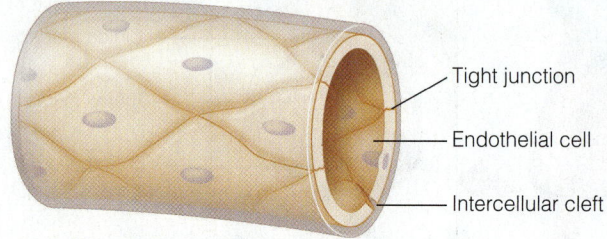

Tight junction
Endothelial cell
Intercellular cleft

(a) Continuous capillary

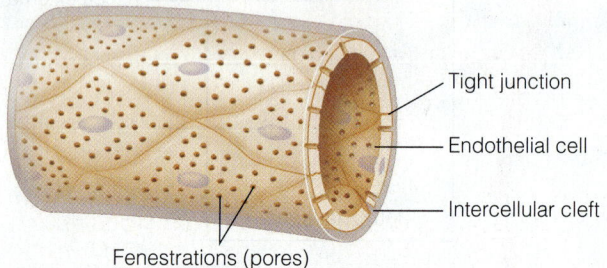

Tight junction
Endothelial cell
Intercellular cleft

Fenestrations (pores)

(b) Fenestrated capillary

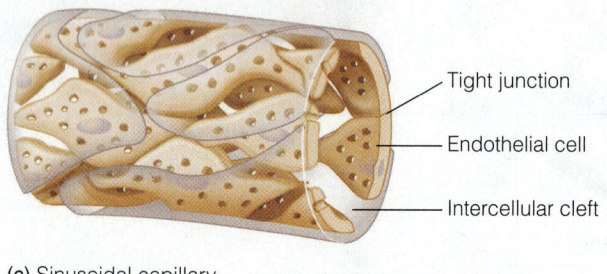

Tight junction
Endothelial cell
Intercellular cleft

(c) Sinusoidal capillary

particular, the tunica media of the veins is much thinner than in the arteries. However, the tunica externa is often more prominent than in the arteries. Veins differ from arteries in that some veins (particularly those in the limbs) contain one-way valves to prevent backflow of blood. The valves are part of the tunica intima. Note that we distinguish arteries and veins by whether they carry blood that is flowing toward or away from the heart, not whether they carry oxygenated or deoxygenated blood. For example, the **pulmonary artery** of mammals, which leads from the heart to the lungs, carries deoxygenated blood, while the **pulmonary vein**, which leads from the lungs to the heart, carries oxygenated blood. In contrast, the aorta carries oxygenated blood, while the **venae cavae** (the large veins leading from the body to the heart) carry deoxygenated blood.

Blood vessels undergo angiogenesis

During the embryonic development of vertebrates, the major vessels of the circulatory system grow into a network of arteries, arterioles, capillaries, venules, and veins, which remains fairly stable throughout adult life. Despite this overall stability, however, the minor vessels undergo constant remodeling throughout life, a process called **angiogenesis**. We now know a great deal about the mechanisms involved in angiogenesis, and these findings are aiding in the search for a treatment for diseases including cancer and heart disease.

Angiogenesis is controlled by both activator and inhibitor molecules that influence the rate of growth and division of vascular endothelial cells. Under normal circumstances, inhibitory factors are dominant, and vascular endothelial cells rarely divide, but when new blood vessels are needed (such as during wound healing), the body secretes angiogenic activator molecules that promote blood vessel growth.

Angiogenesis begins when cells in the region where the blood vessel will develop (the target site) secrete one or more angiogenic growth factors that bind to receptors on the endothelial cells of existing blood vessels. Binding of the growth factor to its receptor activates a signal transduction cascade that helps to dissolve the basement membrane of the endothelium, and causes the endothelial cells to proliferate. The proliferating endothelial cells then migrate out through the holes dissolved in the wall of the existing vessel toward the target site. Specialized membrane proteins called integrins help to pull the sprouting blood vessel forward. Enzymes called matrix metalloproteases help to dissolve the tissues ahead of the advancing endothelial cells, making space for the new blood vessel. Once in place, the endothelial cells join together, forming the tube of the blood vessel, and the other cells of a blood vessel such as smooth muscle are laid down, completing the development of the new vessel.

Low oxygen levels can promote angiogenesis

A number of factors, such as wounding and low oxygen levels (hypoxia) in a tissue can promote angiogenesis. When cells are hypoxic, levels of the protein hypoxia-inducible factor-1 (Hif-1) increase. Hif-1 is part of a transcription factor complex. When the levels of Hif-1 increase, the transcription factor complex moves to the nucleus and binds to the promoters of a variety of hypoxia-inducible genes. One of these genes encodes an angiogenic activator protein called vascular endothelial growth factor (Veg-f). Veg-f binds to receptors on vascular endothelial cells and causes angiogenesis, increasing the density of the **vasculature** in the area. The increased vasculature can supply more oxygen to the tissues, reducing tissue hypoxia. Thus, the angiogenic response to tissue hypoxia acts as a negative feedback loop, maintaining tissue oxygen homeostasis.

Angiogenic activators and inhibitors are currently being studied as possible treatments for diseases such as cancer and coronary artery disease. Cancerous tumors secrete high levels of angiogenic activator molecules, causing new blood vessels to grow to supply the tumor with oxygen and nutrients. Tumor growth depends on this supply, so blocking angiogenesis can halt or slow tumor growth.

Drugs that stimulate angiogenesis are also being tested for treatment of diverse diseases, including coronary artery disease and diabetes. In late-stage diabetes, blood vessels begin to fail, and circulation to the feet can be very poor. As a result, the tissues can become oxygen deprived and die, which may require amputation of the toes or feet. Angiogenic growth factors may help slow the progress of this disease by promoting new blood vessel growth and helping to improve oxygen delivery. This treatment is not a cure, because it does not repair the underlying cause of blood vessel degeneration, but it may reduce the severity of symptoms.

Vertebrate circulatory systems contain one or more pumps in series

Water-breathing fish have a single-circuit circulatory system in which blood flows from the heart through the gills to the body tissues and then back to the heart (Figure 9.17a). Because the heart must pump blood through the gills and tissues in series, some fish (such as hagfish) have a small accessory or caudal heart in the tail that assists blood flow back to the heart. In other species, normal movements of the body help venous return to the heart. In contrast, tetrapods (amphibians, reptiles, birds, and mammals) have two circuits within their circulatory system. This change in circulatory pattern is associated with the colonization of land and the shift to the use of the lungs for gas exchange. The right side of the heart pushes blood through the lungs in the **pulmonary circuit** of the circulatory system, whereas the left side of the heart pushes blood through body tissues in the **systemic circuit** of the circulatory system.

Mammals and birds have completely separated pulmonary and systemic circuits

Although the right and left sides of the heart are grouped together into a single organ, in mammals and birds these two sides of the heart are completely separated. As a result, a mammalian or bird circulatory system is conceptually similar to a single-circuit circulatory system with two pumps in series (Figure 9.17b). Oxygenated blood from the lungs flows to the left heart, which pumps the oxygenated blood to the body. The deoxygenated blood returning from the body flows into the right heart, which then pumps this deoxygenated blood to the lungs.

The completely separated systemic and pulmonary circuits of circulatory systems of mammals and birds are relatively inflexible, because blood cannot be diverted from one part of the system to the other. For example, when a mammal holds its breath, blood must still flow through the lungs, despite the fact that this tissue is not being utilized. However,

FIGURE 9.17 Vertebrate circulatory systems

The structure of vertebrate circulatory systems varies depending on the respiratory strategy of the animal. **(a)** In water-breathing fish, blood travels from the heart through the aorta to the gills and then to the body tissues, and returns to the heart. **(b)** Air-breathing tetrapods have a double-circuit circulatory system with two pumps arranged in series. Blood travels through the left heart to the aorta, which leads to the systemic circuit through the body, returning to the right heart that pumps the blood via the pulmonary artery through the pulmonary circuit through the lungs.

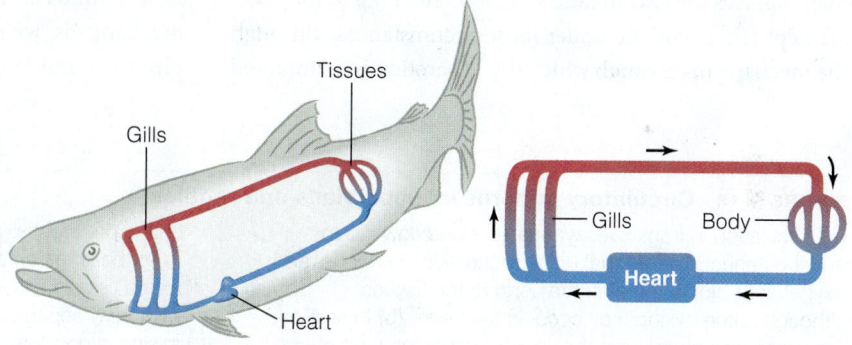

(a) Single-circuit circulatory system

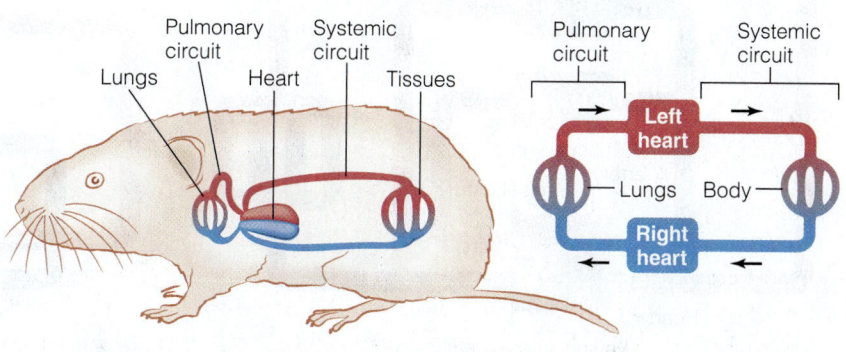

(b) Double-circuit circulatory system

because mammals and birds breathe more or less continuously, the ability to divert flow from the pulmonary circuit has not been an important force shaping the evolution of their circulatory systems.

Having completely separated pulmonary and systemic circuits has one important advantage: It allows pressures to be different in the pulmonary and systemic circuits. But why would having different pressures in the two circuits be an advantage? In the lungs, the capillaries must be very thin to allow effective gas exchange, but if blood flows through these thin capillaries under high pressure, fluid will leak through the capillary walls. When this fluid accumulates it increases the diffusion distance and reduces the efficiency of gas exchange. Therefore, a low-pressure circulatory system through the lungs may be advantageous. In contrast, high pressures are needed to force blood through the long systemic circulatory system. Having separate pulmonary and systemic circuits allows these two differing demands to be met.

Many tetrapods have incompletely separated pulmonary and systemic circuits

Unlike mammals and birds, amphibians and most reptiles have an incompletely divided heart (Figure 9.18). Thus, it is possible for deoxygenated blood from the systemic circuit and oxygenated blood from the pulmonary circuit to mix. In many species the two streams of blood returning to the heart are kept fairly separate under most circumstances, although the mechanisms through which this separation is maintained

are not fully understood. In fact, in some species, such as monitor lizards and pythons, the pulmonary and systemic circuits can maintain substantially different blood pressures. However, because the ventricular chambers of the heart are interconnected, blood can be diverted from the systemic to the pulmonary circuit, or vice versa, if necessary. For example, these animals may divert blood from the pulmonary circuit to the systemic circuit during diving, allowing them to avoid perfusing the inactive lung.

CONCEPT CHECK

7. List the major types of blood vessels in the vertebrates and compare their diameter and wall thickness.

8. How can substances move across capillaries?

9. What are some possible advantages and disadvantages of having completely separated pulmonary and systemic circuits (as in the circulatory systems of birds and mammals)?

The Physics of Circulatory Systems

From the preceding sections it is clear that there is substantial variation in the organization and anatomy of animal circulatory systems. Despite this diversity, however, all animal circulatory systems use similar mechanisms to cause the bulk flow of fluids around the body. In order to understand these mechanisms, we must first review some of the fundamental physics of fluid flow.

FIGURE 9.18 **Circulatory patterns in amphibians and reptiles**

(a) Circulation in frogs. Deoxygenated blood flows to the pulmocutaneous artery that leads to the skin and lungs, and oxygenated blood flows via the aorta to the tissues, although some mixing may occur in the heart. **(b)** In reptiles, deoxygenated blood from the tissues enters the right atrium and is preferentially directed to the lungs. Oxygenated blood from the lungs enters the left atrium and is preferentially directed to the tissues. Oxygenated blood and deoxygenated blood are kept fairly separated under normal circumstances, although mixing is possible.

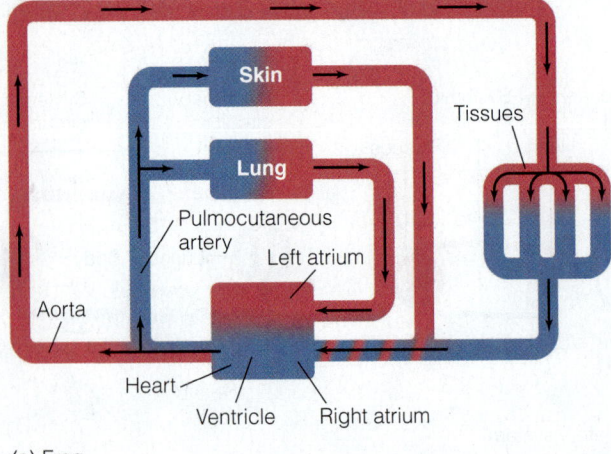

(a) Frog

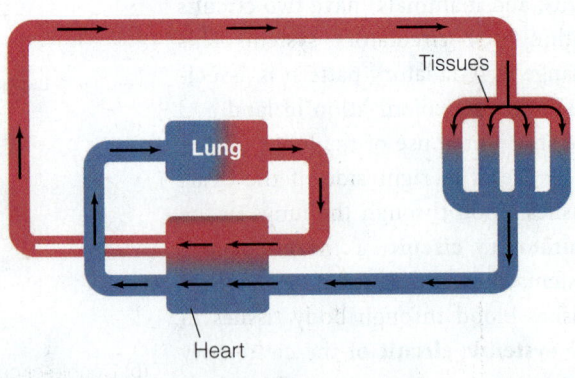

(b) Lizard

Recall from the beginning of the chapter that fluids flow down pressure gradients. Resistance due to friction opposes this movement. We can quantify the relationship between flow, pressure, and resistance in an equation called the **law of bulk flow**:

$$Q = \Delta P/R$$

where Q = flow, P = the pressure gradient, and R = resistance.

The law of bulk flow is very similar to another basic physical principle—Ohm's law—that quantifies the behavior of charge in an electrical circuit. Ohm's law is usually written as $V = IR$ (where V = voltage, I = current, and R = resistance). If we rearrange this equation, we can write $I = V/R$. The electrical current (I) is simply the flow of electrons, and is thus equivalent to fluid flow (Q). The voltage drop across the circuit is the driving force for current movement, and is equivalent to the pressure gradient (P). The electrical resistance is analogous to the frictional resistance of the blood vessels. Ohm's law and the law of bulk flow both quantify a fundamental physical phenomenon that is related to Newton's second law. Substances move because they are acted on by a force, and this movement is impeded by resistance.

Flow is defined as the volume of a fluid that moves past a given point per unit time, and has units such as liters per minute. Flow is, by definition, a rate. But when fluid flows it also moves across a certain distance per unit time—that is, it has a velocity. It is important to bear in mind the difference between flow and velocity. It is possible to have high flow with low velocity, or low flow with high velocity. For example, think about water flowing in a large river such as the Amazon. The Amazon has the highest flow of any river in the world but in many places the water has a rather low velocity because the river can be extremely wide.

You will see a variety of units of pressure used in the physiological literature. The SI unit for pressure is the pascal, or the force per unit area (in newtons per meter squared). Physiologists and physicians often also use non-SI units to express pressure, including millimeters of mercury (mm Hg) and torr (where 1 torr = 1 mm Hg). These older units are the result of the use of mercury-filled manometers for the clinical measurement of blood pressure. Conversion factors among these units can be found in the appendix of this book.

The units for resistance in a circulatory system are complex, and depend upon the units chosen for pressure and flow. For example, a unit for resistance could be $kPa.min/L^{-1}$. In medicine, the most common unit of resistance is the so-called peripheral resistance unit (PRU) in $mm\ Hg.sec/ml^{-1}$.

The radius of a tube affects its resistance

In circulatory systems, the circulating fluid is generally confined within a system of tubes or spaces, such as the blood vessels of vertebrates. We can begin to understand what sets the **resistance** of a blood vessel in the circulatory system by thinking about factors that affect flow through a drinking straw. Is it easier to drink liquids through a very long straw or a shorter straw? What is the difference between drinking through a narrow straw and a wider straw? What is the difference between drinking a milkshake and water (fluids with very different **viscosity**) through a straw? We can quantify these relationships mathematically as follows:

$$R = 8\ L\eta/r^4$$

where R = the resistance of the tube, L = the length of the tube, η = the viscosity of the fluid, and r = the radius of the tube. Substituting this relationship into the law of bulk flow, we obtain **Poiseuille's equation**:

$$Q = \Delta P\pi r^4/8\ L\eta$$

Although real circulatory systems violate almost all of the assumptions of Poiseuille's equation (see Box 9.1: Math in Physiology: Poiseuille's Equation), it still provides a good conceptual summary of the factors that affect the flow of fluids through circulatory systems.

Because resistance is inversely proportional to radius to the fourth power, small changes in the radius of a tube result in large changes in its resistance.

The resistance of a vessel determines the flow

In general, fluids tend to follow the path of least resistance. So, when blood reaches a branching point in the circulatory system, a higher proportion of the flow will be directed along the path with the lowest resistance. Many animals (both vertebrates and invertebrates) can control the flow through their organs by changing the resistance of blood vessels leading to a particular organ. For example, in the vertebrates the radius of the feed arteries and arterioles leading to the capillary beds can be adjusted via vasoconstriction or vasodilation. During vasoconstriction, the radius of the blood vessel decreases, increasing the resistance and reducing the flow through the vessel. During vasodilation the radius of the blood vessel increases, reducing the resistance and increasing the flow. For example, during exercise the arterioles leading to skeletal muscle vasodilate, while arterioles leading to the digestive system vasoconstrict. Because small changes in radius cause large changes in resistance, even modest vasoconstriction and vasodilation can result in large changes in flow.

Because of the law of conservation of mass, the flow through each segment of a circulatory system must be equal. So the total flow in the aorta is the same as the total flow across the capillary beds. Because the law of bulk flow is essentially similar to Ohm's law for electrical current, we can model circulatory systems as simple electrical circuits, and use our knowledge of electrical circuits to understand the

MATH IN PHYSIOLOGY 9.1

POISEUILLE'S EQUATION

Although Poiseuille's equation provides a useful framework for thinking about the physics of circulatory systems, real circulatory systems violate almost all of its assumptions. For example, Poiseuille's equation assumes that the tubes in the system are unbranched and rigid, and that flow involves a simple fluid moving steadily through the tubes. In real circulatory systems, the vessels are branched and are distensible, changing their diameter as pressure changes; flow is often pulsatile, increasing and decreasing with the heartbeat; and the fluid is a complex mixture of plasma and cells.

The degree to which a blood vessel expands in response to increased pressure is called its compliance, C, and is equal to

$$C = \Delta V/\Delta P$$

where V = volume and P = pressure. Vessels with high compliance stretch easily when exposed to pressure, whereas vessels with low compliance stretch less. If we plot the change in volume against the change in pressure of a representative blood vessel, the slope of the line is the compliance of the vessel. The compliance of a blood vessel is not constant; compliance decreases at higher pressures and volumes—vessels become "stiffer" at high pressures. The compliance of a vessel is usually assessed under steady-state conditions, but blood vessels take some time to stretch, a phenomenon known as the *Windkessel effect*. In essence, blood vessels can store the potential energy imparted by pressure, and release it at a later time. As we see later in the chapter, this effect is important in the arteries.

Turbulent flow is relatively rare in the circulatory system, occurring in the heart and at some vessel branching points. In turbulent flow, the fluid moves in a complex pattern of eddies and whorls, oriented in various directions relative to the main axis of flow. In most blood vessels, flow is fairly laminar so that the fluid moves in a linear way along the blood vessel. But the velocity profile of the blood is not identical across the diameter of the vessel. Flow is slower near the walls because of the effects of friction. Poiseuille's equation ignores this effect. In larger vessels, flow is laminar but pulsatile, increasing when the heart contracts, and decreasing between contractions. The end result of this complex flow pattern is that the velocity profile is flatter, and the direction of flow changes as the heart beats.

The complex nature of blood has important effects on its viscosity. The viscosity of the aqueous component of the blood, called plasma, is low (about 1.8 times the viscosity of pure water), but whole blood has a viscosity about three to four times that of water because of the presence of blood cells. Because it is a mixture of components with different viscosities, blood acts as a non-Newtonian fluid; its viscosity varies depending on the size of the tube that it flows through, a phenomenon called the *Fahraeus-Lindqvist effect*. The Fahraeus-Lindqvist effect occurs because blood tends to separate in smaller blood vessels; in these smaller vessels, blood cells get swept into the higher-velocity flow at the center of the vessel, while the fluid close to the walls consists largely of plasma. The "high-viscosity" component at the center of the vessels has only minor interactions with the walls of the vessels, while the "low-viscosity" plasma interacts with the vessel walls, reducing the apparent viscosity of the fluid. In contrast, in very small vessels, blood cells fill almost the entire diameter of the vessel, and have to change shape to squeeze through the small space. Also, in these small vessels the blood cells tend to stick to each other and to the blood vessel walls, and together these three factors greatly increase the apparent viscosity of the fluid.

Despite these (and other) violations of its assumptions, Poiseuille's equation still provides a useful conceptual model of flow through circulatory systems, and helps to explain the architecture of animal circulatory systems.

---

factors that regulate the flow of blood into specific vessels (Figure 9.19).

Like electrical resistors, blood vessels can be arranged in series or in parallel. The total resistance of a circuit with resistors arranged in series is the sum of the individual resistances, or

$$R_T = R_1 + R_2 \ldots$$

However, when resistors are arranged in parallel, the total resistance is determined as follows:

$$1/R_T = 1/R_1 + 1/R_2 + 1/R_3 \ldots$$

When you add resistors in series, the total resistance of the circuit increases, but when you add resistors in parallel, the total resistance of the circuit decreases. In circulatory systems, resistors are arranged both in series and in parallel. Capillary beds, which consist of many small blood vessels in parallel, typically have relatively low resistance to flow. In contrast, the individual arterioles leading to the capillary beds have high resistance and can be used as flow regulators.

In Figure 9.19b, the total flow at point A and point B is the same. However, the amount of flow in each of the parallel blood vessels at point B need not be equal. The

FIGURE 9.19 **Resistors in series and parallel**
Circulatory systems are analogous to electrical circuits with resistors arranged in both series and parallel. **(a)** The total resistance (R_T) of a circuit with resistors arranged in series is the sum of the individual resistances ($R_1 + R_2 + R_3$). **(b)** The total resistance of a group of resistors arranged in parallel decreases with increasing numbers of resistors. Total flow through each point of a circuit (A, B, C, D, E) is equal, but flow divides among the resistors arranged in parallel, depending on the resistance of each branch.

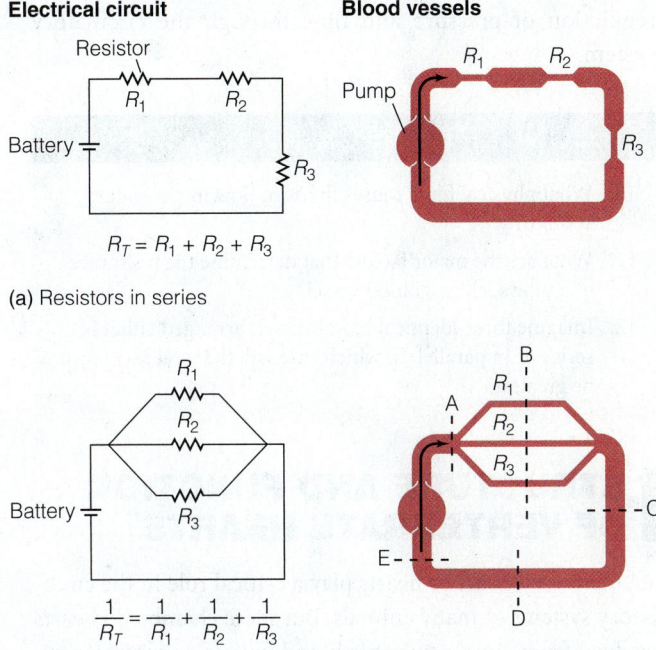

Electrical circuit   **Blood vessels**

(a) Resistors in series

$$R_T = R_1 + R_2 + R_3$$

(b) Resistors in parallel

$$\frac{1}{R_T} = \frac{1}{R_1} + \frac{1}{R_2} + \frac{1}{R_3}$$

mass, the same amount of flow (volume per unit time) must pass through the narrow part of the river as passes through the wide part of the river, but as a result its velocity (distance moved per unit time) must be greater in the narrow channel.

So what happens if a wide river splits into many small channels, such as you might encounter in a river delta? In this case, the velocity of flow in the small channels depends on the total cross-sectional area of the channels. Flow will split up among the channels, so mass will be conserved across the system as a whole, but all of the flow does not have to pass through any one smaller channel. The velocity of flow in the smaller channels will be inversely proportional to the total cross-sectional area of all the channels put together. If there are enough small channels, flow may be slower than in the wide part of the river. Exactly the same reasoning applies to circulatory systems. In areas where a single larger blood vessel splits into many small blood vessels arranged in parallel, the velocity of flow is likely to decrease as the blood enters the many small vessels (assuming that the total cross-sectional area of all the small vessels is greater than that of the single large vessel). For circulatory systems, we can summarize these relationships as follows:

$$\text{Blood velocity} = Q/A$$

where A is equal to the summed cross-sectional area of the blood vessels.

This relationship between velocity and cross-sectional area is significant for a circulatory system, because it takes time for substances to diffuse between the blood and the tissues. Regions of the circulatory system, such as the capillaries, that are involved in the exchange of materials have a very high total cross-sectional area, and so have very low flow velocities, which aids diffusion.

Pressure exerts a force on the walls of blood vessels

The blood pressure within a walled chamber such as a heart or blood vessel exerts a force on the walls of the chamber. This force can be quantified using the law of LaPlace (Figure 9.20), which states that the tension on the walls of a blood vessel is proportional to the blood pressure and the vessel radius according to the following equation:

$$T = aPr$$

where T is the tension on the walls (in N/cm), P is the **transmural pressure**, or the difference between the internal pressure and the external pressure (in Pa), r is the radius of the vessel, and a is a constant ($\frac{1}{2}$ for a cylindrical blood vessel or 1 for a spherical chamber).

The law of LaPlace can be used to understand the structure and function of blood vessels. The law of LaPlace

proportion of flow going through each of the parallel blood vessels depends upon the relative resistances of the blood vessels. As indicated by the law of bulk flow, blood tends to take the path of least resistance; more blood will flow through a low-resistance blood vessel than through one with high resistance. If we know the total flow and the resistance of each of the vessels in parallel, we can calculate the amount of flow going through each vessel, using the law of bulk flow.

Velocity of flow is determined by pressure and cross-sectional area

As discussed above, flow is a measure of the amount of fluid passing a certain point per unit time, which is different from the velocity of flow, which is measured as distance per unit time. The velocity of blood flow in a blood vessel is inversely related to the cross-sectional area of the blood vessel. You can visualize this by thinking about what happens to a volume of water as it flows through narrow and wide parts of the river. Because of the principle of the conservation of

FIGURE 9.20 **The law of LaPlace**

(a) For a thin-walled vessel, the wall tension (*T*) is proportional to the transmural pressure (*P*) times the radius of the vessel.
(b) For a thick-walled vessel, the wall stress (σ) is proportional to the transmural pressure (*P*) and the vessel radius (*r*), but inversely proportional to the wall thickness (*w*).

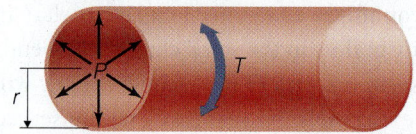

P = Transmural pressure
r = Radius
T = Wall tension

(a) Thin-walled vessel

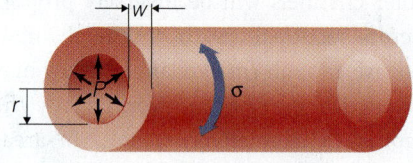

P = Transmural pressure
r = Radius
w = Wall thickness
σ = Wall stress

(b) Thick-walled vessel

shows that the walls of a blood vessel with a larger radius will be exposed to a higher tension than would a blood vessel with a smaller radius. For example, the walls of arteries, which have a large radius, would be exposed to a higher tension than would the walls of the tiny capillaries, simply based on their size. Further increasing the forces on the arterial wall, the transmural pressure in the arteries is greater than the transmural pressure in the capillaries (because blood pressure is highest as blood leaves the heart). Arterial walls must be very thick to withstand this high wall tension, while capillary walls can be very thin because of their small size.

The law of LaPlace can be rewritten to take into account the thickness of the wall of the vessel, as follows:

$$\sigma = Pr/w$$

where σ is the wall stress (in N/cm^2, or Pa), or the force per unit cross-sectional area of the wall, *P* is transmural pressure, *r* is the radius of the vessel, and *w* is the thickness of the wall. From this relationship it is clear that increasing the thickness of the wall of a blood vessel offsets the effects of increasing radius on wall stress. As a result, although the large radius of an artery would result in a high tension on the walls, their thickness reduces the wall stress per unit area, preventing the arteries from bursting due to the pressure exerted on them. From the law of LaPlace, we can also see that capillary walls can only be thin because they have such a small radius.

The law of LaPlace can also be used to understand the forces generated by the heart. A heart with a large radius

must develop more tension within the heart wall to develop the same pressure within the heart (i.e., must undergo a stronger contraction) as would a heart with a smaller radius. Thus, we might expect a greater ratio of heart mass to heart volume in larger hearts.

In the next sections of the chapter, we use these physical principles to understand the functioning of animal circulatory systems. We begin by examining the pumping function of hearts, and then turn to an examination of the regulation of pressure and flow through the circulatory system.

CONCEPT CHECK

10. What physical force causes fluids to flow in circulatory systems?
11. What are the major factors that determine the resistance of a tube such as a blood vessel?
12. Imagine three identical blood vessels arranged either in series or in parallel. In which case will the total resistance be greatest?

STRUCTURE AND FUNCTION OF VERTEBRATE HEARTS

A chambered heart or hearts play a critical role in the circulatory systems of many animals. But these chambered hearts evolved from simple pulsatile blood vessels or tubular peristaltic hearts independently many times in different animal groups. Here we focus on the hearts of vertebrates as an example of these critical pumping structures. We begin with a survey of the anatomy of the heart in various vertebrate groups. Heart anatomy is intimately connected with respiratory mode, and changes in the structure of the heart have occurred in parallel with the transition between an aquatic and a terrestrial mode of life in vertebrates.

Heart Anatomy

Vertebrate hearts have complex walls with four main parts (Figure 9.21). A sac called the **pericardium** surrounds the heart. In some species, such as elasmobranchs, the pericardium is relatively rigid, whereas in other species the pericardium is compliant, and stretches easily as the heart beats. The tough outer layer of the pericardium (the *parietal pericardium*) is made of connective tissue that protects the heart and anchors it to surrounding structures. The pericardium is filled with a small amount of fluid that acts as a lubricant, reducing friction as the heart beats.

The inner layer of the pericardium (the *visceral pericardium*) is continuous with the outer connective tissue of the

FIGURE 9.21 **Structure of vertebrate hearts**

Vertebrate hearts have complex walls consisting of a pericardium, epicardium, myocardium, and endocardium. **(a)** Mammalian myocardium consists largely of compact myocardium. **(b)** In fish and amphibians the myocardium is composed largely of spongy myocardium surrounded by a thin layer of compact myocardium. Spongy myocardium is poorly vascularized and receives oxygen from the blood flowing through the heart, whereas compact myocardium is supplied with oxygen by the coronary arteries.

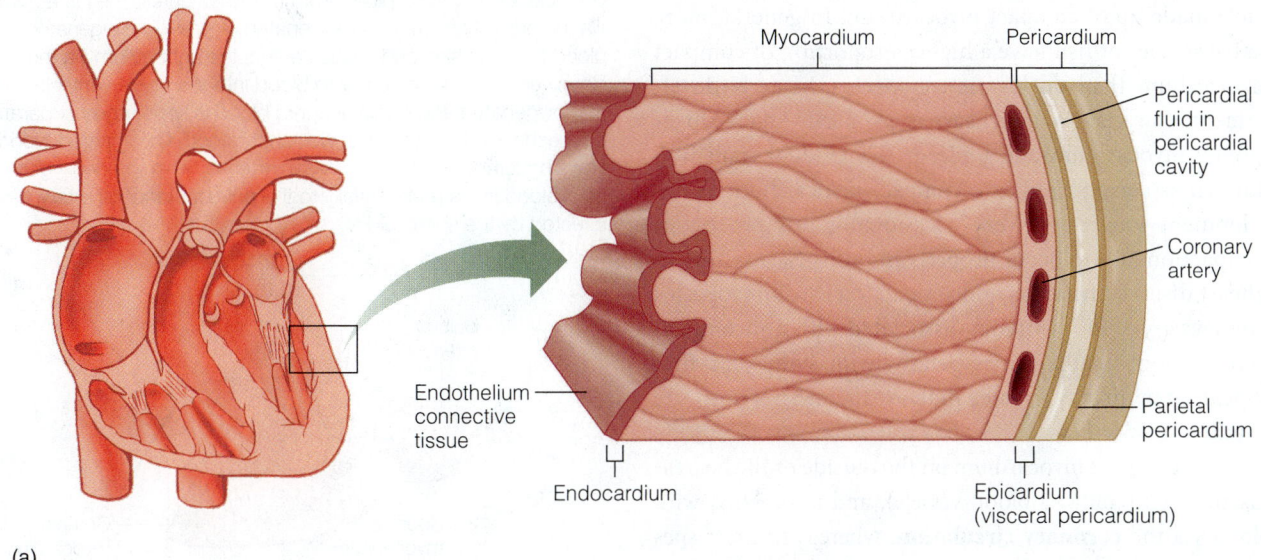

(a)

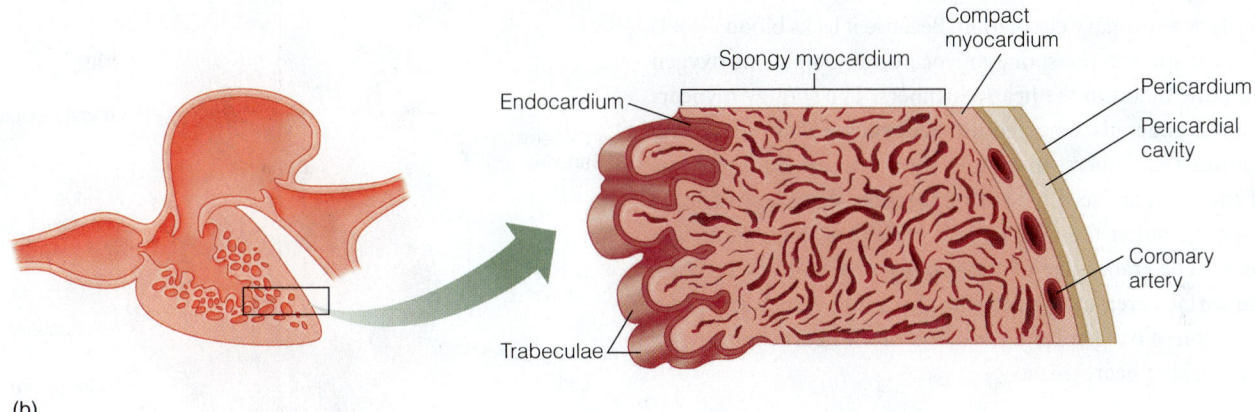

(b)

heart, which is called the **epicardium**. If present, the nerves that regulate the heart are located in the epicardium. In many species there are **coronary arteries** that supply blood to the heart tissues. These vessels originate on the surface of the epicardium and then branch down to penetrate the next layer of the heart—the heart muscle, or **myocardium**. The myocardium is divided into several layers that can be distinguished based on the orientation of the cardiomyocytes (or cardiac muscle cells) in each layer. The innermost lining of the heart is called the **endocardium**, and is composed of a layer of connective tissue covered by a layer of epithelial cells, called the **endothelium**, that lines the chambers of the heart.

This cardiac endothelium is contiguous with the vascular endothelium that lines the blood vessels.

The myocardium can be spongy or compact

The ventricular muscle can be composed of two different types of myocardium: an outer layer of **compact myocardium**, made of tightly packed cells arranged in a regular pattern, and an inner layer of **spongy myocardium** consisting of a meshwork of loosely connected cells. The relative proportion of these two types of myocardium varies among species. In mammals the myocardium is almost entirely compact (Figure 9.21a), whereas in many fish and amphibians it is almost entirely spongy (Figure 9.21b). The ratio of compact to spongy myocardium varies among species of fish and amphibians. For example, many fish have only spongy myocardium, whereas highly active species such as tuna can have as much as 70 percent of their ventricle made up of compact myocardium. In general, more active species of fish have a higher proportion of compact myocardium than do less active species. In early development, the mammalian heart is primarily made up of spongy myocardium and undergoes a gradual transition (known as *compaction*) into compact myocardium as development progresses. Very occasionally, this process of compaction fails to occur properly in humans, resulting in a heart disease known as noncompaction cardiomyopathy. The severity of the symptoms associated with noncompaction cardiomyopathy varies greatly, with symptoms first appearing in infancy in some individuals, and not until late in adult life in others.

The compact myocardium on the outside of the heart is vascularized (contains blood vessels), and is supplied with blood via the **coronary circulation**, whereas in most species the spongy myocardium does not contain blood vessels. Thus, species that lack a compact myocardium also generally lack a coronary circulation. Because it lacks blood vessels in most species, the spongy myocardium obtains its oxygen from the blood in the heart chambers. The spongy myocardium is generally arranged into **trabeculae** that extend into the heart chambers. In fact, in some species the chambers of the heart are so filled with trabeculae that they resemble a sponge rather than the open chambers of the mammalian heart. The trabeculae of the spongy myocardium increase the surface area in contact with the blood, which enhances diffusion of oxygen from the blood in the heart chambers to the working heart tissue.

Fish heart chambers are arranged in series

Recall that most fish are obligate water breathers and have a single-circuit circulatory plan (see Figure 9.17). Associated with this conceptually simple circulatory arrangement, the organization of the heart is also relatively straightforward. The heart of a water-breathing fish consists of four chambers arranged in series (Figure 9.22a). Blood enters the heart via a thin-walled chamber called the **sinus venosus** and flows into the atrium and then into the muscular ventricle. The ventricle pumps the blood into either an elastic structure called the **bulbus arteriosus** (in most bony fish) or a muscular **conus arteriosus** (in elasmobranchs). The single-circuit circulatory system of a fish has the disadvantage that the pressure generated by the heart is largely dissipated as the

FIGURE 9.22 **Cardiac anatomy of fish and frogs**

(a) The heart of a fish is arranged in series. Blood enters the sinus venosus, which pumps blood into the atrium, and then into the muscular ventricle. The ventricle pumps blood via the bulbus arteriosus (in bony fish) or the conus arteriosus (in cartilaginous fish) to the body. **(b)** An amphibian heart has two atria and a single ventricle. Oxygenated blood from the lungs enters the left atrium via the pulmonary vein. Deoxygenated or partially oxygenated blood from the skin and tissues enters the right atrium via the sinus venosus. The atria pump blood into the single ventricle, but the oxygenated and deoxygenated blood is kept largely separate, by mechanisms that are not well understood. Oxygenated blood flows preferentially to the systemic arteries, whereas deoxygenated blood flows preferentially to the pulmocutaneous artery, directed by the spiral fold.

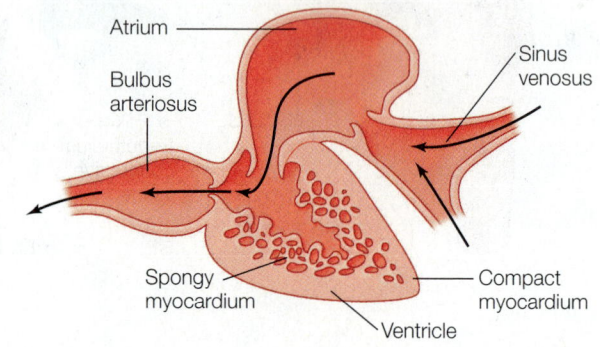

(a) Bony fish heart

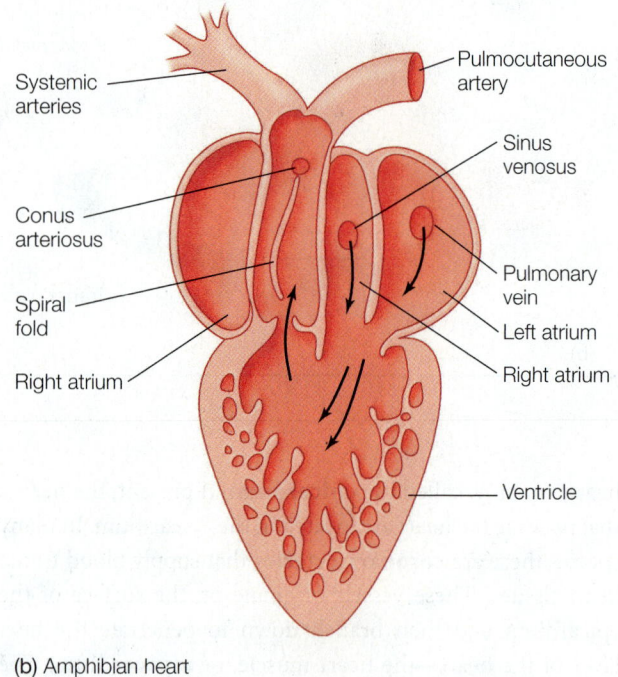

(b) Amphibian heart

blood flows through the gills, and as a result, there is relatively low pressure available to drive blood flow through the tissues. However, this arrangement also makes the presence of a lymphatic system unnecessary in fish because the low pressures in the systemic circulation are insufficient to drive the formation of lymph by ultrafiltration.

Amphibian hearts have three chambers

Amphibians can obtain oxygen from both air and water. As adults, they obtain oxygen from the air via their lungs, but they can also obtain oxygen from the water via the skin. Associated with this respiratory mode, amphibians have a two-circuit circulatory system (see Figure 9.18) and a partially divided heart. The heart has three chambers with two atria and one ventricle (Figure 9.22b). The ventricle of the heart pumps blood via the conus arteriosus into both the pulmonary and systemic circuits of the circulatory system. Oxygenated blood from the lungs returns to the left atrium via the pulmonary vein, while the deoxygenated blood from the systemic circuit mixes with oxygenated blood from the skin (when the amphibian is obtaining oxygen via this route) and returns via veins that empty into the sinus venosus and then into the right atrium. The two atria then supply blood to the single ventricle. The trabeculae within the ventricle help to keep the oxygenated and deoxygenated blood separate, although the mechanisms by which they work are not yet fully understood. In anuran amphibians (frogs and toads) a **spiral fold** within the conus arteriosus is thought to direct deoxygenated blood to the pulmocutaneous artery leading to the lungs and skin and oxygenated blood to the systemic arteries by blocking and unblocking the common entrance to the left and right pulmocutaneous arches.

The lack of complete separation of oxygenated and deoxygenated blood in the amphibian heart has often been considered a disadvantage, as it may result in a decreased supply of oxygen to the tissues. However, viewed from the perspective of the heart, this mixing of oxygenated and deoxygenated blood can be advantageous. In general, amphibians have a relatively limited coronary circulation and a high proportion of nonvascularized spongy myocardium. Thus, much of the heart muscle receives oxygen from the blood within the heart chambers. If all of the blood going to the right side of the ventricle were deoxygenated blood from the body, then the heart muscle on this side would receive very little oxygen. The addition of oxygen from blood returning from the skin, or through mixing of blood between the two sides of the ventricle, may be critical in providing an oxygen supply to the heart.

Most reptiles have five heart chambers

The hearts of most noncrocodilian reptiles are composed of five chambers (Figure 9.23a). As in amphibians, there are two

FIGURE 9.23 Cardiac anatomy of noncrocodilian reptiles

(a) Noncrocodilian reptiles have two atria and three incompletely separated ventricular chambers. **(b)** Diagrammatic view of blood flow through the heart of a noncrocodilian reptile. (Note that the shape of the heart has been "unfolded" so that the atria are shown at the bottom.) Under nonshunting conditions, blood flows from the right atrium to the pulmonary artery, and from the left atrium to the right and left aortas. During a right-to-left (R–L) shunt, some blood from the right atrium enters the aortas, bypassing the lungs. During a left-to-right (L–R) shunt, some blood from the left atrium enters the pulmonary artery, bypassing the tissues.

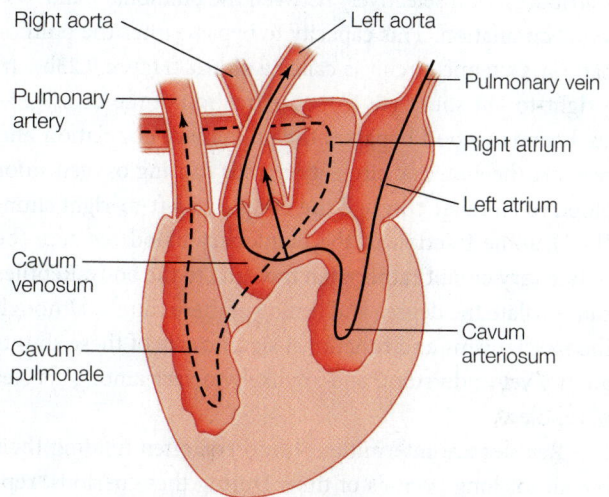

(a) Cardiac anatomy of noncrocodilian reptiles

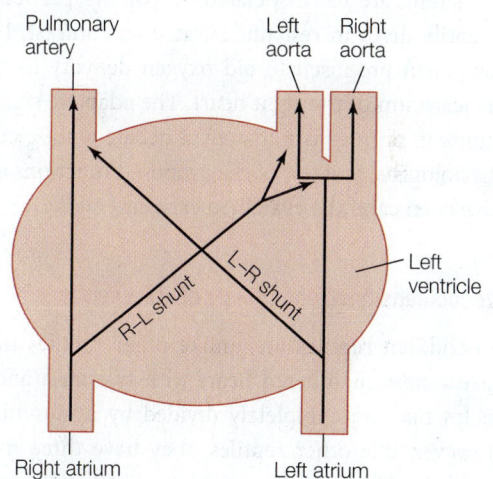

(b) Blood flow through the heart of noncrocodilian reptiles

atria, but the ventricle is divided into three interconnected compartments (the *cavum venosum*, the *cavum pulmonale*, and the *cavum arteriosum*) by muscular ridges, or septa. The conus arteriosus is divided to form the base of three large arteries: the pulmonary artery that leads to the lungs and the right and left aortas that lead to the rest of the body. The pulmonary artery leads from the cavum pulmonale, whereas the aortas lead from the cavum venosum.

Despite their incompletely separated ventricles, reptiles generally maintain separation of oxygenated and deoxygenated blood. Deoxygenated blood enters the right atrium and flows into the cavum venosum and then across the muscular ridge into the cavum pulmonale and out the pulmonary artery. Oxygenated blood enters the left atrium and flows into the cavum venosum and then out the right and left aortas.

As mentioned earlier in this chapter, reptiles can also distribute blood selectively between the pulmonary and systemic circulation. This capacity to bypass either the pulmonary or systemic circuit is called a **shunt** (Figure 9.23b). In a right-to-left shunt (R–L), some fraction of the deoxygenated venous blood bypasses the pulmonary circulation and reenters the systemic circulation, thus causing oxygen-poor blood to circulate through the body. In a left-to-right shunt (L–R), some fraction of the pulmonary blood reenters the pulmonary circuit rather than traveling to the body. Reptiles can regulate the degree and timing of these shunts, although the mechanisms and functional significance of these shunts are not yet understood and are likely to vary among species of reptile.

Reptiles are intermittent breathers, often holding their breath for long periods of time. During these periods, reptiles develop a pronounced R–L shunt, bypassing the pulmonary circulation and directing most of the blood to the body. R–L shunts are also associated with diving, particularly when a reptile dives to rest underwater. In contrast, L–R shunts have been proposed to aid oxygen delivery to the spongy myocardium of the right heart. The adaptive significance of shunts in reptiles is a matter of debate among comparative physiologists, and few of the proposed functions of shunting have been carefully evaluated experimentally.

Crocodilians have completely divided ventricles

Crocodilian reptiles are unlike other reptiles in that they have a four-chambered heart with two atria and two ventricles that are completely divided by a muscular septum. However, like other reptiles, they have three major blood vessels leading away from the heart. The right aorta emerges from the left ventricle, whereas the pulmonary artery and the left aorta emerge from the right ventricle (Figure 9.24). The right aorta sends blood largely to the brain and anterior circulation, whereas the left aorta sends blood largely to the viscera and the posterior parts of the animal. The aortas are connected at two points in the circulatory system: the **foramen of Panizza**, a small opening located at the base of the aortas, near the heart, and an arterial anastomosis located in the abdomen.

FIGURE 9.24 **Cardiac anatomy of a crocodile**

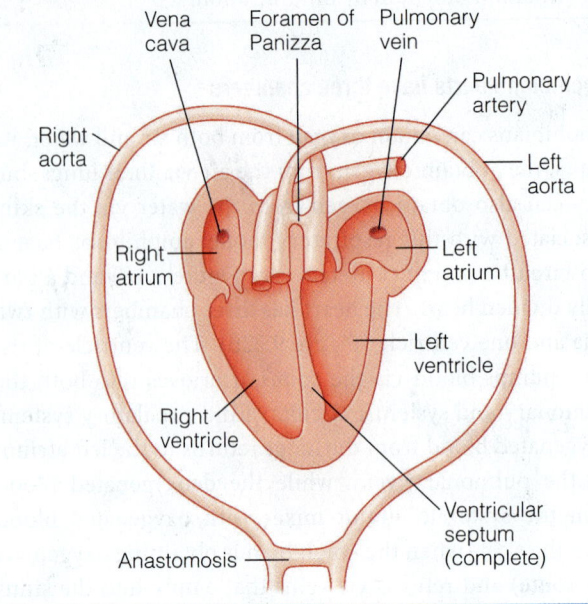

Because of the complete separation of the ventricles, crocodilians cannot shunt blood from the systemic to the pulmonary circulation (a L–R shunt), but R–L shunts are possible (Figure 9.25). When blood pressure in the left and right ventricles is equal, such as might be expected in a resting crocodile breathing air, oxygenated blood from the left ventricle is directed via the right aorta to the brain, while deoxygenated blood flows via the left aorta to the visceral organs, where it may aid in digestion, because this acidic deoxygenated blood can counteract the alkalinization of the blood caused by secretion of digestive acids into the stomach.

FIGURE 9.25 **Pathways of blood flow in a crocodile heart**

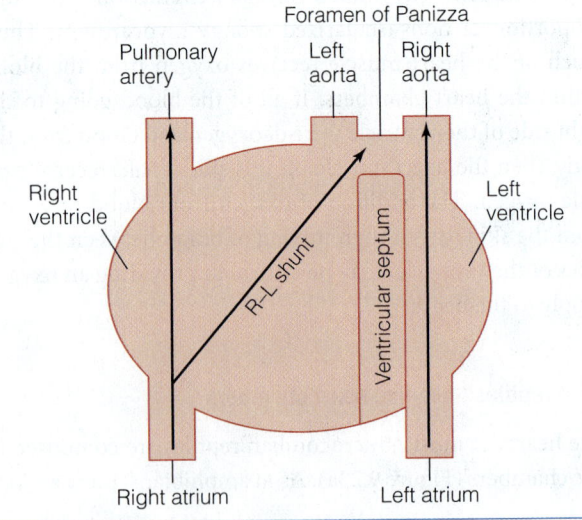

When the animal is active and breathing air, blood pressure is high in the left ventricle compared with the right ventricle. Oxygenated blood flows from the left ventricle both into the right aorta and (via the foramen of Panizza and arterial anastomosis) into the left aorta because the pressure in the right aorta is high compared with the pressure in the left aorta. This prevents deoxygenated blood in the right ventricle from moving into the systemic circulation, and instead it flows almost entirely to the lungs.

The valve at the entrance of the pulmonary artery also helps to control the flow of blood between different parts of the circulatory system. Unlike the passive flaplike valves of other vertebrates, this valve has cog teeth made up of nodules of connective tissue. The cog teeth mesh together, forming a tight seal. The level of epinephrine in the bloodstream controls the position of the teeth in this valve, and thus the valve is controlled actively, rather than simply opening and closing passively in response to pressure changes in the heart. When the crocodile is at rest underwater, and levels of epinephrine are low, the cog teeth close, diverting blood away from the pulmonary artery. When the crocodile is active, the cog teeth open, allowing blood to flow into the lungs.

Crocodiles use the cog valve to shut off the pulmonary system when they dive below the water to rest, allowing them to remain submerged for several hours without perfusing their lungs.

Birds and mammals have four heart chambers

The hearts of mammals and birds are composed of four unobstructed chambers with relatively smooth internal walls (Figure 9.26). The left side of the heart (shown on the right in this ventral view) consists of a thin-walled atrium and a thick-walled ventricle. The right side of the heart also consists of an atrium and ventricle, but the right ventricle has a much thinner wall than the left ventricle. The left ventricle, which pumps blood through the high-resistance systemic circulation, must pump more forcefully than the right ventricle, which pumps blood through the lower-resistance pulmonary circulation. A thick ridge called the intraventricular **septum** separates the two ventricles, while the interatrial septum separates the two atria. These septa are composed of muscle reinforced by connective tissue.

The **atrioventricular (AV) valves** are located between the atria and ventricles and allow blood to flow from the atrium to the ventricle, but not in the reverse direction. The right AV valve, also called the **tricuspid valve**, and the left AV valve, also called the **bicuspid valve**, are attached on the ventricular side to collagenous cords called the **chordae tendineae**. These cords anchor the valves to the **papillary muscles**, and prevent them from opening backward. The **semilunar valves**, located at the exit from the ventricles, prevent blood from flowing backward into the ventricles. The **pulmonary semilunar valve** is located between the right ventricle and the pulmonary artery leading to the lungs. The **aortic semilunar valve** is located between the left ventricle and the aorta, the artery leading to the systemic circulation.

Blood returning to the heart from the body first passes through the superior and inferior venae cavae (superior vena cava and inferior vena cava) into the right atrium. The blood then passes via the right AV, or tricuspid, valve into the right ventricle. The right ventricle pumps the blood through the pulmonary semilunar valve into the pulmonary artery leading to the lungs. The blood travels through the pulmonary capillary bed, where it is oxygenated. It exits the lungs via the pulmonary veins that lead to the left atrium. The blood then travels from the

FIGURE 9.26 Internal anatomy of the mammalian heart

Blood flows from the pulmonary veins into the left atrium and then the left ventricle. The left ventricle pumps blood to the aorta and the systemic circuit of the circulatory system. Blood from the tissues flows via the venae cavae to the right atrium and the right ventricle, which pumps blood to the pulmonary artery and the pulmonary circulation. One-way flow through the heart is ensured by two sets of valves.

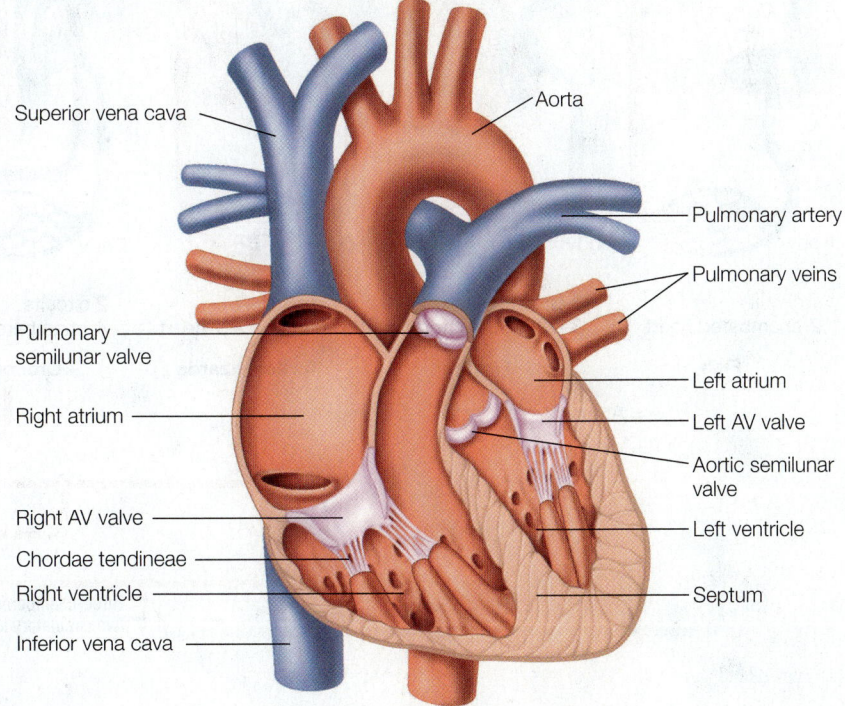

left atrium past the left AV, or bicuspid, valve into the left ventricle. The left ventricle pumps the blood through the aortic semilunar valve into the aorta. The aorta branches into smaller arteries and then arterioles, finally leading to the capillary beds of the systemic circulation. From these capillary beds the blood travels through venules and veins, finally draining into the venae cavae, and returning to the right atrium.

Cardiac anatomy is related to respiratory mode

In vertebrates, the circulatory and respiratory systems are intimately linked; thus it is no surprise that cardiac anatomy is closely related to the respiratory mode of an animal. Changes in heart structure and function across the vertebrates are associated with the colonization of land, the evolution of air breathing, and the evolution of endothermy and high metabolic rate.

Figure 9.27 summarizes the main changes in cardiac anatomy and circulatory organization in vertebrates. Although a single-circuit circulatory system works well for fish, it has limitations in that the maximum blood pressure in the system is limited by the highest blood pressure that can be tolerated by the delicate capillaries of the gills.

Some fish have the ability to come to the surface and breathe air, and many of these species have specialized air-breathing organs for this purpose (for more details see Chapter 11: Respiratory Systems). However, in most species the air-breathing organ is arranged in parallel with the other systemic organs, and oxygenated blood from the air-breathing organ simply mixes with the deoxygenated blood from the other tissues as it returns to the heart. Thus, the general organization of the circulatory system in these fish does not deviate substantially from that of water-breathing fishes. One exception to this pattern is the lungfish, which have a highly developed air-breathing organ and (in some species at least) rather small gills. Lungfish live in habitats where the water can have very low oxygen, and under these conditions these fish are entirely dependent on their lungs for gas exchange. Lungfish hearts have two atria and a partial septum within the ventricle that partially divide the oxygenated blood returning from the lung and the deoxygenated blood returning from the tissues. Although lungfish have a variety of specializations for air breathing, they are aquatic animals that do not venture onto land. However, some species can survive for long periods in air in a dormant state if the pools that they live in dry up. Lungfish are thought to be among the closest living relatives of the terrestrial vertebrates.

FIGURE 9.27   **Summary of vertebrate circulatory and cardiac anatomy**

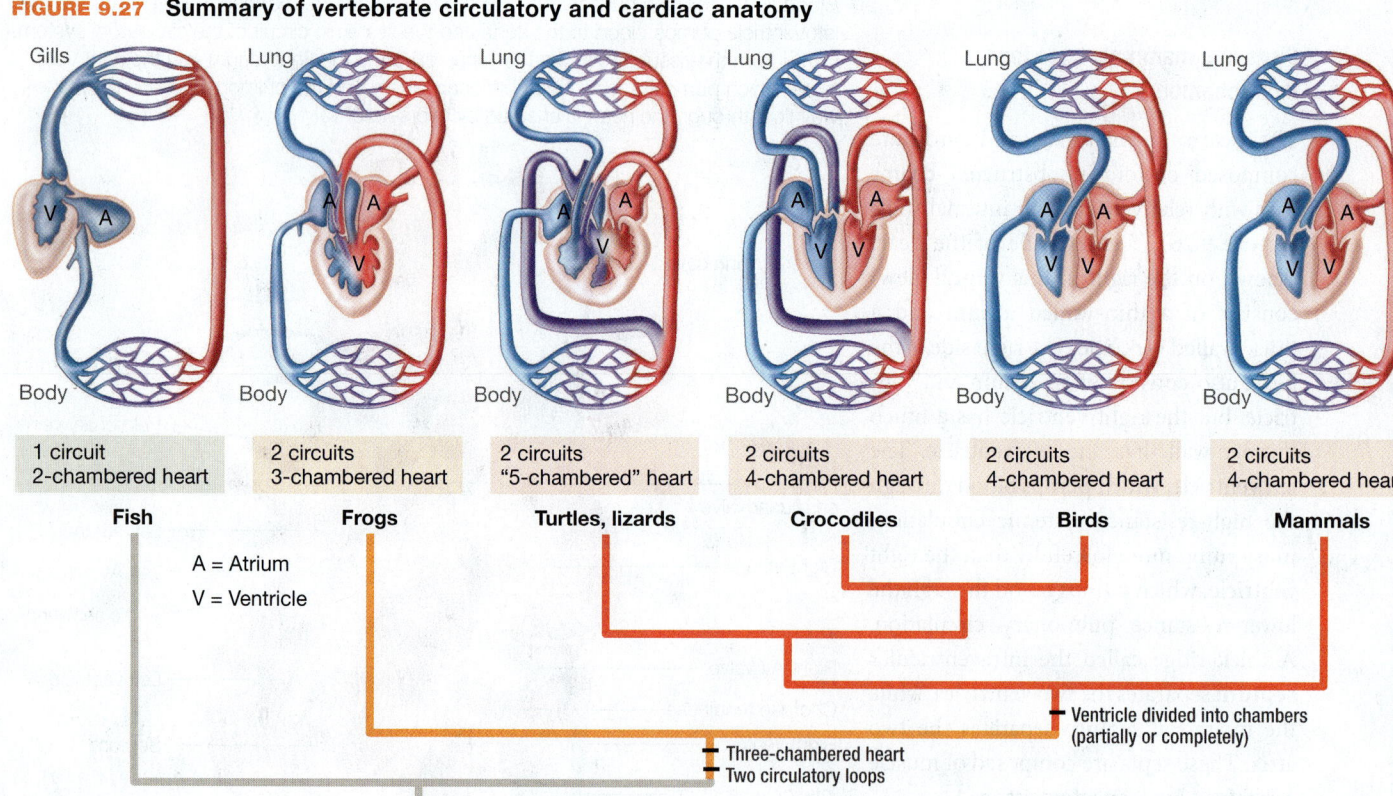

Figure source: Reprinted by permission from Biological Science. (2nd Canadian ed.), Freeman, S., Harrington, M., & Sharp, J., ©2014, Figure 44.24, page 964, Pearson Education Canada: Toronto. Reprinted with permission by Pearson Canada Inc.

The colonization of land by the ancestors of present-day amphibians required a number of changes in the architecture of the circulatory system and heart. Amphibians have two atria and a partially divided ventricle. The pulmocutaneous artery (see Figure 9.18) sends blood to either the lungs (when in air) or the skin (when in water) for gas exchange. Blood from the skin returns to the heart via the systemic circulation (not shown in Figure 9.27), whereas blood from the lungs returns to the heart via the pulmonary circulation. When the animal is air breathing, the heart can maintain almost complete separation of oxygenated and deoxygenated blood, but has the flexibility to bypass the lungs if necessary.

There is a trend of increasing separation of oxygenated and deoxygenated blood in reptiles, birds, and mammals with the evolution of multiple chambers within the ventricle. This separation of the systemic and pulmonary circulation reaches completion in crocodilian reptiles, birds, and mammals, although the complex anatomy of crocodilian blood vessels allows them to retain the capacity to shunt blood away from the lungs, if necessary. This capacity for shunting is lost in birds and mammals. Both birds and mammals are endothermic (maintain a high body temperature through generation of heat; for more details see Chapter 15: Thermal Physiology). Endothermic animals have very high metabolic rates and activity levels, and blood pressure in the systemic circulation must be high to drive blood flow to meet the oxygen demands of the tissues. These pressures would be damaging to the delicate capillaries of the lungs. Thus, the systemic and pulmonary circulation must remain separate to allow the pulmonary circulation to operate at lower pressure.

Cardiac anatomy changes during development

The structures involved in gas exchange change during development. For example, during early embryonic development in fish, most of the gas exchange occurs across the skin, and the gills only gradually take over the primary role in gas exchange as the embryo develops. Similarly, in air-breathing animals, the lungs only assume their primary role in gas exchange after metamorphosis in amphibians, and after hatching or birth in reptiles, birds, and mammals. Thus, as is the case with the phylogenetic patterns of circulatory system evolution, there are substantial changes in the anatomy of the heart during development as the respiratory mode changes. Figure 9.28 summarizes the structural changes in the heart during development of humans, as a representative mammal.

In early fetal development in humans, the heart forms by fusion of two simple heart tubes, resulting in a single tubular heart. The heart tubes then loop and balloon out to form the heart chambers. With the transition from embryo to fetus (at 8–12 weeks after conception in humans), the fetal heart is similar in structure to the heart of an adult. However, there are two critical differences that are related to the respiratory mode of the fetus. A mammalian fetus obtains its oxygen from gas exchange across the placenta. The lungs are not used for gas exchange and little blood flows

FIGURE 9.28   Development of the human heart

Arrows show the direction of blood flow. Days of development are approximate. Note the presence of the ductus arteriosus and the foramen ovale in the fully formed fetal heart that allow blood to bypass the pulmonary circulation.

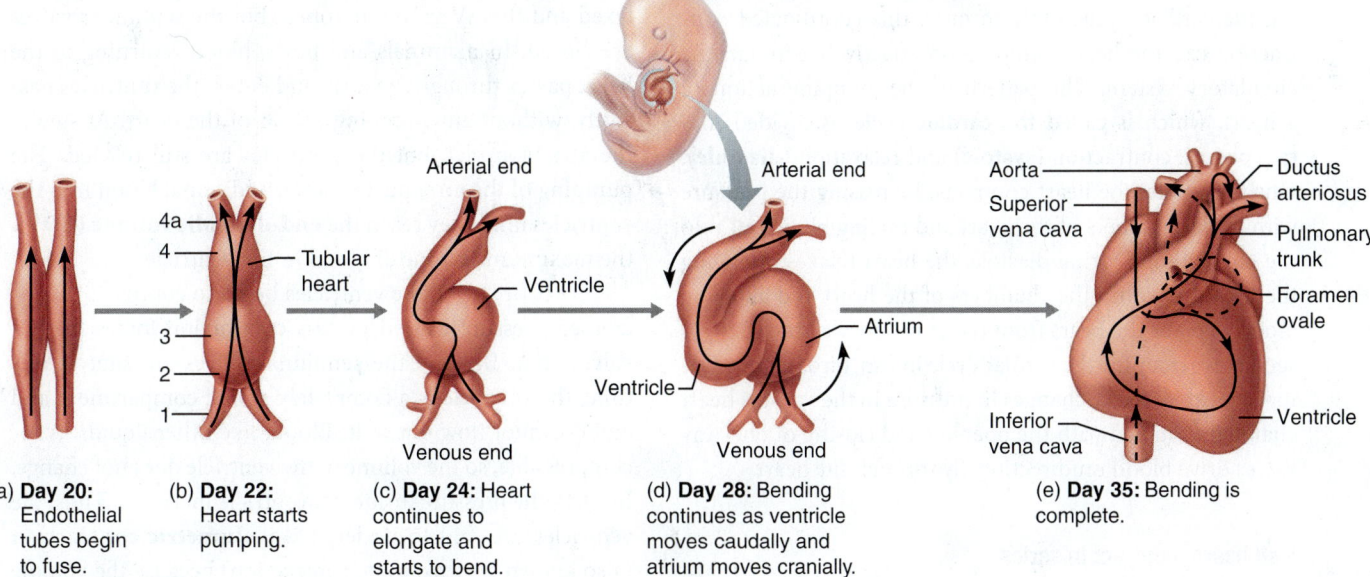

(a) **Day 20:** Endothelial tubes begin to fuse.

(b) **Day 22:** Heart starts pumping.

(c) **Day 24:** Heart continues to elongate and starts to bend.

(d) **Day 28:** Bending continues as ventricle moves caudally and atrium moves cranially.

(e) **Day 35:** Bending is complete.

Figure source: Freeman, Scott, Quillin, Kim, Allison, Lizabeth, *Biological Science*, 5th Ed., ©2014, p. 937. Reprinted And Electronically reproduced by permission of Pearson Education, Inc., Upper Saddle River, New Jersey.

through the pulmonary circulation. Two shunts allow blood to bypass the pulmonary circulation. The *foramen ovale* is a passage between the right and left atrium. It allows most of the blood entering the right side of the heart to pass over to the left atrium to be pumped to the systemic circulation. The *ductus arteriosus* is a connection between the pulmonary artery and the aorta that allows the small volume of blood pumped by the right ventricle to move into the systemic circulation.

Shortly after birth, as the baby takes its first breath and the lungs take over as the organ of gas exchange, both the foramen ovale and ductus arteriosus close. If these ducts do not close properly, the circulatory system may not work efficiently. Failure of the foramen ovale to close is a relatively common developmental defect that may occur in as many as 25 percent of adult humans. If the defect is minor, it has few or no symptoms, as the passage is usually covered with a flexible flap of tissue that effectively blocks most blood from passing between the atria. Patent ductus arteriosus, however, can lead to congestive heart failure if left untreated.

CONCEPT CHECK

13. Which type of animal would you expect to have a higher proportion of spongy myocardium, a fish or a mammal?
14. What is a cardiac shunt, and what are some possible benefits of this process in reptiles?
15. Draw a schematic diagram of the circulatory plan of a mammal similar to that shown on the right side of Figure 9.17b but name and label the position of the heart valves.

The Cardiac Cycle

The vertebrate heart functions as an integrated organ, with each of the chambers contracting at appropriate points during the cardiac cycle. Only through this coordinated contraction can the heart pump blood effectively through the circulatory system. The pattern of the pumping action of a heart, which is called the **cardiac cycle**, is divided into two phases: contraction (**systole**) and relaxation (**diastole**). During systole, the heart contracts, increasing the pressure within the chambers of the heart and forcing blood out into the circulation. During diastole, the heart relaxes, reducing the pressure within the chambers of the heart and allowing blood to enter the heart from the circulatory system. In this section we examine the cardiac cycle in fish, birds, and mammals to explore how changes in pressure in the various heart chambers coupled with the opening and closing of one-way valves drive blood unidirectionally through the heart.

Fish hearts contract in series

During the cardiac cycle of a fish heart, each of the cardiac chambers contracts in series, starting with the sinus venosus.

Contraction of the sinus venosus is unlikely to play an important role in propelling blood through the system because this thin-walled chamber is unable to develop substantial pressure and it lacks a one-way valve to prevent backflow into the circulation. Instead, the primary role of the sinus venosus is to initiate the heartbeat. Following the contraction of the sinus venosus, the atrium contracts. This contraction increases atrial pressure, closing the valve to the sinus venosus, and opening the valve to the ventricle. It is important to note that the valves are passive structures that open and close in response to changes in pressure in the heart chambers, not as a result of active movements of the valves themselves.

The pressure difference between the contracting atrium and the relaxed ventricle then causes blood to flow through the opened valve into the ventricle. Next the muscular ventricle contracts, closing the valve to the atrium and opening the valve to the bulbus arteriosus. Contraction of the muscular ventricle plays the main role in propelling blood through the circulatory system. In bony fish, blood flows from the ventricle into the elastic bulbus arteriosus, causing it to expand. The bulbus arteriosus acts as an elastic energy-storage device that dampens changes in blood pressure and allow more continuous flow of blood. In elasmobranchs, blood flows from the ventricle into the conus arteriosus. Contraction of the conus arteriosus further assists in propelling blood through the body. The elasmobranch conus arteriosus contains several valves that help to ensure unidirectional flow.

The mammalian cardiac cycle is similar to that of fish

Figure 9.29 illustrates the cardiac cycle of a mammalian heart. Because it is a cycle, we can arbitrarily begin our examination of the events at any point. Let's begin at the point labeled step 1. At this point, the atria and ventricles are relaxed and the AV valves are open, but the semilunar valves are closed. In mammals and birds, blood returning to the heart passes through the atria and enters the ventricles passively, without any pumping action of the heart. At step 2, the atria contract, but the ventricles are still relaxed. The pumping of the atria pushes some additional blood into the ventricles until they reach the **end-diastolic volume (EDV)**, the maximum volume of blood in the ventricle.

Next, at step 3, the ventricles begin to contract. The increased pressure caused by this contraction forces the AV valves shut. Because the semilunar valves are shut at this time, the ventricle is a completely sealed compartment and blood cannot flow out of it. Blood, like other liquids, is incompressible, so the volume of the ventricle does not change. Instead, the pressure inside the ventricle increases. Thus, the ventricles are said to undergo **isovolumetric contraction** (also known as isovolumic contraction) because the volume of the chamber does not change. Eventually, the pressure in the ventricles is sufficiently high that it forces open the

FIGURE 9.29 **The cardiac cycle in mammals**

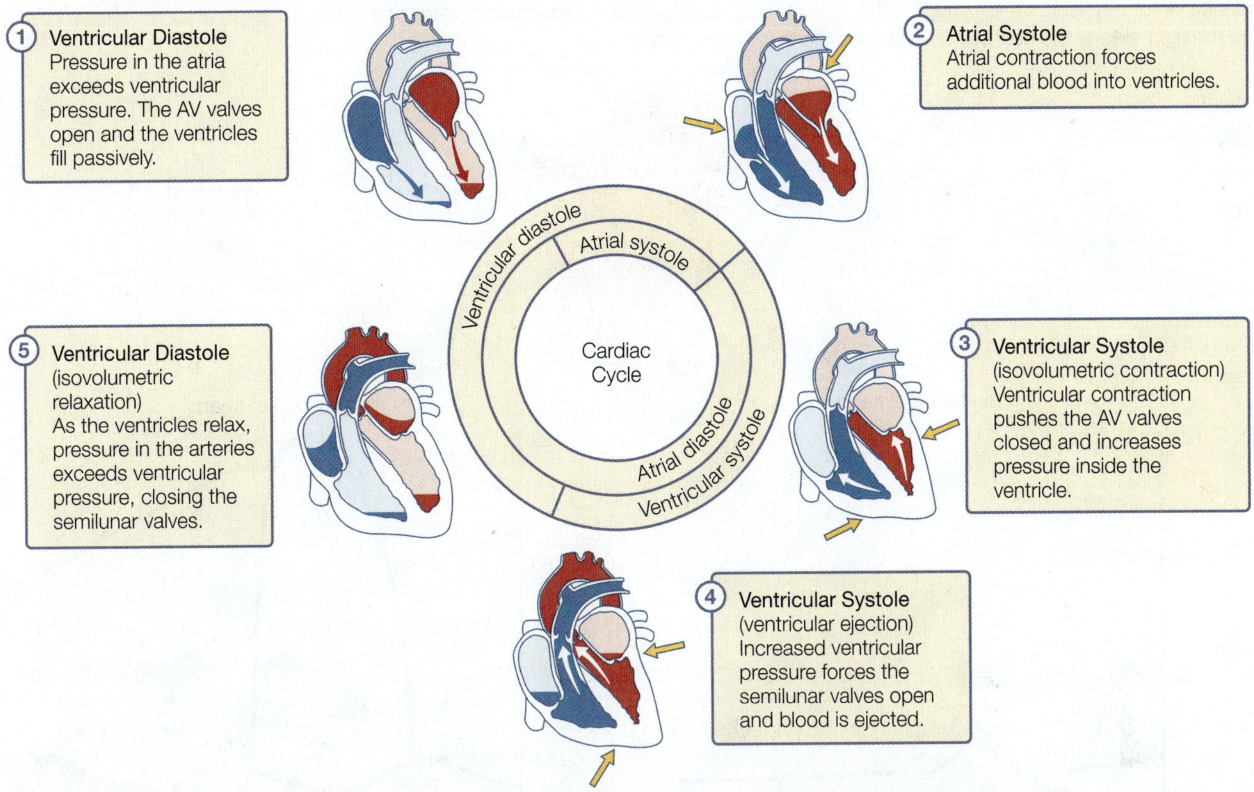

① **Ventricular Diastole**
Pressure in the atria exceeds ventricular pressure. The AV valves open and the ventricles fill passively.

② **Atrial Systole**
Atrial contraction forces additional blood into ventricles.

⑤ **Ventricular Diastole**
(isovolumetric relaxation)
As the ventricles relax, pressure in the arteries exceeds ventricular pressure, closing the semilunar valves.

③ **Ventricular Systole**
(isovolumetric contraction)
Ventricular contraction pushes the AV valves closed and increases pressure inside the ventricle.

④ **Ventricular Systole**
(ventricular ejection)
Increased ventricular pressure forces the semilunar valves open and blood is ejected.

Cardiac Cycle

Ventricular diastole · Atrial systole · Atrial diastole · Ventricular systole

semilunar valves, and blood flows out of the ventricles into the arteries in step 4 of the cardiac cycle: the **ventricular ejection** phase, in which the volume of blood in the ventricle declines. The chordae tendineae prevent the AV valves from being forced open, so blood cannot flow "backward" into the atrium. At this point, the ventricle has reached its minimum volume, or **end-systolic volume (ESV)**. The end-systolic volume is always greater than zero, as the heart does not completely empty itself with each beat. In a healthy human at rest, ESV can be as much as 50 percent of EDV.

At the end of the ventricular ejection phase, the ventricles begin to relax, causing the pressure in the ventricles to drop (step 5). Once the ventricular pressure drops below the pressure in the arteries, the back pressure forces the semilunar valves shut. At this point all the valves are closed, so the volume of the heart does not change, although pressure continues to drop. This step is termed **isovolumetric relaxation**. Throughout ventricular systole, the atria have been in diastole; they have been relaxed and filling with blood. The pressure in the filled atria eventually exceeds the pressure in the relaxing ventricles, and the AV valves pop open, returning the heart to the configuration shown in step 1.

Some vertebrate hearts fill actively

The ventricles of birds and mammals fill passively during diastole, as a result of the relatively low pressure within the ventricle compared with the venous and atrial pressure, with only a small contribution from atrial contraction. But this is not the case for all vertebrates. For example, in fish and some amphibians, the ventricles are primarily filled by contraction of the atrium. In addition, some fishes, including the elasmobranchs, may utilize suction filling of the ventricle, analogous to that seen in the hearts of arthropods, discussed earlier in the chapter. Elasmobranchs have a relatively rigid pericardium. When the ventricle contracts, the volume of pericardial space occupied by the ventricle decreases. This increases pericardial volume and decreases the pressure inside the pericardial cavity. The sinus venosus and atrium are thin-walled chambers, and a very low pressure in the pericardium causes them to expand, reducing the pressure in the atrium and sucking blood into the heart. However, this mechanism will work only if pressure within the pericardium decreases below the pressure in the veins, and cardiovascular physiologists debate whether this mechanism actually operates in elasmobranchs under normal physiological conditions, because it is difficult to measure the exact pressure within the pericardium of a swimming shark.

The right and left ventricles develop different pressures

During the cardiac cycle, the two ventricles of the mammalian heart contract simultaneously, but the left ventricle contracts much more forcefully than the right ventricle, and develops

FIGURE 9.30 **Pressure changes in the heart and arteries of mammals such as humans**

The left side of the heart, which supplies the systemic circuit, develops substantially greater pressures than the right side of the heart, which supplies the pulmonary circuit.

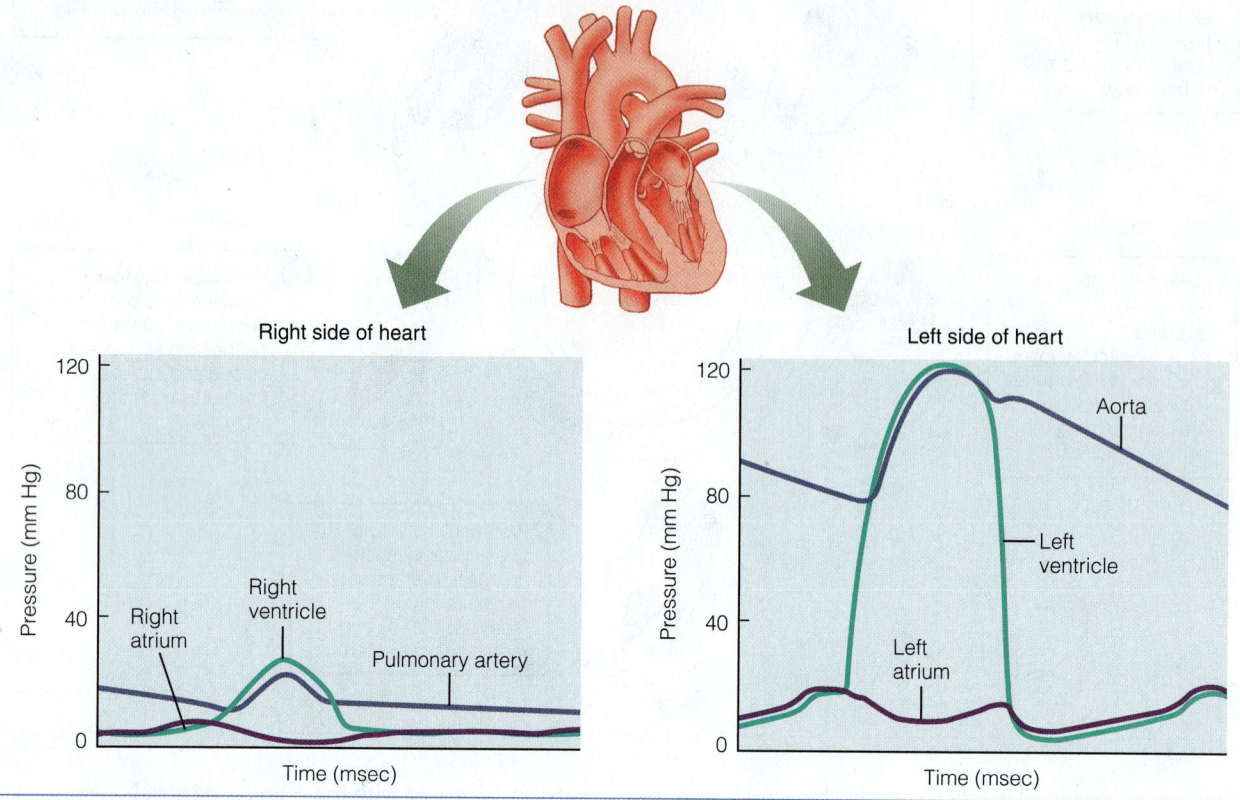

much higher pressure (Figure 9.30). Blood from the left ventricle travels via the aorta to the organs of the body, whereas blood from the right ventricle travels via the pulmonary artery to the lungs. The pulmonary circuit has relatively low total resistance because of the very large number of capillaries arranged in parallel and the relatively short distance traveled. Because the resistance of the circuit is low, the right side of the heart does not need to pump as forcefully to drive blood through the lungs, which protects the delicate blood vessels of the lungs.

CONCEPT CHECK

16. What is isovolumetric (or isovolumic) contraction?
17. What causes the semilunar valves to close during the cardiac cycle in mammals?
18. What is the physiological importance of the difference in pressure generated by the right and left ventricles of the mammalian heart?

Control of Cardiac Contraction

From the preceding discussion it is clear that cardiac contraction must be precisely controlled in order to ensure coordinated unidirectional blood flow through the chambers of the heart. Unlike the neurogenic hearts of the invertebrates that we discussed previously, which require nervous input to initiate contraction, the hearts of some invertebrates and all vertebrate hearts are **myogenic**; their cardiomyocytes can produce spontaneous rhythmic depolarizations that initiate contraction (see Chapter 6: Cellular Movement and Muscles). But in order for the heart to contract in a coordinated way, cardiomyocytes must be electrically coupled via gap junctions so that the depolarization in one cell can spread to adjacent cells, triggering coordinated contractions. The rate of the spontaneous depolarizations varies among cardiomyocytes, with some having a relatively rapid rhythm and others depolarizing more slowly. The cells with the fastest intrinsic rhythm are termed the **pacemaker cells**, because they determine the contraction rate for the entire heart. In fish, the pacemaker cells are located in the sinus venosus, and in other vertebrates they are located in an area of the right atrium and venae cavae called the **sinoatrial (SA) node**, near the junction between these two structures. The sinoatrial node is thought to be evolutionarily related to the sinus venosus of fish.

Pacemaker cells initiate the heartbeat

Although derived from muscle cells, pacemaker cells are small, with few myofibrils, mitochondria, or other organelles, and they do not contract. These cells have an unstable resting membrane potential (called the **pacemaker potential**) that slowly drifts upward from about −60 mV until it reaches threshold (about −40 mV) and initiates an action potential (Figure 9.31). This slow depolarization is, in part, the result of a slow inward movement of sodium, which is called the "funny" current (I_f) because of its unusual behavior. The funny current is the result of the opening of a nonselective cation channel (sometimes called the "funny channel," for consistency with the term *funny current*). This channel opens when the membrane is hyperpolarized, allowing Na^+ to enter the cell. Although this channel is permeable to both Na^+ and K^+, under the voltage conditions at the beginning of the pacemaker potential the current is largely an inwardly directed Na^+ current. The funny channel closes as the membrane gradually depolarizes. In addition, as in all other cells, there is a continuous leak of potassium ions at the resting membrane potential. In pacemaker cells, however, this potassium permeability decreases as the membrane depolarizes due to the gradual closing of a voltage-gated K^+ channel. The slow decrease in potassium movement contributes to the slow depolarization of the cell. The combination of reduced K^+ efflux and increased Na^+ influx causes the pacemaker potential. Particularly in small mammals, a T-type Ca^{2+} channel may also contribute to the depolarization of the pacemaker potential, which may be important for setting the high heart rates of these animals.

When the membrane potential of the pacemaker cell reaches threshold, L-type voltage-gated Ca^{2+} channels open and Ca^{2+} influx increases, causing a further, more rapid, depolarization. Opening of these L-type Ca^{2+} channels results in a depolarization phase that is much less steep than the depolarization of a neural action potential (caused by influx of Na^+ through voltage-gated Na^+ channels; see Chapter 5: Neuron Structure and Function), although it is faster than the depolarization caused by the funny current. About 200 milliseconds after they open, these L-type Ca^{2+} channels begin to close, and K^+ channels open, initiating the repolarization phase of the action potential in the pacemaker cell.

The nervous and endocrine systems can modulate heart rate

The rate of action potentials in the pacemaker sets the heart rate. In most vertebrates, the nervous and endocrine systems can control heart rate by altering the rate of pacemaker potentials in the cells of the sinoatrial node or sinus venosus. Norepinephrine released from sympathetic neurons and epinephrine released from the adrenal medulla bind to adrenergic receptors on the pacemaker cells (Figure 9.32). The receptors stimulate a cAMP-mediated signaling pathway that alters the transport properties of the ion channels in the cell membranes. Funny and Ca^{2+} channels open, increasing the influx of Na^+ and Ca^{2+} ions and increasing the rate of depolarization of the cell. The increased depolarization rate increases the frequency of action potentials in the pacemaker cells, which ultimately increases heart rate. These effects of epinephrine and norepinephrine on the pacemaker cells explain the dangerous side effects of drugs such as ephedrine and the herbal supplement ephedra, which can bind to adrenergic receptors and cause a rapid heart rate.

Acetylcholine, released from parasympathetic neurons, binds to muscarinic receptors on the pacemaker cells of the heart (Figure 9.33). These receptors stimulate a signal transduction pathway that ultimately leads to increased K^+ permeability. The increased K^+ efflux causes the pacemaker cell to hyperpolarize. The pacemaker potential starts at a more negative value, and thus takes longer to reach threshold potential. In addition, binding of acetylcholine to its receptor leads to decreased Ca^{2+} permeability, slowing the rate of the depolarization during a pacemaker potential. Together these

FIGURE 9.31 Pacemaker potentials

In myogenic hearts, the pacemaker cells have an unstable resting membrane potential (the pacemaker potential). Nonselective cation ("funny") channels open, increasing the permeability (P) of the membrane to Na^+, which causes the membrane potential to increase gradually. In small mammals, a T-type Ca^{2+} channel may also contribute to the pacemaker potential. As the membrane approaches threshold, L-type Ca^{2+} channels open, triggering an action potential. After about 200 milliseconds these channels close and K^+ channels open, repolarizing the cell, and the cycle begins again.

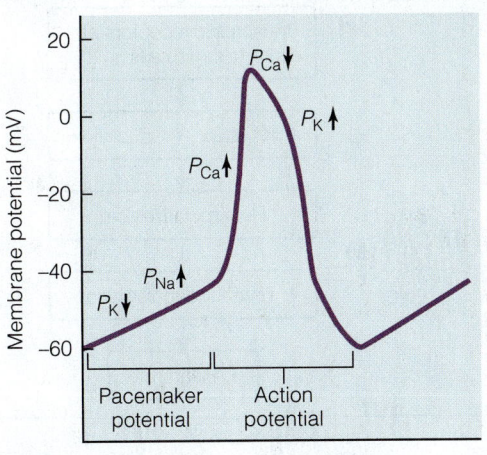

FIGURE 9.32 **The effects of norepinephrine on heart rate**

Norepinephrine increases heart rate by binding to adrenergic receptors, activating an adenylate cyclase (AC) signal transduction pathway that opens cation (funny) and T-type Ca^{2+} channels, increasing the rate of depolarization of the pacemaker potential.

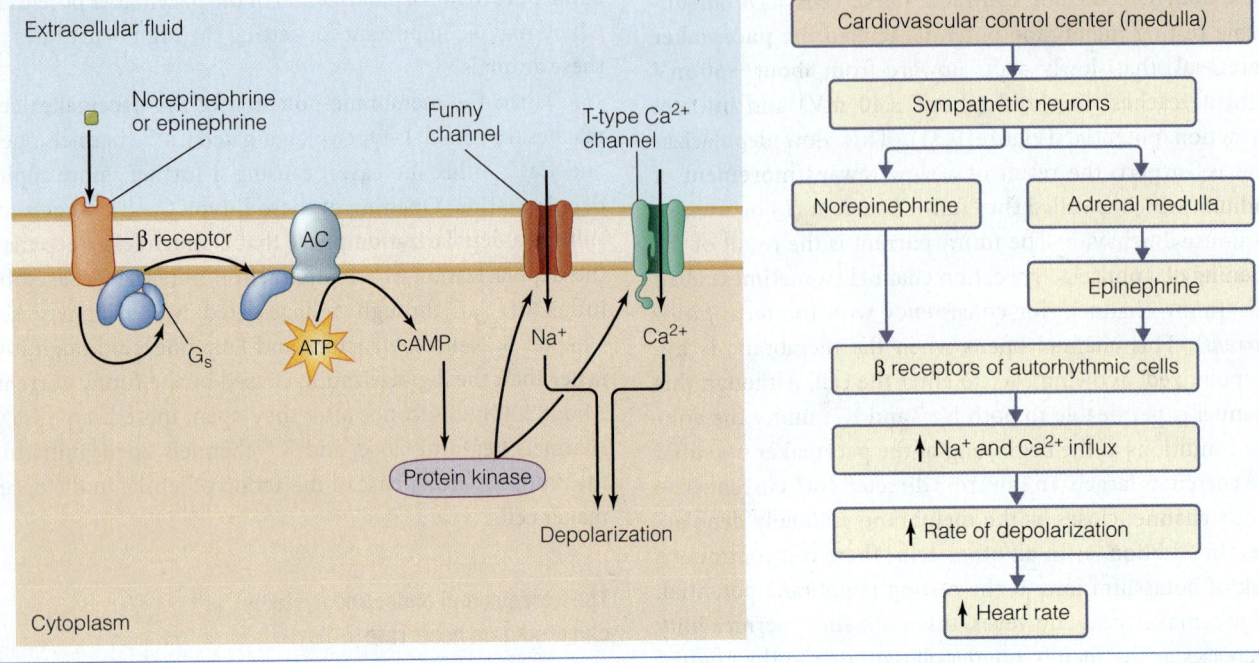

FIGURE 9.33 **The effects of acetylcholine on heart rate**

Acetylcholine decreases heart rate by binding to muscarinic receptors, activating a signal transduction pathway that closes Ca^{2+} channels and opens K^+ channels. This prevents Ca^{2+} ions from entering the cell and allows K^+ ions to exit, causing a net hyperpolarization, which increases the time needed for the pacemaker potential to depolarize the cell to threshold.

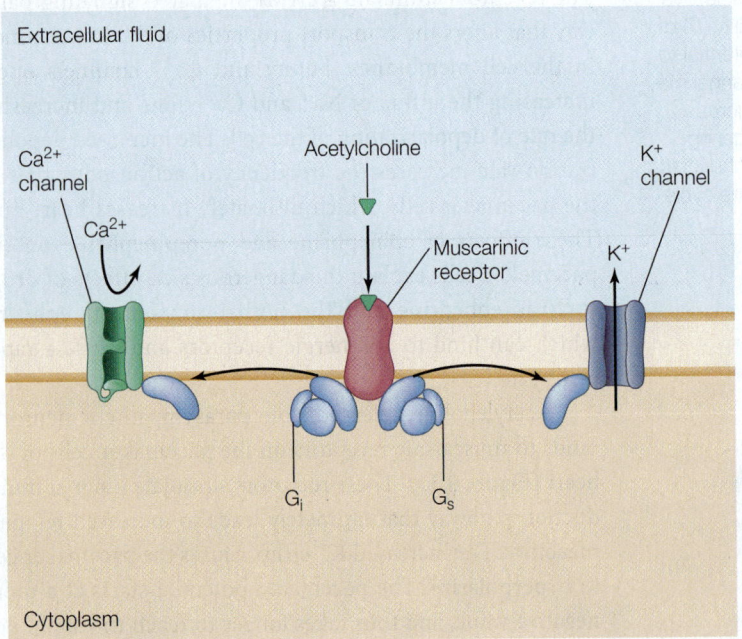

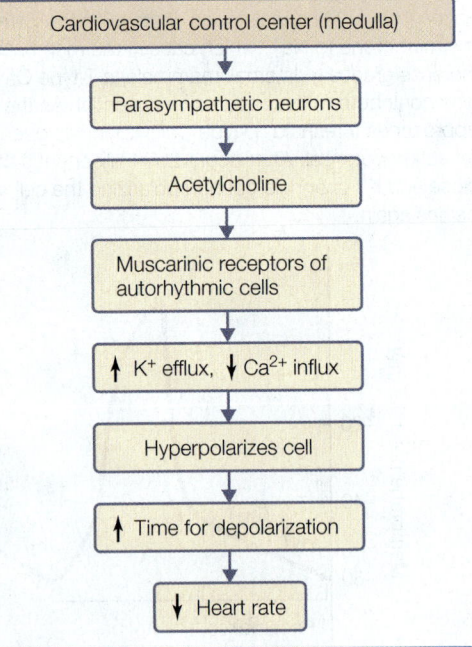

effects decrease the number of depolarizations per unit time, and thus slow the heart rate.

Pacemaker depolarizations can spread via gap junctions

Cardiac cells are electrically connected to each other via gap junctions. Thus, the rhythmic depolarization initiated in the pacemaker cells of the sinus venosus or sinoatrial node can spread from cell to cell via electrotonic current spread. In the adjacent cells, this depolarization triggers action potentials, which can then spread to adjacent cells, propagating the impulse throughout the heart.

Cardiac action potentials have an extended depolarization phase

The action potential of a contractile cardiomyocyte differs from the pacemaker potentials seen in the pacemaker cells of the sinus venosus or sinoatrial node (Figure 9.34). In the contractile cardiomyocytes, the action potential is initiated when a depolarization spreading from an adjacent cell depolarizes the cardiomyocyte beyond the threshold potential of the voltage-gated Na^+ channel. At this point, the voltage-gated Na^+ channels open, causing the rapid depolarization phase of the action potential. In this respect, the action potential of the cardiomyocyte is similar to that in neurons (see Chapter 5: Neuron Structure and Function) and in skeletal muscle cells (see Chapter 6: Cellular Movement and Muscles). However, the action potentials in contractile cardiomyocytes differ from those in skeletal muscles. They have an extended depolarization, called the **plateau phase** (Figure 9.34a). At the time when the voltage-gated Na^+ channel is inactivated (closes), another channel, an L-type voltage-gated Ca^{2+} channel opens, allowing Ca^{2+} to enter the cell. This greatly lengthens the depolarization phase of the action potential in contractile cardiomyocytes. Note that this L-type Ca^{2+} channel is a distinct isoform from the one expressed in the pacemaker cells, accounting for the differences in their behavior.

The plateau phase of the contractile cardiomyocyte action potential corresponds to the refractory period of the cell, in which it cannot generate another action potential. This refractory period lasts almost as long as the entire muscle twitch, preventing new contractions from occurring until the previous one has finished. Thus, unlike skeletal muscle, cardiac muscle cannot go into tetanus—a period of sustained contraction leading to muscle fatigue.

The exact shape and duration of the action potential varies substantially among organisms and among cells from different parts of the heart (Figure 9.34b) as a result of variation in the expression of ion channel isoforms. For example, small

FIGURE 9.34 The action potential in cardiomyocytes

(a) Phases of the action potential. Phase 0: The cell reaches threshold potential and voltage-gated Na^+ channels open, increasing Na^+ permeability (P_{Na}) and depolarizing the cell. Phase 1: The voltage-gated Na^+ channels inactivate and K^+ channels open, causing a transient outward K^+ current, resulting in a slight repolarization. Phase 2: These inward rectifier K^+ channels close and L-type voltage-gated Ca^{2+} channels open, causing the plateau phase of the action potential. Phase 3: L-type voltage-gated Ca^{2+} channels close and K^+ channels open, causing repolarization. Phase 4: The cell returns to the resting membrane potential. **(b)** Pacemaker and action potentials in various types of cardiomyocytes in the mammalian heart. The shapes of the pacemaker and action potentials differ across the parts of the heart as a result of the expression of different channel isoforms.

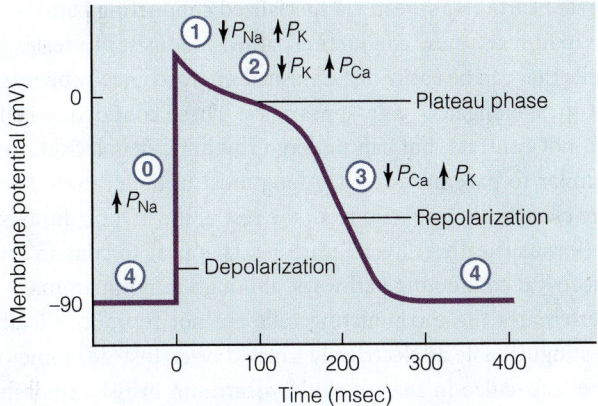

(a) Cardiac action potential

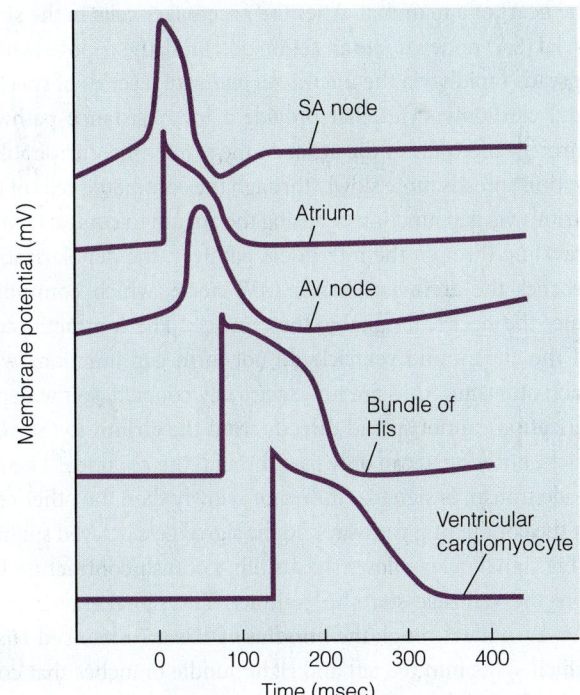

(b) Potentials in various parts of the heart

mammals tend to have a rapid heart rate and cardiac action potentials with shorter plateau phases than large mammals whose hearts beat more slowly.

Conducting pathways spread the depolarization across the heart

In a fish heart, in which the chambers are arranged in a more or less linear way, impulse conduction via gap junctions is sufficient to provide coordinated contraction of the chambers. The depolarizing signal travels via gap junctions from the sinus venosus to the atrium and then to the ventricle, causing them to contract in series. However, in addition to traveling from cell to cell via gap junctions, depolarizations in vertebrate hearts also spread via specialized conducting pathways. In mammals, these conducting pathways consist of a series of cells that can be easily distinguished microscopically because of their elongated, pale appearance. These conducting cells do not contract, but can undergo rhythmic depolarizations, similar to pacemaker cells. Along most of their length they are electrically insulated from the rest of the myocardium by a fibrous sheath. All vertebrate hearts appear to contain fast electrical conducting pathways, although in nonmammalian vertebrates these conducting cells are not morphologically distinguishable as electrically isolated cells. Instead, some of the trabeculae in the spongy myocardium in fish, amphibians, and reptiles appear to play this fast conducting role.

Figure 9.35 shows how electrical signals move through the heart of a mammal. After the pacemaker cells in the sinoatrial (SA) node initiate an action potential, the depolarization spreads rapidly via the *internodal pathway*, a series of specialized cardiomyocytes that provide a low-resistance pathway through the walls of the atria. At the same time, the depolarization spreads more slowly through the contractile cells of the atrium via gap junctions, causing the atrium to contract. After traveling through the internodal pathway, the depolarization reaches the **atrioventricular (AV) node**, which communicates the electrical signal to the ventricle. The contractile cells of the atrium and ventricle do not form gap junctions with each other, and thus are not electrically coupled, so the depolarization cannot spread directly from the atrium to the ventricle, but instead can only pass through the AV node. The AV node transmits signals a little more slowly than the other cells of the conducting pathways, so the signal gets delayed slightly. This signal delay allows the atrium to finish contracting before the ventricle starts to contract. The signal travels from the AV node through the **bundles of His** (pronounced *Hiss*), which splits into the left and right bundle branches that conduct electrical signals to the ventricles. The electrical signal then spreads into a network of conducting pathways called the **Purkinje fibers**. From the Purkinje fibers, the signal spreads from cell to cell in the ventricular myocardium via gap

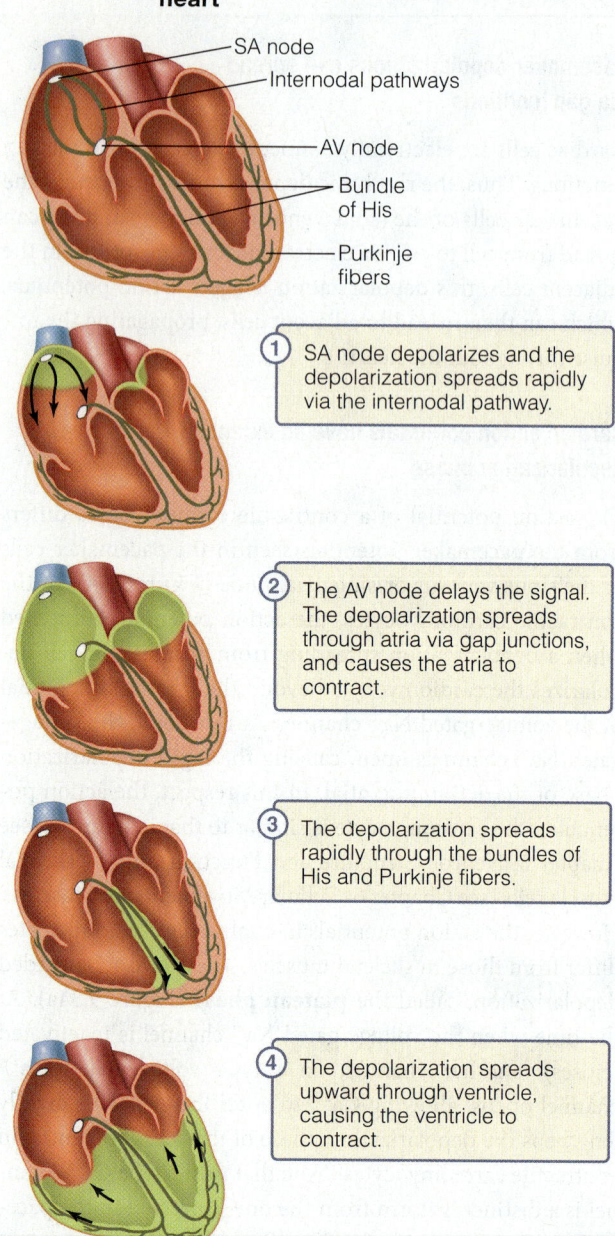

FIGURE 9.35 Electrical conduction in the mammalian heart

- SA node
- Internodal pathways
- AV node
- Bundle of His
- Purkinje fibers

1 SA node depolarizes and the depolarization spreads rapidly via the internodal pathway.

2 The AV node delays the signal. The depolarization spreads through atria via gap junctions, and causes the atria to contract.

3 The depolarization spreads rapidly through the bundles of His and Purkinje fibers.

4 The depolarization spreads upward through ventricle, causing the ventricle to contract.

junctions. The contraction of the ventricle begins at the bottom (or **apex**) of the heart and spreads up through the myocardium, pushing blood upward toward the arteries.

The integrated electrical activity of the heart can be detected with the EKG

The depolarization of cardiac muscle produces a strong electrical signal that travels through the body and can be detected using an instrument called an **electrocardiograph**. These instruments use electrodes applied to various areas on the surface of the body to generate an **electrocardiogram** (abbreviated EKG for the original German spelling, or ECG

FIGURE 9.36 **An EKG tracing**

In the EKG of a normal cardiac rhythm, the P wave indicates atrial depolarization. The QRS complex indicates ventricular depolarization and atrial repolarization, and the T wave indicates ventricular repolarization.

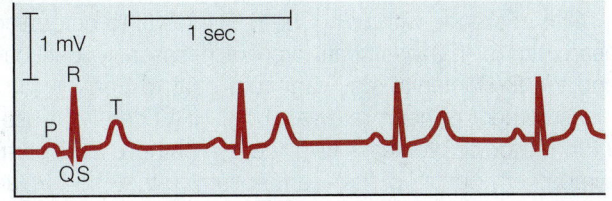

for the English spelling). An EKG is a composite recording of all the action potentials in the various parts of the heart, including the pacemakers, the conducting pathways, and the contractile cells (Figure 9.36). The deflections on the chart are not action potentials, and do not represent specific depolarizations of any given cell. Instead, they are markers of the electrical activity of the heart as a whole. The small **P wave** is the result of the spread of depolarization through the atria. The large **QRS complex** is the result of ventricular depolarization and atrial repolarization. The **T wave** is caused by ventricular repolarization. The EKG can be very useful clinically to diagnose problems with the conducting system or the depolarization of the heart muscle (see Box 9.2: Applications: Using the EKG to Diagnose Heart Conditions).

The heart functions as an integrated organ

The electrical and mechanical events of the heart fit together, allowing the heart to function as an integrated organ (Figure 9.39). At the beginning of the cardiac cycle, the ventricle fills passively. Then the depolarization of the SA node spreads through the atrium, initiating atrial contraction, and pumping some additional blood into the ventricle, which reaches its end-diastolic volume. The depolarization then spreads to the ventricle, which begins to contract. The increased pressure caused by this contraction forces the AV valves shut. Pressure then increases rapidly during the isovolumetric ventricular contraction phase, quickly becoming high enough to open the semilunar valves. The first heart sound is the result of the AV valves shutting and the semilunar valves opening. At this point, the ventricle begins to empty and aortic pressure increases. Initially, pressure in the ventricle continues to increase, despite the reduced volume, because ventricular contraction continues, but ventricular pressure quickly reaches a peak and begins to fall. Shortly thereafter, the ventricle begins to relax, entering ventricular diastole. When ventricular pressure falls below the pressure in the aorta, the aortic valve closes. The closing of the aortic valve causes a brief episode of turbulent flow and a small increase in aortic pressure, called the dicrotic notch. Ventricular pressure falls

rapidly, and once it is lower than atrial pressure, the AV valves open. The second heart sound is the result of the aortic valve closing and the AV valves opening. At this point, blood flows from the atrium into the ventricle, reducing the atrial pressure and initiating ventricular filling.

Cardiac output is the product of heart rate and stroke volume

The amount of blood that the heart pumps per unit time is called the **cardiac output** (CO), and is a product of the **heart rate** (HR) and the amount of blood the heart pumps with each beat, or the **stroke volume** (SV):

$$CO = HR \times SV$$

From this equation you can clearly see that an animal can modulate cardiac output by regulating heart rate, stroke volume, or both of these parameters. We have already seen how the nervous and endocrine systems can modulate heart rate by changing the properties of the pacemaker cells of the sinoatrial node. Decreases in heart rate are termed **bradycardia**, whereas increases in heart rate are termed **tachycardia**. Regulation of heart rate by changes in the rate of depolarization of the sinoatrial node is often referred to as *chronotropy*. Alternatively, the sympathetic nervous system can also increase heart rate by increasing the speed of conduction of the depolarization along the conducting pathways of the heart, a phenomenon known as *dromotropy*.

The nervous and endocrine systems can modulate stroke volume

Both the nervous and endocrine systems can also modulate the **contractility** (the rate and strength of contraction) of the heart by altering some of the properties of cardiac excitation-contraction coupling, a phenomenon known as *inotropy*. If the heart contracts more forcefully, it will pump more blood with each beat, increasing the stroke volume. Norepinephrine released by sympathetic neurons and circulating epinephrine released by the endocrine system increase contractility (Figure 9.40). These signaling molecules bind to β_1 adrenergic receptors on contractile cardiomyocytes. Binding of these molecules to the receptor activates a cAMP-mediated signal transduction pathway that activates a protein kinase that phosphorylates a variety of proteins, resulting in increased contractility via four mechanisms.

- Phosphorylation of L-type Ca^{2+} channels on the cell membrane allows increased Ca^{2+} into the cell in response to depolarization.

- Phosphorylation of proteins in the membrane of the sarcoplasmic reticulum causes it to release more Ca^{2+} into the cytoplasm in response to an action potential.

USING THE EKG TO DIAGNOSE HEART CONDITIONS

The EKG, or electrocardiogram, is an extremely common test that is often a part of a routine physical examination. It is particularly useful for the diagnosis of a variety of heart conditions. Performing an EKG involves applying external electrodes to various parts of the body (Figure 9.37). The heart is a large muscle with a very coordinated pattern of electrical activity. Because body tissues and extracellular fluids can conduct electricity, these signals travel from the heart to all parts of the body, and although the strength of the signal decays with distance from the heart, the tiny residual current can be detected at the skin using electrodes and amplifiers. Clinicians generally perform EKGs on humans using 10 to 12 electrodes, with the electrodes applied to the chest, arms, and hips, but you can generate an interpretable EKG using as few as three electrodes (in humans these electrodes are placed one on each wrist, and one on an ankle, providing a "view" of the heart from three different directions). Diagnostic EKGs are often performed in conjunction with a stress test, in which an individual is asked to exercise on a treadmill or a stationary bike at gradually increasing intensity. These tests help to assess the response of the heart to increased demand from the body. EKGs can also be performed on nonhuman vertebrates and are used routinely both in research and in veterinary medicine in animals ranging from fish to horses.

The first piece of information provided by an EKG is the heart rate. You can calculate heart rate by identifying the large upward spike of the QRS complex, and computing the R–R interval (the time between each heartbeat). This provides the number of seconds per heartbeat. In order to find the heart rate (the number of beats per minute), you simply take the inverse and convert into minutes. A normal resting heart rate in an adult human is generally around 60–80 beats per minute (bpm). Tachycardia is the term used for a higher than normal heart rate, while bradycardia is the term used for a lower than normal heart rate. Highly fit individuals who do regular aerobic exercise tend to have somewhat lower than typical resting heart rates, while individuals with poor physical fitness tend to have higher than typical resting heart rates.

One challenge with using the R–R interval to determine heart rate is that heatbeats are not necessarily identical, and the R–R interval may vary from beat to beat. In fact, measurement of heart rate variability (HRV) can be a useful indicator of problems with the sympathetic and parasympathetic control of the heart. Assuming that the cardiac rhythm is normal, and arrhythmias have been ruled out, low variability in heart rate has been associated with diabetes, coronary artery disease, high blood pressure, and congestive heart failure.

The next important characteristic that can be obtained from an EKG is the type of cardiac rhythm. A normal cardiac rhythm (Figure 9.38a) is called a sinus rhythm, because the heartbeat is being determined by the sinoatrial node. In a normal sinus rhythm there is a P wave associated with each QRS complex and, for an adult human, the P–R interval is between 0.12 seconds and 0.20 seconds (indicating a normal speed of conduction in the conducting pathways of the heart).

Abnormal rhythms, or arrhythmias, can be caused by a variety of problems with the cardiac conduction system.

FIGURE 9.37 **Performing an EKG**

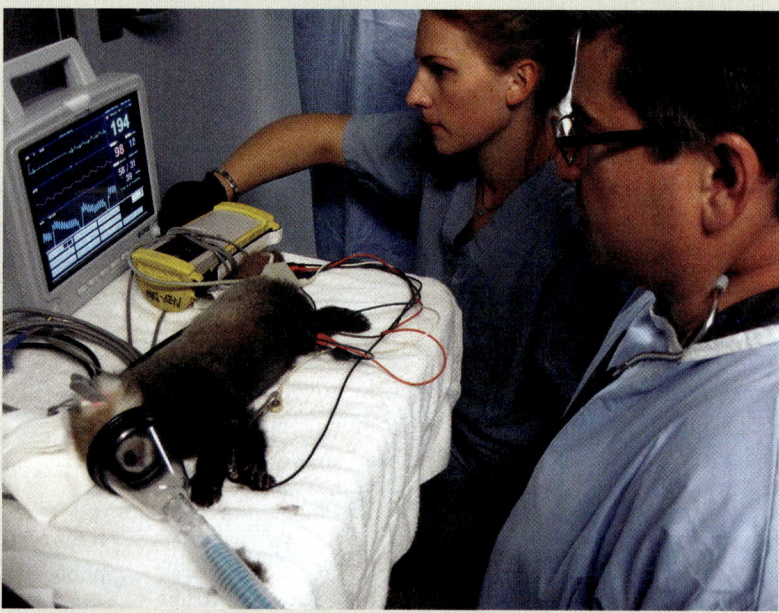

Photo source: Judilee Marrow/AFP/Getty Images/Newscom.

In atrial fibrillation (Figure 9.38b), conduction through the atrium is disturbed and the atria contract in an uncontrolled fashion. On an EKG, atrial fibrillation can be detected by the lack of a clear P wave. In general, the rhythm will also be irregular, with highly variable R–R intervals, and apparent "skipped" beats. Although atrial fibrillation is an indication of a cardiac disorder, it is not usually immediately dangerous. Recall that in humans most ventricular filling is passive, and that atrial contraction only contributes a small amount of additional blood to ventricular filling. Consequently, as long as ventricular contraction remains relatively normal, atrial fibrillation often has few symptoms.

In contrast, ventricular fibrillation (Figure 9.38c), which represents uncoordinated contraction of the ventricle, is potentially deadly because uncoordinated contraction of the ventricle results in ineffective pumping of blood to the tissues. Patients with ventricular fibrillation rapidly lose consciousness, and the associated oxygen deprivation kills tissues such as the brain within a few minutes. Ventricular fibrillation appears as a series of random, apparently unrelated waves in the EKG with no recognizable QRS complex.

Ventricular fibrillation can sometimes be treated using an electronic *defibrillator*. These machines deliver an intense pulse of current to the body, causing all of the cells of the heart to depolarize simultaneously. Defibrillation gives the pacemaker cells of the heart a chance to take over and initiate a normal heartbeat because these cells are likely to be the first to depolarize again following defibrillation. However, defibrillation will not be effective if the pacemaker cells or the conducting pathways have irreversible defects or injuries.

The EKG can also reveal other problems with electrical conduction in the heart that are collectively called heart blocks, or atrioventricular (AV) blocks. These conditions occur when transmission of electrical signals from the atria to the ventricles is impaired. There are three major types of AV block that are distinguished by differences in severity. The mildest, called first-degree AV block, is characterized by a prolonged Q–R interval on the EKG and is associated with few or no symptoms. However, third-degree heart block is characterized by a complete lack of association between the P wave (indicating atrial depolarization) and the QRS complex (indicating ventricular depolarization). Third-degree AV block (Figure 9.38d) can cause fainting, dizziness, and fatigue and must be treated immediately because

FIGURE 9.38 **EKG of normal and abnormal heart rhythms**

(a) Normal heart rhythm, **(b)** atrial fibrillation, **(c)** ventricular fibrillation, and **(d)** third-degree AV block.

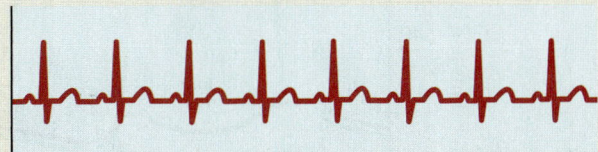

(a) Normal heart rhythm

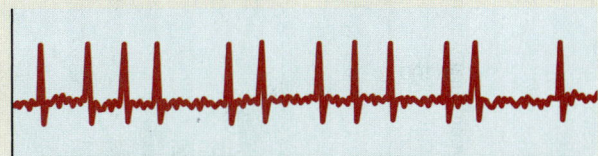

(b) Atrial fibrillation

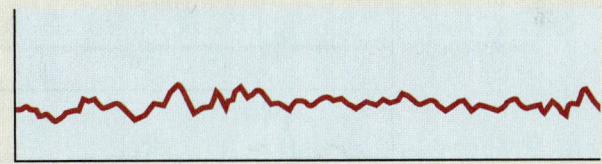

(c) Ventricular fibrillation

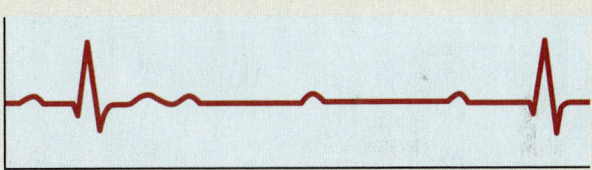

(d) Third-degree AV block

it can lead to fatal arrhythmias such as ventricular fibrillation. Third-degree AV block is generally treated through the implantation of an artificial pacemaker.

References

- Routledge, F. S., Campbell, T. S., Fetridge-Durdle, J. A., & Bacon, S. L. (2010). Improvements in heart rate variability with exercise therapy. *Canadian Journal of Cardiology, 26,* 303–312.

- Thaler, M. S. (2003). *The only EKG book you'll ever need*. Philadelphia, PA: Lippincott Williams & Wilkins.

FIGURE 9.39 **A summary of the electrical and mechanical events of the cardiac cycle**

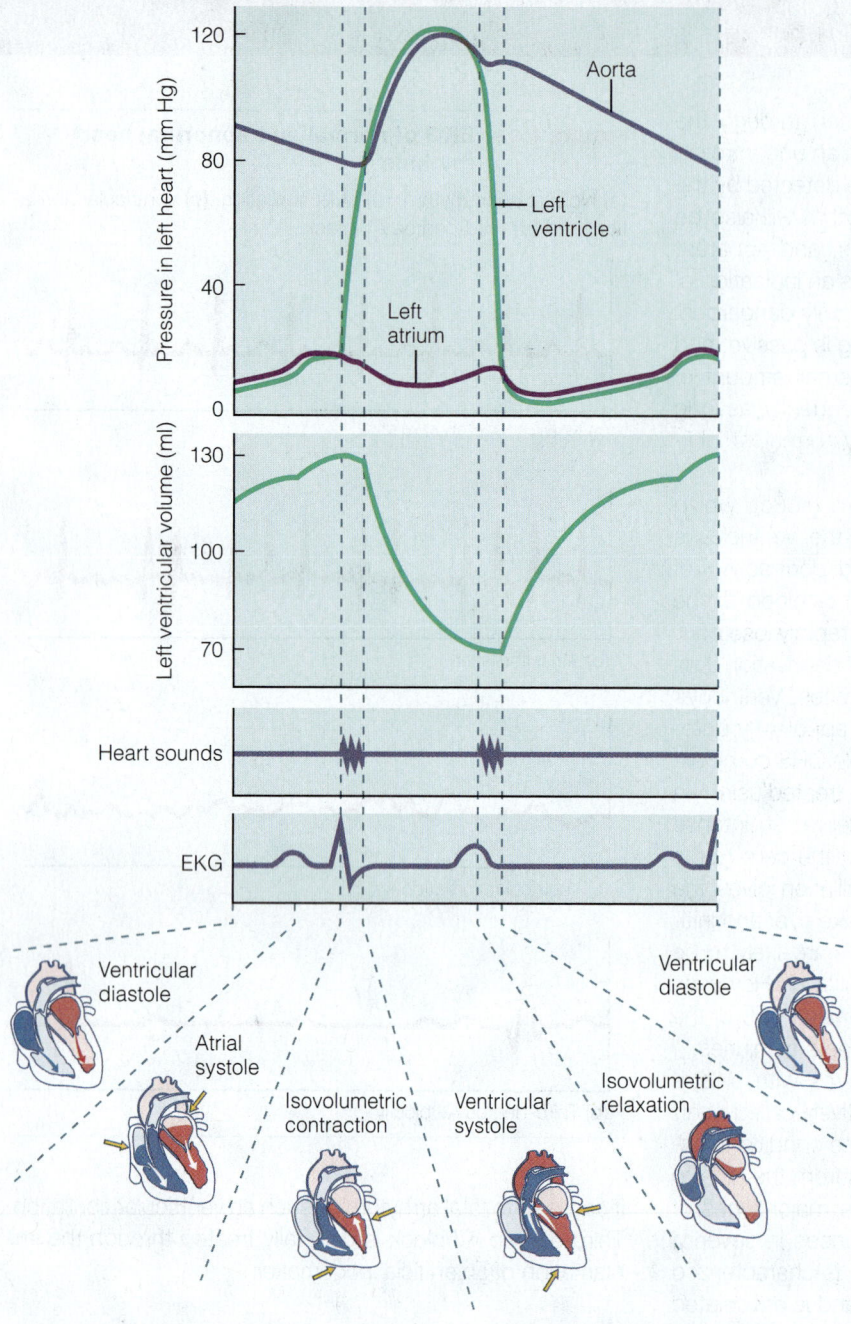

In contrast, stimulation of the parasympathetic nervous system causes a decrease in stroke volume by activating signal transduction pathways that reduce the intracellular Ca^{2+} signal. In mammals, parasympathetic effects are relatively weak in the ventricle, but tend to be strong in the atria.

End-diastolic volume modulates stroke volume

In addition to the extrinsic regulation of heart rate and stroke volume by the nervous and endocrine systems, the heart also undergoes **autoregulation** by intrinsic regulatory mechanisms. If you experimentally increase end-diastolic volume, the ventricle pumps more forcefully, and stroke volume increases (Figure 9.41)—a phenomenon known as the **Frank-Starling effect** (after the two scientists who independently discovered it). The Frank-Starling effect is a result of changes in sensitivity to the calcium that activates muscle contraction due to stretch on the muscle cell. Cardiomyocytes differ from other types of striated muscle in that they are normally shorter than the length needed for optimal contraction so that as you stretch a cardiomyocyte, the strength of contraction increases. When blood enters the ventricle, the increased volume causes the ventricle to stretch, and the more blood that enters the heart at the end of diastole, the greater the degree of stretch. Thus, the end-diastolic volume (the maximum volume during the cardiac cycle) is an index of the amount of stretch imposed on the cardiomyocytes.

The Frank-Starling effect allows the heart to automatically compensate for increases in the amount of blood returning to the heart. Consider what would happen in the absence of the Frank-Starling effect. If stroke volume remained constant in the face of an increase in venous return to the heart, then the heart would pump a smaller fraction of the blood returning to the heart. Assuming that heart rate remained constant, blood would be "left over" in the ventricle after each beat and would slowly build up in the heart, increasing its volume. Eventually, this might cause the ventricles to distend to the

- Phosphorylation of myosin increases the rate of the myosin ATPase, increasing the rate of cross-bridge cycling and the speed of contraction.

- Phosphorylation of the sarcoplasmic reticulum Ca^{2+} ATPase enhances Ca^{2+} reuptake into the sarcoplasmic reticulum, increasing the rate of relaxation.

The net result of these four mechanisms is that the cardiomyocytes contract faster and more strongly in response to sympathetic stimulation, increasing the stroke volume of the heart.

FIGURE 9.40 **Effects of norepinephrine and epinephrine on cardiomyocyte contractility**

Norepinephrine and epinephrine increase contractility by binding to receptors on the cardiomyocyte and activating an adenylate cyclase (AC)–mediated signal transduction pathway that activates protein kinases, which phosphorylate various proteins and cause an increase in the rate and strength of contraction.

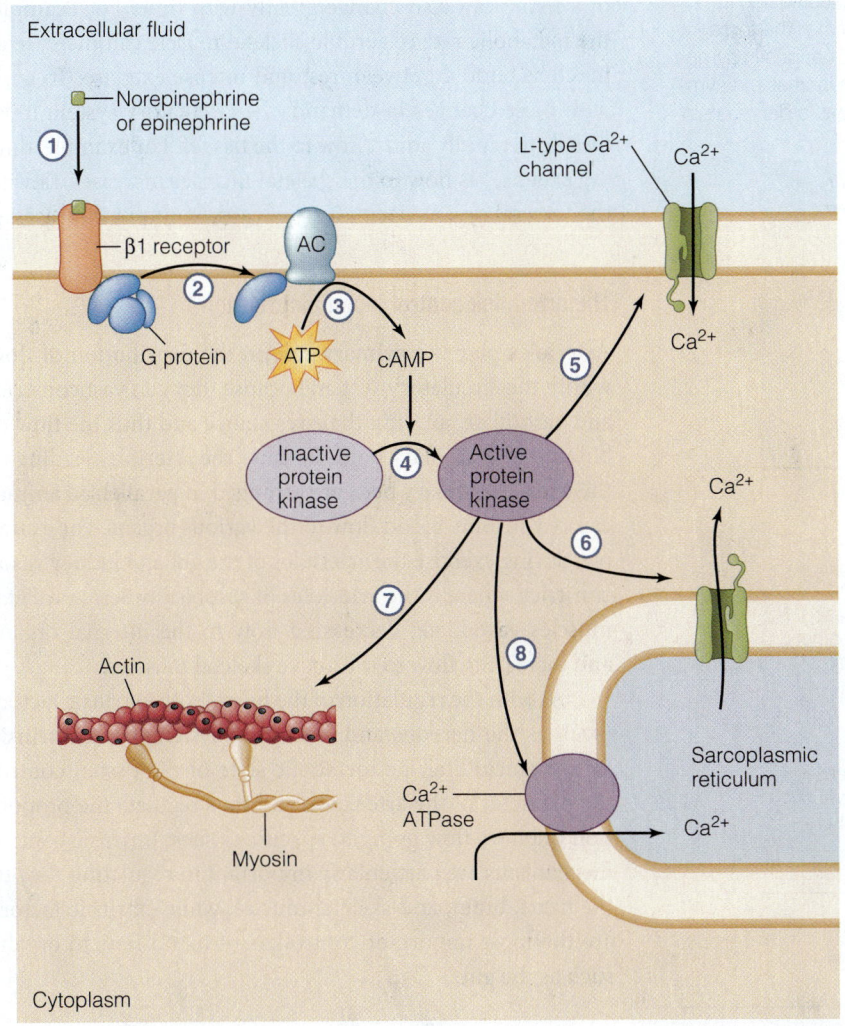

1. Binding of norepinephrine or epinephrine changes the shape of the β1 adrenergic receptor, which activates an associated G protein.

2. The G protein μ subunit activates adenylate cyclase.

3. Adenylate cyclase catalyzes the conversion of ATP to cAMP.

4. The cAMP activates protein kinase A.

5. The protein kinase phosphorylates L-type Ca^{2+} channels, allowing Ca^{2+} to enter the cell, which stimulates contraction.

6. The protein kinase phosphorylates Ca^{2+} channels on the sarcoplasmic reticulum, allowing Ca^{2+} to move to the cytoplasm, which stimulates contraction.

7. The protein kinase phosphorylates myosin, stimulating contraction.

8. The protein kinase phosphorylates the sarcoplasmic Ca^{2+} ATPase, speeding the removal of Ca^{2+} from the cytoplasm during relaxation, which decreases relaxation time.

point that they could no longer contract effectively. Thus, the Frank-Starling effect protects the heart from abnormal increases in volume. Under normal physiological conditions the heart is never stretched to the point that force generation falls. However, this can occur in some pathological situations.

Extrinsic controllers such as the nervous system act in addition to the autoregulatory mechanisms of the Frank-Starling effect; they simply shift the position of the cardiac muscle **length-tension relationship** (Figure 9.41b). Increased sympathetic activity shifts the curve upward (representing an increase in the force of contraction at a given end-diastolic volume), while decreased sympathetic activity shifts the curve downward (representing a decrease in the force of contraction).

CONCEPT CHECK

19. Compare and contrast the molecular events of the action potential in the pacemaker cells of the sinoatrial node to those in a ventricular contractile cardiomyocyte.

20. How does the nervous system modulate heart rate?

21. Why do mammalian hearts have specialized conducting pathways?

REGULATION OF CIRCULATORY FUNCTION

Upon leaving the heart, the blood enters the circulation, which directs and adjusts flow to the various organs according to their metabolic demand. These adjustments in flow

FIGURE 9.41   The Frank-Starling effect

(a) Stroke volume increases as end-diastolic volume increases. When end-diastolic volume is low, cardiomyocytes are shorter than the optimal length needed for maximal contraction. Increasing end-diastolic volume stretches the muscle, increasing its length and increasing force generation. The greater the force generated, the greater the stroke volume. **(b)** Changes in sympathetic activity alter the position of the curve. An increase in sympathetic activity shifts the curve upward, whereas a decrease in activity shifts the curve downward.

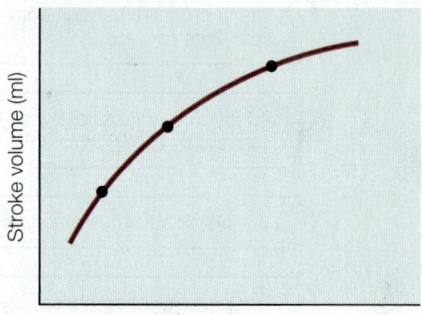

(a) Frank-Starling effect

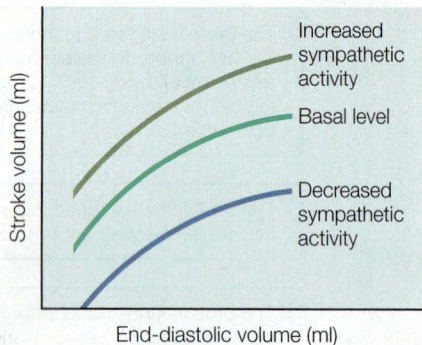

(b) Effects of sympathetic activity on the Frank-Starling effect

are coordinated so that blood pressure is maintained within a fairly narrow range. The homeostatic regulation of blood pressure is critical because the pressure as the blood leaves the heart provides the primary driving force for flow through the circulatory system to critical organs such as the brain. Thus, maintaining this pressure within appropriate limits is one of the most important requirements for the proper functioning of the circulatory system. In this part of the chapter we examine the regulation of blood flow and blood pressure in vertebrate circulatory systems. We conclude the chapter with a discussion of the integrated control of the responses of the circulatory system to exercise.

Regulation of Flow

One fundamental requirement for the proper functioning of the vertebrate circulatory system is the ability to

appropriately direct flow to the organs, depending on their metabolic needs. Tissues that are highly active aerobically have a greater demand for oxygen than do less active tissues, and thus require greater blood flow. The metabolic demands of a tissue can also change greatly with time. For example, the metabolic rate of aerobic skeletal muscle can increase as much as tenfold between rest and intense exercise. To cope with these changes in demand, the circulatory system must be able to rapidly adjust flow to the tissues. For example, during exercise, as flow to the skeletal muscles increases, flow to the visceral organs decreases and cardiac output increases.

The arterioles control blood distribution

Arterioles play the primary role in the distribution of flow within the circulatory system because they can vasoconstrict and vasodilate, altering their resistance and thus the flow of blood to the capillary beds. Because the arterioles leading to the various capillary beds are arranged in parallel, an animal can redistribute blood flow to the various organs. For example, during exercise the arterioles of the gut and kidney vasoconstrict, whereas the arterioles of aerobically active skeletal muscles vasodilate, decreasing flow to the internal organs and increasing flow to the active skeletal muscles.

As with the regulation of the heart, both extrinsic factors (such as the nervous and endocrine systems) and intrinsic factors (including the metabolic state of the tissue) control the diameter of the arterioles, and thus regulate the proportion of blood flow going to specific tissues. Intrinsic control mechanisms are particularly important in regulating flow to the heart, brain, and skeletal muscle, while extrinsic factors are the most important controllers of blood flow to organs such as the gut.

Myogenic autoregulation maintains blood flow

Some of the smooth muscle cells surrounding the arterioles are sensitive to stretch and contract when the blood pressure within the arteriole increases. This **myogenic autoregulation** acts as a negative feedback loop that helps to maintain blood flow to a tissue at a constant level. When flow through the arteriole increases, the pressure on the arteriolar wall increases, stretching the smooth muscle. This stretch causes the smooth muscle to contract, constricting the arteriole. The decrease in arteriolar diameter increases the resistance and decreases the flow, decreasing the pressure, which causes the smooth muscle to relax. Thus, myogenic autoregulation tends to maintain constant blood flow to a tissue. But the metabolic activity of a tissue and its demand for oxygen can vary with time, and thus the need for blood flow varies. For example, when you are sitting still, the muscles of your legs have relatively low demand for oxygen, and little blood flows to them, whereas when you are jogging, your muscles require more oxygen, so more blood must flow to the tissue. Other mechanisms for controlling blood flow come into play when the needs of the tissue change.

Metabolic activity and paracrine signals influence blood flow

The vascular smooth muscle cells surrounding the arterioles are sensitive to the conditions in the extracellular fluid that surrounds them. They contract or relax in response to changes in the concentrations of substances such as oxygen, carbon dioxide, H^+, K^+, and a variety of paracrine signals (Table 9.1). In general, changes in the extracellular fluid

that are associated with increased activity cause vasodilation, while changes that are associated with decreased activity cause vasoconstriction. Thus, decreases in oxygen or increases in carbon dioxide tend to cause vasodilation. Vasodilation increases blood flow to the tissue, bringing more oxygen and carrying away waste products. This reduces the signal to the muscle cell, in a negative feedback loop, stopping the flow from increasing beyond what is needed (Figure 9.42).

Paracrine signaling molecules released from the vascular endothelium also have a profound effect on vascular smooth muscle (Table 9.1). For example, the gas nitric oxide is an important vasodilator. Vascular smooth muscle cells actually release a small amount of nitric oxide all the time,

Table 9.1	Factors influencing vasoconstriction and vasodilation	
Substance	**Source**	**Type**
Vasoconstriction		
Stretch on arteriolar walls	Increased blood pressure	Myogenic autoregulation
Norepinephrine (α receptors on arterioles in most tissues except skeletal and cardiac muscle, which express $\beta2$ receptors)	Sympathetic neurons	Neural
Hydrogen sulphide	Vascular smooth muscle	Paracrine
Endothelin	Vascular endothelium	Paracrine
Serotonin	Platelets	Paracrine
Vasopressin	Posterior pituitary	Endocrine
Angiotensin II	Plasma	Endocrine
Vasodilation		
Hypoxia	Multiple tissues	Metabolite
Increased CO_2	Multiple tissues	Metabolite
H^+	Multiple tissues	Metabolite
K^+	Multiple tissues	Metabolite
Nitric oxide	Endothelium	Paracrine
Hydrogen sulphide	Vascular smooth muscle	Paracrine
Atrial naturietic peptide	Atrial myocardium	Endocrine
Histamine	Mast cells of immune system	Paracrine (systemic actions at high levels)
Substance P	Damaged tissue	Paracrine
Prostacyclin	Damaged tissue	Paracrine
Epinephrine (β receptors in skeletal muscle arterioles)	Adrenal medulla	Endocrine
Acetylcholine (muscarinic receptors)	Parasympathetic neurons leading to erectile tissue of clitoris or penis	Neural
Bradykinin	Multiple tissues	Paracrine
Adenosine	Hypoxic cells	Paracrine

FIGURE 9.42   **The response of arteriolar smooth muscle to an increase in metabolic activity**

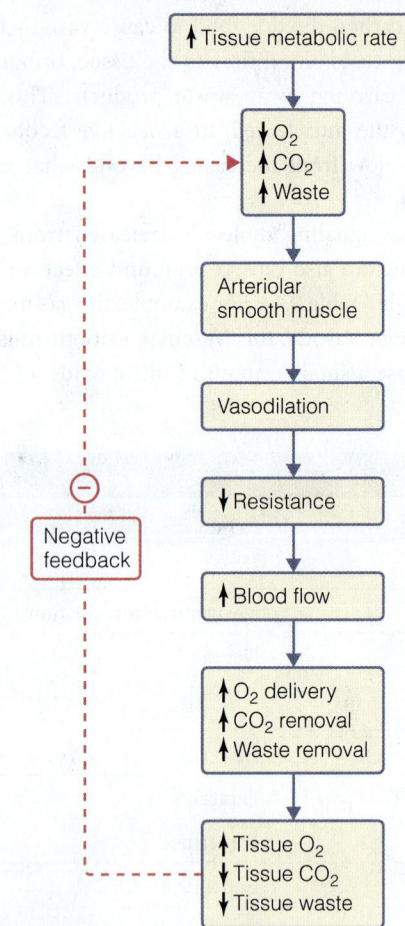

The nervous and endocrine systems regulate arteriolar diameter

In addition to intrinsic and local control mechanisms, the arterioles respond to extrinsic controllers such as the nervous and endocrine systems. The sympathetic nervous system controls the smooth muscle surrounding the arterioles. In vertebrates, the sympathetic nervous system always maintains a certain degree of **vasomotor tone**, constantly sending an electrical signal to the smooth muscles of the arterioles so that the arterioles are always slightly constricted. Increases or decreases in the activity of these sympathetic neurons can alter the degree of vasomotor tone by acting on the smooth muscles surrounding the arterioles. Norepinephrine released from sympathetic neurons binds to α adrenergic receptors on these muscle cells, activating a phosphatidylinositol second messenger system, and causing vasoconstriction. So increases in sympathetic activity tend to cause vasoconstriction, whereas decreases in sympathetic activity tend to cause vasodilation. The smooth muscle in the arterioles of heart and skeletal muscle also express β2 adrenergic receptors. When epinephrine binds to these receptors, it causes vasodilation. However, the relative roles of vasoconstriction due to binding of norepinephrine to α adrenergic receptors and vasodilation due to binding of epinephrine to β2 adrenergic receptors are somewhat unclear, and local and paracrine factors related to muscle metabolic activity are thought to be the primary regulators of vasodilation in skeletal muscle, at least in humans. However, in some species (including mammals such as cats and dogs, but not in humans) skeletal muscle blood vessels are innervated by sympathetic cholinergic neurons that release acetylcholine and cause vasodilation.

As we discussed in Chapter 4: Cell Signaling and Endocrine Regulation, the sympathetic nervous system is stimulated as part of the fight-or-flight response. During this response, the sympathetic nervous system also causes the release of epinephrine and norepinephrine from the adrenal medulla (or the chromaffin cells of fish) into the circulation. These circulating hormones act together with direct sympathetic stimulation of the arterioles to regulate tissue blood flow. The net effect of the activation of the fight-or-flight response is that blood is directed away from organs such as the gut and kidneys, and toward the skeletal muscles and heart, readying the body for action.

Three other hormones also affect vascular smooth muscle. Vasopressin (also called ADH) released from the posterior pituitary gland, and **angiotensin II**, a hormone involved in the regulation of the kidney, promote generalized vasoconstriction, while atrial natriuretic peptide promotes a generalized vasodilation. We discuss these hormones in more detail in Chapter 13: Ion and Water Balance.

The nervous and endocrine systems work together with the paracrine signals that relate to metabolic activity to influence arteriolar diameter and alter blood flow. As a result,

which helps to keep the arterioles dilated. However, nitric oxide production is strongly induced by histamine, bacterial lipopolysaccharides, and other substances that are associated with damage to the vascular endothelium. The increased nitric oxide causes vasodilation, increasing blood flow to damaged areas. This is an important mechanism underlying inflammation. Nitric oxide is also released in the arterioles of skeletal muscles during exercise, causing vasodilation that increases the supply of oxygen to the working muscle.

Nitric oxide activates the enzyme guanylate cyclase in the vascular smooth muscle. Guanylate cyclase catalyzes the conversion of GMP to cGMP, which triggers the muscle cell to relax, causing vasodilation (see Chapter 4: Cell Signaling and Endocrine Regulation). The cGMP is quickly broken down by the enzyme phosphodiesterase, preventing the arteriole from staying permanently dilated and allowing it to constrict or dilate as necessary. The drug sildenafil (Viagra) specifically targets an isoform of phosphodiesterase that is found in the arterioles of the penis. Sildenafil prevents the cGMP from breaking down, prolonging the effects of nitric oxide and causing vasodilation in the vessels of the penis, leading to a sustained erection.

blood flow to each tissue of the body is almost always carefully controlled in order to deliver the amount of blood that the tissue needs.

Regulation of Blood Pressure

As shown in Figure 9.43, blood pressure differs in the different parts of the circulatory system. Notice that blood pressure in the left ventricle also changes greatly over time. During ventricular systole the ventricular pressure is very high, and during diastole it is low. The high systolic pressure in the left ventricle forces blood out into the aorta. The aorta is a large vessel with relatively low resistance, so pressure remains relatively high as blood travels through this and subsequent arteries. Because arterioles are relatively narrow

FIGURE 9.43 **Pressure, velocity, and total cross-sectional area across a vertebrate circulatory system**

Pressure is variable in the ventricle, high and more constant in the arteries, and drops greatly across the arterioles. Blood velocity is inversely proportional to total cross-sectional area of that part of the circulatory system.

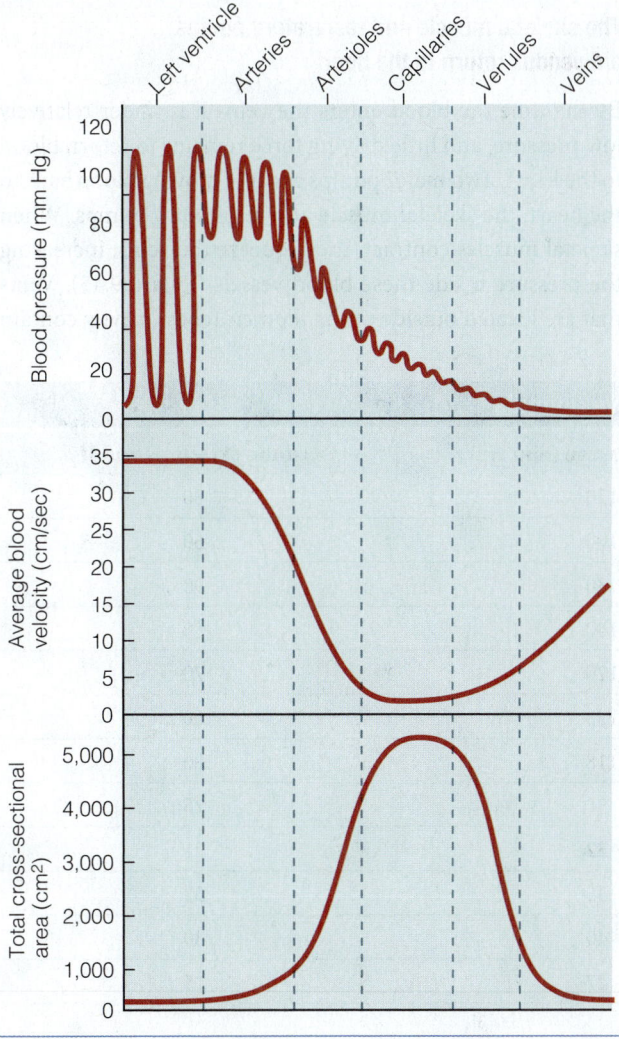

vessels (compared with arteries) and are relatively few in number (compared with capillaries), they have the highest resistance of any part of the circulatory system. Thus, pressure drops greatly as blood travels through the arterioles, and continues to drop as blood proceeds through the capillaries, venules, and veins. By the time the blood returns to the heart, its pressure is barely above ambient. The pressure gradient between the left ventricle and the right atrium causes blood to flow through the system according to the law of bulk flow.

The velocity of blood flow also varies greatly across the circulatory system (see Figure 9.43). Blood velocity is greatest in the arteries and veins, and lowest in the capillaries. Recall from our discussion of the physics of blood flow earlier in this chapter that blood velocity is equal to the blood flow divided by the total cross-sectional area of the vessels in any given portion of the circulatory system. Because of the law of conservation of mass, the flow of blood must be the same in all areas of the circulatory system (or blood would pool), and as you can see from Figure 9.43, the total cross-sectional area of the capillaries is much greater than the total cross-sectional area of any other part of the circulatory system. As a result, the velocity of the blood is lowest in the capillaries. The low velocity of the blood in the capillaries, combined with the thin walls of these blood vessels, allows for efficient exchange of substances between the capillaries and the tissues.

The arteries dampen pressure fluctuations

Notice that the pressure fluctuations in the arteries are far smaller than those in the left ventricle. The aorta (and the bulbus arteriosus of a bony fish) acts as a pressure reservoir and dampens the fluctuations in blood pressure that occur during the cardiac cycle (Figure 9.44). During systole, the ventricle rapidly pushes blood into the aorta. Because the aorta splits into progressively narrower blood vessels, the exit from the aorta has relatively high resistance, so instead of simply flowing out into the rest of the circulatory system, the blood tends to back up and exert pressure on the thick, elastic walls of the aorta. This pressure causes the aorta to expand. Because the walls of the aorta are elastic, they act very much like a spring that stores energy as it is stretched, and releases energy when the tension is removed.

When the heart enters diastole, blood ceases flowing into the aorta. But blood continues to flow out of the aorta into the arterioles, reducing the pressure inside the aorta. This is equivalent to releasing a spring, and the aortic walls snap back into place. This **elastic recoil** propels the blood through the circulatory system and maintains an aortic pressure that is higher than the diastolic pressure in the ventricle, dampening the pressure fluctuations associated with the cardiac cycle. This elastic recoil also helps to maintain relatively continuous flow of blood into the arteries throughout the

FIGURE 9.44 **The aorta as a pressure reservoir**

(a) Blood flows rapidly into the aorta during the ejection phase of ventricular contraction, pushing out on the walls of the aorta and causing it to expand. **(b)** As the heart relaxes, blood flow into the aorta ceases, but flow out into the arterioles continues, reducing the aortic pressure. Elastic recoil of the arterial walls helps to push blood through the vasculature, maintaining pressure and flow.

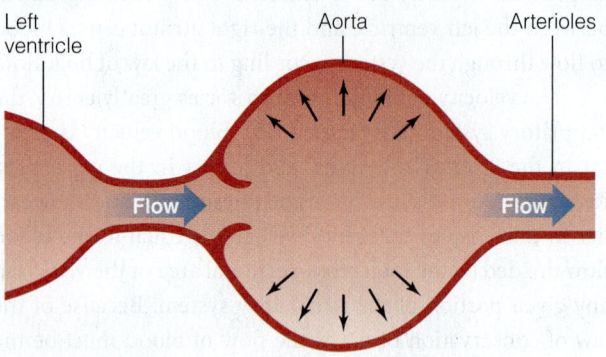

(a) Ventricular contraction

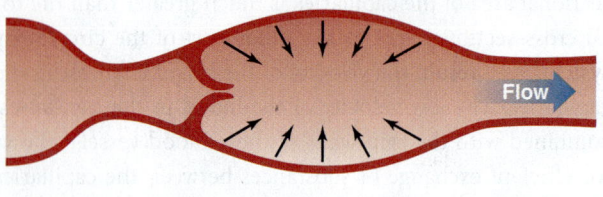

(b) Ventricular relaxation

cardiac cycle. Because of the elastic nature of the aorta, the aortic pressure is higher than the ventricular pressure during some parts of the cardiac cycle, but the aortic semilunar valve prevents backflow of blood from the arteries to the heart.

Mean arterial pressure is determined by systolic and diastolic pressures

The pressure in the aorta is called the **arterial blood pressure**. Although the pressure fluctuations in the aorta are not as large as those in the ventricle, arterial blood pressure still varies with the phases of the cardiac cycle from its maximum, the **systolic pressure**, to its minimum, the **diastolic pressure**. Table 9.2 shows some typical values for systolic and diastolic pressure in a few representative vertebrates. Physiologists often consider the **mean arterial pressure (MAP)**, or the average blood pressure in the arteries across the cardiac cycle, which allows them to ignore the pulsatile nature of blood pressure and apply to the cardiovascular system the simple physical principles of fluid flow. MAP in humans can be approximated as follows:

$$MAP = 2/3 \text{ diastolic pressure} + 1/3 \text{ systolic pressure}$$

Thus, using the data from Table 9.2, we can calculate that the mean arterial pressure in humans is typically around 93 mm Hg at rest. However, the length of diastole varies depending on the heart rate, so at high heart rates MAP is better approximated as the average of systolic and diastolic pressures.

The skeletal muscle and respiratory pumps aid venous return to the heart

By the time the blood enters the veins it is under relatively low pressure, and little driving force remains to return blood to the heart. Two major pumps assist in moving blood back to the heart: the skeletal muscle and respiratory pumps. When skeletal muscles contract, they squeeze the veins, increasing the pressure inside these blood vessels (Figure 9.45). Veins that are located outside of the *thoracic* (chest) cavity contain

Table 9.2 Systolic and diastolic pressure in representative animals		
Species	**Systolic Pressure (mm Hg)**	**Diastolic Pressure (mm Hg)**
Homo sapiens (human)	120	80
Equus caballus (horse)	100	60
Rattus norvegicus (rat)	130	90
Canis familiaris (dog)	140	80
Loxodonta africana (African elephant)	120	70
Columba livia (pigeon)	135	100
Turdus migratorius (robin)	118	80
Pseudemys scripta (turtle—red-eared slider)	31	25
Rana catesbeiana (bullfrog)	32	21
Oncorhynchus mykiss (rainbow trout)	45	33
Ictalurus punctatus (channel catfish)	40	30
Octopus vulgaris (octopus)	27	15

FIGURE 9.45 The skeletal muscle pump

(a) When a skeletal muscle contracts, it puts pressure on the vein, pushing blood in both directions. The resulting pressure opens the proximal one-way valve and closes the distal one-way valve, squeezing blood toward the heart and preventing backflow. **(b)** When the skeletal muscle relaxes, the one-way valves are in the opposite configuration. The relaxation reduces pressure on the distal valve, which opens and allows blood to flow in. Back pressure from the blood in the proximal segment of the vein closes the proximal valve, preventing backflow.

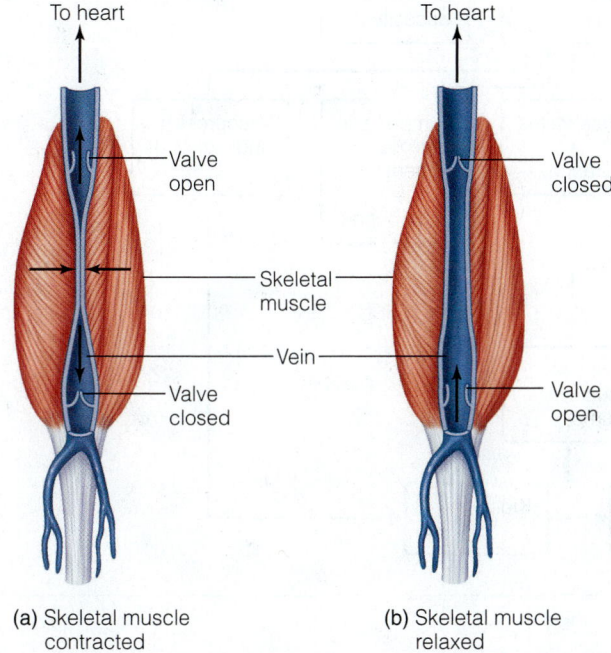

(a) Skeletal muscle contracted

(b) Skeletal muscle relaxed

valves. The increased pressure as a result of the contraction of skeletal muscles forces the valves farthest from the heart to close and the valves closest to the heart to open, pushing blood toward the heart. The rhythmic contraction of this **skeletal muscle pump** helps to drive blood toward the heart, increasing **venous return** to the heart.

Respiratory movements can also help to draw blood toward the heart. As we discuss in more detail in Chapter 11: Respiratory Systems, in terrestrial vertebrates the thoracic cavity expands during inhalation, causing the pressure in the thoracic cavity to drop, and drawing air into the lungs. This low thoracic pressure helps to draw blood into the veins of the thoracic cavity, acting as a **respiratory pump**. During exhalation, the pressure in the thoracic cavity increases, but the valves in the veins outside the thoracic cavity prevent backflow of blood out of the thoracic cavity. Instead, this increased pressure pushes the blood in the other direction, toward the heart.

The veins act as a volume reservoir

The veins have highly compliant walls that stretch easily; small increases in blood pressure lead to large changes in the volume of the veins compared with the volume of the arteries

FIGURE 9.46 Compliance of arteries and veins

Veins are far more compliant than arteries and thus they stretch easily, increasing their volume in response to increases in pressure.

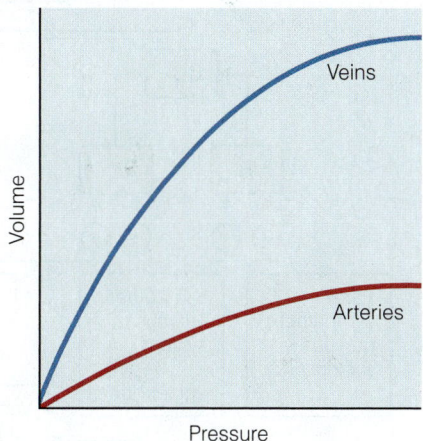

(Figure 9.46). As a result, the veins can act as a volume reservoir for blood. In fact, in mammals the veins typically hold more than 60 percent of the total volume of blood in the body. The sympathetic nervous system regulates the proportion of blood in the venous versus arterial systems by altering the **venomotor tone**. The smooth muscles surrounding the venules and small veins contain adrenergic receptors. Norepinephrine released from sympathetic neurons binds to these receptors, causing the smooth muscle to contract, reducing the diameter of the veins. Because the majority of the blood is contained in these numerous smaller blood vessels, a decrease in the volume of the venules and small veins decreases the volume of the venous reserve. This in turn increases venous return to the heart, increasing cardiac output and forcing blood into the arterial side of the circulation.

Peripheral resistance influences pressure

We can rewrite the law of bulk flow ($Q = \Delta P/R$) as follows to specifically apply to vertebrate circulatory systems:

$$CO = MAP/TPR$$

where cardiac output (CO) is a measure of the total flow (Q) through the system, and TPR (**total peripheral resistance**) is the summed resistances of all the blood vessels in the body and is a measure of the resistance (R) of the circulatory system. We can approximate the pressure gradient across the circulatory system (P) using the mean arterial pressure (MAP). The actual change in pressure across the circulatory system is MAP minus the central venous pressure (CVP, the pressure in the superior vena cava near the right atrium). CVP is usually low relative to MAP, so MAP is approximately equal to the pressure gradient across the circulatory system.

FIGURE 9.47 **Factors affecting mean arterial pressure (MAP)**

CO: cardiac output; TPR: total peripheral resistance; HR: heart rate; SV: stroke volume; EDV: end-diastolic volume.

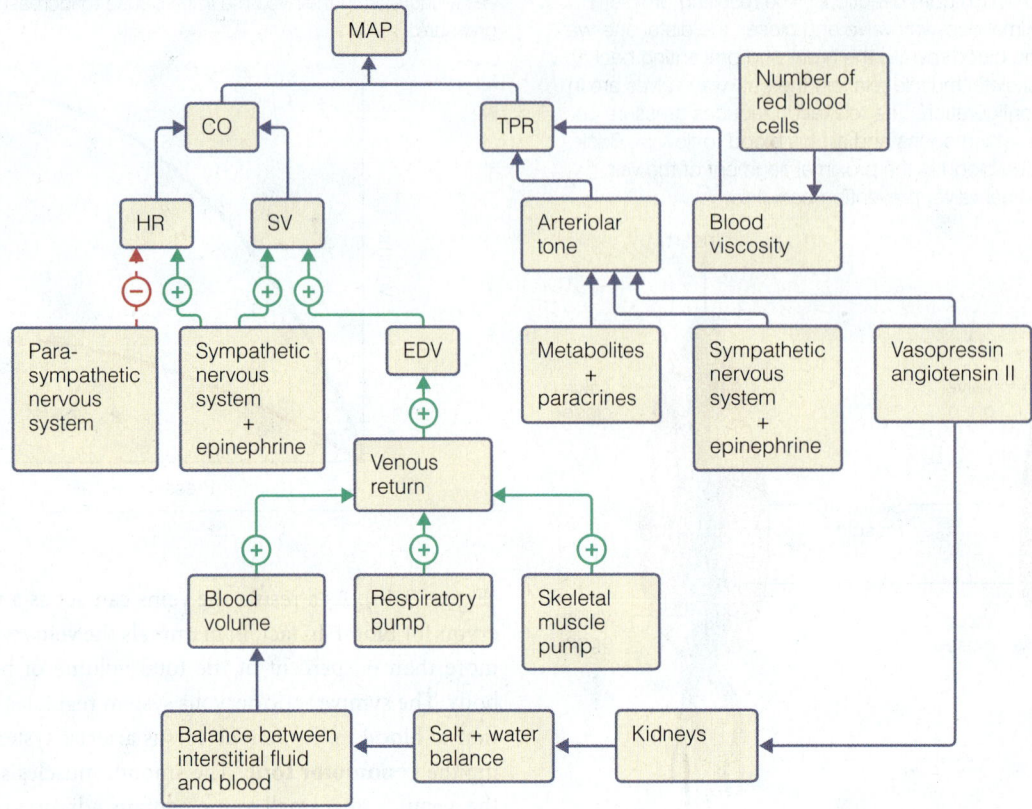

The body varies CO and TPR to maintain MAP within very narrow boundaries. TPR is set primarily by the state of vasoconstriction and vasodilation of the arterioles, which is in turn set largely by the metabolic needs of the tissue. CO (and thus heart rate and stroke volume) varies in response to these changes in TPR in order to maintain MAP within a narrow range. Thus, the metabolic demand of the tissues is the ultimate regulator of the circulatory system. Figure 9.47 provides a summary of the major factors involved in the homeostatic regulation of MAP.

The baroreceptor reflex is the primary means of regulating MAP

Baroreceptors are stretch-sensitive mechanoreceptors that are located in the walls of many of the major blood vessels. The most important of these baroreceptors are located in the carotid artery and aorta, although the large systemic veins, the pulmonary arteries, and the walls of the heart also contain baroreceptors. The carotid artery is the major artery leading to the head, and thus the **carotid body** baroreceptors monitor blood pressure to the brain. The aorta is the primary artery leading to the systemic circulation, so the **aortic body** baroreceptors monitor mean arterial pressure. Together, the

carotid and aortic baroreceptors help regulate mean arterial pressure (MAP) via a reflex called the **baroreceptor reflex** (Figure 9.48). Under normal conditions the carotid and aortic baroreceptors fire a steady stream of action potentials, sending signals via primary afferent neurons to the central nervous system. The **cardiovascular control center** in the medulla oblongata of the central nervous system integrates these inputs, and sends out efferent signals via autonomic neurons that control heart rate, stroke volume, and vasomotor and venomotor tone, thus influencing blood pressure. Increases in blood pressure cause the walls of the arteries to stretch, increasing the firing rate of the baroreceptors, and causing signals that result in a reduction of blood pressure. Decreases in blood pressure cause the walls of the arteries to relax, decreasing the firing rate of the baroreceptors. The decrease in baroreceptor firing causes efferent signals that result in increased blood pressure. Thus, the baroreceptor reflex is a negative feedback loop that homeostatically regulates blood pressure within a relatively narrow range.

Figure 9.48 shows the major steps of the baroreceptor reflex following an increase in blood pressure. Increases in blood pressure stretch the membrane of the baroreceptors in the aortic and carotid bodies, increasing the firing rate of the receptor and the frequency of action potentials traveling

FIGURE 9.48 The baroreceptor reflex response to increased blood pressure

MAP: mean arterial pressure; NE: norepinephrine; SA node: sinoatrial node.

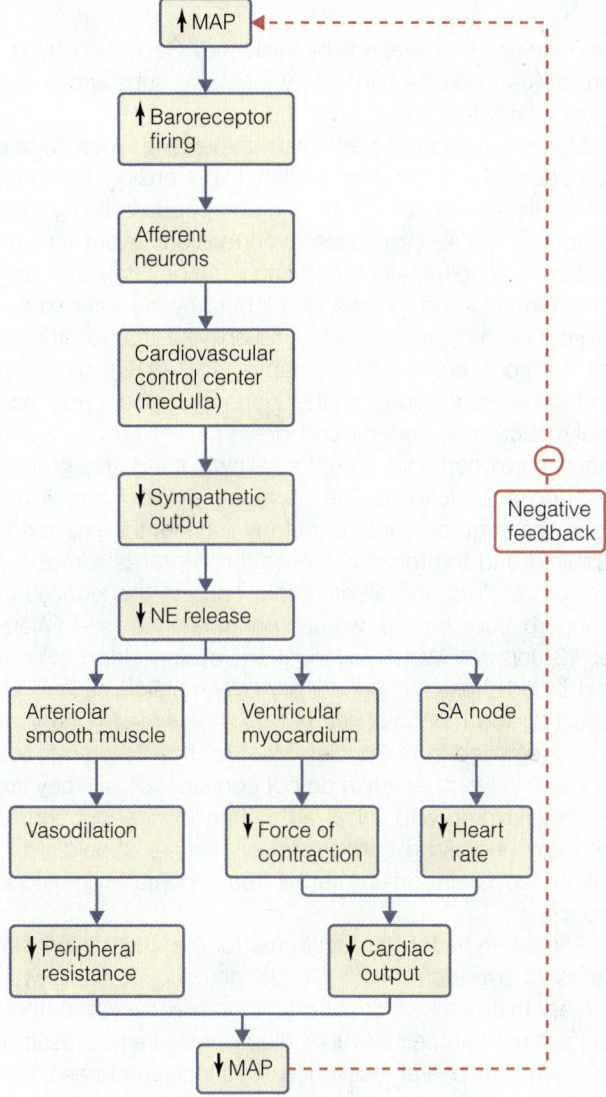

The kidneys also play a role in maintaining blood volume and MAP

Although the baroreceptor reflex plays the most important role in the minute-by-minute regulation of blood pressure, the kidneys play the major role in the long-term regulation of MAP. In a closed system, pressure and volume are intimately related. If you increase the volume of a fluid inside a vessel with a fixed volume, the pressure inside that vessel will increase. (This is the principle behind the isovolumetric contraction of the heart.) Therefore, increases in blood volume will lead to an increase in blood pressure, whereas decreases in blood volume will lead to a decrease in blood pressure. The veins are compliant, and can act as a volume reservoir, but their capacity is not infinite. Any changes in blood volume that exceed the capacity of the veins to act as a buffer will alter blood pressure. The kidneys play a major role in maintaining blood volume, and thus these organs are an important component of the homeostatic regulation of blood pressure. Figure 9.49 illustrates how changes in mean

FIGURE 9.49 The relationship between arterial pressure and blood volume

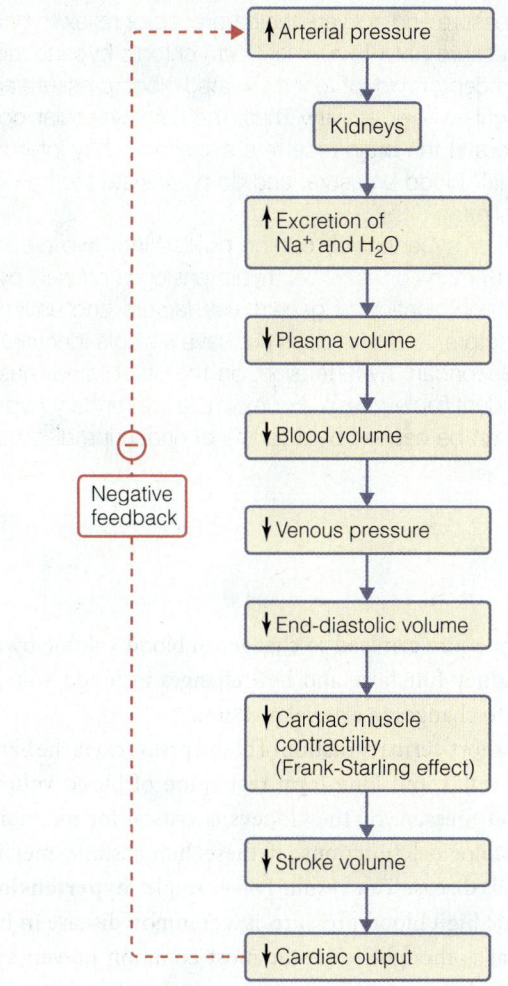

to the **medullary cardiovascular control center** in the central nervous system. The control center integrates the sensory input, and produces an efferent output carried by autonomic neurons. There is a decrease in sympathetic output, resulting in vasodilation. This decrease in sympathetic output in combination with an increase in parasympathetic output results in a decrease in the force of cardiac contraction and a decrease in heart rate. Together, these factors lead to a decrease in peripheral resistance and cardiac output, and a concomitant decrease in blood pressure. The medullary cardiovascular center also decreases the secretion of the hormones vasopressin and angiotensin in response to increased blood pressure. Because these hormones constrict arterioles, decreasing their secretion reduces total peripheral resistance.

Worldwide, approximately 25 percent of the adult population is affected by hypertension, and the prevalence of hypertension is predicted to increase by 60 percent by 2025. At that point, a total of 1.56 billion people could be affected by this disease. Hypertension in adult humans is typically defined as a sustained systolic blood pressure greater than 139 mm Hg and a diastolic blood pressure greater than 89 mm Hg, when measured at rest. Above this level the risk of developing cardiovascular disease rises sharply. Blood pressure in the range of 120–139 mm Hg systolic and 80–89 mm Hg diastolic is classified as prehypertensive, to reflect the fact that the risk of cardiovascular disease rises continuously as blood pressure increases. In addition to the increased risk of cardiovascular disease, hypertension is associated with a variety of other complications, including increased risk of strokes, increased risk of damage to the retina of the eye, and chronic renal failure.

So why don't the baroreceptors detect this increased blood pressure and activate the baroreceptor reflex to bring blood pressure back to normal? With chronic hypertension the baroreceptors adapt to the elevated blood pressure and down-regulate their activity. Thus, the cardiovascular control centers in the brain receive a signal that they interpret as "normal" blood pressure, and do not initiate the baroreceptor reflex.

Cases of hypertension can be divided into two distinct classes. Primary, or essential, hypertension is caused by a complex combination of genetic risk factors and environmental factors, and thus does not have a single identifiable cause. Secondary hypertension, on the other hand, has a specific identifiable cause. For example, secondary hypertension can be caused by a variety of endocrine disorders that increase fluid retention by the kidney. Secondary hypertension can also be caused by ingesting substances that affect kidney function.

Licorice provides a particularly interesting example of a compound that causes secondary hypertension. Ingesting natural licorice, which contains a compound called glycyrrhizic acid (GZA), can cause hypertension severe enough to require hospitalization, and can even be fatal. GZA normally binds to and inactivates 11-beta-hydroxysteroid dehydrogenase (type 2), which is an enzyme that inactivates the hormone cortisol (see Chapter 4: Cell Signaling and Endocrine Regulation). In the kidneys, this enzyme normally inactivates cortisol and prevents it from binding to the mineralocorticoid receptor, allowing this receptor to respond specifically to the hormone aldosterone. If you consume large amounts of natural licorice, the enzyme is inhibited and the mineralocorticoid receptor is stimulated by both cortisol and aldosterone, causing the kidneys to reabsorb sodium and water from the urine (see Chapter 13: Ion and Water Balance), increasing blood volume and blood pressure. Secondary hypertension caused by ingesting too much licorice is rapidly reversed once licorice is removed from the diet. Most licorice-flavored foods available in North America do not contain GZA, as they are actually flavored with anise rather than licorice, but people with any underlying cardiovascular disease should avoid eating foods, including herbal teas, containing natural licorice.

Primary hypertension accounts for the vast majority of cases of hypertension (> 90–95 percent). Patients with primary hypertension usually have normal cardiac output, suggesting that their elevated blood pressure is a result of increased peripheral resistance. This increased peripheral

---

arterial pressure can lead to changes in blood volume by altering kidney function, and how changes in blood volume can lead to changes in arterial pressure.

The short-term regulation of blood pressure via the baroreceptor reflex and long-term regulation of blood volume and blood pressure by the kidneys is critical for maintaining physiological functions. If these homeostatic mechanisms fail, disease can result. For example, **hypertension**, or chronic high blood pressure, is a common disease in humans that is thought to be the most common preventable risk factor for premature death across the globe. Box 9.3:

Challenges to Homeostasis: Hypertension, provides an in-depth look at this common cardiovascular disease.

Blood pressure can force fluid out of the capillaries

In addition to the critical importance of regulating mean arterial pressure in order to maintain the driving force for movement of blood through the vertebrate circulatory system, it is also critical to maintain blood pressure to ensure appropriate fluid balance at the capillaries.

Because of the presence of pores between the cells of the capillary wall, fluids can move from the capillaries to the

resistance is associated with narrowing of the small arteries and arterioles, and possibly by a reduction in the number of capillaries, but it is not clear whether these changes are a cause or an effect of the hypertension. Patients with primary hypertension also often have reduced venous compliance (see Figure 9.46), which can increase peripheral resistance. This reduced compliance may also increase venous return to the heart, which could shift blood volume from the venous to the arterial side of the circulation, resulting in an increase in blood pressure. Patients with essential hypertension also have defects in their vascular endothelium, and typically produce lower levels of the vasodilator nitric oxide, which could contribute to the increase in peripheral resistance, but this is thought to be a consequence, not a cause, of the hypertension. Drugs that target fluid regulation by the kidney can be effective in treating primary hypertension, but the role of changes in kidney function as a cause of the disease is unclear. Thus, the causes of primary hypertension remain poorly understood.

The consequences of chronic hypertension, however, are very well understood. Patients with hypertension maintain normal cardiac output, including normal stroke volume and heart rate. However, the heart must generate this stroke volume while pushing against a much higher mean arterial blood pressure. As a result, the left ventricle increases in size and strength, a process known as hypertrophy. However, the heart eventually gets to a point where it cannot further increase the strength of contraction. At this point, the left ventricle begins to fail. In many cases of hypertension, the blood pressure in the pulmonary circuit remains fairly normal and there is little or no hypertrophy of the right ventricle. If the left ventricle fails while the right ventricle continues pumping relatively normally, blood will "back up" in the lungs, resulting in a condition known as pulmonary edema, in which interstitial fluid accumulates in the lungs. This fluid increases the diffusion distance for gases across the lungs and reduces oxygen exchange. This causes a vicious cycle in which lower oxygen further damages the heart and worsens the pulmonary edema. This disease, known as congestive heart failure, is the leading cause of hospitalization in people over 65 years old in developed countries. Unless treated, congestive heart failure is fatal.

Both lifestyle changes and medical interventions can be used to treat hypertension. Lifestyle changes that are effective include weight loss, increased exercise, and restricting dietary sodium. There are a variety of effective antihypertensive drugs that act on various aspects of cardiovascular physiology. For example, some of these drugs act to vasodilate arterioles and thus reduce peripheral resistance. Other antihypertensive drugs are diuretics that promote water loss at the kidneys, reducing blood volume, and blood pressure. Beta-blockers that reduce heart rate and the force of cardiac contraction can also be useful.

References

- Chobanian, A.V., Bakris, G. L., Black, H. R., Cushman, W. C., Green, L. A., Izzo, J. L., Jr., . . . Roccella, E. J. (2003). Seventh report of the Joint National Committee on Prevention, Detection, Evaluation, and Treatment of High Blood Pressure. *Hypertension, 42*, 1206–1252.

- Kearney, P. M., Whelton, M., Reynolds, K., Muntner, P., Whelton, P. K., & He, J. (2005). Global burden of hypertension: Analysis of worldwide data. *The Lancet, 365*, 217–223.

- Mussalo, H., Vanninen, E., Ikäheimo, R., Laitinen, T., Laakso, M., Länsimies, E., & Hartikainen, J. (2002). Baroreflex sensitivity in essential and secondary hypertension. *Clinical Autonomic Research, 12*, 465–471.

interstitial fluids by bulk flow. This process is particularly important in the kidney, which relies on bulk flow of fluids and filtration in the first step of urine formation, but similar processes occur at all capillaries. Four forces influence the bulk flow of fluids across the capillaries:

1. Hydrostatic pressure in the capillary (P_{cap}) (the transmural pressure)

2. Hydrostatic pressure in the interstitial fluid (P_{if})

3. Osmotic pressure in the capillary (π_{cap})

4. Osmotic pressure in the interstitial fluid (π_{if})

The direction of fluid flow across a capillary wall is the result of the net filtration pressure (NFP), which can be expressed as

$$\text{NFP} = (P_{cap} - P_{if}) - (\pi_{cap} - \pi_{if})$$

This relationship, called the Starling principle of fluid exchange, allows us to quantify the movement of fluid across a capillary. The driving forces are called *Starling forces* after the physiologist Ernest Starling, who discovered this principle in 1896. Note that Ernest Starling is also the codiscoverer of the Frank-Starling law of the heart. The hydrostatic pressure in the capillary is the major driving force pushing fluids from the blood and into the interstitial spaces. If hydrostatic pressure in the capillary is larger than the hydrostatic pressure in the interstitial fluid, then fluids will be forced out of the capillary. Continuous capillaries are permeable only to small molecules, so that plasma proteins and blood cells remain behind in the blood, causing the blood to have a higher osmotic pressure than the interstitial fluid. Because salts and other small molecules are present in roughly equal concentration in the blood and the interstitial fluid, the difference in osmotic pressure between these two compartments is due largely to the presence of proteins in the blood. An osmotic pressure that is due to proteins is termed an **oncotic pressure**. The higher oncotic pressure in the capillaries tends to suck fluids back into the blood. The balance between these two forces influences the rate and direction of fluid movement.

Figure 9.50 illustrates how these forces change as fluids move along capillaries from the arterial side to the venous side. The osmotic pressure of the blood and interstitial fluid remains fairly constant across a capillary bed, but the hydrostatic pressure of the blood declines substantially as it travels from the arterial to the venous end of the capillary bed because of the frictional resistance of the capillary walls. At the arterial end of the capillary the net filtration pressure is positive, indicating that fluid will flow out into the interstitial fluid. At the venous end of the capillary, the net filtration pressure is negative, indicating that fluid will flow back into the capillary.

This balance of forces is true for an idealized capillary, but many capillaries show filtration across their entire length, and some specialized capillaries in the intestinal **mucosa** reabsorb fluids along most of their length. Whatever the capillary, however, the important issue to consider is the balance of Starling forces. Vertebrates have precise control over capillary pressure, mostly through vasoconstriction and vasodilation of the blood vessels leading to capillary beds, and changes in these parameters will lead to changes in the rate of fluid filtration.

Under normal circumstances, in humans almost 20 liters of fluid per day filters out of the capillaries, or almost six times the total volume of the plasma in an average human being. About 17 liters of this fluid is usually reabsorbed into the blood, but this leaves an excess of almost 3 liters of fluid per day that could accumulate in the interstitial fluid.

The lymphatic system returns filtered fluids to the circulatory system

The lymphatic system collects the filtered fluid and returns it to the circulatory system (Figure 9.51). Fluid enters the lymphatic system via the blind-ended *lymphatic capillaries*. The lymphatic capillaries coalesce into progressively larger vessels termed *lymphatic veins* and *lymphatic ducts* that contain valves to prevent backflow of the lymph, and are surrounded by smooth muscle, which propels the lymph forward. In addition, amphibians, reptiles, and the embryos

At the start of the capillary, hydrostatic pressure (P) exceeds capillary osmotic pressure (π), resulting in a net filtration pressure that forces fluid out of the capillary. At the end of the capillary, hydrostatic pressure is less than capillary osmotic pressure, resulting in net reabsorption that returns some of the fluid to the capillary.

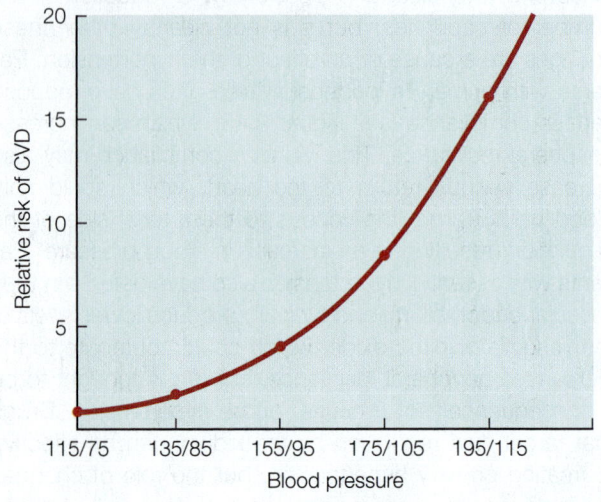

of birds have **lymph hearts** that help to propel the lymph through the body. In birds and mammals, the lymphatic ducts lead to small bean-shaped organs called **lymph nodes**. All vertebrates have lymph nodes in the thoracic cavity, abdomen, and pelvis. In addition, mammals have so-called external lymph nodes located in their necks and at the point where the limbs and torso join (the armpit and groin areas in humans). The lymph nodes filter the lymph, and contain specialized blood cells called **lymphocytes** that kill pathogens and cancerous cells. From the lymph nodes, the filtered lymph travels through the efferent lymphatic vessels. These vessels coalesce into the large *lymphatic ducts* that drain into the circulatory system at the veins of the neck.

Anything that alters the balance between filtration and reabsorption of fluids across the capillary beds or the function of the lymphatic system may lead to accumulation of fluids in the tissues—a condition called **edema**. For example, sitting in one position for a long period of time (such as in an airplane) can reduce blood flow in the veins and cause blood to pool in the capillaries of the ankles and feet. The pooled blood leads to increased capillary hydrostatic pressure, which leads to increased filtration of fluids and ankle edema. Liver disease also affects capillary pressure, because the majority of plasma proteins are produced in the liver. If plasma protein concentration drops, plasma osmotic pressure will drop, reducing the reabsorption of water at the venous end of the capillaries, and increasing net filtration, leading to generalized edema. Alternatively, removal of the lymph nodes (for example, as a part of cancer treatment) can

FIGURE 9.51 Relationship between the mammalian circulatory and lymphatic systems

Some fluid leaving the capillaries enters the lymphatic system. This fluid, called lymph, flows through the lymph nodes and into the lymphatic ducts. The lymphatic ducts return the fluid to the venous part of the circulatory system near the right atrium. The lymphatic ducts contain valves that ensure unidirectional flow.

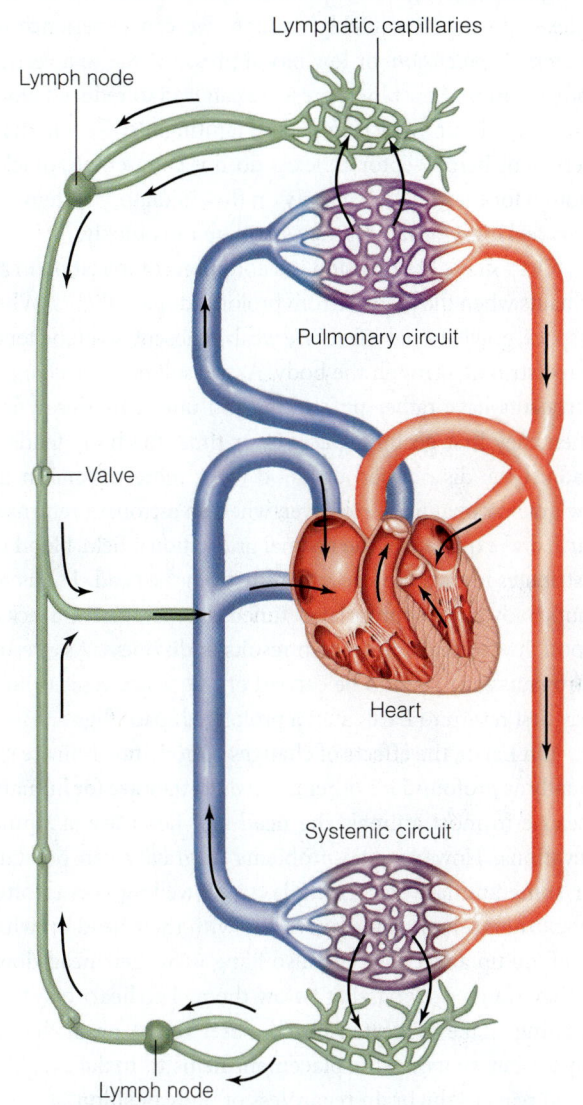

Lymphatic capillaries

Lymph node

Pulmonary circuit

Valve

Heart

Systemic circuit

Lymph node

compromise the function of the lymphatic system, preventing the removal of fluid filtered from the capillaries, which leads to edema of the affected tissues.

Pulmonary edema, in which fluids accumulate in the tissues of the lungs, is one of the most dangerous forms of edema. When fluid accumulates in the lungs, it becomes more difficult for oxygen to diffuse from the lungs to the blood. As a result, pulmonary edema can be fatal. Anything that increases the net filtration pressure in the lung capillaries has the potential to cause pulmonary edema, if the rate of filtration exceeds the rate at which the lymphatic system can remove the fluid. For example, if a heart attack damages the

muscle of the left ventricle but spares the right ventricle, the right side of the heart may pump more blood per beat than the left side of the heart. This causes blood to back up into the lungs, and increases the hydrostatic pressure in the capillaries, which increases the net filtration pressure and can lead to pulmonary edema.

Changes in body position can alter blood pressure and flow

Because of the effects of gravity, an unobstructed vertical column of fluid exerts a pressure, termed the **hydrostatic pressure**, on objects below it (Figure 9.52a). The hydrostatic pressure exerted by a fluid column is thus a function of the effects of gravity and the height of the column. We can express this relationship mathematically as follows:

$$\Delta P = \rho g h$$

where ΔP is the difference in pressure between two points in the fluid column, ρ is the density of the fluid, g is the acceleration due to gravity, and h is the height of the fluid column. As you can see from this equation, hydrostatic pressure is a measure of the gravitational potential energy of the fluid column.

When a person is lying down (Figure 9.52b), this gravitational component is absent, and measured pressure in the feet and head is slightly lower than in the heart. We usually report blood pressure relative to the surrounding atmospheric pressure, so the pressure shown in the figure is actually the amount by which the pressure of the blood exceeds the ambient atmospheric pressure. For example, the mean arterial blood pressure near the human heart is approximately 13.6 kPa, but the actual pressure is 13.6 kPa plus approximately 101 kPa (the atmospheric pressure at sea level), for a total of 114.6 kPa. The pressure gradient between the heart and the rest of the body drives blood flow around the circuit.

In contrast, Figure 9.52c shows the blood pressure in various parts of a human body when standing. When a person is standing, the pressure measured in the ankles is higher than pressure near the heart. If liquids flow from areas of high pressure to areas of low pressure, how can the heart pump blood down to the feet? This anomaly is explained by the fact that the pressure measured in the ankles is the sum of the pressure exerted by the heart plus the hydrostatic pressure exerted by the blood in the circulatory system "pushing down" on the blood in the ankles. The hydrostatic pressure actually represents the gravitational potential energy of the column of blood, and potential energy is highest at the top of the fluid column. Fluids tend to flow from areas of high potential energy to areas of low potential energy. In essence, blood "falls" downward in the circulatory system.

As blood returns up the body to the heart it must move against a gradient of gravitational potential energy. This

FIGURE 9.52 **The effects of gravity on blood pressure**

Blood pressure is generally measured either in kilopascals (kPa), the SI unit of pressure, or in millimeters of mercury (mm Hg), the unit most commonly used in medical diagnostics. 100 mm Hg is equal to 13.3 kPa. **(a)** Hydrostatic pressure is the result of the gravitational potential energy of the fluid column. **(b)** When a human is lying down, arterial blood pressure is highest at the heart and lowest at the feet. **(c)** In a standing human, arterial blood pressure is highest in the feet and lowest in the head.

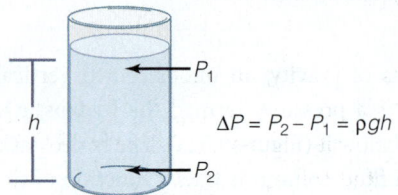

$$\Delta P = P_2 - P_1 = \rho g h$$

(a) Hydrostatic pressure

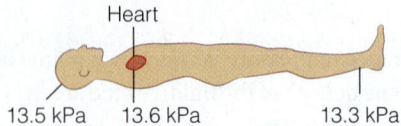

Heart

13.5 kPa   13.6 kPa   13.3 kPa

(b) Measured blood pressure when lying down

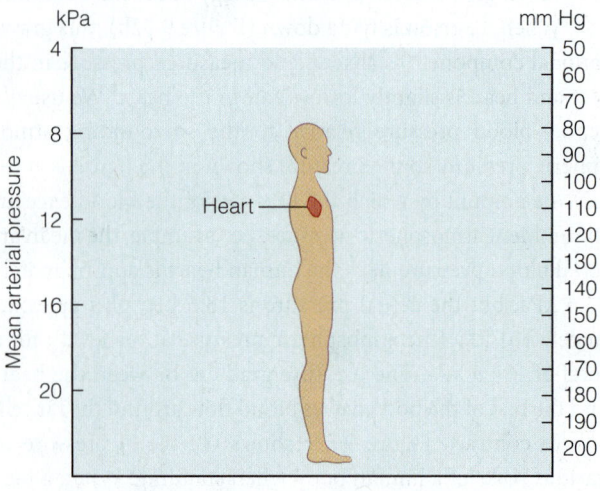

(c) Measured blood pressure when standing

hydrostatic pressure component is absent when a person lies down (as in Figure 9.52b). The skeletal muscle pump and the respiratory pump discussed earlier in this chapter are critical in helping blood to return to the heart against the gravitational potential energy gradient generated when a person is standing.

Changes in body position can cause orthostatic hypotension

When we stand upright, gravity tends to push blood downward because the effects of gravity on the column of blood in the blood vessel exert a hydrostatic pressure on the parts of the circulatory system below. Thus, when we stand up, a certain

amount of blood normally pools in our ankles and legs. This pooling causes a slight decline in venous return to the heart. Because of the Frank-Starling effect, reduced venous return leads to decreased stroke volume and a momentary drop in arterial blood pressure. This drop in blood pressure brings the baroreceptor reflex into play, setting in motion all of the changes that bring blood pressure back to normal. If these reflexes do not act quickly enough, we can experience *orthostatic hypotension*, or low blood pressure due to a vertical body position. Low blood pressure can lead to reduced blood flow to the brain, which can cause fainting. People who have inefficient baroreceptor reflexes do not compensate quickly enough for the effects of gravity on the circulatory system and often feel dizzy or faint if they stand up too quickly.

Orthostatic hypotension is a common complication in astronauts when they return from prolonged space flights. When in space, gravitational effects are weak or absent, so blood tends to redistribute through the body. As a result of these changes, astronauts have rather puffy faces and unusually skinny legs when they first go into space. Over time, the body tends to readjust the distribution of blood to be more normal in the low gravitational field. However, when an astronaut returns to Earth and experiences the normal gravitational field, blood redistributes toward the legs and away from the head. The astronaut's body is not appropriately tuned to cope, causing a lack of blood flow to the brain, which results in dizziness. As a result, astronauts may need to be carried off the space vehicle when they first return to Earth after a prolonged space flight.

On Earth, the effects of changes in body position are not usually as profound for other animals as they are for humans, because in most animals the head and heart are at similar elevations. However, the problems of gravity can be acute for some animals. For example, tree-dwelling snakes often orient themselves almost vertically with their head up when climbing up a tree, but can also hang with their head down as they watch prey passing below them. The heart of a tree-dwelling snake is located much closer to the brain than in most other snakes. This placement helps to make sure that blood reaches the brain regardless of body position.

Very tall animals must have specialized circulatory systems

Physiologists have long been fascinated by the circulatory dynamics of very tall animals, such as the giraffe (Figure 9.53). A giraffe's head can be as much as 2 meters above its heart, while its legs are 2 meters below the heart. Thus, there is a large gravitational potential energy barrier to overcome in pumping blood up to the head. Some physiologists have suggested that some or all of this energy is recovered via a siphon effect, as the blood moves downward back to the heart. However, most comparative physiologists think that this effect is unlikely to be physiologically relevant. Whatever the case, clearly the very

FIGURE 9.53 **The effects of gravity on the circulatory system of a giraffe**

Animals with a very long neck must have relatively high mean arterial pressure at the heart in order to pump blood to the head. The long legs of the giraffe also greatly increase the hydrostatic pressure in the legs, potentially causing a problem with peripheral edema. To combat this high hydrostatic pressure, giraffes have extremely tight skin on their legs that exerts an inward pressure that opposes the hydrostatic pressure due to gravity.

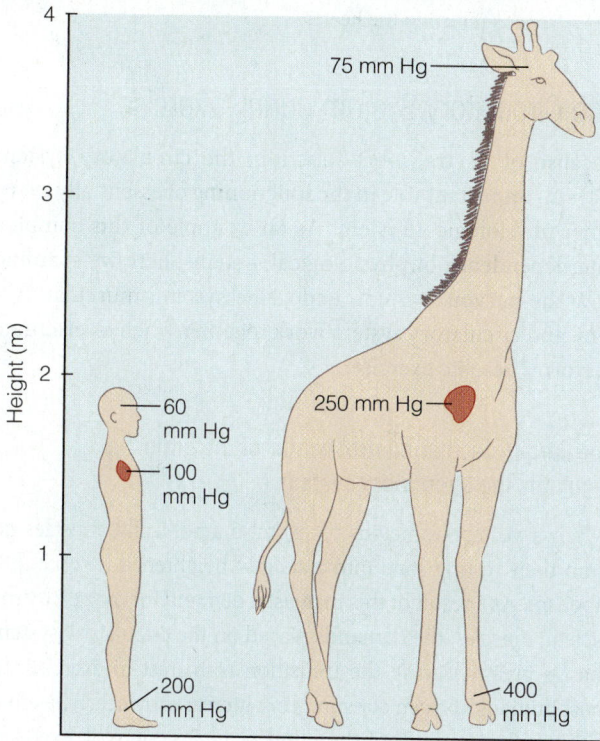

their legs that help to control the flow of blood. But the most important difference between a giraffe and other mammals is that the skin on a giraffe's legs is extremely tight. This tight skin helps the skeletal muscle pump to function efficiently, and increases the interstitial fluid pressure, reducing the risk of edema. Human marathon runners take advantage of a similar principle by wearing compression socks while running.

When a giraffe bends down to drink, the head goes from being several meters above the heart to several meters below it. The resulting increase in the hydrostatic pressure in the head could cause blood to pool in the veins, potentially causing edema in the tissues of the head. Like pulmonary edema, cerebral edema (or accumulation of fluid around the brain) can be life threatening. However, a giraffe has an intricate network of highly elastic blood vessels near the brain that act as a pressure reservoir that expands to accommodate excess blood when the head is lowered, preventing it from pooling in the venous system. In addition, unlike in other mammals, the jugular vein (leading from the head) contains a series of one-way valves that prevent backflow of the blood away from the heart when the giraffe's head is down. Together these mechanisms help to regulate blood flow to the head, regardless of the giraffe's position.

Gravity poses challenges for the structure of circulatory systems in all animals with long necks and legs, not just for giraffes. Consider the sauropod dinosaurs of the Triassic period, which were very large animals with extremely long necks. For example, the neck of a *Brachiosaurus* could reach 9 meters and that of *Mamenchisaurus* 14 meters, which is enormous compared to the 3-meter neck of a giraffe. Of course, it is difficult to study the physiology of animals that are known only from fossils, but we can develop hypotheses based on the phylogenetic relationships of dinosaurs to living animals. Based on the close relationship between dinosaurs and living birds, it is extremely likely that dinosaurs had completely separated systemic and pulmonary circuits in their circulatory systems and a four-chambered heart that could maintain different blood pressures across the two circuits. But what kind of systemic blood pressure would be required to drive flow through the long neck of a sauropod dinosaur to the head? Answering this questions depends on whether sauropod dinosaurs typically held their neck horizontally, allowing them to browse on vegetation at or below the level of their heart, or whether they held their neck vertically, allowing them to browse at the tops of tall trees, as do modern-day giraffes. We can use a physiological approach to assess the likelihood of each of these two possibilities. If you assume that large sauropod dinosaurs routinely held their neck upright, then the circulatory system would have to have had a variety of specializations to pump blood to the head.

Calculations based on the blood pressures of living animals suggest that systemic systolic blood pressure would have to have been as high as 700–750 mm Hg at the heart if the animal routinely held its head up. Blood pressures of

long blood vessels in the neck of a giraffe will have high resistance, and the cardiovascular system of a giraffe must be specialized to cope with pumping blood through the long neck to the head.

A giraffe has an extremely large and muscular heart and the highest blood pressure known for any mammal. With a systolic pressure of up to 280 mm Hg and a diastolic pressure of 180 mm Hg at heart level, its blood pressure is twice that of a typical human. A resting giraffe also has a very high heart rate (about twice that of humans, or approximately 170 beats per minute versus 70 bpm). This observation is particularly surprising because heart rate tends to decrease with size in mammals. These cardiac specializations may be needed to pump blood through the long systemic circuit of a giraffe against a substantial gravitational potential energy gradient.

The high blood pressure of a giraffe combined with the effects of gravity on the hydrostatic pressure within the circulatory system would tend to force blood out of the capillaries into the interstitial fluid in the ankles, causing peripheral edema in the absence of mechanisms to prevent this problem. Giraffes have unusually thick-walled and muscular arteries in

this magnitude are extremely unlikely. The first physiological problem associated with very high blood pressures is that they would cause high rates of fluid filtration at the capillaries, and thus would require very active recovery of this fluid via the lymphatic system. The second, and even more important, physiological issue is that an extremely large heart would have been needed to generate such a high blood pressure. In fact, if you assume that the properties of the heart muscle of sauropod dinosaurs were similar to those of living birds and mammals, then their heart would need to be more than a meter in diameter, and weigh as much as five percent of the total body weight. This would be an astonishing size, given that living species of whales have hearts that make up only 0.5 percent of their body weight. Such a large heart would also require an enormous amount of energy. In fact, it has been estimated that simply fueling the heart would take up more than 60 percent of a large sauropod's resting metabolic rate. Thus, on physiological grounds, it is not possible that large sauropods maintained such high blood pressures.

Given that extremely high blood pressures are unlikely, how could sauropods maintain circulation if they held their heads up? Some suggested mechanisms are the existence of a siphon effect or the presence of auxiliary hearts in the neck. However, there is little evidence that these mechanisms are physiologically feasible or likely to have evolved. Instead, it is far more likely that sauropods held their head in a fairly horizontal position more or less level with the heart most of the time. This would require much lower driving pressure to push blood to the brain, of perhaps 200–300 mm Hg. This is still an impressive level, somewhat higher than that generated by modern-day giraffes (see Figure 9.53), but it is physiologically achievable given the known structure and function of the hearts of extant animals.

The Circulatory System during Exercise

Because of its transport function, the circulatory system plays an important role in the functioning of essentially every other physiological system. As an example of this complex interdependence of physiological systems, here we examine how the nervous system, endocrine system, muscular system, and circulatory system work together when a vertebrate performs aerobic exercise.

The cardiovascular control center of the brain regulates the circulatory system

When a vertebrate begins to exercise aerobically, muscles go from their resting state into a state of heightened aerobic metabolism. As a result of this increased demand for oxygen by the skeletal muscles, the demands placed on the circulatory system change greatly during the transition from rest to exercise. In most humans, oxygen consumption increases by nearly fivefold within a few minutes of the onset of intense aerobic exercise. Figure 9.54 outlines the response of the cardiovascular system to exercise. When we first begin to exercise, mechanoreceptors in our muscles (see Chapter 7: Sensory Systems) detect the change in the tension of the muscle as a result of contraction. These mechanoreceptors send afferent sensory information to our brain, activating the cardiovascular control center in the medulla oblongata. The cardiovascular control center reduces the activity of the parasympathetic nervous system and increases the activity of the sympathetic nervous system, changing the efferent signals going to the heart and the arteriolar smooth muscle surrounding the vessels leading to the exercising muscles.

Cardiac output increases during exercise

The change in parasympathetic and sympathetic activity has dramatic effects on cardiac output. In fact, in humans cardiac output can increase by between four and eight times the value at rest (depending on the type and intensity of the exercise and the fitness of the

FIGURE 9.54   The response of the cardiovascular system to exercise

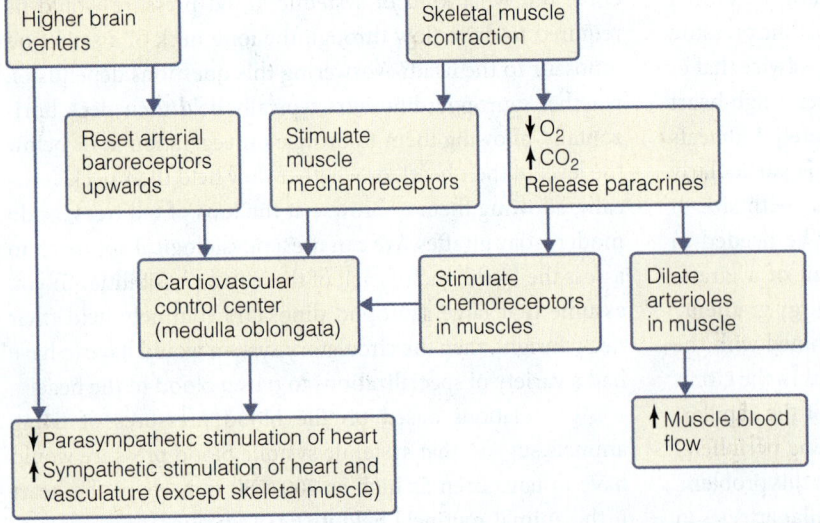

individual). A trained thoroughbred horse can achieve as much as a tenfold increase in cardiac output during maximal exercise. Recall that cardiac output is the product of heart rate and stroke volume. So which of these factors is the most important in causing the increase in cardiac output? At the onset of exercise parasympathetic activity decreases, causing an increase in heart rate. At the same time, the increase in muscular activity and breathing improves the function of the respiratory and skeletal muscle pumps, causing an increase in venous return to the heart. Because of the Frank-Starling effect, the resulting increase in end-diastolic volume causes an increase in stroke volume.

Thus, during the initial stages of exercise, the increases in cardiac output are a result of both increases in heart rate and increases in stroke volume. Next, sympathetic stimulation of the heart increases, resulting in increases in both heart rate and contractility. In principle, the increase in contractility should cause an increase in stroke volume, but the large increase in heart rate reduces the time available for filling of the heart, and limits end-diastolic volume. As a result, during the later stages of exercise in mammals, increases in heart rate contribute more to increases in cardiac output than do increases in stroke volume. In most terrestrial vertebrates, increases in cardiac output in response to exercise are primarily the result of increases in heart rate, with a modest contribution from increases in stroke volume. In contrast, in fish such as salmon, changes in stroke volume play the most important role in causing the increase in cardiac output during exercise. However, not all fish are stroke volume regulators. For example, tuna typically increase cardiac output by increasing heart rate and keeping stroke volume fairly constant. Thus, different animals use different strategies to achieve the same goal: increasing the delivery of oxygen to the working muscles during exercise.

Patterns of blood flow change during exercise

In addition to changes in cardiac output, there are large changes in the patterns of blood flow during exercise. At rest, the skeletal muscles receive only about 20 percent of the total cardiac output, whereas they receive 88 percent of the cardiac output during exercise. Total cardiac output also increases dramatically, so that flow to the skeletal muscles actually increases from about 1.2 liters per minute (l/min) at rest to over 22 l/min during exercise. At the same time, blood flow to organs such as the kidney decreases, both in relative and absolute terms. At rest, approximately 19 percent of the total cardiac output flows through the kidneys (or about 1 l/min), whereas during intense exercise only 1 percent of the total cardiac output flows through the kidneys (or about 0.25 l/min). These changes in blood flow are the result of vasodilation of the arterioles leading to the skeletal muscle and heart and vasoconstriction of the arterioles leading to the other organs. The increase in the activity of the sympathetic nervous system causes a generalized vasoconstriction, as sympathetic neurons release norepinephrine onto the vascular smooth muscle surrounding the arterioles leading to the organs. The norepinephrine binds to its receptors and causes the smooth muscles to contract. In skeletal muscle, however, local release of paracrine factors causes the vascular smooth muscle to relax by opposing the vasoconstrictive effects of adrenergic receptor stimulation. Together, these factors cause an intense local vasodilation, increasing blood flow to the muscles.

Blood pressure changes only slightly during exercise

Recall that mean arterial pressure is the product of cardiac output and total peripheral resistance. During exercise, cardiac output increases greatly, which you might expect to cause a large increase in mean arterial pressure. However, the vasodilation of the arterioles leading to the skeletal muscles more than offsets the vasoconstriction of the arterioles leading to the other organs, so total peripheral resistance falls dramatically. As a result, blood pressure increases only slightly during exercise. Ordinarily, even this modest increase in blood pressure would trigger the baroreceptor reflex, and bring blood pressure back to normal by decreasing cardiac output or total peripheral resistance. Recent data suggest that the afferent signal from the muscle mechanoreceptors changes the set point of the baroreceptor reflex, or alters its sensitivity, allowing blood pressure to increase slightly with exercise.

Higher brain centers are also involved

Feed-forward regulation also plays an important role in the response of the circulatory system to exercise. The circulatory changes that accompany exercise occur more rapidly if you ask an experimental subject to repeatedly contract a muscle, compared to what happens when you electrically stimulate that muscle. This suggests that descending input from higher brain centers helps to cause circulatory changes in anticipation of the need for more oxygen by the working muscles, even before metabolic end products begin to build up. Thus, it is clear that the circulatory responses to exercise represent a delicate integrated response involving the nervous system, the endocrine system, the musculoskeletal system, and the cardiovascular system.

CONCEPT CHECK

25. Drugs called beta-blockers inhibit the actions of the sympathetic nervous system. Predict what taking beta-blockers would do to heart rate and cardiac output during exercise.

26. Why does blood pressure only change slightly during exercise despite the large increase in cardiac output?

SUMMARY

Circulatory systems utilize bulk flow, or the movement of fluids down pressure gradients, for long-distance transport. As a result, the law of bulk flow ($Q = P/R$) is the fundamental law of the circulatory system.

Only a few taxa lack circulatory systems. Some annelids, cephalopod mollusks, and all vertebrates have independently evolved closed circulatory systems, which have generally evolved in parallel with an increased metabolic rate. In vertebrates, two-circuit circulatory systems evolved in conjunction with the colonization of land, but only mammals and birds have completely separated pulmonary and systemic circuits.

Vertebrate hearts are pressure pumps with valves that play a critical role in cardiac function, but that are passive, opening and closing in response to the applied pressure. The contraction of a vertebrate heart is controlled by myogenic pacemaker cells that have an unstable resting membrane potential that initiates the heartbeat. The resulting depolarization spreads through the heart via gap junctions and specialized conducting pathways and coordinates the contraction of the heart. Heart rate and stroke volume are modulated using the nervous and endocrine systems and local factors such as the Frank-Starling relationship.

Flow of blood through the circulatory system is directed using vasoconstriction and vasodilation at the level of the arterioles, which is regulated by local and central factors. The body maintains close homeostatic control over mean arterial pressure by altering cardiac output and total peripheral resistance using the baroreceptor reflex in the short term and volume regulation by the kidneys in the long term. These regulatory mechanisms allow the circulatory system to adjust to changes in demand as a result of factors such as exercise.

REVIEW QUESTIONS

1. **LO1** What are the three primary components that are found in all animal circulatory systems?

2. **LO1** Can decapod crustaceans control the flow of circulatory fluid to different tissues?

3. **LO2** Compare and contrast the circulatory systems of fish, amphibians, and mammals.

4. **LO2** Trace the movement of a drop of blood through the human circulatory system, listing all of the structures it passes (including all of the parts of the heart).

5. **LO3** Use Poiseuille's equation to explain why the circulatory system regulates the distribution of blood to tissues by vasoconstricting or vasodilating arterioles.

6. **LO3** What is the difference between the velocity of the blood and the rate of blood flow? How are these two concepts related?

7. **LO4** Name the layers of the walls of a mammalian heart and describe their structure.

8. **LO4** Compare and contrast the structure of a fish heart with the structure of the mammalian heart.

9. **LO5** What happens to pressure in the left ventricle during left atrial systole?

10. **LO5** Draw a sketch equivalent to Figure 9.30 and indicate the points at which the various valves open. Justify your choices.

11. **LO6** Why is the unstable resting membrane potential of pacemaker cells critical to their function?

12. **LO6** Outline the steps of electrical conduction through the mammalian heart.

13. **LO7** Define heart rate, stroke volume, and cardiac output. Explain how changes in heart rate or stroke volume affect cardiac output.

14. **LO7** What is the importance of the skeletal muscle and respiratory pumps?

15. **LO8** What happens to heart rate, stroke volume, cardiac output, mean arterial pressure, and patterns of blood flow at the onset of exercise in humans?

SYNTHESIS QUESTIONS

1. What are some possible advantages of a double circulation over a single-circuit circulation?

2. Explain the changes in blood pressure as blood flows through the mammalian circulatory system.

3. Aortic blood flow starts to increase only some time after the initiation of ventricular contraction. Similarly, aortic blood flow continues at a relatively high level well into the diastolic period. Explain why.

4. Increased heart rate can greatly reduce diastolic filling time, but has less impact on systolic ejection time. Why?

5. What would happen if the connection between the AV node and the bundle of His were blocked (in a way that didn't directly affect any other parts of the heart)?

6. During an experiment, dogs were given the drug atropine, which abolishes parasympathetic nerve transmission. What effects would you expect on the heart and why?

7. Tom suffers from high blood pressure. Which of the following might help deal with this problem? Remember to explain your answer.
   (a) A drug that stimulates β receptors
   (b) A drug that blocks α receptors
   (c) A drug that blocks β receptors
   (d) A drug that blocks acetylcholine receptors

8. After a heart transplant, there is no direct connection between the nervous system and the heart. However, the cardiac output of patients with heart transplants can vary in response to changes in metabolic demand (such as during exercise). How could this be possible? Would you expect this regulation to be as efficient as in a patient with an intact heart?

QUANTITATIVE QUESTIONS

1. Below is a schematic diagram of the mammalian cardiovascular system.

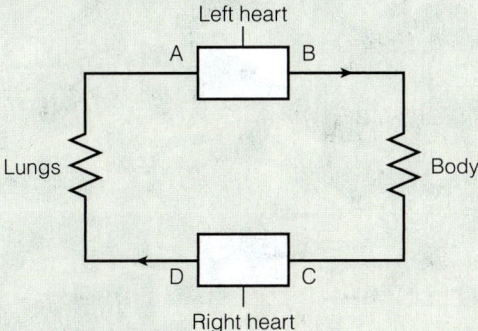

If mean pressure at A = 2 mm Hg, B = 80 mm Hg, C = 5 mm Hg, and D = 10 mm Hg, and cardiac output = 5 l/min, calculate

(a) the resistance of the systemic circulation
(b) the resistance of the pulmonary circulation
(c) What are the units you have used for resistance?

2. The radius of the aorta in humans is about 1×10^{-2} m and the velocity of blood flowing through it is about 0.3 m/sec. What is the average speed of blood in the capillaries, given average capillary diameter is only 8×10^{-6} m, and the total cross-sectional area of the capillaries is about 2×10^{-1} m (the cross-sectional area of a blood vessel is approximately πr^2)?

3. Use this figure to answer the following questions:

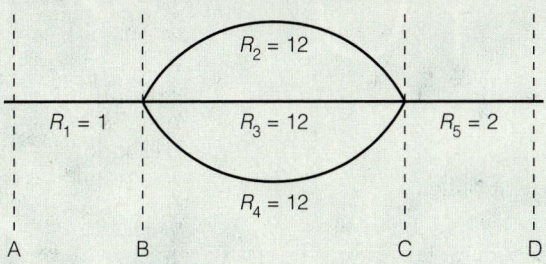

$P_A = 100$ mm Hg
$P_D = 0$ mm Hg

(a) What is the flow through this network?
(b) What are the pressures at points B and C?
(c) What is the flow in vessel 3?
(d) If another vessel is added in parallel to vessels 2–4, with a resistance $R_6 = 18$ mm Hg · min/ml, then what is the flow through the system (assuming ΔP remains the same)?
(e) If vessel 4 becomes completely occluded (blocked) (i.e., R_4 is now infinite), what is the flow through the network?

4. Using the information in Figure 9.39, at what point in the cardiac cycle is ventricular ejection velocity highest?

5. If during exercise heart rate increases from 70 beats/min to 150 beats/min and the stroke volume increases from 70 ml/beat to 120 ml/beat, what will be the difference in cardiac output between rest and exercise?

Learning Objectives

**After reading this chapter,
you should be able to:**

1. Explain how immune cells detect foreign molecules.

2. Identify and characterize the main types of the cells that participate in the innate immune system.

3. Distinguish clearly between innate and adaptive immune systems and describe the phylogenetic distribution of responses of each.

4. Explain the structure and function of immunoglobulins.

5. Distinguish the roles of B cells and T cells.

6. Describe the events in an immune response.

7. Discuss the interaction between the immune system and other physiological systems.

FIGURE 10.1 **Australian rabbits**

Photo source: John Carnemolla/Encyclopedia/Corbis.

ne of the best examples of the negative impact of introduced species is the story of the proliferation of European rabbits in Australia (Figure 10.1). After rabbits were imported and released for food between the late 1700s and the mid-1800s, their populations grew explosively and caused catastrophic consequences for indigenous plants. Despite aggressive hunting, efforts to eradicate the species have largely failed.

In 1950, researchers introduced into rabbit populations a poxvirus called myxoma. The resulting outbreak of this population-level disease killed a high percentage of rabbits throughout Australia. Within 10 years, the original virus had become ineffectual, and subsequent efforts at biological control included other myxoma strains and other viruses. Though there are many lessons to be learned about policies surrounding invasive species and biological control, the changes seen within the virus, the transmission vector, and rabbit populations offer important insights into the evolution of disease resistance and immunity.

The natural host for the myxoma virus is a South American jungle rabbit (*Sylvilagus brasiliensis*), and when infected these animals show very mild symptoms. The virus propagates in infected jungle rabbits, and is transmitted between hosts through insect bites. The virus is also innocuous in several other rabbit species, but when it infects European rabbits (*Oryctolagus cuniculus*), the effects are much more dramatic and usually lethal. Myxomatosis is accompanied by a swollen head, severe skin lesions, and tissue swelling (edema), followed by death 8 to 12 days postinfection. When the virus was introduced to the Australian populations, the first studies were not promising, likely because the mosquito populations were unable to transmit the virus between rabbits. However, by the next summer, the virus had successfully been transmitted throughout some populations, probably due to a seasonal abundance of mosquitoes. Infected populations showed mortality rates as high as 99.8 percent.

There are a number of aspects that make this an interesting immunology story. First, it demonstrates how some pathogens have evolved strong host specificity. Killing your host before it has a chance to transmit the disease is not a stable evolutionary strategy. Second, it illustrates the importance of vector dynamics in pathogen transmission.

Without the appropriate species of vector, a blood-sucking insect in this case, transmission of a virus between animals is improbable. Perhaps most significant to the field of immunology is the story that emerges after the first few years following myxoma inoculations. The virus that was inoculated into the population was capable of killing 99 percent of the exposed rabbits, yet the virus strain that resided in the same rabbit populations seven years later had lost much of its virulence. Infected animals showed only minor symptoms because the rabbits had also been selected to become less sensitive to the virus. Understanding how a species can change its sensitivity to a pathogen has important ramifications for studying the progression of other epizootics (outbreaks of a disease among an animal population other than human) and epidemics (outbreaks of a disease among a human population).

In this chapter we explore the diversity in immunological systems of animals. Though some aspects of immunodefense are broadly conserved across animals, evolution has endowed some lineages with unique capacities to identify and respond to pathogens. These pathways reflect elegant cell-to-cell communication mechanisms, enabled by a circulatory system that delivers immune cells to the correct destination. ◼

LOOKING BACK 10

You may find it helpful to review Chapter 3, where we describe the structural basis of macromolecules, particularly proteins, and the cellular basis of tissues. Chapter 9 describes the organization of the circulatory system, and the relationship between the main circulatory system and the lymphatic system.

▌ OVERVIEW

Animals live in challenging environments, rich in organisms that can cause disease, collectively called pathogens. The first line of defense for most animals is the external surface. This may possess structural defenses to prevent penetration of bacteria, fungi, or viruses. For example, our thickened **stratum corneum** (skin) serves the dual purpose of impeding external pathogens while limiting water loss. Many species secrete mucus, giving the external surface a viscous barrier. Aquatic animals, in particular, use an outer mucus layer to protect their epithelium, increasing the thickness of it if under stress. Terrestrial vertebrates use mucus on their internalized external surfaces, such as the respiratory and digestive tracts. Mucus has a consistency that limits the penetration of microorganisms, and the regular movement of the mucus layer increases the likelihood that the microbes contained within are shed from the body. The epithelial layer may also secrete into its mucus suites of antibacterial enzymes and compounds that kill microorganisms before they enter the body. The epithelial barriers are important components of the host defenses of metazoans, even in animals as simple as cnidarians.

Nevertheless, pathogens inevitably will enter the body, and it falls to the immune system to attack the invader and limit the damage. All animals possess some capacity to recognize and respond to invaders and take defensive measures. The first step is to detect the foreign material; recognition requires an ability to distinguish "self" from "non-self." This system has to be fine tuned in animals that form productive arrangements with "non-self" organisms. For example, cnidarians such as corals permit the invasion of symbiotic protists between their cells while combating potentially pathogenic bacteria. Though we focus our discussion on protection from microorganisms (bacteria, viruses, fungi), the immune system also plays vital roles in defense against parasites and even the animal's own cells, such as cancers and damaged cells. When normal cells become abnormal, the cellular changes allow the immune system to recognize them as non-self, attacking the damaged cells as they would a pathogen. Once recognized, the immune system must be able to neutralize the foreign material. In most cases, this means killing the extracellular pathogen or killing the cell that is infected by the pathogen.

Perhaps the most challenging topic in describing the immune system is the sheer complexity of the types of blood cells involved. Cells can be named for their appearance (**leukocytes**, **granulocytes**), location (lymphocytes), or function (macrophages, **phagocytes**). Cells can also be named for their origin: T cells are produced in the thymus and B cells in bone marrow, though the *B* in B cell is derived from the bursa of Fabricus, the structure in birds where B cells were first identified. Individual cell types may have diverse functions, playing either independent or collaborative roles. Figure 10.2 shows the developmental origins of many of the immune cells that we discuss. As you make your way through this chapter, it may help to refer to Table 10.1, which lists the different types of immune cells and their roles.

FIGURE 10.2   Blood cell formation in mammals

Blood cells are derived from hematopoietic stem cells that can differentiate to form any type of hemocyte. The first round of differentiation forms two cell lines: the myeloid stem cells and the lymphoid stem cells. Most hemocytes are derived from myeloid stem cells. Lymphoid stem cells are the precursors of the lymphocytes.

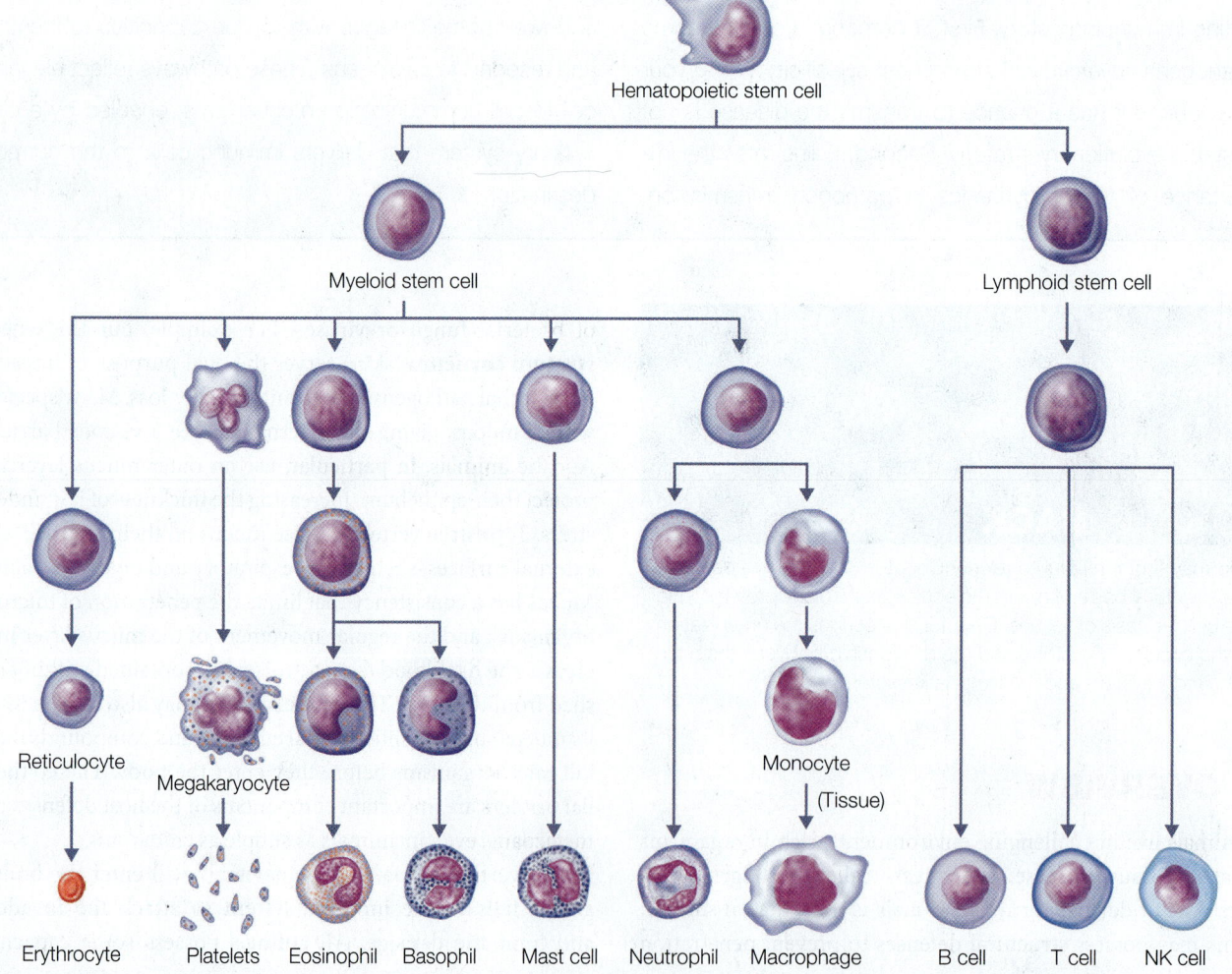

Table 10.1 Immune cells of mammals

Cell Type	Origin, Location, and Function
General terms for cell types	
Antigen-presenting cells (APCs)	Any of the phagocytes that display fragments of phagocytosed material on the outer surface of the cell, where it acts as an antigen for antigen-binding proteins, such as antibodies
Leukocytes	White blood cells include all cells that are not erythrocytes (red blood cells). They include lymphocytes, which spend much of their life in the lymph rather than the plasma.
Phagocytes	Cells that use phagocytosis; may or may not be APC
Lymphoid lineage	
Lymphocytes	Derived from lymphoblasts, these cells include NK cells, B cells, and T cells
Natural killer (NK) cells	Secrete antimicrobial and cytotoxic agents
B cells	Mature B cells produce antibodies. Specialized B cells include memory B cells and plasma cells.
T cells	Mature T cells that stimulate B cells are called helper T cells. Those that produce cytotoxic agents are killer T cells.
Monoblast lineage	
Monocytes	Produced from monoblasts, they circulate through blood and penetrate into tissues. Here they differentiate into macrophages, including dendritic cells.
Macrophages	Produced from monocytes, macrophages ("big eaters") reside in tissues until encountering pathogens, which they phagocytose. They act as APCs when they migrate to lymph nodes. Some researchers make distinctions between types of macrophages based on their anatomical location, cell-surface receptors, or cell shape. Dendritic cells are a specialized form of macrophage.
Myeloid lineage	
Polymorphonuclear (PMN) cells	PMN cells possess a nucleus arranged into lobes. They are also called granulocytes because of the abundance of secretory vesicles. The three types of PMN are neutrophils, basophils, and eosinophils.
Neutrophils	PMN cells that circulate through blood until they detect pathogens. In the tissues, they engage in phagocytosis.
Basophils	PMN cells that circulate through blood until they detect pathogens. In the tissues, they secrete cytokines and proinflammatory agents, particularly histamines.
Eosinophils	PMN cells that circulate through blood until they detect pathogens. In the tissues, they secrete cytotoxic agents and cytokines.
Mast cells	With a granular appearance similar to basophils (though not considered granulocytes), these cells reside in interstitial fluid. They are an important source of histamine, particularly in response to allergens.

There are 2 main types of immune systems, called *innate* and *adaptive*. The **innate immune system** is a collection of defenses that remain ready until needed, then respond without specificity to the type of invader. All but the simplest animals (i.e., sponges) have an innate immune system. Vertebrates also possess an additional layer of defense: the **adaptive immune system**. Both systems depend upon receptors that can detect and bind to macromolecules of pathogens. The main factor that distinguishes the two systems is the ability of the adaptive immune system to modify its response depending on the pathogen. The adaptive immune system has been called an *acquired* or *induced* immune system, because of its ability to increase the intensity of the immune response when a specific foreign body is detected a second time. We adopt the use of the term "adaptive" because it is the one most commonly used by immunologists, though it is important to recognize that "adaptive" means something different here than when used in the evolutionary sense. Invertebrates depend entirely on their innate immune system. Though vertebrates also possess an innate immune system, the adaptive immune system is more important. Furthermore, the innate system of vertebrates has derived roles, working synergistically with the adaptive immune system.

There is a wealth of research on immune systems and our discussion can only scratch the surface. In the following sections, we will discuss the two types of immune systems, considering both the diversity across taxa and the evolutionary origins of the different components. We will conclude with the ways in which the immune system integrates with other physiological systems.

INNATE IMMUNITY

The cells of the innate immune system share three main elements.

1. Cells must recognize the presence of a threat, which requires an ability to distinguish cells from its own body (self) from other material (non-self).

2. Phagocytic cells search out and engulf the foreign body, digesting it in a lysosome. These cells are also responsible for ridding the tissues of debris resulting from normal tissue breakdown.

3. Executioner cells target foreign cells, such as bacteria, or host cells that are infected with pathogens, and secrete cytotoxic compounds that either cause the cell to burst or trigger it to initiate apoptosis.

These basic components have been shown to exist in most animals, though the names of the components differ among taxa. Later in this chapter you will also see that in vertebrates, many of the components of the ubiquitous innate immune system have derived roles in adaptive immunity.

In evolutionary terms, the innate immune system is older than the adaptive immune system, as evident in its taxonomic distribution. Antimicrobial peptides occur in all multicellular organisms, though individual genes may have arisen independently multiple times. Phagocytic cells also occur across taxa, though they have roles that extend beyond immunity. For example, even simple sponges possess phagocytic cells, which contribute to digestion. In cnidarians, both the internal (endodermal) and external (ectodermal) surfaces use chemical defenses such as antimicrobial peptides to protect against microbial pathogens.

Some elements of the innate immune system are more recent. Complement proteins arose more recently, and may be restricted to deuterostome lineages. Though the specifics may differ between taxa, the presence of a vigorous innate immune system enabled the ancestors of vertebrates to evolve a more complex adaptive immune system. In many cases, elements of the innate immune system perform supporting roles in the adaptive immune system, helping to identify and execute pathogens. Conversely, the innate immune system also benefits from the activation of the adaptive immune system. In vertebrates, the two systems work together to generate a more complex immunological defense. One factor that facilitated the evolution of this complexity was the ancestral whole-genome duplications that occurred early in vertebrate evolution. The duplication of genes enabled these ancestors to amplify important immune system genes and diversify function.

Recognition of Pathogens

All types of cells have surface features that give them a unique molecular signature that animals can use to identify pathogens. Many pathogens differ from animal cells in possessing a cell wall. In fungi, the cell wall is made of chitin, whereas in bacteria it is made of complex carbohydrates including lipopolysaccharides, peptidoglycans, and β-glucans. Though viruses lack a cell wall, they possess a viral envelope composed of unique proteins and lipids. As well as surface macromolecules, many of these pathogens possess other unusual molecules, such as the double-stranded RNA genome of some viruses. Some parasitic animals have unique external features, such as the chitinous cuticle of some parasitic worms. You might think that when the parasitic animal has an external surface that seems similar to that of the infected animal, it would be more difficult to detect the parasitic animal as non-self. However, even in such cases, there are important differences between the surfaces of parasites and their hosts at the molecular level. Any of these features can be used as **pathogen-associated molecular patterns**, or **PAMPs**, which can be detected by the animal to initiate an immune response.

Pattern-recognition receptors detect pathogen-associated molecular patterns

The cells of the innate immune system move through the tissues searching for PAMPs. The immune cells possess their own external receptors for PAMPs, called **pattern-recognition receptors** or **PRRs**. When a PRR binds its PAMP, the cell responds by triggering signal transduction pathways that initiate an immune response.

PRRs are typically found on the cell membrane or in the cytoplasm, but they can also be secreted into the plasma. The success of the innate immune system hinges on the animal possessing a wide repertoire of PRRs, enabling the immune cells to recognize diverse pathogens. Central to the variation in PRRs are mechanisms that generate genetic variation, either through mutations or through gene and genome duplications, followed by structural divergence. Thus, most animals have large gene families of PRRs and in many

Table 10.2 Pattern-recognition receptors in animals

| Gene/Protein Family[1] | Taxa | Mechanism of Diversity[2] | | | | Target |
| | | DNA | | RNA | | |
		GF	SR	AS	RE	
Crustins	crustaceans				x	bacteria
Dscam	arthropods			x		bacteria
FREP	mollusks, arthropods	x	x			trematodes, fungi, bacteria
NLR	widespread	x				bacteria
Penaeidins	crustaceans	x				bacteria, fungi
PGRP	widespread					bacteria
RLR	widespread	x				viruses
Sp185/333	echinoderms	x			x	chitin
TLR	widespread	x				bacteria, fungi, viruses, protists
VCBP	cephalochordates	x				chitin

Source: Based on Ghosh J., Lun C. M., Majeske A. J., Sacchi S., Schrankel C. S., & Smith L. C., 2011. Invertebrate immune diversity. *Developmental and Comparative Immunology 35*, 959–974.

[1]Dscam = Down Syndrome cell adhesion molecules; FREP = Fibrinogen-related proteins; NLR = Nucleotide oligomerization domain (Nod)-like receptors; PGRP = peptidoglycan recognition proteins; RLR = retinoic acid–inducible gene (RIG)-1-like receptors; TLR = toll-like receptors; VCBP = Variable domain-containing chitin binding proteins.
[2]GF = gene families; SR = somatic recombination; AS = alternate splicing; RE = RNA editing.

cases individual genes may generate proteins of different sequences through processes such as alternative splicing.

In recent years, the list of known PRRs has grown exponentially, with both new receptors and new variants identified (Table 10.2). Some proteins, such as **toll-like receptors**, or **TLRs**, occur in widely different taxa and may be present in all animals. Typically, animals possess large gene families of TLRs, with subtypes specialized to bind specific pathogen macromolecules. Other PRRs appear to have more limited taxonomic distribution, though it may be that homologues have simply not yet been identified in other taxa. These may exist as gene families within the taxon; but more often, variation in receptor structure arises from nonheritable (somatic) genetic changes and RNA processing. Though we do not discuss any of the PRRs in Table 10.2 in detail, each has an intriguing evolutionary history (what was the ancestral gene?), molecular mechanism (how does amino acid sequence variation arise?), and structural basis (how does it recognize its target?). However, we will consider the near-ubiquitous TLRs in more detail in the next section.

Toll-like receptors activate immune responses

Toll, from the German word for *amazing*, was first identified in fruit flies as a gene involved in normal development, and later was found to play an important role in protection against fungal infection. Toll-like receptors (TLRs) have since been found in almost all animals, playing diverse roles in cell function, including but not limited to the immune response.

Because of its importance in immunity, the TLR gene family is often studied in humans. Each of the 10 TLRs in humans binds a distinct PAMP. Evolutionary analysis of TLRs reveals large, multimember families, and the nature of the families differs widely among taxa. Several of the TLRs in mice have been lost in humans. More than 20 different TLRs have been identified in vertebrates. Fish possess 16 TLRs; some are homologous to those in humans and other tetrapods, whereas a number are unique to fish (including some that are even restricted to specific fish lineages). Within vertebrates, the whole-genome duplications that occurred early in vertebrate evolution may have played a role in the number of gene duplicates available for natural selection. Some early deuterostomes, such as sea urchins and *Amphioxus*, may each possess more than 200 TLRs. The appearance of the adaptive immune system in the early vertebrates probably influenced the evolutionary radiation of the TLR gene family, along with other elements of the innate immune system of vertebrates.

Though the ligands may differ between TLRs, the signal transduction pathway has many conserved features (Figure 10.3). Once the TLR binds its PAMP ligand, the structural changes are transmitted through the transmembrane portion of the receptor, allowing the cytoplasmic domain to recruit specific proteins. These in turn, modify other proteins, which alter the DNA-binding activity or the

FIGURE 10.3 **Toll-like receptors and signaling**

(a) Each TLR possesses an external ligand-binding domain consisting of multiple leucine-rich repeats (LRR), a transmembrane domain (TM), and an internal TIR (toll/interleukin-1 receptor) domain that mediates the signaling cascade. **(b)** Once a PAMP is bound, a signaling cascade begins by recruitment of other adaptor proteins possessing a TIR, activation of transcription factors such as NFκB, and culminating in secretion of cytokines such as interferons, tumor necrosis factor, and interleukins.

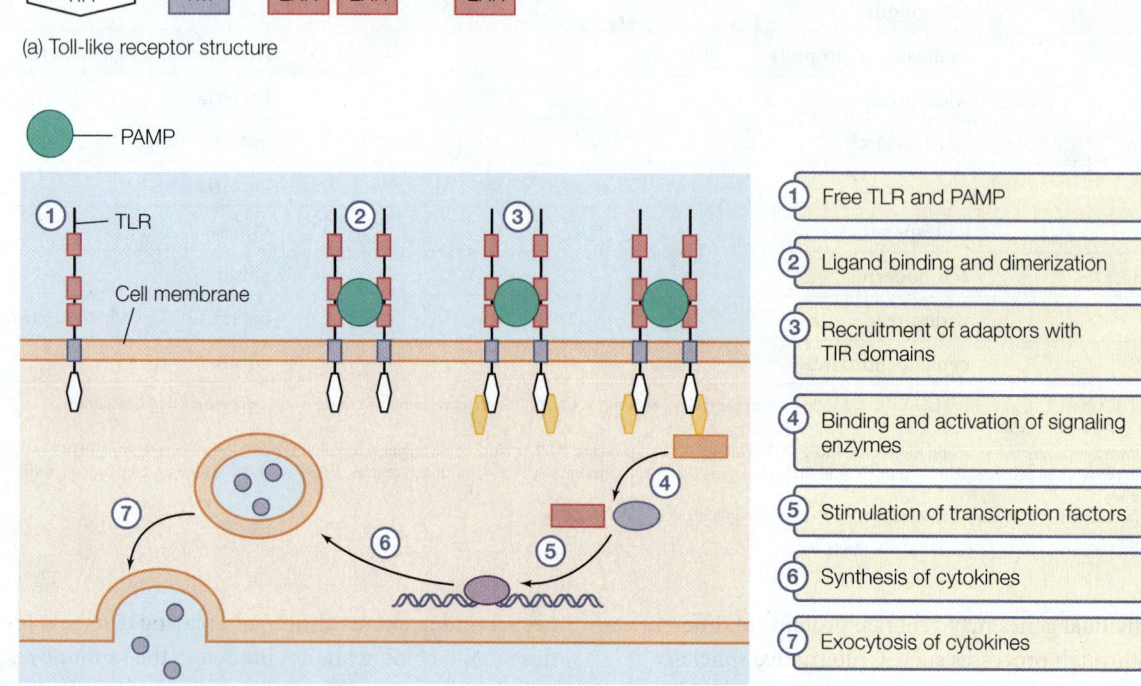

(a) Toll-like receptor structure

①	Free TLR and PAMP
②	Ligand binding and dimerization
③	Recruitment of adaptors with TIR domains
④	Binding and activation of signaling enzymes
⑤	Stimulation of transcription factors
⑥	Synthesis of cytokines
⑦	Exocytosis of cytokines

(b) Toll-like receptor signaling pathway

location of transcription factors that control genes for cytokines: interleukin regulates lymphocyte function, tumor necrosis factor kills animal cells, and interferons interfere with viral replication. The nature of the signaling pathway that results upon activation of a given TLR depends on which of the various adaptor proteins the cell makes. In this way, a TLR may trigger a range of immunological responses.

Phagocytic Cells

Many of the leukocyte types shown in Figure 10.2 use phagocytosis to clear pathogens and cellular debris from the tissues. Much of this foreign material accumulates in the extracellular fluid, and thus many of the phagocytic cells of the immune system reside in the interstitial fluid. The main types of phagocytes involved in the innate immune response are **neutrophils** and **macrophages** (see Table 10.1). Both of these phagocytic cells also participate in the adaptive immune system, but we will consider such functions later in the chapter. Though most animals have phagocytic cells that play a role in the immune system, the names used to describe the cells differ between species and fields. Macrophages, for example, share a common origin but other names are often used to refer to macrophages in specific tissues. In some species, phagocytic cells may have different development origins and go by other names, such as the hemocytes and plasmatocytes of *Drosophila*.

Phagocytic cells engulf and digest foreign cells

Neutrophils, the most abundant of the leukocytes in mammals, are the main phagocytes found in the blood. They display a nucleus with many lobes, giving rise to the name **polymorphonuclear (PMN)** cells. Neutrophils can be distinguished from the other types of PMN cells (basophils and eosinophils) by the histological stain mixture of hematoxylin and eosin (H&E stain). Whereas other PMN cells stain either dark blue (basophils) or bright red (eosinophils), neutrophils stain an intermediate, or neutral, pink. In addition to phagocytosis, neutrophils can kill microbes by secreting antimicrobial agents.

Whereas neutrophils use their abundance to overwhelm microbes, **macrophages** employ a more directed approach to detecting and destroying pathogens. The progenitor of macrophages, called **monocytes**, flow through the circulation until they detect a signal emitted from a damaged region of the tissue. They squeeze between the endothelial cells of the capillaries to invade the surrounding tissue. Once there, they undergo a series of changes that transform the monocyte into a macrophage. As the name suggests, macrophages are large phagocytic cells. They eat bacteria, as do neutrophils, but they are also large enough to ingest the neutrophils themselves, targeting those cells that have ingested or been infected by bacteria.

Active macrophages also secrete chemical signals, or **cytokines**, that induce changes in other cells. When the resulting changes cause the target cell to move, the cytokine is considered a **chemokine** (Figure 10.4). In vertebrates, the important cytokines include tumor necrosis factor α and many members of the interleukin family. Each of these targets specific cells to contribute to the immune response.

Opsonins promote phagocytosis

Recall that some immune cells express membrane PRRs that bind the PAMPs that are expressed by pathogens and displayed on the surface of the pathogen. When the receptor is occupied, a signal transduction cascade ensues in the cell possessing the PRR, which may include secretion of cytotoxic compounds or promotion of phagocytosis. Animals possess another line of defense that depends on detection of PRRs, in this case by soluble proteins that act as PRRs. Instead of initiating a signaling cascade, these PRRs mark the pathogen as a target for phagocytosis by immune cells.

Opsonization is a general term that includes any process that marks a pathogen for phagocytosis by coating it with soluble proteins, collectively **opsonins** (not to be confused with opsins). One of the best examples of an opsonin is **mannose-binding lectin**, a protein secreted from the liver and found circulating throughout the body. Lectin is a general term for a protein that binds a sugar moiety on a glycoprotein, so this protein is named because of its ability to bind mannose-containing glycoproteins. This protein binds specifically to mannose-linked glycoproteins, which are common on microbes, and very rare on healthy animal cells. Thus, mannose-binding lectin is a PRR, which binds to mannose-linked glycoproteins, which act as PAMPs. Mannose-binding lectins are members of a larger group of soluble opsonins known as collectins. Another important opsonin is C-reactive protein, which is a member of the pentraxin family. Like other aspects of the innate immune system, these proteins are widespread in metazoans.

The specific pathways that are induced by binding of soluble PRRs differ widely, but in general, the tagging of a

---

FIGURE 10.4 Secretion of cytokines by macrophages

Macrophages produce and secrete various signaling molecules, including chemokines and other cytokines. These act on suites of cells to stimulate the immune response.

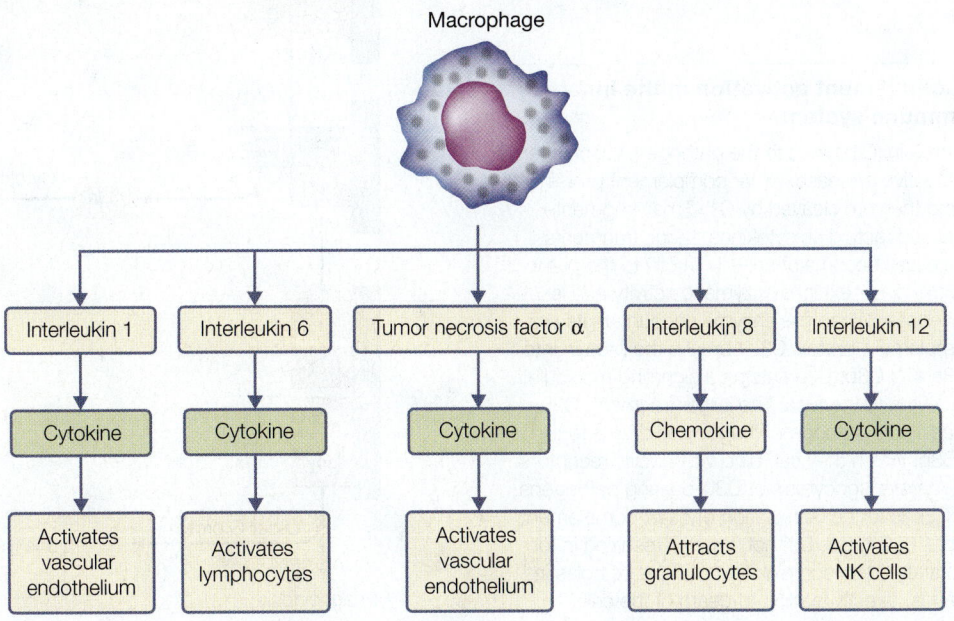

pathogen with soluble PRRs promotes a series of protein–protein interactions that induce phagocytes to bind and engulf the pathogen.

In addition to these PRRs, two other important pathways are included under the umbrella of opsonization. Later in this chapter we consider the function of antibodies, which bind pathogens to facilitate destruction of the cell by the immune system. Another type of opsonization is mediated by a collection of soluble proteins known as complement.

Complement molecules promote other immune processes

Found within the circulation of vertebrates and many invertebrates is a collection of proteins known as **complement**, or the complement system. This name derives from the ability to help other immune components perform their functions. These proteins circulate in an inactive form and become sequentially activated in response to molecular signatures of pathogens.

Once bound to a pathogen, a series of steps leads to activation of the complement. There are three main pathways that are distinguished by the specific proteins involved upstream and downstream of the complex known as C3 convertase. The classical pathway (Figure 10.5) begins when a multifunctional protein, C1, binds the pathogen. Though it is capable of binding the pathogen directly, as shown in Figure 10.5, the activation more commonly occurs when C1 is localized to the pathogen by associating with an antibody attached to a surface antigen from the pathogen. We will discuss the interactions between the complement system and adaptive immunity later in this chapter.

Like so many of the components of the immune system, the origins of complement are difficult to determine with

certainty. One group of complement proteins, C3, C4, and C5, has a shared ancestry and probably diverged from a single gene after the splitting of the deuterostome and protostome lineages. The diversification of these proteins probably arose during the radiation of the deuterostomes. There appear to be no homologues in early chordates and agnathans (jawless vertebrates), but recent studies have shown C3-like proteins in a number of invertebrates, including corals (cnidarians) and horseshoe crabs. These examples are significant because they represent completely different lineages: Corals are cnidarians and lack true tissues, whereas horseshoe crabs and

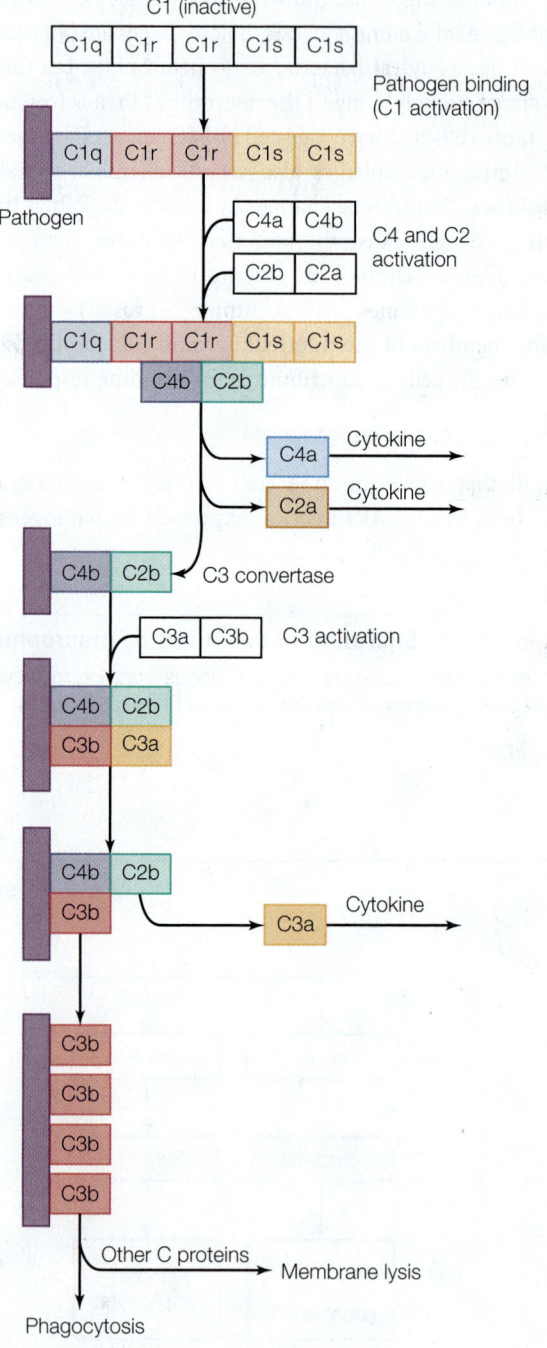

FIGURE 10.5 Complement activation in the innate immune system

The complement protein (C1) binds to the pathogen, which alters parts of C1 into an active protease. Other complement proteins (C2, C4) bind to and then are cleaved by C1. Small fragments (C4a, C2a) are released, acting as cytokines. Large fragments (C2b, C4b) combine and become attached directly to the pathogen surface. Here the dimer exhibits enzymatic activity and is known as C3 convertase. When this enzyme encounters its protein substrate, complement protein C3, it breaks the protein into two fragments: C3a and C3b. C3a acts as a signaling molecule that attracts phagocytes to the area. The larger fragment, C3b, binds to the surface of the pathogen. Phagocytes drawn to the region by C3a find C3b, which they can bind via specific receptors. This interaction triggers phagocytosis of C3b-bearing pathogens. Another action of C3b is further stimulation of other complement proteins (e.g., C5b, C6, C7, C8, C9; not shown), resulting in formation of a membrane-attack complex that can create holes in pathogen membranes, directly leading to death of the cell.

ancient arthropods are protostomes. The exact origin of the complement genes remains uncertain, but the recent proliferation in genomic sequencing has challenged the conventional thinking of the evolutionary origins of the complement system. Later in this chapter, we will return to the complement system to consider its role in adaptive immunity.

CONCEPT CHECK

4. What are the main phagocytic cells?
5. How do phagocytic cells decide what to eat?
6. What is the complement system?

Executing Pathogens in the Innate Immune System

Once a pathogen is detected, the cells of the immune system start the process of recruiting additional cells to the region and activating the various cells that contribute to the response. We have discussed the role of phagocytes in engulfing bacteria, but the defenses are far more complex and include cells that secrete suites of toxic compounds, killing pathogens and infected cells. The entire collection of cells can be directed to a site of infection, triggering broader changes in the vasculature to promote pathogen defense and initiate healing.

Granulocytes and natural killer cells secrete cytotoxic compounds

In mammals, several types of leukocytes act as executioners. Two types of granulocytes, **eosinophils** and **basophils**, are derived from myeloblasts. These cells are typically *granulocytes*, so named because they are rich in secretory vesicles, giving the cell a granular appearance. **Natural killer cells** (NK cells) are derived from lymphoblasts (see Figure 10.2). Each of these is attracted to the area of pathogen attack, and each responds by killing the pathogens or the cells containing the pathogens. The executioners may secrete cytotoxic chemicals to kill the pathogen or induce an infected host cell to undergo apoptosis, trapping viral particles within the cell and subjecting them to controlled degradation.

Though these executioner cells differ in terms of their control and the nature of their contents, there are some similarities in the way they work. Each cell expresses receptors, such as TLR, that await contact with a pathogen. When it detects its target, the signaling pathway triggers secretion of the contents of the storage vesicles, a process called degranulation. The cells have different profiles of cytotoxic compounds, as well as additional products that regulate the immune response, such as cytokines and pro-inflammatory mediators that we discuss in the next section. The cytotoxic compounds act by different mechanisms, targeting specific structures and processes in pathogens. NK cell secretions, for example, include perforins, granzymes, and defensins. These proteins are cytotoxic to bacteria, fungi, and many viruses. Perforins and defensins enter target membranes and form pores, which permits the efflux of intracellular solutes. Granzymes are proteases that attack the cell surface and also enter through the perforin pores, digesting bacterial proteins from within. Eosinophils and basophils also secrete their own cytotoxic chemicals, but they play additional roles in immunoregulation. Both secrete signaling molecules (such as leukotrienes and interleukins) and proteases (such as elastase). Basophils also secrete histamines and play an important role in allergic responses.

Antimicrobial peptides can be secreted by many cell types in all multicellular organisms

The cells involved in the execution of pathogens secrete antimicrobial agents that specifically kill bacteria. More than 1,000 peptides have been identified that are produced by organisms and that possess an ability to kill microbes. Some may act by binding bacterial membranes, forming channels that alter membrane integrity. Others enter a bacterium, where they inactivate vital bacterial proteins to prevent replication or cause death. Some antimicrobial peptides are secreted out of the cell, whereas others are released intracellularly to attack bacteria that have entered the cell.

The best studied of these antimicrobial agents is **defensin**, a small peptide secreted by immune cells. Defensin genes are found across the animal kingdom and even occur in plants, which suggests an ancient evolutionary origin. In mammals, α-defensins are secreted by NK cells, as well as by other cell types, such as neutrophils. The β-defensins are secreted by numerous cells throughout the body, primarily the epithelial cells lining external surfaces, such as the respiratory tract, that constitute the first line of defense.

Antimicrobial peptides play a vital role in the control of microbial growth in many systems. They can be secreted by epithelial cells of most of the tissues that encounter the external world, from the digestive tract to the respiratory surface and even the excretory system. In addition to a role in fighting infections, they may be important in modulating the microbial communities of the small intestine, which play a vital role in digestion.

Inflammation is an early response to pathogens and tissue damage

In the region of a tissue where pathogens have invaded, there is a flurry of activity arising from the actions of the immune system (Figure 10.6). Central to the successful defense against infection is the ability to recruit cells that fight the

FIGURE 10.6 **Cellular responses to pathogens**

(a) Bacteria cross the epithelial layer and enter into the interstitial fluid. Macrophages in the interstitium detect the pathogens
through their PRRs (not shown here). **(b)** The interaction induces
phagocytosis and causes macrophages to degranulate, releasing
the signaling factors stored in vesicles. These include chemokines
to attract other cells, such as NK cells, and cytokines to induce
signaling responses in other cells, such as the endothelium.

(c) Changes in the arterioles permit passage of more blood
through the tissue (signified by extra erythrocytes) and changes
in the endothelium allow more immune cells into the region, and
permit escape of serum from the blood into the interstitium, causing edema (depicted here as a change in the color of the interstitial fluid). Recruitment of more phagocytes and stimulation of
cytotoxic secretions from killer cells combat the bacterial invasion.

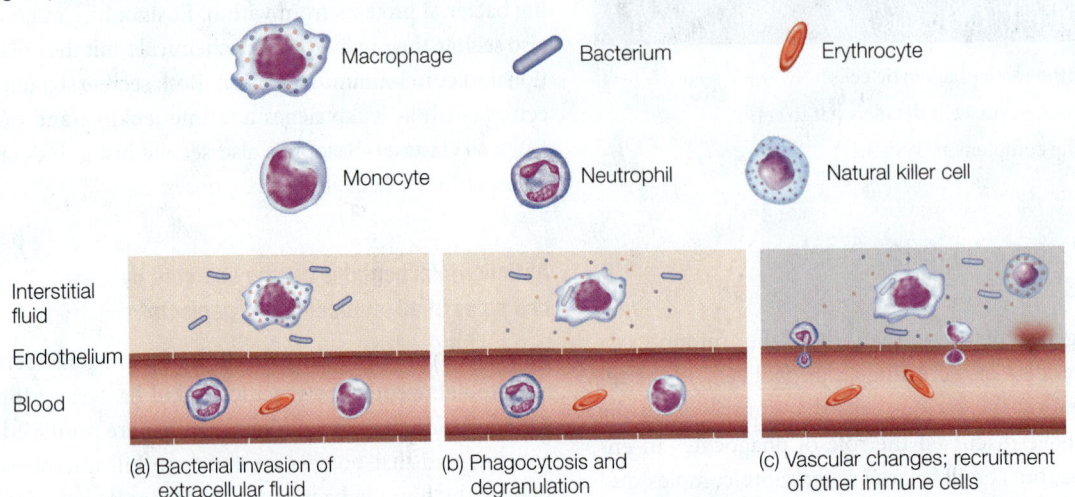

Macrophage   Bacterium   Erythrocyte

Monocyte   Neutrophil   Natural killer cell

Interstitial fluid
Endothelium
Blood

(a) Bacterial invasion of
extracellular fluid

(b) Phagocytosis and
degranulation

(c) Vascular changes; recruitment
of other immune cells

infection and promote the repair of any damage that ensues.
The **inflammatory response** refers to local changes sparked
by tissue damage, including increased blood flow, changes in
vascular permeability to cells and fluids, recruitment of immune cells, and, in some cases, elevated tissue temperature.
The name *inflammation* originated from observations in
humans, where the immune response causes the skin to become red and warm as more blood is delivered to the region.
Other animals may not manifest the inflammatory response
in the same manner; poikilotherms, for example, are unlikely
to experience elevated temperatures locally as a result of altered blood flow.

The detection of the PAMP of a pathogen by a PRR of
an immune cell leads to the secretion of cytokines that act
as inflammatory mediators. Some are chemotactic molecules
that attract other phagocytes to the region. Interleukins, for
example, cause endothelial cells of the capillaries to express
proteins that help recruit leukocytes to the area. Others act
as neurotransmitters or other modifiers of neuronal activity.
For example, histamine released from mast cells sensitizes the
nerves that act as pain receptors. Some affect exocrine glands,
stimulating the secretion of mucus or fluids. Collectively,
these cytokines exert effects that manifest as inflammation,
with five signs: pain, heat, redness, swelling, and impaired
function. Within the vasculature, the cytokines cause arterioles to dilate, permitting more blood into the capillaries,
making the area red. In warm-bodied animals, this permits
more of the warm blood from the body core to perfuse the

cooler body surface, resulting in local warming. The greater
flow through the vasculature allows more of the plasma to
leak into the interstitial fluid, resulting in edema. The endothelial cells of the capillaries also change their permeability by
facilitating the transfer of immune cells across the capillary
wall into the interstitial fluid. Many of the recruited immune
cells release cytokines that stimulate pain receptors, such as
histamine. The fifth sign of inflammation, impaired function,
depends on the location of the tissue damage and the effects
of both the pathogen and the immune response.

The nature of the inflammatory response also differs
among tissues. For example, inflammation causes vascular
smooth muscle to dilate, increasing the **perfusion** through arterioles into capillary beds. However, inflammatory mediators
cause nonvascular smooth muscle to contract. In the respiratory system, the constriction of airways reduces the airflow
into the lungs. The reasons for the differences in the response
are related to both cellular differences in the smooth muscle
and the profile of mediators released by local immune cells.
Later in this chapter we will consider the role of inflammation
in the response of the respiratory system to allergens.

7. What types of cells kill pathogens by secretion of antimicrobial agents and other cytotoxic compounds?

8. What are the five cardinal signs of inflammation and how
do they arise?

ADAPTIVE IMMUNITY OF VERTEBRATES

Both the innate and adaptive immune systems have proteins that bind to specific pathogen molecules. Where they differ is in the ability to selectively amplify clones of cells that produce specific antigen-binding proteins. When a vertebrate is exposed to a novel bacterium, for example, the bacterial surface proteins will be bound by PRRs from the innate system as well as antibodies from the adaptive immune system. Each of these events leads to cellular changes and signal transduction pathways that stimulate immune cells. However, the adaptive immune system is able to identify which immune cells produce the correct antibody and specifically amplify those cells, bolstering the specific immune response. Furthermore, clones of these cells can be retained long term, creating an **immunological memory**. When the animal is exposed to the same pathogen a second time, the innate system responds as before, but the adaptive immune system is primed to mount a more rapid, more dramatic immune response.

The adaptive immune system of vertebrates is extremely complex, with individual proteins (such as antibodies) playing many roles, and a great many types of immune cells collaborating to detect and kill pathogens. Some features of the adaptive immune system are similar across vertebrates. For example, all vertebrates make two types of lymphocytes (B cells and T cells) and do so in different anatomical locations. There are also differences among taxa, such as the mechanism by which diversity arises in the receptors for antigens. Though the adaptive immune system occurs only in vertebrates, the current evidence suggests that it arose at least twice, once in jawless vertebrates (agnathans) and once in jawed vertebrates.

The immune system is often divided between humoral and cellular immunity. The term humoral derives from *humors*, a term that was once used to refer to the various body fluids. Thus, **humoral immunity** refers to those processes mediated by components in solution (e.g., antibodies or complement proteins), while **cellular immunity** refers to processes directly involving cells. Both the innate and adaptive immune systems employ cellular and acellular components, and each has a humoral and a cellular component. Furthermore, the proteins of the humoral response are produced by cells, so the distinction is a bit artificial. Nonetheless, it is useful in delineating the components of the adaptive immune system.

Both humoral and cellular immunity rely on proteins that recognize specific antigens. These proteins belong to the immunoglobulin (Ig) superfamily, and the members share a structural feature known as the Ig domain. These are so named because they were first identified in immunoglobulins, which are more commonly known as antibodies. The basic Ig domain arose early in animal evolution. It was such a useful structure that it was duplicated hundreds of times, becoming part of a great many genes, only some of which have roles in immunity. Many of the Ig superfamily are cell adhesion molecules, surface receptors that allow cells to bind to the extracellular matrix of other cells. Such functions are important in all metazoans, but the evolution of adaptive immunity required coevolution of a series of Ig superfamily members. The complexity and variability of these genes make it difficult to establish the exact evolutionary trajectory of those Ig superfamily members with roles in adaptive immunity: immunoglobulins (usually called antibodies), B-cell receptors (BCR), T-cell receptors (TCR), and major histocompatibility complexes (MHC). These genes share structural and functional features, such as Ig domains and antigen binding. As you will discover, what happens after the antigen binds the Ig superfamily protein depends on the cell bearing the protein and the signaling cascades activated in response to binding.

Central to the utility of these immunity genes is the ability of each to undergo genetic mutations. Before discussing the function of specific Ig superfamily members, we will consider how cells use an Ig gene as the blueprint for a huge repertoire of Ig proteins. Each Ig gene is composed of a series of repeats of four types of DNA fragments: V (variable), D (diversity), J (joining), and C (constant). The gene depicted in Figure 10.7 has n copies each of V, D, J, and **C regions** arranged in clusters. Some of the regions may be as small as six nucleotides. Others are larger, with their own introns.

FIGURE 10.7 Immunoglobulin gene structure

The basic structure of Ig genes includes n repeats of V, D, J, and C regions separated by introns. These are not drawn to scale and introns are not shown. Repeats of the C regions are usually assigned Greek letters (α, δ, ε, γ, μ) rather than numbers.

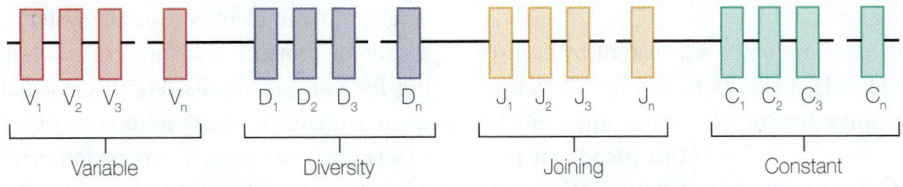

TRANSGENIC MOSQUITOES

Mosquitoes are vectors for transmission of many pathogens, and considerable effort has been invested in mechanisms that would remove them from the chain of transmission. Malaria is a disease of vertebrates arising from infection of the blood with *Plasmodium*, a protist parasite. Each species of *Plasmodium* relies on a specific mosquito vector in which it can develop to the infective stage. Human malaria, which affects hundreds of millions of people, is transmitted by an infected *Anopheles* mosquito. This mosquito first ingests *Plasmodium falciparum* and while in the gut the parasites differentiate to become male microgametes and female macrogametes. After their fusion the zygotes mature into ookinetes, which move through the peritrophic membrane surrounding the food bolus, and enter the digestive tract of the mosquito. Within the mosquito, they continue to develop to form the infective sporozoite, which swims through the hemolymph and invades the salivary glands. These sporozoites are transferred to the human during feeding. The sporozoites then mature and reproduce within the human, giving rise to gametocytes.

The complexity of the life cycle (Figure 10.8) is such that there are

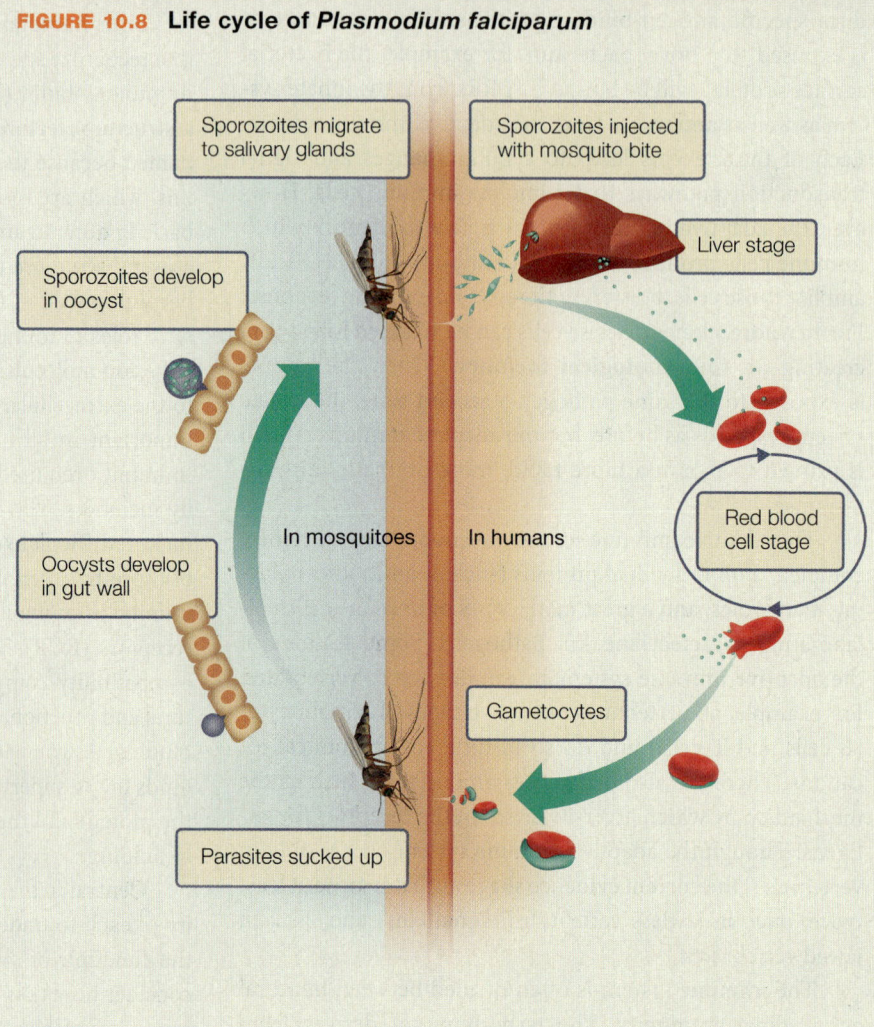

FIGURE 10.8 **Life cycle of *Plasmodium falciparum***

Sporozoites migrate to salivary glands

Sporozoites injected with mosquito bite

Liver stage

Sporozoites develop in oocyst

In mosquitoes

In humans

Red blood cell stage

Oocysts develop in gut wall

Gametocytes

Parasites sucked up

The collection of coding regions, separated by introns, may extend to over 2 million base pairs.

In addition to the V, D, J, and C regions, Ig superfamily genes have regions that encode important structural features. There are regions that designate a protein for secretion, transmembrane domains that affix a receptor to a membrane, and less structured regions that can act as linkers or hinges between regions.

This pattern of repeating units is displayed by each of the genes for antibodies/Ig, BCR, TCR, and MHC, though the numbers and arrangement of the regions differ among genes. Consider, for example, the genes that encode the proteins of an antibody. It is composed of two identical light chains and two identical heavy chains (discussed later in this chapter). Humans have two different light-chain genes (λ, κ), each lacking D regions, and one heavy-chain gene, which possesses almost 30 D regions in the germline.

Humoral Immunity

The cells of the adaptive immune system produce and secrete a suite of proteins that disperse through the body, searching for non-self motifs. We discussed the role of complement proteins in innate immunity, but they also contribute to adaptive immunity. The most important soluble factors in adaptive immunity are antibodies. Much like the recognition

many potential points of attack that could be used to stop the chain of transmission. Approaches have targeted the insect (e.g., insecticides, mosquito nets) or the *Plasmodium* (e.g., antimalarial drugs), yet despite some success, malaria remains a problem worldwide. Some researchers have focused efforts on the physiology of the mosquito, exploring mechanisms to enable the mosquito to prevent its own infection upon feeding. Recently, Anthony James from the University of California at Davis, working with an international team of colleagues, developed a genetic approach to allow the mosquito to attack the sporozoites within the blood meal before they can invade its tissues. These transgenic *Anopheles* mosquitoes express synthetic antibodies against parasite proteins.

The research team evaluated three potential targets: the chitinase enzyme that the parasite uses to break down the peritrophic membrane, an uncharacterized 25kDa protein that appears in development, and a protein that coats the surface of the sporozoite. The team then created genes that encode antibodies able to bind these specific antigens. Recall that natural antibodies consist of multiple protein chains, and antigen specificity arises from structural interactions between the separate chains that make up the variable region. It would be challenging to create **transgenic animals** that produced the appropriate amounts of each chain and assembled them as would happen in a B cell. Genetic engineers have created synthetic variants of antibodies that are encoded by single genes and possess structures that mimic the variable region of natural antibodies. These single-chain variable fragments (scFv) act by binding specific antigens just as would natural antibodies. Mosquito embryos were injected with a solution containing the DNA that encoded the antibody and the RNA for the enzyme that allowed the DNA to integrate stably into the mosquito genome. The researchers' next goal was to express combinations of scFv genes and do so in the right tissues at the correct times.

The transgenic mosquitoes were adept at blocking the transmission of sporozoites. In some combinations, transgenes completely prevented the mosquito from becoming infected after eating blood from an infected host. With such promise in the lab, the next step is to explore options to release these transgenic mosquitoes into the natural environment. If the transgenic mosquitoes were less fit, in an evolutionary sense, than the wild-type mosquitoes, they would fail to prosper in the natural environment. This is why the researchers placed great emphasis on creating transgenic mosquitoes that showed no signs of decline in fitness.

Reference

- Isaacs, A.T., Jasinskiene, N., Tretiakovb, M., Thieryc, I., Zettorc, A., Bourgouinc, C., & James, A. A. (2012). Transgenic *Anopheles stephensi* coexpressing single-chain antibodies resist *Plasmodium falciparum* development. *Proceedings of the National Academy of Sciences (USA)*, *109*, E1922–E1930.

of PAMPs by PRRs of the innate immune system, proteins of the immunoglobulin superfamily are able to recognize pathogen molecules. Whereas PRRs detect specific molecules that are characteristic of pathogens, antibodies recognize short stretches of macromolecular structure that are foreign to the body. **Antigens** are macromolecules, usually protein, that can be bound specifically by antibodies. Even when a particular macromolecule binds an immune protein that is not an antibody, it is often still referred to as an antigen if it has the capacity to bind an antibody.

Antibodies are a powerful tool in the immune system because of their ability to bind specific antigens. Biotechnologists have capitalized on this property by developing numerous analytical tools that rely on antibodies, including immunohistochemistry, enzyme-linked immunosorbant assays (ELISA), and immunoblots. Recently, researchers studying malaria have created transgenes encoding synthetic antibodies in an innovative approach for tackling the transmission of malaria (Box 10.1: Applications: Transgenic Mosquitoes).

Antibodies are composed of variable and constant regions

The structure of an antibody (Figure 10.9) reveals a Y-shaped protein with two arms and a stalk. This three-dimensional shape arises through the arrangement of four

FIGURE 10.9   Antibody structure

Antibodies are composed of four chains, linked together by cross-bridges. Immunologists refer to specific regions of the antibody by subdividing the structure into domains.

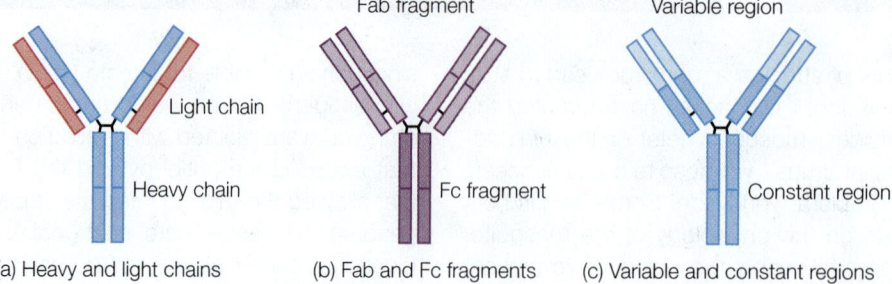

(a) Heavy and light chains   (b) Fab and Fc fragments   (c) Variable and constant regions

---

separate polypeptides: two identical Ig heavy chains and two identical Ig light chains. In select regions, the heavy and light chains are joined by cross-bridges, stabilizing the structure. Some of the earliest studies showed that subjecting the antibody to protease treatment breaks the protein into two regions: The Fab fragment retains the ability to bind antigen, whereas the Fc fragment cannot. Within the Fab fragment, the variable or V region differs between antibodies. The remaining region is conserved in structure among antibodies, and is called the constant or **C region**. The unique specificity of the antibody arises from random mutations affecting the first 110 amino acids of two separate proteins, which collectively determine the structure and binding properties of the V region.

Diversity in immunoglobulins arises through gene recombination

The immune cells that produce antibodies are the B cells. Later in this chapter we will consider the cellular changes that B cells experience as they transform from undifferentiated stem cells into antibody factories. To understand how the collection of B cells generates the repertoire of antibodies,

we have to discuss how the genes are mutated, permitting them to differ between the germline and the specialized cells arising in lymphocyte differentiation.

Recall that antibodies are composed of two Ig light chains and two Ig heavy chains. The Ig genes for a mammal start off as identical in all cells of the body, but in the cells that become lymphocytes, genetic mutations and assembly or conversion processes occur. Thus, a lymphocyte modifies its own Ig genes in unique ways, getting rid of many V, D, and J regions. The gene that remains in that cell possesses a unique VDJ region, in addition to a standard suite of C regions (Figure 10.10). The number and type of many of these regions (V, D, J, and C) differ among species.

The mechanism by which vertebrates accomplish somatic diversification differs among vertebrates. In jawed vertebrates, the key to this genetic hypervariation is a collection of enzymes that are capable of recombining the V, D, and J regions randomly. These regions are flanked by gene segments called recombination signal sequences (RSSs), which are recognized by enzymes known as recombinases. The reason this process is restricted to lymphocyte genes is because only lymphocytes express a recombinase enzyme called recombination activating gene (RAG).

FIGURE 10.10   Recombination of the Ig heavy chain

In the germline, each cell possesses a full collection of V, D, J, and C regions. In this lymphocyte, the genes have been mutated such that the rearranged gene possesses a single copy of each of the V, J, and D regions, plus eight C regions.

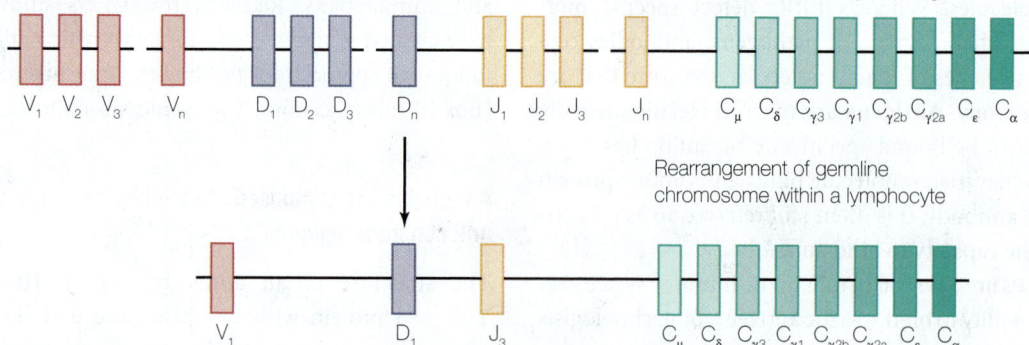

FIGURE 10.11 **Ig heavy chain gene expression**

The gene is transcribed and edited. The pre-mRNA is spliced to remove the unwanted regions, such as introns and exons encoding undesired C minigenes. The cell is able to make

Ig heavy chains with any of the C minigenes (only three of the options are depicted here).

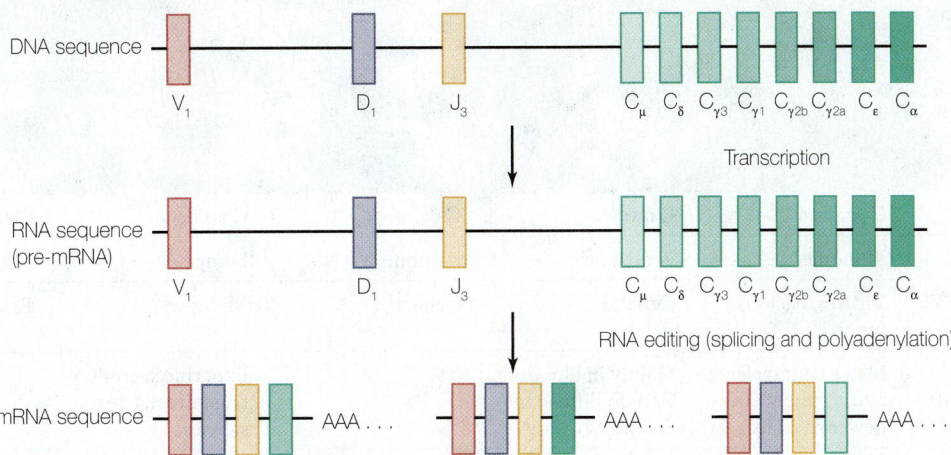

In jawless vertebrates, gene conversion rather than gene recombination is used; the enzyme cytodine deaminase alters the nucleotide sequence of the critical genes, which in these animals encode variable lymphocyte receptors (VLRs). Jawless fish also lack immunoglobulins and use other proteins, called variable lymphocyte receptors (VLRs), to detect the presence of non-self macromolecules. The differences between jawed and jawless fish suggest that the two pathways evolved independently in these two vertebrate lineages.

Antibody classes differ in the C regions

Any B cell has undergone genetic changes that endow it with a unique combination of VDJ regions to produce an Ig. However, each version of the gene possesses a number of C regions. Once the mRNA is produced, the cell uses alternative splicing (see Chapter 3) to create a transcript with the appropriate combinations of C regions (Figure 10.11).

Once the transcript is produced, the B cell uses translation to synthesize the heavy chain protein, then folds it properly and assembles it into the final structure (Figure 10.12).

The ability of a B cell to produce proteins with similar antigen binding but different C regions permits it to synthesize Ig with diverse functions. Mammals have five main classes of immunoglobulins (IgA, IgD, IgE, IgG, and IgM), which differ in the structure of their C regions as well as in their post-translational glycosylations (Table 10.3). Some are better at being detected and bound by phagocytes, others better at recruiting complement proteins or being targeted to **exocrine secretions** such as tears, saliva, or milk. The classes may also differ in the type of pathogen they are best able to attack. Within each class, some species have multiple

variants. For example, humans have four types of IgG and two types of IgA. A single B cell clone may, over the course of its lifetime, produce each class and type of antibody, each possessing the same V, D, and J regions.

The study of the evolution of antibodies has generated many questions about the origin of the diversity seen across vertebrates. Recall that the genes encoding the Ig domain characteristic of Ig superfamily proteins existed long before this namesake. How antibodies arose in early vertebrates remains an open question, though recent genomic studies on diverse vertebrates have helped clarify their evolutionary history. IgM appears to be the most ancient of the Ig genes. It is present in most vertebrates, its structure is very highly conserved, and it is also the first class to be produced in

FIGURE 10.12 **Ig heavy chain synthesis and folding**

In this figure, more detail is provided for the relative sizes of the VDJC minigenes, depicting three different regions of the Cδ region included in the transcript.

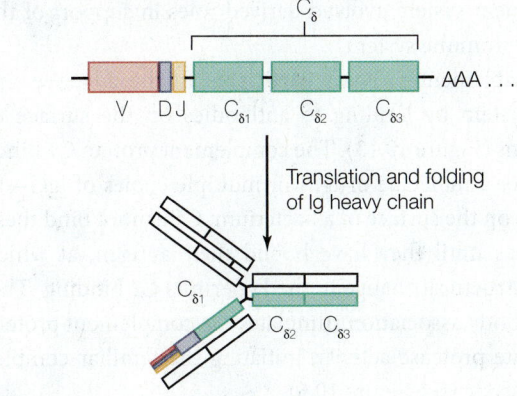

Table 10.3 The five main classes of antibodies in mammals, arranged from most abundant to least abundant in humans. Hexagons denote glycosylation sites.

Structure	(a) IgG	(b) IgM	(c) IgD	(d) IgA	(e) IgE
C regions	C gamma	C mu	C delta	C alpha	C epsilon
Active form	Monomer	Pentamer	Monomer	Dimer	Monomer
Target	Viruses, bacteria, fungi	General	General	Microbes	Parasites, allergens
Location (other than blood)	Maternal transfer to fetus (placenta) and newborn (milk)	Mainly in blood; too large to diffuse into the interstitium		Exocrine secretions (e.g., mucus, tears, saliva)	

early development. IgD also has a wide distribution in vertebrates, but it is highly variable in structure, so much so that in some vertebrate groups, it has been assigned a different name (IgW in *Xenopus*). Studies showing both similarities in structure and a common location within the genome are strong evidence that IgD and IgW are homologues. Nonetheless, there is real diversity in the Ig repertoire of vertebrates. Bony fish, for example, possess the ubiquitous IgM and IgD classes as well as distinct versions called IgT (or IgZ). Birds lack IgD but possess a different antibody, IgY, that is abundant in egg yolk. IgY is also found in reptiles and amphibians.

Complement molecules interact with immunoglobulins

Recall from earlier in this chapter that complement molecules are a collection of proteins that bind pathogen targets to stimulate phagocytosis. The complement system evolved in invertebrates, where it plays a central role in innate immunity. However, in early vertebrates, the components of the complement system evolved derived roles in support of the adaptive immune system.

Complement proteins participate in the adaptive immune system by binding to antibodies on the surface of pathogens (Figure 10.13). The complement protein C1 binds Ig—either a molecule of IgM or multiple copies of IgG—to antigens on the surface of a bacterium. C1 cannot bind these antibodies until they have bound their antigen, at which point a structural change in the Ig permits C1 binding. This C1–antibody association stimulates the complement protein to activate protease activity, initiating the familiar complement cascade (see Figure 10.5).

CONCEPT CHECK

9. What components are considered part of humoral immunity?
10. Is there a distinction between antibodies, immunoglobulins, and the immunoglobulin superfamily?
11. How does complement interact with antibodies?

Cell-Mediated Immunity

The antibodies of humoral immunity are important signals for cells that use this information to gauge the type of response to the presence of antigens. The main cells involved in the cellular immunity are lymphocytes and phagocytes.

The two most common lymphocyte types are **B cells** and **T cells**. Their name reflects their site of synthesis: B in bone marrow, T in the thymus. Each of these lymphocytes differentiates into other subtypes with specific functions. Recall that all vertebrates possess cell-mediated immunity but not all species possess bones and thymus glands. Bony fish, as their name suggests, possess bones but these lack bone marrow. Their B cells are produced in either the head kidney or the spleen. Chondrichthyes and jawless fish lack bones; though cartilaginous fish may produce B cells at various anatomical locations, the site for B cell synthesis in jawless fish is unknown. Both bony fish and cartilaginous fish possess a thymus equivalent, which produces T cells. However, jawless fish lack a thymus gland; it has been shown recently that their T-cell equivalents are produced in regions of the gill termed *thymoids*.

In the innate immune system, phagocytes ingest pathogens and damaged cells, cleaning the interstitial spaces of unwanted material. These cells also play an important role in the adaptive immune system, where some of their prey is

FIGURE 10.13 Complement activation in the adaptive immune system

In the absence of an antigen, antibodies do not bind pathogens, and C1 complement does not bind either monomeric IgG or pentameric IgM. When the antibodies bind antigen, C1 complement binds the antibody, initiating the complement cascade (see Figure 10.5).

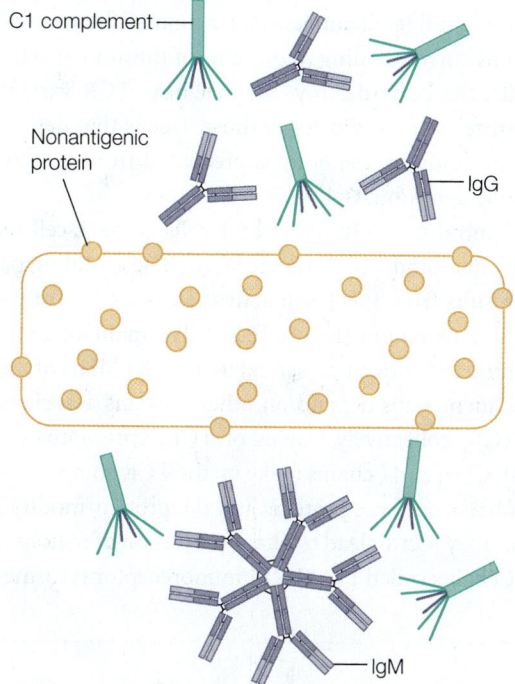

(a) Pathogen lacking antigen: IgG and IgM don't bind

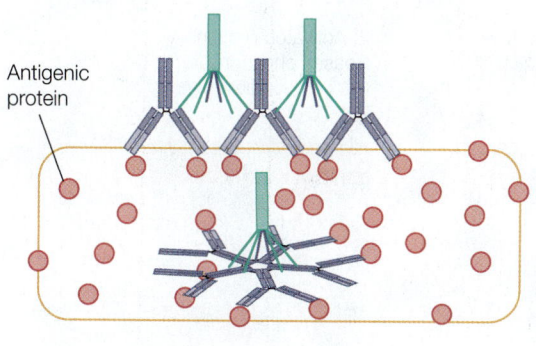

(b) Pathogen with antigen: IgG and IgM bind, recruiting complement

The most important APCs in mammals are B cells and macrophages, which when specialized for APC function are often called dendritic cells.

Once an APC endocytoses the pathogen, it transfers it to a lysosome, where it is partially degraded. The lysosome is then fused with a vesicle containing a membrane protein that can bind the antigen. These proteins are members of the major histocompatibility complex (MHC).[1] When that vesicle is exocytosed, the MHC protein extends outward from the cell, displaying the antigen that is bound to it.

MHC proteins are glycoprotein members of the Ig superfamily, possessing the characteristic Ig domains. As with Ig genes, the potency of MHC function resides in genetic variation. The MHC genes are both polygenic (each individual has many MHC genes) and polymorphic (the population of individuals have different MHC genes).

The MHC genes are colocalized on the chromosome but stretch over several million base pairs of DNA. Within this region are clusters, or classes, of MHC genes. Classes I and II encode the proteins that play the most important roles in immunity. MHC II proteins are expressed in phagocytes, where they participate in presenting antigens derived from ingesting pathogens. MHC I proteins occur in almost all cell types, where they can display antigens arising from intracellular pathogens. For example, when a normal epithelial cell is invaded by a virus, it is able to collect and display viral antigens, notifying the immune system that it is infected.

MHC I and II have similar overall structures, but with distinct subunit organization (Figure 10.14). Both MHC I and II proteins are made from 2 subunits, but in the case of MHC I, only one subunit is encoded by the MHC I locus.

[1]Do not confuse major histocompatibility complex with myosin heavy chain, which shares the abbreviation "MHC."

spared digestion and is exported to the cell surface, where it is displayed to other cells. By displaying antigens on their surface, **antigen-presenting cells (APCs)** inform other immune cells of the presence of a pathogen.

Antigen-presenting cells display fragments of pathogens on the cell surface

Phagocytes acting as APCs participate in the adaptive immune system as efficient interpreters of pathogen invasion.

FIGURE 10.14 MHC I and II proteins

The two classes of MHC differ in subunit composition. The differences in the organization of the domain that binds antigen affect the length of antigen that can be bound.

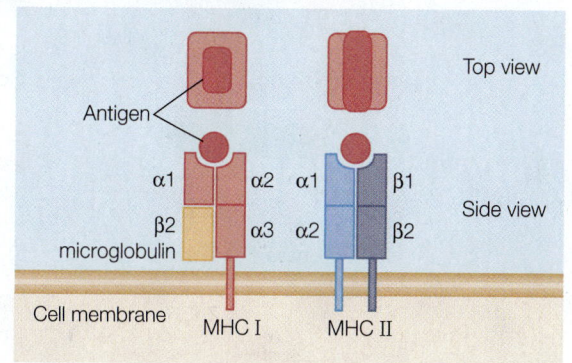

The other subunit is β2 microglobulin. MHC II is a dimer of two MHC II gene products, producing α and β chains. They also differ in how they bind the antigen in the groove at the apex of the receptor. MHC I proteins bind relatively short peptides, typically 8–10 amino acids, by binding both ends. MHC II proteins can bind longer peptides, by interacting at various internal sites, with the two peptide termini extending out of the ends of the groove.

The combination of antigen and MHC creates a surface with a topography that is compatible with receptors expressed by other cells. When a T cell with an appropriate receptor finds its MHC–peptide binding partner, it initiates signal transduction pathways that promote the immune response.

T cells recognize MHC; antigen complexes presented on the surface of other immune cells

T cells search for antigen complexes displayed on APCs. Though they cannot bind free antigen, they bind the antigen-MHC complex, using a surface T-cell receptor (TCR). These receptors are also members of the Ig superfamily, and have structural similarities to the single arms of the Fab region of antibodies. As with antibodies and B-cell receptors (BCRs),

each TCR is capable of binding to a single target, and the collection of different TCRs depends upon the generation of genetic hypervariation through recombination. However, T cells differ from B cells when this genetic variation is generated. B cells constantly undergo somatic hypermutation, whereas T cells undergo such mutations only during early development. Because this process generates receptors capable of binding all antigens, a fraction of these would bind antigens corresponding to proteins of the animal. Thus with T cells, the body destroys all that bear TCR variants that recognize "self," leaving only those T cells that detect "nonself." In doing so, the body is prevented from launching an immune attack on itself.

Central to the function of T cells is the T-cell receptor (TCR) that binds the antigen–MHC. The signaling pathway that results from the T-cell activation is a series of protein–protein interactions (Figure 10.15). The main job of the TCR is to bind the antigen presented to it by the MHC of the APC. Subsequent steps depend on other proteins associated with the TCR; collectively, copies of TCR, coreceptor (CD4 or CD8), CD3, and ζ chains make up the TCR complex. Interactions between these proteins and the protein-modifying enzymes they recruit lead to phosphorylation of regions of CD3 and ζ chains called ITAMs (immunoreceptor tyrosine-based

---

FIGURE 10.15 **T-cell signaling**

Once a T cell binds an antigen attached to an MHC protein, they initiate a signaling cascade that recruits other membrane proteins to form a T-cell receptor complex. After a series of phosphorylation events, the signaling protein ZAP70 is activated, initiating further downstream signaling events within the T cell.

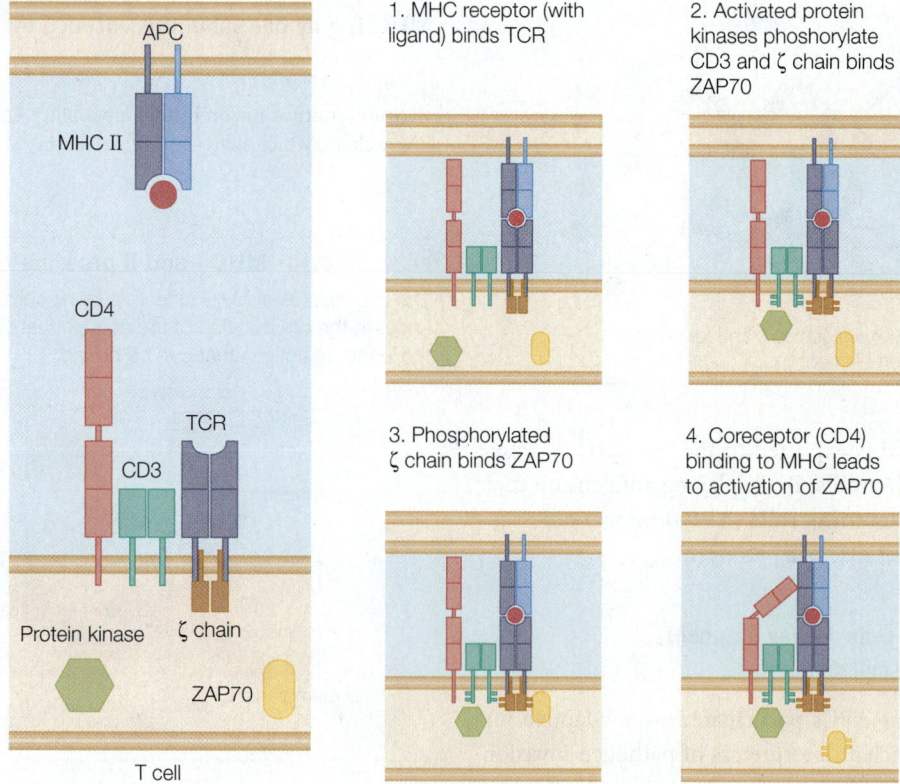

activation motifs). Once the ITAMs are phosphorylated, ZAP70 (or other protein kinases) binds, localizing it near other protein kinases, which can then phosphorylate ZAP70. Once phosphorylated, ZAP70 is active and able to phosphorylate other signaling proteins, ultimately altering gene expression.

The response of the T cell is determined in part by which type of coreceptor it expresses. T cells express either CD4 or CD8 coreceptors. In CD8-bearing T cells, activation of the TCR initiates a signaling pathway that causes the T cell to kill the cell. This would be appropriate when a cell is infected by a bacterium or has become cancerous; the display of the antigen is a signal for the immune system to destroy that cell. Because CD8-bearing T cells kill their targets, they are often called *cytotoxic T cells.* If a T cell possesses CD4, the activation may cause the T cell to synthesize and release cytokines, causing the APC to initiate its own signaling cascade. If that APC is a B cell, this will cause the B cell to terminally differentiate and begin producing antibodies. If the APC is a macrophage, it prompts the cell to destroy the pathogen. Because CD4-bearing T cells prompt other cells into action, they are often called *helper T cells.*

B cells produce antibodies

B cells begin their life in bone marrow as stem cells and then undergo a series of steps that culminate in the production of small, undifferentiated immature B cells. During this phase, they experience patterns of genetic mutations, unique to each cell, that affect the structure of the Ig genes. They also begin to produce the cell-surface receptors that are encoded by the Ig genes. At this point, they are released from the bone marrow and begin circulating through the blood and lymph, awaiting further instructions.

Once they encounter the antigen, they become activated and initiate a series of genetic and structural changes that depend upon signals from other cells (Figure 10.16). Once they bind the antigen on the APC, an individual cell initiates the final differentiation process. Activated B cells undergo monoclonal expansion, followed by somatic hypermutation and final differentiation. These cells have already been selected because their BCR can bind antigen. The hypermutation process allows these clones to experience sequence modifications, perhaps generating a novel clone that is able to bind the antigen more efficiently. At the same time, these cells are primed to undergo programmed cell death. The only way that the B cell can escape cell death is to bind the antigen. This process ensures the death of B cells with detrimental mutations in their

antibody-encoding DNA, while those that are able to bind with highest affinity survive and continue replicating and differentiating. Some will encounter compatible helper T cells, which trigger the final maturation steps.

Some individual cells may undergo terminal differentiation, becoming a plasma cell. These are specialized to produce and secrete large numbers of antibodies. Some cells stop short of terminal differentiation, remaining as **memory B cells**. These cells are held in reserve should the antigen appear in the system at a later point. If the antigen reappears, the memory cells can undergo clonal proliferation and rapidly generate more B cells, some of which differentiate to become plasma cells.

This reserve of memory B cells confers immunological memory, and is the principle behind immunizations. By

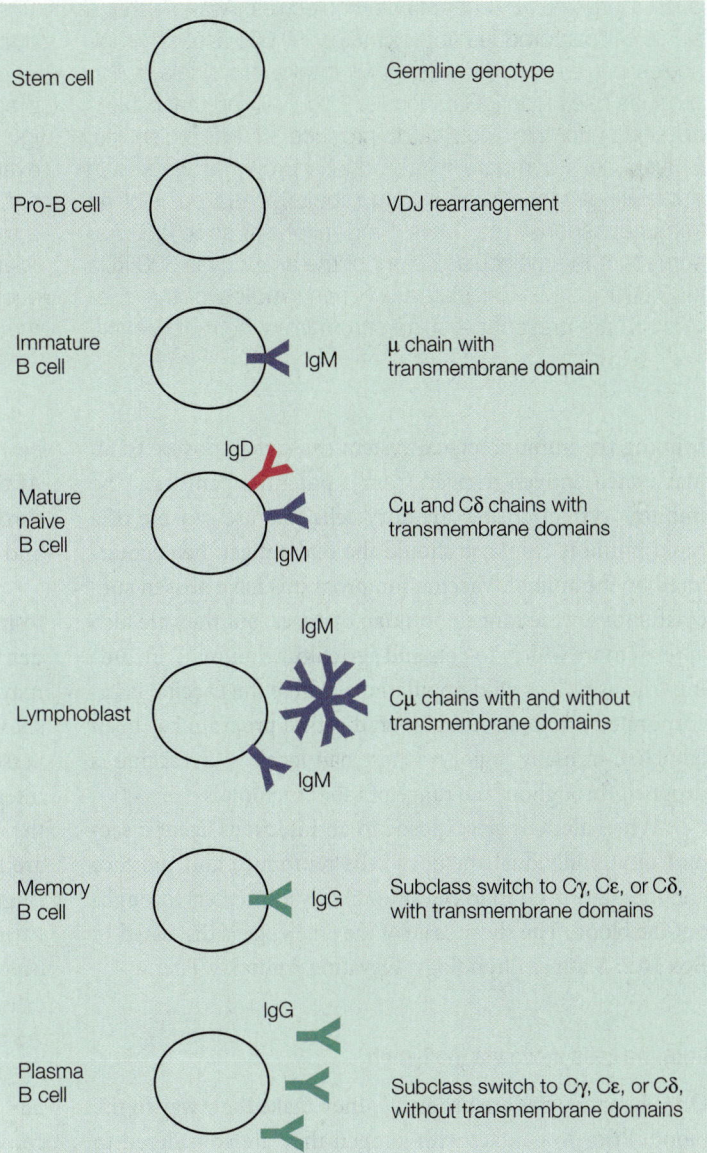

FIGURE 10.16 B-cell activation

Stem cell	Germline genotype
Pro-B cell	VDJ rearrangement
Immature B cell	IgM — μ chain with transmembrane domain
Mature naive B cell	IgD, IgM — Cμ and Cδ chains with transmembrane domains
Lymphoblast	IgM, IgM — Cμ chains with and without transmembrane domains
Memory B cell	IgG — Subclass switch to Cγ, Cε, or Cδ, with transmembrane domains
Plasma B cell	IgG — Subclass switch to Cγ, Cε, or Cδ, without transmembrane domains

Once an animal encounters an antigen, it retains a reserve of memory cells capable of producing the antibody rapidly. In the absence of the antigen, the memory cell is quiescent, and produces very low levels of antibody. When the antigen is encountered a second time, the animal dramatically increases its antibody production. These few cells face the challenge of producing enough antibody to elevate levels in the blood high enough to be effective at detecting antigens anywhere in the body. Consider the antibody dynamics in a relatively small animal like a rabbit. For the calculations that follow, assume that the rabbit is 2 kg and 10 percent of its body mass is serum. The 0.2 kg of serum corresponds to a volume of about 0.2 l.

Let's begin by calculating the ability of a single cell to produce a large number of antibody molecules. Assume that a single cell can produce approximately 10,000 antibody molecules per second. How long will it take this single cell to produce one billion IgG molecules? You will find that it takes about 28 h for this single cell to produce 10^9 IgG molecules.

Next, let's compare this production to what we see in a rabbit. Serum collected from rabbits at the peak of an immune response may have 1 mg/ml of a specific IgG. Assume that the molecular weight of the antibody is 300 kDa (300,000 g/mol). Calculate how many **moles** of the specific IgG are present per ml of serum from the rabbit. Next,

calculate how many molecules of IgG there are per ml of serum. (Hint: Avogadro's number is 6×10^{23}.) Next, calculate how many molecules there are in the 0.2 l of serum possessed by the rabbit.

If it takes 28 hours for a single cell to produce a billion IgG molecules, how long would it take a single cell to achieve the observed IgG level calculated above? Because this number constitutes many lifetimes, the rabbit must solve the problem by producing additional cells capable of producing that IgG. How many cells would be required to produce this amount of antibody in the same 28-h period? If the process began with a single cell, how many doublings would be required to generate this many cells? How long would this take if an immune cell doubled every 20 minutes?

At first glance, it is remarkable that a single cell can produce anything at a rate of 10,000 per second. However, to put this remarkable capacity into context, you must appreciate the challenges associated with producing enough IgG to elevate it to effective levels in an entire rabbit. In this example, it would take 400,000,000 cells to do this in 28 h but only about 30 doublings to obtain this many cells from a single precursor cell. The animal solves this challenge by having multiple copies of specific memory cell clones for each antigen, but also rapidly increasing the number of cells that can participate in the process.

priming the immunological system through exposure to an inactivated antigen derived from a potential pathogen, the immune system creates memory cells that are capable of a rapid immune response should the real antigen be encountered by the animal. Vaccination programs have proven successful for a wide range of human diseases, but they are also applied more widely to pets and agricultural animals, including fish, as well as wild populations, where the vaccine is incorporated into bait. A rabies eradication program has been launched in many regions, where bait laced with vaccine is dropped throughout the range of rabid mammals.

When animals are exposed to an infectious agent a second time, individual memory cells reproduce and produce antibodies in an effort to elevate antibody level (titer) throughout the blood. The sheer scale of the challenge is discussed in Box 10.2: Math in Physiology: Elevating Antibody Titer.

Immune cells move via the lymph

Once lymphocytes are produced, they make their way to the blood. Prior to contact with antigen they are considered to

be *naive lymphocytes*, and remain relatively unspecialized. At this stage they move freely from blood to lymph, passing through capillaries by squeezing between endothelial cells, and from lymph to blood via lymphatic vessels.

During infection, the immune response may be limited to inflammation and the pathogen is dealt with locally. Under more severe conditions, the pathogen and immune cells may move from the affected area. The interstitial fluid of tissues is drained into the lymph, which moves through lymph vessels to lymph nodes. The immune cells move from the interstitial fluid through the lymph, eventually collecting in the lymph nodes. As discussed in Chapter 9, lymph nodes are formed from the intersection of multiple lymph vessels (Figure 9.52). Lymph fluid enters the lymph node from various afferent vessels returning fluid from throughout the body. As it passes through, the lymph node filters out some cells, letting others pass and return to the general circulation via the efferent vessels that drain the lymph nodes.

The role of the lymph nodes is to ensure that the various components of the immune response are physically colocalized. The local cells ensure that antigens encounter lymphocytes, and the various cells involved can communicate with each other to ensure that only the proper cells are amplified, are differentiated, or die. As well, the final products (antibodies, naive lymphocytes, and mature lymphocytes) are returned to the blood via efferent lymph vessels.

Lymphocytes mature in lymph nodes

When the lymph passes through the lymph nodes, the immune cells are segregated to specific regions (Figure 10.17). Antigen-presenting cells (macrophages, plasma cells) accumulate in the medullary region; T cells in the paracortical region; B cells in the lymphoid follicle. Though the exact organization differs among types of lymph nodes, the principle is the same in all. The lymph node removes the antigens from the circulation and ensures that the circulating lymphocytes are exposed to the antigens as they pass through in the lymph. Once they encounter antigen, the B and T lymphocytes are induced to differentiate into effector cells described in previous sections. B cells are located within the lymph node follicle, and when activated their rapid proliferation occurs in regions called germinal centers. Over time, a germinal center will grow rapidly, then deteriorate, leaving a senescent germinal center. During the growing phase, activated B cells undergo monoclonal expansion, followed by somatic hypermutation and final differentiation.

CONCEPT CHECK

12. Distinguish between T cells, B cells, and lymphocytes.
13. How are antigens presented by APCs and how do they initiate a response in other cells?
14. Describe the maturation of B cells.

FIGURE 10.17 Lymph node structure

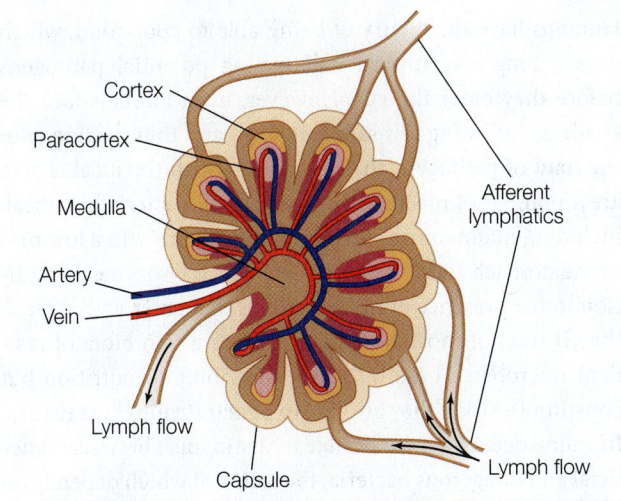

Integration with Other Physiological Systems

In discussing the various components of the innate and adaptive immune systems, it is important to recognize that the individual components rarely work in isolation. Vertebrates use the innate and adaptive immune systems synergistically, with cells of the innate system deriving roles in the adaptive system. Furthermore, the functions of other physiological systems have evolved in parallel with the immune system—affecting it and being affected by it. These complex processes require exquisite communication between cells, enabling coordination of immunodefenses and inducing compensatory changes in other physiological systems.

Allergic responses are stimulated by mast cells

One response that is perhaps most familiar to you is an allergic response (Figure 10.18). Though the allergens are not typically pathogens, they encounter the body, are recognized as non-self, and trigger an immune response. The goal of this response is to protect the body from something foreign, but in most cases allergic responses are overreactions to the threat.

Central to the allergic reaction are **mast cells**. These cells produce a cell membrane receptor with a very high affinity for IgE, which binds the receptor essentially irreversibly, coating the mast cell with IgE. Mast cells are derived from precursors in the bone marrow, and when released into the circulation have an appearance that is very similar to basophils, rich in **secretory granules**. They enter peripheral tissues, taking up residence in specific tissues, such as connective tissue or mucosa. Further maturation occurs, leading to subpopulations that differ in the type of signaling factors they secrete, as well as the profile of other secretory products, such as proteases.

The cytokines released from mast cells lead to the now familiar inflammatory cascade, with changes in vascular permeability, immune cell escape from the circulation, and fluid imbalances (edema). The impact of these local changes depends on the nature of the tissue affected. The response may be as simple as local redness arising from inflammation, to more severe disruption of physiological function. In both the respiratory and digestive systems, there are pronounced effects on smooth muscle, which acts in combination with fluid imbalances and mucus production. In the digestive tract, this effect culminates in diarrhea, and in the respiratory system, bronchioconstriction and an asthmatic response.

These diverse effects throughout the body are possible due to the presence of different histamine receptors (H1, H2, H3, and H4 in humans) and downstream signal transduction pathways. Antihistamines used in allergy medicines work by blocking these receptors, preventing them from responding to local changes in histamine levels, muting the allergic response.

FIGURE 10.18 **Allergic responses**

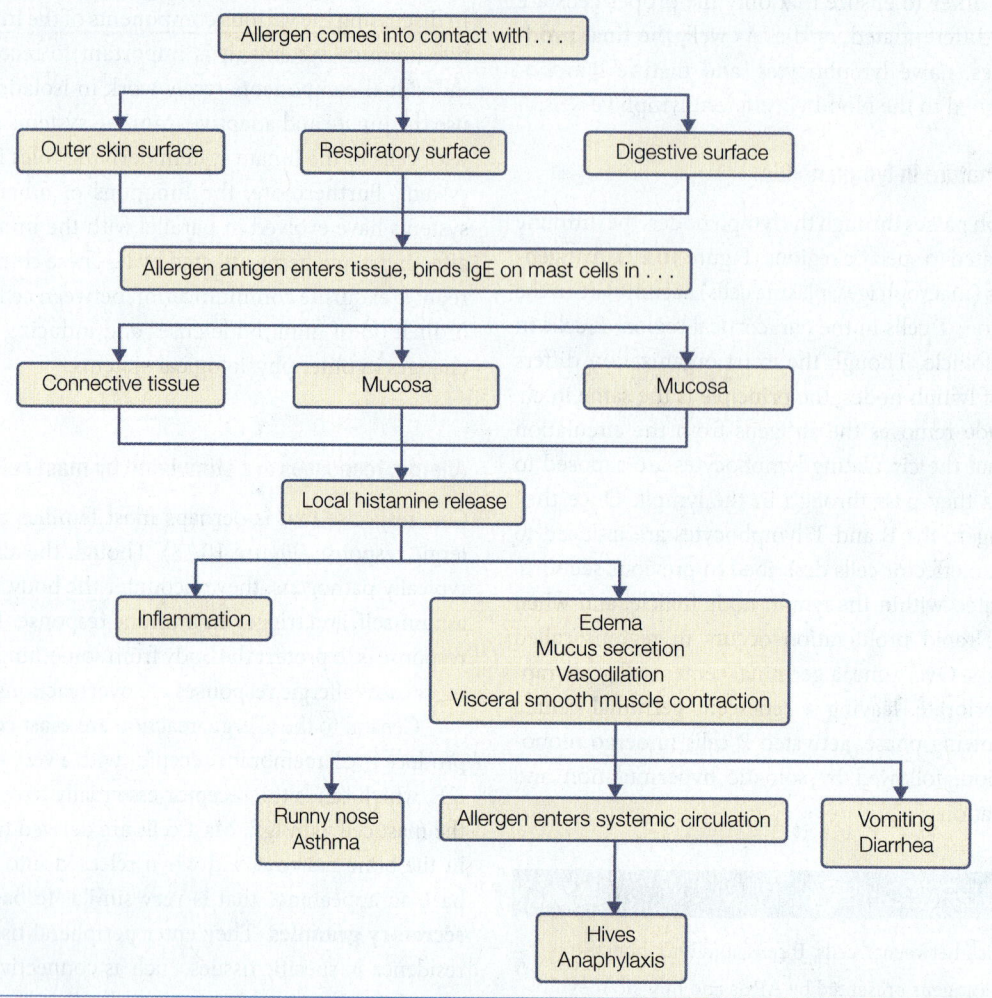

If the allergen passes the external defenses and enters the bloodstream, a systemic response can occur. When the allergen leaves the blood and enters the interstitial fluid of the skin, wide-scale inflammation can result, causing hives. More pervasive effects can lead to a sustained whole-body allergic response, causing anaphylaxis. In some cases, the effects are severe enough to cause respiratory failure and death.

Increases in body temperature impede pathogen replication

Free-living bacteria must be able to survive wide swings in ambient temperature. Many pathogens thrive under thermal conditions that approach the body temperature of their host. Infected animals are able to manipulate body temperature as a means of fighting infection. When a pathogen mounts a localized attack, such as at the site of a cut, the immune response includes an inflammatory response, which (at least in mammals) includes an elevation in temperature in that region. In the accompanying feature (Box 10.3: Challenges to Homeostasis: The Immune System and Thermoregulation)

we discuss the mechanisms by which the components of a local inflammatory response can be used to induce a whole-body response: a **fever**.

The GI tract has immunological defenses

Humans have the luxury of being able to cook food, which goes a long way toward inactivating potential pathogens before they enter the gut. However, most animals face the challenge of eating less sanitized food and thus dealing with the **load** of pathogens that they ingest with the meal. There are a number of mechanisms used to kill bacteria in a meal, including maintaining a strong acid (i.e., one with a low pH) in the stomach and using enzymes such as lysozyme. In addition to the presence of new microbes that enter with a meal, the GI tract of most animals maintains a rich biota of resident microbes. These microbes contribute to nutrition but constitute a risk if they are able to penetrate into host tissues. Immune defenses must be able to distinguish between beneficial and dangerous bacteria, the status of which depends on their location within the GI tract. Not surprisingly, the gut is a major site of immune activity, and the evolution of digestive physiology goes hand in hand with immunoprotection. Common themes emerge from studying diverse animals.

The best way to limit the impact of potential pathogens in the GI tract is to restrict their access to the epithelial layer, though the mechanisms used to do so differ among animals (Figure 10.19). The vertebrate intestinal surface is covered in a viscous layer of mucus, secreted by **goblet cells**. This restricts microbes to the lumen of the intestine. Those microbes that manage to penetrate the mucus layer are assaulted with antimicrobial proteins, such as defensins, that are secreted from the epithelium. They also trigger the adaptive immune system to deploy B cells that produce IgA. After being secreted by the B cells and binding the intestinal pathogens, the IgA crosses the epithelial layer and becomes stationed on the apical surface of the intestinal epithelium.

The sheer number of bacteria in the gut means that any defense barrier will most certainly be breached, at which point a targeted immune response is required. A major challenge in this situation is how to prevent the whole body from responding to a regular, but localized infection. The immunodefenses of the GI tract operate locally, preventing pathogens from entering the systemic body fluids. The various cells of the innate and adaptive immune systems perform the functions we have described, but do so within the confines of the intestinal mucosa. Macrophages that reside in the intestinal mucosa endocytose bacteria. Upon encountering bacteria, several types of immune cells secrete cytokines that activate other immune cells, launching the now familiar immune response of phagocytes and cytotoxic cells.

In humans, there are many diseases that represent a mismatch between digestive physiology and the immune system. Though we have focused on the role of the immune system in protecting us from our gut biota, these bacteria also play a role in regulating our immune system. Under normal circumstances, the gut biota provides a constant, low-level immune signal that keeps the immune system primed and ready to defend against most substantive risks. Under

FIGURE 10.19 **Immunodefenses of the digestive tract**

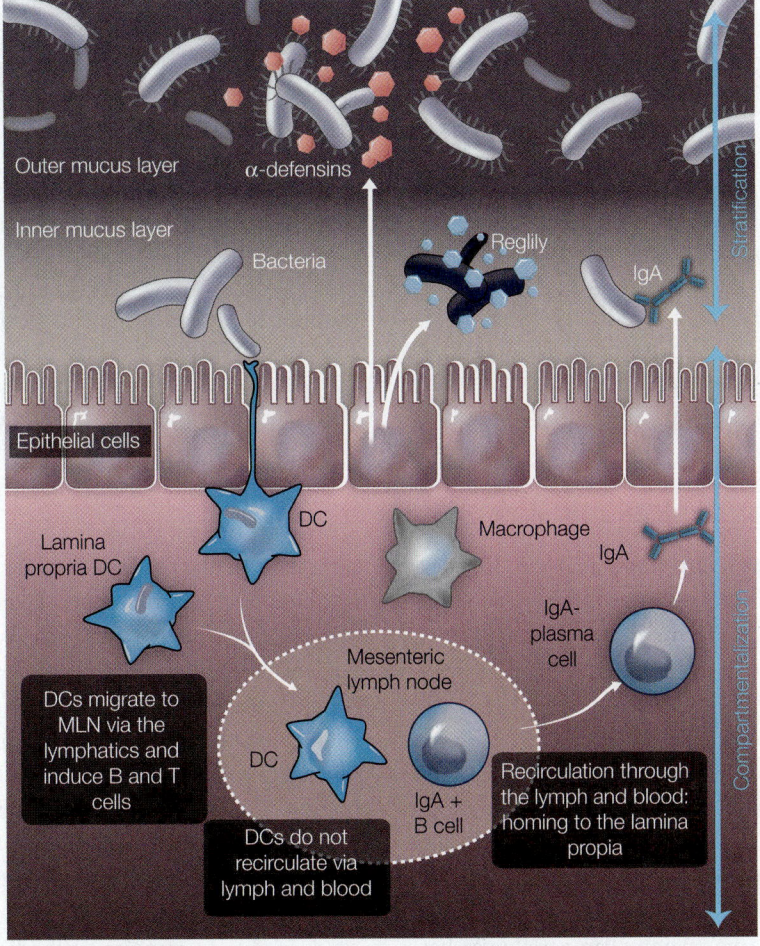

Figure source: Hooper, L. V., Littman, D. R., & Macpherson, A. J. (2012). Figure 1 (pg. 1269) from Interactions between the microbiota and the immune system. *Science, vol. 36,* No. 6086 pp. 1268-1273. DOI: 10.1126/science.1223490. Reprinted with permission from AAAS.

Whether arising from inflammation or a fever, the hyperthermic response serves to improve the ability of the animal to combat the pathogen. You will learn more about the mechanisms animals use to control body temperature in Chapter 15, but regulated **hyperthermia** is an important component of many immunological responses.

Temperature has a direct effect on many physiological processes through effects on thermodynamics. The effects of temperature on a process can be expressed as Q_{10} values, or the van Hoft coefficient. Most immunological processes, such as the rate of movement of or the rate of ingestion by phagocytic immune cells, have Q_{10} values of 2–5, which lie within the range for other cellular and biochemical processes. For these processes, an increase of 2–3°C in regional or systemic temperature would have a relatively minor beneficial effect. However, some aspects of immune function demonstrate Q_{10} values ranging from 100 to 1,000 and would be profoundly enhanced by the degree of hyperthermia seen in inflammation and fever. The process that activates T cells into cytotoxic T cells has a Q_{10} in excess of 100, making this maturation step acutely sensitive to temperature. The hyperthermia arising from an immune response reflects a remarkable coordination between cellular signaling pathways, cardiovascular changes, and central control of body temperature.

The changes in regional body temperature arise from alterations in blood flow due to vasoactive factors, such as histamine and interleukin 1 (Figure 10.20). Vasodilation of arterioles allows more blood into capillary beds. Because many of the surface tissues are cooler than body core temperature, the increase in blood flow may elevate skin temperature by as much as 10°C. The cytokines also alter the permeability of the capillary beds, allowing immune cells in the blood to squeeze between endothelial cells and enter the interstitial fluids. The main features of inflammation are attributable to the changes in the vasculature: redness and warmth due to increased blood flow, and swelling (edema) due to fluids moving from the main circulation through more permeable capillaries into the interstitial fluid.

If a regional infection spreads, or the infection occurs systemically, the animal mounts a more elaborate immune response that includes an increase in body temperature: a fever. The body detects the presence of a pathogen through binding of PAMPs, which in the context of a fever are called *exogenous* **pyrogens**. The macrophages attacking the pathogen secrete cytokines, such as interleukin 1, which works as an *endogenous pyrogen*. It causes other cells to synthesize another factor—a mediator—that exerts its effects on the brain. For example, interleukin 1 induces many cell types in the periphery and in the vasculature of the brain to synthesize prostaglandin E2. It is not yet clear how this mediator crosses the blood-brain barrier (BBB)—it may be through synthesis and secretion by the endothelial cells, or transport across the capillary endothelium—but once across the BBB, prostaglandin E_2 binds to neurons of the hypothalamus, where it alters the neurocircuits that integrate peripheral and central thermal information. The pyrogenic mediator causes the hypothalamus to misinterpret the thermal information. As a result, the brain perceives that the body is too cool, and triggers compensatory heat production and conservation. You will learn more about the mechanisms by which animals alter their thermal biology, such as brown adipose tissue and nonshivering thermogenesis, in Chapter 15. The beneficial effect of hyperthermia in the immune response is likely a very ancient trait,

maladaptive situations, including some immune disorders, the biota may also contribute to either suppressing or exaggerating the systemic immune system.

Some species can transfer immunity to offspring

Antibodies within the blood of females can be transferred to the offspring via several routes. In euthermic mammals, the placenta is a barrier that excludes macromolecules as large as antibodies. However, there is a mechanism to transfer IgG molecules across the placental circulation. As you will learn in Chapter 16, some nonmammalian vertebrates have placental-like support for embryonic development, but it is not known if the placenta mediates transfer of antibodies in these species. In mammals, the more important route of antibody transfer is via the milk. The female secretes IgA, IgE, and IgM into the milk, which are then taken up across the gut of the offspring. In a mature gut, proteins such as antibodies would be denatured by the acidic stomach and broken down by proteases. In the gut of a newborn, these digestive processes are suppressed, preserving large proteins that can then be taken up by transcellular import pathways. Other species are able to feed offspring from parental secretions, but whether these include a transfer of immunological defenses is not yet known.

Birds also transfer antibodies to their offspring. Females deposit antibodies in both the egg yolk and egg white. The chick is able to transfer antibodies from the yolk into the blood. The female deposits IgY, the bird equivalent of IgG, into the yolk. There is also evidence that the chicks can recover antibodies from the egg whites by consuming this material

FIGURE 10.20 **The fever cascade**

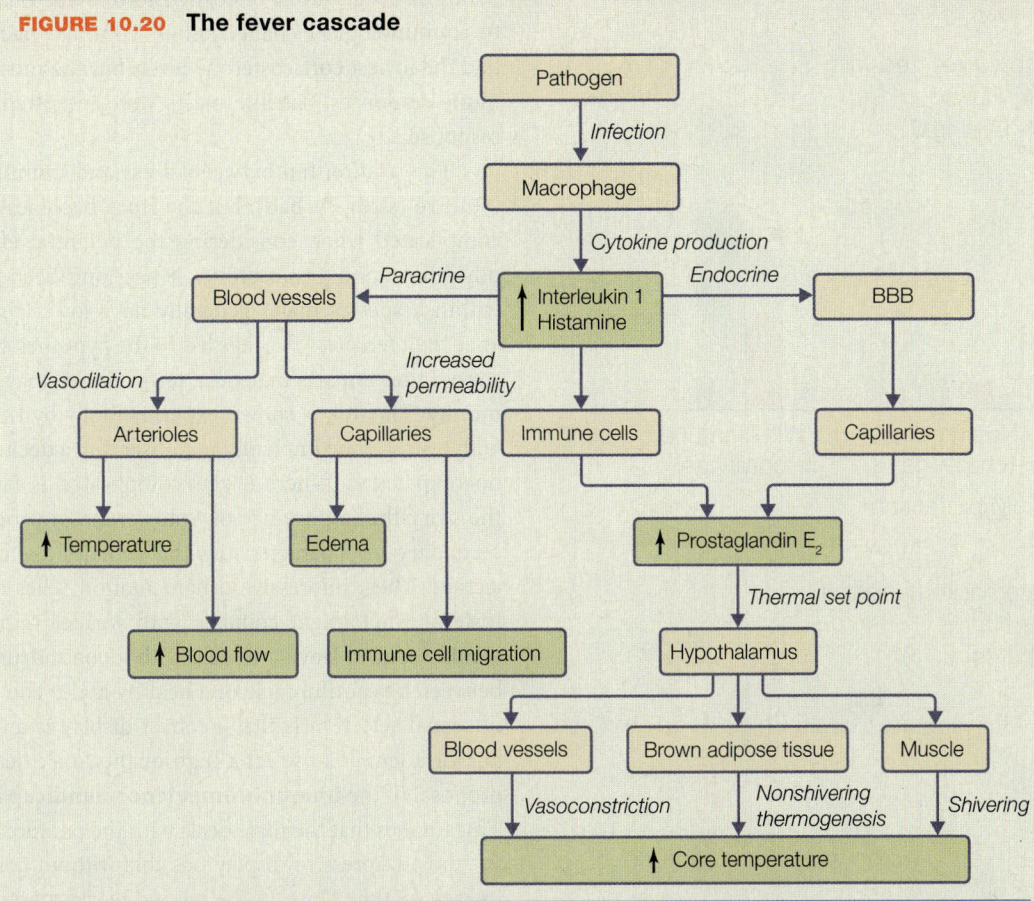

though the mechanisms by which body temperature is elevated differ among lineages.

Vertebrates that cannot use physiological mechanisms to increase body temperature undergo behavioral changes that lead them to move into warmer regions to obtain the immunological benefits of elevated body temperature.

Steroid hormone levels affect the immune system

At one point, most physiologists held that immunity is a powerful advantage, and the more potent the protection, the greater the benefit to the animal. There is now recognition that there are physiological and evolutionary costs to a robust post-hatch. The process by which an egg is created inevitably results in the transfer of some maternal material into the egg, thereby making it available to the embryo. Whether the immunological material exerts any protective effects in these species is not always clear. However, there have been studies on diverse egg-laying species, from reptiles to fish, suggesting that the immune history of the mother influences the immune tolerance of the offspring (Figure 10.21).

immune response. *Immunoecology* is a relatively new field that explores the trade-offs between immunity and other physiological functions, with implications for the success of animals under different environmental conditions. Steroid hormones, such as glucocorticoids and testosterone, have been implicated as critical regulators of trade-offs between immunity and other physiological processes.

Stress, in the general sense, is well known to influence immune function. Whether experiencing psychological stress (such as occurs at exam time), or metabolic stress (such as results from a poor diet), you are more likely to succumb to pathological challenges. The main reason why this relationship exists is because the healthy immune system is negatively affected by the hormones that communicate "stress" to the body. Glucocorticoids, such as cortisol in mammals

FIGURE 10.21 **Maternal transfer of antibodies**

(a) Zebrafish embryos were injected with either a buffer or antibodies to IgM, which depletes those found naturally in the egg. When IgM antibodies are depleted, the embryos are more likely to die from injection of a bacterial pathogen (*Aeromonas*).
(b) When females are immunized, the resulting embryos are more likely to survive an injection of bacteria.

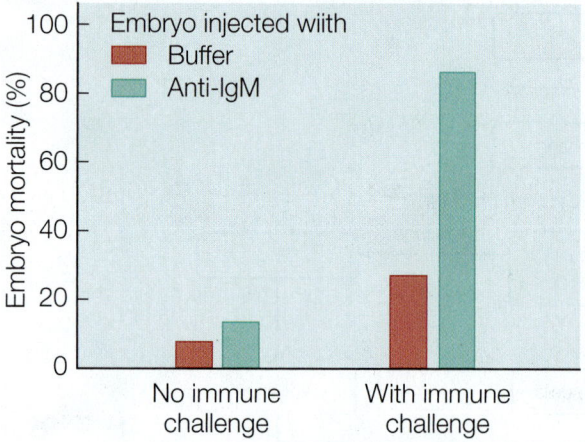

(a) Blocking IgM protection

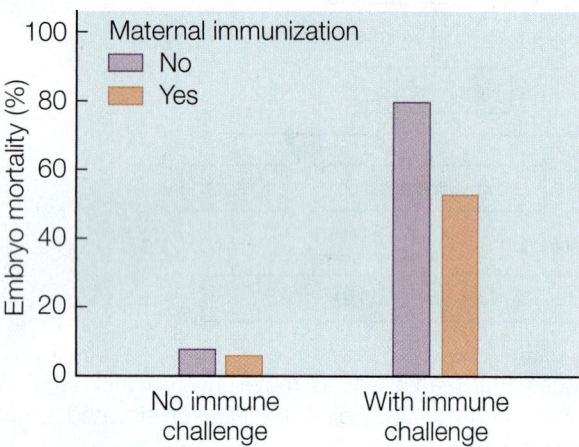

(b) Immunizing females

Figure source: Based on Wang, H., Ji, D., Shao, J., & Zhang, S. (2012). Maternal transfer and protective role of antibodies in zebrafish *Danio rerio*. *Molecular Immunology 51*, 332–336.

and corticosterone in other tetrapods, are produced at greater rates under stress. High glucocorticoid levels inform the body of stressful conditions. In most cases this leads to a switch in energy metabolism, increasing the mobilization of energy reserves and decreasing the overall energetic demands by reducing "nonessential" processes such as protein synthesis. Thus, elevated glucocorticoid levels reduce the synthesis of proteins required in the immune response, such as pro-inflammatory cytokines. As a result, stressed animals generally have blunted immune responses. For example, in a

study of marine iguanas, researchers measured the immune response and levels of corticosterone, comparing males in social groups that differed in their dominance hierarchy. The dominant males defended territories, engaged in elaborate behaviors, and exhibited anatomical ornamentation. These males had high levels of corticosterone but weak responses to immunological challenges. In contrast, bachelor males had the lowest corticosterone levels but the most robust immune responses. Satellite males were intermediate in their response.

The relationship between stress and immunity is fairly intuitive (stress = bad), but the story becomes much more complicated when considering the potential effects of another hormone, testosterone. It has long been known that within a species males generally have lower immunotolerance than females. This has led to the hypothesis that the sex steroid that imparts maleness, testosterone, may depress immunity. The link is shown experimentally by treating males with testosterone implants, and observing a decline in immunocompetence. Where it gets complicated is factoring into the story the importance of testosterone in producing male secondary sex characteristics that females use in sexual selection. Thus, impressive ornamentation relies on high testosterone but might coincide with weaker immunity. This would seem to leave a female with a conundrum: choosing between a beautiful male or a healthy male. The whole point of sexual selection is that a robust display is an honest signal for a female to select a high-quality male, leading to the proposal of the **immunocompetence-handicap hypothesis**. This implies that the male deals with the paradox by building the most impressive display possible without compromising its own health. Thus, in the natural world, only those males with superior immunocompetence can tolerate the negative effects of building impressive displays.

Despite the elegance of the immunocompetence-handicap hypothesis, there has been a lack of consistency in studies that investigate it directly. Researchers argue about whether differences in testosterone alone are sufficient to cause immunosuppression, and many studies have shown that corresponding changes in glucocorticoids may play the greater role in determining immunocompetence.

CONCEPT CHECK

15. Why does your nose run when you have an allergic reaction?

16. How do the resident microbes of the gut escape the immune system?

17. According to the immunocompetence-handicap hypothesis, how would immunity differ between brightly colored and blandly colored males?

SUMMARY

The innate immune system, which uses a nonspecific approach to destroying pathogens, is found in all animals that possess true tissues. It depends on the ability to detect pathogen-associated molecular patterns by cells possessing pathogen recognition receptors. Pathogens may be ingested by phagocytes or killed by cytotoxic secretions from immune cells.

The adaptive immune system, which tailors responses to specific pathogens, evolved in early vertebrates. Humoral immunity relies on antibodies soluble in the blood and lymph. Cellular immunity is mediated by cells that destroy pathogens, either by phagocytosis or secretion of cytotoxic compounds.

B cells produce antibodies that bind to specific antigens on pathogens, initiating a series of responses that target the pathogen and cells affected by the pathogen. T cells may either destroy cells bearing antigens or trigger signaling pathways to support the immune response.

Immune function is integrated into other physiological systems, including respiration, digestion, and thermal biology.

REVIEW QUESTIONS

1. **LO①** Describe the diversity in pathogen recognition receptors.
2. **LO①** What is an antigen?
3. **LO②** Are APCs part of the innate immune system?
4. **LO②** What morphological features distinguish macrophages from basophils?
5. **LO③** Did the innate immune system evolve only once in animals?
6. **LO③** Which of the following animals possess an adaptive immune system: (a) insects, (b) echinoderms, (c) nematodes, (d) agnathans, (e) sharks, (f) salmon?
7. **LO④** What features distinguish the subtypes of antibodies?
8. **LO④** What is the relationship between major histocompatibility complexes, T-cell receptors, B-cell receptors, and antibodies?
9. **LO⑤** What are the various types of B cells, and how do the types differ?
10. **LO⑤** What are the various types of T cells, and how do the types differ?
11. **LO⑥** Describe the inflammatory response from a pathogen entering an abrasion of the skin.
12. **LO⑥** How does an immune response differ if a pathogen is encountered again one year later?
13. **LO⑦** Describe an allergic reaction to an inhaled allergen.
14. **LO⑦** Describe what happens when a gut bacterium penetrates the mucus layer.

SYNTHESIS QUESTIONS

1. In general terms, how do cells differentiate from common precursors to become specialized cells?
2. Describe an experiment that would allow you to distinguish between the effects of glucocorticoids and testosterone as underlying the immunocompetence-handicap hypothesis.
3. Trace the route of a B cell from its site of synthesis to its site of action, considering all of the barriers it crosses.
4. Discuss the role of Ig superfamily proteins in immunity.
5. Trace the immune response from a pathogen entering an abrasion of the skin.

QUANTITATIVE QUESTIONS

1. It is estimated that a mammal requires about 10^{14} different specificities to be able to detect the range of possible "nonself" epitopes. This hypervariability is due in part to VDJ recombination and somatic mutation. Let's consider the relative importance of these processes in calculating how many different antibodies can be made from a light chain (either λ or κ) and a heavy chain.
   (a) If the κ light chain can be made from recombination of 40 different V segments and 5 different J segments, how many VJ combinations are possible?
   (b) If the λ light chain can be made from recombination of 30 different V segments and 5 different J segments, how many VJ combinations are possible?
   (c) How many different light chains can be made through recombination?
   (d) If the heavy chain can be made from 50 different V, 30 different D, and 6 different J segments, how many different heavy chains are possible?
   (e) How many different antibodies are possible solely through recombination of genes for light and heavy chains?
   (f) How does the immune system generate enough different antibodies when only this many can be formed by VDJ recombination?

Learning Objectives

**After reading this chapter,
you should be able to:**

1. Use your knowledge of the physics of gases to explain the structure and function of respiratory systems.

2. Outline the major respiratory strategies of animals.

3. Outline the mechanisms involved in ventilation and gas exchange in water.

4. Outline the mechanisms involved in ventilation and gas exchange in air.

5. Explain how oxygen is transported in circulatory fluids.

6. Explain how carbon dioxide is transported in respiratory fluids.

7. Describe the mechanisms used to regulate ventilation in mammals.

8. Outline how animals respond to hypoxia.

FIGURE 11.1 **Bar-headed geese can fly at very high altitudes**

Photo source: Paul R. Sterry/Nature Photographers Ltd/Alamy.

I f you ascend to the top of Mt. Everest, which reaches 8,850 meters in altitude, you will enter what mountain climbers have termed "the death zone," a region where humans cannot survive for more than a couple of days without supplemental oxygen. Although the percent of oxygen in the air is constant across altitudes, atmospheric pressure declines roughly linearly, so the partial pressure of oxygen also declines. As a result, the air at the summit of Everest has only one-third the oxygen per unit volume compared with the air at sea level, and this level is too low for humans to extract enough oxygen from the environment to support vigorous activity with aerobic metabolism. Even fully acclimatized individuals can only maintain blood oxygen saturation at about 50 percent of normal at the peak of Mt. Everest. At these blood oxygen levels it becomes difficult to perform everyday functions. Your body cannot deliver enough oxygen to supply the needs of your brain, and people tend to get confused and make potentially fatal mistakes and misjudgments. More than 200 climbers have died on

Mt. Everest, and fewer than 5 percent of all the people who have reached the summit of Everest have done so without using bottled oxygen to supplement the thin air at high altitudes.

Although humans cannot function normally when they are at very high altitudes, this is not the case for all animals. Bar-headed geese (*Anser indicus*), such as the ones shown in Figure 11.1, nest and breed on the shores of high-altitude lakes in the Himalayas and the Tibetan plateau. They then migrate to their winter feeding grounds on the shores of lowland lakes in central and southern India. During their migration they fly over the Himalayas, sometimes directly over the summit of Everest, reaching altitudes of nearly 9,400 meters. Airplane pilots have also observed other species of birds at very high altitudes, including whooper swans (*Cygnus cygnus*) at 8,300 meters and bar-tailed godwits

(*Limosa lapponica*) at 6,100 meters. The altitude record for a bird is held by the Ruppell's griffon (*Gyps rueppellii*), obtained when one of these African vultures was sucked into a jet engine at 11,500 meters—more than 2 kilometers higher than the summit of Mt. Everest. Although we do not yet understand the complete suite of adaptations that allow birds to thrive at high altitudes, these animals differ from mammals in their ability to obtain oxygen from the atmosphere, to tolerate low blood oxygen levels, and to cope with changes in blood carbon dioxide and pH.

In this chapter, we will explore the structure and function of the respiratory systems of a diverse range of animals, including humans and bar-headed geese, to see the diversity of strategies that animals use to obtain and transport the critical respiratory gases: oxygen and carbon dioxide. ■

LOOKING BACK 11

Because the respiratory and circulatory systems work together closely to deliver oxygen to tissues, you should review Chapter 9: Circulatory Systems to make sure that you understand the general features of circulatory transport before you begin this chapter. The respiratory system also plays an important role in regulating the pH of the blood, so you also should review Chapter 3: Chemistry, Biochemistry, and Cell Physiology to ensure that you have a good understanding of the nature of acid-base chemistry and pH. At the end of the chapter we discuss how the brain regulates the respiratory system to control the rate and depth of breathing, so it may also be useful to review Chapter 8: Functional Organization of Nervous Systems.

■ OVERVIEW

Most animals depend on mitochondrial respiration to supply the ATP that they need to perform normal cellular functions. During mitochondrial respiration, mitochondria oxidize fuels to produce ATP, consuming oxygen and producing carbon dioxide in the process. Thus, animals must obtain oxygen from the environment and dispose of the resulting carbon dioxide. The entire sequence of events that results in the exchange of oxygen and carbon dioxide between the

external environment of an animal and the mitochondria within its cells is often termed **respiration**. However, we prefer the term **external respiration** to distinguish this process from mitochondrial respiration.

During mitochondrial respiration, mitochondria consume oxygen and act as oxygen sinks, depleting the local concentration of oxygen. Thus, there is an oxygen gradient from the outside of the cell to the mitochondrion. Oxygen molecules move down this gradient into the mitochondria (and carbon dioxide moves in the opposite direction). Unicellular organisms and small multicellular organisms living in aquatic environments can utilize this diffusion gradient to drive gas exchange with the environment (Figure 11.2). Animals that obtain oxygen from air need an additional step: Gaseous oxygen must first dissolve before it can cross the cell membrane.

Diffusion alone is too slow to maintain the rates of gas exchange needed to support the metabolism of larger organisms, because diffusion occurs slowly over long distances (see Chapter 9: Circulatory Systems). Instead, larger organisms rely on a combination of bulk flow and diffusion for gas exchange (Figure 11.2). Some animals, such as sponges and cnidarians, move the external medium (seawater) by bulk flow through an internal body cavity. Oxygen diffuses from the seawater into the cells of the organism, and carbon dioxide diffuses out of the cells into the seawater. The seawater circulating through the body cavity by bulk flow carries the carbon dioxide out into the environment. Insects use a conceptually similar system. In these animals, a series of hollow

FIGURE 11.2 Respiratory strategies of animals

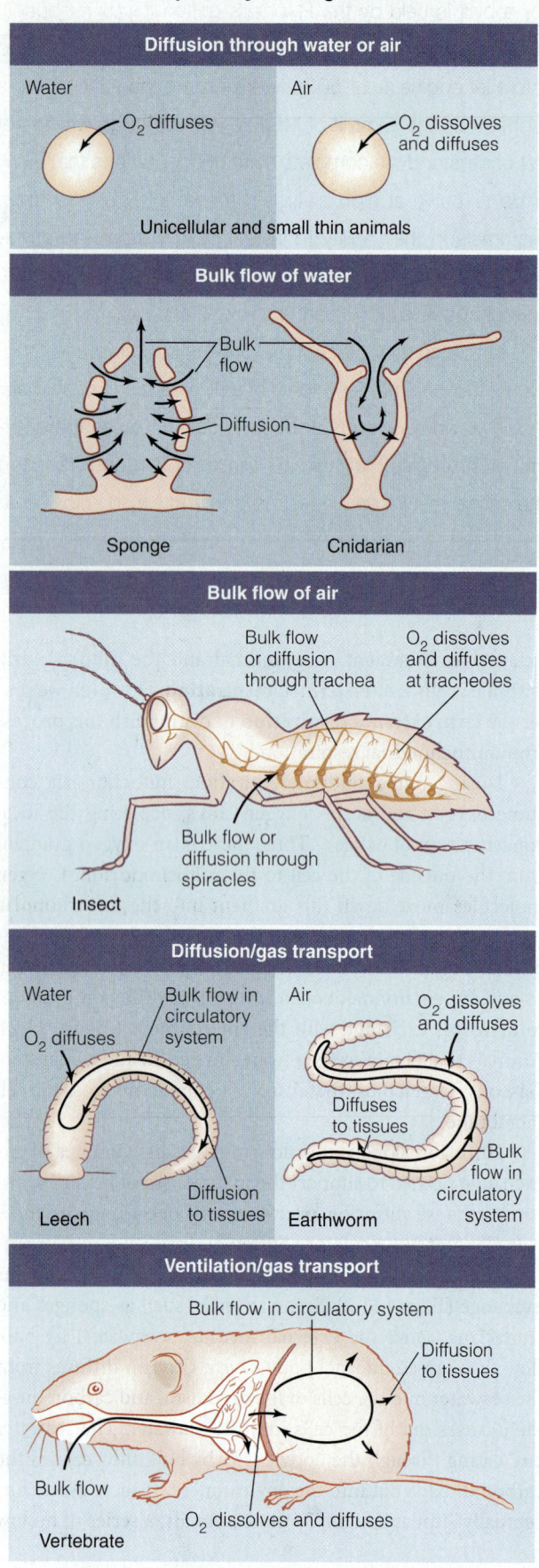

Diffusion through water or air

Water

O₂ diffuses

Air

O₂ dissolves and diffuses

Unicellular and small thin animals

Bulk flow of water

Bulk flow

Diffusion

Sponge

Cnidarian

Bulk flow of air

Bulk flow or diffusion through trachea

O₂ dissolves and diffuses at tracheoles

Bulk flow or diffusion through spiracles

Insect

Diffusion/gas transport

Water

O₂ diffuses

Bulk flow in circulatory system

Air

O₂ dissolves and diffuses

Diffuses to tissues

Diffusion to tissues

Leech

Bulk flow in circulatory system

Earthworm

Ventilation/gas transport

Bulk flow in circulatory system

Diffusion to tissues

Bulk flow

O₂ dissolves and diffuses

Vertebrate

tubes called tracheae penetrate into all parts of the body. Air moves through these tubes either by diffusion or bulk flow, and at the tissues oxygen from the air dissolves in extracellular fluid and diffuses to the mitochondria, while carbon dioxide diffuses out of the cells and into the tracheae, where it moves out to the external environment by either diffusion or bulk flow (depending upon the species).

Many animals have a circulatory system that transports oxygen by bulk flow through the body. In some animals, such as leeches and earthworms, oxygen simply diffuses across the skin and then is carried by bulk flow through the circulatory system, but many organisms have a specialized respiratory organ with a large surface area, either *gills* or *lungs,* which they use for gas exchange. Animals with internal gills or lungs often move the external medium by bulk flow across the respiratory surface—a process called **ventilation**. In these animals, respiration is divided into four steps: (1) bulk flow of the medium across the respiratory surface, (2) diffusion across this surface, (3) bulk flow in the circulatory system (a process termed *gas transport*), and (4) diffusion into the tissues.

In this chapter, we first examine the respiratory strategies used by animals to obtain oxygen from the environment and to dispose of carbon dioxide. Then we take a closer look at the processes of ventilation and gas transport. We end the chapter with a discussion of the regulation of respiratory systems and the response of this system to environmental changes such as high altitude and diving.

■ RESPIRATORY STRATEGIES

Because the processes of diffusion, dissolution, and bulk flow are fundamental in shaping the respiratory strategies of animals, we begin this chapter by focusing on the physical principles that underlie these processes.

The Physics of Respiratory Systems

As we discussed in Chapter 3: Chemistry, Biochemistry, and Cell Physiology, we can quantify the rate of diffusion using the Fick equation:

$$dQ/dt = DA \, (dC/dx)$$

where dQ/dt is the rate of diffusion (or the mass flux—the quantity of substance moving per unit time, e.g., in mol/sec), D is the diffusion coefficient (an index of the ease of diffusion of a particular substance through a given medium, e.g., in cm²/sec), and A is the area of the membrane (e.g., in cm²). Here, we express the Fick equation in terms of dC/dx—the difference in concentration per unit distance (or the concentration gradient). This gradient is more accurately described as an energetic gradient, which may be due to differences in concentration, electrical charge, temperature, or pressure. When we apply the Fick equation to gases, we usually express

FIGURE 11.3 Partial pressure of gases

(a) Molecular collisions of gas molecules exert a pressure on the walls of a container, according to the ideal gas law. Each gas in a mixture contributes to this pressure in proportion to its concentration. **(b)** Henry's law states that gases dissolve in solution according to their partial pressure and solubility. Because the solubility of oxygen in aqueous solutions is low, the concentration of oxygen dissolved in water is much lower than the concentration of oxygen in air, even when the partial pressures in the two media are at equilibrium.

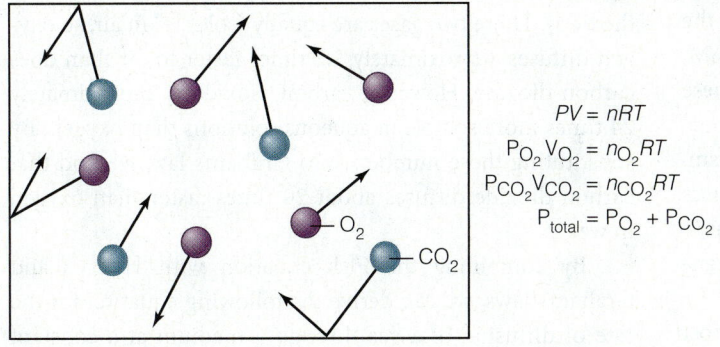

$$PV = nRT$$
$$P_{O_2} V_{O_2} = n_{O_2} RT$$
$$P_{CO_2} V_{CO_2} = n_{CO_2} RT$$
$$P_{total} = P_{O_2} + P_{CO_2}$$

(a) Ideal gas law

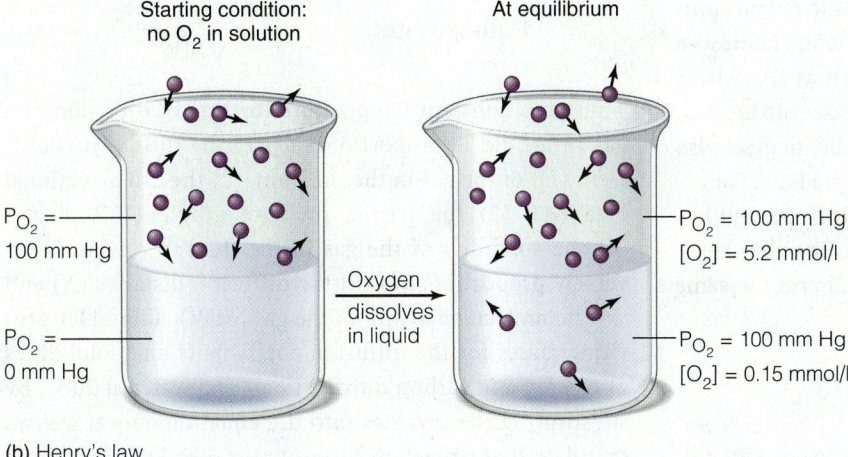

Starting condition: no O_2 in solution

At equilibrium

$P_{O_2} = 100$ mm Hg

$P_{O_2} = 0$ mm Hg

Oxygen dissolves in liquid

$P_{O_2} = 100$ mm Hg
$[O_2] = 5.2$ mmol/l

$P_{O_2} = 100$ mm Hg
$[O_2] = 0.15$ mmol/l

(b) Henry's law

the energy gradient in terms of the pressure gradient of the gas, rather than the concentration gradient, because gases have special properties such that they dissolve, diffuse, and react according to their pressure, not necessarily according to their concentration.

From the Fick equation you can see that the rate of diffusion will be greatest when the diffusion coefficient, area of the membrane, and energy gradients are large, but the diffusion distance is small. These constraints greatly influence the structures of gas-exchange surfaces so that they are typically thin and often fragile, and have a large surface area.

Gases exert a pressure

The total pressure exerted by a gas is related to the number of moles of the gas and the volume of the chamber, according to the *ideal gas law:*

$$PV = nRT$$

where P is the total pressure, V is the volume, n is the number of moles of gas molecules, R is the gas constant, and T is the temperature in Kelvin. Air is a mixture of gases, containing nitrogen (78%), oxygen (21%), argon (0.9%), carbon dioxide (0.03%), and a variety of trace gases. **Dalton's law of partial pressures** states that in a gas mixture each gas exerts its own **partial pressure**. The sum of the partial pressures of the gases in a gas mixture yields the total pressure of the gas mixture (Figure 11.3a). Just as with total pressure, the partial pressure of a gas is proportional to the number of gas molecules.

By rearranging the **ideal gas law** to the form $n/V = P/RT$, we can see that the concentration of the gas (number of moles per unit volume, or n/V) is proportional to the pressure at a constant temperature. If temperature increases, and volume is not fixed, volume will increase, keeping the pressure constant but causing the concentration to change. The effect of temperature on the concentration of a gas is one reason we usually express the Fick equation in terms of pressure when dealing with gases.

Henry's law describes how gases dissolve in liquids

To diffuse into a cell, gas molecules in air must first dissolve in liquid (such as water or extracellular fluid). **Henry's law** states that the amount of gas that will dissolve in a liquid is determined by the partial pressure of the gas and the solubility of the gas in the liquid. We can write Henry's law as follows:

$$[G] = P_{gas} S_{gas}$$

where $[G]$ is the concentration of gas dissolved in the liquid, P_{gas} is the partial pressure of the gas in the atmosphere above the liquid, and S_{gas} is the solubility of the gas in that liquid (Figure 11.3b). The effect of solubility on gas concentration is another reason we usually express the Fick equation in terms of pressure rather than concentration. For example, consider the diffusion of a gas across the cell membrane. Gases are much more soluble in lipids than they are in aqueous solution. When the partial pressures are at equilibrium, and are thus the same in the extracellular fluid outside the cell, in the membrane, and inside the cell, the concentration of gas will actually be higher in the membrane than outside the cell, because of the higher solubility of the gas in the membrane lipids. Despite this concentration gradient, there will be no net movement of gas, because there is no partial pressure gradient.

Notice that Henry's law is actually just a modification of the ideal gas law, where [G] is equivalent to n/V, and $(1/RT)$ represents the solubility of a gas in air. Using these relationships, we can compare the content of oxygen in air with the content of oxygen in water. At sea level at 20°C, the molar concentration of oxygen in air is approximately 9 mM, whereas the concentration of oxygen in water under these conditions is less than 0.3 mM. This difference has important implications for the respiratory strategy of an organism. To obtain the same amount of oxygen, an animal that uses water as its respiratory medium must move 30 times more fluid across its respiratory surface than an equivalent organism that uses air as its respiratory medium.

The solubility of oxygen in water decreases by almost 50 percent when temperature is raised from 0°C to 40°C, causing a large decrease in oxygen concentration. This effect makes it more difficult for aquatic organisms to obtain sufficient oxygen from their environments at high temperatures—a particularly acute challenge for animals such as fish whose body temperature and oxygen demand increase with increasing environmental temperatures. The solubility of gases also decreases with increasing ion concentration in a fluid. For example, the solubility of oxygen in seawater is 20 percent less than in freshwater at the same temperature. Together, these two effects cause seawater at 20°C to have almost the same oxygen content as freshwater at 30°C.

Gases diffuse at different rates

Graham's law states that when gases are dissolved in liquids, the relative rate of diffusion of a given gas is proportional to its solubility in the liquid and inversely proportional to the square root of its molecular weight (MW).

$$\text{Diffusion rate} \quad \text{solubility}/\sqrt{\text{MW}}$$

This relationship has important consequences for the diffusion of respiratory gases. Oxygen is lighter than carbon dioxide (32 atomic mass units compared to 44 for carbon dioxide). These two gases are equally "soluble" in air, so oxygen diffuses approximately 1.2 times faster in air than does carbon dioxide. However, carbon dioxide is approximately 24 times more soluble in aqueous solutions than oxygen. By substituting these numbers into Graham's law, we find that carbon dioxide diffuses about 20 times faster than oxygen in water.

By combining the Fick equation with Henry's and Graham's laws, we can derive the following equation for the rate of diffusion of a gas through a medium at a constant temperature:

$$\text{Diffusion rate} \quad \frac{D \times A \times \quad P_{gas} \times S_{gas}}{X \times \sqrt{\text{MW}}}$$

Thus, at a constant temperature the rate of diffusion of a gas in a fluid is proportional to (1) the diffusion coefficient (D) of the gas in the medium, (2) the cross-sectional area (A), (3) the partial pressure gradient (P_{gas}), and (4) the solubility of the gas in the fluid (S_{gas}), but is inversely proportional to (5) the diffusion distance (X) and (6) the molecular weight of the gas (MW). Table 11.1 provides values for the diffusion coefficients and solubilities of oxygen and carbon dioxide in air and water at 20°C. By substituting these values into the equation above, we can calculate that oxygen diffuses almost 300,000 times more slowly in water than in air at 20°C.

Table 11.1 The physical properties of air and water and their effects on the respiratory gases			
Property	**Air (20°C)**	**Water (20°C)**	**Ratio (Water/Air)**
Oxygen diffusion coefficient (m²/sec × 10⁻⁹)	20,300	2.1	~1:10,000
Carbon dioxide diffusion coefficient (m²/sec × 10⁻⁹)	16,000	1.8	~1:10,000
Oxygen solubility (ml/l)	1,000	33.1	1:30
Carbon dioxide solubility (ml/l)	1,000	930	~1
Oxygen concentration (mM) (at 1 atm)	8.7	0.3	1:30
Carbon dioxide concentration mM (at 1 atm)	.01	0.01	~1
Density (kg/m³)	1.2	998	~800:1
Viscosity (poise × 10⁻²)	0.02	1	50:1

Fluids flow from areas of high to low pressure

Substances move across long distances much more quickly by bulk flow than by diffusion. Thus, the bulk flow of a fluid medium can transport dissolved substances such as gases, moving them across long distances much more quickly than is possible with diffusion alone. Fluids, including both liquids and gases, move by bulk flow if the total pressure in one area differs from the total pressure in another. We have already discussed the factors affecting the bulk flow of liquids in Chapter 9, but for gases, pressure is related to volume according to Boyle's law:

$$P_1V_1 = P_2V_2$$

where P_1 and V_1 equal the initial pressure and volume, and P_2 and V_2 equal the final pressure and volume. Thus, if you increase the volume of a sealed chamber containing a gas, the pressure within that chamber will decrease (Figure 11.4a).

If you then open the chamber to the surrounding atmosphere (which is at higher pressure), the gas will move down the pressure gradient until the external pressure and the pressure inside the chamber are equal, and no further net movement of gas occurs. The lungs of terrestrial animals work in this way. For example, when you breathe in, your chest expands, increasing the volume of your lungs, and decreasing the pressure, causing air to flow into the lungs.

Boyle's law does not apply directly to liquids, because liquids are incompressible (Figure 11.4b); the intermolecular forces holding molecules together in liquid form are too strong to be disrupted by physiologically relevant changes in pressure. However, if you exert a force on a liquid, the pressure within that liquid will change without a change in volume. These pressure changes result in the bulk flow of the liquid from the area of higher pressure to the area of lower pressure.

Resistance opposes flow

Frictional resistance opposes the bulk flow of fluids. The relationship between flow, pressure, and resistance can be quantified using the law of bulk flow ($Q = \Delta P/R$). As in

FIGURE 11.4 **The effects of changes in volume on changes in pressure**

(a) Boyle's law. Increasing the volume of a sealed chamber filled with gas decreases the pressure within the chamber. When the chamber is opened, gas will flow into it down this pressure gradient until the pressures are equalized. **(b)** If you attempt to increase the volume of a sealed chamber containing a liquid, the volume will not change. However, pressure will decrease within the chamber. If you then open the valve, liquid will move into the chamber by bulk flow, increasing the volume of the chamber until the pressures are equalized.

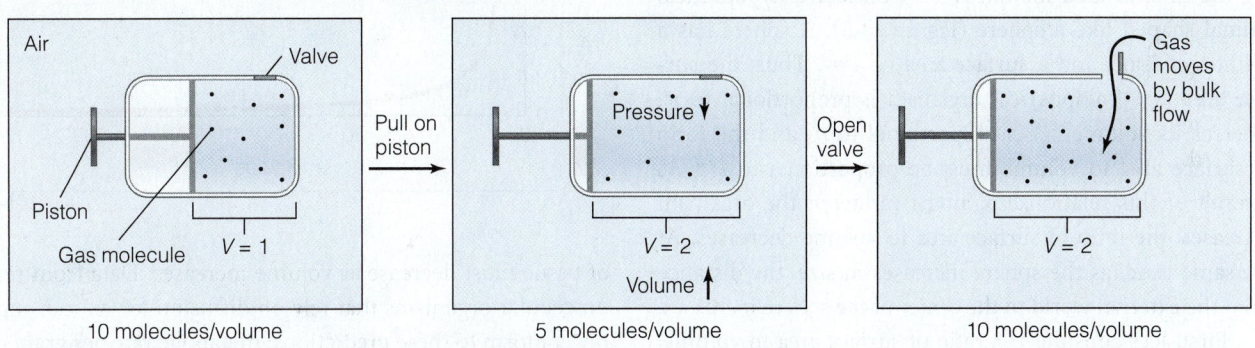

(a) Sealed chamber containing gas (external pressure = 1)

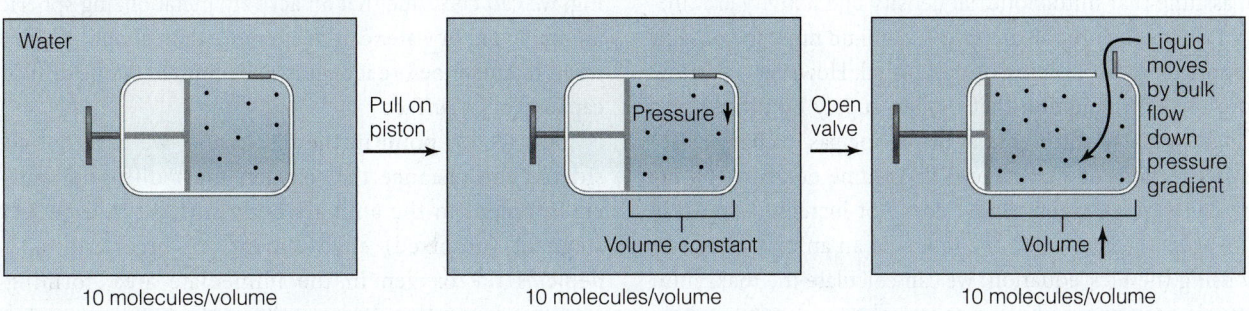

(b) Sealed chamber containing liquid

the circulatory system, flow in respiratory systems often occurs in tubes. In tubes, resistance increases in direct proportion to the length of the tube and the viscosity of the fluid, but decreases in inverse proportion to the radius to the fourth power. Because of this relationship, small increases in the radius of a tube cause large decreases in resistance.

CONCEPT CHECK

1. Use the Fick equation to explain why respiratory surfaces usually have high surface area and are very thin.

2. In a gas mixture consisting of nitrogen, oxygen, and carbon dioxide, if the total pressure is 100 kPa, the partial pressure of nitrogen is 80 kPa, and the partial pressure of carbon dioxide is 0.03 kPa, what is the partial pressure of oxygen?

3. Compare and contrast the bulk flow of liquids and gases.

Types of Respiratory Systems

Only very small animals can rely solely on diffusion of oxygen to support metabolism. As we discussed in Chapter 1: Introduction to Physiological Principles, as organisms grow larger, their ratio of surface area to volume decreases, limiting the area available for diffusion. Moreover, oxygen must diffuse across greater distances within the animal, increasing the time needed for diffusion. Consider a hypothetical animal shaped like a sphere (Figure 11.5). A sphere has a volume of $\frac{4}{3}\pi r^3$, and a surface area of $4\pi r^2$. Thus, the surface area (s) of a spherical organism is proportional to r^2, whereas its volume (v) is proportional to r^3, and the ratio of surface area to volume must be proportional to $1/r$. As a result of this relationship, as the radius of the organism increases, the ratio of surface area to volume decreases. At the same time, as the sphere increases in size, the distance from the external world to the center of the sphere increases.

First, let's consider the ratio of surface area to volume, without addressing the rate of diffusion within the animal. If we assume that mitochondrial density and activity are uniform across the organism, oxygen demand must increase in proportion to the volume of the animal. However, we know from the Fick equation that oxygen supply by diffusion is related to the surface area available for gas exchange. Because the ratio of surface area to volume decreases as radius increases, oxygen supply does not increase as quickly as oxygen demand when the radius of an animal increases. By using the Fick equation, we can calculate the maximum possible oxygen supply to a spherical animal with a given radius, and this oxygen supply must be the upper limit of aerobic metabolic rate.

Because the ratio of surface area to volume decreases as volume increases, the maximum metabolic rate of each gram

FIGURE 11.5   **Relationships between surface area and volume of a sphere**

The ratio of surface area to volume declines as the radius increases.

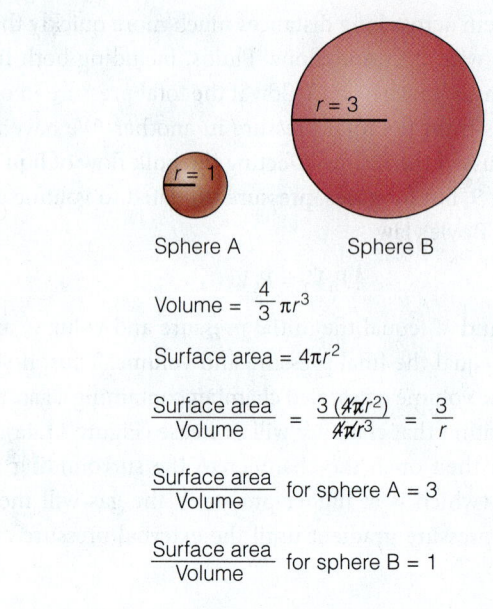

Sphere A   Sphere B

$$\text{Volume} = \frac{4}{3}\pi r^3$$

$$\text{Surface area} = 4\pi r^2$$

$$\frac{\text{Surface area}}{\text{Volume}} = \frac{3\,(4\pi r^2)}{4\pi r^3} = \frac{3}{r}$$

$$\frac{\text{Surface area}}{\text{Volume}} \text{ for sphere A} = 3$$

$$\frac{\text{Surface area}}{\text{Volume}} \text{ for sphere B} = 1$$

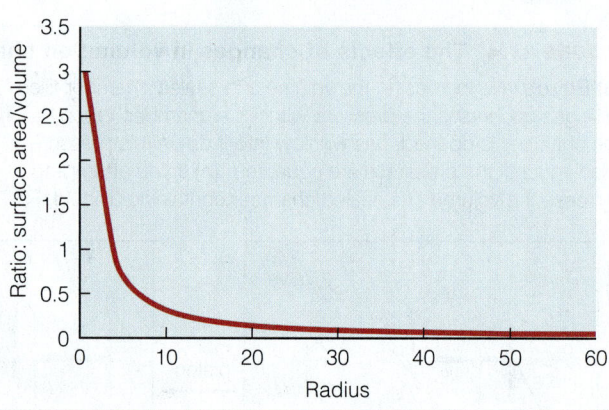

of tissue must decrease as volume increases. Data from real unicellular organisms that rely on diffusion for oxygen supply conform to these predictions; metabolic rate per gram of tissue declines as size increases. In general, using this reasoning, we can conclude that an actively metabolizing spherical animal living in water can be no more than about a millimeter in diameter before it begins to be limited by the diffusing capacity of its surface.

Up to this point in the discussion, we have not considered the distance that oxygen must diffuse from the environment to the animal's body surface. In a perfectly stagnant (unmixed) environment, an organism rapidly depletes the oxygen in the immediate area, forming a stagnant **boundary layer** at its surface. Of course, real environments are almost never entirely still. Instead, environmental fluids typically move by bulk flow as a result of temperature differences or the movement of other organisms through the fluid. These actions mix the fluid and reduce the size of the boundary layer around the organism, reducing the effective diffusion distance between the surface of the organism and the well-mixed regions of the environmental fluid. Environments with more extensive flow will have better mixing than environments with low flow. As a result of this effect, organisms that live in swiftly flowing fluids will have a smaller boundary layer around their surface and can be somewhat larger than organisms that live in motionless fluids. However, the maximum diameter of a spherical organism in a swiftly flowing fluid is still only a few millimeters. Some organisms have cilia or flagella on their surface whose beating causes fluids to move past them by bulk flow, which also acts to reduce the boundary layer, and increases the maximum possible size of a spherical organism.

Very thin animals can rely on diffusion alone for gas exchange

Of course, organisms are not necessarily spherical; their bodies may be long and thin, or their body surface may be highly folded so that the relationships of surface area to volume relevant to spherical animals no longer apply. Under these circumstances, surface area and volume might increase equally as the size of the animal increases. In this case, surface area may be sufficient for diffusion to supply the oxygen needs of even quite large organisms. For example, some soil nematodes (roundworms) can be as much as 7 millimeters long, a few marine species reach 5 centimeters, and some horsehair worms (phylum Nematomorpha) can reach up to 1 meter in length. All of these organisms rely on diffusion across their body surfaces for gas exchange. The marine turbellarian flatworms are among the largest of the animals that rely primarily on diffusion for gas exchange, reaching as much as 60 centimeters in length and 20 centimeters in width.

However, there is an additional factor that must be taken into account when considering the limitations to diffusion. The time needed for diffusion increases with the square of the distance over which a substance must diffuse, according to the following equation:

$$t = x^2/4D$$

where t is the time needed for a given amount of a substance to diffuse across distance x, and D is the diffusion coefficient for the substance. The net result of this relationship is that diffusion occurs rapidly over short distances, but is extremely slow over long distances. None of the species that rely solely on diffusion for gas exchange are more than a few millimeters thick, such that all of the cells of the body are within about a millimeter of the external medium. Organisms that are larger than a few millimeters in thickness must rely on bulk flow to transport gases.

Most animals use one of three major respiratory strategies

Animals that are more than a few millimeters thick use one of three major strategies to facilitate bulk flow of gases from the external environment to every cell in the body: (1) circulating the external medium through the body, (2) diffusion of gases across all or most of the body surface accompanied by transport of gases in an internal circulatory system, or (3) diffusion across a specialized respiratory surface accompanied by circulatory transport (see Figure 11.2). The first strategy is found in the sponges and cnidarians as well as in many terrestrial arthropods. Most aquatic invertebrates, terrestrial annelid worms, and some vertebrates such as frogs and salamanders use the second strategy, which is termed **cutaneous respiration**. The lungless salamanders (family Plethodontidae) are among the largest of animals to rely upon cutaneous respiration. These animals live in moist woodland habitats, and obtain all of their oxygen by diffusion across the skin. The eggs of birds represent a special case of this respiratory strategy. Bird eggs can be extremely large (up to 15 centimeters in diameter in the case of an ostrich egg), but all gas exchange with the environment must occur by diffusion through pores in the eggshell.

The strategy of cutaneous respiration has several limitations. First, the very thin skin necessary to minimize the diffusion distance and maximize the rate of diffusion leaves the animal vulnerable to predation or physical damage. Second, because this thin barrier must remain moist so that dissolved oxygen can diffuse into the cell, animals that use cutaneous respiration are generally confined to aquatic or very moist terrestrial habitats. Third, as a result of these first two constraints, the surface area of the skin is usually quite limited.

Some species that rely on cutaneous respiration have skin with unusually high surface area. For example, the skin of the Lake Titicaca frog (*Telmatobius culeus*) is highly folded to increase the area available for gas exchange (Figure 11.6).

FIGURE 11.6 **Lake Titicaca frog (*Telmatobius culeus*)** These frogs, which live in a high-altitude lake in Peru, use the skin for gas exchange. The highly folded skin surface increases the area of the respiratory surface.

Photo source: Science Source.

Capillaries penetrate into these skin folds, decreasing the diffusion distance between the air and the blood. Similarly, adult male hairy frogs (*Trichobatrachus robustus*) develop a series of highly vascularized hairlike projections of the skin around their thighs and sides of the body during the mating season, when metabolic demands are highest. These projections are thought to increase the surface area available for respiration. However, the strategy of increasing the overall body surface area is rather rare. Instead, many organisms confine their gas exchange with the environment to a small region of the body, but greatly increase the surface area of this region. This specialization allows the respiratory surface to be moist, thin, and have a large surface area, while allowing the rest of the body to be covered with a thick protective layer.

Specialized respiratory surfaces can be classified as either gills or lungs. **Gills** originate as outpocketings (*evaginations*) of the body surface and can be external or located within a respiratory cavity protected by a flap or other covering. **Lungs** originate as infoldings (*invaginations*) of the body surface, forming an internal body cavity that contains the external medium. Gills are most commonly used for gas exchange in water, whereas lungs are most commonly used for gas exchange in air, but as we discuss later in this chapter, there are several exceptions to this general rule.

Gas-exchange surfaces are often ventilated

Most animals ventilate their respiratory surfaces, moving the external medium across the surface by bulk flow. Ventilation of the respiratory surface reduces the formation of static boundary layers that become oxygen depleted, improving the efficiency of gas exchange with the environment. Some animals with external gills rely on natural movements of the water for ventilation, but most species expend energy to actively ventilate their respiratory surfaces.

Nondirectional ventilation occurs when the medium flows past the gas-exchange surface in an unpredictable pattern. Animals that wave their gills through the external medium are an example of those with a nondirectional ventilation pattern. Animals with internalized gills or lungs often utilize **tidal ventilation**. Tidal ventilation occurs when the external medium moves in and out of the respiratory chamber in a back-and-forth movement, whereas in **unidirectional ventilation** the respiratory medium enters the respiratory chamber at one point and exits via another, causing the medium to flow in a single direction across the respiratory surface.

The anatomy of the respiratory surface usually determines the type of ventilation that an animal uses, and thus animals generally do not switch from one ventilatory pattern to another. Instead, animals respond to changes in environmental oxygen or metabolic demands by altering the rate or pattern of ventilation rather than its direction. Table 11.2 describes some of these patterns.

Perfusion of the respiratory surface affects gas exchange

Most animals that have specialized respiratory surfaces also have a circulatory system that moves fluids (such as blood) by bulk flow through the body. The circulatory system allows oxygen from the respiratory surface to be transported across long distances by bulk flow. Just as ventilating the respiratory surface is important for efficient gas exchange, the movement of blood through the respiratory surface can also affect exchange efficiency.

In animals that utilize nondirectional ventilation, the partial pressure of oxygen (P_{O_2}) in the blood leaving the gas exchanger can approach the P_{O_2} in the medium, if the medium is very well mixed (Figure 11.7a). Any factor that increases diffusion distance will decrease oxygen-exchange efficiency, and reduce the P_{O_2} in the blood leaving the gas exchanger (Figure 11.7b). For example, if ventilation is inefficient, an oxygen-depleted boundary layer will form at the respiratory surface, increasing the effective diffusion

Table 11.2	Patterns of ventilation	
Term	**Definition**	**Examples**
Eupnea	Normal breathing	At rest
Apnea	No breathing	During diving in air breathers
Hyperpnea	Increased ventilation frequency or volume associated with increased metabolism	Exercise
Tachypnea	Increased ventilation frequency, usually with a decrease in ventilatory volume	Panting
Dyspnea	Difficult, labored, or uncomfortable	Anxiety or panic attacks, excessive breathing
Hyperventilation	Increased ventilation in excess of that required to meet metabolic needs	Anxiety or panic attacks, blood acid-base disturbance
Hypoventilation	Decreased ventilation	Asthma, various lung diseases

FIGURE 11.7 **Effects of the orientation of the flow of the external medium and the blood on gas-exchange efficiency**

Both the mode of ventilation and the orientation of the flow of the respiratory medium and the blood affect the efficiency of gas exchange. **(a)** In nondirectional ventilation the P_{O_2} of the blood may approach that of the respiratory medium, if diffusion distance is small. **(b)** If diffusion distance increases, efficiency decreases.

(c) In tidally ventilated respiratory structures, and in unidirectionally ventilated respiratory structures with concurrent flow **(d)**, the P_{O_2} of the blood approaches that of the exhaled medium. In unidirectional ventilation with countercurrent **(e)** or crosscurrent **(f)** flow, the P_{O_2} of the blood can be higher than that of the exhaled medium.

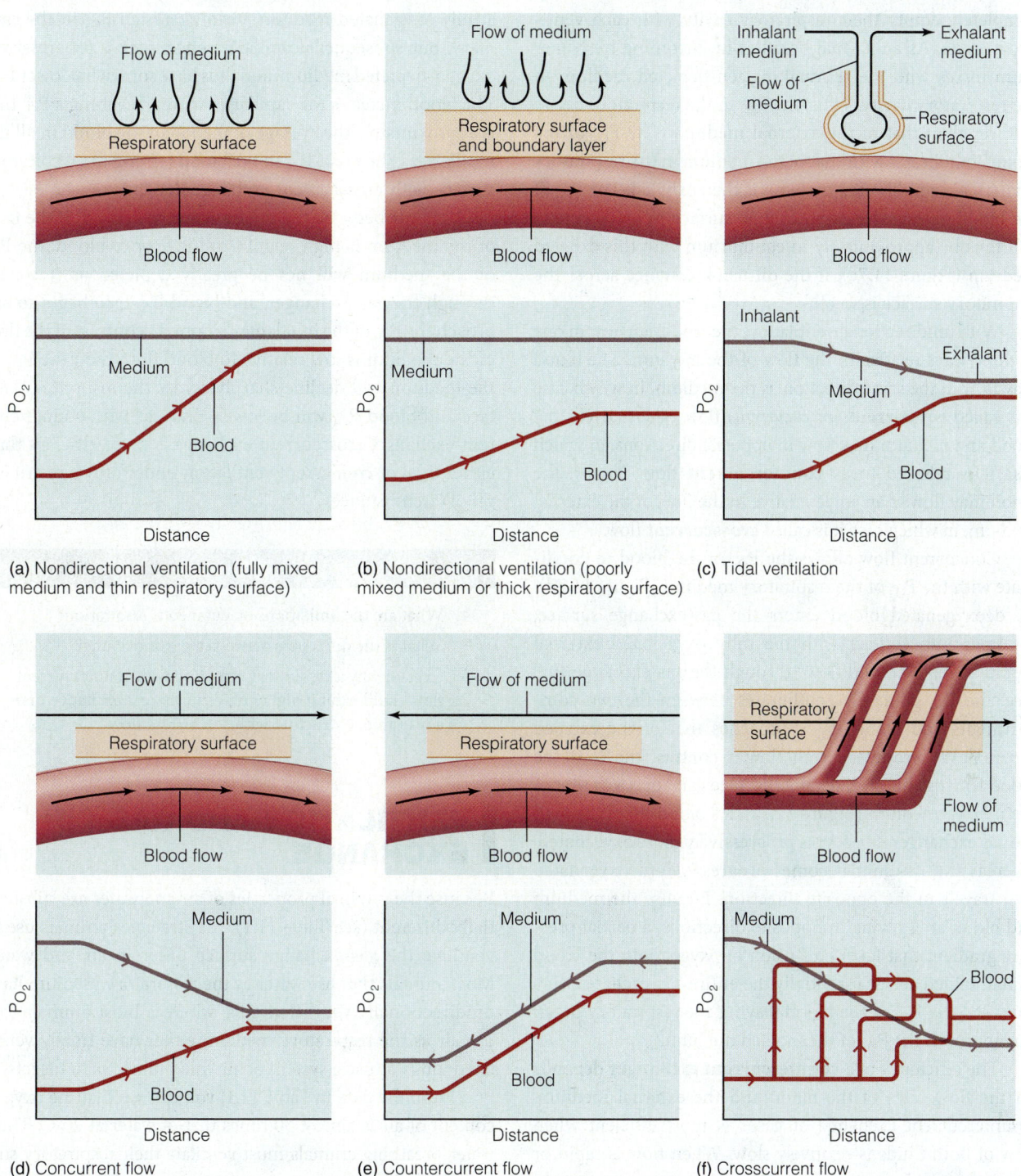

(a) Nondirectional ventilation (fully mixed medium and thin respiratory surface)

(b) Nondirectional ventilation (poorly mixed medium or thick respiratory surface)

(c) Tidal ventilation

(d) Concurrent flow

(e) Countercurrent flow

(f) Crosscurrent flow

Figure source: Based on Piiper, J., & Scheid, P. (1992). Figure 3 from Gas exchange in vertebrates through lungs, gills, and skin. *News in Physiological Sciences, 7:* 199–203.

distance. Similarly, in vertebrates that use cutaneous respiration, the skin is typically much thicker than the lining of other gas-exchange surfaces such as gills or lungs. In these situations, the P_{O_2} in the blood leaving the gas exchanger can be much lower than that in the external medium.

Animals that tidally ventilate are generally unable to completely empty their respiratory cavity with each ventilatory cycle. As an animal breathes in, incoming fresh medium mixes with the residual oxygen-depleted medium in the respiratory cavity. Thus, the P_{O_2} in the respiratory cavity is lower than that of the external medium. The P_{O_2} of the blood equilibrates with that of the medium in the respiratory cavity. This equilibrated medium is then exhaled. The P_{O_2} of the blood exiting the gas-exchange surface in an organism will thus be approximately in equilibrium with this exhaled medium (Figure 11.7c), if the diffusion distance across the respiratory surface is small.

With unidirectional ventilation, the blood can flow in one of three ways relative to the flow of the medium. The blood may flow in the same direction as the medium, in which case it is called **concurrent** (or *cocurrent*) flow. Alternatively, the blood and medium may flow in opposite directions, in which case it is referred to as **countercurrent** flow. Finally, the blood may flow at an angle relative to the flow of the external medium, in which case it is called **crosscurrent** flow.

Concurrent flow allows the P_{O_2} of the blood to equilibrate with the P_{O_2} of the respiratory medium (Figure 11.7d). As deoxygenated blood enters the gas-exchange surface, it comes into contact with the fully oxygenated external medium. As the blood flows through the gas-exchange surface, the P_{O_2} gradually equilibrates between the two compartments and blood P_{O_2} approaches that of the exhaled medium. With countercurrent flow, in contrast, the P_{O_2} of the blood leaving the gas-exchange surface can approach that of the *inhaled* medium (Figure 11.7e). As blood flows through the gas exchanger it becomes progressively more oxygenated, whereas the medium becomes progressively deoxygenated as it travels in the opposite direction. Because the medium and blood are flowing in opposite directions, a partial pressure gradient that favors diffusion of oxygen into the blood is maintained across essentially the entire gas-exchange surface, and the P_{O_2} of the blood leaving the respiratory organ can approach the P_{O_2} of the inhaled medium.

The efficiency of a **countercurrent exchanger** depends on the flow rates of the blood and the external medium. Countercurrent exchange of gases is most efficient when flow of both fluids is relatively slow. When flow is rapid or poorly matched, respiratory systems that use countercurrent flow may not differ substantially in efficiency from systems using concurrent flow.

In crosscurrent flow, multiple capillaries are arranged at an angle to the flow of the external medium. After they exit the gas-exchange surface, these capillaries coalesce into an efferent blood vessel (Figure 11.7f). The P_{O_2} of the efferent vessel leaving the gas-exchange surface is generally higher than would be seen with concurrent flow, but lower than that seen with countercurrent flow. In a crosscurrent system, the first vessel that crosses the gas-exchange surface encounters a fully oxygenated medium, yielding a high P_{O_2} in the capillary, but subsequent capillaries encounter a progressively oxygen-depleted medium, and thus have somewhat lower P_{O_2}. The blood mixes as the capillaries merge, reaching a P_{O_2} that is approximately the average of the P_{O_2} of the blood in all the capillaries. The exact P_{O_2} in the blood leaving the respiratory surface with crosscurrent exchange depends on the relative rates of flow between the medium and the blood. If the flow of the medium is high relative to the flow of blood, the P_{O_2} of the medium will not be greatly depleted as it travels through the gas exchanger, and blood P_{O_2} may begin to approach the P_{O_2} of the inhalant medium. In contrast, if the flow of the medium is low relative to blood flow, then the P_{O_2} of the medium will decline sharply across the respiratory surface and blood P_{O_2} will be lower. Thus, as with countercurrent exchange, crosscurrent exchange is more efficient than either tidal or concurrent ventilation under only a restricted set of circumstances.

CONCEPT CHECK

4. What are the limitations on cutaneous respiration?
5. What is the difference between a gill and a lung?
6. Explain why a respiratory structure with countercurrent flow could exhibit higher efficiency of gas exchange than a respiratory structure with concurrent flow.

VENTILATION AND GAS EXCHANGE

Because the physical properties of air and water are substantially different (see Table 11.1), the strategies animals use to ventilate the gas-exchange surface differ in air and water. Most animals that use water as the respiratory medium have unidirectionally ventilated gills, whereas most animals that use air as the respiratory medium either have tidally ventilated lungs or use a system of air-filled tubes, as in insects.

From the data in Table 11.1, you can see that the oxygen content of air is almost 30 times that of water at 20°C. Thus, water-breathing animals must ventilate their respiratory surface nearly 30 times more vigorously to move the same amount of oxygen across the respiratory surface than do air-breathing animals. Water is also much more dense and viscous than air, and as a result, it takes much more energy to move a volume of water than the same volume of air. In tidal ventilation, an animal must expend energy to reverse the direction of the medium into and then out of the respiratory cavity. With unidirectional ventilation, an organism need only expend energy to move the fluid in a single direction. Unidirectional ventilation is thus less costly than is tidal ventilation. Unidirectional ventilation also makes possible a countercurrent arrangement of blood flow, improving oxygen extraction efficiency. For all of these reasons, aquatic organisms generally have gills that they ventilate unidirectionally.

For animals that use air as the respiratory medium, oxygen availability is high, and the density of the medium is low, so the cost of ventilation is not the primary issue. Instead, these animals face the possibility of evaporation across the respiratory surface, and thus usually have internally located gas-exchange surfaces such as lungs that allow them to recover much of the evaporating water.

The difference in solubility of oxygen and carbon dioxide also has important implications for the relative levels of carbon dioxide in the blood of air and water breathers. Water breathers must ventilate the respiratory surface at a high rate to obtain sufficient oxygen. As a result, they are ventilating more than is necessary to eliminate the carbon dioxide they produce. In contrast, air breathers do not need to ventilate the respiratory surface at such high rates to obtain oxygen, so they do not eliminate as much carbon dioxide as do water breathers. Because of this relative difference in ventilation with respect to carbon dioxide, water breathers typically have an arterial P_{CO_2} that is almost 20 times lower than that seen in air breathers.

Ventilation and Gas Exchange in Water

Animals use a variety of strategies for ventilation and gas exchange in water. Some aquatic animals circulate the external medium through an internal cavity that penetrates throughout the body (Figure 11.8a). In sponges (phylum Porifera) the beating of flagellated cells called choanocytes moves water through a series of pores called *ostia* and into a central cavity called the *spongocoel*. This bulk flow moves the water past essentially all of the cells in the sponge's body. Oxygen diffuses from the water into the cells, while carbon dioxide diffuses out. Water then exits the spongocoel via the osculum. Some flatworms use a similar system. The guts of these species are lined with ciliated flame cells, and the beating of these cilia moves water containing oxygen and food molecules throughout the body.

In cnidarians (jellyfish, corals, sea anemones, and similar animals), muscle contractions move water through the mouth into the gastrovascular cavity (Figure 11.8b), which extends into all parts of the body. As water passes the tissues, oxygen diffuses into the cells, while carbon dioxide diffuses out. Water then flows back out of the gastrovascular cavity via the mouth.

FIGURE 11.8 **Circulation of the external medium through a digestive and respiratory cavity**

(a) The body wall of a sponge is full of pores (ostia) that lead into an inner digestive and respiratory cavity called the spongocoel. The beating of flagellated choanocytes propels water through the ostia into the spongocoel and out the osculum. **(b)** Cnidarians use muscular contractions to propel water into the mouth and through the gastrovascular cavity.

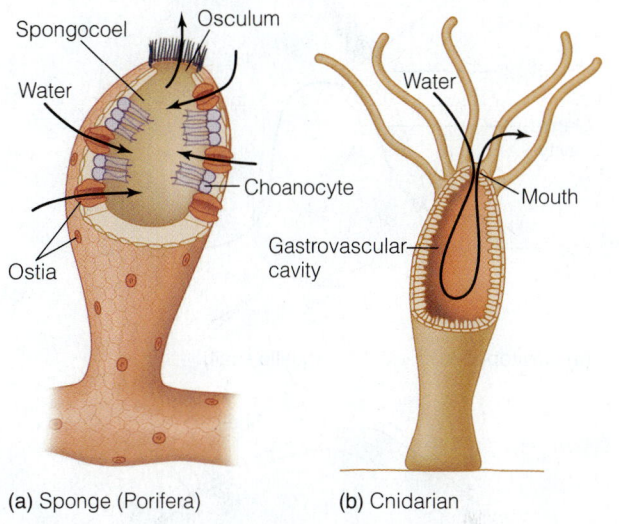

(a) Sponge (Porifera)   **(b)** Cnidarian

Most mollusks ventilate their gills using cilia

All mollusks are built around the same generalized body plan (Figure 11.9). The mantle, an outfolding of the body wall, surrounds the rest of the body, enclosing an internal space called the mantle cavity, which contains the gills, or *ctenidia*. In addition, the mantle itself may act as a respiratory surface in some species. In most mollusks, the gills are ciliated. Beating of these cilia propels water across the gills, allowing unidirectional flow of the external medium. In many species, blood flow through the gills is arranged in a countercurrent pattern to the flow of water. A group of bivalve mollusks known as *lamellibranchs*, which includes clams, mussels, and oysters, have thin, flat, sheetlike gills with multiple filaments that are lengthened and folded to form a series of W-shaped structures with high surface area.

The gills of cephalopod mollusks such as octopuses and squid are not ciliated. Instead, muscular contractions of the mantle propel water unidirectionally through the mantle cavity past the gills, allowing a countercurrent exchange mechanism to function in the gills. This system of ventilating the gills provides very efficient gas exchange, and supports the high metabolic rates of cephalopod mollusks. In some species of cephalopod, water flow through the mantle cavity is used for both respiration and locomotion. By rapidly expelling water out of the mantle cavity via the siphon, a cephalopod such as a squid can move by jet propulsion.

FIGURE 11.9 **Respiratory systems of mollusks**
(a) Aquatic snails ventilate their simple sheetlike gills using cilia.
(b) Lamellibranch mollusks such as clams and mussels have highly modified gills with pores and internal channels. Cilia move the water across the gills by bulk flow. **(c)** Cephalopods ventilate their gills using muscular contractions of the mantle cavity.

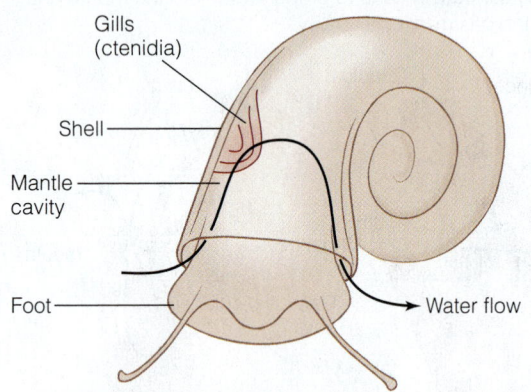

(a) Gastropod mollusk (e.g., aquatic snail)

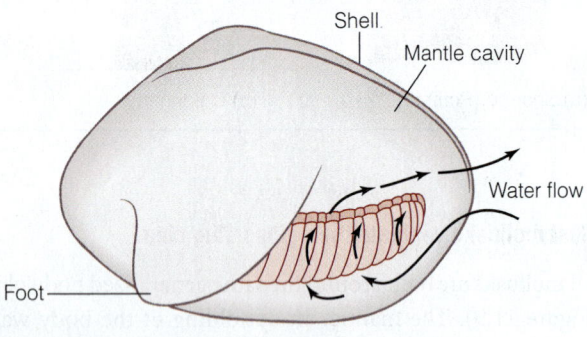

(b) Lamellibranch mollusk (e.g., clam)

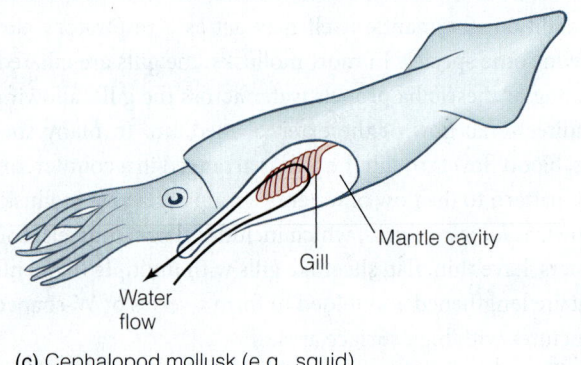

(c) Cephalopod mollusk (e.g., squid)

Crustacean gills are located on the appendages

Crustaceans are the most common of the aquatic arthropods. Filter-feeding species, such as barnacles, or very small species, such as copepods, typically lack gills, and instead rely on diffusion across the body surface for gas exchange. The gills of shrimp, crabs, and lobsters are modified regions of the appendages that are located within a branchial cavity formed by the hard outer covering, or carapace, of the

FIGURE 11.10 **Respiratory systems of crustaceans**
Crustacean gills are modified from the appendages, and are usually located under the carapace. Beating of the scaphognathite (gill bailer) propels water anteriorly through the animal and out an opening near the mouth.

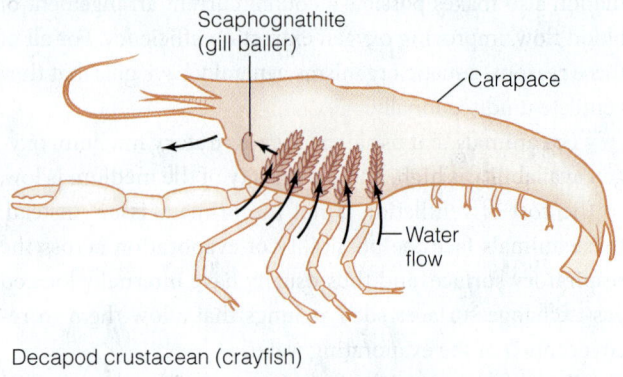

Decapod crustacean (crayfish)

animal (Figure 11.10). Movements of a specialized appendage, the gill bailer or *scaphognathite*, propel water out of the branchial chamber. This movement of water causes a negative pressure within the branchial chamber, which then sucks water across the gills. Various crustaceans have slightly different water-flow patterns. In shrimp, water enters all along the back and side edges of the carapace, whereas in crayfish and lobsters water enters only at the base of the legs, and in crabs water enters only at the base of the claw.

Echinoderms have diverse respiratory structures

Echinoderms (sea stars, sea urchins, brittle stars, sea cucumbers, and their relatives) have diverse respiratory structures (Figure 11.11). Most sea stars and sea urchins use their tube feet for gas exchange. The tube feet are small water-filled tubes with suction cups on the end that are part of the complex water vascular system that echinoderms use for locomotion. Echinoderms suck water into the water vascular system via a sieved opening called the madreporite, and pump this water around the water vascular system to move the tube feet via a hydraulic mechanism. The thin skin of the tube feet, coupled with the water circulating through them, makes them important sites of gas exchange. The tube feet of some sea urchins are specialized for this respiratory function, with a countercurrent flow arrangement.

Sea stars also have external gill-like structures called respiratory papulae scattered across their body surface. The retractable papulae are small tufted evaginations of the body surface that project through holes in the dermal skeleton and function as external gills. The outer surfaces of the papulae are covered with cilia, which beat and ventilate the respiratory surface. Cilia on the inner surface move the internal coelomic fluid by bulk flow, allowing countercurrent exchange. Sea urchins

FIGURE 11.11 **Respiratory systems of echinoderms**
(a) Sea stars use both external gills, called respiratory papulae, and the surface of their tube feet for respiration. **(b)** The respiratory tree of sea cucumbers develops as a pocket leading off the gut, and thus is an invagination of the body surface that should be considered a lung rather than a gill.

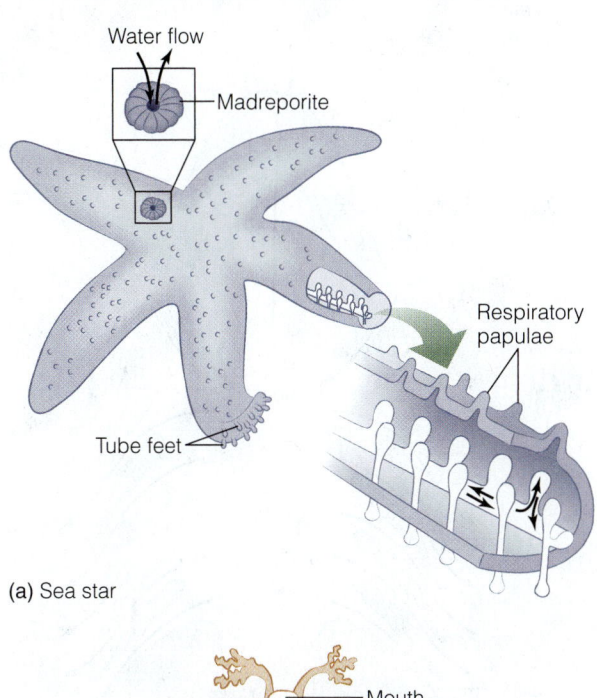

(a) Sea star

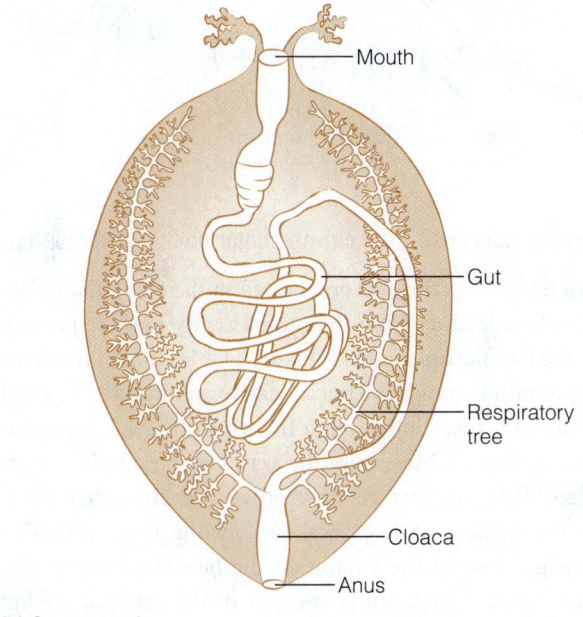

(b) Sea cucumber

FIGURE 11.11 **Respiratory systems of echinoderms**
(a) Sea stars use both external gills, called respiratory papulae, and the surface of their tube feet for respiration. **(b)** The respiratory tree of sea cucumbers develops as a pocket leading off the gut, and thus is an invagination of the body surface that should be considered a lung rather than a gill.

lack papulae, but many species have peristomial gills located around their mouths. Like the papulae of sea stars, these peristomial gills are ventilated by the movements of cilia.

Brittle stars and sea cucumbers have a rather different respiratory strategy. Instead of external gills, their respiratory surfaces are formed by invaginations of the body surface, and thus should more properly be termed lungs. In the brittle stars, these saclike structures are termed bursae, and open to the exterior of the body near the mouth via small slits. The opening of a bursa is usually ciliated, and the beating of these cilia ventilates the respiratory surface. Many sea cucumbers have particularly elaborate invaginated respiratory sacs called *respiratory trees* that connect to the **cloaca**, a portion of the intestine near the anus (Figure 11.11b). Muscular contractions of the cloaca propel water into the trunks and branches, and then the respiratory tree itself contracts to expel water back into the cloaca. Sea cucumbers use this tidally ventilated lung to supplement cutaneous gas exchange.

Feeding lampreys ventilate their gills tidally

Lampreys and hagfish have multiple pairs of gill sacs, located toward the anterior end of the body (Figure 11.12). In the case of hagfish, a muscular pumping structure called the velum propels water through the respiratory cavity. Water enters the pharynx via the single dorsal nostril, and then travels through the gill pouches and out via one or more pairs of outer gill openings (depending on the species). Flow through the gill pouches is unidirectional, and blood flow is arranged in a countercurrent pattern relative to the water flow.

Ventilation in nonfeeding lampreys is thought to be similar to that in hagfish, because lampreys also have a velum that can pump water unidirectionally across the gills. Water flows via the mouth into the pharynx, and then through the gill pouches and out via the outer gill openings. However, adult lampreys are parasitic and feed by tightly attaching their round suckerlike mouth to the skin of a host species such as a bony fish, using their multiple grasping teeth. The lamprey then secretes a substance that dissolves the host tissue, and feeds on the dissolved tissue and blood. When feeding, a lamprey cannot ventilate its gills by unidirectional flow of water through the mouth. Under these circumstances, the lamprey pumps water into the gills via the outer gill openings, and then back out the same way. Thus, a feeding adult lamprey ventilates its gills tidally. The lamprey may continue to use this tidal ventilation between bouts of feeding, or may convert to unidirectional ventilation through the mouth during nonfeeding periods.

Elasmobranchs use a buccal pump for ventilation

The elasmobranchs (sharks, skates, and rays) ventilate their branchial chambers by expanding the volume of the buccal (mouth) cavity (Figure 11.13). This increase in volume sucks fluid into the **buccal cavity** via the mouth and the **spiracles**, a pair of nostril-like structures on the top of the head. The animal then closes its mouth and spiracles, and the muscles surrounding the buccal cavity contract, reducing the volume of the cavity and forcing water past the gills and out via the external gill slits. Thus, the buccal cavity in this species acts

FIGURE 11.12 **Respiratory systems of jawless fishes**

(a) Hagfish ventilate their gills using a muscular velum. Movements of the velum propel water through the mouth across the gills, and out via one or more gill openings. Flow through the gill sacs is unidirectional. **(b)** Lampreys have multiple gill pouches, each with an external opening. Expansion and contraction of the gill pouches ventilates the gills. When the lamprey is feeding (and possibly at other times as well) ventilation of the gill pouches is tidal, with water entering and leaving the gill pouches via the external opening.

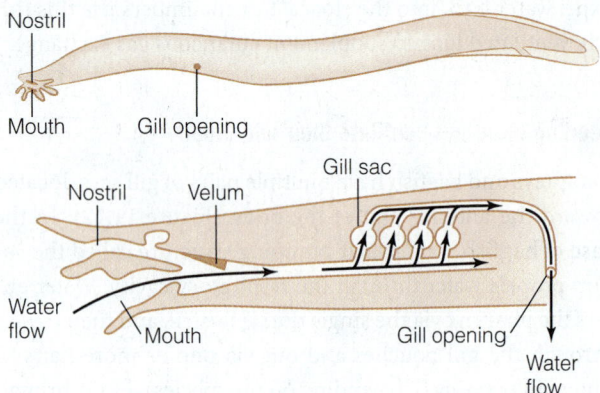

(a) Hagfish (side view and longitudinal section)

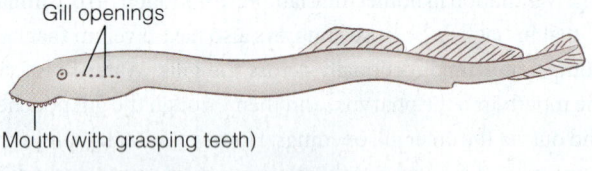

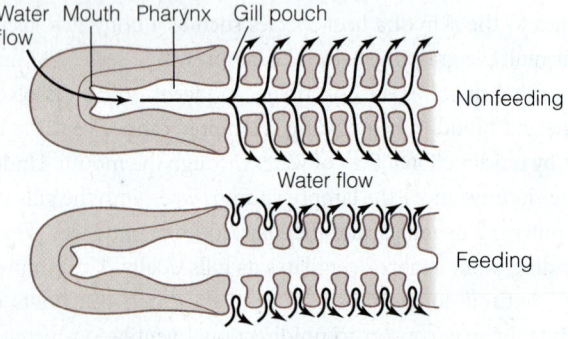

(b) Lamprey (side view and longitudinal section)

FIGURE 11.13 **Respiratory system of sharks**

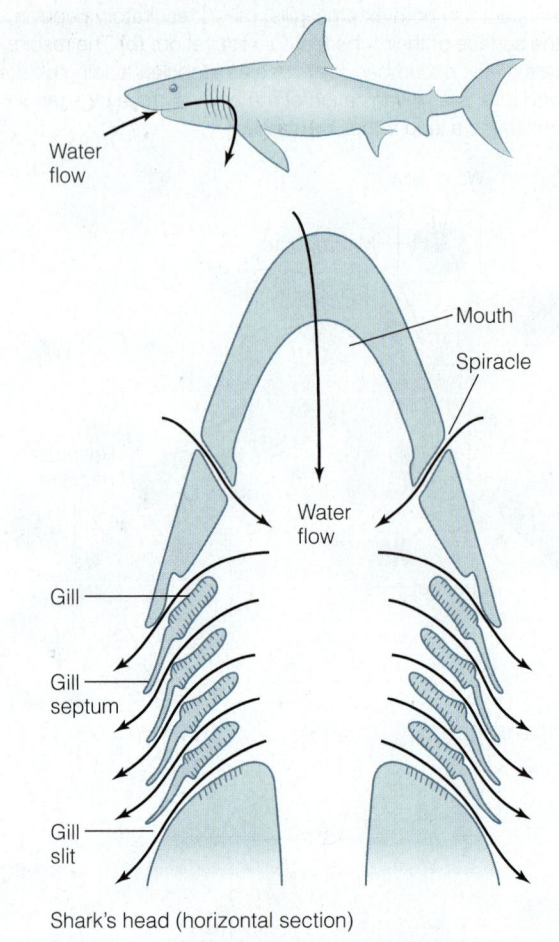

Shark's head (horizontal section)

Teleost fishes use a buccal-opercular pump for ventilation

In a teleost fish the gills are located in the opercular cavities, chambers leading from the buccal cavity that are protected by the flaplike **operculum** (Figure 11.14a). Water flows from the mouth through the buccal cavity and into the opercular cavity, and then out through the slit formed by the operculum. Figure 11.14b shows the ventilatory cycle in a typical teleost fish. The first step in ventilation occurs when the fish lowers the floor of the buccal cavity while its mouth is open. This increase in the volume of the buccal cavity results in a decrease in pressure below that of the external medium, sucking water into the buccal cavity via the mouth. During this phase the operculum is closed, a skeletal muscle pump expands the volume of the opercular cavity, and the pressure in the opercular cavity decreases such that the opercular cavity pressure is below that in the buccal cavity. Thus, there is little or no backflow from the opercular cavity into the buccal cavity during this phase.

During the next phase of the ventilatory cycle, the fish closes its mouth and raises the floor of the buccal cavity. This movement decreases the volume of the buccal cavity,

as both a suction pump and a force pump. Together, these two phases of pumping action cause unidirectional but pulsatile flow across the gills. Blood flow through the gills is arranged in a countercurrent fashion, increasing the efficiency of gas exchange.

To inhale, a shark expands the volume of the buccal cavity, and the resulting decrease in pressure sucks water into the buccal cavity via the mouth and spiracles. The shark then closes its mouth and raises the floor of the buccal cavity, forcing water across the gills.

FIGURE 11.14 **Respiratory systems of teleost fishes**

(a) The gills of a teleost fish are located within the opercular cavity, underneath a muscular flaplike cover called the operculum.

(b) Teleost fish use a buccal-opercular pump that ensures unidirectional and almost continuous flow across the gills.

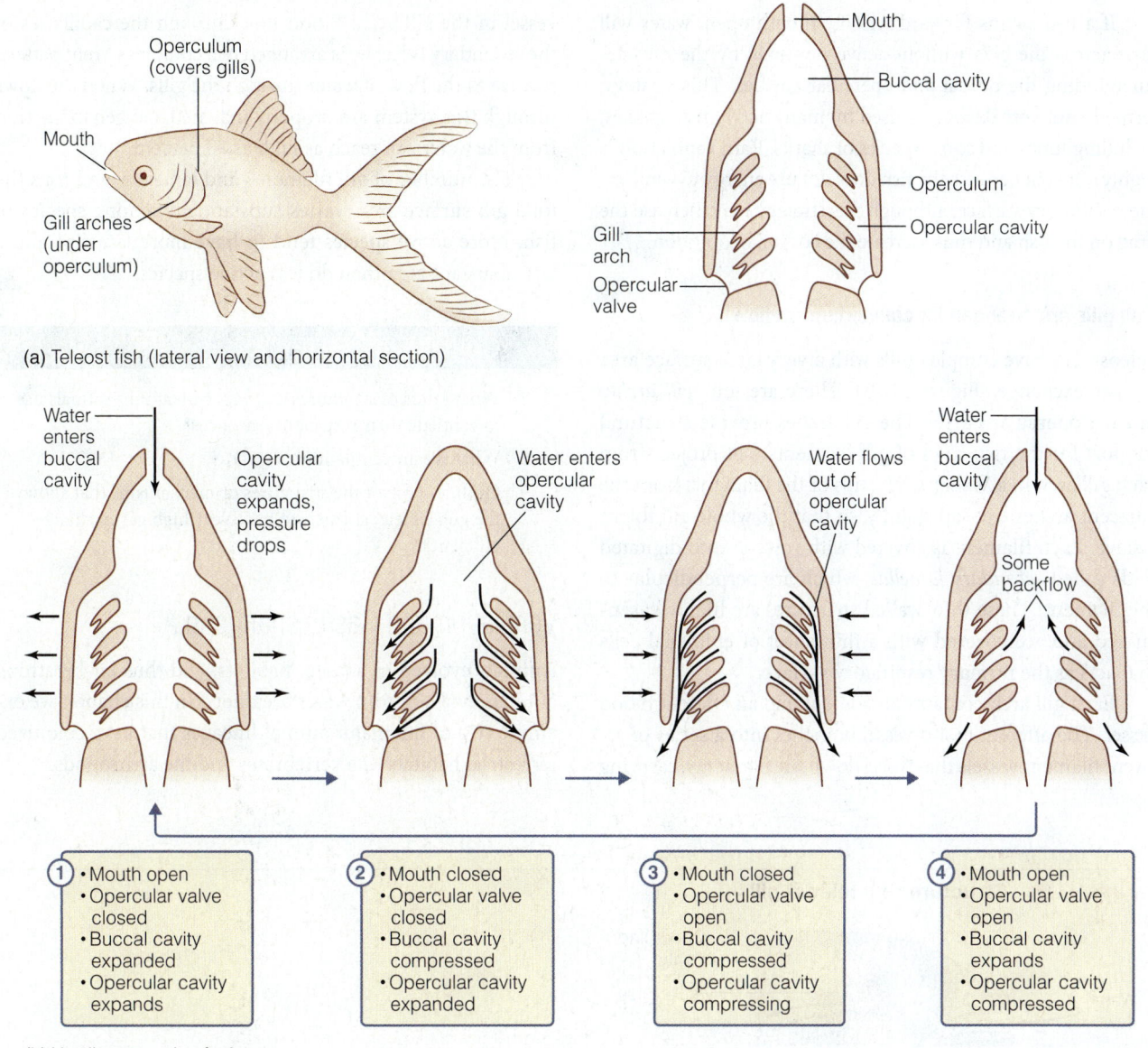

(a) Teleost fish (lateral view and horizontal section)

1
- Mouth open
- Opercular valve closed
- Buccal cavity expanded
- Opercular cavity expands

2
- Mouth closed
- Opercular valve closed
- Buccal cavity compressed
- Opercular cavity expanded

3
- Mouth closed
- Opercular valve open
- Buccal cavity compressed
- Opercular cavity compressing

4
- Mouth open
- Opercular valve open
- Buccal cavity expands
- Opercular cavity compressed

(b) Ventilatory cycle of teleosts

increasing the pressure and pushing water into the expanded opercular cavity. In the next phase of the ventilatory cycle the fish opens its operculum, causing water to flow from the buccal cavity, through the opercular cavity, and out into the environment via the opercular slit. At this stage, the operculum moves inward and begins compressing the opercular cavity, increasing the pressure in the opercular cavity and forcing water out via the open opercular valve. At this point, the pressure within the buccal cavity is still high, so there is little or no backflow from the opercular cavity to the buccal cavity.

The final phase of the ventilatory cycle, which occupies only a small fraction of the total ventilatory cycle, occurs when the fish again opens its mouth and begins to expand the buccal cavity. At this point, the operculum is still compressed, and pressure in the opercular cavity is high. The high opercular pressure continues to force water out into the environment via the opened opercular valve, but because of the lowered pressure in the buccal cavity there may be some backflow of water from the opercular cavity into the buccal cavity. The opercular and buccal cavities then reset to their starting positions. Although there may be brief periods of backflow in the last phase of the ventilatory cycle, flow is generally unidirectional and almost continuous through most of the ventilatory cycle because of the careful coordination of the action of the buccal and opercular pumps. In general, the opercular pump sucks while the buccal pump fills, and the buccal cavity pumps when the opercular cavity empties, reducing the possibility of backflow.

If a fish swims forward with its mouth open, water will flow across the gills without active pumping by the muscles surrounding the buccal and opercular cavities. This strategy, termed **ram ventilation**, is used by many active fish species, including tunas and some species of sharks. Ram ventilation is highly efficient because the fish does not use energy to ventilate the respiratory surface, although this strategy may increase the drag on the fish and thus increase the cost of locomotion.

Fish gills are arranged for countercurrent flow

Teleost fish have complex gills with a very large surface area for gas exchange (Figure 11.15). There are four *gill arches* in each opercular cavity. The gill arches provide structural support for the two rows of gill filaments that project from each gill arch in a V shape. The tips of the filaments from the adjacent arches overlap slightly, so that the whole gill forms a sieve. Each filament is covered with rows of interdigitated folds called *secondary lamellae*, which are perpendicular to the filament. These thin-walled structures are highly vascularized and are covered with a thin sheet of epithelial cells that acts as the primary respiratory surface.

Each gill arch contains an afferent and an efferent blood vessel. The afferent blood vessel branches into a series of afferent filament vessels that travel down the filaments, carrying blood to the respiratory surfaces. The afferent filament vessels then branch into many capillaries where gas exchange takes place. The capillaries then converge into an efferent filament vessel that carries oxygenated blood back to the efferent blood vessel in the gill arch. Blood flow through the capillaries of the secondary lamellae is arranged in a countercurrent pattern relative to the flow of water through the gills. When the flows through this system are properly matched, oxygen extraction from the water can reach as high as 70 percent.

The number of gill filaments and lamellae, and thus the total gill surface area, varies substantially among species of fish. More active species tend to have more lamellae and a larger surface area than do less active species.

CONCEPT CHECK

7. What kinds of structures can water-breathing animals use to ventilate their respiratory surfaces?

8. What is ram ventilation?

9. Outline some of the structures or mechanisms that allow the gills of teleost fishes to have very high gas-exchange efficiency.

Ventilation and Gas Exchange in Air

Animals evolved in aquatic habitats, and thus air-breathing animals evolved from water breathers. In this chapter we examine two of the major animal lineages that have colonized terrestrial habitats: the vertebrates and the arthropods.

FIGURE 11.15 Structure of a teleost gill

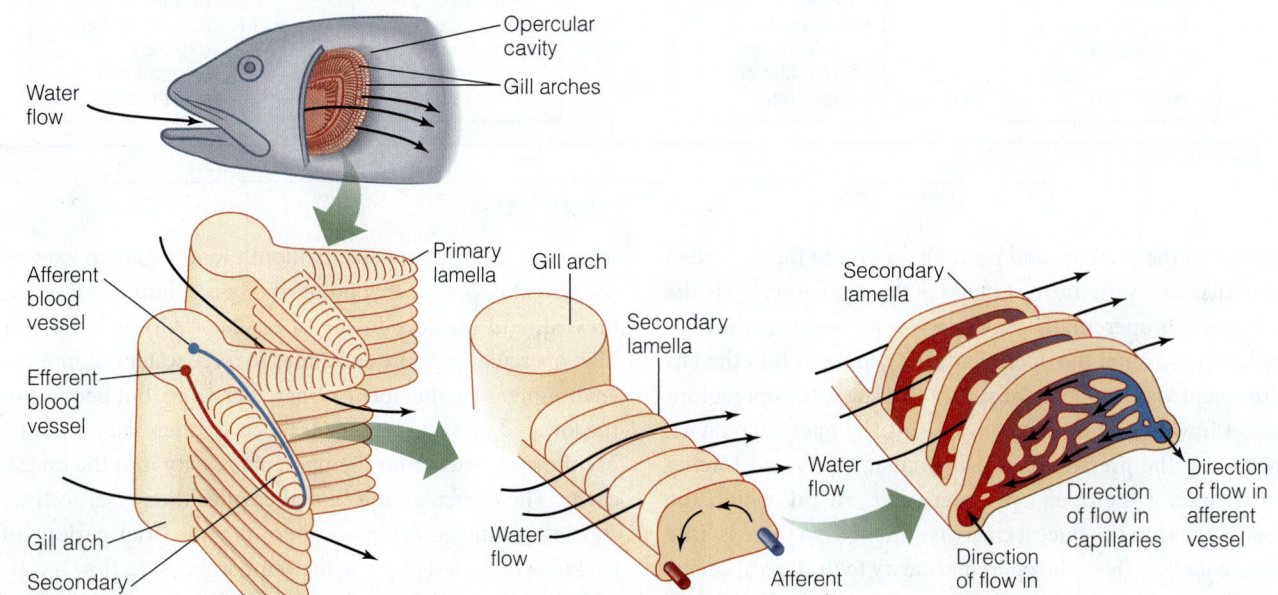

Arthropods use a variety of mechanisms for aerial gas exchange

The respiratory systems of the terrestrial and semiterrestrial crabs are similar in many ways to those of their marine relatives. Like marine crustaceans, these animals have gills located in a branchial cavity, but the gills of terrestrial crabs are stiff so that they do not collapse in air. In addition, the walls of the branchial cavity are often thin and highly vascularized, acting as the primary site of gas exchange in some species. Terrestrial crabs ventilate their branchial cavity in much the same way as do their aquatic relatives; beating of the scaphognathite propels air in and out of the branchial chamber. In some terrestrial crabs, such as the porcelain crabs (genus *Petrolisthes*), the walking legs serve as an accessory respiratory surface. The carapace on part of the walking legs is very thin, allowing gas exchange.

Among the crustaceans, the terrestrial isopods (such as woodlice and sowbugs) have the most extensive specializations for gas exchange with air. In some species, such as the seashore isopod *Ligia*, a thick layer of chitin on one side of the gill provides support, while the other side is a very thin wall specialized for aerial gas exchange. In other species, such as *Armadillidium*, the anterior gills are modified and contain many branching air-filled tubules called *pseudotracheae*. Oxygen in gaseous form diffuses down the pseudotracheae and dissolves in the interstitial fluid. The circulatory system then carries this oxygen to all parts of the body.

Most of the air-breathing chelicerates (spiders, scorpions, and their relatives) have four **book lungs** located within the body cavity (Figure 11.16). Book lungs are derived from the **book gills** of aquatic chelicerates such as horseshoe crabs. Book lungs consist of a series of 10–100 very thin lamellae that project into an air-filled cavity inside the body that opens to the outside via a spiracle. Air diffuses into the cavity via the spiracle and then across the walls of the lamellae into the hemolymph, which then carries the oxygen through the body.

In many spiders, the anterior pair of book lungs is replaced by a **tracheal system**, consisting of a series of air-filled tubes. Some species (such as the Solifugae, or sun spiders) lack book lungs entirely and have only a tracheal system that penetrates into all parts of the body. Species with complex tracheal systems generally make little use of their circulatory systems for gas transport. Instead, oxygen diffuses in gaseous form down the trachea and then dissolves in the interstitial fluid before diffusing into the tissues. The normal body movements of a spider cause changes in the pressure inside the body cavity, which may help to ventilate the trachea. However, some scientists suggest that these movements interfere with gas transport down the trachea, and may reduce ventilation.

Some myriapods (centipedes and millipedes) have tracheal systems similar to those in spiders, but the most extensive tracheal systems are found in insects. As in chelicerates,

FIGURE 11.16 **The book lungs of chelicerates**

Book lungs are composed of a series of thin plates called lamellae. Oxygen from air diffuses across the surfaces of the lamellae into the hemolymph.

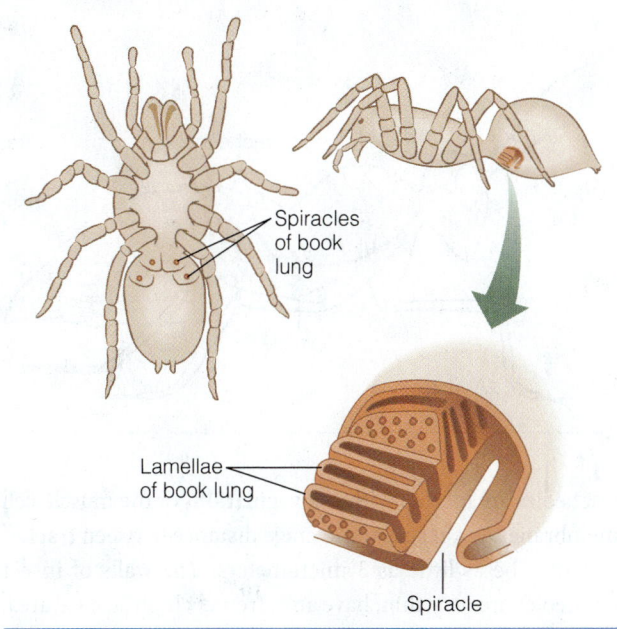

Spiracles of book lung

Lamellae of book lung

Spiracle

the tracheal system of insects is open to the outside air via a series of spiracles, which lead to the air-filled **tracheae** (singular: trachea) that penetrate deep into the body (Figure 11.17). The tracheae branch and divide, terminating in tiny thin-walled structures called **tracheoles**, which can be as small as 0.2 micrometers in diameter. The ends of the tracheoles are filled with circulatory fluid called hemolymph (see Chapter 9: Circulatory Systems). Oxygen dissolves in this fluid, and then diffuses across the thin walls of the tracheoles. The tracheoles penetrate down among individual cells, bringing them into close contact with the mitochondria within these cells. This results in a very low diffusion distance and enhances oxygen delivery.

There is no clear functional distinction between tracheae and tracheoles, but they differ structurally and in size. Tracheae are relatively large tubes that are formed by joining together several epithelial cells. In many species, the walls of the tracheae are reinforced by structures called *taenidia*. These thin bands of cuticle are wrapped in a spiral pattern around the walls of the tracheae. In some species, portions of the tracheae lack taenidia, and instead form air sacs, which are involved in ventilating the tracheal system in these species. In contrast, tracheoles are formed by hollowing out a single cell, and thus have a wall that consists only of two layers of cell membrane. Tracheoles are so numerous that an insect cell is seldom more than a few hundred micrometers, or a few cell diameters, away from the nearest tracheole. In fact, in metabolically active cells such as flight muscle,

FIGURE 11.17 **Insect tracheal systems**

Air enters the tracheae via the spiracles and travels down the progressively branching tubes to the tracheoles. Oxygen then dissolves in the extracellular fluid within the tracheoles and diffuses into the tissues.

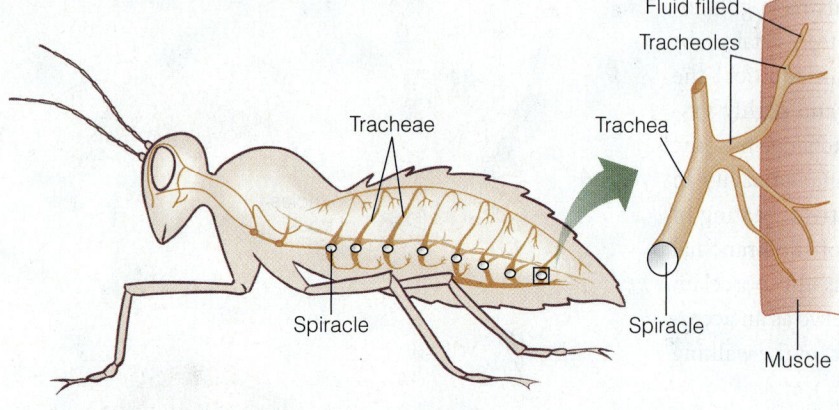

tracheoles are located within invaginations of the muscle cell membrane. As a result, the average distance between tracheoles may be as little as 3 micrometers. The walls of insect tracheoles are very thin, have an extremely high surface area, and are always moist—characteristics required for high-efficiency gas exchange. But because of these factors the tracheoles are also a potential site for water loss, increasing the danger of desiccation, particularly in arid environments. In many species of insects the spiracles can be opened and closed, which seals the tracheal system off from the environment part of the time, potentially reducing water loss.

Tracheal systems provide high-efficiency gas exchange in air because of the high diffusion coefficients of gases in air relative to water. In fact, tracheal systems have evolved independently in several groups of terrestrial arthropods, suggesting that there has been strong natural selection for tracheal-like systems in air. However, tracheal respiratory systems are not very efficient for gas exchange in water.

Tracheal systems are inefficient in water

Although insects evolved on land, some insect groups have secondarily colonized aquatic habitats. Tracheal systems are not very well suited for aquatic respiration, because of the low oxygen content and high density and viscosity of water, and the relatively low rate of diffusion of oxygen in solution. Aquatic insects cope with this problem in two ways. Some insects have structures termed *tracheal gills*, which allow them to extract oxygen from water. Other aquatic insects have developed strategies that permit them to continue to breathe air despite their aquatic habitat.

Like the gills of other species, tracheal gills are evaginations of the body surface, generally arranged in a series of platelike structures. However, tracheal gills are densely packed with sealed air-filled tracheae and tracheoles, covered with only a very thin layer of cuticle. These gills bring the tracheae into very close contact with the water, allowing gas exchange by diffusion. Tracheal gills are generally found in the immature stages of insects and are typical of aquatic **nymphs**, the juvenile stages of insects that do not form pupae. These gills can be located on various parts of the body, including the abdomen, the base of the legs, the anus, and the rectum (the posterior portion of the gut). Mayfly and dragonfly nymphs have tracheal gills on the outside of their abdominal segments, which can be moved to generate ventilatory water currents. Insects with rectal gills pump water in and out of the rectum for ventilation.

Some aquatic insects breathe through siphons

Many species of aquatic insects simply avoid using water as a respiratory medium. For example, some insects such as mosquito larvae remain near the water surface and breathe air through a specialized structure that extends above the surface of the water and acts as a siphon or snorkel (Figure 11.18). To make sure that air and not water will enter the siphon, the spiracles on these respiratory siphons are often covered with water-repellent *hydrofuge hairs*. Some species also have hydrophobic lipids in the tracheoles that repel any water that may enter. Some fly (dipteran) larvae, including *Chrysogaster* and *Notiphila*, and the larvae of the beetle *Donacia* utilize a variant on this siphon strategy. These insects have a sharply

FIGURE 11.18 **Mosquito larvae breathing through siphons**

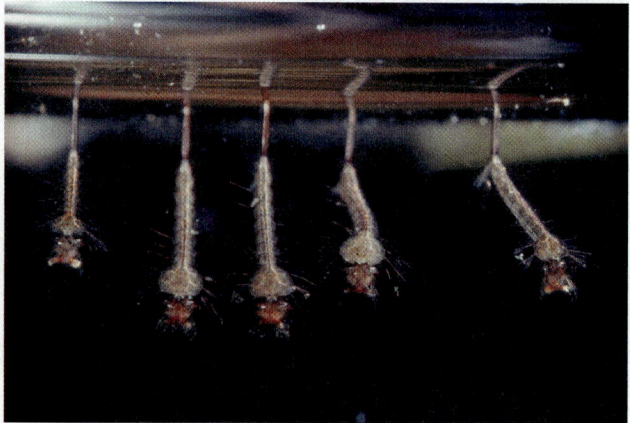

Photo source: Biosphoto/SuperStock.

pointed abdominal siphon, which they use to pierce the surface of aquatic plants and extract the oxygen produced by photosynthesis.

Some aquatic insects carry bubbles of air

Insects that breathe through siphons must remain close to an air source, which imposes severe limitations on their behavior. Many beetles and bugs have adopted a different strategy, that of bubble breathing. These insects dive beneath the surface carrying a conspicuous bubble of air under their wings. This bubble acts as an air supply while the animal is under water. As the animal consumes oxygen from the bubble, the partial pressure of oxygen within the bubble falls lower than that of the surrounding water. As a result, oxygen diffuses down this partial pressure gradient from the water into the air bubble, providing additional oxygen to the animal. Some beetles increase this gas exchange by stirring the water around the bubble with their legs. This reduces the size of the boundary layer around the bubble, and increases oxygen availability.

Because the P_{O_2} within the bubble is lower than that in the water, and the total pressure remains similar to atmospheric pressure, the P_{N_2} within the bubble increases slightly, causing nitrogen to diffuse out of the bubble and into the water. As a result, the bubble gradually shrinks in size over time. Nitrogen is less soluble in water than is oxygen, so nitrogen leaves the bubble more slowly than oxygen enters, but over time the bubble will gradually shrink. Because CO_2 is so soluble in water, it rapidly diffuses out of the bubble, and the CO_2 produced by metabolism does not help to stabilize the size of the bubble.

Diffusion of oxygen into the bubble is a function of the surface area of the bubble (according to the Fick equation), so oxygen delivery declines as the size of the bubble decreases. As a result, these insects must periodically return to the surface to renew their bubble. This problem is even more acute as the insect descends deeper into the water. Hydrostatic pressure increases with depth, causing the volume of the bubble to decrease, which causes an increase in P_{O_2} and P_{N_2} within the bubble. Under these circumstances both oxygen and nitrogen diffuse out of the bubble, causing the size of the bubble to decrease rapidly. Once the P_{O_2} within the bubble drops below the external P_{O_2}, oxygen will start to diffuse into the bubble, and the bubble will shrink more slowly. However, it will continue to decrease in size as nitrogen diffuses into the water, forcing the insect to return to the surface.

Some small aquatic beetles avoid returning to the surface by capturing the oxygen bubbles produced by photosynthesizing algae and adding this gaseous oxygen to their gas bubble. Other bugs and beetles use the strategy of hydrofuge hairs to prevent their bubbles from shrinking. In bugs such as *Aphelocheirus aestivalis* these hairs are arranged into a structure called a plastron, which consists of an extremely dense layer of hydrofuge hairs. These hairs trap air bubbles as a thin film of gas along the surface of the body. The hairs are not collapsible, so the volume of the plastron is fixed. As the air bubble loses nitrogen to the water, the surface tension of the air-water junction between the hairs holds the bubble in place, preventing it from decreasing in size. Thus, the hydrofuge hairs prevent the bubble from collapsing. The bubble then reaches an equilibrium in which its volume is constant, but its internal pressure is reduced. Some species of aquatic insects with plastrons can remain submerged almost indefinitely.

Other aquatic insects maintain large oxygen stores within their bodies. For example, some species of aquatic bugs have hemoglobin molecules in their hemolymph. This hemoglobin is used as an oxygen store that can help aquatic insects remain submerged for prolonged periods.

Many insects actively ventilate the tracheae

The high diffusion coefficient of oxygen in air allows oxygen to diffuse through the tracheal system and still support the metabolic needs of most species of insects. However, many insects also ventilate the tracheal system actively either through contractions of the abdominal muscles or through movements of the thorax. When the abdominal muscles contract, the volume of the abdomen decreases, forcing air out of the tracheae. When the muscles relax, the abdomen springs back to its normal volume, decreasing the pressure within the tracheae, and causing air to move into the tracheae by bulk flow. Similarly, in the thorax as the wings beat, the thoracic muscles contract and relax, changing the volume of the tracheae within the thorax, which causes the air to move in and out of the tracheae by bulk flow. Oxygen then diffuses into the tracheoles, as is the case in species that do not ventilate the tracheae.

The direction of airflow through the tracheal system varies among insects. Insects with relatively simple tracheal systems use tidal ventilation; in others, the flow through the tracheae is unidirectional. For example, in cockroaches and locusts, air enters the anterior spiracles, passing through large longitudinal tracheae and exiting the body via the abdominal spiracles at the rear of the body. This unidirectional ventilation may increase the efficiency of gas exchange by providing a continuous supply of fresh air to the respiratory surfaces, although even in these insects the smaller tracheae that branch off the large longitudinal tracheae are still ventilated tidally. Some flying insects, such as cerambycid (or long-horned) beetles, take advantage of ram ventilation, which is also called *draft ventilation* in insects, to ventilate the large longitudinal tracheae.

Observations of living insects, using a novel technique called synchrotron X-ray imaging, suggest that the volume of the tracheae can change by as much as 50 percent in a rapid cycle of expansion and compression that occurs every one to two seconds (Figure 11.19) and that cannot be accounted for by changes in the volume of the abdomen or thorax. The resulting pressure changes within the tracheae move the air by bulk flow.

Some insects use a ventilatory pattern known as **discontinuous gas exchange**, particularly when they are at rest. Discontinuous gas exchange occurs in three phases (Figure 11.20). During the first phase, called the *closed phase*, the spiracles remain shut, preventing gas exchange with the environment. As a result, the oxygen partial pressure in the tracheoles drops as the mitochondria consume oxygen. However, the partial pressure of carbon dioxide does not increase nearly as much, because the carbon dioxide produced by metabolism reacts with water in the interstitial fluid to form bicarbonate (HCO_3^-). This decline in oxygen without an increase in carbon dioxide causes a slight decrease in the total gas pressure within the tracheae. During the next phase of the respiratory cycle, called the *flutter phase*, the spiracles open and close many times in rapid succession. The low pressure within the tracheae causes air to enter the insect's body, moving by bulk flow down the resulting pressure gradient. Eventually, as carbon dioxide accumulates, and can no longer be stored as HCO_3^-, the partial pressure of carbon dioxide begins to increase. The flutter phase is followed by the *open phase*. At this point in the respiratory cycle, the spiracles open completely, and carbon dioxide is rapidly released.

The adaptive significance of discontinuous gas exchange is a matter of active debate among insect physiologists, and three main hypotheses have been advanced to explain it.

- Discontinuous gas exchange may facilitate tracheal ventilation by causing low total gas pressure within the tracheae, or by inducing a low P_{O_2} that increases the P_{O_2} gradient between the tracheae and the environment, assisting the diffusion of oxygen into the animal. This could be particularly important in insects that spend all or part of their life cycle underground, where environmental P_{O_2} is low and P_{CO_2} is high.

- Discontinuous gas exchange may help to minimize water loss across the tracheae, because water will be lost from the tracheae only during the short open phase of the respiratory cycle.

- Discontinuous gas exchange may protect insects from the harmful effects of oxygen. Although oxygen is necessary for most animal life, it is also a highly reactive chemical that can damage tissues. When an insect's spiracles are fully open, fresh air can diffuse deep into the body, and the P_{O_2} at the ends of the tracheoles approaches 20 kPa. In vertebrates, internal tissues are seldom exposed to P_{O_2} greater than 0.5 kPa, and exposure to high P_{O_2} can cause tissue damage. During discontinuous ventilation the tissues are only exposed to high P_{O_2} during the short open phase, whereas tracheal P_{O_2} remains low during the rest of the ventilatory cycle.

Further research is needed to determine which, if any, of these hypotheses accounts for the evolution of discontinuous gas exchange in insects.

Air breathing has evolved multiple times in vertebrates

Almost 400 species of extant fish are thought to obtain all or part of their oxygen from air, and air breathing is thought to have evolved multiple times within the fishes. As a result of

FIGURE 11.19 X-ray synchrotron images of insect tracheae

A synchrotron, an instrument that can generate an extremely bright beam of light, can be used to generate high-resolution X-ray videos. Using this technique, scientists have been able to visualize the movements of insect tracheae. In some species, the tracheae undergo rapid cycles of expansion and contraction that are independent of movements of the rest of the body. These movements help to ventilate the tracheae. **(a)** X-ray synchrotron image of a Carabid beetle (*Pterostichus stygicus*), **(b)** close-up showing the tracheae, **(c)** tracheae expanded, **(d)** tracheae collapsed during ventilation.

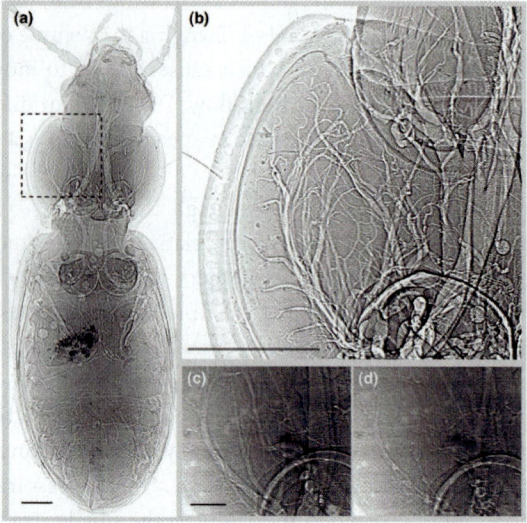

Figure source: Socha JJ, Westneat MW, Harrison JF, Waters JS, Lee WK: Real-time phase-contrast x-ray imaging: a new technique for the study of animal form and function. BMC Biology 2007, 5:6.
Photo source: **(a)** and **(b)** John J Socha/Biomedcentral.

FIGURE 11.20 Discontinuous gas-exchange cycles in insects

Some insects keep their spiracles closed for long periods, only opening them briefly for gas exchange.

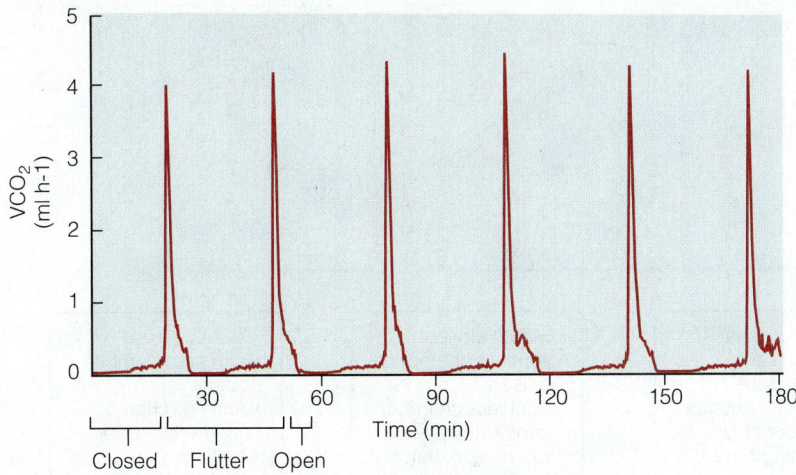

Figure source: Adapted from Hetz, SK & Bradley, TJ. (2005). Figure 2 from Insects breathe discontinuously to avoid oxygen toxicity. *Nature.* Feb 3, 433 (7025): 516–519.

Air-breathing fish ventilate their breathing organs using a buccal force pump similar to those of other fishes (Figure 11.21). They drop the floor of the buccal cavity, and the increase in volume causes a drop in pressure that draws air into the mouth. By closing the mouth and raising the floor of the buccal cavity, the fish then forces air down into the breathing organ. In essence, air-breathing fish simply swallow air.

Amphibians ventilate their lungs using a buccal force pump

Amphibians use cutaneous respiration, external gills, lungs, or some combination of these three methods of gas exchange, depending on whether they are obtaining oxygen from water or from air. Amphibians have relatively simple bilobed lungs that form as outpocketings of the buccal cavity. In some species they may be nothing more than a pair of thin-walled, highly vascularized sacs; however, in the terrestrial frogs and toads, the inner surface of the lungs can be highly folded or divided by partitions called septa, which give the lungs a honeycombed appearance and increase the surface area available for gas exchange.

An amphibian ventilates its lungs using a buccal force pump, similar to that used by air-breathing fish. In the first step of ventilation, the frog expands its buccal cavity, drawing air in through the open **nares** (nostrils) (Figure 11.22). At this point in the ventilatory cycle, the **glottis**, a muscular orifice that acts as a valve for the lungs, is closed. As a result, the fresh air is held in a pocket of the buccal cavity. The frog may make repeated buccal movements to fully refresh the air within the buccal cavity. Next, the glottis opens. Elastic recoil of the lung pushes the spent air into the buccal cavity and out the mouth and nares. Muscle contraction in the chest wall may assist in this exhalation. There is thought to be relatively little mixing of the exhaled stale air with the fresh air held in the buccal cavity because inhaled air is held at the bottom of the buccal cavity, while exhaled air flows out through the upper regions of the buccal cavity. However, the exact degree of mixing is a matter of some debate. The nares then close and the floor of the buccal cavity rises, forcing air from the buccal cavity into the lungs. The glottis then closes as a result of muscular contractions, sealing off the lungs and preventing air from escaping, allowing time for gas exchange.

these independent evolutionary events, fish use a variety of structures for aerial gas exchange. For example, mudskippers have specialized "reinforced" gills that do not completely collapse in air, allowing some limited gas exchange when the fish is out of water. Many fish have specialized *accessory breathing organs* that they use in addition to, or instead of, gills when breathing air. Electric eels use the mouth and pharyngeal cavity for gas exchange. The inside of the mouth is highly vascularized, allowing substantial gas exchange. Some fish, including the armored catfish (*Liposarcus anisitsi*), have a highly modified and vascularized stomach that they use for aerial gas exchange. Many air-breathing fish, including bichirs (*Polypteriformes*), use specialized pockets off the gut for gas exchange.

Lungfish have the most highly developed air-breathing organ of any fish. These lungs are highly complex, covered in folds and pockets that increase their surface area. There are three living genera of lungfish. The Australian lungfish (*Neoceratodus*) has a single lung and relatively well-developed gills, whereas the African lungfish (*Protopterus*) and South American lungfish (*Lepidosiren*) have bilobed lungs and reduced gills. In addition to their highly developed lungs, lungfish have a two-circuit circulatory system with a separate pulmonary circuit. This allows lungfish to separate oxygenated blood coming from the **pulmonary system** and deoxygenated blood coming from the tissues. Animals similar to lungfish are thought to be the common ancestor of the tetrapods (amphibians, reptiles, birds, and mammals).

FIGURE 11.21   The ventilatory cycle in an air-breathing fish

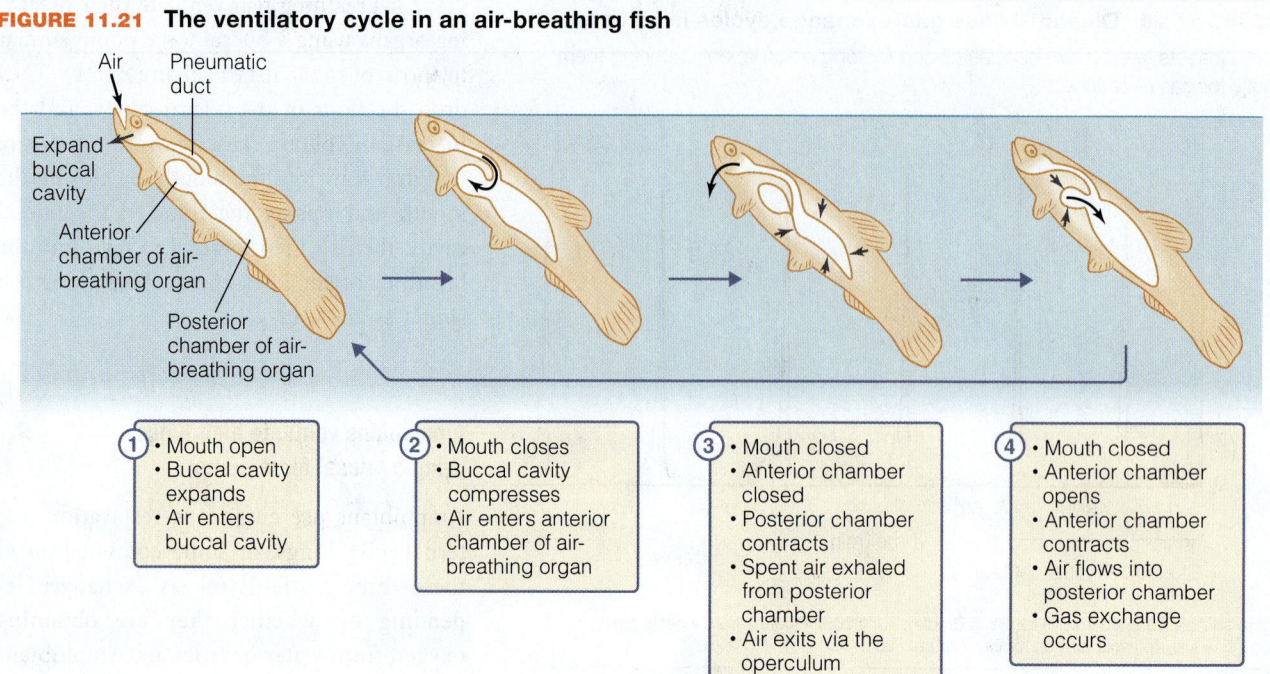

1
• Mouth open
• Buccal cavity expands
• Air enters buccal cavity

2
• Mouth closes
• Buccal cavity compresses
• Air enters anterior chamber of air-breathing organ

3
• Mouth closed
• Anterior chamber closed
• Posterior chamber contracts
• Spent air exhaled from posterior chamber
• Air exits via the operculum

4
• Mouth closed
• Anterior chamber opens
• Anterior chamber contracts
• Air flows into posterior chamber
• Gas exchange occurs

Amphibians are typically intermittent breathers. They often pause for a substantial period before beginning the respiratory cycle again. During the time that the lungs are sealed off by the glottis, a frog may pump air in and out of the buccal cavity multiple times. In fact, amphibians have a diverse ventilatory repertoire. The steps outlined above constitute a *balanced breath*, in which a roughly equal amount of air leaves and then enters the lungs with each ventilatory cycle. But amphibians can also undergo *inflation breaths*, in which the lung deflation step (Figure 11.22, step 2) is reduced or absent, or *deflation breaths*, in which more air leaves the lungs than is pumped back. Further increasing the complexity of amphibian breathing, there are some amphibian species in which the order of the steps differs. For example, aquatic toads such as *Xenopus* first empty both the lungs and the buccal cavity through the open glottis and nares, then draw fresh air into the buccal cavity with the glottis closed, and finally pump this air into the lungs with the glottis open

FIGURE 11.22   The ventilatory cycle in a frog

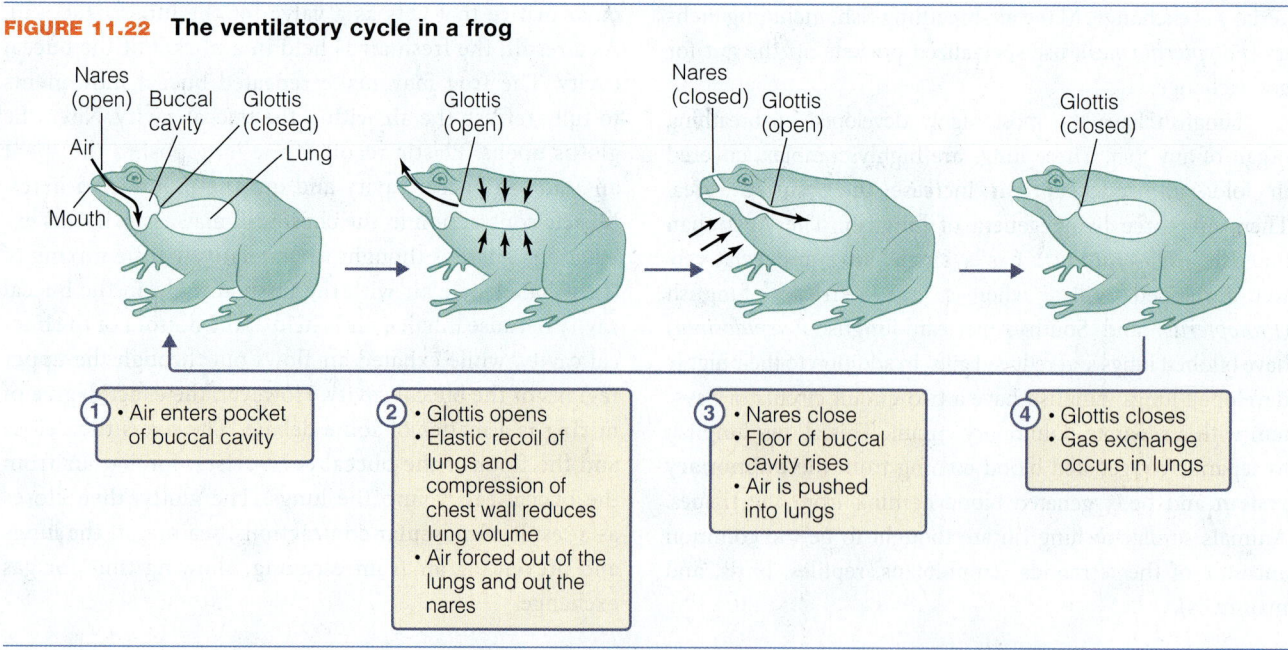

1
• Air enters pocket of buccal cavity

2
• Glottis opens
• Elastic recoil of lungs and compression of chest wall reduces lung volume
• Air forced out of the lungs and out the nares

3
• Nares close
• Floor of buccal cavity rises
• Air is pushed into lungs

4
• Glottis closes
• Gas exchange occurs in lungs

and the nares closed (essentially performing the steps in Figure 11.22 in the order 2, 1, 3, 4).

Reptiles ventilate their lungs using a suction pump

Most reptiles have two lungs, although in snakes one of the lungs may be greatly reduced or absent. The simplest, or *unicameral*, lung is a saclike chamber with a honeycombed wall, similar to the most complex amphibian lungs. In highly active species such as monitor lizards, as well as the turtles and crocodilians, the lungs are divided into many chambers, greatly increasing the surface area available for gas exchange. Each of these *multicameral* lungs has a stiffened tube called a **bronchus** (plural: bronchi) that allows airflow into the chambers of the lung. In some reptiles, the posterior part of the lungs is poorly vascularized, and may act as a bellows to help in lung ventilation.

Reptiles rely on aspiration (suction) pumps to ventilate their lungs, rather than forcing air into the lungs using a buccal pump. This important evolutionary innovation separates the muscles used in feeding from the muscles used in ventilation and is also seen in birds and mammals. In all of these groups, the ventilatory cycle is divided into two phases. During **inspiration** (inhalation), the volume of the chest cavity increases, decreasing the pressure and causing air to enter the lungs. During **expiration** (exhalation), the volume of the chest cavity decreases, increasing the pressure and causing air to exit the lungs.

Reptiles use one of several mechanisms to change the volume of the chest cavity during breathing (Figure 11.23). Snakes and lizards use the intercostal muscles, which are located between the ribs. Contraction of a group of the intercostals lifts the ribs forward and outward, increasing the volume of the chest cavity, sucking air into the lungs. In lizards, the intercostal muscles are also needed for locomotion; when a lizard runs it moves its body back and forth laterally in an S-shaped pattern, a movement that involves the intercostal muscles. Thus, the muscle contractions needed for locomotion may compromise lung ventilation in some species. However, some lizards are known to supplement ventilation with a buccal force pump similar to that used by amphibians, particularly during locomotion.

In turtles and tortoises (Figure 11.23b), the rib cage is fused to the rigid shell, and cannot be moved to ventilate the lungs. Instead, these animals have a pair of sheetlike abdominal muscles that expand and compress the lungs. In addition, movements of the limbs may assist in lung ventilation. However, as with the lizards, during locomotion there may be some conflicts between the motions needed for ventilation and those needed for locomotion. Turtles are not known to use a buccal force pump to assist in ventilating the lungs.

FIGURE 11.23 Lung ventilation in reptiles
(a) Lizards ventilate their lungs using their intercostal muscles.
(b) Chelonians ventilate their lungs using movements of specialized abdominal muscles and the limbs. **(c)** Crocodilians ventilate their lungs using the diaphragmaticus muscles.

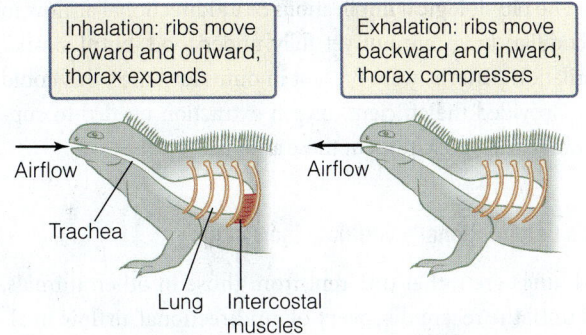

(a) Lung ventilation in lizards

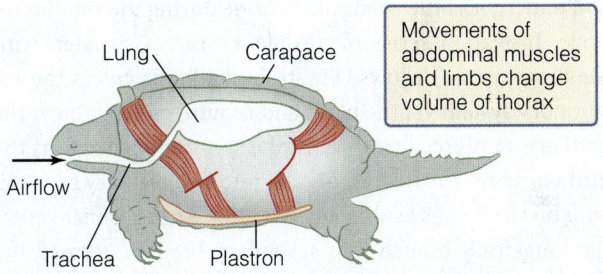

(b) Lung ventilation in chelonians (turtles and tortoises)

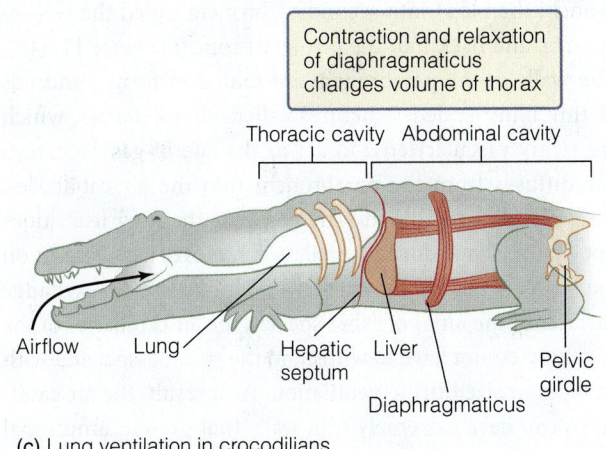

(c) Lung ventilation in crocodilians

In crocodilians (Figure 11.23c), a sheet of connective tissue called the *hepatic septum* is tightly attached to the anterior side of the liver, and divides the visceral cavity into an anterior and a posterior space. The paired diaphragmaticus muscles run from the hepatic septum to the pelvic girdle. When these muscles contract, they pull on the hepatic septum and the liver, decreasing the volume of the abdominal cavity, and increasing the volume of the lungs. This increase in lung volume decreases the pressure in the lungs, and the resulting suction draws air into the lungs. In essence, the liver acts like a piston that helps to alternately compress and expand the lungs. The pistonlike ventilatory mechanism of the crocodilian lung has generally been thought to result in bidirectional ventilation, with air moving into and out of the lung along the same pathway. However, recent studies suggest unidirectional airflow may occur. The physiological implications of unidirectional airflow in crocodilian lungs are not yet fully understood, but if similar ventilation patterns were present in dinosaur lungs, this could have provided the efficient oxygen extraction needed to support high metabolic rates in these animals.

Birds unidirectionally ventilate their lungs

Bird lungs are rather different from those in other animals, and until the recent discovery of unidirectional airflow in alligator lungs, the avian lung was thought to be unique in allowing unidirectional airflow. In birds, the lung itself is stiff and undergoes little change in volume during the ventilatory cycle. Instead, a series of flexible air sacs associated with the lungs act as bellows (Figure 11.24a). Air enters the respiratory system via the nares and mouth, passing down the cartilage-reinforced trachea. At the *syrinx*, which acts as the bird voicebox, the trachea divides into two primary bronchi, with one bronchus leading to each lung. As the bronchi enter the lungs they branch into secondary bronchi, termed the *dorsobronchi*, and then into smaller tubes called **parabronchi** that are arranged in parallel in a hexagonal array. The parabronchi then lead into secondary bronchi called the *ventrobronchi*, and back into the primary bronchi (Figure 11.24b). The walls of the parabronchi are folded to form hundreds of tiny blind-ended structures called *air capillaries*, which are richly vascularized and act as the site of gas exchange. Air diffuses from the parabronchi into the air capillaries, and then into the blood. The fact that the lung itself does not change shape during ventilation removes a constraint on the structure of the air capillaries. Unlike the air-exchange surfaces of the lungs of other species, the air capillaries of the bird lung do not have to withstand the strain associated with changes in size during ventilation. As a result, the air capillaries can have extremely thin walls that present a minimal barrier to gas exchange by diffusion, making the avian lung a very efficient gas-exchange organ.

In birds, ventilation of the lungs requires two cycles of inhalation and exhalation. Because of this ventilatory pattern, airflow across the respiratory surfaces of the lungs is unidirectional and almost continuous. Figure 11.25 follows a single breath of air as it moves through the bird's respiratory system. A bird inhales by expanding the volume of its chest using the rib muscles and muscles attached to the sternum (breastbone). This movement increases the volume of the air sacs, and decreases the pressure within them. Air flows through the trachea and bronchi down this pressure gradient, and moves primarily

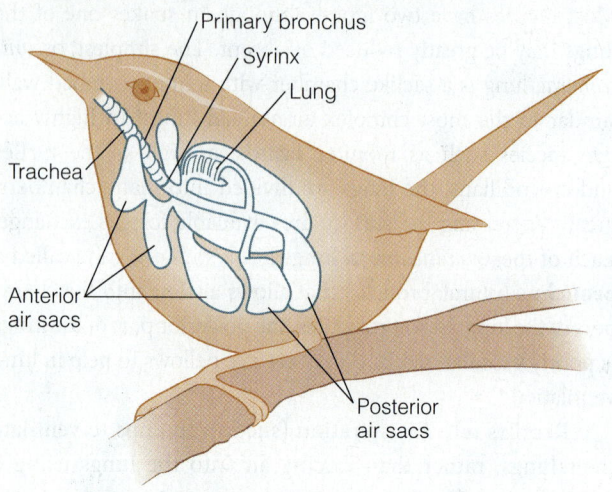

FIGURE 11.24 **Structure of bird lungs**
The respiratory system of birds consists of a pair of rigid lungs and a series of highly extensible air sacs. The stiff lung is made up of hexagonal arrays of parabronchi. Extensions of the parabronchi, called air capillaries, are the site of gas exchange.

(a)

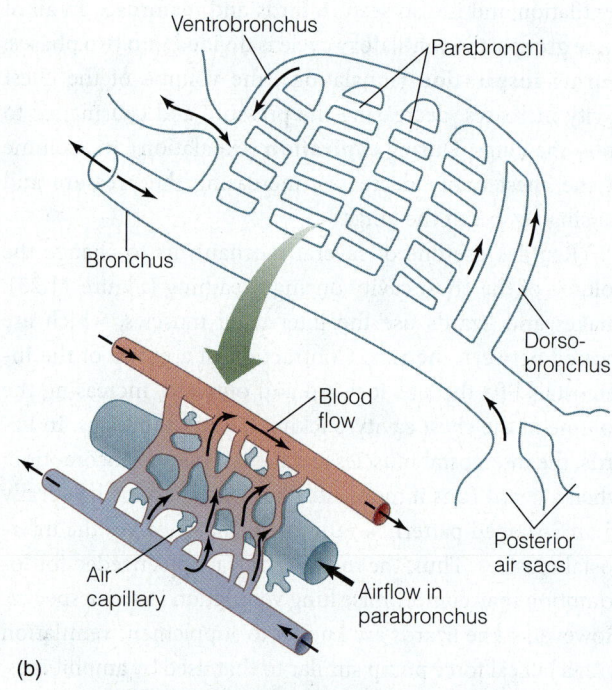

(b)

into the posterior air sacs. There are no physical valves between the bronchi and the lungs, so mechanisms that cause the air to move into the posterior air sacs rather than into the lungs are not fully understood. Unidirectional flow of air is thought to be caused by a combination of a lower pressure in the posterior air sacs relative to the lung and to a phenomenon called *aerodynamic valving* that is a result of the relative diameter of the bronchi and their anatomical arrangement. After inspiration, the bird exhales by compressing its chest, increasing the

FIGURE 11.25 The ventilatory cycle in a bird

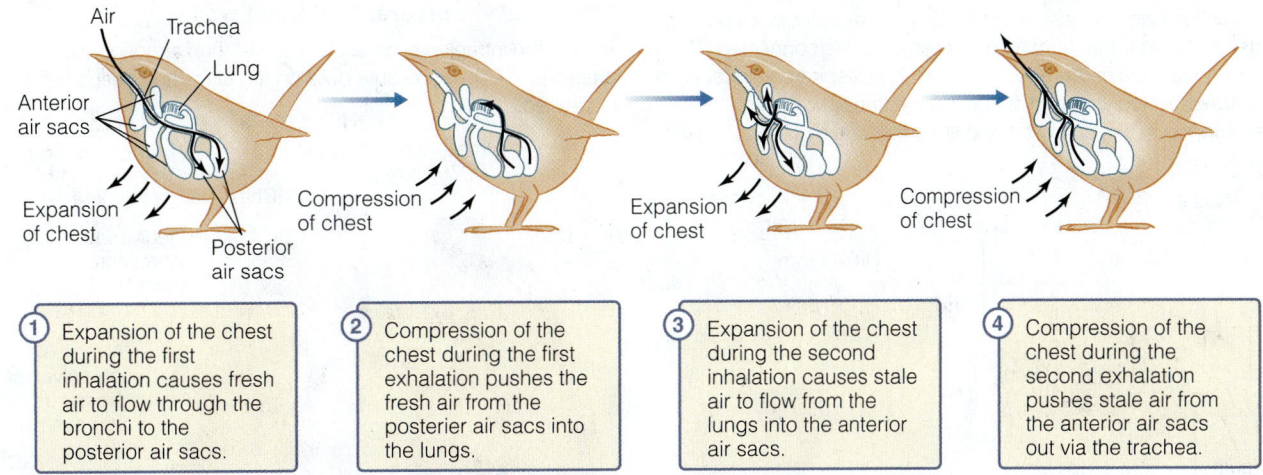

1. Expansion of the chest during the first inhalation causes fresh air to flow through the bronchi to the posterior air sacs.

2. Compression of the chest during the first exhalation pushes the fresh air from the posterier air sacs into the lungs.

3. Expansion of the chest during the second inhalation causes stale air to flow from the lungs into the anterior air sacs.

4. Compression of the chest during the second exhalation pushes stale air from the anterior air sacs out via the trachea.

pressure within the air sacs. This pressure gradient moves air from the posterior air sacs into the lungs. The next inhalation causes this air to move from the lungs into the anterior air sacs. Then, on the next exhalation, the air moves from the anterior air sacs back into the trachea and out the mouth or nares. Note that although we have separated the ventilatory cycle into four steps for clarity, these processes actually occur simultaneously. Both sets of air sacs inflate during inhalation, but fresh air from the environment moves into the posterior air sacs, while stale air from the lungs moves into the anterior air sacs. During exhalation, both sets of air sacs deflate, and fresh air from the posterior air sacs moves into the lungs, while stale air from the anterior air sacs is exhaled out the nares and mouth.

Bird lungs are extremely efficient, and can extract a high percentage of oxygen from the air. In fact, the P_{O_2} of the blood leaving the lungs is typically higher than the P_{O_2} of the exhaled air. As we discussed earlier in the chapter, only a countercurrent or crosscurrent flow pattern in the lungs could account for this observation. To distinguish between these possibilities, respiratory physiologists experimentally reversed the direction of airflow through a bird lung. If the flow was in a countercurrent arrangement, reversing the flow of air should have greatly decreased the oxygen extraction efficiency. Instead, the P_{O_2} of the blood leaving the lung was always higher than the P_{O_2} of the exhaled air, regardless of the direction of airflow. This observation demonstrates that blood flow in a bird lung is arranged in a crosscurrent pattern, providing high oxygen extraction efficiency. Such efficiency may be needed to power flight, and may play a role in the ability of birds to tolerate high altitudes.

The alveoli are the site of gas exchange in mammals

The mammalian respiratory system is located within the chest cavity, or *thorax*, and is divided into an upper respiratory tract, consisting of the mouth, nasal cavity, pharynx, larynx, and trachea, and a lower respiratory tract consisting of the bronchi and gas-exchange surfaces (Figure 11.26). Air enters the lungs via the mouth and nares, passing through the pharynx and larynx, and then entering the cartilage-reinforced trachea. The trachea branches into two primary bronchi, which branch into successively smaller tubes called the secondary and tertiary bronchi, and then **bronchioles**. The bronchioles terminate in thin-walled, blind-ended sacs called **alveoli** that are the site of gas exchange.

The alveolar epithelium is composed of two types of cells. The thin Type I alveolar cells are responsible for gas exchange. The much thicker Type II alveolar cells are responsible for a variety of functions, including maintaining the fluid balance across the lungs and secreting lipoproteins called **surfactants**. The alveoli are wrapped with an extensive capillary network that covers 80–90 percent of the alveolar surface.

Both lungs are surrounded by the **pleural sac** (Figure 11.27), which consists of two layers of cells with a small amount of fluid between them, forming a space called the **pleural cavity**. The pleural fluid lubricates the pleura and allows the two layers to slide past each other during ventilation. The pressure within the fluid of the pleural cavity (or the **intrapleural pressure**) is normally subatmospheric, because the chest wall pulls on the outer layer of the pleura, whereas the elasticity of the lungs tends to pull on the inner layer of the pleura. These two opposing forces result in a subatmospheric pleural pressure.

Low intrapleural pressure plays a critical role in maintaining the integrity of the lungs. Between breaths, the pressure inside the lung at rest is equivalent to atmospheric pressure, and thus is higher than the intrapleural pressure. The relatively low pressure outside the lungs tends to pull the small airways and alveoli open, preventing these fragile structures

FIGURE 11.26 Structure of mammalian lungs

Mammalian lungs consist of conducting airways, not involved in gas exchange, that terminate in a series of interconnected blind-ended sacs called alveoli that form the respiratory surface. The alveoli are polygonal in shape, with flattened walls, and are wrapped in blood vessels and suspended in a collagenous matrix.

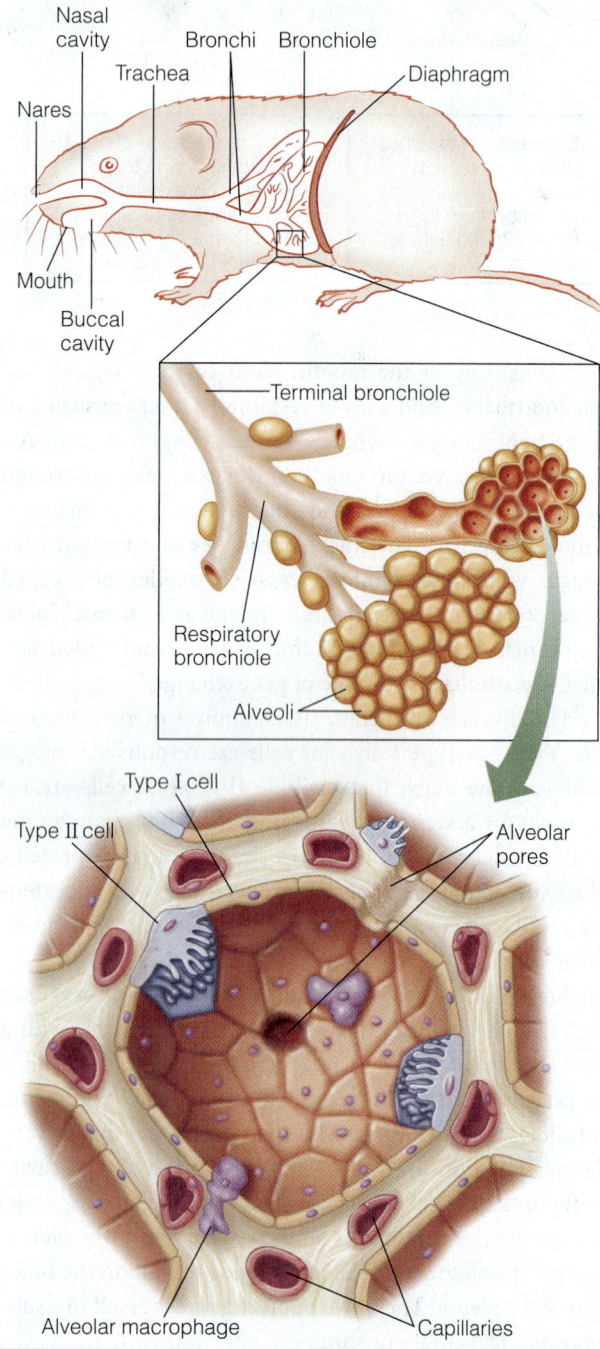

FIGURE 11.27 The relationship between the lungs, pleura, and chest wall

At rest, the intrapleural pressure is lower than atmospheric pressure. This low pressure pulls on the lungs and keeps them expanded.

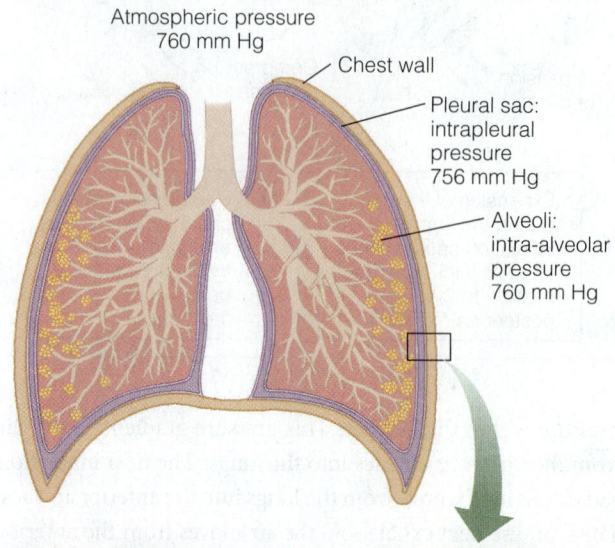

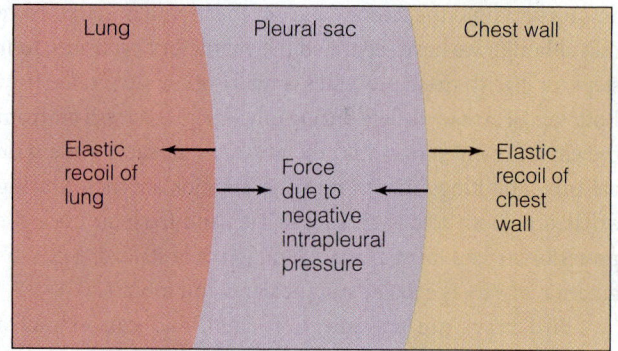

Mammals ventilate their lungs tidally

Mammals exhibit a tidal pattern of ventilation, in which air moves into and out of the lungs via the same pathway. These air movements are driven by pressure gradients, according to the law of bulk flow. Figure 11.28 summarizes the changes in pressure in the relevant compartments of the lungs during quiet breathing. Inspiration begins when somatic motor neurons trigger the contraction of the diaphragm and the external intercostal muscles of the rib cage. These contractions cause the ribs to move outward and upward and the diaphragm to move down, expanding the volume of the thorax. The expansion of the chest cavity pulls on the outer layer of the pleural sac, decreasing the pressure within the pleural cavity. This decrease in intrapleural pressure results in an increase in the pressure difference across the alveolar walls. This increase in the **transpulmonary pressure** gradient causes the lungs to expand, decreasing the pressure in the alveoli. The resulting pressure gradient between the atmosphere and the alveoli causes air to flow into the lungs.

from collapsing in on themselves. If the pleural sac is punctured, the pressure within the pleural cavity increases, and the small airways and alveoli collapse. This condition, known as a *pneumothorax*, causes severe shortness of breath because of the loss of the alveoli as an efficient gas-exchange surface.

Pressure changes in a mammalian lung during quiet breathing

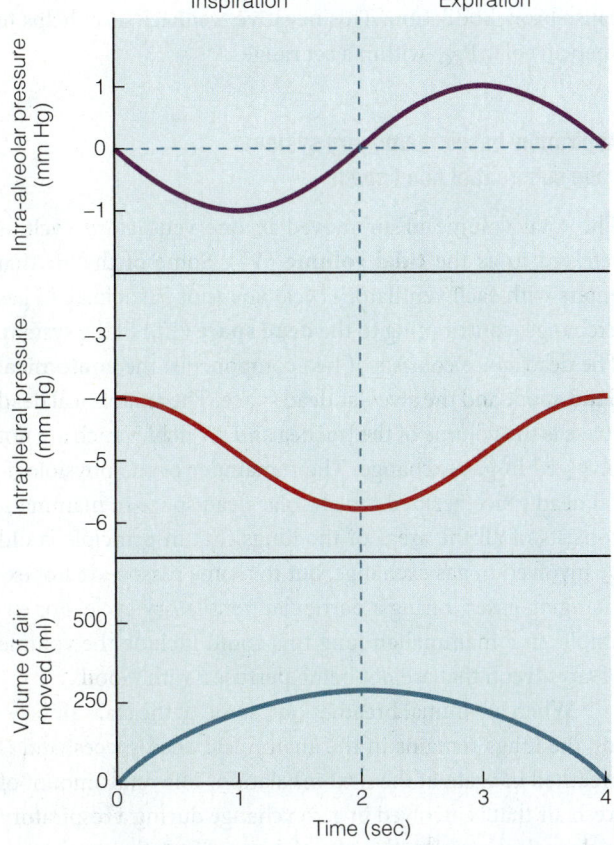

ability of the lungs to reversibly change shape can be quantified using two parameters: **compliance**, which expresses how easy it is to stretch a structure, and **elastance**, which expresses how readily the structure returns to its original shape. Lung compliance is simply defined as the magnitude of change in lung volume produced by a given change in pressure. A highly compliant lung stretches more in response to a pressure change than does a less compliant lung, and can be described by the following equation:

$$C = \Delta V/\Delta P$$

where C is the lung compliance, ΔV is the change in lung volume, and ΔP is the change in transpulmonary pressure. The lower the lung compliance, the harder it is to expand the lungs and the higher the energetic costs of inspiration.

Lung compliance can change as a result of disease. For example, in fibrotic lung disease, which can result from chronic inhalation of asbestos, silicon, or coal dust, scar tissue on the lungs reduces lung compliance and makes inspiration difficult. As a result, individuals with fibrotic lung disease tend to breathe shallowly, and thus must breathe more rapidly in order to obtain sufficient oxygen.

Lung elastance is a measure of the degree of return to resting volume after the lung is stretched. When lung elastance is low, the lungs will not spring back to their original shape when the respiratory muscles relax. As a result, if lung elastance is low, expiration must be active rather than passive. In the disease emphysema, the springy elastin fibers that are normally found in the lungs are destroyed. In individuals with emphysema the lung is easier to inflate (it is more compliant), but its elastance is low, so it will not spring back into shape as well as a healthy lung. Thus, individuals with emphysema have difficulty on expiration, and must expend energy to breathe out even at rest.

Expiration begins when the nerve impulses from the somatic motor neurons that innervate the external intercostal muscles and diaphragm stop. This allows the muscles of the diaphragm and thorax to relax. The thorax then returns to its original position, causing thoracic volume to decrease and intrapleural pressure to increase. Because the lungs contain elastic materials, when they are no longer being actively stretched by the low intrapleural pressure they tend to snap back to their original position. This **elastic recoil** of the lungs decreases lung volume, causing alveolar pressure to increase and air to flow out of the lungs. During rapid and heavy breathing such as that induced by exercise, this passive expiration may not be sufficient for ventilation. Under these circumstances, contraction of the internal intercostal muscles and the abdominal muscles compresses the thorax and actively expels air from the lungs.

The work required for ventilation depends on lung compliance and resistance

The amount of energy needed to ventilate the lungs depends on the elastic properties of the lungs and chest wall and on the resistance to airflow in the pulmonary airways. The

Surfactants increase lung compliance

One important force that resists lung inflation (and thus reduces lung compliance) is surface tension in the thin layer of fluid that lines the small airways and alveoli of the lungs. Surface tension results from hydrogen bonding between water molecules, and provides a cohesive force that causes two wet surfaces to stick together. Surface tension can be altered by the addition of surfactants that disrupt these cohesive forces. Type II alveolar cells secrete lipoprotein surfactants that reduce the surface tension of the fluid layer lining the lungs, thus reducing the tendency of the walls of the small airways and alveoli to stick together. As a result, surfactants make the lung more compliant and easier to stretch. Surfactant secretion from Type II cells is regulated so that stretching these cells (for example, during deep breathing) stimulates surfactant secretion.

The importance of surfactants is often described in terms of the law of LaPlace for spheres as applied to the inflation of individual alveoli. But this represents a misconception of the structure of the alveolus. Alveoli are not spherical, but rather polygonal in shape and are interconnected by alveolar pores, and thus the law of LaPlace for spheres cannot apply. Instead, surface tension along both flat and curved surfaces within the lungs contributes to resistance to lung inflation.

In humans, surfactant synthesis does not begin until relatively late in embryonic development. As a result, babies that are delivered prematurely (more than eight weeks early) do not have sufficient surfactant in their lungs. The lack of surfactant tends to cause the alveoli to collapse, making it very difficult for premature babies to breathe, potentially causing a set of symptoms called respiratory distress syndrome. To learn more how doctors help premature infants to take their first breaths, see Box 11.1: Applications: Treating Respiratory Distress Syndrome in Premature Infants.

Airway resistance affects the work required to breathe

Airway resistance, the force opposing bulk flow of gas through the trachea, bronchi, and bronchioles, is the final determinant of the energy required for breathing. The law of bulk flow and Poiseuille's equation (see Chapter 9: Circulatory Systems) tell us that airway diameter has an extremely large effect on airway resistance. When airway diameter is small, airway resistance is high, and the pressure gradient driving bulk flow must be larger. Thus, airway resistance influences the size of the pressure gradient needed to move air into or out of the lungs. In order to cause air to flow through high-resistance narrowed airways, the lungs must develop a lower intra-alveolar pressure, causing a larger gradient between atmospheric pressure and intra-alveolar pressure, and providing a greater driving force for bulk flow. In order to attain low intra-alveolar pressure, the lungs must develop a large transpulmonary pressure gradient. Because muscular contractions and the resulting change in the volume of the thorax alter the transpulmonary pressure, more energy and thus more work is needed to inflate the lungs when airway diameter is small.

The nervous system, hormones, and paracrine chemical messengers can affect the diameter of the bronchioles. During bronchodilation airway diameter increases, whereas during bronchoconstriction airway diameter decreases. Parasympathetic neurons innervate the smooth muscles surrounding the bronchioles. Stimulation of these neurons causes bronchoconstriction. The paracrine chemical messenger histamine also causes bronchoconstriction. Histamine is released in response to tissue damage or as a result of allergic reactions. Because of this effect of histamine on the bronchioles, severe allergic reactions can cause difficulties in breathing. Circulating epinephrine causes bronchodilation, acting primarily through β receptors in the smooth muscle of the bronchioles. Similarly, high levels of CO_2 in the alveoli cause bronchodilation. This negative feedback loop helps to keep alveolar P_{CO_2} within a set range.

Aspiration-based pulmonary systems have substantial dead space

The total volume of air moved in one ventilatory cycle is referred to as the **tidal volume** (V_T). Some of the air that enters with each ventilatory cycle does not participate in gas exchange, contributing to the **dead space** (V_D) of the system. The dead space consists of two components: the **anatomical dead space** and the alveolar dead space. The anatomical dead space is the volume of the trachea and bronchi, which are not involved in gas exchange. The remainder of the physiological dead space, termed the alveolar dead space in mammals, consists of all the areas of the lungs that in principle could be involved in gas exchange, but for some reason are not exchanging gases during a particular ventilatory cycle. For example, in a mammalian lung this could include the volume of any alveoli that are not being perfused with blood.

When an animal breathes out, some of the stale air leaving the lungs remains in the anatomical dead spaces, and is breathed in again at the next inhalation. The total amount of fresh air that is involved in gas exchange during a respiratory cycle is thus equal to the tidal volume minus the dead space ($V_T - V_D$), and in mammals is symbolized as V_A, or the alveolar ventilation volume. The total effective ventilation of the lungs per unit time is simply this quantity multiplied by the breathing frequency, or respiratory rate (f). Thus, lung ventilation is equal to $f(V_T - V_D)$. Since breathing frequency is usually measured in breaths per minute, this is usually called the alveolar minute ventilation in mammals, and is symbolized as $\dot{V}_A$. The small dot over the V indicates that this is a rate function. High alveolar minute ventilation results in greater gas exchange across the lungs. Increases in the size of the dead space decrease alveolar ventilation at a given tidal volume, and reduce gas exchange. This effect is particularly important for species with very long necks, such as giraffes and some birds (Figure 11.29). These animals have extremely large tidal volumes in order to ensure adequate ventilation of the respiratory surfaces.

Pulmonary function tests measure lung function and volumes

Pulmonary function tests allow clinicians and experimenters to measure both lung volumes and lung function. An instrument called a spirometer can be used to measure the volumes of air inhaled and exhaled under various conditions. When

APPLICATIONS 11.1

TREATING RESPIRATORY DISTRESS SYNDROME IN PREMATURE INFANTS

Respiratory distress was once the leading cause of infant death in North America, particularly in premature infants. Premature infants often struggled to breathe, and would gradually turn blue as their hemoglobin became progressively deoxygenated. Although many of the babies with respiratory distress would soon die, others spontaneously recovered, making this disease a major medical puzzle.

It wasn't until 1959 that Dr. Mary Ellen Avery and her colleague Dr. Jere Mead discovered that the lungs of premature infants do not make sufficient surfactant, and that this lack of surfactant is the primary cause of respiratory distress. This insight has allowed the development of a variety of very effective treatments for respiratory distress syndrome in infants, so that today fewer than 1,000 babies die of respiratory distress syndrome in North America each year.

Doctors now routinely use amniocentesis to determine whether a baby is synthesizing sufficient surfactant prior to birth. In the womb, fetuses make breathing motions that move amniotic fluid into and out of their lungs. If the baby is producing surfactant, components of the complex mixture of lipids and proteins that constitute the surfactant can be found in the amniotic fluid. If the levels of surfactant are low, the best course of treatment is to try to delay the delivery of the baby to allow it more time to develop. This can sometimes be accomplished by making the mother rest or remain in bed.

If birth cannot be delayed, a physician can administer corticosteroid hormones to the mother (see Chapter 4: Cell Signaling and Endocrine Regulation). Because steroids are lipid soluble, they can cross the placenta and affect the fetus. Research on sheep performed in the late 1960s demonstrated that steroid administration accelerates the development of the fetal lung, but it was not until 1993 that steroid administration became a routine treatment for humans. By combining bed rest with steroid treatment, it is often possible to delay delivery of the baby long enough for the corticosteroids to stimulate sufficient surfactant production to prevent respiratory distress syndrome.

If, despite these efforts, a baby is born prematurely and is not making sufficient surfactants, surfactants can be sprayed into the lungs, or administered via artificial ventilation tubes. The earliest work on surfactant therapy used fluids obtained from the lungs of cows, and surfactants derived from natural sources are still commonly used in clinical settings. However, there has been intensive investigation of the components and properties of surfactants in the quest to produce a highly effective artificial surfactant.

Producing artificial surfactants is a far from trivial task, because natural surfactants contain at least 50 different phospholipids and four surfactant proteins. Experiments in mice indicate that knocking out one of these proteins is sufficient to cause fatal respiratory distress in newborns, suggesting that it plays a key role as part of the surfactant. Unfortunately, the highly hydrophobic nature of these proteins makes them difficult to produce *in vitro*. Instead, researchers have been able to identify the active portion of the protein and develop a therapy using these small peptides. However, despite intensive research, artificial surfactants are currently not as effective as surfactants obtained from natural sources, and further research is required before these replacements are likely to be widely used in a clinical setting.

References
- Clements, J. A., & Avery, M. E. (1998). Lung surfactant and neonatal respiratory distress syndrome. *American Journal of Respiratory Critical Care Medicine, 156*, 559–566.
- Curstedt, T., Calkovska, A., & Johansson, J. (2013). New generation synthetic surfactants. *Neonatology, 103*, 327–330.
- Wrobel, S. (2004). Bubbles, babies, and biology: The story of surfactant. *The FASEB Journal, 18*, 1624e.

at rest, most animals do not fully inflate or deflate their lungs with each breath. Thus, the tidal volume is usually much smaller than the maximum possible amount of air that can be inhaled or exhaled. In a typical adult male human, the tidal volume at rest is approximately 500 milliliters (lung volumes are typically about 20 percent less in females), whereas the total lung capacity is nearly 5,800 milliliters (Figure 11.30). The maximal amount of air that can be inhaled over and above the resting tidal volume is termed the *inspiratory reserve volume*, and the tidal volume plus the inspiratory reserve volume is the *inspiratory capacity*. The maximal amount of air that can be forcibly exhaled over and above the resting tidal volume is the *expiratory reserve volume*. By summing the expiratory reserve volume and the inspiratory capacity, we obtain the **vital capacity**, or the maximum amount of air that can be moved into or out of the respiratory system with one breath. Mammals are not able to expel all the air out of their lungs, even with maximal

FIGURE 11.29 **The respiratory system of a whooping crane**

Some birds have an extremely long trachea, which greatly increases the dead space of the respiratory system.

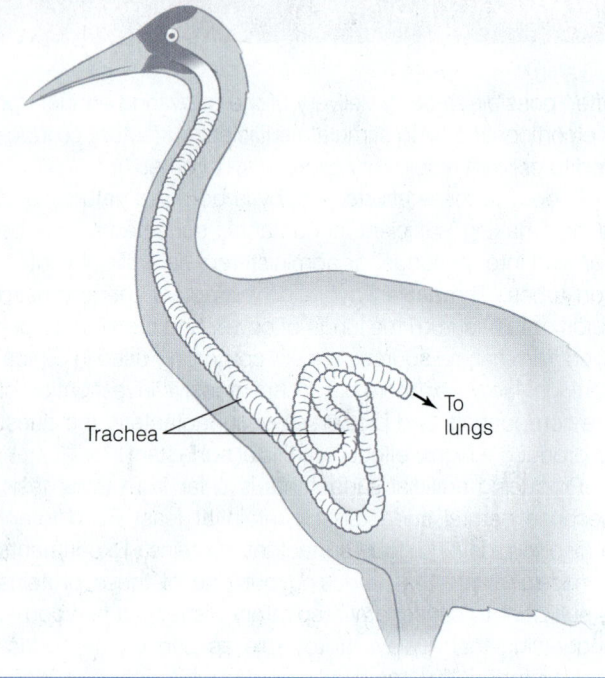

Trachea

To lungs

exhalation. In fact, in humans approximately 1,200 milliliters of air remains in the lungs even at the end of a maximal exhalation. This *residual volume* occurs because the lungs are held stretched against the chest walls by the pleural sac. The **total lung capacity** is the sum of the vital capacity and the residual volume. Box 11.2: Math in Physiology: Pulmonary Function Tests provides more detail about how these parameters are calculated and used to assess lung function.

Ventilation-perfusion matching is important for gas exchange

In order for gas exchange to occur efficiently, the ventilation of the respiratory surface must be matched to the perfusion of the respiratory surface with blood. The **ventilation-perfusion ratio** V_A/Q quantifies this relationship. In a normal human, alveolar ventilation (V_A) is usually around 4–5 liters per minute (l/min), and cardiac output (Q) around 5 l/min, so that V_A/Q is close to 1, on average. The lungs have homeostatic mechanisms to maintain ventilation-perfusion matching at the level of the alveolus. If an alveolus receives little or no fresh air, the P_{O_2} in that alveolus will be low. The low P_{O_2} acts as a signal to the smooth muscle surrounding the arterioles leading to that alveolus. In systemic tissues low P_{O_2}

FIGURE 11.30   **Lung volumes and capacities**

Lung volumes and capacities can be recorded on a spirometer. Inhalation causes the line to deflect upward, whereas exhalation causes the line to deflect downward.

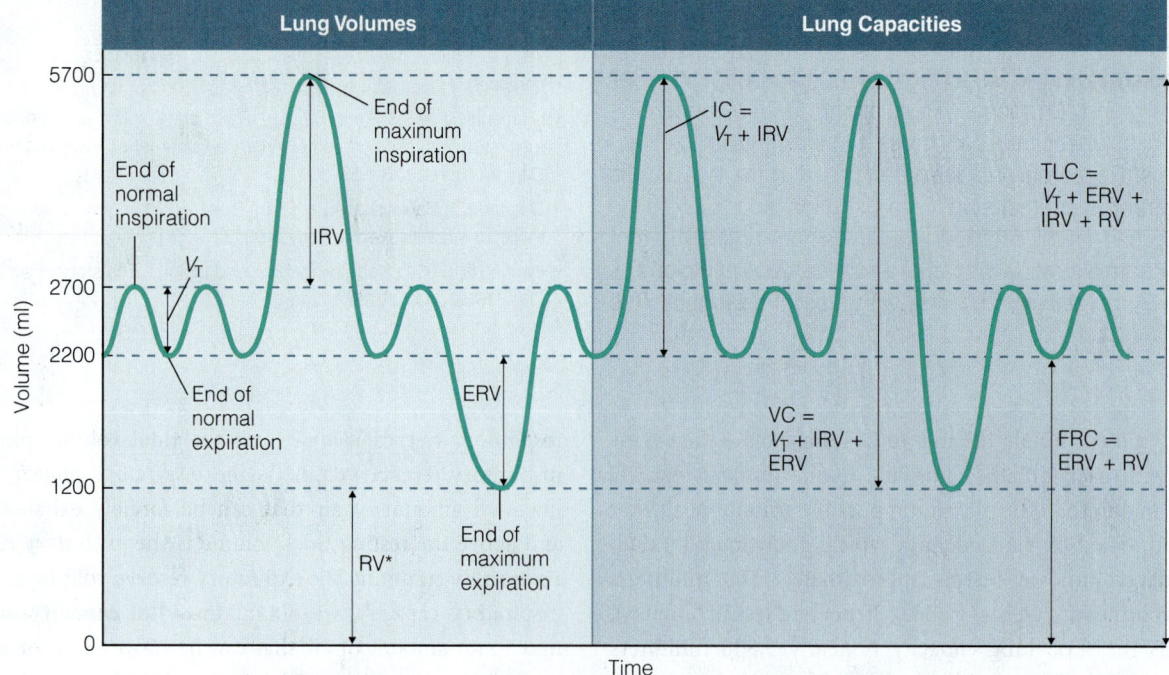

Normal lung volumes and capacities for a healthy 70-kg human male

is a signal for vasodilation, which increases oxygen delivery to the tissues. In contrast, in the lungs, low P_{O_2} causes vasoconstriction, reducing blood flow to areas that are poorly ventilated. This **hypoxic pulmonary vasoconstriction** is the primary means by which the lungs ensure appropriate ventilation-perfusion matching. However, the mechanisms by which the smooth muscle cells of the pulmonary arterioles sense low P_{O_2} and induce contraction are not yet well understood.

CONCEPT CHECK

10. Outline the similarities and differences between the respiratory systems of insects and arachnids (spiders and their relatives).

11. Compare and contrast the mechanisms of ventilation in an air-breathing fish and an amphibian.

12. What is the function of surfactants in the mammalian respiratory system?

13. Explain why bronchoconstriction (for example, during an asthma attack) increases the work required to breathe.

GAS TRANSPORT TO THE TISSUES

Animals such as sponges, cnidarians, and insects, which circulate the external fluid past almost every cell in their bodies, can rely on diffusion to transport gases between the external medium and the tissues. But many animals transport gases using a circulatory system. As we discussed in Chapter 9: Circulatory Systems, animals have exquisite control of their circulatory systems, and can regulate the transport of oxygen and carbon dioxide to and from the tissues by vasoconstricting or vasodilating the blood vessels, altering blood flow. In this section, we look at how animals use circulatory systems to transport both oxygen and carbon dioxide.

Oxygen Transport

Oxygen can be transported from the respiratory surface to the tissues dissolved in the circulatory fluid. But because the solubility of oxygen in aqueous fluids such as plasma is low, the amount of oxygen that can dissolve in the plasma is relatively small. To combat this limitation, the blood of many animals contains specialized *metalloproteins*, which contain metal ions that reversibly bind oxygen. These metalloproteins greatly increase the amount of oxygen that can be carried in the blood. For example, hemoglobin (Hb), the oxygen carrier in vertebrate blood cells, increases the maximum amount of oxygen that blood can carry—or the **oxygen carrying capacity**—by as much as 50-fold.

At the respiratory surface much of the oxygen that diffuses into the blood binds to the metalloprotein oxygen carriers, thereby reducing blood P_{O_2}. By taking this oxygen out of solution, oxygen carriers help to maintain the P_{O_2} gradient across the respiratory surface, improving oxygen extraction. At the tissues, mitochondrial oxygen consumption decreases the P_{O_2} of the blood, causing oxygen to dissociate from the oxygen carrier. This oxygen then diffuses down its P_{O_2} gradient into the cells.

There are three main types of respiratory pigments

The metalloprotein oxygen carriers are often referred to as **respiratory pigments**, because the metal ions that they contain give them a color. In animals, three major types of metalloproteins act as respiratory pigments: hemoglobins, hemocyanins, and hemerythrins.

Hemoglobins, the most common type of respiratory pigment in animals, are found in a wide variety of taxa, including vertebrates, nematodes, some annelids, some crustaceans, and some insects. All hemoglobins consist of at least one molecule of a protein in the **globin** family noncovalently bound to a **heme** molecule, which consists of a **porphyrin** ring containing ferrous iron at the center (Figure 11.31). The iron molecules in hemoglobin give vertebrate blood its reddish color. Globins are structurally diverse, but all share a characteristic tertiary structure called the globin fold, which suggests that these diverse molecules share a common evolutionary history.

In this chapter we focus on the globins found in blood, either within blood cells or extracellularly, but molecules related to the blood hemoglobins are found in many tissues. These hemoglobins are also thought to play a role in oxygen transport and storage. For example, a type of hemoglobin called **myoglobin** is found in muscles, where it helps to provide the oxygen needed for metabolism (see Chapter 6: Cellular Movement and Muscles, and Chapter 12: Locomotion). A related protein called *neuroglobin* is found in neurons. Neuroglobin has been shown to protect neural tissue during periods of hypoxia (low oxygen). Recently, another protein closely related to myoglobin has been identified. This protein, called *cytoglobin*, is found in many tissues, with particularly high expression in the cells of connective tissue. The function of cytoglobin is currently unknown.

Active hemoglobin molecules can be made up of between one and several hundred globin molecules and their associated heme groups. Myoglobin is monomeric, whereas the blood hemoglobins of vertebrates are generally tetrameric, consisting of four globin molecules. The hemoglobins of annelids such as earthworms (*Lumbricus*) contain nearly 150 globin molecules plus a number of linker proteins that do not contain heme. Hemoglobins can be found inside

When performing a pulmonary function test on a person, you place a clip on the subject's nose to prevent air entering the lungs via the sinuses, and the subject breathes through a tight-fitting mouthpiece that is connected to the spirometer. The subject is first asked to breathe normally into the device, and is then asked to inhale as much as possible and exhale as much as possible.

We can characterize lung function with the four lung volumes and four lung capacities (see Figure 11.30). The lung volumes are directly measured, while the lung capacities can be calculated using these volumes. The four main lung volumes are:

- Tidal volume (V_T): The volume breathed in or out during a normal breath at rest
- Inspiratory reserve volume (IRV): The maximum volume of air that can be inhaled beyond the tidal volume
- Expiratory reserve volume (ERV): The maximum volume of air that can be exhaled beyond the tidal volume
- Residual volume (RV): The volume of air remaining in the lungs after a maximal exhalation

The four main lung capacities are calculated from the lung volumes as follows:

- Inspiratory capacity (IC) = V_T + IRV
- Vital capacity (VC) = ERV + V_T + IRV
- Functional residual capacity (FRC) = RV + ERV
- Total lung capacity (TLC) = RV + ERV + V_T + IRV

Clinicians also often calculate the forced expired volume in the first second of maximal expiration (FEV_1), which can be a useful indicator of certain types of lung disease.

Standard spirometers can be used to measure the first three lung volumes, but cannot be used to determine the residual volume. Instead, it must be measured using techniques such as the helium dilution method.

The helium dilution method works by measuring the change in helium concentration between two conditions.

The test uses a sealed spirometer filled with a mixture of helium and oxygen gas at known starting concentrations and volumes. Similar to a regular spirometry test, the subject wears a nose clip and breathes through a mouthpiece connected to the apparatus. Helium is not exchanged across the alveolar-capillary diffusing barrier, so the total amount of helium in the system remains constant, but the volume of the system increases once the subject starts breathing through the mouthpiece because the total volume now includes both the volume of the apparatus and the volume of the lungs. The subject breathes normally into the apparatus for several minutes to allow the helium to equilibrate across the system.

Once the helium has equilibrated across the system, the subject is asked to breathe out maximally (i.e., to empty the lungs as much as possible). The concentration of helium in the system is measured following this deep expiration, and the amount of helium in the apparatus is measured. We can then calculate the residual volume (RV) of the lung as follows:

The amount of a substance is related to the concentration of the substance and the volume of the system according to the formula:

$$\text{Amount} = CV$$

(Where C = concentration and V = volume).

At the beginning of the test (before the subject begins breathing into the apparatus), the lungs are not part of the system, so:

Amount of helium at the beginning of the test = $C_1 V_S$

Where C_1 is the initial concentration of helium and V_S is the volume of the spirometer.

Once the subject starts breathing into the system, we must take into account both the volume of the lungs (V_L) and the volume in the spirometer (V_S). At the end of a forced expiration, V_L is equal to the residual volume (RV). Note that the volume in the spirometer under these final conditions is now greater than it was under the initial conditions

---

blood cells, as in vertebrates, or extracellularly dissolved in the circulatory fluid, as in many invertebrates.

A few families of marine annelids have unusual respiratory pigments called **chlorocruorins**, also known as the green hemoglobins because in dilute solutions they are greenish in color. Some investigators consider the chlorocruorins to be a distinct class of respiratory pigment, but they share many characteristics with the hemoglobins. Chlorocruorins are composed of a globin molecule complexed to

an iron porphyrin. The porphyrin ring in the chlorocruorins differs slightly from heme in that one of the CH=CH$_2$ side chains is replaced with a CHO side chain; however, the globin molecule shares clear phylogenetic relatedness with other invertebrate globins, suggesting that the chlorocruorins are simply a subclass of the hemoglobins.

Hemocyanins are found in both arthropods and mollusks; however, the hemocyanins in these two groups appear to have independent evolutionary origins. Among mollusks,

(because of the volume of the expired breath), so we can designate this volume as V_{Sf}. Therefore:

Amount of helium in the system at the end of the test =
$$C_2 (V_{Sf} + V_L)$$

Because helium is not significantly exchanged across the alveoli, the total amount of helium at the beginning of the test must be the same as the total amount of helium at the end of the test and:

$$C_1 V_1 = C_2 V_2$$

(Where C_1 and V_1 are the initial concentration and volume, and C_2 and V_2 are the final concentration and volume).

Substituting into this equation we find that:

$$C_1 V_S = C_2 (V_{Sf} + V_L)$$

The spirometer measures V_S and V_{Sf}, and we can use a gas analyzer to measure C_1 and C_2 for helium, so we can calculate V_L, which is the RV of the lungs.

Solving for V_L,

$$V_L = (C_1 V_S / C_2) - V_{Sf}$$

With a standard spirometry test and a measure of residual volume such as a helium dilution test, it is possible to measure all of the relevant lung volumes and capacities. These measures can be used as diagnostic tools because lung diseases cause changes in lung volumes and capacities.

Obstructive lung diseases such as asthma and chronic obstructive pulmonary disease (COPD) cause the airways to narrow, increasing resistance to airflow. This is a particular problem during exhalation, because exhalation tends to compress the airways, causing them to narrow even further. As a result, patients with obstructive lung diseases cannot fully empty their lungs and RV increases. Although obstructive lung disease is always associated with an increase in RV, the changes in the other lung volumes can be variable among patients with different types of obstructive lung disease. Thus, a direct measure of RV (for example, from a

helium dilution test) is the best way to diagnose these conditions. However, regular spirometry provides a measure of FEV_1, and decreased FEV_1 is also characteristic of obstructive lung disease. FEV_1 is low in patients with obstructive lung disease because they have particular difficulty when breathing out, so the volume of air that they can exhale in the first second of exhalation is reduced. When FEV_1 relative to vital capacity is less than about 75 percent of normal values, obstructive pulmonary disease is likely.

Restrictive pulmonary diseases differ from obstructive pulmonary diseases in that airway resistance is not increased. Thus FEV_1 is typically fairly normal in these patients. Restrictive lung diseases can be divided into those that cause problems with inspiration and those that cause problems with expiration.

Expiratory problems can be caused by weakness of the abdominal wall, or can be caused by changes in body shape due to obesity or pregnancy. For example, during advanced pregnancy, the presence of the fetus pushes the diaphragm upward, so the mother does not have a lot of scope to push the diaphragm further on exhalation. This can make breathing difficult during late pregnancy. As a result, ERV declines, reducing TLC.

Inspiratory problems can be caused by anything that reduces lung compliance. For example, fibrosis is associated with an accumulation of fibrous "scar tissue" in the lungs, and may be due to exposure to hazardous substances such as asbestos or can be the result of autoimmune disorders or viral infections. This scar tissue makes the lungs less stretchy and more difficult to inflate. However, patients can still make a forced maximal expiration. As a result, ERV may remain fairly normal, but all of the other lung volumes decrease, so total lung capacity decreases.

Reference
• Wanger, J. (2012). *Pulmonary function testing: A practical approach.* (3rd ed.). Burlington, MA: Jones and Bartlett Learning.

they are found in some gastropods, some bivalves, and all cephalopods. Among arthropods, they are present in most crustaceans, arachnids, and centipedes. Hemocyanins do not contain iron, but instead contain copper, which is complexed directly to the protein rather than being part of a heme group. Hemocyanins are very large multimeric proteins consisting of up to 48 individual subunits per molecule. They are usually dissolved in hemolymph, often at high concentrations, rather than being located within blood cells. This

extracellular location poses a strong constraint on the total concentration of hemocyanin because increased hemocyanin concentration results in an increase in the viscosity of the hemolymph, making it more difficult to pump around the body. Because hemocyanins are colorless when deoxygenated and turn blue when oxygenated, the hemolymph of these species appears blue.

Hemerythrins are found in species from four invertebrate phyla (sipunculids, priapulids, brachiopods, and

All hemoglobins consist of one or more globin proteins complexed to an iron-containing porphyrin ring. Most vertebrate hemoglobins are tetramers, composed of four globins and their heme groups. Mammalian hemoglobins are composed of two alpha and two beta globin chains.

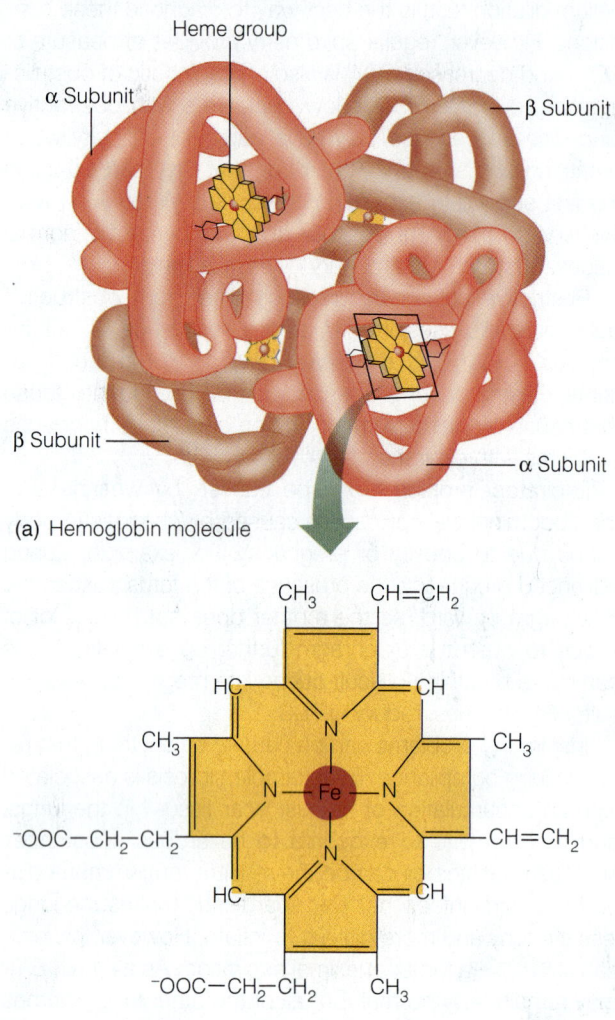

(a) Hemoglobin molecule

(b) Heme group containing iron (Fe)

annelids). However, their distributions within these phyla differ. They are found in essentially all of the sipunculid and priapulid worms, and many of the brachiopods, but in only one family of marine annelids. This unusual phylogenetic distribution is puzzling and may represent a case of convergent evolution. Alternatively, patterns such as this in which closely related genes are present in distantly related taxa may represent a case of horizontal gene transfer in which viruses carry genes from one species into another.

The hemerythrins do not contain heme. Instead, iron is bound directly to the protein via the carboxylate side chains of a glutamate and an aspartate, and the imidazole groups on five histidines. Hemerythrins are generally trimeric or octameric molecules in which each subunit contains two iron ions. Most hemerythrins are found inside circulating coelomic cells and in muscle cells, and thus can be present at high concentrations without increasing the viscosity of the hemolymph. Hemerythrins are colorless when deoxygenated but violet-pink when oxygenated. As a result, the coelomic cells containing hemerythrins are sometimes called pink blood cells.

The significance of the great variety of animal respiratory pigments is not well understood. The respiratory pigments likely represent an example of multiple independent solutions to the common problem of oxygen transport and storage.

Respiratory pigments have characteristic oxygen equilibrium curves

An **oxygen equilibrium curve** shows the relationship between the partial pressure of oxygen in the plasma and the percentage of oxygenated respiratory pigment in a volume of blood (Figure 11.32a). When the partial pressure of oxygen in solution is zero, no oxygen will be bound to the respiratory pigment. As partial pressure increases, more and more pigment molecules will bind oxygen, until the available molecules are fully bound to oxygen. At this point, the blood is said to be **saturated** with oxygen. An oxygen equilibrium curve is thus very much like a hormone-binding curve, discussed in Chapter 3.

We typically express oxygen equilibrium curves in terms of percent saturation, because this allows us to conveniently compare the properties of the respiratory pigments in blood with different amounts of pigment. However, we can also express this relationship in terms of total oxygen content of the blood. Figure 11.32b shows the total oxygen content of blood that contains differing amounts of hemoglobin. As you can see, as the amount of hemoglobin increases, the total amount of oxygen that can be carried in the blood when the hemoglobin is fully saturated also increases, thus increasing the carrying capacity of the blood.

Many animals regulate the amount of respiratory pigment in the blood. For example, in many vertebrates exposure to low environmental oxygen, or hypoxia, triggers red blood cell release or production. For example, in many vertebrates one of the first responses to hypoxia is contraction of an organ called the **spleen**. One of the functions of the spleen is to act as a storage site for red blood cells. Splenic contraction pushes additional red blood cells into the circulation, increasing the **hematocrit** (Hct), a measure of the proportion of blood volume that is occupied by red blood cells. In addition, hypoxia stimulates the production of new red blood cells. Low P_{O_2} stabilizes a protein called HIF-1 (hypoxia inducible factor 1), causing its concentration to increase. When HIF-1 levels are high, the protein acts as a

FIGURE 11.32 **Oxygen equilibrium curves**

(a) The percentage of saturation of a respiratory pigment as a function of oxygen partial pressure. **(b)** The oxygen content of blood as a function of partial pressure for blood with high and low content of respiratory pigment.

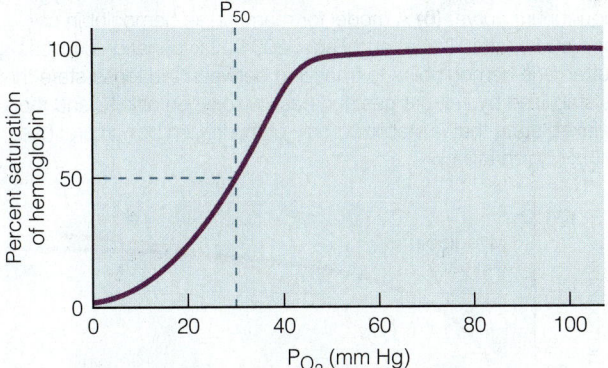

(a) Percentage of respiratory pigment oxygenated

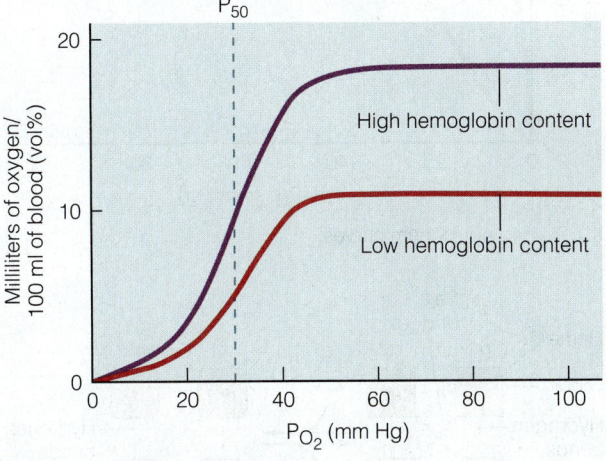

(b) Oxygen content of blood

muscles, although some species express this protein in the heart. Because of the cold, stable temperatures of the Antarctic Ocean (the mean temperature in McMurdo Sound is approximately 1.9°C throughout the year), the metabolic rate and thus the oxygen demand of these fishes is relatively low. In addition, these low temperatures increase the solubility of oxygen in water and plasma, increasing the oxygen concentration of the blood. However, icefish also exhibit a number of physiological adjustments that help to compensate for the lack of hemoglobin. These fish have unusually large hearts and blood vessels, a large blood volume, and increased cardiac output compared with their non-Antarctic relatives. Together, these circulatory adjustments help to increase oxygen delivery in the absence of a respiratory pigment.

The oxygen affinity of a respiratory pigment is a measure of how readily the pigment binds oxygen. We typically express the oxygen affinity of a pigment using a measure termed the **P_{50}**, which is the oxygen partial pressure at which the pigment is 50 percent saturated. The P_{50} of a respiratory pigment is thus analogous to the K_m of an enzyme. Note that the P_{50}, like K_m, has an inverse relationship to affinity. Pigments that require relatively low partial pressures for oxygen to bind (i.e., have a low P_{50}) are said to have high affinity for oxygen, whereas pigments that require relatively high partial pressures for oxygen to bind (i.e., have a high P_{50}) are said to have low affinity.

The P_{50} of a respiratory pigment has important implications for its ability to transport oxygen. For example, a terebellid polychaete worm *Pista pacifica* has three different types of hemoglobin, each with a characteristic P_{50}. It has a giant extracellular hemoglobin with a very low oxygen affinity that circulates through its vascular system, a moderate-affinity hemoglobin that is located within circulating coelomic cells that travel through the interstitial fluid, and a high-affinity myoglobin within the cells of the body wall. These worms live in burrows that can extend almost a meter down in the anoxic (oxygen-free) sediments of mudflats. At high tide, these worms extend their gills out into the well-oxygenated water above the mudflat to obtain oxygen. Oxygen diffuses into the blood vessels of the gills, raising the P_{O_2} of the circulatory fluid. The low-affinity hemoglobin in this circulation readily binds oxygen at the relatively high P_{O_2} seen in the gills. As the blood leaves the gills, this low-affinity hemoglobin passes oxygen to the moderate-affinity hemoglobin in the coelomic cells that circulate through the body cavity and carry oxygen to the tissues. At the body wall, the moderate-affinity hemoglobin passes the oxygen to the high-affinity myoglobin in the muscle cells, providing oxygen to the tissues. Together, these three hemoglobins ensure efficient gas transport from the gills to the tissues of the worm.

In general, species living in low-oxygen environments tend to have lower hemoglobin P_{50} (and thus higher affinity for oxygen) than do species living in normoxic environments.

transcription factor and induces the expression of a number of genes in a variety of tissues, including the gene coding for **erythropoietin**, a hormone that induces the formation of red blood cells. This increase in red blood cell numbers, and thus in hematocrit and hemoglobin concentration, increases the oxygen carrying capacity of the blood.

There is also evolutionary variation among animals in the levels of respiratory pigment in blood. For example, diving mammals have extremely high levels of blood hemoglobin compared with terrestrial mammals, which increases the oxygen carrying capacity of blood and allows it to act as an oxygen store during diving. In contrast, the Antarctic icefish (family Channichthyidae) are unique among the vertebrates in that they do not have any hemoglobin in the blood, and most icefish species have lost the gene coding for hemoglobin. As a result, the blood oxygen carrying capacity of these species is very low. Icefish also lack myoglobin in their skeletal

For example, the bar-headed geese that we discussed at the beginning of the chapter have a hemoglobin with a particularly low P_{50}, and this may be an important adaptation allowing them to function at high altitude. Similarly, the hemoglobins expressed in fetal mammals tend to have lower P_{50} than do the hemoglobins expressed in adults. This difference in P_{50} allows oxygen to be transferred from the maternal circulation to the fetal circulation.

Hemoglobin has extremely high affinity for carbon monoxide, binding with carbon monoxide more than 200 times more readily than with oxygen. As a result, carbon monoxide can interfere with hemoglobin oxygen binding. Thus, exposure to even relatively low levels of carbon monoxide can be fatal, because it decreases the oxygen carrying capacity of the blood, reducing oxygen supply to the tissues.

The shapes of oxygen equilibrium curves differ

Oxygen equilibrium curves can be either hyperbolic or sigmoidal. For example, unlike hemoglobin, myoglobin exhibits a hyperbolic oxygen equilibrium curve (Figure 11.33a). Myoglobin is a monomeric respiratory pigment containing a single heme molecule with one oxygen-binding site. Because each myoglobin molecule binds oxygen independently of other myoglobin molecules, the principles of mass action predict that the equilibrium curve should be hyperbolic in shape.

In contrast, because of their tetrameric structure, vertebrate hemoglobins exhibit a sigmoidal oxygen equilibrium curve. These hemoglobins are composed of two alpha and two beta subunits. Each alpha subunit associates tightly with one of the beta subunits, forming two dimers ($\alpha1\beta1$ and $\alpha2\beta2$) that associate with each other more loosely (see Figure 11.31a). When a hemoglobin molecule is fully deoxygenated, it adopts a rigid conformation termed the tense, or T, state that is stabilized by hydrogen bonds, binding of allosteric effectors, and salt bridges between the subunits (Figure 11.33b). In contrast, fully oxygenated hemoglobin adopts a loose conformation that is termed the relaxed, or R, state. In this conformation, interactions between the subunits are stabilized only by hydrogen bonds. In the T state, hemoglobin has a relatively low affinity for oxygen, but when an oxygen molecule binds to one of the heme groups, the hemoglobin begins a transition from the T to the R state. Binding of oxygen to the iron atom causes the iron to alter its spin state and to move into the plane of the porphyrin ring of the heme group. These movements are transmitted to the globin subunits, and weaken the salt bridges holding the molecule in the tense conformation. Oxygen affinity increases progressively as each oxygen binds and the molecule adopts an increasingly relaxed conformation. The net effect of this cooperative binding (or **cooperativity**) is an oxygen equilibrium curve with a sigmoidal shape.

FIGURE 11.33 **Cooperativity in oxygen binding**
(a) Monomeric respiratory pigments, such as mammalian myoglobin, do not bind oxygen cooperatively and have a hyperbolic oxygen equilibrium curve. Multimeric respiratory pigments, such as mammalian hemoglobin, often display cooperative binding. The result of this cooperative binding is a sigmoidal oxygen equilibrium curve. **(b)** A model for mammalian hemoglobin cooperativity (after Weber and Fago, 2004). Oxygenation causes tetrameric hemoglobins to transition between the tense state that is stabilized by salt bridges and has low oxygen affinity, and the relaxed state that is stabilized only by hydrogen bonds and has high oxygen affinity.

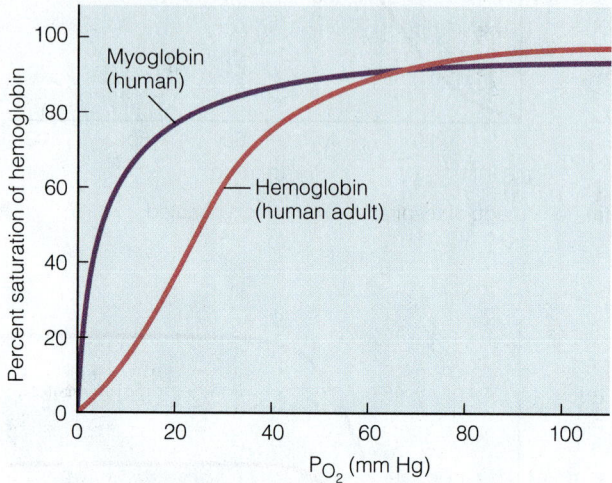

(a) Oxygen equilibrium curves

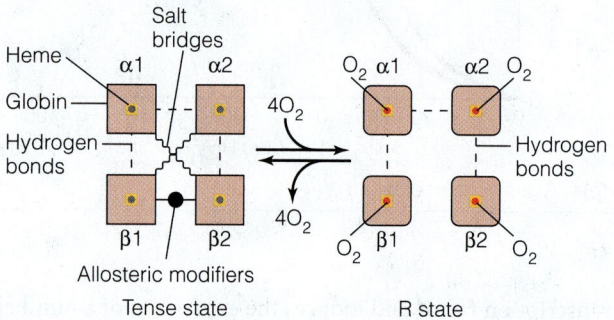

(b) A model for hemoglobin cooperativity

Although most vertebrate hemoglobins conform to this model, the hemoglobins of the jawless fishes (lampreys and hagfish) have an entirely different mechanism. These hemoglobins are monomers when they are oxygenated, and form dimers, trimers, or tetramers when deoxygenated. This shift from a multimeric to a monomeric form also results in a sigmoidal oxygen equilibrium curve.

Blood pH and P_{CO_2} can affect oxygen affinity

Changes in pH and P_{CO_2} alter the shape of the oxygen equilibrium curve for the respiratory pigments in many species, a phenomenon termed the **Bohr effect** or Bohr shift

FIGURE 11.34 **The Bohr effect**

Decreases in pH or increases in CO_2 cause a right shift of the oxygen equilibrium curve.

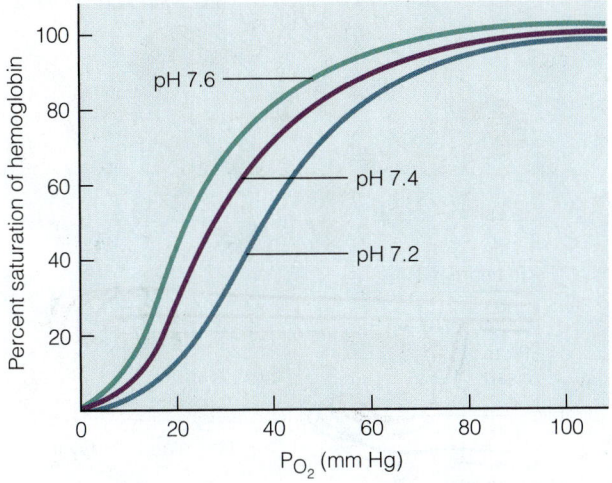

FIGURE 11.35 **Root effect**

The Root effect is seen only in the hemoglobins of some teleost fish and a few species of invertebrates. Decreases in pH cause an exaggerated right shift of the oxygen equilibrium curve, and a decrease in the carrying capacity of the blood.

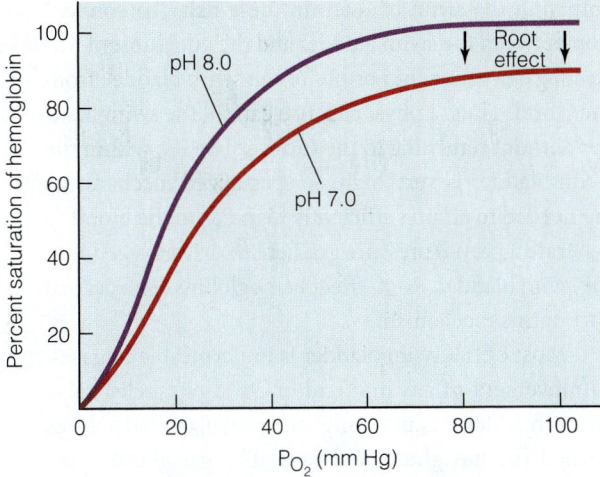

(Figure 11.34). In the Bohr effect, a decrease in pH or increase in P_{CO_2} reduces the oxygen affinity of a respiratory pigment, shifting the oxygen equilibrium curve to the right. Protons (H^+) cause the Bohr effect by binding to the respiratory pigment and causing a conformational change in the protein that alters its oxygen affinity. Thus, protons act as allosteric modulators of these respiratory pigments. The specific sites within respiratory pigments that are responsible for the Bohr effect appear to vary among species. In humans a histidine residue near the C-terminal end of the β subunits is particularly important for the Bohr effect, but this residue does not appear to be involved in the Bohr effect in all species.

Carbon dioxide can cause the Bohr effect through two separate mechanisms. As we discuss in more detail later in the chapter, in blood CO_2 reacts to form a bicarbonate ion (HCO_3^-) and a proton (H^+), and this proton can cause the Bohr effect as described above. Alternatively, carbon dioxide can have a direct effect on the oxygen affinity of respiratory pigments. CO_2 binds to the amine group of the amino acids in the respiratory pigments, forming **carbaminohemoglobin**, with a decreased oxygen affinity.

The Bohr effect facilitates oxygen transport to active tissues. At the respiratory surface, where P_{CO_2} is low and pH is high, the oxygen affinity of the respiratory pigment will be high (the curve will be shifted to the left), facilitating oxygen binding. Metabolizing tissues produce CO_2, so P_{CO_2} and $[H^+]$ in the blood increase at the tissues. This change in P_{CO_2} and pH causes the Bohr effect, decreasing the oxygen affinity of the respiratory pigment, and shifting its oxygen equilibrium curve to the right. This facilitates oxygen release from the respiratory pigment, helping to supply the tissues with oxygen.

The size of the Bohr effect differs among respiratory pigments. For example, the hemoglobins of elasmobranch fishes usually have either no Bohr effect or a very small one, whereas the hemoglobins of mammals and birds usually exhibit modest Bohr effects, and the hemoglobins of many teleost fish have extremely large Bohr effects.

In some crustaceans, cephalopods, and many teleost fishes, increases in P_{CO_2} and decreases in pH cause not only a Bohr effect, but also a reduction in the oxygen carrying capacity of the respiratory pigment (Figure 11.35), a phenomenon called the **Root effect** (or Root shift). In addition to an increase in the P_{50} at low pH, the carrying capacity of a Root-effect hemoglobin decreases greatly due to a decrease in cooperativity among the subunits, releasing oxygen into solution. Thus, Root-effect hemoglobins can act as proton-triggered oxygen pumps, greatly increasing the P_{O_2} of the plasma under low-pH conditions. The mechanisms involved in the Root effect have not been fully characterized, but site-directed mutagenesis and other protein structure-function studies suggest that interactions among several amino acids are involved, and that different amino acids may be important in different species.

Root-effect hemoglobins help to deliver oxygen to the swim bladder

Root-effect hemoglobins are particularly important for delivering oxygen to the retina of the eye and to a gas-filled organ called the **swim bladder**. The low density of the gas in the swim bladder offsets the higher density of the other tissues of the fish, allowing the fish to maintain neutral buoyancy.

In some fish, such as eels and salmon, the swim bladder opens into the gut via the pneumatic duct. These **physostome** fish can fill the swim bladder by gulping air, or empty the swim bladder by burping. The **physoclist** fish use an alternative solution to filling and emptying the swim bladder. In these fish, the connection between the swim bladder and the gut is absent. Instead, gases move into or out of the swim bladder from the blood. Thus, a physoclist fish can fill the swim bladder without returning to the surface. The P_{O_2} within the swim bladder is very high, so specialized mechanisms are needed to attain sufficiently high P_{O_2} in the blood to generate a partial pressure gradient to drive oxygen into the swim bladder. Root-effect hemoglobins are a critical part of this mechanism.

Most of the swim bladder is impermeable to gases, so movement of gas into and out of a physoclist fish's swim bladder occurs only at specialized structures termed the **gas gland** and **oval**. The gas gland is involved in gas secretion into the swim bladder, whereas the oval is involved in gas reabsorption from the swim bladder back into the blood (Figure 11.36).

For oxygen to diffuse into the swim bladder from the blood, the blood P_{O_2} in the gas gland must be greater than that in the swim bladder. To maintain this high P_{O_2}, the tissues of the gas gland produce H^+ ions and CO_2. The resulting decrease in pH and increase in P_{CO_2} cause both a Bohr effect and a Root effect. Because of the Bohr effect, the oxygen affinity of hemoglobin decreases, causing oxygen release from hemoglobin. Because of the Root effect, the oxygen carrying capacity of hemoglobin decreases, also causing oxygen release. The net result of these two effects is that a substantial amount of oxygen dissociates from hemoglobin and dissolves in the blood. This dissolved oxygen now contributes to the P_{O_2} in the blood, increasing the blood P_{O_2} within the gas gland.

The rete mirabile maintains the low pH and high P_{O_2} at the gas gland

The gas gland of physoclist fish is associated with a specialized capillary bed called a **rete mirabile** ("wonderful net" in Latin), or rete. A rete is a bundle of capillaries in which the capillaries are arranged with flow through the arterial and venous vessels in countercurrent. This countercurrent exchanger prevents the loss of oxygen and protons from the gas gland via the venous blood. The rete accomplishes this largely because of the movement of CO_2 from venous to arterial blood, rather than by movement of oxygen. As blood exits the gas gland, it has a high P_{O_2} and very high CO_2 content. This CO_2 diffuses from the venous side of the rete to

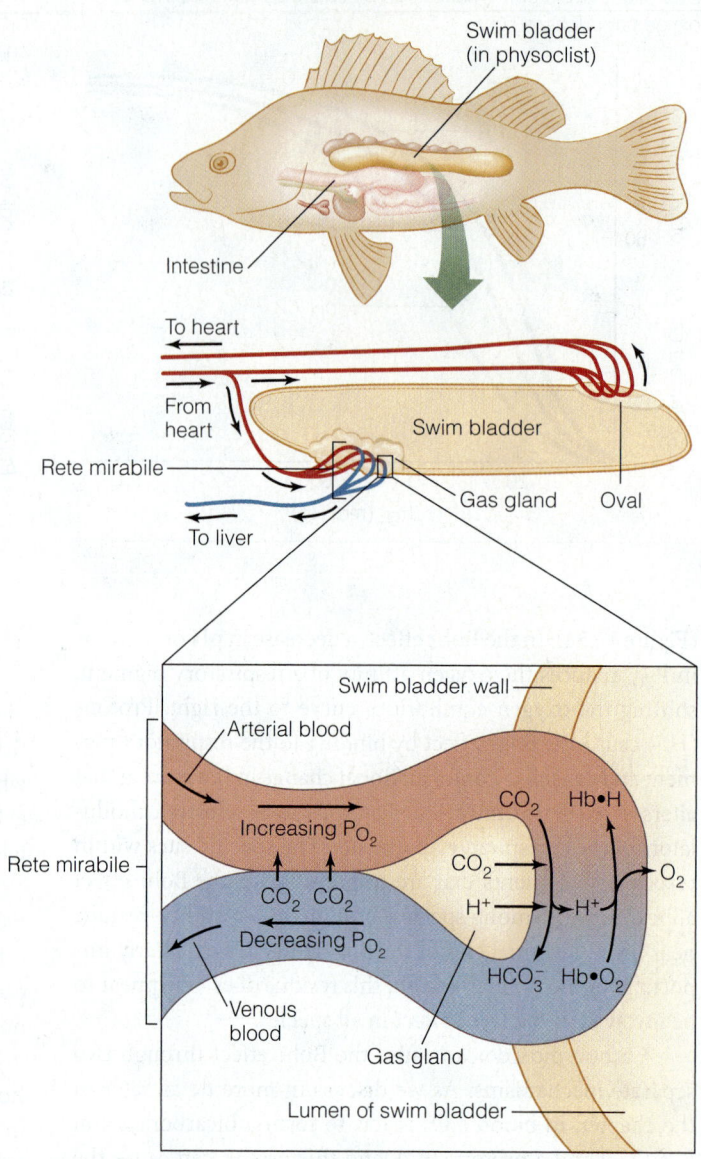

FIGURE 11.36 Mechanism of oxygen loading into a physoclist swim bladder

the arterial side as it passes through the countercurrent exchanger. The increase in CO_2 and the associated drop in pH on the arterial side contribute to the Root and Bohr effects, increasing the P_{O_2} of the blood entering the gas gland. At the same time, the decrease in CO_2 and the associated increase in pH on the venous side cause oxygen to bind to hemoglobin, decreasing the P_{O_2} of the blood.

The longer the rete, the greater the P_{O_2} that can be achieved at the gas gland. Fish that live at great depths must be able to attain high P_{O_2} in the gas gland to force oxygen into the swim bladder. The amount of oxygen in the swim bladder increases with depth, because as depth increases, pressure increases, which decreases the volume of the swim bladder and reduces the buoyancy of the fish. To compensate, fish must add more oxygen into their swim bladder with depth. The length of the rete capillaries, and thus the ability of the fish to maintain a high P_{O_2} in the gas gland, is correlated with the maximum depth that this fish can attain. In some deep-sea fish, such as *Bassozetus*, the rete can be as long as 25 millimeters.

Physoclist fish empty their swim bladder at the oval. Reabsorbing oxygen from the swim bladder is not as physiologically challenging as secreting oxygen into the swim bladder, because oxygen can simply diffuse down its partial pressure gradient from the swim bladder into the blood. In most species, the oval is equipped with a muscular valve so that it can be opened and closed to regulate the amount of gas removed from the swim bladder.

A similar rete system (termed the *choroid rete mirabile*) is present in the eyes of some teleost fish, and may function as an oxygen-concentrating apparatus similar to the rete mirabile of the swim bladder.

The Root effect may also assist in delivering oxygen to systemic tissues

Although the Root effect was traditionally thought to have evolved in teleost fish to support functions such as delivery of oxygen to the retina and the filling of the swim bladder, recent data suggest that it may help in the delivery of oxygen to other tissues as well. During intense exercise, muscles rely on anaerobic metabolism, which results in the production of protons and a decrease in blood pH. Decreases in pH inside the red blood cell cause Root-effect hemoglobins to release oxygen, which would be beneficial because it would deliver additional oxygen to the exercising muscle. However, for many years physiologists ruled out this mechanism because fish with Root-effect hemoglobins also have mechanisms to prevent red blood cell pH from changing when there is a decline in pH that affects the whole body, such as during intense exercise. An exercise-induced **acidosis** decreases blood pH not only in the muscle but also at the gills. If pH inside the red cell is low at the gills, the blood will not be able to pick up sufficient oxygen as it passes through the gills, which would be a major disadvantage to an exercising fish.

Fish with Root-effect hemoglobins express a protein called β-NHE (a Na^+/H^+ exchanger) on the membrane of their red cells. The β-NHE is activated under stressful conditions and helps keep red cell pH constant when plasma pH falls. This prevents the Root effect during stress and protects oxygen uptake at the gills. With this mechanism in place, it seemed unlikely that the Root effect could be involved in helping to deliver oxygen to muscle during exercise, and thus physiologists assumed that the Root effect could only be important in specialized tissues such as the swim bladder that produce a localized acidosis that is not associated with stress. However, recent work suggests that fishes have a

mechanism that short-circuits the β-NHE when the red cell passes through muscle, but allows the β-NHE to function as the red cell passes through the gills. Via this short-circuit mechanism, Root-effect hemoglobins can enhance oxygen delivery to the muscle during exercise without compromising oxygen uptake at the gills.

Temperature affects oxygen affinity

Increases in temperature can decrease the oxygen affinity of respiratory pigments such as hemoglobin in many species, shifting the oxygen equilibrium curve to the right (Figure 11.37). This effect may promote oxygen delivery during exercise. Exercising muscles generate heat, which can increase the local temperature in the blood that perfuses the tissues. As temperature increases, P_{50} increases (oxygen affinity decreases), causing oxygen to dissociate from hemoglobin, and delivering oxygen to the tissue. This temperature effect works together with the Bohr effect to maximize oxygen delivery. Similarly, the temperature of the respiratory surface may decline during exercise if the temperature of the external medium is low. This decrease in temperature increases hemoglobin oxygen affinity, which could promote oxygen uptake. However, even at normal temperatures, blood is typically almost completely saturated with oxygen at the lungs, so this effect is likely to be minor.

Some arctic animals such as reindeer and musk ox have hemoglobins that exhibit small or no temperature effects. In these animals, which live at temperatures as low as −40°C, the temperature in peripheral tissues such as the feet can be as much as 10°C lower than the core body temperature. If their hemoglobin exhibited a typical increase in oxygen affinity with decreasing temperature, oxygen delivery to the tissues might be greatly impaired.

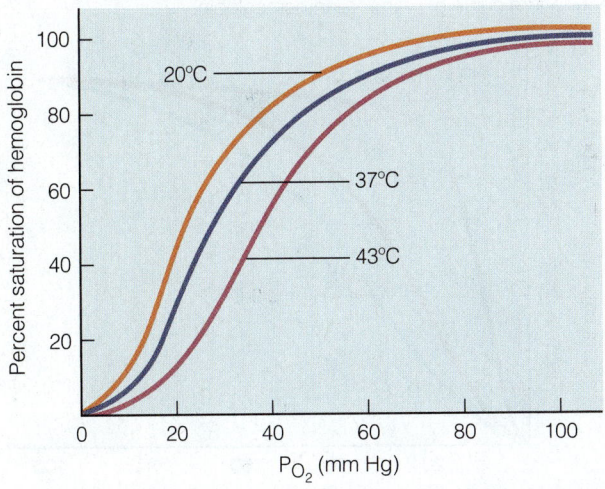

FIGURE 11.37 Effects of temperature on oxygen equilibrium curves

Organic modulators can affect oxygen affinity

A variety of organic compounds can act as modulators of the oxygen affinity of respiratory pigments. In most mammals the compound 2,3-bisphosphoglycerate, also called 2,3-diphosphoglycerate (2,3-DPG), acts as an allosteric regulator of hemoglobin. 2,3-DPG is also the primary allosteric modifier in reptiles (except crocodiles), whereas in most birds inositol pentaphosphate plays this role. In contrast, in most fish (except the cyclostomes), ATP or GTP modulates hemoglobin oxygen affinity. Organic compounds including lactate, urate, and dopamine modulate the arthropod hemocyanins, with increases in these compounds increasing oxygen affinity.

In most mammals, the effect of increased 2,3-DPG is to increase the P_{50} (decrease the oxygen affinity) of hemoglobin (Figure 11.38). Some 2,3-DPG is present within red blood cells at all times, and thus hemoglobin-oxygen binding is somewhat inhibited even at rest. 2,3-DPG levels increase in response to **anemia**, a condition in which hemoglobin levels are low, causing reduced oxygen carrying capacity, which could reduce oxygen delivery to the tissues. Increasing 2,3-DPG levels cause a modest right shift of the oxygen equilibrium curve. This change in P_{50} is not enough to harm oxygen loading at the lungs, but helps oxygen unloading at tissues. As we discuss later in this chapter, a similar effect occurs in some mammals in response to high-altitude hypoxia.

CONCEPT CHECK

14. What is the role of the metal ion that is found in most respiratory pigments?
15. What effect does changing the amount of hemoglobin in the blood have on the P_{50} of a blood sample, and why?
16. Compare and contrast the Root effect and the Bohr effect.

FIGURE 11.38 **Allosteric modulation of oxygen affinity of hemoglobin**

Effects of the organic modulator 2,3-DPG on the oxygen equilibrium curve of mammalian hemoglobin.

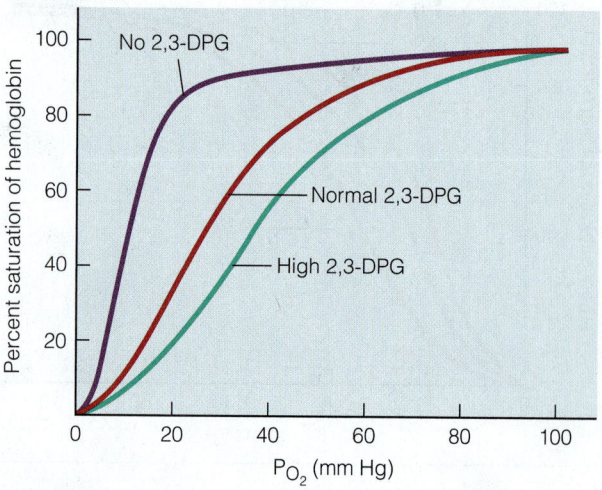

Carbon Dioxide Transport

Mitochondrial respiration produces carbon dioxide that must be transported out of the body. As is the case for oxygen, in very small animals, carbon dioxide can simply diffuse from the tissues to the external environment, but in larger animals, the circulatory system transports carbon dioxide from the tissues to the respiratory surface, where it diffuses into the external environment.

Carbon dioxide is much more soluble in body fluids than is oxygen. However, very little of the CO_2 present in the blood of vertebrates is actually in the form of molecular CO_2. Some of the CO_2 binds to proteins. For example, when CO_2 binds to hemoglobin, it forms carbaminohemoglobin. Carbaminohemoglobin is a significant means of CO_2 transport in mammals, but it may not be significant in other organisms (which have far less hemoglobin).

The majority of the CO_2 is transported as bicarbonate (HCO_3^-). Carbon dioxide reacts spontaneously in water to form carbonic acid (H_2CO_3), which can further dissociate into HCO_3^- and a proton according to the following equation:

$$CO_2 + H_2O \longleftrightarrow H_2CO_3 \longleftrightarrow HCO_3^- + H^+$$

However, the equilibrium constant of this equation lies far to the left, and this spontaneous reaction occurs slowly in aqueous solutions. In animals, an enzyme called **carbonic anhydrase (CA)** catalyzes the formation of HCO_3^-. In contrast to the uncatalyzed reaction, the reaction catalyzed by carbonic anhydrase occurs extremely rapidly. Like the respiratory pigments, carbonic anhydrase is a metalloprotein, but in this case the enzyme contains a zinc ion. Water binds to the zinc ion within the protein, and is dissociated to form H^+ and OH^-. The enzyme then directs the transfer of the OH^- ion to carbon dioxide, forming a bicarbonate ion in the following reaction:

$$CO_2 + H_2O \longleftrightarrow HCO_3^- + H^+$$

In principle, the bicarbonate formed as a result of carbonic anhydrase catalysis could further dissociate into carbonate (CO_3^-) and H^+, but this reaction is not physiologically significant in most animals. Together, molecular CO_2, carbaminohemoglobin, and HCO_3^- make up the total CO_2 content of the blood. In mammals, approximately 70 percent of the blood CO_2 content is in the form of HCO_3^-, whereas 7 percent is present as dissolved CO_2 in solution, and 23 percent is in the form of carbaminohemoglobin.

The carbon dioxide equilibrium curve quantifies carbon dioxide transport

Carbon dioxide equilibrium curves show the relationship between P_{CO_2} and the total carbon dioxide content of the blood, and as such are analogous to oxygen equilibrium

FIGURE 11.39 Carbon dioxide equilibrium curve (human blood)

The carbon dioxide equilibrium curve of most vertebrates differs for oxygenated and deoxygenated blood, a phenomenon called the Haldane effect. The blue line shows the total amount of carbon dioxide in deoxygenated blood. The red line shows the total amount of carbon dioxide in oxygenated blood. The green line shows the portion of that carbon dioxide that is dissolved in the plasma, which does not differ between oxygenated and deoxygenated blood.

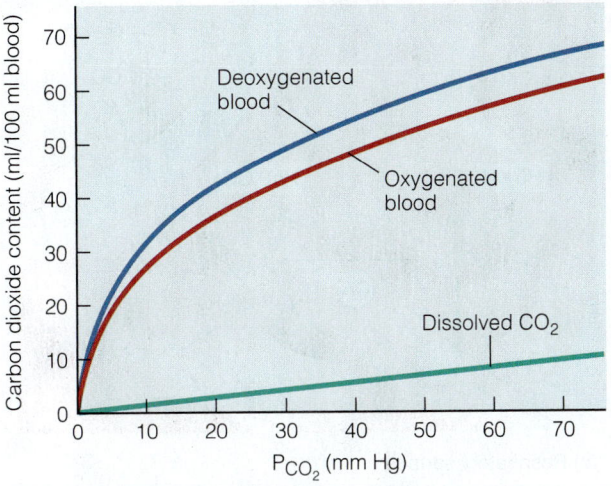

curves (Figure 11.39). However, blood does not become saturated with CO_2; there is a rapid increase in CO_2 content at relatively low P_{CO_2}, and a continued but slower increase as P_{CO_2} rises.

The exact shape of the CO_2 equilibrium curve depends largely on the kinetics of HCO_3^- formation in the blood. In turn, the kinetics of this reaction depend on blood pH, and how well H^+ ions are buffered. To understand this effect we need to recall the principles of buffering and mass action ratios from basic chemistry (see Chapter 3: Chemistry, Biochemistry, and Cell Physiology). We can write the equilibrium constant for the reaction of CO_2 and H_2O as

$$K = \frac{[HCO_3^-][H^+]}{[CO_2]}$$

Because K is a constant, from this equation we can easily see that when $[H^+]$ is high, $[HCO_3^-]$ must decrease, if $[CO_2]$ stays constant. In essence, as pH decreases (and H^+ increases)—for example, as a result of muscle anaerobic metabolism—the CO_2-bicarbonate reaction ($CO_2 + H_2O \rightarrow HCO_3^- + H^+$) will be pushed to the left, decreasing the amount of HCO_3^-. In contrast, as pH increases (and H^+ decreases) the reaction will be pushed to the right, increasing the amount of HCO_3^-. The close relationship between blood pH and carbon dioxide become even more obvious if we log transform this equation, yielding the Henderson-

Hasselbalch equation that we discussed in Chapter 3: Chemistry, Biochemistry, and Cell Physiology:

$$pH = pK + \log\frac{[HCO_3^-]}{[CO_2]}$$

In general, blood is very well buffered. As HCO_3^- forms, the H^+ ions are quickly bound to buffer groups such as the terminal amino groups on proteins, and the imidazole side chains found on amino acids such as histidine. This prevents H^+ from accumulating and allows further HCO_3^- formation. The greater the buffering capacity of the blood, the greater the capacity to form HCO_3^-. For example, human blood is so highly buffered that 99.999 percent of the H^+ formed by the carbonic anhydrase reaction can be buffered. Mammalian hemoglobins have relatively high numbers of histidines, and thus act as effective buffers. In contrast, many fish hemoglobins have few histidines on the surface of the molecule, and thus act as poor buffers. Differences in the buffering capacity of the blood contribute to differences in the shape of the CO_2 equilibrium curve among species.

Blood oxygenation affects CO₂ transport

Deoxygenated blood can carry more CO_2 than can oxygenated blood (see Figure 11.39). In other words, the CO_2 equilibrium curve of deoxygenated blood is shifted to the left, a phenomenon known as the **Haldane effect**. Oxygenated hemoglobin releases H^+ ions. This reduces pH (by increasing the concentration of H^+ ions) and shifts the CO_2-bicarbonate reaction to the left, reducing the amount of HCO_3^- in the blood and reducing the total amount of CO_2 that can be carried. In contrast, deoxygenated hemoglobin tends to bind H^+ ions, increasing the pH and HCO_3^- and increasing the total amount of CO_2 that can be carried. The significance of the Haldane effect is that deoxygenation of hemoglobin at the tissues promotes CO_2 uptake by the blood, whereas oxygenation of hemoglobin at the respiratory surface promotes CO_2 unloading.

Vertebrate red blood cells play a role in CO₂ transport

In vertebrates, carbonic anhydrase is present primarily within the red blood cells, and all of the reactions discussed above occur within these cells rather than in the plasma. However, most of the bicarbonate is actually carried in the plasma. This phenomenon is easiest to understand by working through an example of carbon dioxide transport (Figure 11.40). At the tissues, CO_2 is produced by aerobic metabolism, and rapidly diffuses out of tissues and into the red blood cells. Within the red blood cell, carbonic anhydrase catalyzes the formation of HCO_3^-. The H^+ formed by this reaction binds to hemoglobin. Bicarbonate does not readily diffuse through membranes, but the HCO_3^- ions are moved out of the red blood cell by a chloride-bicarbonate

FIGURE 11.40 **Carbon dioxide transport in vertebrate blood**

(a) Carbon dioxide diffuses from the tissues into the red blood cell. Some binds to hemoglobin, forming carbaminohemoglobin ($Hb \cdot CO_2$). Carbonic anhydrase (CA) within the red blood cell catalyzes formation of HCO_3^-. The HCO_3^- is transported out of the red blood cell in exchange for Cl^- (the chloride shift). The H^+ ions produced by the CA reaction are buffered by hemoglobin.

(b) In the lungs, CO_2 diffuses into the alveoli, and the CA equilibrium shifts to favor the formation of CO_2, reducing the amount of HCO_3^- within the red blood cell. HCO_3^- enters the red blood cell in exchange for Cl^-, and is converted to CO_2, which then diffuses into the alveoli.

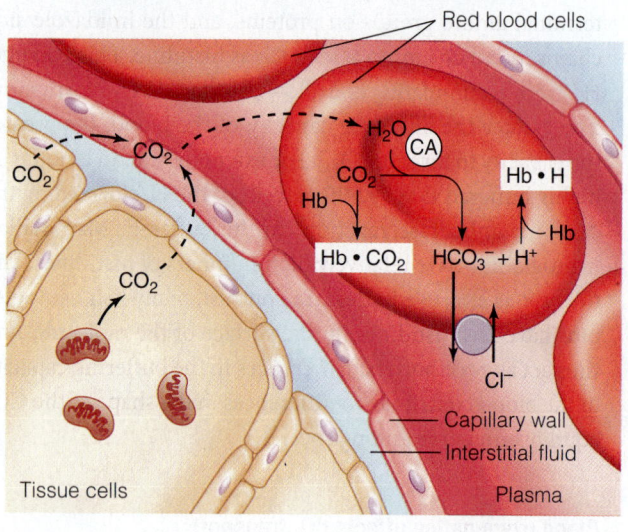

(a) Systemic tissues

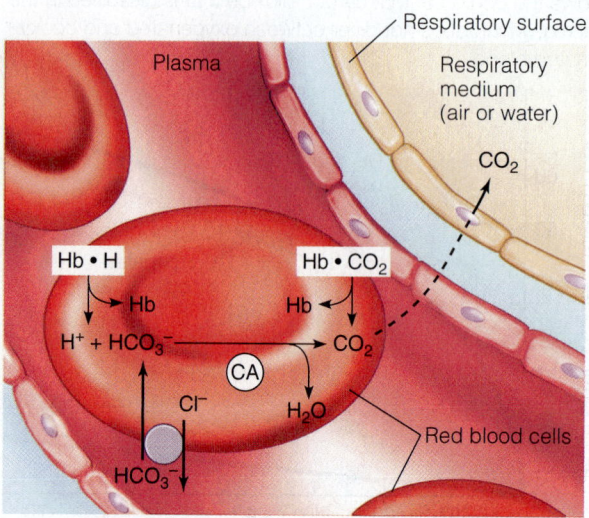

(b) Respiratory surface

exchanger, also called band III. This process of Cl^-/HCO_3^- exchange is known as the **chloride shift**. If this HCO_3^- were not removed, it would build up within the red blood cell and would tend to reverse the carbonic anhydrase reaction. Within the red blood cell, band III and carbonic anhydrase are bound to each other, and another isoform of carbonic anhydrase is linked to band III on the extracellular face of the membrane. Together, these proteins form a **metabolon** (a group of enzymes that work together to perform a function and are spatially localized within the cell). Metabolons allow pathways to function more rapidly than would be possible if the substrates and products had to diffuse through the cell from one enzyme to another.

At the respiratory surface, the P_{CO_2} of the environment is lower than that of blood, and CO_2 diffuses out of the plasma across the respiratory surface. Because of this drop in plasma P_{CO_2}, CO_2 diffuses out of the red blood cell and into the plasma. This decrease in $[CO_2]$ within the red blood cell shifts the CO_2-bicarbonate reaction, causing the band III exchanger to move HCO_3^- ions from the plasma into the red blood cells in exchange for Cl^- (in a reverse chloride shift). The HCO_3^- and H^+ form carbonic acid and then CO_2, and the CO_2 diffuses out of the red blood cell into the plasma and then across the respiratory surface. The location of carbonic anhydrase within the red blood cell increases the total CO_2 carrying capacity of the blood by ensuring that the products of the carbonic anhydrase reaction do not build up

within a single compartment. This forces the CO_2-bicarbonate equilibrium to the right, and increases the amount of CO_2 that is carried as HCO_3^-. In many vertebrates, carbonic anhydrase is also present on the endothelial cells lining tissues such as the lungs. As a result, all of the bicarbonate does not necessarily have to travel via a red blood cell to be converted to CO_2.

The respiratory system can regulate blood pH

Because most proteins have a relatively narrow pH range in which they function effectively, most animals closely regulate intracellular pH. Most animals also regulate the pH of extracellular fluids such as blood, because regulating extracellular pH reduces the regulatory burden on individual cells. For example, in humans the normal pH of blood is approximately 7.4; a pH above 7.7 or below 6.8 can be fatal. Because of the tight linkage between CO_2 and pH through the reaction catalyzed by carbonic anhydrase, which we have already discussed, respiratory systems play an important role in the regulation of pH in extracellular fluids such as blood. Because the partial pressure of a gas, rather than its concentration, is the most physiologically relevant parameter, we can rewrite the Henderson-Hasselbalch equation as follows:

$$pH = pK + \log \frac{[HCO_3^-]}{\alpha CO_2 \times P_{co_2}}$$

where αCO_2 is the solubility of carbon dioxide in the fluid, and P_{CO_2} is the partial pressure of carbon dioxide.

Physiologists use a type of graph called a **pH-bicarbonate plot** (which is sometimes referred to as a Davenport diagram) to describe the interrelationships between P_{CO_2}, HCO_3^-, and pH (Figure 11.41). These diagrams consist of a graph of the relationship between pH (plotted on the x-axis) and $[HCO_3^-]$ (plotted on the y-axis). Onto this graph are superimposed a series of curved diagonal lines called **isopleths**. Each isopleth represents the pH of the plasma as HCO_3^- is varied for a series constant values of P_{CO_2}. A Davenport diagram also includes the blood buffer line, which is an empirically calculated relationship showing the change in blood HCO_3^- when pH is titrated. The blood buffer line depends on the composition of the plasma, and thus varies among species. Under normal circumstances, an animal has typical values of plasma pH, HCO_3^-, and P_{CO_2} that fall on the blood buffer line. For example, for mammals P_{CO_2} is typically 40 mm Hg, plasma pH is 7.4, and $[HCO_3^-]$ is 24 mM.

A pH-bicarbonate plot allows physiologists to visualize what happens to the other parameters in the system when any one parameter is varied. For example, consider what happens when an animal hyperventilates. **Hyperventilation** is defined as alveolar ventilation greater than is needed to

remove the CO_2 produced by metabolism. During hyperventilation plasma P_{CO_2} will fall. As P_{CO_2} declines, pH and HCO_3^- values will shift along the blood buffer line. As a result, pH will increase and HCO_3^- will decrease. In contrast, during **hypoventilation**, alveolar ventilation is less than is needed to remove the CO_2 produced by metabolism. In this case, plasma P_{CO_2} will increase, so pH will decrease and $[HCO_3^-]$ will increase. We can observe a similar phenomenon looking at the data for eels in Figure 11.41. In this case, the eels were put into water with varying carbon dioxide levels, which resulted in increases in plasma P_{CO_2} from the resting value of approximately 5 mm Hg up to a value of 40 mm Hg. In this figure, look at the point at which the blood buffer line crosses the P_{CO_2} isopleths. Under normal conditions, blood pH is about 7.8 and $[HCO_3^-]$ is approximately 13 mM. During acute hypercarbia, when P_{CO_2} rises to 40 mm Hg, blood pH falls to 7.15 and $[HCO_3^-]$ rises to 20 mM.

From a **pH-bicarbonate plot** it is very clear that changes in environmental P_{CO_2} or in ventilation will result in changes in pH. **Respiratory acidosis** occurs when ventilation is insufficient to remove all of the CO_2 produced by metabolism. This results in an increase in blood P_{CO_2} that shifts the carbonic anhydrase reaction to the right, increasing $[H^+]$ and decreasing pH. The new values of pH and HCO_3^- can be estimated from the **Davenport diagram** by moving along the blood buffer line to the point where it intersects the appropriate P_{CO_2} isopleth. In contrast, a **respiratory alkalosis** occurs when ventilation is greater than is needed to remove the CO_2 produced by metabolism, causing a net loss of CO_2, which shifts the carbonic anhydrase reaction to the left, and increases the pH.

Changes in metabolism can also directly affect extracellular pH. During intense exercise, muscles produce H^+ ions. This pH disturbance is often called a lactic acidosis, because intense exercise also produces lactate as a result of anaerobic glycolysis. Because the lactate itself is not the source of the protons, this decrease in pH is more properly referred to as a **metabolic acidosis**. Metabolic acidosis can also occur because of excessive loss of HCO_3^- from the intestine during intense diarrhea, or as a result of kidney failure. In contrast, **metabolic alkalosis** can occur as a result of the loss of excess H^+ from vomiting, or because of a loss of H^+ from the kidneys as a result of kidney failure.

Let's examine what would happen during a metabolic acidosis if P_{CO_2} were held constant. The metabolic protons would react with HCO_3^-, decreasing $[HCO_3^-]$. If P_{CO_2} is held constant, however, the relationship of pH to $[HCO_3^-]$ cannot move off the P_{CO_2} isopleth, and thus the values move off the blood buffer line and pH falls. Of course, animals can adjust their rate and depth of ventilation, which alters P_{CO_2}. These changes can be used to correct pH imbalances. For example, metabolic acidosis causes increased ventilation, inducing a respiratory alkalosis and returning the pH to

FIGURE 11.41 A pH-bicarbonate plot

Sometimes called a Davenport diagram, a pH-bicarbonate plot with P_{CO_2} isopleths can be used to visualize the relationships between pH, HCO_3^-, and P_{CO_2} in a buffered solution. Values shown are for the European eel. When carbon dioxide levels in the water are normal, eels have a P_{CO_2} around 5 mm Hg, plasma pH around 7.8, and $[HCO_3^-]$ is approximately 13 mM. As P_{CO_2} in the water increases, the values for plasma pH and P_{CO_2} shift along the blood buffer line, resulting in acid-base disturbances.

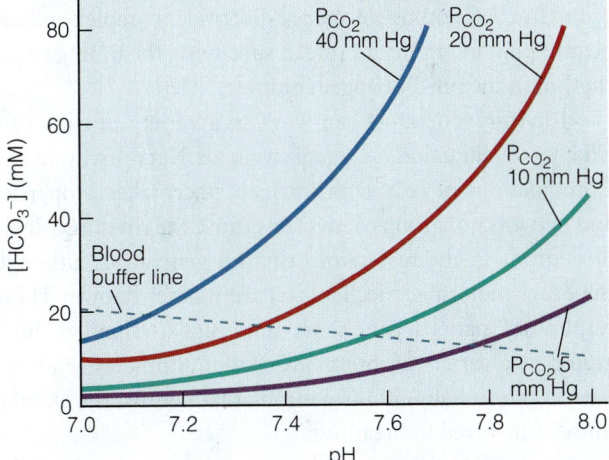

normal values. However, the respiratory system is responsible largely for minute-to-minute regulation of blood pH, while the excretory system plays the major role in long-term regulation (Chapter 13: Ion and Water Balance). In the next section of this chapter, we examine some of the mechanisms by which animals regulate their ventilation, and thus gas exchange and plasma pH.

REGULATION OF VERTEBRATE RESPIRATORY SYSTEMS

Like other physiological systems, respiratory systems are closely regulated in response to changes in both the internal and external environments. Vertebrate respiratory and circulatory systems work together to regulate gas delivery and plasma pH by (1) regulating ventilation, (2) altering oxygen carrying capacity and affinity, and (3) altering perfusion.

Regulation of Ventilation

Ventilation is an automatic rhythmic process that continues even during loss of consciousness. Rhythmically firing groups of neurons within the central nervous system, or *central pattern generators*, initiate ventilatory movements in animals. In the vertebrates, these central pattern generators are located within the medulla of the brain. All vertebrates that have been examined so far have a column of respiratory-related neurons running along each side of the medulla. In bony fish, the central pattern generator is located in the rostral (or anterior) part of the medulla near the neurons that innervate the buccal cavity. Lampreys, amphibians, and mammals, however, appear to have at least two pairs of pattern generators. In mammals, these pattern generators are located in the caudal medulla (Figure 11.42).

The precise mechanisms of respiratory rhythm generation are still not fully understood. In at least some vertebrates, a small region of the caudal medulla called the **pre-Bötzinger complex** is essential for respiratory rhythm generation. The pre-Bötzinger complex is part of a larger structure called the ventral respiratory group that contains other regions that are thought to be involved in respiratory rhythm generation, including the Bötzinger complex (located just anterior to the pre-Bötzinger complex).

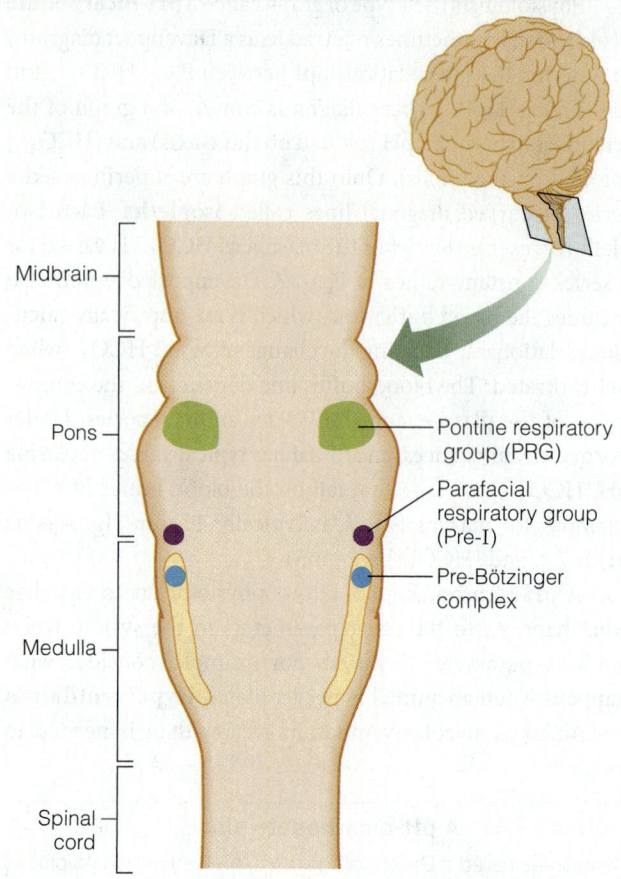

FIGURE 11.42 **Location of the respiratory central pattern generators in mammals**

Labels: Midbrain — Pons — Medulla — Spinal cord — Pontine respiratory group (PRG) — Parafacial respiratory group (Pre-I) — Pre-Bötzinger complex

In addition, another neuronal complex, the **parafacial respiratory group** or pre-I complex, is coupled to the pre-Bötzinger complex. Neurons in the parafacial respiratory group fire before those in the pre-Bötzinger complex and appear to play an important role in specifying the timing of the rhythm in the pre-Bötzinger complex.

Rhythm generators can work in a variety of ways (see Chapter 8: Functional Organization of Nervous Systems). Combinations of cells with intrinsic pacemaker properties and networks of groups of neurons cause the rhythmic firing of neurons in the respiratory rhythm generators, although the exact molecular mechanisms are not yet known. These respiratory pattern generators send signals that are integrated by a variety of interneurons that ultimately send signals to the somatic motor neurons that control the skeletal muscles involved in breathing.

The respiratory pattern generators are regulated by a variety of other brain centers that modulate their output to control the rate and depth of breathing, including areas such as the pontine respiratory group in a region of the brain called the pons. The pontine respiratory group integrates chemosensory information and then sends signals to the respiratory rhythm generators to modulate the rate and depth of breathing.

Chemosensory input influences ventilation

Chemosensory input helps to modulate the output of the central pattern generators. Chemoreceptors detect changes in CO_2, H^+, and O_2 and send afferent sensory information to the brain. Various regions in the brain, including the pontine respiratory group, integrate this information and provide input to the respiratory rhythm generators to modify the rate or depth of breathing. These changes in breathing act by negative feedback to maintain blood P_{CO_2} and P_{O_2} within a narrow range.

Oxygen sensing is of primary importance in water-breathing vertebrates, whereas CO_2 sensing is of primary importance in air-breathing vertebrates. Oxygen levels in water are low compared with those in air, and hypoxia, or lower than normal P_{O_2}, is a common occurrence in aquatic environments. As a result, aquatic organisms must have high ventilation in order to obtain sufficient O_2. These levels of ventilation are usually more than adequate to remove CO_2, and blood CO_2 content is typically low. In contrast, oxygen is generally present at high levels in air, and air-breathing organisms do not need to ventilate at such high levels to obtain oxygen. But as a result, less CO_2 is removed, and total CO_2 content of the blood is typically higher in air breathers than in water breathers.

Water breathers have internal O_2 chemoreceptors that monitor the P_{O_2} of blood within the gills. There are also O_2 chemoreceptors on the surface of the body, particularly in the gill cavity and on the surface of the gills, although the distribution of these receptors may vary among species. The O_2 chemoreceptors send afferent signals to the medulla that modulate the output of the respiratory and cardiac rhythm generators. The efferent signals from these rhythm generators regulate ventilation volume and rate, cardiac output, and the perfusion pattern within the gills. Water breathers also have CO_2/pH chemoreceptors in the gills, although these are thought to be primarily involved in sensing the characteristics of the external medium.

Air-breathing vertebrates have internal CO_2/pH chemoreceptors that monitor either the P_{CO_2} or the pH of the blood. Because of the tight linkage between CO_2 and $[H^+]$ through the carbonic anhydrase equilibrium, it is difficult to establish with any certainty exactly which parameter these chemoreceptors are sensing, although recent evidence suggests that they sense intracellular pH. There are two main clusters of internal CO_2/pH chemoreceptors: **central chemoreceptors**, located in the medulla of the brain, and **peripheral chemoreceptors**, located in specific arteries.

The central chemoreceptors respond to pH changes in the cerebrospinal fluid. Although the blood-brain barrier is relatively impermeable to protons, CO_2 readily diffuses into the cerebrospinal fluid. Carbonic anhydrase within this fluid catalyzes the formation of HCO_3^- and H^+, which stimulates these chemoreceptors. Increases in CO_2 (and thus H^+) stimulate ventilation, whereas decreases in CO_2 (and thus H^+) reduce ventilation.

The peripheral chemoreceptors of mammals sense both P_{O_2} and P_{CO_2}/pH. The **carotid body** chemoreceptors are located in the carotid artery and monitor the composition of blood going to the brain. The **aortic body** chemoreceptors, located in the wall of the aorta, monitor the composition of the blood going to the body. These receptors fire only when plasma P_{O_2} starts to fall below the level required to saturate hemoglobin, which in most animals occurs only during pronounced hypoxia. As a result, the majority of respiratory regulation is accomplished by sensing CO_2/pH, with the central chemoreceptors playing the predominant role.

Figure 11.43 illustrates the role of these chemoreceptors in regulating ventilation when P_{CO_2} increases and pH and P_{O_2} decrease. However, as illustrated in the figure, input from the

FIGURE 11.43   Regulation of ventilation in mammals

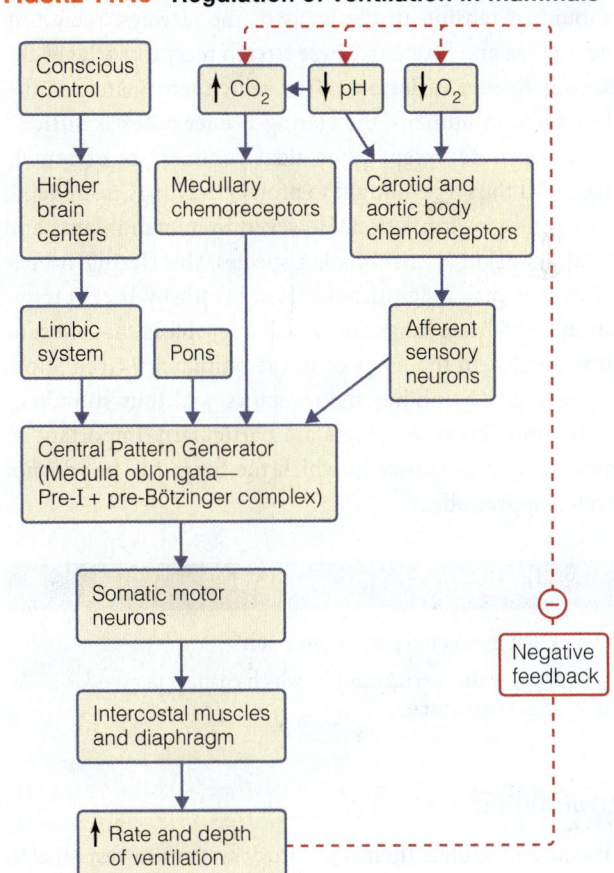

chemoreceptors is only part of the overall regulation of ventilation, and many other factors also play a role.

Other factors regulate breathing

As illustrated in Figure 11.43, breathing is also under the control of higher brain centers in the hypothalamus and cerebrum. For example, we can voluntarily alter our breathing patterns by deciding to hold our breath. However, although we can temporarily override the respiratory centers, we cannot do so indefinitely. If you attempt to hold your breath, eventually the drive to breathe becomes so intense, as a result of the chemoreceptor input into the **medullary respiratory centers**, that you are forced to breathe. Brain centers such as the limbic system can also regulate breathing. When the limbic system is activated, it increases the rate and depth of breathing. The limbic system plays an important role in regulating the autonomic nervous system, including emotional responses such as fear.

A number of mechanosensory reflexes also influence breathing. For example, in mammals irritants such as inhaled particles can stimulate receptors in the airways of the lungs. These mechanoreceptors send a signal to the central nervous system that causes the bronchi to constrict. This protective bronchoconstriction prevents the inhalation of more particles. Another set of mechanoreceptors, the slowly adapting pulmonary stretch receptors, detect the amount of tension in the walls of the airways, including the trachea and bronchi. These stretch receptors trigger the **Hering-Breuer inflation reflex**, which terminates inhalation. In adult humans, the Hering-Breuer reflex is difficult to demonstrate except when tidal volumes are extremely large, and thus it is thought to protect the lungs from being damaged by overinflation. However, in human infants and in adults of other mammalian species, the Hering-Breuer reflex may play a significant role in breath-by-breath regulation. Vertebrate lungs also contain receptors that are sensitive to CO_2 in the lungs or in the pulmonary circulation. Increasing CO_2 inhibits the receptors, and thus stimulates ventilation. These receptors are particularly important in animals such as turtles in which the lungs fill, but do not stretch appreciably.

CONCEPT CHECK

20. What is a central pattern generator?
21. Outline the mechanisms by which changes in blood P_{O_2} affect ventilation.

Environmental Hypoxia

Organisms regulate their respiratory systems in response to changes in both their external and internal environments.

Ventilation rate and breathing frequency typically increase in response to increases in metabolic demand, such as during exercise. Animals may also have to cope with changes in environmental oxygen and carbon dioxide. In aquatic environments, for example, environmental oxygen often varies from the *normoxic* condition. During the day, when photosynthesis is maximal and plants are net oxygen producers, enclosed bodies of water such as ponds, swamps, or tidepools can become *hyperoxic*—supersaturated with oxygen. In contrast, at night when plants are net oxygen consumers, these habitats can become extremely *hypoxic*, and fish living in these areas can experience very low oxygen levels. Terrestrial animals seldom experience hyperoxia, but may experience **hypoxia** within burrows or at high altitudes. You may also come across the term **hypoxemia**—lower than normal arterial blood oxygen content. Hypoxemia can be caused by environmental hypoxia, inadequate ventilation, reduced blood hemoglobin content, and a variety of disease states. The terms **hypercapnia** and **hypocapnia** describe higher or lower than normal P_{CO_2} in either the environment or the blood. Like hypoxia, environmental hypercapnia can occur within enclosed environments such as burrows.

Fish respond to hypoxia in many ways

Many fish have external oxygen chemoreceptors that can detect environmental hypoxia, allowing fish to initiate behavioral or physiological responses to prevent hypoxemia from occurring, for example by moving away from hypoxic water. If this initial strategy fails, environmental hypoxia causes an initial, usually transient, decrease in blood P_{O_2}. This decrease in blood P_{O_2} stimulates the internal O_2 chemoreceptors, causing an increase in ventilation. A fish that ram ventilates typically opens its mouth wider to increase the flow of water over the gills, whereas a fish that uses buccal-opercular pumping increases the rate and depth of these movements. If respiratory adjustments are insufficient to compensate for environmental hypoxia, some types of fish initiate behavioral strategies such as aquatic surface respiration, in which they move to the surface of the water and ventilate their gills with the thin layer of better-oxygenated water at the air-water interface.

Prolonged exposure to hypoxia causes an increase in red blood cell numbers, and thus hemoglobin concentration, increasing oxygen carrying capacity and oxygen extraction from the environment. Some fish can reduce their metabolic rate by reducing their activity level, moving to cooler water to reduce metabolic rate, or actively suppressing their metabolism to conserve energy.

Air breathers can experience high-altitude hypoxia

Most air-breathing organisms only experience low environmental oxygen in specific habitats, such as when diving,

FIGURE 11.44 **The response to high altitude in humans**

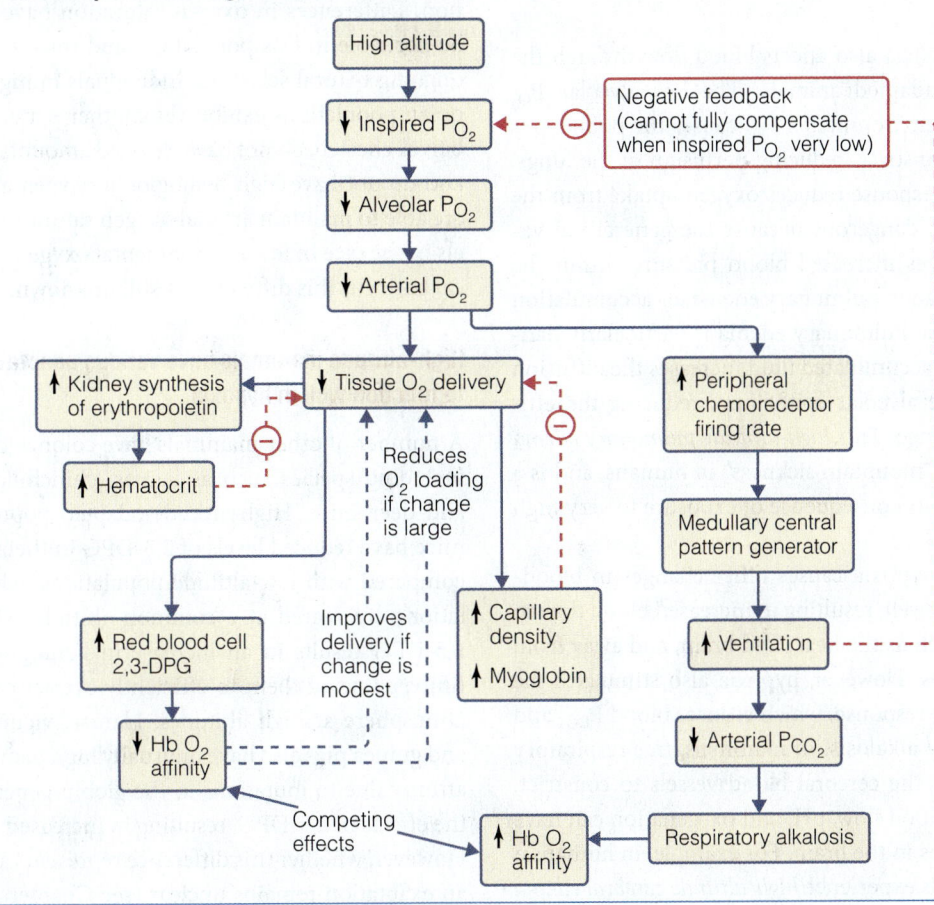

within enclosed spaces such as burrows, or at high altitudes. When low-altitude-adapted animals are brought to high altitudes, they undergo a number of physiological changes, some of which may be involved in acclimatizing to the environmental hypoxia, and some of which may be pathological, if the animals are unable to acclimatize. Figure 11.44 summarizes the responses of lowland-adapted animals, such as humans, experiencing high-altitude hypoxia.

When a low-altitude-adapted mammal experiences high-altitude hypoxia, blood P_{O_2} drops. Arterial chemoreceptors detect this decline in blood P_{O_2}, and send a signal to the medulla to increase the rate and depth of breathing, restoring or partially restoring blood P_{O_2}. Because of the increased ventilation rate, more CO_2 will be lost at the lungs, leading to hypocapnia, or lower than normal blood P_{CO_2}. Recall that, in mammals, blood P_{CO_2} provides the primary drive to breathe. The low blood P_{CO_2} at altitude can cause difficulty with breathing, particularly during sleep when the conscious drive to breathe is removed. Because of the carbonic anhydrase equilibrium, hypocapnia also leads to low $[H^+]$. Thus, the ventilatory response to high altitude causes respiratory alkalosis. Over longer-term exposure to high altitude, this persistent respiratory alkalosis triggers

the kidneys to excrete HCO_3^- in an attempt to homeostatically regulate blood pH.

High-altitude hypoxia also leads to increases in red blood cell numbers by signaling the kidney to produce the hormone erythropoietin. This effect of high altitude is one reason competitive athletes may choose to train at high altitudes or utilize a hypobaric chamber, which provides an artificial low-pressure, low-P_{O_2} environment. It is currently a matter of some debate as to whether this increase in red blood cell numbers (or *polycythemia*) actually assists in acclimatization to altitude. Polycythemia results in an increase in *hematocrit*, the proportion of the blood volume occupied by red blood cells. High hematocrit causes increased blood viscosity, which could impair blood flow through capillaries and interfere with gas exchange at the tissues.

In humans and many other lowland-adapted animals, hypoxia also increases the levels of 2,3-DPG in the red blood cells. Increased 2,3-DPG would, in principle, decrease the oxygen affinity of the blood, which might assist in oxygen unloading at the tissues. However, the respiratory alkalosis associated with hyperventilation generally cancels out this effect, resulting in no net change in hemoglobin oxygen affinity at altitude.

High altitude can cause pathological responses in lowland animals

Environmental hypoxia also affects blood flow through the lungs of lowland-adapted animals. The low alveolar P_{O_2} caused by the low environmental P_{O_2} causes the pulmonary arterioles to vasoconstrict, reducing perfusion of the lungs. This pathological response reduces oxygen uptake from the atmosphere, and is dangerous because the generalized vasoconstriction causes increased blood pressure within the lungs, which can lead to pulmonary edema, or accumulation of fluid in the lungs. Pulmonary edema is particularly dangerous because the accumulated fluid increases the diffusion distance across the alveolar epithelium, reducing the efficiency of gas exchange. This *high-altitude pulmonary edema* is a severe form of "mountain sickness" in humans, and is a potentially dangerous consequence of exposure to very high altitudes.

High-altitude hypoxia causes other changes in blood-flow distribution as well, resulting in increased blood flow to essential tissues such as the heart and brain, and away from less essential tissues. However, hypoxia also stimulates the hypoxic ventilatory response, which reduces blood P_{CO_2} and causes a respiratory alkalosis. In mammals, this respiratory alkalosis can cause the cerebral blood vessels to constrict. These changes in blood flow, pH, and oxygenation can have severe consequences in the brain. For example, in humans a subset of individuals experience *high-altitude cerebral edema* at high altitude. Although the exact physiological causes of this syndrome are not well understood, fluid accumulates in the brain of individuals with this illness, increasing intracranial pressure and disrupting brain function. Individuals with high-altitude cerebral edema become disoriented and confused, and may lose consciousness. Affected individuals must immediately descend to lower altitudes, because cerebral edema can rapidly lead to coma and death.

Some human populations have colonized high altitudes

Populations of indigenous peoples in China, Nepal, Tibet, Ethiopia, and Peru all inhabit altitudes that cause respiratory problems for low-altitude-adapted human populations. We are only just beginning to understand the physiological differences between individuals in these populations and lowland human populations, but the data collected so far suggest that each of these populations uses a different strategy for coping with high altitude. For example, the Quechua of Peru are typically barrel-chested, suggesting a higher than usual lung capacity, and have high hemoglobin levels. In contrast, Tibetan populations are not barrel-chested, and have moderately elevated hemoglobin levels. Individuals in Tibetan populations vary in arterial hemoglobin oxygen saturation, and individuals with higher oxygen saturation have higher offspring survival than individuals with low oxygen saturation. Differences in oxygen saturation have been shown to be heritable in this population, and thus may be subject to ongoing natural selection. Individuals in high-altitude Ethiopian populations exhibit yet another pattern. They are not barrel-chested, do not have elevated amounts of hemoglobin, and do not have high hemoglobin oxygen affinity, but they are able to maintain arterial oxygen saturation at normal levels in the face of low environmental oxygen. The physiological basis for this difference is still unknown.

High-altitude mammals have various adaptations to function well in hypoxia

A number of other mammals have colonized high altitudes, including species such as llamas, chinchillas, guinea pigs, and deer mice. High-altitude-adapted populations of deer mice have reduced levels of 2,3-DPG in their red blood cells compared with low-altitude populations, when both populations are reared at a common altitude. This decrease in 2,3-DPG results in an increase in hemoglobin oxygen affinity, allowing them to efficiently extract oxygen from the atmosphere at high altitudes. Llamas, vicuñas, chinchillas, and guinea pigs also have unusually high hemoglobin oxygen affinity due to mutations in the globin genes that eliminate the effects of 2,3-DPG, resulting in increased oxygen affinity. However, whether this difference represents an adaptation or an exaptation remains unclear (see Chapter 1: Introduction to Physiological Principles).

Birds have a greater tolerance of high-altitude hypoxia than do mammals

Although most birds are found at low altitudes, there are representatives of many avian orders that live at high altitudes or fly at high altitudes. The lung anatomy of birds, including unidirectional ventilation, a very thin gas-exchange surface, and crosscurrent flow, provides extremely efficient gas exchange and oxygen extraction in hypoxia. Birds are also able to tolerate hyperventilation and the resulting hypocapnia and alkalosis much better than can mammals, so they can maximize oxygen extraction at high altitudes. Birds also have increased capacity for gas exchange at their muscles because they have higher capillary density and smaller muscle fibers compared with those of mammals.

Some birds, however, have additional adaptations that allow them to fly at extremely high altitudes. The bar-headed geese (*Anser indicus*) described at the beginning of this chapter are a particularly well-studied example of a high-altitude-adapted animal. To learn more about the specific adaptations of bar-headed geese for flight at high altitude, see Box 11.3: Challenges to Homeostasis: Adaptations to High Altitude in Bar-Headed Geese.

Metabolic suppression is a common response to hypoxia

In low-oxygen environments, animals may be unable to obtain sufficient oxygen to meet the metabolic needs of their tissues. Many animals that can survive environmental hypoxia use a strategy called hypoxic metabolic suppression (or **hypometabolism**), in which they reduce their activity and metabolic needs in parallel with the reduced oxygen supply. This reduction in metabolic rate reduces oxygen demand and may allow an animal to survive for long periods despite environmental hypoxia. For example, some species of turtles make use of hypoxic metabolic suppression to survive long periods under water. Freshwater turtles, such as the painted turtle (*Chrysemys picta*) and the red-eared slider (*Trachemys scripta*) are obligate air breathers, but can remain submerged for long periods—for example, during winter in ice-covered ponds. Some species also bury themselves in anoxic mud. The metabolic rate of a submerged turtle at low temperatures is less than 0.1 percent of the normoxic summer metabolic rate. Part of this metabolic rate depression is a result of the decrease in temperature, but a substantial component is the result of active suppression of metabolism.

The triggers that induce hypoxic metabolic suppression are not yet understood, but one cue may be tissue acidosis. When oxygen supply is not sufficient to meet the metabolic needs of the organism, such as during environmental hypoxia, ATP must be produced using anaerobic pathways. In most animals this involves flux through glycolysis, producing lactate as the metabolic end product. High glycolytic flux results in a metabolic acidosis—an increase in net hydrogen ion production by the cell. A large metabolic acidosis can have dangerous consequences for an organism, because most enzymes are highly sensitive to the pH of the body. Initial exposure to hypoxia results in a modest tissue acidosis. This acidosis can then act as a cue to trigger a reduction in metabolic rate, protecting the animal against further acidosis.

Hypometabolic states are not unique to hypoxic environments. Many organisms use hypometabolism to survive adverse environmental conditions, including low temperature, low food availability, or desiccation, in addition to hypoxia. Although the nature of these conditions is diverse, in each case animals need to reduce metabolic rate to preserve energy stores. **Hibernation** (a long period of metabolic depression associated with cold temperature) and **torpor** (a shorter period of metabolic depression, often seen at night) are particularly interesting hypometabolic states because they occur under normoxic conditions. As animals enter into hibernation or torpor they *voluntarily* reduce ventilation in parallel with the reduction in metabolic rate. Thus, these animals actively reduce both oxygen supply and demand in concert. Many mammalian hibernators, such as ground squirrels, exhibit a pattern of *episodic breathing* during hibernation that includes long periods of **apnea** interspersed with ventilatory bouts. The mechanisms that convert the regularly spaced pattern of mammalian breathing to an episodic pattern during hibernation are not yet understood, but presumably involve changes in the function of the respiratory pacemakers in the medulla.

CONCEPT CHECK

22. What are some of the mechanisms by which fish respond to hypoxia?
23. Why do humans typically become hypocapnic at high altitudes?

Diving

A variety of air-breathing vertebrates, including some mammals, birds, and reptiles, have adopted a fully or partially aquatic mode of life. However, all of these animals remain dependent on air as a respiratory medium, and must be able to actively hunt prey underwater while relying on the oxygen stores that they carry with them as they dive below the surface. The physiology of diving in these animals provides an ideal example of the ways in which the respiratory and circulatory systems are integrated to allow animals to function in their environment.

Sperm whales are the champion divers among the marine mammals, with recorded dives to a depth of more than 2,000 meters and dive lengths of more than an hour. The pinnipeds (seals and sea lions) are also excellent divers. Among pinnipeds, the elephant seals hold the record for both the longest and deepest dives at almost 1,600 meters and nearly 80 minutes. The emperor penguin can dive down to 500 meters, but its dives are typically relatively short, averaging around 3 minutes. Green sea turtles can remain submerged for as long as five hours, although active dives typically average 5–10 minutes.

Anaerobic metabolism takes over at the aerobic dive limit

When an air-breathing vertebrate dives, it must rely on stored oxygen to fuel aerobic metabolism. These onboard stores are typically sufficient for short dives, but cannot sustain metabolism during long dives, and anaerobic metabolism must be used (Figure 11.46). The **aerobic dive limit**—the point at which an animal must either surface to breathe or begin to use anaerobic metabolism—varies greatly among species. For example, adult Weddell seals, which hunt underneath the Antarctic ice sheets, have an aerobic dive limit of about 20 minutes, whereas California sea lions have an aerobic dive limit of only about 5 minutes. In principle, two physiological adjustments can alter the aerobic dive limit: increasing oxygen stores and decreasing oxygen demand.

Bar-headed geese (*Anser indicus*) have been seen flying over the Himalayas at nearly 9,000 meters during their migratory flights, although these birds generally prefer to take an "easier" route through valleys and mountain passes, staying at altitudes below 6,000 meters whenever they can. However, even at 6,000 meters humans cannot perform maximal exercise, whereas these birds are able to fly long distances—a form of locomotion that has a very high oxygen demand.

Consistent with their high-altitude lifestyle, bar-headed geese are remarkable in their ability to tolerate low oxygen. Laboratory studies have shown that they can tolerate severe hypoxia down to a P_{O_2} of about 2.8 kPa, which is equivalent to an elevation of approximately 12,000 meters, or well above the "death zone" for humans.

Understanding the specializations that allow bar-headed geese to fly at high altitudes requires thinking about the entire pathway involved in obtaining oxygen from the environment and delivering it for use in the tissues. This pathway has been termed the *oxygen cascade* (Figure 11.45). The oxygen cascade can be divided into five main steps: (1) ventilation of the respiratory surface, (2) diffusion of O_2 across the respiratory-exchange surface, (3) transport of O_2 in the blood, (4) diffusion of O_2 from the blood to tissue mitochondria, and (5) use of oxygen in the cell. Any or all of these steps could potentially be altered in bar-headed geese compared with their lowland relatives to improve oxygen delivery during high-altitude flight.

Ventilation of the respiratory surface: Like most birds, bar-headed geese are able to tolerate substantial drops in blood P_{CO_2} without reducing ventilation, which is an advantage under hypoxic conditions. However, bar-headed geese are at the extreme even for birds. For example, bar-headed geese breathe more deeply when exposed to severe hypoxia compared with related species of low-altitude birds. In fact, bar-headed geese have the largest ventilatory response to hypoxia of any bird species that has been studied to date.

Diffusion of O_2 across the respiratory-exchange surface: Bar-headed geese have unusually large lungs for their body size compared with lowland birds, which should increase the size of the respiratory-exchange surface. From the Fick equation, we can see that this increase in surface area should lead to an increase in oxygen diffusion capacity.

Transport of O_2 in the blood: One of the best understood adaptations of bar-headed geese to high-altitude flight is an increase in hemoglobin oxygen affinity. This increase in affinity is primarily due to a change in a single amino acid that causes the loss of a hydrogen bond that normally stabilizes the T state of hemoglobin. This change causes the hemoglobin to assume a more relaxed conformation and increases the oxygen affinity of the protein, increasing oxygen loading in hypoxia.

In addition to having high oxygen affinity, the hemoglobin of bar-headed geese also has unusually high temperature sensitivity. Recall that low temperature shifts the hemoglobin oxygen saturation curve to the left, increasing affinity, while higher temperatures shift the curve to the right, decreasing affinity. Temperature declines with altitude, so when bar-headed geese are flying at high altitude the air is very cold. Although animals have a variety of mechanisms to warm the air as they inhale, it is possible that the temperature in the lungs is still somewhat below the body temperature, which would shift the hemoglobin oxygen saturation curve to the left and enhance oxygen uptake. In contrast, the working muscles are likely to be at a higher temperature, which would enhance oxygen delivery to the tissues.

Bar-headed geese may also have specializations in the heart that help to maintain cardiac output and blood circulation during hypoxia. For example, the heart of bar-headed geese has a higher density of capillaries than do the hearts of their lowland relatives, which should improve oxygen delivery to the heart muscle. They also have specializations of an enzyme called cytochrome oxidase in their mitochondria that may help reduce the production of damaging oxygen free radicals during hypoxia, helping to protect cardiac function.

Diffusion of O_2 from the blood to tissue mitochondria: Like all birds, bar-headed geese have higher capillary density and smaller muscle fibers compared with those of mammals, but this trait is particularly extreme in bar-headed geese. Bar-headed geese also differ from their lowland cousins in that within their muscle cells, the mitochondria are located close to the capillaries, rather than deep within the cells near the contractile proteins. This pattern reduces the diffusion distance between the blood and the mitochondria, and from the Fick equation

FIGURE 11.45 **The oxygen transport cascade**

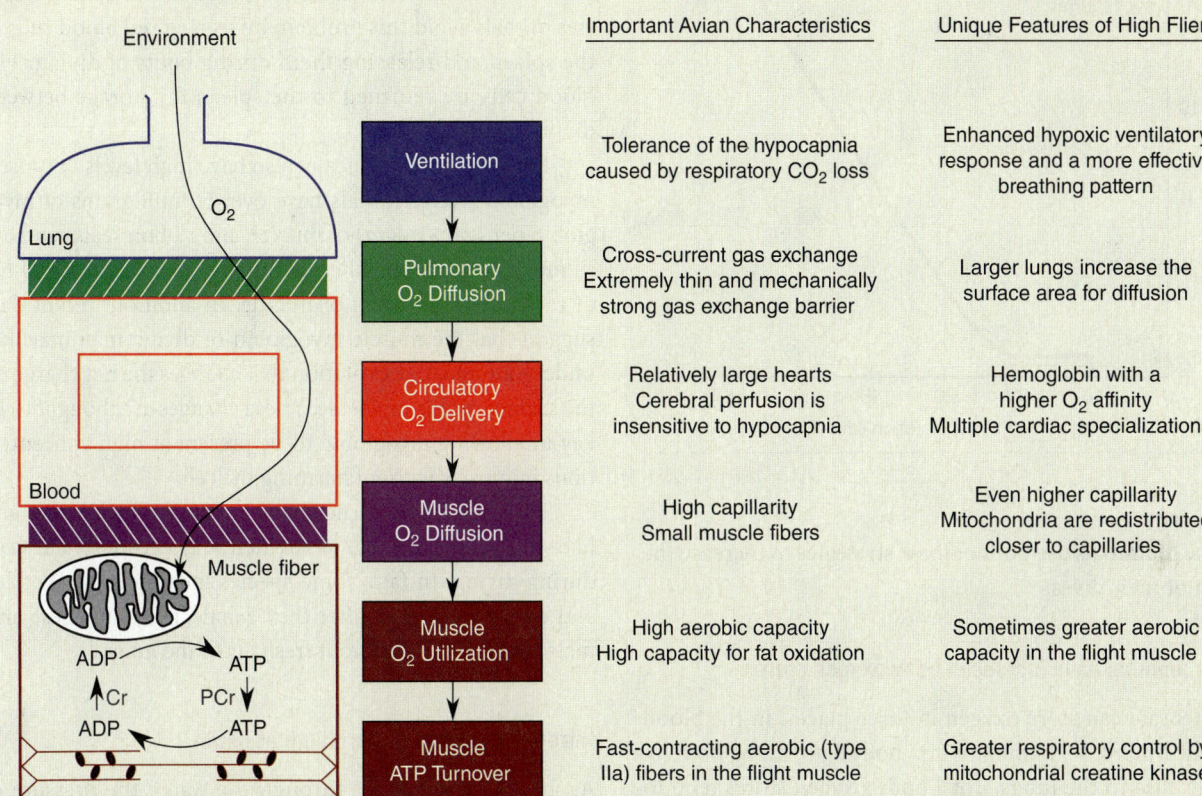

Figure source: Republished with permission of The Company of Biologists Ltd; Society of Experimental Biology (Great Britain), from Figure 2 from Elevated performance: the unique physiology of birds that fly at high altitudes. *Journal of Experimental Biology* 214, 2455–2462, Scott, GR. © 2011; permission conveyed through Copyright Clearance Center, Inc.

we can see that this will increase diffusion capacity for oxygen.

Use of oxygen in the cell: The mitochondria of bar-headed geese are not particularly adapted for operation at low oxygen levels. In fact, their K_m for oxygen is similar to that of their lowland relatives. In addition, bar-headed geese have a higher proportion of highly aerobic muscle fibers, suggesting an increased demand for oxygen compared with lowland geese. One possible reason for this difference is that bar-headed geese might need to have more of these muscle fibers to compensate for the reduction in the power output of each muscle fiber during hypoxia. Alternatively, more aerobic fibers might be needed to power flight at high altitudes where the low density of air reduces the lift produced by the wings.

References

• Hawkes, L. A., Balachandran, S., Batbayar, N., Butler, P. J., Chua, B., Douglas, D. C., . . . Bishop, C. M. (2013). The paradox of extreme high-altitude migration in bar-headed geese, *Anser indicus. Proceedings of the Royal Society of London B, 280*(1750 20122114) (published online before print).

• Meir, J. U., & Milsom, W. K. (2013). High thermal sensitivity of blood enhances oxygen delivery in the high-flying bar-headed goose. *Journal of Experimental Biology, 216*, 2172–2175.

• Scott, G. R., Egginton, S., Richards, J. G., & Milsom, W. K. (2009). Evolution of muscle phenotype for extreme high-altitude flight in the bar-headed goose. *Proceedings of the Royal Society of London B, 276*, 3645–3653.

• Scott, G. R. (2011). Elevated performance: the unique physiology of birds that fly at high altitudes. *Journal of Experimental Biology, 214*, 2455–2462.

• Scott G. R., Schulte, P. M., Egginton, S., Scott, A. L., Richards, J. G., & Milsom, W. K. (2011). Molecular evolution of cytochrome C oxidase underlies high-altitude adaptation in the bar-headed goose. *Molecular Biology and Evolution, 28*, 351–363.

FIGURE 11.46 **Lactate accumulation during diving in Weddell seals**

The aerobic dive limit is the dive time at which lactate begins to accumulate as a result of the switch to anaerobic metabolism.

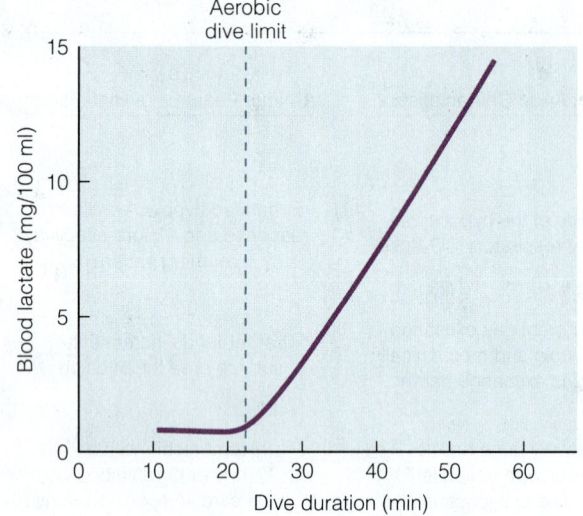

Marine mammals use both of these strategies to increase the length of their dives.

Diving animals have increased body oxygen stores

A vertebrate can store oxygen in three places: in the blood (largely bound to hemoglobin), bound to myoglobin in muscle, and in the lungs. Total body oxygen stores tend to be larger in diving mammals than in terrestrial mammals, although this relationship is most evident in very proficient divers (Figure 11.47). Diving mammals often have high

FIGURE 11.47 **Total body oxygen stores of diving mammals and humans (expressed per kg body mass)**

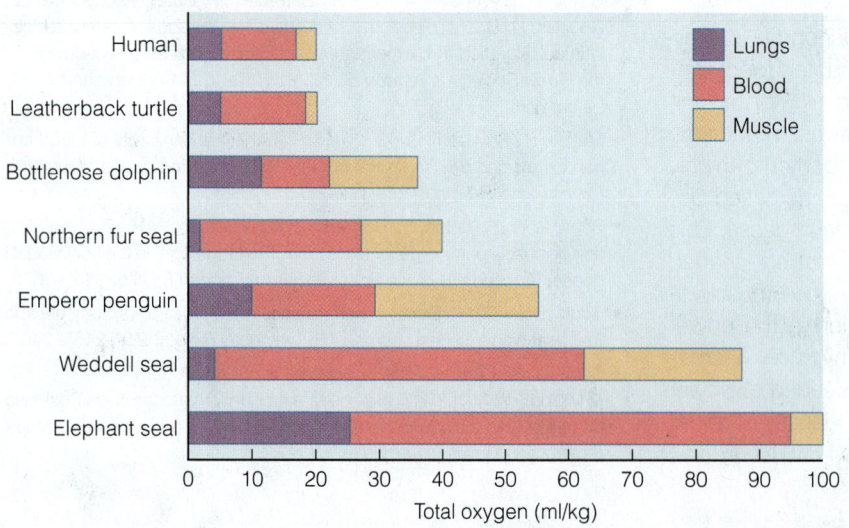

blood volumes and high oxygen carrying capacity, allowing them to store more oxygen in the blood than is typical for a terrestrial mammal. For example, a Weddell seal is able to store almost five times as much oxygen in blood as a human can. Recall from our discussion of the effects of high altitude that polycythemia increases blood viscosity, and can cause difficulties with cardiac function. Some species of seals avoid this problem by storing red blood cells in the spleen and releasing them during bouts of diving. The blood cells are returned to the spleen for storage between diving bouts.

Diving animals typically also have high levels of muscle myoglobin. Weddell seals have over 50 milligrams of myoglobin per gram (mg/g) of muscle, and ribbon seals can have as much as 80 mg/g, whereas humans have about 5–10 mg of myoglobin per gram of muscle. In addition, recent data suggest that the muscle myoglobin of diving mammals has undergone adaptive evolution that changes the net charge on the surface of this molecule. These changes are thought to be key in allowing myoglobin to be present at high concentrations in muscle without harming the cell.

Diving animals do not have unusually large lungs, and likely do not make much use of their lungs as an oxygen store during diving. In fact, some species including the Weddell seal dive immediately after they exhale, and thus these animals swim actively without fresh air in the lungs.

Nitrogen narcosis is a problem at depth

As an animal descends through the water, the pressure of the surrounding water increases. The elevated ambient pressure causes the lungs to decrease in volume. The decrease in volume increases the partial pressure of the gases within the lungs. This effect can be beneficial, because it tends to drive additional oxygen into the circulation, but this benefit comes with a substantial risk: The increased pressure can also drive nitrogen gas into the circulation. This increase in blood nitrogen content can lead to a condition called **nitrogen narcosis**. The symptoms of nitrogen narcosis are similar to those of ingesting alcohol, progressing from an initial feeling of euphoria, through disorientation, and finally to loss of consciousness. Nitrogen gas is thought to act in a way similar to the anesthetic gas nitrous oxide, altering the activity of the nervous system by impairing the action of excitatory NMDA receptors, and enhancing the activity of the inhibitory opioid receptors.

Decompression sickness can occur on ascent

A related condition called "the bends," or decompression sickness, occurs when a diver ascends to the surface too quickly. At depth, nitrogen content of the blood is high. As a diver ascends, this nitrogen will simply diffuse back into the lungs, and can be exhaled. However, if a diver ascends too quickly the nitrogen will come out of solution while still in the blood, forming bubbles. This is similar to what happens when you open a bottle of soda pop. Soda pop is bottled under a high pressure of carbon dioxide. When you open the bottle, the pressure drops abruptly, causing bubbles to form. Bubbles in the blood are not inevitably harmful. They only cause problems if they become large, because large bubbles can lodge in small capillaries, blocking blood flow, or can press on nerve endings, or can become trapped in other enclosed spaces such as the joints. Decompression sickness is associated with a variety of symptoms, the most common of which are pain in the joints and muscles, and neurological problems, including headache and stroke. The risk of nitrogen narcosis and the bends is higher in scuba divers than in free divers, but extreme human free divers, who can descend to depths of over 70 meters, may experience some of these effects. The effects of decompression sickness have been observed in the carcasses of beached sperm whales that have ascended to the surface too rapidly after being startled by sonar signals.

Many diving marine mammals avoid nitrogen narcosis and decompression sickness by exhaling before diving and allowing the lungs (or more properly, the alveoli) to collapse completely as the animal descends. When the alveoli collapse, the residual volume of air in the lungs is pushed back into the conducting airways of the lungs, which do not participate in gas exchange. Thus, blood nitrogen levels in diving seals increase very little, regardless of dive depth. It is less clear how diving birds avoid this problem, because the lungs themselves are rigid. This difference in lung anatomy may explain why few birds dive deeply or for long periods. Laboratory experiments with Adélie penguins suggest that nitrogen levels can increase into the danger zone during unusually long or deep dives.

Marine mammals decrease oxygen demand during a dive

In addition to increasing oxygen stores, marine mammals also readjust oxygen demand during long dives, presumably to conserve oxygen and increase their aerobic dive limit. In fact, experiments on freely diving Weddell seals in nature suggest that the metabolic rate during diving is lower than during nondiving periods, despite the fact that these animals hunt actively while diving. Diving animals use a variety of biomechanical strategies to reduce the costs of locomotion in water. During forced dives in the laboratory, or when a freely diving animal must stay underwater for a prolonged period—for example, to avoid a predator—the animal invokes a series of physiological mechanisms that have been collectively called the **dive response**. During the dive response, arterioles leading to the skeletal muscles, skin, kidneys, and gut constrict, shunting blood away from the muscles and other nonessential organs, and toward the heart and brain. The brain is entirely dependent on aerobic metabolism and cannot survive oxygen deprivation for very long, whereas other tissues can tolerate reduced oxygen supply by reducing metabolic rate and by relying on anaerobic metabolism. At the same time, smooth muscles in the spleen contract, forcing stored red blood cells that are saturated with oxygen out into the circulation. During a forced or long dive, heart rate also slows, matching the reduced circulatory demand. The extent of this **diving bradycardia** is dependent on dive duration in voluntary dives, so that short dives involve little or no bradycardia whereas long dives involve a much greater bradycardia. Particularly profound episodes of bradycardia have been observed in freely diving seals in nature when the seal is forced to remain underwater longer than is typical (for example, by the presence of a predator). In these situations, the cardiovascular dive response allows the seal to conserve its remaining oxygen stores until it can safely return to the surface.

The cardiovascular dive response is not unique to diving mammals, but instead is a fundamental property of all vertebrates. Most animals reduce metabolic rate and redistribute blood flow to essential tissues when they are deprived of oxygen. However, the dive response is typically more profound in diving mammals than in terrestrial animals such as humans.

Diving animals have modified responses to CO_2

Finally, we must consider the effects of the CO_2 that is produced during a dive, and the resulting drop in blood pH. Diving animals appear to have unusually high buffering capacity in the blood, which blunts or prevents large swings in blood pH. In addition, diving mammals have a greatly reduced ventilatory response to CO_2. In humans, the gradual buildup of CO_2 and the resulting decrease in blood pH during apnea act as a very strong stimulus to take a breath. If you have ever tried to swim a long distance underwater, you will have experienced this intense urge to breathe as a result of CO_2 buildup. Diving animals such as seals do not have nearly as strong a response while submerged, which allows them to stay underwater longer without feeling the urge to take a breath.

CONCEPT CHECK

24. Outline at least four characteristics of animals such as seals that allow some species to dive for long periods to great depths.
25. Why do marine mammals such as seals breathe out before a dive?

SUMMARY

Respiratory systems consist of all the structures animals use to obtain oxygen from the environment, and to dispose of carbon dioxide. These systems use a combination of diffusion and bulk flow to transport gases between the environment and the tissues, along the steps of the oxygen cascade from the respiratory surface to the mitochondria. Animals living in air and water utilize differing respiratory strategies, because of the differences in the physical properties of these two media. Gas exchange in water is particularly challenging and is associated with strategies of unidirectional ventilation and countercurrent exchange. Air-breathing mammals have tidally ventilated lungs, but birds have lungs that are unidirectionally ventilated by a series of air sacs. This arrangement allows crosscurrent exchange, and allows the lungs to have a fixed volume, rather than expanding and contracting with each breath, which allows the gas exchange surface to be very thin and makes avian lungs more efficient than mammalian lungs.

Oxygen is carried to the tissues either dissolved in blood or bound to a respiratory pigment such as hemoglobin, hemerythrin, or hemocyanin. Blood can vary in both oxygen affinity and carrying capacity due to variation in the properties of the respiratory pigment among species, or as a result of modulation of the shape of the oxygen equilibrium curve due to changes in blood pH, P_{CO_2}, temperature, and organic molecules such as 2,3-DPG.

Carbon dioxide can be carried in the blood as dissolved CO_2, as HCO_3^-, or bound to proteins such as hemoglobin. Blood CO_2, HCO_3^-, and pH are interrelated via the carbonic anhydrase equilibrium reaction. Blood oxygenation affects CO_2 transport by altering hemoglobin CO_2 binding, and by altering blood pH. Vertebrate red blood cells play an important role in CO_2 transport by separating the reactants and products of the carbonic anhydrase equilibrium, greatly increasing the CO_2 carrying capacity of the blood.

Ventilation is carefully regulated. In the vertebrates, central pattern generators in the medulla initiate ventilation. Chemosensory inputs influence the action of these pattern generators, modulating the rate and depth of breathing, and breathing can also be modulated by conscious control. Environmental hypoxia and diving provide two examples of the ways in which vertebrates regulate their respiratory systems in response to environmental changes.

REVIEW QUESTIONS

1. LO1 Why is diffusion an inefficient respiratory strategy for organisms that are more than a few millimeters thick?

2. LO1 Outline why oxygen uptake is more challenging for animals living in water than for animals living in air.

3. LO2 Compare and contrast the lungs of birds, the lungs of mammals, and the tracheal systems of insects.

4. LO2 Explain how countercurrent flow arrangements can lead to more efficient gas exchange across a respiratory surface.

5. LO2 Compare and contrast the force pumps and aspiration pumps of tetrapod vertebrate respiratory systems.

6. LO3 Provide two examples of types of animals that use cilia to ventilate their respiratory surface.

7. LO3 Name one major difference between the ventilation of the gills in squid and teleost fishes.

8. LO4 Define discontinuous breathing. Why do some insects use this strategy?

9. LO4 Describe the changes in alveolar and intrapleural pressure during a single ventilatory cycle in mammals.

10. LO5 Why does the oxygen equilibrium curve of mammalian hemoglobin have a sigmoidal shape?

11. LO5 How does the Root effect help a physoclist fish to add oxygen to the swim bladder?

12. LO6 What is the significance of the red blood cell for CO_2 transport in vertebrates?

13. LO6 Using the Henderson-Hasselbalch equation, outline what happens to the pH of a poorly buffered aqueous solution when $[CO_2]$ increases.

14. LO7 Outline how chemoreceptors influence ventilation in mammals.

15. LO7 Why is it difficult to distinguish whether chemosensory cells detect P_{CO_2} or pH?

16. LO8 Explain why hypometabolism can be an effective response to hypoxia. What are some disadvantages of this strategy?

17. LO8 What is the "dive response"?

SYNTHESIS QUESTIONS

1. Very few animals that use water as the respiratory medium have lungs. Instead, most water breathers use gills for gas exchange. What functional disadvantages do lungs have in water?

2. Lungless salamanders typically live in moist or humid habitats, and can die if their skin dries out. Explain why it is critical for the skin of lungless salamanders to remain moist.

3. Some species of lungless salamander cannot live in water as adults, and will drown if fully immersed. Why might this occur?

4. In an experiment to determine the role of the air sacs in the avian lung, physiologists tied off an air sac so that gas from that air sac could no longer enter the lung. The experimenters then injected carbon monoxide into the sealed air sac. This manipulation did not decrease the oxygen saturation of hemoglobin in arterial blood. Explain why this was the case, and what this experiment demonstrates about the nature of the air sacs in birds.

5. A woman gets a disease that makes her unable to produce surfactant in her lungs. If she has a normal tidal volume, what can you say about her intrapleural pressure during inspiration?

6. What effects might you expect in a mammal whose major hemoglobin is mutated such that it lacks a Bohr effect?

7. Metabolic rate can increase as much as 40-fold above resting values as a result of feeding in some species of reptiles. In addition, during digestion, a large amount of H^+ is secreted into the stomach, which results in the so-called alkaline tide, a large metabolic alkalosis in which blood pH increases. Outline the likely response of the respiratory system to this increased oxygen demand and pH disturbance.

8. In fish, there is a positive correlation between whole-animal metabolic rate and the surface area of the gill. What might explain this relationship?

9. High-altitude-adapted mammals often do not show as large a pulmonary vasoconstriction in response to low inspired P_{O_2} (environmental hypoxia) as do lowland-adapted mammals. What advantages might this difference have at high altitude?

10. Hemoglobin is typically saturated with oxygen when the blood leaves the lungs. In a person who is doing pull-ups, will hemoglobin release more of the bound oxygen in the quadriceps (leg muscles) or in the biceps (arm muscles)? Describe at least two factors that could cause a difference, if any, in oxygen release between your biceps and quadriceps.

11. Imagine that you take hemoglobin molecules from both a sheep fetus and its mother. You mix equal amounts of these two hemoglobins in an aqueous solution in the presence of oxygen, at a P_{O_2} that is not sufficient to saturate all the hemoglobin sites on the molecules you have added. Given what you know about maternal and fetal hemoglobins, where would you expect to find most of this oxygen bound? How would this compare to the amount of oxygen dissolved in your solution and not bound to hemoglobin? Why?

12. Anxiety can cause a person to hyperventilate (breath rapidly and deeply). This can cause a variety of symptoms, including dizziness and fainting. What changes would you expect in systemic arterial O_2 and CO_2 concentration and pH during an episode of hyperventilation? How (i.e., by what mechanism) might this affect blood flow to the brain? Breathing into a paper bag is often suggested as a treatment for hyperventilation. Do you think this would work? Why or why not?

QUANTITATIVE QUESTIONS

1. The graphs below represent the gas exchange across two hypothetical respiratory surfaces (a and b). One of these surfaces has concurrent flow, and one has countercurrent flow.

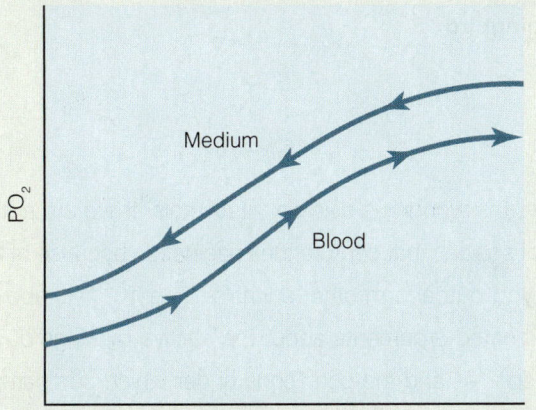

(a) Distance along repiratory surface

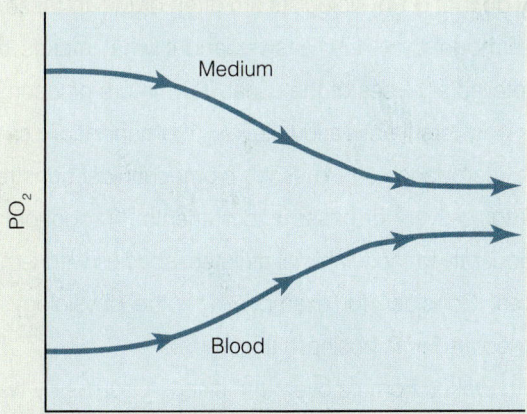

(b) Distance along respiratory surface

(a) Which surface has concurrent flow, and which surface has countercurrent flow?

(b) Based on the data shown, which surface has the most efficient gas exchange?

(c) What might account for this observation?

2. If a mammal has a minute volume of 5,200 ml/min, a breathing frequency of 13 breaths per minute, a vital capacity of 4,600 ml, and an expiratory reserve volume of 1,200 ml, what are the tidal volume and inspiratory reserve volume?

3. As part of a physiology experiment, a human subject is asked to breathe through a hose 1 m long and 3 cm in diameter (the end of the hose is open to the air in the room). What changes would you expect in ventilation rate and tidal volume compared with those measured in the same subject breathing normally? (Explain your answers.)

4. John, Jeff, and Harry are all breathing at different rates and depths. Using the data provided below, who would have the highest P_{O_2} in the blood leaving the lungs? Who would have the lowest? (Show your work.)

	Breathing Rate (Breaths per Minute)	Tidal Volume (ml per Breath)	Dead Space (ml)
John	15	500	200
Jeff	40	250	200
Harry	10	1,000	200

5. Using the Hb-oxygen saturation curve in Figure 11.32a, answer the following questions:
   (a) If P_{O_2} in the lungs is approximately 100 mm Hg, what is the percent saturation of Hb in the pulmonary capillaries?
   (b) If P_{O_2} in the tissues is approximately 5 mm Hg, what is the percent saturation of Hb in the systemic capillaries?

Learning Objectives

**After reading this chapter,
you should be able to:**

1 Explain the importance of different muscle fiber types and arrangements in locomotor systems.

2 Discuss the relationship between energy metabolism and locomotion.

3 Explain how other physiological systems affect locomotion.

4 Explain how skeletal systems are built, and how the arrangements with muscles influence the nature of work.

5 Discuss the different ways animals use anatomy and physiology to overcome environmental constraints in locomotion.

6 Discuss the factors that affect the energetic costs of movement.

FIGURE 12.1 A hummingbird

Photo source: ktsdesign/Fotolia.

Despite the wondrous diversity of animals, there are a number of species that capture the imagination because of their ability to outperform other animals. "Top 10" lists abound, with heated arguments about the relative rankings of various species and the conditions under which comparisons should be made. Each of these animal athletes raises the question: "How can they do that?" Physiologists are often drawn to these elite athletes as experimental models, but any answer about what makes them unusual requires prior detailed analyses of the usual. The nature of locomotor systems means that the answers lie at various levels of organization: special features of the molecular components of muscle, biomechanical constraints to design, and systems for delivery of gases and nutrients. Throughout this chapter we will return frequently to those animal athletes, species with remarkable locomotor capacities. Consider, for example, how the physiology of a hummingbird allows it to go about its business (Figure 12.1).

When a hummingbird wakes from its overnight sleep, it begins by warming its body temperature prior to its first flight. The body initiates breakdown of fat, providing a substrate for its flight muscle, a necessity for it to make its first foraging flight of the day. Shortly after eating its first meal, it transitions to a sugar-burning animal. As the day progresses, the hummingbird flits from flower to flower, hovering over flowers long enough to drink nectar. As you will learn, hovering is possible in hummingbirds because of two special features. First, these animals have relatively large breast muscles that permit the wing to generate lift in both the downstroke and the upstroke. Second, the wings beat extremely fast, upwards of 30 beats a second. The circulatory system is driven by a powerful heart that beats nearly as fast as the wings, generating enough force to move blood through the entire circulatory circuit in about 1 second. The flight muscles are packed with mitochondria, enabling the muscle to produce enough ATP to support the high energy demands of hovering flight. There are even specializations within the mitochondrion, filling them so full of cristae that there is only enough space between to fit one or two molecules of enzyme.

In the hummingbird, parallel adaptations in muscle, nervous, circulatory, digestive, and thermal systems culminate in an exceptional locomotor capacity, and remind us that locomotor physiology is far more complex than simply muscles in action. In this chapter we explore the ways animals integrate muscles into physiological systems to enable animals to move within their environments. ∎

LOOKING BACK 12

You may find it helpful to review Chapter 3, where we describe the nature of energy, the fundamentals of energy metabolism, and the biochemical basis of molecular structures, including the extracellular matrix. Also, Chapter 5 describes how nerves control muscles, Chapter 6 discusses the cellular basis of muscles and muscle diversity, and Chapters 9 and 11 discuss in more detail the control of the blood flow and oxygen delivery.

▌ OVERVIEW

Locomotion is usually defined as the act of moving from one place to another. To an animal physiologist, locomotion is an active process that is initiated and controlled by the animal. Locomotor systems integrate anatomy with several physiological systems. Appendages such as fins, legs, and wings allow animals to interact with the environment to generate or control forces that result in directional movement. The physical organization of muscles into musculoskeletal systems allows animals to translate cellular contraction into whole-animal locomotion. The musculoskeletal system acts in combination with the nervous system to control the position and movement of appendages. Locomotion demands exquisite control of energy metabolism and digestive physiology, mediated by the hormones that regulate fuel assimilation, storage, and mobilization. The respiratory system ensures that oxygen uptake eventually matches the increased oxygen demands that accompany muscle activity. The cardiovascular system delivers fuels to the muscle and removes metabolic end products. The interactions between these systems are summarized in Figure 12.2.

A hallmark of locomotor systems is the ability to respond to changes in demand. This capacity is particularly impressive in animals that undergo long-distance migrations. Prolonged changes in activity (training or detraining) alter the locomotor machinery. Humans are one of the few species that has the luxury of becoming detrained. In the natural world, detrained animals tend to get eaten or starve. Regardless of how fast or how far an animal travels, the ability to move requires coordination of diverse physiological systems.

Superimposed on the control of body movement are the constraints of the environment. Each environment, whether aquatic, aerial, or terrestrial, has physical properties that animals must overcome in order to move.

▌ LOCOMOTOR SYSTEMS

We begin our discussion of locomotor physiology by exploring the nature of the systems that support movement. When we first introduced muscles in Chapter 6, we focused mainly on the control of excitation-contraction coupling. We now turn our attention to the way different types of muscles are integrated into a musculoskeletal system composed of muscles

FIGURE 12.2   **Control of locomotion**
Animals move in response to environmental cues, both favorable (such as food) and unfavorable (such as local hypoxia). Sensory neurons receive the information and signal the central nervous system, which initiates locomotion by signaling via motor neurons to locomotor muscle. The cardiovascular system controls the flow to blood vessels. Metabolites from the digestive system and O_2 from the respiratory system enter the blood and serve the musculoskeletal system.

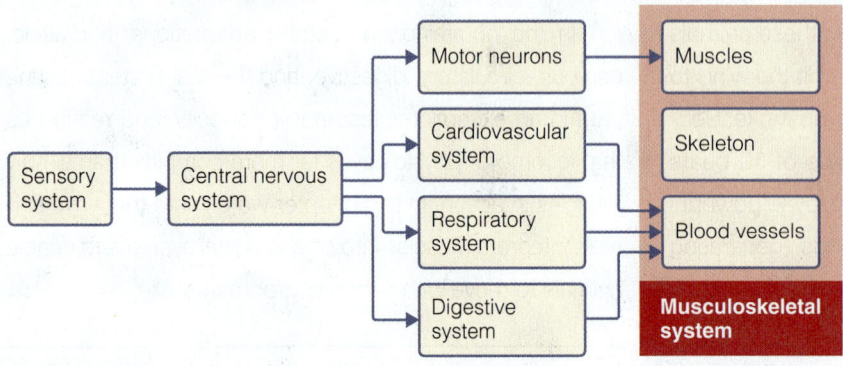

and skeleton, held together by connective tissue, controlled by the nervous system, and nourished by the blood supply. These musculoskeletal systems allow animals to translate changes in cell shape into movement.

Muscle Fiber Types

Most animals rely on muscles to generate the force required to move from place to place. Each style of movement requires muscles that possess appropriate biomechanical properties. The contractile properties of a muscle are determined by the design and organization of the proteins within the myofiber. The properties of contractile proteins alter cross-bridge cycling dynamics. The cellular machinery of excitation-contraction coupling affects the kinetics of contraction and relaxation. The three-dimensional arrangement of sarcomeres determines how much force a skeletal muscle can generate. Through differences in protein properties and structural organization, animals can produce muscles with particular contractile phenotypes that enable animals to move in the environment. Chapter 6 focused on the cellular processes that allow muscles to contract. In the following sections, we discuss how animals incorporate muscles into locomotor systems.

Many invertebrates use simple circular and longitudinal muscles to move

With the exception of the arthropods, most terrestrial invertebrates move by crawling. Simple muscles work in combination with a fluid-filled internal chamber that acts as a **hydrostatic skeleton**, and permits movement of internal fluids to aid in locomotion. Invertebrate locomotor muscles are typically striated, although the myofibers are often organized in ways that differ from vertebrate striated muscles.

Most wormlike invertebrates crawl using overlapping layers of muscle fibers. Nematodes use two layers of fibers running in different orientations along the longitudinal axis (Figure 12.3). When the muscle fibers contract on one side, coelomic fluid is forced into the opposite side and the worm bends. The nematode uses cycles of contraction and relaxation to undulate through the environment.

Earthworms organize locomotor striated muscles into circular and longitudinal layers. This arrangement is reminiscent of the organization of smooth muscles of our digestive tract (see Chapter 14). As with the gut musculature, these muscles allow the animal to produce peristaltic waves of contraction. Earthworms use the same principle, but because they are segmented, each body segment works independently, giving the earthworm a much greater degree of control over movement (Figure 12.4).

Directly beneath the outer layers of the earthworm cuticle and epidermis lies the thin layer of circular muscle. The thicker longitudinal layer of muscle is composed of groups of muscle cells arranged into fan-shaped (pennate) bundles. Each bundle is surrounded by a basement membrane, and bundles are bound together by connective tissue. A ring of

FIGURE 12.3   **Nematode muscles and crawling**
Nematodes move through the soil using undulations. The body bends when overlapping muscle fibers contract on one side of the body and relax on the other side, forcing a redistribution of coelomic fluids.

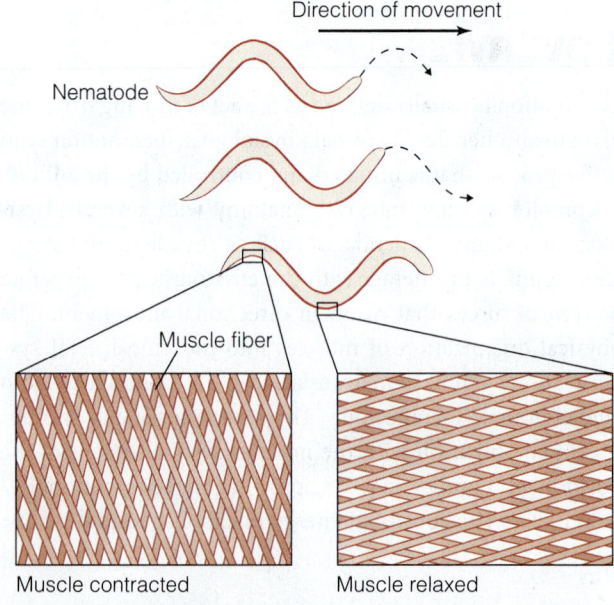

FIGURE 12.4 Earthworm locomotion

(a) Earthworms move using waves of muscle contraction that act in conjunction with the hydrostatic skeleton. Contraction of circular muscle reduces the diameter of the worm and pushes coelomic fluid forward. Longitudinal muscle contraction pulls the posterior segments of the worm forward. **(b)** This pattern of muscle contraction translates into locomotion with the help of a series of hairlike setae that anchor segments of the worm to the substratum. The attachment of setae is under muscular control. Protractor muscles force setae outward to lock onto the substrate. Retractor muscles pull setae back toward the body, releasing the surface. Movement requires coordination of the muscles of the body wall and setae.

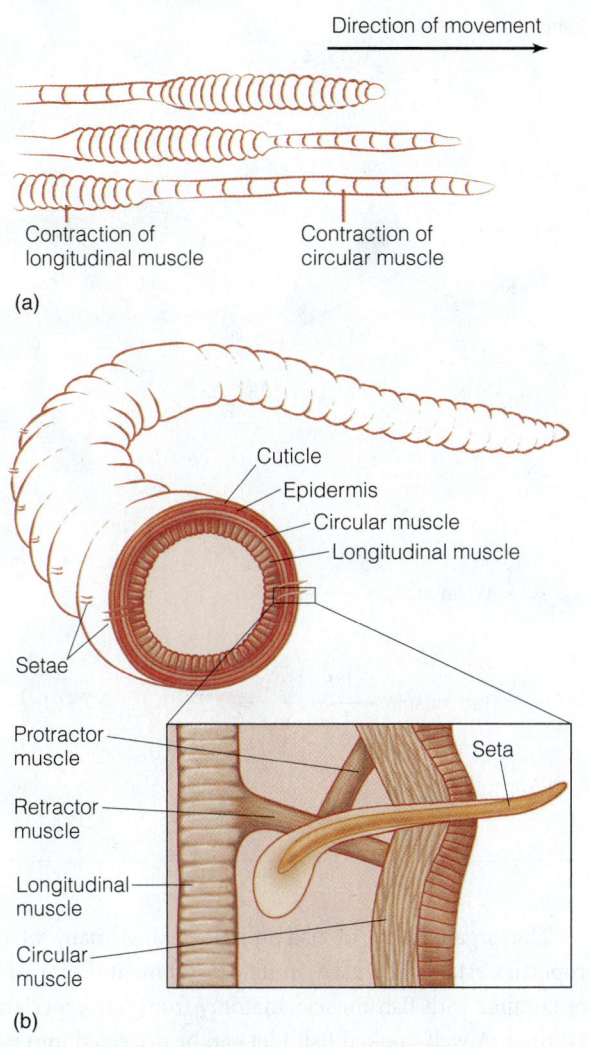

Direction of movement →

Contraction of longitudinal muscle

Contraction of circular muscle

(a)

Cuticle
Epidermis
Circular muscle
Longitudinal muscle

Setae

Protractor muscle
Seta
Retractor muscle
Longitudinal muscle
Circular muscle

(b)

FIGURE 12.5 Squid jet propulsion

(a) Squid produce jet propulsion by forcing water from the body cavity out of a tubelike siphon. Water moves in and out of the body cavity in response to muscular contractions of the body wall, or mantle. **(b)** The mantle is composed of complex, inter-twined layers of muscle fibers. Radial fibers control the thickness of the mantle. The diameter of the mantle is controlled by three layers of circular muscles.

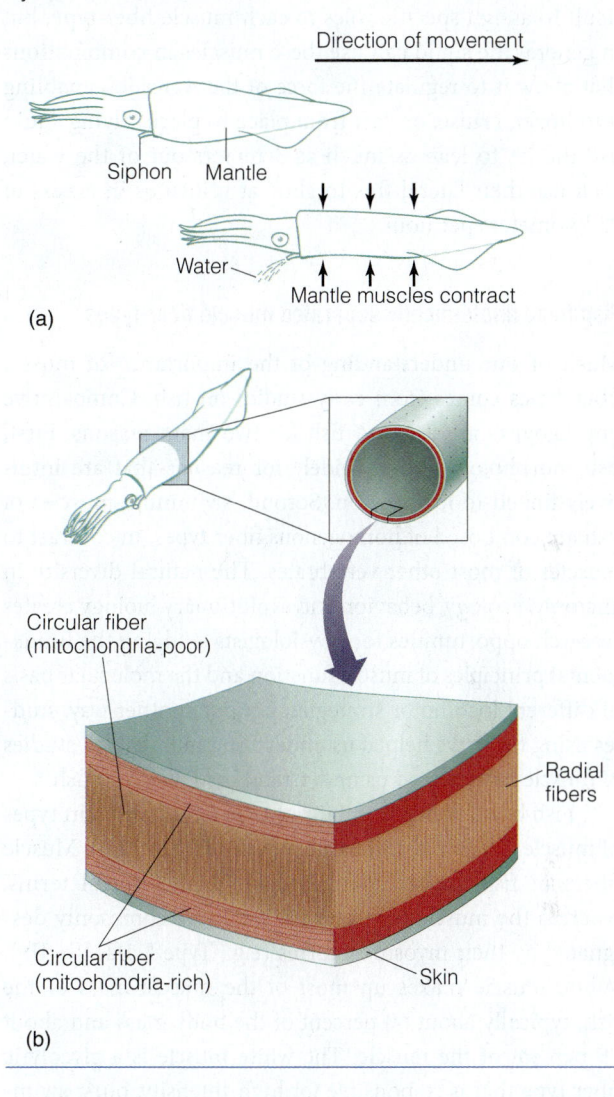

Direction of movement →

Siphon   Mantle

Water
Mantle muscles contract

(a)

Circular fiber (mitochondria-poor)

Radial fibers

Circular fiber (mitochondria-rich)
Skin

(b)

nerves circles the segment, running between muscle layers, with axons extending toward the muscles. When the circular muscle contracts, the coelomic fluid is pushed forward to extend the segment. Once the segment is extended, tiny hairlike projections called setae attach to the soil or other substrate surface. When the longitudinal muscle contracts, the anterior end of the segment remains in place and the posterior part of the segment is pulled forward. The nerve networks coordinate the movement of circular and longitudinal muscles and the patterns of activity in the independent segments.

Squid, the fastest of aquatic invertebrates, also use complementary muscle layers to move, but the arrangement is quite different. The muscles of the outer body wall, or mantle, are intermingled in two planes (Figure 12.5). Radial muscle fibers extend from the inside of the mantle to the outside. Contraction of the radial muscles reduces the thickness of the mantle wall and reduces its circumference. Circular muscle, which surrounds the mantle, is composed of three layers. A thick central layer of muscle with low mitochondrial content is covered on the inside and outside by a thin layer of **mitochondria-rich muscle cells**. Squid use these complex mantle muscles to produce jet propulsion. Water enters the internal chamber when the mantle muscles relax. Upon contraction, water is rapidly ejected out of the mantle cavity through a tube, or siphon, creating a flume of water that pushes the squid forward. In Chapter 4: Neuron Structure and Function, we discussed how the giant axon ensures that electrical stimulation of the mantle muscles occurs in unison to maximize the force of water expulsion. The anatomical complexity of the muscles has made it difficult to assign specific roles to each muscle fiber type, but in general the squid can use these muscles in combinations that allow it to regulate the force of the water jet, enabling it to hover, cruise, or dart from place to place. Flying squid use the jet to leap as much as 3 meters out of the water, then use their lateral fins to glide at velocities in excess of 25 kilometers per hour.

Fish have anatomically separated muscle fiber types

Much of our understanding of the importance of muscle fiber types comes from early studies on fish. Comparative physiologists are lured to fish for two main reasons. First, fish morphology differs widely for reasons that are intuitively linked to locomotion. Second, swimming muscles of fish are composed of homogenous fiber types, in contrast to muscles of most other vertebrates. The natural diversity in anatomy, ecology, behavior, and evolutionary biology creates research opportunities for physiologists studying the fundamental principles of muscle function and the molecular basis of different locomotor strategies. Or, put another way, studies using fish have helped us understand muscle, and studies of muscle have helped us understand the biology of fish.

Fish build their locomotor muscle from two main types of muscle fibers: red and white muscle (Figure 12.6). Muscle fibers of fish are still described by these colorful terms, whereas the muscles of tetrapods are more commonly designated by their myosin isoforms (e.g., Type I, IIa, IIb, IIx). White muscle makes up most of the muscle mass of the fish, typically about 60 percent of the body mass and about 85 percent of the muscle. The white muscle is a glycolytic fiber type that is responsible for high-intensity, burst swimming. Red muscle is usually confined to a narrow ribbon that extends along the side of the animal just under the lateral line. Small patches of red muscle are also found at the base of fins, where they are used to power the fin movements. Red muscle is an oxidative fiber type that supports slow, **steady-state** cruising activity. Many fish have a third type of locomotor muscle called pink muscle that is intermediate in contractile properties. Pink muscle is typically found at the interface between the white and red muscles. Each region of locomotor muscle is virtually homogeneous in fiber type. This anatomical organization is convenient for researchers who study the cellular origins and physiological function of different muscle fiber types.

FIGURE 12.6 **Musculature of fish**

Fish white muscle is composed of more than 100 repeating units called myotomes. They extend backward from the spine, twisting forward as they approach the exterior surface of the fish. Narrow strips of red muscle are found laterally along the length of the fish. Pink muscle (not shown) often separates the red from the white muscle.

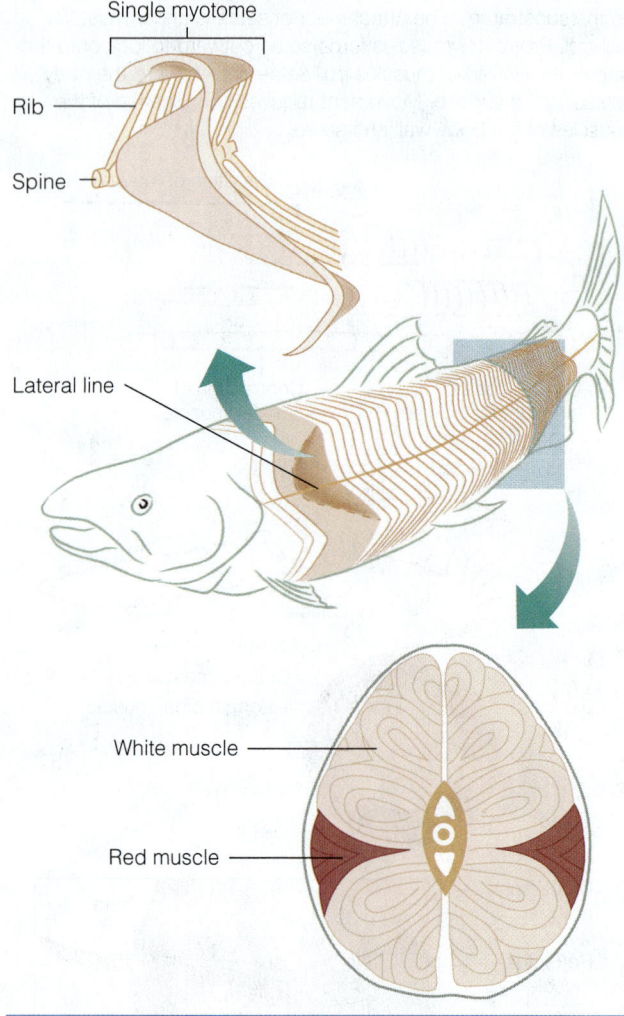

The organization of fish muscle retains many of the properties established early in its development. Many of us are familiar with fish muscle anatomy from our experience at dinner. A well-cooked fish filet can be dissected into parallel layers of white muscle. Each layer is a **myotome**, one of the original segments established early in embryological development. Each myotome contains blocks of parallel white muscle fibers separated by a thin layer of connective tissue called the *myoseptum*. Each myotome is attached to the posterior region of the fish by tendons. The skin also acts as a sheath that connects the different myotomes, helping to integrate the force of the different contractile units. Contraction of a myotome generates force that is transmitted in complex ways to other regions of the body. Force is transferred to the next myotome across myosepta, to the caudal fin along tendons, and to the skin. These forces culminate in movement of the trunk and tail to generate propulsion. Force generation in red muscle also relies on the skin and tendons that insert at the tail. This arrangement converts contractile force directly to movement of the trunk and tail.

The red muscle of tuna is unusual in two important respects that influence force generation. Most species of fish have a thin wedge of red muscle that runs the length of the fish, just beneath the lateral line. Tuna red muscle, however, is not homogenously distributed along the length but rather is concentrated midway along the length of the fish. It is also located deep within the body, close to the spine. Just above, we discussed how the superficial location of red muscle of fish helps with force generation. In this position, it has leverage to bend the body wall. How, then, does the deep red muscle of tuna power its high-velocity swimming? The core of deep red muscle is able to shorten more than the surrounding white muscle. The red muscle tendons connect directly to the caudal fin, allowing more effective force transmission. Because of these efficient tendons, the anterior red muscle can make important contributions to the power of posterior movements, even though the anterior part of the fish does not bend during swimming.

The pattern of locomotor muscle contraction is controlled by motor neurons

The differences in the contractile properties of oxidative (red) and glycolytic (white) muscle enable the animal to produce different types of movement. Although most easily shown in fish, these same general rules apply to tetrapods. Red muscle exhibits its maximal power output at much lower tail-beat frequencies than does white muscle. Consequently, fish use red muscle in slow swimming and white muscle at higher velocities. In living fish, this pattern of sequential activation of muscle contraction, called **recruitment**, is determined by motor neurons, under the control of the central nervous system.

Researchers study muscle recruitment in living fish by fitting them with electromyograph (EMG) electrodes and inducing them to swim at different velocities. The EMG output shows that at low swim speeds, only the red muscle is electrically active (Figure 12.7). As swim speed increases, red muscles are activated more frequently. At still faster speeds, white muscle is activated. At high swim velocities, red muscle may continue to be activated but it doesn't generate much power. Fish can swim continuously for hours at speeds where only red muscle is active. At faster speeds, where white muscle is recruited, fish quickly become exhausted.

The importance of neuronal control of locomotor movement can be illustrated using the lamprey, a primitive

FIGURE 12.7 Swimming velocity and muscle recruitment

(a) Power output of isolated muscle can be assessed over a range of frequencies of electrical stimulation. Red muscle has a lower power output than white muscle, and it generates its optimal power at a lower frequency. **(b)** Electrical activity of red and white muscle in living fish can be measured by electromyography. The different muscle fiber types are recruited at different swim velocities. At low velocities (one body length per second), only red muscle is active. As velocity increases, the frequency of contractions increases. Once swim velocity exceeds a threshold (in this example, two body lengths per second), white muscle is activated. Red muscle continues to contract, but the force it generates contributes little to locomotion at high velocities.

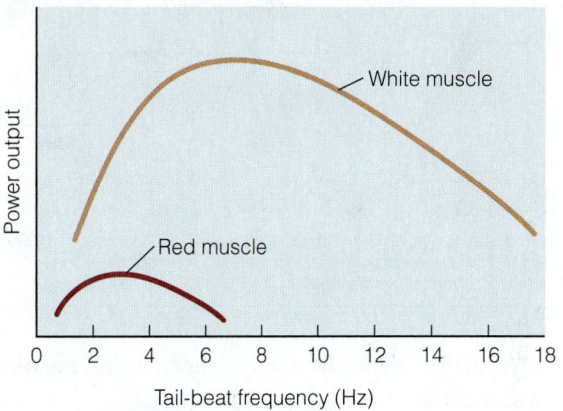

(a)

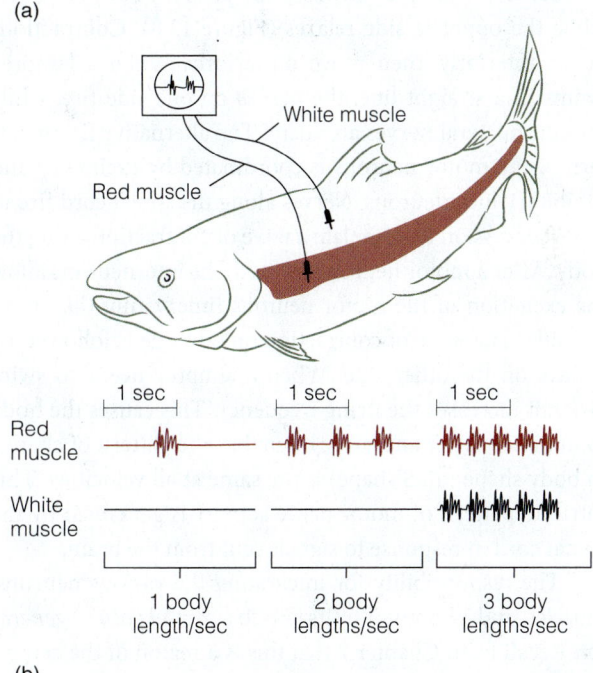

(b)

Figure source: Panel (b): Based on Johnston, I. A. (1981). Structure and function of fish muscles. *Symposia of the Zoological Society of London, 48,* 71–113.

fish that swims by simple snakelike undulations. Like other fish, the lamprey has superficial red muscle and deep white muscle organized into about 100 myotomes. Nerve roots from the corresponding segment of the spinal cord innervate

FIGURE 12.8 **Swimming lamprey**

The lamprey swims by anguilliform movement, using waves of contraction of trunk muscles. Each burst of electrical activity on an EMG recording signifies a muscle contraction. When muscles on one side of the body are activated, the muscles on the opposite side are inhibited. The waveform is generated by sequential activation of muscles along the length of the body.

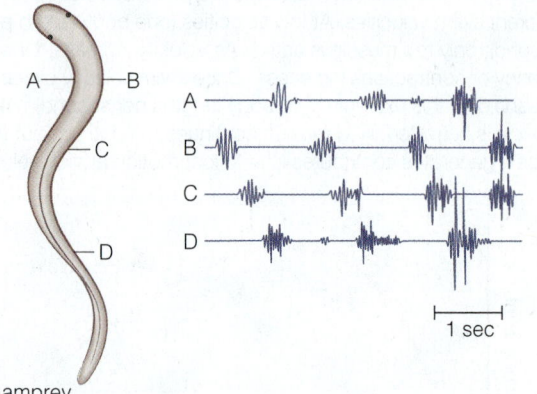

Lamprey

Figure source: Based on Orlovsky, G., Deliagina, T. G., & Grillner, S. (1999). Page 115 from *Neuronal control of locomotion: From mollusc to man.* Oxford, UK: Oxford University Press.

each myotome. Separate nerves innervate the muscles on each side of the fish.

When the lamprey swims, one side of the body contracts while the opposite side relaxes (Figure 12.8). Contractions begin anteriorly, then move posteriorly. When a lamprey swims in a straight line, the nerves on one side fire, while the contralateral nerves are silent. The alternative firing pattern of the motor neurons is coordinated by excitatory and inhibitory interneurons. Nerves along the spinal cord fire in rapid succession to stimulate a wave of contraction along the body. After a motor neuron has fired, the interneurons allow the excitation of the motor neurons innervating the opposite side. The wave of contraction on one side is followed by a wave on the other side. When a lamprey needs to swim faster, it increases the firing frequency. This causes the body to undulate faster and more often, but the pattern of change in body shape (an S shape) is the same at all velocities. This intricate pattern of motor nerve activity is generated by the spinal cord in response to signals sent from the brain.

The responsibility for integrating the various neurons, muscles, and locomotor units falls to a *central pattern generator*. Recall from Chapter 7 that this is a region of the central nervous system that stimulates the right neurons to activate the right muscles at the proper point in a complex movement.

Tetrapods have a multiplicity of fiber types

Fish locomotion using the trunk and tail is relatively simple in terms of both muscle organization and neuronal control. However, once vertebrates made the transition to land,

movement required much more complex locomotor muscles and neuronal controls. Whereas fish can get by with two or three muscle fiber types, tetrapods build individual muscles using combinations of fiber types. The limb musculature of tetrapods is developmentally homologous to the fin musculature of fish. Tetrapods have great diversity in how they use their limbs in movement, but the organization of muscles is similar in amphibians, reptiles, birds, and mammals. Each group of tetrapods draws upon large suites of muscle contractile proteins to create diverse fiber types.

Much of our understanding of tetrapod muscle function comes from studies on the hindlimb muscles that frogs use to jump. Like fish locomotor muscle, the jumping (**extensor**) muscle of a frog is relatively pure in fiber type. Researchers from many physiological disciplines value the frog hindlimb preparation as an experimental tool. Frog extensors are easily removed from the animal and remain stable, enabling researchers to work with the preparation for long periods. Biomechanics researchers focus on the hindlimb because of its activity during jumping. When frogs leap with their strongest contractions, virtually every fiber of the extensor muscles is recruited. Cell biologists use frog extensors because they can isolate intact, single fibers, which facilitates the exploration of cellular and genetic properties.

The diversity in muscle composition in tetrapods is evident at many levels of biological organization. Recall from Chapter 6 that skeletal muscle cells, or myofibers, are multinucleated cells. Each nucleus within a single myofiber usually expresses the same genes for contractile proteins. That is, each myofiber is usually of a pure fiber type because all nuclei within the cell express the same myosin heavy chain isoform gene. However, hundreds of myofibers are combined to make the muscle. In most cases, tetrapod muscles are mosaics of different fiber types (see Figure 6.26). Each fiber is innervated by a motor neuron, and animals have the capability of differentially stimulating sets of myofibers. This permits muscles to conduct different types of activities. Consider the way in which the sciatic nerve controls the contraction of the mosaic gastrocnemius muscle of a frog (Figure 12.9). In the animal, each neuron of the sciatic nerve controls a specific myofiber, and each can be regulated by the animal to induce different patterns of contraction. When an electrical stimulus is applied to the sciatic nerve, the influence of recruitment can be seen by progressively increasing voltage. At low intensity, only a few neurons are stimulated to induce an action potential, and only a few myofibers contract, causing the muscle to display a low force contraction. As stimulation voltage increases, more and more neurons and myofibers are activated, increasing the force of contraction. This growth in force with each contraction is something that happens at the level of the whole muscle through recruitment of additional myofibers. The underlying mechanism is different from the

An isolated sciatic nerve is stimulated electrically, causing the gastrocnemius muscle to contract. As the strength of the stimulus increases, more motor neurons in the nerve are activated, causing more myofibers in the muscle to contract.

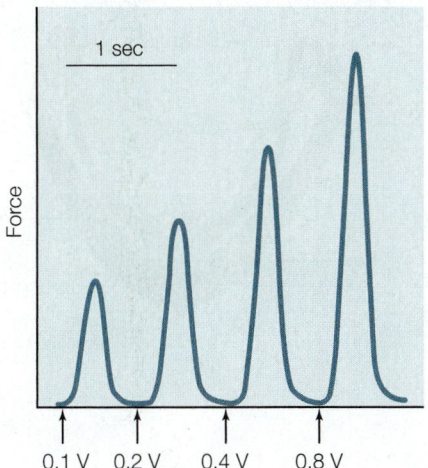

increased force that arises within a single myofiber as a result of high-frequency stimulation (see Figure 6.30).

The ability to build muscle from different motor units, each with their own neuronal stimulation, number of myofibers, and contractile properties is vital to providing animals with locomotor flexibility. The mosaic design of tetrapod muscles is critical in enabling a single muscle to participate in distinct styles of movement. The frog uses its hindlimb muscles to swim, walk, hop, and jump. Mammals use hindlimb muscles to stand, walk, jog, swim, sprint, and jump. Forearm muscles enable birds to use their wings to flap, glide, and undertake complex aerial maneuvers. Though a single muscle is used in different patterns, each of type of movement requires multiple muscles to be used in combination.

Locomotor muscles are organized into locomotor modules and functional groups

Most tetrapods move using cyclical changes in the position of limbs. When a limb bends at a joint, the movement is called **flexion**. The limb straightens during **extension**. Flexion and extension are induced in response to the contraction of separate **antagonistic muscles** (Figure 12.10). For example, when a primate bends its arm (flexion), the biceps muscle contracts while the triceps is relaxed. Extension occurs when the triceps contracts while the biceps is relaxed. Limb movement in support of locomotion typically involves complex combinations of muscles that work together to move each segment of the limb in a coordinated manner.

Consider the muscles used in the mammalian hindlimb during walking. An extensor group of leg muscles works synergistically to move the leg forward; a **flexor** group of muscles works synergistically to pull the leg back. The extensor group includes the soleus and gastrocnemius, which bend the foot; the quadriceps and rectus femoris, which straighten the knee; and the gluteus, which works at the hip to swing the leg forward. The flexor group includes the tibialis anterior, which moves the foot; the hamstring group, which bends the knee; and the iliopsoas, which rotates the leg at the hip. These muscle groups work antagonistically: Contraction of one muscle group requires relaxation of the other muscle group. In addition to the muscles that move the leg, other suites of muscles participate in movement. The fine muscles of the feet work in combination with sensory information collected by proprioceptors in the skin to make fine-scale adjustments in position. The postural muscles of the back and abdomen are recruited to maintain balance during movement. All of the muscles that are responsible for a type of movement are grouped together into a **locomotor module**.

Bird flight musculature is another example of a locomotor module. The musculature that powers flight in birds is derived from the same appendicular musculature that supports the movement of forearms in tetrapods. As in

FIGURE 12.10 Antagonistic muscle groups

A limb straightens when extensor muscles contract and bends when flexor muscles contract. In the forelimb of primates, the biceps is the primary flexor muscle and the triceps is the main extensor muscle.

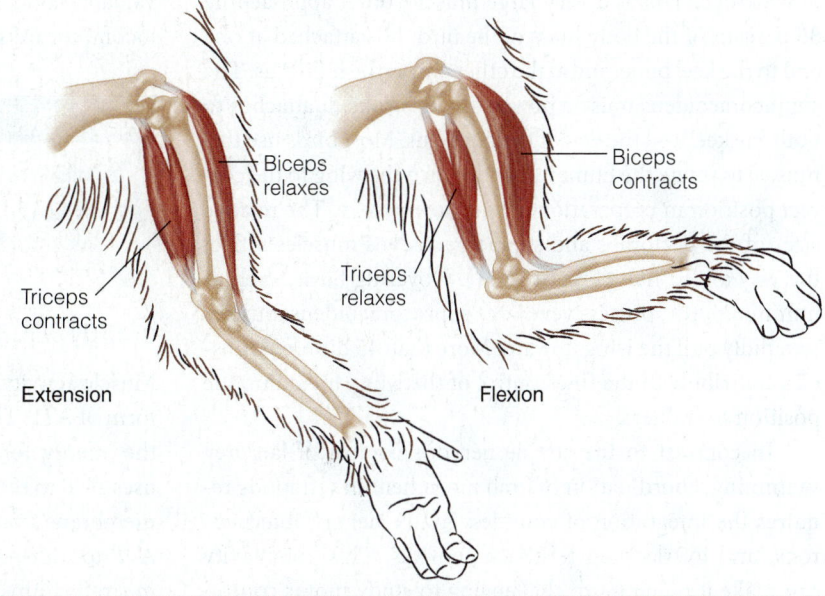

FIGURE 12.11 **Bird flight muscles**

Birds use their pectoralis muscle to power the downstroke, and their supracoracoideus muscle for the upstroke. **(a)** Birds that fly by flapping their wings, such as the seagull, have a very large pectoralis muscle. **(b)** The hovering flight of hummingbirds also requires a strong supracoracoideus muscle because force is generated on both the downstroke and the upstroke.

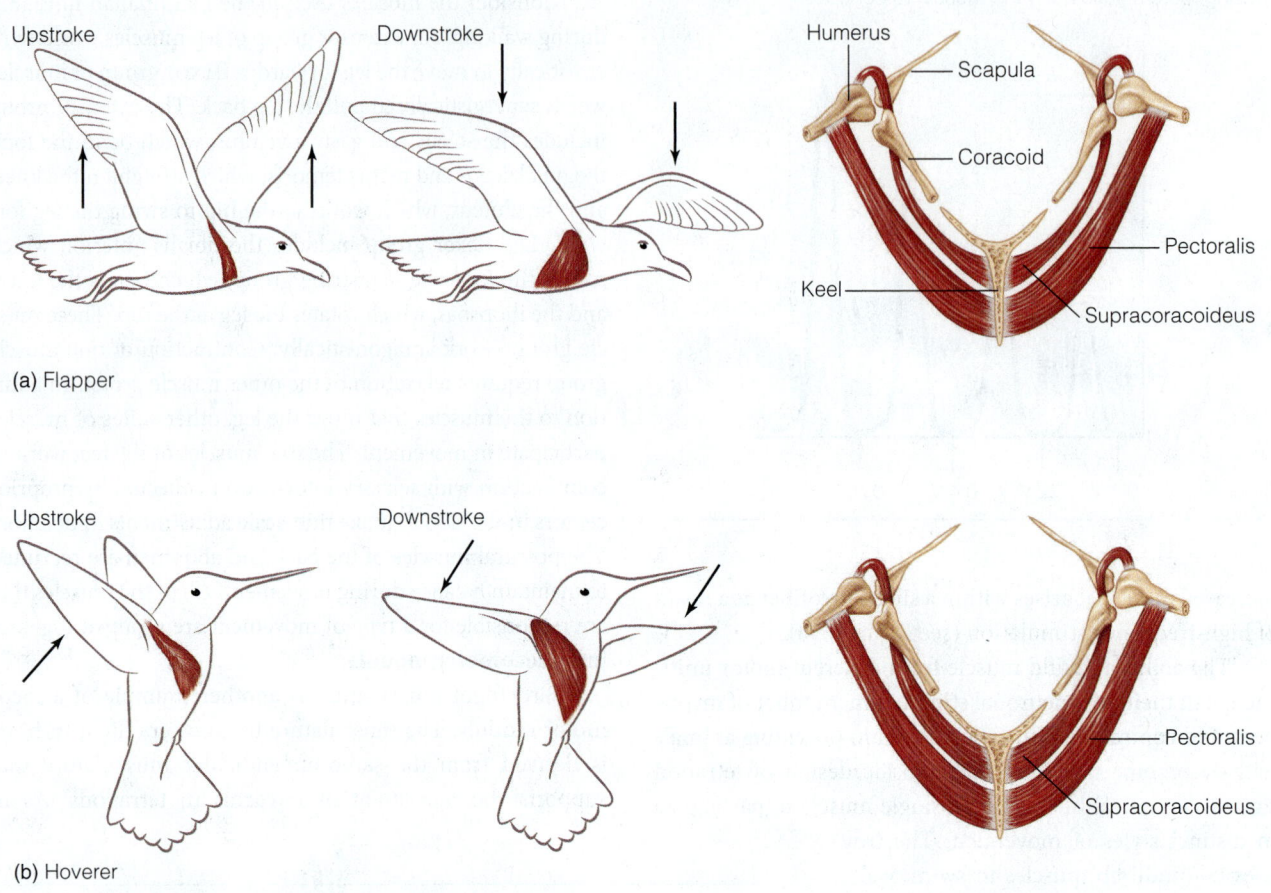

(a) Flapper

(b) Hoverer

other vertebrates, muscles work in antagonistic groups to power wing movements. The pectoralis muscle powers the downstroke. This is a very large muscle, often approaching 35 percent of the body mass of the bird. It is attached at one end to the keel bone, and at the other end to the humerus. The supracoracoideus muscle powers the upstroke. It attaches to both the keel and the end of the humerus. Most birds use this muscle to rotate the humerus, and return the wing to the correct position in preparation for the downstroke. The relative sizes of the pectoralis and supracoracoideus muscles reflect the way a bird flies (Figure 12.11). Hovering birds, such as hummingbirds, possess very large supracoracoideus muscles to rapidly pull the wing upward. More than 45 different muscles contribute to the fine control of the wing, including the position of feathers.

In contrast to the simple nervous control of lamprey swimming, coordination of limb movement in tetrapods requires the integration of countless motor nerves, interneurons, and overlapping feedback controls. This complexity can make it much more challenging to study motor control in tetrapods. For this reason, simple systems such as fish swimming musculature and frog extensor muscles remain valuable tools for exploring neuronal control of vertebrate locomotor muscle.

CONCEPT CHECK

1. What are muscle fiber types and what is recruitment?
2. What is the relationship between a central pattern generator and a locomotor module?

Energy Metabolism

Muscle activity demands a great deal of energy, mainly in the form of ATP. The actinomyosin ATPase uses ATP to provide the energy for cross-bridge cycling. The Na^+/K^+ ATPase uses ATP to reestablish ion gradients across the sarcolemmal membrane after each action potential. The Ca^{2+} ATPase uses ATP to transport cytoplasmic Ca^{2+} back into the sarcoplasmic reticulum. Because working muscles can have high rates of ATP turnover, let's discuss how the unique features of the pathways of energy metabolism are integrated into muscle structure and function.

Glycolysis and mitochondria support different types of locomotion

Muscle contraction is an energetically expensive process, and shortfalls in energy production can compromise locomotion. Muscles meet energy demands using a combination of preformed **phosphagens** and ATP-producing pathways. The preformed phosphagens include the adenylate pool (ATP and ADP) as well as the phosphoguanidine compounds. Vertebrates use phosphocreatine and invertebrates use one or more of phosphoarginine, phosphoglycocyamine, phosphotaurocyamine, or phospholambricine (see Chapter 3). Because these preexisting energy pools can support locomotion only for very short periods, other pathways of ATP production are critical. Most locomotor activity is supported by some combination of anaerobic glycolysis and mitochondrial aerobic metabolism. These two pathways differ in five main respects that determine how they support muscle activity.

1. **Metabolic efficiency.** Oxidative phosphorylation produces more ATP per glucose molecule than does glycolysis (36 versus 2 ATP per glucose). As a result, all muscles rely on oxidative phosphorylation to support metabolism at rest and during recovery from activity. Slow-twitch muscles (such as fish red muscle) rely on oxidative phosphorylation to support muscle activity.

2. **Rate of ATP production.** Though less efficient, glycolysis can generate ATP faster than oxidative phosphorylation. When an animal must move very quickly, ATP must be produced at rates that cannot be met by mitochondria. A cheetah chasing a gazelle relies on glycolysis to provide the ATP that allows it to reach high sprint speeds. Although glycolysis allows the muscle to produce ATP very quickly, limited stores of glycogen mean the less-efficient glycolytic pathway quickly runs out of fuel. Thus, the cheetah must capture its prey within a short period or its muscles will run out of the carbohydrate fuels necessary to support sprinting.

3. **Dependence on oxygen.** In the absence of oxygen, glycolysis is the only option to produce ATP. During high-intensity activity, oxygen cannot be delivered to muscle fast enough to meet ATP demands by mitochondrial metabolism and the tissue becomes functionally hypoxic. Hypoxic muscle relies on internal glycogen stores and produces lactate, metabolic disturbances that must be rectified during recovery.

4. **Fuel diversity.** Glycolysis relies exclusively on carbohydrate, whereas mitochondria can generate energy from oxidation of carbohydrates, lipids (fatty acids), and amino acids. Fuels for muscle activity can be derived directly from the diet or mobilized from intramuscular stores or extramuscular storage depots.

5. **Rate of mobilization.** Muscles possess low levels of fuels that can be oxidized immediately (glucose, fatty acids, glycerol, free amino acids). Muscles consume these fuels rapidly, so animals must mobilize stored fuels to sustain muscle activity. Each type of metabolic fuel can be mobilized at a characteristic rate. When muscle activity begins, glycogen hydrolysis begins within a fraction of a second. If muscle activity continues, other fuel depots are mobilized.

Mitochondrial content influences muscle aerobic capacity

Oxidative phosphorylation is central to the energetics of most muscles, and mitochondrial content is an important determinant of muscle aerobic capacity. Muscle mitochondria are constructed in ways that pack maximal metabolic capacity into minimal space. Many aspects of muscle mitochondrial structure and function are similar across the animal kingdom. Although the mitochondrial content of muscles may vary widely across muscle fiber types, muscle mitochondrial properties are similar across species. However, some exceptional species show specializations that reflect the limits of mitochondrial function and the evolution of aerobic capacity. The network of mitochondria, or reticulum, is particularly well developed in the locomotor muscles of active organisms, allowing the mitochondria to operate as a more efficient electrical network. Antarctic fish also have an extensive mitochondrial reticulum, but in these animals the reticulum may improve the efficiency of oxygen delivery into the cell. Because oxygen dissolves more readily into lipid than water, the interconnected mitochondrial membranes facilitate oxygen delivery into the depths of the cell. This may be an important mechanism to facilitate oxygen delivery into the cell, as many of these animals lack the oxygen-carrying proteins hemoglobin and myoglobin.

The mitochondrial inner membrane structure also reflects the premium on intracellular space. The cristae, which possess the enzymes of oxidative phosphorylation, are densely packed to compress a high catalytic potential into a small space. Each milliliter of mitochondria possesses 20–40 m^2 of inner membrane. Imagine 400–800 pages of a textbook folded into a space the size of the end of your thumb. Some "athletic" species possess more densely packed cristae, sometimes approaching 70 m^2/ml of mitochondria. At this high cristae density there is barely enough space between cristae to fit two molecules of an average mitochondrial matrix enzyme.

Mitochondrial content varies widely among muscle types and species. The sparse mitochondria in glycolytic muscle fibers typically occupy less than 2 percent of the muscle intracellular space. The mitochondrial content of oxidative muscles is usually three- to tenfold greater than that of glycolytic muscles in the same animal. In the flight muscles of insects and hummingbirds, which contract at very high frequencies, almost half of the muscle intracellular volume is occupied by mitochondria. Furthermore, the mitochondria in these animals also possess a very high cristae density. Any mechanism that permits more efficient packing of mitochondrial structures frees up space that can be used for other muscle components, such as myofibrils and SR.

Muscle must recover from high-intensity activity

High-intensity activity is fueled by intramuscular stores of glycogen. As fast-twitch muscles undergo glycolysis, lactate is produced. The muscle becomes exhausted from the combination of energetic shortfalls, ion disturbances, and pH imbalance. To recover from **burst exercise**, muscles must replenish energy stores, including glycogen, ATP, and phosphocreatine. They must also reestablish ion gradients, Ca^{2+} stores, and pH. An important element of recovery is removal of the lactate that results from anaerobic glycolysis. At the end of exercise, lactate can have many different fates (Figure 12.12). Some muscles use lactate as a fuel to rebuild glycogen stores. Other muscles export the lactate for processing by other tissues. Some blood-borne lactate is oxidized by other aerobic tissues, such as the heart. If muscles release lactate into the blood, they must import glucose from the blood to rebuild muscle glycogen stores. Many animals use the *Cori cycle* to replenish muscle glycogen. In this pathway, muscle-derived lactate is imported by the liver, which uses it to resynthesize glucose. Liver glucose is then released into the blood and taken up by muscle, which can use it to produce glycogen. The relative importance of each pathway depends on muscle type and species.

Consider the example of the northern pike, a fish that lives in northern temperate waters. It spends most of its time hiding in the weeds waiting for unsuspecting prey to approach. When it sees a small fish or frog, the pike uses its white muscle to flip its tail. With just a few tail flips, the pike accelerates up to 5 *g*, roughly the equivalent of the acceleration of a fighter jet. If the pike misses its target with the initial thrust, the prey can escape because the pike cannot immediately mount a second attack. Instead, it returns to its hiding spot and begins the long, slow process of metabolic recovery. The northern pike, for example, requires many hours for its muscle to return to the preexercise metabolic state.

Recovery following intense muscle activity requires both metabolic and cellular corrections, each of which requires energy investment. Resynthesis of ATP, phosphocreatine, and glycogen requires oxidative phosphorylation. Energy is also required to reestablish ion distributions across membranes (H^+, Ca^{2+}, K^+, and Na^+). Muscle activity can also cause physical damage to the muscle, which must be repaired

FIGURE 12.12 Lactate metabolism during recovery from activity

High-intensity exercise in glycolytic muscles causes buildup of lactate. When exercise ceases, lactate is removed by many different pathways. Some lactate is used to resynthesize glycogen in the glycolytic muscle. Lactate can also be released into the blood and taken up by the liver, which uses it to produce glucose. Oxidative tissues, such as heart and red muscle, can oxidize lactate as a fuel.

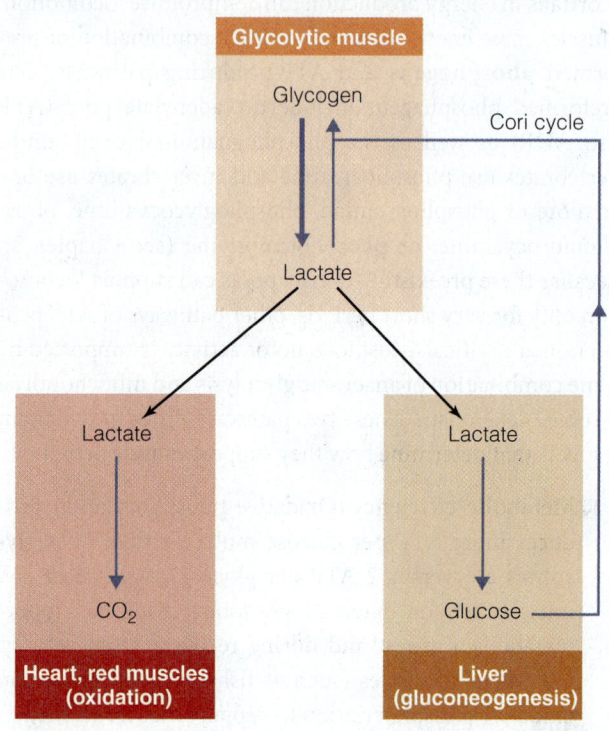

during recovery. The energy for these processes is provided by mitochondrial oxidative phosphorylation. Recovering animals often show elevated postexercise oxygen consumption (EPOC) long after exercise has ceased, a phenomenon call *oxygen debt* (Figure 12.13).

Metabolic transitions accompany prolonged exercise

Locomotor activity poses unique challenges for animals. During activity, muscle cells must produce ATP at high rates. Metabolic fuels, primarily carbohydrate and lipid, must be mobilized from intracellular stores or storage tissues. These metabolic processes must be precisely coordinated to ensure that ATP synthesis matches ATP demand. Consider the following example.

The hovering hummingbird has one of the highest **mass-specific metabolic rates** in the animal kingdom. It must fly to feed, and it must eat in order to fly. It is an extreme example of the sort of metabolic transitions most animals face in integrating nutrient consumption with activity. Each summer morning the hummingbird wakes and flies from flower to flower, drinking nectar. Occasionally, it eats

FIGURE 12.13 **Elevated postexercise oxygen consumption**

Exercise causes a rapid increase in the rate of oxygen consumption. Once exercise ceases, respiration declines but remains elevated above the resting rate for extended periods. The duration of this elevated postexercise oxygen consumption, or oxygen debt, depends on the intensity of exercise and varies among species.

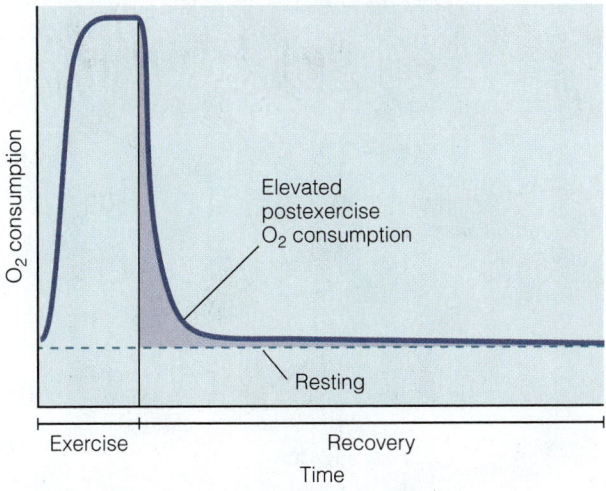

FIGURE 12.14 **Hummingbird flight metabolism**

Hummingbird respiration was monitored by oxygen and CO_2 sensors incorporated into a feeder. The metabolic fuel being oxidized is reflected in the respiratory quotient (RQ), which is the ratio of CO_2 produced to O_2 consumed. At rest, birds oxidize lipid fuels, as indicated by the RQ of 0.7. Once flight begins and feeding commences, the RQ rapidly rises to a value near 1, an indication of carbohydrate oxidation.

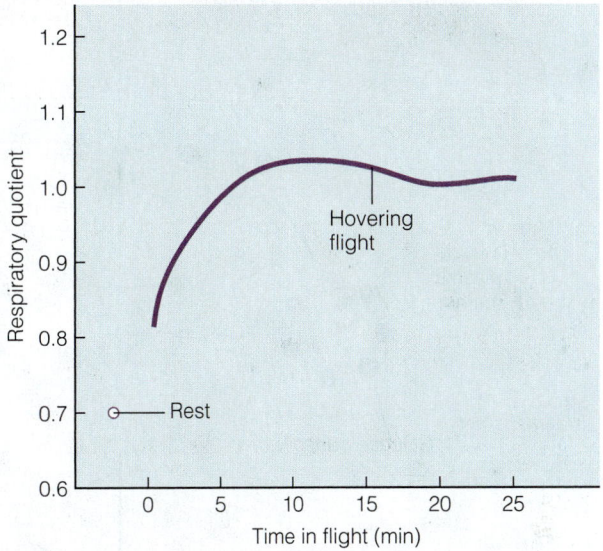

Figure source: Adapted from Suarez, R. K., Lighton, J. R. B., Moyes, C. D., Brown, G. S., Gass, C. L., & Hochachka, P. W. (1990). Figure 2 from Fuel selection in rufous hummingbirds: Ecological implications of metabolic biochemistry. *Proceedings of the National Academy of Sciences USA, Ecology, 87*, pp. 9207–9210. http://www.pnas.org/content/87/23/9207 .full.pdf.

an insect. Most of its waking hours are spent perching. Its nectar diet is almost exclusively sucrose, so you might assume that its metabolic regulation is simple. Looking closer, however, you will discover that complex metabolic control is needed to accommodate the daily changes in feeding, flying, and sleeping. When the hummingbird is actively feeding on summer flowers, it uses dietary carbohydrate to fuel flight muscle metabolism. It stores any extra dietary sucrose as glycogen and lipid. In the evening, the hummingbird cannot feed and must rely on energy reserves to sustain its resting metabolic demands. It also becomes *hypometabolic*, allowing its body temperature to fall to reduce metabolic demands. In the morning, the hummingbird supports its first flight by oxidizing fatty acids mobilized from tissue stores. As soon as it obtains its first nectar meal, its metabolism switches to carbohydrate utilization and lipid storage. The transitions in fuel selection can be monitored by measuring the ratio of CO_2 production to O_2 consumption, known as the *respiratory quotient*, or RQ (Figure 12.14). Each metabolic fuel generates a characteristic RQ: 0.7 for lipids and 1.0 for carbohydrates. This daily cycle continues throughout the feeding season, but as winter approaches many species of hummingbirds reorganize metabolism to prepare for migration. An important step is an increase in their lipid stores. A 3-gram hummingbird may put on 2 grams of fat prior to its migration.

Hormones control fuel oxidation in muscle

All forms of muscle activity require complex control of metabolic fuel utilization. Most animals rely on a combination of carbohydrate and lipid for muscle ATP production. The carbohydrate can be derived from muscle stores, mainly glycogen particles, but circulatory glucose is also an important fuel. Muscle maintains a store of lipid in the form of triglyceride droplets. The blood also provides lipids from breakdown of lipoproteins. As we discussed in Chapter 3, most of the energy for muscle activity is produced when mitochondria oxidize pyruvate, from carbohydrate, and fatty acids, from lipid breakdown. The pathway for muscle metabolic fuel consumption is summarized in Figure 12.15.

Many of the steps in fuel breakdown change in response to activity level. These metabolic transitions are orchestrated by hormones that act on skeletal muscle and fuel storage tissues. During steady-state activity, muscles are promiscuous in their fuel preferences, utilizing whichever fuels are abundant. The levels of metabolic fuels in the blood are determined by the balance of actions of many different hormones, such as insulin, glucagon, catecholamines, and glucocorticoids. Each hormone has effects on storage tissues that influence production or release of fuels. These hormones can also alter the ability of locomotor muscles to use the fuels by altering the levels of transporters and the activities of metabolic enzymes. During low to moderate activity, glucose remains an important

FIGURE 12.15 **Metabolic fuels and exercise**

Exercise is fueled by a combination of carbohydrate and lipid. Some carbohydrate is stored within the muscle in the form of glycogen. Muscles also use glucose from the blood, arising from digestion or glycogen stores in the liver. The main source of lipid for exercise is fatty acids arising from triglyceride breakdown. The muscle has substantial triglyceride stores in the form of lipid droplets. Triglyceride is also delivered to the muscle by the blood in the form of lipoprotein complexes.

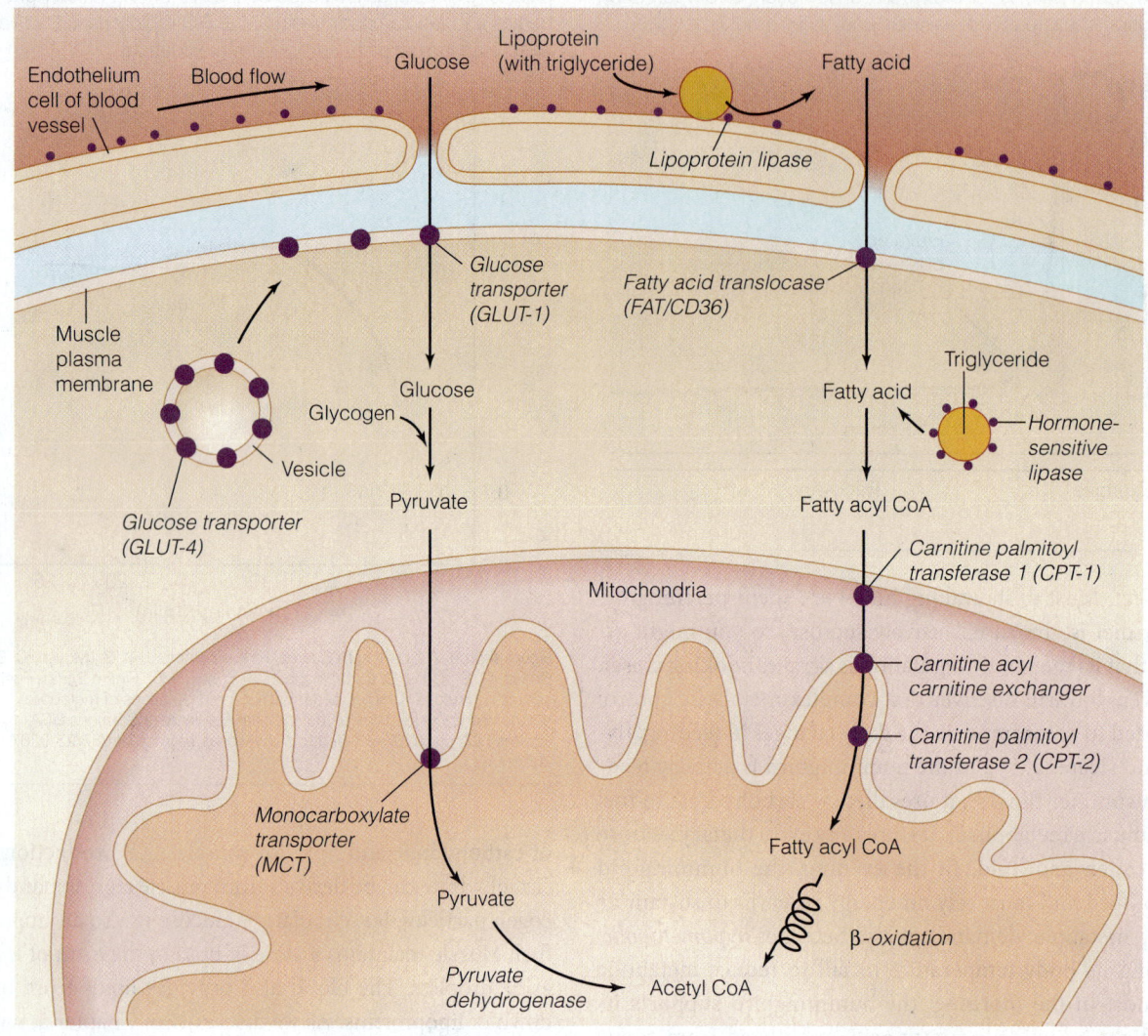

metabolic fuel. Glycogen breakdown is stimulated in muscle and liver. Insulin and cortisol act together to promote liver glycogen breakdown and glucose export into the blood. Insulin enhances glucose uptake by the muscle by stimulating the movement of glucose transporters from intracellular vesicles to the sarcolemma. Whereas glycogen stores in the liver and muscle can be mobilized quickly, lipid fuels are mobilized more slowly. If activity levels are sustained, lipid fuels become increasingly important. Triglyceride mobilization in skeletal muscle and adipose tissue is governed by lipases. In adipose tissue, hormone-sensitive lipase is controlled by corticotropin, epinephrine, norepinephrine, and glucagon. These hormones act through cAMP signaling cascades to activate

protein kinase A, which phosphorylates the lipase. Muscle also possesses hormone-sensitive lipase activity to trigger release of fatty acids directly within muscle. By using hormones that act at the locomotor muscle and at extramuscular storage sites, animals are able to control the flow of metabolic substrates to the ATP-producing machinery.

Given the importance of muscle in whole-animal metabolism, it is not surprising that defects in muscle metabolism can have a profound influence on health. In recent years, changes in diet have led to many issues related to obesity. As we discuss in the accompanying feature (Box 12.1: Applications: Exercise and Type 2 Diabetes Mellitus), exercise has important benefits in reducing the severity or onset of metabolic disorders.

Perfusion and Oxygen Delivery to Muscle

During locomotion, muscles must be supplied with fuels and cleansed of end products. Muscle metabolic rates of some animals are so low that simple diffusion is sufficient to ensure adequate movement of metabolites and gases in and out of the muscle. For example, nematodes and flatworms are able to obtain adequate gas diffusion across the **integument** and no specialized circulatory systems are necessary. Active animals use cardiovascular systems to service muscles, removing metabolic end products and CO_2, and delivering O_2, fuels, and hormones to the muscle. Active insects, such as bees and locusts, use tracheae to deliver oxygen directly to flight muscles, and a muscular heart to push hemolymph through circulatory systems to provide metabolic fuels. Vertebrate skeletal muscle is perfused by much more complicated circulatory networks. In these muscles, arteries branch into successively smaller arterioles, which divide into thin-walled capillaries. Perfusion of muscle depends upon the structure of the capillary networks and the amount of blood that reaches the capillaries.

Capillary networks bring oxygen to vertebrate muscle fibers

Oxygen delivery to muscle is controlled by structural features, such as capillary density, and functional parameters, such as vascular tone and the oxygen affinity of hemoglobin.

Acting in combination with the respiratory and cardiovascular systems, the muscle controls how much blood reaches the intramuscular capillary beds and how much oxygen is extracted from the blood.

Once blood enters the vascular beds of muscle, oxygen may be released from hemoglobin. Recall from Chapter 11: Respiratory Systems that oxygen is released when the P_{O_2} is low or when physiochemical conditions alter the oxygen affinity of hemoglobin. Muscle activity influences oxygen extraction from the blood in several ways. Aerobic metabolism consumes O_2, reducing P_{O_2}. Changes in erythrocyte pH or the levels of regulatory metabolites, such as diphosphoglycerate (DPG) and nucleotides, can cause hemoglobin to release oxygen to the muscle. Once O_2 is released from hemoglobin, the rate of diffusion from the erythrocyte to the muscle mitochondria depends on the steepness of the gradient and the diffusion distance. In some muscles, mitochondria are localized beneath the SR, which would reduce the diffusion limit for oxygen. The diffusion distance is determined largely by capillary geometry. Diffusion distances are short in aerobic muscles, which have small diameters and abundant capillaries. Diffusion distances are greater in glycolytic muscles, which are larger and possess fewer capillaries.

August Krogh first modeled capillary geometry as a cylinder within a cylinder (Figure 12.16a). The inner cylinder represents the capillary that services a volume of muscle, represented by the outer cylinder. His model assumed that (1) each capillary is the only oxygen supply for a surrounding cylinder of tissue, (2) the P_{O_2} at the vessel wall is equal to that of the blood, (3) there is no decline of P_{O_2} along a capillary, (4) oxygen diffuses radially from the capillary, and (5) consumption is uniform in the tissue. The Krogh distance reflects the distance that oxygen can diffuse into surrounding tissue. Using this model, he calculated the dynamics of

FIGURE 12.16 Krogh model of perfusion

(a) The Krogh model of perfusion suggests that each capillary is able to provide adequate oxygen to a volume of surrounding tissue, represented by a cylinder. **(b)** In many situations, the oxygen levels decline along the length of a capillary. This reduces the volume of muscle that can obtain adequate oxygen. Some areas become hypoxic unless other capillaries are close enough to provide oxygen.

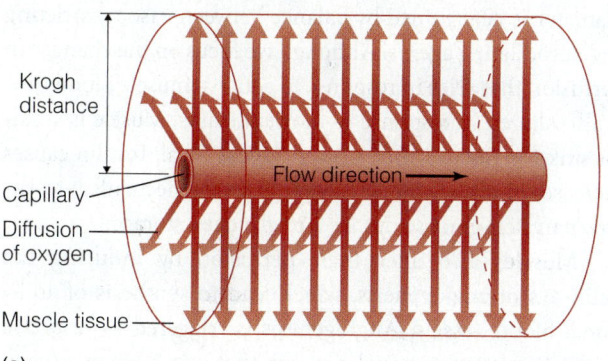

(a)

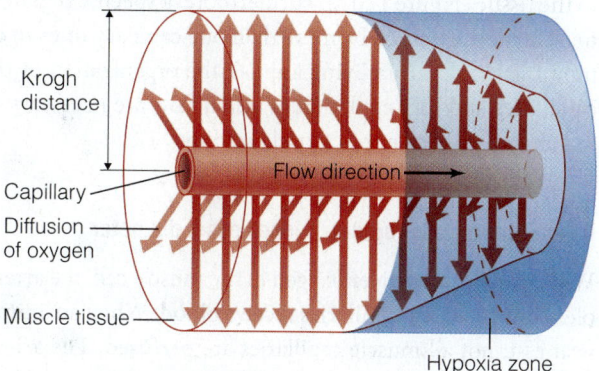

(b)

EXERCISE AND TYPE 2 DIABETES MELLITUS

The feedback and regulatory loops described in the previous section explain how animals ensure that muscle obtains the nutrients required at the required rates. Species differ in the way they manage these relationships because of differences in diet, activity, and evolutionary history. Human disease provides an opportunity to study what happens when normal regulatory relationships become dysfunctional. Understanding the origins of the dysfunction also helps develop approaches that mitigate the negative effects.

The concept of exercise and training is something that is peculiar to humans because our behavior has permitted mismatches between our actions and what our physiology has evolved to do. The recent changes in the nature of the diet and level of activity have created a mismatch that manifests as metabolic disorders. The origins of the evolution of obesity remain vigorously debated. However, there is little doubt that regular physical activity slows the progression of many metabolic disorders. Perhaps the most prevalent of these is type 2 diabetes mellitus (T2DM), in which tissues (skeletal muscle, liver, adipose) become unresponsive

to insulin. In healthy individuals, increases in blood glucose trigger secretion of insulin. Though insulin acts on diverse tissues, skeletal muscle is an important glucose-consuming tissue. As described in Figure 12.15, insulin stimulates the export of glut-4 transporters, improving glucose uptake. In T2DM, skeletal muscle becomes insensitive to the insulin signal, and in failing to respond, more glucose is taken up by tissues, particularly liver and adipose, that convert it to lipid. The increased lipid storage has important consequences for health, including obesity, immunity, inflammation, cardiovascular disease, and hypertension. With the disruption of the negative feedback loop, the pancreatic beta cells increase insulin production to ameliorate the perceived insulin deficiency, and with time this leads to beta cell failure. Just as T2DM may lead to obesity, obesity may also lead to T2DM.

Many studies have shown that exercise delays the onset of T2DM and reduces the subsequent complications. Exercise activity is actually an extraordinarily complex regulatory event. Activity changes metabolites, reactive

oxygen diffusion under various myofiber geometries and physiological conditions.

The Krogh model and more recent variations allow researchers to predict oxygen delivery in relation to fiber geometry and metabolic rate. Many of the constants in the original Krogh model are treated as variables in more recent models. We now know that oxygen levels can decline along the length of the capillary, causing some regions of the muscle to become hypoxic (Figure 12.16b). Capillaries weave back and forth across the muscle; the degree of weaving, or *tortuosity*, increases the transit time for blood cells, allowing longer periods and greater surface area for oxygen to diffuse to the tissue (Figure 12.17). Furthermore, a specific region of muscle may be served by more than one capillary or even by minor arterioles. In a living animal, the organization of the capillaries and the regulation of blood flow are necessary to match oxygen delivery to muscle activity.

Vasoactive agents regulate blood vessel diameter

While capillaries deliver oxygen to the muscle cell, the arterioles control which capillaries receive blood. When an animal is at rest, not all muscle capillaries are perfused. The arterioles that feed the capillaries undergo **vasomotion**, regularly cycling between constriction and dilation. When conditions

demand an increase in blood flow to the muscle, arterioles remain open for longer periods and total blood flow to the capillaries within that muscle increases.

As we discussed in Chapter 9: Circulatory Systems, vasoactive agents alter the contractility of the smooth muscle that lines the arterioles, and thereby determine perfusion through capillaries. Some vasoactive agents, such as insulin, are endocrine hormones produced at distant sites and released into the circulation. There are neurohormonal factors produced locally by nerves, and paracrine factors produced by vascular smooth muscle, endothelium, or the muscle itself. The end products of muscle metabolism, such as pH, oxygen, and CO_2, also exert effects on capillary perfusion. The arteriole diameter is determined by balance between vasoconstricting and vasodilating agents. Although we focus on the changes in perfusion that arise in response to activity, muscle blood flow is also altered in response to nutrient status. Muscle is a major sink for glucose after a high-glucose meal. Insulin causes increases in muscle blood flow as part of a mechanism to enhance muscle glucose uptake and glycogen storage.

Muscles also alter their perfusion by inducing the pathways of angiogenesis, which lead to synthesis of additional blood vessels. Angiogenesis is triggered in response to the persistent regional hypoxia that arises when oxygen demands exceed oxygen delivery. When endothelial cells

oxygen species, and autocrine, paracrine, and endocrine regulators, with effects exerted on the working muscles and many other tissues. A number of studies have used pharmacological agents that mimic the beneficial effects of exercise. Some drugs affect the activity of regulatory enzymes: For example, metformin is a drug that activates AMP-dependent protein kinase (AMPK), an important cellular energy sensor. By activating the enzyme, the cell responds as if it were energy limited, stimulating pathways that increase ATP production. Insulin sensitizers are agents that stimulate the expression of genes that encode diverse enzymes and transporters of intermediary metabolism. Glitazones, for example, stimulate PPARγ, a transcription factor that regulates many genes associated with lipid metabolism.

Drug regimens tend to become less effective with time and they often have negative side effects. However, the benefits of exercise remain effective, and can work synergistically with pharmacological approaches to reduce the effects of T2DM. The main challenge clinically is convincing patients that they should set aside time for regular exercise. Recent studies have explored whether short intervals of high-intensity training offer the same advantages as longer periods of lower-intensity exercise. As well, there is a great deal of variability in how individuals respond to exercise and nutrition. Nutrigenomics is a new field that uses high-throughput genetic analyses to explore the importance of genetic variation in the response to nutritional signals.

References

- Bird, S. R., & Hawley, J. A. (2012). Exercise and type 2 diabetes: New prescription for an old problem. *Maturitas, 72*, 311–316.

- Friedrichsen, M., Mortensen, B., Pehmøller, C., Birk, J. B., & Wojtaszewski, J. F. (2012). Exercise-induced AMPK activity in skeletal muscle: Role in glucose uptake and insulin sensitivity. *Molecular Cellular Endocrinology* (in press).

- Hagberg, J. M., Jenkins, N. T., & Spangenburg, E. (2012). Exercise training, genetics and type 2 diabetes-related phenotypes. *Acta Physiologica, 205*, 456–471.

FIGURE 12.17 Capillary tortuosity

Individual muscle fibers are surrounded by capillary networks that weave back and forth across the surface of the myofiber. The image shown here is the capillary structure from a frog muscle. The capillaries are preserved while the muscle is corroded away from the preparation.

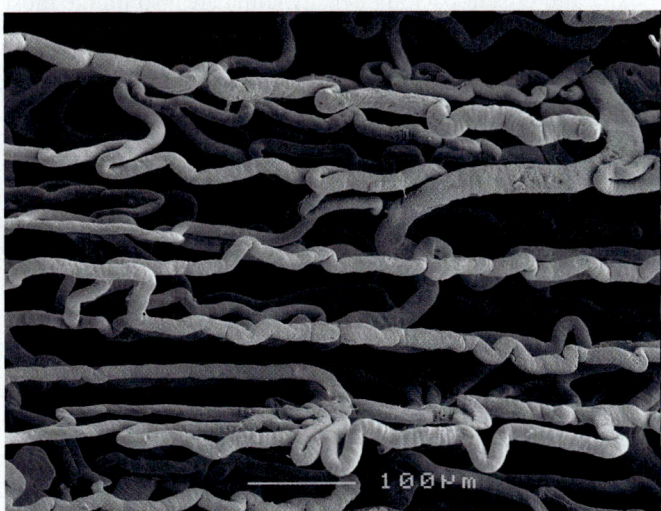

Photo source: Nicholas Hudson and Craig Franklin.

experience hypoxia, levels of the protein hypoxia-inducible factor-1 (Hif-1) increase. This transcription factor triggers the release of the hormone vascular endothelial growth factor (VEGF) into the wall of the blood vessels. When receptors on the vascular smooth muscle cells bind VEGF, the cells proliferate and penetrate the surrounding tissue. The growth of blood vessels into hypoxic regions increases the perfusion of active muscle. The same pathway is used to increase perfusion of muscle regions with damaged or blocked blood vessels.

Myoglobin aids in oxygen delivery and utilization

As we first discussed in Chapter 9, myoglobin is an oxygen-binding heme protein found in aerobic muscles. Myoglobin has two major roles within muscle cells: intracellular oxygen storage and oxygen transport.

Many muscles use myoglobin as an oxygen store. When tissue oxygen levels decrease, myoglobin releases its oxygen for use by muscle mitochondria. Myoglobin concentrations are high in muscles of animals that regularly experience hypoxic conditions. For instance, diving mammals, such as whales and seals, prepare for a dive by saturating myoglobin stores with oxygen. During the dive, oxygen is released from the myoglobin to support muscle activity.

Once oxygen crosses the muscle cell membrane, it is rapidly bound by myoglobin. By reducing the concentration of free oxygen within cells, myoglobin helps maintain the oxygen gradient necessary for oxygen diffusion. Oxygen bound to one myoglobin molecule can be transferred from myoglobin to another molecule to facilitate oxygen diffusion to the mitochondria. Because of this role in facilitating oxygen delivery, muscle myoglobin concentration often parallels muscle mitochondrial content.

The importance of myoglobin in facilitating oxygen delivery remains controversial. Researchers using mathematical modeling of molecular movements of myoglobin maintain that oxygen diffusion is improved by only a small percentage. In an effort to explore the importance of myoglobin in muscle, researchers in the 1990s engineered lines of transgenic mice with the myoglobin gene knocked out. Much to their surprise, they found that these myoglobinless mice were able to exercise as well as wild-type mice. At first, these results seemed to argue against a role for myoglobin in support of muscle activity. Subsequent studies revealed that myoglobinless mice had extensive changes in the vasculature of muscles. Without myoglobin to facilitate oxygen delivery, the muscles adapted by increasing muscle capillarity. From an evolutionary perspective, animals produce myoglobin to reduce the costs of building and maintaining vasculature. This trade-off is best illustrated by the Antarctic fish that lack myoglobin altogether. The absence of myoglobin is tolerated in these species because of their low metabolic rate and the high oxygen content of cold polar waters. This trait has arisen several times in distantly related taxa and by different mechanisms. In some species the myoglobin gene is not transcribed, whereas other species express the gene but do not translate the mRNA into protein.

Locomotor physiology is maximized in animal athletes

When studying integrative locomotor physiology, animal athletes are useful models for studying the limits to aerobic activity. Each animal taxon has a few species that epitomize some aspect of aerobic locomotor performance. Bumblebees and hummingbirds flap wings at exceptionally high frequencies, allowing these animals to hover. Thoroughbred horses and pronghorn antelope run faster than most land animals. Tunas and lamnid sharks swim faster than other fish. To explore the physiological features that accompany exceptional aerobic locomotor performance, we will consider the physiology of tuna.

Body shape is very important for aquatic animals. The streamlined, fusiform body of a tuna is built to move efficiently through water. Many other fish have a general streamlined shape, but the tuna is as close to a perfect teardrop as any fish. The shape of the caudal fin is also unusual, with its narrow caudal peduncle and thin, crescent-shaped (lunate) caudal fin. Tuna also show an unusual swimming style. Even at high speed there is little movement in the trunk. The caudal fin merely bends back and forth at the caudal peduncle. Although the trunk doesn't move during swimming, the muscles within the entire trunk contribute to force generation for the caudal fin. Force is transferred from the muscle to the caudal fin through the myosepta, skin, and tendons.

The tuna meets the energetic demands of rapid swimming with specializations of the respiratory, cardiovascular, and locomotor systems. The gills have a large surface area and thin gill epithelia, structural features that enhance the rate of oxygen exchange. The blood has a high oxygen-carrying capacity, due to higher hematocrit and higher hemoglobin concentrations. Tuna have an extensive coronary circulation that delivers oxygenated arterial blood to the heart, unlike most fish hearts, which must extract oxygen from the venous blood passing through the cardiac chamber. The capillary density of the red muscle can be as much as four times greater than in other fish. Muscle myoglobin content is also high in tuna. Each of these features would seem to enhance the capacity of the fish to extract oxygen from water and deliver it to the mitochondria of the working muscle. The muscle itself has high aerobic capacity. Although the mitochondrial content is similar to that of other species (about 35 percent of cell volume), the mitochondrial cristae are two to three times more densely packed than in other species. Thus, mitochondrial enzymes required for energy production occur at high activities. This high mitochondrial capacity is characteristic of all animal athletes, which may possess exceptional mitochondrial volume density and cristae-packing density. Tuna are also unlike most fish in their thermal physiology. These fish are regional endotherms; they are able to retain muscle heat within the body core. These elevated temperatures increase the kinetics of both contraction and energy metabolism. Tuna thermal physiology is discussed in more detail in Chapter 13: Thermal Physiology.

Tuna are remarkable animals that have provided important information about the structural and physiological constraints on locomotor activity. The evolutionary and developmental origins of these specializations remain to be explored. Interestingly, the lamnid sharks, which include the mako and great white sharks, demonstrate many similarities to tuna. Because these species are only distantly related, the striking similarities between tuna and lamnid sharks are examples of convergent evolution.

Many of the most remarkable animal athletes are those that undertake long-term, steady-state exercise. In the accompanying feature (Box 12.2: Challenges to Homeostasis:

Migration), we compare the disparate biochemical mechanisms that enable hummingbirds and salmon to complete their migrations.

Skeletal Systems

Muscle contraction may provide the force for locomotion, but locomotion requires some form of skeleton to move various forms of appendages. Imagine an isolated muscle contracting on a bench top. It is free to contract and relax, but without connections to some form of skeleton the muscle contraction is reduced to a shape change. Earlier in this chapter we discussed how invertebrates such as worms are able to crawl using muscles that act on fluid-filled chambers that constitute a hydrostatic skeleton. Their muscles contract to cause a change in the distribution of fluids to move the body. Hydrostatic skeletons are also important in other animals. A few species of spiders use a hydrostatic skeleton as a substitute for an antagonistic muscle group. They extend their legs with an infusion of hydrostatic fluid, functionally replacing an extensor muscle group.

A solid skeleton is important in the locomotion of all chordates and most invertebrates, such as echinoderms, arthropods, and mollusks. Invertebrate external skeletons, or **exoskeletons**, can cover the animal completely, as in insects, or only partially, as in mollusks. Internal skeletons, or **endoskeletons**, are most common among vertebrates. The endoskeletons found among some groups of invertebrates, such as sponges and echinoderms, are used for protection and support, not locomotion. The endoskeletons of vertebrates are made of cartilage or bone produced by specialized cells. Hard skeletons are central to locomotor strategies of animals, acting as structural support for appendages, elastic storage devices, or biomechanical levers. Muscles are incorporated into locomotor systems by connections between muscles, and tendons that connect muscles to the skeleton.

Hard skeletons are made from cellular secretions

Most cells secrete suites of macromolecules that make up the extracellular matrix. In soft tissues, the extracellular matrix is the glue that holds cells together. Skeletons are derived from a specialized extracellular matrix produced by secretory cells. They can be made of diverse materials that vary in biophysical properties such as rigidity, flexibility, durability, and inertness.

Most invertebrates possess an external surface layer that helps protect the animal from the environment. The exoskeleton of insects, known as the cuticle, is composed of the carbohydrate chitin, proteins such as sclerotin, water molecules, and phenolic compounds. The cuticle is produced from secretions of a layer of cells that lie beneath the cuticle mounted on the basement membrane. These hypodermal cells secrete long strands of chitin that become embedded in a complex protein matrix. After the chitin and protein secretions are assembled, the cuticle incorporates oxidized phenolic compounds. This final step of exoskeleton assembly, called **sclerotization**, makes the cuticle more rigid by cross-linking proteins in the exoskeleton. Insect muscles are connected to the exoskeleton via myotendon junctions (Figure 12.18). Muscle cells in the flight musculature come into contact with epithelial cells that produce the cuticle. The two cell types link together via cell membrane receptors such as integrins. As the cellular connections mature, the region forms the myotendon junction.

FIGURE 12.18 **Insect cuticle**
The insect exoskeleton is a modified extracellular matrix of underlying hypodermal cells. Muscles are attached to the exoskeleton at myotendon junctions.

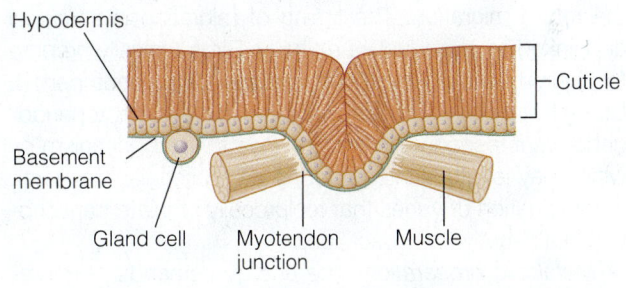

Locomotor strategies are quite complex in insects, and the exoskeleton is used in many different ways to allow these animals to jump, walk, and fly. The insect wing is composed of cuticle, although it has a different composition than the cuticle of the exoskeleton. The insect leg is a series of hollow tubes of exoskeleton. Internal muscles act across joints to cause the leg to bend. Insect flight is controlled by a series of thoracic flight muscles, either direct, indirect, or both. Direct flight muscles attach via ligaments to the base of the wing. Activation of one muscle group (elevators) moves the wing up, whereas activation of the antagonistic muscle group (depressors) moves the wing down (Figure 12.20). These muscles are also called synchronous muscles because muscle activation arises from a neuronal stimulus. Contraction occurs when Ca^{2+} levels rise, and relaxation follows when Ca^{2+} is resequestered in the sarcoplasmic reticulum. Direct muscles are found in primitive insects, such as orthopterans (locusts), coleopterans (beetles), and odonatans (dragonflies). Some insects have another arrangement of flight

One of greatest challenges for an animal to survive is the metabolic stress associated with long-distance migration. Animals that undergo long migrations show a pronounced reorganization of their physiology to prepare for the journey. Suites of hormones respond to environmental cues to reorganize physiological systems and alter normal foraging behavior. Once the migration begins, the animal cannot easily be diverted from its route, frequently forgoing the distractions of feeding. In this feature, we compare two examples in which the animals have evolved different solutions to the stress of migration. Sockeye salmon reach reproductive maturity in seawater, then migrate into freshwater, remarkably to the same streams in which they began. After mating, they die. Ruby-throated hummingbirds make annual migrations between eastern North America and over-wintering grounds in Central America.

Stimulus for migration: Sockeye spend several years in seawater growing in size, storing energy, and preparing for the return migration. The timing of migration is seasonal and linked to reproductive maturity. Birds typically prepare for their southward migration in response to photoperiod. Steroid hormones are also required for this photoperiod-dependent response. In many systems, the mechanism by which day length is interpreted is via a circadian oscillator, a combination of genes that reciprocally regulate transcription in a negative feedback loop.

Metabolic preparation: The energy demands of migration require exquisite coordination from multiple physiological systems. Many animals gorge on food prior to migration, "fattening" for the journey. Fat is the wonder fuel for migration because of its high energetic density and economy of storage (ATP per gram of fuel). A 3-gram hummingbird that deposits 1.5 grams in fat droplets would need to store 15 grams of glycogen particles (five times its body weight!) to achieve the same caloric content.

Feeding during migration: Though hummingbirds feed during migration, many animals (including sockeye) are completely committed to using their nutrient stores during migration, refusing to eat even if they encounter food. Commitment to nonfeeding strategies has several advantages to a migratory animal. In animals that rely on stored fuels, success of the migration does not depend on successful foraging en route. Foraging in unfamiliar environments may put the animal at an increased risk of predation. In many cases, it also permits animals to allow their digestive systems to degrade, reducing the costs of routine metabolism.

Metabolism during migration: The main difference between hummingbirds and sockeye is that only one of them needs to prepare for life after arrival. Hummingbirds have an exceptionally high metabolic rate and it is a priority for them to conserve fuel where possible. When flying across the Gulf of Mexico, they have been reported to stop for a rest on oil rigs. Without feeding, they must be able to complete their migration with onboard lipid supplies. Sometimes these are exhausted and the birds are unable to fly. However, when successful, they can feed on arrival and continue life under more hospitable conditions. Pacific salmon migrate for the purpose of reproduction but shortly after mating they die. Some populations, such as the Fraser River sockeye salmon, may travel more than 1,000 kilometers through stretches of swift currents (Figure 12.19). The pie charts show the relative importance of each metabolic fuel along the migration. Large fat stores fuel the earliest stage of migration but become depleted later in the migration. With most of its major fuel stores reduced, the salmon has no choice but to start breaking down endogenous proteins. The fish then starts to break down its muscles and intestinal tract, releasing the chemical energy stored within the tissues. The salmon first breaks down the white muscle that is no longer needed for high-intensity swimming, but it spares

muscles. They are called indirect muscles because of the way contraction is coupled to wing movement, or asynchronous wing muscles because of the mode of excitation-contraction coupling. Indirect muscle does not attach directly to the wing, but rather changes the position of the wing by altering the shape of the thoracic exoskeleton. Both the wings and the flight muscles attach to the upper region of the thorax known as the *tergum*. When the elevator muscles contract, the tergum is pulled down, a distortion that pulls the wings up and also stretches the antagonistic depressor muscles. After the wing is elevated, the elevator muscles relax, the depressor muscles are activated, and the tergum pops up, pulling the wings down. More derived insects, such as dipterans (flies) and hymenopterans (bees), use indirect flight muscles to power flight, although they use direct muscles to control the fine movements of the wing that allow maneuverability.

Vertebrate skeletons are composed of mineralized calcium

Most vertebrates possess endoskeletons composed of combinations of bone and cartilage. Cartilaginous skeletons are found in the ancient fish, including agnathans (lamprey, hagfish) and chondrichthians (sharks, rays). More recent fish and all tetrapods possess skeletons of bone and cartilage.

Skeletal changes were essential when early vertebrates began the transition to land. Without the support of water,

the red muscle it uses for slow, steady-state swimming. Some amino acids are oxidized within muscle, but many are converted to glucose in the liver. Late in the migration, glycogen and glucose support the vigorous spawning activity. During this entire trip the salmon coordinates its whole body metabolism to make fuels available to working muscle while sparing the reproductive tissues needed for gamete production. By the time the salmon spawns, it has depleted its energy stores and digested its own tissue. Shortly thereafter, the salmon dies.

FIGURE 12.19   Salmon migration

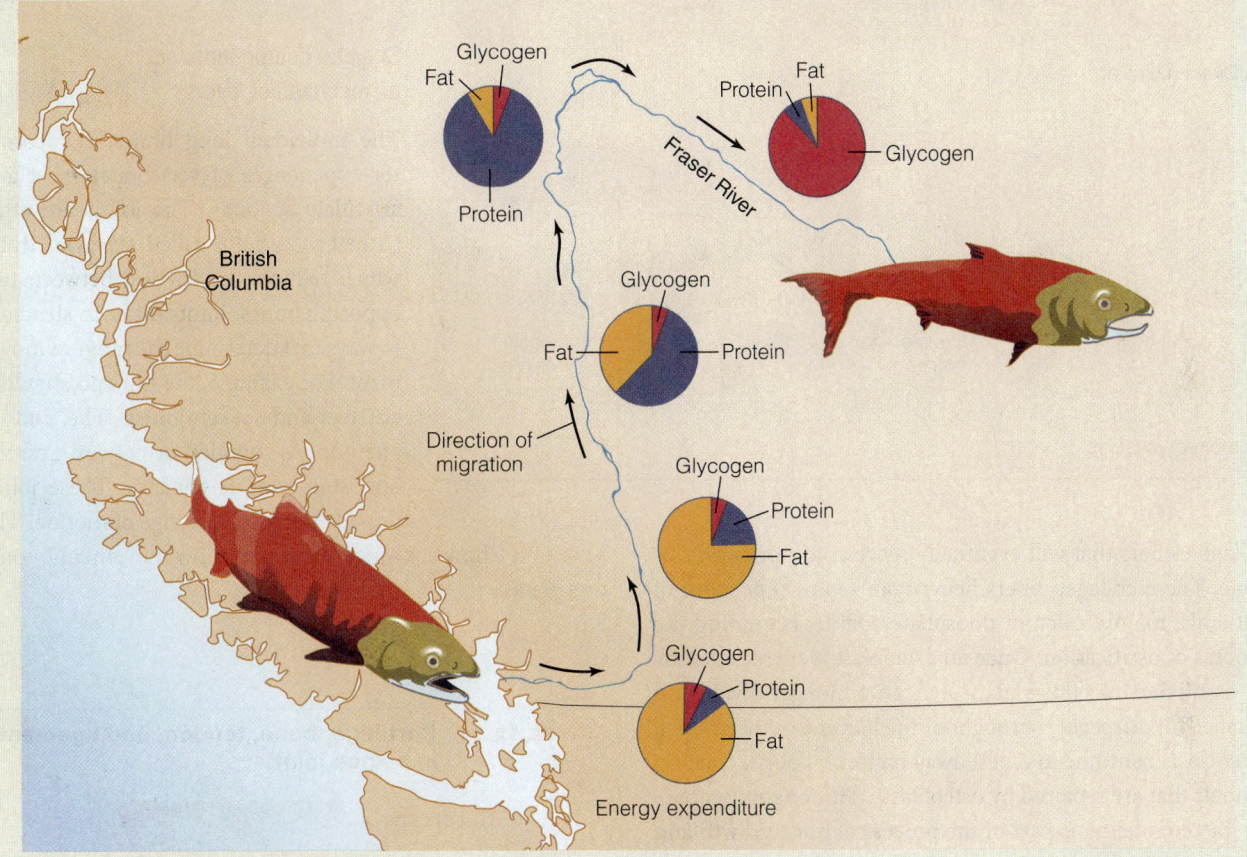

early land animals needed more robust skeletons and specialized musculature to support them against the force of gravity. Birds and bats have secondarily reduced their skeletons to facilitate flight. The properties of the endoskeleton are controlled by **chondrocytes**, the cells that produce cartilage, and **osteoblasts**, the cells that produce bone.

Chondrocytes begin the process of cartilage synthesis early in embryological development. They secrete proteins and proteoglycans, such as chondroitin sulfate, into the extracellular space. These macromolecules make up the extracellular matrix of the chondrocyte. Many different chondrocytes combine their extracellular matrices to produce cartilage. Most vertebrate bones begin as cartilage. As the animal grows and matures, cartilage is broken down and replaced with bone. Mature animals retain cartilage in a few locations within the skeleton, mostly near the ends of long bones where the soft cartilage helps improve the performance of joints.

Mature bone is a living tissue, constantly undergoing remodeling. Bone itself is a collection of multiple cells, cellular secretions, and mineral salts, all enveloped in a fibrous sheath called the periosteum. **Osteoclasts** secrete hydrolytic enzymes to create tunnels into the bone or cartilage. These tunnels allow blood vessels to penetrate the extracellular matrix. When osteoblasts invade the tunnel, they secrete

FIGURE 12.20 **Cross-section through thorax to show direct and indirect flight muscles**

Direct muscles attach to the base of the wing, whereas indirect muscles attach to the thorax. Primitive insects, such as the locust, have only direct muscles. More advanced insects, such as the blowfly, use indirect muscles to power flight, although direct muscles may be used for the fine-scale wing movements needed for maneuverability.

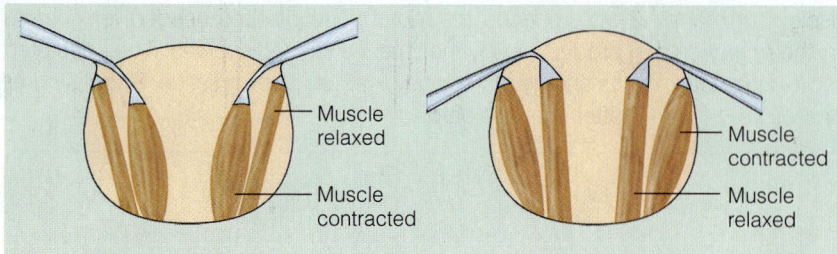

(a) Direct muscles

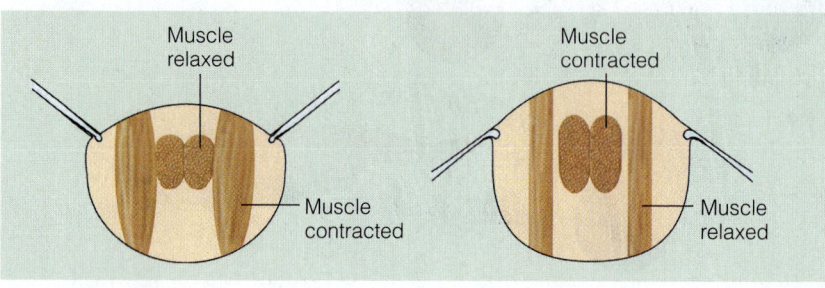

(b) Indirect muscles

Ligaments and tendons have important roles in locomotion. They interconnect the different elements of the musculoskeletal system. They ensure that muscles are correctly positioned and stretched to the appropriate sarcomere length. They also help transmit forces between musculoskeletal elements. For example, when tendons are stretched, their elastic nature permits them to store energy, which can reduce the costs of locomotion.

Skeletal components act as mechanical levers

The individual long bones in locomotor appendages of vertebrates meet and articulate at joints. The joints are often bathed in a fluid, called **synovial fluid**, which reduces the friction between two opposing bones. Joints differ in structure in ways that determine the range of movement. For example, the hip and shoulder are ball-and-socket joints: The end of one bone is rounded or convex, and the opposing bone is concave. These joints provide the greatest range of motion. The knee and elbow are hinge joints and allow movement in only one plane.

collagen fibers that will eventually serve as a framework for bone. These collagen fibers help organize the deposition of minerals, mainly calcium phosphate apatite, beginning the process of ossification. Once an osteoblast is surrounded by an ossified extracellular matrix, it can no longer divide and is called an *osteocyte*. Throughout the lifetime of the animal, osteoclasts continue to digest away regions of bone, creating tunnels that are repaired by osteoblasts. This ongoing capacity for remodeling is part of the process of bone growth and repair. By regulating bone growth and ossification, animals can control the physical properties of bone, such as dimensions and density. For example, these cells build the lighter bones required by flying animals, as well as the heavier bones of large herbivorous land mammals.

Ligaments and tendons hold the musculoskeletal system together (Figure 12.21). **Ligaments** hold one bone to another. They are a type of connective tissue produced when the fibroblasts near the ends of bones secrete long, parallel fibers of collagen linked to proteoglycan. **Tendons** attach muscles to the skeleton. They are composed of connective tissue similar in structure to ligaments. At one end of the tendon, the connective tissue binds to the bone. At the other end, the tendon binds at various points along the belly of the muscle. Tendons connect both ends of the muscle to bones.

FIGURE 12.21 **Cartilage, bone, tendon, and ligament in a knee joint**

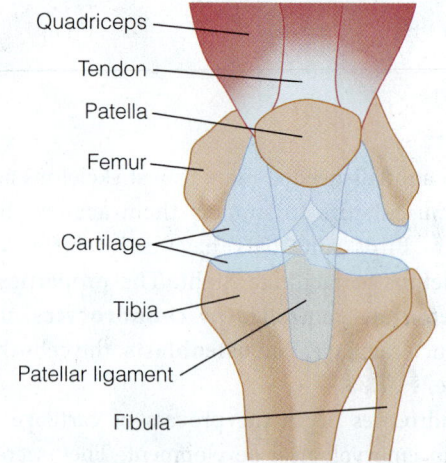

Figure source: Mary Lanning Memorial Hospital. (2007). "Total knee replacement" page from Mary Lanning Memorial Hospital website. Downloaded February 17, 2014 from http://199.184.119.123/stdpg.aspx?id=402.

Muscles work in combination with bones to create levers. When an untethered muscle contracts, it pulls its end toward its middle to generate a linearly compressed movement. When the muscle is attached to a bone, the geometry of the bone and the position of the joint constrain the muscle from its natural range of movement. The contracting muscle pulls the bone, causing it to rotate through an arc. This movement allows the bone to be used as a lever. All mechanical and biological levers have three elements: a fulcrum, a weight, and a force. The fulcrum is the point of rotation, which in the context of locomotion is the joint. The weight is the force exerted by the object to be moved. The force is generated by muscle contraction. If you are bending your arm to pick up a rock, the fulcrum is the elbow, the rock is the weight, and the biceps muscle generates the force.

The mechanics of lever action depend on the relative position of the three elements, as well as the distances between the elements. The distance between the force and the fulcrum is the force arm. In the example of your arm, the force arm is the distance between the elbow and point of insertion of the biceps muscle. The region between the fulcrum and the weight is the weight arm. The mechanical advantage (MA) of a lever is expressed as the ratio of the length of the force arm (L_{FA}) to the length of the weight arm (L_{WA}).

Levers are distinguished based on the relative position of the three elements (Figure 12.22). A crowbar is an example of a class I lever. The lever is long (large L_{FA}) and the fulcrum is close to the weight (small L_{WA}). Thus, this type of lever has a large mechanical advantage; a minimal amount of force can be used to lift a large weight. A wheelbarrow is an example of a class II lever. The weight is between the fulcrum and the force. We can lift quite a bit of weight using a wheelbarrow, but a class II lever does not have as great a mechanical advantage as a class I lever. Most levers in animal locomotion are class III levers. In our arm example, the biceps (force) inserts between the elbow (fulcrum) and hand (weight). Unlike the other types of lever, a class III lever has no mechanical advantage because L_{FA} is always less than L_{WA}. Consequently, class III levers are the least effective in translating muscle force into leverage. These levers are valuable not because of a mechanical advantage but because they can increase the range and velocity of movement. A modest amount of force exerted at a short distance from near the fulcrum causes the mobile end of the lever to move quickly through a much greater distance. In terms of your arm, when the bicep shortens only about 2 centimeters, it causes the hand to rotate through a 50-centimeter arc.

The position of the muscle insertion on the bone, relative to the joint, has important biomechanical ramifications. The relative lengths of the force arm and weight arm determine how efficiently muscle force can translate into leverage and movement. The importance of these relationships is best

FIGURE 12.22 **Levers**

Three classes of levers are distinguished by the relative positions of three elements: the fulcrum, the weight to be lifted, and the point at which force is applied. The part of the lever between the fulcrum and the weight is the weight arm. The force arm is the part of the lever between the fulcrum and the point at which force is applied. The ratio of the length of the force arm (L_{FA}) to that of the weight arm (L_{WA}) is the mechanical advantage.

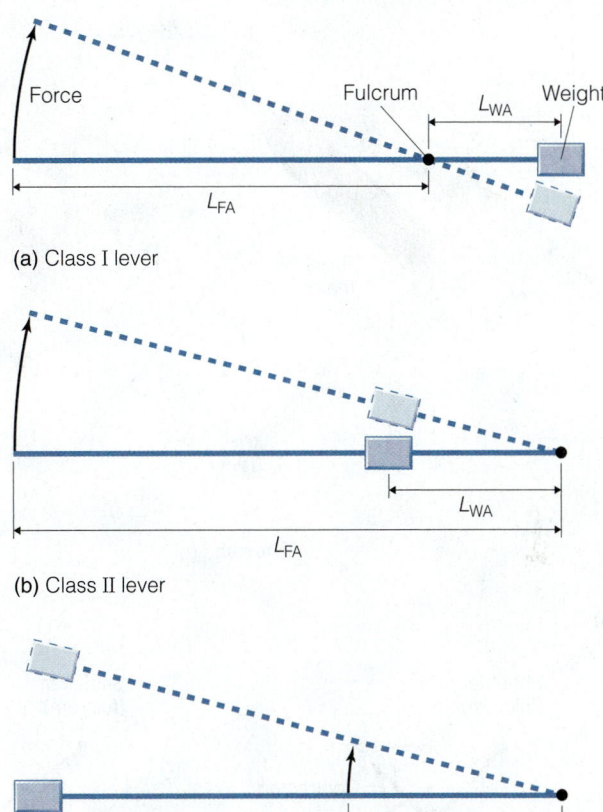

(a) Class I lever

(b) Class II lever

(c) Class III lever

illustrated by considering the morphometry of the legs of animals specialized for different lifestyles. A cheetah is built for speed, whereas a lion is slower but stronger. When the forelegs are drawn to a similar scale, the differences in leg morphometry are more obvious (Figure 12.23). The teres major is the muscle that pulls the foreleg backward, a movement that is used in running and also in prey capture. The teres major attaches much closer to the shoulder joint in a cheetah than in the lion. As a result of these differences in mechanical advantage, the cheetah can move its foreleg faster whereas the lion moves its foreleg with more force.

Skeletons can store elastic energy

Another way that animals use the skeleton in movement is through **elastic storage energy**. When the muscle shortens,

FIGURE 12.23   **Muscle position on the bone**

The geometry of muscles and bones determines the relationship between the force generated by the muscle and the type of movement that results. **(a)** In the cheetah foreleg, the muscle is inserted closer to the joint than in the lion foreleg, when drawn to the same scale. **(b)** When modeled as a lever, the cheetah foreleg can move faster, through a longer arc, but the lion foreleg can generate more forceful movements.

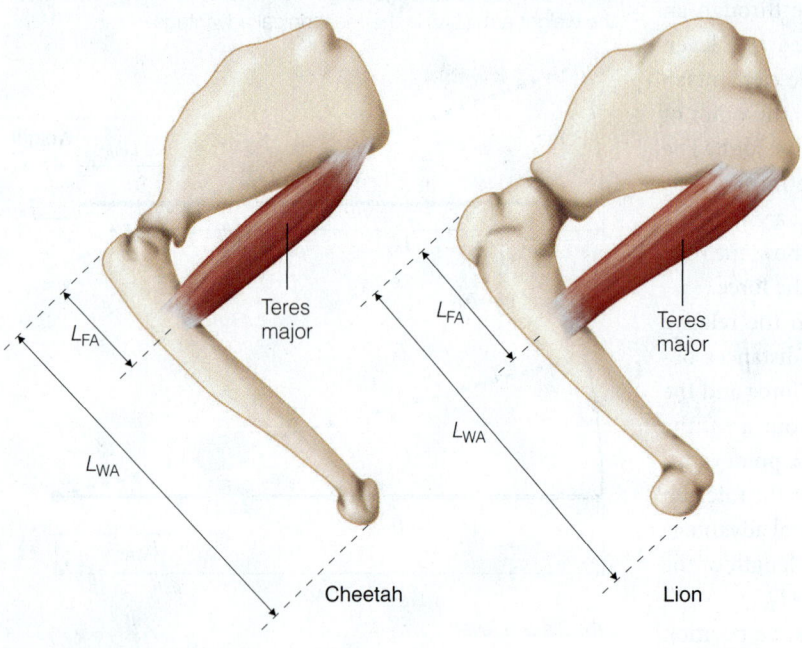

(a)

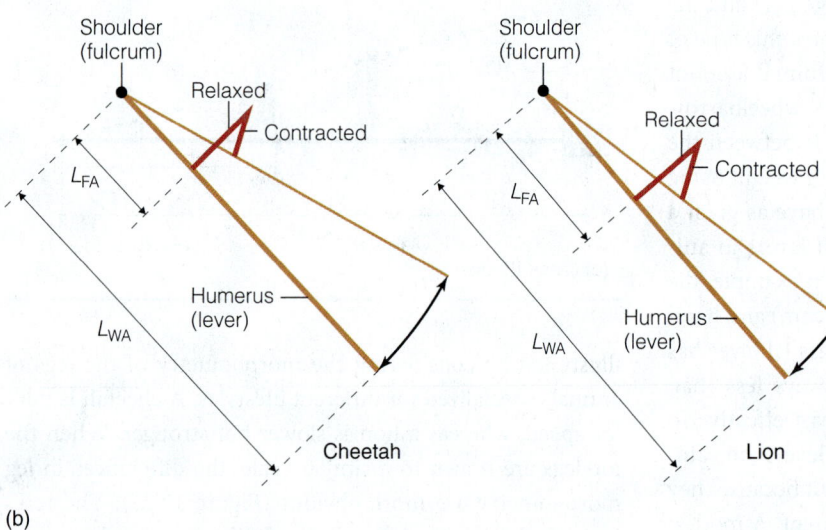

(b)

some of the force that is used to stretch the connective tissue and bend the bones is stored as elastic storage energy. When the muscle relaxes, the elastic storage energy can help the muscle stretch. Vertebrates benefit from elastic storage energy in locomotion, although some animals benefit more than others. The kangaroo uses elastic storage energy to improve the efficiency of locomotion. When the kangaroo first begins to hop, extensor muscles are used to lift the animal off

the ground. When it lands, some of the force is used to distend the muscle and connective tissue, creating a short-term store of elastic energy. Upon recoil, these elastic elements generate force that can be applied toward the next jump. Later in this chapter we discuss how animals use the muscles of the back as elastic energy stores during running.

The importance of elastic storage energy is much more obvious in arthropod locomotion, particularly jumping and flight. In some cases, elastic structures functionally replace antagonistic muscles altogether. For example, many spiders have leg joints that lack extensor muscles. Portions of the exoskeletal plates called **sclerites** span the joint (Figure 12.24). Muscle contraction deforms the sclerites during flexion. When the muscles relax, the sclerites recoil to extend the leg.

Elastic structures were an important evolutionary innovation in arthropod movement. Most invertebrates move with the help of hydrostatic skeletons. As mentioned earlier in this chapter, many extant spiders use fluid movements and hydrostatic pressure to aid in leg extension, augmenting elastic storage energy. However, a strategy that relies on hydrostatic pressure for locomotion has several limitations in rapidly moving animals. The mass of elastic structures is small relative to the mass of the hydrostatic fluid that would be needed to extend a leg. Thus, if legs rely on elastic structures they can be smaller, which saves energy for a moving animal. It also costs the animal metabolic energy to push hydrostatic fluids into the leg. Using an extracellular fluid to generate hydrostatic pressure may also compromise the diffusion of metabolites and respiratory gases in the circulatory system. Thus, structures that rely on elastic storage energy allow arthropods to escape some of the constraints imposed by hydrostatic skeletons.

Muscle function in animal locomotion varies hugely, and all levels of biological organization contribute to this diversity. There are many ways that variations in the molecular and cellular properties of the striated muscles contribute to muscle diversity: motor neuron properties, contraction

FIGURE 12.24 Spider legs

Leg extension occurs in spiders by several mechanisms. Some use movement of hydrostatic fluids to extend the leg (not shown). More commonly, spiders use either **(a)** extensor muscles or **(b)** elastic storage structures that span the leg joint. When leg joints are flexed, the elastic sclerite is deformed. When the muscle relaxes, the sclerite recoils to extend the leg forward.

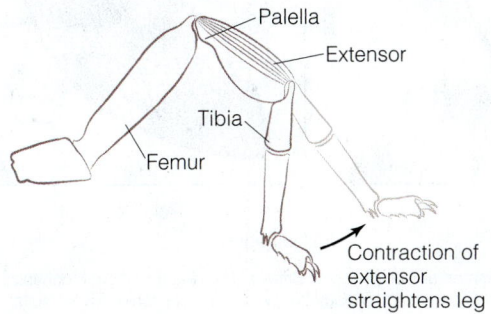

(a) *Heterometrus* (Asian forest spider)

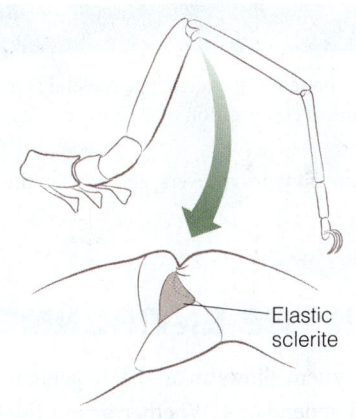

(b) *Eremopus* (sun spider)

Figure source: Republished with permission of The Company of Biologists Ltd; Society of Experimental Biology (Great Britain), from Figure 1 from Mechanics of cuticular elastic energy storage in leg joints lacking extensor muscles in arachnids. Journal of Experimental Biology 206: 771–784, Sensenig, AT, & Shultz, JW. © 2003; permission conveyed through Copyright Clearance Center, Inc.

frequency, motor end plate organization, T-tubules and action potential propagation, SR structure, Ca^{2+} buffering, and thin and thick filament protein isoforms. The arrangement of myofibers into muscles and the material properties of the connective tissue and skeleton are critical elements. Each of these factors affects the muscle dynamics—how the muscles are integrated into the anatomy of the whole animal and how this affects the conversion of muscle contraction to movement.

Work loops determine if a muscle is working as motor, brake, or strut

When muscles are integrated into locomotor systems, many factors affect their ability to do work. Work (W) is the product of force (F) and shortening distance (d). When muscles are mounted in a skeleton, they can be stretched to different lengths, affecting sarcomere length and force. The ability to shorten and generate force may be constrained by either skeletal elements or antagonistic muscles. As mentioned previously, there are situations in which a muscle may be arranged in a manner that generates the most force when external changes are causing it to lengthen. Likewise, activation and relaxation of a muscle may not lead to much change in length. Any of these situations are realistic possibilities for a muscle in a complex musculoskeletal system. To assess the amount of work a muscle performs during contraction and relaxation, the concept of the work loop was developed.

Consider the simplest situation where a relaxed muscle is stretched to a given length. Upon activation, it shortens and during this phase, the force production changes. If the starting length is near the optimal sarcomere length for force production (recall Figure 6.21), then as sarcomeres get shorter, force production decreases. This reduction continues until the muscle contracts to its shortest length. Plotting the force-length relationship generates a curve, and the area under this descending curve ($F \times d$) reflects the work done by the muscle during shortening and is called **positive work** (Figure 12.25a).

During relaxation, the muscle lengthens. Although the lengthening muscle still exerts some force, in this scenario it is less than the force exerted at the same muscle length during contraction. The area under this ascending curve is also a measure of work, but since the length is reduced ($-d$), the work done during relaxation is **negative work** (Figure 12.25b).

The net work done by the muscle is the difference between the positive work and the negative work. Graphically, this is reflected in the area enclosed by the two curves, known as the **work loop** (Figure 12.25c). Superimposed on the loop are arrows that inform whether the upper limits occur during shortening or lengthening. In most cases, the descending curve (during contraction) lies above the ascending curve (during relaxation). If you followed the coordinates of force and length around the graph during such an experiment, you would move around the work loop in a counterclockwise direction. This signifies that a cycle of contraction and relaxation generates net positive work.

Not all myofibers generate positive work during an activation-relaxation cycle. **Isometric muscles** do not change in length ($d = 0$), generate no power (because $P = F \times d/t$), and therefore perform no net work during contraction. Muscles are remarkably plastic and can be arranged into locomotor systems in ways that permit them to serve diverse roles.

Consider the muscles in the front of your thigh and how you use them walking up and down stairs. When walking up stairs, your foot reaches to the next step and these

FIGURE 12.25 **Work loops**

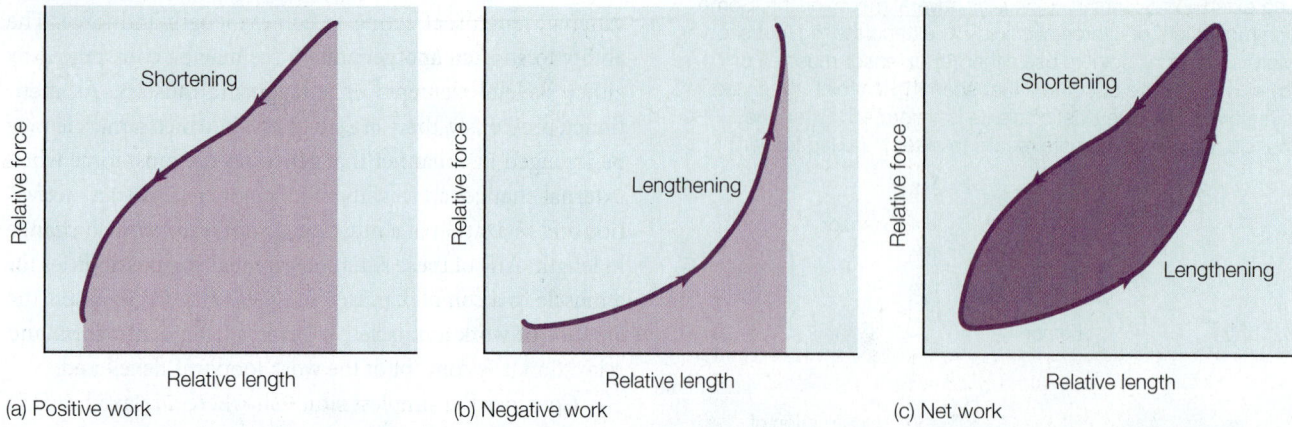

(a) Positive work   (b) Negative work   (c) Net work

Figure source: Republished with permission of The Company of Biologists Ltd; Society of Experimental Biology (Great Britain), from Figure 1 from Mechanics of cuticular elastic energy storage in leg joints lacking extensor muscles in arachnids. *Journal of Experimental Biology* 206: 771–784, Sensenig, AT, & Shultz, JW. © 2003; permission conveyed through Copyright Clearance Center, Inc.

muscles contract to straighten your leg. A work loop done during an activation relaxation cycle would look much like Figure 12.25c, where the most work is done during shortening. In this case you are using these muscles as motors. When you walk down the stairs, your leg begins straight, but as you lower your body, these same muscles are activated to slow your descent. Under this condition, more force is being generated when the muscle is lengthening. Graphically, this would mean the negative work curve lies above the positive work curve. The work loop would run clockwise, signifying net negative work. In this capacity these muscles act as a brake or shock absorber rather than a motor.

There is nothing unusual about the cellular properties of the muscle that causes this relationship. Rather, negative net work arises because of the way the muscle is arranged in the musculoskeletal system and the nature of the anatomical relationships with other muscles during movement. Whether a muscle generates positive or negative work depends on when it is activated during limb movement. If, for example, external forces cause a muscle to compress at a time when it is shortening, the muscle generates much less force than is possible. Many of the muscles that control the fine movements of flying insects produce negative net work. They exert their effects by using contraction to change their mechanical properties, altering how other muscles and the exoskeleton affect the flight system.

In other scenarios, much more complex relations can emerge. In some cases, muscles change little in length during activation, and within the context of the skeleton they act as struts. They are blocks that resist deformation, enabling them to transmit forces between regions. For example, regions of a fish body wall may act as struts when other parts are contracting, transmitting the change in body shape along the animal.

MOVING IN THE ENVIRONMENT

The musculoskeletal system allows an animal to generate force to move its body and appendages. Whether or not this activity translates into locomotion depends on how the animal interacts with the physical environment. The two dominant environmental factors that influence locomotion are gravity and fluid properties. In the following section we discuss the constraints on animal locomotion in terms of these environmental factors. We use this approach rather than describing locomotion in terms of style of movement, such as swimming, jumping, running, walking, and flying. The physiology of locomotion has much more to do with the physical environment than with the pattern of movement of appendages. For example, fleas, frogs, and kangaroos each jump, but the forces that govern their movement are completely different because of their size and the effects of gravity. Conversely, the biomechanics of swimming and flying are quite similar. Both air and water are fluids and obey the same laws of fluid dynamics. Locomotor systems allow animals to move from place to place, overcoming the physical constraints imposed by the environment.

Gravity and Buoyancy

Gravity is the element of the physical environment that has the greatest consequences for locomotor strategies. No animals can escape gravity, but some are less affected by it than others. Gravity exerts its greatest effects on terrestrial animals, which use muscles to solve the biomechanical problems associated with movement on land under the full weight of gravity. Gravity has much less effect on an animal with a body density that approximates that of the environment. Aquatic animals can reduce the effects of gravity by manipulating their body composition.

Body composition influences buoyant density

An object immersed in water tends to float if it is less dense than the water. The tendency to float is *buoyancy,* an upward force that counteracts the effects of gravity. The body density is determined by the body composition. Each component has a characteristic density, measured as specific gravity (Table 12.1). Water is the most abundant molecule in most animals, and therefore body density usually approximates the density of water. Bones and cartilage have the highest density in animals. Proteins are slightly denser than water, whereas lipids are slightly less dense than water. Gases have the lowest density. Many of the soft-bodied marine invertebrates have tissue compositions that confer neutral buoyancy.

Not all aquatic animals need to be buoyant. Benthic animals—those that live on the bottom of aquatic ecosystems—tend to be denser than the surrounding water. This allows them to maintain contact with the bottom without expending energy. However, most aquatic animals possess a body composition that induces either neutral buoyancy or positive buoyancy, allowing them to move through the water column. These animals reduce their overall density by increasing the proportion of less dense constituents, typically lipids or gases.

Lipid accumulations aid buoyancy in zooplankton and chondrichthians

Many species of zooplankton possess large droplets of lipid, typically in the form of wax esters. A wax ester, which is a

Table 12.1 Specific gravity of biomaterials

Biomaterial	Specific Gravity (g/ml)
Bone	3
Cartilage	2
Protein	1.6
Seawater	1.024
Pure water	1.0
Triglyceride	0.90
Squalene	0.86
Oxygen	0.00143

long-chain fatty acid esterified to a long-chain fatty alcohol, is metabolically active. Zooplankton can alter their buoyant density by synthesizing or degrading the wax esters, allowing these animals to slowly alter their buoyancy to change their position in the water column.

Chondrichthians (sharks and rays) also use lipid to increase their buoyancy. They accumulate high levels of the steroid compound squalene in their livers. The amount of lipid is highest in pelagic sharks, which can be neutrally buoyant, and lowest in benthic rays, which are slightly negatively buoyant.

Other aquatic animals with high levels of lipid in their tissues benefit from their buoyancy, although they are accumulated for other purposes. The triglyceride accumulations in fish livers are primarily important in energy metabolism. The lipid found in the thick blubber layer of marine mammals serves as insulation. However, these substantial lipid depots also contribute to buoyancy, thereby reducing the amount of energy needed to remain in the water column.

Gas bladders aid buoyancy in bony fish

Because gas is the least dense material, many aquatic groups have evolved ways to use gas bladders to aid in floatation or buoyancy. The Portuguese man o' war (*Physalia physalis*) shown in Figure 12.26 has a gas-filled *pneumatophore* which accumulates CO_2, permitting it to float on the surface. When threatened from above, the man o' war can rapidly deflate the bladder and sink below the surface.

Many bony fish possess a gas-filled swim bladder that is important in buoyancy, but some fish use the swim bladder as a respiratory organ. It is not yet certain which function arose first. Whereas use of the swim bladder as a lung occurs in many fish taxa, the buoyancy function occurs only in actinopterygian fish. This suggests that swim bladders likely arose first as a primitive lung, and only secondarily as a buoyancy organ.

The swim bladder (Figure 12.27) is derived from an outgrowth of the gastrointestinal tract that appears early in fish development. The gas accumulated in these internal balloons is sufficient to compensate for the negative buoyancy of the remainder of the body. The walls of the swim bladder are flexible, allowing the organ to contract and expand. Guanine crystals embedded in the swim bladder reduce the permeability of the swim bladder to gases. For a fish to be able to use a swim bladder as a buoyancy organ, it must be able to control the volume of gas within the organ. *Physostome fish* have a connection between the gastrointestinal tract and the swim bladder. They increase the volume of the swim bladder by gulping atmospheric air and pushing it through the pneumatic duct that connects the gut to the swim bladder. Similarly, they reduce the swim bladder volume by contracting the smooth muscle that surrounds the bladder and opening

FIGURE 12.26   **Portuguese man o' war**

Photo source: A. N. T./Science Source.

FIGURE 12.27   **Swim bladders**

(a) Physoclist fish inflate the swim bladder by injecting oxygen from the blood into the bladder at a region called the gas gland. Gases can escape the bladder at another vascularized region, called the oval. **(b)** Physostome fish inflate and deflate their swim bladder through a direct connection between the gastrointestinal tract and the swim bladder, called the pneumatic duct.

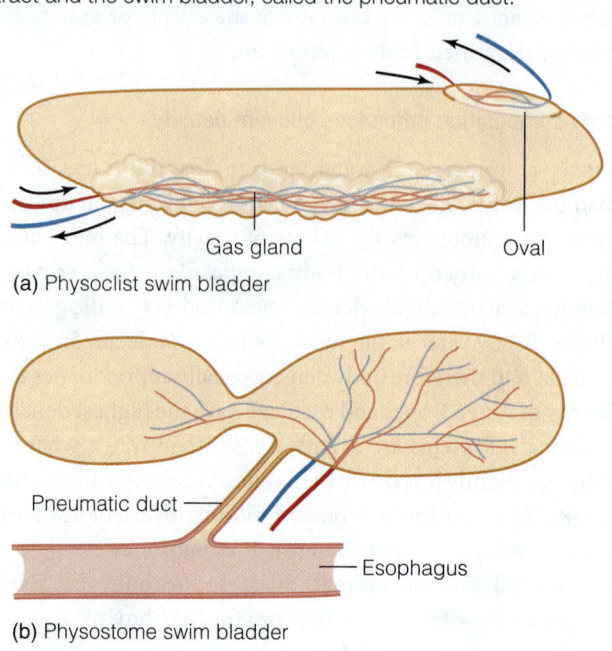

Gas gland   Oval

(a) Physoclist swim bladder

Pneumatic duct

Esophagus

(b) Physostome swim bladder

the pneumatic duct to release air into the gut, where it is burped out of the animal. *Physoclist fish* have lost the direct connection between gut and swim bladder. These fish inflate the swim bladder at a vascularized region of the organ called the *gas gland*. Blood arrives at the gas gland with oxygen loaded onto hemoglobin. When a fish needs to increase the volume of the bladder, the gas gland induces a local acidification, causing hemoglobin to release oxygen. Oxygen unloading is maximized by the countercurrent arrangement of the blood vessels. When a fish needs to reduce the volume of the swim bladder, oxygen is allowed to flow into the blood at a separate vascularized region called the *oval*. Physostome fish may also have a gas gland and an oval, but they are generally reduced in size and less important for gas exchange than the structures in physoclists.

Gas-filled swim bladders reduce the costs of swimming, but they do have functional limitations. The volume of the swim bladder changes in response to hydrostatic pressure. As hydrostatic pressure increases, the volume of a swim bladder shrinks. When the pressure is relieved, the swim bladder expands. Swim bladders are most useful for fish that remain within a narrow range of depths, but they would impair pelagic fish from moving rapidly up and down in the water column. If a deepwater fish comes to the surface too quickly, the volume of its swim bladder can increase so fast that the fish is incapacitated. Many active fish have lost their swim bladders, and instead expend muscle energy to maintain their position in the water column. Although this is more expensive energetically than a swim bladder, it allows the fish to rapidly change depth without suffering a rapid change in swim bladder volume.

CONCEPT CHECK

9. How do the properties of molecules influence their utility in conferring buoyancy?

Fluid Mechanics

An object moving through a fluid creates a complex pattern of flow. The rules that describe the movement of a fluid, called fluid mechanics, apply to both air and water. Animals are able to move through fluids by governing the path of the fluids around them. Some animals are most concerned with moving fluids out of the way to allow efficient movement. The fluids impede movement. Other animals control fluid movements to aid in locomotion. In this situation, the movement of fluids pushes the animal forward or lifts it upward.

Reynolds numbers determine turbulent or laminar flow

A simple way to begin our discussion of fluid mechanics is to consider the forces that act on an object, such as a canoe paddle, moving through water at different speeds and orientations (Figure 12.28). When you move the paddle through water very slowly, the fluid flows over the surface of the blade in smooth layers, a condition called **laminar flow**. If you were to repeat this movement at increasing velocities, you would reach a point where the pattern of flow would become less ordered, resulting in more **turbulent flow**. The costs of locomotion are greatly increased under turbulent flow conditions. The transition from laminar flow to turbulent flow

FIGURE 12.28 Laminar and turbulent flow

As an object such as a canoe paddle moves through water, the fluid is forced around the blade. **(a)** The flow remains laminar at low velocities. **(b)** At greater velocities the flow can become chaotic, resulting in turbulence in the wake of the object. This increases the cost of movement.

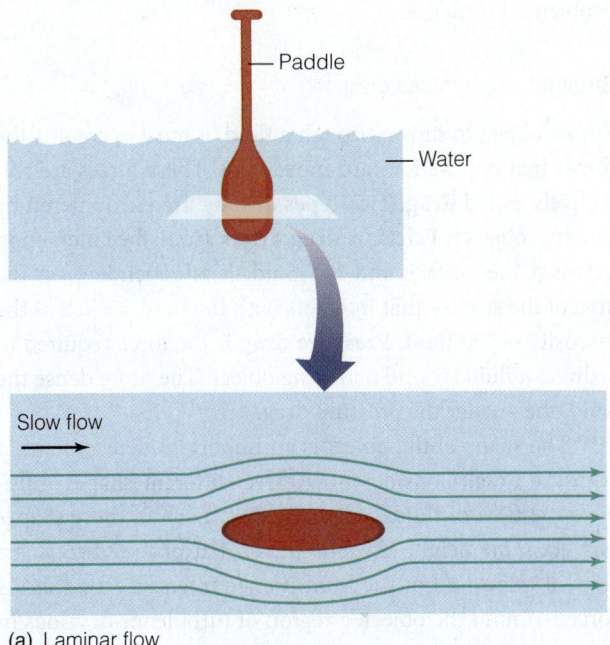

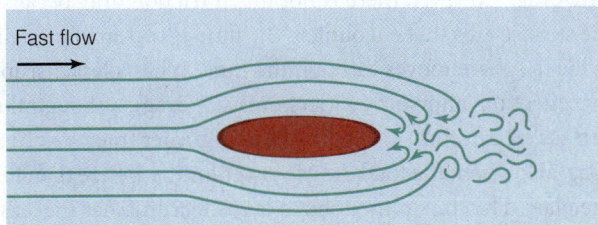

depends upon properties of the fluid (viscosity, density), the object (size, shape), and the movement (velocity, direction). The relationship between these parameters is described by the Reynolds equation. The **Reynolds number** (Re) is calculated as follows:

$$\text{Re} = VL\rho/\mu$$

where V is velocity of movement, L is a linear dimension of the object, ρ is the density of the fluid, and μ is the viscosity of the fluid. The Reynolds number enables researchers to predict such things as how easily an object can glide through a fluid or when movement through a fluid is likely to be turbulent. Our intuitive appreciation of the biological factors that influence locomotion can be traced back to the parameters of the Reynolds equation.

In our example of moving the canoe paddle through water at different velocities, the mathematical explanation for the increase in turbulence is related to the effect of V on Re. The influence of L on Re can be illustrated by changing the orientation of the paddle. Moving it through the water edge first is easier than when the paddle moves face first. In the face-first orientation, the surface of the paddle that first encounters the fluid is much wider. In the calculation of Re, this difference is reflected in values of L (Figure 12.29). To appreciate the impact of density, compare the effort of paddling through air versus water. An object moving through air has a lower Re because air has a lower density (ρ).

FIGURE 12.29 Orientation and turbulent flow

The orientation of objects can influence the formation of turbulence. As the linear dimension encountering the fluid (L) increases, the turbulence also increases. **(a)** When the canoe paddle moves edge first, the lower L value results in less turbulence. **(b)** Moving the paddle blade first increases L and enhances turbulence.

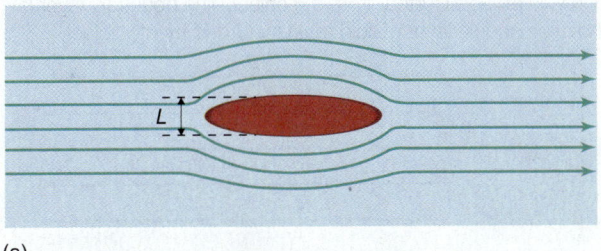

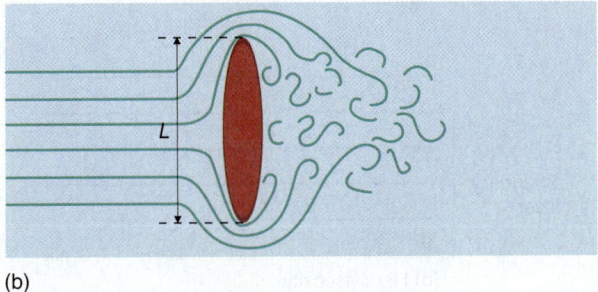

The last parameter in the Reynolds equation, viscosity (μ), requires more explanation. Fluids differ in their ability to flow around an object. When a solution moves across a surface, the molecular layer closest to the surface adheres to the surface and moves with it. The next layer of fluid interacts with the layer of fluid in contact with the surface. The further the distance from the surface, the less the fluid movement is influenced by the surface. The boundary layer is the molecular layer of fluid that is influenced by the surface of the object around which it moves (Figure 12.30). Some fluids are more viscous than others, a physical property that we recognize as the "thickness" of a solution. For example, we perceive honey to be thicker than water. Viscosity influences the movement of an object through a fluid because of the way the fluid interacts with the object to create a boundary layer. If you remove your finger from a bowl of water, it will have a thin coating of water. If you remove your finger from a bowl of honey, a much thicker layer sticks to your finger. Any time you move your finger through a liquid, you carry that layer of fluid along for the ride. It costs you extra energy to carry that layer of honey through the remainder of the honey, known as the bulk phase. Note that fluid viscosity affects animal locomotion, but animals do not have to cope with *changes* in environmental viscosity. The viscosity of water or air varies little under most conditions. Thus, for the Re of an animal in its environment, the most important factors are *V* and *L*.

FIGURE 12.30 Boundary layers

(a) When an object moves through a solution of low viscosity, each layer of laminar flow moves at the same velocity, as indicated by vectors of equal length. **(b)** In solutions of higher viscosity, the layer of laminar flow in contact with the object moves more slowly because of interactions with the object. The impact of the object is reduced further from the object. The boundary layer is the microscopic layer of fluid that is retarded by the object.

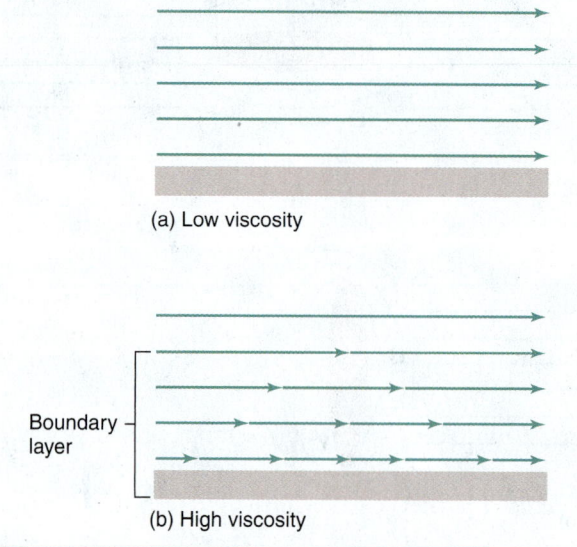

(a) Low viscosity

Boundary layer

(b) High viscosity

The relative importance of viscous and inertial effects determine Re

The thickness of the boundary layer is a property of the fluid, not the moving object. The boundary layer of water is just as thick on a whale as on a small aquatic invertebrate, such as a copepod. The whale expends relatively little energy to carry around the added water because the water layer is trivial in comparison to the size of the whale. However, the costs to the copepod are significant. These fluid layers exert the greatest effects on locomotion of small, slow animals. The magnitude of these **viscous effects** depends on the viscosity of the fluid, the velocity of movement, and the properties of the surface of the animal that interacts with the fluid. These properties include body shape and surface area, the physical composition of the surface, and the nature of appendages. Larger, faster animals are less influenced by viscous effects because of much lower ratios of surface area to mass (Figure 12.31). When a copepod stops swimming, the viscous effects stop forward progression. When a whale stops moving its tail, it has enough momentum to overcome viscous effects. These **inertial effects**, which are dependent on body mass, dominate the movement of larger animals in air and water. The high Re in large animals, however, creates another potential problem: turbulence.

Streamlining reduces drag

For an object to move through a fluid, it must overcome the forces that oppose forward movement. These forces are collectively called **drag**. Two types of drag are encountered by moving objects. **Friction drag** arises from the interaction between the surface and the fluid. It is dependent on the area of the surface that interacts with the fluid, as well as the viscosity of the fluid. **Pressure drag** is the force required to redirect a fluid around a moving object. The more dense the fluid, the greater the pressure drag.

The shape of the object is an important determinant of pressure drag. Consider how three different shapes influence the flow of fluids (Figure 12.32). Each of these shapes has the same height (*L*). The broad, flat plate redirects the flow of almost all of the fluid it encounters. As the fluid is forced around the object, a region of turbulence develops in its wake. Under these conditions, there is a great deal of pressure drag. However, there is not much friction drag because the surface area that encounters the fluid is reasonably small. When a sphere moves through the fluid, it has a less disruptive effect on laminar flow (less pressure drag), although the surface area in contact with the fluid is greater (more friction drag). However, the total drag is lower for the sphere than for the plate. The streamlined shape of the teardrop has the least effect on laminar flow, causing the lowest amount of pressure drag. Although additional friction drag is associated

FIGURE 12.31 Influence of Reynolds number on animal locomotion

The Reynolds number reflects the properties of a fluid and the size and shape of the animal. Larger animals have a higher Reynolds number than smaller animals. Swimmers have a larger Reynolds number than fliers of similar size. The larger the Reynolds number, the more important are inertial effects on locomotion. Viscous effects dominate at low Reynolds numbers.

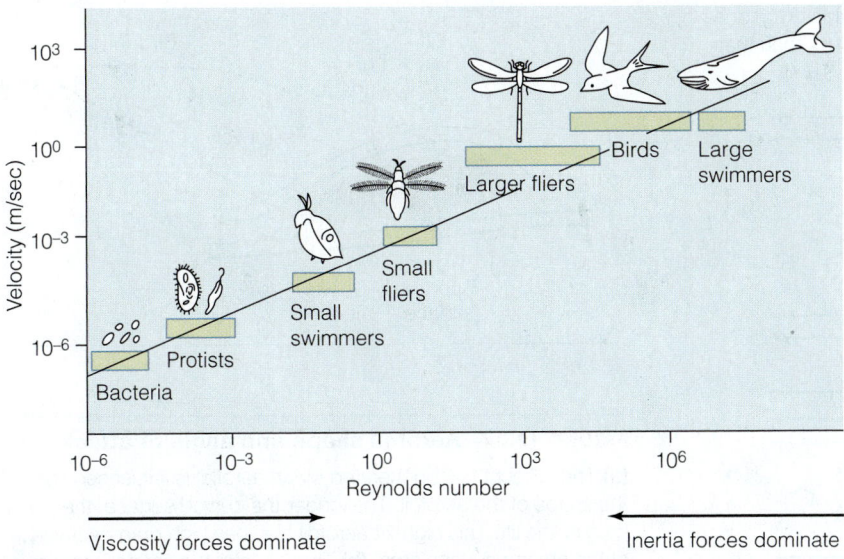

Figure source: Adapted from Nachtigall, W. (1977). On the significance of Reynolds' number and the fluid mechanical phenomena connected to it in swimming physiology and flight biophysics (author's trans. [In German]). *Fortschritte der Zoologie, 24*, 13–56.

with the streamlined shape, the total drag is the lowest of all three shapes.

Streamlining reduces the amount of energy animals require to overcome pressure drag. Although each of the objects shown in Figure 12.32 has a similar value of *L*, they have very different masses. That means that the cost of overcoming drag in a large, streamlined animal is similar to the cost for a much smaller, nonstreamlined animal. Most larger swimmers and fliers have streamlined body shapes that reduce drag.

In addition to streamlining, many of the fastest swimmers and fliers also have modified body surfaces that further reduce friction drag. This increased efficiency is critical for an animal like the dolphin, which can swim through the water at 40 kilometers per hour. The surface of the dolphin is mounted on a layer of tiny pillars that readily change shape when water moves over the surface. When the skin compresses in response to small, localized turbulence, friction drag is minimized as fluids move smoothly over the surface. Another property of dolphin skin allows this animal to avoid a problem that plagues recreational sailors and the navy. Barnacles readily attach to the surface of manufactured vessels, drastically reducing the efficiency of movement through the water. Barnacles cannot attach to the skin of dolphins because of microscopic contours over the surface. This nanoscale terrain prevents the

barnacle from forming a tight seal on the surface, and keeps the dolphin barnacle-free throughout its life.

CONCEPT CHECK

10. Distinguish between viscous forces and inertial forces in relation to animal locomotion.
11. Distinguish between friction drag and pressure drag.

Aerodynamics and Hydrodynamics

Because air and water share similar fluid properties, swimmers and fliers face similar challenges in moving through the environment. Swimmers and fliers must overcome the force of gravity to maintain their vertical position. Their locomotor strategies must be consistent with the physical properties of the fluid, particularly density. Swimmers and fliers both benefit from streamlining and use appendages to control the movement of fluids over the body.

Aerofoils and hydrofoils generate lift

When an object moves through a fluid, the fluid is diverted around the object. This movement, and the changes in pressure that result, are responsible for both defying gravity and generating forward movement, or propulsion. Wings and fins are structures used by animals to control the path of movement of the fluid. Most of these structures have a cross-sectional structure similar to that shown in Figure 12.33. This is the general shape of an **aerofoil**, or in water, a **hydrofoil**. The upper surface is curved. The lower surface is flattened, the front is rounded, and the back tapered. The shape is critical in producing the force required to generate an upward force called **lift**. We will discuss how lift works using an aerofoil as an example, but the same principles apply to hydrofoils.

When the aerofoil moves forward, air collides with the leading edge and causes an increase in air pressure. The air slides upward and is compressed into the air on top of the aerofoil. The airstream continues to flow backward. The upper surface of the aerofoil curves downward, away from the airstream. This causes a region of low air pressure. On the bottom of the aerofoil, the air continues smoothly along the surface. Because of the differences in the airflow, there is a difference in the air pressures over the surfaces of the aerofoil.

FIGURE 12.32 **Streamlining and drag**

Three objects move through a fluid at the same velocity. They have the same cross-sectional profiles, as indicated by a constant value of *L*. The Reynolds number for each object is identical. The shape of the objects influences the amount of pressure and friction drag. The streamlined object has the lowest amount of pressure drag, despite its much greater mass. Although the streamlined object has a larger friction drag, due to its larger surface area, the total drag is much less than that with the plate or the sphere.

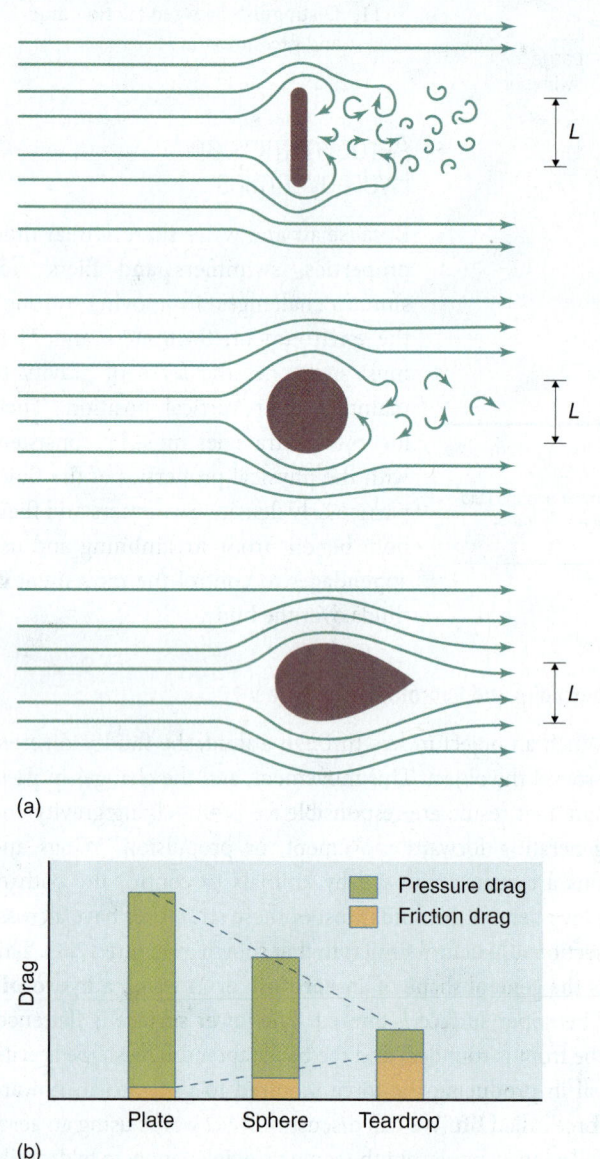

(a)

(b)

FIGURE 12.33 **Aerofoils and hydrofoils**

Many wings and fins possess the shape of an aerofoil or hydrofoil. Shown in cross-section, the upper surface of the aerofoil is curved and tapered downward, whereas the lower surface is flat. The fluid must move faster as it moves over the longer upper surface. This results in an area of low pressure, causing a net upward force known as lift.

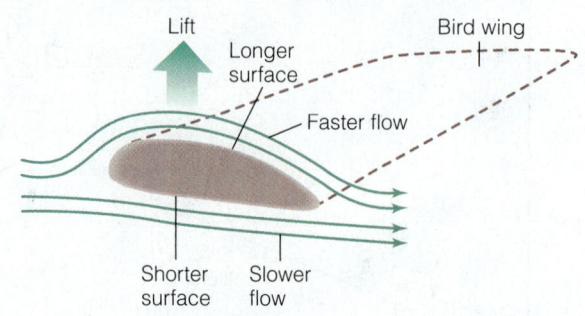

FIGURE 12.34 **Aerofoil shape and angle of attack**

(a) The amount of lift generated by an aerofoil is influenced by the shape of the aerofoil. The longer the curved surface, the greater the lift. This high-lift aerofoil also has high drag because of the greater surface area. **(b)** The angle of the aerofoil relative to horizontal, known as the angle of attack, influences the pattern of fluid flow and consequently lift.

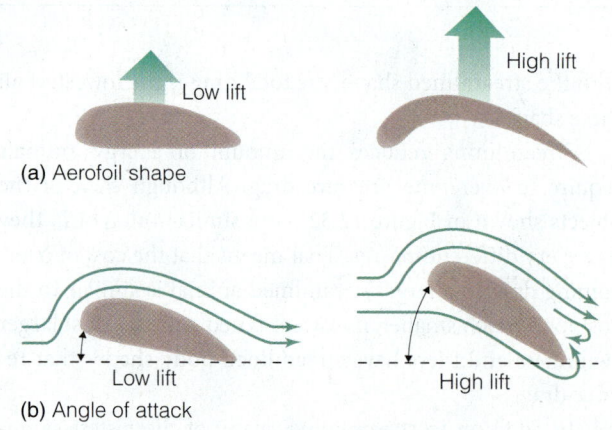

(a) Aerofoil shape

(b) Angle of attack

object size and dimension. Another parameter that affects lift and drag is the **angle of attack**, which is the angle the aerofoil faces relative to the oncoming airflow (Figure 12.34).

Soaring uses lift from natural air currents to overcome gravity

When discussing movement through the air, it is important to distinguish true flight from gliding. In true flight, animals use wings to lift off the ground and remain airborne for long periods. True flight includes flapping flight and hovering flight, where wing movements generate fluid movements that allow the animal to control altitude and velocity. True flight also

This pressure differential equates to a force. Some of the force lifts the aerofoil upward. Some of the force is lost as drag.

The balance between the lift component and the drag component depends on many factors: air speed, air density, wing area, and a coefficient that is specific to each aerofoil. Both the **lift coefficient** (C_l) and **drag coefficient** (C_d) are determined by direct measurement. They are properties of the

includes soaring, where the animal uses stationary wings to generate lift to keep it airborne. Gliding, like soaring, relies on stationary structures to alter fluid movements, but unlike soaring, the animal inevitably descends toward the ground. Gliding is much more widespread in animals because it requires much less anatomical and physiological specialization than does true flight. Any structure that increases surface area can improve the ability to glide. There are many examples of mammals (squirrels, primates) and reptiles (snakes, lizards) that extend flaps of skin from the body to glide (Figure 12.35). Flying squid and flying fish, which don't actually fly, use fins to glide over the surface of water. In each case, the shape or orientation of the gliding structure produces some lift, just not enough to remain aloft indefinitely.

Of all the flying animals, only birds soar. In some large birds, such as the albatross and condor, wing structure is much better suited to soaring flight than flapping flight. The efficiency of soaring is enhanced by strategies that capitalize on natural air movements. Many birds undertake slope soaring, riding on the air currents deflected upward along the topography of the surface. Many sea birds, such as pelicans, use air movements on the surface of water (Figure 12.36). Land birds use wind currents flowing up from ridges to reduce the costs of flight. Soaring birds can also ride upwellings of warm air called thermals. Migratory birds can ride a bubble of air upward to great height, then soar away, heading toward the next thermal. Slope soaring and thermal soaring dramatically reduce the costs of flight. Many birds migrate along routes that take advantage of natural topographic features, covering distances that would not be possible without the metabolic savings of soaring.

True flight arose at least four times

The earliest fliers were insects derived from a single common terrestrial ancestor that first took flight about 350 million years ago. By 290 million years ago, this group had diversified to more than 15 orders of insects. Pterosaurs, or flying dinosaurs, arose about 290 million years ago. They were the first flying vertebrates and rapidly diversified. Birds probably arose from small theropod dinosaurs around 180 million years ago. Bats appeared about 50 million years ago. The geological record tells us that in each of these periods, atmospheric oxygen concentrations were unusually high. A high oxygen level had two effects on animal locomotion. First, the greater availability of oxygen allowed animals to produce ATP at higher rates. Second, the increased atmospheric oxygen level increased the density of air. This allowed animals to generate more lift from the same structures.

Flight is not possible without wings, but the original function of structures that became wings probably had little to do with flight. The wings of insects, which are structurally related to their cuticle, may have arisen to increase the efficiency of gas exchange. Movement of the wings would both increase the movement of gases around the insect spiracles and induce a form of thoracic pumping to increase respiration. The presence of wings in the aquatic ancestors of insects may have allowed a type of movement that eventually gave rise to flight. Some modern stone flies, for example, use their wings to propel themselves across the surface of water. Surface tension keeps them on top of the water, and the wing movement pushes them along the surface. For the vertebrate fliers there is an ongoing debate about whether they first flew from trees (arboreal) or from the ground (cursorial). In the arboreal hypothesis, animals would climb trees or cliffs and then use their wings to gently glide down to the ground. This same strategy is seen in many modern vertebrates. Flying

FIGURE 12.35   Gliding animals

(a) Flying squirrels and **(b)** flying fish are two of the many nonbird species that can glide.

(a)

(b)

Photo source: (a) Nicholas Bergkessel, Jr. / Science Source; (b) feathercollector/ Fotolia.

FIGURE 12.36   Soaring on air currents

Birds can soar on upwardly directed air currents. Sloping land such as ridges can direct air upward. Warm bubbles of air, called thermals, rise upward over land warmed by the sun.

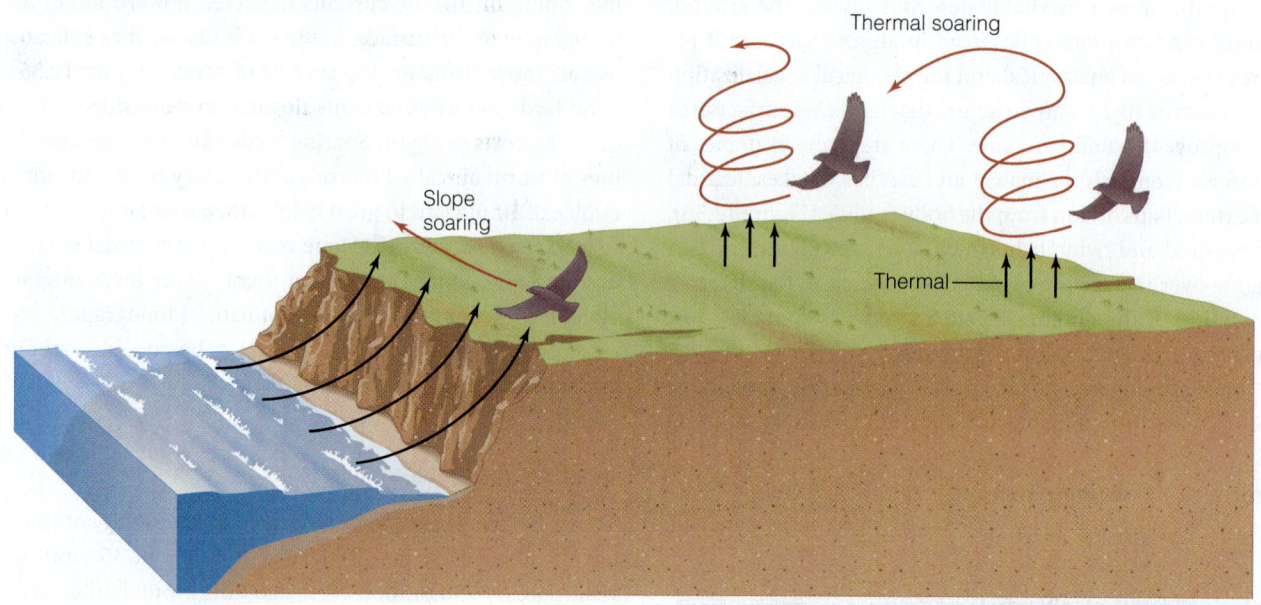

squirrels and flying lizards extend flaps of skin to increase the ability to soar. In the cursorial hypothesis, animals would use their wings to lift off the ground into the air. Modern birds such as quail use their wings to climb trees. They run vertically up trees, flapping their wings in a way that generates reverse lift to push them against the tree for better foot traction.

Feathers are very important in bird flight, helping to guide the flow of air across the wing surface. Early feathers arose in several birdlike reptilian lineages as insulation (see Chapter 15). The structures necessary for flight in modern animals, such as wings, muscles, and feathers, may have arisen for other purposes, but evolution has allowed them to become fine-tuned for flight performance.

Vertebrate wings are modifications of forelimbs and hands, but the origins of insect wings are less obvious. At one point in evolutionary time, prior to the emergence of flight, insects and crustaceans shared a common arthropod ancestor. This ancestor had extra appendages that evolved in different ways in each lineage. In the crustacean lineage, the appendages became epipods, elongated structures that aid in gas exchange. In the insect lineage, the extra appendages became the wings. The same genes that gave rise to insect flight 350 million years ago control the development of the epipods in modern crustaceans and wings in insects.

Fluid movements can generate propulsion

Bird wings are of a size, shape, and orientation to generate lift if the animal is moving relative to the air. If the animal is not moving forward through the air, no lift results. If movement of the fluid relative to the animal is required to generate lift, then how do animals take off or hover, behaviors that would seem to preclude the generation of lift? In other words, how do animals generate the propulsive forces necessary for forward movement?

Swimmers and fliers move their appendages to alter fluid flows to produce propulsive force, or thrust. Whereas lift overcomes body weight and the effects of gravity, thrust overcomes drag. As with other rules of fluid dynamics, the mechanisms of thrust are similar in swimmers and fliers.

To understand how wings and fins generate thrust, let's begin by considering an analogy. Imagine a ball floating stationary in a pool of water. If you were to move your hand gently over the surface of the ball, you would cause the ball to spin. Similarly, when the caudal fin of a fish moves through the water, it causes the fluid to swirl into a circular pattern called a vortex. Moving the fin in one direction causes a clockwise vortex, and moving the fin in the opposite direction causes a counterclockwise vortex. These vortices of fluid movement are a consequence of the transfer of force from the fin to the environment. As the fish moves through the water, the flapping caudal fin leaves a series of interlinked vortices in its wake. These fluid movements ultimately provide the force that propels the fish forward.

The same vortex ring theory applies to flying animals, but wing movements are much more complicated than fin movements. Wings must move in a way that generates both the forward force and the upward force. Lift is a force that arises from wing shape (aerofoil) only when the fluid is flowing over the aerofoil. Lift is adequate to keep a soaring bird aloft, but the situation is much more complex when a wing moves in space. Furthermore, if the animal is not moving forward, how can it generate lift to remain aloft? Most insects move their wings in a pattern that cannot easily generate lift. At the top of the stroke, the wing is nearly vertical above the insect. The wing moves rapidly downward below a horizontal plane, twisting as it moves. The combination of rapid downstroke and a twisting movement generates a large vortex of air movement at the leading edge of the wing. These air movements allow the insect to generate both the upward and the forward force. The situation is fundamentally similar in birds and bats. Downward wing movements generate vortices that can be used to remain aloft and propel the animal forward. In addition, insects and hummingbirds can generate favorable fluid movements during the upstroke, which allows them to hover.

Although researchers have many techniques to visualize the vortices that develop during flight, the exact forces at play remain unclear. The style of movement, the shape of the appendages, and the velocity of movement all affect the nature of the wake and the forces that govern movement.

Fin and wing shapes influence fluid movements

In the previous sections we have described how the physical attributes of body shape, wing, and fin shape influence fluid movements. The diversity in these structures within the animal kingdom reflects the effects of biological properties and the physical environment acting in combination.

Although insects, bats, and birds all fly, their wing shapes are markedly different. Insect wings differ widely in shape and appearance, but they share many features. Typically, the leading edge of the wing is a stiffened structure, whereas most of the wing is a flexible membrane strengthened by an internal framework. During flight, the insect wing distorts, creating complex fluid movements that enable flight. Bat wings, like insect wings, are membranous, but the bones that act as the framework of the wing are jointed. The fine muscles within the wing allow the bat to change the wing shape, which translates into greater maneuverability than is seen in insects. With the elasticity of the membrane, the bat is able to change the dimensions of the wing by as much as 20 percent without incurring a change in the tightness of the membrane. The feathers of the bird wing have specific shapes and positions that allow the wing to better control the path of air over the surface of the wing. Because the feathers overlap and can slide over each other, birds can change the geometry of the wing without compromising the ability of the wing to act as an aerofoil.

While bird wing geometry is similar overall among species, the subtle differences in shape have important ramifications for flight. Let's first consider the relationship between bird wing size and body mass. Because air flows over the entire wing surface, a combination of wingspan (b) and surface area (S) influences lift. Obviously, larger birds need larger wings to generate the lift to remain aloft. However, which is more effective, longer wings or broader ones? Birds of the order Procellariiformes, which includes albatrosses and petrels, differ in size by 400-fold. They share a similar lifestyle, soaring long distances over open ocean. When these birds are drawn scaled to the same wingspan, the importance of wing shape is evident (Figure 12.37). The larger birds have longer and narrower wings. Mathematically, the shape is described as the aspect ratio (Λ), which is calculated as follows:

$$\Lambda = b^2/S$$

The shape of fish fins, which are much more variable in shape than bird wings, enables fish to undertake diverse swimming styles. If we restrict our comparison to the fastest-swimming fish, we can see the importance of fin shape in swimming strategies. Burst swimmers, such as pirarucu, possess thick caudal peduncles with rounded caudal fins of low aspect ratio. Fast steady-state swimmers, such as tuna, possess thin caudal peduncles with crescent-shaped, or

FIGURE 12.37 Wing aspect ratios

The birds shown in this image range almost eightfold in wingspan, but are drawn to the same wingspan to illustrate the differences in wing shape. The horizontal bar represents relative wingspan. The smallest birds have relatively broad wings.

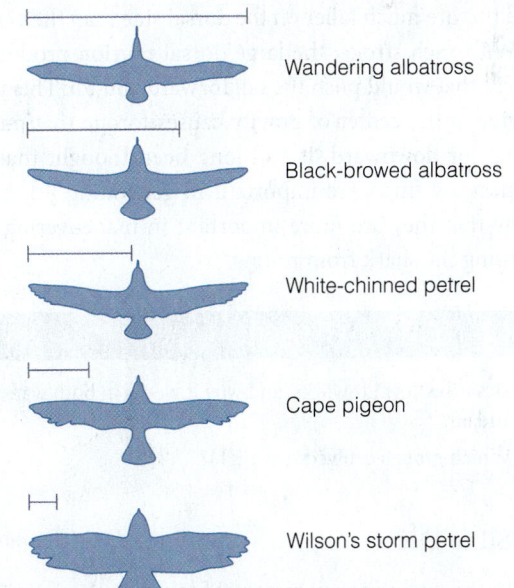

Wandering albatross

Black-browed albatross

White-chinned petrel

Cape pigeon

Wilson's storm petrel

Figure source: Based on Pennycuick, C. J. (1992). Figures 4.4 and 4.5 from *Newton rules biology: A physical approach to biological problems.* New York: Oxford University Press.

FIGURE 12.38   Caudal fin shapes
Shark caudal fins range in shape from nearly symmetrical (homocercal) to strongly asymmetrical (heterocercal).

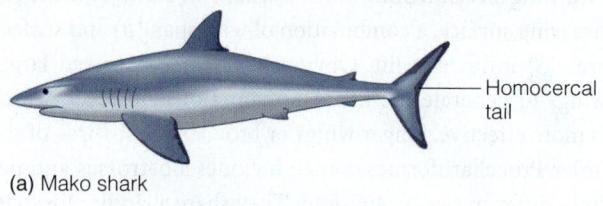

(a) Mako shark

Homocercal tail

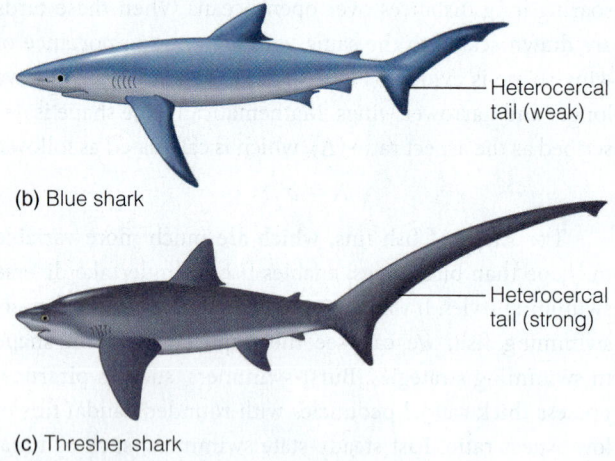

(b) Blue shark

Heterocercal tail (weak)

(c) Thresher shark

Heterocercal tail (strong)

lunate, caudal fins of high aspect ratio. Each of these caudal fins is *homocercal*, or symmetrical above and below the midline. The fastest sharks, such as the mako shark, have homocercal caudal fins, but pronounced heterocercal caudal fins are found in pelagic cruising sharks (Figure 12.38). Many sharks possess asymmetrical caudal fins. These *heterocercal* caudal fins are much taller on the dorsal side than the ventral side. With each stroke, the large dorsal portion produces a net force that would push the tail forward and up. This force posterior to the center of gravity causes torque that pushes the anterior downward. It had long been thought that the rigid pectoral fins were important in generating lift, but it is likely that they are more important in maneuvering and preventing the shark from rolling.

CONCEPT CHECK

12. Describe how lift works, and why it works in both water and air.
13. Which groups evolved true flight?

Terrestrial Life

Early in the evolutionary history of metazoans, all animals lived in aquatic ecosystems. The invasion of land came in at least two waves. Today, the metazoans of terrestrial ecosystems are represented by diverse taxa of invertebrates and vertebrates. Many show vestiges of their aquatic ancestry in semiaquatic lifestyles and aquatic developmental stages. Each lineage faced its own set of challenges with terrestrial life. In previous chapters we have discussed how this invasion required physiological strategies to cope with osmotic and respiratory challenges. In this section we consider how terrestrial animals meet the oppressive challenge of gravity.

Aquatic animals invaded the land several times

Invertebrates invaded land many times, but the most successful group is the arthropods, primarily arachnids (e.g., spiders), myriapods (e.g., centipedes), and hexapods (e.g., insects). The earliest terrestrial invertebrates were probably detritivores, scrambling over the ground eating partially hydrolyzed plant material. Herbivores and carnivores arose later in invertebrate evolution. Each lifestyle requires a different type of locomotor apparatus to meet the challenges of the complex terrestrial world.

Vertebrates were once found only in aquatic ecosystems, when large, shallow marshes dominated the landscape. Then about 370 million years ago the vertebrate invasion of land began. Many fish species had already evolved strong fins that enabled them to move through sunken vegetation. These locomotor modifications helped the first amphibious fish to move on land, facilitating the transition to a terrestrial world. The coelacanth, a fully aquatic fish, is closely related to the early terrestrial invaders and anatomically similar. Many unrelated fish have fin structures that facilitate a semiterrestrial life. These early invaders used paired pectoral and pelvic fins to pull the body along, but the trunk was in direct contact with the ground. Evolution of the appendicular musculature and skeleton allowed animals to become more mobile, as the limbs supported more of the weight of the animal. Improvements in leg musculature, changes in postural muscles, reoriented skeletons, and stronger bones all contributed to the colonization of land and the diversification of land animals. The many species of semiaquatic animals illustrate the type of physiological modifications that are necessary for a terrestrial life.

Amphibious animals that must move on both land and water face the challenge of using the same locomotor apparatus under two different conditions. Eels and snakes use trunk movements to swim in water and crawl over land. Ducks and turtles use their feet to walk on land and paddle in the water. The same locomotor modules are used to move in both environments, but an animal may use the musculature in a way that is specific for each environment. For example, when ducks and turtles are in water, they do not need to use leg muscles to support the body mass. Rather, the leg musculature can extend and contract at a higher frequency during swimming. Eels and snakes use the same undulatory movements both on land and in the water. However, movement on land requires more force because of the effects of gravity. Thus, the undulations of an eel on land may be at the same frequency as in the water, but the eel uses the more powerful white muscle on land, and the more efficient red muscle in the water. Collectively, amphibious animals use combinations of motor patterns and recruitment to utilize the same locomotor modules to move in two worlds.

Metamorphosis remodels anatomy and physiology for terrestrial locomotion

Many animals begin their lives in an aquatic world and then undergo a developmental remodeling of anatomy and physiology to specialize for a terrestrial life. You are probably most familiar with the development of local amphibians, by which fully aquatic tadpoles metamorphose into semiaquatic frogs and terrestrial toads. This developmental transition from aquatic to terrestrial animals is also common in insects. These animals provide vivid examples of the anatomical and physiological differences in locomotor patterns in aquatic and terrestrial animals.

Amphibians provide many interesting examples of how changes in locomotor physiology are integrated into life history strategies. Some amphibians remain aquatic animals throughout their lives, using appendages and a tail to swim through the water or crawl through vegetation. Many frogs and toads undergo metamorphosis. Tadpoles are larval forms of frogs and toads that undergo indirect development. They swim through the water much like a fish that uses its tail and trunk to generate thrust. In the late stages of larval development, changes in thyroid hormone levels trigger remodeling of the locomotor apparatus. Limb buds arise from the body trunk and grow into hindlimbs and forelimbs (Figure 12.39). At maturity, the hindlimb anatomy becomes specialized for a type of movement that enables both swimming and jumping, although unlike mammals, the limb musculature does not support the entire weight of the animal. In some species of frogs, tadpoles can climb onto the back of a parent, which carries its offspring between ponds. Still other species of frogs undergo direct development. Miniature frogs, or froglets, hatch from eggs laid on vegetation. In contrast to tadpoles, these juvenile frogs can swim, climb, or jump from place to place. It is not yet clear how the basic developmental biology of the amphibians' locomotor system has evolved to account for these diverse life history strategies.

FIGURE 12.39 Tadpole metamorphosis

Fully aquatic larval frogs (tadpoles) swim using their tail. Legs begin to grow during metamorphosis: first hindlimbs, then forelimbs. Once the tail is resorbed, the mature frog ventures onto land, using its legs to walk and jump.

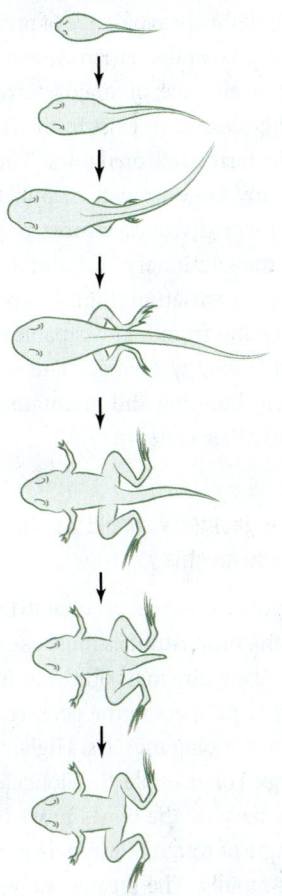

Flightless birds evolved in the absence of terrestrial predators

For many animals, the locomotor machinery must allow movement in more than one environment. Although flying is the most efficient mode of transportation for birds, most birds also spend significant time on the ground. At one extreme are the flightless ratite birds, which include the extant ostrich, emu, and kiwi, as well as the extinct moa and elephant bird (standing 2.5 meters tall and weighing 450 kilograms). Although the evolutionary ancestry of these animals remains uncertain, it is likely that the flightless lineages arose about 40 million years ago. Modern ratites, such as the ostrich, use wings for balance during running and as part of courtship rituals. These birds possess well-developed leg musculature, allowing many species to run at high velocities. Other species of flightless birds appear around the world. The wings of penguins may look like shark fins or seal flippers, but the penguins use their wings to "fly" through the water.

Darwin once commented that there is no greater anomaly in nature than a bird that cannot fly. There may be many reasons for the evolutionary loss of flight. The two most obvious advantages of flight are avoidance of predators and ability to migrate to more favorable environments. Most flightless birds arose in the absence of major terrestrial predators. Populations of flightless birds exist in the Galápagos Islands, which lack major terrestrial predators. The ostrich lives in a region with many large predators, but its large size and powerful kicking legs discourage most predators. Whether considering macroevolutionary variation (flightless species) or microevolutionary variation (flightless populations of one species), the transition from flight-capable to flightless strategies must provide energy savings. The energy that would otherwise be spent building and maintaining wing muscles can be diverted to other systems.

Animals of similar geometry should be able to jump to the same heights

Jumping is a form of locomotion peculiar to terrestrial animals, with specialized anatomy. Animals must use a single muscular contraction to lift the entire mass off the ground. Good jumpers differ from poor jumpers in the geometry of the legs and the strength of the jumping muscles. Higher jumps are possible with longer legs. For example, the elongated tarsals of frogs improve jumping because the bones move through a greater arc for a given angle of rotation. Jumpers must also be able to contract muscles rapidly. The greater the velocity at takeoff, the further the animal can jump.

Animals of different size but similar geometry should be able to jump to the same height. Similar geometry means that the overall dimensions of legs are similar and the mass of the jumping muscle is a constant proportion of body mass. With a constant proportional muscle mass, the velocity at takeoff would be similar, and therefore small and large animals should be able to jump to the same height (Figure 12.40). The reference point when talking about the effects of gravity is the vertical midpoint of the mass of the animal—the center of gravity. Although a small animal may not reach the same height as a large animal, it is able to lift its center of gravity the same distance. These relationships depend on the assumption of similar geometry. When comparing different species, variations in the animal morphology, physiology, and composition come into play, and contribute to differences in the ability to jump.

Fleas are often considered to be exceptional jumpers because they can jump to heights hundreds of times greater than their own height. Small jumping animals, like the flea, face several challenges that are less important for larger animals.

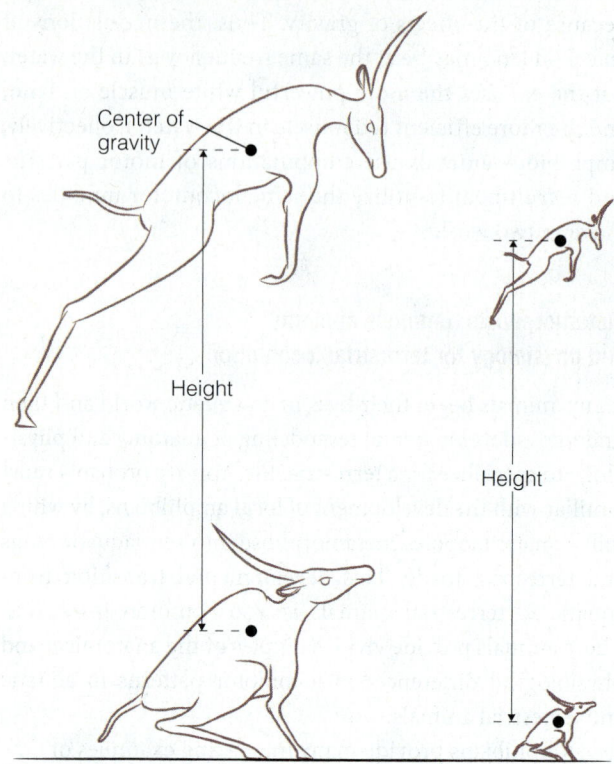

FIGURE 12.40 **Jumping antelope**

Animals of similar geometry should be able to lift their center of gravity the same vertical distance in a jump. The larger animal reaches a greater height because its center of mass begins at a greater distance from the ground.

Center of gravity

Height

Height

Figure source: Newton Rules Biology: A Physical Approach to Biology by Pennycuick (1992) Figure 4.7 (p. 47). By permission of Oxford University Press.

First, viscous effects are more important for small animals. A flea jumping through air faces a drag force similar to what a larger animal might face jumping through water. Second, jumping animals need to move their legs fast enough to reach takeoff velocity. Flea legs are so small that no conventional musculoskeletal combination could reach the required contraction velocity. Fleas avoid this problem by using an unusual mechanism. Muscles power the jump of a flea only indirectly. In the first of two steps, a leg muscle pulls on an internal spring and locks it into the loaded position. Next, a second muscle releases the spring, causing the leg to rapidly extend and the flea to jump. The spring returns to its unloaded position faster than any muscle could induce a contraction.

Terrestrial animals require strong bones and postural musculature

The main challenge in terrestrial locomotion is gravity. In the aquatic world, the natural density of the body imparts some degree of buoyancy that greatly reduces the influence of gravity. However, terrestrial dwellers are much more dense than air, the surrounding fluid. Amphibians and reptiles typically lie directly on the ground, reducing the costs of fighting gravity. However, birds and mammals, as well as extinct dinosaurs, use their limb muscles to lift the body off the ground. This strategy requires anatomical and physiological investments. Bones must be thicker to accommodate the increased force of gravity. Limb musculature must be more extensive to support and move the limbs. Muscle activity is required throughout the body to actively maintain posture. Even the process of standing still requires considerable muscle activity. In the next section we discuss the energetic factors that govern animal locomotion. Although these considerations apply to all animals, they have special relevance for terrestrial animals.

CONCEPT CHECK

14. What locomotor challenges would a fish face if it moved on to land?
15. Under what circumstances would flightless forms of flying animals evolve?

Energetics of Movement

Locomotion is expensive, and many studies in the comparative physiology of locomotion focus on the ways anatomy and physiology are used to minimize the costs of movement. In addition to the long-term costs of building and maintaining locomotor tissues, animals incur short-term costs when they use that machinery to move. The costs of locomotion, which depend on many biological and physical factors, can be expressed in several different terms. The mechanical costs of work can be expressed in units of joules (or calories). The metabolic costs of work are best expressed as ATP turnover (moles of ATP per minute). An estimate of ATP turnover can be obtained from oxygen consumption, but only when the animal is moving slowly enough to justify the assumption that oxidative phosphorylation is providing the ATP. CO_2 production, measured relative to oxygen consumption, provides important information about metabolic fuel selection. Most importantly, these different indices of the cost of locomotion are readily interconverted. Oxygen consumption (V_{O_2}), the most easily measured parameter, can be translated into both metabolic units (ATP) and work units (joules). For example, an animal that consumes 1 milliliter of oxygen generates about 20 joules (J) of energy. The costs of movement depend on many factors, both environmental and functional.

Energy demands of movement can be expressed as total costs or mass-specific costs

There are many ways to assess the energy required for locomotion. Each specific parameter takes into account a different set of concerns that are appropriate to the situation. Calculation of each parameter includes reasonable assumptions that must be kept in mind to properly interpret experimental observations. Let's consider some examples.

An ecological physiologist might be interested in the energetics of a specific migratory bird. The primary question is the relationship between stored energy and the locomotor feat. The experiment may be as simple as weighing birds before and after migration. Analyses of body tissues may be used to assess how specific energy storage depots change as a result of the activity. These measurements could include adipose tissue mass and the lipid and glycogen content of skeletal muscle. For example, the researcher might conclude that flying from one site to another costs x joules of energy, on the basis of the difference in weight and fuel depots.

A more biomechanically oriented physiologist might be most interested in how velocity of movement affects the metabolic costs. Laboratory studies might involve flying this bird species in a wind tunnel to assess the energetic costs of flying at different velocities. Birds may be fitted with gas masks that provide oxygen and capture CO_2. The metabolic demands of exercise are discussed in the context of a specific parameter called **cost of transport (COT)**. The central question in these studies asks how much energy it costs an animal to move a particular distance. The total COT (COT_{total}) is calculated as the metabolic rate divided by locomotor velocity.

$$COT_{total} = (\text{ml of } O_2 \text{ per min})/(\text{m per min})$$
$$= \text{ml of } O_2 \text{ per m}$$

The calculation of COT_{total} does not take into account the resting metabolic rate of the animal. The net COT is the difference between the total metabolic rate and the resting metabolic rate. COT calculations allow a researcher to determine the velocity at which an animal can move to most economically cross a given distance.

Each of the previous examples considers the energetics of movement of specific animals, but in many cases researchers are interested in comparisons between different animals. The most common type of comparison considers the effects of body size on the COT. Larger animals use more energy to move, simply because they are larger and have greater total metabolic demands. When considering the impact of body size, it is common to standardize locomotor parameters to the body size. For example, the metabolic rate measurements may be expressed relative to body mass to compare differences in energetics in two animals of different sizes. Also, studies on fish locomotion often express velocities not in absolute terms (meters per second) but as body lengths per second.

Each of these energetic parameters is useful and important in specific contexts. However, the nuances of each parameter are crucial considerations. Expressing values per animal versus per

MATH IN PHYSIOLOGY 12.3

COT IN COD

The velocity of movement influences the metabolic rate as well as the economy of movement, expressed as cost of transport, or COT (milliliters of O_2 per meter). Experimentally, these relationships are studied by monitoring respiration of an animal that is moving at different velocities. Such studies have been performed with aquatic, aerial, and terrestrial animals. To explore how these measurements are made, consider the following data and analysis modeled after a study on energetics of swimming in Atlantic cod (*Gadus morhua*). The data are realistic in comparison to this study, but simplified to make the equations a bit easier to explain.

In this hypothetical cod, oxygen consumption is measured at different swim speeds. The fish is placed in the respirometer and water flows past the fish at a given velocity (V). In most studies of fish, velocity is expressed relative to body length of the fish, but for convenience here we report V in meters per second (m/s). There is simultaneous measurement of oxygen consumption, which permits the calculation of oxygen consumption rate (J), measured as mg O_2 per min per kg fish. Recall that the direct measure of metabolic rate is in units of heat production (joules), but metabolic rate can be estimated indirectly using oxygen consumption or carbon dioxide production. The experiment yields the following data and graph (Figure 12.41).

How would you calculate COT (mg O_2/kg/m) at different velocities? Divide J (mg O_2/min/kg) by V (m/s), and divide by 60 to correct for the different time units. The data, plotted in Figure 12.41b, can be fitted to a quadratic equation:

$$COT = a + bV + cV^2$$

where a = 0.17, b = −0.22, and c = 0.14. These data show that for this fish, there is a velocity at which COT is a minimum

(COT_{min}). How would you go about finding what V gives the COT_{min}? The first derivative of the equation above allows the calculation of slope at each point along the curve:

$$dCOT/dV = b + 2cV$$

COT_{min} corresponds to the point where the derivative of the COT curve = 0.

$$0 = b + 2cV$$

Therefore, the velocity (V) at COT_{min} is −b/2c or 0.79 km/h.

These relationships allow many predictions, and provide the basis for further experiments that explore the impact of environmental and physiological influences on the energetics of transport. For example, researchers could ask whether COT is affected by water temperature, previous exercise, body size, or any other parameter that could affect the metabolic support for locomotion or the function of muscles.

Questions:
1. How much energy would it cost a 500-gram cod to swim 50 kilometers at the optimal velocity versus 50 percent faster than the optimal velocity?
2. If a locomotor activity has a metabolic cost of 0.20 mg O_2/kg/km, how would you translate this into units of nmol ATP/kg/ km and joules/kg/km? What assumptions do you make in converting between units?

Reference

• Syme, D. A., Gollock, M., Freeman, M. J., & Gamperl, A. K. (2008). Power isn't everything: Muscle function and energetic costs during steady swimming in Atlantic cod (*Gadus morhua*). *Physiological and Biochemical Zoology, 81,* 320–335.

FIGURE 12.41   Cost of transport

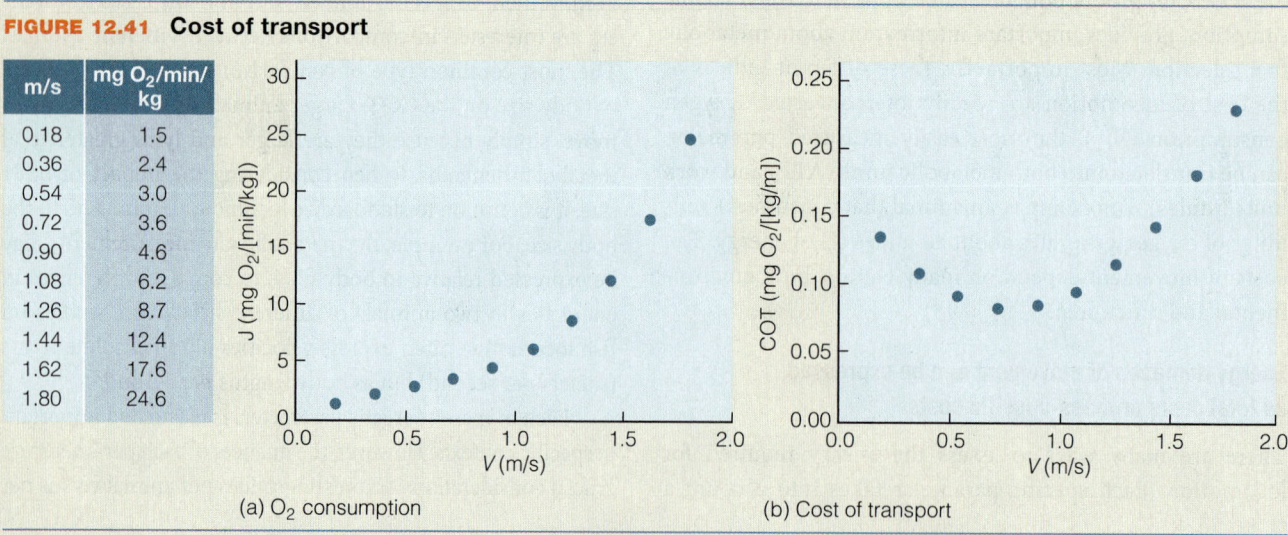

m/s	mg O_2/min/kg
0.18	1.5
0.36	2.4
0.54	3.0
0.72	3.6
0.90	4.6
1.08	6.2
1.26	8.7
1.44	12.4
1.62	17.6
1.80	24.6

(a) O_2 consumption

(b) Cost of transport

gram of animal provides very different information about the energetics. Similarly, each measurement has implicit assumptions about the underlying biochemistry. Although these calculations are intended to provide information about the muscles that underlie locomotor systems, it is important to recognize that other physiological systems, such as respiratory and cardiovascular systems, also incur a cost during locomotion. Box 12.3: Math in Physiology: COT in Cod provides a step-by-step explanation of how COT calculations are determined, and how they can be used to understand the energetics of movement.

Animals change style of movement to alter the costs of locomotion

When given a choice, animals tend to move at a specific velocity called the preferred velocity. You have probably experienced this yourself if you have walked with someone who is shorter or taller. For example, a tall person walking with a small child finds it challenging to walk at the child's pace. Remarkably, the preferred velocity is usually close to the velocity at which the COT is minimal.

The relationships between preferred velocity and minimum COT bring up interesting questions about the evolution of physiology. That animals choose a velocity that is near COT suggests that animals are able to detect conditions that result in maximal efficiency. The sensory feedback mechanisms responsible for the relationship between preferred velocity and COT are not yet clear. Presumably, there is also an evolutionary advantage to a behavior that leads to an animal moving slower than it otherwise could. The immediate benefits are in energy savings, but there may also be the long-term benefit of avoiding muscle damage. When animals move near the maximal possible velocity, the muscles can experience isometric stress. By using muscles well below their capacities, the animal reduces the risk of debilitating musculoskeletal damage. Thus, the ability to change gaits also reduces the chance of injury when moving faster or slower than an optimal velocity.

Many animals use different styles of movement over different ranges of velocity. A famous study that emerged from the laboratory of the late Dick Taylor used ponies to illustrate how animals can change gait to alter the interaction between velocity and energetics. Like many land animals, ponies exhibit distinct styles of moving, or *gaits*. They walk at low speed, trot at intermediate speed, and gallop at the fastest speed. Taylor's group measured the metabolic rate of ponies as they moved with different gaits at increasing velocity (Figure 12.42). When ponies walked at their preferred velocity of 1–1.5 m/sec, they consumed about 300 J/m. If they were forced to move more slowly or quickly using the same walking gait, their COT increased. The same was true of ponies that either trotted or galloped. The energy demands at their chosen velocities were about 300 J/m, regardless of the gait.

FIGURE 12.42 Gait and energy expenditure

Many animals, such as ponies, can move with different running styles, or gaits. Each style of running has an optimal velocity at which the cost of locomotion is minimal.

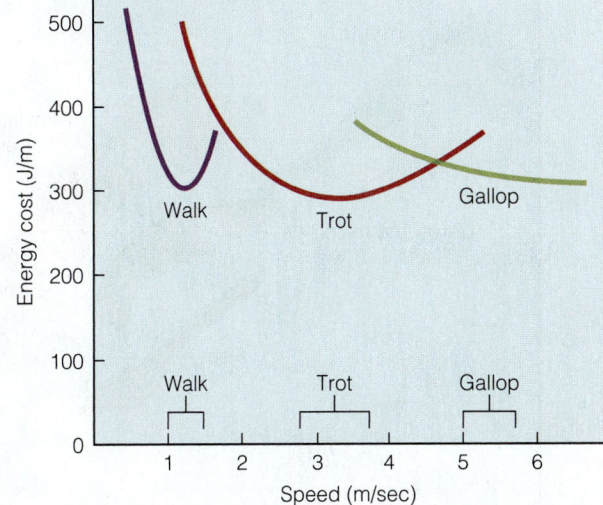

Figure source: Based on Hoyt, D. F., & Taylor, C. R. (1981). Figure 2 (p. 240) from Gait and the energetics of locomotion in horses. *Nature, 292,* 239–240.

Forcing them to move faster or slower than their preferred velocity increased their energy demands. In other words, the minimal COT values were the same in each gait as long as the animals could move at the preferred velocity. A pony that walks, trots, or gallops a distance of 1 km will consume about 300 kJ of energy. The galloping pony will use the energy faster, but it will cover the distance in a shorter period of time.

Gait alters energy expenditures by changing the way locomotor systems are used. Within each gait, the pony uses the same set of muscles over a wide range of velocities. Once the pony reaches a particular threshold velocity, it changes its gait and recruits different combinations of muscles to power different leg movements. The coordination of leg movements also differs between gaits. Walking ponies move left legs in synchrony. Trotting ponies move their diagonal legs in synchrony. Galloping ponies move the hind legs in synchrony, half a cycle out of phase from the front legs. The pattern of leg movement in galloping ponies makes better use of elastic storage energy. When the pony plants its hind legs, it also bends its back, creating and storing elastic tension in the bones and tendons. The release of the stored energy drives the front legs forward. Storing energy in the bones and muscles of the back allows galloping animals to conserve energy. The flexure of the back during running is less obvious in a pony than in other animals. The cheetah, for example, demonstrates a pronounced bend in the back when it sprints.

Environment determines energetic costs

The costs of locomotion differ greatly for swimmers, fliers, and runners, each moving at the optimal velocity

FIGURE 12.43 **Cost of locomotion in air, in water, and on land**

The costs of locomotion are lowest for swimmers and greatest for runners. Within each environment, the mass-specific costs of locomotion decline as animal size increases.

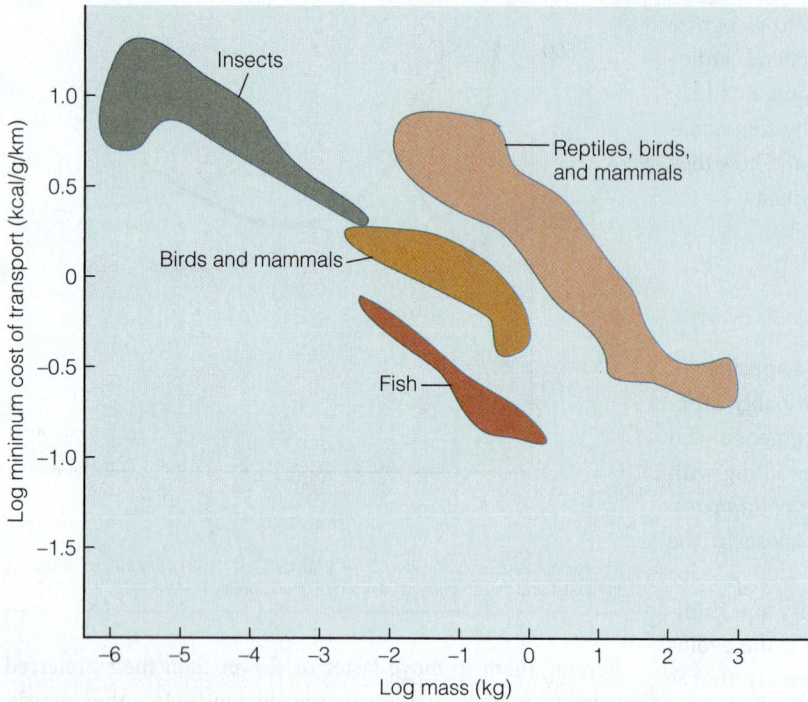

Figure source: Adapted from Tucker, V. A. (1975). The energetic cost of moving about. *American Scientist, 63*, 413–419.

(Figure 12.43). The costs are lowest for swimmers and highest for runners. To travel 1 km, a 1-kg fish would expend about 100 kcal, a 1-kg bird about 300 kcal, and a 1-kg mammal more than 1,000 kcal. Put another way, fliers, swimmers, and runners differ in their mass-specific costs: energy consumed per kilogram of body mass. The reasons for these differences relate to the economy of movement.

Let's start by considering how animals move on land. When an animal walks or runs, energy is required to fight the effect of gravity. When an animal moves one leg forward, its center of gravity drops. Muscular work is required to slow the descent. The center of gravity rises when the rear leg moves forward. More muscular work is required to lift the center of gravity. The cost of moving the center of gravity up and down increases the metabolic rate but does not increase the velocity of forward movement, thus runners have a higher cost of transport. In comparison to a walker, a bicycle rider is able to move much faster and cover the same distance using less energy. One reason is that the bicycle supports the center of gravity and more energy can be used to move the person forward. Similarly, flying is more efficient than walking because the effects of gravity are minimized by lift. Swimmers are the most efficient because they often approach neutral buoyancy, where body composition largely

negates the effects of gravity. Swimming animals require less energy than fliers to move at a given velocity, but fliers are able to move much faster. At high velocities the viscosity and drag of water are insurmountable obstacles for a swimmer.

The environment affects the relationship between velocity and metabolic rate (Figure 12.44). Most terrestrial animals moving with a single gait increase metabolic rate linearly with velocity. The power required to generate faster movement of legs is proportional to velocity. However, this simple linear relationship does not apply to fliers and swimmers.

Flying animals, including insects, bats, and birds, demonstrate more complex relationships between metabolic rate and velocity. Many birds show a U-shaped relationship. Below a critical velocity, some birds must expend additional energy to move wings fast enough to generate the lift required for flight. At the critical velocity, the birds can generate minimal power necessary to remain aloft. However, not all fliers show this relationship. A comparison of three bird species shows three different patterns. The magpie has a shallow curve, using similar power at each velocity. The cockatiel, in contrast, has a pronounced U-shaped curve. The curve for a dove is somewhat intermediate, but at most velocities the dove uses significantly more than the minimal power. The differences between species lie in properties such as wingbeat frequency, wing movement, and wing shape.

Swimming animals typically exhibit an exponential **power-velocity curve**, increasing sharply at higher velocities. Metabolism must provide the energy to support the mechanical power requirements for swimming muscles. The mechanical power required to move an object through water is equal to drag times velocity. For most swimming animals, drag is proportional to velocity squared (drag ∞ velocity^2) and therefore the power requirements for swimming are a function of velocity cubed. This relationship (metabolic rate ∞ velocity^3) accounts for the exponential curve observed experimentally.

Body size affects costs of locomotion

Another factor that emerges from Figure 12.43 is the impact of body size. In mass-specific terms, small animals use more energy to move than do large animals. Consider, for example, the relative costs incurred by three animals that move

FIGURE 12.44 **Work curves for swimmers, fliers, and runners**

The shape of relationship between work and velocity differs widely between animals, due to both the nature of the environment and the locomotor system of the animal. **(a)** Swimmers typically show an exponential relationship, as drag becomes increasingly important at higher velocities. **(b)** The nature of the curve in birds differs widely between species. Species with high drag, perhaps due to elaborate feathers, may expend more energy at most velocities than would a less decorated bird experiencing lower drag. **(c)** Most running animals show an increase in work with the velocity of movement.

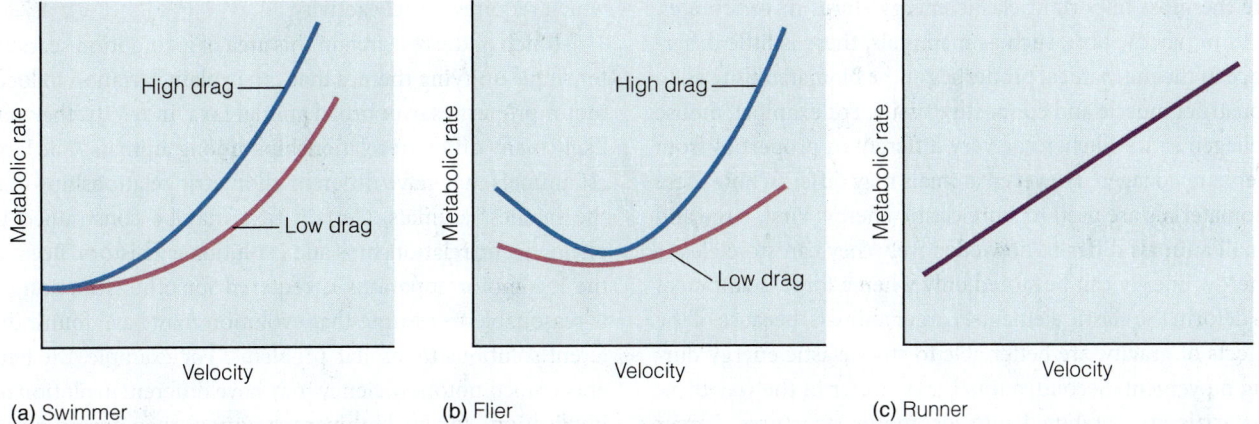

(a) Swimmer   (b) Flier   (c) Runner

Figure source: Data for (a): Pettersson, L. B., & Hedenstrom, A. (2000). Energetics, cost reduction, and functional consequences of fish morphology. *Proceedings of the Royal Society of London, Series B: Biological Sciences, 267*, 759–764. Data for (b): Tobalske, B. W., Hedrick, T. L., Dial, K. P., & Biewener, A. A. (2003). Comparative power curves in bird flight. *Nature, 421*, 363–366.

1 meter. A small insect expends about 1,000 J/kg, a mouse 30 J/kg, and a pony about 3 J/kg. Many confounding factors influence the relationship between body size and costs of transport.

The easiest way for a researcher to study the effects of body size is to examine muscle properties in the widest range of species possible. The famous "mouse to elephant curve" reflects the metabolic properties of mammals over many orders of magnitude. The problem with interpreting this relationship is that mice and elephants differ in many ways, so it is difficult to identify the mechanistic cause of the observed relationships. It is always easier to understand the basis of differences between animals when the species under study are closely related. Thus, researchers can study different sizes of a single species, or a clade of closely related species. However, these comparisons inevitably result in a much narrower range of body sizes. Despite these valid concerns about the importance of considering phylogenetic relatedness, there remains an overriding relationship between body size and cost of movement, one that is apparent across broad taxa and in terrestrial animals, swimmers, and fliers. No single overriding factor is responsible for the greater efficiency of movement in larger animals. Differences in every level of musculoskeletal function and animal locomotion can contribute to the origins of this nearly ubiquitous relationship between body size and the costs of locomotion.

The biomechanical constraints of moving through the environment differentially affect small and large animals.

Aquatic animals, in particular, must overcome the effects of drag. Drag increases with surface area, but power increases with muscle mass, which is reflected in body mass. The ratio of surface area to mass is greater in small animals than in large animals. Thus, as body size increases, the cost of overcoming drag increases but the capacity for power generation increases more. Thus, large animals use less of their muscle capacity to meet the cost of overcoming drag. The differences in drag provide an important insight into the effects of body mass on locomotor costs in aquatic animals, but drag has less significance for flying and terrestrial vertebrates.

As we discussed in Chapter 6, animals can produce muscles using building blocks that are grossly similar in structure but with important differences that influence musculoskeletal function. For example, myosin heavy chain isoforms differ in the relationship between force and ATPase activity. Because a fast-twitch muscle differs from a slow-twitch muscle in the economy of force development, the fiber type recruitment pattern influences the costs of locomotion. Small animals move their legs at a greater frequency than do larger animals. Consequently, a small animal has a greater reliance on fast-twitch fibers, which are less metabolically efficient. Furthermore, the fiber type profile of locomotor muscles differs in large and small mammals. For a given muscle, such as the soleus, large animals have a greater proportion of slow myosins. Thus, both fiber type profile and muscle recruitment patterns contribute to the greater efficiency of locomotion in larger animals.

Important differences also occur in the mechanical properties of muscles in relation to body size. The long bones of mammals, for example, are nearly isometric; the relative shape and size of the bones is similar among mammals of different sizes. However, other aspects of the musculoskeletal system can differ in important ways. Elastic storage energy is an important mechanism that animals can use to increase the efficiency of movement. Bones and connective tissues are the most important elastic energy stores in vertebrates. Within narrow taxa, such as mammals, there is little difference in the mechanical properties of the biomaterials used to construct muscle and connective tissue. For example, mouse collagen is not likely to be very different in properties from elephant collagen. However, animals may differ in how these biomaterials are used to store elastic energy. First, large and small animals differ in how effectively they can store elastic energy. Energy can be stored only when a force is sufficient to deform the elastic elements. Larger animals, because of the effects of gravity, are better able to store elastic energy during movement. Second, animals may differ in the way these materials are combined into locomotor structures. Larger kangaroos, for example, have relatively larger leg muscle tendons than do smaller kangaroos. These larger tendons allow them to store even greater proportions of energy during hopping. The same increase in tendon elastic storage capacity is seen in other mammals, although the effects of body mass are greater in kangaroos.

One of the reasons it is important to compare closely related animals is the potential for fundamental differences in the organization of the musculoskeletal system. Large mammals use less energy in maintaining posture because their appendages are located directly under the body. Appendages that extend more laterally have a lower mechanical advantage, requiring more muscle force to maintain posture. Furthermore, small animals remain in a crouched posture, which requires muscle activity.

Much of the research in this area of locomotion searches for single unifying themes that can explain variation in locomotor properties over broad animal taxa. In reality, there are likely many different relationships among animals. The largest animals may have different allometric relationships than the smallest animals. Certain taxa may be constrained by phylogenetic relationships and evolutionary history. Because the locomotor apparatus is required for other functions, it is reasonable to assume that evolution may have found different solutions to similar problems. For example, the benefits of locomotor efficiency may have different evolutionary implications for an herbivorous animal than for an active predator.

CONCEPT CHECK

16. Why do swimmers have lower costs of transport than fliers?
17. Why do horses switch gaits when velocity changes?

SUMMARY

Locomotion is made possible by using muscles in combination with other physiological processes, particularly nervous, circulatory, and respiratory systems. Movement is supported by energy metabolism, with different profiles of glycolysis and oxidative phosphorylation enabling specialization for different types of movement. Muscles work in combination with a skeleton to translate force development into movement.

The nature of movement depends on the way the animal interacts with the environment, and each environment exerts unique effects as a result of its biophysical properties, primarily density and viscosity. Mechanisms that contribute to buoyancy or lift reduce the energetic costs of animals moving in fluids (air, water). Terrestrial animals use robust musculoskeletal systems to overcome the effects of gravity. The metabolic costs of movement depend on the nature of the environment, velocity, body size, and mode of movement.

REVIEW QUESTIONS

1. **LO 1** Discuss the differences in muscle fiber types that suit them for different types of movement.

2. **LO 1** What is a locomotor module?

3. **LO 2** Why can oxygen consumption be used to measure energy expenditures in moving animals?

4. **LO 2** What are the trade-offs between using glycolysis and oxidative phosphorylation for supporting muscle activity?

5. **LO 3** What is myoglobin and how does it aid in locomotion?

6. **LO 3** How might locomotor muscles be affected by diet?

7. **LO 4** Discuss the role of the vertebrate skeleton in locomotion.

8. **LO 4** Which would generate more lift, the wing of a bird or the fin of a fish, if they were the same dimensions?

9. **LO 5** Why is it more difficult to move through water than air?

10. **LO 5** How do organisms compensate for the effects of gravity?

11. **LO 6** How does body size affect the costs of locomotion in animals?

12. **LO 6** What is a Reynolds number, and why does it matter to a moving animal?

SYNTHESIS QUESTIONS

1. What anatomical and functional features influence the efficiency of movement of oxygen from the erythrocyte to the muscle mitochondria?

2. Many animals alter their physiology in response to frequent bouts of activity. In humans, this is known as a training effect. How would you expect each physiological system to change in response to training?

3. Many marine fish swim into deep, cold water to pursue prey or avoid predators. How does cold temperature influence their ability to swim?

4. Predict the physiological properties of the locomotor system of (a) a cheetah and (b) a tree sloth.

5. Discuss the changes in cardiovascular and respiratory systems that support (a) high-intensity activity and (b) steady-state activity.

6. Discuss the recovery from high-intensity activity. Consider the physiological, physical, and chemical changes that accompany this type of activity and what must happen to prepare the animal for another bout of activity.

QUANTITATIVE QUESTIONS

1. What are the mathematical relationships between power, work, and force? Under what physiological conditions will each of these parameters approach zero?

2. Small-scale models of objects can be constructed to explore how the object moves through fluids. Engineers change the fluid movements to ensure that the Reynolds number remains constant despite the smaller dimensions of the object (L). If an object model is reduced to 1/1,000 of its actual size, how would you change the fluid properties to ensure that the Reynolds number remains constant?

3. Use the following assumptions to answer the subsequent questions about the energy metabolism of a hummingbird on its flight across the Gulf of Mexico:

   - A 2-g hummingbird puts on an additional 1 g of fat.
   - The hummingbird has a mass-specific metabolic rate of 40 ml of O_2 per hour per gram and a total metabolic rate of 120 ml of O_2 per hour per bird. For simplicity, assume that its total metabolic rate remains constant for the duration of the flight.

   - The lipid fuel is palmitate (molecular weight = 256 g per mol), although this ignores the contribution of glycerol from the triglyceride backbone.
   - Oxidation of 2 NADH consumes 1 O_2 and generates 6 ATP, and oxidation of 2 $FADH_2$ consumes 1 O_2 and generates 4 ATP.
   - Though you could translate between milliliters of O_2 and moles of O_2 using the universal gas law ($n = PV/RT$), assume that 1 mole of O_2 occupies 22.4 liters of volume.

   (a) What is the metabolic rate of a hummingbird in terms of ATP consumption in terms of moles of ATP per gram per hour?

   (b) If palmitate is the fuel that supports this activity, what is the rate of palmitate oxidation in terms of moles of palmitate per gram per hour? (Review Chapter 2 to remind yourself of the stoichiometries of NADH and FADH production in β-oxidation of fatty acids.)

   (c) How long would the 1 g of stored fat be able to support flight?

CHAPTER

13 Ion and Water Balance

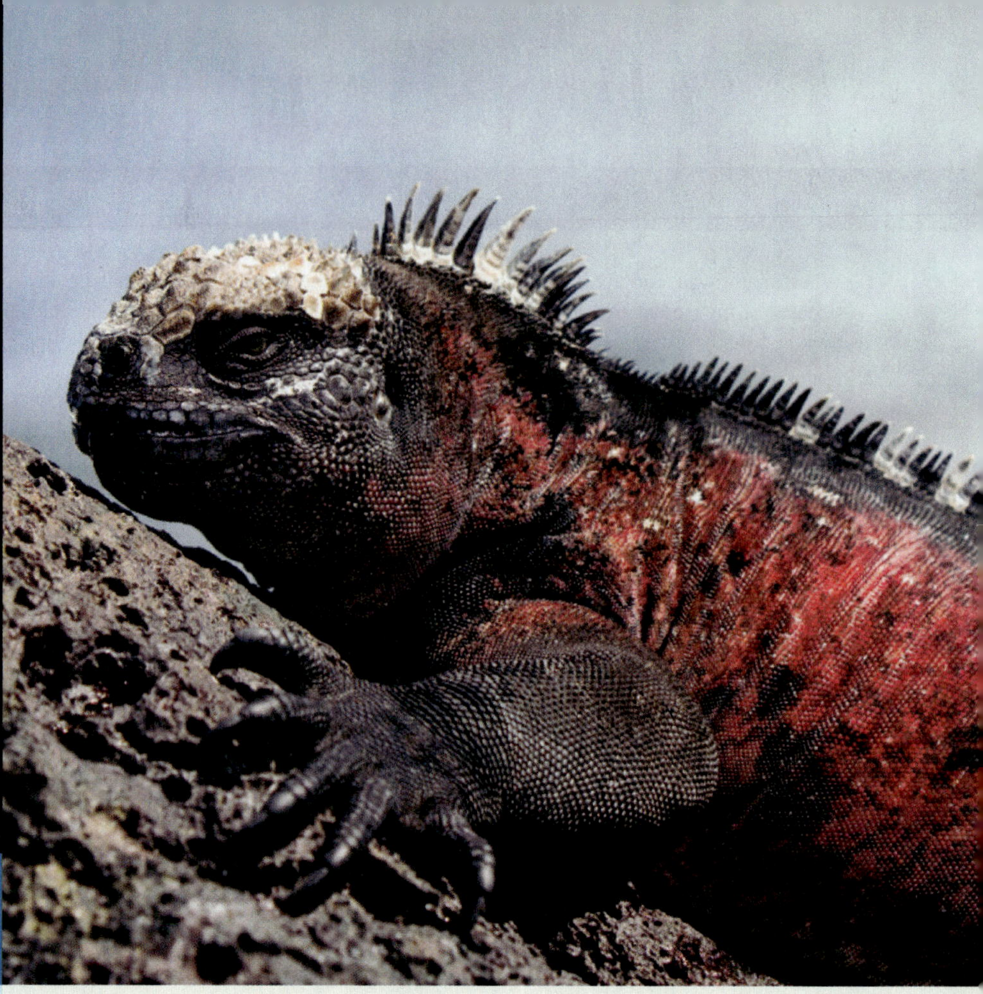

FIGURE 13.1 **A Galápagos marine iguana, *Amblyrhynchus cristatus***

Photo source: demarfa\Fotolia.

Learning Objectives

After reading this chapter, you should be able to:

1. Describe the relationships between external, extracellular, and intracellular compartments.
2. Compare and contrast the strategies used by animals for ionic and osmotic regulation, including osmoconforming, osmoregulating, ionoconforming, and ionoregulating.
3. Contrast the challenges of living in freshwater, seawater, and on land from the perspective of maintaining ion and water balance.
4. Explain the physiological impact of producing different nitrogenous wastes.
5. Demonstrate how the structure of the mammalian kidney relates to its function.
6. Outline the ways in which kidneys help to maintain ion balance.
7. Outline the ways in which kidneys help to maintain water balance.
8. Compare the tissues responsible for controlling excretion and the excretory strategies used by different groups of animals.

Galápagos marine iguanas (*Amblyrhynchus cristatus)*, such as the one shown in Figure 13.1, often have crusty white deposits of salt on top of their head. This salt crust is a by-product of the mechanisms that marine iguanas use to maintain ion and water balance. Although marine iguanas spend much of their time basking on the black lava rocks along the shores of the Galápagos, they feed underwater, diving to graze on dense beds of seaweed and other algae. The seaweed that they eat has a very high salt content, and marine iguanas are also likely to accidentally drink some seawater as they graze. Marine iguanas also passively gain ions from seawater. Iguana blood, like the blood of most vertebrates, has a lower osmolarity than that of seawater, so when a marine iguana dives into seawater, salts tend to diffuse into the body and water tends diffuse out (down their respective concentration gradients). Because iguanas are air breathers, water and ion exchange from seawater across the lungs is not an issue for them, and they have a thick scaly skin that minimizes water loss and ion gain by this route. However, the skin is not completely impermeable. Consequently, at least some ion movement likely occurs across the skin. Similarly, loss of water and gain of ions across areas where the skin is thin, like the nasal passages and the inside of the mouth, is inevitable. The gain of ions from food, from ingested seawater, and from diffusion across the skin poses a problem for the marine iguana: how can it excrete this salt load to maintain ion and water balance?

Like other reptiles, marine iguanas are not capable of producing urine that has a higher ion concentration than that of blood. Thus iguanas cannot use their kidneys to excrete the excess salt that they consume. Instead, marine iguanas have a specialized salt gland in their nose that produces an extremely concentrated salt solution. When startled, marine iguanas sneeze and expel this solution to deter or distract predators (much to the surprise of human visitors to the Galápagos!). Sometimes this solution lands on the iguana's head, where the water evaporates, leaving a salty crust.

In this chapter, you will learn how the Galápagos marine iguana and other animals use diverse osmoregulatory tissues including kidneys, salt glands, and gills to maintain ion and water balance. ■

LOOKING BACK 13

You may find it helpful to review Chapter 2, where we identified the factors that play an important role in the evolution of the sodium-potassium pump. In Chapter 3, we describe the basics of solutions, cellular transport, and the nature of epithelial tissues. Chapter 9 describes the role of the circulatory system in controlling blood volume and pressure, which relates to kidney function.

▮ OVERVIEW

Animals must maintain appropriate levels of solutes and water in their tissues in order to function. The solution inside a cell (intracellular fluid) is controlled to maintain a satisfactory environment for macromolecules. In Chapter 3, we discussed how individual cells regulate their ion and water balance, but many animals also control the ion and water composition of extracellular fluids. Extracellular fluids are the fluids found outside of cells, but within the confines of the animal, such as plasma, lymph, hemolymph, interstitial fluid, and coelomic fluid. The composition of the extracellular fluids is important because it determines electrochemical gradients across the cell's plasma membrane. Epithelial tissues separate the internal fluids from the outside world (Figure 13.2). Animals exchange water and ions with their external environment across these epithelia.

This chapter explores the diverse mechanisms used by animals to control the nature of their extracellular fluids through three intertwined homeostatic processes:

- *Osmotic regulation* is the control of tissue osmotic pressure, which determines the driving force for the movement of water across biological membranes. Animals and cells cannot actively pump water. Osmotic regulation requires the movement of solutes across membranes, altering osmotic gradients.

- *Ionic regulation* is the control of the ionic composition of body fluids. In this chapter we focus on the ions that are important solutes, and therefore relevant to the osmoregulatory strategies. In Chapter 14: Digestion and Energy Metabolism, we discuss some of the pathways by which animals obtain the ions that are important in biosynthesis—trace elements and micronutrients.

- *Nitrogen excretion* is the pathway by which animals excrete ammonia, the toxic nitrogenous end product of protein catabolism. The process for expelling ammonia, or metabolic alternatives such as urea and **uric acid**, is linked to the control of osmotic and ionic homeostasis. The tissues of the excretory system are responsible for collecting nitrogenous waste and expelling it into the environment.

FIGURE 13.2 Tissues as osmotic and ionic barriers

Epithelial tissues separate internal fluid compartments from the external world. In the case of an aquatic animal, such as a mudpuppy, the external (apical) side of the epithelial cell layer interacts directly with the external water, though it can secrete a protective layer of mucus that also traps a layer of water underneath. Intercellular junctions connect epithelial cells together to form a barrier between external and internal fluids. On the internal (basolateral) side of the epithelium, cells are bathed in interstitial fluid trapped between cells. The tissue is fed by capillaries, with vascular endothelial cells separating interstitial fluid from plasma.

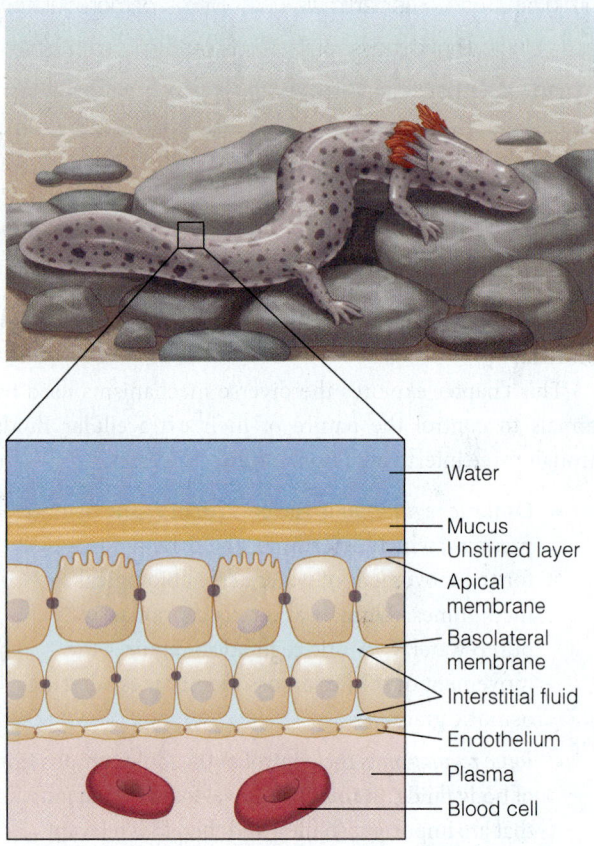

- Water
- Mucus
- Unstirred layer
- Apical membrane
- Basolateral membrane
- Interstitial fluid
- Endothelium
- Plasma
- Blood cell

IONIC AND OSMOTIC REGULATION

Ion and water balance is essential to the function of each physiological system, and every animal has mechanisms to maintain osmotic and ionic properties of their tissues within tolerable ranges. Where animals differ is in (1) the specific tissues that carry the burden of ionic and osmotic balance and (2) the extent to which they tolerate changes in ion and water homeostasis in the extracellular fluids. Though there is considerable diversity in ionic and osmotic regulation between animals, there are unifying themes that have a foundation in the basic chemical, biochemical, and cellular properties. You are encouraged to review the material in Chapter 3 that describes in more detail the following physiochemical properties of solutes and solutions important in osmoregulation and ionoregulation. These properties include:

- Water is the solvent that is used to dissolve the ions and metabolites needed to sustain cells. Changes in the concentration of ions have the potential to affect the structure of macromolecules, which has direct effects on macromolecular function. The concentration of an *individual* solute, such as Na^+, is measured as *molarity* (moles per liter water). The concentration of the *collection* of solutes is measured as *osmolarity*. In comparing two solutions, that with the lower osmolarity is *hypoosmotic*, and that with the higher osmolarity is *hyperosmotic*.

- Cells change volume in response to osmotic gradients across the cell membrane. Cells are able to use ion pumps to transport solutes in or out of the cell to govern electrochemical gradients, but they cannot avoid osmotic equilibrium. A solution that causes a cell to swell is *hypotonic*; a solution that shrinks a cell is *hypertonic*. Changes in cell volume can damage cells directly, sometimes causing cell death. Cell shrinkage can pull cells apart, disrupting the integrity of tissues. Cell swelling can damage tissues and occlude capillaries, altering blood flow through the tissue.

- *Epithelial tissues* form the barrier between the animal and the environment. The nature of the interactions between epithelial cells governs which types of molecules can pass, either between cells (*paracellular transport*) or across cells (*transcellular transport*). Regulation of the transporters determines which ions move where, and the resultant movement of water. Transport epithelia share four basic features that reflect their specialization for transport of ions: high surface area, abundant mitochondria, cell-to-cell interactions, and asymmetrical transporter distribution.

These basic features are important in all animals, but the way an individual animal regulates its internal ionic and osmotic conditions depends upon how evolution has shaped its anatomical features and the nature of the environment.

Individual cells within the body are bathed in extracellular fluid and they reach osmotic equilibrium with this extracellular fluid. The animal, therefore, can help mediate cell volume regulation by controlling the nature of the extracellular fluid that surrounds the cells. Animals determine the composition of their extracellular fluids by regulating net movement, or *flux*, of ions and water across the epithelial tissues that form the barrier between inside and outside. The outer body surface (skin, cuticle), respiratory tissues, and digestive tract each play an active role in control of ion and water movement.

Vertebrates and most invertebrates possess specialized cells or tissues that carry most of the burden of ion and water balance. Vertebrates possess kidneys composed of epithelial tissues that determine the excretion of ions and water. Invertebrates possess their own analogs of kidneys such as the protonephridia and metanephridia of simple invertebrates and the Malpighian tubules of insects. Many lineages possess **extrarenal** ("beyond kidney") tissues that perform essential functions in ion and water balance such as the renal glands of sharks, the salt glands of birds and reptiles, and the gills of fish. Later in this chapter we will discuss the roles of kidneys and extrarenal tissues, but first we will explore the ways in which the environment imposes challenges to ion and water balance.

Strategies for Ionic and Osmotic Regulation

You have probably heard it said that our blood is similar to seawater in its composition. Both are dominated by Na^+ and Cl^- ions, but the actual concentrations of ions are quite different. Table 13.1 compares the osmolarity and ion levels of mammalian blood to that of freshwater, seawater, and salt lakes. The difference between these concentrations means that when an animal with a blood ion composition similar to that of a mammal is immersed in these other fluids, there is a tendency for ions and water to move to equilibrate concentrations. Consider the relative concentrations when a bony fish, which has plasma concentrations similar to that of a mammal, is placed in different aquatic environments. When the fish is in freshwater, it will tend to lose ions and gain water across the body surface. In seawater, that same fish would tend to gain ions and lose water. Without some form of compensation, a fish in freshwater would bloat from uncontrolled uptake of water, and shrivel in seawater as water is lost to the environment. To compensate for these passive

movements of ions and water, fish expend energy to pump ions across epithelial tissues in or out of the animal in an effort to control internal osmolarity and ion profiles.

Terrestrial animals face a near constant pressure of water loss across the body surface and respiratory system. Ions and water must be obtained from the diet, and consequently the digestive tract plays a central role in ion and water balance. Later in this section we will consider the myriad adaptations terrestrial animals use to obtain and retain water, permitting them to inhabit dehydrating environments.

Though the ionic and osmotic characteristics of aquatic and terrestrial environments are diverse, some animal species have gained a foothold in all but the most toxic. The extent to which a particular ionic or osmotic gradient constitutes a physiological burden depends on the ionoregulatory and osmoregulatory strategies of the animal.

Animals may be regulators or conformers

Ionoregulatory and osmoregulatory strategies of animals can be distinguished by (1) the differences between extracellular fluids and external conditions and (2) the extent to which extracellular fluids change when external conditions change. *Conformers* have internal conditions that are similar to the external conditions, even when the external conditions change. *Regulators* defend a nearly constant internal state that is distinct from the external conditions.

An **ionoconformer** exerts little control over the solute profile within its extracellular space. These animals usually live in seawater. Their extracellular fluids resemble seawater in terms of the concentrations of the major cations (Na^+, Ca^{2+}, and Mg^{2+}) and anions (Cl^- and SO_4^{2+}). In contrast to ionoconformers, an **ionoregulator** controls the levels of most of the ions in extracellular fluids, employing a combination of ion absorption and excretion strategies. Regulating the ionic profile of extracellular fluid compartments eases the burden of ionic regulation placed on individual cells.

Fluid	Osmolarity (mOsM)	Ion Concentrations (mM)					
		Monovalent			Divalent		
		Cations		Anions	Cations		Anions
		Na^+	K^+	Cl^-	Ca^{2+}	Mg^{2+}	SO_4^{2-}
Mammalian blood	300	140	4	100	5	2	1
Seawater	1,000	470	10	540	10	53	28
Freshwater	< 5	0.2–0.7	0.03–0.1	0.2–0.7	0.2–2.0	0.05–0.4	0.1–1.0
Salt lakes	50–3000	4–1400	1–10	2–100	3–20	20–150	20–1,200

Table 13.1   Properties of mammalian fluids and aquatic environments

FIGURE 13.3   Osmoregulatory strategies and salinity tolerance

Osmotic strategies can be distinguished by three factors: **(1)** the osmotic gradients between the animal and the water, **(2)** the degree to which internal osmolarity changes in relation to a changing external osmolarity, and **(3)** the degree of tolerance of an osmotic challenge. The four osmotic strategies depicted in this figure can be distinguished by following the internal osmolarity of four animals living in full-strength seawater, then exposed to a decreasing osmolarity until death.

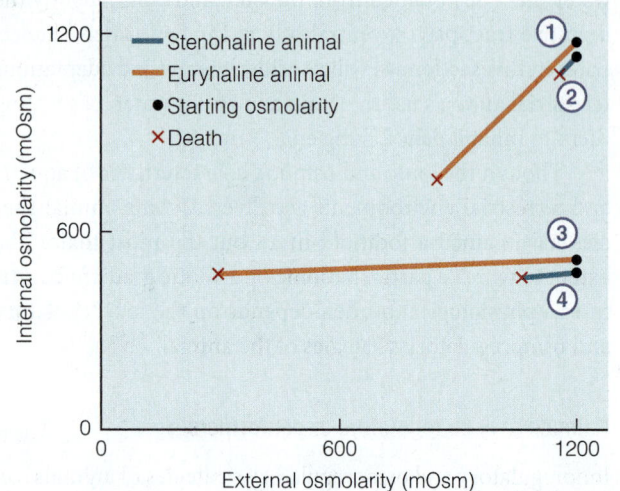

1. Euryhaline osmoconformer allows osmolarity to decrease in parallel with water until death.

2. Stenohaline osmoconformer dies after very modest osmotic disruption.

3. Euryhaline osmoregulator defends a nearly constant internal state but eventually succumbs.

4. Stenohaline osmoregulator can defend its internal osmolarity over a narrow range of external osmolarities.

The internal osmolarity of an **osmoconformer** nears that of the external environment; if external osmotic conditions change, internal osmolarity changes in parallel. An osmoconformer may control the *profile* of extracellular solutes, but the environment imposes the osmolarity. An **osmoregulator** maintains internal osmolarity within a narrow range regardless of the external environment. Depending on the conditions, the animal could have an osmolarity higher or lower than the surrounding water.

We also classify animals according to their ability to tolerate changes in external osmolarity. **Stenohaline** animals can tolerate only a narrow range of salt concentrations, whereas *euryhaline* animals can tolerate widely variant osmolarities. There is no predetermined relationship between the strategy (osmoconforming versus osmoregulating) and the degree of tolerance (euryhaline versus stenohaline) (Figure 13.3). For example, intertidal mollusks are euryhaline osmoconformers, whereas intertidal fish are euryhaline osmoregulators.

The environment provides water in many forms

All animals require a source of water, though some animals have a harder time finding it than others. Freshwater osmoregulators have no problem obtaining the water they need, and in fact must cope with excessive water uptake. Marine osmoregulators must deal with the ion loads that accompany the water they consume. Terrestrial animals consume much of their water in the diet, and generally must find ways to minimize water loss. A few animals have unusual physiological adaptations that allow them to survive various degrees of water deprivation, including dehydration (discussed later in Box 13.1: Challenges to Homeostasis: Life Without Water).

The diet itself is a mixture of water and solutes in various chemical forms. Aquatic animals ingest some liquid water while eating, and they must manage the resulting osmotic and ionic consequences. Many aquatic animals expel the liquid before it enters the gastrointestinal tract. Filter-feeding whales, such as the baleen whale, gulp large volumes of seawater laden with krill, and then use the tongue to compress the meal against the baleen, expelling excess seawater. Many marine animals possess mechanisms that enable them to expel excess salt, allowing them to drink seawater to obtain water. For example, many marine reptiles and birds can drink seawater because they possess specialized salt-secreting glands, discussed in the chapter-opening essay. Without a capacity to rid its body of salt, an animal drinking seawater will become progressively more dehydrated.

Plant and animal tissues are important sources of **dietary water** for animals (see Table 13.2). This water is preformed in the food, either trapped within the solid food or as a liquid component of the meal. An animal cannot absorb all of the dietary water, because it must retain some water to give the **feces** the appropriate consistency for transit through the gastrointestinal tract. Once ingested, many macromolecules undergo hydrolysis as part of the digestive process. Hydrolysis—literally "water splitting"—consumes a water molecule to break a chemical bond. After this minor investment of water early in digestion, subsequent metabolic processes generate water as a result of oxidative phosphorylation (see Figure 3.34); this water is known as **metabolic water**.

Table 13.2 Water and solute content of food	
Nutrient	**Water Content (% of Wet Weight)**
Animal and plant fluids	
Sap and nectar	90–100%
Blood	95%
Milk (most mammals)	87%
Milk (marine mammals)	40%
Fruits and vegetation	80–95%
Plant and animal tissues	
Muscle and animal tissues	50–70%
Seeds and grains	< 10%

Each of the major macromolecules produces about the same amount of metabolic water, expressed per unit of metabolic energy. Based on the same 100 kilocalories of metabolizable energy, carbohydrate produces 15 milliliters of water; protein, 10.5 milliliters of water; and fat, 11.1 milliliters. For an average human, about 10 percent of daily water requirements come from metabolic water production, 60 percent from drinking, and 30 percent from water trapped in solid foods. Many desert animals drink no fluids, and instead obtain their water entirely from solid foods and metabolic water.

Solutes can be classified as perturbing, compatible, or counteracting

In Chapter 3 we introduced the chemistry of solutes and solvents in biological systems. The total concentration of solutes imparts an osmolarity and determines the osmotic gradient across biological membranes, and thereby the direction and magnitude of water movement. In addition to these general osmotic effects of solutes, there are solute-specific effects. Three classes of solutes are distinguished by their effects on the structure and function of macromolecules, such as enzymes (Figure 13.4). *Perturbing solutes* disrupt macromolecular function at normal concentrations found within the animal. These include the inorganic ions found in body fluids, primarily Na^+, K^+, Cl^-, and SO_4^{2+}, as well as some organic solutes, such as charged amino acids (e.g., arginine). **Compatible solutes** have little effect on macromolecular function and can accumulate to high concentration without deleterious effects on cellular processes. The most common compatible solutes in body fluids are polyols (trehalose, glycerol, and glucose) and uncharged amino acids, including several of the amino acids (alanine, glycine, serine, and proline) as well as other amino acids (alanine and taurine). **Counteracting solutes** are deleterious when used on

FIGURE 13.4 Perturbing, compatible, and counteracting solutes

Each type of solute exerts characteristic effects on macromolecular structure and function, such as enzyme kinetics (V_{max} or K_m). **(a)** A perturbing solute is shown to increase the K_m value of a hypothetical enzyme, whereas a compatible solute at the same concentration has no effect on K_m. **(b)** Each counteracting solute has perturbing effects when present alone, but when both are present, the effects are offset. Urea is shown to increase K_m and TMAO decreases K_m, but the combination of the two has no effect.

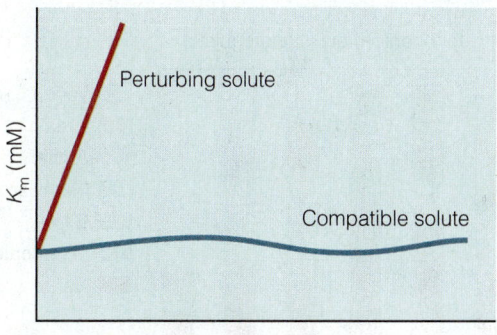

(a) Perturbing and compatible solutes

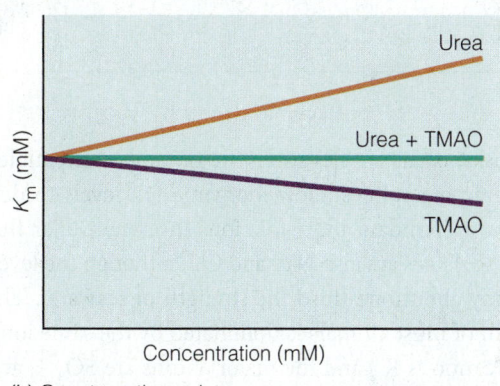

(b) Counteracting solutes

their own, but can be employed in combinations where the deleterious effects of one solute counteract the deleterious effects of the other. For example, urea disrupts hydrophobic interactions and methylamines strengthen hydrophobic interactions. A combination of urea and methylamines allows the effects of one solute to negate the effects of the other solute. The most common methylamines employed by animals are trimethylamine oxide (TMAO), betaine, and sarcosine.

Figure 13.5 summarizes the solute composition of selected animals to illustrate the relative importance of the various solutes in different species and cellular compartments. The extracellular space of most animals is dominated by Na^+ and Cl^-. Marine ionoconformers possess extracellular concentrations of these ions, as well as Mg^{2+} and Ca^{2+}, close to seawater levels. In osmoconforming ionoregulators

FIGURE 13.5 Organic and inorganic solutes in extracellular fluid of animals

Seawater is mainly Na^+ and Cl^-, with lower levels of other ions such as K^+, Mg^{2+}, and Ca^{2+}. Ionoconformers have high levels of Na^+ and Cl^-, whereas the levels of these ions are lower in ionoregulators. Osmoconformers have the same osmolarity as seawater but maintain an inorganic ion profile much like that of an osmoregulator. The remainder of the osmolarity is due to organic solutes, such as urea, amino acids, and methylamines.

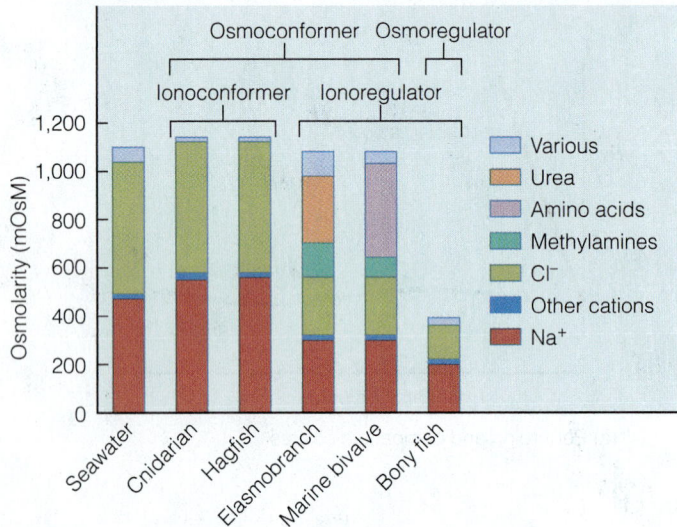

Evolution, Environment, and Osmoregulation

Much of the diversity in the physiology of ion and water balance reflects the evolution of animal lineages. Milestones in early metazoan evolution, such as the formation of tissue layers, changed the ways that ion and water balance could be regulated. As well, animals were able to invade new environmental niches only after they evolved the capacity to control internal conditions in the face of changes in external osmolarity. As we compare the ways extant animals cope with ionic and osmotic challenges in seawater, freshwater, and on land, recognize that different strategies may arise because of distinct evolutionary histories. An understanding of the evolutionary origins of animal lineages gives insight into why animals living in similar environments have completely different approaches to ion and water balance. Because animals evolved in the sea, we will begin our discussion by surveying the osmoregulatory strategies of marine animals.

Marine invertebrates are osmoconformers

Sponges and cnidarians, the simplest of animals, are unable to maintain a distinct extracellular compartment, and therefore the concepts of osmoregulation aren't really applicable. Upon the evolution of three tissue layers, animals created a compartment separated from the external water. Most of the extant invertebrate taxa arose in seawater, and the ancestral state for most lineages included a strategy of osmoconforming.

In osmoconforming marine invertebrates, the internal fluids—both extracellular and intracellular fluids—have an osmolarity that approaches that of seawater. Many of the smallest species are difficult to study because they do not have enough extracellular fluid to collect and analyze. The larger size of polychaete worms (Annelida) has permitted their use as models for studying invertebrate osmotic and ionic regulation. The polychaete worm *Nereis* lives on the sea bottom, but its range extends into intertidal zones where salinity can change as a result of evaporation and freshwater runoff. These animals can tolerate both hypoosmotic and hyperosmotic stress. In each case, they osmoconform, with their coelomic fluid experiencing changes in inorganic salts that parallel seawater. In terms of their extracellular fluids, such invertebrates are also ionoconformers.

Crustaceans show diverse osmotic strategies, but most are marine osmoconforming ionoconformers. The Na^+ and Cl^- concentrations of the extracellular fluid, hemolymph, are nearly identical to the surrounding seawater. Most of these species are also stenohaline, losing ions and dying quickly when moved into freshwater. However, there are euryhaline species, such as the crab *Cancer maenas*, as well as freshwater species, such as the crayfish. These euryhaline and freshwater crustaceans can survive by resisting the loss of ions and movement of water, and are considered osmoregulators and

(mollusks, sharks), elevations in organic compatible and counteracting solutes allow inorganic ion levels to decline. The most abundant inorganic ions in extracellular fluid of osmoregulators are also Na^+ and Cl^-, although the levels are generally about one-third the strength of seawater. The cytoplasm of most animals is dominated by the same ions; the major cation is K^+ and the major anions are SO_4^{2+}, acetate, and Cl^-. Organic solutes occur in all animals but are most abundant in marine osmoconformers. Cartilaginous fish rely on the counteracting solutes: urea and various methylamines such as TMAO, sarcosine, and betaine. Invertebrates possess high concentrations of compatible solutes, mainly amino acids such as alanine, taurine, and proline. These organic solutes confer more than half the osmolarity in marine osmoconformers. When osmolarity changes, the concentrations of organic solutes often change disproportionately, allowing ionic solutes to remain relatively constant.

CONCEPT CHECK

1. What are the main differences in osmotic and ionic composition of freshwater and seawater?
2. What is the difference between perturbing, compatible, and counteracting solutes?
3. What are the different fluid compartments in an animal and how do they communicate?

ionoregulators. The variation within crustaceans is attributed in large part to the utility of the exoskeleton covering the entire body surface. By evolving differences in the permeability of this surface, crustaceans have been able to invade both freshwater and terrestrial biotopes.

A different strategy is shown by mollusks. Though like other invertebrates they are osmoconformers, they are able to remodel their extracellular fluids, accumulating organic compatible solutes, such as free amino acids, to permit the reduction of inorganic perturbing solutes, such as Na^+ and Cl^-. When an intertidal mussel experiences a change in external osmolarity, it osmoconforms, but unlike other invertebrates it changes osmolarity by altering the levels of the organic compatible solutes, particularly free amino acids.

Many of these invertebrate lineages have individual species that have successfully invaded freshwater. For example, there are freshwater mollusks (clams, snails), annelids (leeches), and arthropods (crayfish). Most live their entire life in freshwater, but in the case of insects, the aquatic phase may be restricted to juveniles. In each case, these animals are exceptions in their lineages, being able to survive in ion-poor freshwater as osmoregulators and ionoregulators. They may have mechanisms to prevent water influx, such as an impermeable body surface, or enhanced water excretion. They are also able to efficiently extract ions from freshwater via transport or digestive epithelia.

Most ancient fish are osmoconformers

Major changes in osmoregulation and ionoregulation occurred in the evolution of the ancestors of vertebrates. Like many simple marine invertebrates, the earliest chordates were marine organisms that had little control over the nature of their extracellular fluid composition. Almost 400 mya (million years ago), there were many lineages of marine animals that you might call fish. The modern descendants are remarkably diverse despite being lumped into the category "ancient fish." Modern hagfish, lamprey, and the chondrichthians (rays and sharks) each arose from different agnathan ancestors and their physiological divergence reflects these ancestries being separated for about 400 million years. Modern fish likely arose from still another agnathan ancestor, which accounts for the differences we will discuss in a subsequent section.

The most ancient of these extant fish is the hagfish, though its phylogenetic relationship with other primitive vertebrates remains contentious. The extracellular fluid of the hagfish is similar to seawater in osmolarity, and tracks external osmolarity when changes in salinity arise. The hagfish is a good example of an osmoconformer. Hagfish blood also resembles seawater in monovalent ion (Na^+, Cl^-) concentration, but these animals regulate the levels of divalent ions, including Ca^{2+}, Mg^{2+}, and SO_4^{2-}. Thus, hagfish are considered ionoregulators because of their capacity to maintain reduced levels of divalent cations. Lamprey, an agnathan fish only distantly related to hagfish, is able to control both its internal osmolarity and ionic profile of its extracellular fluids; lamprey is an osmoregulator and an ionoregulator. How lamprey gained this capacity remains unknown, but all species have a freshwater life stage. When a lamprey returns to the sea, it defends a nearly constant internal osmolarity.

Chondrichthians are generally considered osmoconformers because their internal osmolarity changes in parallel with external osmolarity. For example, a euryhaline marine skate moving into brackish estuaries experiences a reduction in plasma osmolarity as water moves into its tissues. However, at any salinity, chondrichthians maintain their extracellular fluids a bit hyperosmotic to the seawater, suggesting a degree of active hyperosmotic regulation. Whether they should be considered osmoconformers or osmoregulators is debatable, but cartilaginous fish are certainly ionoregulators. Their extracellular fluid possesses Na^+ and Cl^- at levels about half that of seawater. Organic solutes increase extracellular fluid osmolarity to nearly match that of seawater. Chondrichthians use the counteracting solute pairs of urea and methylamines, such as TMAO. When chondrichthians move into **brackish water**, the decline in extracellular fluid osmolarity is due almost entirely to loss of the organic solutes, preserving nearly constant ionic composition.

There are some species of chondrichthians that live in freshwater in the Amazon and southeast Asia. These animals have very low levels of organic solutes, and their inorganic ion profile is very similar to bony fish, which we discuss in the next section. These stingrays have lost the ability to use urea as a major solute. When faced with increased salinity, the Amazonian stingray, *Potamotrygon motoro*, increases synthesis of free amino acids to elevate its extracellular osmolarity.

Bony fish are ionoregulators and osmoregulators

Bony fish are thought to have arisen from an agnathan ancestor that had invaded freshwater. This ancestor, like the extant lamprey, needed a greater capacity for ionic control to survive in ion-poor water. Once the lineage committed to tighter osmotic and ionic regulation, it changed how derived bony fish evolved in the face of new osmotic niches. Thus, freshwater and marine bony fish are osmoregulators and ionoregulators because their ancestors invaded freshwater before returning to the sea. A bony fish in salt water will tend to gain ions and lose water across its gills, gut, and skin. Exchange of water and ions across the gills is a particular challenge because the epithelium of the gill must be thin and have a high surface area to allow for efficient gas exchange. To compensate for the loss of water across the gills and other body surfaces, these fish drink seawater. Unfortunately, this strategy only increases their problem of ion gain from the environment. In seawater, bony fish use ion pumps to expel Na^+ and Cl^- across the gills (Figure 13.6a). Freshwater bony fish face the opposite challenge. They lose ions and gain

FIGURE 13.6 **Osmoregulatory strategies of bony fish in (a) seawater and (b) freshwater**

Solid arrows show fluxes that are detrimental because they create an osmoregulatory burden. Dashed arrows identify fluxes that are beneficial, helping the animal maintain ionic and osmotic balance.

(a) Fish in seawater

(b) Fish in freshwater

Photo source: (a) federicocandonifoto/Fotolia; (b) Robert La Salle/Aqua-Photo/Alamy.

water across the gills and skin. They actively take up Na$^+$ and Cl$^-$ across the gills and digestive tract, and get rid of excess water through their kidneys by excreting copious amounts of dilute urine (Figure 13.6b).

The ability to control internal ionic and osmotic properties was essential to the diversification of freshwater bony fish, which now occupy almost every aquatic and semiaquatic niche on the planet, often tolerating inhospitable ionic and osmotic conditions, environments with very high or low pH, extremes in salinity, and even periods of dehydration. For instance, cichlids live in the alkaline waters of Lake Magadi (pH 10) and tambaqui thrive in acidic waters of the Amazon (pH 3.5). Fish can be found in waters of varying salinity, from the hypersaline salt marshes and inland seas, through the oscillating salinity of the intertidal zone, to lakes and rivers that are nearly devoid of essential ions. A few species of fish even survive out of the water. Some tropical catfish walk over land from one temporary pool to another. Other fish enter a period of dormancy, such as the lungfish that bury themselves underground in a mucus cocoon.

Some fish move between freshwater and seawater

There are many examples of marine fish that venture into more dilute estuaries to feed or escape predators. With notable exceptions, such as some skates, these euryhaline animals are osmoregulators, resisting the osmotic stress they encounter on their short-term excursions.

The adaptations that permit animals to spend time in different salinities are impressive, but it is perhaps more remarkable to consider that some animals are **diadromous**, spending part of their lives in freshwater and part of their lives in seawater. There are two types of diadromous strategies: anadromous and catadromous. Salmon and sea lamprey are **anadromous**, living their adult life in the ocean, then migrating to freshwater to reproduce. Conversely, eels are **catadromous**, spend their adulthood in freshwater before migrating to the sea to breed. When the young eels approach adulthood, they migrate back to freshwater. In each case, these fish prepare for their migrations by preadapting to the new osmotic environments. As we will discuss in more detail in a later section, salmon extensively remodel their gill ultrastructure, changing it from a tissue that extracts ions from freshwater into a tissue that extrudes ions into seawater. Though the osmolarity of extracellular fluids of diadromous fish changes somewhat with the movement between freshwater and seawater, the variation is much less than is seen in osmoconformers experiencing the same type of environmental change.

Terrestriality evolved multiple times in animals

The ability to control internal osmolarity independent of external conditions was essential for the success of the animal lineages that invaded land. There were four main, independent invasions of land, where major lineages made a transition from aquatic to terrestrial habitats. The earliest terrestrial invaders were arthropods (Figure 13.7). More than 420 mya, separate arthropod ancestors gave rise to myriapods (centipedes and millipedes), insects, and spiders.

FIGURE 13.7 Evolution of terrestrial arthropods

Terrestrial life arose independently at least three times in arthropods, each time from early crustaceans (protocrustaceans). The unlabeled lines are each lineages of modern crustaceans.

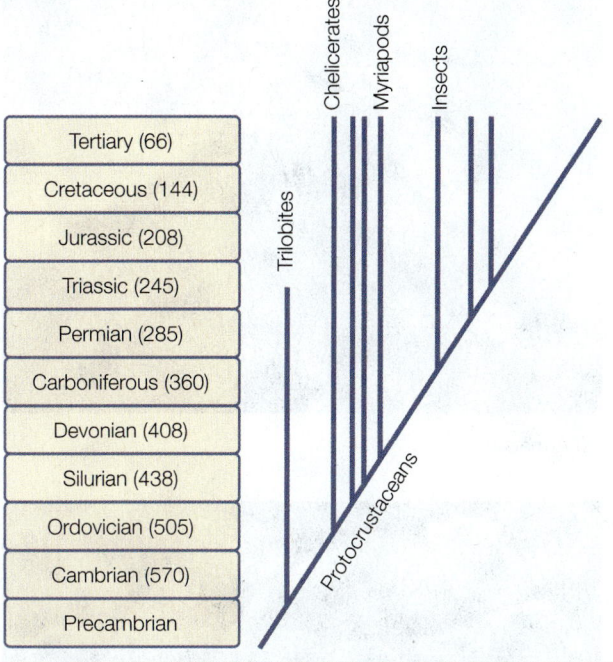

Tertiary (66)	
Cretaceous (144)	
Jurassic (208)	
Triassic (245)	
Permian (285)	
Carboniferous (360)	
Devonian (408)	
Silurian (438)	
Ordovician (505)	
Cambrian (570)	
Precambrian	

Around 400 mya, the fourth invasion occurred when the first amphibian vertebrates ventured onto land. A terrestrial existence puts animals at risk for desiccation, and species that successfully invaded land demonstrate evolutionary adaptations that reduce water loss. For one thing, they need a body surface more resistant to desiccation. No longer able to excrete metabolic wastes directly into the water, they also need an alternative way to dispose of nitrogenous waste. Ion balance, water balance, nitrogen excretion, and pH balance are interdependent processes that must be regulated (and evolve) in parallel to ensure homeostasis. Remarkably, each of these lineages found different solutions to the challenges of a terrestrial existence.

The importance of the homeostatic mechanisms is evident when observing the transitions experienced in amphibious animals as they move from aquatic to terrestrial habitats. For example, amphibians spend early life stages in freshwater, living as ionoregulators. The aquatic larvae (tadpoles) excrete water via their kidney, and obtain ions from both the diet and across the gills. Part of metamorphosis is remodeling the body surface to become less permeable to ions and water, and the kidney transitions from water excretion to water retention.

In most cases, organisms that are successful in occupying terrestrial niches have an ability to limit the loss of water from the body. The first line of defense is the body covering. Whether considering invertebrates or vertebrates, terrestrial animals produce a body surface or integument that resists the passive loss of water.

The integument is an osmotic barrier

Animals reduce the flux of water across the body surface by limiting the water permeability of the epithelial tissues, both internal and external. Some animals reduce this permeability by controlling the number of aquaporin proteins in the plasma membrane. Each aquaporin permits more than a billion water molecules to pass through each second. An epithelial cell with aquaporins may be 100-fold more permeable to water than a cell without aquaporins. The aquaporin levels in the plasma membrane depend on the expression of aquaporin genes and on pathways of intracellular traffic that control the interchange of aquaporins between storage vesicles and the plasma membrane.

Some animals reduce water loss by covering external surfaces with a thick layer of hydrophobic molecules. Mucus—an extracellular secretion of mucopolysaccharides, lipids, and proteins—is an example of such a hydrophobic barrier. Mucus layers on the surface of the lung and gastrointestinal tract reduce water loss across these epithelia. Many semiaquatic animals, such as frogs, use mucus to prevent water loss and keep the skin hydrated. The thick mucus layer of a hibernating lungfish dries to form a water-impermeable cocoon that prevents the animal from dehydrating during the many months of **estivation**. Surface mucus also reduces osmoregulatory costs by trapping a layer of water between the animal and the environment. This layer of water is a microcompartment that acts as an osmotic and ionic buffer zone.

Land animals use more elaborate adaptations in epithelial structure to prevent water loss across the skin. The **keratinocytes** of the skin of terrestrial amphibians and amniotes secrete proteins and modified lipids to form a dense, hydrophobic extracellular matrix. The amniotes, but not the amphibians, possess an additional layer on top of the keratinocytes. This layer, called the **stratum corneum**, is composed of keratinocytes that have differentiated to form another type of cell—a **corneocyte**. During the differentiation process, the cells produce thick bundles of the protein keratin, an intermediate filament of the cytoskeleton. These bundles are, in turn, interconnected by other proteins, such as keratohyalin. The cell then produces a complex layer of proteins, called the *cornified envelope*, which eventually replaces the corneocyte plasma membrane. During cornification, the corneocyte undergoes programmed cell death, and what remains is the keratin network surrounded by the cornified envelope. Extracellular matrix proteins connect these cellular remnants to stacks of lipid molecules called the lamellar membrane.

FIGURE 13.8   **Stratum corneum structure**

The stratum corneum is the thickened external layer of modified epithelium found in mammals. Keratinocytes differentiate into corneocytes, producing a waterproof layer composed of a complex network of intracellular and extracellular proteins, augmented by lipids.

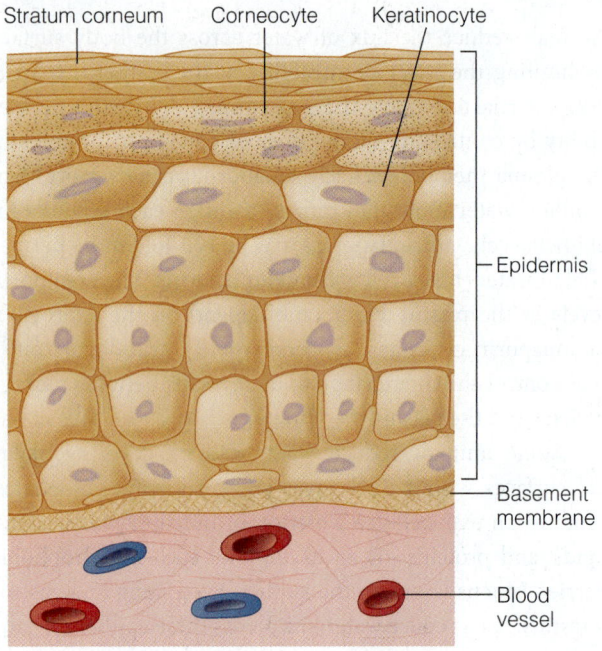

Stratum corneum   Corneocyte   Keratinocyte

Epidermis

Basement membrane

Blood vessel

FIGURE 13.9   **Diversity in the stratum corneum of vertebrate tetrapods**

(a) Armadillo

(b) Horny skin iguana

Photo source: (a) George Holton/Science Source; (b) Dee Breger/Science Source.

Once formed, this mixture of proteins and lipids undergoes a series of enzymatic and chemical processes that modify it into the stratum corneum (Figure 13.8). Although the tissue is dead, it remains responsive to physical changes, triggering the underlying keratinocytes to secrete proteins, lipids, and signaling factors.

The diversity in the properties of vertebrate skin is due mainly to the way the stratum corneum is constructed. The scales of reptiles and birds are composed of interconnected patches of stratum corneum (largely keratin). Mammalian skin is also keratinized, although only a few mammals retain the ancestral "scales," such as the covering on a rodent's tail or an armadillo's shell. Modifications of the keratinized stratum corneum provide terrestrial vertebrates with other structures, such as the scutes on the underbelly of snakes that are used in locomotion and the protective spines of the desert lizards. However, all tetrapods depend on their keratinized stratum corneum to minimize desiccation (Figure 13.9).

The other major group of terrestrial animals, the arthropods, possesses a different type of waterproof integument. The insect **cuticle** is a complex network of hydrophobic molecules that covers all of the external surfaces of insects, including the surfaces of the trachea and gut. The main structural component of the cuticle is the polysaccharide *chitin*. It is synthesized within the cells of the epidermis and

then transported to the extracellular space, where it is chemically modified, crystallized, and combined with other proteins and polysaccharides to obtain the appropriate physical properties. The mature cuticle has very low permeability to water, and is rigid enough to act as an external skeleton for the animal. We discussed the nature of the insect cuticle in greater detail in Chapter 12: Locomotion, considering its role as an exoskeleton in locomotor systems.

The integuments of both tetrapods and terrestrial insects possess an additional layer of lipid that reduces evaporative water loss. The cells of the epidermis secrete these lipids, which then form a continuous coat that acts as a sealant. Birds and mammals possess a thin layer of glycolipid that covers the stratum corneum and fills gaps between cells. The exoskeleton of insects also has a surface coating of long-chain fatty acids and wax esters. In fact, this thin lipid layer gives the insect exoskeleton its resistance to water movement. The ability of the lipid layers to limit water movement depends on the interaction between the lipid molecules, creating a hydrophobic barrier that excludes water. The lipid layer is held together by hydrogen bonds, and as we learned in Chapter 3, an increase in temperature weakens such bonds. Consequently, the lipid layer loses its integrity at higher temperature, greatly enhancing evaporative water loss.

Collectively, the properties of the integument, established by the cells of the epidermis, control the magnitude of water loss. Although we have focused on the outer body covering, the same processes occur across another epithelial tissue: the respiratory surface. The magnitude of respiratory water loss depends on structural features, described for the outer integument, as well as other factors. For example, an air-breathing animal with a high metabolic rate will have higher ventilation rates and therefore greater respiratory water loss than an animal with a lower metabolic rate. Many animals, especially desert animals we discuss in a later feature, possess anatomical adaptations that reduce respiratory water loss.

Desert animals have water-conserving adaptations

Although most terrestrial animals must meet the challenge of obtaining water, the challenge is greatest for animals that live in environments where water is in short supply. When surveying the animals that survive in deserts, we find that the physiological and behavioral strategies are not specific to lineages. Whether studying a desert beetle, lizard, or antelope, we discover similar complex mechanisms to reduce water loss.

Many animals survive in the desert by being better at finding and storing water. Of course, desert animals drink water when they find it, whether in standing pools found in oases, or as dew droplets forming on vegetation. One desert insect, the Namib desert beetle, can harvest water directly from the air. It climbs to the top of sand hills in the early morning and stands on its head. Water condenses on its exoskeleton and falls in rivulets to its mouth. **Preformed water** is also trapped in solid food, such as succulent cacti. Water is also produced during the metabolic breakdown of dietary macromolecules.

Many desert animals, particularly insects, can survive radical changes in tissue water content between dehydration and drinking bouts. Desert beetles swell with water in the rainy season, increasing water content to about 70 percent of body mass. Over the course of the dry season, they may lose as much as 60 percent of this water. Most of this water is lost from the hemolymph; some beetles can tolerate almost complete loss of hemolymph without obvious consequences (the insect hemolymph has no role in delivery of oxygen).

Most desert vertebrates cannot tolerate severe dehydration, but the camel is one exception. When water is available, a 700-kilogram camel can consume as much as 100 kilograms of water in as little as 10 minutes, rehydrating its tissues throughout the body. Similarly, a camel gorges when food is available, storing excess energy in its hump as fat. When deprived of food and water, the camel draws on water stores and degrades the fat in the hump. Eventually, the hump shrinks in size, slumping over to one side as the fat is oxidized to produce energy and metabolic water. Despite the production of metabolic water, camels undergo severe dehydration. In contrast to camels, most desert vertebrates maintain tissue water content within a narrow range using physiological mechanisms that maximize water conservation.

Given the nature of the desert terrain, larger animals, such as the camel, have little hope of finding shade. Instead, physiological strategies help them cope with the direct sunlight. Just as waterproofing of the integument was an important adaptation in the earliest terrestrial invaders, the desert dwellers have evolved superior mechanisms to prevent water flux across the skin. Amphibians and reptiles that live in the desert have skin with a thicker stratum corneum than do those that live in wetter habitats. Birds and mammals—both homeotherms—face an additional risk of dehydration through cutaneous water loss. Generally, large mammals use sweating as a means of cooling under hot conditions. Although birds do not possess sweat glands, cutaneous water loss contributes to cooling. However, to many desert animals conserving water is more urgent than cooling the body. They block **evaporative cooling**, allowing their body temperature to rise. For example, the body temperatures of the oryx (a large antelope) and the camel may exceed 40°C during the heat of the day. These animals do not shed the stored body heat until the cool evening, when the body temperature can fall below 35°C. Interestingly, the featherless neck of ostriches is actually much more permeable to water than is the skin of other birds. This suggests that evaporative cooling is more important to the ostrich than is water conservation.

Other physiological processes, such as ventilation, digestion, and excretion, lead to water loss. Desert animals often have unusual adaptations that reduce this incidental loss of water. Some desert mammals, such as the kangaroo rat, minimize respiratory water loss by passing the expired air over a region of the nose equipped with a countercurrent heat exchanger. This countercurrent heat exchanger cools the surface of the nasal passages, cooling the expired air, allowing water to condense out of the air before it is breathed out, which retains water in the body. The dik-dik, an African antelope that lives in semiarid scrubland, possesses an enlarged nose that acts as a cooling chamber. The kangaroo rat is also able to extract most of the water from its urine and feces prior to excretion. Desert birds and mammals limit

LIFE WITHOUT WATER

Many animals are able to enter a form of suspended animation when water availability plummets. Some terrestrial pulmonate snails, such as *Helix*, withstand dry conditions for months by entering a period of dormancy (*estivation*) in which they lower metabolic rate precipitously and seal off their shell, retarding water loss. In some cases, the snail may lose almost 50 percent of its total body water with prolonged exposure. But because dry mass also decreases proportionally, the percentage of tissue water is fairly constant.

Other species endure a more dramatic loss of water, and their metabolic depression is called anhydrobiosis. Rotifers and tardigrades live and breed in wet moss, but become dehydrated and enter a dormant state when the moss desiccates. When water returns, they rehydrate and become active. Even more tolerant of desiccation are the nematodes that live in the Antarctic. These worms must survive cold stress as well as osmotic stress. The cold, dry air can dehydrate an animal, but these nematodes also experience hyperosmotic stress when melting water dissolves salts, elevating osmolarity as much as fivefold. During dehydration, the water content of the nematode's tissues may decrease from about 75 percent to between 2 percent and 10 percent of body mass. Like the snails, nematodes survive this extreme dehydration in a dormant, hypometabolic state that may last for decades.

The champion of desiccation tolerance is the brine shrimp, *Artemia*. The encysted embryos, often called eggs, are sold as "sea monkeys" with promises that the desiccated animals can be reanimated with the addition of water. If protected from the damaging effects of oxygen, dehydrated brine shrimp eggs can survive hundreds of years in this dehydrated state. Once the eggs hatch, the larvae lose their desiccation tolerance. Brine shrimp inhabit waters that experience periodic dehydration. When water appears, the *Artemia* eggs hatch and larvae mature quickly to initiate a rapid round of reproduction. *Artemia* retains a normal metabolic rate until body water content reaches 50 percent; then metabolic rate declines as more body water is lost. In the final stages, when body water levels are below 1 percent, no evidence of life can be detected. Metabolism essentially stops, as indicated by measurement of metabolic fuel levels, gas exchange, and heat production.

Central to the survival of most species that tolerate anhydrobiosis is accumulation of protective agents, particularly carbohydrates and proteins. For example, when a nematode experiences some desiccation, it produces large amounts of the disaccharide trehalose, which accumulates to levels as high as 15 percent of its dry mass. Trehalose replaces the water molecules in the hydration shell of proteins and other macromolecules, and forms a coating around proteins, lipids, and other macromolecules that stabilizes macromolecular structure. In many species, the ability to survive dehydration correlates with trehalose levels, suggesting that trehalose may be required for survival. Recent studies have gone one step further, to test whether trehalose alone is sufficient to endow cells with desiccation tolerance. Researchers bathed mammalian platelets in trehalose, allowing them to take up the sugar. The platelets were then frozen slowly and dehydrated in this frozen state, reducing water content to about 5 percent of mass. When the freeze-dried platelets were thawed, they remained viable. Transgenic mammalian cells have also been constructed to test the hypothesis that trehalose alone can endow desiccation tolerance. When mouse cells were transfected with two bacterial genes for the enzyme trehalose synthase, they produced very high levels of trehalose (about 100 mM). Unfortunately, these cells could not survive the desiccation process. These studies suggest that trehalose is necessary for desiccation, but that other factors may be required to endow an animal with desiccation tolerance.

References
- Crowe, L. M. (2002). Lessons from nature: The role of sugars in anhydrobiosis. *Comparative Biochemistry and Physiology—Part A: Molecular and Integrative Physiology, 131*, 505–513.
- Møbjerg, N., Halberg, K. A., Jørgensen, A., Persson, D., Bjørn, M., Ramløv, H., & Kristensen, R. M. (2011). Survival in extreme environments: On the current knowledge of adaptations in tardigrades. *Acta Physiologica (Oxford), 202*, 409–420.
- Tunnacliffe, A., Garcia de Castro, A., & Manzanera, M. (2001). Anhydrobiotic engineering of bacterial and mammalian cells: Is intracellular trehalose sufficient? *Cryobiology, 43*, 124–132.
- Wharton, D. A. (2003). The environmental physiology of Antarctic terrestrial nematodes. *Journal of Comparative Physiology, 173B*, 621–628.
- Wolkers, W. F., Tablin, F., & Crowe, J. H. (2002). From anhydrobiosis to freeze-drying of eukaryotic cells. *Comparative Biochemistry and Physiology—Part A: Molecular and Integrative Physiology, 131*, 535–543.

excretory water loss by producing a very concentrated urine. The urine of a dik-dik, for example, is 12 times more concentrated than its plasma. The camel also reduces the degree of dehydration by blocking urination, retaining urea within the tissues until water becomes available.

Each of these examples of desert animal physiology illustrates how animals survive on little water. In contrast to the animals that resist dehydration, some animals survive water stress by tolerating dehydration, in some cases losing all free water, a state known as **anhydrobiosis** (see Box 13.1).

4. Compare the osmotic strategies of marine animals.

5. Explain the changes in osmotic and ionic gradients that would accompany migrations of anadromous and catadromous fish.

6. Describe how desert animals minimize water loss.

Nitrogen Excretion

Another factor that influences osmotic strategies is how the animal disposes of ammonia produced during the breakdown of amino acids. It is a toxic solute that must be excreted, either as ammonia, urea, or uric acid (Figure 13.10). Animals use a variety of strategies to excrete these nitrogenous wastes, and these strategies have important implications for ion and water balance. An animal that excretes most of its nitrogen in the form of ammonia is called an **ammoniotele**. Because ammonia is very toxic, it cannot be stored in the body and must be excreted as a dilute solution, resulting in water loss. Alternative strategies involve energy-dependent production of nitrogenous wastes that can be stored at higher levels, and excreted with less water loss. The two most common alternatives to ammoniotelism are ureotelism and uricotelism. A **ureotele** excretes urea, and a **uricotele** excretes uric acid. Although animals excrete most of their nitrogenous waste in one form, almost every species has the capacity to produce each of these molecules. For example, humans are ureoteles, but they also produce and excrete some ammonia and uric acid.

Each group of animals relies predominantly on a particular strategy (Table 13.3). Among the vertebrates, there are ureoteles (mammals), uricoteles (birds and reptiles), and ammonioteles (amphibians and fish). However, there are many exceptions to these generalizations. There are exceptional species; for example, a few species of bony fish are ureoteles. There are also developmental transitions; for instance, most amphibians excrete ammonia as larva but urea as adults. Other transitions in nitrogenous excretion strategies are triggered by environmental conditions; for example, dehydration causes some lungfish to convert from ammoniotelism to ureotelism. Because the enzymes necessary for ammonia,

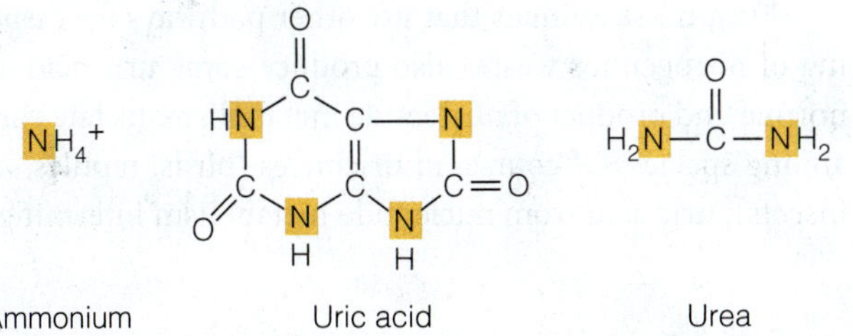

Table 13.3 Nitrogen excretion strategies

Nitrogen Excretion Strategy	Animal Group
Ammonioteles	Simple invertebrates (cnidarians, nematodes)
	Aquatic mollusks
	Agnathans, chondrichthians, bony fish, larval amphibians
Uricoteles	Terrestrial mollusks (snails, slugs), terrestrial arthropods
	Reptiles, birds
Ureoteles	Some larval bony fish, estivating lungfish
	All mammals

urea, and uric acid synthesis exist in most animals, we can assume that the atypical species or developmental changes arise through variation in the control of expression of genes, rather than convergent evolution of novel capabilities.

Ammonia is produced in amino acid metabolism

Ammonia is at the heart of amino acid metabolism. It is used in the synthesis of amino acids by reactions that add ammonia to a carbon skeleton to create an amino acid that can be used in biosynthesis of proteins. When proteins are degraded, the amino acids are broken down to produce carbon skeletons that can be used for energy metabolism. The ammonia that is liberated is toxic and must be either excreted or metabolized into a less toxic form.

The removal and processing of ammonia from amino acids is complex because of the unique structural features of each amino acid. A few amino acids (asparagine, glutamine, glutamate, histidine, serine) can be *deaminated*, with ammonia cleaved from the carbon backbone and released. For most amino acids, aminotransferases transfer their amino group to 2-oxoglutarate, producing glutamate, which can then be deaminated by the enzyme glutamate dehydrogenase (Figure 13.11). In many animals, ammonia produced by glutamate dehydrogenase or other deaminating enzymes is repackaged into a form that is less toxic. Many animal tissues use the enzyme glutamine synthase to transfer ammonia to glutamate, forming glutamine. This amino acid can then be transported to other tissues, where it can be deaminated by the enzyme glutaminase, releasing ammonia and glutamate. This complex cycle of ammonia release, glutamine synthesis, and glutamine **deamination** costs the animal metabolic energy in the form of ATP. However, it gives an animal greater control over the rate and location of ammonia production, which is particularly important in animals that further metabolize ammonia into less toxic nitrogenous compounds bound for excretion.

FIGURE 13.10 Structures of the nitrogenous end products

Ammonium   Uric acid   Urea

FIGURE 13.11   Glutamine metabolism and ammoniagenesis

NH_4^1 from most amino acids is transferred to glutamate through various aminotransferases. The glutamate can then be oxidatively deaminated by glutamate dehydrogenase (GDH). NH_4^1 can also be used by glutamine synthase (GS) to produce glutamine, a convenient molecule to transport ammonia between tissues. Glutamine can then be deaminated by glutaminase.

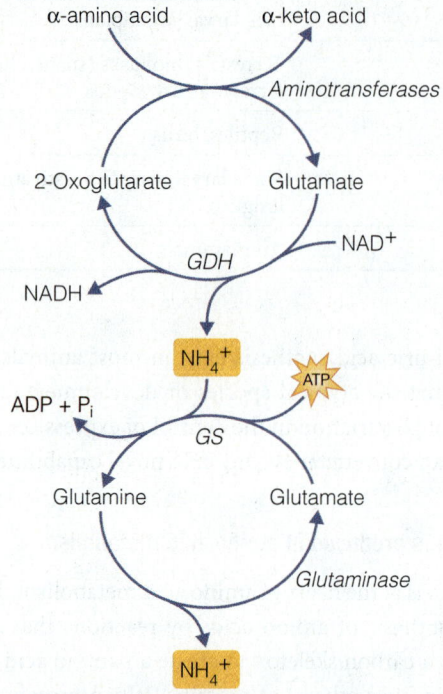

Ammonia can be excreted across epithelial tissues

Metabolic enzymes produce a combination of NH_3 and NH_4^+, but the relative concentrations of the different forms of ammonia in fluids depend on many factors. Because NH_3 is a gas, its concentration in biological fluids depends on how much dissolves into water, which in turn depends on the partial pressure of the gas (P_{NH_3}), its solubility in water, and the temperature. Once dissolved, some NH_3 becomes protonated to form NH_4^+. The balance between these two forms depends on pH. Because the pK_a value for NH_4^+ is approximately 9, at a physiological pH most of the ammonia occurs in the ionized (NH_4^+) form.

Ammonia can cross biological membranes as both NH_3 and NH_4^+, although by different mechanisms. NH_3 can passively diffuse through membranes at a moderate rate. Recently it has been shown that, like water movement, some NH_3 crosses membranes via specific gas channels. Though animals have an NH_4^+/H^+ exchanger, NH_4^+ can also replace K^+ in some transporters, such as NKCC and Na^+/K^+ ATPase, or replace H^+ in the Na^+/H^+ exchanger.

Ammonioteles export the ammonia produced in these reactions across diverse epithelial tissues. In general, the uncharged form, NH_3, crosses membranes, whereas the charged form, NH_4^+, requires specific transporters. Ammoniotelism is most common in animals that live in water. Freshwater fish are typically ammonioteles, excreting most of their nitrogen waste as NH_3. Marine fish can also excrete NH_3, but in these species NH_4^+ excretion across the gills is also important. Some air-breathing fish are able to excrete some ammonia through volatilization of NH_3. Most terrestrial animals release at least some NH_3 across the skin and lung, even if ammoniotelism is not their primary mode of excretion of nitrogenous wastes.

Ammoniotelism has one main advantage: Little additional energy is required to metabolize this nitrogenous waste into a form ready for excretion. However, ammonia excretion is not practical for terrestrial animals because it requires large volumes of water and constant urination to ensure that ammonia levels remain within a tolerable range.

Birds, reptiles, and insects excrete uric acid

The terrestrial invasion by animals necessitated an excretory strategy that permitted nitrogen excretion with little need for water. The earliest evolutionary solution to this problem was uricotelism. Unlike ammonia, uric acid can accumulate in body fluids with few toxic effects. Uricotelism spares water, because uric acid is excreted as anhydrous, white crystals. However, uric acid synthesis does require metabolic energy.

Uric acid is produced by most animals as part of an energy-dependent pathway for nucleotide synthesis (Figure 13.12). Networks of aminotransferases transfer nitrogen from various amino acids to the three amino acids that act as substrates for IMP synthesis: glutamine, glycine, and aspartate. IMP synthesis requires 5 ATP, but an additional high-energy phosphate is required for the conversion of IMP to either AMP or GMP. Both AMP and GMP are broken down to form xanthine. AMP is metabolized to adenosine, inosine, hypoxanthine, and then xanthine, whereas GMP is metabolized to guanosine, guanine, and then xanthine. Some terrestrial arthropods (for example, spiders and scorpions) excrete guanine as a nitrogenous waste product. The xanthine that is produced in these reactions is oxidized to form uric acid. Depending on the species, uric acid may be further metabolized to **allantoin**, allantoic acid, or urea, any of which may be excreted as a nitrogenous waste.

Even those animals that use other pathways for disposing of nitrogenous wastes also produce some uric acid as a normal end product of nucleotide metabolism. Its fate varies among species. Of course, in uricoteles (birds, reptiles, and insects), uric acid from nucleotide metabolism intermingles

FIGURE 13.12 Uric acid metabolism

A complex reaction network uses high-energy phosphate compounds to use amino acids as substrates to produce various nucleotides, and then break those nucleotides down for excretion. This pathway is also an important route of nitrogenous waste production. Amino acid nitrogen is transferred to uric acid, which, depending on the animal, may be excreted or further metabolized to produce other nitrogenous wastes. PRPP: 5-phosphoribosyl-1-pyrophosphate.

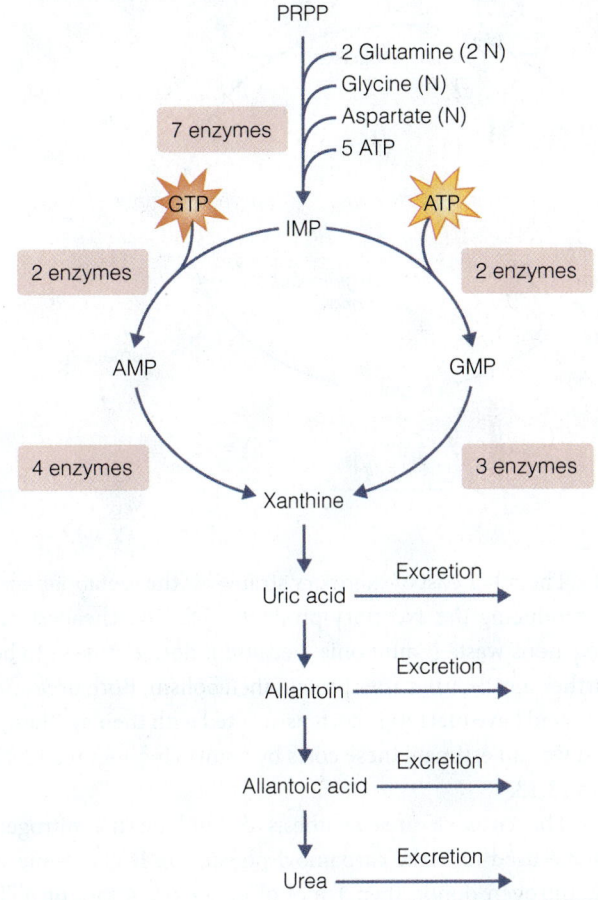

with that produced in nitrogen excretion. However, primates also excrete some uric acid. In other animals, uric acid is further metabolized, then excreted as allantoin (in nonprimate mammals), allantoate (in bony fish), urea (in amphibians and cartilaginous fish), or ammonia (in marine invertebrates).

Multiple, unrelated lineages of animals—vertebrates and invertebrates—share the feature of uricotelism. This striking example of convergent evolution is possible only because the pathway of uric acid synthesis is available to all animals as part of intermediary metabolism. The inherent flexibility of these pathways is evident in the animals that can switch between uricotelism and ammoniotelism, depending on conditions. The amphibious Indian apple snail can switch modes depending on the environment, living as an ammoniotele while in water and a uricotele when on land.

Urea is produced in the ornithine-urea cycle

Long after the first invertebrate and vertebrate uricoteles appeared on the scene, another form of nitrogen excretion—ureotelism—arose in the terrestrial lineages. Urea is the main excretory product of mammals, as well as selected species in other taxa. Urea is produced in some species in the breakdown of uric acid or arginine, but ureoteles produce urea by another pathway, the **ornithine-urea cycle** (Figure 13.13).

The prelude to urea production is the transfer of amino groups from the diverse amino acids to the form that can be used by the enzyme carbamoyl phosphate synthase (CPS). One isoform of CPS (CPS II) is involved in pyrimidine nucleotide synthesis and uses glutamine as a substrate. However, ureotelic animals possess other CPS isoforms (CPS I and CPS III) that are specialized for urea synthesis. The evolutionary origins of the urea cycle are intimately linked to the evolution of the CPS genes. The two CPS forms involved in urea synthesis differ in the N donor; CPS I uses NH_4^1, whereas CPS III uses glutamine. Once carbamoyl phosphate is produced, it enters the ornithine-urea cycle.

In addition to the five enzymes of the ornithine-urea cycle, urea synthesis requires two transporters to shuttle substrates across the mitochondrial membrane: the ornithine/citrulline transporter and the aspartate/glutamate transporter. The division of the pathway between the cytoplasm and mitochondria allows greater control over the fate of metabolites. There is also evidence that metabolites are channeled from one enzyme to the next to avoid the loss of metabolites to other pathways. Arginine, for example, is used in multiple other pathways and must be constrained within the ornithine-urea cycle for efficient urea production.

Urea is made in the liver and released into the blood, where its fate depends on the species. In mammals, urea is collected by the kidney and excreted in the urine. In other animals, urea may be excreted via other routes, such as the fish gill. Urea is carried across the plasma membrane by facilitated diffusion on specific urea transporters. These transporters govern how fast urea crosses membranes in different cell types and regions of the kidney. Active transporters for urea may exist in tissues such as shark gills, although much less is known about such carriers.

The rate of urea production is matched to the rate of protein metabolism, which is high in animals that (1) eat protein-rich diets or (2) degrade body protein during starvation. The rate of urea synthesis is regulated by enzyme quantity and allosteric regulation. First, animals use hormones to regulate the rate of expression of genes that encode the

FIGURE 13.13 **Ornithine-urea cycle**

Amino nitrogen in the form of either glutamine or NH_4^1 is used to produce carbamoyl phosphate, which enters the ornithine-urea cycle.

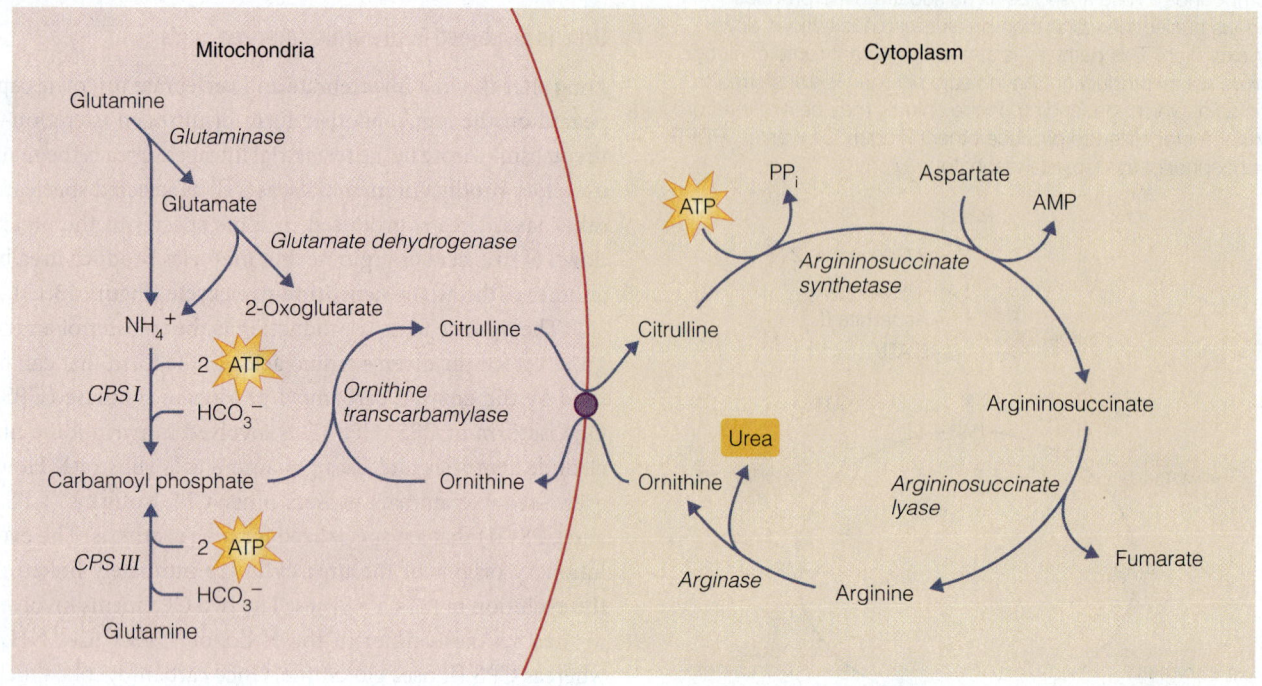

enzymes of the ornithine-urea cycle. Glucagon and gluco-corticoids stimulate the expression of ornithine-urea cycle enzymes, whereas insulin inhibits expression of these genes. Second, animals regulate CPS activity through the allosteric regulator N-acetyl glutamate. When amino acid levels are high, an elevation in glutamate levels increases the activity of the enzyme N-acetyl glutamate synthetase.

Each nitrogenous waste strategy has inherent costs

Excretory strategies have been an important element of many ecophysiological studies. The costs and benefits are clear and can readily be understood in terms of the environmental and ecological constraints on the animal: available water, dietary strategies, and metabolic cost.

Each excretory strategy has implications for water balance, but not all animals within a taxonomic group have the same needs for water conservation. For example, all birds share the reptilian trait of uricotelism, which offers the greatest benefits in terms of water conservation. However, not all birds live in a water-poor environment. Hummingbirds, for instance, eat a diet that is very low in protein and high in water content. They produce very little nitrogenous waste during digestion. Thus, hummingbirds and other nectar feeders can expend the water necessary to make greater use of ammonia excretion. However, even these birds are not truly ammoniotelic—most of their nitrogenous waste is still excreted in the form of uric acid.

The other cost of excretory strategy is the metabolic cost of producing the excretory product itself. The cheapest nitrogenous waste is ammonia, because it does not need to be further metabolized after protein metabolism. Both urea and uric acid have metabolic costs associated with their synthesis, and we can estimate these costs by comparing Figures 13.12 and 13.13.

The costs of urea synthesis depend on the nitrogen source used to make carbamoyl phosphate. If glutamine is the nitrogen donor, then 1 mol of urea costs 4 mol of ATP (i.e., 1 mol of ATP to make glutamine, 2 mol of ATP for carbamoyl phosphate synthesis, and 1 mol of ATP for argininosuccinate synthesis). The pyrophosphate produced in argininosuccinate synthesis is normally hydrolyzed, wasting an additional high-energy phosphate. Thus, the costs of urea synthesis are most often estimated as 5 mol of ATP per mol of urea. In comparison to urea, uric acid costs more to produce (7 ATP) but it also has more nitrogen (4 N). Thus, uric acid (7 ATP; 1.75 ATP/N) is slightly more economical than urea (5 ATP; 2.5 ATP/N). However, uric acid pellets include numerous proteins; because these proteins are lost in the excreta, they represent an indirect cost of uricotelism.

The mode of nitrogen excretion can change with development or environment

The reasons for the occurrence of ureotelism in species other than mammals are not always clear, although it usually coincides with an atypical environmental situation or life history strategy. Let's consider some examples.

Urea production by most teleost fish is normally quite low and an insignificant contribution to nitrogen excretion. Some fish species live most of their life as ureoteles. For example, the Lake Magadi tilapia lives in water with a pH so high that the gill cannot excrete NH_3. In most fish, NH_3 diffusion across the gills is accelerated when external protons ionize NH_3 to form NH_4^+. At a high external pH, well above the pK_a value for NH_3, this reaction is very slow, reducing the rate of NH_3 diffusion. These fish have an active ornithine-urea cycle in the liver, but surprisingly, the muscle also plays an important role in urea synthesis in these fish. Urea is excreted across the gills as the primary form of nitrogenous waste.

Other fish species may adopt a ureotelic strategy, depending on external conditions. For example, as we mentioned earlier in the chapter, lungfish are normally ammonioteles, excreting ammonia into the surrounding water. However, when water levels decrease, the African lungfish (*Protopterus*) burrows into the mud and forms a mucus cocoon. Because the animal cannot excrete ammonia, other pathways must be used for nitrogen excretion. Once exposed to the air, the lungfish rapidly induces the expression of urea cycle enzymes and glutamine synthase, and converts to ureotelism.

The gulf toadfish, *Opsanus beta*, also can convert to ureotelism, typically when it moves to crowded conditions. The urea is stored in the blood and released once or twice daily in short pulses across the gill following the insertion of urea transporters into the gill epithelia. It remains unclear why ureotelism is advantageous in this species. It may serve to reduce the risk of local fouling of water where animals are closely associated together. Alternatively, because many animals use ammonia as a cue to detect prey, urea production may confuse predators. Urea production is more common in the early developmental stages of many ammoniotelic species, including rainbow trout. It is likely that all fish are capable of synthesizing urea, but the species that produce urea as adults likely do so by retaining this embryonic capacity.

Cartilaginous fish produce urea as an osmolyte

Most species that produce a lot of urea do it mainly to excrete nitrogenous wastes. However, some species produce urea but retain it as an osmolyte. For example, the urea concentration in the plasma of the crab-eating frog (*Rana cancrivora*) increases more than 20-fold when the frog is exposed to high salinity. Because the rates of urea excretion do not change, it is likely that urea is serving an important role as an osmolyte.

Urea is an important osmolyte in cartilaginous fish, where it can account for almost half of the tissue osmolarity. At the high concentrations seen in shark blood, urea could disrupt macromolecular structures. However, its effects are counteracted by methylamines, such as TMAO, betaine, and sarcosine, which are also accumulated at high concentrations. By relying on counteracting solutes, sharks can maintain the concentration of inorganic ions (perturbing solutes) at low levels. Although most cartilaginous fish are stenohaline, several species can tolerate some degree of diluted seawater. When a **euryhaline** shark moves from seawater to dilute seawater, it excretes urea as well as some ions. More than 40 species of elasmobranchs can survive in freshwater. Species such as bull sharks may travel from the sea into freshwater lakes, such as Lake Nicaragua, surviving for years before returning to the sea to breed. In freshwater, these sharks lose some of their osmolytes—about 50 percent of urea and 20 percent of Na^+ and Cl^-—yet maintain an osmolarity well above that of other freshwater fish. The Amazonian stingray remains in freshwater all its life, maintaining an osmolarity near that of teleost fish by excreting urea as it is produced.

CONCEPT CHECK

7. What are the costs and benefits of using ammonia, urea, and uric acid as nitrogenous wastes?
8. What substrates are required to produce a molecule of urea?

THE KIDNEY

Most animals maintain ion and water balance using some form of internal organ derived during the development of the embryonic digestive system. Multiple types of cells combine to produce a tubelike structure, or tubule, through which excretory solutions pass from the animal to the external environment. Animals differ in the way the tubule fluid is produced and how it is modified prior to excretion. In some animals, a few simple tubules are sufficient to produce the excretory products. More complex animals, such as vertebrates, combine tubules to form the kidney, which has six roles in homeostasis.

1. **Ion balance.** Sodium levels are an important determinant of extracellular fluid osmolarity. Animals exhibit fluid imbalances if blood $[Na^+]$ is too high (*hypernatremia*) or too low (*hyponatremia*). Potassium balance is important because changes in $[K^+]$ can alter resting membrane potential, which affects the function of excitable tissues such as muscles and neurons. If blood $[K^+]$ is too high (*hyperkalemia*), excitable tissues can undergo spontaneous depolarization, causing cardiac arrhythmias and muscle twitches. Low $[K^+]$, or *hypokalemia*, can cause muscle weakness. The kidney also controls the loss of ions that have important roles as micronutrients, including Ca^{2+}, iron, and trace metals.

2. **Osmotic balance.** The kidneys determine the volume of urine produced, and thereby control water balance. Dehydration results from inadequate consumption of water, or consumption of chemicals known as **diuretics**, which increase water loss in the urine. Conversely, inadequate water excretion can result in high blood pressure and edema.

3. **Blood pressure.** By controlling blood volume, the kidney acts over the long term to regulate blood pressure. It acts in concert with shorter term cardiovascular effectors, such as cardiac contractile properties and peripheral resistance of the vasculature. The volume of the extracellular fluid is under the control of the kidney, through hormones and nerves that integrate cardiovascular conditions with the output of the central cardiovascular control center. Low blood pressure (*hypotension*) compromises the delivery of fuels to tissues with high energy demands, such as the brain and locomotor muscle. High blood pressure (*hypertension*) can compromise the integrity of the microvasculature in vital tissues, putting the animal at risk for a myocardial infarction, stroke, or embolism. Many antihypertensive agents are diuretics, enhancing the production of urine to reduce blood volume.

4. **pH balance.** The kidney augments the respiratory system in controlling the pH of body fluids. The kidney regulates the pH of the extracellular fluid by retaining or excreting H^+ or HCO_3^-. Many of the metabolic and transport pathways of ammonia metabolism also involve acid or base production. The production of urea leads to the consumption of bicarbonate, which also has consequences for whole-body pH regulation.

5. **Excretion.** The kidney plays an important role in the excretion of nitrogenous wastes as well as other water-soluble toxins. Excess water-soluble vitamins, for example, are excreted in the urine.

6. **Hormone production.** The kidney has an important role in the synthesis and release of hormones, such as renin, which controls blood pressure, and erythropoietin, which regulates red blood cell synthesis.

We begin our discussion of the kidney by exploring the structure and function of the mammalian kidney, focusing on its role in the regulation of water and ion balance. Our understanding of animal kidney function benefits from the many studies that examine the role of the kidney in human diseases, such as hypertension. Later in this section we examine the specific properties of kidneys from other species. We conclude by surveying the extrarenal epithelial tissues (such as gills and salt glands) that complement kidney function in some species.

Kidney Structure and Function

The typical mammalian kidney (Figure 13.14) is crescent shaped with two layers: an outer cortex and an inner medulla. The medulla is composed of a number of parallel

FIGURE 13.14   Mammalian kidney

The kidney is composed of two layers, the cortex and the medulla. As urine is produced, it is collected by the minor calyces, which join together to form the major calyx. The urine passes through the ureter into the urinary bladder for storage, eventually leaving the animal through the urethra.

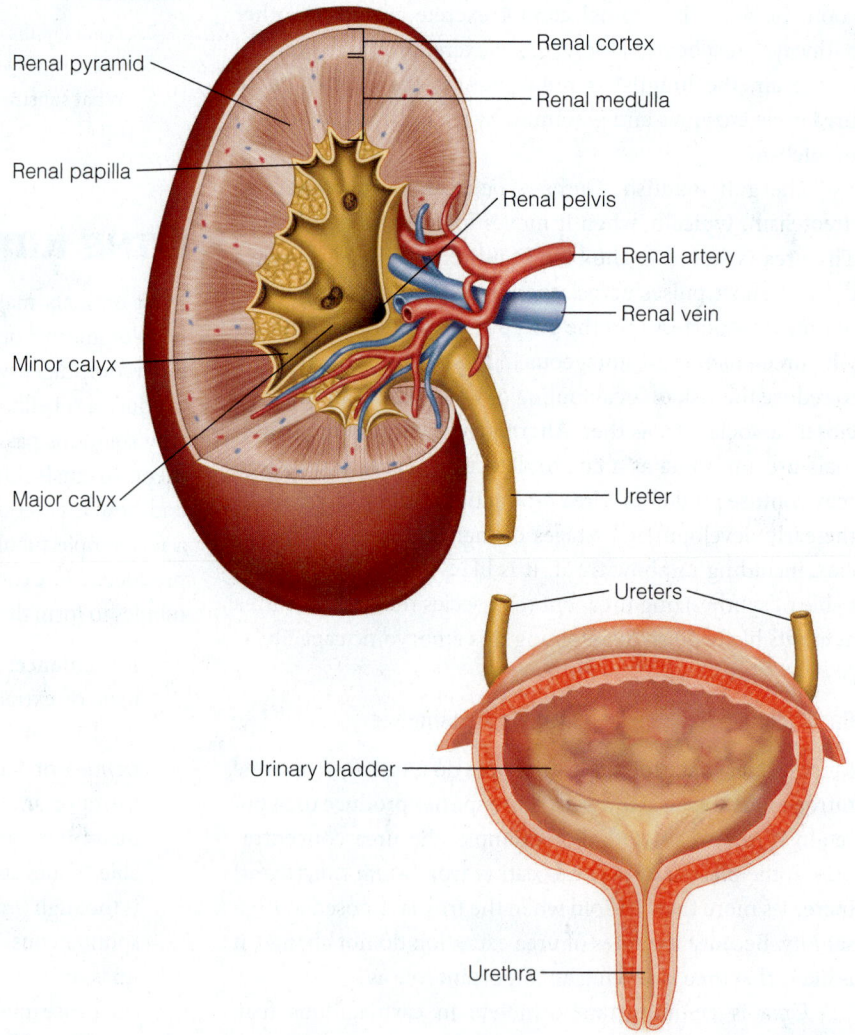

cone-shaped segments called *renal pyramids*. The inner narrow region of each pyramid is called the papilla. Once the urine is formed, it passes into a cavity called the *minor calyx*. Multiple minor calyces drain into the *major calyx*, which in turn empties into the **ureters** that drain the kidney. The ureters empty into the *urinary bladder* where urine is stored. Eventually, the urine is expelled from the bladder through a single **urethra**, a process with the elegant name *micturition*. Kidneys must process tremendous volumes of blood. Even though kidneys make up less than 1 percent of the entire body mass, the blood flow through the kidneys is much greater than that to muscles during heavy exercise. In humans, the kidney may process 4 liters of blood per kilogram each minute but exercising muscle receives only about 0.5 liters per kilogram per minute. Numerous hormones and neurotransmitters ensure that urine composition and release are matched to the physiological needs of the animal. These regulatory factors affect the four processes involved in urine formation: filtration, reabsorption, secretion, and excretion.

loop consisting of a descending limb and an ascending limb. After leaving the loop of Henle, the fluid then enters the **distal tubule**. The fluid from multiple distal tubules drains into a single **collecting duct**, several of which fuse together to form papillary ducts, which in turn empty into the minor calyx of the kidney.

The vasculature of the nephron is central to nephron function, (Figure 13.16). Blood enters the kidney from the renal artery, which branches into smaller vessels that ultimately give rise to the **afferent arteriole** that leads into the capillaries of the glomerulus. After the filtered blood leaves the glomerulus, it passes into an **efferent arteriole**. This arrangement is unlike that of a conventional capillary bed where the venous system is immediately downstream of the capillaries. The efferent arteriole generates enough smooth muscle contraction to maintain a degree of vasoconstriction, causing a higher degree of resistance than could a venule. The blood passes through the efferent arteriole into one of two types of capillary beds. In cortical nephrons, the

The nephron is the functional unit of the kidney

The **nephron** is the main structural and functional unit of the kidney. In a typical kidney, some nephrons (termed *cortical nephrons*) are located relatively high within the renal cortex and extend only a short distance into the renal medulla. Others are longer and extend deep into the renal medulla (these are termed *juxtamedullary nephrons* because they begin fairly deep within the renal cortex near the junction with the medulla) (Figure 13.15).

Each nephron is composed of two regions with differing functions: (1) the **renal corpuscle** (or *Malphigian corpuscle*), which filters the blood, and (2) the **renal tubules**, which modify the filtered fluid by reabsorbing or secreting specific substances. The renal corpuscle is composed of a twisted ball of capillaries called the **glomerulus** and the surrounding **Bowman's capsule**, which is a cuplike expansion of the renal tubules. The renal tubules are formed from a single layer of epithelial cells and can be divided into three regions with differing transport properties. Fluid leaving the Bowman's capsule first enters the **proximal tubule** and then enters the **loop of Henle**, which forms a hairpinlike

FIGURE 13.15 **Nephron structure**

Two types of nephrons are distinguished by their location within the kidney. Though the glomerulus is in the cortex, tubules can penetrate the medulla to different degrees. **(a)** Cortical nephrons are located predominantly in the outer cortex. **(b)** Juxtamedullary nephrons are mainly in the inner medulla.

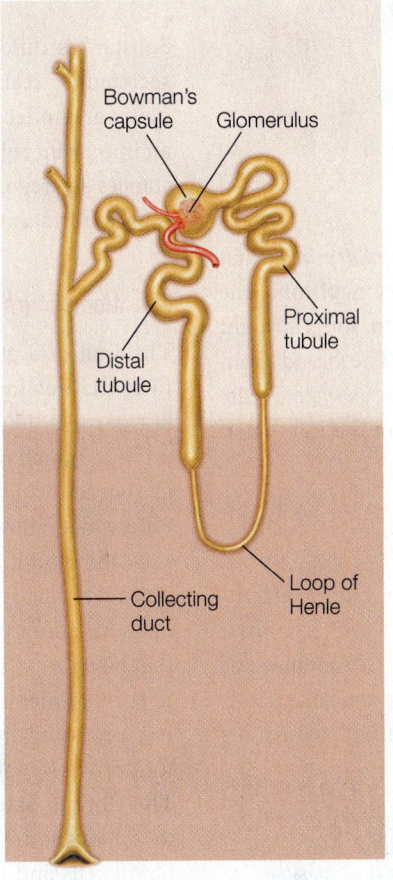

(a) Cortical nephron

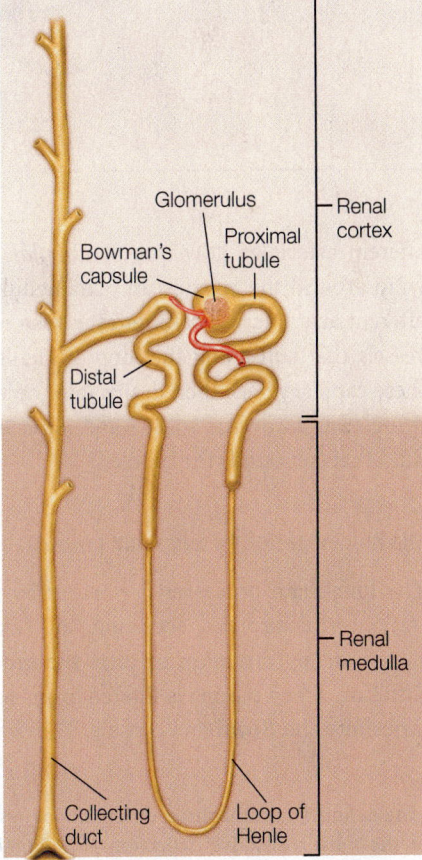

(b) Juxtamedullary nephron

FIGURE 13.16   **Blood vessels of the nephron**

Blood delivered to the kidney by the renal artery passes through smaller arteries and reaches an afferent arteriole that services one nephron. The arteriole diverges into the glomerulus, a network of capillaries within the Bowman's capsule. After leaving the glomerulus, blood enters an efferent arteriole. The efferent arterioles that drain cortical nephrons empty into peritubular capillaries. The efferent arterioles that drain juxtaglomerular nephrons flow into the vasa recta.

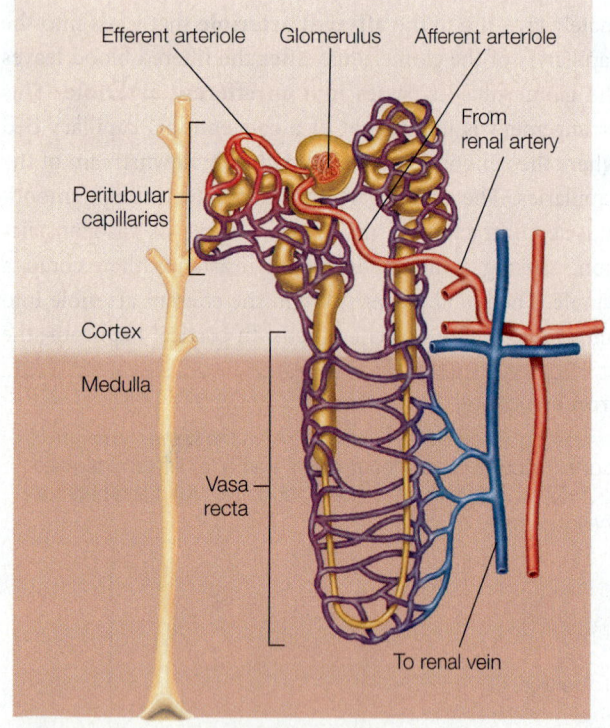

efferent arterioles flow into *peritubular capillary beds* that wrap around the tubules. In juxtamedullary nephrons, the efferent arterioles diverge into the **vasa recta**, long, straight vessels that run along the loop of Henle. The blood from these capillary beds then drains into the venous system, carrying away recovered solutes and water from the interstitial fluid that surrounds the tubule.[1]

The kidney performs four main processes

The four main processes performed by the kidney are filtration, reabsorption, secretion, and excretion. The first step in urine formation involves the process of glomerular filtration, when plasma is filtered from the glomerular capillaries into the Bowman's capsule. This filtration step results

[1]The definition of a nephron differs among researchers. In contrast to the most restrictive definition—the glomerulus and tubule—some researchers include the collecting duct and vasa recta as part of a nephron.

in a fluid, called **primary urine**, with a composition very similar to that of blood, except that it lacks cells and large macromolecules such as proteins (and also has low levels of some small molecules such as calcium and fatty acids that are closely associated with plasma proteins). Note that filtration is not a very selective process, as almost all molecules below a certain size will pass through the filter into the primary urine. The primary urine then passes into the tubules of the nephron, where its composition is altered through the processes of reabsorption and secretion. Reabsorption occurs when a substance is moved from the tubular fluid back into the blood, whereas movement from the blood into the tubular fluid is called secretion. Both reabsorption and secretion are highly selective and can be isolated to particular locations. Thus, only specific substances are moved out of or into the tubular fluid. Together, the processes of reabsorption and secretion act to transform the composition of the primary urine into the urine that is collected in the urinary bladder and excreted.

The four major processes of the kidney act together such that the amount of a substance that is excreted in the urine is equal to the amount filtered plus the amount secreted, minus the amount reabsorbed:

$$\text{Amount excreted} = \text{Amount filtered} + \text{Amount secreted} - \text{Amount reabsorbed}$$

Substances differ in the extent to which they are filtered, secreted, or reabsorbed, and the rates of each of these processes are under physiological control. Thus the kidney plays an important role in maintaining homeostatis for many substances by regulating their excretion through altering the rates of filtration, secretion, and reabsorption.

Filtration occurs at the glomerulus

The wall of a glomerular capillary is a complex biological filter that retains the blood cells and large macromolecules but permits liquid and small molecules in blood to escape into the lumen of the Bowman's capsule (Figure 13.17). The glomerular capillaries are fenestrated (see Figure 9.16), with pores that allow low-molecular-weight molecules to escape the blood. A specialized type of epithelial cell called a **podocyte** covers the outer surface of the capillary. The podocytes have **foot processes**, which are cytoplasmic extensions that help form the filtration structure. The podocyte attaches to the basement membrane, a filamentous extracellular matrix produced by the capillary cells. The gap between the foot processes, about 14 nm wide, is called a **filtration slit**. The fibrous basement membrane spans the filtration slits to act as the biological filter of the glomerulus, excluding blood cells and large proteins, and passing water, ions, and low-molecular-weight molecules.

FIGURE 13.17 Glomerulus

(a) The glomerulus is a network of capillaries that empty much of the fluid from the blood into the Bowman's capsule of the nephron. **(b)** Mesangial cells between the capillaries help control blood flow through the glomerulus. The individual capillaries are composed of loosely connected endothelial cells and are covered on the external surface by podocytes. **(c)** The podocytes issue several foot processes that form filtration slits. **(d)** The podocytes interact with the basement membrane to create a filter that retains blood cells and large proteins in the plasma while permitting the passage of fluids through filtration slits.

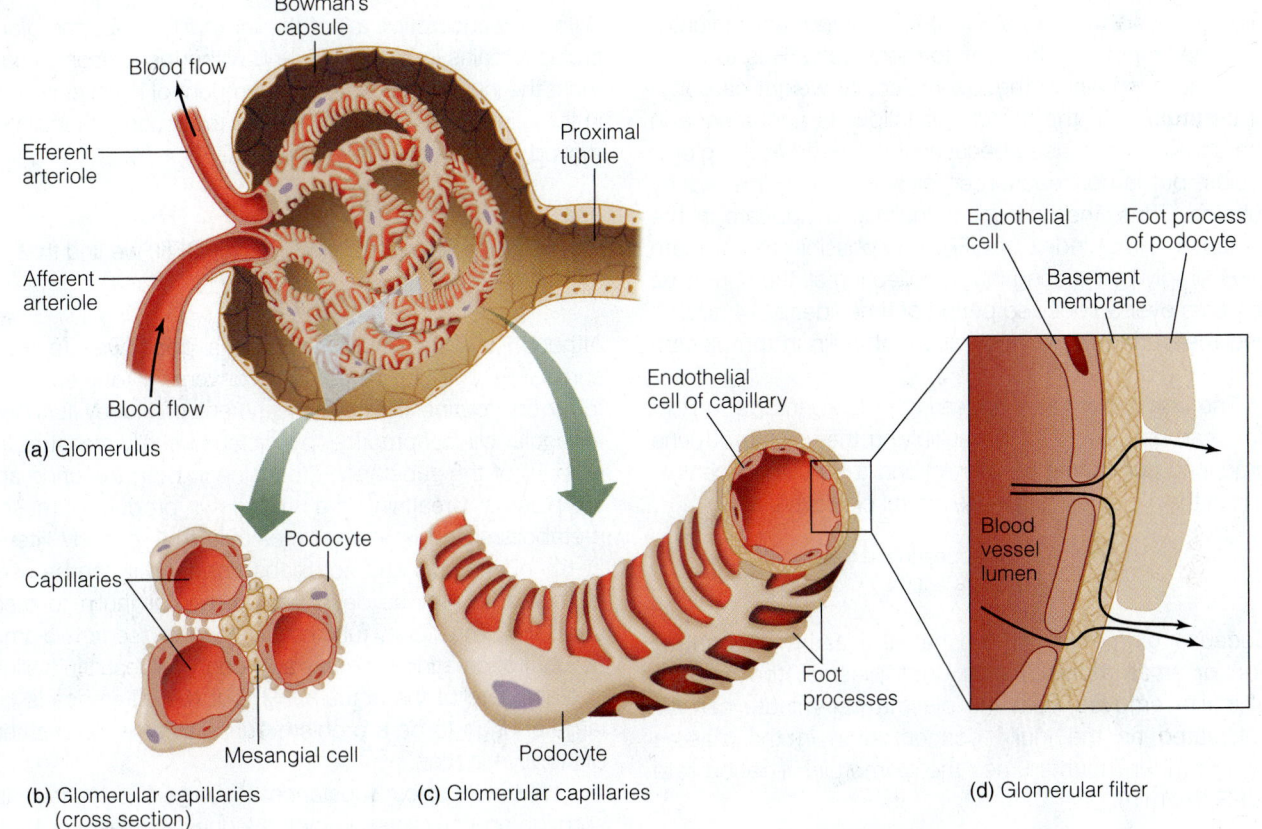

(a) Glomerulus

(b) Glomerular capillaries (cross section)

(c) Glomerular capillaries

(d) Glomerular filter

The **mesangial cells**, similar to smooth muscle cells, wrap around the capillaries of the glomerulus. Contraction of the mesangial cells restricts blood flow to specific vessels within the capillary network, regulating blood pressure within the glomerulus and altering the surface area available for filtration.

Glomerular filtration pressure is affected by hydrostatic pressure and oncotic pressure

The rate at which plasma is filtered at the glomerulus, known as the **glomerular filtration rate**, or **GFR**, is the amount of filtrate produced per minute (see Box 13.2: Math in Physiology: Calculating Glomerular Filtration Rate (GFR) and Renal Clearance). Filtration at the glomerulus occurs by bulk flow of fluids from a region of higher pressure (the glomerulus) to a region of lower pressure (the Bowman's capsule). Thus, the pressure difference between these two regions, or the net glomerular filtration pressure, is an important determinant of GFR. Three main forces act together to set net glomerular filtration pressure: glomerular capillary hydrostatic pressure, Bowman's capsule hydrostatic pressure, and the net oncotic pressure (Figure 13.18).

Let's begin our discussion of these forces by considering an analogy. Imagine a garden hose connected to a standard tap. Midway through the hose, a section of rubber has been perforated with thousands of small holes that act as a filter, allowing water to leak out of the hose. Now consider what happens to the rate of flow through the leaky region of the hose when we alter the system. When the tap is partially closed, less water will flow through the hose and there will be a decrease in the volume of water leaking from the system. Similarly, if you constrict the hose upstream of the leaky region, there will be a decrease in hydrostatic pressure downstream of the constriction and less water will leak through the filter. Conversely, if you constrict the hose downstream of the leaky region, water will tend to "back up" and increase the hydrostatic pressure upstream, which forces

CALCULATING GLOMERULAR FILTRATION RATE (GFR) AND RENAL CLEARANCE

Glomerular filtration rate (GFR) is an important indicator of kidney function. One way to measure GFR is to inject a solution containing the low-molecular-weight carbohydrate **inulin** into the blood and follow its appearance in the urine. Inulin is used because it is filtered at the glomerulus, but is not reabsorbed or secreted by the kidney tubules. Thus, the amount of inulin that appears in the urine is a direct index of GFR. It is possible to calculate GFR simply by injecting inulin, collecting all the urine that appears over a specified period of time (ideally 24 hours), and measuring the concentration of inulin in the plasma and in the urine.

The amount of inulin appearing in the urine per unit of time can be calculated by multiplying the volume of urine produced per minute (V, ml/min) and the inulin concentration in that volume of urine (U, mg/ml or mol/ml).

$$\text{Amount of inulin appearing in the urine} \atop \text{per minute} = V \times U$$

Because glomerular filtrate has the same concentration of small molecules as does plasma, the amount of inulin removed from the plasma per minute can be calculated as the inulin concentration in the plasma (P, mg/ml or mol/ml) times the glomerular filtration rate (GFR, ml/min).

$$\text{Amount of inulin removed from the} \atop \text{blood per minute} = \text{GFR} \times P$$

Without reabsorption, all of the inulin filtered by the glomerulus remains in the tubule, and without secretion to augment the inulin in the lumen, the amount of inulin appearing in the urine per minute (VU) equals the amount of inulin removed from the blood per minute (GFR $\times$ P):

$$VU = \text{GFR} \times P$$

Rearranging the equation to solve for GFR, we find that

$$\text{GFR} = \textbf{\textit{VU/P}}$$

Although injecting inulin provides a good way to measure GFR, it is not particularly convenient to inject inulin for every routine clinical assessment of kidney function. In regular clinical practice, physicians usually measure the amount of the substance creatinine in both the urine and the plasma. Creatinine is a breakdown product of muscle metabolism and is a small molecule that is freely filtered at the glomerulus and not reabsorbed, so it can be used in the same way as described above for inulin to measure GFR. The kidney tubules do, however, secrete a small amount of creatinine, so this approach will result in a slight overestimate of the actual GFR, but the difference is not large enough to be a problem during routine assessment of kidney function.

Unlike inulin, most substances undergo substantial reabsorption and/or secretion by the kidney tubules. For these substances we use equation 4 to redefine a parameter called **renal clearance (C)**, which is the volume of plasma

more water through the filter. In this analogy, the tap represents the heart, the first section of hose represents the afferent arteriole leading to the glomerulus, the perforated region represents the glomerulus, and the last section of hose represents the efferent arteriole. From this analogy we can see that when cardiac output or systemic blood pressure falls or the afferent arteriole constricts, glomerular capillary hydrostatic pressure will tend to decrease, but when the efferent arteriole constricts, glomerular capillary hydrostatic pressure will tend to increase.

The second main force that influences net filtration pressure is Bowman's capsule hydrostatic pressure. In the previous analogy, the water leaked out of the perforated region of the hose into the air and there was little pressure to oppose the free movement of the water out of the holes in the hose. In the tubule, the glomerular filtrate does not

empty into air, but into the Bowman's capsule, which also has a hydrostatic pressure. The hydrostatic pressure of the Bowman's capsule is a force opposing filtration. Thus the net hydrostatic pressure gradient is the glomerular capillary hydrostatic pressure (which is a force driving filtration) minus the Bowman's capsule hydrostatic pressure (which is a force opposing filtration). In a typical mammalian kidney, the hydrostatic pressure within the Bowman's capsule is about 15 mm Hg, while the glomerular capillary hydrostatic pressure is about 60 mm Hg. This difference results in a hydrostatic pressure gradient of about 45 mm Hg that drives fluid through the filter.

The third main force that influences the net filtration pressure is the net oncotic pressure. **Oncotic pressure** is the osmotic pressure that arises because of a protein concentration gradient. Because the filter at the glomerulus

from which a substance is completely removed (cleared) per unit time (ml/min):

$$C = VU/P$$

For substances like inulin, which are neither secreted nor reabsorbed, renal clearance is equal to GFR (compare equation 4 and equation 5). A substance that is secreted will have a clearance rate higher than GFR, and a substance that is reabsorbed will have a clearance rate lower than GFR.

One important point to note about renal clearance is that it is not a measure of the *amount* of a substance removed from the plasma per unit time, but instead has the units of *volume* per unit time. Thinking about clearance in terms of a volume of plasma cleared of a substance is a rather artificial concept, because the kidney does not actually clear 100 percent of a substance from any particular volume of plasma. Instead, when a substance is excreted into the urine, the substance's overall concentration in the plasma is decreased to some extent across all of the plasma, rather than all of the substance being removed from a small portion of the plasma. Thus, clearance is sometimes defined as the "virtual" volume of plasma that would be cleared of a substance per unit time, given a particular plasma concentration of the substance. If you wish to work out the amount of the substance cleared, you simply multiply clearance by the plasma concentration, which gives the amount of the substance cleared per time.

So why do scientists and physicians instead use the "virtual volume" represented by clearance as an index of kidney function, instead of the amount of the substance that is cleared? Filtration at the glomerulus is dependent on the concentration of the substance in the plasma, and will increase or decrease depending on the plasma concentration of the substance, so expressing clearance as a parameter that is scaled to plasma concentration makes physiological sense, and it allows clearance to be meaningfully compared independent of the starting concentration of a substance in the plasma.

CHECK YOUR UNDERSTANDING

1. Work through the equations in this box by substituting in the units associated with each parameter, and checking to see how the units cancel out to yield GFR (or clearance) in ml/min.
2. If the clearance of inulin is measured to be 125 ml/min and the clearance of substance X was measured to be 300 ml/min, would you predict that substance X is reabsorbed, secreted, or neither reabsorbed or secreted by the kidney tubules? Explain your answer.
3. You inject inulin into the blood of a human patient such that the plasma concentration is 0.3 mg/ml. You collect all the urine produced over 24 hours (1,800 ml) and it has an inulin concentration of 30 mg/ml. What is the GFR of this patient?

allows the movement of fluid and small solutes, but prevents the movement of proteins, the concentration of proteins is much higher in the plasma of the glomerulus than in the Bowman's capsule, which results in an oncotic pressure gradient. This oncotic pressure gradient tends to draw fluids back into the glomerular capillary. In a typical mammalian kidney this oncotic pressure is about 30 mm Hg in opposition of filtration.

Taking all of these forces together, the net glomerular filtration pressure can be calculated as:

$$\text{Net glomerular filtration pressure} = P_{GC} - P_{BC} - \pi_{GC}$$

Where P_{GC} is the glomerular capillary hydrostatic pressure, P_{BC} is the Bowman's capsule hydrostatic pressure, and π_{GC} is the oncotic pressure in the glomerular capillaries. In a typical mammalian kidney, the net glomerular filtration pressure is therefore approximately 15 mm Hg (60 mm Hg − 15 mm Hg − 30 mm Hg).

The kidney can maintain GFR across a range of blood pressures

Maintaining a relatively constant GFR is important because the processes involved in the reasborption of salt and water in the tubule are dependent on the rate of flow of fluid through the tubules. The kidney uses three main processes to maintain GFR in the face of changes in blood pressure: myogenic regulation, tubuloglomerular feedback, and mesangial control. Myogenic regulation involves the smooth muscle cells of the kidney vasculature. As described in the previous section, an increase in systemic arterial blood pressure would be expected to increase GFR. However, this increase

FIGURE 13.18 **Glomerular filtration pressures**

The overall pressure for fluid movements is the difference between inward and outward pressures. The hydrostatic pressure gradient, the difference between the mean blood pressure and the hydrostatic pressure of the lumen, favors movement into the lumen of the Bowman's capsule. The oncotic pressure gradient, due to the proteins that remain in the plasma, opposes movement into the lumen.

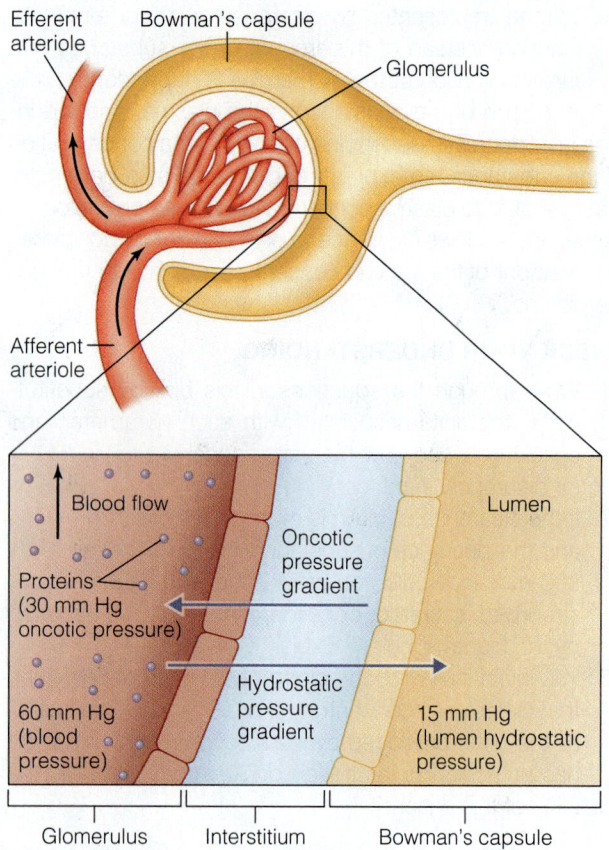

FIGURE 13.19 **Intrinsic control of GFR**

An increase in mean arterial pressure (MAP) triggers a change in glomerular filtration pressure. **(a)** Myogenic regulation controls vasoconstriction by triggering contraction of the vascular smooth muscle of the afferent arterioles. **(b)** The tubuloglomerular feedback loop involves signaling factors released from the macula densa that alter smooth muscle contractility. Two other modes of intrinsic control—mesangial control and pressure natriuresis—are described in the text.

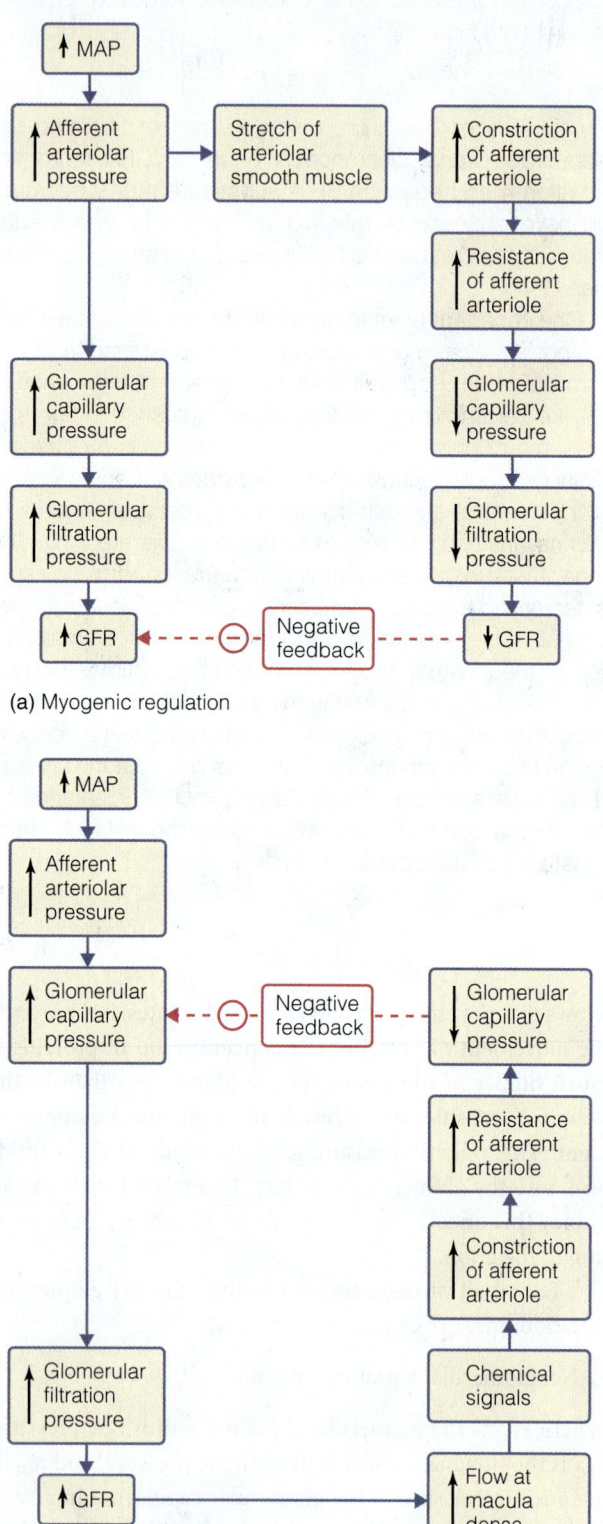

in blood pressure stretches smooth muscle cells in the vascular wall of the afferent arteriole. The deformation of the cytoskeleton and plasma membrane of these smooth muscle cells activates stretch-sensitive ion channels, which results in depolarization of the plasma membrane of smooth muscle cells. This depolarization stimulates the contractile apparatus, increasing tension and causing vasoconstriction. The resultant decrease in blood flow in the afferent vessels reduces hydrostatic pressure, returning GFR to baseline levels (Figure 13.19a). The same system responds in reverse when arterial blood pressure decreases. Smooth muscle relaxes, vasodilation results, and the increase in blood flow increases the hydrostatic pressure and returns GFR to baseline.

In tubuloglomerular feedback, the cells in a region of the distal tubule, called the **macula densa**, contact specialized **juxtaglomerular cells** in the walls of the afferent arterioles (Figure 13.20). When flow through the distal tubule increases, the tubule cells signal the afferent arteriole, causing vasoconstriction, a decrease in hydrostatic pressure, and

FIGURE 13.20 Macula densa and the juxtaglomerular apparatus

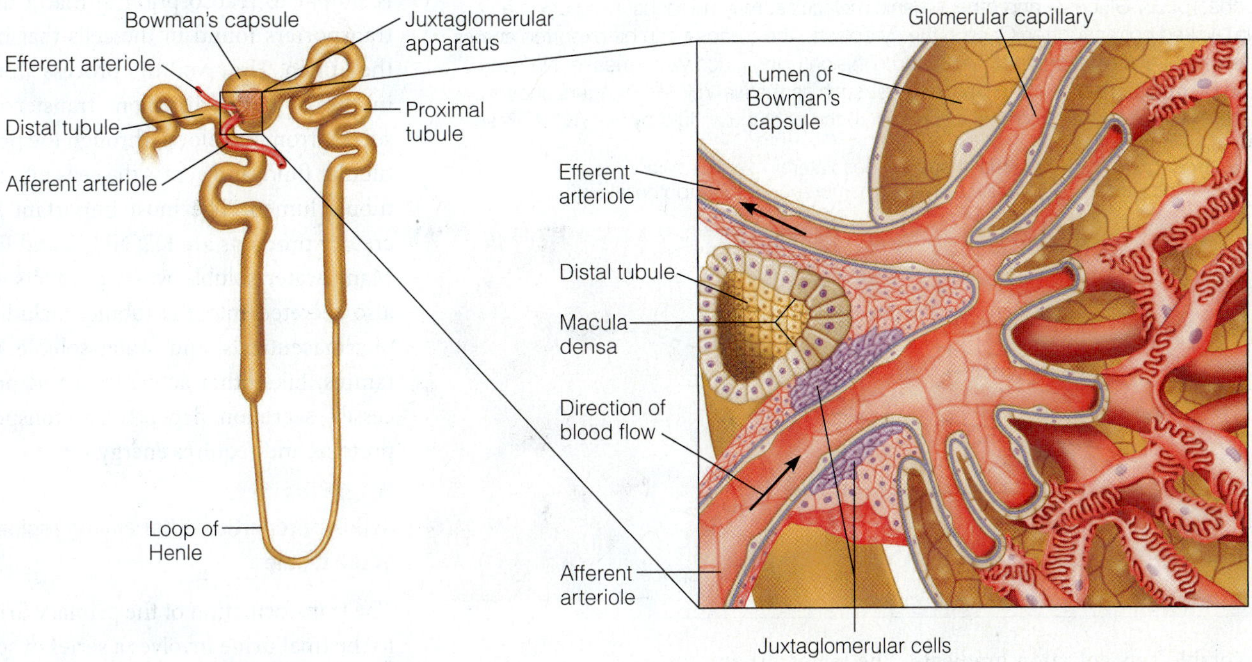

a decrease in GFR (Figure 13.19b). It is not yet clear which factors facilitate this paracrine communication. Myogenic control and tubuloglomerular feedback are two important means of intrinsic control of blood pressure that affect GFR by altering the vasculature.

Unlike myogenic control and tubuloglomerular feedback, mesangial control does not involve changes in filtration pressure. Instead, mesangial control involves changes in the surface area of the filter. When arterial blood pressure increases, which would be expected to increase GFR, the mesangial cells surrounding the blood vessels in the glomerulus are stretched, triggering them to contract. This contraction reduces the surface area of the filter, which tends to reduce GFR back to normal.

The intrinsic pathways—myogenic regulation, tubuloglomerular feedback, and mesangial control—act as negative feedback loops over a relatively narrow range of blood pressures. Other regulators are recruited when blood pressure increases or decreases more significantly or for longer periods, such as in dehydration or following blood loss.

The primary urine is modified by reabsorption and secretion

The *primary urine* that is formed by filtration is essentially isosmotic to blood (about 300 mOsM). As the fluid passes through the tubule, about 99 percent of the volume is recovered. For example, an average-sized human produces about 7.5 liters of primary urine each hour, but generates only about 75 ml of final urine. The remodeling of the primary

urine occurs as it passes through successive regions of the tubule, each with specialized transport capacities. Recall that the tubule wall is composed of a single layer of epithelial cells. Like most epithelial cells, the apical membranes (facing the lumen) and basolateral membranes (facing the interstitium) have specialized profiles of transporters. Also, the cells of the epithelium may be interconnected in ways that form a tight epithelium or a leaky epithelium. Before discussing the roles of each region of the tubule, let's first consider the general features of tubular transport.

Recovery of substances from the lumen of the tubule requires a favorable electrochemical gradient and appropriate transport capacities. Some substances in the primary urine are reclaimed by transepithelial transport, moving from the lumen of the tubule, across the single layer of epithelial cells, into the interstitial fluid (*peritubular fluid*), and ultimately back into the blood. Some hydrophobic solutes cross the tubular epithelium by **passive transport**; as water is removed from the primary urine, concentration gradients are created that can drive hydrophobic solutes back to the blood. Larger molecules in the filtrate, such as small proteins, can be recovered by transcytosis: endocytosis into the epithelial cell and exocytosis into the interstitial fluid. Most molecules, however, are reabsorbed through a combination of facilitated diffusion and active transport, both primary and secondary.

Consider how cells reabsorb sodium and glucose (Figure 13.21). The concentrations of Na^+ and glucose in the primary urine are not different from that of the blood, so the challenge is how to recover these solutes in the absence of

FIGURE 13.21 Reabsorption of glucose and Na⁺

Suites of specific transporters remove solutes from the lumen in the process of reabsorption. Glucose, and other organic molecules, may be reabsorbed using a Na⁺-linked cotransporter. Once in the cytoplasm, the glucose can be exported across the basolateral membrane by facilitated diffusion using glucose permease. Na⁺ can also be reabsorbed by other transporters, such as the Na⁺/H⁺ exchangers shown here. Na⁺ is exported from the cytoplasm to the peritubular fluid by Na⁺/K⁺ ATPase.

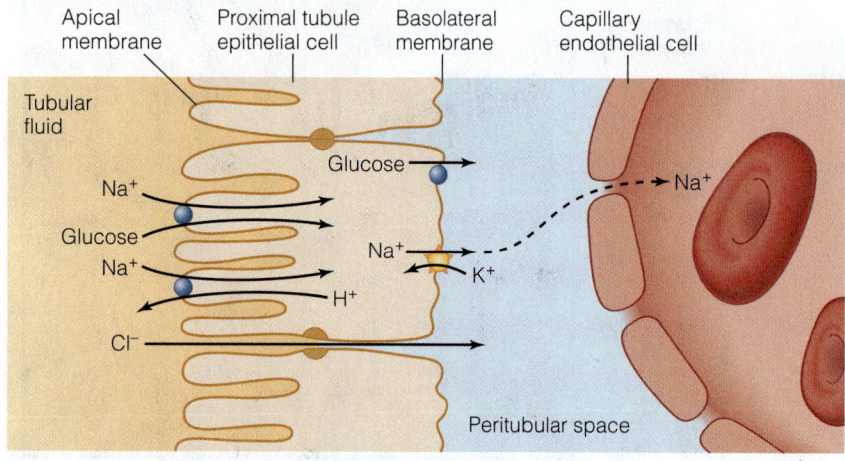

The other way the primary urine is modified is through secretion. Secretion is similar to reabsorption in that it uses transporters found in the cells that line the lumen. However, the process works in the opposite direction, transferring solutes from the blood, through the peritubular fluid, and across the cells into the tubule lumen. The most important secretory products are K^+, NH_4^+, and H^+. Many water-soluble waste products are also secreted into the tubule, including pharmaceuticals and water-soluble vitamins. Like other active transport processes, secretion depends on transport proteins and requires energy.

Cellular properties differ among regions of the tubule

The transformation of the primary urine to the final urine involves a series of specialized regions of the tubule that depend upon cellular specializations (Figure 13.23). Though the tubule wall is a single

favorable concentration gradients. The major driving force underlying the transport is the Na⁺/K⁺ ATPase found in the basolateral membrane. By pumping Na⁺ out of the cell into the interstitial fluid, the nephron cells create a favorable inward Na⁺ electrochemical gradient on the apical side that can be used to drive both Na⁺ uptake and Na⁺-coupled glucose uptake. Na⁺ can cross into the tubule cells by a Na⁺ channel, Na⁺/H⁺ exchanger, or by suites of other carriers that couple the import of organic molecules and Na⁺, including the Na⁺-glucose cotransporter. Concentrating glucose inside the cell creates a favorable outward chemical gradient for glucose; glucose permease allows glucose to cross into the peritubular interstitial fluid via facilitated diffusion. Each of these transport processes requires energy, either in the form of ATP used by the primary active transporters (for example, Na⁺/K⁺ ATPase) or in the form of electrochemical gradients used by secondary active transporters (for example, the Na⁺-glucose cotransporter).

The ability to reabsorb solutes such as glucose is limited by transport capacity. Like many active transporters, the kinetics of the transport machinery can become saturated at high substrate levels (Figure 13.22). This capacity for solute recovery is known as the *renal threshold*. If the amount of substance to be recovered is in excess of the capacity of the transport machinery, some of the substance will escape in the urine. In type 1 diabetes, the levels of glucose can be very high in the blood. When the blood is filtered by the glomerulus, the primary urine also has a very high glucose concentration. Despite the active glucose transporters, the kidney cannot reabsorb all of the glucose, and some is lost in the urine (*glucosuria*).

FIGURE 13.22 Renal threshold

Reabsorption depends on the activity of specific transporters that have a finite maximal capacity. Solutes move from the plasma to the tubule fluid when the blood passes through the glomerulus. If a solute is present at a low concentration in the plasma (and hence the tubule fluid), all of the solute can be recovered during reabsorption. As the concentration of solute increases in the plasma, it becomes more difficult to recover all of the solute from the tubule fluid. When the plasma concentration is so high that the tubule cannot reabsorb all of the solute, some appears in the urine. At still higher concentrations, the solute concentration in the urine increases dramatically.

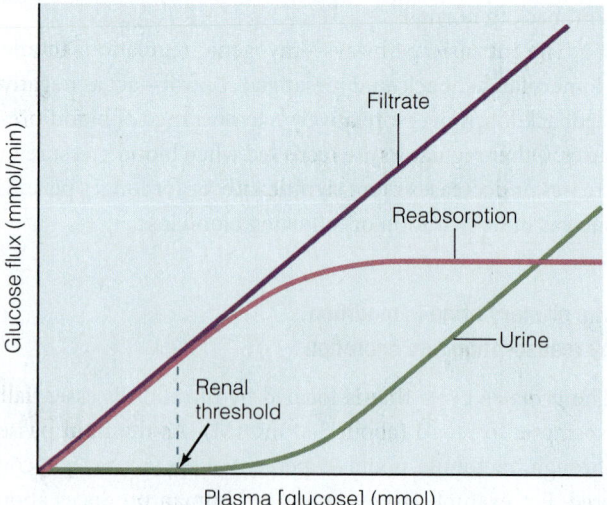

FIGURE 13.23   **Solute and water transport in each region of the nephron**

Each region of the nephron has specific transporters that can reabsorb or secrete molecules.

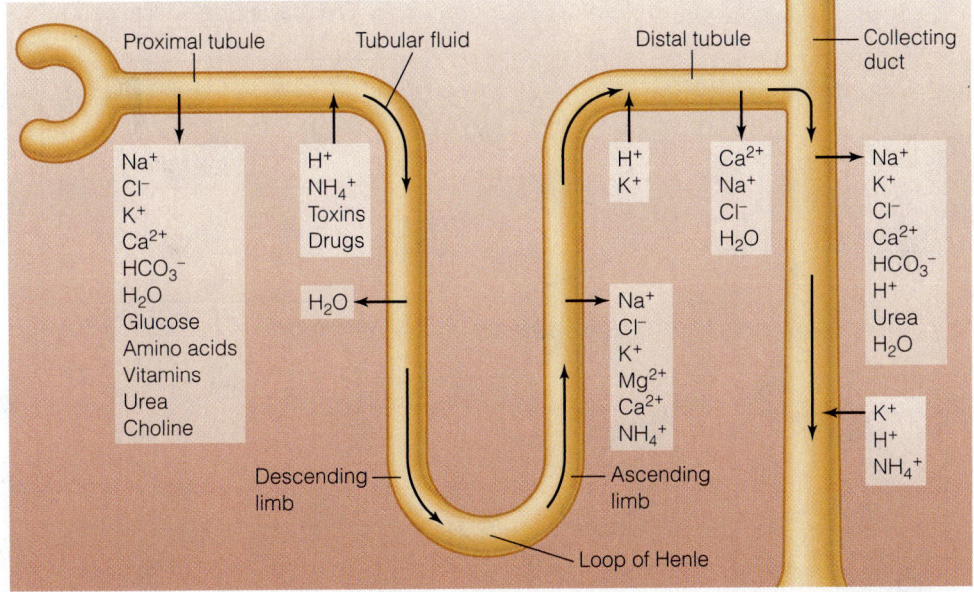

the proximal tubule, most of the epithelial cells of the distal tubule have simple membranes with few microvilli. This type of cell, known as a principal cell, also dominates the cell profile of the collecting duct. The less common intercalated cells are cuboidal epithelial cells with abundant microvilli. Not surprisingly, the functions of principal cells and intercalated cells differ as much as their structures.

The differences in cell type and morphology along the tubule and collecting duct are summarized in Figure 13.24.

layer of epithelial cells connected together by tight junctions, cell morphology and function differ considerably among regions of the tubule.

The proximal tubule can be a simple, straight tube or take a path with many convolutions; for this reason it is sometimes called the *proximal convoluted tubule*. The cells of the proximal tubule are tall cuboidal epithelial cells, with abundant mitochondria and microvilli. As with other epithelial tissues, these features are common in cells that carry out energy-dependent solute transport processes.

The proximal tubule then gives way to the loop of Henle. There is considerable variation in the nature of the loop of Henle among species, and even among nephrons of a single animal. In general, the loop of Henle is divided into a descending limb, a loop, and an ascending limb. The first part of the descending limb of the loop of Henle is composed of cuboidal epithelial cells, much like the proximal tubule. These are gradually replaced with the flatter squamous epithelial cells. The difference in the height of the cuboidal and squamous cells creates a difference in width of the wall, and these regions of the tubule are often distinguished as *thick descending limb* and *thin descending limb*. Further along the tubule, the ascending limb of the loop of Henle becomes thicker as cuboidal epithelial cells predominate. As with the descending limb, the ascending limb may be subdivided as *thin ascending limb* and *thick ascending limb*. These distinctions are made because the differences in cell shape coincide with distinctions in transport properties.

Following the loop of Henle is the distal tubule, which can be simple and straight or long and convoluted. In contrast to

The proximal tubule reabsorbs salts and organic metabolites

The proximal tubule is specialized for transport, and it is the region where most solute and water reabsorption occurs (Figure 13.25). Many solutes are transported from the lumen into proximal tubule epithelial cells via Na^+ cotransporters including organic molecules (glucose, lactate, amino acids, water-soluble vitamins) and inorganic ions (phosphate). These processes are also important in contributing to reabsorption of Na^+. The organic molecules can escape the cell into the interstitial fluid via facilitated diffusion, whereas Na^+ is pumped across the basolateral membrane via the Na^+/K^+ ATPase. The transepithelial electrochemical gradient also drives the paracellular transport of Cl^- from the lumen to the interstitial fluid. As a result of the net movement of ions and solutes from the lumen to the peritubular interstitial fluid, a decrease in osmolarity creates a favorable osmotic gradient for the movement of water. Transepithelial water movement occurs mainly through transcellular transport, mediated by aquaporins, although some paracellular movement of water may also occur. Transgenic mice lacking the gene for aquaporin-1 have a diminished ability to recover tubular fluids and are unable to form a concentrated urine.

Through these interdependent transport processes, the proximal tubule is able to reabsorb almost all organic solutes, most of the phosphate, and 60–75 percent of the Na^+, Cl^-, and water that appear in the primary urine.

The proximal tubule is also the site of secretion of organic anions, organic cations, and water-soluble toxins, including pharmaceutical agents. These molecules are imported into

FIGURE 13.24   Cell type and morphology in the tubule and collecting duct

The wall of the tubule is composed of a single layer of epithelial cells that differ in morphology.

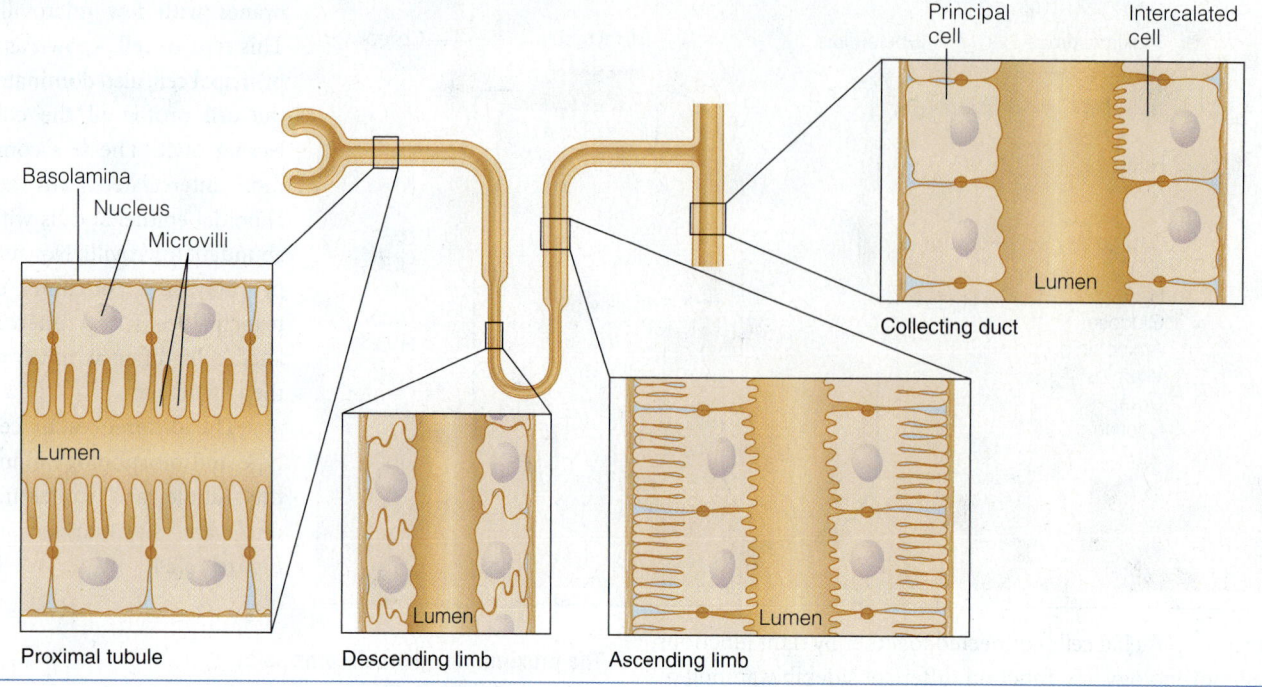

FIGURE 13.25   Transport in proximal tubule cells

OA: organic anion. OC: organic cation.

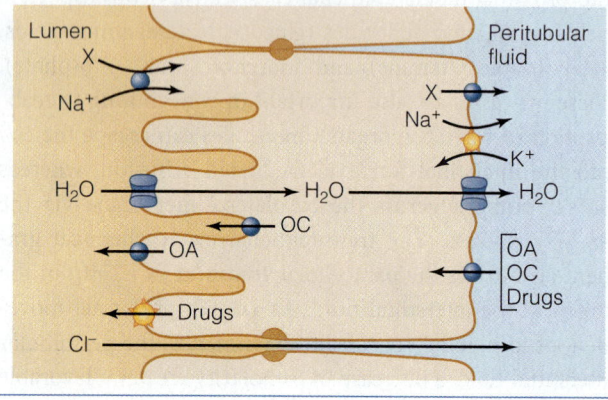

the proximal tubule cells through suites of transporters in the basolateral membrane, then exported into the lumen through apical transporters.

The loop of Henle mediates sequential uptake of water, then salt

When the primary urine has passed through the proximal tubule, the volume has diminished and most of the valuable solutes have been recovered. The remainder of the tubule is responsible for recovering the balance of the solutes and water. The next region encountered by the primary urine is the descending limb of the loop of Henle. This region of the tubule is specialized to transport water, but it is not a major site of transport for solutes. As with the proximal tubule, aquaporins allow water to move across epithelial cells in relation to the osmotic difference from the lumen to the interstitial fluid.

Critical to the water recovery strategy is an osmotic gradient that exists within the medulla (Figure 13.26). At the transition between the proximal tubule and descending loop of Henle, the osmolarity of the interstitial fluid is similar to that of the blood—about 300 mOsM. As the descending loop of Henle goes deeper into the medulla, the osmolarity of the interstitial fluid increases, drawing water from the primary urine across the epithelial cells. With loss of water, but not solutes, the osmolarity of the primary urine increases, reaching a maximum at the loop region of the loop of Henle.

Once the tubule turns and moves back toward the cortex, the epithelial cell transport capacity changes. Instead of expressing aquaporin genes, these epithelial cells express solute transporters. As the tubule passes through the medulla, the interstitial osmolarity decreases. Because the epithelial cells can only transport solutes, the transepithelial gradients drive movements of solutes from the primary urine to the interstitial fluid. As a result of various transporters in the apical and basolateral membranes, there is a net movement of Na^+ and

FIGURE 13.26 Osmotic gradients in the interstitial fluid of the medulla

The loop of Henle passes through osmotic gradients in the medulla. The osmolarity is lowest near the border of the cortex, and increases deeper into the kidney.

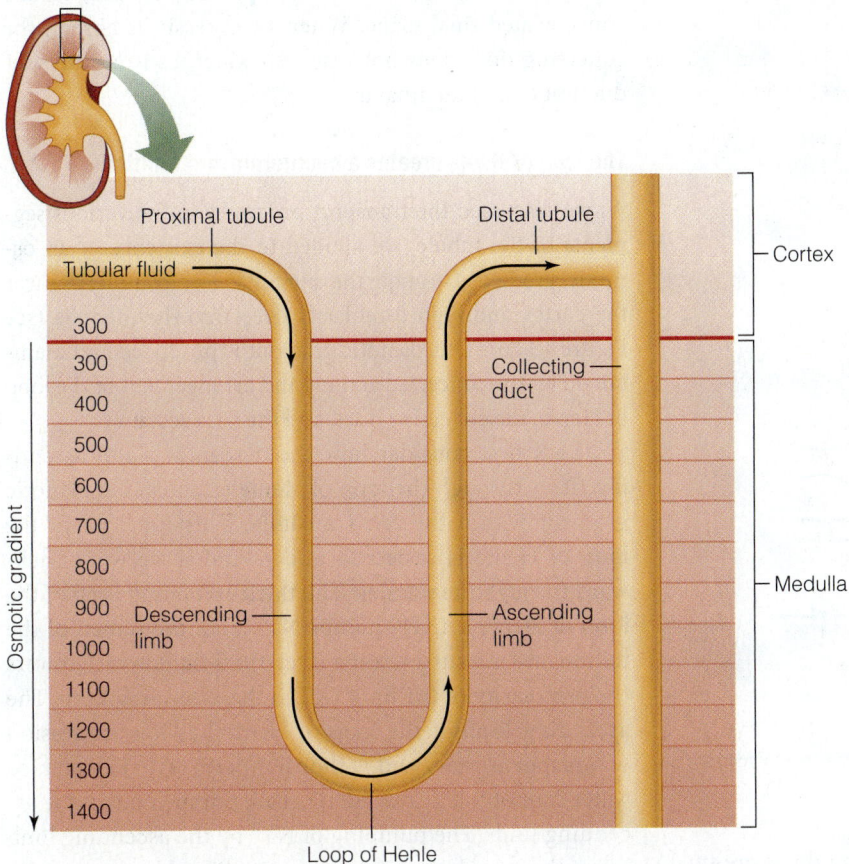

Though the proximal tubule reabsorbs most of the Na^+ and Cl^- appearing in the primary urine, the distal tubule reabsorbs most of the remaining Na^+ and Cl^-. An apical Na^+-Cl^- cotransporter carries the ions into the cell; Na^+ is then exported from the distal tubule epithelial cells via the Na^+/K^+ ATPase, and Cl^- escapes through Cl^- channels.

As with the Na^+ and Cl^-, the proximal tubule is the main site of reabsorption of Ca^{2+} and Mg^{2+}, but the distal tubule is the segment where hormones exert their effects on absorption of the remainder. Ca^{2+} enters the distal tubule epithelial cells through Ca^{2+} channels, and exits into the interstitial fluid via a Na^+/Ca^{2+} exchanger and, to a lesser extent, a Ca^{2+} ATPase.

The distal tubule is an important site for recovery of water, under conditions where water recovery is required. Under normal circumstances, the distal tubule cells have low expression of aquaporin genes. When an animal is dehydrated, hormones such as vasopressin lead to increased expression of aquaporin genes, allowing water recovery from the tubule lumen.

The distal tubule is also the main site of secretion of K^+ into the tubule. As the primary urine moves through the proximal tubule and loop of Henle, about 90 percent of K^+ is reabsorbed. In the distal tubule, the epithelial cells are able to secrete K^+. It is brought into the epithelial cell from the interstitial fluid via Na^+/K^+ ATPase, and moves into the lumen through either a K^+-Cl^- cotransporter or a K^+ channel.

The transport processes in the distal tubule are summarized in Figure 13.28.

Cl^- from the primary urine to the interstitial fluid. On the apical membrane, the NKCC transporter mediates uptake of Na^+, K^+, and Cl^- into the cell. The basolateral membrane transports Na^+ and Cl^- into the interstitial fluid: Na^+ via the Na^+/K^+ ATPase, and Cl^- via Cl^- channels and a K^+-Cl^- cotransporter. An apical K^+ channel allows K^+ imported via NKCC to escape back to the lumen. The transport processes in the ascending limb and descending limb are summarized in Figure 13.27.

The distal tubule mediates K^+ secretion, NaCl reabsorption, and hormone-sensitive water recovery

After fluids leave the loop of Henle, they enter the distal tubule. This region of the tubule is an important site for hormone-mediated regulation of uptake of solutes and water. Hormones produced by the adrenal gland (mineralocorticoids), hypothalamic-pituitary axis (vasopressin, also called antidiuretic hormone), and parathyroid (parathyroid hormone) act on distal tubule epithelial cells to alter levels and activities of transport proteins.

The collecting duct regulates ion and water flux

The collecting ducts traverse the layers of the kidney, connecting the distal tubules of cortical and juxtamedullary nephrons. As they move deeper into the kidney, the profile of cells changes, enabling specialized transport functions in different segments. The principal cells secrete K^+ and reabsorb Na^+, similar to those found in the distal tubule. The intercalated cells are able to secrete H^+ or HCO_3^-, depending on the acid-base status of the animal. H^+ secretion is coupled to K^+ import through a H^+/K^+ ATPase.

FIGURE 13.27 **Transport in the loop of Henle**

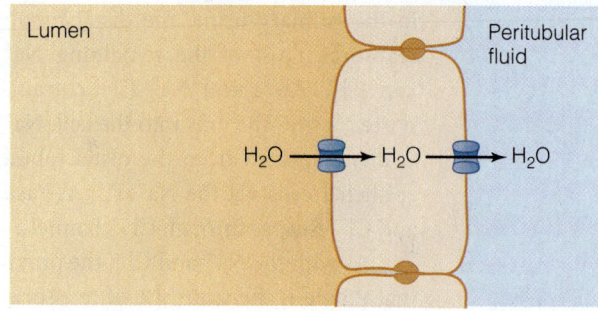

(a) Thin descending limb

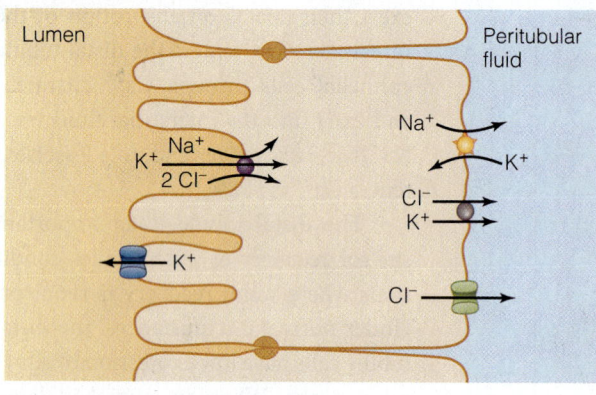

(b) Thick ascending limb

As with the distal tubule, the collecting ducts are important targets of regulatory changes in ion and water movements, including hormone-responsive pathways. Thus, the collecting ducts can be important sites of K^+ secretion or reabsorption, depending on the nature of the primary urine and systemic K^+ homeostasis. When K^+ excretion is needed, secretion by principal cells is stimulated, but when K^+ recovery is needed, reabsorptive pathways

FIGURE 13.28 **Transport in the distal tubule**

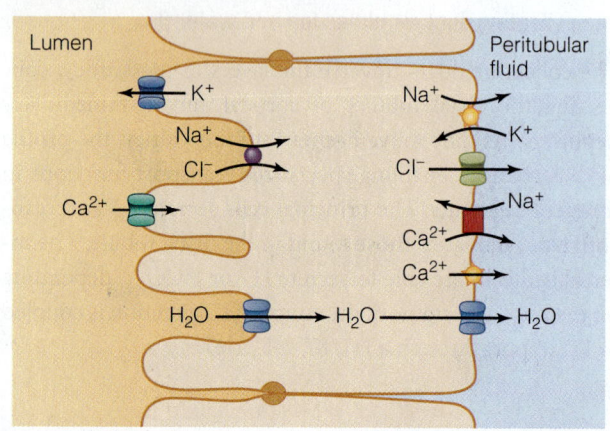

in intercalated cells are stimulated. Similarly, the collecting ducts are the main site of regulated water reabsorption. In the presence of high levels of vasopressin, the collecting duct reabsorbs water from the primary urine to form a concentrated final urine. When vasopressin is absent, the collecting duct does not reabsorb water, causing the production of a dilute final urine.

The loop of Henle creates a countercurrent multiplier

As we discussed the transport processes in the various segments of the tubule, we alluded to the existence of an osmotic gradient through the medulla: low osmolarity near the cortex and high osmolarity deep into the medulla (see Figure 13.26). This osmotic gradient is produced and maintained by the concerted actions and arrangement of the loop of Henle, the collecting duct, and the vasa recta.

Let's first consider how the descending and ascending flows through the loop of Henle establish the osmotic gradient within the renal medulla. This function of the loop of Henle is easiest to understand if we work backward through the tubules. The thick ascending limb of the loop of Henle actively pumps Na^+ from the lumen of the tubule into the surrounding interstitial fluid, which lowers the osmolarity of the fluid within the ascending limb. The ascending limb of the loop of Henle has low expression of aquaporin genes and is thus not permeable to water, so water cannot follow the salts that are pumped out of the ascending limb. The pumping of Na^+ by the ascending limb raises the osmolarity of the interstitial fluid in the medulla compared with the fluid in the descending limb of the loop of Henle.

The descending limb of the loop of Henle is permeable to water, but not to salts. Because the interstitial fluid surrounding the loop has been made more concentrated (due to the active pumping of Na^+ by the ascending limb), water is drawn out of the descending limb into the interstitial fluid, until the osmolarity within the interstitial fluid and the descending limb equilibrate. The ascending limb of the loop of Henle continues to pump ions into the interstitial fluid, so the net effect of these processes is that the osmolarity in the interstitial fluid and in the descending limb of the loop of Henle are higher than that of the fluid in the proximal tubule, and the osmolarity of the fluid in the ascending limb of the loop of Henle is lower than in the proximal tubule. This process, which is termed the *single effect*, results in a modest increase in the osmolarity of the renal medulla compared with the renal cortex. But establishing the very large osmotic gradient within the medulla requires another process. The loop of Henle acts as a **countercurrent multiplier.**

As the name suggests, the countercurrent multiplier of the loop of Henle acts to multiply the single effect to allow the renal medulla to maintain a much larger osmotic gradient than would be possible from ion pumping alone. This multiplication is possible because of the countercurrent arrangement of the descending and ascending limbs of the loop of Henle: Fluid that flows through the descending limb is traveling in the opposite direction to fluid that flows through the ascending limb. Figure 13.29 provides a conceptual example of how the countercurrent multiplier of the kidney works.

In step (a), imagine that the entire loop of Henle is filled with a fluid that has an osmolarity roughly similar to that of blood (note that this does not actually occur in a real nephron, but it provides us with a starting point with which to understand the countercurrent multiplier). As we have already discussed, the thick ascending limb actively pumps Na^+ into the interstitial fluid (step b), but water cannot follow. Instead, water is drawn from the descending limb into the interstitial fluid (step c), so that the fluid in the descending limb and the interstitial fluid equilibrate, but at an osmolarity that is somewhat higher than that of blood because of the Na^+ movement from the ascending limb. This increase in osmolarity in the tubular fluid is the starting point for the countercurrent multiplier, which comes into play when we consider that fluid is continuously flowing through the kidney tubules. As shown in step (d), new fluid flows from the proximal tubule into the descending limb of the loop of Henle, pushing the concentrated fluid around into the base of the ascending limb. In step (e), the ascending limb continues to pump Na^+ into the interstitial fluid, but it is starting from a more concentrated solution, so it is able to generate a higher osmolarity within the interstitial fluid. In the next steps (not shown), more fluid flows into the loop of Henle from the proximal tubule and the process continues, further increasing the osmolarity in the medulla. This process repeats as the fluid flows through the loop of Henle, ultimately establishing a large osmotic gradient in the medulla. The exact extent of this osmotic gradient depends on a variety of factors, including the size of the single effect, the rate of fluid flow through the loop of Henle, and the length of the loop itself.

Vasopressin alters the permeability of the collecting duct

Note that the net effect of countercurrent multiplication is to produce a fluid in the distal tubule that has a lower osmolarity than that of blood. Producing a highly concentrated urine requires that water be reabsorbed from this dilute solution. **Vasopressin**, also known as **antidiuretic hormone** or **ADH**, is the main hormone responsible for recovery of water from the tubule. After this peptide hormone is produced in the cell bodies of hypothalamic neurons, it travels down the neurons to the pituitary gland, where it is released into the circulation. High vasopressin levels increase the reabsorption of water by the collecting duct. Vasopressin alters water uptake by

FIGURE 13.29 Countercurrent multiplication

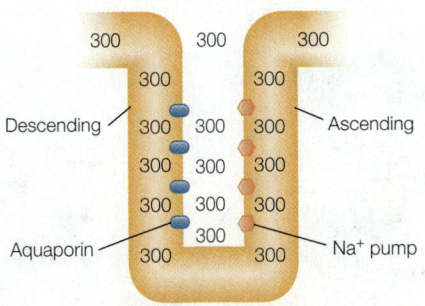

(a) Isoosmotic fluid in tubule (no tubular flow)

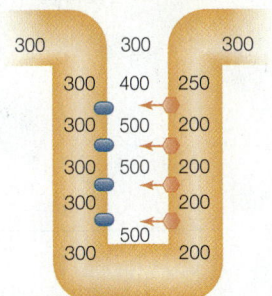

(b) Na⁺ into interstitium (no tubular flow)

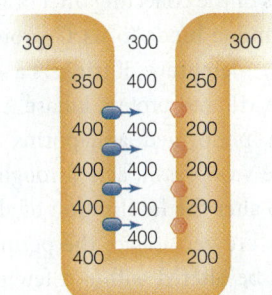

(c) Water into interstitium (no tubular flow)

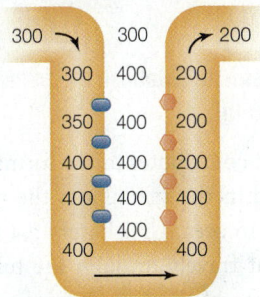

(d) Tubular flow into loop of Henle

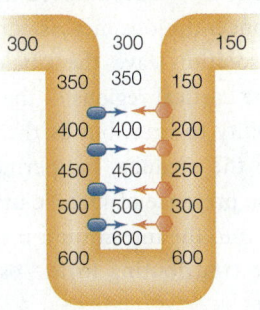

(e) Na⁺ and water movements into interstitium

FIGURE 13.30 **Vasopressin and water permeability**

Vasopressin changes the water permeability of the distal tubule and collecting duct by altering the levels of aquaporins present in the membrane.

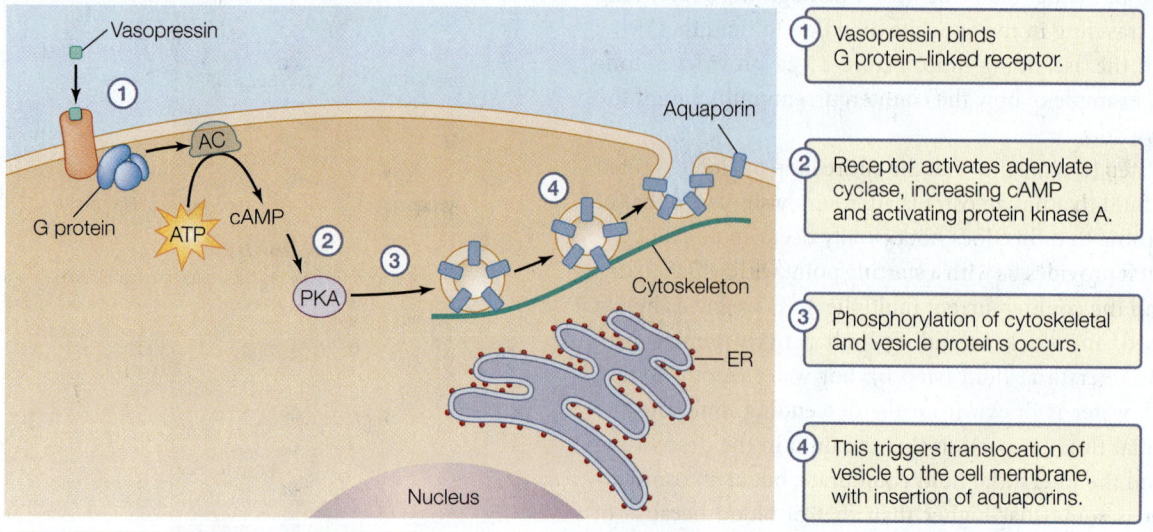

1. Vasopressin binds G protein–linked receptor.

2. Receptor activates adenylate cyclase, increasing cAMP and activating protein kinase A.

3. Phosphorylation of cytoskeletal and vesicle proteins occurs.

4. This triggers translocation of vesicle to the cell membrane, with insertion of aquaporins.

affecting the number of aquaporins in the apical membrane of the principal cells of the collecting duct (Figure 13.30).

When the hormone binds to its G protein–linked receptor in the plasma membrane, it triggers a signaling pathway that acts via cAMP and protein kinase A to translocate vesicles containing preformed aquaporins to the apical membrane. Because vasopressin acts through a G protein–coupled pathway to alter the localization of already existing proteins, its actions are very rapid; the permeability of the collecting duct can be altered within a few minutes. Once vasopressin levels fall, the pathway reverses and aquaporins are removed from the membrane by endocytosis.

Recycling of urea helps to establish the osmotic gradient in the medulla

Another factor that contributes to the formation of the osmotic gradient within the medulla is the permeability of the collecting duct to urea. Urea enters the tubule through the glomerulus, but travels through the tubule with little reabsorption because of the low urea permeability of the tubule. With much of the water removed from the original filtrate, the urea concentrations increase dramatically. The concentrated urea solution leaves the tubule and enters the collecting duct. The cortical regions of the collecting duct have low permeability to urea, but as the collecting duct moves deeper into the medulla, the permeability to urea increases due to the presence of specific urea transporters. Movement of urea into the interstitium increases the local osmolarity, further contributing to the osmotic gradient within the medulla.

The vasa recta maintains the medullary osmotic gradient via a countercurrent exchanger

The osmotic gradient may *arise* along the depth of the medulla through the movement of salts and water between the tubule and the interstitial fluid, but it is *maintained* because the *vasa recta* (see Figure 13.16) works as a *countercurrent exchanger*.[2] In most tissues, capillaries drain the interstitium, collecting solutes and water and emptying them into the blood. The vasculature in the medulla is arranged in a way that it can meet the circulatory needs (O_2 delivery, CO_2 removal) without disrupting the osmotic gradient. Consider what would happen if the blood vessels flowed unidirectionally from the cortex through the medulla and out of the kidney; the blood would draw fluids and solutes out of the kidney, rapidly dissipating the gradient created within the medulla. Instead, the vessels of the vasa recta carry blood into the medulla, then back out of the medulla. As blood leaves the efferent arteriole and enters the vasa recta, it is carried into the medulla, where the higher osmolarity causes it to passively pick up solutes and lose water. As the vessels head back toward the cortex, the decreasing osmolarity causes the blood to lose solutes and gain water. The blood vessels exit the kidney at the junction between cortex and medulla, where interstitial fluid is isosmotic to blood. Thus, the countercurrent arrangement of the vasa recta ensures that the osmotic gradient within the medulla is maintained.

[2]Most commonly, countercurrent exchangers and countercurrent multipliers are distinguished by the need for direct energy investment. That is, exchangers passively transfer molecules (or heat), whereas multipliers require some form of active transport.

Micturition is regulated by reflex and higher pathways

After the urine leaves the kidney, it enters the urinary bladder for storage. The bladder is a hollow sac composed of smooth muscle, with a capacity of approximately 500 milliliters in humans. From the bladder, the urine exits through the urethra. Two sphincters control the flow of urine from the bladder to the urethra. The internal sphincter is composed of smooth muscle and is under the control of the sympathetic and parasympathetic nervous systems. The external sphincter is composed of skeletal muscle and is under voluntary control mediated by the somatic motor nervous system.

The bladder wall contains stretch receptors that are activated once the bladder wall has been stretched. This triggers a signal via sensory neurons to the spinal cord, which in turn stimulates parasympathetic neurons to trigger the contraction of smooth muscle in the walls of the bladder. This increases pressure on bladder contents, and opens the internal sphincter. Simultaneously, there is an inhibition of the somatic motor neurons that normally hold the external sphincter closed. When the balance of stimulatory and inhibitory controls exceeds a threshold, the sphincters opens and urine is released. In human infants, micturition is an entirely reflex process, occurring approximately twenty times each day, and the ability to voluntarily suppress micturition does not develop until about two or three years of age.

CONCEPT CHECK

9. What is the role of the glomerulus in the nephron?
10. Discuss movements of NaCl and water in the segments of the renal tubule.

Roles of the Kidney in Homeostasis

As we discussed earlier in this chapter, the kidney plays a major role in maintaining homeostasis, and is critically important for ion balance, osmotic balance, pH balance, and the regulation of blood pressure. The kidney works closely with other systems, such as the cardiovascular system and the respiratory system, in performing this homeostatic control.

Endocrine hormones have a central role in regulating osmotic and ion balance in mammals, acting on both the cardiovascular system and the nephron itself to alter the nature of the urine. The steroid hormones that affect ion and water balance (mineralocorticoids) act over hours to alter transporter levels in the tubule. The peptide hormones released from the hypothalamic-pituitary axis act much more rapidly. Superimposed on the natural, hormonal controls are dietary factors that affect urine properties: Diuretics stimulate the excretion of water, and antidiuretics reduce the excretion of water. Often, these dietary factors induce maladaptive changes—dehydration or water retention—that must be overcome by intrinsic negative feedback pathways.

Aldosterone regulates sodium and potassium balance

Steroid hormones called mineralocorticoids stimulate Na^+ reabsorption (and secondarily water recovery from the urine) and enhance K^+ excretion. The mineralocorticoids are produced by the adrenal cortex in tetrapods and the interrenal tissue in fish. These tissues, both physically close to the kidney, release aldosterone into the blood. Aldosterone targets the principal cells of the distal tubule and collecting ducts, binding to a cytoplasmic hormone receptor and entering the nucleus to stimulate transcription of genes involved in ion transport (Figure 13.31). The effects of aldosterone manifest over several hours because the process involves gene transcription, translation at the endoplasmic reticulum, processing in the Golgi apparatus, packaging into vesicles, and the fusion of the vesicles with the plasma membrane.

Insight into the role of aldosterone comes from studies of lab rats with the adrenal gland surgically removed (adrenalectomy). Within only a few hours, the rats produce copious volumes of urine, high in Na^+ and low in K^+. As the loss of aldosterone continues unabated, the animal slowly dehydrates as it draws fluids from the extracellular spaces to maintain blood volume and blood pressure.

Aldosterone exerts its effects on K^+, Na^+, and water by stimulating the expression of genes encoding transport proteins. Na^+/K^+ ATPase is produced in the principal cells and sent to the basolateral membrane; K^+ channels and Na^+ channels are produced and targeted to the apical membrane. The interaction between Na^+ and K^+ transport causes the net exchange of plasma K^+ for Na^+ in the urine. The actions of the Na^+/K^+ ATPase increase intracellular $[K^+]$, driving K^+ efflux into the tubule lumen through the K^+ channels. As the Na^+/K^+ ATPase pulls K^+ from the plasma, it expels Na^+ from the cytoplasm. This Na^+ enters the tubule cell through Na^+ channels in the luminal (apical) membrane from the primary urine. Aldosterone exerts no direct effects on water transport (unlike vasopressin); the stimulation of water recovery from the urine is a consequence of the reabsorption of Na^+.

The renin-angiotensin-aldosterone pathway regulates blood pressure

Circulating $[K^+]$ is a major determinant of aldosterone synthesis—another example of a negative feedback loop. However, aldosterone production is also regulated by the hormone angiotensin II in the renin-angiotensin pathway. Juxtaglomerular cells in afferent and efferent arterioles of the nephron secrete the enzyme renin, which converts the

FIGURE 13.31   Aldosterone and ion reabsorption

Aldosterone stimulates the transcription of a variety of genes involved in sodium and potassium transport.

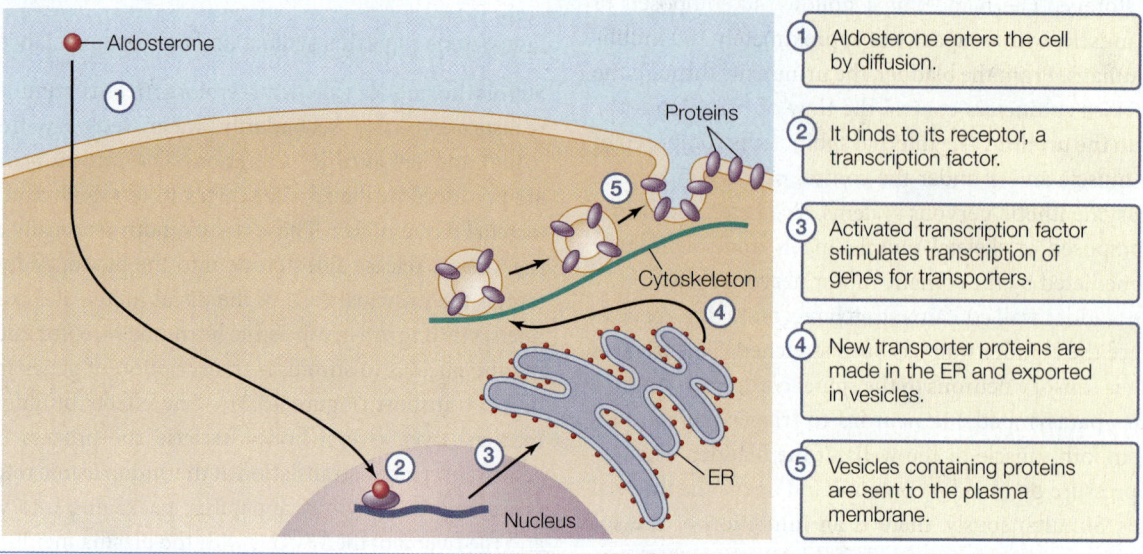

1. Aldosterone enters the cell by diffusion.

2. It binds to its receptor, a transcription factor.

3. Activated transcription factor stimulates transcription of genes for transporters.

4. New transporter proteins are made in the ER and exported in vesicles.

5. Vesicles containing proteins are sent to the plasma membrane.

plasma protein angiotensinogen to angiotensin I. Another enzyme called **angiotensin-converting enzyme**, or ACE, found on the epithelia of blood vessels, converts angiotensin I to angiotensin II. The secretion of renin is controlled in three ways. First, juxtaglomerular cells release renin when blood pressures decline; the juxtaglomerular cells may be baroreceptors themselves, or they may rely on neighboring cells to sense and respond to pressure changes through local signaling factors. Second, decreases in blood pressure activate sympathetic neurons in the cardiovascular control center of the medulla oblongata, triggering an increase in renin secretion. Third, the macula densa cells in the wall of the distal tubule respond to a decrease in urine flow and Na^+ delivery by releasing a paracrine signal that induces the juxtaglomerular cells to increase renin secretion.

Angiotensin II acts at a number of different sites, including the kidney, brain, heart, adrenal cortex, and blood vessels. Recall from Chapter 9: Circulatory Systems that angiotensin II is an important regulator of the cardiovascular system, exerting effects on cardiac growth and angiogenesis. In terms of ion and water balance, angiotensin II stimulates Na^+ reabsorption in the proximal tubule and vasoconstricts postglomerular blood vessels. It can also stimulate the synthesis and release of other hormones that exert their own effects on the kidney to increase solute and water recovery. Angiotensin II increases the synthesis and release of aldosterone from the adrenal cortex and vasopressin from the pituitary.

Natriuretic peptides also play a role in sodium balance

Mammals produce a group of hormones called natriuretic peptides (NPs), which as the name suggests, favor the appearance of Na^+ in the urine. The first natriuretic hormone to be identified was **atrial natriuretic peptide (ANP)**. Cardiac atrial cells produce ANP and excrete it in response to excessive stretch, which would accompany an increase in blood volume. Upon release, ANP travels to the kidney, where it increases Na^+ excretion by several mechanisms dependent upon activation of guanylyl cyclases and cGMP. The natriuretic and diuretic effects of ANP affect both the renal vasculature and tubular function.

The effects of ANP serve to increase the GFR. ANP increases blood flow to the glomerulus, acting on either the afferent glomerular arteriole (vasodilation) or efferent glomerular arteriole (vasoconstriction). It also causes relaxation of the mesangial cells, increasing the surface area available for filtration. It may also target the foot processes of the podocytes, increasing the size of the filtration slits of the glomerulus.

The effects of ANP on renal tubules are mediated through antagonistic effects on other hormones. It decreases aldosterone release by the adrenal cortex, preventing aldosterone from enhancing Na^+ reabsorption in the distal tubule. It decreases renin release, thereby decreasing angiotensin II. In many ways, ANP acts antagonistically to the renin-angiotensin system and the aldosterone pathway. It is also an antagonist of the production and release of vasopressin, reducing water reabsorption in the collecting ducts.

The respiratory system and excretory system contribute to acid-base balance

The concentration of H^+ in both intracellular and extracellular fluids is closely regulated in mammals and many other animals. Sources of H^+ include food and metabolic processes. The largest source of acid in most animals is the production of CO_2 during aerobic respiration. Carbon dioxide is not, itself, an acid, but it combines with water to form carbonic acid, which dissociates into a proton and a bicarbonate ion (HCO_3^-). The reaction shown below can occur spontaneously, but it is catalyzed at a very high rate by the enzyme carbonic anhydrase.

$$CO_2 + H_2O \rightarrow H^+ + HCO_3^-$$

The body copes with changes in acid production through changes in ventilation and by regulating the excretion of H^+ and HCO_3^- at the kidneys. When blood pH falls, an animal will hyperventilate, resulting in a reduction in plasma P_{CO_2}. As P_{CO_2} falls, the carbonic anhydrase equilibrium shifts, and the concentration of H^+ ions in the plasma declines, increasing the pH and restoring homeostasis. The respiratory system plays the major role in regulating body pH, but the kidneys also provide an important component.

Transport processes in each segment of the nephron contribute to changes in the pH of the primary urine as a way of controlling whole-body acid-base balance. Conversely, changes in pH of the primary urine affect the ability of cells to use pH-dependent transporters to recover or secrete ions. The main way that the nephron regulates pH of the urine is through transport and metabolism of H^+, HCO_3^-, and ammonia. For example, metabolic acidosis leads to secretion of H^+ and NH_4^+, and reabsorption of HCO_3^-. Many transporters affect pH by expelling protons into the lumen. For example, apical Na^+/H^+ exchangers recover Na^+ and extrude H^+, acidifying the urine. These exchangers are found in the proximal tubule, ascending limb of the loop of Henle, the distal tubule, and collecting ducts. Some segments also possess proton pumps, such as the H^+ ATPase and H^+/K^+ ATPase of the distal tubule and collecting duct. Overall, proton excretion by the collecting duct plays the greatest role in regulation of acid extrusion by the tubule. Movements of bicarbonate (HCO_3^-) also affect acid-base balance. Many regions have Cl^-/HCO_3^- exchangers that allow cells to recover Cl^-, while alkalinizing the primary urine. The proximal tubule and ascending limb of the loop of Henle are the main sites of HCO_3^- reabsorption.

The tubule epithelial cells that secrete protons derive those protons through the actions of carbonic anhydrase. Protons are exported across the apical membrane into the lumen, whereas HCO_3^- can be exported into the blood via a basolateral Cl^-/HCO_3^- exchanger. The net effect is acidification of the urine and alkalinization of the interstitial fluid. Ammonia production, reabsorption, and secretion affect pH balance. The proximal tubule is an important site of ammonia production, largely from glutamine. Metabolism of glutamine occurs via glutaminase (producing glutamate), glutamate dehydrogenase (producing 2-oxoglutarate), and

TCA cycle enzymes (producing oxaloacetate). Whether the resulting oxaloacetate is completely oxidized in the TCA cycle or used as a gluconeogenic substrate, each glutamine generates two HCO_3^- and two NH_4^+. These reactions have an influence on acid-base balance because the NH_4^+ (an acid) is excreted and HCO_3^- can titrate H^+. Ammonia produced by the proximal tubule is secreted into the lumen, reabsorbed in the ascending limb of the loop of Henle, and secreted in the collecting duct using a combination of transporters. Acid-base balance, as with other renal responsibilities, is regulated directly by prevailing conditions in the tubule lumen and interstitial fluid, as well as by hormones that respond to systemic changes and mediate compensatory responses.

CONCEPT CHECK

11. Compare and contrast how vasopressin and aldosterone regulate kidney function.
12. Describe the relationship between respiration and nitrogen excretion.

Water Intake and Excretion

To maintain water balance, the amount of water entering the body must be balanced with the amount of water leaving the body. The principle routes of water entry in humans are from drinking, from food, and the production of water in metabolic pathways. Humans and other mammals cannot obtain water across the skin or respiratory surfaces, although water movements across these surfaces are common in aquatic vertebrates. The principle routes of water loss in humans are across the respiratory surfaces, the skin, and in the urine. Humans are adapted for terrestrial life, and thus have relatively thick skin and have mechanisms to recover water that is lost across the respiratory surfaces. As a result, the major route for water loss in humans and other mammals is in the urine. When water intake goes down, urine production decreases to compensate, and when water intake increases, urine production goes up.

As we discussed earlier in this chapter, vasopressin is the primary hormone that regulates the volume of urine. When vasopressin levels are high, aquaporins are inserted into the membrane of the collecting duct and water is reabsorbed, resulting in the production of a low volume of highly concentrated urine. When vasopressin levels are low, aquaporins are removed from the membrane of the collecting duct, and water cannot be reabsorbed, resulting in the production of a large volume of dilute urine.

Hypothalamic factors regulate thirst

Water balance is, of course, affected by water consumption. The perception of thirst can arise in response to dehydration or Na$^+$ overload. Hormones that reflect the systemic state of the animal, including the osmotic condition and the cardiovascular state, exert effects on the central nervous system to affect thirst.

The hypothalamus is responsible for sensing the external conditions and controlling thirst. Recall that this region of the brain has an incomplete blood-brain barrier, allowing hypothalamic neurons to detect plasma conditions, including circulating hormones. The osmotic condition is detected by a combination of osmoreceptors and hormone receptors. The osmoreceptors in circumventricular organs monitor the osmolarity of the cerebrospinal fluid that bathes the hypothalamus. Angiotensin II, which exerts water-sparing effects on the kidney, also binds to receptors in this region of the brain. This hypothalamic region then sends signals to the thirst center elsewhere in the hypothalamus, likely the dorsomedial hypothalamic nucleus. Stimulation of the thirst center increases the motivation to drink.

The excretory system interacts with the cardiovascular system to regulate blood pressure

In our discussion of kidney function, we focused on how the kidney produces urine to control water balance. However, the excretory system and cardiovascular system have overlapping responsibilities in regulating blood pressure. The cardiovascular system responds primarily to changes in blood pressure, whereas the excretory system responds to changes in both blood pressure and blood osmolarity. Animals regulate blood pressure by controlling both the volume of blood and its osmolarity, which depend on water and salt fluxes but can vary independently of each other.

Consider how different foods affect water and salt balance, and how the excretory system must respond to maintain homeostasis. If you drink a large amount of water without ingesting anything salty, the total body fluid volume quickly increases and osmolarity decreases. Increasing the volume of urine corrects this situation. Conversely, if you eat salty food without drinking, the osmolarity increases but your body fluid volume remains unaltered. The kidneys must increase the excretion of salt, but retain as much water as possible. Both volume and osmolarity increase if you eat salty food and drink a large amount of liquid at the same time. The kidney must increase both the volume of urine and the total amount of salt in the urine. However, the response to changes in volume and osmolarity is not always this simple. High osmolarity could arise from excessive salt (so a response of salt excretion is appropriate) or dehydration (a response of water consumption is appropriate).

Dehydration is, in fact, the most common cause of disturbances in fluid volume and osmolarity in terrestrial animals. If you were to exercise on a hot day, you would lose water in the sweat and in the expired air. Without drinking, you become dehydrated; blood volume will decrease and osmolarity will increase, with negative effects on the cardiovascular system. The decrease in blood volume leads to decreases in venous return to the heart, cardiac output, and mean arterial blood pressure. Thus, during dehydration, blood pressure drops while blood osmolarity increases.

Various pathways are involved in homeostatic compensation for severe dehydration (Figure 13.32). These pathways involve the cardiovascular system, the renin-angiotensin system, renal mechanisms such as glomerular filtration, and mechanisms coordinated by the hypothalamus.

One of the fastest responses to the decrease in blood pressure is the fluid-shift mechanism. Low blood pressure reduces filtration across the capillaries, and causes fluid to shift from the interstitial space to the blood. This helps to return blood volume and blood pressure to normal.

The decrease in blood pressure as a result of dehydration also reduces the amount of stretch on the carotid and aortic body baroreceptors. This causes them to reduce the frequency of action potentials in the afferent neurons leading to the cardiovascular control center in the medulla oblongata of the brain. This decrease in action potential frequency causes the cardiovascular control center to decrease parasympathetic output and increase sympathetic output, and these changes in turn increase heart rate and the force of cardiac contraction, increasing cardiac output. At the same time, the sympathetic neurons leading to many systemic arterioles stimulate the arteriolar smooth muscle to contract. The resulting vasoconstriction increases total peripheral resistance (TPR). Because mean arterial pressure is equal to cardiac output times total peripheral resistance, these two mechanisms lead to an increase in blood pressure, helping compensate for the decreased blood pressure caused by dehydration.

The decrease in stimulation of the atrial volume receptors and the carotid and aortic body baroreceptors as a result of low blood pressure also has a direct effect on the hypothalamus, increasing vasopressin secretion and thirst. Together, these responses increase water reabsorption by the kidney and water intake, resulting in increased fluid volume and decreased osmolarity.

The decreased blood pressure caused by dehydration also stimulates the juxtaglomerular (JG) cells of the kidney, causing them to increase the secretion of renin. The increased renin increases the conversion of angiotensinogen to angiotensin I. Angiotensin-converting enzyme (ACE) then catalyzes the conversion of angiotensin I to angiotensin II. Simultaneously, the increase in sympathetic output also stimulates the juxtaglomerular cells, further increasing the level of angiotensin II. As we have learned in this chapter and Chapter 9, angiotensin II has wide-ranging effects on the circulatory and excretory systems. Angiotensin II can directly

FIGURE 13.32 **Regulation of blood pressure and kidney function in response to dehydration**

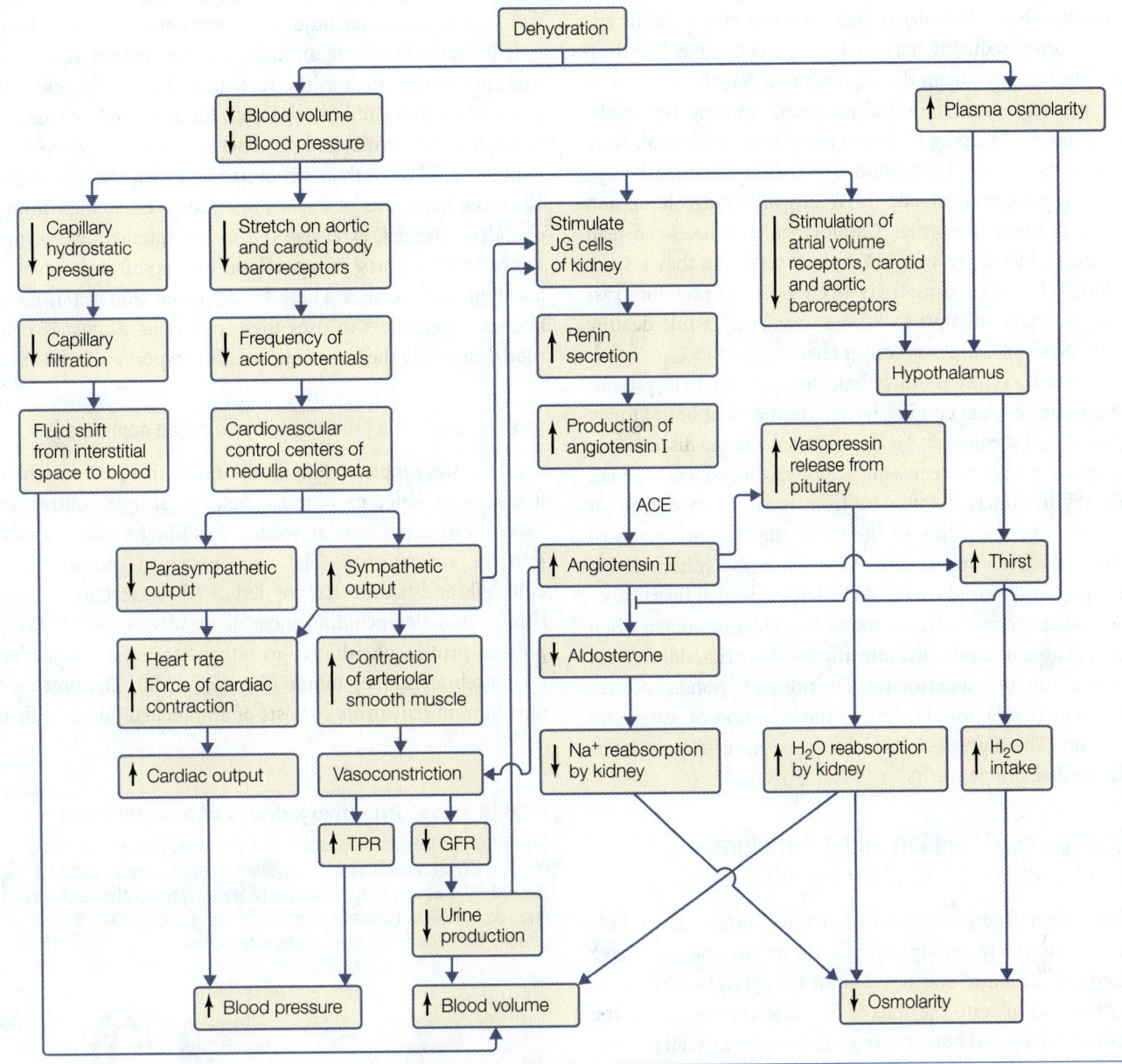

promote the reabsorption of sodium and water at the level of the proximal tubule and indirectly in the distal nephron via the actions of aldosterone released from the adrenal cortex. In dehydration, however, the latter process is blocked due to direct effects of increased plasma osmolarity on the adrenal cortex. Decreased blood pressure also affects glomerular filtration rate (GFR). Lower blood pressure has a small direct effect on GFR, reducing filtration pressure in the glomerulus, and slowing the rate of urine production. However, recall that the glomerular filtration rate is actually rather tightly regulated even in the face of changes in mean arterial pressure, so these direct effects are minor. Instead, increased

sympathetic stimulation (as a result of the decrease in blood pressure) has a major effect. Sympathetic stimulation causes vasoconstriction of the afferent arteriole of the glomerulus, reducing glomerular filtration pressure, and thus GFR and urine production. The reduction in GFR also decreases the flow of fluid through the kidney tubules. The cells in the macula densa detect this decrease in flow and stimulate the juxtaglomerular cells to secrete renin, thus further increasing the levels of angiotensin II.

Most of the mechanisms we have discussed so far involve the stimulus of decreased blood pressure, but increased osmolarity also has important effects. Osmoreceptors in the hypothalamus directly sense the increased osmolarity and stimulate the hypothalamus to release vasopressin as well as stimulate thirst. Osmolarity also has direct effects on the adrenal cortex, reducing the secretion of aldosterone. The drop in aldosterone reduces the expression of Na^+/K^+ ATPase in the membranes of the distal nephron, reducing Na^+ reabsorption, and helping to return osmolarity to normal. Note that reducing Na^+ absorption also reduces water reabsorption, which could impede the return of blood volume and blood pressure to normal. Cardiovascular reflexes can help to restore blood pressure in the short term, but they cannot address changes in osmolarity. In contrast, the excretory system generally attempts to restore osmolarity, while dealing with blood pressure over longer terms.

Because of the intimate links between the two systems, many pathological conditions have elements of both kidney disease and cardiovascular dysfunction. Kidney disease may be either a cause or consequence of cardiovascular disease. Kidney dysfunction can arise from renal artery defects or maladaptive regulation of the renin-angiotensin system or other vasoactive agents. The changes in blood volume create a hypertensive condition that challenges normal heart function. Many people with congestive heart failure worsen when the changes in blood pressure affect kidney function. When cardiac function deteriorates, the kidney responds with renal vasoconstriction, leading to the retention of water and sodium. The increase in blood volume in turn exacerbates the cardiac problems.

Evolutionary Variation in the Structure and Function of Excretory Systems

The cellular composition and functional properties of kidneys vary widely among animals. Up to this point, we have used the structure and function of the typical mammalian kidney to illustrate the role of the different regions of the kidney tubule and how the structural and functional properties produce appropriate urine. Of course, there is no such thing as a typical anything in animals as diverse as vertebrates. The model we described most closely resembles the kidney of a large mammal living on a mixed diet with ample access to fresh water. In other animals, even other mammals, there is considerable variation in kidney structure and function. Armed with an understanding of the roles of each of the main regions of the nephron, we can explore the basis of variation in nephron and kidney structure in other animals, beginning with the invertebrates.

Kidney and kidneylike structures of invertebrates play vital roles in ion and water balance of animals. However, in many species, particularly vertebrates, other tissues augment the role of kidneys. Many species possess extrarenal tissues

that play specialized roles in ion regulation, either importing critical ions from the environment, or exporting excess ions from the extracellular fluid. Such extrarenal tissues include gills in water-breathing animals, and specialized accessory exocrine glands, such as the rectal gland of sharks and salt gland of reptiles and birds. As with kidneys, Malpighian tubules, metanephridia, and protonephridia, these are epithelial tissues. Though their structures differ widely, they share all of the hallmarks of ion-transporting tissues: high mitochondrial content, extensive cell-to-cell interactions, asymmetry in transports in basolateral and apical membranes, and high surface area. These fundamental similarities have allowed researchers to uses these tissues as August Krogh models to study the basic features of transport epithelia.

Invertebrates have primitive kidneys called nephridia

Sponges, the simplest animals, act much like protists when it comes to water excretion. They use simple contractile vacuoles to expel cellular wastes, including water, directly into the environment. The true metazoans possess specific cells and tissues that are dedicated to excretion. Many simple animals, including most of the diverse worm taxa, possess **protonephridia**, a primitive functional analog of the vertebrate kidney tubule (Figure 13.33a). The protonephridium in flatworms consists of a branched tubule with a

---

FIGURE 13.33 **Primitive kidneys of invertebrates**
(a) Primitive invertebrates, such as flatworms, possess protonephridia, which use ciliated or flagellated cells to draw interstitial fluid into the lumen of tubules. **(b)** More advanced invertebrates, such as annelids, possess metanephridia, which collect fluids directly from the circulatory system or coelom.

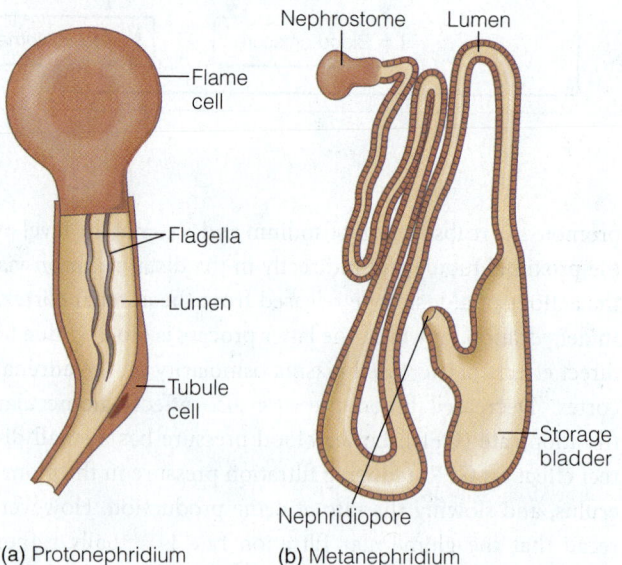

(a) Protonephridium   (b) Metanephridium

pore (nephridiopore) at one end and a cap cell at the other. Fluids are propelled through the duct of the protonephridia by flagella or cilia that extend from specialized cells. Some species have **flame cells**, which possess a tuft of cilia. Other species have **solenocytes**, which possess one or two flagella that extend into the lumen. The role of protonephridia varies among species and in relation to the environment. In general, protonephridia are important in osmoregulation, and are best developed in the freshwater species that must export water. They probably have no role in ammonia excretion in most species that possess protonephridia; these animals excrete ammonia directly across the body surface. The number of protonephridia differs widely among species, from as few as two, with a pair of nephridiopores, to thousands of units.

More complex nephridia, called *metanephridia*, occur in mollusks and annelids. Most mollusks have a single metanephridium, with a sac possessing deeply invaginated walls to increase the surface area (Figure 13.33b). Solutes and water are collected and expelled through a short tube called a ureter. Annelids possess a metanephridium in each body segment. The tubule begins at the nephrostome, which collects fluids from the coelom. The fluid passes through the long tubule, which winds through the body segment. Tubule length depends on habitat; marine species, with little need for water excretion, have shorter tubules than do freshwater species. The **nephridium** passes through the septum between body segments, and joins the body wall at the nephridiopore, releasing waste products from the animal. In some cases, the nephridium expands into a saclike bladder that is able to store fluids.

The cellular structures of these primitive kidneys vary widely among the invertebrates, but the main difference between a protonephridium and a metanephridium is in the relationship with the intracellular fluids. Protonephridia use their beating flagella and cilia to draw interstitial fluid into the lumen of the tubule. In contrast, the duct of a metanephridium has an internal opening that collects body fluids, either blood or coelomic fluid.

One unusual group among the invertebrates are the nematodes. Unlike other worms, nematodes lack nephridia altogether. Their excretory system employs *rennette cells*, which secrete waste into a duct that empties through an excretory pore. Nematodes differ in the morphology of the rennette cells—glandular or tubular—and the extent of the canal system that links the rennette cell to the excretory pore.

Insects use Malpighian tubules and the hindgut for ion and water regulation

In insects, no single tissue fulfills the function of the vertebrate kidney or invertebrate nephridium; water and ion balance in insects is regulated by concerted actions of the **Malpighian tubule** and the hindgut.

The Malpighian tubule is a tubelike structure with a blind sac at one end of a long tube that empties into the hindgut (Figure 13.34). Some insects, such as hemipteran bugs, possess two very long, coiled tubules, whereas other species have many shorter tubules, up to 250 in the locust *Schistocerca*. Although an insect Malpighian tubule is

FIGURE 13.34 Insect Malpighian tubule structure and function

(a) The Malpighian tubules, the insect kidney, empty into the digestive tract. Although many insects have four Malpighian tubules, the numbers can range from two to more than 250. **(b)** The tubule itself is composed of principal cells and stellate cells.

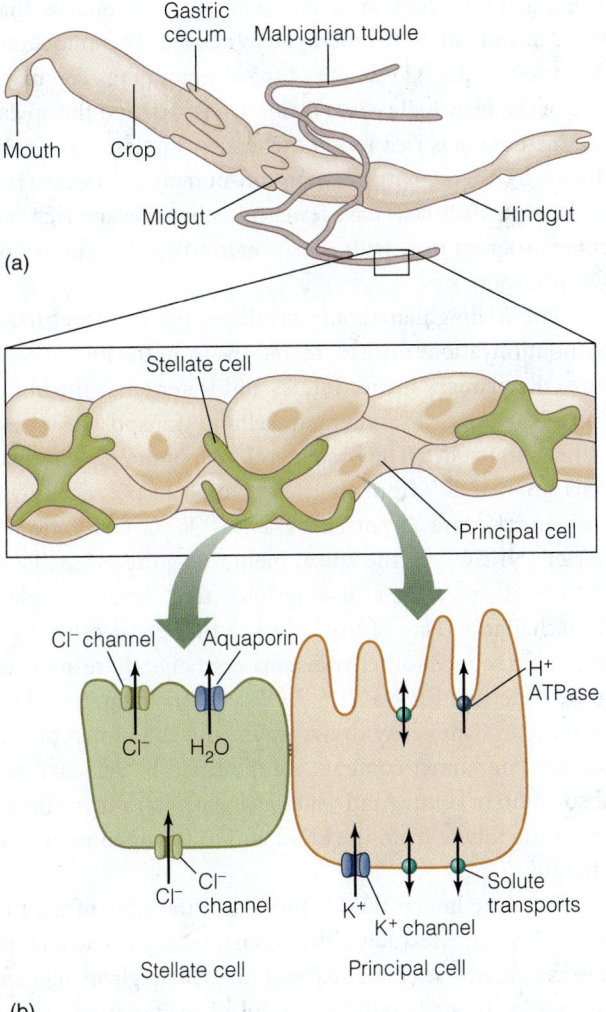

Figure source: Based on O'Donnell, M. J., Dow, J. A., Huesmann, G. R., Tublitz, N. J., & Maddrell, S. H. (1996). Separate control of anion and cation transport in Malpighian tubules of *Drosophila melanogaster.* Page 1172. *Journal of Experimental Biology, 199,* 1163–1175.

typically only one cell layer thick, there is considerable variation among species in the structural complexity, which can be related to the nature of the diet. Insects that consume a great deal of water, such as sap feeders, blood feeders, and carrion feeders, may have more complex structures that improve filtration.

The hindgut, which includes the rectum and rectal gland, receives the flow from the Malpighian tubule. The fluid is typically slightly hypoosmotic to the hemolymph. As it passes into the hindgut, the fluid is further modified by reabsorption and secretion. When it leaves the hindgut, the final osmolarity may be hypoosmotic, isosmotic, or hyperosmotic.

The Malpighian tubule of a typical dipteran (flies and mosquitoes) is composed of two main cell types: large principal cells and small stellate cells. Principal cells, often called secretory cells, possess extensive apical microvilli. The microvilli contain long, slender mitochondria that move in and out of the microvilli as needed. The mitochondria provide the ATP required for ion pumping. The main role of the principal cells is cation transport, and the apical cell membrane is rich in ion exchangers that are ultimately driven by the activity of a proton-pumping ATPase (H^+ ATPase). Stellate cells have fewer mitochondria and lack the complex apical microvilli. Their main role is the control of Cl^- transport.

The Malpighian tubule produces the primary urine without filtration. Instead, secretions from the tubule cells form the primary urine. Solutes and water enter the blind end of the tubule by either paracellular transport or transcellular transport. The basolateral membrane of principal cells imports K^+ from the hemolymph by K^+ channels; Na^+ and K^+ are imported by a Na^+-K^+-2 Cl^- cotransporter (NKCC). At the apical membrane, the H^+ ATPase exports H^1, creating a driving force that can be coupled to exchangers (Na^+/H^+ or K^+/H^+) that expel other cations. Unlike most other transport epithelia, there appears to be little role for Na^+/K^+ ATPase in most species. The increase in osmolarity draws water into the lumen of the tubule. The lumen contents are modified by selective reabsorption of solutes and water as the primary urine flows down the tubule from the blind end to the opening in the hindgut.

Once the lumen fluid is formed in the ends of the tubules, it progresses down the tubule, where it encounters mechanisms of selective reabsorption. Malpighian tubules are not innervated, and the control of secretion and reabsorption is under the control of intrinsic regulators and circulating hormones. Three main classes of diuretic hormones have been identified in insects.

1. *CRF-related diuretic hormones* have structural similarities to vertebrate hormones of the corticotropin-releasing factor (CRF) family, such as urotensin and urocortin. Fifteen different CRF-related diuretic hormones have been identified in insects, ranging in size from 30 to 47 amino acids. These hormones appear to act by stimulating the synthesis of cAMP in Malpighian tubule cells, which activates cation transport at the basolateral and apical regions of the principal cells.

2. *Insect (myo)kinins* are short peptide hormones, usually eight amino acids, that possess a characteristic C-terminal sequence of five amino acids. These hormones act on the stellate cells of the Malpighian tubules, activating phospholipase C to increase the production of IP_3, which in turn causes a release of Ca^{2+} from intracellular stores. This increase in $[Ca^{2+}]$ causes an increase in Cl^- transport into the lumen, although the mechanisms are not yet clear. The movement of Cl^- causes a parallel movement of Na^+ and K^+, leading to a net movement of NaCl and KCl from the hemolymph to the lumen.

3. *Cardioacceleratory peptides* were first identified by their ability to increase the heart rate. However, these hormones also stimulate the secretion of fluid into Malpighian tubules. This diverse family of hormones appears to stimulate phospholipase C in principal cells. The increase in IP_3 and then Ca^{2+} activates a cascade involving Ca^{2+} calmodulin-dependent nitric oxide synthase and guanylyl cyclase. These second messengers and regulatory enzymes lead to an increase in H^+ ATPase activity.

Although these diuretic hormones have been well characterized, much less is known about antidiuretic hormones in insects. Some, called antidiuretic factors, act by reducing the movement of water into the Malpighian tubule. Others, such as neuroparsins and ion-transport peptide, act by increasing water reabsorption in the gut, after the lumen contents empty into the hindgut.

Chondrichthian kidneys produce hypoosmotic urine and retain urea

Recall that sharks have an unusual osmotic strategy among vertebrates, maintaining their body fluids slightly hypertonic to seawater and accumulating urea to high concentrations (300–400 mM). Sharks have two long kidneys lying along the dorsal wall of the body cavity. The kidney tubules are long and complex in structure (Figure 13.35).

The tubules weave back and forth across the kidney to form two layers: a sinus zone where tubules are loosely

FIGURE 13.35 **Variation in the vertebrate kidneys**

Each vertebrate kidney possesses regions specialized for absorption and secretion. However, the dimensions of each region vary among taxa.

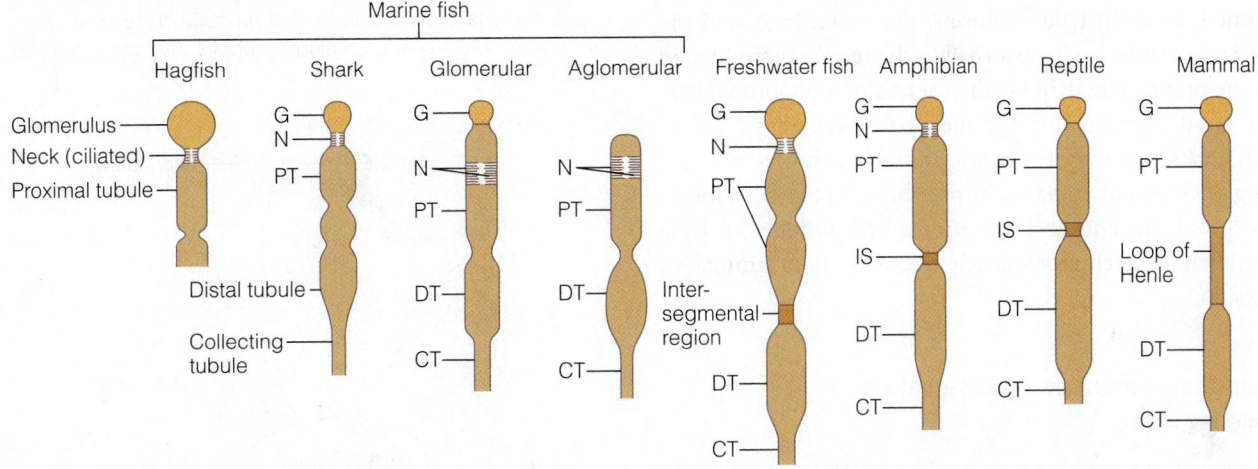

Figure source: Republished with permission of Blackwell Publishing, from *Environmental Physiology of Animals*, from Willmer, P., Stone, G., & Johnston, I. A, p. 109, © 2000; permission conveyed through Copyright Clearance Center, Inc.

packed and separated by fluid, and a more compact zone where tubules are bundled together and wrapped in a membranous sheath. This complex arrangement may set up a countercurrent exchanger that allows the shark kidney tubule to recover as much as 90 percent of the urea from the primary urine. The exact mechanism by which urea is recovered remains unclear, and may occur through active reabsorption via Na^+-urea cotransporters. The urine produced by the shark is slightly hypoosmotic (relative to the shark tissues) and close to the osmolarity of seawater. Sharks that move into dilute seawater reduce their internal osmolarity by producing copious amounts of dilute urine.

The role of the fish kidney differs in freshwater and seawater

In bony fish, two paired kidneys run along the dorsal surface of the inner body cavity. The function of the kidney depends on the osmolarity of the water. The glomerulus, which produces the primary urine, is much larger in freshwater fish than in marine species. The distal tubule, which functions in salt recovery and water excretion, may also be much larger. The kidneys of freshwater fish produce large volumes of hypoosmotic urine.

The kidneys of marine fish play a much-reduced role in ion and water balance. They produce very little urine, which is isosmotic to body fluids. The nephrons of marine fish have a less complex glomerulus, shorter proximal tubules,

and distal tubules that are reduced or absent. Some marine fish lack a glomerulus altogether. These **aglomerular kidneys** occur in species from three unrelated taxa. Because the other species in these taxa have glomerular kidneys, the aglomerular state has evolved at least three separate times in fish.

The amphibian kidney changes in metamorphosis

Like freshwater fish, most amphibians living in water must rid themselves of excess water absorbed from the environment across highly permeable skin. In their aquatic life they have little need for water retention mechanisms. However, when amphibians are on land, they must conserve water. Like freshwater fish, amphibians possess a kidney that lacks a loop of Henle, a structure that enables the mammalian kidney to produce hyperosmotic urine. An amphibian meets the conflicting demands of life on land and in water by (1) regulating the glomerular filtration rate to control the rate of water loss and (2) recovering water from the urine stored in the urinary bladder. Whereas most terrestrial animals use the bladder only for short-term storage of urine prior to micturition, amphibians use the bladder for water storage. The reabsorption process is under the control of the amphibian **homolog** of vasopressin.

The nature of the amphibian kidney changes during development. Larval amphibians, as well as larval fish, have a simple nephron called a **pronephros**. Recall that the mammalian kidney tubule, also known as a metanephros, empties fluid from the circulation directly into the interior of the nephron at the Bowman's capsule. In a pronephric kidney, the filtrate first enters the coelom, then is swept into the pronephric tubules through the nephrostomal funnels. As with true nephrons, the water, ions, and organic molecules are reabsorbed in the tubule and returned to the blood. The urine is then sent along the pronephric duct and expelled through the cloaca. Whereas a mammalian kidney may possess a million nephrons, a larval frog possesses just a pair of pronephros. As the larva metamorphoses to an adult, the pronephros is replaced by a kidney that much more closely resembles the mammalian version.

Terrestrial animals have kidneys that help conserve water

The variations in kidney morphology among reptiles, birds, and mammals reflect different solutions to the challenge of avoiding dehydration. The challenges of reducing water loss are greatest in desert animals, but all terrestrial animals have multiple means of matching kidney function to the constraints of environmental water availability.

Modern reptiles reduce the need for water by producing uric acid as a nitrogenous end product. Because uric acid is insoluble, water is not wasted as a solvent, although some water is used to wash the uric acid down the tubule lumen. This water can be reabsorbed in the cloaca. The reptilian kidney has much reduced glomeruli, and in some species the glomerulus is absent. As with the amphibians, the reptilian nephron lacks a loop of Henle, and therefore cannot produce hyperosmotic urine.

One of the major innovations in terrestrial vertebrate evolution was the loop of Henle. This extended segment between the proximal and distal tubules occurs only in birds and mammals, although birds have some nephrons that lack a loop of Henle. Because of the loop of Henle, most mammals can produce urine with an osmolarity that is about five times greater than the plasma osmolarity.

If it were simply the total length of the loop of Henle that determined the ability to produce concentrated urine, the elephant would be a champion; it has a long loop of Henle simply because its kidney is so large. The best predictor of the ability of the nephron to produce concentrated urine takes into account the size of the kidney. Because the loop of Henle spans the medulla, the potential to produce concentrated urine is best expressed as relative medullary thickness: the width of the medulla relative to the total width of the kidney (Figure 13.36). Mammals that live in environments with abundant water, such as beavers, have a low relative medullary thickness and nephrons with a short loop of

FIGURE 13.36 Relative medullary thickness in mammalian kidneys

Animals that produce a more concentrated urine, such as the kangaroo rat, have nephrons with a longer loop of Henle and a thicker medulla than do animals that produce dilute urine, such as a beaver. Most species, including rabbits, fall between these extremes.

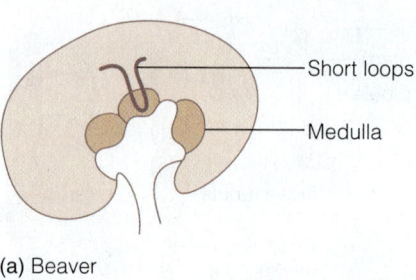

(a) Beaver

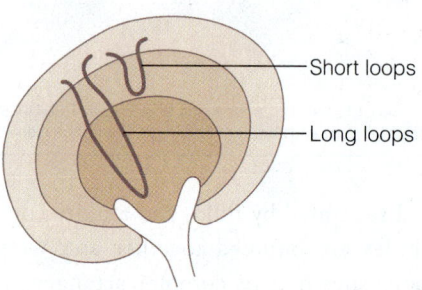

(b) Rabbit

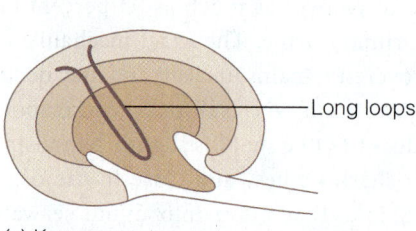

(c) Kangaroo rat

Figure source: Republished with permission of Schmidt-Nielsen, B., & O'Dell, R. (1961). Structure and concentrating mechanism in the mammalian kidney. Page 1121. *American Journal of Physiology* 200, 1119–1124; permission conveyed through Copyright Clearance Center, Inc.

Henle that produce dilute urine. Conversely, mammals that live in very dry environments, such as the kangaroo rat, have a high relative medullary thickness and nephrons with a long loop of Henle that produce highly concentrated urine, typically four to five times more concentrated than that of most mammals.

Fish gills transport ions into and out of the water

Like most transport epithelia, fish gills have several types of cells involved in control of ion and water balance. Perhaps the best-studied system is that of the rainbow trout (Figure 13.37). Mucus-secreting cells are scattered over

FIGURE 13.37   **Cells of the fish gill**

The fish gill is an important site of ion exchange in both freshwater and seawater species. It has multiple cell types, including mucus cells, chloride cells, and pavement cells. SEM, TEM: scanning or transmission electron micrograph.

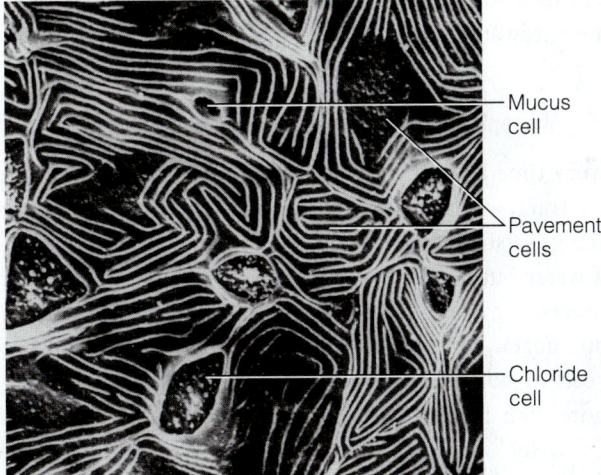

(a) Gill surface (SEM)

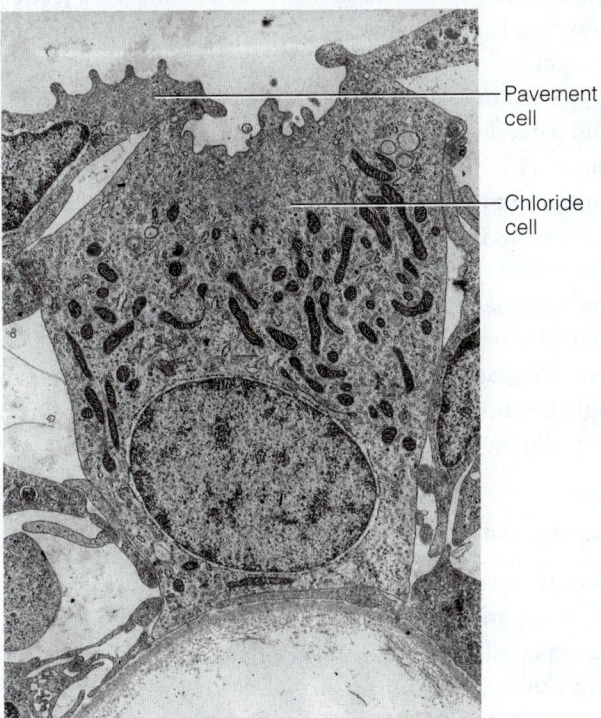

(b) Chloride cell (TEM)

Figure source: (a) Dr. Steve Perry, University of Ottawa; (b) Dr. Steve Perry, University of Ottawa.

the surface of the gill. There are **chloride cells**, which are large cells with abundant mitochondria. Much of the surface is covered by smaller, flattened cells collectively called **pavement cells**. Some pavement cells, like chloride

cells, have numerous mitochondria, whereas others possess fewer mitochondria. It is thought that most of the ion regulation in the gill is mediated by the two types of cells that are rich in mitochondria. These two cell types can be distinguished using histochemical methods that employ a glycoprotein (peanut lectin agglutin, or PNA) that binds carbohydrates on chloride cells that are absent from pavement cells. Thus, chloride cells are often called PNA+ cells, and pavement cells are PNA− cells. In rainbow trout, and perhaps freshwater fish in general, these two types of mitochondria-rich cells mediate different transport processes.

The direction of transport of ions and water depends on the salinity of the water (Figure 13.38a). The gill of a freshwater fish must take up Na^+, Ca^{2+}, and other ions from the water, frequently against steep electrochemical gradients. The PNA− cells take up Na^+ through an apical Na^+ channel. Although there is an unfavorable gradient for Na^+ uptake, these cells create a favorable electrochemical gradient using a H^+ ATPase that acidifies the water in the boundary layer. Once inside the cell, Na^+ is exported to the extracellular fluid by the basolateral Na^+/K^+ ATPase or a Na^+/HCO_3^- exchanger. PNA+ cells import Cl^- into the cell using an apical Cl^-/HCO_3^2 exchanger, which then escapes through basolateral Cl^- channels. In both transport schemes, production of HCO_3^- and H^+ by carbonic anhydrase is essential, providing ions that can be used as counterions or to change pH.

In contrast to freshwater fish, marine fish must avoid excessive ion uptake and limit water loss. The gill is central to ion balance, and chloride cells in particular are critical for excreting ions (Figure 13.38b). The combined actions of the Na^+/K^+ ATPase and the Na^+-K^+-2 Cl^- cotransporter bring K^+ and Cl^- (and some Na^+) into the cell from the blood. The Cl^- channels in the apical membrane allow Cl^- to escape into the seawater, and basolateral K^+ channels allow K^+ to return to the blood. The movement of Cl^- and other ions creates a transepithelial membrane potential (negative on the outside). Na^+ is thought to escape through paracellular channels, driven by the transepithelial membrane potential. This arrangement of transporters is common in other ion-pumping epithelial cells that expel Cl^- from cells, such as the shark rectal gland we discuss later in this chapter.

As you can see, the responsibilities of the ion-pumping cells of the fish gill change depending on the external conditions. *Anadromous* fish, such as salmon, migrate from seawater to freshwater to reproduce. Young salmon grow in freshwater, then migrate to the sea. Prior to migration, the gills of these fish undergo a dramatic cellular reorganization as the ion-pumping properties of the gill cells

FIGURE 13.38 **Ion transport processes in gills of freshwater and marine fish**

Gills possess ion-pumping cells that cause the net uptake of Na^+ and Cl^- in freshwater and the net export of Na^+ and Cl^- in seawater. **(a)** The freshwater gill possesses two types of ion-pumping cells. Acid-secreting cells (PNA$^-$) import Na^+ from the water. Base-secreting cells (PNA$^+$) import Cl^- and Ca^{2+}. **(b)** Gill epithelial cells of marine fish export Cl^- and Na^+.

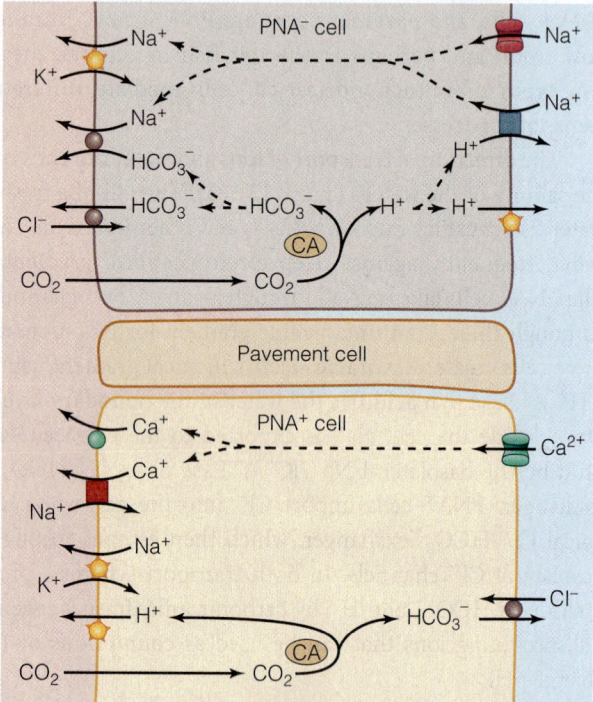

(a) Freshwater trout gill

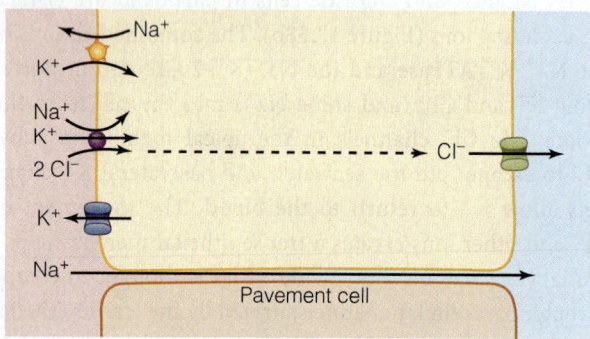

(b) Marine fish gill

Figure source: Based on Perry, S. F., & Gilmour, K. (2006). Acid-base balance and CO_2 excretion in fish: Unanswered questions and emerging models. *Respiratory Physiology & Neurobiology, 154,* 199–215.

prepare for the new environment. Interestingly, the remodeling process, called *smoltification,* occurs before exposure to seawater. It is mediated largely by growth hormone, insulinlike growth factor 1, cortisol, and to a lesser extent thyroid hormone (see Box 13.3: Applications: Conservation Physiology of Salmon). Smoltification also leads to the remodeling of other tissues involved in ion and water balance, including the gastrointestinal tract and probably the kidney. As a consequence of the cellular changes, there is very little ionic and osmotic disturbance when the salmon enter seawater.

Digestive epithelia mediate ion and water transfers

Every time an animal consumes food or water, the digestive tract, with its high surface area, becomes a site of exchange of solutes and water. The diet may be a vital source of water but it may also create an osmotic burden. Many insects, for example, feed on diets rich in water, such as sap, nectar, or blood. Consider the osmotic challenge faced by *Rhodnius,* a blood-sucking bug that consumes more than 12 times its body mass in a single blood meal. Blood-sucking insects must remove the water from the blood meal in order to process the remaining energy-rich macromolecules. Facing similar challenges, a female mosquito begins to urinate shortly after commencing feeding, allowing her to compress the solids of the blood meal in the gut.

Scientists debate the relative importance of transcellular and paracellular transport in water transport across the gut, but it is likely that both processes are important. Transcellular transport is driven by osmotic gradients and facilitated by aquaporins in both basolateral and apical membranes of the epithelium. Paracellular transport occurs when the internal and external fluids are nearly isosmotic. Ions, mainly Na^+ and Cl^-, are secreted into the interstitial space to create an osmotic gradient that drives movement of water across the tight junctions. Once in the interstitial fluid, water makes its way into the blood.

Reptiles and birds possess salt glands

Because freshwater has a very low solute concentration, it creates an inward osmotic pressure that helps drive water uptake. However, animals that drink seawater face two challenges. First, water molecules must be selectively transported across the gut against the osmotic gradient. It is likely that transcellular transport across tight epithelia is important in these animals. Second, the animals must be able to expel the salt that accompanies the seawater consumed in the diet.

Many reptiles and birds possess a **salt gland** that aids in ion and water balance by excreting hyperosmotic solutions of Na^+ and Cl^-. Whether living in the ocean or the desert, species with salt glands can cope without access to

CONSERVATION PHYSIOLOGY OF SALMON

Most sockeye salmon (*Oncorhynchus nerka*) are anadromous. They are hatched in freshwater, live there for a period of time (up to three years), and then undergo the process of smoltification, migrating out to sea where they may spend up to four years before migrating back to freshwater to spawn and die. (All Pacific salmon, including sockeye salmon, have a reproductive strategy known as semelparity: They breed only once and then die shortly thereafter.) The journey up river to spawn is a perilous one, and not all sockeye salmon make it to the breeding grounds. Sockeye salmon do not feed during their upriver migration, so they must rely on "on-board" fuel stores to accomplish the saltwater to freshwater transition, to swim through what can be extremely rapidly flowing rivers, and to court and mate at the spawning grounds.

What makes the difference between a sockeye salmon that spawns successfully and one that does not make it to the breeding grounds? This question is being actively addressed by conservation physiologists (scientists who use physiological research to provide information to assist with decisions about the conservation of species—see Chapter 1 for more detail). Of course, many sockeye salmon are removed from the spawning population due to fishing, but for those that avoid being caught, are released by fisherman, or escape from nets, researchers are now seeking to identify possible physiological differences between fish that are able to spawn successfully and those that are not.

The gill of a salmon must undergo a fundamental transformation as the fish moves between freshwater and salt water. In the case of an adult salmon returning to spawn, the gill must transition from being an ion-secreting epithelium in seawater to an ion-absorbing epithelium in freshwater. In salmon, one clear signature of the shift between these two types of epithelia is a change in the expression of genes encoding the Na^+/K^+ ATPase (sodium pump). The isoform called Na^+/K^+ ATPase α1a is expressed almost exclusively in the freshwater epithelium, while the isoform called Na^+/K^+ ATPase α1b tends to be more highly expressed at the start of seawater entry (such as during smoltification). A series of studies in which sockeye salmon were sampled in seawater and at various points during their upriver migration confirmed that this is also the case in sockeye. When fish move from the ocean into the river, there is an increase in the amount of mRNA coding for Na^+/K^+ ATPase α1a in the gill. This pattern indicates a shift from an ion-secreting to an ion-absorbing "freshwater-type" epithelium with freshwater entry. These changes are thought to be regulated by the hormone prolactin, as prolactin levels in the blood are high both in seawater before migration and during migration in freshwater. Similarly, mRNA levels for the prolactin receptor increase in the gill after entry into freshwater.

To determine whether fish that successfully reach the spawning grounds and breed differ from those that fail to reach the spawning grounds or fail to breed after they arrive, researchers captured sockeye salmon in the ocean prior to their spawning migration or in the river shortly after entry into freshwater. At this point, the fish were implanted with a small radiotransmitter that allowed the researchers to track the movement of the salmon throughout their migration, and a tiny sample of gill tissue was removed and preserved for later analyses of gene expression. Researchers were able to correlate the patterns of gene expression in the gill samples with the probability of a fish surviving to reach the spawning grounds and breed. They discovered that there was a clear "mortality-related signature" of gene expression in the gill that could be used to identify fish that were unlikely to make it successfully to the spawning grounds.

Particularly relevant to the topic of this chapter, fish that did not make it successfully to the spawning grounds to breed tended to undergo the transformation of the gill from an ion-secreting to an ion-absorbing epithelium while they were still in salt water, while fish that made it successfully to the breeding grounds only underwent this gill transformation once they reached freshwater. These data suggest that unsuccessful fish may undergo a premature shift in their osmoregulatory strategy, which might impair their ability to osmoregulate while still in seawater, causing them to enter freshwater in poor condition.

References

- Cooke, S. J., Hinch, S. G., Donaldson, M. R., Clark, T. D., Eliason, E. J., Crossin, G. T., . . . Farrell, A. P. (2012). Conservation physiology in practice: How physiological knowledge has improved our ability to sustainably manage Pacific salmon during up-river migration. *Philosophical Transactions of the Royal Society of London B (Biological Sciences), 367,* 1757–1769.

- Flores, A. M., Shrimpton, J. M., Patterson, D. A., Hills, J. A., Cooke, S. J., Yada, T., . . . Farrell, A. P. (2012). Physiological and molecular endocrine changes in maturing wild sockeye salmon, *Oncorhynchus nerka,* during ocean and river migration. *Journal of Comparative Physiology B, 182,* 77–90.

- Jeffries, K. M., Hinch, S. G., Donaldson, M. R., Gale, M. K., Burt, J. M., Thompson, L. A., . . . Miller, K. M. (2011). Temporal changes in blood variables during final maturation and senescence in male sockeye salmon *Oncorhynchus nerka:* Reduced osmoregulatory ability can predict mortality. *Journal of Fish Biology, 79,* 449–465.

- Miller, K. M., Li, S., Kaukinen, K. H., Ginther, N., Hammill, E., Curtis, J. M., . . . Farrell, A. P. (2011). Genomic signatures predict migration and spawning failure in wild Canadian salmon. *Science, 331,* 214–217.

- Shrimpton, J. M., Patterson, D. A., Richards, J. G., Cooke, S. J., Schulte, P. M., Hinch, S. G., & Farrell, A. P. (2005). Ionoregulatory changes in different populations of maturing sockeye salmon *Oncorhynchus nerka* during ocean and river migration. *Journal of Experimental Biology, 208,* 4069–4078.

FIGURE 13.39 **Salt glands of birds and reptiles**

Some birds and reptiles that live in seawater or the desert are able to excrete Na$^+$ and Cl$^-$ from specialized salt glands.

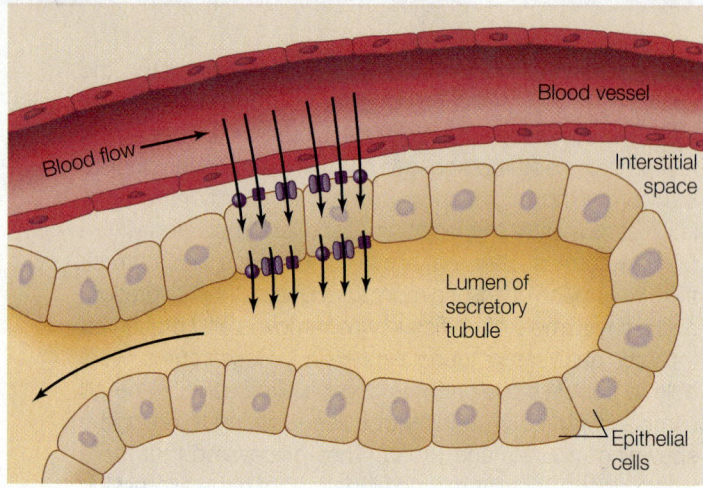

freshwater, deriving water from drinking hypertonic seawater or exclusively from food.

In birds, the salt gland is found in a depression at the base of the beak, and its secretions drain through a canal that runs along the beak and opens at the nostrils. The nasal salt gland secretion can be as much as three times more concentrated than the plasma. Thus, if a bird drinks 30 milliliters of seawater, it can excrete all of the salt in 10 milliliters of salt gland secretion, gaining 20 milliliters of pure water. The salt glands are able to do this by using metabolic energy to create a countercurrent multiplier.

The salt gland is composed of a series of secretory tubules, surrounded by peritubular fluid and a capillary network. The tubule has a closed end and an elongated tube that empties into a collecting duct. Fluids flow from the closed end of the tubule to the open end. A capillary network is arranged in parallel to the tubule, though direction of blood flow is the opposite direction to that of the lumen fluids (Figure 13.39). This countercurrent arrangement of flows is central to the ability of the salt gland to produce a concentrated secretion. The countercurrent multiplier mechanism is as follows: As blood flows toward the closed end of the tubule, salts escape into the interstitial fluid and are taken up by the tubule cells and transferred to the lumen. As a result, the blood becomes progressively more dilute. The interstitial fluid that bathes the tubule cells is in equilibrium with the blood passing over the tubule: low osmolarity near the closed end and high osmolarity near the opening. Thus, the tubule cells near the closed end of the

tubule are exposed to a dilute interstitial fluid and create a dilute lumen fluid. As lumen fluids flow from the closed end to the open end, the surrounding interstitial fluids are increasingly concentrated, and the transcellular transport of salts across the tubule cells causes the lumen fluids to become more concentrated.

The epithelial cells that line the secretory tubule extract salts from the interstitial fluid found between the tubule cells and the blood. The basolateral membrane and apical membrane work in conjunction to produce a hyperosmotic secretion. The basolateral membrane of the epithelial cells brings ions into the cell using the suites of transporters involved in a regulatory volume increase. Conversely, the apical membrane possesses the transporters that are involved in regulatory volume decreases. Although the exact mechanisms remain unclear, the Na$^+$/K$^+$ ATPase, NKCC, K$^+$ channels, and Cl$^-$ channels have all been implicated in the formation of the hyperosmotic secretion. The net result of these activities is the import of Na$^+$ and Cl$^-$ from the plasma and their secretion into the lumen of the tubule. Like other epithelial tissues involved in ion transport, the cells of the secretory tubule have a high content of mitochondria, which produce the ATP needed to pump ions and establish the gradients used by secondary active transport. The ion-secreting machinery of the salt glands is similar in many respects to the transporters used by other salt-secreting epithelia discussed earlier in this chapter, such as the fish gill.

Elasmobranch rectal glands excrete Na$^+$ and Cl$^-$, while retaining urea

Like seabirds, elasmobranchs have an accessory excretory organ that aids in salt excretion. The **rectal gland** is composed of many tubules surrounded by capillaries. Each tubule is composed of a single type of epithelial cell. Like other transport epithelial cells, the cells of the rectal gland tubule have abundant mitochondria and basolateral invaginations, much like microvilli, that increase the surface area for ion exchange with the blood. The tubules are able to transfer NaCl from the blood to the tubule lumen. Though the osmolarity of the tubule secretions is similar to that of the plasma, the secretions have a much higher concentration of NaCl because urea is retained in the blood. Two separate mechanisms are responsible for transepithelial movement of Na$^+$ and Cl$^-$. Tubular epithelial cells actively transport Cl$^-$ from the blood via transcellular transport, whereas Na$^+$ moves between the tubular epithelial cells, from the blood to the tubule lumen, via paracellular transport.

The hypersaline excretions of salt glands form in secretory tubules that are arranged into lobes that drain into collecting ducts. Blood vessels juxtaposed to the secretory tubules flow countercurrent to the flow of fluid through the tubule.

The transport processes carried out by the tubular epithelium function much like those of chloride cells of the teleost gill and the salt gland of birds, using a combination of basolateral NKCC, Na^+/K^+ ATPase, K^+ channels, and apical Cl^- channels. A model for describing the secretion of Cl^- is shown in Figure 13.40. The main source of entry of Cl^- into the epithelial cells is via the NKCC. The inward movements of Na^+ and K^+ are reversed by the action of the basolateral K^+ channels and the exchange of Na^+ for K^+ via the Na^+/K^+ ATPase. Once Cl^- enters the cytoplasm of the epithelial cell, it can escape across the apical plasma membrane through Cl^- channels. The rectal gland is also the site of Na^+ excretion, which moves between cells from the interstitial fluid to the lumen of the tubule. This paracellular transport is driven by the transepithelial electrochemical potential.

Salt secretion by the rectal gland occurs in pulses after a shark has incurred a salt load, either through drinking or eating salt-laden food. The osmotic perturbation triggers release of hormones that stimulate rectal gland secretion. The osmotic and blood volume changes stimulate the release of atrial natriuretic peptide from the heart. We discussed this hormone as it functions in mammals in some detail previously in this chapter, but in sharks atrial natriuretic hormone triggers the release of the neuroendocrine hormone vasoactive intestinal peptide (VIP). When VIP binds to its G protein–linked receptor, it activates adenylate cyclase, increasing cAMP synthesis, which activates protein kinase A (PKA). The main target of PKA in this process is the apical Cl^- channel itself; phosphorylation opens the channel. PKA may also affect intracellular traffic, causing movement of more Cl^- channels to the apical membrane to further increase Cl^- conductance. Though the changes in Cl^- activity probably drive this process, the activity of NKCC is also regulated during stimulation of salt secretion. The efflux of Cl^- causes a regulatory decrease in cell volume and cytoplasmic Cl^- levels. The changes in cell volume trigger phosphorylation of NKCC, which is normally inactive in the basolateral membrane. Although the exact protein kinases that phosphorylate NKCC are not yet established, PKA is not involved. These protein kinases, whatever their nature, may also be activated through hormonal or neuroendocrine factors.

FIGURE 13.40 **Chloride transport in the elasmobranch rectal gland**

The excretion of salt in the shark rectal gland is driven by the secretion of Cl^-. Chloride is imported into the cell from the plasma through the Na^+-K^+-2 Cl^- cotransporter and escapes through Cl^- channels. The entire process is sensitive to hormones such as vasoactive intestinal peptide (VIP), which elevate cAMP levels, activating protein kinase A (PKA).

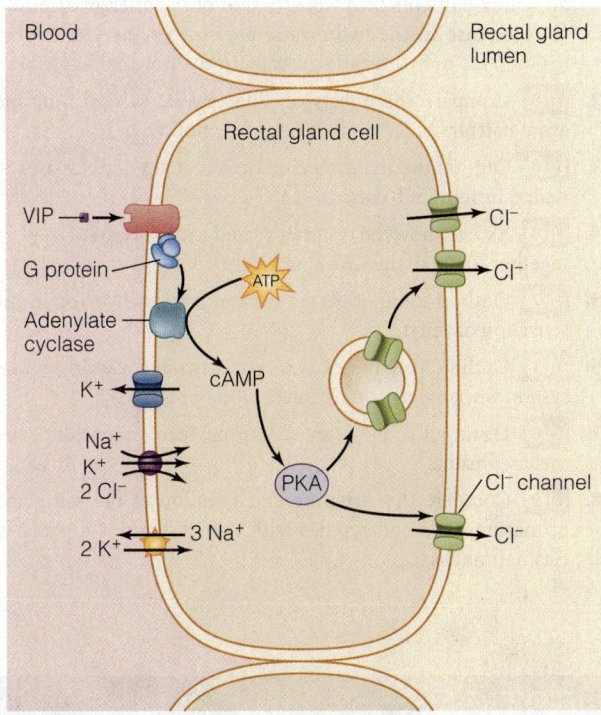

Figure source: Based on Silva, P., Solomon, R. J., & Epstein, F. H. (1997). Transport mechanisms that mediate the secretion of chloride by the rectal gland of *Squalus acanthias. Journal of Experimental Zoology, 279,* 504–508.

CONCEPT CHECK

13. What animals have salt glands?
14. Which extrarenal tissues make use of countercurrent exchangers?

SUMMARY

Epithelial tissues are the interface between internal fluids and the external environment, creating osmotic and ionic barriers, and controlling ion balance, water balance, and nitrogen excretion.

Animals differ in their ability to maintain a constant internal osmolarity (osmoregulators versus osmoconformers) and their ability to tolerate changes in external osmolarity (stenohaline versus euryhaline).

Most aquatic animals (invertebrates, fish, amphibians) primarily excrete NH_3 (i.e., they are ammoniotelic); terrestrial animals are typically either uricotelic (most invertebrates, reptiles, and birds) or ureotelic (mammals).

Kidneys are critical osmoregulatory organs in many animals. The functional unit of the vertebrate kidney is the nephron,

a combination of complex vasculature and renal tubules, consisting of a proximal tubule, loop of Henle, distal tubule, and collecting duct.

Various hormones (such as vasopressin and aldosterone) control kidney function, altering transport in select regions of the tubule, thereby changing the nature of the primary urine.

Changes in plasma osmolarity and volume lead to compensatory changes in thirst centers and kidney function to alter water uptake and excretion of salt and water.

Excretory organs occur throughout animals, from simple protonephridia and metanephridia of invertebrates, to extrarenal excretory tissues of fish (gills), reptiles (salt glands), and cartilaginous fish (rectal gland), to the complex kidneys of vertebrates.

REVIEW QUESTIONS

1. **LO 1** What factors determine the direction and magnitude of water movement from the environment into the individual cells of an animal?

2. **LO 1** Does water move between intracellular and extracellular fluid in a cell under isotonic conditions?

3. **LO 2** How do different types of fish differ in their strategies of ionoregulation and osmoregulation?

4. **LO 2** Compare the costs and benefits of osmoconforming versus osmoregulating.

5. **LO 3** What features might predispose an aquatic animal to living on land?

6. **LO 3** How do different terrestrial animals limit water loss to the environment?

7. **LO 4** What is the relationship between the volume of urine produced and the type of nitrogenous waste excreted by an organism? Explain why this relationship occurs.

8. **LO 4** Compare the energetic costs of producing the different nitrogenous wastes.

9. **LO 5** Discuss how countercurrent systems aid renal function.

10. **LO 5** Describe the structure of a mammalian nephron.

11. **LO 5** In a normal kidney, which of the following would cause an increase in GFR? (a) Constriction of the afferent arteriole, (b) Decrease in the hydrostatic pressure in the glomerulus, (c) Increase in hydrostatic pressure in the Bowman's capsule

12. **LO 6** Compare the effects of aldosterone, vasopressin, and atrial natriuretic factor on kidney function.

13. **LO 6** Outline the main mechanisms that the kidney uses to maintain sodium balance.

14. **LO 6** Explain how the respiratory and excretory systems work together to maintain acid-base balance.

15. **LO 7** Outline some of the endocrine factors involved in the sensation of thirst.

16. **LO 7** Outline how the excretory system and cardiovascular system work together to regulate blood pressure.

17. **LO 8** Distinguish between nephrons, protonephridia, and metanephridia.

18. **LO 8** Compare the structure and function of the salt gland of marine birds and reptiles with that of the rectal gland of elasmobranchs.

SYNTHESIS QUESTIONS

1. Is more water derived from oxidizing glycogen, protein, or lipid?

2. Discuss the integration of the respiratory and excretory systems in controlling pH balance.

3. Describe the role of nerves and muscles in control of ion and water balance.

4. Compare the anatomy, physiology, and life history of a largely terrestrial amphibian, such as a toad, with that of a largely aquatic reptile, such as a sea turtle.

5. Angiotensin-converting enzyme inhibitors (ACE inhibitors) are used to treat high blood pressure. Using a flowchart, explain why these drugs are helpful in treating hypertension.

6. The kidney of a cactus wren is less efficient at concentrating urine than are the kidneys of a kangaroo rat, yet the cactus wren produces less urine. In one or two sentences, explain this apparent contradiction.

7. A person with cirrhosis of the liver has lower than normal levels of plasma proteins (because production of albumin, one of

the major plasma proteins, decreases) and a higher than normal GFR. Explain why a decrease in plasma protein concentration would increase GFR.

8. Most freshwater fish are unable to survive in water with high concentrations of bicarbonate. Draw a diagram of a freshwater fish gill and, using this diagram, outline a possible physiological reason for this observation.

QUANTITATIVE QUESTIONS

1. If an aquaporin can pass 10^9 molecules of water a second, how many channels would be needed to reduce the volume of a 1-μl cell by half in 1 second? (Hint: How many water molecules are in 1 μl of water?)

2. Assuming complete dissociation, which of the following solutions will have the greatest osmolarity: 150 mM glucose, 80 mM NaCl, 90 mM Na_2SO_4, or 210 mM urea?

3. Explain why an individual with a plasma glucose concentration of 375 mg/100 ml of blood will have glucose in the urine. (Note: Normal plasma glucose is approximately 100 mg/100 ml of blood, normal GFR is approximately 180 l/day, and the

kidney's maximal transport rate for glucose is approximately 375 mg/min.)

4. A human patient has a plasma urea concentration of 10 mg/dl, a urine urea concentration of 100 mg/dl, and renal clearance of urea is 65 ml/min. What is the urine flow rate (ml/min) of this patient? Normal urine flow in humans is between 800 and 1,200 ml/day. Is this patient within the normal range?

5. For the patient in question 4, if inulin clearance was 125 ml/min, what does this suggest about the handling of urea in the kidney?

14

Digestion and Energy Metabolism

FIGURE 14.1 **Giant vent worms (*Riftia pachyptila*)**

Photo source: Photo by Craig Cary, Univ. of Delaware/NSF/HOV Alvin 2001©Woods Hole Oceanographic Institution

Most food webs on the planet owe their origins to sunlight, captured by photosynthetic organisms that become food for animals. One environment where the sun plays no role is the deep-sea vent. The fissures in these undersea volcanoes release extremely hot water, rich in sulfides. While the surrounding waters are cold, deep-sea deserts, the vent waters are under-sea oases, with warm water, rich in biodiversity. Though most food webs rely on photosynthetic organisms, chemotrophic bacteria are the nutritional base of deep-sea vent ecosystems, providing food for many species of invertebrates. Some animals, like the vent mussel *Bathymodiolus thermophilus*, collect bacteria from the water by filter feeding. Others, such as the polychaete *Alvinella pompejana*, graze on the thick bacterial mats. These invertebrates, in turn, are food for predatory invertebrates and vertebrates, which live on the fringe of the toxic zone created by the sulfides emanating from the vents. Several animals cultivate chemotrophic bacteria on their body surfaces, essentially farming their food supply.

Some species of animals enter into symbiotic relationships with the chemotrophic bacteria. An extreme version of a symbiotic relationship was discovered in a group of vent animals called giant vent worms (*Riftia pachyptila*) (Figure 14.1). In 1977, the U.S. Navy submersible Alvin was exploring the deep-sea vents of the Pacific Ocean. The researchers with Alvin observed worms with bright red featherlike plumes extending from tubes formed at the interface between toxic sulfide emissions and cold, oxygen-rich seawater. Subsequent research has tried to identify evolutionary affinities for these unusual animals, and it appears that *Riftia pachyptila* is a specialized type of vestimentiferan annelid worm within the annelid family Siboglinidae.

What makes this animal so unusual is that it lacks any digestive tract: no mouth, no anus, no stomach, no intestines! Instead, it derives its nutrients from an organ called a **trophosome**, which is an internal sac filled with chemolithotrophic bacteria. The worm uses its red plume to collect nutrients to deliver to the bacteria, including nitrogen, phosphorus, hydrogen sulfide, oxygen, and carbon dioxide. The hemoglobin of the worm is essential for collecting and transporting both oxygen and hydrogen sulfide to the bacteria. When the bacteria receive the nutrients, they use them to produce the organic substrates needed by the worm for biosynthesis and energy production, primarily sugars and amino acids.

Riftia continues to be studied to address many questions related to the evolution of this peculiar endosymbiotic relationship. However, in the time since the giant vent worms were discovered, researchers have identified other examples of vent animals with endosymbiotic bacteria. The tally now includes multiple other siboglinid worms, several bivalve and gastropod mollusks, nematodes, and sea urchins. In most of these relationships, the symbionts augment dietary nutrients of the host, in contrast to *Riftia*, which has dispensed with a digestive system entirely. Other groups of animals, such as some intestinal parasites, have also lost their digestive system, but a hallmark of animals is the need to feed.

In this chapter, we discuss the evolution and regulation of digestive physiology, exploring the diversity associated with different diets and lifestyles. ■

LOOKING BACK 14

You may find it helpful to review Chapter 3, where we describe the nature of energy, the fundamentals of energy metabolism, and the biochemistry of the macromolecules that serve as nutrients. In Chapter 2 we identify the factors that play an important role in the evolution of the digestive system, such as the development of the coelom. Also, Chapter 5 describes the basic pathways and properties of neurons and how they regulate physiology, which becomes relevant when we discuss how the nervous system controls digestion. Chapter 6 covers the structure and regulation of smooth muscle, which lines the digestive tract of most animals. Chapter 9 describes the organization of the circulatory system, and its role in transport of nutrients between tissues. Finally, in Chapter 10 we discuss the relationship between the gut microbes and the immune system.

■ OVERVIEW

Digestive physiology is concerned with all of the structures, tissues, and processes that contribute to the physical and chemical breakdown of food (Figure 14.2). Digestion begins with the neurosensory machinery utilized to identify food, such as an insect's antennae or a knifefish's electrical sensors. Once food is located in the broad environment, it must be captured using specialized anatomy, such as the lobster's claw, the eagle's talon, or the mosquito's proboscis. Once acquired, food is usually mechanically disrupted with the help of other specialized structures, such as a mammal's teeth or the snail's tongue.

Animals then begin the process of **assimilation** whereby nutrients are broken down, absorbed, and converted into useable forms. The food may be macerated, or softened, by soaking in fluids such as saliva. Chemical digestion begins with the enzymatic processes that convert large food items to macromolecules and small molecules, and releases micronutrients—ions, vitamins, and minerals—from

FIGURE 14.2 **Digestion**

Animals use combinations of sensory and mechanical processes to acquire and ingest food. Vision and smell are central to the feeding strategies of most vertebrates. Once acquired, the food begins to undergo the process of digestion. Frequently, ingestion begins with mechanical disruption in the upper digestive tract, followed by chemical processing of the food material that is required for assimilation. Undigestible material is expelled from the animal.

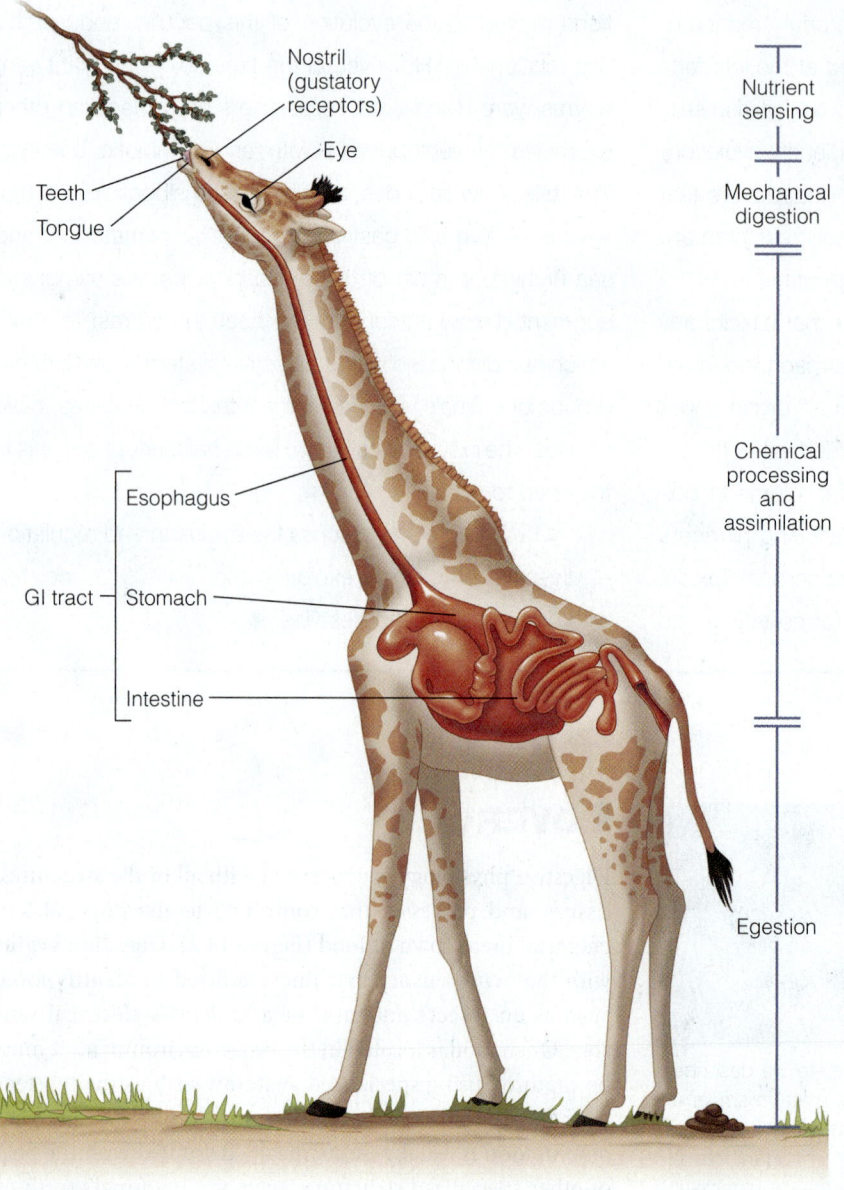

the food. Chemical breakdown is primarily enzymatic and in most cases takes place *outside* the animal. Note that the inner surface of the **gastrointestinal tract** (or GI tract) is contiguous with the external environment. Nutrients are then transported into the animal across the epithelial cells that line the GI tract. The GI tract is wondrous in its complexity. It is composed of many cell types: absorptive cells that take up nutrients, glands that secrete suites of chemicals (mucus, acid, ions, and enzymes), muscles that control the GI tract

shape and motility, and nerves that regulate GI tract function. Once the nutrients are absorbed into the animal, they may be broken down for energy or converted into other forms or stored for later use. Undigested food is expelled from the body by the process of **egestion**.

THE NATURE AND ACQUISITION OF NUTRIENTS

Every organic molecule on the planet possesses chemical energy, yet animals are able to capture this energy from only a small subset of these molecules. Food is a sampling of the external environment, a heterogeneous mixture of digestible and undigestible materials. Nutrients are the external molecules that allow an animal to build and maintain cells. We begin our discussion of digestive physiology by considering the nature of the nutrients.

Nutrients

Ingestion is the primary route that an animal uses to gain access to environmental chemicals. Although many aquatic animals obtain some essential ions by importing them across the external epithelial surfaces, such as the gills and skin, most animals absorb nutrients across the epithelium of the gastrointestinal tract. Some of the assimilated nutrients are degraded to liberate chemical energy; the rest are used as building blocks. Many of the macromolecules that animals need for biosynthesis cannot be synthesized *de novo*, so a dietary source is critical. *Essential nutrients,* those chemicals that must be obtained in the diet, include most vitamins and minerals, as well as several amino acids and fatty acids. *Nonessential nutrients* are those chemicals that the animal can produce from other molecules.

Diets provide energy for activity, growth, maintenance, and reproduction

The diet provides animals with nutrients that can be oxidized for energy. Every diet has an energy content that can be described in the standard units of energy: joules or calories. There must be enough energy in the diet to match the metabolic demands of the animal, also measured in joules or calories. (Recall from Chapter 3 that the layman's use of the term *Calorie* is 1 kilocalorie.)

The energetic needs of an animal depend on many factors. Its long-term metabolic energy consumption reflects the long-term dietary needs for energy. In the short term, energy consumption and utilization frequently fall out of balance, and energy status must be buffered by the use of fuel storage depots. Body size, activity levels, growth rate, reproductive state, and environmental stress are the most important factors that influence the metabolic rate of an animal, and therefore dietary energy demands. These factors also account for the differences in energy demands between species.

Each macromolecule has a corresponding energy content, measured as a *caloric equivalent*. A gram of protein or carbohydrate possesses 4 kilocalories (kcal) of energy, whereas fat has 9 kcal per gram. Thus, for an animal to obtain an equivalent amount of energy, it would have to eat more than twice as much protein as fat. Gross energy is measured experimentally by *calorimetry*. The food material is burned to ash, and the resulting heat production reflects the total energy content. However, not all of the food an animal consumes is digestible (Figure 14.3). If you ate nothing but wood chips (4 kcal/g), you would obtain little energy because you can't digest the plant material to liberate the chemical energy trapped within the cellulose molecules. The gross energy that can be broken down is the **digestible energy**, and the remainder is lost in the feces. Of this digestible energy, only a fraction is **metabolizable energy**, with the remainder of the absorbed nutrients lost in the urine. Much of the metabolizable energy is used by the animal to support maintenance, growth, and reproduction. This is called the **net energy**. The remainder of the metabolizable energy is lost as a result of the digestion process. This energy, called **specific dynamic action (SDA)**, is reflected in the increase in metabolic rate during the digestive process. The SDA, measured as heat production, is a result of the complex events occurring as a result of digestion, including the chemical hydrolysis of food as well as the elevations in metabolic rate of the digestive machinery. Anyone who has overindulged in a holiday meal will recognize the effects of SDA. The heat warms the body, and this in combination with neurotransmitters can induce drowsiness. Many large predators, such as lions and snakes, sleep after gorging in feeding bouts.

The SDA, or *heat increment,* as it is often termed, is an important source of thermal energy for the animal. The heat of digestion is rapidly transferred to the rest of the body by the abundant vasculature that serves the GI tract. Thus, SDA contributes to heat production in endothermic animals, reducing the need for specific thermogenic pathways. For a hummingbird feeding on a cold morning, SDA is an important contribution to whole-body heat production, helping it cope with cold air temperatures as well as cold nectar; ingesting a normal-sized nectar meal at 4°C creates a thermal challenge equivalent to that experienced when the entire hummingbird is at 15°C. In some ectothermic animals, SDA causes local warming to speed the rate of digestion. The bluefin tuna, for example, possesses countercurrent heat exchangers to help retain heat within the GI tract, accelerating digestion.

Vitamins and minerals participate in catalysis

Vitamins are a group of chemically unrelated molecules with diverse functions. For simplicity, they are usually categorized based on their solubility. The fat-soluble vitamins are A, D, E, and K; the water-soluble vitamins include the B family and vitamin C (Table 14.1). Solubility influences both the mode of uptake and the potential toxicity. An animal can consume copious amounts of water-soluble vitamins with little ill effect because any excess is readily excreted in the urine. Fat-soluble vitamins can be problematic, however, because they are stored in lipid depot tissues and can be released in a toxic pulse when fats are mobilized.

Some animals obtain selected vitamins from symbiotic bacteria living in the GI tract. For example, the gut flora of most mammals produce all the vitamin C needed in the diet.

FIGURE 14.3 Dietary energy

Not all food energy is digestible. Undigestible material, such as dietary fiber, is lost in the feces. Some of the nutrients taken up by the gut are lost in the urine, unmetabolized by the animal. A portion of the metabolizable energy is released as heat during the process of digestion. The remainder can be used to fuel activity, growth, reproduction, and other energy-dependent processes necessary for life.

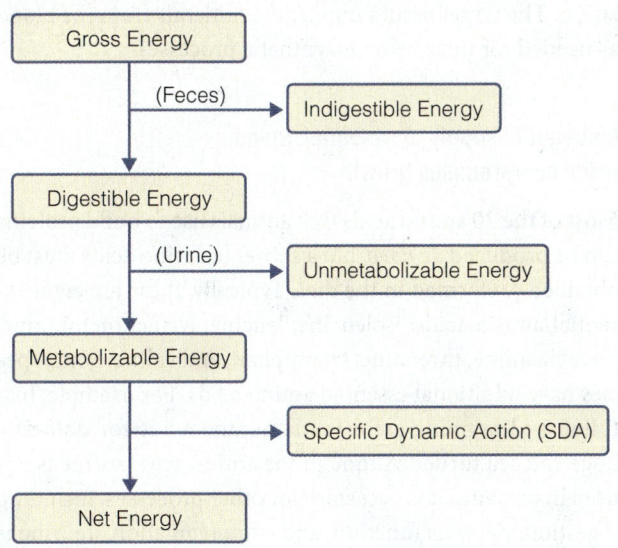

Table 14.1	Vitamins	
Vitamin*	**Functions**	**Deficiency Symptoms**
Fat-soluble vitamins		
A, retinol	Visual pigments, gene regulation	Night blindness, epithelial damage
D, calciferol	Calcium and phosphate absorption	Rickets
E, tocopherol	Antioxidant	Anemia
K, menadione	Blood clotting	Hemophilia
Water-soluble vitamins		
B_1, thiamin	Coenzyme: thiamin pyrophosphate	Beriberi
B_2, riboflavin	Coenzyme: FAD, FMN	Various skin disorders
B_3, niacin	Coenzyme: NAD, NADP	Pellagra
B_5, pantothenic acid	Coenzyme: coenzyme A	Adrenal and reproductive dysfunction
B_6, pyridoxine	Coenzyme: pyridoxyl phosphate	Peripheral neuritis
Biotin	Coenzyme: biotin	Hair loss, skin problems
Folic acid	Coenzyme: tetrahydrofolate	Megaloblastic anemia
B_{12}, cobalamin	Coenzyme: methylcobalamin	Pernicious anemia
C, ascorbic acid	Antioxidant, connective tissue growth	Scurvy

*The vitamins are listed in the form in which they appear in the diet. Some are modified by the animal to produce vital molecules. For example, retinol is converted to retinal to produce the visual pigment.

Humans, unlike most mammals, must obtain their vitamin C preformed in the diet. Fortuitously, some of the pioneering studies on vitamin C were performed on guinea pigs, which also derive vitamin C from the diet. Vitamin absorption is one of the main benefits of an unusual feeding strategy known as *coprophagy*. Rabbits, for example, eat their own feces as a way of regaining vitamins lost in undigestible material. While coprophagy increases the risk for parasites and disease, it provides important nutritional advantages to some animals, including a second opportunity to extract nutrients from the vegetation they eat.

Mineral nutrients are a collection of metallic elements that participate in many aspects of physiology, including osmoregulatory balance, cell signaling, and protein structure. Animal diets differ in mineral content, and many animals face mineral limitations that require more specialized feeding. For example, herbivore diets may be poor in some minerals; large herbivores seek out additional sources of salt, and rodents require additional calcium, which is low in most of the seeds on which rodents typically feed. Aquatic animals obtain many of their essential nutrients directly from the water, transporting them across the gills or skin. Most minerals, however, are absorbed from the diet. Calcium enters the intestinal cell through Ca^{2+} channels and is exported into the blood by Ca^{2+} ATPases. The entire transport process is accelerated in the presence of the protein *calbindin*.

Ca^{2+} uptake is controlled by vitamin D, which regulates the synthesis of calbindin. Phosphorus is imported into the intestinal cells as inorganic phosphate, transported using Na^+ cotransporters. Iron is imported into the cell in the ferrous form (Fe^{2+}) by a nonspecific divalent metal transporter, cotransported with H^+. If the iron arrives in the diet incorporated into heme, it can be transported into the cell in that form. Copper, zinc, and other minerals are also transported into intestinal cells by specific carriers. Once absorbed, these minerals are pumped out of the intestinal cell into the circulation. The target tissues import the minerals from the blood as needed for their own biosynthetic processes.

Inadequate supply of essential amino acids compromises growth

Most of the 20 amino acids that animals use to build proteins can be produced *de novo*, but a subset of amino acids must be obtained preformed in the diet. Typically, there are eight essential amino acids: isoleucine, leucine, lysine, methionine, phenylalanine, threonine, tryptophan, and valine. Some species have additional essential amino acids. For example, histidine and arginine are essential amino acids for domestic dogs and sea turtles. Although the amino acid taurine is not used in proteins, it is necessary for other processes, including digestion, nervous function, and osmoregulation. Taurine is an essential amino acid for several animals, including each of the 30 species of cats examined to date. In other words, don't feed dog food to your cat.

If a diet is persistently deficient in any of the essential amino acids, the animal may experience developmental defects or slower growth. Because dietary protein is the source of these amino acids, *protein quality*—the profile of amino acids in dietary protein—is a critical nutritional concern. Animal tissues provide a higher quality dietary protein than do plant tissues, because they possess an amino acid profile that more closely resembles the needs of other animals. In contrast, plant proteins are often deficient in one or more of the essential amino acids. For example, maize proteins are deficient in lysine and wheat proteins are deficient in tryptophan. An herbivore can avoid amino acid deficiencies by eating plants with different combinations of deficiencies.

Animals require linoleic and linolenic acid in the diet

Animals use lipids for many purposes, including energy production, cellular membranes (phospholipids), and cell signaling (prostaglandins, leukotrienes). They can produce *de novo* a broad suite of fatty acids that differ in chain length and desaturation. For instance, animals can produce palmitate from acetyl CoA using the enzyme fatty acid synthase, then metabolize it into other forms by elongases (which increase fatty acid chain length) and desaturases (which introduce double bonds). However, animals cannot produce sufficient amounts of omega-3 (ω3) and omega-6 (ω6) fatty acids *de novo*. Instead, animals require ω3 and ω6 fatty acids from the diet, typically as linoleic acid (18:2 ω6) and α-linolenic acid (18:3 ω3). Humans can most readily meet ω3 requirements by consuming fish. Fish also obtain their ω3 fatty acids in the diet, derived ultimately from the photosynthetic phytoplankton at the base of the food chain. Plant seeds are the best dietary source of ω6 fatty acids.

Digestion of specific nutrients requires specific enzymes

Digestive enzymes allow animals to convert the complex macromolecules arriving in the diet to forms that can be absorbed by the animal and processed into usable forms. Although the nature of diets is very diverse, most animals rely on the same suites of digestive enzymes.

- *Lipases* release fatty acids from triglycerides (triglyceride lipases) and phospholipids (phospholipases).
- *Proteases* (trypsin, chymotrypsin) break down proteins into shorter polypeptides. *Peptidases* are proteases that cleave successive amino acids from the end of a polypeptide. Amino-peptidases attack the first (N-terminal) peptide bond, whereas carboxy-peptidases attack the last (C-terminal) peptide bond.

A dipeptidase breaks the peptide bond of a dipeptide, producing two amino acids.

- **Amylases** such as dextrinase and glucoamylase break down polysaccharides into oligosaccharides. *Disaccharidases* such as maltase, sucrase, and lactase break down specific disaccharides.
- *Nucleases* break down DNA into nucleotides, which are then broken into nucleosides and nitrogenous bases for absorption.

Not every macromolecule ingested is subjected to the digestive process. Many animals are unable to produce the enzymes needed to assimilate a dietary macromolecule. In some cases, the levels of enzymes can vary among individuals. For example, many humans show an age-dependent reduction in production of lactase, the enzyme that breaks down the disaccharide lactose. When lactose-intolerant people consume milk products, lactose can escape the upper intestine undigested, passing into the lower intestine. The methane-producing gut flora can feast on this rich energy source, much to the discomfort of the individual and displeasure of those in the immediate vicinity.

Many animals incorporate symbiotic organisms into their digestive physiology

Despite their impressive capacity to break down food, many animals benefit from the assistance of symbiotic organisms. Three main types of symbionts participate in digestion. **Enterosymbionts** live within the lumen of the GI tract itself. Because the inside of the gut is contiguous with the external environment, in principle these symbionts live outside the animal tissues. They are called enterosymbionts to distinguish them from **exosymbionts**, which are symbionts that are actively cultivated outside the body. **Endosymbionts** are organisms that grow within the animal, typically embedded between host cells in a tissue or, less often, within a host cell.

Not all symbionts are bacteria. Fungi are important enterosymbionts in many types of plant-eating insects. Leaf-cutter ants feed leaf fragments to exosymbiotic fungi, cultivated by the ant colony. The ants consume both the fungi and the plant material that has been partially degraded by the fungi. Many marine animals form symbiotic relationships with photosynthetic organisms that grow interspersed with their own cells as endosymbionts. Cyanelles are cyanobacteria living in association with sponges. Dinoflagellates live as symbionts of corals. Zooanthellae are small unicellular brown algae that live in cnidarians and some mollusks. Zoochlorellae are green algae that live in association with sponges, cnidarians, flatworms, and some mollusks. These symbionts use photosynthesis to produce carbon skeletons that are taken up by the animal cells. Zooanthellae produce glycerol, and zoochlorellae produce monosaccharides such as glucose and maltose. These symbiotic cells gain protection from predators by living in the confines of the animal tissues. Perhaps the strangest endosymbiotic relationship is seen in the giant vent worm (*Riftia pachyptila*), discussed in our chapter-opening feature (see Figure 14.1).

Enterosymbionts play multiple roles in digestive physiology

Symbionts living within the digestive tract (*enterosymbionts*) provide many services for their host. They produce many organic compounds that can be taken up by the hosts, including vitamins. They are perhaps most valuable for their ability to break down macromolecules that would otherwise be poorly digested, such as cellulose, wax, or chitin. Recent genome-sequencing projects have shown that a number of the species that consume these macromolecules have genes for the enzymes required to break them down. Thus, some plant-feeding insects possess cellulose genes, and some insectivorous bats possess chitinase genes. Evolutionary genomics studies explore the origins of such genes, which occur only sporadically in animal lineages, considering less-conventional mechanisms such as lateral gene transfer. However, even species that possess these unusual enzymes rely heavily on enterosymbionts for digestion.

Cellulose is a poorly digested plant polysaccharide, which in most animals becomes dietary fiber. However, it is as rich in chemical energy as glycogen, and many animals possess mechanisms to digest cellulose. Some invertebrates possess genes for *cellulase*, the enzyme that cleaves the β1-4 glycosidic bond that distinguishes cellulose from glycogen (α1-4) and starch (α1-6) (see Figure 3.20). Most animals that can digest cellulose require enterosymbionts. For example, termites digest wood fibers with the help of protists and fungi. Many species house cellulolytic bacteria in specialized fermentation chambers. Cellulose is broken down to glucose, which can be absorbed by the animal or fermented by the bacteria to produce anaerobic end products, including the volatile fatty acids acetate, butyrate, and propionate. The animals absorb these fermentation products for use in biosynthesis or energy metabolism.

Though cellulose is utilized by many lineages of animals, select groups are able to use enterosymbionts to digest other large macromolecules. Marine animals that feed on plankton can digest the chitin exoskeleton with the help of symbiotic bacteria. Whales hold chitinolytic bacteria in **gastric** ceca. Many animals possess genes encoding chitinases, but these enzymes are used by immune cells that attack chitin-containing pathogens and it is not clear if animals can secrete an endogenous chitinase into the gut, where it would aid in digestion. Another long macromolecule that is undigestible for most animals is wax. However, several species of birds eat the wax found in beehives. Bacteria within their GI tract hydrolyzes the wax into shorter carbon units that can be absorbed by the animal.

Finally, some animals can treat their gut flora as a farm, partially digesting the bacteria as food. These animals secrete the enzyme *lysozyme* into the gut to break down the bacterial cell wall. The lysozyme of ruminants has adapted to function under the harsh conditions of the ruminant fermentation chambers, whereas the lysozyme from most mammals is nonfunctional under these conditions. Interestingly, one lineage of primates, the colobine monkeys, possesses foregut fermentation chambers that allow them to digest vegetation. Their lysozyme structure more closely resembles that of a cow than that of their nearest primate relatives. This example of convergent evolution illustrates the constraints on animal enzyme function, and the opportunities that are afforded animals that can digest an underutilized resource.

The gut bacterial community is essential to proper digestion in humans. As we discuss in Box 14.1: Applications: The Human Microbiome, the maintenance of the gut microbiome is a complex interplay between the diet, the proliferation of favorable gut flora, and the response of the host's immune system.

CONCEPT CHECK

1. How is energy partitioned in an animal's diet?
2. What are the major nutrients in a diet, and what enzymes metabolize them into the forms in which they are transported into the digestive epithelium?
3. How is it that many animals obtain nutrition from eating cellulose, yet lack the enzymes to break it down?

Finding and Consuming Food

You are familiar with the basic dietary strategies seen in animals—carnivory, herbivory, and omnivory—each with its advantages and disadvantages. The physiology of digestion is matched to the chemical and physical nature of the diet. To find the food that matches their dietary needs, animals use neurosensory systems. Some feeding strategies, such as filter feeding, depend on random encounters. Most animals, however, actively seek out and often pursue their food. Once found, the food must be ingested to begin the process of digestion. In the following section, we survey some of the ways animals find diets that suit their nutritional needs.

Animals sense food using chemical, electrical, and thermal cues

The nature of food varies widely among animals, and the mechanisms animals use to detect food are equally diverse. Animals link some form of receptor to a signaling pathway that leads to a behavioral response that alters feeding.

THE HUMAN MICROBIOME

The human GI tract is home for about 100 trillion microbes, which when collected weigh around 2 kilograms. Collectively, they form a microbial ecosystem in which nutrients arrive from the host, competition for resources occurs, and populations grow to capacity. The gut population is a processing plant for the host, digesting macromolecules that would otherwise be undigestible. As discussed in Chapter 10, the massive population of microbes housed in the gut is also a threat to the immunohealth of the animal, and the immune system displays constant vigilance to protect itself from its enterosymbionts. Changes in the gut microbiome can have important consequences for the health of the individual. For example, many people experience a loss of the ability to produce the enzyme lactase. With this deficiency, milk sugar (lactose) cannot be digested and is left for the gut bacteria, which metabolize it to form gases that contribute to nausea, cramping, bloating, diarrhea, and flatulence.

In many cases, disease symptoms are caused when immune system signaling misfires as a result of the gut microbiome. There is some evidence that changes in the GI tract bacteria can trigger autoimmune responses, such as type I diabetes and multiple sclerosis. Some GI tract microflora are pathogenic and do not contribute to digestion. *Helicobacter pylori* is a bacterium that invades the pits of the stomach, causing the damage that culminates in gastric ulcers.

A healthy gut flora is a well-balanced ecosystem, where different types of bacteria compete for resources. Occasionally situations arise in which populations of problematic bacteria become more abundant, causing digestive and other problems. For example, Clostridia is a polyphyletic group of normal bacteria of the gut. They use secretions of phenolic compounds to kill their competitors. If they become too abundant, the phenolic compounds rise and become a danger for the host. The host in turn produces protective sulfur compounds, which could potentially become limiting to the host. The need for a proper gut ecosystem is the basis of the many types of probiotic treatments, in which "good" bacteria (such as lactobacillus and bifidobacteria) are ingested in an effort to remodel the microbiome. Many clinical studies have contributed to the conclusion that a proper gut microbiome can have effects on the brain that influence mood and mental health.

A more dangerous clostridial bacterium is *Clostridium difficile*, which can cause severe digestive dysfunction. It is very difficult to treat with drugs, but there has been some success with fecal transplants. Feces are collected from a healthy individual and transferred to the unhealthy patient via an enema; the bacteria contained in the transplanted material can help reestablish the normal gut flora, outcompeting *C. difficile* and alleviating the symptoms.

In 2008, the U.S. National Institutes of Health launched the Human Microbiome Project to characterize the microbial flora of humans. In addition to the study of the GI tract, the project included surveys of the mouth, skin, vagina, and respiratory tract. It is thought that this information will enable researchers to identify links between specific diseases and microfloral patterns.

References
- Bested, A. C., Logan, A. C., & Selhub, E. M. (2013). Intestinal microbiota, probiotics and mental health: From Metchnikoff to modern advances. Part III: Convergence toward clinical trials. *Gut Pathology, 5*, 4.
- Ettinger G., Burton, J. P., & Reid, G. (2013). If microbial ecosystem therapy can change your life, what's the problem? *Bioessays, 35*, 508–512.

Many animals possess means of detecting the presence of specific chemicals in the environment. The chemical may be a nutrient, and movement toward the source of the nutrient increases the likelihood that the animal will find more food. For example, the cestode (tapeworm) *Hymenolepis diminuta* undergoes diurnal migrations up and down the GI tract of its host, following the nutrients released from a meal under digestion. In other cases, the chemical that is detected may not itself be a nutrient but rather a signal that prey is nearby. For example, when a *Hydra* detects small organic molecules such as proline or reduced glutathione, it waves its tentacles and opens its mouth. As we discussed in Chapter 7, complex animals use *gustatory receptors* and *olfactory receptors* to locate food, determine its palatability, and control the drive to feed (appetite). Herbivorous insects, such as aphids, use gustatory receptors to detect chemicals that either stimulate feeding (phagostimulants) or deter feeding (phagodeterrents). The most important phagostimulants in insects are sugars and amino acids. Plants can deter insects from feeding by releasing secondary metabolites that an insect recognizes as toxic. Gustatory signals are also important in vertebrates. Carrion eaters detect volatile compounds that escape rotting flesh. Sharks are able to detect from great distances chemicals that are normally found in vertebrate blood, a sign of an injured animal. Although the chemical nature of the gustatory stimulants is diverse, each works in combination with a sensory receptor that triggers a signaling cascade ultimately affecting central control of feeding behavior.

Many animals find prey by sensing the energy emitted or reflected from the animal in the form of light, sound, heat, or electricity. A bird of prey, such as the golden eagle, uses its visual system to spot a field mouse moving in a distant meadow. Some insects can detect the infrared light emitted from the warm bodies of potential prey species. Light can also be produced by animals in conjunction with foraging strategies. For example, predatory firefly species attract a prey firefly species by producing a light pattern that mimics the mating signal of the prey. Deep-sea fish use bioluminescent appendages to lure small prey. There are many examples of predator–prey coevolution, in which prey properties such as cryptic color are selected on the ability to confuse the visual system of its predator. Animals that rely on sound energy as a feeding strategy employ a variety of sound detection organs ranging from the mammalian ear to the fish lateral line. The weakly electric knifefish, which lives in the murky waters of the Amazon, uses electromagnetic receptors to detect the muscle activity of potential prey items.

Simple animals digest food within phagocytic vesicles

The simplest of animals, the sponges, obtain nutrients primarily by *phagocytosis,* much like protists such as the amoeba. Sponges subsist on particles of various sizes, ranging from organic debris much smaller than bacteria (50 µm). Water carrying food particles passes through the sponge's network of pores and channels, flowing in currents generated by flagellated cells called choanocytes (Figure 14.4). As the water permeates the animal, it flows through biological filters that sort particles by size. Cells that line the pores,

choanocytes as well as amoebocytes, engulf the particles using phagocytosis. Digestion occurs inside these cells in endocytic vacuoles. Breakdown products are released into the cell, and undigested material is exocytosed out of the cell.

Other metazoans possess something akin to a mouth—an entrance to an internal compartment that carries out digestion. The challenge for many animals is to get the food to the mouth. Cnidarians, such as corals and *Hydra*, use tentacles to capture small prey, such as zooplankton. Once the prey is captured, the tentacle bends to the mouth to release the food. The mouth gapes to permit food to enter the gastrovascular cavity. Movement down the tentacles and into the mouth is aided by a layer of mucus secreted by the epithelial cells. The wall of the gastrovascular cavity is composed of gastrodermal cells, including nutritive cells and enzymatic gland cells (Figure 14.5). The enzymatic gland cells release digestive enzymes that break down prey into a slurry of nutrients. The nutritive cells phagocytose the smaller particles and process them within the endocytotic **food vacuole**, releasing nutrients that escape the gastrodermis and cross the gelatinous mesoglea to supply the diverse cells of the epidermis, including the stinging cells, or *nematocytes*. Once the meal is digested, the animal expels the remaining material from the gastrovascular cavity and feeds again.

Feeding structures are matched to diet

Most animals have some form of specialized mouthparts to assist in feeding. The mouth itself may be lined with hard structures that grasp or cut the food. Some form of extension may also protrude from the mouth to manipulate, disrupt, or suck. Although we typically identify these structures as jaws and tongues, they are extraordinarily diverse in structure and developmental origins.

Some species of invertebrates, such as free-living worms, have a simple mouth that engulfs particles. Most invertebrates have structures associated with the mouth to aid in feeding. For example, some endoparasitic worms, such as the liver fluke, have a mouth that acts as both a siphon and an attachment organ. Although cestodes possess an anterior attachment organ (a combination of suckers and hooks), they have no mouth and, in fact, lack the entire digestive system. These worms absorb nutrients over the outer body surface, which is decorated with spikelike extensions of the cells called microvilli. In many ways, the cestode anatomy resembles a gut turned inside out.

FIGURE 14.4 **Sponge digestion**

Water is brought through channels by the flagellated choanocytes. Food particles are phagocytosed by choanocytes and amoebocytes.

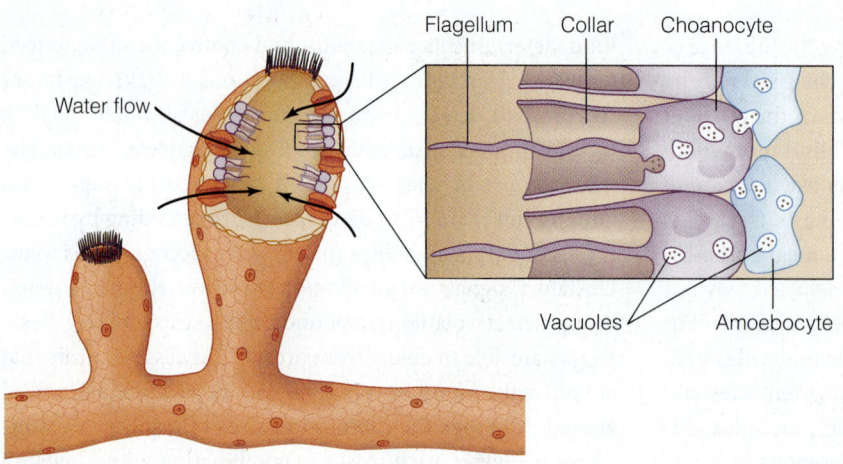

FIGURE 14.5 Cnidarian digestive system

A cnidarian, such as *Hydra*, captures food with its tentacles, and carries it to the mouth in mucous streams. The food passes through the open mouth into the gastrovascular cavity for digestion. Particles are phagocytosed by nutritive cells lining the cavity, and digested in endocytic vacuoles. Nutrients can then diffuse from the nutritive cells of the gastrodermal layer to the other cells of the gastrodermis (gland cells) and epidermis (sensory cells, nematocytes, epithelial cells).

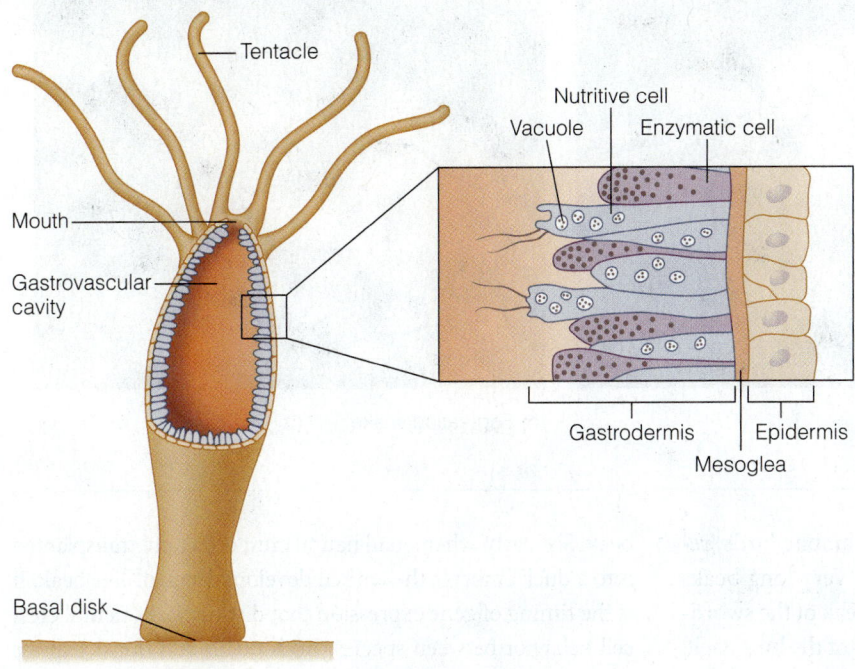

Many animals possess oral appendages that are functionally homologous to a tongue. Snails have a muscular tongue called a *radula*. Sharp protrusions from the radula help the snail to grind, rasp, or cut away chunks of food. Many nectar-eating butterflies and moths possess a long tubelike tongue, or *proboscis*. The insect uncoils its proboscis to reach deep into the throat of flowers to get to the nectar. Flower anatomy often coevolves with butterfly tongues, ensuring that flowers are pollinated by specific species of butterflies. When Darwin studied an unusual orchid from Madagascar, he predicted that a moth would be found that had a tongue long enough to feed on the flower. The Madagascar hawk moth, discovered about 40 years later, has a proboscis that is nearly 30 centimeters long.

Many species possess hardened mouthparts or oral appendages that help penetrate or mechanically disrupt the surface of food. The squid uses a hard beak to bite off chunks of prey captured by its tentacles. Arthropods possess complex mouth segments that help the animals acquire food. A spider uses its *chelicerae* to attack and mechanically disintegrate its prey (Figure 14.6a). Hymenopterans, which include bees and wasps, are chewing insects. The paper wasp, for example, has hinged mandibles that can crush the tough exoskeleton of the insects on which it feeds. Insects of the order Diptera use their mouthparts to suck fluids. For example, fruit flies siphon plant juices from rotting fruit, and mosquitoes extract blood from vertebrates. However, anyone who has been bitten by a large horsefly will be difficult to convince that these dipterans are not biting insects but sucking insects. The horsefly uses hardened mouthparts like scissors to slice through the skin. It can then use its labium to suck the fluids that seep from the wound.

The most important feeding structure of vertebrates is the jaw. With the exception of the primitive agnathans, which lack jaws, all vertebrate mouths are built upon a common plan of paired jaws. As we discussed in Chapter 2, the evolution and development of the head may be the single most important variation to arise in the evolution of vertebrates. The rearrangement of cranial structures gave vertebrates the developmental flexibility to tolerate evolutionary changes in the structure of the head and associated features. This facilitated adaptive radiation by permitting the evolution of feeding structures that allowed vertebrates to succeed in novel niches. Consider, for example, the variations in the organization of the vertebrate jaw. In most species, the upper jaw is immobile and integrated into the skull, whereas the lower jaw is hinged and movable. In contrast, several species have evolved a more mobile upper jaw. Some snakes can separate or disarticulate the jawbones. The egg-eating snake can disarticulate its jaw, allowing it to open its mouth more than four times larger than its normal gape, enabling it to swallow an intact egg (Figure 14.6b). It then uses strong neck muscles to crush the egg against the spine. Once the egg contents slide down the throat, the snake vomits the eggshells.

Bird beaks are composed of keratinized tissue

The beak of a bird is composed of bone covered by overlapping scales called *rhamphotheca*. The cells in this epidermal layer produce a cytoskeleton that is rich in the intermediate filament keratin. When the surface cells die, the layer of keratin remains as a protective surface over the beak. Living cells within this layer constantly repair the keratin layer as it is damaged, particularly at the margins of the beak, which are often abraded during feeding.

Diversity in the beak structure of Galápagos finches was central to Darwin's theories of evolution and natural

FIGURE 14.6 **Feeding appendages**

(a) Spiders have appendages associated with the mouth that aid in holding, manipulating, and disrupting prey. **(b)** Many snakes can separate the upper and lower jaw, expanding the gape to enable the animal to swallow large food items, such as a whole egg.

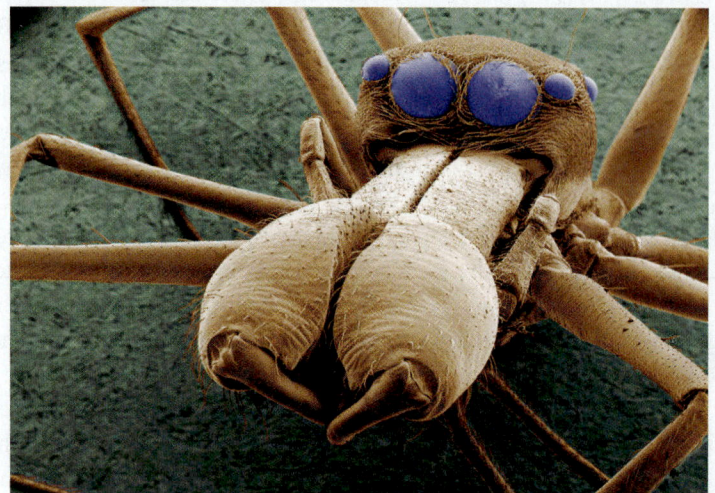

(a) Spider chelicerae

(b) Egg-eating snake

Photo source: For (a) Science Source; (b) Karl H. Switak/Science Source.

selection. Beak morphology is very diverse among birds, reflecting the type of food each bird gathers. Very long beaks can be used to reach deep into flowers; the beak of the sword-billed hummingbird is longer than the body of the bird itself. Flamingos use the beak as a sieve to strain food out of water. Some birds, such as the puffin, possess toothlike ridges on the margins of the beak to assist in tearing apart flesh. It is important to remember that bird beaks serve purposes other than feeding, including vocalization, defense, grooming, and courting. The morphology of beak structure reflects the evolutionary compromises that allow the beak to perform each of its roles. For example, the subtle differences in the beak shape of Darwin's finches can influence the nature of the birdsong, which has important ramifications for territorial behavior and courtship.

Whereas the adaptive significance of bird beak morphology is clear, the developmental and evolutionary determinants of beak shape have only recently been studied. Because a bird emerges from the egg with its beak formed, we know that the factors that establish beak morphology begin well before hatching. Within the first one or two days after fertilization, the bird embryo has established body segments that will eventually give rise to all of the structures of the head (Figure 14.7). Neural crest cells migrate from the forebrain, midbrain, and rhombomeres 1 and 2 to form the beak and associated facial structures. Much of the remarkable diversity in beak structure of different birds can be attributed to the regulation of these neural crest cells in early development. When researchers transplanted neural crest cells from a duck embryo into a quail embryo, the animal developed into a quail with a ducklike

beak. Similarly, when quail neural crest cells were transplanted into a duck embryo, the animal developed a quail-like beak. It is the timing of gene expression that distinguishes neural crest cell behavior between species. Both quails and ducks express the same developmental genes during craniofacial development, but the timing of expression is quite different between species. Although many genes likely contribute to this evolutionary diversity, bone morphogenic protein 4 (Bmp4) accounts for at least part of the intraspecific and interspecific variation seen in nature.

Mammals have bony teeth

Many vertebrates possess oral structures that resemble and function as teeth, but mammalian teeth are structurally unique. Each tooth is composed of a crown, neck, and root (Figure 14.8). The crown extends above the gum, or gingiva; the root is embedded in the gum; and the neck is a narrow region between the crown and the root. A cross section through the tooth reveals the three layers of a typical tooth: enamel, dentin, and pulp. The outer enamel is composed of calcium phosphate crystals integrated into the extracellular matrix. Enamel is so hard that it can be brittle, cracking when an animal bites a hard food. Animal teeth differ in the thickness of the enamel layer as well as its molecular composition. Beneath the enamel is an intermediate layer of dentin and an inner layer of pulp. The dentin is a porous support for the enamel. The pulp is more cellular, and rich in blood vessels and nerves. These two inner layers are living tissues that help build and maintain the tooth.

FIGURE 14.7 **Beak development**

FIGURE 14.7 **Beak development**

In the developing bird embryo, four sequential segments give rise to most of the structures that make up the adult beak: forebrain (fb), midbrain (mb), rhombomere 1 (r1), and rhombomere 2 (r2). Neural crest cells move from the forebrain and midbrain to form the frontonasal region, which becomes the upper beak. Neural crest cells from the midbrain and rhombomeres 1 and 2 migrate to form the mandibular and maxillary regions, which become the lower beak.

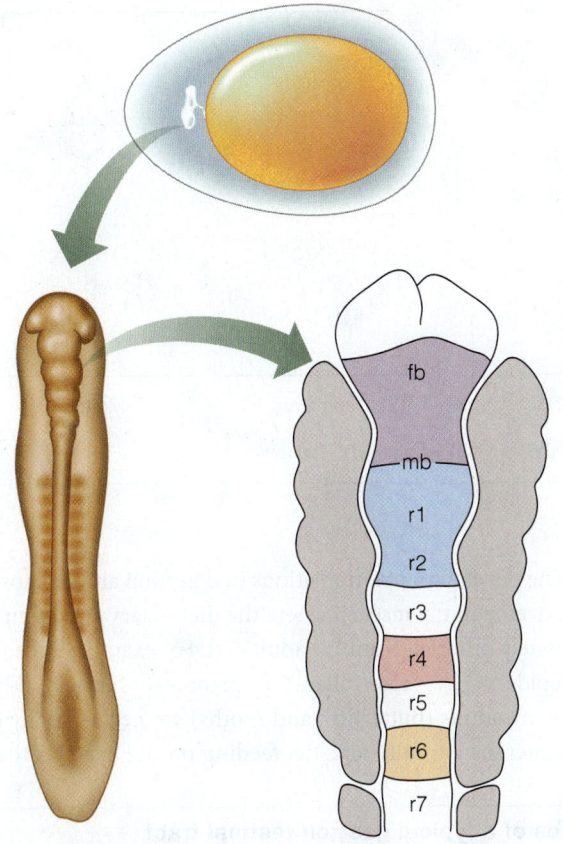

(a) Chick development at day 1 (dorsal view)

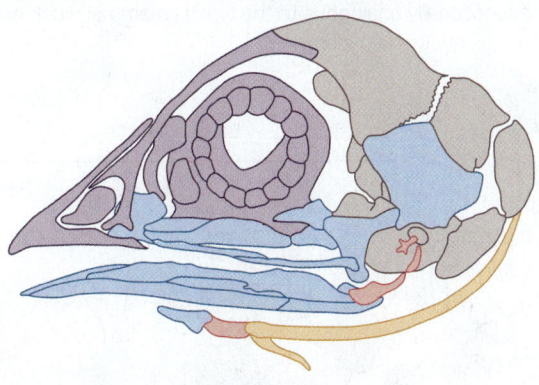

(b) Head structures (lateral view)

Mammals possess four main types of teeth: incisors, canines, premolars, and molars (Figure 14.8b). Incisors and canines are long, sharp teeth that aid in piercing and tearing flesh. The broad, flat molars aid in grinding. Premolars are intermediate in shape and have a role in both tearing and grinding. Like beak morphology, the shape of mammalian

teeth differs markedly in ways that reflect the nature of the diet. The molars of insectivorous bats have sharp cusps and elongated crests to help crack insect exoskeletons. In contrast, fruit bats have molars with broader cusps and basins for crushing plant tissue. There are also many differences in the number of teeth and their growth patterns. Rodents, for example, possess only front incisors and molars; the canines and premolars are lost in early development to make room for the larger incisors and molars. The profile of teeth can also change over the lifetime of an animal. Most mammals replace their teeth once during the lifetime: Early teeth are replaced by the permanent adult teeth. However, monotremes lose their teeth altogether when the animal matures. Most mammalian teeth grow to a predetermined size and then stop growing. In contrast, rodent teeth grow continuously, allowing the tooth to maintain length as it is worn down from continuous grinding.

CONCEPT CHECK

4. Contrast the digestive systems of a sponge and a hydra.
5. Contrast the teeth of a dog and a beaver.
6. Are bird beaks and mammalian teeth living tissue?

DIGESTION AND ASSIMILATION

With an understanding of the nature of nutrients, and the way animals acquire food, we turn our attention now to the ways that an animal uses its digestive system to extract the nutrients from food. We begin with a discussion of the types of cells and tissues that make up digestive systems, and then consider how the animal controls gut function. Hormones and neurotransmitters are central to the control of digestion, ultimately matching whole-animal metabolic needs to feeding behavior, nutrient uptake, storage, and mobilization. These controls are particularly important when the animal experiences physiological challenges and transitions associated with life history patterns, including development and reproduction.

Digestive Systems

The evolutionary history of digestive systems is marked by increasing anatomical and functional specialization. Sponges lack a gut; cnidarians and platyhelminths have blunt-ended sacs or two-way guts, where food enters and leaves through a single opening. With the evolution of the one-way gut, animals were better able to create specialized regions. The nature of these regions varies considerably among animals. Our description of gut regions is based on the terminology used for mammals (Figure 14.9). The mouth opens into the upper

FIGURE 14.8 **Mammalian tooth structure**

(a) The mammalian tooth is composed of three layers. The outer enamel is dead tissue. The inner pulp and intermediate dentin are composed of living cells, nourished by blood vessels, and innervated. The shape and size of the types of teeth vary among species. **(b)** Molars and premolars are generally flattened teeth used for grinding and chewing. Incisors and canines are used for piercing and tearing.

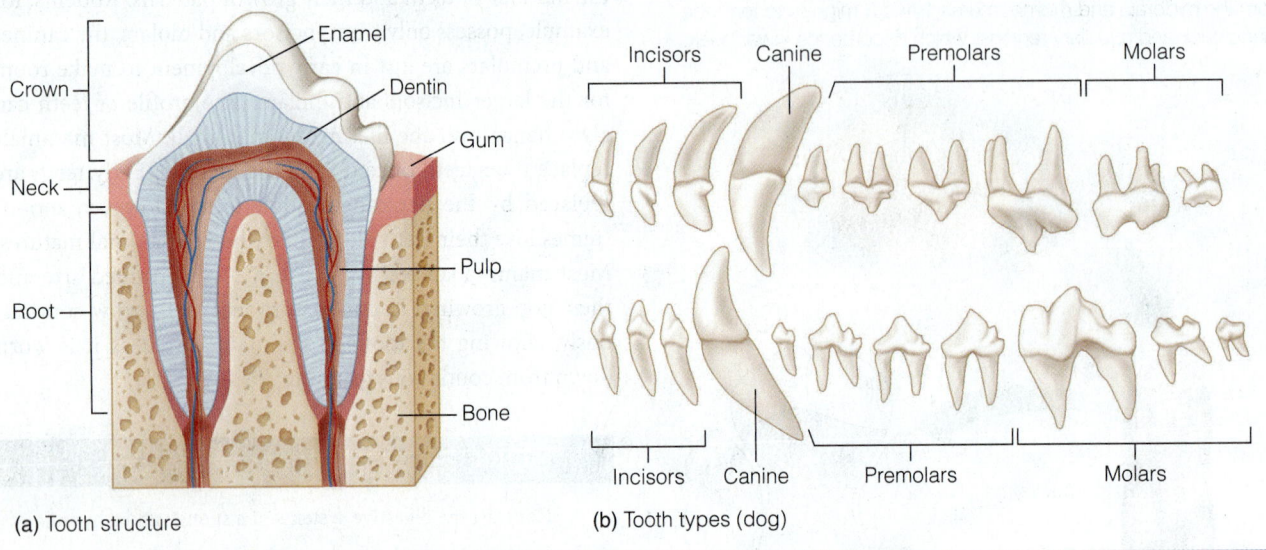

(a) Tooth structure

(b) Tooth types (dog)

region of the GI tract called the pharynx or esophagus. This upper region typically participates in the mechanical breakdown of food. The gastric region or stomach follows; in most animals this is an acidic compartment. The upper intestine, or small intestine, neutralizes the acidic solution released from the stomach, and carries out much of the digestion and nutrient absorption. The upper intestine also receives exocrine secretions from digestive glands: the liver and pancreas in most vertebrates and the hepatopancreas in most invertebrates. The lower intestine, or large intestine, is responsible for reclamation of water and salts. Finally, undigestible material is released through the anus. Most species have side chambers that branch off from the main GI tract. A single chamber is called a **cecum** (plural: ceca). Muscular valves (sphincters) regulate passage through the different compartments.

Superimposed on the evolutionary (interspecies) variation in gut design are modifications that arise in individuals in response to diet and life history. The mammalian diet changes as offspring transition from maternal blood-borne nutrients across the placenta, to mammary gland secretions, to solid food.

The developmental transitions in digestion are perhaps most extreme in the insects, where the diet of larvae is often completely different from the adult diet. For example, most larval lepidopterans (caterpillars) eat plant leafy material, whereas many adults (butterflies and moths) eat nectar. Many larval dipterans are fully aquatic, feeding on the bacteria that live

FIGURE 14.9 **Features of a typical gastrointestinal tract**

Although the exact organization of the GI tract differs among species, most complex animals have regions that are functionally analogous to the typical mammal, such as the horse shown here.

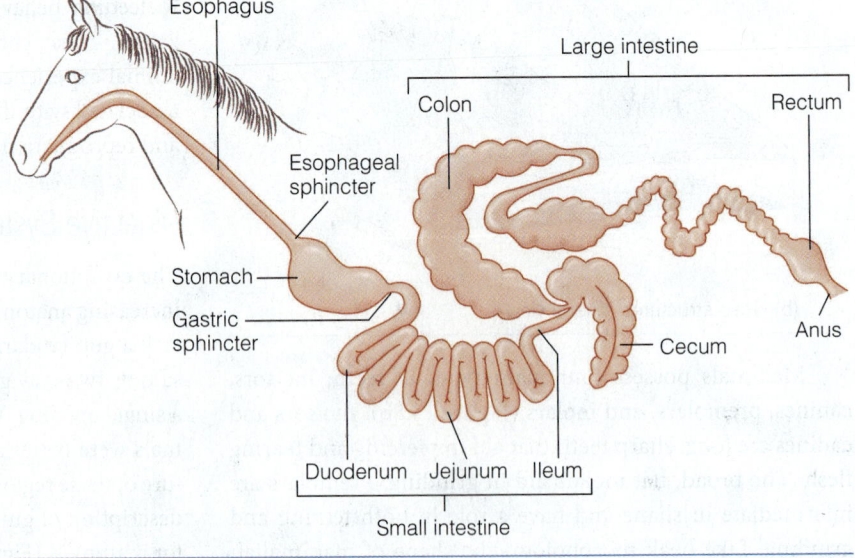

on the surface of stagnant water (mosquitoes) or in the sediment (chironomids). The adults are fully terrestrial, feeding on a wide range of plant and animal material. Remarkably, male and female adult mosquitoes consume different diets; females feed on the blood of vertebrates, from tree frogs to mammals, whereas males drink plant nectar.

Gut complexity is linked to the appearance of the coelom

The nature of the digestive system differs greatly in animals. The simplest of animals—sponges—lack a discrete digestive system. Cnidarians possess a blunt-ended gastrovascular cavity, where food enters and exits through the same opening. With some exceptions, other animals possess some form of gastrointestinal tract, the complexity of which grows with the evolution of the three cell layers and an internal coelom.

Cnidarians are diploblastic, built from two **germ cell** layers that form solid tissues without internal compartments. More advanced animals possess three layers of germ cells—endoderm, mesoderm, and ectoderm. Nemerteans and flatworms remain relatively simple because the three layers of germ cells stick together during development and no coelom forms. The digestive tract of flatworms is, as in cnidarians, a two-way gut; however, the gut itself can be simple or quite complex, with many branches called *diverticula* (Figure 14.10).

The developmental origin of the gut differs among animals in a way that is thought to be diagnostic for evolutionary affinities. Early in gastrulation, a region of the blastula (a hollow ball of cells) migrates inward, causing first a depression and then a pit called the blastopore. In *protostomes*, such as arthropods, annelids, and mollusks, the blastopore becomes the mouth, and the anus forms at a distant site. In *deuterostomes*, such as chordates, hemichordates, and echinoderms, the anus arises from the blastopore, and the mouth is formed second.

The evolutionary and developmental origins of a one-way gut are intimately linked to the appearance of the **coelom**, an internal cavity that arises in a developing embryo. The space between the GI tract and the body wall, known as the *peritoneal cavity*, is one part of the coelom of a vertebrate. There are different types of coeloms that are distinguished by their embryonic origins. A *pseudocoelom* appears in rotifers and nematodes, arising as a gap between the endoderm and mesoderm. All other major animal taxa possess a true coelom arising from layers of the mesoderm. A *schizocoelom* forms when mesoderm splits into two layers, whereas the *enterocoelom* forms when the layer of mesoderm extends, then pinches off from the gut (see Figure 2.7). In general, protostomes possess a schizocoelom and deuterostomes an enterocoelom, though chordates possess a schizocoelom. The appearance of the coelom was important in the evolution of digestive physiology because it allows greater specialization of internal organs.

The early embryonic gut is derived from endoderm, and divided into three regions: foregut, midgut, and hindgut. In the chicken, the gut develops into these regions within four days postfertilization (Figure 14.11). These regions differentiate to form the embryonic gastrointestinal tract. The foregut endoderm gives rise to the esophagus, stomach, and anterior region of the **duodenum** of the small intestine. It also forms buds that develop into the pancreas and liver. The midgut endoderm develops into the posterior part of the duodenum, the remainder of the small intestine (**jejunum** and **ileum**), and much of the large intestine, including cecum, appendix, and part of the colon. The hindgut endoderm develops into the remainder of the colon and the rectum. The properties of these regions continue to change through development and after hatching, matching physiological capacities to the diet.

The digestive systems of complex animals maximize surface area

In the simplest animals with a two-way gut, macromolecule breakdown occurs primarily inside vesicles within the cells. Proteins, complex sugars, and lipids are hydrolyzed, and the end products—amino acids, monosaccharides, and fatty acids—are released directly into the cytoplasm. More complex animals carry out these reactions within the lumen of the

FIGURE 14.10 Flatworm GI tracts

Like the simple animals, such as sponges and cnidarians, the flatworms have two-way guts. **(a)** Most flatworms, such as *Macrostomum*, possess a simple gut with a single sac. **(b)** In some larger flatworms, such as *Dugesia*, the gut can have three or more side branches with lateral diverticula.

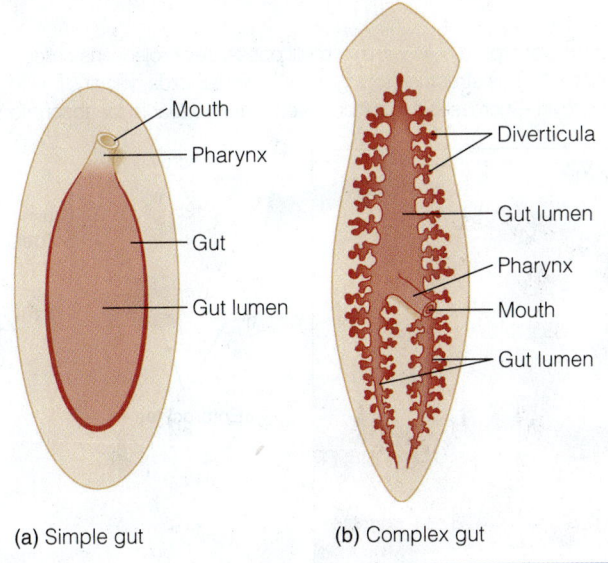

(a) Simple gut   (b) Complex gut

FIGURE 14.11   Gut development

The chicken embryo develops into a chick within 20 days. By day 4, the digestive system has developed enough that major structures are recognizable. The embryonic gut is divided into three sections: foregut, midgut, and hindgut.

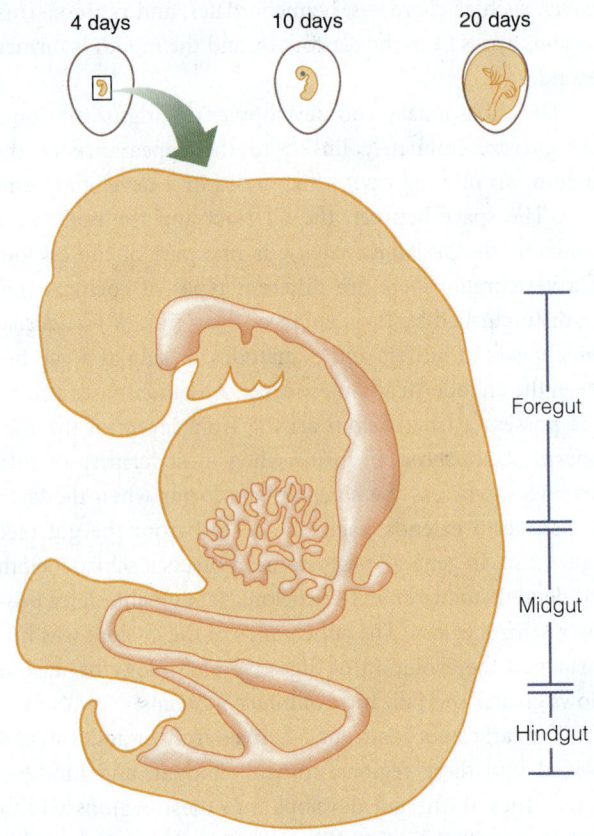

4 days   10 days   20 days

Foregut

Midgut

Hindgut

and nutrient transporters, the process can be slow. Complex animals increase the efficiency of transport by building guts with very large surface areas. This can be achieved by increasing total gut length or increasing surface area for absorption, which can be done at the cellular, tissue, and organ level.

The overall length of the GI tract can be a fraction of the length of the whole animal if it is a simple, straight tube, as seen in agnathans. Alternately, the GI tract can be wrapped around itself, allowing it to be many times longer than the animal. Some species increase the passage time using internal channels. For example, the straight gut of a shark possesses an internal membranous network, called the spiral valve, that increases the functional length of the gut. While most measurements of gut length are performed on dead animals, in the living animal visceral smooth muscle compresses the GI tract into a much shorter tube, so functional length is usually much shorter than maximal length. Nonetheless, the relative length of the gut reflects the digestibility of the diet. Animals with diets that are difficult to digest often have longer guts to increase the efficiency of digestion. For example, carnivores tend to have shorter guts than herbivores because the food is more easily digested. The importance of gut dimensions is best shown by comparing closely related species with differences in diet. The cecum of a grouse, which browses on vegetation, is almost twice the length of the cecum of a similarly sized partridge, which eats seeds.

The surface of the gut has a complex topography that serves to maximize surface area. We see this at the organ level, where the gut has deep circular folds that run around the circumference of the intestine (Figure 14.12). It is also evident at the tissue level, where the surface of the gut tissue is arranged into fingerlike projections called **villi**. The maximization of surface area is even seen at the cellular level. Enterocytes possess microscopic protrusions, supported

digestive tract. The end products of this extracellular digestion must then be taken into the cells lining the gut. Because this uptake step requires many different digestive enzymes

FIGURE 14.12   Intestinal topography

(a) The inner surface of the intestine is a series of folds or ridges that run circularly around the intestine. **(b)** The surface of the tissue is arranged into fields of fingerlike projections called villi. **(c)** Each

of the absorptive cells within the villi possesses projections called microvilli. This structural topography—circular folds, villi, and microvilli—increases the surface area that is available for absorption.

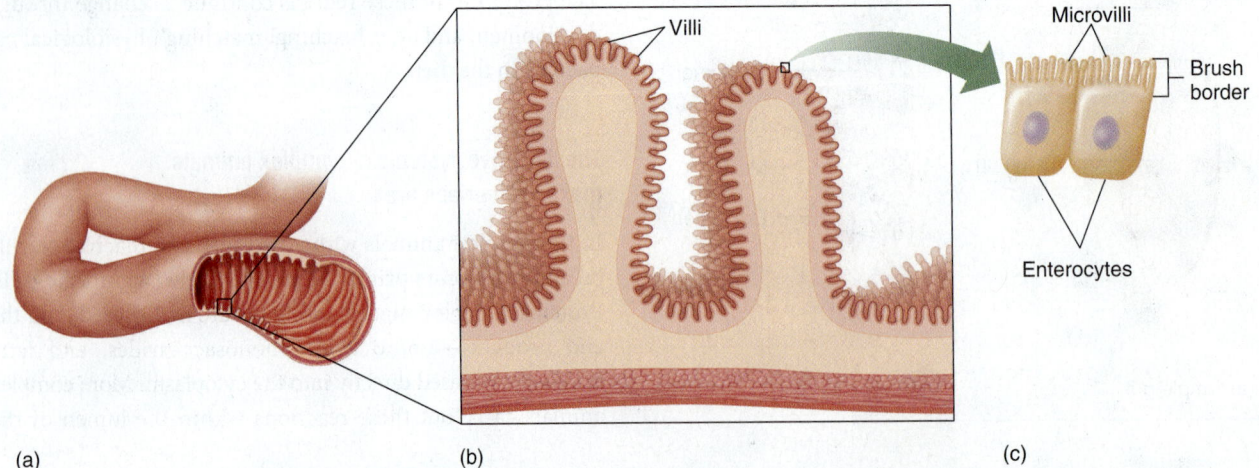

Villi

Microvilli

Brush border

Enterocytes

(a)   (b)   (c)

by the actin cytoskeleton, called **microvilli**. The microvilli cause the surface of the intestinal mucosa to appear fuzzy, which is why the intestinal epithelium is often called the **brush border**. As a result of the circular folds, the villi, and the microvilli, the surface area of the gut is several hundred times greater than it would be if it were composed of flat sheets of smooth cells.

Specialized compartments increase the efficiency of digestion

The efficiency of digestion depends on the ability of the animal to create regions of functional specialization. Even a simple GI tract can have such specializations. Ctenophores (comb jellies) have a simple digestive sac that is elongated and flattened. Food enters the first region of the pharynx, which is acidic, then continues along the pharynx through two basic regions before looping back to exit through the opening that serves as both mouth and anus. With the exception of a small area of confluence, the inward and outward flows are well separated. These specialized sequential compartments allow the two-way gut to function much like a one-way gut, allowing the ctenophore to process multiple prey items in different regions at distinct stages of digestion.

Regional specializations are more developed in animals with a one-way gut. In many cases, muscular valves called sphincters control the passage of food from one compartment to the next. Regional properties are created and maintained by specific types of cells. Some cells alter the pH of the fluids in the lumen by secreting acids or bases. Because most of the macromolecules that appear in food are stable at a pH near neutrality, extremes in pH can enhance their breakdown. Mucus secretions help protect cells and lubricate the surface. Secretory cells release the digestive enzymes—proteases, amylases, lipases, and nucleases—that accelerate chemical breakdown of macromolecules. The absorptive cells in each region also possess specialized transport capacities.

The general plan of the GI tract is similar among vertebrates, but taxa differ in the types of compartments (Figure 14.13). Many species possess extra chambers or modified regions along the GI tract. Birds and bony fish possess ceca that branch from the GI tract and contain bacteria that aid in digestion. The upper GI tract of birds is also more complex than that of other vertebrates. The crop is an outpouching of the esophagus that enables a bird to store partially digested food.

Many species of mammals possess elaborate modifications of the typical gastrointestinal tract that improve the digestibility of plant material. Ruminants (cows, deer, giraffe, goats, and sheep) possess a modified digastric stomach that allows vegetation to be more effectively digested. Ruminants possess a stomach composed of four chambers divided into two functional groups (Figure 14.14). Vegetation passes through the esophagus into the first pair of compartments:

FIGURE 14.13 **Vertebrate gut morphology**

The vertebrate gut differs widely in complexity and length among species. Each group of vertebrates is drawn to the same body length to emphasize the differences in length.

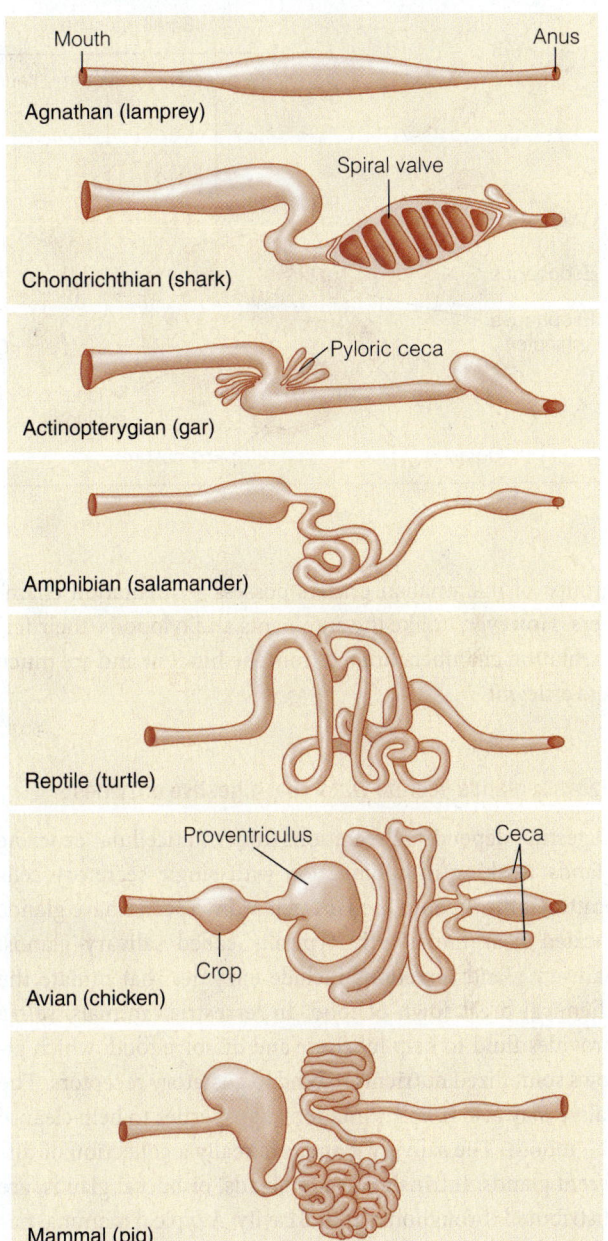

the rumen and reticulum. These interconnected regions house the fermentative bacteria that digest cellulose and produce volatile fatty acids and gases, largely carbon dioxide and methane. The animal can regurgitate food from the rumen back to the mouth, where it can chew the partially degraded material again. When the food returns to the esophagus, it enters the second division, comprising the omasum and abomasum. The abomasum serves as the glandular stomach, secreting digestive enzymes. Like ruminants, the closely related tylopods (camels, llamas) possess a **digastric stomach**, although these animals lack the omasum. Many of the other

FIGURE 14.14 **Ruminants**

Many mammals possess chambers derived from the GI tract that house bacteria that can ferment cellulose. Ruminants, including the cow shown here, possess four chambers.

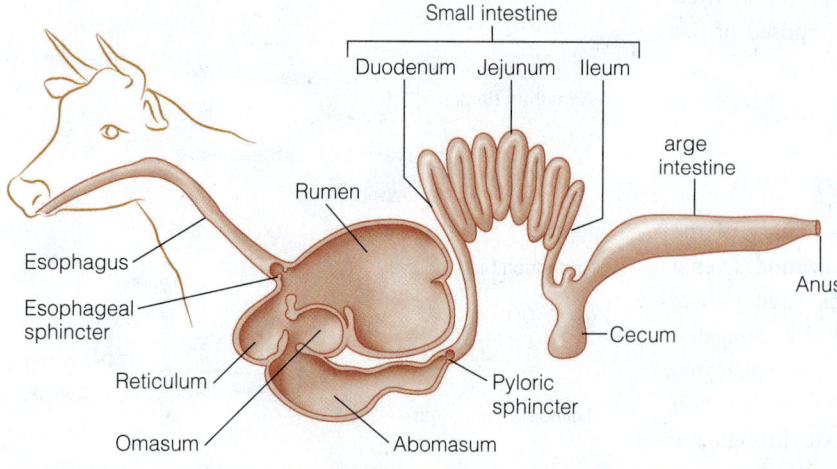

in the mouth. When food is taken into the mouth, the mechanical stimulation triggers pressure-sensitive receptors that send signals to the region of the brainstem that controls serous gland secretions. Similarly, when chemoreceptors detect specific chemicals in the food, a signal is sent to the brain. As Pavlov discovered long ago, animals can also salivate in response to sights and sounds that are associated with food. Salivary gland secretions can also be inhibited. Dehydrated animals use the sympathetic nervous system to restrict blood flow to the salivary glands, preventing secretion. The same sympathetic response induces dry mouth, a response often induced in humans under stressful conditions, such as public speaking.

groups of mammalian grazers possess fermentation chambers. However, unlike the ruminants and tylopods, their fermentation chambers branch from the hindgut and are much less efficient.

Salivary glands secrete water and digestive enzymes

Digestion depends on secretions from multicellular exocrine glands working in conjunction with single secretory cells scattered throughout the GI tract. Many species have glands located near the mouth, typically called salivary glands. Salivary gland secretions include enzymes that initiate the chemical breakdown of food. In terrestrial animals, saliva provides fluid to help lubricate and dissolve food, which allows solubilized nutrients to bind to gustatory receptors. The saliva may also have antimicrobial properties to help cleanse the mouth. The salivary glands are really a collection of different glands. Intrinsic salivary glands, or buccal glands, are distributed throughout the oral cavity. A typical mammal has multiple pairs of extrinsic salivary glands: A dog has parotid glands just anterior to the ear, orbital glands near the eye, mandibular glands near the lower jaw, and sublingual glands beneath the tongue (Figure 14.15). Each of these glands possesses at least two types of cells: mucus-secreting cells and serous cells, which secrete the degradative enzymes.

Because of the high water content of saliva, secretions from these glands impinge on water balance. An average human, for example, might secrete more than 1 liter of water in saliva every day. The rate of secretion from salivary glands is regulated by the parasympathetic system in response to pressure-sensitive receptors and chemoreceptors

The stomach secretes acid and mucus

The surface of the stomach is an epithelium composed of columnar epithelial cells (Figure 14.16). The cells are linked together via *tight junctions* that prevent the leakage of lumen fluids into the tissue. Dotted over the surface of the stomach are deep gastric pits composed of four cell types. *Mucous neck cells*, found near the pit opening, secrete an acid type of mucus. **Parietal cells** in the middle of the pit secrete acid, mainly HCl. **Chief cells** near the base of the pit secrete

FIGURE 14.15 **Salivary glands**

Like most mammals, the dog has multiple sets of salivary glands that secrete liquid and enzymes into the oral cavity.

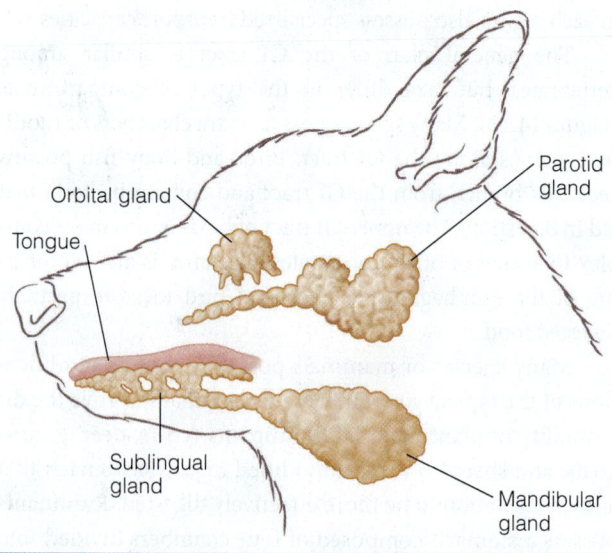

FIGURE 14.16 Stomach cell structure

The smooth surface of the stomach has numerous cavities called gastric pits. These pits are composed of four main cell types that control the secretions of mucus, acid, enzymes, and hormones. They are also the location where *Helicobacter pylori* accumulate.

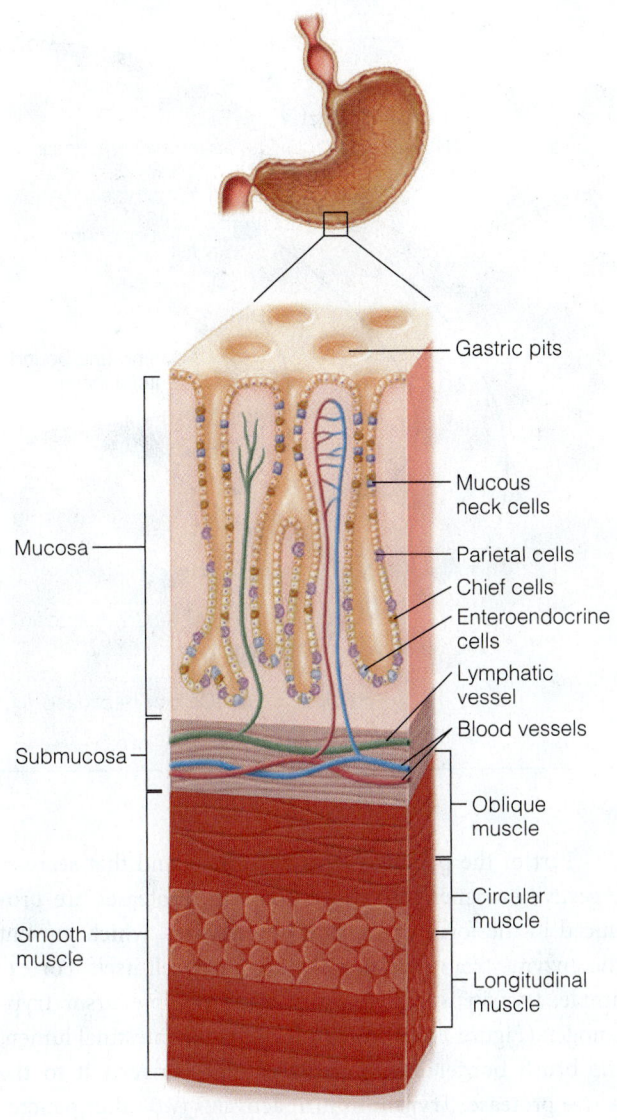

digestive enzymes, primarily the protease pepsin. Finally, *enteroendocrine cells* secrete several hormones into the blood in response to stomach contents. For example, the hormone gastrin is released from enteroendocrine cells into the blood supply of the stomach, inducing secretion by other gastric cells. We discuss the function of other hormones released by enteroendocrine cells later in this chapter when we consider the control of gut motility.

The low pH of the stomach is optimal for many of the gastric enzymes, but it is also harsh enough to kill most bacteria and parasites that enter in the diet, including the bacterium that causes gastric ulcers, **Helicobacter pylori** (see Box 14.1).

This bacterium survives the low pH of the stomach by proliferating deep within the gastric pits, where the pH is higher.

Not all vertebrates have acidic stomachs. The platypus, for example, does not acidify the stomach for reasons that are not yet clear. Another interesting exception is the gastric brooding frog, *Rheobatrachus silus*. It swallows fertilized eggs, which mature in the stomach. The developing young secrete prostaglandin E_2 to inhibit acid secretion. Upon hatching, the tiny frogs hop up the esophagus and escape through the mouth.

The intestine is where most nutrients are hydrolyzed and absorbed

The intestines are also rich in histological diversity. A cross-section through the intestine reveals the four major layers: mucosa, **submucosa**, circular smooth muscle, and longitudinal smooth muscle. The mucosal surface is composed of many cell types, each with distinct roles (Figure 14.17). Much of the mucosa is composed of *enterocytes*, the absorptive cells with abundant microvilli. Mucus-secreting *goblet cells* are scattered among the enterocytes. *Enteroendocrine cells* secrete the hormones that help regulate digestion and nutrient assimilation. At the base of each villus is a region called the **crypt of Lieberkühn**. In addition to enterocytes, each crypt

FIGURE 14.17 Intestinal cell structure

The villi are composed of multiple cell types. Enterocytes are absorptive cells that possess microvilli (not shown). Goblet cells secrete mucus. Interepithelial lymphocytes are T cells that help in immunodefense. Enteroendocrine cells secrete the hormones that control GI tract motility and other aspects of digestion. At the base of the villi are the crypts of Lieberkühn. The epithelial cells within the crypts secrete the intestinal juice. The Paneth cells at the base of the crypt secrete an enzyme that breaks down bacterial cell walls.

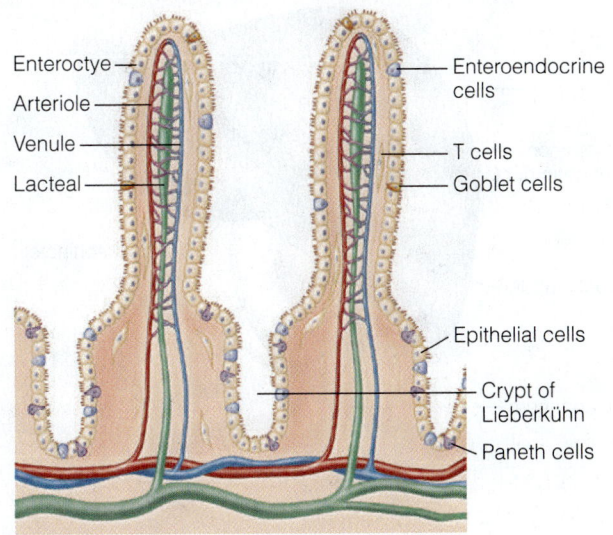

possesses *Paneth cells*, which secrete antimicrobial molecules into the lumen. Adjacent to the Paneth cells are stem cells that divide and differentiate to replenish the other cell types of the intestine. The intestinal submucosa, lying beneath the surface mucosa, is a layer of connective tissue through which blood and lymphatic vessels pass, as well as the nerves that control the GI tract. It also contains the duodenal glands, whose cells secrete basic mucus through ducts that penetrate the epithelium to help neutralize the acid arriving from the stomach. The inner and outer smooth muscle controls the movement of food along the GI tract.

The small intestine also receives secretions of bile from the gallbladder (Figure 14.18). Bile is a complex solution of digestive chemicals and liver waste products. Only two types of molecules in bile have a role in digestion: phospholipids and bile salts. Phospholipids, such as lecithin, aid in the uptake of lipids. **Bile salts** help emulsify fats in the duodenum. They are **amphipathic** molecules with nonpolar regions that bind to fats and polar regions that interact with water. A coating of bile salts helps stabilize the small fat droplets. Liver cells (**hepatocytes**) produce bile and secrete it into small ducts that run adjacent to the hepatocytes. These ducts fuse and empty into the common hepatic duct, which joins the cystic duct from the gallbladder to form the **bile duct**. The gallbladder stores bile until it is needed, then empties into the duodenum via the bile duct.

FIGURE 14.18 Bile production, storage, and secretion

Bile is produced by hepatocytes and released into small adjacent ducts. These ducts collect bile and empty into the common hepatic duct. When the bile duct sphincter is closed, bile is routed through the cystic duct to the gallbladder for storage. When the sphincter opens, bile is released from the gallbladder into the duodenum.

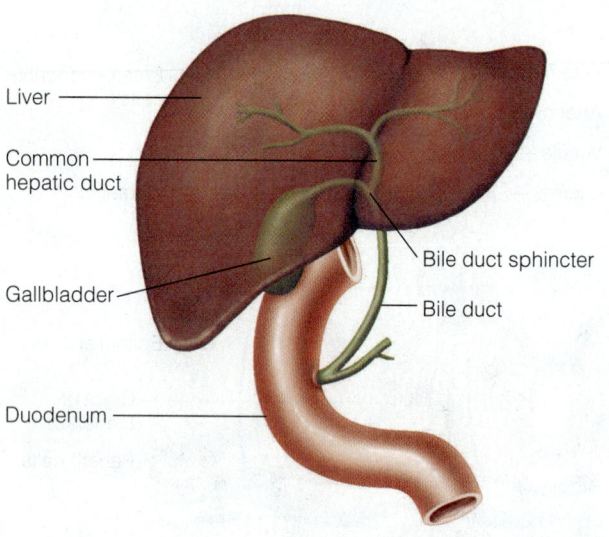

FIGURE 14.19 Trypsinogen cascade

The pancreas secretes three important proteases, all in inactive forms. Trypsinogen is activated by proteolytic cleavage by enterokinase. The activated trypsin then activates chymotrypsinogen and procarboxypeptidase by proteolytic cleavage.

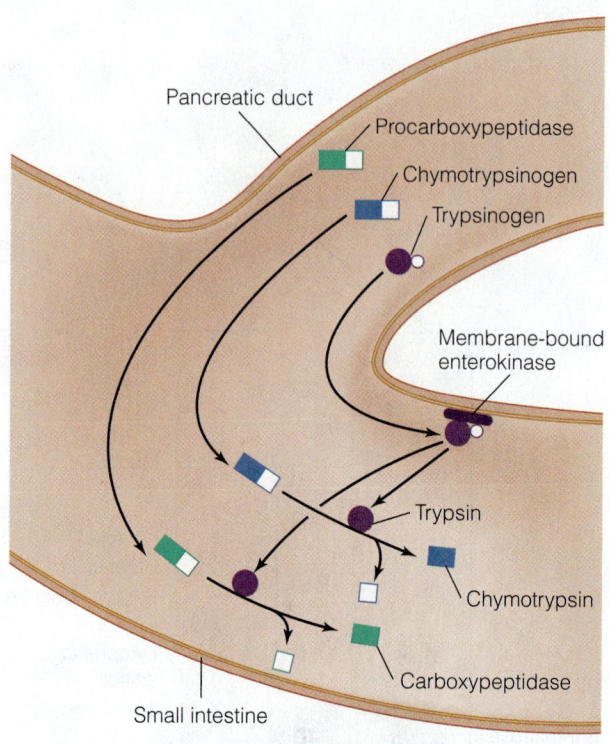

Part of the pancreas is an exocrine gland that secretes digestive enzymes into the duodenum. Proteases are produced in the form of inactive **proenzymes**, which prevent the enzyme from digesting the secretory cell itself. For example, trypsin is secreted as the inactive precursor trypsinogen (Figure 14.19). When it enters the intestinal lumen, the brush border enzyme enterokinase converts it to the active protease. Trypsin in turn activates two other pancreatic enzymes, carboxypeptidase and chymotrypsin. Secreting these enzymes as inactive proenzymes reduces the risk that the pancreas will digest itself. The pancreas also releases enzymes that break down glycogen (amylase), triglycerides (lipase), and nucleic acids (nucleases).

In addition to the enzymes secreted into the gut lumen, there are suites of enzymes produced by the brush border. These enzymes extend into the lumen, but remain tethered to the epithelial surface. These enzymes include disaccharidases (lactase, sucrose, maltase), peptidases (aminopeptidases, carboxypeptidase), and phosphatases (alkaline phosphatase, phosphodiesterase). Collectively, the brush border enzymes and secreted enzymes break down macromolecules into the forms in which they can be assimilated.

Assimilation

The various digestive processes enable nutrients from the diet to be liberated and absorbed at the GI tract epithelium. They are transported from the gut and transferred to the extracellular fluids where they can be imported by storage and target tissues. In this section we discuss the enzymatic pathways responsible for breaking down macromolecules and transporting them into tissues.

Refer to Chapter 3 for coverage of the many ways that molecules can be transported across the plasma membrane. Polar molecules, such as monosaccharides and amino acids, cannot penetrate the plasma membrane at a significant rate, and require specific protein transporters to move them across the plasma membrane. The nature of the transport process for a specific molecule depends on its transmembrane gradient. If there is a favorable concentration gradient, the cell may use a transporter that works by facilitated diffusion. For example, GLUT proteins are carriers that mediate facilitated diffusion of glucose across the plasma membrane. In the liver, GLUT-2 allows glucose out of the cell, whereas in muscle GLUT-1 allows glucose into the cell. In both cases, glucose moves from a higher concentration to a lower concentration. Conversely, if the transport process must proceed against a concentration gradient, the cell must use some form of active transport. For example, amino acids are taken into cells by a carrier protein that is driven by the Na^+ gradient, a form of secondary active transport.

Some nutrients are transported across the plasma membrane via vesicles. Cells engulf regions of the plasma membrane to form vesicles. If the nutrients are in solution, the process is pinocytosis. If the nutrients are particulate, the process is phagocytosis. Similarly, cells can expel nutrients via exocytosis. These pathways of endocytosis and exocytosis are critical for the movement of complex lipids. In many cases, lipids are associated in ways that make it difficult for a membrane carrier to transport one molecule at a time. For example, lipoproteins—complexes of lipid and protein—are exported from cells via exocytosis.

Carbohydrates are hydrolyzed in the lumen and transported by multiple carriers

The main types of carbohydrate consumed by animals are polysaccharides—primarily glycogen, starch, cellulose, and chitin. Disaccharides such as sucrose, lactose, and maltose are also important in some species. Polysaccharides and disaccharides must be broken down to monosaccharides for absorption. The various amylases and disaccharidases at work in the gut ultimately break these larger carbohydrates down to produce monosaccharides, primarily glucose, fructose, and galactose, which are absorbed by the enterocytes of the small intestine (Figure 14.20). Animals use a combination

FIGURE 14.20 Carbohydrate digestion
Starch and glycogen are broken down in the mouth and duodenum by the action of amylase. The resulting disaccharides are further processed in the duodenum by the specific disaccharidases.

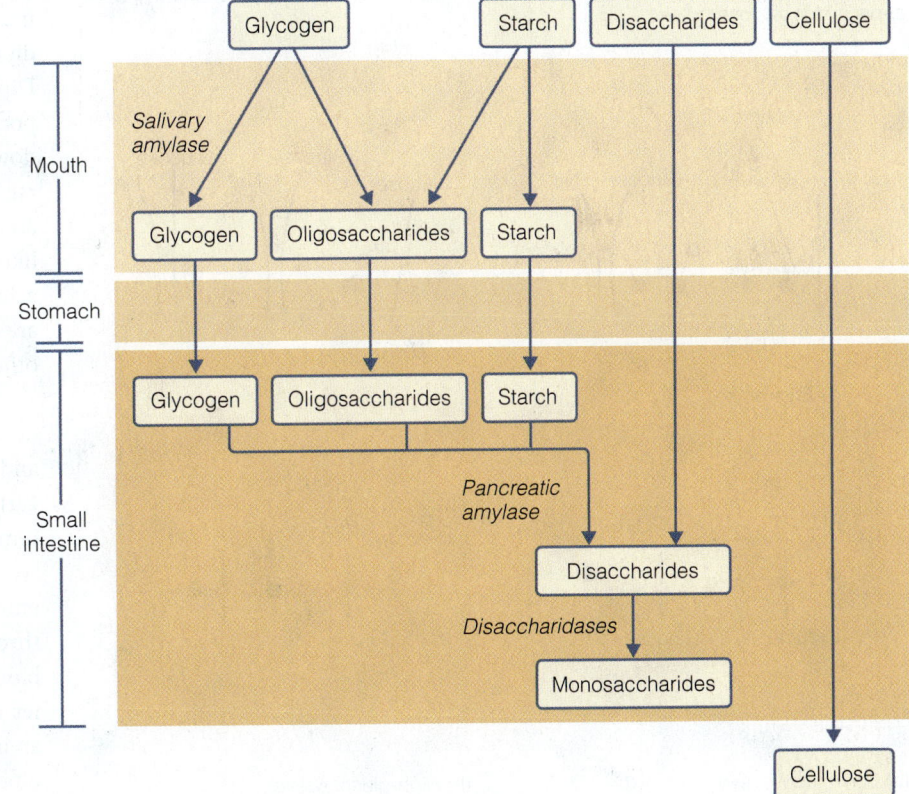

of active transport and facilitated diffusion to carry monosaccharides from the lumen into the intestinal absorptive cells (enterocytes). Glucose and galactose typically enter enterocytes by a Na^+-glucose cotransporter, whereas fructose, which occurs at relatively low concentrations in the cytoplasm, enters the cell via facilitated diffusion.

Many years of study have led to a better understanding of the mechanisms by which the GI tract absorbs glucose. Much of the glucose is transported into intestinal cells by Na^+-glucose cotransporter 1 (SGLT-1). A second type of glucose transport mechanism facilitates the diffusion of glucose into cells during periods of high glucose concentrations in the lumen (Figure 14.21). The carrier is GLUT-2, a member of the large GLUT family of transporters that mediate facilitated diffusion of glucose in various tissues. In brief, when a bolus of glucose first appears in the intestine, transport is mediated primarily by SGLT-1. This transporter also acts as a glucose sensor, triggering a signaling pathway that leads to rapid synthesis of GLUT-2 and intracellular transport of the carrier to the microvilli.

An animal can increase its capacity for glucose transport in several ways, as indicated by interspecies comparisons.

Studies from Jared Diamond's lab at UCLA have shown how SGLT-1 levels can determine the rate of glucose transport. Animals can increase glucose uptake by increasing the total number of SGLT-1 transporters in the gut by (1) producing more transporters per unit surface area of the gut, (2) increasing the surface area of the gut per unit length, or (3) increasing the total length of intestine. Comparisons between species are complicated by phylogenetic differences, as well as dietary differences. Consider the differences in the GI tract of a domestic chicken, which grows quickly, and the guinea jungle fowl, a slow-growing wild relative. These species have a similar surface area (per centimeter of intestine) and capacity for glucose transport (per unit surface area), but the birds differ in gut length. The longer gut of the chicken allows it to assimilate nutrients at greater rates and, as a result, grow faster.

Proteins are broken down into amino acids by proteases and peptidases

The pathway for digestion of proteins begins with extracellular hydrolysis by proteases secreted from the cells of the GI tract and glands associated with the GI tract. Gastric pepsin breaks proteins into large polypeptides. These polypeptides move on to the small intestine, where pancreatic proteases (trypsin, chymotrypsin, and carboxypeptidase) break large polypeptides into small polypeptides, and peptidases of the intestinal lining liberate free amino acids, dipeptides, and tripeptides (Figure 14.22). Dipeptides and tripeptides can be transported into the epithelial cell and broken down cytoplasmically. Free amino acids are carried into the epithelial cells on amino acid–Na^+ cotransporters, much like glucose transport. The free amino acids that are not used by the enterocytes are released into the blood for use by other tissues.

While most proteins are broken down within the lumen of the stomach and small intestine, some proteins are carried into cells intact. First, they are removed from the lumen by endocytosis across the apical membrane of the enterocyte. They can then be carried through the cell and exocytosed into the bloodstream. For example, the antibodies that arrive in the milk consumed by an infant mammal are transported to the blood intact, transferring immunoprotection from the mother.

FIGURE 14.21 Carbohydrate transport into intestinal cells (enterocytes)
(a) Under low-glucose conditions, most glucose import occurs on the Na^+-dependent glucose transporter 1 (SGLT-1). Fructose enters the cell via facilitated diffusion on glucose transporter 5 (GLUT-5). **(b)** When glucose levels rise, GLUT-2 transporters, another type of facilitated diffusion carrier, are translocated to the microvilli, greatly increasing the capacity for glucose uptake.

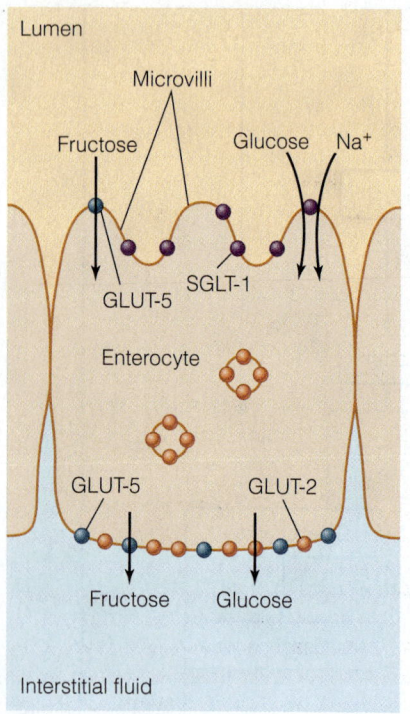

(a) Low-glucose level

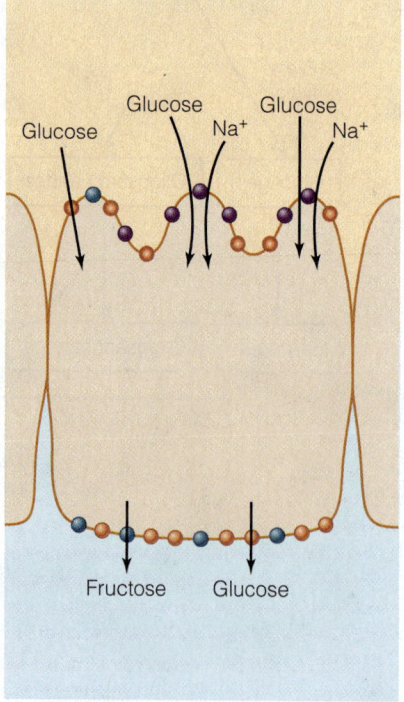

(b) High-glucose level

FIGURE 14.22 **Protein digestion and transport**

In the acidic stomach, pepsin breaks down large proteins into large polypeptides. Proteases from the pancreas (trypsin, chymotrysin, and carboxypeptidase) hydrolyze these polypeptides into smaller polypeptides and peptides. Intestinal aminopeptidases, carboxypeptidases, and dipeptidases complete the proteolysis to produce amino acids.

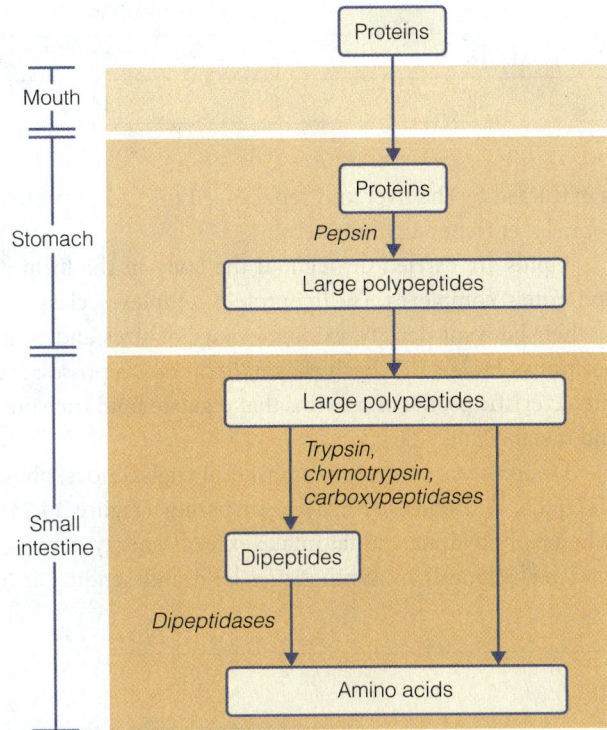

FIGURE 14.23 **Lipid transport across the gut**

Lipids reach the small intestine in the form of large insoluble globules. High pH, bile salts, and phospholipids (lecithin) emulsify the fat into smaller fat droplets. These make their way to the microvilli, where fatty acids and monoacylglycerides can cross into the enterocyte. Inside the enterocyte, the lipids are taken up by the ER and repackaged into vesicles that are secreted from the cell into the surrounding lymph, which is collected in lymph vessels (lacteals).

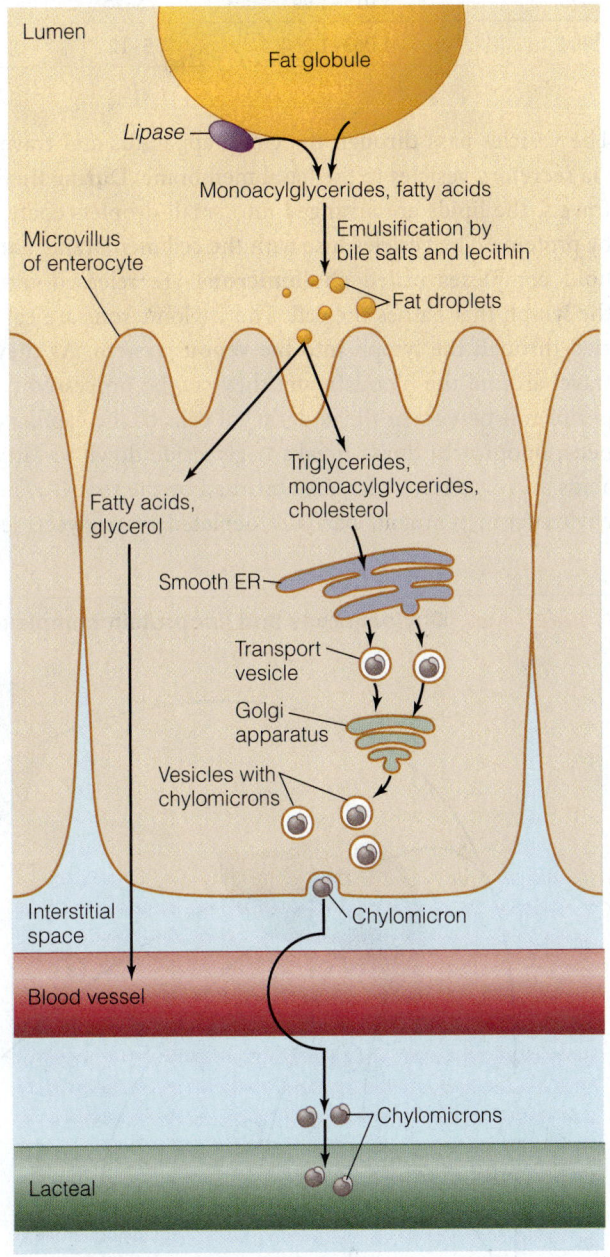

Lipids are transported in many forms

Digestion and import of lipids are complicated by their hydrophobicity. The gastrointestinal tract overcomes the solubility limitations by secreting chemicals that act as lipid emulsifiers. Bile is a mixture of cholesterol, phospholipids, pigments, and salts produced in the liver and secreted into the intestine. The phospholipids, mainly lecithin, act in conjunction with the bile salts to organize the lipids into small droplets called **micelles**. Dietary cholesterol and fat-soluble vitamins form the inner hydrophobic core of the micelle. Fatty acids and monoglycerides coat the hydrophobic core and interact with the outer coating of bile salts and lecithin. The micelles diffuse to the microvilli, where the components simply diffuse off the micelle, crossing the enterocyte cell membrane.

The fate of each lipid depends on its physical properties (Figure 14.23). Short-chain fatty acids and glycerol are sufficiently polar that they can be carried in the blood without assistance. After being taken up by the enterocyte, these molecules cross the basal membrane and enter the blood, where they travel to the liver via the hepatic portal vein. Longer chain fatty acids, monoglycerides, and cholesterol are relatively insoluble and must enter the systemic circulation by a different route. Once in the cytoplasm, the fatty acids and monoglycerides are used to resynthesize triglyceride. The enterocyte smooth endoplasmic reticulum takes up the lipids and packages them into vesicles.

Table 14.2	Lipoprotein composition						
			Composition (% of Total Mass)				
Lipoprotein	Density (g/ml)	Diameter (nm)	Protein	Phospholipid	Triglyceride	Cholesterol
Chylomicron	0.95	75–1200	2	8	86	4
VLDL	1.006	30–80	7	18	58	17
IDL	1.006–1.019	25–35	17	22	22	39
LDL	1.019–1.063	18–25	22	18	8	52
HDL	1.063–1.210	5–12	50	28	8	14

The vesicles pass through the Golgi apparatus and travel via secretory vesicles to the basal membrane. During their travels, the lipids are arranged into small droplets coated by proteins. The vesicles fuse with the cell membrane, and lipid complexes called **chylomicrons** are released into the lymph that bathes the cell. The chylomicrons are carried through the lymph into the venous system. As they travel around the bloodstream, they can be processed by peripheral tissues. In the endothelial cells of the capillary beds, lipoprotein lipase breaks triglyceride down to fatty acids and glycerol, which are absorbed by the tissues. The chylomicron remnant, partially depleted of triglyceride,

is extracted by the liver and repackaged into a lipoprotein complex enriched in cholesterol.

Lipids are carried throughout the body in the form of lipoprotein complexes. The lipoprotein complexes, classified by their buoyant density, exhibit a range of sizes and compositions (Table 14.2). Each class of lipoproteins possesses a characteristic profile of proteins that regulate lipid transport and metabolism.

Lipoproteins control the transfer of triglycerides, phospholipids, and cholesterol between tissues (Figure 14.24). When carbohydrate and fat intake exceeds energy demand, the liver responds by synthesizing lipid and sending it to

FIGURE 14.24 **Chylomicrons and lipoprotein complexes**

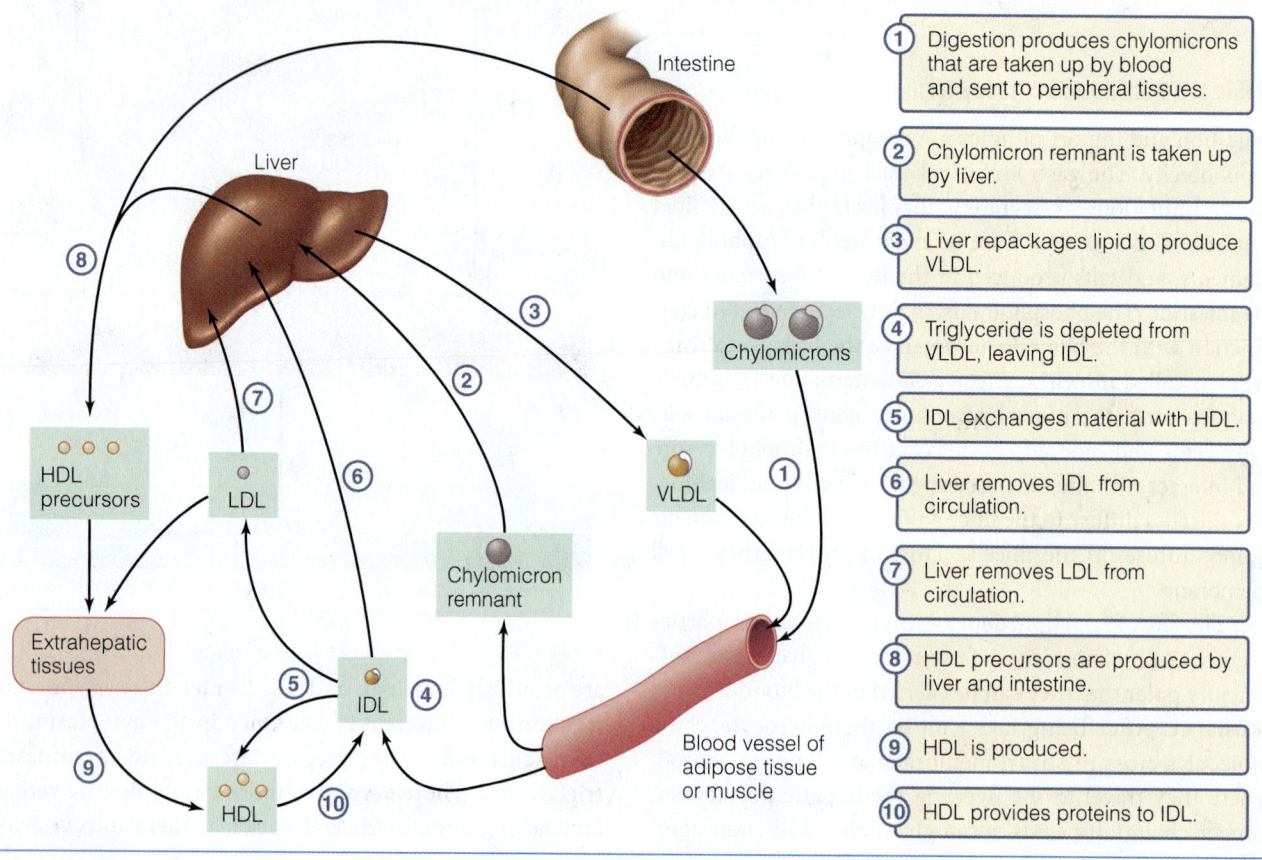

1. Digestion produces chylomicrons that are taken up by blood and sent to peripheral tissues.
2. Chylomicron remnant is taken up by liver.
3. Liver repackages lipid to produce VLDL.
4. Triglyceride is depleted from VLDL, leaving IDL.
5. IDL exchanges material with HDL.
6. Liver removes IDL from circulation.
7. Liver removes LDL from circulation.
8. HDL precursors are produced by liver and intestine.
9. HDL is produced.
10. HDL provides proteins to IDL.

other tissues for storage. The liver produces and releases triglyceride in the form of a very low-density lipoprotein complex (VLDL). As the VLDL moves through the circulation, the triglyceride is hydrolyzed by lipoprotein lipase and is progressively depleted. The fatty acids released in the capillary beds can be stored or oxidized, depending on the specific needs and abilities of the tissue. What was once a triglyceride-rich VLDL becomes an intermediate lipoprotein (IDL), then eventually a cholesterol-rich LDL. The LDL can bind specific receptors on various tissues to unload cholesterol that will be used for membrane synthesis or other biosynthetic pathways. At any point in this cycle, lipoprotein complexes can be returned to the liver for repackaging.

The proteins in the lipoprotein are important in controlling the lipoprotein composition and metabolism. For example, some proteins in the VLDL and LDL complexes regulate lipoprotein lipase. The proteins found in high-density lipoprotein (HDL) are important building blocks for other lipoproteins. For example, HDL donates proteins to the chylomicrons that exit the intestinal lymph, and to VLDL circulating in the blood.

CONCEPT CHECK

10. Where are carbohydrates broken down and absorbed?
11. Where are proteins broken down and absorbed?
12. Where are lipids broken down and absorbed?

▍ DIGESTION AND METABOLISM

Feeding is a necessary evil in the life of most animals; while they must feed to survive, the process of feeding requires considerable energy and may expose the feeder to predation. Feeding strategies evolve to provide an animal with the greatest chance of obtaining nutrients while minimizing the risk to its survival. In terms of digestive physiology, the most significant variables are the nature of the nutrients, the quantity of food consumed in a given period, and how often the food is consumed. Consider a day in the life of a filter feeder. Filter-feeding animals, such as barnacles, are surrounded by their food and feeding is a continuous process, interrupted only when a potential predator is sensed in the proximity. Conversely, some deep-sea fish may encounter food once a year. Many animals feed during a narrow window in their lifetime, and display a life history strategy that is choreographed around this meal.

Much of the chapter to this point discusses how digestive systems are built and regulated. Superimposed on structure and function of digestive physiology is the question of what determines the metabolic demands of the animal. Digestive systems vary in large part because of inherent differences in demand for energy, reflected in the metabolic rate.

Regulating Digestive Systems in Individuals

Animals face the daunting challenge of matching their dietary intake to their short-term metabolic demands, while ensuring an opportunity for long-term development and reproduction. For many complex animals, the drive to feed (appetite) is regulated by the central nervous system (CNS). Input to the CNS comes from environmental factors such as photoperiod, as well as intrinsic signals that reflect the nutrient levels or metabolic status of the animal. Typically, animals feed when their energy needs exceed the metabolic potential of circulating fuels, allowing the animal to avoid drawing on nutrient stores. On top of appetite control, animals regulate the activities of compartments of the digestive system. Physical and chemical information is collected in the gut, which sends signals throughout the body, including the brain and other regions of the gut. The major hormones involved in control of GI tract secretions are summarized in Table 14.3.

The control of appetite has been best studied in mammals because of the implications for human obesity. These studies have identified more than 20 different regulatory factors that link nutrition, metabolism, and feeding. Some regulatory factors are produced in the vicinity of the GI tract, controlling local events and sending signals into the blood to affect other tissues. Hormones released by the GI tract make their way to the hypothalamus, which integrates the information and controls feeding behavior. Three main hormones control appetite: leptin, ghrelin, and peptide YY. These hormones exert effects on multiple target tissues, but in terms of appetite control, their main effects arise through receptors in the hypothalamus. Recall that this region of the brain possesses an incomplete blood-brain barrier, and thus is able to sense the profiles of blood-borne metabolites and small hormones. Leptin is too large to passively move across the endothelium of the capillaries that feed the hypothalamus; it is likely transferred from the blood across the blood-brain barrier through an active transport mechanism.

Hormones control the desire to feed

Leptin is an appetite-suppressing hormone produced in **white adipose tissue** (WAT). It acts as an "adipostat," ensuring that adipose lipid content is stable. When adipose triglyceride levels rise, leptin is secreted and appetite is suppressed. Restoration of adipose lipid stores inhibits leptin secretion and appetite increases. Though leptin exerts an important control over appetite, its effects are mediated over the long term. Over the short term, ghrelin and peptide YY appear to be more important in controlling the desire to eat between meals. Ghrelin is an appetite-stimulating hormone, released from gastric cells when the stomach is empty. Peptide YY is an appetite-reducing hormone, released from enteroendocrine cells when the colon is full.

Table 14.3 Hormonal control of digestion

Regulatory Factor	Source	Stimulates	Inhibits
Acetylcholine	Cholinergic nerves	Gastric secretion	
Adiponectin	Adipose tissue	Appetite	
Cholecystokinin (CCK)	Duodenum	Expulsion of bile from gallbladder, pancreatic enzyme secretion, appetite	
Enkephalin	Duodenum	Gastric acid secretion	Pancreatic enzyme secretion
Epinephrine	Intestinal nerves	Gastric acid secretion	
Epinephrine	Intestinal nerves		Gastric acid secretion
Galanin	Intestinal nerves		Gastric acid secretion
Gastric inhibitory peptide (GIP)	Duodenum		Gastric secretion
Gastrin	Stomach and duodenum	Gastric acid production and secretion	
Gastrin-releasing peptide	Brain	Gastrin secretion	
Ghrelin	Stomach	Appetite	
Glucagon	Duodenum		Pancreatic and intestinal secretion
Glucagon-like peptide-1 (GLP-1)	Jejunum, lower intestine		Appetite
Leptin	Adipose tissue		Appetite
Motilin	Jejunum	Gastric acid secretion	
Pancreatic polypeptide (PP)	Pancreas		Appetite, gastric secretion
Peptide YY (PYY)	Jejunum, lower intestine		Appetite, gastric secretion
Pituitary adenylate cyclase activating polypeptide (PACAP)	Pituitary	Gastric secretion	
Secretin	Duodenum	Water and bicarbonate secretion, bile production	
Somatostatin	Duodenum		Gastric acid secretion, pancreatic secretion, blood flow (vasoconstriction)
Vasoactive intestinal peptide (VIP)	Duodenum	Intestinal blood flow (vasodilation), pancreatic and gastric secretion, intestinal salt secretion	

These hormones exert their effects on the arcuate nucleus of the hypothalamus. Recall that a nucleus is a region where the cell bodies of the neurons are collected. The neurons of the arcuate nucleus send their axons to other neurons in the region, as well as higher centers of the brain that regulate behavior. Some neurons release appetite-stimulating factors, mainly neuropeptide Y (NPY), as well as agouti-related peptide and gamma-aminobutyric acid (GABA). Other neurons release the appetite-suppressing factor proopiomelanocortin (POMC). It is the balance of activity of NPY-releasing neurons and POMC-releasing neurons that determines the appetite signal sent to the higher centers of the brain. This balance is influenced by the hormones that stimulate and inhibit each type of neuron, and how the neurons interact with each other through antagonistic neurotransmitters. Both NPY-releasing neurons and POMC-releasing neurons express leptin receptors, but connections between the receptor and neurotransmitter release are different. Leptin binding to its receptor in NPY-releasing neurons reduces neurotransmitter release, whereas binding to POMC-releasing neurons stimulates neurotransmitter release. Each of these effects contributes to the suppression of appetite in response to leptin. Ghrelin and peptide YY each bind NPY-releasing neurons, though

FIGURE 14.25 **Control of appetite**

Appetite is controlled by the neurons of the arcuate nucleus of the hypothalamus, which interacts with hormones secreted from the GI tract and WAT. Release of the neurotransmitter neuropeptide Y (NPY) stimulates appetite, whereas release of the neurotransmitter proopiomelanocortin (POMC) depresses appetite. These neurons, through their neurotransmitters, affect the appetite centers of the brain directly, or antagonize the release of neurotransmitters from other neurons. Leptin exerts its appetite-suppressing effects by inhibiting NPY-releasing neurons and stimulating POMC-releasing neurons. Appetite is increased by the actions of other hormones on NPY-releasing neurons: Ghrelin stimulates and peptide YY inhibits these neurons.

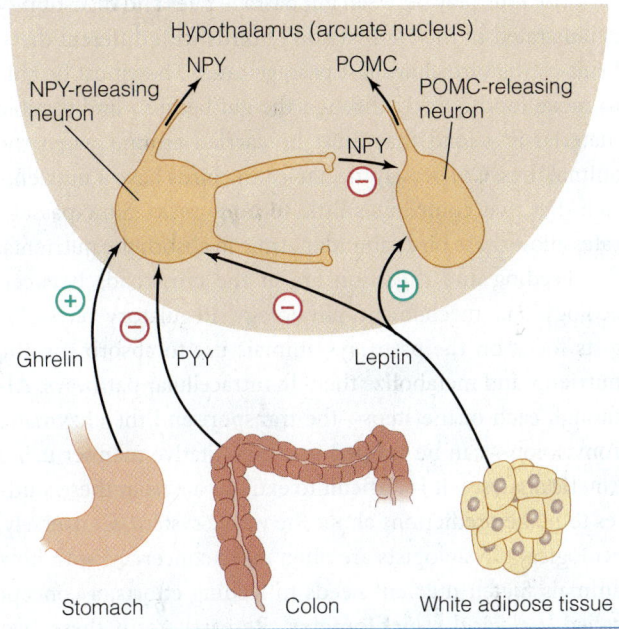

Hormones and neurotransmitters control gastrointestinal secretions

Once food enters the gut, the GI tract secretes a spectrum of chemicals and enzymes that digest the food into forms that can be taken up. Control of these secretions depends on complex regulatory mechanisms that respond to both the anticipation of food and its physical presence in the digestive system. Earlier in this chapter we discussed the nature of GI tract secretions—saliva, acid, mucus, bile, bicarbonate, and digestive enzymes—but not how animals control these secretions.

The stomach is acidified when parietal cells in the gastric lining secrete HCl, or rather both H^+ and Cl^-. Central to the secretion of acid is the activity of the enzyme carbonic anhydrase, which converts CO_2 and H_2O to form H^+ and HCO_3^-. The parietal cells expel protons into the lumen via a proton pump, a K^+/H^+ ATPase. The bicarbonate is exported from the cell to the blood via a Cl^-/HCO_3^- exchanger. The Cl^- then escapes the cell through an apical Cl^- channel. The secretion of acid from parietal cells is triggered when histamine binds to receptors (H_2 receptors) on the parietal cells, to initiate a cAMP cascade that activates the proton pump. The histamine is released by enterochromaffinlike (ECF) cells in the stomach lining. The ECF cells release their histamine in response to gastrin, a peptide hormone produced by neuroendocrine cells (G cells) in the stomach and duodenum, and released in response to adrenergic and cholinergic nerve activity (Figure 14.26). Gastrin also regulates

FIGURE 14.26 **Control of gastric secretion of acid and pepsinogen**

Gastric cells secrete acid (parietal cells) and pepsinogen (chief cells) in response to signals relayed from the central nervous system and from the food itself, acting through chemoreceptors and mechanoreceptors.

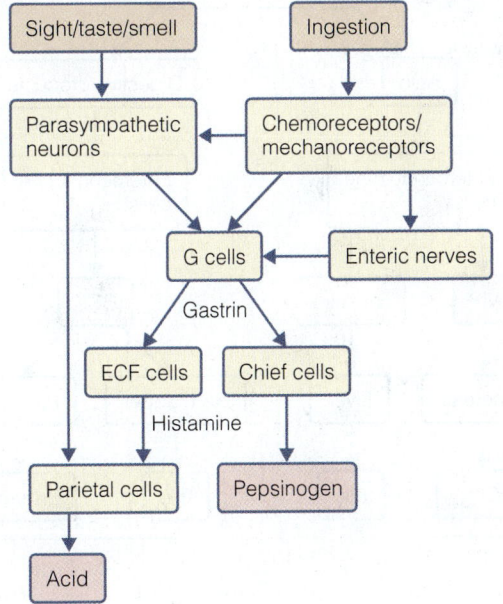

activation of their respective receptors works antagonistically on neurotransmitter release (Figure 14.25).

The factors that control appetite have been studied intensively because of their potential for treatment of obesity. There are many animal models with genetic defects that cause overeating (*hyperphagy*) and obesity. For example, animal models with defects in leptin signaling—loss of the ability to synthesize leptin or its receptor—are obese and exhibit many of the other physiological problems associated with obesity. Unfortunately, strategies to target the leptin signaling cascade in antiobesity treatments have not met with much success. Obese humans actually have very high levels of leptin, yet their appetite is not suppressed, suggesting that the hypothalamus can become resistant to leptin. It is also not yet clear how leptin and other regulators of appetite act in other species of vertebrates with diverse feeding strategies. Frequency of feeding differs widely among animals. Large snakes and deep-sea fish may feed very infrequently, sometimes only once per year. The hormonal and neuronal regulation of appetite is not well studied in such animals.

pepsinogen secretion by chief cells of the gastric mucosa. The contents of the stomach can interact with each of these cells—parietal cells, ECF cells, and G cells—to alter acid secretion. Treatments for excessive acid secretion can target the K^+/H^+ ATPase (proton pump inhibitors) or the histamine receptors (H_2 blockers). Gastrin also controls other secretory cells within the gastric mucosa. For example, gastrin induces chief cells to secrete pepsinogen. The low pH of the stomach activates pepsinogen to form pepsin, a carboxypeptidase, initiating protein degradation.

Once food passes from the stomach to the upper intestine, secretions alter the pH of the bolus and bombard it with a different suite of digestive chemicals. Bicarbonate secretions from the pancreas and bile from the gallbladder neutralize the acidity. The pancreas also secretes digestive enzymes, including amylase, chymotrypsin, carboxypeptidases, aminopeptidases, nucleases, and lipases. When acidic material enters the upper intestine, it triggers duodenal secretion of secretin and vasoactive intestinal peptide (VIP) into the blood, which act at the pancreas to induce secretion of bicarbonate. Other intestinal cells sense the levels of amino acids and fatty acids and secrete cholecystokinin (CCK) into the blood. CCK acts on the pancreas, inducing the secretion of digestive enzymes, and on the gallbladder, inducing contraction of the smooth muscle to eject bile (Figure 14.27).

FIGURE 14.27 Control of intestinal secretion
The acidic fluids that exit the stomach trigger intestinal secretion. The secretions neutralize the acidic fluids (via bicarbonate and bile), and aid in digestion through digestive enzymes (proteases, lipases, nucleases, amylases) and bile, which emulsifies lipids.

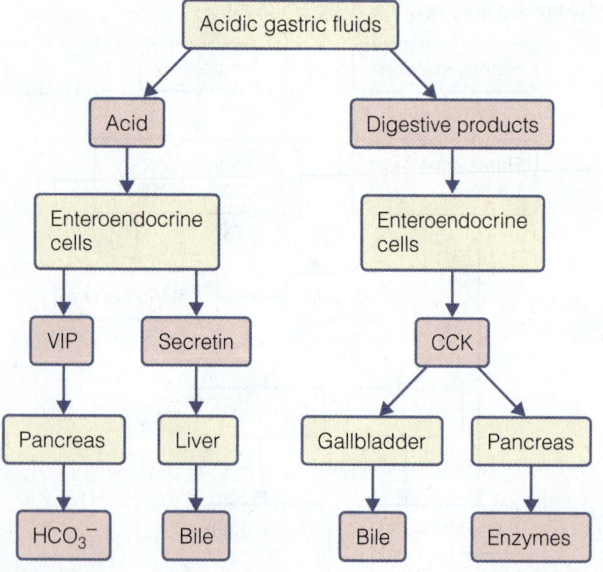

Retention time affects the efficiency of nutrient uptake

As with most physiological systems, muscles and nerves play important roles in regulating the digestive system. Food is moved along the gastrointestinal tract by visceral smooth muscles, which are under the control of nerves and hormones. By increasing gut motility, an animal increases the rate of passage of food down the GI tract, which in turn affects the efficiency of absorption. It must be fast enough to ensure that the animal is not carrying around a mass of undigestible material, but slow enough to allow time for digestion and assimilation.

The interplay between gut passage rates and digestibility is illustrated in the comparison of birds with different diets. Fruit-eating birds have fast passage rates. They must be able to move food quickly through the gut because undigestible material is a load that must be carried around when the animal flies. Conversely, nectar-eating birds have a nutrient-rich diet that contributes little to body mass. Slow passage rates allow these birds abundant time to absorb the nutrients.

Feeding and digestion are at the crossroads between ecology and mechanistic physiology. Regulatory physiologists focus on the pathways animals use to absorb specific nutrients and metabolize them in intracellular pathways. Although each of the steps—the transport and the enzymatic conversion—can be studied in a quantitative manner using kinetic analyses, it is difficult to extrapolate from these studies to make predictions about the whole system. Conversely, ecological physiologists are often more concerned with how animals match nutrient needs to feeding efforts, a concept called *ecological* **stoichiometry**. Researchers in these two fields—regulatory physiology and ecological stoichiometry—were initially separated because of the diversity of nutrients and the complexities of nutrient breakdown, absorption, and assimilation. The two alternate experimental frameworks are brought together in **gut reactor theory**, which allows researchers to use mathematical relationships to make qualitative and quantitative predictions about digestive physiology function and evolution (see Box 14.2: Math in Physiology: Gut Reactor Theory).

Gut motility is regulated by nerves and hormones that act on smooth muscle

Gut motility is controlled by the actions of the two layers of smooth muscle that line the intestinal tract. Each layer of smooth muscle in the GI tract is composed of muscle cells embedded in an extracellular matrix of elastin and collagen molecules, and interconnected into an electrical network that allows the individual cells to contract and relax as a unit. The thin outer longitudinal layer controls intestinal length. The thick inner circular layer, which controls the diameter of the lumen, is arranged into contractile units, each about 1 millimeter long. Gut motility is determined by the contractile activity of the circular smooth muscle. The smooth muscle has a resting contractile tension, or muscle tone, that controls the diameter of the lumen. Tonic contraction is controlled by intrinsic pathways within the muscle cells (myogenic) and by neurotransmitters released from motor nerves (neurogenic). These motor nerves from the CNS do not act directly on smooth muscle, rather feeding into a network of nerves called the *myenteric plexus* (Figure 14.30). The myenteric plexus and the submucosal, or Meissner's, plexus make up the enteric nervous system (see Chapter 8: Functional Organization of Nervous Systems). The myenteric plexus contains the neurons involved in regulating gut motility and enzyme secretion, whereas the submucosal plexus regulates gut blood flow and plays an important role in regulating ion and water transport by the gut. These components of the enteric nervous system work together to regulate gut function.

The gut also changes its contractile state to help propel food through the lumen. **Peristalsis** is a slow wave of contraction that progresses down the GI tract to push food toward the anus. It is controlled by the intrinsic myogenic activity of the smooth muscle cells, but also influenced by *interstitial cells of Cajal* that act as pacemaker cells. Much like the pacemaker cells of the heart, these cells spontaneously depolarize to initiate a wave of depolarization to the smooth muscle cells to which they are attached via gap junctions.

You may be familiar with some of the many regulatory factors that control gut motility. Stimulatory factors include: acetylcholine, adenosine, **bombesin**, cholecystokinin (CCK), gastrin-releasing polypeptide, histamine, motilin, neurokinin A, opioids, prostaglandin E_2, serotonin, SP, and thyrotropin-releasing hormone. Inhibitory factors include: calcitonin gene-regulating protein (CGRP), gamma-aminobutyric acid (GABA), galanin, glucagon, neuropeptide Y, neurotensin, nitric oxide, norepinephrine, pituitary adenylate cyclase–activating polypeptide (PACAP), peptide histidine isoleucine (PHI), peptide YY (PYY), secretin, somatostatin, and vasoactive intestinal peptide (VIP). Some of these factors are endocrine hormones. For example, release of glucagon by the pancreas reduces gut motility, which increases the efficiency of glucose uptake. In addition to endocrine factors, paracrine and autocrine factors are released by secretory cells in the stomach and intestine. For example, serotonin can be released by different secretory cells in the GI tract and act on both smooth muscle and nerves to stimulate GI motility. The nervous control of the GI tract includes signals from the CNS as well as local nerve networks. Centrally, the hypothalamus and spinal cord receive information from nerves in the GI tract that respond to the activity of chemoreceptors and mechanoreceptors. The parasympathetic neurons send signals back to the gut to stimulate motility by releasing acetylcholine; sympathetic neurons inhibit motility by releasing norepinephrine, somatostatin, and neuropeptide Y. The **myenteric** plexus compiles the stimulatory and inhibitory signals, then transmits nervous signals to the smooth muscle.

Because of the overlapping regulatory pathways, the control of gut motility is complex. Consider the mechanism by which one neurotransmitter, acetylcholine, induces contraction. Recall from Chapter 6 that smooth muscle contraction is regulated directly by Ca^{2+} as well as by changes in the phosphorylation state of thick and thin filament proteins. Acetylcholine stimulates contraction in visceral smooth muscle by increasing Ca^{2+} levels. This activates myosin light chain kinase (MLCK), which phosphorylates the myosin light chain of the thick filament. Acetylcholine acts through a type of G protein–linked muscarinic receptor that activates phospholipase C (PLC). This produces two second messengers, diacylglycerol (DAG) and inositol triphosphate (IP_3), which increase cytoplasmic Ca^{2+} levels (Figure 14.31). The IP_3 and its metabolites open Ca^{2+} channels in the sarcoplasmic reticulum to release Ca^{2+}. When protein kinase C binds DAG in the membrane, it phosphorylates and activates Ca^{2+} channels. Acetylcholine also acts via an independent route to impair relaxation. It binds to a second class of muscarinic receptors that inhibits adenylate cyclase, reducing cAMP levels and PKA activity. Because PKA phosphorylates and desensitizes contractile proteins, acetylcholine's actions also favor sensitization of contractile proteins. In the absence of acetylcholine, relaxation is favored because the channels close and Ca^{2+} can be pumped back out of the cytoplasm.

Relaxation is triggered by hormones that act through both Ca^{2+}-dependent and Ca^{2+}-independent routes. The adrenergic effectors, such as epinephrine, bind G protein–linked receptors that activate adenylate cyclase, elevating the level of cAMP and activating PKA. Nitric oxide stimulates guanylyl cyclase, elevating the levels of cGMP and protein kinase G (PKG). Vasoactive intestinal peptide acts through both pathways, increasing the levels of both cAMP and cGMP. Stimulation of PKA and PKG leads to phosphorylation of critical proteins that reduce Ca^{2+} levels and lead to relaxation.

Metabolic Transitions

Animals regulate their dietary intake to ensure that they feed when they require energy for development, growth, reproduction, or activity. As discussed previously, animals are able to use complex signaling pathways to sense their energy

MATH IN PHYSIOLOGY 14.2

GUT REACTOR THEORY

The animal digestive system shares many similarities with the reactors used in industry to convert one set of chemicals to another form. Chemical engineers define three types of chemical reactors that have clear parallels to the animal digestive systems we have discussed: **batch reactors**, tank reactors, and **plug flow reactors** (Figure 14.28).

Batch reactors receive a pulse of precursors and after a period of time convert the precursors into products. This is much like the two-way gut used by cnidarians, which engulfs and digests food particles in a gastrovascular cavity, then expels undigested material. Tank reactors receive a constant infusion of precursors and generate a constant stream of products. The fermentation chambers of some animals, such as the bird cecum or the cow rumen, are examples of tank reactors. In plug flow reactors, a bolus of precursors begins at one end of a tube-shaped reactor and moves through the tube to the other end. The intestine of most animals works in this way, with food exiting the stomach and passing through the tubular intestine to the anus.

Chemical reactor theory allows a researcher to model the digestive process mathematically, to assess the factors that determine the performance of the digestive system. For

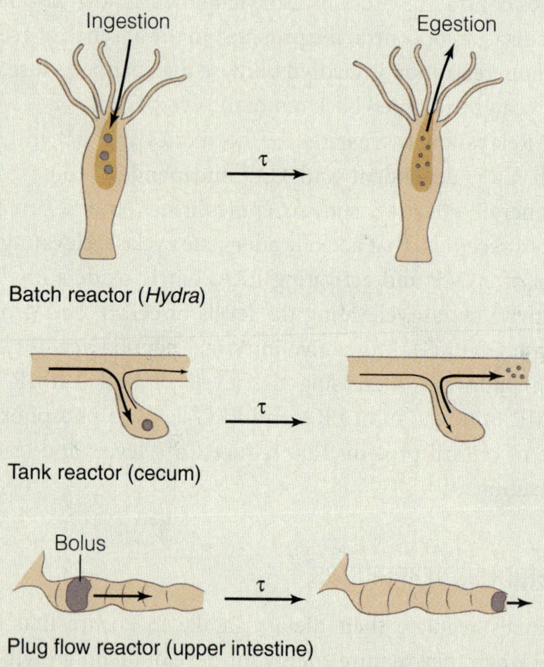

FIGURE 14.29 **Gut uptake rates**

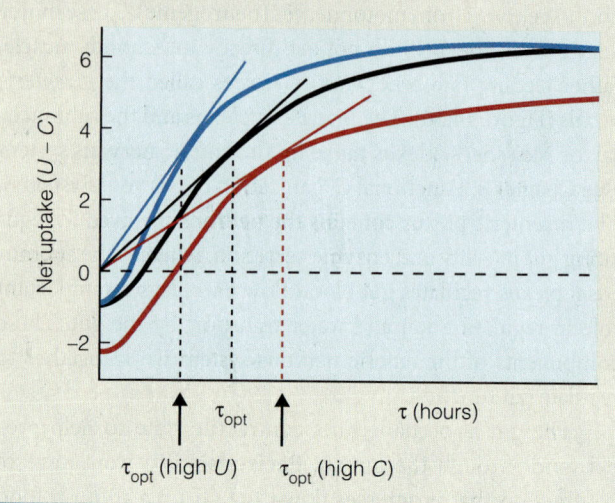

example, if a digestive system works like a batch reactor, then the animal stands to gain the most energy if it digests a single meal to gain the most nutrients in the shortest period of time. If the time is too short, the bolus of food is expelled with many nutrients remaining. If it holds on to the food too long, it may extract more nutrients but it forgoes an opportunity to feed again. Reactor theory can predict the optimal retention time for food by plotting the relationship between net uptake (total uptake U minus foraging costs C) and retention time τ (Figure 14.29). This curve can be used to predict the optimal residence time. Soon after the meal is consumed ($\tau = 0$), the animal has incurred costs (C) but gained no nutrients. As digestion proceeds (τ increases), there is an increase in the slope of the curve. Think of this slope, termed $U'(\tau)$, as the rate at which the animal is gaining nutrients at that point in time. At some point, the slope of the curve reaches its maximum, or $U'(\tau_{opt})$. After a longer period of digestion, nutrients continue to be absorbed but at a diminishing rate. Mathematically, the relationship between these parameters is defined by the equation

$$U'(\tau_{opt}) = (U(\tau_{opt}) - C)/\tau_{opt}$$

Graphically (Figure 14.29), the τ_{opt} value is identified by a line that begins at the origin and intersects the curve at the point where the slope begins to decrease. The red line shows how an increase in foraging costs (C) shifts the entire curve downward; τ_{opt} increases. If it costs more to feed,

FIGURE 14.28 **Gut reactor types**

Ingestion

Egestion

τ

Batch reactor (*Hydra*)

τ

Tank reactor (cecum)

Bolus

τ

Plug flow reactor (upper intestine)

then the animal benefits from assimilating more nutrients from the first meal. Similarly, the blue line shows how uptake increases when a meal is more digestible. The entire curve shifts upward, and a shorter τ_{opt} is predicted.

In the same manner, more complex equations can be used to predict optimal feeding strategies in animals with a digestive system that more closely approximates the plug flow reactor. In many ways, this model is like a series of batch flow reactors, with a given volume of food progressing from one region to the next. Unlike the batch reactor, the plug flow reactor accepts a continuous input, which has two consequences for predicting the gain. First, because the animal feeds continuously, its costs of feeding are spread out over time (in a batch reactor, the feeding costs are incurred first, but the gain is spread out over time). Second, for any given period, multiple meals contribute to the gain.

In recent years, gut reactor theory has been used to confront the biological complexity we discuss in this chapter. First, whereas models generally assume that the uptake rate is a linear function of nutrient concentration, the kinetics are usually more complicated. The impacts of complex kinetics of digestive enzymes and intestine active transporters have only been resolved in simple systems, such as nectar-feeding birds. Second, the volume of the plug is assumed to be constant, but in reality it changes as animals remove fluids from or secrete them into the gut. Third, the models require thorough mixing of the volume, but within the gut there are well-established concentration gradients as a result of transport processes, such as unstirred layers. Fourth, the animal can change the functional length of a gut through smooth muscle activity. Many of the studies that use reactor theory operate on the premise that digestive systems work optimally. For example, it is assumed that animal digestive physiology (feeding behavior and nutrient uptake) strives to reach an optimal retention time. When a diet consists of a single major nutrient, it is plausible that a single τ_{opt} exists. In a complex diet, each type of nutrient might have distinct optimal uptake kinetics, yet the bolus of food progresses through the tubular gut at a single rate. Thus, a single passage rate may be longer than required for some nutrients, and shorter than is necessary for others. The τ_{opt} in some cases may reflect the need to expel undigestible or toxic material, rather than to take up nutrients.

Reactor theoreticians continue to incorporate these important physiological and morphological variables as they develop more sophisticated models to predict digestive physiology and feeding strategies. Reactor theory has been best applied to animals with simple diets. Dr. Carlos Martinez del Rio and his colleagues have used it to study the feeding physiology of nectar-feeding birds. The simplicity of the diet facilitates the testing of mathematical models incorporating plug reactor theory. A nectar-feeding bird converts sucrose to fructose and glucose using the intestinal disaccharidase sucrase. It displays Michaelis-Menton kinetics, with the rate of hydrolysis (r_s) expressed as:

$$r_s = V_{max} \, C_s \, (K_m + C_s)^{-1}$$

where V_{max} is the maximal rate of sucrase averaged along the gut, K_m is the Michaelis-Menton constant, and C_s is the sucrose concentration. The retention time (τ) can be calculated as

$$\tau = [(K_m \ln (C_{s0}/C_{sf}) + (C_{s0} - C_{sf})] \, V_{max}^{-1}$$

where C_{s0} is the initial sucrose concentration and C_{sf} is the final sucrose concentration.

Once τ is known, the gut intake rate (V_0) can be calculated as

$$V_0 = G \tau^{-1}$$

Martinez del Rio and his colleagues then compared this model to actual experimental observations of hummingbirds feeding on different sucrose solutions. The more dilute the sucrose solutions, the larger the volume consumed by the birds. In another study, they used this same approach to find whether feeding behavior reflected an attempt by the bird to match uptake to metabolic demand (compensatory feeding), or rather to ensure an uptake that kept the digestive machinery working at its maximal rate (physiological constraint). Hummingbirds were fed the same range of sucrose solutions, but exposed to different ambient temperatures. The colder temperatures elevated metabolic demands. They found that cold birds drank the same amount of sucrose as warm birds, suggesting a physiological constraint.

References

- Martinez del Rio, C., Schondube, J. E., McWhorter, T. J., & Herrera, L. G. (2001). Intake responses in nectar-feeding birds: Digestive and metabolic causes, osmoregulatory consequences, and coevolutionary effects. *American Zoologist, 41*, 902–915.

- McWhorter, T. J., & Martinez del Rio, C. (2000). Does gut function limit hummingbird food intake? *Physiological and Biochemical Zoology, 73*, 313–324.

FIGURE 14.30   Myenteric plexus

The nerves of the parasympathetic and sympathetic nervous systems send their signals to the myenteric plexus that lies beneath the submucosa. This group of nerves integrates the various signals and sends the appropriate neurotransmitters to the circular smooth muscle to control contraction.

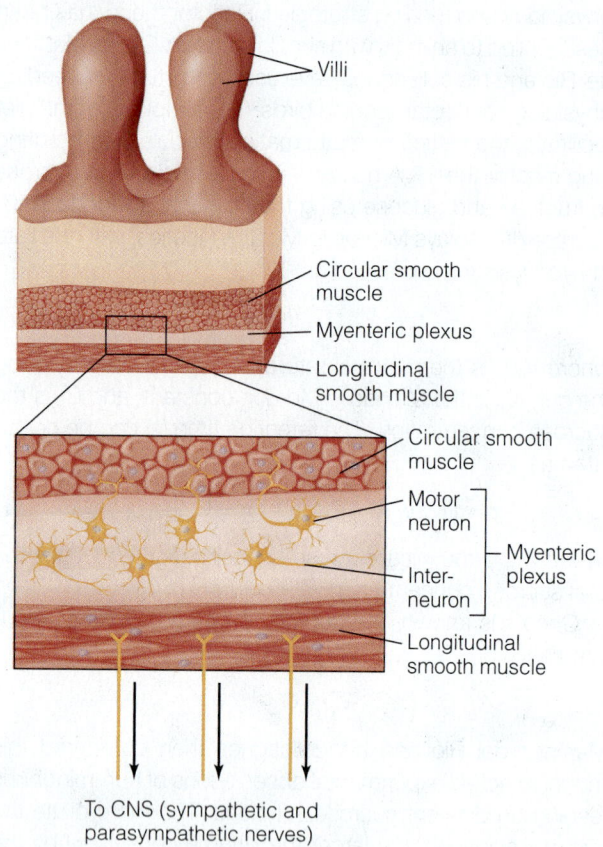

Villi

Circular smooth muscle

Myenteric plexus

Longitudinal smooth muscle

Circular smooth muscle

Motor neuron

Inter- neuron

Myenteric plexus

Longitudinal smooth muscle

To CNS (sympathetic and parasympathetic nerves)

stores and communicate the condition to the brain to advise on appetite. However, there are periods when animals do not feed, and the result is a change in the nature of the nutrient stores and digestive system. For most animals, there is a relatively short, or least predictable, time between meals. Depending on the duration between meals, the animal may show a mild fasting response or a more severe starvation response, where it reorganizes how it meets the body's metabolic demands by breaking down muscle protein. For some animals, periods of food deprivation can be extreme by human standards, and the adaptations to cope with the challenge are remarkable. Many animals have periods in their life history where they increase food intake to prepare for food deprivation. We have touched on this topic in other chapters. In Chapter 12: Locomotion, we discussed the ways in which animals approach the metabolic challenges of migrations. In Chapter 13: Ion and Water Balance we introduced the animals that undertake various forms of dehydration to cope with harsh conditions. In this section, we discuss some

examples of animals that must cope with changes in metabolic demands, regulating the digestive system in concert with peripheral tissues.

Though most animals eat to ensure that their immediate energetic needs are met, there are some scenarios in which animals eat beyond their needs (*hyperphagy*), and undergo rapid weight gain. For example, some birds will experience major weight gain in preparation for migration, when opportunities for feeding are not reliable. Humans, conversely, have become vulnerable to a regulatory imbalance arising from a mismatch between energy input and expenditure. Over the long term, an excess of energy in the diet leads to obesity, a physiological condition that can be quite debilitating (see Box 14.3: Challenges to Homeostasis: Obesity).

During the period immediately after feeding, known as the **postprandial period**, an animal utilizes some nutrients and stores others, enabling it to survive until the next meal. The normal period between meals may be anywhere from seconds to months, depending on the animal and its feeding strategy. In an animal with a high metabolic rate, these energy stores are rapidly expended and the animal enters a starvation period, mobilizing energy stores and even degrading structure. Many animals are subjected to very long periods between meals and possess strategies that combine reducing metabolic demands and more efficiently using the available resources.

For some animals, the food deprivation period may persist for the life of the animal. Many insects have nonfeeding developmental stages. Typically, the early life stages feed actively, storing nutrients for metamorphosis and reproduction. Most pupae of insects do not feed, instead relying on nutrients stored as larvae to reorganize the anatomy and physiological systems. In a few cases, the adult form of an insect is nonfeeding. Mayflies, for example, spend as long as 2.5 years as nymphs, feeding as predators in the debris of waterways. When waters warm in spring, the adult stages emerge and reproduce, then die one or two days later. Adults do not feed, and prior to their emergence the GI tract atrophies, acting as a nutrient store used to support reproductive maturation.

Nutrient stores are regulated between meals

After nutrients pass through the enterocytes to the blood, they may be utilized directly by other tissues or stored in depot tissues. With each meal there is a burst of readily metabolizable carbon fuels that can be oxidized to support the metabolic demands of tissues. In many tissues, the fuels used to support energy metabolism are influenced by the spectrum of fuels in the blood. The vertebrate heart, for example, is capable of oxidizing glucose, lactate, amino acids, or fatty acids, depending on their availability in the blood.

FIGURE 14.31 **Smooth muscle and the control of gut motility**

Acetylcholine (ACh) released from enteric nerves induces contraction of smooth muscle by increasing cytoplasmic Ca^{2+} levels. When it binds to muscarinic receptors, ACh activates phospholipase C (PLC), causing an increase in IP_3, which opens Ca^{2+} channels in the sarcoplasmic reticulum, and DAG, which activates PKC and opens Ca^{2+} channels in the cell membrane. ACh also antagonizes relaxation. It activates muscarinic receptors that bind a G_i protein that inhibits adenylate cyclase, thereby reducing cAMP levels and PKA activity.

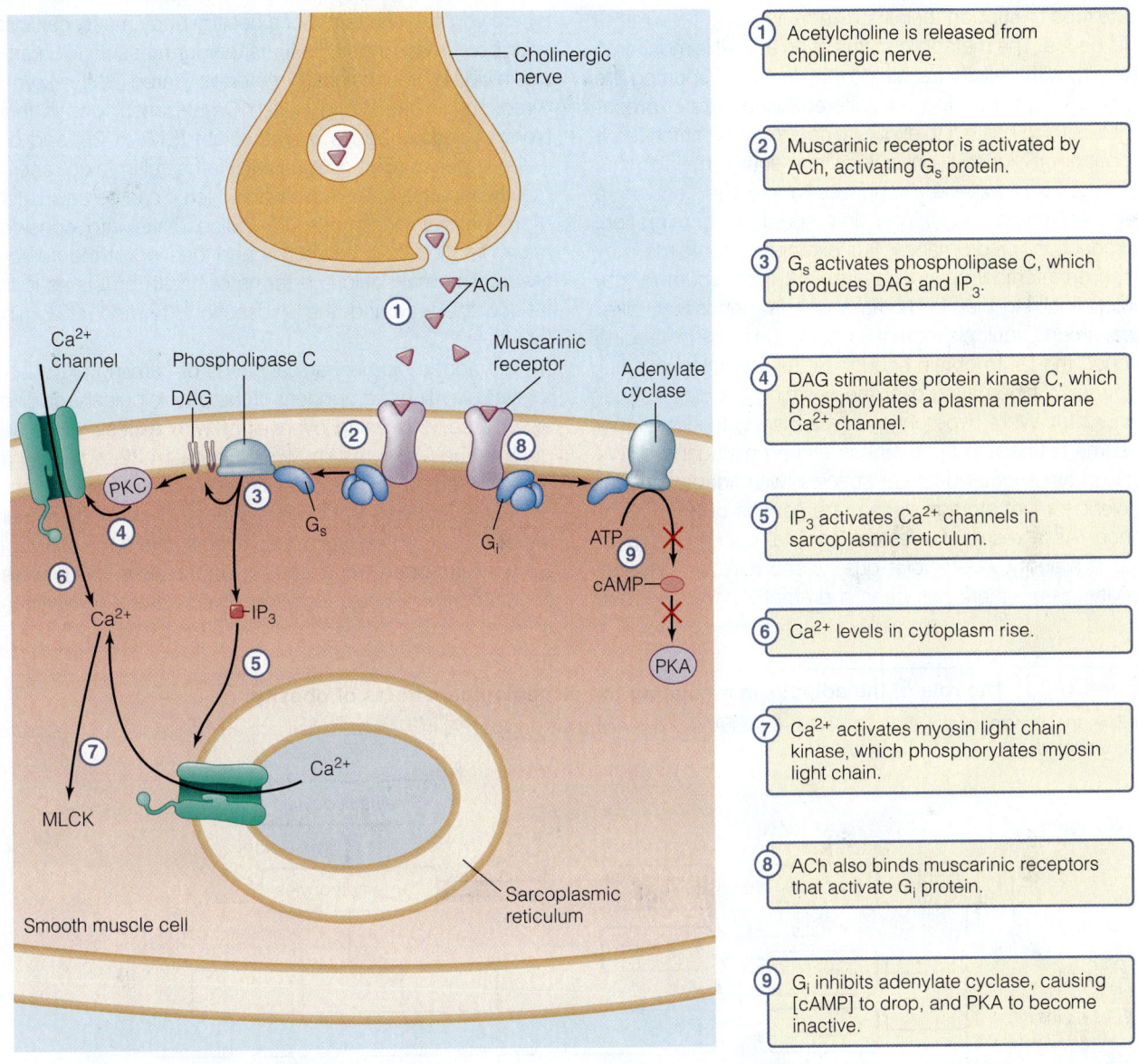

1. Acetylcholine is released from cholinergic nerve.

2. Muscarinic receptor is activated by ACh, activating G_s protein.

3. G_s activates phospholipase C, which produces DAG and IP_3.

4. DAG stimulates protein kinase C, which phosphorylates a plasma membrane Ca^{2+} channel.

5. IP_3 activates Ca^{2+} channels in sarcoplasmic reticulum.

6. Ca^{2+} levels in cytoplasm rise.

7. Ca^{2+} activates myosin light chain kinase, which phosphorylates myosin light chain.

8. ACh also binds muscarinic receptors that activate G_i protein.

9. G_i inhibits adenylate cyclase, causing [cAMP] to drop, and PKA to become inactive.

Immediately after a meal, such tissues have many alternative fuels. Later, however, the levels of nutrients in the blood depend on the action of hormones that control the release of fuels from storage tissues. This regulation is determined primarily by endocrine hormones.

In vertebrates, the immediate fate of dietary nutrients (oxidation, storage, or biosynthesis) depends on the levels of the pancreatic hormones insulin and glucagon, as well as glucocorticoids. During digestion, these hormones act on peripheral tissues to control the pattern of fuel utilization and on storage tissues to control rates of uptake and synthesis. In the postabsorptive animal, these same hormones control the release of fuels from storage depots. When the glucose level is high, as it would be after a meal, pancreatic beta cells are induced to secrete insulin. Insulin acts upon multiple tissues to promote glucose removal from the blood. In skeletal muscle, it enhances glucose uptake by causing translocation of glucose transporters (GLUT-4) to the cell

OBESITY

Most animals face the continuing challenge of finding adequate food to support their short-term and long-term metabolic needs. The metabolic status of an animal is monitored centrally, with deficits translated into "hunger," spurring the animal to search for food despite enduring risks of predation. Evolution has led to exquisite controls that match feeding behavior, digestive physiology, and energy metabolism. Some animals experience phases where they eat more than usual (hyperphagy), often in preparation for migration, reproduction, or dormancy. For example, shorebirds may gorge on intertidal crustaceans before flying south for the winter, doubling their body mass with fat deposition. Likewise, ground squirrels more than double in mass by feeding through the fall to obtain enough fat for insulation and nutrition while hibernating over the seemingly endless Canadian winter. While hyperphagy is essential in the life history of some animals, in humans it is entirely maladaptive. We evolved as a hunter-gatherer species, with adaptations for efficient nutrient storage during rare periods of food abundance. As a result of Western societal changes—higher food availability, poorer diet quality, and reduced physical activity levels—there has been a dramatic increase in the prevalence of obesity in many populations. To discover where you stand in terms of a healthy body mass, calculate your body mass index (BMI): take your mass (in kilograms) and divide by your height (in meters) squared (BMI = kg/m^2). According to the World Health Organization, one in three North American adults is overweight (BMI > 25) and one in ten is obese (BMI > 30). BMI is a useful index of obesity mainly because of the ease with which it can be calculated. More physiologically relevant indices take into consideration the metabolic properties and location of the adipose tissue. The main culprit in terms of health problems is the fat localized around the midsection, termed abdominal (or visceral) fat.

The added biomechanical stress of carrying extra fat is a relatively minor component of the physiological disruption associated with being overweight with excess white adipose tissue (WAT). As shown in Figure 14.32, adiposity affects numerous physiological systems, contributing to many diseases. Adipose metabolism affects whole-body nutrient metabolism, and through these effects, alters the sensitivity to other important regulators of metabolism. WAT is also an endocrine tissue, secreting diverse hormones related

FIGURE 14.32 **The role of the adipose in mediating the physiological effects of obesity**

ANG = angiotensinogen. IL-6 = interleukin-6. NEFA = nonesterified fatty acids. PAI-1 = plasminogen activator inhibitor-1. TNF = tumor necrosis factor.

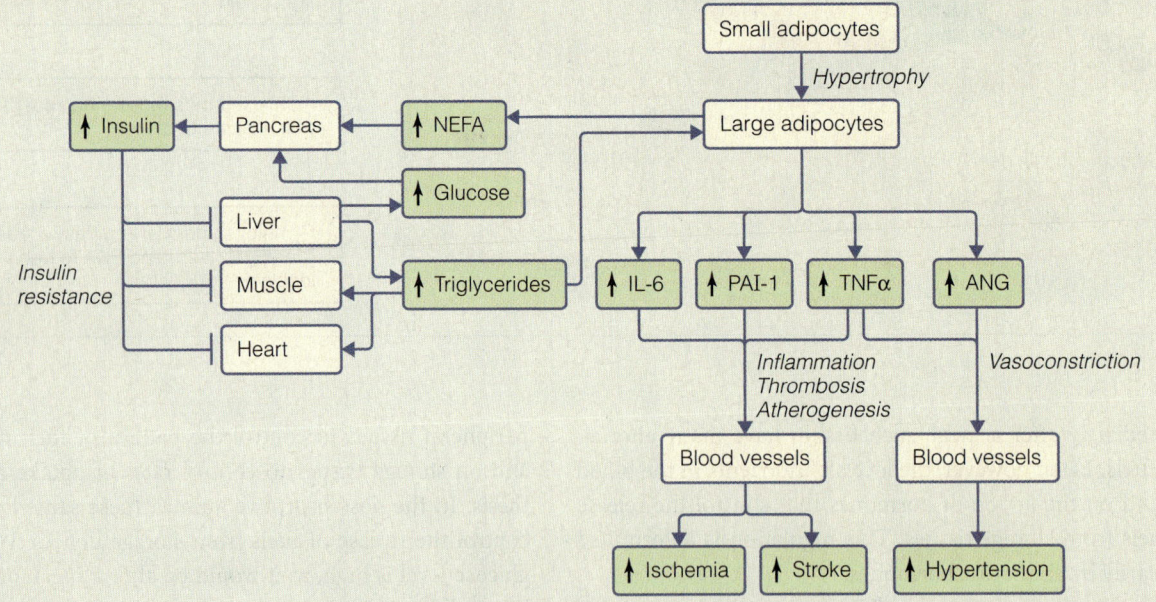

to dietary status (leptin, adiponectin), blood clotting (plasminogen activator inhibitor-1), inflammation (interleukin 6, tumor necrosis factor alpha), and blood pressure (angiotensinogen). In overweight individuals, it is the combination of larger adipocytes and greater total WAT mass that affects the endocrine functions of the tissue.

The main metabolic consequences of obesity are related to disruption of normal insulin signaling. In a healthy individual, an elevated blood glucose level triggers the pancreas to secrete insulin, which in turn promotes glucose uptake by adipose and skeletal muscle, and inhibits hepatic gluconeogenesis. In an obese individual, the pancreas secretes insulin, but despite *hyper-insulinemia*, the target tissues fail to respond to the hormone. As a result of the insulin resistance, glucose is not cleared by metabolism and the blood maintains a very high glucose level (*hyperglycemia*). At the heart of this disorder is insulin resistance in the WAT. In normal adipocytes, high insulin levels signal an "energy-rich" state, causing adipocytes to reduce triglyceride breakdown. In obese individuals, the adipocytes are hypertrophied, and these larger, lipid-rich cells are resistant to the insulin signal and respond by releasing nonesterified fatty acids (NEFA). The reasons for the loss of insulin sensitivity in peripheral tissues are complex. In the liver, it may be caused by metabolic disruption, such as elevated NEFA, or by changes in adipocyte regulatory factors, such as tumor necrosis factor alpha (TNFα). In either case, the loss of insulin sensitivity causes the liver to increase lipid storage, creating a condition known as fatty liver disease. There are also dramatic increases in the triglyceride levels in skeletal muscle and around the heart (*epicardial fat*). It also alters how the liver maintains lipid profiles in the blood; more triglyceride is produced and released to the blood, and there is a reduction in the levels of HDL, the lipoprotein that reduces the negative effects of cholesterol. The main metabolic effects of obesity—high blood glucose, high blood triglyceride, insulin resistance, low HDL—are four of five symptoms of a condition known as *metabolic syndrome* (the fifth symptom, high blood pressure, will be discussed a bit later in this feature). People with three or more of these symptoms are at a much greater risk of cardiovascular disease.

Like the metabolic effects of obesity, the cardiovascular effects are complex. Obese individuals may experience greater risk of numerous cardiovascular disorders. Obesity and insulin resistance interact to cause high blood pressure (*hypertension*). Insulin is a powerful vasodilator, and if obesity makes the vasculature insensitive to its hypotensive effects, hypertension can result. Adipocytes are also a major site of two vasoconstricting factors: angiotensinogen and TNF. These factors act on vasculature and also affect how the kidney regulates blood pressure. Apart from regulating vascular tone, obesity and insulin resistance can also affect vascular structure by increasing endothelial damage, promoting formation of vascular plaques (*atherogenesis*) and clots (*thrombosis*). Again, there may be a metabolic link (such as increased plasma cholesterol), but the main reason for the vascular effects is through the alterations in the regulatory factors released by the WAT. Increases in TNF, interleukin 6, and plasminogen activator inhibitor-1 exert complex effects on the vasculature. They act directly and indirectly to promote inflammation, increasing oxidative damage within the vascular tissue, promoting atherogenesis, thrombosis, and platelet aggregation. Collectively, the vascular effects can contribute to other cardiovascular complications. The combination of atherogenesis and thrombosis increases the risk that plaques and clots will cause vascular blockage and **ischemia**. This could cause a heart attack if the blockage is in the coronary arteries, or a stroke if the blockage is in the circulation of the brain.

In relatively rare situations, an obese phenotype can be traced to genetic variants that affect the perception of hunger or the appropriate control of metabolism. However, the most common cause of obesity is simply eating more kilocalories than your body requires. Fortunately, many of the health problems associated with obesity can be reversed if a person returns to a healthy weight.

References

- Adamczak, M., & Wiecek, A. (2013). The adipose tissue as an endocrine organ. *Seminars in Nephrology, 33*, 2–13.
- De Oliveira Leal, V., & Mafra, D. (2013). Adipokines in obesity. *Clinica Chimica Acta, 419*, 87–96.
- Reaven, G., Abbasi, F., & McLaughlin, T. (2004). Obesity, insulin resistance and cardiovascular disease. *Recent Progress in Hormone Research, 59*, 207–223.

membrane. In adipose, it promotes uptake and conversion of glucose into fatty acids, for long-term storage as triglyceride. In liver, it impairs glycogen breakdown and enhances glycogen synthesis. After the glucose level declines, insulin secretion decreases and glucagon is released by pancreatic alpha cells. This causes mobilization of energy stores—glycogen hydrolysis and triglyceride breakdown—and enhances the rate of gluconeogenesis in liver. Thus, the balance between insulin and glucagon determines the balance between glucose utilization and generation.

Glucocorticoids such as cortisol, corticosterone, and cortisone induce gluconeogenesis while reducing glucose uptake by peripheral tissues such as skeletal muscle. This acts to increase circulating glucose levels to ensure that those tissues that require glucose have a steady supply. Glucocorticoids also mobilize triglycerides, ensuring that fatty acids are available to tissues that are prevented from using glucose, such as skeletal muscle. Whereas insulin and glucagon are most important to metabolic regulation in relation to the nutritional state, glucocorticoids are most important as part of a metabolic stress response. For example, the intense metabolic costs of locomotion and reproductive behaviors are met when the glucocorticoid stress hormones cause mobilization and synthesis of fuels.

Invertebrate nutritional metabolism is best studied in insects, mainly because of their importance as agricultural pests. The main energy store in insects is the fat body. During energy-demanding situations, such as flight, *adipokinetic hormone* (AKH) is released from the *corpora cardiacum*, causing the fat body to mobilize energy stores (Figure 14.33). Lipids are broken down to DAG and fatty acids. Glycogen stores are converted to trehalose. The fat body also releases significant amounts of proline in some species. AdK acts via a G protein–coupled receptor (G_q) to activate phospholipase C (PLC). The increase in IP_3 triggers Ca^{2+} release, which activates Ca^{2+}-sensitive signaling enzymes that activate glycogen phosphorylase and triglyceride lipase. At the same time that AKH enhances lipid and protein breakdown, it inhibits lipid and protein synthesis. Because insect reproduction is intimately linked to nutrition, AKH also inhibits egg production in females.

Prolonged food deprivation can trigger a starvation response

Most animals are able to cope with short periods of food deprivation without incurring metabolic distress. Short-term food deprivation, such as the periods between regular meals, can be met with existing energy resources. If the food-deprivation period persists, the animal reorganizes metabolism to ensure long-term survival. Most vertebrates trigger

FIGURE 14.33 **Hormonal regulation of metabolism in insects**

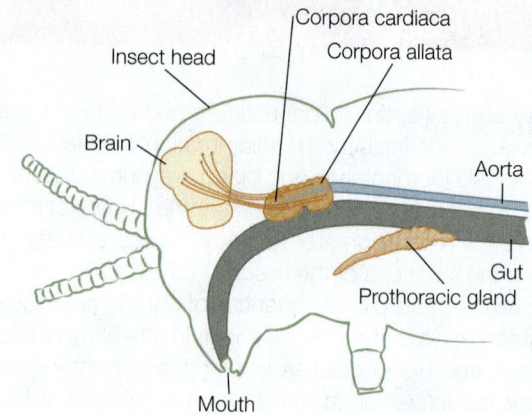

(a) Insect head

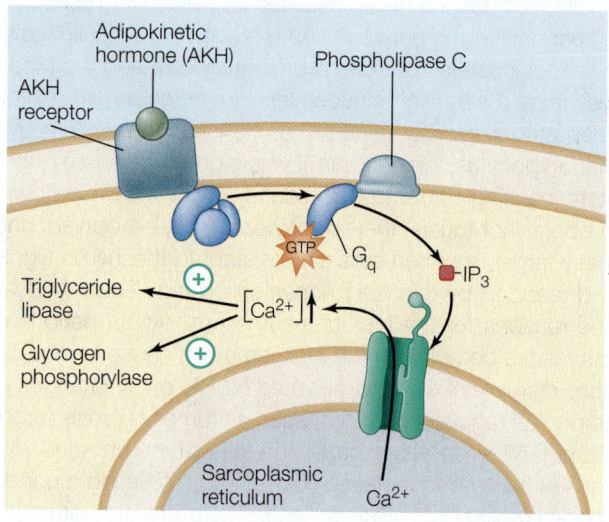

(b) Fat body cell

mechanisms that preserve glucose in order to protect those tissues that rely heavily on glucose to meet energy demands. Nervous tissue, for example, relies almost exclusively on glucose as a fuel. In the early phases of food deprivation, vertebrates mobilize the vast lipid stores in liver and WAT. Muscle, a major consumer of metabolic energy, shifts to rely more heavily on mobilized lipid, reducing the reliance on glucose.

Despite these efforts to conserve glucose, after a time the glycogen stores become depleted and the animal must find a fuel that can be used to produce glucose. After prolonged food deprivation, the animal accelerates the rate of protein breakdown. Because there is no protein store, this usually entails the degradation of the protein structures within cells. One of the earliest tissues to suffer protein degradation is skeletal muscle. Individual myofibers degrade contractile elements in the process of atrophy. When intracellular proteins are degraded by

FIGURE 14.34 **The metabolic cascade of starvation**

When animals are deprived of food, they respond by mobilizing internal energy stores. **(a)** In early starvation of vertebrates, stores of glycogen and triglyceride (TG) provide most of the metabolic needs of tissues. Fatty acids are released from liver and adipose for use in other tissues. **(b)** During late starvation, glycogen reserves are depleted and ketone bodies are produced from fatty acids from adipose and liver, as well as some amino acids derived from muscle proteolysis.

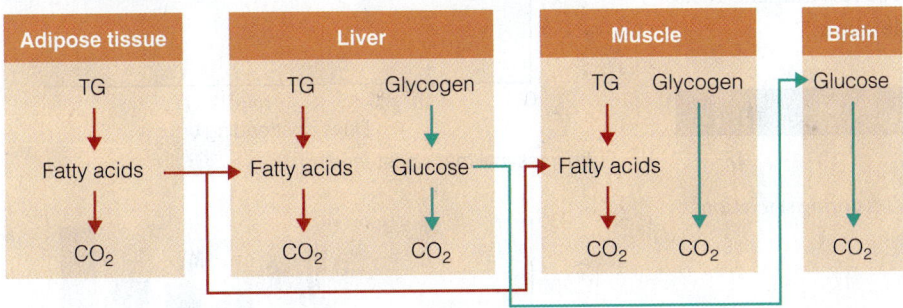

(a) Early starvation

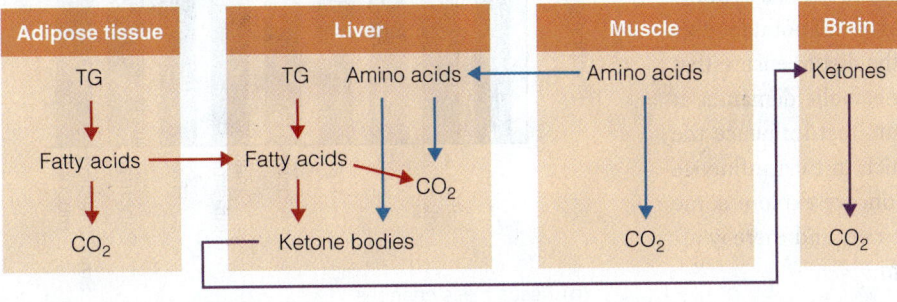

(b) Late starvation

lysosomes and proteasomes, the liberated amino acids can be oxidized for fuel or converted to other molecules, such as ketone bodies, fatty acids, or carbohydrate. These processes can occur either in the muscle itself or after transport of the amino acids to other tissues, primarily liver. Fatty acids can also be converted to ketone bodies, which can then be utilized by tissues that cannot oxidize fatty acids, such as nervous tissue. The main regulatory events that occur during starvation are summarized in Figure 14.34.

The rate at which a starvation response progresses varies widely among species, primarily due to differences in metabolic rate. An animal with a high metabolic rate will deplete its energy stores faster than an animal with a low metabolic rate. Differences in metabolic rate arise in relation to body size, activity levels, and temperature. Because small animals have higher mass-specific metabolic rates than do larger animals, they expend limited energy stores at a faster rate. The energetic state of a hummingbird or shrew after one hour of food deprivation is similar to that of a human who has not eaten for 12 hours. Active animals utilize energy stores faster than similarly sized sedentary animals. For example, a dog

has a metabolic rate that is about twice that of a goat. Even within a single individual, a persistent period of elevated metabolism draws on circulating fuels and stimulates feeding. Prolonged periods of biosynthesis, arising during rapid growth, **gestation**, or lactation, can elevate metabolic rate dramatically. Similarly, the elevation in metabolic rate during muscle activity arising from exercise or shivering stimulates appetite and fuel mobilization. The third factor that affects metabolic rate and nutrient demand is body temperature. An increase in body temperature accelerates the basal metabolic demands and more rapidly depletes available energy, thereby accelerating the rate of progression through the starvation responses.

Pythons may rebuild the digestive tract for each meal

An animal that eats very infrequently must maintain its GI tract in a condition that will allow it to function when needed. Hibernating ground squirrels that have been dormant for more than 12 weeks continue to express the degradative enzymes that would be required to digest a meal. In this way, these animals ensure that they will be able to eat and digest a meal immediately upon emergence from hibernation. However, some animals reduce their energetic costs between meals by allowing the GI tract to degrade. Large predatory snakes, such as the Burmese python, may go months between meals. When a snake feeds, it eats a very large meal. For example, in 1977, villagers in India killed an 18-foot Indian python and recovered the remains of a 45-year-old man. Between these large meals, much of the mucosa and submucosa of the GI tract degrades. The gut becomes thinner and the brush border of the intestine decreases. These structural changes reduce the total surface area of the GI tract and the capacity for nutrient transport. Although the absorptive epithelium is reduced, the GI tract maintains the smooth muscle and nerves that control the gut. Once the animal feeds, the snake rebuilds its GI tract in regions that are just ahead of the bolus of food. Within the first few days after a meal, the mass of the tissues associated with digestion increases dramatically.

The small intestine alone nearly doubles in mass, and other tissues, such as liver and kidney, increase by more than 60 percent in this rapid growth phase (Figure 14.35). The high metabolic cost of rebuilding the gut is an important component of the very high specific dynamic action (SDA) seen in a python digesting a meal; while the costs are great, the cost of rebuilding the GI tract must be less than the costs of maintaining it between unpredictable meals.

CONCEPT CHECK

13. What is the postprandial period?
14. Why do animals produce ketone bodies during starvation?
15. What is a BMI?

Evolutionary Variation in Metabolic Rate

Digestion is regulated to ensure metabolic homeostasis of the animal. Much of what we have discussed to this point focuses on how animals digest and assimilate the diet to ensure that the nutrient and energy needs meet metabolic demands. It is also important to consider the factors that influence the metabolic demands of the animal, which in turn influence the digestive physiology. In this section, we explore some of the factors that influence metabolic rate, and thereby affect the demands of the digestive system.

Metabolic rate can be measured by direct or indirect calorimetry

If *metabolism* is literally the sum of all chemical reactions, then what exactly is meant by metabolic rate (MR) and how is it measured? MR is the overall flux through the pathways of energy production, which matches the rate of energy consumption. In the presence of oxygen, the pathways that lead to production of ATP consume carbon fuels and oxygen (O_2), and produce heat, carbon dioxide (CO_2), and water. Many physiological questions revolve around changes in metabolic rate, and many approaches have been developed to measure the substrates and products of metabolism. **Direct calorimetry** assesses metabolic rate in terms of heat

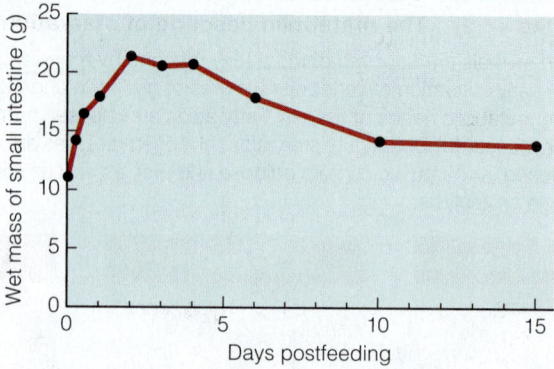

(a) Intestinal mass post-feeding

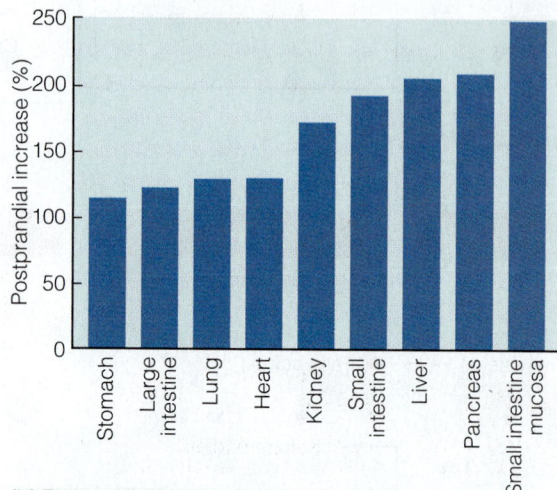

(b) Tissue mass changes

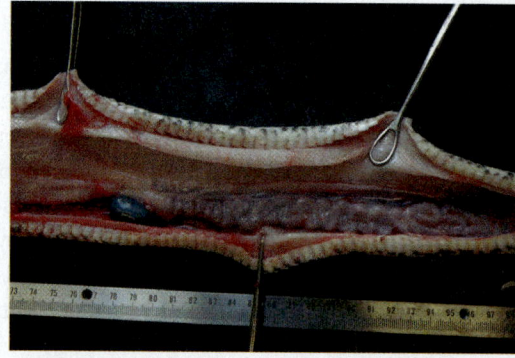

(c) Intestine (pre-fed)

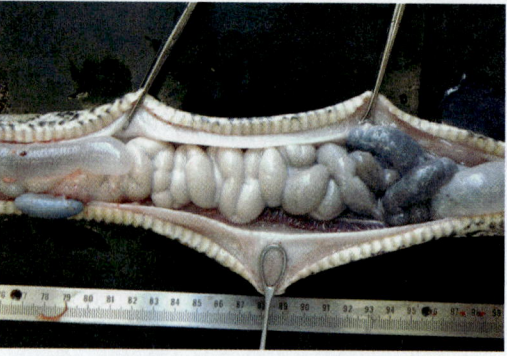

(d) Intestine (post-feeding)

FIGURE 14.35 Python digestion

Large snakes that eat infrequent meals allow their digestive organs to decrease in mass between meals. Organ mass increases rapidly upon feeding. **(a)** Intestinal wet mass doubles within three days postfeeding. **(b)** Other tissues that participate in digestion also increase markedly in the first few days after feeding. The growth in the gut is illustrated by the images of the python digestive tract before **(c)** and after **(d)** a meal.

Photo source: (c–d) Stephen M. Secor.

production, measured in energy units (joules). For purely pragmatic reasons (direct calorimetry requires expensive, specialized equipment), this is the least common way to measure metabolic rate. A more common approach to measuring metabolic rate is **indirect calorimetry**, in which the researcher measures the rate of O_2 consumption or CO_2 production. To infer a metabolic rate from these measurements, it is important to recognize where O_2 is consumed (largely in the electron transport system) and where CO_2 is produced (primarily in the TCA cycle). The quantitative relationship between these three estimates of metabolic rate—heat production, O_2 consumption, and CO_2 production—depends on many factors. You learned earlier in this chapter that the ratio of CO_2 produced to O_2 consumed reflects the metabolic fuel. Likewise, the oxycaloric relationships (O_2 consumed to joules released) depend on the nature of the fuel.

Each of these approaches for measuring metabolic rate requires that the researcher hold an animal under defined conditions. A set of terms has been developed to categorize conditions under which MR is measured.

- **Basal metabolic rate (BMR)** is measured in a homeothermic animal that is unstressed, inactive, at a neutral ambient temperature, and has digested its most recent meal (postasorptive).
- **Standard metabolic rate (SMR)** is similar to the BMR, except that it is measured in a poikilothermic animal at a defined temperature.
- **Resting metabolic rate (RMR)** is measured in either homeotherms or poikilotherms under specific experimental conditions, without specific constraints on activity.

While these experimental conditions yield important information about the physiological hardwiring of an animal, they may not be the best estimates of the animal's metabolic rate under normal conditions. The challenge becomes how to measure the metabolic rate of an animal when you are not able to measure gas exchange.

Field metabolic rate relies upon doubly labeled water

Ecological physiologists are often more interested in long-term metabolic rate of free-ranging animals in the natural setting. One of the most common approaches to measuring **field metabolic rate** (FMR) is the **doubly labeled water** method. Most water in the body is composed of the most common isotopes of hydrogen (^1H) and oxygen (^{16}O). To initiate a doubly labeled water experiment, the animal of interest is captured and injected with small volumes of water composed of less common isotopes of hydrogen (e.g., ^2H)

and oxygen (^{18}O). Over time, the labeled hydrogen is lost from the body primarily as water, through evaporation, respiration, and excretion. Likewise, labeled oxygen is also lost in water, but some is exchanged with the O in CO_2. Thus, the difference between the loss of labeled oxygen and labeled hydrogen reflects the rate of CO_2 production. This method works very well in air-breathing animals, but in water breathers, the rates of water flux are much too great to detect the impact of CO_2 production on isotope ratios.

Maximal sustained MR is about five times greater than RMR

The resting metabolic demands of an animal reflect the costs of body maintenance in the absence of external demands. When challenged, animals can increase their metabolic rates several fold but the greater the elevation in MR, the shorter the duration that it can be sustained. As mentioned in the previous section, researchers measure MR in a variety of contexts.

The maximal sustained metabolic rate is the rate that can be maintained for long periods (days to weeks). Species may differ in terms of the stressor that elicits the maximal rate, but the increase over RMR is typically four- to fivefold. For a laboratory mouse, the highest increase is achieved with lactation but for a wild mouse, it occurs with cold exposure and shivering. Other species reach their maximal sustained MR with physical activity. What is intriguing about these periods of elevated MR is that dietary intake roughly equates with MR, such that the animal does not gain or lose weight rapidly despite very high rates of energy expenditure.

Body size influences metabolic rate

One of the main themes in comparative physiology is the impact of body size on physiological processes. Some processes are isometric: Structures or processes vary in direct proportion to body mass. Metabolic rate is a process that shows a negative allometric relationship. The negative allometric scaling of metabolic rate is depicted in Figure 14.36a.

The scaling of metabolic rate is defined as allometric because it is something other than isometric; it is negative because metabolic rate increases less than proportionally with body mass. As discussed in Chapter 1, the equation defining the relationship between body mass (M) and metabolic rate (B) is explained by the **allometric scaling** equation, also known as **Kleiber's Law**:

$$B = aM^b$$

where a is the normalization coefficient and b the **scaling coefficient**. There is a growing consensus that the value for b is generally close to 0.75 (3/4). Using this relationship, it can be calculated that the metabolic rate of a 20-gram mouse would be about 18 percent that of a 200-gram rat,

FIGURE 14.36 **Allometric scaling of metabolic rate**

(a) The metabolic rates of various mammals are plotted against body weight on a double logarithmic scale. The line of unity shows an isometric relationship. **(b)** The mass-specific metabolic rate is shown for the same mammals, also expressed relative to body mass. The line of unity shows an isometric relationship.

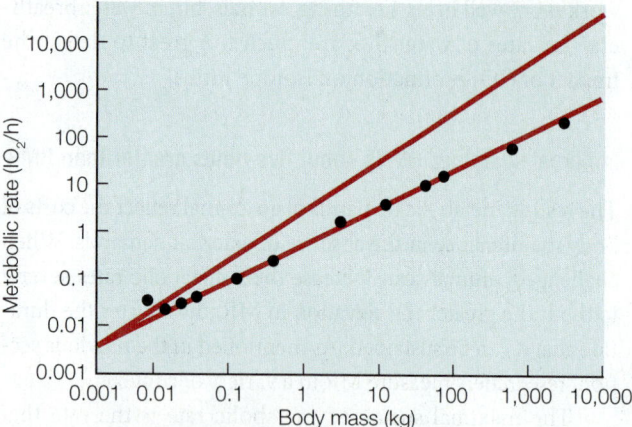

(a) Allometric scaling of metabolic rate

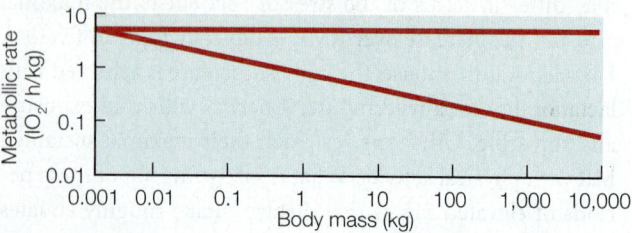

(b) Mass-specific allometric scaling of metabolic rate

Figure source: Based on Schmidt-Nielsen, K. (1997). *Animal hysiology: Adaptation and environment* (5th ed.). Cambridge: Cambridge University Press.

rather than the 10 percent that would be expected if the relationship were isometric.

The relationship can also be expressed in terms of mass-specific scaling (Figure 14.36b). If the scaling coefficient for a whole animal is +0.75, then the mass-specific scaling coefficient is −0.25. Expressing the mass-specific metabolic rate of the mouse would be almost twice (177 percent) that of the rat.

Consider some of the ecological ramifications of the differences in mass-specific metabolic rate. If an environment consists of a limited set of food resources, how the resources are partitioned to animals depends upon their individual metabolic rates and the number of individuals. For example:

- A patch of edible vegetation could support a greater total mass of large animals than small animals because of the differences in their mass-specific metabolic rates.

- 1,000 kilograms of small animals needs a greater ecological range than 1,000 kilograms of large animals.

Scaling relationships have important implications for the energetic, and therefore dietary, needs of animals. Small animals must eat much more food than large animals.

Body temperature affects metabolic rate

Animals exhibit a number of thermal strategies. Metabolic rate changes in animals that experience changes in body temperature (ectotherms), and thus the environmental temperature affects metabolic rate.

The exact relationship between body temperature and metabolic rate depends upon many factors. If you think of whole-body metabolic rate as a chemical reaction, then the sensitivity to temperature is defined as something analogous to activation energy. Recall that the effects of temperature on a chemical reaction is described by the Boltzmann factor, where E_a is activation energy (joules), T is **absolute temperature** (kelvin), and k is the Boltzmann constant (in J/K):

$$\text{Boltzmann factor} = e^{-Ea/kT}$$

For an enzyme, the activation energy (E) relates to the amount of energy needed to push a structural change in the substrate into a form that can be converted to a product.

Applying this concept to a whole animal is much more challenging because an animal's metabolism is the sum of a great many individual chemical events. It is reasonable to assume that the factors that go into calculation of a whole-animal metabolic activation energy would differ widely among animals. For example, some animals may respond to cold passively, allowing their metabolic rate to decline, whereas others may enter torpor and undertake deliberate and extreme reductions in metabolic rate. Their apparent activation energies would differ because of the nature of their physiological responses. Tissues can be differentially affected by temperature, and the global activation energy of the individual will be influenced by difference in tissue composition. As well, once an animal goes beyond its thermal tolerance, metabolic rate will not increase in a manner predicted from lower temperatures.

The metabolic theory of ecology links animal metabolism to ecological relationships

Because both body mass and body temperature have an influence on metabolic rate, which in turn has an impact on demands an animal makes of its dietary environment, there is the potential to combine Kleiber's Law and the Boltzmann factor in a way that takes body mass and body temperature into account.

$$B = aM^b\, e^{-Ea/kT}$$

While this relationship is based on the rules of physics and chemistry, it has been applied to diverse biological systems, largely through the **metabolic theory of ecology** (MTE). The MTE attempts to use this equation to make predictions about larger scale events in biology. It assumes a universal scaling coefficient of 0.75, and thus the equation becomes:

$$B = aM^{0.75} e^{-Ea/kT}$$

The MTE has broad implications for predicting how dietary energy is used within ecosystems. It makes the assumption that there is a strict relationship between the metabolic rate, the food energy assimilated, and that energy being applied to growth and/or reproduction. Thus, higher metabolic rates (from being small bodied or warmer or both) lead to higher rates of individual growth, reproduction, and ultimately population growth. For the most part, the predictions of the MTE have been shown to be reasonable when applied to the real world. However, there are many situations where exceptions are obvious, due to variations previously discussed in predicting the metabolic rate of individuals, such as deviations from the 3/4 scaling coefficient, and complex responses to a thermal environment, which manifest as variable activation energies.

CONCEPT CHECK

16. What might happen if a nectar-eating bird consumed fruit?

17. What is meant by a scaling coefficient = 0.75?

18. What is the metabolic theory of ecology?

SUMMARY

Animals consume nutrients to obtain energy and precursors for biosynthesis, including eight to ten essential amino acids, two classes of essential fatty acids (omega-3 and omega-6), vitamins, and minerals. Animals find food using chemical, thermal, electrical, or visual cues, detected by specific receptors in the nervous system.

Simple animals such as sponges and cnidarians digest food intracellularly, after phagocytosis of particulate matter. More advanced invertebrates break food down into macromolecules extracellularly and transport individual molecules into the gastrointestinal epithelium. Most animals use oral feeding structures to find and ingest food. Evolutionary variation in feeding structures, such as bird beaks and mammalian teeth, permit mechanical disruption of food by grinding, tearing, and shredding.

Although simple invertebrates have short, tubular GI tracts, more complex animals maximize surface area by increasing the undulations of the gut surface, producing fingerlike projections from the surface (villi) and cellular protrusions from the absorptive enterocytes (microvilli). The digestive epithelium in each compartment has special types of secretory cells that release digestive enzymes and control the physical properties with secretions of acid, base, and mucus. Many animals have fermentation chambers prior to the glandular stomach (ruminants) or after the glandular stomach (nonruminants). These specialized compartments house endosymbiotic microbes that possess cellulolytic activity.

Though carbohydrates and proteins are broken down in the gut, most lipids are only partially hydrolyzed, and leave the intestinal cells in the form of chylomicrons. When chylomicrons are gradually stripped of lipids, their remnants are taken up and repackaged into lipoproteins by the liver.

Hormones interpret information from the GI tract and metabolic storage tissues to influence appetite. Once food is ingested, hormones control the secretions by the stomach (acid, pepsin, mucus), pancreas (bicarbonate, proteases, lipases, nucleases), and gallbladder (bile). Smooth muscle of the GI tract controls the rate at which the bolus moves down the digestive tract. Numerous hormones and neurons, acting both locally and centrally, control gut motility.

Animals utilize nutrients that appear in the blood after a meal, oxidizing some directly and metabolizing others into storage forms. Hormones such as insulin and glucagon regulate the fate of the major metabolic fuels. Insulin promotes glucose utilization, whereas glucagon antagonizes the insulin effect. If deprived of food for long periods, a vertebrate initiates a starvation response, converting some of the stored lipids to ketone bodies for use in brain and other tissues that normally rely on glucose for energy.

The metabolic rate of organisms varies in relation to body size and body temperature. The metabolic theory of ecology relates these parameters to make predictions about animal life histories and ecology.

REVIEW QUESTIONS

1. **LO❶** A diet is rich in chemical energy, but not all of this energy is available to the animal. How is energy partitioned in a diet?

2. **LO❶** How does specific dynamic action benefit an animal?

3. **LO❷** How do animals use neurosensory systems to detect food in a complex environment?

4. **LO❷** What role might genetic variation play in the evolution and development of bird beak shape variation?

5. **LO❸** Summarize the basic organization of the vertebrate GI tract. What is the function of each compartment?

6. **LO❸** Discuss the variation in the nature of fermentation chambers.

7. **LO❹** What roles do glands play in the process of digestion?

8. **LO❹** How do animals control the secretions along the gastrointestinal tract?

9. **LO❺** Compare the different pathways for digestion and uptake of the three main classes of macromolecules: lipids, carbohydrates, and proteins.

10. **LO❺** How might an animal alter its ability to import monosaccharides from the gastrointestinal tract?

11. **LO❻** Discuss the fate of glucose during a meal, after a meal, and two days after an animal's meal.

12. **LO❻** What factors might alter the relationship between body mass, body temperature, and metabolic rate?

SYNTHESIS QUESTIONS

1. Discuss situations where digestion and reproduction may be antagonistic processes.

2. An animal that feeds on a large meal undergoes numerous changes that affect its other physiological systems. Discuss how the digestive process impinges on other systems.

3. When wild animals are domesticated, the years of artificial selection can alter the digestive physiology of the animal. Choose an example of a domesticated animal and consider how its digestive physiology might differ from that of its wild ancestors, given the differences in diet and selective pressures.

4. Why is digestion a metabolically expensive process?

5. Follow the path of glucose from the nectar reservoir of a plant to the muscle of a hummingbird. What steps control the rate of this process?

6. What differences in digestive physiology systems would you expect when comparing birds that eat nectar (easy to digest, high energy per gram), seeds (difficult to digest, high energy per gram), or fruit (easy to digest, low energy per gram)?

7. The harsh chemical and enzymatic conditions in the gastrointestinal tract break down nutrients. How do animals protect themselves from their own digestive secretions?

QUANTITATIVE QUESTIONS

1. For the following calculations, assume the following:
   - The generic daily caloric requirements are 2,500 kcal for men, and 2,000 for women.
   - The caloric expenditures for someone with an average lifestyle are attributed to basal metabolic rate (about 70 percent of total), specific dynamic action (10 percent), and physical activity (20 percent).
   - There are 9,000 kcal in 1 kg of fat, and 4,000 kcal in 1 kg of protein or carbohydrate.
   - There are about 7,000 kcal in 1 kg of body mass.
   - A pint of beer has about 200 kcal.
   - You burn about 500 kcal by jogging for 1 h at 10 km/h (though it depends on your weight and the running speed).

   (a) Assuming that your metabolic rate during sleep is equal to your basal metabolic rate (it's actually lower), how many calories did you expend while sleeping for 8 hours? Translate those calories into units of body mass. Did you lose that much weight while you slept? How do respiration and urine production factor into this analysis?

   (b) Assuming no change in basal metabolic rate or SDA, how long would it take to lose 1 kg of body mass (a) by reducing caloric intake by 500 kcal per day or (b) by doubling your physical activity each day?

   (c) If you jogged to your local pub, how far would you have to go to ensure you expended enough calories to maintain caloric balance if you plan to consume two pints of beer?

2. You conduct an experiment to assess the rates of uptake of glucose by bird intestines. One approach is to prepare rings of intestine. You cut across the intestine to create nearly equal-sized pieces, and incubate each ring in a solution of radiolabeled glucose (various concentrations) for 10 minutes. You remove the rings, quickly rinse in fresh saline, and assess the radioactivity in the ring as an index of glucose uptake. You report your raw data in the form of the following table, with the goal of calculating the apparent affinity for glucose (K_m) and the maximum rate of transport (J_{max}, which is analagous to V_{max} for an enzyme).

Ring	1	2	3	4	5	6	7	8	9
Mass (g)	0.12	0.11	0.13	0.10	0.11	0.13	0.09	0.15	0.13
Glucose concentration (mM)	0	0.01	0.02	0.04	0.1	0.2	0.4	0.7	1.0
Glucose uptake (nmol/min/ring)	0	10	30	70	140	230	180	320	330

(a) How and why do you correct for the mass of the intestine?
(b) Plot the data to estimate the K_m and J_{max} for the intestine preparation. (Hint: What is the independent (X) variable? What variable is the dependent (Y) variable?)
(c) Use the linear transformations of the Michaelis-Menton equation (see Chapter 3) to calculate the actual K_m and J_{max} values.

FIGURE 15.1 Opah (*Lampris guttatus*)

Photo source: Southwest Fisheries Science Center, NOAA Fisheries Service.

A high metabolic rate leads to heat production and an increase in body temperature permits a higher metabolic rate. The connection between metabolism and heat production is rooted in chemistry and physics, but that relationship has profound consequences for how thermal physiology evolved.

Before about 200 million years ago (mya), most of the animals on the planet had a body temperature (T_B) determined by the environment, primarily ambient temperature (T_A), a pattern known as *ectothermy*. However, there were a few species, such as large dinosaurs, that were able to retain metabolic heat to elevate T_B above T_A, which is known as *endothermy*. As first discussed in Chapter 1, large animals benefit from a low surface area-to-volume ratio because it reduces heat loss. Though not as large as dinosaurs, several modern large animals, such as leatherback turtles and whale sharks, have some degree of endothermy, unlike their smaller relatives living in the same environment.

The first truly endothermic lineages were mammals and later birds. Though they arose from different reptile ancestors (see Chapter 2), their independent routes to endothermy included convergent evolution of insulation: fur in mammals, feathers in birds. In the mammalian lineage, the ability to retain metabolic heat in small-bodied animals allowed them a nocturnal life, where they avoided predation by larger reptiles. The birds arose from one of several feathered reptilian lineages, but in the bird lineage the feathers were asymmetrical. While serving perfectly well for insulation, these asymmetrical feathers also altered airflows in a way that predisposed them for use in flight. In each of these endothermic lineages, subsequent evolutionary events led to spatial and temporal variations in thermal physiology. With both birds and mammals, select species permit anatomical regions to get cold, and others allow their whole body to cool, decreasing metabolic rate dramatically.

A completely different form of endothermy is seen in select fish, specifically those large enough to attain favorable surface area:volume ratios. This is all the more difficult for fish for two reasons: they live in water, which is more effective at conducting heat from the body, and their circulatory system is configured in a way that brings warm blood from the core to the gills, where it reaches thermal equilibrium with the cooler water. Still, some fish lineages have evolved an ability to maintain parts of the body warm through the use of countercurrent heat exchangers called **retia** (singular, *rete*). Retia are found in the locomotor muscles of large tuna and lamnid sharks and in the GI tract of large billfish. Some fish, such as blue marlin (*Makaira nigricans*) and opah (Figure 15.1), use these circulatory adaptations, in combination with modified muscles called heater organs, to warm regions of the central nervous system.

In this chapter, we explore the diversity in thermal strategies employed by animals. Throughout, we emphasize the relationship between the underlying physical laws of physics and chemistry and the biological adaptations that govern the relationship between an animal and its thermal environment. ◼

LOOKING BACK 15

You may find it helpful to review Chapter 3, where we described the nature of energy, the fundamentals of energy metabolism, and the thermal sensitivity of macromolecular structures. In Chapter 2 we discussed the evolutionary history of the reptiles, which helps you understand the independent origins of thermal physiology of birds and mammals. Chapter 9 described the organization of the circulatory system, and its role in transport of heat between tissues and mediating the exchange of heat between the animal and its environment. In Chapter 12 we discussed the role of muscle in production of metabolic heat, and the nature of neural control of muscle activity. Finally, in Chapter 14 we discussed the relationship between the digestive system and metabolic rate.

▮ OVERVIEW

Thermal energy influences chemical interactions in ways that affect macromolecular structure and biochemical reactions. Consequently, temperature has pervasive effects on all physiological processes. As a result of these temperature effects, every animal displays a thermal strategy: a combination of behavioral, biochemical, and physiological responses that ensures body temperature (T_B) is within an acceptable limit. The most important environmental influence on the thermal strategy (though not the only one) is ambient temperature (T_A). Animals must survive the highest and lowest T_A in their niche (thermal extremes), as well as the changes in T_A (thermal change).

Animals inhabit most thermal niches on the planet (Figure 15.2). The hottest environments exploited by animals are the regions near thermal vents, such as the hydrothermal vents of the deep sea, volcanoes, and geysers. The coldest

FIGURE 15.2 **Thermal niches**

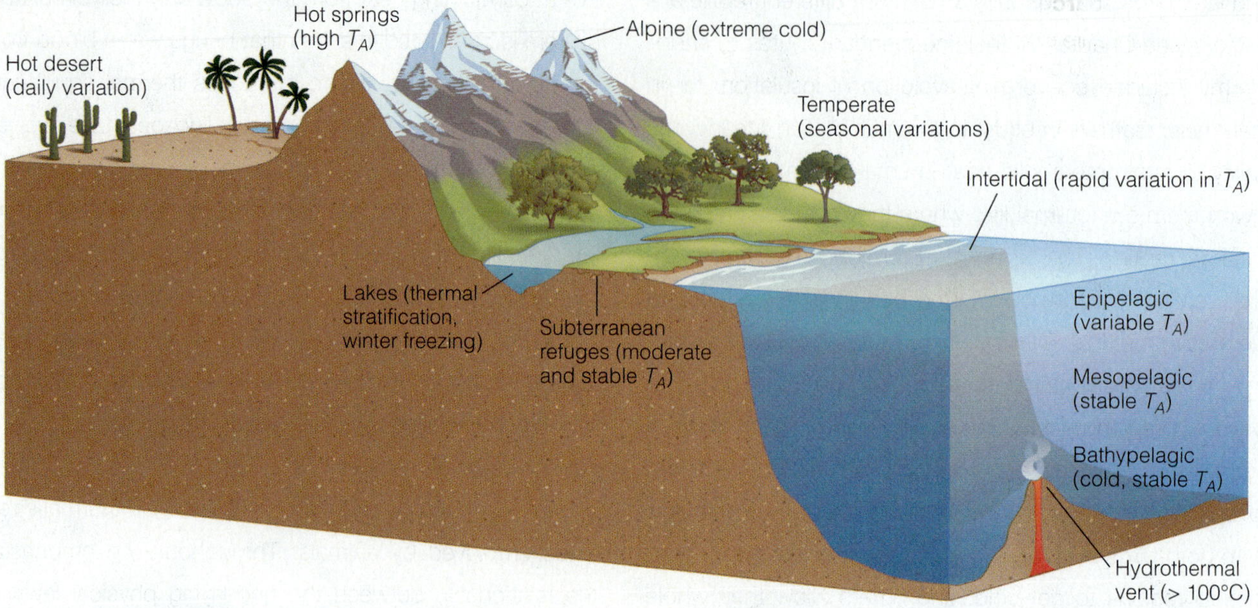

places inhabited by animals are alpine and polar regions. The animals that survive in the extremes of heat and cold are impressive, but the ability to tolerate changing temperature is every bit as challenging physiologically. Environmental temperatures are most variable in terrestrial ecosystems; air temperatures change more rapidly and reach greater extremes than do water temperatures.

Many ecosystems exhibit spatial variation in temperature. Underground refuges are buffered from thermal extremes on the surface. The T_A in alpine regions varies as a result of altitudinal gradients arising over only a few kilometers. Large bodies of water, such as lakes and oceans, can vary in T_A with depth. Deep-ocean (bathypelagic) temperatures are often close to 4°C, whereas midwater (mesopelagic) and surface water (epipelagic) temperatures can be much warmer and more variable. Large temperate lakes may be nearly uniform in temperature, or have sharp demarcations (thermoclines) between top and bottom water, sometimes differing more than 10°C in less than a meter of depth.

Ecosystems can also change in temperature temporally. Terrestrial and aquatic ecosystems in the tropics tend to have a relatively constant T_A, but polar and temperate zones experience seasonal and daily cycles of cold and heat. Air temperatures can change more rapidly than water temperatures, sometimes more than 20°C in a single day. Intertidal animals may experience the heat of a summer day mere seconds before the cold ocean washes over them. Many animals incorporate behavior into their thermal strategy, but animals must also cope with the effects of temperature on biochemistry and physiology.

HEAT EXCHANGE AND THERMAL STRATEGIES

The most important physiological parameter in an animal's thermal physiology is body temperature (T_B). An animal's thermal strategy serves to control the transfer of energy between the animal and the environment. Some animals tolerate wide changes in T_B and the effects of these changes on many physiological processes. Others must use a combination of physiological and behavioral means to ensure that T_B remains nearly constant. As in other physiological systems, both strategies—conforming and regulation—have costs and benefits. The physiological mechanisms that impart a constant T_B use energy. When T_B is allowed to vary, important physiological processes such as development become sensitive to environmental changes. Although T_A has the most obvious impact on animal thermal biology, other routes of heat exchange are also important in many contexts.

Controlling Heat Fluxes

An animal's T_B is a reflection of the thermal energy held within the molecules of the body. Thermal energy can move from the animal to the environment, or from the environment to the animal, depending on temperature gradients. Metabolism—the sum of all biochemical reactions occurring within the body—is the main source of thermal energy in the heat balance equation of most animals. However, other important sources and sinks for thermal energy also affect an animal's thermal budget (Figure 15.3). The thermal

FIGURE 15.3 **Sources and sinks for thermal energy**

The body temperature of an animal is influenced by heat exchange with the environment. This snake is warmed by radiant energy from the sun, as well as thermal energy radiated from its surroundings. The animal exchanges thermal energy through objects and fluids in contact with its external surface (conduction). Movement of the air enhances the efficiency of thermal exchange by convection. The animal itself radiates thermal energy to the surrounding air.

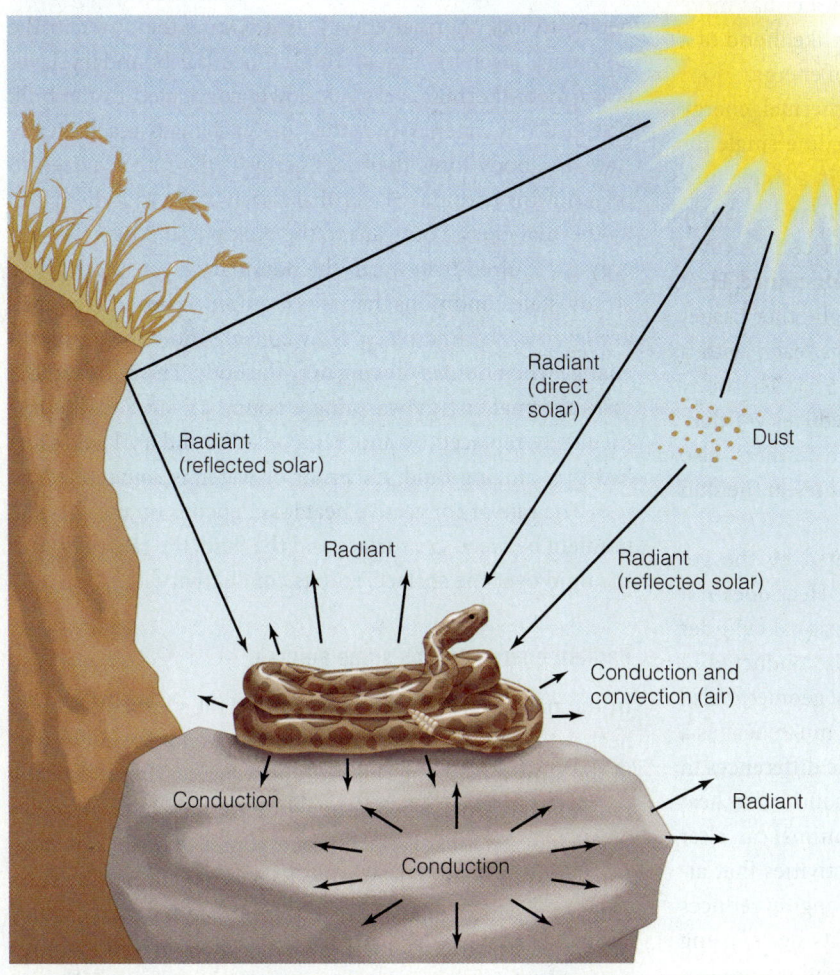

away from the body, or can be warmed as they absorb heat from conductive objects.

- **Convection** is the transfer of thermal energy between an object (the animal in this case) and an external fluid that is moving. For example, warm air feels cooler when it flows over your skin than when the air is still. Most often, convection causes a loss of thermal energy from animals.

- **Radiation** is a general term that refers to the emission of electromagnetic energy from an object. An animal can absorb radiant heat emitted from the surroundings, but can also emit radiant heat from its own surface, a major form of heat loss. The infrared radiation emitted from an object indicates its surface temperature.

- **Evaporation** of water molecules from the surface of an object absorbs thermal energy from the object. Thus, evaporative heat exchange is almost always a heat loss from the animal.

The relative importance and even the direction of heat transfer from each of these parameters differ among animals and conditions. The properties of the animal, including physical composition and color, have a profound influence on the relative importance of these exchanges.

Water has a higher thermal conductivity than air

Conduction is difficult to quantify because of the many factors that affect heat exchange. Let's begin our discussion by considering how conduction is involved in the transfer of thermal energy through a single material, such as a thin metal bar heated at one end. The rate of heat transfer from the warm end to the cool end (heat flux) is described by Fourier's law and the following equation:

$$Q = \frac{\lambda \quad T}{L}$$

where heat flux (Q) depends upon the temperature gradient (ΔT), the distance over which the gradient extends (L), and the thermal conductivity (λ) measured in watts per meter per kelvin (W/m per K). Thermal conductivity is a specific

balance equation takes into consideration all of the routes through which thermal energy, abbreviated as H, can enter or exit the body:

$$H_{total} = \Delta H_{metabolism} + \Delta H_{conduction} + \Delta H_{convection} + \Delta H_{radiation} + \Delta H_{evaporation}$$

If the equation above sums to zero ($H_{total} = 0$), there will be no net change in the thermal energy of the animal and T_B will remain constant. If the flow of thermal energy into the animal exceeds the heat loss, T_B will increase. Each of these routes of thermal energy exchange depends on the thermal properties of the environment as well as the physical properties and physiology of the animal.

- **Conduction** is the transfer of thermal energy from one region of an object or fluid to another. Animals can be cooled when thermal energy is conducted

property of a material. Those objects we think of as *heat sinks* have high thermal conductivity. For example, an aluminum pot feels cold to the touch because it has a high thermal conductivity (210 W/m per K) and readily draws heat from your hand. Similarly, 5°C water feels cooler than 5°C air because water has a thermal conductivity that is 25-fold higher than air (0.58 versus 0.024 W/m per K). Because water has more molecules per unit volume, there is a greater likelihood of a molecular collision that results in a transfer of energy.

The Fourier equation describes how thermal energy moves in a very simple system: heat transfer in a single dimension (from the heat source to heat sink) in a single uniform material. These same parameters (λ, ΔT, and L) apply in thermal biology, but animals are much more complex systems. Consider the influence of **thermal conductance**. Heat is conducted from the internal tissues, through other tissues and fluids, and to the external surroundings, each with a characteristic thermal conductivity (Table 15.1). The body surface layers may possess insulation that reduces conductive heat transfer. Insulation, such as fur and feathers, also increases the distance between the hottest point near the skin and the coldest point in the bulk phase.

Calculations of heat flux are complicated by the geometry of the environment and the animal. Heat does not move from your body through a one-dimensional cylinder of air extending from your skin, but rather is conducted in multiple dimensions from the source. Animal geometry also plays a role. A long, thin animal produces as much heat as a short, round animal of the same mass, but the differences in surface area affect heat exchange. Because conductive heat losses occur across the external surfaces, an animal can alter conductive heat exchange by engaging in activities that alter its effective surface area. For example, a penguin reduces heat loss from the foot by rolling back on its heels, using its tail feathers for balance. Because its tail feathers are less conductive than its feet, less heat is lost. Figure 15.3 shows a snake simultaneously exchanging heat with multiple surfaces. It loses heat via conduction across its upper surface while also exchanging heat through its lower surface in contact with the rock.

Convective heat exchange depends on fluid movements

Imagine yourself immersed in a pool of water that is 10°C colder than your body. Almost immediately, your body begins to lose thermal energy as it warms the water in the boundary layer by almost 10°C. Once the boundary layer is warmed, thermal energy is slowly conducted to the bulk phase of the water. When the heat exchanges reach steady state, the body loses thermal energy at the rate required to rewarm this boundary layer that slowly cools as it dissipates its thermal energy outward to the bulk phase. Much less energy is required to rewarm the boundary layer under these steady-state conditions than was required to heat the boundary layer in the first place. Now consider how the gradients change when fluid is flowing over the body. The body rapidly loses thermal energy warming a boundary layer that is immediately replaced by another, colder boundary layer. Heat lost to a moving fluid, either air or water, is *convective heat loss*. The rate of convective heat loss depends on the thermal gradient between the surface and the fluid, the rate of flow of the fluid over the surface, and its conductivity.

Radiant energy warms some animals

In the natural world, the most important source of radiant heat is the sun. Photons from the sun excite the molecules in the atmosphere, the soil, and the water, warming them by radiant heat. Thus, when animals are warmed by conduction from air, water, or soil, the ultimate source of the heat is radiant energy. But animals can also be warmed directly by solar radiation, which many species accentuate by the behavior known as basking. White body coloration reflects photons in the visible range, and dark coloration absorbs the photons within this range of wavelengths. Animals that bask to warm themselves often possess high levels of black or brown pigments to help absorb thermal energy. As a result of diversity in color, animals in the same area can have markedly different temperatures (Figure 15.4).

In terrestrial systems, the ground warms during the day and then becomes an important source of thermal energy in the form of conduction and radiant heat when the sun sets. Animals also lose thermal energy when they emit radiant heat. Thus, radiant heat may be a net gain or net loss from animals. The relationship that describes radiation from a warm animal is described by the Stefan-Boltzmann equation:

$$P = Ae\delta(T_B^4\ T_A^4)$$

where P is the radiating power, A is its surface area, e is the ability of the object to emit radiation, δ is the Stefan constant, and T the temperature of the body (T_B) or surroundings (T_A)

Table 15.1	Thermal conductivity of materials
Material	**Thermal Conductivity (W/m per K)**
Air	0.02
Snow	0.10
Water	0.59
Rock	1–3
Ice	2.1
Muscle	0.5
Fat	0.2

FIGURE 15.4 Heterogeneity of T_B in the intertidal zone

Infrared photography can be used to compare the body temperature (T_B) of animals. In this image, the mussels are warmer than the starfish because they are better at absorbing radiant energy. The starfish, with its greater surface area, may also be affected more by evaporative cooling.

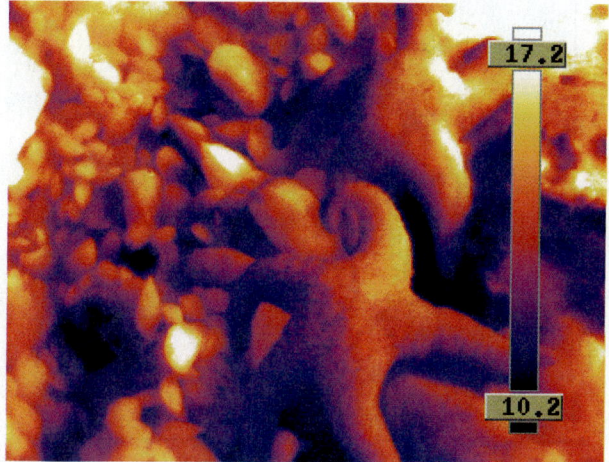

Photo source: Photo by Brian Helmuth, Northeastern University.

in kelvins. Animals can influence their radiant heat loss through changing the nature of the surface (*e*) and the surface area (*A*).

Evaporation induces heat losses

Evaporative cooling arises when fluids draw thermal energy from the body surface as the water molecules make the transition from liquid to vapor. The magnitude of the heat loss depends on the volume of water and its heat of vaporization. It requires more energy to evaporate water from salty sweat than from pure water because the solutes increase the heat of vaporization of water. The efficiency of evaporative cooling also depends on the partial pressure of water vapor in the air. If the air has high humidity, then the water is less likely to evaporate.

Sweating is only one of the ways that animals employ evaporative cooling. When a hippopotamus rolls in the mud of a wet riverbank, the cool mud draws heat from the body (conduction). This is an effective cooling strategy even if the mud is warm: thermal energy is absorbed from the body as the mud dries. Other animals cover their body surfaces with water, such as an elephant that sprays water onto its back or birds that splash in a pool of water. Wet feathers also have a diminished insulatory capacity, allowing more metabolic heat to be lost. Birds that live in hot environments may soak the belly before returning to the nest, allowing the eggs to benefit from evaporative cooling. Kangaroos, which do not produce sweat, lick well-vascularized skin surfaces, which then cool as the saliva evaporates.

Not all evaporative cooling is positive. As discussed in Chapter 13, desert animals must balance the challenges of water balance with the benefits that would accrue from evaporative cooling. Reliance on sweating would enhance dehydration. When semiaquatic animals leave the water, they are typically left with wet body surfaces, causing body temperature to decrease due to evaporative cooling.

Ratio of surface area to volume affects heat flux

The ratio of surface area to volume (see Figure 11.5) can influence all aspects of the heat exchange equation: conduction, convection, radiation, and evaporation. Variation in the ratio is important in several contexts. A given animal may alter its exposed surface area to change heat flux. Dogs stretch out when hot to maximize conductive heat loss to the ground, but roll up when cold to minimize conductive heat loss to the air. Ratios of surface area to volume also come into play when comparing animals of different body dimensions or body mass.

The significance of body size, or more precisely, the ratio of surface area to mass, is apparent in many comparisons. An arctic wolf is about one-tenth the mass of a grizzly bear, but it has twice the ratio of surface area to volume. Although they live in similar niches, the arctic wolf incurs greater thermoregulatory costs because of its size. Similarly, a growing animal increases its body mass faster than its surface area. In general, larger animals lose heat more slowly and retain heat better than do small animals. The effects of body size and shape also manifest themselves in animal evolution. *Bergmann's rule* states that animals living in cold environments tend to be larger than animals in warmer environments. *Allen's rule* states that animals in colder climates tend to have shorter extremities than animals in warmer climates. Thus, mammals or birds living in polar regions or high altitudes tend to be larger and shorter legged than individuals of the same species from more temperate regions. These rules of ecogeography apply to most of the mammals and birds studied to date, but have little relevance to animals that allow T_B to change.

An animal regulates heat exchange by altering the posture of the body to minimize or maximize the exposed surface area. Pythons will roll into a ball to conserve metabolic heat during digestion. When the python, approximately cylindrical in shape, rolls into a ball, its externally exposed surface area decreases by about 85 percent, greatly reducing heat loss.

Animals can also reduce effective surface area by huddling with other animals. Naked mole rats (Figure 15.5) live in burrows at relatively constant temperatures and have a very limited ability to use metabolism to control their body temperature. If housed in groups, they huddle when

FIGURE 15.5   Naked mole rats

Photo source: Science Source.

FIGURE 15.6   Insulation

There is a direct relationship between the thickness of fur and its ability to act as insulation.

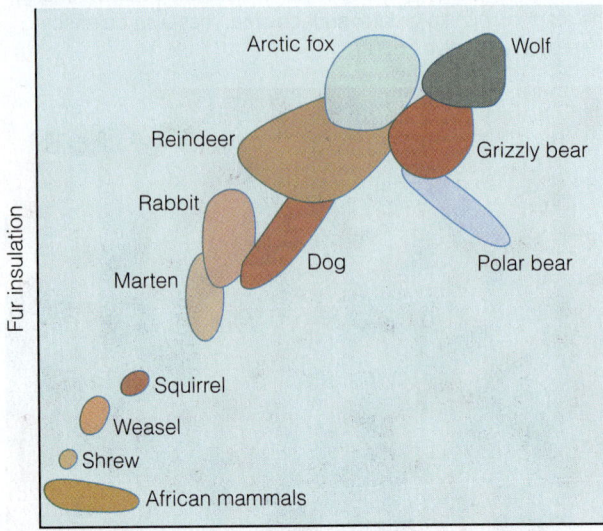

Figure source: Republished with permission of Oxford: Blackwell Science, from *Environmental Physiology of Animals*, Willmer, P., G. Stone, and I. A. Johnston, p. 212, © 2000; permission conveyed through Copyright Clearance Center, Inc.

temperatures drop below about 22°C. This allows them to maintain a relatively constant T_B near 22°C. However, a solitary naked mole rat is unable to defend its T_B at low T_A. When prevented from huddling, its T_B closely reflects T_A, decreasing to as low as 12°C. From the perspective of the individual animal, huddling reduces heat by increasing T_A, replacing cold air with a warm neighbor. From the perspective of the colony, huddling works as a thermoregulatory strategy by reducing ratios of surface area to volume.

Insulation reduces thermal exchange

Internal and external insulation also reduce heat losses by increasing the distance over which a thermal gradient extends (the L in the Fourier equation). Marine mammals have a thick layer of adipose tissue under the skin in the form of blubber. This lipid layer disrupts the flow of thermal energy from the core to the external surface of the animal. More commonly, animals use external insulation to reduce heat loss. Fur and feathers restrict the movement of molecules between the surface of the animal and the bulk phase of the environment. Heat is lost from the animal in proportion to the thermal gradient (T) at the surface of the animal. Molecules of air or water in the insulation layer are warmed by the animal and then trapped within the insulation. The overall temperature gradient from the skin to the bulk phase is the same, but the distance is greater and the animal loses less heat to conduction. The fur also impedes the flow of fluids over the surface of the skin, so there is less convective heat loss.

The effectiveness of insulation depends on its thickness. When faced with cold temperatures, birds (or mammals) can change the orientation of the feathers (or fur) to alter the volume of air trapped within the coat. Similarly, animals that live in colder environments have thicker coats with greater insulating capacity (Figure 15.6). Some species change the

thickness of the external insulation seasonally. Thick coats are a thermoregulatory burden in the warm season, so it is beneficial to shed fur in spring. Because much of hair is composed of dead cells, the cost of rebuilding the coat when temperatures cool is minor in comparison with the metabolic costs the animal would incur trying to cool itself using physiological mechanisms. Mammals alter the nature of their fur coat seasonally, producing a greater density of hairs. Some birds, such as the ptarmigan, produce specialized feathers with an additional shaft to increase the feather density.

CONCEPT CHECK

1. What are the sources and sinks in an equation describing thermal balance?

2. How does insulation reduce heat loss?

3. Why might intertidal animals in the same microenvironment differ in T_B?

Thermal Strategies

There are many remarkable stories in the realm of thermal physiology, with species that are capable of tolerating extreme and rapidly changing temperatures. Consider the deep-sea vent animals discussed in the Chapter 14 opening essay. Some vent dwellers live on the edge of undersea volcanoes, and experience near-instantaneous changes in water temperatures, ranging from superheated vent water to frigid deep-sea water. More familiar may be the temperate zone animals that cope with seasonal changes, and desert animals that survive daily fluctuations. Invertebrates are the most thermotolerant animals in each thermal niche. The hottest deserts are populated by myriads of insects, but only a few vertebrates. Invertebrates can also tolerate the coldest temperatures, often by entering an inactive, dormant state. Once stabilized in this state of "suspended animation," they can survive temperatures far colder than even the coldest natural environments. In contrast, only a few vertebrates, such as the wood frog, can survive subzero body temperatures, frozen in underground refuges.

To understand the distinctions between the various thermal strategies, we begin by distinguishing them using two complementary criteria: the degree of T_B stability and the source of heat (Figure 15.7). The terms *poikilothermy* and *homeothermy* distinguish animals on the stability of their body temperature. *Endothermy* and *ectothermy* distinguish animals on the source of the heat that determines T_B. In the following sections, we explain these terms in more detail, and discuss the many animals that make even these simple distinctions a challenge.

Poikilotherms and homeotherms differ in the stability of T_B

A **poikilotherm** is an animal with a variable T_B—one that varies in response to environmental conditions. A **homeotherm**, in contrast, is an animal with a relatively constant T_B. The distinction between poikilotherm and homeotherm depends on both the properties of the animal and the nature of the environment.

FIGURE 15.7 Thermal strategies

Most animals can be classified as homeothermic endotherms (red) or poikilothermic ectotherms (blue), but there are many exceptions discussed in more detail in the accompanying text.

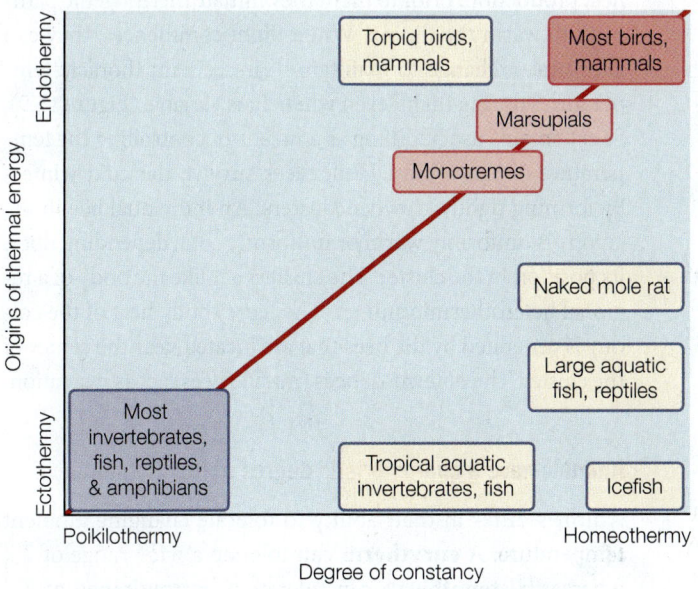

A homeothermic species has a near constant T_B, but the category does not distinguish between a species that achieves constancy through physiological processes versus other means. For example, many Antarctic fish live in waters that are invariably cold and die if subjected to even slightly warmer temperatures. Though fish in general are poikilotherms, these species are fairly defined as homeotherms. In contrast, most eutherian mammals are homeotherms, yet the naked mole rat (see Figure 15.5) allows T_B to change with T_A, and could be considered poikilothermic; it maintains T_B relatively constant by living in underground colonies where T_A changes little. Marsupials and monotremes are considered more poikilothermic than eutherians because they allow T_B to vary over a wider range.

Ectotherms and endotherms differ in the source of body thermal energy

The terms *ectotherm* and *endotherm* distinguish animals by the physiological mechanisms that determine T_B. The environment determines the T_B of an **ectotherm**. An **endotherm** is an animal that generates internal heat to maintain a high T_B. Figure 15.7 provides some examples of animals categorized on the basis of the mechanism that determines T_B.

Both this and the preceding approach to classifying thermal strategies works effectively for most animals. Most birds and mammals can be classified as homeotherms, because T_B is stable, and also as endotherms, because metabolic heat elevates T_B. Most reptiles, amphibians, fish, and invertebrates are poikilotherms, because T_B is variable, and also ectotherms, because the external conditions determine T_B. However, each group of organisms has exceptions. Polar icefish are homeothermic ectotherms; T_B is constant but determined by T_A. Large aquatic ectotherms, such as sea turtles and basking sharks, lack specific metabolic adaptations for heating, but remain warmer than the water by using a favorable surface area-to-volume ratio to retain metabolic heat. As discussed in the next section, there are also exceptions that arise when animals periodically deviate from their normal conditions (*temporal heterotherms*) or keep different parts of the body warmer than T_A (*regional heterotherms*).

Heterotherms exhibit temporal or regional endothermy

Just how constant does T_B have to be for an animal to be considered a homeotherm? In actuality, most animals experience some variation in temperature, either spatially or temporally. Many endothermic animals place greater priority on maintaining certain anatomical regions within very narrow thermal ranges. Typically, homeotherms maintain the central nervous system and internal organs at a more constant temperature, while allowing the periphery to vary. The temperature of these deep, internal regions is often called the *core temperature*. Humans, for example, maintain a near-constant core temperature. However, regions of the human body can experience temperatures much lower than the core T_B. In the cold, humans change blood flow to allow hands and feet to cool to conserve internal heat. Males alter the position of the scrotum to keep spermatogenic tissue from overheating. However, human core T_B can also change under some circumstances. T_B can change in females during the reproductive cycle. It can rise several degrees as a result of a fever. In comparison with other animals, these are relatively minor regional and temporal differences in T_B, and a human is considered an endothermic homeotherm.

In contrast to humans, many other mammals and some birds can undergo dramatic, prolonged changes in T_B. When exposed to cold nighttime temperatures, T_B may decrease by several degrees (Figure 15.8). Hibernating mammals, such as ground squirrels and bats, allow T_B to drop for the winter months. Although these animals allow their bodies to cool, they are still considered endotherms because they produce and retain metabolic heat to maintain T_B above T_A. However, these endothermic animals are more precisely described as **temporal heterotherms**, to reflect the variability in T_B over time. Some ectothermic animals also fit the description of temporal heterotherms. Many large snakes, such as pythons, wind their bodies into a ball after they have ingested their prey. This helps the snake retain the metabolic heat produced by digestion. Temporal **heterothermy** is a strategy that has different benefits for endotherms and ectotherms. It allows an endotherm to conserve energy in cold temperatures by reducing the costs of thermoregulation. It provides an ectotherm with a period of accelerated metabolism to speed digestion, nutrient assimilation, and biosynthesis.

Most ectotherms rapidly lose their metabolic heat to the environment, and consequently cannot elevate T_B much above T_A. However, a **regional heterotherm** can retain heat in certain regions of the body. Billfish, such as marlin and swordfish, are ectotherms but are also able to warm specific regions of the body. Their heater organs produce enough heat near the eye and optic nerves to improve visual clarity when they swim deep into cold waters (see Chapter 6). Large pelagic fish possess countercurrent heat exchangers to conserve the heat of digestion within the body core (see Chapter 14). Tuna and lamnid sharks are able to retain myogenic heat within the muscle. Warming of the red muscle increases metabolic capacity and may improve contractile performance during swimming (see Chapter 12). Thermal gradients occur within the bodies of many animals, but these regional heterotherms have specific physiological mechanisms to produce and retain heat regionally.

Although most insects are ectotherms, some species are regional heterotherms, others temporal heterotherms, and some species are both, depending on the time of year. The largest of flying insects, such as bumblebees, large moths, and cicadas, have a very high metabolic rate in the flight muscles. Thoracic temperature in a large flying insect can increase by more than 10°C, even while other regions of the body remain near T_A. Interestingly, these animals are also able to modulate heat production. Prior to flight they initiate thermogenic pathways to warm the thorax. When flight commences, they can alter heat exchange to maintain near-constant thoracic temperatures during flight, even when T_A is variable (Figure 15.9). Social insects use huddling as a means of controlling the temperature of the colony. Honeybees survive the cold winters by forming tightly crowded clusters. An individual bee in the colony is uniformly warm or uniformly cold, depending upon its position in the cluster. The clusters act like the body of a regional heterothermic animal. The "core" body heat of the colony is generated by the bees that are located near the center of the cluster. The outermost bees (mantle bees) act as insulation.

Animals have a characteristic degree of thermotolerance

Animals differ in their ability to tolerate changing ambient temperature. A **eurytherm** can tolerate a wide range of T_A, whereas a **stenotherm** can tolerate a narrow range of T_A.

FIGURE 15.8 **Short-term cooling in birds**

Many temperate birds, such as the willow tit (*Parus montanus*), allow T_B to decrease when nighttime temperatures decrease. In this experiment, the birds were held at one of three temperatures, each maintained constantly throughout the night. This strategy of temporal heterothermy saves metabolic energy.

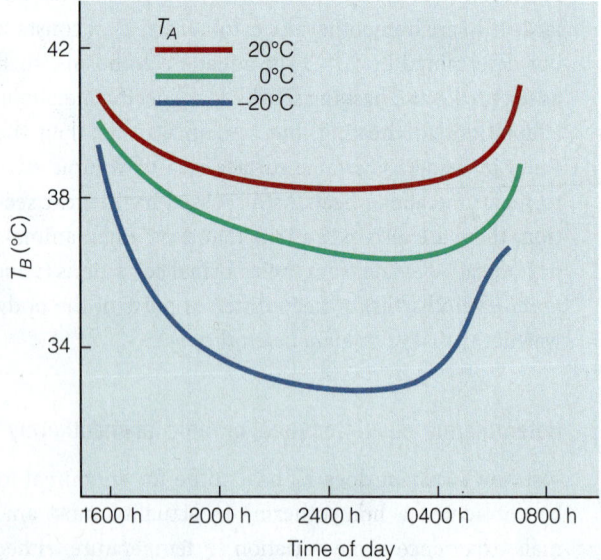

Figure source: Adapted from Different metabolic strategies of northern birds for nocturnal survival. Journal of Comparative Physiology, Part B: Biochemical, Systemic, and Environmental Physiology 156: 655–663, Reinertsen, R.E., & Haftorn, S. (1986). Figure 1a. With permission of Springer Science + Business Media.

FIGURE 15.9 Insect heterotherms

Many large insects are able to conserve metabolic heat that arises when their flight muscles are activated during flight. This warms the thorax while the rest of the body remains near ambient temperature, an example of regional heterothermy.

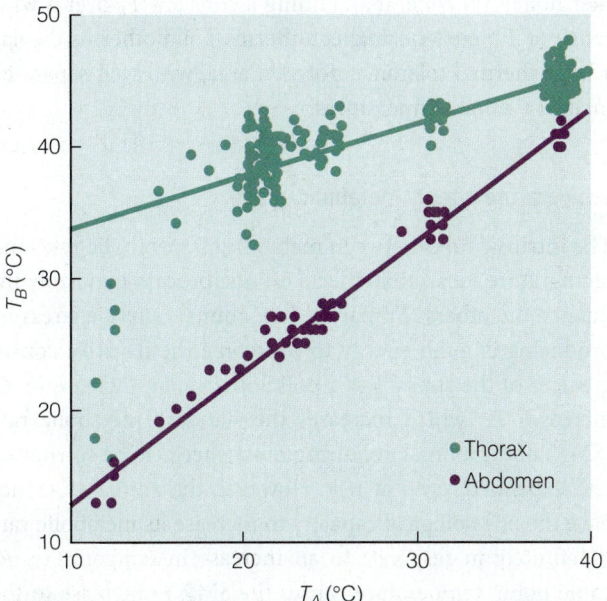

Figure source: From Harrison, J. F., Fewell, J. H., Roberts, S. P., & Hall, H. G. (1996). Figure 2 (p. 89) from Achievement of thermal stability by varying metabolic heat production in flying honeybees. *Science, 274,* 88–90. Reprinted with permission from AAAS.

FIGURE 15.10 Zones of thermal effects of a resting homeotherm

Homeothermic endotherms maintain near-constant body temperature over a wide range of ambient temperatures (purple line). Once ambient temperatures decrease below the lower critical temperature (LCT), the animal must increase its metabolic rate (MR) to generate heat to help maintain a constant T_B. By extending the line explaining the metabolic rate below LCT to the x-axis, the body temperature (T_B) can be obtained as the intercept. Below a certain point, the animal can no longer maintain a constant core temperature and hypothermia results. When ambient temperatures increase past the upper critical temperature (UCT), the animal increases metabolic rate to shed heat. At still higher temperatures, the animal can no longer defend its body temperature and hyperthermia results.

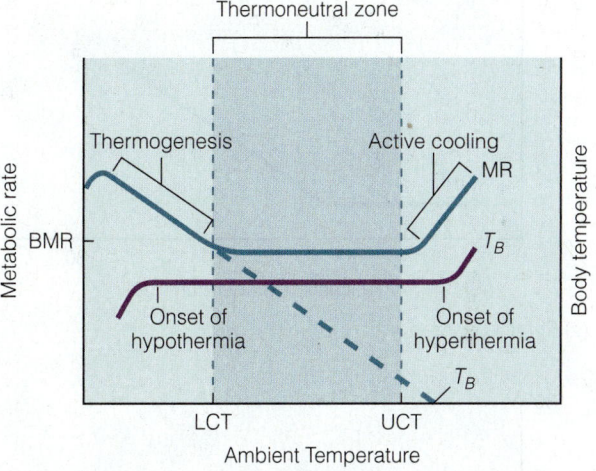

These categories apply to animals regardless of whether they are ectotherms or endotherms.

Physiological strategies for coping with temperature differ in ectotherms and endotherms. For ectotherms, a change in T_A alters T_B and directly changes the rates of many biological processes. In contrast, an endotherm responds to a change in T_A by inducing a compensatory regulatory response. Despite the differences, both endotherms and ectotherms incur physiological costs and consequences when environmental conditions change.

The effects of temperature can be defined in terms of its impact on animal function. An animal typically spends most of its life in a range of temperatures that is optimal for physiological processes. The **thermoneutral zone** of a resting homeothermic endotherm is the range of ambient temperatures where metabolic rate is minimal, which is considered the basal metabolic rate, or BMR (Figure 15.10). If temperatures rise to a point called the **upper critical temperature** (UCT), the metabolic rate rises as the animal induces a physiological response to prevent overheating. If the temperature falls below a **lower critical temperature** (LCT), the metabolic rate rises to increase heat production. For many animals, the T_B can be predicted from the extrapolation of the line that describes the metabolic rate at temperatures below LCT. When faced with a hypothermic challenge, animals

may reduce T_B to maintain homeostasis at metabolic rate. In general, these compensatory responses at high T_A or low T_A allow the animal to maintain a constant T_B, but beyond a point, the animal cannot sustain a constant T_B.

The concept of a thermoneutral zone does not apply to animals that alter T_B, but ectotherms also have ranges of T_A (and T_B) within which growth and reproduction are optimal. Animals actively seek out their *preferred temperature*, a T_A that is within its range for optimal function. At low temperatures, all developmental processes slow because the lower T_A reduces the rate of metabolic reactions. Higher temperatures damage molecules, cells, and tissues, jeopardizing an animal's health. Researchers can assess the thermal tolerance of an ectotherm or a poikilotherm by transferring an animal from its acclimation temperature to a new temperature and assessing survival. The *incipient lethal temperature* is the temperature that has a 50 percent probability of killing the animal within an identified period. The range of tolerance is the difference between the **incipient upper lethal temperature** (IULT) and the **incipient lower lethal temperature** (ILLT) (Figure 15.11).

For ectotherms and poikilotherms, the ability to tolerate temperature changes with thermal history. Many temperate

FIGURE 15.11 **Temperature polygon**

Acclimation affects the incipient upper lethal temperature (IULT) and incipient lower lethal temperature (ILLT) for ectotherms and poikilotherms. The tolerance of an animal is reflected in the area of the polygon created by joining the upper line (IULT, in red) and the lower line (ILLT, in blue). Analysis of a eurythermal fish **(a)** yields a larger polygon than that of a stenothermal fish **(b)**.

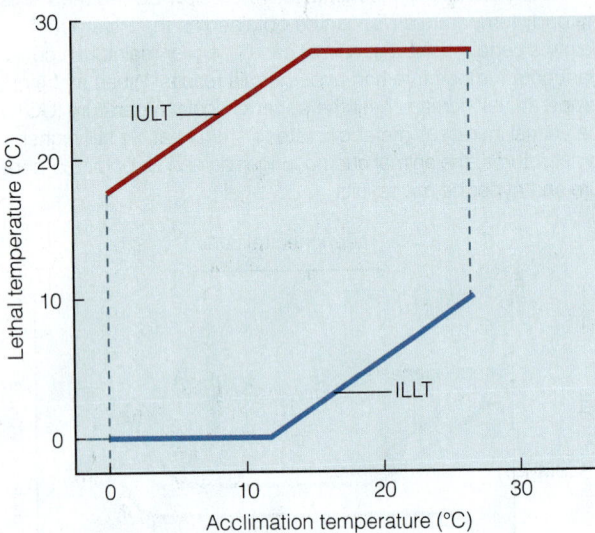

(a) Eurythermal fish

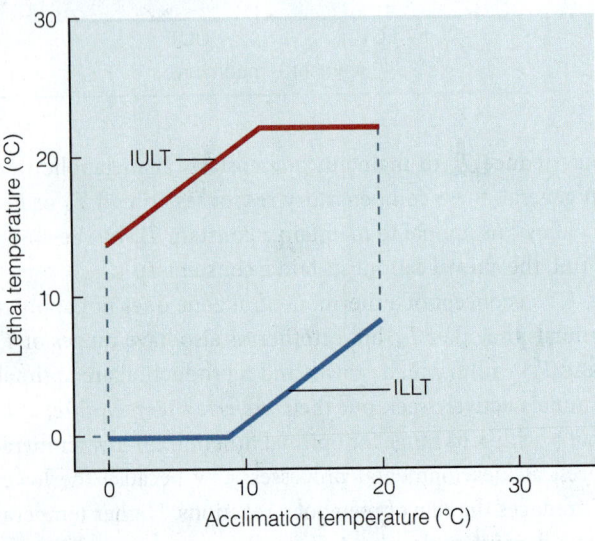

(b) Stenothermal fish

zone animals remodel their cells, tissues, and systems to alter their sensitivity to temperature. Whether responding to temperature (thermal acclimation) or the more complex seasonal changes (seasonal acclimatization), the remodeling response makes the animal better able to cope with the effects of temperature. The impact of thermal history can also be seen in Figure 15.11, where acclimation to a high temperature tends to increase both the ULLT and ILLT. Likewise, acclimation to a low temperature reduces the upper and lower lethal

temperature points. The physiological remodeling in response to temperature may include modifications of cellular features, such as the nature of membranes and levels of critical enzymes, or tissue properties, such as gill surface area.

Eurythermal endotherms/homeotherms possess a wide thermoneutral zone, maintaining a constant T_B over a wide range of T_A; eurythermal ectotherms/poikilotherms display a large thermal tolerance polygon area, with well-separated incipient lethal temperatures.

Temperature affects metabolic scope

The intrinsic links between metabolism, metabolic rate, and temperature mean that effects on one process inevitably influence the others. In many cases, animals survive stress by producing enough energy to overcome the negative consequences of the stress. For a poikilotherm, an increase in T_A increases T_B, which increases the standard metabolic rate (SMR) of the animal, requiring more energy to be consumed and expended, even at rest. However, the animal does not have the physiological capacity to increase its metabolic rate indefinitely in response to an increase in temperature. At some point, temperature causes the SMR to increase to the maximal metabolic rate (MMR), and such an animal would not be able to generate enough energy to do anything more than just survive.

This relationship is articulated in the **oxygen- and capacity-limitation of thermal tolerance** hypothesis (OCLTT). Consider the plight of a poikilothermic animal that experiences an increase in environmental warming (Figure 15.12). Its SMR increases with environmental temperature. The maximal metabolic rate increases likewise, but at some point, called the **pejus temperature** (T_p) the maximal physiological capacity declines as systems deteriorate or fail to meet metabolic demands. At the critical temperature (T_c), the rise in SMR equals the MMR, and the animal has no scope for aerobic activity.

These threshold points are distinct from the incipient lethal temperatures shown in Figure 15.11; the animal dies when it exceeds the IULT or ILLT. In contrast, the OCLTT hypothesis deals with long-term survival of organisms. Short-term deficits in aerobic demand can be met by anaerobic pathways; however, the animal is unable to grow or survive over the long term.

The evolution of thermal tolerance has complex origins

Differences in thermotolerance can be observed in comparisons of populations or species that have evolved in regions separated by latitude, altitude, or other forms of thermal gradients. The ability of an animal to tolerate a lower T_A than its competitor allows the tolerant animal to expand into a

FIGURE 15.12 Oxygen- and capacity-limitation of thermal tolerance

As ambient temperature increases, a poikilotherm experiences increases in standard metabolic rate (SMR) and maximal metabolic rate (MMR). At the pejus temperature (T_p), the MMR begins to decline, eventually reaching the SMR. The upper and lower temperatures beyond which the animal has no aerobic scope are identified as the critical temperatures (T_c).

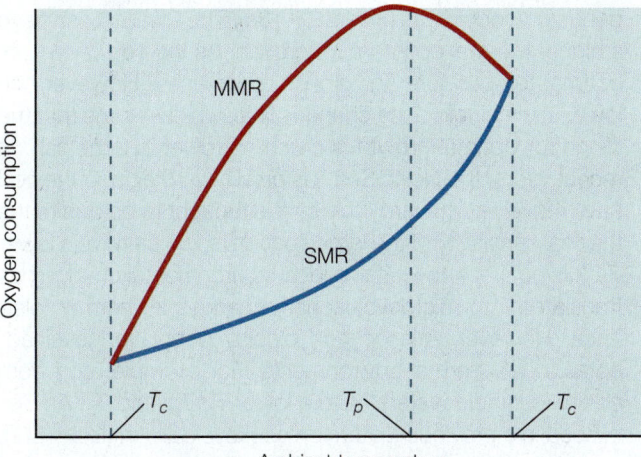

colder environmental niche. Many closely related animals have distinct differences in thermal preferences that contribute to their geographical distributions. Latitudinal patterns are common in both marine and freshwater fish species. Closely related species of barracuda, for example, live at specific latitudes along the Pacific coast with a characteristic average T_A. From north to south, one species gradually replaces another once the average water temperature changes by only 3–8°C. There are also altitudinal patterns seen with terrestrial animals. Many bird species exist in high-altitude and low-altitude populations, each with physiological specializations and morphological differences. The thermal environment resulting from the combination of altitude and latitude also determines the range of many amphibians. Andean tree frogs (*Hyla andina*) can be found at low elevation far from the equator, but closer to the equator they can live at higher altitudes.

The genetic basis of a difference in thermotolerance is not always clear. We can often determine why levels or properties of a single protein differ in two animals in relation to temperature. However, the underlying basis for intricate differences in thermal physiology is more complex. For example, two species of Siberian hamsters, *Phodopus campbelli* and *P. sungorus*, differ in thermal biology in terms of morphology, insulation, behavior, and physiology. Although these are very closely related species, they last shared a common ancestor more than 2 million years ago. A complex trait such as fur density depends on multiple genes, many cell types, and networks of genetic regulators. Furthermore,

the two species may have many genetic differences, but only some of these may influence their thermal biology.

An understanding of the physiological basis of thermotolerance is vital to predicting the effects of global environmental change. In Box 15.1: Applications: Thermal Tolerance and Conservation Biology of Atlantic Cod, we discuss how recent changes in water temperature have influenced populations of Atlantic cod.

CONCEPT CHECK

4. What is the difference between an endotherm and an ectotherm?
5. What is the difference between a homeotherm and a poikilotherm?
6. What is the difference between a regional and a temporal heterotherm?

COPING WITH A CHANGING BODY TEMPERATURE

Although many ectotherms and poikilotherms live in thermally stable environments—underground burrows, tropical rainforests, the deep sea, or a homeotherm's intestine—others must cope with frequent and dramatic changes in T_B. Because of the effects of temperature on macromolecular function and metabolism, ectotherms and poikilotherms must either tolerate or compensate for the complex, often deleterious, effects of changing temperature.

Macromolecular Structure and Metabolism

Of the four classes of macromolecules, only proteins and lipids are substantially affected by temperature over the normal range encountered by animals. Weak bonds (van der Waals forces, hydrogen bonds, and hydrophobic interactions) govern the interactions within and between these macromolecules. Each type of bond has a characteristic response to temperature. Whereas hydrogen bonds and van der Waals forces are disrupted at high temperature, hydrophobic interactions are stabilized at high temperature. Thus, the effects of temperature on macromolecular structures depend on the relative importance of each type of bond.

Animals can remodel membrane fluidity

In Chapter 3, we discussed the structure of cellular membranes and the importance of membrane fluidity. Van der Waals forces hold membrane lipids together. Although the interactions between phospholipids are strong, the membrane must also remain fluid enough to allow proteins to rotate and diffuse laterally within the membrane. Low temperatures cause membrane lipids to solidify, which impairs

THERMAL TOLERANCE AND CONSERVATION BIOLOGY OF ATLANTIC COD

Fish have proven to be a useful model for exploring the potential impact of global environmental change on organisms. Animals in a constant or predictable environment often evolve physiological traits that make them well suited to that environment. As the environment changes, animals are faced with a physiological challenge. As individuals they can survive using physiological responses, and within a population there will be individuals that are better able to tolerate the environmental stressor. If the environmental change is sustained, it is likely that the nature of the population changes. Though dramatic environmental change is possible on a local scale, in most cases the rate of change is sufficiently slow to permit evolution of populations. When the rate is too rapid, populations can become extinct. Global warming is an unusual environmental stressor because it is happening relatively quickly and on a massive scale. In many cases the success or failure of populations can be traced back to physiological properties. In the case of thermal stress, there is growing evidence that survival at high temperatures depends on cardiovascular (supply) limitations. These physiological traits, in turn, influence the natural ranges of animals.

The Atlantic cod (*Gadus morhua*) has a thermal optimum (T_o) of about 5°C, with pejus temperatures (T_p) of 2°C and 7°C. Recall that the T_p is the temperature beyond which the physiology of the animal deteriorates. The North Sea population of this species is able to tolerate temperatures as high as 16°C. Beyond this critical temperature (T_c), the oxygen tension of the venous blood drops dramatically, and heart rate becomes irregular.

The optimum temperature for growth in cod also depends on body mass (Figure 15.13a). The smallest fish have a higher thermal optimum for growth. As the cod grows, its optimal temperature (for growth) decreases. However, the lower thermal tolerance changes little, which means that the range for optimal growth is much narrower in large fish. In recent years, the North Sea has grown warmer, and the cod have moved northward. This shift is thought to be due to the thermal sensitivity of the large spawners, which have a lower T_o. It is not yet known if this local environmental change has translated into microevolutionary changes in thermal tolerance. However, Atlantic cod display population-level adaptation for thermal environments. For example, cod from cooler Icelandic waters have a lower T_o, T_p, and T_c. As discussed in a previous feature on sockeye salmon (Box 12.2), the underlying constraint that limits thermal tolerance may be related to the cardiorespiratory system.

References

- Perry, A. L., Low, P. J., Ellis, J. R., & Reynolds, J. D. (2005). Climate change and distribution shifts in marine fishes. *Science, 308*, 1902–1905.
- Pörtner, H. O., & Knust, R. (2007). Climate change affects marine fishes through the oxygen limitation of thermal tolerance. *Science, 315*, 95–97.
- Pörtner, H. O., Bock, C., Knust, R., Lannig, G., Lucassen, M., Mark, F. C., & Sartoris, F. J. (2008). Cod and climate in a latitudinal cline: Physiological analyses of climate effects in marine fishes. *Climate Research, 37*, 253–270.
- Pörtner, H. O., Schulte, P. M., Wood, C. M., & Schiemer, F. (2010). Niche dimensions in fishes: An integrative view. *Physiological Biochemical Zoology, 83*, 808–826.

FIGURE 15.13 **Thermal optima for cod growth**

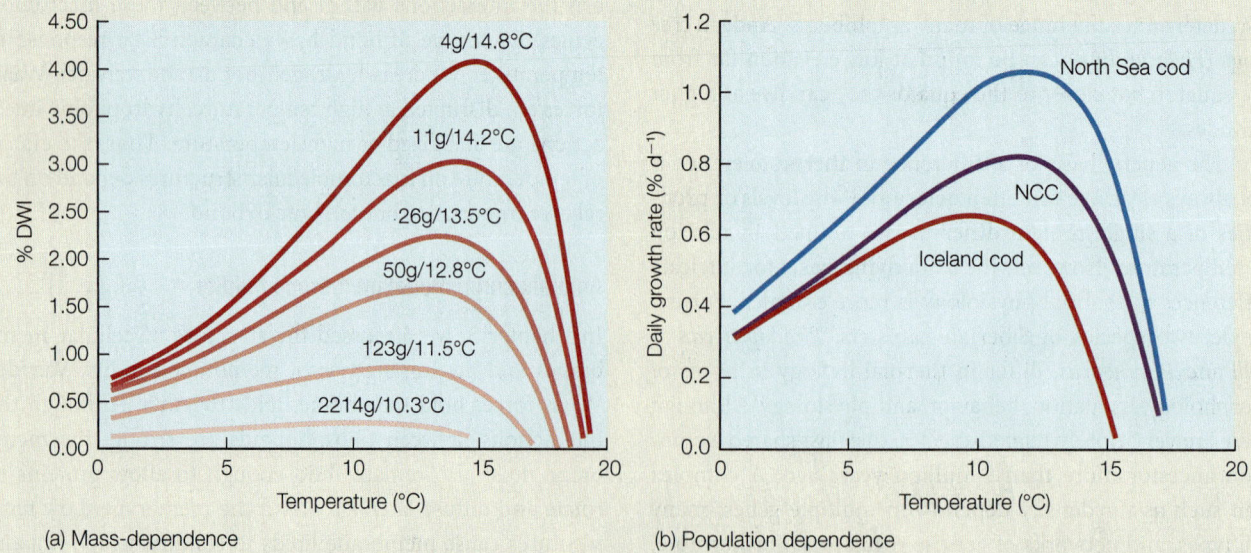

(a) Mass-dependence

(b) Population dependence

Figure source: Adapted from Pörtner, H. O., Bock, C., Knust, R., Lannig, G., Lucassen, M., Mark, F. C., & Sartoris, F. J. (2008). Cod and climate in a latitudinal cline: Physiological analyses of climate effects in marine fishes. *Climate Research, 37,* 253–270. Reprinted by permission from Inter-Research Science Center.

protein movement. Conversely, high temperatures liquefy the membrane, which can compromise its integrity and reduce its effectiveness as a permeability barrier. Cells regulate the balance between the solid *gel* state and the liquid *sol* state.

Ectothermic animals reduce the deleterious effects of temperature by changing the composition of their membranes. In this process, called **homeoviscous adaptation**, cells remodel membranes to preserve fluidity. Three mechanisms target phospholipids (Figure 15.14), and a fourth mechanism alters cholesterol content.

1. **Fatty acid chain length.** Phospholipids with short-chain fatty acids cannot form as many interactions with adjacent fatty acids and therefore are highly mobile. The effectiveness of chain shortening depends upon the fatty acid position on the phospholipid. Due to the three-dimensional structure of a phosphoglyceride, a short-chain fatty acid in position 1 makes a greater contribution to enhancing fluidity than does the same fatty acid in position 2.

2. **Saturation.** Double bonds create a kink in the fatty acid chain that prevents effective bond formation with other fatty acids. With fewer bonds between fatty acid chains, the membrane is more fluid. For example, pure stearic acid (C18:0) becomes liquid only at temperatures above 69°C, whereas oleic acid (C18:1) is liquid at 12°C. The position of the double bond is also critical. A double

bond near the midpoint of the fatty acid chain (as with oleic acid) is more effective than a double bond near the end of the fatty acid chain.

3. **Phospholipid classes.** The difference in the shape of the polar head groups alters the ability of the phospholipids to interact at the surface of the membrane. Phosphatidylcholine (PC) is more common in membranes of warm-acclimated cells, whereas phosphatidylethanolamine (PE) is more common in cold-acclimated cells. The ratio of PC to PE decreases in cold acclimation and adaptation.

4. **Cholesterol content.** A pure phospholipid bilayer is mostly fluid at high temperature and mostly solid at low temperature. Cholesterol has a dual effect that makes it useful in buffering thermal effects on membrane fluidity. Cholesterol in a fluid membrane tends to make it more stable by plugging spaces in between phospholipids, buffering against a loss of integrity at high temperatures. When cholesterol is in a fluid membrane that is being cooled, it disrupts the structure in a way that prevents the membrane from solidifying.

Cells use two general pathways to modify membrane composition in response to temperature: **in situ** modification and *de novo* synthesis. Both pathways require cells to modify the properties of the fatty acids within the fatty acid pool using suites of enzymes that elongate, shorten, saturate, and desaturate fatty acids. Because these enzymes begin with fatty acids derived from the diet, the nature of the diet also affects the profile of fatty acids within the membrane.

Enzymes alter the structure of individual phospholipids directly within the membrane (Figure 15.15). First, phospholipase A removes an acyl chain from membrane phospholipids to form a lysophospholipid. Next, lysophospholipid acyltransferase uses a more appropriate fatty acid (in the form of fatty acyl CoA) to rebuild the phospholipid.

More commonly, membranes are remodeled by endocytosis and exocytosis (see Figure 15.16). The old membrane is removed using endocytosis. Phospholipids are synthesized *de novo* within the endoplasmic reticulum, then packaged into vesicles that fuse with cellular membranes.

Animals remodel membranes to maintain near-constant fluidity

Membrane fluidity is measured in biological membranes using a dye (diphenyl hexatriene) that changes in optical properties in relation to its freedom to move within the membrane (Figure 15.17). When membranes from different species are compared, each exhibits a decrease in fluidity (measured as a change in optical properties) when the membrane is cooled. Taking into consideration the differences in thermal niche, this analysis shows that animals produce membranes that exhibit the same fluidity at the natural temperature. This

FIGURE 15.14 Phospholipid properties and membrane fluidity

Cells change the fluidity of membranes by altering the composition of membrane phospholipids.

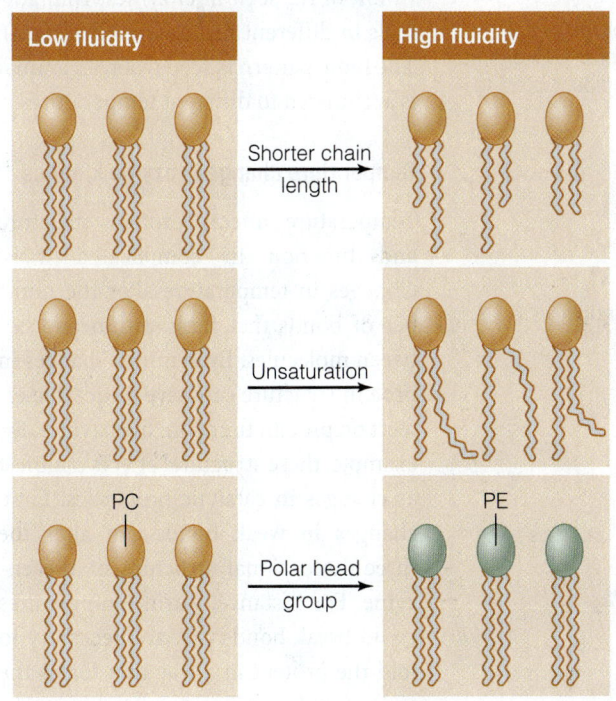

FIGURE 15.15 Phospholipid remodeling

Cells can remodel the phospholipids directly within membranes by removing a fatty acid. A phospholipid is rebuilt by lysophospholipid acyltransferase, which attaches another fatty acid produced by the cell. The fatty acid must first be activated by the esterification of coenzyme A.

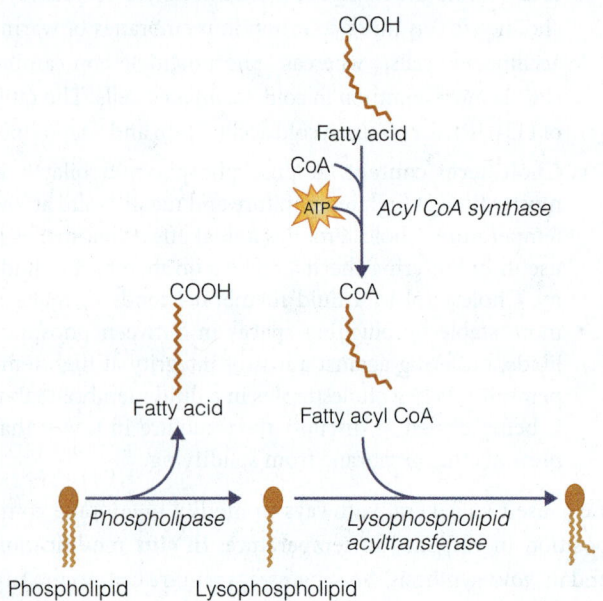

FIGURE 15.17 Conservation of membrane fluidity

Membranes are treated with a dye (diphenyl hexatriene) with optical properties that change in relation to membrane fluidity. Anisotropy is an optical property that reflects the ability of a dye to alter the behavior of plane polarized light. Anisotropy is inversely related to fluidity; at warmer temperatures, a decrease in anisotropy reflects an increase in fluidity. Animals that live in different environments produce membranes that possess a similar fluidity at their normal range of temperatures (indicated by the thickened portion of the lines).

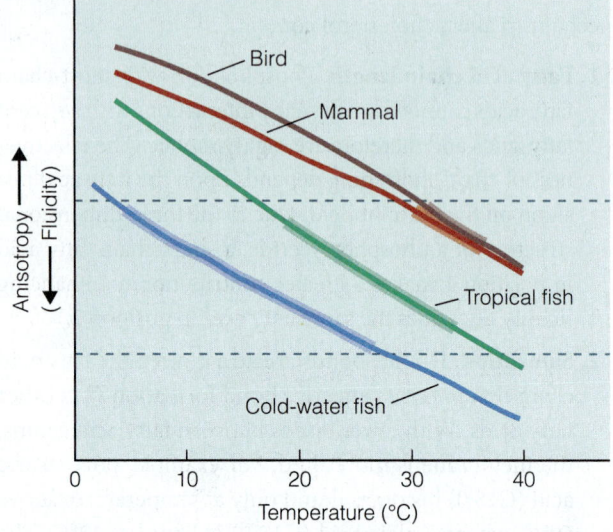

Figure source: Republished with permission of The Company of Biologists Ltd; Society of Experimental Biology (Great Britain), from Figure 1A from Lipid compositional correlates of temperature-adaptive interspecific differences in membrane physical structure. *Journal of Experimental Biology* 203: 2105–2015, Logue, J.A., de Vries, A.L., Fodor, E., & Cossins, A.R., © 2000; permission conveyed through Copyright Clearance Center, Inc.

FIGURE 15.16 Membrane remodeling

Cell membranes are constantly remodeled by endocytosis and exocytosis. When temperature decreases, the cell produces vesicles possessing phospholipids with fatty acids that are shorter and more unsaturated than those in the cell membrane. Over time, the cycles of endocytosis and exocytosis remove undesirable phospholipids, replacing them with more desirable phospholipids.

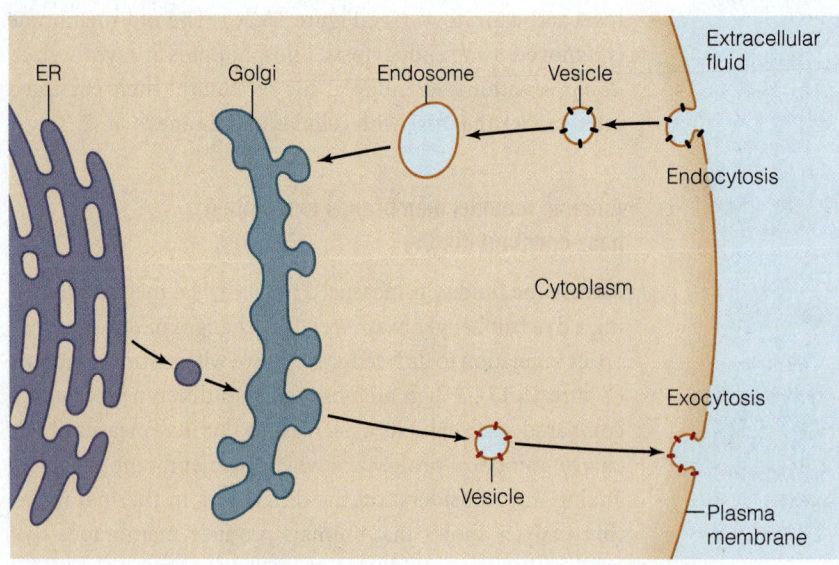

observation is analogous to the conservation of K_m seen in enzymes from animals in different niches (see Chapter 3). The same pattern is seen when an animal is acclimated to different temperatures.

Temperature changes enzyme kinetics

Temperature affects protein structure and function in complicated ways. Changes in temperature alter the number of bonds that form within and between molecules. Even minor changes in protein structure can have noticeable effects on protein function. In enzymes, for example, these structural effects manifest as changes in catalytic properties. First, changes in weak bonds can alter the three-dimensional structure of the enzyme. For instance, warm temperatures could break bonds that are necessary to fold the protein in a way that forms the active site. Second, temperature can alter the ionization state of critical amino acids within the active site. For instance, the amino acid histidine is important in many active sites, and changes in histidine protonation state can alter enzyme substrate affinity. Any increase or decrease in K_m could be disruptive. Third, temperature can alter the ability of the enzyme to undergo the structural changes necessary for catalysis. Enzymes must be rigid enough to maintain the proper conformation, but flexible enough to undertake conformational changes during catalysis. Thus, temperature can affect enzyme kinetics through effects on maximal velocity (V_{max}) or affinities for substrates (K_m), allosteric activators (K_a), and inhibitors (K_i). When animals experience a change in T_B, they may either tolerate the effects on enzyme kinetics or alter metabolic regulation to compensate.

Biochemical reactions are accelerated by higher temperature and reduced at lower temperature. The rate of a chemical reaction depends on the proportion of molecules within the system that possess energy equal to or greater than the activation energy (E_A). As temperature increases, the average kinetic energy of the substrates increases and a greater proportion of molecules has sufficient energy to be converted to products, causing the enzyme velocity to increase (see Figure 3.14). For most enzymes working over a biologically relevant range of temperatures, an increase of 10°C results in a two- to threefold increase in reaction velocity. Researchers express the effects of temperature on rates using an *Arrhenius plot* (see Box 15.2: Math in Physiology: Evaluating Thermal Effects on Physiological Processes Using Q_{10} and Arrhenius Plots).

Evolution may lead to changes in enzyme kinetics

When animals are exposed to suboptimal temperatures for generations, there is the possibility of evolutionary changes in the genes encoding enzymes. We draw again on research with LDH for examples of evolutionary changes that cause differences in enzyme kinetics as well as enzyme synthesis.

Mutations may lead to structural changes in the enzyme that impart a favorable difference in enzyme kinetics. As we learned in Chapter 3, lowering temperature increases the affinity of LDH for its substrate pyruvate (see Figure 3.43). Evolution has led to a fine-tuning of enzyme properties such that subtle structural differences allow each species to possess a similar K_m at its respective normal T_A. This strategy, called *conservation of K_m*, is commonly seen when we compare the effects of temperature on the enzyme kinetics of different animals.

Alternately, mutations in the promoter for an enzyme cause a change in the level of gene expression of an otherwise unchanged enzyme. If such changes are beneficial, they may evolve to become fixed in the population. Killifish live along the eastern coast of North America from Newfoundland to Florida. Within the population as a whole, there are different alleles of the LDH-B gene. One allele predominates in northern populations, while another allele predominates in southern populations. Intermediate populations have both alleles. These alleles have differences in enzyme properties and differ in the level of gene expression. The northern allele is expressed at twofold higher levels than the southern allele, due to mutations in the promoter. The northern fish produce more LDH enzyme molecules, which compensates for the debilitating effects of temperature on enzymatic activity that would occur as a result of living in the colder waters.

Ectotherms can remodel tissues in response to long-term changes in temperature

Many ectothermic animals remodel their cellular machinery to mitigate the effects of variation in T_B. In the laboratory, where the researcher changes only T_A, this remodeling process is called *thermal acclimation*. In the natural world, seasonal transitions in temperature are accompanied by other environmental changes and the response of the animal to complex seasonal changes is called *acclimatization*. In winter, photoperiods get shorter, food may be less abundant, and oxygen levels may change. The complexity of these seasonal environmental changes makes it difficult to link remodeling with the temperature. On one hand, there is uncertainty about the trigger for the remodeling process: Is the change initiated by changes in temperature or by some other factor, such as photoperiod? On the other hand, it is not always clear that the remodeling itself serves to compensate specifically for temperature.

Temperature-dependent remodeling involves combinations of quantitative and qualitative strategies. In Chapter 13, we discussed how ectotherms remodel their muscles in response to temperature. Low temperature may increase the number of mitochondria in muscle, or trigger the hypertrophic growth of the heart. This is an example of a *quantitative* strategy; there is simply more of the same machinery. Muscles can also alter the types of proteins they use to build the contractile machinery. For instance, animals express different myosin isoforms in winter and summer—an example of a *qualitative* strategy.

Surprisingly little is known about the hormones and signaling pathways that cause an ectotherm to remodel its tissues during acclimation and acclimatization. Cold-sensing and warm-sensing neurons are important for detecting temperature, but the links to gene expression are not well known. In some cases, seasonal changes in physiology that mitigate the effects of temperature are triggered by changes in the photoperiod. In Chapter 8, we discussed the importance of the various photoperiod signaling pathways that act through the hypothalamus and pineal glands.

EVALUATING THERMAL EFFECTS ON PHYSIOLOGICAL PROCESSES USING Q_{10} AND ARRHENIUS PLOTS

For many physiological processes, an increase in temperature typically increases the rate of the process. The sensitivity of a reaction to temperature is expressed as the Q_{10} value, which is essentially the ratio between reaction rates at two temperatures, adjusted for a 10°C temperature difference. It is calculated as

$$Q_{10} = \left[\frac{K_2}{K_1}\right]^{[10/(T_2-T_1)]}$$

where the rates of a reaction (K) are compared at two temperatures (1 and 2). Thus, if a rate of 10 units/min (K_1) was observed at 15°C (T_1), and a rate of 20 units/min (K_2) at 25°C (T_2), then

$$Q_{10} = \left[\frac{20}{10}\right]^{[10/(25-15)]} = 2^1 = 2$$

A Q_{10} value for a reaction allows you to make predictions about the potential impact of temperature on reaction rates. A desert lizard may experience a change in temperature of as much as 30°C over a single day, from the midday heat to the cool morning. Consider how temperature affects the maximal activity (V_{max}) of lactate dehydrogenase (LDH) in the lizard muscle as it experiences changes in T_B. Over this time frame, the total number of LDH enzyme molecules does not change appreciably, but the catalytic activity changes with temperature. Assume that LDH displays a $Q_{10} = 2$, and that the lizard tissue at 35°C has an LDH $V_{max} = 400$ U/g tissue (1 unit of enzyme converts 1 μmol of substrate to product each minute). Using the Q_{10} equation, calculate the effects on V_{max} when T_B decreases from 35°C to 25°C, 15°C, and 5°C. Over the course of a single day, changes in T_B mean the desert lizard experiences an eightfold change in its LDH V_{max}. To put this into context, if you were to undergo extensive weight training, your muscle LDH V_{max} might change only twofold.

How does a lizard cope with an eightfold decrease in enzyme activity? Superimposed on the Q_{10} effects are numerous layers of metabolic regulation that ensure that energy metabolism remains in homeostasis. If an individual enzyme is more sensitive to temperature than are other enzymes in the pathway, the cell has several options to increase flux through that step. Most enzymes do not operate near their V_{max}, so changes in flux can arise through changes in substrate or product concentrations. Enzymes can overcome debilitating effects of temperature by changes in kinetic regulation through allosteric effectors or covalent modification.

Another factor to consider is that a reduction in temperature reduces both anabolic and catabolic reactions. It is easy to imagine how an eightfold reduction in LDH capacity might severely impair the capacity to produce ATP by glycolysis. However, rates of ATP synthesis decline in parallel with the rates of ATP utilization, with each step exhibiting a Q_{10} ranging from 2 to 3. Put another way, the animal can tolerate lower rates of muscle ATP production because it slows down and needs less ATP for muscle activity. However, it is important to recognize that $Q_{10} = 2$ is quite different from $Q_{10} = 3$. The levels of ATP in a tissue reflect a balance between rates of synthesis and degradation. If a 10°C decrease in temperature caused ATP synthesis to decrease threefold when ATP demands decreased only twofold, the tissue would be depleted of ATP within seconds or minutes.

The Q_{10} for a process is the best way to express the influence of temperature on reaction rates, but a better approach to exploring the mechanism of action is through an **Arrhenius plot**. In the late 1800s, the chemist Svante Arrhenius described a mathematical approach to exploring the impact of temperature on macromolecular processes. We now use his approach to study processes such as enzymatic reactions, diffusion of molecules, and lipid membrane phase transitions. The sensitivity of a reaction to temperature reflects the activation energy (E_A) of the process. The Arrhenius equation describes the relationship between the

7. What is homeoviscous adaptation?

8. What is conservation of K_m in relation to temperature effects on enzymes?

9. How can an animal alter membrane fluidity?

Life at High and Low Body Temperatures

Animals that can tolerate extreme temperatures can invade and colonize niches that are underexploited by their competitors. Ectothermic animals exposed to thermal challenges must possess mechanisms to mitigate the effects of temperature on macromolecular structure and metabolism. In

activation energy, temperature, and the rate of the process under study:

$$k = Ae^{[-E_a/RT]}$$

More often, the Arrhenius equation is shown as

$$\ln[k] = \ln[A] - E_a/[RT]$$

where k is a rate coefficient, R is the gas constant (8.31447×10^{-3} kJ/K per mol), T is temperature (in degrees kelvin), A is called the pre-exponential factor, and E_a is the activation energy (kJ/mol).

The versatility of the Arrhenius plot allows researchers to describe the thermal behavior of any simple or complex process. Figure 15.18 displays the results of an experiment comparing the effects of temperature on two enzymes.

The researcher varied temperature over a range of interest and measured enzymatic rates. The data she collected could be plotted on a graph with axes chosen from a rearrangement of the Arrhenius equation that generates a linear equation ($y = mx + b$):

$$\ln[k] = -E_a/R \times [1/T] + \ln[A]$$

Plotting $\ln(k)$ versus $1/T$ gives a slope of E_a/R and a y intercept of $\ln(A)$.

This Arrhenius plot illustrates two potential outcomes for an enzyme. For the green line, the data fall along a straight line. The slope of the line reflects the activation energy of the reaction. This is the type of data that would be expected from analysis of a cytosolic (soluble) enzyme such as LDH.

The purple lines show data where one line fits the data at low temperatures, but a different line fits the relationship at high temperatures. The point where the two lines cross is called the **breakpoint**. Because the slope differs between the two lines, we can infer that different activation energies govern the reaction over each temperature range. In many cases, this is due to a mechanistic transition from one

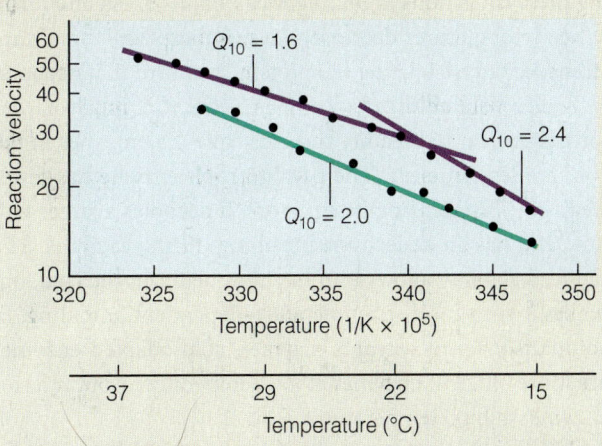

FIGURE 15.18 **Arrhenius plot**

state to another state. If the enzyme under consideration is a membrane enzyme, for instance, the breakpoint might reflect the transition from a liquid to a solid phase. If the process is an enzymatic reaction, the breakpoint might occur at a temperature where a critical bond is broken, converting the enzyme from an efficient catalyst to a less-efficient catalyst or a partially denatured enzyme.

This type of analysis can be used to explore complex processes, such as whole metabolic pathways. However, the results reflect a complex summation of the thermal sensitivities of the various individual steps. Though useful for characterizing the effects of temperature on such pathways, it is much more difficult to assess underlying mechanisms that explain the thermal sensitivity.

Reference

- Metz, J. R., van den Burg, E. H., Bonga, S. E., & Flik, G. (2003). Regulation of branchial Na$^+$/K$^+$ ATPase in common carp *Cyprinus carpio* L. acclimated to different temperatures. *Journal of Experimental Biology, 206*, 2273–2280.

contrast, endothermic animals survive thermal extremes using complex regulatory pathways to maintain a constant T_B. Their existence at extremes is a testament to their physiological capacity to resist the effects of T_A.

Some enzymes display cold adaptation

Earlier in this chapter we discussed how relatively subtle differences in T_A can lead to evolutionary changes in enzyme structure and gene expression. However, the need for enzymatic structural modification is much more pronounced at thermal extremes, particularly at the subzero temperatures encountered in polar seas. Psychrotrophs are organisms that thrive in the extreme cold, in contrast to mesotrophs that live at more moderate temperatures. Animal psychrotrophs, including polar invertebrates and fish, remain active at body temperatures near the point of freezing. Many psychrotrophic organisms possess cold-adapted proteins that function optimally at very low temperatures. Although these enzymes are more stable in the cold, they are rapidly inactivated at slightly higher temperatures.

The catalytic and structural differences between enzymes of psychrotrophs and mesotrophs can be traced to the weak bonds that stabilize enzyme structure. Enzymes undergo pronounced changes in three-dimensional shape during the catalytic cycle, known as protein breathing. During these transitions in folding, weak bonds break and form. When temperatures decrease, most of these weak bonds are strengthened, stabilizing the protein in a form that occupies a smaller volume. In this conformation, it is much harder for the protein to breathe, and consequently enzymes in the cold are less efficient. The psychrotroph enzyme has fewer weak bonds stabilizing its structure; it occupies a larger volume and has an easier time breathing during catalysis. The reduced stability allows it to function better in the cold, but makes it vulnerable to temperature-dependent unfolding. In comparison to mesotroph enzymes, cold-adapted enzymes are more efficient enzymes at low temperatures, but inferior enzymes at high temperatures.

Unique loss-of-function mutations also occur in polar animals. Many Antarctic fish have lost the ability to express functional oxygen-binding proteins, such as hemoglobin and myoglobin. These fish can survive without these oxygen carriers because they have low metabolic rates and the surrounding polar waters are rich in oxygen.

There are many such examples of thermal adaptations of individual selected genes in polar animals. However, more controversial is the question of whether or not polar animals have a fundamentally different organization of metabolism as a result of evolution in the extreme cold. Early studies suggested that polar animals had metabolic rates that were much higher than the metabolic rates of temperate animals measured near 0°C. These observations were used to support a theory that became known as metabolic cold adaptation. It was proposed that thousands of years in the extreme cold led to evolutionary changes that provided these polar animals with an ability to elevate their metabolic rate. Even with years of study it remains unclear whether metabolic cold adaptation is a real phenomenon. The earliest studies were based on comparisons of goldfish and arctic cod. Now that more species have been analyzed using more sophisticated technologies, it seems less likely that metabolic cold adaptation occurs as a general phenomenon. Nonetheless, many studies have identified evolutionary differences and physiological peculiarities in some polar animals.

Stress proteins are induced at thermal extremes

Many proteins are best suited to function over narrow ranges of temperature that span the biological range of the animal.

During the normal structural change that occurs when a protein breathes, the protein is vulnerable to further changes in structure. Occasionally, the protein can unfold or misfold into a nonfunctional conformation. This denatured protein must be repaired or cleared from the cell before it disrupts other cellular functions. Denaturation is a normal process, and cells are able to detect and remove denatured proteins using pathways of protein quality control. These pathways function throughout the lifetime of a cell, but become even more important during times of thermal stress, when denatured proteins can accumulate and kill the cell.

Recall from Chapter 3 that a heat shock protein (Hsp) is a molecular chaperone, which uses the energy of ATP to catalyze protein folding after translation. Chaperones can also help refold proteins that have become denatured as a result of thermal stress. Many cells exposed to extreme temperatures undergo a *heat shock response,* which leads to a dramatic increase in the levels of specific proteins that help repair damaged proteins. During a heat shock, the cell undertakes a rapid increase in the synthesis of several critical heat shock proteins. The cell can halt the transcription and translation of other genes, sparing biosynthetic resources for Hsp synthesis. It stimulates the expression of the Hsp genes by activating a heat shock factor (HSF), a transcription factor that binds to the heat shock elements in the promoters of genes for heat shock proteins. Although there is still some uncertainty about the exact mechanism of activation of HSF, the trigger for the process is thought to involve damaged protein (Figure 15.19). In the absence of thermal stress, most of the cellular HSF is bound to Hsp70 as inactive monomers. When the cell is stressed, the chaperones are lured away from HSF by damaged proteins. The released HSF can then form trimers, which in turn bind the heat shock element on the Hsp genes, activating them. Once the damaged proteins are repaired, Hsp70 is free to bind HSF monomers and reverse the transcriptional activation.

The Hsp response is central to the ability of ectothermic animals to survive brief periods of extreme temperature that often occur within their natural environments. For most species, the Hsp response is induced at temperatures only a few degrees above the typical thermal range. This powerful protective process may be central to the evolution of thermal sensitivities and thermal ranges. If heat shock proteins are protective, why haven't animals evolved greater expression to expand thermal niches? Experiments in fruit flies (*Drosophila*) have shown that elevated Hsp expression comes at a cost. Flies that have evolved extra copies of Hsp70 genes survive better at high temperatures, but at lower temperatures they experience a decrease in fecundity.

Some species have lost their ability to mount a heat shock response. Antarctic fish have lived for thousands of years at 1.96°C. At some point, the species experienced

FIGURE 15.19 **Heat shock response**

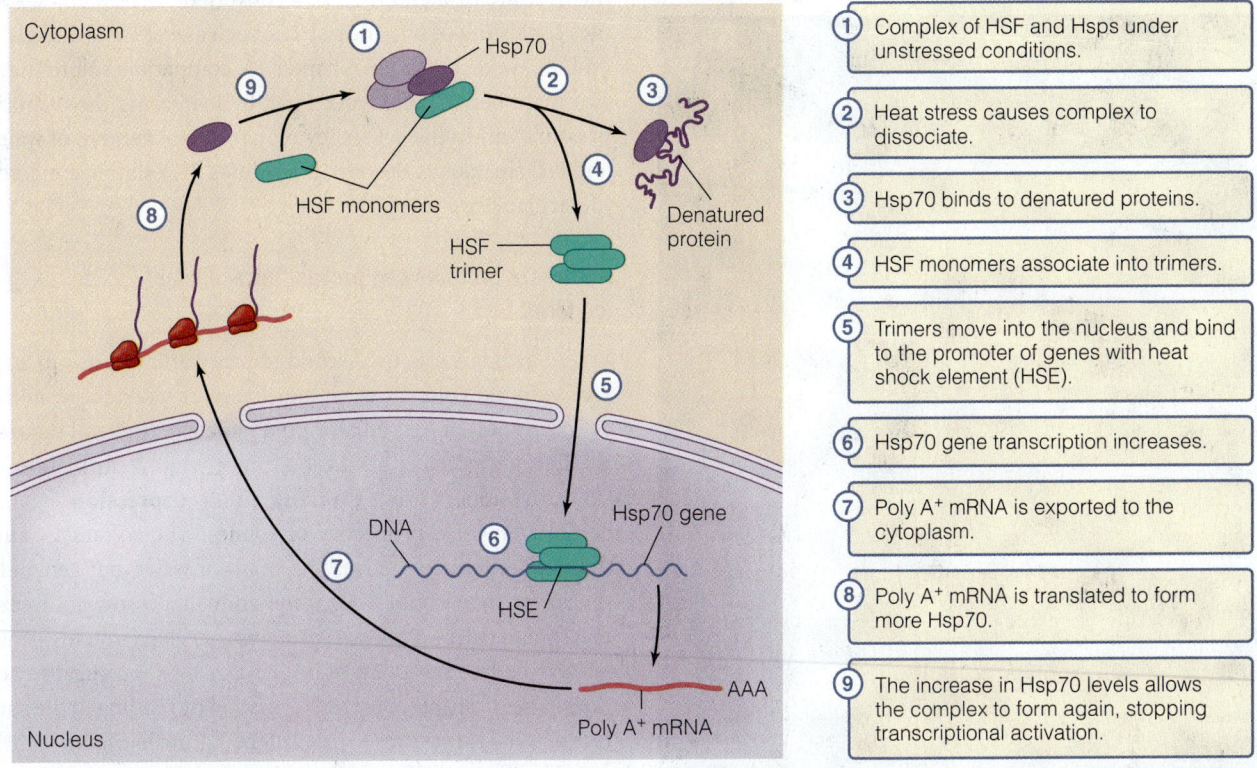

①	Complex of HSF and Hsps under unstressed conditions.
②	Heat stress causes complex to dissociate.
③	Hsp70 binds to denatured proteins.
④	HSF monomers associate into trimers.
⑤	Trimers move into the nucleus and bind to the promoter of genes with heat shock element (HSE).
⑥	Hsp70 gene transcription increases.
⑦	Poly A$^+$ mRNA is exported to the cytoplasm.
⑧	Poly A$^+$ mRNA is translated to form more Hsp70.
⑨	The increase in Hsp70 levels allows the complex to form again, stopping transcriptional activation.

genetic changes that disrupted the capacity to invoke a heat shock response. Because the Antarctic waters remain very constant in temperature, these mutations have no deleterious consequences to the animals. However, when taken out of their natural environment, these fish rapidly succumb to temperatures only a few degrees above 0°C.

Ice nucleators control ice crystal growth in freeze-tolerant animals

Ectotherms that live at freezing temperatures use two strategies to survive the cold: freeze tolerance and freeze avoidance. Freeze-tolerant animals allow their tissues to freeze and even encourage ice to form in the body. Animals that avoid freezing use behavioral and physiological mechanisms to prevent ice crystal formation and growth. To understand why ice is so dangerous, let's consider what happens to water molecules as temperatures decrease.

The freezing point of pure water is 0°C. This is the temperature at which ice could form if enough water molecules cluster together to begin an ice crystal. Below the freezing point, water is on the verge of freezing, awaiting an event that triggers ice formation. When water is below its freezing point, but not yet frozen, it is considered **supercooled**. Pure water, left undisturbed, can be supercooled to almost −40°C before ice forms spontaneously. The trigger for ice formation is a cluster of water molecules that act as a seed for an ice crystal. Alternatively, a macromolecule in solution can act as a **nucleator**, seeding ice crystal formation. Once the ice formation begins, water molecules bind to each face of the growing crystal to create a complex three-dimensional structure.

Ice crystals forming within a tissue have two deleterious effects. First, because ice crystals have points and sharp edges, the growing ice crystal can pierce membranes, killing the cell. Second, ice crystal growth removes surrounding water, causing hyperosmotic stress. If ice forms outside cells, then water is drawn out of cells, causing a hypertonic stress that shrinks the cell, perhaps even killing it. Still, many ectotherms survive freezing (Figure 15.20). Insects such as the goldenrod gall fly (*Eurosta solidaginis*) overwinter in senescent galls on the stems of goldenrod. The stems reach above the snow, and expose the larva to temperatures as low as −55°C. Intertidal bivalves living in northern tidal flats can freeze when exposed to cold air temperatures, then thaw when the warmer water returns at high tide. Several terrestrial vertebrates can also survive freezing. A wood frog in the north temperate zone enters the leaf litter in late fall, in preparation for overwintering. When temperatures drop below freezing, the animal supercools but ice does not form. At still lower temperatures, the animal begins to freeze. First to freeze are the frog's digits. The body core begins to freeze shortly thereafter.

Freeze-tolerant animals usually produce ice nucleators to control the location and kinetics of ice crystal growth.

FIGURE 15.20 **Freeze-tolerant animals**

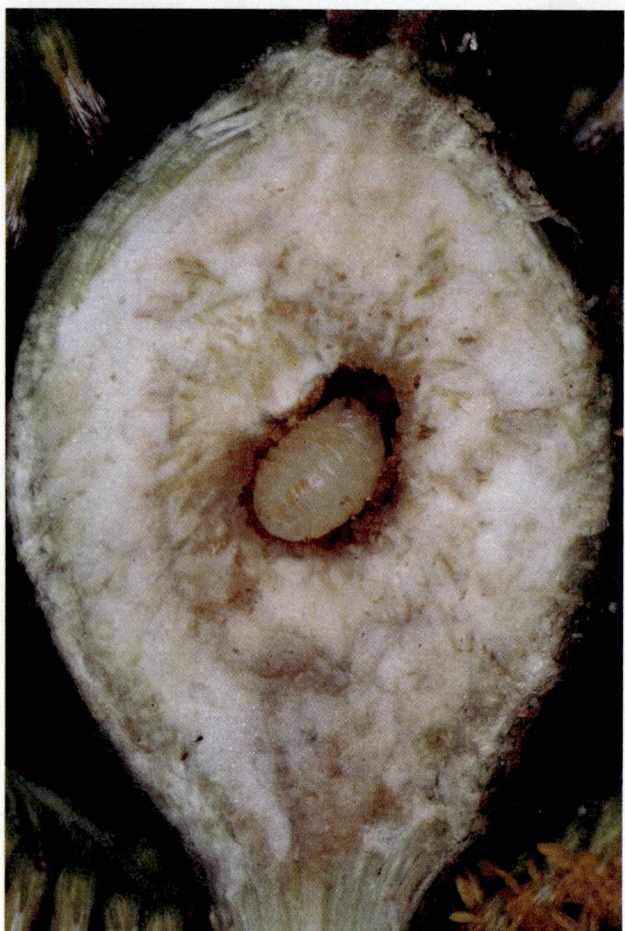

Eurosta in gall

Photo source: Valerie Giles/Science Source.

Ice is most damaging when it forms inside cells, so freeze-tolerant animals secrete nucleators out of the cell. This restricts ice formation to the extracellular fluids, such as hemolymph, and allows the intracellular space to remain liquid. Many different types of molecules can act as nucleators in animals: calcium salts, membrane phospholipids, and long-chain alcohols. However, it is not always clear that these ice nucleators are actually necessary or helpful to freeze-tolerance strategies. For example, the wood frog has an ice nucleator that triggers ice formation at about 7°C. The same ice nucleator is also found in the tissues of frogs that cannot survive freezing. It may induce the formation of ice, but it does not necessarily provide the wood frog with its freeze tolerance. Some nucleators may simply be present for other functions and have no adaptive role in freeze tolerance.

Because ice formation draws water from the cells, freeze-tolerant animals also produce intracellular solutes to

counter the movement of water. Large glycogen reserves of the liver are broken down and converted to compatible solutes consisting of organic polyols, such as trehalose and glycerol. As we discussed in Chapter 13, compatible solutes have two main beneficial effects. First, by increasing the osmotic pressure within the cells, they reduce the movement of water and cell shrinkage. Second, the solutes help stabilize macromolecular structure.

Antifreeze proteins can prevent intracellular ice formation

Freeze avoidance is the second strategy animals use to survive extreme cold. In a car, antifreeze elevates the osmotic concentration of the radiator fluid. Solutes in general depress the freezing point of a solution, preventing ice formation at subzero temperatures. **Freezing point depression** is one of the colligative properties of solutes. The solutes in animal tissues reduce the freezing point of water, but generally not lower than about 2°C. Some animals possess antifreeze macromolecules—typically proteins or glycoproteins—that reduce the freezing point of body fluids by noncolligative actions. They disrupt ice crystal formation by binding to the surface of small ice crystals to prevent their growth (Figure 15.21).

The first **antifreeze protein**, or AFP, was discovered in an Antarctic fish in the 1970s by Dr. Art DeVries. Since then, AFPs have been found in many distantly related taxa of fish, as well as insects and plants. Four classes of AFPs are distinguished by their structure: types I, II, and III, as well as antifreeze glycoproteins, or AFGPs. Interestingly, each of

FIGURE 15.21 **Antifreeze proteins**

Antifreeze proteins bind to the surface of ice crystals to prevent their growth. They bind along the face of the ice crystal, where the protein forms weak bonds with water molecules immobilized in the ice crystal. Because ice growth is very orderly, the presence of the bound protein prevents ice crystal growth.

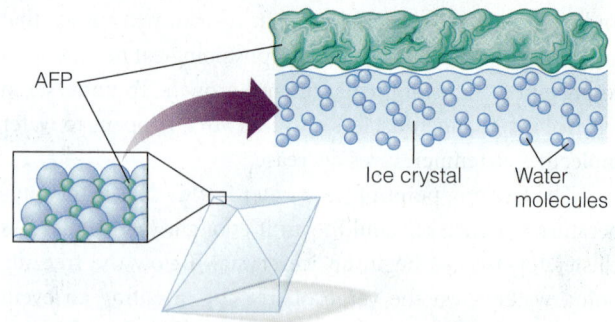

Figure source: Based on Davies, P. L., Baardsnes, J., Kuiper, M. J., & Walker, V. K. (2002). Figure 6 from Structure and function of antifreeze proteins. *Philosophical Transactions of the Royal Society of London, Series B: Biological Sciences, 357,* 927–935.

the classes of AFPs has arisen multiple times in evolution. In fish, AFPs arose less than 20 million years ago. This coincides with recent (in geological terms) sea level glaciation, which probably represented a strong selective pressure on the local marine species. The phylogenetic distribution of AFPs suggests an intriguing evolutionary history.

AFPs provide good examples of parallel evolution. For example, AFP II appears in herring, salmon, and sea ravens, fish from three separate orders. This suggests that AFPs arose multiple times in these lineages but well after the modern species diverged. These AFP II genes may have arisen from similar genes independently in each lineage. The structure of AFP II suggests that the ancestral gene was a Ca^{2+}-dependent lectin, a protein that binds sugars. In structural models, the interaction of a lectin with the hydroxyl groups of sugars is similar to the interaction of AFP with the hydroxyl group of a water molecule.

The evolutionary origins of AFGP are also unusual in terms of protein evolution. The ancestral gene was probably a gene for pancreatic trypsinogen, a digestive protease we introduced in Chapter 14. A region between the first intron and second exon was duplicated not just once but more than 40 times. The resulting gene possessed multiple, tandem sequences that resulted in a repeating Thr-Ala-Ala motif necessary to prevent ice crystal growth. In most cases of gene duplication and divergence, the resulting gene has properties similar to those of the ancestral gene, with relatively subtle differences in function. In the case of AFGP, the resultant gene has a totally distinct function. AFGPs have no protease activity, and trypsinogen has no antifreeze activity.

CONCEPT CHECK

10. Distinguish between freeze-tolerance and freeze-avoidance strategies.
11. Distinguish among nucleators, antifreeze proteins, and stress proteins.
12. What is meant by metabolic cold adaptation?

MAINTAINING A CONSTANT BODY TEMPERATURE

Endothermy is so inextricably intertwined with a high metabolic rate that it is not known which trait arose first. High T_B allows metabolic processes such as growth, development, digestion, and biosynthesis to operate at faster rates, and the higher metabolic rate in turn produces more heat. The ability to become warm bodied requires metabolic pathways to produce heat (**thermogenesis**) as well as physiological mechanisms to retain heat. Most endotherms are also homeotherms

and committed to maintaining a constant T_B. To do so, they must control both thermogenesis and heat exchange. In cold environments, endotherms stimulate thermogenesis and reduce heat loss. In hot environments they increase heat loss, but may also reduce thermogenesis. To control T_B, animals must be able to sense both environmental temperature and body core temperature.

Endothermy, the ability to generate and maintain elevated body temperatures, has arisen several times in the evolutionary history of animals. It goes hand in hand with the capacity to produce heat through metabolism, and therefore activity levels. Most modern birds and mammals have high metabolic rates and are able to maintain their body temperatures well above ambient temperature, often within narrow thermal windows. While both are perceived as "higher vertebrates," birds and mammals arose from separate reptilian ancestors. Thus, endothermy arose independently at least twice. However, fossil evidence suggests that other extinct reptiles may also have been endotherms. The fossil record of the animals in the paleontological period from 200 to 65 million years ago is particularly clear, showing definitive examples of the transitions from reptiles to mammals and birds.

Recall from Chapter 2 that the first mammals appeared approximately 200 million years ago (mya), evolving from small, nocturnal reptiles that were only distantly related to the dinosaurs that would dominate Earth in later years. Fossils dating back to this period reveal the existence of several distinct mammalianlike reptilian lineages. These animals differed from other reptiles by the morphology of the skull and the organization of the teeth. Although most of these lineages disappeared, one group of reptiles called *cynodonts* gave rise to true mammals. The earliest mammals retained the reptilian trait of egg laying, like the modern monotremes, echidna and platypus. By the early Cretaceous period (144 mya), mammals had diversified into several lineages of marsupials and insectivores. When the dinosaurs disappeared about 65 mya, at the end of the Cretaceous period, there was an explosion of mammalian diversification. New species of mammals began to occupy the environmental niches vacated by the dinosaurs. It cannot be said for certain when endothermy arose in the transition from mammalianlike reptiles to true mammals. However, it is likely that the cynodont reptiles were already endothermic. Unlike most other reptiles of the day, cynodonts possessed a bony, secondary palate in the roof of the mouth that would have allowed them to breathe while chewing. This anatomical arrangement is a characteristic of endotherms because they must maintain uninterrupted respiration to sustain high metabolic rates. Cynodonts also appear to have possessed hair, which could have helped insulate their bodies.

Birds, the other group of modern endotherms, also arose from reptiles, although much later than mammals and from different reptilian ancestors. Around the time dinosaurs were declining, several reptilian lineages had already evolved featherlike body coverings. In one group, the theropod dinosaurs (see Figure 2.20) such as *Archaeopteryx*, the feathers were similar in structure to those of modern birds. Their feathers were asymmetrical, a trait that is necessary to be useful in feathered flight. In contrast, the other feathered reptiles of the era, such as *Protarchaeopteryx robusta* and *Caudipteryx zoui*, had symmetrical feathers (Figure 15.22). Because these symmetrical feathers would be useless in flight, they must have arisen in these dinosaurs for other benefits, likely as insulation. Although these other lineages of feathered reptiles became extinct, they were likely also endothermic animals.

Many researchers believe that endothermy arose in other, nonfeathered dinosaur lineages as well. The largest dinosaurs were simply too big to shed metabolic heat, and therefore remained warm-bodied. Many smaller dinosaurs may also have been endothermic. Multiple lines of evidence support the notion that these animals had the high metabolic rates necessary for an endothermic animal. Bone structure and posture suggest rapid rates of locomotion, which in modern animals require high metabolic rates that are possible only in warm-bodied animals. Just as in modern endotherms, many dinosaurs had relatively large brains associated with superior sensory processing. Because brain tissue has a high energy demand, a large brain can have an important influence on the whole-body metabolic rate. Other theories have been raised to support arguments that dinosaurs were endotherms. However, no argument is definitive because of the limitations in using the properties of modern animals as guidelines in predicting the physiological features of these long-extinct animals.

Thermogenesis

Heat production is an inevitable consequence of being alive. An endotherm warms its body using heat that arises as a by-product of other metabolic processes, primarily energy metabolism, digestion, and muscle activity. All animals—endotherms and ectotherms—generate heat during these processes, but only the endotherms possess the physiological adaptations that enable them to retain enough metabolic heat to elevate T_B above T_A.

In addition to the pathways that produce heat as a by-product, endotherms possess specific thermogenic pathways with the main purpose of heat production. Thermogenic pathways rely on *futile cycling*, in which chemical potential energy is spent to generate heat. Most futile cycles involve cycling of ATP hydrolysis and ATP synthesis. Heat is released in ATP hydrolysis to ADP + phosphate, but a great deal more heat is produced when the cell uses intermediary metabolism to regenerate the ATP. Endotherms can enhance heat production either by increasing the rate of ATP turnover or by reducing the efficiency of ATP production. In both cases, most of the metabolic heat arises directly or indirectly from mitochondrial oxidative phosphorylation, discussed at length in Chapter 3. A summary of the main futile cycles we discuss in this section is presented in Figure 15.23.

Shivering thermogenesis results from unsynchronized muscle contractions

Muscle plays a critical role in the thermal budget of endotherms. Because muscle is the most abundant tissue in birds

---

FIGURE 15.22 **Asymmetrical fossilized feather**

Photo source: O. Louis Mazzatenta/National Geographic/Getty Images.

FIGURE 15.23 **Futile cycles and thermogenesis**

(1) Myofibrillar ATPase, recruited during shivering thermogenesis.
(2) Plasma membrane ion (Na$^+$) leakage and pumping.
(3) Nonspecific mitochondrial proton leakage and pumping.
(4) Thermogenin-mediated proton leakage and pumping.
(5) Futile cycling in glycolysis.

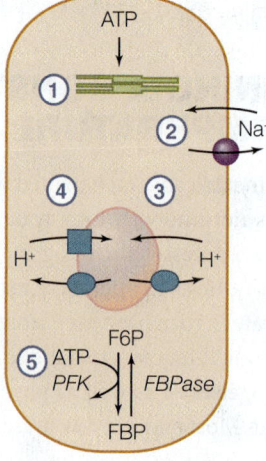

and mammals, it produces considerable heat, even at rest. Locomotion enhances the rate of muscle heat production. However, many birds and mammals can also use skeletal muscle to generate heat by **shivering thermogenesis**.

The act of shivering is controlled by the motor neurons. Individual myofibers contract but the motor units are uncoordinated and the whole muscle undergoes no gross movement. During hypothermia, the shivering response is complex, manifesting a sustained low-intensity shivering with interspersed high-intensity bouts. The low-intensity shivering involves type I fibers, the same muscles that permit low-intensity sustained exercise. Like exercise, this activity is fueled by lipid oxidation. The high-intensity bouts are induced by activation of larger type II fibers, and fueled by glycogen, just as with burst exercise. The balance between low- and high-intensity shivering is regulated by the central nervous system, and is affected by the availability of fuel stores.

Shivering thermogenesis is a strategy that works for short periods of cold exposure, but it is not useful for prolonged cold stress. The mechanics of shivering prevent an animal from using its locomotor muscles to hunt prey or escape predators. Furthermore, if shivering persists, or repeats frequently, the muscles are rapidly depleted of nutrients and they become exhausted, just as they would after high-intensity exercise.

Some insects use metabolic futile cycles to warm flight muscle

Large flying insects, such as bumblebees and some moths, can generate enough heat to warm the thoracic flight muscles, which improves flight muscle performance in terms of energy production, excitation-contraction coupling, and cross-bridge cycling. The high metabolic rate during flight generates abundant heat, enough to warm the flight muscles by several degrees. Remarkably, these insects are even able to warm their flight musculature prior to takeoff.

Three distinct mechanisms allow insects to warm the thorax prior to flight. These same thermogenic pathways also allow social insects to work collectively to warm the hive. The first mechanism is a metabolic futile cycle in carbohydrate metabolism. Within the flight muscle, two opposing enzymes are activated simultaneously: the glycolytic enzyme phosphofructokinase and the gluconeogenic enzyme fructose-1,6-bisphosphatase. The metabolic cycle causes ATP hydrolysis and heat production, but without changes in the levels of the other substrates and products. A second warming mechanism relies on muscle contraction. Two sets of antagonistic flight muscles power wing movements during flight. Bumblebees can induce both sets of muscles to contract simultaneously prior to flight, so that

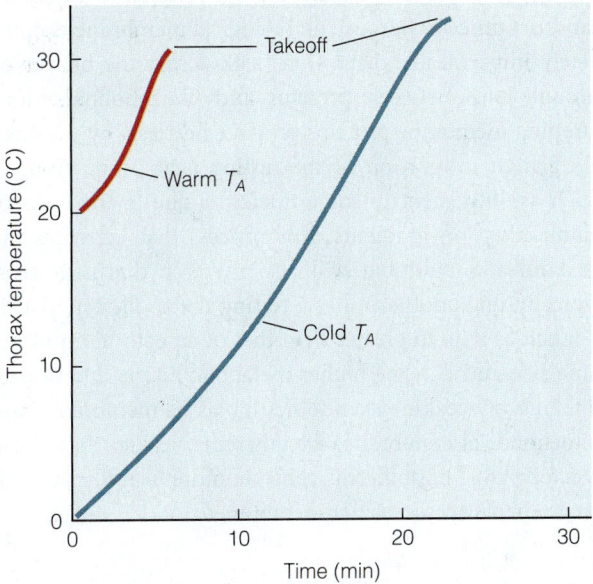

FIGURE 15.24 **Thermogenesis in insect flight muscle**
Many large flying insects can undertake a preflight warm-up, using metabolic futile cycles and muscle activity to elevate thoracic temperatures to a threshold temperature required for flight.

Figure source: Based on Heinrich, B. (1987). Thermoregulation in winter moths. *Scientific American, 256,* 104–111.

energy is expended without productive movement. The third mechanism for heat generation is actual wing movement. The insect moves its wings fast enough to buzz, but controls the frequency and orientation of the wings to avoid generating lift. Collectively, these thermogenic pathways allow the flight muscle to warm up prior to takeoff. There appears to be a critical thoracic temperature that must be achieved before the insect will attempt to fly (Figure 15.24). At high T_A, less of a preflight warm-up is necessary to reach the threshold.

Membrane leakiness enhances thermogenesis

Most cellular membranes maintain an electrochemical gradient arising from differential distribution of ions across the membrane. Cells use chemical energy, usually in the form of ATP, to create these gradients. Consequently, any process that dissipates ion gradients will cause the cell to use chemical energy to reestablish the gradient.

Ion gradients collapse for two main reasons. First, many specific membrane proteins use electrochemical energy to drive other processes such as metabolite transport and biosynthesis. For example, many cells transport glucose and amino acids into the cell using Na^+-dependent cotransporters, causing the cell to use Na^+/K^+ ATPase to pump the Na^+ back out of the cell. The mitochondrial F_1F_o ATPase is another transporter that dissipates ion gradients, in this case the proton motive force. Heat is produced when the mitochondrial electron transport system oxidizes reducing equivalents to regenerate the proton gradient.

The second pathway of ion gradient dissipation is ion leak, in which ion movements are not coupled to any other transport process. Because no biological membrane is completely impermeable, some ions leak across the bilayer or through gaps between proteins and phospholipids. Ion-pumping membrane proteins produce heat as a by-product, and a high proportion of the resting heat production, as much as 50 percent in some tissues, is due to the costs of maintaining ion gradients. Any process that increases the need for ion pumping will also increase thermogenesis. Typically, an endotherm has a resting metabolic rate that is as much as tenfold greater than that of an ectotherm of the same size and T_B. The higher metabolic rate is due in part to membrane leakiness; endotherm plasma membranes and mitochondrial membranes are inherently leakier than those of ectotherms. Endotherms generate more heat to maintain ion gradients across leakier membranes.

Thermogenin enhances mitochondrial proton leak

Mammals possess a unique way of generating heat in specialized deposits of **brown adipose tissue** (BAT), typically located near the back and shoulder region (Figure 15.25). BAT is most important for thermogenesis in small mammals and newborns of larger animals, particularly those that live in cold environments. Its growth and thermogenesis is under the control of the sympathetic nervous system. Norepinephrine released from these nerves causes BAT to grow in cell number (**hyperplasia**) and cell size (**hypertrophy**). Undifferentiated precursor cells are induced to proliferate and then later differentiate into BAT. Triglyceride is synthesized and mitochondria proliferate. BAT heat production is often called **nonshivering thermogenesis (NST)**; while the other pathways we have discussed also differ from shivering, NST is a term usually reserved for BAT-mediated thermogenesis.

The feature that makes BAT unique is the expression of a protein called **thermogenin**. When inserted into the inner mitochondrial membrane, this protein stimulates the rate of mitochondrial respiration and consequently heat production. It works by *uncoupling* mitochondria, dissipating the proton gradient. The oxidation of fuels continues in the electron transport chain, but the protons pumped out of the mitochondria are allowed to return to the mitochondria. Without a proton motive force, the mitochondria cannot produce ATP. However, the reduction of the proton gradient permits respiration to continue at high rates.

Thermogenin was first characterized in the early 1980s and much has been learned about the evolutionary

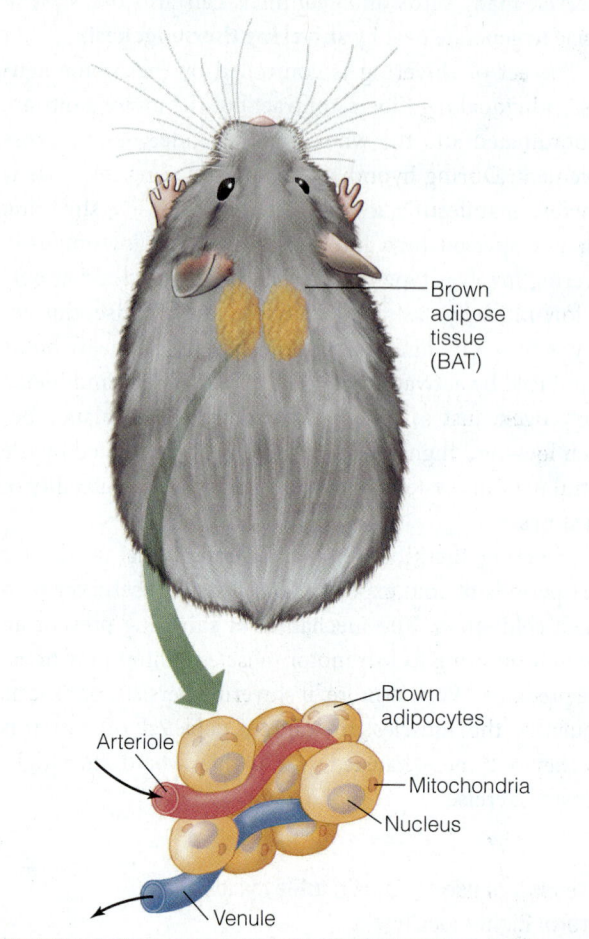

FIGURE 15.25 **Brown adipose tissue in hamsters**
Hamsters possess thick pads of BAT behind the shoulders.

Brown adipose tissue (BAT)

Brown adipocytes

Arteriole

Mitochondria

Nucleus

Venule

origins and physiological functions of uncoupling proteins in vertebrates (see Box 15.3: Challenges to Homeostasis: Evolution and Development of Thermogenin). However, the molecular mechanism by which it induces uncoupling is still not certain. One theory suggests that thermogenin acts as a proton **ionophore**. It picks up protons from the cytoplasm and carries them into the mitochondria, dissipating the proton gradient. An alternative theory suggests that thermogenin dissipates the proton gradient by causing the futile cycling of fatty acids. Thermogenin carries an ionized fatty acid (R-COO⁻) from the mitochondrial side of the inner membrane and flips it across the bilayer to face the cytoplasm. Because of the higher proton concentration (lower pH), the ionized fatty acid is rapidly protonated (R-COOH). In this neutral form it readily flops back into the inner leaflet of the bilayer, where it ionizes again. The complete "flip-flop" cycle causes a proton to be translocated across the inner mitochondrial membrane. Regardless of the molecular mechanism, thermogenin has the dual actions of dissipating the proton gradient and stimulating respiration, thereby generating heat.

EVOLUTION AND DEVELOPMENT OF THERMOGENIN

The story of thermogenin is intriguing because it has a very specific function restricted to select mammals, yet has a deep evolutionary history extending to the origins of vertebrates.

Thermogenin was once thought to be a mammalian evolutionary invention, inextricably linked to the appearance of brown adipose tissue (BAT). It is now known to be one member of the **uncoupling protein** (UCP) gene family. In addition to thermogenin (also called UCP1), mammals express at least two other UCPs. These proteins, UCP2 and UCP3, can increase mitochondrial proton leak, but not enough to cause significant uncoupling or contribute to heat production. Instead, these proteins appear to reduce oxidative stress by preventing production of superoxide anions by mitochondria.

The UCP gene family is ancient, with members in ectothermic animals, such as fish, as well as plants, fungi, and protists. Thermogenin itself has homologs throughout vertebrates, but it is difficult to imagine circumstances that would have led the ectotherm UCP1 homologs to evolve thermogenic functions. Its role in thermogenesis appears to be limited to eutherian mammals.

The picture that has emerged in recent years suggests that the ancestral function of UCP1 was likely similar to that of other UCP paralogs, UCP2 and UCP3. High rates of proton conductance by UCP1 likely arose in mammals. Remarkably, the UCP1 gene appears to have undergone loss-of-function mutations in select mammals, such as the pig. BAT is most important in small animals with unfavorable surface area-to-volume ratios. It has been suggested that large-bodied mammals have little need for nonshivering thermogenesis (NST) and that loss-of-function mutations could be tolerated without negative consequences. Though its role may differ among vertebrates, there is a growing appreciation for the role that it plays in metabolic and thermal homeostasis of humans.

Small mammals, with an unfavorable surface area-to-volume ratio, have the greatest use for BAT. Not surprisingly, BAT is common in small mammals, such as rodents, typically found between the shoulder blades (interscapular). The same type of interscapular BAT is found in infant humans, though this deposit disappears with age. Recently, humans and mice have been shown to possess another type of thermogenic adipose tissue that is intermediate between brown and white, called brite (from *brown/white*) or beige adipose tissue. The brite adipose tissue deposits, identified by high-resolution imaging methods, are found on top of the collarbone (supraclavicular). The differences in the appearance of brown and brite AT reflect different cellular origins. Brown adipocytes arise from the same precursor cells that differentiate to produce skeletal muscle, whereas brite adipocytes are derived from vascular cells within the WAT. Both brown and brite adipocytes are mitochondria-rich cells, but only brown adipocytes express high levels of UCP1 under normal conditions. However, when brite adipocytes are stimulated by hormones that elevate cAMP, they increase the expression of UCP1 and stimulate mitochondrial respiration and

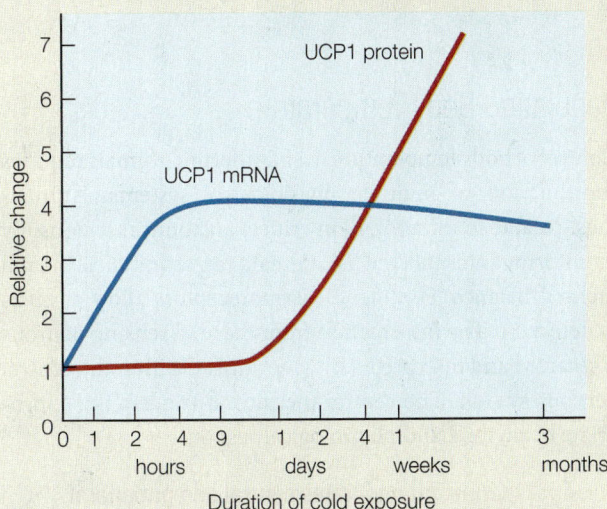

FIGURE 15.26 Changes in UCP1 mRNA and protein with cold exposure in mice

Figure source: Based on Nedergaard, J., & Cannon, B. (2013). UCP1 mRNA does not produce heat. *Biochimica et Biophysica Acta Molecular and Cell Biology of Lipids, 1831,* 943–949.

heat production. A similar response occurs when mice are cold exposed (Figure 15.26). Within hours of cold exposure, the mRNA for UCP1 increases manyfold. However, it takes many days before a corresponding change in UCP1 protein is seen. This delay is due in part to the different kinetics of mRNA and protein synthesis.

Given the role in energy dissipation and heat production, researchers explored the relationship between BAT activity and metabolic diseases, such as obesity and type II diabetes mellitus. In mice, the overexpression of the transcription factor PRDM16, known to increase production of BAT, is protective against diet-induced metabolic dysfunction, including obesity. In humans, the possible therapeutic approaches are being explored, and it is advantageous that there are at least two different types of thermogenic adipose tissue: brown and brite. Their different developmental origins may impart different sensitivities to pharmacological interventions intended to reduce obesity and related metabolic disorders.

References

- Jastroch, M., Wuertz, S., Kloas, W., & Klingenspor, M. (2005). Uncoupling protein 1 in fish uncovers an ancient evolutionary history of mammalian nonshivering thermogenesis. *Physiological Genomics, 22,* 150–156.
- Lidell, M. E., et al. (2013). Evidence for two types of brown adipose tissue in humans. *Nature Medicine, 19,* 631–634.
- Nedergaard, J., & Cannon, B. (2013). UCP1 mRNA does not produce heat. *Biochimica et Biophysica Acta - Molecular and Cell Biology of Lipids, 1831,* 943–949.
- Wu, J., Cohen, P., & Spiegelman, B. M. (2013). Adaptive thermogenesis in adipocytes: Is beige the new brown? *Gene Development, 27,* 234–250.
- Wu, J. et al. (2012). Beige adipocytes are a distinct type of thermogenic fat cell in mouse and human. *Cell, 150,* 366–376.

Regulating Body Temperature

Control of body temperature in endothermic animals requires coordination of multiple physiological systems. Animals must be able to monitor T_B in critical anatomical regions. By monitoring internal core T_B, animals can assess their overall thermal balance. Peripheral thermoreceptors allow animals to detect T_A. The information from thermal sensing neurons is received and interpreted by a thermostat within the central nervous system. The central thermostat triggers the appropriate behavioral and physiological response.

A central thermostat integrates central and peripheral thermosensory information

As we discussed in Chapter 7: Sensory Systems, animals possess different types of neurons to sense and respond to temperature. Temperatures are monitored peripherally and centrally by temperature-sensitive neurons, both cold sensing and warm sensing. Birds and mammals monitor temperature using similar neurons, although the location of the central thermostat differs in the two taxa.

Mammals monitor T_A by peripheral cold-sensitive neurons located in the skin and the viscera. When T_A decreases, peripheral neurons send signals to the hypothalamus (Figure 15.27). The preoptic area of the anterior hypothalamus has both cold-sensing and warm-sensing neurons that monitor core body temperature. Information from the peripheral and the central thermal sensors is integrated in the posterior hypothalamus, which sends signals to the body to alter the rates of heat production and dissipation. The hypothalamus is much more responsive to information from the central thermoreceptors than from the peripheral thermoreceptors. Changes of less than 1°C can excite central thermoreceptors, triggering a rapid hypothalamic response. Conversely, peripheral thermoreceptors may record and respond to a change of several degrees without invoking a hypothalamic response. Surface temperatures can change by several degrees without harming the animal, whereas the temperature of the central nervous system must be more stable.

FIGURE 15.27 **Hypothalamus and thermoregulation**

The hypothalamus is the thermal control center of mammals. It interprets signals from peripheral and central thermosensitive neurons and sends neuronal signals to other tissues, altering heat flux.

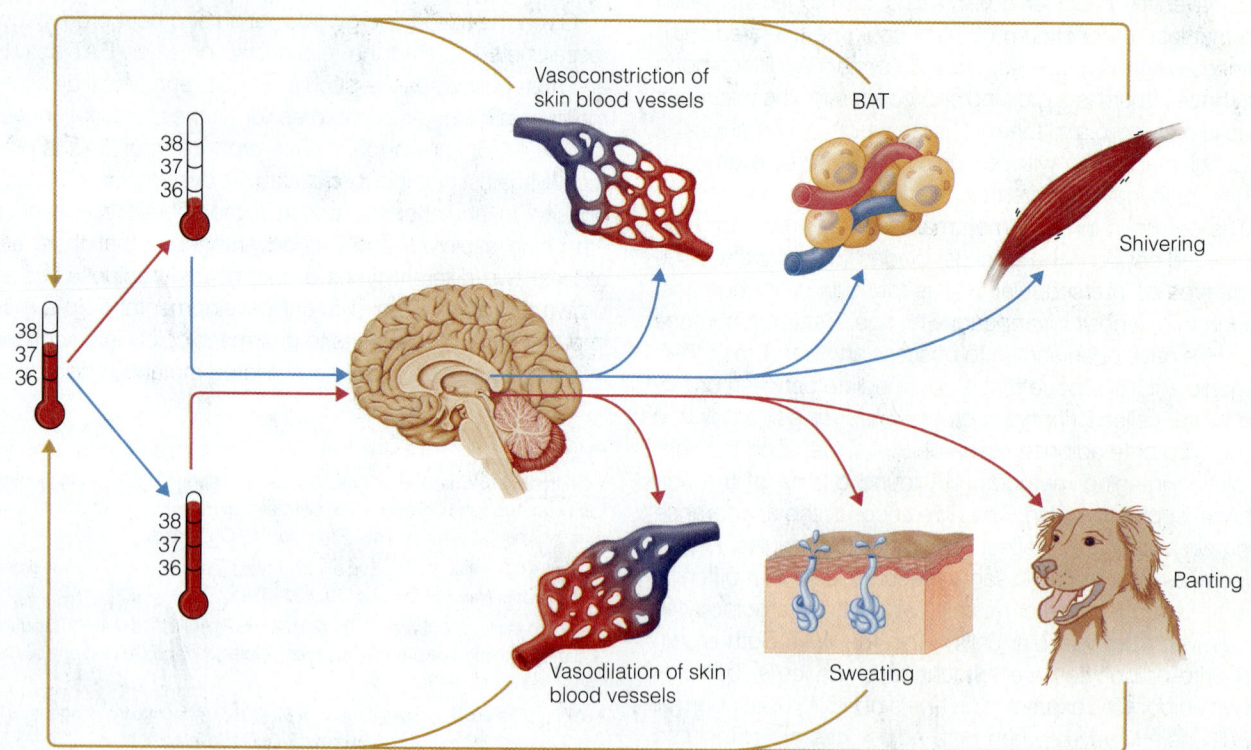

Vasoconstriction of skin blood vessels

BAT

Shivering

Vasodilation of skin blood vessels

Sweating

Panting

Bird T_B regulation is less understood but is clearly different from that of mammals. Heating or cooling the hypothalamus has little effect on the thermoregulatory response of birds. The central thermostat in birds appears to be the spinal cord, not the hypothalamus. However, the thermostat is still responsible for integrating information from central and peripheral thermosensors. When the central thermostat detects changes in temperature, it responds by firing neurons that lead to a compensatory response. Both birds and mammals alter T_B by changing rates of heat production and heat dissipation.

Piloerection reduces heat losses

Earlier in this chapter we discussed how body coverings, such as hair and feathers, act as insulation for endotherms. Because the efficiency of the insulatory layer depends on its thickness, animals can regulate heat loss by changing the orientation of the hair (in mammals) or feathers (in birds). Birds (and mammals) get fluffier in the cold by forcing their feathers (and hair) to orient perpendicular to the body surface. The mechanism by which this orientation is controlled is best understood with mammalian hair, but the position of bird feathers is controlled in a similar way.

Hair itself is a collection of cells that possess abundant keratin, an intermediate filament of the cytoskeleton. The distal end of a hair is primarily dead tissue, but the proximal end is composed of living cells embedded within the hair follicle. Depending on the species, a hair follicle can produce either a single hair shaft or complex combinations of hairs of various lengths and structures. Whereas human hair follicles produce single hairs, dog hair follicles produce a primary guard hair and multiple secondary hairs—soft, fine hairs that form the undercoat of the fur (Figure 15.28). The pit of the hair follicle is composed of epidermal cells. Intimately associated with each hair follicle is a sebaceous gland, which releases complex secretions of lipid (squalene, wax esters, triglyceride, and fatty acids) that form a protective coating on the hair and provide moisturization.

Tiny smooth muscles, called erector muscles, connect each hair follicle to the undersurface of the epidermis. When the erector muscle contracts, the hair is pulled perpendicular, a process termed **piloerection**, so that the fur offers better insulation. The erector muscle contractility is regulated by numerous factors, both blood-borne and neural in origin. The situation is similar in birds, where erector muscles also control the orientation of the feathers.

Changes in blood flow affect thermal exchange

All animals exchange heat at the external surfaces of the body, but they are able to alter the *effectiveness* of surface

FIGURE 15.28 **Hair follicles of a dog**

A hair is produced by cells in the hair follicle. Erector muscles attached to the base of the hair contract in response to neural stimulation, causing the hair to become upright. Sebaceous glands secrete lipids into the follicle ducts.

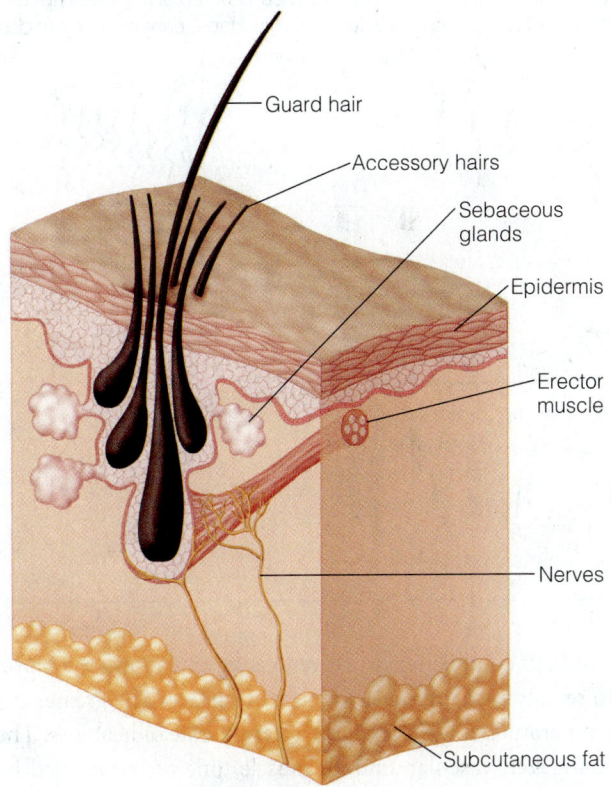

Guard hair
Accessory hairs
Sebaceous glands
Epidermis
Erector muscle
Nerves
Subcutaneous fat

heat exchange by changing the pattern of blood flow. Internal heat is equilibrated throughout the body by the blood. Where blood vessels approach the body surface, they will more readily lose heat. Similarly, increasing the flow of blood through the vessels increases the capacity for heat loss because it warms the surface of the skin, the site of heat loss by conduction, convection, and radiation.

The regulation of the amount of blood flowing into the vasculature is known as the **vasomotor response** (Figure 15.29). Directly under the skin are capillary beds fed by subcutaneous arteries and drained by veins that empty into a network called the *venous plexus*. There is also direct exchange of some blood between the veins and arteries through connections called *arteriovenous anastomoses*, or *metarterioles*. At normal T_B, the sympathetic nervous system constricts the arterioles to reduce blood flow. This tonic constriction is mediated by vascular smooth muscle in response to adrenergic signals. When body temperature rises, there is a loss of tonic constriction and arterioles dilate to allow more blood into the skin vasculature. At the same time, the blood vessels of the anastomoses constrict, forcing more blood to move through the vessels near the skin. The large volume

FIGURE 15.29   Skin vasculature

When blood travels close to the surface of the animal, heat is lost across the skin. When temperatures are cold (left), blood is diverted from the skin through arteriovenous (AV) shunts, called arteriovenous anastomoses, reducing heat loss. When an animal is in a hot environment, shunts are constricted and blood moves through the vessels closer to the skin surface, enhancing heat loss.

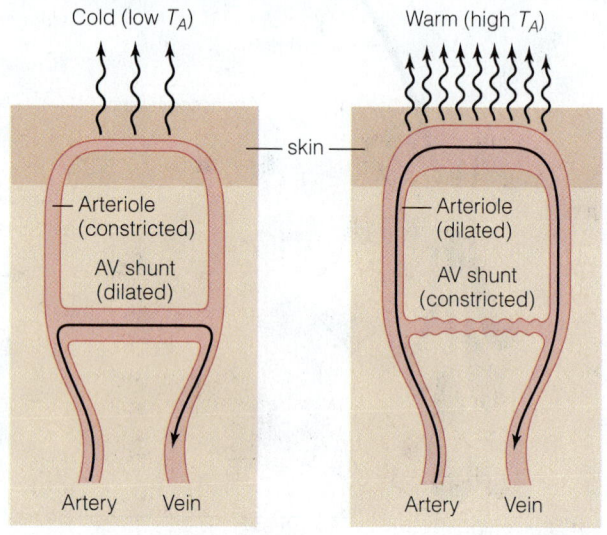

and high compliance of the venous system allows the blood to readily exchange heat to the skin surface. The greater the temperature of the skin, the greater the rate of heat loss. The changes in vascular smooth muscle tone are controlled by the posterior hypothalamus.

Changes in blood flow through these capillary beds allow an endotherm to control heat exchange. The effects are perhaps most obvious in Caucasian humans, whose rapid changes in skin color reflect subdermal blood flow. Exercise increases the core body temperature and triggers an increase in blood flow to the skin, causing it to turn red. Similarly, cold temperatures cause peripheral vasoconstriction, reducing blood flow to the hands and feet, causing them to turn white. Prolonged restriction of blood flow can cause the extremities to turn purple, as the blood pooled in the venous system is slowly deoxygenated.

Countercurrent exchangers in the vasculature help retain heat

In addition to restricting blood flow to the periphery, some animals are able to extract heat from warmed blood and transfer it to cooler blood. This is accomplished by arranging the vasculature into *countercurrent heat exchangers*. The exact arrangement depends upon the animal and the tissue.

Because fish breathe water, any metabolic heat is rapidly lost across the gills. Some regionally heterothermic fish, discussed earlier in this chapter, are active swimmers that produce abundant heat in their red muscle. In tuna, veins leaving the red muscle are juxtaposed to the arteries that supply the red muscle, allowing the transfer of myogenic heat from the veins back to the arteries (Figure 15.30). This allows red muscle to reach temperatures more than

FIGURE 15.30   Countercurrent heat exchangers in tuna muscle

Each heterothermic scombrid species relies on different combinations and numbers of retes to retain heat. Red muscle of bluefin tuna is served by cutaneous arteries and veins that run beneath the skin. From these main vessels, smaller lateral vessels run over the surface of the red muscle, with branches penetrating the muscle. These lateral vessels are arranged in a countercurrent manner, with lateral venules transferring myogenic heat to lateral arterioles.

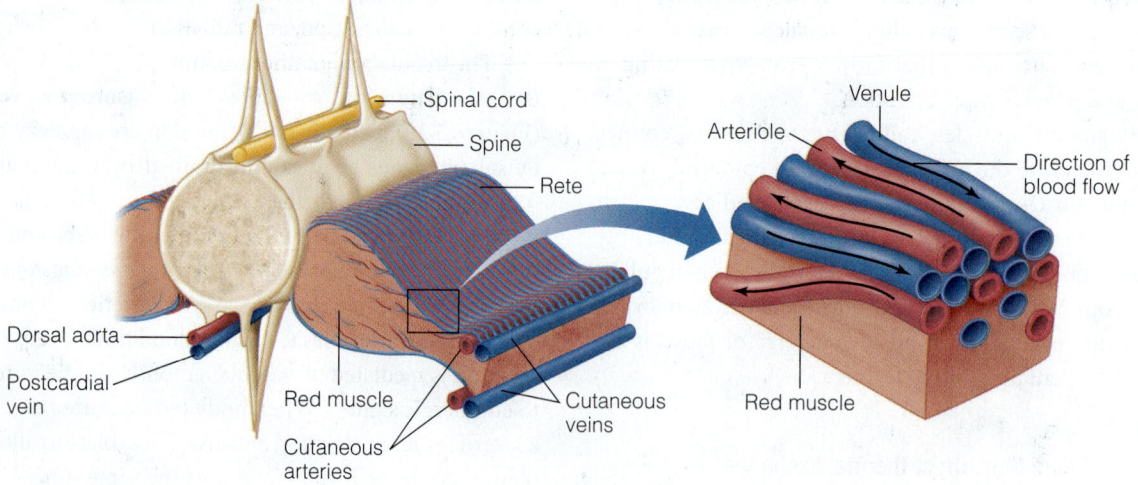

Figure source: Based on Carey, F. G. (1973). Fishes with warm bodies. *Scientific American, 228,* 36–44.

10°C warmer than other tissues, including **white muscle**. Countercurrent heat exchangers are important in other regionally heterothermic fish. As we discussed in Chapter 6, billfish possess a modified eye muscle, called a heater organ, that warms the eye and optical nerves. Countercurrent heat exchangers help retain heat in the optical system. Many large fish, such as bluefin tuna, use countercurrent heat exchangers in the gastrointestinal tract to retain the heat of digestion.

Countercurrent heat exchangers are used by endotherms to reduce heat loss at the periphery. Birds standing on cold surfaces, such as ice, can lose a great deal of heat through the feet (Figure 15.31). They can reduce heat loss by restricting blood flow to the periphery, but over long periods this would cause the peripheral tissues to starve. Countercurrent heat exchangers transfer heat from arteries emerging from the body core to veins returning from the cold periphery. Warming of the venous blood lessens the impact of the peripheral cooling. Also, cooling the arterial blood decreases the thermal gradient across the skin and therefore reduces heat loss.

Sweating reduces body temperature by evaporative cooling

One mode of shedding excess heat is evaporative cooling. In mammals, many species sweat, releasing a mixture of water, salts, and some oils. The salt in sweat raises the boiling point of water, making evaporative cooling more efficient. Loss of water and salts can affect ion and osmoregulation, but animals exposed to hot weather for long periods can change the chemical composition of their sweat to minimize ionic and osmotic problems. They produce a larger volume of sweat with a lower NaCl content, preserving vital salts. Sweating is controlled by the anterior hypothalamus and triggered by activation of the sympathetic nerves that control the activity of sweat glands.

The evolution of sweat as an important route of heat loss was influenced by many factors. Small animals have a favorable ratio of surface area to volume for heat loss, so evaporative cooling is used primarily by larger mammals. In species with fur, sweat glands are present but sweating as a means of thermoregulation is less effective because the fluid simply mats the fur. In primates in general, and humans specifically, the increase in the importance of sweat glands for thermoregulation coincided with the evolution of a hairless skin and large body size.

Panting increases heat loss across the respiratory surface

Another way animals lose heat is through ventilation. The properties that make a respiratory surface good at gas exchange—high vascularity, moist surfaces, and high airflow—also enhance heat loss. Whether respiratory heat loss is beneficial or detrimental depends on the situation. In the cold, birds and mammals minimize heat loss from respiration, but at high T_A, animals may alter their breathing pattern to accentuate heat loss.

Cooling through ventilation is a strategy that must balance respiratory demands with thermoregulation. Cooling is enhanced when animals increase ventilation frequency while reducing tidal volume. Shallow, rapid breathing is a sign that an animal may be overheated. Gular fluttering is a cooling behavior seen in birds, characterized by rapid contraction and relaxation of the throat muscles. Mammals pant. Each of these behaviors cools the animal in multiple ways. First, rapid ventilation increases the heat loss across the respiratory surface by convection. Second, and perhaps more important, the rapid ventilation causes water to evaporate from the surface of the airway, from the pulmonary surface to the tongue. Animals that rely on ventilatory cooling often possess well-vascularized respiratory surfaces that are kept wet through secretions. These ventilatory

---

FIGURE 15.31 **Peripheral vasoconstriction in cold endotherms**

Birds standing on cold surfaces can alter the flow of blood into the feet, reducing heat loss. The blood vessels of the leg and foot are arranged in parallel, allowing the formation of a countercurrent heat exchanger.

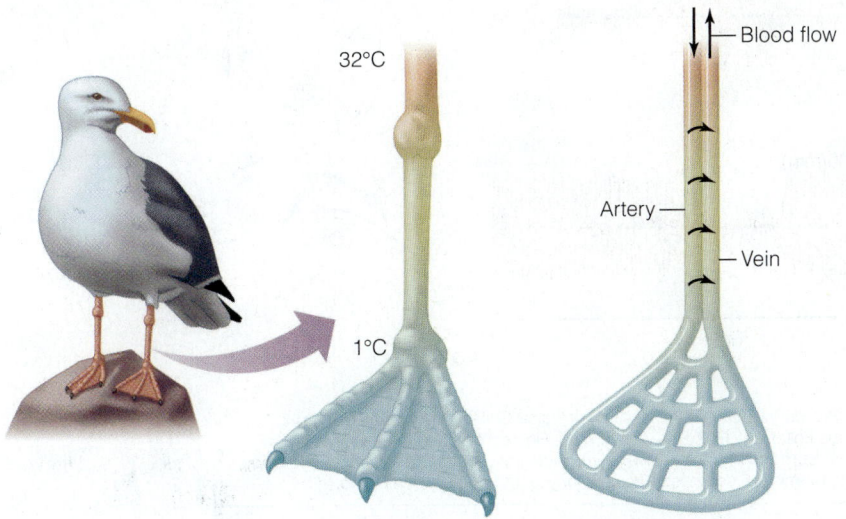

32°C

1°C

Blood flow

Artery

Vein

patterns could alter the nature of the blood gas profile, impinging on respiratory physiology. The increase in ventilation frequency is offset in part by a reduction in tidal volume.

Reindeer provide a good example of the links between respiration and thermoregulation. Although they live in the cold, reindeer are at risk of heat stress because of their large size and thick layer of fur insulation. At normal cold temperatures (10°C), a reindeer breathes through its nose at low frequency. The upper part of the nasal cavity is rich in capillaries, and nasal respiration helps cool the nearby brain regions. When a reindeer becomes too warm, it shifts its respiratory pattern. Breathing frequency increases, and the animal begins to pant through the mouth (Figure 15.32). Although this change in breathing pattern may reduce direct cooling of the brain, it reduces body core temperature more efficiently.

Relaxed endothermy results in hypometabolic states

In previous chapters, we have encountered how endotherms use various forms of hypometabolism to survive adverse conditions. Hummingbirds, for example, undergo a nightly

---

FIGURE 15.32 Heat loss during panting

Like other mammals, reindeer alter breathing to increase heat loss. Reindeer breathe through the nose at low temperatures. The flow of air cools the blood circulating through the vessels that line the nasal cavity. When temperatures increase, reindeer breathe through the mouth and at a faster rate (200–300 breaths per minute).

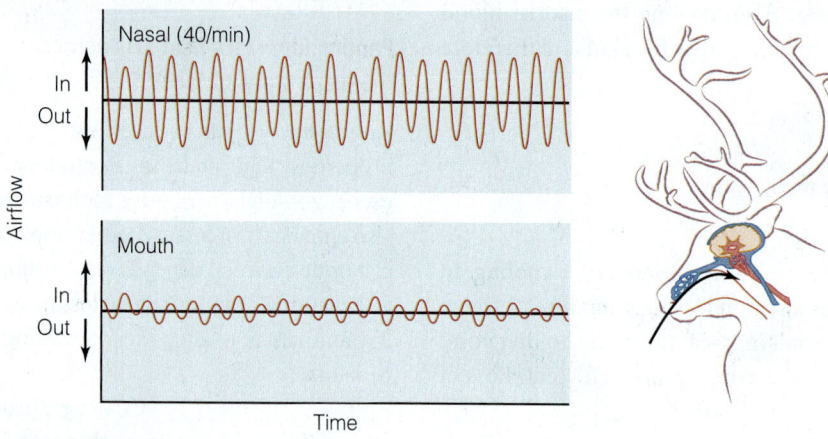

(a) Low temperature

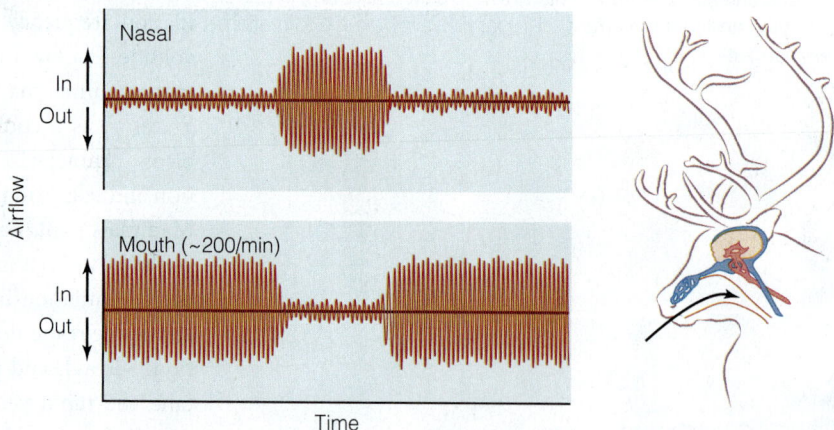

(b) High temperature

Figure source: Republished with permission of American Physiological Society, from Panel (b) graph: Adapted from Aas-Hansen, O., Folkow, L. P., & Blix, A. S. (2000). Figure 1 from Panting in reindeer (*Rangifer tarandus*). *American Journal of Physiology: Regulatory, Integrative, and Comparative Physiology, 279*: R1190–R1195; © 2000. Permission conveyed through Copyright Clearance Center, Inc.

FIGURE 15.33 **Hypometabolic states**

Many endotherms respond to cold temperatures by entering some form of dormancy. Body temperature generally declines in parallel with metabolic rate. The dormancy is called **(a)** hibernation when the metabolic depression lasts for weeks to months or **(b)** torpor when the animal enters a hypometabolic state in daily cycles.

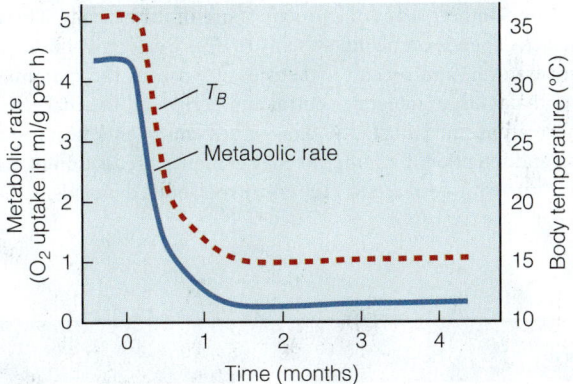

(a) Hibernation

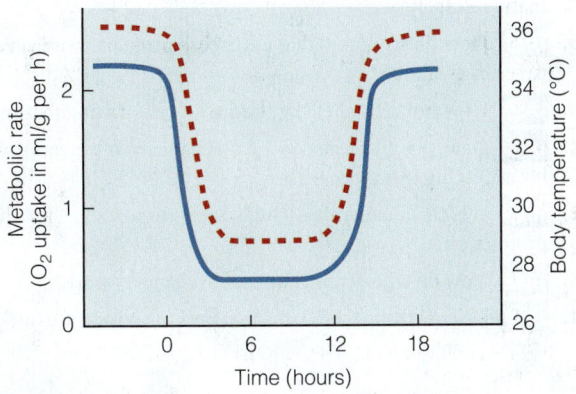

(b) Torpor

and magnitude of reduction in T_B differ among animals and types of dormancy (Figure 15.33). An Arctic squirrel, for example, can allow T_B to fall close to the freezing point. However, even minor reductions in T_B can offer important energetic savings for a dormant animal.

Under normal (euthermic) conditions, mammals and birds maintain T_B within a narrow range. A euthermic animal induces a compensatory response when its central thermostat—the hypothalamus in mammals—senses a decrease in T_B. During periods of relaxed endothermy, the animal recalibrates its central thermostat to recognize and defend a different T_B set point. The endothermic animal may allow T_B to fall close to T_A, well below the euthermic set point. In many species, long periods of dormancy are interrupted by brief periods of arousal. In these episodes, lasting minutes to hours, T_B rises and the animal elevates heart rates and respiration rates, before returning to the hypometabolic condition.

The links between metabolism and T_B regulation make it difficult to establish which parameter causes hypometabolic cooling. For most animals entering dormancy, T_B and metabolic rate decline in parallel, and it is not clear if the colder T_B slows metabolism, or alternately if the slower metabolic heat production causes cooling. In some studies, animals show a reduction in metabolic rate before T_B declines, suggesting that hypometabolism initiates the reduction in T_B. However, in larger animals a delay in cooling upon entering dormancy is due in part to thermal inertia; the large mass and low ratio of surface area to volume delay the impact of reduced thermogenesis, allowing the animal to remain much warmer than T_A even with a reduced metabolic rate.

reduction in metabolic rates. Hibernating mammals also undergo metabolic suppression during the long, cold winter months when food is scarce. Whether a daily dormancy (torpor) or a more prolonged seasonal dormancy (hibernation), the hypometabolic phase is accompanied by a decrease in T_B, a phenomenon called **relaxed endothermy**. The time course

CONCEPT CHECK

16. What regions of the body detect and respond to changes in temperature in mammals?

17. What are the various types of hypometabolism?

18. How do animals control heat flux across the external body surface?

SUMMARY

T_B of an organism depends on the environment (e.g., radiation), anatomy (e.g., shape, insulation), metabolic rate, and heat exchange (e.g., thermal conductance, fluid movement). Thermal strategies are categorized based on the source of heat and the degree of constancy, both temporally and spatially.

Thermal tolerance is influenced by many anatomical and physiological factors, and modified by thermal history. Changes in T_A have greater consequences for ectotherms than for endotherms, altering many aspects of macromolecular structure and metabolism. Temperature alters membrane fluidity and protein structure and function but animals have cellular pathways for minimizing perturbations and mitigating damage.

Poikilotherms that have lived for long periods in extreme cold often possess cold-adapted proteins. Some animals are able to survive freezing by ensuring that it happens in a controlled manner using ice nucleators. Others avoid freezing through antifreeze proteins.

Endothermic animals produce metabolic heat and retain it to elevate T_B above T_A. Their metabolic reactions produce more heat than in ectotherms and they retain more of it internally. Thermal balance depends on neural systems to detect external and internal temperatures, and a central thermostat, such as the mammalian hypothalamus, to integrate central and peripheral thermal sensory information, and adjust physiological systems to alter heat production and retention. Endotherms may combine a reduction in metabolic rate with decreased T_B to reduce metabolic demands.

REVIEW QUESTIONS

1. **LO①** Water at 10°C feels colder than air at 10°C. Why?

2. **LO①** What behaviors reduce heat losses due to (a) conduction; (b) convection?

3. **LO②** Compare and contrast the following terms: homeothermy, poikilothermy, endothermy, and ectothermy.

4. **LO②** Use examples to distinguish between regional heterothermy and temporal heterothermy.

5. **LO③** Why does aerobic scope decline as temperature rises?

6. **LO③** Discuss the different sources of energy an ectotherm can use to raise T_B.

7. **LO④** Why are antifreeze proteins found in marine fish but not freshwater fish?

8. **LO④** Why does a higher temperature generally increase enzymatic rates?

9. **LO⑤** How do we know that antifreeze proteins arose several times in evolution?

10. **LO⑤** How can cells alter the fluidity of cellular membranes?

11. **LO⑥** Compare and contrast the mechanisms of shivering and nonshivering thermogenesis.

12. **LO⑥** Which biochemical steps are responsible for heat production?

13. **LO⑦** How do countercurrent heat exchangers work?

14. **LO⑦** Discuss the mechanisms that permit an increase in T_A to trigger sweating.

SYNTHESIS QUESTIONS

1. Compare the effects of high and low temperature on molecules, cells, tissues, and organisms.

2. How could you convert a stenothermal animal to a eurythermal animal?

3. Summarize the physiological changes that accompany thermal acclimation.

4. Why do endothermic animals need both peripheral and central temperature-sensitive neurons?

5. Thermoregulation requires active control of blood flow through vessels. How do animals dilate some blood vessels while constricting others?

6. What would you expect to happen to blood pressure when a mammal is exposed to cold temperatures?

7. What gene regulatory changes must have accompanied the evolution of brown adipose tissue?

8. Animal color influences many aspects of physiology and ecology. Identify some examples of animals whose color patterns are consistent with a role in thermoregulation.

9. Many mammals grow coats that differ in winter and summer. What factors affect the costs and benefits of seasonal shedding?

10. Compare and contrast the structures of hair and feathers.

QUANTITATIVE QUESTIONS

1. The metabolic rate of a fish heart is studied at various temperatures. The metabolic rate is 20 mol ATP per min per g tissue at 25°C, 8 mol ATP per min per g tissue at 10°C, 4 mol ATP per min per g tissue at 5°C, and 1 mol ATP per min per g tissue at 2°C. Calculate the Q_{10} values over this range of temperatures and offer an explanation for the patterns.

2. The levels of ATP are maintained through a balance between the rates of ATP synthesis and ATP utilization. For a given tissue (e.g., heart) at a given T_B (e.g., 15°C), assume that (a) the rates of ATP synthesis and utilization are both 10 mol/min/g, (b) the rate of ATP synthesis exhibits a $Q_{10} = 2$, (c) the rate of ATP utilization has a $Q_{10} = 2.05$, and (d) the starting ATP level was 5 mol/g tissue. Calculate the change in ATP levels over time that would result if the animal were moved to an environment that caused a 10°C increase in T_B.

3. Recall the Stefan-Boltzmann equation, $P = Ae\delta(T_B^4\ T_A^4)$, where P is the radiating power, A is its surface area, e is the ability of the object to emit radiation, δ is the Stefan constant, and T is the temperature of the body (T_B) or surroundings (T_A) in kelvins. Consider an animal that uses a strategy of changing posture to alter the surface area as a way of controlling heat loss. It assumes a particular posture when it is in an environment that is 5°C below its body temperature. How does it need to change its surface area when it moves to a new environment that is 20°C cooler?

FIGURE 16.1 *Hydra* with lateral bud

Photo source: Biophoto Associates/Science Source.

Sexual reproduction is essential in evolution of organisms because the process of gamete production in parents generates genetic variation in the offspring. This genetic variation is the raw material for natural selection, and increases the likelihood that some variant will be well suited to the demands of a changing environment. Of course, some species have evolved means of asexual reproduction, which is well suited to more stable environments. Clonal reproduction, essentially budding off parts of the adult to generate genetically identical offspring, is used by many invertebrates, such as *Hydra* (Figure 16.1).

Much rarer in animals is a mode of reproduction that combines the benefits of asexual and sexual reproduction. As will be discussed later in this chapter, **parthenogenesis** hijacks the machinery of gametogenesis to allow a female to self-fertilize her own ova. In recent years, the popular press has reported a number of instances of virgin birth in zoo settings where females who may have not recently encountered a male suddenly begin producing offspring. In 2013, Armani the anteater at LEO Zoological Conservation Center in Greenwich, Connecticut gave birth to a pup long after Armani's last encounter with a male. Though originally reported as an example of parthenogenesis, it is more likely a case of delayed implantation. Fertilized embryos from her last encounter with a male likely entered stasis for several months before implanting in the uterus and continuing embryonic development. However, parthenogenesis has been reported in numerous species of birds, snakes, and lizards. For example, Flora is a Komodo dragon at the Chester Zoo in the United Kingdom. She has laid clutches of eggs without ever having encountered a male Komodo dragon.

Though most easily verified in a zoo setting, parthenogenesis has been shown to occur broadly in nature. It is important in many species of invertebrates. For example, when food is abundant a female aphid can use parthenogenesis to rapidly produce 50–100 young aphids. Within only a few days these offspring, which are tiny versions of their mother, reproduce parthenogenically, resulting in an aphid infestation. The whiptail lizard (*Cnemidophorus uniparens*) exists as an entirely female species that reproduces by parthenogenesis.

Cnemidophorus inornatus, its closest relative and likely the ancestral species, reproduces sexually. Remarkably, many of the mating behaviors that occurred in the ancestral species still occur in the parthenogenic species. In the sexual species, a surge of progesterone causes a male to mount a female. In the asexual species, a progesterone surge occurs in an ovulating female, causing her to mount another female. These "mating" behaviors are common in parthenogenic species. In some species, the behaviors are simply a regulatory remnant of their sexual ancestry, but some mating rituals take on new functions. For example, the mating behavior of two parthenogenic females can induce ovulation.

Reproductive physiology captures the imagination of students because many of the traits are so fundamentally different from the more familiar human mode. Though there are common themes when comparing animals, there are also wondrous exceptions. In this chapter, we explore the diversity in reproductive physiology, emphasizing the ways that different systems contribute to successful reproduction in animals. ■

LOOKING BACK 16

You may find it helpful to review Chapter 3 for the basic features of steroid synthesis, the mechanisms that control secretions from cells, and the synthesis of the various macromolecules that contribute to secretions such as milk. Review Chapter 4, where we discuss the basic features of cell signaling pathways, which are critical in reproductive physiology. Some of this chapter also touches on energy metabolism, which we discuss in Chapter 14.

▌ OVERVIEW

The life cycle of an animal begins with a single cell, which divides repeatedly through multicellular stages (**zygote**, blastula, and gastrula) that differentiate to form tissues (morphogenesis). Juvenile forms then undergo further development to reach reproductive maturity (Figure 16.2). The reproductive traits of the individual are usually established in embryonic development, with the acquisition of the primary sex characteristics: the **gonads**. These multicellular tissues include cells that produce the **gametes** as well as somatic tissues that support gamete production (**gametogenesis**). The gonads develop in combination with other physiological and behavioral systems in preparation for mating. Mating behavior may be linked to environmental conditions and often follows complex courtship rituals. Animals then release the gametes—ova or **spermatozoa**—when the chances for successful fertilization are maximized. Spermatozoa, or sperm for short, face many challenges. They must find the **ovum** in a complex environment and outcompete other sperm to be the one that fertilizes the ovum. After fertilization, the embryo grows under the control of its unique genome, a mosaic of its parents. All of the elements of sexual reproduction—sex determination, gametogenesis, mating, fertilization, and development—depend on the coordination of cellular processes in multiple tissues. The responsibility for coordination of these processes falls upon the endocrine hormones.

FIGURE 16.2 **Animal life cycle**

FIGURE 16.2 **Animal life cycle**

This generalized life cycle highlights the developmental stages seen in most animals.

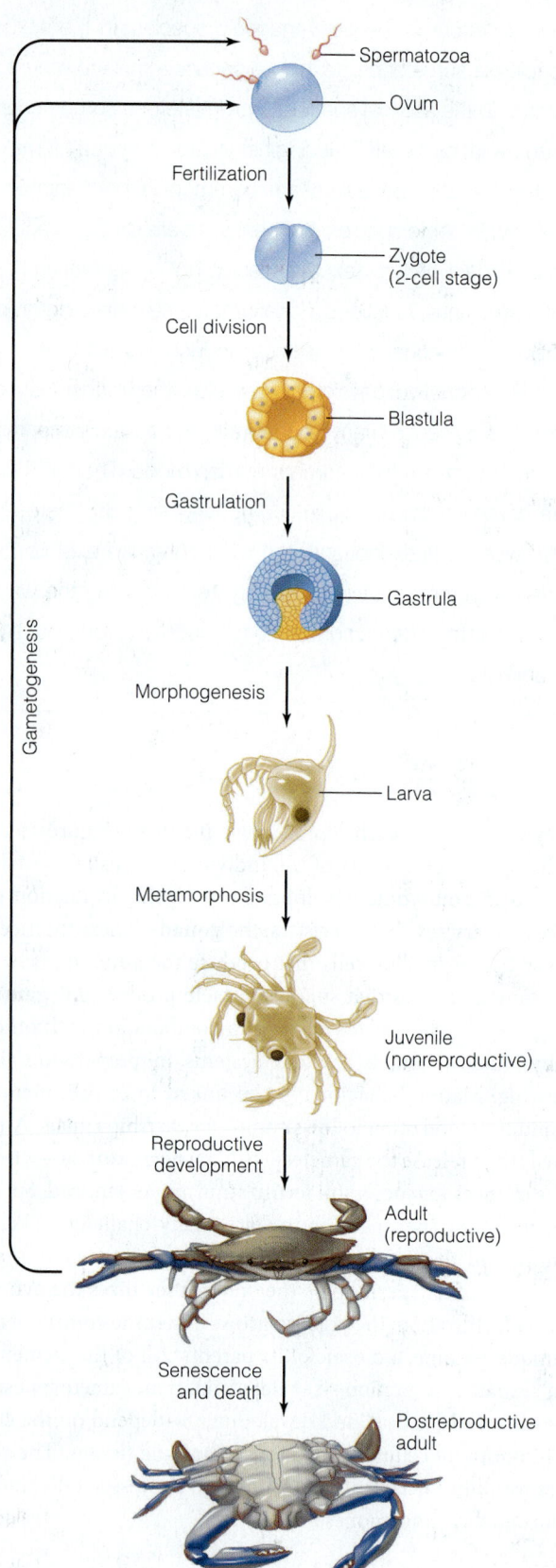

The diversity seen in the life histories of animals is remarkable, given the relative similarity in hormones, cell signaling, and gametogenesis. In this section, we survey the basic features of reproductive physiology, considering modes of reproduction, hormones, gametogenesis, and reproductive anatomy. In the next section, we focus in greater detail on the reproductive physiology of mammals, through ovulation, gestation, parturition, and postpartum care, emphasizing the role of hormones. We conclude this chapter with a brief discussion of patterns of postembryonic development and growth.

REPRODUCTION

Let's begin by considering the aspects of reproduction that are common to most animals. Long before the animals appeared on the scene, the early eukaryotes (for example, the protists) had already evolved a capacity for sexual reproduction. The essence of sexual reproduction is the generation of offspring from two parents, each of which contributes a nearly equal amount of genetic material. The biological concept of "maleness" and "femaleness" is based on the size of the gametes. In sexual reproduction, the gametes are of different size (*anisogametic*): The male has gonads (testes) that produce small gametes (spermatozoa), and the female has gonads (ovaries) that produce large gametes (ova). Gametogenesis occurs through meiosis, although there are important distinctions between spermatozoa production (**spermatogenesis**) and ova production (**oogenesis**). Reproductive systems include the gonads, the reproductive tract through which gametes escape, and the accessory tissues that provide regulatory molecules, nutrients, and fluids.

Sexual reproduction is one of the reasons why animals have been so successful in exploiting diverse ecological niches. The process generates genomic variation at three levels. First, an animal produces gametes with genomes consisting of combinations of chromosomes originally provided by the animal's own parents. For an animal with 23 chromosome pairs, more than 8 million genetically different gametes can be produced by a single individual. Second, during meiosis, chromosomal recombinations can create chromosomes that are hybrids of maternal and paternal chromosomes, further adding to the total number of unique gametes. Third, the diploid offspring produced by fertilization are unique combinations of the different types of variants arising independently from the first two processes in both oogenesis and spermatogenesis. For these reasons, each offspring produced in sexual reproduction is unlike either its siblings or its parents. Thus, sexual reproduction creates a population that is a collection of distinct genotypes—a genetic diversity that is the raw material upon which natural selection acts.

REPRODUCTIVE ENDOCRINOLOGY

Reproductive hormones orchestrate development, sexual maturation, gametogenesis, and mating. There are many common themes in how diverse animals use hormones to control reproduction.

- Complex pathways of negative and positive feedback control hormone synthesis.

- Hormone levels are determined by regulation of synthesis as well as degradation.

- Hormone efficacy is influenced by hormone receptor synthesis in target tissues.

- Males and females of a species use the same suites of hormones, although an individual hormone may have sex-specific functions.

- Hormones with major roles in other physiological systems also have vital functions in reproduction.

Reproductive Hormones

Steroid hormones are critical regulators of animal reproductive physiology. Recall from Chapter 4 that steroid hormones regulate physiology primarily through effects on gene expression. Each steroid hormone binds to a *nuclear hormone receptor*, a protein that heterodimerizes with another DNA-binding protein to form an active transcription factor. Animals mediate the effects of steroid hormones by altering the rates of hormone synthesis, the levels of receptors in target tissues, and the rates of degradation of hormones and receptors, and by producing extracellular proteins that bind steroids. Steroid hormones are all derived from cholesterol, but diverse enzymatic pathways allow animals to produce a range of structurally related specific hormones.

Vertebrates rely on progesterone, androgens, and estrogens

In vertebrates, there is a complex suite of steroid hormones with subtle structural differences that induce unique activities (Figure 16.3). Progesterone is produced from cholesterol

FIGURE 16.3 **Reproductive hormones**

Highlighted areas distinguish chemical differences in closely related hormones.

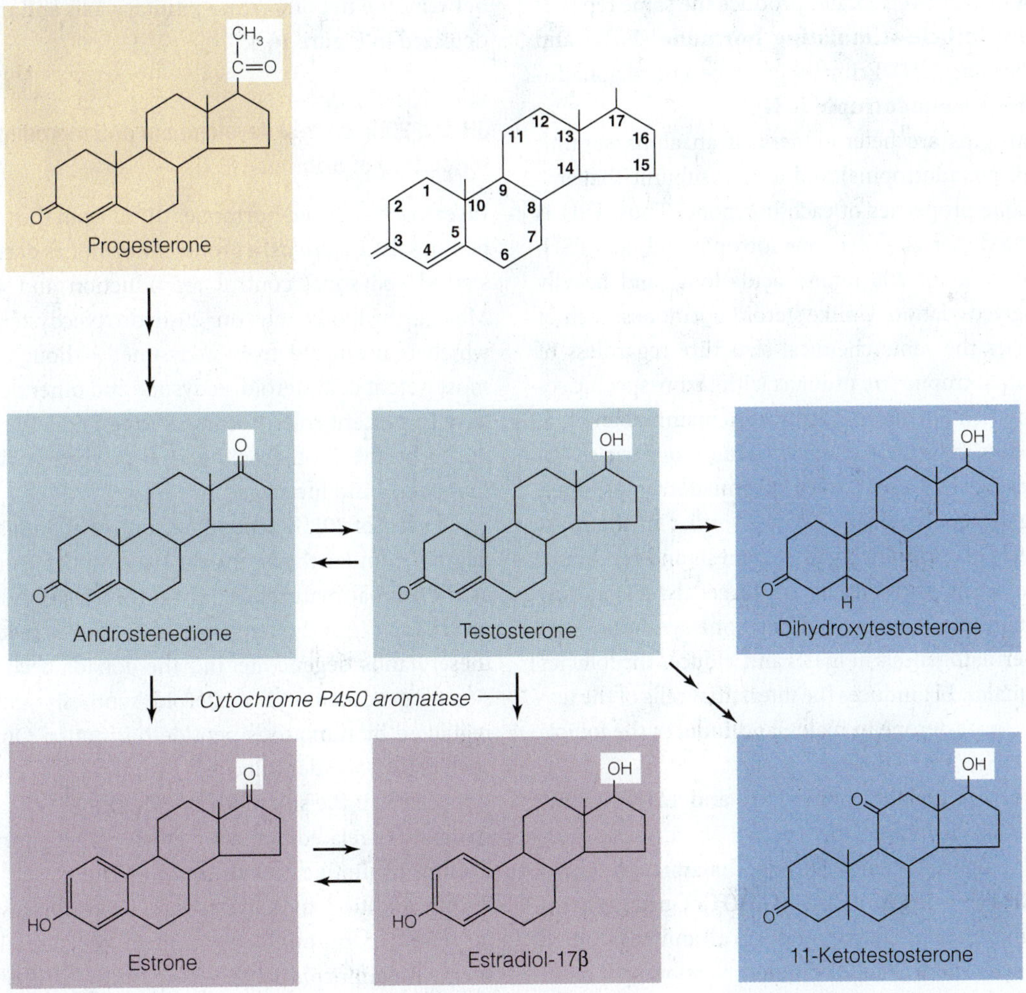

in a number of steroidogenic tissues, including the adrenal gland and gonads. It can escape into the blood, exerting effects in both males and females, or it can be further metabolized to androstenedione. In males, androstenedione is further metabolized to various **androgens**. The most common androgen is testosterone, although other androgens (11-ketotestosterone, androstenedione, and dihydrotestosterone) predominate in some species and processes. Although these are called male hormones, they are also produced in females and serve as the precursors for synthesis of **estrogens**, primarily estrone and **estradiol-17β**.

The rates of production of individual steroids depend largely on the distribution and activity of steroid metabolizing enzymes. Central to steroid metabolism are the **cytochrome P450** enzymes of the endoplasmic reticulum. **Aromatase** is a cytochrome P450 enzyme that metabolizes androgens to estrogens. For example, it converts testosterone to estradiol-17β and androstenedione to estrone.

Gonadotropins control steroid hormone levels

Steroid synthesis in the gonads is controlled by the levels of nonsteroidal hormones produced by the anterior pituitary: **gonadotropins**. Most vertebrates produce the same types of gonadotropins: **follicle-stimulating hormone (FSH)** and *luteinizing hormone (LH)*. Primates produce a third gonadotropin, **chorionic gonadotropin (CG)**.

Gonadotropins are heterodimers of an alpha subunit (shared by all gonadotropins) and a beta subunit that imparts the unique properties of each hormone. Thus, FSH is composed of a dimer of alpha gonadotropin and beta FSH. Each subunit is about 100 amino acids long, and heavily modified by glycosylation. Unlike steroid hormones, each of which possesses the same chemical structure regardless of taxon, the gonadotropins are proteins with taxon-specific sequences. Thus, fish FSH is not identical to mammalian FSH, but the gonadotropins are so named because of their structural similarities. The exact roles of gonadotropins often differ among vertebrate taxa. They are similar in the most general respects of controlling gametogenesis and reproductive maturity, acting both directly on target tissues and indirectly through effects on steroid hormone synthesis. FSH stimulates spermatogenesis in males and induces the follicles to ripen in females. LH induces the interstitial cells of the testes to produce testosterone in males, and induces the follicle to produce estrogens in females.

Release of the gonadotropins FSH and LH from the anterior pituitary is under the control of multiple hormones. The main regulator is a hypothalamic hormone, **gonadotropin-releasing hormone (GnRH)**. GnRH is composed of 10 amino acids (a decapeptide) in all animals studied to date. However, more than 20 different versions of GnRH have been seen in vertebrates, and most species produce two or more versions of GnRH with subtly different effects on target tissues. The primary role of GnRH is in reproduction, but it has other roles as well, such as behavioral control.

GnRH is produced by hypothalamic neurons and released into the portal system that carries hypothalamic factors to the anterior pituitary. The neurons release a burst of GnRH that triggers secretion of LH and FSH. Differences in the way LH and FSH are stored affect the profile of these hormones in the blood. The anterior pituitary stores ample LH in vesicles that can be released in synchrony to induce a pulse of LH in the blood. In contrast, the anterior pituitary stores little preformed FSH, producing FSH on demand in response to GnRH.

The gonadotropins regulate many aspects of reproductive physiology, acting through effects on their primary target tissue, the gonads. In addition to effects on the gametogenic tissues and other gonad functions, they induce the release of estrogens in the female and androgens in the male. These hormones then act on other tissues, including both the primary reproductive tissues (ovaries and testes) as well as those considered secondary sex features (mammary glands, hair follicles, and male sexual displays). These relationships between the hypothalamic-pituitary axis and the gonads are depicted in Figure 16.4.

JH and 20HE control development and reproductive physiology of arthropods

Invertebrate steroid hormones differ from those used by vertebrates. *Ecdysteroids*, a group of hormones derived from the steroid ecdysone, control reproduction and development. Most arthropods rely on 20-hydroxyecdysterone (20HE), which is produced from ecdysone. Although 20HE is the most potent ecdysteroid, ecdysone and other derivatives also have important roles in some species. Ecdysteroids are produced by the prothoracic glands or gonads, depending on the species and life stage.

Levels of 20HE depend on control of both synthesis and degradation. Furthermore, the pathways of synthesis change as the animal matures. A larva produces ecdysteroids in its prothoracic glands, but when the animal metamorphoses, these glands degenerate and the gonads become the main site of production. Ecdysteroid synthesis and release are regulated by numerous peptide hormones. One of the first such regulators identified was *bombyxin*. This hormone, first isolated from the silk moth *Bombyx mori*, is a protein that is structurally related to the vertebrate protein hormones of the insulin/insulinlike growth factor family.

In addition to ecdysteroids, invertebrates use various terpenoid compounds to control reproductive development, metamorphosis, molting, and metabolism. Insects

FIGURE 16.4 Hypothalamic-pituitary axis

The hypothalamus receives signals from the brain and blood-borne hormones, and responds by releasing gonadotropin-releasing hormone into the pituitary. This induces the release of gonadotropins (LH and FSH) into the blood, for transport to the gonads. The gonads respond by increasing steroid hormone synthesis. Ovaries release estrogens and progesterone, which exert effects on primary reproductive tissues, such as the uterus, and secondary sex tissues, such as the mammary glands. In males, the testes release androgens, which exert effects in the testes, but also affect other tissues, including secondary sex organs and muscles.

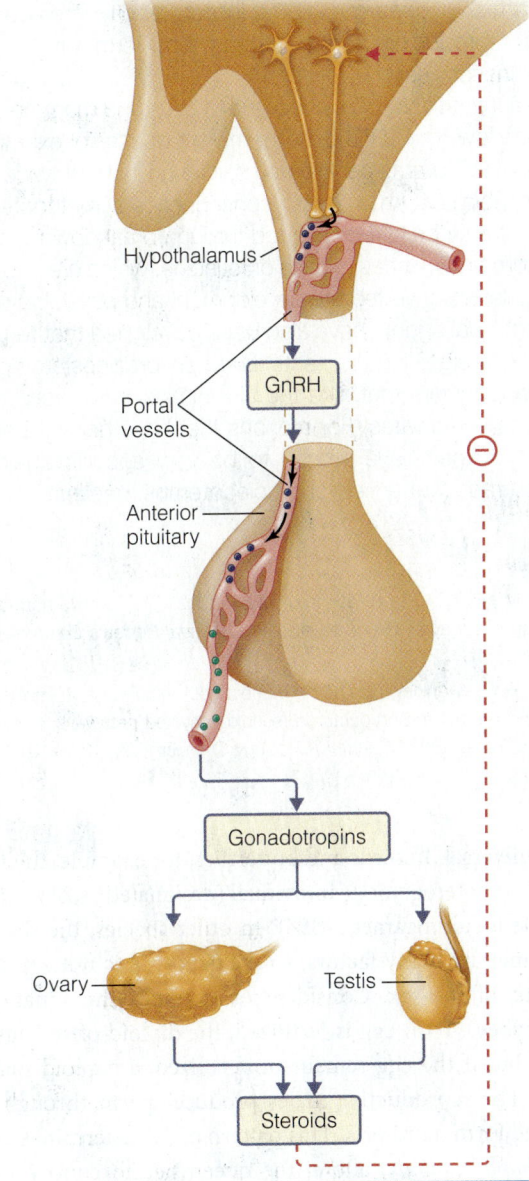

Hypothalamus

GnRH

Portal vessels

Anterior pituitary

Gonadotropins

Ovary   Testis

Steroids

It splits open the exoskeleton, rapidly increases in volume, and then resynthesizes a new, larger exoskeleton. Most insects undergo multiple larval molts prior to adulthood. The last step of development, the emergence of the adult, occurs by one of two alternate routes. In **holometabolous insects**, the last **instar** forms a cocoon, a fibrous external coating around the inner juvenile form, at this stage called a **pupa**. Although it appears dormant, inside the cocoon the pupa is reorganizing its physiological systems in preparation for reproductive maturation. An adult form emerges from the cocoon, although it may need to undergo additional sexual development. In **hemimetabolous insects**, the larval forms, usually called **nymphs**, undergo repeated molts, with the last nymph emerging as an adult. Holometabolous insects include lepidopterans (butterflies), dipterans (flies), and coleopterans (beetles). Odonates (dragonflies), orthopterans (locusts), and true bugs (hemipterans and homopterans) are hemimetabolous.

Juvenile hormone is so named because of its role in maintaining juvenile characteristics in the larvae. It stimulates the synthesis of larval exoskeleton, which differs in molecular composition from the adult exoskeleton. High levels of JH also prevent larvae of holometabolous insects from undergoing pupation. Only when JH levels decline can the larva enter the pupal stage. During the pupal stage, JH levels continue to fall and the pupa develops into the adult form. Once JH levels have fallen to some minimum value, the neurosecretory cells of the brain release another hormone, eclosion hormone, and the adult emerges from the cocoon (eclosion). Upon eclosion, JH assumes a new regulatory role, increasing in concentration to trigger sexual maturation in both the male and the female.

The activity of terpenoids, like 20HE, is controlled by both synthesis and degradation. JH biosynthesis in the **corpus allatum** is regulated by factors released from neurons and neuroendocrine cells. **Allatotropins** are peptide hormones that stimulate JH production and release, whereas **allatostatins** are inhibitory peptide hormones. Insects also control the levels of JH through degradation, using enzyme JH esterase to convert JH to less active metabolites. Thus, an increase in JH esterase activity is one way an insect larva reduces JH levels to allow it to proceed in development.

Exquisite control of JH and ecdysteroids is required to ensure that development occurs at the proper time, usually ensuring that the animal hits developmental milestones at times when they have the appropriate metabolic physiology (e.g., energy stores) and when environmental conditions are optimal. Thus, many efforts for pest control focus on the JH–ecdysteroid axis, introducing antagonists and agonists in an effort to disrupt proper development and reproductive maturation (see Box 16.1: Applications: Pesticides Targeting Insect-Specific Hormonal Pathways).

rely upon **juvenile hormone (JH)**, whereas crustaceans use methyl farnesoate. When an insect egg hatches, a juvenile form (larva) emerges and begins to eat. As the larva grows, it reaches the capacity of its rigid exoskeleton. The first larva, also known as the first instar, undergoes **ecdysis** (molting):

PESTICIDES TARGETING INSECT-SPECIFIC HORMONAL PATHWAYS

Many of the most common insecticides attack insects by disrupting neuronal function. Pyrethroids, for example, are organic compounds that are synthetic variants of pyrethrin, which is a product of pyrethrum plants, such as *Chrysanthemum.* In use for more than 100 years, there is growing concern that these neurotoxic agents have negative effects when escaping into the ecosystem. Given the conservation of neuronal properties across animals, it is not surprising that neurotoxins that work on insects will also work on non-target species, including humans.

Alternative strategies for insect control take advantage of insect-specific physiology in an effort to avoid toxicity for humans and other vertebrates that may come in contact with the agent. The dependence on juvenile hormone (JH) and ecdysteroids is unique to invertebrates, and most important in arthropods. When the levels of these hormones are too high or too low, insects may not be able to metamorphose or reach reproductive maturity. Capitalizing on this vulnerability, several pest management strategies have been developed that revolve around disruption of JH or ecdysteroid signal transduction.

Methoprene has emerged as an important insecticide in many applications. It is the active ingredient in many antiflea treatments used in household pets. It is added to drinking water in many countries to reduce mosquito populations. It is fed to cattle to reduce the numbers of insects that breed in the dung.

It is structurally similar to JH, and is thought to act by binding the JH receptor and enhancing JH signaling. Most effective in larva, the enhanced JH signal prevents the larva from entering the next step in development, such as pupation. Though it does not kill the insect directly, it prevents it from reproducing, which affords long-term protection against insect pests.

The acute toxicity of methoprene to birds and mammals is extremely low. The LD50 dose for mallard ducks, for example is more than 2 grams per kilograms, making it about twice as toxic as table salt. An unknown consequence of methoprene treatment may be effects exerted through breakdown products. Some may act as mimics of retinoids, which are important regulators of vertebrate development and physiology.

Insecticidal agents have also been developed that target ecdysteroid signaling in insects. Bisacylhydrazines are nonsteroidal agonists that, like the JH mimics, have very low toxicity to vertebrates. For reasons that have not yet been elucidated, they have proven to be very specific against lepidopterans (butterflies) and coleopterans (beetles).

References

- Jindra, M., Palli, S. R., & Riddiford, L. M. (2013). The juvenile hormone signaling pathway in insect development. *Annual Reviews Entomology, 58*, 181–204.
- Schoff, P. K., & Ankley, G. T. (2004). Effects of methoprene, its metabolites, and breakdown products on retinoid-activated pathways in transfected cell lines. *Environmental Toxicology Chemistry, 23*, 1305–1310.

CONCEPT CHECK

1. How does the chemical structure of reproductive hormones affect the way their synthesis and secretion is regulated?
2. What are the main hormones in vertebrate reproduction and where are they produced?
3. Contrast the roles of ecdysone and juvenile hormone.

Sex Determination

Sex is strictly defined in relation to gamete size, but a misconception persists that gender is always a result of the presence or absence of the Y chromosome. In mammals, the Y chromosome is called the sex-determining chromosome; a male results when the zygote is heterogametic (XY) and a female when it is homogametic (XX). This pattern, however, is not universal. In birds and butterflies, for example, the female is the heterogametic individual (designated as ZW) and the male is homogametic (ZZ). In other species, the sex is determined by many factors, so the genotype is not a good predictor of the sex. Consider, for example, the situation in honeybees. If an egg is fertilized, the diploid offspring is female, but if the egg remains unfertilized, a haploid male results. The reproductive males produce sperm through a modified form of mitosis. This pattern of sex determination, called *haplo-diploidy*, allows the queen bee to control the numbers of males and females within the colony.

The consequences of being male versus female differ widely among animals. In some species, males and females are nearly indistinguishable physically and in many cases share parental duties equally. There are also many examples of sexual dimorphism. In many birds, for example, the males and females may differ in coloration. In these species (think of peacocks and peahens), color patterns or decorations are meaningful to mates, conferring some indication of the fitness of the potential mate. There are also many examples of extreme sexual dimorphism, where males and females are barely recognizable as the same species. In anglerfish, males live as small parasites on females, waiting for a chance to fertilize eggs. There can also be negative consequences for a male that is smaller and more vulnerable than the female. Male spiders, like the famed black widow, and some midges, are consumed by the female after mating.

Before discussing the specifics of sex and sexual reproduction, we will review the relatively less common scenarios where animals reproduce without sex: **clonal reproduction** and parthenogenesis.

Clonal reproduction is asexual

The genetic diversity arising through sexual reproduction helps animals evolve in changing environments, but for species that live in a relatively constant environment, genomic variation is not necessarily an advantage. Evolution has endowed some sexually reproducing animals with the capacity to reproduce asexually. Corals, for example, reproduce sexually but have evolved the ability for asexual reproduction, producing buds that are clones of the parent. Buds form from somatic tissues of the adults, either male or female. This allows a single individual coral to produce a colony of clones.

Parthenogenesis is a short-circuit of sexual reproduction

Most forms of asexual reproduction in animals are not through clonal mechanisms, but rather by **parthenogenesis** ("virgin birth"). In contrast to cloning, parthenogenesis occurs through the use of ova and the female reproductive system. In contrast to sexual reproduction, no male is involved.

Parthenogenesis allows a single diploid female to use its reproductive tissue to produce offspring that may be diploid or haploid, depending on the pathways involved. The most common pathway of parthenogenesis, called **automictic parthenogenesis** (*automictic* = self-mixing), is a variation on the standard meiotic pathway for oogenesis, proceeding to the point where the secondary **oocyte** is formed (see Figure 16.5). When the secondary oocyte undertakes

the second meiotic division, the second polar body doesn't degrade but instead fertilizes the ovum, resulting in a homogametic zygote. Because the offspring from automictic parthenogenesis is homogametic, the sex of the offspring depends on which of the sexes is homogametic. Thelytoky is a form of automictic parthenogenesis in which a homogametic female (XX) produces females; it lacks the Y allele that is needed to produce a heterogametic male (XY). In contrast, in *arrhenotoky*, heterogametic (WZ) females produce only males (ZZ). If the ovum and second polar body originate from the Z allele, offspring are ZZ males. If the ovum and second polar body arise from the W allele, a nonviable WW genotype is formed. Populations survive by alternating between sexual and parthenogenic reproduction.

Animals may be simultaneous or serial hermaphrodites

Sexual reproduction does not necessarily require genetically separate sexes. Many species are **hermaphrodites**, possessing the capacity to produce both eggs and sperm. Some hermaphrodites, like the earthworm, produce both eggs and sperm at the same time. The testes are in segments that are separated from the segments bearing ovaries. When two earthworms

FIGURE 16.5 Automictic parthenogenesis

In some species, the females reproduce by parthenogenesis when the second polar body fertilizes the ovum. **(a)** In thelytoky, homogametic females produce only female offspring. **(b)** In arrhenotoky, heterogametic females produce male offspring through parthenogenesis.

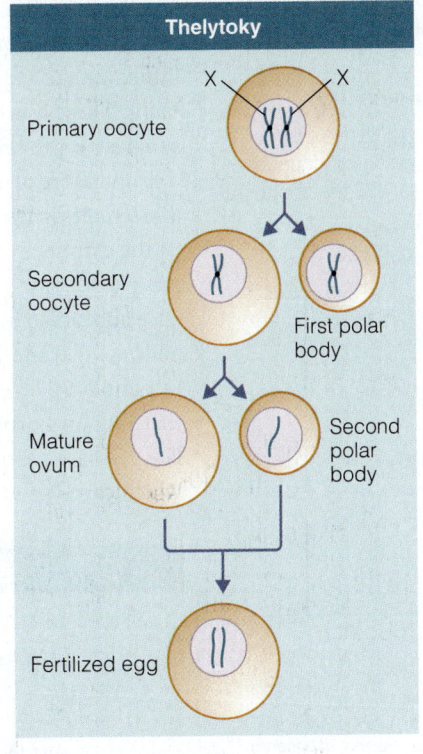
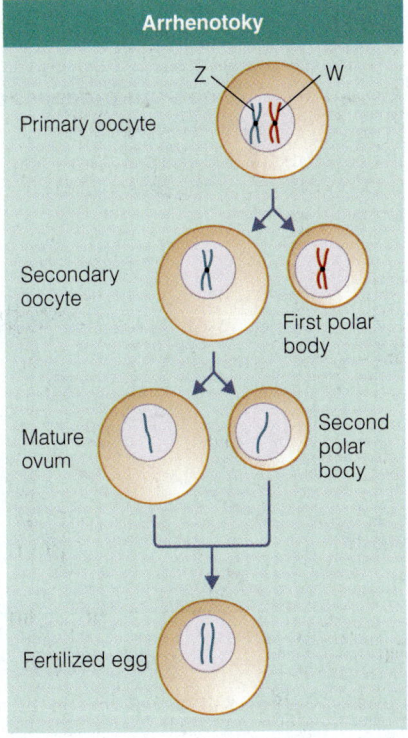

(a)   (b)

copulate, they arrange their ventral sides together, but oriented anterior to posterior. Thus, the spermatogenic tissue is directly against the oogenic region. Although this antiparallel arrangement optimizes the chance of cross-fertilization for both worms, self-fertilization can occur.

Other species are serial hermaphrodites, existing for part of life as one sex but sometimes exercising an option to change to the other sex later in life under some circumstances. *Protogynous* animals are first female (producing eggs), and then become male (producing sperm). *Protandrous* animals are male first, then become female. In many cases, the switch from one sex to the other occurs in response to environmental conditions, including social interactions. For example, as discussed in Chapter 4, some female coral reef fish spontaneously transform into males if the dominant male in the community is removed. The transition from female to male appears to involve a change in the metabolism of the main sex hormones. The male reproductive system is maintained by testosterone and its metabolite 11-ketotestosterone. The female reproductive state is maintained by estradiol-17β. The control of sex is linked to the metabolism of testosterone. In females, testosterone is metabolized to estradiol-17β through a pathway involving the cytochrome P450 enzyme aromatase (see Figure 16.6). When aromatase inhibitors are given to females, they undergo a sex change in little more than two months. The new males possess low levels of estradiol-17β and high levels of testosterone and 11-ketotestosterone. It remains unknown how environmental factors, including social interactions, act through physiological regulators to alter steroid hormone metabolism in the natural setting.

FIGURE 16.6 **Temperature-dependent sex determination**

In painted turtles, the levels of steroid hormones in yolk changes throughout the breeding season, and correlates with the prevalence of females.

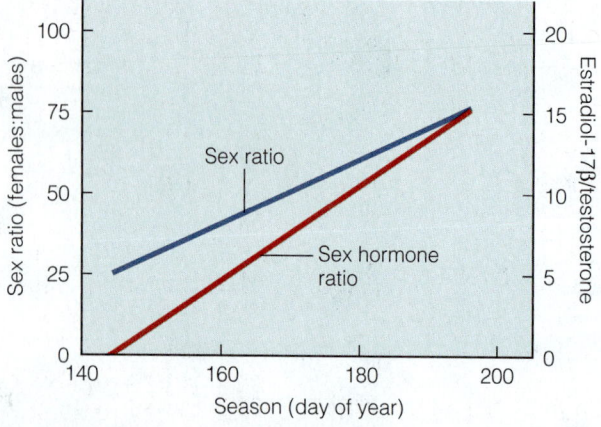

Figure source: Based on Bowden, R. M., Ewart, M. A., & Nelson, C. E. (2000). Figures 1 and 3c from Environmental sex determination in a reptile varies seasonally and with yolk hormones. *Proceedings of the Royal Society of London, Series B: Biological Sciences, 267*, 1745–1749.

Sex is determined in some species by environmental conditions

In most animals, the sex of young is determined by the genotype: presence or absence of sex-determining chromosomes. However, in some species sex is determined by the physical and chemical environment around the developing embryo. The most common form of environmental sex determination is temperature-dependent sex determination (TSD). It is very common in reptiles, occurring in all crocodilians and marine turtles, as well as selected species of lizards and terrestrial turtles. At an intermediate ambient temperature, called the **pivotal temperature**, equal numbers of males and females result. Three main patterns emerge in studies of TSD. Some turtles produce males when temperatures are below the pivotal temperature and females above. Conversely, some lizards produce males when temperatures are high and females at low temperature. A third pattern is seen in crocodiles and alligators: Female offspring dominate at both high and low temperatures, but male offspring are more abundant at intermediate temperatures.

It is not always obvious why one particular sex may be advantageous at a given temperature, and it is not yet certain that the mother actively biases the sex ratio by choosing where to lay her eggs. TSD also poses some risks: If temperature were the only factor that influenced sex, then conditions could arise in which whole populations would become threatened by abnormally high (or low) temperatures, resulting in a preponderance of only one sex in the population. Thus, such species could be at great risk from global climate change.

The sex ratio resulting from TSD is influenced by other factors as well. For example, levels of sex hormones in the yolk influence the pattern of sex determination during development. These hormone levels vary seasonally, imparting a seasonal aspect to the sex ratios. For example, in painted turtles, a temperature of 28°C generates near-equal numbers of males and females in the middle of the breeding season (Figure 16.6). At the extremes of the breeding season, the same temperature can yield 75 percent males or 75 percent females. The difference appears to be linked to the relative levels of estradiol-17β and testosterone in the egg. When eggs have relatively high estradiol-17β levels, the clutch is more female biased. Species that rely on hormones in the yolk as a mechanism to regulate TSD are particularly susceptible to endocrine disruptors, which can alter sex ratios independent of temperature.

CONCEPT CHECK

4. What is the difference between XY and ZW sex determination?
5. What is the difference between clonal reproduction and parthenogenesis?
6. What is temperature-dependent sex determination?

GAMETOGENESIS AND FERTILIZATION

In most species, females produce their lifetime supply of gametes early in life and retain them in a state of developmental quiescence until needed. The term *ovum* typically refers to the unfertilized gamete, without distinguishing between primary oocyte, secondary oocyte, or ovum (see Figure 16.2). In some situations, people may use the terms ovum and egg interchangeably, but in other cases the egg may actually be fertilized and undergoing embryonic growth. The ovum is a single cell, but it is also associated with noncellular material produced by the female reproductive tract.

The three main types of reproductive strategies—ovipary, vivipary, and ovovivipary—are distinguished by the fate of the ova prior to and after fertilization. Different degrees of parental care are roughly commensurate with the three reproductive strategies. **Oviparous** animals expel the ova from the body, and all development occurs externally using the resources within the egg. Fertilization may be external, as in most fish, or internal, as in birds and reptiles. The level of parental care ranges from none to intense. Few insects exhibit parental care, whereas most birds guard eggs and feed young. **Viviparous** animals use internal fertilization, and the young develop within the female body. In early development, the young derive significant resources from the mother. Placental mammals are the most obvious examples of vivipary, but it also occurs in some species of fish, snakes, and skinks. The female reproductive tract produces nutrients for the offspring, which can be a simple slurry of "uterine milk" secreted from the uterus, or more elaborate arrangements that allow the embryo to derive nutrition from the uterine blood vessels. **Ovoviviparous** animals demonstrate features of both ovipary and vivipary. They use internal fertilization, followed by extensive internal development of embryos. While in the uterus, the embryos derive their nutrition from the yolk, rather than the mother. When mature, the eggs hatch within the mother. This strategy is common in fish, including sharks, reptiles, and many invertebrates.

Surprisingly, reproductive mode varies widely within taxa. Some species are able to switch between modes. Brine shrimp, for example, can be ovoviviparous and release free-living young (naupali) or oviparous, laying gastrulae encrusted in a shell (cysts). The reproductive strategy can differ among populations of a single species. The skink *Lerista* has both oviparous and viviparous populations. Among chondrichthians (sharks and rays), some species of skates release fertilized eggs, some sharks are ovoviviparous, and others are viviparous. In several shark species, the ovoviviparous embryo thrives on the nutrients from the egg, but then at some point begins to feed on its brothers and sisters within the reproductive tract—a life history strategy that is difficult to categorize.

Gametogenesis

The gametes are formed by the two-step process of meiosis, and both the process and end products differ between males and females (Figure 16.7). A germ cell (either spermatogonium or oogonium) proliferates in the gonads to create a stock of diploid cells that can undergo gametogenesis. Meiosis begins when each chromosome duplicates; the progression through meiosis differs in males and females.

In oogenesis (Figure 16.7a) the **primary oocyte** grows to a critical size, then becomes quiescent. When the primary oocyte becomes activated later in life, it undergoes an asymmetrical cell division, devoting most of the cytoplasm to a single daughter cell (secondary oocyte). The other, smaller daughter cell, called the first polar body, is usually degraded. The secondary oocyte undergoes another round of asymmetrical cell division, resulting in the ovum and the smaller second polar body, which is also degraded.

In spermatogenesis (Figure 16.7b), the **primary spermatocyte** undergoes cell division to produce two secondary spermatocytes. Meiosis continues and each secondary spermatocyte divides to produce two haploid spermatids.

Ova are produced within follicles of somatic tissue

The female reproductive tract includes the ovary, oviduct, uterus, and gonopore. The ovary is composed of the ova-producing **oogonia** as well as surrounding somatic cells that provide structural and nutritive support for oogenesis. In most species, oogenesis progresses through the primary oocyte stage (see Figure 16.2) early in the life of the female, but the final steps of the process are delayed until later in life. As the oocytes form, the surrounding somatic cells proliferate to form a **follicle** that encapsulates the oocytes. The follicle cells, or **granulosa cells**, secrete the extracellular matrix components that form an acellular layer between the oocyte and follicle cells, called the **zona pellucida**. The entire follicle is surrounded by a basolateral membrane, which in vertebrates is known as the **theca**.

The follicle cells orchestrate oogenesis, including the delayed maturation and ultimate release of the ovum. They communicate with the oocytes by paracrine factors and direct cell-to-cell contacts. Prior to ovulation, a subset of follicles is stimulated to mature (folliculogenesis). The oocyte must first increase in cytoplasmic volume, although the increase in cell size occurs by multiple mechanisms. Vertebrate oocytes grow by accepting biosynthetic precursors from the somatic follicle cells. A different pattern occurs in many invertebrates. In fruit flies, for example, oocytes absorb the cytoplasm of surrounding nurse cells, derived from oogonia that fail to differentiate into oocytes (Figure 16.8).

FIGURE 16.7 Gametogenesis

Oogenesis **(a)** and spermatogenesis **(b)** follow a series of genetic replications, followed by cell divisions. The two alleles for each gene are shown as red and blue chromosomes. The pathways differ in females and males in the fate of the various daughter cells.

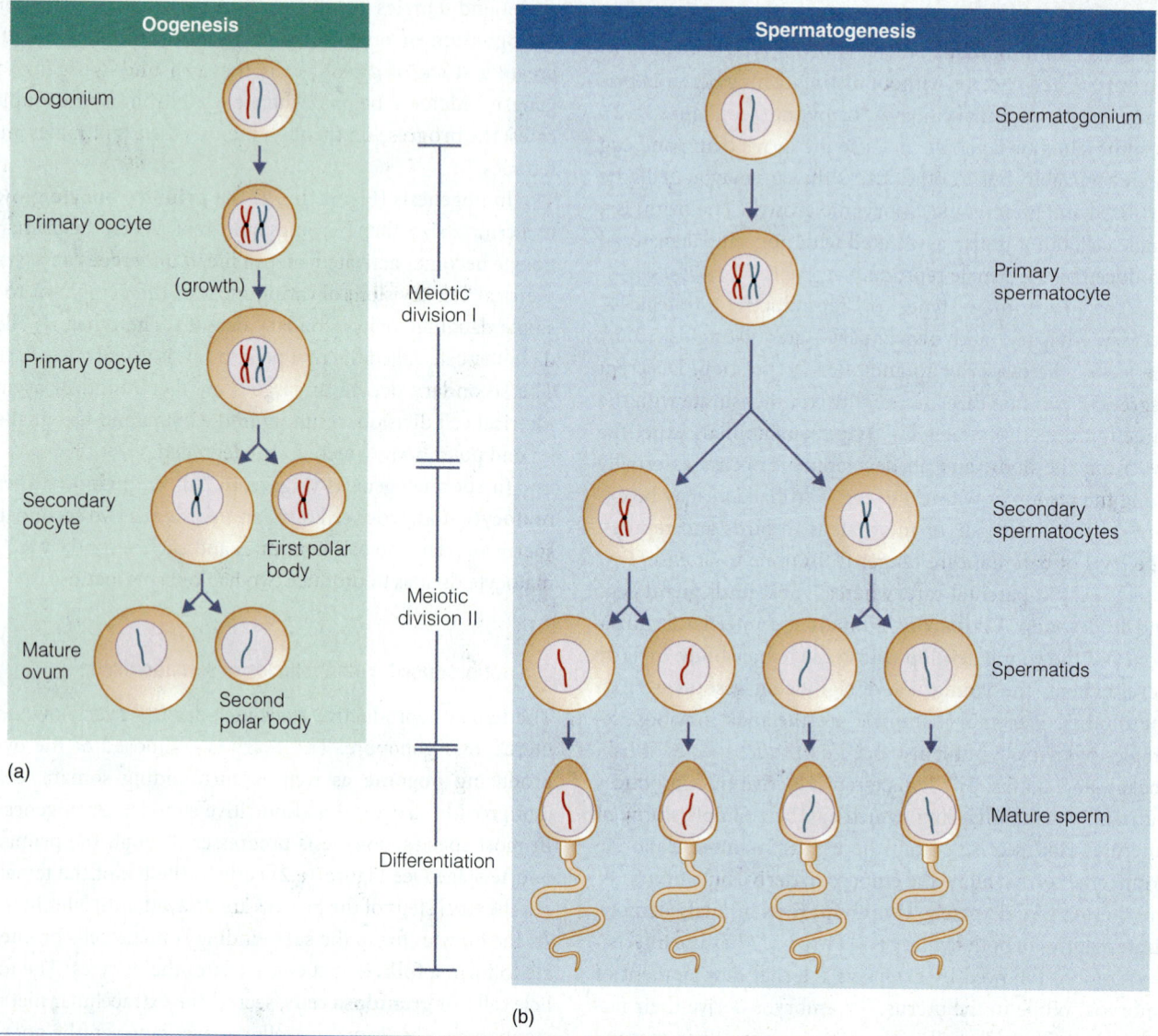

(a)

(b)

When the follicle ruptures, the ovum escapes the ovary and moves into the coelom. In some species, the ova are retained within the coelom. For example, some insects accumulate eggs until the abdomen bursts, killing the female. More commonly, the ovum crosses a short stretch of coelom and enters the opening of the oviduct, called the fallopian tube in mammals. The ovum passes through the oviduct into the uterus. Those species that use internal fertilization retain the ova in the oviduct or uterus. The uterus may be a simple passage, or it may be strong muscular tissue that uses smooth muscle contractions to expel ova, fertilized eggs, or young through the gonopore: the vagina in those species with a dedicated reproductive pore, or a cloaca if the reproductive and excretory systems have a common pore.

The yolk provides building blocks and metabolic precursors

Most animals, with the exception of placental mammals, provide each ovum with a source of nutrients in the form of **yolk**, a complex mixture of proteins and lipids. Most of the macromolecules in yolk are produced outside the oocyte, then sequestered by the oocyte early in oogenesis. Triglyceride from the extracellular fluid passes from the blood between the follicle cells to the oocyte, where it is taken up and stored within vesicles. The yolk possesses many proteins, but **vitellin** is the most abundant. It is produced in the oocyte from **vitellogenin**, a bulky and complex phospholipoglycoprotein that is produced by the insect fat body, the vertebrate liver, and, in some animals, the follicle cells. Vitellogenin is taken up from the extracellular fluid by

FIGURE 16.8   The ovarian follicle

Each oocyte is surrounded by somatic follicle cells. The entire follicle is encapsulated in a thin layer of extracellular matrix (basal lamina). **(a)** Invertebrate oocytes receive cytoplasm from nurse cells through gaps in the plasma membrane. **(b)** Vertebrate follicle cells produce a more extensive extracellular matrix at the apical (zona pellucida) and basolateral (theca) surfaces.

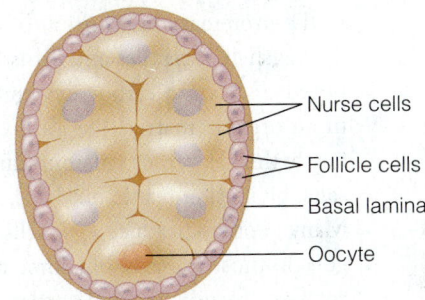

(a) Invertebrate follicle (*Drosophila*)

- Nurse cells
- Follicle cells
- Basal lamina
- Oocyte

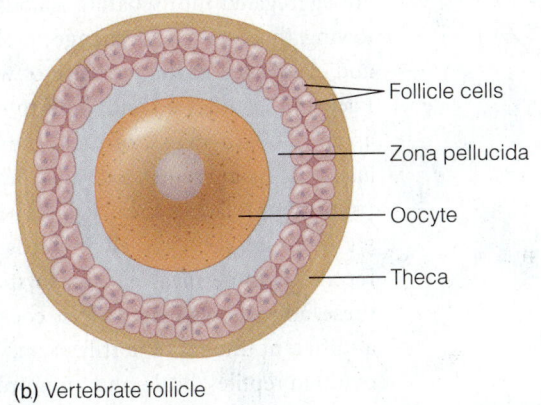

(b) Vertebrate follicle

- Follicle cells
- Zona pellucida
- Oocyte
- Theca

FIGURE 16.9   Vitellogenesis

Animals initiate vitellogenesis in response to external cues, such as an environmental condition or developmental program. The pathways begin centrally within the brain, triggering a hormonal cascade that causes biosynthetic tissues to produce and secrete vitellogenin. This protein passes the follicular cells and is taken up by the oocytes, stored, and then converted to vitellin. Invertebrates and vertebrates differ in the specific hormones and target tissues, but the general features are similar.

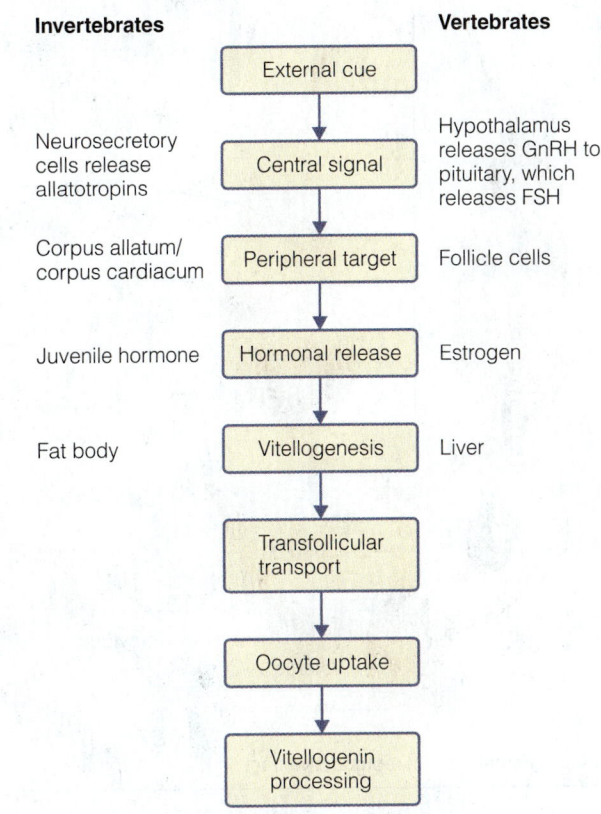

Invertebrates		Vertebrates
	External cue	
Neurosecretory cells release allatotropins	Central signal	Hypothalamus releases GnRH to pituitary, which releases FSH
Corpus allatum/ corpus cardiacum	Peripheral target	Follicle cells
Juvenile hormone	Hormonal release	Estrogen
Fat body	Vitellogenesis	Liver
	Transfollicular transport	
	Oocyte uptake	
	Vitellogenin processing	

endocytosis. The internalized vesicles then coalesce to form larger yolk bodies.

Suites of hormones mediate vitellogenesis. External signals of various forms stimulate the central nervous system to release vitellogenic factors (Figure 16.9). In blood-feeding insects, vitellogenesis begins shortly after the animal consumes a blood meal, at which point a JH surge causes the fat body to produce vitellogenin. In vertebrates, vitellogenin is produced in response to estrogens, primarily estradiol-17β.

Insect eggs are surrounded by a chorion

Oogenesis has been well studied in many insects. In the silk moth, the ova develop in four ovaries (ovarioles), each of which contains in excess of 100 follicles arranged in series. The follicle that is closest to the gonopore undergoes oogenesis first (Figure 16.10). After about 2.5 hours, the next follicle enters oogenesis, and so on along the entire length of each ovariole. Thus, at late stages of oogenesis, a single

ovariole possesses each of the developmental stages separated by about 2.5 hours of development. These stages are divided into three groups: *previtellogenesis, vitellogenesis,* and *choriogenesis.* Ecdysone controls the early development of ovarioles as well as the previtellogenic stages. During previtellogenesis, the follicles have not yet begun to produce yolk. The oocyte then begins to accumulate yolk proteins, marking the onset of the vitellogenic period. The yolk proteins from the fat body are transferred from the hemolymph to the oocyte across the follicle cells. The follicular cells also produce egg-specific proteins that are secreted and taken up by the oocyte. As with the early stages of development, ecdysone controls the production of the egg proteins, although not directly through changes in 20HE levels but rather through induction of a specific type of ecdysteroid receptor. After vitellogenesis has begun, a reduction in 20HE levels causes the follicle cells to begin **chorion** formation (*choriogenesis*). The follicular cells produce and secrete more than 100 types of proteins to construct the chorion. The ovum moves into the

FIGURE 16.10   **Oogenesis in the silk moth**

When the ovarioles of the silk moth undertake oogenesis, the follicles mature in sequence. Each follicle is about 2.5 hours more developed than the follicle next to it. The ova are released and pass down the oviduct into the uterus, where they are fertilized with sperm that was collected and stored in the spermatheca after a previous mating.

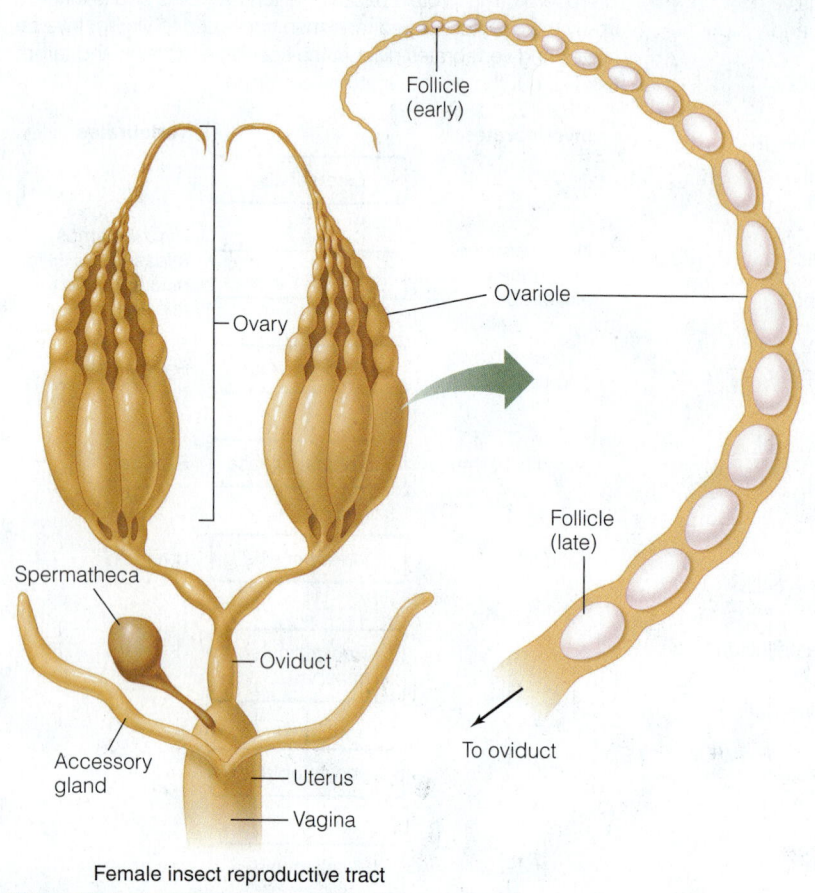

Female insect reproductive tract

The constraint of this strategy is the need for water at all developmental stages. For the ancient vertebrates to be truly terrestrial, they needed a mechanism to reproduce on land. Like the insects, they produced a hardened external shell around the egg that provided support and prevented dehydration. In contrast to the proteinaceous chorion of insects, the eggshell of reptiles and birds is composed of calcium carbonates embedded in an organic matrix. The bird eggshell has a thick layer of calcium carbonate salts, giving it a brittle but hard texture. Many reptiles produce eggshells analogous to those in birds, but some reptiles, such as crocodilians and turtles, have a leathery and pliable eggshell. In these animals, the calcium carbonate crystals are aggregated into separate islands, allowing the eggshell to change in shape and even swell in the presence of water. Each egg is endowed with yolk to serve as an onboard source of fuel. The eggs also possess a viscous, hydrated protein (**albumen**) to act as a shock absorber.

Because the eggshell in birds and reptiles is impermeable, even to sperm, these animals also needed to coevolve a different mode of fertilization. The ovum in reptiles, birds, and monotremes (egg-laying mammals) must be fertilized before the eggshell is formed. Thus, fertilization is internal and the eggshell forms in the oviduct around a fertilized ovum.

Eutherian (placental) and metatherian (marsupial) mammals, of course, have dispensed with the eggshell and solve the challenges of terrestrial life by rearing fertilized ova internally. Nonetheless, each of these terrestrial vertebrate lineages produces embryos that, early in development, produce a complex set of internal membranes and fluid-filled compartments. Reptiles, birds, and mammals are collectively **amniotes**, a name derived from one of the four extraembryonic membranes. We discuss the origins of these membranes later in this chapter.

oviduct, where it is fertilized. Sperm cross this impermeable shell through a tunnel called the micropyle. The fertilized eggs are then laid.

The insects were the first animals to successfully invade land. Central to this invasion was the evolution of an egg that could withstand terrestrial conditions. The chorion is resilient enough to withstand desiccation yet still able to permit the movement of gases (O_2, CO_2). As we see in the next section, the early terrestrial vertebrates faced the same problem but solved it a different way.

Egg structure differs in aquatic and terrestrial vertebrates

Most fish and amphibians produce eggs that are simple in structure. The ovum is physically connected to yolk. As the ovum passes down the reproductive tract, it receives a viscous coating from reproductive tract secretions. The gelatinous eggs are released from the animal into the water unfertilized. In amphibians and fish, the young leave the egg as aquatic larvae and complete their reproductive maturation.

Spermatogenesis requires production of motile gametes

In order to reproduce, male reproductive physiology ensures that sperm are prepared to fertilize the egg once the male engages in activities that bring the gametes in close proximity. For many species, the greatest challenge is finding a mate in order to breed. In some species, reproductive maturation coincides with an ability to sense and respond to mating factors released by one sex to attract the other. Once mates are found, males must be able to deliver sperm that are ready to move to the ovum and fertilize it to initiate embryogenesis.

Leydig cells and Sertoli cells control spermatogenesis

The typical testis produces spermatozoa in seminiferous tubules, which are composed of Leydig cells, Sertoli cells, and spermatozoa at various developmental stages (Figure 16.11). **Leydig cells** are interstitial cells found on the blood side of the basal lamina. They produce the testosterone that controls spermatogenesis. **Sertoli cells** are large cells that fill the gaps between columns of spermatogenic cells. Each Sertoli cell is in contact with about 50 spermatogenic cells. Sertoli cells serve many purposes in spermatogenesis, producing regulatory molecules as well as nutrients that are used for both metabolic energy and biosynthesis. They regulate the testosterone-signaling pathway by producing an androgen-binding protein. They also mediate the response of the testis to FSH, secreting other spermatogenic factors. The main effects of the sex hormones in mammalian males are summarized in Table 16.1.

The progression from **spermatogonia** to spermatids to spermatozoa involves a series of coordinated changes in cellular structure and function, with many of the precursors provided through cytoplasmic bridges that interconnect spermatozoa to neighboring cells. In the final stages of spermatogenesis, a spermatid reorganizes its microtubules to form the axoneme that underlies the flagellum. The length and structure of the flagellum varies widely in animals. It is essentially absent in some species, but can be as long as 6 centimeters, as with the sperm of the fruit fly *Drosophila bifurca*. Spermatozoa then eliminate much of their cytoplasm, leaving small, densely packed cells with abundant mitochondria organized around the base of the axoneme (see Figure 6.9). They also reorganize the DNA in their nuclei,

FIGURE 16.11 Seminiferous tubules
Sperm production is controlled by Sertoli cells of the seminiferous tubules. The Sertoli cells interact through physical connections with spermatogenic cells at various stages, and interact with each other to form a blood-testes barrier. Leydig cells are found in the interstitial space on the blood side of the blood-testes barrier. These cells produce regulatory factors that act on Sertoli cells to control spermatogenesis.

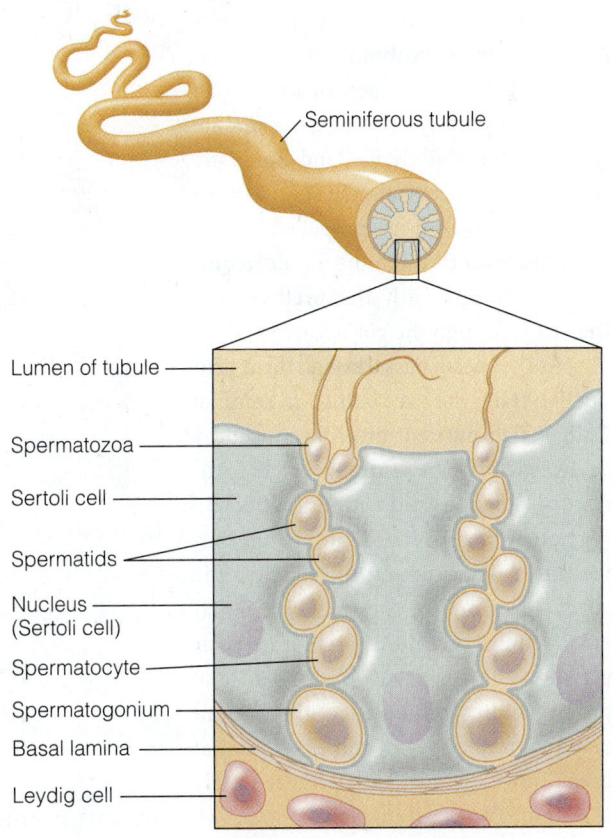

replacing the histones with basic sperm-specific proteins called protamines, which keep the DNA highly condensed and transcriptionally silent.

Table 16.1	Mammalian reproductive hormones in male sexual development and reproduction	
Hormone	**Tissue of Origin**	**Main Targets and Actions**
Sexual maturation		
Androgens	Testes	Secondary sex characteristics: promote axillary hair growth, voice deepening, and libido
Spermatogenesis		
GnRH	Hypothalamus	Anterior pituitary: stimulates LH release, FSH synthesis and release
LH	Anterior pituitary	Leydig cells: stimulates androgen synthesis and release
FSH	Anterior pituitary	Sertoli cells: stimulate spermatogenesis
Androgens	Testes (Leydig cells)	Sertoli cells: stimulate spermatogenesis
Prostaglandins	Seminal vesicles	Uterus of mate: induce changes within the uterus that affect sperm motility

Once these structural changes are complete, the spermatozoa are released from the confines of the Sertoli cells into the lumen of the tubule. From here they progress along the male reproductive tract (Figure 16.12). At this point, the sperm are not capable of either swimming or fertilization, and must undergo a series of modifications. As the sperm pass into the **epididymis**, they further mature. It is in this region that they gain the capacity to swim. The sperm are stored in the epididymis, and fluids are removed to concentrate the sperm into a small volume. They are propelled by cilia along the tract through the **vas deferens**, which connects with the urethra, and then exit through the gonopore.

As the sperm pass through the reproductive tract, they are bathed in seminal fluid, a rich nutrient broth produced by several glands. The **seminal vesicles** produce an alkaline fluid with nutrients and regulatory factors. The high pH neutralizes the acidic ovarian fluid to allow the sperm to swim. The sperm use the nutrients, mainly fructose, as fuel for flagellar activity. The regulatory factors include prostaglandins, which affect the ovarian response to the sperm, and enzymes that break down chemical antagonists to fertilization. The **prostate gland** also secretes nutrients, mainly citrate, as well as enzymes that aid in fertilization. The **bulbourethral gland** secretes mucus that acts as a lubricant.

In some species, the sperm released from the male gonopore are not yet capable of fertilizing an egg. Mammalian sperm, for example, undergo a developmental transition known as **capacitation** only after they enter the female reproductive tract. Once inside, they are exposed to regulatory factors produced by the female that change sperm metabolism, ion regulation, and membrane fluidity, making the sperm capable of fertilizing the ovum.

Reproductive hormones interact with other hormones

In discussing the control of gametogenesis, it should be clear that hormones are extremely important. As with all hormones, reproductive hormones are subject to multiple layers of feedback regulation. Not surprisingly, other physiological processes have the potential to influence reproduction. In turn, reproductive status influences the progression of other physiological processes. Stress is a generic term that can refer

FIGURE 16.12   The male reproductive tract

Sperm released from the wall of seminiferous tubules are carried along the reproductive tract. As they pass through the epididymis and vas deferens, the secretions from the accessory glands provide seminal fluid.

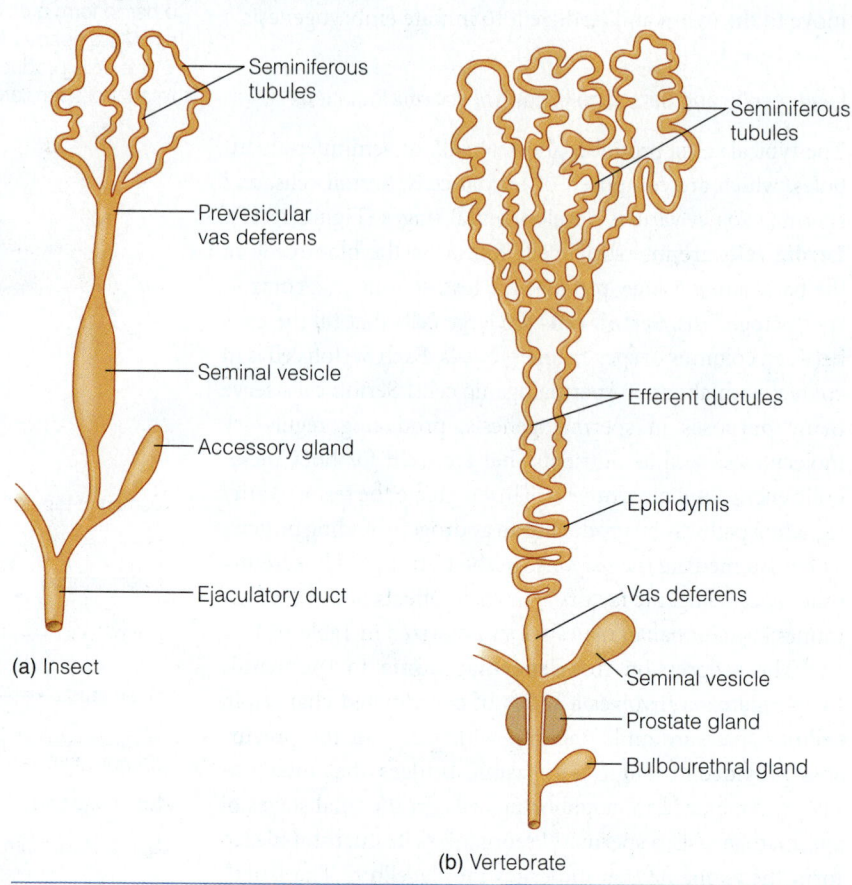

(a) Insect

(b) Vertebrate

to any disruption of normal physiology. It can arise from changes in the physical environment, activity patterns, and interactions with predators, prey, and conspecifics. In the accompanying feature (Box 16.2: Challenges to Homeostasis: Reproduction and Stress), we discuss some of the ways that stress and reproduction interact.

CONCEPT CHECK

7. Compare the three main modes of reproduction in animals (vivipary, ovipary, and ovovivipary).

8. Trace the route of the oocyte from ovary to gonopore. Trace the route of the sperm from seminal vesicle to gonopore.

9. Which cells are the germ cells of males and females? Which cells of the gonads are somatic tissue in males and females?

Mating, Fertilization, and Embryonic Development

There is considerable diversity in the mechanisms by which the sperm are delivered to the ovum. Some species produce

Stress and reproduction are inseparable. Reproduction is a demanding activity that influences other physiological systems and consequently challenges homeostatic regulation. Reproduction disrupts homeostasis and causes stress in two ways. First, it exerts effects on energy metabolism. Reproducing animals incur considerable energetic costs in producing and supporting reproductive systems, provisioning resources for fetal growth, building and maintaining tissues for sexual displays, and enduring physical challenges in competing for mates. Second, reproduction causes stress through *hormonal antagonism*. The glucocorticoids (stress hormones) that trigger mobilization of energy metabolism also exert direct effects on reproductive physiology. The sex hormones also exert their own effects on other systems, which may be advantageous and expensive, but may also be disruptive yet tolerated. Testosterone, in particular, has many effects on nonreproductive physiology. In general, the interactions between reproduction and stress are reciprocal: Reproduction causes stress but stress impairs reproduction. It has been hypothesized that male displays reflect an ability of males to successfully cope with the stresses of reproduction.

The many forms of stress are regulated by the chemical communication network formed by the hypothalamus, the anterior pituitary, and the adrenal cortex (or interrenal cells in vertebrates such as fish). When exposed to an external stress, animals alter hormonal conditions (typically elevated corticosterone) to mobilize fuels, produce glucose, and suppress energy-dependent processes such as growth and reproduction. This defense response allows the animal to survive. Conversely, reproduction itself may create a stressful condition that requires the animal to modify its stress hormone production to gain some of the benefits, like energy production, while curtailing the repressive effects of stress on reproduction. In many cases, the elevation in the levels of hormones such as corticosterone is a necessary component of reproductive physiology. For example, when frogs call, they are engaging in one of the most energetically expensive behaviors seen in ectotherms. The energy for calling is produced when glucocorticoids trigger fuel mobilization, but the calling itself is dependent on testosterone. More testosterone leads to more calling, which demands more energy, which requires elevated glucocorticoids. After a point, glucocorticoids reach such high levels that a stress response ensues, and testosterone production is curtailed.

Animals can influence the steroid-dependent pathways by altering steroid production, by producing steroid-binding proteins, and by altering the profile of steroid hormone receptors. As a result, the magnitude of the stress response can depend on the sex and reproductive state of the animal. Consider the way sex and reproductive state influence how capture manifests as stress in sea turtles. When males

FIGURE 16.13 Plasma corticosterone levels in green sea turtles

Many animals respond to capture by inducing stress hormones, such as corticosterone. The magnitude of the response is influenced by other hormones related to **(a)** sex or **(b)** reproductive state.

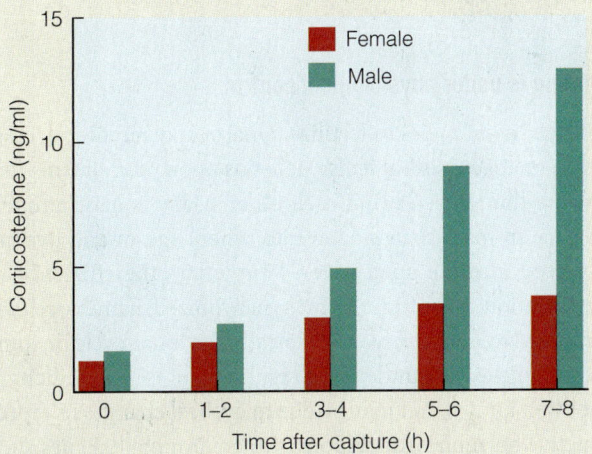

(a) Effect of sex

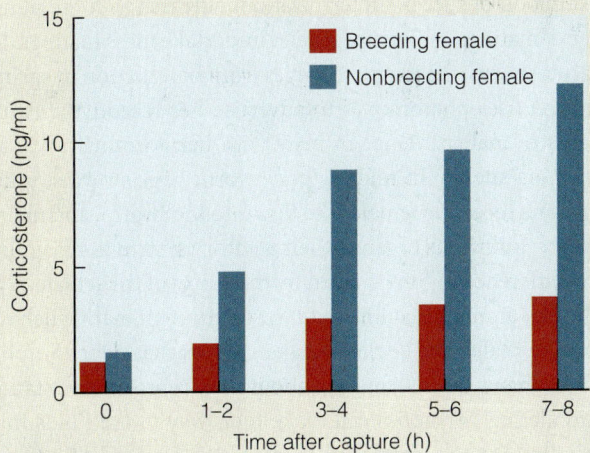

(b) Effect of reproductive status

Figure source: Adapted from Moore, I. T., & Jessop, T. S. (2003). Figure 1a and 1b (p. 43) from Stress, reproduction, and adrenocortical modulation in amphibians and reptiles. *Hormones and Behavior, 43,* 39–47.

and females are captured at sea, males exhibit greater increases in the stress hormone corticosterone. Similarly, nonbreeding females exhibit a greater degree of capture stress than breeding females (Figure 16.13). The hormonal background associated with sex and breeding status influences how other hormones exert their effects.

Reference

• Moore, I. T., & Jessop, T. S. (2003). Stress, reproduction, and adrenocortical modulation in amphibians and reptiles. *Hormones and Behavior, 43,* 39–47.

copious numbers of gametes, casting them into the open environment where a minute proportion of sperm successfully fertilize a few ova. Other animals engage in mating behaviors that bring males and females into close proximity to increase the likelihood of successful fertilization. Some clasp onto mates and release sperm in synchrony to maximize chances of fertilization. Other species use copulatory organs of various configurations, typically associated with the male. Once the sperm have been passed from the male, the individual sperm must find and fertilize the egg, often competing with sperm from other males.

Mating is under physiological control

The ability of males to fertilize females may require successful gametogenesis but it also depends upon mechanisms that ensure that gametes find each other. Many aquatic animals engage in mass spawning events, where sperm and ova are released into the open water. Most often, the efficiency of fertilization is optimized by synchronized gamete release with an environmental cue, typically the lunar cycle or some seasonal cue. The underlying regulation of this periodicity is not well known, but may be due to cyclical changes in reproductive hormones, or responses to environmental cues such as nighttime illumination.

For many species, mating is not a solitary adventure. The likelihood of successful fertilization increases with the number of matings, and many species undertake mass matings. In garter snakes, the female emerges from hibernation in spring and releases pheromones to advertise her receptivity. Hundreds of males attempt to mate with her, forming a ball of writhing snakes. In midges, males form large swarms, waiting for a receptive female. She flies into the swarm, and males use the Johnston's organ of their auditory system to recognize the difference in tone created by the wings of the female.

For animals that interact directly through mating behavior, the males and females make choices that depend upon the exchange of information about their reproductive status. Circulating hormones can make their way to the fluids that an animal expels; animals that are able to detect and interpret the information in the excreta (i.e., feces, urine) and secretions (e.g., pheromones) can advise potential mates to promote an appropriate response. Prior to mating, a porcupine male urinates on a potential mate, and a hippopotamus male uses its tail to fling feces on the female. While these animals may go to great lengths to distribute their message, many animals use urine as a medium for conveying sexual receptivity. For example, when a female dog enters heat, her reproductive status is communicated via the hormones in the urine, which she frequently distributes around her home range.

Many species use elaborate displays to attract the attention of potential mates. In Chapter 10, we discussed the interactions between the immune system and sexual selection. Many of the interactions between reproduction and stress physiology can be traced back to the interactions between testosterone, secondary sex characteristics, and the immune system. High levels of testosterone impair the immune system, compromising immunocompetence. The link is shown experimentally by treating males with testosterone implants. Studies in many species show that increased testosterone augments secondary sex traits but can also make males more susceptible to parasites and disease.

This antagonistic relationship is thought to be one important factor in sexual selection for male displays. The *immunocompetence-handicap hypothesis* suggests that male traits evolve in a way that allows each male to build the most impressive display possible without compromising its own health. Thus, in the natural world only those males with impressive immunocompetence can tolerate the negative effects of building impressive displays. It would not suit a male deer to build such a large display that its immune system declined to the point at which the animal became unhealthy. Because testosterone is linked to male secondary sex traits, many studies have illustrated the relationship between male displays and immunity. For example, male redwing blackbirds sing loud songs at frequent intervals to attract females and defend a territory. The hypertrophy of the muscles required to sing depends on testosterone levels. Male redwing blackbirds with the greatest singing capacity also have stronger immune systems, as indicated by parasite load and blood-borne immune cells.

Male copulatory organs increase the efficiency of sperm transfer

Of the many species that use internal fertilization (arthropods, mammals, reptiles, and some fish), most possess some form of copulatory organ or intromittent organ. Birds, one notable exception, transfer sperm directly from the male's cloaca to the female's cloaca. Many other species possess a copulatory organ that serves as an extension of the male reproductive tract.

Some copulatory organs are simple channels, helping to guide sperm to the female reproductive tract. For example, claspers of male elasmobranchs are pelvic fins that interlock to form a channel that guides sperm to the oviduct. Hemipenes are male copulatory organs seen in many reptiles, flanking the cloaca. The hemipenes are often decorated with barbs or spikes that maximize the duration of penetration. A true penis is distinct from other copulatory organs because it is a direct extension of the male reproductive tract.

The diversity in penis form and function is really quite remarkable. Bedbugs possess a penis that they use like a spear, penetrating the female body wall and releasing sperm into the body cavity that holds the ova. Some flatworms use their penis as a weapon, indulging in fencing matches with other flatworms. As hermaphrodites, these matches are the basis of deciding which worm will be the donor of the sperm, and which the recipient.

In animals that undergo repeated matings, there can be elaborate mechanisms to ensure that the sperm of an individual male will successfully fertilize ova at the exclusion of other males. Apart from the intrauterine mechanisms of sperm competition, discussed in a later section, some males use their penis to deliver a mating plug that physically blocks the female reproductive tract. Many mammals, such as select primates and rodents, and some arthropods, such as spiders and scorpions, produce secretions that are mixtures of long-chain lipids. These are secreted as liquids and then solidify, plugging the tract or gluing the walls together.

Erection is controlled by vascular changes in the penis

The mammalian penis changes its blood distribution to create the hydrostatic pressure needed for a shape change (erection) that facilitates penetration. Many mammals also have a bone within the penis called an *os penis* or *baculum*. This allows the male to penetrate the female before the penis becomes erect. After penetration, the penis engorges, locking it into the vagina to maximize the probability of successful sperm transfer. An erectogenic stimulus, usually visual in nature, triggers the firing of neurons in the brain that transmit signals to the vasculature that feeds the penis. This activates the enzyme nitric oxide synthase (NOS), resulting in production of the gaseous neurotransmitter nitric oxide (NO) (Figure 16.14). Recall from Chapter 6 that smooth muscle contractility is under complex control by signaling pathways

FIGURE 16.14 Control of erection in a mammalian penis

Drugs marketed to combat erectile dysfunction in human males target this signaling pathway. Sildenafil (Viagra), for example, inhibits the phosphodiesterase 5 (PDE5) of vascular smooth muscle. Because PDE5 breaks down cGMP, sildenafil allows cGMP levels to rise, permitting the changes in the vascular smooth muscle that are needed to respond to an erectogenic stimulus.

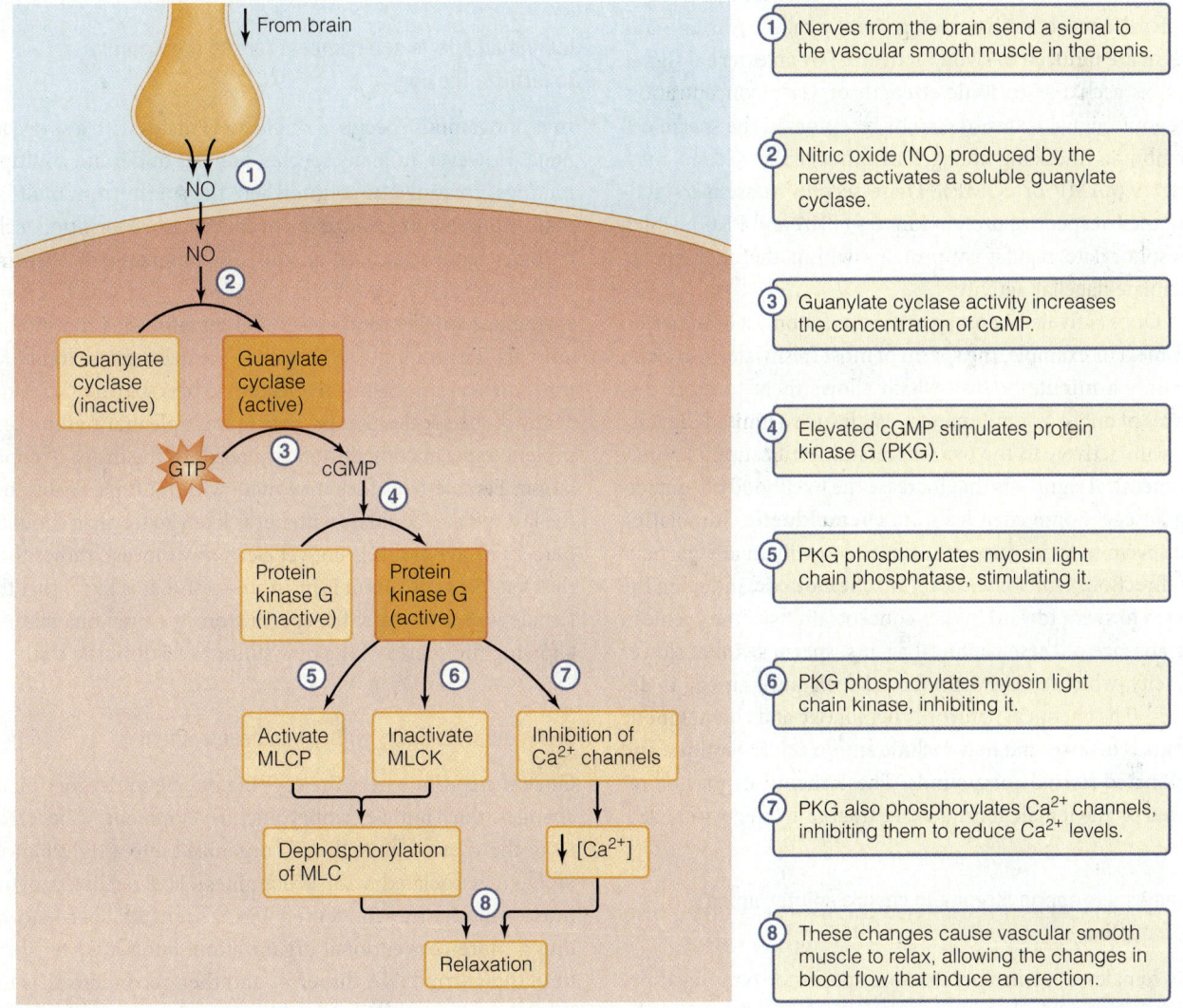

1. Nerves from the brain send a signal to the vascular smooth muscle in the penis.

2. Nitric oxide (NO) produced by the nerves activates a soluble guanylate cyclase.

3. Guanylate cyclase activity increases the concentration of cGMP.

4. Elevated cGMP stimulates protein kinase G (PKG).

5. PKG phosphorylates myosin light chain phosphatase, stimulating it.

6. PKG phosphorylates myosin light chain kinase, inhibiting it.

7. PKG also phosphorylates Ca^{2+} channels, inhibiting them to reduce Ca^{2+} levels.

8. These changes cause vascular smooth muscle to relax, allowing the changes in blood flow that induce an erection.

that affect the thick and thin filaments. As we discussed in Chapter 9, in the vascular smooth muscle of the penis, NO binds guanylate cyclase, stimulating it to increase cGMP production, which activates cGMP-dependent protein kinase G (PKG). PKG phosphorylates critical proteins to favor smooth muscle relaxation. It phosphorylates Ca^{2+} channels, inhibiting them to reduce cytoplasmic Ca^{2+} levels. PKG phosphorylates thick and thin filament proteins to desensitize the contractile apparatus. PKG may also phosphorylate K^+ channels to hyperpolarize the cell. Upon relaxation of the arteriolar smooth muscle, blood flows into the penis, filling the surrounding spongy tissue and causing an increase in blood volume that compresses surrounding veins. The combination of increased blood inflow and reduced venous return causes the penis to engorge.

Sperm alter activity in response to chemokinetic and chemotaxic molecules

Depending on the reproductive strategy, ejaculation may propel the sperm into freshwater, saltwater, or the fluid of the female reproductive tract, generally called ovarian fluid. Sperm are induced to swim (activated) by an external signal, such as a change in ionic strength or Ca^{2+} concentration. The ionic signal is transduced by receptors in the sperm cell membrane, inducing changes in intracellular second messengers (cAMP or cGMP). These second messengers activate their respective protein kinases (PKA and PKG), which phosphorylate regulatory proteins within the axoneme to stimulate flagellar activity.

Once activated, most sperm swim for only a brief period of time. For example, the sperm of most freshwater fish swim for only a minute or two, which allows them to cross distances of only a few millimeters. With such a limited capacity to swim actively to the ova, successful fertilization may rely on chemical signposts that increase the likelihood of contacting an egg. Some chemicals are **chemokinetic**, stimulating the sperm to swim faster but not necessarily in any particular direction. Other chemicals are **chemotaxic**, inducing the sperm to swim toward higher concentrations of the agent. In the absence of these chemical agents, sperm swim at slower velocity, which conserves onboard fuels until an egg is detected. The chemical nature of chemotaxic and chemokinetic agents is diverse, and may include amino acids, peptides, and sulfonated steroid compounds. These chemicals may be released by the female reproductive tract or by the ovum itself.

Females use sperm storage to ensure uninterrupted reproduction

The females of some species store sperm for prolonged periods in specialized compartments within the reproductive tract. Sperm storage enables a female to fertilize her ova long after mating, which is adaptive in animals that might encounter mates infrequently. Some species mate before the female has reached reproductive maturity, and sperm storage allows her to bridge the gap between the mating and gonadal maturation. Sperm can be stored for long periods. Fruit flies store sperm for little more than a week. However, mated female honeybees can retain viable sperm for several years. Some large snakes in captivity have laid fertilized eggs five years after mating.

The anatomical strategies for sperm storage are diverse. Reptiles possess sperm storage tubules that branch from the uterus, or in some species, the vagina. Preovulatory surges in estrogens trigger contraction of smooth muscle that expels the stored sperm from the tubules and into the oviduct, where they can fertilize the egg. Insects possess a more elaborate sperm storage organ called the spermatheca. The length of the spermatheca reflects the length of the sperm. In *Drosophila bifurca*, the females have very long spermathecae to accommodate the 5-cm-long sperm.

Individual sperm can compete for the opportunity to fertilize the egg

In monogamous species, a single male mates with a single female. However, in many species, females undertake multiple matings, creating a situation where the sperm from multiple males compete to fertilize the ova. DNA fingerprinting technologies have been used to study the parentage of offspring in many taxa. It is now clear that *polyandry*, in which the offspring in a single brood have different fathers, is common in animals. The multiple matings also create an opportunity for the female to use chemical effectors to bias sperm utilization. Many of the species that partake in multiple matings may experience sperm competition as a result of the order of copulation. Female fruit flies may mate with multiple males, but the last male to copulate with her is likely to fertilize about 80 percent of the ova. It is not yet clear why the last, rather than the first, bolus of sperm is most successful. It is likely that the female is able to expel the sperm from the previous mating, allowing the sperm of the new suitor to fertilize the ova.

Some animals delay embryonic development

Once the sperm enters the egg, the oocyte undergoes many changes that initiate embryonic development. The DNA from the sperm enters the cell organized into a tight bundle of DNA associated with protamines. The fertilized ovum must remodel the condensed DNA from the spermatozoa into a more conventional organization. Soon after fertilization, the sperm DNA disperses and then recondenses as the protamines are replaced by histones. Once organized into nucleosomes, the paternal DNA within the oocyte can become transcriptionally active. At this early stage, the oocyte has two separate genomes: the maternal pronucleus and the paternal pronucleus. The fertilized ovum undergoes many rounds of cell division to reach the **blastocyst** stage. Soon afterward the various germ layers form, which differentiate to form the complex tissues that ultimately form the embryo. In most species, the embryonic development continues until the young escapes the confines of the egg or reproductive tract. A few species interrupt normal development, pausing at an early phase of embryogenesis. Such a delay allows animals to ensure that embryogenesis proceeds at the appropriate time to ensure hatching or birth occurs under favorable environmental conditions.

Brine shrimp are crustaceans that live in salt-rich water, such as Utah's Great Salt Lake. As discussed earlier in this chapter, brine shrimp can reproduce through ovovivipary or ovipary. The embryos of brine shrimp develop to the gastrula stage, at which point they can delay further development until environmental conditions are adequate. As discussed in Chapter 13, these brine shrimp cysts can undergo metabolic arrest and survive very long periods without water.

More than 100 species of mammals can control embryogenesis through **delayed implantation**. The fertilized ovum develops to the early blastocyst stage (100–400 cells) in the uterus, but implantation in the uterine wall is delayed, retarding further development. Some mammals, such as seals, have an obligate period of delayed implantation, whereas other species can use delayed implantation opportunistically. For example, a rodent may copulate shortly after giving birth to a litter, then delay implantation of the embryos for several weeks. In mammals, the delay can be a few days or weeks or as long as 11 months, as in the river otter.

Postfertilization development relies on maternal factors

Early embryonic development is a period during which the control of cellular processes is transferred from two independent parental genomes to the integrated genome of the offspring. In the earliest phase, cellular changes are governed by maternal factors that existed preformed in the ovum. This includes hormones (androgens and estrogens) that exert regulatory effects on developmental variables, such as sex determination. Gradually, the cellular control transfers to the embryo, when the contributions from paternal genes begin to influence the developmental pattern. In mammals, this transition from maternal to embryonic control occurs at about the two-cell stage. In lower vertebrates and invertebrates, the maternal control extends until the embryo consists of thousands of cells. Even after the paternal genes become active, factors present in the oocyte can continue to play an important role well into embryological development.

The division of the genomes of the two parents allows for differential modification patterns that influence later development, through the process known as *gene imprinting*. Under normal conditions, each diploid cell is able to produce mRNA from either the maternal or paternal allele of a gene. Before the maternal and paternal genomes merge into a single nucleus, a small subset of the genes may be modified in a way that prevents the maternal or paternal allele from being expressed. Furthermore, this imprinted gene remains transcriptionally silent throughout development, while the allele of the gene derived from the other parent is expressed. Most of the genes subject to imprinting encode proteins critical for normal growth and neurobehavior, such as insulinlike growth factor 2 (IGF-2) and its regulators. These hormonal pathways control embryonic growth, so the embryo is at the center of an interesting evolutionary conflict. The embryo possesses genes from both father and mother, but the costs of producing and raising the embryo are borne largely by the mother. Thus, it is in the best interest of the father to pass on genes that induce rapid embryonic growth; his offspring thrive but the mother bears the costs of rapid embryonic growth. Conversely, it is in the interest of the mother to curtail growth to a manageable level. Within the embryo, the parental genomes have conflicting goals, and patterns of gene imprinting on maternal and paternal alleles of genes for growth regulatory proteins determine the trajectory of embryonic development.

Amniotes produce four extraembryonic membranes early in development

Soon after fertilization, the embryo of amniotes produces sheets of cells that separate from the embryo to form the four extraembryonic membranes: chorion,[1] amnion, allantois, and yolk sac. These membranes grow in size as the embryo develops (Figure 16.15). The chorion, the outermost membrane that lies beneath the albumen, acts as a gas exchange surface. The amnion encloses the embryo. As the embryo develops, the amnion fills with fluids that act as a hydraulic cushion and provide a favorable ionic and osmotic environment for the embryo. The allantois is a membranous outpouching of the primitive gut. During development, it becomes vascularized, delivering gases between the embryonic circulation and the outer surface layers. In birds and reptiles, the allantois is also a storage sac for nitrogenous waste, mainly uric acid. The yolk sac surrounds the yolk, secreting digestive enzymes that break the yolk down into macromolecules that can be transferred to the embryo. The animal grows within the egg until it reaches a point where it can break through the shell.

---

[1]The term *chorion* is a general one that refers to an outer layer of an extraembryonic structure. The chorions of insects and amniotes are unrelated in origin and composition.

FIGURE 16.15 **The amniote egg**

Once the ovum of an amniote is fertilized, it undergoes cell division. Most of these cells form the embryo, but four sheets of cells separate from the embryonic tissue to form the extraembryonic membranes—the chorion, amnion, allantois, and yolk sac—that enclose compartments for storage of nutrients (yolk sac), fluids (amniotic space), and wastes (allantoic cavity).

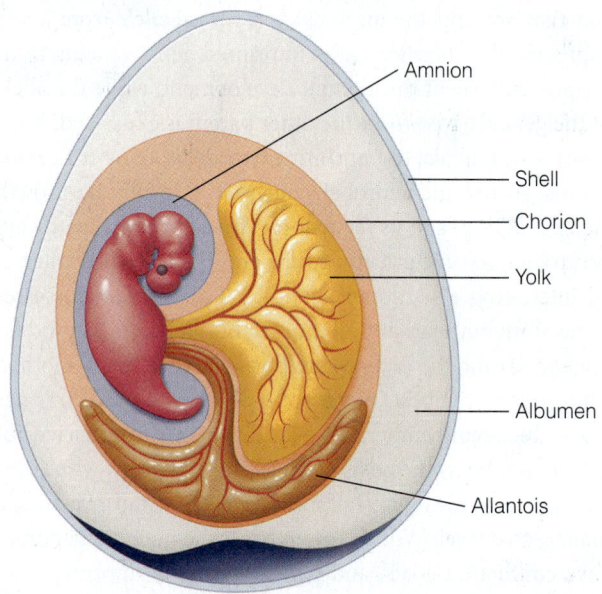

Amnion

Shell

Chorion

Yolk

Albumen

Allantois

Although nonmonotreme mammals lack the hardened shell of other terrestrial vertebrates, they are also amniotes and the embryo possesses all of the same membranes. Later in this chapter, we will elaborate on the origins and roles of these membranes in mammalian reproduction.

CONCEPT CHECK

10. What is delayed implantation?
11. What is gene imprinting and what does it affect?
12. What are the four extraembryonic tissues in amniotes?

REGULATING REPRODUCTION AND DEVELOPMENT IN MAMMALS

Despite common themes, some of which were discussed earlier in this chapter, there is amazing diversity in reproductive biology of animals. In the next section, we focus on mammals, discussing the pathways that coordinate the events in the uterus and ovaries.

Coordinating the Ovarian and Uterine Cycles

The physiological processes that prepare a female to ovulate and support a subsequent pregnancy involve a series of ovarian and uterine events that are highly regulated by hormones. Some mammals, such as camels and their relatives, ovulate only in response to mating. This pattern, known as **induced ovulation**, leads to simultaneous changes in the uterus. However, for most mammals, females experience an **estrous cycle**, where regular changes in hormones coordinate mating behavior with ovarian and uterine changes.

Mammals differ in the number and timing of estrous cycles. *Monoestrous* mammals, such as canines, undergo a single estrous cycle each year. *Polyestrous* mammals undergo estrous cycles throughout the year, although they may breed only during certain seasons. Humans and other primates are polyestrous animals, although the estrous cycle is more commonly known as the **menstrual cycle**. Some people make a distinction between estrous and menstrual cycles based upon female behavior; a species has an estrous cycle if the female demonstrates a period of intense interest in mating that coincides with a specific part of the ovulatory cycle. For example, dogs and cats go into *heat* at a specific point of the estrous cycle; they exhibit anatomical and behavioral changes that "inform" potential mates that they are ovulating and interested in copulation. Conversely, human females exhibit interest in copulation at many phases of the reproductive cycle and show few outward signs of ovulation. Other people distinguish a menstrual cycle from an estrous cycle by the magnitude of the uterine tissue loss (**menses**) at the end of a cycle. Although most species exhibit cyclical changes in the uterine wall, and many show evidence of vaginal discharge, the relative volume is much greater in primates.

Hormones control the ovarian and uterine cycles

Hormones control the cyclical maturation of follicles, ovulation, and the parallel changes in the uterine wall. With the exception of humans, most mammalian species coordinate ovulation and copulation; the same hormones that regulate ovulation induce external and behavioral displays that announce they are receptive to copulation. The hypothalamus releases gonadotropin-releasing hormone (GnRH) into the portal blood vessels, causing the anterior pituitary to secrete pulses of gonadotropins (LH and FSH), which in turn cause the gonads to produce steroids (progesterone and estradiol-17β). Another hormone that plays a role in the regulation of ovulation is **inhibin**. A peptide hormone of the TGF-β family of cytokines, inhibin is released by the mature follicle cells and exerts multiple effects. It has endocrine effects at the hypothalamic-pituitary axis, inhibiting the release of FSH. It also has autocrine and paracrine effects at the ovary, inhibiting the production of estrogen. (*Estrogen* is a general term that does not distinguish between the various estrogens. Although estradiol-17β is the most important estrogen in most mammals, the other estrogens such as estrone contribute to estrogen signaling.) These hormones interact through both positive and negative feedback cycles. The hormones that drive follicular events cause other physiological and behavioral changes in the female.

The estrous cycle is composed of four phases: estrus, metestrus, diestrus, and proestrus. The first day of estrus is demarked by the onset of interest in mating, typically identified by the nature of social interactions or the assumption of mating postures in the presence of males. In the ensuing sections, we discuss the control of ovarian and uterine events from the human perspective, where the ovulatory cycle is discussed as two phases of two weeks each. The **follicular phase** begins on the first day of menses. The **luteal phase** begins after ovulation. Keep in mind that the general features are similar among mammals, but there is considerable variation in the details. For example, not all human females show a standard 28-day ovulatory cycle. A normal cycle is considered somewhere between 25 and 35 days. It can vary within and among women as a result of diet, stress, and exercise. The shortest ovulatory cycle in mammals, seen in the golden hamster, is 4 days. In humans, the ovarian and uterine changes are tightly linked in each reproductive cycle. However, in many species, the nature of the cycles and linkage between them may depend on copulation, where the mechanical stimulation of the vagina induces hormonal changes that in turn affect the ovarian and/or uterine changes. For example, some species use copulation to trigger the rupture of the follicles (ovulation), and other species are programmed to ovulate cyclically but modify the uterus only in response to copulation.

The follicular phase of ovulation is driven by FSH

We begin our discussion late in the luteal phase, when the levels of estrogen and progesterone decline by mechanisms clarified later in this section (Figure 16.16). Recall that these hormones suppress the release of GnRH from the hypothalamus, and thereby minimize gonadotropin release from the anterior pituitary. Thus, once the levels of progesterone and estrogen fall below a critical threshold, hypothalamic GnRH is secreted into the blood, stimulating the anterior pituitary to secrete gonadotropins; LH increases slowly, whereas FSH increases more rapidly.

These two hormones act on different cell types of the ovary to coordinate the maturation of the follicle and the metabolism of sex hormones. The rise in FSH causes the granulosa cells to proliferate. As the follicle grows in size, the outermost layer of granulosa cells differentiates to form the theca. One function of the mature follicle is to produce the appropriate amount of progesterone and estrogen. The extrafolliclar cells of the ovary (interstitial cells) produce and release progesterone; some escapes into the blood and some makes its way to the theca of maturing follicles. The theca cells use the progesterone to produce androgens, some of which makes its way to the inner granulosa cells, where it is used to produce estrogen. This difference in steroid synthesis among ovarian cells is due to the expression of the genes for the enzymes of steroid metabolism. Differentiating theca cells express LH receptors, enabling them to respond to LH by expressing the appropriate genes for androgen synthesis, as well as aromatase.

Early in the follicular phase, many follicles mature in parallel. As the collection of follicles grows, estrogen secretion increases. The elevated estrogen in the blood exerts negative feedback on the hypothalamic-pituitary axis, blocking GnRH release from the hypothalamus and production of LH and FSH by the anterior pituitary. The decline in estrogen and the increase in inhibin act together to suppress FSH release. With FSH levels plummeting, most of the follicles are unable to sustain their own development and undergo **atresia**, a form of apoptosis. However, a subset of follicles, called dominant follicles, matures to the point where they can sustain maturation despite falling FSH. It is not yet clear if the dominant follicles escape the effects of plummeting FSH by increasing the number of FSH receptors, or by modulating the local signaling environment to make FSH more effective. Regardless of the mechanism, the dominant follicles continue to mature, with the granulosa cells growing in number while awaiting the signal for ovulation.

Ovulation and the luteal phase follow an LH surge

The negative feedback interaction between estrogen and the hypothalamic-pituitary axis is essential for follicle maturation and selection of the dominant follicle. However, in the late follicular phase, the hypothalamic-pituitary axis reorganizes its signaling pathways in a way that reverses the effects of estrogen. Instead of impairing GnRH release, estrogen stimulates GnRH release.

Of the gonadotropins, the most important hormone for late follicular maturation is LH. The growing follicle continues to produce estrogen, which in turn enhances LH release, an example of positive feedback. The dramatic increase in LH, called the *LH surge*, causes the granulosa cells to secrete several factors that support oocyte maturation. Paracrine signaling factors induce the oocyte to complete its meiotic pathway, generating the ovum. Enzymes are secreted to digest the extracellular matrix between the follicle cells. The follicle weakens and ruptures to release the ovum. Just prior to ovulation, the follicle cells increase the production of progesterone. Ovulation marks the beginning of the luteal phase. Depending on the species, the transition from estrus to metestrus occurs either slightly before or slightly after ovulation.

After ovulation, the remnants of the follicle continue to play an important role in hormone synthesis. Driven by the LH surge, the follicle undergoes a change in structure, increasing

FIGURE 16.16 **Ovulation cycle in mammals**

The estrous cycle is divided into proestrus (P), estrus (E), metestrus (M), and diestrus (D), or alternatively, the follicular and luteal phases. The exact relationships differ among species, but in general estrus coincides with ovulation, the demarcation between the follicular and luteal phases. The figure shows two ovulatory cycles, the first ending without fertilization and the second with fertilization.

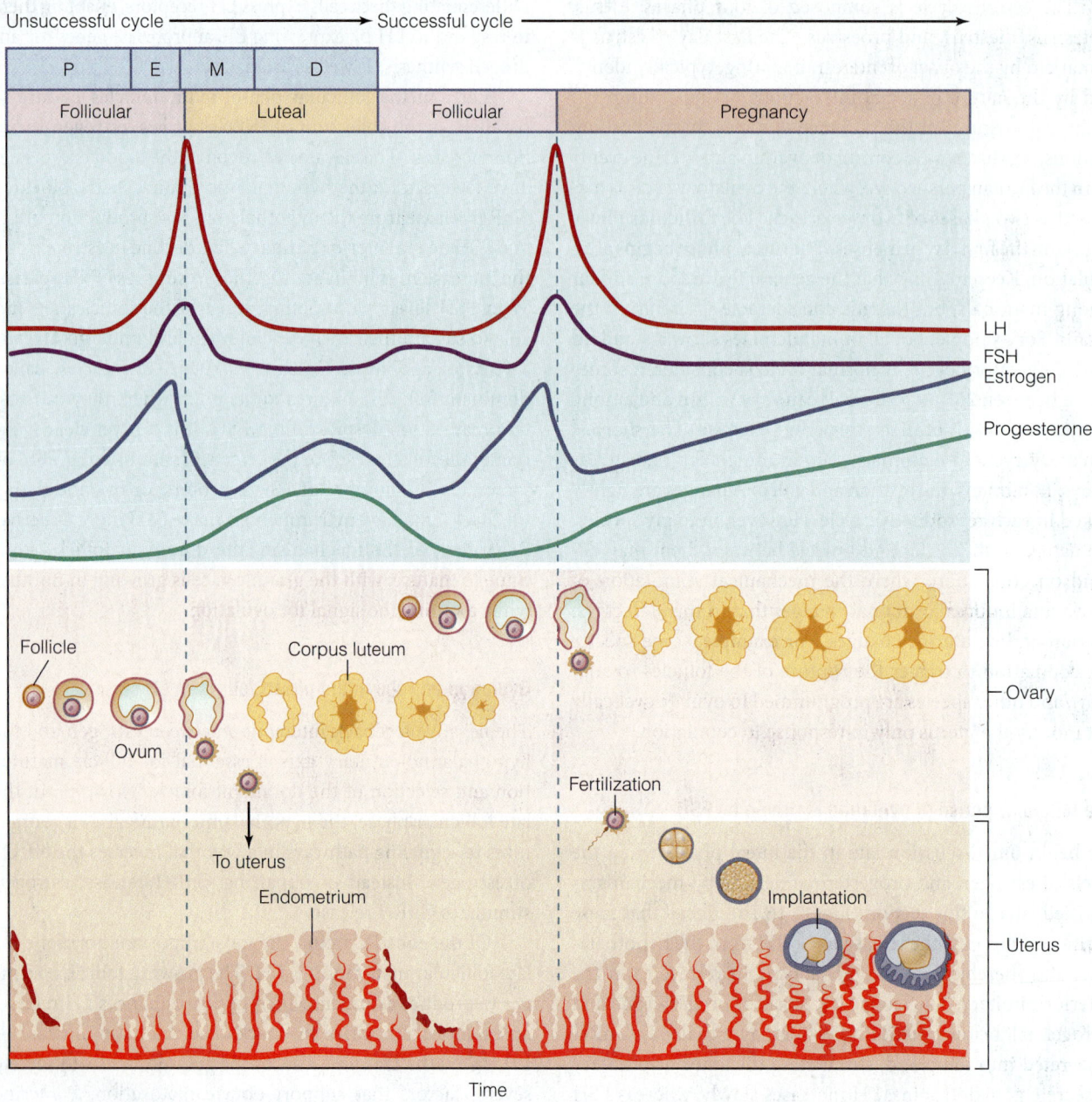

Figure source: Adapted from McNaught, A. B., & Callander, R. (1975). *Illustrated physiology.* New York: Churchill Livingstone.

in size and complexity as capillaries and fibroblasts penetrate the structure. The remnants of the ruptured follicle appear as a dense yellow body in the ovary known as the **corpus luteum** (which roughly translates as "yellow body"). The corpus luteum maintains the ability to synthesize and secrete large amounts of progesterone and lesser amounts of estrogen. These hormones ensure that the uterine wall changes in preparation for implantation.

In the luteal phase of the cycle, the corpus luteum sustains steroid hormone secretion for a time, but estrogen and progesterone levels begin to decline. What happens next depends on whether a fertilized ovum implants in the uterus. If the ovum is not fertilized, progesterone levels continue to decline and the next ovulatory cycle begins. Before considering what happens when the ovum is fertilized, we will consider the relationship between the ovulatory cycle and the changes in the uterine wall.

The endometrial cycle parallels the ovulatory cycle

The events in the ovulation cycle are coordinated with changes in the uterine cycle, through shared sensitivity to steroid hormones. The uterus is composed of a layer of smooth muscle (**myometrium**) covered by a layer of epithelial tissue (**endometrium**). When the ovulatory cycle is in the follicular phase, the endometrial cycle is in the *proliferative phase*. The endometrium thickens as epithelial, immune, and glandular cells replicate (hypertrophy), with blood vessels growing in parallel to ensure vascularization. The luteal phase of the ovulatory cycle coincides with the *secretory phase* of the endometrial cycle. The endometrial cells secrete numerous regulatory factors, including cytokines and prostaglandins, that ensure the uterus is prepared for implantation of the growing embryo.

The hormones involved in regulating the ovulatory and endometrial cycles of female mammals are summarized in Table 16.2. The birth control pill, developed in the early 1960s, is a combination of hormones that impairs ovulation, fertilization, and implantation. Although exact compositions differ among brand names, most birth control pills are composed of chemical analogs of estrogen and progesterone. Because maturation of follicles in the late luteal phase is possible only after progesterone levels decline, the elevated progesterone levels prevent ovulation, essentially by convincing the ovary that the female is pregnant. In addition to its effects on ovulation, the pill also thickens the cervical mucus layer, impairing sperm movement into the uterus, thus reducing the likelihood of fertilization if ovulation does occur. If ovulation and fertilization occur, the pill also reduces the likelihood of successful implantation because it impairs endometrial growth. The pill should not be confused with emergency contraception known as the "morning–after pill." This treatment consists of very high doses of progesterone, estrogens, or both, thereby preventing ovulation.

The regular cycle of ovulation changes when an ovum is fertilized. The embryonic tissues and placenta gradually become an endocrine gland, taking over the central control of hormone levels to ensure that the fetus matures to the point that it can be expelled from the uterus in the process of **parturition**.

A placenta forms after a fertilized ovum implants in the uterine wall

A fertilized ovum begins the process of cell division and continues to divide for several days. It sheds the zona pellucida, and then the remaining cells form the blastocyst. Groups of cells differentiate to form the embryonic structures. The outermost cells differentiate to form the **trophoblast** (Figure 16.17). Then the embryo attaches to the uterine wall to begin the process of implantation. Trophoblast cells proliferate and invade the endometrium, forming an association

Table 16.2	Mammalian reproductive hormones in females in the ovulatory cycle	
Hormone	**Tissue of Origin**	**Main Targets and Actions**
Sexual maturation, puberty, and menarche		
Estrogens	Ovary	Secondary sex characteristics: promote fat deposition, maturation of ovaries and mammary glands
Androgens	Ovary	Adrenal gland: secondary sex characteristics: promote axillary hair growth and libido
Follicular phase		
GnRH	Hypothalamus	Anterior pituitary: controls LH release, FSH synthesis and release
LH	Anterior pituitary	Ovarian follicle: triggers ovulation
FSH	Anterior pituitary	Ovarian follicle: stimulates estrogen synthesis and follicle maturation
Estrogens	Ovarian follicle	Ovarian follicle: stimulates proliferation of granulosa cells
		Endometrium: stimulates proliferation of endometrial cells, sensitization to progesterone, angiogenesis
		Hypothalamic-pituitary axis: reduces gonadotropin levels by negative feedback
Luteal phase		
Estrogens	Corpus luteum	Hypothalamus–anterior pituitary: inhibits GnRH release, reducing release of FSH and LH from anterior pituitary to prevent folliculogenesis
Progesterone	Corpus luteum	Uterus: promotes maturation of endometrium and reduces uterine smooth muscle contractility
Inhibin	Corpus luteum	Hypothalamus–anterior pituitary: impairs FSH synthesis and release

FIGURE 16.17   **Embryonic development in the uterus of a placental mammal**

Cell division begins once the egg is fertilized, which usually occurs in the oviduct. Implantation begins after the blastocyst binds to the uterine wall. Cells in the outer blastocyst layer, the trophoblast, invade the endometrium of the uterus and begin to form the placenta. The extraembryonic membranes develop, and the amniotic cavity increases in volume. The timeline shown in this figure is for a primate.

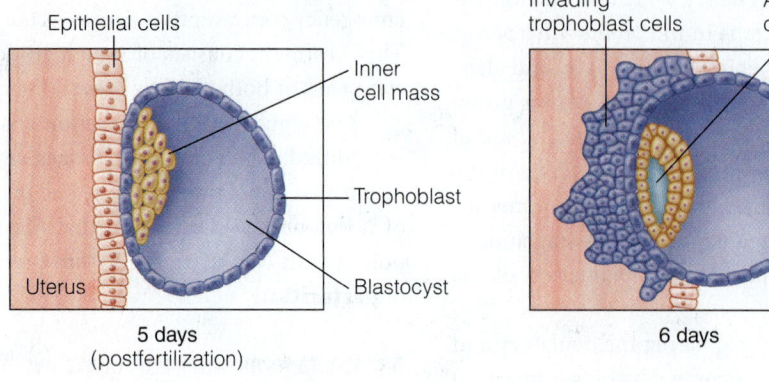

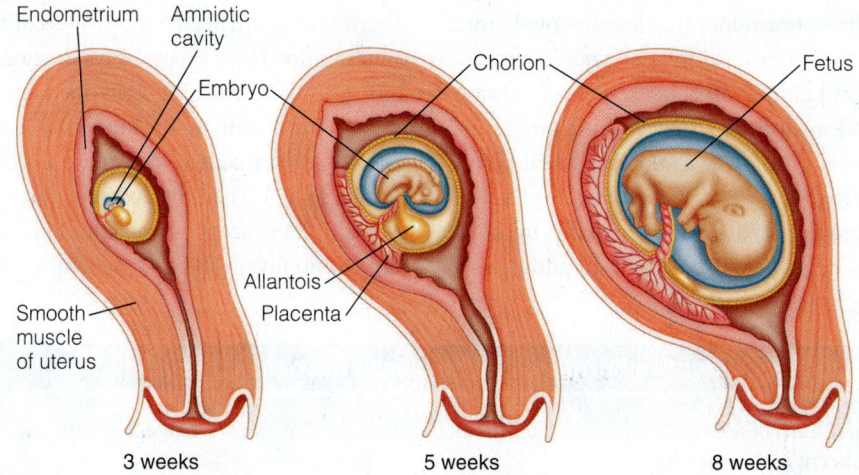

that will develop into the placenta. The trophoblast cells differentiate to form the chorion. At the same time, the inner cell mass of the blastocyst continues to divide and differentiate. First, a gap appears between cells to form the amniotic cavity. The cells that surround the amniotic cavity differentiate to form the amnion. The remaining cells of the blastocyst inner cell mass form the embryo, which grows to become the fetus.

Central to the development of the fetus is the placenta. It is the interface between mother and fetus, and is composed of cells derived from both. For the first third of the pregnancy, the placenta has a vital endocrine function. The region of the placenta that was derived from the chorion secretes chorionic gonadotropin (CG). Early pregnancy tests rely on detection of very low levels of human CG (hCG). Like LH, another gonadotropin, CG targets the corpus luteum in the ovary to ensure that it continues to secrete estrogen and progesterone. These hormones are vital to the remodeling of the mother's physiology necessary to sustain the pregnancy and prepare her for parturition and subsequent maternal care. Later in the pregnancy, the placenta itself becomes the main source of progesterone and estrogen, and the corpus luteum degenerates. In some mammals, the corpus luteum remains the main source of steroid hormones throughout the pregnancy.

The duration of gestation varies widely among mammals. Altricial species (those giving birth to large litters of poorly developed young) have shorter gestation periods than precocial species (those having fewer, well-developed offspring). For animals of similar body size, the gestation period for a precocial species is about three times longer than that for an altricial species. Body size also plays a role (Figure 16.18).

Maternal changes in physiology accompany pregnancy

Over the duration of the pregnancy, the female undergoes broad suites of physiological changes. Many of the changes serve to alter the female to deal with the added metabolic costs of fetal growth.

FIGURE 16.18 **Gestation period and body size in mammals**

Larger mammals have longer gestation times. Precocial mammals have longer gestation times than similarly sized altricial mammals.

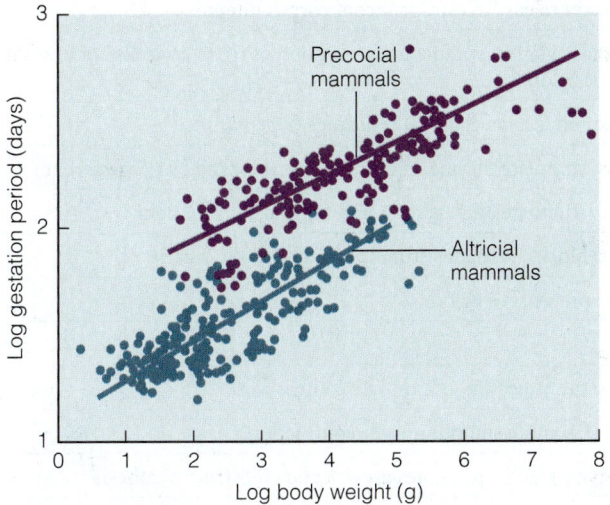

Figure source: Reprinted by permission from Evolutionary Studies, Martin, R.D. (1989). Size, shape, and evolution. In Evolutionary Studies: A *Centenary Celebration of the Life of Julian Huxley*, ed. M. Keynes, pp. 96–141. London: Eugenics Society. Reproduced with permission of Palgrave Macmillan.

There are increases in blood volume with a decrease in blood pressure, arising from reduced peripheral resistance. There is also an increase in cardiac output, arising from both increases in heart rate and stroke volume driven by reduced vagal tone. The dramatic changes in the cardiovascular system also lead to unpredictable fluctuations in blood pressure.

The additional weight, its effects on posture, and a regulatory environment that supports fetal growth lead to marked changes in the musculoskeletal system. There are changes in digestive physiology to cope with an increase in nutritional requirements, including elevated vitamin needs.

Contractions of uterine smooth muscle induce parturition

The uterus has thick walls of smooth muscle (*myometrium*) underlying the endometrium. As the fetus develops, the elevated levels of progesterone and estrogens remodel the uterine smooth muscle to prepare for parturition. The high levels of estrogens enhance the contractile strength of the muscle. They also induce the expression of the genes encoding the receptor for oxytocin, which has an important role in parturition. While the smooth muscle grows in strength, progesterone disrupts excitation-contraction coupling to prevent the smooth muscle from contracting prematurely.

Parturition begins in response to a series of hormonal changes. The levels of progesterone decline, allowing the strong uterine muscles to contract. At the onset of labor, fetal cells produce oxytocin, which acts on the placenta to induce

the release of prostaglandins. At the same time, the mounting stress in the mother triggers the hypothalamic-pituitary axis, causing the release of oxytocin from her own posterior pituitary. Prostaglandins and oxytocin act on the uterine smooth muscle directly to induce contractions that begin to propel the infant along the uterus. In a clinical setting, labor can be induced by injection with oxytocin. As labor progresses, the additional stress triggers the release of even more oxytocin, further strengthening the contractions, an example of positive feedback regulation.

Soon after the young is born, the placenta is expelled. During gestation, the placenta was a major source of estrogen and progesterone. At this point, the female experiences a rapid decline in estrogen and progesterone production as a result of the loss of this endocrine gland. Once the fetus is born, the maternal physiology begins the process of postpartum recovery from birth, and simultaneously initiates the early steps of maternal care, including milk production. The hormones involved in regulating parturition and postpartum events are summarized in Table 16.3.

CONCEPT CHECK

13. What are the main phases of the mammalian female ovulatory and endometrial cycles?
14. What hormones are produced by the ovarian tissue during the ovulatory cycle?
15. Provide examples of negative and positive feedback in the regulation of the ovulatory cycle.

Postnatal Growth and Development

Tightly regulated molecular mechanisms coordinate embryological development, orchestrating the remarkable changes that happen prior to the point at which an egg hatches or a fetus is born. The field of evolution of development, or evo-devo, focuses on mechanisms that are broadly conserved across organisms, and identifies those responsible for specific patterns of morphogenesis. The specifics of embryonic development are beyond the scope of this chapter. Instead, we pick up the story of mammalian embryonic development at parturition. The transition from the relatively sheltered life inside a uterus to the harsh realities of the external world necessitates dramatic changes in the physiology of the infant, aided in part by continued parental care.

Prolactin also controls parental care of offspring

Apart from its effects on milk production, prolactin also influences maternal behavior. Pregnancy and lactation lead to a remodeling of the hormonal regulatory pathways, including hormone production and hormone receptor expression. In

Table 16.3 Mammalian reproductive hormones in pregnancy and parturition		
Hormone	**Tissue of Origin**	**Main Targets and Actions**
Pregnancy		
Chorionic gonadotropin	Placenta	Stimulates release of estrogen from corpus luteum
Estrogens	Placenta	Mammary glands: stimulate proliferation of secretory cells but prevent milk secretion
		Cervix: reduces mechanical resistance (ripens)
		Uterus: stimulate uterine smooth muscle (blocked by progesterone)
		Uterus: stimulate angiogenesis and mitotic division in endometrium
Progesterone	Placenta	Uterus: blocks estrogen's stimulation of smooth muscle
		Ovary: prevents ovulation
Parturition		
Oxytocin	Posterior pituitary	Uterus: promotes smooth muscle contraction
Prostaglandins	Placenta	Uterus: promote smooth muscle contraction
Prolactin	Anterior pituitary	Mammary glands: promotes growth and colostrum synthesis
Postpartum events		
Oxytocin	Posterior pituitary	Mammary glands: promotes smooth muscle contraction
Prolactin	Anterior pituitary	Mammary glands: stimulates growth and milk synthesis

mammals, prolactin and steroid hormones work in conjunction to alter the biochemistry of the brain and behavior of the female. This remodeling process begins in pregnancy and continues during lactation. Virgin females that are exposed to unrelated newborns may gradually acquire maternal behaviors and adopt the infant. The acquisition of maternal behavior is related to the increase in prolactin synthesis and expression to prolactin receptors in the medial preoptic area of the hypothalamus. In mice with their prolactin receptors knocked out, females show less interest in caring for their own young and less willingness to adopt other pups. Interestingly, females that have had multiple experiences birthing and rearing infants often show a reduction in prolactin levels relative to novices. It is thought that maternal behaviors in these females are sustained through greater sensitivity of the hypothalamus to prolactin.

The prevalence of maternal care in animals is rationalized by evolutionary arguments that only the mother can be certain of parentage of the offspring, so the father's energy is best spent copulating. Paternal care occurs in some mammals, primarily canines, rodents, and a few primates. Interestingly, paternal care also appears to be controlled by prolactin. In Djungarian hamsters, paternal care may begin at parturition, with fathers acting as midwives by assisting with the birth of the pups. During early pup growth, the fathers may help groom the offspring, retrieve wandering pups, and assist in thermoregulation. Remarkably, the mates of pregnant females experience hormonal changes that alter their paternal behavior. The degree (and skill) of paternal behavior is linked to both hormonal changes and experience. Among those

species of mammals that exhibit paternal care, attending fathers usually have higher levels of prolactin in the blood than do nonpaternal males. The superior skills and attention demonstrated by experienced males may also be due to higher prolactin levels. Interestingly, prolactin has also been implicated in other species that exhibit paternal care, including many fish and birds. It is not yet known how prolactin affects the central nervous system to influence paternal behavior.

Milk is a secretory product of mammary glands

Mammals are unique in possessing mammary glands that enable a female to produce milk for her offspring, driven by the hormone prolactin. Although a remarkable adaptation, the mammalian mammary gland has many parallels. As mentioned earlier in this chapter, some species produce secretions that feed the offspring while still in the reproductive tract, such as the uterine milk of ovoviviparous fish. Several non-mammalian species produce nutrients for their free-living offspring. For example, pigeons produce **crop milk**, a secretion produced by the upper gastrointestinal tract and regurgitated into the mouths of the chicks. Interestingly, crop milk secretion is also induced by prolactin. In fact, there is some evidence that other examples of parental secretion of nutrients, as with some fish species, may also be regulated by prolactin.

Milk is produced by the mammary gland, and in almost all cases only the female produces milk. In the mid-1990s, researchers in Malaysia discovered that males of the local fruit bat species could produce and secrete milk. Even human males can undergo changes that induce their quiescent mammary glands to produce milk. Most commonly this is due to pathological changes in endocrine tissues, but there have been verified reports of lactation in pubescent males, and even documented cases of adult men producing enough milk to suckle an infant.

The hormone that controls milk production in mammals is prolactin, a peptide hormone released from the anterior pituitary gland. Interestingly, the role of prolactin in mammals is a variation on its role in other vertebrates, including regulation of secretory functions, ion and water balance, and even behavior. During pregnancy, estrogen produced by the corpus luteum, and later the placenta, induces prolactin release. Prolactin prepares the mammary gland for milk production by increasing mammary gland mass and ensuring that the biosynthetic machinery is in place. During pregnancy, the high levels of progesterone and estrogen suppress the actual production of milk. Only after the levels of estrogen and progesterone decline during parturition does the mammary gland produce milk.

Several features of mammary glands are shared among all mammals. Like sebaceous glands, mammary glands are associated with hair follicles. The mammary glands are composed of both exocrine cells, which secrete the milk, and myoepithelial cells, which control the secretions. The milk itself is a mixture of fluids and macromolecules released from exocrine cells under the control of prolactin. However, the three groups of mammals differ in the complexity of the secretion and the anatomical structure of the gland itself. The monotreme mammary gland consists of convoluted tubes that lie beneath the ventral skin of the female. There are no teats or nipples to localize secretions; the milk oozes through the ducts onto the mother's fur, where it pools in surface indentations. Marsupials have a more complex mammary gland with discrete teats. The young locate the teat and suck it into the mouth, where it engorges to fill the oral cavity, locking the pup into position. Eutherian mammals possess complex mammary glands that are networks of lobes grouped into alveoli, with ducts that empty through an external teat (Figure 16.19). Unlike marsupials, the young of eutherian mammals can attach and detach at will. Behavioral interactions associated with feeding help establish a social bond between mother and offspring.

Mammary gland secretions include two novel products, casein and lactose

Mammary gland secretions are the source of water, salts, and nutrients for the infant, but the nature of the milk changes with time. The earliest secretions from the mammary gland, called *colostrum*, are rich in immunoprotective agents, growth factors, minerals, and vitamins A and D. The colostrum also has a trypsin inhibitor that protects the vital proteins in the colostrum from digestion in the infant's

FIGURE 16.19 **Synthesis of mammary gland secretions**

The secretory units of the mammary gland are the alveoli. They produce casein (milk protein) and lactose (milk sugar) in the ER-Golgi network, secreting it into the milk duct via exocytosis. Lipid droplets accumulate within the mammary epithelial cells through synthesis and uptake from adipocytes. Some proteins are taken up from the blood and carried by transcytosis across the epithelial cell and secreted into the milk duct.

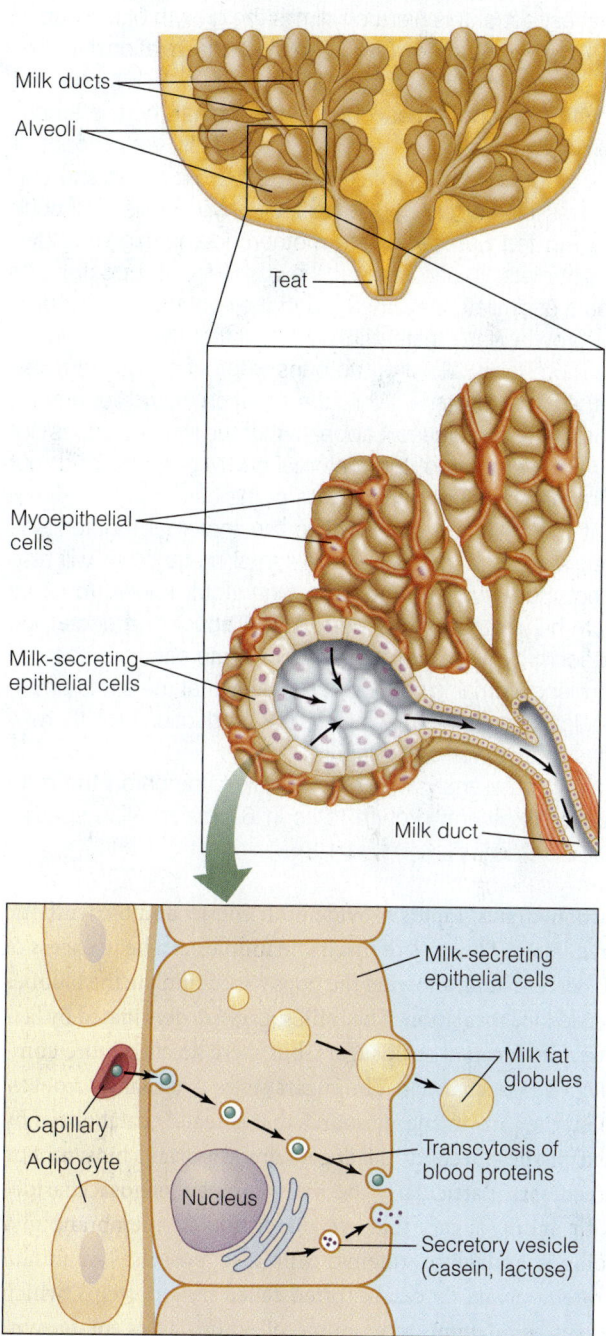

gastrointestinal tract. At this point in development, the infant's gastrointestinal tract is able to transport antibodies intact, transferring them to its own circulation.

As the colostrum is depleted by the infant, the mammary gland produces a milk that is much richer in lipids and

The growth rate of a nursing newborn depends on the milk delivered from the mother, which in turn depends on the nutrient availability from the diet. One question to ask is, what aspect of this hierarchy limits the growth of the pups?

Many researchers have explored the relationship between maternal metabolic energy intake (MEI) and the growth of young. It has long been held that there is a central limitation to milk energy output. That is, the amount of milk produced by a female is limited by how fast she can process dietary energy. To test this hypothesis, Valencak and Ruf fed European hare mothers (dams) high- or low-quality diets, expecting that the dams fed the poorer diet would assimilate less energy and their young (pups) would not grow as fast. Instead, they found that the dams simply ate more food, allowing the pups to grow as fast as those of the well-fed dams. While the situation may differ among mammals, in this case it appears that the limitation does not lie with the ability of the maternal gut to process food, but rather the metabolic capabilities of the dam.

If the limitation is related to the maternal metabolism, then any factor that affects maternal metabolism will also affect the growth of the pups. One factor known to affect maternal metabolism is body size. Though the underlying reason why whole-animal metabolic rate shows a size dependency remains unknown, it is likely that the same physiological constraints may affect milk production, and thereby affect growth rates of offspring.

In a meta-analysis, Alexander Riek compared the metabolic fluxes and growth rates in 62 mammalian species differing in body mass. A subset of those data is shown in Table 16.4.

One way to look at these data is to ask if there is a size dependency (scaling) of growth rate. To calculate a scaling coefficient for growth rate, log-transform the data for body mass (M) and growth rate (R). The scaling equation ($R = M^b + a$) becomes $\log R = b \log M + \log a$, where b is the scaling coefficient. This relationship, shown in Figure 16.18, produces a value of $b = 0.79$, which is fairly close to the scaling coefficient of -0.75 seen for other metabolic processes.

When Dr. Reik used the full data set, he found a scaling coefficient closer to 0.82, which he concludes differed significantly from the expected value of 0.75, suggesting that the value we find differs from that of a larger data set. What we would like you to appreciate is the potential influence of species selection on the outcome from the plotting of the scaling coefficient. For example:

1. How would the derived scaling coefficient change if the data for the hooded seal is added to the data set? (M = 42.5 kg, MEI = 248,900 kJ/d, R = 5,900 g/day)
2. How would the equation change if the other two seals were removed from the regression?

Apart from learning about size dependence of metabolic processes, this exercise also illustrates the potential influence of experimental choices around species selection. Which animals are included in studies is often based on practical limitations; however, researchers are compelled

carbohydrates. Lipids provide both energy and biosynthetic precursors. The milk of marine mammals can be in excess of 60 percent lipid, allowing the pups to accumulate the blubber needed for insulation. The milk sugars are dominated by lactose (often called milk sugar), but there are also more complex oligosaccharides. The sugars serve two main purposes. First, they are an energy source that is readily catabolized by fetal tissues. Second, the sugars are important biosynthetic precursors, particularly the more complex oligosaccharides with amino sugars that are important for membrane glycolipids and glycoproteins. Milk also possesses abundant protein, primarily casein (often called milk protein), which serves as an important source of amino acids for biosynthesis. This protein is highly phosphorylated, enabling it to bind Ca^{2+}. Almost 90 percent of the Ca^{2+} in the infant diet is locked into the structure of casein particles.

The two novel products found in the milk—lactose and casein—have origins that are intimately linked with the evolution of mammals. Lactose is produced by the enzyme *lactose synthase*, which is a complex of two proteins: galactosyltransferase and α-lactalbumin. Galactosyltransferase, which is found throughout eukaryotes, is one of the many enzymes that catalyze glycosylation reactions in the Golgi apparatus, adding galactose to various macromolecules, including proteins and lipids. However, in the mammary gland, the galactose acceptor for galactosyltransferase is glucose, and the disaccharide lactose is produced. This unique capacity is conferred by the second subunit of lactose synthase, α-lactalbumin. This subunit is structurally related to another enzyme, lysozyme. Thus, the capacity to produce lactose may have arisen only after the duplication of a lysozyme gene early in the mammalian lineage. The duplicated gene subsequently mutated into a form that could dimerize with galactosyltransferase to form the unique enzyme lactose synthase.

The protein casein most closely resembles the β-chain of fibrinogen, a serum protein that is involved in clotting of blood. Interestingly, the most primitive mammary glands produce a secretion that is primarily derived from

Table 16.4	Metabolic fluxes and growth rates in mammalian species differing in body mass		
	Body Mass (kg)	**Metabolic Energy Intake (kJ/d)**	**Growth Rate (g/day)**
American mink *Mustela vison*	0.092	121	4.8
Meerkat *Suricata suricatta*	0.108	184	6
Striped skunk *Mephitis mephitis*	0.161	222	4.9
Domestic cat *Felis catus*	0.347	263	8.1
Domestic dog *Canis lupus familiaris*	1.2	1,072	37
Northern fur seal *Callorhinus ursinus*	13.7	16,860	111
Australian fur seal *Arctocephalus pusillus*	19.8	13,700	58
American black bear *Ursus americanus*	40	9,739	351
Hooded seal *Cystophora cristata*	42.5	248,900	5,900
Brown bear *Ursus arctos*	61.7	14,751	605

to ensure that the conclusions are not unduly influenced by the choice of species. This may be affected by the inclusion or exclusions of outliers, which may be species for which the data are simply experimentally flawed or genuinely different. Elsewhere we have alluded to the importance of considering the phylogenetic relatedness of species. By statistically taking into account the phylogenetic distance between groups using phylogeny-independent contrasts, it is possible to separate effects due to phylogeny from those due to body mass. For example, seals collectively may have

a different relationship between lactation and growth that supersedes the effects of body mass.

References

- Riek, A. (2007). Relationship between milk energy intake and growth rate in suckling mammalian young at peak lactation: An updated meta-analysis. *Journal of Zoology, 274*, 160–170.
- Valencak, T. G., & Ruf, T. (2009). Energy turnover in European hares is centrally limited during early, but not during peak lactation. *Journal of Comparative Physiology B, 179*, 933–943.

presynthesized components of the blood, including fibrinogen. More advanced mammals rely primarily on molecules produced directly in the mammary gland. Thus, it is thought that evolution led to a shift from provision of serum proteins, such as fibrinogen, to production of fibrinogenlike proteins produced directly within the gland. The mammary gland is an excellent example of the way evolutionary processes produce something novel by modifying existing genes and anatomical structures. The production of milk and the nature of the mammary gland reflect an integration of unique aspects of biochemistry, physiological regulation, and anatomical structure.

Milk energy output influences infant growth rate

Production of milk is an extremely expensive metabolic process: The maternal physiology must process dietary energy and mobilize internal stores to produce large volumes of energy-rich nutrients. The metabolic costs to the female are

impressive, and evolutionary processes are thought to lead to behaviors that balance out the costs to the female with the benefits to the young. The balance sheet also must be justifiable over the lifetime of the female, meaning that the investment for any particular litter can be less than the maximal that is supportable physiologically.

During lactation, females in some species can elevate their metabolic rates as much as sixfold. The milk produced is transferred to the infant(s) to contribute to extremely rapid growth rates. Given the costs, one question that has intrigued physiologists has been the limits to the relationship between milk production and infant growth rates. Animals that eat more, or eat better quality food, are able to support faster growth rates of their offspring. However, at some point, females reach a limit, beyond which they cannot produce additional milk. The nature of this limit is not clear, and may differ between species, but it seems to be a result of general physiological limitations, either in the ability of the digestive tract to process nutrients, or mammary gland biosynthetic capacity. Sustaining such high rates of metabolism can be damaging to the female, and the limits to milk production may reflect a longer term strategy to limit milk production for one brood to ensure that females are able to rise to the challenge for subsequent broods.

Mammals differ in terms of the strategy for milk delivery and growth. Some seals, for example, compress the lactation into a very short period with remarkable transfer of energy and growth. Hooded seal pups weigh about 40 kilograms and have a gross energy intake from milk of 250 MJ/day, which supports growth at a rate of 6 kilograms per day. For a 40-kilogram human, this would require consumption of about 15 liters of milk per day. The same-sized seals would consume a lower volume of milk because of the higher energy content of seal milk, but the energy transfer from mother's milk to pup growth is remarkable.

Apart from examples where individual species or groups of species have peculiar strategies, there are more generalized relationships between species. Body mass, which we know to have a profound effect on metabolism, also exerts effects on milk production and infant growth (see Box 16.3: Math in Physiology: Scaling of Milk Production).

Early postnatal development requires remodeling of each physiological system

Even the most precocious mammals begin life in a physiologically vulnerable condition. They have developed in the comfort of the uterus, sustained by the maternal systems. Upon parturition, the mammal must gain responsibility for its own homeostatic processes, which requires maturation of all physiological systems.

In embryogenesis, the heart forms from a tubelike structure that recruits cardiomyocytes to the region to form the cardiac muscle. As the heart grows in mass, it also increases its contraction rate. Once the infant is born, the cardiovascular system undergoes the equivalent of an exercise training response, with the heart remodeling to gain strength to meet the greater demands of self-sufficiency.

The respiratory system transitions from a quiescent state in utero to supporting active ventilation. When born near term, the respiratory system must spring into action, taking on the immediate responsibility for gas exchange and eventually other physiological functions such as vocalization,

thermal exchange, and immunodefense activities, such as coughing and sneezing.

The immune system also matures. At first, the infant benefits from passive immunity acquired from the mother via milk. With time, the innate and acquired immune systems mature. The gut microbiota also changes dramatically, with microbes being acquired from the food and cultivated within the infant gut. The digestive tract grows in complexity. The permeability of the lining decreases commensurate with a reduction in ability to take up intact proteins from the diet, such as maternal antibodies. With time, food diversifies, and the full complement of digestive enzymes is needed.

The muscular and locomotor systems also change dramatically. Precocial species, such as horses, are born capable of supporting their own weight, and very quickly moving around the environment. More altricial species undergo a slow transformation into an active individual, with increases in muscle contractile properties. The skeletal system grows in size and individual bones become more ossified.

As a result of surface area-to-volume ratios, small mammals have greater challenges in maintaining constant body temperature. This presents a problem for species whose infants are born both small and metabolically immature, exacerbated by environmental conditions that pose a thermal challenge. Metabolic energy expended by the infant to thermoregulate comes at a cost of growth rate. Small mammals, such as rodents, produce pups that are so small that thermoregulatory costs are prohibitive. For newborn mice experiencing a cold challenge, it would be futile to attempt to use metabolic energy for thermogenesis, so in the early days of their life, they do not respond to cold stress. As they grow, they increase their mass-specific metabolic rates, and soon use energy for both rapid growth and thermogenesis. Once a critical size is reached, the extraordinary costs of thermogenesis decline, and energy expenditure declines. For larger animals, these early metabolic and thermoregulatory transitions occur in utero, and animals are born capable of thermoregulation.

CONCEPT CHECK

16. Compare the roles of prolactin in males and females.
17. What is crop milk?
18. What are the main components of milk?

SUMMARY

The hypothalamic-pituitary axis in conjunction with gonadal steroid hormones control vertebrate reproduction. The neurons of the hypothalamus secrete gonadotropin-releasing hormone in the region of the anterior pituitary, which responds by secreting luteinizing hormone and follicle-stimulating hormone. These control the

release of reproductive steroid hormones. In contrast, arthropods use terpenoid hormones and 20-hydroxyecdysone to control reproduction and development. In all animals, hormonal pathways are controlled by synthesis and degradation of both hormones and receptors.

Some animals reproduce by asexual reproduction, either clonal or parthenogenic, but most animals use sexual reproduction. Males make small gametes (sperm), and females make large gametes (ova). Sex may be determined by genotype, as in the XY system or ZW system, or by environment, as in temperature-dependent sex determination.

Oviparous animals expel either ova (external fertilization) or fertilized eggs (internal fertilization), allowing the embryo to develop externally. Ovoviviparous animals retain fertilized eggs internally. Viviparous animals bear live young, which develop internally and derive nutrition from the maternal tissues. Many animals have mechanisms to alter the timing of fertilization and development. Females of some species can store sperm for long periods after mating to ensure uninterrupted reproduction. Once the ovum is fertilized, factors derived from the ovum control early development.

Amniote embryos produce four cellular extraembryonic membranes: chorion, allantois, amnion, and yolk sac. These membranes play similar roles in amniotes, but in placental mammals, the chorion interacts with the maternal tissue to create the placenta.

In mammals, the follicle ruptures, releasing the ovum. The remaining follicular cells differentiate to form the corpus luteum, which continues to produce estrogens and progesterone. Once fertilized, the ovum implants in the uterine wall and grows. The remnant of the follicle becomes the corpus luteum, which produces steroids in response to hypothalamic and, in primates, chorionic gonadotropins, sustaining the pregnancy. With time, the corpus luteum degrades and the placenta maintains synthesis of progesterone and estrogens.

The steroid hormones (estrogen and progesterone) and peptide hormones (prolactin and oxytocin) prepare the female for parturition and postnatal care. Milk, a secretory product of mammary glands, is unique to mammals, allowing the female to transfer nutrients to the young. Prolactin controls milk production, as well as both maternal and paternal behavior.

REVIEW QUESTIONS

1. **LO 1** Compare the roles of steroid hormones in the reproduction of vertebrates and invertebrates.

2. **LO 1** What is the impact of using (steroid) hormones that are lipid soluble?

3. **LO 2** Discuss how chromosomes determine sex of animals.

4. **LO 2** What factors might alter sex ratios in natural populations?

5. **LO 3** Compare the features of ovipary, ovovivipary, and vivipary.

6. **LO 3** Compare the pathways of gametogenesis in males versus females.

7. **LO 4** Choose examples of male sexual displays and discuss the cellular mechanisms that animals would use to produce the features.

8. **LO 4** What is sperm competition?

9. **LO 5** How does a sperm reach the genetic material of an ovum in (a) an insect egg and (b) a chicken egg?

10. **LO 5** What animals might be expected to use delayed implantation?

11. **LO 6** Discuss how hormones regulate the ovulatory cycle of mammals.

12. **LO 6** Discuss the diverse roles of smooth muscle in mammalian reproductive physiology.

13. **LO 7** Discuss the steps that would have been required for the evolution of milk secretion in placental mammals.

14. **LO 7** What differences might you expect in the milk of a platypus and of a seal?

SYNTHESIS QUESTIONS

1. Embryos derive nutrition from yolk, except in placental mammals. Discuss the benefits and risks of the two modes of nutrient delivery.

2. Why are animals with temperature-dependent sex determination at risk from endocrine disruptors?

3. Both yolk and milk are products of cellular secretion. Compare their pathways for synthesis and secretion.

4. Males and females develop from genomes that are the same, except for a few genes on the sex determination chromosome. Discuss how the same cellular machinery is used differently in males versus females.

5. Using only mammalian examples, discuss the energetic tradeoffs for K-type versus r-type life history strategies.

6. Apart from affecting swimming energetics, how might sperm tail length be evolutionarily advantageous or disadvantageous?

QUANTITATIVE QUESTION

1. Sperm of most fish are released into the water and commence swimming to find an egg. The duration of swimming activity can be as short as a couple of minutes or may continue for several hours. If a sperm swims at a velocity of 100 μm/sec and continues swimming for 2 minutes, how far will it swim? What is the significance of your result in relation to mating strategies of fish?

Glossary

A-band (or **anisotropic band**) The region of a muscle sarcomere where the thick filaments occur.

absolute refractory period The period during and immediately following an action potential in which an excitable cell cannot generate another action potential, no matter how strong the stimulus.

absolute temperature A measure of temperature in kelvins, where 0 K (absolute zero) is the temperature at which there is no atomic or molecular movement. 1 unit on the Kelvin scale equals 1° on the Celsius scale. 0 K = −273°C.

acclimation A persistent but reversible change in a physiological function that occurs as a result of an alteration in an environmental parameter, such as temperature or photoperiod. Acclimation usually occurs as a result of an experimental manipulation (see also *acclimatization*).

acclimatization A reorganization of physiological functions that occurs as a result of complex environmental changes, such as season or altitude (see also *acclimation*).

accommodation The process by which an eye changes its focal length. Accommodation allows the eye to produce a focused image of objects at different distances.

acetyl CoA An activated form of acetate that serves as the entry point for carbon into the TCA cycle.

acetylcholine A neurotransmitter found in most animal species in many types of neurons, including motor neurons and the autonomic ganglia of vertebrates.

acetylcholinesterase An enzyme that catalyzes the breakdown of acetylcholine into choline and acetate.

acid A chemical that donates a proton (see also *base*).

acidosis A decrease in pH arising through respiration (respiratory acidosis) or metabolism (metabolic acidosis).

acrosome A vesicle in sperm that contains digestive enzymes that enable the sperm to penetrate the outer layers of an ovum.

acrosome reaction The exocytosis of the enzyme-laden acrosomal vesicle of sperm in response to contact with the ovum.

actin G-actin is a monomeric protein that can be polymerized to construct filamentous actin (F-actin). Actin is the basis of both cytoskeletal microfilaments (composed of the α-actin isoform of G-actin) and skeletal thin filaments (composed of the β-actin isoform of G-actin) (see also *myosin*).

actinomyosin The combination of actin and myosin, joined by a cross-bridge.

action potential A relatively large-amplitude, rapid change in the membrane potential of an excitable cell as a result of the opening and closing of voltage-gated ion channels; involved in transmitting signals across long distances in the nervous system.

activation energy (E_A) The energetic barrier that must be reached before a reactant can be transformed into a product.

activation gate One of the two gates that open and close voltage-gated sodium channels (see also *inactivation gate*).

active site A region of an enzyme that binds the substrate and undergoes conformational changes to catalyze the reaction.

active state The phase of a cross-bridge cycle in which myosin is attached to actin and generating force.

active transport Protein-mediated movement of a substance across a membrane with the utilization of some form of energy. Primary active transport uses ATP. Secondary active transport uses an electrochemical gradient (see also *facilitated diffusion, passive transport*).

acuity The ability to resolve fine detail of a stimulus.

acute response The rapid phase of response to an external or internal change in conditions, usually within seconds to minutes.

adaptation Used in two contexts in physiology: (1) a change in the genetic structure of a population as a result of natural selection; (2) a reversible change in a physiological parameter that provides a beneficial response to an environmental change. Evolutionary and comparative physiologists prefer to use only the first definition.

adaptation See *receptor adaptation*.

adaptive immune system The components of the immune system that deal with specific pathogens, in contrast to the innate immune system, which deals with pathogens more generally. Central to the adaptive (or acquired) immune system is receptors that bind to specific molecular motifs, initiating an immune response.

adenine A purine nitrogenous base component of nucleotides, including nucleic acids.

adenosine A nucleoside composed of adenine and the sugar deoxyribose, important as a signaling molecule.

adenosine diphosphate (ADP) A nucleotide composed of the nucleoside adenine with two phosphate groups, with a single high-energy phosphodiester bond.

adenosine triphosphate (ATP) A nucleotide composed of the nucleoside adenine with three phosphate groups, with two high-energy phosphodiester bonds.

adenylate cyclase (adenylyl cyclase) The enzyme that converts ATP to cyclic AMP.

adequate stimulus The stimulus modality to which a sensory receptor is the most sensitive.

adhesion plaque A membrane protein complex that anchors thin filaments to the membrane.

adipose tissue A tissue composed of fat cells (adipocytes) that produce and store lipid.

ADP See *adenosine diphosphate*.

adrenal cortex See *adrenal gland*.

adrenal gland A gland near the kidney, which in mammals is composed of an outermost layer (the adrenal cortex) and an inner layer (adrenal medulla).

adrenergic receptor A G protein–linked cell membrane receptor that binds norepinephrine preferentially, with a lower affinity for epinephrine.

adrenal medulla See *adrenal gland*.

adrenergic receptors Receptors for the catecholamines norepinephrine and epinephrine.

adrenoreceptors See *adrenergic receptors*.

aerobic Occurring in, or depending on, the presence of oxygen.

aerobic dive limit The maximum length of a dive prior to any increase in blood lactate levels.

aerobic scope The ratio of the maximal aerobic metabolic rate to the basal metabolic rate, typically in the range of 3–10.

aerofoil A surface, teardrop shaped in profile, that moves through air to generate lift. An aerial version of a hydrofoil.

afferent Leading toward a region of interest (see also *efferent*).

afferent arteriole An arteriole that enters the glomerulus of a kidney tubule.

afferent division The part of the peripheral nervous system that conducts sensory information from sensory receptors and organs toward the central nervous system.

afferent neuron A neuron that conducts a signal from the periphery to an integrating center (see also *sensory neuron*).

affinity A measure of the degree of attraction between a ligand and a molecule that binds the ligand (see also K_m).

affinity constant (or K_a) Reciprocal of the dissociation constant.

after-hyperpolarization phase A prolonged hyperpolarization following an action potential.

aglomerular kidney A derived form of kidney, with tubules that lack a glomerulus, found in many lineages of marine fish.

agonist A substance that binds to a receptor and initiates a signaling event. May include both the natural endogenous ligand as well as pharmaceutical agents that mimic the natural substance.

albumen A protein found in eggs that cushions the embryo.

albumin A binding globulin (carrier protein) that is one of the primary proteins of vertebrate plasma; makes a major contribution to blood osmotic pressure.

aldosterone Mineralocorticoid hormone secreted by the adrenal cortex. Its main function is to alter the levels of Na^+ and K^+ in the urine, secondarily affecting water transport.

alkaloids A large group of compounds derived from plants that have pharmacological effects in animals.

alkalosis The condition of being alkaline (see also *metabolic alkalosis, respiratory alkalosis*).

allantoic membrane One of four membranes in an amniote egg.

allantoin An intermediate in nucleotide breakdown and uric acid synthesis; an important form of nitrogenous waste for some animals.

allatostatin A neuropeptide hormone in arthropods that inhibits the corpus allatum from secreting juvenile hormone.

allatotropin A neuropeptide hormone in arthropods that stimulates the corpus allatum to secrete juvenile hormone.

alleles Different forms of the same protein that are encoded by the same gene but differ slightly in primary sequence.

allelochemical A chemical produced by one species that affects the growth, survival, or reproduction of other species.

allometry (or **allometric scaling**) The pattern seen when comparing structural or functional parameters in relation to body size.

allostasis The process by which stability is achieved through changes in physiological systems. In contrast to homeostasis, this emphasizes that aspects of physiology actively change to maintain constancy in other parameters.

allosteric regulator A molecule that binds an enzyme at a site distinct from the substrate binding site to regulate activity.

allosteric site A region of an enzyme, distinct from the active site, that binds a molecule other than the substrate or product, triggering a structural change that alters the catalytic properties of the enzyme.

allozyme An allelic variant of an enzyme.

alpha-helix (α-helix) A secondary structure of protein or DNA in which the molecule twists in a characteristic pattern, with structure stabilized by hydrogen bonds between adjacent regions.

alternative splicing One of the processes that can result in different mRNAs being coded by a single gene. Different exons of the gene are spliced out in each mRNA, resulting in a number of possible combinations.

alveoli (singular: **alveolus**) The site of gas exchange in mammalian lungs.

ambient External or environmental conditions, such as ambient temperature.

amine A class of molecules based on ammonia, with a side group substituting for at least one N atom.

amino acid Organic molecules with at least one amino group and at least one carboxyl group. The amino acids that are used to build proteins are α-amino acids.

ammonia A general term that includes both NH_3 and NH_4^+ (ammonium), potent neurotoxins.

ammoniotele An animal with an excretory strategy in which more than half of the nitrogen is excreted as ammonia (see also *ureotele, uricotele*).

amniote Vertebrates with an amnion, namely reptiles, birds, and mammals.

amphibolic pathway A metabolic pathway that both synthesizes (catabolic) and degrades (anabolic) metabolites.

amphipathic A molecule with both hydrophobic and hydrophilic parts.

amplification An exponential increase in activity from one step of a pathway to the next; typically used in the context of signal transduction pathways.

ampulla Any saclike enlargement of a tube or duct, such as the terminal ends of the semicircular canals of the inner ear of vertebrates or the modified neuromasts of the lateral line system in sharks and rays (see *ampullae of Lorenzini*).

ampullae of Lorenzini A series of pits found on the noses of sharks and rays acting as polymodal receptors that detect both electrical and mechanical stimuli.

amygdala A part of the limbic system of the vertebrate brain that is involved in emotional responses such as fear and anger.

amylase An enzyme that breaks down starch (amylose, amylopectin).

anabolic pathways (or **anabolism**) Metabolic reactions or pathways that build complex molecules from simpler molecules.

anadromous The life history strategy of an animal living most of its life in the sea, then returning to freshwater to reproduce (see also *catadromous*).

anaerobic Without oxygen. Pertains to an environment without oxygen, or a pathway that occurs in the absence of oxygen (see also *aerobic*).

anaplerotic pathway (or **anaplerosis**) A metabolic reaction that replenishes intermediates of pathways.

anastomosis A convergence of two or more branches of a tubular structure; e.g., a direct connection between two arteries in the circulatory system.

anatomical dead space The portion of a respiratory structure that cannot participate in gas exchange (e.g., the trachea and bronchi).

androgens Steroid hormones structurally related to testosterone that control masculine features.

anemia A condition in which the number of erythrocytes or hemoglobin in the blood is lower than normal.

angiogenesis Synthesis of new blood vessels, often in response to local hypoxia.

angiotensin II A peptide hormone that controls blood pressure. Its precursor is angiotensinogen, which is cleaved by renin to form angiotensin I. This decapeptide is cleaved to the final form, angiotensin II, an octapeptide.

angiotensin-converting enzyme (ACE) An enzyme that converts angiotensin I to angiotensin II.

angle of attack The angle at which a surface meets the fluid it encounters, as with aerofoils and hydrofoils.

anhydrobiosis Literally "life without water," this refers to the physiological responses that permit animals to survive in the absence of water.

anion An ion with a negative charge.

anoxic See *anaerobic*.

antagonist A substance that binds to a receptor but does not stimulate a signaling event. Antagonists interfere with the binding of the natural ligand.

antagonistic controls For a given step or pathway, sets of controls that exert opposing effects.

antagonistic muscle A muscle that opposes the movement of another muscle.

anterior pituitary gland The anterior lobe of the pituitary gland of vertebrates, also called the adenohypophysis; secretes tropic hormones.

antidiuretic A substance that induces a reduction in urine volume.

antidiuretic hormone (ADH) Also known as vasopressin, by increasing the permeability of the collecting duct of the nephron, this peptide hormone regulates physiological processes that help conserve water, and reduce the loss of water in the urine.

antifreeze protein A protein that disrupts the growth of ice crystals, allowing an organism to survive subzero temperatures.

antigen A substance, usually a protein, that induces the formation of an antibody that can bind the antigen.

antigen-presenting cells (APCs) These immune cells ingest pathogens or foreign material, digest it into smaller fragments, and exocytose the material to display it on the cell surface as an antigen. Recognition of the material by other cells triggers an immune response.

antiport (or **exchanger**) A transport protein that exchanges one ion (or molecule) for another ion (or molecule) on the opposite side of a membrane.

anus The sphincter through which feces exit the gastrointestinal tract.

aorta The major artery exiting the heart.

aortic body A sensory structure located in the vertebrate aorta that contains baroreceptors and chemoreceptors.

aortic semilunar valve The valve between the left ventricle and the aorta of the mammalian cardiovascular system.

apex The bottom of the heart in mammals.

apical The end of a structure opposite the base.

apical membrane The end of the cell furthest from the basolateral membrane; the membrane oriented away from the circulatory system.

apnea A period without breathing.

apocrine A type of secretion whereby the cell sheds the apical region of plasma membrane as part of a signaling pathway.

apoenzyme The proteinaceous part of an enzyme.

aquaporin A large tetrameric channel that allows the passage of water through the plasma membrane.

aqueous humor A thin, watery fluid found in the vertebrate eye between the cornea and the lens.

arginine phosphate A major phosphagen in invertebrates, which performs the same role as creatine phosphate in vertebrates.

aromatase See *cytochrome P450 aromatase*.

Arrhenius plot A curve relating temperature to activity, enabling the calculation of activation energy.

arterial blood pressure See *mean arterial pressure*.

arteriole A small branch of the arterial network immediately preceding a capillary bed (see *venule*).

artery A large blood vessel carrying blood away from the heart.

asexual reproduction Production of offspring without the fertilization of an ovum by a sperm (see also *automictic parthenogenesis*).

assimilation Conversion of dietary nutrients into metabolizable fuels.

assimilation efficiency Proportion of dietary nutrients successfully assimilated.

astrocytes Vertebrate glial cells that help to support and regulate the action of neurons in the central nervous system.

asynchronous flight muscle A muscle in which a single neuronal stimulation causes multiple cycles of contraction and relaxation.

ATP See *adenosine triphosphate*.

ATP-binding cassette A common structural motif found in diverse proteins that binds ATP.

ATPase A class of proteins, including enzymes and transporters, that couples ATP hydrolysis to a mechanical or chemical process.

ATPS Standardized reference condition for measuring gas volumes: ambient temperature, pressure, and saturated with water.

atresia The programmed cell death (apoptosis) of follicles other than the dominant follicle that matures during the ovulatory cycle.

atrial natriuretic peptide (ANP) A peptide hormone produced in the heart that exerts effects on ion and water balance that tend to reduce blood pressure. It increases urine volume and Na^+ excretion.

atrioventricular node (AV node) Part of the conducting pathways of the mammalian heart; delays conduction of the electrical signal between the atrium and ventricles.

atrioventricular (AV) valves Valves located between the atrium and the ventricle of vertebrate hearts.

atrium (plural: **atria**) One of the chambers of a heart. Blood moves from the atrium to the ventricle.

atrophy Loss of tissue mass as a result of dying cells; often seen with locomotor muscle in response to prolonged periods of inactivity.

August Krogh principle Principle that for every biological problem, there is an organism on which it can most conveniently be studied.

autocrine A type of cell signaling in which a single cell signals another cell of the same type, including itself.

automictic parthenogenesis Production of offspring by a female in which the second polar body fuses with the ovum to produce a diploid offspring.

autonomic division (of the nervous system) See *autonomic nervous system.*

autonomic ganglia Ganglia of the vertebrate peripheral nervous system.

autonomic nervous system Part of the vertebrate peripheral nervous system that controls largely involuntary functions such as heart rate. It is divided into three main branches: the sympathetic, parasympathetic, and enteric nervous systems.

autoregulation Regulation of an organ by intrinsic mechanisms (within the same organ). For example, regulation of the force of cardiac contraction by the pressure exerted by the blood within the heart (see *Frank-Starling effect*).

autotrophy An organism that synthesizes its own nutrients from inorganic material, using the energy of the sun (photoautotroph) or inorganic reactions (chemoautotrophs).

Avogadro's number The number of molecules in a mole (6.02252×10^{23}).

axoaxonic synapse A synapse formed between the axon terminal of one neuron and the axon of another neuron (at any point along its length).

axodendritic synapse A synapse formed between the axon terminal of one neuron and the dendrite of another neuron.

axon A projection of the cell body of a neuron that is involved in carrying information, usually in the form of action potentials, from the cell body to the axon terminal.

axon hillock The junction between the cell body and axon of a neuron. In many neurons, the axon hillock is the site of action potential initiation, acting as the trigger zone for the neuron.

axon terminal The distal end of an axon that forms a synapse with an effector cell or neuron.

axon varicosity A type of synapse in which the presynaptic cell releases neurotransmitter at a series of swellings along the axon.

axonal transport Cytoskeletal-mediated movement of organelles and vesicles along the length of an axon.

axonemal dyneins Motor proteins that enable the sliding of microtubules in cilia and flagella.

axoneme The microtubule-based structure that underlies flagella and cilia.

axosomatic synapse A synapse formed between the axon terminal of one neuron and the soma (cell body) of another neuron.

B cells Lymphocytes that are produced in the bone marrow (mammals) and bursa of Fabricus (birds), recognized by their expression of B cell receptors that bind to antigens.

baroreceptor A receptor that senses pressure (by sensing the resulting stretch on the cell membrane).

baroreceptor reflex A homeostatic feedback loop that regulates blood pressure. Pressure sensors in the heart and arterial system detect changes in blood pressure and send sensory feedback to the central nervous system that causes physiological responses that return blood pressure back to the normal range.

basal lamina The extracellular matrix underlying a sheet of epithelial cells; part of the connective tissue formed largely by fibroblasts.

basal metabolic rate (BMR) The metabolic rate of a homeothermic animal at rest, at a thermal neutral temperature, and post-absorptive (see also *resting metabolic rate, standard metabolic rate*).

basal nuclei Interconnected groups of gray matter within the mammalian brain.

base A molecule that accepts a proton, or otherwise causes a reduction in proton concentration through effects on the dissociation of water.

basement membrane See also *basal lamina.*

basilar membrane The location of the auditory hair cells in the mammalian cochlea.

basophil A type of white blood cell that releases histamine; involved in the vertebrate immune response.

batch reactor A chemical reactor in which nutrients enter and exit through the same opening; nutrients are retained in the reactor and digested; the undigested material is then expelled, and replaced by another batch of nutrients to be processed.

behavioral thermoregulation The use of behavior to control the body temperature of a poikilotherm, or to reduce the costs of thermoregulation for a homeotherm.

beta-oxidation (β-oxidation) Pathway of fatty acid catabolism that produces acetyl CoA and reducing equivalents.

beta-sheet (β-sheet) Protein folding pattern in which stretches of amino acids are aligned along another amino acid stretch. This secondary structure is stabilized by hydrogen bonds.

bicuspid valve The valve between the left atrium and the left ventricle of the mammalian heart (also called the mitral valve).

bilateral symmetry A body form in which the body can be divided by a single plane such that the right and left sides are approximate mirror images.

bile A thick, yellow-green fluid composed of salts, pigments, and lipids produced by the liver and stored by the gallbladder; when released into the small intestine it neutralizes gastric acid and aids in the digestion of nutrients, particularly lipids.

bile duct The connection between the liver and the small intestine.

bile pigments Nondigestible breakdown products of porphyrins, including the hemes found in hemoglobin and cytochromes.

bile salts Cholic acid conjugated with amino acids, primarily glycine and taurine; assist in emulsification of lipid within the small intestine.

binocular vision The ability to compare the images coming from two eyes to produce three-dimensional perception.

binocular zone The area of overlap between the right and left visual fields of a vertebrate that allows depth perception.

biogenic amine A class of neurotransmitters derived from amino acids including the catecholamines and dopamine.

bioluminescence The production of light by living organisms.

bipolar neuron A neuron with two main processes leading from the cell body, one of which conveys signals toward the cell body, and one of which conveys signals away from the cell body.

blastema A mass of cells that can proliferate and differentiate to regenerate damaged tissues or organs.

blastocoel The cavity formed by the inpouching of the blastocyst, which eventually forms the alimentary canal.

blastocyst In mammals, the blastula continues development to form the blastocyst. It contains an inner cell mass and an outer layer of cells: the trophoblast.

blastula One of the early developmental stages of animals prior to the formation of the embryonic germ layers. In many animals, this consists of a hollow ball of about 100 cells.

bleaching The fading of a photopigment following absorption of energy from photons. In the case of the retinal-opsin complex, absorption of energy from light causes retinal to dissociate from opsin. Opsin is not pigmented, and thus the photopigment loses its color.

blood The circulatory fluid in animals with closed circulatory systems. Generally contains proteins, ions, organic molecules, and various cell types.

blood-brain barrier A specialized protective barrier made up of glial cells that separates the circulatory system and the central nervous system in vertebrates.

blood vessels Tubes that carry blood through an animal's body.

blubber Subcutaneous lipid deposits of marine mammals, which provide thermal insulation.

Bohr effect A change in hemoglobin oxygen affinity due to a change in pH.

bolus A volume of material introduced into a flow-through system that moves through the system as a unit, with some dispersion along the way; often used in the context of a bolus of food moving through the gastrointestinal tract.

bombesin A hormone that regulates release of gastrointestinal hormones and control of gastrointestinal motility in vertebrates.

bond energy The energy required to form a chemical bond.

bone In vertebrates, a solid structure composed of mineralized extracellular matrix of osteocytes; with cartilage and tendon, it constitutes the skeleton.

book gills The respiratory surfaces of water-breathing chelicerates such as horseshoe crabs.

book lungs The respiratory surfaces of some air-breathing chelicerates such as spiders and scorpions.

boundary layer The region of a solution that is in direct contact or otherwise influenced by a surface; often called an unstirred layer.

Bowman's capsule A cup-shaped expansion of the vertebrate kidney tubule; surrounds the glomerulus.

brackish water Water that is intermediate between freshwater and seawater; typically found in estuaries, salt marshes, or isolated ponds.

bradycardia A heart rate that is slower than normal.

brain A large grouping of ganglia that act as a sophisticated integrating center. Typically located toward the anterior end of the body in the cephalic (head) region.

brainstem A portion of the vertebrate central nervous system that connects the cerebrum of the brain to the spinal cord; contains the pons and medulla, the sites of the respiratory and cardiovascular control centers.

branchial Relating to gills.

breakpoint Refers to a transition in a relationship, usually indicating the point of convergence of two lines with different slopes; used specifically with Arrhenius plots to show a change in the effects of temperature on a structure or process over different ranges.

Broca's area A region in the frontal lobe of the brain of humans that is involved in speech production.

bronchi (singular: **bronchus**) Airways of vertebrate lungs leading from the trachea to the bronchioles.

bronchioles The smallest branches of the airways of mammalian lungs; lead to the terminal alveoli.

brood spot A well-vascularized, featherless region on the underside of birds that is important for warming developing eggs.

brown adipose tissue Also known as brown fat, a thermogenic tissue found in many small mammals, often in the back or neck region. Abundant mitochondria in the brown adipocytes possess thermogenin, a protein that uncouples oxidative phosphorylation to enhance heat production.

brush border Abundant microvilli on epithelial cells in the gastrointestinal tract, giving the tissue a microscopic brushlike appearance.

BTPS Standardized reference conditions for measuring gas volumes: body temperature, atmospheric pressure, and saturated with water.

buccal cavity Mouth cavity.

buffer Chemicals which, when placed in solution, confer on the solution an ability to resist changes in pH when acid or base is added.

bulbourethral gland A mucus-secreting accessory gland of the male reproductive tract.

bulbus arteriosus The outflow tract of the heart in bony fishes; nonmuscular and elastic (see also *conus arteriosus*).

bulk flow The movement of a fluid as a result of a pressure or temperature gradient.

bulk phase (or **bulk solution**) The volume of solution that is beyond the influence of the surfaces (see also *boundary layer*).

bundle of His One of the conducting pathways of the mammalian heart.

burst exercise High-intensity exercise powered by glycolytic muscle fibers; can continue for only short periods, until glycogen stores are exhausted.

C region The part of an antibody that is constant in sequence and structure.

cable properties The electrical properties of axons.

calcitonin A thyroid hormone that helps regulate Ca^{2+} levels, typically opposing the effects of parathyroid hormone, lowering plasma Ca^{2+} levels.

calcium-induced calcium release A mode of muscle activation where calcium crossing the sarcolemma through a Ca^{2+} channel causes a Ca^{2+} channel in the sarcoplasmic reticulum to open.

caldesmon A calcium-binding protein important in the regulation of smooth muscle contractility.

calmodulin A calcium-sensing protein involved in many signal transduction pathways.

caloric deficit The condition in which energy derived from the diet is less than energetic expenditure, resulting in net loss of energy by the animal.

calorie A unit of heat equal to 4.2 joules; nutritional literature may refer to the unit Calorie, which is equivalent to 1,000 calories. The unit of heat required to raise 1 g of water at 1 atm by 1°C.

calorimetry The measurement of heat production as an index of metabolic rate.

calsequestrin A calcium-binding protein that allows a muscle to concentrate Ca^{2+} within the sarcoplasmic reticulum.

cAMP (cyclic AMP) A second messenger produced by adenylate cyclase; most important action is the stimulation of protein kinase A.

capacitation A maturation step experienced by sperm after they encounter fluids from the female reproductive tract.

capillary The smallest of the blood vessels in a closed circulatory system; the site of exchange of materials with the tissues.

capillary beds A collection of capillaries.

carbaminohemoglobin Hemoglobin bound to carbon dioxide.

carbohydrate A group of organic molecules that share a preponderance of hydroxyl groups (see also *disaccharide, monosaccharide, polysaccharide*).

carbonic anhydrase (CA) An enzyme that catalyzes the conversion of carbon dioxide and water to bicarbonate and protons.

carboxyhemoglobin Hemoglobin bound to carbon monoxide.

cardiac cycle The complete sequence of events from one heartbeat to the next (see *systole* and *diastole*).

cardiac muscle A form of striated muscle that occurs in the heart.

cardiac output The volume of blood pumped by the heart per unit time; the product of heart rate and stroke volume.

cardiomyocyte A muscle cell found in the heart.

cardiovascular control center A region of the brain within the medulla oblongata that is involved in regulating heart rate and blood pressure.

cardiovascular system An alternate term for the circulatory system of animals such as vertebrates. Consists of the heart, blood, and blood vessels.

carotid body A structure located in the carotid artery leading to the head of vertebrates; contains baroreceptors and chemoreceptors.

carotid rete A network of blood vessels that cools the brain.

carrier protein (or **binding protein; binding globulin**) Blood proteins that help to transport hydrophobic molecules (such as steroid hormones) in the blood.

carrier-mediated transport All forms of transport across membranes that require a protein.

cartilage In vertebrates, a semisolid structure composed of the extracellular matrix of chondrocytes; the major component of the skeleton of chondrichthians but important in other vertebrates as a cushion between joints.

catabolic pathway (or **catabolism**) A metabolic pathway that degrades macromolecules into smaller molecules.

catadromous A life history strategy of fish (e.g., eels) in which the adult migrates from freshwater to seawater to breed (see also *anadromous*).

catalysis The progression of a chemical reaction that proceeds with the help of a catalyst.

catalyst A molecule that accelerates chemical reactions but is not changed in the process.

catalytic constant (k_{cat}) The number of reactions catalyzed by a single molecule of enzyme per second.

catecholamines The biogenic amines epinephrine and norepinephrine.

cation An ion with a positive charge.

caudal A location near the posterior of an animal.

cecum A blind-ended sac that carries out digestive reactions in the gastrointestinal tract.

cell body See *soma*.

cell membrane See *plasma membrane*.

cellular immunity A subdivision of the immune system that relies upon cells, rather than noncellular elements, such as antibodies. (Also known as cell-mediated immunity.)

cellular membranes A general term that refers to the collection of membranes within a cell, including plasma membrane and organelle membranes.

cellulose A glucose polymer that serves a structural role in plants; indigestible by most animals without the assistance of symbionts.

central chemoreceptors A group of chemoreceptors located in the medulla of vertebrate brains.

central lacteal A small, saclike vessel in an intestinal villus; collects lipids that cross the intestinal epithelium.

central nervous system The portion of the nervous system containing the primary integrating centers. In vertebrates it consists of the brain and spinal cord. In invertebrates, it consists of the brain, the major ganglia, and the connecting commissures.

cephalic Toward the anterior end of an animal.

cephalization An evolutionary trend toward the centralization of nervous and sensory functions at the anterior end of the body (in the head).

cerebellum A part of the vertebrate hindbrain that is involved in maintaining balance and coordinating voluntary muscle movement.

cerebral cortex Outer surface of the vertebrate brain.

cerebral hemispheres Paired structures of the cerebrum (part of the vertebrate forebrain). The cerebral hemispheres are the most obvious structures of a mammalian brain.

cerebral ventricle See *ventricle*.

cerebrospinal fluid (CSF) A fluid contained within the meninges that surrounds the brain and spinal cord of vertebrates.

cerebrum The largest part of the mammalian forebrain.

cGMP See *cyclic GMP*.

cGMP phosphodiesterase An enzyme that cleaves cGMP, producing GMP.

channel A transport protein that facilitates the movement of specific ions or molecules across a cellular membrane down an electrochemical gradient.

chaperone protein See *molecular chaperone*.

chemical energy The energy associated with the reorganization of the chemical structure of a molecule.

chemical gradient An area across which the concentration of a chemical differs, often across a membrane.

chemical synapse A junction between a neuron and another cell in which the signal is transmitted across the synapse in the form of a neurotransmitter.

chemoautotroph An organism that uses inorganic chemical energy to convert organic sources of carbon and nitrogen into biosynthetic building blocks.

chemokine A cytokine that induces a cell to move.

chemokinetic An increase in nondirectional movement in response to the detection of a chemical.

chemoreceptor Used to describe either a cell containing chemoreceptive proteins, or the proteins themselves. Chemicals such as hormones, odorants, and tastants bind specifically to chemoreceptor proteins, altering their conformation and causing a signal within the chemoreceptor cell.

chemotaxic Movement toward higher concentrations of a chemical.

chief cell The secretory cells of the gastric epithelium that release pepsin.

chitin A polymer of N-acetyl glucosamine used by arthropods to construct the exoskeleton.

chloride cell An ion-pumping cell of fish gill epithelium (also called a mitochondria-rich cell).

chloride shift The exchange of chloride and bicarbonate across the erythrocyte membrane.

chlorocruorin A type of hemoglobin found in some annelids; known as the green hemoglobins.

choanocytes Flagellated cells of sponges that resemble the protist choanoflagellates.

choanoflagellates Flagellated protists that resemble the sponge cells known as choanocytes.

cholesterol A steroid compound produced from isoprene units; present in cellular membranes and acts as a precursor for steroid hormones.

cholinergic receptor A receptor that binds the signaling molecule acetylcholine. Cholinergic receptors can be divided into nicotinic and muscarinic receptors.

chondrocytes The cells that produce cartilage.

chordae tendineae Chordlike tendons that connect the atrioventricular valves of the mammalian heart to the papillary muscles and prevent the valve from opening backwards.

chorion The outer protein layer of an insect egg; the outer membrane of a vertebrate ovum.

chorionic gonadotropin (CG) A third gonadotropin of vertebrates, produced by the placenta but only in primates.

choroid A highly pigmented layer of tissue located under the retinal pigment epithelium of the vertebrate eye.

chromaffin cells Cells that secrete the hormone epinephrine (adrenaline). In mammals they are located in the compact adrenal medulla, but in other vertebrates they are more dispersed.

chromophore A molecule that is able to absorb light. In photoreception, the chromophore absorbs the energy from incoming photons and undergoes a conformational change, which sends a signal to an associated G protein, in the first step of visual phototransduction.

chromosome A single, contiguous polymer of DNA found within the genome.

chylomicron A large lipoprotein complex that carries lipid from the digestive tract through the circulation to processing and target tissues.

cilia (singular: **cilium**) Microtubule-based extensions from a cell that move in a wavelike pattern.

ciliary body A part of the vertebrate eye that secretes the aqueous humor.

ciliary muscle The muscle that controls the shape of the lens of the vertebrate eye; involved in producing a focused image.

ciliary photoreceptors One of two types of animal photoreceptor cells. Vertebrate photoreceptors belong to this class (see also *rhabdomeric photoreceptors*).

circadian rhythm Regular changes in gene expression, biochemistry, physiology, and behavior that cycle with a period of approximately 24 hours. Endogenous circadian rhythms persist even in constant darkness.

circulatory system A group of organs and tissues involved in moving fluids through the body; consists of one or more pumping structures and a series of tubes or other spaces through which fluid can move.

citric acid cycle See *tricarboxylic acid cycle*.

clathrin A triskelion-shaped (three-armed) protein that coats some types of vesicles; vesicle formation begins with a clathrin-coated pit, which enlarges to form a clathrin-coated vesicle.

clearance See *renal clearance*.

cloaca The distal portion of the hindgut in some fishes, amphibians, birds, and reptiles; in these species both excretory and reproductive products are emitted into the cloaca, and leave the body via a single opening.

clonal reproduction A form of asexual reproduction whereby an animal produces a genotypically identical offspring (a clone).

closed circulatory system A circulatory system in which the blood remains within a series of enclosed blood vessels throughout the circulation.

cnida Within a cnidocyte, the subcellular capsule that houses the harpoon that is launched when the cnidocyte is stimulated.

cnidocyte The cells found in cnidarians that possess the cnida and the other structures needed to detect a physical disturbance and trigger the cnida to fire. One type of cnidocyte is a nematocyst.

cochlea Spiral structure in the inner ear of mammals; contains the organs of hearing. Less elaborate, but present in birds as the cochlear duct. Derived from the lagena of other vertebrates.

cochlear duct The part of the inner ear of birds that is involved in hearing; equivalent to the mammalian cochlea, but is present as a straight tube, rather than a spiral coil.

coelom The internal compartment of coelomate animals that forms between two layers of mesoderm.

coenzymes Organic cofactors.

coenzyme A A coenzyme derived from the vitamin pantothenic acid.

cofactors Nonprotein components of enzymes, including metals, coenzymes, and prosthetic groups.

coitus Sexual intercourse.

collagen A trimeric protein found in extracellular matrix. It interacts with other collagen molecules to form rigid fibers or durable sheets.

collecting duct The tube that receives the fluid from the distal tubules of the nephron and empties into the minor calyx of the kidney.

colligative properties Four properties of a solute that are due solely to the concentration of solutes, and not their chemical nature.

colloidal osmotic pressure See *oncotic pressure*.

colon A region of the large intestine primarily responsible for water resorption.

compact myocardium One of the two types of heart muscle (see also *spongy myocardium*), consisting of tightly packed cells arranged in a regular pattern; the predominant form of muscle in the mammalian heart.

compatible solute A solute that, at high concentration, does not disrupt protein structure or enzyme kinetics.

competitive inhibitors A mode of enzyme inhibition in which a molecule competes with the substrate for the active site on the enzyme; competitive inhibitors have the effect of reducing the apparent substrate affinity without affecting V_{max}.

complement Part of the immune system, this collection of proteins found in the blood augments the innate immune system response, and in some cases also helps promote the adaptive immune system.

compliance A measure of the ability of a hollow structure (e.g., blood vessel, lung) to stretch in response to an applied pressure.

compound eye A type of eye seen in arthropods; consists of many individual photoreceptive structures.

concurrent An anatomical arrangement of the flow across a gas-exchange surface where the flow of the respiratory medium is in the same direction as the flow of blood through the gas-exchange surface.

conduction Transfer of heat from one object to another object or a fluid.

cone A type of vertebrate photoreceptor cell (see also *rod*). Cones are typically responsible for color vision in bright light.

conformer A strategy whereby the physicochemical properties of an animal (e.g., temperature and osmolarity) parallel those of the environment.

conservation of K_m A pattern in which enzymes from different animals share a similar K_m when assayed under conditions that approximate those that occur in the animal.

constitutive Usually describes a gene for a protein that is expressed at near-constant levels regardless of conditions; can be applied to the protein itself, as in "a constitutive enzyme."

continuous capillaries The most common type of capillary, found in organs such as skin and muscle; these capillaries have low permeability because they are surrounded by a complete basement membrane and most of the intercellular contacts are sealed by tight junctions, although this seal is not complete, allowing fluids and small molecules to pass from the blood to the interstitial fluid.

contractile summation When different motor units are recruited to increase the force of contraction of a muscle.

contractility A measure of cardiac performance related to the ability of the heart muscle to contract.

conus arteriosus The outflow tract of the heart ventricle in elasmobranchs, lungfish, and amphibians; muscular and valved (see also *bulbus arteriosus*).

convection Fluid circulation driven by temperature gradients; a special case of bulk flow.

convergence A pattern in a neural pathway in which multiple presynaptic neurons form synapses with a single postsynaptic neuron.

convergent evolution The independent evolution of similar traits in distantly related or unrelated taxa.

cooperativity A phenomenon demonstrated by multimeric proteins in which binding of a ligand to one protein subunit increases the likelihood of binding to other subunits. Seen in vertebrate blood hemoglobins.

cornea The clear outer surface of an eye. The cornea of an insect ommatidium and a vertebrate eye are analogous structures, but they are not homologous.

corneocyte A cell type derived from keratinocytes that forms the stratum corneum of the skin.

coronary artery Artery that supplies blood to the heart in vertebrates.

coronary circulation The blood vessels that supply oxygenated blood to the heart of vertebrates.

corpus allatum (plural: **corpora allata**) A paired neurohemal organ in arthropods that secretes juvenile hormone.

corpus callosum A thick band of axons that connects the right and left hemispheres of the vertebrate brain.

corpus cardiacum (plural: **corpora cardiaca**) A paired neurohemal organ in arthropods that secretes adipokinetic hormone.

corpus luteum The remnants of a mammalian ovarian follicle that grows in size and becomes an endocrine organ that secretes hormones in support of embryonic development.

cortex The surface or outer layer of an organ (e.g., the cortex of the kidney; the cerebral cortex; cortical bone).

cortisol A steroid hormone that is produced in response to stress in mammals and fish.

cost of transport (COT) The energetic cost for an animal to cross a given distance.

cotransporter See *symport.*

counteracting solutes Pairs of solutes that act in conjunction to offset the detrimental effects that would arise if either solute were present alone.

countercurrent A situation in which two fluids flow in opposite directions on either side of an exchange surface.

countercurrent exchanger A structure in which two fluids flow in opposite directions on either side of an exchange surface, allowing high-efficiency exchange of materials purely by passive means; e.g., heat exchange in a rete.

countercurrent multiplier A structure in which two fluids flow in opposite directions on either side of an exchange surface, allowing high-efficiency exchange of materials by active means; e.g., ion concentration in the loop of Henle.

covalent bonds Strong chemical bonds involving the sharing of electrons between two atoms.

covalent modification Alteration of a macromolecule by the addition (or removal) of another molecule by forming (or breaking) a covalent bond; e.g., glycosylation, methylation, acetylation, and phosphorylation.

cranial nerves A group of vertebrate nerves that originate in the brain. Vertebrates have 12 or 13 pairs of cranial nerves depending on the species.

creatine phosphate A high-energy phosphate compound used to store energy and to facilitate its transfer from the sites of energy production (mitochondria) to the sites of utilization, such as myofibrils.

cristae The highly convoluted inner membrane of mitochondria.

critical thermal maximum The highest environmental temperature tolerated by an animal.

crop milk Produced by some birds, a regurgitated slurry of nutrients arising from ingested material augmented by secretions.

cross-bridge The linkage of a myosin head to an actin subunit; an essential step in actinomyosin mechanoenzyme activity.

crosscurrent A situation in which the flow of the respiratory medium is at an angle to the flow of blood through the exchange surface; seen in bird lungs.

crypt of Lieberkühn A pit at the base of intestinal villi.

cryptobiosis A dormant state in which an animal experiences a severe (but reversible) metabolic depression during adverse conditions.

cryptochrome A blue light–sensitive flavoprotein; involved in circadian rhythms and magnetoreception.

cutaneous respiration Gas exchange across the skin.

cuticle The outer layer of the arthropod exoskeleton; composed of chitin and proteins.

cyclic AMP (cAMP) Cyclic adenosine monophosphate formed by the action of adenylate cyclase; a second messenger that activates protein kinase A.

cyclic GMP (cGMP) Cyclic guanosine monophosphate formed by the action of guanylate cyclase; a second messenger that activates protein kinase G.

cytochromes Metalloproteins produced from porphyrins that are central to many enzymatic reactions, including the mitochondrial electron transport chain (cytochromes a, a_3, b, c) and cytochrome P450 enzymes.

cytochrome P450 aromatase An enzyme in steroid metabolism that converts androgens to estrogens.

cytokines Hormones that trigger cell division.

cytoplasm Soluble and particulate interior of a cell, excluding the nucleus.

cytosine A nucleoside composed of cytidine and a ribose sugar.

cytoskeleton Intracellular protein network of microtubules, microfilaments, and intermediate filaments.

cytosol Fluid portion of the cytoplasm, also known as intracellular fluid.

Dalton's law of partial pressures The total pressure of a gas mixture is the sum of the partial pressures of the constituent gases.

dead space The portion of the respiratory system containing gas that does not participate in gas exchange; the sum of the anatomical and physiological dead spaces.

deamination Removal of an amino group from a molecule, usually an amino acid.

defecation The expulsion of feces.

defensin A widespread protein that is cytotoxic to microbial pathogens, incorporated into the pathogen cell membrane to create a pore that permits movement of ions, killing the target cell.

dehydrogenase A class of enzymes that involves an exchange of electrons between a substrate and product.

delayed implantation A reproductive strategy in which a fertilized ovum fails to implant in the uterus, thereby delaying embryonic growth until external conditions are favorable.

denature The loss of three-dimensional structure (unfolding) of a complex macromolecule, such as protein or nucleic acid.

dendrites The branching extensions of a neuronal cell body that carry signals toward the cell body.

dendritic A tree-like pattern of branching.

dendrodendritic synapse A synapse formed between the dendrites of two neurons.

deoxyhemoglobin Hemoglobin that is not bound to oxygen.

deoxyribonucleic acid See *DNA.*

depolarization A change in the membrane potential of a cell from its normally negative resting membrane potential to a more positive value; a relative increase in the positive charge on the inside of the cell membrane.

depolarization-induced ca²⁺ release A mode of muscle activation in which calcium crossing the sarcolemma through a Ca^{2+} channel causes a depolarization of the membrane, which directly opens a Ca^{2+} channel in the sarcoplasmic reticulum.

depolarization phase The initial part of an action potential during which the electrical difference across the membrane becomes smaller (the membrane potential becomes less negative).

desmosome A type of cell-cell junction common in epithelial tissues.

diabetes mellitus A metabolic condition involving defects in insulin secretion or signal transduction that lead to abnormal regulation of blood glucose. There are two main types of diabetes mellitus: insulin-dependent (type 1) and non-insulin-dependent (type 2).

diacylglycerol (DAG, or diglyceride) A second messenger in the phosphatidylinositol signaling system.

diadromous A life history strategy of fish that includes movement from freshwater to seawater to breed (catadromous) or vice versa (anadromous).

diaphragm A sheetlike group of muscles that separates the thoracic and abdominal cavities of mammals.

diastole The portion of the cardiac cycle in which the heart is relaxing.

diastolic pressure The arterial blood pressure during cardiac diastole.

dichromats Vertebrates with two types of receptors involved in color vision that detect different parts of the visible spectrum.

dietary water Water that comes into the animal preformed, in contrast to water that arises during the digestive process (metabolic water).

diffusion The net movement of a molecule throughout the available space from an area of high concentration to an area of low concentration.

diffusion coefficient A parameter that reflects the ability of an ion or molecule to diffuse.

diffusion gradient See *electrochemical gradient.*

diffusivity The ability of solutes to move through a solution by diffusion.

digastric stomach A two-compartment stomach found in ruminants; each of the two compartments is further divided into two chambers.

digestible energy The proportion of ingested energy that can be further processed, leaving only indigestible material.

digestion The breakdown of nutrients in the gastrointestinal tract.

digestive enzymes Hydrolytic enzymes secreted into the lumen of the gastrointestinal tract by the digestive epithelium and accessory glands.

dihydropyridine receptor (DHPR) The Ca^{2+} channel found in muscle plasma membrane, so named because of its ability to bind members of the dihydropyridine class of drugs.

dimer A combination of two monomers, typically in the context of protein structure. A homodimer has two identical monomers, and a heterodimer has two dissimilar monomers.

diploblastic A reference to the two germinal cell layers that are characteristic of cnidarians and ctenophores.

dipnoan A group of sarcopterygian fish commonly called lungfish, most closely related to the fish ancestor of amphibians.

dipole A molecule with both partial positive (δ^+) and partial negative (δ^-) charges resulting from the asymmetrical distribution of electrons.

direct calorimetry Measurement of heat production; in the context of animal physiology, a measure of metabolic rate.

disaccharide A sugar composed of two monosaccharides.

discontinuous gas exchange A ventilatory pattern seen in some insects in which prolonged periods of apnea are followed by brief but rapid ventilation of the tracheal system.

dissociation constant (K_d) A measure of the tendency of a complex to dissociate into its components; calculated as the ratio of the product of the concentrations of the dissociated components to the concentration of the complex once the reaction reaches equilibrium (e.g., for the reaction AB Δ A + B, K_d = [A][B]/[AB]).

distal A location furthest from a point of reference. Opposite of proximal.

distal tubule The region of a vertebrate kidney tubule just before the collecting tubules.

disulfide bridge A covalent bond between two sulfhydryl groups, denoted as –S–S–; also known as a disulfide bond.

diuresis The process of urine formation.

diuretic An agent that promotes urine formation.

dive response A collection of physiological responses to forced diving in air-breathing animals.

divergence A pattern in a neural pathway in which a single presynaptic neuron forms synapses with multiple postsynaptic neurons.

diving bradycardia A reduction in heart rate as a result of submergence in air-breathing animals.

DNA (deoxyribonucleic acid) A polymer of nucleotides that acts as the genetic template.

DNA microarray A high-throughput method of analyzing DNA or RNA.

Donnan equilibrium The chemical equilibrium reached between two solutions separated from each other by a membrane permeable to some of the ions in the solutions.

dopamine A neurotransmitter (biogenic amine) produced in various regions of the vertebrate brain.

dormancy A general term for hypometabolic states accompanied by a reduction in activity (see also *estivation, hibernation,* and *torpor*).

dorsal horn A region of gray matter within the spinal cord located on the dorsal side.

dorsal root The dorsal of the two branches of a vertebrate spinal nerve as it enters the spinal cord. Contains afferent neurons.

dorsal root ganglion Clusters of afferent cell bodies of neurons in the spinal nerves. Located adjacent to the spinal cord.

doubly labeled water An isotopic variant of water (H_2O), where a less common isotope is used for both ^1H (^2H or ^3H) and ^{16}O (^{18}O). Used to measure field metabolic rate.

down-regulation A decrease in the amount or activity of a protein or process; e.g., a decrease in receptor number or activity on a target cell (see also *up-regulation*).

drag A force that resists the forward movement through a fluid through interactions with the surface of an object.

drag coefficient A dimensionless parameter that is used to measure the amount of resistance as an object moves through a fluid.

dual breather An animal that can breathe either air or water. Also called a bimodal breather.

duodenum The most proximal region of the small intestine, directly following the stomach.

duty cycle In cytoskeletal movement, the proportion of time in a cross-bridge cycle that a motor protein binds its cytoskeletal tract.

dynamic range The range between the minimum and maximum signal that can be discriminated by a sensory receptor.

dynein Motor protein that works in combination with microtubules, usually moving in the minus direction (see also *kinesin*).

dynein arms The motor proteins that extend from microtubules in the axoneme of cilia and flagella.

dyspnea The sensation of difficulty with breathing.

EC coupling Excitation contraction coupling refers to the steps between depolarization of the muscle cell membrane (excitation) and the activation of that muscle (contraction).

eccrine gland A type of exocrine gland characterized by a long coiled duct that delivers secretions from the secretory region to the surface.

ecdysis The periodic shedding of the exoskeleton of invertebrates (molting).

ecdysone One of the ecdysteroid hormones of arthropods that is responsible for controlling many aspects of development, including ecdysis.

ecdysteroids The general name for ecdysone and its active metabolites, such as 20-hydroecdysone.

echolocation Detecting objects based on the reflection of sound waves; used by organisms such as whales and bats.

eclosion The process whereby an adult insect emerges from its cocoon.

ectoderm The outermost of the primary germ layers in a developing embryo that eventually gives rise to tissue such as the nervous system.

ectopic pacemaker A pacemaker in an abnormal location.

ectotherm An animal with body temperature determined primarily by external factors, including but not limited to ambient temperature (see also *endotherm*).

edema Excess accumulation of fluid in a tissue.

effective refractory period The time period in which an excitable tissue cannot be stimulated due to changes in the membrane potential.

effector An organ or cell such as a muscle that responds to stimulation from the nervous system.

efferent Leading away from a structure; e.g., efferent neurons carry signals from the central nervous system to the periphery; efferent arterioles carry blood away from the glomerulus of the kidney.

efferent arteriole The arteriole that emerges from the glomerulus of the kidney tubule.

efferent division The part of the peripheral nervous system that consists of efferent neurons.

efferent neuron A neuron that conducts impulses from an integrating center to an effector.

efflux Movement of a substance outward, usually in the context of movement out of a cell or tissue.

egestion Expulsion of undigested food (feces) from the digestive tract.

eicosanoids A type of short-lived chemical signaling molecule.

elasmobranch fish One of two groups of cartilaginous fish, including skates, rays, and sharks. The other group of cartilaginous fish is holocephalans (ratfish).

elastance A measure of how readily a structure returns to its original shape after having been stretched.

elastic recoil Movement as a result of the release of elastic storage energy.

elastic storage energy Energy stored within a deformed object, which is released when the object regains its relaxed configuration.

electrical gradient A charge gradient across a membrane arising from unequal distribution of charged particles.

electric organ A trans-differentiated muscle of fish that generates electric pulses for detecting objects or defense.

electrical energy The energy associated with gradients of charged particles.

electrical synapse A junction between neurons in which the signal is transmitted as an electrical charge rather than via a neurotransmitter (see also *chemical synapse*).

electrocardiogram (ECG, EKG) A recording of the electrical activity of the heart.

electrocardiograph An instrument that measures electrical potentials on the body surface as an indication of the electrical activity of the heart (see *electrocardiogram*).

electrochemical gradient A gradient composed of the concentration gradient of an ion and the membrane potential; the driving force for the movement of that ion across the membrane.

electrochemical potential difference ($\Delta\mu$) The driving force for movement of a substance across a membrane as a result of the electrical and chemical gradients across the membrane (see *electrochemical gradient*).

electrogenic A transport process that results in a change in electrical charge across a membrane.

electrolyte A charged solute, such as Na^+, K^+, and Cl^-.

electron transport system (ETS) A series of protein complexes with mobile carriers that produce a proton gradient across the inner mitochondrial membrane. It builds the gradient by pumping protons as it transfers electrons from reducing equivalents to oxygen, forming water.

electroneutral A transport process that does not change the electrical charge across a membrane.

electroreceptor A sensory receptor that responds to electric fields or discharges.

electrotonic conduction See electrotonic current spread.

electrotonic current spread The passive conduction of charge along a cell membrane.

elevated postexercise oxygen consumption (EPOC) A period of elevated metabolic rate thought to be necessary to allow the muscle to recover from ionic and metabolic disturbances that arose as a result of intense exercise.

emergence A phenomenon in which the patterns and properties of a complex system are the result of the interactions of the component parts of that system, and are not necessarily predictable from the operation of those components in isolation.

emergent properties Traits of an organism that are the result of the phenomenon of emergence across levels of organization.

empirical An observation arising from direct measurement of a parameter.

encephalization quotient (EQ) The ratio of actual brain size to predicted brain size based on body size; suggested as a way to compare intelligence between species.

end-diastolic volume (EDV) The volume of blood in the heart at the end of diastole; the maximum volume reached during the cardiac cycle.

end-systolic volume (ESV) The volume of blood in the heart at the end of systole; the minimum volume reached during the cardiac cycle.

endergonic reaction A reaction that requires an input of free energy, for which G is positive.

endocardium The internal layer of the heart.

endocrine A signaling pathway in which the signaling molecule is released into the blood and affects a distant cell of a different type.

endocrine disruptor An environmental chemical (often humanmade) that alters cell signaling by acting as an analogue or antagonist of an endocrine hormone.

endocrine gland Type of gland that secretes hormones into the blood.

endocrine system The collective name for the group of glands and other tissues that secrete hormones into the circulatory system.

endocytosis Invagination of the plasma membrane resulting in the formation of a vesicle; used to internalize membrane proteins or capture extracellular solids (phagocytosis) or liquids (pinocytosis).

endoderm The innermost primary germ layer in a developing embryo; eventually gives rise to tissues such as the external surfaces, including the gut lining.

endolymph The fluid in the inner ear of vertebrates.

endometrium The innermost layer of the uterus composed of well-vascularized epithelial tissue; see also *myometrium*.

endoplasmic reticulum (ER) An intracellular organelle that forms a network through which secretory products and plasma membrane components pass.

endoskeleton More commonly referred to as the skeleton, an internal framework of bones, cartilage, and tendons that provides support and resistance for muscular movement.

endosymbiont An organism that lives within another organism.

endosymbiosis A relationship whereby an organism lives within another cell or organism, and both parties benefit from the relationship.

endothelium The innermost layer of blood vessels.

endotherm An animal that generates and retains heat internally.

endothermic reaction A reaction that has a positive H, requiring heat.

end-systolic volume (ESV) The volume of blood in the heart at the end of systole; the minimum volume of blood that the heart contains during the cardiac cycle.

energetics The study of processes that involve the interconversion of energy.

energy The ability to do work.

energy metabolism The sum of metabolic reactions that pertain to the production or utilization of energy.

enteric branch (also enteric division; enteric nervous system) Part of the vertebrate autonomic nervous system involved in regulating the activity of the gut.

enterosymbiont A symbiotic organism that lives within the gastrointestinal tract.

enthalpy The heat content of a system, symbolized as H. Chemical reactions are often expressed as a change in enthalpy (H).

entropy A thermodynamic parameter that reflects the degree of disorder in a system.

environmental estrogen An estrogenlike *endocrine disruptor*.

enzyme A biological catalyst composed of protein (sometimes RNA), frequently incorporating a cofactor into its structure.

enzyme induction An increase in the levels of an enzyme: one way to achieve an increase in catalytic activity.

enzyme kinetics The collection of parameters that describe functional properties of enzymes, including maximal velocity (V_{max}) and affinity (K_m).

eosinophil A type of white blood cell that is involved in the immune response to parasites an in allergic reactions.

ependymal cells Cells that line the ventricles of the brain.

epicardium The outer layer of the heart in vertebrates.

epididymis The structure where sperm mature and are stored in the vertebrate testis.

epigenetic inheritance Modifications of DNA without a change in the DNA sequence that can be transmitted from parent to offspring.

epinephrine A catecholamine that can act as a hormone or neurotransmitter and is involved in the stress response; also called adrenaline.

epithalamus A region of the vertebrate brain that contains the pineal body.

epithelium The outermost cellular layer of eumetazoans.

equilibrium For a chemical reaction, the state in which there is no net change in the reactants; products and substrates continue to interconvert, but at equal rates.

equilibrium constant (K_{eq}) The mass action ratio of a chemical reaction when the reaction is at equilibrium.

equilibrium potential The membrane potential at which an ion is at its equilibrium distribution across a membrane.

eructation Gaseous release from the stomach (belching).

erythrocyte A type of vertebrate blood cell that contains hemoglobin (red blood cell).

erythropoiesis Production of red blood cells from erythroblasts, usually in specialized erythropoietic tissues.

erythropoietin A hormone released from the kidney that induces erythropoiesis.

esophagus The passage from the oral cavity (mouth) to the stomach.

essential nutrient A nutrient that cannot be made by the animal and therefore must be obtained from the diet.

esterase An enzyme that breaks an ester bond.

estivation A form of dormancy in which the reduced metabolic rate occurs in response to dehydration.

estradiol-17β The dominant estrogen in most species.

estrogens A class of steroid hormones that act predominantly in females to stimulate reproductive maturation and control the reproductive cycle.

estrous cycle A reproductive cycle composed of four phases: proestrus, estrus, metestrus, and diestrus.

ethology The study of animal behavior.

Eumetazoans Animals, excluding sponges and placozoans.

eupnea Normal breathing.

euryhaline Tolerant of a wide range of external salinities, or more precisely osmolarities.

eurytherm An animal that is tolerant of a wide range of external temperatures.

evaporation Volatilization of liquid water to gaseous water, with the absorption of heat.

evaporative cooling The heat loss that results when heat is absorbed from the body to enable surface water to evaporate.

evolution The process of descent with modification, or genetic change in taxa over time; may be adaptive, maladaptive, or neutral.

exchanger See *antiport*.

excitable cell A cell that is capable of producing an action potential.

excitation-contraction coupling (or EC coupling) The processes that link external stimulation of a muscle to the activation of actinomyosin ATPase, resulting in muscle contraction.

excitatory postsynaptic potential (EPSP) An excitatory potential in a postsynaptic cell.

excitatory potential A change in the membrane potential in an excitable cell that increases the probability of action potential initiation in that cell.

exergonic reaction A reaction that requires an input of free energy, for which G is positive.

exocrine gland A type of gland that releases its secretions via a duct (usually into the external environment).

exocrine secretions Secretions from exocrine glands; include chemical messengers and substances such as mucus, slime, and silk.

exocytosis The transport of vesicles to, and subsequent fusion with, the plasma membrane; serves to secrete vesicle contents into the extracellular space or to introduce proteins into the plasma membrane.

exon A region of DNA that codes for a protein.

exoskeleton An external rigid structure on the outside of many invertebrates that serves to restrict the movement of water and provide a solid framework that controls animal shape and provides resistance needed for locomotion.

exosymbiont A symbiotic organism that lives outside the animal.

exothermic reaction A reaction that has a negative H value, releasing heat.

expiration Exhalation.

extension A movement that causes a limb to straighten across a joint, usually caused by contraction of an extensor muscle.

extensor A muscle that causes a limb to straighten across a joint (extension).

external respiration The process by which animals exchange gases with the environment to supply oxygen to the mitochondria and to remove the resulting carbon dioxide (see also *respiration*).

extracellular digestion Breakdown of nutrients in the outside of the cell resulting from secretion of digestive enzymes.

extracellular fluids The fluids outside of a cell but contained within the limits of the organism.

extracellular matrix The protein and glycosaminoglycan network found outside cells; includes cartilage, bone, and connective tissue.

extrarenal Occurring in a tissue other than the kidney.

extremophiles Organisms that tolerate environmental extremes, such as temperature, salinity, and pressure.

eye A complex organ that detects light.

facilitated diffusion A mode of transport in which a protein allows an otherwise impermeable entity to cross a membrane down its electrochemical gradient.

fast axonal transport Process by which neurotransmitter-containing vesicles are moved from the cell body to the axon terminal of a neuron; requires molecular motors.

fast-glycolytic (FG) muscle fibers Muscle cells with a biochemical and mechanical protein profile suited to short-duration, high-intensity contractions that rely on glycolysis for energy; typically muscle fibers that express type IIb myosin.

fast-oxidative glycolytic (FOG) muscle fibers Muscle cells with a biochemical and mechanical protein profile suited to contraction of intermediate duration and intensity; rely on a combination of glycolysis and oxidative phosphorylation for energy. Typically muscle fibers that express type IIa or II x/d myosin isoforms.

feces The undigested matter expelled from the gastrointestinal tract.

feedback A regulatory mechanism whereby a step late in a pathway causes a change earlier in the pathway, either decreasing use of the pathway (negative feedback) or increasing its use (positive feedback).

fenestrated capillaries Capillaries with relatively high permeability because of the presence of perforations (fenestrae) through the cells of the capillary wall; found in tissues such as parts of the kidney, the endocrine organs, and the intestine.

fever A period of elevated whole body temperature that arises from an immune response, typically as a result of some form of infection. Behavioral fever results when a poikilothermic animal responds to an immunological challenge by moving into an environment that increases body temperature.

fibroblasts Cells that have a major role in producing the extracellular matrix of most soft tissues.

Fick equation The equation relating diffusive flux to the energetic gradient (concentration, partial pressure, electrical, etc.) driving diffusion.

field metabolic rate (FMR) The metabolic rate of a free-roaming animal, usually measured using doubly labelled water.

filopodia Thin, fingerlike extensions of the cell, supported by the actin cytoskeleton.

filtrate The solution that passes through a filter, such as the primary urine that passes through the glomerulus.

filtration slit The gap between the podocytes that permits movement of fluid into the tubule, excluding cells, particles, and macromolecules that are too large.

flagella (singular: **flagellum**) Microtubule-based extensions from a cell that move in a whiplike pattern; usually present alone or in pairs.

flame cells The flagellated cells within a protonephridium that generate movements that bring fluids into the structure.

flexion A movement of a limb that causes the limb to bend at the joint (caused by a flexor muscle).

flexor A muscle that causes a limb to bend at the joint (flexion).

fluid mosaic model The model of a lipid bilayer membrane that includes multiple types of lipids and proteins and allows for their free rotation and lateral movement.

fluidity The degree of free movement of membrane entities within the membrane; often assessed using the dye DPH, which exhibits an anisotropy that depends on membrane fluidity.

fluorescence Absorbance of a high-energy (low-wavelength) light followed by release of a lower-energy (longer-wavelength) light.

flux Flow of material through a pathway.

follicle A multicellular unit composed of somatic tissue surrounding an ovum.

follicle-stimulating hormone (FSH) One of the two major gonadotropins of vertebrates; causes the ovarian follicle to mature.

follicular phase That portion of the ovulatory cycle where a follicle matures to release the ovum.

food vacuole A phagocytic vesicle that fuses with other vesicles and processing organelles to digest the nutrients.

foot processes Long projections of podocytes in Bowman's capsule that create the filtration slits.

foramen of Panizza A structure that connects the left and right aorta in the crocodile heart.

forebrain The anterior portion of the vertebrate brain, consisting of the telencephalon and diencephalon. Also called the prosencephalon.

founder effect A phenomenon in which the genotypic distribution of a population is a result of historical events that caused the population to be established by a small number of individuals; often associated with a reduction in genetic diversity.

fovea A small region in the center of the retina of a vertebrate eye that is responsible for high-acuity vision.

Frank-Starling effect An increase in the force of cardiac contraction in response to increasing venous return to the heart.

free energy The energy in a system that is available to do work.

freezing-point depression A reduction in the temperature at which a solution freezes; e.g., in the presence of antifreeze molecules.

friction drag The resistance that arises as an object moves through a fluid as a result of the interaction between the surface and the fluid.

futile cycle A combination of enzymatic reactions or processes that lead to net breakdown of ATP and/or release of heat without changes in the carbon substrates.

G protein Type of trimeric membrane protein, associated with specific transmembrane receptors, that plays a role in signal transduction. G proteins bind guanine nucleotides; when bound to GDP the G protein is inactive, but when bound to GTP it is active. The alpha subunit of the G protein moves through the membrane and acts in subsequent steps in the signal transduction pathway.

G protein–coupled receptor A transmembrane receptor that interacts with a G protein.

GABA (gamma-aminobutyric acid) A neurotransmitter; primarily inhibitory in the vertebrate central nervous system.

gallbladder An organ that stores bile produced in the liver.

gamete The germ cell of sexually reproducing species; small gametes are sperm and large gametes are ova.

gametogenesis Production of mature gametes in the ovary or testis.

ganglion (plural: **ganglia**) A cluster of neuronal cell bodies. Ganglia act as integrating centers.

ganglion cell An interneuron in the retina of vertebrates.

gap junction Aqueous pore between two cells that allows ions and small molecules to move freely from cell to cell; formed by proteins called connexins in the vertebrates and innexins in the invertebrates.

gas gland A region of the vasculature of the swim bladder that secretes gases.

gastric Pertaining to the stomach.

gastrointestinal tract The digestive tract, alternately termed GI tract, or intestinal tract.

gastrovascular cavity A space that performs the functions of digestion and circulation; found in organisms such as cnidarians.

gene A region of DNA that, when transcribed, encodes a protein or an RNA.

gene duplication The process of DNA mutation by which a genome can acquire an additional copy of genes.

generator potential A change in the membrane potential in the sensory terminal of a primary afferent neuron. It is a graded potential proportional to the signal intensity. If it exceeds threshold, it will trigger action potentials in the axon of the sensory neuron.

genetic drift A change in gene frequencies in a population over time as a result of random events.

genome All of the genetic material of an organism; the complete set of DNA in both the nucleus and mitochondria.

genotype The specific genetic makeup of an organism.

germ cell A cell that produces the haploid gametes of a sexually reproducing species.

gestation The period of embryonic development within the uterus of a viviparous or ovoviviparous species.

giant axons Unusually large-diameter axons that are present in some invertebrates and vertebrates.

gills Respiratory surfaces that originate as outpocketings of the body surface; generally used for gas exchange in water.

gland A specialized organ that secretes hormones.

glial cells (glia) A group of several types of cells that provide structural and metabolic support to neurons.

gliocytes A type of invertebrate glial cell.

gliotransmitters Chemicals released from glial cells that influence communication among neurons and glia.

globin The protein component of hemoglobins.

globulins A type of protein found in blood. Alpha and beta globulins are transport proteins; gamma globulins are involved in the immune system.

glomerular filtration rate (GFR) The total amount of filtrate per unit time passing through the glomeruli into the tubules of the kidneys.

glomerulus A knot-like cluster of capillaries that acts as a biological filter in the nephrons of many vertebrate kidneys. It permits fluids and small molecules to pass freely from the plasma to the tubule lumen.

glottis A small flap of tissue located between the pharynx and trachea of air-breathing vertebrates.

glucagon A hormone produced by the vertebrate pancreas that inhibits glycogen synthesis and stimulates glycogen breakdown, resulting in an increase in blood glucose.

glucocorticoids Steroid hormones involved in the stress response that regulate carbohydrate, protein, and lipid metabolism.

gluconeogenesis The production of glucose from noncarbohydrate precursors; the main part of the pathway is a reversal of glycolysis, enabled by three enzymes that bypass the two irreversible steps in glycolysis.

glycogen A glucose polysaccharide that forms the main carbohydrate energy store of animals.

glycogenesis Synthesis of glycogen from glucose or glycolytic intermediates.

glycogenolysis The breakdown of glycogen to form glucose-6-phosphate.

glycolipid A glycosylated lipid common in the extracellular side of some plasma membranes.

glycolysis The breakdown of carbohydrates to form pyruvate, or when oxygen is limiting, other end products such as lactate.

glycoprotein A protein that has been modified by the addition of carbohydrates.

glycosaminoglycan A nonproteinaceous component of the extracellular matrix.

glycosuria High levels of glucose in the urine.

glycosylation The addition of carbohydrate groups to proteins, lipids, or carbohydrates within the endoplasmic reticulum or Golgi apparatus.

goblet cell A goblet-shaped mucus-secreting cell found in the intestinal and respiratory surfaces.

Goldman equation The equation that predicts the membrane potential across a cell membrane resulting from the distribution of multiple ions in relation to their permeabilities.

Golgi apparatus An intracellular organelle involved in the processing of proteins prior to export.

gonadotropin A hormone that regulates the activity of reproductive tissues; FSH and LH are the main gonadotropins in vertebrates, and allatotropin and allatostatin are the main gonadotropins in arthropods.

gonads The organs that produce the gametes in males (testes) and females (ovaries).

gonadotropin-releasing hormone (GnRH) A hypothalamic hormone that regulates the release of follicle-stimulating hormone (FSH) and luteinizing hormone (LH) from the pituitary of vertebrates.

gonadotropins A family of proteins, including follicle-stimulating hormone (FSH), luteinizing hormone (LH), and chorionic gonadotropin (CG).

graded potential Changes in the membrane potential of a cell that vary in magnitude with the stimulus intensity; results from the opening and closing of ion channels.

Graham's law Describes the rate of diffusion of a gas in liquid; states that the rate of diffusion of a gas is proportional to its solubility and inversely proportional to the square root of its molecular mass.

granular cells See *juxtaglomerular cells*.

granulosa cells The inner layer of somatic cells of a follicle that surround the primary oocyte.

gray matter Areas of the vertebrate central nervous system that are rich in cell bodies (see also *white matter*).

growth factor A group of peptide hormones that stimulate cells to proliferate (hyperplasia) or grow in size (hypertrophy).

growth hormone A peptide hormone derived from the anterior pituitary that mediates somatic cell growth.

guanine A purine nitrogenous base component of nucleotides, including nucleic acids.

guanosine A nucleoside of guanine and a ribose sugar.

guanosine triphosphate (GTP) A high-energy phosphate compound in energy metabolism; also the substrate for guanylate cyclase, forming the second messenger cGMP.

guanylate cyclase Enzyme that converts GTP to cGMP in response to signaling molecules such as nitric oxide; has soluble and membrane-bound forms.

gustation Detection of ingested chemicals: the sense of taste.

gustducin A G protein–coupled receptor involved in the sense of taste that detects sweet tastants.

gut reactor theory Mathematical explanation of the optimal function of various types of digestive tracts, modeled after chemical reactors.

gyri (singular: **gyrus**) Wrinkles on the surface of the brains of many mammals.

H zone The central region of a sarcomere corresponding to the location of the thick filaments where there is no overlap with thin filaments; the H zone reduces in size upon contraction.

habituation A process by which repeated stimulation of a neuron results in a decreased response.

hair cell Ciliated sensory cells of vertebrates that react to mechanical stimuli (particularly to vibrations). They are the basis of the senses of hearing and balance, and of the lateral line systems of fishes and amphibians.

Haldane effect The effect of oxygen on hemoglobin–carbon dioxide binding.

half-life A period of time required for half of a population of molecules to be converted to another form; often applied to radioactive decay.

heart A muscular pumping structure.

heart rate The number of times the heart beats in a given period of time; typically measured as beats per minute.

heat The kinetic energy associated with the movement of atoms and molecules.

heat capacity The amount of thermal energy required to increase the temperature of 1 g of a substance by 1°C.

heat of vaporization The heat needed to cause a liquid to become gaseous, expressed per unit mass.

heat shock proteins A class of molecular chaperones that increase in abundance in response to elevated temperature; the term includes members of genetically related proteins that are constitutive and do not increase in expression in response to thermal stress.

heater tissues A general term for tissues that serve to elevate regional or systemic temperature of an animal, such as the heater organ of billfish.

Helicobacter pyloric A bacterium that infects gastric pits, creating conditions that can lead to a gastric ulcer.

hematocrit The proportion of whole blood that is occupied by red blood cells.

heme A metal-binding porphyrin derivative that is incorporated into enzymes (e.g., cytochromes) and nonenzyme proteins (e.g., hemoglobin).

hemerythrin An iron-containing respiratory pigment found in sipunculids, priapulids, brachiopods, and annelids; lacks heme.

hemimetabolous insect Type of insect that possesses immature stages (nymphs) that resemble the adults, except in lacking fully formed wings (see also *holometabolous insect*).

hemocoel Collective name for the sinuses in the open circulatory systems of many invertebrates.

hemocyanin A respiratory pigment found in arthropods and mollusks consisting of one or more protein molecules complexed directly to copper molecules.

hemocytes Generalized term for blood cells. Most commonly used for the blood cells of invertebrates.

hemoglobin A respiratory pigment consisting of a globin protein complexed to an iron-containing porphyrin molecule called heme.

hemolymph The circulatory fluid of arthropods.

hemopoietic factor A regulatory protein that induces the synthesis of red blood cells; erythropoietin, for example.

Henderson-Hasselbalch equation The mass action equation for the dissociation of carbonic acid (H_2CO_3) to bicarbonate (HCO_3^-) and hydrogen ions (H^+); important in respiratory physiology.

Henry's law One of the ideal gas laws; describes the dissolution of a gas in a liquid, stating that the amount of gas dissolved in a liquid is related to the partial pressure and the solubility of that gas.

hepatocyte The dominant cell type in a liver.

hepatopancreas An invertebrate tissue that serves the same roles as the vertebrate liver and pancreas.

Hering-Breuer inflation reflex A respiratory reflex that reduces breathing in response to overinflation of the lungs; involved in the termination of a breath.

hermaphrodite An animal that possesses both male and female reproductive tissues either simultaneously or sequentially.

hertz A frequency of 1 per second (1 Hz = $1 \sec^{-1}$).

heterodimer A quaternary structure of two dissimilar monomers.

heterothermy A thermal strategy in which the body temperature (T_B) varies either spatially or temporally.

heterotrimeric G protein See *G protein*.

hexose A general name for monosaccharides with six carbons; includes glucose and fructose.

hibernation A form of dormancy that occurs as a result of low ambient temperature and persists for long periods.

hindbrain The posterior portion of the vertebrate brain, consisting of the cerebellum and brainstem.

hippocampus A part of the vertebrate brain that is involved in the formation of memories.

histamine An amino acid; a regulatory molecule that is released from mast cells in response to an immunological challenge.

histone A protein that reversibly binds to DNA, altering its ability to be transcribed.

holocrine secretion A type of secretion in which entire cells burst, releasing their internal contents.

holometabolous insect An insect in which juvenile stages, dissimilar from the adult, undergo dramatic metamorphosis.

homeostasis A state of internal constancy that is maintained as a result of active regulatory processes.

homeothermy A thermal strategy of an animal (a homeotherm) that has a relatively constant body temperature (T_B).

homeoviscous adaptation A process whereby cells alter the composition of cellular membranes to ensure that fluidity remains constant to compensate for the effects of a change in the external environment.

homing A movement that returns an animal to its home range.

homodimer A molecule composed of two identical subunits.

homologs Genes that are descended from a common ancestor, without intervening duplication events (see also *paralogs, orthologs*).

homology Similar in structure and/or function due to shared ancestry.

homoplasy A trait shared by taxa as a result of convergent evolution rather than shared ancestry.

hormone Type of chemical messenger that is carried in the blood and thus can act across long distances. Classically defined as a substance released from an endocrine gland and active at very low concentrations.

humoral immunity The fluid elements of the immune system that do not involve cells.

hydration shell A coating of water bound to the surface of an ion or molecule.

hydrofoil A surface, teardrop shaped in profile, that moves through water to generate lift. An aquatic version of an aerofoil.

hydrogen bond A class of weak (noncovalent) bond in which an electropositive hydrogen atom is shared by two electronegative atoms.

hydrolysis The breaking of a covalent bond by introducing a water molecule; –H is added to one product and –OH to the other.

hydrophilic A molecule is hydrophilic ("water loving") if it dissolves more easily in water than in an organic phase, such as a lipid bilayer.

hydrophobic A molecule is hydrophobic ("water hating") if it dissolves more easily in a lipid phase than in water.

hydrophobic interactions Weak interaction between two nonpolar groups or molecules arising through their mutual aversion to water.

hydrostatic pressure Pressure exerted by a fluid at rest.

hydrostatic skeleton A closed water-filled sac that acts as a semisolid support for an animal.

hydroxyl ion OH^-.

hypercapnia Higher than normal carbon dioxide levels.

hyperglycemia An elevated blood glucose level.

hyperosmotic A solution that has a higher osmolarity than another solution.

hyperplasia An increase in the number of cells in a tissue or organ.

hyperpnea Rapid breathing.

hyperpolarization A change in the membrane potential of a cell from its normally negative resting membrane potential to a more negative value; a relative increase in the negative charge on the inside of the cell membrane.

hypertension A condition in which arterial blood pressure is elevated above the normal level.

hyperthermia An elevation in body temperature (T_B) above a desired point.

hypertonic A solution that has a combination of osmolarity and solute profile that leads to the efflux of water from the cell, resulting in a decrease in cell volume.

hypertrophy An increase in the size of cells in a tissue or organ.

hyperventilation Breathing rate or depth that is greater than needed for either oxygen supply or carbon dioxide removal.

hypocapnia Lower than normal carbon dioxide levels.

hypoglycemia Low levels of glucose in the blood.

hypometabolism A period when metabolic rate is lower than the normal resting rate.

hypoosmotic A solution that has a lower osmolarity than another solution.

hypothalamic-pituitary portal system A system of blood vessels within the hypothalamus and pituitary that carries hypothalamic hormones to the pituitary, where they regulate the release of pituitary hormones.

hypothalamus A region of the vertebrate forebrain that is involved in controlling body temperature, thirst, hunger, and many other physiological processes. Regulates the function of the pituitary.

hypothermia A decrease in body temperature (T_B) below a desired point.

hypotonic A solution that has a combination of osmolarity and solute profile that leads to the influx of water into the cell, resulting in an increase in cell volume.

hypoventilation Breathing rate or depth that is less than required for adequate gas exchange. For air breathers this usually involves insufficient breathing to allow the removal of carbon dioxide, rather than insufficient for oxygen supply; causes elevated blood carbon dioxide (hypercapnia) and respiratory acidosis.

hypoxemia Lower than normal blood oxygen levels.

hypoxia Lower than normal oxygen; usually referring to environmental oxygen levels (see also *hypoxemia*).

hypoxic pulmonary vasoconstriction Reduction of the diameter of the blood vessels in the lungs in response to low levels of oxygen in the lungs.

I-band (isotropic band) The region of a muscle sarcomere where the thin filaments that span a Z-disk do not overlap with the thick filament.

ice-nucleating agent A molecule or particle that initiates the formation of ice at a sub-freezing temperature.

ideal gas law The relationship between pressure, volume, and gas concentration.

ileum The last section of the small intestine, connecting the jejunum to the large intestine.

imidazole group The amino group found in histidine and other compounds that exhibits a pK value near physiological pH, and is therefore important in the buffering of the pH of body fluids.

immunocompetence-handicap hypothesis A hypothesis that suggests displays are physiologically expensive and they are as elaborate as the animal can tolerate without compromising its health.

immunological memory After exposure to a pathogen, animals with acquired immunity retain the cells needed to produce antibodies to that specific antigen. When the antigen reappears, the cells can rapidly proliferate and produce antibody.

in situ An in vitro condition in which the parameter under investigation is in a realistic setting.

in vitro Occurring outside a living animal or cell.

in vivo Occurring within a living animal or cell.

inactivation gate One of the two gates that open and close voltage-gated sodium channels.

incipient lower lethal temperature (ILLT) For a poikilotherm acclimated to a given temperature, it is the lowest temperature that can be tolerated.

incipient upper lethal temperature (IULT) For a poikilotherm acclimated to a given temperature, it is the highest temperature that can be tolerated.

incus (anvil) One of the three small bones of the mammalian middle ear.

indirect calorimetry Estimation of metabolic rate (heat production) using consumption of oxygen or production of carbon dioxide.

induced ovulation Ovulation that is triggered in response to an external stimulus, such as copulation.

inducible Usually refers to a gene that can increase in expression in response to regulatory conditions; can be applied to the encoded protein itself, as in "an inducible enzyme."

inertial effects The forces that resist a change in the movement of an object. Combines with viscous effects to determine the Reynolds number.

inflammation A element of an immune response associated with local heat production.

inflammatory response Local changes sparked by tissue damage, including increased blood flow, changes in vascular permeability to cells and fluids, recruitment of immune cells, and in some cases, elevated tissue temperature.

ingested energy Term used to describe the total energy content of a diet, includes both digestible energy and indigestible energy.

inhibin A hormone involved in the regulation of follicle-stimulating hormone (FSH).

inhibitory postsynaptic potential (IPSP) An inhibitory potential in a postsynaptic cell.

inhibitory potential A change in the membrane potential that makes an excitable cell (neuron or muscle) less likely to generate an action potential.

innate immune system A type of immune system found in all animals. One of two components of the immune system of vertebrates (see *adaptive immune system*).

inner ear A series of membranous sacs that contain the organs of hearing and balance in vertebrates.

inner hair cells One of two types of hair cells found in the organ of Corti in the inner ear of mammals; involved in the sense of hearing (see also *outer hair cells*).

inorganic ion An ion lacking carbon atoms.

inositol trisphosphate (IP$_3$) A second messenger in the phosphatidylinositol signaling system.

inspiration Inhalation.

instar A juvenile form of an insect that resembles the adult form in gross appearance.

insulation An external or superficial layer of material that reduces the heat loss from the animal to the environment, such as fur, feathers, and blubber.

insulin Peptide hormone that homeostatically regulates blood glucose levels; released in response to increased blood glucose.

integral membrane protein A protein that is embedded within a cellular membrane, and can only be released with detergent treatment that disrupts the membrane.

integrating center The part of the nervous system that takes in afferent sensory information and processes it to send out efferent signals; for example, the brain.

integrins A class of dimeric transmembrane proteins that is important in the interactions betweens cells and the extracellular matrix, mediating both adhesion and cell signaling.

integument The outer layer of an animal, usually derived from epithelial cells and their secretions.

intercalated disc The intercellular contact between cardiomyocytes composed of gap junctions and desmosomes.

intercellular fluid See *interstitial fluid.*

intermediate filaments One class of proteins that are used to make up the cytoskeleton.

interneuron A neuron that makes synaptic connections between other neurons.

internode The region of axonal membrane that is covered with the myelin sheath.

interstitial fluid The component of the extracellular fluid that exists between cells.

intracellular receptors Receptors that are located inside the cell, rather than the cell membrane.

intrapleural pressure The pressure within the pleural cavity that surrounds the lungs of mammals.

intrinsic protein See *integral membrane protein.*

intron A region of DNA that is always spliced out of the mRNA following transcription.

inulin A molecule that is used to assess glomerular filtration rate because it is neither secreted nor recovered by the kidney tubule.

ion An atom or molecule with a net charge.

ion channels Transmembrane proteins that permit transfer of ions or molecules through an aqueous pore down an electrochemical gradient.

ionic bond A weak bond between an anion and a cation.

ionoconformer An animal with an internal ion profile that resembles the ion composition of the external water.

ionophore A molecule that forms pores within membranes, allowing specific ions to cross.

ionoregulator An animal that maintains an internal ion profile independent of the ion composition of the external water.

ionotropic receptor A receptor protein that acts as a gated ion channel.

iris A ring of tissue located immediately in front of the lens of a vertebrate eye that controls the amount of light entering the eye by altering the size of the pupil.

ischemia A reduction in blood flow, depriving a tissue of oxygen and nutrients.

islets of Langerhans Clusters of endocrine cells in the pancreas that produce the hormones glucagon and insulin.

isocortex The outer layer of the forebrain in mammals.

isoelectric point The pH at which an ionizable molecule exhibits no net charge.

isoform A protein that has the same function as another protein but differs in primary sequence either because it is encoded by a different gene, or because it results from alternative promoter usage or differential splicing (contrast with *alleles*).

isometric contraction A muscular contraction that results in force production without a change in length.

isometric muscles Muscles that are arranged in a way that contraction does not lead to a change in length.

isopleth A contour line showing the value of a function of two variables connecting the points where the function has a particular value; e.g., the relationship between pH and bicarbonate concentration as described by the Henderson-Hasselbalch equation.

isosmotic Describes two solutions with the same osmolarity.

isotonic A solution with a profile and concentration of solutes that does not result in a change in the volume of a cell.

isotonic contraction A muscular contraction that results in shortening without force production.

isovolumetric contraction (or **isovolumic contraction**) A phase during the cardiac cycle in which the heart contracts, but does not eject blood because the valves are closed, and thus does not change in volume.

isovolumetric relaxation A phase of the cardiac cycle when the ventricle relaxes without a change in volume.

isozyme An isoform of an enzyme.

jejunum An intermediate region of the small intestine, flanked by an anterior duodenum and a posterior ileum.

joule A measure of energy equal to a Watt exerted for 1 second (1 J = 1 W s).

juvenile hormone (JH) A class of invertebrate hormones derived from isoprenes; secreted from the corpus allatum, JH maintains juvenile traits.

juxtaglomerular apparatus A group of cells located near the distal tubule and the glomerular afferent arterioles.

juxtaglomerular cells Secretory cells of the afferent glomerular arterioles that respond to low blood pressure by secreting renin (also known as granular cells).

k_{cat} See *turnover number.*

keratan A glycosaminoglycan found in the extracellular matrix.

keratin Cytoskeletal protein that forms one type of intermediate filament; common in hair, nails, and feathers.

keratinocytes Epithelial cells of outermost layer of skin that produce keratin.

ketogenesis The production of ketone bodies.

ketolysis The breakdown of ketone bodies to form acetyl CoA.

ketone bodies Substances such as acetone, acetoacetate, and hydroxybutyrate and other products derived from acetyl CoA; produced by fatty acid oxidation under food deprivation conditions.

kidney An organ responsible for producing urine, thereby regulating the levels of nitrogenous wastes, extracellular fluid solute properties, and osmolarity.

kinesin A motor protein associated with microtubules (see also *dynein*).

kinetic energy The energy associated with movement.

kinocilium The long cilium of a mammalian hair cell (involved in the detection of sound).

Kleiber's Law The observation that metabolic rate is related to body mass to the exponent 0.75.

K_m See *Michaelis constant.*

knockout An animal that has been subjected to genetic manipulation leading to the inability to express a native gene.

Krebs cycle See *tricarboxylic acid cycle.*

K-type strategy A life history strategy whereby an animal produces few offspring and invests heavily in their development (see also *r-type strategy*).

lactation Production and release of milk from the mammalian mammary gland.

lagena An extension of the saccule of the inner ear of vertebrates; small in reptiles and amphibians but extended to form the cochlear duct in birds and the cochlea in mammals.

lamella A general term referring to a morphology that resembles stacks of leaves.

lamellipodia Flat, sheetlike extensions of the cell, supported by the actin cytoskeleton.

laminar flow A pattern in which the layers of fluid move in parallel, usually relative to the surface of an object.

larva A pre-adult developmental stage that bears little resemblance to the adult form.

latch state A condition in smooth muscle in which force is generated with less than expected ATP consumption; usually attributed to a more efficient mechanism of crossbridge cycling.

lateral inhibition Process by which a sensory stimulus at one location inhibits the activity of adjacent neurons. Lateral inhibition enhances contrast and improves edge detection in sensory systems.

lateral line system A mechanoreceptive organ in fishes and amphibians that senses vibrations in the water surrounding the animal. Contains hair cells grouped into structures called neuromasts.

law of bulk flow Physical principle that states that fluids flow down pressure gradients, and that this flow is opposed by the resistance of the system; flow = pressure gradient/resistance.

leak channel A passive ion channel in the cell membrane that allows the movement of ions down their concentration gradients.

leaky epithelia An epithelial layer with cell-cell connections that permit paracellular transport.

length constant (λ) A mathematical constant that expresses the distance that electrotonic current can spread along the membrane of a neuron; the distance over which a change in membrane potential decreases to 37% of its original value.

lengthening contraction A type of muscle contraction in which external forces cause the muscle to lengthen while force is being generated.

length-tension relationship Describes the influence of sarcomere length on force development in muscle; muscle generates optimal force when sarcomere length is about 2 μm (in most muscles), and tension declines at higher or lower sarcomere lengths.

lens A clear object that can refract light. In the eye, the lens bends incoming light rays, helping to form a focused image on the retina.

leukocytes Vertebrate white blood cells; cells in blood that are involved in the immune system.

Leydig cell A testosterone-producing cell interspersed in the interstitium of the testes.

lift An upward force creating changes in pressure associated with movement over surfaces of an aerofoil/hydrofoil.

lift coefficient A property of a surface that expresses its ability to generate lift.

ligament A form of connective tissue that joins two bones.

ligand A chemical that specifically and reversibly binds to a receptor or enzyme.

ligand-gated ion channel An ion channel that opens or closes in response to the binding of a specific chemical.

limbic system A group of structures in the vertebrate brain that is involved in processes including emotions and memory.

Lineweaver-Burk equation A plot of the reciprocals of reaction velocity ($1/V$) and substrate concentration ($1/[S]$); generates a linear relationship for enzymes with hyperbolic kinetics.

lipase An enzyme that breaks down lipid; includes triglyceride lipases, lipoprotein lipase, and phospholipase.

lipid A class of organic molecules that share hydrophobicity; includes fatty acids, phospholipids, triglycerides, and steroids.

lipid bilayer The model for a plasma membrane in which the hydrophobic faces of two monolayers of phospholipids are associated.

lipid raft A thickened region of the plasma membrane; often accumulates cholesterol, phospholipids with long chain fatty acids, and proteins with long transmembrane domains.

lipogenesis Conversion of fatty acids and glycerol to acylglycerides including monoacylglycerides, diacylglycerides, triglycerides, and phospholipids.

lipolysis Breakdown of acylglycerides and phospholipids.

lipophilic Hydrophobic or nonpolar.

lipoprotein A complex of lipids and proteins; central to the transport of lipids between tissues.

load A force that opposes muscle contraction.

locomotor module A set of musculoskeletal components that work together to perform a single function, such as flying.

long-term potentiation A long-lasting enhancement of the postsynaptic response as a result of high-frequency stimulation of the presynaptic neuron.

loop of Henle A region of a mammalian kidney tubule that connects the proximal and distal tubule; central to the production of hyperosmotic urine.

lower critical temperature (LCT) The lowest environmental temperature at which a homeotherm can survive for long periods; the lower limit of its thermoneutral zone.

lumen The internal cavity of a multicellular unit, such as a kidney tubule or gastrointestinal tract.

lungs Respiratory surfaces that originate as invaginations of the body surface. Generally used for gas exchange in air.

luteal phase The portion of an ovulatory cycle after the follicle has expelled the ovum and before a second follicle matures.

lymph A fluid consisting of an ultrafiltrate of blood and immune cells that travels through the lymphatic system of vertebrates.

lymph hearts The pumping structures of the lymphatic system, present only in some vertebrates (including fish, amphibians, and reptiles).

lymph nodes Small bean-shaped organs found in various locations in the lymphatic system of tetrapods; they filter lymphatic fluid and produce lymphocytes.

lymphatic system In the vertebrates, a network of vessels or sinuses (depending upon the species) that carries lymph back to the primary circulatory system. In many species it also performs an immune function.

lymphocytes Leukocytes that are involved in adaptive immunity in vertebrates.

lysosomes Organelles responsible for the breakdown of damaged and unnecessary membranous compartments and membrane proteins.

macula densa A group of cells in the juxtaglomerular apparatus that senses the sodium chloride concentration of the tubular fluid.

macrophage A type of white blood cell that ingests foreign invaders and dead or dying cells.

magnetite A crystalline aggregation of a magnetic metal (usually iron); found in some magnetoreceptors.

magnetoreceptor A sensory receptor that responds to magnetic fields.

malleus (hammer) One of the three small bones of the mammalian middle ear involved in transmitting sound vibrations to the inner ear.

Malpighian tubule The functional equivalent of a kidney tubule in insects, releasing the urine into the gut.

mannose-binding lectin A protein secreted from the liver into the blood, which binds to mannose moieties of pathogens, enabling the pathogen to be recognized, an example of opsonization.

mantle cavity A cavity formed by the body wall (mantle) of mollusks; generally contains the respiratory structures.

mass action ratio Ratio of products to substrates; when more than one product (or substrate) is involved, their concentrations are multiplied together. When a reaction is at equilibrium, the mass action ratio equals the equilibrium constant (K_{eq}).

mass-specific metabolic rate The metabolic rate of an animal (usually described as oxygen consumption) expressed relative to body mass.

mast cells Immune cells that release histamine when stimulated.

mastication Mechanical disruption of food in an oral cavity (chewing).

maximum velocity (V_{max}) The maximal enzymatic rate calculated from a substrate-velocity curve; can be estimated by the enzymatic rate observed when product is absent and substrate concentrations are optimal.

mean arterial pressure (MAP) The weighted average of the systolic and diastolic pressures, taking into account the relative length of each of these phases of the cardiac cycle.

mechanical energy A form of energy arising from the movement or position of an object; can be either kinetic energy (as in a moving leg) or potential energy (as in a loaded spring).

mechanogated channel (or *mechanically gated channel*) An ion channel that opens or closes in response to the stress (or stretch) on a membrane.

mechanoreceptor A sensory receptor that detects forces applied to cell membranes (such as touch or pressure). Can be used to describe either the receptor protein or cells containing these receptors.

medulla oblongata A region of the vertebrate brainstem containing centers that regulate heart rate, breathing depth and frequency, and blood pressure. Also called the medulla.

medullary cardiovascular control center The region within the medulla that regulates cardiac function.

medullary respiratory center The region within the medulla that regulates breathing depth and frequency.

melanopsin A photopigment found in the retinal ganglion cells of the vertebrate eye.

melatonin A hormone found in all animal groups that regulates sleep-wake cycles.

melting point The temperature at which a solid can become a liquid; when the melting point and the freezing point are not the same temperature, this hysteresis suggests the presence of a solute that acts in a noncolloidal manner, such as an antifreeze protein.

membrane fluidity A state that allows the two-dimensional movement of lipids and proteins within a lipid bilayer membrane.

membrane potential The electrical gradient across a cellular membrane.

membrane recycling The exchange of membrane lipids and protein between the plasma membrane and the internal membrane network.

memory B cells A subclass of B cell lymphocytes that become quiescent but retain the ability to produce specific antibodies, conferring immunological memory.

menarche The age at which a female mammal with a menstrual cycle experiences her first menstruation.

meninges Membranes covering the vertebrate central nervous system. Mammals have three meninges; birds, reptiles, and amphibians have two; and fish have one.

menses In female mammals, the periodic shedding of the endometrial layer of uterine tissue that occurs if there is no implantation of a fertilized ovum; also known as *menstruation*.

menstrual cycle The estrous cycle of humans and some other primates.

menstruation See *menses*.

mesangial cells Contractile cells between the capillaries of the glomerulus, which control blood flow, and thereby control blood pressure within the glomerulus.

mesencephalon See *midbrain*.

mesoderm The middle of the three primary germ layers in a developing embryo; eventually gives rise to tissues such as bone, muscle, and connective tissue.

messenger RNA See *mRNA*.

metabolic acidosis or alkalosis A decrease or increase, respectively, in blood pH as a result of metabolic activity.

metabolic depression A reduction in metabolic rate below resting levels; associated with a period of dormancy.

metabolic flux The flow rate through a metabolic pathway.

metabolic rate The rate of heat production by a tissue or organism, usually approximated by oxygen consumption or carbon dioxide production.

metabolic theory of ecology An extension of the theory of allometric scaling of metabolic rate with body size that attempts to make predictions about processes at higher levels of biological organization (e.g., populations and communities).

metabolic water The water produced by the metabolic breakdown of macromolecules.

metabolism The sum of all chemical reactions in a biologic entity.

metabolizable energy The proportion of digestible energy retained by the body; the remainder is unmetabolizable energy lost in excretory products.

metabolon A group of enzymes that are spatially localized within the cell and perform a function together.

metabotropic receptor A receptor that signals via a signal transduction pathway (see also *ionotropic receptor*).

metalloprotein A protein with a metal ion integrated into its structure; enzymatic metalloproteins typically involve their metal in oxidation-reduction reactions.

metamer In developmental biology, this refers to a body segment.

metamorphosis The transition between distinct developmental stages, typically from a larva to an adult.

metazoan A multicellular animal.

methemoglobin An oxidized form of hemoglobin that can no longer carry oxygen.

micelle A lipid monolayer that rolls onto itself to form a sphere with a hydrophobic inner core and hydrophilic exterior.

Michaelis constant (K_m) The concentration of substrate that yields half maximal velocity in an enzymatic reaction.

Michaelis-Menten equation $V = V_{max} \times [S]/([S] + K_m)$.

microclimate The external environment within a confined space, typically distinct from the broader conditions, such as a subterranean burrow; typically used to describe the conditions experienced by an organism (see also *microenvironment*).

microelectrode A very small electrode used to record electrical signals from cells.

microenvironment Like a microclimate, but can apply to the environment surrounding anything from individual molecules to whole animals.

microfilaments A polymer of β-actin used to construct the cytoskeleton.

microglia One of the glial cells of the vertebrate central nervous system.

microtubule A large, hollow tube consisting of a polymerized tubulin; used to build the cytoskeleton.

microtubule-associated protein (MAP) A protein that binds to microtubules to alter structural or functional properties.

microtubule-organizing center (MTOC) A multiprotein complex near the center of the cell from which microtubules grow.

microvilli Fingerlike extensions from individual cells, supported by microfilaments, which serve to increase surface area.

micturition Urination.

midbrain The middle portion of the vertebrate brain consisting of the tectum and tegmentum. Also called the mesencephalon.

middle ear A part of the vertebrate ear that consists of the tympanic membrane and one or more small bones (in mammals, the incus, malleus, and stapes) that help to amplify sounds.

milieu intérieur The internal environment of a cell or organism.

mineralocorticoids Steroid hormones involved in water and ion balance.

mirror neurons A neuron that is active when an organism performs a particular action and also when it observes another organism performing that action.

mitochondria Organelles within most eukaryotic cells that produce energy by oxidative phosphorylation; organized in many tissues as a network or reticulum.

mitochondria-rich muscle cell Usually refers to the epithelial cells specialized for ion pumping, which have abundant mitochondria to meet the energy demands of active transport (see also *chloride cell*).

M-line The midpoint of a sarcomere where the thick filament lacks myosin heads.

mobile element A region of DNA that can be excised and inserted elsewhere within the genome.

model organism A species that is widely used in biological research because it has properties that make it particularly suitable for research purposes (see *August Krogh principle*).

molal (molality) Moles of an ion or molecule expressed relative to kilograms of solvent (usually water).

molar (molarity) Moles of an ion or molecule expressed relative to liters of solvent (usually water).

mole 6.02252×10^{23} molecules of a substance; the molecular weight of a substance is the mass of one mole of that substance.

molecular chaperone A protein that uses the energy of ATP hydrolysis to help fold or stabilize denatured proteins; includes heat shock proteins.

molecular phylogeny The evolutionary relationships among organisms as reconstructed based on molecular sequence data.

monoacylglyceride (or monoglyceride) A single fatty acid esterified to a glycerol molecule.

monocyte A large white blood cell that, in the tetrapod immune system, ingests foreign particles such as microbes; when it leaves the blood stream it differentiates into a macrophage.

monogastric stomach An animal that has a stomach with one (usually acidic) compartment.

monomer A single subunit of a multimer, such as a dimer or trimer.

monosaccharide A sugar, usually composed of a 6-carbon (sometimes 5-carbon) ring, such as glucose.

monounsaturated fatty acid A fatty acid with a single double bond.

monozygotic Arising from a single zygote.

morphology The shape or form of an organism.

motor end plate The location on a muscle that forms synapses with a motor neuron; the muscle side of a neuromuscular junction.

motor neuron A neuron that transmits signals from the central nervous system to skeletal muscles.

motor proteins Mechanoenzymes, such as myosin, that use the energy of ATP hydrolysis to move along cytoskeletal tracks.

motor unit A group of muscle fibers under the control of a single neuron.

mRNA Messenger RNA; the form of RNA that is used as a template during translation to form protein.

mucin The lipopolysaccharide that is the main component of mucus.

mucosa Refers to the inside layer of a tissue or organ, often that surface exposed to the lumen of an organ, such as the gastrointestinal tract (see also *serosa*).

multipolar neuron A nerve cell with a single axon and many dendrites.

mucous cells Cells that secrete a complex mucopolysaccharide onto the surface of a tissue; goblet cells are a type of mucous cell found in the intestinal and respiratory surfaces.

mucus A mucopolysaccharide mixture secreted from specialized epithelial cells onto the external surface of a tissue.

multipolar neurons Neurons with many processes leading from the cell body; most of these processes are dendrites, but one may be an axon.

muscarinic acetylcholine receptors G protein–coupled receptors that bind acetylcholine.

muscle A multicellular tissue composed of myocytes, fibroblasts, and vascular cells; the contraction of the myocytes leads to force generation or shortening.

muscle fiber A single muscle cell; can be mononucleated (as in cardiomyocytes) or multinucleated (as in skeletal muscle fibers).

muscle myosin Myosin II, which is the myosin isoform found in muscle.

muscle spindle A muscle stretch receptor.

mutation A heritable alteration in the nucleotide sequence of genomic DNA.

myelin See *myelin sheath*.

myelin sheath The insulating wrappings of vertebrate axons that are composed of multiple layers of glial cell plasma membrane. Invertebrate axons have analogous wrappings, but they are not generally termed a myelin sheath.

myelination The process of forming the myelin sheath around a vertebrate axon.

myenteric plexus A network of neurons found within the smooth muscle of the gastrointestinal tract that controls its muscular and secretory actions.

myoblast A mononucleated, proliferating cell that can differentiate to form a muscle cell.

myocardium The muscle of the heart.

myocyte A general term for a muscle cell, including smooth muscle cells, cardiomyocytes, and myofibers.

myofiber A multinucleated skeletal muscle fiber.

myofibril A long bundle of actin, myosin, and associated proteins in muscle cells.

myogenic Refers to something originating in the muscle, as in myogenic autoregulation of blood flow or myogenic muscle, which triggers its own activation.

myogenic autoregulation Regulation of blood flow via contraction of vascular smooth muscle that is regulated by processes intrinsic to the muscle.

myogenic muscle Muscles whose contraction is initiated by processes intrinsic to the muscle or organ. For example, a myogenic heart contracts spontaneously without input from the nervous system.

myoglobin A type of hemoglobin found in muscle.

myometrium The smooth muscle layers of the uterus.

myosin A large multigene family of ATP-dependent motor proteins that work in conjunction with actin. The thick filament of muscle is composed of myosin, which is organized into hexamers consisting of two myosin heavy chains (MHC) and four myosin light chains (two regulatory MLC and two essential MLC).

myosin heavy chain The motor protein that interacts with actin.

myosin light chain A protein that binds the motor protein myosin II, regulating its structure or function.

myosin light chain kinase (MLCK) An enzyme associated with hexameric myosin that phosphorylates myosin light chain.

myosin light chain phosphatase (MLCP) An enzyme associated with hexameric myosin that dephosphorylates myosin light chain.

myotome A repeating segment in the body musculature of adult fish; also, the embryonic form of muscle derived from a body segment, or somite.

myotube An early stage of muscle differentiation in which multiple myoblasts fuse together to form a multinucleated contractile tubular cell.

Na$^+$/K$^+$ ATPase An ion transporter that expels 3 Na$^+$ out of a cell and imports 2 K$^+$, driven by the energy of ATP hydrolysis.

NaCaX Sodium-calcium exchanger; a type of ion exchanger.

nares Nostrils.

natriuretic Leading to the appearance of sodium in the urine.

natural killer cells A type of lymphocyte that is part of the innate immune system of vertebrates that is capable of killing tumors or cells infected with viruses without prior stimulation by the immune system.

near-equilibrium reaction A reaction in which the products and substrates in vivo are near the concentrations that would arise if the enzymatic reaction were to reach equilibrium. The reaction is regulated by changes in the concentrations of substrates and products.

negative feedback loop A regulatory mechanism whereby a step late in a pathway causes a decrease in the activity of a step earlier in the pathway to reduce the flow through the pathway.

negative feedback regulation A type of regulation in which the output of a pathway tends to decrease the activity of earlier steps in the pathway (see negative feedback loop).

negative work Work that arises when the muscle is lengthening.

nematocyst The stinging cell of cnidarians.

nephridium A primitive type of kidney tubule found in some invertebrates, such as annelids and mollusks; can also refer to the embryonic kidney of vertebrates.

nephron The multicellular unit of the kidney, consisting of the tubule and the vasculature that serves it, typically a glomerulus.

Nernst equation An expression that describes the ion concentration gradient across a permeable membrane in relation to the voltage when the system is at equilibrium.

nerve A cordlike structure composed of a collection of neuronal axons grouped together by connective tissues.

nerve net Description of the structure of the nervous system of cnidarians.

nervous system Network of neurons and their supporting cells.

net energy The proportion of metabolizable energy that is retained by the body, excluding that lost to specific dynamic action.

neurogenic A contraction that occurs in response to a nervous stimulus.

neurogenic muscle A muscle that is activated by neuronal stimulation.

neurohemal organ A region of multiple neurons that secrete hormones into the blood.

neurohormone A chemical messenger released from a neuron into the blood.

neuromast A structure consisting of a cup filled with a viscous gel and several hair cells; the functional unit of the lateral line system of fishes and amphibians.

neuromodulators Substances that alter neurotransmission, and thus regulate the action of neurotransmitters.

neuromuscular junction The synapse between a motor neuron and a skeletal muscle cell.

neurons (nerve cells) Specialized cells in the nervous system that communicate using chemical and electrical signals. Many, but not all, neurons are excitable cells that generate action potentials.

neuropeptides Polypeptides that act as neurotransmitters.

neurosecretory cell Neurons that produce and secrete neurohormones into the blood, typically in a region called a neurohemal organ.

neurotransmitter A chemical messenger released from a neuron into the synaptic cleft.

neutral evolution Changes in gene frequency in a population over time that are solely the result of random mutation and that are not shaped by forces such as natural selection.

neutral The pH at which the concentration of H$^+$ equals that of OH$^-$.

neutrophils The most common type of white blood cell in the vertebrate immune system.

nicotinic ACh receptors Ligand-gated ion channels that open in response to acetylcholine binding.

nitric oxide A gaseous neurotransmitter and paracrine chemical signal that is involved in regulating many physiological processes; important vasodilator in vertebrates.

nitrogen narcosis A state of altered consciousness similar to alcohol intoxication that can occur in humans when they dive to depths greater than 30 m while breathing air.

nociceptor (or nocioceptor) A sensory receptor that responds to noxious stimuli of various types (e.g., extreme heat or cold, extreme pressure, harmful chemicals, tissue damage); pain receptor.

nocturnal Active at night.

nodes of Ranvier A gap of exposed axonal membrane between two regions of myelin sheath.

noncompetitive inhibition A mode of enzyme inhibition in which a molecule inhibits an enzyme by acting at a site distant from the active site; noncompetitive inhibitors can increase the K_m or reduce the V_{max}.

noncovalent bond Includes four types of weak bonds that stabilize macromolecular structure.

nondirectional ventilation Anatomical arrangement of the respiratory system in which the medium flows across the respiratory surface in a random or unpredictable direction.

nonpolar Having low solubility in water or other polar solvents.

nonshivering thermogenesis (NST) Production of heat by chemical means without muscle contraction. Typically refers to heat production by brown adipose tissue; however, there are other means of NST.

norepinephrine (or noradrenaline) A catecholamine neurotransmitter; in vertebrates, released by the sympathetic nervous system.

nuclease An enzyme that hydrolyzes nucleic acids; includes DNases and RNases.

nucleator (or nucleating agent) A molecule or particle that triggers the formation of ice at subzero temperatures.

nuclei (brain) A cluster of cell bodies within the brain that act as an integrating center.

nucleoside A molecule composed of a nitrogenous base (purine or pyrimidine) linked to a ribose or deoxyribose sugar.

nucleotide A nucleoside with one or more phosphate groups, such as ATP.

nymph The larval form of a hemimetabolous insect that resembles in most respects the adult form of the insect, except lacking functional wings.

obliquely striated muscle A muscle where striations run obliquely to the axis of shortening.

odorant Molecules that can be detected by the sense of smell.

odorant-binding protein Proteins found in the mucus of the nasal epithelium that bind to odorants and transfer them to odorant receptors.

odorant receptor protein A G protein–coupled receptor involved in the detection of odorants and thus the sense of smell.

olfaction Detection of environmental chemicals from outside the body: the sense of smell.

olfactory bulb A part of the vertebrate forebrain that is involved in processing olfactory sensations.

oligodendrocyte A vertebrate glial cell that forms the myelin sheath of a neuron in the central nervous system.

ommatidium (plural: ommatidia) The functional unit of the arthropod compound eye.

oncotic pressure The osmotic pressure of blood that is due to the concentration of large macromolecules, primarily protein.

oocyte One of the intermediate stages in the process of producing an ovum during meiosis.

oogenesis The production of an ovum.

oogonia (singular: oogonium) After the primordial germ cell enters the ovary, it differentiates into an oogonium, which undergoes multiple rounds of mitosis before entering meiosis.

open circulatory system A circulatory system in which the blood passes through one or more unbounded spaces called sinuses.

operculum The stiffened flaplike cover of the gills of bony fishes.

opsin A family of G proteins that is involved in visual phototransduction.

opsonins Proteins that bind to pathogens, enabling them to be better recognized by immune cells.

opsonization The addition of opsonins to pathogens.

optic chiasm Area in the vertebrate brain where the optic nerves cross.

optic lobe Either of the two lobes of the vertebrate midbrain that are involved in visual processing; also, in arthropods the regions of the brain involved in processing signals from the compound eyes.

organ of Corti Located in the cochlea of the inner ear; contains the hair cells that are involved in the sense of hearing.

ornithine-urea cycle A pathway by which urea is produced from nitrogen arising from ammonia or glutamine.

orphan receptors Receptors whose ligand and function is not known; identified based on structural similarity to known receptors.

orthologs Genes in different species that are related by direct descent as a result of a speciation event.

osmoconformer An animal that exhibits an internal osmolarity that parallels that of the external environment.

osmolarity Analogous to molarity, it is the concentration of osmolytes in a solution (osmoles per liter); abbreviated OsM.

osmole One mole of osmotically active solutes.

osmolyte An osmotically active solute; any solute that has a significant effect on osmotic pressure.

osmoregulator An animal that exhibits an internal osmolarity that is controlled independently of the osmolarity of the external environment.

osmosis The movement of water across a membrane from an area with a high activity of water to an area with low activity of water.

osmotic pressure A force arising due to the tendency of water to move by osmosis.

osteoblast A bone precursor cell.

osteoclast A type of cell that dissolves and reabsorbs bone.

ostia (singular: **ostium**) An anatomical term for a small opening.

otolith A small mineralized granule (usually calcium carbonate) in the inner ear of vertebrates. Involved in the sense of balance.

outer ear External portion of the vertebrate ear (consisting of the pinna and auditory canal in mammals).

outer hair cells One of two types of hair cells found in the organ of Corti in the inner ear of mammals; involved in amplifying sound and protecting the inner hair cells from loud sounds.

oval A structure that is used in gas reabsorption from the swim bladder of a fish back into the blood.

oval window Membrane between the middle ear and the inner ear of vertebrates. Vibrates to transmit sound to the inner ear.

oviparous An animal that produces eggs that hatch outside the body.

ovoviviparous An animal that holds its eggs inside the body until the eggs hatch, and then releases active young.

ovulation The release of an ovum following the rupture of a follicle.

ovum The larger of the two gametes of a sexually reproducing species. Although an ovum is often defined as the gamete produced by a female, in reality this definition is backward: an individual is a female if it has gonads that can produce an ovum.

oxidant A molecule that accepts an electron from another molecule (the reductant). In doing so, the oxidant becomes reduced.

oxidation A chemical reaction whereby a molecule donates an electron to another molecule, becoming oxidized.

oxidative phosphorylation (OXPHOS) The process by which mitochondria produce ATP from the oxidation of reducing equivalents (NADH, $FADH_2$). The electron transport chain expels protons from the mitochondria to produce a proton motive force, which is then used by the F_1F_0 ATPase to produce ATP.

oxyconformer An animal that exhibits a respiratory rate that declines when oxygen pressure declines.

oxygen carrying capacity The maximum amount of oxygen that can be carried by blood. Includes both dissolved oxygen and oxygen bound to respiratory pigments.

oxygen debt See *excess postexercise oxygen consumption*.

oxygen- and capacity-limitation of thermal tolerance The hypothesis that an organism's thermal tolerance is limited by its ability to supply and utilize oxygen at extreme temperatures.

oxygen dissociation curve See *oxygen equilibrium curve*.

oxygen equilibrium curve A curve showing the relationship between P_{O_2} and the oxygen saturation of blood containing a respiratory pigment.

oxygen-transport pigment See *respiratory pigments*.

oxyregulator An animal that exhibits a constant respiratory rate despite a decline in oxygen pressure.

oxytocin A peptide hormone produced by the anterior pituitary; induces the contraction of smooth muscle during parturition.

P_{50} The partial pressure at which a respiratory pigment is 50 percent saturated with oxygen.

pacemaker A cell or group of cells whose output of action potentials occurs in a rhythmic pattern.

pacemaker cell An excitable cell that spontaneously fires action potentials in a rhythmic pattern.

pacemaker potentials Spontaneous depolarizations of the resting membrane potential that ultimately trigger action potentials within pacemaker cells.

Pacinian corpuscle A type of vertebrate skin mechanoreceptor.

pancreas A vertebrate organ that produces endocrine hormones including insulin and glucagon and also produces exocrine secretions that are involved in digestion.

pancreatic beta cells Cells within the vertebrate pancreas that secrete the hormone insulin.

panting A mode of thermoregulation whereby an increase in the frequency of respiration enhances heat loss from the body core.

papillary muscles Muscles connected to the chordae tendineae of the mammalian heart that help to anchor the atrioventricular valves.

parabronchi Smallest airways of a bird lung.

paracellular pathway The pathway via which paracellular transport occurs.

paracellular transport Passage of solutes or water between cells; in most epithelial tissues, tight junctions and other cell-cell junctions prevent paracellular movement of fluids.

paracrine A type of chemical messenger that is involved in local signaling between nearby cells; paracrine messengers move through the interstitial fluid by diffusion.

parafacial respiratory group A group of neurons in the vertebrate brain that is involved in the generation of respiratory rhythms.

parallel evolution The evolution of a shared underlying trait in similar ways in two distinct but related lineages.

paralogs Genes that are the result of a gene duplication event within a lineage (see also *homologs, orthologs*).

parasympathetic nervous system Part of the vertebrate autonomic nervous system; generally active during periods of rest; releases acetylcholine onto target organs.

parathyroid glands Glands located on the posterior surface of the thyroid gland that release parathyroid hormones in response to changes in extracellular calcium.

parathyroid hormone Peptide hormone that regulates blood calcium levels.

parietal cells The acid-secreting cells within the gastric mucous membrane.

parthenogenesis A mode of asexual reproduction whereby offspring are produced by a female as a result of a variation on the meiotic pathway. Because meiosis is involved, chromosomal recombination is possible and the parthenogenic offspring are not clones of the parent.

partial pressure The pressure exerted by one of the gases in a gas mixture. The sum of the partial pressures of all the gases in a mixture gives the total pressure.

partition coefficient A measure of the relative ability of a solute to dissolve in two different solutes, such as oil and water.

parturition The birthing process by which offspring of viviparous and ovoviviparous females are expelled from the reproductive tract.

parvalbumin A Ca^{2+}-binding protein in the cytoplasm of some muscles, which buffers Ca^{2+} levels to accelerate relaxation.

passive diffusion A type of passive transport that does not require a protein carrier.

passive transport Movement across a cell membrane without an energy investment other than the chemical gradient of the transported molecule; includes both passive diffusion and facilitated diffusion.

patch clamping A method used by neurobiologists to study the function of ion channels, in which the voltage or current across a small patch of membrane is manipulated using a small glass microelectrode applied to the surface of the cell.

pathogen-associated molecular patterns, or PAMPs Molecules arising from pathogens that can be recognized as foreign by immune cells.

pattern generator A group of neurons whose rhythmic firing coordinates a rhythmic physiological process or behavior, such as breathing or locomotion.

pattern-recognition receptors, or PRRs Proteins produced by the immune system that bind PAMPs.

pavement cells Cells within the gills of fish that are responsible for gas exchange.

pejus temperature The temperatures at which physiological processes start to decline in function when temperature is above or below the optimum for function.

pentose A five-carbon monosaccharide, such as ribose and deoxyribose.

peptide bond A carbon-nitrogen bond ($-C-N-$); most common in polymers of amino acids.

perfusion Movement of fluid through a tissue (e.g., flow of blood through a capillary bed).

pericardium The sac surrounding a heart.

pericyte cell Contractile cells that wrap around capillaries.

perilymph The fluid found in the cochlea of the inner ear.

peripheral chemoreceptors Chemoreceptors located in the aortic and carotid bodies of vertebrates that detect changes in blood chemistry.

peripheral membrane protein A protein that is weakly bound to the membrane through an interaction with a lipid or integral membrane protein.

peripheral nervous system (PNS) All of the neurons outside of the central nervous system.

peripheral resistance See *total peripheral resistance*.

peristalsis The rhythmic contractions of intestinal smooth muscle; involved in propelling a bolus of food along the gastrointestinal tract and in moving blood through the circulatory systems of some animals.

permeability The ability of a molecule to cross a barrier, such as a membrane.

permease A transporter that mediates facilitated diffusion, but is neither a channel nor a porin.

pH scale A measure of acidity, expressed as the negative $\log_{10}$ of the proton concentration.

pH-bicarbonate plot (Davenport diagram) A graphical depiction of the relationship between the pH and bicarbonate concentration of a solution. Usually used to describe these relationships in arterial blood.

phagocyte A cell that carries out phagocytosis.

phagocytosis The endocytosis of large particles from the extracellular space.

phasic muscle A type of muscle that undergoes rapid contractions and relaxations; a twitch muscle.

phasic receptor A sensory receptor that produces action potentials only during part of the stimulus (usually at stimulus onset and removal).

phenotype The physical characteristics of an organism; the result of an interaction between the genotype and the environment.

phenotypic plasticity Production of different phenotypes by a single genotype as a result of environmental cues; may be reversible or irreversible (see also *acclimation*).

pheromones Chemical messengers released by an animal into the environment that have an effect on another animal of the same species.

phosphagens Energy-rich compounds that transfer energy in reactions in which a large change in free energy results when a phosphate bond is broken.

phosphatase An enzyme that removes a phosphate group from a molecule; important in signal transduction pathways because it reverses the phosphorylations catalyzed by kinases.

phosphocreatine See *creatine phosphate*.

phosphodiester bond –P–O–P–.

phosphodiesterase An enzyme that breaks down the phosphodiester bonds of cyclic nucleotides such as cAMP and cGMP.

phosphoglycerides The major class of phospholipids of biological membranes, consisting of a glycerol backbone, two fatty acids, and a polar head group linked to the glycerol via phosphate.

phospholipase An enzyme that breaks down phospholipids, releasing either diacylglycerol, polar head groups, or fatty acids, depending on the type of phospholipase.

phospholipids Phosphoglycerides and sphingolipids.

phosphorylation The addition of a phosphate group via a kinase, expending ATP (e.g., a protein kinase catalyzes the phosphorylation of a protein).

phosphorylation cascade A type of signal transduction pathway that involves multiple phosphorylation steps.

phosphorylation potential An expression of energy status; the mass action ratio for an ATPase reaction ($[ATP]/[ADP][P_i]$).

photon The fundamental particle of electromagnetic radiation. Streams of photons can have differing wavelengths, in which case the resulting radiation is given different names (e.g., X-rays, gamma rays, visible light).

photoperiod The length of the light and dark phases of a day.

photopigments Molecules specialized for detecting photons; consist of a chromophore and an associated protein.

photoreceptors Sensory receptors that detect photons with wavelengths in the visible spectrum (i.e., light). Can be used to describe either the receptor proteins or the cells that contain them.

phototaxis Movement in response to light, either toward (positive phototaxis) or away (negative phototaxis).

phylogenetic Pertaining to phylogeny.

phylogeny A hypothesis regarding the evolutionary relationships among organisms; can be based on the analysis of various types of data (e.g., molecular, morphological).

physiological dead space The volume of a respiratory organ that is not involved in gas exchange; consists of both the anatomical dead space and the volume of any regions that, although capable of acting as gas exchange

surfaces, do not participate in gas exchange (e.g., unperfused or unventilated alveoli).

physoclist Any fish whose swim bladder lacks a connection to the gut.

physostome Any fish whose swim bladder is connected to the gut via a tube.

piloerection The movement of hair or feathers perpendicular to the skin in response to muscular contraction.

pilomotor Related to the nerves and muscles that change the orientation of hair.

pineal complex Consists of the pineal gland and related structures; involved in melatonin secretion and the establishment of circadian rhythms.

pineal gland An endocrine organ located in the brain of vertebrates. In nonmammalian vertebrates it is light sensitive. See *pineal complex*.

pinna The cartilaginous structures forming the outer ear of mammals.

pinocytosis The endocytosis of fluids by the plasma membrane (see also *phagocytosis*).

pit organs The highly sensitive thermoreceptive organs of some snakes.

pituitary gland A hormone-secreting organ located at the base of the vertebrate brain; connected to the hypothalamus.

pivotal temperature In an animal with environmental sex determination, it is a temperature at which equal numbers of males and females result.

place coding Mechanism by which the inner ear detects the pitch (frequency) of a sound. Different areas of the basilar membrane of the inner ear respond to each pitch, converting the frequency information into location (place) information.

placenta In eutherian mammals, the membrane derived from the embryonic chorion that encircles the embryo, acting as the interface between embryonic and maternal tissues.

plane polarized light When light arrives at a detector, it typically exhibits waves that run at all angles. Polarizing filters permit the passage of light waves that run in a specific angle (plane), generating plane-polarized light.

plasma The liquid fraction of vertebrate blood.

plasma membrane The lipid bilayer membrane that encircles a cell.

plasticity The ability to change or remodel a physiological process or structure, as in neural plasticity. See also *phenotypic plasticity*.

plateau phase The phase of a cardiac action potential characterized by a sustained depolarization as a result of calcium influx.

pleiotropy A phenomenon in which a single gene is responsible for multiple, seemingly independent phenotypes.

pleural cavity The space between the pleural sacs surrounding the lungs of vertebrates. Low pressure in the pleural cavity helps to keep the lungs from collapsing.

pleural sacs A series of membranes that surround the lungs of vertebrates. The pleural sacs enclose the pleural cavity.

plexus A complex network of blood vessels or nerves.

plug-flow reactor A type of chemical reactor in which the inflow moves as a bolus through the tubelike reactor.

pN The pH at which a zwitterion has no net charge.

podocyte Cells surrounding the capillaries of the glomerulus, with footlike extensions that form the filtration slits.

poikilothermy A thermoregulatory strategy whereby an animal (a poikilotherm) allows

body temperature (T_B) to vary, usually in relation to the ambient conditions.

Poiseuille's equation An equation describing the relationship between the flow, pressure, and resistance of a fluid moving through a rigid tube, including the factors influencing resistance (length, cross-sectional area, and viscosity).

polar See *hydrophilic*.

polymer A chain of repeating molecules, such as a polysaccharide or a polypeptide.

polymodal receptors Sensory receptor cells that can detect more than one type of stimulus.

polymorphonuclear (PMN) cells White blood cells of the immune system that possess multilobed nuclei.

polypeptide A chain of amino acids linked by peptide bonds.

polyphenism A form of irreversible phenotypic plasticity, generally involving alternative developmental pathways.

polypnea Rapid breathing.

polysaccharide A chain of monosaccharides linked by glycosidic bonds.

polysynaptic Involving more than two synapses; used in the context of reflex pathways.

polyunsaturated fatty acid A fatty acid with two or more double bonds along the carbon chain.

pons A region of the vertebrate brain that communicates information between the brainstem and the higher brain centers. Works with the medulla to regulate breathing.

population coding A phenomenon in which information about a stimulus is encoded in the pattern of firing of multiple neurons.

porin A channel that permits the facilitated diffusion of large molecules; e.g., aquaporin is a porin that transports water.

porphyrins Organic ring structures that bind metals, primarily iron but also copper; heme is the most common type of porphyrin in animals.

portal system Two capillary beds connected by a portal vein (e.g., hypothalamic pituitary portal system; intestinal liver portal system).

portal vein A blood vessel that carries blood from one capillary bed to another; part of a portal system.

positive feedback loop A regulatory mechanism whereby a step late in a pathway causes an increase in the activity of a step earlier in the pathway to increase the flow through the pathway.

positive work Work performed during muscle shortening.

posterior pituitary Lobe of the pituitary gland; secretes antidiuretic hormone and oxytocin; also called the neurohypophysis.

postganglionic neuron A vertebrate autonomic neuron has its synapse in the peripheral autonomic ganglia, and extends an axon out into the periphery; forms a synapse with a preganglionic neuron.

postprandial period A period of altered metabolism after a meal has been eaten.

postsynaptic cell A cell (either a neuron or effector) that receives a signal from a presynaptic cell across a synapse.

post-tetanic potentiation (PTP) A phenomenon in which a postsynaptic cell will respond with an unusually large change in membrane potential for several minutes following repeated action potentials in the presynaptic cell.

potential energy The energy that is available in a static system; elastic storage energy is a form of potential energy.

power The rate of doing work.

power-velocity curve The relationship between the velocity of muscle shortening and the force of contraction.

power stroke The part of a cross-bridge cycle in which structural changes in myosin alter the relative position of the actin filament.

pre-Bötzinger complex The primary respiratory rhythm generator of mammals.

preformed water The water that arrives in the diet as a liquid or trapped within solid foods; distinct from metabolic water that is produced during the digestion of foods.

preganglionic neuron A vertebrate autonomic neuron that has its cell body in the central nervous system and forms synapses in the peripheral ganglia.

preprohormone Large inactive polypeptide that is a precursor to a peptide hormone (see also *prohormone*).

pressure A force applied to a unit area of a surface.

pressure drag The resistance that arises as an object moves through a fluid as a result of the interaction with the leading edge of the surface encountering the fluid.

presynaptic cell A neuron that transmits a signal across a synapse to a postsynaptic cell.

primary active transport Active transport that uses chemical or light energy directly, such as an ion-pumping ATPase; distinct from secondary active transport, in which an entity is driven by electrochemical transmembrane gradients of another entity being transported.

primary follicle A follicle that continues to develop to release an ovum, unlike other follicles that degrade and die during the maturation process (atresia).

primary oocyte The products of oogonia that have undergone the first meiotic division to become a diploid cell that will eventually produce an ovum.

primary spermatocyte The products of spermatogonia that have undergone the first meiotic division to become a diploid cell that will eventually produce a spermatozoan.

primary structure The sequence of a polymer without consideration of how it folds; typically refers to the amino acid sequence of a protein.

primary urine The initial contents of the lumen of a nephron. In vertebrates that possess a glomerulus, the primary urine is the filtrate.

proboscis A single extension from the head, typically superior to the oral opening; the nose.

proenzyme A catalytically inactive precursor for an enzyme; usually undergoes proteolytic processing to become the active enzyme.

progenote The last universal common ancestor of all organisms.

progesterone A steroid hormone involved in embryogenesis in all vertebrates; also regulates the menstrual cycle and pregnancy in mammals.

prohormone A polypeptide formed by the cleavage of a preprohormone; a precursor to the formation of a peptide hormone.

prolactin An anterior pituitary hormone that is responsible for milk production in mammals, and more general roles in ion and water balance in other vertebrates.

pronephros A simple kidney equivalent of larval forms of some amphibians and fish.

proprioceptor A sensory receptor that provides information about body position and movement.

prosencephalon See *forebrain*.

prostate gland A gland accessory associated with the reproductive tract of male vertebrates.

prosthetic group A nonprotein component of an enzyme or other protein; e.g., a coenzyme (an organic prosthetic group) or a metal.

protease An enzyme that breaks peptide bonds of proteins to generate polypeptides or amino acids.

proteasome A cytoplasmic multiprotein complex that degrades damaged proteins tagged with a ubiquitin molecule.

protein A polymer of amino acids, usually folded into complex secondary structures.

protein kinase An enzyme that attaches a phosphate to a protein, using a molecule of ATP for energy and as a phosphate source.

protein phosphatase An enzyme that removes a phosphate group from a protein.

proteoglycan A molecule composed of protein and glycosaminoglycan.

proteolysis The breakdown of proteins, usually by hydrolytic cleavage of peptide bonds by a protease.

prothoracic glands A pair of endocrine glands that secrete hormones that regulate ecdysis.

protist Any one of a diverse collection of distantly related eukaryotic unicellular microorganisms.

protofilament A single chain of tubulin that exists prior to the formation of sheets or microtubules.

proton motive force The electrochemical gradient arising from proton pumping by the mitochondrial electron transport chain.

protonephridia Excretory organs consisting of a tubule-like structure; found in organisms that lack a coelom or vascular system (e.g., platyhelminths).

protonephridium A simple kidney tubule-like structure, typically with a flame cell to generate fluid movements.

protostomes The group of animals that, during embryogenesis, have a blastopore that becomes the mouth, such as mollusks, annelids, and arthropods.

protozoans An historical term to describe the phyla of early single-celled eukaryotes known now as protists.

proximal tubule The region of a mammalian or avian kidney tubule that lies between the Bowman's capsule and the descending limb of the loop of Henle.

proximate cause The immediate or direct cause of an organismal structure, function, or behavior; usually refers to the developmental or physiological mechanism (see also *ultimate cause*).

pulmonary artery Blood vessel leading from the heart to the lungs of mammals that carries deoxygenated blood.

pulmonary circuit The part of the tetrapod circulatory system that carries blood from the heart to and from the lungs.

pulmonary semilunar valve The valve between the right ventricle and the pulmonary artery of the mammalian cardiovascular system.

pulmonary system A respiratory system consisting of lungs and the associated vasculature.

pulmonary vein Blood vessel leading from the lungs to the heart of mammals that carries oxygenated blood.

pupa A developmental stage in hemimetabolous insects that separates the larva from the adult; can include a period of quiescence.

pupil An opening in the center of a camera-type eye through which light enters.

purine A class of nitrogenous bases with two rings; includes guanine and adenine.

Purkinje fibers The terminal branches of the conducting fibers of the mammalian heart.

P wave One of the waveforms of an electrocardiogram; represents the depolarization of the atria.

pyloric sphincter The sphincter that regulates movement of material from the stomach to the duodenum.

pyrimidine A class of nitrogenous bases with one ring; includes cytosine, thymine, and uracil.

pyrogen An entity that causes a homeotherm to mount an immune response that culminates in a fever.

Q_{10} A value that reflects the impact of a 10°C change in temperature on an enzymatic or metabolic process; also known as the temperature coefficient.

QRS complex One of the waveforms of an electrocardiogram; represents the depolarization of the ventricles.

quaternary structure The three-dimensional arrangement of a protein composed of multiple monomeric units.

radial symmetry A body plan in which any plane through the animal from oral/anterior to aboral/posterior generates mirror images.

radiant energy Thermal energy released from an object in relation to its temperature.

radiant heat transfer The emission of thermal energy from a warm object to cooler surroundings.

radiation The emission of energy from an object.

ram ventilation A ventilatory strategy in which the forward movement of the animal provides the propulsive force needed for bulk flow of the ventilatory medium across the respiratory surface. Seen in some fishes and insects.

range fractionation A strategy in which groups of sensory neurons work together to increase the dynamic range of a receptor organ. Each neuron has an overlapping, but not identical, dynamic range, allowing a wider range of stimulus intensities to be coded by the population of receptors.

rate constant The factor that allows the prediction of an enzymatic rate based on the concentration of the substrates.

reaction norm The range of phenotypes that can be produced by a given genotype when it is exposed to different environments.

reactive oxygen species (ROS) A free radical in which the unpaired electron is associated with an oxygen atom.

receptive field The area of the body that, when stimulated by an incoming sensory stimulus, affects the activity of a sensory neuron.

receptor A protein or cell that can detect an incoming stimulus.

receptor adaptation The process by which sensory receptor cells become less sensitive to sensory signals as signal duration increases.

receptor potential A graded change in the membrane potential within an epithelially derived sensory receptor cell. The receptor potential triggers the release of neurotransmitter onto a primary afferent neuron, causing a postsynaptic graded potential. If this postsynaptic potential exceeds threshold, it will trigger action potentials in the axon of the primary afferent neuron.

receptor proteins Proteins specialized for the detection of signals.

receptor enzymes Defining feature of a class of signal transduction pathways in which the receptor acts as an enzyme that catalyzes a chemical reaction when activated.

recruitment The stimulation of different collections of muscle fibers in response to different activity patterns.

rectal gland An organ found in cartilaginous fish that secretes salt to aid in osmotic regulation.

redox balance (reduction-oxidation balance) A condition in which there is no net change in the ratio of reduced to oxidized reducing equivalents, typically $NADH/NAD^+$.

redox shuttle A multienzyme pathway used to transfer the energy of reducing equivalents from glycolysis into the mitochondria for oxidation.

redox status The relative levels of reduced to oxidized molecules of interest; typically applied to metabolic biochemistry (e.g., $NADH/NAD^+$) but can also be used to reflect the degree of oxidative stress.

reducing equivalents $NAD(P)H$ or $FADH_2$.

reductant A molecule that donates an electron to another molecule (the oxidant). In doing so, the reductant becomes oxidized.

reduction A chemical reaction whereby a molecule accepts an electron from another molecule, becoming reduced.

reductionism A philosophical approach that asserts that complex processes can be understood in terms of their components.

reflex arc A simple neural circuit that does not involve the conscious centers of the brain.

reflex control pathway See *reflex arc*.

reflex behaviors Behaviors that do not require conscious input from the central nervous system (see *reflex arc*).

refraction The bending of light as it passes from one medium to another.

refractive index The degree to which a material refracts light.

refractory period A period in which an excitable cell is less likely to generate an action potential (see also *absolute refractory period, relative refractory period*).

regional heterothermy A thermoregulatory strategy in which regions of an animal's body exhibit significantly different temperatures.

regulators Animals that maintain a degree of constancy in an internal physiochemical parameter (e.g., osmolarity or temperature) despite external changes in the parameter.

regurgitation The expulsion of stomach contents back up the esophagus into the oral cavity.

relative refractory period A period immediately following the absolute refractory period in which an excitable cell will generate an action potential only if exposed to a suprathreshold (unusually large) stimulus.

relaxed endothermy A thermal strategy in which an endothermic animal allows its body temperature to fall for a period of time.

renal Pertaining to the kidney.

renal clearance The removal of an entity from the plasma by the kidney.

renal corpuscle A structure consisting of the glomerulus and Bowman's capsule of a nephron in the vertebrate kidney.

renal tubule Within a nephron, it is the tube composed of a single layer of transport epithelium. It is also known as a kidney tubule. It is the single filtration unit of the vertebrate kidney.

repolarization phase A return of the membrane potential of a cell toward the resting membrane potential following a depolarization or hyperpolarization.

residuals The difference between the observed values and the values that would be predicted based on an underlying function. Often computed in the context of allometric scaling.

resistance, electrical The force opposing the flow of charge through an electrical circuit.

resistance, vascular The force opposing the flow of blood through the circulatory system.

respiration The process by which mitochondria consume oxygen and produce carbon dioxide (see also *external respiration*).

respiratory acidosis or alkalosis Decrease or increase in blood pH as a result of changes in blood carbon dioxide (usually as a result of changes in ventilation).

respiratory chain See *electron transport system*.

respiratory pigments Metalloproteins that act as oxygen transport and storage molecules (e.g., hemoglobin).

respiratory pump A mechanism that helps to pump blood back to the heart via the venous system as a result of the reduced pressure in the chest cavity during the inspiration phase of lung ventilation.

respiratory quotient (RQ) The ratio of CO_2 produced to O_2 consumed; indicative of the type of fuel being utilized. An RQ of 0.7 indicates fatty acids are the fuel, whereas an RQ of 1.0 suggests carbohydrates are being oxidized.

resting membrane potential The membrane potential of an excitable cell when action potentials or graded potentials are not being generated.

resting metabolic rate (RMR) The metabolic rate of an animal at rest under experimentally defined conditions (see also *basal metabolic rate, standard metabolic rate*).

rete mirabile A network of blood vessels that serve to retain heat via countercurrent exchange.

retia (singular: rete) Networks of blood vessels or nerves.

retina A layer of light-sensitive cells that lines the back of eyes.

retinal A derivative of vitamin A that acts as the light-absorbing chromophore in animal photopigments.

reversal potential The membrane potential at which there is no net movement of an ion through open ion channels.

Reynolds number A dimensionless number associated with an object that reflects how smoothly a fluid flows over the surface of the object.

rhabdomeric photoceptors One of two types of animal photoreceptor cells. Arthropod photoreceptors are rhabdomeric (see also *ciliary photoreceptors*).

rhodopsin A photopigment consisting of the protein opsin chemically linked to a vitamin A derivative called retinal.

rhombencephalon See *hindbrain*.

ribonucleic acid See *RNA*.

ribosomal RNA See *rRNA*.

ribosome A complex of RNA and protein that carries out protein synthesis.

rigor A state of skeletal muscle in which cross-bridges remain intact because ATP has been depleted from the cell.

RNA A polymer of ribonucleic acids similar to DNA except that they contain ribose in place of deoxyribose and uracil in place of thymine; includes mRNA, tRNA, and rRNA. Involved in transferring information from DNA and in protein synthesis.

RNase An enzyme that degrades RNA either from the end (exonuclease) or internally (endonuclease).

rod A type of vertebrate photoreceptor cell. In mammals, rods are responsible for vision in dim light (see also *cone*).

Root effect A change in the oxygen carrying capacity of blood as a result of changes in pH.

round window Membrane at the end of the cochlea; acts as a pressure release for the fluid of the inner ear.

rRNA The form of RNA that is incorporated into the riboprotein complex known as a ribosome.

r-selection A life history strategy whereby parents invest minimally in large numbers of offspring; best suited to rapidly exploit underutilized niches.

r-type strategy A reproductive strategy where parents produce numerous offspring, with relatively little investment in their care.

ryanodine receptor (RYR) A Ca^{2+} channel found in the sarcoplasmic reticulum of muscle, which allows Ca^{2+} to escape into the cytoplasm to initiate muscle contraction.

saccule A region of sensory cells within the inner ear.

saliva A solution of enzymes, salts, and water secreted into the oral cavity to lubricate, dissolve, and disrupt food.

salt A neutral molecule composed of an inorganic anion and inorganic cation linked by an ionic bond, such as NaCl (table salt).

salt gland An extrarenal gland found in some marine and desert vertebrates that secrete Na^+ and Cl^- to reduce body salt content.

saltatory conduction The mode of conduction of action potentials in myelinated axons in which action potentials appear to jump from one node of Ranvier to the next.

sarcolemma The cell membrane of a muscle.

sarcomere The contractile unit of striated muscle, typically measured from one Z-disk to the next.

sarcomere length The distance between two Z-disks of a sarcomere.

sarcoplasm The cytoplasm of a muscle cell; also known as myoplasm.

sarcoplasmic reticulum The endoplasmic reticulum of muscle.

satellite cells A population of omnipotent stem cells found on the surface of striated muscle. When stimulated, satellite cells can enter myogenesis to repair or replace muscle.

saturated (1) For respiratory pigments, hormone receptors, and carrier proteins, refers to a situation in which all available proteins are bound to their ligand. (2) For fatty acids, refers to fatty acid chains that lack double bonds.

saturated fatty acid A fatty acid with no double bonds.

scaling The relationship between a parameter, such as metabolic rate, and body size.

scaling coefficient The slope of a plot of log body mass against log parameter of interest, such as metabolic rate.

Schwann cell A type of glial cell in the vertebrates that forms the myelin sheath around axons in the peripheral nervous system.

sclera Tough outer surface of a vertebrate eye.

sclerites Platelike sections of an invertebrate exoskeleton.

sclerotization The hardening of the arthropod exoskeleton arising from formation of cross-links between proteins.

SDA See *specific dynamic action.*

second messenger A short-lived intracellular messenger that acts as an intermediate in a signal transduction pathway.

secondary active transport Transport of a molecule across a membrane against its electrochemical gradient, driven by the cotransport of another molecule along its electrochemical gradient.

secondary structure The folding pattern of a macromolecule; an alpha-helix is an example of the secondary structure of protein and DNA.

secretagogue A chemical that induces the secretion of another chemical, usually a cell signaling factor such as a hormone.

secretory granules Vesicles of secretory product stored within a cell, prepared for release when the cell receives the appropriate signal.

selectivity filter A part of an ion channel that determines the type of ion that can pass through the pore of the channel.

semicircular canals Structures of the inner ear responsible for the sense of balance and body orientation; part of the vestibular apparatus.

semilunar valves The valves between the ventricles and the arteries of the vertebrate heart.

seminal vesicles A pair of glands that store sperm and secrete nutrients and fluids that form the semen, emptying it into the vas deferens upon ejaculation.

semipermeable membrane A membrane that allows the free movement of some molecules but impedes the movement of others.

sensillum (plural: **sensilla**) Sense organs in the insect cuticle. Involved in the senses of taste, smell, touch, and hearing.

sensitization A process by which the response of a neuron to a stimulus is increased.

sensory adaptation See *receptor adaptation.*

sensory modality The category of sensory input that a sensory system detects (e.g., light, sound, pressure).

sensory neuron A neuron that conveys sensory information from the periphery to the central nervous system (see also *afferent neuron*).

sensory receptor A tissue, cell, or protein that detects incoming sensory information.

sensory transduction The process of converting incoming sensory information to changes in cell membrane potential.

sensory units The smallest unit of a sensory response defined by all of the receptor endings of a single afferent neuron.

septum Any structure that divides two tissues or cavities.

SERCA The sarcoplasmic/endoplasmic calcium ATPase.

series elastic components Elements of a structure that can store elastic energy when they are deformed.

serosa Referring to the outer layer of a tissue or organ (see also *mucosa*).

serotonin A neurotransmitter (biogenic amine) involved in setting mood and regulating blood flow to the brain.

Sertoli cells Elongated cells in the seminiferous tubules of the testis that nourish the spermatids during spermatogenesis.

serum Blood plasma after the clotting factors have been removed.

set point In a homeostatically controlled system, the level at which the regulated variable is maintained.

sexual reproduction A process in which two cells (each with half the normal genetic complement as a result of meiosis and recombination) fuse to form one descendant cell.

shivering thermogenesis Heat production through uncoordinated stimulation of skeletal muscle contractile units.

shunt A pathway that allows flow of blood between the pulmonary and systemic circuits of a tetrapod circulatory system.

signal transduction pathways Biochemical pathways in which a change in conformation of a receptor protein in the target cell is converted to a change in the activity of that cell.

sinoatrial node (SA node) A remnant of the sinus venosus found at the top of the right atrium of the mammalian heart.

sinus venosus The chamber leading to the atrium of the heart in nonmammalian vertebrates.

sinusoidal capillaries A specialized type of fenestrated capillary with larger intercellular gaps and an incomplete basement membrane that result in extremely high permeability; found only in organs such as liver and bone marrow.

skeletal muscle A general term to describe the striated muscle that works in conjunction with the endoskeleton.

skeletal muscle pump A process by which rhythmic contraction of the skeletal muscles in the limbs helps to drive venous return of blood to the heart.

skull The bone or cartilage that surrounds the brain of a vertebrate.

sliding filament model A theory that describes the interaction between actin and myosin during cross-bridge cycling.

smooth muscle A type of muscle that has an irregular arrangement of thick and thin filaments, and thus lacks sarcomeres.

SNARES Proteins involved in the fusion of vesicles to the cell membrane.

sodium-potassium pump See $Na^+/K^+ ATPase.$

solenocytes The cells that create fluid movements at the end of a protonephridium. Similar to flame cells, but possess one or two flagella rather than a tuft of cilia.

solubility coefficient Parameter describing the ability of a gas to dissolve in a liquid.

solute The particles (ions or molecules) dissolved in a solution.

solution The fluid in which solutes are dissolved.

solvent The liquid in which solutes are dissolved.

soma The cell body of a neuron, containing the nucleus.

somatic motor division (of the nervous system) The portion of the vertebrate peripheral nervous system that controls skeletal muscle.

sonic muscles A general term for diverse muscles that are involved in sound production.

spatial summation The process by which graded potentials at different points in the membrane (occurring at the same time) combine to influence the net graded potential of a cell.

specific dynamic action (SDA) The heat produced during the digestive process; also known as the heat increment.

spermatogenesis Production of spermatozoa.

spermatogonia (singular: **spermatogonium**) After the primordial germ cell enters the testes, it differentiates into a spermatogonium, which undergoes multiple rounds of mitosis before entering meiosis.

spermatozoa The smaller gamete in a sexually reproducing species; sperm.

sphincter A ring of smooth muscle that controls the diameter of an opening, controlling passage from one region to the next.

sphingolipid One class of phospholipid based on a sphingosine backbone.

spinal cord Part of the vertebrate central nervous system extending from the base of the skull through the vertebrae of the spine. The spinal cord is continuous with the hindbrain.

spinal nerves A series of paired nerves that exit at regular intervals along the spinal column.

spiracles Small openings leading to the respiratory system; spiracles are the primary opening to the tracheal system of insects. The same word is used for a nonhomologous structure in elasmobranch fishes that provides an alternate opening for the buccal-opercular cavities.

spiral fold Structure in the amphibian heart that allows oxygenated blood to flow preferentially to the systemic arteries.

spleen A vertebrate organ that is involved with the immune, lymphatic, and circulatory systems. It can act as a storage site for red blood cells, and removes damaged cells from the circulation. It also generates immune cells called lymphocytes.

spongy myocardium Type of heart muscle found primarily in nonmammalian vertebrates consisting of a meshwork of loosely connected cells.

standard conditions Accepted external conditions under which physical parameters are assessed; may refer to pressure, temperature, concentration, or other such parameters.

standard metabolic rate (SMR) The metabolic rate of a poikilothermic animal at rest and post-absorptive, measured at a defined external temperature. (see also *basal metabolic rate, resting metabolic rate*).

stanniocalcin A polypeptide hormone that acts in the kidney and gut to regulate calcium and phosphate.

stapes (stirrup) One of the three small bones of the mammalian middle ear.

Starling curve See *Frank-Starling effect.*

statocyst Hollow, fluid-filled sense organ in invertebrates that detects the orientation of the body with respect to gravity.

statolith Small dense granule (usually of calcium carbonate) found in statocysts.

steady state A condition in which there is flux through a reaction or pathway without a change in the concentration of intermediates.

stenohaline An animal that is tolerant of a narrow range of external salinities.

stenotherm An animal that is tolerant of a narrow range of ambient temperatures.

stereocilia The specialized cilia of vertebrate hair cells; involved in the sense of hearing.

stereopsis The ability to see in three dimensions.

steroid hormones A large class of hormones derived from cholesterol.

steroids A diverse group of nonpolar organic molecules composed of multiple carbon rings.

stoichiometry The quantitative relationship between two entities.

stomach A general term for an anterior region of a gastrointestinal tract, typically characterized by acidic digestion processes.

stratum corneum The outer layer of the epidermis of tetrapods, consisting mainly of corneocytes.

striated muscle A class of muscle that possesses thick and thin filaments organized into regular arrays; includes cardiac muscle and skeletal muscle.

stroke volume The volume of blood pumped by the heart in a single beat.

submucosa The tissue layer that lies beneath the mucosal layer.

substrate-level phosphorylation An enzymatic reaction that produces a high-energy phosphate.

sulci (singular: **sulcus**) The folds on the surface of the brain in some mammals.

summation See *spatial summation, temporal summation.*

supercooling The reduction of temperature of a fluid below its freezing point but without the formation of ice.

suprachiasmatic nucleus (SCN) A region within the hypothalamus of the brain that is responsible for regulating circadian rhythms.

surface tension The force of adhesion that binds molecules of a fluid together at the interface with air.

surfactant Substance that lowers the surface tension of liquids; secreted in the lungs of vertebrates.

swim bladder A gas-filled organ that fish use for buoyancy compensation.

sympathetic division See *sympathetic nervous system.*

sympathetic nervous system Part of the vertebrate autonomic nervous system; active during periods of stressful activity; releases the neurotransmitters epinephrine and norepinephrine onto target organs.

symport A transporter that carries two or more entities across a cell membrane in the same direction; also known as a cotransporter.

synapse The junction between a neuron and another neuron or effector cell; consists of a presynaptic cell, the synaptic cleft, and a postsynaptic cell.

synaptic cleft The extracellular space between a presynaptic cell and a postsynaptic cell at a synapse.

synaptic depression A decrease in neurotransmitter release in response to repeated action potentials.

synaptic facilitation An increase in neurotransmitter release in response to repeated action potentials.

synaptic plasticity The capacity of synapses to change their structure and function.

synaptic transmission The process of transmitting information across a neural synapse.

synaptic vesicles Neurotransmitter-containing vesicles that release neurotransmitter into a synapse.

synaptotagmin A protein involved in the trafficking of neurotransmitter-containing vesicles to the membrane of the axon terminal.

syncytium A multinucleated cell that arises from the fusion of multiple cells.

synovial fluid The viscous fluid found between skeletal joints, serving as a lubricant to reduce friction.

synergism A situation in which two agents or processes have a combined effect greater than the sum of the effects of the two agents or processes applied individually.

systemic circuit The part of the tetrapod circulatory system that carries blood from the heart to the body and back.

systole The phase of the cardiac cycle in which the heart is contracting.

systolic pressure The arterial blood pressure during systole.

tachycardia Rapid heartbeat.

tactile receptors Receptors on the skin that are sensitive to touch.

tagmata In segemented animals, a group of segments that are joined together and share a function, such as head, thorax, or abdomen of insects.

tank reactor In gut reactor theory, a type of gut in which nutrients flow into the gut where they are mixed with gut contents, and simultaneously the gut expels fluids that consist of partially degraded nutrients.

tapetum A layer of tissue found in the eye of many vertebrates; involved in reflecting light.

tastants Chemicals that are detected by the sense of taste.

taste bud Structure involved in gustation in the vertebrates.

TCA cycle See *tricarboxylic acid cycle.*

T cells A class of lymphocytes that is produced in the thymus.

tectum Dorsal region of the vertebrate midbrain involved in coordinating visual and auditory responses.

tegmentum An area within the brainstem of the vertebrate brain.

teleost fish The most common subclass of the bony fishes.

temperature coefficient See Q_{10}.

temporal heterothermy A thermal strategy whereby a homeothermic animal exhibits periods of poikilothermy, typically to allow a reduction in metabolic rate; also known as relaxed endothermy.

temporal summation The process by which graded potentials occurring at slightly different times combine to influence the net graded potential of the cell.

tendon The connection between a muscle and a bone.

tension, muscular The force produced by a contracting muscle.

terminal cisternae An enlargement of the sarcoplasmic reticulum near the muscle plasma membrane, specifically T-tubules.

tertiary structure The three-dimensional structure of a macromolecule, stabilized by numerous weak bonds.

testosterone A steroid hormone that stimulates the development of male characteristics.

tetanus The sustained contraction of a muscle arising from multiple stimulations in close succession.

tetrapods Vertebrates with four limbs, including amphibians, reptiles, birds, and mammals.

thalamus One of the basal ganglia of the vertebrate brain that relays sensory information to the cerebral cortex.

theca The outer layer of somatic cells surrounding a follicle, separated from the inner granulosa cells by a basal lamina.

thermal conductance The transfer of thermal energy either within an object or from one object to another.

thermal energy Energy associated with heat production.

thermodynamics A branch of physics that deals with the relationship between heat and other forms of energy.

thermogenesis Heat production.

thermogenin The mitochondrial uncoupling protein found in mammalian brown adipose tissue.

thermoneutral zone The range of ambient temperatures over which an animal does not need to alter metabolic processes to maintain internal constancy.

thermoreceptor A sensory receptor that responds to temperature.

thermoregulation The physiological strategy an animal uses to control temperature within the desired range.

thick filament A polymer of about 300 myosin dimers that produces the contractile force in muscle.

thin filament A muscle-specific α-actin polymer similar in structure to a microfilament; serves as a framework that translates actinomyosin activity into force generation.

threshold of detection The minimum level of a stimulus that can be detected by a sensory receptor.

threshold potential The critical value of the membrane potential in an excitable cell to which the membrane must be depolarized in order for an action potential to be initiated.

threshold stimulus The smallest stimulus that can provoke a response in a cell.

thyroid hormone An iodine-containing hormone produced by the thyroid gland that is involved in the regulation of metabolism.

tidal ventilation A form of ventilation where inhaled and exhaled medium moves along the same pathway.

tidal volume The volume of a respiratory medium moved into or out of a respiratory structure during a single breath.

tight epithelia An epithelial layer with cell–cell connections that limit or prevent paracellular transport.

tight junction A type of intercellular connection that is capable of preventing the free movement of molecules between the cells.

time constant (t) A parameter that characterizes the rate of decay of a change in the membrane potential.

tip link Part of the hair cell in the inner ear and neuromast of vertebrates.

tissue An aggregation of related cells linked together by various types of intercellular connections.

titin A very large protein that runs along the thin filament in striated muscle, determining its length and orienting into the sarcomere.

toll-like receptors, or TLRs An ancient group of receptors found on cells of the innate immune system, responsible for detection of pathogens.

tonic muscle A muscle type with a slow contraction that persists for long periods (see also *phasic muscle*).

tonic receptor A receptor that produces action potentials throughout the duration of a stimulus.

tonicity The property of an extracellular solution that determines whether a cell will swell or shrink.

torpor A type of dormancy characterized by a relatively short period of hypometabolism.

total lung capacity The volume of air in the lungs at the end of a maximal inspiration; the maximum amount of air that can be held in the lungs.

total peripheral resistance The net resistance of the vasculature.

totipotent stem cell An embryonic cell that has the capacity to differentiate into any type of cell when given the appropriate cell signaling information.

trabeculae Any partition that divides or partially divides a cavity.

trachea (plural: **tracheae**) The single large airway leading to the paired bronchi of vertebrate lungs; also, the nonhomologous respiratory structures that are the main conducting airways in arthropod tracheal systems.

tracheal system The respiratory structures of insects and some other groups of air-breathing arthropods.

tracheoles The terminal structures of arthropod tracheal systems across which gas exchange takes place.

tracts Groupings of axons within the central nervous system of vertebrates.

transcellular transport Movement of solutes or water across a cell layer through the cell itself, typically crossing both apical and basolateral cell membranes.

transcription RNA synthesis using the DNA template of a gene.

transcytosis Vesicular transport of materials across a cell.

transducin An inhibitory G protein involved in visual signal transduction in the vertebrates.

transfer RNA See *tRNA*.

transgenic animal An animal that has been genetically modified to possess a heritable mutation.

transition state A temporary, intermediate state in the conversion of substrate to product when a molecule obtains enough energy to reach the activation energy barrier.

translation Protein synthesis using ribosomes and mRNA template.

transmembrane receptor A receptor protein that spans the cell membrane; consists of an extracellular domain, a transmembrane domain, and an intracellular domain.

transmural pressure The pressure difference across the wall of a chamber (e.g., a blood vessel, heart, or airway).

transpirational water loss Water loss arising from gas exchange across the respiratory surface.

transpulmonary pressure The difference between the intra-alveolar pressure and the intrapleural pressure in mammalian lungs.

transverse tubule See *T-tubule*.

triacylglycerol (or **triglyceride**) Three fatty acids esterified to a glycerol molecule.

tricarboxylic acid (TCA) cycle The cyclical mitochondrial pathway that oxidizes acetyl CoA to form 3 NADH, 1 $FADH_2$, and 1 GTP; the pathway that produces most of the CO_2 arising from metabolism.

trichromatic color vision The system of three different photoreceptors by which humans and some other animals obtain color vision.

tricuspid valve The valve between the right atrium and right ventricle of the mammalian heart.

trimer A molecule composed of three subunits.

tRNA (or **transfer RNA**) A cloverleaf-shaped RNA molecule that binds a particular amino acid and participates in translation, binding to a three-nucleotide sequence of mRNA (codon) to transfer the amino acid to a growing polypeptide.

triploblastic Having three primary germ layers.

trophoblast An outer layer of cells derived from the mammalian blastocyst that forms the interface between the fertilized ovum and the uterine wall.

trophosome Found in the body of vent worms, this sac contains endosymbiotic bacteria.

tropic hormones (or **trophic hormones**) Hormones that cause the release of other hormones.

tropomyosin A regulatory protein that stretches across seven actin monomers in a thin filament, controlling myosin's access to its binding site on the thin filament.

troponin A trimeric regulatory protein bound to tropomyosin. It responds to high $[Ca^{2+}]$ by inducing tropomyosin to move into a position that allows myosin to bind actin.

T-tubule An extension of the plasma membrane (sarcolemma) of some muscles that serves to improve the conduction of the action potential into the fiber.

tubulin The monomeric protein subunit of microtubules, itself a dimer of alpha-tubulin and beta-tubulin.

tunica externa Outer layer of the wall of a vertebrate blood vessel.

tunica intima Inner layer of the wall of a vertebrate blood vessel.

tunica media Middle layer of the wall of a vertebrate blood vessel.

turbulent flow A disordered pattern of fluid flow over the surface of an object that reduces the efficiency of movement of the object through the fluid.

turnover number The number of times a single enzyme molecule completes a reaction cycle each second; also known as the catalytic constant (k_{cat}).

turnover rate The number of catalytic events in a given period of time. For an individual enzyme, it is synonymous with the catalytic constant (k_{cat}). It can also be used to describe the rate of synthesis and degradation of a metabolite, such as ATP.

T wave The portion of an electrocardiogram (EKG) that represents the repolarization of the ventricle.

twitch fibers Muscle fibers that undergo a rapid contraction/relaxation cycle (a twitch), in contrast to tonic fibers.

twitch muscle A muscle that contracts and relaxes once after each neuronal stimulus; a **phasic muscle**.

tympanal organ Sensory receptor involved in hearing in insects; insect ears.

tympanic membrane Thin membrane that separates the outer ear from the middle ear. Helps to transfer sound vibrations to the inner ear.

ubiquitin A small protein that is added to damaged proteins to mark them for degradation by the proteasome.

UCP See *uncoupling protein*.

ultimate cause Why an organism has a particular structure, function, or behavior; usually involves understanding the evolutionary advantage of the trait (see also *proximate cause*).

ultrafiltration Process of filtration of a fluid through a size-selective membrane under pressure; used to form the primary filtrate of the vertebrate kidney. Also causes the formation of lymph from blood in vertebrates.

ultraviolet light Short-wavelength light ($<$ ~300 nm); its high energy can damage macromolecules.

uncoupling (of oxidative phosphorylation) When mitochondrial respiration continues without the production of ATP.

uncoupling protein (UCP) A class of proteins, which includes thermogenin (UCP1), that act by dissipating the mitochondrial proton motive force.

unidirectional ventilation A type of ventilation in which the inhaled medium enters the ventilatory system by one route and exits via a different route.

unipolar neuron A neuron with one process leading from the cell body; this process generally splits into two branches, one conveying information toward the cell body and one conveying information away from the cell body.

uniporter A class of transporter that carries a single entity (ion, atom, molecule) with each transfer.

unitary displacement The distance a single motor protein moves during a cross-bridge cycle.

unsaturated fatty acid A fatty acid with one or more double bonds.

upper critical temperature (UCT) The highest temperature at which a homeothermic animal can live for extended periods; the upper limit of the thermoneutral zone.

up-regulation Increase in protein number or activity in a target cell (see also *down-regulation*).

urea A nitrogenous waste possessing two nitrogen atoms per molecule.

ureotele An animal with an excretory strategy in which urea dominates the nitrogenous wastes.

ureter The tube connecting the kidney to the bladder.

urethra The tube carrying urine from the urinary bladder to the excretory opening.

uric acid A nitrogenous waste possessing four nitrogen atoms per molecule.

uricolytic pathway A pathway of breakdown of uric acid present in all animals.

uricotele An animal with an excretory strategy in which uric acid is the dominant nitrogenous waste.

urine A solution of nitrogenous waste produced by the kidney or kidneylike tissues.

utricle A part of the vertebrate inner ear.

vagus nerve The 10th cranial nerve of vertebrates; in mammals, innervates the pharynx, larynx, trachea, lungs, heart, esophagus, and intestinal tract; contains motor, parasympathetic, and sensory neurons.

van der Waals force A type of weak bond forming from the mutual attraction of the nuclei of two atoms in a molecule.

vas deferens The duct through which sperm are carried from the sites of synthesis in the epididymis to the ejaculatory opening.

vasa recta The straight blood vessels arranged in a hairpin loop that run from kidney cortex to medulla and back to the cortex. The countercurrent arrangement allows removal of salts and water from the peritubule interstitium while maintaining intramedullary osmotic gradients.

vascular endothelium Thin layer of cells that lines blood vessels.

vasculature The blood vessels of the circulatory system.

vasoconstriction Narrowing of a blood vessel as a result of contraction of the vascular smooth muscle; decreases local blood flow.

vasodilation Widening of a blood vessel as a result of relaxation of the vascular smooth muscle; increases local blood flow.

vasomotion Change in the diameter of blood vessels; also known as angiokinesis.

vasomotor response The changes in diameter of blood vessels in response to vasodilatory or vasoconstricting factors; also known as the angiokinetic response.

vasomotor tone The degree of contraction of the smooth muscles surrounding the arterioles (see also *venomotor tone*).

vasopressin See *antidiuretic hormone*.

veins Blood vessels that return blood to the heart. In vertebrates, blood flows from the capillaries into venules and then into veins.

venae cavae (singular: **vena cava**) A large vein that carries deoxygenated blood to the heart of vertebrates.

venomotor tone The degree of contraction of the smooth muscles surrounding the veins (see also *vasomotor tone*).

venous return The return of blood to the vertebrate heart via the venous system.

ventilation Active movement of the respiratory medium (air or water) across the respiratory surface.

ventilation-perfusion ratio (or **ventilation-perfusion matching**) The relationship between the ventilation (flow of respiratory medium) and the perfusion (flow of blood) at a respiratory surface.

ventral horns The gray matter portions of the spinal cord that extend to the front.

ventricle A fluid-filled sac or cavity (e.g., the spaces in the center of the vertebrate brain; the muscular pumping chambers of the vertebrate heart).

ventricular ejection The process of pumping blood out of the ventricles of the heart.

venules Small blood vessels located between capillaries and veins.

vertebral column The series of vertebrae extending from the base of the skull to the tip of the tail in vertebrates.

vesicle A membrane-bound compartment that buds off from the intracellular membranous network, often encased in coat proteins such as clathrin.

vestibular apparatus The organ of balance in the vertebrates.

villi Undulations and folds in a tissue that serve to increase surface area; most commonly seen in the gastrointestinal tract.

viscosity An internal property of a fluid that results in resistance to flow. Thick liquids have high viscosity.

viscous effects The antagonism to movement of an object due to the interaction of its surface with the fluid through which it moves. Combines with inertial effects to determine the Reynolds number.

visual cortex A part of the vertebrate brain that is responsible for processing visual signals.

visual field The area that is visible to an eye, without changing eye position.

vital capacity The maximum amount of respiratory medium that can be moved into or out of the respiratory system with each breath.

vitamin A dietary compound that serves as a precursor for prosthetic groups of proteins, particularly enzymes.

vitellin The dominant protein found in yolk produced from vitellogenin.

vitellogenin The major protein in the yolk of an egg.

vitreous humor A thick gel that fills the space between the lens and the retina of the vertebrate eye.

viviparous Animal whose offspring develop internally and are released as active young (see *oviparous* and *ovoviviparous*).

V_{max} The maximal rate of catalysis by an enzyme; arises when all substrates are at optimal (saturating) concentrations and prior to the formation of product.

V_{O2max} The maximal sustainable rate of oxygen consumption exhibited by an animal. The experimental means to assess V_{O2max} differs among disciplines.

volatile fatty acids Fatty acids of chain length less than 2–6 carbons; also known as short chain fatty acids.

voltage clamp A technique used by neurophysiologists to study ion channel function in which the membrane potential is held constant.

voltage-gated ion channel A membrane protein containing an aqueous pore that can be opened in response to changes in the membrane potential.

vomeronasal organ A vertebrate sense organ adjacent to the mouth and nasal cavities that is involved in detecting pheromones.

VU/P ratio The ratio of an ion or molecule concentration in the urine (U) versus the plasma (P).

weak bonds Ionic bonds, hydrogen bonds, van der Waals forces, and hydrophobic interactions.

Wernicke's area Part of the human brain that is involved in the understanding of written and spoken language.

white adipose tissue A lipid storage tissue of mammals; distinct from brown adipose tissue. Other vertebrates lack brown adipose tissue, and white adipose tissue is typically referred to simply as "adipose tissue."

white matter Areas of the vertebrate central nervous system that are rich in axons (see also *gray matter*).

white muscle A muscle fiber type specialized for rapid, high-intensity contractions that continue for a short duration; usually composed of type IIb myosin isoforms.

work The transfer of energy that occurs when force is exerted on a body to cause it to move.

work loop A method used to assess whether a muscle is performing positive or negative work.

xeric A dry, dehydrating environment.

yolk A deposit of lipid and protein (largely vitellin) associated with an ovum.

Z-disk The protein plate at the end of a sarcomere that serves as the insertion site of actin thin filaments.

zona pellucida A thickened glycoprotein extracellular matrix of a mammalian ovum; it binds the sperm to initiate the acrosomal reaction.

zwitterion A molecule with groups that can become positive and others that can become negative.

zygote The single cell arising from the fertilization of an ovum by a sperm.

Animal Index

Page references ending with *fig* indicate an illustrated figure; with *t* indicate a table; with *p* indicate a photograph; with *n* indicate a footnote.

A

Acoelomates, 26, 26*fig*
Actinocoryne contractilis, 204
Actinopterygians, 29, 30*fig*
Adélie penguin, 495
African claw-toed frog, 211*fig*
African lungfish, 463, 559
Agnathans
    evolution of, 28–29
    gut morphology of, 607*fig*
    skeletons of, 516
Agouti, 323*fig*
Albatross, 529, 531*fig*
Algae, 203–204, 597
Alligator, 314*fig*
Altricial animals, 692
Alvinella pompejana, 592
Amblyrhynchus cristatus, 542
American mink, 697*t*
Amniotes, 25, 31
Amphibians, 31
    brain structure of, 324*fig*
    circulatory patterns in, 372*fig*
    gut morphology of, 607*fig*
    hearts of, 378*fig*, 379
    kidneys of, 583–584
    locomotor systems of, 532–533
    ventilation in, 463–464
Amphioxus, 366
Amphiprion percula, 342, 342*p*
Amphiuma, 362
Anadromous animals, 550, 585
Anapsids, 31, 31*fig*
Andean tree frog, 645
Anemones, 24, 182, 316*fig*
Animals
    altricial, 692
    anadromous, 550, 585
    anoxia-tolerant, 65
    catadromous, 550
    desert, 553–554
    diadromous, 550
    freeze-tolerant, 653–654, 654*p*
    hypoxia-tolerant, 65
    oviparous, 677
    ovoviviparous, 677
    precocial, 692
    protandrous, 676
    protogynous, 676
    thin, 449
    viviparous, 677
Annelids, 25, 26*fig*
    cephalization in, 315
    circulatory system of, 363, 363*fig*
    nervous system organization in, 314*fig*
    segmented bodies of, 27

Anopheles, 427
Anoxia-tolerant animals, 65
Anser indicus, 443
Antarctic icefish, 477
Antelope, 514
Anthozoa, 24
Ants, 293, 597
Ape, 301
Aphid, 669
Aplysia californica, 344–345, 345*fig*–346*fig*
Aquatic snail, 454*fig*
Arabidopsis thaliana, 34*fig*
Archaea, 21
Archaeopteryx, 656
Arctic fox, 640*fig*
Arctocephalus pusillus, 697*t*
Armadillidium, 459
Armadillo, 552*p*
Artemia, 554
Arthropods, 25
    circulatory systems of, 363–364, 364*fig*
    compound eyes in, 293–294, 294*fig*
    metamerism and tagmatization of, 27–28
    nervous systems of, 314*fig*, 315–316
    pattern-recognition receptors in, 419*t*
    segmental ganglia in, 315–316
    steroid hormones in, 145–146
    terpenoids in, 146
    terrestrial evolution of, 551*fig*
    See also Crustaceans; Insects
Asteroidea, 28
Atlantic cod, 536, 646, 646*fig*
Australian fur seal, 697*t*
Australian lungfish, 463

B

Bacteria
    cell walls of, 418
    cyanobacteria, 597
    pattern-recognition receptors in, 419*t*
    purple bacteria, 21
Balaenoptera musculus, 356
Baleen whale, 286
Bar-headed geese, 442*p*, 443, 490, 492–493
Barracuda, 645
Bar-tailed godwits, 443
Bassozetus, 481
Bathymodiolus thermophilus, 592
Bats
    hibernation by, 642
    little big-eared bat, 256, 256*p*
Bay scallop, 288
Bears
    black bear, 697*t*
    brown bear, 697*t*
    grizzly bear, 640*fig*
    polar bear
        body temperature of, 16*p*
        endocrine disruptors in, 108
        insulation of, 640*fig*

Beaver, 584*fig*
Bedbug, 684
Bee, 514, 516
Beetles, 461, 515, 553
Bichirs, 463
Billfish, 253, 253*fig*
Birds
    altitude tolerance of, 443, 490
    beaks of, 601–602
    brain structure of, 324*fig*
    circulatory circuits of, 371–372
    evolution of, 32, 529
    flightless, 533–534
    flight muscles of, 505–506, 506*fig*
    hearts of, 381–382
    immunity transfer to offspring, 438–439
    inner ears of, 281*fig*
    lungs of, 466*fig*
    migratory, 305
    salt glands of, 586, 588, 588*fig*
    short-term cooling in, 642*fig*
    sleep patterns of, 311
    uric acid excretion in, 556–557
    ventilation in, 466–467, 467*fig*
    See also Hummingbirds; *specific bird*
Bivalve mollusks, 453
Black bear, 697*t*
Black-browed albatross, 531*fig*
Black ghost knifefish, 306*p*
Blue marlin, 635
Blue mussel, 654*p*
Blue shark, 532*fig*
Blue whale, 157, 356–357
Boa constrictor, 304
Bony fish, 29, 31
Bottlenose dolphin, 310–311, 310*p*, 494*fig*
Box jellies, 24
Brachiosaurus, 409
Branchiostoma lanceolatum, 205
Brine shrimp, 554, 687
Brittle star, 28, 455
Brown bear, 697*t*
Bullfrog, 400*t*
Bumblebee, 514
Butterfly, 146, 601

C

Caenorhabditis elegans
    genome of, 125
    graded potentials in, 174
    nervous system of, 312
    obliquely striated muscle of, 249
    olfactory mechanisms of, 268
    touch receptors of, 273*fig*
California newt, 170
Calliactis parasitica, 315, 316*fig*
Callorhinus ursinus, 697*t*
Cancer magister, 360*fig*
Canis latrans, 11, 12*fig*
Cape pigeon, 531*fig*

Subject Index

Page references ending with *fig* indicate an illustrated figure; with *t* indicate a table; with *p* indicate a photograph; with *n* indicate a footnote.

A

A-band, 225
Absolute refractory period, 167
Accessory breathing organs, 463
Acclimation, 17, 644, 649
Acclimatization, 17, 644, 649
Accommodation, 295
Acetic acid, 50*t*
Acetylcholine (ACh), 110, 178, 197*t*, 616*t*
    heart rate and, 387, 388*fig*
    synthesis and recycling of, 178*fig*
Acetylcholine receptors, 198–199
Acetylcholinesterase, 178
Acetylcholinesterase inhibitors, 179
Acetyl CoA
    energy carried by, 57*fig*
    fatty acids produced from, 66–67
    production of, 71*fig*
    in TCA cycle, 71–72
ACh. *See* Acetylcholine
Acid, 50*t*
    carbon dioxide as source of, 577
    secretion of, 608–609, 617*fig*
    water pH and, 49–50
    See also Amino acids; Fatty acids; *specific acid*
Acid-base balance, 576–577
Acrosome, of sperm, 220*fig*
Acrosome reaction, 218
ACTH. *See* Adrenocorticotropic hormone
Actin, 85, 217
    function of, 223*t*
    myosin and, 218–219
    networks of, 219*fig*
    polymerization of, 218
    structure of, 218*fig*
Actino-myosin activity, 219–222
    Ca^{2+} in, 228–229
    ionic events in, 230*fig*
    regulation of, 229*fig*
Action potentials, 102, 157
    after-hyperpolarization phase of, 167
    Ca^{2+} channels and, 185
    in cardiac and skeletal muscles, 236*fig*
    in cardiomyocytes, 389, 389*fig*
    conduction of, 172, 173*fig*
    depolarization phase of, 166
    frequency of, 176–178, 176*fig*
    graded potentials and, 164–165, 167*t*
    Hodgkin-Huxley theory of, 154–155
    long-distance signals of, 172–174
    refractory periods of, 167, 236–237
    repolarization phase of, 166
    in striated muscle, 234–236, 235*fig*
    unidirectional, 174–176
    in various organisms, 203–205
    voltage-gated Na^+ and K^+ channels and, 171–172, 172*fig*

Activation energy (E_A), 42, 53, 53*fig*, 630
Activation gate, 168, 169*fig*
Active site, 53
Active transport, 80–81, 81*fig*
Acuity, 261
Adaptation, 12–13
    to altitude, 490
    to cold, 651–652
    homeoviscous, 78, 647
    in intertidal zone, 3
    receptor, 264
Adaptive immune system, 417, 425, 431*fig*
Additivity, of hormones, 139–140, 139*fig*
Adenosine, 197*t*
Adenylate cyclase, 129*fig*
Adequate stimulus, 260
ADH. *See* Antidiuretic hormone
Adhesion plaques, 245
Adipokinetic hormone (AKH), 626
Adiponectin, 616*t*
Adipose, 624*fig*
Adipose tissue
    brite, 659
    brown, 658, 658*fig*
    white, 615, 624–625
Adrenal cortex, 143
Adrenal glands, 143, 149*fig*
Adrenal medulla, 143
Adrenergic receptors, 199–201, 203*t*
Adrenocorticotropic hormone (ACTH), 350
Aerobic dive limit, 491
Aerodynamics, 527
Aerofoils, 527–528, 528*fig*
Afferent arteriole, 561
Afferent division, of peripheral nervous system, 312
Afferent neurons, 180, 258
Affinity constant, 115
After-hyperpolarization phase, 167
Aglomerular kidneys, 583
Agonists, 113
Air
    bubbles of, 461
    COT in, 538*fig*
    gas exchange in, 458–473
    physical properties of, 446*t*
    thermal conductivity of, 637–638, 638*t*
    ventilation in, 458–473
Air capillaries, 466
Airway resistance, 470
AKH. *See* Adipokinetic hormone
Albumin, 107, 361
Aldosterone, 35, 575, 576*fig*
Aliphatic chains, 66
Allantois, 687, 688*fig*
Allatostatins, 673
Allatotropins, 673
Alleles, 94
Allelochemicals, 100
Allen's rule, 639

Allergic response, 435, 436*fig*
Allometric scaling, 9, 629, 630*fig*
Allostasis, 16
Allosteric modulation, of oxygen affinity, 482*fig*
Allosteric regulators, 56–57
Allozymes, 94
Alternative splicing, 93
Altitude
    human adaptation to, 490
    hypoxia and, 488–490
    oxygen and, 440–443
Altricial species, 692
Alveoli, 467–468
Amacrine cells, 296
Ambient temperature (T_A), 635
Amines, 109
Amino acid metabolism, 555
Amino acids, 197*t*
    growth and, 596–597
    proteins built from, 59
Ammonia, 555–556
Ammoniagenesis, 556*fig*
Ammoniotele, 555–556, 555*t*
Ammonium, 50*t*, 555*fig*
Amnion, 687, 688*fig*
Amniotes, 687–688, 688*fig*
Amoeboid movement, 223*t*
AMP-dependent protein kinase (AMPK), 513*fig*
Amphibolic metabolic pathway, 51
AMPK. *See* AMP-dependent protein kinase
Amplifier enzymes, 126–127
Ampulla, 281, 282*fig*
Ampullae of Lorenzini, 260, 304
Amygdala, 327
Amylases, 597
Amylopectin, 62*fig*
Amylose, 62*fig*
Anabolic metabolic pathway, 51
Anabolism, 76
Anadromous animals, 550, 585
Analogy, 14, 14*fig*
Anaplerotic pathway, 71
Anastomoses, 368
Ancestral gene duplications, 95–96
Androgens, 671–672, 671*fig*, 681*t*, 691*t*
Anemia, 482
Angiogenesis, 370–371, 512
Angle of attack, 528, 528*fig*
Anguilliform movement, 504*fig*
Anhydrobiosis, 554
Animal athletes, 514
Animalcules, 208*p*
Animals
    anadromous, 550, 585
    catadromous, 550
    common traits among, 12
    desert, 553–554
    diadromous, 550
    endocrine system complexity in, 144
    euryhaline, 546